Proceedings of the Twenty-Ninth AAAI Conference on Artificial Intelligence and the

Twenty-Seventh Innovative Applications of Artificial Intelligence Conference

Volume One

25–30 January 2015
Austin, Texas USA

Palo Alto, California
AAAI Press

AAAI Press
2275 East Bayshore Road, Suite 160
Palo Alto, California 94303

ISBN 978-1-57735-698-1 Six-volume set
ISBN 978-1-57735-699-8 Volume One
ISBN 978-1-57735-700-1 Volume Two
ISBN 978-1-57735-701-8 Volume Three
ISBN 978-1-57735-702-5 Volume Four
ISBN 978-1-57735-703-2 Volume Five
ISBN 978-1-57735-704-9 Volume Six

ISSN 2159-5399 (Print)
ISSN 2374-3468 (Online)

Printed on acid free paper.

Manufactured in the United States of America

Contents

VOLUME ONE

AAAI Organization / xliv

Conference Committees / xlvii

Awards / lxxiv

Sponsors / lxxvi

AAAI Preface / lxxvii
Blai Bonet and Sven Koenig

IAAI Preface / lxxix
David Gunning and Peter Yeh

Invited Talks / lxxx
Michael Bowling, Drew Bagnell, Oren Etzioni, Lise Getoor, Rayid Ghani, Geoffrey Hinton, Meinolf Sellmann

Special Invited Presentations / lxxxiii
AAAI-15 Shakey Celebration: *Ed Feigenbaum, Peter Hart, and Nils Nilsson*
AAAI-15 Debate on Autonomous Weapons: *Ron Arkin and Stephen Goose*

AAAI-15 Technical Papers

AI and the Web

Efficient Top-*k* Shortest-Path Distance Queries on Large Networks by Pruned Landmark Labeling / 2
Takuya Akiba, Takanori Hayashi, Nozomi Nori, Yoichi Iwata, Yuichi Yoshida

Inferring Same-as Facts from Linked Data: An Iterative Import-by-Query Approach / 9
Mustafa Al-Bakri, Manuel Atencia, Steffen Lalande, Marie-Christine Rousset

A Personalized Interest-Forgetting Markov Model for Recommendations / 16
Jun Chen, Chaokun Wang, Jianmin Wang

Will You "Reconsume" the Near Past? Fast Prediction on Short-Term Reconsumption Behaviors / 23
Jun Chen, Chaokun Wang, Jianmin Wang

VELDA: Relating an Image Tweet's Text and Images / 30
Tao Chen, Hany M. SalahEldeen, Xiangnan He, Min-Yen Kan, Dongyuan Lu

On Information Coverage for Location Category Based Point-of-Interest Recommendation / 37
Xuefeng Chen, Yifeng Zeng, Gao Cong, Shengchao Qin, Yanping Xiang, Yuanshun Dai

Visually Interpreting Names as Demographic Attributes by Exploiting Click-Through Data / 44
Yan-Ying Chen, Yin-Hsi Kuo, Chun-Che Wu, Winston H. Hsu

A New Granger Causal Model for Influence Evolution in Dynamic Social Networks: The Case of DBLP / 51
Belkacem Chikhaoui, Mauricio Chiazzaro, Shengrui Wang

An Axiomatic Approach to Link Prediction / 58
Sara Cohen, Aviv Zohar

Perceiving Group Themes from Collective Social and Behavioral Information / 65
Peng Cui, Tianyang Zhang, Fei Wang, Peng He

Predicting the Demographics of Twitter Users from Website Traffic Data / 72
Aron Culotta, Nirmal Kumar Ravi, Jennifer Cutler

High-Performance Distributed ML at Scale through Parameter Server Consistency Models / 79
Wei Dai, Abhimanu Kumar, Jinliang Wei, Qirong Ho, Garth Gibson, Eric P. Xing

An EBMC-Based Approach to Selecting Types for Entity Filtering / 88
Jiwei Ding, Wentao Ding, Wei Hu, Yuzhong Qu

Trust Models for RDF Data: Semantics and Complexity / 95
Valeria Fionda, Gianluigi Greco

Extended Property Paths: Writing More SPARQL Queries in a Succinct Way / 102
Valeria Fionda, Giuseppe Pirrò, Mariano P. Consens

Lower and Upper Bounds for SPARQL Queries over OWL Ontologies / 109
Birte Glimm, Yevgeny Kazakov, Ilianna Kollia, Giorgos Stamou

FACES: Diversity-Aware Entity Summarization Using Incremental Hierarchical Conceptual Clustering / 116
Kalpa Gunaratna, Krishnaprasad Thirunarayan, Amit Sheth

TrustSVD: Collaborative Filtering with Both the Explicit and Implicit Influence of User Trust and of Item Ratings / 123
Guibing Guo, Jie Zhang, Neil Yorke-Smith

A Stochastic Model for Detecting Heterogeneous Link Communities in Complex Networks / 130
Dongxiao He, Dayou Liu, Di Jin, Weixiong Zhang

Prajna: Towards Recognizing Whatever You Want from Images without Image Labeling / 137
Xian-Sheng Hua, Jin Li

Kernel Density Estimation for Text-Based Geolocation / 145
Mans Hulden, Miikka Silfverberg, Jerid Francom

Cross-Modal Image Clustering via Canonical Correlation Analysis / 151
Cheng Jin, Wenhui Mao, Ruiqi Zhang, Yuejie Zhang, Xiangyang Xue

Modeling with Node Degree Preservation Can Accurately Find Communities / 160
Di Jin, Zheng Chen, Dongxiao He, Weixiong Zhang

Estimating Temporal Dynamics of Human Emotions / 168
Seungyeon Kim, Joonseok Lee, Guy Lebanon, Haesun Park

Uniform Interpolation and Forgetting for *ALC* Ontologies with ABoxes / 175
Patrick Koopmann, Renate A. Schmidt

Using Matched Samples to Estimate the Effects of Exercise on Mental Health from Twitter / 182
Virgile Landeiro Dos Reis, Aron Culotta

Consistent Knowledge Discovery from Evolving Ontologies / 189
Freddy Lécué, Jeff Z. Pan

Multi-Document Summarization Based on Two-Level Sparse Representation Model / 196
He Liu, Hongliang Yu, Zhi-Hong Deng

COT: Contextual Operating Tensor for Context-Aware Recommender Systems / 203
Qiang Liu, Shu Wu, Liang Wang

Effectively Predicting Whether and When a Topic Will Become Prevalent in a Social Network / 210
Weiwei Liu, Zhi-Hong Deng, Xiuwen Gong, Frank Jiang, Ivor W. Tsang

Content-Based Collaborative Filtering for News Topic Recommendation / 217
Zhongqi Lu, Zhicheng Dou, Jianxun Lian, Xing Xie, Qiang Yang

A Tri-Role Topic Model for Domain-Specific Question Answering / 224
Zongyang Ma, Aixin Sun, Quan Yuan, Gao Cong

Handling owl:sameAs via Rewriting / 231
Boris Motik, Yavor Nenov, Robert Piro, Ian Horrocks

Incorporating Assortativity and Degree Dependence into Scalable Network Models / 238
Stephen Mussmann, John Moore, Joseph J. Pfeiffer III, Jennifer Neville

Using Description Logics for RDF Constraint Checking and Closed-World Recognition / 247
Peter F. Patel-Schneider

Approximating Model-Based ABox Revision in DL-Lite: Theory and Practice / 254
Guilin Qi, Zhe Wang, Kewen Wang, Xuefeng Fu, Zhiqiang Zhuang

Leveraging Social Foci for Information Seeking in Social Media / 261
Suhas Ranganath, Jiliang Tang, Xia Hu, Hari Sundaram, Huan Liu

Extracting Bounded-Level Modules from Deductive RDF Triplestores / 268
Marie-Christine Rousset, Federico Ulliana

Question/Answer Matching for CQA System via Combining Lexical and Sequential Information / 275
Yikang Shen, Wenge Rong, Zhiwei Sun, Yuanxin Ouyang, Zhang Xiong

A Hybrid Approach of Classifier and Clustering for Solving the Missing Node Problem / 282
Sigal Sina, Avi Rosenfeld, Sarit Kraus, Navot Akiva

Recommending Positive Links in Signed Social Networks by Optimizing a Generalized AUC / 290
Dongjin Song, David A. Meyer

Causal Inference via Sparse Additive Models with Application to Online Advertising / 297
Wei Sun, Pengyuan Wang, Dawei Yin, Jian Yang, Yi Chang

Sampling Representative Users from Large Social Networks / 304
Jie Tang, Chenhui Zhang, Keke Cai, Li Zhang, Zhong Su

Relating Romanized Comments to News Articles by Inferring Multi-*Glyphic* Topical Correspondence / 311
Goutham Tholpadi, Mrinal Kanti Das, Trapit Bansal, Chiranjib Bhattacharyya

Mining User Intents in Twitter: A Semi-Supervised Approach to Inferring Intent Categories for Tweets / 318
Jinpeng Wang, Gao Cong, Wayne Xin Zhao, Xiaoming Li

Burst Time Prediction in Cascades / 325
Senzhang Wang, Zhao Yan, Xia Hu, Philip S. Yu, Zhoujun Li

Clustering-Based Collaborative Filtering for Link Prediction / 332
Xiangyu Wang, Dayu He, Danyang Chen, Jinhui Xu

Mining Query Subtopics from Questions in Community Question Answering / 339
Yu Wu, Wei Wu, Zhoujun Li, Ming Zhou

DynaDiffuse: A Dynamic Diffusion Model for Continuous Time Constrained Influence Maximization / 346
Miao Xie, Qiusong Yang, Qing Wang, Gao Cong, Gerard de Melo

A Probabilistic Model for Bursty Topic Discovery in Microblogs / 353
Xiaohui Yan, Jiafeng Guo, Yanyan Lan, Jun Xu, Xueqi Cheng

On the Scalable Learning of Stochastic Blockmodel / 360
Bo Yang, Xuehua Zhao

RAIN: Social Role-Aware Information Diffusion / 367
Yang Yang, Jie Tang, Cane Wing-ki Leung, Yizhou Sun, Qicong Chen, Juanzi Li, Qiang Yang

Collaborative Topic Ranking: Leveraging Item Meta-Data for Sparsity Reduction / 374
Weilong Yao, Jing He, Hua Wang, Yanchun Zhang, Jie Cao

Robust Image Sentiment Analysis Using Progressively
Trained and Domain Transferred Deep Networks / 381
Quanzeng You, Jiebo Luo, Hailin Jin, Jianchao Yang

Are Features Equally Representative? A Feature-Centric Recommendation / 389
Chenyi Zhang, Ke Wang, Ee-peng Lim, Qinneng Xu, Jianling Sun, Hongkun Yu

Incorporating Implicit Link Preference into Overlapping Community Detection / 396
Hongyi Zhang, Irwin King, Michael R. Lyu

Retweet Behavior Prediction Using Hierarchical Dirichlet Process / 403
Qi Zhang, Yeyun Gong, Ya Guo, Xuanjing Huang

Exploring Key Concept Paraphrasing Based on Pivot Language Translation for Question Retrieval / 410
Wei-Nan Zhang, Zhao-Yan Ming, Yu Zhang, Ting Liu, Tat-Seng Chua

Representation Learning for Aspect Category Detection in Online Reviews / 417
Xinjie Zhou, Xiaojun Wan, Jianguo Xiao

Applications

Person Identification Using Anthropometric and Gait Data from Kinect Sensor / 425
Virginia O. Andersson, Ricardo M. Araujo

R1SVM: A Randomised Nonlinear Approach to Large-Scale Anomaly Detection / 432
Sarah M. Erfani, Mahsa Baktashmotlagh, Sutharshan Rajasegarar, Shanika Karunasekera, Chris Leckie

Personalized Tag Recommendation through Nonlinear Tensor Factorization Using Gaussian Kernel / 439
Xiaomin Fang, Rong Pan, Guoxiang Cao, Xiuqiang He, Wenyuan Dai

A Multivariate Timeseries Modeling Approach to Severity of Illness Assessment
and Forecasting in ICU with Sparse, Heterogeneous Clinical Data / 446
Marzyeh Ghassemi, Marco A. F. Pimentel, Tristan Naumann, Thomas Brennan, David A. Clifton, Peter Szolovits, Mengling Feng

Probabilistic Graphical Models for Boosting Cardinal and Ordinal Peer Grading in MOOCs / 454
Fei Mi, Dit-Yan Yeung

Efficient Computation of Semivalues for Game-Theoretic Network Centrality / 461
Piotr L. Szczepański, Mateusz K. Tarkowski, Tomasz P. Michalak, Paul Harrenstein, Michael Wooldridge

Embedded Unsupervised Feature Selection / 470
Suhang Wang, Jiliang Tang, Huan Liu

Learning User-Specific Latent Influence and Susceptibility from Information Cascades / 477
Yongqing Wang, Huawei Shen, Shenghua Liu, Xueqi Cheng

Cognitive Modeling

Kickback Cuts Backprop's Red-Tape: Biologically Plausible Credit Assignment in Neural Networks / 485
David Balduzzi, Hastagiri Vanchinathan, Joachim Buhmann

An Agent-Based Model of the Emergence and Transmission of a Language System for the Expression of Logical Combinations / 492
Josefina Sierra-Santibáñez

Cognitive Systems

Moral Decision-Making by Analogy: Generalizations versus Exemplars / 501
Joseph A. Blass, Kenneth D. Forbus

AffectiveSpace 2: Enabling Affective Intuition for Concept-Level Sentiment Analysis / 508
Erik Cambria, Jie Fu, Federica Bisio, Soujanya Poria

Dialogue Understanding in a Logic of Action and Belief / 515
Alfredo Gabaldon, Pat Langley

Automated Construction of Visual-Linguistic Knowledge via Concept Learning from Cartoon Videos / 522
Jung-Woo Ha, Kyung-Min Kim, Byoung-Tak Zhang

Bayesian Affect Control Theory of Self / 529
Jesse Hoey, Tobias Schröder

Heuristic Induction of Rate-Based Process Models / 537
Pat Langley, Adam Arvay

Spontaneous Retrieval from Long-Term Memory for a Cognitive Architecture / 544
Justin Li, John Laird

Learning Plausible Inferences from Semantic Web Knowledge by Combining Analogical Generalization with Structured Logistic Regression / 551
Chen Liang, Kenneth D. Forbus

Ontology-Based Information Extraction with a Cognitive Agent / 558
Peter Lindes, Deryle W. Lonsdale, David W. Embley

Extending Analogical Generalization with Near-Misses / 565
Matthew D. McLure, Scott E. Friedman, Kenneth D. Forbus

Automatic Ellipsis Resolution: Recovering Covert Information from Text / 572
Marjorie McShane, Petr Babkin

Inference Graphs: Combining Natural Deduction and Subsumption
Inference in a Concurrent Reasoner / 579
Daniel R. Schlegel, Stuart C. Shapiro

An Entorhinal-Hippocampal Model for Simultaneous Cognitive Map Building / 586
Miaolong Yuan, Bo Tian, Vui Ann Shim, Huajin Tang, Haizhou Li

An Association Network for Computing Semantic Relatedness / 593
Keyang Zhang, Kenny Q. Zhu, Seung-won Hwang

Computational Sustainability and AI

Influence-Driven Model for Time Series Prediction from Partial Observations / 601
Saima Aman, Charalampos Chelmis, Viktor K. Prasanna

Sharing Rides with Friends: A Coalition Formation Algorithm for Ridesharing / 608
Filippo Bistaffa, Alessandro Farinelli, Sarvapali D. Ramchurn

Best-Response Planning of Thermostatically Controlled Loads under Power Constraints / 615
Frits de Nijs, Matthijs T. J. Spaan, Mathijs M. de Weerdt

FutureMatch: Combining Human Value Judgments and
Machine Learning to Match in Dynamic Environments / 622
John P. Dickerson, Tuomas Sandholm

Energy Disaggregation via Learning 'Powerlets' and Sparse Coding / 629
Ehsan Elhamifar, Shankar Sastry

Pattern Decomposition with Complex Combinatorial Constraints: Application to Materials Discovery / 636
*Stefano Ermon, Ronan Le Bras, Santosh K. Suram, John M. Gregoire,
Carla P. Gomes, Bart Selman, Robert B. van Dover*

Learning Large-Scale Dynamic Discrete Choice Models of Spatio-Temporal
Preferences with Application to Migratory Pastoralism in East Africa / 644
*Stefano Ermon, Yexiang Xue, Russell Toth, Bistra Dilkina, Richard Bernstein, Theodoros Damoulas, Patrick Clark,
Steve DeGloria, Andrew Mude, Christopher Barrett, Carla P. Gomes*

A Nonparametric Online Model for Air Quality Prediction / 651
Vitor Guizilini, Fabio Ramos

Power System Restoration with Transient Stability / 658
Hassan Hijazi, Terrence W.K. Mak, Pascal Van Hentenryck

Aggregating Electric Cars to Sustainable Virtual Power Plants:
The Value of Flexibility in Future Electricity Markets / 665
Micha Kahlen, Wolfgang Ketter

Energy Usage Behavior Modeling in Energy Disaggregation via Marked Hawkes Process / 672
Liangda Li, Hongyuan Zha

HVAC-Aware Occupancy Scheduling / 679
BoonPing Lim, Menkes van den Briel, Sylvie Thiébaux, Scott Backhaus, Russell Bent

Data Analysis and Optimization for (Citi)Bike Sharing / 687
Eoin O'Mahony, David B. Shmoys

Towards Optimal Solar Tracking: A Dynamic Programming Approach / 695
Athanasios Aris Panagopoulos, Georgios Chalkiadakis, Nicholas R. Jennings

Risk Based Optimization for Improving Emergency Medical Systems / 702
Sandhya Saisubramanian, Pradeep Varakantham, Hoong Chuin Lau

Predisaster Preparation of Transportation Networks / 709
Hermann Schichl, Meinolf Sellmann

SmartShift: Expanded Load Shifting Incentive Mechanism for Risk-Averse Consumers / 716
Bochao Shen, Balakrishnan Narayanaswamy, Ravi Sundaram

Incentivizing Users for Balancing Bike Sharing Systems / 723
Adish Singla, Marco Santoni, Gábor Bartók, Pratik Mukerji, Moritz Meenen, Andreas Krause

A Simulator of Human Emergency Mobility following Disasters: Knowledge Transfer from Big Disaster Data / 730
Xuan Song, Quanshi Zhang, Yoshihide Sekimoto, Ryosuke Shibasaki, Nicholas Jing Yuan, Xing Xie

Real-Time Predictive Optimization for Energy Management in a Hybrid Electric Vehicle / 737
Alexander Styler, Illah Nourbakhsh

VOLUME TWO

Game Playing and Interactive Entertainment

Automatic Generation of Alternative Starting Positions for Simple Traditional Board Games / 745
Umair Z. Ahmed, Krishnendu Chatterjee, Sumit Gulwani

Continuity Editing for 3D Animation / 753
Quentin Galvane, Rémi Ronfard, Christophe Lino, Marc Christie

Game Theory and Economic Paradigms

Assessing the Robustness of Cremer-McLean with Automated Mechanism Design / 763
Michael Albert, Vincent Conitzer, Giuseppe Lopomo

Online Learning and Profit Maximization from Revealed Preferences / 770
Kareem Amin, Rachel Cummings, Lili Dworkin, Michael Kearns, Aaron Roth

Approximating Optimal Social Choice under Metric Preferences / 777
Elliot Anshelevich, Onkar Bhardwaj, John Postl

Justified Representation in Approval-Based Committee Voting / 784
Haris Aziz, Markus Brill, Vincent Conitzer, Edith Elkind, Rupert Freeman, Toby Walsh

Audit Games with Multiple Defender Resources / 791
Jeremiah Blocki, Nicolas Christin, Anupam Datta, Ariel D. Procaccia, Arunesh Sinha

Learning Valuation Distributions from Partial Observations / 798
Avrim Blum, Yishay Mansour, Jamie Morgenstern

Sequence-Form Algorithm for Computing Stackelberg Equilibria in Extensive-Form Games / 805
Branislav Bosansky, Jirí Cermák

Combining Compact Representation and Incremental Generation in Large Games with Sequential Strategies / 812
Branislav Bosansky, Albert Xin Jiang, Milind Tambe, Christopher Kiekintveld

Strategic Voting and Strategic Candidacy / 819
Markus Brill, Vincent Conitzer

A Faster Core Constraint Generation Algorithm for Combinatorial Auctions / 827
Benedikt Bünz, Sven Seuken, Benjamin Lubin

Price Evolution in a Continuous Double Auction Prediction Market with a Scoring-Rule Based Market Maker / 835
Mithun Chakraborty, Sanmay Das, Justin Peabody

Computing Nash Equilibrium in Interdependent Defense Games / 842
Hau Chan, Luis E. Ortiz

Fair Information Sharing for Treasure Hunting / 851
Yiling Chen, Kobbi Nissim, Bo Waggoner

Conventional Machine Learning for Social Choice / 858
John A. Doucette, Kate Larson, Robin Cohen

The Complexity of Recognizing Incomplete Single-Crossing Elections / 865
Edith Elkind, Piotr Faliszewski, Martin Lackner, Svetlana Obraztsova

A Unifying Hierarchy of Valuations with Complements and Substitutes / 872
Uriel Feige, Michal Feldman, Nicole Immorlica, Rani Izsak, Brendan Lucier, Vasilis Syrgkanis

Do Capacity Constraints Constrain Coalitions? / 879
Michal Feldman, Ofir Geri

A Mechanism Design Approach to Measure Awareness / 886
Diodato Ferraioli, Carmine Ventre, Gabor Aranyi

Facility Location with Double-Peaked Preferences / 893
Aris Filos-Ratsikas, Minming Li, Jie Zhang, Qiang Zhang

Elicitation for Aggregation / 900
Rafael M. Frongillo, Yiling Chen, Ian A. Kash

A Complexity Approach for Core-Selecting Exchange with Multiple Indivisible Goods under Lexicographic Preferences / 907
Etsushi Fujita, Julien Lesca, Akihisa Sonoda, Taiki Todo, Makoto Yokoo

Security Games with Protection Externalities / 914
Jiarui Gan, Bo An, Yevgeniy Vorobeychik

Strategy-Proof and Efficient Kidney Exchange Using a Credit Mechanism / 921
Chen Hajaj, John P. Dickerson, Avinatan Hassidim, Tuomas Sandholm, David Sarne

Hedonic Coalition Formation in Networks / 929
Martin Hoefer, Daniel Vaz, Lisa Wagner

Matching with Dynamic Ordinal Preferences / 936
Hadi Hosseini, Kate Larson, Robin Cohen

On a Competitive Secretary Problem / 944
Anna Karlin, Eric Lei

Controlled School Choice with Soft Bounds and Overlapping Types / 951
Ryoji Kurata, Masahiro Goto, Atsushi Iwasaki, Makoto Yokoo

Optimal Personalized Filtering against Spear-Phishing Attacks / 958
Aron Laszka, Yevgeniy Vorobeychik, Xenofon Koutsoukos

Stable Invitations / 965
Hooyeon Lee, Yoav Shoham

The Pricing War Continues: On Competitive Multi-Item Pricing / 972
Omer Lev, Joel Oren, Craig Boutilier, Jeffrey S. Rosenschein

Cooperative Game Solution Concepts that Maximize Stability under Noise / 979
Yuqian Li, Vincent Conitzer

Congestion Games with Distance-Based Strict Uncertainty / 986
Reshef Meir, David Parkes

On the Convergence of Iterative Voting: How Restrictive Should Restricted Dynamics Be? / 993
Svetlana Obraztsova, Evangelos Markakis, Maria Polukarov, Zinovi Rabinovich, Nicholas R. Jennings

Voting Rules As Error-Correcting Codes / 1000
Ariel D. Procaccia, Nisarg Shah, Yair Zick

Analysis of Equilibria in Iterative Voting Schemes / 1007
Zinovi Rabinovich, Svetlana Obraztsova, Omer Lev, Evangelos Markakis, Jeffrey S. Rosenschein

Incentives for Subjective Evaluations with Private Beliefs / 1014
Goran Radanovic, Boi Faltings

Envy-Free Cake-Cutting in Two Dimensions / 1021
Erel Segal-Halevi, Avinatan Hassidim, Yonatan Aumann

Truthful Mechanisms without Money for Non-Utilitarian Heterogeneous Facility Location / 1029
Paolo Serafino, Carmine Ventre

A Graphical Representation for Games in Partition Function Form / 1036
Oskar Skibski, Tomasz P. Michalak, Yuko Sakurai, Michael Wooldridge, Makoto Yokoo

A Stackelberg Game Approach for Incentivizing Participation in
Online Educational Forums with Heterogeneous Student Population / 1043
Rohith D. Vallam, Priyanka Bhatt, Debmalya Mandal, Y. Narahari

Mechanism Design for Team Formation / 1050
Mason Wright, Yevgeniy Vorobeychik

Exploring Information Asymmetry in Two-Stage Security Games / 1057
Haifeng Xu, Zinovi Rabinovich, Shaddin Dughmi, Milind Tambe

Balanced Trade Reduction for Dual-Role Exchange Markets / 1064
Dengji Zhao, Sarvapali D. Ramchurn, Enrico H. Gerding, Nicholas R. Jennings

Optimal Machine Strategies to Commit to in Two-Person Repeated Games / 1071
Song Zuo, Pingzhong Tang

Heuristic Search and Optimization

Optimal Column Subset Selection by A-Star Search / 1079
Hiromasa Arai, Crystal Maung, Haim Schweitzer

Limitations of Front-to-End Bidirectional Heuristic Search / 1086
Joseph K. Barker, Richard E. Korf

Incremental Weight Elicitation for Multiobjective State Space Search / 1093
Nawal Benabbou, Patrice Perny

Complexity Results for Compressing Optimal Paths / 1100
Adi Botea, Ben Strasser, Daniel Harabor

Two Weighting Local Search for Minimum Vertex Cover / 1107
Shaowei Cai, Jinkun Lin, Kaile Su

Efficient Benchmarking of Hyperparameter Optimizers via Surrogates / 1114
Katharina Eggensperger, Frank Hutter, Holger H. Hoos, Kevin Leyton-Brown

Convergent Plans for Large-Scale Evacuations / 1121
Caroline Even, Victor Pillac, Pascal Van Hentenryck

Initializing Bayesian Hyperparameter Optimization via Meta-Learning / 1128
Matthias Feurer, Jost Tobias Springenberg, Frank Hutter

Stochastic Local Search for Satisfiability Modulo Theories / 1136
Andreas Fröhlich, Armin Biere, Christoph M. Wintersteiger, Youssef Hamadi

Lagrangian Decomposition Algorithm for Allocating Marketing Channels / 1144
Daisuke Hatano, Takuro Fukunaga, Takanori Maehara, Ken-ichi Kawarabayashi

Recursive Best-First Search with Bounded Overhead / 1151
Matthew Hatem, Scott Kiesel, Wheeler Ruml

Reusing Previously Found A* Paths for Fast Goal-Directed Navigation in Dynamic Terrain / 1158
Carlos Hernández, Roberto Asín, Jorge A. Baier

Pruning Game Tree by Rollouts / 1165
Bojun Huang

Solving Distributed Constraint Optimization Problems Using Logic Programming / 1174
Tiep Le, Tran Cao Son, Enrico Pontelli, William Yeoh

Value-Directed Compression of Large-Scale Assignment Problems / 1182
Tyler Lu, Craig Boutilier

On Unconstrained Quasi-Submodular Function Optimization / 1191
Jincheng Mei, Kang Zhao, Bao-Liang Lu

Improved Local Search for Binary Matrix Factorization / 1198
Seyed Hamid Mirisaee, Eric Gaussier, Alexandre Termier

A Theoretical Analysis of the Optimization by Gaussian Continuation / 1205
Hossein Mobahi, John W. Fisher III

Solving Hard Stable Matching Problems via Local Search and Cooperative Parallelization / 1212
Danny Munera, Daniel Diaz, Salvador Abreu, Francesca Rossi, Vijay Saraswat, Philippe Codognet

BDD-Constrained Search: A Unified Approach to Constrained Shortest Path Problems / 1219
Masaaki Nishino, Norihito Yasuda, Shin-ichi Minato, Masaaki Nagata

Exploiting Variable Associations to Configure Efficient Local Search in Large-Scale Set Partitioning Problems / 1226
Shunji Umetani

Resilient Upgrade of Electrical Distribution Grids / 1233
Emre Yamangil, Russell Bent, Scott Backhaus

TDS+: Improving Temperature Discovery Search / 1241
Yeqin Zhang, Martin Müller

Massively Parallel A* Search on a GPU / 1248
Yichao Zhou, Jianyang Zeng

Human Computation and Crowd Sourcing

Novel Mechanisms for Online Crowdsourcing with Unreliable, Strategic Agents / 1256
Praphul Chandra, Yadati Narahari, Debmalya Mandal, Prasenjit Dey

Acquiring Speech Transcriptions Using Mismatched Crowdsourcing / 1263
Preethi Jyothi, Mark Hasegawa-Johnson

Incentive Networks / 1270
Yuezhou Lv, Thomas Moscibroda

Collaboration in Social Problem-Solving: When Diversity Trumps Network Efficiency / 1277
Diego V. Noble, Marcelo O. R. Prates, Daniel S. Bossle, Luís C. Lamb

CrowdWON: A Modelling Language for Crowd Processes Based on Workflow Nets / 1284
David Sánchez-Charles, Victor Muntés-Mulero, Marc Solé, Jordi Nin

On the Impossibility of Convex Inference in Human Computation / 1291
Nihar B. Shah, Dengyong Zhou

Crowdsourcing Complex Workflows under Budget Constraints / 1298
Long Tran-Thanh, Trung Dong Huynh, Avi Rosenfeld, Sarvapali D. Ramchurn, Nicholas R. Jennings

Efficient Task Sub-Delegation for Crowdsourcing / 1305
Han Yu, Chunyan Miao, Zhiqi Shen, Cyril Leung, Yiqiang Chen, Qiang Yang

Humans and AI

When Suboptimal Rules / 1313
Avshalom Elmalech, David Sarne, Avi Rosenfeld, Eden Shalom Erez

Providing Arguments in Discussions Based on the Prediction of Human Argumentative Behavior / 1320
Ariel Rosenfeld, Sarit Kraus

Predicting Emotion Perception across Domains: A Study of Singing and Speaking / 1328
Biqiao Zhang, Emily Mower Provost, Robert Swedberg, Georg Essl

Integrated Systems

Learning to Manipulate Unknown Objects in Clutter by Reinforcement / 1336
Abdeslam Boularias, J. Andrew Bagnell, Anthony Stentz

Bayesian Active Learning-Based Robot Tutor for Children's Word-Reading Skills / 1343
Goren Gordon, Cynthia Breazeal

RANSAC versus CS-RANSAC / 1350
Geun-Sik Jo, Kee-Sung Lee, Devy Chandra, Chol-Hee Jang, Myung-Hyun Ga

Game-Theoretic Approach for Non-Cooperative Planning / 1357
Jaume Jordán, Eva Onaindia

Pattern-Based Variant-Best-Neighbors Respiratory Motion Prediction Using Orthogonal Polynomials Approximation / 1364
Kin Ming Kam, Shouyi Wang, Stephen R. Bowen, Wanpracha Chaovalitwongse

Toward Mobile Robots Reasoning Like Humans / 1371
Jean Oh, Arne Suppé, Felix Duvallet, Abdeslam Boularias, Luis Navarro-Serment, Martial Hebert, Anthony Stentz, Jerry Vinokurov, Oscar Romero, Christian Lebiere, Robert Dean

Integration and Evaluation of a Matrix Factorization Sequencer in Large Commercial ITS / 1380
Carlotta Schatten, Ruth Janning, Lars Schmidt-Thieme

Going Beyond Literal Command-Based Instructions: Extending Robotic Natural Language Interaction Capabilities / 1387
Tom Williams, Gordon Briggs, Bradley Oosterveld, Matthias Scheutz

CORPP: Commonsense Reasoning and Probabilistic Planning, as Applied to Dialog with a Mobile Robot / 1394
Shiqi Zhang, Peter Stone

Tackling Mental Health by Integrating Unobtrusive Multimodal Sensing / 1401
Dawei Zhou, Jiebo Luo, Vincent Silenzio, Yun Zhou, Jile Hu, Glenn Currier, Henry Kautz

Knowledge Representation and Reasoning

Ontology Module Extraction via Datalog Reasoning / 1410
Ana Armas Romero, Mark Kaminski, Bernardo Cuenca Grau, Ian Horrocks

Tractable Interval Temporal Propositional and Description Logics / 1417
Alessandro Artale, Roman Kontchakov, Vladislav Ryzhikov, Michael Zakharyaschev

Action Language *BC*+: Preliminary Report / 1424
Joseph Babb, Joohyung Lee

LARS: A Logic-Based Framework for Analyzing Reasoning over Streams / 1431
Harald Beck, Minh Dao-Tran, Thomas Eiter, Michael Fink

Partial Meet Revision and Contraction in Logic Programs / 1439
Sebastian Binnewies, Zhiqiang Zhuang, Kewen Wang

Pearl's Causality in a Logical Setting / 1446
Alexander Bochman, Vladimir Lifschitz

Grounded Fixpoints / 1453
Bart Bogaerts, Joost Vennekens, Marc Denecker

Solving and Explaining Analogy Questions Using Semantic Networks / 1460
Adrian Boteanu, Sonia Chernova

asprin: Customizing Answer Set Preferences without a Headache / 1467
Gerhard Brewka, James Delgrande, Javier Romero, Torsten Schaub

Exploiting Parallelism for Hard Problems in Abstract Argumentation / 1475
Federico Cerutti, Ilias Tachmazidis, Mauro Vallati, Sotirios Batsakis, Massimiliano Giacomin, Grigoris Antoniou

A Syntax-Independent Approach to Forgetting in Disjunctive Logic Programs / 1482
James P. Delgrande, Kewen Wang

Towards Tractable and Practical ABox Abduction over Inconsistent Description Logic Ontologies / 1489
Jianfeng Du, Kewen Wang, Yi-Dong Shen

On Computing Explanations in Argumentation / 1496
Xiuyi Fan, Francesca Toni

Parallelized Hitting Set Computation for Model-Based Diagnosis / 1503
Dietmar Jannach, Thomas Schmitz, Kostyantyn Shchekotykhin

Splitting a Logic Program Revisited / 1511
Jianmin Ji, Hai Wan, Ziwei Huo, Zhenfeng Yuan

On Elementary Loops and Proper Loops for Disjunctive Logic Programs / 1518
Jianmin Ji, Hai Wan, Peng Xiao

XPath for DL Ontologies / 1525
Egor V. Kostylev, Juan L. Reutter, Domagoj Vrgoc

An Abstract View on Modularity in Knowledge Representation / 1532
Yuliya Lierler, Miroslaw Truszczynski

Learning Partial Lexicographic Preference Trees over Combinatorial Domains / 1539
Xudong Liu, Mirek Truszczynski

From Classical to Consistent Query Answering under Existential Rules / 1546
Thomas Lukasiewicz, Maria Vanina Martinez, Andreas Pieris, Gerardo I. Simari

Belief Revision with General Epistemic States / 1553
Hua Meng, Hui Kou, Sanjiang Li

Incremental Update of Datalog Materialisation: The Backward/Forward Algorithm / 1560
Boris Motik, Yavor Nenov, Robert Piro, Ian Horrocks

Logic Programming in Assumption-Based Argumentation Revisited —
Semantics and Graphical Representation / 1569
Claudia Schulz, Francesca Toni

Minimizing User Involvement for Accurate Ontology Matching Problems / 1576
Anika Schumann, Freddy Lécué

Projection in the Epistemic Situation Calculus with Belief Conditionals / 1583
Christoph Schwering, Gerhard Lakemeyer

Belief Revision Games / 1590
Nicolas Schwind, Katsumi Inoue, Gauvain Bourgne, Sébastien Konieczny, Pierre Marquis

Interactive Query-Based Debugging of ASP Programs / 1597
Kostyantyn Shchekotykhin

Exploring the $KD45_n$ Property of a Kripke Model after the Execution of an Action Sequence / 1604
Tran Cao Son, Enrico Pontelli, Chitta Baral, Gregory Gelfond

Answering Conjunctive Queries over *EL* Knowledge Bases with Transitive and Reflexive Roles / 1611
Giorgio Stefanoni, Boris Motik

How Many Diagnoses Do We Need? / 1618
Roni Stern, Meir Kalech, Shelly Rogov, Alexander Feldman

The Relative Expressiveness of Abstract Argumentation and Logic Programming / 1625
Hannes Strass

A Comparison of Qualitative and Metric Spatial Relation Models for Scene Understanding / 1632
Akshaya Thippur, Chris Burbridge, Lars Kunze, Marina Alberti, John Folkesson, Patric Jensfelt, Nick Hawes

On the Role of Canonicity in Knowledge Compilation / 1641
Guy Van den Broeck, Adnan Darwiche

Knowledge Forgetting in Circumscription: A Preliminary Report / 1649
Yisong Wang, Kewen Wang, Zhe Wang, Zhiqiang Zhuang

Instance-Driven Ontology Evolution in DL-Lite / 1656
Zhe Wang, Kewen Wang, Zhiqiang Zhuang, Guilin Qi

Structured Embedding via Pairwise Relations and Long-Range Interactions in Knowledge Base / 1663
Fei Wu, Jun Song, Yi Yang, Xi Li, Zhongfei Zhang, Yueting Zhuang

A Logic for Reasoning about Game Strategies / 1671
Dongmo Zhang, Michael Thielscher

Existential Rule Languages with Finite Chase: Complexity and Expressiveness / 1678
Heng Zhang, Yan Zhang, Jia-Huai You

VOLUME THREE

Machine Learning Applications

Variational Inference for Nonparametric Bayesian Quantile Regression / 1686
Sachinthaka Abeywardana, Fabio Ramos

Sample-Targeted Clinical Trial Adaptation / 1693
Ognjen Arandjelovic

A Sparse Combined Regression-Classification Formulation for Learning a
Physiological Alternative to Clinical Post-Traumatic Stress Disorder Scores / 1700
Sarah M. Brown, Andrea Webb, Rami S. Mangoubi, Jennifer G. Dy

Marginalized Denoising for Link Prediction and Multi-Label Learning / 1707
Zheng Chen, Minmin Chen, Kilian Q. Weinberger, Weixiong Zhang

Structured Sparsity with Group-Graph Regularization / 1714
Xin-Yu Dai, Jian-Bing Zhang, Shu-Jian Huang, Jia-Jun Chen, Zhi-Hua Zhou

Content-Aware Point of Interest Recommendation on Location-Based Social Networks / 1721
Huiji Gao, Jiliang Tang, Xia Hu, Huan Liu

Constructing Models of User and Task Characteristics from Eye Gaze Data for User-Adaptive Information Highlighting / 1728
Matthew Gingerich, Cristina Conati

Automatic Assessment of OCR Quality in Historical Documents / 1735
Anshul Gupta, Ricardo Gutierrez-Osuna, Matthew Christy, Boris Capitanu, Loretta Auvil, Liz Grumbach, Richard Furuta, Laura Mandell

PD Disease State Assessment in Naturalistic Environments Using Deep Learning / 1742
Nils Yannick Hammerla, James M. Fisher, Peter Andras, Lynn Rochester, Richard Walker, Thomas Plötz

Identifying At-Risk Students in Massive Open Online Courses / 1749
Jiazhen He, James Bailey, Benjamin I. P. Rubinstein, Rui Zhang

Exploiting Determinism to Scale Relational Inference / 1756
Mohamed-Hamza Ibrahim, Christopher Pal, Gilles Pesant

Scalable and Interpretable Data Representation for High-Dimensional, Complex Data / 1763
Been Kim, Kayur Patel, Afshin Rostamizadeh, Julie Shah

Using Supervised Learning to Uncover Deep Musical Structure / 1770
Phillip B. Kirlin, David D. Jensen

Nonstationary Gaussian Process Regression for Evaluating Clinical Laboratory Test Sampling Strategies / 1777
Thomas A. Lasko

Tensor-Based Learning for Predicting Stock Movements / 1784
Qing Li, LiLing Jiang, Ping Li, Hsinchun Chen

Sub-Merge: Diving Down to the Attribute-Value Level in Statistical Schema Matching / 1791
Zhe Lim, Benjamin I. P. Rubinstein

A Regularized Linear Dynamical System Framework for Multivariate Time Series Analysis / 1798
Zitao Liu, Milos Hauskrecht

Generalized Singular Value Thresholding / 1805
Canyi Lu, Changbo Zhu, Chunyan Xu, Shuicheng Yan, Zhouchen Lin

Lazier Than Lazy Greedy / 1812
Baharan Mirzasoleiman, Ashwinkumar Badanidiyuru, Amin Karbasi, Jan Vondrák, Andreas Krause

Inertial Hidden Markov Models: Modeling Change in Multivariate Time Series / 1819
George D. Montañez, Saeed Amizadeh, Nikolay Laptev

Algorithm Selection via Ranking / 1826
Richard J. Oentaryo, Stephanus Daniel Handoko, Hoong Chuin Lau

Propagating Ranking Functions on a Graph: Algorithms and Applications / 1833
Buyue Qian, Xiang Wang, Ian Davidson

On Vectorization of Deep Convolutional Neural Networks for Vision Tasks / 1840
Jimmy SJ. Ren, Li Xu

Learning Hybrid Models with Guarded Transitions / 1847
Pedro Santana, Spencer Lane, Eric Timmons, Brian Williams, Carlos Forster

Transaction Costs-Aware Portfolio Optimization via Fast Löwner-John Ellipsoid Approximation / 1854
Weiwei Shen, Jun Wang

Coupled Interdependent Attribute Analysis on Mixed Data / 1861
Can Wang, Chi-Hung Chi, Wei Zhou, Raymond Wong

Exploring Social Context for Topic Identification in Short and Noisy Texts / 1868
Xin Wang, Ying Wang, Wanli Zuo, Guoyong Cai

Modeling Status Theory in Trust Prediction / 1875
Ying Wang, Xin Wang, Jiliang Tang, Wanli Zuo, Guoyong Cai

Swiss-System Based Cascade Ranking for Gait-Based Person Re-identification / 1882
Lan Wei, Yonghong Tian, Yaowei Wang, Tiejun Huang

An SVD and Derivative Kernel Approach to Learning from Geometric Data / 1889
Eric Wong, J. Zico Kolter

Mining User Interests from Personal Photos / 1896
Pengtao Xie, Yulong Pei, Yuan Xie, Eric Xing

Integrating Image Clustering and Codebook Learning / 1903
Pengtao Xie, Eric Xing

Stable Feature Selection from Brain sMRI / 1910
Bo Xin, Lingjing Hu, Yizhou Wang, Wen Gao

Forecasting Collector Road Speeds under High Percentage of Missing Data / 1917
Xin Xin, Chunwei Lu, Yashen Wang, Heyan Huang

Large-Margin Multi-Label Causal Feature Learning / 1924
Chang Xu, Dacheng Tao, Chao Xu

Exploiting Task-Feature Co-Clusters in Multi-Task Learning / 1931
Linli Xu, Aiqing Huang, Jianhui Chen, Enhong Chen

Temporally Adaptive Restricted Boltzmann Machine for Background Modeling / 1938
Linli Xu, Yitan Li, Yubo Wang, Enhong Chen

On Machine Learning towards Predictive Sales Pipeline Analytics / 1945
Junchi Yan, Chao Zhang, Hongyuan Zha, Min Gong, Changhua Sun, Jin Huang, Stephen Chu, Xiaokang Yang

Bayesian Approach to Modeling and Detecting Communities in Signed Network / 1952
Bo Yang, Xuehua Zhao, Xueyan Liu

Colorization by Patch-Based Local Low-Rank Matrix Completion / 1959
Quanming Yao, James T. Kwok

Sparse Bayesian Multiview Learning for Simultaneous
Association Discovery and Diagnosis of Alzheimer's Disease / 1966
Shandian Zhe, Zenglin Xu, Yuan Qi, Peng Yu

A Closed Form Solution to Multi-View Low-Rank Regression / 1973
Shuai Zheng, Xiao Cai, Chris Ding, Feiping Nie, Heng Huang

A Nonconvex Relaxation Approach for Rank Minimization Problems / 1980
Xiaowei Zhong, Linli Xu, Yitan Li, Zhiyuan Liu, Enhong Chen

Multiagent Systems

An Empirical Study on the Practical Impact of Prior Beliefs over Policy Types / 1988
Stefano V. Albrecht, Jacob W. Crandall, Subramanian Ramamoorthy

Scalable Planning and Learning for Multiagent POMDPs / 1995
Christopher Amato, Frans A. Oliehoek

Multi-Agent Pathfinding as a Combinatorial Auction / 2003
Ofra Amir, Guni Sharon, Roni Stern

Cooperating with Unknown Teammates in Complex Domains:
A Robot Soccer Case Study of Ad Hoc Teamwork / 2010
Samuel Barrett, Peter Stone

Cognitive Social Learners: An Architecture for Modeling Normative Behavior / 2017
Rahmatollah Beheshti, Awrad Mohammed Ali, Gita Sukthankar

Multi-Agent Path Finding on Strongly Biconnected Graphs / 2024
Adi Botea, Pavel Surynek

Verification of Relational Multiagent Systems with Data Types / 2031
Diego Calvanese, Marco Montali, Giorgio Delzanno

Verifying and Synthesising Multi-Agent Systems against One-Goal Strategy Logic Specifications / 2038
Petr Čermák, Alessio Lomuscio, Aniello Murano

Elections with Few Voters: Candidate Control Can Be Easy / 2045
Jiehua Chen, Piotr Faliszewski, Rolf Niedermeier, Nimrod Talmon

Cupid: Commitments in Relational Algebra / 2052
Amit K. Chopra, Munindar P. Singh

Automated Analysis of Commitment Protocols Using Probabilistic Model Checking / 2060
Akin Günay, Song Songzheng, Yang Liu, Jie Zhang

Fast Convention Formation in Dynamic Networks Using Topological Knowledge / 2067
Mohammad Rashedul Hasan, Anita Raja, Ana Bazzan

Distributed Multiplicative Weights Methods for DCOP / 2074
Daisuke Hatano, Yuichi Yoshida

A Counter Abstraction Technique for the Verification of Robot Swarms / 2081
Panagiotis Kouvaros, Alessio Lomuscio

Generalization Analysis for Game-Theoretic Machine Learning / 2089
Haifang Li, Fei Tian, Wei Chen, Tao Qin, Zhi-Ming Ma, Tie-Yan Liu

SCRAM: Scalable Collision-Avoiding Role Assignment with
Minimal-Makespan for Formational Positioning / 2096
Patrick MacAlpine, Eric Price, Peter Stone

Plurality Voting under Uncertainty / 2103
Reshef Meir

Multi-Robot Auctions for Allocation of Tasks with Temporal Constraints / 2110
Ernesto Nunes, Maria Gini

Distributing Coalition Value Calculations to Coalition Members / 2117
Luke Riley, Katie Atkinson, Paul E. Dunne, Terry R. Payne

Fully Proportional Representation with Approval Ballots:
Approximating the MaxCover Problem with Bounded Frequencies in FPT Time / 2124
Piotr Skowron, Piotr Faliszewski

Finding a Collective Set of Items: From Proportional Multirepresentation to Group Recommendation / 2131
Piotr Skowron, Piotr Faliszewski, Jérôme Lang

Solving Games with Functional Regret Estimation / 2138
Kevin Waugh, Dustin Morrill, J. Andrew Bagnell, Michael Bowling

NLP and Knowledge Representation

Learning Word Representations from Relational Graphs / 2146
Danushka Bollegala, Takanori Maehara, Yuichi Yoshida, Ken-ichi Kawarabayashi

Ranking with Recursive Neural Networks and Its Application to Multi-Document Summarization / 2153
Ziqiang Cao, Furu Wei, Li Dong, Sujian Li, Ming Zhou

Refer-to-as Relations as Semantic Knowledge / 2160
Song Feng, Sujith Ravi, Ravi Kumar, Polina Kuznetsova, Wei Liu, Alexander C. Berg, Tamara L. Berg, Yejin Choi

Surveyor: A System for Generating Coherent Survey Articles for Scientific Topics / 2167
Rahul Jha, Reed Coke, Dragomir Radev

Automatically Creating a Large Number of New Bilingual Dictionaries / 2174
Khang Nhut Lam, Feras Al Tarouti, Jugal Kalita

Learning Entity and Relation Embeddings for Knowledge Graph Completion / 2181
Yankai Lin, Zhiyuan Liu, Maosong Sun, Yang Liu, Xuan Zhu

Sense-Aware Semantic Analysis: A Multi-Prototype Word Representation Model Using Wikipedia / 2188
Zhaohui Wu, C. Lee Giles

Phrase Type Sensitive Tensor Indexing Model for Semantic Composition / 2195
Yu Zhao, Zhiyuan Liu, Maosong Sun

NLP and Machine Learning

Predicting Peer-to-Peer Loan Rates Using Bayesian Non-Linear Regression / 2203
Zsolt Bitvai, Trevor Cohn

A Novel Neural Topic Model and Its Supervised Extension / 2210
Ziqiang Cao, Sujian Li, Yang Liu, Wenjie Li, Heng Ji

Unsupervised Word Sense Disambiguation Using Markov Random Field and Dependency Parser / 2217
Devendra Singh Chaplot, Pushpak Bhattacharyya, Ashwin Paranjape

Dataless Text Classification with Descriptive LDA / 2224
Xingyuan Chen, Yunqing Xia, Peng Jin, John Carroll

Topic Segmentation with an Ordering-Based Topic Model / 2232
Lan Du, John K. Pate, Mark Johnson

A Stratified Strategy for Efficient Kernel-Based Learning / 2239
Simone Filice, Danilo Croce, Roberto Basili

Weakly-Supervised Grammar-Informed Bayesian CCG Parser Learning / 2246
Dan Garrette, Chris Dyer, Jason Baldridge, Noah A. Smith

Unsupervised Phrasal Near-Synonym Generation from Text Corpora / 2253
Dishan Gupta, Jaime Carbonell, Anatole Gershman, Steve Klein, David Miller

Local Context Sparse Coding / 2260
Seungyeon Kim, Joonseok Lee, Guy Lebanon, Haesun Park

Recurrent Convolutional Neural Networks for Text Classification / 2267
Siwei Lai, Liheng Xu, Kang Liu, Jun Zhao

Joint Anaphoricity Detection and Coreference Resolution with Constrained Latent Structures / 2274
Emmanuel Lassalle, Pascal Denis

Fast and Accurate Prediction of Sentence Specificity / 2281
Junyi Jessy Li, Ani Nenkova

Learning to Mediate Perceptual Differences in Situated Human-Robot Dialogue / 2288
Changsong Liu, Joyce Y. Chai

Contrastive Unsupervised Word Alignment with Non-Local Features / 2295
Yang Liu, Maosong Sun

Never-Ending Learning / 2302
Tom Mitchell, William Cohen, Estevam Hruschka, Partha Talukdar, Justin Betteridge, Andrew Carlson, Bhavana Dalvi, Matt Gardner, Bryan Kisiel, Jayant Krishnamurthy, Ni Lao, Kathryn Mazaitis, Tahir Mohamed, Ndapa Nakashole, Emmanouil Antonios Platanios, Alan Ritter, Mehdi Samadi, Burr Settles, Richard Wang, Derry Wijaya, Abhinav Gupta, Xinlei Chen, Abulhair Saparov, Malcolm Greaves, Joel Welling

The Utility of Text: The Case of Amicus Briefs and the Supreme Court / 2311
Yanchuan Sim, Bryan R. Routledge, Noah A. Smith

A Family of Latent Variable Convex Relaxations for IBM Model 2 / 2318
Andrei Simion, Michael Collins, Clifford Stein

Online Bayesian Models for Personal Analytics in Social Media / 2325
Svitlana Volkova, Benjamin Van Durme

Microblog Sentiment Classification with Contextual Knowledge Regularization / 2332
Fangzhao Wu, Yangqiu Song, Yongfeng Huang

Learning Greedy Policies for the Easy-First Framework / 2339
Jun Xie, Chao Ma, Janardhan Rao Doppa, Prashanth Mannem, Xiaoli Fern, Thomas G. Dietterich, Prasad Tadepalli

Jointly Modeling Deep Video and Compositional Text to Bridge Vision and Language in a Unified Framework / 2346
Ran Xu, Caiming Xiong, Wei Chen, Jason J. Corso

Ordering-Sensitive and Semantic-Aware Topic Modeling / 2353
Min Yang, Tianyi Cui, Wenting Tu

NLP and Text Mining

Target-Dependent Churn Classification in Microblogs / 2361
Hadi Amiri, Hal Daume III

Chinese Common Noun Phrase Resolution:
An Unsupervised Probabilistic Model Rivaling Supervised Resolvers / 2368
Chen Chen, Vincent Ng

English Light Verb Construction Identification Using Lexical Knowledge / 2375
Wei-Te Chen, Claire Bonial, Martha Palmer

Gazetteer-Independent Toponym Resolution Using Geographic Word Profiles / 2382
Grant DeLozier, Jason Baldridge, Loretta London

Mining User Consumption Intention from Social Media
Using Domain Adaptive Convolutional Neural Network / 2389
Xiao Ding, Ting Liu, Junwen Duan, Jian-Yun Nie

Generating Event Causality Hypotheses through Semantic Relations / 2396
Chikara Hashimoto, Kentaro Torisawa, Julien Kloetzer, Jong-Hoon Oh

A Neural Probabilistic Model for Context Based Citation Recommendation / 2404
Wenyi Huang, Zhaohui Wu, Chen Liang, Prasenjit Mitra, C. Lee Giles

Extracting Verb Expressions Implying Negative Opinions / 2411
Huayi Li, Arjun Mukherjee, Jianfeng Si, Bing Liu

Topical Word Embeddings / 2418
Yang Liu, Zhiyuan Liu, Tat-Seng Chua, Maosong Sun

Towards Knowledge-Driven Annotation / 2425
Yassine Mrabet, Claire Gardent, Muriel Foulonneau, Elena Simperl, Eric Ras

Semantic Lexicon Induction from Twitter with Pattern Relatedness and Flexible Term Length / 2432
Ashequl Qadir, Pablo N. Mendes, Daniel Gruhl, Neal Lewis

Word Segmentation for Chinese Novels / 2440
Likun Qiu, Yue Zhang

Using Frame Semantics for Knowledge Extraction from Twitter / 2447
Anders Søgaard, Barbara Plank, Hector Martinez Alonso

Learning to Recommend Quotes for Writing / 2453
Jiwei Tan, Xiaojun Wan, Jianguo Xiao

Extracting Adverse Drug Reactions from Social Media / 2460
Andrew Yates, Nazli Goharian, Ophir Frieder

An Unsupervised Framework of Exploring Events on Twitter: Filtering, Extraction and Categorization / 2468
Deyu Zhou, Liangyu Chen, Yulan He

VOLUME FOUR

Novel Machine Learning Algorithms

A Probabilistic Covariate Shift Assumption for Domain Adaptation / 2476
Tameem Adel, Alexander Wong

Efficient Active Learning of Halfspaces via Query Synthesis / 2483
Ibrahim Alabdulmohsin, Xin Gao, Xiangliang Zhang

Budgeted Prediction with Expert Advice / 2490
Kareem Amin, Satyen Kale, Gerald Tesauro, Deepak Turaga

Model-Based Reinforcement Learning in Continuous Environments Using Real-Time Constrained Optimization / 2497
Olov Andersson, Fredrik Heintz, Patrick Doherty

Unsupervised Cross-Domain Transfer in Policy Gradient Reinforcement Learning via Manifold Alignment / 2504
Haitham Bou Ammar, Eric Eaton, Paul Ruvolo, Matthew E. Taylor

Aligning Mixed Manifolds / 2511
Thomas Boucher, Clifton J. Carey, Sridhar Mahadevan, Melinda Darby Dyar

Deep Modeling Complex Couplings within Financial Markets / 2518
Wei Cao, Liang Hu, Longbing Cao

Structural Learning with Amortized Inference / 2525
Kai-Wei Chang, Shyam Upadhyay, Gourab Kundu, Dan Roth

A Convex Formulation for Spectral Shrunk Clustering / 2532
Xiaojun Chang, Feiping Nie, Zhigang Ma, Yi Yang, Xiaofang Zhou

Learning Relational Kalman Filtering / 2539
Jaesik Choi, Eyal Amir, Tianfang Xu, Albert J. Valocchi

Policy Tree: Adaptive Representation for Policy Gradient / 2547
Ujjwal Das Gupta, Erik Talvitie, Michael Bowling

Collaborative Filtering with Localised Ranking / 2554
Charanpal Dhanjal, Stéphan Clémençon, Romaric Gaudel

Random Gradient Descent Tree: A Combinatorial Approach for SVM with Outliers / 2561
Hu Ding, Jinhui Xu

An Adaptive Gradient Method for Online AUC Maximization / 2568
Yi Ding, Peilin Zhao, Steven C.H. Hoi, Yew Soon Ong

Graph-Sparse LDA: A Topic Model with Structured Sparsity / 2575
Finale Doshi-Velez, Byron C. Wallace, Ryan Adams

Bayesian Maximum Margin Principal Component Analysis / 2582
Changying Du, Shandian Zhe, Fuzhen Zhuang, Yuan Qi, Qing He, Zhongzhi Shi

Modelling Class Noise with Symmetric and Asymmetric Distributions / 2589
Jun Du, Zhihua Cai

Optimizing Bag Features for Multiple-Instance Retrieval / 2596
Zhouyu Fu, Feifei Pan, Cheng Deng, Wei Liu

Learning Sparse Representations from Datasets with Uncertain Group Structures: Model, Algorithm and Applications / 2603
Longwen Gao, Shuigeng Zhou

Spectral Clustering Using Multilinear SVD: Analysis, Approximations and Applications / 2610
Debarghya Ghoshdastidar, Ambedkar Dukkipati

Pathway Graphical Lasso / 2617
Maxim Grechkin, Maryam Fazel, Daniela Witten, Su-In Lee

Concurrent PAC RL / 2624
Zhaohan Daniel Guo, Emma Brunskill

Discriminative Feature Grouping / 2631
Lei Han, Yu Zhang

Learning Multi-Level Task Groups in Multi-Task Learning / 2638
Lei Han, Yu Zhang

Localized Centering: Reducing Hubness in Large-Sample Data / 2645
Kazuo Hara, Ikumi Suzuki, Masashi Shimbo, Kei Kobayashi, Kenji Fukumizu, Milos Radovanovic

Expressing Arbitrary Reward Functions as Potential-Based Advice / 2652
Anna Harutyunyan, Sam Devlin, Peter Vrancx, Ann Nowé

Active Learning by Learning / 2659
Wei-Ning Hsu, Hsuan-Tien Li

Kernelized Online Imbalanced Learning with Fixed Budgets / 2666
Junjie Hu, Haiqin Yang, Irwin King, Michael R. Lyu, Anthony Man-Cho So

Approximate MaxEnt Inverse Optimal Control and Its Application for Mental Simulation of Human Interactions / 2673
De-An Huang, Amir-massoud Farahmand, Kris M. Kitani, J. Andrew Bagnell

Maximin Separation Probability Clustering / 2680
Gao Huang, Jianwen Zhang, Shiji Song, Zheng Chen

The Dynamic Chinese Restaurant Process via Birth and Death Processes / 2687
Rui Huang, Fengyuan Zhu, Pheng-Ann Heng

Self-Paced Curriculum Learning / 2694
Lu Jiang, Deyu Meng, Qian Zhao, Shiguang Shan, Alexander G. Hauptmann

Outlier-Robust Convex Segmentation / 2701
Itamar Katz, Koby Crammer

Fast Gradient Descent for Drifting Least Squares Regression, with Application to Bandits / 2708
Nathan Korda, Prashanth L.A., Rémi Munos

Spectral Learning of Predictive State Representations with Insufficient Statistics / 2715
Alex Kulesza, Nan Jiang, Satinder Singh

A Generalized Reduced Linear Program for Markov Decision Processes / 2722
Chandrashekar Lakshminarayanan, Shalabh Bhatnagar

Don't Fall for Tuning Parameters: Tuning-Free Variable Selection in High Dimensions with the TREX / 2729
Johannes Lederer, Christian J. Müller

On the Equivalence of Linear Discriminant Analysis and Least Squares / 2736
Kibok Lee, Junmo Kim

Multi-Tensor Completion with Common Structures / 2743
Chao Li, Qibin Zhao, Junhua Li, Andrzej Cichocki, Lili Guo

Large-Scale Multi-View Spectral Clustering via Bipartite Graph / 2750
Yeqing Li, Feiping Nie, Heng Huang, Junzhou Huang

Integrating Features and Similarities: Flexible Models for Heterogeneous Multiview Data / 2757
Wenzhao Lian, Piyush Rai, Esther Salazar, Lawrence Carin

Shift-Pessimistic Active Learning Using Robust Bias-Aware Prediction / 2764
Anqi Liu, Lev Reyzin, Brian D. Ziebart

Unidimensional Clustering of Discrete Data Using Latent Tree Models / 2771
April Hua Liu, Leonard K. M. Poon, Nevin L. Zhang

Low-Rank Multi-View Learning in Matrix Completion for Multi-Label Image Classification / 2778
Meng Liu, Yong Luo, Dacheng Tao, Chao Xu, Yonggang We

Support Consistency of Direct Sparse-Change Learning in Markov Networks / 2785
Song Liu, Taiji Suzuki, Masashi Sugiyama

Low-Rank Similarity Metric Learning in High Dimensions / 2792
Wei Liu, Cun Mu, Rongrong Ji, Shiqian Ma, John R. Smith, Shih-Fu Chang

Large Margin Metric Learning for Multi-Label Prediction / 2800
Weiwei Liu, Ivor W. Tsang

Absent Multiple Kernel Learning / 2807
Xinwang Liu, Lei Wang, Jianping Yin, Yong Dou, Jian Zhang

Eigenvalues Ratio for Kernel Selection of Kernel Methods / 2814
Yong Liu, Shizhong Liao

Parallel Gaussian Process Regression for Big Data:
Low-Rank Representation Meets Markov Approximation / 2821
Kian Hsiang Low, Jiangbo Yu, Jie Chen, Patrick Jaillet

Noise-Robust Semi-Supervised Learning by Large-Scale Sparse Coding / 2828
Zhiwu Lu, Xin Gao, Liwei Wang, Ji-Rong Wen, Songfang Huang

The Hybrid Nested/Hierarchical Dirichlet Process and
Its Application to Topic Modeling with Word Differentiation / 2835
Tengfei Ma, Issei Sato, Hiroshi Nakagawa

UT Austin Villa 2014: RoboCup 3D Simulation League Champion via Overlapping Layered Learning / 2842
Patrick MacAlpine, Mike Depinet, Peter Stone

The Queue Method: Handling Delay, Heuristics, Prior Data, and Evaluation in Bandits / 2849
Travis Mandel, Yun-En Liu, Emma Brunskill, Zoran Popovic

V-MIN: Efficient Reinforcement Learning through Demonstrations and Relaxed Reward Demands / 2857
David Martínez, Guillem Alenyà, Carme Torras

The Boundary Forest Algorithm for Online Supervised and Unsupervised Learning / 2864
Charles Mathy, Nate Derbinsky, José Bento, Jonathan Rosenthal, Jonathan Yedidia

Using Machine Teaching to Identify Optimal Training-Set Attacks on Machine Learners / 2871
Shike Mei, Xiaojin Zhu

Learning Relational Sum-Product Networks / 2878
Aniruddh Nath, Pedro Domingos

Tensor-Variate Restricted Boltzmann Machines / 2887
Tu Dinh Nguyen, Truyen Tran, Dinh Phung, Svetha Venkatesh

Probabilistic Attributed Hashing / 2894
Mingdong Ou, Peng Cui, Jun Wang, Fei Wang, Wenwu Zhu

Obtaining Well Calibrated Probabilities Using Bayesian Binning / 2901
Mahdi Pakdaman Naeini, Gregory F. Cooper, Milos Hauskrecht

Detecting and Tracking Concept Class Drift and Emergence in Non-Stationary Fast Data Streams / 2908
Brandon S. Parker, Latifur Khan

Detecting Change Points in the Large-Scale Structure of Evolving Networks / 2914
Leto Peel, Aaron Clauset

Adaptive Sampling with Optimal Cost for Class-Imbalance Learning / 2921
Yuxin Peng

Multi-Objective Reinforcement Learning with Continuous Pareto Frontier Approximation / 2928
Matteo Pirotta, Simone Parisi, Marcello Restelli

Pareto Ensemble Pruning / 2935
Chao Qian, Yang Yu, Zhi-Hua Zhou

Leveraging Features and Networks for Probabilistic Tensor Decomposition / 2942
Piyush Rai, Yingjian Wang, Lawrence Carin

Doubly Robust Covariate Shift Correction / 2949
Sashank Jakkam Reddi, Barnabás Póczos, Alex Smola

Clustering Longitudinal Clinical Marker Trajectories from Electronic Health Data:
Applications to Phenotyping and Endotype Discovery / 2956
Peter Schulam, Fredrick Wigley, Suchi Saria

SP-SVM: Large Margin Classifier for Data on Multiple Manifolds / 2965
Bin Shen, Bao-Di Liu, Qifan Wang, Yi Fang, Jan P. Allebach

Spectral Label Refinement for Noisy and Missing Text Labels / 2972
Yangqiu Song, Chenguang Wang, Ming Zhang, Hailong Sun, Qiang Yang

Unsupervised Feature Learning through Divergent Discriminative Feature Accumulation / 2979
Paul A. Szerlip, Gregory Morse, Justin K. Pugh, Kenneth O. Stanley

Agnostic System Identification for Monte Carlo Planning / 2986
Erik Talvitie

Optimizing the CVaR via Sampling / 2993
Aviv Tamar, Yonatan Glassner, Shie Mannor

The Winograd Schema Challenge / 4024
Leora Morgenstern, Charles L. Ortiz, Jr.

VOLUME SIX

AAAI-15 Senior Member Papers

Blue Sky Ideas

Speech Adaptation in Extended Ambient Intelligence Environments / 4027
Bonnie J. Dorr, Lucian Galescu, Ian Perera, Kristy Hollingshead-Seitz, David Atkinson, Micah Clark, William Clancey, Yorick Wilks, Eric Fosler-Lussier

Intelligent Agents for Rehabilitation and Care of Disabled and Chronic Patients / 4032
Sarit Kraus

Mechanism Learning with Mechanism Induced Data / 4037
Tie-Yan Liu, Wei Chen, Tao Qin

Emerging Architectures for Global System Science / 4042
Michela Milano, Pascal Van Hentenryck

Blended Planning and Acting: Preliminary Approach, Research Challenges / 4047
Dana S. Nau, Malik Ghallab, Paolo Traverso

Impact of Modeling Languages on the Theory and Practice in Planning Research / 4052
Jussi Rintanen

Steering Evolution Strategically: Computational Game Theory and Opponent Exploitation for Treatment Planning, Drug Design, and Synthetic Biology / 4057
Tuomas Sandholm

Towards a Programmer's Apprentice (Again) / 4062
Howard Shrobe, Boris Katz, Randall Davis

Conducting Neuroscience to Guide the Development of AI / 4067
Jeffrey Mark Siskind

Challenges in Resource and Cost Allocation / 4073
Toby Walsh

Explaining Watson: Polymath Style / 4078
Wlodek Zadrozny, Valeria de Paiva, Lawrence S. Moss

Machine Teaching: An Inverse Problem to Machine Learning and an Approach toward Optimal Education / 4083
Xiaojin Zhu

Building Strong Semi-Autonomous Systems / 4088
Shlomo Zilberstein

Summary Talks

Achieving Intelligence Using Prototypes, Composition, and Analogy / 4093
Vinay K. Chaudhri

Towards User-Adaptive Information Visualization / 4100
Cristina Conati, Giuseppe Carenini, Dereck Toker, Sébastien Lallé

Languages for Mining and Learning / 4107
Luc De Raedt

Compile! / 4112
Pierre Marquis

On the Diagnosis of Cyber-Physical Production Systems: State-of-the-Art and Research Agenda / 4119
Oliver Niggemann, Volker Lohweg

Abstraction for Solving Large Incomplete-Information Games / 4127
Tuomas Sandholm

Semantic Representation / 4132
Lenhart Schubert

AAAI-15 Student Papers

Student Abstracts

A Succinct Conceptualization of the Foundations for a Network Organization Paradigm / 4140
Saad Alqithami

A Goal-Based Model of Personality for Planning-Based Narrative Generation / 4142
Julio César Bahamón, Camille Barot, R. Michael Young

Leveraging Common Structure to Improve Prediction across Related Datasets / 4144
Matt Barnes, Nick Gisolfi, Madalina Fiterau, Artur Dubrawski

Stochastic Blockmodeling for Online Advertising / 4146
Li Chen, Matthew Patton

Query Abduction for $ELH_{\bot}$ Ontologies / 4148
Mahsa Chitsaz, Zhe Wang, Kewen Wang

A Multi-Pass Sieve for Name Normalization / 4150
Jennifer D'Souza

A Sequence Labeling Approach to Deriving Word Variants / 4152
Jennifer D'Souza

Predicting the Quality of User Experiences to Improve Productivity and Wellness / 4154
Priya Lekha Donti, Jacob Rosenbloom, Alex Gruver, James C. Boerkoel Jr.

Modelling Individual Negative Emotion Spreading Process with Mobile Phones / 4156
Zhanwei Du, Yongjian Yang, Chuang Ma, Yuan Bai

Active Learning for Informative Projection Retrieval / 4158
Madalina Fiterau, Artur Dubrawski

Placing Influencing Agents in a Flock / 4160
Katie Genter, Peter Stone

Characterizing Performance of Consistency Algorithms by
Algorithm Configuration of Random CSP Generators / 4162
Daniel J. Geschwender, Robert J. Woodward, Berthe Y. Choueiry

Finding Meaningful Gaps to Guide Data Acquisition for a Radiation Adjudication System / 4164
Nick Gisolfi, Madalina Fiterau, Artur Dubrawski

Dealing with Trouble: A Data-Driven Model of a Repair Type for a Conversational Agent / 4166
Sviatlana Höhn

On Manipulablity of Random Serial Dictatorship in Sequential Matching with Dynamic Preferences / 4168
Hadi Hosseini, Kate Larson, Robin Cohen

Language Independent Feature Extractor / 4170
Young-Seob Jeong, Ho-Jin Choi

Coupled Collaborative Filtering for Context-Aware Recommendation / 4172
Xinxin Jiang, Wei Liu, Longbing Cao, Guodong Long

Sorted Neighborhood for the Semantic Web / 4174
Mayank Kejriwal, Daniel P. Miranker

Effect of Spatial Pooler Initialization on Column Activity in Hierarchical Temporal Memory / 4176
Mackenzie Leake, Liyu Xia, Kamil Rocki, Wayne Imaino

Acronym Disambiguation Using Word Embedding / 4178
Chao Li, Lei Ji, Jun Yan

Learning Word Vectors Efficiently Using Shared Representations and Document Representations / 4180
Qun Luo, Weiran Xu

Just-in-Time Hierarchical Constraint Decomposition / 4182
Valentin Mayer-Eichberger

Every Team Deserves a Second Chance: Identifying When Things Go Wrong / 4184
Vaishnavh Nagarajan, Leandro Soriano Marcolino, Milind Tambe

Active Advice Seeking for Inverse Reinforcement Learning / 4186
Phillip Odom, Sriraam Natarajan

Designing Vaccines that Are Robust to Virus Escape / 4188
Swetasudha Panda, Yevgeniy Vorobeychik

"Is It Rectangular?" Using I Spy as an Interactive, Game-Based Approach to Multimodal Robot Learning / 4190
Natalie Paige Parde, Michalis Papakostas, Konstantinos Tsiakas, Rodney D. Nielsen

A New Computational Intelligence Model for Long-Term
Prediction of Solar and Geomagnetic Activity / 4192
Mahboobeh Parsapoor, John Brooke, Bertil Svensson

GEF: A Self-Programming Robot Using Grammatical Evolution / 4194
Charles Peabody, Jennifer Seitzer

Planning with Numeric Timed Initial Fluents / 4196
Chiara Piacentini, Maria Fox, Derek Long

Combining Ontology Class Expression Generation with Mathematical Modeling for Ontology Learning / 4198
Jedrzej Potoniec, Agnieszka Lawrynowicz

Improving Cross-Domain Recommendation through Probabilistic Cluster-Level Latent Factor Model / 4200
Siting Ren, Sheng Gao, Jianxin Liao, Jun Guo

Representation Discovery for MDPs Using Bisimulation Metrics / 4202
Sherry Shanshan Ruan, Gheorghe Comanici, Prakash Panangaden, Doina Precup

Graphical Representation of Assumption-Based Argumentation / 4204
Claudia Schulz

Actionable Combined High Utility Itemset Mining / 4206
Jingyu Shao, Junfu Yin, Wei Liu, Longbing Cao

Spatio-Temporal Signatures of User-Centric Data: How Similar Are We? / 4208
Samta Shukla, Aditya Telang, Salil Joshi, L. Venkat Subramaniam

Multimedia Data for the Visually Impaired / 4210
Niket Tandon, Shekhar Sharma, Tanima Makkad

Improving Microblog Retrieval from Exterior Corpus by
Automatically Constructing a Microblogging Corpus / 4212
Wenting Tu, David Cheung, Nikos Mamoulis

Time-Sensitive Opinion Mining for Prediction / 4214
Wenting Tu, David Cheung, Nikos Mamoulis

Self-Organized Collective Decision-Making in a 100-Robot Swarm / 4216
Gabriele Valentini, Heiko Hamann, Marco Dorigo

Handling Uncertainty in Answer Set Programming / 4218
Yi Wang, Joohyung Lee

Combining Machine Learning and Crowdsourcing for Better Understanding Commodity Reviews / 4220
Heting Wu, Hailong Sun, Yili Fang, Kefan Hu, Yongqing Xie, Yangqiu Song, Xudong Liu

What Is the Longest River in the USA? Semantic Parsing for Aggregation Questions / 4222
Kun Xu, Sheng Zhang, Yansong Feng, Songfang Huang, Dongyan Zhao

Accelerating SAT Solving by Common Subclause Elimination / 4224
Yaowei Yan, Chris E. Gutierrez, Jeriah Jn-Charles, Forrest Sheng Bao, Yuanlin Zhang

Global Policy Construction in Modular Reinforcement Learning / 4226
Ruohan Zhang, Zhao Song, Dana H. Ballard

Touchless Telerobotic Surgery - Is It Possible at All? / 4228
Tian Zhou, Maria Eugenia Cabrera, Juan Pablo Wachs

Doctoral Consortium

Modeling Eye Movements when Reading Microblogs / 4231
Maria Barrett, Anders Søgaard

Exploiting the Structure of Distributed Constraint Optimization Problems / 4233
Ferdinando Fioretto

Realistic Assumptions for Attacks on Elections / 4235
Zack Fitzsimmons

Social Hierarchical Learning / 4237
Bradley Hayes

Multivariate Conditional Anomaly Detection and Its Clinical Application / 4239
Charmgil Hong, Milos Hauskrecht

Probabilistic Planning with Risk-Sensitive Criterion / 4241
Ping Hou

Entity Resolution in a Big Data Framework / 4243
Mayank Kejriwal

Non-Classical Planning for Robotic Applications / 4245
Scott Kiesel

Transfer Learning-Based Co-Run Scheduling for Heterogeneous Datacenters / 4247
Wei Kuang, Laura E. Brown, Zhenlin Wang

HVAC-Aware Occupancy Scheduling (Extended Abstract) / 4249
Boon-Ping Lim

Scalable Agent Modeling for Large Multiagent Systems / 4251
Carrie Rebhuhn

Explaining Answer Set Programming in Argumentative Terms / 4253
Claudia Schulz

Optimal Multi-Agent Pathfinding Algorithms / 4255
Guni Sharon

Multi-Agent Team Formation: Solving Complex Problems by Aggregating Opinions / 4257
Leandro Soriano Marcolino

Scaling-Up Inference in Markov Logic / 4259
Deepak Venugopal

Risk-Aware Scheduling throughout Planning and Execution / 4261
Andrew J. Wang

AAAI-15 Demonstration Papers

Demonstrations

A Planning-Based Assistance System for Setting Up a Home Theater / 4264
Pascal Bercher, Felix Richter, Thilo Hörnle, Thomas Geier, Daniel Höller, Gregor Behnke, Florian Nothdurft, Frank Honold, Wolfgang Minker, Michael Weber, Susanne Biundo

On Correcting Misspelled Queries in Email Search / 4266
Abhijit Bhole, Raghavendra Udupa

Towards Cognitive Automation of Data Science / 4268
Alain Biem, Maria A. Butrico, Mark D. Feblowitz, Tim Klinger, Yuri Malitsky, Kenney Ng, Adam Perer, Chandra Reddy, Anton V. Riabov, Horst Samulowitz, Daby Sow, Gerald Tesauro, Deepak Turaga

Tartanian7: A Champion Two-Player No-Limit Texas Hold'em Poker-Playing Program / 4270
Noam Brown, Sam Ganzfried, Tuomas Sandholm

CrowdMR: Integrating Crowdsourcing with MapReduce for AI-Hard Problems / 4272
Jun Chen, Chaokun Wang, Yiyuan Bai

VecLP: A Realtime Video Recommendation System for Live TV Programs / 4274
Sheng Gao, Dai Zhang, Honggang Zhang, Jianxin Liao, Chao Huang, Yongsheng Zhang, Jun Guo

Multi-Agent Dynamic Coupling for Cooperative Vehicles Modeling / 4276
Maxime Guériau, Romain Billot, Nour-Eddin El Faouzi, Salima Hassas, Frédéric Armetta

Cognitive Master Teacher / 4278
Raghu Krishnapuram, Luis A. Lastras, Satya Nitta

Visualizing Inference / 4280
Henry Lieberman, Joseph Henke

Bottom-Up Demand Response by Following Local Energy Generation Voluntarily / 4282
Tobias Linnenberg, Alexander Fay, Michael Kaisers

Visualization Techniques for Topic Model Checking / 4284
Jaimie Murdock, Colin Allen

Salient Object Detection via Objectness Proposals / 4286
Tam V. Nguyen

Gene Selection in Microarray Datasets Using Progressively Refined PSO Scheme / 4288
Yamuna Prasad, K. K. Biswas

World WordNet Database Structure: An Efficient Schema for Storing Information of WordNets of the World / 4290
Hanumant Redkar, Sudha Bhingardive, Diptesh Kanojia, Pushpak Bhattacharyya

The Network Data Repository with Interactive Graph Analytics and Visualization / 4292
Ryan A. Rossi, Nesreen K. Ahmed

DeepTutor: An Effective, Online Intelligent Tutoring System that Promotes Deep Learning / 4294
Vasile Rus, Nobal B. Niraula, Rajendra Banjade

Inferring Latent User Properties from Texts Published in Social Media / 4296
Svitlana Volkova, Yoram Bachrach, Michael Armstrong, Vijay Sharma

Circumventing Robots' Failures by Embracing Their Faults:
A Practical Approach to Planning for Autonomous Construction / 4298
Stefan Witwicki, Francesco Mondada

Crowd Motion Monitoring with Thermodynamics-Inspired Feature / 4300
Xinfeng Zhang, Su Yang, Yuan Yan Tang, Weishan Zhang

Virtual Agent Demonstrations

Cerebella: Automatic Generation of Nonverbal Behavior for Virtual Humans / 4303
Margot Lhommet, Yuyu Xu, Stacy Marsella

Scheherazade: Crowd-Powered Interactive Narrative Generation / 4305
Boyang Li, Mark O. Riedl

SimSensei Demonstration: A Perceptive Virtual Human Interviewer for Healthcare Applications / 4307
Louis-Philippe Morency, Giota Stratou, David DeVault, Arno Hartholt, Margaux Lhommet, Gale Lucas, Fabrizio Morbini, Kallirroi Georgila, Stefan Scherer, Jonathan Gratch, Stacy Marsella, David Traum, Albert Rizzo

LOL — Laugh Out Loud / 4309
Florian Pecune, Beatrice Biancardi, Yu Ding, Catherine Pelachaud, Maurizio Mancini, Giovanna Varni, Antonio Camurri, Gualtiero Volpe

Using Social Relationships to Control Narrative Generation / 4311
Julie Porteous, Fred Charles, Marc Cavazza

Interactive Narrative Planning in *The Best Laid Plans* / 4313
Stephen G. Ware, R. Michael Young, Phillip Wright, Christian Stith

What's Hot Talks

What's Hot Abstracts

Knowledge Representation and Reasoning: What's Hot / 4316
Chitta Baral, Giuseppe De Giacomo

What's Hot in Crowdsourcing and Human Computation (HCOMP) / 4318
Jeffrey P. Bigham

BDDs Strike Back (in AI Planning) / 4320
Stefan Edelkamp, Peter Kissmann, Álvaro Torralba

What's Hot in the SAT and ASP Competitions / 4322
Marijn J. H. Heule, Torsten Schaub

What Is Hot in CHI / 4324
Wei Li

AIBIRDS: The Angry Birds Artificial Intelligence Competition / 4326
Jochen Renz

RoboCup@Home — Benchmarking Domestic Service Robots / 4328
Sven Wachsmuth, Dirk Holz, Maja Rudinac, Javier Ruiz-del-Solar

Data Science for Social Good: 2014 KDD Highlights / 4330
Wei Wang

Index / 4333

AAAI Organization

Officers

AAAI President
Thomas G. Dietterich (Oregon State University, USA)

AAAI President-Elect
Subbarao Kambhampati (Arizona State University, USA)

Past President
Manuela Veloso (Carnegie Mellon University, USA)

Secretary-Treasurer
Ted Senator (Leidos, USA)

Councilors

(through 2015)
Carla Gomes (Cornell University, USA)
Julia Hirschberg (Columbia University, USA)
Eduard Hovy (University of Southern California Information Sciences Institute, USA)
Henry Lieberman (MIT Media Lab, USA)

(through 2016)
Sven Koenig (University of Southern California, USA)
Francesca Rossi (University of Padova, Italy)
Sylvie Thiebaux (The Australian National University, NICTA, Australia)
Brian Williams (Massachusetts Institute of Technology, USA)

(through 2017)
Sonia Chernova (Worcester Polytechnic Institute, USA)
Vincent Conitzer (Duke University, USA)
Boi Faltings (École polytechnique fédérale de Lausanne, Suisse)
Stephen Smith (Carnegie Mellon University, USA)

Standing Committees

Awards, Fellows, and Nominating Chair
Manuela Veloso (Carnegie Mellon University, USA)

Conference Chair
Shlomo Zilberstein (University of Massachusetts Amherst, USA)

Conference Outreach Chair
Henry Lieberman (MIT Media Lab, USA)

Finance Chair
Ted Senator (Leidos, USA)

International Committee Chair
Toby Walsh (NICTA, The Australian University, Australia)

Membership Chair
Eduard Hovy (USC Information Sciences Institute, USA)

Publications Chair
David Leake (Indiana University, USA)

Symposium Committee Cochairs
Matthew E. Taylor, Chair (Washington State University, USA)
Gita Sukthankar, Cochair (University of Central Florida, USA)

AAAI Press

Editor-in-Chief
Anthony Cohn (University of Leeds, UK)

General Manager
David M. Hamilton (The Live Oak Press, LLC, USA)

AI Magazine

Editor-in-Chief
David Leake (Indiana University, USA)

Competition Reports Coeditors
Sven Koenig (University of Southern California, USA)
Robert A. Morris (NASA Ames Research Center, USA)

Reports Editor
Robert A. Morris (NASA Ames Research Center, USA)

Managing Editor
David M. Hamilton (The Live Oak Press, LLC, USA)

Conference Committees

AAAI Conference Committee Chair
Shlomo Zilberstein (University of Massachusetts Amherst, USA)

AAAI-15 Program Cochairs
Blai Bonet (Universidad Simón Bolívar, Venezuela)
Sven Koenig (University of Southern California, USA)

IAAI Chair and Cochair
David Gunning (PARC, USA)
Peter Z. Yeh (Nuance Communications, USA)

AI and the Web Track Cochairs
Axel Polleres (Vienna University of Economics and Business, Austria)
Pascal Hitzler (Wright State University USA)

Cognitive Systems Track Cochairs
Kenneth Forbus (Northwestern University, USA)
Paul Rosenbloom (University of Southern California, USA)

Computational Sustainability Track Cochairs
Douglas Fisher (Vanderbilt University, USA)
Zico Kolter (Carnegie Mellon University, USA)
Barry O'Sullivan (University College Cork, Ireland)

Integrated Systems Track Cochairs
Patrick Doherty (Linkoping University, Sweden)
Gal Kaminka (Bar Ilan University, Israel)

Senior Member Track Cochairs
Ariel Felner (BenGurion University, Israel)
Jérôme Lang (Université ParisDauphine, France)

What's Hot Cochairs
Esra Erdem (Sabanci University, Turkey)
Michael Thielscher (University New South Wales, Australia)

Tutorial Cochairs
Emma Brunskill (Carnegie Mellon University, USA)
Mausam (Indian Institute of Technology, India)

Workshop Cochairs
WengKeen Wong (Oregon State University, USA)
Daniel Lowd (University of Oregon, USA)

Student Abstract and Poster Cochairs
Sriraam Natarajan (Indiana University, USA)
Daniele Magazzeni (King's College London, UK)
Sebastian Sardina (RMIT, Australia)

General Student Activities Cochairs
William Yeoh (New Mexico State University, USA)
Nathan Sturtevant (University of Denver, USA)

Women's Mentoring Breakfast
Marie desJardins (University of Maryland, Baltimore County, USA)
Amy McGovern (University of Oklahoma, USA)
Kiri Wagstaff (Jet Propulsion Laboratory, USA)

Demonstrations Chair
Carlos Linares Lopez (Universidad Carlos III de Madrid, Spain)

Robotics Cochairs
George Konidaris (Massachusetts Institute of Technology, USA)
Brad Knox (Massachusetts Institute of Technology, USA)
Nick Hawes (University of Birmingham, UK)

Shakey Celebration Chair
Ben Kuipers (University of Michigan, USA)

RoboCup Exhibition Cochairs
Peter Stone (University of Texas, Austin, USA)
Daniel Lee (University of Pennsylvania, USA)

Computer Game Showcase
Robert Holte (University of Alberta, Canada)
Ryan Hayward (University of Alberta, Canada)
Nathan Sturtevant (University of Denver, USA)
Martin Mueller (University of Alberta, Canada)

General Game-Playing Competition
Bertrand Decoster (Stanford University, USA)
Michael Genesereth (Stanford University, USA)

Video Competition Cochairs
Sabine Hauert (Massachusetts Institute of Technology, USA)
Mauro Birattari (Universite Libre de Bruxelles, Belgium)

Virtual Agents Exhibit
Marc Cavazza (Teesside University, UK)

Fundraising Cochairs
Vasant Honavar (Pensylvania State University, USA)
Sandip Sen (The University of Tulsa, USA)

Publicity and Social Media Chair
Yixin Chen (Washington University in St. Louis, USA)

Funding Information Session Cochairs
Berthe Choueiry (University of Nebraska-Lincoln, USA)
Sandip Sen (University of Tulsa)

Debate on Autonomous Weapons Cochairs
Stuart Russell (University of California, Berkeley, USA)
Toby Walsh (NICTA and University of New South Wales, Australia)

AAAI-15 Advisory Board

Carla E. Brodley (Northeastern University, USA)
Marie desJardins (University of Maryland, Baltimore County, USA)
Jörg Hoffmann (Saarland University, Germany)
Michael Littman (Brown University, USA)
Bart Selman (Cornell University)
Peter Stone (University of Texas at Austin, USA)

AAAI-15 Senior Program Committee

Eneko Agirre (University of the Basque Country, Spain)
Fahiem Bacchus (University of Toronto, Canada)
Chitta Baral (Arizona State University, USA)
Chris Beck (University of Toronto, Canada)
Craig Boutilier (University of Toronto, Canada)
Ronen Brafman (Ben-Gurion University, Israel)
Emma Brunskill (Carnegie Mellon University, USA)
Paul Buitelaar (Insight – National University of Ireland, Galway, Ireland)
Philipp Cimiano (University of Bielefeld, Germany)
Vincent Conitzer (Duke University, USA)
Fabio Cozman (Universidade de São Paulo, Brazil)
Bernardo Cuenca Grau (University of Oxford, UK)
Adnan Darwiche (University of California, Los Angeles, USA)
Luc De Raedt (Katholieke Universiteit Leuven, Belgium)
Bonnie Dorr (University of Maryland, College Park, USA)
Michel Dumontier (Stanford University, USA)
Jennifer Dy (Northeastern University, USA)
Stefan Edelkamp (University of Bremen, Germany)
Ulle Endriss (ILLC, University of Amsterdam, Netherlands)
Marcello Federico (FBK, Italy)
Ariel Felner (BenGurion University, Israel)
Alan Fern (Oregon State University, USA)
Johannes Fürnkranz (TU Darmstadt, Germany)
Hector Geffner (ICREA and Universitat Pompeu Fabra, Spain)
Enrico Giunchiglia (DIST – University of Genova, Italy)
Robert Givan (Purdue University, USA)
Carla Gomes (Cornell University, USA)
Jonathan Gratch (University of Southern California, Institute for Creative Technologies, USA)
Russ Greiner (University of Alberta, Canada)
Claudio Gutierrez (Universidad de Chile, Chile)
Patrik Haslum (ANU, Australia)
Milos Hauskrecht (University of Pittsburgh, USA)
Nick Hawes (University of Birmingham, UK)
Conor Hayes (Insight Centre for Data Analytics, NUI Galway, Ireland)
Martial Hebert (Carnegie Mellon University, USA)
Malte Helmert (University of Basel, Switzerland)
Carlos Hernández Ulloa (Universidad Católica de la Santísima Concepción, Chile)
Jorg Hoffmann (Saarland University, Germany)
Robert Holte (University of Alberta, Canada)

Vasant Honavar (Pennsylvania State University, USA)
Holger Hoos (University of British Columbia, Canada)
Anthony Hunter (University College London, UK)
Alex Ihler (University of California, Irvine, USA)
Krzysztof Janowicz (University of California, Santa Barbara, USA)
Leslie Kaelbling (Massachusetts Institute of Technology, USA)
Meir Kalech (Ben-Gurion University, Israel)
Subbarao Kambhampati (Arizona State University, USA)
Kevin Knight (Information Sciences Institute, University of Southern California, USA)
Craig Knoblock (Information Sciences Institute, University of Southern California, USA)
Sarit Kraus (Bar Ilan University, Israel)
Andreas Krause (ETH Zurich, Switzerland)
Jérôme Lang (LAMSADE, CNRS, Université Paris Dauphine, France)
Kathryn Laskey (George Mason University, USA)
Freddy Lecue (IBM Research, Dublin Research Center, Ireland)
Jens Lehmann (Universität Leipzig, Germany)
Yves Lespérance (York University, Canada)
Vladimir Lifschitz (University of Texas, USA)
Maxim Likhachev (Carnegie Mellon University, USA)
Alessio Lomuscio (Imperial College London, UK)
Ines Lynce (INESC-ID/IST, University of Lisbon, Portugal)
Shaul Markovitch (Technion – Israel Insitute of Technology, Israel)
Sheila Mcilraith (University of Toronto, Canada)
Michela Milano (DEIS Universita' di Bologna, Italy)
Marie-Laure Mugnier (University of Montpellier (LIRMM / INRIA), France)
Ram Nevatia (University of Southern California, Institute for Robotics and Intelligent Systems, USA)
Barry O'Sullivan (4C, University College Cork, Ireland)
David Poole (University of British Columbia, Canada)
Ariel Procaccia (Carnegie Mellon University, USA)
Guilin Qi (Southeast University, China)
Francesca Rossi (University of Padova, Italy and Harvard University, USA)
Dan Roth (University of Illinois at Urbana-Champaign, USA)
Scott Sanner (NICTA, Australia)
David Sarne (Bar-Ilan University, Israel)
Dale Schuurmans (University of Alberta, Canada)
Prasad Tadepalli (Oregon State University, USA)
Peter van Beek (University of Waterloo, Canada)
Pascal Van Hentenryck (NICTA, Australia)
Maria Esther Vidal (Universidad Simon Bolivar, Venezuela)
Toby Walsh (NICTA and UNSW, Australia)
Bonnie Webber (University of Edinburgh, UK)
Kilian Weinberger (Washington University in St. Louis, USA)
Michael Wellman (University of Michigan, USA)
Shimon Whiteson (University of Amsterdam, Netherlands)
Michael Wooldridge (University of Oxford, UK)
Tianbao Yang (University of Iowa, USA)
Scott Wen-Tau Yih (Microsoft Research, USA)
Neil Yorke-Smith (American University of Beirut, Lebanon)

Weixiong Zhang (Washington University in St. Louis, USA)
Shlomo Zilberstein (University of Massachusetts, Amherst, USA)

AAAI-15 Program Committee
Mouaddib Abdel-Illah (GREYC Université de Caen, France)
Karim Abou-Moustafa (University of Alberta, Canada)
Rui Abreu (University of Porto, Portugal)
Maribel Acosta (Institute AIFB, Karlsruhe Institute of Technology, Germany)
Fayyaz-Ul-Amir Afsar (Colorado State University, USA)
Nitish Aggarwal (Insight-Centre NUI Galway, Ireland)
John Mark Agosta (C9 Inc, USA)
Thomas Ågotnes (University of Bergen, Norway)
Bilal Ahmed (Tufts University, USA)
Sandip Aine (Indraprastha Institute of Information and Technology, India)
Stéphane Airiau (LAMSADE – Université Paris-Dauphine, France)
H. Levent Akin (Bogazici University, Turkey)
Alexandre Albore (Onera, France)
Vidal Alcázar (Universidad Carlos III de Madrid, Spain)
Natasha Alechina (University of Nottingham, UK)
Christopher Amato (Massachusetts Institute of Technology, USA)
Leila Amgoud (IRIT – CNRS, France)
Eyal Amir (University of Illinois Urbana-Champaign, USA)
Saeed Amizadeh (Yahoo Labs, USA)
Bo An (Nanyang Technological University, Singapore)
Renzo Angles (Universidad de Talca, Chile)
Carlos Ansótegui (Universitat de Lleida, Spain)
Grigoris Antoniou (United Kingdom)
Alessandro Antonucci (IDSIA, Switzerland)
Raman Arora (Johns Hopkins University, USA)
Yoav Artzi (University of Washington, USA)
Roberto Javier Asín Achá (Universidad Católica de la Santísima Concepción, Chile)
John Atkinson (Universidad de Concepcion, Chile)
Katie Atkinson (University of Liverpool, UK)
Martin Atzmueller (University of Kassel, Germany)
Guillaume Aucher (University of Rennes 1/INRIA, France)
Nathalie Aussenac-Gilles (IRIT- CNRS, Toulouse, France)
Haris Aziz (NICTA and UNSW, Australia)
Joscha Bach (Massachusetts Institute of Technology, USA)
Yoram Bachrach (Microsoft Research, Cambridge, UK)
Christer Bäckström (Linköping University, Sweden)
Jean-François Baget (INRIA and LIRMM, France)
Jorge Baier (Pontificia Universidad Católica de Chile, Chile)
Marcello Balduccini (Drexel University, USA)
David Balduzzi (Victoria University of Wellington, New Zealand)
Tina Balke (University of Surrey, UK)
Jerry Ball (US Air Force, USA)
Arindam Banerjee (University of Minnesota, USA)

Elias Bareinboim (University of California, Los Angeles, USA)
Ken Barker (IBM Research, USA)
Pietro Baroni (University of Brescia, Italy)
Leliane N. Barros (Universidade de São Paulo, Brazil)
Roman Bartak (Charles University in Prague, Czech Republic)
Nicola Basilico (Università degli Studi di Milano, Italy)
Samik Basu (Iowa State University, USA)
Iyad Batal (GE Global Research, USA)
Gustavo E. A. P. A. Batista (University of São Paulo, Brazil)
Dorothea Baumeister (University of Duesseldorf, Germany)
Ana L. C. Bazzan (Universidade Federal do Rio Grande do Sul, Brazil)
Michael Beetz (University of Bremen, Germany)
Ramon Bejar Torres (Universitat de Lleida, Spain)
Kostas Bekris (Rutgers University, USA)
Francesco Belardinelli (Universite d'Evry, France)
Mikhail Belkin (Ohio State University, USA)
Vaishak Belle (University of Toronto, Canada)
Marc Bellemare (United Kingdom)
Heni Ben Amor (Georgia Institute of Technology, USA)
Shai Ben-David (University of Waterloo, Canada)
Yoshua Bengio (University of Montreal, Canada)
Russell Bent (Los Alamos National Laboratory, USA)
J. Benton (Smart Information Flow Technologies, USA)
Pascal Bercher (Ulm University, Germany)
Tanya Berger-Wolf (University of Illinois at Chicago, USA)
Leopoldo Bertossi (Carleton University, Canada)
Philippe Besnard (CNRS / IRIT, France)
Christian Bessiere (University of Montpellier, France)
Aurélie Beynier (University of Pierre and Marie Curie (Paris 6), LIP6, France)
Meghyn Bienvenu (CNRS and Université Paris-Sud, France)
Mustafa Bilgic (Illinois Institute of Technology, USA)
Jeffrey A. Bilmes (University of Washington, USA)
Mauro Birattari (IRIDIA, Université Libre de Bruxelles, Belgium)
Eva Blomqvist (Linköping University, Sweden)
Maria Luisa Bonet (Universitat Politecnica de Catalunya, Spain)
Alessio Bonfietti (University of Bologna, Italy)
Kalina Bontcheva (University of Sheffield, UK)
Richard Booth (University of Luxembourg, Luxembourg)
Georgeta Bordea (Insight, National University of Ireland, Galway, Ireland)
Lucas Bordeaux (Microsoft Research, UK)
Daniel Borrajo (Universidad Carlos III de Madrid, Spain)
Johan Bos (University of Groningen, Netherlands)
Adi Botea (IBM Research, Ireland)
Sylvain Bouveret (LIG – Grenoble INP, France)
Michael Bowling (University of Alberta, Canada)
Levi Boyles (University of Oxford, UK)
Loreto Bravo (Universidad de Concepción, Chile)
Francois Bremond (PULSAR, INRIA, Sophia Antpolis, France)

Will Bridewell (Naval Research Laboratory, USA)
Markus Brill (Duke University, USA)
Jan Broersen (Utrecht University, Netherlands)
Ken Brown (University College Cork, Ireland)
Michael Brown (National University of Singapore, Singapore)
Daniel Bryce (SIFT, LLC, USA)
Jiajun Bu (Zhejiang University, China)
Olivier Buffet (INRIA / LORIA, France)
Lorenz Bühmann (University of Leipzig, Germany)
Hung Bui (NLU Lab, Nuance, USA)
Carlos Buil Aranda (Pontificia Universidad Católica de Chile, Chile)
Darius Burschka (Technische Universität München, Germany)
Dídac Busquets (Imperial College London, UK)
Pedro Cabalar (University of Corunna, Spain)
Shaowei Cai (Institute of Software, Chinese Academy of Sciences, China)
Andrea Calì (University of London, Birkbeck College, UK)
Martin Caminada (University of Aberdeen, UK)
Amparo E. Cano (Knowledge Media Institute, The Open University, UK)
Claire Cardie (Cornell University, USA)
David Carral (Wright State University, USA)
Miguel Carrasco (Universidad Adolfo Ibañez, Chile)
Sofia Ceppi (Microsoft Research, UK)
Volkan Cevher (EPFL, Switzerland)
Ayan Chakrabarti (Toyota Technological Institute at Chicago, USA)
Mithun Chakraborty (Washington University in St. Louis, USA)
Nilanjan Chakraborty (Carnegie Mellon University, USA)
Georgios Chalkiadakis (Technical University of Crete, Greece)
Nathanael Chambers (United States Naval Academy, USA)
Kai-Wei Chang (University of Illinois, USA)
Vinay Chaudhri (SRI International, USA)
Kamalika Chaudhuri (University of California San Diego, USA)
Nitesh V. Chawla (University of Notre Dame, USA)
Michelle Cheatham (Wright State University, USA)
Rama Chellappa (University of Maryland, USA)
Bryant Chen (University of California, Los Angeles, USA)
Cuiting Chen (TU Delft, Netherlands)
Hubie Chen (Universidad del País Vasco and Ikerbasque, Spain)
Lei Chen (Hong Kong University of Science and Technology, Hong Kong)
Minmin Chen (Criteo Lab, USA)
Ping Chen (UMB, USA)
Wenlin Chen (Washington University in St. Louis, USA)
Xiaoping Chen (University of Science and Technology of China, China)
Yiqiang Chen (Institute of Computing Technology, Chinese Academy of Sciences, China)
Yixin Chen (Washington University in St. Louis, USA)
Zheng Chen (Washington University in St. Louis, USA)
Jian Cheng (Institute of Automation, Chinese Academy of Sciences, China)
Sonia Chernova (Worcester Polytechnic Institute, USA)
Colin Cherry (National Research Council Canada, Canada)

Yann Chevaleyre (Universite Paris Nord, France)
Arthur Choi (University of California, Los Angeles, USA)
Jaesik Choi (Ulsan National Institute of Science and Technology, Korea, The Republic of)
Yejin Choi (University of Washington, USA)
Anustup Choudhury (Sharp Laboratories of America, USA)
Christos Christodoulopoulos (University of Illinois, USA)
Geoffrey Chu (University of Melbourne, Australia)
Gokberk Cinbis (INRIA, Turkey)
Jens Classen (RWTH Aachen University, Germany)
Sharlee Climer (Washington University in St. Louis, USA)
Shay Cohen (USA)
Amanda Coles (King's College London, UK)
Andrew Coles (King's College London, UK)
Alexandra Coman (Ohio Northern University, USA)
Martin Cooper (IRIT – Universite Paul Sabatier, France)
Oscar Corcho (Universidad Politécnica de Madrid, Spain)
Jason Corso (University of Michigan, USA)
Gabriella Cortellessa (ISTC-CNR, Italy)
Fabrizio Costa (University of Freiburg, Germany)
Michael Cox (Wright State University, USA)
Jacob Crandall (Masdar Institute of Science and Technology, United Arab Emirates)
Broderick Crawford (Pontificia Universidad Catolica de Valparaiso, Chile)
Marco Cristani (University of Verona, Italy)
Mark Crowley (Oregon State University, USA)
Isabel Cruz (University of Illinois at Chicago, USA)
Philippe Cudré-Mauroux (University of Fribourg, Switzerland)
Peng Cui (Tsinghua University, China)
Naresh Cuntoor (Intelligent Automation Inc., USA)
James Cussens (University of York, UK)
Aba-Sah Dadzie (University of Birmingham, UK)
Claudia D'Amato (University of Bari, Italy)
Theodoros Damoulas (New York University, USA)
Mariana Damova (Mozaika, Bulgaria)
Kostas Daniilidis (University of Pennsylvania, USA)
Mathieu D'Aquin (Knowledge Media Institute, the Open University, UK)
Jnaneshwar Das (University of Pennsylvania, USA)
Kamalika Das (NASA, USA)
Sanmay Das (Washington University in St. Louis, USA)
Mehdi Dastani (Utrecht University, Netherlands)
Jessica Davies (IST Austria, Austria)
Artur D'Avila Garcez (City University London, UK)
Ernest Davis (New York University, USA)
Larry Davis (University of Maryland, College Park, USA)
Cassio De Campos (Queen's University Belfast, UK)
Giuseppe De Giacomo (Sapienza Universita' di Roma, Italy)
Kurt De Grave (KU Leuven, Belgium)
Johan de Kleer (PARC, A Xerox Company, USA)
Fernando De La Torre (Carnegie Mellon University, USA)

James Delgrande (Simon Fraser University, Canada)
Daniel Delling (Microsoft Research Silicon Valley, USA)
David Demirdjian (Aquifi, inc., USA)
Marc Denecker (KU Leuven, Belgium)
Nate Derbinsky (Wentworth Institute of Technology, USA)
Debadeepta Dey (Carnegie Mellon University, USA)
Paramveer Dhillon (Massachusetts Institute of Technology, USA)
M. Bernardine Dias (Carnegie Mellon University, USA)
Jilles Steeve Dibangoye (Université de Lyon, France)
Sven Dickinson (University of Toronto, Canada)
Bistra Dilkina (Georgia Institute of Technology, USA)
Chrysanne Dimarco (University of Waterloo, Canada)
Vania Dimitrova (University of Leeds, UK)
Yannis Dimopoulos (University of Cyprus, Cyprus)
Tommaso Di Noia (Politecnico di Bari, Italy)
Chris Ding (University of Texas at Arlington, USA)
Wei Ding (University of Massachusetts Boston, USA)
Josip Djolonga (Switzerland)
Minh Do (NASA Ames Research Center, USA)
Carlotta Domeniconi (George Mason University, USA)
Justin Domke (NICTA, Australia)
Carmel Domshlak (Technion – Israel Institute of Technology, Israel)
Janardhan Rao Doppa (Oregon State University, USA)
Derek Doran (Wright State University, USA)
Gary Doran (Case Western Reserve University, USA)
Prashant Doshi (University of Georgia, USA)
Ivan Dotu (Boston College, USA)
Agostino Dovier (The University of Udine, Italy)
Bruce Draper (Colorado State University, USA)
Chris Drummond (Canada)
Marek Druzdzel (University of Pittsburgh, Bialystok University of Technology, USA)
Jianfeng Du (Guangdong University of Foreign Studies, China)
Paul Dunne (University of Liverpool, UK)
Eric Eaton (University of Pennsylvania, USA)
Thomas Eiter (Vienna University of Technology, Austria)
Carl Henrik Ek (Royal Institute of Technology, Sweden, Sweden)
Hoda Eldardiry (Palo Alto Research Center, USA)
Ahmed Elgammal (Rutgers Univeristy, USA)
Charles Elkan (University of California, San Diego, USA)
Edith Elkind (University of Oxford, UK)
Tapio Elomaa (Tampere University of Technology, Finland)
David Elson (Google, USA)
Yagil Engel (Microsoft Research, Israel)
Esra Erdem (Sabanci University, Turkey)
Stefano Ermon (Cornell University, USA)
Patricia Everaere (LIFL-Université Lille1, France)
Wolfgang Faber (University of Huddersfield, UK)
Andrew Fagg (University of Oklahoma, USA)

Piotr Faliszewski (AGH University of Science and Technology, Poland)
Boi Faltings (École Polytechnique Fédérale de Lausanne, Switzerland)
Ali Farhadi (University of Washington, USA)
Cristina Feier (University of Oxford, UK)
Alexander Feldman (General Diagnostics, Netherlands)
Ariel Felner (Ben-Gurion University, Israel)
Serge Fenet (LIRIS CNRS UMR 5205 / Université Lyon 1, France)
Zheyun Feng (USA)
Miriam Fernandez (Knowledge Media Institute, UK)
Marcelo Finger (Universidade de São Paulo, Brazil)
Felix Fischer (UK)
Pierre Flener (Uppsala University, Sweden)
Achille Fokoue (IBM Research, USA)
Jeremiah Folsom-Kovarik (Soar Technology, Inc., USA)
Marco Fossati (Fondazione Bruno Kessler, Italy)
James Foulds (University of California, Santa Cruz, USA)
Enrico Franconi (Free University of Bozen-Bolzano, Italy)
Eibe Frank (University of Waikato, New Zealand)
Simone Fratini (European Space Agency – ESA/ESOC, Germany)
Scott Friedman (SIFT, LLC, USA)
Zachary Friggstad (University of Alberta, Canada)
Alex Fukunaga (The University of Tokyo, Japan)
Tim Furche (Oxford University, UK)
Alfredo Gabaldon (Carnegie Mellon University-Silicon Valley, USA)
Christian Gagne (Laval University, Canada)
Avigdor Gal (Technion – Israel Institute of Technology, Israel)
Kobi Gal (Ben Gurion University, Israel)
Andrew Gallagher (Cornell University, USA)
Fabien Gandon (Inria, France)
Vijay Ganesh (University of Waterloo, Canada)
Aldo Gangemi (Université Paris 13 and CNR-ISTC, France and Italy)
Sam Ganzfried (Carnegie Mellon University, USA)
Yong Gao (UBC Okanagan, Canada)
Nicola Gatti (Politecnico di Milano, Italy)
Marco Gavanelli (University of Ferrara, Italy)
Andrew Gelfand (Mitsubishi Electric Research Labs, USA)
Enrico Gerding (University of Southampton, UK)
Alfonso Gerevini (University of Brescia, Italy)
Carmen Gervet (Université de Savoie, LISTIC, France)
Malik Ghallab (France)
Mina Gheiratmand (University of Alberta, Canada)
Chiara Ghidini (FBK-irst, Italy)
Yolanda Gil (Information Sciences Institute, University of Southern California, USA)
Roxana Girju (University of Illinois, USA)
François Goasdoué (Univ. Rennes 1, France)
Lluis Godo (Artificial Intelligence Research Institute, IIIA – CSIC, Spain)
Ashok Goel (Georgia Institute of Technology, USA)
Robby Goetschalckx (Oregon State University, USA)

Vibhav Gogate (The University of Texas at Dallas, USA)
Claudia V. Goldman (General Motors, Israel)
Robert P. Goldman (SIFT, LLC, USA)
Judy Goldsmith (University of Kentucky, USA)
Dan Goldwasser (University of Maryland, USA)
Carla Gomes (Cornell University, USA)
Boqing Gong (University of Southern California, USA)
Shaogang Gong (Queen Mary University of London, UK)
Benjamin Good (TSRI, USA)
Andrew Gordon (University of Southern California, USA)
Dilan Gorur (USA)
Alexandra Goultiaeva (University of Toronto, Canada)
Laurent Gourves (lamsade, France)
Umberto Grandi (University of Toulouse, France)
Alban Grastien (NICTA, Australia)
Gianluigi Greco (University of Calabria, Italy)
Charles Gretton (NICTA, Australia)
Roderich Gross (The University of Sheffield, UK)
Davide Grossi (University of Liverpool, UK)
Christophe Guéret (Data Archiving and Networked Services (DANS), Netherlands)
Tias Guns (KU Leuven, Belgium)
Mingyu Guo (University of Adelaide, Australia)
Yuhong Guo (Temple University, USA)
Shekhar Gupta (Palo Alto Research Center, USA)
Iryna Gurevych (Darmstadt University of Technology, Germany)
Julian Gutierrez (University of Oxford, UK)
Patricia Gutierrez (IIIA CSIC, Spain)
Andras Gyorgy (University of Alberta, Canada)
Peter Haase (fluid Operations, Germany)
Hannaneh Hajishirzi (University of Washington, USA)
Riad Hammoud (BAE Systems, USA)
Jiawei Han (University of Illinois at Urbana-Champaign, USA)
Marc Hanheide (University of Lincoln, UK)
Sanda Harabagiu (Human Language Technology Research Institute, University of Texas at Dallas, USA)
Maaike Harbers (Delft University of Technology, Netherlands)
Paul Harrenstein (University of Oxford, UK)
Andreas Harth (AIFB, Karlsruhe Institute of Technology, Germany)
Seyed Hamed Hassani (ETHZ, Switzerland)
Sabine Hauert (University of Bristol, UK)
Nick Hawes (UK)
Noam Hazon (Ariel University, Israel)
Emmanuel Hebrard (LAAS, CNRS, France)
Fredrik Heintz (Linköping University, Sweden)
Lane Hemaspaandra (University of Rochester, USA)
Joachim Hertzberg (University of Osnabrueck, Germany)
Andreas Herzig (IRIT-CNRS, France)
Marijn Heule (The University of Texas at Austin, USA)
Tom Hinrichs (Northwestern University, USA)

Julia Hockenmaier (University of Illinois, USA)
Robert Hoehndorf (King Abdullah University of Science and Technology, Saudi Arabia)
Rinke Hoekstra (VU University Amsterdam/University of Amsterdam, Netherlands)
Jesse Hoey (University of Waterloo, Canada)
Johannes Hofbauer (Technische Universität München, Germany)
Michael Hofbaur (JOANNEUM RESEARCH, Austria)
Matthew W. Hoffman (University of Cambridge, UK)
Katja Hofmann (Microsoft, UK)
Aidan Hogan (DCC, Universidad de Chile, Chile)
Geoffrey Hollinger (Oregon State University, USA)
Jaakko Hollmén (Aalto University School of Science, Finland)
Yu Hong (Soochow University, China)
Anthony Hoogs (Kitware, Inc., USA)
Matthew Horridge (Stanford University, USA)
Ian Horrocks (University of Oxford, UK)
Katja Hose (Aalborg University, Denmark)
Shahriar Hossain (USA)
Andreas Hotho (University of Wuerzburg, Germany)
Estevam Hruschka Junior (UFSCar – Federal University of São Carlos, Brazil)
Wei Hu (Nanjing University, China)
Yingjie Hu (University of California, Santa Barbara, USA)
Yuheng Hu (Arizona State University, USA)
Liang Huang (City University of New York (CUNY), USA)
Qixing Huang (Stanford University, USA)
Ruihong Huang (Stanford University, USA)
Frank Hutter (University of Freiburg, Germany)
Eero Hyvönen (Aalto University, Finland)
Jaime Ide (Stony Brook University, USA)
Alex Ihler (University of California, Irvine, USA)
Petar Iliev (LORIA, France)
Daniela Inclezan (Miami University, USA)
Katsumi Inoue (NII, Japan)
Hiroshi Ishikawa (Waseda University, Japan)
Volkan Isler (University of Minnesota, USA)
Takayuki Ito (Nagoya Institute of Technology, Japan)
David Jacobs (University of Maryland, College Park, USA)
Manish Jain (University of Southern California, USA)
Prateek Jain (IBM TJ Watson Research Center, USA)
Nathalie Japkowicz (University of Ottawa, Canada)
Matti Järvisalo (University of Helsinki, Finland)
Christopher Jefferson (University of St. Andrews, UK)
David Jensen (University of Massachusetts Amherst, USA)
Anja Jentzsch (Hasso Plattner Institut, Germany)
Arnav Jhala (University of California, Santa Cruz, USA)
Albert Xin Jiang (Trinity University, USA)
Randolph M. Jones (SoarTech, USA)
Catholijn Jonker (Delft University, The Netherlands)
Anders Jonsson (Universitat Pompeu Fabra, Spain)

Peter Jonsson (Linkoping University, Sweden)
Kshitij Judah (Oregon State University, USA)
Frederic Jurie (Université de Caen Basse Normandie, France)
Vishnu Kamalnath (Microsoft Research, USA)
Ece Kamar (Microsoft Research, USA)
Amin Karbasi (Yale University, USA)
Marcel Karnstedt (Bell Labs Ireland, Alcatel-Lucent, Ireland)
Ian Kash (Microsoft Research Cambridge, UK)
George Katsirelos (INRA, Toulouse, France)
Thomas Keller (University of Freiburg, Germany)
Jack Kelly (Imperial College London, UK)
Eamonn Keogh (University of California Riverside, USA)
Gabriele Kern-Isberner (TU Dortmund University, Germany)
Kristian Kersting (TU Dortmund University, Germany)
Peter Key (Microsoft Research, UK)
Eliahu Khalastchi (Ben-Gurion University, Israel)
Roni Khardon (Tufts University, USA)
Christopher Kiekintveld (University of Texas at El Paso, USA)
Philip Kilby (NICTA and ANU, Australia)
Jin-Dong Kim (Database Center for Life Science, Japan)
Junmo Kim (Korea Advanced Institute of Science and Technology, Korea, The Republic of)
Angelika Kimmig (KU Leuven, Belgium)
Akihiro Kishimoto (IBM Research – Ireland, Ireland)
Peter Kissmann (Universität des Saarlandes, Germany)
Zeynep Kiziltan (University of Bologna, Italy)
Arto Klami (University of Helsinki, Finland)
Szymon Klarman (Centre for Artificial Intelligence Research, UKZN and CSIR Meraka, South Africa)
Matthew Klenk (Palo Alto Research Center, USA)
Roman Klinger (University of Stuttgart, Germany)
Pavel Klinov (University of Ulm, Germany)
Matthias Klusch (DFKI, Germany)
Ross Knepper (Massachusetts Institute of Technology, USA)
Matthias Knorr (CENTRIA, Universidade Nova de Lisboa, Portugal)
W. Bradley Knox (Massachusetts Institute of Technology, USA)
Magnus Knuth (Hasso Plattner Institute, University of Potsdam, Germany)
Levente Kocsis (MTA SZTAKI, Hungary)
Philipp Koehn (Johns Hopkins University, USA)
Andrey Kolobov (Microsoft Research, USA)
Greg Kondrak (University of Alberta, Canada)
Boris Konev (University of Liverpool, UK)
George Konidaris (Duke University, USA)
Sébastien Konieczny (CRIL – CNRS, France)
Ioannis Konstas (UK)
Roman Kontchakov (Birkbeck College, UK)
Stefan Kopp (University of Bielefeld, Germany)
Moshe Koppel (Bar-Ilan University, Israel)
Kevin Korb (Monash University, Australia)
Richard Korf (University of California, Los Angeles, USA)

Frederic Koriche (CRIL, Universite de Lille, Nord de France, France)
Egor V. Kostylev (University of Oxford, UK)
Lars Kotthoff (University College Cork, Ireland)
Adila A. Krisnadhi (Wright State University, USA and Universitas Indonesia, Indonesia)
Anastassia Kuestenmacher (Bonn-Rhein-Sieg University, Germany)
Oliver Kullmann (Swansea University, UK)
Akshat Kumar (University of Massachusetts, Amherst, USA)
Gautam Kunapuli (UtopiaCompression Corporation, USA)
Kyros Kutulakos (University of Toronto, Canada)
Sergei O. Kuznetsov (National Research University Higher School of Economics, Russian Federation)
Jonas Kvarnström (Linköping University, Sweden)
Branislav Kveton (Technicolor Labs, USA)
Philippe Laborie (IBM, France)
John Laird (University of Michigan, USA)
Gerhard Lakemeyer (RWTH Aachen University, Germany)
Kiran Lakkaraju (Sandia National Laboratories, USA)
Patrick Lambrix (Linköping University, Sweden)
Christoph Lampert (I.S.T. Austria, Austria)
Marc Lanctot (Google DeepMind, UK)
Terran Lane (University of New Mexico, USA)
Ivan Laptev (INRIA, France)
Kate Larson (University of Waterloo, Canada)
Wallace Lawson (Naval Research Lab, USA)
Alessandro Lazaric (SequeL Project, INRIA Lille-Nord Europe, France)
Daniel Le Berre (CNRS – Université d'Artois, France)
Christian Lebiere (Carnegie Mellon University, USA)
Honglak Lee (University of Michigan, USA)
Jimmy Lee (The Chinese University of Hong Kong, Hong Kong)
Joohyung Lee (Arizona State University, USA)
Joonseok Lee (Georgia Institute of Technology, USA)
Joao Leite (CENTRIA, Universidade Nova de Lisboa, Portugal)
Levi Lelis (Universidade Federal de Viçosa, Brazil)
Nicola Leone (University of Calabria, Italy)
Marius Leordeanu (Romania)
Vincent Lepetit (TU Graz, Austria)
James Lester (North Carolina State University, USA)
Joshua Letchford (Sandia National Laboratories, USA)
Martin Leucker (University of Lübeck, Germany)
Cane Wing-Ki Leung (Huawei Noah's Ark Lab, Hong Kong)
Bin Li (NICTA, Australia)
Chu-Min Li (Université de Picardie Jules Verne, France)
Fangtao Li (Google Research, USA)
Hongdong Li (Australian National University, Australia)
Jason Jingshi Li (The Australian National University, Australia)
Nan Li (D.E. Shaw and Co., L.P, USA)
Ping Li (China)
Wenjie Li (Hong Kong Polytechnic University, Hong Kong)
Wu-Jun Li (Nanjing University, China)

Fangzhen Lin (HKUST, Hong Kong)
Raz Lin (Bar-Ilan University, Israel)
Zhouchen Lin (Peking University, China)
Carlos Linares Lopez (Universidad Carlos III de Madrid, Spain)
Marius Lindauer (University of Freiburg, Germany)
Haibin Ling (Temple University, USA)
Nir Lipovetzky (Australia)
Francesca Alessandra Lisi (Università degli Studi di Bari "Aldo Moro", Italy)
Qiang Liu (University of California, Irvine, USA)
Tie-Yan Liu (Microsoft Research Asia, China)
Ting Liu (Harbin Institute of Technology, China)
Weiru Liu (Queen's University Belfast, UK)
Yan Liu (University of Southern California, USA)
Yang Liu (University of Texas at Dallas, USA)
Yongmei Liu (Sun Yat-sen University, China)
Yun-En Liu (University of Washington, USA)
Yang Liu First (Tsinghua University, China)
Daniel Lizotte (University of Waterloo, Canada)
Jorge Lobo (ICREA and Universitat Pompeu Fabra, Spain)
Kate Lockwood (USA)
Brian Logan (University of Nottingham, UK)
Michele Lombardi (DISI, University of Bologna, Italy)
Derek Long (King's College London, UK)
Nuno Lopes (IBM Research, Smarter Cities Technology Centre, Dublin, Ireland)
Vanessa Lopez (IBM Research, Ireland)
Manuel López-Ibáñez (IRIDIA, Université Libre de Bruxelles, Belgium)
Andrea Loreggia (University of Padova, Italy)
Daniel Lowd (University of Oregon, USA)
Eneldo Loza Mencía (Knowledge Engineering Group, TU Darmstadt, Germany)
Tyler Lu (University of Toronto, Canada)
Benjamin Lubin (Boston University, USA)
Thomas Lukasiewicz (University of Oxford, UK)
Sean Luke (George Mason University, USA)
Carsten Lutz (Universität Bremen, Germany)
Michael Lyu (The Chinese University of Hong Kong, Hong Kong)
Yue Ma (Theoretical Computer Science, TU Dresden, Germany)
Patrick MacAlpine (University of Texas at Austin, USA)
Alan Mackworth (University of British Columbia, Canada)
Richard Maclin (University of Minnesota Duluth, USA)
Anders Madsen (HUGIN EXPERT, Denmark)
Daniele Magazzeni (King's College London, UK)
Sridhar Mahadevan (University of Massachusetts, USA)
Mehrdad Mahdavi (Toyota Technological Institute at Chicago, USA)
Frederick Maier (Institute for Artificial Intelligence, USA)
Donato Malerba (Università degli Studi di Bari "Aldo Moro", Italy)
Maria Maleshkova (Germany)
Brandon Malone (University of Helsinki, Helsinki Institute for Information Technology, Finland)
Suresh Manandhar (University of York, UK)

Travis Mandel (University of Washington, USA)
Prashanth Mannem (Oregon State University, USA)
Vasco Manquinho (INESC-ID, IST/University of Lisbon, Portugal)
Felip Manya (IIIA-CSIC, Spain)
Marco Maratea (University of Genova, Italy)
Enrico Marchioni (UK)
Daniel Marcu (Information Sciences Institute, University of Southern California, USA)
Radu Marinescu (IBM Research, Ireland)
Lluís Màrquez (Qatar Computing Research Institute, Qatar)
Pierre Marquis (CRIL-CNRS and Universit d'Artois, France)
Stacy Marsella (Institute for Creative Technologies, University of Southern California, USA)
Marcos Martinez-Romero (University of A Coruña, Spain)
Manish Marwah (HP Labs, USA)
Franco Mascia (Université Libre de Bruxelles, Belgium)
Nicholas Mattei (NICTA and University of New South Wales, Australia)
Robert Mattmüller (University of Freiburg, Germany)
Denis Maua (Universidade de São Paulo, Brazil)
Nicolas Maudet (Université Paris 6, France)
David McDonald (SIFT, LLC, USA)
Kathleen McKeown (Columbia University, USA)
Neville Mehta (Oregon State University, USA)
Christian Meilicke (University of Mannheim, Germany)
Reshef Meir (Harvard University, USA)
Francisco S. Melo (Instituto Superior Tecnico/INESC-ID, Portugal)
Eitan Menahem (IBM Cyber Security Center of Excellence, Israel)
Pablo Mendes (IBM Research Almaden, USA)
Felipe Meneguzzi (Pontifical Catholic University of Rio Grande do Sul, Brazil)
Aditya Menon (NICTA, Australia)
Tekin Meriçli (Carnegie Mellon University, USA)
Pedro Meseguer (Institut d'Investigacio en Intel.ligencia Artificial, CSIC, Spain)
Giorgio Metta (Italian Institute of Technology, Italy)
Thomas Meyer (Centre for Artificial Intelligence Research, UKZN and CSIR Meraka, South Africa)
Roberto Micalizio (Universita' di Torino, Italy)
Tomasz Michalak (University of Oxford, UK)
Laurent Michel (University of Connecticut, USA)
Ian Miguel (University of St. Andrews, UK)
Michela Milano (Italy)
David Mitchell (Simon Fraser University, Canada)
Joseph Modayil (University of Alberta, Canada)
Sanjay Modgil (King's College London, UK)
Pascal Molli (University of Nantes – LINA, France)
Marco Montali (Free University of Bozen-Bolzano, Italy)
Claire Monteleoni (George Washington University, USA)
Joris Mooij (University of Amsterdam, Netherlands)
Roser Morante (VU University Amsterdam, Netherlands)
Leora Morgenstern (Leidos, USA)
Alessandro Moschitti (University of Trento, Italy)
Boris Motik (University of Oxford, UK)

Martin Mueller (University of Alberta, Canada)
Christian Muise (University of Melbourne, Australia)
Sayan Mukherjee (Duke University, USA)
Aniello Murano (Universita' di Napoli "Federico II", Italy)
Lihi Naamani-Dery (Ariel University, Israel)
Sriram Narasimhan (University of California, Santa Cruz, USA)
Massimo Narizzano (STAR-Lab, DIST, University of Genova, Italy)
Nina Narodytska (University of Toronto and University of New South Wales, Canada)
Alex Nash (Northrop Grumman, USA)
Sriraam Natarajan (Indiana University, USA)
Roberto Navigli (Sapienza Universita' di Roma, Italy)
Ani Nenkova (University of Pennsylvania, USA)
Axel-Cyrille Ngonga Ngomo (University of Leipzig, Germany)
Patrick Nguyen (Metanautix, Inc, USA)
Vinh Nguyen (The University of Melbourne, Australia)
Feiping Nie (University of Texas at Arlington, USA)
Thomas Dyhre Nielsen (Aalborg University, Denmark)
Mathias Niepert (University of Washington, USA)
Oliver Niggemann (Hochschule Ostwestfalen-Lippe, Germany)
Jordi Nin (Universitat Politecnica de Catalunya and Barcelona Supercomputing Center, Spain)
Ko Nishino (Drexel University, USA)
Raz Nissim (Yahoo Labs, Israel)
Peter Novák (Delft University of Technology, Netherlands)
Tim Oates (University of Maryland Baltimore County, USA)
Svetlana Obraztsova (NTUA, Greece)
Simon O'Callaghan (NICTA, Australia)
Angelo Oddi (ISTC-CNR, Italian National Research Council, Italy)
Henrik Ohlsson (University of California, Berkeley, and C3 Energy, USA)
Jason O'Kane (University of South Carolina, USA)
Naoaki Okazaki (Tohoku University, Japan)
Frans Oliehoek (University of Amsterdam, Netherlands and University of Liverpool, United Kingdom)
Albert Oliveras (Technical University of Catalonia, Spain)
Eoin O'Mahony (Cornell University, USA)
Santiago Ontañón (Drexel University, USA)
Francesco Orabona (Yahoo Labs, NY, USA)
Giorgio Orsi (University of Oxford, UK)
Pedro Ortega (USA)
Luis Ortiz (Stony Brook University, USA)
Barry O'Sullivan (University College Cork, Ireland)
David Page (University of Wisconsin, Madison, USA)
Maurice Pagnucco (The University of New South Wales, Australia)
Tapio Pahikkala (University of Turku, Finland)
Ana Paiva (INESC-ID and Instituto Superior Técnico, University of Lisbon, Portugal)
Hector Palacios (Universitat Pompeu Fabra, Spain)
Jeff Z. Pan (University of Aberdeen, UK)
Rong Pan (Sun Yat-Sen University, China)
Thiago A. S. Pardo (University of São Paulo, Brazil)
Devi Parikh (Virginia Tech, USA)

Bijan Parsia (University of Manchester, UK)
Andrea Passerini (University of Trento, Italy)
Becky Passonneau (Columbia University, USA)
Peter Patel-Schneider (Nuance, USA)
Fabio Patrizi (Sapienza Università di Roma, Italy)
Jason Pazis (Duke University, USA)
Justin Pearson (Uppsala University, Sweden)
Michal Pechoucek Czech Republic)
Federico Pecora (Örebro University, Sweden)
Marieke Peeters (Delft University of Technology, Netherlands)
Bernhard Peischl (Technische Universität Graz, Austria)
Wojciech Penczek (IPI PAN and University of Podlasie, Poland)
Jian Peng (Toyota Technological Institute of Chicago, USA)
Yuxin Peng (Peking University, China)
David Pennock (Microsoft Research, USA)
Roberto Perdisci (University of Georgia, USA)
Jorge Pérez (Universidad de Chile, Chile)
Nathalie Pernelle (LRI-Universit Paris SUD, France)
Federico Pernici (University of Florence, Italy)
Patrice Perny (LIP6, France)
Gilles Pesant (Ecole Polytechnique de Montreal, Canada)
Catia Pesquita (University of Lisbon, Portugal)
Ron Petrick (University of Edinburgh, UK)
Marek Petrik (IBM Corporation, USA)
Bernhard Pfahringer (University of Waikato, New Zealand)
Joseph Pfeiffer (Purdue University, USA)
Mike Phillips (Carnegie Mellon University, USA)
Karim Pichara (Pontificia Universidad Catolica de Chile, Chile)
Reinhard Pichler (Vienna University of Technology, Austria)
Andreas Pieris (Vienna University of Technology, Austria)
Ingo Pill (Graz University of Technology, Austria)
Wei Ping (University of California, Irvine, USA)
Giuseppe Pirrò (University of Koblenz-Landau, Germany)
Mihail Pivtoraiko (GRASP Laboratory, University of Pennsylvania, USA)
Erion Plaku (Catholic University of America, USA)
Barbara Poblete (University of Chile, Chile)
Maria Polukarov (University of Southampton, UK)
Heather Pon-Barry (Mount Holyoke College, USA)
David Poole (University of British Columbia, Canada)
Fred Popowich (Simon Fraser University, Canada)
Daniele Porello (Institute for Cognitive Sciences and Technologies, ISTC, CNR, Italy)
Julie Porteous (Teesside University, UK)
Rui Prada (Instituto Superior Técnico, Universidade Técnica de Lisboa, Portugal)
Doina Precup (McGill University, Canada)
Valentina Presutti (STLab (ISTC-CNR), Italy)
Greg Provan (University College Cork, Ireland)
James Pustejovsky (Brandeis University, USA)
Yanjun Qi (University of Virginia, USA)

Tao Qin (Microsoft Research Asia, China)
Novi Quadrianto (University of Sussex, UK)
Claude-Guy Quimper (Université Laval, Canada)
Zinovi Rabinovich (Mobileye Vision Technologies Ltd., Israel)
Iyad Rahwan (Masdar Institute of Science and Technology, United Arab Emirates)
Franco Raimondi (Middlesex University, UK)
Naren Ramakrishnan (Virginia Tech, USA)
Miguel Ramírez (RMIT University, Australia)
Jan Ramon (KU Leuven, Belgium)
Huzefa Rangwala (George Mason University, USA)
Siamak Ravanbakhsh (University of Alberta, Canada)
Balaraman Ravindran (Indian Institute of Technology Madras, India)
Soumya Ray (Case Western Reserve University, USA)
Igor Razgon (Birkbeck, University of London, UK)
Jean-Charles Regin (University of Nice-Sophia Antipolis / I3S / CNRS, France)
Mark Reid (The Australian National University and NICTA, Australia)
Andrea Rendl (NICTA and Monash University, Australia)
Juan L. Reutter (Pontificia Universidad Católica, Chile)
Kate Revoredo (UNIRIO, Brazil)
Francesco Ricca (University of Calabria, Italy)
Elisa Ricci (Università di Perugia, Italy)
Mark Riedl (Georgia Institute of Technology, USA)
German Rigau (IXA Group, UPV/EHU, Spain)
Fabrizio Riguzzi (University of Ferrara, Italy)
Jussi Rintanen (Aalto University, Finland)
Alan Ritter (The Ohio State University, USA)
Frank E. Ritter (Penn State, USA)
David Roberts (North Carolina State University, USA)
Mark Roberts (Naval Research Laboratory, USA)
Marko Robnik-Sikonja (University of Ljubljana, FRI, Slovenia)
Odinaldo Rodrigues (King's College London, UK)
Juan Antonio Rodriguez Aguilar (IIIA-CSIC, Spain)
Mariano Rodriguez-Muro (IBM Research, USA)
Gabriele Röger (University of Basel, Switzerland)
Alex Rogers (University of Southampton, UK)
Andrea Roli (Alma Mater Studiorum – Universita' di Bologna, Italy)
Raquel Ros (Imperial College, UK)
Jeffrey S. Rosenschein (The Hebrew University of Jerusalem, Israel)
Benjamin Rosman (Council for Scientific and Industrial Research, South Africa)
Arun Ross (Michigan State University, USA)
Paolo Rosso (Technical University of Valencia, Spain)
Volker Roth (University of Basel, Switzerland)
Jörg Rothe (Universitaet Duesseldorf, Germany)
Marie-Christine Rousset (University of Grenoble, France)
Marco Roveri (FBK-irst, Italy)
Matthew Rowe (Lancaster University, UK)
Alla Rozovskaya (Columbia University, USA)
Jianhua Ruan (The University of Texas at San Antonio, USA)

Michel Rueher (University of Nice – Sophia Antipolis, France)
Wheeler Ruml (University of New Hampshire, USA)
Nicholas Ruozzi (Columbia University, USA)
Sasha Rush (Massachusetts Institute of Technology, USA)
Maytal Saar-Tsechansky (The University of Texas at Austin, USA)
Regis Sabbadin (INRA, France)
Marta Sabou (MODUL University Vienna, Austria)
Martin Sachenbacher (Technische Universität München, Germany)
Harald Sack (University of Potsdam, Germany)
Alessandro Saetti (University of Brescia, Italy)
Abdallah Saffidine (The University of New South Wales, Australia)
Alessandro Saffiotti (Örebro University, Sweden)
Tomoya Sakai (Nagasaki University, Japan)
Chiaki Sakama (Wakayama University, Japan)
Miguel A. Salido (Universitat Politecnica de Valencia, Spain)
Venkatesh Saligrama (Boston University, USA)
Rajhans Samdani (Google Inc., USA)
Horst Samulowitz (IBM Research, USA)
Rahul Savani (University of Liverpool, UK)
Bastin Tony Roy Savarimuthu (University of Otago, New Zealand)
Paul Scerri (Carnegie Mellon University, USA)
Thomas Scharrenbach (University of Zurich, Switzerland)
Torsten Schaub (University of Potsdam, Germany)
Pierre Schaus (UCLouvain, Belgium)
Thomas Schiex (INRA, France)
Stefan Schlobach (Vrije Universiteit Amsterdam, Netherlands)
Lars Schmidt-Thieme (University of Hildesheim, Germany)
Lenhart Schubert (University of Rochester, USA)
Peter Schüller (Marmara University, Turkey)
Christian Schulte (KTH Royal Institute of Technology, Sweden)
Oliver Schulte (Simon Fraser University, Canada)
Anika Schumann (IBM Research, Ireland)
Andreas Schutt (National ICT Australia, and The University of Melbourne, Australia)
Alexander Schwing (University of Toronto, Canada)
Paul Scott (NICTA, Australia)
Stephen Scott (University of Nebraska, USA)
Sandip Sen (University of Tulsa, USA)
Juan F. Sequeda (University of Texas at Austin, USA)
Luciano Serafini (Fondazione Bruno Kessler, Italy)
Sven Seuken (University of Zurich, Switzerland)
Julie Shah (Massachusetts Institute of Technology, USA)
Onn Shehory (IBM Haifa Research Lab, Israel)
Saeedeh Shekarpour (Bonn University, Germany)
Daniel Sheldon (University of Massachusetts, USA)
Dou Shen (United States)
Yelong Shen (Microsoft, USA)
Solomon Eyal Shimony (Ben-Gurion University, Israel)
David Shmoys (Cornell University, USA)

Mei Si (Rensselaer Polytechnic Institute (RPI), USA)
Jaime Simão Sichman (Universidade de São Paulo, Brazil)
Carles Sierra (The Artificial Intelligence Research Institute, Spain)
Leonid Sigal (Disney Research, USA)
Avirup Sil (IBM Research, NY, USA)
David Silver (Google[X], USA)
Guillermo Ricardo Simari (Universidad Nacional del Sur in Bahia Blanca, Argentina)
Laurent Simon (Labri, Bordeaux Institute of Technology, France)
Helmut Simonis (Ireland)
Sameer Singh (University of Washington, Seattle, USA)
Adish Singla (ETHZ, Switzerland)
Parag Singla (Indian Institute of Technology Delhi, India)
Tomas Singliar (Amazon.com, USA)
Oskar Skibski (Institute of Informatics, University of Warsaw, Poland)
Elizabeth Sklar (University of Liverpool, UK)
Piotr Skowron (University of Warsaw, Poland)
Sebastian Skritek (Vienna University of Technology, Austria)
John Slaney (Australian National University, Australia)
Arkadii Slinko (The University of Auckland, New Zealand)
Kevin Small (Amazon, USA)
David E. Smith (NASA Ames Research Center, USA)
Shirin Sohrabi (IBM Research, USA)
Mauricio Solar (Universidad Tecnica Federico Santa Maria, Chile)
Christine Solnon (LIRIS CNRS UMR 5205 / INSA Lyon, France)
Tran Cao Son (New Mexico State University, USA)
Le Song (Georgia Tech, USA)
Yangqiu Song (University of Illinois at Urbana-Champaign, USA)
Troels Bjerre Sørensen (IT-University of Copenhagen, Denmark)
Ricardo Soto (Pontificia Universidad Catolica de Valparaiso, Chile)
Mikhail Soutchanski (Ryerson University, Canada)
Matthijs Spaan (Delft University of Technology, Netherlands)
Marc Spaniol (Max-Planck-Institut für Informatik, Germany)
Alessandro Sperduti (University of Padua, Italy)
Vivek Srikumar (Stanford University, USA)
Rupesh Srivastava (Switzerland)
Steffen Staab (University of Koblenz-Landau, Germany)
Giorgos Stamou (National Technical University of Athens, Greece)
Gerald Steinbauer (Graz University of Technology, Austria)
Kostas Stergiou (University of Western Macedonia, Greece)
Roni Stern (Ben Gurion University of the Negev, Israel)
Umberto Straccia (ISTI-CNR, Italy)
Carlo Strapparava (FBK-irst, Italy)
Heiner Stuckenschmidt (University of Mannheim, Germany)
Peter J. Stuckey (University of Melbourne, Australia)
Thomas Stützle (Université Libre de Bruxelles, Belgium)
Nathan Sturtevant (University of Denver, USA)
Alex Styler (Carnegie Mellon University, USA)
Jimeng Sun (IBM, USA)

Peter Sunehag (Australian National University, Australia)
Pedro Szekely (USC/Information Sciences Institute, USA)
Armando Tacchella (Università di Genova, Italy)
Hideaki Takeda (National Institute of Informatics, Japan)
Ichiro Takeuchi (Nagoya Institute of Technology, Japan)
Kartik Talamadupula (Arizona State University, USA)
Erik Talvitie (Franklin and Marshall College, USA)
Pingzhong Tang (Tsinghua University, China)
Danny Tarlow (UK)
Christine Task (Purdue University, USA)
Matthew E. Taylor (Washington State University, USA)
Dan Tecuci (Siemens Corporate Research, USA)
Florent Teichteil-Königsbuch (ONERA, France)
Pankaj Telang (North Carolina State University, USA)
Stefanie Tellex (Brown University, USA)
John Thangarajah (RMIT University, Australia)
Jordan Thayer (Smart Information Flow Technologies, USA)
Georgios Theocharous (Adobe, USA)
Sylvie Thiebaux (ANU, Australia)
Matthias Thimm (Universität Koblenz-Landau, Germany)
David R. Thompson (Jet Propulsion Laboratory, California Instittue of Technology, USA)
Yuandong Tian (USA)
Taiki Todo (Kyushu University, Japan)
Julian Togelius (Denmark)
David Tolpin (University of Oxford, UK)
Liila Torabi (USA)
Luis Torgo (University of Porto, Portugal)
ÃÅlvaro Torralba (Saarland University, Germany)
Gianluca Torta (Università di Torino, Italy)
Craig A. Tovey (Georgia Tech, USA)
Felipe Trevizan (NICTA, Australia)
Michael Trick (Carnegie Mellon University, USA)
Rudolph Triebel (Technische Universität München, Germany)
Nicolas Troquard (Laboratory for Applied Ontology, Italy)
Mirek Truszczynski (University of Kentucky, USA)
Ivor Tsang (QCIS, University of Technology, Sydney, Australia)
Kewei Tu (ShanghaiTech University, China)
Zhuowen Tu (University of California, San Diego, USA)
Paolo Turrini (Imperial College London, UK)
Oncel Tuzel (Mitsubishi Electric Research Labs, USA)
Federico Ulliana (Montpellier University, France)
Jacopo Urbani (Vrije Universiteit Amsterdam, Netherlands)
Daniel Urieli (The University of Texas at Austin, USA)
Karina Valdivia (São Paulo University, Brazil)
Michal Valko (INRIA Lille – Nord Europe, France)
Petko Valtchev (Université du Québec à Montréal, Canada)
Marco Valtorta (University of South Carolina, USA)
Menkes Van Den Briel (NICTA, Australia)

Guy Van den Broeck (KU Leuven, Belgium)
Lucy Vanderwende (Microsoft Research, USA)
Marc Van Dongen (University College Cork, Ireland)
Hado Van Hasselt (Google DeepMind, UK)
Willem-Jan Van Hoeve (Carnegie Mellon University, USA)
Matthijs van Leeuwen (KU Leuven, Belgium)
Martijn Van Otterlo (Radboud University Nijmegen, Netherlands)
Harm van Seijen (University of Alberta, Canada)
Pradeep Varakantham (Singapore Management University, Singapore)
Stavros Vassos (Sapienza University of Rome, Italy)
Prasanna Velagapudi (Carnegie Mellon University, USA)
Miroslav N. Velev (Aries Design Automation, USA)
Manuela Veloso (Carnegie Mellon University, USA)
Kristen Brent Venable (Tulane University and IHMC, USA)
Joel Veness (Google DeepMind, UK)
Ruben Verborgh (Ghent University – iMinds, Belgium)
Paul Vernaza (Carnegie Mellon University, USA)
Johanna Völker (University of Mannheim, Germany)
Yevgeniy Vorobeychik (Vanderbilt University, USA)
Slobodan Vucetic (Temple University, USA)
Kiri Wagstaff (Jet Propulsion Laboratory, USA)
Richard Wallace (University College Cork, Ireland)
Haofen Wang (East China University of Science and Technology, China)
Kewen Wang (Griffith University, Australia)
Minlue Wang (University of Birmingham, UK)
Ning Wang (Curious Lab LLC, USA)
Yang Wang (University of Manitoba, Canada)
Yuyang Wang (Amazon, USA)
Tandy Warnow (University of Illinois at Urbana-Champaign, USA)
Renata Wassermann (University of São Paulo, Brazil)
Ian Watson (University of Auckland, New Zealand)
Ingo Weber (NICTA, Australia)
Martin Wehrle (University of Basel, Switzerland)
Adrian Weller (University of Cambridge, UK)
Ji-Rong Wen (Renmin University of China, China)
Patrick Westphal (Universität Leipzig, Germany)
Gerhard Widmer (Johannes Kepler University Linz, Austria)
Christopher Wilkens (Yahoo Labs, USA)
Mary-Anne Williams (Innovation and Enterprise Research Lab, UTS, Australia)
Mark C. Wilson (University of Auckland, New Zealand)
Christoph M. Wintersteiger (Microsoft Research, UK)
Gerhard Wohlgenannt (WU Vienna, Austria)
Stefan Woltran (Vienna University of Technology, Austria)
Weng-Keen Wong (Oregon State University, USA)
Peter Wood (Birkbeck, University of London, UK)
Kristian Woodsend (University of Edinburgh, UK)
Fei Wu (Zhejiang University, China)
Feng Wu (University of Science and Technology of China, China)

Jiewen Wu (IBM Research, Ireland)
Lei Wu (GE Global Research, USA)
Zheng Wu (The Mathworks, Inc., USA)
Josiane Xavier Parreira (Siemens, Austria)
Lirong Xia (Rensselaer Polytechnic Institute, USA)
Hui Xiong (Rutgers University, USA)
Linli Xu (University of Science and Technology of China, China)
Wei Xu (University of Pennsylvania, USA)
Zhao Xu (Fraunhofer SCAI, Germany)
Bishan Yang (Cornell University, USA)
Fangkai Yang (Schlumberger Ltd, USA)
Zhirong Yang (Aalto University, Finland)
Angela Yao (Switzerland)
Roland Yap (National University of Singapore, Singapore)
William Yeoh (New Mexico State University, USA)
Jinfeng Yi (IBM Thomas J. Watson Research Center, USA)
Alper Yilmaz (The Ohio State University, USA)
Yiming Ying (University of Exeter, UK)
Jay Young (United Kingdom)
Chun-Nam Yu (United States)
Yaoliang Yu (University of Alberta, Canada)
Changhe Yuan (Queens College/City University of New York, USA)
Yisong Yue (Disney Research, USA)
François Yvon (LIMSI/CNRS, France)
Fabio Zambetta (RMIT University, Australia)
Alessandro Zanarini (ABB Switzerland, Corporate Research Center, Switzerland)
Marina Zanella (University of Brescia, Italy)
Pablo Zegers (Universidad de los Andes, Chile)
Shaodan Zhai (United States)
Changshui Zhang (Tsinghua University, China)
Chongjie Zhang (Massachusetts Institute of Technology, USA)
Dongmo Zhang (University of Western Sydney, Australia)
Guo-Qiang Zhang (Case Western Reserve University, USA)
Jie Zhang (Nanyang Technological University, Singapore)
Junjie Zhang (Wright State University, USA)
Kai Zhang (Lawrence Berkeley National Laboratory, USA)
Lijun Zhang (Nanjing University, China)
Nevin L. Zhang (The Hong Kong University of Science and Technology, Hong Kong)
Shiqi Zhang (The University of Texas at Austin, USA)
Xinhua Zhang (NICTA and Australian National University, Australia)
Yan Zhang (University of Western Sydney, Australia)
Yu Zhang (Arizona State University, USA)
Xiangfu Zhao (Zhejiang Normal University, China)
Yu Zheng (Microsoft Research Aisa, China)
Feng Zhou (Carnegie Mellon University, USA)
Ming Zhou (Microsoft, China)
Rong Zhou (Palo Alto Research Center, Inc, USA)
Zhi-Hua Zhou (Nanjing University, China)

Jun Zhu (Tsinghua University, China)
Hankz Hankui Zhuo (Sun Yat-sen University, China)
Yair Zick (Carnegie-Mellon University, USA)
Brian Ziebart (University of Illinois at Chicago, USA)
Albrecht Zimmermann (INSA Lyon, France)
Antoine Zimmermann (école des Mines de Saint-étienne, France)
Martin Zinkevich (Google, Inc., USA)
Larry Zitnick (Microsoft, USA)

IAAI-15 Program Committee Members

Carl Andersen (Raytheon BBN Technologies, USA)
Mark Boddy (Adventium Labs, USA)
Markus Bohlin (SICS Swedish ICT AB, Sweden)
Andy Chun (City University of Hong Kong, Hong Kong)
James Crawford (Orbital Insight, USA)
Matt Gaston (Carnegie Mellon University, USA)
Christopher Geib (Drexel University, USA)
Karen Haigh (BBN Technologies, USA)
Neil Jacobstein (Singularity University, USA)
Brian Kettler (Lockheed Martin Advanced Technology Labs, USA)
Jana Koehler (Lucerne University of Applied Sciences and Art, Switzerland)
Robert Neches (Robert Neches Consulting Services, USA)
Bob Price (PARC, a Xerox company, USA)
Nestor Rychtyckyj (Ford Motor Company, USA)
Ted Senator (Leidos, USA)
Mohak Shah (Bosch Research, USA)
Hideo Shimazu (NEC Solution Innovators, Japan)
Reid Smith (i2k Connect LLC, USA)
David Stracuzzi (Sandia National Laboratories, USA)
Ramasamy Uthurusamy (General Motors Corporation (Retired), USA)
G. Michael Youngblood (PARC, a Xerox company, USA)

Student Abstract Program Committee Members

Natasha Alechina (University of Nottingham, UK)
Roman Bartak (Charles University, Czech Republic)
Christian Bauckhage (Fraunhofer IAIS, Germany)
Elizabeth Black (King's College London, UK)
Sylvain Bouveret (Grenoble Informatics Laboratory, France)
Rui Camacho (University of Porto, Portugal)
Michael Cashmore (King's College London, UK)
Hubie Chen (Universidad del País Vasco and IKERBASQUE, Spain)
Stefania Costantini (Università di L'Aquila, Italy)
Fabio Cozman (University of São Paulo, Brazil)
Stephen Cranefield (University of Otago, New Zealand)
Mehdi Dastani (Utrecht University, Netherlands)
Jesse Davis (K.U. Leuven, Belgium)
Sarah Jane Delany (Dublin Institute of Technology, Ireland)
Giuseppe Della Penna (Università di L'Aquila, Italy)

Janardhan Rao Doppa (Washington State University, USA)
Esra Erdem (Sabanci University, Turkey)
Shaheen Fatima (Loughborough University, UK)
Guillaume Infantes (ONERA, France)
Tushar Khot (University of Wisconsin-Madison, USA)
Angelika Kimmig (KU Leuven, Belgium)
Udo Kruschwitz (University of Essex, UK)
Wenwen Li (Arizona State University, USA)
Francesca Alessandra Lisi (University of Bari, Italy)
Weiru Liu (Queen's University Belfast, UK)
Brian Logan (University of Nottingham, UK)
Fabio Mercorio (University of Milano Bicocca, Italy)
Simon Miles (King's College London, UK)
Eva Onaindia (Universitat Politecnica de Valencia, Spain)
Andrea Orlandini (National Research Council of Italy (ISTC-CNR), Italy)
Jeff Z. Pan (University of Aberdeen, UK)
Ron Petrick (School of Informatics, University of Edinburgh)
Franco Raimondi (Middlesex University, UK)
Achim Rettinger (Karlsruhe Institute of Technology, Germany)
Scott Sanner (NICTA / Australian National University, Australia)
Vítor Santos Costa (Universidade do Porto, Portugal)
Carles Sierra (Spanish National Research Council, Spain)
Ameet Soni (Swarthmore College, USA)
Peter Sunehag (Australian National University, Australia)
Matthias Thimm (Universität Koblenz-Landau, Germany)
Anni-Yasmin Turhan (Dresden University of Technology, Germany)
Wamberto Vasconcelos (University of Aberdeen, UK)
Martin Wehrle (University of Basel, Switzerland)
Martha White (Indiana University, USA)
Stefan Woelfl (University of Freiburg, Germany)

Doctoral Consortium Program Committee

Noa Agmon (Bar-Ilan University, Israel)
David W. Aha (Naval Research Laboratory, USA)
Bo An (Nanyang Technological University, Singapore)
Philip Chan (Florida Institute of Technology, USA)
Brad Clement (Jet Propulsion Laboratory, California Institute of Technology, USA)
Mark Core (University of Southern California, Institute for Creative Technologies, USA)
Sanmay Das (Washington University in St. Louis, USA)
Edith Elkind (University of Oxford, UK)
Yolanda Gil (University of Southern California / Information Sciences Institute, USA)
Maria Gini (University of Minnesota, USA)
Benjamin Hirsch (EBTIC/Khalifa University, United Arab Emirates)
Ayanna Howard (Georgia Institute of Technology, USA)
Daniele Magazzeni (King's College London, UK)
Tim Miller (University of Melbourne, Australia)
Jeffrey S. Rosenschein (The Hebrew University of Jerusalem, Israel)
Bill Smart (Oregon State University, USA)

Sebastian Stein (University of Southampton, UK)
Pradeep Varakantham (Singapore Management University, Singapore)
Toby Walsh (NICTA and UNSW, Australia)

AAAI-15 Demonstrations Program Committee

Mark Boddy (Adventium Labs, USA)
Steven Chien (Jet Propulsion Laboratory, USA)
Minh Do (NASA Ames Research Center, USA)
Simone Fratini (European Space Agency, Germany)
Robert P. Goldman (SIFT, LLC, USA)
Akihiro Kishimoto (IBM Research, Ireland)
Jorge Ocón (GMV, Spain)
Nicola Policella (European Space Agency, Germany)

AI Video Competition Program Committee

David Aha (Navy Center for Applied Research in Artificial Intelligence, USA)
Vinay K. Chaudhri (SRI International, USA)
Anders Lyhne Christensen (University Institute of Lisbon, Portugal)
Nikolaus Correll (University of Colorado, USA)
Marco Dorigo (Université Libre de Bruxelles, Belgium)
Babak Esfandiari (Carleton University, Canada)
Michael Floyd (Knexus Research, USA)
Roderich Gross (University of Sheffield, UK)
Mitja Jermol (JSI, Slovenia)
Ramon Lopez de Mantaras (CSIC, Spain)
András Lõrinc (Eötvös Loránd University, Hungary)
Rehan O'Grady (Université Libre de Bruxelles, Belgium)
Ray Perrault (SRI International, USA)
Alessandro Saffiotti (University of Örebro, Sweden)
Angela Schoellig (University of Toronto, Canada)
Michael T. Tolley (Harvard University, USA)
Kiri L. Wagstaff (Jet Propulsion Laboratory, USA)
David C. Wilson (University of North Carolina, USA)
Alan Winfield (University of West of England)
G. Michael Youngblood (PARC, a Xerox Company, USA)

Technical Support

Gaëtan Podevijn (IRIDIA, Université Libre de Bruxelles)

Awards

Outstanding Paper Awards

This year, AAAI's Conference on Artificial Intelligence honored the following two papers, which exemplify high standards in technical contribution and exposition by regular and student authors. In addition, the program committee selected one paper for honorable mention in each category, based on their overall high quality and outstanding contribution.

AAAI-15 Outstanding Paper Award

From Non-Negative to General Operator Cost Partitioning
Florian Pommerening, Malte Helmert, Gabriele Röger and Jendrik Seipp

Honorable Mention

Predicting the Demographics of Twitter Users from Website Traffic Data
Aron Culotta, Nirmal Kumar Ravi, Jennifer Cutler

AAAI-15 Outstanding Student Paper Award

Surpassing Human-Level Face Verification Performance on LFW with GaussianFace
Chaochao Lu and Xiaoou Tang

Honorable Mention

Sparse Bayesian Multiview Learning for Simultaneous Association Discovery and Diagnosis of Alzheimer's Disease
Shandian Zhe, Zenglin Xu, Yuan Qi and Peng Yu

Special Computing Community Consortium (CCC) Blue Sky Awards

AAAI-15, in cooperation with the CRA Computing Community Consortium (CCC), honored three papers in the Senior Member track that presented ideas and visions that can stimulate the research community to pursue new directions, such as new problems, new application domains, or new methodologies. The recipients of the 2015 Blue Sky Idea travel awards, sponsored by the CCC, are as follows.

Intelligent Agents for Rehabilitation and Care of Disabled and Chronic Patients
Sarit Kraus

Emerging Architectures for Global System Science
Michela Milano and Pascal Van Hentenryck

Machine Teaching: An Inverse Problem to Machine Learning and an Approach toward Optimal Education
Xiaojin Zhu

Outstanding Program Committee Members

Each year, AAAI recognizes several outstanding senior program committee and program committee members for their distinguished service on the committee. These individuals went above and beyond the expectations for the role, showing exceptional judgment, clarity, knowledgeability, and leadership in reaching a consensus decision while serving on the committee.

Outstanding Senior Program Committee Members

Vincent Conitzer (Duke University, USA)
Robert Holte (University of Alberta, Canada)
Francesca Rossi (University of Padova, Italy)

Outstanding Program Committee Members

Christopher Amato (Massachusetts Institute of Technology, United States)
Travis Mandel (University of Washington, United States)
Nicholas Mattei (NICTA and University of New South Wales, Australia)
Ingo Pill (Graz University of Technology, Austria)
Erik Talvitie (Franklin & Marshall College, United States)
Paul Vernaza (Carnegie Mellon University, United States)
Xinhua Zhang (University of Alberta, Canada)

Sponsors

Platinum Sponsor

National Science Foundation

AI Journal

Baidu

Gold Sponsor

Infosys

Silver Sponsor

Microsoft Research

Bronze Sponsors

BigML

Disney Research

Google

NSERC Canadian Field Robotics Network (NCFRN)

University of Southern California/Information Sciences Institute

Yahoo Labs!

General Sponsors

ACM/SIGAI

CRA Computing Community Consortium (CCC)

David E. Smith

In Cooperation

University of Texas at Austin Computer Science Department

IEEE Robotics and Automation Society

RoboCup Federation

AAAI-15 Preface

Welcome to the Twenty-Ninth AAAI Conference on AI, the inaugural winter AAAI conference. AAAI-15 features many of the traditional AAAI events but also many innovations, including special programs that celebrate the past and look into the future. The doctoral consortium, workshops, tutorials and open house (that reaches out to the general public) precede the technical program, which includes the different AAAI-15 conference tracks and the Innovative Applications of AI Conference during the days and special events and poster sessions in the evenings. The poster sessions (with food, in lieu of a banquet) feature poster presentations, software and hardware demonstrations and a variety of special exhibits, including a virtual-agent exhibition and a computer-game showcase. The conference this year is colocated with the ACM SIGAI Career Network and Conference.

The main technical track is augmented by topical tracks on AI and the Web, Cognitive Systems, Computational Sustainability, and Integrated Systems. The Integrated Systems track provides a home for research that combines two or more distinct component technologies in an integrated manner that demonstrates added value either formally or empirically. The main technical and topical tracks of AAAI-15 received 1,991 submissions, the largest number in the history of the conference and about 40 percent more than the main technical track of AAAI-14 (that held the record previously), demonstrating that the scope and influence of AI continue to grow. Two highlights of the AAAI-15 submission process were the resubmission policy for substantially improved versions of declined AAAI-14 submissions and the opportunity for authors to request the automatic submission of declined AAAI-15 submissions to AAAI-15 workshops specified by them.

Our review process was the standard one for the AAAI conference series, although with a simplified review form. Each submission was initially assigned to at least three program committee (PC) members and one senior program committee (SPC) member to oversee the review process. Authors had an opportunity to comment on the reviews, providing input for a round of discussions between the SPC and PC members. Additional PC members were assigned to submissions in controversial cases as decided by the SPC members. The SPC members then made recommendations on which submissions to accept and the type of presentation for accepted submissions (either talk or poster), and the authors were notified of the decisions. Reviews and additional feedback (in form of metareviews written by SPC members, in those cases where the SPC members thought that the authors would benefit from them) were provided to the authors as well. Overall, 539 submissions were accepted for publication, for an acceptance rate of 27 percent. Accepted submissions are either presented as 15-minute talks (including 3 minutes of discussion) or posters (with 2-minute advertising talks), depending on the breadth of interest by the AAAI-15 audience as determined by the SPC members and the available time slots – resulting in 239 talks and 300 poster presentations.

The topical emphasis of AAAI-15 is robotics, because it provides exciting applications for AI research that can be of great benefit to society. We started collaborations with the IEEE Robotics and Automation Society, the Robotics: Science and Systems Foundation and the RoboCup Federation to introduce AI researchers to current developments in the robotics research community and to attract additional robotics researchers to AAAI-15 and introduce them to current developments in the AI research community. We are very grateful to the robotics cochairs, who spent an extraordinary amount of effort on coordinating and, in many cases, organizing the many robotics activities. Funding from the National Science Foundation was crucial in establishing activities such as the celebration of the Shakey project — an historic project at the interface of AI and robotics (with Ed Feigenbaum, Peter Hart and Nils Nilsson), a robotics exhibition including RoboCup exhibition matches, two workshops on Research Issues at the Boundary of AI and Robotics (which will compile a list of recommendations to funding agencies, professional organizations and individual researchers for how to push the boundary of AI and robotics further) and Knowledge, Skill and Behavior Transfer in Autonomous Robots, two robotics tutorials on RoboCup and Robot Learning from Demonstration, an invited talk on AI, Machine Learning and Robotics: Interplay and Interaction, a track with 10 selected talks from the 2014 Robotics: Science and Systems conference, and a track with 13 talks and accompanying posters by robotics fellowship students (Ph.D. students from robotics labs who want to learn about AI techniques of relevance to robotics).

AAAI-15 is concerned with the impact of AI on society, the responsible and sustainable transfer of technology from research groups to industry and the general appreciation of AI at large. Several activities are related to these important issues, such as the open house, a topical track on Computational Sustainability, a tutorial on AI and Technological Unemployment, two workshops on AI and Ethics and Computational Sustainability and a debate on Autonomous Weapons (with Stephen Goose and Ronald Arkin, moderated by the AAAI president).

AAAI-15 features a variety of additional tracks not yet mentioned: The senior member track provides an opportunity for established AI researchers to address the AI community and consists of senior member summary talks (on well-developed bodies of research or important new research areas) and blue sky idea talks (on ideas and visions that stimulate the research community to pursue new directions), whose awards are sponsored by the Computing Community Consortium. The what's hot track consists of invited presentations that present research highlights from other AI conferences and AI competitions. Finally, the invited talk track consists of the Joint AAAI/IAAI invited talk by Oren Etzioni, AAAI invited talks by Drew Bagnell, Michael Bowling, Lise Getoor, Geoffrey Hinton and Meinolf Sellmann and an IAAI invited talk by Rayid Ghani.

Several additional activities add excitement to the conference. For example, AAAI-15 has a funding information session during which program directors from several federal funding agencies describe their programs, a community meeting during which the AAAI president explains upcoming AAAI initiatives to the AAAI-15 attendees, a video competition, the General Game Playing Competition and an electronic job market organized in cooperation with the ACM Special Interest Group on AI. AAAI-15 also features additional innovations. For example, it uses a smart-phone app to augment the program brochure and uses social media channels on Facebook, Twitter, Linkedin and Flickr. The AAAI-15 attendees are also able to vote on a variety of awards, such as the best demonstration award, best student abstract talk award, best video award and best poster award.

AAAI-15 extends the traditional student activities. We are very grateful to the student activity and outreach cochairs, who spent an extraordinary amount of effort on coordinating and, in some cases, organizing the many student activities. For example, AAAI-15 offers a doctoral consortium, student abstract and poster program (with a 3-minute presentation contest), women's mentoring breakfast, lunch with a AAAI fellow program, a tutorial on How To Be a Ph.D. Student, highlighting of easily accessible papers in the program (with opportunities to meet their authors), student travel coordination, a student volunteer program and social opportunities such as a game night, research speed dating event and newcomer lunch. Awards designated exclusively for students include the best student paper award and the best student abstract talk award. AAAI-15 also recognizes the research performed by undergraduate students by presenting undergraduate co-authors of papers in the main technical and topical tracks of AAAI-15 with certificates.

AAAI-15 required a tremendous amount of work by a large number of people, especially due to the large number of submissions and activities. Thus, our organizing committee, SPC and PC were much larger than usual. We would like to thank all of them for their dedicated efforts — particularly when the work load ended up at the high end of our predictions! As in previous years, the AAAI staff members put an enormous amount of effort into making all of the local arrangements and managing all administrative aspects of the technical program. We received a tremendous amount of support especially from Carol Hamilton, Keri Harvey and Colleen Boyce. Additional thanks go to Mike Hamilton at The Live Oak Press, LLC for his work on producing these proceedings and other conference materials. We also made use of the wisdom and counsel of two AAAI Presidents (first Manuela Veloso and then Tom Dietterich), the AAAI Conference Committee (chaired by first Subbarao Kambhampati and then Shlomo Zilberstein) and our AAAI-15 advisory board (consisting of the PC chairs of the past three AAAI conferences).

In closing, we wish to express our gratitude for the dedication of the hundreds of people who put effort into making AAAI-15 a success, including the sponsors and especially the authors. Without you, there would be no basis for the conference. It has been a pleasure to serve at the head of this huge undertaking and we hope that you will enjoy the results.

– *Blai Bonet and Sven Koenig*
AAAI-15 Program Cochairs

Welcome to the Twenty-Seventh Annual Conference on

IAAI-15 Preface

the Innovative Applications of Artificial Intelligence (IAAI-15), the premier conference focusing on applied AI research ranging from exciting new potential applications to innovative deployments of AI technology.

IAAI is colocated with AAAI and their paper presentations and invited talks are coordinated. This enables conference attendees to seamlessly move between conferences fostering interest in applied AI research while keeping track of the latest results of AI research.

IAAI-15 presents papers in three tracks: deployed applications, emerging applications, and challenge problems. The deployed applications track focuses on fielded AI applications that distinguish themselves for their innovative use of AI technology. This year we have six papers in this track, including descriptions of the AI technology used for detecting procurement and healthcare fraud, activity planning for lunar orbital missions, performing position assignment in the enterprise, modeling protest events in social media, and a special 30-history of one of AI's longest running applications – the Process Diagnosis System (PDS).

The emerging applications track focuses on areas in which AI technology can have a practical impact. This year we have 13 papers in this track, covering topics on entity recognition, combining qualitative logic and crowdsourcing, machine learning and storm models, learning route preferences, collaborative planning, citizen science, cyber defense, sketch understanding for music education, and skill identification.

This year we've added a new track on Challenge Problems, which will include three papers proposing grand challenges for AI: the Winograd Challenge in commonsense reasoning, the Aristo Challenge in elementary school science, and a challenge in large-scale flow cytometry.

We have an outstanding lineup of invited speakers. Oren Etzioni will present the joint AAAI/IAAI-15 talk on the Allen Institute for Artificial Intelligence. Rayid Ghani will present an IAAI-15 invited talk on his work as the Director of the Center for Data Science at the University of Chicago.

The Innovative Applications of Artificial Intelligence Conference could not take place without the generous help of many people. In particular, we appreciate the hard work and dedication of the IAAI-15 program committee, the invited speakers, and the authors of the technical papers, without whom the technical program would not exist. We also want to acknowledge the professional administrative and planning expertise of Carol Hamilton, Keri Harvey, and the entire AAAI staff. They keep the conference production schedule on track, are wonderful to work with, and make this conference possible. We hope you enjoy the conference!

– David Gunning and Peter Yeh
IAAI 2015 Conference Chair and Cochair

Invited Talks

IAAI-15 /AAAI-15 Joint Invited Talk

You Can't Play 20 Questions with Nature and Win

Oren Etzioni (Allen Institute for Artificial Intelligence)

The machine learning paradigm, and deep learning methods in particular, have achieved phenomenal results in recent years. We need to leverage and extend these methods to address grand AI challenges such as the automated acquisition of common-sense knowledge, and machine reading of text. My talk will describe the ambitious research program at the Allen Institute of AI (AI2), which aims to address these challenges in collaboration with the AI community. I will describe our key projects: Aristo — which learns from textbooks and reasons over learned knowledge to answer standardized test questions, and Semantic Scholar — which aims to utilize AI methods to revolutionize the search for academic papers.

Oren Etzioni is CEO of the Allen Institute for Artificial Intelligence, and a professor at the University of Washington's Computer Science Department. He has received the Robert Engelmore Memorial Award (2007), the IJCAI Distinguished Paper Award (2005), AAAI Fellow (2003), and a National Young Investigator Award (1993). He was also the founder of several companies including Farecast (sold to Microsoft in 2008) and Decide (sold to eBay in 2013), and is the author of more than 100 technical papers that have garnered roughly 22,000 citations. Etzioni received his Ph.D. from Carnegie Mellon University in 1991, and his BA from Harvard in 1986.

AAAI-15 Invited Talk

Artificial Intelligence, Machine Learning and Robotics: Interplay and Interaction

Drew Bagnell (Carnegie Mellon University)

My talk will focus on theoretical and algorithmic ideas in machine learning and AI, and their origin in problems of robotics. Much of my talk will focus on no-regret online learning methods in machine learning and the critical role of interaction for learning in robotics.

I will highlight the tremendous impact robotics has had in identifying key learning problems and suggesting algorithmic techniques; additionally, I'll consider the remarkable tools that have been developed within AI and learning to address hard robotics problems. I'll discuss a variety of machine learning techniques of increasing sophistication from the most familiar classification problems, to structured prediction, and to imitation learning. I will also address how to make reinforcement learning and learning control practical in robotics. Throughout, we will look at case studies in learning dexterous manipulation, activity forecasting of drivers and pedestrians, and imitation learning of robotic locomotion and rough-terrain navigation. These case studies highlight key challenges in applying AI and learning algorithms in practical settings.

J. A. (Drew) Bagnell is an associate professor at Carnegie Mellon University's Robotics Institute, National Robotics Engineering Center and Machine Learning Department. His interests in AI range from algorithmic and basic theoretical development to delivering fielded learning-based systems. Bagnell directs the Learning, AI, and Robotics Laboratory (LAIRLab) within the Robotics Institute. He also serves as the director of the Robotics Institute Summer Scholars program, a summer research experience in robotics for undergraduates throughout the world. Bagnell and his groups have received research awards in both the robotics and machine learning communities including at the International Conference on Machine Learning, Robotics Science and Systems, and International Conference on Robotics and Automation. His current projects focus on machine learning for dexterous manipulation, decision making under uncertainty, ground and aerial vehicle control, robot perception and computer vision. Prior to joining the faculty, Bagnell received his doctorate as an NSF Graduate Fellow at Carnegie Mellon in 2004 and completed undergraduate studies with highest honors in electrical engineering at the University of Florida.

AAAI-15 Invited Talk

von Neumann's Dream

Michael Bowling (University of Alberta)

Chess has long served as the measure of progress for artificial intelligence. However, at the very beginning of computing and artificial intelligence, John von Neumann dreamt of a different game: "Real life is not like [chess]. Real life consists of bluffing, of little tactics of deception, of asking yourself what is the other man going to think I mean to do. And that is what games are about in my theory." The game von Neumann hinted at is poker, and it played a foundational role in his formalization of game theory. Shortly after launching the field of game theory, he practically abandoned his new discipline to focus on the budding field of computing. He saw computers as the way to make his mathematics workable. Now, over 70 years later with both significant advances in computing and game theoretic algorithms, von Neumann's dream is now a reality. Heads-up limit Texas hold'em poker, the smallest variant of poker played by humans, is essentially solved. In this talk, I will discuss how we accomplished this landmark result, along with the substantial scientific advances in our failed attempts along the way.

Michael Bowling is a professor of computing science at the University of Alberta. His research focuses on artificial intelligence, machine learning, and game theory; and he is particularly fascinated by the problem of how computers can learn to play games through experience. Bowling is the leader of the Computer Poker Research Group, which has built some of the strongest poker playing programs in the world. In 2008, one of these programs, Polaris, defeated a team of top professional poker players in two-player, limit Texas Hold'em, becoming the first program to defeat poker pros in a meaningful competition. His research has been featured on the television programs Scientific American Frontiers, National Geographic Today, and Discovery Channel Canada; in the New York Times and Wired; and twice in exhibits at the Smithsonian Museums in Washington, D.C.

AAAI-15 Invited Talk

Using Statistics and Semantics to Solve Big (Graph) Data Problems

Lise Getoor (University of California, Santa Cruz)

Big data problems benefit from modeling both structure and uncertainty, so there is a growing need for tools to develop large, complex probabilistic models. These tools should combine high-level knowledge representation with general purpose, scalable algorithms for learning and inference. In this talk, I will survey some of the recent work from the statistical relational learning community on learning and inference in richly-structured, multi-relational network data. I will highlight both important developments and opportunities in which ideas from AI can have great impact on upcoming challenges within the machine learning, data science and data mining communities.

Lise Getoor is a professor in the Computer Science Department at the University of California, Santa Cruz. Her research areas include machine learning and reasoning under uncertainty, with an emphasis on graph and network data. She is a AAAI Fellow, serves on the Computing Research Association and International Machine Learning Society boards, was cochair of ICML 2011, is a recipient of an NSF Career Award and eight best paper and best student paper awards. She received her PhD from Stanford University, her MS from the University of California, Berkeley, and her BS from the University of California, Santa Barbara, and was a professor at the University of Maryland, College Park from 2001–2013.

AAAI-15 Invited Talk

Deep Learning

Geoffrey Hinton (University of Toronto and Google Inc.)

I will give a brief history of deep learning explaining what it is, what kinds of task it should be good for and why it was largely abandoned in the 1990's. I will then describe how ideas from statistical physics were used to make deep learning work much better on small datasets. Finally I will describe how deep learning is now used by Google for speech recognition and object recognition and how it may soon be used for machine translation.

Geoffrey Hinton received his PhD in artificial intelligence from Edinburgh in 1978. He spent five years at Carnegie-Mellon. In 1987 he moved to the Department of Computer Science at the University of Toronto. Since 2013, he has been splitting his time between the University of Toronto and Google. He was one of the researchers who introduced the back-propagation algorithm. His other contributions to neural network research include Boltzmann machines, distributed representations, time-delay neural nets, mixtures of experts, variational learning, products of experts and deep belief nets. His students used deep learning to change the way in which speech recognition and object recognition are done.

AAAI-15 Invited Talk

Intelligent Decisions

Meinolf Sellmann (IBM T. J. Watson Research Center)

At its best intelligence creates aesthetic and beauty, yet from a utilitarian perspective intelligence primarily serves the purpose of making better decisions. Today's prescriptive decision support systems are most effective when applied to specific recurring operational problems. Recent advances in AI technology have revived the vision of commercially viable cooperative strategic decision support systems. These cognitive systems integrate information retrieval, knowledge representation, interactive modelling, as well as social and self-learning capabilities with logic reasoning and probabilistic decision making under uncertainty. I provide a snapshot of the current technology status by showcasing several projects that ultimately aim at intelligent human-in-the-loop decision making.

Meinolf Sellmann is senior manager for data curation in the cognitive computing department at IBM Watson Research. He received his doctorate degree from Paderborn University from where he went on to Cornell University as postdoctoral associate and Brown University as assistant professor. Sellmann has published over 60 articles in international conferences and journals with central contributions in symmetry breaking, global constraints, the integration of mathematical and constraint programming, search, autonomous algorithm configuration, and algorithm portfolios. He served as conference chair of CP 2007, PC chair of CPAIOR 2013, and associate editor of the Informs Journal on Computing. He received an NSF Early Career Award in 2007 and IBM Outstanding Technical Innovation Awards in 2013 and 2014. Based on their meta-algorithmic research, for four years in a row Sellmann and his team won at international SAT and MaxSAT solver competitions, among others for the overall most efficient parallel SAT Solver in 2013, and three first places at the 2014 MaxSAT Evaluation.

IAAI-15 Invited Talk

Data Science for Social Good: Using Your Powers To Make a Social Impact!

Rayid Ghani (University of Chicago)

The past few years have seen an increasing demand for machine learning/data mining/data science powers. That's wonderful for us data scientists but wouldn't the world be so much better if we also used our computational and analytical powers for social good? In this talk, I'll give examples from work going on around the world including from the summer fellowship program we started at University of Chicago on Data Science for Social Good to show that there are a lot of important social problems in the world that could use our help — from helping students graduate high school to helping disaster victims to improving health.

Rayid Ghani is the director of the Center for Data Science and Public Policy at the University of Chicago. He is also the cofounder of Edgeflip, an analytics and social media startup that is focused on helping nonprofits and social causes. Previously, Ghani was the chief scientist for the Obama 2012 election campaign focusing on analytics, data, and technology.

Ghani is focused on education, research, and developing approaches to use data and analytics for social causes, both with Edgeflip and the University of Chicago. He created and runs the Eric and Wendy Schmidt Data Science for Social Good Summer Fellowship, which brings together aspiring data scientists to work on data science projects in partnership with governments and nonprofits.

Special Invited Presentations

AAAI-15 Panel

The Shakey Celebration

Panelists: Ed Feigenbaum, Peter Hart, and Nils Nilsson

Shakey the Robot, conceived fifty years ago, was a seminal contribution to AI. Shakey perceived its world, planned how to achieve a goal, and acted to carry out that plan. This was revolutionary. We gather to celebrate Shakey, and to gain insights into how the AI revolution moves ahead. The Shakey Celebration will include a panel with Ed Feigenbaum, Peter Hart, and Nils Nilsson, along with other highlights of this historic project.

AAAI-15 Debate

Debate on Autonomous Weapons

Participants: Ron Arkin (Georgia Institute of Technology) and Stephen Goose (Human Rights Watch)

Moderator: Thomas G. Dietterich (Oregon State University)

Mankind is facing a step change in how wars will be fought as fully autonomous weapons are in the process of being developed that could be deployed in the field. The United Nations Convention on Certain Conventional Weapons (CCW) is considering an international ban on such weapons. The debate serves as part of a process by which the AI community might form and voice its opinion on such matters.

Ronald C. Arkin is a regents' professor, director of the Mobile Robot Laboratory, and associate dean for Research in the College of Computing at Georgia Tech. He served as STINT visiting professor at KTH in Stockholm, sabbatical chair at the Sony IDL in Tokyo, and the Robotics and AI Group at LAAS/CNRS in Toulouse. His research interests include behavior-based reactive control and action-oriented perception for mobile robots and unmanned aerial vehicles, hybrid deliberative/reactive software architectures, robot survivability, multiagent robotic systems, biorobotics, human-robot interaction, robot ethics, and learning in autonomous systems. His latest book is Governing Lethal Behavior in Autonomous Robots. Arkin serves on numerous journal editorial boards and is the series editor for The MIT Press book series *Intelligent Robotics and Autonomous Agents.* He has provided expert testimony to the United Nations, the International Committee of the Red Cross, the Pentagon and others on Autonomous Systems Technology. Arkin served on the Board of Governors of the IEEE Society on Social Implications of Technology, the IEEE RAS AdCom, and is founding cochair of IEEE RAS TC on Robot Ethics. He is a distinguished lecturer for the IEEE Society on social implications of technology and a Fellow of the IEEE.

Stephen Goose, executive director of Human Rights Watch's Arms Division, was instrumental in bringing about the 2008 convention banning cluster munitions, the 1997 treaty banning antipersonnel mines, the 1995 protocol banning blinding lasers, and the 2003 protocol requiring clean-up of explosive remnants of war. He and Human Rights Watch cofounded the International Campaign to Ban Landmines (ICBL), which received the 1997 Nobel Peace Prize. Goose created the ICBL's Landmine Monitor initiative, the first time that nongovernmental organizations around the world have worked together in a sustained and coordinated way to monitor compliance with an international disarmament or humanitarian law treaty. In 2013, he and Human Rights Watch cofounded the Campaign to Stop Killer Robots. Before joining Human Rights Watch in 1993, Goose was a US congressional staffer and a researcher at the Center for Defense Information. He has a master's degree in International Relations from the Johns Hopkins School of Advanced International Studies and a BA in History from Vanderbilt University.

Moderator Thomas G. Dietterich is the president of the Association for the Advancement of Artificial Intelligence.

AI and the Web

Efficient Top-k Shortest-Path Distance Queries on Large Networks by Pruned Landmark Labeling

Takuya Akiba[†], **Takanori Hayashi**[†], **Nozomi Nori**[‡], **Yoichi Iwata**[†] and **Yuichi Yoshida**[§‖]
†The University of Tokyo, 113-0033, Tokyo, Japan ‡Kyoto University, 606-8501, Kyoto, Japan
§National Institute of Informatics, 101-8430, Tokyo, Japan
‖Preferred Infrastructure, Inc., 113-0033, Tokyo, Japan
{t.akiba,thayashi,y.iwata}@is.s.u-tokyo.ac.jp, nozomi@ml.ist.i.kyoto-u.ac.jp, yyoshida@nii.ac.jp

Abstract

We propose an indexing scheme for top-k shortest-path distance queries on graphs, which is useful in a wide range of important applications such as network-aware searches and link prediction. While many efficient methods for answering standard (top-1) distance queries have been developed, none of these methods are directly extensible to top-k distance queries. We develop a new framework for top-k distance queries based on *2-hop cover* and then present an efficient indexing algorithm based on the recently proposed *pruned landmark labeling* scheme. The scalability, efficiency and robustness of our method is demonstrated in extensive experimental results. Moreover, we demonstrate the usefulness of top-k distance queries by applying them to link prediction, the most fundamental graph problem in the AI and Web communities.

Introduction

The shortest-path distance between vertices in a network is a fundamental concept in graph theory and is widely applied in the AI and Web communities. For example, because the distances between vertices indicate the relevance among the vertices, they can identify other users or contents that best match a user's intent in socially-sensitive searches (Vieira et al. 2007; Yahia et al. 2008; Maniu and Cautis 2013). In context-aware searches, they are used to assign higher ranks to web pages more related to the currently visited web page (Ukkonen et al. 2008; Potamias et al. 2009).

However, there is a fundamental drawback of basing relevance on distance alone. Specifically, distances should be integers and the diameters of real-world networks are typically small (Watts and Strogatz 1998). Such small diameter greatly reduce the number of possible distances and preclude the full use of the underlying structure.

This problem is clearly depicted in Figure 1. In each graph in the figure, the distance between the pair of black vertices is four. Hence, based on distance alone, the black pairs in all three graphs have the same similarity. However, the pair in graph (c) seems more tightly connected than the pairs in graphs (a) and (b), since this pair is connected by a greater number of shortest paths.

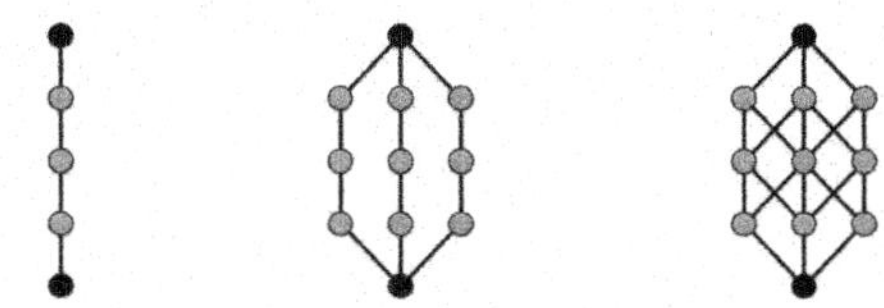

Figure 1: Examples of connection between two vertices.

Table 1: Distances and top-k distances between the two black vertices in Figure 1.

Graph	(Top-1) Distance	Top-k Distances
(a)	4	[4, 6, 6, 6, 6, 8, 8, ...]
(b)	4	[4, 4, 4, 6, 6, 6, 6, ...]
(c)	4	[4, 4, 4, 4, 4, 4, 4, ...]

This intuitive concept can be naturally implemented by adopting the *top-k shortest paths* and *top-k distances* (formally defined later). Table 1 presents the top-k distances between the pair of black vertices in each graph of Figure 1. Although the pairs in each graph are separated by the same distance, their top-k distances markedly vary, providing a potential means of distinguishing these three graph structures.

However, determining the top-k distances between vertices is computationally expensive. The naive approach is to apply a variant of Dijkstra's algorithm that visits the same vertex k times. This approach consumes $O((n+m)k)$ and $O((n \log n + m)k)$ time on unweighted and weighted graphs, respectively, where n and m are the numbers of vertices and edges, respectively. In the above-mentioned applications, the top-k distances must be interactively computed for many vertex pairs on large social and web graphs, requiring a much faster algorithm. Eppstein (Eppstein 1998) improved the time complexity to $O(n+m+k)$ and $O(n \log n + m+k)$ on unweighted and weighted graphs respectively, but his algorithm remains prohibitively slow.

Contribution

To resolve this issue, we propose an indexing method for answering the top-k distances. The proposed method is an indexing method, i.e., it first constructs a data structure called an *index* from a graph and then top-k distances between arbitrary pairs of vertices are rapidly obtained using the index. To our knowledge, we present the first indexing method to top-k distance inquiry.

Our method is built on the recently proposed *pruned landmark labeling*, an indexing scheme that answers shortest-path distances (Akiba, Iwata, and Yoshida 2013). However, modifying this method to answer top-k distances is nontrivial because the number of paths becomes crucial, bringing the new challenge of carefully avoiding double counts. Moreover, it requires several interesting ideas in order to keep the scalability.

As shown later in our experiments, our method can construct indices from large graphs comprising millions of vertices and tens of millions of edges within a reasonable running time. Having obtained the indices, we can compute the top-k distances within a few microseconds, six orders of magnitude faster than existing methods, which require a few seconds to compute these distances.

Moreover, to illustrate the importance of the top-k distances, we apply our method to the *link prediction problem* (Liben-Nowell and Kleinberg 2003), a well-studied problem in AI and Web communities. We empirically show that the support vector machine (SVM) with the top-k distances as its feature outperforms a number of baseline methods including singular value decomposition and random walk with restart. We emphasize that our indexing method enables the first use of the top-k distances for such tasks. The results also indicate the feasibility of top-k distances in other tasks, such as network-aware searching.

Our implementation of the proposed indexing method is publicly available from the first author's web page. We hope that our public code will enable further exploration of top-k distances in various applications.

Related Work

Distance Indices. Although numerous indexing methods for computing shortest-path distances have been proposed (Cheng and Yu 2009; Xiao et al. 2009; Wei 2010; Akiba, Sommer, and Kawarabayashi 2012; Jin et al. 2012; Fu et al. 2013; Akiba, Iwata, and Yoshida 2013), none of these methods can directly answer top-k distance queries.

Pruned Labeling Algorithms. Pruned labeling was first proposed for distance queries on complex networks (Akiba, Iwata, and Yoshida 2013). Then, specialization and extensions have been proposed for reachability queries on directed acyclic graphs (Yano et al. 2013), distance queries on road networks (Akiba et al. 2014), and distance queries on dynamic graphs (Akiba, Iwata, and Yoshida 2014).

Other Vertex Similarities. The performance of applications related to graph mining can also be enhanced by features other than top-k distances, such as *random walk with restart (RWR)*. As straightforward iterative algorithms are precluded by their high computational cost, several approximation methods have been proposed (Jeh and Widom 2003; McSherry 2005; Sun et al. 2005; Tong, Faloutsos, and Pan 2006). Despite sacrificing accuracy for efficiency, these methods remain prohibitively time-expensive for computing the RWR scores for many vertex pairs on large networks in real-time applications, such as network-aware searches.

Similar arguments apply to other walk-based similarities such as *SimRank* (Jeh and Widom 2002) and *commuting time* (Lovász 1996). In contrast, as we shall experimentally demonstrate, such large networks are efficiently handled by our method for answering top-k distances. We also believe that top-k distances provide features with different properties from them, which can be used as complementary features for those other vertex similarities.

Some of *graph kernels* (Smola and Kondor 2003), in particular, those based on the *graph Laplacian* such as the *regularized Laplacian kernel* can also be used to assign relevance scores for vertex pairs (Ito et al. 2005). However, the computational cost of graph kernels is even more infeasible for large graphs.

Preliminaries

The current study focus on networks that are modeled as graphs. To simplify our discussion, we consider only undirected and unweighted graphs first. However, as discussed later, our method is easily extendible to directed and weighted graphs.

Let $G = (V, E)$ be a graph with a vertex set V and an edge set E. We denote the number of vertices $|V|$ and the number of edges $|E|$ by n and m, respectively. We assume that vertices are uniquely represented by integers, enabling natural comparisons of two vertices $u, v \in V$ by expressions such as $u < v$ or $u \leq v$.

An *internal vertex* of a path refers to a vertex in the path that is not an endpoint of it. Let $\mathcal{P}$ be a set of paths. The *i-th shortest path in $\mathcal{P}$* refers to the i-th path in P, ordered by length, where ties are broken arbitrarily.

For a pair of vertices (s, t), let $\mathcal{P}_{st}$ be the set of all (unnecessarily simple) paths between s and t. For a vertex v, let $\mathcal{P}_{st}^{>v}$ be the set of paths in $\mathcal{P}_{st}$ whose internal vertices are all larger than v. Similarly, let $\mathcal{P}_{st}^{\not>v}$ be the set of paths in $\mathcal{P}_{st}$ such that at least one internal vertex is smaller than or equal to v. Then for two vertices s and t, the *i-th shortest path between s and t* is the i-th shortest path in $\mathcal{P}_{st}$. Let $d_{i\text{-th}}(s, t)$, $d_{i\text{-th}}^{>v}(s, t)$, and $d_{i\text{-th}}^{\not>v}(s, t)$ denote the length of the i-th shortest path in $\mathcal{P}_{st}$, $\mathcal{P}_{st}^{>v}$, and $\mathcal{P}_{st}^{\not>v}$, respectively. If the size of the corresponding set is less than i, then we set them to ∞. We define $d_{i\text{-th}}^{\geq v}(s, t)$ and $d_{i\text{-th}}^{\not\geq v}(s, t)$ similarly.

Problem Definition

In this paper, we propose an indexing method that, given a graph G and a positive integer k, construct an index to quickly answer the following query.

Problem 1 (Top-k Distance Query).
Given: *A pair of vertices (s, t).*
Answer: *An array $(d_{1\text{st}}(s, t), d_{2\text{nd}}(s, t), \ldots, d_{k\text{-}th}(s, t))$.*

Proposed Method

This section describes our proposed method and show its correctness. We also suggest several important techniques for practical performance enhancement.

Data Structure

The data structure and query algorithm of the proposed method are based on the general framework of *2-hop cover* (Cohen et al. 2002), which is designed for standard (top-1) distance queries. However, as normal distance queries do not consider the number of paths, the main challenge in processing top-k distance queries is preventing multiple counts of the same path. To this end, we require a more involved framework.

For each vertex v, our method precomputes and stores the following two labels:

- *Distance label* $L(v)$, comprising a set of pairs (u, δ) of a vertex and a path length. If we gather lengths in $L(v)$ associated with a vertex u, they should form the sequence $(d^{>v}_{\text{1st}}(v,u), d^{>v}_{\text{2nd}}(v,u), \ldots, d^{>v}_{\ell\text{-th}}(v,u))$ for some $1 \leq \ell \leq k$.
- *Loop label* $C(v)$, constituting a sequence of k integers $(\delta_1, \delta_2, \ldots, \delta_k)$. This sequence should equal $(d^{\geq v}_{\text{1st}}(v,v), d^{\geq v}_{\text{2nd}}(v,v), \ldots, d^{\geq v}_{k\text{-th}}(v,v))$.

An *index* is a pair $I = (L, C)$, where L and C are the sets of distance labels $\{L(v)\}_{v \in V}$ and loop labels $\{C(v)\}_{v \in V}$, respectively.

Query Algorithm

Given an index $I = (L, C)$ and a pair of vertices (s, t), we compute the top-k distances between s and t as follows. First, we compute the following multiset.

$$\begin{aligned}\Delta(I, s, t) = \{\delta_{sv} + \delta_{vv} + \delta_{vt} \mid (v, \delta_{sv}) \in L(s),\\ \delta_{vv} \in C(v), (v, \delta_{vt}) \in L(t)\}.\end{aligned}$$

Intuitively, we first move from s to v, then loop back to v several steps later, and finally move from v to t. Note that from the definition of distance labels and loop labels, every internal vertex in the path from s to t (except v itself) is larger than v.

Let $\text{QUERY}(I, s, t)$ denote the smallest k elements in the multiset $\Delta(I, s, t)$. If $|\delta(I, s, t)| < k$, the remaining entries are filled with ∞. Our answer to the query (s, t) is $\text{QUERY}(I, s, t)$.

Indexing Algorithm

Our index constructing algorithm is summarized in Algorithm 1. We first compute the loop label $C(v)$ for every vertex v. We then construct the distance labels L by conducting a *pruned BFS* from each vertex.

Algorithm for Computing Loop Labels. We construct the loop labels as follows. For each vertex v, using vertices larger than or equal to v, we perform a modified version of breadth first search (BFS). In the BFS, each vertex may be visited up to k times. The first k visits to the vertex v gives the distance sequence $d^{\geq v}_{\text{1st}}(v,v), d^{\geq v}_{\text{2nd}}(v,v), \ldots, d^{\geq v}_{k\text{-th}}(v,v)$.

Algorithm 1 Indexing Algorithm

```
procedure ConstructIndex(G)
    for i = 1 to n do Compute C(v_i) using the modified BFS.
    L(v) ← ∅ for all v ∈ V.
    for i = 1 to n do PrunedBFS(G, v_i).
    return (C, L).
```

Algorithm 2 Pruned Top-k BFS from $v \in V$.

```
1: procedure PrunedBFS(G, v)
2:     Q ← a queue with only one element (v, 0).
3:     while Q is not empty do
4:         Dequeue (u, δ) from Q.
5:         if δ < max (Query((L, C), v, u)) then
6:             Add (v, δ) to L(u).
7:             for all w ∈ V such that (u, w) ∈ E, w > v do
8:                 Enqueue (w, δ + 1) onto Q.
```

The modified BFS returns to the starting vertex long before all vertices in the graph have been visited. Consequently, the running time is very small in practice and empirically estimated as $O(nk)$ in total from experiments.

Algorithm for Computing Distance Labels. We assume that vertices in V are ordered as $v_1, v_2, \ldots, v_n$. Then for each $1 \leq i \leq n$, we perform a *pruned BFS* from v_i (Algorithm 2). The pruned BFS is essentially a modified version of the BFS from v that visits the same vertex at most k times. The crucial difference is the non-trivial pruning; that is, when visiting a vertex u at distance δ, the process is discontinued if δ is larger than or equal to the k-th shortest distance computable by the current index (L, C) (Line 5).

We roughly estimate the time complexity. Let l be the average size of labels. We visit $O(nl)$ vertices in total, traversing $O(\frac{m}{n})$ edges on average and evaluating a query in $O(l)$ time (by using the fast pruning technique introduced later). Thus, the total time complexity of this part is $O(ml + nl^2)$. In our experiments, l was a few hundred.

Proof of Correctness

The correctness of our method is shown as follows. Let L_i denote the set of distance labels L after the i-th pruned BFS from v_i. We define $L_0(v) = \emptyset$ for any v. Let I_i denote pair (L_i, C) of the partially constructed set of distance labels and the set of loop labels. We prove the following lemma.

Lemma 1. *For every integer i where $0 \leq i \leq n$, and every pair of vertices (s, t), $\text{QUERY}(I_i, s, t) = (d^{\not> v_i}_{\text{1st}}(s,t), d^{\not> v_i}_{\text{2nd}}(s,t), \ldots, d^{\not> v_i}_{k\text{-th}}(s,t))$ holds.*

Proof. We prove the claim by induction on i. When $i = 0$, we have $\text{QUERY}(I_i, s, t) = (\infty, \infty, \ldots, \infty)$ and the claim clearly holds. Suppose that the claim holds for every $i' < i$. For a fixed pair of vertices (s, t) where $s \neq t$, we validate the claim for i and the pair (s, t).

Note that we can already compute $\text{QUERY}(I_{i-1}, s, t) = (d^{\not> v_{i-1}}_{\text{1st}}(s,t), d^{\not> v_{i-1}}_{\text{2nd}}(s,t), \ldots, d^{\not> v_{i-1}}_{k\text{-th}}(s,t))$. Let $\mathcal{P}$ denote the set of paths P such that (i) P is in $\mathcal{P}^{> v_{i-1}}_{st}$, (ii) P passes through v_i, and (iii) the length of P is smaller than

$d_{k\text{-th}}^{\not> v_{i-1}}(s,t)$. Let $\mathcal{P}'$ be the first k elements in $\mathcal{P}$. It suffices to show that, after the i-th pruned BFS, we can also compute the distances of paths in $\mathcal{P}'$.

Let $P \in \mathcal{P}'$. We can split P into three parts P_{sv_i}, $P_{v_iv_i}$, and P_{v_it}. Here, P_{sv_i} denotes the subsequence of P from s to the first appearance of v_i in P, $P_{v_iv_i}$ denotes the subsequence of P from the first appearance of v_i to the final appearance of v_i in P, and P_{v_it} denotes the subsequence of P from the last appearance of v_i in P to t. Note that $P_{v_iv_i}$ must be among the first k elements in $\mathcal{P}_{v_iv_i}^{>v_i}$; otherwise shorter k paths are possible and $P \in \mathcal{P}'$ is contradicted. Hence, $C(v_i)$ must include the length of $P_{v_iv_i}$.

Now we observe that the BFS from v_i along path P_{v_it} is not pruned in the i-th pruned BFS (and similarly for P_{sv_i}). To illustrate by contradiction, suppose that the BFS is pruned at some vertex u on path P_{v_it}. In this case, there exist at least k paths in $\mathcal{P}_{v_iu}^{\not> v_{i-1}}$ shorter than δ, where δ is the distance from v_i to u in the BFS. For each of these k paths, we concatenate P_{sv_i}, $P_{v_iv_i}$, and the suffix of P_{v_it} from u to t. Then, we obtain k paths in $\mathcal{P}_{st}^{\not> v_{i-1}}$ that are shorter than P, and therefore shorter than $d_{k\text{-th}}^{\not> v_{i-1}}(s,t)$ from condition (iii). Hence, we reach a contradiction. □

Corollary 1. *At the end of Algorithm 1, we can correctly answer top-k distance queries using the constructed index.*

Techniques for Efficient Implementation

We introduce several key techniques for practical performance improvement.

Vertex Ordering Strategy. By properly selecting the order of vertices from which we conduct pruned BFSs, our pruning can drastically reduce the search space and label sizes by exploiting the structure of real-world networks, greatly enhancing the efficiency of the proposed method. This is possible because the real networks contain highly centralized vertices (sometimes called *hubs*). As a heuristic vertex ordering strategy, vertices are selected in order of decreasing degrees. Further discussion is provided in (Akiba, Iwata, and Yoshida 2013).

Fast Pruning. When constructing distance labels, many queries are evaluated for pruning. However, when conducting a pruned BFS from a vertex v, queries are limited to "Are there more than k paths of length less than δ between v and u?" Given this restriction, we can reduce the query time. For each vertex w in the distance label of v, we can precompute the number $c_{w,\delta'}$ of paths between v and w of length not exceeding δ' using the loop label $C(w)$. Suppose that we have reached vertex u in the pruned BFS conducted from v. We can then compute the number of paths between v and u of length less than δ as $\sum_{(w,\delta',c)\in L(u)} c \cdot c_{w,\delta-\delta'}$.

Merged Queue Entries. When a (pruned) BFS is performed from a vertex v, rather than pair (u, δ), which denotes the existence of a path of length δ between v and u, triplets (u, δ, c) are pushed onto the queue. These triples specify that c paths of length δ exist between v and u, This technique enables the simultaneous handling of many paths, and significantly reduces the number of pushes onto the queue. Hence, it significantly reduces the running time.

Merged Label Entries. Related to the above technique, instead of pairs (u, δ), which denotes that there is a path of length δ between v and u, triplets (u, δ, c) are stored in distance labels. These triplets indicate that c paths of length δ exist between v and u. A similar technique is applicable to loop labels.

Extensions

Directed graphs. If the input graph is a directed graph, we compute and store two distance labels $L_{\mathrm{IN}}(v)$ and $L_{\mathrm{OUT}}(v)$ for each vertex v, where $L_{\mathrm{IN}}(v)$ and $L_{\mathrm{OUT}}(v)$ contain the distances from and to v, respectively.

Weighted graphs. For weighted graphs, we can replace the pruned BFS by pruned Dijkstra's algorithm. In this scheme, the queue used in Algorithm 2 is replaced by a priority queue. The time complexity becomes $O(ml + nl(\log n + l))$.

Experimental Evaluation

In this section, we show the scalability, efficiency and robustness of the proposed method by experimental results using real-world networks.

Setup

Environment. All experiments were conducted on a Linux server with Intel Xeon X5670 (2.93 GHz) and 48 GB of main memory. The proposed method was implemented in C++. The implementation will be made publicly available online.

Datasets. The target applications of the proposed method are graph mining tasks such as network-aware searching and link prediction. Therefore, our experiments were conducted on publicly available real-world social and web graphs[1][2][3][4][5]. The sizes and types of these graphs are listed in Table 2. We treated all the graphs as unweighted undirected graphs.

Algorithms. As there are no previous indexing methods for top-k distances, the proposed method was evaluated against the following two algorithms without precomputation.

- The first is the BFS-based naive approach, which uses a FIFO queue in the graph search, but which allows at most k visits to each vertex. This algorithm was also implemented in C++ by the authors.
- The second is Eppstein's algorithm (Eppstein 1998), which theoretically attains near-optimal time complexity. We adopted the C++ implementation of Jon Graehl[6].

[1] http://lovro.lpt.fri.uni-lj.si/support.jsp

[2] http://grouplens.org/datasets/hetrec-2011/

[3] http://snap.stanford.edu/

[4] http://socialnetworks.mpi-sws.org/datasets.html

[5] http://law.di.unimi.it/datasets.php (Boldi and Vigna 2004)

[6] http://www.ics.uci.edu/ eppstein/pubs/p-kpath.html

Table 2: Dataset information and performance of the proposed and existing methods on real-world datasets ($k = 8$).

Dataset				Top-k PLL (this work)			BFS	Eppstein
Name	Type	$\|V\|$	$\|E\|$	Indexing time	Index size	Query time		
Facebook-1	Social	334	2,218	13.7 ms	178.6 KB	1.9 μs	227.1 μs	378.4 μs
Last.fm	Social	1,892	12,717	125.3 ms	1.3 MB	1.7 μs	1.6 ms	7.5 ms
GrQc	Social	5,242	14,496	152.9 ms	2.7 MB	1.6 μs	2.2 ms	7.3 ms
HepTh	Social	9,877	25,998	631.2 ms	7.8 MB	2.2 μs	5.5 ms	16.5 ms
CondMat	Social	23,133	186,936	3.2 s	26.4 MB	3.1 μs	15.2 ms	158.8 ms
Facebook-2	Social	63,732	1,545,686	239.0 s	716.8 MB	15.2 μs	117.6 ms	2.7 s
YouTube-1	Social	1,157,828	4,945,382	624.3 s	2.3 GB	5.1 μs	1.5 s	7.0 s
YouTube-2	Social	3,238,848	18,512,606	1627.1 s	9.6 GB	3.9 μs	5.0 s	41.1 s
NotreDame	Web	325,729	1,497,134	52.3 s	617.7 MB	2.9 μs	249.8 ms	1.7 s
Stanford	Web	281,903	2,312,497	42.5 s	230.0 MB	1.7 μs	454.9 ms	2.9 s
BerkStan	Web	685,230	7,600,595	108.7 s	1.0 GB	1.9 μs	643.3 ms	10.8 s
Indo	Web	1,382,906	16,539,644	2695.3 s	6.0 GB	12.1 μs	1.4 s	25.4 s

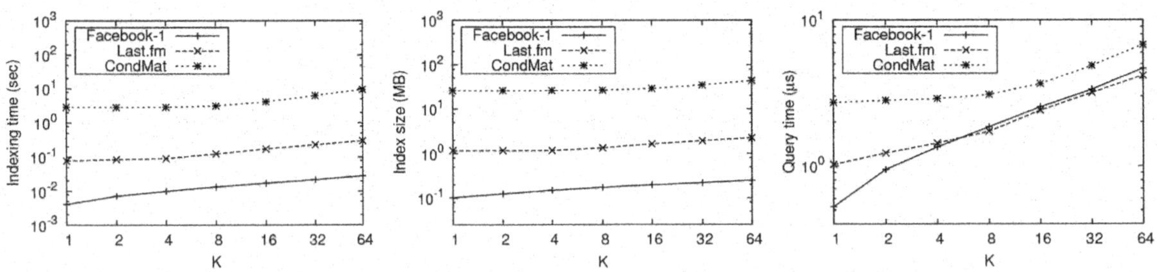

(a) Indexing time (b) Index size (c) Query time

Figure 2: Effect of k on indexing time, index size, and query time.

Indexing Time and Index Size

The high scalability of the proposed method is evident from the index construction time and constructed index size reported in Table 2. Indices were constructed from large social and web graphs comprising tens of millions of edges (YouTube-2 and Indo) in one hour. The index sizes are below 10 GB, easily accommodated by the main memories of modern commodity computers.

While the index construction of all datasets was consistently efficient, we observe that the indexing time does not depend on graph size alone. The efficiency of the proposed method relies on the efficiency of pruning, and is thus related to network properties such as degree distribution and clustering coefficient. However, because the graphs of real-world social, web, computer and biological networks exhibit similar qualitative properties, the proposed method is robust and consistently efficient. The same argument is valid for index size.

Figure 2a and 2b illustrate the effect of k on the indexing time and index size in the proposed method. Both are relatively insensitive to the value of k.

Query Time

The proposed method generally answers queries within microseconds, very much faster than the other algorithms (Table 2). Indeed for the largest dataset, YouTube-2, the query time was six orders of magnitude faster than those of the BFS-based and Eppstein algorithms. In our experiments the BFS-based method was faster than Eppstein's algorithm. This is due to the big constant factor hidden in the O-notation of the time complexity of Eppstein's algorithm, as it involves complex data structure manipulation.

Figure 2c plots the query time as a function of k. Although the query time increased with k, it remained sufficiently fast at high k.

Application to Link Prediction

This section demonstrates the usefulness of the proposed method by applying it to the link prediction problem (Liben-Nowell and Kleinberg 2003). In particular, we confirm that top-k distances can contribute to prediction precision improvement. Note that our indexing method enables the first use of the top-k distances for such tasks, because top-k distances must be computed for many pairs of vertices during training and evaluation.

We selected link prediction as it is one of the most fundamental and popular problems on graphs in the AI and Web communities. However, the results suggest the applicability of top-k distances to other graph tasks such as network-aware searching.

Table 3: Predictive performance (AUC) of the method based on top-k distances and several baseline methods on the link prediction problem. Statistically significant winners (by paired t-test with $p < 0.05$) are highlighted in bold font.

Dataset	CN	Jaccard	Adamic	Preferential	Combined	SVD	RWR	Top-k	Top-1
Facebook-1	0.806	0.812	0.817	0.754	0.890	0.792	0.873	**0.901**	0.808
Facebook-2	0.776	0.777	0.777	0.875	0.755	0.823	**0.949**	0.931	0.931
Last.fm	0.596	0.597	0.603	0.831	0.861	0.644	0.844	**0.876**	0.802
GrQc	0.658	0.658	0.658	0.709	0.793	0.791	0.802	**0.824**	0.799
HepTh	0.546	0.546	0.547	0.686	0.714	0.774	0.779	**0.817**	0.775
CondMat	0.763	0.763	0.764	0.749	0.877	0.875	0.900	**0.929**	0.896

Setup

Prediction Settings. We randomly sampled 60% edges for training and reserved the remaining 40% for evaluation. The task was to predict the hidden evaluation edges given training edges. The sampling, prediction and evaluation procedures were performed 10 times on each datasets.

As an evaluation metric for predictive performance, we used *AUC* (area under the ROC curve). Generally, AUC is defined as the probability of predictions for positive examples larger than those for negative ones in test set. Since the tested datasets contain only positive, our investigation constitutes a "positive-and-unlabeled" case. Therefore, in our AUC evaluation, our test set is regarded as a subset of positive links. Withholding these links, we applied the evaluated methods to the dataset, treating the withheld links as no-links. We evaluated AUC as the probability that a randomly sampled withheld link has a higher predicted relational strength than a randomly sampled no-link vertex pair.

Method Based on Top-k Distances. We used the top-k distances as features in a support vector machine (SVM). More precisely, assuming $(\delta_1, \delta_2, \ldots, \delta_k)$ as the top-k distances of a vertex pair, we defined the features of the pair as k values, where the i-th value is given by $1/\sqrt{\delta_i}$. The value of k was tuned among $\{2^0, 2^1, \ldots, 2^6\}$, using one sample as a development dataset. Moreover, for each dataset we tested both linear SVM and non-linear SVM (with the RBF kernel) and selected the better performing one using the development dataset. The results on the development dataset are not included in the actual evaluation.

Baseline Methods. As baseline methods, we selected four methods commonly used in link prediction; (1) *CN* (Common neighbors), (2) *Jaccard*, (3) *Adamic*, (4) *Preferential* (Preferential Attachment). The scores of these methods were used as link scores. We also considered (5) a *Combined* method, in which the link scores of the four baseline methods were used as the features in SVM. We further compared our method with (6) *SVD* (singular value decomposition) (Golub and Loan 1996) and (7) *RWR* (Random Walk with Restart), and (8) *Top-1* distance. In SVD, the link score is calculated by cosine similarity based on the latent vectors. The number of latent dimension in SVD was tuned among $\{2^0, 2^1, \ldots, 2^8\}$, again using one sample as a development dataset. We adopted the RWR parameters of (He et al. 2004; Tong, Faloutsos, and Pan 2006). More specifically, the restart probability was set to 0.95 and the number of iterations was set to 50. The top-1 distance method corresponds to the above method with $k = 1$; its purpose was to evaluate the true importance of the top-k $(k > 1)$ distances.

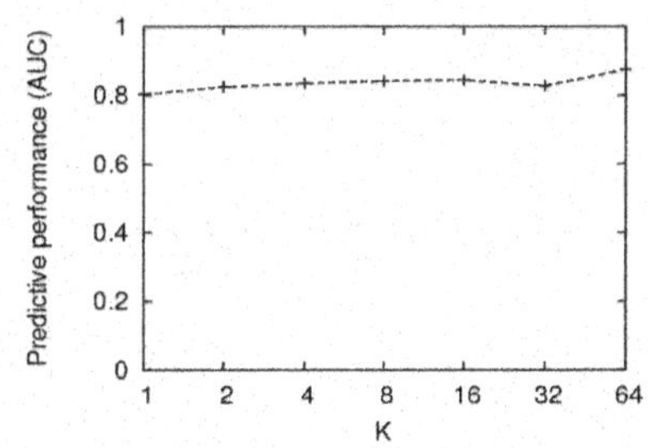

Figure 3: Effect of k on AUC, evaluated on the Last.fm dataset

Datasets. We used the six smaller social networks extracted from the graphs in the previous section, as some of the baseline methods (such as RWR) were too computationally expensive.

Results

Predictive Performance. Table 3 shows the mean AUCs for each method and dataset. The top-k distance method outperformed all the other methods for almost all the datasets. The exception was Facebook-2, for which the method based on top-k distances performed comparably to the top performer, RWR. Moreover, in most of the datasets, the top-k distances yielded higher performance than the top-1 (usual) distance.

Parameter Sensitivity. We experimentally studied the effect of the parameter k. Figure 3 plots the AUCs of the proposed method for the Last.fm dataset with k $\{2^0, 2^1, \ldots, 2^6\}$. We observe that the predictive performance was stable with respect to k.

Conclusion

In this study, we proposed a new indexing method that quickly answers top-k distance queries on large networks. Indeed, we present the first practical indexing method for top-k distances. The efficiency, scalability and robustness of the method was evaluated in extensive experiments on real-world social and web graphs. Moreover, by applying the method to link prediction, we indicated the practicability of top-k distance queries to various applications.

Acknowledgments

Takuya Akiba, Nozomi Nori and Yoichi Iwata are supported by Grant-in-Aid for JSPS Fellows (256563, 269329 and 256487, respectively). Takanori Hayashi and Yuichi Yoshida are supported by JST, ERATO, Kawarabayashi Large Graph Project. Yuichi Yoshida is supported by JSPS Grant-in-Aid for Young Scientists (B) (No. 26730009) and MEXT Grant-in-Aid for Scientific Research on Innovative Areas (No. 24106003).

References

Akiba, T.; Iwata, Y.; Kawarabayashi, K.; and Kawata, Y. 2014. Fast shortest-path distance queries on road networks by pruned highway labeling. In *ALENEX*, 147–154.

Akiba, T.; Iwata, Y.; and Yoshida, Y. 2013. Fast exact shortest-path distance queries on large networks by pruned landmark labeling. In *SIGMOD*, 349–360.

Akiba, T.; Iwata, Y.; and Yoshida, Y. 2014. Dynamic and historical shortest-path distance queries on large evolving networks by pruned landmark labeling. In *WWW*, 237–248.

Akiba, T.; Sommer, C.; and Kawarabayashi, K. 2012. Shortest-path queries for complex networks: exploiting low tree-width outside the core. In *EDBT*, 144–155.

Boldi, P., and Vigna, S. 2004. The webgraph framework I: compression techniques. In *WWW*, 595–602.

Cheng, J., and Yu, J. X. 2009. On-line exact shortest distance query processing. In *EDBT*, 481–492.

Cohen, E.; Halperin, E.; Kaplan, H.; and Zwick, U. 2002. Reachability and distance queries via 2-hop labels. In *SODA*, 937–946.

Eppstein, D. 1998. Finding the k shortest paths. *SIAM J. Computing* 28(2):652–673.

Fu, A. W.-C.; Wu, H.; Cheng, J.; Chu, S.; and Wong, R. C.-W. 2013. Is-label: an independent-set based labeling scheme for point-to-point distance querying on large graphs. *PVLDB* 6(6):457–468.

Golub, G. ., and Loan, C. . 1996. *Matrix Computations*. Johns Hopkins Studies in the Mathematical Sciences.

He, J.; Li, M.; jiang Zhang, H.; Tong, H.; and Zhang, C. 2004. Manifold-ranking based image retrieval. In *MM*, 9–16.

Ito, T.; Shimbo, M.; Kudo, T.; and Matsumoto, Y. 2005. Application of kernels to link analysis. In *KDD*, 586–592.

Jeh, G., and Widom, J. 2002. Simrank: a measure of structural-context similarity. In *KDD*, 538–543.

Jeh, G., and Widom, J. 2003. Scaling personalized web search. In *WWW*, 271–279.

Jin, R.; Ruan, N.; Xiang, Y.; and Lee, V. 2012. A highway-centric labeling approach for answering distance queries on large sparse graphs. In *SIGMOD*, 445–456.

Liben-Nowell, D., and Kleinberg, J. 2003. The link prediction problem for social networks. In *CIKM*, 556–559.

Lovász, L. 1996. Random walks on graphs: A survey. In *Combinatorics, Paul Erdős is Eighty*, volume 2. János Bolyai Mathematical Society. 353–398.

Maniu, S., and Cautis, B. 2013. Network-aware search in social tagging applications: Instance optimality versus efficiency. In *CIKM*, 939–948.

McSherry, F. 2005. A uniform approach to accelerated pagerank computation. In *WWW*, 575–582.

Potamias, M.; Bonchi, F.; Castillo, C.; and Gionis, A. 2009. Fast shortest path distance estimation in large networks. In *CIKM*, 867–876.

Smola, A. J., and Kondor. 2003. Kernels and regularization on graphs. In *COLT*, 144–158.

Sun, J.; Qu, H.; Chakrabarti, D.; and Faloutsos, C. 2005. Neighborhood formation and anomaly detection in bipartite graphs. In *ICDM*, 418–425.

Tong, H.; Faloutsos, C.; and Pan, J.-Y. 2006. Fast random walk with restart and its applications. In *ICDM*, 613–622.

Ukkonen, A.; Castillo, C.; Donato, D.; and Gionis, A. 2008. Searching the wikipedia with contextual information. In *CIKM*, 1351–1352.

Vieira, M. V.; Fonseca, B. M.; Damazio, R.; Golgher, P. B.; Reis, D. d. C.; and Ribeiro-Neto, B. 2007. Efficient search ranking in social networks. In *CIKM*, 563–572.

Watts, D. J., and Strogatz, S. H. 1998. Collective dynamics of 'small-world' networks. *Nature* 393(6684):440–442.

Wei, F. 2010. Tedi: efficient shortest path query answering on graphs. In *SIGMOD*, 99–110.

Xiao, Y.; Wu, W.; Pei, J.; Wang, W.; and He, Z. 2009. Efficiently indexing shortest paths by exploiting symmetry in graphs. In *EDBT*, 493–504.

Yahia, S. A.; Benedikt, M.; Lakshmanan, L. V. S.; and Stoyanovich, J. 2008. Efficient network aware search in collaborative tagging sites. *PVLDB* 1(1):710–721.

Yano, Y.; Akiba, T.; Iwata, Y.; and Yoshida, Y. 2013. Fast and scalable reachability queries on graphs by pruned labeling with landmarks and paths. In *CIKM*, 1601–1606.

Inferring Same-as Facts from Linked Data: An Iterative Import-by-Query Approach

Mustafa Al-Bakri,[1,2] **Manuel Atencia,**[1,2,3] **Steffen Lalande,**[4] and **Marie-Christine Rousset**[1,2,5]
[1] Univ. Grenoble Alpes, LIG, 38000, Grenoble, France
[2] CNRS, LIG, 38000, Grenoble, France
[3] Inria, 38330, Montbonnot-Saint-Martin, France
[4] Institut National de l'Audiovisuel, 94366, Bry-sur-Marne, France
[5] Institut Universitaire de France, 75005, Paris, France
Mustafa.Al-Bakri@imag.fr, Manuel.Atencia@inria.fr, slalande@ina.fr, Marie-Christine.Rousset@imag.fr

Abstract

In this paper we model the problem of data linkage in Linked Data as a reasoning problem on possibly decentralized data. We describe a novel import-by-query algorithm that alternates steps of sub-query rewriting and of tailored querying the Linked Data cloud in order to import data as specific as possible for inferring or contradicting given target same-as facts. Experiments conducted on a real-world dataset have demonstrated the feasibility of this approach and its usefulness in practice for data linkage and disambiguation.

1 Introduction

Linked Data promotes exposing, sharing and connecting data and knowledge in the Semantic Web (Bizer, Heath, and Berners-Lee 2009). Data linkage is a crucial task in Linked Data. In particular, it is very important to correctly decide whether two URIs refer to the same real-world entity. Most existing approaches are based on numerical methods that return weighted owl:sameAs links, among which those with higher weights are likely (but not guaranteed) to be correct.

In contrast, like a few other works (Saïs, Pernelle, and Rousset 2009; Hogan et al. 2012), we propose a rule-based approach equipped with full reasoning to infer all *certain* same-as facts that are logically entailed from a given set of domain constraints and facts. Our main contribution is a novel algorithm, called Import-by-Query, that enables the scalable deployment of such an approach in the decentralized setting of Linked Data. The main challenge is to identify the data, possibly distributed over several datasets, useful for inferring owl:sameAs and owl:differentFrom facts of interest. Compared to the approach reported in (Hogan et al. 2012), relying on a global import obtained by a breadth-first crawl of the Linked Data cloud, we perform a selective import while guaranteeing completeness for the inference of the targeted owl:sameAs and owl:differentFrom facts.

For doing so, the import-by-query algorithm that we have designed alternates steps of sub-query rewriting and of tailored querying of the Linked Data cloud to import data as specific as possible to infer owl:sameAs and owl:differentFrom facts. It is an extension of the well-known query-subquery algorithm for answering Datalog queries over deductive databases. Experiments conducted on a real-world dataset have demonstrated the feasibility of this approach and its usefulness in practice for data linkage and disambiguation.

Section 2 illustrates our approach by example, while Section 3 positions it w.r.t. existing work. In Section 4 the problem that we consider is formally stated. Our import-by-query algorithm is described in Section 5. Then Section 6 reports on experimental results, and Section 7 concludes the paper.

2 Illustrative Scenario

We describe here a simplified scenario inspired by the task of disambiguation of named entities in a large real-world RDF documentary catalog produced by the French National Audiovisual Institute (INA), and that we have used in our experiments (Section 6).

Figure 1 shows an extract of the INA vocabulary and a sample of RDF triples from the INA dataset.[1] Any person entity is an instance of the class ina:PhysicalPerson, which has two subclasses: ina:Person and ina:VideoPerson. The class ina:Person is used for representing French personalities while ina:VideoPerson is used for identifying person entities that play a role in a video. INA experts want to disambiguate individuals within ina:Person, and link these individuals to the ones of ina:VideoPerson.

Three homonymous persons are described in Figure 1, all named "Jacques Martin": ina:per1, ina:per2 and ina:per3. It is unknown if these entities represent the same or different persons, but some additional information is given: ina:per1 is known to be the presenter of a program recorded in the video ina:vid1 whose title is "Le Petit Rapporteur", whereas ina:per2 and ina:per3 have dates of birth "1933-06-22" and "1921-09-25", respectively.

[1] We have slightly modified the INA vocabulary (e.g. translating French terms into English terms) for the sake of readability.

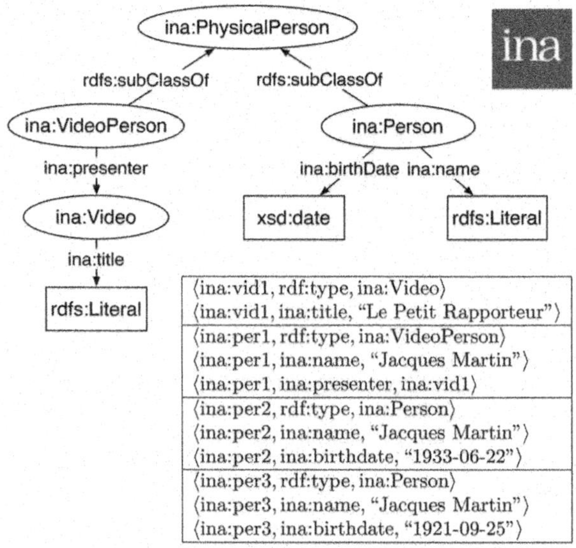

Figure 1: An extract of INA vocabulary and RDF facts.

Our approach to disambiguating the person entities ina:per1, ina:per2 and ina:per3 consists in exploiting domain knowledge and constraints, as well as general properties of owl:sameAs and owl:differentFrom, all this knowledge being expressed in a uniform way by rules. Table 1 shows rules which, for the purpose of this simplified scenario, we can assume they have been validated by INA experts. R1-R3 are domain-specific rules. R1 expresses that ina:birthdate is functional. This rule can be used to infer that ina:per2 and ina:per3 are different because they have different dates of birth. R2 expresses that ina:name and ina:birthdate form a key (within the INA dataset), and R3 the fact that two persons who have the same name and presented programs recorded in videos with the same title must be the same. R2 and R3 indeed could be useful for deciding if ina:per1 refers to the same person as ina:per2 or ina:per3, but some information is missing: the date of birth of ina:per1 is not known, or whether ina:per2 or ina:per3 are presenters and of which programs.

The above missing information can be completed thanks to external data coming from DBpedia. In Figure 2, we show DBpedia facts describing the DBpedia person entity db:per1, and an extract of the DBpedia vocabulary. Rules R4 and R5 in Table 1 translate mappings from the INA and DBpedia vocabularies. Specifically, these mappings state that ina:name and ina:birthdate are equivalent to foaf:name and foaf:birthdate, respectively, and that the composition of ina:presenter and ina:title is equivalent to db:presenter. Let us assume that rules R4 and R5 have been validated by INA experts too. With these rules it can be inferred that db:per1 is the same as ina:per1 because they have the same name and they have presented a program with the same title; and that db:per1 is the same as ina:per2 since they have the same name and birthdate. Therefore, by transitivity of same-as (rule R6 in Table 1), it can be inferred that ina:per1 is the same as ina:per2, and, since ina:per2 is different from ina:per3 then (due to R7) ina:per1 is different from ina:per3 too.

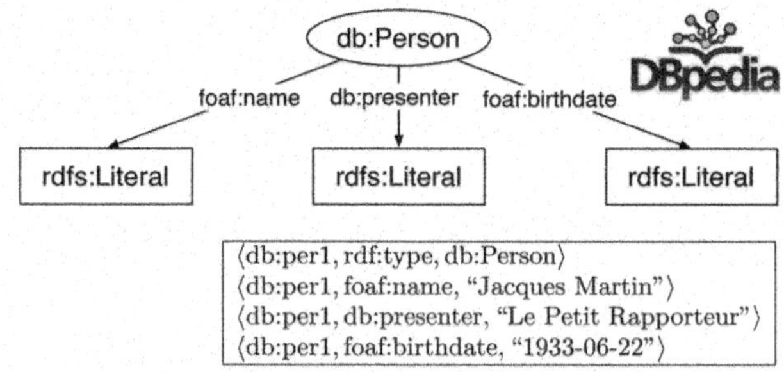

Figure 2: An extract of DBpedia vocabulary and RDF facts.

To avoid downloading the complete DBpedia, and, more generally, the whole Linked Open Data (something that is not practical), our import-by-query approach generates, for each targeted owl:sameAs fact, a sequence of external sub-queries as specific as possible to obtain just the missing facts. The external sub-queries generated by our algorithm for the particular query ⟨ina:per1, owl:sameAs, ina:per2⟩ in our example are shown in Figure 3.

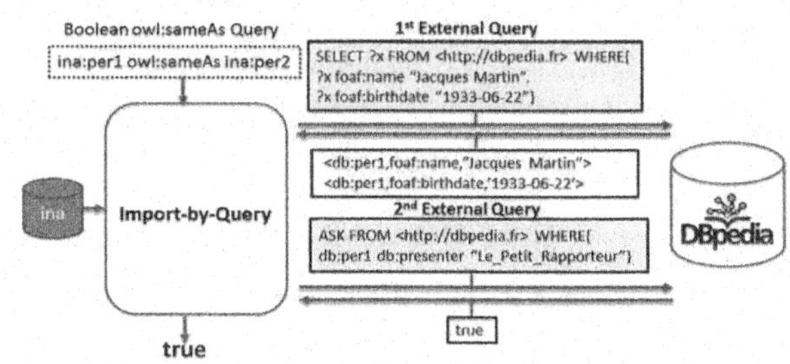

Figure 3: The resultant external sub-queries submitted to DBpedia and their returned answers.

3 Related work

There exists a considerable number of systems that (semi)automatically perform data linkage (Ferrara, Nikolov, and Scharffe 2011). Most of these approaches define or learn metrics to compare entities based on similarities between the values of all or some of their properties. What distinguishes our approach from the majority of these systems is that they are not declarative, with the inherent limitation to be difficult to extend or adapt to new settings with new properties.

There are few existing declarative approaches, in which the comparison methods can be specified by users in the form of (XML) specifications, like in Silk (Volz et al. 2009), or rules, like in LN2R (Saïs, Pernelle, and Rousset 2009) and Hogan et al. (Hogan et al. 2012). Silk specifications can be seen as logical rules along with built-in functions for computing and aggregating similarity degrees between property values. However, these rules are not fully exploited in Silk. More specifically, the possible chaining between rules is not handled by Silk, which makes it incomplete for the task of

Rules
R1 : $\langle ?x1, \text{ina:birthdate}, ?b1\rangle, \langle ?x2, \text{ina:birthdate}, ?b2\rangle, \langle ?b1, \text{notEqualTo}, ?b2\rangle \Rightarrow \langle ?x1, \text{owl:differentFrom}, ?x2\rangle$
R2 : $\langle ?x1, \text{ina:name}, ?n\rangle, \langle ?x2, \text{ina:name}, ?n\rangle, \langle ?x2, \text{ina:birthdate}, ?b\rangle, \langle ?x1, \text{ina:birthdate}, ?b\rangle \Rightarrow \langle ?x1, \text{owl:sameAs}, ?x2\rangle$
R3 : $\langle ?x1, \text{ina:name}, ?n\rangle, \langle ?x2, \text{ina:name}, ?n\rangle, \langle ?x1, \text{ina:presenter}, ?v1\rangle, \langle ?x2, \text{ina:presenter}, ?v2\rangle, \langle ?v1, \text{ina:title}, ?t\rangle, \langle ?v2, \text{ina:title}, ?t\rangle \Rightarrow \langle ?x1, \text{owl:sameAs}, ?x2\rangle$
R4 : $\langle ?x1, \text{ina:name}, ?n\rangle, \langle ?x2, \text{foaf:name}, ?n\rangle, \langle ?x1, \text{ina:presenter}, ?v\rangle, \langle ?v, \text{ina:title}, ?t\rangle, \langle ?x2, \text{db:presenter}, ?t\rangle \Rightarrow \langle ?x1, \text{owl:sameAs}, ?x2\rangle$
R5 : $\langle ?x1, \text{ina:name}, ?n\rangle, \langle ?x2, \text{foaf:name}, ?n\rangle, \langle ?x1, \text{ina:birthdate}, ?b\rangle, \langle ?x2, \text{foaf:birthdate}, ?b\rangle \Rightarrow \langle ?x1, \text{owl:sameAs}, ?x2\rangle$
R6 : $\langle ?x1, \text{owl:sameAs}, ?x2\rangle, \langle ?x2, \text{owl:sameAs}, ?x3\rangle \Rightarrow \langle ?x1, \text{owl:sameAs}, ?x3\rangle$
R7 : $\langle ?x1, \text{owl:sameAs}, ?x2\rangle, \langle ?x2, \text{owl:differentFrom}, ?x3\rangle \Rightarrow \langle ?x1, \text{owl:differentFrom}, ?x3\rangle$
R8 : $\langle ?x1, \text{ina:name}, ?n1\rangle, \langle ?x2, \text{foaf:name}, ?n2\rangle, \langle ?n1, \text{built-in:name-similar}, ?n2\rangle, \langle ?x1, \text{ina:birthdate}, ?b\rangle, \langle ?x2, \text{foaf:birthdate}, ?b\rangle \Rightarrow \langle ?x1, \text{owl:sameAs}, ?x2\rangle$

Table 1: Rules in the INA illustrative scenario.

discovering all the same-as facts that can be logically inferred. As a result, neither Silk nor LIMES (Ngomo and Auer 2011) (similar to Silk in its principles) would discover that ina:p1 is the same as ina:p2 in our illustrative scenario.

LN2R (Saïs, Pernelle, and Rousset 2009) and Hogan et al. (Hogan et al. 2012) come with a complete forward-reasoner and thus guarantee to infer all the same-as facts (and all the different-from facts for LN2R) that can be logically entailed from the rules and facts given as input. Except LN2R, these systems consider using remote data sources to discover links. Unlike our approach, though, the external RDF facts that are loaded to complete local data are obtained either by a global import (of the whole RDF graph of a reference dataset such as DBpedia) or as an incoming data stream produced by a Linked Data crawler. This raises scalability issues that are bypassed either by light-weight incomplete reasoning like in Silk, or by using intensive computational resources requiring clusters of machines like in (Hogan et al. 2012). Instead, our import-by-query algorithm builds iteratively SPARQL queries for importing from external sources in Linked Data the necessary and sufficient data for resolving the link query.

4 Problem statement

We first recall the ingredients of Linked Data and then we define what we call a deductive RDF dataset to capture several ontological constraints expressing data semantics.

RDF datasets in Linked Data

An RDF dataset in Linked Data is defined by a URL u and a set F of RDF facts that are accessible as URL through a query endpoint. We will denote by $ds(u)$ the set F of RDF facts that can be queried at the URL u.

An RDF fact is a triple $t = \langle s, p, o\rangle$ where the subject s is either a URI or a blank node, the predicate p is a URI, and the object o may be either a URI, a blank node or a literal. We will denote the vocabulary used in $ds(u)$ by $voc(u)$, i.e., the names of predicates used to declare triples in the dataset accessible at the URL u.

Queries over RDF datasets in Linked Data

Queries over Linked Data are SPARQL **conjunctive queries** entered through a given query endpoint accessible at a given URL. In this paper, we use a simplified notation for SPARQL queries, and, without loss of generality, we consider that all variables are distinguished.

A query $q(u)$ asked to an RDF dataset identified by (and accessible at) the URL u is a conjunction of **triple patterns** denoted by $TP_1(v_1), \ldots, TP_k(v_k)$ where each triple pattern $TP_i(v_i)$ is a triple $\langle s^v, p^v, o^v\rangle$ in which the subject s^v, the predicate p^v, or the object o^v can be variables: v_i is the set of variables appearing in the triple pattern. Variables are denoted by strings starting by '?'. $TP_i(v_i)$ is a **ground** triple pattern if its set of variables v_i is empty (denoted by $TP_i()$). A ground triple pattern corresponds to a RDF fact. A **boolean query** is a conjunction of ground triple patterns. For instance, the second SPARQL query of Figure 3 in the previous section become in this simplified notation:

q(http://dbpedia.fr):
⟨ db:per1, db:presenter, "Le_Petit_Rapporteur" ⟩.

The evaluation of a query $q(u)$: $TP_1(v_1), \ldots, TP_k(v_k)$ over the dataset $ds(u)$ consists in finding substitutions θ assigning the variables in $\bigcup_{i\in[1..k]} v_i$ to constants (i.e., identifiers or literals) such that $TP_1(\theta.v_1), \ldots, TP_k(\theta.v_k)$ are RDF facts in the dataset.

The corresponding answer is equally defined as the tuple of constants assigned by θ to the variables or as the set of corresponding RDF facts $TP_1(\theta.v_1), \ldots, TP_k(\theta.v_k)$ that will be denoted by $\theta.q(u)$. In the remainder of the paper, we will adopt the latter definition. The answer set of the query $q(u)$ against the dataset $ds(u) = F$ is thus defined as:

$$Answer(q(u), F) = \bigcup_{\{\theta \mid \theta.q(u) \subseteq F\}} \{\theta.q(u)\}$$

For a **boolean query** $q(u)$, either the answer set is not empty and we will say that the query is evaluated to **true**, or it is empty and we will say that it evaluated to **false**.

For a query $q(u)$ to have a chance to get an answer when evaluated over the dataset $ds(u)$, it must be **compatible with** the vocabulary used in this dataset, i.e., (a) the predicates appearing in the triple patterns of $q(u)$ must belong to the set $voc(u)$ of predicates known to occur in $ds(u)$, (b) the URIs appearing as constants in the triple patterns of $q(u)$ must have u as prefix.

In accordance with SPARQL queries allowing different FROM clauses, a conjunctive query can in fact specify several entry points $u_1, \ldots, u_n$ of datasets over which the query to be evaluated. We will denote such a query $q(u_1, \ldots, u_n)$. The above definitions of answers and compatibility can be generalized appropriately by replacing the dataset $ds(u)$ by the union $\bigcup_{i\in[1..n]} ds(u_i)$ of the specified datasets.

Deductive RDF datasets

In order to capture in a uniform way semantic constraints that can be declared on top of a given RDF dataset, but also possibly mappings between local predicates and external predicates within the vocabulary of other datasets, and domain knowledge provided by domain experts, we consider that RDF datasets can be enriched with Datalog rules of the form: $Cond_r \Rightarrow Conc_r$, in which the condition $Cond_r$ is a conjunction of triple patterns (i.e., a conjunctive query) and the conclusion $Conc_r$ is a triple pattern. We consider **safe** rules, i.e., rules such that all the variables in the conclusion are also in the condition. Datalog rules on top of RDFS facts capture most of the OWL constraints used in practice, while guaranteeing a polynomial data complexity for reasoning and query answering.

A deductive RDF dataset $dds(u)$ accessible at the URL u is thus a local knowledge base $\langle F, R\rangle$ made of a set of RDF facts F and a set R of rules. The application of rules allows to infer new facts that are logically entailed from $F \cup R$. A rule r can be applied to F if there exists a substitution θ such that $\theta.Cond_r \subseteq F$ and the result of the rule application is $F \cup \{\theta.Conc_r\}$. These new facts can in turn trigger rules and infer additional facts. From a finite set of facts F and a finite set of safe rules R, the set of facts that can be inferred is finite and can be computed as the least fixed point of immediate consequence operator T_R defined as follows:

$$T_R(F) = F \cup \bigcup_{r \in R} \{\theta.Conc_r | \theta.Cond_r \subseteq F\}$$

Let $F_0 = F$, and for every $i \geq 0$, let $F_{i+1} = T_R(F_i)$. There exists a unique least fixed point F_n (denote by $SAT(F, R)$) such that for every $k \geq n$ $F_k = T_R(F_n)$, i.e., there exists a step in the iterative application of the immediate consequence operator for which no new fact is inferred.

The evaluation of a query $q(u) : TP_1(v_1), \ldots, TP_k(v_k)$ over a deductive dataset $dds(u)$ consists in finding substitutions θ such that the facts $TP_1(\theta.v_1), \ldots, TP_k(\theta.v_k)$ can be **inferred** from the deductive dataset, or equivalently belong to the result $SAT(F, R)$ of the facts that can be inferred from F and R:

$$Answer(q(u), \langle F, R\rangle) = Answer(q(u), SAT(F, R))$$

Thus, a **boolean query** $q(u)$ is evaluated to **true** if and only if $q(u) \in SAT(F, R)$, i.e., if and only if $\langle F, R\rangle \vdash q(u)$, where $\vdash$ is the standard notation for logical inference.

Within the vocabulary of a deductive dataset, we distinguish the extensional predicates (EDB predicates for short) that appear in the triplets of the dataset F, from the intentional predicates (IDB predicates) that appear in conclusion of some rules in R. Like in deductive databases, and without loss of generality (i.e., by possibly renaming predicates and adding rules), we suppose that these two sets are disjoint. We will denote ODB predicates the *external* predicates (i.e., defined in a different namespace than the considered deductive dataset) that possibly appear in the dataset or in the rules. These predicates are the core of Linked Data in which a good practice is to re-use existing reference vocabularies. We suppose (again, without loss of generality) that the set of ODB predicates is disjoint from the set of IDB predicates (but not necessarily from the set of EDB predicates).

The problem that we consider can now be formally stated.

Given a deductive dataset $dds(u) = \langle F, R\rangle$, and a boolean query $q(u)$ the local evaluation of which gives an empty answer set (i.e., $\langle F, R\rangle \not\vdash q(u)$), we aim to construct a set of external queries $q_1(u_1), \ldots, q_k(u_k)$ for which we can guarantee that the subsets of external facts resulting from their evaluation over the (possibly huge) external datasets are sufficient to answer the initial query. More formally:

$$\langle F \cup_{i \in [1..k]} Answer(q_i(u_i), ds(u_i)), R\rangle \vdash q(u)$$
$$\text{iff } \langle F \cup_{i \in [1..k]} ds(u_i), R\rangle \vdash q(u)$$

The more specific the external queries are, the less external facts have to be added and stored to the local dataset and therefore the more interesting a proposed approach is to solve this problem.

5 The iterative Import-by-Query Algorithm

We now describe the algorithm that we have designed and implemented for solving the problem stated above.
Given an input boolean same-as query q, a deductive dataset $\langle F, R\rangle$, and a set $\bar{u}$ of query entry points to external datasets, Import-by-Query iteratively alternates steps of sub-query rewriting based on backward chaining and of external query evaluation.

Each sub-query rewriting step is realized by an adaptation of the *Query-Subquery* algorithm (Vieille 1986; Abiteboul, Hull, and Vianu 1995) that is a set-oriented memoing backward chaining method (Hinkelmann and Hintze 1993) used in deductive databases for evaluating Datalog programs. This results in the *Query-External-Subquery* (*QESQ* for short) algorithm. For space limitation, here we just explain its main principles, compared to *Query-Subquery*, when applied to a list SG of subgoals. QESQ handles the subgoals built on EDB or IDB predicates exactly like *Query-Subquery*, i.e., iteratively removes subgoals built on EDB predicates if they can be matched with local facts, propagates the corresponding substitutions to the remaining subgoals, replaces a subgoal g built on an IDB predicate by the list of partially instantiated conditions of a rule whose conclusion can be matched to g. As for the subgoals on ODB predicates, they are handled by QESQ before the subgoals on IDB predicates, and if and once all the subgoals built on EDB predicates have been removed, and after the corresponding substitutions are applied to the remaining subgoals in the list. These ODB subgoals are conjuncted to obtain an external query q_{ext}, the compatibility of which must be checked w.r.t. $\bar{u}$ to be considered further. QESQ then treats the remaining list SG_{idb} of subgoals on IDB predicates just as *Query-External-Subquery*, i.e., triggers the recursive call $QESQ(SG_{idb})$. It will return as output either **true** or **false** (if it has enough local information to infer a result to the input boolean query), or a set of external queries that, if compatible with the vocabulary of the given external datasets, are then conjuncted with q_{ext} to constitute the output returned by QESQ(SG). As a result QESQ ($\{q\}$) succeeds in handling locally the goal q using F and R just like *Query-Subquery* and then the process is stopped and the result returned by Import-by-Query is **true** or **false** accordingly, or it produces a set $\{q_1(\bar{u}_1), \ldots, q_k(\bar{u}_k)\}$ of external queries the evaluation of which is likely to bring missing facts to F for proving the goal q using R. If this set is empty, the process is stopped and the result returned by Import-by-Query is **false**.

Each evaluation step simply consists in choosing one of the external query $q_i(\bar{u}_i)$ produced by the sub-query rewriting step and to submit it to Linked Data through the specified query entry points. The result is either an empty set (negative result) or a set of external facts (positive result) that can be added to the current local dataset. In both cases, the result is memorized in an associated answer table for the sub-query $q_i(\bar{u}_i)$ that will be thus marked as an already processed subgoal for which the (positive or negative) result is known and can be directly exploited later on. If the result is positive, a new iteration of Import-by-Query is started on the same input except for the set of facts F that is enriched with the facts obtained as the result of the evaluation of the external query $q_i(\bar{u}_i)$. If the result is negative, another external query $q_j(\bar{u}_j)$ in the set produced by the current call to QESQ is evaluated. If the evaluation of all the external queries in the set returns 'false', then the process is stopped and the result returned by Import-by-Query on q is **false**.

The termination of the Import-by-Query algorithm relies on the termination of QESQ, which is guaranteed by the same memoing technique as *Query-Subquery* (i.e., by handling goal and answer tables for each ODB and IDB predicate). The soundness and completeness of the Import-by-Query algorithm results from the soundness and completeness of *Query-Subquery* (Vieille 1986) and from the observation that the result produced by *Query-Subquery*, if applied to the same input in which the ODB predicates are just considered as additional EDB predicates, would be the same as the one produced by Import-by-Query. The reason is that the only difference of Import-by-Query is to replace successive matching of atomic goals against the facts by matching *all at once* the atomic goals composing the external queries produced by QESQ. This does not impact the global boolean result of the sequence of goal matching.

Combining forward and backward chaining

Like any backward chaining method, Import-by-Query (and its main component QESQ) re-starts from scratch for each new goal it tries to solve, even if the facts and the rules remain unchanged. The intermediate subgoals generated and handled by QESQ can be simplified if the input rules are replaced by their (partial) instantiations obtained by the propagation of the facts into (the conditions of) the rules.

Fact propagation is a forward chaining method used in inference engines such as RETE (Forgy 1982) for rule-based systems. It avoids redundant evaluation of same conditions appearing in several rules by memorizing, for each fact f, which condition it satisfies in which rule (possibly already partially instantiated by facts previously propagated), and the corresponding variable substitution that is then applied to all the remaining conditions of the rules.

In our setting, we perform fact propagation as a preprocessing step of the Import-by-Query algorithm, by computing at the same time the set $SAT(F, R)$ of facts that can be inferred locally, and the set $PI(F, R)$ of partial instantiations of the rules in R. This forward reasoning step can be summarized as follows, where $SAT(F, R)$ is initialized as F and $PI(F, R)$ is initialized as R:

- **FOR** each f in $SAT(F, R)$
  FOR each rule $Cond_r \Rightarrow Conc_r$ in $PI(F, R)$ having a condition c that can be matched with f, i.e., there exists θ such that $\theta.c = f$
  - $*$ **IF** c is the only condition in $Cond_r$ **THEN** add $\theta.Conc_r$ to $SAT(F, R)$
  - $*$ **ELSE** add to $PI(F, R)$ the rule obtained from $\theta.Cond_r \Rightarrow \theta.Conc_r$ by removing the condition $\theta.c$ (that is satisfied by the fact f).
- Remove from $PI(F, R)$ those rules whose condition contains EDB predicates that are not ODB predicates (and thus cannot be satisfied by local facts).
- **RETURN** $\langle SAT(F, R), PI(F, R) \rangle$

Each partially instantiated rule r_i returned in $PI(F, R)$ is issued from an input rule r in which some conditions have been matched to facts f_1, ..., f_k that have been inferred before (and added to $SAT(F, R)$), and thus allows us to infer the same conclusion as the input rule r on any set of facts including f_1, ..., f_k. The result $SAT(F, R) \cup PI(F, R)$ is then logically equivalent to the input deductive dataset $F \cup R$ for inferring facts on IDB predicates from the union of F and a set OF of external facts (with ODB predicates), i.e. for every fact f an external set of facts OF:

$$\langle F \cup OF, R \rangle \vdash f \text{ iff } \langle SAT(F, R) \cup OF, PI(F, R) \rangle \vdash f$$

Therefore, it can be equivalently used for proving goals by checking whether they belong to $SAT(F, R)$, or for rewriting goals by applying $QESQ$ to the $PI(F, R)$ (instead of the original R).

6 Experiments

We have conducted experiments on a real deductive dataset composed of 35 rules and ~6 million RDF facts from INA dataset. The rules may be found at http://goo.gl/NfR12w. Most of the 35 rules capture local knowledge in the domain (functional properties and keys declared as schema constraints, and rules provided by INA experts), mappings between INA and DBpedia vocabularies, and general properties of owl:sameAs and owl:differentFrom. Some of the rules of our experiments involve a built-in predicate (called built-in:name-similar) to allow slight differences when comparing literal values corresponding to person names (e.g. R8 in Table 1). This predicate depends on a built-in function which checks if the similarity of the two name strings is above a given threshold. In all our experiments we used edit distance and 0.99 as a threshold. Other built-in predicates involved in the rules are not-equal, less-or-equal, sum, etc.

It is worth noting that the 35 rules can be extended or modified without the need of changing the algorithmic machinery of our approach.

Experimental Goals and Set-Up

The goal of our experiments was threefold: (1) to show that external information available in Linked Open Data is useful to infer owl:sameAs and owl:differentFrom facts within

INA referenced persons, and, thus, to disambiguate local homonyms; (2) to assess the gain in reduced imported facts of our Import-by-Query approach compared to approaches based on forward reasoning only; and (3) to evaluate the runtime of our Import-by-Query algorithm and the possible amortized gain if fact propagation is performed beforehand.

The external datasets from Linked Open Data with which the INA vocabulary shares terms are DBpedia.org and DBpedia.fr. The baseline for evaluating our two first goals is a set of 0.5 million external facts obtained by downloading from DBpedia.org and DBpedia.fr (using their SPARQL endpoints) all the facts about entities having the same name as one of the homonyms in the INA dataset. We applied a preprocessing step on the original INA dataset to keep only the facts on predicates appearing in the rules conditions. The resulting dataset contains almost 1.15 million of RDF facts and will be the INA dataset referred to henceforth.

Our algorithms have been implemented in SWI-Prolog. All the evaluations were done on a machine with an Intel i7 Quad-core processor and 6 GB of memory.

Experimental Results

For evaluating our first goal, we applied (using our forward reasoner) the set of 35 rules to (a) the INA dataset only and (b) the union of the INA dataset with the baseline external facts, and then we compared the number of owl:sameAs and owl:differentFrom facts on INA homonyms we obtained.

The rules applied to the INA dataset only allowed to infer 2 owl:sameAs facts and 108 owl:differentFrom facts, compared to the 4,884 owl:sameAs and 9,764 owl:differentFrom facts inferred when the external facts were added to the process. This clearly demonstrates the benefit of using external information from Linked Open Data for local disambiguation. These resulting 14,648 facts are guaranteed to be correct under the assumption that both rules and data are correct. However, since this is not ensured for DBpedia data, we asked INA experts to evaluate a random sample of 500 of such facts, and all of them were assessed to be true.[2]

The rule expressing owl:sameAs transitivity is crucial for inferring all the owl:sameAs facts that cannot be inferred locally. More generally, full reasoning is very important to discover owl:sameAs and owl:differentFrom facts. In order to show this, we applied Silk to the same two datasets (the INA dataset only, and the union of the INA dataset with the baseline external facts). For doing so, we first had to translate our rules into the Silk specification language. It is not possible, however, to translate into Silk our rules concluding on owl:differentFrom atoms. Thus, we focused on the rules leading to owl:sameAs inference. Among the 4,884 owl:sameAs facts discovered by our full forward reasoner, Silk (which does not perform full reasoning) only discovered 88, i.e. less than 2% of the total. This shows that inference is important for data linkage.

For evaluating our second experimental goal, we took as reference boolean queries the above sample of 500 owl:sameAs and owl:differentFrom facts, and we applied our import-by-query algorithm to each of these boolean queries. The number of external facts imported by our algorithm for all boolean queries was 6,417, which makes, on average, 13 imported facts per boolean query. In contrast, the total number of baseline external facts needed to conclude the boolean queries with the forward reasoner was much higher ($\sim$500,000). This shows that our import-by-query algorithm reduces drastically the number of imported facts needed for disambiguating local data.

Concerning the runtime evaluation, the import-by-query algorithm requires 3 iterations on average — it successively outputs and evaluates 3 external sub-queries (each of them being produced by calling QESQ) — before termination. It takes on average 186 s per boolean query when applied to the initial set of rules and the local dataset. This drops to 7 s when it is applied to the partially instantiated rules obtained by fact propagation beforehand, which means a gain in time of 179 s ($\sim$96%). With respect to the fact propagation, we propagated all facts involving properties of class ina:Person. This took 191 s but it is done only once for all queries, and its cost is amortized very fast, as shown by the above numbers.

[2]For copyright reasons, we are not allowed to expose the whole INA dataset. However, 100 of the 500 facts from the sample, and corresponding INA data, may be found at http://goo.gl/amm1fJ and http://goo.gl/zBrqH5.

7 Conclusion

We have proposed a novel approach for data linkage based on reasoning and adapted to the decentralized nature of the Linked Data cloud. This approach builds on the formal and algorithmic background of answering Datalog queries over deductive databases, that we have extended to handle external rewriting when local answers cannot be obtained. In contrast with existing rule-based approaches for data linkage (Saïs, Pernelle, and Rousset 2009; Hogan et al. 2012) based on forward reasoning to infer same-as facts, Import-by-Query is a backward chaining algorithm that imports *on demand* only external facts useful to infer target same-as facts handled as boolean queries. Our experiments have shown that this approach is feasible and reduces the number of facts needed to be imported. Compared to the depth-first approach sketched in (Abiteboul et al. 2005) for distributed Query-Subquery, our QESQ algorithm generates external rewriting in a breadth-first way.

Performing fact propagation beforehand in order to apply Import-by-Query to a set of more specific rules than the original ones is an optimization close to the ones proposed in QueryPIE (Urbani et al. 2011) for efficient backward reasoning on very large deductive datasets. One important difference, though, is that in the QueryPIE setting, the problem of handling recursive rules can be fully delegated to forward reasoning because all the facts are given and the recursive rules concern a well identified subset of them (so called terminological facts). Another major difference is that Import-by-Query performs query rewriting if no local answer is obtained from the input deductive dataset.

The import-by-query approach in (Grau and Motik 2012) is limited to ABox satisfiability queries used as oracles in Tableau-based reasoning. Compared to the many recent works on ontology-based data access initiated by (Calvanese et al. 2007), in which query rewriting is done independently of the data, we have designed a *hybrid* approach that alternates (external) query rewriting and (local) query answering. We plan to look into this hybrid approach further, in particular to deal with ontological constraints expressible in Datalog$^{+}_{-}$ (Calì, Gottlob, and Lukasiewicz 2012).

The interest of our rule-based approach is that it is generic and declarative: new rules can be added without changing the algorithmic machinery. At the moment the rules that we consider are certain. As a result, the same-as facts that they allow to infer are guaranteed to be correct (under the assumption that the input data does not contain erroneous facts). This is crucial to get automatically same-as facts that are certain, in particular when the goal of discovering same-as links is data fusion, i.e. replacement of two URIs by a single one in all relevant facts. Another added-value to get certain same-as and different-from facts is to find noisy data thanks to contradictions. However, in many cases, domain knowledge is not 100% sure such as pseudo-keys (Atencia, David, and Scharffe 2012) and probabilistic mappings (Tournaire et al. 2011). Data itself may be uncertain due to trust and reputation judgements towards data sources (Atencia, Al-Bakri, and Rousset 2013). Handling uncertain domain knowledge should enable to discover more same-as facts that may be true even if inferred with some uncertainty. We plan to extend our rule-based approach to model any kind of data and rules uncertainty as probabilities within the framework of Probabilistic Datalog (Fuhr 2000).

Acknowledgments

This work has been partially supported by the Qualinca project sponsored by the French National Research Agency under grant number ANR-2012-CORD-012, the LabEx PERSYVAL-Lab (ANR-11-LABX-0025-01), and by grant TIN2011-28084 of the Ministry of Science and Innovation of Spain, co-funded by the European Regional Development Fund (ERDF).

References

Abiteboul, S.; Abrams, Z.; Haar, S.; and Milo, T. 2005. Diagnosis of asynchronous discrete event systems: datalog to the rescue! In *Proceedings of the Twenty-fourth ACM SIGACT-SIGMOD-SIGART Symposium on Principles of Database Systems, June 13-15, 2005, Baltimore, Maryland, USA*, 358–367. ACM.

Abiteboul, S.; Hull, R.; and Vianu, V. 1995. *Foundations of Databases*. Addison-Wesley.

Atencia, M.; Al-Bakri, M.; and Rousset, M. 2013. Trust in networks of ontologies and alignments. *Journal of Knowledge and Information Systems*. Doi: 10.1007/s10115-013-0708-9.

Atencia, M.; David, J.; and Scharffe, F. 2012. Keys and pseudo-keys detection for web datasets cleansing and interlinking. In *Knowledge Engineering and Knowledge Management - 18th International Conference, EKAW 2012, Galway City, Ireland, October 8-12, 2012. Proceedings*, volume 7603 of *LNCS*, 144–153. Springer.

Bizer, C.; Heath, T.; and Berners-Lee, T. 2009. Linked Data - The story so far. *International Journal on Semantic Web and Information Systems* 5(3):1–22.

Calì, A.; Gottlob, G.; and Lukasiewicz, T. 2012. A general datalog-based framework for tractable query answering over ontologies. *Journal of Web Semantics* 14:57–83.

Calvanese, D.; De Giacomo, G.; Lembo, D.; Lenzerini, M.; and Rosati, R. 2007. Tractable reasoning and efficient query answering in description logics: The *DL-Lite* family. *Journal of Automated Reasoning* 39(3):385–429.

Ferrara, A.; Nikolov, A.; and Scharffe, F. 2011. Data linking for the semantic web. *International Journal on Semantic Web and Information Systems* 7(3):46–76.

Forgy, C. 1982. Rete: A fast algorithm for the many patterns/many objects match problem. *Artificial Intelligence* 19(1):17–37.

Fuhr, N. 2000. Probabilistic datalog: implementing logical information retrieval for advanced applications. *Journal of the American Society for Information Science* 51(2):95–110.

Grau, B. C., and Motik, B. 2012. Reasoning over ontologies with hidden content: The import-by-query approach. *Journal of Artificial Intelligence Research (JAIR)* 45:197–255.

Hinkelmann, K., and Hintze, H. 1993. Computing cost estimates for proof strategies. In *Extensions of Logic Programming, 4th International Workshop, ELP'93, St. Andrews, U.K., March 29 - April 1, 1993, Proceedings*, volume 798 of *LNCS*, 152–170. Springer.

Hogan, A.; Zimmermann, A.; Umbrich, J.; Polleres, A.; and Decker, S. 2012. Scalable and distributed methods for entity matching, consolidation and disambiguation over linked data corpora. *Journal of Web Semantics* 10:76–110.

Ngomo, A. N., and Auer, S. 2011. LIMES - A time-efficient approach for large-scale link discovery on the web of data. In *IJCAI 2011, Proceedings of the 22nd International Joint Conference on Artificial Intelligence, Barcelona, Catalonia, Spain, July 16-22, 2011*, 2312–2317. IJCAI/AAAI.

Saïs, F.; Pernelle, N.; and Rousset, M. 2009. Combining a logical and a numerical method for data reconciliation. *Journal on Data Semantics* 12:66–94.

Tournaire, R.; Petit, J.; Rousset, M.; and Termier, A. 2011. Discovery of probabilistic mappings between taxonomies: principles and experiments. *Journal on Data Semantics* 15:66–101.

Urbani, J.; van Harmelen, F.; Schlobach, S.; and Bal, H. E. 2011. QueryPIE: backward reasoning for OWL horst over very large knowledge bases. In *The Semantic Web - ISWC 2011 - 10th International Semantic Web Conference, Bonn, Germany, October 23-27, 2011, Proceedings, Part I*, volume 7031 of *LNCS*, 730–745. Springer.

Vieille, L. 1986. Recursive axioms in deductive databases: the query/subquery approach. In *Expert Database Conf.*, 253–267.

Volz, J.; Bizer, C.; Gaedke, M.; and Kobilarov, G. 2009. Silk - A link discovery framework for the web of data. In *Proceedings of the WWW2009 Workshop on Linked Data on the Web, LDOW 2009, Madrid, Spain, April 20, 2009.*, volume 538 of *CEUR Workshop Proceedings*. CEUR-WS.org.

Proceedings of the Twenty-Ninth AAAI Conference on Artificial Intelligence

A Personalized Interest-Forgetting Markov Model for Recommendations *

Jun Chen, Chaokun Wang and **Jianmin Wang**
School of Software, Tsinghua University, Beijing 100084, P.R. China.
chenjun14@mails.thu.edu.cn, {chaokun, jimwang}@tsinghua.edu.cn

Abstract

Intelligent item recommendation is a key issue in AI research which enables recommender systems to be more "human-minded" when generating recommendations. However, one of the major features of human — forgetting, has barely been discussed as regards recommender systems. In this paper, we considered people's forgetting of interest when performing personalized recommendations, and brought forward a personalized framework to integrate interest-forgetting property with Markov model. Multiple implementations of the framework were investigated and compared. The experimental evaluation showed that our methods could significantly improve the accuracy of item recommendation, which verified the importance of considering interest-forgetting in recommendations.

Introduction

Recommender systems have been so common in people's daily lives as it has become increasingly difficult for people to find items which are interesting and useful to them in the era of big data. As a representative of the most successful recommendation methods, the family of collaborative filtering has been seeking ways to reconstruct people's preferences from their feedbacks on previous consumptions (Koren 2009). The modeling of user preferences is essential for systems to better "understand" people. However, understanding is never enough for intelligent recommender systems which are supposed to be more "human-minded". Recommendations could be more accurate and personalized if the system behaves like the person who is using it.

One of the most prominent features of human beings is the memory forgetting (Averell and Heathcote 2011; Ebbinghaus 1885). People's memory on a certain object is not permanent and is losing from time to time unlike that of computers. When returning back from breaks, the quality of people's work negatively correlates with the length of break while positively correlates with the levels of experience that people achieved before the breaks (Anzanello and Fogliatto 2011). Similar to memory, we believe that people's interest on items also shares the feature of forgetting as time elapses. In this paper, we address the item recommendation problem from a novel perspective that incorporates people's forgetting of interest. Specifically, we integrate the interest-forgetting mechanism with Markov model which is widely used in the existing recommendation methods.

Why interest-forgetting is important? Forgetting is like a filter that removes the out-of-date and the irrelevant-to-present information from people's mind. However, this property of human agents has barely been considered in recommender systems in the literature to the best of our knowledge. The forgetting of interest shares similar concept with those of the context-aware recommendations (Wang, Rosenblum, and Wang 2012; Hariri, Mobasher, and Burke 2012) and the temporal recommendations (Koren 2009; Xiang et al. 2010) where people's long-term interest is usually weakened or ignored compared with their short-term interest in recommendations. However, the interest-forgetting in our work puts its focus on simulating people's mind activities for decision making other than only understanding user contexts. Interest-forgetting enables recommender systems to behave more like real people, which will further lead to more accurate recommendations. In addition, it is obvious that different people have different ways in forgetting interest, e.g., the speed of forgetting, the initial amount of interest as well as the relearning rate. To personalize the interest-forgetting for different people is also a vital problem.

Why integrate with Markov model? Many item recommendation applications have been observed with the first-order Markov property or high-order ones (Rendle, Freudenthaler, and Schmidt-Thieme 2010; Cheng et al. 2013). In a Markov chain, discrete stochastic states are represented by random variables, which is naturally in line with the interest-forgetting mechanism that the older the item occurs in the consumption history, the larger amount of interest on it will be lost. Besides, Markov models have successfully been applied in recommender systems due to their solid mathematical foundations (Raftery 1985; Dimitrakakis 2010; Begleiter, El-Yaniv, and Yona 2004). Thus, it is sensible and straightforward to integrate interest-forgetting with Markov model for intelligent recommendations.

Challenges and Contributions To address the issue of performing personalized recommendation considering interest-forgetting with Markov model, we are confronted

*Corresponding author: Chaokun Wang.

with two big challenges: (1) It is nontrivial to determine the appropriate model of interest-forgetting. The existing research on memory forgetting have explored many forms of forgetting mechanisms (Averell and Heathcote 2011; Anzanello and Fogliatto 2011). Unfortunately, there is no prior work to validate which one suits people's forgetting of interest better. (2) The way to integrate interest-forgetting with Markov model is unclear. The Markov model is a probabilistic representation of transitions between states like people's choices. Thus, the interest-forgetting also needs to be interpreted in a probabilistic manner.

In this paper, we attempt to tackle these challenges and address this recommendation problem. The major contributions of this paper are summarized as follows:

- We considered the forgetting of interest in the item recommendation problem, which has barely been mentioned in the literature. We also integrated the interest-forgetting mechanism with Markov models towards a "human-minded" recommender system.
- A personalized framework for interest-forgetting Markov model was brought forward in this paper, together with multiple implementations of the experience and the retention components in the framework.
- The experimental evaluation showed that our methods could significantly improve the accuracy of item recommendation compared with the state-of-the-art.

Related Works

Markov models have enjoyed a wide popularity in the recommender system community for decades. In the simplest form, the first-order Markov chain has been successfully applied in the next-basket recommendation (Rendle, Freudenthaler, and Schmidt-Thieme 2010) and the successive point-of-interest recommendation (Cheng et al. 2013) where agents' next choices are considered only relevant to the last step. To break the limitations of first-order Markov chain on the simple dependency between states, high-order Markov models (Raftery 1985) and variable-order Markov models (Begleiter, El-Yaniv, and Yona 2004; Dimitrakakis 2010) are also brought forward in the literature where agents' next movements are dependent on multiple states in previous steps. As the number of order increases, the scale of states in high/variable-order Markov models is exponentially expanded, which leads to ineffectiveness in recommendations (Yang et al. 2010). To deal with the scalability problem, one solution is to multiply a stepwise parameter to the state-to-state transition probabilities while overlooking the set-to-state transitions (Raftery 1985). Bonnin's *n*-gram statistical language method (Bonnin, Brun, and Boyer 2010) also attempts to compute recommendations based on Markov models, but it is a domain-dependent approach on web navigation, which may not be applied in general situations.

Recommender systems are supposed to be intelligent and know human agents well. Unlike computers, people are confronted with unintended memory forgetting (Ebbinghaus 1885). The forgetting/learning curves have been studied to explore the relationship between the quality of people's work and the interruption (Nembhard and Osothsilp 2001; Jaber and Bonney 1997; Anzanello and Fogliatto 2011; Averell and Heathcote 2011). Intuitively, it is sensible to incorporate forgetting into the modeling of intelligent agents in systems. (Packer, Gibbins, and Jennings 2011) employs a semantic forgetting algorithm to remove the infrequently used or cheap to relearn concepts to obtain more workable space and therefore diminish response time. Forgetting is considered as a filter to remove the unnecessary, erroneous and out-of-date information to allow for high performance (Freedman and Adams 2011).

Although there are many existing recommendation methods based on Markov models (Rendle, Freudenthaler, and Schmidt-Thieme 2010; Shani, Heckerman, and Brafman 2005; Yang et al. 2010), very few have considered the forgetting of interest to the best of our knowledge. (Zhao, Sheng, and Zhang 2012) models users' drifting interest in temporal recommendations, which factorizes the ratings by employing Ebbinghaus forgetting curve in computing rating deviation. However, it is subject to the user ratings while ours is not and our work doesn't address recommendation as a rating prediction problem, either.

A Personalized IFMM Framework

In this section, we bring forward a novel framework for personalized **I**nterest-**F**orgetting **M**arkov **M**odel, *abbr.* **IFMM**, to broaden the item recommendation research based on Markov models. We incorporate both experience and forgetting effects of people's interest into Markov models to allow for more accurate modeling on agents' behaviors.

Problem Formulation

Let $\mathcal{X} = \{x_1, x_2, ..., x_{|\mathcal{X}|}\}$ denote the set of items (e.g. music, movie, book) in the given data set, and $\mathcal{U} = \{u_1, u_2, ..., u_{|\mathcal{U}|}\}$ be the set of agents (a.k.a. users) in the system. Under the Markov model setting, we formulate the item recommendation as: Given an observing sequence of items $\mathcal{X}^{u,t} \subseteq \mathcal{X}$, which have already been consumed by agent u at time t, recommend Top-N unseen items for u at next time $t+1$ while each item x in the Top-N list should maximize the following recommendation probability:

$$P(x|\mathcal{X}^{u,t}) = P(X^u_{t+1} = x|X^u_t = x^u_t, ..., X^u_1 = x^u_1), \quad (1)$$

where $\mathcal{X}^{u,t} = \{x^u_t, ..., x^u_1\}$, x^u_i is the item consumed by u at time i, while X^u_i is a random variable representing an arbitrary item in $\mathcal{X}$.

λ-VOM

Basically, the above is a variable-order Markov model (VOM) problem (Begleiter, El-Yaniv, and Yona 2004) since the length t of the observing sequence is not fixed and varies with input. However, as (Raftery 1985) puts it, a high order of Markov chain (HOM) usually leads to exponential expansion on the number of states, e.g., $|\mathcal{X}|^{k+1}$ parameters for a k-order Markov chain. Moreover, high order Markov chains also suffer from the sparsity of transitions in the given data set, which usually leads to ineffectiveness in modeling the behaviors of agents. VOM is also confronted with these limitations of HOM. Thus, similar to (Raftery 1985), we simplify the expression of $P(x|\mathcal{X}^{u,t})$ by only multiplying a balancing component λ on each one-step transition probability:

$$P(x|\mathcal{X}^{u,t}) \propto \sum_{j=1}^{t} \lambda_j^{u,t} P(X_{t+1}^u = x | X_{t+1-j}^u = x_{t+1-j}^u) \quad (2)$$
$$= \sum_{j=1}^{t} \lambda_j^{u,t} P(x|x_{t+1-j}^u),$$

where $P(x|x_{t+1-j}^u)$ represents the one-step transition probability from item x_{t+1-j}^u to item x. We consider the one-step transition probability $P(x_i|x_j), \forall x_i, x_j \in \mathcal{X}$ to be fixed for all agents so that the whole number of states as well as parameters could be greatly reduced. Therefore, the λ component should be user-specific (u), time-aware (t) and step-aware (j) in this work (see Eq. 2). We call this model λ-VOM, which forms the basis of our IFMM framework.

Personalized IFMM Framework

So as to improve Markov models to better understand and behave more like the agents in the system, we attempt to incorporate the agents' *memory of interest* on items into Markov models, especially the λ-VOM. The major factor of memory is *forgetting* (or the counterpart *learning*), which plays a great role in agents' behaviors (Averell and Heathcote 2011). The strength of memory is the interplay of both agents' prior experience and amount of forgetting on the items (Wright 1936). Similarly, we believe that agents' interest on items is also influenced by prior experience and forgetting as their memory do. Let $\Upsilon_x^{u,t}$ ($1 \leq \Upsilon_x^{u,t} \leq 2$) be the prior experience of agent u on item x at time t, and $\Phi_x^{u,t}$ ($0 \leq \Phi_x^{u,t} \leq 1$) be the retention of u's interest on x at time t. We fairly set the base values of $\Upsilon_x^{u,t}$ and $\Phi_x^{u,t}$ as 1 where no interest on x is lost while u has only consumed x once before t. However, the experience $\Upsilon_x^{u,t}$ monotonically increases as the agent repeats the consumptions on that item, while the retention of interest $\Phi_x^{u,t}$ is monotonically decreasing as the interval between the time of the consumption on x and t gets larger. Due to the different monotonic properties of $\Upsilon_x^{u,t}$ and $\Phi_x^{u,t}$ as with elapsed time, they naturally have different value ranges, but are still of the same range length.

In our personalized IFMM framework, we combine the λ-VOM and the effect of interest-forgetting ($\Upsilon_x^{u,t}$ and $\Phi_x^{u,t}$) together by defining the λ component in λ-VOM as:

$$\lambda_j^{u,t} = \Upsilon_{x_{t+1-j}^u}^{u,t} \Phi_{x_{t+1-j}^u}^{u,t}, \quad (3)$$

where x_{t+1-j}^u is the item consumed by u at time $t+1-j$ ($1 \leq j \leq t$). Next, we attempt to find proper mathematical expressions of $\Upsilon_x^{u,t}$ and $\Phi_x^{u,t}$ as well as the one-step transition probability between items, so that the item with the largest probability (see Eq. 4) will be the one that agent u finds the most interesting among all the items.

$$P(x|\mathcal{X}^{u,t}) \propto \sum_{j=1}^{t} \Upsilon_{x_{t+1-j}^u}^{u,t} \Phi_{x_{t+1-j}^u}^{u,t} P(x|x_{t+1-j}^u). \quad (4)$$

Suppose each agent u has a set of observing sequences $\mathcal{X}^u = \{\mathcal{X}^{u,t_1}, ..., \mathcal{X}^{u,t_u}\}$, e.g., a set of music playlists, or a set of check-in sequences separated by months. Let Θ denote the set of parameters in the personalized IFMM framework. Then, we define our optimization problem to obtain the optimal Θ^* as follows:

$$\Theta^* = \underset{\Theta}{\text{argmax}} \prod_{u \in \mathcal{U}} \prod_{\mathcal{X}^{u,t} \in \mathcal{X}^u} P(x|\mathcal{X}^{u,t}). \quad (5)$$

The goal of this problem is to maximize the probability of predicting the last item given the rest of an observing sequence $\mathcal{X}^{u,t}$. To solve this optimization problem, we employ the maximum a posteriori (MAP) estimation on the following log-likelihood function:

$$\Theta^* = \underset{\Theta}{\text{argmax}}\, \mathcal{L} = \sum_{u \in \mathcal{U}} \sum_{\mathcal{X}^{u,t} \in \mathcal{X}^u} \ln(P(x|\mathcal{X}^{u,t})) \quad (6)$$
$$= \sum_{u \in \mathcal{U}} \sum_{\mathcal{X}^{u,t} \in \mathcal{X}^u} \ln(\sum_{j=1}^{t} \Upsilon_{x_{t+1-j}^u}^{u,t} \Phi_{x_{t+1-j}^u}^{u,t} P(x|x_{t+1-j}^u)),$$
$$s.t. \quad 1 \leq \Upsilon_x^{u,t} \leq 2, 0 \leq \Phi_x^{u,t} \leq 1, 0 \leq P(x|x_{t+1-j}^u) \leq 1.$$

Furthermore, the gradient of the log-likelihood $\mathcal{L}$ with respect to the model parameters is given by:

$$\frac{\partial \mathcal{L}}{\partial \Theta} = \sum_{u \in \mathcal{U}} \sum_{\mathcal{X}^{u,t} \in \mathcal{X}^u} \quad (7)$$
$$\frac{\sum_{j=1}^{t} (\frac{\partial \Upsilon_{x_{t+1-j}^u}^{u,t}}{\partial \Theta} \Phi_{x_{t+1-j}^u}^{u,t} + \frac{\partial \Phi_{x_{t+1-j}^u}^{u,t}}{\partial \Theta} \Upsilon_{x_{t+1-j}^u}^{u,t}) P(x|x_{t+1-j}^u)}{\sum_{j=1}^{t} \Upsilon_{x_{t+1-j}^u}^{u,t} \Phi_{x_{t+1-j}^u}^{u,t} P(x|x_{t+1-j}^u)}.$$

Given a training set containing observing sequences of agents, we can iteratively update the parameters Θ using the gradient ascent method. Once the (near) optimal Θ is obtained, our IFMM framework allows for personalized recommendations based on Eq. 4. In the next section, we will introduce the specifications of our IFMM framework, especially the inferences of $\Upsilon_{x_{t+1-j}^u}^{u,t}$ and $\Phi_{x_{t+1-j}^u}^{u,t}$.

Framework Specifications

In our personalized IFMM framework, the recommendation probability of an arbitrary item depends on three components — experience, interest retention and one-step transition probability as shown in Eq. 4.

One-Step Transition Probability

The one-step transition probabilities between two items under the personalized IFMM framework are supposed to be fixed. Since λ-VOM is used in the framework, we define the one-step transition probability from item x_j to item x_i as:

$$P(x_i|x_j) = \frac{\sum_{u \in \mathcal{U}} \sum_{\mathcal{X}^{u,t} \in \mathcal{X}^u} \mathbb{1}_{\{x_j, x_i\} \subseteq \mathcal{X}^{u,t}}}{\sum_{u \in \mathcal{U}} \sum_{\mathcal{X}^{u,t} \in \mathcal{X}^u} \mathbb{1}_{x_j \in \mathcal{X}^{u,t}}}, \quad (8)$$

where $\mathbb{1}_{cond}$ is the indicator function, and it returns 1 if *cond* is satisfied, or otherwise returns 0. $\{x_j, x_i\} \subseteq \mathcal{X}^{u,t}$ represents the condition that $\{x_j, x_i\}$ is a subsequence of $\mathcal{X}^{u,t}$ (x_i appears after x_j in $\mathcal{X}^{u,t}$). This expression of one-step transition probability defines how often that item x_i will be observed after the occurrence of item x_j in a same sequence.

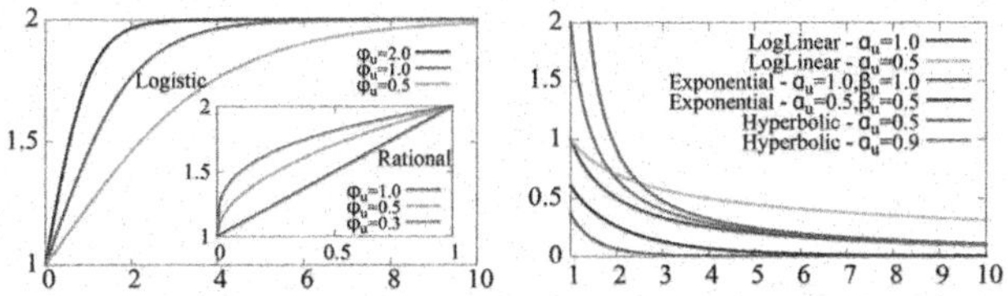

(a) Experience curves

(b) Retention curves

Figure 1: Examples of experience curves and interest retention curves.

Experience

The value of experience $\Upsilon_x^{u,t}$ represents the familiarity of agent u on item x at time t. The larger the value of $\Upsilon_x^{u,t}$ is, the more likely that u's choices will be affected by x at time t. Intuitively, agent u's experience on item x should be monotonically increasing with the number of consumptions on x by u. Thus, $\Upsilon_x^{u,t}$ could be considered as a function of the frequency $f_{u,t}(x)$ of u's consumption on item x by time t. Since the value of experience is bounded by 1 (lower) and 2 (upper) in the framework, we employ the logistic function to define experience:

$$\Upsilon_x^{u,t} = \frac{2}{1+e^{-\phi_u f_{u,t}(x)}} \qquad (f_{u,t}(x) \geq 0, \phi_u \geq 0), \quad (9)$$

where ϕ_u is u's personalized parameter for experience. To explore the proper selection of experience function in another way, we also bring forward a rational function of experience definition:

$$\Upsilon_x^{u,t} = 1 + (f_{u,t}(x))^{\phi_u} \quad (0 \leq f_{u,t}(x) \leq 1, 0 \leq \phi_u \leq 1), \quad (10)$$

where the frequencies of item consumptions are normalized by u's total consumptions before time t. Fig. 1(a) shows some examples of experience curves with both logistic function (Eq. 9) and rational function (Eq. 10). The larger the value of ϕ_u is, the steeper the curve will be for logistic function, but in contrast, the more gradual the curve will be for rational function.

In the personalized IFMM framework, the gradient of experience concerning the parameter ϕ_u is given by:

$$\frac{\partial \Upsilon_x^{u,t}}{\partial \phi_u} = \begin{cases} \frac{2 f_{u,t}(x) e^{-\phi_u f_{u,t}(x)}}{(1+e^{-\phi_u f_{u,t}(x)})^2}, & \text{Logistic function} \\ (f_{u,t}(x))^{\phi_u} \ln(f_{u,t}(x)), & \text{Rational function} \end{cases} . \quad (11)$$

In both cases, the value of experience $\Upsilon_x^{u,t}$ is always bounded by 1 and 2. The implementations of experience can also be replaced by other definitions. In this work, we evaluate our framework with these two experience expressions.

Interest Retention

Interest retention is also the core of our personalized IFMM framework. The memory retention problem has been well studied in the form of forgetting/learning curves in the literature (Anzanello and Fogliatto 2011; Averell and Heathcote 2011; Jaber and Bonney 1997; Ebbinghaus 1885). According to the review in (Anzanello and Fogliatto 2011), the major mathematical expressions of retention can be classified into three categories: log-linear model, exponential model and hyperbolic model. Similarly, as for agents' interest retention on items, we also bring forward three definitions with respect to the memory retention expressions.

Log-Linear Model Let x_{t+1-j}^u denote the item consumed by agent u at time $t+1-j$ $(1 \leq j \leq t)$ in an observing sequence of length t, and $\Phi_{x_{t+1-j}^u}^{u,t}$ be u's interest retention on x_{t+1-j}^u at time $t+1$ (the recommendation step). The log-linear definition of interest retention based on (Wright 1936) is as follows:

$$\Phi_{x_{t+1-j}^u}^{u,t} = C_u j^{-\alpha_u}, \quad (12)$$
$$1 \leq j \leq t; 0 \leq \alpha_u \leq 1; 0 < C_u \leq 1,$$

where α_u and C_u are u's personalized parameters which are also bounded. As the number of time steps gets further from now (i.e., j increases), the interest retention decreases accordingly. The gradients of $\Phi_{x_{t+1-j}^u}^{u,t}$ w.r.t. parameters are:

$$\frac{\partial \Phi_{x_{t+1-j}^u}^{u,t}}{\partial \alpha_u} = -C_u j^{-\alpha_u} \ln(j), \quad (13)$$

$$\frac{\partial \Phi_{x_{t+1-j}^u}^{u,t}}{\partial C_u} = j^{-\alpha_u}. \quad (14)$$

Exponential Model The exponential definition of interest retention is based on (Knecht 1974), and the mathematical form is:

$$\Phi_{x_{t+1-j}^u}^{u,t} = C_u j^{-\alpha_u} e^{-\beta_u j}, \quad (15)$$
$$1 \leq j \leq t; 0 \leq \alpha_u, \beta_u \leq 1; 0 < C_u \leq 1.$$

Similarly, α_u, β_u and C_u are u's bounded personalized parameters. The gradients w.r.t. these parameters are given by:

$$\frac{\partial \Phi_{x_{t+1-j}^u}^{u,t}}{\partial \alpha_u} = -C_u j^{-\alpha_u} e^{-\beta_u j} \ln(j). \quad (16)$$

$$\frac{\partial \Phi_{x_{t+1-j}^u}^{u,t}}{\partial \beta_u} = -C_u j^{1-\alpha_u} e^{-\beta_u j}. \quad (17)$$

$$\frac{\partial \Phi_{x_{t+1-j}^u}^{u,t}}{\partial C_u} = j^{-\alpha_u} e^{-\beta_u j}. \quad (18)$$

Hyperbolic Model The hyperbolic definition of interest retention is based on (Mazur and Hastie 1978) with personalized parameters α_u and C_u,

$$\Phi_{x_{t+1-j}^u}^{u,t} = \frac{C_u}{j-\alpha_u}, 0 \leq \alpha_u < 1, 0 < C_u \leq 1. \quad (19)$$

Similar to other models, the gradients of interest retention with regard to α_u and C_u are:

$$\frac{\partial \Phi_{x_{t+1-j}^u}^{u,t}}{\partial \alpha_u} = \frac{C_u}{(j-\alpha_u)^2}. \quad (20)$$

$$\frac{\partial \Phi_{x_{t+1-j}^u}^{u,t}}{\partial C_u} = \frac{1}{j-\alpha_u}. \quad (21)$$

In the above models, C_u is the personalized maximum interest retention value of user u. α_u in Log-Linear model and Exponential model, and β_u in Exponential model, are the personalized decaying parameters representing the interest forgetting speeds of users. The larger the values of these parameters are, the faster the interest is lost. Besides, α_u in Hyperbolic model compensates the number of consumption steps, and it personalizes the start step of interest forgetting.

Fig. 1(b) illustrates some examples of interest retention models. For simplicity, the scale parameter C_u here is set to 1.0. We can see that the curves of hyperbolic model are the steepest ones, and those of exponential model are the closest to the horizontal axis. The values on the log-linear curves are relatively higher but also not so differentiable between each other by contrast. In addition, the set of parameters Θ in our framework consists of all the personalized parameters in the definitions of experience and interest retention, such as ϕ_u, α_u, β_u and C_u in this paper. These personalized parameters are randomly initialized in the range $[0.0, 1.0]$ except for the ϕ_u of non-normalized experience which is randomly drawn from absolute $N(0, 0.1)$. By using the learning method introduced in the framework, we can further perform personalized recommendations based on Eq. 4.

Experiments

Experimental Settings

We conducted experiments on the large scale music listening data set collected from Last.fm (Celma 2010). Music recommendation is commonly used in people's daily lives (Wang, Rosenblum, and Wang 2012), and people's listening behaviors are a mixture of new songs and the old songs in the playlists (Anderson et al. 2014). Thus, music recommendation is a typical representative of application scenarios of the personalized IFMM framework. This data set contains 16,986,614 listening records from 992 users on 964,463 songs. We partitioned the listening history of each user into sessions (*a.k.a.* observing sequences) based on a timeout threshold like 1 hour which is the default in our experiments. The threshold measures the maximum acceptable interval between two adjacent records in time order to be considered in the same session. Meanwhile, the listening records whose duration is less than 30 seconds are considered as dislikes of users, and are removed before further experiments.

We evaluated our methods with two experience implementations and three interest retention implementations, i.e., NM+LL, NM+EX, NM+HY, NO+LL, NO+EX and NO+HY where NM, NO, LL, EX and HY represent normalized experience (logistic function), non-normalized experience (rational function), log-linear retention, exponential retention and hyperbolic retention, respectively. We compared our method with the state-of-the-art item recommendation methods, i.e., the Markov-based ones like FPMC (Rendle, Freudenthaler, and Schmidt-Thieme 2010; Cheng et al. 2013) and TSPR (Haveliwala 2002), the graph-based preference fusion STG (Xiang et al. 2010), as well as the sequential pattern based method SEQ (Hariri, Mobasher, and Burke 2012). The sequential pattern based method was evaluated with different supports and window sizes, e.g.,

Table 1: Hit ratios of the proposed methods.

Method	Top10	Top30	Top50	Top70	Top90	Top100
NM+LL	0.3288	0.4163	0.4536	0.4756	0.4919	0.4983
NM+EX	0.3335	0.4189	0.4553	0.4766	0.4924	0.4983
NM+HY	**0.3954**	**0.4573**	0.4816	0.4962	0.5068	0.5113
NO+LL	0.3289	0.4164	0.4537	0.4757	0.4921	0.4984
NO+EX	0.3345	0.4198	0.4557	0.4769	0.4927	0.4987
NO+HY	0.3935	**0.4573**	**0.4834**	**0.4991**	**0.5109**	**0.5154**

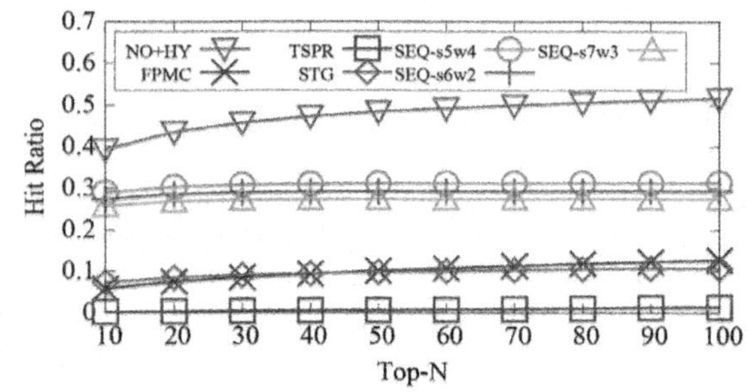

Figure 2: Comparisons on the accuracy of recommendation.

SEQ-s5w4 means the method with support as 5 and window size as 4. Since IFMM framework doesn't solve recommendations as a rating prediction problem and there are also no ratings in the Lastfm dataset, we don't consider those rating-oriented approaches, e.g. timeSVD++ (Koren 2009) and NMF, as appropriate comparative ones to our method.

Overall Accuracy Performance

We first evaluated the overall accuracy performance of our proposed methods and the baselines. In the evaluation, we used 80% of each user's observing sequences to learn the personalized parameters in the IFMM framework as well as the parameters of the comparative models. Then, the other 20% observing sequences were used to test the performance by predicting the last song in each test observing sequence while using its rest as input.

Table 1 shows the hit ratios of the proposed methods in the accuracy evaluation under different length of recommendation list. Generally, all the proposed methods exhibit promising accuracy performance in the experiment. As for the choice of retention expressions, we observed that HY methods outperformed the other methods in this evaluation. Meanwhile, the ones with log-linear retention and exponential retention showed similar performance in accuracy. As for the choice of experience expressions, there is not much difference between the hit ratios of methods with normalized experience and non-normalized experience compared with the methods with different retention expressions. Although experience and interest retention are both essential factors in people's forgetting process, this comparison indicates that interest retention is more important than experience on people's listening choices in the Lastfm data set.

Next, we compared the accuracy performance between our methods and the baselines. NO+HY is selected as the representative of our methods since it shows the best perfor-

Table 2: Value distributions of the learned parameters with respect to each method in the experiments. Ranges of parameter values are represented with parentheses.

(a) Value distribution of Normalized ϕ_u.

Method	[0.0,0.2)	[0.2,0.4)	[0.4,0.6)	[0.6,0.8)	[0.8,1.0]
NM+LL	0.945	0.011	0.012	0.014	0.018
NM+EX	0.937	0.015	0.014	0.014	0.020
NM+HY	0.945	0.013	0.009	0.022	0.011

(b) Value distribution of Non-Normalized ϕ_u.

Method	[0.0,2.0)	[2.0,4.0)	[4.0,6.0)	[6.0,8.0)	[8.0,∞)
NO+LL	0.111	0.484	0.403	0.002	0.000
NO+EX	0.128	0.657	0.213	0.002	0.000
NO+HY	0.174	0.492	0.333	0.001	0.000

(c) Value distribution of α_u.

Method	[0.0,0.2)	[0.2,0.4)	[0.4,0.6)	[0.6,0.8)	[0.8,1.0]
NM+LL	0.810	0.066	0.056	0.049	0.019
NM+EX	0.755	0.077	0.080	0.060	0.028
NM+HY	0.877	0.061	0.034	0.020	0.008
NO+LL	0.831	0.052	0.059	0.037	0.021
NO+EX	0.760	0.079	0.068	0.053	0.040
NO+HY	0.889	0.064	0.026	0.018	0.003

(d) Value distribution of β_u.

Method	[0.0,0.2)	[0.2,0.4)	[0.4,0.6)	[0.6,0.8)	[0.8,1.0]
NM+EX	0.696	0.084	0.095	0.085	0.040
NO+EX	0.700	0.093	0.101	0.067	0.039

(e) Value distribution of C_u.

Method	[0.0,0.2)	[0.2,0.4)	[0.4,0.6)	[0.6,0.8)	[0.8,1.0]
NM+LL	0.005	0.019	0.030	0.046	0.900
NM+EX	0.002	0.013	0.037	0.056	0.892
NM+HY	0.003	0.023	0.030	0.053	0.891
NO+LL	0.004	0.021	0.032	0.050	0.893
NO+EX	0.006	0.021	0.027	0.057	0.889
NO+HY	0.002	0.013	0.036	0.051	0.898

mance among the 6 proposed methods (see Table 1). Fig. 2 illustrates the comparison results where we can see NO+HY dominates all the baselines under different length of recommendation list. The absolute improvement of NO+HY is about 10% to 20% compared with the best of the baselines. The sequential pattern based methods showed competitive results by reaching hit ratios around 30%, while FPMC, STG and TSPR are not observed with high accuracy in the experiments. In all, our method can significantly improve the accuracy of item recommendations in the experiments.

Personalized Parameters

We analyzed the value distributions of the learned personalized parameters in our methods to explore the functionality of parameters as shown in Table. 2. The values of parameters are grouped and represented with parentheses. For instance, in Table 2(a), the value 0.018 in the cell with respect to method NM+LL and parameter range [0.8,1.0] means there are about 1.8% of users whose normalized ϕ_u values fall between [0.8,1.0] when computed with method NM+LL. By comparing the distributions of experience parameter ϕ_u in

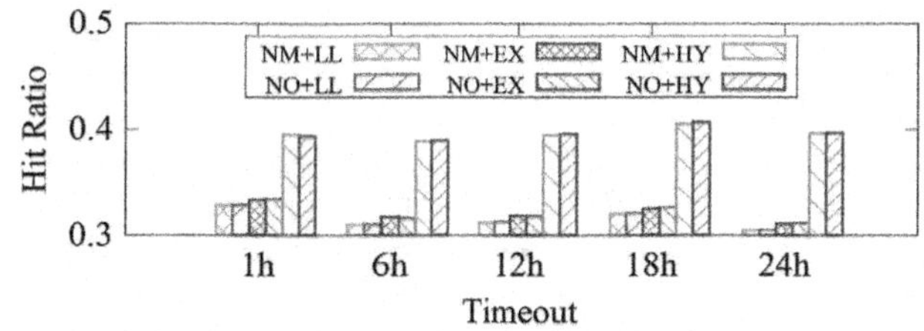

(a) Top-10 recommendations.

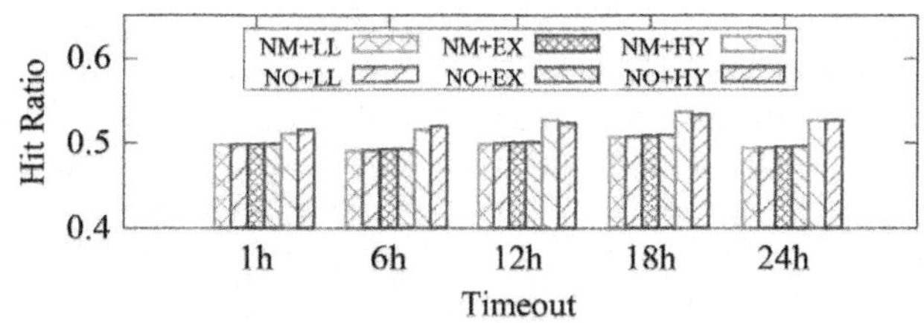

(b) Top-100 recommendations.

Figure 3: The impact of timeout on the performance.

Table. 2(a) and Table. 2(b), we can see that for the NM methods, most users have the normalized ϕ_u values between $[0.0,0.2)$, which are not very differentiable. While for the NO methods, a large number of users show their ϕ_u values around $2.0 - 4.0$, which leads to wider difference in contrast.

Table. 2(c) shows the distribution of α_u from the retention expressions. Many users tend not to be personalized on this parameter since the α_u values of about 75% – 90% users are within $[0.0,0.2)$. However, the fractions of α_u-less-personalized users are different where the EX methods have lower fractions while the HY methods have higher ones.

Similarly, Table. 2(d) shows the distribution of β_u value from the exponential retention expression. The personalization on β_u is more significant compared to the other parameters although there are still 70% users having β_u within $[0.0,0.2)$. However, the fractions of personalized users contribute to the improvement in the recommendation accuracy.

Besides, the distribution of C_u parameter from the retention expressions is shown in Table. 2(e). C_u is a scaling parameter which controls the maximum interest retention a user has. Unsurprisingly, most users have $C_u > 0.8$ while a small fraction of users have smaller C_u values.

From the above analysis, we know that not all users tend to be personalized enough in all dimensions. In contrast, different human agents tend to be personalized on different aspects. However, even only one personalized parameter exists among the above for any human agent, the recommendation results will be much different. The diversified personalization ways may be one of the reasons why our methods outperformed the baselines in the accuracy as shown in Fig. 2.

Timeout

We also evaluated the performance of our methods as with the change of timeout which partitions the observing sequences along the history of people's consumptions. Timeout influences the general length of observing sequences, i.e., the order of λ-VOM. A larger timeout will usually lead to longer sequences which incorporate more contextual information into user "contexts" for next-step recommendations. As illustrated in Fig. 3 of the impact of timeout on the recommendation accuracy, we found slight fluctuations on hit ratios of our methods as timeout changes for both Top-10 and Top-100 recommendations. In our experiments, the best choice of timeout seems to be about 18 hours from Fig. 3. However, the overall performance of our methods is not apt to be significantly affected by the setting of timeout.

In sum, the experiments showed that our methods under the IFMM framework can significantly improve the item recommendations with diversified personalization strategies, and the performance of our methods is stable and promising. Besides, the time complexity of online recommendation using IFMM framework is linear to the length of the observing sequence and the number of transferable items, which makes IFMM efficient and scalable. The IFMM framework is applicable as long as the consumption time (or order) information is available regardless of the type of items. However, for scenarios where few reconsumption behaviors on a same item from a same user are observed, e.g. movie, IFMM still works since the interest retention could be computed though the experience would always be 1.

Our methods is not vulnerable to new users because we can assume several consumptions randomly or based on popularity for new users, and recommend items to them. As long as consumptions are generated, we can remove the assumptions and leave the real consumptions in the observing sequences. As for new items, our method may need to recalculate the transition probabilities in a batch mode periodically. However, only the transition probabilities of items in the new batch of observing sequences will be updated, which means only a local updating is required.

Conclusions and Future Work

In this paper, we attempted to incorporate the forgetting of interest into Markov models to better simulate the decisions of intelligent agents for personalized recommendations. To address this issue, we brought forward a framework of personalized interest-forgetting Markov model as well as the specifications of the framework. The experimental evaluations showed that our methods could significantly improve the item recommendation accuracy. In the future, we prospect this framework to behave in a human way to compute recommendations, i.e. human intelligent features should be incorporated into this framework, especially the mind activities like learning, forgetting and relearning.

Acknowledgments

This work was supported in part by the National Natural Science Foundation of China (No. 61373023, No. 61170064, No. 61133002) and the National High Technology Research and Development Program of China (No. 2013AA013204).

References

Anderson, A.; Kumar, R.; Tomkins, A.; and Vassilvitskii, S. 2014. The dynamics of repeat consumption. In *WWW*, 419–430.

Anzanello, M. J., and Fogliatto, F. S. 2011. Learning curve models and applications: Literature review and research directions. *Int J Ind Ergonom* 41:573–583.

Averell, L., and Heathcote, A. 2011. The form of the forgetting curve and the fate of memories. *J Math Psychol* 55:25–35.

Begleiter, R.; El-Yaniv, R.; and Yona, G. 2004. On prediction using variable order markov models. *J Artif Intell Res* 22:385–421.

Bonnin, G.; Brun, A.; and Boyer, A. 2010. *Skipping-based collaborative recommendations inspired from statistical language modeling*. InTech.

Celma, O. 2010. *Music Recommendation and Discovery in the Long Tail*. Springer. chapter 3.

Cheng, C.; Yang, H.; Lyu, M. R.; and King, I. 2013. Where you like to go next: successive point-of-interest recommendation. In *IJCAI*, 2605–2611.

Dimitrakakis, C. 2010. Bayesian variable order markov models. In *AISTATS*, 161–168.

Ebbinghaus, H. 1885. *Memory: A Contribution to Experimental Psychology*. New York by Teachers College, Columbia University.

Freedman, S., and Adams, J. 2011. Filtering data based on human-inspired forgetting. *IEEE Trans Syst Man Cybern B Cybern* 41(6):1544–1555.

Hariri, N.; Mobasher, B.; and Burke, R. 2012. Context-aware music recommendation based on latent topic sequential patterns. In *RecSys*, 131–138.

Haveliwala, T. H. 2002. Topic-sensitive pagerank. In *WWW*, 517–526.

Jaber, M. Y., and Bonney, M. 1997. A comparative study of learning curves with forgetting. *Appl Math Model* 21(8):523–531.

Knecht, G. 1974. Costing, technological growth and generalized learning curves. *Oper Res Quart* 25(3):487–491.

Koren, Y. 2009. Collaborative filtering with temporal dynamics. In *KDD*, 447–456.

Mazur, J., and Hastie, R. 1978. Learning as accumulation: a reexamination of the learning curve. *Psychol Bull* 85(6):1256–1274.

Nembhard, D. A., and Osothsilp, N. 2001. An empirical comparison of forgetting models. *IEEE Trans Eng Manag* 48(3):283–291.

Packer, H. S.; Gibbins, N.; and Jennings, N. R. 2011. An on-line algorithm for semantic forgetting. In *IJCAI*, 2704–2709.

Raftery, A. E. 1985. A model for high-order markov chains. *J Roy Statist Soc Ser B* 47(3):528–539.

Rendle, S.; Freudenthaler, C.; and Schmidt-Thieme, L. 2010. Factorizing personalized markov chains for next-basket recommendation. In *WWW*, 811–820.

Shani, G.; Heckerman, D.; and Brafman, R. 2005. An MDP-based recommender system. *J Mach Learn Res* 6:1265–1295.

Wang, X.; Rosenblum, D.; and Wang, Y. 2012. Context-aware mobile music recommendation for daily activities. In *ACM Multimedia*, 99–108.

Wright, T. 1936. Factors affecting the cost of airplanes. *J. Aeronaut. Sci.* 3(2):122–128.

Xiang, L.; Yuan, Q.; Zhao, S.; Chen, L.; Zhang, X.; Yang, Q.; and Sun, J. 2010. Temporal recommendation on graphs via long- and short-term preference fusion. In *KDD*, 723–732.

Yang, Q.; Fan, J.; Wang, J.; and Zhou, L. 2010. Personalizing web page recommendation via collaborative filtering and topic-aware markov model. In *ICDM*, 1145–1150.

Zhao, L.; Sheng, F.; and Zhang, B. 2012. Collaborative filtering based on user's drifting interests. *IJACT* 4(15):336–345.

Proceedings of the Twenty-Ninth AAAI Conference on Artificial Intelligence

Will You "Reconsume" the Near Past? Fast Prediction on Short-Term Reconsumption Behaviors *

Jun Chen, Chaokun Wang and **Jianmin Wang**
School of Software, Tsinghua University, Beijing 100084, P.R. China.
chenjun14@mails.thu.edu.cn, {chaokun, jimwang}@tsinghua.edu.cn

Abstract

The short-term reconsumption behaviors, i.e. "reconsume" the near past, account for a large proportion of people's activities every day and everywhere. In this paper, we firstly derived four generic features which influence people's short-term reconsumption behaviors. These features were extracted with respect to different roles in the process of reconsumption behaviors, i.e. users, items and interactions. Then, we brought forward two fast algorithms with the linear and the quadratic kernels to predict whether a user will perform a short-term reconsumption at a specific time given the context. The experimental results show that our proposed algorithms are more accurate in the prediction tasks compared with the baselines. Meanwhile, the time complexity of online prediction of our algorithms is $O(1)$, which enables fast prediction in real-world scenarios. The prediction contributes to more intelligent decision-making, e.g. potential revisited customer identification, personalized recommendation, and information re-finding.

Introduction

People's reconsumption behaviors exist everywhere and happen every day. We loop our favourite songs while searching for the newly released music tracks from our favourite artists. We eat regularly at our favourite restaurants while experiencing fresh tastes at the new restaurants recommended by our friends. People's consumptions of items, e.g., songs, restaurants and web pages, consist of both novelty-seeking behaviors and reconsumption behaviors which are alternated now and then (Anderson et al. 2014). Thus, an interesting question is: Are these seemingly random behaviors, especially the reconsumption behaviors predictable?

(Anderson et al. 2014) proposed a method to predict what will most likely be reconsumed given the premise that the user is surely about to perform a reconsumption. However, this assumption leaves the more fundamental problem blank, i.e. whether or not a user will reconsume at a specific time. Answering the "whether" question is no inferior than answering the "what" question. If whether a user will reconsume could be predicted, then different data processing strategies would be used by systems, e.g., web revisitation or novel web exploration, recommendation from the past or from the unobserved. The "whether" problem can be considered as a *switch* that opens the doors of two disjoint problems and narrows the problem domains therein.

The prediction on whether or not a user will reconsume at a specific time is of broad interest. In recommendation tasks (Bobadilla et al. 2013), the prediction results help recommender systems understand whether the novel unobserved items or the already consumed items are more appropriate to be recommended at a specific time. In web browsers, the prediction results suggest whether or not the visited web pages should be cached for later revisitation (Adar, Teevan, and Dumais 2008). In commercial business, the prediction results enable restaurants and supermarkets to identify potential revisited customers who are further delivered with coupons (Han, Back, and Barrett 2009). Furthermore, inside mobile phones, the prediction could also help the system decide whether or not the pre-launching of that application is necessary out of the considerations for efficiency and user friendliness (Xia and Lam 2012).

Similar to the taxonomy of web revisitations by Adar *et al.* (Adar, Teevan, and Dumais 2008), the general reconsumption behaviors of human can also be classified into the short-term reconsumptions (fast group), the medium-term reconsumptions (medium group) and the long-term reconsumptions (slow group). In this paper, we mainly focus on the study of the **S**hort-**T**erm **REC**onsumption behaviors, *abbr.* STREC behaviors (i.e., reconsume the near past). The dynamics of STREC behaviors make it more difficult and important to study compared with the long-term and the medium-term reconsumption behaviors. The prediction of people's STREC behaviors is nontrivial and is confronted with a number of challenges: First, STREC behaviors are more prone to change with time compared with long-term reconsumption behaviors, which makes it more difficult to model the dynamics. Second, STREC behaviors are seemingly random and they are likely to be influenced by multiple factors like users, items and user-item interactions. Third, people may have different STREC behavior preferences in different domains, and it is difficult to extract general domain-independent patterns to represent people's STREC behaviors.

In this paper, we studied people's STREC behaviors in a

*Corresponding author: Chaokun Wang.

domain-independent way. Four prominent features were extracted given the user's recent consumption history. Two fast algorithms were proposed by solving an optimization problem to predict whether or not a user will perform a reconsumption at a specific time based on these features.

We summarize our main contributions as follows:

- We analyzed the major domain-independent factors in influencing people's STREC behaviors. The factors in the analysis covered the user aspect, the item aspect and the interactional aspect between users and items.
- The problem of the binary prediction on people's STREC behaviors, i.e., whether or not a user will perform a reconsumption given the user's consumption history, was presented and formulated. To the best of our knowledge, the problem has not been studied in a domain-independent way in the literature.
- Two fast prediction algorithms were proposed based on these domain-independent features to address the above problem. The proposed methods can be further improved by simply appending more domain-specific features to our feature vectors.
- The experimental results showed that the proposed methods demonstrated promising effectiveness and efficiency in the prediction. They outperformed the reference approaches using the state-of-the-art classifiers in the prediction experiment.

Related Work

People's reconsumption behaviors are observed frequently in many fields. We introduced several studies on people's reconsumption behaviors in this section.

Web Revisitation. As a major kind of reconsumption types, the web revisitation has been well studied (Adar, Teevan, and Dumais 2008; Liu et al. 2012; Yu et al. 2013), where people revisit the web pages that have already been visited before. People usually conduct web revisitation through the browsers' URL auto-completion, bookmarks, history sidebars, back and forward buttons (Kawase, Papadakis, and Herder 2011; Kawase, Herder, and Nejdl 2011). Zhang and Zhao (Zhang and Zhao 2011) found that about 39.3% of web page views are revisitations, and the proportion could be higher (about 59.6%) when considering the tab-switches in web browsers as revisitations. Generally, people tend to revisit the popular web pages and those which have recently been viewed (Catledge and Pitkow 1995).

Repeat Queries. Repeat queries, a.k.a. reconsumption of web queries, account for a large amount of web search traffic (Tyler and Teevan 2010). For example, about 40% web queries are repeat queries in the Yahoo's searching logs (Teevan et al. 2007). People frequently type the same queries in the web search engine to re-find exactly the same information they have viewed before or to follow the updated information on the topics they have explored (Teevan et al. 2007). Compared with the repeat queries in web search, the query repetition rate is reported higher (55.76%) in the short-text corpus — Twitter (Teevan, Ramage, and Morris 2011). People are likely to use repeat queries on Twitter to monitor topics over time.

Information Re-finding. Information re-finding is another challenging topic in people's reconsumption behaviors, where people attempt to re-find the information they have come across before. One of the most common scenarios of information re-finding is to re-find past emails (Elsweiler, Baillie, and Ruthven 2011). It is reported that about 55% selections on messages in email clients are re-finding behaviors (Elsweiler, Harvey, and Hacker 2011). (Elsweiler, Harvey, and Hacker 2011) used a generalized linear model to identify if the sequence of operations in the email client contains a re-finding behavior. The problem they have addressed is different from ours in this paper. They focused on identifying re-finding behaviors among the past consumptions rather than predicting the future, and they used the features related to operations in email clients, e.g., the selections on email entries and the opening of folders, instead of the domain-independent features used in this paper.

People's reconsumption behaviors are also observed in other fields like the repeat purchase (Chiu et al. 2012; Weisberg, Te'eni, and Arman 2011), the revisitation on restaurants from customers (Han, Back, and Barrett 2009; Park and Jang 2014) as well as the repeat social choice (Sarma et al. 2012). To the best of our knowledge, the most related work with ours is the analysis on the dynamics of reconsumptions (Anderson et al. 2014), in which the authors found that the quality of items and the recency effect have significant impacts on people's choice of items for reconsumption given the premise that the system already knows the user will perform a reconsumption. By contrast, our work attempts to predict whether a user will reconsume at a specific time, which is exactly the study on their premise. As far as we know, this is the first work addressing the domain-independent prediction on people's short-term reconsumption behaviors.

Preliminaries

In this work, we use a sliding window along the sequence of each user's consumptions ordered by time. The sliding window always maintains the k most recent consumptions for each user, and the length of the window k is fixed. As the user performs a new consumption, the sliding window takes a step forward. Thus, the sliding window also represents the updated user "context" to some extent. There are several basic concepts in our work:

Definition 1 *A consumption transaction t is a random variable representing an arbitrary item. The consumption history of user u is represented by a sequence of consumption transactions, $T_u = \{t_1^u, t_2^u, ..., t_{|T_u|}^u\}$.*

Definition 2 *A k-length sliding window, denoted as W_k, is a queue which maintains the k most recent consumption transactions of a user till now. Once the user issues a new transaction t on an arbitrary item, t is pushed into the tail of W_k. Meanwhile, if the number of transactions in W_k exceeds the limit k, the head transaction of W_k is popped.*

The sliding window W_k consists of no more than k consumption transactions. Based on the use of sliding window, we can formally define the STREC behaviors:

Definition 3 *Given the k-length sliding window W_k of a user by now and a new consumption transaction t, we call t a STREC behavior, iff $t \in W_k$. Otherwise, t is considered as a novel consumption.*

According to Definition 3, whether or not consumption transaction t is a STREC behavior is influenced by the setting of k. To investigate people's STREC behaviors, k is usually not large so that only the repetitions on the recent consumptions are considered. Thus, we formulate the problem of the binary prediction of STREC behaviors as below:

Definition 4 *Given the k-length sliding window $W_k^{u,t}$ of user u right before performing consumption transaction t, the problem of the* binary prediction of STREC behaviors *is to predict whether or not $t \in W_k^{u,t}$ where t is unknown.*

In this work, we use k-last-visited items to define sliding window rather than the elapsed time because the continuity makes the time bound hard to determine in real-world scenarios, and the k-last-visited items are representative enough for people's (re)consumption contexts.

Binary STREC Behavior Prediction

In this section, we first introduce the four generic features that we propose to represent user's reconsumption context. Then, two fast prediction methods are discussed.

Feature Extraction

So as to model people's willingness to reconsume, we propose the following features: (1) item popularity, (2) item reconsumption ratio, (3) user reconsumption ratio, and (4) window repeat ratio. These features correspond to the three major aspects regarding STREC behaviors, i.e. item aspect (1-2), user aspect (3) and interactional aspect (4).

Item Popularity The quality of items has an important effect upon the reconsumption behaviors (Anderson et al. 2014), and the items with high quality are usually much more likely to be reconsumed. Item popularity (*abbr.* IP) is an ideal measurement of the quality of each item.

Let $freq(x)$ be the frequency of item x in the given data set. We measure the popularity of item x as its fraction of the maximum item frequency in the data set,

$$h_{IP}(x) = \frac{log(1 + freq(x))}{\max_{y \in \mathbf{X}} log(1 + freq(y))}, \quad (1)$$

where $\mathbf{X}$ is the item set. The log operator is used to adjust the skewed distribution of item popularity. To represent the given sliding window W_k, we used the average popularity:

$$h_{IP}(W_k) = \frac{1}{|W_k|} \sum_{x \in W_k} h_{IP}(x). \quad (2)$$

By analyzing the relationship between $h_{IP}(W_k)$ and people's reconsumption willingness, we find that the probability of reconsumption increases as the average item popularity of sliding window increases.

Item Reconsumption Ratio As another way to explore the intrinsic item factors upon STREC behaviors, it is a straightforward intuition that the different reconsumption ratios of items also lead to different probabilities to perform reconsumptions. The absolute item reconsumption ratio is defined as its probability to be observed as a reconsumption along the user consumption transaction sequences,

$$h_{AIRR}(x) = log(1 + \frac{\sum_{u \in \mathbf{U}} \sum_{t \in T_u} \mathbb{1}_{t=x \wedge t \in C_k^{u,t}}}{\sum_{u \in \mathbf{U}} \sum_{t \in T_u} \mathbb{1}_{t=x}}), \quad (3)$$

where $\mathbf{U}$ is the user set, T_u is the consumption transaction sequence of user u, $\mathbb{1}_{cond}$ is the indicator function which returns 1 when $cond$ is satisfied, and otherwise returns 0. Similar to the definition of the item popularity, the value of the absolute item reconsumption ratio is also adjusted by a log operator.

The relative item reconsumption ratio is defined as the fraction of the maximum absolute item reconsumption ratio in the data set,

$$h_{IRR}(x) = \frac{h_{AIRR}(x)}{\max_{y \in \mathbf{X}} h_{AIRR}(y)}. \quad (4)$$

We use the average item reconsumption ratio (*abbr.* IRR) of a sliding window as another metric,

$$h_{IRR}(W_k) = \frac{1}{|W_k|} \sum_{x \in W_k} h_{IRR}(x). \quad (5)$$

In our experiments, we found that people's reconsumption probability is also increasing as the average item reconsumption ratio of sliding window gets larger.

User Reconsumption Ratio The user preference plays a key role in people's behaviors (Zhang, Wang, and Wang 2014), and the preferences are usually diverse among the crowds (Jung, Hong, and Kim 2005). The user factor is absolutely an important signal in analyzing people's STREC behaviors. For example, many people have brand loyalty and re-purchase on a few brands frequently (Chiu et al. 2012).

However, it is nontrivial to model every user aspect related to the personalities and preferences. We use the simple and straightforward feature of the user factor, i.e., user reconsumption ratio, to analyze how STREC behaviors can be affected by different user personalities and preferences. The ratio is defined as the probability that a user performs a reconsumption along her consumption transaction sequence,

$$h_{URR}(u) = \frac{\sum_{t \in T_u} \mathbb{1}_{t \in W_k^{u,t}}}{|T_u|}. \quad (6)$$

User reconsumption ratio (*abbr.* URR) is not time-aware, and it should be a static and intrinsic feature of user. A larger value of this feature indicates that the user is more likely to perform a reconsumption.

Window Repeat Ratio Besides the item factors and the user factor, we also explored the impact of the interactional factor upon people's STREC behaviors. Given a k-length sliding window W_k, we would like to know if the total number of reconsumption times in W_k influences people's reconsumption behavior in the next step. This feature is based on the hypotheses that people may get satiated with reconsuming several items again and again, or on the contrary, the compact reconsumptions increase the probability to perform another reconsumption again like the "Mathew Effect" (Merton 1968) in people's STREC behaviors.

Let $DS(W_k)$ be the set of *distinct* items in W_k, and $1 \leq |DS(W_k)| \leq k$. We use the proportion of the reconsumptions in the current sliding window to measure the window repeat ratio (*abbr.* WRR),

$$h_{WRR}(W_k) = 1 - \frac{|DS(W_k)|}{k}. \quad (7)$$

Obviously, $0 \leq h_{WRR}(W_k) < 1$. The larger the value of $h_{WRR}(W_k)$ is, the more compact the reconsumptions are in the sliding window. In our experiments, we found that the reconsumption probability is almost linear to the value of window repeat ratio in the current sliding window. This observation meets the hypothesis that "the rich get richer" effect also exists in people's STREC behaviors.

Fast Prediction Methods

In this paper, we attempt to combine all the four generic features to predict people's STREC behaviors. Given the k-length sliding window $W_k^{u,t}$ of user u right before performing consumption transaction t, we construct a vector $\mathbf{x}_{u,t} = \{h_{IP}(W_k^{u,t}), h_{IRR}(W_k^{u,t}), h_{URR}(u), h_{WRR}(W_k^{u,t})\}^T$ combining all the factors mentioned above together. Next, we propose two fast binary prediction methods with the linear and the quadratic kernels, respectively, to address our problem in this paper.

Linear Method Firstly, we use a linear hyperplane to separate the points in the 4-dimensional feature space. Our linear method predicts the probability of u's new consumption transaction t to be a reconsumption with the probability $\Pr_{\mathcal{L}}(u,t) = \mathbf{w}^T\mathbf{x}_{u,t}$, $s.t.$, $\sum_i \mathbf{w}_i = 1$. $\mathbf{x}_{u,t}$ is the aforementioned feature vector which represents the user's consumption "context", and $\mathbf{w}$ is the vector representing the hyperplane. So as to get the optimal hyperplane, it naturally leads to the following optimization problem,

$$\underset{\mathbf{w}^*_{\mathcal{L}}}{\text{argmin}}\, \mathcal{L}(\mathbf{w}) = \sum_{u\in\mathbf{U}}\sum_{t\in T_u}(\mathbf{w}^T\mathbf{x}_{u,t} - \mathbb{1}_{t\in W_k^{u,t}})^2, \quad (8)$$
$$s.t. \sum_i \mathbf{w}_i = 1,$$

where $W_k^{u,t}$ is the k-length sliding window of user u just before performing a new unknown consumption transaction t. Since the value of each dimension in $\mathbf{x}_{u,t}$ is between 0 and 1, the value of $\mathbf{w}^T\mathbf{x}_{u,t}$ will therefore be limited in the range $[0.0, 1.0]$. To solve this optimization problem, we rewrite the objective function $\tilde{\mathcal{L}}$ by adding a Lagrange multiplier,

$$\underset{\mathbf{w}^*_{\tilde{\mathcal{L}}}}{\text{argmin}}\, \tilde{\mathcal{L}}(\mathbf{w}) = \sum_{u\in\mathbf{U}}\sum_{t\in T_u}(\mathbf{w}^T\mathbf{x}_{u,t} - \mathbb{1}_{t\in W_k^{u,t}})^2 + \lambda\sum_i \mathbf{w}_i. \quad (9)$$

We solve this problem using the gradient method by updating the hyperplane vector step by step using the following updating rule,

$$\frac{\partial\tilde{\mathcal{L}}(\mathbf{w})}{\partial\mathbf{w}_i} = \sum_{u\in\mathbf{U}}\sum_{t\in T_u} 2\mathbf{x}_{u,t,i}(\mathbf{w}^T\mathbf{x}_{u,t} - \mathbb{1}_{t\in W_k^{u,t}}) + \lambda. \quad (10)$$

Our linear method works by separating the points representing reconsumptions and novel consumptions in the 4-dimensional feature space with a linear hyperplane. If $\Pr_{\mathcal{L}}(u,t) > \frac{1}{2}$ for user u just before performing a new consumption transaction t, our linear method will predict t to be a reconsumption.

Quadratic Method In our experiments of the four generic features, we observed that people would be more likely to perform a reconsumption if any one of the four features is large enough. Thus, we believe it is better to separate the feature points using a hypersphere like a four dimensional ellipsoid. The probability of user u's new consumption transaction t being a reconsumption should be $\Pr_{\mathcal{Q}}(u,t) = \sqrt{\mathbf{w}^T diag(\mathbf{x}_{u,t})^2\mathbf{w}}$. We bring forward our quadratic method by solving the following quadratic optimization problem:

$$\underset{\mathbf{w}^*_{\mathcal{Q}}}{\text{argmin}}\, \mathcal{Q}(\mathbf{w}) = \sum_{u\in\mathbf{U}}\sum_{t\in T_u}(\sqrt{\mathbf{w}^T diag(\mathbf{x}_{u,t})^2\mathbf{w}} - \mathbb{1}_{t\in W_k^{u,t}})^2, \quad (11)$$
$$s.t. \mathbf{w}^T\mathbf{w} = 1,$$

where $diag(\mathbf{x}_{u,t})$ is the diagonal matrix representation of vector $\mathbf{x}_{u,t}$. Similarly, this optimization problem can be solved by adding the Lagrange multiplier to the new objective function $\tilde{\mathcal{Q}}(\mathbf{w})$,

$$\underset{\mathbf{w}^*_{\tilde{\mathcal{Q}}}}{\text{argmin}}\, \tilde{\mathcal{Q}}(\mathbf{w}) = \sum_{u\in\mathbf{U}}\sum_{t\in T_u}(\sqrt{\mathbf{w}^T diag(\mathbf{x}_{u,t})^2\mathbf{w}} - \mathbb{1}_{t\in W_k^{u,t}})^2 + \lambda\mathbf{w}^T\mathbf{w}. \quad (12)$$

The vector hypersphere is updated using the following rule,

$$\frac{\partial\tilde{\mathcal{Q}}(\mathbf{w})}{\partial\mathbf{w}_i} = \sum_{u\in\mathbf{U}}\sum_{t\in T_u} 2(\sqrt{\mathbf{w}^T diag(\mathbf{x}_{u,t})^2\mathbf{w}} - \mathbb{1}_{t\in W_k^{u,t}}) \frac{2\mathbf{x}^2_{u,t,i}\mathbf{w}_i}{\sqrt{\mathbf{w}^T diag(\mathbf{x}_{u,t})^2\mathbf{w}}} + 2\lambda\mathbf{w}_i$$
$$= \sum_{u\in\mathbf{U}}\sum_{t\in T_u} 4\mathbf{x}^2_{u,t,i}\mathbf{w}_i(1 - \frac{\mathbb{1}_{t\in W_k^{u,t}}}{\sqrt{\mathbf{w}^T diag(\mathbf{x}_{u,t})^2\mathbf{w}}}) + 2\lambda\mathbf{w}_i. \quad (13)$$

If $\Pr_{\mathcal{Q}}(u,t) > \frac{1}{2}$ for user u just before performing a new consumption transaction t, our quadratic method will predict t to be a reconsumption.

The proposed methods are efficient in the tasks of the binary prediction of STREC behaviors. The time complexity of online computation of four features and the prediction probability is $O(1)$ since a priority queue is used as the sliding window moves forward and the values can be obtained

Table 1: Statistics of the data sets.

Data Set	#.Users	#.Items	#.Transactions
Lastfm	992	964,463	16,986,614
BrightKite	51,406	772,966	4,747,281
Gowalla	107,092	1,280,969	6,442,892
ManicTime	44	22,808	253,283

by simply subtracting old ones and adding new ones. There is no need to re-compute these features by enumerating the window again online. In contrast, the only time-consuming part is to learn the hyperplane and the hypersphere in our methods, which however, can be finished and updated offline in a batch mode periodically. Thus, our methods are very efficient in the binary prediction.

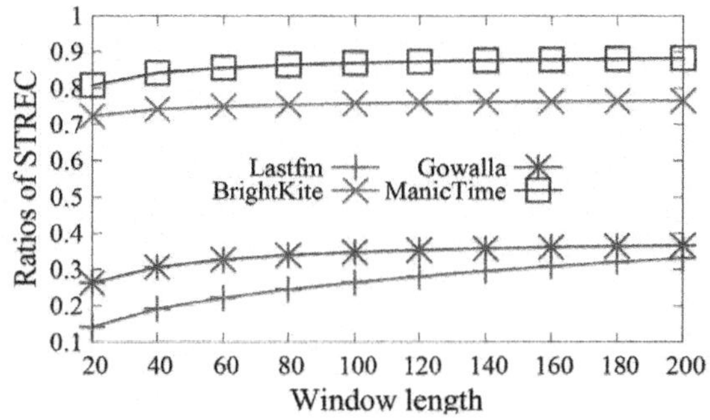

Figure 1: The ratios of the STREC behaviors of four data sets under different sliding window length.

Experiments

Data Sets

We used four data sets to evaluate the performance of our prediction algorithms. The statistics of these data sets are shown in Table 1.

Lastfm. This publicly available data set is a collection of people's listening records on Last.fm (Celma 2010). People listen to music frequently in their daily lives. The listening records are the mixture of novel songs and loops of previously heard songs.

BrightKite. This publicly available data set contains people's check-ins at different locations (Cho, Myers, and Leskovec 2011). People's repeat check-ins at the same location which is recognized by the location-id or the coordinates, can be considered as reconsumptions.

Gowalla. Gowalla was a location-based social network available. This data set contains users' check-ins of locations (Cho, Myers, and Leskovec 2011). Similar to BrightKite, people's repeat check-ins at the same location are considered as reconsumptions. However, Gowalla has nearly twice the number of users and items compared with BrightKite, and this is also the sparsest data set in our experiments. Besides, the overall reconsumption ratio of Gowalla is very different from that of BrightKite (see Fig. 1).

ManicTime. To broaden the types of reconsumption data in our analysis, we also collected a new data set which contains the using logs of people's desktop applications on PCs. We recruited 44 college students to conduct the rewarding experiments. Each of the volunteers installed the time management tool — ManicTime [1], on their personal computers. This tool monitors the using logs like the launching time, the shutdown time and the lasting period of each application without interrupting the daily work of users. All the volunteers agreed to keep this tool running as a background service and collect logs for at least one month. They are assured that the users will be anonymized and the data will be used only for research purpose. In this data collection, the repeat use on the same application by a same user is considered as reconsumptions.

[1] http://www.manictime.com

Experimental Settings

To the best of our knowledge, there is no prior work directly addressing the problem of predicting whether a user will perform a reconsumption. Therefore, we used the state-of-the-art classifiers — the support vector machine (SVM) and the discriminant analysis (DA) using our proposed features as the comparisons to our proposed methods in this paper. Since we presented both the linear and the quadratic methods, we also evaluated the SVM and DA with the linear and the quadratic kernel functions, and they are denoted as SVM-L, SVM-Q, DA-L and DA-Q, respectively. The parameters in SVM and DA are tuned in advance to maximize their prediction accuracy on each data set. Besides, our proposed methods are denoted by ST-L (linear method) and ST-Q (quadratic method), respectively.

STREC Behavior Prediction

According to Definition 3, whether or not a consumption transaction is considered as a STREC behavior can be affected by the length of sliding window. Windows of different lengths lead to different definitions of STREC behaviors as well as different ground truth in our evaluations on the same data sets. Thus, we firstly compared these prediction methods under the same setting of window length.

Table 2 shows the results of predicting whether or not a new transaction is a STREC behavior in all data sets when the window length $k = 20$. TP, TN, FN and FP represent True-Positive, True-Negative, False-Negative and False-Positive, respectively. Thus, the values of $\frac{TP}{TP+TN}$ and $\frac{FN}{FN+FP}$ can be used to measure the ability of the methods to identify the reconsumption behaviors and the novel consumption behaviors, respectively. Furthermore, the overall prediction accuracy of these methods can be evaluated by $\frac{TP+FN}{TP+TN+FN+FP}$.

We can see that ST-L and ST-Q have the dominating overall prediction accuracy on all the four data sets and their performance is stable and promising. ST-Q has the highest prediction accuracy 0.7741 in the BrightKite set, and ST-L outperforms the other methods in the Lastfm, the Gowalla and the ManicTime sets by reaching the prediction accuracy, 0.8799, 0.7526 and 0.8090, respectively. The limitation of our proposed methods is the hypothesis that the fea-

Table 2: Results of predicting reconsumption behaviors. TP, TN, FN, FP represent True-Positive, True-Negative, False-Negative, False-Positive, respectively. (k=20.)

(a) The Lastfm set.

Method	TP/(TP+TN)	FN/(FN+FP)	(TP+FN)/(TP+TN+FN+FP)
DA-L	0.6095	0.9098	0.8662
DA-Q	**0.6321**	0.8762	0.8407
SVM-L	0.0	**1.0**	0.8548
SVM-Q	0.0	**1.0**	0.8548
ST-L	0.3467	0.9704	**0.8799**
ST-Q	0.3078	0.9762	0.8791

(b) The BrightKite set.

Method	TP/(TP+TN)	FN/(FN+FP)	(TP+FN)/(TP+TN+FN+FP)
DA-L	0.6237	0.8650	0.6985
DA-Q	0.5773	**0.8927**	0.6751
SVM-L	0.7409	0.7110	0.7316
SVM-Q	0.9181	0.1772	0.6885
ST-L	0.8840	0.5282	0.7738
ST-Q	0.8649	0.5719	**0.7741**

(c) The Gowalla set.

Method	TP/(TP+TN)	FN/(FN+FP)	(TP+FN)/(TP+TN+FN+FP)
DA-L	0.5901	0.7523	0.7084
DA-Q	0.6029	0.7246	0.6916
SVM-L	0.4351	0.8444	0.7336
SVM-Q	**0.9968**	0.0008	0.2704
ST-L	0.2978	0.9214	**0.7526**
ST-Q	0.2975	0.9210	0.7523

(d) The ManicTime set.

Method	TP/(TP+TN)	FN/(FN+FP)	(TP+FN)/(TP+TN+FN+FP)
DA-L	0.7585	0.5485	0.7157
DA-Q	0.7824	0.5082	0.7265
SVM-L	0.0	**1.0**	0.2038
SVM-Q	**0.9949**	0.0531	0.8030
ST-L	0.9731	0.1681	**0.8090**
ST-Q	0.9767	0.1514	0.8085

ture points in the proposed 4-dimensional space are separable. According to the results of the prediction experiments, both of the separations worked effectively. Meanwhile, we also observed that the SVM methods are prone to over-learn and lead to biased prediction results, e.g. either all positive or all negative. By contrast, our methods could balance the prediction results better.

Impacts of Window Length

People's consumption transactions may or may not be identified as STREC behaviors under different settings of window length according to Definition 3. Fig. 1 illustrates the overall ratios of STREC behaviors with respect to different settings of window length of the four data sets. The changes of STREC behavior ratio of BrightKite, Gowalla and ManicTime, are all very smooth as the window length increases, which means most people are not likely to reconsume what have been consumed far from now. This observation is also a proof that the recency effect is significant in the location check-ins and the use of desktop pplications. In contrast, the STREC ratio of Lastfm increases quickly from 0.14 (k = 20) to 0.33 (k = 200). It means we are likely to reconsume a music track that was heard long ago, which may result from that we usually have a playlist when listening to music, and only perform reconsumptions after listening through the whole playlist.

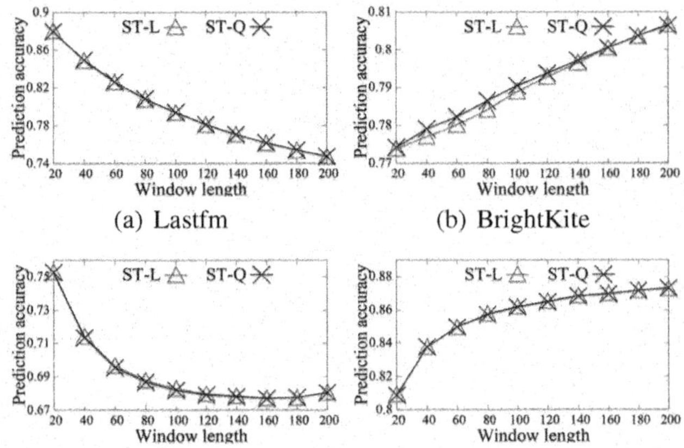

(a) Lastfm (b) BrightKite (c) Gowalla (d) ManicTime

Figure 2: The prediction accuracy under different settings of window length of the four data sets.

The accuracy of binary STREC predictions under different settings of window length is illustrated in Fig. 2. We can see that the accuracy performance of ST-L and ST-Q is very similar regardless of the change of window length. In addition, the accuracy performance of our methods is also subject to the overall reconsumption ratios as illustrated in Fig. 1. It will be the most difficult (with the least accuracy) to predict STREC behaviors if the overall reconsumption ratio is around 50% under a certain setting of window length, and vice versa.

Analysis of Learned Parameters

Next, we analyzed the parameters of our methods obtained by solving the optimization problems to study the relative importance of each generic feature. The parameters of the hyperplane and the hypersphere are shown in Fig. 3. The values of parameters in each vector **w** are their fractions of the maximum value in **w**, i.e., $\frac{\mathbf{w}_i}{\max_j \mathbf{w}_j}$.

For the parameters of the linear method, we can see that the IRR and the WRR dimensions are significant in the binary prediction in the Lastfm set, while the IRR and the URR dimensions are both significant in the Gowalla and the ManicTime sets. In the BrightKite set, the most significant dimension is the IP by contrast. Different from the quadratic method, parameters of the linear method have the possibility to be negative, e.g., the IP dimension in Fig. 3(a).

For the parameters of the quadratic method, we observed similar trend in the BrightKite and the ManicTime that the importance of the IP, the IRR, the URR and the WRR dimensions is in descending order. Besides, the most significant dimension of the Gowalla set is the URR dimension,

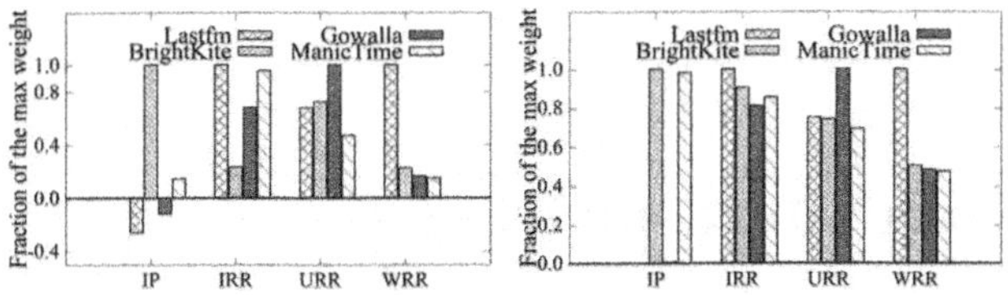

(a) ST-L Parameters (b) ST-Q Parameters

Figure 3: The learned parameters of the hyperplane and the hypersphere of our methods. Parameters are shown as their fractions of the maximum value in each vector $\mathbf{w}$. ($k = 20$)

while the IRR and the WRR dimensions seem to be the most important in the Lastfm set.

Based on the discussion on the experiments, we can see that our methods are effective and efficient in solving the binary prediction of STREC behaviors.

Conclusion and Future Work

In this paper, we addressed the problem of predicting whether or not people would perform a reconsumption at a specific time. Four generic features were derived based on people's recent (re)consumption behaviors. We also proposed two fast binary prediction algorithms w.r.t. the linear and the quadratic kernels. The experimental results showed that our methods are effective in the prediction compared with the reference methods using the state-of-the-art classifiers. In the future, we will expand our current work to further predict which item will most probably be reconsumed when our methods foresee the happening of a reconsumption behavior. Then, both the "*whether*" and "*what*" questions about people's reconsumption behaviors will be answered.

Acknowledgments

This work was supported in part by the National Natural Science Foundation of China (No. 61373023, No. 61170064, No. 61133002) and the National High Technology Research and Development Program of China (No. 2013AA013204).

References

Adar, E.; Teevan, J.; and Dumais, S. T. 2008. Large scale analysis of web revisitation patterns. In *CHI*, 1197–1206.

Anderson, A.; Kumar, R.; Tomkins, A.; and Vassilvitskii, S. 2014. The dynamics of repeat consumption. In *WWW*, 419–430.

Bobadilla, J.; Ortega, F.; Hernando, A.; and Gutiérrez, A. 2013. Recommender systems survey. *Knowledge-Based Systems* 46:109–132.

Catledge, L. D., and Pitkow, J. E. 1995. Characterizing browsing strategies in the world-wide web. *Computer Networks and ISDN Systems* 27(6):1065–1073.

Celma, O. 2010. *Music Recommendation and Discovery in the Long Tail*. Springer. chapter 3.

Chiu, C.-M.; Hsu, M.-H.; Lai, H.; and Chang, C.-M. 2012. Re-examining the influence of trust on online repeat purchase intention: The moderating role of habit and its antecedents. *Decision Support Systems* 53:835–845.

Cho, E.; Myers, S. A.; and Leskovec, J. 2011. Friendship and mobility: User movement in location-based social networks. In *KDD*, 1082–1090.

Elsweiler, D.; Baillie, M.; and Ruthven, I. 2011. What makes re-finding information difficult? a study of email re-finding. In *ECIR*, 568–579.

Elsweiler, D.; Harvey, M.; and Hacker, M. 2011. Understanding re-finding behavior in naturalistic email interaction logs. In *SIGIR*, 35–44.

Han, H.; Back, K.-J.; and Barrett, B. 2009. Influencing factors on restaurant customers' revisit intention: The roles of emotions and switching barriers. *International Journal of Hospitality Management* 28(4):563–572.

Jung, S. Y.; Hong, J.-H.; and Kim, T.-S. 2005. A statistical model for user preference. *TKDE* 17(6):834–843.

Kawase, R.; Herder, E.; and Nejdl, W. 2011. Beyond the usual suspects: context-aware revisitation support. In *ACM conference on Hypertext and hypermedia*, 27–36.

Kawase, R.; Papadakis, G.; and Herder, E. 2011. Supporting revisitation with contextual suggestions. In *JCDL*, 227–230.

Liu, J.; Yu, C.; Xu, W.; and Shi, Y. 2012. Clustering web pages to facilitate revisitation on mobile devices. In *IUI*, 249–252.

Merton, R. K. 1968. The mathew effect in science. *Science* 159(3810):56–63.

Park, J.-Y., and Jang, S. 2014. Revisit and satiation patterns: Are your restaurant customers satiated? *International Journal of Hospitality Management* 38:20–29.

Sarma, A. D.; Gollapudi, S.; Panigraphy, R.; and Zhang, L. 2012. Understanding cyclic trends in social choices. In *WSDM*, 593–602.

Teevan, J.; Adar, E.; Jones, R.; and Potts, M. 2007. Information re-retrieval: repeat queries in yahoo's logs. In *SIGIR*, 151–158.

Teevan, J.; Ramage, D.; and Morris, M. R. 2011. Twittersearch: a comparison of microblog search and web search. In *WSDM*, 35–44.

Tyler, S. K., and Teevan, J. 2010. Large scale query log analysis of re-finding. In *WSDM*, 191–200.

Weisberg, J.; Te'eni, D.; and Arman, L. 2011. Past purchase and intention to purchase in e-commerce: The mediation of social presence and trust. *Internet Research* 21(1):82–96.

Xia, B., and Lam, I. 2012. Adaptive termination and pre-launching policy for improving application startup time. US Patent App. 13/161,703.

Yu, C.; Balakrishnan, R.; Hinckley, K.; Moscovich, T.; and Shi, Y. 2013. Implicit bookmarking: Improving support for revisitation in within-document reading tasks. *Int. J. Human-Computer Studies* 71:303–320.

Zhang, H., and Zhao, S. 2011. Measuring web page revisitation in tabbed browsing. In *CHI*, 1831–1834.

Zhang, J.; Wang, C.; and Wang, J. 2014. Learning temporal dynamics of behavior propagation in social networks. In *AAAI*, 229–236.

VELDA: Relating an Image Tweet's Text and Images

Tao Chen,[1] **Hany M. SalahEldeen,**[2] **Xiangnan He**[1] **Min-Yen Kan,**[1,3] **Dongyuan Lu**[1]
[1]School of Computing, National University of Singapore
[2]Department of Computer Science, Old Dominion University
[3]NUS Interactive and Digital Media Institute, Singapore
{taochen, xiangnan, kanmy, ludy}@comp.nus.edu.sg hany@cs.odu.edu

Abstract

Image tweets are becoming a prevalent form of social media, but little is known about their content – textual and visual – and the relationship between the two mediums. Our analysis of image tweets shows that while visual elements certainly play a large role in image-text relationships, other factors such as emotional elements, also factor into the relationship. We develop Visual-Emotional LDA (VELDA), a novel topic model to capture the image-text correlation from multiple perspectives (namely, visual and emotional).

Experiments on real-world image tweets in both English and Chinese and other user generated content, show that VELDA significantly outperforms existing methods on cross-modality image retrieval. Even in other domains where emotion does not factor in image choice directly, our VELDA model demonstrates good generalization ability, achieving higher fidelity modeling of such multimedia documents.

1 Introduction

Smartphones with cameras have morphed traditional text-only user generated content into multimedia. *Image tweets* – microblog posts which embed images – enable a viewer to see the world through someone else's eyes. Their multimedia form attracts larger viewership and prolongs their half-life as compared to their poorer cousins – text only posts – in Sina *Weibo* (Zhao et al. 2012), the dominant microblog platform in China, and have been found to be 35% more retweetable than text-only tweets in Twitter[1].

These posts are fast becoming the *de facto* standard on such microblog platforms. They constitute over 45% of overall traffic in Weibo (Chen et al. 2013) and have seen rapid adoption in Twitter. How about image-only tweets? While a picture may be worth a thousand words, image-only posts are still rare: over 99% of tweets with images are also accompanied by text (Chen et al. 2013).

A natural set of questions emerge that our work attempts to address. Why do people post image tweets? What is the nature of the relationship between the text and image? And, given the answers to these questions, can we design a model that explains how image tweets could be generated?

[1]https://blog.twitter.com/2014/what-fuels-a-tweets-engagement

Figure 1: A visually relevant image tweet from Twitter (left) and an emotionally relevant image tweet from Weibo (right).

Through a corpus analysis, Chen et al. (2013) identified image and text in the microblog can be either visually or emotionally correlated. To validate this, we surveyed image tweets authors, and discovered images are used for visual purpose (*i.e.*, both image and text mention the same physical object) as well as for enhancing the emotion of the post (see Figure 1 for both examples). However, current multi-modal models only capture a single factor in modeling image-text correspondence.

Our paper's key contribution is to address this modeling gap by introducing Visual–Emotional LDA (VELDA), a novel topic model that captures image–text correlations through multiple evidence sources (namely, visual and emotional, yielding the method's namesake). On experiments with both English (Twitter) and Chinese (Weibo) image tweets and other forms of user generated content, VELDA yields significantly improved modeling over the other existing methods on cross-modality image retrieval. Even in other domains where emotion does not factor in image choice directly, VELDA demonstrates good generalization ability, modeling these multimedia documents much better than existed methods. Finally, we apply VELDA in a real-world task of automated microblog illustration, selecting a relevant image from an image collection.

2 Related Work

The duality of image and text has been a recurring topic of study in the multimedia area. Uncovering and modeling the relationship between the two mediums has been a key area of study. One method is to map the multimodal data into a shared space such that the distance between two similar objects is minimized. Under this approach, Canonical Correlation Analysis (CCA) (Hotelling 1936) and its extensions are often utilized (Rasiwasia et al. 2010; Sharma et al. 2012). CCA finds a pair of linear transformations to maximize the correlations between two variables (*i.e.*, image and text), jointly reducing the dimensionality of the two heterogeneous representations of the same data.

An alternative method employs probabilistic latent topic modeling to learn the joint distribution of the multi-modal data. These approaches are based on extensions of Latent Dirichlet Allocation (LDA) (Blei, Ng, and Jordan 2003), a generative model to discover underlying topics that generate the documents and the topic distribution within each document. The seminal work of Barnard et al. (2003) proposed multi-modal LDA that aimed to capture the association of two modalities at the topic level, assuming the two are generated from the same topic distribution. Later, Blei and Jordan (2003) proposed correspondence LDA (hereafter, Corr-LDA; Figure 2) to model text and image differently, where the image is assumed as the primary medium and generated first via standard LDA; then, conditioned on image's topics, the text is generated. In this sense, Corr-LDA assumes the topics of the two modalities have a one-to-one correspondence. To relax such constraint, Putthividhy, Attias, and Nagarajan (2010) proposed a topic-regression multi-modal LDA to learn a regression from the topics in one modality to those in the other. In real-world scenarios, much of free text may only be loosely associated to an accompanying image, and in some datasets, some documents may lack images or text. To address these shortcomings, Jia, Salzmann, and Darrell (2011) proposed Multi-modal Document Random Field (MDRF) that connects the documents based on intra- or inter-modality topic similarity. The resultant learned topics are shared across connected documents, encoding the correlations between different modalities. In a separate line of work, multiple modal LDAs have been generalized to non-parametric models (Yakhnenko and Honavar 2009; Virtanen et al. 2012; Liao, Zhu, and Qin 2014), which alleviates the need to choose the number of topics *a priori*.

Although the prior work is comprehensive, we have found that image tweets can exhibit and be explained from multiple perspectives. Current models assume that the relationship between an image and text can only be attributed to a single (*e.g.*, visual) model. Our proposed method extends LDA to cater for this key characteristic in the generative process.

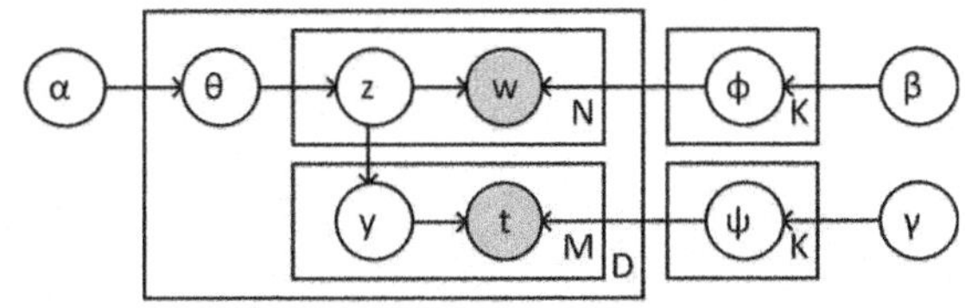

Figure 2: Correspondence LDA (Corr-LDA), where the N plate specifies visual words and the M plate specifies individual words in the text. Y, the topic assignments of textual words, are conditioned on Z, the topic assignments of N visual words.

3 Visual-Emotional LDA

To understand how image tweets are generated, we first turn to their authors. Prior work by Chen et al. (2013) identified three image-text correlations, namely, visually relevant, emotionally relevant and irrelevant (*e.g.*, noisy image tweets). To test whether their findings are corroborated by actual users (their study was limited to corpus analysis), we recruited 109 *Weibo* users (62 females and 47 males) from the popular Chinese crowdsourcing site *Zhubajie*[2]. Respondents were asked to fill out a questionnaire on their image posting behavior. In the question of "Why do you embed an image in a tweet?", 66.6% of respondents post images primarily for enhancing their text's emotion, while a much smaller 29.4% did so to provide a visually corresponding artifact as mentioned in the text. Our survey validates the hypothesis that *emotional correlation is also a prominent image–text relation in microblog posts*[3].

To achieve high fidelity modeling of the image-text relationship in image tweets, we must account for multiple channels. We propose Visual-Emotional LDA (VELDA) as a generative model that incorporates the suggested emotional aspect in modeling image tweets. In the following, we first detail VELDA's model formulation, and then describe its parameter estimation process.

3.1 Model Formulation

Figure 3 shows the graphical representation of VELDA. In VELDA, each image tweet has three modalities – the textual tweet, and the visual and the emotional view of the image. Similar to other topic modeling methods, we model the three modalities as discrete features, which are referred as textual words, visual words, and emotional words, respectively (the feature extraction process is detailed later in Section 4.2).

Following Corr-LDA, we correlate image and text in the latent topic level, such that the topic of each textual word corresponds to an image topic; the major difference is that in VELDA, we have two heterogeneous views of an image – visual and emotional. To decide which image view a textual word corresponds to, we introduce a switch variable r. When $r = 0$, the textual word is visually related to the image and thus sampling its topic y from the empirical image-visual topic distribution $\tilde{\theta^V}$; likewise $r = 1$ indicates emotional relevance, sampling from the empirical image-emotional topic distribution $\tilde{\theta^E}$. While we could also introduce $r = 2$ to capture attribution to both visual and emotional correlation, the resultant modeling complexity would be changed from linear $(K + E)$ to quadratic $(K \times E)$. To keep the model simple, we did not do so.

[2]http://www.zhubajie.com

[3]While the survey was limited to Chinese *Weibo* users, we believe this correlation also holds for other microblog sites and cultures.

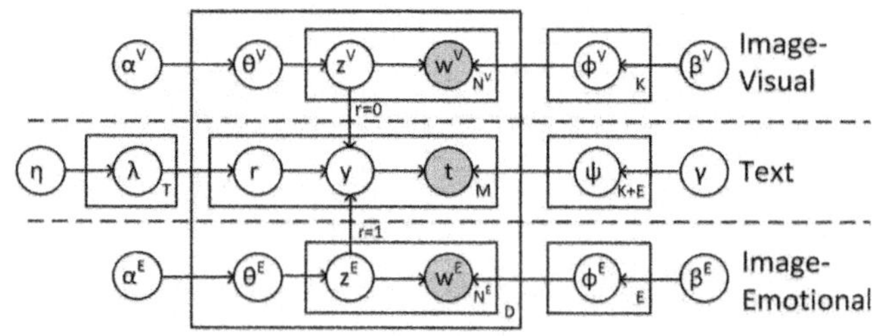

Figure 3: Visual-Emotional LDA's generative model.

Intuitively, the assignment of r should be term-sensitive — some textual words (*e.g.*, a physical object) are more likely to correspond to visual objects within an image, while others tend to reflect the emotion and atmosphere of an image. As such, the switch variable r is personalized for each textual word and sampled from a relevance distribution λ. The overall generative story is summarized as follows, where specific notations are explained in Table 1[4]:

1. For each textual word $t = 1, ..., T$, sample a relevance distribution $\lambda \sim \text{Dir}(\eta)$.
2. For each image–visual topic $k = 1, ..., K$, sample the topic word distribution $\phi^V \sim \text{Dir}(\beta^V)$. Similarly for image–emotional topic e and textual topic l.
3. For each image tweet $d = 1, ..., D$, sample its image–visual topic distribution $\theta_d^V \sim \text{Dir}(\alpha^V)$ and image–emotional topic distribution $\theta_d^E \sim \text{Dir}(\alpha^E)$.
   (a) For each visual word $w_n^V, n = 1, ..., N_d^V$:
      i. Sample topic assignment $z_n^V \sim \text{Mult}(\theta_d^V)$
      ii. Sample visual word $w_n^V \sim \text{Mult}(\phi_{z_n^V}^V)$
   (b) For each emotional word $w_n^E, n = 1, ..., N_d^E$:
      i. Sample topic assignment $z_n^E \sim \text{Mult}(\theta_d^E)$
      ii. Sample emotional word $w_n^E \sim \text{Mult}(\phi_{z_n^E}^E)$
   (c) For each textual word $t_m, m = 1, ..., M$:
      i. Sample relevance type $r_m \sim \text{Mult}(\lambda_{t_m})$
      ii. if $r_m = 0$:
         A. Sample a topic $y_m \sim \text{Unif}(z_1^V, ..., z_{N_d^V}^V)$
         B. Sample a word $t_m \sim \text{Mult}(\psi_{k=y_m})$
      iii. if $r_m = 1$:
         A. Sample a topic $y_m \sim \text{Unif}(z_1^E, ..., z_{N_d^E}^E)$
         B. Sample a word $t_m \sim \text{Mult}(\psi_{e=y_m})$

3.2 Parameter Estimation

In VELDA, we need to infer six sets of parameters: three topic-word distribution (ϕ^V, ϕ^E and ψ for image-visual, image-emotional and text, respectively), two document-topic distribution (θ^V and θ^E for image-visual and image-emotional, respectively), and the relevance distribution of textual words λ. As with LDA, exact inference of the parameters is intractable; so approximate inference is applied.

We adopt Gibbs sampling to estimate the model parameters, due to its simplicity in deriving update rules and effectiveness in dealing with high-dimensional data. The basic idea of Gibbs sampling is to sequentially sample all variables from the targeted distribution when conditioned on the current values of all other variables and the data. For example, to estimate the image-visual topic distribution θ^V, we need to sequentially sample its latent topic variable z^V. To sample for z_i^V (where $i = (d, n)$ representing the n-th word of the d-th document), we condition on the current value of all other variables.

[4] We use the abbreviation Dir(·), Mult(·) and Unif(·) to denote the Dirichlet, Multinomial and Uniform distribution, respectively.

Table 1: Notations used in VELDA.

Symbol	Description
K, E	number of image-visual and image-emotional topics, respectively.
D, T, C, S	number of tweets, unique textual words, unique image-visual words, and unique image-emotional words, respectively.
α^V, α^E, β^V, β^E, γ, η	hyperparameters of Dirichlet distributions.
θ^V, θ^E	$D \times K$, $D \times E$ matrices indicating image-visual, image-emotional topic distribution, respectively
ϕ^V, ϕ^E	$K \times C$, $E \times S$ matrices indicating image-visual, image-emotional topic-word distribution, respectively
ψ	a $(K + E) \times T$ matrix indicating textual topic-word distribution.
λ	a $T \times 2$ matrix indicating textual word's relevance distribution.
$M_{d,t}$, $N_{d,c}^V$, $N_{d,s}^E$	number of textual words, image-visual words, and image-emotional words in the d-th tweet.
$M_{d,z}$	number of textual words in d-th tweet that are assigned to topic z.
$N_{d,k}^V$, $N_{d,e}^E$	number of image-visual, image-emotional words in d-th tweet that are assigned to visual topic k, emotional topic e, respectively.
$M_{t,r}$	number of times that textual word t is assigned to relevance r.

$$P(z_i^V = k | W^V, W^E, T, Z_{-i}^V, Z^E, Y, R) \propto \frac{N_{k,c,-i}^V + \beta_c^V}{N_k^V + C\beta^V - 1} \cdot (\frac{N_{d,k}^V}{N_{d,k,-i}^V})^{M_{d,k}} \cdot \frac{N_{d,k,-i}^V + \alpha_k^V}{N_d^V + K\alpha^V - 1}. \quad (1)$$

Similarly, we can derive the sampling rule for z_i^E:

$$P(z_i^E = e | W^V, W^E, T, Z^V, Z_{-i}^E, Y, R) \propto \frac{N_{e,s,-i}^E + \beta_s^E}{N_k^E + S\beta^E - 1} \cdot (\frac{N_{d,e}^E}{N_{d,e,-i}^E})^{M_{d,e}} \cdot \frac{N_{d,e,-i}^E + \alpha_e^E}{N_d^E + E\alpha^E - 1}. \quad (2)$$

Next, we sample the latent topics y of the textual words based on the topic assignment of image–visual and image–emotional. Note that for each latent topic y_i, there is a switch variable r_i that states whether it is sampled from image–visual topics or image–emotional topics. If y_i is sampled from image–visual topics, it implies that the sampled r_i was 0, and vice versa. As such, we need to sample based on the joint distribution of y_i and r_i, which leads to:

$$\begin{aligned} &P(r_i = 0, y_i = k | W^V, W^E, T, Z^V, Z^E, Y_{-i}, R_{-i}) \\ &\propto \frac{M_{k,t,-i} + \gamma}{M_k + T\gamma - 1} \cdot \frac{M_{t,r=0,-i} + \eta}{M_t + 2\eta - 1} \cdot \frac{N_{d,k}^V}{N_d^V}, \\ &P(r_i = 1, y_i = e | W^V, W^E, T, Z^V, Z^E, Y_{-i}, R_{-i}) \\ &\propto \frac{M_{e,t,-i} + \gamma}{M_e + T\gamma - 1} \cdot \frac{M_{t,r=1,-i} + \eta}{M_t + 2\eta - 1} \cdot \frac{N_{d,e}^E}{N_d^E}. \end{aligned} \quad (3)$$

Iterative execution of the above sampling rules until a steady state results allows us to obtain the values of the latent variables. Finally, we estimate the six sets of parameters by the following equations:

$$\theta^V_{k,d} = \frac{N^V_{k,d} + \alpha^V}{N^V_d + K\alpha^V}, \quad \theta^E_{e,d} = \frac{N^E_{e,d} + \alpha^E}{N^E_d + E\alpha^E}, \quad \phi^V_{k,c} = \frac{N^V_{k,c} + \beta^V}{N^V_k + C\beta^V},$$
$$\phi^E_{e,s} = \frac{N^E_{e,s} + \beta^E}{N^E_e + S\beta^E}, \quad \psi_{z,t} = \frac{M_{z,t} + \gamma}{M_z + T\gamma}, \quad \lambda_{r,t} = \frac{M_{r,t} + \eta}{M_t + 2\eta}. \tag{4}$$

3.3 Discussion

At first glance, VELDA looks complicated, having more parameters than LDA and Corr-LDA. Essentially, it is a well-formed extension of Corr-LDA that adds an emotional view of images and the relevance indicators for textual words. In our experiments, we observed that the larger parameter space does not adversely affect convergence – parameter estimation for VELDA is rather fast, with the Gibbs sampler usually converging within 100 iterations. VELDA's calculation is also compatible with distributed computation strategies for Gibbs sampling (Wang et al. 2009), making VELDA applicable to large-scale data.

One may note that the structure of VELDA — its separation of both the visual and emotional views of images, and the introduction of switch variable r — is generic. Both image views are simply copies of the standard LDA entwined to the text via r. Additional views of the image–text relation are easily modeled by simply introducing an additional LDA generative process, adjusting the switching variable and dimension of the textual topics accordingly. The derivations of the existing image parts of the model are unchanged, just incurring additional updating rules for any new factors.

4 Evaluation

We evaluated VELDA in modeling the generation of image tweets against several baseline methods. Although VELDA was conceived to model image tweets, we claim it is also applicable to other related image–text correlation tasks. As such, we investigated how VELDA fares in modeling other general domain image–text pairs. To this end, we collected image tweets from two microblog platforms — Weibo and Twitter — and image-text pairs from Google and Wikipedia. In the following, we describe the collected datasets, our feature extraction process, the evaluation criteria, and conclude by discussing the experiments and their results.

4.1 Datasets

We collected five image–text datasets (see Table 2). The first four have a common basis for collection – constructed by a list of queries, so we describe this basis first. Previous work by Chen et al. (2013) released a collection of 4K image tweets curated from Weibo with human image–text relation annotations following their categorization scheme (*i.e.*, visually relevant, emotionally relevant and irrelevant). Though these labels were assigned at the tweet level, only certain words were found to be visual (emotional) indicators. Based on their work, we construct potential visual (emotional) queries by extracting the most frequent textual words

Table 2: Demographics of the five datasets.

	Weibo	Twitter	G-Zh	G-En	POTD
Size	22,782	16,427	38,806	26,903	2,524
Text language	Chinese	English	Chinese	English	English
Best settings for VELDA	K=100, E=60	K=40, E=80	K=80, E=50	K=100, E=100	K=40, E=80

from the categorized visual (emotional) image tweets, discarding stop words. In total, we obtain 353 words from visually relevant tweets (*e.g.*, bread, sunset), 133 words from emotionally relevant tweets (*e.g.*, worry, love), and use each single word as a query.

1. **Weibo**. We sent each query as a hashtag in Weibo's search interface to obtain up to 1,000 most recent image tweets. For the final dataset, we discarded queries with less than 40 results, randomly sampled 100 image tweets for those with more than 100 results, and kept those with 40 to 100 results, which resulted in a set of 22,782 image tweets.
2. **Twitter**. Following the same pipeline, we constructed 16,427 image tweets from Twitter using the same base queries. As the queries were originally in Chinese, we translated them into English using Google Translate. Our spot checks show the translated words are acceptable.

3 & 4. **Google-Zh** and **Google-En**. Image tweets vary greatly in quality for both text and images. We also want to assess VELDA performance on "prominent" images returned from an image search engine. We sent the Chinese and English (translated) text queries to Google Image Search. We obtained 38,806 and 26,903 images and their associated text snippet for Chinese and English, respectively. Since these are from the general web and are curated by the search engine, we expect these image–text pairs to be somewhat higher in quality than the image tweets.

5. **Wikipedia POTD**. At the high end of the quality spectrum is the "Picture of the Day" (POTD) collection, a set of of daily featured pictures accompanied by a short description from Wikipedia[5]. Unlike the other four datasets, POTD concentrates on high-quality, manually-curated academic topics. We collected the daily pictures and their corresponding descriptions from 1 Nov 2004 to 11 Jun 2014, obtaining a total of 2,524 image-text pairs.

4.2 Feature Extraction

We extract textual words from image's textual description, and another two sets of features from the image to represent its visual semantics and emotional semantics, respectively. We adopt current best practices to generate features for each modality. Since VELDA requires all features to be discrete, we represent all three sets of features as bags-of-words.

Text Features. For Chinese text, we first pass the text through a Chinese word segmentation program. Then both Chinese and English text are assigned Part-of-Speech (POS) tags. English words are additionally stemmed. We apply a frequency filter to omit words that occur in fewer than 10 (5 in the case of POTD, due to its small size) documents, drop

[5] http://en.wikipedia.org/wiki/Wikipedia:Picture_of_the_day

stop words and further discard closed-class words, leaving only open-class words – nouns, verbs, adjectives and adverbs. This helps to reduce the noise by removing words that are potentially irrelevant to the image. We then discard short documents with less than four words. Applying this process resulted in 6714, 2802, 8382, 4794, and 3224 unique words for Weibo, Twitter, Google-Zh, Google-En and POTD datasets, respectively.

Visual Features. We adopt the standard Scale-Invariant Feature Transform (SIFT; Lowe 2004) descriptors to represent the visual semantics of an image and follow the tradition of quantizing SIFT descriptors to yield discrete words by means of a visual codebook learned by k-means. To better capture the image characteristics in each dataset, we trained two separate visual codebooks: one for the POTD dataset and another for the four datasets based on the common basis. Each codebook thus consists of 1000 visual words.

Emotional Features. The feature representation of image emotions (*a.k.a.*, sentiment or affect) has been investigated in many works. Color-based features have proved to be simple yet effective (Valdez and Mehrabian 1994; Colombo, Del Bimbo, and Pala 1999; Machajdik and Hanbury 2010; Jia et al. 2012; Yang et al. 2013). We adopt 22 color-based features from the state-of-art work (Machajdik and Hanbury 2010), summarized in Table 3. To turn an image into a bag of emotional words, we first segment each image into patches by a graph-based algorithm (Felzenszwalb and Huttenlocher 2004), and then extract the 22 features for each patch. Similar to the procedure of constructing visual words, one million emotional patches were randomly sampled to learn 1000 clusters via k-means. Finally, each patch is quantized into one of the 1000 emotional words. As with the visual words, we trained two separate emotional codebooks for images from POTD and images from the other datasets.

Table 3: Features used to represent image emotions.

Name	Dim.	Description
Saturation	2	Mean and standard deviation of saturation.
Brightness	2	Mean and standard deviation of brightness.
Hue	4	Mean hue and angular dispersion, with and without saturation weighted.
Color Names	11	Amount of black, blue, brown, green, gray, orange, pink, purple, red, white and yellow (van de Weijer, Schmid, and Verbeek 2007).
Pleasure, Arousal, Dominance	3	One set of affective coordinates, calculated from brightness and saturation, following (Valdez and Mehrabian 1994).

4.3 Experimental Settings

A good model of image–text relations should be able to help generate one given the other. We set the task as cross-modal retrieval: given the text of an image tweet, attempt to retrieve its accompanying image from an image dataset. Specifically, given a textual query $T = t_1, ..., t_N$, VELDA computes a relevance score for an image i by the following formula:

$$\begin{aligned} score_i &= P(T|\theta_i^V, \theta_i^E) = \prod_{n=1}^{N} P(t_n|\theta_i^V, \theta_i^E) \\ &= \prod_{n=1}^{N} (\lambda_{t_n,0} \sum_{k=1}^{K} \psi_{k,t_n} \theta_{i,k}^V + \lambda_{t_n,1} \sum_{e=1}^{E} \psi_{e,t_n} \theta_{i,e}^E) \end{aligned} \tag{5}$$

where θ_i^V and θ_i^E are the visual and emotional topic distribution for a test image i, and λ is the textual word's relevance distribution learned during training.

As there is only one ground-truth match for each textual query (*i.e.*, the original image accompanying the post), we consider the position of the ground-truth image in the ranked list as an evaluation metric. Following (Jia, Salzmann, and Darrell 2011), we consider an image as correctly retrieved if it appears in the top t percent of the image test collection created from the text in the corresponding post.

We compare VELDA against a **random** baseline and two state-of-the-art image–text correlation algorithms – **Corr-LDA** (Blei and Jordan 2003) and **LDA-CCA** (Rasiwasia et al. 2010). Corr-LDA computes the score of an image given a text query similar to Eq. 5. In LDA-CCA, two standard LDA models are first trained for texts and visual images individually; *i.e.*, an image-text pair is represented as two independent topic distributions. Then Canonical Correlation Analysis (CCA) projects the two distributions to a shared latent space where the correlation between image-text pairs is maximized. For each textual query, the images are ranked to minimize the distance with the query in the shared space.

We randomly split each dataset into 90% as training set and the remaining 10% as testing set. Our development testing showed that VELDA operated well over a wide range of hyperparameter settings. As such, we fix the six sets of hyperparameters to relatively standard settings: α^V=1, α^E=1, β^V=0.1, β^E=0.1, γ = 0.1, and η = 0.5. We then tune the number of visual topics (K) and emotional topics (E) in a grid search for each dataset (see Table 2 for the detailed settings). We similarly optimize the Corr-LDA and LDA-CCA baselines by searching for their best parameter settings.

4.4 Results and Analysis

Results on the cross-modal image retrieval tasks on the five datasets are shown in Figure 4. Each plot depicts the retrieval errors averaged over all testing queries in a specific dataset. For all five datasets, a one-tailed paired t-test with threshold 0.001 revealed that VELDA's performance gain is statistically significant. For POTD, we have additionally overlaid Jia et al.'s MDRF results, as taken from their paper. The MDRF results are not strictly comparable – our dataset is larger by 537 documents (approximately 20% larger) and we do not have their extracted features – but we feel that they are indicative of MDRF's performance, and further help to show VELDA's competitive performance.

For all graphs, better performance is equated with lower error rate (curves closer to the bottom left corner). From Figure 4, we see that the error rate of VELDA drops dramatically when increasing the retrieval results to first 10%. In particular, more than 20% of ground truth images appear in the very early positions of the ranked list (*e.g.*, the top 0.8% for Weibo). For concrete comparison, we focus on recall on the top 10% level, reported separately in Table 4. Compared to Corr-LDA (the strongest baseline), our proposed VELDA significantly improves retrieval performance by 20.6%, 31.6%, 25.8%, 22.4% for Weibo, Google-Zh, Google-En and POTD, respectively. For the POTD dataset,

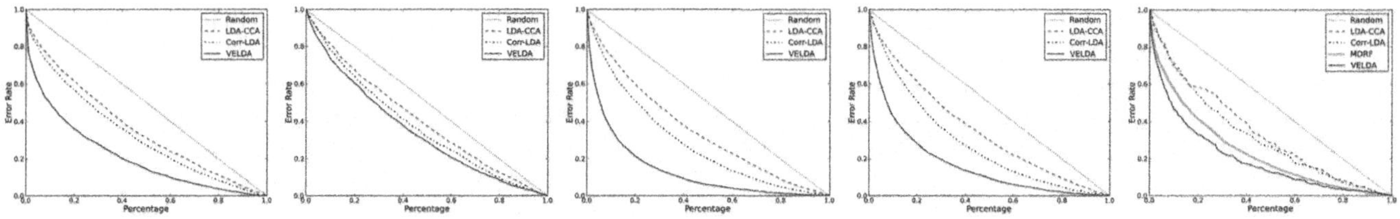

(a) Weibo (b) Twitter (c) Google-Zh (d) Google-En (e) Wikipedia POTD

Figure 4: Retrieval error rate by the percentage of the ranked list considered. Curves closer to the axes represent better performance.

Table 4: Percentage of images correctly retrieved in the top 10% of the ranked list. The difference between VELDA and any of the two other methods is statistically significant with the one-tailed paired t-test ($p < 0.001$).

	Weibo	Twitter	G-Zh	G-En	POTD
LDA-CCA	25.6%	18.8%	25.0%	25.6%	28.8%
Corr-LDA	29.8%	22.0%	32.1%	31.2%	31.2%
VELDA	**50.4%**	**26.6%**	**63.7%**	**57.0%**	**53.6%**

Table 5: VELDA's performance broken down by query type.

	Weibo	Twitter	G-Zh	G-En
Visual queries	53.8%	28.1%	69.8%	61.6%
Emotional queries	39.5%	22.1%	47.0%	45.4%

VELDA outperforms MDRF by 8%. In this dataset, though emotion is not the primary reason for choosing the images, it might be an implicit factor, *e.g.*, nature related articles prefer images that are bright and tranquil.

We note the lower performance of all methods on Twitter. We attribute this to the brevity of Twitter: each Twitter image tweet has only 6.7 textual words on average (after text processing), far shorter than the other datasets (*e.g.*, 18.9 for Weibo). This passes little textual information to the model, making the image-text correlation learning difficult. Even in such sparse data scenarios, VELDA still betters Corr-LDA and LDA-CCA by 4.6% and 7.8%, respectively.

We further break down VELDA's performance by query type, as shown in Table 5. We find all the other four datasets show the same trend that VELDA performs better in image-text pairs from visual queries than those from emotional ones. As the query type is a good indicator of the image-text correlation type (visual or emotional), this trend partially implies that learning image-text's emotional correlation is more difficult than the visual correlation.

To apply our VELDA model to other domains, the major parameter to tune is the hyperparameter η, which determines the relevance distribution (λ) of textual words, while other parameters can be easily set with standard LDA heuristic rules. So we further investigate the impact of η. Theoretically speaking, large (small) η makes the relevance distribution λ more skewed (balanced). From Figure 5, we see that VELDA's performance remains relatively stable for varying values of η. This insensitivity to η shows that VELDA is robust and does not require careful tuning to perform well.

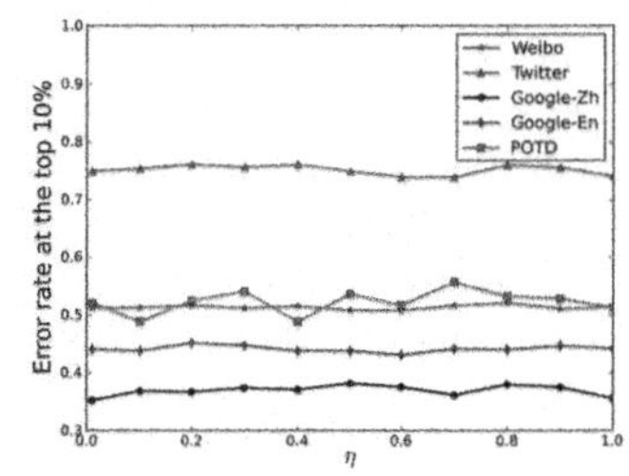

Figure 5: Parameter η versus error rate for top 10% retrieval.

[Have some #nuts at noon] Nuts such as walnuts, peanuts, sunflower seeds, hazelnuts, cedar nuts and chestnuts, should be part of our daily diet. They are rich in Omega-3 and Omega-6 fatty acids and are essential for good health and have anti-aging benefits too.

#Upset I am hungry but I cannot eat now as I have to wait for someone else. What if there is a blackout now? Let me amuse myself by reading up some jokes.

The worries and problems that other people are facing always seem so minuscule and in-significant. However, when you come face to face with the same problems, you will realise that it is not possible to just laugh it off. #painful

Figure 6: Three (translated) Weibo posts, along with VELDA's top 4 (from top left to bottom right) suggested illustrations.

Finally, in Figure 6, we show three typical Weibo posts (translated to English) and their top four recommended images by VELDA. As we can see, for the very visual tweet that mentions many physical objects, *e.g.*, the top example post, our suggested illustrations not only accurately correspond to objects, but also cover a few varieties (*e.g.*, capturing three different nuts in the top four illustrations). For sentimental tweets, *e.g.*, the bottom example post, our recommended images match the emotions of the text well. This suggests a real possibility of applying VELDA to an automated microblog illustration task.

5 Conclusion

Image tweets match text with image to help convey a unified message. We examine the image–text correlation and its modeling for cross-modality image retrieval, in both microblog posts as well as other image–text datasets.

We discover that an image tweet's image and text can be related in different modes, not limited to visual relevance but including emotional relevance. A key contribution is our development of Visual-Emotional LDA (VELDA), a novel topic model that captures such two image–text correlations. Experiments on both English and Chinese image tweets show that VELDA significantly outperforms baseline methods. VELDA also demonstrates its robustness and generalization, being applicable not only to its intended domain of image tweets but also general image–text datasets.

In the future, we may develop a mobile application to assist users discover and use visually and emotionally relevant images to adorn their textual posts. In a separate vein of work, we hope to validate VELDA as a generic model that can apply to other instances of multimedia correspondence. Moreover, the current VELDA regards image's visual and emotion as two independent views, it will be interesting to explore how these two are correlated with each other.

Acknowledgments

This research is supported by the Singapore National Research Foundation under its International Research Centre @ Singapore Funding Initiative and administered by the IDM Programme Office. We also would like to thank our colleagues, Kazunari Sugiyama, Jun-Ping Ng, Jovian Lin and Jingwen Bian, for the discussions.

References

Barnard, K.; Duygulu, P.; Forsyth, D.; de Freitas, N.; Blei, D. M.; and Jordan, M. I. 2003. Matching Words and Pictures. *Journal of Machine Learning Research* 3:1107–1135.

Blei, D. M., and Jordan, M. I. 2003. Modeling Annotated Data. In *Proceedings of the 26th Annual International ACM SIGIR Conference on Research and Development in Informaion Retrieval*, SIGIR '03, 127–134.

Blei, D. M.; Ng, A. Y.; and Jordan, M. I. 2003. Latent Dirichlet Allocation. *Journal of Machine Learning Research* 3:993–1022.

Chen, T.; Lu, D.; Kan, M.-Y.; and Cui, P. 2013. Understanding and Classifying Image Tweets. In *Proceedings of the 21st ACM International Conference on Multimedia*, MM '13, 781–784.

Colombo, C.; Del Bimbo, A.; and Pala, P. 1999. Semantics in visual information retrieval. *IEEE MultiMedia* 6(3):38–53.

Felzenszwalb, P. F., and Huttenlocher, D. P. 2004. Efficient Graph-Based Image Segmentation. *International Journal of Computer Vision* 59(2):167–181.

Hotelling, H. 1936. Relations Between Two Sets of Variates. *Biometrika* 28(3-4):321–377.

Jia, J.; Wu, S.; Wang, X.; Hu, P.; Cai, L.; and Tang, J. 2012. Can We Understand Van Gogh's Mood? Learning to Infer Affects from Images in Social Networks. In *Proceedings of the 20th ACM International Conference on Multimedia*, MM 12.

Jia, Y.; Salzmann, M.; and Darrell, T. 2011. Learning Cross-modality Similarity for Multinomial Data. In *Proceedings of the 2011 International Conference on Computer Vision*, ICCV '11, 2407–2414.

Liao, R.; Zhu, J.; and Qin, Z. 2014. Nonparametric Bayesian Upstream Supervised Multi-modal Topic Models. In *Proceedings of the 7th ACM International Conference on Web Search and Data Mining*, WSDM '14, 493–502.

Lowe, D. G. 2004. Distinctive Image Features from Scale-Invariant Keypoints. *International Journal of Computer Vision* 60(2):91–110.

Machajdik, J., and Hanbury, A. 2010. Affective Image Classification Using Features Inspired by Psychology and Art Theory. In *Proceedings of the 18th ACM International Conference on Multimedia*, MM '10, 83–92.

Putthividhy, D.; Attias, H.; and Nagarajan, S. 2010. Topic Regression Multi-modal Latent Dirichlet Allocation for Image Annotation. In *Proceedings of the 23rd IEEE Conference on Computer Vision and Pattern Recognition*, CVPR '10, 3408–3415.

Rasiwasia, N.; Costa Pereira, J.; Coviello, E.; Doyle, G.; Lanckriet, G. R.; Levy, R.; and Vasconcelos, N. 2010. A New Approach to Cross-modal Multimedia Retrieval. In *Proceedings of the 18th ACM International Conference on Multimedia*, MM '10, 251–260.

Sharma, A.; Kumar, A.; Daume, H.; and Jacobs, D. W. 2012. Generalized Multiview analysis: A Discriminative Latent Space. In *Proceedings of the 25th IEEE Conference on Computer Vision and Pattern Recognition*, CVPR '12, 2160–2167.

Valdez, P., and Mehrabian, A. 1994. Effects of Color on Emotions. *Journal of Experimental Psychology: General* 123(4):394–409.

van de Weijer, J.; Schmid, C.; and Verbeek, J. 2007. Learning color names from real-world images. In *Proceedings of the 20th IEEE Conference on Computer Vision and Pattern Recognition*, CVPR '07, 1–8.

Virtanen, S.; Jia, Y.; Klami, A.; and Darrell, T. 2012. Factorized Multi-Modal Topic Model. In *Proceedings of the 28th Conference on Uncertainty in Artificial Intelligence*, UAI '12, 843–851.

Wang, Y.; Bai, H.; Stanton, M.; Chen, W.-Y.; and Chang, E. Y. 2009. PLDA: Parallel Latent Dirichlet Allocation for Large-Scale Applications. In *Proceedings of the 5th International Conference on Algorithmic Aspects in Information and Management*, AAIM '09, 301–314.

Yakhnenko, O., and Honavar, V. 2009. Multi-Modal Hierarchical Dirichlet Process Model for Predicting Image Annotation and Image-Object Label Correspondence. In *Proceedings of the 2009 SIAM International Conference on Data Mining*, SDM '09, 283–293.

Yang, Y.; Cui, P.; Zhu, W.; and Yang, S. 2013. User Interest and Social Influence Based Emotion Prediction for Individuals. In *Proceedings of the 21st ACM International Conference on Multimedia*, MM '13, 785–788.

Zhao, X.; Zhu, F.; Qian, W.; and Zhou, A. 2012. Impact of Multimedia in Sina Weibo: Popularity and Life Span. In *Joint Conference of 6th Chinese Semantic Web Symposium (CSWS'12) and the First Chinese Web Science Conference (CWSC'12)*.

On Information Coverage for Location Category Based Point-of-Interest Recommendation

Xuefeng Chen,[1] Yifeng Zeng,[2] Gao Cong,[3] Shengchao Qin,[2] Yanping Xiang,[1] Yuanshun Dai[1]

[1]School of Computer Science and Engineering, University of Electronic Science and Technology of China, China
{cxflovechina, xiangyanping, uestcdaiys}@gmail.com
[2]School of Computing, Teesside University, UK, {Y.Zeng, S.Qin}@tees.ac.uk
[3]School of Computer Engineering, Nanyang Technological University, Singapore, gaocong@ntu.edu.sg

Abstract

Point-of-interest (POI) recommendation becomes a valuable service in location-based social networks. Based on the norm that similar users are likely to have similar preference of POIs, the current recommendation techniques mainly focus on users' preference to provide accurate recommendation results. This tends to generate a list of homogeneous POIs that are clustered into a narrow band of location categories (like food, museum, etc.) in a city. However, users are more interested to taste a wide range of flavors that are exposed in a global set of location categories in the city. In this paper, we formulate a new POI recommendation problem, namely top-K location category based POI recommendation, by introducing information coverage to encode the location categories of POIs in a city. The problem is NP-hard. We develop a greedy algorithm and further optimization to solve this challenging problem. The experimental results on two real-world datasets demonstrate the utility of new POI recommendations and the superior performance of the proposed algorithms.

Introduction

The increasing popularity of location-based social networks (LBSNs), e.g., *Foursquare*, *GyPSii* and *Loopt*, encourages more and more users to share their experience for point-of-interest (POI) in a cyber world (Zheng 2011; Zheng et al. 2010a). When users visit a POI such as store, museum, *etc.*, they post their physical locations, comments and tips that compose a set of *check-in* data in the registered LBSNs. The quick aggregation of data naturally generates valuable service of POI recommendation that instructs users on exploring new places.

Most of the existing work on POI recommendation discovers users' preference implicitly through relating similar users on previous check-in activities in LBSNs (Konstas, Stathopoulos, and Jose 2009; Ye et al. 2011b; Ye, Liu, and Lee 2012; Yuan et al. 2013), and offers a list of POIs to users. Due to the limited budget (like time, money, etc.), users may visit K POIs that are ranked in terms of their *relevance* to users' preference in the recommendation. The recommendation, called *conventional top-K POIs* in this paper, tends to generate a set of homogeneous POIs (e.g., all about restaurant), which are often similar to the majority of the POIs visited by the previous users. However, users are often interested to be recommended with a set of heterogeneous POIs that can cover the different types (e.g., food, sports, etc) of locations in the targeted city.

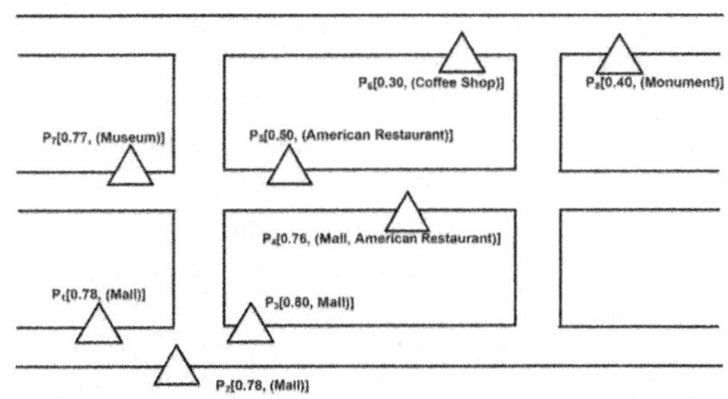

Figure 1: A place with eight POIs (Δ). Each POI is denoted by one tuple in which the number scores its relevance to a user and the term describes its location category.

Considering the example of eight potential POIs in Fig. 1, the top-3 POIs, $\{P_1, P_2, P_3\}$, are highly scored as they are the most relevant to the user's historical check-ins. However, the resulting recommendation is rather monotonic and concentrates only on *mall* in a new place. In contrast, the POIs, $\{P_3, P_4, P_7\}$, would be a better recommendation list as they achieve high relevance scores and simultaneously provide more flavor of the city, including mall, restaurant and museum, to users. For instance, tourists would like to enjoy shopping while browsing through museums or historical monuments around the city. The recommendation needs to consider a wide range of location categories that provide global features of the city. Note that LBSNs, such as *Foursquare*, categorize locations in a city and personalize the POI search. Hence improving information coverage on different categories is to exploit valuable information in LBSNs thereby providing a better POI recommendation.

As recognized in *Foursquare*, most of locations in a city can be categorized into different types such as mall, Austrian restaurant, coffee shop and so on [1], and these categories represent different characteristics of the city. Users would like to explore new types of locations that have not been visited by them. In Fig. 2, we confirm this observation in two real-

[1]https://developer.foursquare.com/categorytree

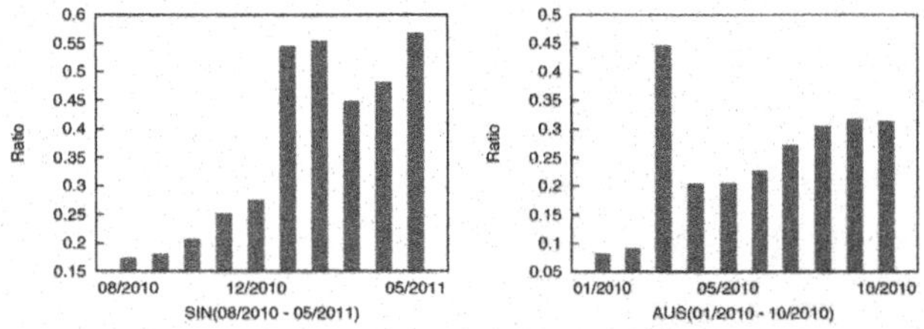

Figure 2: Ratio reports users' incline to exploring new location categories over time.

world datasets containing check-ins in Singapore (SIN) and Austin (AUS) respectively over one time period. We compute the ratio of new location categories (in contrast to those in the previous month) to all ones visited by an user for each month and report the average value for all users. Fig. 2 shows that the users explore around 25-30% (Y-axis: Ratio) new location categories for most of the months (X-axis: Month) in both datasets. The peaks appear due to a significantly larger number of check-ins made in the particular months. The existing POI recommendation methods tend to recommend a user the POIs that belong to the same set of categories as those visited by the user.

In this paper, we aim to improve the conventional top-K POIs on information coverage of location categories in the recommendation. We formulate the issue as one multi-objective optimization problem solving which recommends top-K location category based POIs (LC-POIs). The top-K LC-POIs optimize both their information coverage of a place and their relevance to users in the recommendation.

Following the same spirit of user-based collaborative filtering methods (Zheng et al. 2010b; Ye et al. 2011b), we compute relevance of POIs by gauging users' similarity based on their previous check-in activities. The technique has been well studied and adapted successfully in POI recommendation. Meanwhile, as optimizing information coverage expects a list of POIs to jointly enclose different location categories in a place, we resort to information coverage function for the computation purpose (El-Arini et al. 2009). Since all locations are categorized into several types in check-ins, we compute the degree to which one POI covers a category by counting how often the POI is checked as the category in the data. It represents the popularity of the POI labelled by the category in a city. We further weight the coverage degree with the category popularity.

Solving top-K LC-POIs problem is rather challenging as in principle we need to enumerate all possible sets of K POIs that can be retrieved from check-ins. However, we observe that the objective function, which models both information coverage and relevance, satisfies attractive property of submodularity (Nemhauser, Wolsey, and Fisher 1978) and monotony. By exploiting the property, we propose a greedy algorithm that is guaranteed to produce a near-optimal solution of top-K LC-POIs. To speed up the recommendation, we improve the efficiency of greedy algorithm by pruning the POIs with low relevance and information coverage. We also evaluate performance of the proposed algorithm on two real-world datasets.

Related Work

Most of POI recommendations follow the classical user-based collaborative filtering techniques that score POIs in terms of similarity between users' check-in activities (Zheng et al. 2010b; 2009; Ye, Yin, and Lee 2010). The techniques are further improved by taking into account social and geographical influence in the recommendation (Gao, Tang, and Liu 2012; Ye, Liu, and Lee 2012; Cheng et al. 2012; Liu et al. 2013).

Location content becomes an important input for improving LBSN service as it provides more semantic information to recommender systems (Ye et al. 2011a; Bao, Zheng, and Mokbel 2012; Liu and Xiong 2013). To overcome the data sparsity problem, Yin *et al.* (Yin et al. 2013) utilized local features (e.g., attractions and events) to improve the model learning and inference procedure for the recommendation purpose. In parallel, Ye *et al.* (Ye, Zhu, and Cheng 2013) exploited region categories to predict the most likely location of users given their previous activities. In this paper, location categories are considered as important features in the recommended POIs, which become another dimension on evaluating recommendation performance.

One relevant topic is on the diversity of recommendation systems (Zhou et al. 2010; Zhang and Hurley 2008; Yu, Lakshmanan, and Amer-Yahia 2009). Qin and Zhu (Qin and Zhu 2013) used an entropy regularizer to characterize the item diversity in order to improve the top-K prediction. Lathia *et al.* (Lathia et al. 2010) exploited the temporal characteristics of user ratings and improved the diversity of recommended lists. Yin *et al.* (Yin et al. 2011) focused on mining and ranking the diversified trajectory pattern in social media while Zhang *et al.* (Zhang et al. 2014) diversified the spatial search results to improve service in road networks. To be best of our knowledge, the diversity of POI recommendations has not been explored so far. Our work may contribute into attractive research on diversifying POI recommendations.

Problem Formulation

Existing POI recommendation techniques compute a score for each POI and recommend the highly ranked ones. As the recommended POIs are computed based on most of users' personally relevant information, we call the resulting scores as the $relevance$ measurement in the recommendation. We will utilize the well-developed techniques to compute the relevance function.

Finding top-K LC-POIs is to optimize the relevance and information coverage of a set of POIs based on check-in data. We provide a sample of check-ins in Table 1. As some of the previously available check-ins lack proper categories, we locate the POIs through the reference of latitude and longitude and label them with the well-defined category hierarchy in *Foursquare*.

We first choose the state-of-art POI recommendation technique to compute the relevance function. Subsequently, we formally develop information coverage function and define

Table 1: Sample of User Check-in Sequences.

User-ID	Check-in Time	POI-ID	(Lati., Long.)	Category
user-1	20120603, 17:23	POI-2	(1.31,103.85)	*Mall*
user-2	20120605, 08:23	POI-1	(1.31,103.85)	*Zoo*
user-1	20120703, 22:23	POI-3	(1.29,103.84)	*Bar*
...	...	...	...	...

a multi-objective optimization problem for top-K LC-POIs recommendation. We prove hardness of the new recommendation problem.

POI Relevance

As suggested in most of the previous research, the relevance computation follows user-based collaborative filtering methods and can be implemented in a unified framework (Ye et al. 2011b). It is further improved by considering the temporal information in check-ins (Yuan et al. 2013).

Let $L = \{l_1, \cdots, l_m\}$ be a set of POIs. For a given user u at time t, we compute the relevance score for a POI in Eq.1.

$$R(l_j) = \alpha \times c^t_{u,t,l_j} + (1-\alpha) \times c^s_{u,t,l_j} \quad (1)$$

where c^t_{u,t,l_j} is the recommendation score that user u will visit l_j at time t and is computed based on the similarity of users' check-in activities, c^s_{u,t,l_j} the spatial influence of u's previously visited POIs and α the tuning parameter. Time t can be some day, e.g., Monday, or a particular time, e.g., night.

The relevance score $R(L)$ for a set of POIs is the sum of scores for all POIs. It is computed in Eq. 2.

$$R(L) = \sum_{l_j \in L} R(l_j) \quad (2)$$

Note that the relevance function in Eq. 2 is one of the state-of-the-art methods (UST: the user-spatial-temporal unified framework) for POI recommendation (Yuan et al. 2013). It recommends conventional top-K POIs based on the relevance factor. Our proposed method is equally applicable if other methods of computing the relevance are used.

Information Coverage

Information coverage considers how a set of POIs, $L = \{l_1, \cdots, l_m\}$, collectively enclose different location categories derived from check-ins. In general, one category contains a set of POIs and one POI may be labelled with multiple categories in check-ins. The degree to which one POI covers a category reflects the popularity of the POI in the corresponding category. The larger degree of covering all categories, the more information the set of POIs provide in the recommendation. A POI enjoys different popularity of being in one category when it is checked at different time points. We consider time-aware information coverage in this paper.

Let $A = \{a_1, \cdots, a_q\}$ be a set of location categories and $w^t_{a_q}$(>0) the weight of category a_q at time t. We compute the information coverage of a set of POIs in Eq. 3.

$$I(L) = \textstyle\sum_{a_q \in A} w^t_{a_q} cov^t_{a_q}(L) \quad (3)$$

where $cov^t_{a_q}(L)$ measures the degree to which category a_q is covered by at least one POI in the set L at time t. Thus we compute $cov^t_{a_q}(L)$ below.

$$cov^t_{a_q}(L) = 1 - \textstyle\prod_{l_j \in L}[1 - cov^t_{a_q}(l_j)] \quad (4)$$

where $cov^t_{a_q}(l_j)$ is the degree to which POI l_j covers the category a_q at t.

The popularity of a POI labelled by the category a_q is implied by the number of checks-in that the POI receives at a_q. To equally prioritize POIs with a high volume of check-ins, we compute $cov^t_{a_q}(l_j)$, which is proportional to users' check-ins of l_j in the average check-ins labelled by a_q, in Eq. 5.

$$cov^t_{a_q}(l_j) = min[\frac{nc^t_{l_j^{a_q}}}{\frac{1}{\sum_{l_j} 1} \times \sum_{l_j} nc^t_{l_j^{a_q}}}, 1] \quad (5)$$

where $nc^t_{l_j^{a_q}}$ is the number of check-ins that are made at l_j and labelled by category a_q at time t. $\sum_{l_j} 1$ is the number of POIs visited at time t and $\sum_{l_j} nc^t_{l_j^{a_q}}$ counts all check-ins labelled by a_q at t. $cov^t_{a_q}(l_j)$ is 1 if $nc^t_{l_j^{a_q}}$ exceeds the average number of check-ins labelled by a_q.

Example 1. *Given 3 POIs (l_1, l_2 and l_3) labelled by a_q in one city, the numbers of check-ins are 50, 100 and 150 respectively on l_1, l_2 and l_3 at time t. Hence the average number of check-ins labelled by a_q is 100 for POIs at time t. Subsequently we get: l_1 covers a_q with a degree 0.5 while l_2 and l_3 cover a_q completely (with a degree 1).*

In general, a city is featured by its local attractions of categories that become common in check-ins. To offset the focused categories, we adapt the TF-IDF (Term Frequency-Inverse Document Frequency) technique to compute the category weight $w^t_{a_q}$ in Eq. 6.

$$w^t_{a_q} = \frac{nc^t_{a_q}}{\sum_{a_q} nc^t_{a_q}} \times (lg \frac{\sum_{a_q} z^t_{a_q}}{z^t_{a_q}} + \tau) \quad (6)$$

where $nc^t_{a_q}$ ($=\sum_{l_j} nc^t_{l_j^{a_q}}$) is the number of check-ins labelled by a_q at t and $z^t_{a_q}$ counts the number of city in which at least one POI is labelled by a_q at t. We set $\tau = \frac{1}{\sum_{a_q} z^t_{a_q}}$ to maintain a positive value of $w^t_{a_q}$.

As the information coverage function needs to consider the joint influence of a set of POIs, it differs from the relevance function (in Eq. 2) that can be calculated separately for each POI.

Top-K LC-POIs Recommendation

We proceed to formulate the top-K LC-POIs recommendation problem. The two factors, namely relevance and information coverage, are objectives that shall be balanced when we expect to optimize the recommendation list. For a given user u, the problem is to find a set of POIs that maximize the scoring function $\sigma(L)$ by computing their relevance and information coverage in check-in data. Formally the top-K

LC-POIs recommendation is modeled as one multi-objective optimization problem below.

$$\begin{aligned}&\textbf{Given}: \mathcal{D}, K, \beta, u, t\\&\textbf{Objective}:\\&max_{L\subseteq\mathcal{D},|L|=K}\ \sigma(L) = (1-\beta)\times R(L) + \beta\times I(L)\end{aligned} \tag{7}$$

where $L \subseteq \mathcal{D}$ retrieves all POIs, denoted as $POI\text{-}ID$, from check-in data $\mathcal{D}$, and $\beta(\geq 0)$ is a tradeoff between relevance and information coverage measurements.

The limited number (K) of POIs to be recommended is supplied by a user who may have limited budget (e.g., time and money) in a visit. Another parameter β is determined by the user's plan on either exploiting some areas (following her/his personal experience) or exploring the entire city (tasting all flavor of a city). Intuitively, β is set to be small when the user has visited the city for several times and expects to focus on some specific areas in a new visit. This however depends on the user's personal interests.

We observe that the top-K LC-POIs recommendation is a complex combinatorial optimization problem with two objectives. We prove it to be NP-hard.

Proposition 1. *The top-K LC-POIs recommendation problem formulated in Eq.7 is NP-hard.*

Proof. We develop the proof by converting the problem into a unit cost version of the budgeted maximum coverage problem (Khuller, Moss, and Naor 1999). Given a unit cost version of the budgeted maximum coverage (UBMC) problem instance φ : a collection of sets $S = \{S_1, S_2, \cdots, S_m\}$ with a unit cost C, a domain of elements $X = \{x_1, x_2, \cdots, x_n\}$ with associated weights $\{w_1, w_2, \cdots, w_n\}$, and a budget B, we can construct a top-K LC-POIs recommendation problem instance ω by setting $\beta = 1$, $K = \lfloor B/C \rfloor$ and $I(S')$ corresponds to the total weight of the elements covered by S'. Hence, S' is the set having a maximum weight in φ iff S' is the top-K LC-POI set of ω. As the UBMC problem has been proved to be NP-hard, the top-K LC-POIs recommendation problem is NP-hard as well. ■

Property Analysis and Greedy Algorithm

It is rather difficult to solve the top-K LC-POIs recommendation problem. By leveraging the monotone submodularity of the scoring function ($\sigma(L)$ in Eq. 7), we present a greedy algorithm to find top-K LC-POIs and improve its efficiency.

Monotone Submodularity

Let $\mathcal{V}$ be a finite set. A set of function F: $\mathcal{V} \rightarrow \mathbb{R}$ is called *submodular* if it satisfies the *diminishing returns* property (Nemhauser, Wolsey, and Fisher 1978), $F(B\bigcup s) - F(B) \geq F(\hat{B}\bigcup s) - F(\hat{B})$, for all $B \subseteq \hat{B} \subseteq \mathcal{V}$ and $s \notin B$. $F(B\bigcup s) - F(B)$ is the *marginal increase* of F when an element s is added into B. Submodularity characterizes the notion that supplementing elements to a small set B provides more than doing it to a larger set $\hat{B}$.

To prove the monotone submodularity of $\sigma(L)$, we first analyze the properties of $R(L)$ and $I(L)$ respectively. The relevance analysis is straightforward because $R(L)$ computes scores for every POI independently in Eq. 1.

Proposition 2. *The relevance function $R(L)$ is monotone and submodular.*

Proof. Let $L_1 \subseteq L_2 \subseteq L$ and $l_i \in L$. For any $l_i \notin L_1$, we compute

$$R(L_1\bigcup l_i) - R(L_1) = [R(L_1) + R(l_i)] - R(L_1) = R(l_i)$$

As the relevance score for a POI is nonnegative, $R(L)$ is monotone. Similarly, we have $R(L_2\bigcup l_i) - R(L_2) = R(l_i)$. This leads to $R(L_1\bigcup l_i) - R(L_i) \geq R(L_2\bigcup l_i) - R(L_2)$. Hence the relevance function $R(L)$ is submodular. ■

Intuitively, users know more about a city when they visit more places in a city. However, visiting one place after traveling a small part of the city provides more knowledge to them than visiting the place after traveling a larger part of the city. This indicates the property of information coverage function on the monotone submodularity. We formulate it in Proposition 3.

Proposition 3. *The information coverage function $I(L)$ is monotone and submodular.*

Proof. Let $L_1 \subseteq L_2 \subseteq L$ and $l_i \in L$. For any L_1 and $l_i \notin L_1$, we compute

$$\begin{aligned}&cov^t_{a_q}(L_1\bigcup l_i) - cov^t_{a_q}(L_1) = \textstyle\prod_{l_j\in L_1}(1-cov^t_{a_q}(l_j)) - \\&\textstyle\prod_{l_j\in L_1\bigcup l_i}(1-cov^t_{a_q}(l_j)) = cov^t_{a_q}(l_i)\prod_{l_j\in L_1}(1-cov^t_{a_q}(l_j))\end{aligned}$$

Since both $cov^t_{a_q}(l_i)$ and $cov^t_{a_q}(l_j)$ are in the range [0,1], we get $cov^t_{a_q}(L_1\bigcup l_i) \geq cov^t_{a_q}(L_1)$. Thus $cov^t_{a_q}(L)$ is monotone. We proceed to compute

$$\begin{aligned}&[cov^t_{a_q}(L_1\bigcup l_i) - cov^t_{a_q}(L_1)] - [cov^t_{a_q}(L_2\bigcup l_i) - cov^t_{a_q}(L_2)]\\&= cov^t_{a_q}(l_i)\textstyle\prod_{l_j\in L_1}(1-cov^t_{a_q}(l_j))(1-\prod_{l_j\in L_2-L_1}(1-cov^t_{a_q}(l_j))\end{aligned}$$

We have $cov^t_{a_q}(L_1\bigcup l_i) - cov^t_{a_q}(L_1) \geq cov^t_{a_q}(L_2\bigcup l_i) - cov^t_{a_q}(L_2)$. Hence $cov^t_{a_q}(L)$ is submodular.

In Eq. 3, $I(L)$ is a linear combination of $cov^t_{a_q}(L)$ weighted by $w^t_{a_q}$(>0). The monotone submodularity is closed under a linear combination with a nonnegative weight. This concludes that the information coverage function is monotone submodularity. ■

Given the above propositions, we obtain the attractive property of the scoring function $\sigma(L)$ in Proposition 4.

Proposition 4. *The scoring function $\sigma(L)$ is monotone submodularity.*

Proof. It follows that $\sigma(L)$ is a linear combination of $R(L)$ and $I(L)$ both of which are monotone submodularity and the weighting parameter β is nonnegative. ■

Greedy Algorithm and Its Optimization

Greedy Algorithm. As shown in Proposition 1, finding top-K LC-POIs is NP-hard in the recommendation. However, the monotone submodularity property suggests a greedy algorithm with theoretical guarantees for maximizing a multi-objective function (Nemhauser, Wolsey, and Fisher 1978). In Alg. 1, the greedy algorithm starts with an empty set of POI (line 1) and repeatedly adds the POI incurring the largest marginal score increase to the POI set L until $|L| =$

K (lines 5-7). The algorithm can achieve near-optimal solutions of top-K LC-POIs with a (1-$\frac{1}{e}$) approximation on the optimal score.

Since the greedy algorithm needs to check all of the POI candidates in every round (line 6), the time complexity is $\mathcal{O}[K|\mathcal{D}|\mathcal{T}(\sigma(L))$, where $|\mathcal{D}|$ is the size of check-in data and $\mathcal{T}(\sigma(L))$ the run time for computing the scoring function.

Pruning Optimization. The large size of check-ins ($|\mathcal{D}|$) prevents a quick response from the greedy algorithm on finding top-K LC-POIs in real time. We improve its efficiency by pruning the POIs having a small relevance and information coverage value. The operations of *Pruning Optimization* are embedded in the greedy algorithm (lines 2-4). The POI to be pruned has a smaller value of $\sigma(l_i)$ compared to the score $R(l_k)$ of the Kth POI that is ranked by the relevance measurement in check-ins. With a general setting of $K \ll |\mathcal{D}|$, the operations prune a significantly large number of POIs. Meanwhile, the pruning maintains the solution quality of the greedy algorithm. We prove the property.

Algorithm 1: Greedy Algorithm with Pruning Optimization

Input: $\mathcal{D}, K, \beta, u, t$
Output: A set of POIs, L, with $|L|$=K
1 Initialize L=$\emptyset$;
2 Compute $\sigma(l_i)$ for each $l_i \in \mathcal{D}$;
3 Rank $\mathcal{D}$ in decreasing order of $R(l_i)$;
4 Prune the POI set $L_{pru} = \{l_i|\sigma(l_i) < (1-\beta) \times R(l_K)\}$ where l_K is the Kth POI ranked by the relevance score;
5 **for** $j = 1$ **to** K **do**
6 $\quad l_j \leftarrow argmax_{l_j}\ [\sigma(L \bigcup l_j) - \sigma(L)]$;
7 $\quad L \leftarrow L \bigcup l_j$;
8 **return** L;

Proposition 5. *Pruning Optimization preserves the solution quality of the greedy algorithm.*

Proof. Assume that there exists a POI $l_a \in L_{pru}$ belonging to top-K LC-POIs recommendation $L_{K-1} \bigcup l_a$, where L_{K-1} is top-$(K-1)$ LC-POIs recommendation. Let L_{rel} be top-K relevant POIs set (containing the first K POIs of sorted $\mathcal{D}$ in line 3 of Alg. 1), l_b be the POI meeting $l_b \in L_{rel}$ and $l_b \notin L_{K-1} \bigcup l_a$. As $(1-\beta) \times R(l_a) + \beta \times I(l_a) < (1-\beta) \times R(l_b)$, $\sigma(L_{K-1} \bigcup l_a) < \sigma(L_{K-1}) + (1-\beta) \times R(l_a) + \beta \times I(l_a) < \sigma(L_{K-1}) + (1-\beta) \times R(l_b) < \sigma(L_{K-1} \bigcup l_b)$. Thus, we get a better K POIs recommendation $L_{K-1} \bigcup l_b$, it contradicts the assumption. This implies that each POI in L_{pru} is not a candidate of top-K LC-POIs. Hence it is safe for Pruning Optimization to prune the POIs. ■

Experimental Study

We conducted a series of experiments to study the top-K LC-POIs recommendation problem and demonstrated performance of the proposed approaches compared to state-of-the-art recommendation techniques.

Experimental Settings

Datasets. We used two real-world check-in datasets. One was collected from $Foursquare$ which was made in Singapore between Aug. 2010 and Jul. 2011 (Yuan et al. 2013). The other one is from *Gowalla* which was made in Austin between Nov. 2009 and Oct. 2010 (Cho, Myers, and Leskovec 2011). Each check-in contains the aforementioned attributes in Table 1. To fill in the missing values of $Category$, we implemented the tool based on the $Foursquare$ APIs. For both datasets, we removed users who have checked in fewer than 5 POIs, and then removed POIs that were checked by fewer than 5 users. After preprocessing, the $Foursquare$ dataset has 189,306 check-ins made by 2,321 users at 5,412 POIs, and the *Gowalla* dataset contains 201,525 check-ins made by 4,630 users at 6,176 POIs. For each user, we randomly mark off 20% of his/her visited POIs as the testing data to evaluate the recommendation methods. The recommendation is done for a user given a specific time Day. To compute Eq. 6, we extracted *Gowalla* check-ins made in 162 cities from the dataset provided by *Cho et. al* (Cho, Myers, and Leskovec 2011).

Comparative Recommendation Techniques. We implemented both the greedy algorithm (GA) and its improved version with the pruning optimization (GA+PO) to find top-K LC-POIs. Additionally, we adopt the CELF optimization (Leskovec et al. 2007), which is widely used to improve the efficiency of GA, in the implementation of GA+PO. For the comparison purpose, we implemented a random algorithm (Random) which selects K POIs from the dataset randomly and repeats the procedure for a sufficient number of times (10,000). Note that all of the four algorithms recommend top-K LC-POIs.

To demonstrate the quality of top-K LC-POIs, we implemented the state-of-the-art method (UST) that recommends conventional top-K POIs solely based on the relevance score. All methods are implemented in JAVA, and experiments are conducted on a Windows PC with a 4-core Intel i7-3770 3.4GHz CPU and 8 GB memory.

Performance Metrics. The evaluated recommendation methods aim to find top-K LC-POIs to the targeted user by computing the scoring function and then rank candidate POIs accordingly. We employ the Shannon entropy (Cover and Thomas 1991) as a measurement (div@K) to show the category diversity of the recommended POIs in Eq. 8.

$$div@K = -\frac{\sum_{a_q} \frac{|l_j^{a_q}|}{K} ln(\frac{|l_j^{a_q}|}{K})}{lnK} \tag{8}$$

where $|l_j^{a_q}|$ is the number of POIs labelled by the category a_q.

Meanwhile we use pre@K and rec@K to measure how many POIs in the recommended POIs correspond to the hold-off POIs in the testing data and how many POIs in the hold-off POIs in the testing set are returned as the recommended POIs respectively (Yuan et al. 2013).

Performance of Methods

Effectiveness of Methods. We compare the recommendation quality of three methods (GA, UST and Random) with the settings of β=0.3 and 0.2 respectively in Foursquare and Gowalla. Note that GA and its enhanced versions (GA+PO and GA+PO+CELF) recommend the same top-K LC-POIs.

Fig. 3 shows that GA improves the diversity of UST by around 35% in *Foursquare* and 13% in *Gowalla*. Meanwhile, it keeps around 97% precision and recall of UST on both datasets. Although Random achieves the best diversity, it leads to an extremely low recommendation precision and recall. Overall the results demonstrate that Random can not offer a good recommendation while GA improves the category diversity of UST significantly and achieve similar precision and recall as UST does.

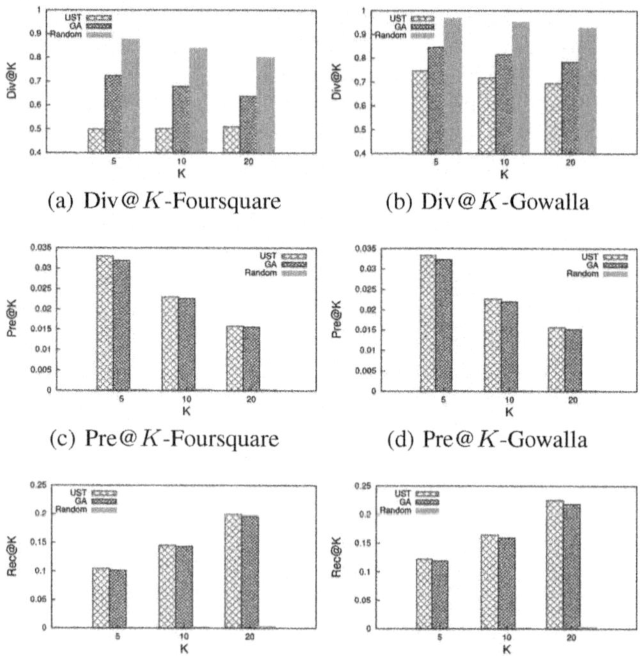

(a) Div@K-Foursquare (b) Div@K-Gowalla

(c) Pre@K-Foursquare (d) Pre@K-Gowalla

(e) Rec@K-Foursquare (f) Rec@K-Gowalla

Figure 3: Comparison of the diversity, precision and recall of top-K POIs recommended by the methods.

Efficiency of Methods. We compare the methods (GA, GA+PO and GA+PO+CELF) based on run time each takes to identify top-K LC-POIs in two datasets. Fig. 4 shows the run time of the methods varying β with $K = 15$. GA consumes much more time than other methods. A large β shrinks the pruned POI set, which results in the increase of the run time for GA+PO. Fig. 5 exhibits the run time of the methods varying K with a fixed β (0.3 on Foursquare and 0.2 on Gowalla). The run time of GA+PO and GA+PO+CELF is small and stable while the run time of GA grows quickly as K increases.

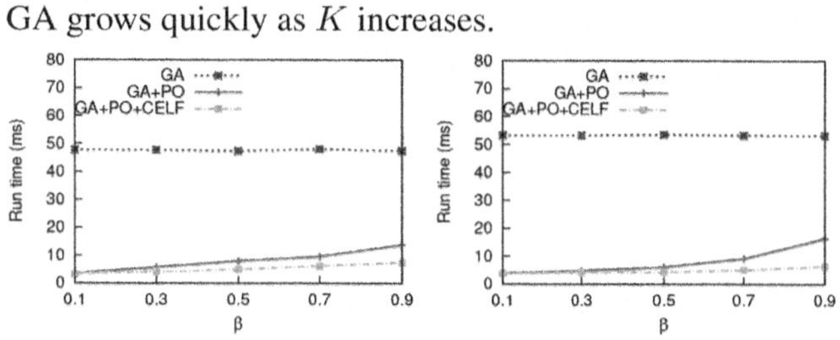

(a) Foursquare and $K = 15$ (b) Gowalla and $K = 15$

Figure 4: Comparison of methods varying β on run time

Effect of Parameter β. The parameter β balances the relevance and information coverage factors in the POI recommendation. If $\beta = 0$, top-K LC-POIs become conventional top-K POIs, and if $\beta = 1$, top-K LC-POIs maximize the information coverage. Fig. 6 shows the effect of β with $K = 5$ on the recommendation. With the increase of β, the diversity grows while the precision and recall decrease. Tuning β in this fashion allows top-K LC-POIs to be customized and optimized for needs of different users or communities.

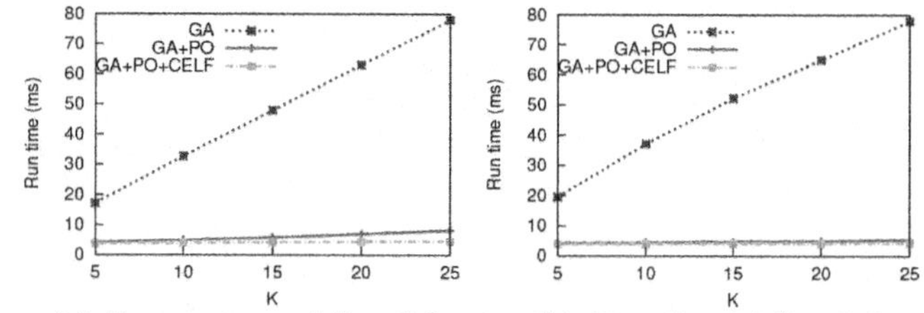

(a) Foursquare and $\beta = 0.3$ (b) Gowalla and $\beta = 0.2$

Figure 5: Comparison of methods varying K on run time.

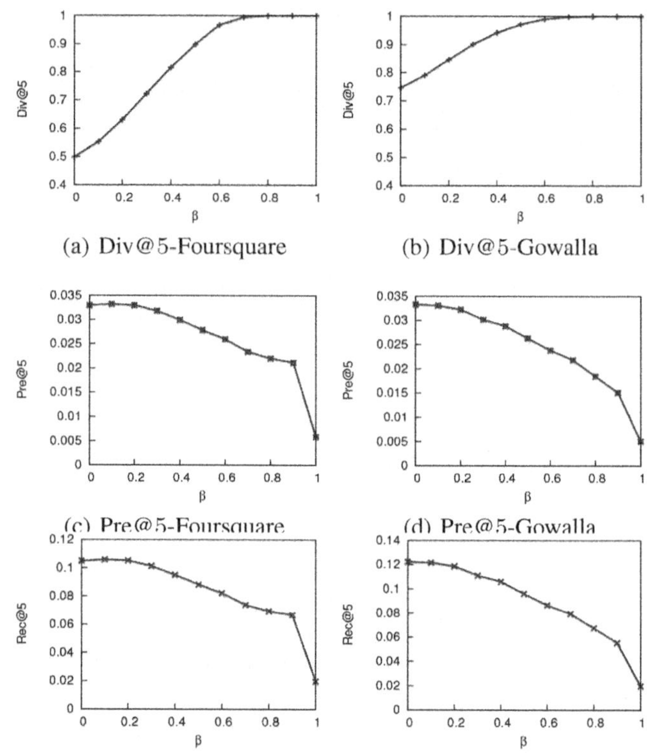

(a) Div@5-Foursquare (b) Div@5-Gowalla

(c) Pre@5-Foursquare (d) Pre@5-Gowalla

(e) Rec@5-Foursquare (f) Rec@5-Gowalla

Figure 6: Effect of parameter β with $K = 5$.

Conclusion

With the observation of users' interests in exploring new location categories, we improve the POI recommendation by introducing information coverage into the recommendation measurement. We formulate the top-K LC-POIs recommendation problem and prove its monotone submodularity property. To solve the new problem, we propose a greedy algorithm with $(1-\frac{1}{e})$ theoretical bound and improve it using one pruning optimization. We empirically demonstrate the quality of top-K LC-POIs recommendation as well as the performance of our proposed methods. Further research can be conducted on improving POI recommendation through users' explicit feedback in LBSNs.

Acknowledgements

Part of this work was done during Xuefeng's visit to Teesside University, sponsored by Teesside University and its University Research Fund (URF). Yuanshun is the corresponding author. Gao Cong was supported in part by the MOE AcRF Tier 2 Grant (ARC30/12).

References

Bao, J.; Zheng, Y.; and Mokbel, M. F. 2012. Location-based and preference-aware recommendation using sparse geo-social networking data. In *Proceedings of the 20th International Conference on Advances in Geographic Information Systems*, 199–208. ACM.

Cheng, C.; Yang, H.; King, I.; and Lyu, M. R. 2012. Fused matrix factorization with geographical and social influence in location-based social networks. In *AAAI*, volume 12, 1.

Cho, E.; Myers, S. A.; and Leskovec, J. 2011. Friendship and mobility: user movement in location-based social networks. In *Proceedings of the 17th ACM SIGKDD international conference on Knowledge discovery and data mining*, 1082–1090. ACM.

Cover, T. M., and Thomas, J. A. 1991. *Elements of Information Theory*. New York, USA: Wiley-Interscience.

El-Arini, K.; Veda, G.; Shahaf, D.; and Guestrin, C. 2009. Turning down the noise in the blogosphere. In *Proceedings of the 15th ACM SIGKDD international conference on Knowledge discovery and data mining (KDD)*, 289–298.

Gao, H.; Tang, J.; and Liu, H. 2012. gscorr: Modeling geo-social correlations for new check-ins on location-based social networks. In *Proceedings of the 21st ACM International Conference on Information and Knowledge Management (CIKM)*, 1582–1586.

Khuller, S.; Moss, A.; and Naor, J. S. 1999. The budgeted maximum coverage problem. *Information Processing Letters* 70(1):39–45.

Konstas, I.; Stathopoulos, V.; and Jose, J. M. 2009. On social networks and collaborative recommendation. In *Proceedings of the 32Nd International ACM SIGIR Conference on Research and Development in Information Retrieval (SIGIR)*, 195–202.

Lathia, N.; Hailes, S.; Capra, L.; and Amatriain, X. 2010. Temporal diversity in recommender systems. In *Proceedings of the 33rd International ACM SIGIR Conference on Research and Development in Information Retrieval (SIGIR)*, 210–217.

Liu, B., and Xiong, H. 2013. Point-of-interest recommendation in location based social networks with topic and location awareness. In *SDM*, 396–404. SIAM.

Liu, B.; Fu, Y.; Yao, Z.; and Xiong, H. 2013. Learning geographical preferences for point-of-interest recommendation. In *Proceedings of the 19th ACM SIGKDD international conference on Knowledge discovery and data mining*, 1043–1051. ACM.

Nemhauser, G.; Wolsey, L.; and Fisher, M. 1978. An analysis of the approximations for maximizing submodular set functions. *Mathematical Programming* 14:265–294.

Qin, L., and Zhu, X. 2013. Promoting diversity in recommendation by entropy regularizer. In *Proceedings of the Twenty-Third International Joint Conference on Artificial Intelligence (IJCAI)*, 2698–2704.

Ye, M.; Shou, D.; Lee, W.-C.; Yin, P.; and Janowicz, K. 2011a. On the semantic annotation of places in location-based social networks. In *Proceedings of the 17th ACM SIGKDD International Conference on Knowledge Discovery and Data Mining (KDD)*, 520–528.

Ye, M.; Yin, P.; Lee, W.-C.; and Lee, D.-L. 2011b. Exploiting geographical influence for collaborative point-of-interest recommendation. In *Proceedings of the 34th International ACM SIGIR Conference on Research and Development in Information Retrieval (SIGIR)*, 325–334.

Ye, M.; Liu, X.; and Lee, W.-C. 2012. Exploring social influence for recommendation: A generative model approach. In *Proceedings of the 35th International ACM SIGIR Conference on Research and Development in Information Retrieval (SIGIR)*, 671–680.

Ye, M.; Yin, P.; and Lee, W.-C. 2010. Location recommendation for location-based social networks. In *Proceedings of the 18th SIGSPATIAL International Conference on Advances in Geographic Information Systems (GIS)*, 458–461.

Ye, J.; Zhu, Z.; and Cheng, H. 2013. What's your next move: User activity prediction in location-based social networks. In *Proceedings of the SIAM International Conference on Data Mining (SDM)*, 171–179.

Yin, Z.; Cao, L.; Han, J.; Luo, J.; and Huang, T. S. 2011. Diversified trajectory pattern ranking in geo-tagged social media. In *Proceedings of the SIAM International Conference on Data Mining (SDM)*, 980–991.

Yin, H.; Sun, Y.; Cui, B.; Hu, Z.; and Chen, L. 2013. Lcars: A location-content-aware recommender system. In *Proceedings of the 19th ACM SIGKDD International Conference on Knowledge Discovery and Data Mining (KDD)*, 221–229.

Yu, C.; Lakshmanan, L.; and Amer-Yahia, S. 2009. It takes variety to make a world: Diversification in recommender systems. In *Proceedings of the 12th International Conference on Extending Database Technology: Advances in Database Technology (EDBT)*, 368–378.

Yuan, Q.; Cong, G.; Ma, Z.; Sun, A.; and Thalmann, N. M. 2013. Time-aware point-of-interest recommendation. In *Proceedings of the 36th International ACM SIGIR Conference on Research and Development in Information Retrieval*, 363–372.

Zhang, M., and Hurley, N. 2008. Avoiding monotony: Improving the diversity of recommendation lists. In *Proceedings of the ACM Conference on Recommender Systems (RecSys)*, 123–130.

Zhang, C.; Zhang, Y.; Zhang, W.; Lin, X.; Cheema, M. A.; and Wang, X. 2014. Diversified spatial keyword search on road networks. In *Proceedings of the 17th International Conference on Extending Database Technology (EDBT)*, 367–378.

Zheng, Y.; Zhang, L.; Xie, X.; and Ma, W.-Y. 2009. Mining interesting locations and travel sequences from gps trajectories. In *Proceedings of the 18th International Conference on World Wide Web (WWW)*, 791–800.

Zheng, V. W.; Zheng, Y.; Xie, X.; and Yang, Q. 2010a. Collaborative location and activity recommendations with gps history data. In *Proceedings of the 19th International Conference on World Wide Web (WWW)*, 1029–1038.

Zheng, V. W.; Cao, B.; Zheng, Y.; Xie, X.; and Yang, Q. 2010b. Collaborative filtering meets mobile recommendation: A user-centered approach. In *Proceedings of the Twenty-Fourth AAAI Conference on Artificial Intelligence (AAAI)*, 236–241.

Zheng, Y. 2011. Location-based social networks: Users. *Computing with Spatial Trajectories* 243–276.

Zhou, T.; Kuscsik, Z.; Liu, J.-G.; Medoa, M.; Wakeling, J. R.; and Zhang, Y. C. 2010. Solving the apparent diversity-accuracy dilemma of recommender systems. In *Proceedings of the National Academy of Sciences (PNAS)*, 4511–4515.

Visually Interpreting Names as Demographic Attributes by Exploiting Click-Through Data

†‡Yan-Ying Chen, †Yin-Hsi Kuo, †Chun-Che Wu, †Winston H. Hsu
†National Taiwan University, Taipei, Taiwan
‡FX Palo Alto Laboratory, Inc., California, USA
{yanying,kuonini,kenwu0721}@gmail.com, whsu@ntu.edu.tw

Abstract

Name of an identity is strongly influenced by his/her cultural background such as gender and ethnicity, both vital attributes for user profiling, attribute-based retrieval, etc. Typically, the associations between names and attributes (e.g., people named "Amy" are mostly females) are annotated manually or provided by the census data of governments. We propose to associate a name and its likely demographic attributes by exploiting click-throughs between name queries and images with automatically detected facial attributes. This is the first work attempting to translate an abstract name to demographic attributes in visual-data-driven manner, and it is adaptive to incremental data, more countries and even unseen names (the names out of click-through data) without additional manual labels. In the experiments, the automatic name-attribute associations can help gender inference with competitive accuracy by using manual labeling. It also benefits profiling social media users and keyword-based face image retrieval, especially for contributing 12% relative improvement of accuracy in adapting to unseen names.

Figure 1: We aim at associating a human name such as "Amy Liu" with its likely visual attributes by exploiting click-throughs in web image search logs under a novel visual-data-driven manner without intensive labeling efforts and adaptive to unseen names.

Introduction

Human attributes (gender, age, ethnicity, etc.) are vital to semantically characterize a person or demographics of a community. This nature makes it valuable for marketing (Aaker 1997), personalization (Cheng et al. 2011), surveillance system (Vaquero et al. 2009), face image search (Kumar, Belhumeur, and Nayar 2008), social computing (Liu, Zamal, and Ruths 2012) and more human-centric research. The preliminary studies have achieved convincing results in attribute prediction of a person by analyzing his/her tweets (Burger et al. 2012), face images (Cheng et al. 2011) and user names (Mislove et al. 2012); however, in general circumstances people may hide most attribute contexts because of privacy issues.

Since users tend to keep their online profiles private (Dey, Jelveh, and Ross 2012), name is the most reachable piece of personal information among these contexts. The problem we address is – given a name, associating and predicting its likely demographic attributes, particularly, the gender and ethnicity attributes discussed in this paper. As shown in Figure 1[1], given a person named "Amy Liu," the person is likely an Asian female. Name makes the first impression of a person because naming conventions are strongly influenced by culture, e.g., first name and gender, last name and location of origin. Typically, the associations between names and the two attributes are available by referring to demographics maintained by governments (Burger et al. 2012; Mislove et al. 2012) and manually labeling attributes based on profile photos of sampled social media users (Liu, Zamal, and Ruths 2013). The former is limited in regional census data and not general to more countries. The latter has major concerns in time and cost when it adapts to large-scale data.

Different from the traditional manners, we propose to associate name and attribute by exploiting click-throughs between text queries and face images in web search logs, where the names are extracted from queries and the attributes are detected from face images automatically. In this paper, a *click-through* means when one of the URLs returned by a text query has been clicked to view a web image it di-

[1]The face images presented in this paper are under Creative Commons Licenses.

rects to (Beeferman and Berger 2000). The mechanism delivers two messages, (1) the association between a query and an image is based on viewers' clicks, that is, human intelligence from web-scale users; (2) users may have considerable knowledge to the associations because they might be partially aware of what they are looking for and search engines are getting much better at satisfying user intent. Both characteristics of click-throughs reduce the concerns of incorrect associations. Meanwhile, the Internet users' knowledge enables discovering name-attribute associations with high generality to more countries and without relying on regional census data that might not be freely accessible.

Because click-throughs may suffer from data sparsity problem (Craswell and Szummer 2007; Cao et al. 2010) and always have new instances out of the existing coverage, both leading to a large proportion of unseen names – the names lacking associations with any images in click-through data. We further propose to predict attributes of unseen names by using search snippets, the informative texts that appear under every search result and summarize what and why the page is relevant to the given query. Note that, the labels for training attribute classifiers of unseen names solely rely on the automatic association by using click-throughs. For evaluations, we only use English names; however, we believe that the method can scale to more communities by incorporating natural language processing for more languages.

In the experiments, we demonstrate how the learned attribute classifiers of names can contribute to keyword-based face image retrieval and cross-domain gender inference. The accuracy is increasing with the incremental knowledge of crowds taken into account. In summary, our contributions include, (1) proposing a novel visual-data-driven approach to associate a human name with its likely demographic attributes by using click-throughs; (2) proposing to predict attributes of unseen names by using search snippets; (3) showing the effectiveness of name-attribute associations in improving keyword-based face image retrieval especially for the queries comprising unseen names; (4) demonstrating the capability of the name-attribute associations in cross-domain gender inference.

The system overview is illustrated in Figure 2. In the rest of the paper, the literature survey is introduced first, followed by the description of click-through data. The proposed name-attribute association and attribute prediction for unseen names are then presented. Finally, the experiments are discussed, closing with a conclusion.

Related Work

Our main idea is motivated by these preliminary studies: (1) a click-through can be viewed as a weak indication of relevance with user judgment (Song, Miao, and Shen 2011; Joachims 2002); (2) certain human attributes are intuitively understandable through visual appearance of a person (Liu, Zamal, and Ruths 2013); (3) semantic attribute is cross-domain and adaptive to unseen (or new) classes (Lampert, Nickisch, and Harmeling 2014). We first review how click-through data are used in previous literature, followed by the challenges in obtaining attribute labels and identifying new classes by semantic attributes.

Click-through data have been leveraged for optimizing information retrieval (Joachims 2002; Cao et al. 2010), interpreting implicit feedback (Joachims 2005; Chen et al. 2011) and query suggestion (Beeferman and Berger 2000). It acts as additional and free contexts beyond content and associates relevant items even across multiple modals such as image and text. Song, Miao, and Shen (2011) propose an efficient multiple instance learning approach to automatically produce high relevance labels for pairs of query and URL. Jain and Varma (2011) propose to improve the performance of keyword-based image retrieval by click-through data. Yao et al. (2013) propose an economic way for video tagging by understanding user searching behavior through clicks. Different from the previous work where click-throughs only contribute document (image) level association, we propose to leverage visual-based face attribute detection to achieve attribute level association with name queries.

Attribute labels are not easily available on the Internet because users would like to protect their privacy and hide the details of their profiles (Dey, Jelveh, and Ross 2012). Some studies have tried to empirically determine attributes of a user by observing the user generated textual content in one form or another (Burger et al. 2012; Pennacchiotti and Popescu 2011). Liu, Zamal, and Ruths (2013) propose to collect gender labels of Twitter users by hiring Turkers to label each user's gender based on his/her profile photo. However, paid crowdsourcing is relatively harder to scale up to big data. Conversely, the public click-throughs are nearly free, and with more clicks the incorrect annotation can be reduced considerably. Meanwhile, visual content, particularly face, has become more important for knowledge extraction and representation with the prevalence of images and videos on the Internet (Hasan and Pal 2014).

Attributes that carry semantics are beneficial for zero-shot learning which targets the classification when no training data for a new class are available. Lampert, Nickisch, and Harmeling (2014) propose to identify unseen objects based on high-level semantic attributes such as the object's color or shape. Chen, Gallagher, and Girod (2013) propose attribute-based approach to predict the most possible name given a face image. In contrast to recognizing attributes or names for given image content, we intend to translate a name (class) to semantic attributes by how the crowd think it should look like.

Data Collection

We need massive annotated data for inferring the associations between names and demographic attributes. Instead of collecting data manually, we leverage click-throughs in web search logs that can be viewed as weak annotations. In the experiments, we utilize a new large-scale real-world click data set publicly released by Microsoft Research and Bing (Hua et al. 2013). They sampled from one-year click logs of the Bing image search engine and formed the dataset – **Clickture-Lite**, which contains 23 million click data with 1 million unique images. Each of the click-through data (θ) consists of <image ID, query text, number of clicks> (cf. Figure 2) with 11.7 million unique query texts.

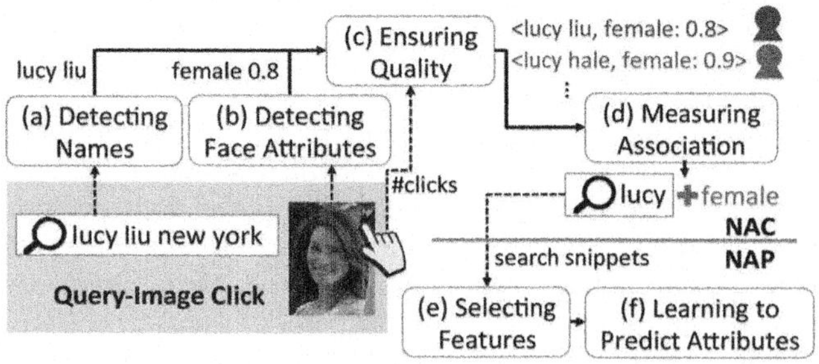

Figure 2: The proposed framework with two major parts – name-attribute association by clicks (NAC) and attribute prediction for unseen names (NAP). Given a query-image click, (a) the name in the query and (b) the face attributes in the image are detected automatically to form an association. (c) The clicks contributed by the Internet users are leveraged to ensure quality of association. (d) Assuming each full name represents one person, the association of a (first/last) name and an attribute is measured by considering the attribute probability of persons with the same first/last name. For unseen names, (e) we collect search snippets as features and exploit the associations obtained by NAC (a to d) as labels for learning attribute detectors (f).

Name-Attribute Association by Clicks (NAC)

Seeing the importance of semantic attributes and their close relationship with a name, we would like to address the problem – given a name n_i, associating its likely gender and ethnicity attributes. We leverage our click-through data θ as observation to measure the name-attribute association $P(a_j|n_i;\theta)$ of each attribute a_j given a name n_i. The name-attribute association $P(a_j|n_i;\theta)$ is a statistical measurement that can be interpreted as a prior probability of attributes for an identity with that name. As shown in Figure 2, four major steps (a) detecting names, (b) detecting face attribute, (c) ensuring quality by clicks and (d) measuring name-attribute associations are proposed to infer the likely attributes of a given name.

Detecting Names: We construct a name dictionary to detect names in queries. First, we collect a list of celebrity names available on the Internet [2], totally 2,221 names denoted as C. Each name is split into words, typically a first name and a last name, resulting in 1,164 first names and 1,681 last names denoted as F and L, respectively. To enrich the name dictionary, we combine each first name in F and each last name in L, which can cover nearly two million name combinations. Given a query, we then extract any names in C or any consecutive words where the former one in F and the latter one in L. The queries comprising any of the two million names in our dictionary are used to infer associations. Without loss of generality, we further address the unseen names out of this coverage in the next section.

Detecting Face Attributes: On the part of image, we leverage a visual-based approach to automatically detect face attributes. First, we localize the faces in an image by face detection (Viola and Jones 2001), totally 495,585 faces detected from 328,838 images. For each of the detected faces, we use the four face attribute classifiers $a_j \in$ {gender, Asian, African, Caucasian} (Kumar, Belhumeur, and Nayar 2008), to predict the probability $P_v(a_j|d_t)$ for a binary outcome of each attribute a_j appearing in a given face d_t. Each attribute classifier is learned by Support Vector Machines (SVMs) using four kinds of low-level features, Local Binary Pattern (LBP), Gabor filter, Histogram of Oriented Gradient and Grid Color Moments extracted from face images. The average accuracy of face attribute detection is around 80% (Kumar, Belhumeur, and Nayar 2008).

Ensuring Quality of Query-Image Pairs: The ambiguous mappings between multiple names in a query and multiple faces in an image may induce incorrect name-attribute associations. To eliminate the ambiguity, we only keep the query-image pair if the query has exactly one name n_i and the image has exactly one face d_t (cf. the example query-image pair in Figure 2), each corresponding to the probabilities of attributes $P_v(a_j|d_t)$ detected from the face d_t. In addition, the number of clicks for a query-image pair can be thought as the agreement among users such that it can be used to confirm the correctness of a name-attribute association. In our experiments, a query-image pair should be clicked at least twice to ensure the quality of association. The converted name-face pair is referred as $< n_i, d_t >$.

Measuring Probability of Association: We measure the probability of a name-attribute association $P(a_j|n_i)$ of a name n_i and an attribute a_j by averaging attribute probability $P_v(a_j|d_t)$ of all images for a name.

$$P(a_j|n_i) = \frac{\sum_{d_t \in d'} P_v(a_j|d_t)}{|d'|}, \quad (1)$$
$$d' = \{d_t | \forall < n_h, d_t >, n_h = n_i\}.$$

A name n_i may consist of a first name $n_i^{(f)}$ and a last name $n_i^{(l)}$; for example, "Michael Jordan" comprise the first name "Michael" and the last name "Jordan." In such case, we separate $P(a_j|n_i)$ to $P(a_j|n_i^{(f)})$ and $P(a_j|n_i^{(l)})$. Like the example in Figure 2, there may exist more than one full names with the same first name, e.g., "Lucy Liu," "Lucy Hale" and "Lucy Gordon" all have the same first name "Lucy." Assuming that a full name represents a person, the association probability $P(a_j|n_i^{(f)})$ of a first name $n_i^{(f)}$ and an attribute a_j can be measured by averaging $P(a_j|n_i)$ of the full names n' comprising the same first name $n_i^{(f)}$.

$$P(a_j|n_i^{(f)}) = \frac{\sum_{n_h \in n'} P(a_j|n_h)}{|n'|}, \quad (2)$$
$$n' = \{n_h | \forall n_h, n_h^{(f)} = n_i^{(f)}\}.$$

The association probability for last name $P(a_j|n_i^{(l)})$ follows the same formulation. The higher $|n'|$ means more reference persons are sampled as the observations, that is, the association probability is more statistically convincing. The number of reference persons is sort of confidence for the association and its impact is discussed in the experiments.

[2] http://www.posh24.com/celebrities/

Attribute Prediction for Unseen Names (NAP)

We further target predicting attributes of the unseen names which lack click-throughs with any images in observation data. Because of limited information in the very short text of a name, we crawl additional contexts of a name to further predict its attributes. The query expansion technique (Sahami and Heilman 2006) is adopted to acquire the snippets of each name returned by the search engine as the features (Figure 2 (e)). The automatic name-attribute associations via click-throughs are exploited as the pseudo labels for learning attribute classifiers of names (Figure 2 (f)). The output is a probability $\hat{P}(a_j|n_i)$ for a binary classifier of each attribute a_j given a name n_i.

Selecting Differential Features: We use the approach extensively used in prior studies (Burger et al. 2012; Liu, Zamal, and Ruths 2012) to select discriminative text features for specified classes. We convert all the snippets to lowercase and split words with space and punctuation. All the split words are then lemmatized to group the different inflected forms of a word as a single item (Bird 2006). The split words are formed as a corpus for extracting unigrams and bigrams. The k most differential unigrams and bigrams found in the snippets of each class are selected as features. For a binary attribute classifier with two classes, the most differential features have higher difference of term frequency in the snippets for one class versus those in the opposite one. Some examples of the selected features are presented in Figure 6. Finally, the selected differential unigrams and bigrams are collected as a vocabulary S for feature extraction.

Learning to Predict Attributes: Based on the vocabulary S, we extract the features for search snippets of each name. The features of a name constitute an indicator vector, each indicating the presence of a term in S. The attribute label of each name in training data is annotated by automatic associations by using NAC. The binary attribute classifier of a name is then learned by SVM (Chang and Lin 2011) with Radial Basis Function as kernel. The cost and gamma parameters are optimized by grid search. Given a new coming name which has not yet been clicked, we can predict its likely attributes by feeding the features extracted from its search snippets to the learned attribute classifier.

Experiments

Evaluation Data Sets and Metrics

We organize the evaluation with four major parts (1) the accuracy of the name-attribute associations, (2) the accuracy of attribute prediction for unseen names, (3) the ranking quality of keyword-based image retrieval and (4) the accuracy of cross-domain gender inference improved by the automatic name-attribute associations. All of the experiments are evaluated in publicly available benchmarks introduced as below.

Demographics from Government (GT): We refer to the 1,000 popular female names and 1,000 popular male names from the real demographics provided by the U.S. Social Security Administration [3]. The associations of names and ethnicity are collected from the U.S. Census [4], totally 1,000 popular last names.

Bing Image Search Development Data (Bing-D): The Clickture-Lite provides a development set with relevance labels for evaluating image retrieval. Based on the development set, we construct 4 subsets – CQ-S, CQ, PQ, PQ-S – for detailed evaluations. CQ-S retains the queries comprising at least one full name appearing in the name dictionary. CQ further includes the queries comprising **Partial Names** – at least one first or last name in the dictionary. In addition to CQ, PQ includes **Unseen Names** that are out of the dictionary. The **Ambiguous Names**, e.g., multiple names or names of cartoon and game characters, are excluded from PQ to form PQ-S. The performance is evaluated by discounted cumulative gain at 25 (DCG_{25}) for each query. The setting and detailed numbers are presented in Table 2.

Twitter User Data (TU): We use the canonical gender-labeled Twitter data (Liu, Zamal, and Ruths 2013) to evaluate how much our gender-name associations can contribute to gender inference for Twitter users. Totally 10,788 users and their user names are included for evaluation, totally 6,903 females and 3,885 males. Each gender label is decided by Turkers based on the user's profile photo.

Figure 3: The tag cloud of male (left) and female (right) names. The larger size the name has, the higher probability the persons with the name are likely of that gender.

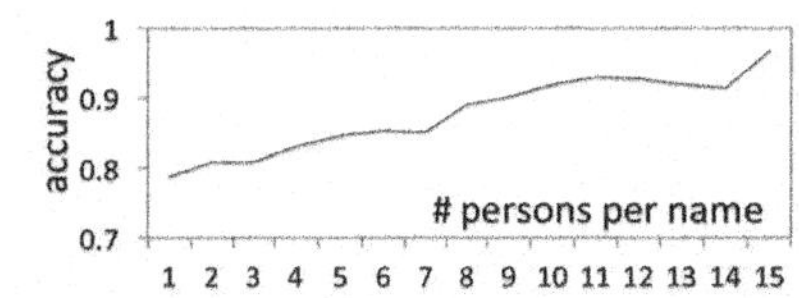

Figure 4: The accuracy of name-gender associations by clicks. The results show that the association accuracy improves saliently if more reference persons (more web search logs contributed by crowds) are taken into account.

Evaluation of Name-Attribute Association (NAC)

Figure 3 shows the tag clouds of male (left) and female (right) names, where the size of names is decided by the name-male and name-female probabilities $P(a_j|n_i^{(f)})$ (cf. Eq. 2), respectively. The top 3 names having the highest associations with the male attribute are "William," "Thomas" and " Russell" while the top 3 ones for female are "Ann,"

[3]http://www.ssa.gov/OACT/babynames/

[4]http://www.census.gov/

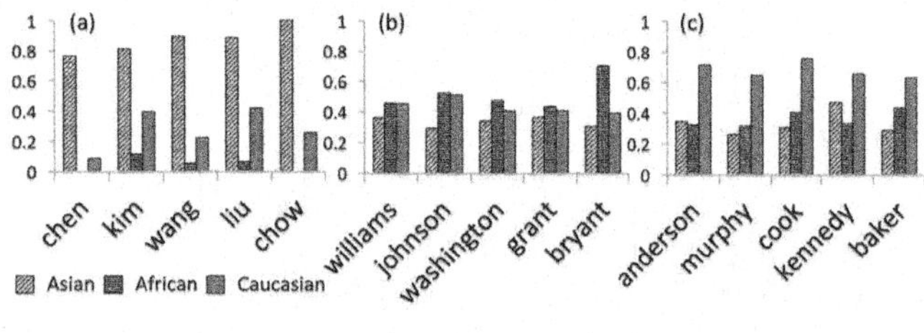

Figure 5: The attribute probabilities given the five sampled popular last names of three different races in the U.S. government data (GT). For the Asian last names (a), the estimated association probability with the Asian attribute is much higher than that with the other ethnicity attributes.

(a)	his, actor, online, game, he, company, team, men, sport	latest news, his stage, stock chart, name after, against other
(b)	her, she, actress, facebook, photo, model, girl, like, fashion, woman	american actress, her father, her work, show off, photo gallery

Figure 6: The example differential terms in the snippets searched by male names (a) and female names (b). The left and right are unigram and bigram features, respectively.

"Danielle," and "Kimberly." The persons who have these names are likely to be males/females. It is intuitive that more reference persons are considered in statistics, more accurate results we might have. We use the (GT) data set as the ground truth and control the minimum number of reference persons for a name (n' in Eq. 2) from 1 to 15. As shown in Figure 4, the names with at least one reference person can reach 79.64% in accuracy and the accuracy is constantly increasing for the names with more reference persons.

We present our results in terms of ethnicity including Asian, African and Caucasian. The race distribution are much more unbalanced because we now only target English language communities. One more problem is visual-based attribute detection for three races are more challenging compared to gender attribute detection. The results among the most race-specific last names still tell the interesting relations between last name and race. We select 5 popular names for Asian, African and Caucasian, respectively, based on the real demographics in (GT) data. Note that, most of them are relatively popular names rather than race-specific names, because most of the last names in the U.S. census data are not that specific to a certain race. Figure 5 reports the probability yielded by three binary classifiers, each corresponding to a race attribute. The probability of association with the Asian attribute (a) is much higher than that with the other race attributes. For the African (b) and Caucasian (c), the differences are not that significant, perhaps because the mix-race groups are more common for these two race communities in our training data.

Evaluation of Attribute Prediction for Unseen Names (NAP)

We present the experiments for predicting attributes for an unseen name, *where its name-attribute association in the training data is not available*. However, because the association between name and race is not that differentiable, it is less effective to train attribute classifiers by the less reliable associations. Therefore, we only address how well the gender attribute of an unseen name can be predicted.

Table 1: Attrbuite prediction for unseen names. The accuracy of NAP can reach 75% by cross-validation (NAP-CV) and 77% by testing the government data (NAP-GT) that is comparative to automatic associations by clicks (NAC-GT).

method	NAP-CV	NAP-GT	NAC-GT
Accuracy	75.76%	77.25%	79.64%

We first select the differential words from the search snippet data crawled by using name as query. The differential terms in snippets searched by male and female names are presented in Figure 6 (a) and (b). Most snippets comprise the short introduction or profiles of celebrities, brands or social media users. The snippets regarding celebrities usually have gender-specific pronouns like "he" or "she" as well as their professions such as "actress." A name might represent a brand, which may not be directly related to human. However, an interesting finding is that these brand names are human-attribute-specific. For example, the name "Laura" is a brand name of woman clothing such that its descriptions comprise the word "woman" much frequently. For the snippets from user names in social media, the content may reveal their interests and favors. Among these interests, "game," "sport" and "fashion" are more differential over gender groups.

To evaluate the accuracy of the proposed prediction approach (NAP), we conduct experiments over our snippet data set labeled by automatic name-gender association. Table 1 shows the accuracy reaches 75.76% in cross-validation manner (NAP-CV). We again use the (GT) data as the ground truth to evaluate how precisely the predicted gender can match the real demographics. The accuracy (NAP-GT) reaches 77.25% which is comparative to name-gender association (NAC-GT).

Image Retrieval by Name Attributes

Translating a name into semantic attributes poses a new opportunity for keyword-based image retrieval. The attributes are helpful to rerank the retrieved images; for example, given a query with only female names, suppressing the images with males can improve the precision in top ranks. We compare our methods with the two previous studies, (1) **IR** (Hua et al. 2013) is the text-based initial ranking provided by (Bing-D); (2) **FR** (Ahonen, Hadid, and Pietikäinen 2004) is the ranking measured by face recognition, totally 6,762 identity classifiers trained by the web images weakly labeled by names in queries. As Table 2 shows, the proposed NAC, NAP and their combination NAC+NAP (using NAP for unseen names; otherwise, using NAC) can consistently improve image retrieval accuracy compared to the baseline IR in all the experiment settings. Although the DCG_{25} of FR is better than NAC and NAP, FR only works for the queries

Table 2: The setting of test sets (Bing-D) and the average DCG_{25}. 'yes' and 'no' indicates whether a test set comprises the Partial, Unseen or Ambiguous Names. 'N/A' means the method cannot deal with the corresponding test set. The results show that the proposed gender inference (NAC+NAP) can deal with general test cases while the baseline (FR) cannot. It also consistantly improves the retrieval accuracy compared to the baseline (IR), even reaching 12% relative gain.

Data Set	CQ-S	CQ	PQ	PQ-S
#queries	62	92	300	153
#images	5,825	7,599	30,835	22,573
Partial Name	no	yes	yes	yes
Unseen Name	no	no	yes	yes
Ambiguous Name	yes	yes	yes	no
IR	0.491	0.481	0.436	0.501
FR	0.511	N/A	N/A	N/A
NAC	0.500	0.499	N/A	N/A
NAP	0.498	0.502	0.467	0.565
NAC+NAP	0.500	0.503	0.468	0.563

with full names in the name dictionary while our method NAC+NAP can cope with more queries (e.g., PQ and PQ-S) even they comprise Partial Names, Unseen Names or Ambiguous Names. For the queries without Ambiguous Names, the relative improvement of NAC+NAP can further reach 12% compared to the baseline IR.

The example search results are shown in Figure 7. Because Eva Amurri Martino participates in a comedy film starring Adam Sandler and Andy Samberg, the initial ranking results contain lots of images related to the film (left of (a)). By considering attributes, the images with female are promoted to top ranks (right of (a)). However, we might not be able to improve human-related queries beyond face such as (c). Nevertheless, the proposed method can provide an essential cue for further improvement and is complementary to the existing methods that consider visual similarity only.

User Profiling by Name Attributes

The name-gender associations by clicks in Bing image search logs also benefit gender inference for Twitter users. Twitter user name is not of strict naming convention like personal name. It could be a simple name or name combination with special symbols and of more free forms. To extract the informative parts, we split a user name by any punctuation or space to get one or more terms and transform them in lower case. Then we match each term with the name set included in the automatic name-gender associations by NAC and use the corresponding probability to represent the likely gender of the user name. If a Twitter user name is matched with multiple names, we assign it with the average attribute probability of the names that it is comprised of.

To demonstrate the accuracy of gender inference, we use the publicly available gender-labels for Twitter users (TU) as the ground truth. We remove the user names without any

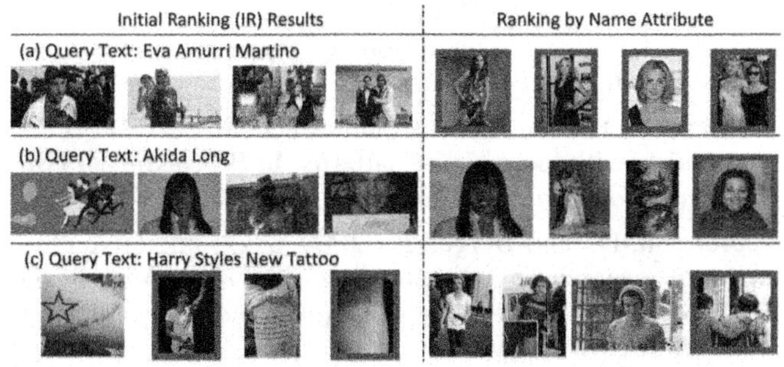

Figure 7: Examples for image ranking results. The blue rectangles indicate correct results. (a)(b) Based on the name attribute prediction, we can estimate whether the query is related to female and filter out those irrelevant male images. (c) Our proposed method might fail if the name query intended for information beyond face but it might be enhanced combining with intention classification methods.

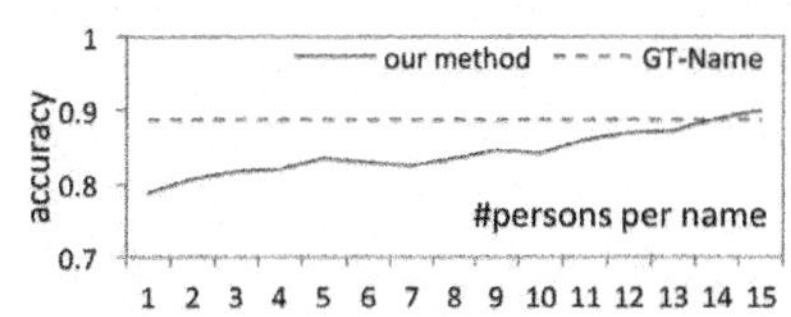

Figure 8: Gender inference for Twitter users. By considering the associations with more reference persons, the accuracy of our method is steadily increasing and comparable with the baseline (GT-Name) that uses data from U.S. census.

terms matched with our name set, totally 5,320 user names remained for evaluation. As shown in Figure 8, our method can reach more than 80% in accuracy. By considering the name-gender associations with more reference persons, the accuracy is steadily increasing and comparative with the accuracy of the baseline (GT-Name) by using name-gender associations from the U.S. government (Liu, Zamal, and Ruths 2013). That again confirms that the proposed name-gender association by click-throughs is convincing to measure prior knowledge for gender inference even in different domains (names in web search logs vs. Twitter user names).

Conclusion and Future Work

To sum up, we propose the first work to interpret a name to demographic attributes in visual-data-driven manner by using publicly available web search logs. The proposed framework is adaptive to incrementally updated data and general to names for more countries and even unseen names lacking click-throughs with any images. Finally, we demonstrate how the automatic associations can improve keyword-based face image retrieval and cross-domain gender inference. With the idea of visual interpretation, we are going to address more names beyond human, e.g., animal, plants and places. For example, the flower species named with "Grevillea" are mostly brightly colored and petal-less (visually perceivable attributes) due to the common genus in biology.

References

Aaker, J. L. 1997. Dimensions of brand personality. In *Journal of Marketing Research*.

Ahonen, T.; Hadid, A.; and Pietikäinen, M. 2004. Face recognition with local binary patterns. In *Proceedings of the European Conference on Computer Vision (ECCV)*.

Beeferman, D., and Berger, A. 2000. Agglomerative clustering of a search engine query log. In *Proceedings of the ACM SIGKDD Conference on Knowledge Discovery and Data Mining (SIGKDD)*.

Bird, S. 2006. Nltk: the natural language toolkit. In *Proceedings of the COLINGACL on Interactive presentation sessions*.

Burger, J. D.; Henderson, J.; Kim, G.; and Zarrella, G. 2012. Discriminating gender on twitter. In *Proceedings of the Conference on Empirical Methods on Natural Language Processing (EMNLP)*.

Cao, B.; Shen, D.; Wang, K.; and Yang, Q. 2010. Clickthrough log analysis by collaborative ranking. In *Proceedings of the AAAI Conference on Artificial Intelligence (AAAI)*.

Chang, C.-C., and Lin, C.-J. 2011. LIBSVM: A library for support vector machines. *ACM Transactions on Intelligent Systems and Technology*. Software available at http://www.csie.ntu.edu.tw/~cjlin/libsvm.

Chen, W.; Ji, Z.; Shen, S.; and Yang, Q. 2011. A whole page click model to better interpret search engine click data. In *Proceedings of the AAAI Conference on Artificial Intelligence (AAAI)*.

Chen, H.; Gallagher, A. C.; and Girod, B. 2013. What's in a name? first names as facial attributes. In *Proceedings of the IEEE Conference on Computer Vision and Pattern Recognition (CVPR)*.

Cheng, A.-J.; Chen, Y.-Y.; Huang, Y.-T.; Hsu, W. H.; and Liao, H.-Y. M. 2011. Personalized travel recommendation by mining people attributes from community-contributed photos. In *Proceedings of the ACM International Conference on Multimedia (ACM MM)*.

Craswell, N., and Szummer, M. 2007. Random walks on the click graph. In *Proceedings of the ACM SIGIR Conference on Research & Development on Information Retrieval (SIGIR)*.

Dey, R.; Jelveh, Z.; and Ross, K. 2012. Facebook users have become much more private: A large-scale study. In *Proceedings of the IEEE International Workshop on Security and Social Networking (SESOC)*.

Hasan, M. K., and Pal, C. 2014. Experiments on visual information extraction with the faces of wikipedia. In *Proceedings of the AAAI Conference on Artificial Intelligence (AAAI)*.

Hua, X.-S.; Yang, L.; Wang, J.; Wang, J.; Ye, M.; Wang, K.; Rui, Y.; and Li, J. 2013. Clickage: Towards bridging semantic and intent gaps via mining click logs of search engines. In *Proceedings of the ACM International Conference on Multimedia (ACM MM)*.

Jain, V., and Varma, M. 2011. Learning to re-rank: Query-dependent image re-ranking using click data. In *Proceedings of the International World Wide Web Conference (WWW)*.

Joachims, T. 2002. Optimizing search engines using clickthrough data. In *Proceedings of the ACM SIGKDD Conference on Knowledge Discovery and Data Mining (SIGKDD)*.

Joachims, T. 2005. Accurately interpreting clickthrough data as implicit feedback. In *Proceedings of the ACM SIGIR Conference on Research & Development on Information Retrieval (SIGIR)*.

Kumar, N.; Belhumeur, P.; and Nayar, S. 2008. Facetracer: A search engine for large collections of images with faces. In *Proceedings of the European Conference on Computer Vision (ECCV)*.

Lampert, C. H.; Nickisch, H.; and Harmeling, S. 2014. Attribute-based classification for zero-shot visual object categorization. *IEEE Transactions on Pattern Analysis and Machine Intelligence*.

Liu, W.; Zamal, F. A.; and Ruths, D. 2012. Using social media to infer gender composition of commuter populations. In *Proceedings of the International AAAI Conference on Weblogs and Social Media (ICWSM) Workshop on When the City Meets the Citizen*.

Liu, W.; Zamal, F. A.; and Ruths, D. 2013. What's in a name? using first names as features for gender inference in twitter. In *Proceedings of the AAAI Spring Symposium*.

Mislove, A.; Lehmann, S.; Ahn, Y.-Y.; Onnela, J.-P.; and Rosenquist, J. N. 2012. Understanding the demographics of twitter users. In *Proceedings of the International AAAI Conference on Weblogs and Social Media (ICWSM)*.

Pennacchiotti, M., and Popescu, A.-M. 2011. A machine learning approach to twitter user classification. In *Proceedings of the International AAAI Conference on Weblogs and Social Media (ICWSM)*.

Sahami, M., and Heilman, T. D. 2006. A web-based kernel function for measuring the similarity of short text snippets. In *Proceedings of the International World Wide Web Conference (WWW)*.

Song, H.; Miao, C.; and Shen, Z. 2011. Generating true relevance labels in chinese search engine using clickthrough data. In *Proceedings of the AAAI Conference on Artificial Intelligence (AAAI)*.

Vaquero, D. A.; Feris, R. S.; Tran, D.; Brown, L.; Hampapur, A.; and Turk, M. 2009. Attribute-based people search in surveillance environments. In *Proceedings of the IEEE Winter Conference on Applications of Computer Vision (WACV)*.

Viola, P., and Jones, M. 2001. Rapid object detection using a boosted cascade of simple features. In *Proceedings of the IEEE Conference on Computer Vision and Pattern Recognition (CVPR)*.

Yao, T.; Mei, T.; Ngo, C.-W.; and Li, S. 2013. Annotation for free: Video tagging by mining user search behavior. In *Proceedings of the ACM International Conference on Multimedia (ACM MM)*.

A New Granger Causal Model for Influence Evolution in Dynamic Social Networks: The Case of DBLP

Belkacem Chikhaoui, Mauricio Chiazzaro, Shengrui Wang
Prospectus Laboratory, Department of Computer Science
University of Sherbrooke, Canada
{belkacem.chikhaoui, mauricio.chiazzaro, shengrui.wang}@usherbrooke.ca

Abstract

This paper addresses a new problem concerning the evolution of influence relationships between communities in dynamic social networks. A weighted temporal multigraph is employed to represent the dynamics of the social networks and analyze the influence relationships between communities over time. To ensure the interpretability of the knowledge discovered, evolution of the influence relationships is assessed by introducing the Granger causality. Through extensive experiments, we empirically demonstrate the suitability of our model for studying the evolution of influence between communities. Moreover, we empirically show how our model is able to accurately predict the influence of communities over time using random forest regression.

Introduction

Users in real-world social networks are organized into communities that are distinguished by number of users, preferences and interests, social influence, etc. (Zhang et al. 2013). Discovering and estimating social influence, with the aim of understanding how users affect each other, is an important research issue that has received considerable attention from the AI research community (Belák, Lam, and Hayes 2012; Mehmood et al. 2013; Zhang et al. 2013). In fact, detecting influential users in social networks and assessing their influence makes it possible to study information propagation in the network, which is very helpful in developing online advertisements, marketing campaigns and recommender systems (Barbieri and Bonchi 2014; Ye, Liu, and Lee 2012).

Much research has been conducted recently on detecting communities and studying influence in social networks (Chen, Wang, and Yang 2009; Leskovec, Lang, and Mahoney 2010). Detecting communities provides insight into the structure of the social network, whereas detecting influential users allows us to understand information dynamics and propagation and network evolution. Different types of influence have been proposed, such as pairwise influence (Goyal, Bonchi, and Lakshmanan 2010; Yin and Zhang 2012), social influence locality (Zhang et al. 2013), community influence (Belák, Lam, and Hayes 2012; Mehmood et al. 2013), topic influence (Liu et al. 2012; 2010; Tang et al. 2009), indirect influence (Kim, Newth, and Christen 2013; Shuai et al. 2012), and external influence (Myers, Zhu, and Leskovec 2012). However, these influence measures have been proposed for the purpose of detecting influential users and are not intended for assessing the influence between communities. Moreover, none of these measures studies the evolution of influence over time. With the rapid growth of social networks, detecting communities without assessing their overall influence in the network is now considered insufficient. This in turn suggests the need to study how communities influence each other and how this influence evolves over time. Finally, studying influence at the community level may reveal many more interesting patterns than merely looking at pairwise influence between users. These points constitute the major rationale for the work reported here.

In this paper, we propose an effective model for analyzing influence evolution in dynamic social networks. A weighted temporal multigraph is employed in order to represent the dynamics of social networks. The evolution of influence between communities is then assessed by incorporating the Granger causality (Granger 1969). Our model also makes it possible to predict the influence between communities using random forest regression. The combination of these methods yields an integrated framework for studying and predicting influence evolution. The major contributions of this paper can be summarized as follows:

1. Proposing an effective model for influence evolution using the Granger causality.

2. Combining weighted temporal multigraphs and the Granger causality for representing dynamic social networks and studying the evolution of inter-community influence.

3. Predicting the influence between communities over time using random forest regression.

The rest of the paper is organized as follows. First, we give an overview of related work in Section 2. Section 3 describes the proposed model in terms of weighted temporal multigraph representation, influence evolution and prediction. The results of our experiments on real social network datasets are presented in Section 4. Finally, Section 5 presents our conclusions.

Related work

In this section we discuss related work in the area of influence detection and assessment. We will focus mainly on influence between communities and its evolution over time.

Much research has been done in the social network field over the last decade. One of the most important areas of research in social networks concerns community detection and influential user extraction (Belák, Lam, and Hayes 2012; Liu et al. 2012; Mehmood et al. 2013; Chen, Wang, and Yang 2009; Zhang et al. 2013). Community detection allows one to pinpoint groups of users with common interests, tastes or goals (Dietz 2009), while influential user extraction allows one to locate those individuals that play a central role in the social network. Such users are those having high values of centrality or betweenness centrality (Kazuya, Wei, and Xiang-yang 2008).

Despite the considerable body of research on community detection, little work has been reported on assessing the influence between communities. Mehmood et al. (Mehmood et al. 2013) propose a community-level social influence measure for assessing the strength of influence between two different communities in directed social networks. Belák et al. (Belák, Lam, and Hayes 2012) propose a framework for cross-community influence analysis in discussion fora. The authors use the in-degree measure to assess the influence. Liu et al. (Liu et al. 2010) propose a topic-level influence in social networks. The authors also propose a method for calculating direct and indirect influence in social networks. Dietz et al. (Dietz, Bickel, and Scheffer 2007) propose an unsupervised prediction of citation influence in publication repositories. However, their model deals with the influence between papers and does not study the influence between communities.

Although existing models study influence between users or communities, none of them provides effective solutions to understand and predict the evolution of influence between communities in dynamic social networks. In this paper, we propose an effective model for studying the evolution of inter-community influence over time. Moreover, we build a method in our model to predict the influence between communities.

Our proposed model

In order to study the evolution of inter-community influence, our model needs a structure capable of representing the dynamics of the social network and displaying its state at each time instant. We resort to a multigraph formalism representation as a means to address this need and facilitate the assessment of influence evolution.

Weighted Temporal Multigraph

With the rapid evolution of social networks and their dynamics, basic graphs are unable to show the different aspects of the network dynamics. For this reason, we adapt the multigraph formalism in order to represent the dynamics of social networks. A multigraph is a graph in which multiple edges are permitted between two nodes. The rationale for using the

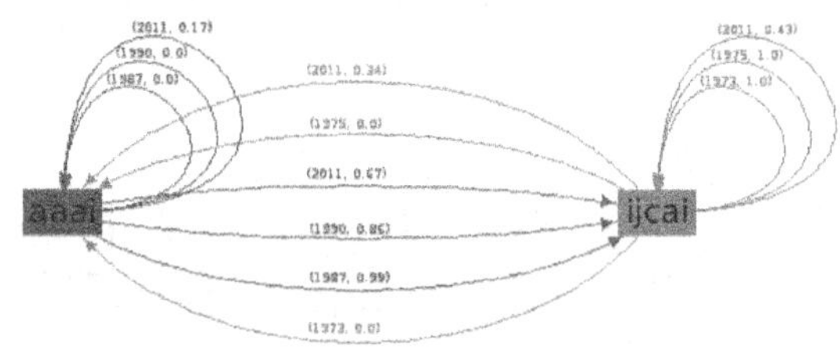

Figure 1: Example of a weighted temporal multigraph showing citation relationships between two communities, AAAI and IJCAI, in the DBLP dataset. Each edge here is marked by the time instant and its weight, the latter being calculated by Equation 1.

multigraph representation is twofold: 1) it allows us to represent the temporal progression of the social network; and 2) it is a good visualization tool for the social network dynamics. In addition, in our model, a node represents a community as a whole and not an individual user, which is an extremely information-rich representation compared to classical graphs. As a result, our model deals with multigraphs of communities, which constitutes a new method of assessing influence evolution.

Given that influence between communities can be quantified and measured, we resort to the weighted temporal multigraph (WTMG) to represent the social network dynamics. A WTMG is a multigraph in which a weight (typically a real number) has been assigned to every edge at a time instant. Formally, we define a weighted temporal multigraph as $G = (V, E, T, W)$, where V is the set of nodes, $E \subseteq V \times T \times V \times W$ denotes a set of edges, T is a finite set of time instants, and W is a real-value function from E to the real numbers $\mathbb{R}^+$. A weighted temporal edge e in G is defined as an ordered quadruple $e = (u, v, t, w)$, where $u, v \in V$, with u possibly equal to v, are the origin and destination nodes, t is the time instant for the node u, and w is the weight of the edge e, which can be written as $w = W(e)$.

Figure 1 shows an example of a weighted multigraph, where the nodes represent two communities of the artificial intelligence discipline, the AAAI and IJCAI conferences.

As shown in Figure 1, the multigraph is a compact representation of graphs evolving over time. A node in a weighted temporal multigraph will have a matrix of influence values between itself and the other nodes at each time instant. The matrix of influence can be reduced to a vector of influence by accumulating and normalizing the influence values with respect to a time instant. As a consequence, each community $u \in G$ can be presented as a chronologically ordered series of influence vectors over time. To illustrate this point, without loss of generality, let the AAAI and IJCAI conferences be two artificial intelligence communities in the graph G of the DBLP dataset. Let the function $W()$ be the number of citations of the papers of one conference by the papers of the other conference for each year. If no citation is reported between the two conferences at a particular time instant, then the edge weight will simply be zero. The Figure 2 illustrates citation relationships between the AAAI and IJCAI communities at different time instants in the DBLP and Arnet Miner

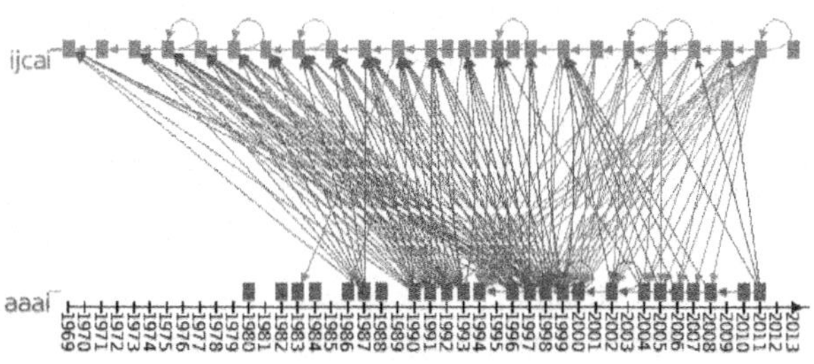

Figure 2: Citation relationships between the two communities AAAI and IJCAI in the DBLP and Arnet Miner datasets.

datasets.

As shown in Figure 2, each pair of nodes will have two chronologically ordered series of influence values over time. For example, at each time instant t_i, a community $u \in G$ will have a certain number of citations $\{N(j \rightarrow u, t_i) | j \in v\}$ of another community $v \in G$. Each community is composed of a certain number of papers. Therefore, a normalized citation weight is computed to represent the citation influence (CI) (Dietz, Bickel, and Scheffer 2007) between the two communities at a particular time instant t_i. Note that the citation influences $u \rightarrow v$ and $v \rightarrow u$ are different and should both be computed using the following formula:

$$CI(u \rightarrow v, t_i) = \frac{\sum_{j \in v} N(j \rightarrow u, t_i)}{M_{v,t_i}}, \quad (1)$$

where $N(j \rightarrow u, t_i)$ represents the number of citations of community u by a paper $j \in v$ at time instant t_i, and M_{v,t_i} represents the number of all citations made by community v from the other communities in graph G at time instant t_i. The citation influence values obtained at each time instant will be used to study the influence evolution, as described in the next section. Table 1 shows the citation influence values computed between the AAAI and IJCAI communities using Equation 1 at different time instants. The labels in Table 1 reflect the year in which an article from one community was published, assuming that article cited the other community articles published in any year (current or previous).

Table 1: $CI(AAAI \rightarrow IJCAI)$ and $CI(IJCAI \rightarrow AAAI)$ values computed using Equation 1.

	1991	**1993**	**1997**	**1999**	**2005**	**2011**
AAAI→IJCAI	0.854	0.947	0.698	0.401	0.055	0.666
IJCAI→AAAI	0.032	0.142	0.416	0.787	0.471	0.335

As shown in Table 1, the value (0.854) of the citation influence AAAI → IJCAI obtained during 1991 can be interpreted as indicating that 85.4 % of the citations made by the IJCAI community are from the AAAI community. Similarly, only 3.2 % of the citations made by the AAAI community are from the IJCAI community.

Influence Evolution Analysis

Influence between communities is a challenging research issue and little work has been reported on detecting the influence between communities. Moreover, studying the evolution of influence in dynamic social networks is a new problem. We propose an effective method for studying the evolution of influence between communities. Our method is based on the use of the Granger causality (Granger 1969) to infer influence evolution.

The rationale for incorporating the Granger causality in assessing influence evolution is twofold. First, it helps develop a more effective model for discovering hidden knowledge from the data. Secondly, it makes the discovered knowledge more interpretable from both the statistical and the semantic standpoints. The Granger causality has gained tremendous success across many domains due to its simplicity, robustness, extendability and it involves no hypothesis about the data (Ioannis, David, and Wan 2000). The Granger causality was initially developed for analyzing the effect of one time series on another. Formally, suppose we have two stationary time series $CI(u \rightarrow v) = \{CI(u \rightarrow v)(t)_{t \in T}\}$ and $CI(v \rightarrow u) = \{CI(v \rightarrow u)(t)_{t \in T}\}$ and we intend to study whether one influences (Granger causes) the other or not. The regression formulation of Granger causality states that $CI(u \rightarrow v)$ influences (Granger causes) $CI(v \rightarrow u)$ if the past values of $CI(u \rightarrow v)$ are helpful in predicting the future values of $CI(v \rightarrow u)$. If there is no influence between the two time series, the null hypothesis holds. The two regression formulas are presented below:

$$H_0 : CI(v \rightarrow u)(t) = \sum_{l=1}^{L} a_l CI(v \rightarrow u)(t-l) + \epsilon_1 \quad (2)$$

$$H_1 : CI(v \rightarrow u)(t) = \sum_{l=1}^{L} a_l CI(v \rightarrow u)(t-l) + \sum_{l=1}^{L} b_l CI(u \rightarrow v)(t-l) + \epsilon_2, \quad (3)$$

where L is the maximal time lag, a_l and b_l are the regression variable coefficients, and ϵ_1 and ϵ_2 are the residual terms, which are independent and identically distributed according to a standard Gaussian $N(0;\sigma^2)$. If Equation 3 is a significantly better model than Equation 2, we conclude that time series $CI(u \rightarrow v)$ Granger causes time series $CI(v \rightarrow u)$. Among other techniques, the models above can be tested using the Granger Sargent test (Granger 1969), defined as follows:

$$F = \frac{(RSS_{\epsilon_1} - RSS_{\epsilon_2})/L}{(RSS_{\epsilon_2})/(n-2L)} \sim F(L, n-2L), \quad (4)$$

where RSS_{ϵ_1} is the "restricted" residual sum of squares under H_0 , RSS_{ϵ_2} is the "unrestricted" residual sum of squares under H_1, and n is the number of observations. The Granger causality is assessed for the two time series $CI(u \rightarrow v)$ and $CI(v \rightarrow u)$ in both directions in order to discover whether the influence between them is bi-directional or uni-directional. Thus, by using the Granger causality principle, we will be able to assess the evolution of the influence between communities at each time instant.

Influence Prediction

Predicting the influence between communities over time involves evaluating the influence that one community might exert on the other at a specific time instant. For instance, what is the predicted value of the influence that community AAAI might exert on community IJCAI during the year 2015? Computing the predicted influence value is challenging. We use a random-forest-based regression method to predict the influence between two communities. Random-forest-based regression has been proved to be effective in terms of prediction accuracy (Khan 2014). Our method utilizes the weighted temporal multigraph state at time t in order to predict the state at $t+1$. It proceeds by first learning the evolution of inter-community influence values and then predicting the future influence between communities using the learned model.

Formally, a random forest is a predictor consisting of a collection of tree-structured predictors $\{h(\mathbf{x}, \Theta_k), k = 1, 2, ..., K\}$, where $\mathbf{x}$ represents the observed input vector of length p with associated random vector $\mathbf{X}$ and Θ_k are independent and identically distributed (iid) random vectors. Each tree $h(\mathbf{x}, \Theta_k)$ is constructed employing a different bootstrap sample of the training dataset, using the algorithm in (Breiman 2001). As we mentioned above, since our goal is to predict the influence between two communities, we focus on the regression aspect for which we have a numerical output, Y (Segal 2004).

A random forest for regression is an unweighted average over the collection $\bar{h}(\mathbf{x}) = (1/K)\sum_{k=1}^{K} h(\mathbf{x}, \Theta_k)$. According to (Segal 2004), as $k \to \infty$, the law of large numbers ensures that the following holds:

$$E_{\mathbf{X},Y}(Y - \bar{h}(\mathbf{X}))^2 \to E_{\mathbf{X},Y}(Y - E_{\Theta}h(\mathbf{X}, \Theta))^2 \quad (5)$$

The quantity $E_{\mathbf{X},Y}(Y - E_{\Theta}h(\mathbf{X}, \Theta))^2$ is the prediction error of the random forest, designated as PE_f^*. The average prediction error for an individual tree $h(\mathbf{X}, \Theta)$ can be computed as follows:

$$PE_{tree}^* = E_{\Theta}E_{\mathbf{X},Y}(Y - h(\mathbf{X}, \Theta))^2 \quad (6)$$

Validation

This section presents the datasets used and discusses the results obtained for the evolution and prediction of influence between communities.

Dataset

To validate our proposed model, we used the DBLP dataset, which contains information about articles, authors, conferences, and dates. However, it does not provide information about citation relationships between papers. We therefore augmented the DBLP dataset with paper citation information by incorporating the Arnet Miner citation network dataset. We merged the two datasets based on the article title to form one complete, rich network dataset. Table 2 shows the details of each dataset.

In our work, we selected well-known research disciplines such as Artificial Intelligence (AI), Data Mining (DM) and Human Computer Interaction (HCI) to validate our proposed model. In each discipline, top-ranked conferences, according to the Microsoft conference ranking system, have been selected as the communities for which influence evolution and prediction are evaluated.

Table 2: Datasets used for validation

	Number of papers	Citations	Date
DBLP	2 712 770	No citations	08-08-2014
Arnet Miner	2 244 021	4 354 534	25-05-2014

Influence Evolution

Influence evolution is assessed between each pair of conferences in each discipline. Before assessing the influence evolution using the Granger causality, we computed all of the citation influences between all conferences at each time instant using formula 1. The values computed for citation influence between communities provide the basis on which the evolution of that influence is assessed using the Granger causality. Figure 3 on the next page shows a graphical representation of the distribution of citations between all communities in the AI and DM disciplines.

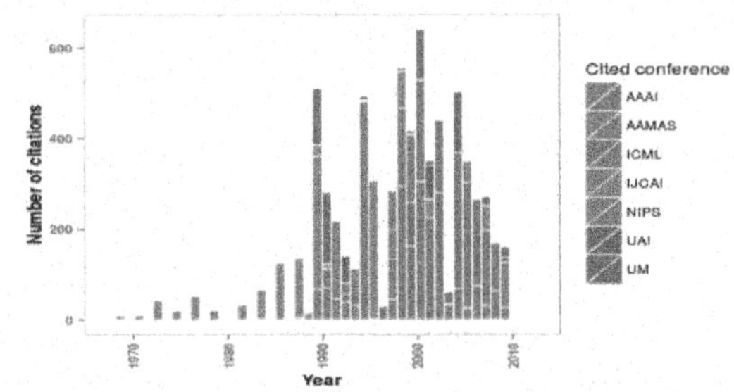

(a) AI

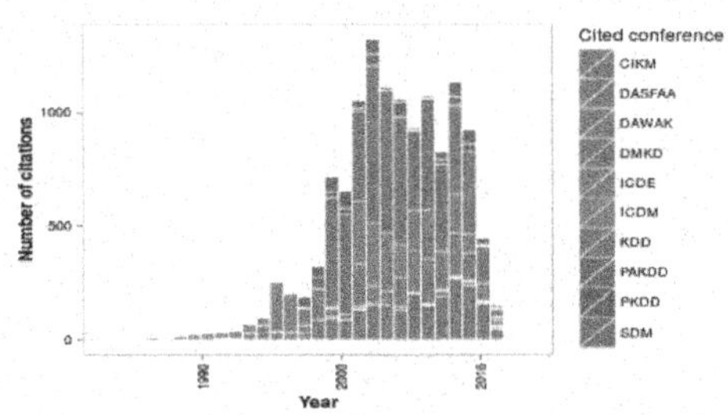

(b) DM

Figure 3: Citation values of communities at each time instant for each discipline.

To assess the influence evolution, we performed two types of validation: 1) a validation using all the citation influence values computed for all time instants, and 2) a validation using citation influence values computed for intervals between time instants to track the influence evolution.

Influence Evolution Using All Time Instants In this validation, we used the citation influence values computed between communities for all time instants. The influence evolution is assessed between each pair of communities. For example, to assess the influence evolution between communities AAAI and IJCAI, we computed the citation influence values using formula 1 for the AAAI community by taking the AAAI $\stackrel{Cites}{\rightarrow}$ IJCAI citations for all time instants (i.e., from 1969 to 2013). Similarly, we computed the citation influence values for the IJCAI community by taking the IJCAI $\stackrel{Cites}{\rightarrow}$ AAAI citations for all time instants.

Once the citation influence vectors have been computed, the Granger causality can be assessed. We computed the F-statistic and P-values in order to assess the Granger causality. Then, based on these results, the direction of influence between each pair of communities is established. Tables 3, 4 and 5 show the influence relationships obtained between each pair of communities for each discipline.

Table 3: Influence relationships obtained for the AI discipline.

	F-value	P-value	Influence direction
AAAI $\stackrel{Cites}{\rightarrow}$ ICML	0.1729	0.6800	
ICML $\stackrel{Cites}{\rightarrow}$ AAAI	**5.4735**	**0.0251**	**AAAI$\longmapsto$ICML**
AAAI $\stackrel{Cites}{\rightarrow}$ IJCAI	**7.0334**	**0.0010**	**IJCAI$\longmapsto$AAAI**
IJCAI $\stackrel{Cites}{\rightarrow}$ AAAI	0.0511	0.9843	
ICML $\stackrel{Cites}{\rightarrow}$ UAI	**4.0914**	**0.0154**	**UAI$\longmapsto$ICML**
UAI $\stackrel{Cites}{\rightarrow}$ ICML	3.1663	0.0392	
UAI $\stackrel{Cites}{\rightarrow}$ IJCAI	**5.4709**	**0.0251**	**IJCAI$\longmapsto$UAI**
IJCAI $\stackrel{Cites}{\rightarrow}$ UAI	4.1302	0.0497	
UM $\stackrel{Cites}{\rightarrow}$ IJCAI	**49.4017**	**1.6462e-10**	**IJCAI$\longmapsto$UM**
IJCAI $\stackrel{Cites}{\rightarrow}$ UM	2.4947	9.8434e-02	

Table 4: Influence relationships obtained for the DM discipline.

	F-value	P-value	Influence direction
CIKM $\stackrel{Cites}{\rightarrow}$ DAWAK	**18.4613**	**0.0001**	**DAWAK$\longmapsto$ CIKM**
DAWAK $\stackrel{Cites}{\rightarrow}$ CIKM	0.2210	0.8046	
CIKM $\stackrel{Cites}{\rightarrow}$ ICDE	**5.4344**	**0.0177**	**ICDE$\longmapsto$ CIKM**
ICDE $\stackrel{Cites}{\rightarrow}$ CIKM	0.7044	0.5708	
DMKD $\stackrel{Cites}{\rightarrow}$ ICDE	**51.6178**	**2.1726e-06**	**ICDE$\longmapsto$ DMKD**
ICDE $\stackrel{Cites}{\rightarrow}$ DMKD	0.0455	8.3364e-01	
DMKD $\stackrel{Cites}{\rightarrow}$ KDD	**6.5576**	**0.0209**	**KDD$\longmapsto$ DMKD**
KDD $\stackrel{Cites}{\rightarrow}$ DMKD	1.7726	0.2017	
DMKD $\stackrel{Cites}{\rightarrow}$ PKDD	**11.1662**	**0.0015**	**PKDD$\longmapsto$ DMKD**
PKDD $\stackrel{Cites}{\rightarrow}$ DMKD	0.1078	0.8985	
KDD $\stackrel{Cites}{\rightarrow}$ DASFAA	**3.9801**	**0.0448**	**DASFAA$\longmapsto$ KDD**
DASFAA $\stackrel{Cites}{\rightarrow}$ KDD	0.6789	0.5242	
PAKDD $\stackrel{Cites}{\rightarrow}$ CIKM	**5.3874**	**0.0182**	**CIKM$\longmapsto$ PAKDD**
CIKM $\stackrel{Cites}{\rightarrow}$ PAKDD	1.7249	0.2247	
PAKDD $\stackrel{Cites}{\rightarrow}$ ICDE	**7.8417**	**0.0058**	**ICDE$\longmapsto$PAKDD**
ICDE $\stackrel{Cites}{\rightarrow}$ PAKDD	0.0764	0.9268	
PAKDD $\stackrel{Cites}{\rightarrow}$ PKDD	**19.4611**	**0.0004**	**PKDD$\longmapsto$ PAKDD**
PKDD $\stackrel{Cites}{\rightarrow}$ PAKDD	0.0227	0.8819	
SDM $\stackrel{Cites}{\rightarrow}$ KDD	**81.9723**	**2.4255e-07**	**KDD$\longmapsto$ SDM**
KDD $\stackrel{Cites}{\rightarrow}$ SDM	0.1208	9.4570e-01	

As shown in tables 3, 4 and 5, our model is able to determine which community of a pair of communities is more influential. For example, in the AI discipline, the re-

Table 5: Influence relationships obtained for the HCI discipline.

	F-value	P-value	Influence direction
CHI $\stackrel{Cites}{\rightarrow}$ HCI	0.2581	0.6160	
HCI $\stackrel{Cites}{\rightarrow}$ CHI	**7.3180**	**0.0123**	**CHI$\longmapsto$ HCI**
CHI $\stackrel{Cites}{\rightarrow}$ HUC	1.4453	0.2410	
HUC $\stackrel{Cites}{\rightarrow}$ CHI	**5.3463**	**0.0296**	**CHI$\longmapsto$ HUC**
CSCW $\stackrel{Cites}{\rightarrow}$ IUI	1.4379	0.2421	
IUI $\stackrel{Cites}{\rightarrow}$ CSCW	**9.3921**	**0.0053**	**CSCW$\longmapsto$ IUI**
CSCW $\stackrel{Cites}{\rightarrow}$ UIST	1.1675	0.2906	
UIST $\stackrel{Cites}{\rightarrow}$ CSCW	**7.2489**	**0.0127**	**CSCW$\longmapsto$ UIST**
ECSCW $\stackrel{Cites}{\rightarrow}$ HUC	**4.0247**	**0.0331**	**HUC$\longmapsto$ ECSCW**
HUC $\stackrel{Cites}{\rightarrow}$ ECSCW	0.2218	0.8028	
HCI $\stackrel{Cites}{\rightarrow}$ HUC	0.1673	0.6860	
HUC $\stackrel{Cites}{\rightarrow}$ HCI	**13.8550**	**0.0010**	**HCI$\longmapsto$ HUC**
HUC $\stackrel{Cites}{\rightarrow}$ IUI	1.5109	0.2437	
IUI $\stackrel{Cites}{\rightarrow}$ HUC	**5.6946**	**0.0105**	**HUC$\longmapsto$ IUI**
HUC $\stackrel{Cites}{\rightarrow}$ UIST	**5.9564**	**0.0089**	**UIST$\longmapsto$ HUC**
UIST $\stackrel{Cites}{\rightarrow}$ HUC	0.2873	0.7531	
ISWC $\stackrel{Cites}{\rightarrow}$ IUI	**4.9097**	**0.0178**	**IUI$\longmapsto$ ISWC**
IUI $\stackrel{Cites}{\rightarrow}$ ISWC	0.2254	0.8000	

sults show that the AAAI community significantly influences the ICML community, based on the F-values ($5.4735 > 0.1729$) and P-values ($0.0251 < 0.6800$) computed for ICML $\stackrel{Cites}{\rightarrow}$ AAAI and AAAI $\stackrel{Cites}{\rightarrow}$ ICML respectively. Therefore, the AAAI community can be considered as an influential community in the AI discipline. Consequently, one of the potentials of our model is the ability to detect influential communities using the Granger causality tests. To this end, we propose the following definition for an influential community:

Definition 1 *Let $CI(u \rightarrow v)$ and $CI(v \rightarrow u)$ be two citation influence vectors. Community u is influential if $CI(u \rightarrow v)$ Granger causes $CI(v \rightarrow u)$, and the P-value $\leq \epsilon$*

For example, if $\epsilon = 0.03$, the communities IJCAI, AAAI and UAI can be considered as influential communities in the AI discipline. The same observations can be generalized for the DM and HCI disciplines. We choose $\epsilon = 0.03$ to indicate that the results are highly significant. The communities KDD, ICDE, DAWAK, PKDD and CIKM are thus the influential communities in the DM discipline. Similarly, the communities CHI, HCI, CSCW, HUC, UIST and IUI are the influential communities in the HCI discipline.

Influence Evolution Using Time Intervals The purpose of this validation is to show how the influence between communities evolves over time. To this end, we computed the Granger causality between each pair of communities for different time intervals. For example, for the AI discipline, we computed the Granger causality for the intervals 1969 to 2009 and 1969 to 2010 (the influence results for the time interval 1969 to 2011 are presented in Table 3). The results obtained allow us to understand how the influence between communities evolves from the first time interval to the last. Tables 6 and 7 show the results obtained for the influence between each pair of communities in the AI discipline for each time interval.

Table 6: Influence results obtained for the AI discipline for the time interval 1969 to 2009.

	F-value	P-value	Influence direction
AAAI $\overset{Cites}{\rightarrow}$ ICML	0.2402	0.6272	
ICML $\overset{Cites}{\rightarrow}$ AAAI	**4.5101**	**0.0412**	**AAAI⟼ICML**
AAAI $\overset{Cites}{\rightarrow}$ IJCAI	**7.9633**	**0.0016**	**IJCAI⟼AAAI**
IJCAI $\overset{Cites}{\rightarrow}$ AAAI	0.0711	0.9315	
ICML $\overset{Cites}{\rightarrow}$ UAI	0.2567	6.1576e-01	
UAI $\overset{Cites}{\rightarrow}$ ICML	**29.7501**	**4.8242e-06**	**ICML⟼UAI**
UAI $\overset{Cites}{\rightarrow}$ IJCAI	**5.9411**	**0.0203**	**IJCAI⟼UAI**
IJCAI $\overset{Cites}{\rightarrow}$ UAI	4.3208	0.0454	
UM $\overset{Cites}{\rightarrow}$ IJCAI	**57.9152**	**5.0014e-11**	**IJCAI⟼UM**
IJCAI $\overset{Cites}{\rightarrow}$ UM	5.0955	1.2441e-02	
AAAI $\overset{Cites}{\rightarrow}$ UAI	1.3887	0.2675	
UAI $\overset{Cites}{\rightarrow}$ AAAI	**3.4245**	**0.0312**	**AAAI⟼UAI**

Table 7: Influence results obtained for the AI discipline for the time interval 1969 to 2010.

	F-value	P-value	Influence direction
AAAI $\overset{Cites}{\rightarrow}$ ICML	0.3087	0.5821	
ICML $\overset{Cites}{\rightarrow}$ AAAI	**5.0843**	**0.0306**	**AAAI⟼ICML**
AAAI $\overset{Cites}{\rightarrow}$ IJCAI	**8.2204**	**0.0013**	**IJCAI⟼AAAI**
IJCAI $\overset{Cites}{\rightarrow}$ AAAI	0.0453	0.9557	
ICML $\overset{Cites}{\rightarrow}$ UAI	**23.4571**	**6.2522e-07**	**UAI⟼ICML**
UAI $\overset{Cites}{\rightarrow}$ ICML	5.3754	9.9034e-03	
UAI $\overset{Cites}{\rightarrow}$ IJCAI	**5.4526**	**0.0255**	**IJCAI⟼UAI**
IJCAI $\overset{Cites}{\rightarrow}$ UAI	3.9706	0.0543	
UM $\overset{Cites}{\rightarrow}$ IJCAI	**59.9145**	**2.2366e-11**	**IJCAI⟼UM**
IJCAI $\overset{Cites}{\rightarrow}$ UM	5.2113	1.1191e-02	

The results reported in Tables 6 and 7 clearly show how the influence values change between communities at each time interval. For example, for ICML$\overset{Cites}{\rightarrow}$AAAI, the F-value increased from 4.5101 in 2009, to 5.0843 in 2010, to 5.4735 in 2011. Similarly, the P-value decreased from 0.0412 in 2009, to 0.0306 in 2010, to 0.0251 in 2011. This means that the community AAAI is gaining influence for the ICML community. An important observation can be made for UAI$\overset{Cites}{\rightarrow}$ICML. Indeed, the F-value decreased from 29.7501 in 2009 to 5.3754 in 2010. Similarly, the P-value increased from $4.8242e-06$ in 2009 to $9.9034e-03$ in 2010. This variation indicates a change in the direction of the influence between the two communities: i.e., in 2009, **ICML $\longmapsto$ UAI**, while in 2010, **UAI $\longmapsto$ ICML**. The influence direction **ICML $\longmapsto$ UAI** established in 2009 has been re-established again in 2011, as shown in Table 3. This example clearly demonstrates that our model is able to study and analyze the evolution of influence between communities. Table 6 also shows that the AAAI community influences the UAI community (**AAAI⟼UAI**) in 2009. However, this influence relationship no longer holds in 2010 (F-value = 0.5400, P-value = 0.4674) and 2011 (F-value = 0.3067, P-value = 0.5831).

Influence Prediction

An influence prediction is calculated for each pair of communities, and the results are averaged for each discipline. We used ten-fold cross-validation for training and test. We computed the Correlation Coefficient (CC), the Mean Absolute Error (MAE) and the Root Mean Squared Error (RMSE) in order to measure the accuracy of our model. For comparison purposes, we used two other regression models, the linear regression model and the multilayer perceptron model, to highlight the suitability and performance of our random forest regression model compared with the two other models. The rational of using these methods is that the linear regression is considered as the reference regression model, and the multilayer perceptron is the most commonly used model for comparing regression methods given its performance and reliability. Table 8 shows the results obtained for the three models.

Table 8: Influence prediction results by discipline using RF(Random Forest), LR(Linear Regression) and MP(Multilayer Perceptron).

	AI			DM			HCI		
	CC	MAE	RMSE	CC	MAE	RMSE	CC	MAE	RMSE
RF	**0.811**	**0.068**	**0.138**	**0.876**	**0.042**	**0.090**	**0.950**	**0.024**	**0.062**
LR	0.618	0.107	0.188	0.816	0.055	0.107	0.927	0.0317	0.075
MP	0.712	0.127	0.180	0.799	0.061	0.116	0.906	0.051	0.089

As shown in Table 8, our model achieves the highest coefficient of correlation of the three models. Moreover, our model results in lower prediction error than the others. This demonstrates the efficiency of our model and its suitability for predicting the influence between communities.

Conclusion

In this paper we have investigated a new problem concerning the evolution of influence between communities in dynamic social networks. We have proposed a new model, based on the Granger causality, for studying influence evolution. Our model utilizes a weighted temporal multigraph to represent the dynamics of the social network. The evolution of inter-community influence was studied by incorporating the Granger causality and utilizing the influence values computed between communities at each time instant. We have also proposed a method based on random forest regression to predict the influence between communities.

We have illustrated the effectiveness and suitability of our model through extensive experiments on the DBLP dataset. The experimental results demonstrate that our model is able to study influence evolution over time and that it can accurately predict the influence between communities by minimizing the prediction error.

It will be interesting in the future to conduct more experiments using other dynamic social networks such as Facebook, Youtube and Twitter, and study the evolution of the influence between online communities.

References

Barbieri, N., and Bonchi, F. 2014. Influence maximization with viral product design. In *SDM*.

Belák, V.; Lam, S.; and Hayes, C. 2012. Cross-community influence in discussion fora. In *ICWSM*.

Breiman, L. 2001. Random forests. *Mach. Learn.* 45(1):5–32.

Chen, W.; Wang, Y.; and Yang, S. 2009. Efficient influence maximization in social networks. In *Proceedings of the 15th ACM SIGKDD International Conference on Knowledge Discovery and Data Mining*, KDD '09, 199–208. New York, NY, USA: ACM.

Dietz, L.; Bickel, S.; and Scheffer, T. 2007. Unsupervised prediction of citation influences. In *Proceedings of the 24th International Conference on Machine Learning*, ICML '07, 233–240. New York, NY, USA: ACM.

Dietz, L. 2009. Modeling shared tastes in online communities. In *NIPS Workshop on Applications for Topic Models: Text and Beyond*.

Goyal, A.; Bonchi, F.; and Lakshmanan, L. V. 2010. Learning influence probabilities in social networks. In *Proceedings of the Third ACM International Conference on Web Search and Data Mining*, WSDM '10, 241–250. New York, NY, USA: ACM.

Granger, C. W. J. 1969. Investigating causal relations by econometric models and cross-spectral methods. *Econometrica* 37(3):424–438.

Ioannis, A.; David, A.; and Wan, M. M. 2000. Non-linear granger causality in the currency futures returns. *Economics Letters* 68(1):25 – 30.

Kazuya, O.; Wei, C.; and Xiang-yang, L. 2008. Ranking of closeness centrality for large-scale social networks. In *Frontiers in Algorithmics*, 186–195.

Khan, I. 2014. Bias-corrected quantile regression forests for high-dimensional data. In *Proceedings of the 13th International Conference on Machine Learning and Cybernetics*. IEEE.

Kim, M.; Newth, D.; and Christen, P. 2013. Modeling direct and indirect influence across heterogeneous social networks. In *Proceedings of the 7th Workshop on Social Network Mining and Analysis*, SNAKDD '13, 9:1–9:9. New York, NY, USA: ACM.

Leskovec, J.; Lang, K. J.; and Mahoney, M. 2010. Empirical comparison of algorithms for network community detection. In *Proceedings of the 19th International Conference on World Wide Web*, WWW '10, 631–640. New York, NY, USA: ACM.

Liu, L.; Tang, J.; Han, J.; Jiang, M.; and Yang, S. 2010. Mining topic-level influence in heterogeneous networks. In *Proceedings of the 19th ACM International Conference on Information and Knowledge Management*, CIKM '10, 199–208. New York, NY, USA: ACM.

Liu, L.; Tang, J.; Han, J.; and Yang, S. 2012. Learning influence from heterogeneous social networks. *Data Mining and Knowledge Discovery* 25(3):511–544.

Mehmood, Y.; Barbieri, N.; Bonchi, F.; and Ukkonen, A. 2013. Csi: Community-level social influence analysis. In *ECML/PKDD (2)*, 48–63.

Myers, S. A.; Zhu, C.; and Leskovec, J. 2012. Information diffusion and external influence in networks. In *Proceedings of the 18th ACM SIGKDD International Conference on Knowledge Discovery and Data Mining*, KDD '12, 33–41. New York, NY, USA: ACM.

Segal, M. R. 2004. Machine learning benchmarks and random forest regression. Technical report, Center for Bioinformatics & Molecular Biostatistics. UC San Francisco.

Shuai, X.; Ying, D.; Jerome, B.; Shanshan, C.; Yuyin, S.; and Jie, T. 2012. Modeling indirect influence on twitter. *IJSWIS* 8(4):20–36.

Tang, J.; Sun, J.; Wang, C.; and Yang, Z. 2009. Social influence analysis in large-scale networks. In *Proceedings of the 15th ACM SIGKDD International Conference on Knowledge Discovery and Data Mining*, KDD '09, 807–816. New York, NY, USA: ACM.

Ye, M.; Liu, X.; and Lee, W.-C. 2012. Exploring social influence for recommendation: A generative model approach. In *Proceedings of the 35th International ACM SIGIR Conference on Research and Development in Information Retrieval*, SIGIR '12, 671–680. New York, NY, USA: ACM.

Yin, Z., and Zhang, Y. 2012. Measuring pair-wise social influence in microblog. In *Privacy, Security, Risk and Trust (PASSAT), 2012 International Conference on and 2012 International Confernece on Social Computing (SocialCom)*, 502–507.

Zhang, J.; Liu, B.; Tang, J.; Chen, T.; and Li, J. 2013. Social influence locality for modeling retweeting behaviors. In *Proceedings of the Twenty-Third International Joint Conference on Artificial Intelligence*, IJCAI'13, 2761–2767. AAAI Press.

Proceedings of the Twenty-Ninth AAAI Conference on Artificial Intelligence

An Axiomatic Approach to Link Prediction

Sara Cohen and **Aviv Zohar**
Rachel and Selim Benin School of Computer Science and Engineering,
Hebrew University of Jerusalem,
Jerusalem, Israel
{sara, avivz}@cs.huji.ac.il

Abstract

Link prediction functions are important tools that are used to predict the evolution of a network, to locate hidden or surprising links, and to recommend new connections that should be formed. Multiple link prediction functions have been developed in the past. However, their evaluation has mostly been based on experimental work, which has shown that the quality of a link prediction function varies significantly depending on the input domain. There is currently very little understanding of why and how a specific link prediction function works well for a particular domain. The underlying foundations of a link prediction function are often left informal—each function contains implicit assumptions about the dynamics of link formation, and about structural properties that result from these dynamics.

We draw upon the motivation used in characterizations of ranking algorithms, as well as other celebrated results from social choice, and present an axiomatic basis for link prediction. This approach seeks to deconstruct each function into basic axioms, or properties, that make explicit its underlying assumptions. Our framework uses "property templates" that can be considered as general choices made by a function designer, such as what score is assigned to a 2-vertex graph, which vertices are irrelevant to the score, how removing edges or contracting vertices affects the score, and more. Using this framework, we fully characterize four well known link prediction functions and show that they are in fact derived from different variants of a single basic set of property templates.

1 Introduction

Link prediction functions are widely used in a variety of fields where complex networks are naturally studied. Uses range from applications in social networks to discover hidden or surprising connections and to suggest possible "friends" to users, through collaborative filtering (Huang, Li, and Chen 2005), scientific collaboration networks, biological and chemical networks, and more.

Several link prediction functions exist, each inspired by different underlying principles of network formation and creation (Leskovec et al. 2008; Qiu, He, and Yen 2011). Such functions have mostly been evaluated empirically, and have usually been found to work well in practice on specific data sets, while performing less favorably on others (Liben-Nowell and Kleinberg 2007). This is not surprising given that different dynamics often take part in the formation of networks from diverse domains. However, this also means that given a specific domain, there is currently no way to predict which functions are likely to work well over this domain. Some attempts have been made to train functions (Al Hasan et al. 2006) in order to automatically choose a well-performing function.

Except for a few notable exceptions (e.g. (Sarkar, Chakrabarti, and Moore 2011)), most link prediction functions do not have strong theoretical underpinnings, and it is not always clear which properties they uphold. In this work, we apply an *axiomatic approach* to the characterization of link prediction functions, in an attempt to formalize their underlying assumptions and basic components. This can be helpful in the future in determining whether a specific function would be a good choice for a specific domain (by seeing whether the underlying assumptions are compatible), and can also be useful as a starting point for defining new link prediction functions.

The axiomatic approach has been widely used in the context of social choice, including celebrated results such as Arrow's impossibility result (Arrow 1951), and the Gibbard-Satterthwaite theorem (Gibbard 1973; Satterthwaite 1975). Axiomatic treatments of this flavor, that expose deep impossibilities, show us the limits of what voting rules and preference aggregation can achieve: certain sets of desirable properties (or axioms) cannot all be satisfied within a single voting rule. Compromises must therefore be made when choosing which rule to use.

A second flavor of axiomatization is to find characterization results for algorithms or rules (e.g., axiomatization of the Shapley value in cooperative game theory (Shapley 1953)). Such characterizations show how a set of properties uniquely determines the rule or algorithm to be used, implying again that any property not already satisfied by the algorithm will not be added without the loss of another.

A clear progression from these classic results extends to the domain of other algorithms that rank, for example, ranking the vertices in a graph in order to determine their centrality or "importance". Such is the case with the PageRank algorithm, that was originally constructed to rank individual pages in the web-graph to aid in finding relevant search results. An axiomatic treatment for PageRank was given in (Altman and Tennenholtz 2005). Other similar works include axiomatizations of selection from within the electorate, which is also formalized in a graph structure (Alon et al. 2011), personalized ranking systems that rank vertices differently from the perspective of the ranker (which is yet another node in the graph) (Altman and Tennenholtz 2010), tie strength in social networks (Gupte and Eliassi-Rad 2012), and trust based recommendation systems (Andersen et al. 2008). Finally, work has also been performed on axiomatic treatments of collaborative filtering (Pennock et al. 2000).

Our own work focuses, for the first time, on axiomatizations of link prediction functions. In contrast to previous work, these functions do not rank vertices, but rather pairs of vertices (potential edges), in order to ascertain which ones are likely to exist or to appear in the graph. As is standard, we use link prediction functions that provide a numerical score to each such pair. This, in turn, implies a ranking of vertices that is generated by sorting all pairs by their scores.

The main contributions of our paper are as follows:

- We present a set of axioms (properties), in the format of "templates," allowing us to express natural and intuitive properties over specific types of graphs. Our axioms have a plug-and-play flavor, in that they can be instantiated in different manners, depending on the desired ranking properties. For example, an irrelevance property is defined using a function that trims away irrelevant portions of the graph that do not affect the score for a pair of vertices. Choosing different instantiations changes the property but maintains its primary function: to focus attention on the part of the graph that is influential and to specify which parts are not. We include a brief description of the intuition behind each axiom along with its definition.
- We show that different subsets of axioms can be used to fully characterize standard link prediction functions. Thus, while our axioms ostensibly consider limited types of graphs, they imply ranking functions over arbitrary graphs. In particular, we fully characterize four standard link prediction functions, namely, hitting time, the Katz score (Katz 1953), shortest path and reliability.

2 Formal Framework

Graphs. In the following, G denotes a simple directed graph (with no self-edges), with vertices V_G and edges E_G. We use $\Gamma^i_G(v)$ and $\Gamma^o_G(v)$ to denote the set of incoming and outgoing neighbors, respectively, of v. We denote $\Gamma_G(v) = \Gamma^i_G(v) \cup \Gamma^o_G(v)$. We say that v is a *source* if $\Gamma^i_G(v) = \emptyset$ and a *sink* if $\Gamma^o_G(v) = \emptyset$.

We will sometimes also consider graphs with weights on the vertices and edges. Intuitively, a vertex weight $\nu_G(v)$ is used to indicate properties of v, such as its importance or its likelihood of failure. An edge weight $\varepsilon_G(u, v)$ is used to represent properties such as the closeness of the relationship between u and v or the probability of using this relationship when disseminating information.

We will say that G has *independent probabilistic* edge weights if $0 \leq \varepsilon_G(u, v) \leq 1$ for all $(u, v) \in E_G$. We will say that G has *normalized probabilistic* edge weights if *(1)* $0 \leq \varepsilon_G(u, v) \leq 1$ for all u, v, and *(2)* for all u it holds that $\sum_{v \in \Gamma^o_G(u)} \varepsilon_G(u, v) = 1$. Intuitively, the former is used to allow each edge to be chosen independently of the others, while the latter models a probability distribution over outgoing edges.

Link Prediction Functions. *Link prediction functions* associate pairs of vertices in a graph with a number that indicates how likely it is for a link to form (or to exist) between these vertices. Some functions use lower values to infer a greater likelihood, while others use greater values. We use $\mathbb{R}_+$ to denote the non-negative real numbers, and $\mathbb{R}^\top_+$ to denote $\mathbb{R}_+ \cup \{\top\}$, where $\top$ is a special symbol, such that for all $c \in \mathbb{R}^\top_+$, we have $c + \top = \top + c = c \cdot \top = \top \cdot c = \top$, as well as $\min\{c, \top\} = c$ and $\max\{c, \top\} = \top$.

A *link prediction function* f associates every triple G, u, v, where $u, v \in V_G$, with a value in $\mathbb{R}^\top_+$. If $f(G, u, v) \neq \top$, we say that f is *finite* with respect to G, u, v. Otherwise, we say that f is *infinite* with respect to G, u, v. We use *fin*(f) to denote the (possibly infinite) set of triples for which $f(G, u, v)$ is finite.

We demonstrate the notion of a link prediction function with several well-known examples.

Function 2.1 (Weighted Distance). *One simple method to predict links from u to v in G is simply by examining the shortest weighted distance from u to v, denoted* $\mathrm{wdist}(G, u, v)$. *Note that if v is not reachable from u, the value $\top$ is returned, and also note that a lower value indicates that a link is more likely to form.*

Function 2.2 (Reliability). *Another method for predicting links is based on the notion of* network reliability. *Each vertex v and each edge e is associated with an independent probability of non-failure $\nu_G(v)$ and $\varepsilon_G(e)$, respectively. Note that G has independent probabilistic edge weights. Then, we can measure the likelihood of a link from u to v simply by computing the probability that a path exists from u to v, when u does not fail, i.e.,*

$$\mathrm{rlbty}(G, u, v) = P(v \textit{ is reachable from } u \mid u \textit{ did not fail}) .$$

This function gives greater likelihood to link formation when it returns higher values.

Function 2.3 (Katz). *The* Katz measure *(Katz 1953) is a well-known method of measuring the closeness of a pair of vertices u and v in a graph G, and is used for link prediction:*[1]

$$\mathrm{katz}^\beta(G, u, v) = \sum_{l=0}^{\infty} \beta^l \cdot |\mathrm{Paths}^l(G, u, v)| \tag{1}$$

where $\mathrm{Paths}^l(G, u, v)$ *is the set of paths of length precisely l from u to v in G, and $0 < \beta < 1$. The parameter β is used to give lower weight to paths that are longer.*

[1] A more standard formulation of Katz has the summation starting at paths of length one. To simplify the exposition, we use the given version, with the summation starting at paths of length zero. We note, however, that it is straightforward to adapt our results to summations starting at one.

Note that katz^β *may be undefined for pairs of vertices* u, v *in a graph* G. *In particular, this occurs when the summation does not converge, in which case we define* $\mathrm{katz}^\beta(G, u, v) = \top$. *We note that these cases can easily be characterized, in the following fashion (Liben-Nowell and Kleinberg 2007). Let* G *be a graph, and* u, v *be vertices in* G. *Let* $G^{u,v}$ *be the subgraph of* G *containing* u, v, *and precisely those vertices and edges that participate in some path from* u *to* v. *Let* $A^{u,v}$ *be the adjacency matrix for* $G^{u,v}$ *and* $I^{u,v}$ *be the identity matrix with the same dimension as* $A^{u,v}$. *Then, it is well known that* $\mathrm{katz}^\beta(G, u, v) \neq \top$ *if and only if* $I^{u,v} - \beta A^{u,v}$ *is invertible, i.e.,*

$$fin(\mathrm{katz}^\beta) = \{(G, u, v) \mid I^{u,v} - \beta A^{u,v} \text{ is invertible}\}.$$

Moreover, if $(G, u, v) \in fin(\mathrm{katz}^\beta)$, *then the matrix*

$$K = (I^{u,v} - \beta A^{u,v})^{-1} \tag{2}$$

satisfies that $K_{i,j} = \mathrm{katz}^\beta(G, v_i, v_j)$, *where* v_i *and* v_j *are the* i*-th and* j*-th vertices in* $G^{u,v}$. [2]

Function 2.4 (Hitting Time). Hitting time *is another well known link prediction function. Intuitively, a random walk starting at vertex* u *iteratively moves to a neighbor chosen uniformly at random. The hitting time* $\mathrm{hit}(G, u, v)$ *from* u *to* v *is the expected number of steps required for a random walk starting at* u *to first reach* v. *A slightly more expressive version of hitting time, which we will use in this paper, considers weighted graphs with probabilities associated with edges, i.e., graphs have normalized probabilistic edge weights. A random walk now chooses a neighbor* w *of* u *at random, with probability* $\varepsilon_G(u, w)$.

We say that v *is* strongly reachable *from* u *in* G, *written* $u \rightsquigarrow_G v$, *if for every node* w *that is reachable from* u *without traversing* v, *it holds that* v *is reachable from* w. *Intuitively, if* $u \rightsquigarrow_G v$, *then every path starting at* u *can eventually reach* v.

It is immediately obvious that

- *If* $u \not\rightsquigarrow_G v$, *then the hitting time from* u *to* v *is not finite, written* $\mathrm{hit}(G, u, v) = \top$.
- *Otherwise,* $\mathrm{hit}(G, u, v)$ *is*

$$\begin{cases} 0 & u = v \\ 1 + \sum_{w \in \Gamma_G^o(u)} \varepsilon_G(u, w) \cdot \mathrm{hit}(G, w, v) & u \neq v \end{cases}$$

3 Link Prediction Axioms

In this paper, we will focus on *axioms* (also called *properties*) that link prediction functions may satisfy. These axioms typically consider special cases of graphs, and specify how to compute a link prediction function based on a reduction to a smaller (or simpler) graph. Interestingly, we will show that although the axioms only explicitly deal with special cases, they can often completely characterize the behavior of a link prediction function on an arbitrary graph. This characterization by means of special cases allows a deeper understanding of the underlying principles of various functions, and can also be a source of inspiration for additional functions.

In the following f is a link prediction function. We will consider graphs G for which both ν_G and ε_G are defined.

Pair Graphs. We first focus on graphs G containing only a pair of vertices u, v, and either a single edge from u to v, or no edge at all. We call G a *pair graph.* The Pair Graph property defines the scoring function for the simplest non-trivial case, and so imbues meaning to the edge and vertex weights, as well as to the existence of an edge.

Suppose there is an edge from u to v. In this case, it is natural to use the likelihood of taking edge (u, v), along with the value of the vertex v, to define $f(G, u, v)$. On the other hand, if there is no edge in G, then there is no indication in the graph that a link should form from u to v. In this case, $f(G, u, v)$ is given the worst possible score. We observe that the notion of a "worst" possible score can differ from function to function, as there are those for which higher scores indicate greater likelihood, while there are those who behave in the opposite manner. Therefore, the following property is parameterized by a value $\Box \in \mathbb{R}_+^\top$ representing this worst possible score.

Property 1. PAIR GRAPH: ($\Box$-PG). *We say that* f *satisfies the* $\Box$-PG property *if whenever* G *is a pair graph,*

$$f(G, u, v) = \begin{cases} \varepsilon_G(u, v) \cdot \nu_G(v) & (u, v) \in E_G \\ \Box & E_G = \emptyset \end{cases}$$

Alternatives for Source Vertices. We now consider the special case in which we are interested in computing $f(G, u, v)$ when u is a source vertex. This case essentially defines the meaning of alternative edges emanating from the source vertex. Is the best score among the different routes chosen (as in the case of a message taking the shortest path to its destination)? Or is a weighted combination of scores considered (for example in case of an undirected message travelling at random)?

We will provide two different properties that are used to model functions in which edge weights are normalized, or are arbitrary.

Suppose that $w \in \Gamma_G^o(u)$. We use G_w to denote the graph derived by *(1)* removing all outgoing edges from u, other than (u, w) *(2)* defining ν_{G_w} to be equal to ν_G, and *(3)* defining ε_{G_w} to be equal to ε_G. We call G_w the *same probability* alternative graph for G, u, w.

We say that G'_w is the *propagated probability* alternative graph for G, u, w, if G'_w is defined in the same manner as G_w, except that we have $\varepsilon_{G'_w}(u, w) = 1$. Intuitively, G'_w represents the graph in which we have "chosen" to use some edge (u, w) to reach v from u, and, hence, the probability is modified. Figure 1 (a) demonstrates these graph transformations.

The following properties express $f(G, u, v)$ as a function of same probability or propagated probability alternative graphs. Since there are many different useful ways in which these values can be combined to derive $f(G, u, v)$,

[2] Since the standard formation of Katz sums paths starting from length one, this formula appears in the literature as $(I - \beta A)^{-1} - I$.

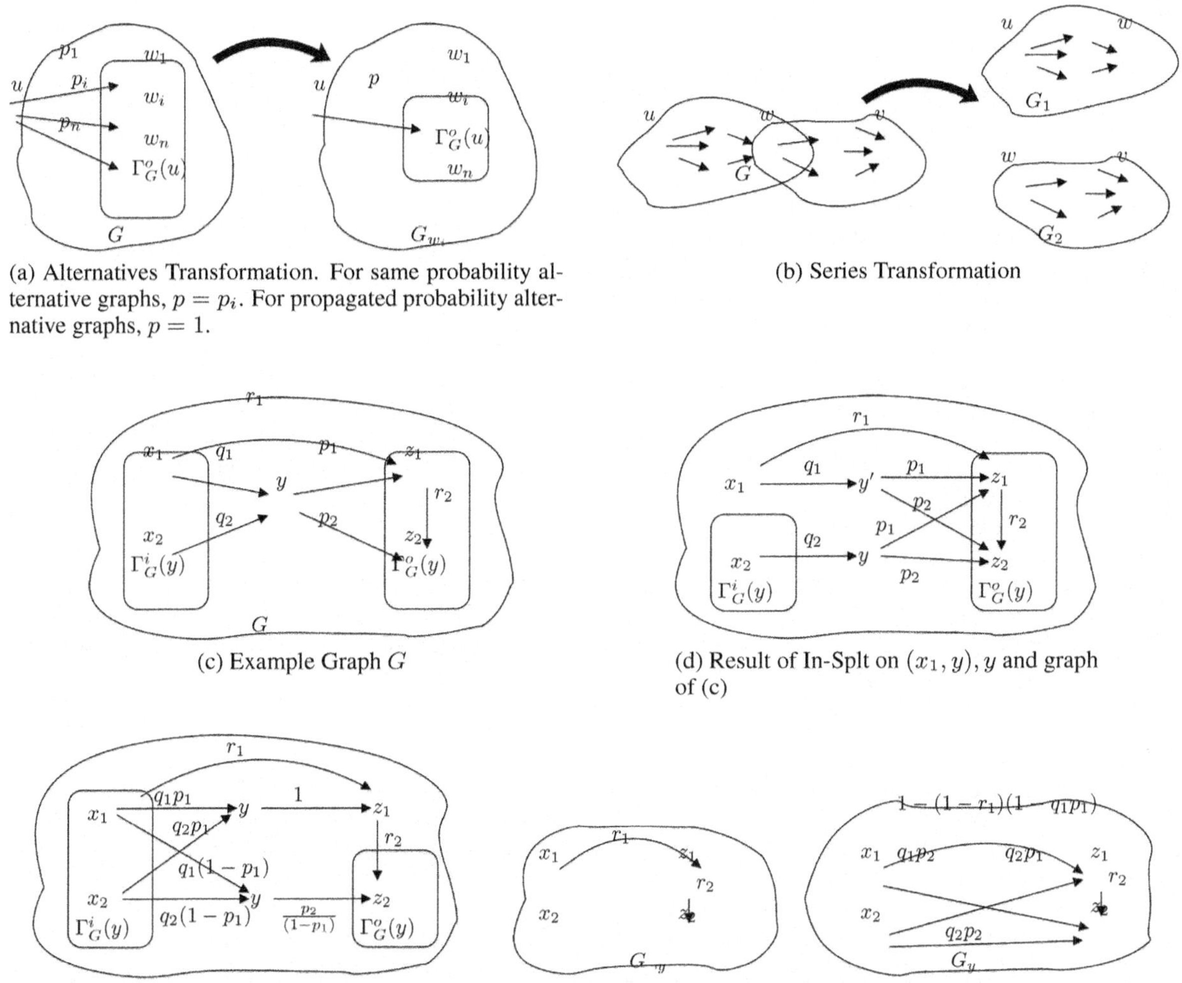

(a) Alternatives Transformation. For same probability alternative graphs, $p = p_i$. For propagated probability alternative graphs, $p = 1$.

(b) Series Transformation

(c) Example Graph G

(d) Result of In-Splt on $(x_1, y), y$ and graph of (c)

(e) Result of PropOut-Splt on $(y, z_1), y$ and graph of (c)

(f) Result of RemV on graph of (c) with y

Figure 1: Illustration of Properties.

our properties are parameterized by an aggregate function α. (An aggregate function receives a set of values and returns a single value.)

Property 2. ALTERNATIVE GRAPHS: (α-SAMEALT, α-PROPALT). *We say that f satisfies the α-*SameAlt property *if whenever u is a source vertex in G, then*

$$f(G, u, v) = \alpha(\{f(G_w, u, v) \mid w \in \Gamma^o_G(v)\}),$$

where G_w is the same probability alternative graph for G, u, w.

*We say that f satisfies the α-*PropAlt property *if whenever u is a source vertex in G, then*

$$f(G, u, v) = \alpha(\{\varepsilon_G(u, w) \cdot f(G_w, u, v) \mid w \in \Gamma^o_G(v)\}),$$

where G_w is the propagated probability alternative graph for G, u, w.

Series Graphs. Sometimes it is possible to split a graph G with vertices u, v into two graphs connected in sequence through a single vertex. Decomposing the graph in this way reveals the effect of chaining graphs (and paths). Does the likelihood of a connection decay as distance is added, such as in the case of rumor travelling in a social network? Is the effect additive or multiplicative?

Formally, let G_1 and G_2 be graphs such that:

- u is in G_1 and v is in G_2;
- there is a single vertex w in both G_1 and G_2, and w is a sink in G_1 or a source in G_2.

When w is a sink (source) in G_1, we will say that G_1 and G_2 are *w-sink (w-source) series* graphs *covering G, u, v.*

Since w is, in essence, a single point of division between u and v, it is natural to express $f(G, u, v)$ as a function of $f(G_1, u, w)$ and $f(G_2, w, v)$. Different such functions can be useful, and thus, the following properties are parameterized by a binary operation $\oplus$.

Property 3. SINK (SOURCE) SERIES: ($\oplus$-SNK, $\oplus$-SRC).

We say that f satisfies the $\oplus$-Snk property *(resp. the* $\oplus$-Src property*) if whenever G_1 and G_2 are w-sink (resp. w-source) series graphs covering G, u, v, then*

$$f(G, u, v) = f(G_1, u, w) \oplus f(G_2, w, v)\,.$$

This property is demonstrated in Figure 1 (b).

Splitting Vertices. We now consider graphs in which there is some vertex y (different from u and v) that has multiple incoming or outgoing edges. The following properties express $f(G, u, v)$ in terms of $f(G', u, v)$ where G' is a graph derived from G in which y has been split into two vertices. A single incoming (resp. outgoing) edge of the original vertex is reconnected to only one copy, while the other outgoing (resp. incoming) edges are replicated and connected to both vertices.

Intuitively, this property reveals the process occurring at each vertex. Suppose for example, messages (or rumors, or infections) come in through several incoming edges. Is this message identical? Does it get sent out through all outgoing edges (as is the case with infections)? Or does it get forwarded along a single outgoing edge? We determine this by removing an edge from the vertex and preserve as much as possible of the structure. The basic operation used to derive G' is called an *incoming* or *outgoing split*, and is defined next.

We start with incoming splits. Let $e = (x, y)$ be an edge in G. We say that G' is the *e, y-split* of G if the following three conditions hold. First, $V_{G'} = V_G \cup \{y'\}$ where y' is a new vertex. Second, $E_{G'}$ is derived from E_G by replacing edge e with (x, y') (thereby leaving y with less incoming edges than before), and adding an edge (y', z) for every $z \in \Gamma^o_G(y)$. Finally, if $\pi : V_{G'} \to V_G$ is the identity on V_G and maps y' to y, then for all vertices w and edges e', we define $\nu_{G'}(w) = \nu_G(\pi(w))$ and $\varepsilon_{G'}(e') = \varepsilon_G(\pi(e'))$. Figure 1 (d) demonstrates this transformation on the graph in Figure 1 (c).

Property 4. INCOMING SPLIT: (IN-SPLT). *We say that f satisfies the* In-Splt property *if whenever G' is the e, y-split of G for some $y \neq u$, $y \neq v$ and incoming edge e of y, then*

$$f(G, u, v) = f(G', u, v)\,.$$

Outgoing splits are somewhat more intricate, due to the different ways in which the probability weights attached to edges can change. We consider two different options: leaving the probabilities unchanged, or propagating probabilities so that the probabilities of entire paths being taken do not change. Let $e = (y, z)$ be an edge in G. Let G' be the graph such that *(1)* $V_{G'} = V_G \cup \{y'\}$ where y' is a new vertex and *(2)* $E_{G'}$ is derived from E_G by replacing edge e with (y', z) (thereby leaving y with less outgoing edges than before), and adding an edge (x, y') for every $x \in \Gamma^i_G(y)$. Let $\pi : V_{G'} \to V_G$ be the identity on V_G and map y' to y.

We say that G' is the *same probability e, y-split of G* if for all vertices w and edges e', we have $\nu_{G'}(w) = \nu_G(\pi(w))$ and $\varepsilon_{G'}(e') = \varepsilon_G(\pi(e'))$. We say that G' is the *propagated probability e, y-split of G* if for all vertices w and edges $e' = (w_1, w_2)$, we have $\nu_{G'}(w) = \nu_G(\pi(w))$ and

- if $w_1 = y'$ (and thus $w_2 = z$), then $\varepsilon'_G(w_1, w_2) = 1$;
- if $w_1 = y$, then $\varepsilon'_G(w_1, w_2) = \varepsilon_G(w_1, w_2)/(1 - \varepsilon_G(y, z))$;
- if $w_2 = y'$, then $\varepsilon'_G(w_1, w_2) = \varepsilon_G(w_1, y) \cdot \varepsilon_G(y, z)$;
- if $w_2 = y$, then $\varepsilon'_G(w_1, w_2) = \varepsilon_G(w_1, y) \cdot (1 - \varepsilon_G(y, z))$;
- otherwise $\varepsilon_{G'}(e') = \varepsilon_G(\pi(e'))$.

where $e = (y, z)$. The result of a propagated probability e, y split of the graph of Figure 1 (c) appears in Figure 1 (e).

Using these two types of outgoing splits, we define additional properties.

Property 5. OUTGOING SPLIT: (SAMEOUT-SPLT, PROPOUT-SPLIT). *We say that f satisfies the* SameOut-Splt property *(resp. the* PropOut-Split property*) if whenever G' is the same probability (resp. propagated probability) e, y-split of G for some $y \neq u$, $y \neq v$ and outgoing edge e of y, then*

$$f(G, u, v) = f(G', u, v)\,.$$

Removing Vertices. While the previous property considered splitting vertices, we now consider removing vertices completely from a graph. This is useful, in particular, when the weights on vertices and edges indicate their probability of failure, or some probability that they will transmit an infection further.

Let G be a graph and y be a vertex in G. We use $G_{\neg y}$ to denote the graph derived by removing y and all its adjacent edges from G. We use G_y to denote the graph derived by following the same process as for $G_{\neg y}$, and then adding in the edge (x, z) for all $x \in \Gamma^i_G(y)$, $z \in \Gamma^o_G(y)$ with $\varepsilon_{G_y}(x, z) = \varepsilon_G(x, y) \cdot \varepsilon_G(y, z)$. In order to remain with a simple graph, we do two final corrections to G_y. First, we remove any self edges that have been created. Second, if there are two edges e_1, e_2, with weights p_1, p_2, between the same two vertices, we only retain a single edge e, and define $\varepsilon_{G_y}(e) = 1 - (1 - p_1) \cdot (1 - p_2)$. Figure 1 (f) demonstrates this transformation on the graph in Figure 1 (c).

Property 6. REMOVING VERTICES: (REMV). *We say that f satisfies the* RemV property *if whenever $y \neq u$, $y \neq v$ the following holds:*

$$f(G, u, v) = \nu_G(y) \cdot f(G_y, u, v) + (1 - \nu_G(y)) \cdot f(G_{\neg y}, u, v).$$

Irrelevant Portions of Graph. Our final property is used to state that certain portions (vertices and/or edges) are irrelevant when computing $f(G, u, v)$. This property is important as it can focus the attention on a smaller portion of the graph. Different link prediction functions may deem different portions of the graph as irrelevant. For example, katz$^\beta$ can ignore edges that are not on any path from u to v, while wdist can ignore edges that are not on any simple path from u to v. Thus, the following property is parameterized by a *relevance function* $\Upsilon(G, u, v)$ which returns a subgraph of G that should not be ignored when computing $f(G, u, v)$. We note that the weights on the subgraph $\Upsilon(G, u, v)$ will be renormalized, if G has normalized probabilistic edge weights.

Every link prediction function will satisfy this property when the relevance function is chosen as the identity function on graphs. However, some link prediction functions will satisfy this property with richer functions. Furthermore, relevance functions are selected to be almost "obvious", for example, unreachable vertices, or vertices that are not on any path between the pair we are scoring.

Property 7. RELEVANT SUBGRAPH: (Υ-REL). *We say that f satisfies the* Υ-Rel property *if for all G, u, v, it holds that* $f(G,u,v) = f(\Upsilon(G,u,v),u,v)$.

4 Characterizing Link Prediction Functions

We now show that the axioms presented can be used to uniquely characterize several standard link prediction functions. For this we will need to instantiate the property parameters with a variety of values. We use *min* and *max* to denote the aggregation function minimum and maximum, respectively. We also define the following relevance functions:

- $\Upsilon_{path}(G,u,v)$: Returns the subgraph of G containing u,v and all vertices and edges that participate in a path from u to v;
- $\Upsilon_{\text{spath}}(G,u,v)$: Returns the subgraph of G containing u,v and all vertices and edges that participate in a *simple* path from u to v;
- $\Upsilon_{\text{fpath}}(G,u,v)$: Returns the subgraph of G containing u,v and all vertices and edges that participate in a path from u to v that does not contain v more than once.

Due to lack of space, proofs are omitted.

Theorem 4.1. *Let G be a graph with weights on edges and the constant weight function of 1 on vertices. Let u,v be vertices in G. There is a single link prediction function f satisfying the properties $\top$-PG,* min-*SameAlt, +-Snk and* Υ_{spath}*-Rel, and this function is precisely* $\text{wdist}(G,u,v)$.

We note that wdist also satisfies +-Src, In-Splt and SameOut-Splt, but these properties are not needed to characterize wdist. (An alternative characterization to the one given in Theorem 4.1 can use +-Src instead of +-Snk.)

Theorem 4.2. *Let G be a graph with probabilities on vertices and independent probabilistic weights on edges. Let u,v be vertices in G. There is a single link prediction function f satisfying the properties* 0*-PG, RemV and* Υ_{spath}*-Rel, and this function is precisely* rlbty.

The function rlbty also satisfies max-Alt, but this property is not required for the characterization. For the special case where all probabilities are 1 or 0, we observe that rlbty becomes rchblty (reachability) which gives a score of 1 if v is reachable from u, and 0 otherwise. For this reason, rchblty satisfies the properties from Theorem 4.2 (as well as max-Alt). It also satisfies $\times$-Snk, $\times$-Src, In-Splt and SameOut-Splt. An alternative characterization to that given here for rlbty uses an additional axiom to reduce the graph to one with 0/1 weights, and then uses the above-mentioned axioms for rchblty. We omit further details due to lack of space.

Theorem 4.3. *Let G be a graph with the constant weight function of 1 on vertices and the constant weight function of β on edges. Let u,v be vertices in G. There is a single link prediction function f satisfying the properties* 0*-PG,* $\sum$*-SameAlt,* $\times$*-Snk,* $\times$*-Src, In-Splt, SameOut-Splt,* Υ_{path}*-Rel, and and this function is precisely* $\text{katz}^{\beta}(G,u,v)$.

Theorem 4.4. *Let G be a graph with normalized probabilistic edge weights and the constant weight function of 1 on vertices. Let u,v be vertices in G. There is a single link prediction function f satisfying the properties $\top$-PG,* $\sum$*-PropAlt, +-Snk, In-Splt, PropOut-Splt,* Υ_{fpath}*-Rel, and this function is precisely* $\text{hit}(G,u,v)$.

Theorems 4.1–4.4 are proven in two parts. First we show that each of the link prediction functions of interest satisfies the given properties (e.g., we show that wdist satisfies $\top$-PG, *min*-SameAlt, +-Snk). This is usually not difficult and requires a careful analysis of the behavior of the link ranking functions on the the special graphs specified in the properties.

The second part of each proof is to show that the set of given properties uniquely defines the specific link prediction function (i.e., there exist no additional functions satisfying the set of properties). This type of proof is typically more intricate. For wdist, we prove the required by induction on the length of the longest simple path from u to v. For rlbty, we show uniqueness by induction on the number of vertices in G. The proof for katz^{β} involves applying a series of graph transformations and an analysis that formulates the score returned by link prediction functions satisfying the properties of Theorem 4.3 as a matrix equation that coincides with the definition of katz^{β}, i.e., $(I^{u,v} - \beta A^{u,v})^{-1}$. Finally, to show the second part of hit, we again apply a series of graph transformations and analysis to derive a function coinciding with hit.

5 Conclusions and Future Work

We have presented an axiomatization framework for a class including several link prediction functions and have shown their characterizations. These axioms shed light on the underlying principles of the various functions. Thus, they can also be seen as a starting point to develop additional link prediction functions (or to enrich those that have been studied in the past).

In the future, we intend to develop new link prediction functions using instantiations of the properties in different ways, and to test their quality on a variety of domains, with different principles of network formation. We will also look for new and appealing properties, and check for impossibility results for certain combinations of properties. In addition, many other link prediction functions are known in the literature, and further axiomatic treatment for these is of interest. Additional link prediction functions to be considered include, among others, preferential attachment, triadic closure, and Adamic-Adar, as well as network-link scoring domains coming from sociology, such as balance theory.

6 Acknowledgements

Sara Cohen was supported by the Israel Science Foundation (Grant 1467/13) and the Ministry of Science and Technology (Grant 3-8710). Aviv Zohar was supported by the Israel Science Foundation (Grants 616/13, and 1773/13), and by the Israel Smart Grid (ISG) Consortium.

References

Al Hasan, M.; Chaoji, V.; Salem, S.; and Zaki, M. 2006. Link prediction using supervised learning. In *SDM06: Workshop on Link Analysis, Counter-terrorism and Security*.

Alon, N.; Fischer, F.; Procaccia, A.; and Tennenholtz, M. 2011. Sum of us: Strategyproof selection from the selectors. In *Proceedings of the 13th Conference on Theoretical Aspects of Rationality and Knowledge*, 101–110. ACM.

Altman, A., and Tennenholtz, M. 2005. Ranking systems: the pagerank axioms. In *Proceedings of the 6th ACM conference on Electronic commerce*, 1–8. ACM.

Altman, A., and Tennenholtz, M. 2010. An axiomatic approach to personalized ranking systems. *Journal of the ACM (JACM)* 57(4):26.

Andersen, R.; Borgs, C.; Chayes, J.; Feige, U.; Flaxman, A.; Kalai, A.; Mirrokni, V.; and Tennenholtz, M. 2008. Trust-based recommendation systems: an axiomatic approach. In *Proceedings of the 17th international conference on World Wide Web*, 199–208. ACM.

Arrow, K. J. 1951. 1963. social choice and individual values. *Wiley, New York.*

Gibbard, A. 1973. Manipulation of voting schemes: a general result. *Econometrica: journal of the Econometric Society* 587–601.

Gupte, M., and Eliassi-Rad, T. 2012. Measuring tie strength in implicit social networks. In *Web Science 2012*, 109–118.

Huang, Z.; Li, X.; and Chen, H. 2005. Link prediction approach to collaborative filtering. In *Proceedings of the 5th ACM/IEEE-CS joint conference on Digital libraries*, 141–142. ACM.

Katz, L. 1953. A new status index derived from sociometric analysis. *Psychometrika* 18(1):39–43.

Leskovec, J.; Backstrom, L.; Kumar, R.; and Tomkins, A. 2008. Microscopic evolution of social networks. In *Proceedings of the 14th ACM SIGKDD International Conference on Knowledge Discovery and Data Mining*, KDD '08, 462–470. New York, NY, USA: ACM.

Liben-Nowell, D., and Kleinberg, J. 2007. The link-prediction problem for social networks. *J. Am. Soc. Inf. Sci. Technol.* 58(7):1019–1031.

Pennock, D. M.; Horvitz, E.; Giles, C. L.; et al. 2000. Social choice theory and recommender systems: Analysis of the axiomatic foundations of collaborative filtering. In *AAAI/IAAI*, 729–734.

Qiu, B.; He, Q.; and Yen, J. 2011. Evolution of node behavior in link prediction. In *AAAI*.

Sarkar, P.; Chakrabarti, D.; and Moore, A. W. 2011. Theoretical justification of popular link prediction heuristics. In *IJCAI Proceedings-International Joint Conference on Artificial Intelligence*, volume 22, 2722.

Satterthwaite, M. A. 1975. Strategy-proofness and arrow's conditions: Existence and correspondence theorems for voting procedures and social welfare functions. *Journal of economic theory* 10(2):187–217.

Shapley, L. S. 1953. A value for n-person games. contribution to the theory of games. *Annals of Mathematics Studies* 2:307–317.

Perceiving Group Themes from Collective Social and Behavioral Information

Peng Cui, Tianyang Zhang
Department of Computer Science
Tsinghua University, Beijing, China

Fei Wang
Department of Computer Science
University of Connecticut, USA

Peng He
Department of Social Network Operation
Tencent Technology, Shenzhen, China

Abstract

Collective social and behavioral information commonly exists in nature. There is a widespread intuitive sense that the characteristics of these social and behavioral information are to some extend related to the themes (or semantics) of the activities or targets. In this paper, we explicitly validate the interplay of collective social behavioral information and group themes using a large scale real dataset of online groups, and demonstrate the possibility of perceiving group themes from collective social and behavioral information. We propose a REgularized miXEd Regression (REXER) model based on matrix factorization to infer hierarchical semantics (including both group category and group labels) from collective social and behavioral information of group members. We extensively evaluate the proposed method in a large scale real online group dataset. For the prediction of group themes, the proposed REXER achieves satisfactory performances in various criterions. More specifically, we can predict the category of a group (among 6 categories) purely based on the collective social and behavioral information of the group with the Precision@1 to be 55.16% , without any assistance from group labels or conversation contents. We also show, perhaps counterintuitively, that the collective social and behavioral information is more reliable than the titles and labels of groups for inferring the group categories.

Introduction

Collective social and behavioral information commonly exists in nature, e.g. groups of birds, insects and fishes coordinate their moves and speeds so that they can move together. Humans, as a typical social species, show a variety of social and behavioral information. The synchronization of applause in concerts, the formation of consensus in social groups, the common social attributes of the audience of a certain movie are easily recognizable examples. There is a widespread intuitive sense that the characteristics of these social and behavioral information are to some extend related to the themes (or semantics) of the activities or targets. For example, the style of applause synchronization in piano concerts should be quite different from that in rock concerts. But it has been difficult to evaluate this question quantitatively since it requires a setting where various social and behavioral information happen in a shared environment. In recent years, social networks, especially the online social groups, digitally and continuously record the collective behaviors and social profiles of users, as well as the themes of social groups in an unprecedented level. This provides precious opportunities to investigate the link between the collective social and behavioral information of group members and the group themes. The interplay between semantics and human behaviors is of significant interest to both academia to understand human collective behaviors and industry to serve customers more intelligently.

Social groups and the collective behaviors of their members have been studied in sociology for many years (Shaw 1971)(Barsade 2002), and most of them focus on the offline social groups and collective behaviors themselves and hardly investigate their relations with semantics. In recent years, it arouses considerable research interests in computer science to study social groups and collective behaviors in a large scale and with finer resolution. (Backstrom et al. 2006)(Kairam, Wang, and Leskovec 2012) studied the dynamic mechanisms of online groups, including group formation, growth, evolution and demise. In (Danescu-Niculescu-Mizil et al. 2013), the effects of users' susceptibility to linguistic change on their lifecycles in groups was investigated. (Qiu, Zhu, and Jiang 2013) exploited user behaviors and group information to regularize the topic categorization of online documents. Also, (Sachan et al. 2012) used content (semantics) and user interaction behaviors to assist community (group) discovery in social networks. These works either study the dynamics of social group themselves, or using the social and behavior information in social groups to assist community detection or topic categorization. In contrast, the goal of this paper is to demonstrate the possibility of perceiving group themes directly from collective social and behavioral information.

Online social groups, which are established, owned and maintained by group owners, is a feature in many social network platforms to provide interest- and niche-specific networks within the larger and more diverse global social networks. Normally, a group owner should select a category from a predefined category list for the group under establishment, name it with a group title and label it with several words to represent the theme of the group. Then other users can apply to or freely join the group to create, post, comment or read contents in the group. The revealing of the links between semantics and collective social and behavioral information can at least benefit the identification of group themes with the assistance of social and behavioral information. However, the group themes can be represented in different granularity levels. For example, the theme of the FIFA World Cup group can be represented by "interest related - sports related - football related - FIFA World CUP". In order to infer the rich hierarchical semantics from social behavioral information, it is required to study the learning model that can incorporate multiple types of relations, including semantic relations across different semantic levels and the relations between semantics and social behavioral information.

In this paper, we extract a set of effective social and behavioral features for group theme prediction. We further propose a REgularized miXEd Regression (REXER) method based on matrix factorization to predict group themes with hierarchical semantics (including both group categories and label sets) from collective social behavioral information of group members, where flexible regularizers are imposed to alleviate the problems brought by sparse and noisy data. We validate the discoveries and evaluate the prediction performances of REXER in a large scale real online group dataset, which is collected from an MSN-style instant message platform in China. We have in total 50,000 online groups with 5,549,570 group members, the social profiles of these group members and their behavior information for on month. The experimental results show that the proposed REXER achieves satisfactory performances in group theme prediction. More specifically, we can predict the category of a group (among 6 categories) purely based on the collective social and behavioral information of the group with the Precision@1 to be 55.16% , without any assistance from group labels or conversation contents. We also show, perhaps counterintuitively, that the collective social and behavioral information is more reliable than the titles and labels of groups for inferring the group categories.

Data and Features

In this section, we will introduce the characteristics of the dataset and introduce the social and behavioral features for group theme prediction.

Data Description

The online group dataset is collected from the real social network platform QQ, an MSN-style instant messenger in China with more than 500 million users. According to our statistics, there are around 100 million online groups that are generated and maintained by users. In this paper, we randomly select 50 thousand online groups with 5,549,570 unique anonymized users. For each user, we have their profile information (e.g. sexuality, age, geo-location etc.), and their behaviors (e.g. their participating behaviors in group conversations, and the timestamps of these behaviors) for one month. Besides, we know the friendship relations between group members. (Note that online groups are overlays on the global social network. Any pair of members in one group may or may not have friendship relation in the social network.) In total, we have 91,600,486 user participating behaviors, and 69,272,454 social relations.

In the dataset, there are 6 categories for these groups (as listed in Table 1), and each group belongs to one category. These categories can be used as the themes of groups. When a group is established, a title and a short description will be assigned to the group, from which we can extract labels to represent more detailed themes than categories. Thus, we use standard LDA (Latent Dirichlet Allocation) model to categorize them into 30 label sets after removing the high-frequency and low-frequency labels,, and use these label sets to represent the detailed theme of groups. For abbreviation, we only list the descriptions and representative labels for 14 label sets in Table 2, and the following visualizations are based on these 14 label sets. Note that most label sets are interpretable, except some ones mixing several topics together, e.g. the No. 12 label set.

No.	Categories
1	Friends
2	Housing
3	Game
4	People
5	Education
6	Industry

Table 1: Description of categories for online groups.

Social Features

We suppose that most groups in a given theme have similar distributions on some collective (i.e. group level) social features. Here we first extract the following collective social features.

- **Friendship Relational Density (FriDty)**. It is calculated by the ratio of the number of group member pairs that have friendship relation to the number of all possible group member pairs. Intuitively, a group with high friendship relational density is more relation driven rather than topic driven.
- **Sex Ratio (SexRto)**. It is calculated by the ratio of the number of male members to the total number of members.
- **Average Age (AvgAge)**. It is calculated in a normal way except that the outliers in user profiles are filtered, such as the age of 0 and 99 years.
- **Variance of Age (VarAge)**. Here we use standard deviation to represent the variance of age.
- **Geo-Affinity (GeoAff)**. We first find out the geographical area (province-level in our case) that include the largest number of group members, and calculate the ratio of the number of group members in that area to the total number of group members.

These features are in different scales. In order to make these feature values comparable, we normalize all these features into the rage of $[0, 1]$.

No.	Label Set Description	Representative Words
1	Mobile and Telecom Agent	Mobile, Recharge Card, Telecom, 3G, Mobile Phone
2	Business	Corporation, Taobao, Product, E-Commerce, Marketing
3	Online Game	Game, Community, Entertainment, Forum, Hero
4	Middle School	Class, Friendship, Middle School, Teacher, Love
5	University	University, Student Union, College, Sports, Community
6	Stock Market	Stock, Investment, Gold, Security, Buy and Sell
7	Organizations	Organization, Techniques, Business, Government Officer, Experience
8	Living Areas	House Owner, Photo, Living Area, Property Management, Group Buy
9	Blogs	Family, Blog, Accountant, Network, Software
10	House	Building, Living Area, Garden, Building Level, Buy House
11	Middle School Alumni	Middle School, Memory, Address List, Old School, Emotion
12	Mixed	Game, Classmate, Community, Engineering, Mechanic
13	Engineering	Engineering, Training, Cost of Manufacturing, Construction, Channel
14	Education	Children, Parents, Teacher, English, Training

Table 2: Description of label sets for online groups.

Behavioral Features

We suppose that most groups in a given theme have similar distributions on some collective behavioral features. Thus we first extract the following collective behavioral features.

- **Mobile Conversation Ratio (MobRto)**. It represents the proportion of conversation participating behaviors that are generated through mobile phones.
- **No-response Conversation Ratio (NoReRto)**. It represents the proportion of conversations that do not get any responses from other group members, where no-response conversation is determined by a waiting duration of three hours.
- **Night Conversation Ratio (NgtRto)**. It represents the proportion of conversations that are generated between 8pm to 11pm each day.
- **Degree of Conversational Dominance (DegDom)**. We first figure out three most active users that generate most conversations, and calculate the proportion of conversations that are generated by these 3 active users to represent the degree of conversational dominance.

We normalize all these features into the rage of $[0, 1]$.

Group Theme Prediction

In this section, we will present the method of perceiving group themes from social and behavioral information. First we introduce some symbols and notations that will be used through out the paper.

Notations and Problem Statement

As stated in the introduction, the problem we focus on is to infer the themes of online groups from the collective social and behavioral information of group members. In this paper, the group themes is represented in both category level (coarser semantic granularity) and label level (finer semantic granularity). Thus, the problem is how to infer the category and labels for a group given the features extracted from the social and behavioral information in the group.

Suppose we have N groups. Each group belongs to one of the M categories, and corresponds to some of the K labels. Then we have the Group-Category matrix $\mathbf{M} \in \mathbb{R}^{N\times M}$, and the Group-Label matrix $\mathbf{Y} \in \mathbb{R}^{N\times K}$. As the matrix $\mathbf{M}$ and $\mathbf{Y}$ are incomplete and noisy, we aim to complete them based on social and behavioral information. Here we represent each group by P-dimensional social and behavioral features by concatenating social and behavioral features into vectors, then we have the group feature matrix $\mathbf{G} \in \mathbb{R}^{N\times P}$. We assume these social and behavioral features are correlated with group labels, thus we use $\mathbf{A} \in \mathbb{R}^{P\times K}$ to denote the Feature-Label matrix. Meanwhile, as label is a more fine-grained way to represent group themes in contrast with group categories, we assume that there should be a mapping between labels and categories, and use $\mathbf{R} \in \mathbb{R}^{M\times K}$ to denote the Category-Label matrix.

In this way, the problem of perceiving group themes from collective social and behavioral information is transformed into the matrix completion problem on $\mathbf{Y}$ and $\mathbf{M}$.

Problem Formulation

As stated above, group themes can be represented by both categories and labels. We assume that the social and behavioral features are correlated with labels rather than categories. As the labels are in finer granularity than category, the correlation between social behavioral features and group categories can be transited by labels. Thus, given the observed Group-Label matrix $\mathbf{Y}$, one objective is to find an optimal Feature-Label matrix $\mathbf{A}$ to approximate $\mathbf{Y}$ by minimizing $||\mathbf{Y} - \mathbf{GA}||_F^2$. In order to leverage both labeled groups and unlabeled groups, we impose a constraint on the loss in a similar way as semi-supervised learning.

$$\mathcal{J}_1 = ||\mathbf{\Omega}(\mathbf{Y} - \mathbf{GA})||_F^2 \tag{1}$$

where $\mathbf{\Omega}$ is a diagonal matrix, such that

$$\Omega_{ii} = \begin{cases} 1, & \text{if the label of the } i\text{-th group is available} \\ 0, & \text{otherwise} \end{cases} \tag{2}$$

The second objective is to find an optimal Category-Label matrix $\mathbf{R}$ to approximate the Group-Category matrix $\mathbf{M}$ by minimizing

$$\mathcal{J}_2 = ||\mathbf{\Lambda}(\mathbf{M} - \mathbf{GAR}^T)||_F^2 \tag{3}$$

where $\mathbf{\Lambda}$ is a diagonal matrix, such that

$$\Lambda_{ii} = \begin{cases} 1, & \text{if the category of the } i\text{-th group is available} \\ 0, & \text{otherwise} \end{cases} \tag{4}$$

As $\mathbf{Y}$ and $\mathbf{M}$ are very sparse, the learned model is quite easy to be overfitting. In order to further improve the prediction performance, we further impose two regularizers on the main objectives under the following assumptions:

- Any two groups that have similar group members, which can be measured by the number of common members or the number of similar members in profiles, should have similar labels.
- The mapping between labels and categories should be sparse, i.e. each category should have only a small number of representative labels.

For the first assumption, we have the third objective:

$$\mathcal{J}_3 = ||\mathbf{W} - \mathbf{A}^T\mathbf{G}^T\mathbf{GA}||_F^2 \tag{5}$$

where $\mathbf{W} \in \mathbb{R}^{N\times N}$ is the group similarity matrix.

For the second assumption, we simply use $L-1$ norm to regularize the Category-Label mapping matrix $\mathbf{R}$.

$$\mathcal{J}_4 = ||\mathbf{R}||_1 \tag{6}$$

By combining $\mathcal{J}_1$ to $\mathcal{J}_4$ together, we propose the REgularized miXed Regression (REXER) model, and we can get $\mathbf{A}$ and $\mathbf{R}$ by minimizing:

$$\mathcal{J} = ||\mathbf{\Omega}(\mathbf{Y} - \mathbf{GA})||_F^2 + \lambda_1||\mathbf{\Lambda}(\mathbf{M} - \mathbf{GAR}^T)||_F^2 + \lambda_2||\mathbf{W} - \mathbf{A}^T\mathbf{G}^T\mathbf{GA}||_F^2 + \sigma||\mathbf{R}||_1 \tag{7}$$

Optimization Algorithm

Before deriving any details, we define the following matrices

$$\widetilde{\mathbf{Y}} = \mathbf{\Omega Y},\ \widetilde{\mathbf{G}} = \mathbf{\Omega G},\ \widehat{\mathbf{M}} = \mathbf{\Lambda M},\ \widehat{\mathbf{G}} = \mathbf{\Lambda G} \tag{8}$$

Then

$$\min_{\mathbf{A},\mathbf{R}} ||\widetilde{\mathbf{Y}} - \widetilde{\mathbf{G}}\mathbf{A}||_F^2 + \lambda_1||\widehat{\mathbf{M}} - \widehat{\mathbf{G}}\mathbf{AR}^T||_F^2 + \lambda_2||\mathbf{W} - \mathbf{GAA}^T\mathbf{G}^T||_F^2 + \sigma||\mathbf{R}||_1 \tag{9}$$

There are only two group of variables, $\mathbf{A}$ and $\mathbf{R}$. We adopt an *Block Coordinate Descent* (BCD) strategy to solve it. Each time we fix one group of variable and solve the other. When fixing $\mathbf{A}$, the problem of solving $\mathbf{R}$ is to minimize

$$\mathcal{J}_{\mathbf{R}} = \lambda_1||\widehat{\mathbf{M}} - \widehat{\mathbf{G}}\mathbf{AR}^T||_F^2 + \sigma||\mathbf{R}||_1 \tag{10}$$

which is a standard ℓ_1 norm regularized least squares problem and can be solved with any LASSO solver.

Fixing $\mathbf{R}$ solving $\mathbf{A}$ is much more complicated, we need to minimize

$$\mathcal{J}_{\mathbf{A}} = ||\widetilde{\mathbf{Y}} - \widetilde{\mathbf{G}}\mathbf{A}||_F^2 + \lambda_1||\widehat{\mathbf{M}} - \widehat{\mathbf{G}}\mathbf{AR}^T||_F^2 + \lambda_2||\mathbf{W} - \mathbf{A}^T\mathbf{K}_G\mathbf{A}||_F^2 \tag{11}$$

where the first term

$$\mathcal{J}_{\mathbf{A}}^1 = ||\widetilde{\mathbf{Y}} - \widetilde{\mathbf{G}}\mathbf{A}||_F^2 = tr(\widetilde{\mathbf{Y}}^T\widetilde{\mathbf{Y}}) - 2tr(\widetilde{\mathbf{Y}}^T\widetilde{\mathbf{G}}\mathbf{A}) + tr(\mathbf{A}^T\widetilde{\mathbf{K}}_G\mathbf{A}) \tag{12}$$

the second term

$$\mathcal{J}_{\mathbf{A}}^2 = ||\widehat{\mathbf{M}} - \widehat{\mathbf{G}}\mathbf{AR}^T||_F^2 = tr(\widehat{\mathbf{M}}^T\widehat{\mathbf{M}}) - 2tr(\mathbf{R}\widehat{\mathbf{M}}^T\widehat{\mathbf{G}}\mathbf{A}) + tr(\mathbf{RA}^T\widehat{\mathbf{K}}_G\mathbf{AR}^T) \tag{13}$$

the third term

$$\begin{aligned}\mathcal{J}_{\mathbf{A}}^3 &= ||\mathbf{W} - \mathbf{GAA}^T\mathbf{G}^T||_F^2 \\ &= tr(\mathbf{W}^T\mathbf{W}) - 2(\mathbf{A}^T\mathbf{G}^T\mathbf{WGA}) \\ &+ tr(\mathbf{A}^T\mathbf{G}^T\mathbf{GAA}^T\mathbf{G}^T\mathbf{GA})\end{aligned} \tag{14}$$

The partial gradient of those three term with respect to $\mathbf{A}$ are

$$\nabla_{\mathbf{A}}\mathcal{J}_{\mathbf{A}}^1 = -2\widetilde{\mathbf{G}}^T\widetilde{\mathbf{Y}} + 2\widetilde{\mathbf{K}}_G\mathbf{A} \tag{15}$$

$$\nabla_{\mathbf{A}}\mathcal{J}_{\mathbf{A}}^2 = -2\widehat{\mathbf{G}}^T\widehat{\mathbf{M}}\mathbf{R}^T + 2\widehat{\mathbf{K}}_G\mathbf{ARR}^T \tag{16}$$

$$\nabla_{\mathbf{A}}\mathcal{J}_{\mathbf{A}}^3 = -4tr(\mathbf{G}^T\mathbf{WGA}) + 4(\mathbf{K}_G\mathbf{AA}^T\mathbf{K}_G\mathbf{A}) \tag{17}$$

Therefore

$$\nabla_{\mathbf{A}}\mathcal{J}_A = \nabla_{\mathbf{A}}\mathcal{J}_{\mathbf{A}}^1 + \lambda_1\nabla_{\mathbf{A}}\mathcal{J}_{\mathbf{A}}^2 + \nabla_{\mathbf{A}}\mathcal{J}_{\mathbf{A}}^2 \tag{18}$$

Then we can adopt gradient descent to solve $\mathbf{A}$. The whole algorithm is summarized in Algorithm 1.

Algorithm 1 REgurlarized miXEd Regression (REXER)

Require: Tradeoff parameters $\lambda_1 > 0, \lambda_2 > 0, \sigma > 0$, Group-Category matrix $\mathbf{M}$, Group-Label matrix $\mathbf{Y}$, Group-Feature matrix $\mathbf{G}$, group similarity matrix $\mathbf{W}$, step size $0 < \alpha_{\mathbf{A}} < 1$.

```
Initialize Label-Feature matrix A^(0) and Category-Label matrix R^(0)
Calculate the current value of J^(0) ← J(A^(0), R^(0)) with Equation (7)
Initialize the iteration variable k ← 0
repeat
    k ← k + 1
    Update R^(k) by solving J_R(A^(k-1)) in Equation (10) with standard LASSO solver
    Initialize the iteration variable l ← 0
    Calculate the current value of J_A^(0)(A^(k-1), R^(k)) using Equation (11)
    repeat
        l ← l + 1
        Calculate ∇_A J_A^(l-1) using Equation 18.
        Update Ā^(l) ← A^(l-1) − α_A ∇_A J_A^(l-1)
        Calculate J_A^l(Ā^(l), R^(k)) using Equation (11)
    until J_A^l(Ā^(l), R^(k)) converged
    Update A^(k) ← Ā^(l)
    Calculate J^(k) ← J(A^(k), R^(k))
until J^(k) converged
Output: A = A^(k), R = R^(k)
```

We analyze the model complexity for each BCD iteration, which includes two parts:

- **Fixing A, solving R.** This is standard LASSO problem and the complexity is $O(KNM \min(N, M))$
- **Fixing R, solving A.** This step require Gradient Descent (GD) iterations, each GD step evaluating the gradient takes $O(4PNK + NMK + P^2N + PN^2 + KM^2 + 4P^2K + PK^2)$ time, evaluating the objective function loss takes $O(K^2P)$ time. Out of the GD iterations, evaluating $\mathbf{K}_G$ takes $O(NP^2)$ time.

Experiments

In this section, we will present the empirical study results on the REXER method for group theme prediction.

Experimental Settings

Training and Testing. In this paper, the problem of group theme prediction is transformed into category prediction and label set prediction. In order to evaluate the prediction performance of REXER, we randomly select 20% groups and hide their corresponding category and label set information from $\mathbf{Y}$ and $\mathbf{M}$. After learning $\mathbf{A}$ and $\mathbf{R}$ from the remaining 80% entries, we reconstruct $\mathbf{Y}$ and $\mathbf{M}$ and calculate the loss on the hidden entries. For all the following experiments, we conduct 20-folds testing and report average results with standard deviation.

Groundtruth. As each group belongs to only one category, the groundtruth can be naturally derived from the data. For the label sets, as we derive them by applying LDA on the labels of groups, we directly use the topic relevance score of a group over label sets (i.e. categorized topics in LDA) as the groundtruth on label sets for the group. In order to filter the trivial topic distributions, we set a threshold on the topic relevance score, and the scores that are below the threshold will be set to 0.

No.	RMSE	MAE	Rank
1	0.295 ± 0.008	0.210 ± 0.005	1.864 ± 0.124
2	0.371 ± 0.005	0.276 ± 0.003	2.667 ± 0.221
3	0.280 ± 0.007	0.195 ± 0.0040	1.386 ± 0.090
4	0.331 ± 0.014	0.230 ± 0.010	2.0890 ± 0.170
5	0.384 ± 0.006	0.283 ± 0.004	2.619 ± 0.153
6	0.331 ± 0.010	0.244 ± 0.009	1.748 ± 0.145
All	0.327 ± 0.002	0.234 ± 0.002	1.969 ± 0.037

Table 3: Category prediction performances.

Evaluation Criteria. In the following experiments, we will use RMSE (Root Mean Square Error) and MAE (Mean Average Error) to calculate the reconstruction loss of $\mathbf{Y}$ and $\mathbf{M}$ on the testing entries, which evaluates the prediction performance in value aspect. We will also evaluate the ranking performance by using Average Rank. Finally, we calculate the Precision@K to evaluate the prediction accuracy on the top recommended options, which is important in applications such as group recommendation and search.

Parameter Setting. In the proposed REXER method, we have 3 parameters in total, including λ_1, λ_2 and σ. For the parameter setting, we use grid search to get the optimal parameters $\lambda_1 = 1.3, \lambda_2 = 0.2, \sigma = 0.13$.

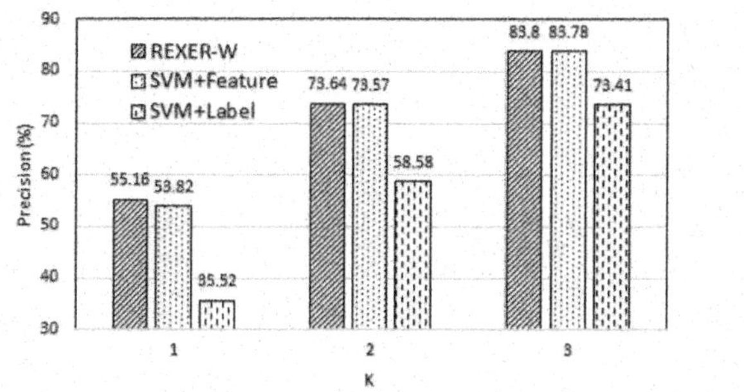

Figure 1: Precision@K for category prediction from REXER-W, SVM+Label, and SVM+Feature.

Predicting Group Category

We first evaluate the performance of REXER in category prediction. The experimental results are shown in Table 3. It can be seen that REXER can produce good results in both value approximation and ranking aspect. A perfect prediction will result in the average rank to be 1, our result 1.97 is satisfactory, especially considering that the predictions are purely based on social and behavioral information without any assistance from the labels and conversational contents of groups. Among the 6 categories, better predictions can be achieved for categories on Friends, Game and Industry. Comparatively, categories on Housing and Education are more challenging to predict.

No.	RMSE	MAE	Rank
All	0.198 ± 0.002	0.099 ± 0.003	12.8 ± 0.4

Table 4: Label set prediction performances.

In order to demonstrate the predictive power of collective social and behavioral information as well as the advantage of REXER model, we conduct comparative study by using SVM, an standard and effective multi-class classification tool, as the baseline method. Here we use SVM in two ways. First, we represent a group with its labels' distribution on the label sets which is derived from LDA, and denote it as SVM+Label. Also, we represent a group with its collective social and behavioral features, and denote it as SVM+Feature. As the group similarity information implied in matrix $\mathbf{W}$ cannot be straightforwardly incorporated into SVM model, in order to make the comparison fair, we remove the $\mathbf{W}$ from REXER to form REXER-W that is purely based on social and behavioral features. Then we calculate the Precision@K for REXER-W, SVM+Feature and SVM+Label methods, and the experimental results are shown in Figure 1. It is obvious that SVM+Feature can achieve much higher precision than SVM+Label. We attribute the weak predicting power of group labels to their deficiencies of noisy and free-style, especially in the social network environment. Comparatively, collective social and behavioral features show robust and good performance on category prediction because of the commonly existed and distinguishable collective social and behavioral synchronies among groups of different themes. Also, REXER-

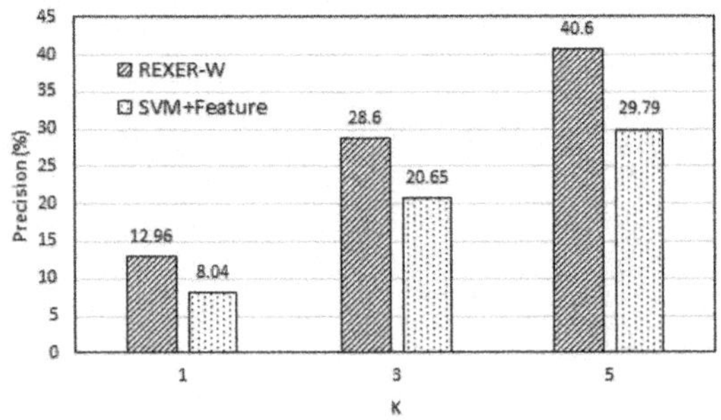

Figure 2: Precision@K for Label set prediction from REXER-W and SVM+Feature.

W achieves the best performances among the three models, especially in Precision@1.

Predicting Group Labels

We then evaluate the performance of REXER on label set prediction. The experimental results are shown in Table 4. Note that the overall results are averaged from 30 label sets. It can be seen that REXER can produce good results on RMSE and MAE, but the ranking results are not very satisfactory. According to our observation, the potential cause of this is due to the severe unbalance between label sets. For example, the label set No. 13 is a mixed label set and does not show very distinguishable social and behavioral information, but it includes 17% of all groups, thus the prediction results of groups are prone to be this label set, which would cause a better average rank in this label set while sacrificing other label sets.

The Precision@K for label set prediction is also shown in Figure 2. Here we compare REXER-W with SVM+Feature, and the results demonstrate that the proposed REXER-W model can achieve much higher precision than SVM+Feature in all cases, which demonstrates the advantages of REXER in predicting fine-granularity group themes. We attribute this significant improvement of REXER to the consideration of the duality between category and label sets. The group categories impose constraints on label sets by $\mathbf{R}$, and the label sets impose constraints on social and behavioral features by $\mathbf{A}$ so that the generation process of the observed data can be better approximated.

In order to look into the label set prediction, we plot the prediction confusion matrix in Figure 3. Here the confusion matrix is generated in the following way. Suppose we have a confusion matrix $\widehat{\mathbf{C}}$, where $\widehat{\mathbf{C}}_{i,j}$ means the number of groups that are with groudtruth label set i and are correctly (if $i = j$) or erroneously (if $i \neq j$) classified into label set j. For a predicted group, if the groundtruth labelset k is among the top 3 predicted label sets l, m, n, then $\widehat{\mathbf{C}}_{k,k} + 1$. Else, $\widehat{\mathbf{C}}_{k,l} + 1$, $\widehat{\mathbf{C}}_{k,m} + 1$, and $\widehat{\mathbf{C}}_{k,n} + 1$. Finally, we normalize $\widehat{\mathbf{C}}$ by columns into $\mathbf{C}$ so that the sum of each column in $\mathbf{C}$ is equal to 1. Thus, $\mathbf{C}_{i,j}, (i \neq j)$ means the probability of a group with label set i being misclassified into label set j. From diagonal elements in Figure 3, we can see that the group label sets are well predicted in most cases. Of course

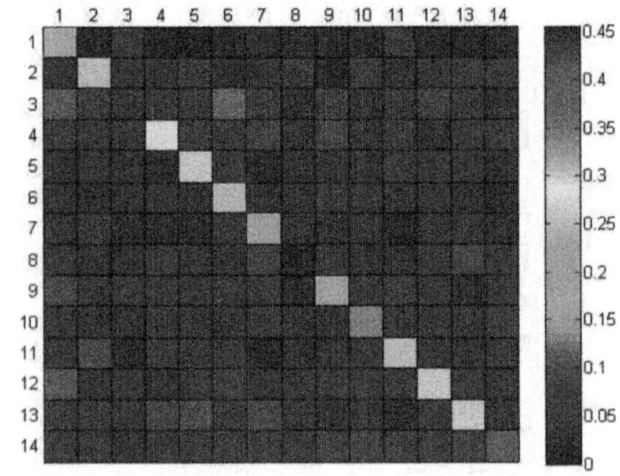

Figure 3: The confusion matrix of label set prediction.

there are some obvious confusion pairs. For example, $\mathbf{C}_{3,6}$ indicates that groups on Online Game are easy to be misclassified into Stock Market, as they share several common social and behavioral synchronies, such as low friendship density, and high degree of conversation dominance. The groups on Middle School are easy to be misclassified into University, Organizations and School Alumni (indicated by $\mathbf{C}_{4,5}$, $\mathbf{C}_{4,7}$, and $\mathbf{C}_{4,11}$).

Conclusion

In this paper, we aim to understand the interplay between semantics and collective social and behavioral information, and explore the possibility of perceiving semantics from the content-agnostic social and behavioral information. By studying a large scale real online group dataset, we discover the commonly existed social and behavioral information among groups in each theme and further propose the REXER method to predict hierarchical group themes, including both group categories and label sets, from collective social and behavioral information. We extensively evaluate the proposed REXER and achieve satisfactory prediction performances on both category prediction and label set prediction.

Acknowledgement

This work was supported by National Program on Key Basic Research Project, No. 2015CB352300, No. 2011CB302206; National Natural Science Foundation of China, No. 61370022, No. 61472444 and No. 61210008; International Science and Technology Cooperation Program of China, No. 2013DFG12870. Thanks for the support of NExT Research Center funded by MDA, Singapore, under the research grant, WBS:R-252-300-001-490 and the research fund of Tsinghua-Tencent Joint Laboratory for Internet Innovation Technology.

References

Backstrom, L.; Huttenlocher, D.; Kleinberg, J.; and Lan, X. 2006. Group formation in large social networks: membership, growth, and evolution. In *Proceedings of the 12th ACM*

SIGKDD international conference on Knowledge discovery and data mining, 44–54. ACM.

Barsade, S. G. 2002. The ripple effect: Emotional contagion and its influence on group behavior. *Administrative Science Quarterly* 47(4):644–675.

Danescu-Niculescu-Mizil, C.; West, R.; Jurafsky, D.; Leskovec, J.; and Potts, C. 2013. No country for old members: User lifecycle and linguistic change in online communities. In *Proceedings of the 22nd international conference on World Wide Web*, 307–318. International World Wide Web Conferences Steering Committee.

Kairam, S. R.; Wang, D. J.; and Leskovec, J. 2012. The life and death of online groups: Predicting group growth and longevity. In *Proceedings of the fifth ACM international conference on Web search and data mining*, 673–682. ACM.

Qiu, M.; Zhu, F.; and Jiang, J. 2013. It is not just what we say, but how we say them: Lda-based behavior-topic model. In *2013 SIAM International Conference on Data Mining (SDM'13)*. SIAM.

Sachan, M.; Contractor, D.; Faruquie, T. A.; and Subramaniam, L. V. 2012. Using content and interactions for discovering communities in social networks. In *Proceedings of the 21st international conference on World Wide Web*, 331–340. ACM.

Shaw, M. E. 1971. Group dynamics: The psychology of small group behavior.

Predicting the Demographics of Twitter Users from Website Traffic Data

Aron Culotta and **Nirmal Kumar Ravi**
Department of Computer Science
Illinois Institute of Technology
Chicago, IL 60616
aculotta@iit.edu, nravi@hawk.iit.edu

Jennifer Cutler
Stuart School of Business
Illinois Institute of Technology
Chicago, IL 60616
jcutler2@stuart.iit.edu

Abstract

Understanding the demographics of users of online social networks has important applications for health, marketing, and public messaging. In this paper, we predict the demographics of Twitter users based on whom they follow. Whereas most prior approaches rely on a supervised learning approach, in which individual users are labeled with demographics, we instead create a distantly labeled dataset by collecting audience measurement data for 1,500 websites (e.g., 50% of visitors to gizmodo.com are estimated to have a bachelor's degree). We then fit a regression model to predict these demographics using information about the followers of each website on Twitter. The resulting average held-out correlation is .77 across six different variables (gender, age, ethnicity, education, income, and child status). We additionally validate the model on a smaller set of Twitter users labeled individually for ethnicity and gender, finding performance that is surprisingly competitive with a fully supervised approach.

1 Introduction

Social media are increasingly being used to make inferences about the real world, with application to politics (O'Connor et al. 2010), health (Dredze 2012), and marketing (Gopinath, Thomas, and Krishnamurthi 2014). Understanding the demographic makeup of a sample of social media users is critical to further progress in this area, as it allows researchers to overcome the considerable selection bias in this uncontrolled data. Additionally, this capability will help public messaging campaigns ensure that the target demographic is being reached.

A common approach to demographic inference is supervised classification — from a training set of annotated users, a model is fit to predict user attributes from the content of their writings (Argamon et al. 2005; Schler et al. 2006; Rao et al. 2010; Pennacchiotti and Popescu 2011; Burger et al. 2011; Rao et al. 2011; Al Zamal, Liu, and Ruths 2012). This approach has a number of limitations: collecting human annotations is costly and error-prone; many demographic variables of interest cannot easily be labeled by inspecting a profile (e.g., income, education level); by restricting learning to a small set of labeled profiles, the generalizability of the classifier is limited. Additionally, most past work has focused on text as the primary source of evidence, making limited use of network evidence.

In this paper, we use regression to predict six demographic variables (gender, age, ethnicity, education, income, and child status) of a set of Twitter users based solely on whom they follow. Rather than using a standard supervised approach, we construct a distantly labeled dataset consisting of web traffic demographic data from Quantcast.com. By pairing web traffic data for a site with the followers of that site on Twitter.com, we fit a regression model between a set of Twitter users and their expected demographic profile.

With this data, we explore several questions:

RQ1. Can the demographics of a set of Twitter users be inferred from network information alone? We find across six demographic variables an average held-out correlation of .77 between the web traffic demographics of a website and that predicted by a regression model based on the site's Twitter followers. We can learn, for example, that high-income users are likely to follow The Economist and young users are likely to follow PlayStation.

RQ2. Can a regression model be extended to classify individual users? Using a hand-labeled validation set of users annotated with gender and ethnicity, we find that the regression model is competitive with a fully-supervised approach.

RQ3. How much follower information is needed for inference? We find that the identities of only 10 followed accounts per user, chosen at random, is sufficient to achieve 90% of the accuracy obtained using 200 followed accounts.

In the remainder of the paper, we will first review related work, then describe the data collected from Twitter and QuantCast and the feature representation used for the task; next, we will present regression and classification results; finally, we will conclude and outline directions for future work.[1]

[1] Code is available here: https://github.com/tapilab/aaai-2015-demographics.

2 Related Work

Predicting attributes of social media users is a growing area of interest, with recent work focusing on age (Schler et al. 2006; Rosenthal and McKeown 2011; Nguyen, Smith, and Ros 2011; Al Zamal, Liu, and Ruths 2012), sex (Rao et al. 2010; Burger et al. 2011; Liu and Ruths 2013), race/ethnicity (Pennacchiotti and Popescu 2011; Rao et al. 2011), and personality (Argamon et al. 2005; Schwartz et al. 2013). Other work predicts demographics from web browsing histories (Goel, Hofman, and Sirer 2012).

The majority of these approaches rely on hand-annotated training data, require explicit self-identification by the user, or are limited to very coarse attribute values (e.g., above or below 25-years-old).

A related lightly supervised approach includes Chang et al. (2010), who infer user-level ethnicity using name/ethnicity distributions provided by the Census; however, that approach uses evidence from first and last names, which are often not available, and thus are more appropriate for population-level estimates. Rao et al. (2011) extend this approach to also include evidence from other linguistic features to infer gender and ethnicity of Facebook users; they evaluate on the fine-grained ethnicity classes of Nigeria and use very limited training data. More recently, Mohammady and Culotta (2014) trained an ethnicity model for Twitter using county-level supervision.

There have been several studies predicting population-level statistics from social media. Eisenstein, Smith, and Xing (2011) use geolocated tweets to predict zip-code statistics of race/ethnicity, income, and other variables using Census data; Schwartz et al. (2013) similarly predict county health statistics from Twitter. However, none of this prior work attempts to predict or evaluate at the user level.

The primary methodological novelties of the present work are its use of web traffic data as a form of weak supervision and its use of follower information as the primary source of evidence. Additionally, this work considers a larger set of demographic variables than prior work, and predicts a much more fine-grained set of categories (e.g., six different age brackets instead of two or three used previously).

3 Data

3.1 Quantcast

Quantcast.com is an audience measurement company that tracks the demographics of visitors to millions of websites. This is accomplished by using cookies to track the browsing activity of a large panel of respondents (Kamerer 2013).

We sampled 1,532 websites from Quantcast and downloaded statistics for six demographic variables:

- **Gender:** Male, Female
- **Age:** 18-24, 25-34, 35-44, 45-54, 55-64, 65+
- **Income:** $0-50k, $50-100k, $100-150k, $150k+
- **Education:** No College, College, Grad School
- **Children:** Kids, No Kids
- **Ethnicity:** Caucasian, Hispanic, African American, Asian

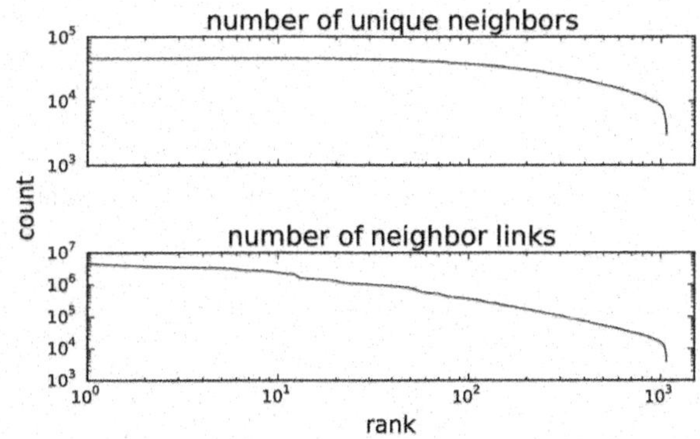

Figure 1: Rank-order frequency plots of the number of neighbors per account and the number of links to all neighbors per account.

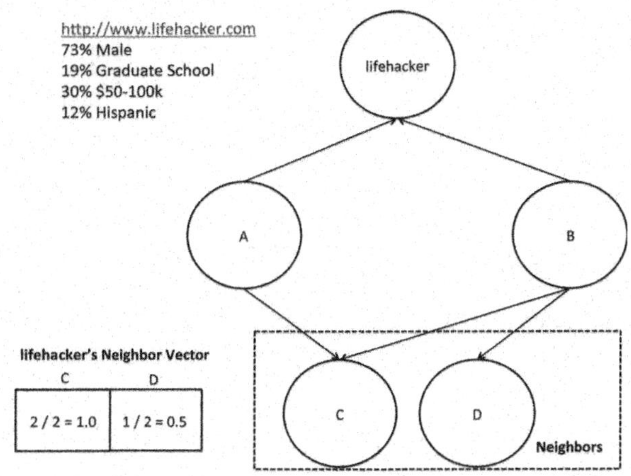

Figure 2: Data model. We collect QuantCast demographic data for each website, then construct a **Neighbor Vector** from the Twitter connections of that website, based on the proportion of the company's followers that are friends with each neighbor.

Each variable represents the estimated percentage of visitors to a website with a given demographic.

3.2 Twitter

For each website collected in the previous step, we executed a script to search for its Twitter account, then manually verified it; 1,066 accounts from the original set of 1,532 were found. An assumption of this work is that the demographic profiles of followers of a website on Twitter are correlated with the demographic profiles of visitors to that website. While there are undoubtedly biases introduced here (e.g., Twitter users may skew younger than the web traffic panel), in aggregate these differences should have limited impact on the final model.

For each account, we queried the Twitter REST API to sample 120 of its followers, using `followers/ids` request. This sample is not necessarily uniform. The Twitter

API documentation states that "At this time, results are ordered with the most recent following first — however, this ordering is subject to unannounced change and eventual consistency issues."

For each of these followers, we then collected up to 5,000 of the accounts they follow, called *friends*, using the `friends/ids` API request. Thus, for each of the original accounts from Quantcast, we have up to ($120 * 5K = 600K$) additional accounts that are two hops from the original account (the friend of a follower). We refer to these discovered accounts as *neighbors* of the original Quantcast account.

Of course, many of these accounts will be duplicates, as two different followers will follow many of the same accounts (i.e., *triadic closure*) — indeed, our core assumption is that the number of such duplicates represents the strength of the similarity between the neighbors.

For each of the original accounts, we compute the fraction of its followers that are friends with each of its neighbors and store this in a *neighbor vector*. For example, suppose a Quantcast account A has two followers B and C; B follows D and E; and C follows D and F. Then the neighbor vector for A is $\{(D, 1), (E, .5), (F, .5)\}$. This suggests that A and D are closer neighbors than A and E. Figure 2 depicts this representation.

The resulting dataset consists of 1.7M unique neighbors of the original 1,532 accounts. To reduce dimensionality, we removed neighbors with fewer than 100 followers, leaving 46,622 unique neighbors with a total of 178M incoming links. Figure 1 plots the number of unique neighbors per account as well as the number of neighbor links per account.

4 Analysis

4.1 Regression

For each Quantcast site, we pair its demographic variables with its neighbor vector to construct a regression problem. Thus, we attempt to predict the demographic profile of the followers of a Twitter account based on the friends of those followers.

Due to the high dimensionality and small number of examples, we use elastic net regularization, which combines both L1 and L2 penalties. Furthermore, since each output variable consists of dependent categories (e.g., age brackets), we use a multi-task variant of elastic net to ensure that the same features are selected by the L1 regularizer for each category. We use the implementation of `MultiTaskElasticNet` in `scikit-learn` (Pedregosa and others 2011).[2]

Recall that standard linear regression selects coefficients β to minimize the squared error on a list of training instances $\{\mathbf{x}_i, y_i\}_{i=1}^N$, for feature vector $\mathbf{x}_i$ and expected output y_i.

$$\beta^* \leftarrow \text{argmin}_\beta \sum_{i=1}^{N} (y_i - \beta^T \mathbf{x}_i)^2$$

Lasso imposes an L1 regularizer on β, while ridge regression imposes an L2 regularizer on β. Elastic net combines both penalties:

$$\beta^* \leftarrow \text{argmin}_\beta \frac{1}{N} \sum_{i=1}^{N} (y_i - \beta^T \mathbf{x}_i)^2 + \lambda_1 ||\beta||_1 + \lambda_2 ||\beta||_2^2$$

where λ_1 and λ_2 control the strength of L1 and L2 regularizers, respectively. The L1 regularizer encourages sparsity (i.e., many 0 values in β), while the L2 regularizer prevents β values from becoming too large.

Multi-task elastic net extends elastic net to groups of related regression problems (Obozinski, Taskar, and Jordan 2006). E.g., in our case, we would like to account for the fact that the regressions for "No College", "College", and "Grad School" are related; thus, we would like the sparse solutions to be similar across tasks (that is, L1 should select the same features for each task).

Let $\beta^{(j)}$ be the coefficients for task j, and let $\beta_k = (\beta_k^{(1)} \dots \beta_k^{(M)})^T$ be the vector of coefficients formed by concatenating the coefficients for the kth feature across all M tasks. Then multi-task elastic net objective enforces that similar features are selected across tasks:

$$\beta^* \leftarrow \text{argmin}_\beta \sum_{j=1}^{M} \frac{1}{N_j} \sum_{i=1}^{N_j} (y_i^{(j)} - \beta^{(j)T} \mathbf{x}_i^{(j)})^2 + \lambda_1 \sum_{k=1}^{p} ||\beta_k||_1 + \lambda_2 ||\beta||_2^2$$

where N_j is the number of instances for task j and p is the number of features.

Regression Results We perform five-fold cross-validation and report the held-out correlation coefficient (r) between the predicted and true demographic variables. Figure 3 displays the resulting scatter plots for each of the 19 categories for 6 demographic variables.

We can see that overall the correlation is very strong: .77 on average, ranging from .55 for the 35-44 age bracket to .89 for Male and African American. All of these correlation coefficients are significant using a two-tailed t-test ($p < 0.01$), with a Bonferroni adjustment for the 19 comparisons. These results indicate that the neighbor vector provides a reliable signal of the demographics of a group of Twitter users.

To further examine these results, Table 1 displays the accounts with the 5 largest coefficients per class according to the fit regression model. These contain many results that match common stereotypes: sports accounts are correlated with men, video game accounts are correlated with younger people, financial news accounts are correlated with greater income, and parenting magazines are correlated with people who have children. There also appear to be some geographic effects, as California-related accounts are highly weighted for both Hispanic and Asian categories. There seems to be good city-level resolution — Los Angeles accounts (*latimes*, *Lakers*) are more strongly correlated with Hispanics, whereas San Francisco accounts (*SFGate*, *SFist*, *SFWeekly*) are more strongly correlated with Asians.

Finally, we compare multi-task elastic net with the single-task variant of elastic net and ridge regression (with regularization parameters tuned as before). Table 2 shows a large

[2] After tuning on a validation set for one task, we fix alpha=$1e-5$ and l1_ratio=0.5.

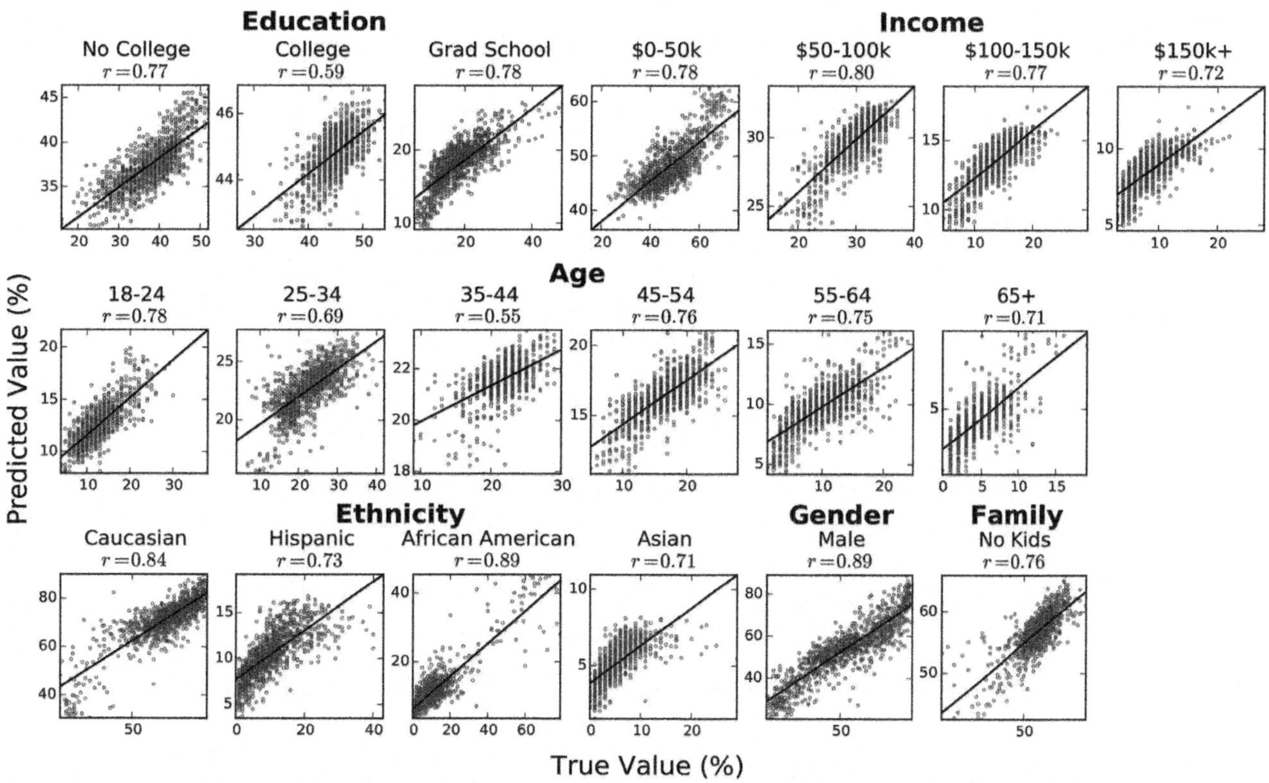

Figure 3: Scatter plots of the true demographic variables from Quantcast versus those predicted from the neighbor vector, along with the held-out correlation coefficient (r).

Model	Average Correlation
multi-task elastic net	0.772
elastic net	0.769
ridge	0.671

Table 2: Average held-out correlation across all demographic variables for three competing regression models.

improvement from ridge to elastic net, and a more modest improvement when using the multi-task formulation.

4.2 Classification

The regression results suggest that the neighbor vector of an account is highly predictive of the demographics of its followers. In this section, we provide additional validation using data manually annotated at the user level.

Many of the demographic variables are difficult to label at the individual level — e.g., income or education level is rarely explicitly mentioned in either a profile or tweet. Indeed, an advantage of the approach here is that aggregate statistics are more readily available for many demographics of interest that are difficult to label at the individual level. For validation purposes, we focus on two variables that can fairly reliably be labeled for individuals: ethnicity and gender.

These were collected as follows: First, we used the Twitter Streaming API to obtain a random sample of users, filtered to the United States (using time zone and the place country code from the profile). From six days' worth of data (December 6-12, 2013), we sampled 1,000 profiles at random and categorized them by analyzing the profile, tweets, and profile image for each user. We categorized 770 Twitter profiles into one of four ethnicities (Asian, African American, Hispanic, Caucasian). Those for which ethnicity could not be determined were discarded (230/1,000; 23%).[3] The category frequency is Asian (22), African American (263), Hispanic (158), Caucasian (327). To estimate inter-annotator agreement, a second annotator sampled and categorized 120 users. Among users for which both annotators selected one of the four categories, 74/76 labels agreed (97%). There was some disagreement over when the category could be determined: for 21/120 labels (17.5%), one annotator indicated the category could not be determined, while the other selected a category. Gender annotation was done automatically by comparing the first name provided in the user profile with the U.S. Census list of names by gender.[4] Ambiguous names were removed.

For each user, we collected up to 200 of their friends using the Twitter API. We removed accounts that restricted access

[3]This introduces some bias towards accounts with identifiable ethnicity; we leave an investigation of this for future work.

[4]http://www.census.gov/genealogy/www/freqnames.html

Category	Value	Top Accounts
Gender	Male	AdamSchefter, SportsCenter, espn, WIRED, mortreport
	Female	TheEllenShow, Oprah, MarthaStewart, Pinterest, FoodNetwork
Age	18-24	PlayStation, IGN, RockstarGames, Ubisoft, steam_games
	25-34	azizansari, louisck, lenadunham, mindykaling, WIRED
	35-44	TMZ, Oprah, BarackObama, andersoncooper, cnnbrk
	45-54	cnnbrk, FoxNews, AP, CNN, ABC
	55-64	FoxNews, cnnbrk, AP, WSJ, WhiteHouse
	65+	FoxNews, cnnbrk, WSJ, AP, DRUDGE_REPORT
Income	\$0-50k	YouTube, PlayStation, IGN, RockstarGames, KevinHart4real
	\$50-100k	cnnbrk, espn, SportsCenter, AP, WSJ
	\$100-150k	WSJ, TheEconomist, nytimes, washingtonpost, Forbes
	\$150k+	WSJ, TheEconomist, nytimes, Forbes, BloombergNews
Education	No College	YouTube, PlayStation, RockstarGames, katyperry, KevinHart4real
	College	ConanOBrien, louisck, danieltosh, azizansari, WIRED
	Grad School	NewYorker, nytimes, TheEconomist, WSJ, washingtonpost
Children	No Kids	NewYorker, StephenAtHome, nytimes, TheEconomist, WIRED
	Has Kids	parentsmagazine, parenting, TheEllenShow, thepioneerwoman, HuffPostParents
Ethnicity	Caucasian	FoxNews, jimmyfallon, TheEllenShow, blakeshelton, cnnbrk
	Hispanic	latimes, Lakers, SFGate, kobebryant, SFist
	African American	KevinHart4real, Drake, iamdiddy, Tip, kendricklamar
	Asian	SFGate, SFist, TechCrunch, WIRED, SFWeekly

Table 1: Accounts with the highest estimated coefficients for each category.

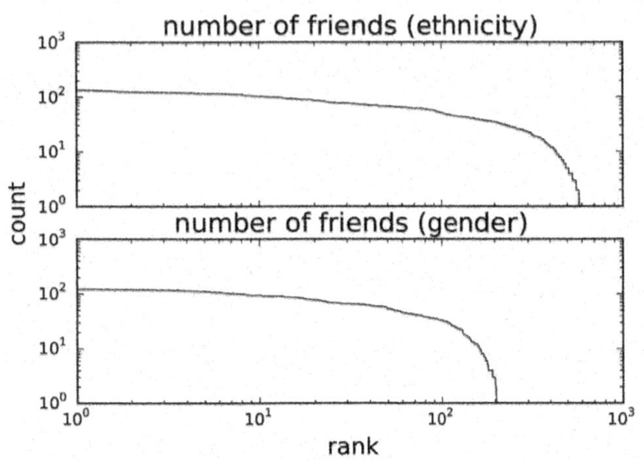

Figure 4: Rank-order frequency plots of the number of friends per user in each of the labeled datasets (ethnicity, gender). These friends are restricted to one of the 46,622 accounts used in the regression experiments.

to friend information; we also removed the Asian users due to the small sample size, leaving a total of 615 users. For classification, each user is represented by the identity of their friends (up to 200). Only those friend accounts contained in the 46,622 accounts used for the regression experiments were retained. Figure 4 shows the number of friends per user for each dataset.

As a baseline, we trained a logistic regression classifier with L2 regularization, using a binary representation of each user's friends. To repurpose the regression model to perform classification, we must modify the coefficients returned by regression. We first compute the z-score of each coefficient with respect to the other coefficients for that category value. E.g., all coefficients for the *Male* class are adjusted to have mean 0 and unit variance. This makes the coefficients comparable across labels. Furthermore, we set to 0 any negative coefficient. To classify each user, we then compute the sum of coefficients for each friend, and select the class with maximum value.

Classification Results Figure 5 displays the macro-F1 value for ethnicity (three classes) and gender (two classes). The regression model is fit using only the Quantcast data, while the classification model uses three-fold cross-validation using the labeled user accounts. We compare the regression approach with logistic regression using an increasingly larger number of labeled examples.

For gender, the regression model outperforms the classification approach, which is surprising given that the regression model does not have any hand-labeled profiles for training. For ethnicity, the regression approach outperforms classification until over half of the labeled data is used to fit the classification approach, after which the classification approach dominates. In general, the accuracy of the two approaches is comparable.

Sensitivity to number of friends Finally, we investigate how much information we need about a user before we can make an accurate prediction of their demographics. Whereas the previous results considered up to 200 friends of each user, we consider smaller numbers of friends to determine how the number of friends collected affects accuracy. Figure 6 displays the macro-F1 value for trials in which the number of friends per user is one of

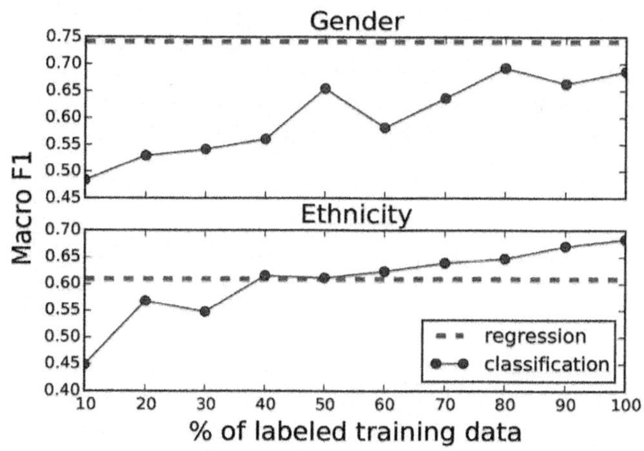

Figure 5: Classification results comparing a standard logistic regression classifier (`classification`), trained using cross-validation, versus the proposed approach (`regression`), which is fit solely on statistics from Quantcast, with no individually labeled data.

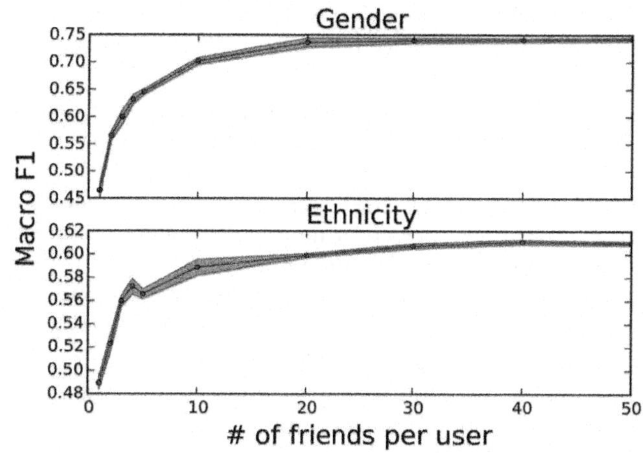

Figure 6: Macro F1 as the number of friends per user increases (with standard errors).

$\{1, 2, 3, 4, 5, 10, 20, 30, 40, 50\}$ (values greater than 50 did not significantly increase accuracy). The friends are sampled at random, and the results are averaged over five trials. We can see that accuracy plateaus quickly: for both tasks, the F1 score using only 10 friends is within 5% of the score using all 200 friends.

This result has implications for scalability — Twitter API rate limits make it difficult to collect the complete social graph for a set of users. Additionally, this has important privacy implications; revealing even a small amount of social information also reveals a considerable amount of demographic information. Twitter users concerned about privacy may wish to disable the setting that makes friend identity information public.

5 Conclusion

In this paper, we have shown that Twitter follower information provides a strong source of information for performing demographic inference. Furthermore, pairing web traffic demographic data with Twitter data provides a simple and effective way to train a demographic inference model without any annotation of individual profiles. We have validated the approach both in aggregate (by comparing with Quantcast data) and at the individual level (by comparing with hand-labeled annotations), finding high accuracy in both cases. Somewhat surprisingly, the approach outperforms a fully-supervised approach for gender classification, and is competitive for ethnicity classification.

In the future, we will test the generalizability of this approach to new groups of Twitter users. For example, we can collect users by city or county and compare the predictions with the Census demographics from that geographic location. Additionally, we will investigate ways to combine labeled and unlabeled data using semi-supervised learning (Quadrianto et al. 2009; Ganchev et al. 2010; Mann and McCallum 2010).

References

Al Zamal, F.; Liu, W.; and Ruths, D. 2012. Homophily and latent attribute inference: Inferring latent attributes of twitter users from neighbors. In *ICWSM*.

Argamon, S.; Dhawle, S.; Koppel, M.; and Pennebaker, J. W. 2005. Lexical predictors of personality type. In *In proceedings of the Joint Annual Meeting of the Interface and the Classification Society of North America*.

Burger, J. D.; Henderson, J.; Kim, G.; and Zarrella, G. 2011. Discriminating gender on twitter. In *Proceedings of the Conference on Empirical Methods in Natural Language Processing*, EMNLP '11, 1301–1309. Stroudsburg, PA, USA: Association for Computational Linguistics.

Chang, J.; Rosenn, I.; Backstrom, L.; and Marlow, C. 2010. ePluribus: ethnicity on social networks. In *Fourth International AAAI Conference on Weblogs and Social Media*.

Dredze, M. 2012. How social media will change public health. *IEEE Intelligent Systems* 27(4):81–84.

Eisenstein, J.; Smith, N. A.; and Xing, E. P. 2011. Discovering sociolinguistic associations with structured sparsity. In *Proceedings of the 49th Annual Meeting of the Association for Computational Linguistics: Human Language Technologies - Volume 1*, HLT '11, 1365–1374. Stroudsburg, PA, USA: Association for Computational Linguistics.

Ganchev, K.; Graca, J.; Gillenwater, J.; and Taskar, B. 2010. Posterior regularization for structured latent variable models. *J. Mach. Learn. Res.* 11:2001–2049.

Goel, S.; Hofman, J. M.; and Sirer, M. I. 2012. Who does what on the web: A large-scale study of browsing behavior. In *ICWSM*.

Gopinath, S.; Thomas, J. S.; and Krishnamurthi, L. 2014. Investigating the relationship between the content of online word of mouth, advertising, and brand performance. *Marketing Science*. Published online in Articles in Advance 10 Jan 2014.

Kamerer, D. 2013. Estimating online audiences: Understanding the limitations of competitive intelligence services. *First Monday* 18(5).

Liu, W., and Ruths, D. 2013. What's in a name? using first names as features for gender inference in twitter. In *AAAI Spring Symposium on Analyzing Microtext*.

Mann, G. S., and McCallum, A. 2010. Generalized expectation criteria for semi-supervised learning with weakly labeled data. *J. Mach. Learn. Res.* 11:955–984.

Mohammady, E., and Culotta, A. 2014. Using county demographics to infer attributes of twitter users. In *ACL Joint Workshop on Social Dynamics and Personal Attributes in Social Media*.

Nguyen, D.; Smith, N. A.; and Ros, C. P. 2011. Author age prediction from text using linear regression. In *Proceedings of the 5th ACL-HLT Workshop on Language Technology for Cultural Heritage, Social Scie nces, and Humanities*, LaTeCH '11, 115–123. Stroudsburg, PA, USA: Association for Computational Linguistics.

Obozinski, G.; Taskar, B.; and Jordan, M. 2006. Multi-task feature selection. *Statistics Department, UC Berkeley, Tech. Rep.*

O'Connor, B.; Balasubramanyan, R.; Routledge, B. R.; and Smith, N. A. 2010. From tweets to polls: Linking text sentiment to public opinion time series. *ICWSM* 11:122–129.

Pedregosa, F., et al. 2011. Scikit-learn: Machine learning in Python. *Machine Learning Research* 12:2825–2830.

Pennacchiotti, M., and Popescu, A.-M. 2011. A machine learning approach to twitter user classification. In Adamic, L. A.; Baeza-Yates, R. A.; and Counts, S., eds., *ICWSM*. The AAAI Press.

Quadrianto, N.; Smola, A. J.; Caetano, T. S.; and Le, Q. V. 2009. Estimating labels from label proportions. *J. Mach. Learn. Res.* 10:2349–2374.

Rao, D.; Yarowsky, D.; Shreevats, A.; and Gupta, M. 2010. Classifying latent user attributes in twitter. In *Proceedings of the 2nd International Workshop on Search and Mining User-generated Contents*, SMUC '10, 37–44. New York, NY, USA: ACM.

Rao, D.; Paul, M. J.; Fink, C.; Yarowsky, D.; Oates, T.; and Coppersmith, G. 2011. Hierarchical bayesian models for latent attribute detection in social media. In *ICWSM*.

Rosenthal, S., and McKeown, K. 2011. Age prediction in blogs: A study of style, content, and online behavior in pre- and post-social media generations. In *Proceedings of the 49th Annual Meeting of the Association for Computational Linguistics: Human Language Technologies - Volume 1*, HLT '11, 763–772. Stroudsburg, PA, USA: Association for Computational Linguistics.

Schler, J.; Koppel, M.; Argamon, S.; and Pennebaker, J. W. 2006. Effects of age and gender on blogging. In *AAAI 2006 Spring Symposium on Computational Approaches to Analysing Weblogs (AAAI-CAAW)*, 06–03.

Schwartz, H. A.; Eichstaedt, J. C.; Kern, M. L.; Dziurzynski, L.; Ramones, S. M.; Agrawal, M.; Shah, A.; Kosinski, M.; Stillwell, D.; Seligman, M. E.; et al. 2013. Characterizing geographic variation in well-being using tweets. In *Seventh International AAAI Conference on Weblogs and Social Media*.

Proceedings of the Twenty-Ninth AAAI Conference on Artificial Intelligence

High-Performance Distributed ML at Scale through Parameter Server Consistency Models

Wei Dai, Abhimanu Kumar, Jinliang Wei, Qirong Ho*, Garth Gibson and Eric P. Xing
School of Computer Science, Carnegie Mellon University
*Institute for Infocomm Research, A*STAR
twdai,abhimank,jinlianw,garth,epxing@cs.cmu.edu, hoqirong@gmail.com

Abstract

As Machine Learning (ML) applications embrace greater data size and model complexity, practitioners turn to distributed clusters to satisfy the increased computational and memory demands. Effective use of clusters for ML programs requires considerable expertise in writing distributed code, but existing highly-abstracted frameworks like Hadoop that pose low barriers to distributed-programming have not, in practice, matched the performance seen in highly specialized and advanced ML implementations. The recent Parameter Server (PS) paradigm is a middle ground between these extremes, allowing easy conversion of single-machine parallel ML programs into distributed ones, while maintaining high throughput through relaxed "consistency models" that allow asynchronous (and, hence, inconsistent) parameter reads. However, due to insufficient theoretical study, it is not clear which of these consistency models can really ensure correct ML algorithm output; at the same time, there remain many theoretically-motivated but undiscovered opportunities to maximize computational throughput. Inspired by this challenge, we study both the theoretical guarantees and empirical behavior of *iterative-convergent ML algorithms* in existing PS consistency models. We then use the gleaned insights to improve a consistency model using an "eager" PS communication mechanism, and implement it as a new PS system that enables ML programs to reach their solution more quickly.

Introduction

The surging data volumes generated by internet activity and scientific research (Dean et al. 2012) put tremendous pressure on Machine Learning (ML) methods to scale beyond the computation and memory limit of a single machine. With very large data sizes (Big Data), a single machine would require too much time to process complex ML models (Ahmed et al. 2012; Ho et al. 2013; Cipar et al. 2013; Cui et al. 2014; Li et al. 2014), and this motivates or even necessitates distributed-parallel computation over a cluster of machines. A popular approach is *data parallelism*, in which the data is partitioned and distributed across different machines, which then train the (shared) ML model using their local data. One of the primary challenges in data parallelism is designing software systems to share the ML model across a cluster of commodity machines, in a manner that is theoretically well-justified, empirically high-performance, and easy-to-program all at the same time — and a highly promising solution is the titular "Parameter Server" (PS) paradigm, which ML practitioners have been turning to in recent years (Ahmed et al. 2012; Ho et al. 2013; Cipar et al. 2013; Cui et al. 2014; Li et al. 2014).

Many general-purpose Parameter Server (PS) systems (Ho et al. 2013; Cipar et al. 2013; Cui et al. 2014) provide a Distributed Shared Memory (DSM) solution to the issue of Big Data in ML computation. DSM allows ML programmers to treat the entire cluster as a single memory pool, where every machine can read/write to any model parameter via a simple programming interface; this greatly facilitates the implementation of distributed ML programs, because programmers may treat a cluster like a "supercomputer" that can run thousands of computational threads, without worrying about low-level communication between machines. It should be noted that not all PS systems provide a DSM interface; some espouse an arguably less-convenient push/pull interface that requires users to explicitly decide which parts of the ML model need to be communicated (Li et al. 2014), in exchange for potentially more aggressive efficiency gains.

A major motivation behind the parameter server architecture is the opportunities it offers — without forcing users to use complicated distributed programming tools — to explore various relaxed consistency models for controlled asynchronous parallel execution of machine learning programs, in an effort to improve overall system efficiency. Central to the legitimacy of employing such inconsistent models — which in theory would cause erroneous outcomes — is the iterative-convergent nature of ML programs, which presents unique opportunities and challenges that do not manifest in traditional database applications. One of the most interesting opportunities is that iterative-convergent ML programs exhibit limited error-tolerance in the parameter states, a point that is confirmed by the theoretical and empirical success of stochastic subsampling (e.g. minibatch methods) or randomized algorithms, which are prominently represented in the large-scale ML literature (Ahmed et al. 2012; Ho et al. 2013; Gemulla et al. 2011; Kumar et al. 2014). The key challenge is to determine *why* error tolerance allows inconsistent execution models to accelerate distributed-parallel execution of ML algorithms on Big Data (while still producing correct answers), which in turn teaches us *how* to construct better execution models that not only have superior theoretical properties, but also enable more efficient systems designs.

Recent works (Niu et al. 2011; Ho et al. 2013; Kumar et al. 2014) have introduced relaxed consistency models to trade off between parameter read accuracy and read throughput, and show promising speedups over fully-consistent models. Their success is underpinned by the aforementioned error-tolerant nature of ML, that "plays nicely" with relaxed synchronization guarantees — and in turn, relaxed synchronization allows system designers to achieve higher throughput, compared to fully-consistent models. These progresses notwithstanding, we still possess limited understanding of (1) how relaxed consistency affects the convergence rate and stability of distributed ML algorithms, and (2) what opportunities remain undiscovered or unexploited to seek better trade-offs between the performance of the distributed ML algorithm (how much progress it makes per iteration, which can be compromised by relaxed consistency), and the throughput of the PS system (how many iterations can be executed per second, which increases with relaxed consistency). Contemporary PS literature has focused most on system optimizations for PSes, using various heuristics like async relaxation (Chilimbi et al. 2014) and uneven update propagation based on parameter values (Li et al. 2014), but lacks a thorough formal analysis of such trade-offs. In this paper, we investigate these issues from an ML-theoretic standpoint, and provide principled insights on how system behaviors influence algorithmic outcomes, as well as insights on how to improve PS design thereupon. Concretely, we examine the theoretical and empirical behavior of PS consistency models from several interesting angles, such as the distribution of stale reads and the impact of staleness on solution stability. We then apply the learnt insights to design a more efficient consistency model and, accordingly, a new PS system that outperforms its predecessors.

We begin with an in-depth examination of a Value-Bounded Asynchronous Parallel (VAP) model, which we formulated to encapsulate an appealing idea that can be shown to represent an ideal, gold-standard parallelization strategy in terms of theoretical behavior (high progress per ML algorithm iteration). Unfortunately, although the basic idea of VAP was attempted in (Li et al. 2013), mathematically the VAP principle can be only approximated, because bounding the value of in-transit updates amounts to tight synchronization. Without well-defined system guarantees, theses system artifacts built on approximate VAP are difficult to formally characterize. We then propose an Eager Stale Synchronous Parallel (ESSP) model, a variant of the Stale Synchronous Parallel (SSP, a bounded-iteration model that is fundamentally different from VAP) model introduced in (Ho et al. 2013), and formally show that ESSP offers a comparable guarantee to that of the ideal VAP, but represents a practical and easily realizable PS scheme for data-parallelization. Specifically, we establish expectation and variance bounds for both ESSP and VAP, and show that ESSP attains qualitatively the same guarantees as VAP, but with an arguably easier-to-control parameter (staleness versus value-bound), and significantly stronger guarantees than that of the original SSP. The variance bounds in particular provide a deeper characterization of convergence (particularly solution stability) under SSP and VAP, which is not possible with existing PS theory that is focused only on expectation bounds (Ho et al. 2013). Upon this new theory, we develop an efficient implementation of ESSP and shows that it outperforms SSP in convergence (both real time and per iteration) by reducing the average staleness, consistent with our theoretical results. This ESSP implementation will be made available soon as part of the Petuum project (www.petuum.org), an open-source framework for distributed Machine Learning.

Taking a broader view of recent large-scale ML efforts, we see our work as complementing *model-parallel* efforts (Lee et al. 2014; Kumar et al. 2014) that directly partition ML parameters for parallel updates (as opposed to PS-supported data-parallellism, where every data partition updates the *whole* parameter state). While the theoretical underpinnings of model-parallelism seem quite different from the data-parallel analysis espoused in this paper, we conjecture that the two types of parallelism are in fact compatible, and can be practically applied, as well as theoretically analyzed, in tandem. Since data-parallelism solves the issue of large data, while model-parallelism addresses massive ML model sizes, it seems only natural that their combination should yield a highly-promising solution to the Big ML challenge, where both data and model sizes greatly exceed the computational and memory capacity of a single machine. We expect the results presented in this paper will provide a desirable theoretical and systems paradigm for studying this promising direction in future work.

Parameter Server and Data Parallelism

We now make precise the data-parallel computation model and the parameter server (PS) abstraction that facilitates large-scale data-parallel computation. In data-parallel ML the data set D is pre-partitioned or naturally stored on worker machines, indexed by $p = 1, ..., P$ (Fig. 1a). Let D_p be the p-th data partition, $A^{(t)}$ be the model parameters at clock t, the data-parallel computation executes the following update equation until some convergence criteria is met:

$$A^{(t)} = F(A^{(t-1)}, \sum_{p=1}^{P} \Delta(A^{(t-1)}, D_p))$$

where $\Delta()$ performs computation using full model state $A^{(t-1)}$ on data partition D_p. The sum of intermediate results from $\Delta()$ and current model state $A^{(t-1)}$ are aggregated by $F()$ to generate the next model state. For stochastic gradient (SGD) algorithms like the one used in this paper for matrix factorization, $\Delta()$ computes the gradient and the update is $A^{(t)} = A^{(t-1)} + \eta \sum_{p=1}^{P} \Delta(A^{(t-1)}, D_p)$ with η being the step size. The second example application in this paper is topic model (LDA) using collapsed Gibbs sampling. In this case $\Delta()$ increments and decrements the sufficient

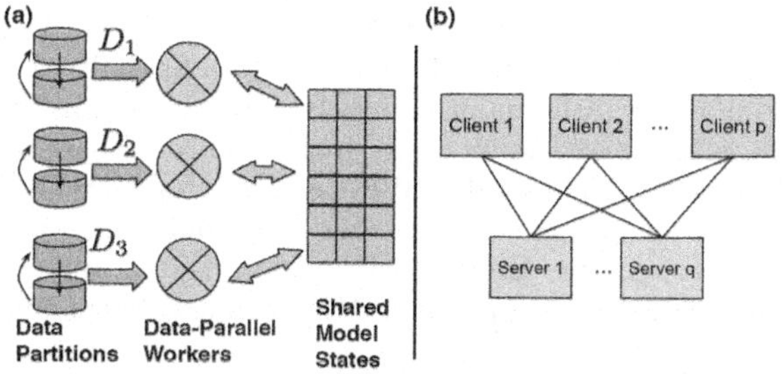

Figure 1: (a) Illustration of data parallelism. (b) Parameter server topology. Servers and clients interact via a bipartite topology. Note that this is the logical topology; physically the servers can collocate with the clients to utilize CPU on all machines.

statistics ("word-topic" counts) according to the sampled topic assignments. This update equation can also express variational EM algorithms $A^{(t)} = \sum_{p=1}^{P} \Delta(A^{(t-1)}, D_p)$. To achieve data-parallel ML computation, we need to (1) make model state A available to all workers, and (2) accumulate the Δ updates from workers. A Parameter Server (PS) serves these needs by providing a distributed shared memory interface (a shared key-value store using a centralized storage model). The model parameters A are stored on the server, which can be distributed and thus not limited by a single machine's memory (Fig. 1b). The worker machines access the entire model state on servers via a key-value interface. This distributed shared memory provided by the PS can be easily retrofitted to existing single-machine multithreaded ML programs, by simply replacing reads/updates to the model parameters with read/update calls to the PS. Because inter-machine communication over networks is several orders of magnitude slower than CPU-memory communication in both bandwidth and latency, one challenge in implementing an efficient PS is to design consistency models for efficient reads/updates of model parameters.

Consistency Models for Parameter Servers

A key idea for large-scale distributed ML is to carefully trade off parameter consistency for increased parameter read throughput (and thus faster algorithm execution), in a manner that guarantees the final output of an ML algorithm is still "correct" (meaning that it has reached a locally-optimal answer). This is possible because ML algorithms are *iterative-convergent* and *error-tolerant*: ML algorithms will converge to a local optimum even when there are errors in the algorithmic procedure itself (such as stochasticity in randomized methods).

In a distributed-parallel environment, multiple workers must simultaneously generate updates to shared global parameters. Hence, enforcing strong consistency (parameters updates are immediately reflected) quickly leads to frequent, time-consuming synchronization and thus very limited speed up from parallelization. One must therefore define a relaxed consistency model that enables low-synchronization parallelism while closely approximating the strong consistency of sequential execution. The insight is that, to an iterative-convergent ML algorithm, inconsistent parameter reads have essentially the same effect as errors due to the algorithmic procedure — implying that convergence to local optima can still happen even under inconsistent reads, *provided the degree of inconsistency is carefully controlled.* We now explain two possible PS consistency models, and the trade-offs they introduce.

The ideal but hard-to-realize Value-bounded Asynchronous Parallel (VAP) model

We first introduce Value-bounded Asynchronous Parallel (VAP), an ideal model that directly approximates strong consistency (e.g. in the sequential setting) by bounding the difference in *magnitude* between the strongly consistent view of values (i.e. values under the single-thread model) and the actual parameter views on the workers. Formally, let $\mathbf{x}$ represent all model parameters, and assume that each worker in the ML algorithm produces additive updates ($\mathbf{x} \leftarrow \mathbf{x} + \mathbf{u}$, where $\mathbf{u}$ is the update)[1]. Given P workers, we say that an update $\mathbf{u}$ is *in transit* if $\mathbf{u}$ has been seen by $P-1$ or fewer workers — in other words, it is yet visible by all workers. Update $\mathbf{u}$ is no longer in transit once seen by all workers. The VAP requires the following condition:

VAP condition: Let $\mathbf{u}_{p,i}$ be the updates from worker p that are in transit, and $\mathbf{u}_p := \sum_i \mathbf{u}_{p,i}$. VAP requires that, whenever any worker performs a computation involving the model variables $\mathbf{x}$, the condition $||\mathbf{u}_p||_\infty \leq v_{thr}$ holds for a specified (time-varying) value bound parameter v_{thr}. In other words, the aggregated in-transit updates from all workers cannot be too large.

To analyze VAP, we must identify algorithmic properties common to ML algorithms. Broadly speaking, most ML algorithms are either *optimization-based* or *sampling-based.* Within the former, many Big Data ML algorithms are stochastic gradient descent-based (SGD), because SGD allows each worker to operate on its own data partition (i.e. no need to transfer data between workers), while the algorithm parameters are globally shared (hence a PS is necessary). SGD's popularity makes it a good choice for grounding our analysis — in later section, we show that VAP approximates strong consistency well in these senses: (1) SGD with VAP errors converges *in expectation* to an optimum; (2) the parameter *variance* decreases in successive iterations, guaranteeing the quality and stability of the final result.

While being theoretically attractive, the VAP condition is too strong to be implemented efficiently in practice: before any worker can perform computation on $\mathbf{x}$, it must ensure that the in-transit updates from all other workers sum to at most v_{thr} component-wise due to the max-norm. This poses a chicken-and-egg conundrum: for a worker to ensure the VAP condition holds, it needs to know the updates from all other workers — which, in general, requires the same amount of communication as strong consistency, defeating the purpose of VAP. While it may be possible to relax the

[1]This is common in algorithms such as gradient descent ($\mathbf{u}$ being the gradient) and sampling methods.

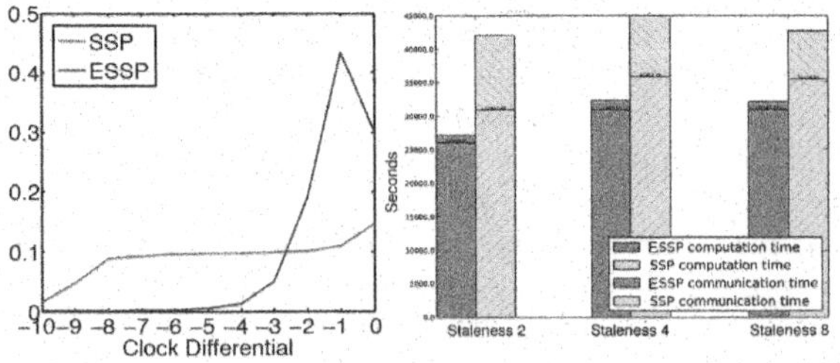

Figure 2: *Left:* Empirical staleness distribution from matrix factorization. X-axis is (parameter age - local clock), y-axis is the normalized observation count. Note that on Bulk Synchronous Parallel (BSP) system such as Map-Reduce, the staleness is always -1. We use rank 100 for matrix factorization, and each clock is 1% minibatch. The experiment is run on a 64 node cluster. *Right:* Communication and Computation breakdown for LDA. The lower part of the bars are computation, and the upper part is communication.

VAP condition for specific problem structures, in general, value-bounds are difficult to achieve for a generic PS.

Eager Stale Synchronous Parallel (ESSP)

To design a consistency model that is practically efficient while providing correctness guarantees, we consider an iteration-based consistency model called Stale Synchronous Parallel (SSP) (Ho et al. 2013) that can be efficiently implemented in PS. At a high level, SSP imposes bounds on *clock*, which represents some unit of work in an ML algorithm, akin to iteration. Given P workers, SSP assigns each worker a clock c_p that is initially zero. Then, each worker repeats the following operations: (1) perform computation using shared parameters $\mathbf{x}$ stored in the PS, (2) make additive updates $\mathbf{u}$ to the PS, and (3) advance its own clock c_p by 1. The SSP model limits fast workers' progress so that the clock difference between the fastest and slowest worker is $\leq s$, s being a specified staleness parameter. This is achieved via:

SSP Condition (informal): Let c be the clock of the fastest workers. They may not make further progress until all other workers' updates $\mathbf{u}_p$ that were made at clocks at or before $c - s - 1$ become visible.

We present the formal condition in the next section. Crucially, there are multiple update communication strategies that can meet the SSP condition. We present *Eager SSP (ESSP)* as a class of implementations that eagerly propagate the updates to reduce empirical staleness beyond required by SSP. ESSP does not provide new guarantees beyond SSP, but we show that by reducing the average staleness ESSP achieves faster convergence theoretically and empirically.

To show that ESSP reduces the staleness of parameter read, we can empirically measure the staleness of parameter reads during PS algorithm execution. Fig. 2 (left) shows the distribution of parameter staleness observed in matrix factorization implemented on SSP and ESSP. Our measure of staleness is a "clock differential": when a worker reads a parameter, the read parameters reflect updates from other worker 0 or more clocks behind. Clock differential simply measures this clock difference. Under SSP, the distribution of clock differentials is nearly uniform, because SSP "waits until the last minute" to update the local parameter cache. On the other hand, ESSP frequently updates the local parameter caches via its eager communication, which reduces the negative tail in clock differential distribution — this improved staleness profile is ESSP's most salient advantage over SSP. In the sequel, we will show that better staleness profiles lead to faster ML algorithm convergence, by proving new, stronger convergence bounds based on average staleness and the staleness distributions (unlike the simpler worst-case bounds in (Ho et al. 2013)).

Our analyses and experiments show that ESSP combines the strengths of VAP and SSP: (1) ESSP achieves strong theoretical properties comparable to VAP; (2) ESSP can be efficiently implemented, with excellent empirical performance on two ML algorithms: matrix completion using SGD, and topic modeling using sampling. We also show that ESSP achieves higher throughput than SSP, thanks to system optimizations exploiting ESSP's aggressive scheduling.

Theoretical Analysis

In this section, we theoretically analyze VAP and ESSP, and show how they affect ML algorithm convergence. For space reasons, all proofs are placed in the appendix. We ground our analysis on ML algorithms in the stochastic gradient descent (SGD) family (due to its high popularity for Big Data), and prove the convergence of SGD under VAP and ESSP. We now explain SGD in the context of a matrix completion problem.

SGD for Low Rank Matrix Factorization

Matrix completion involves decomposing an $N \times M$ matrix D into two low rank matrices $L \in \mathbb{R}^{N \times K}$ and $R \in \mathbb{R}^{K \times M}$ such that $LR \approx D$ gives the prediction of missing entries in D, where $K << \min\{M, N\}$ is a user-specified rank. The ℓ_2-penalized optimization problem is:

$$\min_{L,R} \sum_{(i,j) \in D_{obs}} ||D_{ij} - \sum_{k=1}^{K} L_{ik} R_{kj}||^2 + \lambda(||L||_F^2 + ||R||_F^2)$$

where $|| \cdot ||_F$ is the Frobenius norm and λ is the regularization parameter. The stochastic gradient updates for each observed entry $D_{ij} \in D_{obs}$ are

$$L_{i*} \leftarrow L_{i*} + \gamma(e_{ij} R_{*j}^{\top} - \lambda L_{i*})$$
$$R_{*j}^{\top} \leftarrow R_{*j} + \gamma(e_{ij} L_{i*}^{\top} - \lambda R_{*j})$$

where L_{i*}, R_{*j} are row and column of L, R respectively, and $L_{i*} R_{*j}$ is the vector product. $e_{ij} = D_{ij} - L_{i*} R_{*j}$. Since L, R are being updated by each gradient, we put them in the parameter server to allow all workers access them and make additive updates. The data D_{obs} are partitioned into worker nodes and stored locally.

VAP We formally introduce the VAP computation model: given P workers that produce updates at regular intervals which we call "clocks", let $\mathbf{u}_{p,c} \in \mathbb{R}^n$ be the update from worker p at clock c applied to the system state $\mathbf{x} \in \mathbb{R}^n$ via $\mathbf{x} \leftarrow \mathbf{x} + \mathbf{u}_{p,c}$. Consider the update sequence $\hat{\mathbf{u}}_t$ that orders the updates based on the global time-stamp they are generated. We can define "real-time sequence" $\hat{\mathbf{x}}_t$ as

$$\hat{\mathbf{x}}_t := \mathbf{x}_0 + \sum_{t'=1}^{t} \hat{\mathbf{u}}_{t'}$$

assuming all workers start from the agreed-upon initial state $\mathbf{x}_0$. (Note that $\hat{\mathbf{x}}_t$ is different from the parameter server view as the updates from different workers can arrive the server in a different order due to network.) Let $\breve{\mathbf{x}}_t$ be the noisy view some worker w sees when generating update $\hat{\mathbf{u}}_t$, i.e., $\hat{\mathbf{u}}_t := G(\breve{\mathbf{x}}_t)$ for some function G. The VAP condition guarantees

$$||\breve{\mathbf{x}}_t - \hat{\mathbf{x}}_t||_\infty \le v_t = \frac{v_0}{\sqrt{t}} \tag{1}$$

where we require the value bound v_t to shrink over time from the initial bound v_0. Notice that $\breve{\mathbf{x}}_t - \hat{\mathbf{x}}_t$ is exactly the updates *in transit* w.r.t. worker w. We make mild assumptions to avoid pathological cases.[2]

Theorem 1 *(SGD under VAP, convergence in expectation) Given convex function $f(\boldsymbol{x}) = \sum_{t=1}^{T} f_t(\boldsymbol{x})$ such that components f_t are also convex. We search for minimizer $\boldsymbol{x}^*$ via gradient descent on each component ∇f_t with step-size $\breve{\eta}_t$ close to $\eta_t = \frac{\eta}{\sqrt{t}}$ such that the update $\hat{\boldsymbol{u}}_t = -\breve{\eta}_t \nabla f_t(\breve{\boldsymbol{x}}_t)$ is computed on noisy view $\breve{\boldsymbol{x}}_t$. The VAP bound follows the decreasing v_t described above. Under suitable conditions (f_t are L-Lipschitz and bounded diameter $D(x\|x') \le F^2$),*

$$R[X] := \sum_{t=1}^{T} f_t(\breve{\boldsymbol{x}}_t) - f(\boldsymbol{x}^*) = \mathcal{O}(\sqrt{T})$$

and thus $\frac{R[X]}{T} \to 0$ as $T \to \infty$.

Theorem 1 implies that the worker's noisy VAP view $\breve{\mathbf{x}}_t$ converges to the global optimum $\mathbf{x}^*$, as measured by f, in expectation at the rate $\mathcal{O}(T^{-1/2})$. The analysis is similar to (Ho et al. 2013), but we use the real-time sequence $\hat{\mathbf{x}}_t$ as our reference sequence and VAP condition instead of SSP. Loosely speaking, Theorem 1 shows that VAP execution is unbiased. We now present a new bound on the variance.

Theorem 2 *(SGD under VAP, bounded variance) Assuming $f(\boldsymbol{x})$, $\breve{\eta}_t$, and v_t similar to theorem 1 above, and $f(\boldsymbol{x})$ has bounded and invertible Hessian, Ω^* defined at optimal point $\boldsymbol{x}^*$. Let $\mathrm{Var}_t := \mathbb{E}[\breve{x}_t^2] - \mathbb{E}[\breve{x}_t]^2$ (Var_t is the sum of component-wise variance[3]), and $\breve{g}_t = \nabla f_t(\breve{x}_t)$ is the gradient, then:*

$$\mathrm{Var}_{t+1} = \mathrm{Var}_t - 2cov(\hat{\boldsymbol{x}}_t, \mathbb{E}^{\Delta_t}[\breve{g}_t]) + \mathcal{O}(\delta_t) \tag{2}$$
$$+ \mathcal{O}(\breve{\eta}_t^2 \rho_t^2) + \mathcal{O}^*_{\delta_t} \tag{3}$$

near the optima $\boldsymbol{x}^*$. The covariance $cov(\boldsymbol{a}, \boldsymbol{b}) := \mathbb{E}[\boldsymbol{a}^T\boldsymbol{b}] - \mathbb{E}[\boldsymbol{a}^T]\mathbb{E}[\boldsymbol{b}]$ uses inner product. $\delta_t = ||\boldsymbol{\delta}_t||_\infty$ and $\boldsymbol{\delta}_t = \breve{\boldsymbol{x}}_t - \hat{\boldsymbol{x}}_t$. $\rho_t = ||\breve{\boldsymbol{x}}_t - \boldsymbol{x}^*||$. Δ_t is a random variable capturing the randomness of update $\hat{\boldsymbol{u}}_t = -\eta_t \breve{\boldsymbol{g}}_t$ conditioned on $\hat{\boldsymbol{x}}_t$ (see appendix).

$cov(\hat{\mathbf{x}}_t, \mathbb{E}^{\Delta_t}[\breve{g}_t]) \ge 0$ in general as the change in $\mathbf{x}_t$ and average gradient $\mathbb{E}^{\Delta_t}[\breve{g}_t]$ are of the same direction. Theorem 2 implies that under VAP the variance decreases in successive iterations for sufficiently small δ_t, which can be controlled via VAP threshold v_t. However, the VAP condition requires tight synchronization as $\delta_t \to 0$. This motivates our following analysis of the SSP model.

SSP We return to the (p, c) index. Under the SSP worker p at clock c only has access to a noisy view $\tilde{\mathbf{x}}_{p,c}$ of the system state ($\tilde{\mathbf{x}}$ is different from the noisy view in VAP $\breve{\mathbf{x}}$). Update $\mathbf{u}_{p,c} = G(\tilde{\mathbf{x}}_{p,c})$ is computed on the noisy view $\tilde{\mathbf{x}}_{p,c}$ for some function $G()$. Assuming all workers start from the agreed-upon initial state $\mathbf{x}_0$, the SSP condition is:

SSP Bounded-Staleness (formal): For a fixed staleness s, the noisy state $\tilde{\mathbf{x}}_{p,c}$ is equal to

$$\tilde{\mathbf{x}}_{p,c} = \mathbf{x}_0 + \underbrace{\left[\sum_{c'=1}^{c-s-1}\sum_{p'=1}^{P} \mathbf{u}_{p',c'}\right]}_{\text{guaranteed pre-window updates}} + \underbrace{\left[\sum_{(p',c')\in\mathcal{S}_{p,c}} \mathbf{u}_{p',c'}\right]}_{\text{best-effort in-window updates}},$$

for some $\mathcal{S}_{p,c} \subseteq \mathcal{W}_{p,c} = \{1, ..., P\} \times \{c - s, ..., c + s - 1\}$ which is some subset of updates in the $2s$ window issued by all P workers during clock $c - s$ to $c + s - 1$. The noisy view consists of (1) guaranteed pre-window updates for clock 1 to $c - s - 1$, and (2) best-effort updates indexed by $\mathcal{S}_{p,c}$.[4] We introduce a clock-major index t:

$$\tilde{\mathbf{x}}_t := \tilde{\mathbf{x}}_{(t \bmod P), \lfloor t/P \rfloor} \qquad \mathbf{u}_t := \mathbf{u}_{(t \bmod P), \lfloor t/P \rfloor}$$

and analogously for $\mathcal{S}_t$ and $\mathcal{W}_t$. We can now define a reference sequence (distinct from $\hat{\mathbf{x}}_t$ in VAP) which we informally refers to as the "true" sequence:

$$\mathbf{x}_t = \mathbf{x}_0 + \sum_{t'=0}^{t} \mathbf{u}_{t'} \tag{4}$$

The sum loops over workers ($t \bmod P$) and clocks $\lfloor t/P \rfloor$. Notice that this sequence is unrelated to the server view.

Theorem 3 *(SGD under SSP, convergence in expectation (Ho et al. 2013), Theorem 1) Given convex function $f(\boldsymbol{x}) = \sum_{t=1}^{T} f_t(\boldsymbol{x})$ with suitable conditions as in Theorem 1, we use gradient descent with updates $\boldsymbol{u}_t = -\eta_t \nabla f_t(\tilde{\boldsymbol{x}}_t)$ generated from noisy view $\tilde{\boldsymbol{x}}_t$ and $\eta_t = \frac{\eta}{\sqrt{t}}$. Then*

$$R[X] := \sum_{t=1}^{T} f_t(\tilde{\boldsymbol{x}}_t) - f(\boldsymbol{x}^*) = \mathcal{O}(\sqrt{T})$$

and thus $\frac{R[X]}{T} \to 0$ as $T \to \infty$.

[2] To avoid pathological cases where a worker is delayed indefinitely, we assume that each worker's updates are finitely apart in sequence $\hat{\mathbf{u}}_t$. In other words, all workers generate updates with sufficient frequency. For SGD, we further assume that each worker updates its step-sizes sufficiently often that the local step-size $\breve{\eta}_t = \frac{\eta}{\sqrt{t-r}}$ for some bounded drift $r \ge 0$ and thus $\breve{\eta}_t$ is close to the global step size schedule $\eta_t = \frac{\eta}{\sqrt{t}}$.

[3] $\mathrm{Var}_t = \sum_{i=1}^{d} \mathbb{E}[\breve{x}_{ti}^2] - \mathbb{E}[\breve{x}_{ti}]^2$

[4] In contrast to (Ho et al. 2013), we do not assume read-my-write.

Theorem 3 is the SSP-counterpart of Theorem 1. The analysis of Theorem 3 only uses the worst-case SSP bounds. However, in practice many updates are much less stale than the SSP bound. In Fig 2 (left) both implementations have only a small portion of updates with maximum staleness.

We now use moment statistics to further characterize the convergence. We begin by decomposing $\tilde{\mathbf{x}}_t$. Let $\bar{u}_t := \frac{1}{P(2s+1)} \sum_{t' \in \mathcal{W}_t} ||\mathbf{u}_{t'}||_2$ be the average of ℓ_2 of the updates. We can write the noisy view $\tilde{\mathbf{x}}_t$ as

$$\tilde{\mathbf{x}}_t = \mathbf{x}_t + \bar{u}_t \gamma_t \quad (5)$$

where $\gamma_t \in \mathbb{R}^d$ is a vector of random variables whose randomness lies in the network communication. Note that the decomposition in eq. 5 is always possible since $\bar{u}_t = 0$ iff $\mathbf{u}_{t'} = \mathbf{0}$ for all updates $\mathbf{u}_{t'}$ in the $2s$ window. Using SSP we can bound $\bar{u}_t$ and γ_t:

Lemma 4 $\bar{u}_t \leq \frac{\eta}{\sqrt{t}} L$ *and* $\gamma_t := ||\gamma_t||_2 \leq P(2s+1)$.

Therefore $\mu_\gamma = \mathbb{E}[\gamma_t]$ and $\sigma_\gamma = var(\gamma_t)$ are well-defined. We now provide an exponential tail-bound characterizing convergence in finite steps.

Theorem 5 *(SGD under SSP, convergence in probability) Given convex function* $f(\boldsymbol{x}) = \sum_{t=1}^T f_t(\boldsymbol{x})$ *such that components* f_t *are also convex. We search for minimizer* $\boldsymbol{x}^*$ *via gradient descent on each component* ∇f_t *under SSP with staleness parameter* s *and* P *workers. Let* $\boldsymbol{u}_t := -\eta_t \nabla_t f_t(\tilde{\boldsymbol{x}}_t)$ *with* $\eta_t = \frac{\eta}{\sqrt{t}}$*. Under suitable conditions (*f_t *are L-Lipschitz and bounded divergence* $D(x||x') \leq F^2$*), we have*

$$P\left[\frac{R[X]}{T} - \frac{1}{\sqrt{T}}\left(\eta L^2 + \frac{F^2}{\eta} + 2\eta L^2 \mu_\gamma\right) \geq \tau\right] \leq \exp\left\{\frac{-T\tau^2}{2\bar{\eta}_T \sigma_\gamma + \frac{2}{3}\eta L^2(2s+1)P\tau}\right\}$$

where $R[X] := \sum_{t=1}^T f_t(\tilde{x}_t) - f(x^*)$*, and* $\bar{\eta}_T = \frac{\eta^2 L^4 (\ln T + 1)}{T} = o(T)$.

This means that $\frac{R[X]}{T}$ converges to $O(T^{-1/2})$ in probability with an exponential tail-bound. Also note that the convergence is faster for smaller μ_γ and σ_γ.

We need a few mild assumptions on the staleness γ_t in order to derive variance bound:

Assumption 1 γ_t *are i.i.d. random variable with well-defined mean* μ_γ *and variance* σ_γ.

Assumption 2 γ_t *is independent of* $\boldsymbol{x}_t$ *and* $\boldsymbol{u}_t$.

Assumption 1 is satisfied by Lemma 4, while Assumption 2 is valid since γ_t are only influenced by the computational load and network bandwidth at each machine, which are themselves independent of the actual values of the computation ($\mathbf{u}_t$ and $\mathbf{x}_t$). We now present an SSP variance bound.

Theorem 6 *(SGD under SSP, decreasing variance) Given the setup in Theorem 5 and assumption 1-2. Further assume that* $f(\boldsymbol{x})$ *has bounded and invertible Hessian* Ω^* *at optimum* $\boldsymbol{x}^*$ *and* γ_t *is bounded. Let* $\mathrm{Var}_t := \mathbb{E}[\tilde{\boldsymbol{x}}_t^2] - \mathbb{E}[\tilde{\boldsymbol{x}}_t]^2$, $\boldsymbol{g}_t = \nabla f_t(\tilde{\boldsymbol{x}}_t)$ *then for* $\tilde{\boldsymbol{x}}_t$ *near the optima* $\boldsymbol{x}^*$ *such that* $\rho_t = ||\tilde{\boldsymbol{x}}_t - \boldsymbol{x}^*||$ *and* $\xi_t = ||\boldsymbol{g}_t|| - ||\boldsymbol{g}_{t+1}||$ *are small:*

$$\mathrm{Var}_{t+1} = \mathrm{Var}_t - 2\eta_t cov(\boldsymbol{x}_t, \mathbb{E}^{\Delta_t}[\boldsymbol{g}_t]) + \mathcal{O}(\eta_t \xi_t) \quad (6)$$

$$+ \mathcal{O}(\eta_t^2 \rho_t^2) + \mathcal{O}^*_{\gamma_t} \quad (7)$$

where covariance $cov(\boldsymbol{a}, \boldsymbol{b}) := \mathbb{E}[\boldsymbol{a}^T \boldsymbol{b}] - \mathbb{E}[\boldsymbol{a}^T]\mathbb{E}[\boldsymbol{b}]$ *uses inner product.* $\mathcal{O}^*_{\gamma_t}$ *are high order (≥ 5th) terms involving* $\gamma_t = ||\gamma_t||_\infty$. Δ_t *is a random variable capturing the randomness of update* $\boldsymbol{u}_t$ *conditioned on* $\boldsymbol{x}_t$ *(see appendix).*

As argued before, $cov(\mathbf{x}_t, \mathbb{E}^{\Delta_t}[\boldsymbol{g}_t]) \geq 0$ in general. Therefore the theorem implies that Var_t monotonically decreases over time when SGD is close to an optima.

Comparison of VAP and ESSP

From Theorem 2 and 6 we see that both VAP and (E)SSP decrease the variance of the model parameters. However, VAP convergence is much more sensitive to its tuning parameter (the VAP threshold) than (E)SSP, whose tuning parameter is the staleness s. This is evident from the $O(\delta_t)$ term in Eq. 3, which is bounded by the VAP threshold. In contrast, (E)SSP's variance only involves staleness γ_t in high order terms $\mathcal{O}^*_{\gamma_t}$ (Eq. 7), where γ_t is bounded by staleness. This implies that staleness-induced variance vanishes quickly in (E)SSP. The main reason for (E)SSP's weak dependency on staleness is because it "factors in" the SGD step size: as the algorithm approaches an optimum, the updates automatically become more fine-grained (i.e. their magnitude decreases), which is conducive for lowering variance. On the other hand, the VAP threshold forces a minimum size on updates, and without adjusting this threshold, the VAP updates cannot become more fine-grained.

An intuitive analogy is that of postmen: VAP is like a postman who only ever delivers mail above a certain weight threshold δ. (E)SSP is like a postman who delivers mail late, but no later than s days. Intuitively, the (E)SSP postman is more reliable than the VAP postman due to his regularity. The only way for the VAP postman to be reliable, is to decrease the weight threshold. This is important when the algorithm approaches convergence, because the algorithm's updates become diminishingly small. However, there are two drawbacks to decreasing δ: first, much like step-size tuning, it must be done at a carefully controlled rate — this requires either specific knowledge about the ML problem, or a sophisticated, automatic scheme (that may also be domain-specific). Second, as δ decreases, VAP produces more frequent communication and reduces the throughput.

In contrast to VAP, ESSP does not suffer as much from these drawbacks, because: (1) the SSP family has a weaker theoretical dependency on the staleness threshold (than VAP does on its value-bound threshold), thus it is usually unnecessary to decrease the staleness as the ML algorithm approaches convergence. This is evidenced by (Ho et al. 2013), which achieved stable convergence even though they did not decrease staleness gradually during ML algorithm execution. (2) Because ESSP proactively pushes out fresh parameter values, the distribution of stale reads is usually close to zero-staleness, regardless of the actual staleness threshold used (see Fig. 2) — hence, fine-grained tuning of the staleness threshold is rarely necessary under ESSP.

ESSPTable: An efficient ESSP System

Our theory suggests that an ESSP implementation using eager parameter updates should outperform a SSP implementation using stalest parameters, when network bandwidth is sufficient. To verify this, we implement ESSP in Parameter Server (PS), which we call ESSPTable.

PS Interface: ESSPTable organizes the model parameters as tables, where each parameter is assigned with a row ID and column ID. Rows are the unit of parameter communication between servers and clients; ML applications can use one of the default types or customize the row data-structure for maximal flexibility. For example, in LDA, rows are word-topic vectors. In MF, rows in a table are rows in the factor matrices.

In ESSPTable each computation thread is regarded as a worker by the system. The computation threads execute application logic and access the global parameters stored in ESSPTable through a key-value store interface—read a table-row via `GET` and write via `INC` (increment, i.e. addition). Once a computation thread completes a clock tick, it notifies the system via `CLOCK`, which increments the worker's clock by 1. As required by the SSP consistency , a `READ` issued by a worker at clock c is guaranteed to observe all updates generated in clock $[0, c - s - 1]$, where s is the user-defined staleness threshold.

Ensuring Consistency: The ESSPTable client library caches previously accessed parameters. When a computation thread issues a `GET` request, it first checks the local cache for the requested parameters. If the requested parameter is not found in local cache, a read request is sent to the server and a call-back is registered at the server.

Each parameter in the client local cache is associated with a clock c_i. $c_i = t$ means that all updates from all workers generated before clock t have already been applied to this parameter. c_i is compared with the worker's clock c_p. Only if $c_i > c_p - s$, the requested parameter is returned to the worker. Otherwise, the reader thread is blocked until an up-to-date parameter is received from the server.

Communication Protocol: The updates generated by computation threads are coalesced since they are commutative and associative. These updates are sent to the server at the end of each clock tick. The server sends updated parameters to the client through call-backs. When a client request a table-row for the first time, it registers a call-back on the server. This is the only time the client makes read request to the server. Subsequently, when a server table's clock advances from getting the clock tick from all clients, it pushes out the table-rows to the respective registered clients. This differs from the SSPTable in (Ho et al. 2013) where the server passively sends out updates upon client's read request (which happens each time a client's local cache becomes too stale). The call-back mechanism exploits the fact that computation threads often revisit the same parameters in iterative-convergent algorithms, and thus the server can push out table-rows to registered clients without clients' explicit request. Our server-push model causes more eager communication and thus lower empirical staleness than SSPTable in (Ho et al. 2013) as shown in Fig. 2 (left).

We empirically observed that the time needed to communicate the coalesced updates accumulated in one clock is usually less than the computation time. Thus computation threads usually observe parameters with staleness 1 regardless of the user-specified staleness threshold s. That relieves the burden of staleness tuning. Also, since the server pushes out updated parameters to registered clients in batches, it reduces the overall latency from sending each parameter separately upon clients' requests (which is the case in SSPTable). This improvement is shown in our experiments.

Experiments

We show that ESSP improves the speed and quality of convergence (versus SSP) for collapsed gibbs sampling in topic model and stochastic gradient descent (SGD) in matrix factorization. Furthermore, ESSP is robust against the staleness setting, relieving the user from worrying about an additional tuning parameter. The experimental setups are:

- **ML Models and algorithms:** LDA topic modeling (using a sparsified collapsed Gibbs sampling in (Yao, Mimno, and McCallum 2009)) and Matrix Factorization (using stochastic gradient descent (Koren 2009)). Both algorithms are implemented using ESSPTable's interface. For LDA we use 50% minibatch in each `Clock()` call, and we use log-likelihood as measure of training quality. For MF we use 1% and 10% minibatch in each `Clock()` and record the squared loss instead of the ℓ_2-penalized objective. The step size for MF is chosen to be large while the algorithm still converges with staleness 0.
- **Datasets** Topic model: New York Times ($N = 100m$ tokens, $V = 100k$ vocabularies, and $K = 100$ topics). Matrix factorization: Netflix dataset ($480k$ by $18k$ matrix with $100m$ nonzeros.) Unless stated otherwise, we use rank $K = 100$ and regularization parameter $\lambda = 0.1$.
- **Compute cluster** Matrix factorization experiments were run on 64 nodes, each with 2 cores and 16GB RAM, connected via 1Gbps ethernet. LDA experiments were run on 8 nodes, each with 64 cores and 128GB memory, connected via 1Gbps ethernet.

Speed of Convergence: Figure 3 shows the objective over iteration and time for LDA and matrix factorization. In both cases ESSP converges faster or comparable to SSP with respect to iteration and run time. The speed up over iteration is due to the reduced staleness as shown in the staleness profile (Figure 2, left). This is consistent with the fact that in SSP, computation making use of fresh data makes more progress (Ho et al. 2013). Also it is worth pointing out that large staleness values help SSP substantially but much less so for ESSP because ESSP is less sensitive to staleness.

Robustness to Staleness: One important tuning knob in SGD-type of algorithms are the step size. Step sizes that are too small leads to slow convergence, while step sizes

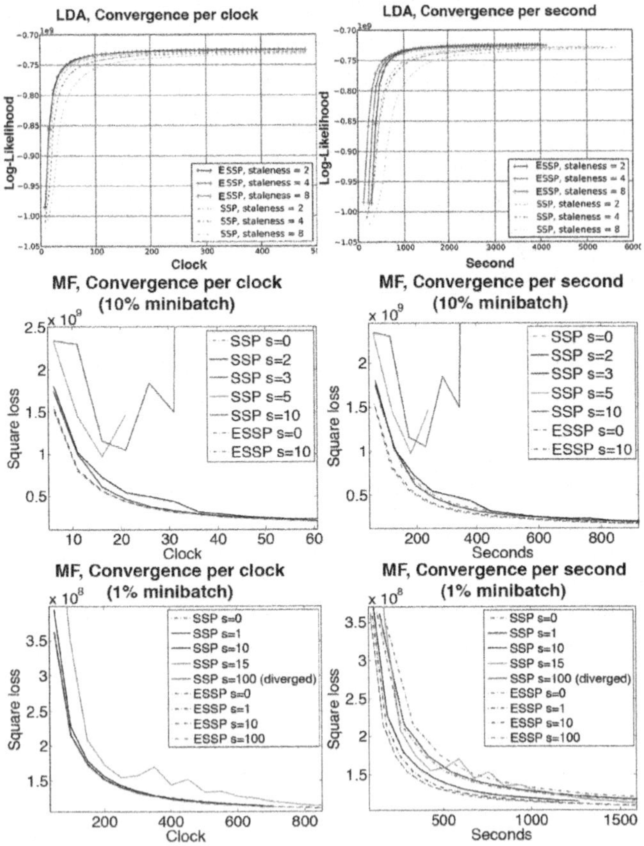

Figure 3: Experimental Results. The convergence speed per iteration and per second for LDA and MF.

that are too large cause divergence. The problem of step size tuning is aggravated in the distributed settings, where staleness could aggregate the updates in a non-deterministic manner, causing unpredictable performance (dependent on network congestion and the machine speeds). In the case of MF, SSP diverges under high staleness, as staleness effectively increases the step size. However, ESSP is robust across all investigated staleness values due to the concentrated staleness profile (Fig. 2, left). For some high SSP staleness, the convergence is "shaky" due to the variance introduced by staleness. ESSP produces lower variance for all staleness settings, consistent with our theoretical analyses. This improvement largely reduced the need for user to tune the staleness parameter introduced in SSP.

System Opportunity In addition to faster convergence per iteration, ESSP provides opportunities for system to optimize the communication. By sending updates preemptively, ESSP not only reduces the staleness but also reduces the chance of client threads being blocked to wait for updates; in essence, ESSP is a more "pipelined" version of SSP. Figure 2 (right) shows the breakdown of communication and compuation time for varying staleness. This contributes to the overall convergence per second in Figure 3, where ESSP has larger margin of speed gain over SSP than the convergence per iteration.

Related Work and Discussion

Existing software that is tailored towards *distributed* (rather than merely single-machine parallel), scalable ML can be roughly grouped into two categories: general-purpose, programmable libraries or frameworks such as GraphLab (Low et al. 2010) and Parameter Servers (PSes) (Ho et al. 2013; Li et al. 2013), or special-purpose solvers tailored to specific categories of ML applications: CCD++ (Yu et al. 2012) for Matrix Factorization, Vowpal Wabbit for regression/classification problems via stochastic optimization (Langford, Li, and Strehl 2007), and Yahoo LDA as well as Google plda for topic modeling (Wang et al. 2009).

The primary differences between the general-purpose frameworks (including this work) and the special-purpose solvers are (1) the former are user-programmable and can be extended to handle arbitrary ML applications, while the latter are non-programmable and restricted to predefined ML applications; (2) because the former must support arbitrary ML programs, their focus is on improving the "systems" code (notably, communication and synchronization protocols) to increase the efficiency of *all ML algorithms*, particularly through the careful design of consistency models (graph consistency in GraphLab; iteration/value-bounded consistency in PSes) — in contrast, the special-purpose systems combine both systems code improvements and *algorithmic* (i.e. mathematical) improvements tailor-made for their specific category of ML applications.

As a paper about general-purpose distributed ML, we focus on consistency models and systems code, and we deliberately use (relatively) simple algorithms for our benchmark applications, for two reasons: (1) to provide a fair comparison, we must match the code/algorithmic complexity of the benchmarks for other frameworks like GraphLab and SSP PS (Ho et al. 2013) (2) a general-purpose ML framework should not depend on highly-specialized algorithmic techniques tailored only to specific ML categories. General-purpose frameworks should *democratize distributed ML* in a way that special-purpose solvers cannot, by enabling those ML applications that have been under-served by the distributed ML research community to benefit from cluster computing. Since our benchmark applications are kept algorithmically simple, they are unlikely to beat the special-purpose solvers in running time — but we note that many algorithmic techniques featured in those solvers can be applied to our benchmark applications due to the general-purpose nature of PS programming.

In (Li et al. 2013), the authors propose and implement a PS consistency model that has similar theoretical guarantees to the ideal VAP model presented herein. However, we note that their implementation does not strictly enforce the conditions of their consistency model. Their implementation implicitly assumes zero latency for transmission over network, while in a real cluster, there could be arbitrarily long network delay. In their system, reads do not wait for delayed updates, so a worker may compute with highly inconsistent parameters in the case of congested network.

On the wider subject of Big Data, Hadoop (Borthakur 2007) and Spark (Zaharia et al. 2010) are popular programming frameworks which ML applications have been developed on. To our knowledge, there is no work showing that Hadoop or Spark have superior ML algorithm performance compared to frameworks designed for ML like GraphLab and PSes (let alone the special-purpose solvers). The main difference is that Hadoop/Spark only feature strict consistency, and do not support flexible consistency models like graph- or bounded-consistency; but Hadoop and Spark ensure program portability, reliability and fault tolerance at a level that GraphLab and PSes have yet to match.

Acknowledgement

This work is supported by DARPA XDATA FA87501220324, NSF IIS1447676, and ONR N000141410684.

References

Ahmed, A.; Aly, M.; Gonzalez, J.; Narayanamurthy, S.; and Smola, A. J. 2012. Scalable inference in latent variable models. In *WSDM*, 123–132.

Borthakur, D. 2007. The hadoop distributed file system: Architecture and design. *Hadoop Project Website* 11:21.

Chilimbi, T.; Suzue, Y.; Apacible, J.; and Kalyanaraman, K. 2014. Project adam: Building an efficient and scalable deep learning training system. In *11th USENIX Symposium on Operating Systems Design and Implementation (OSDI 14)*, 571–582. Broomfield, CO: USENIX Association.

Cipar, J.; Ho, Q.; Kim, J. K.; Lee, S.; Ganger, G. R.; Gibson, G.; Keeton, K.; and Xing, E. 2013. Solving the straggler problem with bounded staleness. In *HotOS '13*. Usenix.

Cui, H.; Cipar, J.; Ho, Q.; Kim, J. K.; Lee, S.; Kumar, A.; Wei, J.; Dai, W.; Ganger, G. R.; Gibbons, P. B.; Gibson, G. A.; and Xing, E. P. 2014. Exploiting bounded staleness to speed up big data analytics. In *2014 USENIX Annual Technical Conference (USENIX ATC 14)*, 37–48. Philadelphia, PA: USENIX Association.

Dean, J.; Corrado, G.; Monga, R.; Chen, K.; Devin, M.; Le, Q.; Mao, M.; Ranzato, M.; Senior, A.; Tucker, P.; Yang, K.; and Ng, A. 2012. Large scale distributed deep networks. In *NIPS 2012*.

Gemulla, R.; Nijkamp, E.; Haas, P. J.; and Sismanis, Y. 2011. Large-scale matrix factorization with distributed stochastic gradient descent. In *KDD*, 69–77. ACM.

Ho, Q.; Cipar, J.; Cui, H.; Kim, J.-K.; Lee, S.; Gibbons, P. B.; Gibson, G.; Ganger, G. R.; and Xing, E. P. 2013. More effective distributed ml via a stale synchronous parallel parameter server. In *NIPS*.

Koren, Y. 2009. Matrix factorization techniques for recommender systems. *IEEE Computer* 42(8):30–37.

Kumar, A.; Beutel, A.; Ho, Q.; and Xing, E. P. 2014. Fugue: Slow-worker-agnostic distributed learning for big models on big data. In *Proceedings of the Seventeenth International Conference on Artificial Intelligence and Statistics*, 531–539.

Langford, J.; Li, L.; and Strehl, A. 2007. Vowpal wabbit online learning project.

Lee, S.; Kim, J. K.; Zheng, X.; Ho, Q.; Gibson, G. A.; and Xing, E. P. 2014. Primitives for dynamic big model parallelism. In *Advances in Neural Information Processing Systems (NIPS)*.

Li, M.; Yang, L. Z. Z.; Xia, A. L. F.; Andersen, D. G.; and Smola, A. 2013. Parameter server for distributed machine learning. *NIPS workshop*.

Li, M.; Andersen, D. G.; Park, J. W.; Smola, A. J.; Ahmed, A.; Josifovski, V.; Long, J.; Shekita, E. J.; and Su, B.-Y. 2014. Scaling distributed machine learning with the parameter server. In *Operating Systems Design and Implementation (OSDI)*.

Low, Y.; Gonzalez, J.; Kyrola, A.; Bickson, D.; Guestrin, C.; and Hellerstein, J. M. 2010. Graphlab: A new parallel framework for machine learning. In *Conference on Uncertainty in Artificial Intelligence (UAI)*.

Niu, F.; Recht, B.; Ré, C.; and Wright, S. J. 2011. Hogwild!: A lock-free approach to parallelizing stochastic gradient descent. In *NIPS*.

Wang, Y.; Bai, H.; Stanton, M.; Chen, W.-Y.; and Chang, E. Y. 2009. Plda: Parallel latent dirichlet allocation for large-scale applications. In *Proceedings of the 5th International Conference on Algorithmic Aspects in Information and Management*, AAIM '09, 301–314. Berlin, Heidelberg: Springer-Verlag.

Yao, L.; Mimno, D.; and McCallum, A. 2009. Efficient methods for topic model inference on streaming document collections. In *Proceedings of the 15th ACM SIGKDD international conference on Knowledge discovery and data mining*, KDD '09, 937–946. New York, NY, USA: ACM.

Yu, H.-F.; Hsieh, C.-J.; Si, S.; and Dhillon, I. S. 2012. Scalable coordinate descent approaches to parallel matrix factorization for recommender systems. In *ICDM*, 765–774.

Zaharia, M.; Chowdhury, N. M. M.; Franklin, M.; Shenker, S.; and Stoica, I. 2010. Spark: Cluster computing with working sets. Technical Report UCB/EECS-2010-53, EECS Department, University of California, Berkeley.

An EBMC-Based Approach to Selecting Types for Entity Filtering

Jiwei Ding, Wentao Ding, Wei Hu and Yuzhong Qu
National Key Laboratory for Novel Software Technology,
Nanjing University, Nanjing 210023, China
{jiweiding,wentaoding}@outlook.com, {whu,yzqu}@nju.edu.cn

Abstract

The quantity of entities in the Linked Data is increasing rapidly. For entity search and browsing systems, filtering is very useful for users to find entities that they are interested in. Type is a kind of widely-used facet and can be easily obtained from knowledge bases, which enables to create filters by selecting at most K types of an entity collection. However, existing approaches often fail to select high-quality type filters due to complex overlap between types. In this paper, we propose a novel type selection approach based upon Budgeted Maximum Coverage (BMC), which can achieve integral optimization for the coverage quality of type filters. Furthermore, we define a new optimization problem called Extended Budgeted Maximum Coverage (EBMC) and propose an EBMC-based approach, which enhances the BMC-based approach by incorporating the relevance between entities and types, so as to create sensible type filters. Our experimental results show that the EBMC-based approach performs best comparing with several representative approaches.

Introduction

Along with the rapid growth of the Linked Data, many Web search and browsing activities are centered on entities. General users often use entity search or browsing systems, such as Libra Academic Search (Nie et al. 2007) and Falcons (Cheng and Qu 2009), to look for entities that they are interested in. However, it might be difficult for users to find the entities they want when search results contain large amount of entities. Therefore, entity filtering is demanded by users to ease their tasks.

Faceted search systems provide filters in different facets for interactive search and browsing (Sah and Wade 2013). Since type can be seen as an important facet (Tonon et al. 2013), a group of filters can be created by selecting values in this facet. In many publicly-accessible knowledge bases such as DBpedia and Yago, entities are associated with multiple types. The number of types related to the whole entity collection can be very large, while the number of filters in a group is limited to a positive integer K. How to select at most K types to make up a group of filters in entity search or browsing systems is worth studying.

Let us take an answer set to the question *"chess players who died in the same place they were born in"* as an example. The resulted entity collection consists of 45 chess players, each of which has at least 13 Yago types.

To the best of our knowledge, the most commonly used approach in faceted search is to count values in terms of their occurrence frequency, which means to rank types by their coverage rate in our problem. The following list shows a group of filters generated by this approach.

ChessPlayer (44)
Contestant (44)
Player (44)
Rival (19)
Intellectual (18)

However, we argue that this group of filters are not good enough. Although it covers most of entities in the collection, some types like *"Player"* is not suitable for filtering, since it covers too many entities. Furthermore, the overlap between types is not considered in this approach, e.g., *"Contestant"* and *"Player"*, which is another main cause to this drawback.

Some approaches are proposed to reduce the overlap between selected types, such as Maximum Marginal Relevance (MMR) (Carbonell and Goldstein 1998), but they still cannot avoid selecting types like *"ChessPlayer"*, which covers almost all of the entities. Some other approaches (Hearst 2006; Cheng and Qu 2009) also provide their solutions, but all of them suffer from a serious drawback, that is, they cannot provide sensible types, in other words, users cannot decide how close in perception the entity they want is relevant to a type. For example, the filter *"ChessOlympiadCompetitors (16)"* is more sensible than *"Intellectual (18)"*.

In this paper, we use the Budgeted Maximum Coverage (BMC) model (Khuller, Moss, and Naor 1999) to achieve an integral optimization for the coverage quality of selected types, which increases the coverage rate and reduces the overlap at the same time. To decrease the influence of the selected types covering too many or too few entities, we design a cost function on candidate types based on the coverage rates of types. Furthermore, we define the Extended Budgeted Maximum Coverage (EBMC) optimization problem and propose an EBMC-based approach, which enhances the BMC-based approach by incorporating the relevance between entities and types. In our implemented method, we leverage the type hierarchy to measure the relevance of an entity with its associated types. Our experimental results show that the EBMC-based approach performs best in overall comparing with other methods. For the "chess players" example, the type filters selected by the EBMC-based approach are shown below. This group of types is much more sensible than the previous one.

ChessOlympiadCompetitors (16)
ChessTheoreticians (15)
SovietChessPlayers (14)
GermanChessPlayers (4)
EnglishChessPlayers (5)

The rest of this paper is structured as follows. Section 2 reviews related work. In Section 3, we propose an approach based on BMC. In Section 4, we define EBMC and propose an approximation algorithm to solve it. Also, an EBMC-based approach is proposed. In Section 5, we evaluate the two proposed approaches by comparing them with three others on various entity collections. Finally, Section 6 concludes the paper with future work.

Related Work

Our work is related to faceted search since type is often considered as an important kind of facets. To the best of our knowledge, the most commonly used approach for selecting values in a facet is based on occurrence frequency. However, this approach is not suitable for selecting types since there often exists high overlap between different types.

MMR (Carbonell and Goldstein 1998) is a diversity-based re-ranking approach, which is mainly used for re-ranking search results or summarizing documents. We may use this approach here to minimize overlap and increase the coverage at the same time. However, this approach still does not work well because it cannot avoid types that covers too generally or too specifically.

Falcons Object Search (Cheng and Qu 2009) is a search engine for objects in the Linked Data. It gives a simple solution to this problem, which selects types according to coverage rate mainly, and ensures that class inclusion relation never holds between any pair of selected types. However, this approach may lead to a low coverage percentage when the number of selected types is limited to K, and sometimes suffers from providing inadequate types.

An alternative solution to this problem is "hierarchical faceted category", since types form a hierarchy naturally. However, the type hierarchy is sometimes too detailed, which means it may cost users too many clicks before they get the filtering condition they want. In the "chess player" example, at least 4 clicks are needed between the type *"Player"* and a specific type *"EnglishChessPlayers"*.

Another line of related work is entity type ranking. TRank (Tonon et al. 2013) proposes different kinds of ranking approaches and evaluates the efficiency, but these approaches cannot be applied to entity collection directly.

Besides, our work is also related to tag recommendation if we broadly treat types as tags. Xu et al. exploit collaborative tagging information to recommend tags (Xu et al. 2006). Their recommendation algorithm attempts to minimize the overlap among the recommended tags to allow for high coverage of multiple facets. However, this algorithm can only be used for a single entity and needs much user tagging information.

Selecting Types Based on BMC

In this section, we firstly introduce the well-known BMC optimization problem and its approximation algorithm. Then, we transform our problem to the BMC form, and mainly focus on how to assign costs to different types.

Budgeted Maximum Coverage Problem

Notice that our problem can be seen as selecting at most K types to cover most of the entities in the collection, we can formalize our type selection problem by the BMC optimization problem (Khuller, Moss, and Naor 1999), which is defined as follows:

Definition 1 (The Budgeted Maximum Coverage Problem). *A collection of sets $S = \{S_1, S_2, \dots, S_m\}$ with associated costs $\{c_i\}_{i=1}^m$ is defined over a domain of elements $X = \{x_1, x_2, \dots, x_n\}$ with associated weights $\{w_i\}_{i=1}^n$. The goal is to find a collection of sets $S' \subseteq S$, such that the total cost of elements in S' does not exceed a given budget L, and the total weight of elements covered by S' is maximized.*

Although BMC is an NP-hard problem, several efficient approximation algorithms have been developed. By comparing the approximation ratio and the time complexity of these algorithms, we consider the $(1 - \frac{1}{\sqrt{e}})$ approximation algorithm with time complexity $O(m^2 n)$ provided by (Khuller, Moss, and Naor 1999) to be best for our work.

The BMC-Based Approach

To formalize our problem, entities can be regarded as elements in BMC. Set S_i is defined as a set of entities that are associated with $type_i$, and we may simply represent this set by $type_i$. Without loss of generality, we set budget L to 1 to simplify the formalization. The weight of each entity can be set by its popularity, its relevance to the query, or simply 1 so that all entities are treated equally.

As for the cost of a type, it should be set by how appropriate it is to be selected as a filter, which can be inferred from the coverage rate of the type filter. In our problem, a good group of filters consists at most K types with similar coverage rate and little overlap between each other. A type with huge coverage rate may be too vague and leads to a large overlap with other selected types, while a type with little coverage rate may not contain the entity wanted by the users. So in the ideal case, the K type filters are orthogonal, each of which covers $\frac{1}{K}$ entities. Since the overlap between types cannot be avoided in practice, it is suggested that the ideal coverage rate R can be chosen between $\frac{1}{K}$ and $\frac{2}{K}$. A power function is considered to be the punishment for the types covering too many or too few entities. Lastly, we set $\frac{1}{K+1}$ as a lower bound of the cost for each type, which ensures that no more than K types would be selected by the approach. On the whole, the cost function can be defined as follows:

$$\left|\frac{|S_i|}{|S|} - R\right|^\alpha + \frac{1}{K+1}, \tag{1}$$

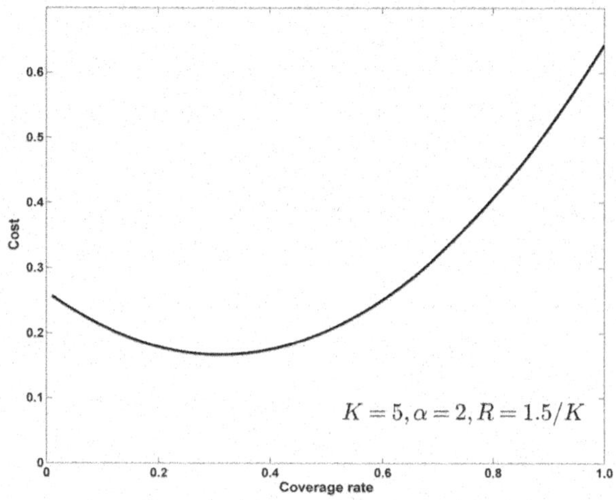

Figure 1: An example of cost function

where R is the ideal coverage rate for each type that can be set by application developers, and α is a parameter varying from different K or different datasets, which can be tuned by training. An example of cost function is shown in Figure 1.

Selecting Types Based on EBMC

In this section, we firstly analyze the drawback of the BMC-based approach. Then, we give a formal definition of the EBMC optimization problem and propose a $(1-\frac{1}{\sqrt{e}})$-approximation algorithm. Finally, a type selection approach based on EBMC is presented.

Drawback of the BMC-Based Approach

By transforming the type selection problem to the BMC problem, we can decrease the effect of selecting types that cover too many or too few entities. However, this approach can still be improved since the binary type coverage function does not characterize how relevant a type is to an entity, e.g., the weight of covering *"VasilySmyslov"* by *"SovietChessPlayers"* is the same as covering it by *"Player"* in BMC. If these two types cover similar entities in an entity collection, the BMC-based approach would choose either of them. But the type *"SovietChessPlayers"* is more informative and also easy to understand, which means it is more suitable for being a filter. To realize this improvement, we generalize the set in BMC to fuzzy set, which leads to the EBMC problem.

Extended Budgeted Maximum Coverage Problem

Now, we define the EBMC problem as follows:

Definition 2 (The Extended Budgeted Maximum Coverage Problem). *Let $S=\{S_1,S_2,\ldots,S_m\}$ be a collection of fuzzy sets defined over a domain of elements $X=\{x_1,x_2,\ldots,x_n\}$. Each fuzzy set has a cost $\{c_i\}_{i=1}^m$ while each element has a weight $\{w_i\}_{i=1}^n$. $f(S_i,x_j)$ is defined as the grade of membership of x_j in S_i. The goal is to find a collection of fuzzy sets $S'\subseteq S$, such that the total cost of S', denoted by $c(S')$, does not exceed a given budget L, while the total weight $w(S')$ is maximized.*

Where $c(S')$ and $w(S')$ are defined by the following formulae, respectively.

$$c(S')=\sum_{S_i\in S'} c_i \tag{2}$$

$$w(S')=\sum_{j=1}^{n}\left(w_j\cdot \max\{f(P,x_j)|P\in S'\}\right). \tag{3}$$

Obviously, the EBMC problem is a generalization of BMC. EBMC can also be treated as a specific case of the Generalized Maximum Coverage problem (GMC) (Cohen and Katzir 2008). However, the GMC problem is so complex that even the simplest algorithm mentioned in that paper has a high time complexity of $O(m^2n\cdot f(n,\epsilon))$ and a non-constant approximation ratio of $\frac{e-1}{2e-1}-\epsilon$, where $O(f(n,\epsilon))$ is the time complexity of an FPTAS approximation algorithm of the knapsack problem of n items. Our evaluation with GMC shows that it does not work for real-time applications when n and m reach 100.

An Approximation Algorithm for the EBMC Problem

Following the idea of the approximation algorithm for solving BMC, we give an approximation algorithm for EBMC, as shown in Algorithm 1.

Algorithm 1: Approximation algorithm for EBMC

$G\leftarrow\emptyset$; $C\leftarrow 0$; $U\leftarrow S$
repeat
    Select $S_i\in U$ that maximizes $\frac{(w(G\cup\{S_i\})-w(G))}{c_i}$;
    if $C+c_i\le L$ **then**
        $G\leftarrow G\cup\{S_i\}$;
        $C\leftarrow C+c_i$;
    $U\leftarrow U\setminus\{S_i\}$;
until $U=\emptyset$;
Select a fuzzy set T that maximizes $w(\{T\})$ over S;
if $w(G)\ge w(\{T\})$ **then**
    return G;
else
    return $\{T\}$;

We give a brief result to show that the main properties of the BMC problem still holds after introducing the concept of fuzzy set, and the time complexity of Algorithm 1 is still $O(m^2n)$. We proved that the algorithm is $(1-\frac{1}{\sqrt{e}})$-approximate. The detailed version of proof is provided in Appendix A.

Here, we give two properties of the EBMC model, which form the basis of the proof.

Lemma 1. *For any two collections of fuzzy sets A and B:*

$$w(A)+w(B)\ge w(A\cup B). \tag{4}$$

Lemma 2. *For any two collections of fuzzy sets A and B:*

$$w(A) - w(B) \leq \sum_{P \in A \setminus B} (w(B \cup \{P\}) - w(B)). \quad (5)$$

Let l be the number of fuzzy sets in G, and S_{G_i} be the ith fuzzy set added into G. $S_{G_{l+1}}$ is defined as the first fuzzy set from an optimal solution OPT selected but not added to G by the algorithm. In the following two lemmas we present some properties of the greedy approach.

Lemma 3. *After each iteration* $i = 1, \ldots, l$,

$$w(G_i) - w(G_{i-1}) \geq \frac{c(\{S_{G_i}\})}{L} \cdot (w(OPT) - w(G_{i-1})). \quad (6)$$

Lemma 4. *After each iteration* $i = 1, \ldots, l$,

$$w(G_i) \geq \Big(1 - \prod_{k=1}^{i} (1 - \frac{c(\{S_{G_k}\})}{L})\Big) \cdot w(OPT). \quad (7)$$

Now we can prove the approximation ratio and the time complexity of the algorithm.

Theorem 1. *Algorithm 1 achieves an approximation factor of* $(1 - \frac{1}{\sqrt{e}}) \approx 0.393469$.

Theorem 2. *The time complexity of Algorithm 1 is* $O(m^2 n)$, *where* $m = |S|$ *and* $n = |X|$.

The EBMC-Based Approach

The cost for types and the weight for entities can be set the same as in the BMC-based approach. By the modeling capability of EBMC, we can use the membership function to describe the relevance between the set and elements, which is different from the binary value in BMC.

To describe the relevance between types and entities, the hierarchy of types should be considered. Notice that the types and their hierarchy form a directed acyclic graph, which can be converted to a Hasse diagram since the hierarchy of types is a partially ordered relation. Then, we add the entities as vertices to the graph. For each entity added in, only minimal types of the entity are considered adjacent to it. Now the distance between an entity and a type can be defined as the distance of their corresponding vertices in this graph, denoted by $dist(type_i, entity_j)$ (If $type_i$ cannot reach $entity_j$, $dist(type_i, entity_j) = \infty$). The larger distance between a type and an entity is, the less relevant they are. So, we formalize the relevance function as follows:

$$f(S_i, x_j) = rel(type_i, entity_j) = \left(\frac{1}{2}\right)^{dist(type_i, entity_j)-1}. \quad (8)$$

As an example, the relevance of an entity with its types is depicted in Fig.2. The membership value of f(*SovietChessPlayers*, *VasilySmyslov*) is 1 since they are directed adjacent, and f(*Player*, *VasilySmyslov*) $= \frac{1}{4}$ since the length of shortest directed path between them is 3. f(*AmericanChessPlayers*, *VasilySmyslov*) $= 0$ because that there is no directed path from entity "*VasilySmyslov*" to type "*AmericanChessPlayers*".

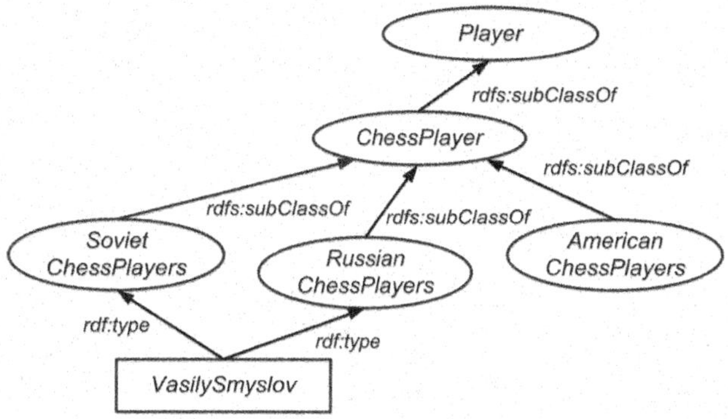

Figure 2: The relevance of an entity with its types

There are many other state-of-the-art approaches that can assess the relevance of an entity with respect to a type (or a facet), such as (Vandic, Frasincar, and Kaymak 2013) and (Liberman and Lempel 2012). We are going to incorporate these approaches in the future.

Evaluation

In this section, we report our evaluation of the proposed approaches, which is conducted on a PC with an Intel Xeon 3.2GHz CPU and 2GB JVM.

Entity Collections

We select the entity collections from Task 1 of the Question Answering over Linked Data campaign (QALD-4).[1] There are 250 questions in total, in which 181 have answer type "Resource". All the resources can be found in DBpdeia 3.9, so do their Yago types as well. Resources without any Yago types or questions having less than 20 answers are removed. The answer lists for the remaining 29 questions are used as entity collections in our evaluation. In average, a collection contains 180 entities (at least 20 entities and at most 1,125 entities), with 8,928 associated types in total. We randomly choose 4 entity collections for parameter tuning, while the rest ones are used for testing.[2]

Task

Given a collection of entities and their types, each participating approach selects no more than K types, which are considered as a group of filters for the given collection. We set $K = 5$ and $K = 8$ in our evaluation. For smaller K, it is not sufficient for filtering, while larger K is difficult for humans to judge its accuracy.

Comparative Approaches

In our evaluation, we compare the BMC-based and EBMC-based approaches, together with 3 alternatives: the CR-based approach, the MMR-based approach, and the one used in Falcons. We briefly introduce them as follows.

[1] http://greententacle.techfak.uni-bielefeld.de/~cunger/qald/

[2] Detailed information about these collections is available at http://ws.nju.edu.cn/ebmc/

The CR-based approach is widely used in faceted search, which selects types in terms of the descending order of their coverage rates. This approach is considered as the baseline in our evaluation.

The MMR-based approach is an improvement of selecting types by coverage rate. It uses a diversity-based re-ranking technique to increase coverage rate and decrease overlap simultaneously. Let U be the set of all types, S be the set of selected types, and λ be the weighting factor to balance the coverage rate and overlap, MMR can be calculated by the following equation:

$$MMR = \underset{T_i \in U \setminus S}{\arg\max} \Big[\lambda \cdot \big(CoverageRate(T_i) - (1-\lambda) \cdot \max_{T_j \in S} Overlap(T_i, T_j)\big)\Big], \quad (9)$$

where $CoverageRate(T_i)$ computes the coverage rate of type T_i, while $Overlap(T_i, T_j)$ computes the Jaccard coefficient of two entity sets covered by types T_i and T_j, respectively. Therefore, MMR maximizes the coverage rate when λ approaches 1, and minimizes the overlap when λ approaches 0. We test $\lambda = 0.1, 0.3, 0.5, 0.7, 0.9$ and set it to 0.3, since it achieves the best performance in our evaluation.

The approach used in Falcons selects types one by one in terms of their coverage rates, and skips a type if it is a subclass of any selected types. If a user had already selected some types as a previous filtering condition, only the subclasses of these types can be further selected. In our evaluation, there is no previous filtering condition so that all types are involved in the candidate list.

The BMC-based and EBMC-based approaches are implemented just as we described in the previous sections. We simply set the ideal coverage rate $R = 1.5/K$, and test parameter α from 1.00 to 3.00, step by 0.25, for various K. Considering the performance of the two approaches on the entity collections, we set $\alpha = 2.00$ for $K = 5$, and $\alpha = 2.50$ for $K = 8$ in this evaluation.

Measurement

Since there are too many types in the candidate type list, it is too hard for human to select K types for each entity collection. Instead, we invite 10 judges who are all CS graduate students to evaluate the quality of the filters generated by different approaches. Each judge is presented with a collection of entities and their types, and is asked to assess filters on 20 entity collections, so that each entity collection with certain K is assessed by 4 judges. They score 1 point to 5 point on the following 5 dimensions:

- Coverage rate ($1 = low$, $5 = high$)
- Overlap ratio ($1 = high$, $5 = low$)
- No. of types ($1 = too\ few$, $5 = almost\ matches\ K$)
- Sensibility ($1 = non\text{-}sensible$, $5 = sensible$)
- Overall ($1 = bad$, $5 = good$)

The dimension "Coverage rate" and "Overlap ratio" are generally considered by almost all the approaches. Since some approaches could select too few types, the dimension "No. of types" is added. The dimension "Sensibility" is particularly designed to assess the difference between the EBMC-based approach and others. A type is sensible if its meaning is accurate, concrete and easy to be understood by humans, which is important to the usefulness of filters. Additionally, we add the "Overall" dimension to achieve comprehensive assessment of the filters.

Table 1: Average scores of the approaches ($K = 5$)

	CR	MMR	Falcons	BMC	EBMC
Coverage rate	4.37 (0.37)	4.57 (0.33)	**4.63** (0.35)	4.37 (0.44)	3.95 (0.48)
Overlap ratio	1.95 (0.42)	2.09 (0.40)	2.68 (0.55)	3.12 (0.50)	**3.39** (0.49)
No. of types	4.18 (0.18)	**4.20** (0.16)	3.79 (0.44)	2.78 (0.57)	3.46 (0.47)
Sensibility	2.75 (0.71)	2.74 (0.60)	2.77 (0.54)	2.63 (0.42)	**3.71** (0.38)
Overall	2.84 (0.45)	2.80 (0.56)	2.96 (0.53)	2.60 (0.40)	**3.55** (0.29)

Table 2: Average scores of the approaches ($K = 8$)

	CR	MMR	Falcons	BMC	EBMC
Coverage rate	4.32 (0.43)	**4.54** (0.41)	4.51 (0.32)	4.33 (0.38)	3.87 (0.40)
Overlap ratio	1.96 (0.49)	2.08 (0.52)	2.80 (0.74)	3.62 (0.61)	**4.00** (0.46)
No. of types	**4.43** (0.18)	**4.43** (0.17)	3.41 (0.56)	3.41 (0.62)	4.11 (0.55)
Sensibility	2.64 (0.66)	2.77 (0.74)	2.73 (0.85)	3.12 (0.58)	**4.14** (0.42)
Overall	2.64 (0.60)	2.73 (0.54)	2.71 (0.67)	3.11 (0.49)	**4.06** (0.41)

Results

Table 1 shows the average scores of the five approaches on different dimensions in the case of $K = 5$, and Table 2 shows the scores for $K = 8$. The average of the standard deviations among different judges for different entity collections is also shown in the table with parentheses. We observe that the results for $K = 5$ and $K = 8$ are quite consistent, and our EBMC-based approach performs best in general among all the five approaches.

By comparing these type selection approaches, we find that the CR-based approach has a high coverage rate, and can provide enough types in most cases. However, it does not consider the problem of overlap, which severely affect the quality of the filters. The MMR-based approach increases the coverage rate and decreases the overlap comparing with the CR-based one, but it still does not work well because it cannot avoid selecting types covering too many entities. The approach in Falcons decreases the overlap to some extent and keeps a relatively high coverage rate, but it fails to select enough types sometimes. Our BMC-based approach decreases the overlap ratio successfully and has a better performance when more types are selected. The EBMC-based approach improves a lot on giving more sensible types with less overlap, but costs a small loss on coverage rate.

The standard deviations show that the scores given by different judges for the same task are quite similar, which means the judges reach an agreement on each dimension to some extent. Furthermore, Repeated Measures ANOVA indicates that the differences between the EBMC and other approaches in overall are statistically significant ($p < 0.03$) both for $K = 5$ and 8. Additionally, the EBMC-based approach can generate filters per case within 1 second, which demonstrates its efficiency.

We also tried to evaluate different approaches with DBpedia types. Generally speaking, for a large number of entity collections, DBpedia has only less than 10 (even duplicated) types, and most of them cover almost the whole entity collection, which led to similar results between all participating approaches, and it might be unnecessary to select types for filtering in this situation. We are going to consider other type sources for testing our approach in the future.

In overall, the EBMC-based approach is shown as the best to select type filters in our evaluation.

Conclusion

In this paper, we studied how to select types for entity filtering. Our main contributions are as follows:

- We modeled the K type selection problem as the BMC problem, which pursues integral optimization for the coverage quality of type filters. Accordingly, we proposed a cost function on candidate types, which increases the chance of selecting types with appropriate coverage rates.
- We defined a new model, EBMC, which extends the capability of BMC by incorporating fuzzy set. Moreover, we designed an approximation algorithm for EBMC, which achieves the same approximation ratio and time complexity as those of BMC.
- We proposed an EBMC-based approach to selecting type filters, which incorporates the relevance between entities and types by leveraging type hierarchy. Our evaluation results show that the EBMC-based approach tends to select sensible types with superior quality.

In future work, we look forward to applying EBMC to other problems such as entity summarization. We also want to design new algorithms for EBMC with a higher approximation ratio while keeping an acceptable time complexity.

Acknowledgments

This work is supported in part by the National Natural Science Foundation of China (NSFC) under Grant Nos. 61170068, 61223003 and 61370019. We would like to thank Dr. Gong Cheng for his valuable suggestion on the design of our experiments, and Yong Wang for his help on evaluation. We are also grateful to all participants in the evaluation for their time and effort.

Appendix A: Proof of Approximation Ratio and Running Time of Algorithm 1

Proof of Lemma 1.

$$\begin{aligned} w(A\cup B) &= \sum_{j=1}^{n}\big(w_j\cdot \max\{f(P,x_j)\mid P\in A\cup B\}\big) \\ &\le \sum_{j=1}^{n}\big(w_j\cdot \max\{f(P,x_j)\mid P\in A\}\big) \\ &\quad +\sum_{j=1}^{n}\big(w_j\cdot \max\{f(P,x_j)\mid P\in B\}\big) \\ &= w(A)+w(B). \end{aligned}$$

□

Proof of Lemma 2.

$$\begin{aligned} & w(A)-w(B) \\ =& \sum_{j=1}^{n}\Big(w_j\cdot\big(\max_{Q\in A} f(Q,x_j)-\max_{Q\in B} f(Q,x_j)\big)\Big) \\ \le& \sum_{j=1}^{n}\Big(w_j\cdot\sum_{P\in A\setminus B}\big(\max_{Q\in B\cup\{P\}} f(Q,x_j)-\max_{Q\in B} f(Q,x_j)\big)\Big) \\ =& \sum_{P\in A\setminus B}\big(w(B\cup\{P\})-w(B)\big). \end{aligned}$$

□

Proof of Lemma 3.
According to Lemma 2, we have $w(OPT)-w(G_{i-1})\le \sum_{P\in OPT\setminus G_{i-1}}(w(G_{i-1}\cup\{P\})-w(G_{i-1}))$. Because S_{G_i} is selected by the greedy strategy, we have $\frac{w(G_{i-1}\cup\{P\})-w(G_{i-1})}{c(\{P\})}\le\frac{w(G_i)-w(G_{i-1})}{c(\{S_{G_i}\})}$ for each $P\in OPT\setminus G_{i-1}$. Thus,

$$\begin{aligned} & w(G_i)-w(G_{i-1}) \\ =& \frac{c(\{S_{G_i}\})}{c(OPT)}\cdot\frac{\sum_{P\in OPT}c(\{P\})}{c(\{S_{G_i}\})}\cdot(w(G_i)-w(G_{i-1})) \\ \ge& \frac{c(\{S_{G_i}\})}{L}\cdot\sum_{P\in OPT\setminus G_{i-1}}\Big(\frac{c(\{P\})}{c(\{S_{G_i}\})}\cdot(w(G_i)-w(G_{i-1}))\Big) \\ \ge& \frac{c(\{S_{G_i}\})}{L}\cdot\sum_{P\in OPT\setminus G_{i-1}}(w(G_{i-1}\cup\{P\})-w(G_{i-1})) \\ \ge& \frac{c(\{S_{G_i}\})}{L}\cdot\big(w(OPT)-w(G_{i-1})\big). \end{aligned}$$

□

Proof of Lemma 4.
Basis. When $i=1$, $w(\{S_{G_1}\})\ge\frac{c(\{S_{G_1}\})}{L}\cdot w(OPT)$, because the ratio $\frac{w(\{S_{G_1}\})}{c(G_1)}$ is maximum over all sets.

Inductive hypothesis. For $i=1,\ldots,p-1$, we have $w(G_i)\ge\Big(1-\prod_{k=1}^{i}\big(1-\frac{c(\{S_{G_k}\})}{L}\big)\Big)\cdot w(OPT)$.

Inductive step. When $i = p$,

$$\begin{aligned}
w(G_p) &= w(G_{p-1}) + \big(w(G_p) - w(G_{p-1})\big)\\
&\geq w(G_{p-1}) + \frac{c(\{S_{G_p}\})}{L} \cdot \big(w(OPT) - w(G_{p-1})\big)\\
&= (1 - \frac{c(\{S_{G_p}\})}{L}) \cdot w(G_{p-1}) + \frac{c(\{S_{G_p}\})}{L} \cdot w(OPT)\\
&\geq (1 - \frac{c(\{S_{G_p}\})}{L})\Big(1 - \prod_{k=1}^{p-1} (1 - \frac{c(\{S_{G_k}\})}{L})\Big) \cdot w(OPT)\\
&\quad + \frac{c(\{S_{G_p}\})}{L} \cdot w(OPT)\\
&= \Big(1 - \prod_{k=1}^{p} (1 - \frac{c(\{S_{G_k}\})}{L})\Big) \cdot w(OPT).
\end{aligned}$$

Thus, $w(G_i) \geq \Big(1 - \prod_{k=1}^{i} (1 - \frac{c(\{S_{G_k}\})}{L})\Big) \cdot w(OPT)$. □

Proof of Theorem 1.
Case 1. For some $S_k \in S$, $w(\{S_k\}) \geq \frac{1}{2} \cdot w(OPT)$. We have $\frac{w(\{T\})}{w(OPT)} \geq \frac{w(\{S_k\})}{w(OPT)} \geq \frac{1}{2}$.

Case 2. For all $S_k \in S$, $w(\{S_k\}) < \frac{1}{2} \cdot w(OPT)$.

Case 2.1 $c(G) < \frac{L}{2}$. Then $\forall S_k \notin G.\ c_k > \frac{L}{2}$, implying that there is at most one fuzzy set in $OPT \setminus G$ because of $c(OPT) \leq L$. We have $w(G) \geq w(OPT \cap G) \geq w(OPT) - w(OPT \setminus G) > \frac{1}{2} \cdot w(OPT)$.

Case 2.2 $c(G) \geq \frac{L}{2}$. According to Lemma 4, we have $w(G_i) \geq \Big(1 - \prod_{k=1}^{i} (1 - \frac{c(\{S_{G_k}\})}{L})\Big) \cdot w(OPT)$. Because $c(G) = \sum_{i=1}^{l} c(\{S_{G_i}\}) \geq \frac{L}{2}$. We have $\Big(1 - \prod_{k=1}^{l} (1 - \frac{c(\{S_{G_k}\})}{L})\Big) \geq \Big(1 - (1 - \frac{1}{2l})^{l}\Big)$, which implies

$$\begin{aligned}
w(G_l) &\geq \Big(1 - \prod_{k=1}^{l} (1 - \frac{c(\{S_{G_k}\})}{L})\Big) \cdot w(OPT)\\
&\geq \Big(1 - (1 - \frac{1}{2l})^{l}\Big) \cdot w(OPT)\\
&\geq (1 - \frac{1}{\sqrt{e}}) \cdot w(OPT).
\end{aligned}$$

So, the weight of the collection generated by Algorithm 1 is proved to be at least $(1 - \frac{1}{\sqrt{e}}) \cdot w(OPT)$ in each of the cases. □

Proof of Theorem 2.
In each iteration, we need to check all the fuzzy sets in U to get S_{G_i}, which means no more than m fuzzy sets will be checked. Regarding the time complexity of adding a new fuzzy set P into S', the addition weight $w(S' \cup \{P\}) - w(S')$ can be calculated by $\sum_{j=1}^{n} \big(w_j \cdot \max\{f(Q, x_j) \mid Q \in (S' \cup \{P\})\}\big) - \sum_{j=1}^{n} \big(w_j \cdot \max\{f(Q, x_j) \mid Q \in S'\}\big)$, which can be done in $O(n)$ time. Thus, each iteration takes $O(mn)$ time, and the running time in total is $O(m^2 n)$ since U will be empty after m iterations. □

References

Carbonell, J., and Goldstein, J. 1998. The use of MMR, diversity-based reranking for reordering documents and producing summaries. In *Proceedings of 21st Annual International ACM SIGIR Conference on Research and Development in Information Retrieval*, 335–336. ACM Press.

Cheng, G., and Qu, Y. 2009. Searching linked objects with Falcons: Approach, implementation and evaluation. *International Journal on Semantic Web and Information Systems* 5(3):49–70.

Cohen, R., and Katzir, L. 2008. The generalized maximum coverage problem. *Information Processing Letters* 108(1):15–22.

Hearst, M. A. 2006. Clustering versus faceted categories for information exploration. *Communications of the ACM* 49(4):59–61.

Khuller, S.; Moss, A.; and Naor, J. 1999. The budgeted maximum coverage problem. *Information Processing Letters* 70(1):39–45.

Liberman, S., and Lempel, R. 2012. Approximately optimal facet selection. In *Proceedings of the ACM Symposium on Applied Computing, SAC 2012, Riva, Trento, Italy, March 26-30, 2012*, 702–708.

Nie, Z.; Ma, Y.; Shi, S.; Wen, J.; and Ma, W. 2007. Web object retrieval. In *Proceedings of 16th International World Wide Web Conference*, 81–90. ACM Press.

Sah, M., and Wade, V. 2013. Personalized concept-based search and exploration on the web of data using results categorization. In *Proceedings of 10th Extended Semantic Web Conference*, 532–547. Springer.

Tonon, A.; Catasta, M.; Demartini, G.; Cudre-Mauroux, P.; and Aberer, K. 2013. TRank: Ranking entity types using the web of data. In *Proceedings of 12th International Semantic Web Conference*, 640–656. Springer.

Vandic, D.; Frasincar, F.; and Kaymak, U. 2013. Facet selection algorithms for web product search. In *22nd ACM International Conference on Information and Knowledge Management, CIKM'13, San Francisco, CA, USA, October 27 - November 1, 2013*, 2327–2332.

Xu, Z.; Fu, Y.; Mao, J.; and Su, D. 2006. Towards the semantic web: Collaborative tag suggestions. In *Proceedings of WWW 2006 Workshop on Collaborative Web Tagging*.

Trust Models for RDF Data: Semantics and Complexity*

Valeria Fionda and Gianluigi Greco
Department of Mathematics and Computer Science,
University of Calabria, Italy
{fionda,ggreco}@mat.unical.it

Abstract

Due to the openness and decentralization of the Web, mechanisms to represent and reason about the reliability of RDF data become essential. This paper embarks on a formal analysis of RDF data enriched with trust information by focusing on the characterization of its model-theoretic semantics and on the study of relevant reasoning problems. The impact of trust values on the computational complexity of well-known concepts related to the entailment of RDF graphs is studied. In particular, islands of tractability are identified for classes of acyclic and nearly-acyclic graphs. Moreover, an implementation of the framework and an experimental evaluation on real data are discussed.

1 Introduction

The Resource Description Framework (RDF) is the basic representation language for the Semantic Web, where data is exposed as a set of triples expressing the properties that hold among a given universe of resources, identified by URIs (Hayes and Patel-Schneider 2014). In fact, RDF is not suited, in its basic form, to represent meta-information. Therefore, efforts have been made to define extensions for dealing with time (Gutierrez, Hurtado, and Vaisman 2007), provenance (Dividino et al. 2009), fuzzy (Straccia 2009), and trust (Hartig 2009; Tomaszuk, Pak, and Rybinski 2013). These ad-hoc extensions come in the form of annotations over the triples and general frameworks for annotated Semantic Web data have been proposed, too (Udrea, Recupero, and Subrahmanian 2010; Zimmermann et al. 2012).

In this paper, we consider RDF data enriched with trust information, and we study specific reasoning problems that arise within this setting. Indeed, RDF links between resources can be unilaterally set and be part of any data source as in the spirit of Tim Berners Lee's words: "Anyone can say anything about any topic and publish it anywhere". However, the lack of central control on the publishing of RDF data on the Web can have an impact on their accuracy, and it therefore becomes essential to associate trust information to data and being able to reason about them. To this end, the starting point of our analysis is the trust model proposed by (Hartig 2009), who firstly advocated the need of a uniform way to rate the trustworthiness of RDF data and of mechanisms to access and use these ratings. In fact, the analysis of (Hartig 2009) has been mainly carried out from the conceptual viewpoint, so that a number of the properties of the trust model, related to semantic and complexity issues, remain unexplored. In this paper we fill the gap.

In more detail, we first propose a model-theoretic semantics for the trust model by (Hartig 2009). The semantics is based on the concept of *trust aggregation functions*, which are functions designed to aggregate trust values coming from different RDF triples (Section 3.1). We then analyze the computational properties exhibited by the proposed framework (Section 3.2), and it turns out that:

- ▶ Even simple reasoning problems, such as checking whether there is a model for a given RDF graph, become intractable, formally NP-hard, in presence of trust information for general trust aggregation functions.

Motivated by the above bad news, we focus on specific classes of trust aggregation functions computable via binary *trust operators*, in the spirit of the general framework for annotated RDF data by (Zimmermann et al. 2012) and some proposals in relational (Karvounarakis and Green 2012) and RDF databases (Buneman and Kostylev 2010) where commutative semirings are considered. Within these classes, we analyze the concepts of *entailment*, *equivalence*, and *core* as suitable adaptations of corresponding concepts for RDF data (Gutierrez et al. 2011) and we study their intrinsic computational complexity (Section 4). It turns out that:

- ▶ The syntactic restriction introduced by trust operators is a key for the tractability of the reasoning problems in presence of trust information.
- ▶ While *entailment*, *equivalence*, and *core* are grounded on the semantics of the representation language, tight syntactic characterizations can be exhibited for them.
- ▶ Islands of tractability for these concepts can be singled out based on the structural properties of the interactions among the data. In particular, tractability can be established for acyclic or nearly-acyclic RDF graphs.

Finally, we point out that the trust framework and all the algorithms proposed in the paper have been implemented

*V. Fionda's work was supported by the European Commission, the European Social Fund and the Calabria region. G. Greco's work was also supported by a Kurt Gödel Research Fellowship, awarded by the Kurt Gödel Society.

and are made available in a prototype system.[1] We conducted experiments on real data in order to assess the applicability of the approach and the effectiveness of the algorithmic solutions. Implementation issues and experimental results are also discussed in the paper (Section 5).

2 Preliminaries

RDF Graphs. Let $\mathcal{U}$ and $\mathcal{B}$ be two disjoint infinite sets of *URI references* and *blank node identifiers*, respectively. An *RDF triple* has the form (s, p, o), where $s \in \mathcal{U} \cup \mathcal{B}$ is the *subject*, $p \in \mathcal{U}$ is the *property* (also called *predicate*), and $o \in \mathcal{U} \cup \mathcal{B}$ is the *object*.[2] The intuitive meaning is that the property p holds between the subject s and the object o (Hayes and Patel-Schneider 2014). A set $\mathcal{G}$ of RDF triples is usually called an RDF *graph*. Indeed, an RDF triple can be viewed as a directed edge, from the subject to the object nodes, labeled with the corresponding property (i.e., URI reference). In the paper, we deal with *simple* RDF graphs only, i.e., we do not specify any ad-hoc semantics for the properties occurring in the triples of $\mathcal{G}$.

Semantics of RDF graphs. An *interpretation* $\mathcal{I}$ over $\mathcal{U}$ is a tuple $\langle Res, Prop, PVal, Int\rangle$ where: (i) Res is a non-empty set of resources; (ii) $Prop$ is a non-empty set of property names, not necessarily disjoint from Res; (iii) $PVal : Prop \to 2^{Res \times Res}$ is a function that assigns a subset of $Res \times Res$ to each property name in $Prop$; and (iv) $Int : \mathcal{U} \to Res \cup Prop$ is an interpretation mapping that assigns a resource or property name to each element of $\mathcal{U}$.

$\mathcal{I}$ is a *model* of an RDF graph $\mathcal{G}$ if there is a blank node assignment $A : \mathcal{B} \to Res$, in the following referred to as the *witness* of $\mathcal{I}$, such that: for each triple $(s, p, o) \in \mathcal{G}$, $Int(p) \in Prop$ and $(Int_A(s), Int_A(o)) \in PVal(Int(p))$, where $Int_A(x) = Int(x)$ if $x \in \mathcal{U}$, and $Int_A(x) = A(x)$ if $x \in \mathcal{B}$. Note that blank nodes are interpreted existentially via the underlying witness A.

3 Trust Framework

In this section, we illustrate the trust framework to enrich standard RDF graphs with trust values, inspired by the approach proposed by (Hartig 2009). We also define its model-theoretic semantics and study its complexity. In the following, if h is a function, we denote by $\mathtt{dom}(h)$ its domain and, by slightly abusing notation, for each element $z \notin \mathtt{dom}(h)$, we write $h(z) = \phi$, where ϕ is a distinguished symbol acting as a neutral element. If $\langle z_1, .., z_m\rangle$ is a tuple of values, then $\langle h(z_1), .., h(z_m)\rangle$ is shortened to $h(\langle z_1, ..., z_m\rangle)$.

3.1 Syntax and Semantics of t-Graphs

The *trustworthiness* of an RDF triple $t = (s, p, o)$ is a value indicating to what extent t is believed or disbelieved to be true. A trust-enriched RDF graph (short: *t-graph*) is a pair $\langle \mathcal{G}, w\rangle$ where $\mathcal{G}$ is an RDF graph, and w is a real-valued *trust function* such that:

[1] See http://trdfreasoner.wordpress.com

[2] *Literals* are not considered, as they do not play a role in the formal analysis at the given abstraction level (Gutierrez et al. 2011).

Figure 1: Examples of t-graphs.

- $\mathtt{dom}(w)$ is a set of RDF triples; here, the symbol ϕ associated with any triple outside the domain is meant to denote that the trust value of t is unknown;
- for each $t \in \mathtt{dom}(w)$, $-1 \leq w(t) \leq 1$ holds. Intuitively, the value 1 (resp., -1) represents the maximum belief (resp., disbelief) in the information encoded by the triple. A value of 0 represents absolute uncertainty on the reliability of the corresponding triple.

Note that $\mathtt{dom}(w) \supseteq \mathcal{G}$ is not enforced to hold. So, a tuple $t \in \mathcal{G}$ might have no associated trust value. In particular, $w(t) = \phi$ is different from $w(t) = 0$, as discussed by (Hartig 2009).

Example 1 Two t-graphs are illustrated in Figure 1. For instance, in $\langle \mathcal{G}_1, w_1\rangle$ we have that $w_1((\mathtt{A\_Time\_To\_Kill}, \mathtt{author}, \mathtt{John\_Grisham})) = 0.8$ and $\mathtt{dom}(w_1) = \mathcal{G}_1 \setminus \{(\mathtt{A\_Time\_To\_Kill}, \mathtt{genre}, \mathtt{Legal\_thriller})\}$. ◁

In many cases, we need to aggregate the trust values that come from different RDF triples, even possibly from the entire RDF graph. To this end, we consider *trust aggregation functions*, i.e., functions taking as input a multiset (i.e., a set where repetitions are allowed) of elements in $[-1, 1] \cup \{\phi\}$ and producing an aggregate value in $[-1, 1] \cup \{\phi\}$. The specific choice of the trust aggregation function f depends on the requirements of the application at hand. However, as ϕ is a neutral element with respect to f, we consistently assume that $f(S) = f(S \cup \{\phi\})$ holds, for each S.[3]

As a concrete choice, we might aggregate values by taking the minimum one, if a *cautious* function $f_{\min}$ is used where the trust value of a set of triples is equal to the trust value of the least trusted triple. The *brave* perspective is instead given by the function $f_{\max}$ taking the maximum value.

Example 2 Consider again $\langle \mathcal{G}_1, w_1\rangle$ in Figure 1. According to the *cautious* perspective, we have $f_{\min}(\{w_1(t) \mid t \in \mathcal{G}_1\}) = \min\{w_1(t) \mid t \in \mathcal{G}_1\} = $-0.2. According to the *brave* perspective, $f_{\max}(\{w_1(t) \mid t \in \mathcal{G}_1\}) = \max\{w_1(t) \mid t \in \mathcal{G}_1\} = 0.8$. ◁

The trust framework illustrated so far is essentially taken from (Hartig 2009), where however a formal model-theoretic semantics is not proposed. Our first contribution is to extend the concept of model to t-graphs in a way that it is parametric w.r.t. the trust aggregation function f.

Definition 1 (f-models) Let $\mathcal{I} = \langle Res, Prop, PVal, Int\rangle$ be an interpretation, and let $\bar{\sigma} = \sigma_{y|y \in Prop}$ be a family of real-valued functions with $\mathtt{dom}(\sigma_y) \subseteq PVal(y)$, for each $y \in Prop$, i.e., σ_y assigns trust values to pairs $(s, o) \in PVal(y)$. The pair $\langle \mathcal{I}, \bar{\sigma}\rangle$ is an *f-model* of a t-graph $\langle \mathcal{G}, w\rangle$ if there is a blank node assignment $A : \mathcal{B} \to Res$ such that:

[3] Operations over sets are hereinafter transparently applied to multisets, by taking multiplicity of elements into account.

(1) $\mathcal{I}$ is a model of $\mathcal{G}$, with A being the associated witness;

(2) for each $(s,p,o) \in \mathcal{G}$, $\sigma_{Int(p)}(Int_A(s), Int_A(o)) = f(\{\sigma_{Int(p)}(Int_A(s), Int_A(o))\} \cup S)$, where

$$S = \bigcup_{\substack{(s',p',o') \in \mathcal{G} \text{ such that} \\ Int_A((s,p,o)) = Int_A((s',p',o'))}} \{w((s',p',o'))\}.$$

□

Note that, according to our approach, standard interpretations are equipped with real-valued functions that provide an interpretation to trust values. Indeed, condition (1) is the standard definition of model for RDF graphs, while condition (2) is specific for trust values. In order to get an intuition, observe that, for the maximization function, condition (2) prescribes that the value assigned via $\bar{\sigma}$ to each "interpreted" triple in any model has to be an upper bound for the trust values of the RDF triples that are mapped into it.

Example 3 Consider again $\langle \mathcal{G}_1, w_1\rangle$ in Figure 1. Let $\langle \mathcal{I}, \bar{\sigma}\rangle$ be the pair such that: $\sigma_p(s,o) = w_1((s,p,o))$, $\forall (s,p,o) \in \texttt{dom}(w_1)$; $\sigma_p(s,o)=0$, $\forall (s,p,o) \in \mathcal{G}_1 \setminus \texttt{dom}(w_1)$; and where $\mathcal{I} = \langle Res, Prop, PVal, Int\rangle$ is an interpretation whose resources and property names directly correspond to URI references and properties, respectively:

- *Res*={`John_Grisham`, `author`, `A_Time_To_Kill`, `Legal_thriller`, `genre`};
- *Prop*={`author`, `genre`},
- *PVal*(`author`)={(`A_Time_To_Kill`, `John_Grisham`)}, *PVal*(`genre`)= {(`A_Time_To_Kill`, `Legal_thriller`)};
- *Int* is the identity function;

Note that $\langle \mathcal{I}, \bar{\sigma}\rangle$ is an $f_{\max}$-model of the t-graph $\langle \mathcal{G}_1, w_1\rangle$ in Figure 1, whose witness is the blank node assignment A with A(`_:b1`)=`A_Time_To_Kill`. Instead, observe that $\langle \mathcal{I}, \bar{\sigma}\rangle$ is not an $f_{\min}$-model. Indeed, we have that $\sigma_{\texttt{genre}}$(`A_Time_To_Kill`, `Legal_thriller`)=0 and since A is the only possible blank node assignment, we obtain that min{$\sigma_{\texttt{genre}}$(`A_Time_To_Kill`, `Legal_thriller`), w_1(`A_Time_To_Kill`, `genre`, `Legal_thriller`), w_1(`_:b1`, `genre`, `Legal_thriller`)}=min{0, ϕ,-0.2}= -0.2 $\neq$ 0 ◁

3.2 Complexity Analysis

The framework illustrated so far is general enough to fit a number of application domains. However, there is a price to be paid for this generality, which comes in the form of the intrinsic complexity of the basic reasoning problem arising with the concept of f-model. In fact, it is well-known and easy to see that, given an interpretation $\mathcal{I}$ and an RDF graph $\mathcal{G}$, deciding whether $\mathcal{I}$ is a model of $\mathcal{G}$ is NP-complete in general, but it is feasible in polynomial time if $\mathcal{G}$ is acyclic. Opposed to this goods news, it turns out that deciding whether $\langle \mathcal{I}, \bar{\sigma}\rangle$ is an f-model of $\langle \mathcal{G}, w\rangle$ (according to Definition 1) is intractable even over acyclic graphs.

Formally, let CHECK$_{f,\mathcal{C}}$ be the problem receiving as input a pair $\langle \mathcal{I}, \bar{\sigma}\rangle$ and a t-graph $\langle \mathcal{G}, w\rangle$ with $\mathcal{G}$ belonging to the class $\mathcal{C}$ of RDF graphs, and asking to decide whether $\langle \mathcal{I}, \bar{\sigma}\rangle$ is an f-model of $\langle \mathcal{G}, w\rangle$. Then, the following holds.

Theorem 1 *Assume that f is a polynomial-time computable function. Then,* CHECK$_{f,\mathcal{C}}$ *is* NP*-complete. Hardness holds even if $\mathcal{C}$ is the class of all acyclic RDF t-graphs.*

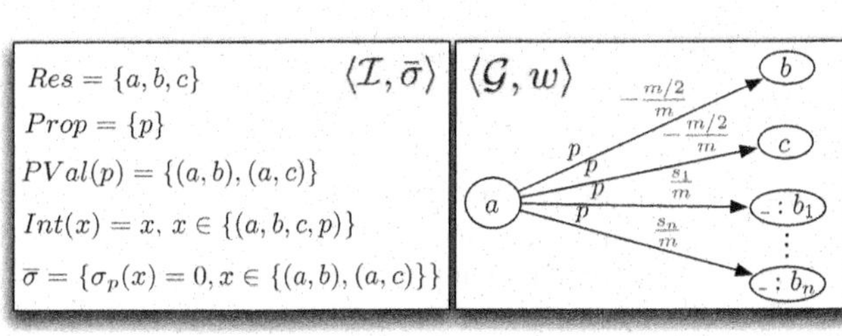

Figure 2: Example construction in the proof of Theorem 1.

Proof Sketch. NP-hardness can be shown via a reduction from the PARTITION problem of deciding whether there is a way to partition a multiset $S = \{s_1, s_2, \ldots, s_n\}$ of integers into two multisets S_1 and S_2 such that the sum of the numbers in S_1 equals the sum of the numbers in S_2.

Based on S, we build the f-model checking instance $(\langle \mathcal{I}, \bar{\sigma}\rangle, \langle \mathcal{G}, w\rangle)$ reported in Figure 2 with f being the average function, where blank nodes $\_{:}b_i \in \mathcal{G}$ are in one-to-one correspondence with the numbers $s_i \in S$, and where the trust values (normalized by the factor $m = \sum_{s_i \in S} s_i$) are given by the weights associated with the edges. Eventually, one can check that $\langle \mathcal{I}, \bar{\sigma}\rangle$ is an f-model of $\langle \mathcal{G}, w\rangle$ if, and only if, the answer to the PARTITION instance is positive. Indeed, $\langle \mathcal{I}, \bar{\sigma}\rangle$ is a model if, and only if, blank nodes (hence numbers) can be partitioned in two groups, mapped to nodes b and c, respectively, whose trust values sum up to $1/2$. □

4 Trust Aggregation Operators

In order to circumvent the above intractability, we have to focus on specific kinds of trust aggregation functions. Our choice is to consider functions that can be built on top of binary operators, enjoying algebraic properties which are very often considered in the literature.

Definition 2 (trust operator) A *trust (aggregation) operator* $\oplus$ is a binary operator defined over $[-1,1] \cup \{\phi\}$ and satisfying the following axioms:

1. $\oplus$ is a binary closed operator, i.e., $\oplus : [-1,1] \cup \{\phi\} \times [-1,1] \cup \{\phi\} \mapsto [-1,1] \cup \{\phi\}$;
2. $\oplus$ is associative, i.e., $\forall v, v', v'' \in [-1,1] \cup \{\phi\}$, the equation $(v \oplus v') \oplus v'' = v \oplus (v' \oplus v'')$ holds;
3. ϕ is the identity element, i.e., $\forall v \in [-1,1] \cup \{\phi\}$, the equation $v \oplus \phi = \phi \oplus v = v$ holds.
4. $\preceq$, defined as $v \preceq v'$ if, and only if, $v \oplus v' = v$, is a partial order over $([-1,1] \cup \{\phi\}, \oplus)$ that is compatible with $\oplus$, i.e., if $v \preceq v'$ then $v \oplus v'' \preceq v' \oplus v''$, $\forall v, v', v'' \in [-1,1] \cup \{\phi\}$;

Therefore, $([-1,1] \cup \{\phi\}, \oplus, \preceq)$ is an Ordered Monoid with the partial order $\preceq$. Moreover, we require that the following two additional axioms are satisfied:

5. $\oplus$ is idempotent, i.e., $\forall v \in [-1,1] \cup \{\phi\}$, $v \oplus v = v$ (in fact, this means that $\preceq$ is reflexive);
6. $\oplus$ is commutative, i.e., $\forall v, v' \in [-1,1] \cup \{\phi\}$, the equation $v \oplus v' = v' \oplus v$ holds. □

In the following, the symbol "$\oplus$" will always refer to a trust operator. A derived property of "$\oplus$" is stated below.

Proposition 1 (decomposability) *Let* v, v', v'' *be in* $[-1, 1] \cup \{\phi\}$. *Then,* $v \preceq v' \oplus v'' \Leftrightarrow v \preceq v'$ *and* $v \preceq v''$.

Proof. ($\Rightarrow$) Observe that $v \preceq v' \oplus v''$ implies $v = v \oplus v' \oplus v''$. Since $\preceq$ is compatible with $\oplus$, we have $v \oplus v' \preceq v \oplus v' \oplus v'' \oplus v'$, which implies $v \oplus v' = v \oplus v' \oplus v \oplus v' \oplus v'' \oplus v'$. By commutativity and idempotence, we obtain $v \oplus v' = v \oplus v' \oplus v''$, that is, $v \oplus v' = v$ and thus $v \preceq v'$. A similar reasoning applies to show that $v \preceq v''$.

($\Leftarrow$) Since $\preceq$ is compatible with $\oplus$, $v \preceq v'$ (resp., $v \preceq v''$) implies $v \oplus v'' \preceq v' \oplus v''$ (resp., $v \oplus v \preceq v'' \oplus v$). By commutativity and idempotence, we obtain $v = v \oplus v \preceq v \oplus v''$. Then, by transitivity, we derive $v \preceq v' \oplus v''$. □

A trust operator $\oplus$ naturally induces the trust aggregation function $f_\oplus$ such that, for each multiset S of elements in $[-1, 1] \cup \{\phi\}$, $f_\oplus(S) = \oplus_{v \in S}\, v$. Note that this is well-defined, as $\oplus$ is commutative and associative (so the order is immaterial). Moreover, note that min and max are trust operators. Hence, the notation $f_{\min}$ and $f_{\max}$ used in the previous section is consistent. Now, we claim that, by dealing with trust operators, no unexpected complexity blow up occurs. The result is a simple adaptation of a stronger technical result discussed in Theorem 6. Here, we just stress that the average aggregation function is not expressible via binary operators, so that the result below does not apply to it—indeed, we already know from the proof of Theorem 1 that this operator quickly leads to intractability.

Theorem 2 *If* $\mathcal{A}$ *is a class of acyclic RDF graphs, then* $\text{CHECK}_{f_\oplus, \mathcal{A}}$ *is feasible in polynomial time.*

Now that trust operators have been shown to be computationally well-designed, we proceed to analyze their properties. In particular, we shall next focus on concepts playing a relevant role in the analysis of RDF redundancies. Before doing so, we point out that the specialization of Definition 1 to a function $f_\oplus$, for any given trust operator $\oplus$, nicely fits the concept of model designed by (Zimmermann et al. 2012) for the framework of annotated RDF graphs–in its turn inspired by (Kifer and Subrahmanian 1992). In fact, it can be checked that our results smoothly apply to that general framework for annotated RDF graphs, too.

More abstractly, our framework is also related to a number of works where commutative *semirings* are used to record the provenance of query results when dealing with annotated data (Karvounarakis and Green 2012; Buneman and Kostylev 2010). With this respect, note that semirings have two different kinds of operations: *(i)* the addition operation (corresponding to our aggregation function) that is used to combine annotations (in our case, trust values) referring to the same tuple; *(ii)* the product operation that is used to join annotations of different tuples in the context of *query answering* (more generally, reasoning about RDF schema). As we do not care about querying mechanisms (or RDF schema reasoning) in the paper, it is enough to focus on the addition operation only. In fact, entailment check and core computation on RDF data with annotated triples has been not considered in such related works, and our results smoothly apply to the semiring-based models, too.

4.1 Entailment for t-Graphs

We start the analysis by presenting a generalization of the concept of *entailment* for t-graphs.

Definition 3 ($\oplus$-entailment) Let $\langle \mathcal{G}_1, w_1 \rangle$ and $\langle \mathcal{G}_2, w_2 \rangle$ be two t-graphs. Then, $\langle \mathcal{G}_1, w_1 \rangle$ $\oplus$*-entails* $\langle \mathcal{G}_2, w_2 \rangle$ (denoted by $\langle \mathcal{G}_1, w_1 \rangle \models \langle \mathcal{G}_2, w_2 \rangle$, if $\oplus$ is understood) if every $f_\oplus$-model of $\langle \mathcal{G}_1, w_1 \rangle$ is also a $f_\oplus$-model of $\langle \mathcal{G}_2, w_2 \rangle$. □

Entailment has been studied for RDF graphs (without trust functions) and syntactic characterizations are known for it (Gutierrez et al. 2011). So, it is natural to look for similar characterizations in our context. To this end, we say that a function $\mu : \mathcal{U} \cup \mathcal{B} \to \mathcal{U} \cup \mathcal{B}$ is a URI preserving *mapping* if $\mu(u) = u$, for each $u \in \mathcal{U}$ as defined in (Gutierrez et al. 2011). For an RDF graph $\mathcal{G}$, let $\mu(\mathcal{G})$ be the set of triples $\{\mu(t) \mid t \in \mathcal{G}\}$ resulting from the application of μ. By exploiting the results of (Gutierrez et al. 2011) in our context, the following can be obtained.

Theorem 3 *Let* w_ϕ *be the function such that* $\texttt{dom}(w_\phi) = \emptyset$. *Then,* $\langle \mathcal{G}_1, w_\phi \rangle \models \langle \mathcal{G}_2, w_\phi \rangle$ *if, and only if, there is a URI preserving mapping* μ *with* $\mu(\mathcal{G}_2) \subseteq \mathcal{G}_1$.

Proof Sketch. Let $\langle \mathcal{I}, \bar{\sigma} \rangle$ be an interpretation and $\mathcal{G}$ an RDF graph. If $\langle \mathcal{I}, \bar{\sigma} \rangle$ is an $f_\oplus$-model of $\langle \mathcal{G}, w_\phi \rangle$, then for each triple $(s, p, o) \in \mathcal{G}$, $\sigma_{Int(p)}(Int_A(s), Int_A(o)) \preceq \phi$ must hold, being ϕ the identity element. Thus, Definition 1 reduces to the standard concept of model for RDF graphs, i.e., $\oplus$ plays no role. The result then follows by (Gutierrez et al. 2011). □

To extend the result to arbitrary trust functions, we need to introduce some restrictions on the allowed mappings, which are meant to recast Definition 1 in purely syntactic terms.

Definition 4 ($\oplus$-preserving mappings) Let $\langle \mathcal{G}_1, w_1 \rangle$ and $\langle \mathcal{G}_2, w_2 \rangle$ be two t-graphs. A mapping $\mu : \mathcal{U} \cup \mathcal{B} \to \mathcal{U} \cup \mathcal{B}$ is $\oplus$*-preserving for* $\langle \mathcal{G}_1, w_1 \rangle$ *w.r.t.* $\langle \mathcal{G}_2, w_2 \rangle$ if μ is URI preserving, $\mu(\mathcal{G}_2) \subseteq \mathcal{G}_1$ and, for each $t \in \mathcal{G}_2$, $w_1(\mu(t)) \preceq w_2(t)$. □

Example 4 Consider again the two t-graphs in Figure 1. If μ is a URI preserving mapping such that $\mu(\texttt{\_:b2}) = \texttt{\_:b1}$ or $\mu(\texttt{\_:b2}) = \texttt{A\_Time\_To\_Kill}$, then μ is min-preserving for $\langle \mathcal{G}_1, w_1 \rangle$ w.r.t. $\langle \mathcal{G}_2, w_2 \rangle$. ◁

We next show that the entailment for t-graphs is intimately related with the existence of $\oplus$-preserving mappings.

Theorem 4 $\langle \mathcal{G}_1, w_1 \rangle$ $\oplus$*-entails* $\langle \mathcal{G}_2, w_2 \rangle$ *if, and only if, there is a* $\oplus$*-preserving mapping for* $\langle \mathcal{G}_1, w_1 \rangle$ *w.r.t.* $\langle \mathcal{G}_2, w_2 \rangle$.

Proof Sketch. Assume that $\langle \mathcal{G}_1, w_1 \rangle \models \langle \mathcal{G}_2, w_2 \rangle$, and consider the Herbrand interpretation (Hayes and Patel-Schneider 2014) $\langle \mathcal{H} = \langle Res, Prop, PVal, Int \rangle, \bar{\sigma} \rangle$ of $\mathcal{G}_1$, such that for each $(s, p, o) \in \mathcal{G}_1$, $\sigma_p(s, o) = w_1((s, p, o))$. By construction, $\langle H, \bar{\sigma} \rangle$ is an $f_\oplus$-model of $\langle \mathcal{G}_1, w_1 \rangle$ with the identity function $A_{\mathcal{H}}$ as witness. Since $\langle \mathcal{G}_1, w_1 \rangle \models \langle \mathcal{G}_2, w_2 \rangle$, $\langle \mathcal{H}, \bar{\sigma} \rangle$ is an $f_\oplus$-model of $\langle \mathcal{G}_2, w_2 \rangle$, for some witness A'. Let μ be the mapping such that $\mu(x) = Int_{A'}(x)$. All the triples of $\mathcal{G}_2$ are interpreted through μ as triples of $\mathcal{G}_1$ and, thus, $\mu(\mathcal{G}_2) \subseteq \mathcal{G}_1$. Moreover, one can check that μ is $\oplus$-preserving, due to the decomposability property (cf. Proposition 1).

Let now μ be a $\oplus$-preserving mapping and let $\langle \mathcal{I}, \bar{\sigma} \rangle$ be an $f_\oplus$-model of $\langle \mathcal{G}_1, w_1 \rangle$, whose witness is A. The blank

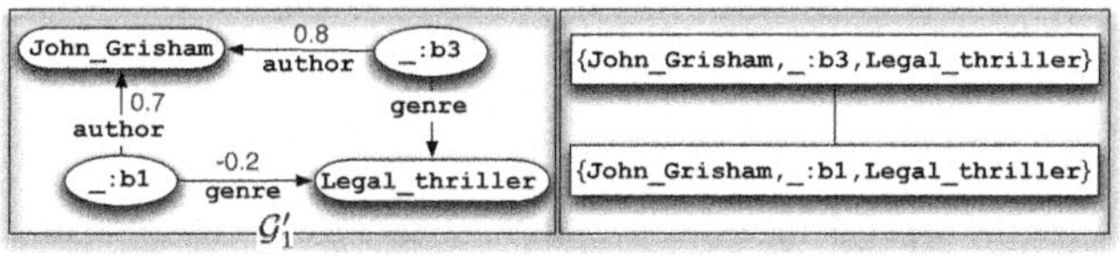

Figure 3: Structures in Example 6.

node assignment $B(x){=}A(\mu(x))$ is a witness for $\langle \mathcal{I}, \bar{\sigma}\rangle$ being an $f_\oplus$-model of $\langle \mathcal{G}_2, w_2\rangle$. □

Example 5 Recall from Example 4 that a min-preserving mapping exists for the t-graphs in Figure 1. Moreover, we claim that $\langle \mathcal{G}_1, w_1\rangle \models \langle \mathcal{G}_2, w_2\rangle$ holds. Indeed, whatever $f_{\min}$-model $\langle I, \bar{\sigma}\rangle$ of $\langle \mathcal{G}_1, w_1\rangle$ must be such that $\min\{\sigma_{Int(\texttt{author})}(\texttt{A\_Time\_To\_Kill}, \texttt{John\_Grisham}),$ $w_1((\texttt{A\_Time\_To\_Kill}, \texttt{author}, \texttt{John\_Grisham}))\} \leq 0.8$. So, $\langle I, \bar{\sigma}\rangle$ is also an $f_{\min}$-model of $\langle \mathcal{G}_2, w_2\rangle$ with witness the blank node assignment $A(\texttt{\_:b2}){=}\texttt{A\_Time\_To\_Kill}$. ◁

Note that Theorem 4 generalizes the syntactic characterization of entailment defined for RDF graphs (Gutierrez et al. 2011) in presence of trust information. Besides its own conceptual relevance, the result plays an important role for a deeper analysis of the complexity of the setting.

Let $\oplus$-ENTAILMENT be the problem receiving as input a pair $\langle \mathcal{G}_1, w_1\rangle$ and $\langle \mathcal{G}_2, w_2\rangle$ and asking whether $\langle \mathcal{G}_1, w_1\rangle$ $\oplus$-entails $\langle \mathcal{G}_2, w_2\rangle$. Since the size of $\oplus$-preserving mappings is polynomially bounded, the following is easily seen to hold,[4] with the hardness trivially deriving from the corresponding one over RDF graphs (Gutierrez et al. 2011).

Theorem 5 *$\oplus$-ENTAILMENT is* NP*-complete.*

Note that Theorem 5 tells us that trust operators provide a method to deal with trust values without representing a source of additional complexity w.r.t. the basic RDF setting.

However, the fact that even the basic setting of RDF graphs without trust values is intractable is clearly not satisfying in general, and motivates the analysis of special classes of RDF and t-graphs. In particular, as often done in the literature, we next focus on nearly-acyclic graphs as they can be formalized via the concept of *tree decomposition*.

Definition 5 A tree decomposition of an RDF graph $\mathcal{G}$ is a pair $\langle T, \chi\rangle$, where $T = (V, E)$ is a tree and χ is a labeling function associating each vertex $v \in V$ with a set of nodes of $\mathcal{G}$ such that for each triple $(s,p,o) \in \mathcal{G} \setminus \{(s,p,o) \in \mathcal{G} \mid \{s,p,o\} \subseteq \mathcal{U}\}$, i.e., for each triple involving blank nodes, the following properties hold:

- there is a vertex $v \in V$ such that $\chi(v) \supseteq \{s, o\}$; and
- the sets of vertices $\{v \in V \mid s \in \chi(v)\}$ and $\{v \in V \mid o \in \chi(v)\}$ induce two connected subtrees over T.

The *width* of $\langle T, \chi\rangle$ is the value $\min_{v\in V} |\chi(v)| - 1$. The *treewidth* of an RDF graph $\mathcal{G}$, denoted by $tw(\mathcal{G})$, is the minimum width over all its possible tree decompositions. □

[4] In the results, we assume the usual computation model with unit costs for all operations involving numbers (in particular, for their manipulation via the $\oplus$ operator).

Note that edge orientation is immaterial in the above notion. Moreover, triples that do not contain blank nodes do not play any role no matter of their interconnections. As an example, the two graphs in Figure 1 have both treewidth 1, i.e., they are acyclic, while the undirected version of $\mathcal{G}_1$ (including the triples without blank nodes) contains a cycle.

Example 6 Consider the graph $\mathcal{G}_1'$ shown on the left of Figure 3, which is obtained from $\mathcal{G}_1$ by just replacing the resource $\texttt{A\_Time\_To\_Kill}$ with a blank node. The (undirected version of the) graph contains a cycle over edges including blank nodes. Indeed, its treewidth is 2, as it is witnessed by the tree decomposition shown on the right. ◁

Let $\oplus$-ENTAILMENT$_\mathcal{C}$ be the restriction of the problem $\oplus$-ENTAILMENT where $\mathcal{G}_2$ (but not necessarily $\mathcal{G}_1$) belongs to a given class $\mathcal{C}$. We next show that this problem is tractable over classes of bounded treewidth, hence generalizing the tractability of RDF graphs (without trust values) having bounded treewidth (Pichler et al. 2008). Hereinafter, $\mathcal{T}_k$ is the class of RDF graphs whose treewidth is k at most.

Theorem 6 *Let $k > 0$ be a fixed natural number. Then, $\oplus$-ENTAILMENT$_{\mathcal{T}_k}$ is computable in polynomial time.*

Proof Sketch. Given two t-graphs $\langle \mathcal{G}_1, w_1\rangle$ and $\langle \mathcal{G}_2, w_2\rangle$ such that $tw(\mathcal{G}_2){=}k$, $\langle \mathcal{G}_1, w_1\rangle {\models} \langle \mathcal{G}_2, w_2\rangle$ can be checked in polynomial time with an adaptation of the algorithm presented in (Pichler et al. 2008). Let $\langle T, \chi\rangle$ be one of the tree decompositions of $\langle \mathcal{G}_2, w_2\rangle$ with width k. T is visited according to a post-order depth-first traversal, i.e., from the leaves to the root, by associating to each node v the set of $\oplus$-preserving mappings μ such that $\mu(\mathcal{G}_v){\subseteq}\mathcal{G}_1$, where $\mathcal{G}_v{\subseteq}\mathcal{G}_2$ contains all the triples of $\mathcal{G}_2$ whose subject or object belong to $\chi(v)$. The sets are propagated from the children to the parent via left semi joins. At the end, if the root has a non empty set of mappings, then $\langle \mathcal{G}_1, w_1\rangle {\models} \langle \mathcal{G}_2, w_2\rangle$. □

As a specialization of the above result, we get that $\oplus$-ENTAILMENT$_\mathcal{C}$ is tractable on any class $\mathcal{C}$ of graphs that do not involve at all blank nodes—so that the notion of treewidth trivializes because $\mathcal{G} \setminus \{(s,p,o) \in \mathcal{G} \mid \{s,p,o\} \subseteq \mathcal{U}\} = \emptyset$, for each $\mathcal{G} \in \mathcal{C}$. Note that, unlike the standard setting of RDF graphs, even this basic result is not immediate in our setting because of the presence of trust functions.

4.2 Cores of t-Graphs

Another concept we would like to explore is the *core*. Indeed, when reasoning about RDF data redundancy, it plays a fundamental role by providing a "normal form" for graphs. Before introducing the concept of core of a t-graph, let us introduce a related notion.

Definition 6 A t-graph $\langle \mathcal{G}, w\rangle$ is *$\oplus$-lean* if there is no $\oplus$-preserving mapping for $\langle \mathcal{G}', w\rangle$ w.r.t. $\langle \mathcal{G}, w\rangle$, $\forall \mathcal{G}' \subset \mathcal{G}$. □

We are now ready to define the concept of $\oplus$-core.

Definition 7 ($\oplus$-core) Let $\langle \mathcal{G}, w\rangle$ be a t-graph. A *$\oplus$-core* of $\langle \mathcal{G}, w\rangle$ is a t-graph $\langle \mathcal{G}', w\rangle$ with $\mathcal{G}' \subseteq \mathcal{G}$ and such that: *(i)* there is a $\oplus$-preserving mapping for $\langle \mathcal{G}', w\rangle$ w.r.t. $\langle \mathcal{G}, w\rangle$; and *(ii)* $\langle \mathcal{G}', w\rangle$ is $\oplus$-lean. □

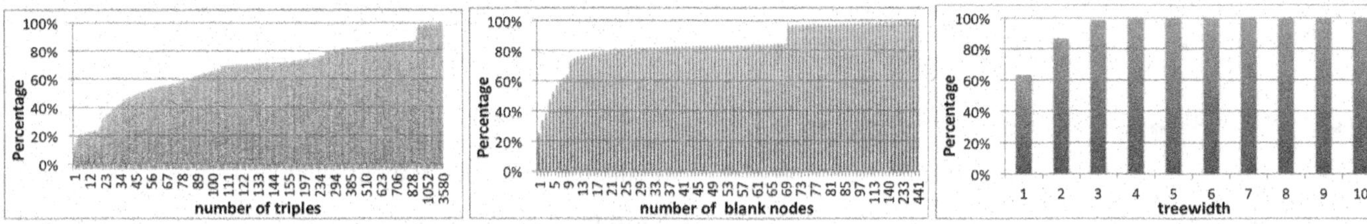

Figure 4: Distribution of RDF graphs in the dataset.

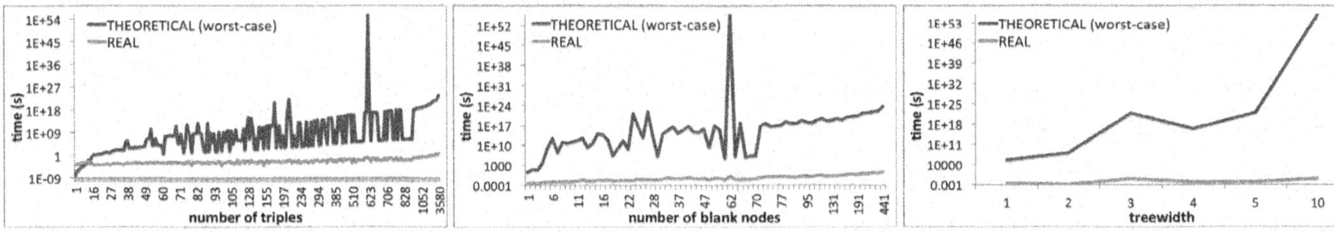

Figure 5: Running time of $\oplus$-entailment checking.

Note that the above definition reduces to the standard one for RDF graphs (Hayes and Patel-Schneider 2014), by getting rid of the function w. In fact, it is well-known that every RDF graph $\mathcal{G}$ has a core, that all its cores are *equivalent* (in fact, *isomorphic*), and that any core of $\mathcal{G}$ is equivalent to $\mathcal{G}$ itself. It is immediate to see that the latter property is preserved in presence of trust values.

Proposition 2 *If* $\langle \mathcal{G}', w\rangle$ *is a* $\oplus$-core *of* $\langle \mathcal{G}, w\rangle$, *then* $\langle \mathcal{G}', w\rangle$ *and* $\langle \mathcal{G}, w\rangle$ *are* $\oplus$*-equivalent, i.e.,* $\oplus$*-entail each other.*

Proof. By Theorem 4, $\langle \mathcal{G}', w\rangle$ and $\langle \mathcal{G}, w\rangle$ are $\oplus$-equivalent if, and only if, there is a $\oplus$-preserving mapping μ for $\langle \mathcal{G}, w\rangle$ w.r.t. $\langle \mathcal{G}', w\rangle$ and a $\oplus$-preserving mapping μ' for $\langle \mathcal{G}', w\rangle$ w.r.t. $\langle \mathcal{G}, w\rangle$. The existence of μ' is guaranteed by point *(i)* in Definition 7, whereas μ can be just the identity function. □

In order to show that the other properties are preserved as well, we need some elaborations.

Theorem 7 *Every t-graph* $\langle \mathcal{G}, w\rangle$ *has a* $\oplus$*-core. Moreover, any two cores of* $\langle \mathcal{G}, w\rangle$ *are* $\oplus$*-equivalent.*

Proof Sketch. Let $\langle \mathcal{G}', w\rangle$ and $\langle \mathcal{G}'', w\rangle$ be two $\oplus$-cores of $\langle \mathcal{G}, w\rangle$ and μ' (resp., μ'') be the $\oplus$-preserving mapping for $\langle \mathcal{G}', w\rangle$ (resp., $\langle \mathcal{G}'', w\rangle$) w.r.t. $\langle \mathcal{G}, w\rangle$. Since $\oplus$ is decomposable and $\mathcal{G}'\subseteq\mathcal{G}$, μ'' is also $\oplus$-preserving for $\langle \mathcal{G}'', w\rangle$ w.r.t. $\langle \mathcal{G}', w\rangle$. Because of Theorem 4, we have $\langle \mathcal{G}', w\rangle\models\langle \mathcal{G}'', w\rangle$. Symmetrically, we could derive that $\langle \mathcal{G}'', w\rangle\models\langle \mathcal{G}', w\rangle$, hence the cores are $\oplus$-equivalent. As for the existence, let $\mu_1,\ldots,\mu_n$ be a maximal sequence such that μ_i, for each $i\in\{1,\ldots,n-1\}$, is $\oplus$-preserving for $\langle \mathcal{G}_{i+1}, w\rangle$ w.r.t. $\langle \mathcal{G}_i, w\rangle$, where $\mathcal{G}_{i+1}=\mu_i(\mathcal{G}_i)\subset\mathcal{G}_i$ and $\mathcal{G}_1=\mathcal{G}$. Such a sequence is finite because it is a succession of contractions of the original graph. It can be shown that the composition $\circ$ of two $\oplus$-preserving mappings is $\oplus$-preserving and thus, the composition $\mu^*=\mu_1\circ\ldots\circ\mu_n$ is $\oplus$-preserving for $\langle \mathcal{G}_n, w\rangle$ w.r.t. $\langle \mathcal{G}, w\rangle$, where $\mathcal{G}_n=\mu^*(\mathcal{G})\subseteq\mathcal{G}$. By the maximality of the sequence, $\langle \mathcal{G}_n, w\rangle$ is lean, and hence it is a $\oplus$-core. □

Note that the proof of the existence of a core is actually constructive. This is the key to establish the following result.

Theorem 8 *Let k be a fixed natural number. A* $\oplus$*-core of any* $\langle \mathcal{G}, w\rangle$ *with* $\mathcal{G}\in\mathcal{T}_k$ *can be computed in polynomial time.*

Proof Sketch. The $\oplus$-core can be computed via an adaptation of the method in (Gottlob and Nash 2008) by iteratively trying to contract $\mathcal{G}$ by removing one blank node and all the triples involving it (thus obtaining a proper subgraph $\mathcal{G}'$ of $\mathcal{G}$) and by checking in polynomial time (by Theorem 6) if $\langle \mathcal{G}, w\rangle$ $\oplus$-entails $\langle \mathcal{G}', w\rangle$. After all blank nodes have been checked, the last valid contraction $\langle \mathcal{G}', w\rangle$ is the $\oplus$-core. □

5 Implementation and Evaluation

The trust framework has been implemented as an extension of the Jena API (http://jena.apache.org) and can be downloaded at http://trdfreasoner.wordpress.com. It provides classes to represent and manage trust values associated to RDF statements and implements some trust aggregation functions. Both algorithms for $\oplus$-entailment checking and $\oplus$-core computation have been implemented by relying on the LibTW library (http://www.treewidth.com) to compute tree decompositions.

Evaluation. An empirical study on the usage of blank nodes in RDF data on the Web has been recently carried out by (Hogan et al. 2014) on the BTC dataset (Harth 2012), by showing that the 44.9% of RDF graphs feature at least one blank node and the majority of them contain acyclic (62.3%) or nearly-acyclic (37.7% with treewidth equals to 2) structures on which Theorem 6 and Theorem 8 apply. In our experiments, we have considered again the BTC dataset, by focusing on the 10 top publishers of blank nodes as reported in (Hogan et al. 2014) and by randomly sampling ~1K RDF graphs from them. Figure 4 reports some statistics about the resulting dataset D w.r.t. the number of triples, blank nodes and treewidth as cumulative bar charts.

For each RDF graph in D, we generated 5 t-graphs with random trust values, computed the $\oplus$-core of each of them and checked the $\oplus$-entailment between each pair. In addition, we computed the $\oplus$-core of each graph in D by considering all trust values equal to 1. Running times have been compared with the (worst-case) theoretical estimates that can be derived by analyzing the algorithms.[5] Results for $\oplus$-entailment checking are reported in logarithmic scale in Figure 5 where they are compared with the theoretical estimates—experiments have been executed on an PC Intel Core i7 2,8 GHz, 16GB RAM. Trends are almost identical for $\oplus$-core computation. Running times are reported w.r.t. the number of triples (nt), number of blank nodes (nb) and treewidth (tw). For each input configuration, we executed 5 runs and computed the running time as the average of the 3 running times obtained by excluding the lowest and highest ones. For each parameter $p \in \{nt, nb, tw\}$, D has been partitioned such that all the graphs in the same partition have the same value of p (e.g., as for tw, $\mathcal{G}_i$ and $\mathcal{G}_j$ belong to the same partition if, and only if, $tw(\mathcal{G}_i) = tw(\mathcal{G}_j)$). For each value of p, we computed the real and theoretical running times as the average on all the graphs of the corresponding partition. As can be noted both algorithms perform much faster than the worst-case theoretical bounds.

6 Discussion and Conclusions

The use of RDF helps improving productivity and efficiency in terms of data dissemination and integration, by automatizing processes with minimal human intervention. However, the presence of incorrect and unreliable data can negatively affect decision processes and cause economic damages. By associating trust values to RDF data, some of these issues can be mitigated. However, having trust values alone is not enough. Indeed, since RDF is the backbone of the Semantic Web, making reasoning problems tractable when dealing with such a large volume of data is essential. This paper contributed in this direction by defining a formal framework (and a prototype system) for reasoning about trust values and by singling out islands of tractability (for classes of acyclic and nearly-acyclic graphs) for the most basic problems arising therein.

References

Buneman, P., and Kostylev, E. 2010. Annotation algebras for RDFS. In *The Second International Workshop on the role of Semantic Web in Provenance Management (SWPM-10)*.

Dividino, R. Q.; Sizov, S.; Staab, S.; and Schueler, B. 2009. Querying for provenance, trust, uncertainty and other meta knowledge in RDF. *J. Web Sem.* 7(3):204–219.

Gottlob, G., and Nash, A. 2008. Efficient core computation in data exchange. *J. ACM* 55(2).

[5] In fact, both algorithms are easily seen to be polynomial in the size of the input graphs and exponential in the treewidth.

Gutierrez, C.; Hurtado, C. A.; Mendelzon, A. O.; and Prez, J. 2011. Foundations of Semantic Web databases. *J. Comput. Syst. Sci.* 77(3):520–541.

Gutierrez, C.; Hurtado, C.; and Vaisman, A. 2007. Introducing time into RDF. *IEEE Transactions on Knowledge and Data Engineering* 19(2):207–218.

Harth, A. 2012. Billion Triples Challenge data set. Downloaded from http://km.aifb.kit.edu/projects/btc-2012/.

Hartig, O. 2009. Querying Trust in RDF Data with tSPARQL. In *6th Annual European Semantic Web Conference (ESWC2009)*, 5–20.

Hayes, P., and Patel-Schneider, P. 2014. RDF 1.1 Semantics. W3C recommendation.

Hogan, A.; Arenas, M.; Mallea, A.; and Polleres, A. 2014. Everything you always wanted to know about blank nodes. *Web Semantics: Science, Services and Agents on the World Wide Web* In press.

Karvounarakis, G., and Green, T. J. 2012. Semiring-annotated data: queries and provenance? *SIGMOD Record* 41(3):5–14.

Kifer, M., and Subrahmanian, V. S. 1992. Theory of Generalized Annotated Logic Programming and its Applications. *J. Log. Program.* 12(3&4):335–367.

Pichler, R.; Polleres, A.; Wei, F.; and Woltran, S. 2008. dRDF: Entailment for Domain-Restricted RDF. In *ESWC*, volume 5021 of *Lecture Notes in Computer Science*, 200–214. Springer.

Straccia, U. 2009. A Minimal Deductive System for General Fuzzy RDF. In Polleres, A., and Swift, T., eds., *RR*, volume 5837 of *Lecture Notes in Computer Science*, 166–181. Springer.

Tomaszuk, D.; Pak, K.; and Rybinski, H. 2013. Trust in RDF Graphs. In Morzy, T.; Hrder, T.; and Wrembel, R., eds., *ADBIS*, volume 186 of *Advances in Intelligent Systems and Computing*, 273–283. Springer.

Udrea, O.; Recupero, D. R.; and Subrahmanian, V. S. 2010. Annotated RDF. *ACM Trans. Comput. Log.* 11(2).

Zimmermann, A.; Lopes, N.; Polleres, A.; and Straccia, U. 2012. A general framework for representing, reasoning and querying with annotated Semantic Web data. *Web Semantics: Science, Services and Agents on the World Wide Web* 11:72–95.

Extended Property Paths: Writing More SPARQL Queries in a Succinct Way*

Valeria Fionda[1], Giuseppe Pirrò[2] and Mariano P. Consens[3]
[1] DeMaCS, University of Calabria, Italy
[2] WeST, University of Koblenz-Landau, Germany
[3] MIE, University of Toronto, Canada

Abstract

We introduce Extended Property Paths (EPPs), a significant enhancement of SPARQL property paths. EPPs allow to capture in a succinct way a larger class of *navigational queries* than property paths. We present the syntax and formal semantics of EPPs and introduce two different evaluation strategies. The first is based on an algorithm implemented in a custom query processor. The second strategy leverages a translation algorithm of EPPs into SPARQL queries that can be executed on existing SPARQL processors. We compare the two evaluation strategies on real data to highlight their pros and cons.

1 Introduction

Motivated by the spread of graph-like data, the area of graph databases has received renewed attention. SPARQL, the W3C standard query language for data in RDF, has recently been enhanced with *property paths* (Harris and Seaborne 2013) to support graph navigation capabilities. The regular-expression-like syntax of property paths enables to write SPARQL navigational queries in a more *succinct* way and extend the matching of triple patterns to arbitrary length paths.

However, property paths offer limited navigation capabilities; queries like "*Find my exclusive friends*", that is, my friends that are not friend of any of my friends, cannot be expressed. To enhance the expressive power of property paths and enable to write more navigational queries in a succinct way, we introduce Extended Property Paths (EPPs). In designing EPPs we identified a core of new features and investigated how to make available such features; indeed, one can devise a custom query processor like in (Alkhateeb, Baget, and Euzenat 2009; Fionda and Pirrò 2013) and/or leverage existing (SPARQL) processors. The goal of this paper is to discuss the design and implementation of EPPs.

Related Work. Graph query languages have been deeply studied (Wood 2012). It emerged that for certain classes of languages, like Conjunctive Regular Path Queries (CRPQs) (Barceló et al. 2012; Alkhateeb, Baget, and Euzenat 2009), the evaluation problem can become too expensive, making the class unattractive for practical purposes. Hence, restricted classes of languages like acyclic CRPQs and Nested Regular Expressions (NREs) (Pérez, Arenas, and Gutierrez 2010) have been proposed. NREs are at the core of navigational languages for RDF such as nSPARQL (Pérez, Arenas, and Gutierrez 2010) and NautiLOD (Fionda, Gutierrez, and Pirrò 2012). Languages like `TriAL` (Libkin, Reutter, and Vrgoč 2013), `TriQ` (Arenas, Gottlob, and Pieris 2014) and NEMODEQ (Rudolph and Krötzsch 2013) are grounded on (extensions of) Datalog. Other expressive languages like SPARQLeR (Kochut and Janik 2007) and *extended* CRPQs (Barceló et al. 2012) focus on discovering paths.

In terms of expressiveness, Barceló et al. (Barceló, Pérez, and Reutter 2012) showed that NREs *cannot express* queries involving, for instance, path conjunction. SPARQL property paths are even less expressive than NREs because of the lack of nesting and tests also within (arbitrary length) paths. `TriAL` can capture queries not captured by NREs and nSPARQL. However, NREs/nSPARQL queries can be evaluated in linear time. Arenas et al. (Arenas, Gottlob, and Pieris 2014) studied the relationships between `TriQ`, `TriAL` and NEMODEQ in terms of Datalog$^{\pm}$ programs (Cali et al. 2010). Fletcher et al. (Fletcher et al. 2011) compared the expressiveness of navigational languages by considering different sets of features. We compare EPPs with closely-related languages in Section 3.3.

EPPs extend the expressive power of SPARQL property paths and NREs-based languages with new features such as *path conjunction*, *path negation* and *powerful types of tests*. These features are partially available in the W3C standard language XPath 2.0 used to query tree-like data (Berglund et al. 2010). From a concrete point of view, with EPPs we faced two main challenges: *(i)* how to make EPPs a conservative extension of SPARQL property paths; *(ii)* how to make EPPs readily available in existing SPARQL processors.

1.1 EPPs by Example

We now give an overview of EPPs via a concrete example. The syntax and semantics of EPPs will be discussed in detail

*V. Fionda's work was supported by the European Commission, the European Social Fund and the Calabria region. G. Pirrò was partially supported by the EU Framework Programme for Research and Innovation under grant agreement no. 611242 (Sense4us).

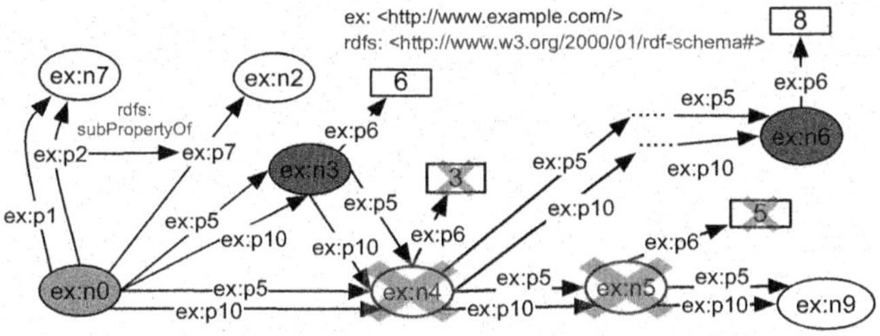

Figure 1: An example of RDF graph.

in Section 2.

Example 1 (Extended Property Paths). By considering the graph in Fig. 1, find pairs of nodes[1] (n_i, n_j) simultaneously connected via two paths: one labeled as p_5 and the other labeled as p_{10}; moreover, from n_j an edge labeled as p_6 that leads to nodes having value <6 must not exists.

NREs-based languages (and PPs) *cannot* express such request due to the lack of path conjunction/negation. With EPPs it can be expressed as:

$$?x\ ((p_5\&p_{10}){\sim}(p_5\&\&TP(\_o, p_6\&\&T(\_o{<}6))))\ ?y$$

The path conjunction & enables to check that both paths p_5 and p_{10} connect n_i with n_j, while path negation ~ enables to discard from the set of nodes satisfying the first path those that also satisfy the second one. Note also that SPARQL property paths and NREs-based languages *lack tests like* TP, to check the existence of a path (via p_6) to nodes having value <6.

The evaluation of the EPP expression with the algorithm described in Section 3 starts from all the *bindings* of the variable ?x; we discuss the case ?x→n_0. From n_0, the evaluation of the first path ($p_5\&p_{10}$) enables to reach n_3. The second path (negated via ~) is evaluated again from n_0 and consists in the logical AND (via &&) of two tests. The first test checks for the existence of an edge p_5, which leads to n_3. The second test (i.e., TP) includes: *(i)* the position in the RDF triple from which the test starts; *(ii)* a path. The position symbol _o means that the test starts from the object of the previous navigational step, that is, the object of the triple (n_0, p_5, n_3). From n_3, another logical AND of two tests is evaluated. The first one checks the existence of an edge p_6 and enables to reach the node 6. The second AND, which starts from the object of the previous step (i.e., 6), checks that the value is <6; in this case the test fails and n_3 *is not* included in the results of the negated path. Conversely, n_4 satisfies the test, it is included in the results of the negated path and thus, it is not a valid binding for ?y when considering ?x→n_0.

Overall, for ?x→ n_0 we get ?y→ n_3 meaning that from n_0 the navigation of the graph according to the expression enabled to reach n_3.

We have also devised a translation procedure (see Section 3.2) of EPPs into SPARQL. The translation of Example 1 is shown in Fig. 2; here, ?o_0_0_1_0_1_0 is a variable automatically generated by the translation. The advantage of the translation is that the query in Fig. 2 can be executed on *existing SPARQL processors*. From the syntactic point of view, the advantage of using EPPs to write navigational queries instead of writing them directly into pure SPARQL is that the same request can be expressed more succinctly and without the need to deal with intermediate variables.

```
SELECT DISTINCT ?x ?y WHERE {
   { ?x p5 ?y. ?x p10 ?y. }
   MINUS
   { ?x p5 ?y.
     FILTER EXISTS
     { ?y p6 ?o_0_0_1_0_1_0.
       FILTER( ?o_0_0_1_0_1_0 < 6 ) }}}
```

Figure 2: Translation into SPARQL of Example 1.

1.2 Contributions and Organization

The contributions of this paper are the following: *(i)* EPPs a language more expressive than NREs-based languages and SPARQL property paths; *(ii)* a concise syntax and a formal semantics for EPPs *(iii)* an algorithm for the evaluation of EPPs and an implementation in a custom query processor; *(iv)* a formalization and implementation of a translation procedure of EPPs into SPARQL; *(v)* a comparison between the custom query processor and Jena ARQ (for EPPs translated into SPARQL).

EPPs can be seen as a language per se, which goes beyond NREs-based languages and SPARQL property paths. Moreover, EPPs serve also the purpose of capturing a larger fragment of pure SPARQL *navigational queries* in a *succinct* way. To the best of our knowledge, EPPs are the first proposal covering both aspects.

The remainder of the paper is organized as follows. Section 2 presents EPPs; syntax and semantics. Section 3 introduces an evaluation algorithm for EPPs and the translation of EPPs into SPARQL. The implementation and evaluation of EPPs are discussed in Section 4. We conclude in Section 5.

2 Extended Property Paths

Let **U** (URIs), **B** (blank nodes), **L** (literals), and $\mathcal{V}$ (variables, starting withe the '?' symbol) be four pairwise disjoint, countably infinite sets. An *RDF triple* is a tuple of the form $\langle s, p, o\rangle \in (\mathbf{U}\cup\mathbf{B})\times\mathbf{U}\times(\mathbf{U}\cup\mathbf{B}\cup\mathbf{L})$. An RDF graph $\mathcal{G}$ is a set of triples. We indicate by $nodes(\mathcal{G}) \subseteq \mathbf{U}\cup\mathbf{B}\cup\mathbf{L}$ the set of URIs, blank nodes and literals that appear as subject or object of some triples in $\mathcal{G}$. Moreover, $\mathcal{T} \subseteq \mathbf{U}\cup\mathbf{B}\cup\mathbf{L}$ is the set of terms of $\mathcal{G}$.

2.1 Extended Property Paths Syntax

The syntax of EPPs is reported in Table 1.

Commonalities with SPARQL property paths (PPs)
The first line of the syntax covers the syntax of PPs (Harris and Seaborne 2013) (section 9.1); moreover, (Negated) PropertySets like '!(u_1 ||...^u_n')' that are

[1]The prefix ex: is omitted for sake of space.

```
          epp ::=  '^' epp | epp '+' | epp '?' | epp'*' | epp '/' epp | epp '|' epp | '(' epp ')' |
                   [pos]^1 test [pos]^2 | epp '&' epp | epp '~' epp
         test ::=  '!' test | test '&&' test | test '||' test | '(' test ')' | base
         base ::=  uri | 'TP('pos ',' epp ')' | 'T('EExp')'
EBuiltInCall ::=  BuiltInCall | pos
          pos ::=  '_s' | '_p' | '_o'
```

Table 1: Syntax of EPPs expressions. [1]If omitted is _s; [2]If omitted is _o.

R1	$\mathbf{E}[\![\hat{\ }\mathtt{epp}]\!]^{\mathcal{G}}$	:=	$\{(\mathtt{u},\mathtt{v}) : (\mathtt{v},\mathtt{u}) \in \mathbf{E}[\![\mathtt{epp}]\!]^{\mathcal{G}}\}$
R2	$\mathbf{E}[\![\mathtt{epp_1}/\mathtt{epp_2}]\!]^{\mathcal{G}}$	:=	$\{(\mathtt{u},\mathtt{v}) : \exists \mathtt{w}\ (\mathtt{u},\mathtt{w}) \in \mathbf{E}[\![\mathtt{epp_1}]\!]^{\mathcal{G}} \wedge (\mathtt{w},\mathtt{v}) \in \mathbf{E}[\![\mathtt{epp_2}]\!]^{\mathcal{G}}\}$
R3	$\mathbf{E}[\![(\mathtt{epp})^{*}]\!]^{\mathcal{G}}$	:=	$\{(\mathtt{u},\mathtt{u}) \mid \mathtt{u} \in \mathit{nodes}(\mathcal{G})\} \cup \bigcup_{i=1}^{\infty} \mathbf{E}[\![\mathtt{epp}_i]\!]^{\mathcal{G}} \mid \mathtt{epp_1} = \mathtt{epp} \wedge \mathtt{epp}_i = \mathtt{epp}_{i-1}/\mathtt{epp}$
R4	$\mathbf{E}[\![(\mathtt{epp})^{+}]\!]^{\mathcal{G}}$	:=	$\bigcup_{i=1}^{\infty} \mathbf{E}[\![\mathtt{epp}_i]\!]^{\mathcal{G}} \mid \mathtt{epp_1} = \mathtt{epp} \wedge \mathtt{epp}_i = \mathtt{epp}_{i-1}/\mathtt{epp}$
R5	$\mathbf{E}[\![(\mathtt{epp})?]\!]^{\mathcal{G}}$	:=	$\{(\mathtt{u},\mathtt{u}) \mid \mathtt{u} \in \mathit{nodes}(\mathcal{G})\} \cup \mathbf{E}[\![\mathtt{epp}]\!]^{\mathcal{G}}$
R6	$\mathbf{E}[\![(\mathtt{epp_1} \vert \mathtt{epp_2})]\!]^{\mathcal{G}}$	:=	$\{(\mathtt{u},\mathtt{v}) : (\mathtt{u},\mathtt{v}) \in \mathbf{E}[\![\mathtt{epp_1}]\!]^{\mathcal{G}} \vee (\mathtt{u},\mathtt{v}) \in \mathbf{E}[\![\mathtt{epp_2}]\!]^{\mathcal{G}}\}$
R7	$\mathbf{E}[\![(\mathtt{epp_1}\&\mathtt{epp_2})]\!]^{\mathcal{G}}$	:=	$\{(\mathtt{u},\mathtt{v}) : (\mathtt{u},\mathtt{v}) \in \mathbf{E}[\![\mathtt{epp_1}]\!]^{\mathcal{G}} \wedge (\mathtt{u},\mathtt{v}) \in \mathbf{E}[\![\mathtt{epp_2}]\!]^{\mathcal{G}}\}$
R8	$\mathbf{E}[\![(\mathtt{epp_1} \sim \mathtt{epp_2})]\!]^{\mathcal{G}}$	:=	$\{(\mathtt{u},\mathtt{v}) : (\mathtt{u},\mathtt{v}) \in \mathbf{E}[\![\mathtt{epp_1}]\!]^{\mathcal{G}} \wedge (\mathtt{u},\mathtt{v}) \notin \mathbf{E}[\![\mathtt{epp_2}]\!]^{\mathcal{G}}\}$
R9	$\mathbf{E}[\![\mathtt{pos_1}\ \mathtt{test}\ \mathtt{pos_2}]\!]^{\mathcal{G}}$	:=	$\{(P_m(\mathtt{pos_1},\mathtt{t}), P_m(\mathtt{pos_2},\mathtt{t}))) \mid \text{triple } \mathtt{t} \in \mathcal{G} \wedge \mathbf{E}_{\mathcal{T}}[\![\mathtt{test}]\!]_t^{\mathcal{G}}\}$
R10	$\mathbf{E}_{\mathcal{T}}[\![\mathtt{u}]\!]_{\mathtt{t}}^{\mathcal{G}}$	:=	$P_m(\_p,\mathtt{t}) = \mathtt{u}$
R11	$\mathbf{E}_{\mathcal{T}}[\![\mathtt{T(EExp)}]\!]_{\mathtt{t}}^{\mathcal{G}}$	:=	$\mathtt{EvalSPARQLBuilt\text{-}in(EExp,t)}$
R12	$\mathbf{E}_{\mathcal{T}}[\![\mathtt{TP(pos,epp)}]\!]_{\mathtt{t}}^{\mathcal{G}}$	:=	$\exists v : (P_m(\mathtt{pos},\mathtt{t}), v) \in \mathbf{E}[\![\mathtt{epp}]\!]^{\mathcal{G}}$
R13	$\mathbf{E}_{\mathcal{T}}[\![\mathtt{test_1}\&\&\mathtt{test_2}]\!]_{\mathtt{t}}^{\mathcal{G}}$	:=	$\mathbf{E}_{\mathcal{T}}[\![\mathtt{test_1}]\!]_{\mathtt{t}}^{\mathcal{G}} \wedge \mathbf{E}_{\mathcal{T}}[\![\mathtt{test_2}]\!]_{\mathtt{t}}^{\mathcal{G}}$
R14	$\mathbf{E}_{\mathcal{T}}[\![\mathtt{test_1} \Vert \mathtt{test_2}]\!]_{\mathtt{t}}^{\mathcal{G}}$	:=	$\mathbf{E}_{\mathcal{T}}[\![\mathtt{test_1}]\!]_{\mathtt{t}}^{\mathcal{G}} \vee \mathbf{E}_{\mathcal{T}}[\![\mathtt{test_2}]\!]_{\mathtt{t}}^{\mathcal{G}}$
R15	$\mathbf{E}_{\mathcal{T}}[\![!\mathtt{test}]\!]_{\mathtt{t}}^{\mathcal{G}}$	:=	$\neg \mathbf{E}_{\mathcal{T}}[\![\mathtt{test}]\!]_{\mathtt{t}}^{\mathcal{G}}$

Table 2: Formal semantics of EPPs expressions.

a combination of forward/reverse predicates in a (negated) set are expressible in the EPPs syntax via the productions `test` $\rightarrow$ `base` $\rightarrow$ `u`. Note that EPPs use the symbol '||' while PPs use '|'.

New features introduced by Extended Property Paths
The following *additional* features are introduced: path conjunction ($\mathtt{epp_1}\&\mathtt{epp_2}$), path negation ($\mathtt{epp_1}{\sim}\mathtt{epp_2}$) and different types of tests (`test`) *within* a path, also by specifying the *starting* and *ending* positions (`pos`). EPPs enable to test from each of the subject, predicate and object positions in RDF triples, mapped in the syntax to _s, _p and _o, respectively. Positions do not need to be always specified; by default a test starts from the subject (_s) and ends on the object (_o) of a triple.

Tests (`test`) can be of different types and can be combined by using the logical operators AND (&&), OR (||) and NOT (!). A test can be a simple check for the existence of a URI or a *nested* EPP, i.e., `TP(pos, epp)`, which corresponds to the evaluation of `epp` starting from a position `pos` (of the last triple traversed) and whose evaluation returns true if, and only if, there exists at least one node that can be reached via `epp`. A base test (production `base`) can be of type `T`, which is a SPARQL boolean expression; here, `EExp` (not reported here for sake of space) extends the production [110] in the SPARQL grammar[2] where `BuiltInCall`[3] is substituted with `EBuiltInCall`, which enables to use in EPPs tests available in SPARQL as built-in conditions also augmented with positions (`pos`). Built-in conditions are constructed using elements of the set $\mathbf{U} \cup \mathbf{L}$ and constants, logical connectives ($\neg$, $\wedge$, $\vee$), (in)equality symbol(s) (=,<,>,≤,≥), unary (e.g., `isURI`,) and binary (e.g., `STRSTARTS`) functions.

[2]http://www.w3.org/TR/sparql11-query/\#rExpression

[3]http://www.w3.org/TR/sparql11-query/\#rBuiltInCall

2.2 Extended Property Paths Semantics

The semantics (shown in Table 2) for the interpretation of an EPP expression `epp` on a graph $\mathcal{G}$ uses two functions: *(i)* $\mathbf{E}[\![\mathtt{epp}]\!]^{\mathcal{G}}$ defined as a binary relation $(\mathtt{u},\mathtt{v})$ such that `u` and `v` are nodes in $\mathcal{G}$ and `v` is reachable from `u` via a path in $\mathcal{G}$ satisfying `epp`; and *(ii)* $\mathbf{E}_{\mathcal{T}}[\![\mathtt{test}]\!]_{\mathtt{t}}^{\mathcal{G}}$ defined as a boolean function, which evaluates `true` if, and only if, the triple `t` satisfies the test `test`. The semantics also uses the position mapping function P_m defined as follows:

Definition 2 (Position mapping function). Let $\mathtt{t}{=}\langle \mathtt{x},\mathtt{y},\mathtt{z}\rangle$ be a triple pattern, $\{\mathtt{x},\mathtt{y},\mathtt{z}\} \subseteq \mathcal{T} \cup \mathcal{V}$. The position mapping function $P_m(\mathtt{pos},\mathtt{t})$ is defined as: *(i)* $P_m(\_s,\mathtt{t}) = \mathtt{x}$, *(ii)* $P_m(\_p,\mathtt{t}) = \mathtt{y}$ *(iii)* $P_m(\_o,\mathtt{t}) = \mathtt{z}$.

P_m selects one among the subject, predicate and object of a triple on the basis of the value of `pos`. Consider the triple $\langle \mathtt{u_1},\mathtt{p_1},\mathtt{u_2}\rangle$ and the test $\mathtt{T}(\_p{=}\mathtt{p_1})$; this instantiates P_m as $P_m(\_p,\langle \mathtt{u_1},\mathtt{p_1},\mathtt{u_2}\rangle){=}\mathtt{p_1}$, which checks $\mathtt{p_1}{=}\mathtt{p_1}$ returning true while testing $\mathtt{T}(\_o{=}\mathtt{u_3})$ gives false.

3 Algorithms and Complexity

This section presents two strategies for the evaluation of EPPs expressions. The first via an ad-hoc algorithm; the second one via a translation into SPARQL queries that can be executed on existing processors.

```
Function EVALUATE(n, epp, G)
Input: node n, expression epp, graph G; Output: node set Res.
if epp = (epp1)* then
    return CLOSURE(n, epp1, G, {}, 0)
else if epp = (epp1)+ then
    return CLOSURE(n, epp1, G, {}, 1)
else
    return BASE(n, epp, G))
```

```
Function CLOSURE(n, epp, G, Res, l)
Input: node n, EPPs expression epp, graph G, node set Res, lower bound l;
Output: node set Res.
if l = 1 then
    S = EVALUATE(n, epp, G)
else
    S = {n}
while S ≠ ∅ do
    n = extractNode(S) /* extract one node */
    if n ∉ Res then
        Res = Res ∪ {n}
        S = S ∪ EVALUATE(n, epp, G)
return Res
```

```
Function BASE(n, epp, G)
Input: node n, EPPs expression epp, graph G; Output: node set Res.
1: if epp = epp1|epp2 then
2:     return EVALUATE(n, epp1, G) ∪ EVALUATE(n, epp2, G)
3: if epp = epp1/epp2 then
4:     Res' := EVALUATE(n, epp1, G)
5:     Res = {}
6:     for all nodes n' ∈ Res' do
7:         Res = Res ∪ EVALUATE(n', epp2, G)
8:     return Res
9: if epp = epp1&epp2 then
10:     return EVALUATE(n, epp1, G) ∩ EVALUATE(n, epp2, G)
11: if epp = epp1 ~ epp2 then
12:     return EVALUATE(n, epp1, G) \ EVALUATE(n, epp2, G)
13: if epp = epp1? then
14:     return {n} ∪ EVALUATE(n, epp1, G)
15: if epp = pos1testpos2 then
16:     Res = {}
17:     for all triple t ∈ G s.t. Pm(pos1, t) = n do
18:         if EVALTEST(t, test, G) then
19:             Res = Res ∪ {Pm(pos1, t), Pm(pos2, t)}
20:     return Res
```

```
Function EVALTEST(t, test, G)
Input: triple t, graph G; Output: true if t satisfy test.
if test = test1&&test2 then
    return EVALTEST(t, test1, G) ∧ EVALTEST(t, test2, G)
if test = test1||test2 then
    return EVALTEST(t, test1, G) ∨ EVALTEST(t, test2, G)
if test =!test1 then
    return ¬EVALTEST(t, test1, G)
if test = u then
    return Pm(_p, t) = u
if test = TP(pos, epp) then
    return EVALUATE(Pm(pos, t), epp, G) ≠ ∅
if test = T(EExp) then
    return EvalSPARQLBuilt-in(EExp, t)
```

Figure 3: EPPs evaluation algorithm.

3.1 Recursion-based Algorithm

The algorithm for the evaluation of an EPP expression starts by invoking EVALUATE (Fig. 2), which receives as input a graph $\mathcal{G}$, an expression `epp` and a node n. If `epp` is non recursive (i.e., it does not contain the closure operators '+' and '*') then it is given as input to the function BASE, which considers the various forms of syntactic expressions. For recursive expressions the algorithm uses the function CLOSURE. Finally, the boolean function EVALTEST handles the different types of `test`.

The result of the evaluation of an EPP expression `epp` from a node n is a set of pairs of nodes (n,n_r) where nodes n_r are reachable from n via paths satisfying `epp`.

We now discuss the complexity of the algorithm. We assume $\mathcal{G}$ to be stored by its adjacency list. In particular, for each `t` $\in \mathcal{T}$, a Hashtable is maintained where the set of keys is the set of predicates `p` such that there exists a triple in $\mathcal{G}$ having as subject `t` and as predicate `p`, and the set of values are lists of objects `o` reachable by traversing `p`-predicates from `t`. We assume that given `t` and a predicate `p` the set of nodes reachable can be accessed in time $O(1)$. An additional Hashtable is used for inverse navigation, that is, for navigation starting on the object and ending on the subject. Both structures use space $O(|\mathcal{G}|)$. Let $|\texttt{epp}|$ be the size of the EPP expression `epp`.

Theorem 3 Given the EPP expression `epp`, an RDF graph $\mathcal{G}$ and a node $n \in \mathcal{G}$ the evaluation of $\mathrm{E}[\![\texttt{epp}]\!]^{\mathcal{G}}$ can be performed in time $O(|\mathcal{G}| \cdot |\texttt{epp}|) + c_{\texttt{EExp}}$.

Proof: [SKETCH] The function EVALUATE is recursively called on each sub-expression of the `epp` in input; if such sub-expressions are not recursive (i.e., do not contain '*', '+'), EVALUATE is invoked at most $O(|\texttt{epp}|)$ times. The base cases (lines 15-19 of function BASE) require to consider at most all the edges for all the nodes; this can be done in time $O(|\mathcal{G}|)$. If `epp` is recursive, the function CLOSURE is executed at most $O(nodes(\mathcal{G}))$ times; the procedure EVALUATE is invoked for each node in the worst case. When evaluating a subexpression from a node we use *memoization* to store its result (i.e., the set of reachable nodes) thus avoiding to recompute the same expression from the same node multiple times. Memoization guarantees that the total time required by CLOSURE is $O(|\texttt{epp}| \cdot |\mathcal{G}|)$. As for *nested* expressions, memoization enables to mark nodes of the graph satisfying a given subexpression.

Path conjunction and negation, corresponding to intersection and difference of set of nodes respectively (line 10 and 12 of BASE), can be computed in time $O(|\mathcal{G}|)$ by using a (prefect) hash function as the graph is known beforehand. As for tests, their cost is constant for *logical operators* and simple URI checking. The complexity is parametric wrt the cost of other SPARQL-based built-in conditions `EExp` ($c_{\texttt{EExp}}$). Finally, observe that with memoization the space complexity is $O(|\texttt{epp}| \cdot nodes(\mathcal{G})^2)$. □

3.2 Translation into SPARQL

The W3C spec. (Harris and Seaborne 2013) *informally* mentions the fact that non-recursive property paths can be evaluated via a *translation* into equivalent SPARQL algebraic forms. However, no formal proof of the correctness and completeness of such translation is provided. Recursive property paths are handled in the standard via auxiliary functions called `ALP` (Harris and Seaborne 2013). With EPPs

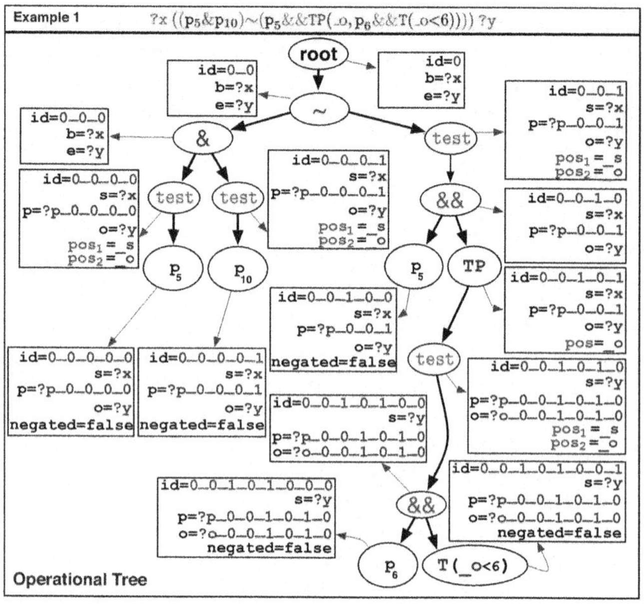

Figure 4: *Operational tree* for Ex. 1 after propagation.

(that are meant to extend property paths) we adopted a similar approach. In what follows, we give an overview of how *non-recursive* EPPs (NREPPs) are translated into SPARQL queries. For recursive EPPs we modified the ALP function defined in the W3C standard where subexpressions in recursive calls to ALP are evaluated via the SPARQL translation.

The NREPPtoSPARQL translation

Let $\mathcal{P}$=(α, epp, β), $\alpha, \beta \in \mathcal{T} \cup \mathcal{V}$ be a NREPP pattern. The translation algorithm $\mathcal{A}^t$ uses a structure called *operational tree* built from the *parse tree* of $\mathcal{P}$. The operational tree associated to $\mathcal{P}$ is an ordered, labeled, rooted tree with node attributes reflecting the operational structure of $\mathcal{P}$. We now give a high level overview of the three phases of the translation algorithm $\mathcal{A}^t$:

$\mathbf{R_m}$	$\Theta^{\mathcal{P}}$(root)	:='SELECT DISTINCT' root.b root.e '{ WHERE {' $\Theta^{\mathcal{P}}$(root.*child*(1)) '}}'
R0	$\Gamma(n)$	:=n.s n.p n.o'.'
R1	$\Theta^{\mathcal{P}}(n^{\hat{}})$	:=$\Theta^{\mathcal{P}}(n.child(1))$
R2	$\Theta^{\mathcal{P}}(n^{/})$	:=$\Theta^{\mathcal{P}}(n.child(1))\ \Theta^{\mathcal{P}}(n.child(2))$
R3	$\Theta^{\mathcal{P}}(n^{\vert})$	:='{'$\Theta^{\mathcal{P}}(n.child(1))$'} UNION{'$\Theta^{\mathcal{P}}(n.child(2))$'}'
R4	$\Theta^{\mathcal{P}}(n^{\&})$	:=$\Theta^{\mathcal{P}}(n.child(1))\ \Theta^{\mathcal{P}}(n.child(2))$
R5	$\Theta^{\mathcal{P}}(n^{\sim})$	:='{'$\Theta^{\mathcal{P}}(n.child(1))$'} MINUS{'$\Theta^{\mathcal{P}}(n.child(2))$'}'
R6	$\Theta^{\mathcal{P}}(n^{\mathtt{test}})$	:= $\Theta^{t}(n.child(1))$
R7	$\Theta^{t}(n^{u})$	:=$\Gamma(n)$ 'FILTER('n.p['!']'= u)'[a]
R8	$\Theta^{t}(n^{\mathrm{T(EExp)}})$	:=$\Gamma(n)$ 'FILTER'['!']'(' EExp')'[a]
R9	$\Theta^{t}(n^{\mathrm{TP}})$	:=$\Gamma(n)$ 'FILTER'['NOT'] 'EXISTS'{$\Theta^{\mathcal{P}}(n.child(1))$'}'[a]
R10	$\Theta^{t}(n^{\&\&})$	:=$\Theta^{t}(n.child(1))\ \Theta^{t}(n.child(2))$
R11	$\Theta^{t}(n^{\Vert})$	:='{'$\Theta^{t}(n.child(1))$'} UNION{'$\Theta^{t}(n.child(2))$'}'

Figure 5: Translation rules. [a]If the node in input has the attribute negated=true use '!' (resp., 'NOT').

(i) Building of the operational tree

Consider a NREPP pattern $\mathcal{P}$. In the operational tree associated to $\mathcal{P}$, nodes are of two types: *(i) operational nodes* (labeled with $\sim, \&, /, |, \hat{}$) and *(ii) test nodes* (labeled with test[4], ||, &&, TP, u, T(EExp)). Each node n_i in the operational tree has a single parent and its children are an ordered set. Moreover, n_i has an attribute id whose unique value is computed as the *concatenation* of the parent's id and n_i's position in the ordered set of children. The operational tree for Example 1 is shown in Fig. 4.

(ii) Propagation of variables and terms[5]

The key point is the propagation of variable names and RDF terms (kept in nodes' attributes). This is done by traversing the operational tree top-down and propagating attributes from each parent node to its children.

(iii) Application of the translation rules

This phase always starts by applying rule $\mathbf{R_m}$ in Fig. 5 on the root of the operational tree. This generates the outermost part of the final rewritten query into the SPARQL syntax. The translation proceeds by applying rules at each node of the operational tree visited according to a pre-order depth-first traversal.

For instance, in Fig. 4, after the root, the node with id=0_0 and labeled with $\sim$ is visited. This causes the triggering of rule R5, which enables to generate another (internal) chunk of the final SPARQL query. Node 0_0 is an operational node representing path negation $\sim$. As it can be noted, our translation procedure uses the SPARQL MINUS operator to reflect the semantics of EPPs dealing with path negation. The semantics of nodes representing EPPs test (e.g., 0_0_1_0_1) is reflected into SPARQL via the FILTER operator.

Correctness of the translation

In order to prove the correctness of the translation of NREPPs into SPARQL we have defined a SPARQL based semantics (not reported here for sake of space) where conjunction (&) and negation ($\sim$) are translated into join ($\bowtie$) and difference ($\setminus$) of (multi)sets of solution mappings (Pérez, Arenas, and Gutierrez 2009). Let $[\![\mathcal{P}]\!]^{\mathcal{G}}_{epps}$ denote the SPARQL-based semantics of EPPs, where $\mathcal{P}$ is an NREPP pattern, and $[\![\mathcal{S}]\!]^{W3C}_{\mathcal{G}}$ denote the SPARQL W3C semantics (Harris and Seaborne 2013), where $\mathcal{S}$ is a SPARQL query. The following theorem shows the correctness of the translation.

Theorem 4 The translation algorithm $\mathcal{A}^t$ is correct and runs in polynomial time in the size of the expression to be translated. Moreover, for any RDF graph $\mathcal{G}$ given $\mathcal{P}$ it holds that $[\![\mathcal{P}]\!]^{epps}_{\mathcal{G}}$=$[\![\mathcal{S}]\!]^{W3C}_{\mathcal{G}}$, where $\mathcal{S}$=$\mathcal{A}^t(\mathcal{P})$ is the query produced by translating $\mathcal{P}$.

Proof: [SKETCH] $\mathcal{A}^t$ is polynomial as it requires one scan of the operational tree (whose size is polynomial in the size of the EPP expression). As for the correctness, it is enough to prove that the propagation of variable names and RDF terms in the operational tree is correct. This proof can be

[4]In the syntax it coresponds to $\mathtt{pos}_1$ test $\mathtt{pos}_2$.

[5]Negation (!) for test nodes is propagated top-down when building the tree via the attribute negated.

done by structural induction on the depth of the operational tree. Finally, the semantic equivalence can be proved by associating to all types of EPP patterns the corresponding semantics as per SPARQL specification (Harris and Seaborne 2013). □

Complexity of the translated queries. Consider a NREPP `epp` in a pattern $\mathcal{P}$ and its translation into SPARQL $\mathcal{S}_{\texttt{epp}}$. Clearly, the complexity of evaluating $\mathcal{S}_{\texttt{epp}}$ depends on the fragment of SPARQL used in the translation. In particular (see Fig. 5) we make usage of `SELECT`, `UNION`, `MINUS` and `FILTER` and we *do not* use `OPTIONAL`. The complexity of this and other SPARQL fragments has been studied in (Pérez, Arenas, and Gutierrez 2009).

Summary. EPPs can be seen as a language per se and can be evaluated by implementing the algorithm in Fig. 3 in a custom processor, thus being independent from existing SPARQL processors. EPPs can also be seen as a conservative extension of SPARQL property paths and, thanks to the translation algorithm, can be evaluated on existing SPARQL processors. We have implemented both strategies; their pros and cons will be discussed in Section 4.

3.3 Comparison with Related Languages

As the goal of EPPs is to extend the expressive power of SPARQL property paths (PPs) and NREs-based languages, we compared such proposals with EPPs; Table 3 summarizes the (informal) comparison. We consider the following features of EPPs: path conjunction (&), path negation (~), nesting (TP), tests over node values (`test`) and usage of positions (`pos`). As it can be observed, PPs are the least expressive language; they do not support any of the new features of EPPs. This motivated our choice of *extending* PPs as described in Section 2.1. As for NREs, they clearly support nesting but neither other types of tests (e.g., node equality) nor path conjunction/negation as discussed in (Barceló, Pérez, and Reutter 2012).

Language	&	~	TP	`test`	`pos`
EPPs	**Yes**	**Yes**	**Yes**	**Yes**	**Yes**
PPs	No	No	No	No	No
NREs	No	No	**No**	No	No
nSPARQL	**Yes**	**Yes**	**Yes**	No	**Yes**

Table 3: Comparison of EPPs with related languages.

As for nSPARQL (based on NREs), it supports path conjunction and negation only via the SPARQL algebra; it also supports nesting and positions. However, it does not allow to test (in)equalities of nodes reached with a nested expression. EPPs support logical combination of tests representing nesting and tests representing (in)equalities as well as *safe*-negation[6]. Note that neither PPs nor NREs nor nSPARQL can express Example 1. nSPARQL supports positions by transforming an RDF graph into another graph where *navigational axes* (similar to those defined in XPath) are made explicit. On the other hand, EPPs do not require any transformation. In the syntax of EPPs, positions enable to perform *edge to node* traversals allowing to reach the node representing the predicate of a triple whence it is possible to traverse e.g. the property hierarchy. Finally, we want to emphasize that EPPs are syntactically compatible with PPs and are the only language, which thanks to the `NREPPtoSPARQL` translation, can be used in existing SPARQL processors.

4 Implementation and Evaluation

We have implemented both a custom query processor for EPPs and the `NREPPtoSPARQL` translation[7].

Dataset and query set. We used a crawl of the FOAF social network (~500MBs) obtained from the BTC2012[8] by traversing from the URI of T. Berners-Lee (TBL) `foaf:knows` predicates up to distance 4. We call the resulting graph $\mathcal{G}^F$, which has ~4M triples. We created 4 groups $G_i, i \in \{1,...,4\}$ of EPP expressions each with 3 queries; this gives a queryset Q of 12 queries. The experiments have been performed on an Intel i5 machine with 8GBs RAM. Results are the average of 5 runs after removing lowest and highest values.

Experiment 1: Running time
For each `epp` $\in Q$ we generated the corresponding SPARQL query $\mathcal{S}_{\texttt{epp}}$ via the algorithm described in Section 3.2. We measured the execution time for each `epp` $\in Q$ with *our processor* and the execution time for $\mathcal{S}_{\texttt{epp}}$ in *Jena ARQ*[9]. Fig. 6 shows the running times. The number of results ranges from ~50 to ~8000.

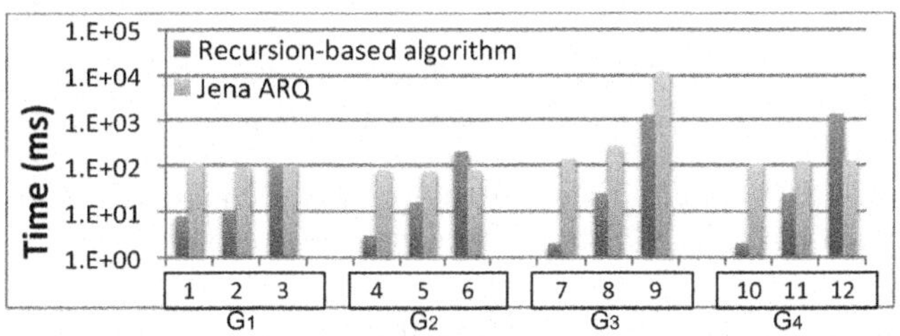

Figure 6: EPPs-custom-processor vs. Jena ARQ.

As it can be observed, for G_1, which contains queries asking for friends of TBL up to distance 3, our evaluator performs better than ARQ at distance 1 and 2; at distance 3 times are comparable. The group G_2 additionally considers a test based on *nesting*. Again, our evaluator performs better at distance 1 and 2; at distance 3 it shows a higher running time. In G_3, which considers *negation* (e.g., *exclusive friends* at various distances) our approach performs consistently better. Finally, in G_4 that includes conjunction (to ask for *mutual* friends at various distances) our approach performs better at distance 1 and 2 and obtains a higher running time at distance 3.

[6]The first element must be positive path.

[7]Available at http://extendedpps.wordpress.com

[8]http://km.aifb.kit.edu/projects/btc-2012

[9]http://jena.apache.org

The complexity of the algorithm described in Section 3 is lower than that of Jena ARQ, which implements SPARQL. However, our evaluation suggests that for real-world data and natural queries (e.g., mutual friends) working with the translation of EPPs and using existing processors is still useful. Hence, the advantage of our approach is that navigational queries can be written in a succinct way via the EPPs syntax and execute after their translation via `NREPPtoSPARQL`. Anecdotally, while the EPP asking for mutual friends at distance 3 contains ∼200 characters, the SPARQL query (obtained from the translation) contains ∼700 characters. Moreover, when writing the SPARQL query one has also to deal with a large number of variables that need to be consistently joined.

Experiment 2: Translation overhead
We compared the elapsed times of our `NREPPtoSPARQL` with the `SPARQLtoALGEBRA` translation of Jena ARQ. We used 28 queries generated in two steps. We started with 4 base expressions plus a fifth one combining them. Second, starting from them we generated increasingly longer expressions. We found that our `NREPPtoSPARQL` translation performs comparably (in the order of ms) to the existing `SPARQLtoALGEBRA` translation.

5 Conclusions and Future Work

We introduced Extended Property Paths (EPPs), a significant extension of SPARQL property paths. We have provided an algorithm for their evaluation and also a translation procedure into SPARQL.

EPPs bring some benefits: *(i)* users can leverage their syntax to write more expressive *navigational* queries in a succinct way; *(ii)* EPPs are immediately available into existing SPARQL processors. Our study opens some research questions such as investigating properties of the translation (e.g., minimality) and studying optimization techniques. Also containment of EPPs is an open question.

References

Alkhateeb, F.; Baget, J.-F.; and Euzenat, J. 2009. Extending SPARQL with Regular Expression Patterns (for querying RDF). *J. Web Semantics* 7(2):57–73.

Arenas, M.; Gottlob, G.; and Pieris, A. 2014. Expressive Languages for Querying the Semantic Web. In *Proc. of the 33rd symposium on Principles of Database Systems*, 14–26. ACM.

Barceló, P.; Libkin, L.; Lin, A. W.; and Wood, P. T. 2012. Expressive Languages for Path Queries over Graph-Structured Data. *ACM Transactions on Database Systems* 37(4):31.

Barceló, P.; Pérez, J.; and Reutter, J. L. 2012. Relative Expressiveness of Nested Regular Expressions. In *Proc. of the 6th Alberto Mendelzon International Workshop on Fundations of Data Management*, 180–195.

Berglund, A.; Boag, S.; Chamberlin, D.; Fernández, M.; Kay, M.; Robie, J.; and Siméon, J. 2010. XML Path Language (XPath) 2.0, W3C.

Cali, A.; Gottlob, G.; Lukasiewicz, T.; Marnette, B.; and Pieris, A. 2010. Datalog+/-: A Family of Logical Knowledge Representation and Query Languages for New Applications. In *Proc. of the 25th Annual IEEE Symposium on Logic in Computer Science*, 228–242. IEEE.

Fionda, V., and Pirrò, G. 2013. Querying Graphs with Preferences. In *Proc.of the 22nd ACM international conference on Conference on Information & Knowledge Management*, 929–938. ACM.

Fionda, V.; Gutierrez, C.; and Pirrò, G. 2012. Semantic Navigation on the Web of Data: Specification of Routes, Web Fragments and Actions. In *Proc. of the 21st International Conference on World Wide Web*, 281–290. ACM.

Fletcher, G. H.; Gyssens, M.; Leinders, D.; Van den Bussche, J.; Van Gucht, D.; Vansummeren, S.; and Wu, Y. 2011. Relative Expressive Power of Navigational Querying on Graphs. In *Proc. of the 14th International Conference on Database Theory*, 197–207. ACM.

Harris, S., and Seaborne, A. 2013. SPARQL 1.1 Query Language, W3C.

Kochut, K., and Janik, M. 2007. SPARQLeR: Extended SPARQL for Semantic Association Discovery. In *Proc. of the 4th European Semantic Web Conf.*, 145–159.

Libkin, L.; Reutter, J.; and Vrgoč, D. 2013. TriAL for RDF: Adapting Graph Query Languages for RDF Data. In *Proc. of the 32nd Symposium on Principles of Database Systems*, 201–212. ACM.

Pérez, J.; Arenas, M.; and Gutierrez, C. 2009. Semantics and Complexity of SPARQL. *ACM Transactions on Database Systems* 34(3).

Pérez, J.; Arenas, M.; and Gutierrez, C. 2010. nSPARQL: A Navigational Language for RDF. *J. Web Semantics* 8(4):255–270.

Rudolph, S., and Krötzsch, M. 2013. Flag & check: Data Access with Monadically Defined Queries. In *Proc. of the 32nd Symposium on Principles of Database Systems*, 151–162. ACM.

Wood, P. T. 2012. Query Languages for Graph Databases. *SIGMOD Rec.* 41(1).

Lower and Upper Bounds for SPARQL Queries over OWL Ontologies

Birte Glimm and **Yevgeny Kazakov**
University of Ulm, Germany
<firstname.surname>@uni-ulm.de

Ilianna Kollia and **Giorgos Stamou**
National Technical University of Athens, Greece
ilianna2@mail.ntua.gr, gstam@cs.ntua.gr

Abstract

The paper presents an approach for optimizing the evaluation of SPARQL queries over OWL ontologies using SPARQL's OWL Direct Semantics entailment regime. The approach is based on the computation of lower and upper bounds, but we allow for much more expressive queries than related approaches. In order to optimize the evaluation of possible query answers in the upper but not in the lower bound, we present a query extension approach that uses schema knowledge from the queried ontology to extend the query with additional parts. We show that the resulting query is equivalent to the original one and we use the additional parts that are simple to evaluate for restricting the bounds of subqueries of the initial query. In an empirical evaluation we show that the proposed query extension approach can lead to a significant decrease in the query execution time of up to four orders of magnitude.

Introduction

Query answering—the computation of answers to users' queries w.r.t. ontologies and data—is an important task in the context of the Semantic Web. Ontologies formulated in the Web Ontology Language OWL (Motik, Patel-Schneider, and Parsia 2009) correspond to Description Logic (DL) knowledge bases (KBs) (Baader et al. 2007), i.e., to theories in a decidable fragment of First-Order Logic. Many Description Logic reasoners support some form of query answering, but while much effort has been spent on optimizing standard reasoning tasks for expressive DLs, e.g., the computation of subsumption relations between concepts (unary predicates), less attention has been given to optimizing the evaluation of more complex query patterns. The need for an efficient evaluation of complex queries over OWL ontologies becomes more urgent with the standardization of the SPARQL 1.1 Entailment Regimes (Glimm and Ogbuji 2013), which extend the SPARQL Query Language (Harris and Seaborne 2013) with the capability of querying also for answers that are entailed by the queried ontology, whereas without entailment regimes only explicitly stated knowledge is taken into account. In this paper, we propose a way of exploiting the knowledge in the ontology to more efficiently evaluate complex queries over OWL 2 DL ontologies under the OWL Direct Semantics entailment regime of SPARQL 1.1.

Since computing the answers to a query over an expressive knowledge base is computationally very costly, approximation techniques have been proposed that use a weakened version of the KB to compute a lower bound (yields sound but potentially incomplete results) and a strengthened version to compute an upper bound (yields complete but potentially unsound results) for the query answers (Zhou et al. 2014; Pan, Thomas, and Zhao 2009; Ren, Pan, and Zhao 2010). The weakened and strengthened versions are typically approximated in a simpler logic, for which more efficient reasoning algorithms can be used. Another well-known technique is to compute the bounds from a pre-model, i.e., a complete and clash-free tableau generated by a DL reasoner (Kollia and Glimm 2012). Facts that are derived deterministically are used as lower bound, while also non-deterministically derived facts are considered for the upper bound. For simple queries, the lower bound allows for simply reading off the answers, while answers in the "gap", i.e., potential answers in the upper but not the lower bound, usually have to be checked individually by performing a consistency check with a fully fledged OWL 2 DL reasoner. Following Zhou et al. (2014), we refer to the technique of first computing lower and upper bounds and then checking the answers in the gap as *hybrid approach*. Since performing many consistency checks is unlikely to work well in practice, Zhou et al. also propose optimizations such as extracting relevant fragments of the ontology for checking a potential answer and an adaptation of the summarization technique (Dolby et al. 2009; 2007).

In this paper, we also follow the hybrid approach, but we significantly extend the form of allowed queries. Furthermore, we present a way of using the knowledge in the ontology to extend the query such that the additionally added parts allow for better query planning and an overall faster query evaluation. Compared to query evaluation with standard static query planning (Kollia and Glimm 2013) our empirical analysis with a prototypical implementation shows an improvement of up to four orders of magnitude in the query execution times due to the proposed optimizations.

The idea of modifying the query for better query planning and evaluation has been presented before in the database community. However, the proposed methods do not involve background knowledge, they rather present query approximations that are based on query forms with better complexity characteristics for query evaluation (like acyclicity, bounded treewidth, etc.) (Barceló, Libkin, and Romero 2012), or on queries expressed in less expressive query languages (for example without self-joins) (Fink and Olteanu 2011), or on queries for which the answers have been pre-computed (views) (Halevy 2001). On the other hand, there is a lot of work for query extension using semantic data descriptions, but mainly in the area of information retrieval focusing more on the representation of the query context for query expansion and refinement, and not on faster query evaluation (Bhogal, Macfarlane, and Smith 2007; Munir, Odeh, and McClatchey 2012; Luna, Revoredo, and Cozman 2010; Grootjen and van der Weide 2006).

Preliminaries

SPARQL's basic building blocks are so-called basic graph patterns (BGPs), which can then be combined using operators such as `UNION` or filters using the `FILTER` keyword. While the evaluation of BGPs is performed over the queried ontology, all other operators simply combine solutions obtained by evaluating the BGPs. Hence, we focus on the evaluation of BGPs in this paper. In the context of the OWL Direct Semantics Entailment Regime of SPARQL 1.1 (Glimm and Ogbuji 2013), BGPs correspond to "extended" OWL ontologies/KBs, where one can use variables in place of concept names (unary predicates), role names (binary predicates) or individual names (constants), which is why we next define the syntax of "extended" KBs in the DL $\mathcal{ALC}$ of which standard $\mathcal{ALC}$ KBs are a subset.

Definition 1 (Syntax). *The* syntax of an extended $\mathcal{ALC}$ knowledge base *or* query *is defined using a signature (T_C, T_R, T_I), consisting of countably infinite disjoint sets T_C of* concept terms, *T_R of* role terms, *and T_I of* individual terms. *The set T_C (T_R, T_I) consists of the disjoint union of countably infinite sets of* concept (role, individual) names *N_C (N_R, N_I) and* concept (role, individual) variables *V_C (V_R, V_I). We further allow for the two special concepts $\top$ and $\bot$. Complex concept templates can be composed from these basic elements by using negation ($\neg C$), conjunction ($C_1 \sqcap C_2$), disjunction ($C_1 \sqcup C_2$), or by quantification over a role ($\forall r.C$ and $\exists r.C$) with $C_{(i)} \in T_C$ and $r \in T_R$. An* axiom template *(short: template) has the form $C \sqsubseteq D$, $C(t)$, or $r(t, t')$ with C, D concept templates, r a role term, and t, t' individual terms. If a concept template or an axiom template does not contain any variable, we call it* ground *or simply a* concept *or an* axiom.

An extended knowledge base *$\mathcal{K} = \mathcal{T} \cup \mathcal{A}$ is a finite set of axiom templates, where $\mathcal{T}$ is an* extended TBox *consisting of axiom templates of the form $C \sqsubseteq D$ and $\mathcal{A}$ is an* extended ABox *consisting of the remaining axiom templates. A (standard)* knowledge base *(short: KB) is an extended knowledge base that does not contain variables, that is, a set of axioms.*

A query *q is a set of templates and the size $|q|$ of q is the number of templates in q. If q contains only templates of the form $A(t)$ or $r(t, t')$ with $A \in N_C$, $r \in N_R$, and $t, t' \in T_I$, we call q a* conjunctive instance query. *We denote by vars(q) the set of all (concept, role, and individual) variables occurring in q. If vars(q) $= \emptyset$, we call q a* ground *or* Boolean query.

$$
\begin{aligned}
\mathcal{K} &= \mathcal{T} \cup \mathcal{A}, \text{ where} \\
\mathcal{T} &= \{B \sqsubseteq A \sqcup C,\ \exists r.B \sqsubseteq C\} \\
\mathcal{A} &= \{A(a),\ B(b),\ r(a, b),\ A(d)\} \\
q &= \{A(x), \exists r.Y(x), Y \sqsubseteq B\}
\end{aligned}
$$

$$r \in N_R,\ \{A, B, C\} \subseteq N_C,\ \{a, b, c, d\} \subseteq N_I,\ Y \in V_C,\ x \in V_I$$

Figure 1: The (standard) knowledge base $\mathcal{K}$ and the query q used in the examples of this paper.

Note that the above definition can easily be extended to allow for more expressive Description Logics constructors such as nominals (concepts defined as an enumeration of individuals), role chains (e.g., for expressing transitivity), or (qualified) cardinality constraints (counting quantifiers in First-Order Logic) (Horrocks, Kutz, and Sattler 2006). We omit the introduction of these features for brevity, but the presented results are straightforwardly applicable.

Example 1. *Figure 1 gives an example of a standard knowledge base $\mathcal{K}$ and a query q. The knowledge base $\mathcal{K} = \mathcal{T} \cup \mathcal{A}$ consists of two TBox axioms and four ABox axioms. The query q consists of three axiom templates containing variables vars(q) $= \{x, Y\}$, where x is an individual variable, and Y is a concept variable.*

The query answers are then mappings such that the query instantiated by the mappings yields axioms that are entailed by the queried knowledge base. To make this more precise, we next define the semantics of (extended) KBs and queries.

Definition 2 (Semantics). *An* interpretation *$\mathcal{I} = (\Delta^\mathcal{I}, \cdot^\mathcal{I})$ consists of a non-empty set $\Delta^\mathcal{I}$, the* domain *of $\mathcal{I}$, and an* interpretation function *$\cdot^\mathcal{I}$, that assigns to each $A \in N_C$ a subset $A^\mathcal{I} \subseteq \Delta^\mathcal{I}$, to each $r \in N_R$ a binary relation $r^\mathcal{I} \subseteq \Delta^\mathcal{I} \times \Delta^\mathcal{I}$, and to each $a \in N_I$ an element $a^\mathcal{I} \in \Delta^\mathcal{I}$. We further have $\top^\mathcal{I} = \Delta^\mathcal{I}$ and $\bot^\mathcal{I} = \emptyset$. The interpretation is extended to (ground) complex concepts as follows: $(\neg C)^\mathcal{I} = \Delta^\mathcal{I} \setminus C^\mathcal{I}$, $(C \sqcap D)^\mathcal{I} = C^\mathcal{I} \cap D^\mathcal{I}$, $(C \sqcup D)^\mathcal{I} = C^\mathcal{I} \cup D^\mathcal{I}$, $(\forall r.C)^\mathcal{I} = \{\delta \in \Delta^\mathcal{I} \mid \langle \delta, \delta' \rangle \in r^\mathcal{I} \rightarrow \delta' \in C^\mathcal{I}\}$, $(\exists r.C)^\mathcal{I} = \{\delta \in \Delta^\mathcal{I} \mid \exists \delta' \in C^\mathcal{I} : \langle \delta, \delta' \rangle \in r^\mathcal{I}\}$.*

An interpretation $\mathcal{I}$ satisfies *a (ground) axiom α (notation: $\mathcal{I} \models \alpha$) as follows: $\mathcal{I} \models C \sqsubseteq D$ if $C^\mathcal{I} \subseteq D^\mathcal{I}$, $\mathcal{I} \models C(a)$ if $a^\mathcal{I} \in C^\mathcal{I}$, and $\mathcal{I} \models r(a, b)$ if $\langle a^\mathcal{I}, b^\mathcal{I} \rangle \in r^\mathcal{I}$. $\mathcal{I}$ is a* model *of a (standard) knowledge base $\mathcal{K}$ (notation: $\mathcal{I} \models \mathcal{K}$) if $\mathcal{I} \models \alpha$ for every axiom $\alpha \in \mathcal{K}$. If such a model for $\mathcal{K}$ exists, we say that $\mathcal{K}$ is* consistent. *$\mathcal{K}$* entails *an axiom α (notation: $\mathcal{K} \models \alpha$) if $\mathcal{I} \models \alpha$ for every model $\mathcal{I}$ of $\mathcal{K}$.*

A mapping *is a (partial) function $\mu \colon V_C \cup V_R \cup V_I \rightarrow N_C \cup N_R \cup N_I$ such that $\mu(x) \in N_C$ for each $x \in V_C$, $\mu(x) \in N_R$ for each $x \in V_R$, and $\mu(x) \in N_I$ for each $x \in V_I$. We use dom(μ) to denote the* domain *of a function μ. Two mappings μ_1 and μ_2 are* compatible *if $\mu_1(x) = \mu_2(x)$ for every $x \in$ dom(μ_1) $\cap$ dom(μ_2). In this case,* the union of μ_1 and μ_2 *is the mapping $\mu = \mu_1 \cup \mu_2$ with dom(μ) $=$ dom(μ_1) $\cup$ dom(μ_2)*

defined by $\mu(x) = \mu_1(x)$ *for* $x \in dom(\mu_1)$ *and* $\mu(x) = \mu_2(x)$ *for* $x \in dom(\mu_2)$*. If* M_1 *and* M_2 *are two sets of mappings then the* join of M_1 and M_2 *is the set of mappings* $M_1 \bowtie M_2 = \{\mu_1 \cup \mu_2 \mid \mu_1 \in M_1, \mu_2 \in M_2, \mu_1$ *and* μ_2 *are compatible*$\}$.

Given a query q*, we denote with* $\mu(q)$ *the result of replacing each variable* $x \in dom(\mu)$ *with* $\mu(x)$*. If* $vars(q) \subseteq dom(\mu)$*, we write* $\mathcal{I}, \mu \models q$ *if* $\mathcal{I}$ *satisfies every (ground) axiom template of* $\mu(q)$*. A mapping* μ *is a* certain answer *for a query* q *over a (standard) KB* $\mathcal{K}$*, written* $\mathcal{K}, \mu \models q$*, if* $\mathcal{I}, \mu \models q$ *for each* $\mathcal{I}$ *such that* $\mathcal{I} \models \mathcal{K}$*. We set* $\mathsf{ans}(\mathcal{K}, q) = \{\mu \mid \mathcal{K}, \mu \models q, dom(\mu) = vars(q)\}$*. Queries* q_1 *and* q_2 *are* equivalent w.r.t. $\mathcal{K}$ *if* $\mathsf{ans}(\mathcal{K}, q_1) = \mathsf{ans}(\mathcal{K}, q_2)$.

Note that if $q = q_1 \cup q_2$ then $\mathsf{ans}(\mathcal{K}, q) = \mathsf{ans}(\mathcal{K}, q_1) \bowtie \mathsf{ans}(\mathcal{K}, q_2)$.

Example 2. *It is easy to check that the KB* $\mathcal{K}$ *in Figure 1 has a model* $\mathcal{I} = (\Delta^\mathcal{I}, \cdot^\mathcal{I})$ *with* $\Delta^\mathcal{I} = \{d_1, d_2, d_3, d_4\}$, $a^\mathcal{I} = d_1$, $b^\mathcal{I} = d_2$, $c^\mathcal{I} = d_3$, $d^\mathcal{I} = d_4$, $A^\mathcal{I} = \{d_1, d_2, d_4\}$, $B^\mathcal{I} = \{d_2\}$, $C^\mathcal{I} = \{d_1\}$*, and* $r^\mathcal{I} = \{\langle d_1, d_2 \rangle\}$*. Note that* $\mathcal{I} \models A(a)$ *but* $\mathcal{I} \not\models B(a)$*. Hence,* $\mathcal{K} \not\models A \sqsubseteq B$*. Thus, for the mapping* μ *with* $\mu(Y) = A$*, we have* $\mathcal{K}, \mu \not\models \{Y \sqsubseteq B\}$*. The same also holds for every* μ *with* $\mu(Y) \in \{C, \top\}$*. Thus,* $\mathsf{ans}(\mathcal{K}, \{Y \sqsubseteq B\}) = \{\bot, B\}$*. Similarly, one can show that* $\mathsf{ans}(\mathcal{K}, \{A(x)\}) = \{\mu \mid \mu(x) \in \{a, d\}\}$ *since* $\mathcal{K} \models A(a)$, $\mathcal{K} \models A(d)$*, but* $\mathcal{K} \not\models A(b)$ *and* $\mathcal{K} \not\models A(c)$*, and that* $\mathsf{ans}(\mathcal{K}, \{\exists r.Y(x)\}) = \{\mu \mid \mu(x) = a, \mu(Y) \in \{B, \top\}\}$ *since* $\mathcal{K} \models \exists r.B(a)$ *and* $\mathcal{K} \models \exists r.\top(a)$*, but* $\mathcal{K} \not\models \exists r.A(a)$, $\mathcal{K} \not\models \exists r.B(b)$*, etc. Hence, for* $q = \{A(x), \exists r.Y(x), Y \sqsubseteq B\}$ *in Figure 1 we obtain* $\mathsf{ans}(\mathcal{K}, q) = \mathsf{ans}(\mathcal{K}, \{A(x)\}) \bowtie \mathsf{ans}(\mathcal{K}, \{\exists r.Y(x)\}) \bowtie \mathsf{ans}(\mathcal{K}, \{Y \sqsubseteq B\}) = \{\mu \mid \mu(x) = a, \mu(Y) = B\}$.

Bounds for Queries and Subqueries

Since entailment checking is the standardized reasoning task for OWL reasoners, a naive way to evaluate queries is to instantiate the query with all possible query mappings and check entailment of the resulting axioms using an OWL reasoner. Since the number of possible mappings can be very large, this method is not efficient even with small queries. Therefore, practical algorithms try to reduce the number of entailment tests by determining using other techniques, which mappings can or cannot satisfy the query. We present this general idea using the notion of a query bound.

Definition 3 (Query Bound). *Let* $\mathcal{K}$ *be a knowledge base and* q *a query. A* bound for q w.r.t. $\mathcal{K}$ *is a pair of sets* $[\mathcal{L}; \mathcal{U}]$ *of mappings such that* $\mathcal{L} \subseteq \mathsf{ans}(\mathcal{K}, q) \subseteq \mathcal{U}$*. We call* $\mathcal{L}$ *the* lower *and* $\mathcal{U}$ *the* upper bound *for* q *over* $\mathcal{K}$*. The bound* $[\mathcal{L}; \mathcal{U}]$ *is* exact *if* $\mathcal{L} = \mathcal{U}$ *(and hence* $= \mathsf{ans}(\mathcal{K}, q)$*).*

We usually assume that $\mathcal{K}$ is fixed and refer to bounds for queries without mentioning $\mathcal{K}$.

Example 3. *Consider again the KB* $\mathcal{K}$ *in Figure 1. Since* $\{A(a), A(d)\} \subseteq \mathcal{K}$ *we have* $\mathcal{K} \models A(a)$ *and* $\mathcal{K} \models A(d)$*. Hence* $\mathsf{ans}(\mathcal{K}, \{A(x)\})$ *contains at least all* μ *such that* $\mu(x) \in \{a, d\}$*. That is, we can find the lower bound* $\mathcal{L} = \{\mu \mid \mu(x) \in \{a, d\}\}$ *for the query* $\{A(x)\}$ *over* $\mathcal{K}$ *without performing any tests.*

To find an upper bound for $\{A(x)\}$*, consider the model* $\mathcal{I}$ *constructed in Example 2. Note that* $\mathcal{I} \not\models A(c)$*. Thus, from this model alone one can conclude that* $\mathcal{K} \not\models A(c)$ *and hence that* $\mathsf{ans}(\mathcal{K}, \{A(x)\}) \subseteq \{\mu \mid \mu(x) \in \{a, b, d\}\}$*. Thus, the set* $\mathcal{U} = \{\mu \mid \mu(x) \in \{a, b, d\}\}$ *provides an upper bound for the query* $\{A(x)\}$ *over* $\mathcal{K}$*.*

Although the model $\mathcal{I}$ *can be similarly used for finding an upper bound for complex templates, such as* $\{\exists r.Y(x)\}$*, in general it can only be found by iterating over all possible mappings for* x *and* Y *and checking which instances of this template are entailed by the model. Therefore, in practice, one does not compute the bounds for complex templates.*

The bounds for the query $\{Y \sqsubseteq B\}$ *can be computed by classifying the knowledge base and retrieving subsumption relationships with concept* B*. Since for classification one usually needs to consider just the (relatively small) TBox* $\mathcal{T}$*, the bounds for this query can be computed exactly. That is, in our example we have* $\mathcal{L} = \mathcal{U} = \{\bot, B\}$*.*

Query bounds can be also extracted by weakening and strengthening of the knowledge bases in tractable fragments (Zhou et al. 2014). Lower query bounds for simple instance queries can also be obtained by inspecting which assertions are derived deterministically when testing satisfiability of $\mathcal{K}$ using (hyper-)tableau procedures (Kollia and Glimm 2012). Using the computed bounds for simple queries, one can derive the bounds for more complex queries as follows.

Lemma 1. *Let* $q = q_1 \cup q_2$, $[\mathcal{L}_1; \mathcal{U}_1]$ *be a query bound for* q_1 *and* $[\mathcal{L}_2; \mathcal{U}_2]$ *a query bound for* q_2*. Then* $[\mathcal{L}_1 \bowtie \mathcal{L}_2; \mathcal{U}_1 \bowtie \mathcal{U}_2]$ *is a query bound for* $q_1 \cup q_2$*.*

Proof. It is easy to show that if $M_1 \subseteq M_1'$ and $M_2 \subseteq M_2'$ are sets of mappings then $M_1 \bowtie M_2 \subseteq M_1' \bowtie M_2'$. Since $\mathsf{ans}(\mathcal{K}, q_1 \cup q_2) = \mathsf{ans}(\mathcal{K}, q_1) \bowtie \mathsf{ans}(\mathcal{K}, q_2)$, from $\mathcal{L}_1 \subseteq \mathsf{ans}(\mathcal{K}, q_1) \subseteq \mathcal{U}_1$ and $\mathcal{L}_2 \subseteq \mathsf{ans}(\mathcal{K}, q_2) \subseteq \mathcal{U}_2$ we obtain $\mathcal{L}_1 \bowtie \mathcal{L}_2 \subseteq \mathsf{ans}(\mathcal{K}, q_1 \cup q_2) \subseteq \mathcal{U}_1 \bowtie \mathcal{U}_2$. □

The above lemma gives rise to a query answering algorithm that first retrieves the query bounds for each axiom template in the query. Second, the join of all query bounds is computed. Third, the mappings that are in the upper but not in the lower bound are checked using an OWL reasoner. Since computing a join of (potentially large) sets of mappings can be expensive, one can instead try to reduce the bounds for axiom templates using other parts of the query.

Definition 4 (Subquery Bound). *If* $q = q_1 \cup q_2$*, then we say that* q_1 *is a* subquery *of* q*. The pair of sets* $[\mathcal{L}_1; \mathcal{U}_1]$ *is a* subquery bound for q_1 *in* q over $\mathcal{K}$ *if* $\mathcal{L}_1 \subseteq (\mathsf{ans}(\mathcal{K}, q_1) \cap \mathcal{U}_1)$ *and* $\mathsf{ans}(\mathcal{K}, q) = (\mathsf{ans}(\mathcal{K}, q_1) \cap \mathcal{U}_1) \bowtie \mathsf{ans}(\mathcal{K}, q_2)$*.*

Intuitively, a subquery bound provides a range for those answers of the subquery q_1 that are sufficient to evaluate the query q. If the query $q = q_1 \cup q_2$ is clear from the context, we usually call $[\mathcal{L}_1; \mathcal{U}_1]$ a subquery bound of q_1 without mentioning q (and $\mathcal{K}$ as for query bounds). Clearly, if $q = q_1 \cup q_2$ and $[\mathcal{L}_1; \mathcal{U}_1]$ is a query bound for q_1, then it is also subquery bound for q_1 in q. The converse property does not hold as shown in the next example.

Example 4. *Consider* $\mathcal{K}$ *from Figure 1 and* $q = q_1 \cup q_2$ *with* $q_1 = \{A(x)\}$ *and* $q_2 = \{\exists r.Y(x)\}$*. As shown in Example 2,* $\mathsf{ans}(\mathcal{K}, q_1) = \{\mu \mid \mu(x) \in \{a, d\}\}$ *and* $\mathsf{ans}(\mathcal{K}, q_2) = \{\mu \mid \mu(x) = a, \mu(Y) \in \{B, \top\}\}$*. It is easy to see that* $\mathsf{ans}(\mathcal{K}, q) = \mathsf{ans}(\mathcal{K}, q_1) \bowtie \mathsf{ans}(\mathcal{K}, q_2) = \mathsf{ans}(\mathcal{K}, q_2)$*.*

Now, consider $\mathcal{L}_1 = \mathcal{U}_1 = \{\mu \mid \mu(x) = a\}$. Clearly, $\mathcal{L}_1 \subseteq \mathsf{ans}(\mathcal{K}, q_1) \cap \mathcal{U}_1$. Also, $(\mathsf{ans}(\mathcal{K}, q_1) \cap \mathcal{U}_1) \bowtie \mathsf{ans}(\mathcal{K}, q_2) = \mathcal{U}_1 \bowtie \mathsf{ans}(\mathcal{K}, q_2) = \mathsf{ans}(\mathcal{K}, q_2) = \mathsf{ans}(\mathcal{K}, q)$. Hence $[\mathcal{L}_1; \mathcal{U}_1]$ is a subquery bound for q_1 in q. It is, however, not a query bound for q_1 since $\mathsf{ans}(\mathcal{K}, q_1) \not\subseteq \mathcal{U}_1$.

Lemma 2. *Let $q = q_1 \cup q_2 \cup q_3$ and let $[\mathcal{L}_1; \mathcal{U}_1]$, $[\mathcal{L}_2; \mathcal{U}_2]$ be subquery bounds for q_1 and q_2 w.r.t. q, respectively. Then $\mathsf{ans}(\mathcal{K}, q) = (\mathsf{ans}(\mathcal{K}, q_1) \cap \mathcal{U}_1) \bowtie (\mathsf{ans}(\mathcal{K}, q_2) \cap \mathcal{U}_2) \bowtie \mathsf{ans}(\mathcal{K}, q_3)$.*

Proof. Clearly, $(\mathsf{ans}(\mathcal{K}, q_1) \cap \mathcal{U}_1) \bowtie (\mathsf{ans}(\mathcal{K}, q_2) \cap \mathcal{U}_2) \bowtie \mathsf{ans}(\mathcal{K}, q_3) \subseteq \mathsf{ans}(\mathcal{K}, q_1) \bowtie \mathsf{ans}(\mathcal{K}, q_2) \bowtie \mathsf{ans}(\mathcal{K}, q_3) = \mathsf{ans}(\mathcal{K}, q)$, so it remains to show the converse $\mathsf{ans}(\mathcal{K}, q) \subseteq (\mathsf{ans}(\mathcal{K}, q_1) \cap \mathcal{U}_1) \bowtie (\mathsf{ans}(\mathcal{K}, q_2) \cap \mathcal{U}_2) \bowtie \mathsf{ans}(\mathcal{K}, q_3)$.

Since $[\mathcal{L}_1; \mathcal{U}_1]$ is a subquery bound for q_1, $\mathsf{ans}(\mathcal{K}, q) = (\mathsf{ans}(\mathcal{K}, q_1) \cap \mathcal{U}_1) \bowtie \mathsf{ans}(\mathcal{K}, q_2 \cup q_3) = (\mathsf{ans}(\mathcal{K}, q_1) \cap \mathcal{U}_1) \bowtie \mathsf{ans}(\mathcal{K}, q_2) \bowtie \mathsf{ans}(\mathcal{K}, q_3)$. Hence, for every $\mu \in \mathsf{ans}(\mathcal{K}, q)$ there exist $\mu_1 \in \mathsf{ans}(\mathcal{K}, q_1) \cap \mathcal{U}_1$, $\mu_2 \in \mathsf{ans}(\mathcal{K}, q_2)$, and $\mu_3 \in \mathsf{ans}(\mathcal{K}, q_3)$ that are compatible such that $\mu = \mu_1 \cup \mu_2 \cup \mu_3$. Likewise, since $[\mathcal{L}_2; \mathcal{U}_2]$ is a subquery bound for q_2, there exist $\mu'_1 \in \mathsf{ans}(\mathcal{K}, q_1)$, $\mu'_2 \in \mathsf{ans}(\mathcal{K}, q_2) \cap \mathcal{U}_2$, and $\mu'_3 \in \mathsf{ans}(\mathcal{K}, q_3)$ that are compatible such that $\mu = \mu'_1 \cup \mu'_2 \cup \mu'_3$. Since $\mathrm{dom}(\mu_i) = \mathrm{vars}(q_i) = \mathrm{dom}(\mu'_i)$ $(1 \leq i \leq 3)$, from $\mu_1 \cup \mu_2 \cup \mu_3 = \mu'_1 \cup \mu'_2 \cup \mu'_3$ we obtain $\mu_1 = \mu'_1$, $\mu_2 = \mu'_2$, and $\mu_3 = \mu'_3$. In particular $\mu = \mu_1 \cup \mu'_2 \cup \mu_3 \in (\mathsf{ans}(\mathcal{K}, q_1) \cap \mathcal{U}_1) \bowtie (\mathsf{ans}(\mathcal{K}, q_2) \cap \mathcal{U}_2) \bowtie \mathsf{ans}(\mathcal{K}, q_3)$, which proves $\mathsf{ans}(\mathcal{K}, q) \subseteq (\mathsf{ans}(\mathcal{K}, q_1) \cap \mathcal{U}_1) \bowtie (\mathsf{ans}(\mathcal{K}, q_2) \cap \mathcal{U}_2) \bowtie \mathsf{ans}(\mathcal{K}, q_3)$. □

Theorem 1 illustrates how the bound of one subquery (q_1) can be reduced using the bound of another subquery (q_2). Note that the subqueries q_1 and q_2 can be arbitrary, e.g., empty, singleton templates or sets of possibly overlapping templates.

Theorem 1. *Let $q = q_1 \cup q_2 \cup q_3$, let $[\mathcal{L}_1; \mathcal{U}_1]$, $[\mathcal{L}_2; \mathcal{U}_2]$ be subquery bounds for q_1 and q_2 w.r.t. q, respectively, and let $M_1 \subseteq \mathcal{U}_1$ be such that $M_1 \bowtie \mathcal{U}_2 = \emptyset$. Then $[\mathcal{L}_1 \setminus M_1; \mathcal{U}_1 \setminus M_1]$ is also a subquery bound for q_1.*

Proof. Clearly, if $\mathcal{L}_1 \subseteq (\mathsf{ans}(\mathcal{K}, q_1) \cap \mathcal{U}_1)$ then $\mathcal{L}_1 \setminus M_1 \subseteq (\mathsf{ans}(\mathcal{K}, q_1) \cap (\mathcal{U}_1 \setminus M_1))$. It remains, therefore, to show that $\mathsf{ans}(\mathcal{K}, q) = (\mathsf{ans}(\mathcal{K}, q_1) \cap (\mathcal{U}_1 \setminus M_1)) \bowtie \mathsf{ans}(\mathcal{K}, q_2) \bowtie \mathsf{ans}(\mathcal{K}, q_3)$. By Lemma 2, $\mathsf{ans}(\mathcal{K}, q) = (\mathsf{ans}(\mathcal{K}, q_1) \cap \mathcal{U}_1) \bowtie (\mathsf{ans}(\mathcal{K}, q_2) \cap \mathcal{U}_2) \bowtie \mathsf{ans}(\mathcal{K}, q_3) = (\mathsf{ans}(\mathcal{K}, q_1) \cap (\mathcal{U}_1 \setminus M_1)) \bowtie (\mathsf{ans}(\mathcal{K}, q_2) \cap \mathcal{U}_2) \bowtie \mathsf{ans}(\mathcal{K}, q_3) \cup (\mathsf{ans}(\mathcal{K}, q_1) \cap M_1) \bowtie (\mathsf{ans}(\mathcal{K}, q_2) \cap \mathcal{U}_2) \bowtie \mathsf{ans}(\mathcal{K}, q_3) = (\mathsf{ans}(\mathcal{K}, q_1) \cap (\mathcal{U}_1 \setminus M_1)) \bowtie (\mathsf{ans}(\mathcal{K}, q_2) \cap \mathcal{U}_2) \bowtie \mathsf{ans}(\mathcal{K}, q_3)$ since $(\mathsf{ans}(\mathcal{K}, q_1) \cap M_1) \bowtie (\mathsf{ans}(\mathcal{K}, q_2) \cap \mathcal{U}_2) \bowtie \mathsf{ans}(\mathcal{K}, q_3) \subseteq M_1 \bowtie \mathcal{U}_2 \bowtie \mathsf{ans}(\mathcal{K}, q_3) = \emptyset$. □

Example 5. *Consider the knowledge base $\mathcal{K}$ and the query $q = \{\exists r.Y(x), A(x), Y \sqsubseteq B\}$ from Figure 1. Assume that we have found the query bound $[\mathcal{L}_2; \mathcal{U}_2]$ for $q_2 = \{A(x)\}$ as in Example 3, namely, $\mathcal{L}_2 = \{\mu \mid \mu(x) \in \{a, d\}\}$ and $\mathcal{U}_2 = \{\mu \mid \mu(x) \in \{a, b, d\}\}$. As mentioned before, $[\mathcal{L}_2; \mathcal{U}_2]$ is also a subquery bound for q_2 in q. Let $[\mathcal{L}_1; \mathcal{U}_1]$ be the trivial subquery bound for $q_1 = \{\exists r.Y(x)\}$ in q, i.e., $\mathcal{L}_1 = \emptyset$ and $\mathcal{U}_1 = \{\mu \mid \mu(x) \in \{a, b, c, d\}, \mu(Y) \in \{\bot, A, B, C, \top\}\}$. Furthermore, let $M_1 = \{\mu \mid \mu(x) = c\}$. Clearly, $M_1 \bowtie \mathcal{U}_2 = \emptyset$. Hence, by Theorem 1, $[\mathcal{L}_1 \setminus M_1; \mathcal{U}_1 \setminus M_1] = [\emptyset; \{\mu \mid \mu(x) \in \{a, b, d\}, \mu(Y) \in \{\bot, A, B, C, \top\}\}]$ is also a subquery bound for q_1 in q. Similarly, using the (exact) query bound $[\mathcal{L}_3; \mathcal{U}_3]$ for $q_3 = \{Y \sqsubseteq B\}$ with $\mathcal{L}_3 = \mathcal{U}_3 = \{\mu \mid \mu(Y) \in \{\bot, B\}\}$, one can further reduce the upper bound for q_1 to $\{\mu \mid \mu(x) \in \{a, b, d\}, \mu(Y) \in \{\bot, B\}\}$.*

Improving Bounds via Query Extension

As seen from the previous section, subquery bounds can be improved using bounds of other subqueries of this query. Thus, if a query q can be extended to an *equivalent* query $q \cup q'$, the number of reasoner calls performed for evaluating the axiom templates in q can be reduced using q'. In this section we consider a method by which one can extend queries based on a ground version of q together with axioms from the queried knowledge base. The proposed query extension method is similar to the method for deciding containment between conjunctive queries (Calvanese, De Giacomo, and Lenzerini 2008), with the main difference (apart from allowing concept and role variables) that instead of checking query containment, we construct a query contained in the given query ourselves.

Theorem 2 (Query Extension). *Let $\mathcal{K}$ be a knowledge base, q a query, and μ a mapping with $dom(\mu) = vars(q)$ such that for each $x \in dom(\mu)$, $\mu(x)$ does not occur in $\mathcal{K}$ and for each $x, y \in dom(\mu)$, $x \neq y$ implies $\mu(x) \neq \mu(y)$. Then for every query q' such that $vars(q') \subseteq dom(\mu)$ and $\mathcal{K} \cup \mu(q) \models \mu(q')$, we have $\mathsf{ans}(\mathcal{K}, q) = \mathsf{ans}(\mathcal{K}, q \cup q')$.*

Proof. Clearly, $\mathsf{ans}(\mathcal{K}, q \cup q') \subseteq \mathsf{ans}(\mathcal{K}, q)$, so it remains to show that $\mathsf{ans}(\mathcal{K}, q) \subseteq \mathsf{ans}(\mathcal{K}, q \cup q')$. Take any $\mu' \in \mathsf{ans}(\mathcal{K}, q)$, i.e., $\mathcal{K} \models \mu'(q)$. To prove that $\mu' \in \mathsf{ans}(\mathcal{K}, q \cup q')$, we need to show that $\mathcal{K} \models \mu'(q \cup q')$. Since $\mathcal{K} \models \mu'(q)$, it is left to prove that $\mathcal{K} \models \mu'(q')$. Let ρ be such that $\mu'(x) = \rho(\mu(x))$ for every $x \in \mathrm{vars}(q) = \mathrm{dom}(\mu)$. That is, ρ replaces each value of $\mu(x)$ with the corresponding value of $\mu'(x)$. Since $\mu(x) \neq \mu(y)$ for each $x \neq y$, $x, y \in \mathrm{dom}(\mu)$, such function ρ always exists. Then $\mathcal{K} \cup \mu(q) \models \mu(q')$ implies $\rho(\mathcal{K} \cup \mu(q)) \models \rho(\mu(q')) = \mu'(q')$. Since $\rho(\mathcal{K} \cup \mu(q)) = \rho(\mathcal{K}) \cup \rho(\mu(q))$, $\rho(\mathcal{K}) = \mathcal{K}$ (because $\mu(x)$ does not occur in $\mathcal{K}$ for every $x \in \mathrm{dom}(\mu)$) and $\mathcal{K} \models \mu'(q) = \rho(\mu(q))$, we obtain $\mathcal{K} \models \mu'(q')$ what was required to show. □

Example 6. *For the KB $\mathcal{K} = \mathcal{T} \cup \mathcal{A}$ and query $q = \{A(x), \exists r.Y(x), Y \sqsubseteq B\}$ in Figure 1, consider a mapping μ such that $\mu(x) = a_x$, $\mu(Y) = A_Y$ with $a_x \in N_I, A_Y \in N_C$. Clearly the conditions of Theorem 2 are satisfied. Note that $\mathcal{T} \cup \mu(q) = \{B \sqsubseteq A \sqcup C, \exists r.B \sqsubseteq C, A(a_x), \exists r.A_Y(a_x), A_Y \sqsubseteq B\} \models C(a_x)$. Thus, for $q' = \{C(x)\}$, we have $\mathcal{K} \cup \mu(q) \models C(a_x) = \mu(q')$, and by Theorem 2, the query q has the same answers for $\mathcal{K}$ as the extended query $q \cup q' = \{A(x), \exists r.Y(x), Y \sqsubseteq B, C(x)\}$.*

Using Theorem 2, the improved algorithm for evaluating a query q over a knowledge base $\mathcal{K}$ can now be described as follows:

1. Replace every (concept, role, individual) variable in q with a fresh distinct (concept, role, individual) name. Let μ be the mapping that performs this replacement.
2. Add the resulting axioms $\mu(q)$ to $\mathcal{K}$ and perform materialization, i.e., compute all concept assertions $A(a)$, role

manually created gold standard.

The structure of the paper is as follows. In the next sections, we discuss related work, define the problem, and present the FACES approach. Then we explain the evaluation of the system and discuss the results. Finally, we conclude with suggestions for future research.

Related Work

Summarization tasks can be categorized into *extractive* and *non-extractive* methods. Extractive summaries choose a subset of the features for the summary whereas non-extractive summaries include reformulation of the extracted facts. We focus on extractive summaries at the entity level.

(Cheng, Tran, and Qu 2011) introduced and defined the problem of entity summarization in RDF graphs and showed its usefulness in quick identification of an entity. Their system, called RELIN, generalizes the PageRank algorithm to select both related and informative features. The problem with RELIN's random surfer, which selects both related and informative features, is that it tends to emphasize central themes and similar features of an entity because of the centrality based ranking mechanism of PageRank. SUMMARUM (Thalhammer and Rettinger 2014) is an entity summarization system for DBpedia that is also based on PageRank and utilizes the global popularity of resources gleaned with the help of information from the corresponding Wikipedia pages. Note that, neither RELIN nor SUMMARUM focus on diversity in the summary whereas our approach does. (Thalhammer, Knuth, and Sack 2012) proposed an approach that utilizes usage data for creating entity summaries and evaluated it in the movie domain where they could find user ratings for movies. Such an approach is hard to generalize because usage data may not be readily available for entities. We do not utilize any usage data. (Xu, Cheng, and Qu 2014) created entity summaries to facilitate coreference resolution and consider pairs of entities when creating summaries. Hence, it is different from our approach, RELIN, and SUMMARUM.

Ranking in the Semantic Web is closely related to entity summarization as the latter task can be perceived as selecting the top k features from an RDF graph. Various ranking algorithms exist in the literature for RDF graphs including TripleRank (Franz et al. 2009) that ranks triples, SemRank (Anyanwu, Maduko, and Sheth 2005) that ranks associations, (Ding et al. 2005) that ranks documents, and TRank (Tonon et al. 2013) that ranks concepts. These approaches incorporate ranking algorithms for different reasons. For example, TripleRank (Franz et al. 2009) groups triples using tensors and link analysis. TripleRank's goal is to rank and identify authoritative sources for a given entity. The facet or latent grouping concept that we introduce in FACES is different from facets in TripleRank as TripleRank's grouping is based on authority whereas FACES's is based on semantic overlap of the expanded terms of the features. Also, (Cheng, Tran, and Qu 2011) pointed out that it is hard to align the TripleRank approach to the entity summarization problem but its authoritative ranking is similar to RELIN where centrality dominates. Grouping in RDF datasets has been investigated in upper level ontology creation (Zhao and Ichise 2012) and property alignment (Gunaratna et al. 2013), but these groupings are different from what we explored in FACES. We find *conceptually similar* groups (explained later) that are not just related (i.e., object value overlap of RDF triples) (Zhao and Ichise 2012) or equivalent (Gunaratna et al. 2013) groups.

Diversity has been shown to be useful in creating graphical entity summarization (Sydow, Pikuła, and Schenkel 2013), which is different from entity summarization as it produces a graph (includes neighboring entities) rather than a set of features. They pick 'lexicographically different' property names to achieve diversity in the summary using syntactic measures (e.g., *birthPlace* and *deathPlace* are different in their context) whereas FACES groups them together (i.e., significantly beyond string similarity). FACES differs from the existing entity summarization and ranking systems to create both concise and comprehensive summaries. We hypothesize that diversity makes the summary provide a more complete picture of the entity (i.e., comprehensive) when subjected to a length constraint (i.e., concise) environment.

Problem description

Informal problem statement: An entity is usually described using conceptually diverse set of facts to improve coverage. We want to select a *'representative'* subset of this set in a good summary to uniquely identify the entity.

We review below preliminaries introduced in (Cheng, Tran, and Qu 2011) for completeness.

Preliminaries

A data graph is a graph based data model, which describes entities using properties and their values. It consists of sets of entities (E), literals (L), and properties (P). An entity e ($e \in E$) is described in a data graph using property-value pairs $(a, v) \in P$ x $(E \cup L)$.

Definition 1 ***(data graph)*** *A data graph is a digraph* $G = \langle V, A, Lbl_V, Lbl_A\rangle$, *where (i)* V *is a finite set of nodes, (ii)* A *is a finite set of directed edges where each* $a \in A$ *has a source node* $Src(a) \in V$, *a target node* $Tgt(a) \in V$, *(iii)* $Lbl_V : V \mapsto E \cup L$ *and (iv)* $Lbl_A : A \mapsto P$. Lbl_V *and* Lbl_A *are labeling functions that map nodes to entities or literals and edges to properties, respectively.*

Definition 2 ***(feature)*** *A feature* f *is a property-value pair where* $Prop(f) \in P$ *and* $Val(f) \in E \cup L$ *denote the property and the value of the feature* f, *respectively. An entity* e *has a feature* f *in a data graph* $G = \langle V, A, Lbl_V, Lbl_A\rangle$ *if there exists* $a \in A$ *such that* $Lbl_A(a) = Prop(f)$, $Lbl_V(Src(a)) = e$ *and* $Lbl_V(Tgt(a)) = Val(f)$.

Definition 3 ***(feature set)*** *Given a data graph* G, *the feature set of an entity* e, *denoted by* $FS(e)$, *is the set of all features of* e *that can be found in* G.

An entity summary is a subset of all features that belong to that entity.

Definition 4 ***(entity summary)*** *Given an entity* e *and a positive integer* $k < |FS(e)|$, *summary of entity* e *is* $Summ(e, k) \subset FS(e)$ *such that* $|Summ(e, k)| = k$.

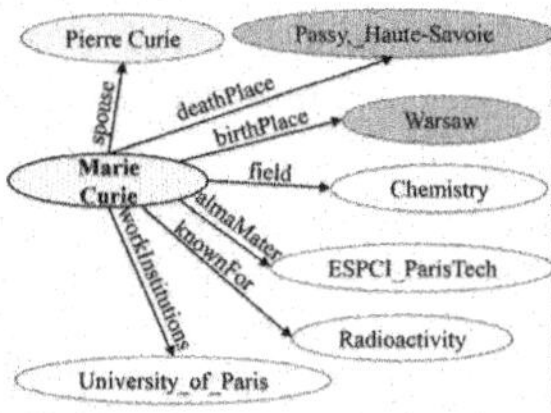

Entity - Marie Curie				
Feature Set	Facets	Features	Property	Value
FS	F1	f1	spouse	Pierre_Curie
	F2	f2	birthPlace	Warsaw
		f3	deathPlace	Passy,_Haute-Savoie
	F3	f4	almaMater	ESPCI_ParisTech
		f5	workInstitutions	University_of_Paris
		f6	knownFor	Radioactivity
		f7	field	Chemistry

Summary 1 (normal) : {f2, f3, f4}
Summary 2 (faceted) : {f1, f2, f6}

Figure 1: Facets of entity - Marie Curie. Values for conceptually similar features are in the same color pattern.

Consider the entity Marie Curie taken from DBpedia as shown in Figure 1. We omit namespaces of the URIs for the clarity of presentation. Then a summary for the entity Marie Curie can be created selecting a subset of the features. E.g., Summary 1 and Summary 2 are two summaries of length 3 that can be created for the entity Marie Curie.

Faceted entity summaries

In general, different properties represent different aspects of an entity. E.g., Summary 2 in Figure 1 has two features having *knownFor* and *spouse* properties where they represent different aspects of the entity. The first represents an intangible value and the second represents a human; one talks about the entity's professional background and the other about its personal life. Based on this observation, we can formalize facets of an entity in terms of its feature set.

Definition 5 ***(facet)*** *Given an entity e, a set of facets $F(e)$ of e is a partition of the feature set $FS(e)$. That is, $F(e)$ = $\{C_1, C_2, ...C_n\}$ where $C_i \subseteq FS(e)$. Each C_i is called a facet of e.*

Our hypothesis is that the feature set of an entity can be divided into conceptually orthogonal groups, approximated by the facets, using a partitioning (clustering) algorithm (we will explain the details in the next section). Furthermore, a facet can be viewed as a *hidden variable*. See Figure 1. {F1, F2, F3} is a partition of the feature set FS. Note that the features within each facet are similar than those between facets. I.e., the features that are expressed through *KnownFor* and *Field* properties are *conceptually similar* because they both talk about the entity's professional life. But features having *birthPlace* and *knownFor* properties are conceptually dissimilar as they represent completely different information to each other. Next, we define *Faceted Entity Summary* for an entity based on facets.

Definition 6 ***(faceted entity summary)*** *Given an entity e and a positive integer $k < |FS(e)|$,* faceted entity summary of *e, FSumm(e, k), is a collection of features such that FSumm(e, k) $\subset$ FS(e), |FSumm(e, k)| = k, and if k > |F(e)| then $\forall X \in$ F(e) $\Rightarrow X\cap$ FSumm(e, k) $\neq \emptyset$ else $\forall X \in$ F(e) $\Rightarrow |X\cap$ FSumm(e, k) $| \leq 1$.*

Informally, if the number of facets is n and the size of the summary is k, *at least one feature* from each facet is included in the summary when $k > n$. If $k \leq n$, then *at most one feature* from each facet is included in the summary. E.g., a faceted summary of length 3 for the entity Marie Curie can be {f1, f2, f6} as shown in Figure 1.

Approach

The FACES approach generates faceted entity summaries that are both *concise* and *comprehensive*. Conciseness is about selecting a small number of facts. Comprehensiveness is about selecting facts to represent all aspects of an entity that improves coverage. Diversity is about selecting facts that are orthogonal to each other so that the selected few facts enrich coverage. *Hence, diversity improves comprehensiveness when the number of features to include in a summary is limited.* Conciseness may be achieved by ranking and filtering techniques. But creating summaries that satisfy both conciseness and comprehensiveness constraints simultaneously is not a trivial task. It needs to recognize facets of an entity so that the summary can represent as many facets (diverse and comprehensive) as possible without redundancy (concise). The number and nature of facets (corresponding to abstract concepts) in a feature set is not known a priori for an entity and is hard to guess without human intervention or explicit knowledge. Therefore, a supervised or unsupervised clustering (partitioning) algorithm with prescribed number of clusters to seek cannot be used in this context. Next, we describe the three main algorithms in our approach: *partitioning feature set into facets, ranking features within facets, and generating faceted entity summaries.*

Partitioning feature set

Our goal is to partition the feature set $FS(e)$ of an entity e. To achieve this goal, we adapted the Cobweb (Fisher 1987), an incremental system for hierarchical conceptual clustering. The algorithm embodies a top-down approach and creates a concept hierarchy where each node represents a concept with a probabilistic explanation/description. I.e., it clusters items utilizing attribute-value pairs associated with them and the clustering depends on the probability of attribute-value pairs for the items in each part of the partition. Further, it maximizes intra-cluster similarity and inter-cluster dissimilarity of items being clustered. This is closely related to the decisions that humans make in partitioning tasks (Fisher 1987). We chose this algorithm because: (1) it is hierarchical and hence the number of clusters need not be known a priori, (2) it creates groups for specific concepts, and (3) it is influenced by heuristics that humans use for grouping based on probability. Cobweb is also efficient compared to other hierarchical clustering algorithms (e.g., single-link, complete-link) because it is incremental.

Cobweb has been designed to work with attribute-value pairs for objects such as 'height - 6 ft' and 'weight - 120 pounds' for a person. In our problem, there are two attributes associated with each feature f: property and value. Values of these attributes are $Prop(f)$ and $Val(f)$, respectively. Moreover, Cobweb uses a heuristic measurement called *Category Utility (CU)* to determine partitions in the hierarchy by measuring partition quality. Let C_p be a node in the hierarchy with a set of features and has child clusters (partition) $C_1, C_2, .., C_n$. Then *CU* of partition $\{C_1, C_2, .., C_n\}$ of C_p can be computed as in Equation 1.

$$CU(C_p) = \frac{\sum_{x=1}^{n} P(C_x) \sum_{i=1}^{2} [P(A_i, V_i|C_x)^2 - P(A_i, V_i|C_p)^2]}{n} \quad (1)$$

$P(C_x)$ is the probability of a random feature belonging to child cluster C_x and (A_i, V_i) is the ith attribute-value pair of the new feature being clustered. When a new feature is to be positioned in the hierarchy, Cobweb starts from the root node and performs one of the following operations based on the maximum *CU* score at each level until the new feature is settled in the hierarchy. They are: (1) *Insert* operation that inserts the feature into an existing cluster, (2) *Create* operation that creates a new cluster for the feature, (3) *Merge* operation that combines two clusters into one, and (4) *Split* operation that divides an existing cluster into several clusters. Cobweb uses a cut-off threshold to decide when to stop in the hierarchy and inherits agglomerative and divisive characteristics from merge and split operations, respectively. Furthermore, the split operation can be used to undo a merge operation performed earlier and vice versa.

CLASSIT (Gennari, Langley, and Fisher 1989) is a variation of Cobweb that is used in the text clustering domain, but requires a normal distribution for the values of the attributes. CLASSIT has been shown applicable in the document clustering context with the use of Katz's distribution where rich term distributions can be found (Sahoo et al. 2006). We do not have such a rich term distribution as in (Wang and Li 2010; Sahoo et al. 2006) for documents and hence it is difficult to use the CLASSIT implementation. Therefore, we adapt and modify the original Cobweb for our problem.

Input to the Cobweb is the feature set $FS(e)$ of an entity e and each feature f should have sufficient attribute-value pairs so that the *CU* function can group them accurately in the hierarchy. Each feature, modeled as two attribute-value pairs, does not have adequate details to group conceptually similar features. Hence, we expand the property and value of each feature f to get a set of words $WS(f)$ in such a way that expanded terms can be used to glean higher level abstract meaning. The terms in the word set can be mapped to attribute-value pairs required by the algorithm by mapping words in the word set to 1 and those not in the word set to 0.

Our partitioning algorithm uses labels associated with URIs. If labels are not available, the local name of the URIs are utilized. For the property name expansion, we first tokenize property name and remove stop words. Then we retrieve higher level abstract terms for the tokenized words. For the value expansion, we retrieve typing information (classes assigned to the resource), tokenize them, remove stop words, and expand them to include higher level abstract terms of the tokenized words. Tokenizing includes processing camelcase, spaces, punctuations, underscores etc. Then we add output of the property name and value expansion steps of feature f into a single word set $WS(f)$. See Figure 2 for example. In our implementation, we used hypernyms as the abstract terms taken from WordNet[1], a widely

[1]http://wordnet.princeton.edu/

Feature (f)	Property expansion	Value expansion	Word set (WS(f))
birthPlace:Warsaw	{*birthPlace*, *birth*, *place*, beginning, point, area, locality, ..}	{*place*, *PopulatedPlace*, populated, point, area, locality, ..}	{*birthPlace*, *birth*, *place*, *PopulatedPlace*, beginning, populated, point, area, locality, ..}

Figure 2: Feature expansion example. Terms taken from WordNet as hypernyms are underlined.

used online lexical database. Note that any service similar to WordNet could be used for this purpose. We are interested in using hypernyms because we need conceptually similar feature groups as facets from the clustering algorithm. If typing information is not available in the dataset or for the value (such as data-type property), an external knowledge source such as Wikipedia[2] can be used.

We modified the original Cobweb *CU* implementation designed for nominal attributes shown in Equation 1 and adapted it to use only the terms in the word set $WS(f)$ for a feature f (omit 0 or 1). See Equation 2. W_i is a word appearing in $WS(f)$.

$$CU(C_p) = \frac{\sum_{x=1}^{n} P(C_x) \sum_{i} [P(W_i|C_x)^2 - P(W_i|C_p)^2]}{n} \quad (2)$$

Ranking features

Our approach ranks features that appear within each facet locally, and hence, related features do not affect the ranking result, unlike graph based ranking algorithms. A specific ranking algorithm influenced by the *tf-idf* technique has been used to get the top features from each facet to form the faceted summary. For a feature f and the value v of f, the ranking takes into consideration the informativeness/uniqueness (reflected using idf) of f ($Inf(f)$), and popularity (reflected using tf) of v ($Po(v)$). $Inf(f)$ is defined in Equation 3. N is the total number of entities in the data graph G. $Po(v)$ is the number of distinct triples in the data graph G that has the matching value v. Following the IR tradition we take the log of this value as expressed in Equation 4.

The ranking of features within a facet is then the product of the informativeness of the feature and popularity of the value as defined in Equation 5. Our intuition is that a feature (property-value pair) should be relatively rare (i.e., informative) to be interesting and not the property alone. Also when the value is popular in the dataset, it tends to help form a more human readable summary.

$$Inf(f) = log(\frac{N}{|\{e|f \in FS(e)\}|}) \quad (3)$$

$$Po(v) = log|\{triple\ t|\exists\, e, f : t \text{ "appears in" } G \ and\ t \equiv (e\ Prop(f)\ Val(f))\ and\ Val(f) = v\}| \quad (4)$$

[2]http://www.wikipedia.org/ has category hierarchy that can be used similar to class labels

$$Rank(f) = Inf(f) * Po(Val(f)) \quad (5)$$

Generating faceted entity summary

Given the feature set $FS(e)$ of an entity e and a positive integer $k < |FS(e)|$, the process of faceted entity summary creation can be stated as follows. (1) First, each feature f in $FS(e)$ is enriched to have a wordset $WS(f)$. (2) The enriched feature set $FS(e)$ is input to the partitioning algorithm to create facets. The algorithm yields a dendrogram (hierarchical tree) for $FS(e)$ and it is cut at a desired level to get the facet set $F(e)$ of $FS(e)$. (3) Then, features in each facet are ranked using the ranking algorithm. (4) The top ranked features from each facet are picked according to Definition 6 to form the faceted entity summary of length k. In this implementation, we avoid picking features that have the same property name from each facet when $k > |F(e)|$.

Evaluation

We evaluate the FACES approach in two orthogonal ways: (1) Evaluate the quality of the summaries in comparison to the state-of-the-art systems using a gold standard. (2) Evaluate summary quality by user preference. We evaluate FACES against RELIN that outperformed earlier entity summarization tools and SUMMARUM which is DBpedia specific. We did not choose domain specific summarization tools like (Thalhammer, Knuth, and Sack 2012) as they are not applicable in general and require additional domain specific usage data. We do not consider the graphical entity summarization (Sydow, Pikuła, and Schenkel 2013) approach as it is different from an entity summarization captured by RELIN and FACES.

We selected the DBpedia dataset for our evaluation as it was the benchmark dataset selected in (Cheng, Tran, and Qu 2011) and contains entities that belong to different domains. We created a gold standard for the evaluation due to unavailability of the evaluation data of RELIN (as confirmed by the authors of RELIN). We randomly selected 50 entities[3] from DBpedia (English version 3.9) that have at least 17 distinct properties per entity. The average number of distinct features per entity is 44. Further, RELIN's results and user agreement for ideal summaries are not the same as those reported in (Cheng, Tran, and Qu 2011) because of the differences in the test set. We filtered out schema information and dataset dependent details such as *dcterms:subject*, *rdf:type*, *owl:sameAs*, *wordnet_type* and *Wikipedia related links* to ease manual evaluation and further they do not express facts about the entities. We extracted object-type properties for this dataset as the original set of triples is too large for manual evaluators, they are cleaner than data-type properties, and they contain more interesting information. Further, use of object-type properties is consistent with SUMMARUM, and hence enables a meaningful comparison. We asked 15 human judges with background in Semantic Web to select 5 and 10 feature length summaries for each of the entities. These are referred from now on as the *ideal summaries*. They were not given specific information about any system and asked to select a summary that can better represent the entity (facilitate quick identification). We provided them the Wikipedia page link of each entity in case they needed additional information about an unfamiliar entity. Each entity has at least 7 ideal summaries from 7 different judges and this comprises the gold standard for evaluation. All experiments were performed using a Core i7 3.4 GHz Desktop machine with 12 GB of RAM. We replicated DBpedia dataset locally and used caches for RELIN as mentioned in (Cheng, Tran, and Qu 2011). More details about the approach and gold standard dataset can be found at our web page[4].

Evaluation with the gold standard

Our objective is to show that faceted entity summaries produce results that are closer to human judgment. We configured FACES that produces the best possible results and RELIN according to its recorded optimal configuration. We empirically determined to cut FACES cluster hierarchies at level 3 which gave good results. We also set the cut-off threshold of Cobweb to 5, which gave the optimal results. For RELIN, we set the jump probability and number of iterations to 0.85 and 10, respectively. Authors of RELIN provided the source code of RELIN in absence of the evaluation data to replicate the environment. We replaced Google search service with Sindice API[5] as Google search API is no longer free of charge. Sindice indexes the LOD data and is adequate for this purpose. Further, we collected Google API and Sindice API search hits for a small random sample (5 entities) and applied RELIN to both API search hits. The results confirmed that the difference is negligible.

$$Agreement = \frac{2}{n(n-1)} \sum_{i=1}^{n} \sum_{j=i+1}^{n} |Summ_i^I(e) \cap Summ_j^I(e)| \quad (6)$$

$$Quality(Summ(e)) = \frac{1}{n} \sum_{i=1}^{n} |Summ(e) \cap Summ_i^I(e)| \quad (7)$$

We use the evaluation metrics used in (Cheng, Tran, and Qu 2011). When there are n ideal summaries denoted by $Summ_i^I(e)$ for $i = 1, .., n$ and an automatically generated summary denoted by $Summ(e)$ for entity e, the agreement on ideal summaries is measured by Equation 6 and the quality of the automatically generated summary is measured by Equation 7. In other words, quality of an entity summary is its average overlap with the ideal summaries for the entity. Our evaluation results and statistics are presented in Table 1. We modified the original RELIN algorithm to discard duplicate properties and named it as RELINM in Table 1. The modification did not yield much improvement in the results

[3]Selected entities are from the domains of politician, actor, scientist, song, film, country, city, river, company, game, etc

[4]http://wiki.knoesis.org/index.php/FACES

[5]http://sindice.com/developers/searchapiv3

System	Evaluation 1 - Gold standard					Evaluation 2 - User preference	
	k = 5			k = 10		User preference	
	Quality	FACES % ↑	Time/Entity	Quality	FACES % ↑	User study 1	User study 2
FACES	**1.4314**	NA	**0.76 sec.**	**4.3350**	NA	**84%**	**54%**
RELIN	0.4981	187 %	10.96 sec.	2.5188	72 %	NA	NA
RELINM	0.6008	138 %	11.08 sec.	3.0906	40 %	16%	16%
SUMMARUM	1.2249	17 %	NA	3.4207	27 %	NA	30%
Agreement	1.9168			4.6415			

Table 1: Evaluation of the summary quality and FACES %↑ = 100 * (FACES result - Other system result) / (Other system result) for k=5 and k=10, respectively, and average time taken per entity for k=5 for Evaluation 1. Evaluation 2 measures user preference % for each system. (NA stands for Not Applicable)

and this was to test whether re-ranking mechanisms can improve RELIN results. We ran each algorithm for all the 50 entities 5 times and recorded the average time taken per entity in seconds. According to the results, FACES achieved 138% and 40% increase in quality against RELINM and 187% and 72% increase in quality against RELIN, and 17% and 27% increase in quality against SUMMARUM for k=5 and k=10, respectively. Even though FACES achieves superior results compared to RELIN, it does not compromise its efficiency. FACES is much more efficient (14 times faster) than RELIN as shown in Table 1 in summary computation (i.e., running time). Time for SUMMARUM is not applicable (NA) as we get results from a web service but can be assumed to be similar to RELIN. FACES can be further improved to compute summaries on the fly.

We conducted the *paired t-test* to confirm the significance of the FACES's mean summary quality improvements over others. For $k = 5$ and $k = 10$, P values for FACES against RELINM are 2.04E-10 and 1.92E-14 and for FACES against SUMMARUM are 0.029 and 3.71E-7. When P values are less than 0.05, the results are statistically significant.

Evaluation of user preference

We carried out two blind user evaluations (users didn't know which system produced which summaries) to see how users rated summaries created by FACES, RELINM, and SUMMARUM. We randomly selected 10 instances from our evaluation sample and created $k = 5$ length summaries and had 69 users participate in total. The results are shown in Table 1. For the first user evaluation, we showed them summaries of FACES and RELINM side by side and asked them to select the best summary that helped them to identify the entity. The users average preference was 84% for FACES and 16% for RELINM. This shows that unique properties alone are not desirable to humans. In the second user evaluation, we showed users all three system summaries and their preferences were 54%, 16%, and 30% for FACES, RELINM, and SUMMARUM, respectively. This shows that users sometimes prefer popularity as in SUMMARUM but not in all the cases. RELINM got almost the same percentage in both experiments reflecting that users preferred unique features for some entities. Moreover, results suggest that users like a balanced (unique and popular) and diversified approach like in FACES and confirm our claim that the diversity makes summaries more human friendly.

Discussion

In summary, our evaluation shows that FACES performs better in all cases. It was able to achieve 138% and 40% increase over RELINM and 17% and 27% increase over SUMMARUM in summary quality for k=5 and k=10, respectively. The results of the paired t-test confirms that FACES results are not random and consistently outperforms the other two systems. FACES achieves this by its non-trivial facet identification process and persistence in selecting a diverse summary based on the facets. Note that agreements between ideal summaries are not very high in the sample dataset due to the large number of distinct features present in each entity (see Table 1). The second evaluation shows that the faceted summaries are desirable to human users.

FACES behaves similar to an ordinary summarization algorithm such as RELIN and SUMMARUM when there are few facets available. It behaves as if it is ranking a flat list of features. A key reason why RELIN (including RELINM), which is based on PageRank that exploits both informativeness and relatedness measures, underperforms is that the summary can include redundant and correlated features. This also affects SUMMARUM. The redundancy comes at the expense of reduced coverage. We address this limitation by emphasizing diversity to suppress redundant features[6] and improve coverage by identifying facets to pick representative features. Figure 3 shows entity summary examples generated by the three approaches.

We observed that sometimes FACES clusters features differently from what we expect. For example, *spouse* property of Barack Obama is clustered into a facet that contains *vicePresident* property. This happens because sometimes typing information of values is too specific[7] and affects the clustering process. Moreover, FACES performs better in almost all cases according to the second evaluation except for some specific entities. E.g., *Usain Bolt* is an Olympic athlete with many records. Some users preferred facts about his 100 meter records over his 200 meter records, while both information were present in a facet. FACES can generate either of the two facts in a summary (based on a subjective ranking within a facet) and the tie can be broken. We can further investigate how to effectively combine diversity, uniqueness, and popularity of features as the user preference varies. Fur-

[6] May not be syntactically the same but conceptually similar

[7] *Michelle Obama*'s typing information is similar to a politician

FACES	RELINM	SUMMARUM
<birthPlace, Warsaw>	<isPrimaryTopicOf, Marie_Curie>	<birthPlace, Poland>
<workInstitutions, University of Paris>	<wasDerivedFrom, oldid=547107936>	<birthPlace, Warsaw>
<field, Physics>	<knownFor, Polonium>	<birthPlace, Russian_Empire>
<spouse, Pierre Curie>	<almaMater, ESPCI>	<field, Physics>
<deathPlace, Passy, Haute-Savoie>	<deathPlace, Passy, Haute-Savoie>	<field, Chemistry>

Figure 3: Entity summaries for the entity Marie Curie by each system. $k = 5$ and the size of feature set is 39.

thermore, clustering phase of FACES can be tuned for fine grained grouping by modifying the enrichment process. E.g., adding hyponyms to the word set makes features containing *birthPlace* and *stateOfOrigin* properties fall into different facets.

Conclusion

We have investigated how to create entity summaries that are *concise* and *comprehensive* for the purpose of quick identification of an entity. We adapted a well known incremental hierarchical conceptual clustering algorithm for entities (in RDF format) to identify facets (that addressed diversity) and developed intra-cluster ranking algorithm for features (that addressed uniqueness and popularity) to create *faceted entity summaries*. We showed that faceted entity summaries created by combining diversity, uniqueness, and popularity are better representatives for an entity and closer to ideal ones. Our approach shows superior results (improvement in summary quality in the range 17% - 187%) and does not require pre-computation of values like the existing systems. In future, we plan to investigate facet ranking, which facets to select and how many features to pick from each facet in creating "personalized" and "balanced" summaries.

Acknowledgments

This work was supported by the National Science Foundation under award 1143717 III: EAGER Expressive Scalable Querying over Linked Open Data.

References

Anyanwu, K.; Maduko, A.; and Sheth, A. 2005. Semrank: ranking complex relationship search results on the semantic web. In *Proceedings of the 14th international conference on World Wide Web*, 117–127. ACM.

Auer, S.; Lehmann, J.; Ngomo, A.-C. N.; and Zaveri, A. 2013. Introduction to linked data and its lifecycle on the web. In *Reasoning Web. Semantic Technologies for Intelligent Data Access*. Springer. 1–90.

Cheng, G.; Tran, T.; and Qu, Y. 2011. Relin: relatedness and informativeness-based centrality for entity summarization. In *The Semantic Web–ISWC 2011*. Springer. 114–129.

Ding, L.; Pan, R.; Finin, T.; Joshi, A.; Peng, Y.; and Kolari, P. 2005. Finding and ranking knowledge on the semantic web. In *The Semantic Web–ISWC 2005*. Springer. 156–170.

Fisher, D. H. 1987. Knowledge acquisition via incremental conceptual clustering. *Machine learning* 2(2):139–172.

Franz, T.; Schultz, A.; Sizov, S.; and Staab, S. 2009. Triplerank: Ranking semantic web data by tensor decomposition. In *The Semantic Web-ISWC 2009*. Springer. 213–228.

Gennari, J. H.; Langley, P.; and Fisher, D. 1989. Models of incremental concept formation. *Artificial intelligence* 40(1):11–61.

Gunaratna, K.; Thirunarayan, K.; Jain, P.; Sheth, A.; and Wijeratne, S. 2013. A statistical and schema independent approach to identify equivalent properties on linked data. In *Proceedings of the 9th International Conference on Semantic Systems*, 33–40. ACM.

Mani, I. 2001. *Automatic summarization*, volume 3. John Benjamins Publishing.

Nenkova, A., and McKeown, K. 2012. A survey of text summarization techniques. In *Mining Text Data*. Springer. 43–76.

Sahoo, N.; Callan, J.; Krishnan, R.; Duncan, G.; and Padman, R. 2006. Incremental hierarchical clustering of text documents. In *Proceedings of the 15th ACM international conference on Information and knowledge management*, 357–366. ACM.

Sydow, M.; Pikuła, M.; and Schenkel, R. 2013. The notion of diversity in graphical entity summarisation on semantic knowledge graphs. *Journal of Intelligent Information Systems* 41(2):109–149.

Thalhammer, A., and Rettinger, A. 2014. Browsing dbpedia entities with summaries. In *The Extended Semantic Web Conference 2014. Poster & Demo.*

Thalhammer, A.; Knuth, M.; and Sack, H. 2012. Evaluating entity summarization using a game-based ground truth. In *The Semantic Web–ISWC 2012*. Springer. 350–361.

Tonon, A.; Catasta, M.; Demartini, G.; Cudré-Mauroux, P.; and Aberer, K. 2013. Trank: Ranking entity types using the web of data. In *The Semantic Web–ISWC 2013*. Springer. 640–656.

Wang, D., and Li, T. 2010. Document update summarization using incremental hierarchical clustering. In *Proceedings of the 19th ACM international conference on Information and knowledge management*, 279–288. ACM.

Xu, D.; Cheng, G.; and Qu, Y. 2014. Facilitating human intervention in coreference resolution with comparative entity summaries. In *The Semantic Web: Trends and Challenges*. Springer. 535–549.

Zhao, L., and Ichise, R. 2012. Graph-based ontology analysis in the linked open data. In *Proceedings of the 8th International Conference on Semantic Systems*, 56–63. ACM.

Proceedings of the Twenty-Ninth AAAI Conference on Artificial Intelligence

TrustSVD: Collaborative Filtering with Both the Explicit and Implicit Influence of User Trust and of Item Ratings

Guibing Guo, Jie Zhang, Neil Yorke-Smith*
School of Computer Engineering, Nanyang Technological University, Singapore
*American University of Beirut, Lebanon; and University of Cambridge, UK
{gguo1,zhangj}@ntu.edu.sg, *nysmith@aub.edu.lb

Abstract

Collaborative filtering suffers from the problems of data sparsity and cold start, which dramatically degrade recommendation performance. To help resolve these issues, we propose *TrustSVD*, a trust-based matrix factorization technique. By analyzing the social trust data from four real-world data sets, we conclude that not only the explicit but also the implicit influence of both ratings and trust should be taken into consideration in a recommendation model. Hence, we build on top of a state-of-the-art recommendation algorithm SVD++ which inherently involves the explicit and implicit influence of rated items, by further incorporating both the explicit and implicit influence of trusted users on the prediction of items for an active user. To our knowledge, the work reported is the first to extend SVD++ with social trust information. Experimental results on the four data sets demonstrate that our approach TrustSVD achieves better accuracy than other ten counterparts, and can better handle the concerned issues.

Introduction

Incorporating trust into recommender systems has demonstrated potential to improve recommendation performance (Yang et al. 2013; Fang, Bao, and Zhang 2014), and to help mitigate some well-known issues, such as *data sparsity* and *cold start* (Guo, Zhang, and Thalmann 2012). Such trust-aware approaches are developed based on the phenomenon that friends often influence each other by recommending items. However, even the best performance reported by the latest work (Fang, Bao, and Zhang 2014) can be inferior to that of other state-of-the-art models which are merely based on user-item ratings. For instance, a well-performing trust-based model (Yang et al. 2013) obtains 1.0585 on data set Epinions.com in terms of Root Mean Square Error (RMSE), whereas the performance of a user-item baseline (see Koren (2008), Sect. 2.1) can achieve 1.0472 in terms of RMSE.[1]

To investigate this phenomenon, we conduct an empirical trust analysis based on four real-word data sets (FilmTrust, Epinions, Flixster and Ciao) through which two important observations are concluded. First, trust information is also very sparse, yet complementary to rating information. Hence, focusing too much on either one kind of information may achieve only marginal gains in predictive accuracy. Second, users are strongly correlated with their trust neighbors whereas they have a weakly positive correlation with their *trust-alike* neighbors (e.g., friends). Given that very few trust networks exist, it is better to have a more general trust-based model that can well operate on both trust and trust-alike relationships. These observations motivate us to consider both explicit and implicit influence of ratings and of trust in a trust-based model. The influence can be explicit (real values of ratings and trust) or implicit (who rates what (for ratings) and who trusts whom (for trust)). The implicit influence of ratings has been demonstrated useful in providing accurate recommendations (Koren 2008). We will later show that implicit trust can also provide added value over explicit trust.

Thus we propose a novel trust-based recommendation model *TrustSVD*. Our approach builds on top of a state-of-the-art model SVD++ (Koren 2008) where both the explicit and implicit influence of user-item ratings are involved to generate predictions. To the authors' knowledge, our work is the first to extend SVD++ with social trust information. Specifically, on one hand the implicit influence of trust (who trusts whom) can be naturally added to the SVD++ model by extending the user modeling. On the other hand, the explicit influence of trust (trust values) is used to constrain that user-specific vectors should conform to their social trust relationships. This ensures that user-specific vectors can be learned from their trust information even if a few or no ratings are given. In this way, the data sparsity and cold start issues can be better alleviated. Our novel model thus incorporates both explicit and implicit influence of item ratings as well as user trust. In addition, a weighted-λ-regularization technique is used to further avoid over-fitting for model learning. Experimental results on the four real-world data sets demonstrate that our approach achieves significantly better accuracy than other trust-based counterparts as well as other ratings-only well-performing models (ten approaches in total), and is more capable of coping with cold start situations.

Related Work

Trust-aware recommender systems have been widely studied, given that social trust provides an alternative view of user preferences other than item ratings (Guo, Zhang, and

[1] Smaller RMSE values indicate better predictive accuracy. Result reported by the recommendation toolkit MyMediaLite (mymedialite.net/examples/datasets.html).

Yorke-Smith 2014). Specifically, Ma et al. (2008) propose a social regularization method (*SoRec*) by considering the constraint of social relationships. The idea is to share a common user-feature matrix factorized by ratings and by trust. Ma, King, and Lyu (2009) then propose a social trust ensemble method (*RSTE*) to linearly combine a basic matrix factorization model and a trust-based neighborhood model together. Ma et al. (2011) further propose that the active user's user-specific vector should be close to the average of her trusted neighbors, and use it as a regularization to form a new matrix factorization model (*SoReg*). Jamali and Ester (2010) build a new model (*SocialMF*) on top of SoRec by reformulating the contributions of trusted users to the formation of the active user's user-specific vector rather than to the predictions of items. Yang et al. (2013) propose a hybrid method (*TrustMF*) that combines both a truster model and a trustee model from the perspectives of trusters and trustees, that is, both the users who trust the active user and those who are trusted by the user will influence the user's ratings on unknown items. Tang et al. (2013) consider both global and local trust as the contextual information in their model, where the global trust is computed by a separate algorithm. Yao et al. (2014) take into consideration both the explicit and implicit interactions among trusters and trustees in a recommendation model. Fang, Bao, and Zhang (2014) stress the importance of multiple aspects of social trust. They decompose trust into four general factors and then integrate them into a matrix factorization model. All these works have shown that a matrix factorization model regularized by trust outperforms the one without trust. That is, trust is helpful in improving predictive accuracy. However, it is also noted that even the latest work (Fang, Bao, and Zhang 2014) can be inferior to other well-performing ratings-only models. To explain this phenomenon, we next conduct a trust analysis to investigate the value of trust in recommender systems.

Trust Analysis

Four data sets are used in our analysis and also our later experiments: Epinions (trustlet.org/wiki/Epinions_datasets), FilmTrust (www.librec.net/datasets.html), Flixster (www.cs.sfu.ca/~sja25/personal/datasets/) and Ciao (www.public.asu.edu/~jtang20/datasetcode/truststudy.htm). All the four data sets contain both item ratings and social relationships specified by active users. The ratings in Epinions and Ciao are integers from 1 to 5, while those in the other data sets are real values, i.e., [0.5, 4.0] for FilmTrust, [0.5, 5.0] for Flixster both with step 0.5. Note that trust is asymmetric in Epinions, FilmTrust and Ciao whereas it is symmetric in Flixster. A subset of the Flixster data set is used in this paper to avoid memory-consuming issues. The data set statistics are illustrated in Table 1. Two important observations are concluded from these data sets.

Observation 1 *Trust information is very sparse, yet is complementary to rating information.*

On one hand, as shown in Table 1, the density of trust is much smaller than that of ratings in Epinions, FilmTrust and Flixster whereas trust is only denser than ratings in Ciao. Both ratings and trust are very sparse across all the data sets.

Table 1: Statistics of the four data sets

Feature	Epinions	FilmTrust	Flixster	Ciao
users	40,163	1,508	53,213	7,375
items	139,738	2,071	18,197	99,746
ratings	664,824	35,497	409,803	280,391
density	0.051%	1.14%	0.04%	0.03%
trusters	33,960	609	47,029	6,792
trustees	49,288	732	47,029	7,297
trusts	487,183	1,853	655,054	111,781
density	0.029%	0.42%	0.03%	0.23%

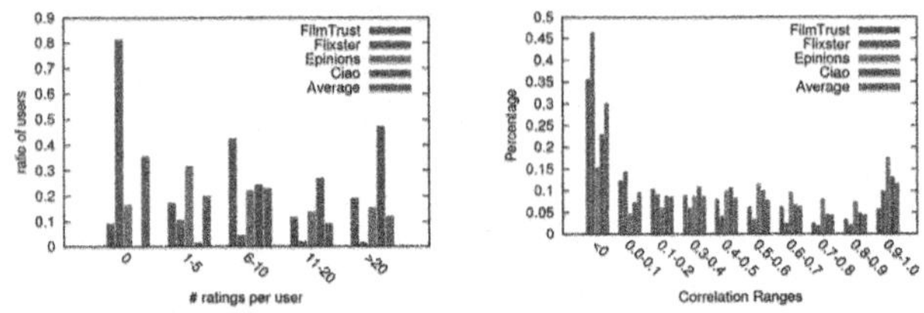

(a) (b)

Figure 1: (a) The distribution of ratio of users who have issued trust statements w.r.t. the number of ratings that they each have given. (b) The correlations between a user's ratings and those of her trusted neighbors in all the data sets.

In this regard, a trust-aware recommender system that focuses too much on trust (rather than rating) utility is likely to achieve only marginal gains in recommendation performance. In fact, the existing trust-based models consider only the explicit influence of ratings. That is, the utility of ratings is not well exploited. In addition, the sparsity of explicit trust also implies the importance of involving implicit trust in collaborative filtering. On the other hand, trust information is complementary to the rating information. Figure 1a shows that: (1) A portion of users have not rated any items but are socially connected with other users. (2) For the *cold-start* users who have rated few items (less than 5 in our case), trust information can provide a complementary part of source of information with ratio greater than 10% on average. (3) The *warm-start* users who have rated a lot of items (e.g., > 20) are not necessary to specify many other users as trustworthy (12% on the average). Although having differing distributions across the data sets, trust can be a complementary information source to item ratings for recommendations.

This observation motivates us to consider both the explicit and implicit influence of ratings and trust, making better and more use of ratings and trust to resolve the concerned issues.

Observation 2 *A user's ratings have a* ***weakly positive correlation*** *with the average of her social neighbors under the concept of trust-alike relationships, and a* ***strongly positive correlation*** *under the concept of trust relationships.*

Next, we consider the influence of trust in rating prediction, i.e., the influence of trusted neighbors on the active user's rating for a specific item, a.k.a. *social influence*. Specifically, we calculate the Pearson correlation coefficient (PCC) between a user's ratings and the average of her social neighbors. The results are presented in Figure 1b, indicating that: (1) A weakly positive correlation is observed between a user's ratings and the average of the social neighbors in FilmTrust (mean 0.183) and Flixster (0.063). The distributions of the two data sets are similar. Flixster adopts the symmetric friendship relationships whereas trust is directed. Although FilmTrust adopts the concept of trust (with values from 1 to 10), the publicly available data set contains only binary values (such degrading may cause much noise). We regard these relationships as *trust alike*, i.e., the social relationships that are similar with, but weaker (or more noisy) than social trust. (2) Under the concept of trust relationships, on the contrary, a user's ratings are strongly and positively correlated with the average of trusted neighbors. Specifically, a large portion (17.63% in Epinions, 13.14% in Ciao) of user correlations are in the range of $[0.9, 1.0]$, and (resp. 54.70%, 39.14%) of user correlations are greater than 0.5. The average correlation is 0.446 in Epinions, and 0.322 in Ciao. Since PCC values are in the range of $[-1, 1]$, values of 0.446 and 0.322 indicate decent correlations. In the social networks with relatively weak trust-alike relationships (e.g., friendship), implicit influence (i.e., binary relationships) may be more indicative than explicit (but noisy) values for recommendations. Hence, a trust-based model that ignores the implicit influence of ratings and trust may lead to deteriorated performance if being applied to such cases.

The second observation suggests that incorporating both the explicit and implicit influence of ratings and trust may promote the generality of a trust-based model to both trust and trust-alike social relationships. Our approach presented next is constructed based on these two observations.

TrustSVD: A Trust-based Model

Problem Definition

The recommendation problem in this paper is to predict the rating that a user will give to an unknown item, based on both a user-item rating matrix and a user-user trust matrix. Suppose that a recommender system includes m users and n items. Let $R = [r_{u,i}]_{m\times n}$ denote the user-item rating matrix, where each entry $r_{u,i}$ represents the rating given by user u on item i. For clarity, we preserve symbols u, v for users, and i, j for items. Let I_u denote the set of items rated by user u. Let p_u and q_i be a d-dimensional latent feature vector of user u and item i, respectively. The essence of matrix factorization is to find two low-rank matrices: user-feature matrix $P \in \mathbb{R}^{d\times m}$ and item-feature matrix $Q \in \mathbb{R}^{d\times n}$ that can adequately recover the rating matrix R, i.e., $R \approx P^\top Q$, where $P^\top$ is the transpose of matrix P. Hence, the rating on item j for user u can be predicted by the inner product of user-specific vector p_u and item-specific vector q_j, i.e., $\hat{r}_{u,j} = q_j^\top p_u$. In this regard, the main task of recommendations is to predict the rating $\hat{r}_{u,j}$ as close as possible to the ground truth $r_{u,j}$. Formally, we can learn the user- and item-feature matrices by minimizing the following loss (objective) function:

$$\mathcal{L}_r = \frac{1}{2}\sum_u \sum_{j\in I_u} (q_j^\top p_u - r_{u,j})^2 + \frac{\lambda}{2}\Big(\sum_u \|p_u\|_F^2 + \sum_j \|q_j\|_F^2\Big),$$

where $\|\cdot\|_F$ denotes the Frobenius norm, and λ is a parameter to control model complexity and to avoid over-fitting.

On the other hand, suppose that a social network is represented by a graph $\mathcal{G} = (\mathcal{V}, \mathcal{E})$, where $\mathcal{V}$ includes a set of m nodes (users) and $\mathcal{E}$ represents the directed trust relationships among users. We can use the adjacency matrix $T = [t_{u,v}]_{m\times m}$ to describe the structure of edges $\mathcal{E}$, where $t_{u,v}$ indicates the extent to which users u trusts v. We denote p_u and w_v as the d-dimensional latent feature vector of truster u and trustee v, respectively. We limit the trusters in the trust matrix and the active users in the rating matrix to share the same user-feature space in order to bridge them together. Hence, we have truster-feature matrix $P^{d\times m}$ and trustee-feature matrix $W^{d\times m}$. By employing the low-rank matrix approximation, we can recover the trust matrix by $T \approx P^\top W$. Thus, a trust relationship can be predicted by the inner product of a truster-specific vector and a trustee-specific vector $\hat{t}_{u,v} = w_v^\top p_u$. The matrices P and W can be learned by minimizing the following loss function:

$$\mathcal{L}_t = \frac{1}{2}\sum_u \sum_{v\in T_u} (w_v^\top p_u - t_{u,v})^2 + \frac{\lambda}{2}\Big(\sum_u \|p_u\|_F^2 + \sum_v \|w_v\|_F^2\Big),$$

where T_u is the set of users trusted by user u.

The TrustSVD Model

In line with the two observations of the previous section, our TrustSVD model is built on top of a state-of-the-art model known as SVD++ proposed by Koren (2008). The rationale behind SVD++ is to take into consideration user/item biases and the influence of rated items other than user/item-specific vectors on rating prediction. Formally, the rating for user u on item j is predicted by:

$$\hat{r}_{u,j} = b_u + b_j + \mu + q_j^\top \Big(p_u + |I_u|^{-\frac{1}{2}} \sum_{i\in I_u} y_i\Big),$$

where b_u, b_j represent the user and item biases, respectively; μ is the global average rating; and y_i denotes the implicit influence of items rated by user u in the past on the ratings of unknown items in the future. Thus, user u's feature vector can be also represented by the set of items she rated, and finally modeled as $(p_u + |I_u|^{-\frac{1}{2}} \sum_{i\in I_u} y_i)$ rather than simply as p_u. Koren (2008) has shown that integrating implicit influence of ratings can well improve predictive accuracy.

Previously, we have stressed the importance of trust influence for better recommendations, and its potential to be generalized to trust-alike relationships. Hence, we can enhance the trust-unaware SVD++ model by incorporating trust influence. Specifically, the implicit effect of trusted users on item ratings can be considered in the same manner as rated items, given by:

$$\begin{aligned}\hat{r}_{u,j} &= b_u + b_j + \mu \\ &+ q_j^\top \Big(p_u + |I_u|^{-\frac{1}{2}} \sum_{i\in I_u} y_i + |T_u|^{-\frac{1}{2}} \sum_{v\in T_u} w_v\Big),\end{aligned}$$

where w_v is the user-specific latent feature vector of users (trustees) trusted by user u, and thus $q_j^\top w_v$ can be explained by the ratings predicted by the trusted users, i.e., the influence of trustees on the rating prediction. In other words, the inner product $q_j^\top w_v$ indicates how trusted users influence user u's rating on item j. Similar to ratings, a user's feature vector can be interpreted by the set of users whom she trusts, i.e., $|T_u|^{-\frac{1}{2}} \sum_{v\in T_u} w_v$. Therefore, a user u is further modeled by $(p_u + |I_u|^{-\frac{1}{2}} \sum_{i\in I_u} y_i + |T_u|^{-\frac{1}{2}} \sum_{v\in T_u} w_v)$ in the social rating networks, considering the influence of both rated items and trusted users. The objective function to minimize is then given as follows:

$$\mathcal{L} = \frac{1}{2}\sum_u \sum_{j\in I_u} \left(\hat{r}_{u,j} - r_{u,j}\right)^2 + \frac{\lambda}{2}\Big(\sum_u b_u^2 + \sum_j b_j^2 + \sum_u \|p_u\|_F^2 + \sum_j \|q_j\|_F^2 + \sum_i \|y_i\|_F^2 + \sum_v \|w_v\|_F^2\Big).$$

To reduce the model complexity, we use the same regularization parameter λ for all the variables. Finer control and tuning can be achieved by assigning separate regularization parameters to different variables, but it may result in great complexity when comparing with different models.

In addition, as explained earlier, we constrain that the user-specific vectors decomposed from the rating matrix and those decomposed from the trust matrix share the same feature space in order to bridge both matrices together. In this way, these two types of information can be exploited in a unified recommendation model. Specifically, we can regularize the user-specific vectors p_u by recovering the social relationships with other users. The new objective function (without the other regularization terms) is given by:

$$\mathcal{L}=\frac{1}{2}\sum_u \sum_{j\in I_u}(\hat{r}_{u,j} - r_{u,j})^2 + \frac{\lambda_t}{2}\sum_u \sum_{v\in T_u}(\hat{t}_{u,v} - t_{u,v})^2,$$

where $\hat{t}_{u,v} = w_v^\top p_u$ is the predicted trust between users u and v, and λ_t controls the degree of trust regularization.

Further, as suggested by Yang et al. (2013), a technique called weighted-λ-regularization can be used to help avoid over-fitting when learning parameters. In particular, they consider more penalties for the users who rated more items and for the items which received more ratings. However, we argue that such consideration may force the model to be more biased towards popular users and items. Instead, in this paper we adopt a distinct strategy that the popular users and items should be less penalized (due to smaller chance to be over-fitted), and cold-start users and *niche items* (those receiving few ratings) should be more regularized (due to greater chance to be over-fitted). Therefore, the new loss function to minimize is obtained as follows:

$$\begin{aligned}\mathcal{L} = &\frac{1}{2}\sum_u \sum_{j\in I_u} \left(\hat{r}_{u,j} - r_{u,j}\right)^2 + \frac{\lambda_t}{2}\sum_u \sum_{v\in T_u}\left(\hat{t}_{u,v} - t_{u,v}\right)^2 \\ &+ \frac{\lambda}{2}\sum_u |I_u|^{-\frac{1}{2}} b_u^2 + \frac{\lambda}{2}\sum_j |U_j|^{-\frac{1}{2}} b_j^2 \\ &+ \sum_u \left(\frac{\lambda}{2}|I_u|^{-\frac{1}{2}} + \frac{\lambda_t}{2}|T_u|^{-\frac{1}{2}}\right)\|p_u\|_F^2 \\ &+ \frac{\lambda}{2}\sum_j |U_j|^{-\frac{1}{2}}\|q_j\|_F^2 + \frac{\lambda}{2}\sum_i |U_i|^{-\frac{1}{2}}\|y_i\|_F^2 \\ &+ \frac{\lambda}{2}|T_v^+|^{-\frac{1}{2}}\|w_v\|_F^2,\end{aligned} \tag{1}$$

where U_j, U_i are the set of users who rate items j and i, respectively; and T_v^+ is the set of users who trust user v. Since the active user has rated a number of items and specified other users as trustworthy, the penalization on user-specific vector p_u takes into account both cases.

Model Learning

To obtain a local minimization of the objective function given by Equation 1, we perform the following gradient descents on b_u, b_j, p_u, q_j, y_i and w_v for all the users and items.

$$\begin{aligned}\frac{\partial \mathcal{L}}{\partial b_u} &= \sum_{j\in I_u} e_{u,j} + \lambda |I_u|^{-\frac{1}{2}} b_u \\ \frac{\partial \mathcal{L}}{\partial b_j} &= \sum_{u\in U_j} e_{u,j} + \lambda |U_j|^{-\frac{1}{2}} b_j \\ \frac{\partial \mathcal{L}}{\partial p_u} &= \sum_{j\in I_u} e_{u,j} q_j + \lambda_t \sum_{v\in T_u} e_{u,v} w_v \\ &\quad + (\lambda |I_u|^{-\frac{1}{2}} + \lambda_t |T_u|^{-\frac{1}{2}}) p_u \\ \frac{\partial \mathcal{L}}{\partial q_j} &= \sum_{u\in U_j} e_{u,j}\Big(p_u + |I_u|^{-\frac{1}{2}}\sum_{i\in I_u} y_i \\ &\quad + |T_u|^{-\frac{1}{2}}\sum_{v\in T_u} w_v\Big) + \lambda |U_j|^{-\frac{1}{2}} q_j \\ \forall i\in I_u, \frac{\partial \mathcal{L}}{\partial y_i} &= \sum_{j\in I_u} e_{u,j} |I_u|^{-\frac{1}{2}} q_j + \lambda |U_i|^{-\frac{1}{2}} y_i \\ \forall v\in T_u, \frac{\partial \mathcal{L}}{\partial w_v} &= \sum_{j\in I_u} e_{u,j} |T_u|^{-\frac{1}{2}} q_j + \lambda_t e_{u,v} p_u + \lambda |T_v^+|^{-\frac{1}{2}} w_v\end{aligned} \tag{2}$$

where $e_{u,j} = \hat{r}_{u,j} - r_{u,j}$ indicates the rating prediction error for user u on item j, and $e_{u,v} = \hat{t}_{u,v} - t_{u,v}$ is the trust prediction error for user u towards user v.

In the cold-start situations where users may have only rated a few items, the decomposition of trust matrix can help to learn more reliable user-specific latent feature vectors than ratings-only matrix factorization. In the extreme case where there are no ratings at all for some users, Equation 2 ensures that the user-specific vector can be trained and learned from the trust matrix. In this regard, incorporating trust in a matrix factorization model can alleviate the cold start problem. By considering both explicit and implicit influence of trust rather than either one alone, our model can better utilize trust to further mitigate the concerned issues.

Complexity Analysis

The computational time of learning the TrustSVD model is mainly taken by evaluating the objective function $\mathcal{L}$ and its gradients against feature vectors (variables). The time to compute the objective function $\mathcal{L}$ is $O(d|R| + d|T|)$, where d is the dimensionality of the feature space, and $|R|, |T|$ refer to the number of observed entries. Due to the sparsity of rating and trust matrices, the values will be much smaller than the matrix cardinality. The computational complexities for gradients $\frac{\partial \mathcal{L}}{\partial b_u}, \frac{\partial \mathcal{L}}{\partial b_j}, \frac{\partial \mathcal{L}}{\partial p_u}, \frac{\partial \mathcal{L}}{\partial q_j}, \frac{\partial \mathcal{L}}{\partial y_i}, \frac{\partial \mathcal{L}}{\partial w_v}$ in Equation 2 are $O(d|R|), O(d|R|), O(d|R| + d|T|), O(d|R| + d|T|), O(d|R|k)$ and $O(d|R|p + d|T|p)$, where k, p are the average number of ratings and trust statements received by an item and a user, respectively. Hence, the overall computational complexity in one iteration is $O(d|R|c+d|T|c)$, where $c = \max(p, k)$. Due to $c \ll |R|$ or $|T|$, the overall computational time is linear with respect to the number of observations in the rating and trust matrices. To sum up, our model has potential to scale up to large-scale data sets.

Experiments and Results

Data Sets. The four data sets presented in Table 1 are used.

Cross-validation. We use 5-fold cross-validation for learning and testing. Specifically, we randomly split each data set into five folds and in each iteration four folds are used as the

Table 2: Performance comparison in two testing views, where * indicates the best performance among all the other methods, and column 'Improve' indicates the relative improvements that our approach TrustSVD achieves relative to the * results.

All	Metrics	UserAvg	ItemAvg	PMF	RSTE	SoRec	SoReg	SocialMF	TrustMF	SVD++	TrustSVD	Improve
FilmTrust	MAE	0.636	0.725	0.714	0.628	0.628	0.674	0.638	0.631	0.613*	**0.609**	0.65%
$d = 5$	RMSE	0.823	0.927	0.949	0.810	0.810	0.878	0.837	0.810	0.804*	**0.789**	1.87%
	MAE	0.636	0.725	0.735	0.640	0.638	0.668	0.642	0.631	0.611*	**0.607**	0.65%
$d = 10$	RMSE	0.823	0.927	0.968	0.835	0.831	0.875	0.844	0.819	0.802*	**0.787**	1.87%
Epinions	MAE	0.930	0.928	0.979	0.950	0.882	0.994	0.825	0.818	0.818*	**0.804**	1.71%
$d = 5$	RMSE	1.203	1.094	1.290	1.196	1.114	1.315	1.070	1.069	1.057*	**1.043**	1.32%
	MAE	0.930	0.928	0.909	0.958	0.884	0.932	0.826	0.819	0.818*	**0.805**	1.59%
$d = 10$	RMSE	1.203	1.094	1.197	1.278	1.142	1.232	1.082	1.095	1.057*	**1.044**	1.23%
Flixster	MAE	0.729*	0.858	0.814	0.751	0.750	0.820	0.770	0.890	0.794	**0.726**	0.41%
$d = 5$	RMSE	0.979*	1.088	1.076	0.975	0.974	1.087	0.994	1.146	1.062	**0.948**	3.17%
	MAE	0.729*	0.858	0.769	0.784	0.785	0.785	0.784	1.116	0.821	**0.727**	0.27%
$d = 10$	RMSE	0.979*	1.088	1.009	1.015	1.018	1.034	1.009	1.441	1.091	**0.950**	2.97%
Ciao	MAE	0.781	0.760	0.920	0.767	0.765	0.899	0.749	0.742*	0.752	**0.723**	2.56%
$d = 5$	RMSE	1.031	1.026	1.206	1.020	1.013	1.183	0.981*	0.983	1.013	**0.955**	2.65%
	MAE	0.781	0.760	0.822	0.763	0.761	0.815	0.749*	0.753	0.748	**0.723**	3.47%
$d = 10$	RMSE	1.031	1.026	1.078	1.013	1.010	1.076	0.976*	1.014	1.001	**0.956**	2.05%

Cold Start	Metrics	UserAvg	ItemAvg	PMF	RSTE	SoRec	SoReg	SocialMF	TrustMF	SVD++	TrustSVD	Improve
FilmTrust	MAE	0.709	0.722	0.814	0.680	0.670*	0.881	0.697	0.674	0.677	**0.661**	1.34%
$d = 5$	RMSE	0.979	0.911	1.079	0.884	0.857*	1.104	0.916	0.867	0.897	**0.853**	0.47%
	MAE	0.709	0.722	0.767	0.674	0.668*	0.771	0.680	0.687	0.680	**0.663**	0.75%
$d = 10$	RMSE	0.979	0.911	1.009	0.900	0.897*	1.034	0.907	0.900	0.905	**0.853**	4.91%
Epinions	MAE	1.047	0.852*	1.451	1.051	0.892	1.398	0.884	0.891	0.889	**0.868**	-1.88%
$d = 5$	RMSE	1.430	1.127	1.770	1.266	1.138	1.735	1.133	1.125*	1.162	**1.105**	1.78%
	MAE	1.047	0.852	1.153	0.981	0.846*	1.139	0.857	0.853	0.891	**0.868**	-2.60%
$d = 10$	RMSE	1.430	1.127*	1.432	1.313	1.180	1.437	1.152	1.176	1.166	**1.108**	1.69%
Flixster	MAE	0.869	0.906	1.097	0.872	0.872	1.058	0.881	0.901	0.868*	**0.855**	1.50%
$d = 5$	RMSE	1.155	1.114	1.390	1.097	1.096*	1.358	1.103	1.138	1.122	**1.066**	2.74%
	MAE	0.869*	0.906	0.949	0.889	0.892	0.951	0.884	0.976	0.869*	**0.858**	1.27%
$d = 10$	RMSE	1.155	1.114	1.206	1.137	1.144	1.218	1.112*	1.328	1.112*	**1.070**	3.78%
Ciao	MAE	0.829	0.735*	1.033	0.957	0.789	1.173	0.774	0.752	0.759	**0.729**	0.82%
$d = 5$	RMSE	1.138	1.005	1.334	1.113	0.998	1.430	1.001	0.954*	1.039	**0.953**	0.10%
	MAE	0.829	0.735	0.926	0.803	0.730*	0.949	0.741	0.770	0.749	**0.721**	1.23%
$d = 10$	RMSE	1.138	1.005	1.191	1.014	1.031	1.214	0.978*	1.096	1.020	**0.962**	1.64%

training set and the remaining fold as the test set. Five iterations will be conducted to ensure that all folds are tested. The average test performance is given as the final result.

Evaluation Metrics. We adopt two well-known metrics to evaluate predictive accuracy, namely mean absolute error (MAE) and root mean square error (RMSE), defined by:

$$\text{MAE} = \frac{\sum_{u,j} |\hat{r}_{u,j} - r_{u,j}|}{N}, \ \text{RMSE} = \sqrt{\frac{\sum_{u,j} (\hat{r}_{u,j} - r_{u,j})^2}{N}}$$

where N is the number of test ratings. Smaller values of MAE and RMSE indicate better predictive accuracy.

Testing Views. Two data set views are created for testing. First, the *All* view indicates that all ratings are used as the test set. Second, the *Cold Start* view means that only the users who rate less than five items will be involved in the test set. Similar testing views are also defined and used in (Guo, Zhang, and Thalmann 2012; Yang et al. 2013).

Comparison Methods. Three kinds of approaches are compared with our method **TrustSVD**[2]: (1) Baselines: **UserAvg** and **ItemAvg** make predictions by the average of ratings that are given by the active user and received by the target item, respectively; (2) Trust-based models: **SoRec** (Ma et al. 2008), **RSTE** (Ma, King, and Lyu 2009), **SoReg** (Ma et al. 2011), **SocialMF** (Jamali and Ester 2010), **TrustMF** (Yang et al. 2013) and **Fang's** (Fang, Bao, and Zhang 2014); (3) Ratings-only state-of-the-art models: **PMF** (Salakhutdinov and Mnih 2008) and **SVD++** (Koren 2008).

Parameter Settings. The optimal experimental settings for each method are determined either by our experiments or suggested by previous works. Specifically, the common settings are $\lambda = 0.001$, and the number of latent features $d = 5/10$, the same as all the previous trust-based models. The other settings are: (1) RSTE: $\alpha = 0.4$ for Epinions, and 1.0 for the others; (2) SoRec: $\lambda_c = 0.1, 1.0, 0.001, 0.01$ corresponding to FilmTrust, Epinions, Flixster and Ciao, respectively; (3) SoReg: $\beta = 1.0$ for Flixster and 0.1 for the others; (4) SocialMF, TrustMF: $\lambda_t = 1$; (5) SVD++: $\lambda = 0.1, 0.35, 0.03, 0.1$ (resp.); (6) TrustSVD: $\lambda = 1.2, \lambda_t = 0.9$ for FilmTrust, $\lambda = 0.9, \lambda_t = 0.5$ for Epinions, $\lambda = 0.8, \lambda_t = 0.5$ for Flixster, and $\lambda = 0.5, \lambda_t = 1$ for Ciao.

[2]Source code is included in the LibRec library at www.librec.net.

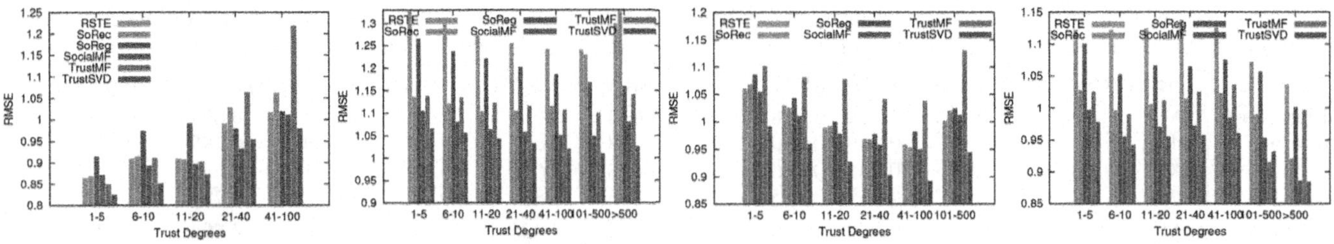

(a) FilmTrust (b) Epinions (c) Flixster (d) Ciao

Figure 2: Performance comparison on users with different trust degrees ($d = 10$) [best viewed in color]

Table 3: Comparing with (Fang, Bao, and Zhang 2014)

Fang's vs. **TrustSVD**	**Epinions** $d=5$	**Epinions** $d=10$	**Ciao** $d=5$	**Ciao** $d=10$	**FilmTrust** $d=5$	**FilmTrust** $d=10$
MAE	0.806	0.814	0.737	0.745	0.616	0.625
	0.804	**0.805**	**0.723**	**0.723**	**0.609**	**0.607**
RMSE	1.047	1.059	0.972	0.985	0.793	0.810
	1.043	**1.044**	**0.955**	**0.956**	**0.789**	**0.787**

Comparison with other models. The experimental results are presented in Table 2. For all the comparison methods in the testing view of *All*, SVD++ outperforms the other comparison methods in FilmTrust and Epinions, and UserAvg performs the best in Flixster. This implies that these trust-based approaches cannot always beat other well-performing ratings-only approaches, and even simple baselines in trust-alike networks (i.e., FilmTrust and Flixster). Only in Ciao, trust-based approach (SocialMF) gives the best performance. On the contrary, our approach TrustSVD is consistently superior to the best approach among the others across all the data sets. Although the percentage of relative improvements are small, Koren (2010) has pointed out that even small improvements in MAE and RMSE may lead to significant differences of recommendations in practice.

For all the comparison methods in the testing view of *Cold Start*, SoRec and SVD++ perform respectively the best in FilmTrust and Flixster (trust-alike), while no single approach works the best in Epinions and Ciao (trust). Generally, our approach performs better than the others both in trust and trust-alike relationships. Although some exceptions are observed in Epinions in terms of MAE, TrustSVD is more powerful in terms of RMSE. Since all the trust-based models aim to optimize the square errors between predictions and real values, RMSE is more indicative than MAE, and thus TrustSVD still has best performance overall.

Besides the above-compared approaches, some new trust-based models have been proposed recently. The most relevant model is presented in (Fang, Bao, and Zhang 2014); for clarity, we denote it by *Fang's*. It is reported to perform better than other trust-based models and than SVD++ (except in Ciao). Table 3 shows the comparison between Fang's and our approach TrustSVD. The results of Fang's approach are reported in (Fang, Bao, and Zhang 2014), and directly re-used in our paper. Note that we sampled more data for Flixster than Fang's, and thus their experimental results are not comparable. Table 3 clearly shows that our approach performs better than Fang's in terms of both MAE and RMSE.

One more observation from Tables 2 and 3 is that the performance of TrustSVD when $d = 5$ is very close to that when $d = 10$, indicating the reliability of our approach with respect to the feature dimensionality. We ascribe this feature to the consideration of both the explicit and implicit influence of ratings and trust in a unified recommendation model.

In conclusion, the experimental results indicate that our approach TrustSVD outperforms the other methods in predicting more accurate ratings, and that its performance is reliable with different number of latent features.

Comparison in trust degrees. Another series of experiments are conducted to investigate the performance on users with different trust degrees. The trust degrees refer to the number of trusted neighbors specified by a user. We split the trust degrees into seven categories: 1-5, 6-10, 11-20, 21-40, 41-100, 101-500, >500. The results of trust-based models are illustrated in Figure 2, where we only present the performance in RMSE when $d = 10$ due to space limitation; similar trends in other cases. In general, our approach TrustSVD consistently achieves the best performance in the cases of different trust degrees. Paired t-tests (confidence 0.95) shows that such improvements are statistically significant ($p<10^{-5}$) in three data sets but not in FilmTrust (details are omitted to save space). Two possible explanations can be made: (1) FilmTrust has a smaller data size than the others; (2) due to the noise arising from converting real-valued trust to binary trust, the trust may be less useful in FilmTrust than in the others as indicated in (Fang, Bao, and Zhang 2014).

Conclusion and Future Work

This paper proposed a novel trust-based matrix factorization model which incorporated both rating and trust information. Our analysis of trust in four real-world data sets indicated that trust and ratings are complementary to each other, and both pivotal for more accurate recommendations. Our novel approach, TrustSVD, takes into account both the explicit and implicit influence of ratings and trust information when predicting ratings of unknown items. A weighted-λ-regularization technique was adapted and used to further regularize the user- and item-specific latent feature vectors. Comprehensive experimental results showed that our approach TrustSVD outperformed both trust- and ratings-based methods in predictive accuracy across different testing views and across users with different trust degrees. For future work, we intend to further improve the proposed model by considering both the influence of trusters and trustees.

Acknowledgements

Guibing Guo thanks the Institute for Media Innovation for a PhD grant at Nanyang Technological University, Singapore.

The work is also partially supported by the MoE AcRF Tier 2 Grant M4020110.020.

References

Fang, H.; Bao, Y.; and Zhang, J. 2014. Leveraging decomposed trust in probabilistic matrix factorization for effective recommendation. In *Proceedings of the 28th AAAI Conference on Artificial Intelligence (AAAI)*, 30–36.

Guo, G.; Zhang, J.; and Thalmann, D. 2012. A simple but effective method to incorporate trusted neighbors in recommender systems. In *Proceedings of the 20th International Conference on User Modeling, Adaptation and Personalization (UMAP)*, 114–125.

Guo, G.; Zhang, J.; and Yorke-Smith, N. 2014. Leveraging multiviews of trust and similarity to enhance clustering-based recommender systems. *Knowledge-Based Systems (KBS)* in press.

Jamali, M., and Ester, M. 2010. A matrix factorization technique with trust propagation for recommendation in social networks. In *Proceedings of the 4th ACM Conference on Recommender Systems (RecSys)*, 135–142.

Koren, Y. 2008. Factorization meets the neighborhood: a multifaceted collaborative filtering model. In *Proceedings of the 14th ACM SIGKDD International Conference on Knowledge Discovery and Data Mining (KDD)*, 426–434.

Koren, Y. 2010. Factor in the neighbors: Scalable and accurate collaborative filtering. *ACM Transactions on Knowledge Discovery from Data (TKDD)* 4(1):1:1–1:24.

Ma, H.; Yang, H.; Lyu, M.; and King, I. 2008. SoRec: social recommendation using probabilistic matrix factorization. In *Proceedings of the 31st International ACM SIGIR Conference on Research and Development in Information Retrieval (SIGIR)*, 931–940.

Ma, H.; Zhou, D.; Liu, C.; Lyu, M. R.; and King, I. 2011. Recommender systems with social regularization. In *Proceedings of the 4th ACM International Conference on Web Search and Data Mining (WSDM)*, 287–296.

Ma, H.; King, I.; and Lyu, M. 2009. Learning to recommend with social trust ensemble. In *Proceedings of the 32nd International ACM SIGIR Conference on Research and Development in Information Retrieval (SIGIR)*, 203–210.

Salakhutdinov, R., and Mnih, A. 2008. Probabilistic matrix factorization. In *Advances in Neural Information Processing Systems (NIPS)*, volume 20, 1257–1264.

Tang, J.; Hu, X.; Gao, H.; and Liu, H. 2013. Exploiting local and global social context for recommendation. In *Proceedings of the 23rd International Joint Conference on Artificial Intelligence (IJCAI)*, 2712–2718.

Yang, B.; Lei, Y.; Liu, D.; and Liu, J. 2013. Social collaborative filtering by trust. In *Proceedings of the 23rd International Joint Conference on Artificial Intelligence (IJCAI)*, 2747–2753.

Yao, W.; He, J.; Huang, G.; and Zhang, Y. 2014. Modeling dual role preferences for trust-aware recommendation. In *Proceedings of the 37th International ACM SIGIR Conference on Research & Development in Information Retrieval (SIGIR)*, 975–978.

A Stochastic Model for Detecting Heterogeneous Link Communities in Complex Networks

Dongxiao He[1], Dayou Liu[2*], Di Jin[1], Weixiong Zhang[3,4]

[1]School of Computer Science and Technology, Tianjin University, Tianjin 300072, China, [2]College of Computer Science and Technology, Jilin University, Changchun 130012, China, [3]Department of Computer Science and Engineering, Washington University, St. Louis, MO 63130, USA, [4]Institute for Systems Biology, Jianghan University, Wuhan, Hubei 430056, China

hedongxiao@tju.edu.cn, liudy@jlu.edu.cn, jindi@tju.edu.cn, weixiong.zhang@wustl.edu

Abstract

Discovery of communities in networks is a fundamental data analysis problem. Most of the existing approaches have focused on discovering communities of nodes, while recent studies have shown great advantages and utilities of the knowledge of communities of links. Stochastic models provides a promising class of techniques for the identification of modular structures, but most stochastic models mainly focus on the detection of node communities rather than link communities. We propose a stochastic model, which not only describes the structure of link communities, but also considers the heterogeneous distribution of community sizes, a property which is often ignored by other models. We then learn the model parameters using a method of maximum likelihood based on an expectation-maximization algorithm. To deal with large complex real networks, we extend the method by a strategy of iterative bipartition. The extended method is not only efficient, but is also able to determine the number of communities for a given network. We test our approach on both synthetic benchmarks and real-world networks including an application to a large biological network, and also compare it with two existing methods. The results demonstrate the superior performance of our approach over the competing methods for detecting link communities.

1. Introduction

Many complex systems in the real world exist in the form of networks, such as social networks, biological networks, and the Internet, which are collectively referred to as complex networks. One of the main problems in the study of complex networks is the detection of community structures (Girvan and Newman 2002), which has drawn a great deal of interest. Although no common definition has been agreed upon, a community within a network is usually considered as a group of nodes that are densely connected with respect to the rest of the network. In the past few years, many different approaches have been proposed to uncover network community structures, as reviewed in (Fortunato 2010; Xie, Kelley, and Szymanski 2013).

Although previous research on community detection has been mainly focusing on finding communities of nodes, several recent works considered finding communities of links (Ahn, Bagrow, and Lehmann 2010; Evans and Lambiotte 2009; Evans and Lambiotte 2010; Kim and Jeong 2011; Pan et al. 2011; He et al. 2012). In many real networks, link communities are often more informative and intuitive than node communities, because links usually have unique identities, while nodes typically have multiple roles. In a social network, for instance, most individuals belong to multiple communities such as families, friends, and co-workers, while the link between two individuals often exists for a dominant reason which may represent family ties, friendship, or professional relationships. Furthermore, multiple links connecting to a node may belong to distinct link communities, so that the node can be assigned to multiple communities of links. Accordingly, overlapping communities of nodes, another attractive topic in community detection (Palla et al. 2005), could be detected as a natural byproduct of link communities.

Thanks to the good performance and sound theoretical basis, stochastic models constitute a promising technique for identifying modular properties of networks, and thus have been actively researched (Newman 2012). However, most of them focused on the detection of node communities (Wang et al. 2011; Psorakis et al. 2011; Zhang and Yeung 2012; Ren et al. 2009; Shen, Cheng, and Guo 2011; Karrer and Newman 2011; Zhang, Wang, and Ahn 2013), with only one exception for detecting link communities (Ball, Karrer, and Newman 2011). However, like most stochastic models, Ball's model requires the number of communities to be given and is computationally inefficient, so that its applicability is limited, particularly for large-scale networks. More importantly, it fails to describe heterogeneous distributions of community sizes of real networks, providing distorted resulting link communities.

* Corresponding author

Therefore, much needs to be done for stochastic models for link community detection.

In this work, we introduce a stochastic model for link communities, namely LM (link model), which considers the heterogeneity of link community sizes when describing community structures. We learn the parameters of this model using a maximum likelihood method based on an expectation-maximization algorithm. We then extend the above method, by introducing a scheme of iterative bipartition, to link model with iterative bipartition (LMBP). Our new LMBP method can not only autonomously determine the number of communities but is also efficient. Therefore it is applicable to large networks. Our experimental results show that LMBP outperforms two related competing methods on both synthetic and real-world networks for detecting link communities.

2. Related Work

A number of approaches to the detection of link communities in networks have been proposed. (Ahn, Bagrow, and Lehmann 2010) used a hierarchical clustering with similarity between links to build a dendrogram to describe hierarchical link structures. In order to obtain the most relevant communities, they introduced a link density function to determine the best level to cut the tree to determine the number of communities. (Evans and Lambiotte 2009; Evans and Lambiotte 2010) transformed a given network into a line graph based on several types of random walk, and detected link communities by applying some existing algorithms for node partitioning to the line graph. (Kim and Jeong 2011) extended the map equation method (Rosvall and Bergstrom 2008), which was originally developed for node communities, to link community detection by assigning the communities to links instead of nodes, modifying the encoding rule for the random walk to represent this change in the community structure, and proposing the corresponding map equation for the link community. (Pan et al. 2011) proposed a local-based method for finding natural link communities through expanding a selected seed to optimize a local function. (He et al. 2012) presented a stochastic process based on a link-node-link random walk to unfold the community structure of links, and then utilized the local mixing properties of the Markov chain to extract emerged link communities.

Moreover, stochastic models provided a promising technique for identifying communities from networks, which has been actively researched (Newman 2012). Several model-based methods have been proposed; they were based on a blockmodel or its variations and employed different inference algorithms, e.g., expectation-maximization and nonnegative matrix factorization, to derive the number of communities. Nevertheless, most of these methods focused on the detection of node communities (Wang et al. 2011; Psorakis et al. 2011; Zhang, and Yeung 2012; Ren et al. 2009; Shen, Cheng, and Guo 2011; Karrer and Newman 2011; Zhang, Wang, and Ahn 2013). One exception for detection of link communities that we are aware of is the algorithm designed by (Ball, Karrer, and Newman 2011). While Ball's model seemed to have a high similarity with the one that we proposed here, there are several key differences. Compared with Ball's model, the most salient feature of ours is its high flexibility. In our model, the size of a link community is modeled by a set of parameters ω_z. This enables it to better describe the heterogeneous community sizes, such as that following a power law distribution which often appears in the real world. This feature, lacking in Ball's model, allows us to better characterize community structures of links of real-world networks. Moreover, our extended LMBP method does not need the number of communities a *priori*, which in contrast is required by the Ball's method BModel. LMBP is also more efficient than BModel. Therefore, compared with BModel, our LMBP method is more suitable for large networks, a necessity for real-world applications.

3. The Methods

We first introduce a model for the description of link communities, and then present a method based on maximum-likelihood estimation to learn the model parameters. For clarity, we present an example to illustrate the method. We then extend the basic method to make it more suitable for large real networks.

3.1 Stochastic Model

We define a stochastic model of link communities to characterize networks with a given number n of vertices and m undirected edges divided among a given number c of communities. Taking the notion of *soft* membership of links, the model is parameterized by two sets of parameters, ω_z's and θ_{iz}'s. Here, ω_z denotes twice the expected number of links in community z, which is defined as the sum of all expected counts of z-links (links in community z) that a node connects to, and θ_{iz} denotes the probability that community z selects node i when generating edges, which is defined as the expected proportion of z-links node i connects to in this community. Thus, we have $\sum_z \omega_z = 2m$ and $\sum_i \theta_{iz} = 1$.

Based on the model above, an edge $<i, j>$ can be generated as follows. A link community z is chosen with size ω_z, and within community z, nodes i and j are selected with probabilities θ_{iz} and θ_{jz}, respectively, to form an edge. Consequently, the expected number of links between nodes i and j in community z is

$$\hat{A}_{ij}^{z} = \omega_z \theta_{iz} \theta_{jz} \,. \tag{1}$$

Summing over communities z, the expected number of link between i and j can be written as

$$\hat{A}_{ij} = \sum_z \hat{A}_{ij}^{z} = \sum_z \omega_z \theta_{iz} \theta_{jz} \,. \tag{2}$$

Under this model, link communities will appear with the generating of networks. Intuitively, two nodes i and j which have large values of ω_z, θ_{iz} and θ_{jz} for some value of z have a high probability of being connected by a link within community z. Thus, groups of such nodes will tend to be connected by relatively dense webs of z-links, and these sets of edges correctly form the link communities we expect to see.

Formally, assume that the community assignments are represented by a set of variables R_{ij}^z's, where R_{ij}^z denotes the fraction that a link <i, j> belongs to community z. Then we have

$$R_{ij}^z = \frac{\hat{A}_{ij}^z}{\hat{A}_{ij}} = \frac{\omega_z\theta_{iz}\theta_{jz}}{\sum_s \omega_s\theta_{is}\theta_{js}}, \qquad (3)$$

As the soft membership of communities cannot be used directly, we simply assign each link <i, j> to community r satisfying $r = \mathrm{argmax}_z \{R_{ij}^z, z=1,2,\ldots,c\}$, and then derive a hard partition of links.

3.2 Parameter Learning

Since the (stochastic) model parameters for a given network are unknown, we need to learn the parameters in order to infer the link communities in the network. This can be done by maximizing a likelihood function that the network was presumably generated from the model. Since the number of links between two nodes is given in the expectation of a Poisson distribution (Karrer and Newman 2011; Ball, Karrer, and Newman 2011), the probability of generating a graph G with adjacency matrix $(A_{ij})_{n\times n}$ by the model specified in (2) is

$$P(G\mid\omega,\theta) = \prod_{i,j} \frac{\left(\sum_z \omega_z\theta_{iz}\theta_{jz}\right)^{A_{ij}}}{A_{ij}!} \exp\left(-\sum_z \omega_z\theta_{iz}\theta_{jz}\right). \qquad (4)$$

The best fit between the given network G and its expected network in (2) can be achieved by maximizing the likelihood function in (4).

Likelihood maximization does not typically work directly with the likelihood itself, but with its logarithm. Taking the log of (4), rearranging, and dropping additive and multiplicative constants, we derive the log-likelihood

$$L = \sum_{ij} A_{ij} \log\left(\sum_z \omega_z\theta_{iz}\theta_{jz}\right) - \sum_{ijz} \omega_z\theta_{iz}\theta_{jz}. \qquad (5)$$

Direct maximization of this expression by differentiating leads to a set of nonlinear implicit equations for ω_z and θ_{iz} that seem to be difficult to solve. Here we adopt an expectation-maximization (EM) algorithm (Dempster, Laird, and Rubin 1977). We apply Jensen's inequality to (5), and obtain

$$L \ge \bar{L} = \sum_{ijz} \left(A_{ij} q_{ij,z} \log \frac{\omega_z\theta_{iz}\theta_{jz}}{q_{ij,z}} - \omega_z\theta_{iz}\theta_{jz} \right), \qquad (6)$$

where the probabilities $q_{ij,z}$ can be freely chosen, provided they satisfy $\sum_z q_{ij,z} = 1$. Especially, the exact equality can always be achieved by making a particular choice $q_{ij,z}=\omega_z\theta_{iz}\theta_{jz}/\sum_s\omega_s\theta_{is}\theta_{js}$. Thus, it follows that the double maximization of the new function $\bar{L}$ with respect to both the model parameters (ω_z and θ_{iz}) and the probabilities ($q_{ij,z}$) is equivalent to maximizing the original log-likelihood L with respect to the model parameters alone. Given the optimal model parameters ω_z and θ_{iz}, the optimal values of probabilities $q_{ij,z}$ are given by

$$q_{ij,z} = \frac{\omega_z\theta_{iz}\theta_{jz}}{\sum_s \omega_s\theta_{is}\theta_{js}}, \qquad (7)$$

since these are the values that give the inequality in (6) an exact equality. Meanwhile, given the optimal probabilities $q_{ij,z}$, the optimal values of model parameters ω_z and θ_{iz} can be found by maximizing $\bar{L}$ with the constraints $\sum_z \omega_z = 2m$ and $\sum_i \theta_{iz} = 1$. Introducing Lagrange multipliers ρ and γ_z to incorporate these constraints, the Lagrange form of $\bar{L}$ is

$$\tilde{L} = \bar{L} + \rho\left(\sum_z \omega_z - 2m\right) + \sum_z \gamma_z \left(\sum_i \theta_{iz} - 1\right). \qquad (8)$$

By differentiating (8), the optimal values of ω_z and θ_{iz} are given as

$$\omega_z = \sum_{ij} A_{ij} q_{ij,z}; \quad \theta_{iz} = \frac{\sum_j A_{ij} q_{ij,z}}{\sum_{kj} A_{kj} q_{kj,z}}. \qquad (9)$$

Maximizing the log-likelihood L is now equivalent to simultaneously solving (7) and (9), which can be done iteratively by choosing a random set of initial values and alternating back and forth between the two equations. The EM algorithm implemented here is guaranteed to converge under the above conditions.

Notice that the $q_{ij,z}$ are only defined for node pairs i, j that are actually connected in the network (so that $A_{ij} = 1$), and hence there are only as many of them as there are observed edges. Thus the time to evaluate (7) once is $O(mc)$, where m is the number of edges and c the number of communities. Similarly, the time for calculating (9) once is $O(mc)$ as we only need to consider the observed edges. Therefore, the time complexity of our method is $O(Tmc)$, where T is the number of iterations to convergence.

3.3 An Illustrative Example

We now illustrate the idea of our method using a simple example shown in Figure 1 and Table 1.

The given network G is in Figure 1(a). Under our model, given the parameters ω_z's and θ_{iz}'s such as that in Table 1, we can form the expected graphs of all the link communities in G according to (1), which are shown in Figure 1(b) and (c). Further, we can form the expected graph of the whole network G according to (2), which is an ensemble of the expected graphs of all its communities, shown in Figure 1(d). However, the model parameters are unknown, they must first be learned in order to find the communities in the network. To this end, we consider network G and its expected graph by optimizing (4), and then get the best ω_z's and θ_{iz}'s, as shown as Table 1. Thereafter, we infer the community structure of links according to (3), which perfectly matches the ground-truth given in Figure 1(a).

Table 1: *The learned model parameters ω_z's and θ_{iz}'s*

	ω_z	θ_{iz}			
		i=1	i=2	i=3	i=4
z=1	19.99992	0.2	0.2	0.2	0.2
z=2	20.00008	5.20E-07	5.36E-07	5.19E-07	5.04E-07
	θ_{iz}				
	i=5	i=6	i=7	i=8	i=9
z=1	0.199999	1.39E-09	1.36E-09	1.43E-09	8.37E-10
z=2	0.200001	0.199999	0.199999	0.199999	0.199999

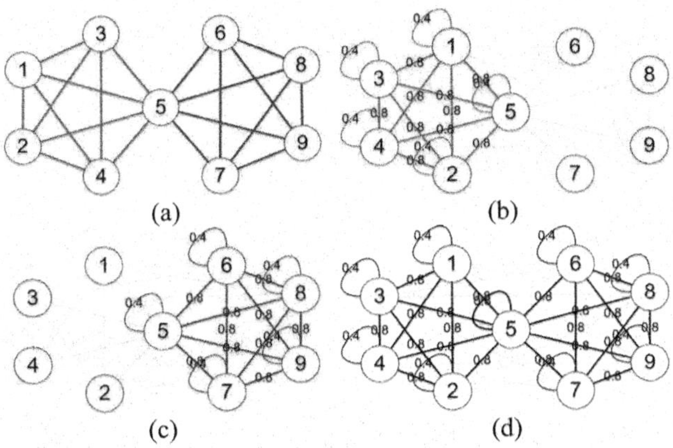

Figure 1: *An illustration of our method for identifying the community structure of links.* ***(a)*** *The given network G with two link communities (in red and blue).* ***(b)*** *and* ***(c)*** *The expected graph of the red and blue link community, respectively.* ***(d)*** *The expected graph of G, which is an ensemble of the expected graphs of its red and blue communities. The width of a link corresponds to its expected values, and values smaller than 1.0e-3 are omitted.*

3.4 A Practical Extension

The method discussed above can be improved. A drawback of our basic method is that it offers no criterion for determining the value of parameter c, i.e., the number of communities in a network. This is also a common problem suffered by all exiting methods based on stochastic models. A statistical model selection method can be, in principle, applied to stochastic models to find the number of communities (Brunet et al. 2004; Tan and Févotte 2012). Such a model selection method is too computationally demanding to be desirable to any but some small networks (Ball, Karrer, and Newman 2011). Even if the number c of communities is given, because large networks often have large values of c, the convergence rate of the core learning algorithms, such as expectation maximization and nonnegative matrix factorization, will become very slow. This is also a crucial limitation for the existing model-based methods when dealing with large real networks. It remains an open problem whether an accurate and efficient model selection method can be developed for large real networks (Karrer and Newman 2011).

To mitigate the above problems, we extend our original method LM (link model) to "link model with iterative bipartition", or LMBP for short. In LMBP, we first divide a network into two link modules using LM with community number $c = 2$, and then recursively subdivide the two parts. In dividing a subnetwork, we isolate it from the rest of the network and perform a 'nested' LMBP on it, resulting in a partition of the subnetwork with two smaller link communities. For each partition, we decide whether to accept a bipartition based on the quality of the resulting link partition. We summarize the algorithm LMBP using the following recursive algorithm:

Algorithm P = LMBP(G) // G is a graph, P is a link partition of G

1. $P = \{E(G)\}$; // $E(G)$ denotes the edge set of G
2. Divide G into two link modules N_1 and N_2 by LM;
// $E(N_1) \cap E(N_2) = \Phi$, $E(N_1) \cup E(N_2) = E(N)$
3. If the link partition quality cannot be improved by this bipartition, return P;
// the quality function is to be introduced later
4. P_1 = LMBP(N_1);
5. P_2 = LMBP(N_2);
6. Return $P = P_1 \cup P_2$.

We now consider the termination condition for the repetitive process of subdividing the links of network G, so as to obtain a superior link community structure. Several measures for community structures exist, most of which were developed for node communities (Fortunato 2010; Newman and Girvan 2004; Lancichinetti et al. 2011). Fortunately, partition density D (Ahn, Bagrow, and Lehmann 2010) was specially designed for link communities. Here we adopt it as our quality metric, i.e., we iteratively bipartition each (sub)network until the density D cannot be further improved to determine the acceptance of the bipartition.

For a network with m links and n nodes, $P = \{P_1, P_2, \ldots, P_c\}$ is a partition of the links into c communities. The number of links in community z, P_z, is $m_z = |P_z|$. The number of induced nodes, the nodes that those links connect to, is $n_z = |\cup_{eij \in Pz,} \{i, j\}|$. The link density D_z of P_z is

$$D_z = \frac{m_z - (n_z - 1)}{n_z(n_z - 1)/2 - (n_z - 1)}. \quad (10)$$

This is m_z normalized by the minimum and maximum numbers of links among n_z connected nodes. Thus, $D_z = 1$ when P_z is a clique, or $D_z = 0$ when P_z is a tree. In particular, we assume that $D_z = 0$ if $n_z = 2$ without loss of generality. In essence, D_z measures how 'clique-ish' versus 'tree-ish' that P_z is. Then, the partition density, D, is the average of D_z, weighted by the fraction of links that are present:

$$D = \frac{2}{m}\sum_z m_z \frac{(m_z - n_z + 1)}{(n_z - 2)(n_z - 1)}. \quad (11)$$

4. Experiments

In order to evaluate the performance of our method LMBP, we tested it on synthetic networks and widely used real-world networks. The synthetic networks allow us to test LMBP's ability to detect known communities, while the real networks allow us to assess its performance in practice. As an application, we applied LMBP to a large biological network.

In our analysis, we compared LMBP with two well-known and closely related methods. The first (denoted as BModel) is a model-based method for link communities proposed by (Ball, Karrer, and Newman 2011), and the second (denoted as LC) is the notable method of link communities proposed by (Ahn, Bagrow, and Lehmann 2010). To the best of our knowledge, LMBP and BModel are the only two methods based on stochastic models for link communities, and LMBP and LC are the only two hierarchical methods using partition density D (Ahn, Bagrow, and Lehmann 2010) as a quality metric to detect link communities. Note that BModel needs the number c of communities as a given parameter, thus we used the community number obtained by our LMBP as its input. Besides, the LMBP and BModel converge to local minima, thus we ran each of them 20 times and reported the best results.

4.1 Synthetic Networks

Several benchmarks of synthetic network have been proposed for node communities (Girvan and Newman 2002; Lancichinetti, Fortunato, and Radicchi 2008; Lancichinetti and Fortunato 2009). In contrast, only one benchmark, to our knowledge, has been designed for testing algorithms for link community detection (Ball, Karrer, and Newman 2011), which we used in this evaluation. We also employed two accuracy measures introduced in (Ball, Karrer, and Newman 2011), namely "Fraction of Vertices Classified Correctly (FVCC)" and "Jaccard index", to compare the planted community structures of a network and the ones delivered by the algorithms compared. Notice that LC does not appear here, because it often finds very small communities, and fails to detect the communities defined in this benchmark.

Following (Ball, Karrer, and Newman 2011), the parameter setting for this benchmark is given as follows. The networks have n = 10000 nodes each, divided into two overlapping (link) communities. We placed x nodes in the first community only, i.e., these nodes have connections exclusively within the community, y nodes in the second community only, and the remaining $z=n-x-y$ nodes in both communities, with equal numbers of connections to nodes in these two communities on average. We set the expected degree of all nodes to a fixed value $<k>$. We also varied the parameters x, y, z, and $<k>$ to generate networks with stark community structures or no structure at all, so as to vary the difficulty of the network instances posed to the algorithms.

We performed three sets of tests. In the first set of experiments, we fixed the size of the overlap between the communities at z = 500, divided the remaining nodes evenly (i.e., x = y = 4750), and varied the value of $<k>$ from 1 to 15 with an increment of 1. For the second set of tests, we again set the overlap at z = 500 but fixed $<k>$ = 10 and varied the ratio between x and y. Finally, for the third set of tests, we set $<k>$ = 10, constrained x and y to be equal, and varied the amount of overlap z.

As BModel requires the number of communities to be given, we set the number of communities for BModel to 2, the actual number of communities. For fairness, the first bipartition result from LMBP was used for comparison with BModel. In Figure 2, we show the fraction of corrected classified nodes by the two algorithms for each of the three sets of experiments. To be considered correctly classified, a node's membership in both communities must be reported correctly by an algorithm. As shown in Figure 2, LMBP outperforms BModel in terms of FVCC accuracy in all the three tests. This may be mainly due to our parameter ω_2, which controls the size of each link community, and thus makes our model more flexible to describe link communities compared with Ball's model.

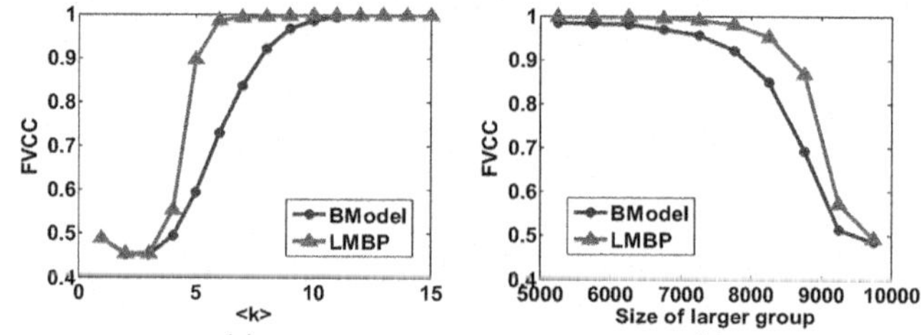

(a) (b)

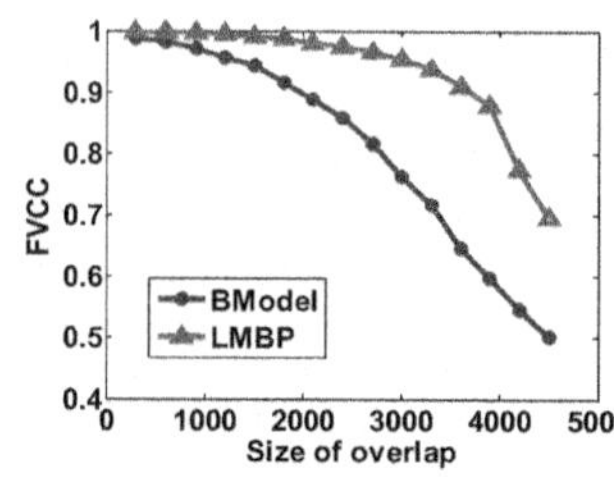

(c)

Figure 2: *Comparison of LMBP and BModel in the three sets of synthetic networks, measured by the fraction of vertices classified correctly. **(a)** FVCC accuracy as a function of the expected degree <k> of all nodes. **(b)** FVCC as a function of the size of the larger community. **(c)** FVCC as a function of the amount of overlap between the two communities.*

Furthermore, we adopted the Jaccard index to compare the two algorithms' ability for identifying overlapping (link) communities using the same sets of network instances. Let S be the set of truly overlapping nodes and V be the set of predicted overlapping nodes, the Jaccard index is $J = |S \cap V|/|S \cup V|$. This index is a standard measure of similarity between sets that rewards accurate identification of the overlap while penalizes both false positives and false negatives. Figure 3 shows the result comparing the two algorithms. As shown, LMBP is also superior to BModel in all the three sets of experiments. This result is similar to the results in Figure 2, and they both confirm the validity of LMBP.

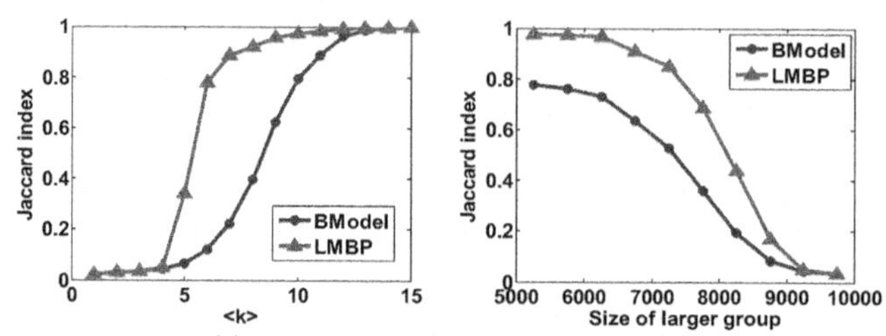

(a) (b)

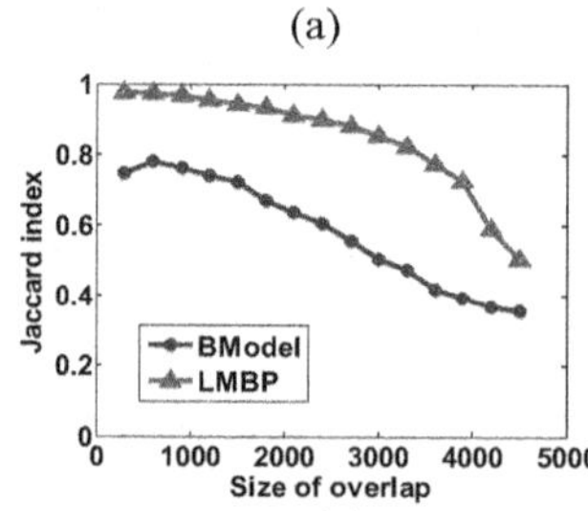

(c)

Figure 3: *Comparison of LMBP and BModel in the three sets of synthetic networks measured by the Jaccard index. **(a)** Jaccard index as a function of the expected degree <k>. **(b)** Jaccard index as a function of the size of the larger community. **(c)** Jaccard index as a function of the amount of overlap.*

4.2 Real Networks

As real-world networks may have some unique topological properties not present in synthetic ones, we considered some widely used real networks to compare these algorithms. All the networks we used here were obtained from Newman's website (Newman, 2013), except that 'protein-protein interaction' and 'word association' that were from (Palla et al. 2005). We adopted the partition density D (Ahn, Bagrow, and Lehmann 2010), discussed earlier, as the quality metric for comparison.

Table 2 shows the result comparing our method LMBP with BModel and LC on these real-world networks. As shown, LMBP has the best performance on 13 of the 16 networks in terms of partition density D, BModel performs the best on two networks, and LC performs the best on one network. This result shows the superior performance of our method over the others methods on real-world networks.

Table 2: *Comparison of three methods for detecting link communities on real networks. Here, the greater a D-value, the better. In the table, '–' denotes run time >48 hours or the program ran out of memory.*

Datasets	n	m	c (Ours)	partition density D		
				LMBP	BModel	LC
Zachary's karate club	34	78	19	**0.5405**	0.4496	0.2847
Dolphin social network	62	160	29	**0.3308**	0.3199	0.3155
High school friendship	69	220	41	**0.4932**	0.4576	0.3600
Les Miserables	77	254	27	**0.6772**	0.5518	0.5765
Political books	105	441	90	**0.5151**	0.4958	0.2866
Word adjacencies	112	425	82	**0.2863**	0.2701	0.0632
American college football	115	613	98	0.5432	**0.5508**	0.5500
Jazz musicians collaborations	198	2,742	181	**0.6234**	0.6033	0.4155
C. Elegans neural	297	2,148	308	**0.4067**	0.3553	0.0823
E. coli metabolic	453	2,025	412	0.5626	**0.5983**	0.3333
E-mail network URV	1,133	5,451	910	**0.3846**	0.3186	0.1018
Political blogs	1,490	16,717	921	**0.2690**	0.1971	0.1204
Network science collaborations	1,589	2,742	518	**0.8207**	0.7517	0.6937
Power grid	4,941	6,594	58	0.0344	-3.1e-4	**0.1370**
Protein-protein interaction	2,640	6,600	917	**0.2740**	0.2217	0.1705
Word association	5,017	29,148	5,335	**0.2687**	–	0.0767

4.3 Application

The large real network we considered as an application is the protein-protein interaction (PPI) network of budding yeast *Saccharomyces cerevisiae* (Palla et al. 2005; Xenarios et al. 2000). It contains 2,640 nodes (proteins) and 6,600 links (physical interactions between pairs of proteins).

We used the Gene Ontology (GO) terms (Ashburner et al. 2000), the most elaborate gene function annotations, as domain metadata for quality assessment. The GO terms include information on functions and cellular locations of a gene and biological pathways that a gene may be involved in. The biological significance of a community of genes (nodes) can be measured by the GO terms enriched in the genes in the community. Enrichment of GO terms can be evaluated by a hyper-geometric test (Altman 1991), providing a GO term a p-value to quantify the significance of the term. To quantify the biological significance of a community structure, we used as quality metric the average number of significantly enriched GO terms with p-values less than a given threshold for all communities. The larger this average number of significant GO terms, the more biologically significant the community structure is.

As shown in Figure 4, our method LMBP identified PPI community structures with many more significant GO terms than the LC method and with slightly more significant GO terms than the BModel method under all 10 different p-value thresholds tested. It serves as an additional example of the consistent superior performance of our method over the competing methods compared.

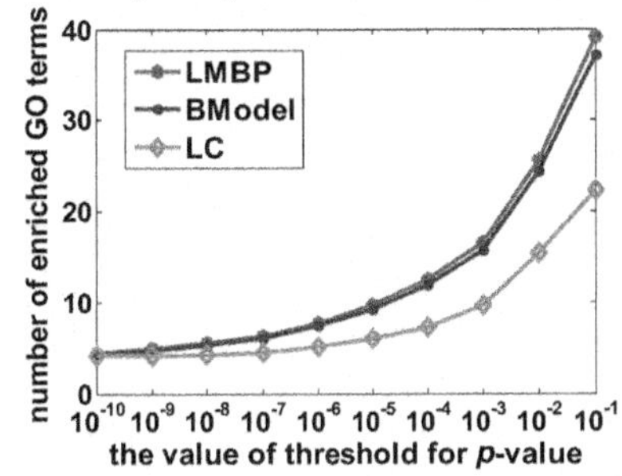

Figure 4: *Comparison of LMBP with BModel and LC on budding yeast PPI network.*

5. Conclusions

We proposed a stochastic model, namely Link-Model or LM, to not only describe the structure of link communities but also deal with heterogeneous sizes of community structures. In our method, we learned the model parameters by a combination of likelihood optimization and expectation-maximization. We extended the basic method by an iterative bipartition to autonomously determine the number of communities. The new method, named as LMBP, is more suitable for large, real networks. We tested LMBP and compared it with two existing competing methods on synthetic benchmark problems and real-world networks including a large biological network. Experimental results demonstrated the superior performance of our method over the competing methods for the detection of link communities in large networks.

There are other quality metrics for link communities (e.g., the extended map equation (Kim and Jeong 2011)) which may be also suitable for our iterative bipartition procedure. We will include in our software an option for choosing different quality metrics to make our method more applicable to various problems. Besides, we will use our method to analyze multimedia and social networks, and try to unfold significant community structures in real life.

Acknowledgments

The work was supported in part by National Basic Research Program (973 Program) of China (2013CB329301), Natural Science Foundation of China (61303110, 61133011, 61373035 and 31300999), National High Technology Research and Development Program (863 Program) of China (2013AA013204), the municipal government of Wuhan, Hubei, China (2014070504020241 and the Talent Development Program), and an internal research grant of Jianghan University, Wuhan, China, as well as by United States National Institutes of Health (R01GM100364).

References

Ahn, Y. Y.; Bagrow, J. P.; and Lehmann, S. 2010. Link Communities Reveal Multiscale Complexity in Networks. *Nature* 466(7307): 761-764.

Altman, D. G. eds. 1991. *Practical Statistics for Medical Research*. London, UK: Chapman& Hall/CRC.

Ashburner, M.; Ball, C. A.; Blake, J. A.; Botstein, D.; Butler, H.; Cherry, J. M.; Davis, A. P.; Dolinski, K.; Dwight, S. S.; Eppig, J. T.; Harris, M. A.; Hill, D. P.; Issel-Tarver, L.; Kasarskis, A.; Lewis, S.; Matese, J. C.; Richardson, J. E.; Ringwald, M.; Rubin, G. M.; Sherlock, G. 2000. Gene Ontology: Tool for the Unification of Biology. *Nature Genetics* 25(1): 25-29.

Ball, B.; Karrer, B.; and Newman, M. E. J. 2011. Efficient and Principled Method for Detecting Communities in Networks. *Physical Review* E 84(3): 036103.

Brunet, J. P.; Tamayo, P.; Golun, T. R.; and Mesirov, J. P. 2004. Metagenes and Molecular Pattern Discovery Using Matrix Factorization. *Proceedings of National Academy of Sciences of the United States of America* 101(12): 4164-4169.

Dempster, A. P.; Laird, N. M.; and Rubin, D. B. 1977. Maximum-likelihood from Incomplete Data via the EM Algorithm. *Journal of the Royal Statistical Society: Series B (Methodological)* 39(1): 1-38.

Evans, T. S.; and Lambiotte, R. 2009. Line Graphs, Link Partitions, and Overlapping Communities. *Physical Review* E 80(1): 016105.

Evans, T. S.; and Lambiotte, R. 2010. Line Graphs of Weighted Networks for Overlapping Communitie. *The European Physical Journal* B 77(2): 265-272.

Fortunato, S. 2010. Community Detection in Graphs. *Physics Reports* 486(3-5): 75-174.

Girvan, M.; and Newman M. E. J. 2002. Community Structure in Social and Biological Networks. *Proceedings of National Academy of Sciences of the United States of America* 99(12): 7821-7826.

He, D.; Liu, D.; Zhang, W.; Jin, D.; and Yang, B. 2012. Discovering Link Communities in Complex Networks by Exploiting Link Dynamics. *Journal Statistical Mechanics: Theory and Experiment* 2012: P10015.

Karrer, B.; and Newman, M. E. J. 2011. Stochastic Blockmodels and Community Structure in Networks. *Physical Review* E 83(1): 016107.

Kim, Y.; and Jeong, H. 2011. Map Equation for Link Communities. *Physical Review* E 84(2): 026110.

Lancichinetti, A.; Fortunato, S.; and Radicchi, F. 2008. Benchmark Graphs for Testing Community Detection Algorithms. *Physical Review* E 78(4): 046110.

Lancichinetti, A.; and Fortunato, S. 2009. Benchmarks for Testing Community Detection Algorithms on Directed and Weighted Graphs with Overlapping Communities. *Physical Review* E 80(1): 016118.

Lancichinetti, A.; Radicchi, F.; Ramasco, J. J.; and Fortunato, S. 2011. Finding Statistically Significant Communities in Networks. *PLoS ONE* 6(4): e18961.

Newman M. E. J.; and Girvan M. 2004. Finding and Evaluating Community Structure in Networks. *Physical Review* E 69(2): 026113.

Newman, M. E. J. 2012. Communities, Modules and Large-scale Structure in Networks. *Nature Physics* 8: 25-31.

Newman, M. E. J. 2013. Real-world Network Data in Newman's Homepage. http://www-personal.umich.edu/~mejn/netdata/

Palla, G.; Derenyi, I.; Farkas, I.; and Vicsek, T. 2005. Uncovering the Overlapping Community Structures of Complex Networks in Nature and Society. *Nature* 435(9): 814-818.

Pan, L.; Wang, C.; Xie, J.; and Liu, M. 2011. Detecting Link Communities Based on Local Approach. In *Proceedings of the 23rd IEEE International Conference on Tools with Artificial Intelligence,* 884-886. Piscataway, NJ, USA: IEEE Press.

Psorakis, I.; Roberts, S.; Ebden, M.; and Sheldon, B. 2011. Overlapping Community Detection Using Bayesian Non-negative Matrix Factorization. *Physical Review* E 83(6): 066114.

Ren, W.; Yan, G.; Liao, X.; and Xiao, L. 2009. Simple Probabilistic Algorithm for Detecting Community Structure. *Physical Review* E 79(3): 036111.

Rosvall, M.; and Bergstrom, C. T. 2008. Maps of Random Walks on Complex Networks Reveal Community Structure. *Proceedings of National Academy of Sciences of the United States of America* 105(4): 1118-1123.

Shen, H.; Cheng, X.; and Guo, J. 2011. Exploring the Structural Regularities in Networks. *Physical Review* E 84(5): 056111.

Tan, V. Y. F.; and Févotte, C. 2013. Automatic Relevance Determination in Nonnegative Matrix Factorization with the β-divergence. *IEEE Transactions on Pattern Analysis and Machine Intelligence* 35(7): 1592-1605.

Wang, F.; Li, T.; Wang, X.; Zhu, S.; and Ding, C. H. Q. 2011. Community Discovery Using Nonnegative Matrix Factorization. *Data Mining and Knowledge Discovery* 22(3): 493-521.

Xenarios, I.; Rice, D. W.; Salwinski L.; Baron M. K.; Marcotte E. M.; Eisenberg D. 2000. DIP: the Database of Interacting Proteins. *Nucleic Acids Research* 28(1): 289-291.

Xie, J.; Kelley S.; and Szymanski B. K. 2013. Overlapping Community Detection in Networks: The State-of-the-Art and Comparative Study. *ACM Computing Survey* 45(4): Article No. 43.

Zhang, Z.; Wang, Y.; and Ahn, Y. Y. 2013. Overlapping Community Detection in Complex Networks Using Symmetric Binary Matrix Factorization. *Physical Review* E 87(6): 062803.

Zhang, Y.; and Yeung, D.-Y. 2012. Overlapping Community Detection via Bounded Nonnegative Matrix Tri-factorization. In *Proceedings of the 18th ACM SIGKDD International Conference on Knowledge Discovery and Data Mining*, 606-614. New York, NY, USA: ACM Press.

Combined Recognition

The proposed system combines model based recognition and search based recognition into one recognition engine.

A variety of learning models can be applied to build recognition models. The deep neural network model gives the best recognition results on ImageNet dataset. Fisher vector as feature plus online SVM also got good results in non-neural-network based approaches. In this paper, to make it easier to compare and reimplementation, we adopt online SVM approach though the dimension of the features we are using is much lower than a typical Fisher Vector. We trains M models for the M entities via online SVM, and the algorithm is briefly described as below. More details about the SGD based online SVM learning can be found in (Crammer et al. 2001 and 2006).

To build image index, we extract up to 300 T2S2 visual words per image. We then build an inverted index that maps each visual word to a list of images. The algorithm for using the inverted index to do recognition is as follows:

Algorithm 1: Search based image recognition

Input: An image I, and an inverted index *Index*
1: Extract visual words from I, denoted as $\{\boldsymbol{w}_i\}$.
2: For each $\boldsymbol{w}_i$, find the list of images in the *Index*, denoted by: $\boldsymbol{L}_i = \{(\boldsymbol{I}_{ij}, \boldsymbol{h}_{ij})\}$, where $\boldsymbol{h}_{ij}$ is the visual words count in image $\boldsymbol{I}_{ij}$.
3: Merge $\{\boldsymbol{L}_i\}$ by summing up the visual word hit counts of the same images, and order the images by the hit counts in descending order:

$$\textbf{sum}\ \{\boldsymbol{h}_{ij}\}\ \text{group by}\ \boldsymbol{I}_{ij}\ \textbf{from}\ \{\boldsymbol{L}_i\}\ \textbf{order by}\ \boldsymbol{h}_{ij}. \quad (3)$$

4: Get the entity names for the top images in the list and output it as the recognition result, and the confidence score is estimated by the number of hits divided by the number of visual words.

Combined Recognition

Most image recognition works use model based approaches and very few researchers reported search based approaches (Wang et al. 2007). The advantage of model based approach is that the learned models are "abstract" representations of the entities and are powerful to handle object models with reasonable variations. On the other hand, the disadvantage is that some outstanding "prototypes" will not be captured by the abstracted models if the amount of training data for these prototypes is not sufficient. These "prototypes" actually can be well handled by search based approaches if near duplicates and/or partial duplicates can be found in the training set. Search based approaches also scale better as the index operation is less expensive than model recognition.

In the proposed image recognition system, we attempt to combine both approaches, aiming at leveraging the large amount of automatically selected training data in a more effective way. There are two difficulties in combining these two approaches.

First, search based approach requires a training set with high accuracy and large coverage at the same time. However, these two requirements are contradict to each other. Second, it is unclear on how to combine the outputs from model based classification and inverted index search. The predicted scores for the candidate labels in the classification results are often not in accordant with the probabilities whether the corresponding predictions are correct. Theoretic research in combing the two results are still under developing. In Prajna, we propose the following empirical approach to estimate a "relative confidence score" for model based classification and calibrate it with the weighted confidence score from search based recognition.

The basic idea is to estimate how "significant" the classification score is by comparing the score with all other scores from the model vectors of other entities. A naive way to get a relative confidence score of a prediction is to compare the score of the top one result and that of the second result. Larger difference indicates higher relative confidence score and vice versus. However, multiple entity names may be related to one particular image. For example, for a picture of a lion and tiger, the scores of lion and tiger may be both high and close to each other. To solve this, we check more than one consecutive pairs and also take the "similarity" of the entity pairs into account. Suppose the prediction scores of top n entities are $t_1, t_2, \ldots, t_n$, then the relative confidence score of this prediction is defined as:

$$C^{(r)} = \max\{t_i\} + \alpha \max\{t_i - t_{i+1}\} - \beta \sum_{i \neq j} \frac{D(E_i, E_j)}{|t_i - t_j| + \gamma}. \quad (4)$$

On the right side of equation (3), the first term aims to keep the information in the original prediction score, the second term promote predictions with outstanding scores, and the third term penalizes predictions that give similar scores to "distinct" entities, where the distance between two entities is estimated by the average pair-wise cluster distances. (α, β, γ) are empirical numbers. By using the relative confidence score, the combine recognition scheme becomes:

Algorithm 2: Combined recognition

1: Prediction by model based classification.
2: Get relative confidence score $\boldsymbol{C}^{(r)}$ for the prediction. If $\boldsymbol{C}^{(r)}$ is bigger than a threshold, then output result. Otherwise, go to 3.
3: Get an entity list by searching over the index. Calculate a weighted confidence scores. If the top score is higher than $\boldsymbol{\eta C}^{(r)}$, output the search based recognition result; otherwise, output model based recognition results. $\boldsymbol{\eta}$ is an empirical parameter.

System Level Considerations

In this section, we will discuss system-level considerations, particularly on how to scale out the system and make the system extensible.

Distributed Computing

A large number of image can be collected from search engines and social media portals. For example, for an entity set with 1000 entities, if we collect 6000 images per entity, there will be 6 million images in total. If we are dealing with multiple entity sets, the computation cost can be huge. It is usually impractical for the entire computation be completed in one machine in a reasonable period of time. To solve this, we used a map-reduce based distributed system with thousands of nodes to complete most of the tasks. Different parallelization methods are applied for different steps according to the natural and complexity of the processes, as shown in Figure 4. For example, feature extraction and within entity clustering can be easily executed using direct parallelization approach; inter-cluster feature extraction and inter-entity propagation need to be run in divide and merge manner; Online SVM training can be parallelized using divide and aggregate strategy.

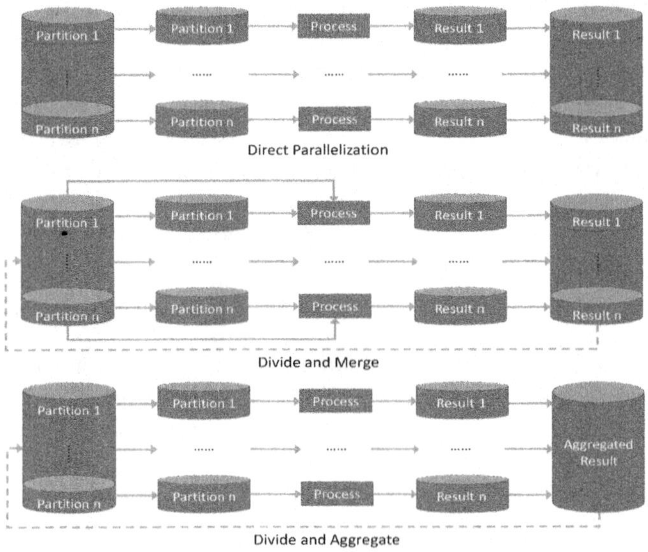

Figure 4. Three parallelization strategies.

Extending Entity Set on the Fly

If some entities that are related to the current entity set are not supported by the current image recognition system, it is easy to add the new entities into the existing system, because that all the steps, including getting image list, downloading, feature extraction, clustering, cluster feature extraction, cluster classification, inverted indexing, and SVM model training, can be done incrementally. Therefore, new entities can be added to the system at low computation and time cost.

Handling Multiple Entity Sets

Though we mainly use "Seattle", an outdoor scenery entity set as example, the system described can work on arbitrary entity set selected by the users. We have also considered the problem to make Prajna work for more than one entity sets at the same time in one system. The primary issue is how to determine the right entity sets (one or more) to do the combined recognition when there are multiple models and indexes available in the system.

There are a few potential approaches that can be adopted here. One approach is to use a multi-layer classification, in which a top layer classifier determines which entity subsets are to be further applied. An alternative approach is to use inverted indexes to determine which entity set should be used. That is, we will search for the given image from the indexes of all entity sets, and the entity subsets that have the most number of matched images or visual words will be selected. A third approach is to run classifications on all entity sets, and compare the relative confidence scores to pick one or more entity sets. We can also combine one or more of the above approaches to fuse the recognition result.

Experiments

The Prajna system has a large number of components. Due to space limit, we will focus on evaluating how image selection and combined recognition improve the overall recognition accuracy.

Evaluation Datasets

Four entity sets are used for evaluation: ImageNet animal subset, Disneyland attractions, Seattle attractions and Aquarium sea creatures. For ImageNet subset, we select all the animal related entities from the ImageNet 1K dataset 0, which has 163 synsets. The reason to pick ImageNet dataset is that it has a manually labeled training set, validation set and test set, so we can compare and evaluate the accuracy of the system built upon unlabeled data. For Seattle entity set, we manually labeled 5000 images obtained from Google image search as the test dataset. Due to the high cost of manual labeling, for the other two entity sets, clicked images from Clickture-Full dataset (Hua 2013) is used as the test data.

For ImageNet dataset, there are 1.3M images in the training set, 50K images in the evaluation set, as well as 150K image in test set for the 1000 synsets. After selecting all the images that are associated with the 163 animal related synsets, we get 211.9K images for training, 8.15K for validation, and 24.45K for testing. For the click data from Clickture, we use the corresponding animal names to retrieve the clicked images in Clickture.

Up to 6150 images per entity are collected, among which (up to) 6000 are from Flickr and 150 are from Bing image search. For ImageNet animal subsets, each individual animal name of a synset is used as one query and then the search results of all the queries for the same synset are merged.

Performance Comparison

In the first experiment, we compare different image selection approaches on the ImageNet animal subset. We will also compare our results with the ones based on ImageNet labeled training data and clicked data in Clickture. As there is no other published research for dealing with highly-noisy labelled web image data, we do not compare our approaches with existing approaches in the literature.

Evaluation on ImageNet animal subset

Table 1 shows the experimental settings in terms of the sources of the training data, image selection approaches, as well as the recognition engines. All evaluations are run on the ImageNet test set.

There are indeed quite a few parameters need to set empirically, which is inevitable for a complex real-world end-to-end system. Thanks to the high computation power of the computer cluster, a parameter sweeping procedure is done to find the best parameters on the ImageNet validation dataset based on experimental setting 10 in Table 1. The below table shows the parameters as well as the sweeping intervals. To speed up parameter sweeping, clustering and propagation results are stored as intermediate data and then different parameters are applied in image selection, learning and combined recognition steps. The best parameters obtained on the validate set is 0.15, 0.8, 0.9, 20, 0.01, 3, 7, and 0.9.

Table 1. Experiment settings.

ID	Training Set/Image Selection	Recog. Engine
Ex01	ImageNet training set (animal subset)	Model + Index
Ex02	Clickture-Full	Model + Index
Ex03	Flickr/Bing unfiltered	Model + Index
Ex04	Flickr/Bing + cluster selection	Model + Index
Ex05	Flickr/Bing + propagation	Model + Index
Ex06	Flickr/Bing + cluster selection/propagation	Model
Ex07	Flickr/Bing + cluster selection/propagation	Index
Ex08	Flickr only + cluster selection/ propagation	Model + Index
Ex09	Bing only + cluster selection/ propagation	Model + Index
Ex10	Flickr/Bing + Cluster selection/ propagation	Model + Index

Table 2. Parameter sweeping.

ID	Parameter	Range	Interval
Th1	Cluster based selection classifier	[-1.0, 1.0]	0.05
Th2	Intra-entity propagation selection	[0.1, 1.0]	0.1
Th3	Inter-entity propagation selection	[0.1, 1.0]	0.1
Th4	Online SVM partition number	[20, 50]	5
Th5	Learning rate	[0.001, 0.1]	10 times
Th6	Rounds of learning on each node	[1, 10]	1
Th7	Rounds of model averaging	[1, 20]	1
Th8	Relative confidence threshold	[0.5, 4]	0.1

Table 3 shows the recognition accuracy on the ImageNet test set (animal subset) and the actual size of training data used. From this table, it can be observed that: (1) Ex10, the final proposed approach, gives the second highest recognition accuracy. It is slightly lower than the accuracy based on the ImageNet manually labeled data. The result shows leveraging large amount of noisy data on the Internet with a selection step is a promising solution to automatically generate training data, thus potentially we can expand image recognition to any given set of entities as long as we can collect sufficient number of images from the Internet (and the entities are somewhat model-able by the visual features). From Ex10, even the cleaned data set is not as accurate as the manually labeled one, but it has a larger amount of data, which provides useful additional variation to build an effective classifier. The gap between Ex01 and Ex10 may also indicates that there is still room to improve in the image selection step. (2) Ex03 has much lower accuracy than Ex10, which shows image selection is essential to ensure the quality of the training data. (3) Ex02 is worse than Ex01, Ex06, Ex08 and Ex10, which proves the volume and variations of clicked data are not sufficient to capture the visual variations of the entities. (4) Ex10 is better than Ex04 and Ex05, which shows combining clustering based selection and propagation based selection boosts the accuracy. The difference between Ex04 and 05 shows clustering based selection is more effective for noise removal. An explanation is that propagation based approach is less effective when the noise level is high. (5) Ex10 is better than Ex06 and Ex07, which means combining model-based recognition and search-based recognition improves the recognition performance. (6) Ex10 is better than Ex08 and Ex09, which shows both Flickr data and Bing data contributes to the performance and Flickr contributes more due to more images from Flickr crawling.

Table 3. Experiment results.

ID	Train. Image	Sel. Ratio	Top 1 Acc.	Top 5 Acc.
Ex01	211.9K	-	0.52581	0.80822
Ex02	69.7K	-	0.28290	0.54233
Ex03	1311.1K	100%	0.37146	0.60123
Ex04	920.3K	70.2%	0.47894	0.75431
Ex05	1101.8K	84.0%	0.42540	0.68417
Ex06	808.9K	61.7%	0.46030	0.73106
Ex07	808.9K	61.7%	0.20112	0.46978
Ex08	750.3K	64.6%	0.48133	0.77686
Ex09	98.5K	66.7%	0.32986	0.57636
Ex10	808.9K	61.7%	0.51526	0.79648

Evaluation on Other Datasets

In the second experiment, we evaluate the accuracy of the proposed framework on the other three entity sets: Seattle attractions on a manually labeled dataset and click dataset from Clickture, Disneyland attractions and Aquarium sea creatures on Clickture dataset. The focus is on evaluating the image selection approaches as there are no sufficient manually labeled training datasets for these three entity sets,

Table 3 shows the evaluation results on these three entity sets under setting Ex10 (with image selection) and Ex03 (no image selection). It is observed that image selection step pays a significant role in improving the final recognition accuracy. In addition, we can see that with the increase of the size of the entity set, the recognition accuracy decreases significantly. One reason that Disneyland entity set has low recognition rate is that many entities have limited number of images collected from the Internet (especially from Flickr), such as "Café Rix" (a restaurant in Disneyland park, 12 image) and "BouTiKi" (a store, 48 images).

In the above experiments, the manually labeled dataset and click dataset are both derived from search engines, which is not a perfect evaluation setting for Prajna as most of the images we are using to train the system are from Flickr, which have a different image-label characteristics (e.g., containing many personal photos). Search results and click log data also contain image types that do not usually present in Flickr, e.g., clipart images. That explains why we get better accuracy on animal set compared with these three entity sets. In addition, if we train DNN recognition models directly from the filtered training data, we should get a higher recognition accuracy.

Table 3. Results on Seattle, Disneyland & Aquarium.

Entity Set (#)	Selection	Test Set	Top 1 Acc.	Top 5 Acc.
Seattle (106)	Yes	Manual 5K	0.47813	0.73902
	No		0.32342	0.54239
	Yes	Clickture 2.4K	0.40517	0.65297
	No		0.29368	0.51980
Disneyland (623)	Yes	Clickture 112.8K	0.25834	0.50322
	No		0.10136	0.23169
Aquarium (239)	Yes	Clickture 46.9K	0.37253	0.61458
	No		0.26878	0.51970

Conclusion

In this paper, we proposed an end-to-end system "Prajna" to mine knowledge from the Internet and build image recognition systems with minimal human involvement. Potentially the system can recognize any given set of entities as long as we can collect sufficient large number of (noisy) image data from the Internet. The basic idea is to automatically select relevant and informative training data from the noisy data by leveraging the intrinsic characteristics of the data distribution as well as the correlations among images and labels. We apply well known distributed computing strategies so that it is feasible to build a recognition engine for a given set of entities in a reasonable period of time.

Prajna uses the entire Internet as a knowledge base (though noisy) to mine structured knowledge of image data. We believe that this is a promising direction to build real-world image recognition systems as well as to power recognition related applications (such as photo tagging). Prajna represents our first attempt to build image recognition system from web data, and there are still rooms to improve for many Prajna modules. For example, we can potentially adapt selection parameter according to the distribution of the original noisy dataset; make use of the textual metadata of the images; use more sophisticated approaches to combine model based approach and search based approach; balance computation cost on each node to further speed up the system building process; learn entity set specific features for recognition; automate approaches to form an entity set for a given topic; estimate the accuracy of the recognition system without labeled data, etc.. We hope this work will inspire more researchers and groups to use web data to mine structured knowledge.

References

Ahn, L. von; Dabbish, L. 2004. Labeling images with a computer game. SIGCHI.

Chua, T.-S.; et al. 2009. NUS-WIDE: A Real-World Web Image Database from National University of Singapore. ACM CIVR.

Chen, X.; Shrivastava, A.; Gupta, A. 2013. NEIL: Extracting Visual Knowledge from Web Data. ICCV.

Crammer, K.; Singer, Y. 2001. On the Algorithmic Implementation of Multi-Class SVMs. JMLR, Vol 2, pp. 265-292.

Crammer, K.; Dekel, O.; Keshet, J.; Shalev-Shwartz, S.; Singer, Y. 2006. Online Passive-Aggressive Algorithms. JMLR, Vol 7.

Deng, J.; et al. 2009. ImageNet: A Large-Scale Hierarchical Image Database. IEEE Computer Vision and Pattern Recognition.

Divvala, S.K.; et al. 2014. Learning Everything about Anything: Webly-Supervised Visual Concept Learning. CVPR.

Griffin, G.; Holub, A.; and Perona, P.. 2007. Caltech-256 object category dataset. Technical Report 7694, Caltech.

Hall, K. B.; Gilpin, S.; Mann, G. 2010. MapReduce/Bigtable for Distributed Optimization. NIPS Workshop on Learning on Cores, Clusters, and Clouds.

Hua, X.-S.; et al. Clickage: Towards Bridging Semantic and Intent Gaps via Mining Click Logs of Search Engines. 2013. ACM MM.

Hsu, W. H.; et a;. 2007. Video Search Reranking through Random Walk over Document-Level Context Graph. ACM Multimedia.

Jing, Y. S.; and Baluja, S. 2008. VisualRank: Applying PageRank to Large-Scale Image Search. Transon Pattern Analysis and Machine Intelligence.

Krizhevsky, A.; Sutskever, I.; Hinton , G.E. 2012. ImageNet Classification with Deep Convolutional Neural Networks. NIPS.

Le, Q.; Ranzato, M.; Monga, R.; Devin, M.; Chen, K.; Corrado, G.; Dean, J.; Ng, A. 2012. Building high-level features using large scale unsupervised learning. ICML.

Li, X. R.; Snoek, C. G. M.; and Worring, M. 2008. Learning Tag Relevance by Neighbor Voting for Social Image Retrieval. In Proceedings of the ACM ICMR.

Liu, D.; Hua, X.-S.; Yang, L.; Wang, M.; Zhang, H.-J. 2009. Tag Ranking. WWW.

Liu, D.; et al. 2011. Image Retagging via Collaborative Tag Propagation. IEEE Transaction on Multimedia (TMM), 13(1):82-91.

Russell, B.; et al. 2007. LabelMe: a database and web-based tool for image annotation. International Journal of Computer Vision.

Tang, J.; Yan, S.; Hong, R.; Qi, G.-J.; and Chua, T.-S. 2009. Inferring semantic concepts from community-contributed images and noisy tags. ACM Multimedia.

Tian, X.; Yang, L.; Wang, J.; Yang, Y.; Wu, X.; Hua, X.-S. 2008. Bayesian Video Search Reranking. ACM Multimedia.

Torralba, A.; Fergus, R.; and Freeman, W. 2008. 80 million tiny images: A large data set for nonparametric object and scene recognition. PAMI, 30(11):1958–1970.

Wang, X.-J.; Zhang, L.; Jing, F.; Ma, W.-Y. 2007. AnnoSearch: Image Auto-Annotation by Search. CVPR.

Winder, S.; Brown, M. 2007. Learning Local Image Descriptors. IEEE CVPR.

Weston, J. ; Makadia, A.; and Yee H. 2013. Label Partitioning For Sublinear Ranking. ICML.

Weston, J.; Bengio, S.; Usunier, N. 2011. Wsabie: Scaling Up To Large Vocabulary Image Annotation. Intl. Joint Conference on Artificial Intelligence (IJCAI).

Proceedings of the Twenty-Ninth AAAI Conference on Artificial Intelligence

Kernel Density Estimation for Text-Based Geolocation

Mans Hulden
University of Colorado Boulder
mans.hulden@colorado.edu

Miikka Silfverberg
University of Helsinki
miikka.silfverberg@helsinki.fi

Jerid Francom
Wake Forest University
francojc@wfu.edu

Abstract

Text-based geolocation classifiers often operate with a grid-based view of the world. Predicting document location of origin based on text content on a geodesic grid is computationally attractive since many standard methods for supervised document classification carry over unchanged to geolocation in the form of predicting a most probable grid cell for a document. However, the grid-based approach suffers from sparse data problems if one wants to improve classification accuracy by moving to smaller cell sizes. In this paper we investigate an enhancement of common methods for determining the geographic point of origin of a text document by kernel density estimation. For geolocation of tweets we obtain a improvements upon non-kernel methods on datasets of U.S. and global Twitter content.

Introduction

Text-based geolocation has received much attention recently. This is partly attributable to the availability of large geotagged datasets through Wikipedia and Twitter, which allows the evaluation of possibilities of geolocating a document solely through its text content.

The problem of geolocating a document has often been approached as a supervised classification problem where the task is to associate a document with a discrete cell of the earth's surface, given some previous training data for which the coordinates are known. Many standard classification approaches such as Naive Bayes can be directly adapted to address the problem of placing a document of unknown origin on a geodesic grid. The grid-based approach has also been shown to be quite competitive (Serdyukov, Murdock, and Van Zwol 2009; Wing and Baldridge 2011; Roller et al. 2012) with other more complex models, such as ones based on topic modeling (Eisenstein et al. 2010; Eisenstein, Ahmed, and Xing 2011) and more involved feature engineering (Han, Cook, and Baldwin 2012). However, discretizing the world into fixed-size bins entails a trade-off between accuracy and the amount of data available—the smaller and potentially more accurate the grid becomes, the more acute is the data sparsity problem for each cell. This has been partly addressed by work such as Roller et al. (2012), which uses a grid that adaptively shrinks in size so that each cell accommodates roughly the same number of training documents. In this work we address the data sparsity problem through smoothing out relevant features on a geodesic grid by kernel density estimation, while maintaining the grid model. We show that kernel density estimation offers consistent and robust results compared with completely discretized models. The amount of bookkeeping is also minimal compared with many other methods to handle grid data sparsity.

The paper is laid out as follows: first, we examine the basic geolocation of text documents using Naive Bayes and Kullback-Leibler divergence, and also introduce our adaptation of kernel density estimation to these methods. In the following sections we present the data and the details behind our experiments for geolocation using the U.S. GEOTEXT data set and a global WORLDTWEETS data set. This is followed by the results and discussion.

Geolocation on a geodesic grid

In the current work we discretize the earth's surface into square cells C that come in various sizes depending on the experiment; $10° \times 10°, 5° \times 5°, 2° \times 2°, 1° \times 1°$, and $0.5° \times 0.5°$.

Under this model, we treat geolocating a text document as a classification task where the object is to place an unknown text document in the most appropriate cell $\hat{c} \in C$. In our experiments, the features we use for classification are simply the individual words in a document. Although we only use words, there is in principle no reason why additional features, linguistic and non-linguistic (Eriksson et al. 2010; Youn, Mark, and Richards 2009), could not be integrated in the methods described below.

We briefly look at two popular approaches for classifying documents on a grid—Naive Bayes and Kullback-Leibler divergence—and discuss our adaptation of these to use kernel density estimates. Other classification methods can naturally be used. However, given the large number of classes in the task (e.g. 259,200 for $0.5° \times 0.5°$ granularity), simpler methods such as Naive Bayes are more practicable.

Applications

Since the Twitter platform started providing information about the geographic location of tweeters based on self-

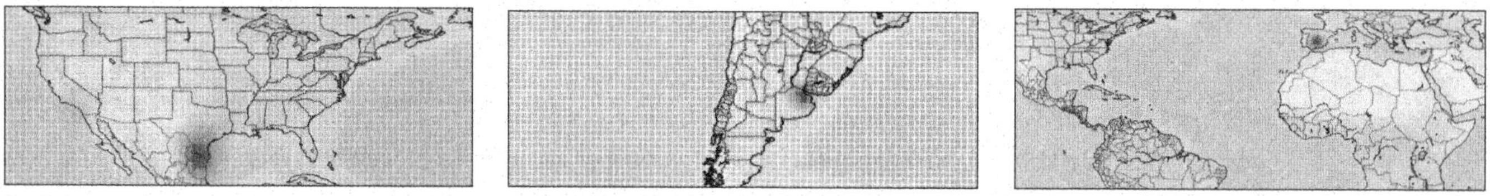

`lmao no` **`mames`**

`porque no te vas a cagar` **`boludo`** `despues queres que hablee`

`venga,` `va mañana me animo a ir con coleta`

Figure 1: Classification output identifying Spanish dialects and regional usage (Mexican, Argentine, and Peninsular Spanish) in three tweets using the WORLDTWEETS corpus. The most geographically indicative words are boldfaced.

reports or built-in GPSs in devices, we have witnessed a flurry of creative applications that take advantage of this new resource. Most applications involve supervised learning algorithms that identify tweet locations from words. The topics of investigation have included the study of language variation along various dimensions: socioeconomic (Alis and Lim 2013), regional (Hong et al. 2012; Kondor et al. 2013), and social variables of language (Eisenstein 2013). Others have tapped into the opportunities of supporting language and cultural education through knowledge of the geographic origin of tweets (Grosseck and Holotescu 2008; Borau et al. 2009). The possibility of identifying disaster and crisis tweets has also been researched (Corvey et al. 2012). One of the intended applications of the current work is the ability to perform fine-grained dialect distinctions automatically, providing opportunities for automatic text classification on non-tweet material. Figure 1 shows an example output of our tweet location classifier tool GEOLOC, discussed in this paper, when trained on tweets from around the globe and provided with short Spanish-language tweets from Mexico, Argentina, and Spain.

Multinomial Naive Bayes

To geolocate a document with words $w_1, \ldots, w_n$ using Naive Bayes and words as features, we assume the standard document classification approach of estimating

$$\hat{c} = \underset{c \in C}{\operatorname{argmax}} \hat{P}(c) \prod_i \hat{P}(w_i|c) \tag{1}$$

The prior probability of a document originating from a cell $\hat{P}(c)$ is obtained by observing the number of documents emanating from a cell in the training data, divided by the total document count $|T|$.[1]

$$\hat{P}(c) = \frac{\#(t,c) + \alpha}{|T| + \alpha|C|} \tag{2}$$

Likewise, the conditional estimate $\hat{P}(w_i|c)$ is obtained from the counts of words found in training documents in a particular cell.

$$\hat{P}(w_i|c) = \frac{\#(w_i,c) + \beta}{\sum_{j \in V} \#(w_j,c) + \beta|V|} \tag{3}$$

[1] We use $\#()$ to denote counts.

Here, α and β are our cell and word priors, respectively, and V is the vocabulary seen during training.

Kullback-Leibler divergence

In classifying with Kullback-Leibler (KL) divergence, we try to find a cell whose word distribution matches the distribution of the document. Using the definition of KL-divergence

$$KL(P||Q) = \sum_i P(i) log \frac{P(i)}{Q(i)} \tag{4}$$

we assume P to be the document's distribution of words and Q a given earth cell's distribution of words. Then, for a current document D to be classified, we estimate the probability of the ith word P_{di} to be $\#(w_i \text{ in } D)/|D|$, and the divergence becomes

$$\sum_i P_{di} \log(\frac{P_{di} \sum_{j \in V} \#(w_j,c) + \beta|V|}{\#(w_i,c) + \beta}) \tag{5}$$

using the same quantities as in Naive Bayes for the distribution of a cell's words $\hat{P}(w_i|c)$ in the denominator. Classifying a document entails finding the cell with minimum KL-divergence.

Kernel density estimation

As mentioned above, when geolocating documents with the above methods, using smaller grid sizes leads to an immediate sparse data problem since very few features/words are observed in each cell. The idea behind kernel density estimation is to smooth out the counts of documents and words over a larger region, while simultaneously being able to maintain a small cell size for accurate location classification. Figure 3 illustrates this smoothing effect by showing the distribution of a feature as a single point (in red) and as a density resulting from kernel density estimation.

To this end, when estimating $\hat{P}(c)$ and $\hat{P}(w_i|c)$ in the Naive Bayes and KL-divergence classification, instead of counts, we assign each document and feature a mass in a cell based on a Gaussian that is centered on the actual location where that feature or document was observed. We use a two-dimensional spherical (isotropic) Gaussian kernel to assign mass to each cell: the Gaussian has its means centered at the latitude and longitude of the observation, and each cell

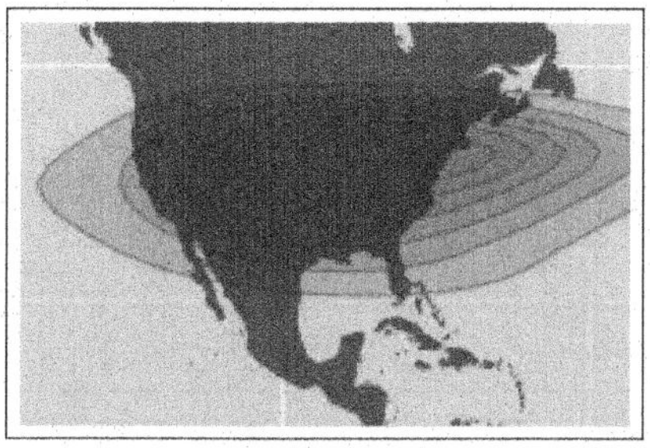

Figure 2: Aggregate density for an English word occurring throughout the United States.

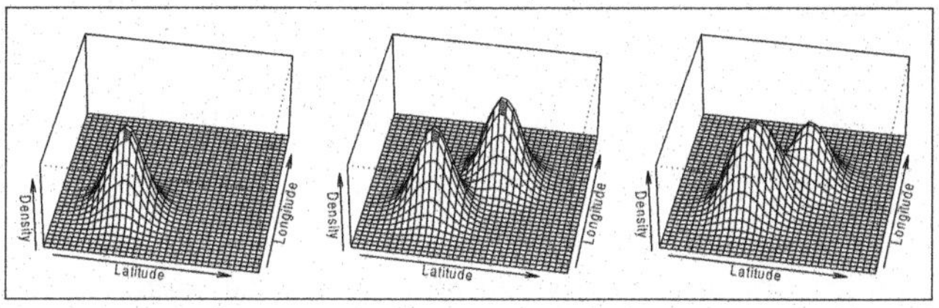

Figure 3: Illustration of areal smoothing effect for features with kernel density estimation, showing the how the contribution of a word feature is spread out over a large area.

receives the corresponding density measured at that cell's midpoint. We then replace our earlier count-based estimates with the respective kernel-based ones:

$$\hat{P}(c) = \frac{\hat{f}_H(t, c) + \alpha}{|T| + \alpha|C|} \tag{6}$$

and

$$\hat{P}(w_i|c) = \frac{\hat{f}_H(w_i, c) + \beta}{\sum_{j \in V} \hat{f}_H(w_j, c) + \beta|V|} \tag{7}$$

Here, the kernel function $\hat{f}_H$ is simply the sum of the relevant individual Gaussians at the midpoint (x, y) of cell c of the form

$$f(x, y) = \frac{1}{2\pi\sigma^2} e^{\frac{-\left((x-\mu_x)^2+(y-\mu_y)^2\right)}{2\sigma^2}} \tag{8}$$

where μ_x and μ_y are the observation coordinates.

We assume a spherical kernel function as a good preliminary evaluation entry point to the overall usefulness of kernel density methods as spherical Gaussians can be calculated quickly and only have one parameter to tune.[2]

Data

For our first experiments, we have used the GeoText geotagged corpus. GeoText is a corpus of 377,616 geotagged tweets originating within the United States by 9,475 users recorded from the Twitter API in March 2010, as documented in Eisenstein et al. (2010). A document in the dataset

[2]The only tunable parameter is a single standard deviation σ, expressing the width of the dispersion of mass of an observation.

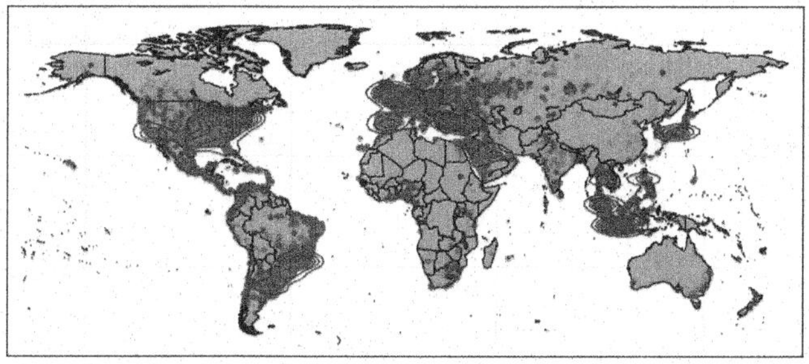

Figure 4: Density map of 1 million tweets sampled from the larger WorldTweets dataset.

consists of all tweets from a single user, concatenated. We use the training/test/dev splits that come with the dataset and are used elsewhere, yielding 5,685 documents in the training set and 1,895 documents in the development and test sets. While the corpus is relatively small—the raw data occupying 54MB—it has the advantage of public availability.[3]

For the second experiment, we used a larger global set of geolocated tweets, WorldTweets, collected during three weeks beginning at the end of January 2014. The set contains 4,870,032 randomly selected geotagged tweets from a wide variety of languages and locations around the globe (as seen in figure 4). We held out 10,000 tweets for development and 10,000 for testing. In this data set, each tweet was considered a separate document (unlike GeoText where tweets from one user are combined into one document).

Preprocessing of both the GeoText and WorldTweets textual data included a basic cleanup and tokenization by simply replacing all non-alphanumeric symbols (except `#`, `@`, `'`) with single spaces, lowercasing all Latin characters, and segmenting on whitespace.

Replication

The program code and relevant instructions for running all experiments are available at our website.[4] We release the main program, GeoLoc, as a stand-alone utility for geolocating arbitrary documents using the methods described in this paper, and also the WorldTweets dataset.

Details

In classifying tweet documents using the above methods we also consider some additional useful implementation details that other authors have taken advantage of.

When classifying a document in a cell $\hat{c}$, we will not assign the actual midpoint coordinates of the cell to the document. Rather, we will use the centroid of all documents in that cell seen during training time. Using a centroid instead of the midpoint of a most likely cell to estimate location has been noted to yield good results (Roller et al. 2012), which is confirmed by our experiments on the development set.

[3]Unfortunately, some larger data sets, such as UTGeo2011 (Roller et al. 2012), are not publicly available.

[4]http://geoloc-kde.googlecode.com

To include a word type in the model, we require a minimum number of occurrences of it during training. Such a threshold has been found to have a large impact by other authors (Wing and Baldridge 2011). Additionally for the GEOTEXT corpus experiments,, we use a list of 572 stopwords for English that we ignore during training. The list originates in the *Textgrounder* project (Roller et al. 2012). In all tests, unknown words during classification are simply discarded, as our preliminary tests on the development set showed consistently worse results with attempts to model unknown word distributions.

Tuning

We tune the following parameters for the density estimation method: (1) the standard deviation of the two-dimensional Gaussian: σ, (2) the vocabulary threshold h, (3) the prior β for words. The document/cell prior α is fixed at 1.

Methods

We tune the parameters on the development set separately for both the standard and density-based methods. In total, we report on four models: NAIVEBAYES—Standard Naive Bayes, KULLBACK-LEIBLER—KL-divergence, NAIVEBAYES$_{kde2d}$—Naive Bayes using kernel density estimation, and KULLBACK-LEIBLER$_{kde2d}$—KL-divergence using kernel density estimation, each described above. In all approaches, we tune for mean location error (rather than median). Table 2 shows the mean errors on the development sets in kilometers with varying vocabulary thresholds and grid sizes. As a baseline, we use the strategy of always choosing the cell with largest document count seen in training.

A coarse grid search over σ, β, and h (threshold) was used to fix σ, after which a finer-grained 3d grid search was used to tune β , h (0-20), and the grid size in degrees (0.5,1,2,5,10) (part of it is shown in table 2). The cell prior α was fixed from the beginning at 1.0 as it has very little effect on the GEOTEXT datasets where documents are long and the prior gets quickly overwhelmed by the data as one 'document' consists of many concatenated tweets from a single user.

	Grid size				
Thr.	0.5°	1°	2°	5°	10°
0	895.0	889.1	900.8	914.0	1029.8
2	800.2	797.5	798.6	832.7	1029.0
3	753.5	748.9	752.1	795.6	1030.0
5	760.7	**747.7**	756.2	782.1	1021.6
10	789.5	788.91	785.8	783.6	1002.9
20	894.4	887.1	890.7	873.0	1014.1

Table 2: Mean error (km) on the development set for the Naive Bayes classifier with kernel density estimation using different vocabulary thresholds and grid resolutions.

Results

The main results of our experiments of the test set of GEOTEXT are given in table 1. Following the results from tuning on the development set, the grid sizes were set to 5 degrees for the non-kernel experiments and 1 degree for the kernel-based ones—for comparison, we also report the kernel-based version results on a 5-degree grid size. Overall, the effect of the kernel-based approach is reflected primarily in the mean error distance, while the median error is roughly similar in both types of approaches. Also, there is little significant difference between the Naive Bayes and KL-divergence approaches. We see an improvement to prior work on the same data set both as regards the mean error and the median error. The KL-divergence without kernel density estimation produces the smallest median error at 333.4km, while NAIVEBAYES$_{kde2d}$ yields the smallest mean error at 764.8km. The fact that KL-divergence slightly outperforms Naive Bayes in the non-kernel setting is a result also found in Wing and Baldridge (2011).

We note, however, that the GEOTEXT data set appears to be too limited and non-standardized to be used for very reliable comparison between algorithms and methods, especially that of different authors. We found large fluctuations of performance on the development set based on text preparation factors such as text normalization, whether to retain user name and hashtag references that sometimes occur within tweets, punctuation removal strategy, and lowercasing. Indeed, these factors were often more important than the specific choice of algorithm, which motivates repetition of the test on the larger WORLDTWEETS. As mentioned above, in our final experiments, the tweets were used as is, with only lowercasing, punctuation removal and tokenization.

In the results for the larger global data set (table 3), WORLDTWEETS, we see a much larger, consistent improvement with the kernel density method, with the Naive Bayes kernel density classifier producing the smallest mean and median error.

The kernel-based methods require a much larger model. This is because for each word, the density for that word in each cell for the whole grid needs to be stored. Naturally, these matrices containing the densities are relatively sparse and have significant weight only near the means of the observation and hence occupy little space individually. Despite the larger model size, the kernel-based methods are not significantly slower at classification time. If classification speed is less of an issue compared with memory, the kernels can also be calculated on-demand. Doing so slows down classification time to roughly 0.5s per document from 0.04s when pre-calculated (at 1° × 1°) on GEOTEXT.

Discussion

The general areal smoothing approach presented here could also be extended to include frameworks where several individually inaccurate sources of knowledge are combined to yield a location prediction. This could include IP address information, discussion topic information, census data, and similar material. Under such scenarios, the density measure could be of arbitrary shape—e.g. the precise known area of an IP address pool, boundaries of a city, boundaries of a time

Method	Mean error(km)	Median error(km)	Grid size	Threshold
Most frequent cell	1157.4	756.5	5°	N/A
NAIVEBAYES	855.0	352.3	5°	5
KULLBACK-LEIBLER	802.0	**333.4**	5°	5
NAIVEBAYES$_{kde2d}$	**764.8**	357.2	1°	5
KULLBACK-LEIBLER$_{kde2d}$	781.2	380.0	1°	5
NAIVEBAYES$_{kde2d}$	767.0	397.1	5°	5
KULLBACK-LEIBLER$_{kde2d}$	767.3	400.0	5°	5

Table 1: Performance of different methods on the test set of GEOTEXT.

Method	Mean(km)	Median(km)
Most frequent cell	10929.8	11818.9
NAIVEBAYES	2678.9	637.0
KULLBACK-LEIBLER	2777.6	681.2
NAIVEBAYES$_{kde2d}$	**2429.0**	**531.7**
KULLBACK-LEIBLER$_{kde2d}$	2691.0	578.0

Table 3: Performance of different methods on the test set of WORLDTWEETS. Grid size is 1° and word threshold 5 throughout.

zone—and still integrated into a probabilistic model where Gaussians are used to model the uncertainty of geographic origin of an individual word.

An area of further investigation is also to evaluate the individual contribution of components that other authors have found to enhance accuracy; these include integration of topic models into the task (Eisenstein et al. 2010), k-d trees splitting of grid cells (Roller et al. 2012), n-gram information (Priedhorsky, Culotta, and Del Valle 2014) as well as exploiting tweet metadata such as user profile information (Han, Cook, and Baldwin 2013; 2014) and IP information (Backstrom, Sun, and Marlow 2010) in various ways.

In the current work, no effort has been made to constrain feature dispersion to known land masses. Including such information could also provide gains in accuracy, especially for fine-grained grid sizes. Likewise, more general linear (and other discriminative) classifiers—though more costly to train with very large amounts of data—may profit from the areal smoothing presented in this paper.

Conclusion

We have shown that a kernel-based method alleviates some of the sparse data problems associated with geolocating documents on a discretized surface modeled as a geodesic grid and allows for the use of much smaller grids with less data. The kernel estimation can also be postponed until classification time, avoiding the storage of large models, at the cost of slightly slower classification. In such a case, the resulting model sizes are roughly comparable with those produced by strictly grid-based methods.

Using a kernel-based method significantly improves the mean error on the WORLDTWEETS data set, even when combined with a relatively simple Naive Bayes or KL-divergence based classifier.

References

Alis, C. M., and Lim, M. T. 2013. Spatio-temporal variation of conversational utterances on Twitter. *PloS one* 8(10):e77793.

Backstrom, L.; Sun, E.; and Marlow, C. 2010. Find me if you can: Improving geographical prediction with social and spatial proximity. In *Proceedings of the 19th International Conference on World Wide Web*, WWW '10, 61–70. New York, NY, USA: ACM.

Borau, K.; Ullrich, C.; Feng, J.; and Shen, R. 2009. Microblogging for language learning: Using Twitter to train communicative and cultural competence. In *Advances in Web Based Learning–ICWL 2009*. Springer. 78–87.

Corvey, W. J.; Verma, S.; Vieweg, S.; Palmer, M.; and Martin, J. H. 2012. Foundations of a multilayer annotation framework for Twitter communications during crisis events. In *LREC*, 3801–3805.

Eisenstein, J.; Ahmed, A.; and Xing, E. P. 2011. Sparse additive generative models of text. In *Proceedings of the 28th International Conference on Machine Learning (ICML-11)*, 1041–1048.

Eisenstein, J.; O'Connor, B.; Smith, N. A.; and Xing, E. P. 2010. A latent variable model for geographic lexical variation. In *Proceedings of the 2010 Conference on Empirical Methods in Natural Language Processing*, 1277–1287. Cambridge, MA: Association for Computational Linguistics.

Eisenstein, J. 2013. What to do about bad language on the Internet. In *HLT-NAACL*, 359–369.

Eriksson, B.; Barford, P.; Sommers, J.; and Nowak, R. 2010. A Learning-based Approach for IP Geolocation. In *Passive and Active Measurement*, 171–180.

Grosseck, G., and Holotescu, C. 2008. Can we use Twitter for educational activities. In *4th international scientific conference, eLearning and software for education, Bucharest, Romania*.

Han, B.; Cook, P.; and Baldwin, T. 2012. Geolocation prediction in social media data by finding location indicative words. *Proceedings of COLING 2012: Technical Papers* 1045–1062.

Han, B.; Cook, P.; and Baldwin, T. 2013. A stacking-based approach to Twitter user geolocation prediction. In *ACL (Conference System Demonstrations)*, 7–12.

Han, B.; Cook, P.; and Baldwin, T. 2014. Text-based Twitter user geolocation prediction. *J. Artif. Intell. Res.(JAIR)* 49:451–500.

Hong, L.; Ahmed, A.; Gurumurthy, S.; Smola, A. J.; and Tsioutsiouliklis, K. 2012. Discovering geographical topics in the Twitter stream. In *Proceedings of the 21st international conference on World Wide Web*, 769–778. ACM.

Kondor, D.; Csabai, I.; Dobos, L.; Szule, J.; Barankai, N.; Hanyecz, T.; Sebok, T.; Kallus, Z.; and Vattay, G. 2013. Using robust pca to estimate regional characteristics of language use from geo-tagged Twitter messages. In *Cognitive Infocommunications (CogInfoCom), 2013 IEEE 4th International Conference on*, 393–398. IEEE.

Priedhorsky, R.; Culotta, A.; and Del Valle, S. Y. 2014. Inferring the origin locations of tweets with quantitative confidence. In *Proceedings of the 17th ACM conference on Computer supported cooperative work & social computing*, 1523–1536. ACM.

Roller, S.; Speriosu, M.; Rallapalli, S.; Wing, B.; and Baldridge, J. 2012. Supervised text-based geolocation using language models on an adaptive grid. In *Proceedings of the 2012 Joint Conference on Empirical Methods in Natural Language Processing and Computational Natural Language Learning*, 1500–1510. Jeju Island, Korea: Association for Computational Linguistics.

Serdyukov, P.; Murdock, V.; and Van Zwol, R. 2009. Placing flickr photos on a map. In *Proceedings of the 32nd international ACM SIGIR conference on Research and development in information retrieval*, 484–491. ACM.

Wing, B., and Baldridge, J. 2011. Simple supervised document geolocation with geodesic grids. In *Proceedings of the 49th Annual Meeting of the Association for Computational Linguistics: Human Language Technologies*, 955–964. Portland, Oregon, USA: Association for Computational Linguistics.

Youn, I.; Mark, B.; and Richards, D. 2009. Statistical Geolocation of Internet Hosts. In *Computer Communications and Networks*, 1–6.

Proceedings of the Twenty-Ninth AAAI Conference on Artificial Intelligence

Cross-Modal Image Clustering via Canonical Correlation Analysis

Cheng Jin, Wenhui Mao, Ruiqi Zhang, Yuejie Zhang, Xiangyang Xue
School of Computer Science, Shanghai Key Laboratory of
Intelligent Information Processing, Fudan University, Shanghai, China
{jc, 13210240099, 12210240075, yjzhang, xyxue}@fudan.edu.cn

Abstract

A new algorithm via Canonical Correlation Analysis (CCA) is developed in this paper to support more effective cross-modal image clustering for large-scale annotated image collections. It can be treated as a bi-media multimodal mapping problem and modeled as a correlation distribution over multimodal feature representations. It integrates the multimodal feature generation with the Locality Linear Coding (LLC) and co-occurrence association network, multimodal feature fusion with CCA, and accelerated hierarchical *k*-means clustering, which aims to characterize the correlations between the inter-related visual features in images and semantic features in captions, and measure their association degree more precisely. Very positive results were obtained in our experiments using a large quantity of public data.

Introduction

With the massive explosion of annotated image data on the Web, methods to seamlessly handle the complex structures of image data to achieve more efficient organization and management have become an important research focus (Datta et al. 2008; Rasiwasia et al. 2010). Usually, an annotated image is exhibited in a multimodal form, that is, both semantic and visual. Thus, integrating multimodal information sources to enable cross-modal image clustering has been the core component. However, due to the semantic gap, there may be significant differences and independence among visual images and textual captions, which leads to the huge difficulty and uncertainty in making full use of the relations between the visual features (in images) and semantic features (in captions) (Fan et al. 2012).

To achieve effective cross-modal image clustering, three inter-related issues should be addressed simultaneously: 1) the valid coding and discovery of valuable multimodal features to characterize visual images and textual captions more reasonably, 2) multimodal feature fusion to identify better multimodal correlations between the visual features in images and semantic features in captions, and 3) appropriate clustering methods to speed up the cross-modal clustering process. To address the first issue, it is very important to leverage large-scale annotated images for robust visual coding and semantic mining to achieve more comprehensive multimodal feature representation. To address the second issue, it is very interesting to develop new algorithms for fusing multimodal features and efficiently exploiting the correlations among attributes of different modalities in annotated images. To address the third issue, it is critical to explore an appropriate clustering mechanism with high efficiency but no sacrifice of clustering accuracy.

Based on the above observations, a novel scheme is developed in this paper to facilitate more effective cross-modal image clustering for large-scale annotated image collections. Our scheme significantly differs from other earlier work as follows. a) The visual feature generation based on Locality Linear Coding (LLC) can achieve a smaller quantization error and better coding stability. The semantic feature generation based on a co-occurrence association network can exploit the inter-term statistical co-occurrence associations to learn the semantic feature representations. b) The multimodal feature fusion based on Canonical Correlation Analysis (CCA) has a strong ability to characterize the multimodal correlations between the visual features in images and semantic features in captions. c) The specified accelerated hierarchical *k*-means clustering is exploited to face scalability problems when scaling up to large-scale annotated images. d) A new cross-modal image clustering framework is built by integrating the above feature representation, fusion, and clustering mechanisms.

How to integrate multimodal features for image clustering is an open issue because it is hard to provide a base to multiple similarities among the images which are calculated from multiple features in different modalities. The main contribution of our work is that we effectively apply CCA to enable cross-modal image clustering, which has provided a more reasonable base for us to integrate visual similarity with semantic similarity by determining an optimal correlated projection space. Thus such cross-modal clustering can be treated as a bi-media multimodal mapping problem, and modeled as a correlation distribution over multimodal feature representations, where the most important task is creating the multimodal association between visual and semantic features and measuring the degree to which they are related. We have obtained very positive results in our experiments to demonstrate our observations.

Related Work

Image clustering is not a novel task, but has been the subject of extensive research in areas such as multimedia information processing and retrieval (Chaudhuri et al. 2009; Yang et al. 2010). Earlier research placed the main emphasis on unimodal approaches, where the clustered images shared a single modality (Pan et al. 2004; Goldberger, Gordon, and Greenspan 2006). However, because of considering only visual or textual information in annotated images, such methods often demonstrate a poor performance (Chen, Wang, and Dong 2010; Jia, Salzmann, and Darrell 2011). Recently, closer attention has been given to methods that rely on both low-level visual and high-level semantic features, that is, grouping together visually similar and semantically related images. Thus, there has been increasing research interest in combining multiple information sources and exploiting the multimodal information in annotated images to support precise image clustering.

In recent years, some related research has used the textual information that accompanies an image. Bekkerman and Jeon (2007) introduced the powerful *Comraf* framework to cluster multimedia collections, in which they exploited the multimodal nature of multimedia collections from multiple views or modalities. Moëllic, Haugeard, and Pitel (2008) studied an image clustering process for descriptors of different natures, using textual information and visual features based on bags-of-SIFT descriptors. Rege, Dong, and Hua (2008) addressed the problem of Web image clustering by the simultaneous integration of visual and textual features from a graph partitioning perspective. Yang et al. (2009) presented image clustering as an example to illustrate how unsupervised learning can be improved by transferring knowledge from auxiliary heterogeneous data. Chen, Wang, and Dong (2010) presented a semi-supervised approach for image co-clustering based on non-negative matrix factorization. Fu et al. (2011) presented a multi-modal constraint propagation approach to exploiting pairwise constraints for constrained clustering tasks on multi-modal datasets. Hamzaoui, Joly, and Boujemaa (2011) proposed a new multi-source shared neighbors scheme applied to multi-modal image clustering.

Unfortunately, none of these approaches have provided good solutions for the following three important issues. (a) **Multimodal Information Exploration for Discovering Multimodal Features** – Most existing image clustering techniques typically focus on the traditional visual feature representation and the oversimplified utilization of the limited textual information. They may not stress an in-depth consideration of more reasonable coding methods for the low-level visual features involved in images or exploit all the information to acquire more comprehensive high-level semantic features contained in captions. These approaches may be restricted to the use of the limited annotation tags corresponding to salient objects in the images, while discarding the wealth of information and its connotations in the captions. An attractive paradigm is to improve the unimodal-based model by using multimodal information and performing a deep exploration for the construction of both a visual and semantic feature space. The captioned images could be well represented in this multimodal space and beneficial to image clustering. (b) **Inter-related Correlation Measure for Multimodal Feature Fusion** – Most existing related approaches focus on exploiting information from different modalities separately, and the inter-related correlations between different modalities are completely ignored. Although some advances have been reported on multimodal image clustering, they have usually involved the fusion of features from different modalities into a single vector, or learning different models for different modalities and fusing their output. Cross-modal correlations could provide helpful hints on mining multimodal information for image clustering. Establishing multimodal associations between low-level visual features and high-level semantic attributes may shed light on the captioned image understanding and clustering. Thus, the explicit modeling of cross-modal correlations between visual and semantic features becomes very important. From the viewpoint of multimodal feature exploitation and fusion, it's a significant way to combine both visual and semantic abstractions for images and captions in a joint space and establish a multimodal joint modeling. **(3) Clustering Optimization for Time Efficiency** – Building an appropriate optimized clustering mechanism to make clustering, especially cross-modal clustering, scalable to large-scale annotated images is an important challenge. However, most existing unimodal or multimodal clustering schemes have no in-depth consideration of such a mechanism. Some accelerated clustering strategies can be employed in controlling both the time and memory cost within a more reasonable range.

To tackle the above obstacles, we have developed a novel framework by integrating the visual feature generation with LLC and semantic feature generation with co-occurrence association network (i.e., mining valuable multimodal feature information), the CCA-based multimodal feature fusion (i.e., bridging the semantic gap between visual contents and semantic annotations), and the accelerated hierarchical *k*-means clustering (i.e., fusing the optimization strategy to improve the clustering efficiency). In our study, we realized that an annotated image usually appears with multiple correlated semantic concepts and spans multimodal associations in both visual and conceptual levels. Our CCA-based cross-modal image clustering aims at exploring valuable multimodal correlations involved in images and their annotations to improve the reasoning ability for clustering. It's a new attempt on exploiting such feature generation, fusion and clustering optimization strategies, especially CCA, on cross-modal image clustering.

Multimodal Feature Generation

The multimodal information is the significant expression and exhibition for image content, that is, the visual and semantic description in each annotated image. Thus to acquire the cross-modal correlation between visual images and textual captions, the multimodal features in annotated images should be detected and represented more precisely.

Visual Feature Generation

Each image can be represented by using the SIFT descriptor under the Bag-of-Features (BoF) framework (Csurka et al. 2004). However, such a kind of feature usually occupies the large storage space and requires much more computational cost in a high-dimensional space. Some coding methods have been proposed to project the higher dimensional features into a sparse presentation, such as Vector Quantization (VQ) (Sivic and Zisserman 2003), Sparse coding (SC) (Yang et al. 2009) and Local Coordinate Coding (LCC) (Yu, Zhang, and Gong 2009). However, these manners may produce larger quantization error and lose the correlations between codes. Thus to achieve more precise visual description of images, it's very useful to establish an efficient coding manner to achieve dimension reduction and reduce the computational cost.

First, each SIFT descriptor is viewed as a visual word, and assigned one or a few feature points in the codebook based on the coding algorithm according to the codebook. Compared to the traditional methods, Locality Linear Coding (LLC) can generate the coding result by searching the k-nearest neighbors and require the less computational cost (Wang et al. 2010). As the main strategy for feature coding, LLC is incorporated into our visual feature extraction.

Assume that S is a set of D-dimensional visual words extracted from an image with N entries, $S=[s_1, s_2, ..., s_N]\in R^{D\times N}$. Given a codebook with M entries, $B=[b_1, b_2, ..., b_M]\in R^{D\times M}$. Each word is converted into a M-dimensional code to generate the final image representation by Formula (1), which is the approximated method of LLC for fast coding.

$$\arg\min_{C} \sum_{i=1}^{N} \|s_i - c_i b_i\|^2, \ s.t.\ 1^T c_i = 1, \forall i \qquad (1)$$

where b_i only contains a small group of local bases that are the nearest neighbors of s_i in the codebook B. The coding result C is constructed quickly and then the global features of images can be obtained, while the local information is ignored. In order to characterize the local features for images more accurately, the LLC is combined with the Spatial Pyramid Matching (SPM), which partitions images into increasingly fine spatial sub-regions and computes the local features from each sub-region (Lazebnik, Schmid, and Ponce 2006). Typically, this coding manner consists of $2^l\times 2^l$ subregions in each level, l=0, 1, 2. Thus the similarity based on SPM between two images u and v can be calculated as shown in Formula (2).

$$Sim(u, v) = \sum_{l=0}^{L-1} \sum_{i=0}^{2^{2l}-1} Dist(F(u_l^i), F(v_l^i)) \qquad (2)$$

Where $F(u^i{}_l)$ and $F(v^i{}_l)$ denote the coding result of SIFT features, that is, the ith sub-region in the lth sub-region level of two images u and v; and L means the max level of SPM.

Semantic Feature Generation

To obtain more accurate semantic formulation for annotated images, the co-occurrence association network and optimal semantic feature coding are both constructed to assist in getting more coherent semantic feature representations.

a. Co-occurrence Association Network Construction

Our co-occurrence association network is automatically generated from large-scale annotated images to characterize the co-occurrence correlations between a large number of semantic concepts of interest (i.e., annotation tags). Such a network can provide a good environment for: (a) discovering more meaningful co-occurrence associations among annotation tags; (b) acquiring more abundant semantic descriptions for annotated images; (c) assisting the semantic feature coding optimization more effectively.

Our association network consists of: (1) large amounts of semantic concepts of interest; and (2) their inter-concept co-occurrence association relations. Intuitively, semantic concepts of interest related to an annotated image should be some concept terms associated with the prominent objects or scenes in this image and play important roles in making discrimination between different objects and scenes in different images. Thus the selected semantic concepts of interest focus on the key terms with high frequency in image annotations from *Flickr* and class names from *Caltech* 256 commonly used in computer vision.

We hope our association network could fuse the important semantic concept association information involved in annotations. Thus the flat construction criterion is considered to achieve more precise characterization of the inter-concept semantic association relations in large-scale annotated image collections. For two semantic concepts of interest, their association relation consists of the flat association relation because of their co-occurrences in image collections, e.g., the higher co-occurrence probability corresponds to the stronger association relation. Even if there are no obvious semantic relations among some co-occurrence concepts, it's still easy for people to relate these concepts together, such as "*monkey*" and "*banana*". Thus the co-occurrence probability between two semantic concepts of interest SC_i and SC_j can be computed according to Formula (3), which indicates what percentage of images annotated by both SC_i and SC_j in the images with SC_i or SC_j.

$$Pco(IMG\_Set_{SC_i}, IMG\_Set_{SC_j}) = \frac{|IMG\_Set_{SC_i} \cap IMG\_Set_{SC_j}|}{|IMG\_Set_{SC_i} \cup IMG\_Set_{SC_j}|} \qquad (3)$$

where IMG_Set_{SCi} and IMG_Set_{SCj} denote two image sets that contain SC_i and SC_j as one annotation tag respectively.

Each semantic concept of interest on the co-occurrence association network can be linked with all the other associated concepts on the network. Eliminating the weak inter-concept links can allow concentrating on the most significant association relations. Thus each concept is linked with the most relevant concepts with stronger flat semantic association relation. The co-occurrence association network for our whole image database is shown in Figure 1.

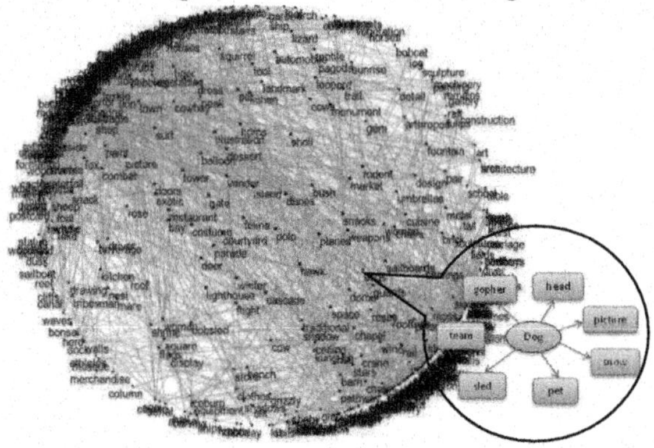

Figure 1. The co-occurrence association network for our image database.

b. Optimal Semantic Feature Coding

To obtain the better quantization for semantic features, the statistical method based on *tf-idf* is incorporated to construct the optimal semantic feature coding, by which the annotation tags (i.e., semantic concepts of interest) could have different importance degrees in different images.

Assume S is an image dataset with the size of N, which contains D different annotation tags in total, Q^i_j means the quantization result of the ith annotation tag Tag_i in the jth image Img_j. Considering that the annotation tags in different images have different importance metrics, we let $Q^i_j=0$ if $Tag_i \notin Img_j$. Otherwise, if $Tag_i \in Img_j$, we achieve coding the image annotation set according to Formula (4).

$$Q^j_i = \frac{1}{\sum_{k=0}^{D} BL_{Img_j}(Tag_k)} \cdot \log \frac{N}{\sum_{p=1}^{N} BL_{Img_p}(Tag_i)} \quad (4)$$

where $BL_{Img_i}(Tag_k)$ is 1 when Tag_k belongs to Img_j, otherwise is 0; and $BL_{Img_p}(Tag_i)$ has the similar definition.

The above algorithm can be considered as the basic model for the initial *tf-idf*-based semantic feature generation. However, the common fact is that there are limited annotation tags in an image caption. If only considering such annotation tags to construct the semantic feature representation, there may cause the restricted or even sparse semantic feature description for an annotated image. It's worth noting that the frequent co-occurrence tags related to the original tags in an image caption can be very beneficial to the semantic information enhancement or supplement for constructing more complete semantic expression for the image. The desirable situation is that more strongly related tags can be explored to the semantic description for an image as possible. Thus, to further acquire more accurate semantic feature representation, the initial semantic feature coding optimization can be implemented based on the co-occurrence associations among different annotation tags on our co-occurrence association network, as shown in Formula (5). The main purpose of such an optimization strategy is to exploit both the explicit semantic information (i.e., the original annotation tags in image caption) and the implicit semantic information (i.e., the related tags with the strong co-occurrence association relations on our co-occurrence association network) for ensuring more accurate and comprehensive formulation of semantic feature.

$$\arg\min_{C^i_j} \sum_{j=1}^{N} \sum_{i=1}^{D} \left(\left\| C^i_j - Q^i_j \right\|^2 + \sum_{k=1}^{D} w_{ik} \left\| C^i_j - C^k_j \right\|^2 \right), \ s.t., 0 \le C^i_j \le 1 \quad (5)$$

where Q_j can be understood as the initial *tf-idf*-based semantic feature vector for the jth image, Q^i_j is the ith feature in Q_j; C_j can be understood as the optimized semantic feature vector for the jth image, C^i_j is the ith feature in C_j; $||C^i_j - Q^i_j||^2$ means that the feature coding optimization should keep the characteristics of the initial *tf-idf*-based feature, and the difference between the optimized feature and the initial feature should as small as possible; $||C^i_j - C^k_j||^2$ means that if an annotation tag has the strong co-occurrence association with the original annotation tag on our co-occurrence association network, it can contribute to the semantic feature representation for the corresponding image and the discrepancy between the semantic features for these two tags should as small as possible; and w_{ik} indicates the weight between two annotation tags (i.e., semantic concepts of interest) of SC_i and SC_k on the co-occurrence association network, and defined as:

$$w_{ik} = \begin{cases} P_{co}(IMG\_Set_{SC_i}, IMG\_Set_{SC_k}), & P_{co}(IMG\_Set_{SC_i}, IMG\_Set_{SC_k}) > \tau \\ 0, & P_{co}(IMG\_Set_{SC_i}, IMG\_Set_{SC_k}) \le \tau \end{cases} \quad (6)$$

where τ is a predefined threshold value.

To guarantee the valid solution for Formula (5), it can be transformed into a simplified form for each image in Formula (7), which is a convex optimization problem.

$$\arg\min_{C^i} \sum_{i=1}^{D} \left(\left\| C^i - Q^i \right\|^2 + \sum_{k=1}^{D} w_{ik} \left\| C^i - C^k \right\|^2 \right), \ s.t., 0 \le C^i \le 1 \quad (7)$$

Through computing the derivative with respect to C^i and set it to 0, we can obtain Formula (8) after some algebra.

$$C^i = \frac{1}{\left(1+\sum_{k=1}^{D} w_{ik}\right)} * Q_i + \frac{1}{\left(1+\sum_{k=1}^{D} w_{ik}\right)} * \sum_{k=1}^{D} w_{ik} * C^k \quad (8)$$

Thus for all the annotation tags in an annotated image, the following Formula (9) can be obtained.

$$\begin{bmatrix} C^1 \\ \vdots \\ C^i \\ \vdots \\ C^D \end{bmatrix} = \begin{bmatrix} \frac{Q^1}{\left(1+\sum_{k=1}^{D} w_{1k}\right)} \\ \vdots \\ \frac{Q^i}{\left(1+\sum_{k=1}^{D} w_{ik}\right)} \\ \vdots \\ \frac{Q^D}{\left(1+\sum_{k=1}^{D} w_{Dk}\right)} \end{bmatrix} + \begin{bmatrix} \frac{w_{11}}{\left(1+\sum_{k=1}^{D} w_{1k}\right)} & \cdots & \frac{w_{1i}}{\left(1+\sum_{k=1}^{D} w_{1k}\right)} & \cdots & \frac{w_{1D}}{\left(1+\sum_{k=1}^{D} w_{1k}\right)} \\ \vdots & \ddots & \vdots & \ddots & \vdots \\ \frac{w_{i1}}{\left(1+\sum_{k=1}^{D} w_{ik}\right)} & \cdots & \frac{w_{ii}}{\left(1+\sum_{k=1}^{D} w_{ik}\right)} & \cdots & \frac{w_{iD}}{\left(1+\sum_{k=1}^{D} w_{ik}\right)} \\ \vdots & \ddots & \vdots & \ddots & \vdots \\ \frac{w_{D1}}{\left(1+\sum_{k=1}^{D} w_{Dk}\right)} & \cdots & \frac{w_{Di}}{\left(1+\sum_{k=1}^{D} w_{Dk}\right)} & \cdots & \frac{w_{DD}}{\left(1+\sum_{k=1}^{D} w_{Dk}\right)} \end{bmatrix} * \begin{bmatrix} C^1 \\ \vdots \\ C^i \\ \vdots \\ C^D \end{bmatrix} \quad (9)$$

The above operation can be iteratively performed until a certain condition is met. The final $(C^1, \ldots, C^i, \ldots, C^D)$ is the optimized feature representation for the given image.

Multimodal Feature Fusion

The multimodal feature fusion based on Canonical Correlation Analysis (CCA) is implemented to exploit multiple features of annotated images and explore the multimodal associations between visual property features and semantic expression features. To make a clear presentation, we first introduce the canonical correlation model, and then develop our CCA-based multimodal feature fusion mechanism.

Revisit of Canonical Correlation Analysis (CCA)

The CCA algorithm is a classic statistical method to multiview and multi-scale analysis for multiple data sources, which has received much attention in the field of cross-media/cross-modal processing (Cao et al. 2009; Gordoa et al. 2012). It aims at finding linear projections for different types of data with the maximum correlation, which can provide a linear function learning method by projecting different types of data into a high dimension feature space (Gong et al. 2012). The difference between CCA and other closely related approaches is that CCA learns two separate encodings with the objective that the learned encodings are as correlated as possible, and such different objectives may have advantages in different settings. Thus CCA, which could obtain more accurate highly abstract expression of real data via the complex linear transformation, is introduced to make a better solution for multimodal feature fusion in cross-modal image clustering. We emphasize on building a novel cross-modal feature representation for image clustering, which combines canonical correlations of multimodal (visual and semantic) features.

Integrating Multimodal Features with CCA

For integrating multi-modal features to cross-modal features with CCA, it aims at projecting the multimodal features with different modalities on multiple views into a common subspace and making sure that the correlation between visual and semantic features could be maximized.

Let *IMG* be the set of annotated images that consists of N samples; $V \in R^{D_V * N}$ is the centered visual feature matrices for *IMG* and $S \in R^{D_S * N}$ represents the centered semantic feature matrices, D_V and D_S are the dimensionality values for these two matrices, generally $D_V \neq D_S$. The following projection can be considered, as shown in Formula (10).

$$CCA_{VV} = VV^T, \quad CCA_{SS} = SS^T, \quad CCA_{VS} = VS^T, \quad CCA_{SV} = SV^T \tag{10}$$

To find a projection relation between the visual feature space and semantic feature space that could maximize the correlation between different feature views, the following Formula (11) is adopted to achieve such a goal.

$$\arg\max_{p \in R^{DV}, q \in R^{DS}} p^T CCA_{VS} q, \quad s.t., \ p^T(CCA_{VV} + \rho I)p = 1, \ q^T(CCA_{SS} + \rho I)q = 1 \tag{11}$$

where the small regularization factor ρ is used to avoid the numerically ill-conditioned problem; p and q are the projection directions that force the data from V and S into the common space; and I denotes an identity matrix. Hence, we can obtain the set of the projection matrix $P=\{p_1, p_2, \ldots, p_R\}$ and $Q=\{q_1, q_2, \ldots, q_R\}$ by transforming it to a symmetric eigenvalue problem. The ith component p_i and q_i can be calculated by the following Formula (12).

$$\begin{aligned}(CCA_{VV} + \rho I)^{-1} CCA_{VS} (CCA_{SS} + \rho I)^{-1} CCA_{SV} p_i &= \lambda_i^2 p_i \\ (CCA_{SS} + \rho I)^{-1} CCA_{SV} (CCA_{VV} + \rho I)^{-1} CCA_{VS} p_i &= \varphi_i^2 q_i\end{aligned} \tag{12}$$

where λ^2_i and φ^2_i represent the ith eigenvalue. We can project the feature vectors of V and S into a common space based on the matrices of $P \in R^{D_V * R}$ and $Q \in R^{D_S * R}$. Thus we can embed the multi-modal features (i.e., visual features and semantic features) into a subspace that can generate the final cross-modal feature *MF* as shown in Formula (13).

$$MF = \alpha V^T * P + (1-\alpha) S^T * Q \tag{13}$$

where α is a constant parameter in [0, 1]. Compared to the common feature concatenation, such a linear weighting can achieve the lower dimensional feature representation without the sacrifice of the clustering performance.

In fact, for the visual and semantic features involved in each annotated image, they belong to different feature spaces with different dimensions, and have no direct associations. Our CCA-based multimodal feature fusion can provide a relatively perfect feature representation with associations between various features in different modalities for cross-modal image clustering, which can mitigate the problem of semantic gap to a certain extent and achieve the better clustering with multimodal feature associations.

Accelerated Hierarchical *K*-means Clustering

Since our cross-modal image clustering orients to large-scale annotated image collections, the number of image class may reach up to hundreds, thousands, or even tens of thousands. To describe multimodal attributes for each annotated image, hundreds of feature points of interest can be extracted from each image to compose the associated high-dimensional feature vector representation. Thus for facilitating the better solution of cross-modal image clustering, it's meaningful to build an efficient optimized clustering mechanism with the ability to work with large dataset, high-dimensional data, reasonable time complexity, etc.

The most popular method for image clustering is the *k*-means algorithm, which has been widely applied in the field of image processing (Elkan 2004; Arai and Barakbah 2007; Hamerly 2010). It has the relatively fast computation speed, and can gradually converge to the best situation with the execution of iteration. The superiority of *k*-means is that even if the convergence process for clustering need execute thousands of iterations, the solution close to the final convergence results can be obtained just after dozens of iterations. However, k-means also has the obvious defect, that is, the convergence effect is very sensitive to the selection of initial starting points, which leads to the difficulty to reach global optimum, but only in local minimum. The initial cluster is generated randomly in k-means, thus the unique clustering results cannot be guaranteed. Meanwhile, due to the fact that most distance calculations in k-means are redundant, if a point is far away from a cluster center, it's not necessary to calculate the exact distance between this point and the center in order to confirm that this point should not be assigned to the center. Such redundant calculations may usually consume more computational cost. Thus in our cross-modal image clustering, the Accelerated Hierarchical K-means Clustering (AHKMC) algorithm is adopted to determine the initial centers for the accelerated k-means, which combines the idea of hierarchical clustering and accelerated k-means to satisfy various restrictions under the condition of huge amounts of data and make the suitable optimization for cutting down the computational cost. The basic framework of AHKMC is shown as follows.

Algorithm 1 AHKMC(multimodal feature point set *MFS*)
1: **for** $p = 1$ to P **do**
2: $CK_p \leftarrow$ random(MFS, K)
3: $IC_p \leftarrow$ Accelerated K-means Clustering AKMC(MFS, CK_p)
4: $FC \leftarrow$ *all elements in* $IC_p, p \in [1, P]$
5: **while** $|FC| > K$ **do**
6: Merge(FC_i, FC_j), $\underset{i \neq j \text{ and } i, j \in [1, |FC|]}{\arg\min} CDist(FC_i, FC_j)$
//$CDist$(,) is a distance metric defined on center-center pairs
7: **return** AKMC(MFS, FC)

Algorithm 2 AKMC(multi-modal feature point set *MFS*, initial center set *C*)
1: **for** i=1 to $|MFS|$ **do**
2: $Center(i) \leftarrow \arg\min\{Dist(MFS_i, C_j)\}$
//$Center(i)$ is the index of the center to which MFS_i is assigned
//$Dist$(,) is a distance metric defined on point-center pairs
3: **while** not converged **do**
4: $C \leftarrow$ new centers C' except the first iteration; UPDATE($Center(i)$, C)
5: **for** i=1 to $|MFS|$ **do**
6: **if** $Dist(C_{Center(i)}, MFS_i) + Dist(C'_{Center(i)}, C_{Center(i)}) < BFC_{Center(i)}$, **continue**
//BFC_j denotes the first bound of centers
7: **if** $Dist(C_{Center(i)}, MFS_i) < BSC_{Center(i)} - 1/2 * Dist(C'_{Center(i)}, C_{Center(i)})$, **continue**
//BSC_j denotes the second bound of centers
8: **for** j=1 to $|C|$ **do**
9: **if** $Dist(C'_{Center(i)}, MFS_i) < 1/2 * Dist(C'_{Center(i)}, C'_j)$, **continue**
10: **else if** $Dist(C'_{Center(i)}, MFS_i) > Dist(C'_j, MFS_i)$, $Center(i) \leftarrow j$
11: **return** C'

Algorithm 3 UPDATE($Center(i)$, C)
1: **for** j=1 to $|C|$ **do**
2: $C' \leftarrow avg_{Center(i)=j}\{MFS\}$
3: **for** j=1 to $|C|$ **do**
4: $BFC_j \leftarrow 1/2 * \min_{j \neq j' \text{ and } j, j' \in [1, |C'|]} \{Dist(C'_j, C'_{j'})\}$, $BSC_j \leftarrow 1/2 * \min_{j \neq j' \text{ and } j \in [1, |C|], j' \in [1, |C'|]} \{Dist(C_j, C'_{j'})\}$

It's important to note that our AHKMC algorithm can achieve the significant acceleration effect through filtering out some avoidable redundant calculations with the characteristic of triangle inequality. The first bound for the first triangle inequality in Line 6 of Algorithm 2 is set based on Lemma 1 in (Elkan 2004; Hamerly 2010). The second bound is a novel boundary check condition for the second triangle inequality in Line 7, which is proposed under consideration for further refining effective calculations. Its derivation process is described in detail as follows. According to the principle of triangle inequality, for any three points x, y and z, $d(x, z) < d(x, y) + d(y, z)$ and $d(x, z) > d(x, y) - d(y, z)$, where $d($, $)$ is a distance metric function. Assume in Algorithm 2, x is a point, a and b are two centers in C (i.e., the center in the previous iteration), a' and b' are two centers in C' (i.e., the center in the current iteration), as shown in Figure 2. Thus for the triangle $\Delta axb'$, $d(x, b') > d(a, b') - d(x, a)$; and for $\Delta axa'$, $d(a, a') + d(x, a) > d(x, a')$. If $d(a, b') - d(x, a) > d(a, a') + d(x, a)$, i.e., $d(x, a) < 1/2 * (d(a, b') - d(a, a'))$, then $d(x, b') > d(x, a')$.

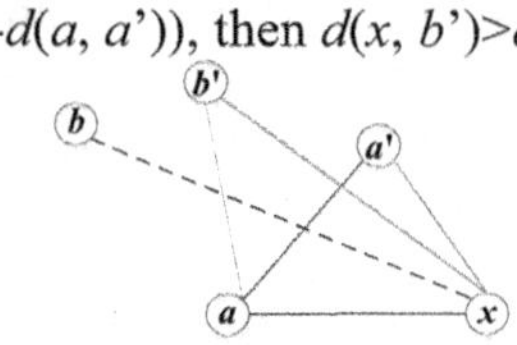

Figure 2. An instantiation for the second bound in Line 7 of Algorithm 2.

Experiment and Analysis

Dataset and Evaluation Metrics

Our dataset is established based on two benchmark datasets of *Corel30k* and *Nus-Wide*. To evaluate the performance, we employ the benchmark metric of *Normalized Mutual Information* (*NMI*) and two metrics of *Average Clustering Accuracy* (*ACA*) and *Average Clustering Entropy* (*ACE*). The higher value of *NMI* or *ACA* appears better clustering, but the lower *ACE* indicates the excellent clustering.

$$NMI(\Omega, C) = \frac{I(\Omega, C)}{(H(\Omega) + H(C))/2} \quad (14)$$

where Ω is the cluster set after clustering; C is the ground-truth cluster set; I=(Ω, C) represents the mutual information; and $H(\Omega)$ and $H(C)$ denote the entropy values.

$$ACA(\Omega) = \frac{\sum_{i=1}^{|\Omega|} CA(\omega_i)}{|\Omega|}, CA(\omega_i) = \frac{\sum_{k=0}^{|\omega_i|} \delta(TagSet(Img_i), Topic(\omega_i))}{|\omega_i|} \quad (15)$$

$$\delta(TagSet(Img_i), Topic(\omega_i)) = \begin{cases} 1, & iff\ Topic(\omega_i) \in TagSet(Img_i) \\ 0, & ff\ Topic(\omega_i) \notin TagSet(Img_i) \end{cases}$$

where $CA(\omega_i)$ indicates the clustering accuracy for the cluster ω_i, $TagSet(Img_i)$ is the tag set for the image Img_i; $Topic(\omega_i)$ is a concept that has the highest correlation with ω_i,; and $\delta(TagSet(Img_i), Topic(\omega_i))$ is to judge whether the annotation for an image in the cluster contains the most important concept that can be representative of this cluster.

$$ACE(\Omega) = \frac{\sum_{i=1}^{|\Omega|} CE(\omega_i)}{|\Omega|}, CE(\omega_i) = -\sum_{l=1}^{M} (P(tag_l) \ln P(tag_l)) \quad (16)$$

where M is the number of different tags in the same cluster; and $P(tag_l)$ is the occurrence probability of the lth tag in ω_i.

Experiment on Parameter Setting

To show the effect of the important parameter α in Formula (13) on the whole clustering performance, we compare the performance rising speeds for different settings of α, as shown in Figure 3. It can be observed that on *Corel30k*, the *NMI*, *ACA* and *ACE* have no significant fluctuations under different settings of α. This implies the smaller correlation gap between the visual and semantic feature spaces obtained on this dataset. However, the different situation appears on *Nus-Wide*. The *NMI* and *ACA* decrease with α increasing while the *ACE* rises, which means the weak consistency between two modalities in such a dataset. Thus we set α as 0.3 to make a trade-off for better performance.

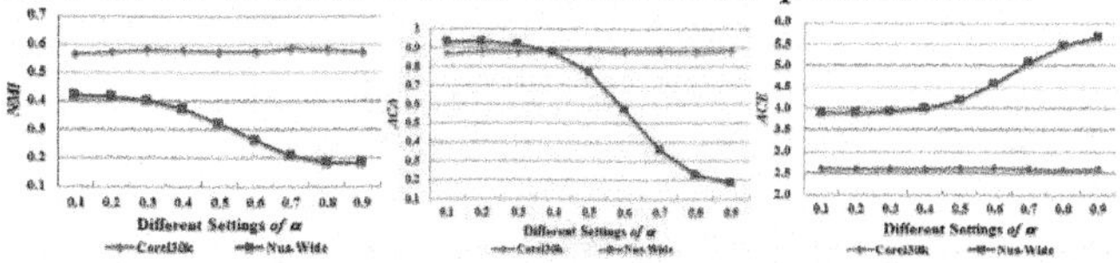

Figure 3. The experimental results for different settings of α.

Experiment on Cross-modal Image Clustering

Our modal is created by integrating Multimodal Feature Generation (MFG) [Visual/Semantic Feature Generation (VFG/SFG)], Multimodal Feature Fusion (MFF) and AHKMC. To investigate the effect of each part, we introduce three evaluation patterns: 1) *Baseline(MFG_VFG)* [*BMV*]; 2) *Baseline(MFG_SFG)* [*BMS*]; and 3) *Baseline(MFG_VFG&SFG)+MFF* [*BMV&S+MFF*]. The experimental results are shown in Figure 4, 5 and 6.

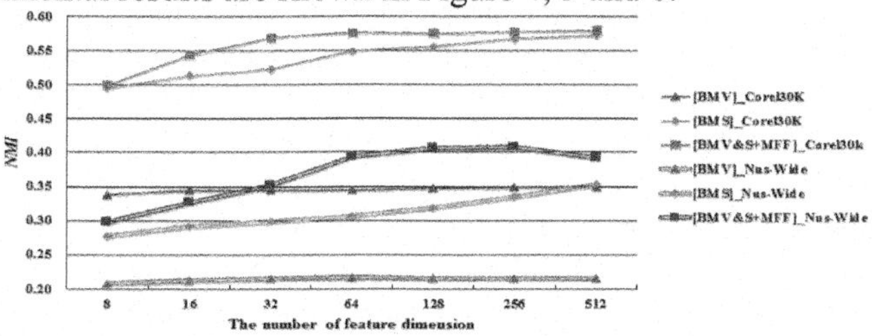

Figure 4. The experimental results for *NMI* on *Corel30k* and *Nus-Wide*.

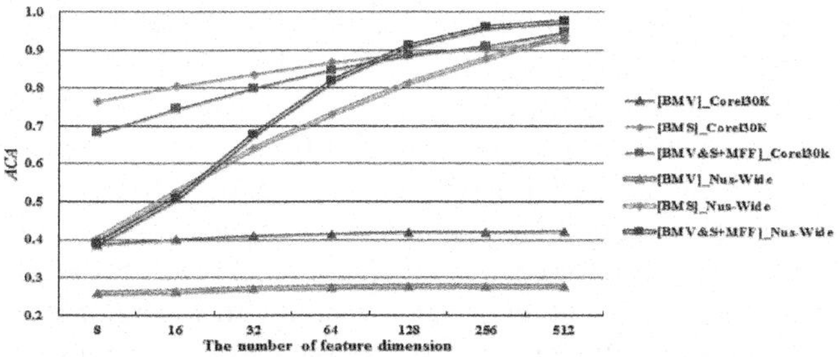

Figure 5. The experimental results for *ACA* on *Corel30k* and *Nus-Wide*.

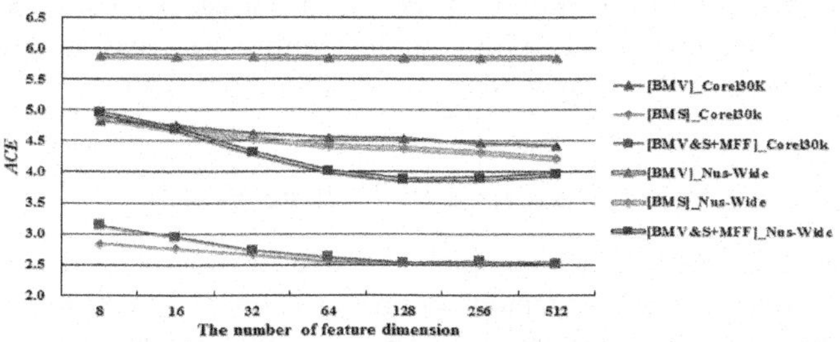

Figure 6. The experimental results for *ACE* on *Corel30k* and *Nus-Wide*.

It can be seen from Figure 4 that on *Corel30k* and *Nus-Wide*, we can obtain the best *NMI* value of 0.5802 in the evaluation pattern of fusing *Baseline* with *MFG_VFG*, *MFG_SFG* and *MFF*. In comparison with the baseline model using unimodal visual information, the performance could be greatly promoted by successively adding *MFG_SFG* and *MFF*, which confirms the obvious advantage of our cross-modal clustering. Compared two baseline models using unimodal visual and semantic feature information, the performance with semantic feature generation appears better, which shows the beneficial effect of semantic feature on image clustering. Compared two models with unimodal semantic and multimodal feature information, our cross-modal clustering can still gain the significant advantage for the performance on both *Corel30k* and *Nus-Wide*. Compared the results for different numbers of feature dimension, we can observe that with the dimension increasing, the performance gradually becomes pretty good. These results are consistent with what we expect considering more valuable multimodal feature information. Compared the results on *Corel30k* and *Nus-Wide*, the results on *Nus-Wide* appear less performant due to the differences between these two datasets. *Corel30k* is a relatively small-scale dataset with normative and consistent annotations and the images in the same cluster have the higher visual similarity, while *Nus-Wide* from *Flickr* is a relatively large-scale dataset with more obvious characteristics of social annotated images, such as noisy tag, redundant tag, missing tag, etc. As shown in Figure 5 and 6, the same conclusions as above can be drawn from the *ACA* and *ACE* on *Corel30k* and *Nus-Wide*, which show the consistence of our model on different indicators. All these observations indicate that the CCA-based multimodal feature fusion have more positive effect on image feature description, which can exactly yield the significant performance improvement more than only considering the unimodal feature representation. It can be found that our cross-modal manner is obviously superior to the traditional unimodal methods and more suitable for the optimized clustering in the complicated environment of social annotated images.

In addition, to explore the efficiency advantage of our framework with AHKMC, we focus on making a comparison of the time cost between the accelerated clustering in AHKMC and the general *k*-means clustering under the same settings of initial condition. The curves of clustering time are shown in Figure 7. With the number of feature dimension increasing, the general *k*-means manner can get the fast clustering within 313 and 16,304 seconds on *Corel30k* and *Nus-Wide* respectively. In contrast, the accelerated clustering time in AHKMC can be dramatically decreased to 63% (196 seconds) and 81% (13,200 seconds) of those with the general *k*-means clustering on *Corel30k* and *Nus-Wide* respectively, which gives no side-effects on the performance and contributes the better efficiency.

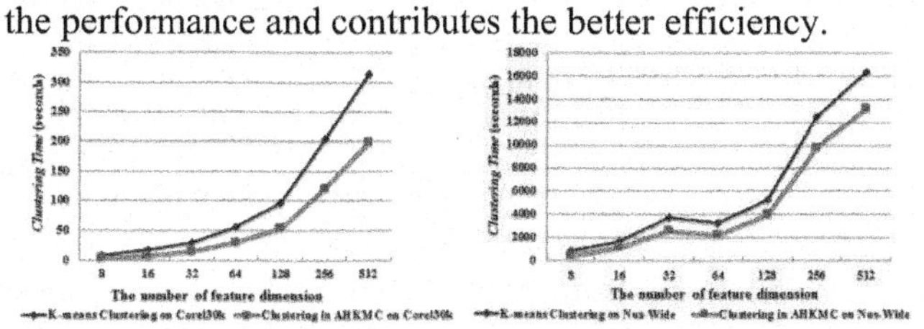

Figure 7. The comparison results for clustering time.

It's worth noting that in our optimized clustering algorithm, the in-depth multimodal analysis is available and presents more impactful ability for discovering the meaningful multimodal features and correlations. Our framework can not only significantly improve the clustering performance via CCA, but also greatly reduce the time cost via AHKMC. The same conclusions can be drawn from the different sets of *Corel30k* and *Nus-Wide*, which show the consistence of our model on different data sources. An instantiation of some clusters is shown in Figure 8.

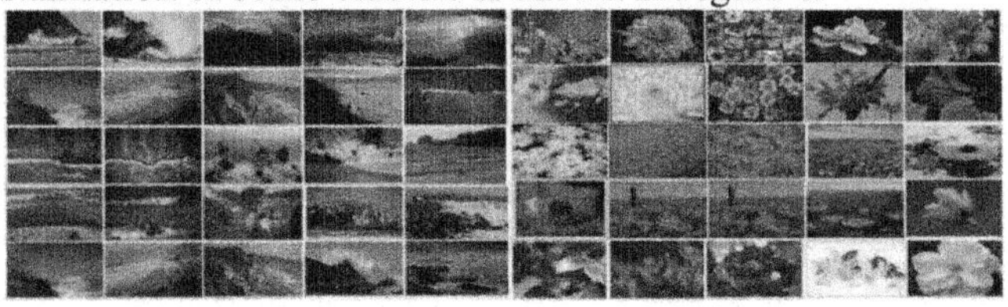

waves *flowers*

Figure 8. An instantiation of some cross-modal clusters.

Comparison with Existing Approaches

Compared to the common image clustering methods in recent years, our approach is a new exploration for taking full advantage of CCA to integrate multimodal information in clustering large-scale annotated images. To give full exhibition to the superiority of our model, we have performed a comparison between our and the other classical approaches for the past few years. Rege et al. (2009) (*Rege*) and Fu et al. (2011) (*Fu*) are analogous with ours, and were accomplished on the same dataset of *Corel30k* and a tailored subset of *Nus-Wide* (26,965 images, selecting one image every other ten images). This is because it must take a massive memory to implement *Rege&Fu* on the original *Nus-Wide*. The results are presented in Table 1, which reflect the difference of power among three approaches.

Dataset	Approaches		Feature Dimensions	Evaluation Metrics		
				NMI	*ACA*	*ACE*
Corel30k	**Rege *et al.* (2009) (*Rege*)**		**-**	**0.4724**	**0.7096**	**3.3587**
	Fu *et al.* (2011) (*Fu*)		**320**	**0.2314**	**0.4488**	**3.2375**
	Our Approach	***Baseline [BMV]***	**512**	**0.3495**	**0.4219**	**4.4281**
		Baseline [BMS]	**512**	**0.5727**	**0.9259**	**2.5578**
		BMV&S [MFG] +MFF+AHKMC	8	0.5004	0.6809	3.1387
			16	0.5443	0.7447	2.9469
			32	0.5692	0.7992	2.7302
			64	0.5766	0.8468	2.6235
			128	0.5755	0.8855	2.5343
			256	0.5780	0.9106	2.5539
			512	**0.5802**	**0.9463**	**2.5041**
Nus-Wide	**Rege *et al.* (2009) (*Rege*)**		**-**	**0.2542**	**0.1258**	**5.2656**
	Fu *et al.* (2011) (*Fu*)		**704**	**0.1365**	**0.2807**	**4.1142**
	Our Approach	***Baseline [BMV]***	**512**	**0.2155**	**0.2768**	**5.8589**
		Baseline [BMS]	**512**	**0.3627**	**0.9388**	**4.2252**
		BMV&S [MFG] +MFF+AHKMC	8	0.2973	0.3879	4.9599
			16	0.3269	0.5078	4.6864
			32	0.3515	0.6779	4.3076
			64	0.3937	0.8192	4.0111
			128	0.4066	0.9116	3.8776
			256	0.4081	0.9591	3.8956
			512	**0.3927**	**0.9757**	**3.9612**

Table 1. The comparison results between our and the other approaches.

It can be found from Table 1 that the best performance can be acquired on *Corel30k* and *Nus-Wide* by our approach. Compared the results of *Rege/Fu* and our baseline model with *VFG*, we can find the better performance appears in *Rege/Fu*. However, when integrating *MFG_VFG*, *MFG_SFG*, *MFF* and *AHKMC*, we can acquire the obviously better performance than those of *Rege/Fu* with lower feature dimensions. As the numbers of dimension are set as 16 and 64 on *Corel30k* and *Nus-Wide* respectively, all the values of *NMI*, *ACA* and *ACE* based on our approach have been dramatically higher than those based on *Rege/Fu*. With the feature dimension increasing, our approach reveals more significant advantage. This indicates that our approach is superior to *Rege/Fu*, and further confirms the prominent roles of *MFG* and *MFF* in cross-modal clustering, which implies that our model is exactly a better way for determining multimodal associations among images.

Analysis and Discussion

Through the analysis for the clustering results, it can be found that our cross-modal clustering quality is highly related to the following aspects. (1) The clustering effect is closely associated with the preprocessing for annotated images. It's easier to introduce error or noisy detections for visual and semantic feature information, which will seriously affect the whole clustering performance. (2) There is abundant information connotation involved in visual image. It's empirically realized that only using visual features is not sufficient for well formulating the distinguishability among image classes. The intensive visual feature expression can be utilized to further improve the clustering effectiveness and stableness. (3) There are different multimodal attributes among different annotated images. Although more obvious performance superiority has been exhibited via our CCA-based multimodal feature fusion, it's very beneficial to exploit an adaptive fusion between visual and semantic feature for each annotated image. (4) Some annotated images present an extreme vision with wrong or even without any valid annotations. With very limited useful annotation information and too much noises, it's hard for such images to successfully implement precise cross-modal clustering. This may be the most stubborn problem.

Conclusions and Future Work

A new framework is implemented to exploit multimodal correlations among annotated images to enable more effective cross-modal clustering. The in-depth feature analysis is established for characterizing the multimodal attributes for annotated images. The CCA-based multimodal feature fusion is introduced to acquire the specified multimodal feature expressions. The AHKMC manner is exploited to solve the efficiency for optimized clustering. Our future work will focus on making our system available online, so that more Internet users can benefit from our research.

Acknowledgments

This work is supported by National Science & Technology Pillar Program of China (No. 2012BAH59F04), National Natural Science Fund of China (No. 61170095), Zhuoxue Program of Fudan University, and Shanghai Leading Academic Discipline Project (No. B114). Yuejie Zhang is the corresponding author.

References

Arai, K., and Barakbah, A.R. 2007. Hierarchical K-means: An Algorithm for Centroids Initialization for K-means, Reports of the Faculty of Science and Engineering, 36(1):25-31.

Bekkerman, R., and Jeon, J. 2007. Multi-modal Clustering for Multimedia Collections. In *Proceedings of CVPR 2007*, 1-8.

Cao, L.L.; Yu, J.; Luo, J.B.; and Huang, T.S. 2009. Enhancing Semantic and Geographic Annotation of Web Images via Logistic Canonical Correlation Regression. In *Proceedings of MM 2009*, 125-134.

Chaudhuri, K.; Kakade, S.M.; Livescu, K.; and Sridharan, K. 2009. Multiview Clustering via Canonical Correlation Analysis. In *Proceedings of ICML 2009*, 129-136.

Chen, Y.H.; Wang, L.J.; and Dong, M. 2010. Non-negative Matrix Factorization for Semisupervised Heterogeneous Data Coclustering. *IEEE Transactions on Knowledge and Data Engineering* 22(10):1459-1474.

Csurka, G.; Dance, C.; Fan, L.; Willamowski, J.; and Bray, C. 2004. Visual Categorization with Bags of Keypoints. In *Proceedings of ECCV Workshop on Statistical Learning in Computer Vision*, 59-74.

Datta, R.; Joshi, D.; Li, J.; and Wang, J.Z. 2008. Image Retrieval: Ideas, Influences, and Trends of the New Age. *ACM Computing Surveys* (*CSUR*) 40(2), Article 5.

Elkan, C. 2004. Using the Triangle Inequality to Accelerate K-means. In *Proceedings ICML 2003*, 3:147-153.

Fan, J.P.; He, X.F.; Zhou, N.; Peng, J.Y.; and Jain, R. 2012. Quantitative Characterization of Semantic Gaps for Learning Complexity Estimation and Inference Model Selection. *IEEE Transactions on Multimedia* 14(5):1414-1428.

Fu, Z.H.; Ip, H.H.S.; Lu, H.T.; and Lu, Z.W. 2011. Multi-modal Constraint Propagation for Heterogeneous Image Clustering. In *Proceedings of MM 2011*, 143-152.

Goldberger, J.; Gordon, S.; and Greenspan, H. 2006. Unsupervised Image-Set Clustering Using an Information Theoretic Framework. *IEEE Transactions on Image Processing* 15(2):449-458.

Gong, Y.; Lazebnik, S.; Gordo, A.; and Perronnin, F. 2012. Iterative Quantization: A Procrustean Approach to Learning Binary codes for Large-scale Image Retrieval. *IEEE Transactions on Pattern Analysis and Machine Intelligence* 35(12):2916-2929.

Gordoa, A.; Rodriguez-Serrano, J.A.; Perronnin, F.; and Valveny, E. 2012. Leveraging Category-level Labels for Instance-level Image Retrieval. In *Proceedings of CVPR 2012*, 3045-3052.

Hamerly, G. 2010. Making K-means Even Faster. In *Proceedings of SIAM 2010*, 130-140.

Hamzaoui, A.; Joly, A.; and Boujemaa, N. 2011. Multi-source Shared Nearest Neighbours for Multi-modal Image Clustering. *Multimedia Tools and Applications* 51(2):479-503.

Jia, Y.Q.; Salzmann, M.; and Darrell, T. 2011. Learning Cross-modality Similarity for Multinomial Data. In *Proceedings of ICCV 2011*, 2407-2414.

Lazebnik, S.; Schmid, C.; and Ponce, J. 2006. Beyond Bags of Features: Spatial Pyramid Matching for Recognizing Natural Scene Categories. In *Proceedings of CVPR 2006*, 2:2169-2178.

Moëllic, P.A.; Haugeard, J.E.; and Pitel, G. 2008. Image Clustering based on a Shared Nearest Neighbors Approach for Tagged Collections. In *Proceedings of CIVR 2008*, 269-278.

Pan, J.Y.; Yang, H.J.; Faloutsos, C.; and Duygulu, P. 2004. Automatic Multimedia Cross-modal Correlation Discovery. In *Proceedings of SIGKDD 2004*, 653-658.

Rasiwasia, N.; Pereira, J.C.; Coviello, E.; Doyle, G.; Lanckriet, G.R.G.; Levy, R.; and Vasconcelos, N. 2010. A New Approach to Cross-modal Multimedia Retrieval. In *Proceedings of MM 2010*, 251-260.

Rege, M.; Dong, M.; and Hua, J. 2008. Graph Theoretical Framework for Simultaneously Integrating Visual and Textual Features for Efficient Web Image Clustering. In *Proceedings of WWW 2008*, 317-326.

Sivic, J., and Zisserman, A. 2003. Video Google: A Text Retrieval Approach to Object Matching in Videos. In *Proceedings of ICCV 2003*, 2:1470-1477.

Wang, J.J.; Yang, J.C.; Yu, K.; Lv, F.J.; Huang, T.; and Gong, Y.H. 2010. Locality-constrained Linear Coding for Image Classification. In *Proceedings of CVPR 2010*, 3360-3367.

Yang, Q.; Chen, Y.Q.; Xue, G.R.; Dai, W.Y.; and Wan, W.G. 2009. Image Co-clustering with Multi-modality Features and User Feedbacks. In *Proceedings of MM 2009*, 1-9.

Yang, Y.; Xu, D.; Nie, F.P.; Yan, S.C.; and Zhuang, Y.T. 2010. Image Clustering Using Local Discriminant Models and Global Integration. *IEEE Transactions on Image Processing* 35(12):2761-2773.

Yang, J.C.; Yu, K.; Gong, Y.H.; and Huang, T. 2009. Linear Spatial Pyramid Matching Using Sparse Coding for Image Classification. In *Proceedings of CVPR 2009*, 1794-1801.

Yu, K.; Zhang, T.; and Gong, Y.H. 2009. Nonlinear Learning Using Local Coordinate Coding. In *Proceedings of NIPS 2009*, 1-8.

Modeling with Node Degree Preservation Can Accurately Find Communities

Di Jin[1], Zheng Chen[2], Dongxiao He[1], Weixiong Zhang[2,3]

[1]School of Computer Science and Technology, Tianjin University, Tianjin 300072, China, [2]Department of Computer Science and Engineering, Washington University, St. Louis, MO 63130, USA, [3]Institute for Systems Biology, Jianghan University, Wuhan 430056, China
{jindi, hedongxiao}@tju.edu.cn, {zheng.chen, weixiong.zhang}@wustl.edu

Abstract

An important problem in analyzing complex networks is discovery of modular or community structures embedded in the networks. Although being promising for identifying network communities, the popular stochastic models often do not preserve node degrees, thus reducing their representation power and applicability to real-world networks. Here we address this critical problem. Instead of using a blockmodel, we adopted a random-graph null model to faithfully capture community structures by preserving in the model the expected node degrees. The new model, learned using nonnegative matrix factorization, is more accurate and robust in representing community structures than the existing methods. Our results from extensive experiments on synthetic benchmarks and real-world networks show the superior performance of the new method over the existing methods in detecting both disjoint and overlapping communities.

1. Introduction

Most networks, such as social and biological networks, are better organized and represented in communities or modules, where nodes within a community are relatively densely connected and nodes across communities are sparsely linked (Girvan and Newman 2002). Due to its utility in unraveling complex structures in networks from diverse fields, ranging from social sciences, engineering to biology and medicine, identification of communities in complex networks has attracted much attention in recent years (Fortunato 2010). Much effort has been devoted to developing methods for community detection. These methods can be grouped into that for finding disjoint communities (Girvan and Newman 2002; Blondel et al. 2008; Rosvall and Bergstrom 2008) and those for finding overlapping communities (Palla et al. 2005; Lancichinetti, Fortunato and Kertesz 2009; Ahn, Bagrow and Lehmann 2010).

Among the existing methods for community discovery are stochastic models of communities, which offer an effective technique for network analysis and has attracted much attention lately (Newman 2012). Several model-based methods have been proposed (Wang et al. 2011; Psorakis et al. 2011; Zhang and Yeung 2012; Ren et al. 2009; Shen, Cheng and Guo 2011; Karrer and Newman 2011; Ball, Karrer and Newman 2011), most of which are based on the popular stochastic blockmodel (Nowicki and Snijders 2001). In a simple form of the stochastic blockmodel, each of n nodes of a network is assigned to one of c communities, and two nodes are connected with a probability depending on the community memberships of the nodes. To be concrete, the stochastic blockmodel of a network of n nodes can be represented by a $c\times c$ probability matrix $\omega = (\omega_{g_i g_j})$, where g_i is the community that node i belongs to and $\omega_{g_i g_j}$ is the probability that an edge is introduced between nodes i and j.

Although simple, this blockmodel ignores variation of node degrees and thus does not preserve node degrees of a network to be modeled, rendering the model unsuitable for real networks (Karrer and Newman 2011). Node degrees of a real-world network are typically distinct from that of a random graph; node degrees of a real-world network often exhibit a power-law distribution (Barabasi and Albert 1999). Neglect or improper formulation of node degrees can result in inaccurate network structures and thereby affecting the quality of a community discovery algorithm.

The idea of preserving node degrees was proposed by (Karrer and Newman 2011). However, their model itself does not preserve node degrees; this is achieved by additional inference, which limits its generality. This critical issue has not been addressed adequately in the existing methods that adopt or extend the blockmodel, as discussed in Sec. 5. Here, we attempted to address this issue. In our study, we did not use the blockmodel. Rather, we introduced a new stochastic model atop a popular random-graph null model, i.e., null model of modularity (Newman and Girvan 2004). Using probabilistic community membership, our new model can not only describe those community structures that the original null model failed to capture, but also hold the property of retaining the expected node degrees in the model to be the same as in the original network. The community structure was learned by fitting the model to the given network. Our model preserves node degrees by itself without inference, and hence it doesn't have to rely on specialized inference algorithms for this task. As a result, the new model and its companion network community discovery method are effective in discovering intrinsic and subtle community structures of many real-world networks.

This paper is organized as follows. We first show the importance of preserving node degrees by an example. We then introduce the new model and discuss the new MNDP method. We present experimental results thereafter. Finally, we discuss the related works and conclude this work.

2. A Motivating Example

We examine here the well-known "karate club" (Zachary 1977) to show the importance of preserving node degrees. This network has been considered as the *de facto* model for network analysis. It represents the relationships among the 34 members of a karate club. The club is known to have split into two groups or communities as a result of a dispute, and the members of each group are known.

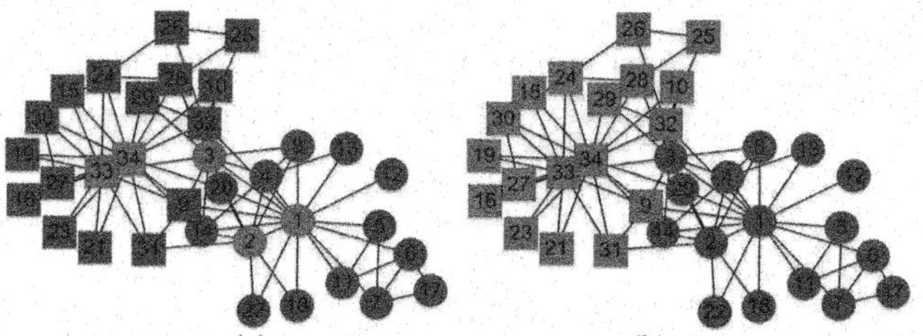

(a) (b)

Figure 1: The Zachary's "karate club" network. The two node shapes represent the two actual communities reported: the club administrator's (square) and the instructor's (circle). **(a)** The two communities, in red and blue, reported by the basic blockmodel. **(b)** The two communities, also in red and blue, correctly identified by our model that is able to preserve node degrees.

The basic blockmodel (Nowicki and Snijders 2001) found two communities (Fig. 1(a)), which are drastically different from the two actual groups of the club. The main problem of this model, as correctly pointed out by others (Karrer and Newman 2011), is that it fails to preserve node degrees so that it erroneously splits the club members into a group with (red) nodes of high degrees and another with (blue) nodes of low degrees.

On the contrary, our model correctly split the club members into two groups that perfectly match the actual network communities (Fig. 1(b)). The success of our model on this well-known network, as well as on other networks to be discussed in later sections, is mainly from faithfully modeling heterogeneous node degrees in the model (see Fig. 2 and Table 1). Besides, our result here is also better than that of the Karrer's degree-corrected blockmodel (Fig. 1(b) in (Karrer and Newman 2011)). The reason may be that: we adopt the random-graph null model while Karrer used the stochastic blockmodel; our model itself preserves node degrees while Karrer's model achieved this by specialized inference (see Sec. 5 for discussion).

3. The Method

We first describe the new model, discuss its properties, and then introduce an algorithm to learn the model parameters.

3.1 Stochastic Model

Consider an undirected graph of n nodes, $G = (V, E)$, represented by an adjacency matrix A. Assume that the nodes can be partitioned into c communities using a probabilistic group membership variable S, where S_{iz} is the probability that node i belongs to community z, subject to $\sum_z S_{iz} = 1$.

Given S_{iz}, network G can be viewed as an ensemble of c probabilistic communities, $\{C_1, C_2, \ldots, C_c\}$, where every node has a probabilistic membership in each community C_z. The degree of node i within community C_z can be defined as $d_{iz} = d_i S_{iz}$, where d_i is the degree of node i in G. Since C_z corresponds to only one community, it can be regarded as a random graph with no community structure. A popular random-graph null model, namely null model of modularity (Newman and Girvan 2004), is suitable for characterizing a probabilistic community. This null model describes random graphs with no communities where edges are rewired randomly among the nodes. We used the null model of modularity to describe each C_z with the given node degrees $\{d_{1z}, d_{2z}, \ldots, d_{nz}\}$, so that we preserved node degrees in each of the probabilistic communities. In this null model, the expected number of links (or expected link weight) between nodes i and j in C_z can be written as

$$\hat{w}_{ij}^z = d_{iz} d_{jz} / \sum_k d_{kz} . \tag{1}$$

Taking all the communities $\{C_z | z=1,2,..,c\}$ into consideration, the expected number of links between nodes i and j in the model can be written as

$$\hat{w}_{ij} = \sum_z \hat{w}_{ij}^z = \sum_z \left(d_{iz} d_{jz} / \sum_k d_{kz} \right) . \tag{2}$$

However, the community membership S_{iz} is unknown in advance, and it needs to be inferred by fitting the model parameters d_{iz} to the given network, which will be discussed in Sec. 3.3. When the parameters d_{iz} are available, the community membership S_{iz} can then be inferred by

$$S_{iz} = d_{iz} / \sum_r d_{ir} = d_{iz} / d_i . \tag{3}$$

Both hard and overlapping communities can be derived from the probabilistic community membership, S_{iz}. Specifically, to derive a hard partition, node i can be assigned to community $r = argmax_z \{S_{iz}, z=1,2,\ldots,c\}$. To construct a structure with overlapping communities, the strategy of (Zhang and Yeung 2012) can be adopted, i.e., the entries in vector $\{S_{i1}, S_{i2}, \ldots, S_{ic}\}$ are first scaled to values in [0, 1], and those entries whose rescaled values exceed a threshold are set to 1, or 0 otherwise. Then we can use a suitable quality metrics of communities to determine the threshold.

3.2 Model Properties

The new model consists of a set of probabilistic communities, each of which is considered to be a random graph and represented by a null model of modularity. The new model can in essence be regarded as a generalization to the null model of modularity. It not only incorporates the ability of describing communities which the original null model does not have, but also holds the property, as with the original model, that fixes the expected node degrees to be the same as that of the observed network, as captured by Proposition 1 below. Our model naturally describes the distributions of heterogeneous node degrees, making it more robust for complex network community structures than the blockmodels, which do not have this property.

Proposition 1. *In our model, the expected graph of G preserves the same node degrees as in the observed network G (see Appendix for proof).*

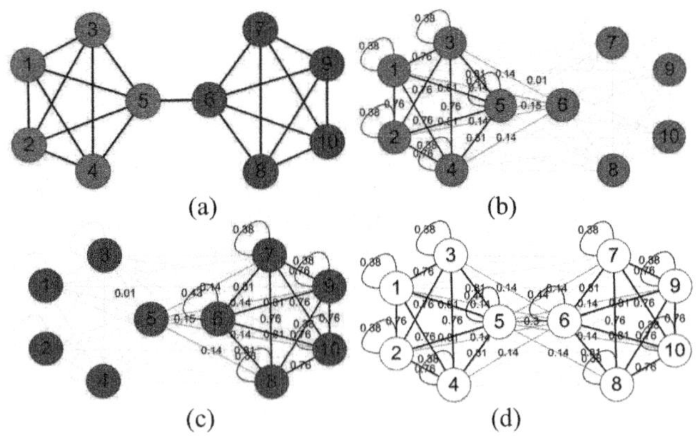

Figure 2: An example illustrating some properties of the model with network parameters d_{iz} listed in Table 1. **(a)** A given network G with two communities shown in red and blue. **(b)** and **(c)** The expected graphs of the red and blue communities, each of which is described by a null model of modularity. **(d)** The expected graph of G that combines the expected graphs of the two communities. The width of a link corresponds to its expected values; the links with values smaller than 1.0e-2 are omitted.

Table 1: The parameters d_{iz} used in Fig 2 and learned by NMF

d_{iz}	$i=1$	$i=2$	$i=3$	$i=4$	$i=5$
$z=1$	3.999949	3.999974	3.999975	3.999972	4.253827
$z=2$	5.12E-05	2.63E-05	2.45E-05	2.76E-05	0.746173
d_{iz}	$i=6$	$i=7$	$i=8$	$i=9$	$i=10$
$z=1$	0.748089	7.14E-04	7.39E-04	7.02E-04	6.89E-04
$z=2$	4.251911	3.999286	3.999261	3.999298	3.999311

Here we offer an example, shown in Fig. 2 and in Table 1, to illustrate our model of a small network. The red and blue communities are indexed by 'z=1' and 'z=2' in Table 1, respectively. Firstly, consider the within-community nodes, e.g., nodes 3 and 4. As d_{31} and d_{41} are both large, the expected number of red links between them is large ($\hat{w}^1_{3,4}$ =0.76), so that the expected number of links between nodes 3 and 4 is large as well ($\hat{w}_{3,4}$ = 0.76). On the other hand, consider the nodes in different communities, such as nodes 3 and 7. As d_{71} is very small, although d_{31} is large, the expected number of red links between these two nodes is still small ($\hat{w}^1_{3,7}$ <1.0e-2); similarly, the expected number of blue links between them is also small ($\hat{w}^2_{3,7}$ < 1.0e-2). Thus, the expected number of links between nodes 3 and 7 is much smaller than that between 3 and 4 ($\hat{w}_{3,7} << \hat{w}_{3,4}$). This result correctly matches the intuition that intra-cluster connectivities are dense than inter-cluster connectivities.

More importantly, by preserving node degrees our model is consistent with the observation that nodes with high degrees are, with all other things being equal, more likely to be connected among themselves than those with low degrees. In Fig. 1(d), for instance, as node 5 has a larger degree than node 3, $\hat{w}_{5,4} = 0.81 > \hat{w}_{3,4} = 0.76$. Intuitively, two nodes of high degrees are more likely to be connected than two nodes of low degrees. Thus, by incorporating such observations, we can faithfully describe heterogeneous node degrees and accurately find communities.

3.3 Parameter Learning

The model is specified by a set of parameters d_{iz} of node degrees in the communities, for n nodes i =1,2,…,n and c communities z=1,2,…,c. These parameters have to be learned from the data of the given network G. The problem of fitting the model to the data of G can be cast as the following optimization problem,

$$\min_{d_{iz}\geq 0} \left\|A-\hat{A}\right\|_F^2 = \sum_{ij}\left(w_{ij} - \sum_z\left(d_{iz}d_{jz}/\sum_k d_{kz}\right)\right)^2 \quad s.t.\ \sum_z d_{iz} = d_i \qquad (4)$$

where $\|.\|_F$ denotes Frobenius norm. The best fit between the expected graph with adjacency $\hat{A} = (\hat{w}_{ij})_{n\times n}$ and a given network G with adjacency $A = (w_{ij})_{n\times n}$ can be achieved by optimizing (4). We give a nonnegative matrix factorization (NMF) method to solve the optimization in (4).

We first introduce an auxiliary matrix X, where X_{iz} is

$$X_{iz} = d_{iz} / \sqrt{\sum_j d_{jz}} \,. \qquad (5)$$

Function (4) can be written as a constrained NMF problem,

$$\min_{X\geq 0} \left\|A - XX^{\mathrm{T}}\right\|_F^2, \quad st.\ XX^{\mathrm{T}}1_n = d \,, \qquad (6)$$

where $d = (d_1, d_2,\ldots, d_n)^{\mathrm{T}}$. It is nontrivial to directly optimize (6) with the hard constraints. We relax this optimization problem by introducing a penalty term that represents the hard constraints into the objective function, arriving at minimizing the following objective function,

$$O(X) = \frac{1}{2}\left\|A - XX^T\right\|_F^2 + \frac{\lambda}{2}\left\|XX^T 1_n - d\right\|_2^2 \qquad (7)$$

where λ is a hyperparameter that reflects the importance of the hard constraints. Violation to more hard constraints incurs a higher penalty to the objective function. In our experiments, we first get an initial value of X_0 by setting λ = 0. Then we restart the optimization with $X = X_0$ and let λ to a relatively large number, e.g., 1000, to minimize the chance of violating the degree constraints. The purpose of the initialization is to restrict the search for a model to start from some good approximations. Similar to other forms of NMF, the objective function in (7) is not convex w.r.t. X, so that it is computationally intractable to find global minima. Therefore, the gradient descent method is adopted to search for local minima, which can be implemented in a multiplicative updating algorithm similar to the method for SNMF (Wang et al. 2011). In order to derive the updating rule, a Lagrange multiplier matrix Θ for the nonnegative constraints on X is introduced to (7), resulting in the following equivalent objective function,

$$\mathcal{L}(X) = Tr(XX^TXX^T)/4 - Tr(A^TXX^T)/2$$
$$+\lambda Tr(1_n^TXX^TXX^T1_n)/2 - \lambda Tr(1_n^TXX^Td) + Tr(\Theta^TX)$$

For any stationary state, we have

$$\partial\mathcal{L}/\partial X = XX^TX - AX + \lambda 1_n 1_n^T XX^TX$$
$$+\lambda XX^T1_n1_n^TX - \lambda 1_n d^TX + \lambda d 1_n^TX + \Theta$$

Using complementary slackness condition $(\Theta)_{ik}(X)_{ik} = 0$, we have the following equation,

$$(XX^TX - AX + \lambda 1_n 1_n^T XX^TX + \lambda XX^T1_n1_n^TX - \lambda 1_n d^TX$$
$$+ \lambda d1_n^TX)_{ik}(X)_{ik} = 0.$$

This leads to the following update rule for X:

$$X_{ik} = X_{ik}\left(\frac{\left((A + \lambda 1_n d^T + \lambda d 1_n^T)X\right)_{ik}}{\left(XX^TX + \lambda 1_n 1_n^T XX^TX + \lambda XX^T1_n1_n^TX\right)_{ik}}\right)^{\frac{1}{4}} \quad (8)$$

When the update rule converges, shown in Theorem 1 below, the solution satisfies the Karush-Kuhn-Tucker (KKT) conditions (Boyd and Vandenberghe 2004).

Theorem 1. *Function O in (7) is non-increasing under the updating rule in (8). O is invariant under these updates if and only if X becomes stationary (see Appendix for proof).*

Finally, when the method converges, the parameters d_{iz} of the model can be computed using (5) as follows,

$$d_{iz} = X_{iz}\sqrt{\sum_j d_{jz}} = X_{iz}\sum_j X_{jz}\,. \quad (9)$$

Notice that, the time to calculate AX, $1_n(d^TX)$, $d(1_n^TX)$, $X(X^TX)$, $1_n(1_n^TXX^TX)$ and $X(X^T1_n)(1_n^TX)$ in (8) is $2mc$, $2nc$, $2nc$, $2nc^2$, $4nc$ and $4nc$, respectively, where n is the number of nodes, m is the number of edges and c is the number of clusters. So the time to evaluate (8) once is $O(mc+nc^2)$, and hence the time complexity of MNDP is $O(T(mc+nc^2))$, where T is the iteration number for convergence. As the number of communities is much smaller than network size (i.e., $c << m, n$), our method scales well to large networks.

4. Experiments

To test the performance of our MNDP, we evaluated it on synthetic and real networks. We also compared it with four related methods, i.e., Karrer's method (Karrer and Newman 2011), Ball's method (Ball, Karrer and Newman 2011), SNMF (Wang et al. 2011) and BNMTF (Zhang and Yeung 2012). Karrer's method considers node degrees, but it adopts likelihood probability as objective function which is optimized by local search. Ball's method was designed for link partitions (overlapping communities) and extended to node partitions with node degrees being taken into consideration. SNMF and BNMTF use squared loss objective functions and adopt NMF for optimization. Since the methods compared converge to local minima, we ran each method 20 times and reported the best result. We compared them in terms of hard partitions and overlapping communities. Besides, we compared them on a large weighted network to assess their applicability to weighted networks.

4.1 Synthetic Networks

Two types of synthetic benchmarks, one with disjoint communities (Lancichinetti, Fortunato and Radicchi 2008) and the other with overlapping communities (Lancichinetti and Fortunato 2009), were proposed. Here we considered them in our experiments. The node degrees and community size of a LFR benchmark graph follow power law distributions, a property that most real-world networks share. We did not compare the results of BNMTF here because it cannot finish in 100 hours on every trial attempted.

4.1.1 LFR Benchmark with Disjoint Communities

Proposed by (Lancichinetti, Fortunato and Radicchi 2008), this type of benchmark is designed to detect disjoint communities. We adopted the widely used Normalized Mutual Information (NMI) index as the quality metric in our study.

Following the parameter setting as the LFR benchmark used in (Lancichinetti, Fortunato and Radicchi 2008), we considered networks with 1000 nodes and the minimum community size c_{min} of 10 or 20. We varied the mixing parameter μ, which specifies the fraction of the links of a node connecting to nodes outside of the node's community, from 0 to 0.8 with an increment of 0.05. The remaining parameters were kept fixed: the average degree d was set to 20, the maximum degree d_{max} to $2.5{\times}d$, the maximum community size c_{max} to $5{\times}c_{min}$, the exponent of power-law distribution of node degrees τ_1 to -2 and community size τ_2 to -1. This design space led to two sets of benchmarks.

Fig. 3 shows the accuracy of each algorithm in NMI as a function of the mixing parameter μ. As shown, our MNDP outperformed Karrer's method, Ball's method and SNMF, especially when μ is in the range of 0.5 to 0.7.

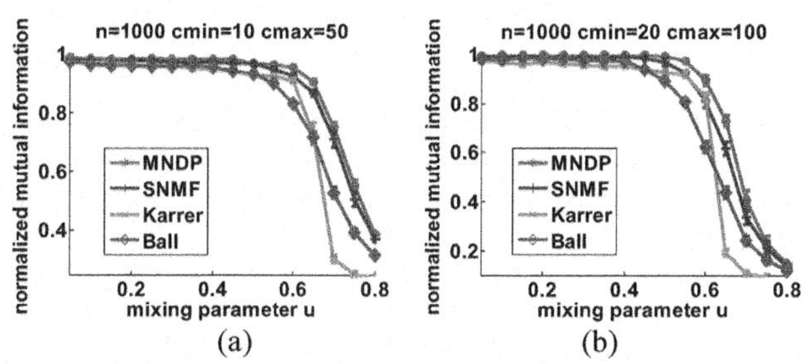

Figure 3: Comparison of different methods in terms of NMI accuracy on the LFR benchmark of disjoint communities. Error bars show the standard deviations estimated from 50 graphs. Shown are results on networks of **(a)** small communities (c_{min} = 10, c_{max} = 50) and **(b)** large communities (c_{min} = 20, c_{max} = 100).

4.1.2 LFR Benchmark with Overlapping Communities

This type of benchmark for overlapping communities was proposed by (Lancichinetti and Fortunato 2009). We used the generalized NMI (GNMI) (Lancichinetti, Fortunato and Kertesz 2009) as accuracy metric. Here we did not include Karrer's method, as it cannot find overlapping structures, nor Ball's method as it finds highly overlapped structures, thus failing to detect clusters defined in this benchmark.

Adopting the same parameter setting as for the LFR benchmark in (Lancichinetti and Fortunato 2009), we used networks with 1000 nodes, the minimum community size c_{min} of 10 or 20, the mixing parameter μ of 0.1 or 0.3, and varying fraction of overlapping (o_n/n) from 0 to 0.5 with an increment of 0.05. The remaining parameters were fixed: the average node degree d was set to 20, the maximum degree d_{max} to $2.5\times d$, the maximum community size c_{max} to $5\times c_{min}$, the number of communities that an overlapping node belongs to (denoted as o_m) to 2, the exponents of the power-law distribution of node degrees τ_1 to -2 and community sizes τ_2 to -1, resulting in four sets of benchmarks.

Fig. 4 shows the results comparing MNDP and SNMF in terms of the GNMI index. As shown, MNDP outperforms SNMF on all four sets of benchmarks. Particularly, when overlapping (o_n/n) is larger, MNDP performs better.

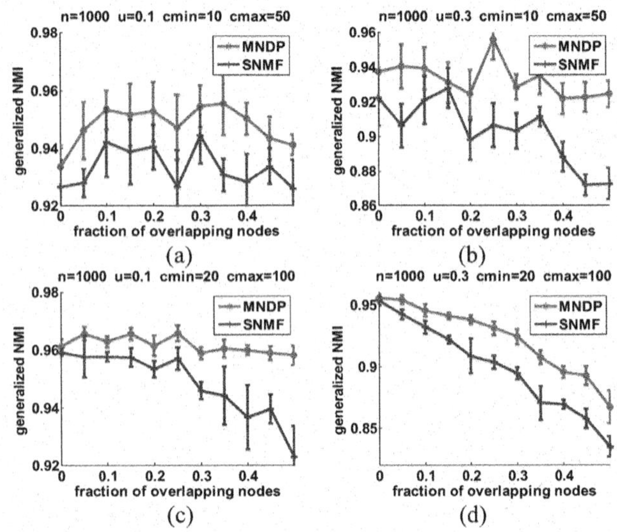

Figure 4: The GNMI accuracy of each algorithm as a function of the fraction of overlapping nodes. Shown are results on networks of **(a)** small mixing parameter & small communities ($\mu = 0.1$, $c_{min} = 10$, $c_{max} = 50$), **(b)** big mixing parameter & small communities ($\mu = 0.3$, $c_{min} = 10$, $c_{max} = 50$), **(c)** small mixing parameter & big communities ($\mu = 0.1$, $c_{min} = 20$, $c_{max} = 100$) and **(d)** big mixing parameter & big communities ($\mu = 0.3$, $c_{min} = 20$, $c_{max} = 100$).

4. 2 Real-World Networks

Many real-world networks have distinct topological properties from synthetic networks so that different network analysis methods may render performance on such networks different from that on synthetic networks. We compared the algorithms on two types of real-world networks, i.e., networks with known community structures and networks with actual community structures unknown. We included networks with disjoint and overlapping communities, as well as a large weighted network in comparison.

4.2.1 Networks with Known Community Structures

The real networks analyzed (Newman 2013; Xie, Kelley and Szymanski 2013) and the methods compared are listed in Table 2. For comparison on networks with known community structures, we adopted the NMI index as the quality metric. As shown in the table, the new method MNDP has the best performance on five of the seven networks, and is also competitive with the other methods on the left two networks. On average, our method is 6.7543%, 3.9414%, 1.2814% and 2.5186% more accurate than Karrer's method, Ball's method, SNMF and BNMTF, respectively.

Table 2: Accuracies of 5 methods compared, in NMI index, on 7 networks. 'Friendship6' and 'friendship7' have the same network, but are described by different "true" community structures.

Datasets	n	m	c	NMI index (%)				
				MNDP	Karrer	Ball	SNMF	BNMTF
Zachary's karate club	34	78	2	**100**	83.72	**100**	**100**	**100**
Dolphin social network	62	160	2	**88.88**	**88.88**	81.41	81.41	81.41
High school friendship6	69	220	6	**79.30**	77.02	78.08	78.64	71.22
High school friendship7	69	220	7	84.26	**85.10**	83.93	82.11	84.30
Political books	105	441	3	53.01	54.20	53.39	**56.48**	51.18
American college football	115	613	12	**92.42**	87.06	91.34	90.38	**92.42**
Political blogs	1,490	16,717	2	**71.07**	45.68	53.20	70.95	70.78

4.2.2 Networks with no Known Community Structures

These five methods were further compared on real-world networks whose community structures are unknown (Newman 2013; Nelson, McEvoy and Schreiber 2013). The results are in Table 3. As no "true" community structure is known, Louvain method (Blondel et al. 2008), which is regarded as one of the best algorithms for community detection by (Fortunato 2010), was applied to estimate the numbers of communities that were used by the 5 methods. Because some of the algorithms compared are able to find both disjoint and overlapping community structures, we used two widely used quality metrics: the modularity Q (Newman and Girvan 2004) for evaluating hard partitions and the generalized map equation L for testing overlapping communities (Esquivel and Rosvall 2011). Because Louvain method was designed to optimize Q, it is not surprising that it is able to derive higher Q-values. Besides, as Louvain method is unable to find overlapping communities, we did not include it in comparison here.

Table 3: Some real-world networks without ground-truths.

Datasets	n	m	c (Louvain)
Les Miserables	77	254	6
Word adjacencies	112	425	7
Jazz musicians collaborations	198	2,742	4
C. Elegans neural	297	2,148	5
E. coli metabolic	453	2,025	10
E-mail network URV	1,133	5,451	11
Network Science collaborations	1,589	2,742	277
Power grid	4,941	6,594	39
Word association (unweighted)	5,018	55,234	12
Word association (weighted)	5,018	55,234	30

Table 4: The comparison of community detection algorithms on several real networks. The greater a Q-value, the better; and the smaller a L-value, the better. '–' denotes run time >100 hours. Karrer's method cannot find overlapping communities. Karrer's method and Ball's method cannot deal with weighted networks.

Datasets	Modularity Q (disjoint)					Map equation L (overlaps)			
(abbr)	MNDP	Karrer	Ball	SNMF	BNMTF	MNDP	Ball	SNMF	BNMTF
Les Mis	0.5434	0.4575	0.5211	0.5453	**0.5487**	**4.7283**	4.8922	4.7640	4.7713
Adjnoun	**0.2712**	-0.1041	0.2594	0.2672	0.2634	6.6474	6.7941	6.6869	**6.6397**
Jazz	**0.4377**	0.3696	0.4352	0.4348	0.4347	**6.8327**	6.9121	6.8465	6.8506
Neural	**0.3811**	0.2617	0.3638	0.3701	0.3689	**7.6108**	7.7163	7.6276	7.6893
Metabolic	0.3796	0.2656	0.3689	**0.3879**	0.3834	7.6252	7.7358	**7.5434**	7.6129
Email	**0.5154**	0.5126	0.4814	0.5007	0.4685	**8.6075**	9.0586	8.6202	8.7130
Netscience	**0.8336**	0.6402	0.7296	0.7986	0.7592	5.2338	**3.7445**	5.2922	6.7284
Power	**0.8683**	0.1796	0.6641	0.8649	–	**8.1487**	8.8804	8.1512	–
Word_u	0.3613	**0.4595**	0.3625	0.3546	–	**11.7068**	12.2743	11.7225	–
Word_w	**0.5190**	*NaN*	*NaN*	0.5030	–	**10.4104**	*NaN*	10.4499	–

The results are in Table 4. As shown, MNDP has the best performance on seven of the ten networks in terms of modularity Q. On average, our method is 0.1722, 0.0451, 0.0083 and 0.0193 better than Karrer's method, Ball's method, SNMF and BNMTF, respectively. As Q-values are normally in the range of 0.3 to 0.8 (Newman and Girvan 2004), MNDP obviously outperforms the existing methods. In terms of map equation L, MNDP has the best performance on seven of the ten networks. On average, our method is 0.0963, 0.0153 and 0.2456 bits better than Ball's method, SNMF and BNMTF, respectively. It is known that the improvement of L is typically very small near optimal solutions (see Table II of (Kim and Jeong 2011)), thus our improvement here is also nontrivial. Furthermore, we used the unweighted and weighted versions of the 'word association' network in the comparison. The performance of each method on the weighted network is much better than that on unweighted network. This suggests that edge weights contain additional information of the networks, and thus it is important for an algorithm to be able to incorporate weight information in the weighted networks. Importantly, MNDP outperformed the other two NMF-based methods on both unweighted and weighted versions of this network.

5. Related Works

Several model-based methods have been developed, most of which are built atop the stochastic blockmodel or its variations and employ different optimization methods for model learning. For instance, some works extend the basic blockmodel by introducing soft community membership and use nonnegative matrix factorization (NMF) or its variations as the optimization methods to learn model parameters. In particular, (Wang et al. 2011) use a squared loss and a symmetric nonnegative matrix factorization (SNMF) to minimize the loss function. (Psorakis et al. 2011) adopt generalized KL-divergence as the loss function, and develop a Bayesian nonnegative matrix factorization (BNMF) for optimization. (Zhang and Yeung 2012) remove the constraint that the sum of probabilities for each node belonging to different communities equals to 1 to better model overlapping structures. Further, they use both squared loss and KL-divergence as the loss functions, and devise a bounded nonnegative matrix tri-factorization (BNMTF) for optimization. While these methods are all based on NMF with soft membership, they do not preserve node degrees, which may distort the community detection results.

There are also other works that adopt similar models (Ren et al. 2009; Shen, Cheng and Guo 2011; Karrer and Newman 2011; Ball, Karrer and Newman 2011). However, rather than using loss functions, they adopt likelihood probabilities as the objectives, and take different algorithmic approaches, e.g., Expectation-Maximization algorithm, to learn the models. Of particular interest is the Karrer's method (Karrer and Newman 2011), which attempts to preserve node degrees. However, it does not preserve the node degrees in its model, but achieves this objective by a special inference algorithm, which may limit its generality. Specifically, the expected degree of node i in Karrer's model is $\sum_j \theta_i \theta_j \omega_{g_i g_j}$, which is not necessary equal to node i's degree d_i. For example, if we use squared loss instead of Poisson distribution to fit Karrer's model to the given network, its property of preserving node degree will be lost. In contrast, the model in our MNDP preserves node degrees by itself with no inference, which makes it a generalized model for this problem. Specifically, the expected degree of node i in our model is $\sum_j \left(d_{iz} d_{jz} / \sum_k d_{kz} \right)$, which is equal to node i's degree d_i without any inference (proof in Proposition 1). Furthermore, Karrer's model is an extension of blockmodel to correct node degrees by using a block matrix ω (discussed in Sec. 1) to specify relationships among communities. It has two objective functions to fit: communities and disassortative structures. In contrast, our model is a generalization to the null model of modularity to incorporate community structures, which does not use any types of block matrices. It has one objective (i.e. communities) to fit, which may improve the ability to detect communities. Moreover, Karrer's model focuses on hard clustering that can only detect disjoint communities, while our model uses soft community membership and thus is able to find both disjoint and overlapping communities. Finally, Karrer's model cannot handle weighted networks as it uses Poisson distribution to derive the objective function, while our model can handle weighted networks.

The work proposed by (Ball, Karrer and Newman), which can be considered as a relaxation to Karrer's degree-corrected blockmodel, is also related. Nevertheless, Ball's model was initially designed for link communities and then extended to node communities. In contrast, our model focused on node communities. Furthermore, Ball's model is parameterized by parameters θ_{iz}'s, where θ_{iz} denotes that node i to have links in community z; and then it takes $\theta_{iz}\theta_{jz}$ as the expected number of links in community z connecting nodes i and j. In comparison, our model is parameterized by parameters d_{iz}'s, where d_{iz} is the expected node degree of i in community z; and takes $d_{iz} d_{jz} / \sum_k d_{kz}$ as the expected number of links between nodes i and j in community z, following the null model of modularity. In short, these two models use different ideas to describe communities. Specifically, if we map $d_{iz} = \theta_{iz} \sum_j \theta_{jz}$, Ball's model assigns a node to a community for which $d_{iz}/\sum_{j=1}^{n} d_{jz}$ is the largest, while our model assigns a node to a community for which $d_{iz}/\sum_{r=1}^{c} d_{ir}$ is the largest, resulting in two different types of community structures. More importantly, similar to Karrer's model, Ball's model does not preserve node degrees by itself. Specifically, the expected degree of node i in Ball's model is $\sum_j \theta_{iz}\theta_{jz}$, which may not be equal to node i's degree d_i. When using squared loss instead of Poisson distribution to fit the Ball's model to the given network, its objective function will be $\| A - XX^{\mathrm{T}} \|_F^2$, which is a basic NMF and will not preserve node degrees. Finally, Ball's model cannot deal with weighted networks.

We used the null model of modularity to describe probabilistic communities because of its simplicity and good performance. Some other random models with given degree sequence (e.g., that due to Havel-Hakimi (Havel 1955; Hakimi 1962)) may also be suitable for this task. We will include these models in our framework in the future. Our model offers no criterion for determining the number of communities, which is a critical parameter for analyzing community structures. This is a common drawback shared by almost all model methods (Newman 2012). The methods of statistical model selection (Brunet et al. 2004; Tan and Févotte 2012) may in principle be used to address this issue; nevertheless it is too computationally demanding to be useful for any but some small graphs (Ball, Karrer and Newman 2011). More research is needed to address this issue, a direction we plan to pursue in future research.

6. Conclusion

We studied the importance of preserving node degrees for identifying community structures in complex networks. We developed a novel model and an efficient algorithm for finding such structures. They can be used to identify both overlapping and disjoint communities and are applicable to weighted networks. The new model generalizes the null model of modularity (Newman and Girvan 2004) and utilizes probabilistic community memberships to characterize community structures. In our method, we introduced a squared loss function based on this extended model, and optimized the model parameters using a NMF approach.

Our extensive experimental comparison of the new method and four existing competing methods on synthetic benchmarks and real-world networks demonstrated the superior performance of the new MNDP method in detecting both disjoint and overlapping communities.

Acknowledgments

The work was supported by National Basic Research Program (973 Program) of China (2013CB329301, 2012CB316301), Natural Science Foundation of China (61303110, 61271128, 61133011, 31300999), Major Project of National Social Science Fund (14ZDB153), the municipal government of Wuhan, China (2014070504020241 and the Talent Development Program), an internal grant of Jianghan University, Wuhan, China, and United States National Institutes of Health (R01GM100364).

Appendices

A1. Proof of Proposition 1

Let d_i be the degree of node i in G. Given an arbitrary set of variables d_{iz}, subject to $\sum_z d_{iz} = d_i$, which correspond to our model parameters, then using (2) the degree of node i in the expected graph of G can be inferred as

$$\hat{d}_i = \sum_j \hat{w}_{ij} = \sum_j \sum_z \left(d_{iz} d_{jz} / \sum_k d_{kz} \right)$$
$$= \sum_z \left(d_{iz} \sum_j d_{jz} \right) / \sum_k d_{kz} = \sum_z d_{iz} = d_i ,$$

which equals to node i's degree in the observed network G.

A2. Proof of Theorem 1

We adopt the auxiliary function approach used in Expectation-Maximization and NMF. The basic idea is to construct an auxiliary function $C(X,\tilde{X})$ such that:

$O(X) = C(X,X) \le C(X,\tilde{X}) \le C(\tilde{X},\tilde{X}) = O(\tilde{X})$

If we can minimize $C(X,\tilde{X})$ w.r.t to X, then we are guaranteed to drive $O(X)$ down. Note that,

$$O(X) = Tr(XX^T XX^T)/4 - Tr(A^T XX^T)/2$$
$$+\lambda Tr(1_n^T XX^T XX^T 1_n)/2 - \lambda Tr(1_n^T XX^T d)$$
$$\le Tr(P\tilde{X}\tilde{X}^T)/4 + \lambda Tr(P 1_n 1_n^T \tilde{X}\tilde{X}^T)/2 - Tr(A^T XX^T)/2$$
$$-\lambda Tr(d 1_n^T XX^T) \text{ (by Lemma 6 of (Wang et al. 2011))}$$
$$\le Tr(R^T \tilde{X}\tilde{X}^T \tilde{X})/4 + \lambda Tr(R^T 1_n 1_n^T \tilde{X}\tilde{X}^T \tilde{X})/4$$
$$+ \lambda Tr(\tilde{X}^T 1_n 1_n^T \tilde{X}\tilde{X}^T R)/4 - Tr(Z^T A\tilde{X}) - \lambda Tr(Z^T d 1_n^T \tilde{X})$$
$$- \lambda Tr(\tilde{X}^T d 1_n^T Z) - Tr(\tilde{X}^T A\tilde{X})/2 - \lambda Tr(\tilde{X}^T d 1_n^T \tilde{X})$$
$$\text{(by Lemma 7 and 3 of (Wang et al. 2011))}$$
$$\equiv C(X,\tilde{X}),$$

where $P_{kl} = [XX^T]_{kl}^2/[\tilde{X}\tilde{X}^T]_{kl}$, $R_{ik} = [X]_{ik}^4/[\tilde{X}]_{ik}^3$, and $Z_{ij} = \tilde{X}_{ij}\ln(X_{ij}/\tilde{X}_{ij})$. The equality holds when $X = \tilde{X}$. Then $C(X,\tilde{X})$ satisfied the conditions of being an auxiliary function for $O(X)$. So we can define the updating rules as:

$$X^{(t+1)} = \min_X C(X, X^{(t)})$$

$$\frac{\partial C(X,\tilde{X})}{\partial X_{ik}} = \frac{X_{ik}^3}{\tilde{X}_{ik}^3} [\tilde{X}\tilde{X}^T \tilde{X} + \lambda 1_n 1_n^T \tilde{X}\tilde{X}^T \tilde{X} + \lambda \tilde{X}\tilde{X}^T 1_n 1_n^T \tilde{X}]_{ik}$$
$$- \frac{\tilde{X}_{ik}}{X_{ik}} [A\tilde{X} + \lambda d 1_n^T \tilde{X} + \lambda 1_n d^T \tilde{X}]_{ik} = 0$$

Thus we get the update rule for X as in (8).

References

Ahn, Y. Y.; Bagrow, J. P.; and Lehmann, S. 2010. Link communities reveal multiscale complexity in networks. *Nature* 466: 761-764.

Ball, B.; Karrer, B.; and Newman, M. E. J. 2011. Efficient and principled method for detecting communities in networks. *Phys. Rev.* E 84: 036103.

Barabasi, A.; and Albert, R. 1999. Emergence of scaling in random networks. *Science* 286: 509-512.

Blondel, V. D.; Guillaume, J. L.; Lambiotte, R.; and Lefebvre, E. 2008. Fast unfolding of communities in large networks. *J. Stat. Mech.* 2008: P10008.

Boyd, S., and Vandenberghe, L. eds. 2004. *Convex optimization.* Cambridge, UK: Cambridge University Press.

Brunet, J-P.; Tamayo, P.; Golun, T. R.; and Mesirov, J. P. 2004. Metagenes and molecular pattern discovery using matrix factorization. *Proc. Natl. Acad. Sci.* 101: 4164-4169.

Danon, L.; Duch, J.; Diaz-Guilera, A.; and Arenas, A. 2005. Comparing community structure identification. *J. Stat. Mech.* 2005: P09008.

Esquivel, A. V.; and Rosvall, M. 2011. Compression of flow can reveal overlapping-module organization in networks. *Physical Review* X 1: 021025.

Fortunato, S. 2010. Community detection in graphs. *Phys. Rep.* 486: 75-174.

Girvan, M.; and Newman, M. E. J. 2002. Community structure in social and biological networks. *Proc. Natl. Acad. Sci.* 99: 7821-7826.

Havel, V. 1955. A remark on the existence of finite graphs. *Časopis pro pěstování matematiky (in Czech)* 80: 477-480.

Hakimi, S. L. 1962. On realizability of a set of integers as degrees of the vertices of a linear graph. *Journal of the Society for Industrial and Applied Mathematics* 10: 496-506.

Karrer, B.; and Newman, M. E. J. 2011. Stochastic blockmodels and community structure in networks. *Phys. Rev.* E 83: 016107.

Kim, Y.; and Jeong, H. 2011. Map equation for link communities. *Phys Rev* E 84: 026110.

Lancichinetti, A.; Fortunato, S.; and Kertesz, J. 2009. Detecting the overlapping and hierarchical community structure in complex networks. *New J. Phys.* 11: 033015.

Lancichinetti, A.; Fortunato, S.; and Radicchi, F. 2008. Benchmark graphs for testing community detection algorithms, *Phys. Rev.* E 78: 046110.

Lancichinetti, A.; and Fortunato, S. 2009. Benchmarks for testing community detection algorithms on directed and weighted graphs with overlapping communities. *Phys. Rev.* E 80: 016118.

Nelson, D. L.; McEvoy, C. L.; and Schreiber, T. A. 2013. The University of South Florida, word association, rhyme, and word fragment norms. http://w3.usf.edu/FreeAssociation/

Newman, M. E. J.; and Girvan, M. 2004. Finding and evaluating community structure in networks. *Phys. Rev.* E 69: 026113.

Newman, M. E. J. 2012. Communities, modules and large-scale structure in networks. *Nature Physics* 8: 25-31.

Newman, M. E. J. 2013. Real-world network data in Newman's hompage. http://www-personal.umich.edu/~mejn/netdata/

Nowicki, K.; and Snijders, T. A. B. 2001. Estimation and prediction for stochastic blockstructures. *Journal of the American Statistical Association* 96: 1077-1087.

Palla, G.; Derenyi, I.; Farkas, I.; and Vicsek, T. 2005. Uncovering the overlapping community structures of complex networks in nature and society. *Nature* 435: 814-818.

Psorakis, I.; Roberts, S.; Ebden, M.; and Sheldon, B. 2011. Overlapping community detection using Bayesian non-negative matrix factorization. *Phys. Rev.* E 83: 066114.

Ren, W.; Yan, G.; Liao, X.; and Xiao, L. 2009. Simple probabilistic algorithm for detecting community structure. *Phys. Rev.* E 79: 036111.

Rosvall, M.; and Bergstrom, C. T. 2008. Maps of random walks on complex networks reveal community structure. *Proc. Natl. Acad. Sci.* 105: 1118-1123.

Shen, H.; Cheng, X.; and Guo, J. 2011. Exploring the structural regularities in networks. *Phys. Rev.* E 84: 056111.

Tan, V. Y. F.; and Févotte, C. 2012. Automatic relevance determination in nonnegative matrix factorization with the β-divergence. *IEEE Transactions on Pattern Analysis and Machine Intelligence* 35: 1592-1605.

Wang, F.; Li, T.; Wang, X.; Zhu, S.; and Ding, C. H. Q. 2011. Community discovery using nonnegative matrix factorization. *Data Mining and Knowledge Discovery* 22: 493-521.

Xie, J.; Kelley, S.; and Szymanski, B. K. 2013. Overlapping community detection in networks: the state of the art and comparative study. *ACM Comput Surv* 45: Article No. 43.

Zachary, W. W. 1977. An information flow model for conflict and fission in small groups. *J Anthropol Res* 33: 452-473.

Zhang, Y.; and Yeung, D. 2012. Overlapping community detection via bounded nonnegative matrix tri-factorization. *In Proceedings of the 18th ACM SIGKDD international conference on Knowledge discovery and data mining*, 606-614. New York, NY: ACM Press.

Proceedings of the Twenty-Ninth AAAI Conference on Artificial Intelligence

Estimating Temporal Dynamics of Human Emotions

Seungyeon Kim* and **Joonseok Lee*** and **Guy Lebanon†** and **Haesun Park***
*College of Computing, Georgia Institute of Technology, Atlanta, GA, USA
†Amazon, Seattle, WA, USA
{seungyeon.kim, jlee716}@gatech.edu, glebanon@gmail.com, hpark@cc.gatech.edu

Abstract

Sentiment analysis predicts a one-dimensional quantity describing the positive or negative emotion of an author. Mood analysis extends the one-dimensional sentiment response to a multi-dimensional quantity, describing a diverse set of human emotions. In this paper, we extend sentiment and mood analysis temporally and model emotions as a function of time based on temporal streams of blog posts authored by a specific author. The model is useful for constructing predictive models and discovering scientific models of human emotions.

1 Introduction

Sentiment analysis predicts the presence of a positive or negative emotion $y \in \mathbb{R}$ in a document x. Recent attempts (Mishne 2005; Kim et al. 2013) generalize sentiment analysis by introducing a multivariate response variable $y \in \mathbb{R}^d$, which corresponds to a more complex emotional state. For example, a classical model from psychology examines a two-dimensional emotional quantity in which the first dimension corresponds to sentiment and the second corresponds to the level of engagement (`aroused` vs. `calm`). Sentiment analysis and its generalizations are important tools in industry, attracting a considerable amount of attention from the research community.

The analysis of human emotions based on text has focused mostly on static analysis, that is the analysis of documents solely based on its own content ignoring temporal dependences. This paper explores a temporal model for human emotions that applies to a sequential stream of text documents written by the same author across different time points. Our model is somewhat similar to Brownian motion and the Kalman filter and generalizes the latent space emotion model in Kim et al. (2013).

Most papers on sentiment analysis use movie or item reviews, which are poorly suited to temporal modeling. Reviews relate to specific stationary truth and are unlikely to significantly change based on the time of authoring. Blog posts, however, are free expressions of the author's emotions and thus depend more on the time of authoring. Therefore, we demonstrate a temporal model on data consisting of time-stamped blog posts. We construct the sentiment or emotion ground truth from an emotion label for the text.

The temporal model is useful in two ways. First, it leads to a predictive model that estimates the current emotional state of the author within a specific time context. This predictive model is more accurate than static analysis, which ignores time information. Second, the model is useful in confirming or refuting psychological models concerning human emotions and their dependency on time. Specifically, we reexamine the circadian rhythm model from psychology and investigate its higher order generalizations and its variance across multiple individuals.

2 Related Work

Most sentiment or mood analysis work focus on extracting a richer set of features in a single document; it is somewhat orthogonal to our contribution. Pang and Lee (2008) and Liu (2012) are good surveys of this field. Mishne (2005), Généreux and Evans (2006), and Keshtkar and Inkpen (2009) are also notable as they extended binary sentiment to multivariate emotions using multiclass classifiers. Kim et al. (2013) is the most closely aligned to our work because of its similar multi-dimensional latent variable formulation.

Several studies have devoted to the temporal variation of sentiment even though they have not examined inter-document dependencies. Mishne and Maarten (2006) explored a trend of emotions, yet they did not include temporal dependencies in their model. Mao and Lebanon (2007; 2009) introduced temporal variation in topics and sentiments within a single document.

Supervised and temporal topic models are also similar to our model. Supervised topic models (Blei and McAuliffe 2007; Ramage et al. 2009) include similar graphical models except for their use of discrete latent variables and lack of temporal dependencies. Temporal topic models (Blei and Lafferty 2006; Wei, Sun, and Wang 2007; Wang, Blei, and Heckerman 2009; Hong et al. 2011), by contrast, do not use supervised label information. Conditional Random Field (CRF) (Lafferty, Pereira, and McCallum 2001) includes both dependencies; however, it does not use specific time information. Additional examples of temporal modeling of text documents include Lebanon, Mao, and Dillon (2007); Mao, Dillon, and Lebanon (2007); Lebanon and Zhao (2008).

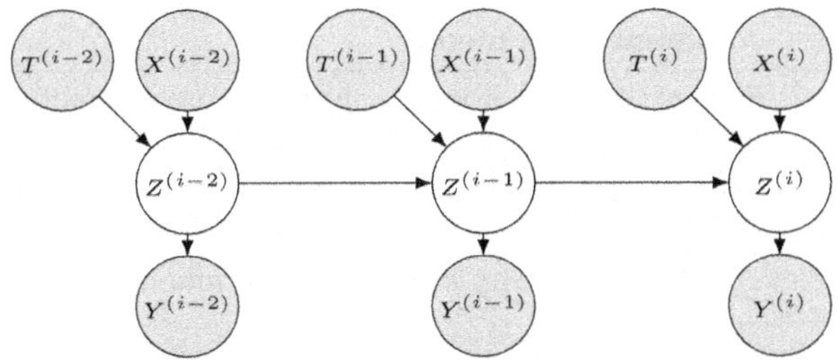

Figure 1: Graphical model of the temporal sentiment analysis model. X denote sequence of documents, T is the corresponding authoring time, Y is for the sentiment, and Z is the continuous latent variable. See text for details.

The psychological community has not employed such graphical models; however, it has devoted a great deal of effort to explore human emotions. Note that *emotion*, *affect*, and *mood* have distinguishable meanings in psychology, but we use them here interchangeably. Watson and Tellegen (1985) introduced the dimensional structures of emotions. Lewis and Granic (2002) and Verduyn et al. (2009) described the temporal dynamics of moods. Murray, Allen, and Trinder (2002) and Golder and Macy (2011) explored periodic phenomena in temporal progression of moods. Papers in the psychology literature build models mostly based on data from a limited set of human surveys. Our approach is to leverage the internet by analyzing user-generated content such as blog posts.

Our work differs from previous studies in primarily three ways. First, unlike sentiment or mood analysis work, we employ temporal dependencies between documents. Second, our work assumes continuous embedding while other supervised topic models assume a discrete set of labels (multi-class). Third, we use specific time information rather than only ordering between documents, which is covered in CRF.

3 Temporal Dynamics of Binary Sentiment

We augment the standard dataset in sentiment analysis $\{(X^{(i)}, Y^{(i)}), i = 1, \ldots, n\}$ with time stamps $T^{(i)} \in \mathbb{R}$, representing the time document $X^{(i)}$ was authored. We assume that the documents are represented as feature vectors $X^{(i)}$. The feature vector can have any document-level features such as bag-of-words or even sophisticated autoencoder features. The response variables $Y^{(i)} \in \{-1, +1\}$ are binary sentiment polarity values. We additionally assume a latent variable $Z^{(i)} \in \mathbb{R}$ associated with $X^{(i)}$ and $Y^{(i)}$ representing a continuous sentiment concept.

The introduction of the continuous latent variable serves several roles: (i) it is easier to construct temporal models in continuous state space, and (ii) the framework conveniently generalizes to mood analysis where there are a large number of emotions embedded in a low dimensional continuous space (we explore this generalization in the next section).

We assume that $Z|Y$ follows a Gaussian distribution in $\mathbb{R}$, implying that Y is a (stochastic) discretization of Z. We also assume that $Z|X$ follows a linear regression model and that $Z^{(1)}, \ldots, Z^{(n)}$ follow a Markov chain with Gaussian conditional distributions $Z^{(i)}|Z^{(i-1)}$. The formal definition appears below and the graphical model appears in Figure 1.

1. $X^{(i)} \to Z^{(i)} \to Y^{(i)}$ forms a Markov chain ($Y^{(i)}$ is independent of $X^{(i)}$ given $Z^{(i)}$).
2. The distribution of $Z|Y$ is a Gaussian with appropriate mean and variance:
$$\{Z^{(i)}|Y^{(i)} = y\} \sim \mathcal{N}(y, \sigma_y^2),\ y \in \{-1, +1\}.$$
3. The distribution of $Z|X$ follows a linear regression model (assuming the document X is represented as a vector)
$$\{Z^{(i)}|X^{(i)} = x\} \sim \mathcal{N}(\theta^\top x, \epsilon^2),\ X^{(i)}, \theta \in \mathbb{R}^k. \quad (1)$$
4. The latent variables follow a Markov chain with Gaussian conditionals. ($\Delta T = T^{(i)} - T^{(i-1)}$)
$$\{Z^{(i)}|Z^{(i-1)}\} \sim \mathcal{N}(Z^{(i-1)}, \beta\Delta T) \quad (2)$$

Assumptions 3 and 4 above can be combined to produce

$$\{Z^{(i)}|X^{(i)}, Z^{(i-1)}\} \sim \mathcal{N}(\mu^{(i)}, \sigma^{(i)})$$
$$\text{where } \sigma^{(i)} = \left((\beta\Delta T)^{-1} + \epsilon^{-2}\right)^{-1}$$
$$\mu^{(i)} = \sigma^{(i)} \left((\beta\Delta T)^{-1} Z^{(i-1)} + \epsilon^{-2}\theta^\top X^{(i)}\right).$$

For simplicity, we consider (above and in the sequel) the time points $T^{(i)}$ to be non-random, and we therefore omit them in the probability notations for example $P(Z^{(i)}|X^{(i)})$ rather than $P(Z^{(i)}|X^{(i)}, T^{(i)})$. This is analogous to fixed design in regression analysis, as opposed to random design.

We emphasize the following characteristics. First, low-dimensional latent variable $Z^{(i)}$ solely determines polarity $Y^{(i)}$ ($Y^{(i)}$ is independent of high-dimensional $X^{(i)}$ given $Z^{(i)}$). Second, $Z^{(i)}$ has a distribution that centered at $Z^{(i-1)}$ with a variance that increases with ΔT, which is in agreement with psychological observations as well as standard models in the time series literature. Third, as we do not specify $p(X)$, our model is a discriminative model. It is similar to standard discriminative structured classifiers (such as CRF) with an additional constraint for inter-document dependency by β and ΔT. It matches our intuition as temporal proximity tends to imply proximity in sentiment (for blog posts written by the same author).

3.1 Learning and Using the Model

Parameters $\eta = (\theta, \beta, \mu_y, \sigma_y)$ can be estimated by maximizing the conditional likelihood, $p(Y|X)$, of observed data.

We consider two alternatives to handle documents written by different authors: (i) estimating a single set of parameters for all authors, and (ii) estimating separate parameters for each author. In the first approach, the model is universal and can capture generic trends. The second approach fits specialized models for each author. While the first approach appears more limited than the second, it is particularly useful when some authors do not have sufficient labeled data. In either case, we maximize the likelihood function for the observed data, which integrates over the latent variables.

In the first case above, we estimate the parameter by maximizing the total sum of conditional log-likelihood (temporal dependencies only holds for each author). Denoting the set of authors by A and an individual author as $a \in A$, we have

$$\eta = \arg\max_{\eta} \sum_{a \in A} \ell(\eta, a) \tag{3}$$

$$\begin{aligned} \ell(\eta, a) &= \log p_\eta(y_a^{(1)}, \ldots, y_a^{(n)} | x_a^{(1)}, \ldots, x_a^{(n)}) \\ &= \log \int_z p_\theta(z^{(1)} | x_a^{(1)}) \cdot \prod_{i=2}^{n} p_{\theta,\beta}(z^{(i)} | z^{(i-1)}, x_a^{(i)}) \\ &\cdot \prod_{i=1}^{n} p_{\mu_y,\sigma_y}(y_a^{(i)} | z^{(i)}) dz, \end{aligned} \tag{4}$$

where $x_a^{(i)}$ and $y_a^{(i)}$ denote documents and labels associated with a specific author $a \in A$ and the integral over z represents integration over the latent variables $z^{(i)}$. In the second case, the log-likelihood is the same as above except that we have multiple terms of log-likelihood for each author with different parameters $\eta_a, a \in A$. It can possibly describe behaviors of an author in depth (some authors may have stronger temporal dependency or lesser).

Inference To predict the most likely polarity of a given temporal document (in test time), we compute below the most likely value. Note that we use the previous time stamped documents to improve the estimation accuracy.

$$\hat{y}^{(i)} = \arg\max_{y^{(i)}} p(y^{(i)} | x^{(i)}, \ldots, x^{(1)}) \tag{5}$$

$$\begin{aligned} &= \arg\max_{y^{(i)}} \int \cdots \int p(y^{(i)} | z^{(i)}) \\ &\cdot \prod_{j=1}^{i} p(z^{(j)} | x^{(j)}, z^{(j-1)}) dz^{(1)} \ldots dz^{(i)}. \end{aligned} \tag{6}$$

Approximation and Implementation There are several approaches for computing (4) including numeric integration, Laplace approximation, and Markov Chain Monte Carlo (MCMC). We use a simpler approximation that replaces the Gaussian distribution over Z with a Dirac's delta centered at the most likely value of z. This approximation replaces the integral with the integrand, evaluated at the most likely value of the latent variable. Naturally, the approximation quality increases as the variance of the Gaussian decreases.

$$\int \mathcal{N}(z; z^*, \sigma) g(z) dz \approx c(\sigma) \int \delta(z - z^*) g(z) dz = c(\sigma) g(z^*).$$

Applying this approximation to (4) we get:

$$\begin{aligned} \ell &\approx \log p(y^{(1)}, \ldots, y^{(n)}, z^{(1)} = z^{*(1)}, \ldots | x^{(1)}, \ldots, x^{(n)}) \\ &= \sum_{i=1}^{n} \log p_\theta(z^{*(1)} | x^{(1)}) + \sum_{i=2}^{n} \log p_{\theta,\beta}(z^{*(i)} | z^{*(i-1)}, x^{(i)}) \\ &+ \sum_{i=1}^{n} \log p_{\mu_y,\sigma_y}(y^{(i)} | z^{*(i)}) \end{aligned} \tag{7}$$

where
$$\begin{aligned} z^{*(i)} &= \arg\max_z p(z^{*(i)} | z^{*(i-1)}, x^{(i)}) p(y^{(i)} | z^{*(i)}) \\ &= \left({\sigma^{(i)}}^{-1} + {\sigma_y}^{-1}\right)^{-1} \left({\sigma^{(i)}}^{-1} \mu^{(i)} + {\sigma_y}^{-1} \mu_y\right). \end{aligned}$$

$\pm$	**Assignments of moods**
+1	excited, pleased, good, cheerful, amused, hopeful, bouncy, chipper, thoughtful, accomplished
-1	cold, exhausted, sleepy, tired, bored, sick, sore, uncomfortable, depressed, sad, annoyed

Table 1: Polarity assignments of moods

The maximum likelihood estimator for θ, $\hat{\theta} = \arg\max_\theta$

$$\left[\log p(z^{*(1)} | x^{(1)}) + \sum_{i=2}^{n} \log p(z^{*(i)} | z^{*(i-1)}, x^{(i)})\right]$$

is conveniently given in closed form. Since the conditional probabilities are Gaussian, the MLE is equivalent to a least squares linear regression model $\theta^\top X = W$ where $X = [x^{(1)}, \ldots, x^{(n)}]$ and $W \in \mathbb{R}^n$ is

$$W = \begin{bmatrix} z^{*(1)} \\ \vdots \\ \epsilon^2 \left[\left((\beta \Delta T)^{-1} + \epsilon^{-2} \right) z^{*(i)} - (\beta \Delta T)^{-1} z^{*(i-1)} \right] \\ \vdots \end{bmatrix}.$$

After obtaining the MLE $\hat{\theta}$, we can fix that parameter value and compute the MLE for the remaining parameters $(\hat{\beta}, Z^*, \hat{\mu}_y, \hat{\sigma}_y)$ using standard gradient based optimization. We then re-calculate $\hat{\theta}$ and iterate until convergence.

The approximation above can also be used in test time prediction. It proceeds as above by replacing the integrals over the latent variables Z by the integrand evaluated at the most likely value of the latent variables.

3.2 Experiment

Dataset Most standard sentiment analysis datasets (Pang, Lee, and Vaithyanathan 2002; Wiebe, Wilson, and Cardie 2005; Ganu, Elhadad, and Marian 2009) focus on a sentiment concept corresponding to opinions or reviews on specific topics. This sentiment concept is unlikely to vary significantly with time as much because it reflect the author's opinion about a specific issue (however, see Koren (2009) that discovers some temporal effects in movie reviews). We choose instead to model blog posts, which depend more significantly on time.

We gathered data by crawling a popular blog service, Livejournal[1] from May 2010 to July 2011. Livejournal provides time-stamps as well as emotion annotation that reflect the author's mood of a single blog post (one annotation per one blog post). The authors are offered the use of a wide range of emoticons and also offers a free text emotion annotation. The crawling resulted in two million documents authored by 315K authors, and about 20% of the authors annotated their posts with such annotation.

Since most authors do not provide more than 2 documents (the median number of blog post by an author), we selected

[1]http://www.livejournal.com

Methods	F1	Accuracy
temporal sentiment method	**0.7596**	**0.8058**
temporal linear-chain CRF	0.7130	0.7742
temporal VARX(1)	0.6554	0.7172
non-temporal logistic regression	0.7109	0.8016
non-temporal SVM	0.6555	0.7557
non-temporal SLDA	0.5093	0.7379
non-temporal naive Bayes	0.6915	0.7373

Table 2: Test set F1 and accuracy results for predicting sentiment polarity. Bold face shows statistically significant improvement over other competitors (t-test, 95% confidence).

the top 50 most frequently publishing authors. We also had to remove spam authors who kept posting the same content repeatedly with random emotions. We finally obtained 19 authors with 64 different emotions after removing rare emotions that appeared in less than 20 documents.

We want to note that most authors don't write frequently, which makes estimating their emotion harder. For example, the 50th most active author had only 52 documents for training. It is a common case when we handle social media data. We expect our method that exploits temporal dependencies to lead to a more accurate model than non-temporal models in this sparse setting.

In this section, we converted the emotions to polarity labels $\{-1, +1\}$, while ignoring neutral emotions as indicated by Table 1. This procedure yielded 6,295 documents with 0.27:0.73 (negative:positive) class distributions. Section 4.1 describes experiments on the entire set of emotions including the neutral emotions.

For document-level features, $X^{(i)}$, we selected negation-handled term frequencies. Specifically, we tokenized and stemmed (Krovetz) the documents, and added new features for negated words as is commonly done in sentiment analysis (Kennedy and Inkpen 2006). For example, this implies that negation words like "not" or "isn't" followed by "good" will yield negated tokens such as "not-good." This procedure yielded 43,910 features. To create the final document representation, we used the square root of the normalized term frequency of the tokens since (i) it is closely associated with the Hellinger distance and the multinomial Fisher geometry that have nice theoretical properties (Čencov 1982), and (ii) it often leads to improved modeling accuracy (see Lafferty and Lebanon (2005), Lebanon (2005a; 2005c; 2005b), and Dillon et al. (2007) for examples of using Hellinger distances in text modeling and interpreting it in terms of information geometry).

It is possible other sophisticated features such as dependency tree features or auto encoder features can be used for $X^{(i)}$; however, the term frequency feature is sufficient for demonstrating the model and contrasting it with standard sentiment analysis models. Our main contribution is presenting the manifold Z which is applicable regardless of the document-level feature extraction.

A few statistics concerning the dataset are: (i) the average document length is 71 words (± 89), (ii) most documents (55%) have less than 50 words, (iii) there are a few very long documents (0.01%) with more than 500 words, and (iv) the average word length is 8.33 characters. This denotes our blog posts are relatively sparser than other popular sentiment dataset such as the movie review dataset (Pang, Lee, and Vaithyanathan 2002).

Methods	Time (sec)
temporal sentiment method	16.96
temporal linear-chain CRF	3352.81
temporal VARX(1)	9.17
non-temporal logistic regression	48.39
non-temporal SVM	27.26
non-temporal SLDA	1047.59
non-temporal naive Bayes	1.07

Table 3: Training time comparison of each method

Classification One of the primary tasks in sentiment analysis is predicting the sentiment polarity $Y \in \{-1, +1\}$ of a document X. Table 2 compares seven different methods in sentiment prediction with our model using shared parameters across all authors (Equation 3). With larger dataset, we may use author-specific parameters to improve the accuracy.

We compare our temporal sentiment method with non-temporal classification baselines including a well known supervised topic model (Supervised Latent Dirichlet Allocation[2] (Blei and McAuliffe 2007)), SVM[3], logistic regression with L_2 regularization, and naive Bayes classifier. We also compare our model with temporal models such as Conditional Random Field[4] (Lafferty, Pereira, and McCallum 2001) and VARX(1)[5], $y^{(t)} = a + X^{(t)}\beta + Ay^{(t-1)}$, which is the most relevant vector autoregressive model. The inputs of VARX(1) model are given $\{-1, +1\}$ accordingly and the output is interpreted as a binary classification by its polarity.

Training and test set were split 50:50 by post-by-post random (not author-based). Post orderings of each author were recovered using timestamps $T^{(i)}$ and author ID after the split. All regularization parameters were chosen by a validation set on training examples using grid search of 5 candidates. We tried various sizes of latent topics on SLDA (2 to 20) and included the best result.

Our model demonstrates statistically significant improvement in both F1 measure and classification accuracy (t-test with 100 random trials) compared to all non-temporal methods and other temporal methods. SLDA performed relatively poorly especially on F1, perhaps due to the extreme sparsity. CRF and VARX(1) do not explicitly model the time gap (ΔT) between observations and rather only consider the ordering of the time stamps unlike the proposed model. This explains the lower performance of CRF, which is generally considered a top performing model.

[2]Gibbs sampling implementation: https://github.com/michaelchughes/SuperTopicModels

[3]LibSVM (ν-SVM, RBF kernel): http://www.csie.ntu.edu.tw/~cjlin/libsvm/

[4]Linear-chain CRF from Kevin Murphy: http://www.cs.ubc.ca/~murphyk/Software/CRF/crf.html

[5]Matlab implementation

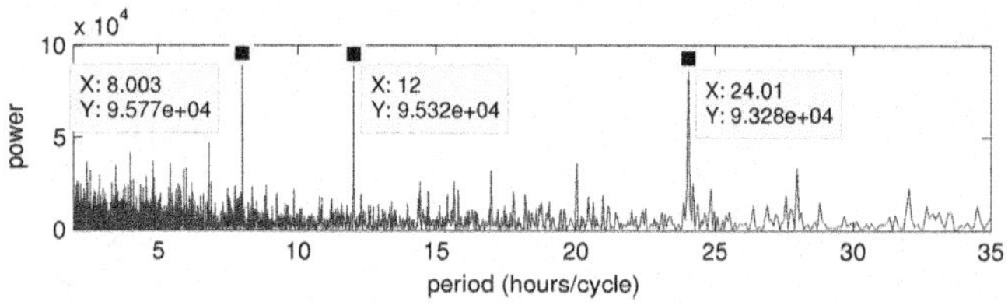

Figure 2: Fourier components of the latent variable in the global model. There are three significant periodic components representing the periods: 8 hours, 12 hours, and 24 hours (circadian rhythm).

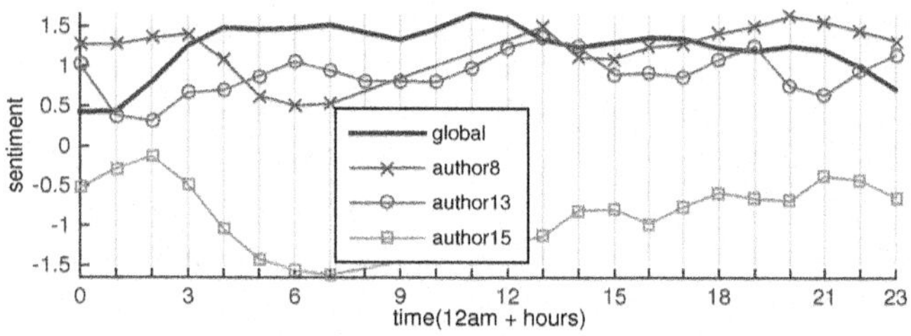

Figure 3: Hourly pattern of global sentiment and selected authors. The y axis correspond to the latent variable of the model (higher values correspond to stronger positive sentiment). See text for details.

Table 3 shows average training time of each methods. Our method (temporal sentiment) takes much shorter time to train the model compared to methods that have comparable performance (such as CRF, SVM or logistic regression). In fact, it is far faster than CRF and SLDA, which are considered to be one of the state-of-the-art methods.

Periodicity The temporal model can also be used for analyzing temporal variations in the emotions of authors. Figure 2 investigates the periodic behavior of the temporal sentiment by displaying the Fourier components of the latent variable. The x axis of the graph measures period (one over frequency) rather than traditional Fourier frequency for better interpretation in our context.

The peaks in graph show significant periodic components at 8 hours, 12 hours, and 24 hours. Interestingly, the strong 24 hours periodicity matches the circadian rhythm discovery from chronobiology and psychology research (Murray, Allen, and Trinder 2002; Golder and Macy 2011). Specifically, this confirms the work of (Murray, Allen, and Trinder 2002) that explored a circadian component in positive affect. The confirmation is noteworthy as our model was constructed from blog posts, while they surveyed human subjects in a controlled environment.

Hourly Pattern From Figure 2, we found 24 hours of periodicity. We investigate this finding further by visualizing hourly average sentiment values (as measured by the latent variable) for models trained on data of specific authors and for the globally-trained model (Figure 3).

The figure shows interesting observations that agree our intuition. First, the trend of global model is well aligned with generic daily schedules. Four local maxima at 6am, 11am, 16pm and 20pm match to positive daily events: wake-up time, lunch break, office closing time, and dinner time. There are notable minima in late night (0am-3am) and the end of lunch break (1pm). The highest and lowest sentiment values are achieved around noon and midnight, respectively. Second, some authors have different temporal patterns, which may indicate different time zones or different life styles. For example, author 8 and 15 exhibit low sentiment in the early morning and high sentiment late at night. Third, the hourly trend shows characteristics of an author. A sentiment structure of author 15 shows an overall lower sentiment compared to others. When we manually visit the actual blog site of the author, we observed many negative annotations. These observations can be useful in psychological studies as well as marketing and advertisement sciences.

4 Temporal Dynamics of Multivariate Emotions

We now extend the temporal dynamics model to the case where a richer concept describing a diverse set of emotions rather than having a one dimensional polarity. Such emotions, for example `happy`, `sad`, `excited`, and `tired` are correlated with the polarity, but they offer an opportunity to construct a more fine grained model of the author's emotion.

Since there is a relatively large set of possible emotions, and these emotions are related to one another, we avoid constructing a separate temporal dynamics model for each individual binary emotion. Instead, we extend the formalism of Kim et al. (2013), where a large set of emotions are embedded in a low dimensional Euclidean space. We thus generalize the model of the previous section by increasing the dimensionality of the latent variable Z. We make use of the same notation as Section 3, but now $Y^{(i)} \in \{1, 2, \ldots, |C|\}$, and the latent variable is a vector $Z^{(i)} \in \mathbb{R}^l$.

The largest difference between our work with Kim et al. (2013) is that their work lacks temporal dependence. They assume blog posts are independent from each other while our model makes better use of data considering previous observations. Another difference is that we consider both individual-level and global-level emotion manifolds, as described in the previous section.

The assumptions in Section 3 are now extended to adapting multivariate emotions. Assumption 2 now has a multivariate Gaussian instead of the univariate Gaussian: $\{Z^{(i)}|Y^{(i)} = y\} \sim \mathcal{N}(\mu_y, \Sigma_y)$; the centroids ($\mu_y$) correspond to $\{-1, +1\}$ from the previous section that described positive and negative polarity in the latent space. Assumption 3 is extended to multi-response regression: $\{Z^{(i)}|X^{(i)} = x\} \sim \mathcal{N}(\Theta x, \epsilon^2 \mathsf{I}), \Theta \in \mathbb{R}^{l \times k}$, and a spherical covariance is used instead of a scalar in Assumption 4: $\{Z^{(i)}|Z^{(i-1)}\} \sim \mathcal{N}(Z^{(i-1)}, \beta \cdot \Delta T \cdot \mathsf{I})$.

We additionally introduce the fifth and last assumption similar to that in Kim et al. (2013).

5. $\forall y \in C$, distances between $\{\mathsf{E}[Z^{(i)}|Y^{(i)} = y]\}$ are similar to the corresponding distances in $\{\mathsf{E}[X^{(i)}|Y^{(i)} = y]\}$.

This assumption enables us to estimate μ_y, Σ_y by multidimensional scaling (MDS) on empirical averages corresponding to $\mathsf{E}[X|Y = y]$.

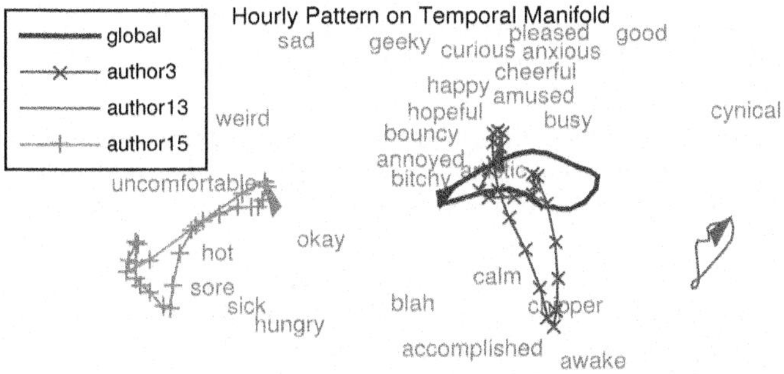

Figure 4: Hourly trends of global model and selected authors on the first two dimensions of the manifold (smoothed). Gray words show $\mathsf{E}[Z|Y = y]$. The arrow shows the start of the day (12am) and direction of the progression of each circle. There is clear separation between day and night time.

It is worth mentioning our model incorporates two different types of proximities: temporal proximities between $Z^{(i)}$ and $Z^{(i-1)}$ and spatial proximities between $\mathsf{E}[Z^{(i)}|Y^{(i)}]$ and $\mathsf{E}[X^{(i)}|Y^{(i)}]$. We also expect the dimensionality l of the latent space $Z^{(i)}$ to be smaller than the number of emotions $l \ll |C|$ and much smaller than the dimensionality of $X^{(i)}$. This means that $Z^{(i)}$ serves as a latent low-dimensional variable that connects two observed high dimensional variables.

To estimate the model, we start by MDS to estimate μ_y, Σ_y. The dimension of latent space Z is bounded by $|C| - 1$ consequently. We then follow the maximum likelihood procedure and approximation as described in the previous section.

4.1 Experiments

Dataset We now consider full emotion labels (including all neutral emotions) from Section 3.2. The data contains 11,659 documents with 43,910 features and 64 emotions. The label frequencies varied between 0.0018 (21 documents) to 0.1441 (1680 documents), with an average label frequency of 0.0156 (182 documents).

Hourly Pattern Figure 4 shows temporal trajectories of the latent variable in several models based on individuals, as well as a global model on the first two dimensions of the model. The first two dimensions seem to capture sentiment level (horizontally) and energy level (vertically). Gray words show centroids of corresponding emotion labels.

The global model shows a progression from negative sentiment (left side) to positive sentiment (right side) from 12am, and the progression is reversed later on 12pm similar to Figure 3. Each author shows their unique progression style and location. For example, author 15 is exceptional in its location (close to negative emotions) and its progression (counter-clockwise) as opposed to the frequently observed clockwise progression; this means the author has emotional transitions in an opposite order to most people.

Classifying Emotions We now consider the task of predicting the emotion of a given text document. Compared to classifying a binary sentiment polarity, predicting the multiclass emotion concept is difficult due to the large number of interrelated emotions, some of which having only a small set of labeled documents.

	Macro F1	Accuracy
temporal model (proposed)	**0.2552**	0.4381
non-temporal model	0.2522	0.4370
logistic regression	0.1618	0.4329
SLDA	0.1131	0.3358
naive Bayes	0.0103	0.1405

Table 4: Test set F1 and accuracy results for predicting emotion among 64 emotions. Bold face shows statistically significant improvement over other competitors (t-test, 95% confidence). See text for details.

Table 4 shows the test set classification performance of predicting the emotion (out of a set of $|C| = 64$ possible emotions). We compared our temporal model with global parameter setting, the non-temporal model (Kim et al. 2013), SLDA (Blei and McAuliffe 2007), logistic regression, and naive Bayes. CRF failed to converge in weeks of running time. Details of experimental configuration remain the same as in Section 3.2 except that (i) the size of latent topics on SLDA was varied from $2 \cdot |C|$ to $5 \cdot |C|$ and (ii) the experiment was repeated 50 times by random split.

The improvement in classification accuracy is noticeable, but not statistically significant; however, the improvement in macro F1 is statistically significant. This is notable as our class distribution is highly unbalanced and F1 is the measure that is often regarded as more informative than accuracy in the multiclass case with unbalanced class frequencies.

Above, the dimension of the latent space l is $|C| - 1$. However, reducing the dimensionality to $0.7|C|$, $0.45|C|$, and $0.19|C|$ reduces the accuracy of the full model to 90%, 80%, and 70% respectively. This shows that the manifold includes most of its information in only a few dimensions. This classification experiment includes tiny classes that have a few documents (minimum 20 documents). When we performed the same experiment while excluding tiny classes (minimum 100 documents), the non-temporal method (Kim et al. 2013) performed better in terms of emotion classification accuracy. We conclude that our model is well suited to handling small classes, which is often the case in self reported mood data.

5 Summary

We presented a temporal statistical model for modeling binary sentiment polarity values and multivariate emotions. Our model uses temporally-dependent continuous latent variables in order to capture relationships between various emotions and observations. We examined a wide variety of applications, including sentiment or emotion prediction of time-stamped documents and scientific research into the temporal variations of human emotions. Our experimental results demonstrate improved statistical modeling and confirmation of discoveries from the psychology literature concerning the static and temporal structure of human emotions.

Acknowledgments

This work was supported in part by NSF Grant CCF-1348152 and DARPA XDATA Grant FA8750-12-2-0309. Any opinions, findings and conclusions or recommendations expressed in this material are those of the authors and do not necessarily reflect the views of the funding agencies.

References

Blei, D., and Lafferty, J. 2006. Dynamic topic models. In *Proc. of the International Conference on Machine Learning*.

Blei, D., and McAuliffe, J. 2007. Supervised topic models. *Advances in Neural Information Processing Systems*.

Čencov, N. N. 1982. *Statistical Decision Rules and Optimal Inference*. American Mathematical Society.

Dillon, J.; Mao, Y.; Lebanon, G.; and Zhang, J. 2007. Statistical translation, heat kernels, and expected distances. In *Uncertainty in Artificial Intelligence*, 93–100. AUAI Press.

Ganu, G.; Elhadad, N.; and Marian, A. 2009. Beyond the stars: Improving rating predictions using review text content. In *International Workshop on the Web and Databases*.

Généreux, M., and Evans, R. 2006. Distinguishing affective states in weblog posts. In *AAAI Spring Symposium on Computational Approaches to Analyzing Weblogs*.

Golder, S., and Macy, M. 2011. Diurnal and seasonal mood vary with work, sleep, and daylength across diverse cultures. *Science* 333(6051):1878–1881.

Hong, L.; Yin, D.; Guo, J.; and Davison, B. 2011. Tracking trends: incorporating term volume into temporal topic models. In *Proc. of International Conference on Knowledge Discovery and Data mining*.

Kennedy, A., and Inkpen, D. 2006. Sentiment classification of movie reviews using contextual valence shifters. *Computational Intelligence* 22(2):110–125.

Keshtkar, F., and Inkpen, D. 2009. Using sentiment orientation features for mood classification in blogs. In *IEEE International Conference on Natural Language Processing and Knowledge Engineering*.

Kim, S.; Li, F.; Lebanon, G.; and Essa, I. 2013. Beyond sentiment: The manifold of human emotions. In *Proc. of the International Conference on Artificial Intelligence and Statistics*.

Koren, Y. 2009. Collaborative filtering with temporal dynamics. In *Proc. of International Conference on Knowledge Discovery and Data mining*.

Lafferty, J., and Lebanon, G. 2005. Diffusion kernels on statistical manifolds. *Journal of Machine Learning Research* 6:129–163.

Lafferty, J.; Pereira, F.; and McCallum, A. 2001. Conditional random fields: probabilistic models for segmenting and labeling sequence data. In *Proc. of the International Conference on Machine Learning*.

Lebanon, G., and Zhao, Y. 2008. Local likelihood modeling of the concept drift phenomenon. In *Proc. of the 25th Intrenational Conference of Machine Learning*.

Lebanon, G.; Mao, Y.; and Dillon, J. 2007. The locally weighted bag of words framework for documents. *Journal of Machine Learning Research* 8:2405–2441.

Lebanon, G. 2005a. Axiomatic geometry of conditional models. *IEEE Transactions on Information Theory* 51(4):1283–1294.

Lebanon, G. 2005b. Information geometry, the embedding principle, and document classification. In *Proc. of the 2nd International Symposium on Information Geometry and its Applications*, 101–108.

Lebanon, G. 2005c. *Riemannian Geometry and Statistical Machine Learning*. Ph.D. Dissertation, Carnegie Mellon University, Technical Report CMU-LTI-05-189.

Lewis, M. D., and Granic, I. 2002. *Emotion, development, and self-organization: Dynamic systems approaches to emotional development*. Cambridge University Press.

Liu, B. 2012. Sentiment analysis and opinion mining. *Synthesis Lectures on Human Language Technologies* 5(1).

Mao, Y., and Lebanon, G. 2007. Isotonic conditional random fields and local sentiment flow. In *Advances in Neural Information Processing Systems 19*, 961–968.

Mao, Y., and Lebanon, G. 2009. Generalized isotonic conditional random fields. *Machine Learning* 77(2-3):225–248.

Mao, Y.; Dillon, J.; and Lebanon, G. 2007. Sequential document visualization. *IEEE Transactions on Visualization and Computer Graphics* 13(6):1208–1215.

Mishne, G., and Maarten, R. 2006. Capturing global mood levels using blog posts. In *AAAI Symposium on Computational Approaches to Analysing Weblogs*.

Mishne, G. 2005. Experiments with mood classification in blog posts. In *Workshop on Stylistic Analysis Of Text For Information Access*.

Murray, G.; Allen, N.; and Trinder, J. 2002. Mood and the circadian system: Investigation of a circadian component in positive affect. *Chronobiology international* 19(6):1151–1169.

Pang, B., and Lee, L. 2008. Opinion mining and sentiment analysis. *Found. Trends Inf. Retr.* 2:1–135.

Pang, B.; Lee, L.; and Vaithyanathan, S. 2002. Thumbs up?: sentiment classification using machine learning techniques. In *Proc. of the Conference on Empirical Methods in Natural Language Processing*.

Ramage, D.; Hall, D.; Nallapati, R.; and Manning, C. 2009. Labeled lda: A supervised topic model for credit attribution in multi-labeled corpora. In *Proc. of the Conference on Empirical Methods in Natural Language Processing*.

Verduyn, P.; Delvaux, E.; Coillie, H. V.; Tuerlinckx, F.; and Mechelen, I. V. 2009. Predicting the duration of emotional experience: Two experience sampling studies. *Emotion* 9(1):83.

Wang, C.; Blei, D.; and Heckerman, D. 2009. Continuous time dynamic topic models. In *Proc. of Uncertainty in Artificial Intelligence*.

Watson, D., and Tellegen, A. 1985. Toward a consensual structure of mood. *Psychological bulletin* 98(2):219–235.

Wei, X.; Sun, J.; and Wang, X. 2007. Dynamic mixture models for multiple time-series. In *International Joint Conferences on Artificial Intelligence*.

Wiebe, J.; Wilson, T.; and Cardie, C. 2005. Annotating expressions of opinions and emotions in language. *Language Resources and Evaluation* 39(2):165–210.

Proceedings of the Twenty-Ninth AAAI Conference on Artificial Intelligence

Uniform Interpolation and Forgetting for $\mathcal{ALC}$ Ontologies with ABoxes

Patrick Koopmann and Renate A. Schmidt
School of Computer Science, The University of Manchester,
Oxford Road, Manchester M13 9PL, United Kingdom

Abstract

Uniform interpolation and the dual task of forgetting restrict the ontology to a specified subset of concept and role names. This makes them useful tools for ontology analysis, ontology evolution and information hiding. Most previous research focused on uniform interpolation of TBoxes. However, especially for applications in privacy and information hiding, it is essential that uniform interpolation methods can deal with ABoxes as well. We present the first method that can compute uniform interpolants of any $\mathcal{ALC}$ ontology with ABoxes. ABoxes bring their own challenges when computing uniform interpolants, possibly requiring disjunctive statements or nominals in the resulting ABox. Our method can compute representations of uniform interpolants in $\mathcal{ALCO}$. An evaluation on realistic ontologies shows that these uniform interpolants can be practically computed, and can often even be presented in pure $\mathcal{ALC}$.

Introduction

Ontologies are knowledge bases that are used in diverse applications ranging from medicine, bio-informatics and software development to the semantic web. They are used to define and store conceptual information about a domain of interest, and are usually represented using a description logic. Often, an ontology consists of a TBox and an ABox. The TBox, containing terminological information, defines concepts and relations. The ABox, containing factual information, uses these defined concepts and relations to make assertions about individuals.

Uniform interpolation allows for information that is irrelevant for a new context, or that should be hidden from certain users, to be removed from an ontology. This is done by restricting the set of concept and relation symbols that occur in the ontology, preserving all entailments of the original ontology that are expressible in the restricted signature. An alternative view of uniform interpolation is forgetting. The aim of forgetting is to eliminate a set of concept and role symbols from an ontology in such a way that all entailments in the remaining signature are preserved.

Uniform interpolation has numerous applications, of which we give some examples; more examples can be found in Lutz and Wolter (2011) and Ludwig and Konev (2014).

Ontology Reuse. Often, only a subset of the vocabulary of an existing ontology is relevant for a particular application. Uniform interpolants can be used to extract small subsets of existing ontologies to reuse them in specialized contexts. **Ontology Analysis.** By computing a restricted view that uses only a limited set of symbols of interest, hidden relations between concepts and individuals are made explicit (Konev, Walther, and Wolter 2009). **Logical Difference.** Applying changes to an ontology can lead to undesired new entailments regarding already defined concepts. The new entailments in the common signature of two ontologies are referred to as logical difference (Konev, Walther, and Wolter 2008). The logical difference can easily be computed by checking for entailment of the axioms of the respective uniform interpolants (Ludwig and Konev 2014). **Information Hiding.** In applications where ontologies are accessed by multiple users, it is critical that confidential information is sufficiently protected (Grau 2010). This can be solved by sharing a uniform interpolant of the original ontology, where confidential concepts and relations have been eliminated.

Given its importance for all these applications, uniform interpolation has recently gained a lot of attention in the literature. First methods for simpler description logics such as DL-Lite (Wang et al. 2010) and $\mathcal{EL}$ (Konev, Walther, and Wolter 2009; Lutz, Seylan, and Wolter 2012; Nikitina and Rudolph 2014), as well as for more expressive ones such as $\mathcal{ALC}$ (Wang et al. 2014; Ludwig and Konev 2014; Koopmann and Schmidt 2013c), $\mathcal{ALCH}$ (Koopmann and Schmidt 2013a) and even $\mathcal{SHQ}$ (Koopmann and Schmidt 2014a) have been devised. However, none of the methods for the more expressive description logics works without limitations if ABoxes are involved.

Especially for privacy and information hiding applications, we believe support for ABoxes is important if uniform interpolation is to be used effectively. In a lot of cases, confidential information will be stored as facts in ABoxes or databases used in connection with ontologies. For instance, Grau (2010) mentions shared patient data records, for which hiding information is indispensable in order to preserve the privacy of the patients. So far no method is able to deal with these situations properly, if the data are to be shared.

The first method for uniform interpolation in $\mathcal{ALC}$, presented in Wang et al. (2009), already considers ontologies with ABoxes. This method is based on computing the disjunctive normal form of its input, which makes it unpractical for large ontologies. Later methods for expressive description logics presented in Ludwig and Konev (2014) and Koopmann and Schmidt (2013c; 2013a; 2014a) employed saturation based reasoning techniques to achieve practicality, but only apply to TBoxes. Moreover, it turns out that the original approach by Wang et al. (2009) cannot compute the right uniform interpolant for all ABoxes. In order to preserve all entailments in the desired signature of an ontology with ABox, it is necessary to use a more expressive description logic than $\mathcal{ALC}$ for the uniform interpolant.

Uniform interpolation and forgetting are tasks much more difficult than standard reasoning tasks. Not all uniform interpolants can be finitely represented using standard description logics, and it has been shown that the size of a uniform interpolant of a TBox can be triple exponential with respect to the input TBox, if represented in $\mathcal{ALC}$ (Lutz and Wolter 2011). For $\mathcal{ALC}$ TBoxes, finite representations can be obtained by extending the underlying description logic with fixpoint expressions (using $\mathcal{ALC}\nu$), or by allowing additional symbols in the uniform interpolant (Koopmann and Schmidt 2013c). This is however not sufficient if ABoxes are involved, as our results show. If we want to preserve all entailments in the desired signature, we have to represent the uniform interpolant in an extended language such as $\mathcal{ALC}\nu$ with disjunctive ABoxes or $\mathcal{ALCO}\nu$.

The method presented in this paper is based on a method for $\mathcal{ALCH}$ TBoxes from Koopmann and Schmidt (2013a), which is extended in non-trivial ways. First, we extend the calculus with unification based reasoning. As a by-product, we develop a decision procedure for $\mathcal{ALC}\nu$ ontologies with disjunctive ABoxes. Second, in order to represent the result in $\mathcal{ALCO}$ with classical ABoxes, we devise a method to approximate disjunctive $\mathcal{ALC}$ ABoxes into classical $\mathcal{ALCO}$ ABoxes in the same signature that preserve all classical $\mathcal{ALC}$ entailments. This method is also of interest for applications other than uniform interpolation.

To summarize, the contributions of this work are the following: (1) We define a new resolution-based decision procedure for $\mathcal{ALC}\nu$ ontologies with disjunctive ABoxes. (2) Based on this procedure, we define a method to compute uniform interpolants of $\mathcal{ALC}\nu$ ontologies with disjunctive ABoxes. This method is both able to forget concept and role symbols. By using helper concepts, these uniform interpolants can be represented in pure $\mathcal{ALC}$ with disjunctive ABoxes. (3) We define a method for efficiently transforming $\mathcal{ALC}$ ontologies with disjunctive ABoxes into classical $\mathcal{ALCO}$ ontologies that preserve all entailments in $\mathcal{ALC}$. (4) Based on these methods, we develop the first method that is able to compute uniform interpolants of all $\mathcal{ALC}$ ontologies with ABoxes, and represent them as $\mathcal{ALCO}$ ontologies. (5) We evaluated the method on realistic ontologies, showing that it is indeed practical, and that in most cases even $\mathcal{ALC}$ is sufficient to represent uniform interpolants of $\mathcal{ALC}$ ontologies with ABoxes.

Detailed proofs of all theorems can be found in the long version of the paper (Koopmann and Schmidt 2014c). A preliminary version was presented at the 2014 Description Logic Workshop (Koopmann and Schmidt 2014b).

Description Logics

In this section, we recall the description logics $\mathcal{ALC}$ and $\mathcal{ALCO}$, and introduce $\mathcal{ALC}\nu$ with disjunctive ABoxes. Let N_c, N_r, N_i and N_v be pairwise disjoint sets of *concept symbols*, *role symbols*, *individuals* and *concept variables*. An $\mathcal{ALC}$ *concept* is an expression of the form A, $\neg C$, $C \sqcup D$, $C \sqcap D$, $\exists r.C$, $\forall r.C$, where $A \in N_c$, $r \in N_r$ and C, D are $\mathcal{ALC}$ concepts. An $\mathcal{ALC}$ *TBox* is a finite set of *general concept inclusion axioms* (GCIs) of the form $C \sqsubseteq D$, where C, D are $\mathcal{ALC}$ concepts. A *classical* $\mathcal{ALC}$ *ABox* is a set of *concept assertions* of the form $C(a)$, and *role assertions* of the form $r(a, b)$, where C is any $\mathcal{ALC}$ concept, $r \in N_r$ and $a, b \in N_i$. We refer to GCIs, concept assertions and role assertions collectively as *axioms*. A *classical* $\mathcal{ALC}$ *ontology* is a tuple $\langle \mathcal{T}, \mathcal{A} \rangle$, where $\mathcal{T}$ is an $\mathcal{ALC}$ TBox and $\mathcal{A}$ an $\mathcal{ALC}$ ABox. The semantics of $\mathcal{ALC}$ is defined as usual (see, e.g., Baader and Nutt (2007)). We write $\mathcal{O} \models \alpha$, where $\mathcal{O}$ is an ontology and α any GCI, concept assertion or role assertion, to denote that α is true in every model of $\mathcal{O}$.

A *greatest fixpoint* is a concept of the form $\nu X.C[X]$, where $X \in N_v$ and $C[X]$ is a concept in which X occurs as a concept symbol, but only positively, e.g., under an even number of negations. $\mathcal{ALC}\nu$ extends $\mathcal{ALC}$ with greatest fixpoints, which are only allowed to occur positively in concept assertions and on the right hand side of GCIs. Due to this condition, least fixpoints cannot be equivalently expressed in $\mathcal{ALC}\nu$. Intuitively, $\nu X.C[X]$ represents the most general concept C_ν, with respect to the concept inclusion relation, for which $C_\nu \equiv C[C_\nu]$ holds, where $C[C_\nu]$ is the result of replacing X in $C[X]$ by C_ν. For a formal definition of the semantics of fixpoint expressions, we refer to Calvanese, De Giacomo, and Lenzerini (1999).

A *disjunctive* $\mathcal{ALC}\nu$ *ABox* is a classical $\mathcal{ALC}\nu$ ABox that additionally contains *disjunctive concept assertions* of the form $C_1(a_1) \vee \ldots \vee C_n(a_n)$, where for $1 \leq i \leq n$, $a_i \in N_i$ and C_i is any $\mathcal{ALC}\nu$ concept. The semantics is as expected: $\mathcal{O} \models C_1(a_1) \vee \ldots \vee C_n(a_n)$ iff $\mathcal{O} \models C_i(a_i)$ for some $i \in \{1, \ldots, n\}$. A *general* $\mathcal{ALC}$ *(*$\mathcal{ALC}\nu$*) ontology* is a tuple $\langle \mathcal{T}, \mathcal{A} \rangle$, where $\mathcal{A}$ is a disjunctive ABox.

The description logics $\mathcal{ALCO}$ and $\mathcal{ALCO}\nu$ extend respectively $\mathcal{ALC}$ and $\mathcal{ALC}\nu$ with *nominal concepts* of the form $\{a\}$, $a \in N_i$. They allow to reference specific individuals in concepts and can be used in any combination with the other operators. For the semantics of $\mathcal{ALCO}$ and $\mathcal{ALCO}\nu$, we again refer to Baader and Nutt (2007) and Calvanese, De Giacomo, and Lenzerini (1999).

Uniform Interpolation

We now define $\mathcal{ALC}$ uniform interpolants formally. A *signature* is any subset $\mathcal{S}$ of $N_c \cup N_r$. The signature $sig(E)$ denotes the concept and role symbols occurring in E, where E ranges over concepts, axioms and ontologies.

Definition 1. *Let $\mathcal{O}$ be a classical $\mathcal{ALC}$ ontology and $\mathcal{S}$ a signature. An ontology $\mathcal{O}^\mathcal{S}$ is an $\mathcal{ALC}$* uniform interpolant of $\mathcal{O}$ for $\mathcal{S}$ *iff the following conditions hold:*

1. *$sig(\mathcal{O}^\mathcal{S}) \subseteq \mathcal{S}$.*
2. *For any $\mathcal{ALC}$ axiom α with $sig(\alpha) \subseteq \mathcal{S}$, $\mathcal{O}^\mathcal{S} \models \alpha$ iff $\mathcal{O} \models \alpha$.*

Note that we do not require an $\mathcal{ALC}$ uniform interpolant $\mathcal{O}^{\mathcal{S}}$ to be itself a classical $\mathcal{ALC}$ ontology. In particular, $\mathcal{O}^{\mathcal{S}}$ can also be an $\mathcal{ALCO}\nu$ ontology or an $\mathcal{ALC}\nu$ ontology with disjunctive concept assertions.

Before we describe our method for computing $\mathcal{ALC}$ uniform interpolants, we start in a generalized setting, namely, general $\mathcal{ALC}\nu$ uniform interpolants.

Definition 2. *Let $\mathcal{O}$ be a general $\mathcal{ALC}\nu$ ontology and $\mathcal{S}$ a signature. $\mathcal{O}^{\mathcal{S}}$ is a* general $\mathcal{ALC}\nu$ uniform interpolant *of $\mathcal{O}$ for $\mathcal{S}$, iff*

1. *$sig(\mathcal{O}^{\mathcal{S}}) \subseteq \mathcal{S}$ and*
2. *For any $\mathcal{ALC}\nu$ axiom or disjunctive concept assertion α with $sig(\alpha) \subseteq \mathcal{S}$, $\mathcal{O}^{\mathcal{S}} \models \alpha$ iff $\mathcal{O} \models \alpha$.*

It is easy to verify that the conditions in Definition 2 imply those in Definition 1. The converse does not hold, since a general $\mathcal{ALC}\nu$ uniform interpolant might entail disjunctive concept assertions, which are not necessarily preserved by classical $\mathcal{ALC}$ uniform interpolants. General $\mathcal{ALC}\nu$ uniform interpolants have the nice property that they can always be represented as general $\mathcal{ALC}\nu$ ontologies themselves:

Theorem 1. *Let $\mathcal{O}$ be any $\mathcal{ALC}\nu$ ontology, and $\mathcal{S}$ any signature. Then there exists a finite general $\mathcal{ALC}\nu$ ontology $\mathcal{O}^{\mathcal{S}}$, which is a uniform interpolant of $\mathcal{O}$ for $\mathcal{S}$.*

The validity of this theorem follows from the correctness of the method that we describe in the next sections.

Normalized Ontologies

Our approach is based on a method for computing uniform interpolants of $\mathcal{ALCH}$ TBoxes, introduced in Koopmann and Schmidt (2013a). A key ingredient of this method is that TBox axioms are represented in a certain normal form. We extend this presentation with variables and constants in order to incorporate ABox axioms.

Definition 3. *Let $N_d \subseteq N_c$ be a set of specific concept symbols called* definers. *A* concept literal *is a concept of the form A, $\neg A$, $\exists r.D$ or $\forall r.D$, where $A \in N_c$, $r \in N_r$ and $D \in N_d$. An ontology $\mathcal{O}$ is in* normal form *if every axiom is a role assertion, or a* clause *of one of these two forms, where L_i is a concept literal and $a_i \in N_i$ for $1 \leq i \leq n$.*

1. TBox clause: $L_1(x) \vee \ldots \vee L_n(x)$
2. ABox clause: $L_1(a_1) \vee \ldots \vee L_n(a_n)$

We view clauses as sets of literals, that is, they do not have duplicate literals and their order is not important. Furthermore, every clause is allowed to contain maximally one literal of the form $\neg D(x)$ and no literal of the form $\neg D(a)$, where $D \in N_d$ and $a \in N_i$.

A TBox clause $L_1(x) \vee \ldots \vee L_n(x)$ represents the equivalent GCI $\top \sqsubseteq L_1 \sqcup \ldots \sqcup L_n$. The symbol x occurring in TBox clauses is referred to as a *variable*. Observe that one variable x is sufficient in our representation. We call elements of the set $N_i \cup \{x\}$ *terms*.

Any general $\mathcal{ALC}\nu$ ontology can be transformed into normal form using the following rules, applied from left to right, where $\mathsf{Q} \in \{\forall, \exists\}$, $D \in N_d$ is fresh, $C[X]$ contains a concept variable X, and $C[D]$ denotes the result of replacing X in $C[X]$ by D.

1. $C_1 \vee \mathsf{Q}r.C_2(t_1) \quad \Leftrightarrow C_1 \vee \mathsf{Q}r.D(t_1), \neg D(x) \vee C_2(x)$
2. $C_1 \vee \mathsf{Q}r.\nu X.C_2[X](t_1) \Leftrightarrow C_1 \vee \mathsf{Q}r.D(t_1), \neg D(x) \vee C_2[D](x)$
3. $C_1 \vee \nu X.C_2[X](t_1) \Leftrightarrow C_1 \vee D(t_1), \neg D(x) \vee C_2[D](x)$

These rules are justified by Ackermann's Lemma (Ackermann 1935) and a generalization (Nonnengart and Szałas 1995), which show that the transformation preserves the same models modulo interpretation of the definer concepts. The transformation introduces only finitely many fresh definers.

Any ontology in normal form can be converted back into a general $\mathcal{ALC}\nu$ ontology without definers by applying the rules in the other direction. This is ensured by the last conditions in Definition 3. Whereas the transformations from left to right can just be applied to concepts as they are, the transformations from right to left require $\neg D(x)$ to be the only negative occurrence of the definer D in the ontology. This is achieved by grouping TBox clauses containing the same negative literal $\neg D(x)$ into one TBox axiom $\neg D(x) \vee C$. This is possible since negative definer literals only occur in TBox clauses, and since every TBox clause contains maximally one negative definer literal.

Example 1. *Let $\mathcal{O}_1 = \{A \sqsubseteq \forall r.(B \sqcap C)$, $r(a,b)$, $s(a,b)$, $\neg(A \sqcap B)(b)\}$. For the normal form, we have to replace $(B \sqcap C)$ in the first axiom by a new definer D_1. The normal form of $\mathcal{O}_1$ is $\mathcal{N}_1 = \{\neg A(x) \vee (\forall r.D_1)(x)$, $\neg D_1(x) \vee B(x)$, $\neg D_1(x) \vee C(x)$, $r(a,b)$, $s(a,b)$ $\neg A(b) \vee \neg B(b)\}$.*

The set of clauses $\mathcal{N}_2 = \{B(b) \vee (\forall r.D_1)(a)$, $\neg D_1(x) \vee A(x)$, $\neg D_1(x) \vee (\exists r.D_1)(x)\}$, $D_1 \in N_d$, is transformed into the general $\mathcal{ALC}\nu$ ontology $\mathcal{O}_2 = \{B(b) \vee (\forall r.\nu X.(A \sqcap \exists r.X))(a)\}$ without definers.

Our method for forgetting concept and role symbols works on the normal form representation of the input ontology. The definers are eliminated afterwards using the right to left transformations above.

The Calculus

Uniform interpolants are computed by saturating an ontology in normal form using the rules of the calculus shown in Figure 1. Before we describe the rules, a few notions have to be introduced.

Our normal form allows for a very simple form of unification. In our setting, given two terms t_1 and t_2, the *unifier* of t_1 and t_2 is a substitution that replaces t_1 by t_2, or vice versa. Two terms t_1 and t_2 only have a unifier if $t_1 = x$, $t_2 = x$ or $t_1 = t_2$. For example, the terms a and b do not have a unifier, and the unifier of a and x is $\sigma = [x \mapsto a]$. Applied to a clause $C = A(x) \vee B(x)$, this unifier produces the clause $C\sigma = A(a) \vee B(a)$.

To preserve the normal form, the calculus introduces new definers dynamically. More specifically, given two definers D_1 and D_2, a definer D_{12} representing $D_1 \sqcap D_2$ is introduced by adding the two clauses $\neg D_{12}(x) \vee D_1(x)$ and $\neg D_{12}(x) \vee D_2(x)$. These two clauses correspond to the TBox axiom $D_{12} \sqsubseteq D_1 \sqcap D_2$. New definers are only introduced if necessary. By reusing already introduced definers, we maximally introduce 2^n many new definers, where n

Resolution

$$\frac{C_1 \vee A(t_1) \quad C_2 \vee \neg A(t_2)}{(C_1 \vee C_2)\sigma}$$

Role Propagation

$$\frac{C_1 \vee (\forall r.D_1)(t_1) \quad C_2 \vee (\mathsf{Q}r.D_2)(t_2)}{(C_1 \vee C_2)\sigma \vee \mathsf{Q}r.D_{12}(t_1\sigma)}$$

Existential Role Restriction Elimination

$$\frac{C \vee (\exists r.D)(t) \quad \neg D(x)}{C}$$

Role Instantiation

$$\frac{C_1 \vee (\forall r.D)(t_1) \quad r(t_2, b)}{C_1\sigma \vee D(b)}$$

where $\mathsf{Q} \in \{\exists, \forall\}$, σ is the unifier of t_1 and t_2 if it exists, D_{12} is a possibly new definer representing $D_1 \sqcap D_2$ and $C_1 \vee C_2$ contains maximally one literal of the form $\neg D(x)$ and no literal of the form $\neg D(a)$.

Figure 1: The rules of the calculus.

is the number of definers in the normalized input. This results in a double exponential bound on the number of derived clauses, and guarantees termination of our method.

The first three rules in Figure 1 are generalizations of the rules used in Koopmann and Schmidt (2013a). Whereas the original calculus has only rules for TBox clauses, we extend them using unification to make them applicable for cases where the premises contain one or more ABox clauses. In addition, since an ABox can contain role assertions, we need a rule that propagates information for universal role restrictions $\forall r.D$ along role assertions. This is achieved by the role instantiation rule. Observe that, for a role assertion $r(a, b)$, the rule is only applicable to clauses of the form $C \vee (\forall r.D)(x)$ or $C \vee (\forall r.D)(a)$.

The side conditions of the rules ensure that only clauses in the normal form are derived. This way, we ensure that any derived set of clauses can be transformed back into an $\mathcal{ALC}\nu$ ontology without definers. Clauses of the form $\neg D(a) \vee C$ do not need to be derived, as is shown in the correctness proofs in the long version of this paper.

Example 2. *Take the clause set $\mathcal{N}_1$ from Example 1. We can apply role instantiation on $\neg A(x) \vee (\forall r.D_1)(x)$ and $r(a, b)$, using the unifier $[x \mapsto a]$, and infer the clause $\neg A(a) \vee D_1(b)$. With the same unifier, we can apply resolution on $D_1(b)$ in this clause and derive $\neg A(a) \vee B(b)$ and $\neg A(a) \vee C(b)$. Resolution on $\neg A(a) \vee B(b)$ and $\neg A(b) \vee \neg B(b)$ derives $\neg A(a) \vee \neg A(b)$, where the unifier is $[b \mapsto b]$.*

Theorem 2. *For any general $\mathcal{ALC}\nu$ ontology $\mathcal{O}$, $\mathcal{O}$ is unsatisfiable iff the empty clause can be derived in finitely many steps from its normal form representation using the rules of the calculus.*

Proof (sketch). Termination follows from the fact that, starting from a set $\mathcal{N}$ of n $\mathcal{ALC}$ clauses, maximally $O(2^{2^n})$ many clauses can be derived. A derivation of the empty clause embodies a direct contradiction. If the empty clause cannot be derived, we can adapt the model construction used in Koopmann and Schmidt (2013c) to build a model based on the saturated set of clauses. Consequently, $\mathcal{N}$ has a model and is satisfiable. □

Uniform Interpolation in Normal Form

Let $\mathcal{N}$ be any ontology in normal form, $\mathcal{S}$ any signature, and $\mathcal{N}^*$ the saturation of $\mathcal{N}$ using the rules of the calculus. The *clausal representation $\mathcal{N}^{\mathcal{S}}$ of the uniform interpolant of $\mathcal{N}$ for $\mathcal{S}$* is the smallest set of clauses $C \in \mathcal{N}^*$ with $sig(C) \subseteq \mathcal{S} \cup N_d$ that satisfy at least one of the following conditions:

1. $C \in \mathcal{N}$.
2. C is the result of applying a rule on a literal that is not in $\mathcal{S} \cup N_d$.
3. C contains a definer D that occurs in another clause in $\mathcal{N}^{\mathcal{S}}$.

It can be shown that every entailment α of $\mathcal{N}$ with $sig(\alpha) \subseteq \mathcal{S}$ is also entailed by $\mathcal{N}^{\mathcal{S}}$. Condition 1 ensures that we keep all clauses that were in the desired signature from the beginning. Condition 2 ensures that we preserve all possible inferences in $\mathcal{S}$ that involve symbols outside $\mathcal{S}$. It is possible that these inferences are made possible by applications of the role propagation rule. If this is the case, $\mathcal{N}^{\mathcal{S}}$ contains introduced definers. This is taken care of by Condition 3, which ensures that $\mathcal{N}^{\mathcal{S}}$ is closed under introduced definers. To be more specific, any existential or universal restrictions that refer to these introduced definers, and any clauses of the form $\neg D_{12}(x) \vee C(x)$ that are necessary to preserve the meaning of D_{12}, belong to $\mathcal{N}^{\mathcal{S}}$. This ensures that all entailments in $\mathcal{S}$ are still preserved after the elimination of all definers using the normal form transformation rules described in an earlier section.

Given any general $\mathcal{ALC}\nu$ ontology $\mathcal{O}$ and any signature $\mathcal{S}$, this is how a general $\mathcal{ALC}\nu$ uniform interpolant $\mathcal{O}^{\mathcal{S}}$ is computed: (1) $\mathcal{O}$ is transformed into a set $\mathcal{N}$ of clauses in normal form. (2) For $\mathcal{N}$, we compute the set $\mathcal{N}^{\mathcal{S}}$ defined above using the rules of the calculus. (3) Finally, we eliminate all definers by applying the normal form transformation rules from right to left. We have the following theorem.

Theorem 3. *Let $\mathcal{O}$ be any general $\mathcal{ALC}\nu$ ontology and $\mathcal{S}$ any signature. The described method always terminates and the returned ontology, $\mathcal{O}^{\mathcal{S}}$, is a general $\mathcal{ALC}\nu$ uniform interpolant of $\mathcal{O}$ for $\mathcal{S}$. Furthermore, $\mathcal{O}^{\mathcal{S}}$ is in the worst case of size $O(2^{2^n})$, where n is the size of $\mathcal{O}$.*

Example 3. *Let $\mathcal{O}_1$ and $\mathcal{N}_1$ be is as in Example 1 and $\mathcal{S} = \{A, C, r, s\}$. We already computed all inferences for $\mathcal{N}_1$ in Example 2. Following the above conditions, we have that the clausal representation of the uniform interpolant of $\mathcal{O}_1$ for $\mathcal{S}$ is $\mathcal{N}_1^{\mathcal{S}} = \{\neg A(x) \vee (\forall r.D_1)(x), \neg D_1(x) \vee C(x), r(a, b), s(a, b), \neg A(a) \vee \neg A(b)\}$. After eliminating the only definer D_1, we obtain a uniform interpolant of $\mathcal{O}_1$ for $\mathcal{S}$, which is $\mathcal{O}_1^{\mathcal{S}} = \{A \sqsubseteq \forall r.C, r(a, b), s(a, b), \neg A(a) \vee \neg A(b)\}$.*

Representing the Result in $\mathcal{ALCO}$

Since all classical $\mathcal{ALC}$ ontologies are also $\mathcal{ALC}\nu$ ontologies, the method can be used for computing a finite uniform interpolant of any $\mathcal{ALC}$ ontology, but in an extended language, because these uniform interpolants may contain greatest fixpoint concepts and disjunctive concept assertions. These are not supported by standard description logic reasoners or the web ontology standard language OWL. For this reason, it is of interest to represent the uniform interpolant in a more common description logic.

If a definer can only be eliminated by introducing a fixpoint, we can omit this elimination and keep the corresponding cyclic definer concept. As a result, we obtain an ontology that is not completely in the desired signature, but preserves all entailments we are interested in. The cyclic definers that stay in the ontology can be seen as helper concepts that "simulate" the greatest fixpoints and make a finite representation possible, despite cycles in the TBox. For applications that require the uniform interpolant to be completely in the desired signature, e.g. logical difference, the fixpoint can be approximated by bounded iterative unfolding, as described in Koopmann and Schmidt (2013c).

Another problem is illustrated by the uniform interpolant $\mathcal{O}_1^{\mathcal{S}}$ computed in Example 3. Due to the clause $\neg A(a) \vee \neg A(b)$, and because a and b are connected by the two role assertions $r(a, b)$ and $s(a, b)$, one can verify that $\mathcal{O}_1^{\mathcal{S}} \models (\neg A \sqcup \exists r.(\neg A \sqcap E) \sqcup \exists s.(\neg A \sqcap \neg E))(a)$, for any $\mathcal{ALC}$ concept E. These cannot be captures by a finite classical $\mathcal{ALC}$ ontology. However, in $\mathcal{ALCO}$, we can capture them by the concept assertion $(\neg A \sqcup \exists r.(\neg A \sqcap \{b\}))(a)$, taking into account the role assertions $r(a, b)$ and $s(a, b)$ in the uniform interpolant. (Another solution, using a technique from Areces et al. (2003), involves the introduction of additional roles for each disjunction. But this approach unnecessarily extends the signature of the uniform interpolant.)

If all individuals occurring in an ABox clause C are connected to some root individual a via a chain of role assertions, C can be represented as a classical $\mathcal{ALCO}$ concept assertion on a in the same way as in the example. We call these concept assertions $\mathcal{ALCO}$ *convertible*. If an ABox clause C is not $\mathcal{ALCO}$ convertible, we cannot express C as a classical concept assertion, but C might still contribute to the entailment of other classical concept assertions. To compute a set of clauses that can be fully translated into $\mathcal{ALCO}$, and that preserves all entailments which are classical $\mathcal{ALC}$ axioms, we use our calculus in a similar way as for computing uniform interpolants. Let $\mathcal{N}$ be any set of clauses and $\mathcal{N}^*$ the saturation of $\mathcal{N}$. The set $\mathcal{N}^{conv}$ is the smallest set of clauses $C \in \mathcal{N}^*$ that are $\mathcal{ALCO}$ convertible and satisfy at least one of the following conditions:

1. $C \in \mathcal{N}$.
2. C is the conclusion of any rule application on a clause that is not $\mathcal{ALCO}$ convertible.

$\mathcal{N}^{conv}$ preserves all entailments of $\mathcal{N}$ that are representable as classical $\mathcal{ALC}$ axioms. $\mathcal{N}^{conv}$ can be transformed into an $\mathcal{ALCO}$ ontology without definers, and all remaining disjunctive concept assertions can be represented as classical concept assertions using nominals.

Theorem 4. *Let $\mathcal{N}$ be any ontology in normal form. Then, the described method for approximating disjunctive concept assertions computes an $\mathcal{ALC}$ or $\mathcal{ALCO}$ ontology $\mathcal{O}$ with classical ABox, and we have for any classical $\mathcal{ALC}$ axiom α without definers that $\mathcal{O} \models \alpha$ iff $\mathcal{N} \models \alpha$.*

By combining this technique with our method for computing general $\mathcal{ALC}\nu$ uniform interpolants, we can compute $\mathcal{ALC}$ uniform interpolants in $\mathcal{ALCO}\nu$ with classical ABoxes for any $\mathcal{ALC}$ input ontology. Furthermore, by keeping definers that can only be eliminated using fixpoints, we can represent all uniform interpolants as classical $\mathcal{ALCO}$ ontologies.

Evaluation

To investigate practicality of our approach, we have implemented a prototype using the OWL API[1] and some of the optimisations mentioned in Ludwig and Konev (2014) and Koopmann and Schmidt (2013b). Experiments were conducted on a set of ontologies taken from the NCBO BioPortal[2] and the Oxford Ontology[3] repositories, which we restricted to axioms fully expressible in $\mathcal{ALC}$, where domain and range restrictions were interpreted as corresponding $\mathcal{ALC}$ axioms. For a detailed description of these repositories, see Matentzoglu, Bail, and Parsia (2013). The experiments have been performed on a desktop PC with Intel Core i7 350GHz CPU and 8 GB RAM.

To obtain a set of ontologies that test the ABox processing of our method and can be evaluated in reasonable time, we selected ontologies according to the following criteria: They (1) could be downloaded and parsed by the OWL API without errors, (2) contain more ABox axioms than TBox axioms, (3) are consistent, (4) contain at least 100 TBox axioms, (5) contain at least 80% TBox axioms that are in $\mathcal{ALC}$, (6) contain at least one axiom that is in $\mathcal{ALC}$ but not in $\mathcal{EL}$, and (7) contain at most 40,000 axioms. The selected ontologies are listed in Table 1, which shows the number of TBox axioms, ABox axioms, concept symbols and role symbols for each ontology. CCON, CTX, ICPS, ICF and SSE were taken from the NCBO BioPortal repository, whereas 00104, 00596, 00597 and 00773 were taken from the Oxford Ontology repository.

For the experiments, our assumption has been that the targeted applications require either uniform interpolants for relatively big signatures (e.g., logical difference, information hiding) or for relatively small signatures (e.g., ontology analysis). We therefore generated for each ontology 350 signatures which included any concept or role symbol with a probability of 90% (forgetting about 10% of all symbols), and 350 signatures which included any concept or role symbol with a probability of 10% (forgetting about 90% of all symbols). We then computed uniform interpolants for these signatures represented as $\mathcal{ALCO}$ ontologies with classical ABoxes. For each experimental run, the timeout was 30 minutes.

[1] http://owlapi.sourceforge.net/

[2] http://bioportal.bioontology.org/

[3] http://www.cs.ox.ac.uk/isg/ontologies/

Ontology	TBox	ABox	Concepts	Roles
CCON	214	364	86	28
CTX	364	1,553	290	22
ICPS	953	4,254	432	135
ICF	1,991	17,223	1,596	41
SSE	267	2,323	243	18
00104	1,157	2,451	1,094	6
00596	2,257	2,658	2,023	19
00597	2,887	3,646	2,341	25
00773	581	2,334	244	83

Table 1: The input ontologies.

Ontology	Timeouts	Duration	TBox	ABox
CCON	1.1%	14.1 sec.	89.1%	92.0%
CTX	4.0%	72.6 sec.	87.5%	153.5%
ICPS	21.1%	11.1 sec.	243.2%	81.0%
ICF	0.0%	13.0 sec.	86.6%	38.1%
SSE	0.0%	1.9 sec.	85.3%	99.5%
00104	0.0%	8.2 sec.	87.9%	97.8%
00596	0.0%	10.6 sec.	85.3%	89.4%
00597	6.6%	108.8 sec.	167.6%	91.1%
00773	0.0%	3.9 sec.	109.2%	104.2%

Table 2: Uniform interpolants for symbols selected with 90% probability.

The results are shown in Table 2 and 3, where we show the number of timeouts, the average duration of each successful run, and the percentage of the average number of TBox and ABox axioms in the computed uniform interpolants in comparison to those in the input ontologies. For the uniform interpolants that included any symbol with a probability with 90%, each ABox axiom contained on average 2.6 symbols, whereas each TBox axiom contained on average 8.5 symbols (counting concept symbols, role symbols, individuals and operators). For the uniform interpolants that included any symbol with a probability of 10%, each ABox axiom contained on average 2.4 symbols and each TBox axiom 13.5 symbols. As the table shows, many uniform interpolants that included symbols with a probability of 10% only had small TBoxes. This can be explained by the small number of symbols present in these ontologies, which restricts the number of axioms that can be expressed.

Most concept assertions used just one concept symbol, whereas a few used simple concept disjunctions or role restrictions. On the other hand, the structure of the TBox axioms was affected more, especially in uniform interpolants with small signatures. Whereas a lot of axioms had simple forms such as $A \sqsubseteq B$, $A \sqsubseteq \exists r.B$ or $A \sqcup B \sqcup C \sqsubseteq \bot$, some would involve deep nestings of role restrictions. We also noticed that more complex axioms sometimes contained redundant information that was not detected by our prototype. A typical example are patterns such as $A \sqcap (\neg A \sqcup C)$, that could have been simplified using further resolution steps. In general, the majority of axioms was still easily human readable.

Ontology	Timeouts	Duration	TBox	ABox
CCON	0.0%	4.0 sec.	3.3%	62.5%
CTX	91.7%	607.1 sec.	3.5%	28.2%
ICPS	19.1%	28.2 sec.	68.4%	465.7%
ICF	0.0%	7.4 sec.	4.5%	11.2%
SSE	0.0%	23.4 sec.	3.3%	28.3%
00104	0.0%	2.4 sec.	3.7%	48.0%
00596	0.0%	10.4 sec.	3.5%	10.5%
00597	51.1%	705.5 sec.	179.8%	11.4%
00773	0.0%	24.9 sec.	29.1%	286.3%

Table 3: Uniform interpolants for symbols selected with 10% probability.

Only uniform interpolants of the ontologies CCON, 00597 and 00773 contained cyclic definers. Of their uniform interpolants, only 7.2% contained cyclic definers. Interestingly, no uniform interpolant made use of nominals. The reason is that the ontologies of our corpus only contained few role assertions, and imposed a relatively simple structure. However, in 25.3% of cases we had to use our method for eliminating disjunctive ABox statements, which always succeeded without introducing nominals. Hence, eliminating all non $\mathcal{ALCO}$ convertible clauses quickly resulted in clause sets fully representable in $\mathcal{ALC}$.

As the tables show, the results varied considerably depending on the structure of the ontology, and the size was not the only determining factor. For example, CTX has only 290 TBox axioms, but caused in 91.7% of the cases timeouts when computing small uniform interpolants. Analysis of the signatures that caused timeouts showed that in most cases just a small number of symbols was responsible, whereas the majority of concepts could be eliminated very quickly. In practical applications, one might therefore consider to extend the desired signature by one or two symbols, determined by some heuristics, if the computation turns out to be too expensive and the application allows it.

Conclusion and Future Work

We have presented a new method for computing uniform interpolants of $\mathcal{ALC}$ ontologies with ABoxes. Though the problem is complex and theoretical results show the target language needs to be slightly more expressive, our experiments show that in most cases uniform interpolants can be computed in reasonable time and do not fall outside the boundary of $\mathcal{ALC}$.

We are currently extending the approach to more expressive description logics, allowing for role hierarchies, transitive roles, inverse roles or cardinality restrictions. Even though our prototype already uses optimisations, further optimisations would strengthen the approach further, especially for ontologies with large ABoxes, but also for computing smaller axioms.

Acknowledgments

Patrick Koopmann is supported by an EPSRC doctoral training award.

References

Ackermann, W. 1935. Untersuchungen über das Eliminationsproblem der mathematischen Logik. *Mathematische Annalen* 110(1):390–413.

Areces, C.; Blackburn, P.; Hernández, B. M.; and Marx, M. 2003. Handling Boolean ABoxes. In *Proc. DL'03*, volume 81 of *CEUR Workshop Proceedings*. CEUR-WS.org.

Baader, F., and Nutt, W. 2007. Basic description logics. In Baader, F.; Calvanese, D.; McGuiness, D. L.; Nardi, D.; and Patel-Schneider, P. F., eds., *The Description Logic Handbook*. Cambridge University Press, second edition. chapter 2.

Calvanese, D.; De Giacomo, G.; and Lenzerini, M. 1999. Reasoning in expressive description logics with fixpoints based on automata on infinite trees. In *Proc. IJCAI '99*, 84–89. Morgan Kaufmann.

Grau, B. C. 2010. Privacy in ontology-based information systems: A pending matter. *Semantic Web* 1(1-2):137–141.

Konev, B.; Walther, D.; and Wolter, F. 2008. The logical difference problem for description logic terminologies. In *Automated Reasoning*. Springer. 259–274.

Konev, B.; Walther, D.; and Wolter, F. 2009. Forgetting and uniform interpolation in large-scale description logic terminologies. In *Proc. IJCAI '09*, 830–835. AAAI Press.

Koopmann, P., and Schmidt, R. A. 2013a. Forgetting concept and role symbols in $\mathcal{ALCH}$-ontologies. In *Proc. LPAR'13*, volume 8312 of *LNCS*, 552–567. Springer.

Koopmann, P., and Schmidt, R. A. 2013b. Implementation and evaluation of forgetting in $\mathcal{ALC}$-ontologies. In *Proc. WoMO'13*, volume 1081 of *CEUR Workshop Proceedings*, 37–48. CEUR-WS.org.

Koopmann, P., and Schmidt, R. A. 2013c. Uniform interpolation of $\mathcal{ALC}$-ontologies using fixpoints. In *Proc. FroCoS'13*, volume 8152 of *LNCS*, 87–102. Springer.

Koopmann, P., and Schmidt, R. A. 2014a. Count and forget: Uniform interpolation of $\mathcal{SHQ}$-ontologies. In *Proc. IJCAR'14*, volume 8562 of *LNCS*, 434–448. Springer.

Koopmann, P., and Schmidt, R. A. 2014b. Forgetting and uniform interpolation for $\mathcal{ALC}$-ontologies with ABoxes. volume 1193 of *CEUR Workshop Proceedings*, 245–257. CEUR-WS.org. Proc. DL'14.

Koopmann, P., and Schmidt, R. A. 2014c. Uniform interpolation and forgetting for $\mathcal{ALC}$ ontologies with ABoxes—long version. eScholar uk-ac-man-scw:240525, The University of Manchester, UK.

Ludwig, M., and Konev, B. 2014. Practical uniform interpolation and forgetting for $\mathcal{ALC}$ TBoxes with applications to logical difference. In *Proc. KR'14*. AAAI Press.

Lutz, C., and Wolter, F. 2011. Foundations for uniform interpolation and forgetting in expressive description logics. In *Proc. IJCAI '11*, 989–995. AAAI Press.

Lutz, C.; Seylan, I.; and Wolter, F. 2012. An automata-theoretic approach to uniform interpolation and approximation in the description logic $\mathcal{EL}$. In *Proc. KR'12*, 286–296. AAAI Press.

Matentzoglu, N.; Bail, S.; and Parsia, B. 2013. A snapshot of the OWL web. In *Proc. ISWC'13*. Springer. 331–346.

Nikitina, N., and Rudolph, S. 2014. (non-) succinctness of uniform interpolants of general terminologies in the description logic $\mathcal{EL}$. *Artificial Intelligence* 215:120–140.

Nonnengart, A., and Szałas, A. 1995. A fixpoint approach to second order quantifier elimination with applications to correspondence theory. Technical report.

Wang, K.; Wang, Z.; Topor, R.; Pan, J.; and Antoniou, G. 2009. Concept and role forgetting in $\mathcal{ALC}$ ontologies. 666–681.

Wang, Z.; Wang, K.; Topor, R. W.; and Pan, J. Z. 2010. Forgetting for knowledge bases in DL-Lite. *Ann. Math. Artif. Intell.* 58(1–2):117–151.

Wang, K.; Wang, Z.; Topor, R. W.; Pan, J. Z.; and Antoniou, G. 2014. Eliminating concepts and roles from ontologies in expressive descriptive logics. *Computational Intelligence* 30(2):205–232.

Proceedings of the Twenty-Ninth AAAI Conference on Artificial Intelligence

Using Matched Samples to Estimate the Effects of Exercise on Mental Health from Twitter

Virgile Landeiro Dos Reis and **Aron Culotta**
Department of Computer Science
Illinois Institute of Technology
Chicago, IL 60616
vlandeir@hawk.iit.edu, aculotta@iit.edu

Abstract

Recent work has demonstrated the value of social media monitoring for health surveillance (e.g., tracking influenza or depression rates). It is an open question whether such data can be used to make causal inferences (e.g., determining which activities lead to increased depression rates). Even in traditional, restricted domains, estimating causal effects from observational data is highly susceptible to confounding bias. In this work, we estimate the effect of exercise on mental health from Twitter, relying on statistical matching methods to reduce confounding bias. We train a text classifier to estimate the volume of a user's tweets expressing anxiety, depression, or anger, then compare two groups: those who exercise regularly (identified by their use of physical activity trackers like Nike+), and a matched control group. We find that those who exercise regularly have significantly fewer tweets expressing depression or anxiety; there is no significant difference in rates of tweets expressing anger. We additionally perform a sensitivity analysis to investigate how the many experimental design choices in such a study impact the final conclusions, including the quality of the classifier and the construction of the control group.

1 Introduction

Social media are increasingly used for tracking health concerns such as influenza (Lampos and Cristianini 2010; Culotta 2010; Paul and Dredze 2011; Signorini, Segre, and Polgreen 2011; Sadilek, Kautz, and Silenzio 2012), E. coli (Stewart and Diaz 2012), Adderall use (Hanson et al. 2013), dental pain (Heaivilin et al. 2011), insomnia (Jamison-Powell et al. 2012) and depression (De Choudhury et al. 2013). See Dredze (2012) for an overview. This approach provides an attractive complement to traditional survey approaches; it is cheaper, faster, and typically provides larger sample sizes, making it particularly appealing for monitoring diseases with rapid transmission rates.

While health tracking has been well studied, little efforts have been made to use social media data for a potentially more powerful health application: Web scale observational studies. Epidemiologists commonly conduct observational studies using survey data or health screenings to estimate causal effects when more rigorous controlled studies are infeasible or unethical — e.g., measuring the health effects of living in proximity to waste landfill sites.

Because subjects are not randomly assigned to experimental and control groups, observational studies do not have the same internal validity of randomized controlled trials, making them susceptible to the correlation/causation fallacy. That is, the observed difference in groups may be due to variables other than that proposed by the scientific hypothesis. As a result, many statistical techniques have been developed to estimate causal effects from observational data — for example, stratification and matching (Winship and Morgan 1999). These approaches all assume the presence of some observable covariates (e.g., demographics) that are predictive of group assignment.

In this paper, we take initial steps to explore the potential of Web-scale observational studies in the context of a specific health hypothesis: *Does exercise improve mood?* This question has been studied using traditional small study designs in psychology and psychiatry, where the evidence suggests that vigorous physical activity can alleviate symptoms of mild depression, improve self-image and social skills, and reduce anxiety (Taylor, Sallis, and Needle 1985). Traditional studies are typically limited by cost to small sample sizes and brief time windows. Social media provides a potential new data source to conduct such observational studies.

We develop an experimental framework to test this hypothesis using Twitter data, focusing on three research questions:

RQ1. **Can we accurately annotate users according to mood and physical activity?** We train a text classifier that identifies three different mood states (Hostility, Dejection, Anxiety) with 87% accuracy. Additionally, we use the increased popularity of activity tracking applications (e.g., Nike+) to identify physically active users.

RQ2. **How can we identify a suitable control set of users?** We provide an exact matching approach that identifies users with similar characteristics as the physically active set of users (based on gender, location, and online activity).

RQ3. **How sensitive are the results to choice of control**

set and quality of the classifier? We find that a more naive selection of a control group leads to inflated estimates of causal effects; additionally, we find that poor classifier accuracy can make it difficult to identify significant differences between groups.

As classifying online users by mental health or mood has been studied previously (De Choudhury, Counts, and Horvitz 2013; Li, Wang, and Hovy 2014), our primary contributions are (1) a new matching methodology for studies of online users, (2) an empirical comparison of the effect that control group selection has on the study conclusions, (3) a demonstration of this methodology for investigating the relationship between exercise and mood.

In the remainder of the paper, we first summarize related work, then describe our methodology for data collection, matching, and mood classification. We present and discuss the results, then conclude with future work.[1]

2 Related Work

Of the many recent studies inferring health from social media (Lampos and Cristianini 2010; Culotta 2010; Paul and Dredze 2011; Signorini, Segre, and Polgreen 2011; Heaivilin et al. 2011; Dredze 2012; Jamison-Powell et al. 2012; Sadilek, Kautz, and Silenzio 2012; Stewart and Diaz 2012; Hanson et al. 2013; Culotta 2013; De Choudhury et al. 2013; De Choudhury, Counts, and Horvitz 2013), perhaps the most aligned with our vision is Sadilek and Kautz (2013), who infer adverse health symptoms (coughing, headaches) from Twitter data and correlate them with environmental variables. While they do include some socio-economic control variables in a regression model, these are at the population level (zip-code), not individual covariates.

While most social media-based point prevalence work has made no attempt to control for confounding bias, Gayo-Avello (2011) emphasizes the importance of this bias, and provides evidence that age bias can affect attempts to predict political elections from Twitter sentiment. Additionally, Schonlau et al. (2009) use propensity score matching to adjust for selection bias in web surveys. Recent work has performed controlled experiments (Kohavi et al. 2009) and quasi-experiments (Oktay, Taylor, and Jensen 2010) on social media systems, though not for health studies, and not with experimental variables inferred from text.

More recently, Murnane and Counts (2014) identified Twitter users who attempted to quit smoking, then identified attributes that distinguished those who succeeded from those who did not. For example, they found that those who did not succeed posted more frequently and used less positive language, while those who succeed had greater social connectivity. This provides a great example of the promise of social media for this type of observational study, as well as the difficulty of estimating causal effects from noisy, online data.

[1] Code is available here: https://github.com/tapilab/aaai-2015-matching.

3 Methods

Below we describe our approach to sample users for the physically active (experimental) group and a control group, as well as how we classify messages according to mood.

3.1 Detecting Physically Active Users

We first identify a set of users who are physically active. Recently, a number of physical activity monitoring applications have been developed that allow one to record progress toward fitness goals. One feature of such applications is the ability to broadcast to others one's exercise activities. For example, `runmeter` allows one to broadcast the distance and time of a run.

We manually identified 10 hashtags for activity tracking applications: `runkeeper`, `nikeplus`, `runtastic`, `endomondo`, `mapmyrun`, `strava`, `cyclemeter`, `fitstats`, `mapmyfitness`, `runmeter`. We collect 123K tweets matching one of these 10 hashtags over a 10 day period (5/21/2014-5/31/2014) from 67K unique users. From these 67K users, we remove those who follow more than 5,000 accounts and those which are followed by more than 5,000 accounts. This is made in order to:

1. remove marketing accounts: physical activity tracking applications tend to do self promotion using Twitter;
2. to avoid a large number of calls to the Twitter API while collecting information about a unique user.

3.2 Matching

Below we first motivate the need for matching, then describe our procedure for identifying a matched control group.

Let H_i be a binary random variable representing a potential health outcome for individual i, e.g., $H_i = 1$ can indicate that individual i has high anxiety. In a typical observational study, individuals are categorized into two groups: the *treatment* group G_t is exposed to conditions that are hypothesized to affect the health outcome H (e.g., physical activity); the *control* group G_c is unexposed. Group assignment is indicated by a superscript: H_i^t is the health outcome for individual i in the treatment group, and H_j^c is the outcome for individual j in the control group.

The main quantity of interest is the *treatment effect*, the difference in outcome introduced by treatment: $\tau_i = H_i^t - H_i^c$. Of course, an individual i cannot be assigned to both groups simultaneously, so we can observe only one of H_i^t and H_i^c for each individual i. As a result, the average treatment effect is instead used, typically estimated by

$$\bar{\tau} = \bar{H}^t - \bar{H}^c \quad (1)$$

where $\bar{H}^t = \frac{1}{|G_t|}\sum_{i \in G_t} H_i^t$ and $\bar{H}^c = \frac{1}{|G_c|}\sum_{i \in G_c} H_i^c$. That is, the treatment effect is estimated by the difference between the mean outcomes of the two groups.

The key difference between an observational study and a randomized experiment is that in an observational study individuals are not randomly assigned to treatment and control groups. Because of this, the estimate in Equation 1 is susceptible to *omitted variable bias* when there exist confounding variables that influence both treatment and outcome. For example, if people who exercise regularly have higher income

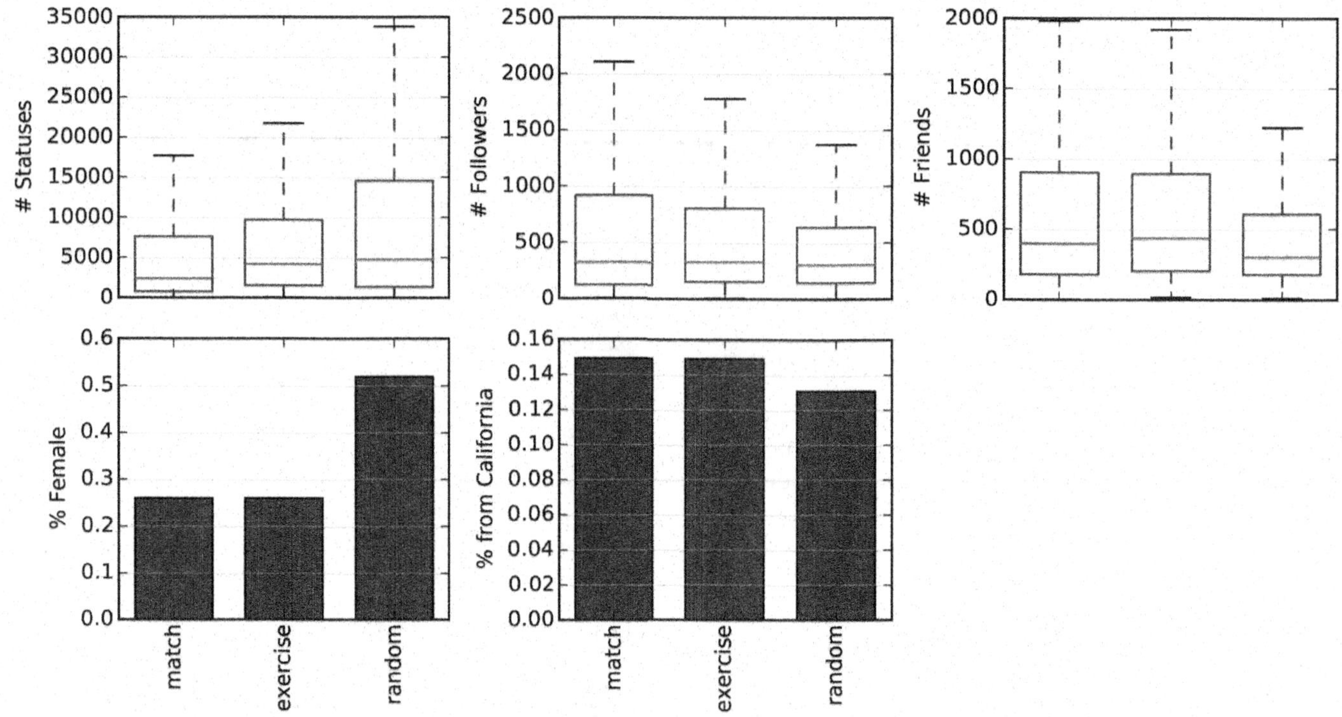

Figure 1: A comparison of various attributes of the experimental group (exercise), the matched control group, and a random control group, indicating that the matching procedure results in a control group more similar to the experimental group.

levels on average, then selecting a control group uniformly at random may over-estimate the treatment effect, since those with lower income levels may also have lower health outcomes on average. Thus, the choice of control group can dramatically impact the estimated treatment effect.

Standard approaches to reducing omitted variable bias include matching, stratification, and regression modeling (Winship and Morgan 1999). All of these methods assume that one can first measure a set of k potentially confounding variables (*covariates*) $Y_{i1} \ldots Y_{ik}$ for each individual i. Common covariates used in health studies include age, education, race/ethnicity, gender, and health-related behaviors such as smoking and alcohol consumption. These covariates can then be included as control variables in a regression model or used to filter or weight samples in the control group as in stratification or matching.[2]

In this work, we use matching to identify a control group that is similar to the experimental group. For each user i in the experimental group, we search for a "virtual twin" on Twitter using the following procedure:

1. Identify the set of *friends* of i (F_i) defined as the set of accounts j such that j follows i and i also follows j.
2. Filter F_i by removing accounts that do not have the same gender as i. To determine gender, we compared the first name provided in the user profile with the U.S. Census list of names by gender[3]. Ambiguous names are removed: a name is ambiguous if it appears in both the male and female census with frequencies that differ from less than a given ϵ (we use $\epsilon = 0.1$).
3. Filter F_i to those accounts with the same city/state as i. We restrict our study to the U.S., using heuristics to parse the (potentially noisy) location field of the user's profile. If no city and state match, an account with just a matching state is accepted.
4. Rank the remaining elements of F_i according to the number of tweets, followers, and friends. We compute the cosine similarity between these values for i and for each element of F_i, after first taking the log of each value.
5. Select the element of F_i with the highest cosine similarity for inclusion in the control group.
6. Check that the selected match m for i is not using any physical activity tracker. If it appears that m uses such an application, we remove m and i respectively from the control and treatment group.

Physically active users for whom we cannot find a suitable match are removed from the pool (e.g., if we cannot infer the gender or location of u, they are removed). In the end, we select 1,161 physically active users for the experimental group and 1,161 users for the control group.

To assess the quality of this matching procedure, we compare the attributes of the control and experimental groups

[2] Note however that a 'hidden bias' can still exist when unobserved variables affect treatment and outcome simultaneously.

[3] http://www.census.gov/genealogy/www/freqnames.html

with a random selection of 236 Twitter users from the U.S. for whom we could infer gender and location. Figure 1 shows that while the number of statuses (tweets) and followers is similar between the experimental (exercise) and random groups, random users tend to have many fewer friends than either the control or experimental groups. Furthermore, the random group has over twice as many female users as the other groups, and a much different geographic distribution. For comparison, we display just the fraction of users from California, which is the most common state in the data.

As location and gender are very likely to be confounding variables, these results indicate that the process of sampling social media users can have a large impact on the final results.

3.3 Mood classification

In this section, we describe our classifier to annotate tweets by mood.

Data annotation The final variable we must infer is the mood of a user. We build a text classifier to label each tweet on three mood states: **Anger/Hostility**, **Depression/Dejection**, **Tension/Anxiety**.

Building on prior work (Bollen, Mao, and Zeng 2011), we begin with the Profile of Mood States (POMS) (McNair, Heuchert, and Shilony 2003), a psychology questionnaire commonly used to assess the mood of respondents. This contains 35 total terms corresponding to one of the three mood states above. While previous work in sentiment analysis uses keywords themselves for classification (Wilson et al. 2005), we find that the polysemy and variety of usage on Twitter makes this approach too inaccurate for our purposes. Instead, we perform supervised classification, using these 35 as a seed set to collect tweets for annotation.

For each term from POMS, we search through a sample of tweets to collect contexts in which the term appears. We next compute context vectors for each term, consisting of the frequencies of unigrams in a 3-word window from each appearance. Finally, we compute similar vectors for words in an expanded vocabulary, and identify the closest n terms to the original word, using cosine similarity. For each mood state, then, we expand the term list to 100 terms.

With these 300 terms, we then search Twitter for 10 examples of each term. We then annotate each message as expressing zero or more of the three mood states. (A second annotator labeled 100 of the tweets, resulting in 75% overlap.)

This process yields 2,367 total annotated tweets: 229 are labeled positive for the Anger/Hostility dimension, 369 for the Depression/Dejection dimension, and 381 for the Tension/Anxiety dimension.

Features We tokenize each tweet by splitting on whitespace and retaining punctuation and stop words. In addition to unigrams and bigrams, we also include features from the 2001 Linguistic Inquiry and Word Count (LIWC) lexicon (Pennebaker, Francis, and Booth 2001) and emoticons. LIWC contains 74 categories and 2,300 word patterns (which includes exact matches as well as prefixes like *awake**). This lexicon was developed over a number

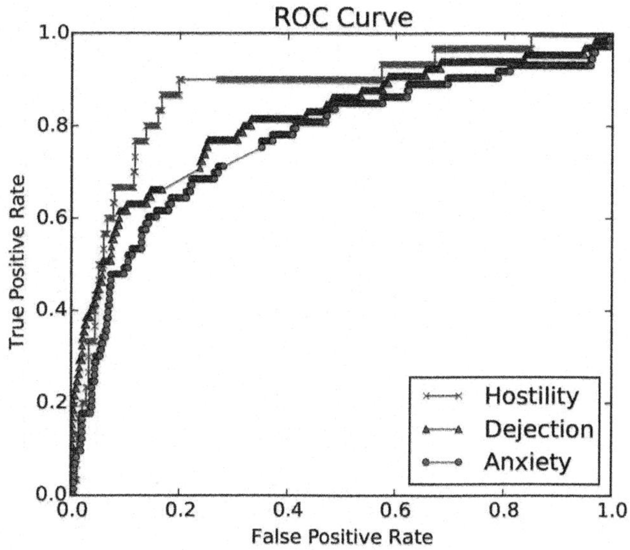

Figure 2: ROC curve for classifying tweets according to mood state.

Category	Accuracy	Precision	Recall	F1
Hostility	.901	.490	.358	.410
Dejection	.870	.620	.447	.514
Anxiety	.850	.551	.372	.442
Average	.874	.554	.392	.455

Table 1: Classification results (on tweets already matching a set of mood-related keywords).

of years to identify categories that capture emotional and cognitive cues of interest to health, sociology, and psychology. It has been used in numerous studies (James W Pennebaker 2003), including Twitter studies (Qiu et al. 2012; Schwartz and others 2013; De Choudhury et al. 2013).

Classifier We first perform a pilot study in which we vary the number of features from 80 to 800, comparing Decision Tree, K-neighbors, Logistic Regression, Naive Bayes, and SVM classifiers. (We use the `scikit-learn` implementations (Pedregosa and others 2011).) From this study, we select a Logistic Regression classifier, using feature selection to retain the top 160 features. Figure 2 displays the ROC curve for this classifier using 10-fold classification.

Table 1 shows the results for each category. We note that this classifier is evaluated on tweets that already contain at least one of the 300 POMS-related words identified in the previous section, so this accuracy indicates how well the classifier can disambiguate tweets that likely contain a mood state.

Table 2 shows the highest weighted coefficients for each class according to the classifier. Terms in typewriter font (`Anger` and `Sad`) indicate LIWC categories. We can see that the LIWC category is a top feature in two of the three classes. Also, bigrams appear to help here, particularly those beginning with "so" (e.g., "so tired", "so sick", "so annoy-

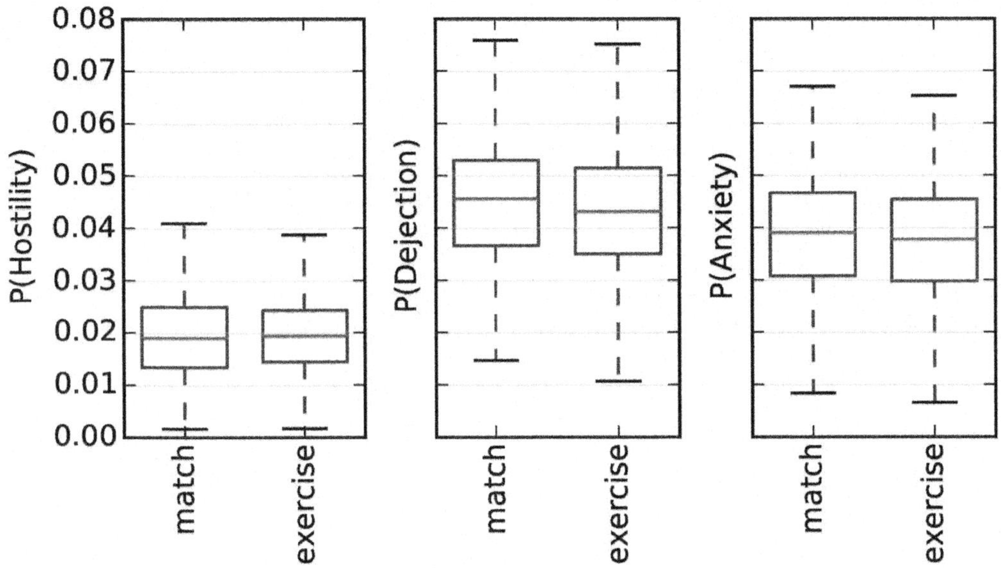

Figure 3: The results comparing the mood of users who are physically active versus a matched control group, indicating that the active group has lower rates of Dejection and Anxiety tweets. See Table 3 for significance levels.

Category	Terms
Hostility	upset, hate, so mad, fucking, irritated, shut, ive, freakin, `Anger`, your, dumb, ignorant, to die, rude, why would
Dejection	somebody, depressed, `Sad`, bored, exhausted, tired of, lazy, so tired, ive been, so sick, so depressing, get out, pain, sick, everyones
Anxiety	disgusted, shut, why cant, nervous, of this, fuck, paranoid, teacher, hate, cranky, rude, so annoying, tomorrow im, fucking, irritated

Table 2: The top 15 terms per category, ranked by fitted coefficients.

ing").

We use this classifier to annotate each user in the control and experimental groups with the level of each mood. We do this by computing the fraction of tweets from a user that are classified as positive for each class. We remove retweets as well as auto-generated tweets from consideration.

4 Results

Figure 3 shows the box-plots for the mood classifications for the experimental (exercise) and matched control groups. The y-axis is the class probability per user (the fraction of tweets assigned positive classification labels). We see that overall that Dejection and Anxiety tweets are more common than Hostility tweets. Furthermore, it appears that the control group has higher values for Dejection and Anxiety, but lower values for Hostility.

To test for significance, we use a Wilcoxon signed-rank test. Table 3 displays the results. This table reports the estimated difference in mood between the exercise and control groups. E.g., the -2.7% value in column 2 means that physically active Twitter users posted on average 2.7% fewer anxious tweets than a matched user (a relative difference). The Random Control and 50% Training Data columns use a different control set and less accurate classifier (discussed below). Bold values are those found to be statistically significant by the Wilcoxon signed-rank test ($p < 0.05$).

The "Matched Control" results in Table 3 indicate that the experimental group has a significantly lower incidence of Dejection and Anxiety tweets; the difference in Hostility tweets is not significant. These results are further validated by the psychology literature, which in small studies has found reduced incidence of anxiety and depression symptoms in highly active individuals. While it is difficult to directly compare our results to the psychology literature, for reference, exercise has been found to reduce the rate of self-reported anxiety (roughly 1 point on a 5-point scale) (Taylor, Sallis, and Needle 1985). It is suspected, however, that these differences are temporary (possibly due to endorphins). An attractive property of studies of social media is that it may be easier to study such effects over time, which we leave for future work.

4.1 Effects of control group

Table 3 also reports the results comparing the experimental group to the randomly selected control group (Random Control). We can see that such a comparison greatly overstates the effects — the experimental group has significantly lower rates of all mood classes, and the magnitude of the difference is 2-20 times that for the matched control group.

	Matched Control		Random Control		50% Training Data	
Category	**% Change**	**p-value**	**% Change**	**p-value**	**% Change**	**p-value**
Hostility	0.9	0.53	**-21.1**	9.2E-17	1.3	0.47
Dejection	**-3.9**	7.8E-4	**-5.4**	1E-4	**-2.0**	0.016
Anxiety	**-2.7**	0.02	**-7.9**	3.6E-6	0.1	0.64

Table 3: Estimated effect sizes of exercise on mood, using a Wilcoxon signed-rank test. The matched control provides a much more conservative estimate as compared to using a random control set. The results can also be sensitive to the accuracy of the classifier — using only half the training data removes the effect for Anxiety.

These results have implications for other studies that use social media data to make inferences about differences in population groups. It is important that we adjust for the selection bias introduced by the creation of the control and experimental groups. For example, Figure 1 indicates that the random control group has roughly twice as many female users as the exercise group. Given the observed lexical variation between genders on social media (Bamman, Eisenstein, and Schnoebelen 2014), this will confound hypothesis testing, since many factors other than exercise are contributing to the observed difference in mood. By matching based on gender and the other attributes described in Section 3.2, we can reduce the impact of such confounders.

4.2 Effects of classifier accuracy

Finally, Table 3 reports the results comparing the experimental group to the matched control group, but instead using a classifier trained on only 50% of the annotated data. The purpose of this sensitivity analysis was to determine how classifier quality affected the final results. We can see that effects for two of the three classes actually became stronger (Hostility and Detection), while the effect for Anxiety grew weaker (and changed sign). Taken together, this sensitivity analysis highlights the importance of the experimental design choices in conducting such studies.

5 Conclusion and Future Work

We have presented an observational study of the effect of exercise on mood using only social media data. The results of our analysis suggest that there is a smaller incidence of tweets classified as Dejection or Anxiety for users who are physically active, as determined by their use of physical activity trackers. We have also performed a sensitivity analysis which reveals the importance of selecting a realistic control group.

There are a number of limitations, most notably the fact that there is imperfection both in the assignment of users to control and experimental groups (e.g., users who exercise but do not use one of the 10 tracking apps may end up in the control group) and in the outcome variable (i.e., the mood classifier). As such imperfections are inherent to any attempt at Web observational studies, in future work we will investigate multiple imputation methods (Schafer 1999) to incorporate this uncertainty directly into hypothesis testing. Additionally, in future work we will compare alternative matching strategies, such as propensity score matching (Winship and Morgan 1999).

References

Bamman, D.; Eisenstein, J.; and Schnoebelen, T. 2014. Gender identity and lexical variation in social media. *Journal of Sociolinguistics* 18(2):135–160.

Bollen, J.; Mao, H.; and Zeng, X. 2011. Twitter mood predicts the stock market. *Journal of Computational Science* 2(1):1–8.

Culotta, A. 2010. Towards detecting influenza epidemics by analyzing Twitter messages. In *Workshop on Social Media Analytics at the 16th ACM SIGKDD Conference on Knowledge Discovery and Data Mining*.

Culotta, A. 2013. Lightweight methods to estimate influenza rates and alcohol sales volume from twitter messages. *Lang. Resour. Eval.* 47(1):217238.

De Choudhury, M.; Gamon, M.; Counts, S.; and Horvitz, E. 2013. Predicting depression via social media. In *ICWSM*.

De Choudhury, M.; Counts, S.; and Horvitz, E. 2013. Predicting postpartum changes in emotion and behavior via social media. In *Proceedings of the SIGCHI Conference on Human Factors in Computing Systems*, CHI '13, 32673276. New York, NY, USA: ACM.

Dredze, M. 2012. How social media will change public health. *IEEE Intelligent Systems* 27(4):81–84.

Gayo-Avello, D. 2011. Don't turn social media into another 'Literary digest' poll. *Commun. ACM* 54(10):121128.

Hanson, C. L.; Burton, S. H.; Giraud-Carrier, C.; West, J. H.; Barnes, M. D.; and Hansen, B. 2013. Tweaking and tweeting: Exploring twitter for nonmedical use of a psychostimulant drug (adderall) among college students. *Journal of Medical Internet Research* 15(4):e62.

Heaivilin, N.; Gerbert, B.; Page, J.; and Gibbs, J. 2011. Public health surveillance of dental pain via twitter. *Journal of Dental Research* 90(9):1047–1051. PMID: 21768306 PMCID: PMC3169887.

James W Pennebaker, M. R. M. 2003. Psychological aspects of natural language. use: our words, our selves. *Annual review of psychology* 54:547–77.

Jamison-Powell, S.; Linehan, C.; Daley, L.; Garbett, A.; and Lawson, S. 2012. "I can't get no sleep": Discussing #insomnia on Twitter. In *Proceedings of the SIGCHI Conference on Human Factors in Computing Systems*, CHI '12, 15011510. New York, NY, USA: ACM.

Kohavi, R.; Longbotham, R.; Sommerfield, D.; and Henne, R. M. 2009. Controlled experiments on the web: survey and practical guide. *Data Mining and Knowledge Discovery* 18(1):140–181.

Lampos, V., and Cristianini, N. 2010. Tracking the flu pandemic by monitoring the social web. In *2nd IAPR Workshop on Cognitive Information Processing (CIP 2010)*, 411–416.

Li, J.; Wang, X.; and Hovy, E. 2014. What a nasty day: Exploring mood-weather relationship from twitter. In *Proceedings of the 23rd ACM International Conference on Conference on Information and Knowledge Management*, 1309–1318. ACM.

McNair, D.; Heuchert, J.; and Shilony, E. 2003. Research with the profile of mood states (poms) 1964–2002: A comprehensive bibliography. *MHC, Toronto* 7–8.

Murnane, E. L., and Counts, S. 2014. Unraveling abstinence and relapse: smoking cessation reflected in social media. In *Proceedings of the 32nd annual ACM conference on Human factors in computing systems*, 1345–1354. ACM.

Oktay, H.; Taylor, B. J.; and Jensen, D. D. 2010. Causal discovery in social media using quasi-experimental designs. In *Proceedings of the First Workshop on Social Media Analytics*, 1–9. ACM.

Paul, M. J., and Dredze, M. 2011. You are what you tweet: Analyzing twitter for public health. In *Fifth International AAAI Conference on Weblogs and Social Media*.

Pedregosa, F., et al. 2011. Scikit-learn: Machine learning in Python. *Machine Learning Research* 12:2825–2830.

Pennebaker, J.; Francis, J.; and Booth, R. 2001. Linguistic inquiry and word count: LIWC 2001. *World Journal of the International Linguistic Association*.

Qiu, L.; Lin, H.; Ramsay, J.; and Yang, F. 2012. You are what you tweet: Personality expression and perception on twitter. *Journal of Research in Personality* 46(6):710–718.

Sadilek, A., and Kautz, H. 2013. Modeling the impact of lifestyle on health at scale. In *Proceedings of the Sixth ACM International Conference on Web Search and Data Mining*, WSDM '13, 637646. New York, NY, USA: ACM.

Sadilek, A.; Kautz, H.; and Silenzio, V. 2012. Predicting disease transmission from geo-tagged micro-blog data. In *Twenty-Sixth AAAI Conference on Artificial Intelligence*.

Schafer, J. L. 1999. Multiple imputation: a primer. *Statistical methods in medical research* 8(1):3–15.

Schonlau, M.; Soest, A. v.; Kapteyn, A.; and Couper, M. 2009. Selection bias in web surveys and the use of propensity scores. *Sociological Methods & Research* 37(3):291–318.

Schwartz, H. A., et al. 2013. Characterizing geographic variation in well-being using tweets. In *Seventh International AAAI Conference on Weblogs and Social Media (ICWSM)*.

Signorini, A.; Segre, A. M.; and Polgreen, P. M. 2011. The use of twitter to track levels of disease activity and public concern in the U.S. during the influenza a H1N1 pandemic. *PLoS ONE* 6(5):e19467.

Stewart, A., and Diaz, E. 2012. Epidemic intelligence: For the crowd, by the crowd. In Brambilla, M.; Tokuda, T.; and Tolksdorf, R., eds., *Web Engineering*, number 7387 in Lecture Notes in Computer Science. Springer Berlin Heidelberg. 504–505.

Taylor, C. B.; Sallis, J. F.; and Needle, R. 1985. The relation of physical activity and exercise to mental health. *Public health reports* 100(2):195.

Wilson, T.; Hoffmann, P.; Somasundaran, S.; Kessler, J.; Wiebe, J.; Choi, Y.; Cardie, C.; Riloff, E.; and Patwardhan, S. 2005. Opinionfinder: A system for subjectivity analysis. In *Proceedings of hlt/emnlp on interactive demonstrations*, 34–35. Association for Computational Linguistics.

Winship, C., and Morgan, S. L. 1999. The estimation of causal effects from observational data. *Annual Review of Sociology* 25:pp. 659–706.

Consistent Knowledge Discovery from Evolving Ontologies

Freddy Lécué
IBM Dublin Research Center, Ireland
freddy.lecue@ie.ibm.com

Jeff Z.Pan
University of Aberdeen, UK
jeff.z.pan@abdn.ac.uk

Abstract

Deductive reasoning and inductive learning are the most common approaches for deriving knowledge. In real world applications when data is dynamic and incomplete, especially those exposed by sensors, reasoning is limited by dynamics of data while learning is biased by data incompleteness. Therefore discovering consistent knowledge from incomplete and dynamic data is a challenging open problem. In our approach the semantics of data is captured through ontologies to empower learning (mining) with (Description Logics) reasoning. Consistent knowledge discovery is achieved by applying generic, significative, representative association semantic rules. The experiments have shown scalable, accurate and consistent knowledge discovery with data from Dublin.

Introduction and Related Work

Knowledge discovery, as an area focusing upon methodologies for extracting knowledge through deduction (a priori) or from data (a posteriori), has been largely studied in Database and Artificial Intelligence. Deductive reasoning e.g., logic reasoning (Reiter 1980) gains logically knowledge from pre-established (certain) knowledge statements, while inductive inference such as data mining (Agrawal, Imielinski, and Swami 1993) or learning (Fanizzi, d'Amato, and Esposito 2010; Völker and Niepert 2011) discovers (uncertain) knowledge by generalizing from initial information.

Data is dynamic, incomplete, especially when exposed through sensors (Labrinidis and Jagadish 2012). Tracking phenomena with multiple sensor readings is a challenging problem. From traffic diagnosis (Lécué 2012), systems monitoring (Song et al. 2014) to disease transmission prediction (Sadilek, Kautz, and Silenzio 2012), all are examples of scenarios where consistent knowledge needs to be derived from dynamic, incomplete data. Reasoning is strongly restricted by dynamics, variance, noisiness of data, enforcing knowledge to be regularly revisited (Anicic et al. 2011). Recent works in stream reasoning (Valle et al. 2009) handle the dynamics of semantic querying but are very limited in reasoning, and fail in recovering knowledge from data. Although (Lécué and Pan 2013) exposed benefits in combining reasoning and learning, the shortcomings are lack of scalability, over-specification of rules, non-integration to reasoning systems. On the other hand inductive learning is limited by the large fluctuation of rules abstraction and its (high) theoretical complexity. Learning is also heavily biased by data incompleteness and inconsistency, making knowledge subject to incorrectness (Dietterich and Michalski 1981). They follow classic (raw) data mining techniques i.e., identification of patterns using distance metrics (Ramaswamy, Rastogi, and Shim 2000) between syntactic values. (Srikant and Agrawal 1995) capture such patterns through frequent itemset mining (Agrawal et al. 1996). Their approach discovers recurring sequences of syntactic items and implication rules among those items e.g., rules "*buying milk* implies *buying bread* with a confidence of 70%" are learnt in market basket analysis. (Dehaspe and Raedt 1997) constrain all rules to be represented following inductive logic programming (ILP), which significantly improve scalability. Although metrics have been used to measure the *quality* of the derived rules, previous approaches fail in deriving scalable, accurate, and consistent knowledge. In this respect (Galárraga et al. 2013) tackles the scalability issue when performing rule mining on semantic data but does not in the context of evolving data.

We address *"discovery of consistent knowledge from dynamic semantic data"*. Given continuous knowledge, how do we capture a minimal albeit representative set of time-evolving trends to discover accurate, consistent knowledge? The semantics of data is captured through OWL (*Web Ontology Language*) ontologies, which are underpinned by Description Logics (DL) (Baader and Nutt 2003). Key contributions include: (1) We design the first algorithm to learn DL rules, which are strictly more expressive than DL axioms and Datalog rules. (2) By exploiting the expressiveness of DL rules, we introduce the notions of significative, representative association DL rules, enabling precise identification of fundamental rules. The benefits of combining learning and reasoning, validated in experiments, are: (i) logical representation of learnt rules, (ii) classification, and abstraction of rules, (iii) tight integration of rules in reasoning; (iv) scalability, (v) accuracy of consistent knowledge discovery.

Next section reviews the adopted logic and rule representation together with dynamic ontology (knowledge). Then we present inductive learning in dynamic ontologies. The next section presents how representative rules drive consistent knowledge discovery. Finally, we report experiments with real data from Dublin City and draw some conclusions.

$SocialEvent \sqcap \exists type.Music \sqsubseteq Event \sqcap \exists disruption.Steady$	(1)
$SocialEvent \sqsubseteq Event$	(2)
$Incident \sqcap \exists impact.Serious \sqsubseteq Event \sqcap \exists disruption.High$	(3)
$Road \sqcap \exists adj.(\exists occur.(\exists disruption.High)) \sqsubseteq DisruptedRoad$	(4)
$BusRoad \sqcap \exists travel.Long \sqsubseteq Road \sqcap \exists with.CongestedBus$	(5)
$Road \sqcap \exists with.Bus \sqsubseteq BusRoad$ (6) $\quad Road(r_0)$	(7)
$Steady \sqsubseteq High$ (8) $\quad Stop \sqsubseteq Long \sqsubseteq Abnormal$	(9)
$Bus(b_1)$ (10) $\quad Bus(b_2)$ (11) $\quad Bus(b_3)$	(12)
$Road(r_1)$ (13) $\quad Road(r_2)$ (14) $\quad Road(r_3)$	(15)
$adj(r_0, r_1)$ (16) $\quad adj(r_0, r_2)$ (17) $\quad adj(r_0, r_3)$	(18)

Figure 1: $\mathcal{O} \doteq \langle \mathcal{T}, \mathcal{A} \rangle$. Sample of TBox $\mathcal{T}$ and ABox $\mathcal{A}$.

R_1	If $X \sqsubseteq A,\ A \sqsubseteq B$ then $X \sqsubseteq B$
R_2	If $X \sqsubseteq A_1, \cdots A_n,\ A_1 \sqcap \cdots \sqcap A_n \sqsubseteq B$ then $X \sqsubseteq B$
R_3	If $X \sqsubseteq A,\ A \sqsubseteq \exists r.B$ then $X \sqsubseteq \exists r.B$
R_4	If $X \sqsubseteq \exists r.A,\ A \sqsubseteq A',\ \exists r.A' \sqsubseteq B$ then $X \sqsubseteq B$
R_5	If $X \sqsubseteq \exists r.A,\ A \sqsubseteq \bot$ then $X \sqsubseteq \bot$
R_6	If $X \sqsubseteq \exists r.A,\ r \sqsubseteq s$ then $X \sqsubseteq \exists s.A$
R_7	If $X \sqsubseteq \exists r_1.A,\ A \sqsubseteq \exists r_2.B,\ r_1 \circ r_2 \sqsubseteq r_3$ then $X \sqsubseteq \exists r_3.B$

Table 1: $\mathcal{EL}^{++}$ TBox Completion Rules (no datatypes).

Background

Evolving and static background knowledge are represented using an ontology. We focus on DL to define ontologies since it offers good reasoning support for most of its expressive families and compatibility to W3C standard OWL 2. We illustrate our work with DL $\mathcal{EL}^{++}$ (Baader, Brandt, and Lutz 2005). The selection of this DL fragment, which is the logic behind the basis of many more expressive DL, has been guided by (i) the semantics expressed by data in our application cf. Experimental Results, lessons learned, (ii) its polynomial time reasoning (satisfiability, subsumption) when combined with $\mathcal{EL}^{++}$ rules. We review (i) DL basics of $\mathcal{EL}^{++}$, (ii) $\mathcal{EL}^{++}$ atomsets and rules, (iii) evolving ontologies and the underlying reasoning.

Description Logics $\mathcal{EL}^{++}$

A signature Σ, noted $(\mathcal{N}_C, \mathcal{N}_R, \mathcal{N}_I)$ consists of 3 disjoint sets of (i) atomic concepts $\mathcal{N}_C$, (ii) atomic roles $\mathcal{N}_R$, and (iii) individuals $\mathcal{N}_I$. Given a signature, the top concept $\top$, the bottom concept $\bot$, an atomic concept A, an individual a, an atomic role expression r, $\mathcal{EL}^{++}$ concept expressions C and D in $\mathcal{C}$ can be composed with the following constructs:

$$\top \mid \bot \mid A \mid C \sqcap D \mid \exists r.C \mid \{a\}$$

The DL ontology $\mathcal{O} \doteq \langle \mathcal{T}, \mathcal{A} \rangle$ is composed of a TBox $\mathcal{T}$, and an ABox $\mathcal{A}$. A TBox is a set of concept and role axioms. $\mathcal{EL}^{++}$ supports General Concept Inclusion axioms (GCIs e.g. $C \sqsubseteq D$), Role Inclusion axioms (RIs e.g., $r \sqsubseteq s$). An ABox is a set of concept assertion axioms e.g., $C(a)$, role assertion axioms e.g., $R(a, b)$, individual in/equality axioms e.g., $a \neq b$, $a = b$. In this paper, we assume acyclic TBoxes which entail finitely instance statements.

Example 1. ***(TBox and ABox Concept Assertion Axioms)*** *Figure 1 presents (i) a TBox $\mathcal{T}$ where $DisruptedRoad$ (4) denotes the concept of "roads which are adjacent to an event causing high disruption", (ii) concept assertions (16–18) denoting the individual r_0 having $r_{i,1 \le i \le 3}$ as adjunct roads.*

Table 1 sketches some completion rules (Baader, Brandt, and Lutz 2005) that are used to classify $\mathcal{EL}^{++}$ TBox $\mathcal{T}$ and entail subsumption. Reasoning with such rules is PTime-Complete (Baader, Brandt, and Lutz 2008).

$\mathcal{EL}^{++}$ Atom, Atomsets, Binding and Rule

We consider $\mathcal{EL}^{++}$ with (i) concept expressions $\mathcal{C}$, role names $\mathcal{N}_R$, individual names $\mathcal{N}_I$, and (ii) a countable set of first-order variables $\mathcal{V}$.

Atomset: Given terms $x_1, x_2 \in \mathcal{V} \cup \mathcal{N}_I$, a concept (role) atom is a formula $C(x_1)$ ($R(x_1, x_2)$) with $C \in \mathcal{C}$ ($R \in \mathcal{N}_R$). We use finite sets (*atomsets*) $\mathbb{B}$ of (concepts, roles) atoms for representing conjunction $\forall \vec{x}. \bigwedge B$ where $\vec{x} \doteq x_1, \cdots, x_n \in \mathcal{V}$ are variables of atoms $B \in \mathbb{B}$ which could be shared.

Atomset Binding: Atomsets can be seen as conjunctive queries (Glimm et al. 2007) without non-distinguished variables. The arity of an atomset is the number of variables in an atomset. We write $\mathcal{T}, \mathcal{A} \models \mathbb{B}[\vec{a}]$ to denote that $\vec{a} \in \mathcal{N}_I$ is an answer to query $\mathbb{B}$. In other words the variables $\vec{x}$ of atomset $\mathbb{B}$ are bound (mapped) by $\vec{a}$. In the rest of the paper we used the terms *answer* and *binding* interchangeably. $bind(\mathbb{B}, \mathcal{T} \cup \mathcal{A})$ is the set of all bindings to $\mathbb{B}$ w.r.t. $\mathcal{T}$, $\mathcal{A}$.

Example 2. ***(Atomset & Binding w.r.t. $\mathcal{O}$ in Figure 1)*** *Given atomset $\mathbb{B} \doteq \{adj(x, r_1)\}$, $bind(\mathbb{B}, \mathcal{O})$ is $\{(r_0)\}$.*

Atomset Containment: Let $\mathcal{T}$ be a TBox, $\mathbb{B}, \mathbb{C}$ atomsets with the same arity. Then $\mathbb{B}$ is contained in $\mathbb{C}$ w.r.t. $\mathcal{T}$, written $\mathbb{B} \subseteq_{\mathcal{T}} \mathbb{C}$, if for all consistent ABoxes $\mathcal{A}$ w.r.t. $\mathcal{T}$, we have $bind(\mathbb{B}, \mathcal{T} \cup \mathcal{A}) \subseteq bind(\mathbb{C}, \mathcal{T} \cup \mathcal{A})$.

Example 3. ***(Atomset Containment w.r.t. $\mathcal{O}$ in Figure 1)*** *Let $\mathbb{B}$, $\mathbb{C}$ be atomsets $\{(1)\}$ and $\{(2)\}$; $\mathcal{A}'$ be $\{Event(e_1), Event(e_2), SocialEvent(e_1)\}$. $\mathbb{B} \subseteq_{\mathcal{T}} \mathbb{C}$ for $\mathcal{A}'$ since all bindings (answers) of $\mathbb{B}$ are also bindings of $\mathbb{C}$.*

$$SocialEvent(x) \quad (1) \qquad\qquad Event(x) \quad (2)$$

$\mathcal{EL}^{++}$ Rules: $\mathcal{EL}^{++}$ rules (Krötzsch, Rudolph, and Hitzler 2008) extends $\mathcal{EL}^{++}$ expressivity while maintaining polynomial time complexity of many typical inference problems. Given atomsets $\mathbb{B}$, $\mathbb{H}$, and all variables $\vec{x} \in \mathcal{V}$ of atomset $\mathbb{B} \cup \mathbb{H}$, an $\mathcal{EL}^{++}$ *rule* is a formula $\mathbb{B} \twoheadrightarrow \mathbb{H}$, such that $\mathbb{B}$ is cycle free and does not contain atom of the form $R(x, x)$.

Example 4. ***($\mathcal{EL}^{++}$ Rule)*** *Below rule denotes "if x_3 is adjacent to a x_2 where a highly disruptive event x_1 occurs then buses are congested in x_3". $\{(5)\}$ is atomset $\{(Road \sqcap \exists with.CongestedBus)(x_3)\}$.*

$$(Event \sqcap \exists disruption.High)(x_1) \wedge \quad (3)$$
$$occur(x_2, x_1) \wedge adj(x_3, x_2) \quad (4)$$
$$\twoheadrightarrow (Road \sqcap \exists with.CongestedBus)(x_3) \quad (5)$$

Dynamics of Knowledge as Evolving Ontologies

We represent dynamics of knowledge by an evolution of ontologies in Definition 1 (Huang and Stuckenschmidt 2005).

$\mathcal{P}_0^9(5) : (Event \sqcap \exists disruption.High)(e_1),\quad occur(r_1, e_1)$	(24)
$\mathcal{Q}_0^9(5) : (Road \sqcap \exists travel.Long)(r_1)$	(25)
$\mathcal{R}_0^9(5) : with(r_1, b_1)$	(26)
$\mathcal{P}_0^9(6) : (SocialEvent \sqcap \exists type.Music)(e_2),\quad occur(r_2, e_2)$	(27)
$\mathcal{Q}_0^9(6) : (Road \sqcap \exists travel.Abnormal)(r_2)$	(28)
$\mathcal{R}_0^9(6) : with(r_2, b_2)$	(29)
$\mathcal{P}_0^9(7) : (Incident \sqcap \exists impact.Serious)(e_3),\quad occur(r_3, e_3)$	(30)
$\mathcal{Q}_0^9(7) : (Road \sqcap \exists travel.Stop)(r_3)$	(31)
$\mathcal{R}_0^9(7) : with(r_3, b_3)$	(32)

Figure 2: Evolving Ontologies $\mathcal{P}_0^9(i)$, $\mathcal{Q}_0^9(i)$, $\mathcal{R}_0^9(i)_{i \in \{5,6,7\}}$.

Definition 1. ***(DL $\mathcal{L}$ Evolving Ontology)***
A DL $\mathcal{L}$ evolving ontology $\mathcal{P}_m^n$ from point of time m to point of time n is a sequence of (sets of) Abox axioms $(\mathcal{P}_m^n(m), \mathcal{P}_m^n(m+1), \cdots, \mathcal{P}_m^n(n))$ w.r.t a static TBox $\mathcal{T}$ in a DL $\mathcal{L}$ where $m, n \in \mathbb{N}$ and $m < n$.

$\mathcal{P}_m^n(i)$ is a snapshot of an evolving ontology $\mathcal{P}_m^n$ at time i, referring to ABox axioms with respect to a TBox in $\mathcal{L}$. We will consider evolving ontologies $\mathcal{P}_0^n$ for the sake of clarity.

Example 5. ***(DL $\mathcal{EL}^{++}$ Evolving Ontology)***
Figure 2 illustrates $\mathcal{EL}^{++}$ evolving ontologies $\mathcal{P}_0^9$, $\mathcal{Q}_0^9$, $\mathcal{R}_0^9$, related to events, travel time, buses, through snapshots at time $i \in \{5, 6, 7\}$. Their dynamic knowledge is captured by evolving ABox axioms e.g., (27) captures e_2 as "a social music event occurring in r_2" at time 6 of $\mathcal{P}_0^9$.

By applying rules in Table 1 on static knowledge $\mathcal{T}$, evolving ontology $\mathcal{P}_0^n$, snapshot-specific axioms are inferred.

Example 6. ***(Reasoning in Evolving Ontology)***
(6), (7), as dynamic knowledge are entailed from axioms of $\mathcal{O}$ in Figure 1 and evolving ontologies $\mathcal{P}_0^9$, $\mathcal{Q}_0^9$, $\mathcal{R}_0^9$ in Figure 2 (cf. references to axioms A in $\models^{(A)}$), by applying completion rules in Table 1 (cf. references to rules R in $\models_R$). E.g., r_0 and r_3 are respectively entailed to be roads with: (i) disruptions, (ii) some congested buses, both at time 7.

$$\mathcal{O}, \mathcal{P}_0^9(7) \models^{(3)\text{-}4),(7),(18),(30)}_{R_1,R_2,R_3,R_7} DisruptedRoad(r_0) \quad (6)$$

$$\mathcal{O}, \mathcal{Q}_0^9 \cup \mathcal{R}_0^9(7) \models^{(5\text{-}6),(9),(12),(31\text{-}32)}_{R_1,R_2,R_3,R_4} \exists with.CongestedBus(r_3) \quad (7)$$

ABox axioms (31) in $\mathcal{Q}_0^9$, (32) in $\mathcal{R}_0^9$ are both required to fire GCIs (5–6) and entail (34). We say that (34) emphasizes an "*association*" ($\twoheadrightarrow$ in Figure 3) of $\mathcal{Q}_0^9$, $\mathcal{R}_0^9$ through (5–6) in $\mathcal{T}$. Thus dynamic knowledge can be entailed by axioms from single (6) but also "*associated*" (7) evolving ontologies.

Inductive Reasoning in Evolving Ontologies

Axioms which enable knowledge association e.g., (5–6) are rarely modeled a priori in a background knowledge $\mathcal{T}$ because of the uncertainty of evolving ontologies. An association of $\mathcal{P}_0^9$ (events) with $\mathcal{Q}_0^9$ (travel time) or $\mathcal{R}_0^9$ (buses information) cannot be derived a priori but only a posteriori by analyzing data. Indeed (5–6) are specific to cities subject to changes. Capturing such "*rules*" (e.g., dashed $\twoheadrightarrow$ in Figure 3) in $\mathcal{T}$ would certainly extend the reasoning impact since they capture evolving knowledge. They could be used for inducing missing knowledge in $\mathcal{Q}_0^9$ or $\mathcal{R}_0^9$. *How to discover*

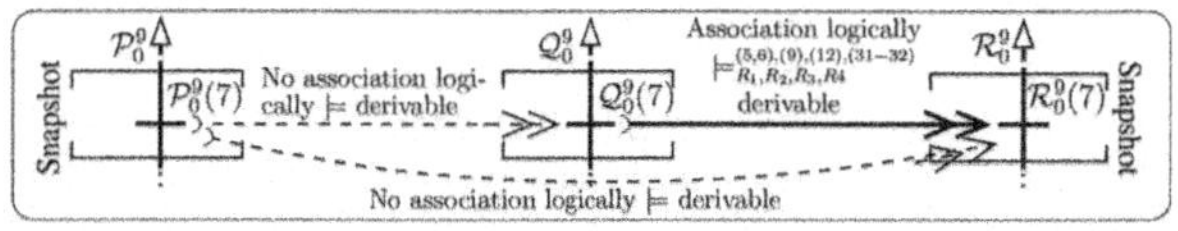

Figure 3: How to Discover an Association ($\twoheadrightarrow$) of Evolving Ontologies $\mathcal{Q}$, $\mathcal{R}$ at time 7 with respect to $\mathcal{T}$?

knowledge association across evolving ontologies $\mathcal{P}$ and $\mathcal{R}$ or $\mathcal{Q}$ at time 7 with respect to $\mathcal{T}$? We tackle this problem by mining knowledge associations as $\mathcal{EL}^{++}$ rules.

Association $\mathcal{EL}^{++}$ Rules

We revisit the concept of association rules (Agrawal, Imielinski, and Swami 1993) in the context of evolving ontologies through an $\mathcal{EL}^{++}$ rule-based representation.

Definition 2. ***(Association $\mathcal{EL}^{++}$ Rule)***
Let $\langle \mathcal{T}, \mathcal{A} \rangle$ be $\mathcal{EL}^{++}$ axioms, $\mathcal{P}_0^n$, $\mathcal{Q}_0^n$ be $\mathcal{EL}^{++}$ evolving ontologies, $\mathbb{B}$, $\mathbb{H}$ be atomsets where the set of variables in $\mathbb{H}$, or $var(\mathbb{H})$, is a subset of the variables in $\mathbb{B}$. An association $\mathcal{EL}^{++}$ rule in $\mathcal{P}_0^n \times \mathcal{Q}_0^n$ is a DL $\mathcal{EL}^{++}$ rule $\mathbb{B} \twoheadrightarrow \mathbb{H}$ (identified by atomset $\mathbb{B} \cup \mathbb{H}$) such that $\exists i \in [0, n]$: $bind(\mathbb{B}, \mathcal{T} \cup \mathcal{A} \cup \mathcal{P}_0^n(i))|_{var(\mathbb{H})} = bind(\mathbb{H}, \mathcal{T} \cup \mathcal{A} \cup \mathcal{Q}_0^n(i))$.

Definition 2 identifies an association as an $\mathcal{EL}^{++}$ rule between atomsets $\mathbb{B}$, $\mathbb{H}$ if they have the same bindings for their variables across two evolving ontologies at a time i. Contrary to (Lécué and Pan 2013), representing association as an arbitrary combination of ABox axioms, we consider $\mathcal{EL}^{++}$ rule as a broader framework. Indeed it supports (i) associations which can be modeled by $\mathcal{EL}^{++}$ rules, (ii) more generic rules since variables are accepted in atoms of $\mathcal{EL}^{++}$ rules, instead of only allowing constants in the other case, (iii) native combination of $\mathcal{EL}^{++}$ rule and axioms. In addition rules could be evaluated with respect to their bindings.

Example 7. ***(Association $\mathcal{EL}^{++}$ Rule)***
The rule (3-5) in Example 4 illustrates an association $\mathcal{EL}^{++}$ rule from $\mathcal{P}_0^9$ to $\mathcal{Q}_0^9 \cup \mathcal{R}_0^9$. The atomset of this rule is bound at time 5 by $\{(e_1, r_0, r_1)\}$ and 7 by $\{(e_3, r_0, r_3)\}$.

We measure the interestingness of association rules by adapting the concepts of *support* (Definition 3) and *confidence* (Definition 5) introduced in the database community.

Definition 3. ***(Atomset Support)***
Given axioms $\mathcal{O} \doteq \langle \mathcal{T}, \mathcal{A} \rangle$, an evolving ontology $\mathcal{P}_0^n$, atomset $\mathbb{B}$, the support of $\mathbb{B}$, noted $\sigma(\mathbb{B})$, in $[0, 1]$ is defined by:

$$\sigma(\mathbb{B}) \doteq \frac{|\{i \in [0, n] \mid \exists \vec{a} \in \mathcal{N}_I : \mathcal{O}, \mathcal{P}_0^n(i) \models \mathbb{B}[\vec{a}]\}|}{n+1} \quad (8)$$

where the expression $|S|$ refers to the cardinality of S.

The support of atomset $\mathbb{B}$ is the proportion of snapshots where $\mathbb{B}$ has at least one binding $\vec{a}$ in $\mathcal{A} \cup \mathcal{P}_0^n$ with respect to $\mathcal{T}$. Since $\mathbb{B}$ may have multiple bindings in $\mathcal{A} \cup \mathcal{P}_0^n$ at any time $i \in [0, n]$, we capture their number in Definition 4.

Definition 4. ***(Atomset Weight)***
Given $\mathcal{EL}^{++}$ axioms $\mathcal{O} \doteq \langle \mathcal{T}, \mathcal{A} \rangle$, evolving ontology $\mathcal{P}_0^n$

Ontology		$\mathcal{P}_5^7$		$\mathcal{Q}_5^7$		$\mathcal{R}_5^7$	$\mathcal{Q}_5^7 \cup \mathcal{R}_5^7$
Atomset $\mathbb{B}$		{(21)}	{(22)}	{(28)}*	{(31)}*	{(32)}*	{(23)}
Variable $\mathcal{V}$		(x_1)	(x_1, x_2, x_3)	(x_3)	(x_3)	(x_4, x_3)	(x_3)
Binding at Time	5	$\{(e_1)\}$	$\{(e_1, r_1, r_0)\}$	$\{(r_1)\}$		$\{(b_1, r_1)\}$	$\{(r_1)\}$
	6	$\{(e_2)\}$	$\{(e_2, r_2, r_0)\}$	$\{(r_2)\}$		$\{(b_2, r_2)\}$	
	7	$\{(e_3), (e_4)\}$	$\{(e_3, r_3, r_0), (e_4, r_3, r_0)\}$	$\{(r_3)\}$	$\{(r_3)\}$	$\{(b_3, r_3)\}$	$\{(r_3)\}$
$\sigma(\mathbb{B})$		1	1	1	1/3	1	2/3
$\omega(\mathbb{B})$		4	4	3	1	3	2

[*] From now on all terms $\mathcal{N}_I$ of (28), (31-32) are free variables in $\mathcal{V}$.

Table 2: Binding, Support and Weight of Atomsets $\mathbb{B}$.

and atomset $\mathbb{B}$, the weight of $\mathbb{B}$, noted $\omega(\mathbb{B})$, is defined by:

$$\omega(\mathbb{B}) \doteq \sum_{i=0}^{n} |\{\vec{a} \in \mathcal{N}_I \mid \mathcal{O}, \mathcal{P}_0^n(i) \models \mathbb{B}[\vec{a}]\}| \tag{9}$$

Example 8.*(Atomsets Support and Weight)* *Let $\mathcal{P}_5^7$, $\mathcal{Q}_5^7$, $\mathcal{R}_5^7$ be $\mathcal{P}_0^9$, $\mathcal{Q}_0^9$, $\mathcal{R}_0^9$ restricted to $[5,7]$ where ABox statements related to e_4 extends $\mathcal{P}_5^7$ at time 7 cf. Table 2. This table illustrates the support σ, weight ω of atomsets e.g., $\{(5)\}$ is bound in $\mathcal{Q}_5^7 \cup \mathcal{R}_5^7$ at time 5 by $\{(r_1)\}$ and 7 by $\{(r_3)\}$, but not at time 6, thus $\sigma(\{(5)\})$ is 2/3. The number of bindings of $\{(5)\}$, noted $\omega(\{(5)\})$, is 2 in $\mathcal{Q}_5^7 \cup \mathcal{R}_5^7$.*

Definition 5. ***(Confidence of an Association $\mathcal{EL}^{++}$ Rule)*** *Let $\mathbb{B} \twoheadrightarrow \mathbb{H}$ be an association $\mathcal{EL}^{++}$ rule in $\mathcal{P}_0^n \times \mathcal{Q}_0^n$. The confidence γ of $\mathbb{B} \twoheadrightarrow \mathbb{H}$ in $(0,1]^2$ is:*

$$\gamma(\mathbb{B} \twoheadrightarrow \mathbb{H}) \doteq \left(\frac{\sigma(\mathbb{B} \cup \mathbb{H})}{\sigma(\mathbb{B})}, \frac{\omega(\mathbb{B} \cup \mathbb{H})}{\omega(\mathbb{B})} \right) \tag{10}$$

$\sigma(\mathbb{B} \cup \mathbb{H})$, $\omega(\mathbb{B} \cup \mathbb{H})$ are support and weight of $\mathbb{B} \twoheadrightarrow \mathbb{H}$ i.e., respectively: the proportion of snapshots in $\mathcal{P}_0^n \cup \mathcal{Q}_0^n$ where $\mathbb{B} \cup \mathbb{H}$ has at least one binding, and its number of bindings.

The confidence is defined as the percentage of (i) snapshots in $\mathcal{P}_0^n \cup \mathcal{Q}_0^n$ where $\mathbb{B} \cup \mathbb{H}$ has at least a binding with regard to those where $\mathbb{B}$ has a binding, and (ii) bindings of $\mathbb{B} \cup \mathbb{H}$ in $\mathcal{P}_0^n \cup \mathcal{Q}_0^n$ with regard to those which bind $\mathbb{B}$. That is, they represent complementary conditional probabilities:

$$p(\mathcal{O}, \mathcal{Q}_0^n(i) \models \mathbb{H}[\vec{a}] \mid \mathcal{O}, \mathcal{P}_0^n(i) \models \mathbb{B}[\vec{a}]|_{var(\mathbb{H})}) \tag{11}$$

evaluated with respect to the number of (i) snapshots and (ii) bindings i.e., respectively σ- and ω-related entry of (10).

Example 9. ***(Confidence of an Association $\mathcal{EL}^{++}$ Rule)*** *Confidence $\gamma(\mathbb{B} \twoheadrightarrow \mathbb{H})$ with $\mathbb{B}$:{(3), (4)}, $\mathbb{H}$:{(5)} is:*

$$\left(\frac{\sigma(\{(3),(4),(5)\})}{\sigma(\{(3),(4)\})}, \frac{\omega(\{(3),(4),(5)\})}{\omega(\{(3),(4)\})} \right) \text{ i.e., } \left(\frac{2/3}{3/3}, \frac{3}{4} \right)$$

$\mathbb{B} \twoheadrightarrow \mathbb{H}$ is correct in 2/3 of time $[5,7]$ and its atomset $\mathbb{B} \cup \mathbb{H}$ is bound by 3/4 of bindings of atomset $\mathbb{B}$: $\{(3),(4)\}$.

Remark 1. ***(Rule Confidence and Ordering)*** *The level of confidence of rules can be compared by analyzing their supports and weights since confidence is defined as a tuple (Definition 5) e.g., $\gamma(\mathbb{B}_1 \twoheadrightarrow \mathbb{H}_1) > \gamma(\mathbb{B}_2 \twoheadrightarrow \mathbb{H}_2)$ if*

$$\frac{\sigma(\mathbb{B}_1 \cup \mathbb{H}_1)}{\sigma(\mathbb{B}_1)} > \frac{\sigma(\mathbb{B}_2 \cup \mathbb{H}_2)}{\sigma(\mathbb{B}_2)} \qquad \frac{\omega(\mathbb{B}_1 \cup \mathbb{H}_1)}{\omega(\mathbb{B}_1)} > \frac{\omega(\mathbb{B}_2 \cup \mathbb{H}_2)}{\omega(\mathbb{B}_2)}$$

If conflict e.g., value of 1st element of $\gamma(\mathbb{B}_1 \twoheadrightarrow \mathbb{H}_1)$ is better than 1st element of $\gamma(\mathbb{B}_2 \twoheadrightarrow \mathbb{H}_2)$ but worse for 2nd element, we compare a weighted average of normalised components.

Mining Association $\mathcal{EL}^{++}$ Rules

Mining $\mathcal{EL}^{++}$ rules consists in generating all rules with a minimum support $\sigma_{\min}$, confidence $\gamma_{\min}$, weight $\omega_{\min}$. This can be decomposed (Agrawal, Imielinski, and Swami 1993) by: (i) finding all significant atomsets i.e., atomsets with support, weight above $\sigma_{\min}$, $\omega_{\min}$, (ii) using them to generate rules that meet $\gamma_{\min}$. Algorithm 1 revisits WARMR (Dehaspe and Raedt 1997) to support $\mathcal{EL}^{++}$ atomsets bindings, containment and weight. It finds all significant atomsets by exploiting the lattice structure the containment relation $\subseteq_{\mathcal{T}}$ is imposing on the space of atomsets to perform a breadth-first search. $\mathcal{S}_k$ refers to the set of significant atomsets mined at depth k in the lattice while $\mathcal{C}_k$ is the set of potential candidates for $\mathcal{S}_k$. Their elements are called k-atomsets i.e., atomsets of k atoms. Initially (line 4) the set of significant 1-atomsets $\mathcal{S}_1$ is determined. A subsequent pass (line 5), say pass k, consists of two phases. First (line 6), the significant atomsets $\mathcal{S}_{k-1}$ found in the $(k-1)^{th}$ pass are used to generate the candidate atomsets $\mathcal{C}_k$, using Algorithm 2. $\mathcal{P}_0^n$ is then analyzed (line 7) to determine support (line 10) and weight (line 11) of candidates $\mathbb{C} \in \mathcal{C}_k$, when bound in $\mathcal{P}_0^n$ (line 9).

Algorithm 1: `atomsets-mining`$\langle \mathcal{O}_0^n, \sigma_{\min}, \omega_{\min} \rangle$.

```
1  Input: EL++ axioms O ≐ ⟨T, A⟩; EL++ evolving ontology
      P_0^n; Min. threshold of support σ_min and weight ω_min.
2  Result: Set of significant atomsets.
3  begin
4    S_1 ← Set of significant 1-atomsets; % Initialization
5    foreach k ≥ 2 | S_{k-1} ≠ ∅ do % k-atomsets on top of k-1 ones
6      C_k ← atomsets-gen⟨S_{k-1}⟩; % k-atomsets Candidates
7      foreach point of time i ∈ [0, n] do % Snapshot P_0^n(i)
8        % Atomsets with bindings ā in P_0^n(i)
9        foreach C ∈ C_k | ∃ā : T, A ∪ P_0^n(i) ⊨ C[ā] do
10         count(C) ← count(C) + 1; % Needed for σ(C)
11         ω(C) ← ω(C) + |{ā | T, A ∪ P_0^n(i) ⊨ C[ā]}|;
12     % Only significant atomsets are considered
13     S_k ← {C ∈ C_k | count(C)/(n+1) ≥ σ_min, ω(C) ≥ ω_min};
14   return ⋃_k S_k;
```

Algorithm 2 generates candidate $(k+1)$-atomsets from significant k-atomsets. In join-step (lines 5-7) where atomsets are sorted in their lexicographic order ($\preceq_{lex}$), $\mathcal{S}_k$ is combined with itself on the basis of its k common atoms. In the prune-step, we discard all atomsets that have a subset which does meet $\sigma_{\min}$, $\omega_{\min}$ i.e., not in $\mathcal{S}_k$ (line 10). It is trivial to show that any atomset in $\mathcal{C}_{k+1}$ is significant only if all subsets of size k are also significant by revisiting the results of (Agrawal et al. 1996) for $\mathcal{EL}^{++}$ atomsets. Thus line 10 maintains completeness. We also prune $(k+1)$-atomsets which are redundant i.e., already contain(ed by) $\mathcal{S}_k$ (line11).

The complexity of Algorithm 1 is $\Theta(|\mathbb{S}|^2 \times (n+1))$ where $|\mathbb{S}|$ is the number of atoms in $\mathcal{P}_0^n$. The prune-step in Algorithm 2 controls the exponential growth of atomsets.

Example 10. (Atomset Mining - Case $k = 2$) *Let $\{(3)\}$,$\{(4)\}$,$\{(2)\}$ be significant 1-atomsets. After the join-step of Algorithm 2 we obtain 2-atomsets*

Algorithm 2: Atomsets Generation: `atomsets-gen`$\langle \mathcal{S}_k \rangle$

1 **Input**: A terminology $\mathcal{T}$; Set of $\mathcal{S}$ignificant k-atomsets $\mathcal{S}_k$.
2 **Result**: Set of $\mathcal{C}$andidate $(k+1)$-atomsets $\mathcal{C}_{k+1}$.
3 **begin**
4 % *Join-step of k-atomsets from the same level k to obtain* $\mathcal{C}_{k+1}$
5 $\mathcal{C}'_{k+1} \leftarrow \{\{S_1, ..., S_k, T_k\} \mid \{S_1, ..., S_{k-1}, S_k\} \in \mathcal{S}_k,$
6 $\{S_1, ..., S_{k-1}, T_k\} \in \mathcal{S}_k,$
7 $S_k \preceq_{lex} T_k\}$
8 % *Prune-step of* $(k+1)$*-atomsets*
9 $\mathcal{C}_{k+1} \leftarrow \mathcal{C}'_{k+1} \setminus \{\ \{S_1, ..., S_k, T_k\} \mid$
10 $(i)\ \exists \mathbb{S} \subseteq \{S_1, ..., S_k, T_k\}$ with $|\mathbb{S}| = k$ such that $\mathbb{S} \notin \mathcal{S}_k$,
11 $(ii)\ \{T_k\} \subseteq_{\mathcal{T}} (\supseteq_{\mathcal{T}}) \{S_k\}\ \}$ % *Redundant k-atomsets*
12 **return** $\mathcal{C}_{k+1}$;

$\{(3),(4)\}, \{(4),(2)\}, \{(3),(2)\}$. *The last one is discarded during pruning (line 11) since* $\{(3)\} \subseteq_{\mathcal{T}} \{(2)\}$.

For generating $\mathcal{EL}^{++}$ rules with minimum confidence (Definition 5), we refer to `ap-genrules` (Agrawal et al. 1996). This procedure for large itemsets, with minor modifications e.g., rules representation (Definition 2), applies to significant atomsets. Its complexity is $\Theta(\max_k |\mathcal{S}_k| \times k)$, where $|\mathcal{S}_k|$ is the number of significant k-atomsets.

Knowledge Discovery in Evolving Ontologies

Knowledge is discovered by (i) determining its representative rules (Definition 7), and (ii) exploiting their combination with background knowledge (Algorithm 3).

Representative Association $\mathcal{EL}^{++}$ Rules

Although measures of support, weight, confidence largely pruned uninteresting rules, the remaining ones are not necessarily all fundamental to discover new knowledge. Indeed some can be logically derived from a minimal set of rules, which represents the "*representative*" inductive rules. Definition 7 formalizes this concept of representative rule by refining the notion of "*cover*" (Zaki 2000) in Definition 6.

Definition 6. ***(Association*** $\mathcal{EL}^{++}$ ***Rules Cover)***
Let $\mathcal{R}$ *be association* $\mathcal{EL}^{++}$ *rules. The cover of a rule* $\rho : \mathbb{B} \twoheadrightarrow \mathbb{H}$ *in* $\mathcal{R}$ *is defined by* $\Gamma(\rho) \doteq \{\mathbb{A} \twoheadrightarrow \mathbb{H} \text{ in } \mathcal{R} \mid \mathbb{A} \subseteq_{\mathcal{T}} \mathbb{B}\}$.

The rule ρ, covering rules in $\Gamma(\rho)$, synthesizes all rules deriving same consequents as ρ from any contained antecedents. It captures all rules which convey to similar knowledge but requiring more specific knowledge than ρ.

Definition 7. ***(Representative Association*** $\mathcal{EL}^{++}$ ***Rules)***
A set of representative association DL rules of $\mathcal{R}$*, denoted by* $\mathcal{R}^*$*, is defined by* $\{\rho \in \mathcal{R} \mid \nexists \rho' \in \mathcal{R},\ \rho' \neq \rho,\ \rho \in \Gamma(\rho')\}$.

A set of representative association DL rules is a least set of rules covering (Definition 6) all rules in $\mathcal{R}$. It captures a synthesis set of $\mathcal{R}$, which is required to derive any rule in $\mathcal{R}$. Thus all rules in a cover can be derived from their representative rule by atomset containment.

Proposition 1. ***(Minimum Support, Weight of Rules in*** $\mathcal{R}^*$***)***
$\sigma(\rho^*) \geq \sigma_{min}$ *and* $\omega(\rho^*) \geq \omega_{\min}$ $\forall \rho^* \in \mathcal{R}^*$ *iff* $\exists \rho \in \mathcal{R} \mid$ *(i)* $\sigma(\rho) \geq \sigma_{min}$*, (ii)* $\omega(\rho) \geq \omega_{\min}$ *and (iii)* $\rho \in \Gamma(\rho^*)$.

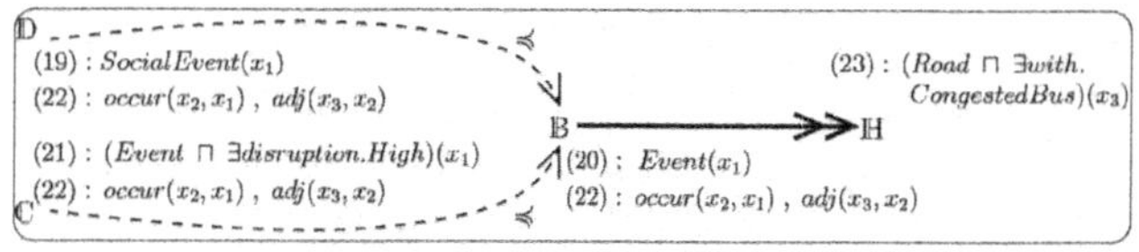

Figure 4: $\mathbb{B} \twoheadrightarrow \mathbb{H}$ as Representative Rule of $\mathbb{C} \twoheadrightarrow \mathbb{H}$, $\mathbb{D} \twoheadrightarrow \mathbb{H}$.

Proposition 1 states that any representative rule has minimum support, weight if it covers a rule with minimum support, weight. The proof is trivial per Definitions 6 and 7.

Example 11. ***(Rules Cover and Representative Rules)***
Let $\mathcal{R}$ *be* $\{(2),(4)\} \twoheadrightarrow \{(5)\}$, $\{(1),(4)\} \twoheadrightarrow \{(5)\}$, $\{(3),(4)\} \twoheadrightarrow \{(5)\}$ *in Figure 4. The first rule covers the last two since antecedents* (1), (3) *are contained by* (2) *cf. Examples 3, 10 while their consequent are similar.* $\mathcal{R}^*$ *is* $\{(2),(4)\} \twoheadrightarrow \{(5)\}$*, covering the other two rules.*

The semantics of atomsets is crucial to prune large sets of rules through its representative rules. The more semantic relations (atomsets containment) among evolving ontologies the more (resp. less) covered (resp. representative) rules.

Consistent Inductive Knowledge Discovery (CIKD)

Algorithm 3 presents our general approach `CIKD` for inducing consistent knowledge from $\mathcal{P}_0^n$ to $\mathcal{Q}_0^n$ at time i.

All significant rules $\mathcal{R}$ in $\mathcal{P}_0^n \times \mathcal{Q}_0^n$, which are generated from significant atomsets (line 5), are identified by adapting `ap-genrules` (Agrawal et al. 1996) in line 7. Besides atom(sets) to be substituted by item(sets), our revisited definitions of support and confidence needs to be applied. Its representative rules $\mathcal{R}^*$ are then elaborated (line 8). Proposition 1 ensures minimum support, weight. All representative rules $\rho : \mathbb{B} \twoheadrightarrow \mathbb{H}$, filtered by confidence (line 10), are evaluated at time i of $\mathcal{P}_0^n$, $\mathcal{Q}_0^n$ (line 13). We checked consistency of $\mathcal{Q}_0^n(i)$ with knowledge $\mathbb{H}$ derived from ρ, especially for all bindings $\vec{a}$ of $\mathbb{B}$ with respect to $\mathcal{P}_0^n(i)$. This ensures that only consistent knowledge $\mathbb{H}(\vec{a})$ is derived from $\mathbb{B}(\vec{a})$ and added to $\mathcal{Q}_0^n(i)$. This condition validates the consistent combination TBox, ABox, rules axioms at time i of $\mathcal{P}_0^n$, $\mathcal{Q}_0^n$.

Its complexity is polynomial since (i) the representative rules generation (lines 4-8) is polynomial in the number of snapshots, atoms (line 5 i.e., Algorithms 1,2), k-atomsets (line 7), rules (Definition 7); (ii) their consistency checking (line 13), together with (iii) atomset binding, containment are polynomial in $\mathcal{EL}^{++}$ (Bienvenu, Lutz, and Wolter 2012).

Example 12. ***(Consistent Knowledge Discovery)***
Suppose $\mathcal{Q}_5^7$, $\mathcal{R}_5^7$ *not exposed at time 5 due to defective sensors.* $\mathcal{R}_5^7(5)$ *cannot be deduced from* $\mathcal{T}$ *neither* $\mathcal{P}_5^7(5)$*. So we apply Algorithm 3 with e.g.,* $\langle \mathcal{T}, \mathcal{P}_5^7, \mathcal{R}_5^7, 5, 2/3, 2, (2/3, 3/4) \rangle$*. This leads to the representative rule (among others) in Example 11, which derives consistent knowledge in* $\mathcal{R}_5^7(5)$*:* $(Road \sqcap \exists with.CongestedBus)(r_1)$*. Applying the same approach to* $\mathcal{R}_5^7(6)$ *ends up with consistent but not accurate knowledge, hence the use of support, weight, confidence.*

Experimental Results

We report (i) scalability, (ii) accuracy of Algorithm 3 (noted [A3]). The experiments have been conducted on a server of

Algorithm 3: CIKD$\langle \mathcal{T}, \mathcal{P}_0^n, \mathcal{Q}_0^n, i, \sigma_{\min}, \omega_{\min}, \gamma_{\min}\rangle$

1 **Input**: Terminology $\mathcal{T}$; Evolving Ontologies $\mathcal{P}_0^n$, $\mathcal{Q}_0^n$; Time i; Min. support $\sigma_{\min}$, weight $\omega_{\min}$, confidence $\gamma_{\min}$.
2 **Result**: Consistent knowledge $\mathcal{Q}_0^n(i)$ induced from $\mathcal{P}_0^n \times \mathcal{Q}_0^n$.
3 **begin**
4 % $\mathcal{S}$: *Set of significant atomsets in evolving ontology* $\mathcal{P}_0^n \cup \mathcal{Q}_0^n$
5 $\mathcal{S} \leftarrow$ atomsets-mining$\langle \mathcal{P}_0^n \cup \mathcal{Q}_0^n, \sigma_{\min}, \omega_{\min}\rangle$;
6 % $\mathcal{R}$: *Set of rules in* $\mathcal{P}_0^n \times \mathcal{Q}_0^n$ *with minimum confidence* $\gamma_{\min}$
7 $\mathcal{R} \leftarrow$ ap-genrules$\langle \mathcal{S}, \mathcal{P}_0^n \times \mathcal{Q}_0^n, \gamma_{\min}\rangle$; % *Version adapted*
8 $\mathcal{R}^* \leftarrow \{\rho \in \mathcal{R} \mid \nexists \rho' \in \mathcal{R},\ \rho' \neq \rho,\ \rho \in \Gamma(\rho')\}$; % *Definition 7*
9 % *All representative rules* $\rho : \mathbb{B} \twoheadrightarrow \mathbb{H}$ *with highest confidence*
10 **foreach** *rule* $\rho : \mathbb{B} \twoheadrightarrow \mathbb{H}$ *in* $\mathcal{R}^* \mid \nexists \rho' \in \mathcal{R}^*, \gamma(\rho') > \gamma(\rho)$ **do**
11 % *Consistency of rule* ρ *at time* i *of* $\mathcal{P}_0^n \times \mathcal{Q}_0^n$
12 **if** $\mathcal{T} \cup \mathcal{Q}_0^n(i) \cup \{\mathbb{H}(\vec{a})\} \not\models \top \sqsubseteq \bot$
13 $\left(\forall \vec{a} \mid \mathcal{T} \cup \mathcal{P}_0^n(i) \models \mathbb{B}[\vec{a}]|_{var(\mathbb{H})}\right)$
14 % $\mathcal{Q}_0^n(i)$ *and knowledge* $\mathbb{H}[\vec{a}]$ *from inductive reasoning*
15 **then** $\mathcal{Q}_0^n(i) \leftarrow \mathcal{Q}_0^n(i) \cup \{\mathbb{H}[\vec{a}]\}$; ;
16 **return** $\mathcal{Q}_0^n(i)$;

DataSet	Size (Mb / Day)	#Axioms / Update	#RDF Triples / Update
[a] Weather	3	53	318
[b] Travel Time	43	270	810
[c] Incident	0.1	81	324
[d] Event	9.5	480	1,150
[e] Bus	120	3,000	12,000

Table 3: Dynamic Data / Evolving Ontologies Details.

4 Intel(R) Xeon(R) X5650, 2.67GHz cores, 6GB RAM.

• **Context:** Dynamic data: [a] weather, [b] travel time, [c] incident, [d] event, [e] bus location in Dublin (Table 3) is transformed in $\mathcal{EL}^{++}$ using mapping techniques. We used a fixed (off-line) window of $n = 4,320$ snapshots (48 hours) for mining. We considered an ontology $\mathcal{T}$ of 55 concepts and 19 roles. The objective is to derive the status of buses (by mining $\mathcal{EL}^{++}$ rules across semantic data i.e., association of types of weather, travel condition, incident, events, bus delays) when not retrievable (due to 34% of missing data).

• **Scalability Result:** Figure 5 reports scalability of [A3] ($(\sigma_{\min}, \omega_{\min}, \gamma_{\min})$ being $(1/2, n, (2/3, 3/4))$) and compares its computation time with (Dehaspe and Raedt 1997) using inductive logic noted [D97], (Srikant and Agrawal 1995) using basic taxonomies noted [S95] and (Lécué and Pan 2013) using ABox axioms-related rules noted [L13]. The evaluation is achieved on different (i) variations of $\mathcal{T}$ i.e., $\mathcal{T}[0]$, $\mathcal{T}[50]$, $\mathcal{T}[100]$ capturing a proportion of 0%, 50%, 100% of GCIs, RIs of $\mathcal{T}$, (ii) number of evolving ontologies $|s|$ i.e., $\{1, 3, 5\}$ for respectively [e], [c,d,e], [a,b,c,d,e] in Table 3. The scalability of all approaches decreases with the number of evolving ontologies, axioms. [D97] is the most scalable (when $|s| > 1$) since it supports pruning strategies. Its performance remains unchanged for any variation of $\mathcal{T}$ since no semantics is supported. [S95], [A3] improve their scalability by clustering rules using semantics, which highly reduces the number of representative rules for [A3]. The off-line version of [L13] is the least scalable since knowledge discovery is based on the high number significant rules. Our approach outperforms (i) [S95] when numerous evolving ontologies occur, (ii) [D97] when more semantics is captured by $\mathcal{T}$.

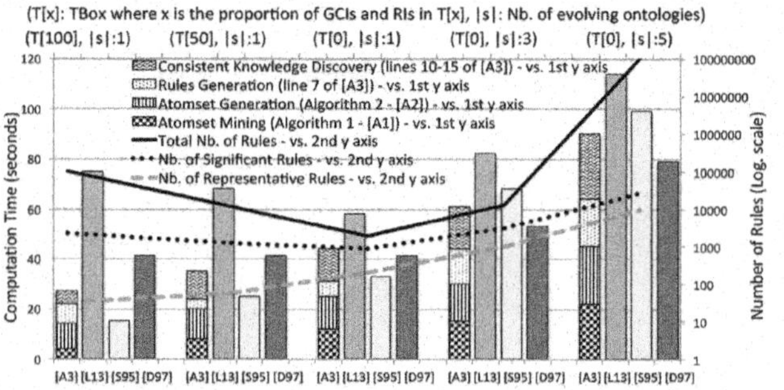

Figure 5: Scalability. 1st x axis: Approaches on 5 Test Cases. 1st y axis: Computation Time in Seconds. 2nd x axis: 5 Types of Semantic and Evolving Ontologies Configurations. 2nd y axis: Search Space of Association Rules.

	c_1	c_2	c_3	c_4	c_5	c_6	c_7	c_8
$\sigma_{\min}$	.4	.4	.4	.4	.8	.8	.8	.8
$\gamma_{\min}$	(.4, .4)	(.4, .8)	(.8, .4)	(.8, .8)	(.4, .4)	(.4, .8)	(.8, .4)	(.8, .8)

Table 4: Support $\sigma_{\min}$, Confidence $\gamma_{\min}$ Configuration.

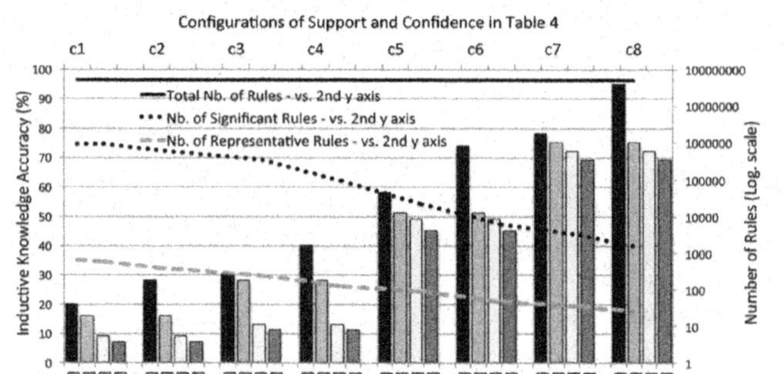

Figure 6: Accuracy. 1st x axis: Approaches on 8 Test Cases. 1st y axis: Accuracy of Discovered Knowledge. 2nd x axis: 8 Types of Support / Confidence Configurations (Table 4).

• **Accuracy Result:** Figure 6 reports accuracy with Table 4 as configuration. The weight is interpreted in [A3]. $\mathcal{T}[50]$ and all ontologies are considered. Accuracy is measured by validating induced knowledge over 10,000 past situations where buses status is known. All approaches are compared as they expose similar results with different representation. [A3] outperforms all approaches, even significantly when (i) weight associated to confidence $\gamma_{\min}$ is higher than .4, (ii) support $\sigma_{\min}$ is .8. The experiments v.s. [L13] show that genericity, representativeness, weight of rules largely contribute in reducing their quantity while improving quality.

• **Lessons Learnt:** The semantics of rules and its atomsets together with representativeness benefits classical rules mining approaches. Our approach, as a variant of [L13], [D97], [S95], benefits from (i) [L13] to discover association, (ii) [D97] to prune atomsets (for scalability), (iii) [S95] to capture their semantics (for consistency, accuracy). The scalability (accuracy) of knowledge discovery is negatively (positively) impacted by the number of data sources, snapshots, axioms c.f. Algorithms 1, 2. Their number are critical as they drive heterogeneity in rules, which could improve accuracy, but not scalability. It would be worst with more expressive DLs due to binding and containment checks.

Conclusion and Future Work

Our approach, combining inductive and deductive reasoning, discovers consistent knowledge by mining and applying association $\mathcal{EL}^{++}$ rules across DL-augmented dynamic data. Existing approaches learn knowledge from raw data while we exploit its semantics and consistency during the learning phase. Semantics was essential for (i) capturing consistent knowledge across evolving ontologies, (ii) raising its accuracy, (iii) improving scalability through identification of representative rules. Experiments have shown scalable, accurate, consistent knowledge discovery in Dublin.

In future work we will investigate scalable and incremental re-adjustment of rules in a context of streaming data.

References

Agrawal, R.; Mannila, H.; Srikant, R.; Toivonen, H.; and Verkamo, A. I. 1996. Fast discovery of association rules. In *Advances in Knowledge Discovery and Data Mining*. AAAI/MIT Press. 307–328.

Agrawal, R.; Imielinski, T.; and Swami, A. N. 1993. Mining association rules between sets of items in large databases. In *SIGMOD Conference*, 207–216.

Anicic, D.; Fodor, P.; Rudolph, S.; and Stojanovic, N. 2011. Ep-sparql: a unified language for event processing and stream reasoning. In *Proceedings of the 20th international conference on World wide web*, 635–644. ACM.

Baader, F., and Nutt, W. 2003. In *The Description Logic Handbook: Theory, Implementation, and Applications*.

Baader, F.; Brandt, S.; and Lutz, C. 2005. Pushing the el envelope. In *IJCAI*, 364–369.

Baader, F.; Brandt, S.; and Lutz, C. 2008. Pushing the el envelope further. In *OWLED*.

Bienvenu, M.; Lutz, C.; and Wolter, F. 2012. Query containment in description logics reconsidered. In *KR*.

Dehaspe, L., and Raedt, L. D. 1997. Mining association rules in multiple relations. In *ILP*, 125–132.

Dietterich, T. G., and Michalski, R. S. 1981. Inductive learning of structural descriptions: Evaluation criteria and comparative review of selected methods. *Artificial intelligence* 16(3):257–294.

Fanizzi, N.; d'Amato, C.; and Esposito, F. 2010. Induction of concepts in web ontologies through terminological decision trees. In *ECML/PKDD (1)*, 442–457.

Galárraga, L. A.; Teflioudi, C.; Hose, K.; and Suchanek, F. M. 2013. AMIE: association rule mining under incomplete evidence in ontological knowledge bases. In *22nd International World Wide Web Conference, WWW '13, Rio de Janeiro, Brazil, May 13-17, 2013*, 413–422.

Glimm, B.; Horrocks, I.; Lutz, C.; and Sattler, U. 2007. Conjunctive query answering for the description logic shiq. In *IJCAI*, 399–404.

Huang, Z., and Stuckenschmidt, H. 2005. Reasoning with multi-version ontologies: A temporal logic approach. In *ISWC*, 398–412.

Krötzsch, M.; Rudolph, S.; and Hitzler, P. 2008. Description logic rules. In *ECAI*, 80–84.

Labrinidis, A., and Jagadish, H. 2012. Challenges and opportunities with big data. *Proceedings of the VLDB Endowment* 5(12):2032–2033.

Lécué, F., and Pan, J. Z. 2013. Predicting knowledge in an ontology stream. In *IJCAI*.

Lécué, F. 2012. Diagnosing changes in an ontology stream: A dl reasoning approach. In *AAAI*.

Ramaswamy, S.; Rastogi, R.; and Shim, K. 2000. Efficient algorithms for mining outliers from large data sets. In *ACM SIGMOD Record*, volume 29, 427–438. ACM.

Reiter, R. 1980. A logic for default reasoning. *Artificial intelligence* 13(1):81–132.

Sadilek, A.; Kautz, H. A.; and Silenzio, V. 2012. Predicting disease transmission from geo-tagged micro-blog data. In *AAAI*.

Song, X.; Zhang, Q.; Sekimoto, Y.; and Shibasaki, R. 2014. Intelligent system for urban emergency management during large-scale disaster. In *AAAI*, 458–464.

Srikant, R., and Agrawal, R. 1995. Mining generalized association rules. In *VLDB*, 407–419.

Valle, E. D.; Ceri, S.; van Harmelen, F.; and Fensel, D. 2009. It's a streaming world! reasoning upon rapidly changing information. *IEEE Intelligent Systems* 24(6):83–89.

Völker, J., and Niepert, M. 2011. Statistical schema induction. In *The Semantic Web: Research and Applications - 8th Extended Semantic Web Conference, ESWC 2011, Heraklion, Crete, Greece, May 29-June 2, 2011, Proceedings, Part I*, 124–138.

Zaki, M. J. 2000. Generating non-redundant association rules. In *KDD*, 34–43.

Proceedings of the Twenty-Ninth AAAI Conference on Artificial Intelligence

Multi-Document Summarization Based on Two-Level Sparse Representation Model

He Liu, Hongliang Yu, Zhi-Hong Deng*
Key Laboratory of Machine Perception (Ministry of Education),
School of Electronics Engineering and Computer Science, Peking University, Beijing 100871, China
lhdgriver@gmail.com, yuhongliang324@gmail.com, zhdeng@cis.pku.edu.cn

Abstract

Multi-document summarization is of great value to many real world applications since it can help people get the main ideas within a short time. In this paper, we tackle the problem of extracting summary sentences from multi-document sets by applying sparse coding techniques and present a novel framework to this challenging problem. Based on the data reconstruction and sentence denoising assumption, we present a two-level sparse representation model to depict the process of multi-document summarization. Three requisite properties is proposed to form an ideal reconstructable summary: **Coverage**, **Sparsity** and **Diversity**. We then formalize the task of multi-document summarization as an optimization problem according to the above properties, and use simulated annealing algorithm to solve it. Extensive experiments on summarization benchmark data sets DUC2006 and DUC2007 show that our proposed model is effective and outperforms the state-of-the-art algorithms.

Introduction

Multi-document summarization is the process of generating a short version of given materials to indicate its main ideas. As the number of documents on the web exponentially increases, text summarization has attracted a growth of attention since it can help people get the topic within a short time.

Most existing studies are extraction-based methods. The extraction approaches usually use a rank model to select sentences from original text set. However, these methods suffer from severe problem that top-ranked sentences tend to convey much redundant information. Although some methods tried to reduce the redundancy (Li et al. 2009), finding balance between wide coverage and minimum redundancy is a non-trivial task.

In this paper, an ideal summary is assumed to represent the whole document set, namely, by reading the summarization instead of the whole set one can understand the general idea of the original documents. Rank models merely provide important sentences by score, and hence are not able to cover all aspects of the original corpus. Inspired by data compression and reconstruction(Simon, Snavely, and Seitz 2007a; Yang et al. 2013; Yu et al. 2014), a good summary should recover the whole documents, or in other words, reconstruct the whole documents. Based on the assumption, we think a good summary should meet three key requirements: **Coverage**, **Sparsity** and **Diversity**. **Coverage** means the extracted summary can conclude every aspect of all documents. Similar to (He et al. 2012), we use non-negative linear combination to represent the relations between sentences in the document set and the summary sentences. The relation can help to reconstruct the original document set by summary sentences. **Sparsity** means one certain sentence in the document set should be precisely represented by only a small number of summary sentences. Intuitively, multi-document set always have one central topic and some sub-topics, indicating that the summary sentences should also be categorized into groups. Each sentence in the document set should only be represented by summary sentences in the same group. On the contrary, not all summary sentences can be used to reconstruct one certain sentence although all of them are important. Otherwise we will bring in noise since some summary sentences are irrelevant. To enforce the sparsity property, we introduce sparse coding, a powerful tool, for denoising (Elad and Aharon 2006). **Diversity** means to eliminate redundancy. As stated above, document set can often be divided into some sub-topics, and thus we capture the overall view of the document set if we introduce diversity into our model. In this paper, we use the correlation of the least different summary sentence pairs to measure diversity.

Based on these three requisites, we design a two-level sparse representation model to tackle the multi-document summarization problem:

- *Level-1*: The summary set is a sparse representation of the original document set.
- *Level-2*: Each sentence in the candidate set is sparsely reconstructed by the summary set.

The model is illustrated in Figure 1. We denote the set of all the sentences in the original document set as candidate set, and the set of all the summary sentences as summary set. The summary set is selected from the candidate set. Similar to (Yang et al. 2013), the two-level sparse representation model we introduced is NP-hard, we use simulated annealing algorithm to get the summarization.

To our knowledge, this is the first paper that utilizes cover-

*Corresponding author

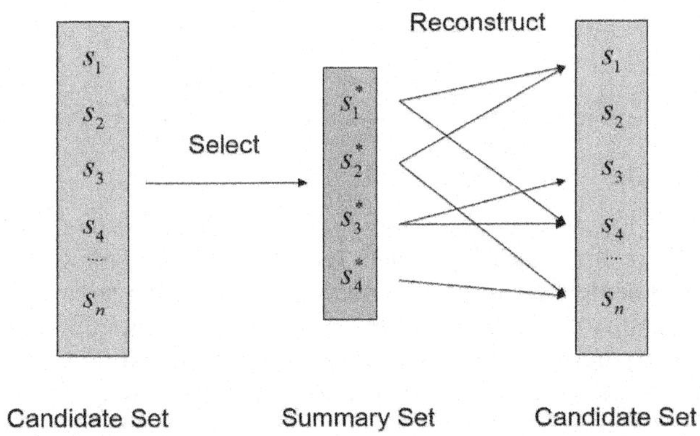

Figure 1: **two-level sparse representation model**

age, sparsity and diversity together in multi-document summarization. We test our model on DUC2006 and DUC2007 data sets and the results show that our approach can perform effectively and efficiently.

Related Work

Multi-document summarization aims at reducing the long documents into short length sentences, which helps readers quickly grasp the general information of the document set. Though over the past 50 years, the problem has been addressed from many different perspective in varying domains and using various paradigms, it is still a non-trivial task.

There are two main approaches in text summarization : text abstraction and text extraction.

Text abstraction build an internal semantic representation and then use natural language generation (Reiter, Dale, and Feng 2000) techniques to create a summary that is closer to what a human might generate. Such a summary might contain words not explicitly present in the original documents(Qian and Liu 2013). Though abstraction method uses smaller units such as words and phrases, it may contain more information than extraction method, but it suffers from poor readability and low efficiency, which is critical for online summarization.

Text extraction means to identify the most relevant sentences in one or more documents. Most existing systems use rank model to select the sentences with highest scores to form the summarization. They differ in the rules they used to compute the salient scores. The important parts are often retrieved by using some natural language processing and heuristics methods(Luhn 1958; Simon, Snavely, and Seitz 2007b). More advanced techniques consider the rhetorical structure(Marcu 1997) and semantic relationships(Gong and Liu 2001) and there are also some machine learning models(Kupiec, Pedersen, and Chen 1995). (Conroy and O'leary 2001) model the problem of extracting a sentence from a document using hidden Markov model(HMM). Graph based models like PageRank(Brin and Page 1998) and HITS(Kleinberg 1999) build similarity graph of sentences, and use influence propagation algorithms to give each sentence a score. One of the disadvantages in above techniques is that they seem to ignore the redundancy and coverage in summarization.

Sparse coding is proved to be very useful in image processing(denoting, in painting, super resolution) :(Yu, Sapiro, and Mallat 2012; Mairal, Elad, and Sapiro 2008; Yang et al. 2013) and object recognition:(Yang et al. 2009; Boureau et al. 2011). It was first introduced into document summarization in (He et al. 2012). They represent each sentence as a non-negative linear combination of the summary sentences. But they do not consider the sparsity of the summarization. We design a two-level sparse representation model to extract multi-document summarization. The original document set is sparsely represented by summary sentences. Each sentence in the original document set is sparsely represented by the summary sentences. In other words, we represent each sentence as a non-negative linear combination of only some of the summary sentences. Our experiments show that sparsity is critical for high quality summarizations.

Proposed Model

Preliminary

In this section, we give the notations we use in this paper. We denote the corpus of documents as $C_{corpus} = \{Doc_1, Doc_2, \dots\}$, in which Doc_i denotes the ith document in C_{corpus}. Each document is made up of a set of sentences, all of which form the **candidate set** $S = \{\mathbf{s}_1, \mathbf{s}_2, \dots, \mathbf{s}_n\}$, where $\mathbf{s}_i \in R^d$ is the term-frequency vector for sentence i, and d is the number of distinct terms in the **candidate set**. The task of multi-document summarization is to select a small number of sentences $S^* = \{\mathbf{s}_1^*, \mathbf{s}_2^*, \dots, \mathbf{s}_k^*\}$ from the **candidate set** which best describe the subjects. Note that $k \ll n$ and $S^* \subset S$. Here, we denote S^* as **summary set**.

MDS-Sparse Model

In this section, we describe the details of our proposed framework MDS-Sparse (***M****ulti-****D****ocument* ***S****ummarization based on Two-Level* ***Sparse*** *Representation Model*).

The most challenging part is to properly model summaries. We observe that an effective multi-document summarization should meet three key requirements:

1. **Coverage.** Most existing extraction methods focus on selecting top ranked sentences, which are considered important in the whole document set. But in real life, a good summarization should not only contain the main ideas of the whole topic, it should conclude the whole document set. The summary sentences should represent the other sentences. Like (He et al. 2012), we find summary sentences that can best reconstruct other sentences by non-negative linear combination.

2. **Sparsity.** As multi-document texts often describe one central topic and some sub-topics, the sentences can be categorized into groups. Accordingly, we can only use summary sentences in the same group to conclude one certain sentence in the document set. Instead of using traditional classification methods, we use sparse coding technologies to impose the sparsity of the representation.

In fact, our model incorporate a two-level sparse representation model : (1) The **summary set** is the sparse representation of the **candidate set** (2) All sentences in the **candidate set** is sparsely represented by the **summary set**, which means only some of the sentences in the **summary set** is used when constructing one sentence in the **candidate set**.

3. **Diversity.** A topic which contains many documents usually contains one core topic and some subtopics. A good summarization should not only find the most obvious topic, but also other sub-topics that help us better understand the whole document set. Thus we use the correlation of the least different summary sentence pairs to eliminate redundancy and improve diversity.

Coverage By treating the problem of multi-document summarization as the issue of data reconstruction, each sentence in the original **candidate set** can be approximately reconstructed by a non-negative weighted linear combination of the **summary set**.

Given a sentence $\mathbf{s}_i \in S$, MDS-Sparse represents it as a non-negative linear combination of the **summary set**.

$$\begin{aligned} &\mathbf{s}_i \approx \sum_{j=1}^{k} a_{ji}\mathbf{s}_j^* \\ &s.t. \quad a_{ji} \geq 0, \end{aligned} \tag{1}$$

where $a_{ji} \geq 0$ is the coefficient of the linear combination. To be specific, a_{ji} is a measurement of the correlation between s_i and s_j^*. To evaluate the coverage of the summary, we define the reconstruction error in L_2-norm:

$$re(\mathbf{s}_i) = \|\mathbf{s}_i - \sum_{j=1}^{k} a_{ji}\mathbf{s}_j^*\|_2^2 \tag{2}$$

Then the loss function is the global reconstruction error of the summary set:

$$\begin{aligned} J &= \min_{\mathbf{S}^*, \mathbf{A}} \sum_{i=1}^{n} re(\mathbf{s}_i) \\ &= \min_{\mathbf{S}^*, \mathbf{A}} \sum_{i=1}^{n} \|\mathbf{s}_i - \sum_{j=1}^{k} a_{ji}\mathbf{s}_j^*\|_2^2 \\ s.t. &\quad a_{ji} \geq 0, \end{aligned} \tag{3}$$

where $\mathbf{S}^*$ is the matrix of the summary sentences and $\mathbf{A}$ is the matrix of a_{ji}.

Sparsity As stated before, our framework is a two-level sparse representation model. Each sentence in the **summary set** may contain different aspects of the core topic, and other sentences should be covered by only some of them. So we put sparsity restriction on $a_{:i}$, the columns of coefficient matrix, to ensure that each sentence is reconstructed by a small number of the summary sentences. Here we impose L_0-norm on each $a_{:i}$

$$\begin{aligned} J &= \min_{\mathbf{S}^*, \mathbf{A}} \sum_{i=1}^{n} \|\mathbf{s}_i - \sum_{j=1}^{k} a_{ji}\mathbf{s}_j^*\|_2^2 + \lambda \sum_{i=1}^{n} \|a_{:i}\|_0 \\ s.t. &\quad a_{ji} \geq 0, \quad \lambda > 0, \end{aligned} \tag{4}$$

where L_0-norm controls the sparsity of $\mathbf{A}$ hence each sentence in the **candidate set** is represented by a small number of sentences in the **summary set**. Given the general intractability of the L_0-norm problem, we replace the L_0-norm with L_1-norm since L_1-norm problem is tractable and the two norms is known to yield similar results. The loss function therefore becomes:

$$\begin{aligned} J &= \min_{\mathbf{S}^*, \mathbf{A}} \sum_{i=1}^{n} \|\mathbf{s}_i - \sum_{j=1}^{k} a_{ji}\mathbf{s}_j^*\|_2^2 + \lambda \sum_{i=1}^{n} \|a_{:i}\|_1 \\ s.t. &\quad a_{ji} \geq 0, \quad \lambda > 0 \end{aligned} \tag{5}$$

Diversity The summary sentences should be diverse, since we expect a summarization to involve many different subjects. In the objective function, we add the maximized correlation score rather than the average correlation score because the diversity of a summary is determined by the least different sentence pairs; while the mean value measurements do not guarantee that the member of any pair differs from each other to some degree(Yang et al. 2013). Our loss function now becomes:

$$\begin{aligned} J = &\min_{\mathbf{S}^*, \mathbf{A}} \sum_{i=1}^{n} \|\mathbf{s}_i - \sum_{j=1}^{k} a_{ji}\mathbf{s}_j^*\|_2^2 \\ &+ \lambda \sum_{i=1}^{n} \|a_{:i}\|_1 + \beta max_{j \neq k} corr(\mathbf{s}_j^*, \mathbf{s}_k^*) \\ s.t. &\quad a_{ji} \geq 0, \quad \lambda > 0, \quad \beta > 0 \end{aligned} \tag{6}$$

The correlation function is defined below:

$$corr(\mathbf{s}_i^*, \mathbf{s}_j^*) = \frac{(\mathbf{s}_i^* - \overline{\mathbf{s}_i^*})(\mathbf{s}_j^* - \overline{\mathbf{s}_j^*})}{\sigma_i \sigma_j}, \tag{7}$$

where $\overline{\mathbf{s}^*}$ is the mean value of the vector and σ is the standard deviation.

Algorithm

The optimization problem defined in Eq.(6) is NP-hard(Yang et al. 2013). We use the simulated annealing algorithm to find the near optimal solution.

The overview of MDS-Sparse.

1. We set the initial temperature and create a random initial solution
2. The algorithm begins to loop until the stop criterion is met. Usually either the system has sufficiently cooled, or the system has not been promoted for certain number of iterations.
3. We fix the **summary set** to find a better coefficient matrix **A** that minimizes the reconstruction error.
4. From here we select a neighbor of each summary sentence by making a small change to our current **summary set**.

5. We then decide whether to move to that neighbor solution.
6. Finally, we decrease the temperature and continue looping (step to 2).

Algorithm 1 MDS-Sparse Algorithm

```
Input: candidate set S, the number of summary sentences
    k, sparse coefficient λ, correlation coefficient β, k = 0,
    J is the loss function, S* is initialized randomly. T_stop
    is the temperature that the annealing algorithm will stop.
Output: summary set S*
1: while T_k > T_stop do
2:   A ← SparseCoding(S, S*)
3:   if J(S, A, T_k) < J_opti then
4:     J_opti ← J(S, A, S*_k)
5:     S*_opti ← S*_k
6:   else
7:     rej ← rej + 1
8:     if ref ≥ MaxConseRej then
9:       return S*_opti
10:    end if
11:  end if
12:  for all s* in S*_k do
13:    tmp ← Update_S*(s*, T_k)
14:    if Accept(s*, tmp, S*_k, T_k) then
15:      S*_{k+1} ← S*_{k+1} ∪ tmp
16:    else
17:      S*_{k+1} ← S*_{k+1} ∪ s*
18:    end if
19:  end for
20:  T_{k+1} ← Update_T(k)
21:  k ← k + 1
22: end while
23: return S*_opti
```

We first randomly select a temporary **summary set** and then use them to sparsely represent the original **candidate set**. We can fix the diversity part to constant since the temporary **summary set** is now fixed. Our loss function can be represented as:

$$
\begin{aligned}
J = \min_{\mathbf{S}^*, \mathbf{A}} & \sum_{i=1}^{n} \|\mathbf{s}_i - \sum_{j=1}^{k} a_{ji}\mathbf{s}_j^*\|_2^2 \\
& + \lambda \sum_{i=1}^{n} \|a_{:i}\|_1 + Constant \\
s.t. \quad & a_{ji} \geq 0, \quad \lambda > 0, \quad \beta > 0
\end{aligned}
\tag{8}
$$

The above convex optimization problem can be solved using multiplicative algorithm(Hoyer 2002). ,

$\cdot *$ and $\cdot /$ are element-wise multiplication and division respectively. A is calculated iteratively until convergence is met.

We randomly select neighbors from temporally selected sentences (temporary **summary set**). We iteratively update each sentence in this set by searching from its neighbors by using function **Update_S*** in line 13.

Algorithm 2 SparseCoding(S^*, S)

```
Input: candidate set S, summary set S*
Output: coefficient matrix A
initialize A with 1/k
while t < 100 do
  A^{t+1} = A^t · *(S*^T S) · /(S*^T S* A^t + λ1)
  if norm(A^{t+1} − A^t) < 0.01 then
    break
  end if
  t ← t + 1
end while
return A^t
```

The search range in **Update_S*** decreases monotonically as the temperature goes down. It shrinks rapidly at earlier iterations and decreases slowly in later steps, since as the iteration steps increase, the algorithm searches more locally to find the optimal solution.

The **Accept** function in line 14 is adopted to judge whether a replacement of the summary sentence is acceptable. Some replacements that fail to lower the loss function also have a chance to be accepted since they serve to allow exploring more of the possible space of solutions.

Experiments

Experimental Setup

Datasets In this study, we use the standard summarization benchmark DUC2006 and DUC2007 for evaluation. Document Understanding Conference (DUC) has organized yearly evaluation of document summarization. DUC2006 contains 50 document sets while DUC2007 contains 45 document sets. Every document set has 25 news articles. Each document set consists of several articles written by various authors, which is also the ground truth of the evaluation. Every sentence is either used in its entirety or not at all for constructing a summary. The length of a result summary is limited by 250 tokens(whitespace delimited).

Evaluation Metric We use the Rouge(Lin 2004) evaluation toolkit, which is adopted by DUC for automatic summarization evaluation. It measures summary quality by counting overlapping units such as the n-gram, word sequences and word pairs between the candidate summary and the reference summary. As mentioned in (He et al. 2012), Rouge-N is defined as follows:

$$
Rouge\text{-}N = \frac{\sum_{S \in Ref} \sum_{gram_n \in S} CountMatch(gram_n)}{\sum_{S \in Ref} \sum_{gram_n \in S} Count(gram_n)} \tag{9}
$$

where n stands for the length of the n-gram, Ref is the set of reference summaries. *CountMatch*($gram_n$) is the maximum number of n-grams co-occurring in a candidate summary and a set of reference summaries, and *Count*($gram_n$) is the number of n-grams in the reference summaries. Among the evaluation methods implemented in Rouge, Rouge-1 focuses on the occurrence of the same words between candidate summary and reference summary, while Rouge-2 and

Rouge-SU4 focus more on the readability of the candidate summary. We use these three metrics in the experiment.

Compared methods We compare our MDS-Sparse with several state-of-the-art text extraction methods described briefly as follows:

1. **Random** selects sentences randomly from the **candidate set**.
2. **Lead** (Simon, Snavely, and Seitz 2007b) first sort all the documents chronologically and then select sentences from each document one by one.
3. **LSA** (Gong and Liu 2001) applies the singular value decomposition (SVD) on the terms-frequency matrix, then selects sentences with highest eigenvalues.
4. **DSDR** (He et al. 2012) represents each sentence as a non-negative linear combination of the summary sentences. And it uses sparse coding to select the summary sentences.

Preprocessing

In this subsection, we describe how we convert the raw documents to fit into our mathematical models.

Firstly we erase the html tag from the raw document. Secondly we segment the documents into sentences. The problem of sentence segmentation is non-trivial. In English and some other languages, using punctuation, particularly the full stop character is a reasonable approximation. However even in English this problem is not simple due to the use of the full stop character for abbreviations, which may or may not also terminate a sentence. For example, *Mr.* with a full stop character is not a sentence in *"Mr. Smith went to the shops."* Fortunately, there are already mature tools we can use the tackle this challenge. We use splitta [1], which uses SVM as classifier to separate sentences. On splitta's homepage, the reported error rates on test news data are near 0.25%. After sentence segmentation, we eliminate the stopwords and use porter stemming algorithm [2] to stem each sentence. And finally, we create a term-frequency vector for every sentence. All the sentences form the **candidate set**.

Experimental Results

In this subsection, we give the results of the experiments and the analysis.

Overall performance Table 1 and Table 2 are the overall performance comparison of MDS-Sparse against other algorithms. Rouge generates three kinds of scores: precision, recall and F-measure. To compare different approaches, we employ F-measure, a widely used measurement which combines precision and recall, to fully disclose the performance of different algorithms.

MDS-Sparse+div denotes our algorithm incorporated with diversity component (We set $\beta = 1000$ through experiments). MDS-Sparse-div denotes our algorithm without diversity ($\beta = 0$). The scores in bold are the highest ones

Algorithm	Rouge-1	Rouge-2	Rouge-SU4
Random	0.28047	0.04613	0.08785
Lead	0.30758	0.04836	0.08652
LSA	0.24415	0.03022	0.07097
DSDR	0.32034	0.04585	0.09804
MDS-Sparse+div	0.34034	**0.05233**	**0.10730**
MDS-Sparse-div	**0.34439**	0.05122	0.10717

Table 1: Average F-measure performance on DUC2006. MDS-Spsarse+div and MDS-Sparse-div denote MDS-Sparse with diversity and MDS-Sparse without diversity respectively.

Algorithm	Rouge-1	Rouge-2	Rouge-SU4
Random	0.30199	0.04628	0.08763
Lead	0.31188	0.0576	0.10201
LSA	0.25977	0.04062	0.08338
DSDR	0.32641	0.04876	0.10245
MDS-Sparse+div	0.35258	0.05479	0.11233
MDS-Sparse-div	**0.35399**	**0.06448**	**0.11669**

Table 2: Average F-measure performance on DUC2007. MDS-Sparse+div and MDS-Sparse-div denote MDS-Sparse with diversity and MDS-Sparse without diversity respectively.

in the column. From Table 1 and Table 2, it is obvious that MDS-Sparse outperforms other algorithms significantly.

Except MDS-Sparse, DSDR performs better than other algorithms, and it may be because DSDR also uses sparse coding. But it did not consider that one certain sentence should be sparsely represented by a small number of summary sentences, which is considered in our model. Besides, selecting the leading sentences (Lead) is a little better than just selecting sentences randomly. It may be caused by that article writers tend to put the conclusion sentences at the beginning of the document. Among all the six summarization algorithms, LSA shows the poorest performance on both data sets. LSA directly applies SVD on the term-frequency matrix and chooses those sentences with the largest indexes along the orthogonal latent semantic directions. Such sentences may be important of matrix decomposition, but it seems not helpful for human understanding.

Rouge-1 focuses on the occurrence of the same words between candidate summary and reference summary, while Rouge-2 and Rouge-SU4 focus more on the readability of the candidate summary. Since our work uses a two-level sparse representation model which is more close to real life, our model obtains highest scores in all three measurements. MDS-Sparse+div and MDS-Sparse-div act almost the same. This may be caused by that we adopt the non-negative linear combination of the summary sentences for reconstructing the candidate set. As mentioned in (He et al. 2012), the non-negative weighted combination might means addition of the summary sentences, and therefore, our framework incorporates diversity naturally.

Efficiency In addition, the speed of our methods is quite competitive. Note that we do not consider other algorithms, because both of MDS-Sparse and DSDR adopt sparse cod-

[1] https://code.google.com/p/splitta/

[2] http://tartarus.org/martin/PorterStemmer

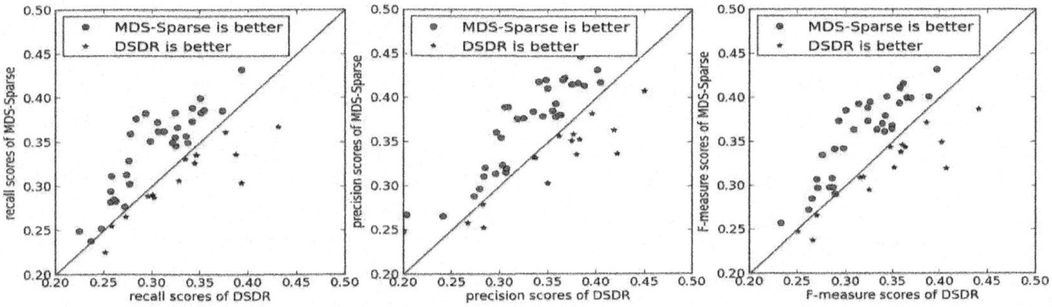

Figure 2: **The Rouge recall, precision, F-measure scores of MDS-Sparse and DSDR on each document set of DUC2006, the circles denote MDS-Sparse are better than DSDR, while the stars denote otherwise.**

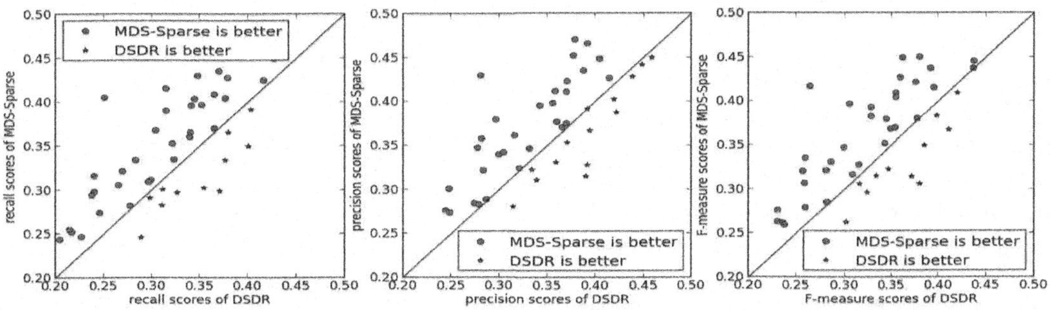

Figure 3: **The Rouge recall, precision, F-measure scores of MDS-Sparse and DSDR on each document set of DUC2007, the circles denote MDS-Sparse are better than DSDR, while the stars denote otherwise.**

ing approach. The experiments were performed on a 2.4GHz PC machine (Intel Core2 P8600) with 4GB of memory, running on an Ubuntu12.04 operating system. The average running time of DSDR on one document set is 4334.7s, while MDS-Sparse is 38.9s. Our algorithm runs two orders of magnitude faster than DSDR.

Evaluations on Different Topics In subsection , we discussed the overall performance of MDS-Sparse and other algorithms. In this subsection, we will focus on the topic-level comparison of the algorithms. We only compare MDS-Sparse+div (β = 1000 through experiments) and DSDR since both of them outperform other algorithms significantly and both use sparse coding framework to solve the summarization problem.

In Figure 2 and Figure 3, we compare the topic-level superiority of MDS-Sparse (We set $\beta = 1000$ through experiments) and DSDR in all the three measurements (recall, precision and F-measure). Each of the red circles and the blue stars denotes one document set which describes one topic in the document sets. The document set is a red circle when MDS-Sparse performs better than DSDR, otherwise a blue star. It is obvious that MDS-Sparse outperforms DSDR on both DUC2006 and DUC2007 data sets. The number of red circles is much more than that of blue stars.

Conclusion

In this paper, we propose a novel model to tackle the problem of multi-document summarization. We first investigate three requisite properties of an ideal summarization. Then a two-level sparse representation model is devised to extract all the salient sentences. In our model, the task of multi-document summarization is regarded as a document reconstruction problem which contains diversity naturally. Extensive experiments on standard datasets show that our methods is quite effective.

Recently a lot of new researches on text summarization like storyline generation and hierarchical summarization have attracted much attention. It would be of great interests to extend our model to tackle these relevant emerging tasks.

Acknowledgments

This work is supported by National Natural Science Foundation of China (Grant No. 61170091).

References

Boureau, Y.-L.; Le Roux, N.; Bach, F.; Ponce, J.; and LeCun, Y. 2011. Ask the locals: multi-way local pooling for image recognition. In *Computer Vision (ICCV), 2011 IEEE International Conference on*, 2651–2658. IEEE.

Brin, S., and Page, L. 1998. The anatomy of a large-scale hypertextual web search engine. *Computer networks and ISDN systems* 30(1):107–117.

Conroy, J. M., and O'leary, D. P. 2001. Text summarization via hidden markov models. In *Proceedings of the 24th annual international ACM SIGIR conference on Research and development in information retrieval*, 406–407. ACM.

Elad, M., and Aharon, M. 2006. Image denoising via sparse and redundant representations over learned dictionaries. *Image Processing, IEEE Transactions on* 15(12):3736–3745.

Gong, Y., and Liu, X. 2001. Generic text summarization using relevance measure and latent semantic analysis. In *Proceedings of the 24th annual international ACM SIGIR conference on Research and development in information retrieval*, 19–25. ACM.

He, Z.; Chen, C.; Bu, J.; Wang, C.; Zhang, L.; Cai, D.; and He, X. 2012. Document summarization based on data reconstruction. In *AAAI*.

Hoyer, P. O. 2002. Non-negative sparse coding. In *Neural Networks for Signal Processing, 2002. Proceedings of the 2002 12th IEEE Workshop on*, 557–565. IEEE.

Kleinberg, J. M. 1999. Authoritative sources in a hyperlinked environment. *Journal of the ACM (JACM)* 46(5):604–632.

Kupiec, J.; Pedersen, J.; and Chen, F. 1995. A trainable document summarizer. In *Proceedings of the 18th annual international ACM SIGIR conference on Research and development in information retrieval*, 68–73. ACM.

Li, L.; Zhou, K.; Xue, G.-R.; Zha, H.; and Yu, Y. 2009. Enhancing diversity, coverage and balance for summarization through structure learning. In *Proceedings of the 18th international conference on World wide web*, 71–80. ACM.

Lin, C.-Y. 2004. Rouge: A package for automatic evaluation of summaries. In *Text Summarization Branches Out: Proceedings of the ACL-04 Workshop*, 74–81.

Luhn, H. P. 1958. The automatic creation of literature abstracts. *IBM Journal of research and development* 2(2):159–165.

Mairal, J.; Elad, M.; and Sapiro, G. 2008. Sparse representation for color image restoration. *Image Processing, IEEE Transactions on* 17(1):53–69.

Marcu, D. 1997. From discourse structures to text summaries. In *Proceedings of the ACL*, volume 97, 82–88. Citeseer.

Qian, X., and Liu, Y. 2013. Fast joint compression and summarization via graph cuts. In *EMNLP*, 1492–1502.

Reiter, E.; Dale, R.; and Feng, Z. 2000. *Building natural language generation systems*, volume 33. MIT Press.

Simon, I.; Snavely, N.; and Seitz, S. M. 2007a. Scene summarization for online image collections. In *ICCV*, volume 7, 1–8.

Simon, I.; Snavely, N.; and Seitz, S. M. 2007b. Scene summarization for online image collections. In *ICCV*, volume 7, 1–8.

Yang, J.; Yu, K.; Gong, Y.; and Huang, T. 2009. Linear spatial pyramid matching using sparse coding for image classification. In *Computer Vision and Pattern Recognition, 2009. CVPR 2009. IEEE Conference on*, 1794–1801. IEEE.

Yang, C.; Shen, J.; Peng, J.; and Fan, J. 2013. Image collection summarization via dictionary learning for sparse representation. *Pattern Recognition* 46(3):948–961.

Yu, H.; Deng, Z.-H.; Yang, Y.; and Xiong, T. 2014. A joint optimization model for image summarization based on image content and tags. In *Twenty-Eighth AAAI Conference on Artificial Intelligence*.

Yu, G.; Sapiro, G.; and Mallat, S. 2012. Solving inverse problems with piecewise linear estimators: from gaussian mixture models to structured sparsity. *Image Processing, IEEE Transactions on* 21(5):2481–2499.

COT: Contextual Operating Tensor for Context-Aware Recommender Systems

Qiang Liu, Shu Wu, Liang Wang
Center for Research on Intelligent Perception and Computing, National Laboratory of Pattern Recognition
Institute of Automation, Chinese Academy of Sciences, China
{qiang.liu, shu.wu, wangliang}@nlpr.ia.ac.cn

Abstract

With rapid growth of information on the internet, recommender systems become fundamental for helping users alleviate the problem of information overload. Since contextual information can be used as a significant factor in modeling user behavior, various context-aware recommendation methods are proposed. However, the state-of-the-art context modeling methods treat contexts as other dimensions similar to the dimensions of users and items, and cannot capture the special semantic operation of contexts. On the other hand, some works on multi-domain relation prediction can be used for the context-aware recommendation, but they have problems in generating recommendation under a large amount of contextual information. In this work, we propose Contextual Operating Tensor (COT) model, which represents the common semantic effects of contexts as a contextual operating tensor and represents a context as a latent vector. Then, to model the semantic operation of a context combination, we generate contextual operating matrix from the contextual operating tensor and latent vectors of contexts. Thus latent vectors of users and items can be operated by the contextual operating matrices. Experimental results show that the proposed COT model yields significant improvements over the competitive compared methods on three typical datasets, i.e., Food, Adom and Movielens-1M datasets.

Introduction

With rapid growth of available information on the internet, users are getting in trouble with the problem of information overload. Recommender systems have become important for helping user to select interesting information in many Web applications such as social networks, e-commerce, online reading, review websites and so on. Nowadays, with enhanced ability of systems in collecting information, a great amount of contextual information in recommender systems has been collected. The contextual information in real-world application includes location, time, weather, companion and so on. These kinds of contexts have significant effect on the user behavior. For instance, a man may like to watch cartoon with his children while may like to watch romantic movies with his wife. He may prefer to read novels during weekend while may tend to read professional books during weekdays.

Due to the fundamental effect of contextual information in recommender systems, many different kinds of context modeling methods have been developed. Some existing works (Karatzoglou et al. 2010; Rendle et al. 2011) incorporate the contextual information in a factorization model via treating the context as one or several dimensions which have similar properties as dimensions of users and items. However, treating contexts as same as users and items, these methods cannot model the semantic operation of contexts. Moreover, some works on multi-domain relation prediction (Zhang, Agarwal, and Chen 2011; Jamali and Lakshmanan 2013) can also be implemented for the context-aware recommendation. These methods incorporate transfer matrix to map latent vectors of entities from one domain to another domain. To deal with context-aware recommendation, using transfer matrix, latent vectors can be mapped from one context to another context. However, since there are multiple contexts in the real world (e.g., location, time, companion), using a transfer matrix for each specific context combination, these methods have problem in confronting with large amount of contextual information.

To overcome the shortages mentioned above, we propose a novel context modeling method, which uses contextual operating tensor to capture the operation of contexts. In the research of natural language processing, a noun has semantic information as a latent vector, and an adjective has semantic operation on nouns as an operating matrix (Baroni and Zamparelli 2010). For instance, in the phrase "excellent product", the noun "product" has a latent vector, while the adjective "excellent" has the semantic operating matrix which operate the vector of the noun "product". Thus, the phrase "excellent product" has a new latent vector which represents a positive attitude to the "product". In this work, we assume that context combinations have similar properties of adjectives and can operate the latent characteristics of entities. For instance, when a man is with children, the context of this companion operates his latent interests, and then he may like to watch cartoons. Here, for the context combination in a user-item rating behavior, we use contextual operating matrix to represent the semantic operation. Inspired by (Socher et al. 2013) in simplifying the matrix-vector operation, we use contextual operating tensor to capture common effects of contexts. Besides, we represent each context combination as a latent vector, and then multiply it with the tensor to generate the operating matrix. The main contributions of this work are listed as follows:

- We model the contextual information as the semantic operation on entities, which presents a novel perspective on modeling of the contextual information.
- We use contextual operating tensor to capture the common semantic effects of contexts, and latent vectors to capture the specific properties of contexts. Then the contextual operating matrix can be generated from them.
- Experiments conducted on three real datasets show that COT is effective and evidently outperforms the state-of-the-art context-aware models.

Related Works

In this section, we review some related works on matrix factorization and state-of-the-art context-aware models.

Matrix Factorization

Matrix Factorization (MF) (Mnih and Salakhutdinov 2007; Koren, Bell, and Volinsky 2009; Koren and Bell 2011) has become the state-of-the-art approach to recommender systems. The basic objective of MF is to factorize a user-item rating matrix into two low rank matrices, each of which represents the latent factors of users or items. The original rating matrix can be approximated via the multiplying calculation.

MF has been extended nowadays. SVD++ (Koren 2008) combines the neighborhood model with matrix factorization model in one prediction function. Treating time information as a special context, timeSVD++ (Koren 2010) and tensor factorization (Xiong et al. 2010) are proposed, which achieve the state-of-the-art performance in the time-aware recommendation. Factorization machine (FM) (Rendle 2010) models all interactions between pairs of variables with the target by using factorized interaction parameters. FM is a flexible model for recommendation, and other state-of-the-art factorization models including SVD++ and timeSVD++ can be implemented using FM by defining the input data or features (Rendle 2012).

Context-aware Recommender Systems

Contextual information has been proved to be useful for recommender systems (Palmisano, Tuzhilin, and Gorgoglione 2008; Adomavicius and Tuzhilin 2011), and many context-aware recommendation methods have been developed. According to the survey of (Adomavicius and Tuzhilin 2011), these methods can be categorized into pre-filtering, post-filtering and context modeling. Employing pre-filtering or post-filtering strategies, conventional methods (Adomavicius et al. 2005; Baltrunas and Ricci 2009; Panniello et al. 2009) utilize contextual information to drive data selection or adjust the resulting set. These ad-hoc methods may work in practice, but they require the supervision and the fine-tuning in all steps of recommendation (Rendle et al. 2011).

The context modeling approaches, which use the contextual information directly in the model, have become popular. Recent works on context modeling have focused on integrating contextual information with user-item rating matrix and building models based on factorization models. Multiverse recommendation (Karatzoglou et al. 2010) represents the user-item rating matrix with contextual information as a user-item-context rating tensor, which is factorized with Tucker decomposition (Tucker 1966). And FM is easily applicable to a wide variety of context by specifying only the input data (Rendle et al. 2011). However, these methods treat contexts as one or several dimensions besides the dimensions of users and items, and cannot capture the special semantic operation of contexts.

Research on multi-domain relation prediction can also be used for the context-aware recommendation. Collective Matrix Factorization (CMF) (Singh and Gordon 2008) factorizes the rating matrix in each domain, and the latent vectors of some entities are shared among different domains. CMF can also be applied in social rating networks (Yang et al. 2011) and attribute-aware relation prediction (Lippert et al. 2008). The work of (Zhang, Agarwal, and Chen 2011) considers user attributes as priors for user latent vectors, and a transfer matrix is used to generate latent vectors from the original ones. Similarly, Heterogeneous Matrix Factorization (HeteroMF) (Jamali and Lakshmanan 2013) generates context-specific latent vectors of entities using a context-dependent transfer matrix and the original latent vectors of entities. However, for context-aware recommendation, with a transfer matrix for each context combination, these methods cannot be implemented for real applications with large amount of contextual information.

Proposed COT Model

In this section, we introduce our proposed contextual operating tensor model. We introduce the notations at first, then present the proposed model thoroughly, and finally describe the process of parameter inference.

Notations

In typical recommender systems, there are users and items denoted by $U = \{u_1, u_2, ...\}$ and $V = \{v_1, v_2, ...\}$. The latent vectors of user i and item j can be denoted by $u_i \in \mathbb{R}^d$ and $v_j \in \mathbb{R}^d$. There are multiple contexts $\mathcal{C}_1, ..., \mathcal{C}_n$, such as location, time, companion and so on. A context value c is a variable of the context $\mathcal{C}$, and a specific combination $\{c_{1,k}, ..., c_{n,k}\}$ is named context combination k. The latent vector of the context value $c_{m,k}$ is denoted as $h_{m,k} \in \mathbb{R}^{d_c}$, then the context combination k can be represented as a latent matrix $H_k = [h_{1,k}, ..., h_{n,k}] \in \mathbb{R}^{d_c \times n}$.

In this work, the rating that user i provides to item j under the context combination k can be written as $r_{i,j,k}$. Note that, in some cases, i and j can be the same entity. For example, in social network, both i and j are users.

Contextual Operating Matrix

In typical matrix factorization methods, latent vectors of users and items are constant with varying contexts. But in

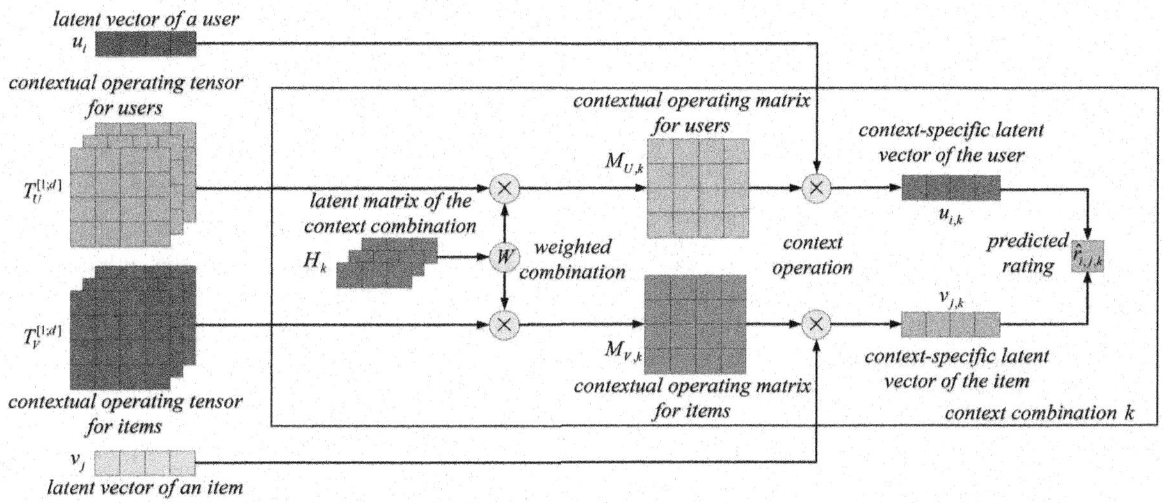

Figure 1: Overview of our proposed COT model. Contextual operating tensors and latent vectors of entities are shown on the left side, and the computational procedure under each context combination is illustrated in the square.

real-world applications, user interests and item properties are changed with different context combinations. Here, we use context-specific latent vectors for users and items under different context combinations. Then, the matrix factorization equation can be rewritten as:

$$\hat{r}_{i,j,k} = \omega_0 + \omega_i + \omega_j + \sum_{m=1}^{n} \omega_{m,k} + u_{i,k}^T v_{j,k} \ , \quad (1)$$

where ω_0 denotes the global bias, ω_i and ω_j denote the biases of user i and item j, $\omega_{m,k}$ is the bias of the context value $c_{m,k}$, $u_{i,k}$ and $v_{j,k}$ are context-specific latent vectors of user i and item j under the context combination k.

Similar to a phrase of noun and adjective, where the noun has semantic information and the adjective has semantic operation on the noun, in recommender systems, entities have rich semantic information and contexts act like adjectives which have the operation on entities. For example, companion with children can make users would like to watch cartoons, and romantic films become popular during Valentine's Day. We use two contextual operating matrices for a specific context combination. These matrices describe how a context combination affects the properties of entities and how context-specific latent vectors of users and items can be generated from their original ones. Here, we can calculate context-specific latent vectors as:

$$u_{i,k} = M_{U,k} u_i \ , \quad (2)$$

$$v_{j,k} = M_{V,k} v_j \ , \quad (3)$$

where $M_{U,j}$ and $M_{V,j}$ are both $d \times d$ matrices, denoting the contextual operating matrices for users and items under the context combination k.

Contextual Operating Tensor

As discussed above, with two contextual operating matrices for each context combination, the number of parameters will grow rapidly as the number of context combinations grows. Besides, different contexts share similar common semantic effects, for example, both weekend and being at home can make you would like to read novels. Context operation can be represented as a unity of common semantic effects and specific properties of contexts. Therefore, it will be wonderful and plausible if we can generate contextual operating matrices from several basic matrices which represent some common semantic effects of contexts. In this way, we can not only reduce the number of parameters to be estimated, but also model the underlying characteristics of contexts. Here, incorporating contextual operating tensors, we have:

$$M_{U,k} = a_k^T T_U^{[1:d]} \ , \quad (4)$$

$$M_{V,k} = a_k^T T_V^{[1:d]} \ , \quad (5)$$

where $T_U^{[1:d]}$ and $T_V^{[1:d]}$ are both $d_c \times d \times d$ tensors, denoting the contextual operating tensors for users and items. Representing the context combination k, a_k is a d_c dimensional latent vector, which is a weighted combination of latent vectors of each context value:

$$a_k = H_k W \ , \quad (6)$$

where W is a n dimensional vector, indicating the weights of each context, and each column of H_k denotes the latent vector of each context value under the context combination k. Then, substituting the Equation (4-6) into the context-specific latent vectors of users and items in Equation (2-3), we have:

$$u_{i,k} = (H_k W)^T T_U^{[1:d]} u_i \ , \quad (7)$$

$$v_{j,k} = (H_k W)^T T_V^{[1:d]} v_j \ , \quad (8)$$

Equation (7-8) can be calculated as:

$$u_{i,k} = \begin{bmatrix} (H_k W)^T T_{U,1}^{[1:d]} u_i \\ \cdots \\ (H_k W)^T T_{U,d}^{[1:d]} u_i \end{bmatrix} , \quad (9)$$

$$v_{j,k} = \begin{bmatrix} (H_k W)^T T_{V,1}^{[1:d]} v_j \\ \cdots \\ (H_k W)^T T_{V,d}^{[1:d]} v_j \end{bmatrix} , \quad (10)$$

where $T_{U,m}^{[1:d]}$ and $T_{V,m}^{[1:d]}$ denote the mth slices of the tensor $T_U^{[1:d]}$ and $T_V^{[1:d]}$, and each slice is a $d_c \times d$ matrix.

With such a computation, the contextual operating tensor can relate latent vectors of entities and latent vectors of contexts. Each slice of contextual operating tensor can capture a specific type of common semantic operation on users or items.

After discussing our model above, the overall rating prediction function for COT can be written as:

$$\hat{r}_{i,j,k} = \omega_0 + \omega_i + \omega_j + \sum_{m=1}^{n} \omega_{m,k} + \Bigg[\underbrace{\overbrace{(H_k W)^T T_U^{[1:d]}}^{M_{U,k}} u_i}_{u_{i,k}} \Bigg]^T \underbrace{\overbrace{(H_k W)^T T_V^{[1:d]}}^{M_{V,k}} v_j}_{v_{j,k}} . \quad (11)$$

As shown in Figure 1, under each context combination k, the contextual operating matrix $M_{U,k}$ or $M_{V,k}$ is a certain combination of all types of semantic operation described in contextual operating tensor $T_U^{[1:d]}$ or $T_U^{[1:d]}$. In addition, latent factor of context combination k is represented as a weighted combination of columns in the latent matrix H_k. Therefore, the context-specific latent vectors $u_{i,k}$ and $v_{j,k}$ are the latent vectors u_i and v_j under the context operation captured by $M_{U,k}$ and $M_{V,k}$.

Parameter Inference

We have already introduced our model mathematically in the previous section. Now, to accomplish the parameter inference, we need to minimize the following objective function:

$$\begin{aligned} \min_{U,V,H,T,W} J = & \sum_{\langle i,j,k \rangle \in \Omega} (r_{i,j,k} - \hat{r}_{i,j,k})^2 \\ & + \tfrac{\lambda}{2}(||U||^2 + ||V||^2 + ||H||^2 + ||T||^2 + ||W||^2) \end{aligned} , \quad (12)$$

where Ω denotes the train set, and λ is a parameter to control the regularizations, which can be determined using 5-fold cross validation.

The derivations of J with respect to all the parameters can be calculated as:

$$\frac{\partial J}{\partial u_i} = -2 \sum_{\langle i,j,k \rangle \in \Omega} l_{i,j,k} \left(\sum_{m=1}^{d} T_{U,m}^{[1:d]} v_{i,k,m} \right)^T H_k W + \lambda u_i ,$$

$$\frac{\partial J}{\partial v_j} = -2 \sum_{\langle i,j,k \rangle \in \Omega} l_{i,j,k} \left(\sum_{m=1}^{d} T_{V,m}^{[1:d]} u_{j,k,m} \right)^T H_k W + \lambda v_j ,$$

$$\frac{\partial J}{\partial T_{U,m}^{[1:d]}} = -2 \sum_{\langle i,j,k \rangle \in \Omega} l_{i,j,k} H_k W u_i^T v_{j,k,m} + \lambda T_{U,m}^{[1:d]} ,$$

$$\frac{\partial J}{\partial T_{V,m}^{[1:d]}} = -2 \sum_{\langle i,j,k \rangle \in \Omega} l_{i,j,k} H_k W v_j^T u_{i,k,m} + \lambda T_{V,m}^{[1:d]} ,$$

$$\frac{\partial J}{\partial H_k} = -2 \sum_{\langle i,j,k \rangle \in \Omega} l_{i,j,k} Q_{i,j,k} W^T + \lambda H_k ,$$

$$\frac{\partial J}{\partial W} = -2 \sum_{\langle i,j,k \rangle \in \Omega} l_{i,j,k} H_k^T Q_{i,j,k} + \lambda W ,$$

where $u_{i,k,m}$ and $v_{j,k,m}$ denote the mth components of latent vector $u_{i,k}$ and $v_{j,k}$, $l_{i,j,k}$ and $Q_{i,j,k}$ are two intermediate variables which are computed as follows:

$$l_{i,j,k} = (r_{i,j,k} - \hat{r}_{i,j,k}) ,$$

$$Q_{i,j,k} = \left(T_U^{[1:d]} u_i\right) v_{j,k} + \left(T_V^{[1:d]} v_j\right) u_{j,k} .$$

After calculating all the derivations, a solution of J in Equation (12) can be obtained by using stochastic gradient descent, which has been widely used in recommender systems (Koren, Bell, and Volinsky 2009; Koren and Bell 2011).

Experiment

In this section, we empirically investigate the performance of COT. First we describe the datasets and settings in our experiments, then report and analyze the experiment results.

Experiment Datasets

Our experiments are conducted on three real datasets.

- **Food dataset** (Ono et al. 2009) is collected from a restaurant. There are two contexts: *virtuality* describes if the situation in which the user rates is virtual or real, and *hunger* captures how hungry the user is.
- **Adom dataset** (Adomavicius et al. 2005) is collected on a movie website and has rich contextual information. There are five contexts: *companion* captures who the user watches the movie with, *when* shows whether the user watches the movie at weekend, *release* indicates whether the user watches the movie on first release, *rec* captures how will the user recommend the movie, and *where* indicates whether the user watches the movie in the theater.
- **Movielens-1M**[1] is collected from a movie recommender system Movielens[2]. There is no explicit contextual information, but the timestamp can be split into two contexts: *hour* and *day*.

Compared Methods

We compare COT model with four state-of-the-art models.

- **SVD++** (Koren 2008) is a context-unaware model which is used as a baseline in our experiments. We use LibFM[3] to implement the method.

[1] http://grouplens.org/datasets/

[2] http://movielens.org/

[3] http://www.libfm.org/

Table 1: Performance comparison on three datasets and two kinds of splitting, measured by RMSE and MAE ($d = 8$, $d_c = 4$).

	Food Dataset				Adom Dataset				Movielens-1M			
	All Users		Cold Start		All Users		Cold Start		All Users		Cold Start	
	RMSE	MAE	RMSE	MAE	RMSE	MAE	RMSE	MAE	RMSE	MAE	RMSE	MAE
SVD++	1.155	0.948	1.278	1.086	2.782	2.093	3.421	2.436	0.942	0.721	1.248	0.956
Multiverse	1.063	0.841	1.121	0.921	1.833	1.383	2.168	1.556	0.883	0.669	1.025	0.771
FM	1.055	0.845	1.115	0.918	1.852	1.446	2.125	1.563	0.878	0.672	1.001	0.766
HeteroMF	1.072	0.862	1.136	0.932	2.084	1.552	2.384	1.782	0.902	0.686	1.072	0.792
COT	**1.002**	**0.792**	**1.098**	**0.898**	**1.726**	**1.367**	**2.056**	**1.518**	**0.841**	**0.645**	**0.987**	**0.759**

- **Multiverse Recommendation** (Karatzoglou et al. 2010) is a state-of-the-art model and has been shown to outperform other context-aware recommendation models on the Food dataset and the Adom dataset.
- **FM** (Rendle et al. 2011) is applicable to the contextual information by specifying the input data. We also use LibFM as its implementation.
- **HeteroMF** (Jamali and Lakshmanan 2013) uses transfer matrix to model the contextual information. Each specific context combination has a transfer matrix in HeteroMF.

Evaluation Metrics

To measure the performance of rating prediction, we use the most popular metrics, Root Mean Square Error (RMSE) and Mean Average Precision (MAE):

$$RMSE = \sqrt{\frac{\sum\limits_{(i,j,k)\in\Omega_{test}} (r_{i,j,k} - \hat{r}_{i,j,k})^2}{n_{test}}}, \quad (13)$$

$$MAE = \frac{\sum\limits_{(i,j,k)\in\Omega_{test}} |r_{i,j,k} - \hat{r}_{i,j,k}|}{n_{test}}, \quad (14)$$

where Ω_{test} denotes the test set, and n_{test} denotes the number of ratings in test set. The smaller the value, the better the performance.

Experiment Methodology

To examine the performance on all users and cold start users, we adopt two different ways to split the datasets.

- **All Users**: We randomly sample about 10% of the ratings from the original dataset to create the test set, and the remaining 90% ratings are treated as the train set.
- **Cold Start**: We randomly sample some users from the original dataset then select less than three of their ratings as the train set, and leave all remaining ratings as the test set. The numbers of ratings of each user in test set are randomly decided. Also, the test set covers about 10% of the original dataset, and the train set covers about 90%.

Performance Comparison

Table 1 illustrates all the experiment results measured by RMSE and MAE on three datasets and two kinds of splitting. This table shows that COT achieves the best results consistently, which demonstrates the effectiveness of using contextual operating tensor to model the contextual information. On all users splitting, comparing with the best performance of other models, COT improves the RMSE values by 5.2%, 6.0% and 4.2% on the Food, Adom and Movelen-1M datasets respectively. On cold start splitting, the improvements become 1.5%, 3.2% and 1.0%. COT improves greatly on the Adom dataset, which proves COT to be particularly helpful for the dataset with rich contextual information. Through all the experiments, context-aware models outperform the context-unaware model SVD++, which demonstrates the importance of the utilization of contextual information in recommender systems. Multiverse Recommendation and FM achieve close performance on all the datasets. On Food and Movielens-1M datasets, HeteroMF performs close to Multiverse Recommendation and FM, but fails on the Adom dataset. This may be because HeteroMF needs to estimate too many transfer matrices with rich contextual information in the Adom dataset.

Moreover, we compute and illustrate the RMSE improvements of the context-aware models comparing with SVD++ in the left part of Figure 2. We can observe that, on all three datasets, the RMSE improvements are larger on cold start splitting than those on all users splitting. This shows that the contextual information is more important in the cold start situation and can be used to compensate for the lack of history information.

The convergence curves are illustrated in the right part of Figure 2. The convergence curves show that the RMSE of COT becomes stable after about 30 iterations. These indicate that COT has a satisfactory convergence rate and can be trained rapidly and effectively in practical applications.

Analysis of Contexts

As we discussed in the section of the COT model, each slice of contextual operating tensor represents one kind of common operation. With larger difference among all the slices, the contextual operating tensor is more powerful in modeling the context operation. Similar to the content diversity measuring the difference among content of movies (Nguyen et al. 2014), we use a metric *matrix diversity* measuring the

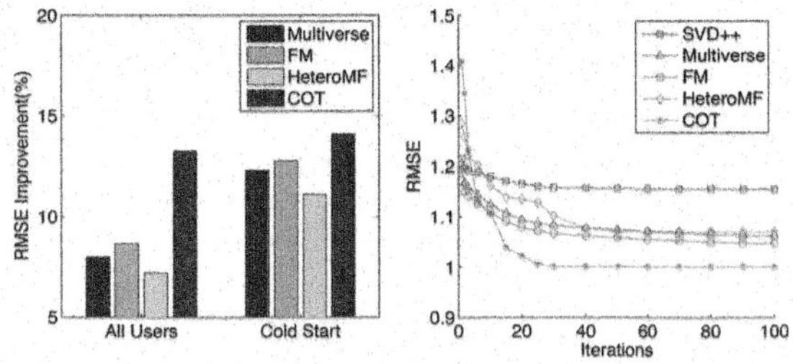

(a) Food Dataset

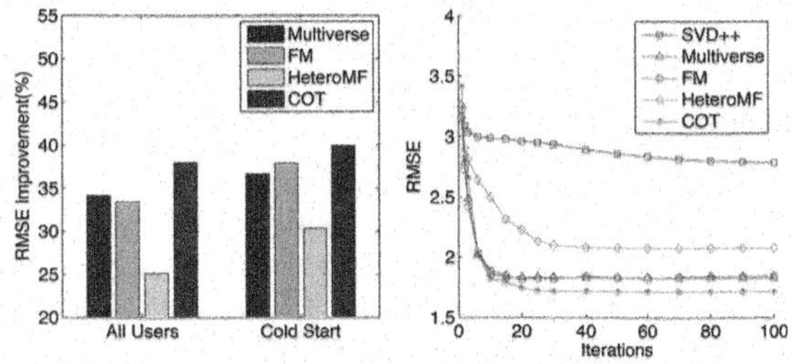

(b) Adom Dataset

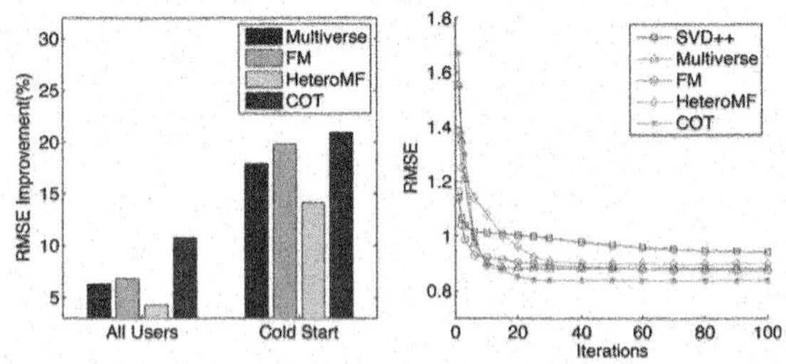

(c) Movielens-1M

Figure 2: Performance comparison on three datasets. The left part illustrates the RMSE improvement of the context-aware models compared to SVD++. The right part illustrates the convergence curves of the models.

difference among all slices. Matrix diversity is defined as average RMSE of all slice pairs of tensor. Figure 3 illustrates how matrix diversity of the contextual operating tensors changes with increasing number of iterations. The figure shows that values of matrix diversity increase when the number of iterations grows from 1 to about 30. After the iteration 30, the values of matrix diversity become stable. Besides, we can see that COT achieves convergence in Figure 2 at the same time as the values of matrix diversity converged in Figure 3 on three datasets. These evidences indicate that in the training process, when matrix diversity achieves stable results, COT achieves the best performance. Moreover, the final value of matrix diversity on the Adom dataset is larger than those on the other two datasets. This may be because richer contextual information on the Adom dataset has more powerful operating ability in changing the properties of users and items.

The weights of different contexts captured by W on three datasets are illustrated in Figure 4. The figure shows that the context *hunger* is more important than *virtuality* on the Food dataset, and *day* is more important than *hour* on Movielens-1M. These observations follow our intuition. For the Adom

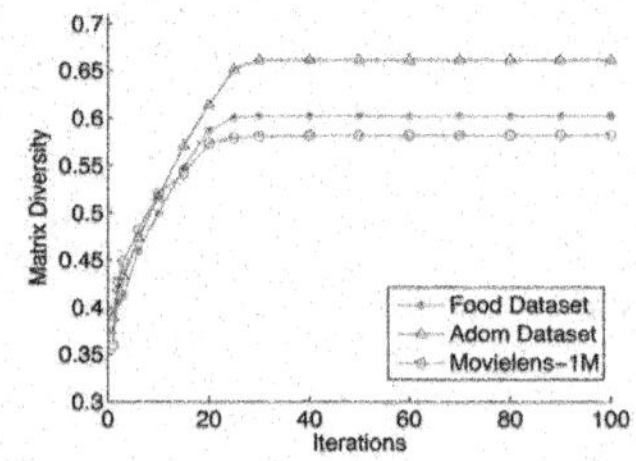

Figure 3: Matrix diversity of tensor T_U and T_V with increasing number of iterations on three datasets.

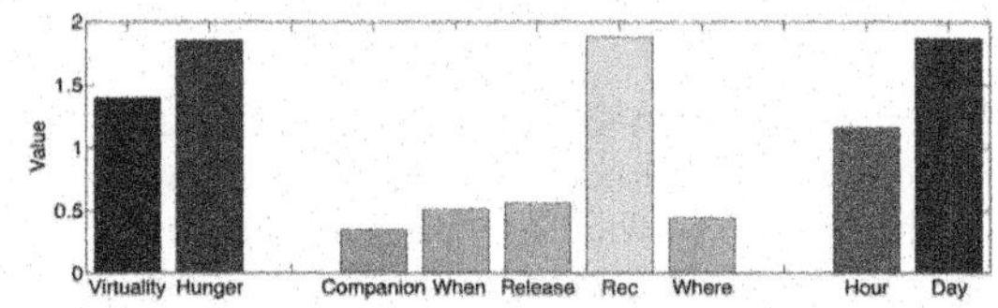

Figure 4: Weights of different contexts on three datasets.

dataset, the context *rec* has much higher weight and becomes the dominant context. This may be because the context *rec*, which indicates how will the user recommend the movie, has high relevance with the final rating.

Impact of Parameters

As shown in Figure 5, we study the model performance with varying dimensionalities of entity vector d and context vector d_c on the Food dataset. With increasing d and d_c, the value of RMSE decreases at first, then stays nearly stable after $d = 5$ and $d_c = 3$. The parameter d_c can be selected in a large range, which means that the performance of COT doesn't rely on parameter selection very much. Since the performances of COT with different parameter values selected from these ranges are very similar, in previous subsection, we only illustrate the results with $d = 8$ and $d_c = 4$ on three datasets for simplicity.

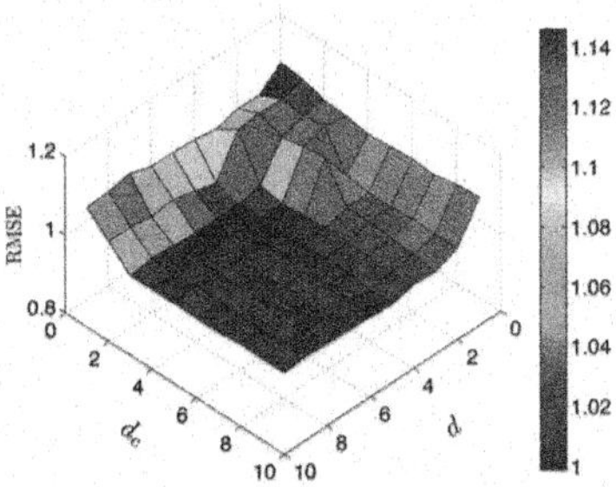

Figure 5: Performance of COT on the Food dataset with varying dimensionalities d and d_c.

Conclusion

In this paper, a novel context-aware recommendation method, i.e. COT, is proposed. In COT, the context is converged to be a vector and the common semantic effects of contexts are captured by a contextual operating tensor. Besides, the semantic operation of a context combination on entities, i.e., users and items, are captured by a contextual operating matrix, which can be generated from the contextual operating tensor and latent vectors of contexts. The experimental results on three real datasets show that COT outperforms the state-of-the-art context-aware models and can well reveal the relationship between contexts and entities.

Acknowledgments

This work is jointly supported by National Basic Research Program of China (2012CB316300), National Natural Science Foundation of China (61403390, 61175003, 61135002) and Hundred Talents Program of CAS.

References

Adomavicius, G., and Tuzhilin, A. 2011. Context-aware recommender systems. In *Recommender systems handbook*. Springer. 217–253.

Adomavicius, G.; Sankaranarayanan, R.; Sen, S.; and Tuzhilin, A. 2005. Incorporating contextual information in recommender systems using a multidimensional approach. *ACM Transactions on Information Systems (TOIS)* 23(1):103–145.

Baltrunas, L., and Ricci, F. 2009. Context-based splitting of item ratings in collaborative filtering. In *Proceedings of the third ACM conference on Recommender systems*, 245–248. ACM.

Baroni, M., and Zamparelli, R. 2010. Nouns are vectors, adjectives are matrices: Representing adjective-noun constructions in semantic space. In *Proceedings of the 2010 Conference on Empirical Methods in Natural Language Processing*, 1183–1193. Association for Computational Linguistics.

Jamali, M., and Lakshmanan, L. 2013. Heteromf: recommendation in heterogeneous information networks using context dependent factor models. In *Proceedings of the 22nd international conference on World Wide Web*, 643–654. International World Wide Web Conferences Steering Committee.

Karatzoglou, A.; Amatriain, X.; Baltrunas, L.; and Oliver, N. 2010. Multiverse recommendation: n-dimensional tensor factorization for context-aware collaborative filtering. In *Proceedings of the fourth ACM conference on Recommender systems*, 79–86. ACM.

Koren, Y., and Bell, R. 2011. Advances in collaborative filtering. In *Recommender Systems Handbook*. Springer. 145–186.

Koren, Y.; Bell, R.; and Volinsky, C. 2009. Matrix factorization techniques for recommender systems. *Computer* 42(8):30–37.

Koren, Y. 2008. Factorization meets the neighborhood: a multifaceted collaborative filtering model. In *Proceedings of the 14th ACM SIGKDD international conference on Knowledge discovery and data mining*, 426–434. ACM.

Koren, Y. 2010. Collaborative filtering with temporal dynamics. *Communications of the ACM* 53(4):89–97.

Lippert, C.; Weber, S. H.; Huang, Y.; Tresp, V.; Schubert, M.; and Kriegel, H.-P. 2008. Relation prediction in multirelational domains using matrix factorization. In *Proceedings of the NIPS 2008 Workshop: Structured Input-Structured Output, Vancouver, Canada*.

Mnih, A., and Salakhutdinov, R. 2007. Probabilistic matrix factorization. In *Advances in neural information processing systems*, 1257–1264.

Nguyen, T. T.; Hui, P.-M.; Harper, F. M.; Terveen, L.; and Konstan, J. A. 2014. Exploring the filter bubble: the effect of using recommender systems on content diversity. In *Proceedings of the 23rd international conference on World wide web*, 677–686. International World Wide Web Conferences Steering Committee.

Ono, C.; Takishima, Y.; Motomura, Y.; and Asoh, H. 2009. Context-aware preference model based on a study of difference between real and supposed situation data. In *User Modeling, Adaptation, and Personalization*. Springer. 102–113.

Palmisano, C.; Tuzhilin, A.; and Gorgoglione, M. 2008. Using context to improve predictive modeling of customers in personalization applications. *Knowledge and Data Engineering, IEEE Transactions on* 20(11):1535–1549.

Panniello, U.; Tuzhilin, A.; Gorgoglione, M.; Palmisano, C.; and Pedone, A. 2009. Experimental comparison of pre-vs. post-filtering approaches in context-aware recommender systems. In *Proceedings of the third ACM conference on Recommender systems*, 265–268. ACM.

Rendle, S.; Gantner, Z.; Freudenthaler, C.; and Schmidt-Thieme, L. 2011. Fast context-aware recommendations with factorization machines. In *Proceedings of the 34th international ACM SIGIR conference on Research and development in Information Retrieval*, 635–644. ACM.

Rendle, S. 2010. Factorization machines. In *Data Mining (ICDM), 2010 IEEE 10th International Conference on*, 995–1000. IEEE.

Rendle, S. 2012. Factorization machines with libfm. *ACM Transactions on Intelligent Systems and Technology (TIST)* 3(3):57.

Singh, A. P., and Gordon, G. J. 2008. Relational learning via collective matrix factorization. In *Proceedings of the 14th ACM SIGKDD international conference on Knowledge discovery and data mining*, 650–658. ACM.

Socher, R.; Perelygin, A.; Wu, J. Y.; Chuang, J.; Manning, C. D.; Ng, A. Y.; and Potts, C. 2013. Recursive deep models for semantic compositionality over a sentiment treebank. In *Proceedings of the Conference on Empirical Methods in Natural Language Processing (EMNLP)*, 1631–1642. Association for Computational Linguistics.

Tucker, L. R. 1966. Some mathematical notes on three-mode factor analysis. *Psychometrika* 31(3):279–311.

Xiong, L.; Chen, X.; Huang, T.-K.; Schneider, J. G.; and Carbonell, J. G. 2010. Temporal collaborative filtering with bayesian probabilistic tensor factorization. In *SDM*, volume 10, 211–222. SIAM.

Yang, S.-H.; Long, B.; Smola, A.; Sadagopan, N.; Zheng, Z.; and Zha, H. 2011. Like like alike: joint friendship and interest propagation in social networks. In *Proceedings of the 20th international conference on World wide web*, 537–546. ACM.

Zhang, L.; Agarwal, D.; and Chen, B.-C. 2011. Generalizing matrix factorization through flexible regression priors. In *Proceedings of the fifth ACM conference on Recommender systems*, 13–20. ACM.

Effectively Predicting Whether and When a Topic Will Become Prevalent in a Social Network

Weiwei Liu[1,2], **Zhi-Hong Deng**[1*], **Xiuwen Gong**[3], **Frank Jiang**[4] and **Ivor W. Tsang**[2]
[1]Key Laboratory of Machine Perception (Ministry of Education),
School of Electronics Engineering and Computer Science, Peking University, Beijing 100871, China
[2]Center for Quantum Computation and Intelligent Systems, University of Technology, Sydney, Australia
[3]School of Mathematics and Computer Science, Anhui Normal University, Wuhu, China
[4]School of Engineering and IT, University of New South Wales, Australia
liuweiwei863@gmail.com, zhdeng@cis.pku.edu.cn, gongxiuwen@gmail.com,
F.Jiang@adfa.edu.au, ivor.tsang@uts.edu.au

Abstract

Effective forecasting of future prevalent topics plays an important role in social network business development. It involves two challenging aspects: predicting whether a topic will become prevalent, and when. This cannot be directly handled by the existing algorithms in topic modeling, item recommendation and action forecasting. The classic forecasting framework based on time series models may be able to predict a hot topic when a series of periodical changes to user-addressed frequency in a systematic way. However, the frequency of topics discussed by users often changes irregularly in social networks. In this paper, a generic probabilistic framework is proposed for hot topic prediction, and machine learning methods are explored to predict hot topic patterns. Two effective models, *PreWHether* and *PreWHen*, are introduced to predict whether and when a topic will become prevalent. In the *PreWHether* model, we simulate the constructed features of previously observed frequency changes for better prediction. In the *PreWHen* model, distributions of time intervals associated with the emergence to prevalence of a topic are modeled. Extensive experiments on real datasets demonstrate that our method outperforms the baselines and generates more effective predictions.

Introduction

Forecasting (Brockwell and Davis 2002) has emerged as an important activity in economics, commerce, marketing, statistics and various branches of science. Most of the existing methods are based on time series analysis. Examples of time series include daily stock prices, monthly accidental deaths, annual rainfall, and the market index. Predictive patterns to be discovered in such time series may consist of (a) increasing or decreasing trends, (b) seasonal patterns, (c) apparent sharp changes, and (d) outlying observations. Several literatures (Brillinger 1981; Madsen 2008) have studied the internal mechanisms of generating such time series. However, these methods cannot be used to predict whether a topic will become prevalent and when it will become popular in social networks.

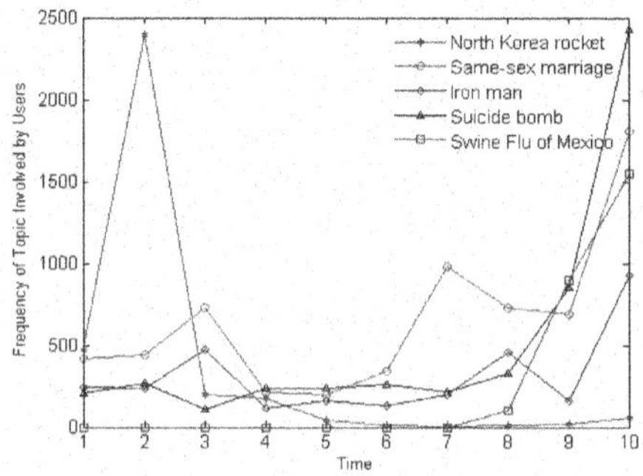

Figure 1: The frequency of topic addressed by users in social networks

Other typical time series forecasting models include Autoregressive (AR) models, integrated (I) models, and moving average (MA) models (Gershenfeld 1999). These models depend linearly on historical data. Combining these models produces models such as autoregressive moving average (ARMA) and autoregressive integrated moving average (ARIMA) (Prado and West 2010; Box and Jenkins 1990). However, when applied to topic modeling, these models effectively predict a hot topic on condition that a full cycle is observed when a series periodically changes. This condition is inconsistent with the practices of topic evolution, in which frequency with which a topic series is discussed by users often changes irregularly. For example, we divide April 2009 into 10 equal time windows; five hot topics are detected in this month, and the frequency of these topics is counted in every time window. The results are shown in Figure 1. These hot topics do not exhibit clear predictability, and it is ineffective to analyze the patterns of these hot topics. Another well-recognized aspect is to effectively predict a topic as

*Corresponding author

early as possible to capture important events or outcomes, in particular, to determine whether and when a topic will become popular. The existing methods (Gershenfeld 1999; Chen et al. 2002; Palpanas et al. 2004) focus on predicting the topic frequency based on the observed historical appearance frequency of the topic. These methods face a number of challenges in practice; for example, they cannot address the following scenarios: (1) With the three-day frequency of a topic involved in a social network, will it become a hot topic in the near future? To address this question, both qualitative and quantitative analysis is necessary. For instance, many web-sites recommend the Top 10 hot news, movies or music based on the sum of the click rate over a recent period of time. However, if the change in click rate is big, or there is an apparent sharp change in the click rate, an item may suddenly become popular even though the sum of the click rate is low. Our experimental results show that these methods are not effective in predicting whether a topic is hot.

Once we can predict whether a topic will become hot in the near future, another question arises: (2) When will a topic become hot and interesting to many users (rather than individuals) in a social network? A quantitative answer to this question challenges the existing time series-based forecasting models which need intensive human interaction before an answer can be reached, and recommendation methods (Konstan and Riedl 2012; Jannach 2011) which focus on recommending items for individual users and consistent changes. Although it appears that we predict when a topic will become hot based on the observed increased rate of frequency of involvement with this topic by users within a few days, our experimental results with this method have proved to be mostly invalid, except for determining that the change in topic frequency is smooth. This is inconsistent with the reality in social networks, in which topic frequency changes stochastically.

This work addresses the above problems of predicting whether and when a topic will become hot. Motivated by the assumption that the trend of a topic's popularity at the current moment is relevant to the behaviors of the topic in the previous time period, we propose a generic probabilistic framework which incorporates the pattern of topic evolution identified in the previous time period into the prediction of its dynamics at the current time. Two effective probabilistic models are then built to address the above questions, i.e. predicting whether and when a topic will become hot. Specifically, the *PreWHether* model is proposed to simulate the extracted features of previously observed topic dynamics, which determine whether it will become hot. The *PreWHen* model further models the distributions of time intervals from the emergence of the topic to its prevalence by using the Gamma distribution, which can identify when a topic becomes popular.

Related Work

Evolution of Topics A number of methods have been proposed for analyzing the temporal evolution of topics in document collections, such as the dynamic topic model (DTM) (Blei and Lafferty 2006), topics over time (TOT) (Xuerui and Andrew 2006), trend analysis model (TAM) (Kawamae 2011). DTM extends the classic state space models to specify a statistical model of topic evolution and then develops efficient approximate posterior inference techniques for determining the evolving topics from a sequential collection of documents.

Forecasting Actions Agarwal, Chen, and Elango (2009) exploit the Gamma-Poisson model to estimate click-through rates (number of clicks per display) in the context of content recommendation. Matsubara et al. (2012) introduce the TriMine method which automatically finds patterns in huge collections of complex events and forecasts future events. Tan et al. (2010) propose a Noise Tolerant Time-varying Factor Graph Model (NTT-FGM) for modeling and predicting social actions. NTT-FGM simultaneously models social network structure, user attributes and user action history for better prediction of users' future actions. Shi et al. (2009) study the pattern of user participation behaviors, and the feature factors that influence such behaviors on different forum data sets.

The above methods make use of time series analysis to predict a personal action such as whether a user will discuss specific topic on his microblogs (tweets), or how many clicks will be received the next day from a specific user. They aim to gain more insights into the micro-level for forecasting actions. Our work mainly focuses on finding macro-level mechanisms for predicting whether and when a topic will become hot in social networks.

Time Series Pattern Discovery Time series has been used for similarity search and pattern discovery in series and sequence data (Matsubara, Sakurai, and Yoshikawa 2009; Sakurai, Faloutsos, and Yamamuro 2007). For instance, Papadimitriou, Brockwell, and Faloutsos (2004) apply wavelet transform to capture patterns of time series and introduce a method of discovering optimal local patterns in Papadimitriou and Yu (2006), which concisely describes the main trends in a time series. Approaches for regression on time series and streams include Chen et al. (2002) and Palpanas et al. (2004). They both estimate the best fit of a given function for forecasting rules in time series.

The above methods address the following problem: Given a time series which exhibits a clear periodicity, how can a pattern which concisely describes the main trends in the series be learned. In social networks, the topic frequency series discussed by users often do not exhibit a clear periodicity. It is likely that topic frequency series does not form a continuous sequence, rather, it has only a small number of values. This makes it difficult to use the above methods to predict hot topic trends, and especially to address the whether and when problems.

Problem Statement

In this section, we formalize the problem of forecasting whether and when a topic will become hot in a social network in the near future. We divide a month into T time windows and the length of every time window is t hours. Given a topic which first emerges at the i-th time window, and its frequency of appearing in the network at i-th,$\cdots$,$i+m$-th time windows, if the topic is not prevalent at $i+m$-th time window, the task here is to forecast whether it will become hot and at which future time window. We formalize the problem as follows.

Let K be a set of topics, $K = \{k_i | k_i$ is the set of keywords$\}$. $x_{k_i,j}$ denotes the frequency of topic k_i involved at the j-th time window. We define a hot topic as follows:

Definition 1. *(Hot Topic) Let* $S = \sum_{j=0}^{m} x_{k_i,j}, 0 \leq m \leq T$. *If* $S \geq \alpha$ *(where* α *is the threshold), then topic* k_i *is a hot topic.*

Assume users in the network first talk about topic k_i at the j-th time window. We get the time series data, $\{x_{k_i,j}, \cdots, x_{k_i,m}\}$, $j < m < T$. If $\sum_{t=j}^{m} x_{k_i,t} < \alpha$, we aim to forecast whether topic k_i will become a hot topic at a later time window based on features of the time series data. We use vector $X = (x^1_{k_i}, \cdots, x^n_{k_i})$ to denote the features of the observed time series data. For example, we can use the sum, growth rate, mean and variance and so on as the features of the time series data. Accordingly, we state Problem 1 as follows.

Problem 1. *(Whether a Topic Hot) We observe the time series data* $\{x_{k_i,j}, \cdots, x_{k_i,m}\}$, $j < m < T$. *If* $\sum_{t=j}^{m} x_{k_i,t} < \alpha$, *we aim to forecast whether topic* k_i *will be hot at a later time window based on* X *which is the feature vector of the time series data. That is, whether* $\exists \epsilon, m < \epsilon \leq T$, *to satisfy* $\sum_{t=j}^{\epsilon} x_{k_i,t} \geq \alpha$.

If a topic is predicted to be a hot one, we aim to forecast when it becomes hot. This leads to Problem 2.

Problem 2. *(When a Topic Will Become Hot) Given a hot topic* k_i *which emerges at* j*-th time window, we aim to find* η*-th* $(j \leq \eta \leq T)$ *time window, satisfying* $\sum_{t=j}^{\eta} x_{k_i,t} \geq \alpha$.

In our experiments, we divide a month into 90 time windows and the length of every time window is 8 hours ($T = 90$, $t = 8$). For every topic, we set a fixed length of observed time series data. Suppose users in the network first talk about topic k_i at the j-th time window, then let us observe the evolution of the topic within 9 time windows $\{x_{k_i,j}, \cdots, x_{k_i,j+8}\}$ (namely three days). In our framework, we consider the choice of 3 features that are usually used in statistics and practice(i.e. sum, average rate of change and standard deviation), to measure the topic evolution, so the feature vector X is denoted as: $X =$ (sum, average rate of change, standard deviation), where sum$= \sum_{t=j}^{j+8} x_{k_i,t}$, average rate of change$= \frac{1}{8} \cdot \sum_{t=j}^{j+7} \frac{x_{k_i,t+1} - x_{k_i,t}}{x_{k_i,t}}$, standard deviation$= \sqrt{\frac{1}{9} \cdot \sum_{t=j}^{j+8} (x_{k_i,t} - \hat{\mu})^2}$ where $\hat{\mu}$ is the mean of $\{x_{k_i,j}, \cdots, x_{k_i,j+8}\}$.

Proposed Models

The PreWHether Model

Here we specify and present an effective model, *PreWHether*, for predicting whether a topic will become hot. Let C_1 denote a hot topic, and C_0 represent a topic that is not hot. Given topic k_i and the feature vector X, a more powerful approach to forecasting Problem 1 is to model the posterior probability distributions $p(C_0|X)$ and $p(C_1|X)$. These two distributions are then used to make an optimal decision.

Based on Bayes' theorem, the posterior probability $p(C_1|X)$ can be written as

$$p(C_1|X) = \frac{p(C_1)p(X|C_1)}{p(C_1)p(X|C_1) + p(C_0)p(X|C_0)} \quad (1)$$

If the likelihood and prior probability distributions in Eq.(1) are obtained, we can determine Problem 1. Below, we discuss how to model the likelihood and prior probability distributions in Eq.(1).

The dimension of feature vector X of topic k_i is 3: *sum* denoted as $x^1_{k_i}$, *average rate of change* denoted as $x^2_{k_i}$, *standard deviation* denoted as $x^3_{k_i}$. Assume $x^1_{k_i}, x^2_{k_i}, x^3_{k_i}$ are mutual conditionally independent given C_1 or C_0. The likelihood probability $p(X|C_1)$ can be written as

$$p(X|C_1) = p(x^1_{k_i}|C_1) \cdot p(x^2_{k_i}|C_1) \cdot p(x^3_{k_i}|C_1) \quad (2)$$

We analyze the features of sum, average rate of change, standard deviation and model likelihood probability distributions for these three dimension variables respectively.

By observing the data characteristics of topic evolution, we find that the probability of topic k_i which belongs to C_1 is proportional to $x^1_{k_i}$. If the propagation sources of topic k_i are influential on the whole network, there will be more people talking about this topic, and $x^1_{k_i}$ will become bigger. If the topic is interesting to people, more people will focus on this topic at the initial time windows, so we obtain much bigger $x^1_{k_i}$. We suppose there are two factors controlling $x^1_{k_i}$: one is related to the propagation sources of the topic, while the other is related to the attraction of the topic to people. Suppose $x^1_{k_i}$ is a continuous variable, we use the Beta distribution to model the likelihood of probability distributions. The shape of the probability density function of the Beta distribution changes with different parameter settings. We can use the increasing function to model $p(x^1_{k_i}|C_1)$ and the decreasing function to model $p(x^1_{k_i}|C_0)$. The different parameters denote different classes.

We observe that $x^2_{k_i}$ tends to have concentrated distribution at different intervals for different classes. Assume that $x^2_{k_i}$ is a continuous variable. Considering that $x^2_{k_i}$ varies from negative infinity to positive infinity, we can use Gaussian distribution to model $p(x^2_{k_i}|C_1)$ and $p(x^1_{k_i}|C_0)$.

We also observe that $x^3_{k_i}$ tends to have concentrated distribution at different intervals for different classes. Assume that $x^3_{k_i}$ is a continuous variable. Since $x^3_{k_i}$ is nonnegative, and we need an unimodal distribution to characterize it, the Gamma distribution is frequently used to model $p(x^3_{k_i}|C_1)$ and $p(x^3_{k_i}|C_0)$.

To keep the notation clean, we denote topic k_i by i. Suppose we have a data set $D = (x_i^1, x_i^2, x_i^3, t_i)$ where $i = 1, \cdots, n$. Here $t_i = 1$ denotes class C_1 and $t_i = 0$ denotes class C_0. Let the prior class probability be $p(C_1) = \beta$, so that $p(C_0) = 1 - \beta$. a, b, μ, σ, c, d are the parameters which describe each distribution. i.e. μ, σ stand for the mean and variance of Gaussian distribution; a, b and c, d represent the shape and scale parameters of Beta and Gamma distribution respectively. For a feature vector $X = \{x_i^1, x_i^2, x_i^3\}$ from class C_1, we have $t_i = 1$ and hence

$$\begin{aligned} &p(X, C_1) = p(C_1)p(X|C_1) \\ &= \beta \cdot Beta(x_i^1|a_1, b_1) \cdot N(x_i^2|\mu_1, \sigma_1) \cdot Gamma(x_i^3|c_1, d_1) \end{aligned} \tag{3}$$

Similarly for class C_0, we have $t_i = 0$ and hence

$$\begin{aligned} &p(X, C_0) = p(C_0)p(X|C_0) \\ &= (1 - \beta) \cdot Beta(x_i^1|a_0, b_0) \cdot N(x_i^2|\mu_0, \sigma_0) \\ &\cdot Gamma(x_i^3|c_0, d_0) \end{aligned} \tag{4}$$

To keep the notation clean, we write $\omega_1 = (a_1, b_1, \mu_1, \sigma_1, c_1, d_1)$ and $\omega_0 = (a_0, b_0, \mu_0, \sigma_0, c_0, d_0)$. Thus the likelihood function is given by

$$\begin{aligned} &p(D|\beta, \omega_1, \omega_0) \\ &= \prod_{i=1}^{n} [\beta \cdot Beta(x_i^1|a_1, b_1) \cdot N(x_i^2|\mu_1, \sigma_1) \\ &\cdot Gamma(x_i^3|c_1, d_1)]^{t_i} \cdot [(1 - \beta) \cdot Beta(x_i^1|a_0, b_0) \\ &\cdot N(x_i^2|\mu_0, \sigma_0) \cdot Gamma(x_i^3|c_0, d_0)]^{1-t_i} \end{aligned} \tag{5}$$

$\beta, \omega_1, \omega_0$ can be obtained by solving the problem

$$\begin{aligned} &\max \ln p(D|\beta, \omega_1, \omega_0) \\ &s.t. \quad a_1 > 0, b_1 > 0, a_0 > 0, b_0 > 0 \\ &\qquad \sigma_1 > 0, \sigma_0 > 0, 0 \le \beta \le 1 \\ &\qquad c_1 > 0, d_1 > 0, c_0 > 0, d_0 > 0 \end{aligned} \tag{6}$$

Estimation of parameters. Because the likelihood probability $p(X|C_1)$ and $p(X|C_0)$ are the product of three factors and the parameters of Beta distribution, Gaussian distribution and Gamma distribution are mutually independent in Eq.(6). We estimate the respective parameters of the three distributions accordingly.

Let $L(x_i^1; \beta, a_1, b_1, a_0, b_0) = \prod_{i=1}^{n} (\beta \cdot Beta(x_i^1|a_1, b_1))^{t_i} \cdot [(1-\beta) \cdot Beta(x_i^1|a_0, b_0)]^{1-t_i}$. For estimating the parameters of the Beta distribution, we need to solve the problem below:

$$\begin{aligned} &\min - \ln L(x_i^1; \beta, a_1, b_1, a_0, b_0) \\ &s.t. \quad a_1 > 0, b_1 > 0, a_0 > 0, b_0 > 0 \\ &\qquad 0 \le \beta \le 1 \end{aligned} \tag{7}$$

The solution to Eq.(7) is unique, computable and consistent.

Based on Hölder's inequality (Hewitt and Stromberg 1965), we have the following two theorems:

Theorem 1. *(Log-convex for beta function) Let $x > 0$, $y > 0$, the Beta function can be written as*

$$B(x, y) = \int_0^1 u^{x-1} \cdot (1 - u)^{y-1} du \tag{8}$$

Then $B(x, y)$ is a log-convex function of x and y.

Assume that $f_i, 1 \le i \le n$ are convex functions, and $w_i \ge 0, 1 \le i \le n$

$$f = \sum_{i=1}^{n} w_i \cdot f_i \tag{9}$$

Then Eq.(9)) is a convex function.

Based on Theorem 1 and Eq.(9)), we have the following theorem:

Theorem 2. *(Convexity for Eq.(7)) The optimization problem of maximizing the log of the Beta distribution function represented by Eq.(7) is a convex optimization problem.*

Let $L(x_i^2, x_i^3; \mu_1, \sigma_1, \mu_0, \sigma_0, c_1, d_1, c_0, d_0) = \prod_{i=1}^{n} N(x_i^2|\mu_1, \sigma_1)^{t_i} \cdot N(x_i^2|\mu_0, \sigma_0)^{1-t_i} \cdot Gamma(x_i^3|c_1, d_1)^{t_i} \cdot Gamma(x_i^3|c_0, d_0)^{1-t_i}$. To estimate the parameters of Gaussian and Gamma distributions, we solve the problem

$$\begin{aligned} &\min - \ln L(x_i^2, x_i^3; \mu_1, \sigma_1, \mu_0, \sigma_0, c_1, d_1, c_0, d_0) \\ &s.t. \quad \sigma_1 > 0, \sigma_0 > 0 \\ &\qquad c_1 > 0, d_1 > 0, c_0 > 0, d_0 > 0 \end{aligned} \tag{10}$$

We can get a local optimal solution of Eq.(10).

The PreWHen Model

We describe an effective model, *PreWHen*, for predicting when a topic will become a hot topic. We observe the time series of hot topics in the data set. Most of the topics tend to become hot at a constant time window from their first emergence in the network. Assume topic k_i emerges at the j-th time window, and it becomes hot at η-th ($j \le \eta \le T$) time window which means that $\sum_{t=j}^{\eta} x_{k_i,t} \ge \alpha$. Let x denote the difference between $x_{k_i,\eta}$ and $x_{k_i,j}$ for all the hot topic, $x = x_{k_i,\eta} - x_{k_i,j}$. Assume x is continuous variable. Since x is nonnegative, we use unimodal Gamma distribution to characterize it. Let Δx be a small interval of x. We set the length of Δx to 1.

$$p(x) \cong Gamma(x|\varphi, \chi) \cdot \Delta x \tag{11}$$

We need to estimate the parameters in Eq.(11). The maximum likelihood estimation of the Gamma distribution function is used to estimate φ and χ. Let $L(x_i; \varphi, \chi) = \prod_{i=1}^{n} Gamma(x_i|\varphi, \chi)$. Given observations $x_1, \cdots, x_n$, the problem is

$$\begin{aligned} &\min - \ln L(x_i; \varphi, \chi) \\ &s.t. \quad \varphi > 0, \chi > 0 \end{aligned} \tag{12}$$

Eq.(12) is not a convex optimization problem, so we adopt a local optimal solution.

A topic will be a hot one at the interval of the Gamma distribution mode in the maximum probability.

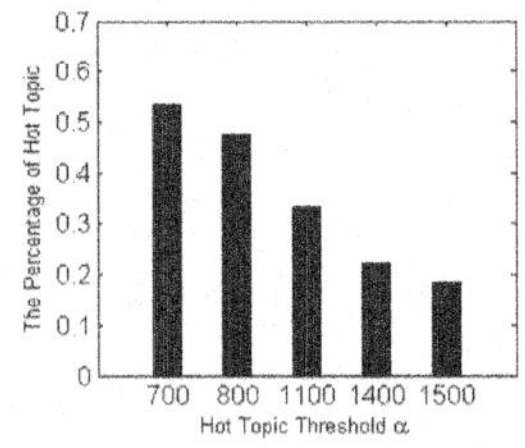

Figure 2: The percentage of hot topics with different hot topic thresholds α

Hot Topic Prediction

We develop the *PreWHether* and *PreWHen* models to discover hot topic patterns based on the previous time series data of hot topics. Given a new topic k_{new} and its corresponding time series data $\{x_{k_i,j}, \cdots, x_{k_i,m}\}$, we can predict whether the topic is hot based on the learned hot topic patterns. Firstly, we calculate the feature vector of topic k_{new}, $X = (x^1_{k_{new}}, x^2_{k_{new}}, x^3_{k_{new}})$; We then compute $p(C_1|X)$ and $p(C_0|X)$ based on the learned parameters. Lastly, we calculate $p(C_1|X)$ with $p(C_0|X)$. If $p(C_1|X)$ is bigger than $p(C_0|X)$, we predict it as a hot topic; otherwise, it is not a hot topic. Assuming that topic k_{new} is a hot one, we predict it will become hot at the interval of the Gamma distribution mode in the maximum probability based on the learned *PreWHen* model.

Experimental Evaluation

Data Sets

The data sets are from Meme Tracker[1](Leskovec, Backstrom, and Kleinberg 2009). They consist of a set of (P, Ti, Q), P is the URL which denotes users, Ti is the time point, Q is the text that a user P typed at time point Ti. We extract the data from August 2008 to April 2009. Every month is divided into 90 time windows and the length of every time window is 8 hours.

We extract the news topic from a website [2], and keywords reflecting different topics are extracted. If text Q involves keywords that reflect a specific topic k_i by user P, we consider that P talks about k_i at the corresponding time point Ti. For every month, we extract 15 news topics and corresponding keywords for every topic. We count the frequency of every topic that is involved by users for 90 time windows and observe whether these topics are hot. The total number of topics extracted is 120.

Performance Evaluation for PreWHether

The percentage of hot topics for different hot topic thresholds is shown in Figure 2. We see the percentage of hot topics decrease with the increase of the hot topic threshold α. Assuming the percentage of hot topics is between 20% and 50%, we select 800, 1100 and 1400 as the values of the hot topic threshold α.

[1]http://snap.stanford.edu/data/memetracker9.html

[2]http://www.infoplease.com

Table 1: The mean of Precision, Recall and F1-Measure with hot topic threshold $\alpha = 800$

	M-Precision	M-Recall	M-F1-Measure
3→1	0.5510	0.7026	0.6176
4→1	0.6282	0.7831	0.6971
5→1	0.6722	0.8958	0.7680
6→1	0.6566	0.9444	0.7746
7→1	0.6350	0.9167	0.7503

Baseline Methods. The existing algorithms in recommendation systems, topic modeling, and time series can be used to handle the whether and when problems discussed in this paper. As our proposed approach is based on time series analysis, we compare our method with the following methods of predicting whether a topic will become hot:

Naive: Recommended the top 20 per cent of topics to users as hot topics based on the sum of frequency observed in 9 time windows of topics which have user involvement from the emergence of these topics.

Ar: Autoregressive (AR(4)) model is used to predict the topic frequency of the 10-th time window from its emergence. The top 20 percent topics are regarded as hot based on the values pedicted by the AR(4) model. We used the same three features for the *PreWHether* model to train the AR model.

Regre-3: Polynomial regression model with degree 3 is used to model the topic frequency of the observed 9 time windows from emergence. In this model, a topic is judged to be hot or not in a step by step process until the answer is obtained.

Evaluation Metrics. We evaluate the proposed method in terms of Precision, Recall and F1-Measure, and compare it with the baseline methods to validate the effectiveness of the proposed method.

We have 9 months' topics in total. Let $\alpha = 800$. Topics of 7 months are treated as the training set to predict the next month's topics. First, we use the data set of the first to the seventh month as the training set to predict the eighth month's topics and compute Precision, Recall, and F1-Measure. Then the data set of the second to eighth month is used as the training set to predict the ninth month's topics and compute Precision, Recall, and F1-Measure. Last, we separately calculate the mean of Precision, Recall, and F1-Measure. In our experiment, the topic data of 3 months, 4 months, 5 months and 6 months respectively is used as a training set to predict the corresponding next month's topics, and we obtain similar results. The experiment results are shown in Table 1, and M-Precision, M-Recall and M-F1-Measure denote the mean of Precision, Recall, and F1-Measure respectively. 7→1 means that the topic data of 7 months is used as a training set to predict the next month's topics. The meanings of 3→1, 4→1, 5→1 and 6→1 are similar to the 7→1. Table 1 shows that the M-F1-Measure increases and the M-F1-Measure of 5→1 almost equals to that of 6→1 and 7→1. We therefore execute the next experiment under the condition of 5→1. Let $\alpha = 800$, we use the *PreWHether* model to predict the sixth, seventh,

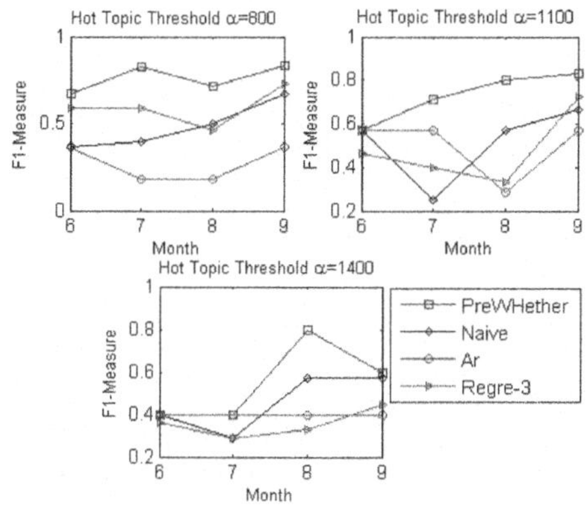

Figure 3: The performance evaluation for *PreWHether* and baseline methods

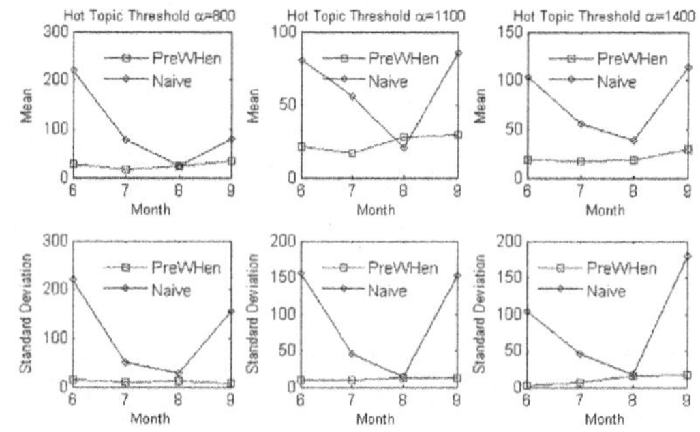

Figure 4: The performance evaluation for *PreWHen* against baseline methods

eighth and ninth month topics based on the previous five months of topic data and compute the corresponding Precision, Recall, and F1-Measure for each predicted month. Baseline methods are also used to predict the sixth, seventh, eighth and ninth month topics and we obtain the corresponding Precision, Recall and F1-Measure. The experiments of $\alpha = 1100, 1400$ are similar to $\alpha = 800$. Figure 3 shows the prediction performance of different approaches based on the three different hot topic thresholds α with the following observations. Due to the page limitation, we only report the performance of F1-Measure here in Figure 3. The month in the x-axis of Figure 3 is the ground-truth month value.

Performance Comparison. We can see that our model *PreWHether* consistently achieves better performance than the baseline methods. In terms of F1-Measure, *PreWHether* achieves more than +60% with $\alpha = 800, 1100$. Even though the number of hot topics in the training dataset is fewer when $\alpha = 1400$, our method still mostly achieves an F1-Measure of +40%. Given the experiments shown in Figure 3, not all baselines do not work better than the proposed method in all cases. The Naive and Ar methods depend on only one metric of the past few frequency values of a single series to address Problem 1. The series of hot topic frequency discussed by users does not change periodically through time and the observed data is very limited. As a result, these methods cannot achieve a better prediction for Problem 1. Regre-3 may have a good fit to a set of past data, but it is not the most useful model for predicting future values. Fitting past values and forecasting future values are two quite different things. The regression models do not work well for solving Problem 1. The hot topic trends of one month are related to hot topic patterns of several previous months, and our approach incorporates the information of hot topic patterns of several previous months to mine more effective hot topic patterns. In summary, our model effectively makes better predictions than the baseline approaches.

Performance Evaluation for PreWHen

Evaluation Metrics. Given a hot monthly topic, we separately forecast the time window in which this topic will become hot by our method and the Naive method, the deviation between the predicted value and true value is then obtained. We forecast all hot topics of one month, and use the Mean and Standard Deviation of these deviations to evaluate the performance of *PreWHen* against the Naive method.

Certain models require step by step judgement until the time window for a hot topic is achieved. Therefore, we do not use these models to tackle Problem 2.

Let $\alpha = 800$, we use *PreWHen* and the Naive method respectively to predict when topics of the sixth month become hot, and compute the corresponding Mean and Standard Deviation, likewise for the seventh, eighth and ninth months. Both methods are separately tested based on patterns of the previous five months of hot topics and the rise rate of the observed frequency in 9 time windows of each hot topic. The experiments of $\alpha = 1100, 1400$ are similar to $\alpha = 800$. Figure 4 shows the prediction performance of two approaches on three different hot topic thresholds α.

Performance Comparison. Our method *PreWHen* consistently achieves better performance. In terms of Mean, the average deviation of our method is smaller than the baseline method by fifty. In terms of Standard Deviation, our approach fluctuates a little, while the Naive method fluctuates much more than ours. The baseline method works well in predicting hot topics of the eighth month. This is because the average rise rate of frequency of these hot topics tends to be smooth, whereas such a case seldom appears. The proposed method provides effective answers for Problem 2.

Conclusions

In this paper, we discuss two practical but challenging issues, i.e., forecasting whether and when a topic will become a hot topic in a social network. Limited existing research can be directly applied to address these problems, due to the uncertainty and restricted information from the related data characteristics and the involvement of the community in a network. In this paper, a generic probabilistic framework has been presented to discover a hot topic evolution pattern for the effective prediction of the topic prevalence. Two effective probabilistic models, *PreWHether* and *PreWHen*, have been learned to solve the proposed problems. Substantial experiments on real datasets show that our method outperforms the baselines and makes much better predictions.

Acknowledgments

This research was supported by the Project 61170091 supported by National Natural Science Foundation of China and the Australian Research Council Future Fellowship FT130100746.

References

Agarwal, D.; Chen, B.-C.; and Elango, P. 2009. Spatio-temporal models for estimating click-through rate. In *WWW*, 21–30.

Blei, D. M., and Lafferty, J. D. 2006. Dynamic topic models. In *ICML*, 113–120.

Box, G. E. P., and Jenkins, G. 1990. *Time Series Analysis, Forecasting and Control*. San Francisco, CA: Holden-Day, Incorporated.

Brillinger, D. R. 1981. *Time series : data analysis and theory*. San Francisco, CA: Holden-Day.

Brockwell, P., and Davis, R. 2002. *Introduction to Time Series and Forecasting*. New York: Springer.

Chen, Y.; Dong, G.; Han, J.; Wah, B. W.; and Wang, J. 2002. Multi-dimensional regression analysis of time-series data streams. In *VLDB*, 323–334.

Gershenfeld, N. A. 1999. *The Nature of Mathematical Modeling*. Cambridge: Cambridge University Press.

Hewitt, E., and Stromberg, K. 1965. *Real and abstract analysis. A modern treatment of the theory of functions of a real variable*. New York: Springer-Verlag.

Jannach, D. 2011. *Recommender systems : an introduction*. New York: Cambridge University Press.

Kawamae, N. 2011. Trend analysis model: trend consists of temporal words, topics, and timestamps. In *WSDM*, 317–326.

Konstan, J. A., and Riedl, J. 2012. Recommender systems: from algorithms to user experience. *User Modeling and User-Adapted Interaction* 22:101–123.

Leskovec, J.; Backstrom, L.; and Kleinberg, J. M. 2009. Meme-tracking and the dynamics of the news cycle. In *KDD*, 497–506.

Madsen, H. 2008. *Time Series Analysis*. London: CRC Press.

Matsubara, Y.; Sakurai, Y.; Faloutsos, C.; Iwata, T.; and Yoshikawa, M. 2012. Fast mining and forecasting of complex time-stamped events. In *KDD*, 271–279.

Matsubara, Y.; Sakurai, Y.; and Yoshikawa, M. 2009. Scalable algorithms for distribution search. In *ICDM*, 347–356.

Palpanas, T.; Vlachos, M.; Keogh, E. J.; Gunopulos, D.; and Truppel, W. 2004. Online amnesic approximation of streaming time series. In *ICDE*, 339–349.

Papadimitriou, S., and Yu, P. S. 2006. Optimal multi-scale patterns in time series streams. In *SIGMOD*, 647–658.

Papadimitriou, S.; Brockwell, A.; and Faloutsos, C. 2004. Adaptive, unsupervised stream mining. *VLDB J.* 13(3):222–239.

Prado, R., and West, M. 2010. *Time Series: Modelling, Computation and Inference*. London: CRC Press.

Sakurai, Y.; Faloutsos, C.; and Yamamuro, M. 2007. Stream monitoring under the time warping distance. In *ICDE*, 1046–1055.

Shi, X.; Zhu, J.; Cai, R.; and Zhang, L. 2009. User grouping behavior in online forums. In *KDD*, 777–786.

Tan, C.; Tang, J.; Sun, J.; Lin, Q.; and Wang, F. 2010. Social action tracking via noise tolerant time-varying factor graphs. In *KDD*, 1049–1058.

Xuerui, W., and Andrew, M. 2006. Topics over time: A non-markov continuous-time model of topical trends. In *KDD*, 424–433.

Content-Based Collaborative Filtering for News Topic Recommendation

Zhongqi Lu[†], **Zhicheng Dou**[*], **Jianxun Lian**[‡], **Xing Xie**[‡] and **Qiang Yang**[†]
[†]Hong Kong University of Science and Technology, Hong Kong
[*]Renmin University of China, Beijing, China
[‡]Microsoft Research, Beijing, China
[†]{zluab, qyang}@cse.ust.hk, [*]dou@ruc.edu.cn, [‡]{v-lianji, xing.xie}@microsoft.com

Abstract

News recommendation has become a big attraction with which major Web search portals retain their users. Two effective approaches are Content-based Filtering and Collaborative Filtering, each serving a specific recommendation scenario. The Content-based Filtering approaches inspect *rich contexts* of the recommended items, while the Collaborative Filtering approaches predict the interests of *long-tail users* by collaboratively learning from interests of related users. We have observed empirically that, for the problem of news topic displaying, both the rich context of news topics and the long-tail users exist. Therefore, in this paper, we propose a Content-based Collaborative Filtering approach (CCF) to bring both Content-based Filtering and Collaborative Filtering approaches together. We found that combining the two is not an easy task, but the benefits of CCF are impressive. On one hand, CCF makes recommendations based on the rich contexts of the news. On the other hand, CCF collaboratively analyzes the scarce feedbacks from the long-tail users. We tailored this CCF approach for the news topic displaying on the Bing front page and demonstrated great gains in attracting users. In the experiments and analyses part of this paper, we discuss the performance gains and insights in news topic recommendation in Bing.

Introduction

News topic recommendation has been an important attraction offered by many major web portals, such as Yahoo! (*www.yahoo.com*), Excite (*www.excite.com*), MSN (*www.msn.com*), Bing (*www.bing.com*) and AOL (*www.aol.com*). News displaying provides an important service that can help keeping the users on the portals. Therefore, it is important for these search portals to understand users' interests and display the "right" news at the right time.

Brute-force recommendation methods such as expert edited rules had been adopted traditionally (Bobadilla et al. 2013), but had shown poor performance due to two major challenges. The first and traditional challenge is that users often prefer to view new items. When a piece of news is just emerging, the recommender system may find it hard to tell whether users are interested in it or not, as the topic may not be in the users' history. A typical solution is Content-based Filtering, where the contents of the news are analyzed before presented to the users. When the users have sufficient news reading records, Content-based Filtering approaches can usually perform well. The second major challenge is due to the scarce clicking feedbacks from users. Because news reading usually may not be the main functions for the web portals, users do not intend to see the news at these portals, even though the news may be of interest to them. A solution to this problem lies in the fact that there are always users who read some news, and these users may serve as a basis to help to predict the interests of the long-tail users. This intuition leads to the Collaborative Filtering approach.

Web search portals are starting to recognize the importance of news topic recommendation, where both previously mentioned challenges exist. We propose to bring both Content-based Filtering approach and Collaborative Filtering approach together to make recommendations. Intuitively, the key to both approaches is to find similarities and do clustering implicitly. Content-based Filtering approach relies on the similarity of contexts and clusters the items, while Collaborative Filtering approach finds similarity in user-item links and clusters the links. A difficulty is that these two kinds of similarities are measured under absolutely different scales and cannot be simply summed up.

In this paper, we propose to combine both similarities by a neighborhood model. Specifically, from the contexts of news, we obtain similarity between items. In the optimization phase, we cluster the user-item links by jointly considering the similarity between items. In our proposed model, we combine both advantages of the Content-based Filtering approach and the Collaborative Filtering approach. We present a kernel to capture the contextual information in the news and then integrate the kernel into a Collaborative Filtering framework. On one hand, the proposed model tries to understand the emerging news by learning the contextual meanings. On the other hand, by clustering with the similarity of the user-item links, the long-tail users are properly handled.

In the following, we start by discussing the related works. Then we introduce some preliminary notations and frameworks. We illustrate the motivation by presenting a unique Bing news topic recommendation setting, and then propose our Content-based Collaborative Filtering (CCF) approach, focusing on the two previously mentioned challenges. Finally, we demonstrate the experimental results on the Bing

[*]Corresponding author

portal and discuss our insights from the application.

Related Works

This paper proposed Content-based Collaborative Filtering to recommend news for users. In particular, we would like to use both the contexts of news and the interests of related users to predict a user's news reading interests, so that the proper piece of news could be recommended. The work is mostly related to content based recommendation, collaborative filtering and implicit feedbacks.

Collaborative Filtering is an approach of making automatic prediction (filtering) about the interests of a user by collecting interests from many related users (collaborating). Some of the best results are obtained based on matrix factorization techniques (Marlin 2003; Koren, Bell, and Volinsky 2009; Singh and Gordon 2008). Collaborative Filtering methods are usually adopted when the historical records for training are scarce.

Content-based Filtering Content-based recommender systems try to recommend items similar to those a given user has liked in the past(Lops, De Gemmis, and Semeraro 2011). The common approach is to represent both the users and the items under the same feature space. Then similarity scores could be computed between users and items. The recommendation is made based on the similarity scores of a user towards all the items. The Content-based Filtering methods usually perform well when users have plenty of historical records for learning.

Hybrid of CF and Content-based Filtering As a first attempt to unify Collaborative Filtering and Content-based Filtering, (Basilico and Hofmann 2004) proposed to learn a kernel or similarity function between the user-item pairs that allows simultaneous generalization across either user or item dimensions. This approach would do well when the user-item rating matrix is dense (e.g. 6% as reported by (Basilico and Hofmann 2004)). However in most current recommender system settings, the data are rather sparse, which would make this method fail.

The uses of item contents to help the recommendation tasks are widely adopted in various recommendation settings recently. (San Pedro and Karatzoglou 2014) proposed to extend the supervised Latent Dirichlet Allocation model to model expertise in collaborative question answering communities with application to question recommendation. (Liu et al. 2014) proposed to augment item features by a virtual profile based on observed user-item interactions in LinkedIn. As far as we are concerned, our work is the pioneer to retrieve the rich contexts as recommended items to users.

Implicit Feedback is originated from the area of information retrieval and the related techniques have been successfully applied in the domain of recommender systems (Kelly and Teevan 2003; Rendle et al. 2009; Koren 2008; Oard, Kim, and others 1998). The implicit feedbacks are usually inferred from user behaviors, such as browsing items, marking items as favourite, etc. Intuitively, the implicit feedback approach is based on the assumption that the implicit feedbacks could be used to regularize or supplement the explicit training data. From this point of view, our work proposes an effective implicit feedback for the recommender systems during the sale events.

News Recommendation News Recommendation is an application of recommender system techniques and/or Natural Language Processing(NLP) techniques. As a popular service and an important application to retain users, the industry puts much efforts in News Recommendation researches (Das et al. 2007; Li et al. 2010). The initial attempts (Mittermayer and Knolmayer 2006) are NLP oriented. Some works (Kompan and Bieliková 2010) adopt the content-based approach. Some (Das et al. 2007) adopt the Collaborative Filtering approach.

Preliminary

Notations

In this section, we first introduce some general notations in this paper. Other specific notations of the proposed method will be further introduced in the subsequent sections. We adopt special indexing letters for distinguishing users from items: For users, we use u, v; For news items, we use i, j. The set of users is denoted by U, while the set of the news items is denoted by I. A rating r_{ui} indicates the preferences by user u of news item i, where higher values mean stronger preferences. The observed value for the user u over item i, i.e. (u, i), is represented as r_{ui}, and the predicted value is represented as $\hat{r}_{ui}$. We use the superscript $^\top$ to denote the transport of a matrix.

Latent Factor Models

Latent factor models comprise an important approach to Collaborative Filtering. A major advantage of the latent factor models is to tackle the data sparseness issue. We will focus on the models that are induced by the Singular Value Decomposition (SVD) on the user-item preference matrix. A typical model associates each user u with a user-factor vector p_u, and each item i with an item-factor vector q_i. The prediction is given by

$$\hat{r}_{ui} = b_{ui} + p_u^\top q_i$$

where b_{ui} denotes a baseline estimate for an unknown rating r_{ui}:

$$b_{ui} = \mu + b_u + b_i$$

and μ is the overall average rating, b_u and b_i indicate the observed deviations of user u and item i, respectively.

Neighborhood Models

The neighborhood models estimate unknown ratings based on recorded ratings of either like-minded users or similar items. While the neighbor selection could be either item-oriented or user-oriented, in our work, we focus on an item-oriented method. The user-oriented method could be derived in a similar way. As suggested by (Koren 2008), we model the latent factors of an item i by its neighbors $N(\theta, i)$, based on the similarity measure θ. Specifically, $N(\theta, i)$ could be a neighborhood selection function, which returns the neighbors of i when their similarity measured by θ exceeds certain

Figure 1: Front page of Bing in the U.S. market, the bottom of which is used for news topic recommendation.

boundary. The prediction is given by

$$\hat{r}_{ui} = b_{ui} + p_u^\top (q_i + \mid N(\theta, i) \mid^{-\frac{1}{2}} \sum_{j \in N(\theta,i)} \theta_{ij} y_j) \quad (1)$$

where the term $q_i + \mid N(\theta, i) \mid^{-\frac{1}{2}} \sum_{j \in N(\theta,i)} \theta_{ij} y_j$ is defined as the latent factors of an item i, y_j is another set of latent factors to describe the neighbor items of i, and θ_{ij} is the interpolation weights to measure the similarity between the item i and j.

News Topic Recommendation

Bing Search and News Reading

While providing the web search function, the Bing[1] also makes news topic recommendations in the bottom of the webpage. Figure 1 demonstrates a snapshot for the front page of Bing. As we could see in the snapshot, each piece of news is represented by a few keywords decorated by a picture, which are chosen by the human editors as a summary of the news. When clicking, the users will be leaded to a search result page, where the queries are the keywords about the news.

From our statistics, more than half of the recommended news topics will be replaced the next day. Therefore, the recommendation of news is challenged by the cold start issue. However the cold start issues about the news may not affect human readers. Although the news is emerging from time to time, users could have a big picture in mind about the briefing (and/or the backgrounds) of the news by reading the keywords for the news. This big picture is instantiated by the documents in the search result page. A proper recommender system should also take this big picture into consideration when making recommendations.

[1]The news topic recommendation function is currently only available in the U.S. market - http://www.bing.com/?mkt=en-us

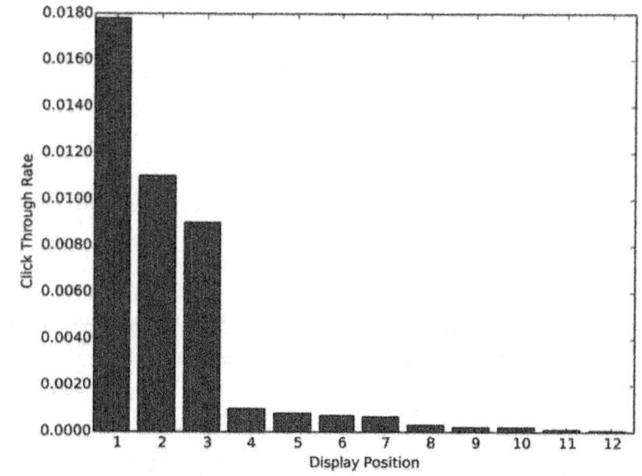

Figure 2: Click Through Rate (CTR) for different positions in news topic recommendation.

Data Analysis of News Reading at Bing

In order to make proper news topic recommendations, we first conduct the data analysis in the news reading settings. We sampled $30,000$ users in Bing and randomly provided news topic recommendations to them in a time span of 5 days, so that the users' feedbacks truly reflect the user's preferences, without the affects of display positions or news rankings etc.

From the statistics, we found the average visit per user of the front page of Bing is less than 1.5 in a day, while the average Click Through Rate (CTR) for any news items is 0.007. Empirically, this indicates that the collected data may not be able to construct traditional recommendation models effectively, due to the sparseness of training data.

Further, we investigate the CTR on different positions. In Figure 1, we have already demonstrated the layout of the news displays. Starting from the left most news item, we mark its position as 1 and the rest of the positions are marked in order. Then we calculate the CTR for each of the positions. The statistics is shown in Figure 2. Because the news items are randomly presented to the users in each position, the content in each position shall not be biased. We found the left most position have the highest CTR. Besides, most of the click behaviours happen in the left three positions. This indicates that the position bias exists in the news topic recommendation of Bing, as it is in the Web search (Craswell et al. 2008).

In order to better serve the users, we would like them to see and click on the news of their concerns. Based on the above observations, it is desirable to place the most interested news on the left most position, while the displays of news in other positions may not be much important. For the ease of experiments and evaluations, we set our objective of recommendation in this work as recommending the most interesting news to users in the left most position.

Content-based Collaborative Filtering Approach

In the following, we describe our proposed method for making news topic recommendations based on both the rich contexts and the collaborative filtering.

Based on the neighborhood models as described in Section *Neighborhood Models*, we derive the collaborative approach. The prediction of user u's interests on an item i is given by

$$\hat{r}_{ui} = b_{ui} + p_u^\top (q_i + \eta) \tag{2}$$

where $b_{ui} = \mu + b_u + b_i$, $\eta = \mid N(\theta, i) \mid^{-\frac{1}{2}} \sum_{j \in N(\theta,i)} \theta_{ji} y_j$. In general, θ is the similarity measure between two items. Under the Bing news topics recommendation setting, θ measures the similarity between two rich bodies of contexts (two sets of documents), which should consider both the semantics and the word frequencies. Fisher kernel would be a desirable choice of such measure. We will discuss the details about this measure of similarity between queries in the next section.

Now we propose to model the latent feature of item i as $q_i + \mid N(\theta, i) \mid^{-\frac{1}{2}} \sum_{j \in N(\theta,i)} \theta_{ji} y_j$. We use the item vector q_i to represent the latent feature from the item i itself, and the latent feature vector is complemented by a weighted sum $\mid N(\theta, i) \mid^{-\frac{1}{2}} \sum_{j \in N(\theta,i)} \theta_{ji} y_j$, which describes the item i by the latent features of those items from general search logs.

The model parameters associated with the prediction rule in 2 are learnt by solving the regularized least squares problem

$$\begin{aligned} \min_{b_\star, p_\star, q_\star, y_\star} \quad \sum\nolimits_{(u,i)} \quad & \Big(\big(r_{ui} - \mu - b_u - b_i - p_u^\top (q_i + \eta)\big)^2 \\ & + \lambda_1 b_u^2 + \lambda_2 b_i^2 + \lambda_3 \|p_u\|^2 + \lambda_4 \|q_i\|^2 \\ & + \lambda_5 \sum_{j \in N(\theta,i)} \|y_j\|^2 \Big) \end{aligned} \tag{3}$$

where $\lambda_\star$ are regularization constants.

We estimate the model parameters by minimizing the regularized squared error function through stochastic gradient descent. To ease the presentation, we define $e_u i = r_u i - \hat{r}_u i$. We randomly shuffle the user-item pairs in the training set κ and loop over κ to update the parameters. For a particular user-item pair (u, i), we update the parameters by moving in the opposite direction of the gradient, yielding:

$$\begin{aligned} b_u &\leftarrow b_u + \gamma_1 (e_{ui} - \lambda_1 b_u) \\ b_i &\leftarrow b_i + \gamma_2 (e_{ui} - \lambda_2 b_i) \\ p_u &\leftarrow p_u + \gamma_3 (e_{ui}(q_i + \eta) - \lambda_3 p_u) \\ q_i &\leftarrow q_i + \gamma_4 (e_{ui} p_u - \lambda_4 q_i) \\ \forall j &\in h(A, i): \\ y_j &\leftarrow y_j + \gamma_5 (e_{ui} p_u \mid N(\theta, i) \mid^{-\frac{1}{2}} \theta_{ji} - \lambda_5 y_j) \end{aligned}$$

where $\gamma_\star$ are constants for the step size.

Measure of similarity between queries θ_{ij}

Since queries are usually very short texts, we adopt a search engine to help understand the similarity between two queries. With the search engine, we first enrich the meaning of the queries with the textual search results, i.e. the documents related to the queries. Then the similarity between two queries is quantified with both the semantic of the documents and the frequencies of their words.

Following the work of (Hofmann 2000), to measure the similarity between two collections of documents, we would like to derive a Fisher kernel function (Jaakkola, Haussler, and others 1999) from the Probabilistic Latent Semantic Analysis (PLSA) model (Hofmann 1999).

Let us consider a collection of documents d_i, and a collection of the words $\{c_n\}$. We define the log-probability of d_i by the probability of all the word occurrences in d_i normalized by length of the document set

$$l(d_i) = \sum_n [\hat{P}(c_n \mid d_i) log \sum_k P(c_n \mid z_k) P(z_k \mid d_i)] \tag{4}$$

where z_k is the latent features, $\hat{P}(c_n \mid d_i) = \frac{COUNT(d_i, c_n)}{\sum_m COUNT(d_i, c_m)}$. Notice that by defining $l(d_i)$ as in Eq.4, $l(d_i)$ is directly correlated to the Kullback-Leibler divergence between the empirical distribution $\hat{P}(c_n \mid d_i)$ and the distribution from PLSA model.

In order to derive the Fisher Kernel, we compute the Fisher information and Fisher scores. By the definition, the Fisher score $u(d_i; \theta)$ is set to be the gradient of $l(d_i)$ with respect to θ. For simplicity, we make the same assumption as in (Hofmann 2000) that the Fisher information matrix approximates to the identity matrix. Above all, the Fisher Kernel of two sets of documents d_i and d_j with respect to the parameter set θ is given by

$$\mathcal{K}(d_i, d_j) = \langle u(d_i; \theta), u(d_j; \theta) \rangle \tag{5}$$

where $\langle \cdot, \cdot \rangle$ denotes the inner product operator. Notice that we have two choices for the parameter sets, i.e. $P(z_k)$ and $P(c_n \mid z_k)$. Due to the limits of spaces, we omit the detailed derivation of the gradients and present the results. The similarity measure due to the parameters $P(z_k)$ is given by

$$\mathcal{K}_1(d_i, d_j) = \sum_k \frac{P(z_k \mid d_i) P(z_k \mid d_j)}{P(z_k)} \tag{6}$$

And the similarity measure due to the parameters $P(c_n \mid z_k)$ is given by

$$\begin{aligned} &\mathcal{K}_2(d_i, d_j) = \\ &\sum_n [\hat{P}(c_n \mid d_i) \hat{P}(c_n \mid d_j) \sum_k \frac{P(z_k \mid d_i, c_n) P(z_k \mid d_j, c_n)}{P(c_n \mid z_k)}] \end{aligned} \tag{7}$$

where $P(z_k \mid d_i)$, $P(z_k)$, $P(z_k \mid d_i, c_n)$ and $P(c_n \mid z_k)$ are obtained from the estimation of the PLSA model in (Hofmann 1999).

The $\mathcal{K}_1$ kernel computes a "semantic" overlap between the two queries via the analysis of two sets of documents, while the $\mathcal{K}_2$ kernel handles the empirical word distributions. We sum the outputs of both measures to produce the similarity θ_{ij}:

$$\theta_{ij} = \rho \mathcal{K}_1(d_i, d_j) + (1 - \rho)\mathcal{K}_2(d_i, d_j) \quad (8)$$

where ρ is the weighting constant to balance the "semantic" overlap and the empirical word distributions when calculating the similarity. And the subscripts i, j is used to index the news items, i.e. $i, j \in I$ and I denotes the index set of the news topics.

External Search Queries as Auxiliary Data

As discussed in a previous section , because of the limited number of view and click behaviours, it would be helpful to use some auxiliary data to help building the links between different pieces of news.

From Bing search, we have plenty of external queries and their search results. In the settings of Bing news topic recommendation as we have discussed, we are presenting news topic recommendations in a format of search result, and a recommendation algorithm is proposed based on the analyzing of search results. Therefore, it is natural to integrate the external search queries and their search results into our proposed model.

As a preliminary attempt to extend our proposed model, we augment the learning of θ. In the previous section, θ is learned to measure the similarity between two queries in the news set I. We introduce the external search query set I', so that θ is learned based on both I and I'. Formally from Equation 8, we obtain θ_{ij}, where $i, j \in \{I, I'\}$. Then this larger θ is used in our previous model.

Experiments

Experimental Settings

In the experiments, we are applying our CCF approach on the Bing news reading dataset. To collect for the dataset, we sampled $30,000$ users. In order to eliminate the bias of position as mentioned in Section *Data Analysis in News Reading at Bing*, we randomly displayed news to these users in the period of data collection. The data collections lasted for 5 days. During the data collection, there are 183 pieces of news displayed on the front page of Bing. We retrieved at least 8 documents for each of the news from Bing search engine and in total there are 1793 documents. To train the model, we adopt the data in the first 3 days. And to test, we use the data in the rest 2 days.

As we have discussed in Section *Data Analysis in News Reading at Bing*, improving the overall users' experiences is equivalent to refining users' satisfaction on the left most position for news display, which is also adopted in the previous news topic recommendation researches (Li et al. 2010). Therefore, in the experiments, we focus on the feedbacks from the left most position.

Performance Comparisons

As discussed previously, to measure the performance, we use the "root-mean-square error" (RMSE) on the left most position of the news displays as the evaluation matric throughout the experiments:

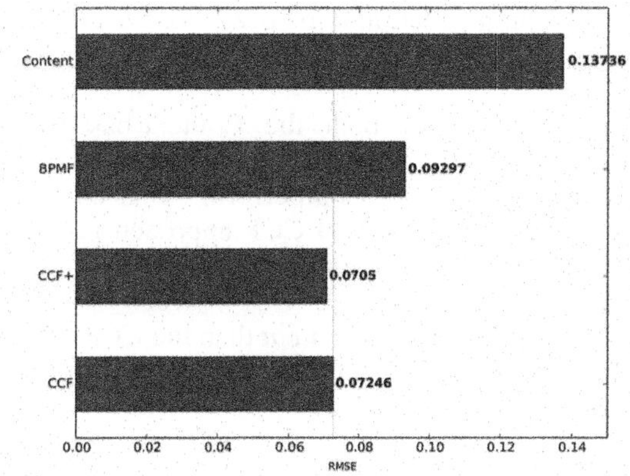

Figure 3: Performance comparison for different recommendation methods.

$$RMSE = \sqrt{\sum_{u=1}^{m}\sum_{i=1}^{n} I_{ui}(\mathbf{R}_{ui} - \hat{\mathbf{R}}_{ui})^2 / \mid I \mid}$$

where $\mathbf{R}_{ui}$ and $\hat{\mathbf{R}}_{ui}$ represent the true and the predicted values for the user-item scores respectively. I_{ui} is the indicator function which is equal to 1 if user u browsed item i, and 0 otherwise. In our settings, the RMSE indicates the difference between users' true interests towards the news in the left most position and the predicted ones. The smaller RMSE means better performance of the method.

Other than *CCF*, we compare with the following methods:

- *BPMF* (Salakhutdinov and Mnih 2008). BPMF is a classical Collaborative Filtering approach, using fully Baysian treatment of the Probabilistic Matrix Factorization. It is generally considered to be one of the most effective method when the training data is sparse.
- *Content* As surveyed by (Lops, De Gemmis, and Semeraro 2011), the most effective content-based document recommendation method calculate the document similarity based on both the keyword-based vector space model and the semantic analysis. In our experiments, we use the similarity measure θ, as described in a previous section. This could be considered as an effective Content-based Filtering method.
- *CCF+* We use *CCF+* to denote the extension of the CCF approach, which is discussed in Section *External Search Queries as Auxiliary Data.* These external contents come from the Bing general search. They includes about 1000 general search queries and the resulting documents.

The comparison is shown in Figure 3. Because there are much more negative training samples (exposed but not clicked) than the positive samples in the dataset, the absolute value of RMSE is not very meaningful. As a dummy baseline under the measure of RMSE, we report the RMSE for random recommendation to be 0.20736. We are expecting the relative decreasing of RMSE for a more effective method.

As a combination of both the Content-based Filtering approach and the Collaborative Filtering approach, the *CCF/CCF+* approaches outperform. This empirically demonstrates that our proposed CCF approach is effective in the Bing news topic recommendation settings. Besides, the extended CCF approach, i.e. *CCF+*, leads to more improvements over *BPMF* and *Content* than the *CCF* does. We will further discuss this observation together with another finding in the following sections.

Effectiveness of Contents

We inspect the effectiveness of the contents in helping the Content-based Collaborative Filtering. The results are shown in Figure 4. In figure 4, the x-axis represents number of average resulting documents returned from search. The y-axis represents the RMSE value. For BPMF, it is a pure CF method and does not use search results as inputs. For Content, we use all available search results as inputs. Therefore, for both BPMF and Content methods, which are discussed in Section *Performance Comparisons*, the values in y-axis are constant. However, as a variation of Content method, we use different numbers of documents for each piece of news when learning the similarity between the news. With the increasing number of documents for each piece of news, better results are achieved, as expected. In the extreme case when the number of documents equals zero, the recommendation becomes random.

For the CCF methods, we use different numbers of documents for each piece of news when learning the θ. When the number of documents equals zero, the CCF method reduces to a Collaborative Filtering one, which has similar performance with *BPMF*. Besides, with the increasing number of documents for each piece of news, there is a trend of constant decreasing of RMSE for *CCF*. Due to the system limitations, we kept a limited number of logged documents for each piece of news. But this trend might be served as a good hint for future refinements in the real world applications.

Notice that for the *CCF+*, which uses external contents, we do not report the results of increasing external contents, because the performance gain is not significant in our experiments. There might be some good results when the amount of external contents is increased to the real world scale, i.e. thousands of Terabytes of records, because the general search results might contain the news related documents. However, because this is not the key point of this research and due to lack of the computational power, we would like to save this issue to the future works.

Discussions about Contents in CCF

From Figure 3, we notice that the extended CCF approach, i.e. *CCF+*, leads to more improvements over *BPMF* and *Content* than the *CCF* does. This indicates that the general search queries and resulting documents could be used into the CCF framework, which is an interesting finding. However, from Figure 4 in the experiments of increasing the number of documents for each piece of news, the trend of

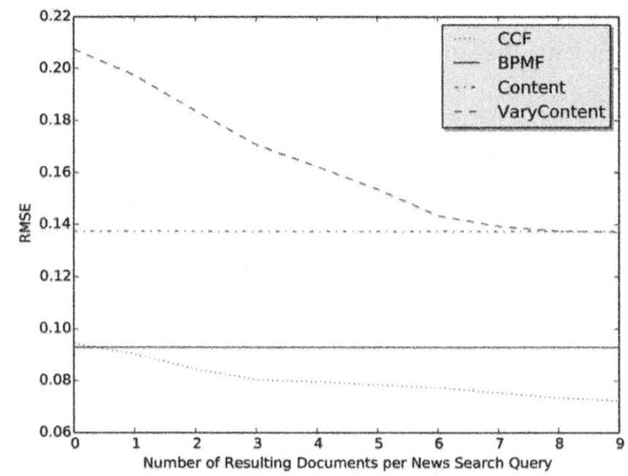

Figure 4: Change the number of news related documents for each piece of news.

performance gain for *CCF* may indicate when larger number of documents for each piece of news is provided, the performance could be further increased. The two observations leads to two possible directions to the future works: either to find good resources to obtain news related documents, or to develop better methods to mine the general search results, which obviously contains much news related documents. Under the framework of CCF, we admit that the performance gain of *CCF+* over *CCF* might be larger, if some methods could be proposed to more effectively transfer the knowledge from the general search queries to the news topic recommendation settings. We hope this preliminary attempts in the CCF framework could inspire future works.

Another concern is that will some noisy contents lead to bad performance in the CCF approaches? For the CCF approach in this work, we use θ to measure the similarity between two pieces of news, and only the similar piece of news shall be used in the CCF methods. As described in Section *Measure of similarity between queries* θ_{ij}, we define kernels to consider both the semantics and the words distributions in measuring the similarity. This similarity checking strategy would ensure no noisy contents would be used in the learning of the CCF models, although the computational complexity might be an issue.

Conclusions

We proposed the Content-based Collaborative Filtering (CCF) approach for the news topic recommendation in Bing. By utilizing the rich contexts and focusing on the long-tail users, the proposed CCF combines both the advantages of Content-based Filtering approach and the features of Collaborative Filtering approach. This CCF is designed for the settings like Bing news topic recommendation, where a piece of news could be interpreted by rich contexts, such as the querying results. We have demonstrated the performance gains of the CCF approaches over the others in our Bing news displaying dataset. Under this CCF framework, we discussed our insights towards the news topic recommendation for today's web portals.

Acknowledgments

The research has been supported in part by China National 973 Project 2014CB340304 and Hong Kong RGC Projects 621013, 620812 and 621211.

References

Basilico, J., and Hofmann, T. 2004. Unifying collaborative and content-based filtering. In *Proceedings of the twenty-first international conference on Machine learning*, 9. ACM.

Bobadilla, J.; Ortega, F.; Hernando, A.; and Gutiérrez, A. 2013. Recommender systems survey. *Knowledge-Based Systems* 46:109–132.

Craswell, N.; Zoeter, O.; Taylor, M.; and Ramsey, B. 2008. An experimental comparison of click position-bias models. In *Proceedings of the 2008 International Conference on Web Search and Data Mining*, 87–94. ACM.

Das, A. S.; Datar, M.; Garg, A.; and Rajaram, S. 2007. Google news personalization: scalable online collaborative filtering. In *Proceedings of the 16th international conference on World Wide Web*, 271–280. ACM.

Hofmann, T. 1999. Probabilistic latent semantic indexing. In *Proceedings of the 22nd annual international ACM SIGIR conference on Research and development in information retrieval*, 50–57. ACM.

Hofmann, T. 2000. Learning the similarity of documents: An information-geometric approach to document retrieval and categorization.

Jaakkola, T.; Haussler, D.; et al. 1999. Exploiting generative models in discriminative classifiers. *Advances in neural information processing systems* 487–493.

Kelly, D., and Teevan, J. 2003. Implicit feedback for inferring user preference: a bibliography. In *ACM SIGIR Forum*, volume 37, 18–28. ACM.

Kompan, M., and Bieliková, M. 2010. Content-based news recommendation. In *E-commerce and web technologies*. Springer. 61–72.

Koren, Y.; Bell, R.; and Volinsky, C. 2009. Matrix factorization techniques for recommender systems. *Computer* 42(8):30–37.

Koren, Y. 2008. Factorization meets the neighborhood: a multifaceted collaborative filtering model. In *Proceedings of the 14th ACM SIGKDD international conference on Knowledge discovery and data mining*, 426–434. ACM.

Li, L.; Chu, W.; Langford, J.; and Schapire, R. E. 2010. A contextual-bandit approach to personalized news article recommendation. In *Proceedings of the 19th international conference on World wide web*, 661–670. ACM.

Liu, H.; Goyal, A.; Walker, T.; and Bhasin, A. 2014. Improving the discriminative power of inferred content information using segmented virtual profile. In *Proceedings of the 8th ACM Conference on Recommender systems*, 97–104. ACM.

Lops, P.; De Gemmis, M.; and Semeraro, G. 2011. Content-based recommender systems: State of the art and trends. In *Recommender systems handbook*. Springer. 73–105.

Marlin, B. M. 2003. Modeling user rating profiles for collaborative filtering. In *NIPS*.

Mittermayer, M.-A., and Knolmayer, G. 2006. *Text mining systems for market response to news: A survey*. Institut für Wirtschaftsinformatik der Universität Bern.

Oard, D. W.; Kim, J.; et al. 1998. Implicit feedback for recommender systems. In *Proceedings of the AAAI workshop on recommender systems*, 81–83. Wollongong.

Rendle, S.; Freudenthaler, C.; Gantner, Z.; and Schmidt-Thieme, L. 2009. Bpr: Bayesian personalized ranking from implicit feedback. In *Proceedings of the Twenty-Fifth Conference on Uncertainty in Artificial Intelligence*, 452–461. AUAI Press.

Salakhutdinov, R., and Mnih, A. 2008. Bayesian probabilistic matrix factorization using markov chain monte carlo. In *Proceedings of the 25th international conference on Machine learning*, 880–887. ACM.

San Pedro, J., and Karatzoglou, A. 2014. Question recommendation for collaborative question answering systems with rankslda. In *Proceedings of the 8th ACM Conference on Recommender systems*, 193–200. ACM.

Singh, A. P., and Gordon, G. J. 2008. Relational learning via collective matrix factorization. In *Proceedings of the 14th ACM SIGKDD international conference on Knowledge discovery and data mining*, 650–658. ACM.

Proceedings of the Twenty-Ninth AAAI Conference on Artificial Intelligence

A Tri-Role Topic Model for Domain-Specific Question Answering

Zongyang Ma Aixin Sun Quan Yuan Gao Cong
School of Computer Engineering, Nanyang Technological University, Singapore 639798
{zma4, qyuan1}@e.ntu.edu.sg {axsun, gaocong}@ntu.edu.sg

Abstract

Stack Overflow and MedHelp are examples of domain-specific community-based question answering (CQA) systems. Different from CQA systems for general topics (*e.g.*, Yahoo! Answers, Baidu Knows), questions and answers in domain-specific CQA systems are mostly in the same topical domain, enabling more comprehensive interaction between users on fine-grained topics. In such systems, users are more likely to ask questions on unfamiliar topics and to answer questions matching their expertise. Users can also vote answers based on their judgements. In this paper, we propose a Tri-Role Topic Model (TRTM) to model the tri-roles of users (*i.e.*, as askers, answerers, and voters, respectively) and the activities of each role including composing question, selecting question to answer, contributing and voting answers. The proposed model can be used to enhance CQA systems from many perspectives. As a case study, we conducted experiments on ranking answers for questions on Stack Overflow, a CQA system for professional and enthusiast programmers. Experimental results show that TRTM is effective in facilitating users getting ideal rankings of answers, particularly for new and less popular questions. Evaluated on nDCG, TRTM outperforms state-of-the-art methods.

Introduction

In community-based question answering (CQA) systems for general topics (*e.g.*, Yahoo! Answers, Baidu Knows), users may ask questions of any topic, *e.g.*, "*What is Paris famous for?*". To answer this question, no much professional knowledge is needed. In domain-specific CQA systems (*e.g.*, Stack Overflow, MedHelp), professional knowledge is required to answer questions like "*How does ruby on rails handle requests?*" from Stack Overflow, and "*How do I know when skipped heart beats are dangerous?*" from MedHelp. While a lot of studies have been carried out on CQA for general topics (Xu, Ji, and Wang 2012; Li, Shen, and Grant 2012; Dror et al. 2011). There are limited studies on domain-specific CQA systems.

Domain-specific CQA systems have recently attracted a lot of users and accumulated a large number of domain-specific questions and answers. For example, Stack Overflow, for professional and enthusiast programmers, has over 2 million registered users and more than 7 million questions as at Apr 2014, according to Wikipedia. Users who have questions which require professional knowledge are more likely to source for help in domain-specific CQA systems, because these systems enable comprehensive interaction between users on fine-grained domain-specific topics. However, there is a lack of study on the formal modeling of users' activities in a unified framework. In this study, we consider and model users' activities with their tri-roles (*i.e.*, *asker*, *answerer*, and *voter*) in a probabilistic framework at topic level. A topic-level modeling for users' activities benefits many applications in CQA such as ranking answers for questions, and expert finding.

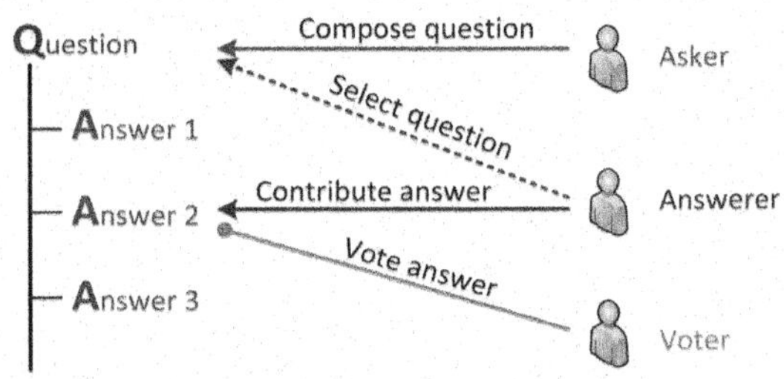

Figure 1: The tri-roles of a user and the activities

Illustrated in Figure 1, in a typical domain-specific CQA system like Stack Overflow, users may perform activities as three roles.

- **Asker**. To ask a question of unfamiliar topics, a user composes the question and waits for answers to this question.
- **Answerer**. If a user believes that she has the knowledge to answer this question, she contributes an answer. Note that, there is an *implicit* question selection activity where an answerer performs a self-assessment whether she has the knowledge to answer this question. The question selection activity is indicated by the dotted line in Figure 1.
- **Voter**. In CQA systems, users are often allowed to vote for the answers to a question, based on their judgements.

Note that, a user may perform the three roles (*i.e.*, asker, answerer, or voter) simultaneously across different questions in a CQA system.

In this paper, we propose a probabilistic Tri-Role Topic Modeling (TRTM) which makes use of the three roles of users for modeling users' activities and for mining fine-grained topics in domain-specific CQA systems. Our model is an extension of Probabilistic Latent Semantic Analysis (PLSA), which assumes that each document has a mixture of topics and each word of the document is sampled from its related topic (Hofmann 1999). Here, a document can be a question or an answer.

As aforementioned, a user composes questions in her unfamiliar topics, and contributes answers if she believes that she has the right knowledge. Users also vote positively for answers that well address the questions. We therefore argue that the topic distributions of the asker role and the answerer role of the same user could be very different (*e.g.*, unfamiliar topics vs familiar topics). Moreover, if an answer receives a large number of positive votes, then the answer is believed to be of similar topic distribution with the question. TRTM therefore assigns each user an asker role and an answerer role; each role has its own topic distribution. TRTM also implicitly models the voter role of users, which has no explicit topic distributions but contributes to constraining topical matching between questions and answerers. As the result, TRTM generates not only topic distributions of questions and answers, but also topic distributions of askers and answerers. TRTM makes three assumptions: (1) An asker and all the questions composed by her share similar topic distributions; (2) An answerer and all the answers contributed by her share similar topic distributions; and (3) An answerer's topic distribution is more similar to that of the questions answered by her, if her answers to these questions receive many positive votes.

To evaluate the effectiveness of our model, we apply TRTM to the application of ranking answers for questions. A popular question may receive many answers within a short period. The task of ranking answers is to rank the best answers to top positions before waiting for users' votes as the latter might take a long time. TRTM outperforms two state-of-the-art baselines on real data collected from Stack Overflow on this task. TRTM can also be utilized in many applications such as expert finding and similar question searching.

Related Work

We briefly overview the studies on Stack Overflow, and then survey topic models on CQA systems.

Stack Overflow. Anderson *et al.* (2012) found that in Stack Overflow, expert users are likely to answer questions more quickly, and a higher activity level of a question benefits all answerers of this question to increase their reputation level. Based on some extracted features from Stack Overflow, they attempted to predict the long-term value of a question and whether a question has been sufficiently answered. Their results show that votes indicate a user's expertise level on a specific topic. This is consistent with the modeling of votes in our proposed TRTM. Subsequently, Anderson *et al.* (2013) observed that badge mechanism in Stack Overflow steers users to increase their participation in answering questions. Question deletion in Stack Overflow was studied in (Correa and Sureka 2014), where 47 features were used to predict whether a question will be deleted. The quality of question content is found to be the main factor.

Dalip *et al.* (2013) proposed to rank answers of a question in Stack Overflow using Learning to Rank (L2R), a supervised approach. The L2R model is learned from the feature vector representations of question-answer pairs. Each pair is represented by features in 8 groups (*e.g.*, user features, structure features, style features). Answers of new coming questions are then predicted by the trained L2R model. Note that, L2R is a supervised approach. In our work, we focus on a generative probabilistic model, which is unsupervised in nature, to model the three roles of users and their activities.

Most germane to our work is the Topic Expertise Model (TEM) proposed in (Yang et al. 2013). TEM is a LDA-based model to jointly model topics and expertise of users. Gaussian mixture hybrid is used to model votes. TRTM is significantly different from TEM because TRTM considers and models the three roles of users. Our experimental results confirm that modeling three roles of users benefits the mining fine-grained topics of users. TEM was evaluated on three applications: expert finding, similar question searching, and ranking answers for questions. Nevertheless, the problem definition of ranking answers is different from ours. In (Yang et al. 2013), only answers from answerers that appear in training data can be ranked. In our problem definition, answers from new answerers can also be ranked.

Topic models on CQA systems. A body of literature exists on topic modeling in CQA context. Existing work can be classified into PLSA-based models (Xu, Ji, and Wang 2012; Wu, Wang, and Cheng 2008) and LDA-based models (Ji et al. 2012; Zhou et al. 2012; Guo et al. 2008).

Xu *et al.* (2012) proposed Dual-Role Model (DRM) to recommend questions to matching users in Yahoo! Answers. DRM is a PLSA-based model and it models the asker role and answerer role of users, but not the voter role. Through DRM, the authors showed clear distinctions between the two roles of users. Compared to TRTM, other than ignoring the voter role, DRM cannot directly generate topic distributions of askers and answerers although the two roles are considered in the modeling. An Incremental PLSA is proposed in (Wu, Wang, and Cheng 2008) for question recommendation in Wenda. The model considers users' long-term interests and short-term interests for question matching.

Ji *et al.* (2012) presented a LDA-based model for question retrieval. The model outperforms translation models on the task by using topics discovered from Yahoo! Answers. A user-topic model treating all documents of a user (*i.e.*, questions and answers) as an aggregated document was proposed in (Zhou et al. 2012). The user-topic model was applied for finding expert users in CQA and it outperforms PageRank (Page et al. 1999). Guo *et al.* (2008) extended LDA using category information in Yahoo! Answers to return expert lists for new questions. Their generative model is able to discover latent topics in the content of questions and answers and the latent interests of users. The experimental results evidence the capability of topic models for recommendation problems in CQA systems.

Table 1: Notations

Symbol	Description
U	Collection of askers $u \in U$
V	Collection of answerers $v \in V$
Q	Collection of questions $q \in Q$
A	Collection of answers $a \in A$
Z	Collection of topics $z \in Z$
W	Word vocabulary of questions
E	Word vocabulary of answers
Q_u	Set of questions composed by u
Q_v	Set of questions answered by v
A_v	Set of answers contributed by v
V_q	Set of answerers to question q
s_q^a	Voting score of answer a to question q
$n(q,w)$	Number of occurrences of $w \in W$ in q
$n(a,e)$	Number of occurrences of $e \in E$ in a

Tri-Role Topic Model

We start with the notations used in our model, summarized in Table 1. We then present the Tri-Role Topic Model (TRTM) and its inference algorithm.

Notations

Let Q and A be the set of questions and the set of answers respectively. W is the word vocabulary of questions and E is the word vocabulary of answers. Let U be the set of askers (*i.e.,* users who ever asked questions), and let V denote the set of answerers (*i.e.,* users who ever answered questions). Note that, a user can be an asker for one question and be an answerer of another question, *i.e.,* $U \cap V \neq \Phi$. We further use Q_u to denote the set of questions composed by asker u, and use Q_v to denote the set of questions answered by answerer v. The set of answers contributed by v is denoted by A_v.

An answer a, contributed by answerer v to question q, may receive zero or more votes. As a vote can be either positive or negative, the aggregated number of votes to an answer may be negative. For easy processing, we compute a *voting score* for answer a to question q as $s_q^a = x - x_{min} + 0.5$, where x is raw aggregated vote for this answer and x_{min} is the lowest vote of an answer in our data collection, and 0.5 is a constant to ensure $s_q^a > 0$. In other word, s_q^a is the aggregated votes of an answer shifted to positive region.

Model Description

In TRTM, each user has three roles: an asker, an answerer, and a voter. As discussed earlier, different from a question or an answer, a vote is not associated with any textual content. Moreover, votes become meaningful only when the number of votes is large. We therefore do not model the voter role explicitly in TRTM. Instead, voting is used to constrain the topic distributions in our model.

TRTM models four types of topic distributions. Let z denote topic. The four types of topic distributions are: (i) $p(z|u)$, topic distribution of asker u, (ii) $p(z|v)$, topic distribution of answerer v, (iii) $p(z|q)$, topic distribution of question q, and (iv) $p(z|a)$, topic distribution of answer a. Note that, TRTM assumes that each question or answer has multiple topics and each word is sampled from its corresponding topic with probability $p(w|z)$ or $p(e|z)$. Regarding topic distributions, we make the following three assumptions (**A1**, **A2**, and **A3**) in TRTM. Note that **A1** and **A3** are also adopted in (Xu, Ji, and Wang 2012).

- **A1**: An asker u and all the questions composed by her Q_u share similar topic distributions.
- **A2**: An answerer v and all the questions answered by her Q_v, share similar topic distributions. The degree of similarity in the topic distributions between v and Q_v is reflected by the voting scores of her answers. If an answer to question q by v receives a large voting score, then most users believe that this answer well addresses the question; hence answerer v has the expertise in answering this question q. v and q therefore share more similar topic distributions. Here, we use the *voter* role of users (*i.e.,* those who are not answerers or the asker) to constrain the topic distributions between the answerer and her questions. In simple words, an answerer's topic distribution is more similar to that of the questions answered by her, if her answers to these questions receive more positive votes.
- **A3**: An answerer v and all the answers contributed by her A_v share similar topic distributions.

In TRTM, we adopt the *exponential KL-divergence (eKL)* function to model the relationship between two topic distributions. Proposed in (Kim, Park, and Shim 2013), the eKL function is the combination of exponential probability densities and KullbackLeibler divergence. For two k-dimensional probability distributions μ and θ and a given scalar λ, $eKL(\theta, \lambda, \mu)$ is defined as:

$$eKL(\theta, \lambda, \mu) = \lambda e^{-\lambda KL(\mu||\theta)}$$

where $KL(\mu||\theta)$ is $\sum_k \mu_k \log(\mu_k/\theta_k)$. The properties of the $eKL(\theta, \lambda, \mu)$ function include: (i) with a fixed λ, the eKL value increases with the degree of similarity between μ and θ, and (ii) with a larger λ, the exponential probability densities decrease faster when increasing the value of $KL(\mu||\theta)$.

The generative process of TRTM is divided into three sub-procedures, namely (i) composing question, (ii) selecting question to answer, and (iii) contributing answer.

Composing question. An asker u composes a question $q \in Q_u$ with probability $eKL(u, \alpha, q)$, where α is a scalar. When topic distributions of u and q are more similar, u is more likely to compose question q because of interest matching (Assumption **A1**). Next, for each word w in q, a topic z is sampled with probability $p(z|q)$, and then w is generated based on $p(w|z)$.

Selecting question to answer. The probability of an answerer v choosing to answer a question $q \in Q_v$ is modeled as $eKL(v, \beta \cdot s_q^a, q)$, where s_q^a is the voting score and β is a scalar. Recall that in Assumption **A2**, the degree of similarity in the topic distributions between v and Q_v is reflected by the voting scores of her answers. The larger the voting score s_q^a, the sharper the curve of $eKL(v, \beta \cdot s_q^a, q)$, which means that the eKL assigns a higher probability when the distance between v and q gets smaller.

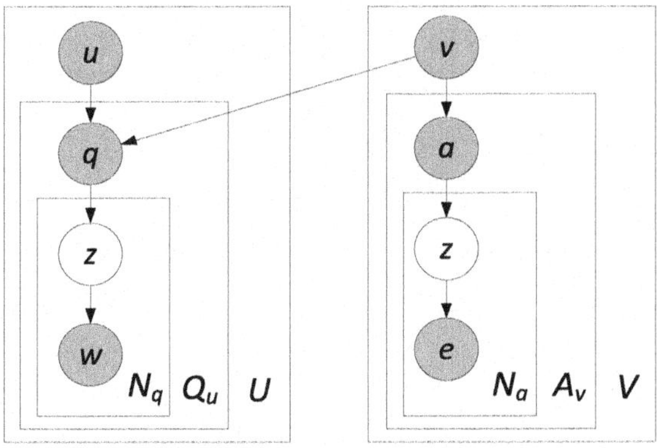

Figure 2: Tri-Role Topic Model. Note that the voter role of user is modeled implicitly, and the plate model does not show s_q^a.

Contributing answer. An answerer v contributes an answer $a \in A_v$ with probability $eKL(v, \tau, a)$, where τ is a scalar. Based on Assumption **A3**, v prefers to contribute a if the topical similarity between v and a is high. Next, for each word e in a, a topic z is sampled with probability $p(z|a)$, and then e is generated with $p(e|z)$.

The graphical representation of the TRTM model is shown in Figure 2 and the generative process is summarized as follows:

- For each question $q \in Q_u$
  - For each answer $a \in A_v$ of question q
    - ∗ Asker u composes question q with probability $eKL(p(z|q), \alpha, p(z|u))$
    - ∗ For each word w in q
      - · Draw a topic z from $p(z|q)$
      - · Draw a word w from $p(w|z)$
    - ∗ Answerer v selects to answer question q with probability $eKL(p(z|q), \beta \cdot s_q^a, p(z|v))$
    - ∗ Answerer v contributes answer a with probability $eKL(p(z|a), \tau, p(z|v))$
    - ∗ For each word e in a
      - · Draw a topic z from $p(z|a)$
      - · Draw a word e from $p(e|z)$

The Inference Algorithm of TRTM

Given question set Q composed by U and answer set A by answerers from V, we obtain the likelihood of the data in Equation 1.

$$\begin{aligned} L = & \prod_{u \in U} \prod_{q \in Q_u} eKL\Big(p(z|q), \alpha, p(z|u)\Big) \\ & \prod_{u \in U} \prod_{q \in Q_u} \prod_{w \in W} \Big[\sum_z p(w|z)p(z|q)\Big]^{n(q,w)} \\ & \prod_{v \in V} \prod_{q \in Q_v} eKL\Big(p(z|q), \beta \cdot s_q^a, p(z|v)\Big) \\ & \prod_{v \in V} \prod_{a \in A_v} eKL\Big(p(z|a), \tau, p(z|v)\Big) \\ & \prod_{v \in V} \prod_{a \in A_v} \prod_{e \in E} \Big[\sum_z p(e|z)p(z|a)\Big]^{n(a,e)} \end{aligned} \tag{1}$$

The exact inference of Equation 1 is intractable. We propose an Expectation-Maximization (EM) algorithm to appropriately infer TRTM. The EM algorithm has two steps: E-step and M-step. The E-step calculates the expectation of the hidden variables *i.e.,* $p(z|q, w)$ and $p(z|a, e)$ in TRTM.

- **E-step:**

$$\begin{aligned} p^{k+1}(z|q,w) &= \frac{p^k(w|z)p^k(z|q)}{\sum_{z' \in Z} p^k(w|z')p^k(z'|q)} \\ p^{k+1}(z|a,e) &= \frac{p^k(e|z)p^k(z|a)}{\sum_{z' \in Z} p^k(e|z')p^k(z'|a)} \end{aligned}$$

The M-step maximizes the log-likelihood (see Equation 1). The following probabilities are calculated: $p(w|z)$, $p(e|z)$, $p(z|u)$, $p(z|q)$, $p(z|a)$, and $p(z|v)$.

- **M-step:**

$$\begin{aligned} p^{k+1}(w|z) &= \frac{\sum_{q \in Q} n(q,w)p^{k+1}(z|q,w)}{\sum_{w' \in W} \sum_{q \in Q} n(q,w')p^{k+1}(z|q,w')} \\ p^{k+1}(e|z) &= \frac{\sum_{a \in A} n(a,e)p^{k+1}(z|a,e)}{\sum_{e' \in E} \sum_{a \in A} n(a,e')p^{k+1}(z|a,e')} \\ p^{k+1}(z|u) &= \frac{[\prod_{q \in Q_u} p^{k+1}(z|q)]^{1/|Q_u|}}{\sum_{z' \in Z} [\prod_{q \in Q_u} p^{k+1}(z'|q)]^{1/|Q_u|}} \end{aligned}$$

The calculation of the probabilities $p(z|q)$, $p(z|a)$, and $p(z|v)$ are shown in Table 2 for presentation clarity. We iteratively compute probabilities of **E-step** and **M-step** until achieving convergent log-likelihood (see Equation 1). k represents the kth iteration of EM algorithm. Note that, in **M-step**, we first calculate $p(z|q)$ and $p(z|a)$, then calculate $p(z|u)$ and $p(z|v)$.

Experiment

We evaluate the proposed TRTM model on Stack Overflow data[1]. Although the model can be used to enable multiple applications, due to page limit, we report one case study for the application of ranking answers for questions.

[1] http://blog.stackoverflow.com/category/cc-wiki-dump/

Table 2: **M-step** (continued) for computing $p(z|v)$, $p(z|q)$, and $p(z|a)$

$$p^{k+1}(z|v) = \frac{\left[\prod_{q\in Q_v} p^{k+1}(z|q)^{\beta\cdot s_q^a} \prod_{a\in A_v} p^{k+1}(z|a)^{\tau}\right]^{1/(\sum_{q\in Q_v}\beta\cdot s_q^a+\tau|A_v|)}}{\sum_{z'\in Z}\left[\prod_{q\in Q_v} p^{k+1}(z'|q)^{\beta\cdot s_q^a} \prod_{a\in A_v} p^{k+1}(z'|a)^{\tau}\right]^{1/(\sum_{q\in Q_v}\beta\cdot s_q^a+\tau|A_v|)}}$$

$$p^{k+1}(z|q) = \frac{\sum_{w\in W} n(q,w)p^{k+1}(z|q,w) + \sum_{u\in U_q}\alpha p^k(z|u) + \sum_{v\in V_q}\beta\cdot s_q^a\cdot p^k(z|v)}{\sum_{z'\in Z}\left\{\sum_{w\in W} n(q,w)p^{k+1}(z'|q,w) + \sum_{u\in U_q}\alpha p^k(z'|u) + \sum_{v\in V_q}\beta\cdot s_q^a\cdot p^k(z'|v)\right\}}$$

$$p^{k+1}(z|a) = \frac{\sum_{e\in E} n(a,e)p^{k+1}(z|a,e) + \sum_{v\in V_a}\tau p^k(z|v)}{\sum_{z'\in Z}\left\{\sum_{e\in E} n(a,e)p^{k+1}(z'|a,e) + \sum_{v\in V_a}\tau p^k(z'|v)\right\}}$$

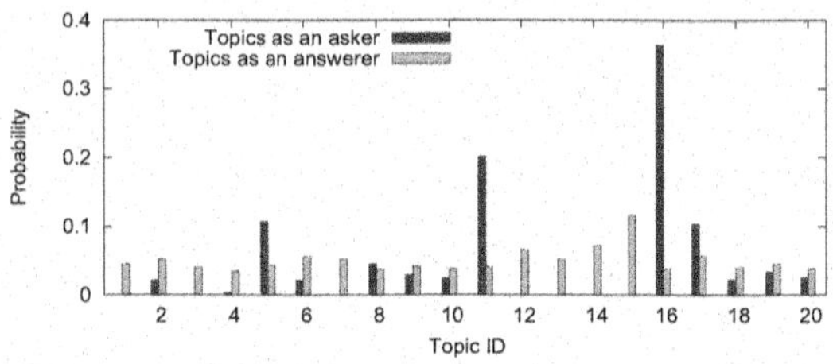

Figure 3: Topic distributions of asker role and answerer role from the same example user

Data Set. Questions and answers from Stack Overflow posted between Jan 01, 2011 and Mar 31, 2011 are used as training data; questions and answers published from Apr 01, 2011 to Sep 06, 2013 are used as test data.

We preprocess the training data by removing questions and answers from inactive users. More specifically, a user is inactive if the total number of questions and answers posted by her is smaller than 80, as defined in (Yang et al. 2013). After preprocessing, the training data contains 16,141 questions from 868 askers and 180,394 answers from 1,184 answerers. Note that a user could play a single role (*i.e.*, an asker or an answerer). The vocabulary size for questions is 21,760 and that for answers is 85,889. The raw aggregated vote is in the range of -10 to 359.

For test data, questions with fewer than 5 answers are removed, because answer ranking is more meaningful if a question has a large number of answers. As the result, the test data contains 20,834 questions and 150,320 answers. Note that, the askers and answerers in the test data may not appear in the training data.

We experimentally set the hyperparameters of TRTM: $\alpha = 100$, $\beta = 100$, $\tau = 100$. We evaluated different number of topics $|Z|$ = 10, 20, and 40.

Topic Discovery

Discovered by TRTM, we randomly select 5 topics of questions and 5 topics of answers as examples, shown in Tables 3(a) and 3(b) respectively. The top-10 words based on $p(w|z)$ and $p(e|z)$ respectively are listed for each topic. Observe that TRTM captures some major topics of questions and answers in Stack Overflow. Questions related to Java programming (Topic 8) and Web development (Topic 14) are frequently asked. Process and thread (Topic 13) and Server client programming (Topic 20) are prevalent in answers. Note that, the vocabulary sets of the questions and of the answers are significantly different. Naturally, the number of words in all answers to a question is much larger than the words in the question itself. More importantly, there are more technical terminologies in answers than that in questions.

Table 3: Example topics by TRTM from Stack Overflow

(a) Example question topics with topic ID and words

ID	Top-10 words with highest generative probability
6	file error window install reference build directory js header include
8	app java process compile org template apache module map default
12	image project script photo folder null get collection assembly generate
14	php div tag run html load link content element use
18	data create database select custom ve use answer please size

(b) Example answer topics with topic ID and words

ID	Top-10 words with highest generative probability
1	change memory compile program language address python stack git branch
5	string page example html look jquery instead url javascript content
8	application java request access cache compile load log map api
13	thread bit process result field template loop message format single
20	name server service net project client source standard connection header

We also show topic distributions of a randomly selected user for her asker and answerer roles in Figure 3. Observe that the topic distributions of the two roles are significantly different. For instance, topics 11 and 16 have large $p(z|u)$ in her question topic distribution. For the answer topic distribution, topic 15 has the largest probability $p(z|v)$. This indicates that this user is less familiar with questions of topics 11 and 16 but she has the expertise in providing answers for topic 15. TRTM is capable of distinguishing question and answer topic distributions for users as askers and answerers.

Ranking Answers for Questions

A popular question could receive many answers within a very short period. However, given the short time period, there might be lack of enough votes to help the asker to select the high quality answers, because the answers may be from a domain the asker is unfamiliar with. Timely ranking answers for questions benefits askers in quickly getting high-quality answers.

Problem definition. Given a question q and its answer set A_q, the task of *ranking answers* is to rank answers $a \in A_q$ such that the top-ranked answers best address q. In this sense, we assume that the best answers for a question are the ones sharing most similar topic distributions with the question. The answers are then ranked by topical similarities to the question, and the topics of a's and q are learned using topic models, TRTM or other baseline models.

The *topical similarity* (TS) between a question q and an answer a is evaluated using Jensen-Shannon divergence,

$$TS(q, a) = JSD(\theta_q, \theta_a)$$

where θ_q and θ_a represent the topic distributions of question q and answer a respectively.

$$\theta_q \approx p(\boldsymbol{w}_q|z) = \sum_{w \in \boldsymbol{w}_q} p(w|z)$$

$$\theta_a \approx p(\boldsymbol{e}_a|z) = \sum_{e \in \boldsymbol{e}_q} p(e|z)$$

In above equations, $\boldsymbol{w}_q$ and $\boldsymbol{e}_q$ are word vectors for question q and answer a respectively.

Baseline methods. Latent Dirichlet Allocation (**LDA**) is a standard technique for topic analysis in document collections (Blei, Ng, and Jordan 2003). Here, a virtual document is created for each user by aggregating all her questions and answers, and then LDA is employed to learn the hidden topics (*i.e.*, $p(w|z)$). Topic Expertise Model (**TEM**) is a very recent model proposed in (Yang et al. 2013). Considered as a state-of-the-art baseline, TEM jointly models user topical interests and expertise in a probabilistic model. TEM has been evaluated on Stack Overflow data and has been applied for the task of answer ranking but with a different problem setting in (Yang et al. 2013)[2]. For both LDA and TEM, the topical similarity is computed in a similar way as in TRTM.

Evaluation measure. We use normalized discounted cumulative gain (nDCG) to evaluate the list of ranked answers, following (Yang et al. 2013). Here, the ground-truth ranking of the answers to a question is the ranking by the number of aggregated votes of the answers. The number of aggregated votes is also used to define the degree of relevance of each item in a rank, required by the nDCG measure. $nDCG@M$ for the top-M ranked answers of test question q computed as follows:

$$nDCG(q, M) = \frac{1}{IDCG(q, M)} \sum_{i=1}^{M} \frac{2^{rv_{q,i}} - 1}{\log_2(i+1)}$$

[2] In TEM, only the answers from the answerers that appear in training data are ranked. In our proposed solution, we utilize the words in an answer (*i.e.*, $p(z|w)$) where the answerer may not appear in the training data.

Table 4: nDCG of the three models; the best result for each topic number setting ($|Z|$=10, 20, 40) is in boldface.

$\lvert Z\rvert$	Model	$nDCG@1$	$nDCG@5$	$nDCG@10$	$nDCG$
10	TRTM	**0.3273**	**0.6448**	**0.6759**	**0.6762**
	TEM	0.3005	0.6281	0.6607	0.6611
	LDA	0.3026	0.6296	0.6618	0.6622
20	TRTM	**0.3405**	**0.6518**	**0.6824**	**0.6828**
	TEM	0.3052	0.6303	0.6630	0.6633
	LDA	0.3093	0.6331	0.6651	0.6654
40	TRTM	**0.3380**	**0.6506**	**0.6806**	**0.6810**
	TEM	0.3106	0.6333	0.6657	0.6660
	LDA	0.3195	0.6411	0.6719	0.6722

where $rv_{q,i}$ is the number of aggregated votes received by the answer ranked at the i-th position; $IDCG(M, q)$ is the normalization factor for the discounted cumulative gain of the ideal ranking of the top-M answers for question q. Then $nDCG@M$ is the average of $nDCG(q, M)$ over all questions in the test data.

Experimental results The $nDCG@M$'s of the three models with $|Z| = 10$, 20, and 40 topics are reported in Table 4 where M=1, 5, 10, and all answers. The following three observations are made from the results.

- TRTM performs better than both baseline methods TEM and LDA, for all different settings on number of topics and on all M settings. Particularly, on $nDCG@1$, TRTM outperforms TEM by 11.6% and LDA by 10.1% respectively. The results evidence the effectiveness of our proposed model.
- All models with 20 topics yield best results, which suggests that 20 is a more appropriate number of topics on this dataset. On the other hand, all the three models are relatively not very sensitive to topic number setting.
- LDA slightly outperforms TEM. One possible reason is that TEM assumes each question (resp. each answer) has only one unique topic, which is not appropriate in modeling Stack Overflow data, where some questions and answers are fairly long and may cover multiple topics.

Conclusion and Future Work

In this paper, we propose a Tri-Role Topic Model to model the tri-roles of users (*i.e.*, askers, answerers, and voters) in CQA systems and the activities of each role (*i.e.*, composing question, selecting question to answer, contributing, and voting answers). Our model is capable of mining four topic distributions of asker, answerer, question, and answer, respectively. We demonstrate the effectiveness of our model in discovering topics from Stack Overflow and also in addressing the problem of ranking answers for questions on the same dataset.

As a part of future work, we expect to model the rich temporal patterns of users in CQA systems. We observe that different users prefer to answer questions at different time point of a day and different day of a week. Incorporating temporal patterns of users has great potential in modeling users' activities more accurately.

References

Anderson, A.; Huttenlocher, D.; Kleinberg, J.; and Leskovec, J. 2012. Discovering value from community activity on focused question answering sites: A case study of stack overflow. In *KDD*, 850–858. ACM.

Anderson, A.; Huttenlocher, D.; Kleinberg, J.; and Leskovec, J. 2013. Steering user behavior with badges. In *WWW*, 95–106.

Blei, D. M.; Ng, A. Y.; and Jordan, M. I. 2003. Latent dirichlet allocation. *J. Mach. Learn. Res.* 3:993–1022.

Correa, D., and Sureka, A. 2014. Chaff from the wheat: Characterization and modeling of deleted questions on stack overflow. In *WWW*, 631–642.

Dalip, D. H.; Gonçalves, M. A.; Cristo, M.; and Calado, P. 2013. Exploiting user feedback to learn to rank answers in Q&A forums: A case study with stack overflow. In *SIGIR*, 543–552. ACM.

Dror, G.; Koren, Y.; Maarek, Y.; and Szpektor, I. 2011. I want to answer; who has a question?: Yahoo! answers recommender system. In *KDD*, 1109–1117. ACM.

Guo, J.; Xu, S.; Bao, S.; and Yu, Y. 2008. Tapping on the potential of Q&A community by recommending answer providers. In *CIKM*, 921–930. ACM.

Hofmann, T. 1999. Probabilistic latent semantic indexing. In *SIGIR*, 50–57. ACM.

Ji, Z.; Xu, F.; Wang, B.; and He, B. 2012. Question-answer topic model for question retrieval in community question answering. In *CIKM*, 2471–2474. ACM.

Kim, Y.; Park, Y.; and Shim, K. 2013. DIGTOBI: A recommendation system for digg articles using probabilistic modeling. In *WWW*, 691–702.

Li, Z.; Shen, H.; and Grant, J. E. 2012. Collective intelligence in the online social network of Yahoo! answers and its implications. In *CIKM*, 455–464. ACM.

Page, L.; Brin, S.; Motwani, R.; and Winograd, T. 1999. The pagerank citation ranking: Bringing order to the web. Technical Report 1999-66, Stanford InfoLab.

Wu, H.; Wang, Y.; and Cheng, X. 2008. Incremental probabilistic latent semantic analysis for automatic question recommendation. In *RecSys*, 99–106. ACM.

Xu, F.; Ji, Z.; and Wang, B. 2012. Dual role model for question recommendation in community question answering. In *SIGIR*, 771–780. ACM.

Yang, L.; Qiu, M.; Gottipati, S.; Zhu, F.; Jiang, J.; Sun, H.; and Chen, Z. 2013. CQArank: Jointly model topics and expertise in community question answering. In *CIKM*, 99–108. ACM.

Zhou, G.; Lai, S.; Liu, K.; and Zhao, J. 2012. Topic-sensitive probabilistic model for expert finding in question answer communities. In *CIKM*, 1662–1666. ACM.

Handling owl:sameAs via Rewriting

Boris Motik, Yavor Nenov, Robert Piro and **Ian Horrocks**
Department of Computer Science, Oxford University
Oxford, United Kingdom
forename.lastname@cs.ox.ac.uk

Abstract

Rewriting is widely used to optimise owl:sameAs reasoning in materialisation based OWL 2 RL systems. We investigate issues related to both the correctness and efficiency of rewriting, and present an algorithm that guarantees correctness, improves efficiency, and can be effectively parallelised. Our evaluation shows that our approach can reduce reasoning times on practical data sets by orders of magnitude.

1 Introduction

RDF (Manola and Miller 2004) and SPARQL (Harris and Seaborne 2013) are increasingly being used to store and access semistructured data. An OWL ontology (Motik, Patel-Schneider, and Parsia 2012) is often used to enhance query answers with tuples implied by the ontology and data, and the OWL 2 RL profile was specifically designed to allow for tractable rule-based query answering (Motik et al. 2012). In practice, the latter often involves using a forward chaining procedure in which the *materialisation* (i.e., all consequences) of the ontology and data is computed in a preprocessing step, allowing queries to be evaluated directly over the materialised triples. This technique is used by systems such as Owlgres (Stocker and Smith 2008), WebPIE (Urbani et al. 2012), Oracle's RDF store (Wu et al. 2008), OWLIM SE (Bishop et al. 2011), and RDFox (Motik et al. 2014a).

One disadvantage of materialisation is that the preprocessing step can be costly w.r.t. both the computation and the storage of entailed triples. This problem is exacerbated when materialisation requires equality reasoning—that is, when the owl:sameAs property is used to state equalities between resources. OWL 2 RL/RDF (Motik et al. 2012, Section 4.3) axiomatises the semantics of owl:sameAs using rules such as $\langle s', p, o \rangle \leftarrow \langle s, p, o \rangle \wedge \langle s, \text{owl:sameAs}, s' \rangle$ that, for each pair of equal resources r and r', 'copy' all triples between r and r'. It is well known that such 'copying' can severely impact both the materialisation size and time (Kolovski, Wu, and Eadon 2010); what is less obvious is that the increase in computation time due to duplicate derivations may be even more serious (see Section 3).

In order to address this problem, materialisation based systems often use some form of *rewriting*—a well-known technique for theorem proving with equality (Baader and Nipkow 1998; Nieuwenhuis and Rubio 2001). In the OWL 2 RL setting, rewriting consists of choosing one representative from each set of equal resources, and replacing all remaining resources in the set with the representative. Variants of this idea have been implemented in many of the above mentioned systems, and they have been shown to be very effective on practical data sets (Kolovski, Wu, and Eadon 2010).

Although the idea of rewriting is well known, ensuring its correctness (i.e., ensuring that the answer to an arbitrary SPARQL query is the same with and without rewriting) is not straightforward. In this paper we identify two problems that, we believe, have been commonly overlooked in existing implementations. First, whenever a resource r is rewritten in the data, r must also be rewritten in the rules; hence, the rule set cannot be assumed to be fixed during the course of materialisation, which is particularly problematic if computation is parallelised. Second, it is a common assumption that SPARQL queries can be efficiently evaluated over the materialisation by rewriting them, evaluating them over the rewritten triples, and then 'expanding' the answer set (i.e., substituting all representative resources with equal ones in all possible ways). However, such an approach can be incorrect when SPARQL queries are evaluated under bag semantics, or when they contain builtin functions.

We address both issues in this paper and make the following contributions. In Section 3 we discuss the problems related to owl:sameAs in more detail and show how they can lead to both increased computation costs and incorrect query answers. In Section 4 we present an algorithm that generalises OWL 2 RL materialisation, can also handle SWRL rules (Horrocks et al. 2004), rewrites rules as well as data triples, and is *lock-free* (Herlihy and Shavit 2008). The latter means that at least one thread always makes progress, ensuring that the system is less susceptible to adverse thread scheduling decisions and thus scales better to many threads. In Section 5 we show how to modify SPARQL query processing so as to guarantee correctness. Finally, in Section 6 we present a preliminary evaluation of an implementation of our algorithms in the open-source RDFox system. We show that rewriting can reduce the number of materialised triples by a factor of up to 7.8, and can reduce materialisation time by a factor of up to 31.1 on a single thread, with the time saving being largely due to the elimination of duplicate derivations. Our approach also parallelises computation very well in practice,[1] providing a speedup of up to 6.7 with eight physical cores, and up to 9.6 with 16 virtual cores.[2]

Due to space constraints, in this paper we have only been able to present a high level description of our algorithms, but detailed formalisations and correctness proofs are provided in a technical report (Motik et al. 2014b). The implemented system and all test data sets are available online.[3]

2 Preliminaries

A *term* is a *resource* (i.e., a constant) or a variable. Unless otherwise stated, s, p, o, and t are terms, and x, y, and z are variables. An *atom* is a triple of terms $\langle s, p, o\rangle$ called the *subject*, *predicate*, and *object*, respectively. A *fact* (or *triple*) is a variable-free atom. A *rule* r is an implication of the form (1), where $\mathsf{h}(r) := \langle s, p, o\rangle$ is the *head*, $\mathsf{b}(r) := \langle s_1, p_1, o_1\rangle \wedge \ldots \wedge \langle s_n, p_n, o_n\rangle$ is the *body*, and each variable in $\mathsf{h}(r)$ also occurs in $\mathsf{b}(r)$.

$$\langle s, p, o\rangle \leftarrow \langle s_1, p_1, o_1\rangle \wedge \ldots \wedge \langle s_n, p_n, o_n\rangle \quad (1)$$

A *program* P is a finite set of rules, and $P^\infty(E)$ is the *materialisation* of P on a finite set of *explicit* (i.e., extensional or EDB) facts E (Abiteboul, Hull, and Vianu 1995).

Two styles of OWL 2 RL reasoning are known, corresponding to the RDF- and DL-style semantics of OWL. In the RDF style, an ontology is represented using triples stored with the data in a single RDF graph, and a fixed (i.e., independent from the ontology) set of rules is used to axiomatise the RDF-style semantics (Motik et al. 2012, Section 4.3). While conceptually simple, this approach is inefficient because the fixed program contains complex joins. In the DL style, the rules are derived from and depend on the ontology (Grosof et al. 2003), but they are shorter and contain fewer joins. This approach is complete only if the ontology and the data satisfy conditions from Section 3 of (Motik, Patel-Schneider, and Parsia 2012)—an assumption commonly met in practice. Rewriting can be used with either style of reasoning, but we will use the DL style in our examples and evaluation because the rules are more readable and their evaluation tends to be more efficient.

3 Problems with owl:sameAs

In this section we discuss, by means of an example, the problems that the owl:sameAs property poses to materialisation-based reasoners. The semantics of owl:sameAs can be captured explicitly using program $P_\approx$, consisting of rules ($\approx_1$)–($\approx_5$), which axiomatises owl:sameAs as a congruence relation (i.e., an equivalence relation satisfying the replacement property). We call each set of resources all of which are equal to each other an owl:sameAs-*clique*.

$$\langle x_i, \mathsf{owl{:}sameAs}, x_i\rangle \leftarrow \langle x_1, x_2, x_3\rangle, \text{ for } 1 \leq i \leq 3 \quad (\approx_1)$$

$$\langle x_1', x_2, x_3\rangle \leftarrow \langle x_1, x_2, x_3\rangle \wedge \langle x_1, \mathsf{owl{:}sameAs}, x_1'\rangle \quad (\approx_2)$$

$$\langle x_1, x_2', x_3\rangle \leftarrow \langle x_1, x_2, x_3\rangle \wedge \langle x_2, \mathsf{owl{:}sameAs}, x_2'\rangle \quad (\approx_3)$$

$$\langle x_1, x_2, x_3'\rangle \leftarrow \langle x_1, x_2, x_3\rangle \wedge \langle x_3, \mathsf{owl{:}sameAs}, x_3'\rangle \quad (\approx_4)$$

$$\mathsf{false} \leftarrow \langle x, \mathsf{owl{:}differentFrom}, x\rangle \quad (\approx_5)$$

OWL 2 RL/RDF (Motik et al. 2012, Section 4.3) also makes owl:sameAs symmetric and transitive, but those rules are redundant as they are instances of ($\approx_2$) and ($\approx_4$).

Rules ($\approx_1$)–($\approx_5$) can lead to the derivation of many equivalent triples, as we demonstrate using an example program P_{ex} containing rules (R)–(F_3); these correspond directly to SWRL rules, but one could equally use slightly more complex rules obtained from OWL 2 RL axioms.

$$\langle x, \mathsf{owl{:}sameAs}, \mathsf{{:}USA}\rangle \leftarrow \langle \mathsf{{:}Obama}, \mathsf{{:}presidentOf}, x\rangle \quad (R)$$

$$\langle x, \mathsf{owl{:}sameAs}, \mathsf{{:}Obama}\rangle \leftarrow \langle x, \mathsf{{:}presidentOf}, \mathsf{{:}USA}\rangle \quad (S)$$

$$\langle \mathsf{{:}USPresident}, \mathsf{{:}presidentOf}, \mathsf{{:}US}\rangle \quad (F_1)$$

$$\langle \mathsf{{:}Obama}, \mathsf{{:}presidentOf}, \mathsf{{:}America}\rangle \quad (F_2)$$

$$\langle \mathsf{{:}Obama}, \mathsf{{:}presidentOf}, \mathsf{{:}US}\rangle \quad (F_3)$$

On $P_{ex} \cup P_\approx$, rule (R) derives that :USA is equal to :US and :America, and rules ($\approx_1$)–($\approx_4$) then derive an owl:sameAs triple for each of the nine pairs involving :USA, :America, and :US. The total number of derivations, however, is much higher: we derive each triple once from rule ($\approx_1$), three times from rule ($\approx_2$), once from rule ($\approx_3$),[4] and three times from rule ($\approx_4$); thus, we get 66 derivations in total for the nine owl:sameAs triples. Analogously, rule (S) derives that :Obama and :USPresident are equal, and rules ($\approx_1$)–($\approx_4$) derive the two owl:sameAs triples 22 times in total. These owl:sameAs triples lead to further inferences; for example, from (F_1), rules ($\approx_2$) and ($\approx_4$) infer 2×3 triples with subject :Obama or :USPresident, and object :USA, :America, or :US. Each of these six triples is inferred three times from rule ($\approx_2$), once from rule ($\approx_3$), and three times from rule ($\approx_4$), so we get 36 derivations in total.

Thus, for each owl:sameAs-clique of size n, rules ($\approx_1$)–($\approx_4$) derive n^2 owl:sameAs triples via $2n^3 + n^2 + n$ derivations. Moreover, each triple $\langle s, p, o\rangle$ with terms in owl:sameAs-cliques of sizes n_s, n_p, and n_o, respectively, is 'expanded' to $n_s \times n_p \times n_o$ triples, each of which is derived $n_s + n_p + n_o$ times. This duplication of facts and derivations is a major source of inefficiency.

To reduce these numbers, we can choose a representative resource for each owl:sameAs-clique and then *rewrite* all triples—that is, replace all resources with their representatives (Stocker and Smith 2008; Urbani et al. 2012; Kolovski, Wu, and Eadon 2010; Bishop et al. 2011). For example, after applying rule (R), we can choose :USA as the representative of :USA, :US and :America, and, after applying rule (S), we can choose :Obama as the representative of :Obama and :USPresident. The materialisation of P_{ex} then contains only the triple $\langle \mathsf{{:}Obama}, \mathsf{{:}presidentOf}, \mathsf{{:}US}\rangle$ and, as we show in Section 4, the number of derivations of owl:sameAs triples drops from over 60 to just 6.

[1] Datalog reasoning is PTIME complete in the size of the data, and it is thus believed that sequential computation will be required in some cases.

[2] In *hyperthreading*, each virtual core has its own architectural state, but several virtual cores share the execution resources of one physical core.

[3] https://krr-nas.cs.ox.ac.uk/2015/AAAI/RDFox/Equality/

[4] Rule ($\approx_1$) derives $\langle \mathsf{owl{:}sameAs}, \mathsf{owl{:}sameAs}, \mathsf{owl{:}sameAs}\rangle$, so we can map variable x_2 to owl:sameAs in rule ($\approx_3$).

Since owl:sameAs triples can be derived continuously during materialisation, rewriting cannot be applied as preprocessing; moreover, to ensure that rewriting does not affect query answers, the resulting materialisation must be equivalent, modulo rewriting, to $[P_{ex} \cup P_{\approx}]^{\infty}(E)$. Thus, we may need to continuously rewrite both triples and rules: rewriting only triples can be insufficient. For example, if we choose :US as the representative of :USA, :US and :America, then rule (S) will not be applicable, and we will fail to derive that :USPresident is equal to :Obama. To the best of our knowledge, no existing system implements rule rewriting; certainly OWLIM SE and Oracle's RDF store do not,[5] and so rewriting in these systems is *not* guaranteed to preserve query answers.

Note that the problem is less acute when using a fixed rule set operating on (the triple encoding of) the ontology and data, but it can still arise if owl:sameAs triples involve rdf: or owl: resources (with a fixed rule set, these are the only resources occurring in rule bodies).

4 Parallel Reasoning With Rewriting

The algorithm by Motik et al. (2014a) used in the RDFox system implements a fact-at-a-time version of the seminaïve algorithm (Abiteboul, Hull, and Vianu 1995): it initialises the set of facts T with the input data E, and then computes $P^{\infty}(E)$ by repeatedly applying rules from P to T using N threads until no new facts are derived. The objective of our approach is to adapt the RDFox algorithm to use rewriting and thus reduce both the size of T and the time required to compute it, while ensuring that an arbitrary SPARQL query can be answered over the resulting facts as if the query were evaluated directly over $[P \cup P_{\approx}]^{\infty}(E)$. To achieve this, we use a mapping ρ that maps resources to their representatives. For α a fact, a rule, or a set thereof, $\rho(\alpha)$ is obtained by replacing each resource r in α with $\rho(r)$; moreover, $T^{\rho} := \{\langle s,p,o\rangle \mid \langle \rho(s),\rho(p),\rho(o)\rangle \in T\}$ is the *expansion* of T with ρ. To promote concurrency, we update ρ in a lock-free way, using *compare-and-set* primitives to prevent thread interference. Moreover, we do not lock ρ when computing $\rho(\alpha)$; instead, we only require $\rho(\alpha)$ to be at least as current as α just before the computation. For example, if ρ is the identity as we start computing $\rho(\langle a,b,a\rangle)$, and another thread makes a' the representative of a, then $\langle a,b,a\rangle$, $\langle a',b,a\rangle$, $\langle a,b,a'\rangle$, and $\langle a',b,a'\rangle$ are all valid results.

We also maintain queues R and C of rewritten rules and resources, respectively, for which also use lock-free implementations as described by Herlihy and Shavit (2008).

To extend the original RDFox algorithm with rewriting, we allow each thread to perform three different actions. First, a thread can extract a rule r from the queue R of rewritten rules and apply r to the set of all facts T, thus ensuring that changes to resources in rules are taken into account.

Second, a thread can rewrite outdated facts—that is, facts containing a resource that is not a representative of itself. To avoid iteration over all facts in T, the thread extracts a resource c from the queue C of unprocessed outdated resources, and uses indexes by Motik et al. (2014a) to identify each fact $F \in T$ containing c. The thread then removes each such F from T, and it adds $\rho(F)$ to T.

Third, a thread can extract and process an unprocessed fact F in T. The thread first checks whether F is outdated (i.e., whether $F \neq \rho(F)$); if so, the thread removes F from T and adds $\rho(F)$ to T. If F is not outdated but is of the form $\langle a, \text{owl:sameAs}, b\rangle$ with $a \neq b$, the thread chooses a representative of the two resources, updates ρ, and adds the other resource to queue C. The thread derives a contradiction if F is of the form $\langle a, \text{owl:differentFrom}, a\rangle$. Otherwise, the thread processes F by partially instantiating the rules in P containing a body atom that matches F, and applying such rules to T as described by Motik et al. (2014a).

Rewriting rules is nontrivial: RDFox uses an index to efficiently identify rules matching a fact, and the index may need updating when ρ changes. Updating the index in parallel would be very complex, so we perform this operation serially: when all threads are waiting (i.e., when all facts have been processed), a single thread updates P to $\rho(P)$, reindexes it, and inserts the updated rules (if any) into the queue R of rules for reevaluation. This is obviously a parallelisation bottleneck, but our experiments have shown that the time used for this process is not significant when programs are of moderate size.

Parallel modification of T can also be problematic, as the following example demonstrates: (1) thread A extracts a current fact F; (2) thread B updates ρ and deletes an outdated fact F'; and (3) thread A derives F' from F and writes F' into T, thus undoing the work of thread B. This could be solved via locking, but at the expense of parallelisation. Thus, instead of physically removing facts from T, we just mark them as outdated; then, when matching the body atoms of partially instantiated rules, we simply skip all marked facts. All this can be done lock-free, and we can remove all marked facts in a postprocessing step.

Our rewriting algorithm is presented in full in the accompanying technical report (Motik et al. 2014b). Theorem 1 states several important properties of our algorithm that, taken together, ensure the algorithm's correctness; a detailed formalisation of the algorithm and a proof of the theorem are provided in the technical report.

Theorem 1. *The algorithm terminates for each finite set of facts E and program P. Let ρ be the final mapping and let T be the final set of unmarked facts.*

1. *$\langle a, \text{owl:sameAs}, b\rangle \in T$ implies $a = b$—that is, ρ captures all equalities.*
2. *$F \in T$ implies $\rho(F) = F$—that is, T is minimal.*
3. *$T^{\rho} = [P \cup P_{\approx}]^{\infty}(E)$—that is, T and ρ together represent $[P \cup P_{\approx}]^{\infty}(E)$.*

Example

Table 1 shows six steps of an application of our algorithm to the example program P_{ex} from Section 3 on one thread. Some resource names have been abbreviated for convenience, and $\approx$ abbreviates owl:sameAs. The $\triangleright$ symbol identifies the last fact extracted from T. Facts are numbered for easier referencing, and their (re)derivation is indicated on the

[5] Personal communication.

right: $R(n)$ or $S(n)$ means that the fact was obtained from fact n and rule R or S; moreover, we rewrite facts immediately after merging resources, so $W(n)$ identifies a rewritten version of fact n, and $M(n)$ means that a fact was marked outdated because fact n caused ρ to change.

We start by extracting facts from T and, in steps 1 and 2, we apply rule R to facts 2 and 3 to derive facts 4 and 5, respectively. In step 3, we extract fact 4, merge :America into :USA, mark facts 2 and 4 as outdated, and add their rewriting, facts 6 and 7, to T. In step 4 we merge :USA into :US, after which there are no further facts to process. Mapping ρ, however, has changed, so we update P to contain rules (R') and (S'), and add them to the queue R.

$$\langle x, \text{owl:sameAs}, \text{:US}\rangle \leftarrow \langle \text{:Obama}, \text{:presidentOf}, x\rangle \quad (R')$$
$$\langle x, \text{owl:sameAs}, \text{:Obama}\rangle \leftarrow \langle x, \text{:presidentOf}, \text{:US}\rangle \quad (S')$$

In step 5 we evaluate the rules in queue R, which introduces facts 9 and 10. Finally, in step 6, we rewrite :USPresident into :Obama and mark facts 1 and 9 as outdated. At this point the algorithm terminates, making only six derivations in total, instead of more than 60 derivations when owl:sameAs is axiomatised explicitly (see Section 3).

5 Rewriting and SPARQL Query Answering

Given a set of unmarked facts T and mapping ρ, we can answer a SPARQL query Q correctly by evaluating Q in the expansion T^ρ, but that is inefficient because it 'duplicates' join evaluation for equal triples. An attempt at an improvement would be to evaluate $\rho(Q)$ in T and expand the result—that is, for each answer μ obtained by evaluating $\rho(Q)$ in T, output each answer ν such that $\rho(\nu(x)) = \mu(x)$ for each variable x in the domain of μ. However, using the example program P_{ex} from Section 3, we show that such an approach is *not* complete. Note that, after we finish the materialisation of P_{ex}, we have $\rho(x) = \text{:US}$ for each $x \in \{\text{:USA}, \text{:AM}, \text{:US}\}$ and $\rho(x) = \text{:Obama}$ for each $x \in \{\text{:USPresident}, \text{:Obama}\}$.

The first problem is due to the *bag* semantics of SPARQL, where repeated answers matter. Let Q_1 be as follows:

```
SELECT ?x WHERE { ?x :presidentOf ?y }
```

On T^ρ, query Q_1 produces answers $\mu_1 = \{?x \mapsto \text{:Obama}\}$ and $\mu_2 = \{?x \mapsto \text{:USPresident}\}$, each of which is repeated three times—once for each match of $?y$ to :USA, :US, or :America. In contrast, on T, query $\rho(Q_1)$ yields only one occurrence of μ_1, and its expansion produces one occurrence of μ_2; we thus obtain all answers, but not with the correct cardinalities. This problem arises because variable $?y$ is projected out, so the final expansion step does not take into account the number of times each binding of $?y$ contributes to the result. To solve this problem, we must modify the projection operator to output each projected answer as many times as there are resources in the projected owl:sameAs-clique(s). Thus, we can answer Q_1 as follows: we match the triple pattern of $\rho(Q_1)$ to T as usual, obtaining one answer $\nu_1 = \{?x \mapsto \text{:Obama}, ?y \mapsto \text{:US}\}$; then, we project $?y$ from ν_1 to obtain three occurrences of μ_1 since the owl:sameAs-clique of :US is of size three; finally, we expand each occurrence of μ_1 to μ_2 to obtain all six results.

The second problem is due to SPARQL builtin functions. For example, let Q_2 be as follows:

```
SELECT ?y WHERE {
    ?x :presidentOf :US .
    BIND(STR(?x) AS ?y)
}
```

On T^ρ, query Q_2 produces answers $\tau_1 = \{?y \mapsto \text{"}Obama\text{"}\}$ and $\tau_2 = \{?y \mapsto \text{"}USPresident\text{"}\}$; in contrast, on T, query $\rho(Q_2)$ yields only τ_1, which does not expand into τ_2 because strings "Obama" and "USPresident" are not equal. To solve this problem, we must expand answers *before* evaluating builtin functions. Thus, we can answer Q_2 as follows: we match the triple pattern of $\rho(Q_2)$ to T as usual, obtaining $\kappa_1 = \{?x \mapsto \text{:Obama}\}$; then, we expand κ_1 to $\kappa_2 = \{?x \mapsto \text{:USPresident}\}$; next, we evaluate the BIND expression and extend κ_1 and κ_2 with the respective values for $?y$; finally, we project $?x$ to obtain τ_1 and τ_2. Since we have already expanded $?x$, we should not repeat the projected answers as many times as there are elements in the owl:sameAs-clique for $?x$; instead, we output each projected answer only once to obtain the correct answer cardinalities.

6 Evaluation

We have implemented our approach in RDFox, allowing the system to handle owl:sameAs via rewriting (REW) or the axiomatisation (AX) from Section 3. We then compared the performance of materialisation using these two approaches. In particular, we investigated the scalability of each approach with the number of threads, and we measured the effect that rewriting has on the number of derivations and materialised triples.

Test Data Sets. We used five test data sets, each consisting of an OWL 2 DL ontology and a set of facts. The data sets were chosen because they contain axioms with the owl:sameAs property leading to interesting inferences. Four data sets were derived from real-world applications.

- Claros has been developed in an international collaboration between IT experts and archaeology and classical art research institutions with the aim of integrating disparate cultural heritage databases.[6]
- DBpedia is a crowd-sourced community effort to extract structured information from Wikipedia and make this information available on the Web.[7]
- OpenCyc is an extensive ontology about general human knowledge. It contains hundreds of thousands of terms organised in a carefully designed ontology and can be used as the basis of a wide variety of intelligent applications.[8]
- UniProt is a subset of an extensive knowledge base about protein sequences and functional information.[9]

[6]http://www.clarosnet.org/XDB/ASP/clarosHome/

[7]http://www.dbpedia.org/

[8]http://www.cyc.com/platform/opencyc/

[9]http://www.uniprot.org/

Table 1: An Example Run of Materialisation on P_{ex} and One Thread

Step 1			Step 2			Step 3		
1	⟨:USPres, :presOf, :US⟩		1	⟨:USPres, :presOf, :US⟩		1	⟨:USPres, :presOf, :US⟩	
▷2	⟨:Obama, :presOf, :Am⟩		2	⟨:Obama, :presOf, :Am⟩		2	~~⟨:Obama, :presOf, :Am⟩~~	$M(4)$
3	⟨:Obama, :presOf, :US⟩		▷3	⟨:Obama, :presOf, :US⟩		3	⟨:Obama, :presOf, :US⟩	
4	⟨:Am, ≈, :USA⟩	$R(2)$	4	⟨:Am, ≈, :USA⟩		▷4	~~⟨:Am, ≈, :USA⟩~~	$M(4)$
			5	⟨:US, ≈, :USA⟩	$R(3)$	5	⟨:US, ≈, :USA⟩	
						6	⟨:Obama, :presOf, :USA⟩	$W(2)$
						7	⟨:USA, ≈, :USA⟩	$W(4)$

Step 4			Step 5			Step 6		
1	⟨:USPres, :presOf, :US⟩		1	⟨:USPres, :presOf, :US⟩		1	~~⟨:USPres, :presOf, :US⟩~~	$M(9)$
3	⟨:Obama, :presOf, :US⟩	$W(6)$	3	⟨:Obama, :presOf, :US⟩		3	⟨:Obama, :presOf, :US⟩	
▷5	~~⟨:US, ≈, :USA⟩~~	$M(5)$	8	⟨:US, ≈, :US⟩	$R'(3)$	8	⟨:US, ≈, :US⟩	
6	~~⟨:Obama, :presOf, :USA⟩~~	$M(5)$	9	⟨:USPres, ≈, :Obama⟩	$S'(1)$	▷9	~~⟨:USPres, ≈, :Obama⟩~~	$M(9)$
7	~~⟨:USA, ≈, :USA⟩~~	$M(5)$	10	⟨:Obama, ≈, :Obama⟩	$S'(3)$	10	⟨:Obama, ≈, :Obama⟩	$W(9)$
8	⟨:US, ≈, :US⟩	$W(5,7)$						

The ontologies of all data sets other than DBpedia are not in the OWL 2 RL profile, so we first discarded all axioms outside OWL 2 RL, and then we translated the remaining axioms into rules as described in (Grosof et al. 2003).

Our fifth data set was UOBM (Ma et al. 2006)—a synthetic data set that extends the well-known LUBM (Guo, Pan, and Heflin 2005) benchmark. We did not use LUBM because neither its ontology nor its data uses the owl:sameAs property. The UOBM ontology is also outside OWL 2 RL; however, instead of using its OWL 2 RL subset, we used its *upper bound* (Zhou et al. 2013)—an unsound but complete OWL 2 RL approximation of the original ontology; thus, all answers that can be obtained from the original ontology can also be obtained from the upper bound, but not the other way around. Efficient materialisation of the upper bound was critical for the work by Zhou et al. (2013), and it has proved to be challenging due to equality reasoning.

The left-hand part of Table 2 summarises our test data sets: column 'Rules' shows the total number of rules, column 'sA-rules' shows the number of rules containing the owl:sameAs property in the head, and column 'Triples before' shows the number of triples before materialisation.

Test Setting. We conducted our tests on a Dell computer with 128 GB of RAM and two Xeon E5-2643 processors with a total of 8 physical and 16 virtual cores, running 64-bit Fedora release 20, kernel version 3.13.3-201. We have not conducted warm and cold start tests separately since, as a main-memory system, the performance of RDFox should not be affected by the state of the operating system's buffers. For the AX tests, we extended the relevant program with the seven rules from Section 3. In all cases we verified that the expansion of the rewritten triples is identical to the triples derived using the axiomatisation.

Effect of Rewriting on Total Work. In order to see how rewriting affects the total amount of work, we materialised each test data set in both AX and REW modes while collecting statistics about the inference process; the results are shown in the right-hand part of Table 2. Column 'Triples after' shows the number of triples after materialisation; in the case of REW tests, we additionally show the number of unmarked triples (i.e., of triples relevant to query answering). Column 'Memory' shows the total memory use as measured by RDFox's internal counters. Column 'Rule appl.' shows the total number of times a rule has been applied to a triple, and column 'Derivations' shows the total number of derivations. Column 'Merged resources' shows the number of resources that were replaced with representatives in the course of materialisation. Finally, row 'factor' shows the ratio between the respective values in the AX and the REW tests.

As one can see, the reduction in the number of the derived triples is correlated with the number of rewritten constants: on UniProt there is no observable reduction since only five resources are merged; however, equalities proliferate on OpenCyc and so rewriting is particularly effective. In all cases the numbers of marked triples are negligible, suggesting that our decision to mark, rather than delete triples does not have unexpected drawbacks. In contrast, the reduction in the number of rule applications and, in particular, of derivations is much more pronounced than the reduction in the number of derived triples.

Effect of Rewriting on Materialisation Times. In order to see how rewriting affects materialisation times, we measured the wall-clock times needed to materialise our test data sets in AX and REW modes on 1, 2, 4, 8, 12, and 16 threads. For each test, we report average wall-clock time over three runs. Table 3 shows our test results; column 'sec' shows the materialisation time in seconds, column 'spd' shows the speedup over the single-threaded version, and column '$\frac{\text{AX}}{\text{REW}}$' shows the speedup of REW over AX.

As one can see from the table, RDFox parallelises computation exceptionally well in both AX and REW modes. When using the eight physical cores of our test server, the speedup is consistently between six and seven, which suggests that the lock-free algorithms and data structures of RDFox are very effective. We believe that the more-than-linear speedup on Claros is due to improved memory locality resulting in fewer CPU cache misses. The speedup continues to increase with hyperthreading, but is less pronounced:

Table 2: Test Data Sets Before and After Materialisation

	Rules	sA-rules	Triples before	Mode	Triples after: unmarked	Triples after: total	Memory (GB)	Rule appl.	Derivations	Merged resources
Claros	1312	42	19M	AX	102M		4.5	867M	11,009M	
				REW	79.5M	79.7M	3.6	149M	128M	12,890
				factor		1.28x	1.28x	5.8x	85.5x	
DBPedia	3384	23	113M	AX	139M		6.9	934M	895M	
				REW	136M	136M	7.0	44.5M	37M	7,430
				factor		1.2x	0.99x	21.0x	24.4x	
OpenCyc	261,067	3,781	2.4M	AX	1,176M		35.9	7,832M	12,890M	
				REW	141M	142M	4.6	309M	281M	361,386
				factor		7.8x	7.8x	25.3x	45.9x	
UniProt	451	60	123M	AX	228M		15.1	1,801M	1,555M	
				REW	228M	228M	15.1	262M	183M	5
				factor		1.0x	1.0x	6.9x	8.5x	
UOBM	279	4	2.2M	AX	36M		1.2	332M	16,152M	
				REW	9.4M	9.7M	0.4	33.8M	4,256M	686
				factor		3.2x	3.2x	9.9x	3.8x	

Table 3: Materialisation Times with Axiomatisation and Rewriting

Test	Claros					DBpedia					OpenCyc				
Threads	AX		REW		AX/REW	AX		REW		AX/REW	AX		REW		AX/REW
	sec	spd	sec	spd		sec	spd	sec	spd		sec	spd	sec	spd	
1	2042.9	1.0	65.8	1.0	31.1	219.8	1.0	31.7	1.0	6.9	2093.7	1.0	119.9	1.0	17.5
2	969.7	2.1	35.2	1.9	27.6	114.6	1.9	17.6	1.8	6.5	1326.5	1.6	78.3	1.5	16.9
4	462.0	4.4	18.1	3.6	25.5	66.3	3.3	10.7	3.0	6.2	692.6	3.0	40.5	3.0	17.1
8	237.2	8.6	9.9	6.7	24.1	36.1	6.1	5.2	6.0	6.9	351.3	6.0	23.0	5.2	15.2
12	184.9	11.1	7.9	8.3	23.3	31.9	6.9	4.1	7.7	7.7	291.8	7.2	56.2	2.1	5.5
16	153.4	13.3	6.9	9.6	22.3	27.5	8.0	3.6	8.8	7.7	254.0	8.2	52.3	2.3	4.9

Test	UniProt					UOBM				
Threads	AX		REW		AX/REW	AX		REW		AX/REW
	sec	spd	sec	spd		sec	spd	sec	spd	
1	370.6	1.0	143.4	1.0	2.6	2696.7	1.0	1152.7	1.0	2.3
2	232.3	1.6	86.7	1.7	2.7	1524.6	1.8	599.6	1.9	2.5
4	129.2	2.9	46.5	3.1	2.8	813.3	3.3	318.3	3.6	2.6
8	74.7	5.0	25.1	5.7	3.0	439.9	6.1	177.7	6.5	2.5
12	61.0	6.1	19.9	7.2	3.1	348.9	7.7	152.7	7.6	2.3
16	61.9	6.0	17.1	8.4	3.6	314.4	8.6	137.9	8.4	2.3

virtual cores do not provide additional execution resources, and so they mainly compensate for CPU stalls due to cache misses. The AX mode seems to scale better with the number of threads than the REW mode, and we believe this to be due to contention between threads while accessing the map ρ. Only OpenCyc in REW mode did not scale particularly well: OpenCyc contains many rules, so sequentially updating P and the associated rule index when ρ changes becomes a significant parallelisation bottleneck. Finally, since the materialisation of Claros with more than eight threads in REW mode takes less than ten seconds, these results are difficult to measure and are susceptible to skew.

Our results confirm that rewriting can significantly reduce materialisation times. RDFox was consistently faster in the REW mode than in the AX mode even on UniProt, where the reduction in the number of triples is negligible. This is due to the reduction in the number of derivations, mainly involving rules ($\approx_1$)–($\approx_5$), which is still significant on UniProt. In all cases, the speedup of rewriting is typically much larger than the reduction in the number of derived triples (cf. Table 2), suggesting that the primary benefit of rewriting lies in less work needed to match the rules, rather than, as commonly thought thus far, in reducing the number of derived triples. This is consistent with the fact that the speedup of rewriting was not so pronounced on UniProt and UOBM, where the reduction in the number of derivations was less significant.

Our analysis of the derivations that RDFox makes on UOBM revealed that, due to the derived owl:sameAs triples, the materialisation contains large numbers of resources connected by the :hasSameHomeTownWith property. This property is also symmetric and transitive so, for each pair of connected resources, the number of times each triple is derived by the transitivity rule is quadratic in the number of connected resources. This leads to a large number of duplicate derivations that do *not* involve equality. Thus, although it is helpful, rewriting does not reduce the number of deriva- tion in the same way as, for example, on Claros, which explains the relatively modest speedup of REW over AX.

7 Conclusion

In this paper we have investigated issues related to the use of rewriting in materialisation based OWL 2 RL systems, and have shown how these issues can lead to both increased computation costs and incorrect query answers. We have addressed these issues by presenting algorithms that guarantee the correctness of query answers for any input ontology and data set. Moreover, we have implemented our algorithms in the RDFox system, a preliminary evaluation of which has shown that our approach parallelises computation very well in practice and can reduce materialisation times on practical data sets by orders of magnitude.

Acknowledgements

This work was supported by the EPSRC projects MaSI^3, Score! and DBOnto, and by the EU FP7 project Optique.

References

Abiteboul, S.; Hull, R.; and Vianu, V. 1995. *Foundations of Databases*. Addison Wesley.

Baader, F., and Nipkow, T. 1998. *Term Rewriting and All That*. Cambridge University Press.

Bishop, B.; Kiryakov, A.; Ognyanoff, D.; Peikov, I.; Tashev, Z.; and Velkov, R. 2011. Owlim: A family of scalable semantic repositories. *Semantic Web* 2(1):33–42.

Grosof, B. N.; Horrocks, I.; Volz, R.; and Decker, S. 2003. Description Logic Programs: Combining Logic Programs with Description Logic. In *Proc. WWW*, 48–57.

Guo, Y.; Pan, Z.; and Heflin, J. 2005. LUBM: A benchmark for OWL knowledge base systems. *Journal of Web Semantics* 3(2–3):158–182.

Harris, S., and Seaborne, A. 2013. SPARQL 1.1 Overview. W3C Recommendation. http://www.w3.org/TR/sparql11-overview/.

Herlihy, M., and Shavit, N. 2008. *The Art of Multiprocessor Programming*. Morgan Kaufmann.

Horrocks, I.; Patel-Schneider, P. F.; Boley, H.; Tabet, S.; Grosof, B.; and Dean, M. 2004. SWRL: A semantic web rule language combining OWL and RuleML. W3C Member Submission. http://www.w3.org/Submission/SWRL/.

Kolovski, V.; Wu, Z.; and Eadon, G. 2010. Optimizing Enterprise-Scale OWL 2 RL Reasoning in a Relational Database System. In *Proc. ISWC*, 436–452.

Ma, L.; Yang, Y.; Qiu, Z.; Xie, G. T.; Pan, Y.; and Liu, S. 2006. Towards a Complete OWL Ontology Benchmark. In *Proc. ESWC*, 125–139.

Manola, F., and Miller, E. 2004. RDF primer. W3C Recommendation. http://www.w3.org/TR/rdf-primer/.

Motik, B.; Cuenca Grau, B.; Horrocks, I.; Wu, Z.; Fokoue, A.; and Lutz, C. 2012. OWL 2 Web Ontology Language Profiles (Second Edition). W3C Recommendation. http://www.w3.org/TR/owl2-profiles/.

Motik, B.; Nenov, Y.; Piro, R.; Horrocks, I.; and Olteanu, D. 2014a. Parallel materialisation of Datalog programs in centralised, main-memory RDF systems. In *Proc. of the 28th Nat. Conf. on Artificial Intelligence (AAAI 14)*, 129–137. AAAI Press.

Motik, B.; Nenov, Y.; Piro, R.; and Horrocks, I. 2014b. Handling owl:sameAs via Rewriting. arXiv:cs/1411.3622.

Motik, B.; Patel-Schneider, P. F.; and Parsia, B. 2012. OWL 2 Web Ontology Language Structural Specification and Functional-style Syntax (Second Edition). W3C Recommendation. http://www.w3.org/TR/owl2-syntax/.

Nieuwenhuis, R., and Rubio, A. 2001. Paramodulation-Based Theorem Proving. In Robinson, A., and Voronkov, A., eds., *Handbook of Automated Reasoning*, volume I. Elsevier Science. chapter 7, 371–443.

Stocker, M., and Smith, M. 2008. Owlgres: A Scalable OWL Reasoner. In *Proc. OWLED: Experiences and Directions Workshop*, 26–27.

Urbani, J.; Kotoulas, S.; Maassen, J.; van Harmelen, F.; and Bal, H. E. 2012. WebPIE: A Web-scale Parallel Inference Engine using MapReduce. *Journal of Web Semantics* 10:59–75.

Wu, Z.; Eadon, G.; Das, S.; Chong, E. I.; Kolovski, V.; Annamalai, M.; and Srinivasan, J. 2008. Implementing an Inference Engine for RDFS/OWL Constructs and User-Defined Rules in Oracle. In *Proc. ICDE*, 1239–1248.

Zhou, Y.; Cuenca Grau, B.; Horrocks, I.; Wu, Z.; and Banerjee, J. 2013. Making the most of your triple store: query answering in OWL 2 using an RL reasoner. In *Proc. WWW*, 1569–1580.

Proceedings of the Twenty-Ninth AAAI Conference on Artificial Intelligence

Incorporating Assortativity and Degree Dependence into Scalable Network Models

Stephen Mussmann[1,2]* and **John Moore**[1]* and **Joseph J. Pfeiffer III**[1] and **Jennifer Neville**[1]
Departments of Computer Science and Statistics[1], and Mathematics[2]
Purdue University, West Lafayette, IN
Email: {somussma, moore269, jpfeiffer, neville}@purdue.edu
*Authors contributed equally

Abstract

Due to the recent availability of large complex networks, considerable analysis has focused on understanding and characterizing the properties of these networks. Scalable generative graph models focus on modeling distributions of graphs that match real world network properties and scale to large datasets. Much work has focused on modeling networks with a power law degree distribution, clustering, and small diameter. In network analysis, the *assortativity* statistic is defined as the correlation between the degrees of linked nodes in the network. The assortativity measure can distinguish between types of networks—social networks commonly exhibit positive assortativity, in contrast to biological or technological networks that are typically disassortative. Despite this, little work has focused on scalable graph models that capture assortativity in networks.

The contributions of our work are twofold. First, we prove that an unbounded number of pairs of networks exist with the same degree distribution and assortativity, yet different joint degree distributions. Thus, assortativity as a network measure cannot distinguish between graphs with complex (nonlinear) dependence in their joint degree distributions. Motivated by this finding, we introduce a generative graph model that explicitly estimates and models the joint degree distribution. Our *Binned Chung Lu* method accurately captures both the joint degree distribution and assortativity, while still matching characteristics such as the degree distribution and clustering coefficients. Further, our method has subquadratic learning and sampling methods that enable scaling to large, real world networks. We evaluate performance compared to other scalable graph models on six real world networks, including a citation network with over 14 million edges.

1 Introduction

Networks are commonly used as a representation for understanding complex systems. For example, interactions of physical systems (e.g., internet topology), biology (e.g., protein interactions), the Web (e.g., hyperlink structure) and social networks (e.g., Facebook, email) can be represented as networks. This has led to considerable interest in understanding these networks and constructing generative network models that can capture a wide range of network behavior. Generally speaking, generative graph models are used to reason about observed graph structures by constructing graphs that are, ideally, structurally similar to an input graph. The methods use an input (observed) graph to estimate parameters of the model, then the learned parameters are used to generate a new network by drawing a sample from the model. A variety of scalable generative network models exist that capture common network structure such as a power law degree distribution, small diameter and clustering coefficients (Chung and Lu 2002; Kolda et al. 2013; Leskovec et al. 2010; Pfeiffer III et al. 2012).

However, the *assortativity* of a network, or the tendency for vertices to form connections with other vertices of similar degree, is largely overlooked in these modeling efforts. This is surprising in the sense that assortativity typically reflects the network type: social networks generally have positive assortativity, while biological and technological networks are generally disassortative (i.e., negative assortativity) (Stanton and Pinar 2011). Thus, the assortativity in a network can provide significant insight into the type of complex network observed, making it a popular statistic within social network analysis (Newman 2002; Zhou et al. 2012).

Although assortativity is rarely directly modeled, it may be produced as a byproduct of the modeling process. For example, the Block Two-Level Erdos Renyi (BTER) model (Kolda et al. 2013) groups clusters of vertices with similar degree together in such a way that the vertices *within* a cluster have higher probability of linking to each other; this representation produces networks with high clustering and assortativity. However, this approach cannot produce disassortative networks and moreover, the assortativity and clustering cannot be varied independently, since they are tied together in the process. Stanton and Pinar (2011) explicitly model the joint degree distribution of a network, which generalizes the assortativity summary statistic. However, their approach that directly models the entire joint degree distribution is quadratic in the number of unique degrees in the network, and their model cannot easily model other network statistics (e.g., clustering).

In this work, we explore two aspects of this problem. First, we formally discuss the relationship between the assortativity of a network and its joint degree distribution. Namely, we prove that assortativity alone cannot summarize the joint degree distribution of a network: even networks with identical degree distributions and assortativity can have provably different joint degree distributions. Second, we develop a *Binned Chung Lu* (BCL) generative graph model that can *learn* assortativity patterns from an input graph and reflect them accurately in the sampled networks. Specifically, we enhance the Chung Lu (CL) family of models (Chung and Lu 2002; Pfeiffer III et al. 2012) to learn and incorporate a model of the joint degree distribution (JDD)—using a coarse *binning* technique to summarize the JDD with a small number of parameters and a statistical accept-reject sampling process that augments the original CL model to sample networks to match the the observed patterns in the JDD. Unlike previous approaches, our BCL method can accurately *learn* and model a wide range of joint degree distributions (i.e., with both positive and negative assortativity). Moreover, since our binning approach provably matches the coarse JDD of the original network, it will also coarsely preserve the assortativity. We also prove that our BCL approach maintains the same expected degree distributions as the baseline CL model and remains scalable (i.e., subquadratic). Our contributions can be summarized as follows:

- Introduction of a coarse binning technique to capture the joint degree distribution and assortativity found in a range of real world networks.
- Proof that assortativity cannot distinguish joint degree distributions, including a constructive proof for an infinite class of graphs and an illustrative real-world example.
- Development of an accept-reject sampling process to efficiently sample networks with a prescribed JDD and assortativity, and a method to efficiently learn the corresponding model parameters.
- Proofs that our BCL approach only incurs an extra subquadratic learning and constant sampling cost.
- Proofs that our model and sampling algorithm preserves the degree distribution and bin frequencies (i.e., approximate JDD).

Our BCL approach is general enough to use with any CL model, but for this paper we implement and experiment with two different baseline models: Fast Chung Lu with Binning (FCLB), which extends the Fast Chung Lu model of (Kolda et al. 2013), and Transitive Chung Lu with Binning (TCLB), which extends the Transitive Chung Lu model of (Pfeiffer III et al. 2012). We apply our methods to six network datasets and show they are able to accurately capture assortativity (significantly better than baseline methods) while maintaining other graph properties of the original models. Additionally, to empirically demonstrate the scalability of the models, we apply them to learn and sample from a Patents dataset with 14 million edges.

In the following section, we outline the notation used, introduce the Chung Lu model with its variants, and discuss related work. Section 3 discusses assortativity in detail. Section 4 outlines our BCL method and analyzes its characteristics. In section 5, we compare BCL experimental to competing models. We conclude in section 6.

2 Notation and Background

Let a graph $G = \langle \mathbf{V}, \mathbf{E} \rangle$ define a set of *vertices* or nodes $\mathbf{V}$, with a corresponding set of edges $\mathbf{E} \subseteq \mathbf{V} \times \mathbf{V}$. We denote the individual edges $e_{ij} \in \mathbf{E}$ where $e_{ij} = (v_i, v_j)$. As the graph is undirected, $e_{ij} \in \mathbf{E}$ if and only if $e_{ji} \in \mathbf{E}$. Let D_i be the degree of node v_i in the graph. Let M be the total number of edges in the graph. Note that $|\mathbf{E}| = 2M$ since each undirected edge corresponds to two elements in $\mathbf{E}$. We refer to the number of nodes of each degree as the degree distribution of the graph.

Assortativity is a graph measure defined in (Newman 2002); formally, it is the correlation of degrees across edges observed in the network. Define $T_\beta(e_{ij}) = D_i$ and $T_\epsilon(e_{ij}) = D_j$. Intuitively, $\{T_\beta(e) | e \in \mathbf{E}\}$ is the distribution of degrees of the startpoints of edges in graph G, while $\{T_\epsilon(e) | e \in \mathbf{E}\}$ is the distribution of degrees of the endpoints in graph G. The assortativity is the Pearson correlation coefficient for these variables:

$$\mathcal{A} = \frac{cov(\{T_\beta(e), T_\epsilon(e) | e \in \mathbf{E}\})}{\sqrt{var(\{T_\beta(e) | e \in \mathbf{E}\})} \cdot \sqrt{var(\{T_\epsilon(e) | e \in \mathbf{E}\})}} \quad (1)$$

Note that as the graph is undirected, the variances of the random variables are equal; however, the *covariance* can widely vary depending on the network structure (as we will explore in detail in Section 3). A more in depth discussion of assortativity can be found in (Newman 2002).

Chung-Lu Models

The Chung Lu models are a family of models such that the expected degree of a vertex in a sampled network is equal to the degree of the node in the original network (Chung and Lu 2002). Chung Lu models define the marginal probability of an edge to be proportional to the product of the endpoint degrees normalized by a constant; i.e., $(D_i D_j)/2M$.

The structural assumptions of the model enable a fast sampling method for sparse networks; although the model defines a set of edge probabilities quadratic in the number of vertices, efficient sampling algorithms exist that are linear in the number of edges. This Fast Chung Lu (FCL) algorithm (Pinar, Seshadhri, and Kolda 2011) generates a graph by repeatedly sampling proportional to their defined probabilities and adds them to the network. Let G be an observed graph and π be a normalized degree distribution ($\pi(i) = D_i/2M$). For M iterations, the FCL algorithm samples twice from π to select an i, j pair and then adds the edge e_{ij} to the output graph G'. FCL provably samples a given network's degree distribution in expectation. However, for most graphs, the observed clustering coefficient is much higher than what is generated by FCL.

In contrast, the Transitive Chung Lu (TCL) graph model extends the simple FCL method to incorporate *transitivity* into the sampling process (Pfeiffer III et al. 2012). In particular, TCL is a mixture model: with probability $1 - \rho$ it samples an edge using FCL, but with probability ρ performs a two hop random walk across the current network sample. Starting at a vertex v_i, once it takes two random steps it places an edge between v_i and the endpoint v_j. Thus, TCL incorporates transitivity into the network distribution by inserting triangles at a higher probability. This adjustment provably maintains the degree distribution, but allows TCL to accurately model the clustering of real world networks. TCL has a simple and scalable learning algorithm, meaning that it already can accurately learn p from large scale networks. Further, TCL provably samples twice from the corresponding marginal degree distributions, which will be an important criteria for this work. Our method will be able to be used with TCL, allowing us to model large scale networks' degree distributions, clustering coefficients and joint degree distributions.

Attributed Graph Models

Recently, the *Attributed Graph Model* (Pfeiffer III et al. 2014) was proposed as an extension to generative graph models to allow for jointly modeling the dependencies between vertex attributes and network structure. This method augments generative graph models to incorporate correlated attributes while accurately maintaining patterns in the graph structure. In that work, *accept-reject* sampling was used to keep proposed FCL and TCL edges from being inserted into a final network if they did not match the desired correlations (with some probability). This representation provably samples from the set of edges conditioned on the vertex attributes, and has scalable learning and sampling algorithms for determining the acceptance probabilities given an attributed network. In this work, we expand on this to prove that higher order graph statistics (namely, the joint degree distribution) can be efficiently learned and sampled while maintaining lower order statistics (degree, clustering).

Accept-reject sampling is a framework used in statistics (Liang, Liu, and Carrol 2010) that we will employ in our BCL method. In particular, given a proposal distribution Q' that is easy to sample from, we wish to use Q' to sample from a more complex target distribution Q. Using accept reject sampling, we can repeatedly draw from Q' but only *accept* the sample some of the time. In particular, for each value x that is drawn from Q', we flip a Bernoulli coin with probability proportional to $\frac{Q(x)}{Q'(x)}$ and only accept the sample x if the Bernoulli trial is a success. In particular the probability that x is sampled is $A(x) = \frac{Q(x)}{Q'(x)Z}$, where Z is a constant such that $\forall\, x,\ A(x) \leq 1$. Note that as samples are drawn from $Q'(x)$, the resulting distribution (after the rejection process) is simply $Q(x)$.

3 Assortativity in Graph Models

Assortativity is a measure of the correlation among the degrees of linked nodes in a network (Newman 2002). It is a popular measure used to categorize and understand the structure of a network, since different types of networks have varying amounts of assortativity. For example, social networks tend to have positive assortativity while biological and technological networks tend to have negative assortativity (Stanton and Pinar 2011). See Table 1 for the assortativity ($\mathcal{A}$) we observed across six networks of varying sizes that we considered in this work, ranging from 0.18 to -0.29 (the details on each is discussed in Section 5).

Graph	Nodes	Edges	$\mathcal{A}$	$\hat{\mathcal{A}}_{TCL}$
Facebook Wall	444,829	1,014,542	-0.297	-0.0021
Purdue Email	54,076	880,693	-0.1161	-0.0092
Gnutella	36,682	88,328	-0.1034	0.0006
Epinions	75,865	385,418	0.0226	-0.0363
Rovira Email	1,133	5,451	0.0782	-0.0200
Patents	2,745,762	13,965,410	0.1813	0.0004

Figure 1: Network Statistics

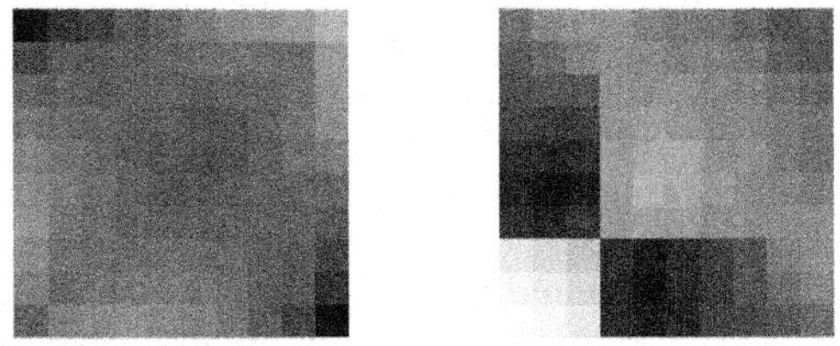

(a) Purdue Email (b) Gnutella

Figure 2: Joint degree distribution representations $\mathcal{B}$; $k=10$.

However, despite its popularity as a graph measure, assortativity can fail to capture important dependencies in the joint degree distribution. This is because it measures degree correlation and thus focuses on linear relationships. Consider the real-world examples depicted in Figures 2.a-b, which illustrate the joint degree distributions of the Purdue email and Gnutella networks respectively. To (coarsely) visualize the joint degree distribution, we divide the degrees of a graph G into k quantiles that we refer to as $\mathbf{B}_k = [B_1, B_2, ..., B_k]$. In Figure 2, we use $k = 10$. Let $b(D)$ be a function that returns the set membership in $\mathbf{B}_k$ for a given degree D. We can now construct a $k \times k$ matrix $\mathcal{B}$ to represent the joint degree distribution, where each cell i, j counts the number of edges between nodes with degrees in B_i and those with degree B_j. In other words, an edge e_{ij} would be counted in cell $[b(D_i), b(D_j)]$. When visualizing $\mathcal{B}$, we use a gray scale intensity plot to indicate the number of edges in each cell (i.e., a cell without any edges will be colored white and a cell with the largest amount of edges will be close to black).

Assuming the axes of $\mathcal{B}$ are ordered by increasing degree, as we do above, these plots show information related to assortativity. If the darker boxes form a line with a positive slope, the graph will have positive assortativity. In contrast, if the dark boxes form a line with a negative slope, the graph will have negative assortativity. More precisely, the *binned* plots are a histogram approximation to the full joint degree distribution; they graphically represent the dependencies between the various degrees in the network.

The Purdue Email and Gnutella datasets have similar assortativity values of -0.1161 and -0.1034, respectively. However, their joint degree distributions are quite different as can be seen in Figures 2.a-b. These examples illustrate evidence in support our claim that the single dimensional measure of assortativity does not fully capture the dependencies we observe in joint degree distributions in real networks.

To expand on this individual example, we prove in Theo-

D	A	B
1	8910	8910
5	1782	1782
10	176	176

(a) Degrees

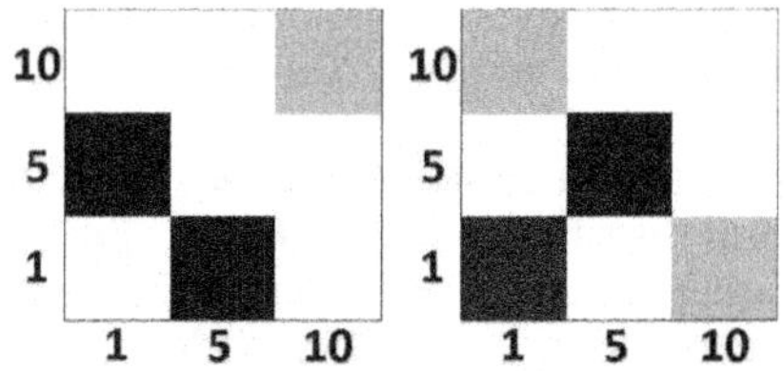

(b) Graph A (c) Graph B

Figure 3: (a) Degree distribution; (b-c) Joint degree distribution representations $\mathcal{B}$; $k = 3$.

rem 1 that there are infinitely many pairs of graphs with the same assortativity and degree distribution, but maximally different joint degree distributions (Proof in Appendix).

Theorem 1. *Let A_w, B_w be two networks comprised of graphlets, where w parameterizes the size and counts of the graphlets. There exist an infinite set of pairs of graphs $\{A_w, B_w\}$ such that for any $w \geq 2$, A_w and B_w have the same degree distribution, the same assortativity, but infinite KL-Divergence between their joint degree distributions.*

As an example of a pair of graphs that are covered by Thm. 1, we construct two Graphs A and B with $w = 5$. The graphs are composed of disconnected subgraphs that are either stars or cliques. Graph A consists of 1782 stars of size 5 and 16 cliques of size 11. Graph B consists of 176 stars of size 10, 297 cliques of size 6, and 3575 cliques of size 2. Both of these graphs have the exact same degree distribution (see Table 3.a) and the same assortativity: $\mathcal{A} = \frac{9}{187}$. However, Figures 3.b-c show that the two graphs have very different joint degree distributions, despite their identical assortativity and degree distributions. Further, as the two joint degree distributions have disjoint support, the KL-Divergence between them is infinite. Next, we propose a novel approach to modeling assortativity in networks that considers dependencies in the full joint distribution.

4 Binning Chung Lu

Most generative graph models are not able to reproduce assortativity, and even fewer model negative assortativity. For example, although Chung Lu (CL) models preserve other network statistics, the processes produce no correlation between the degrees of edge endpoints. This results in network samples with near zero assortativity (see Figure 1). We now propose the Binning Chung Lu (BCL) method to model assortativity in networks.

Generally speaking, our BCL methods use an existing edge-by-edge generative graph model (such as FCL or TCL) to *propose* possible edges from their respective distributions. BCL then filters, or conditionally accepts, a subset of the proposed edges into a final network sample. By estimating the correct acceptance probabilities, the final accepted edge samples are provably from the desired joint degree distribution. Our approach is a form of accept reject sampling and general enough to augment any Chung Lu model. In this paper, we implement our approach using both FCL and TCL—referring to them as FCLB and TCLB respectively.

More specifically, BCL expands on the binning visualization introduced in the previous section. First, BCL creates a "degree vector", where the pair (D_i, v_i) is inserted in the vector D_i times. We then sort this vector by the degrees of the vertices, followed by dividing the vector into k equal segments, or *quantiles*. These quantiles correspond to the bins discussed in the visualization from the previous section: every vertex v_i is assigned to its corresponding bin, or quantile, as determined by the vertex's degree D_i. Similarly, the vertices contained within a bin B_p are the vertices with degrees in the pth quantile of the degree vector. Then the $k \times k$ matrix $\mathcal{B}$ represents the count of the number of observed edges e_{ij} that fall in a particular cell indexed by $[b(D_i), b(D_j)]$.

Given $\mathcal{B}$, which is our coarse, *binned* representation of the joint degree distribution, we can outline an accept-reject sampling method to extend a given FCL or TCL model. Formally, the original CL model is a proposal distribution Q': FCL and TCL are chosen due to their scalable sampling processes. We define the target distribution Q to be a network distribution with the same binned joint degree distribution as the input graph.

To implement BCL, we first compute the bin representation $\mathbf{B}_k$ and associated $\mathcal{B}$ from an input graph G. We then generate a graph G' from the CL model, using G as input, and compute the resulting joint degree distribution $\mathcal{B}'$ from G' (using $\mathbf{B}_k$). With $\mathcal{B}$ and $\mathcal{B}'$, we estimate the acceptance probabilities A:

$$R(m,n) = \frac{\#\{e_{ij} \in \mathbf{E} \mid b(D(i)) = m \wedge b(D(j)) = n\}}{\#\{e_{ij} \in \mathbf{E}' \mid b(D(i)) = m \wedge b(D(j)) = n\}} = \frac{\mathcal{B}_{mn}}{\mathcal{B}'_{mn}}$$

$$A(m,n) = \frac{R(m,n)}{\max_{mn} R(m,n)} = \frac{R(m,n)}{R_{max}}$$

We refer to the sampling process of the CL model as $\pi(\Theta)$. Thus, we sample two nodes i, j from π and after each sample, determine whether to accept or reject the edge e_{ij} depending on the corresponding bin's acceptance probability. We repeat this process until we have sampled as many edges as the original graph.

This process is described in Algorithm 1. G is the original graph, π is the CL model, and Θ is the parameters for the CL model. Note that we must first generate a preliminary graph using the CL model so that we can compute the acceptance probabilities. For a proposed edge e_{ij} (line 7), $A(b(D_i), b(D_j))$ returns the acceptance probability from the appropriate cell of $\mathcal{B}$ (Line 8). Lastly, lines 9-12 determine whether to accept the proposed edge into the final set.

In the next subsection, we prove that our BCL approach maintains the original degree distributions as guaranteed by FCL and TCL, while also modeling the true joint degree distribution of the original network and (by extension) the assortativity.

Analysis of Binning Chung Lu Models

In this section, we prove the following key theorems:

- **Theorem 2:** In expectation, the Binning Chung Lu models provably sample from the original coarse JDD.

Algorithm 1 Binning Chung Lu Method(G, π, Θ, k)

Compute $k \times k$ bin frequencies $\mathcal{B}$ from G
Generate G' from π, using G and Θ
Compute $k \times k$ bin frequencies $\mathcal{B}'$ from G'
Compute $A(m,n)$ from $\mathcal{B}$ and $\mathcal{B}'$
Create empty graph G^{BCL}
while $|E^{BCL}| \leq |E|$ **do**
  $<i,j>=$ edge sampled using $\pi(\Theta)$
  $a = A(b(D_i), b(D_j))$
  $r = bernoulli\_sample(a)$
  if $r = 1$ **then**
    $E^{BCL} = E^{BCL} \cup e_{ij}$
  end if
end while
$return(G^{BCL})$

- **Theorem 3:** The expected degree of a node sampled using Binning Chung Lu models equals the original degree.

These proofs exploit a key relationship between the Chung Lu graph models and the defined quantiles; namely, the Chung Lu graph models sample uniformly from the coarse JDD representation. In the following Lemma, we use this to derive the probability a given sample from a Chung Lu model is accepted by Binning Chung Lu. This is subsequently used to prove both Theorem 2 and 3.

Lemma 1. *In BCL, if the edges are sampled from a Chung Lu model, the marginal probability that an edge sample is accepted is* $\frac{1}{R_{max}}$.

Proof. First, the acceptance probability is equivalent to marginalizing over all the acceptance probabilities for each e_{ij}. Let k_1, k_2 indicate a particular bin index. Then:

$$
\begin{aligned}
P(\text{accepted}) &= \sum_{e_{ij}} P(e_{ij}) P(\text{accepted}|e_{ij}) \\
&= \sum_{e_{ij}} \frac{D_i D_j}{(2M)(2M)} \sum_{k_1,k_2} \frac{\mathbb{I}[e_{ij} \in R(k_1,k_2)] \cdot R(k_1,k_2)}{R_{max}} \\
&= \frac{1}{R_{max}} \sum_{k_1,k_2} \sum_{e_{ij} \in Bin(k_1,k_2)} \frac{D_i D_j}{(2M)(2M)} R(k_1,k_2) \\
&= \frac{1}{R_{max}} \sum_{k_1,k_2} \sum_{e_{ij} \in Bin(k_1,k_2)} \frac{D_i D_j}{(2M)(2M)} \frac{\mathcal{B}_{k_1 k_2}}{\mathcal{B}'_{k_1 k_2}}
\end{aligned}
$$

The edge probabilities can be further split by their respective quantiles $Qu(k_1), Qu(k_2)$, i.e., $Qu(k) = \{v_i | b(D_i) = B_k\}$:

$$
\begin{aligned}
P(\text{accepted}) &= \frac{1}{R_{max}} \sum_{k_1} \sum_{k_2} \left(\sum_{i \in Qu(k_1)} \frac{D_i}{2M} \right) \left(\sum_{j \in Qu(k_2)} \frac{D_j}{2M} \right) \frac{\mathcal{B}_{k_1 k_2}}{\mathcal{B}'_{k_1 k_2}} \\
&= \frac{1}{R_{max}} \frac{1}{k} \frac{1}{k} \sum_{k_1} \sum_{k_2} \frac{\mathcal{B}_{k_1 k_2}}{\mathcal{B}'_{k_1 k_2}}
\end{aligned}
$$

As Chung Lu models have uniform bin distribution $\forall\, k_1, k_2$, we have $\mathcal{B}'_{k_1 k_2} = \frac{2M}{k^2}$. Thus:

$$
P(\text{accepted}) = \frac{1}{R_{max}} \frac{1}{k} \frac{1}{k} \frac{k^2}{2M} \sum_{k_1} \sum_{k_2} \mathcal{B}_{k_1,k_2}
$$

As the sum over all the bin frequencies is $2M$, we simplify the above to recover $P(\text{accepted}) = \frac{1}{R_{max}}$. □

Using the above lemma, we show that although the proposal distribution (FCL or TCL) proposes edges from a uniform joint degree distribution, the edges *accepted* into the network sample provably model the joint degree distribution of the original network.

Theorem 2. *For a graph G^{BCL} generated by BCL, the expected edge frequency in bin $\mathcal{B}^{BCL}_{k_1 k_2}$ is equal to the frequency in bin $\mathcal{B}_{k_1 k_2}$, from the original input graph G.*

Proof. The probability of accepting an edge in a bin is:

$$
\begin{aligned}
P(\text{edge in } \mathcal{B}^{BCL}_{k_1 k_2}) &= \sum_{e_{ij} \in \mathcal{B}^{BCL}_{k_1 k_2}} P(e_{ij} \text{ sampled}) A(k_1, k_2) \\
&= \sum_{e_{ij} \in \mathcal{B}^{BCL}_{k_1 k_2}} 2 \frac{D_i D_j}{(2M)(2M)} \frac{R(k_1,k_2)}{R_{max}}
\end{aligned}
$$

Summing over quantiles:

$$
\begin{aligned}
&P(\text{edge in } \mathcal{B}^{BCL}_{k_1 k_2}) \\
&= \frac{2}{R_{max}} \left(\sum_{i \in Qu(k_1)} \frac{D_i}{2M} \right) \left(\sum_{j \in Qu(k_2)} \frac{D_j}{2M} \right) \frac{\mathcal{B}_{k_1 k_2}}{\mathcal{B}'_{k_1 k_2}}
\end{aligned}
$$

Chung Lu models have uniform bin distribution so $\mathcal{B}'_{k_1 k_2} = \frac{2M}{k^2}$ and further by definition, the sum of degrees are uniformly distribution among the k quantiles:

$$
\begin{aligned}
P(\text{edge in } \mathcal{B}^{BCL}_{k_1 k_2}) &= \frac{2\mathcal{B}_{k_1,k_2}}{R_{max}} \frac{1}{k} \frac{1}{k} \frac{k^2}{2M} \\
&= \frac{\mathcal{B}_{k_1,k_2}}{R_{max} M}
\end{aligned}
\tag{2}
$$

The overall acceptance probability is $\frac{1}{R_{max}}$ from Lemma 1, meaning the expected number of draws to insert a single edge is R_{max}. Therefore, the expected number of total draws from the underlying CL model is MR_{max}. Thus, combined with Equation 2, the expected number of edges in $\mathcal{B}^{BCL}_{k_1,k_2}$ is equal to $\mathcal{B}_{k_1,k_2}$.

□

Thus, the resulting graph samples will have edges drawn from the coarse joint degree distribution representation that parameterizes the original network G. By extension, the assortativity (which is simply a statistic of the joint degree distribution) of the generated networks G^{BCL} will approximately match that of G. Additionally, our BCL method preserves the modeled expected degree distribution.

Theorem 3. *For a graph G^{BCL} generated by BCL, the expected degree of a node i is D_i, the degree of the node in the original graph G.*

Proof. First, we derive the probability of accepting a sampled edge incident to node i (within bin $b(D_i)$) for a given node i:

$$P(\text{edge incident to } i \text{ accepted})$$
$$= \sum_j P(e_{ij}) P(\text{accepted}|e_{ij})$$
$$= \sum_{k' \in [1..k]} \sum_{j \in Qu(k')} P(e_{ij}) A(b(D_i), k')$$
$$= \sum_{k' \in [1..k]} \sum_{j \in Qu(k')} 2 \frac{D_i D_j}{(2M)(2M)} \frac{R(b(D_i), k')}{R_{max}}$$

Summing over the quantile $B_{k'}$ of node j:

$$P(\text{edge incident to } i \text{ accepted})$$
$$= \frac{D_i}{R_{max} M} \sum_{k' \in [1..k]} \left(\sum_{j \in Qu(k')} \frac{D_j}{2M} \right) \frac{\mathcal{B}_{b(D_i),k'}}{\mathcal{B}'_{b(D_i),k'}}$$
$$= \frac{D_i}{R_{max} M} \frac{1}{k} \frac{k^2}{2M} \sum_{k' \in [1..k]} \mathcal{B}_{b(D_i),k'}$$

Because of the definition of quantiles, the marginal bin frequencies are uniform: $\frac{2M}{k}$

$$P(\text{edge incident to } i \text{ accepted}) = \frac{D_i}{R_{max} M} \frac{1}{k} \frac{k^2}{2M} \frac{2M}{k}$$
$$= \frac{D_i}{R_{max} M}$$

As in the proof of Theorem 2, the expected number of total draws from the underlying CL model is is MR_{max}. Therefore, the expected number of edges incident to node i, and thus the degree of node i, is D_i. □

Runtime Complexity

For a given CL algorithm, let the sampling complexity be $O(M \cdot \lambda)$, where λ is strictly sublinear. For a given k number of bins, the learning step must first (a) construct the degree vector and (b) sort the degree vector. Next, it must (c) construct the k^2 bins, (d) sample a network from the model, and (e) insert all the edges into the appropriate bin. Thus, the total cost is $O(M \log M + k^2 + M \cdot \lambda)$. If the chosen model is scalable and k is a constant, the total learning time is subquadratic. To sample a network, each accept-reject lookup costs $O(1)$, and we have a geometric acceptance distribution. Since the mean of a geometric distribution is a constant, the expected total sampling cost remains $O(M \cdot \lambda)$.

5 Experiments

Experiments were performed to assess the algorithms and to assess how varying the amount of binning effects error rates. To empirically evaluate the models, we learned model parameters from real-world graphs and then generated new graphs using those parameters. We then compared the network statistics of the generated graphs with those of the original networks.

Datasets

We used six different datasets to evaluate our experimental results. Their node and edge counts can be found in Figure 1, with all networks being cast into an undirected and unweighted representation.

First, we study two email datasets: a small publicly available dataset from an email network of students at University Rovira i Virgili in Tarragona (RoviraEmail) (Guimer et al. 2003), and a large email network from Purdue University (Email). Each dataset is a collection of SMTP logs representing when users send an email to one another, with every email sent representing a link between instances.

The next two networks we study are examples of social networks, with a collection of Facebook wall postings (FacebookWall) and the publicly available Epinions trust network (Epinions) (Richardson, Agrawal, and Domingos 2003).

Another dataset is Gnutella, a publicly available Peer2Peer network where users are attempting to find seeds for file sharing (Ripeanu, Iamnitchi, and Foster 2002). In a Peer2Peer network, a user queries its peers to determine if they can seed a file. If not, the peer refers them to other users who might have a file. This repeats until a seed is found.

Lastly, we study a publicly available citation network of US Patents (Leskovec, Kleinberg, and Faloutsos 2005). Nodes in this network are published patents, while edges indicate where one patent cited the other. This is a large network, with over 10 million citations between 2 million edges and demonstrates the scalability of our proposed methods.

Models Compared

We compare our proposed methods against three baselines: FCL, TCL and the Block Two-Level Erdos-Renyi (BTER) model[1] (Kolda et al. 2013). The BTER model groups vertices with similar degrees into blocks with high probability, resulting in networks with a high amount of clustering and positive assortativity. As a result, BTER cannot model networks where the assortativity is independent of the clustering, meaning augmenting BTER with our Binning Chung Lu method would interfere with the clustering that BTER models. In contrast, the degree and clustering statistics of FCL and TCL are independent from the assortativity. Thus, we implement our augmentation to both the FCL and TCL models, creating the FCLB and TCLB methods. We demonstrate how, in particular, TCLB can jointly capture the degree distribution, clustering, joint degree distributions and assortativity, in contrast to any of the baseline methods.

Methodology

We ran experiments on six real world datasets using five different algorithms. For evaluation, we compared the graphs generated by the algorithms using the complementary cumulative distribution function for both the degree distribution and the distribution of local clustering coefficients. We also compared the assortativity coefficient and the joint degree distributions visually. To compare the distributions, we choose a binning number of 10 bins and plot the original and generated graphs' joint degree distribution.

[1]Downloaded from $www.sandia.gov/\ tgkolda/feastpack$

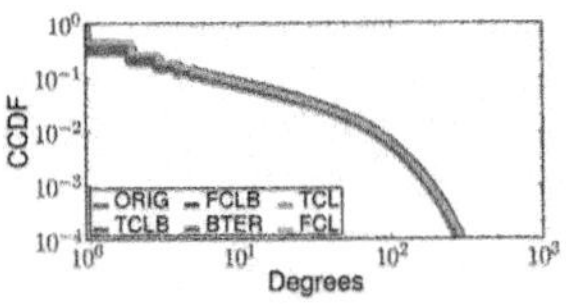

(a) Facebook Wall

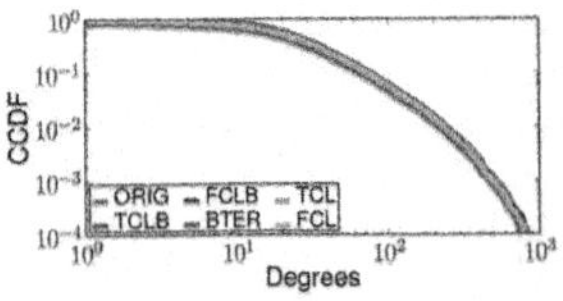

(b) Purdue Email

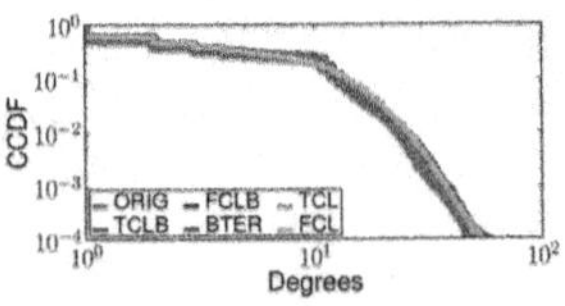

(c) Gnutella

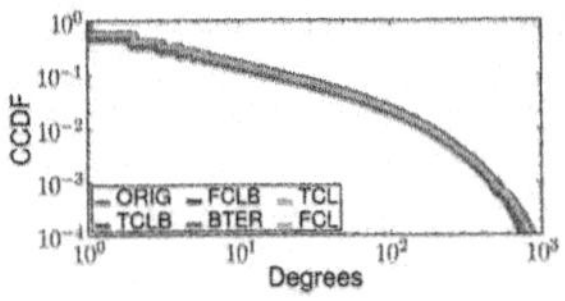

(d) Epinions

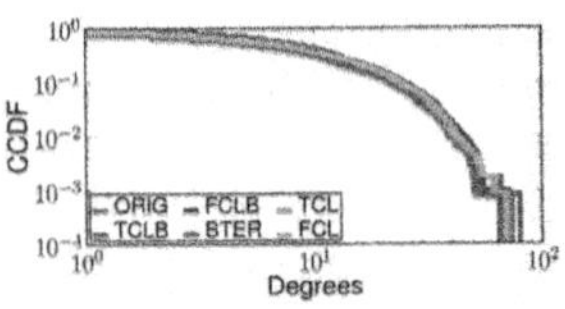

(e) Rovira

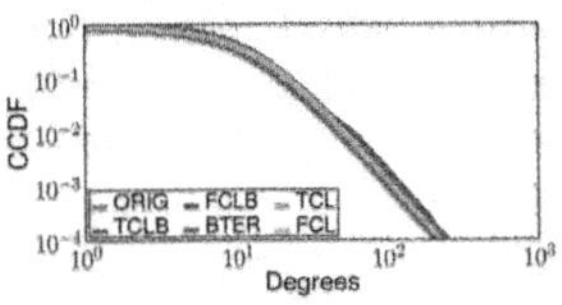

(f) Patents

Figure 4: Degree Distributions

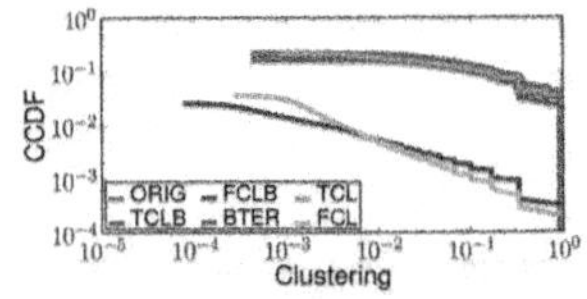

(a) Facebook Wall

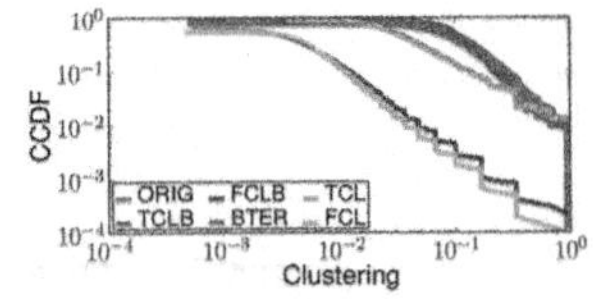

(b) Purdue Email

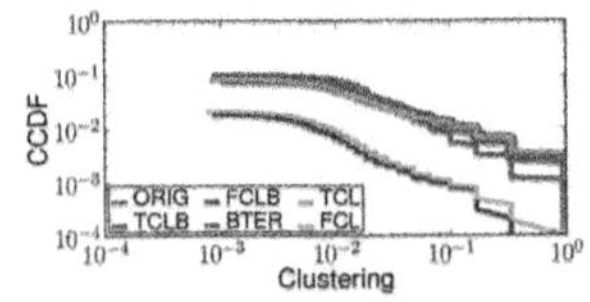

(c) Gnutella

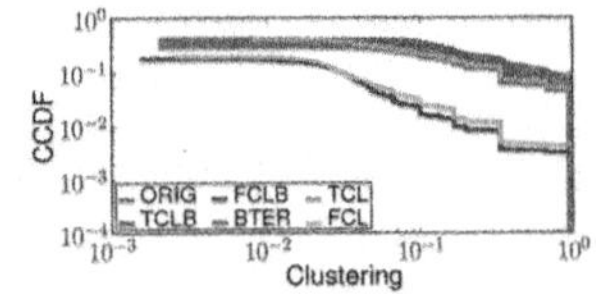

(d) Epinions

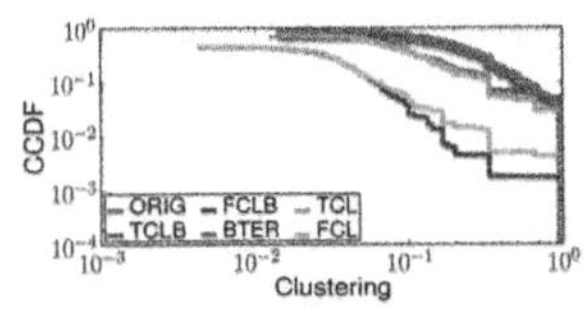

(e) Rovira

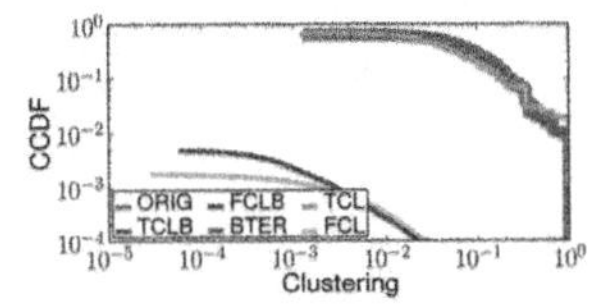

(f) Patents

Figure 5: Clustering Coefficients

Results

To begin, Figure 4 demonstrates that all the compared methods closely model the degree distributions of the datasets. In the next figure, Figure 5, we demonstrate that only TCL, TCLB and BTER preserve the local clustering coefficients found in the original network. As expected, the FCL method fails to model the clustering found in the datasets; this is reflected in FCLB, which only captures the assortativity of the FCL model provided to it. Thus, the binning models (FCLB and TCLB) reflect the underlying proposal distributions (FCL and TCL) and preserve the corresponding statistics that each model .

In Figure 6, we plot the joint degree distributions for all six of our datasets. FCLB and TCLB are able to capture not only the correct assortativity coefficient, but also accurately model the joint degree distribution. In contrast, BTER creates a joint degree distribution with a linear degree correlation.

Correspondingly, we present the assortativity of each of the models for each of the datasets in Figure 7.a. In particular, the non-binning Chung Lu models have assortativity very close to zero. However, FCLB and TCLB closely match the assortativity for all datasets. Although BTER exhibits positive assortativity, it doesn't model the assortativity found in the corresponding real world networks.

In order to test the impact of the 10 bin selection, we compare *error* rates for FCLB and TCLB on the Gnutella dataset as we vary the bin size (Figure 7.b-c) The error we use is the *skew*-divergence to measure the difference between the model distribution and the original data distribution (Lee 2001). The skew-divergence is used as it has a slight mixture between the two distributions, meaning that there is always support between the measures (unlike KL Divergence). We generate 25 different graphs and take the mean and standard deviations (bars) of error rates at various points, measuring the error for the degree distribution, joint degree distribution and clustering coefficients. In addition to the binning methods (solid lines, plotted by means), we give the original models' values for each statistic (dashed lines). First, we see that the degree distribution for the binning models are not significantly different from the original models until a relatively large number of bins are used (50 or more). However, the joint degree distribution quickly improves over the baseline models, with considerably less error when only 5 bins are used. Additionally, the clustering coefficient distribution is not significantly different from the original model. Hence, our models are largely stable over a variety of binning choices, maintaining the original degree distribution and clustering of a given model and additionally modeling joint degree distribution.

Lastly, we plot the rejection rates for the binning models, as we vary the number of bins used, in Figure 7.d. Note that the original Chung Lu models sample from the edge distribution M times. Let $\alpha_{rejection}$ be the rejection rate. Since the acceptance of an edge has a geometric distribution, we can conclude that the binning version samples from the edge distribution $\frac{M}{1-\alpha_{rejection}}$ on average. Thus, even with large amounts of rejection for the large bins (100), the binned version is only 5x longer than the original model. For smaller bin sizes, which also accurately model the joint degree distribution, the rejection rate is considerably less (around 2x rejection rate). Thus, with a constant factor of extra samples we are able to accurately model the joint degree distribution, while maintaining the degree distribution and clustering. Empirically, the Patents dataset containing 14 million edges ran in under 20 minutes with only 10 bins.

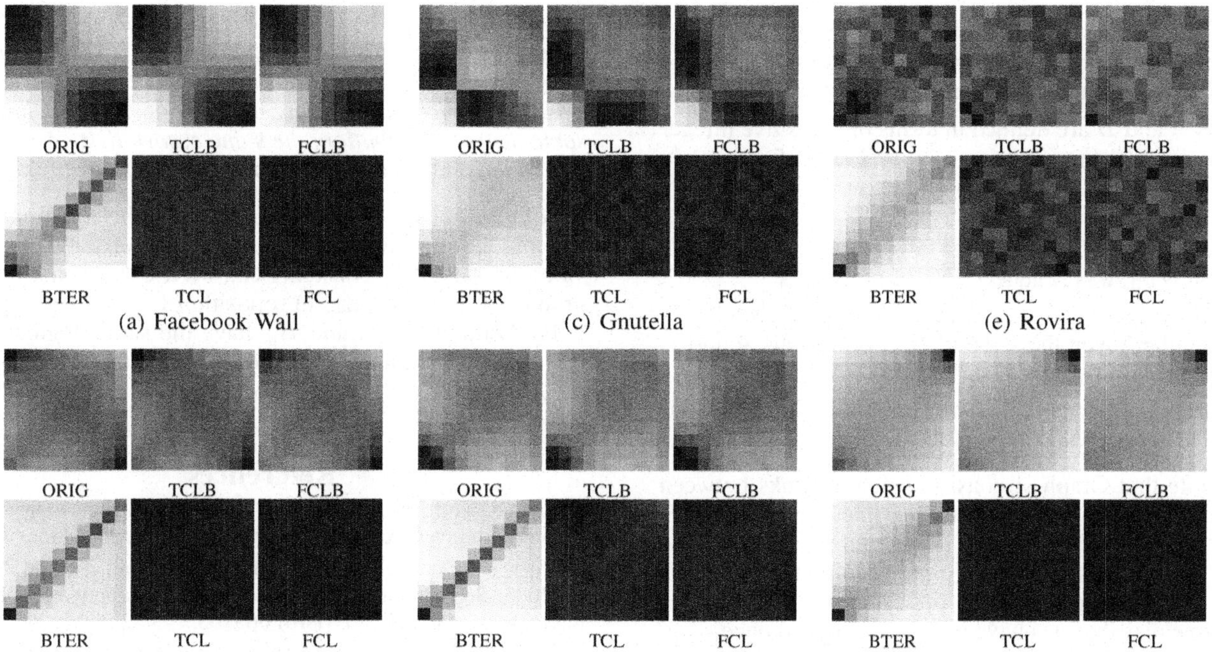

(a) Facebook Wall (c) Gnutella (e) Rovira

(b) Purdue Email (d) Epinions (f) Patents

Figure 6: Visualization of joint degree distribution representations $\mathcal{B}$; $k = 10$.

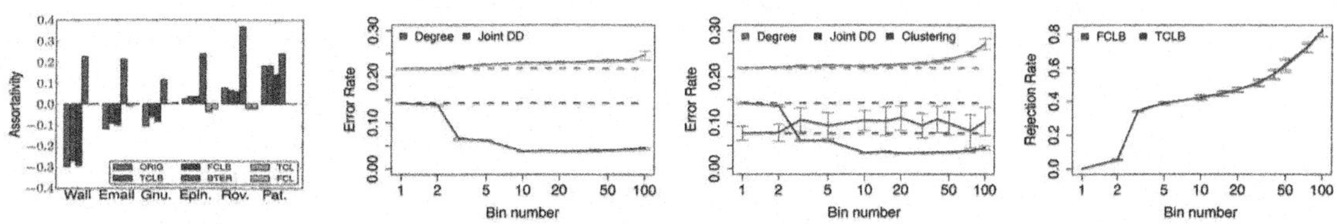

(a) Assortativity (b) FCLB Error Rates (c) TCLB Error Rates (d) Rejection Rates

Figure 7: (a) shows assortativity for the datasets and algorithms. The effect of varying bin sizes for (b) FCLB and (c) TCLB. (d) illustrates the rejection rates for each.

6 Conclusions

In this work, we presented the BCL extension to the Chung Lu family of models. We began with a discussion of the assortativity statistic commonly used in social network analysis, and demonstrated that existing random network models are unable to model it. We next discussed that the assortativity is only a linear summary statistic of the joint degree distribution, demonstrating that real world networks with similar assortativity coefficients but largely different joint degree distributions exist. Further, we proved that there are an infinite number of graphs with the same degree distribution and assortativity, yet different joint degree distributions. This motivated our solution: the coarse binning technique to capture the joint degree distribution of a network. Using accept reject sampling, this binning method can pair with any existing Chung Lu model to preserve the assortativity, degree distribution and clustering, without increasing the runtime complexity.

We implemented our method with both the FCL and TCL models, with the corresponding TCLB capturing the degree distribution, clustering, assortativity and joint degree distribution better than any baselines. We tested this implementation on six large, real world networks, including a Patents dataset with nearly 14 million edges. Our BCL representation empirically preserves an underlying model's statistics while incorporating the true joint degree distribution. Future work includes expanding our methods to scalably model additional graph statistics, all while provably maintaining guarantees of current network models.

Acknowledgements

This research is supported by NSF under contract numbers IIS-1149789, CCF-0939370 and IIS-1219015, and the undergraduate research *Channels Scholars Program*, from the Center for the Science of Information (CCF-0939370).

Appendix

This section provides the detailed proof for Theorem 1.The proof states there are infinitely many pairs of graphs (name A and B) with the following three conditions:

- **Lemma 2**: Graphs A, B have equal degree distributions.

- **Lemma 3**: Graphs A and B have the same assortativity.
- **Proposition 1**: The joint degree distributions of graphs A and B have infinite KL divergence.

Graphs A and B are defined in terms of a positive integer w, where $w \geq 2$. In particular, A and B are defined solely in terms of stars and cliques that relate to w:

Graph A	Graph B
N_S w-stars	N_{2s} 2w-stars
N_{2c} (2w+1)-cliques	N_C (w+1)-cliques
	N_p Pairs

In particular, given the same $w \geq 2$, the graphs A and B have different joint degree distributions.

Proposition 1. *For any $w \geq 2$, the joint degree distributions of Graphs A and B have infinite KL-Divergence.*

Proof. Note that Graph A consists solely of links between nodes of degree 1 to w, and $2w$ to $2w$. In contrast, Graph B consists solely of links between nodes of degree $2w$-1, w to w, and 1 to 1. These sets are disjoint, meaning neither graph has full (or any) support of the opposite graph. Thus, the joint degree distributions have infinite KL-Divergence. □

Next, we define values for the parameters of A and B that result in the same degree distributions between the two networks (computation omitted for space).

Lemma 2. *For any $w \geq 2$, if $N_S = 2(w+1)(2w+1)(2w-1)^2$ and $N_{2s} = (w+1)(2w+1)(w-1)^2$ and $N_C = 2(2w+1)(2w-1)^2$ and $N_{2c} = (w+1)(w-1)^2$ and $N_p = w^2(w+1)(2w+1)(3w-2)$, then graphs A and B have identical degree distributions.*

For an undirected graph, the first moments of these two distributions are identical.

Definition 1. *For a bidirectional graph G, let:*

$$\mu_G = \frac{\sum_{e \in \mathbf{E}} T_*(e)}{|\mathbf{E}|} = \frac{\sum_{e_{ij} \in \mathbf{E}} D_i}{|\mathbf{E}|}$$
$$\sigma_G^2 = \frac{\sum_{e \in \mathbf{E}} (T_*(e) - \mu_G)^2}{|\mathbf{E}|} = \frac{\sum_{e_{ij} \in \mathbf{E}} (D_i - \mu_G)^2}{|\mathbf{E}|}$$

where $* \in \{\beta, \epsilon\}$ This occurs due to the symmetry of a bidirectional network: for every $e_{ij} \in \mathbf{E}$ there is a corresponding $e_{ji} \in \mathbf{E}$.

Lastly, although the variances of $T_\beta(e)$ and $T_\epsilon(e)$ are equal, the covariance between them is not equal to the variance. We use this to define the assortativity.

Definition 2. *The assortativity of a network is defined as the covariance of two variables divided by the standard deviation of each. Thus,*

$$\mathcal{A}_G = \frac{cov(\{T_\beta(e), T_\epsilon(e) | e \in \mathbf{E}\})}{\sigma_G \cdot \sigma_G} = \frac{\sum_{e_{ij} \in \mathbf{E}} (D_i - \mu_G)(D_j - \mu_G)}{\sigma_G^2}$$

With these defined, the next lemma proves values for graphs A and B are equal (computation omitted for space).

Lemma 3. *For any $w \geq 2$, if N_S, N_{2s}, N_C, N_{2c}, and N_p are defined as in Lemma 2, then graphs A and B have identical assortativity values.*

We now combine Lemmas 1 and 2 (matching Degree Distribution and Assorativity) with Proposition 1 (infinite KL divergence in the joint degree distribution).

Theorem 1. *Let A_w, B_w be two networks comprised of graphlets, where w parameterizes the size and counts of the graphlets. There exist an infinite set of pairs of graphs $\{A_w, B_w\}$ such that for any $w \geq 2$, A_w and B_w have the same degree distribution, the same assortativity, but infinite KL-Divergence between their joint degree distributions.*

Proof. We construct $\{A_w, B_w\}$ by using the equations from Lemma 2 and w to find N_S, N_{2s}, N_C, N_{2c}, and N_p. The value of these five constants can be used to construct two graphs, A_w and B_w, as in Proposition 1.

By Lemma 2, A_w and B_w have the same degree distribution. By Lemma 3, A_w and B_w have the same assortativity. Finally, by Proposition 1, A_w and B_w have infinite KL-divergence. □

References

Chung, F., and Lu, L. 2002. The average distances in random graphs with given expected degrees. *Internet Mathematics* 1.

Guimer, R.; Danon, L.; Diaz-Guilera, A.; Giralt, F.; and Arenas, A. 2003. Self-similar community structure in a network of human interactions. *Phys. Rev. E* 68(6):065103.

Kolda, T. G.; Pinar, A.; Plantenga, T.; and Seshadhri, C. 2013. A scalable generative graph model with community structure. arXiv:1302.6636. revised March 2013.

Lee, L. 2001. On the effectiveness of the skew divergence for statistical language analysis. In *Proceedings of Artificial Intelligence and Statistics (AISTATS)*, 65–72.

Leskovec, J.; Chakrabarti, D.; Kleinberg, J.; Faloutsos, C.; and Ghahramani, Z. 2010. Kronecker graphs: An approach to modeling networks. *J. Mach. Learn. Res.*

Leskovec, J.; Kleinberg, J.; and Faloutsos, C. 2005. Graphs over time: Densification laws, shrinking diameters and possible explanations. In *In KDD*, 177–187. ACM Press.

Liang, F.; Liu, C.; and Carrol, R. J. 2010. *Advanced Markov chain Monte Carlo methods: learning from past samples.* Wiley Series in Computational Statistics. New York, NY: Wiley.

Newman, M. E. J. 2002. Assortative mixing in networks. *Physical Review Letters* 89(20):208701.

Pfeiffer III, J. J.; La Fond, T.; Moreno, S.; and Neville, J. 2012. Fast generation of large scale social networks while incorporating transitive closures. In *Fourth ASE/IEEE International Conference on Social Computing (SocialCom).*

Pfeiffer III, J. J.; Moreno, S.; La Fond, T.; Neville, J.; and Gallagher, B. 2014. Attributed graph models: Modeling network structure with correlated attributes. In *Proceedings of the 23rd International World Wide Web Conference (WWW 2014).*

Pinar, A.; Seshadhri, C.; and Kolda, T. G. 2011. The similarity between stochastic kronecker and chung-lu graph models. *CoRR* abs/1110.4925.

Richardson, M.; Agrawal, R.; and Domingos, P. 2003. Trust management for the semantic web. In *Proceedings of the Second International Semantic Web Conference*, 351–368.

Ripeanu, M.; Iamnitchi, A.; and Foster, I. 2002. Mapping the gnutella network. *IEEE Internet Computing* 6(1):50–57.

Stanton, I., and Pinar, A. 2011. Constructing and sampling graphs with a prescribed joint degree distribution. *CoRR* abs/1103.4875.

Zhou, D.; Stanley, H. E.; D'Agostino, G.; and Scala, A. 2012. Assortativity decreases the robustness of interdependent networks. *Phys. Rev. E* 86:066103.

Using Description Logics for RDF Constraint Checking and Closed-World Recognition

Peter F. Patel-Schneider
Nuance Communications
1198 East Arques Avenue, Sunnyvale, California, U. S A.
pfpschneider@gmail.com

Abstract

RDF and Description Logics work in an open-world setting where absence of information is not information about absence. Nevertheless, Description Logic axioms can be interpreted in a closed-world setting and in this setting they can be used for both constraint checking and closed-world recognition against information sources. When the information sources are expressed in well-behaved RDF or RDFS (i.e., RDF graphs interpreted in the RDF or RDFS semantics) this constraint checking and closed-world recognition is simple to describe. Further this constraint checking can be implemented as SPARQL querying and thus effectively performed.

There has recently been considerable attention paid to the problem of validating RDF (Cyganiak, Wood, and Lanthaler 2014) or RDFS information. There are several commercial systems that provide facilities for RDF validation, including TopQuadrant's SPIN (TopQuadrant 2011) and Clark&Parsia's Stardog ICV (Pérez-Urbina, Sirin, and Clark 2012; Clark&Parsia 2014). There are several proposals for specifying the desired form of RDF information, such as Resource Shapes (Ryman 2014). In 2013 W3C held an RDF Validation Workshop (W3C 2013) to gauge interest in the area, and W3C has started a new working group on RDF validation (W3C 2014).

Just what, however, is RDF validation?

Some accounts and systems (such as Stardog ICV) identify RDF validation with satisfying integrity constraints, similar to checking database integrity constraints. In this account, there are conditions (constraints) placed on instances of classes, such as requiring that every person has a name and an address, both strings. The defining characteristic here is that explicit information is needed to satisfy the integrity constraint. To pass the constraint that a person has a name it is necessary to provide a particular string for the name of the person, and not just state that the person has some unknown name.

Other accounts and proposals, such as OSLC Resource Shapes (Ryman, Hors, and Speicher 2013) (used by the Open Services for Lifecycle Collaboration community) and ShEx (Prud'hommeaux 2014; Solbrig and Prud'hommeaux 2014), identify RDF validation more with recognition, similar to determining whether an individual belongs to a Description Logic (Baader et al. 2010) description. For example one might define shape that requires a name and an address and then ask which individuals satisfy the shape's constraint. Here, in contrast to the previous situation, the validation is divorced from any type information in the data. Again, however, there is the requirement that explicit information is needed to match the shape—a particular name must be provided, not just information that there must be one.

As shown in this paper, Description Logics can be used to provide the necessary framework for both checking constraints and providing closed-world recognition facilities, and thus cover most of what SPIN and ShEx provide.

Why then are there claims (Ryman, Hors, and Speicher 2013; Fokoue and Ryman 2013) that OWL (Motik, Patel-Schneider, and Parsia 2012)—the Semantic Web Description Logic—is inadequate for these purposes? There are several aspects of the standard view of Description Logics that might not be consonant with constraints and the kind of recognition that might be desired. However, Description Logic syntax and semantics, and their instantiation in OWL, can serve as the basis for RDF constraint checking and closed-world recognition. The only change required is to consider a closed-world variation of the Description Logic semantics. Then the development of RDF constraint checking and closed-world recognition is easy.

The Basic Idea

Closed-World Recognition

Let's first look at recognition. In recognition we want to determine whether a particular node in an RDF graph matches some criteria. For example, John in the RDF graph[1]

```
ex:John foaf:name "John"^^xsd:string .                    (1)
ex:John foaf:phone "+19085551212"^^xsd:string .
ex:John exo:friend ex:Bill .
ex:John exo:friend ex:Willy .
```

matches the ShEx shape

[1] Turtle (Prud'hommeaux and Carothers 2014) will be used for writing RDF graphs throughout this paper. Prefix and base statements will generally be omitted.

$$\{ \textit{foaf:name xsd:string}, \quad \textit{foaf:phone xsd:string}, \quad \textit{exo:friend}\,[2] \,\} \tag{2}$$

because John has a string value for his name, a string value for his phone, and two friends.

Determining whether an individual belongs to a Description Logic concept is also recognition. The Description Logic description[2] corresponding to the ShEx Shape (2) is

$$= 1\ \textit{foaf:name} \sqcap \forall \textit{foaf:name.xsd:string} \sqcap \; = 1\ \textit{foaf:phone} \sqcap \forall \textit{foaf:phone.xsd:string} \sqcap \; = 2\ \textit{exo:friend} \tag{3}$$

So it seems that Description Logics can easily handle ShEx recognition. Although the ShEx syntax is somewhat more compact here, as ShEx has constructs that combine number restrictions and value restrictions, the Description Logic syntax is not verbose and is quite reasonable.

However, John does not match (3) in the standard semantics of Description Logic. This is precisely because in this standard reading, *and in RDF*, the absence of information is not information about absence. In the standard Description Logic reading, and also in RDF, John could have more than one name as far as the information in the above RDF graph is concerned. Many Description Logics (and, again, RDF too) also do not assume that different names refer to different individuals. So Bill and Willy could be the same person as far as the information in the above RDF graph is concerned.

It turns out that expressive Description Logics have facilities to explicitly state information about absence and information about differences and thus can be used to state complete information, at least on a local level. For example, if we add information to (1) stating that John has only one name and phone, that John's only friends are Bill and Willy, *and* that Bill is not the same as Willy, as in

$$\textit{ex:John} \in\ \leq 1\ \textit{foaf:name}$$
$$\textit{ex:John} \in\ \leq 1\ \textit{foaf:phone}$$
$$\textit{ex:John} \in \forall \textit{exo:friend}.\{\textit{ex:Bill}, \textit{ex:Willy}\}$$
$$\textit{ex:Bill} \neq \textit{ex:Willy}$$

then John does match (3).

So it is not that Description Logics (including OWL) do not perform recognition as in ShEx, it is just that Description Logics do not make the assumption that absence of information is information about absence. In expressive Description Logics (again including OWL) it is possible to explicitly state what comes implicitly from the assumption that absence of information is information about absence.

However, suppose that we want to make this assumption generally? We could manually add a lot of axioms like the ones above, but this is both tedious and error-prone, and thus not at all a viable solution. Instead we can proceed by making the assumption that if the truth of some fact cannot be determined from the information given, then that fact is false. This is often called the closed world assumption or negation by failure, as the failure to prove some fact is used to support its falsity. There is a very large body of work on this topic (see the Related Work section for pointers into this work) and there are many tricky questions that arise with respect to closure in any sophisticated formalism, and expressive Description Logics (including OWL) are indeed sophisticated. As well, reasoning in expressive Description Logics that also have closed world facilities is extremely difficult, even in simple cases.

[2]The abstract syntax (Baader et al. 2010) for Description Logics—a compact but non-ASCII syntax—will be used throughout this paper.

Fortunately RDF and RDFS are unsophisticated and inexpressive, so neither the tricky questions nor the reasoning difficulties arise if all information comes in the form of RDF triples interpreted under the RDF or RDFS semantics (Hayes and Patel-Schneider 2014). The basic idea is to treat the triples (and their RDF or RDFS consequences, if desired) as completely describing the world. In this treatment

1. if a triple is not present then it is false and
2. different IRIs denote different individuals.

This is precisely the same idea that underlies model checking, where a model is a finite set of ground first-order facts and everything else is false. First-order inference is undecidable, but determining whether a first-order sentence is true in one particular model (model checking) is much, much easier.

In this way it is possible to use the Description Logic syntactic and semantic machinery to define how to recognize descriptions under the same assumptions that underlie ShEx. The only change from the standard Description Logic setup is to define how to go from an RDF graph to the Description Logic model that the RDF graph embodies. Definitions, even recursive definitions, can also be handled.

This is all quite easy and conforms to a common thread of both theoretical and practical work. It also matches the theoretical underpinning of Stardog ICV (Pérez-Urbina, Sirin, and Clark 2012; Clark&Parsia 2014). Further, the approach can be implemented by translation into SPARQL queries, showing that it is practical. (There may be some constructs of very expressive description logics that do not translate into SPARQL queries when working with complete information, but at least the Description Logic constructs that correspond to the usual recognition conditions do so translate.)

Constraint Checking

Constraint checking does not appear to be part of the services provided by Description Logics. This has lead to claims that OWL cannot be used for constraint checking. However inference, which is the core service provided by Description Logics, and constraint checking are indeed very closely related.

Inference is the process of determining what follows from what has been stated. Inference ranges from simple (John is a student, students are people, therefore John is a person) to the very complex (involving reasoning by cases, *reductio ad absurdum*, or even noticing that an infinite sequence of inferences will not produce any useful information). Determining whether a constraint holds is just determining whether the constraint follows from the given information.

Figure 1: Data for Example

ex:Amy rdf:type exo:UniStudent .	*ex:Amy exo:enrolled ex:SUNYOrange* .	*ex:Amy exo:friend ex:Bill* .
ex:Amy foaf:name "Amy"^^*xsd:string* .	*ex:Bill exo:enrolled ex:ReindeerPoly* .	*ex:Amy exo:friend ex:John* .
ex:Bill rdf:type exo:UniStudent .	*ex:Bill exo:enrolled ex:HudsonValley* .	*ex:Bill exo:friend ex:Amy* .
ex:Bill foaf:name "Bill"^^*xsd:string* .	*ex:John exo:enrolled ex:ReindeerPoly* .	*ex:Bill exo:friend ex:John* .
ex:John rdf:type exo:GrStudent .	*ex:Susan exo:enrolled ex:ReindeerPoly* .	*ex:John exo:friend ex:Amy* .
ex:John foaf:name "John"^^*xsd:string* .	*ex:Susan exo:enrolled ex:SUNYOrange* .	*ex:John exo:friend ex:Bill* .
ex:John exo:supervisor ex:Len .	*ex:Susan exo:enrolled ex:HudsonValley* .	*ex:John exo:friend ex:Len* .
ex:Susan rdf:type exo:Person .	*ex:Len exo:affiliation ex:ReindeerPoly* .	*ex:Len exo:friend ex:Amy* .
ex:Susan foaf:name "Susan"^^*xsd:string* .	*ex:Len exo:affiliation ex:SUNYOrange* .	*ex:Len exo:friend ex:Susan* .
ex:Len rdf:type exo:Faculty .	*ex:SUNYOrange rdf:type exo:ResOrg* .	
ex:Len foaf:name "Len"^^*xsd:string* .	*ex:HudsonValley rdf:type exo:Uni* .	

Figure 2: RDFS Ontology for Example

foaf:name rdfs:range xsd:string .	*exo:enrolled rdfs:domain exo:UniStudent* .
exo:UniStudent rdfs:subClassOf exo:Person .	*exo:enrolled rdfs:range exo:Uni* .
exo:GrStudent rdfs:subClassOf exo:UniStudent .	*exo:supervisor rdfs:domain exo:GrStudent* .
exo:Faculty rdfs:subClassOf exo:Person .	*exo:supervisor rdfs:range exo:Faculty* .
exo:Uni rdfs:subClassOf exo:Organization .	*exo:affiliation rdfs:domain exo:Person* .
exo:ResOrg rdfs:subClassOf exo:Organization .	*exo:affiliation rdfs:range exo:Organization* .

Figure 3: Constraints and Recognition Axioms for Example

1 *exo:Person* $\sqcap$ *exo:Organization* $\equiv \{\}$	7 *exo:Faculty* $\sqsubseteq\ \leq 5$ *exo:supervisor*$^-$.*exo:GrStudent*
2 *exo:Person* $\sqsubseteq\ = 1$ *foaf:Name* $\sqcap\ \forall$*foaf:Name.xsd:string*	8 *exo:Uni* $\sqsubseteq\ \geq 2$ *exo:enrolled*$^-$
3 *exo:UniStudent* $\sqsubseteq\ \geq 1$ *exo:enrolled* $\sqcap\ \forall$*exo:enrolled.exo:Uni*	9 *exo:GrStudent*$\vert$ *exo:enrolled* $\sqsubseteq$ *exo:supervisor* $\circ$ *exo:affiliation*
4 *exo:GrStudent* $\sqsubseteq\ = 1$ *exo:enrolled* $\sqcap\ \forall$*exo:enrolled.exo:ResOrg*	
5 *exo:Faculty* $\sqsubseteq\ \geq 1$ *exo:affiliation* $\sqcap\ \forall$*exo:affiliation.exo:Uni*	*ex:HecticStudent* $\equiv\ \geq 3$ *exo:enrolled*
6 *exo:Faculty* $\sqsubseteq\ \leq 1$ *exo:affiliation.exo:ResOrg*	*ex:StudentFriend* $\equiv\ \geq 2$ *exo:friend.ex:StudentFriend*

Again, however, constraint checking is generally done with respect to complete information. So, to determine whether the constraint

$$\begin{aligned} &\textit{ex:John} \in \textit{exo:Person} \sqcap \\ &\quad = 1\ \textit{foaf:name} \sqcap \forall \textit{foaf:name.xsd:string} \sqcap \\ &\quad = 1\ \textit{foaf:phone} \sqcap \forall \textit{foaf:phone.xsd:string} \sqcap \\ &\quad = 2\ \textit{exo:friend} \end{aligned} \tag{4}$$

is valid in the presence of (locally) complete information such as

ex:John $\in$ *exo:Person*
ex:John foaf:name "John"^^*xsd:string* .
ex:John $\in\ = 1$ *foaf:name*
ex:John foaf:phone "+19085551212"^^*xsd:string* .
ex:John $\in\ = 1$ *foaf:phone*
ex:John exo:friend ex:Bill .
ex:John exo:friend ex:Willy .
ex:John exo:friend ex:Susan .
ex:John $\in \forall$*exo:friend.*$\{$*ex:Bill*, *ex:Willy*, *ex:Susan*$\}$
ex:Bill $\neq$ *ex:Willy*
ex:Bill $\neq$ *ex:Susan*
ex:Susan $\neq$ *ex:Willy*

is simply a matter of determining whether the constraint follows from the information. (Generally constraints like (4) are written to handle all the members of a class as in

$$\begin{aligned} &\textit{exo:Person} \sqsubseteq \\ &\quad = 1\ \textit{foaf:name} \sqcap \forall \textit{foaf:name.xsd:string} \sqcap \\ &\quad = 1\ \textit{foaf:phone} \sqcap \forall \textit{foaf:phone.xsd:string} \sqcap \\ &\quad = 2\ \textit{exo:friend} \end{aligned}$$

instead of just a single node, but the principle is the same.)

So a way to do constraints in Description Logics is to first set up complete information, and then just perform inference. This approach has been explored in the context of letting certain roles be completely specified as in a database (Patel-Schneider and Franconi 2012). Other approaches to constraints in Description Logics (de Bruijn et al. 2005; Motik, Horrocks, and Sattler 2009; Tao et al. 2010; Donini, Nardi, and Rosati 2002; Sengupta, Krisnadhi, and Hitzler 2011) are considerably more complex, as they deal with the complexities that arise when there are multiple ways to complete the information. However, all these approaches largely agree when there is only a single way to complete the information.

Setting up complete information is just what was done above for closed-world recognition, so this technique can also be used for constraint checking. Of course, this doesn't mean that you have to implement Description Logic inference with complete information the same way that you need to with incomplete information. In fact, as above, constraint checking can be implemented as SPARQL queries.

Example

Here is a small example of how Description Logic constructs can be used for constraint checking. There are three separate kinds of information in the example. The RDF triples in Figure 1 provide the data for the example. The RDFS ontology in Figure 2 provides the organization of the data. The Description Logic axioms in Figure 3 provide the constraints to be validated against the data and the ontology and the classes vocabulary for closed-world recognition.

The constraints are all satisfied, except for one, as follows:

1. Nothing can be inferred to be both a person and an organization, and so persons and organizations are disjoint.
2. Every object that can be inferred to be a person (i.e., students and faculty) has a single name provided, and that name is a string, so every person has exactly one name in the closure.
3. All students (and graduate students) are enrolled in universities—the range of *exo:enrolled* is *exo:Uni*, which makes the typing part of the constraint redundant here.
4. Reindeer Poly is not specified to be a research organization, so although John is enrolled exactly once the constraint on graduate students being enrolled in research organizations is not satisfied.
5. All faculty (Len) are affiliated with only universities.
6. All faculty (again only Len) are affiliated with at most one research organization, as Reindeer Poly is not specified to be a research organization and Len is only affiliated with SUNY Orange and Reindeer Poly.
7. All faculty supervise fewer than five graduate students, as the only faculty (Len) only supervises one student (John).
8. Each university (SUNY Orange, Reindeer Poly, and Hudson Valley) has at least two students enrolled in it, because Amy, Bill, John, and Susan are different individuals.
9. For every graduate student enrollment (*exo:enrolled* domain-restricted to *exo:GrStudent*) there is a supervisor of the graduate student affiliated with the university. This constraint uses an auxiliary non-recursive equivalence definition.

The only hectic student is Susan, as she is the only person with at least three enrollments. However, Amy, Bill, and John all belong to *ex:StudentFriend* because when maximally interpreting *ex:StudentFriend* they each have at least two friends who belong to *ex:StudentFriend.* Len does not belong to *ex:StudentFriend* even though he has two friends, because Susan has too few friends and cannot belong to *ex:StudentFriend.*

One might want to validate that domain and range types are not inferred, but are instead explicitly stated in the data. This can be done by using a version of the ontology without the domain and range statements and validating against a set of constraints that just have the removed domain and range statements. In the example, this would detect that Susan was not stated to be a student, violating the domain constraint for *exo:enrolled*; that SUNY Orange and Reindeer Poly were not stated to be universities, violating the range constraint for *exo:enrolled*; and that Reindeer Poly was not stated to be an organization, violating the range constraint for *exo:affiliation.* All other domain and range constraints would be satisfied, as some required class memberships would be inferred from the subclass statements.

Related Work

The closest work in a technical sense is the work of Patel-Schneider and Franconi (2012). In that work some properties and classes were considered as closed, which turned description logic axioms involving those properties and classes into constraints. RDF and RDFS are very similar to a situation where all properties and classes are closed. The current paper adds the idea of closed-world recognition, which was only implicit in the previous work, and maximal extensions, which provide a much better treatment of recursive definitions, particularly in the monotone case.

The work of Motik, Horrocks, and Sattler (2009) and of Tao *et al.* (2010) both divide up axioms into regular axioms and constraints. They both also permit general Description Logic axioms, not just RDF or RDFS graphs as here. To handle full Description Logic information requires a much more complex construction, involving minimal interpretations. Neither consider closed-world recognition. Tao *et al.* use SPARQL queries as a partial translation of their constraints and forms a basis for Stardog ICV.

The work of Sengupta, Krisnadhi, and Hitzler (2011) uses circumscription as the mechanism to minimize interpretations. It is otherwise similar to the previous efforts. The work of Donini, Nardi, and Rosati (2002) uses autoepistemic constructs within axioms to model constraints, and is thus quite different from the approach here. OWL Flight (de Bruijn et al. 2005) is a subset of OWL where axioms are given meaning as Datalog constraints. Again, as an expressive Description Logic is handled the construction is more complex than the one here. RDFUnit (Kontokostas et al. 2014) has a component that turns RDFS axioms and simple OWL axioms into SPARQL queries that check for data that does not match the axiom and so is somewhat similar to this work. However, there is no notion that RDFUnit is turning ontology axioms into constraints that cover the entire meaning of the axiom.

Shex (Solbrig and Prud'hommeaux 2014) uses very different mechanisms. It builds up shapes, which are akin to definitions of classes, and gives them meaning by a translation into a recursive extension of Z over an abstraction of RDF graphs. Entire documents or document portions are then matched against these shapes.

The Details, but Not All the Details

Description Logic Semantics

The semantics of Description Logics are generally given as a model theory, as for OWL DL (Motik, Patel-Schneider, and Parsia 2012). OWL DL has a complex semantics, as far as Description Logics go, to cover all its constructs and to make it more compatible with RDF. The semantics here will follow the semantics of OWL, with the exception that any property can have both individuals, e.g., *ex:John*, and data values, e.g., "John"^^*xsd:string*, as values.

The fundamental building block of Description Logics semantics is interpretations, which provide a meaning for the primitive constructs in terms of a particular domain of discourse. The meaning of an individual name, such as *ex:John*, is an element of this domain, here that element that we think of as being John. Literal values, such as "John"^^*xsd:string*, are treated specially—their meaning is determined by their datatype. The meaning (or interpretation) of a named concept such as *exo:person*, is a subset of the domain, here those individuals that we might think of as people. The meaning of a named property, such as *exo:friend*, is a set of pairs over the domain, here those pairs that we might think of as being the friend-of relationship. The meaning of non-primitive constructs, such as the description $= 2$ *exo:friend*, are built up from these primitives, resulting here in the set of domain elements that are related to exactly two domain elements via the meaning of *exo:friend*.

Axioms, such as *ex:John* $\in$ *exo:Person*, are true precisely when the meaning of their parts satisfies a particular relationship, here that the meaning of *ex:John* is an element of the meaning of *exo:Person*. There are some other aspects to this simple story, to handle the differences between individuals, e.g., *ex:John*, and data values, e.g., "John"^^*xsd:string*, and to make reasoning over some constructs easier. A Description Logic model of a set of axioms (including what we might call facts), is then just an interpretation that makes all the axioms true.

Canonical Interpretations of RDF Graphs

In an interpretation everything is specified, so each interpretation has complete information. The basic idea is thus to construct an interpretation making just the triples in an RDF graph true and then work with that single interpretation. In this way information that is absent from the RDF graph is considered false.

We can think of most RDF graphs as sets of Description Logic axioms, particularly as we are ignoring the common Description Logic division of properties into properties that have objects that are individuals and properties that have objects that are data values.[3] This correspondence breaks down in two areas: 1/ when the built-in RDF and RDFS vocabulary is used in unusual ways (e.g., making *rdfs:subClassOf* a sub-property of *rdfs:subPropertyOf*), and 2/ if reasoning about individuals can affect reasoning about classes (e.g., forcing two individuals that are also classes to be the same). The abuse and extension of the built-in RDF and RDFS vocabulary is rare, so we just exclude these RDF graphs from our account. (Particular extensions of the RDF and RDFS vocabulary could be built in to an extension of the approach given here.) In RDF and RDFS, but not in OWL, reasoning about individuals can affect reasoning about classes. This is also rare, so we will not handle these inferences.

Definition 1 *Given an RDF graph G with no ill-formed literals and no triples stating membership in a datatype, we construct the canonical Description Logic interpretation of G as follows.*

1. *Datatypes are formed for all the datatypes in the graph, and given meaning in the usual way.*
2. *The domain of the interpretation consists of the non-literal nodes of the RDF graph plus the properties in the graph and the mapping for nodes is the identity mapping. (One might think that this is not an appropriate way to construct an interpretation, as it sets the meaning of ex:John to ex:John, not anything that we might think of as being John, but as far as the formal machinery is concerned, the actual domain elements are not important.)*
3. *The set of literal values is constructed in the usual way from the datatypes. An extra copy of the integers is added to ensure an infinite number of literal values.*
4. *Classes are formed for each node in the graph that has an* rdf:type *link with it as an object or belongs to* rdfs:Class *and their extensions are the set of nodes for which* rdf:type *triples link them to the class.*
5. *Properties (note that we are ignoring the Description Logic division of properties) are formed for each predicate in the graph and also for each node that belongs to* rdf:Property, *and their extensions are the set of pairs taken from triples in the graph with the property as predicate.*

So from the initial RDF graph in this paper, we end up with a canonical interpretation with six domain elements, *ex:John*, *ex:Bill*, *ex:Willy*, *foaf:name*, *foaf:phone*, and *exo:friend*. The interpretation of *foaf:name* consists of just $\langle$*ex:John*, "*John*"$\rangle$ The interpretation of *foaf:phone* consists of just $\langle$*ex:John*, "*+19085551212*"$\rangle$. The interpretation of *exo:friend* consists of $\langle$*ex:John*, *ex:Bill*$\rangle$ and $\langle$*ex:John*, *ex:Willy*$\rangle$.

For constraints and descriptions that use only vocabulary in the RDF graph all we do is work with this interpretation and consider whether the constraint axiom is true in this interpretation so the development is easy. It is obvious that *ex:John* belongs to the interpretation of the first Description Logic description given above, as expected.

Evaluating constraints on the canonical interpretation of a graph is essentially the same as evaluating them on the graph itself. Systems that evaluate constraints on an RDF graph, like ShEx, thus work in a manner very similar to the approach taken here.

Extending to New Classes

For closed-world recognition, it is useful to define new classes, as in

ex:PurePerson $\equiv\ \geq 1$ *exo:friend* $\sqcap$
$\forall$*exo:friend.ex:PurePerson*

There are several possibilities for the meaning of new classes that are recursively defined. The new classes could be interpreted as broadly as possible, as narrowly as possible, or in any consistent manner.

It appears in ShEx that such classes as to be interpreted as broadly as possible. For example, in the RDF graph

ex:John exo:friend ex:Bill .
ex:Bill exo:friend ex:John .

[3] This division has been made so that reasoners do not have to worry about data values having properties, but if we are constructing models this is not a problem. It is easy to revise the treatment here to bring back this division.

the ShEx approach would be that both *ex:John* and *ex:Bill* belong to *ex:PurePerson*. We will take this approach here and interpret new classes as broadly as possible

New classes are handled by considering extensions of the interpretations defined as above. An extension of an interpretation is a new interpretation 1/ with the same domain as the original interpretation, and 2/ that has the same meaning for all individuals, named classes, and named properties in the original interpretation. The extension is allowed to have new named classes, but not new named properties or new individuals. New individuals are not allowed because some Description Logic constructs are sensitive to the set of individuals. New properties are not allowed because they may increase the computational complexity of closed-world recognition.

An interpretation is an extended canonical model of an RDF graph with respect to a set of constraints if it is an extension of the canonical model of the RDF graph and is a model of the constraints.

To interpret recursively defined classes as broadly as possible not all extended canonical models are considered, only maximal ones. An model is maximal among a set of models if there is no other model in the set that 1/ interprets all classes as supersets of their interpretation in the maximal model, and 2/ interprets at least one class as a strict superset of its interpretation in the maximal model.

An individual is recognized as belonging to a description if its interpretation belongs to the interpretation of the description in all maximal extended canonical models.

It turns out that there is only one (up to isomorphism) maximal extended canonical model of the above definition of *ex:PurePerson*. In this model both *ex:John* and *ex:Bill* are in the extension of *ex:PurePerson*. If all new classes are monotone in all the other new classes (i.e., if the extension of some class grows then no other class extensions shrink) then there is always exactly one maximal extension.[4]

RDF and RDFS Semantics

So everything looks fine. We go from an RDF graph to a slightly modified Description Logic interpretation and from there perform constraint checking by determining whether a set of Description Logic axioms are satisfied in the interpretation or in a set of maximal extensions of the interpretation. We can also perform closed-world recognition by determining the interpretation of the new defined classes in the axioms and these classes can even be defined recursively.

However, there is one missing part of the story. If the RDF graph includes triples that trigger RDF or RDF inferences that are not already in the RDF graph the interpretation will not look like an RDF (or RDFS) interpretation. For example, if the RDF graph is

ex:John rdf:type exo:Student .
exo:Student rdfs:subClassOf exo:Person .

our canonical interpretation states that *ex:John* does not belong to *exo:Person*, which goes against the RDFS meaning of the above graph.

[4]Proof sketches of claims here and later in the paper are in an extended version of this paper available at *arxiv.org/abs/1411.4156*.

Fortunately, it is relatively easy to recover from this problem. All that is needed is to add all the RDF (or RDFS) consequences to the graph. Yes, there are an infinite number of these consequences, but our formal development does not care whether the graph is finite or infinite. For complexity analysis and implementation it is not hard to come up with a finite representation of these consequences, like the one initially done by ter Horst (2005), and make the minor fixups needed to determine correct answers from the answers gleaned from this finite approximation.

This all works because the RDF (or RDFS) consequences of an RDF graph can be represented as an RDF graph. OWL consequences cannot be so represented, as the consequences in OWL can be disjunctive. This requires working with minimal equality and minimal models or some other way to single out only the desired interpretations as in previous work on Description Logic constraints, making the formal development much harder and presenting many more choices that have to be justified.

Complexity

It is easy to see that checking axioms against an interpretation is polynomial, as long as there is no new vocabulary in the axioms or no recursive definitions. The formulae corresponding to the axioms are just model checked against the interpretation.

If there are monotone recursive definitions then checking constraints and performing closed-world recognition can be done using techniques from Datalog, such as magic sets. For example, the extension of a recursively-defined class can first be computed ignoring the recursive portion. Violations of the recursive portion can then be checked and objects iteratively removed from the class. These techniques cannot be used for non-monotone recursive definitions, as expanding one class or property might reduce another.

Implementation

The work of Tao *et al.* (2010) shows that the standard Description Logic constraints can be partly implemented as SPARQL queries when no new vocabulary is used. Tao *et al.* worked in a general OWL setting, where their approach is sound but not complete, but in an RDF setting the approach is both sound and complete, because there is only a single model that needs to be considered. This approach forms the basis of Stardog ICV (Clark&Parsia 2014). Indeed Stardog ICV is an implementation of the approach described in this paper showing how the approach to constraints here can be implemented by a translation to SPARQL. The work here can thus also be thought of as a simpler definition of the underpinning of Stardog ICV. Recent work at Mannheim by Thomas Bosch (see *https://github.com/boschthomas/OWL2-SPIN-Mapping*) translates OWL descriptions interpreted as constraints into SPARQL using a similar approach, providing a different implementation.

Non-recursive closed-world recognition can be handled by using nested or repeated SPARQL queries. Monotone recursive closed-world recognition can be implemented using Datalog techniques. Non-monotone recursive closed-world recognition is more complex and cannot be handled in the same way. This indicates that excluding non-monotone recursive closed-world recognition could be a reasonable stance to take.

Conclusion

Description Logics can indeed be used for both the syntax and semantics of constraint checking and closed-world recognition in RDF, by employing an analogue of model checking, and much of both constraint checking and closed-world recognition can be effectively implemented using a translation to SPARQL queries. The main difference between closed-world recognition and constraint checking is that the former either has no axioms or only uses axioms defining names that do not occur in the RDF graph whereas constraint checking uses axioms that relate concepts appearing in the RDF graph to descriptions.

By restricting our information to be RDF or RDFS, i.e, working in situations where there is a unique minimal model, we obtain a simpler formulation, easy implementation, and good performance as compared to previous work in this area. The approach here can be easily extended to other subsets of OWL that have a unique minimal model. An OWL profile with this property is OWL RL (Motik et al. 2012).

References

Baader, F.; Calvanese, D.; McGuinness, D. L.; Nardi, D.; and Patel-Schneider, P. F., eds. 2010. *The Description Logic Handbook: Theory, implementation, and applications*. Cambridge University Press, 2nd edition.

Clark&Parsia. 2014. Stardog integrity constraint validation. *http://docs.stardog.com/icv*.

Cyganiak, R.; Wood, D.; and Lanthaler, M. 2014. RDF 1.1 concepts and abstract syntax. W3C Recommendation, *http://www.w3.org/TR/rdf-concepts/*.

de Bruijn, J.; Polleres, A.; Lara, R.; and Fensel, D. 2005. OWL DL vs. OWL Flight: Conceptual modeling and reasoning for the semantic web. In *Proceedings of the Fourteenth World Wide Web Conference*, 623–632. ACM Press.

Donini, F. M.; Nardi, D.; and Rosati, R. 2002. Description logics of minimal knowledge and negation as failure. *ACM Transactions on Computational Logic* 3(2):177–225.

Fokoue, A., and Ryman, A. 2013. OSLC resource shape: A linked data constraint language. In W3C (2013). *http://www.w3.org/2001/sw/wiki/images/b/b7/RDFVal_Fokuoe_Ryman.pdf*.

Hayes, P., and Patel-Schneider, P. F. 2014. RDF 1.1 semantics. W3C Recommendation, *http://www.w3.org/TR/rdf11-mt/*.

Kontokostas, D.; Westphal, P.; Auer, S.; Hellmann, S.; Lehmann, J.; Cornelissen, R.; and Zaveri, A. J. 2014. Test-driven evaluation of linked data quality. In *Proceedings of the Twenty-Third World Wide Web Conference*, 747–758. ACM Press.

Motik, B.; Grau, B. C.; Horrocks, I.; Wu, Z.; Fokoue, A.; and Lutz, C. 2012. OWL 2 Web Ontology Language: Profiles (second edition). W3C Recommendation, *http://www.w3.org/TR/owl2-profiles*.

Motik, B.; Horrocks, I.; and Sattler, U. 2009. Bridging the gap between OWL and relational databases. *Journal of Web Semantics* 7(2):74–119.

Motik, B.; Patel-Schneider, P. F.; and Parsia, B. 2012. OWL 2 web ontology language: Structural specification and functional-style syntax. W3C Recommendation, *http://www.w3.org/TR/owl2-syntax/*.

Patel-Schneider, P. F., and Franconi, E. 2012. Ontology constraints in incomplete and complete data. In *Proceedings of the Eleventh International Semantic Web Conference*, 444–459. Springer.

Pérez-Urbina, H.; Sirin, E.; and Clark, K. 2012. Validating RDF with OWL integrity constraints. *http://docs.stardog.com/icv/ics-specification.html*.

Prud'hommeaux, E., and Carothers, G. 2014. RDF 1.1 turtle: Terse RDF triple language. W3C Recommendation, *http://www.w3.org/TR/turtle/*.

Prud'hommeaux, E. 2014. Shape expressions 1.0 primer. W3C Member Submission, *http://www.w3.org/Submission/shex-primer/*.

Ryman, A. G.; Hors, A. J. L.; and Speicher, S. 2013. OSLC resource shape: A language for defining constraints on linked data. In Bizer, C.; Heath, T.; Berners-Lee, T.; Hausenblas, M.; and Auer, S., eds., *Proceedings of the WWW2013 Workshop on Linked Data on the Web*. *http://ceur-ws.org/Vol-996/papers/ldow2013-paper-02.pdf*.

Ryman, A. 2014. Resource shape 2.0. W3C Member Submission, *http://www.w3.org/Submission/shapes/*.

Sengupta, K.; Krisnadhi, A.; and Hitzler, P. 2011. Local closed world semantics: Grounded circumscription for OWL. In *Proceedings of the Tenth International Semantic Web Conference*, 617–632. Springer.

Solbrig, H., and Prud'hommeaux, E. 2014. Shape expressions 1.0 definition. W3C Member Submission, *http://www.w3.org/Submission/shex-defn/*.

Tao, J.; Sirin, E.; Bao, J.; and McGuinness, D. L. 2010. Integrity constraints in OWL. In *Proceedings of the Twenty-Fourth National Conference on Artificial Intelligence*, 1443–1448. American Association for Artificial Intelligence.

ter Horst, H. J. 2005. Completeness, decidability and complexity of entailment for RDF Schema and a semantic extension involving the OWL vocabulary. *Journal of Web Semantics* 3(2-3):79–115.

TopQuadrant. 2011. SPIN—modeling vocabulary. W3C Member Submssion, *http://www.w3.org/Submission/spin-modeling/*.

W3C. 2013. W3C RDF validation workshop report. *http://www.w3.org/2012/12/rdf-val/*.

W3C. 2014. W3C RDF data shapes charter. *http://www.w3.org/2014/data-shapes/charter*.

Proceedings of the Twenty-Ninth AAAI Conference on Artificial Intelligence

Approximating Model-Based ABox Revision in DL-Lite: Theory and Practice

Guilin Qi[1,2] Zhe Wang[3] Kewen Wang[3] Xuefeng Fu Zhiqiang Zhuang[3]
[1] School of Computer Science and Engineering, Southeast University, China
[2] State Key Lab for Novel Software Technology, Nanjing University, Nanjing, China
[3] School of Information and Communication Technology, Griffith University, Australia

Abstract

Model-based approaches provide a semantically well justified way to revise ontologies. However, in general, model-based revision operators are limited due to lack of efficient algorithms and inexpressibility of the revision results. In this paper, we make both theoretical and practical contribution to efficient computation of model-based revisions in DL-Lite. Specifically, we show that maximal approximations of two well-known model-based revisions for DL-Lite$_{\mathcal{R}}$ can be computed using a syntactic algorithm. However, such a coincidence of model-based and syntactic approaches does not hold when role functionality axioms are allowed. As a result, we identify conditions that guarantee such a coincidence for DL-Lite$_{\mathcal{FR}}$. Our result shows that both model-based and syntactic revisions can co-exist seamlessly and the advantages of both approaches can be taken in one revision operator. Based on our theoretical results, we develop a graph-based algorithm for the revision operators and thus graph database techniques can be used to compute ontology revisions. Preliminary evaluation results show that the graph-based algorithm can efficiently handle revision of practical ontologies with large data.

Introduction

The latest version of OWL (Ontology Web Language) recommended by W3C is OWL 2[1], which has three profiles with fine-tuned expressive power to support tractable reasoning. OWL 2 QL, one of the three profiles, is designed for ontology-based data access. The logic that underpins OWL 2 QL is DL-Lite, which is a family of tractable description logics[2]. With the development of the Semantic Web, more and more data are published as linked data, and the data is often accompanied with lightweight ontologies[3] which provide extended vocabularies and logical constraints for the data. With new data published and incorporated into the existing data, one typical problem is how to deal with logical inconsistencies caused by the violation of the constraints posed by the ontologies. This problem can be formalized as the problem of ABox revision in description logics, which deals with the removal of assertions in the old ABox to accommodate the new ABox and to resolve inconsistencies, under the assumption that the new ABox is more reliable.

Recently, there has been an increasing interest in ontology revision in DL-Lite. Some model-based revision operators in DL-Lite are proposed (Qi and Du 2009; Kharlamov and Zheleznyakov 2011), which select models of newly received ontology that are 'closest' to the existing ontology. However, model-based operators for ontology revision often suffer from two drawbacks: the inexpressibility problem, i.e., in general, the result of revision cannot be expressed in the same DL, and the computation problem, i.e., the computation of revision is inefficient except for some special cases. In (Calvanese et al. 2010), the authors propose a syntactic algorithm for ABox revision in DL-Lite$_{\mathcal{FR}}$ which runs in polynomial time. It has been shown in (Kharlamov, Zheleznyakov, and Calvanese 2013) that for a fragment of DL-Lite$_{core}$, the core language of DL-Lite, this algorithm outputs the result of two model-based revision operators. However, this result is only shown to hold for the restricted language. An open problem is whether the equivalence of model-based and syntactic revisions still holds in more expressive languages, such as DL-Lite$_{\mathcal{FR}}$, and whether similar result holds for other model-based revision operators.

In this paper, we present the first theoretical work on approximation of two well-known model-based revision operators in DL-Lite$_{\mathcal{FR}}$, as well as a practical graph-based algorithm and some experimental results. We first show that the result of the syntactic revision algorithm given in (Kharlamov, Zheleznyakov, and Calvanese 2013) can be used to approximate two model-based revision operators in DL-Lite$_{\mathcal{R}}$. While both revision operators suffer from the inexpressibility problem, their approximations can be computed efficiently. We then give a counterexample to illustrate that our results on approximation breaks down when role functionality axioms are included. In order to accommodate role functionality axioms, we propose to either disallow the appearance of some role names or modify the syntactic algorithm by removing some axioms. On the practical aspect, we propose a way of implementing the algorithm by transforming a DL-Lite$_{\mathcal{FR}}$ ontology to a graph, and making use of graph database techniques to compute ontology revisions.

[1] http://www.w3.org/TR/owl2-profiles/

[2] http://dl.kr.org/

[3] Here we take ontologies as schema of the data.

Preliminary evaluation results show that the graph-based revision algorithm is able to deal with practical ontologies with large data efficiently.

Preliminaries

In this section, we first briefly recall some basics of DL-Lite and then introduce two model-based revision operators.

DL-Lite

We start with the introduction of DL-Lite$_{core}$, the core language for the DL-Lite family. The complex concepts and roles of DL-Lite$_{core}$ are defined as follows: (1) $B ::= A \mid \exists R$, (2) $R ::= P \mid P^-$, (3) $C ::= B \mid \neg B$, where A denotes an atomic concept, P an atomic role, B a basic concept, and C a general concept.

In DL-Lite$_{core}$, an ontology $\mathcal{O} = \langle \mathcal{T}, \mathcal{A} \rangle$ consists of a TBox $\mathcal{T}$ and an ABox $\mathcal{A}$, where $\mathcal{T}$ is a finite set of *concept inclusion assertions* of the form: $B \sqsubseteq C$; and $\mathcal{A}$ is a finite set of *membership assertions* of the form: $A(a)$, $P(a,b)$. DL-Lite$_{\mathcal{FR}}$ extends DL-Lite$_{core}$ with inclusion assertions between roles of the form $R \sqsubseteq E$ where E is a role or its inverse and functionality on roles or on their inverses of the form $(\texttt{Func}\ R)$. To keep the logic tractable, whenever a role inclusion $R_1 \sqsubseteq R_2$ logically follows from $\mathcal{T}$, neither $(\texttt{Func}\ R_2)$ nor $(\texttt{Func}\ R_2^-)$ can appear in it. We call assertions of the form $B_1 \sqsubseteq \neg B_2$ as negative inclusions (NIs). We use $\mathrm{adom}(\mathcal{O})$ to denote the set of all constants occurring in $\mathcal{O}$.

The semantics of DL-Lite is defined in a standard way. Following the work given in (Calvanese et al. 2010), we assume that all interpretations are defined over the same infinite countable domain Δ. Given an interpretation $\mathcal{I}$ and an assertion α, $\mathcal{I} \models \alpha$ denotes that $\mathcal{I}$ is a *model* of α. An interpretation is called a *model* of an ontology $\mathcal{O}$, iff it is a model for each assertion in $\mathcal{O}$. We use $\mathrm{Mod}(\mathcal{O})$ to denote the set of all models of $\mathcal{O}$. An ontology is satisfiable if it has at least one model. An ontology $\mathcal{O}$ logically implies an assertion α, written $\mathcal{O} \models \alpha$, if all models of $\mathcal{O}$ are also models of α. The deductive closure of an ABox $\mathcal{A}$, denoted $cl_{\mathcal{T}}(\mathcal{A})$, is the set of all ABox assertions α such that $\mathcal{T} \cup \mathcal{A} \models \alpha$.

Model-based revision operators in DL-Lite

Given an ontology $\mathcal{O} = \langle \mathcal{T}, \mathcal{A} \rangle$ and a new ABox $\mathcal{N}$, suppose $\mathcal{O}$ is consistent and $\mathcal{T} \cup \mathcal{N}$ is consistent. The problem of ABox revision is, how to modify $\mathcal{A}$ (by deletion or insertion of assertions) such that $\mathcal{T} \cup \mathcal{N}$ is consistent with the modified ABox? We reformulate the definition of model-based revision operators given in (Calvanese et al. 2010; Kharlamov, Zheleznyakov, and Calvanese 2013). Since we have assumed that all the interpretations are defined over the same domain Δ, we can consider an interpretation as a set of atoms. Given two interpretations $\mathcal{I}$ and $\mathcal{J}$, the set of atoms that are assigned different truth values is denoted as $\mathrm{diff}(\mathcal{I},\mathcal{J}) = \mathcal{I} \ominus \mathcal{J}$, where $\mathcal{I} \ominus \mathcal{J} = (\mathcal{I} \setminus \mathcal{J}) \cup (\mathcal{J} \setminus \mathcal{I})$ is the symmetric difference between $\mathcal{I}$ and $\mathcal{J}$. $\mathrm{diff}(\mathcal{I},\mathcal{J})$ can be extended to two ontologies $\mathcal{O}$ and $\mathcal{O}'$ as $\mathrm{diff}(\mathcal{O},\mathcal{O}') = \{\mathrm{diff}(\mathcal{I},\mathcal{J}) | \mathcal{I} \models \mathcal{O},\ \mathcal{J} \models \mathcal{O}'\}$.

We introduce two well-known distance functions given in the literature (see (Katsuno and Mendelzon 1992) and (Kharlamov, Zheleznyakov, and Calvanese 2013)).

$$\mathrm{dist}_{\subseteq}(\mathcal{I},\mathcal{J}) = \mathrm{diff}(\mathcal{I},\mathcal{J}) \text{ and } \mathrm{dist}_{\#}(\mathcal{I},\mathcal{J}) = |\mathrm{diff}(\mathcal{I},\mathcal{J})|.$$

Furthermore, let $\mathrm{dist}_{\subseteq}(\mathcal{O},\mathcal{O}')$ be the set of minimal elements in $\mathrm{diff}(\mathcal{O},\mathcal{O}')$ w.r.t. the set inclusion and $\mathrm{dist}_{\#}(\mathcal{O},\mathcal{O}') = min_{\mathcal{I}\models\mathcal{O},\mathcal{J}\models\mathcal{O}'} \mathrm{dist}_{\#}(\mathcal{I},\mathcal{J})$.

Based on these two distance functions, we can define two revision operators in a model-theoretic way as follows.

Definition 1. *Given an ontology $\mathcal{O}$ and an ABox $\mathcal{N}$, define*
$\mathrm{Mod}(\mathcal{O} \circ_{\subseteq} \mathcal{N}) = \{\mathcal{J} \in \mathrm{Mod}(\langle\mathcal{T},\mathcal{N}\rangle) \mid$ *there exists* $\mathcal{I} \in \mathrm{Mod}(\mathcal{O})$ *s.t.* $\mathrm{dist}_{\subseteq}(\mathcal{I},\mathcal{J}) \in \mathrm{dist}_{\subseteq}(\mathcal{O},\langle\mathcal{T},\mathcal{N}\rangle)\}$.
$\mathrm{Mod}(\mathcal{O} \circ_{\#} \mathcal{N}) = \{\mathcal{J} \in \mathrm{Mod}(\langle\mathcal{T},\mathcal{N}\rangle) \mid$ *there exists* $\mathcal{I} \in \mathrm{Mod}(\mathcal{O})$ *s.t.* $\mathrm{dist}_{\#}(\mathcal{I},\mathcal{J}) = \mathrm{dist}_{\#}(\mathcal{O},\langle\mathcal{T},\mathcal{N}\rangle)\}$.

In DL-Lite, for any set $\mathcal{M}$ of interpretations, we may not be able to find an ontology whose models are exactly those interpretations in $\mathcal{M}$. Therefore, the notion of sound approximation is defined in (Kharlamov, Zheleznyakov, and Calvanese 2013).

Definition 2. *(Kharlamov, Zheleznyakov, and Calvanese 2013) Let $\mathcal{M}$ be a set of models and $\mathcal{D}$ a DL. We say that a $\mathcal{D}$ ontology $\mathcal{O}$ is a* sound $\mathcal{D}$-approximation *of $\mathcal{M}$ if $\mathcal{M} \subseteq \mathrm{Mod}(\mathcal{O})$. Furthermore, such an ontology $\mathcal{O}$ is a* maximal sound $\mathcal{D}$-approximation *if for every* sound $\mathcal{D}$-approximation *$\mathcal{O}'$ of $\mathcal{M}$ it holds that* $\mathrm{Mod}(\mathcal{O}') \not\subset \mathrm{Mod}(\mathcal{O})$.

Approximating Model-based ABox Revision in DL-Lite$_{\mathcal{R}}$

In this section we show that the approximations of two model-based revision operators $\circ_{\subseteq}$ and $\circ_{\#}$ coincide with the syntactic revision operator introduced in (Kharlamov, Zheleznyakov, and Calvanese 2013) for DL-Lite$_{\mathcal{R}}$. Given a DL-Lite$_{\mathcal{FR}}$ ontology $\mathcal{O} = \langle\mathcal{T},\mathcal{A}\rangle$ and ABox $\mathcal{N}$, an algorithm, denoted as AtAlg, is given in (Kharlamov, Zheleznyakov, and Calvanese 2013) (see Algorithm 1). The algorithm AtAlg determines a *syntactic ABox revision* operator defined as $\mathcal{O} \circ_{MCS} \mathcal{N} = \mathcal{T} \cup \mathcal{N} \cup \mathrm{AtAlg}(\mathcal{O},\mathcal{N})$.

Algorithm 1: $\mathrm{AtAlg}(\mathcal{O},\mathcal{N}))$

Data: DL-Lite$_{FR}$ ontology $\mathcal{O} = \langle\mathcal{T},\mathcal{A}\rangle$ and ABox $\mathcal{N}$
Result: A set of ABox assertions

```
begin
    A' = ∅; X := cl_T(A);
    repeat
        choose some g ∈ X; X:= X \ {g};
        if {g} ∪ N ⊭_T ⊥ then
            A' := A' ∪ {g};
    until X=∅ ;
    return A';
end
```

The following theorem shows that $\mathcal{O} \circ_{MCS} \mathcal{N}$ is a maximal sound approximation of $\mathcal{O} \circ \mathcal{N}$ in DL-Lite$_{\mathcal{R}}$, for $\circ = \circ_{\#}$ and $\circ = \circ_{\subseteq}$.

Theorem 1. *Let $\mathcal{O} = \langle \mathcal{T}, \mathcal{A} \rangle$ be an ontology in DL-Lite$_{\mathcal{R}}$ and $\mathcal{N}$ a new ABox. $\mathcal{O} \circ_{MCS} \mathcal{N}$ is a maximal sound DL-Lite$_{\mathcal{R}}$-approximation of both $\mathcal{O} \circ_{\subseteq} \mathcal{N}$ and $\mathcal{O} \circ_{\#} \mathcal{N}$.*

Proof. (Sketch) Let $M_{\subseteq} = \text{Mod}(\mathcal{O} \circ_{\subseteq} \mathcal{N})$ and $M_{MCS} = \text{Mod}(\mathcal{O} \circ_{MCS} \mathcal{N})$. For any $\mathcal{J} \in M_{\subseteq}$, clearly $\mathcal{J} \models \mathcal{T} \cup \mathcal{N}$. We only need to show that $\mathcal{J} \models \text{AtAlg}(\mathcal{O}, \mathcal{N})$. We show this by absurdity. Suppose there exists $f^* \in \text{AtAlg}(\mathcal{O}, \mathcal{N})$ such that $\mathcal{J} \not\models f^*$. Since $\mathcal{J} \in M_{\subseteq}$, there exists $\mathcal{I} \models \mathcal{O}$ (thus $\mathcal{I} \models f^*$) such that $\text{dist}_{\subseteq}(\mathcal{I}, \mathcal{J})$ is minimal among all pairs of models of $\mathcal{T} \cup \mathcal{N}$ and $\mathcal{O}$. We construct a model $\mathcal{I}'$ of $\mathcal{O}$ and a model $\mathcal{J}'$ of $\mathcal{T} \cup \mathcal{N}$ such that $\text{diff}_{\subseteq}(\mathcal{I}', \mathcal{J}') \subset \text{diff}_{\subseteq}(\mathcal{I}, \mathcal{J})$. In DL-Lite, a standard method to construct a model is to use the notion of a chase. If we take $\mathcal{I}' = chase_{\mathcal{T}}(\mathcal{A})$ and $\mathcal{J}' = chase_{\mathcal{T}}(\mathcal{N})$, where $chase_{\mathcal{T}}(\mathcal{A})$ is the chase of $\mathcal{A}$ w.r.t. $\mathcal{T}$, then we may not have $\text{diff}_{\subseteq}(\mathcal{I}', \mathcal{J}') \subset \text{diff}_{\subseteq}(\mathcal{I}, \mathcal{J})$. Let us look at an example: let $\mathcal{O} = \langle \mathcal{T}, \mathcal{A} \rangle$, $\mathcal{T} = \{A \sqsubseteq \exists R, B \sqsubseteq \neg \exists R^-\}$ and $\mathcal{A} = \{A(c), R(c,d)\}$, and an ABox $\mathcal{N} = \{B(d)\}$. Clearly, $chase_{\mathcal{T}}(\mathcal{A}) = \mathcal{A}$ and $chase_{\mathcal{T}}(\mathcal{N}) = \mathcal{N}$. However, we can find $\mathcal{I} = \{A(c), R(c,d), R(c,e)\}$ and $\mathcal{J} = \{B(d), A(c), R(c,e)\}$ and we can check that $\text{diff}_{\subseteq}(\mathcal{I}, \mathcal{J})$ is minimal w.r.t. the set inclusion. That is, we should add $R(c,e)$ to the model of $\mathcal{A} \cup \mathcal{T}$ and we should add $A(c)$ and $R(c,e)$ to the model of $\mathcal{N} \cup \mathcal{T}$. Based on this intuition, we propose the following method to construct $\mathcal{I}'$ and $\mathcal{J}'$. We first take $\mathcal{I}_1 = chase_{\mathcal{T}}(\mathcal{A})$ and $\mathcal{J}_1 = chase_{\mathcal{T}}(\mathcal{N})$, we then update $\mathcal{J}_1$ using $\mathcal{I}_1$ by adding those $A(c)$ and $P(c,d)$ in $\mathcal{I}_1$ that are not in conflict with $\mathcal{N}$ w.r.t. $\mathcal{T}$ to $\mathcal{J}_1$. Suppose we get $\mathcal{J}_2$. We then update $\mathcal{I}_1$ by $\mathcal{J}_2$, and so on, until we get a fixed point. We can check that $\text{diff}_{\subseteq}(\mathcal{I}', \mathcal{J}') \subset \text{diff}_{\subseteq}(\mathcal{I}, \mathcal{J})$, which is a contradiction. □

One may wonder if $\mathcal{O} \circ_{MCS} \mathcal{N}$ is the syntactic counterpart of $\text{Mod}(\mathcal{O} \circ \mathcal{N})$, for $\circ = \circ_{\subseteq}$ or $\circ = \circ_{\#}$. The following example shows that this is not the case.

Example 1. *Given an ontology $\mathcal{O} = \langle \mathcal{T}, \mathcal{A} \rangle$, where $\mathcal{T} = \{A \sqsubseteq \neg \exists P\}$ and $\mathcal{A} = \{A(c)\}$, and an ABox $\mathcal{N} = \{\exists P(c)\}$. Then $cl_{\mathcal{T}}(\mathcal{A}) = \{A(c)\}$ and $\text{AtAlg}(\mathcal{O}, \mathcal{N}) = \emptyset$. So $\mathcal{O} \circ_{MCS} \mathcal{N} = \mathcal{T} \cup \mathcal{N}$. It is easy to check that $\mathcal{J} = \{P(c,d), P(c,e)\}$ and $\mathcal{J}' = \{P(c,d)\}$ are two models of $\mathcal{T} \cup \mathcal{N}$. Thus they are both models of $\mathcal{O} \circ_{MCS} \mathcal{N}$. The chase of $\mathcal{A}$ w.r.t. $\mathcal{T}$ is $\mathcal{I} = \{A(c)\}$. We have $\text{diff}(\mathcal{I}, \mathcal{J}') \subset \text{diff}(\mathcal{I}, \mathcal{J})$ (resp. $|\text{diff}(\mathcal{I}, \mathcal{J}')| < |\text{diff}(\mathcal{I}, \mathcal{J})|$). Since $\mathcal{J}$ or $\mathcal{J}'$ cannot be expanded with $A(c)$ and any model of $\mathcal{T} \cup \mathcal{A}$ must contain $A(c)$ and can be expanded with neither $P(c,d)$ nor $P(c,e)$, $\text{diff}(\mathcal{I}_i, \mathcal{J}') \subset \text{diff}(\mathcal{I}_i, \mathcal{J})$ (resp. $|\text{diff}(\mathcal{I}_i, \mathcal{J}')| < |\text{diff}(\mathcal{I}_i, \mathcal{J})|$) for any model $\mathcal{I}_i$ of $\mathcal{T} \cup \mathcal{A}$. Thus, $\mathcal{J}$ cannot be a model of $\mathcal{O} \circ \mathcal{N}$, for $\circ = \circ_{\subseteq}$ or $\circ = \circ_{\#}$.*

According to Theorem 1 and Example 1, we can show that operators $\circ_{\subseteq}$ and $\circ_{\#}$ suffer from the problem of inexpressibility, i.e., $\text{Mod}(\mathcal{O} \circ \mathcal{N})$ is not axiomatizable in DL-Lite$_{\mathcal{R}}$.

Approximating model-based revision in DL-Lite$_{\mathcal{FR}}$

We consider the question if Theorem 1 still holds when functionality axioms are included. Unfortunately, the following example gives a negative answer to this question.

Example 2. *Given an ontology $\mathcal{O} = \langle \mathcal{T}, \mathcal{A} \rangle$, where $\mathcal{T} = \{A \sqsubseteq \exists R, B \sqsubseteq \neg \exists R^-, (\texttt{Func } R)\}$ and $\mathcal{A} = \{A(c), B(e), R(c,d)\}$, and an ABox $\mathcal{N} = \{B(d)\}$. Then $cl_{\mathcal{T}}(\mathcal{A}) = \{A(c), B(e), R(c,d), \exists R(c)\}$ and $\text{AtAlg}(\mathcal{O}, \mathcal{N}) = \{A(c), B(e), \exists R(c)\}$. So $\mathcal{O} \circ_{MCS} \mathcal{N} = \mathcal{T} \cup \{A(c), B(d), B(e), \exists R(c)\}$. Consider the following four interpretations:*

$\mathcal{I} = \{A(c), R(c,d), B(e)\}$;

$\mathcal{J}_1 = \{(B(d), B(e), A(c), R(c,f)\}$;

$\mathcal{J}_2 = \{B(d), B(e)\}$;

$\mathcal{J}_3 = \{B(d), A(c), R(c,e)\}$.

It is easy to check that $\mathcal{I}$ is a model of $\mathcal{T} \cup \mathcal{A}$ and $\mathcal{J}_i$ $(i = 1,2,3)$ are models of $\mathcal{T} \cup \mathcal{N}$. We have $\text{diff}(\mathcal{I}, \mathcal{J}_1) = \{B(d), R(c,d), R(c,f)\}$, $\text{diff}(\mathcal{I}, \mathcal{J}_2) = \{A(c), B(d), R(c,d)\}$ and $\text{diff}(\mathcal{I}, \mathcal{J}_3) = \{B(d), B(e), R(c,d), R(c,e)\}$. Thus, $\text{dist}_{\#}(\mathcal{I}, \mathcal{J}_1) = \text{dist}_{\#}(\mathcal{I}, \mathcal{J}_2) = 3$. Any model of $\mathcal{T} \cup \mathcal{A}$ must contain $A(c)$, $R(c,d)$ and $B(e)$ and any model of $\mathcal{T} \cup \mathcal{N}$ must contain $B(d)$. Since $R(c,d)$ and $B(d)$ are in conflict w.r.t. $\mathcal{T}$, any model $\mathcal{I}$ of $\mathcal{T} \cup \mathcal{A}$ and any model $\mathcal{J}$ of $\mathcal{T} \cup \mathcal{N}$ will not contain both of them. For any such $\mathcal{J}$, suppose it contains $A(c)$, then it will contain $R(c, y_{new})$ where y_{new} is a fresh individual. Since $(\texttt{Func } R) \in \mathcal{T}$, $R(c, y_{new})$ cannot exist in any model $\mathcal{I}$ of $\mathcal{T} \cup \mathcal{A}$. Thus, $\text{diff}(\mathcal{I}, \mathcal{J})$ must contain $R(c,d)$, $B(d)$ and $R(c, y_{new})$. If $\mathcal{J}$ does not contain $A(c)$, then $\text{diff}(\mathcal{I}, \mathcal{J})$ must contain $R(c,d)$, $B(d)$ and $A(c)$. Therefore, $\mathcal{J}_2$ and $\mathcal{J}_3$ are models of $\mathcal{O} \circ_{\#} \mathcal{N}$. Clearly, $\mathcal{J}_3$ is not a model of $\text{AtAlg}(\mathcal{O}, \mathcal{N})$. So it is not a model of $\mathcal{O} \circ_{MCS} \mathcal{N}$. Since $\mathcal{J}_2$ is not a model of $A(c)$, $A(c)$ cannot be inferred from $\mathcal{O} \circ_{\#} \mathcal{N}$. Similarly, we can show that $\mathcal{J}_1$, $\mathcal{J}_2$ and $\mathcal{J}_3$ are models of $\mathcal{O} \circ_{\subseteq} \mathcal{N}$. Since $\mathcal{J}_1$ is not a model of $B(e)$ and $\mathcal{J}_3$ is not a model of $A(c)$, neither $A(c)$ nor $B(e)$ can be inferred from $\mathcal{O} \circ_{\subseteq} \mathcal{N}$. Thus, Theorem 1 does not hold for DL-Lite$_{\mathcal{FR}}$.

To see why adding functionalities on roles or their inverses causes the inexpressibility problem, we analyze Example 2 again. Since $(\texttt{Func } R)$ exists, when applying the model construction method given in the proof of Theorem 1, we cannot update models of $\mathcal{O}$ and $\mathcal{T} \cup \mathcal{N}$ successfully because of the functionality constraints. For example, when constructing the chase of $\mathcal{A}$ w.r.t. $\mathcal{T}$, we need to add $R(c, x_{new})$ to the chase of $\mathcal{N}$ w.r.t. $\mathcal{T}$. However, since $(\texttt{Func } R)$) exists, we may not be able to do that. Based on this analysis, we define a notion called *triggered roles*, which are role names that causes the inexpressibility problem.

Definition 3. *(Set of triggered roles). Let $\mathcal{O} = \langle \mathcal{T}, \mathcal{A} \rangle$ be an ontology in DL-Lite$_{\mathcal{FR}}$ and $\mathcal{N}$ a new ABox. The set of* triggered roles *in $\mathcal{O}$, denoted as $\text{TR}[\mathcal{O}, \mathcal{N}]$, is the set of all roles that satisfy one of the following conditions:*

- *Condition 1: (1) $(\texttt{Func } P) \in \mathcal{T}$, (2) $P(c,d) \in cl_{\mathcal{T}}(\mathcal{A})$, and $\mathcal{A} \setminus \{P(c,d)\} \models_{\mathcal{T}} \exists P(c)$, and (3) $\mathcal{N} \cup \{\exists P(c)\} \not\models_{\mathcal{T}} \bot$ and $\mathcal{N} \cup \{\exists P^-(d)\} \models_{\mathcal{T}} \bot$, where $c, d \in \text{adom}(\mathcal{O})$.*
- *Condition 2: (1) $(\texttt{Func } P) \in \mathcal{T}$, (2) $P(c,d) \in cl_{\mathcal{T}}(\mathcal{A})$, and $\mathcal{A} \setminus \{P(c,d)\} \models_{\mathcal{T}} \exists P^-(d)$, and (3) $\mathcal{N} \cup \{\exists P^-(d)\} \not\models_{\mathcal{T}} \bot$ and $\mathcal{N} \cup \{\exists P(c)\} \models_{\mathcal{T}} \bot$, where $c, d \in \text{adom}(\mathcal{O})$.*

We show that if the set of triggered roles is empty, then $\mathcal{O} \circ_{MCS} \mathcal{N}$ is an approximation of $\mathcal{O} \circ \mathcal{N}$, for $\circ = \circ_{\subseteq}$ or $\circ = \circ_{\#}$.

Theorem 2. *Let $\mathcal{O} = \langle\mathcal{T}, \mathcal{A}\rangle$ be an ontology in DL-Lite$_{\mathcal{FR}}$ and $\mathcal{N}$ a new ABox. If $\mathrm{TR}[\mathcal{O},\mathcal{N}] = \emptyset$, then we have $\mathrm{Mod}(\mathcal{O} \circ \mathcal{N}) \subseteq \mathrm{Mod}(\mathcal{O} \circ_{MCS} \mathcal{N})$, for $\circ = \circ_{\subseteq}$ or $\circ = \circ_{\#}$. Otherwise, we cannot have $\mathrm{Mod}(\mathcal{O} \circ \mathcal{N}) \subseteq \mathrm{Mod}(\mathcal{O} \circ_{MCS} \mathcal{N})$, for $\circ = \circ_{\subseteq}$ or $\circ = \circ_{\#}$.*

If the set of triggered roles is not empty, then we can modify $\mathcal{O} \circ_{MCS} \mathcal{N}$ such that it is an approximation of $\mathcal{O} \circ \mathcal{N}$, for $\circ = \circ_{\subseteq}$ or $\circ = \circ_{\#}$. Consider Example 2, $\mathcal{J}_2$ is a model of $\mathcal{O} \circ \mathcal{N}$, but it may not be a model of $A(c)$ and $R(c,d)$, where R is a triggered role. However, it is easy to check that $\mathcal{J}_2$ is a model of $\mathrm{AtAlg}(\mathcal{O},\mathcal{N}) \setminus \{A(c), R(c,d)\}$. This inspired us to give a method to compute the maximal approximation of $\mathcal{O} \circ \mathcal{N}$, for $\circ = \circ_{\subseteq}$ or $\circ = \circ_{\#}$. The idea is to remove $\exists P(c)$ and those assertions that can infer it from $\mathrm{AtAlg}(\mathcal{O},\mathcal{N})$ for each triggered role P. We need a lemma that generalizes Proposition A.1 given in (Kharlamov, Zheleznyakov, and Calvanese 2013).

Lemma 1. *Let $\mathcal{T} \cup \mathcal{A}$ be a consistent DL-Lite$_{\mathcal{FR}}$ ontology and let $g = \exists R(c)$. If $\mathcal{A} \models_{\mathcal{T}} \exists R(c)$, then there exists a membership assertion $f \in \mathcal{A}$ such that $f \models_{\mathcal{T}} \exists R(c)$.*

Lemma 1 infers that each justification for $\exists R(c)$ contains only one membership assertion, where a justification for $\exists R(c)$ is the minimal subset of $\mathcal{A}$ that can entail $R(c)$. We define the notion of removing set of an assertion of the form $\exists R(c)$, which consists of all membership assertions that infer $\exists R(c)$.

Definition 4. *(Removing set) Let $\mathcal{O} = \langle\mathcal{T}, \mathcal{A}\rangle$ be an ontology and $\mathcal{N}$ be an ABox in DL-Lite$_{\mathcal{FR}}$. Suppose $\mathcal{A} \models_{\mathcal{T}} \exists R(c)$. The* removing set *of $\exists R(c)$, denoted as $\mathrm{remove}_{\mathcal{T}}(\exists R(c))$, is defined as*

$$\mathrm{remove}_{\mathcal{T}}(\exists R(c)) = \{f \in \mathrm{AtAlg}(\mathcal{O},\mathcal{N}) | \{f\} \models_{\mathcal{T}} \exists R(c)\}.$$

In Example 2, we have $\mathrm{remove}_{\mathcal{T}}(\exists R(c)) = \{A(c), R(c,d), \exists R(c)\}$.

Theorem 3. *Let $\mathcal{O} = \langle\mathcal{T}, \mathcal{A}\rangle$ be an ontology in DL-Lite$_{\mathcal{FR}}$ and $\mathcal{N}$ a new ABox. Suppose $\mathrm{TR}[\mathcal{O},\mathcal{N}] \neq \emptyset$. Let $\mathrm{AtAlg}(\mathcal{O},\mathcal{N})_{new} = \mathrm{AtAlg}(\mathcal{O},\mathcal{N}) \setminus \cup_{R \in \mathrm{TR}[\mathcal{O},\mathcal{N}]} \mathrm{remove}_{\mathcal{T}}(\exists R(c))$ and $\mathcal{O}' = \mathcal{T} \cup \mathcal{N} \cup \mathrm{AtAlg}(\mathcal{O},\mathcal{N})_{new}$. Then $\mathcal{O}'$ is a maximal approximation of $\mathcal{O} \circ_{\#} \mathcal{N}$ but it is not an approximation of $\mathcal{O} \circ_{\subseteq} \mathcal{N}$.*

Proof. (Sketch) We cannot apply the same method to construct models of $\mathcal{T} \cup \mathcal{A}$ and $\mathcal{T} \cup \mathcal{N}$ as in the proof of Theorem 1. We give a new method to construct models as follows. The construction of $\mathcal{I}_1$ and $\mathcal{J}_1$ is the same as the proof of Theorem 1. However, when updating $\mathcal{J}_1$ using $\mathcal{I}_1$, we need to exclude those role assertions where the role is in $\mathrm{TR}[\mathcal{O},\mathcal{N}]$. □

A Graph-based Algorithm for ABox Revision in DL-Lite

In the previous section, we have shown that the result of the revision operator given in (Kharlamov, Zheleznyakov, and Calvanese 2013) can be used to approximate the result of two model-based revision operators in DL-Lite$_{\mathcal{FR}}$. A variant of this operator is given in (Calvanese et al. 2010), which is defined by a more practical algorithm called *FastEvo*. This algorithm runs in polynomial time. However, as Algorithm AtAlg, it needs to compute the ABox closure w.r.t. the TBox, which will hinder their applicability for ontologies with large ABoxes. In this section, we propose a revision algorithm that does not compute the ABox closure beforehand and it can utilize state of the art graph databases to compute the result of revision. Before we give the algorithm, we present a revision operator that removes one assertion from each *minimal inconsistent subset* of $\mathcal{A}$ w.r.t. $\mathcal{N}$ and $\mathcal{T}$.

Definition 5. *Given an ontology $\mathcal{O} = \langle\mathcal{T}, \mathcal{A}\rangle$ and an ABox $\mathcal{N}$. A minimal inconsistent subset (MIS) $\mathcal{D}$ of $\mathcal{A}$ w.r.t. $\mathcal{N}$ and $\mathcal{T}$ is a sub-ABox of $\mathcal{A}$ which satisfies (1) $\mathcal{D} \cup \mathcal{T} \cup \mathcal{N}$ is inconsistent; (2) $\forall \mathcal{D}' \subset \mathcal{D}$, $\mathcal{D}' \cup \mathcal{T} \cup \mathcal{N}$ is consistent. We denote the set of all the MISs of $\mathcal{A}$ w.r.t. $\mathcal{N}$ by $MIS_{\mathcal{N}}(\mathcal{A})$ (we omit $\mathcal{T}$ to simplify the notation).*

Example 3. *(originally from (Giacomo et al. 2009)) Given an ontology $\mathcal{O} = \langle\mathcal{T}, \mathcal{A}\rangle$ and a new ABox $\mathcal{N}$, where $\mathcal{T} = \{\exists WillPlay \sqsubseteq AvailablePlayer, AvailablePlayer \sqsubseteq Player, Injured \sqsubseteq \neg AvailablePlayer\}$, $\mathcal{A} = \{WillPlay(Peter, game06)\}$, $\mathcal{N} = \{Injured(Peter)\}$. It is easy to check that there exists one MIS of $\mathcal{A}$ w.r.t. $\mathcal{N}$: $\{WillPlay(Peter, game06)\}$.*

According to (Calvanese et al. 2010), every MIS of $\mathrm{MIS}_{\mathcal{N}}(\mathcal{A})$ contains only one assertion. Thus, to restore consistency, we can simply remove $\cup_{\mathcal{D}_i \in MIS_{\mathcal{N}}(\mathcal{A})} \mathcal{D}_i$. However, this may delete much more information than necessary. Consider Example 1 again, we can find that Peter is injured implies that he is not an available player anymore, but he remains a player, and this would not be captured by simply removing $\cup_{\mathcal{D}_i \in MIS_{\mathcal{N}}(\mathcal{A})} \mathcal{D}_i$. Consequently, we will add $Player(Peter)$ to the result of revision as it does not contradict $\mathcal{N} \cup \mathcal{T}$ and it can be inferred from $\cup_{\mathcal{D}_i \in MIS_{\mathcal{N}}(\mathcal{A})} \mathcal{D}_i \cup \mathcal{T}$.

Definition 6. *Given an ontology $\mathcal{O} = \langle\mathcal{T}, \mathcal{A}\rangle$ and an ABox $\mathcal{N}$, a maximal consistent set S of $cl_{\mathcal{T}}(\cup_{\mathcal{D}_i \in MIS_{\mathcal{N}}(\mathcal{A})} \mathcal{D}_i)$ w.r.t. $\mathcal{N}$ is a sub-ABox of $cl_{\mathcal{T}}(\cup_{\mathcal{D}_i \in MIS_{\mathcal{N}}(\mathcal{A})} \mathcal{D}_i)$ which satisfies (1) $S \cup \mathcal{T} \cup \mathcal{N}$ is consistent; (2) $\forall \alpha \in cl_{\mathcal{T}}(\cup_{\mathcal{D}_i \in MIS_{\mathcal{N}}(\mathcal{A})} \mathcal{D}_i)$ and $\alpha \notin S$, $S \cup \{\alpha\} \cup \mathcal{T} \cup \mathcal{N}$ is inconsistent.*

Definition 7. *Given an ontology $\mathcal{O} = \langle\mathcal{T}, \mathcal{A}\rangle$ and an ABox $\mathcal{N}$. The revision operator $\circ_{MIS}$ for $\mathcal{O}$ is defined as follows:*

$$\mathcal{O} \circ_{MIS} \mathcal{N} = \mathcal{T} \cup (\mathcal{A} \setminus \cup_{\mathcal{D}_i \in MIS_{\mathcal{N}}(\mathcal{A})} \mathcal{D}_i) \cup S \cup \mathcal{N}$$

We can show that the deductive closure of the resulting ABox of our operator is the same as the ABox obtained by operator $\circ_{MCS}$ and the revision operator defined by algorithm *FastEvo* given in (Calvanese et al. 2010).

Theorem 4. *Given an ontology $\mathcal{O} = \langle\mathcal{T}, \mathcal{A}\rangle$ and an ABox $\mathcal{N}$ in DL-Lite$_{\mathcal{FR}}$, suppose $\mathcal{O} \circ_{MIS} \mathcal{N} = \langle\mathcal{T}, \mathcal{A}', \mathcal{N}\rangle$, where $\mathcal{A}' = (\mathcal{A} \setminus \cup_{\mathcal{D}_i \in MIS_{\mathcal{N}}(\mathcal{A})} \mathcal{D}_i) \cup S$, then $\mathcal{T} \cup cl_{\mathcal{T}}(\mathcal{A}') \cup \mathcal{N} = \mathcal{O} \circ_{MCS} \mathcal{N}$.*

A Graph-based Algorithm

Given a DL-Lite ontology $\mathcal{O}$ over a signature Σ, which can be partitioned into two disjoint signatures, Σ_P, containing symbols for atomic elements, i.e., atomic concept and atomic roles, and Σ_C, containing symbols for individuals, the digraph $G_{\mathcal{O}} = \langle N, E \rangle$ constructed from ontology $\mathcal{O} = \langle \mathcal{T}, \mathcal{A} \rangle$ over the signature Σ as follows:

(1) for each atomic concept B in Σ_P, N contains the node B;

(2) for each atomic role P in Σ_P, N contains the node $P, P^-, \exists P, \exists P^-$;

(3) for each concept inclusion $B_1 \sqsubseteq B_2 \in T$, E contains the $arc(B_1, B_2)$;

(4) for each role inclusion $P_1 \sqsubseteq P_2 \in T$, E contains the $arc(P_1, P_2), arc(P_1^-, P_2^-)$, $arc(\exists P_1, \exists P_2), arc(\exists P_1^-, \exists P_2^-)$;

(5) for each individual c in Σ_C, N contains leaf node c;

(6) for each concept membership assertion $B(c) \in \mathcal{A}$, E contains $arc(c, B)$;

(7) for each role membership assertion $P(a, b)$, N contains node $(a, b), (b, a)$, and E contains the $arc((a, b), P), arc((b, a), P^-), arc(a, \exists P), arc(b, \exists P^-)$;

In our graph, each node represents a basic concept or a basic role, while each arc represents an inclusion assertion or a membership assertion, i.e. the start node of the arc corresponds to the left-hand side of the inclusion assertion (resp. individual or individual-pair of the membership assertion) and the end node of the arc corresponds to the right-hand side of the inclusion assertion (resp. concept or role of the membership assertion). Items (4) and (7) are used to ensure that the information represented in the ontology is preserved by the graph.

Algorithm 2: GraphRevi($\mathcal{T}$, $\mathcal{A}$, $\mathcal{N}$)

Input: TBox $\mathcal{T}$ and ABoxes $\mathcal{A}, \mathcal{N}$, each consistent with $\mathcal{T}$
Output: $\mathcal{T} \cup (\mathcal{A} \backslash D) \cup M \cup \mathcal{N}$
1 **begin**
2 $D = \emptyset$;
3 $M = \emptyset$;
4 $A_{all} = \mathcal{A} \cup \mathcal{N}$;
5 **for** *each* $(functR) \in \mathcal{T}$ **do**
6 **if** $\{R(a, b), R(a, c)\} \subseteq A_{all}$ **then**
7 **if** $R(a, b) \notin \mathcal{N}$ **then**
8 $D = D \cup \{R(a, b)\}$;
9 **else**
10 $D = D \cup \{R(a, c)\}$;
11 **construct** $G_{\langle \mathcal{T}, A_{all} \backslash D \rangle} = \langle V, E \rangle$;
12 $D = D \cup Search(G_{\langle \mathcal{T}, A_{all} \backslash D \rangle}, \mathcal{A})$;
13 $M = cl_{\mathcal{T}}(D) \backslash D$;
14 **construct** HG $G_{\langle \mathcal{T}, M \cup \mathcal{A}_1 \rangle} = \langle V, E \rangle$;
15 $M = M \backslash Search(G_{\langle \mathcal{T}, M \cup \mathcal{A}_1 \rangle}, M)$;
16 **return** $\mathcal{T} \cup (\mathcal{A} \backslash D) \cup M \cup \mathcal{N}$;
17 **end**

Algorithm 3: Search(G, $\mathcal{A}$)

Data: Graph:G; ABox:$\mathcal{A}$
Result: finite set of membership assertions N
begin
$N = \emptyset$;
for *each* $\neg X \in V$ **do**
$U = leafChild(X) \cap leafChild(\neg X)$;
for *each* $a \in U$ **do**
for *each* $v \in (Children(X) \cup Children(\neg X) \cup \{X\})$ **do**
if $v(a) \in \mathcal{A}$ **then**
if $v(a) = \exists R(a)$ **then**
for *each* $R(a, b) \in \mathcal{A}$ **do**
$N = N \cup \{R(a, b)\}$;
else
$N = N \cup \{v(a)\}$;
return N;
end

We now introduce algorithm *GraphRevi* (see Algorithm 2), which takes $\mathcal{O} = \langle \mathcal{T}, \mathcal{A} \rangle$ and $\mathcal{N}$ as its input. The algorithm can be explained as follows. Let $\mathcal{A}_{all} = \mathcal{A} \cup \mathcal{N}$ (line 4). It first computes the set D of all the membership assertions in $\mathcal{A}$ that are in conflict with functionality axioms and $\mathcal{N}$ (lines 5-10). It then constructs a digraph from $\langle \mathcal{T}, \mathcal{A}_{all} \backslash D \rangle$ and uses function *Search* to compute the set of all the membership assertions in $\mathcal{A}$ that are in conflict with some negative inclusion assertions of the form $B \sqsubseteq \neg B'$ and some assertions in $\mathcal{N}$, and use this set to update D (see Algorithm 3). Thus, D is actually $\cup_{A_i \in MIS_{\mathcal{N}}(\mathcal{A})} A_i$. Let $M = cl_{\mathcal{T}}(D) \backslash D$ (lines 11-12). The algorithm deletes all the membership assertions in M that are in conflict with NI assertions and $\mathcal{N}$ (lines 13-15). Finally, $\mathcal{T} \cup (\mathcal{A} \backslash D) \cup M \cup \mathcal{N}$ is the result of revision (line 16).

Example 4. *Given an ontology $\mathcal{O} = \langle \mathcal{T}, \mathcal{A} \rangle$ and a new ABox $\mathcal{N}$, where $\mathcal{T} = \{(\texttt{Func}\ R), R \sqsubseteq R_1, \exists R^- \sqsubseteq B, A \sqsubseteq C, C \sqsubseteq \neg D, B \sqsubseteq \neg C\}$, $\mathcal{A} = \{R(a, b), C(d), A(e)\}$, $\mathcal{N} = \{R(a, f), A(b), D(d)\}$.*

1. *$A_{all} = \mathcal{A} \cup \mathcal{N} = \{R(a, b), C(d), A(e), R(a, f), A(b), D(d)\}$ (see Algorithm 2 line 4);*
2. *$D = \{R(a, b)\}$ (see Algorithm 1 lines 5-10);*
3. *By constructing digraph $G_{\langle \mathcal{T}, A_{all} \backslash D \rangle}$ (see Figure 1), we can obtain that $D = \{R(a, b), C(d)\}$(see Algorithm 2 lines 11-12);*
4. *$M = cl_{\mathcal{T}}(D) \backslash D = \{R_1(a, b), B(b), A(e), C(e)\}$ (see Algorithm 2 line 13);*
5. *By constructing digraph $G_{\langle \mathcal{T}, M \cup \mathcal{N} \rangle}$ (similar to Figure 1), then we can know that $M = \{R_1(a, b), A(e), C(e)\}$(see Algorithm 2 lines 14-15);*
6. *The result is: $\mathcal{T} \cup \{R(a, f), A(b), D(d), R_1(a, b), A(e), c(e)\}$ (see Algorithm 2 line 16).*

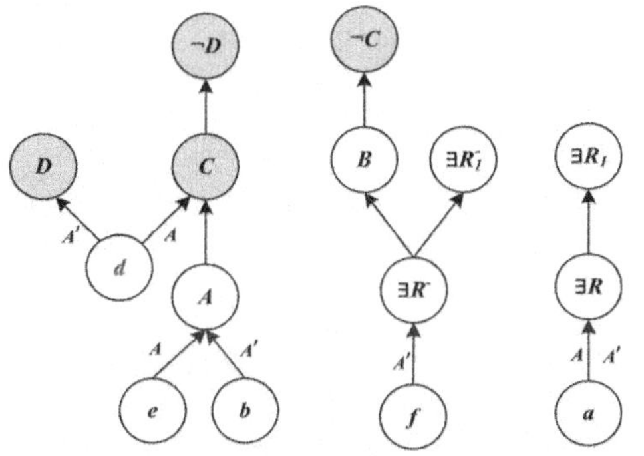

Figure 1: Digraph $G_{\langle \mathcal{T}, \mathcal{A}_{all} \setminus D \rangle}$ of Example 4

Table 1: Generated ABoxes

Data	univ4-1	univ4-2	univ6-1	univ6-2
#axiom	636086	635581	876342	879631
Data	**univ8-1**	**univ8-2**	**univ10-1**	**univ10-2**
#axiom	1139949	1138337	1415102	1416326

Theorem 5. *Algorithm 2 runs in polynomial time. Given an ontology* $\mathcal{O} = \langle \mathcal{T}, \mathcal{A} \rangle$ *and an ABox* $\mathcal{N}$*, we have* $\mathcal{O} \circ_{MIS} \mathcal{N} = GraphRevi(\mathcal{T}, \mathcal{A}, \mathcal{N})$.

Experimental Results

We have implemented our graph-based algorithm for ABox revision in Java. We first transform a DL-Lite ontology into a graph and store it in a Neo4j graph database, which is an open-source and high-performance graph database supported by Neo Technology. We also implemented the revision algorithm presented in (Calvanese et al. 2010) using Neo4j, which we denote as *FastEvo*.

We conducted some experiments on a data set constructed from UOBM benchmark ontology[4] (see Table 1 for details of the data set). We generated ABoxes by using the UOBM generator. We divided each generated ABox into two parts. We used the Random class of Java to control the dividing procedure. Since the original UOBM ontologies are consistent, we modified them by inserting some "inconsistency-generating" axioms, such as disjointness axioms. We generated different percentage of the disjoint classes for each university ontology. After that, for each pair of disjoint concepts or roles, we generated a common instance or pair of instances and added the two conflicting assertions to two ABoxes partitioned from an ABox.

All experiments have been performed on a PC with Intel Corei5-2400 3.1 GHz CPU and 6GB of RAM, running Microsoft window 7 operating system, and Java 1.7 with 6GB of heap space.

We did four experiments to compare the execution time of GraphRevi and *FastEvo*. The results of our experiments are shown in Table 2. According to Table 2, GraphRevi outperforms *FastEvo* when the number of universities and the

[4]http://www.cs.ox.ac.uk/isg/tools/UOBMGenerator/

Table 2: Execution Time (s) of ABox Revision

#univ	Disjointness(%)	GraphRevi	FastEvo
4	20	17.693	51.66
	30	26.591	68.702
	40	41.423	110.251
6	20	19.802	69.001
	30	27.874	86.685
	40	44.833	135.518
8	20	23.353	89.606
	30	31.070	105.483
	40	49.313	167.695
10	20	26.309	119.781
	30	33.945	133.852
	40	59.798	201.149

percentage of disjointness axioms are increasing. In many cases, GraphRevi is 4 to 5 times faster than *FastEvo*. When the percentage of the disjointness axioms is low, GraphRevi runs very efficiently, i.e., in less than 30 seconds. Another observation is that with the increasing percentage of disjointness axioms, GraphRevi becomes less efficient, this is because it takes more time to find the membership assertions in $\mathcal{A}$ that are in conflict with $\mathcal{N}$ w.r.t. $\mathcal{T}$. We also observe that in almost all the test cases, GraphRevi can finish the computation in less than 60 seconds (even when 10 universities are considered). Furthermore, GraphRevis performs well for ontologies with 12 universities, but FastEvol cannot handle them.

Related Work

This work is closely related to the work presented in (Calvanese et al. 2010) and (Kharlamov, Zheleznyakov, and Calvanese 2013). In (Calvanese et al. 2010), the authors propose an ABox revision algorithm *FastEvol* for DL-Lite$_{\mathcal{FR}}$ ontologies, but no implementation is provided. Our experimental results show that our graph-based algorithm significantly outperforms *FastEvol*. It is proven in (Kharlamov, Zheleznyakov, and Calvanese 2013) that $Mod(\mathcal{O} \circ_{MCS} \mathcal{N})$ and $Mod(\mathcal{O} \circ_{\#} \mathcal{N})$ coincide on a fragment of DL-Lite$_{core}$. In this paper, we show that while this result does not hold in the full DL-Lite$_{core}$, $\mathcal{O} \circ_{MCS} \mathcal{N}$ is a maximal approximation of the model-based revision $\mathcal{O} \circ_{\#} \mathcal{N}$ in DL-Lite$_{\mathcal{R}}$.

Revision of DL-based ontologies has been widely discussed in the literature. Most of the work on model-based revision in DLs is devoted to proving the inexpressibility of model-based revision operators (see (Qi and Du 2009), (Calvanese et al. 2010) and (Grau et al. 2012) for example). However, very few of them discuss the approximation of model-based revision. One exception is the work in (Wang, Wang, and Topor 2010), where a revision operator is defined by a new semantics called *features*. However, feature-based revision also suffers from the inexpressibility problem and the algorithm to approximating the result of revision is intractable and is inefficient to deal with large ABoxes. Recently, there are some works on TBox revision based on a new semantics, called *type semantics* (see (Zhuang et al.

2014) and (Wang et al. 2015)).

Another line of work is to adapt the well-known AGM (Alchourrón, Gärdenfors and Markinson) framework to DLs (see (Flouris, Plexousakis, and Antoniou 2005), (Flouris et al. 2006) and (Ribeiro et al. 2013)) and adapt Hansson's postulates for revision (see (Hansson 1999)) to DLs (Ribeiro and Wassermann 2007). However, model-based revision operators are not discussed.

Most of practical revision operators proposed in the literature are syntax dependant, i.e., if two logically dependant ontologies are revised by another ontology, the results of revision may not be logically equivalent. Representative work on syntax-based revision operators can be found in (Haase et al. 2005), (Halaschek-Wiener, Katz, and Parsia 2006) and (Qi et al. 2008). Syntax-based revision operators are not fine-grained because an axiom is removed even if only part of it is involved in the inconsistencies. In this work, we prove that a syntactic revision operator can be used to approximate two model-based revision operators in DL-Lite$_{\mathcal{R}}$, and fill the gap between syntax-based revision and model-based revision.

Conclusion

In this paper, we presented some theoretical work on approximation of model-based ABox revision operators in DL-Lite$_{\mathcal{FR}}$ and proposed an algorithm for computing the result of approximation efficiently. On the theoretical aspect, we discussed whether the result of the syntactic revision algorithm given in (Kharlamov, Zheleznyakov, and Calvanese 2013) can be used to approximate the result of two model-based revision operators. We showed that this property holds in DL-Lite$_{\mathcal{R}}$ but fails in DL-Lite$_{\mathcal{FR}}$ when role functionality axioms are included. In the failure case, we showed that the property still holds if we disallow "triggering roles" in the TBox. We also showed that the result of a modification of the syntactic algorithm can be used to approximate the result of one of the model-based revision operators. On the practical aspect, we proposed a graph-based algorithm that can output the same result as algorithm *FastEvol* but does not need to compute the ABox closure w.r.t. the TBox beforehand. Our algorithm applies new methodology to perform revision using graph databases. We implemented a revision system based on the graph-based algorithm, called GraphRevi, and conducted experiments over a benchmark dataset. Preliminary experimental results show that our system can handle the revision of large DL-Lite ABoxes efficiently and outperforms *FastEvol*.

As a future work, we will optimize our system by exploring distributed index. As another future work, we will work on approximation of ABox revision in other DL-Lite languages, such as DL-Lite$_{bool}^{\mathcal{N}}$.

Acknowledgement

This work was partially supported by NSFC grant 61272378 and Australian Research Council (ARC) under DP130102302 and DP1093652.

References

Calvanese, D.; Kharlamov, E.; Nutt, W.; and Zheleznyakov, D. 2010. Evolution of dl-lite knowledge bases. In *Proc. of ISWC*, 112–128.

Flouris, G.; Huang, Z.; Pan, J.; Plexousakis, D.; and Wache, H. 2006. Inconsistencies, negations and changes in ontologies. In *Proc. of AAAI*, 1295–1300.

Flouris, G.; Plexousakis, D.; and Antoniou, G. 2005. On applying the AGM theory to DLs and OWL. In *Proc. of ISWC*, 216–231.

Giacomo, G. D.; Lenzerini, M.; Poggi, A.; and Rosati, R. 2009. On instance-level update and erasure in description logic ontologies. *J. Log. Comput.* 19(5):745–770.

Grau, B. C.; Ruiz, E. J.; Kharlamov, E.; and Zhelenyakov, D. 2012. Ontology evolution under semantic constraints. In *Proc.of KR*, 137–147.

Haase, P.; van Harmelen, F.; Huang, Z.; Stuckenschmidt, H.; and Sure, Y. 2005. A framework for handling inconsistency in changing ontologies. In *Proc. of ISWC*, 353–367.

Halaschek-Wiener, C.; Katz, Y.; and Parsia, B. 2006. Belief base revision for expressive description logics. In *Proc. of OWL-ED*.

Hansson, S. 1999. *A Textbook of Belief Dynamics: Theory Change and Database Updating*. Kluwer Academic Publishers.

Katsuno, H., and Mendelzon, A. 1992. Propositional knowledge base revision and minimal change. *Artif. Intell.* 52(3):263–294.

Kharlamov, E., and Zheleznyakov, D. 2011. Capturing instance level ontology evolution for DL-Lite. In *Proc. of ISWC*, 321–337.

Kharlamov, E.; Zheleznyakov, D.; and Calvanese, D. 2013. Capturing model-based ontology evolution at the instance level: The case of dl-lite. *J. Comput. Syst. Sci.* 79(6):835–872.

Qi, G., and Du, J. 2009. Model-based revision operators for terminologies in description logics. In *Proc. of IJCAI*, 891–897.

Qi, G.; Haase, P.; Huang, Z.; Ji, Q.; Pan, J.; and Völker, J. 2008. A kernel revision operator for terminologies–algorithms and evaluation. In *Proc. of ISWC*. 419–434.

Ribeiro, M. M., and Wassermann, R. 2007. Base revision in description logics - preliminary results. In *Proc. of IWOD*, 69–82.

Ribeiro, M. M.; Wassermann, R.; Flouris, G.; and Antoniou, G. 2013. Minimal change: Relevance and recovery revisited. *Artificial Intelligence* 201:59–80.

Wang, Z.; Wang, K.; Zhuang, Z.; and Qi, G. 2015. Instance-driven ontology evolution in DL-Lite. In *Proc. of AAAI, to appear*.

Wang, Z.; Wang, K.; and Topor, R. W. 2010. A new approach to knowledge base revision in DL-Lite. In *Proc. of AAAI*, 369–374.

Zhuang, Z.; Wang, Z.; Wang, K.; and Qi, G. 2014. Contraction and revision over DL-Lite tboxes. In *Proc. of AAAI*, 1149–1156.

Leveraging Social Foci for Information Seeking in Social Media

Suhas Ranganath
srangan8@asu.edu
Arizona State University

Jiliang Tang
Jiliang.Tang@asu.edu
Arizona State University

Xia Hu
Xia.Hu@asu.edu
Arizona State University

Hari Sundaram
hs1@illinois.edu
University of Illinois Urbana Champaign

Huan Liu
Huan.Liu@asu.edu
Arizona State University

Abstract

The rise of social media provides a great opportunity for people to reach out to their social connections to satisfy their information needs. However, generic social media platforms are not explicitly designed to assist information seeking of users. In this paper, we propose a novel framework to identify the social connections of a user able to satisfy his information needs. The information need of a social media user is subjective and personal, and we investigate the utility of his social context to identify people able to satisfy it. We present questions users post on Twitter as instances of information seeking activities in social media. We infer soft community memberships of the asker and his social connections by integrating network and content information. Drawing concepts from the social foci theory, we identify answerers who share communities with the asker w.r.t. the question. Our experiments demonstrate that the framework is effective in identifying answerers to social media questions.

Information seeking is defined as "A conscious effort to acquire information in response to a need or gap in knowledge" (Case 2012). Online social media makes it easier for users to reach out to a large number of friends, leading people to use them to seek information from their social connections. This gives rise to a distinct way for online information seeking, wherein the information needs expressed are subjective and personal to the asker. An interesting way people leverage online social media to seek information is by asking questions through their status messages (Morris, Teevan, and Panovich 2010). This phenomenon is prevalent in social media platforms like Twitter and Facebook and has received considerable attention in recent literature (Efron and Winget 2010a; Paul, Hong, and Chi 2011; Lampe et al. 2014).

However, unlike dedicated Q&A platforms, generic social media sites like Twitter and Facebook are not designed for information seeking (Paul, Hong, and Chi 2011). Questions are not archived, thus finding people who answered similar questions in the past is difficult. Questions are buried among other content produced by the social connections of a potential answerer. Designing algorithmic frameworks to identify answerers to social media questions will help to bridge the information gap of users and increase user satisfaction. This framework can also help enhance Twitter search by making it personalized to the asker.

Information need of social media user is subjective or personal, unlike traditional Q&A platforms like Stackoverflow, and hi social context is useful to find appropriate people able to satisfy it (Hecht et al. 2012). Also, users with higher tie strength with the asker were shown to better satisfy information needs in social media (Panovich, Miller, and Karger 2012). For example, to assist a person looking to get a new hairstyle, finding people from his social connections who share related context with him can be more useful to him than finding web pages related to hair salons.

This task faces several challenges. The questions are textual while the social context of the asker can involve network information. Integrating such kind of heterogeneous information will help to efficiently utilize social context to identify answerers to social media questions. Each social media user has many social connections and produces a lot of content leading to significant issues of scalability. Finally, the social context of the asker related to the question needs to be determined and appropriately utilized in order to identify suitable answerers.

In sociological literature, the social foci theory postulates that interactions between people are organized around relevant entities known as foci (Feld 1981). A focus can be the activities, interests, and various affiliations of a user. Different groups of social connections of a user share different foci with him. For example, from Fig. 1(a) we see that the user shares an interest of sports with his connections in green, an interest of music with his connections in yellow and academic interests with his connections in red.

Inspired by the social foci theory we propose that, people in social media sharing social foci related to the question with the asker are suitable to answer them. Illustrative examples of questions are given in Fig. 1(b). The asker of Q1 is seeking assistance in his math homework, and this might be best responded by users sharing academic foci with him. Q2 is seeking opinions on an NFL game, and this might be best provided by his connections sharing foci related to sports with the asker. Similarly, Q3 might be best answered by connections sharing music related foci with the asker.

In this paper, we propose a framework to investigate the utility of social context derived from network and content in-

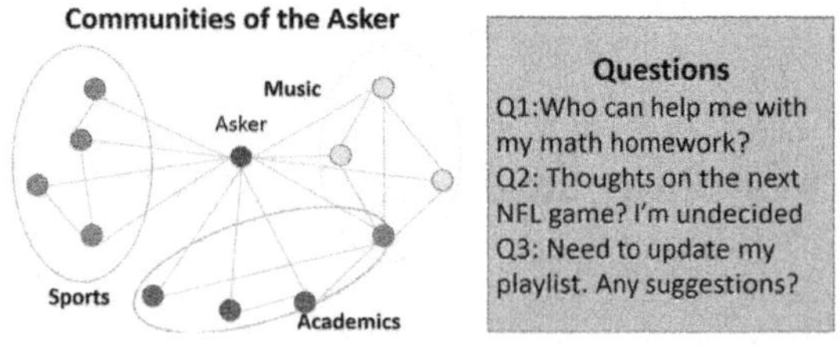

(a) (b)

Figure 1: (a) Different foci a user shares with his social connections. (b) Questions of users. Users sharing different foci with the asker are more likely to answer related questions.

formation in identifying answerers to social media questions. Informed by the concepts of social foci theory illustrated in Fig. 1, we utilize social context of an asker related to the question, and demonstrate that the framework is effective in identifying answerers for social media questions. Specifically, we address the following questions: How to utilize the network and content information of the asker and his social connections to better identify answerers for social media questions? Are approaches based on shared context in the question domain useful in identifying answerers to different kinds of social media questions?

The main contributions of our work are as follows:

- Formally defining the problem of finding suitable users to answer questions in online social media platforms,
- Proposing a framework to exploit network and content information to identify answerers to questions, and
- Conducting experimental evaluations of the framework on a dataset of social media questions.

Related Work

Social media questions have received considerable attention in research communities (Yang et al. 2011; Efron and Winget 2010b; Lee et al. 2012). An analytical study on questions asked and the answers received in Twitter is presented in (Morris, Teevan, and Panovich 2010; Paul, Hong, and Chi 2011). They indicated that subjective questions were the most prevalent and the trust users have on their friends was the primary factor for asking questions. A study of questions and responses received in Facebook was conducted in (Gray et al. 2013; Ellison et al. 2013) and bridging social capital was proposed to be a strong motivation for Q&A activity in social media. These works give interesting insights to the question answering process in social media, but do not focus on identifying answerers to these questions.

Systems to identify answerers for social media questions adopt different methods such as matching question content with profile information (Hecht et al. 2012) and using crowdsourced technology (Jeong et al. 2013). Social search architectures and empirical models to route questions to answerers using different kinds of social information are discussed in (Horowitz and Kamvar 2010; Nandi et al. 2013). These works are meant to demonstrate social search systems and hence do not contain any experimental evaluations.

A related line of research is the study of community Q&A systems like Yahoo! Answers (Adamic et al. 2008) and Quora (Wang et al. 2013a). Content from existing Q&A sessions are used to rank answerers by NLP techniques. (Jurczyk and Agichtein 2007) uses link structure to find authoritative answerers for a question category. (Zhou et al. 2012) and (Yang et al. 2013) combine network and content information to identify authoritative users as answerers. The environment for social media questions is different as the candidate answerers are themselves connected via social relations. Systems utilizing question categories (Zhu et al. 2013) cannot be applied as they are not explicitly known in generic social media. Social expertise systems (Pal and Counts 2011; Bozzon et al. 2013) identify subject matter experts in social media. Social media questions are subjective and personal might require answerers who share social context with the asker rather than subject matter experts.

Another related field to our work is the application of social foci theory in social media. Social foci theory has received attention in several domains such as relational learning (Tang and Liu 2009) and structural hole theory (Burt 2009). Recently, social foci theory has been used to derive community memberships using both node and edge attributes (Yang, McAuley, and Leskovec 2013). To the best of our knowledge, this is the first work that has utilized concepts from social foci theory to identify answerers for social media questions.

Problem Definition

We first describe some general notations. Boldface uppercase letters (e.g $\mathbf{X}$) denote matrices and boldface lowercase letters (e.g. $\mathbf{x}$) denote vectors. $\mathbf{X}_{ij}$ signifies the element in the ith row and j^{th} column of matrix $\mathbf{X}$ and the ith row of a matrix $\mathbf{X}$ is denoted by $\mathbf{X}_i$. Similarly $\mathbf{x}_i$ denotes the ith element of vector $\mathbf{x}$ and $\mathbf{x}_y$ denotes a vector $\mathbf{x}$ corresponding to the quantity y. We denote the Frebonius norm of a matrix $\mathbf{X}$ as $||\mathbf{X}||_F = \sqrt{\sum_{i,j} \mathbf{X}_{ij}^2}$.

We now define some terms related to the questions asked, the network and content of the asker and his social connections. We define attributes of a question q as the set of words used in the question i.e. $\mathbf{w}_q = [w_{q1}, w_{q2}, ..., w_{ql}]$. Since we are dealing with subjective questions, the asker marking the answer to be useful or publicly acknowledging the answerer gives the evidence of its acceptance.

Let A denote the asker of the question q and $\mathbf{f}_A = [f_1, f_2, ..., f_m]$ denote the social connections of A and m is the number of social connections of A. We define the egonetwork of each asker A as consisting of the asker, the social connections of the asker and the links among his social connections. The egonetwork of asker A, $\mathbf{N} \in \mathbb{R}^{(m+1)\times(m+1)}$ is given by

$$\mathbf{N}_{ij} = \begin{cases} 1 & \text{directed edge from } f_j \text{ to } f_i, i \neq j, i,j \in \{A, f_A\} \\ 0 & \text{otherwise} \end{cases}$$

We collect the status messages of the asker and his social connections. We apply basic preprocessing steps such as removal of stop words and stemming. We then define the user-word matrix $\mathbf{S} \in \mathbb{R}^{(m+1)\times w}$ of asker A as

$$\mathbf{S}_{ij} = \begin{cases} \text{num*tfidf}_j & \text{if user } u_i \text{ has used word } w_j \text{ num times} \\ 0 & \text{if user } u_i \text{ has not used the word } w_j, \end{cases}$$

where num is the number of times the user u_i has used the word w_j, w is the total number of words used by the asker and his social connections and $tfidf_j$ is the tf-idf score of word w_j. A single user will only use a small subset of the total number of words, resulting in $\mathbf{S}$ being sparse.

With the terminologies and the notations described above, we formally define the problem as follows *"Given a question q, an asker A, the network neighborhood of the asker $\mathbf{f}_A$, find a suitable set of people among $\mathbf{f}_A$ whose responses for the question q that the asker accepts"*.

Information Seeking via Social Foci

In this section, we describe our framework to identify answerers for social media questions in detail. First, we infer social foci memberships of the asker and his social connections from their network and content information. We then compute the overlap in foci memberships of the asker and his social connections in the question domain to identify answerers to these questions.

Modeling Content Information

We model the content information to infer major foci of the asker and his social connections. We draw from Non-negative Matrix Factorization (NMF) presented in (Seung and Lee 2001) to infer foci from the user-word matrix $\mathbf{S} \in \mathbb{R}^{(m+1)\times w}$. We factorize the matrix $\mathbf{S}$ into two low dimensional sparse non-negative matrices, $\mathbf{U} \in \mathbb{R}^{(m+1)\times k}$ and $\mathbf{P} \in \mathbb{R}^{w\times k}$ such that $k \ll m$ by solving the following optimization problem.

$$\min_{\mathbf{U}\geq 0, \mathbf{P}\geq 0} ||\mathbf{S} - \mathbf{U}\mathbf{P}^{\mathrm{T}}||_F^2 \tag{1}$$

Here, k is the number of latent foci in the neighborhood of the asker and m is the number of his social connections. $\mathbf{U}$ denotes the latent foci membership of the asker and his social connections and $\mathbf{P}$ denotes the latent foci memberships of words. The correlation between foci memberships of the words can be obtained by the overlap in the corresponding rows of $\mathbf{P}$. The constraints $\mathbf{U} \geq 0$ and $\mathbf{P} \geq 0$ denote that the matrices have all non-negative elements. The non-negativity ensures an intuitive decomposition of the matrix into its constituent parts.

Integrating Network Information

In a social setting, the interests or affiliations of an user are correlated with the interests of his social connections, thereby affecting his memberships to different foci (Feld 1981). This notion is also supported by network homogeneity (Marsden 1988), which says that people connected to each other display similar interests and affiliations. Therefore, it is essential to utilize network structure to determine foci memberships of the asker and his social connections.

To utilize the network structure, we first factorize the ego network of the asker $\mathbf{N}$ into two low rank non-negative matrices $\mathbf{U} \in \mathbb{R}^{(m+1)\times k}$ and $\mathbf{V} \in \mathbb{R}^{k\times k}$ s.t. $k \ll m$ by solving the following optimization problem.

$$\min_{\mathbf{U}\geq 0, \mathbf{V}\geq 0} ||\mathbf{N} - \mathbf{U}\mathbf{V}\mathbf{U}^{\mathrm{T}}||_F^2, \tag{2}$$

where $\mathbf{U}$ contains the membership of the asker and his social connections to different latent foci and $\mathbf{V}$ contains the correlations between the foci. The constraints $\mathbf{U} \geq 0$ and $\mathbf{V} \geq 0$ denote that the matrices have only non-negative elements.

We then integrate network and content information to infer the foci membership of the asker and his social connections by formulating the following optimization problem.

$$\begin{aligned}\min_{\mathbf{U}\geq 0, \mathbf{V}\geq 0, \mathbf{P}\geq 0} \quad & \alpha||\mathbf{S} - \mathbf{U}\mathbf{P}^{\mathrm{T}}||_F^2 + \beta||\mathbf{N} - \mathbf{U}\mathbf{V}\mathbf{U}^{\mathrm{T}}||_F^2 \\ & + \gamma(||\mathbf{U}||_F^2 + ||\mathbf{V}||_F^2 + ||\mathbf{P}||_F^2)\end{aligned} \tag{3}$$

Here $\mathbf{U}$ contains the latent foci membership of the asker and his connections obtained by integrating network and content information, $\mathbf{P}$ shows the latent foci memberships of the words and $\mathbf{V}$ represents the correlation between the latent foci. $||\mathbf{U}||_F^2$, $||\mathbf{V}||_F^2$, and $||\mathbf{P}||_F^2$ are regularization terms introduced to prevent overfitting and γ is the positive parameter for control the proportions of the regularization terms. The constraints $\mathbf{U} \geq 0$, $\mathbf{V} \geq 0$, and $\mathbf{P} \geq 0$ denote that the matrices do not contain negative elements. α and β are positive parameters to control the effects of content and network proportions respectively.

We draw from the concepts of the social foci theory illustrated in Fig. 1 to propose that users sharing a large amount of foci memberships with the asker in the question domain can effectively answer social media questions. The shared foci memberships of the asker with his social connections is given by the overlap between their corresponding rows in $\mathbf{U}$. The question domain in the latent foci space is obtained by combining the rows of $\mathbf{P}$ corresponding to the words in the question. Before formalizing these notions, we optimally derive the latent matrices $\mathbf{U}$, $\mathbf{V}$ and $\mathbf{P}$ by solving Eq. (3).

Deriving the Optimal Latent Matrices

The problem presented in Eq. (3) belongs to a class of constrained convex minimization problems. Motivated by (Ding et al. 2006), we describe an algorithm to find optimal solutions for $\mathbf{U}$, $\mathbf{V}$ and $\mathbf{P}$. The key idea is to optimize the objective with respect to one variable while fixing others. The three variables are iteratively updated until convergence.

From Eq.(3), we let

$$\begin{aligned}\mathcal{J} = \; & \alpha||\mathbf{S} - \mathbf{U}\mathbf{P}^{\mathrm{T}}||_F^2 + \beta||\mathbf{N} - \mathbf{U}\mathbf{V}\mathbf{U}^{\mathrm{T}}||_F^2 + \\ & \gamma(||\mathbf{U}||_F^2 + ||\mathbf{V}||_F^2 + ||\mathbf{P}||_F^2)\end{aligned} \tag{4}$$

We then take the Lagrangian of the objective function $\mathcal{J}$. Let the Lagrange multiplier for the constraints $\mathbf{U} \geq 0$, $\mathbf{V} \geq 0$, and $\mathbf{P} \geq 0$ be Λ_u, Λ_v, and Λ_p respectively. Then

$$\mathcal{L} = \mathcal{J} + tr(\Lambda_u \mathbf{U}^{\mathrm{T}}) + tr(\Lambda_v \mathbf{V}^{\mathrm{T}}) + tr(\Lambda_p \mathbf{P}^{\mathrm{T}}) \tag{5}$$

We compute the partial derivatives of the lagrangian $\mathcal{L}$ with respect to $\mathbf{U}$, $\mathbf{V}$, and $\mathbf{P}$ keeping the other variables fixed as shown below.

$$\begin{aligned}\frac{\partial \mathcal{L}}{\partial \mathbf{U}} &= 2(\alpha(-\mathbf{S}\mathbf{P} + \mathbf{U}\mathbf{P}^{\mathrm{T}}\mathbf{P}) + \beta(-\mathbf{N}^{\mathrm{T}}\mathbf{U}\mathbf{V} - \mathbf{N}\mathbf{U}\mathbf{V}^{\mathrm{T}} \\ &\quad + \mathbf{U}\mathbf{V}\mathbf{U}^{\mathrm{T}}\mathbf{U}\mathbf{V}^{\mathrm{T}} + \mathbf{U}\mathbf{V}^{\mathrm{T}}\mathbf{U}^{\mathrm{T}}\mathbf{U}\mathbf{V}) + \gamma\mathbf{U}) + \Lambda_u \\ \frac{\partial \mathcal{L}}{\partial \mathbf{V}} &= 2(\beta(-\mathbf{U}^{\mathrm{T}}\mathbf{N}\mathbf{U} + \mathbf{U}^{\mathrm{T}}\mathbf{U}\mathbf{V}\mathbf{U}^{\mathrm{T}}\mathbf{U}) + \gamma\mathbf{V}) + \Lambda_v \\ \frac{\partial \mathcal{L}}{\partial \mathbf{P}} &= 2(\alpha(-\mathbf{S}^{\mathrm{T}}\mathbf{U} + \mathbf{P}\mathbf{U}^{\mathrm{T}}\mathbf{U}) + \gamma\mathbf{P}) + \Lambda_p.\end{aligned} \tag{6}$$

Substituting the KKT complementary conditions in Eq. (6) and rearranging we get the following update rules for latent matrices $\mathbf{U}$, $\mathbf{V}$, and $\mathbf{P}$.

$$\mathbf{U}_{ij} \leftarrow \mathbf{U}_{ij}\sqrt{\frac{\alpha\mathbf{SP} + \beta(\mathbf{N}^{\mathrm{T}}\mathbf{UV} + \mathbf{NUV}^{\mathrm{T}})}{\alpha\mathbf{UP}^{\mathrm{T}}\mathbf{P} + \beta(\mathbf{UVU}^{\mathrm{T}}\mathbf{UV}^{\mathrm{T}} + \mathbf{UV}^{\mathrm{T}}\mathbf{U}^{\mathrm{T}}\mathbf{UV}) + \gamma\mathbf{U}}}$$
$$\mathbf{V}_{ij} \leftarrow \mathbf{V}_{ij}\sqrt{\frac{\beta\mathbf{U}^{\mathrm{T}}\mathbf{NU}}{\beta(\mathbf{U}^{\mathrm{T}}\mathbf{UVU}^{\mathrm{T}}\mathbf{U}) + \gamma\mathbf{V}}}$$
$$\mathbf{P}_{ij} \leftarrow \mathbf{P}_{ij}\sqrt{\frac{\alpha\mathbf{S}^{\mathrm{T}}\mathbf{U}}{\alpha\mathbf{PU}^{\mathrm{T}}\mathbf{U} + \gamma\mathbf{P}.}} \tag{7}$$

The optimization algorithm is summarized in Steps 1-7 in **Algorithm 1**. The square root on the update rules is added to ensure convergence (Ding, Li, and Jordan 2008). The correctness and convergence of the rules can be proved by the axillary function method (Lee and Seung 2000).

Identifying Answerers from Foci Information

We now identify relevant answerers from the social connections of the asker using the latent matrices $\mathbf{U}$,$\mathbf{V}$ and $\mathbf{P}$. We first extract the words from the question attribute vector $\mathbf{w}_{\mathrm{q}}$ and obtain the foci memberships of each word from the corresponding rows in matrix $\mathbf{P}$. We then compute the domain of the question in the latent foci space as a combination of individual word membership vectors as

$$\mathbf{d}_{\mathrm{q}} = \sum_{\mathrm{w}_i \epsilon \mathbf{w}_{\mathrm{q}}} \mathbf{P}_i, \tag{8}$$

where $\mathbf{d}_{\mathrm{q}}$ represents the domain of the question q in the latent foci space and w_i is the word corresponding to the ith row of $\mathbf{P}$.

We next compute the foci memberships of the asker and his social connections in the question domain. The Hadamard product of two vectors is the pointwise product of their respective elements, and it exactly captures this notion. For each question, we compute the Hadamard product of the row of $\mathbf{U}$ corresponding to the asker, $\mathbf{U}_{\mathrm{A}}$ and the vector representing the question domain $\mathbf{d}_{\mathrm{q}}$.

$$\mathbf{g}_{\mathrm{A}} = \mathbf{U}_{\mathrm{A}} \circ \mathbf{d}_{\mathrm{q}}, \tag{9}$$

where $\mathbf{g}_{\mathrm{A}}$ contains the foci membership of the asker in the domain of the question. Similarly, we compute the foci memberships of each social connection of the asker in the domain of the question q by

$$\mathbf{g}_{\mathrm{f_m}} = \mathbf{U}_{\mathrm{f_m}} \circ \mathbf{d}_{\mathrm{q}}, \tag{10}$$

where $\mathrm{f_m}$ is the mth social connection of the asker, $\mathbf{U}_{\mathrm{f_m}}$ is the row of matrix $\mathbf{U}$ corresponding to $\mathrm{f_m}$ and $\mathbf{g}_{\mathrm{f_m}}$ contains the foci membership of $\mathrm{f_m}$ w.r.t the domain of the question.

Finally, we find the overlap in foci memberships of the asker and his social connections in the question domain as

$$\mathbf{rs}(\mathrm{q}, \mathrm{A}, \mathrm{f_m}) = sim(\mathbf{g}_{\mathrm{A}}, \mathbf{g}_{\mathrm{f_m}}), \tag{11}$$

where $\mathbf{rs}(\mathrm{q}, \mathrm{A}, \mathrm{f_m})$ denotes the score of the answerer $\mathrm{f_m}$ to the question q by the asker A. We sort the answerers according to their score and return them to the asker as a ranked list, $\mathbf{ra}$. Results with different similarity metrics is presented in Table 2. The method for identifying answerers from foci information is summarized in Steps 8-11 in **Algorithm 1**. The quantity $\mathbf{rs}(\mathrm{q}, \mathrm{A}, \mathrm{f_m})$ signifies the context in terms of network and content shared between asker A and his social connection $\mathrm{f_m}$ in the domain of question q.

Algorithm 1: Automatic Identification of Answerers to Social Media Questions

Input: Question q of asker (A), friends and followers of A, $\mathbf{f}_{\mathrm{A}} = [\mathrm{f}_1, \mathrm{f}_2, ..., \mathrm{f_m}]$, Egonetwork of the asker ($\mathbf{N}$), user-word matrix of the asker and his connections ($\mathbf{S}$) and $\{\alpha, \beta, \gamma, k\}$
Output : A ranked list of the potential answerers $\mathbf{ra}$
1: Initialize $\mathbf{U}$, $\mathbf{V}$, $\mathbf{P}$ randomly
2: **while** not convergent **do**
3: update
4: $\mathbf{U}_{ij} \leftarrow \mathbf{U}_{ij}\sqrt{\frac{\alpha\mathbf{SP}+\beta(\mathbf{N}^{\mathrm{T}}\mathbf{UV}+\mathbf{NUV}^{\mathrm{T}})}{\alpha\mathbf{UP}^{\mathrm{T}}\mathbf{P}+\beta(\mathbf{UVU}^{\mathrm{T}}\mathbf{UV}^{\mathrm{T}}+\mathbf{UV}^{\mathrm{T}}\mathbf{U}^{\mathrm{T}}\mathbf{UV})+\gamma\mathbf{U}}}$
5: $\mathbf{V}_{ij} \leftarrow \mathbf{V}_{ij}\sqrt{\frac{\beta\mathbf{U}^{\mathrm{T}}\mathbf{NU}}{\beta(\mathbf{U}^{\mathrm{T}}\mathbf{UVU}^{\mathrm{T}}\mathbf{U})+\gamma\mathbf{V}}}$
6: $\mathbf{P}_{ij} \leftarrow \mathbf{P}_{ij}\sqrt{\frac{\alpha\mathbf{S}^{\mathrm{T}}\mathbf{U}}{\alpha\mathbf{PU}^{\mathrm{T}}\mathbf{U}+\gamma\mathbf{P}}}$
7: **end while**
8: $\mathbf{w}_{\mathrm{q}} = [\mathrm{w_{q1}}, \mathrm{w_{q2}}, ..., \mathrm{w_{ql}}]$, $\mathbf{d}_{\mathrm{q}} = \sum_{\mathrm{w}_i \epsilon \mathbf{w}_{\mathrm{q}}} \mathbf{P}_i$
9: $\mathbf{g}_{\mathrm{A}} = \mathbf{U}_{\mathrm{A}} \circ \mathbf{d}_{\mathrm{q}}$, $\mathbf{g}_{\mathrm{f_m}} = \mathbf{U}_{\mathrm{f_m}} \circ \mathbf{d}_{\mathrm{q}}$
10: $\mathbf{rs}(\mathrm{q}, \mathrm{A}, \mathrm{f_m}) = sim(\mathbf{g}_{\mathrm{A}}, \mathbf{g}_{\mathrm{f_m}})$
11: ra=sort($\mathbf{rs}$)

Time Complexity

The highest time cost results from updating the latent matrices in steps 4-6. In the updating terms, the complexity of the terms $\mathbf{SP}$ and $\mathbf{S}^{\mathrm{T}}\mathbf{U}$ is low due to sparsity of $\mathbf{S}$. The terms $\mathbf{N}^{\mathrm{T}}\mathbf{UV}$, $\mathbf{NUV}^{\mathrm{T}}$ and $\mathbf{U}^{\mathrm{T}}\mathbf{NU}$ have a complexity of $\mathrm{O}(\mathrm{mk}^2)$ where m is the number of friends and k is the number of latent dimensions due to the sparsity of $\mathbf{N}$. The terms $(\mathbf{U}(\mathbf{V}(\mathbf{U}^{\mathrm{T}}\mathbf{U})\mathbf{V}^{\mathrm{T}})$, $(\mathbf{U}(\mathbf{V}^{\mathrm{T}}(\mathbf{U}^{\mathrm{T}}\mathbf{U})\mathbf{V})$ and $((\mathbf{U}^{\mathrm{T}}\mathbf{U})\mathbf{V}(\mathbf{U}^{\mathrm{T}}\mathbf{U}))$ has a complexity of $\mathrm{O}(\mathrm{mk}^2)$ when computed as shown in the brackets. The complexity of $\mathbf{PU}^{\mathrm{T}}\mathbf{U}$ and $\mathbf{UP}^{\mathrm{T}}\mathbf{P}$ is $\mathrm{O}((\mathrm{w}+\mathrm{m})\mathrm{k}^2)$ where w is the number of words. Therefore, the overall complexity of a single iteration is $\mathrm{O}((\mathrm{w}+\mathrm{m})\mathrm{k}^2)$, which is low owing to the few number of latent dimensions. In addition, notice that steps 1-7 can be computed offline and only steps 8-10 are computed when the question is asked, further reducing the time required to identify answerers for a given question.

Experiments

In this section, we first present a dataset of questions posted on Twitter and then conduct experiments to answer the following questions that help in understanding the framework better: How does the proposed framework perform in comparison to existing baselines? What is the effect of the amount of network and content information on the performance of the framework?

Dataset

The dataset consists of subjective questions from the social media platform Twitter. We follow the literature on questions in Twitter (Morris, Teevan, and Panovich 2010) to construct a keyword set related to subjective questions. We append "?" to each keyword to collect questions from the Twitter Streaming API. Texts having "?" in online content are shown to be ques-

Parameter	Statistics
# of Questions	1065
# of Askers	1026
# of Selected Answers	1450
# of Followers and Friends of the askers	966,117
Median # of Followers and Friends per asker	588
Median # Tweets per user	479

Table 1: Dataset containing questions posted in Twitter with statistics related to network and content information.

tions with high precision (Cong et al. 2008). We deem replies to have been accepted by the asker if he has marked it as "favorite" or acknowledged the answerer by using "thanks" or "thank you". We mark the users who provided these answers as the ground truth for each question following (Hecht et al. 2012). Some important statistics of the dataset are given in Table 1. The first question was posted on Dec 27, 2013 and the last one on Jan 15, 2014. We use the methods in the public Twitter API to collect the friends, followers and public status messages of the asker to obtain the asker's social connections and their interests (Kumar, Morstatter, and Liu 2013). We use the data to construct the ego network $\mathbf{N}$ and user-word matrix $\mathbf{S}$ for each asker.

Experiment Settings

We introduce the following metrics to evaluate the performance of our framework: The Mean Reciprocal Rank (MRR) (Radev et al. 2002) is a measure of the overall likelihood of the framework to identify an answerer for a question, the Mean Average of Precision (MAP) (Bian et al. 2008) measures the potential satisfaction of the asker with the top K results and the Normalised Discounted Cumulative Gain (NDCG)@K considers the order within the top K rankings (Wang et al. 2013b).We use the following baselines to evaluate the performance of our framework.

Random: We randomly order the friends and followers of the asker 100 times and return the mean ordering.

Aardvark (Horowitz and Kamvar 2010): This paper describes a search engine which directed questions posted on the system to users with formulation to compute affinity with the asker and interest in the question topics. It does not consider the network structure and also does not contain experimental evaluations of its formulation.

Content based Methods (Riahi et al. 2012): The paper focuses on community Q&A like Yahoo! Answers and compares the similarity of the question topic with the interests of the answerers derived only from the their content. The interests were inferred by two topic models: LDA and the Segmented Topic Model (STM) (Du, Buntine, and Jin 2010).

Topic Sensitive Page Rank (Zhou et al. 2012): This paper employs a PageRank based approach to find subject matter experts in the question topic by combining network and content information of the potential answerers. The paper identifies topical authorities not considering the shared context between the asker and the answerers.

Shared Foci: This baseline measures the effect of shared user context. It computes the shared foci memberships of the asker and his social connections derived from either network (α=0) or content (β=0) information. The question information is not taken into consideration. This also helps in evaluating methods using only network structure.

Method	MRR	MAP@5	NDCG@5
Random	1.20%	1.12%	0.25%
Content-LDA	1.56%	1.46%	0.30%
Content-STM	1.93%	2.27%	0.50%
TSPR	1.64%	1.63%	0.45%
Aardvark	2.11%	2.53%	0.50%
Shared Foci (Network)	3.43%	3.66%	0.97%
Shared Foci (Content)	3.60%	3.87%	1.17%
Our Model (Cosine)	3.91%	4.63%	1.25%
Our Model (PCC)	3.80%	4.73%	1.31%
Our Model (Euclidean)	4.36%	5.54%	1.41%

Table 2: Comparison of performance of the proposed framework with baselines.

For initial experiments, we set the parameters in Eq. (3) as follows. The regularization parameter is set at γ=0.01. The number of topics in the baselines and the number of foci k is set as 50. For initial evaluation of the framework, we choose α=1 and β=1. The performance for different values of α and β will be presented in future subsections.

Performance Evaluation

The results of the evaluations are presented in Table 2. From Table 2, we can see that the proposed framework has outperformed the baselines by a considerable margin. We conducted a paired t-test to compare the performance of our framework with that of the baselines, and the results indicated the difference between them is significant. We make the following observations from the table.

The proposed framework gives more than 300% improvement over random selection. We can see that simple formulations like the one in Aardvark that considers social network information performs on par with complex topical models using only content such as STM. The proposed framework also performs significantly better than methods identifying subject matter experts as answerers such as TSPR. This emphasizes the importance of social context to identify answerers to social media questions.

Considering shared foci between the asker and the answerer improves the performance over methods like Aardvark not utilizing community memberships. This shows the effectiveness of using social foci to exploit social context. Incorporating question information to consider the overlap only in the foci related to the question gives further improvement in the performance.

In summary, by designing approaches based on shared social context and exploiting the structure of social ties, the proposed framework can effectively identify answerers for social media questions in the dataset. Next, we wish to understand the effect of content and network information on the performance of our framework

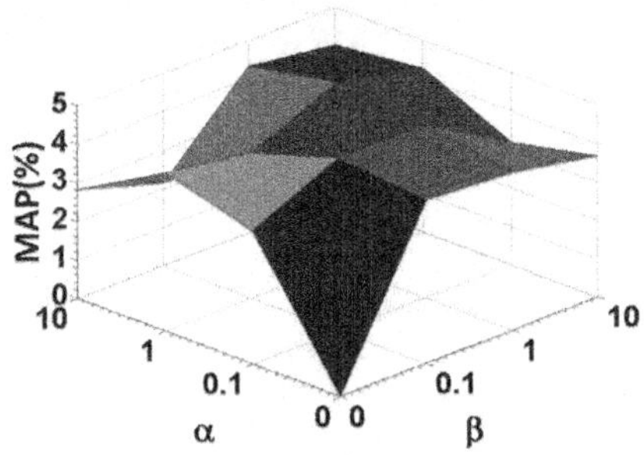

Figure 2: Effect of variation of content and network proportions on the framework performance for MAP.

Effect of Content and Network Information

In the model presented in Eq. (3), α and β control the proportion of the network and content information respectively. In order to evaluate the framework for different proportions of content and network, we set $\alpha = [0.1, 1, 10]$ and $\beta = [0, 0.1, 1, 10]$ and plot the values for MAP in Fig. 2 arbitrarily using cosine similarity as the similarity metric. We make the following observations from the figure.

A general trend in Fig. 2 is a peak at the main diagonal of the α and β axes and an off-diagonal dip. This shows that the framework works best for nearly equal proportions of network and content information. The MAP value is greater than 3% for all α and β except for low proportions of network information ($\alpha = 10$, $\beta = [0, 0.1]$). This emphasizes the importance of social connections of the asker for identifying answerers to social media questions. The lowest performance across all parameter values is more than twice than random ordering indicating the effectiveness of the framework for low relative proportions of content or network information. Overall, the MAP value is above 3% for different combinations of α and β indicating the effectiveness of the framework for a wide range of parameter values.

In summary, the framework performs well over different proportions of network and content and is robust to their variation. An appropriate combination of network and content information can optimize the effectiveness of the framework for identifying answerers to social media questions.

Performance across Question Categories

Literature on social media questions has identified kinds of questions people ask on Twitter. Recommendation, opinions, factual and rhetorical questions are popular questions asked on Twitter (Morris, Teevan, and Panovich 2010; Paul, Hong, and Chi 2011). We select four categories related to subjective questions, "Suggestions", "Opinion", "Favor", and "Rhetorical", and evaluate our framework in identifying answerers for different question categories.

We employed human labelling to assign category labels to questions. Three people independently labeled the questions, and the labels were assigned using majority selection. Employing this procedure, 93.5% of the questions were assigned to either of the four categories and the framework was evaluated on them. The results of the evaluations are presented in Table 3. The distribution of different question categories is given in the first column. The performance for different categories is listed in the other columns. The improvement over (Horowitz and Kamvar 2010), the nearest baseline not a part of our method, for different question categories is shown in the brackets.

Categories	Parts	MRR	MAP@5
Suggestions	39.83%	4.27%(+2.23%)	4.68%(+1.78%)
Opinion	16.42%	2.67%(+1.43%)	2.38%(+1.61%)
Favor	30.51%	3.65%(+1.55%)	4.39%(+1.01%)
Rhetorical	6.74%	1.75%(+1.17%)	0%(+0%)

Table 3: Performance for different question categories.

From the table, we see that the framework gives considerable improvements over all the selected question categories. A paired t-test suggested that the improvements are significant indicating that the framework is effective in finding answerers to a wide range of question categories in Twitter. The best performance can be seen in "Suggestions" and "Favor" categories and the performance in "Opinions" is relatively lower. These results suggest that identifying answerers for the "Opinion" category might depend on additional factors such as similarity of views in a given topic. The framework gives the lowest performance for questions in the "Rhetorical" category. Rhetorical questions are classified as conversational questions in the literature (Harper, Moy, and Konstan 2009). They might be used as an expression of opinion or to initiate a conversation and not to express an information need.

Conclusion and Future Work

Online social media provides a new platform for people seeking information from their social connections. Social media questions represent a form of information seeking behavior of users. Questions are subjective and personal to the asker, and his social context is useful to identify answerers. We draw from sociological theories to present a novel framework to infer the shared context between the asker and the answerers in the question domain. We evaluate the framework on questions on Twitter and demonstrate its effectiveness in identifying answerers. The framework is robust to a wide range of proportions of network and content information and categories of social media questions. The paper provides the first framework with experimental evaluations to identify answerers to questions in social media.

Frameworks exist to identify answerers to factual questions prevalent in community Q&A platforms like Yahoo Answers and StackOverflow. Incorporating concepts from them will enable us to tackle more diverse questions. During situations like natural disasters, social media users propagate requests for help throughout the network. Identifying answerers in these situations will require an understanding of information propagation and information seeking behavior. Identifying users providing misinformation to questions in social media will help to increase the effectiveness of social media as a quality information source.

Acknowledgements

This material is based upon work supported by, or in part by, Office of Naval Research (ONR) under grant number

N000141010091.

References

Adamic, L. A.; Zhang, J.; Bakshy, E.; and Ackerman, M. S. 2008. Knowledge sharing and yahoo answers: everyone knows something. In *WWW*.

Bian, J.; Liu, Y.; Agichtein, E.; and Zha, H. 2008. Finding the right facts in the crowd: factoid question answering over social media. In *WWW*.

Bozzon, A.; Brambilla, M.; Ceri, S.; Silvestri, M.; and Vesci, G. 2013. Choosing the right crowd: expert finding in social networks. In *EDBT*. ACM.

Burt, R. S. 2009. *Structural holes: The social structure of competition*. Harvard university press.

Case, D. O. 2012. *Looking for information: A survey of research on information seeking, needs and behavior*. Emerald Group Publishing.

Cong, G.; Wang, L.; Lin, C.-Y.; Song, Y.-I.; and Sun, Y. 2008. Finding question-answer pairs from online forums. In *SIGIR*.

Ding, C.; Li, T.; Peng, W.; and Park, H. 2006. Orthogonal nonnegative matrix t-factorizations for clustering. In *KDD*.

Ding, C.; Li, T.; and Jordan, M. I. 2008. Nonnegative matrix factorization for combinatorial optimization: Spectral clustering, graph matching, and clique finding. In *ICDM*.

Du, L.; Buntine, W.; and Jin, H. 2010. A segmented topic model based on the two-parameter poisson-dirichlet process. *JMLR*.

Efron, M., and Winget, M. 2010a. Questions are content: a taxonomy of questions in a microblogging environment. *ASIST*.

Efron, M., and Winget, M. 2010b. Questions are content: A taxonomy of questions in a microblogging environment. *ASIST*.

Ellison, N. B.; Gray, R.; Vitak, J.; Lampe, C.; and Fiore, A. T. 2013. Calling all facebook friends: Exploring requests for help on facebook. In *ICWSM*.

Feld, S. L. 1981. The focused organization of social ties. *AJS*.

Gray, R.; Ellison, N. B.; Vitak, J.; and Lampe, C. 2013. Who wants to know?: question-asking and answering practices among facebook users. In *CSCW*.

Harper, F. M.; Moy, D.; and Konstan, J. A. 2009. Facts or friends?: distinguishing informational and conversational questions in social q&a sites. In *CHI*.

Hecht, B.; Teevan, J.; Morris, M. R.; and Liebling, D. J. 2012. Searchbuddies: Bringing search engines into the conversation. *ICWSM*.

Horowitz, D., and Kamvar, S. D. 2010. The anatomy of a large-scale social search engine. In *WWW*.

Jeong, J.-W.; Morris, M. R.; Teevan, J.; and Liebling, D. 2013. A crowd-powered socially embedded search engine. *ICWSM*.

Jurczyk, P., and Agichtein, E. 2007. Discovering authorities in question answer communities by using link analysis. In *CIKM*.

Kumar, S.; Morstatter, F.; and Liu, H. 2013. *Twitter Data Analytics*. Springer.

Lampe, C.; Gray, R.; Fiore, A. T.; and Ellison, N. 2014. Help is on the way: Patterns of responses to resource requests on facebook. In *CSCW*. ACM.

Lee, D. D., and Seung, H. S. 2000. Algorithms for non-negative matrix factorization. In *NIPS*.

Lee, U.; Kang, H.; Yi, E.; Yi, M.; and Kantola, J. 2012. Understanding mobile q&a usage: An exploratory study. In *CHI*.

Marsden, P. V. 1988. Homogeneity in confiding relations. *Social networks*.

Morris, M. R.; Teevan, J.; and Panovich, K. 2010. What do people ask their social networks, and why?: a survey study of status message q&a behavior. In *CHI*.

Nandi, A.; Paparizos, S.; Shafer, J. C.; and Agrawal, R. 2013. With a little help from my friends. In *ICDE, 2013*.

Pal, A., and Counts, S. 2011. Identifying topical authorities in microblogs. In *WSDM*. ACM.

Panovich, K.; Miller, R.; and Karger, D. 2012. Tie strength in question & answer on social network sites. In *CSCW*.

Paul, S. A.; Hong, L.; and Chi, E. H. 2011. Is twitter a good place for asking questions? a characterization study. In *ICWSM*.

Radev, D. R.; Qi, H.; Wu, H.; and Fan, W. 2002. Evaluating web-based question answering systems. *Ann Arbor*.

Riahi, F.; Zolaktaf, Z.; Shafiei, M.; and Milios, E. 2012. Finding expert users in community question answering. In *WWW companion*.

Seung, H., and Lee, D. 2001. Algorithms for non-negative matrix factorization. *NIPS*.

Tang, L., and Liu, H. 2009. Relational learning via latent social dimensions. In *KDD*.

Wang, G.; Gill, K.; Mohanlal, M.; Zheng, H.; and Zhao, B. Y. 2013a. Wisdom in the social crowd: an analysis of quora. In *WWW*.

Wang, Y.; Wang, L.; Li, Y.; He, D.; Liu, T.-Y.; and Chen, W. 2013b. A theoretical analysis of ndcg type ranking measures. *arXiv preprint arXiv:1304.6480*.

Yang, J.; Morris, M. R.; Teevan, J.; Adamic, L. A.; and Ackerman, M. S. 2011. Culture matters: A survey study of social q&a behavior. *ICWSM*.

Yang, L.; Qiu, M.; Gottipati, S.; Zhu, F.; Jiang, J.; Sun, H.; and Chen, Z. 2013. Cqarank: jointly model topics and expertise in community question answering. In *CIKM*, 99–108. ACM.

Yang, J.; McAuley, J.; and Leskovec, J. 2013. Community detection in networks with node attributes. *ICDM*.

Zhou, G.; Lai, S.; Liu, K.; and Zhao, J. 2012. Topic-sensitive probabilistic model for expert finding in question answer communities. In *CIKM*.

Zhu, H.; Chen, E.; Xiong, H.; Cao, H.; and Tian, J. 2013. Ranking user authority with relevant knowledge categories for expert finding. *WWW*.

Proceedings of the Twenty-Ninth AAAI Conference on Artificial Intelligence

Extracting Bounded-Level Modules from Deductive RDF Triplestores

Marie-Christine Rousset
Univ. Grenoble Alpes
CNRS, LIG, 38000, Grenoble, France
IUF (Institut Universitaire de France)
marie-christine.rousset@imag.fr

Federico Ulliana
Université de Montpellier II
CNRS, LIRMM, 34000, Montpellier, France
GrahpIK Team, INRIA Sophia-Antipolis
ulliana@lirmm.fr

Abstract

We present a novel semantics for extracting *bounded-level* modules from RDF ontologies and databases augmented with safe inference rules, à la Datalog. Dealing with a recursive rule language poses challenging issues for defining the module semantics, and also makes module extraction algorithmically unsolvable in some cases. Our results include a set of module extraction algorithms compliant with the novel semantics. Experimental results show that the resulting framework is effective in extracting expressive modules from RDF datasets with formal guarantees, whilst controlling their succinctness.

Introduction

The Semantic Web consolidated a legacy of ontologies and databases today seen as *reference systems* for building new Semantic Web applications. To illustrate, consider a medical application for anatomy, whose goal is to showcase the structure of the human body, the most common pathologies and diseases, and the scientists that contributed to their study. A structural description of human anatomy can be drawn from FMA[1] or My Corporis Fabrica (MyCF).[2] A taxonomy of clinical terms about diseases can be extracted from SNOMED, [3] while biographical informations about scientists implied in studies can be taken from DBPedia.[4] These reference system contain knowledge that can be *reused* to minimize the introduction of errors in the application. However, it is inconvenient to integrate in the application the whole datasets, as they contain complementary data and ontology axioms that are logically redundant. It is thus preferable to extract lightweight fragments of these reference systems - the *modules* - that are relevant for the application, and then to build on top of them.

While extracting modules from ontologies has been largely investigated for Description Logics (DL) (Grau et al. 2008; Konev et al. 2008), module extraction from RDF triplestores has received little attention. Yet, more and more huge RDF datasets are flourishing in the Linked Data and some of them, like DBPedia or YAGO (Suchanek, Kasneci, and Weikum 2007), are increasingly reused in other more specialized datasets. RDF is a graph data model based on triples accepted as the W3C standard for Semantic Web data, with a simple ontology language, RDF Schema (RDFS). The W3C proposed OWL for writing expressive ontologies based on DL constructors. Whereas OWL is often seen as an extension of RDFS, this is not exactly the case. Both RDFS and the RDF query language (SPARQL) feature the possibility of accessing *at the same time* the ontology data and schema, by making variables ranging over classes or properties. This *domain meta-modeling* goes beyond the first-order setting typically considered in DL (De Giacomo, Lenzerini, and Rosati 2011). As a consequence, DL modularization frameworks are not applicable to popular RDF datasets like DBpedia or YAGO. Also, the clear separation between the ABox and the TBox made in DL to define the semantics of modules is not appropriate for RDF where facts and schema statements can be combined within a single RDF triplestore to accommodate heterogeneous knowledge from the Web. Another limit of the current approaches is that the existing semantics do not allow to limit the *size* of the extracted modules. As discussed in (Grau et al. 2008), the risk in practice is to output large portions of the initial ontologies, thus jeopardizing the gains of modularization.

Contributions. As a **first** contribution, we propose a unifying framework for RDF ontologies and databases we call *deductive RDF triplestores*, which is based on RDF triplestores equipped with safe Datalog inference rules. This rule language allows to capture in a uniform manner OWL constraints that are useful in practice, such as property transtivity or symmetry, but also *domain-specific* rules with practical relevance for users in many domains of interest.

The **second** and main contribution of the paper is a parametric semantics for bounded-level modules allowing to effectively control their size. We employ a notion of *level of detail* for modules in such a *deductive* setting. For example, a signature $(\mathsf{subClassOf}, \mathsf{partOf})^3[\mathsf{eye}]$ limits the module-data extracted from a triplestore, by allowing to retrieve a description of all subclasses and subparts of the eye up to three levels.

[1] fma.biostr.washington.edu
[2] www.mycorporisfabrica.org
[3] www.ihtsdo.org/snomed-ct
[4] www.dbpedia.org

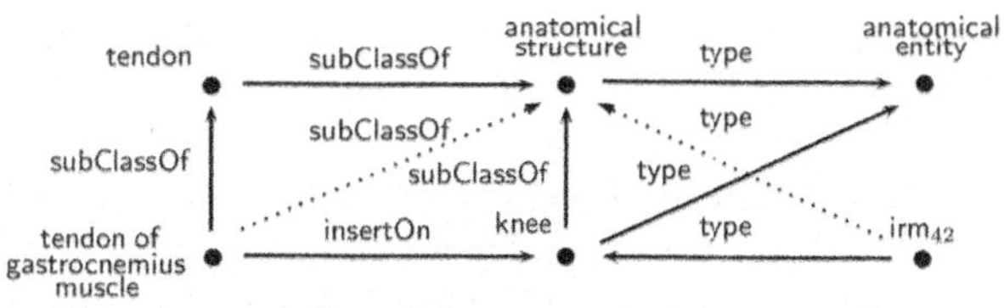

t(tendon, subClassOf, anatomical_structure)
t(anatomical_structure, type, anatomical_entity)
t(tendon_gastr._muscle, insertOn, knee)
t(tendon_gastr._muscle, subClassOf, tendon)
t(knee, subClassOf, anatomical_structure)
t(knee, type, anatomical_entity)
t(irm$_{42}$, type, knee)

Figure 1: Triplestore D_1

The modules in our framework are constituted of both *data* and *rules* entailed by a reference system. Dealing with recursive Datalog rules makes properly defining the parametric modules challenging, and module extraction algorithmically unsolvable in some cases. Therefore, we focus on a class of rules meeting a mild condition on indirect recursion. This is still expressive enough to state for instance transitivity rules. As a **third** contribution, we then provide sound and complete module extraction algorithms, and outline their complexity. Our approach has been implemented on top of an RDF engine and experimentally tested. Proofs and experiment details are reported in (Rousset and Ulliana 2014).

Deductive RDF Triplestores

Data Along the lines of (Calì, Gottlob, and Pieris 2011) and (Libkin, Reutter, and Vrgoc 2013), we assume an infinite universe of constants CONST, which forms the triplestore domain, and an infinite set of variables VARS used in rules. We range over constants by a, b, p, q. We denote by x, y, z and $\bar{x}, \bar{y}, \bar{z}$, variables and sequences of variables belonging to VARS, respectively. A *term*, denoted by u, v is either a constant or a variable. We define RDF triplestores as relational databases over a schema restricted to a single ternary relation $t(\cdot,\cdot,\cdot)$. An atomic formula t is of the form $\mathrm{t} = t(u_1, u_2, u_3)$, with u_i a term. A *triplestore* D is a finite set of atoms of the form $t(u_1, u_2, u_3)$ with $u_i \in$ CONST. Triplestores essentially represent RDF graph data over a relational vocabulary. A path $p_{(u_0,u_n)} = t(u_0, v_1, u_1), t(u_1, v_2, u_2), \ldots, t(u_{n-1}, v_n, u_n)$ is a sequence of atoms where each u_i, v_i are terms. The *length* of a path is the number of its atoms, here $|p_{(u_0,u_n)}| = n$.

Figure 1 presents an RDF triplestore, together with its graph version. The example is inspired by the MyCF ontology (Palombi et al. 2014), which classifies digital representation of human body parts, acquired by IRMs or tomographies, according to anatomical knowledge. For instance, the type edge connecting irm$_{42}$ with knee, corresponds to the triplestore atom t(irm$_{42}$, type, knee), which is the standard RDF syntax for class membership.

Rules Deductive triplestores are equipped with safe Datalog rules. These are first-order logic formulas of the form $\forall \bar{x}\bar{y}.\, \phi(\bar{x}, \bar{y}) \to t(\bar{x})$ where $\bar{x}$ and $\bar{y}$ are sequences of variables belonging to VARS, and $t(\bar{x})$ and $\phi(\bar{x}, \bar{y})$ are an atom and a conjunction of atoms over the ternary relation $t(\cdot,\cdot,\cdot)$, constituting the *head* and the *body* of a rule, respectively. We denote a rule by r and a set of rules by R. To illustrate, the rules for class subsumption
$r_1 : t(x, \mathsf{type}, y), t(y, \mathsf{subClassOf}, z) \to t(x, \mathsf{type}, z)$
$r_2 : t(x, \mathsf{subClassOf}, y), t(y, \mathsf{subClassOf}, z)$
$\to t(x, \mathsf{subClassOf}, z)$
on D_1 entail that irm$_{42}$ has type anatomical_structure, and that a subclass of this last one is tendon_gastr._muscle.

Datalog supports recursion by design. A rule r is said to be recursive if its conclusion unifies with one of its premises. In this work, we consider sets of rules where recursion is limited to recursive rules, like

$r_1 : t(x, \mathsf{hasPart}, y) \to t(y, \mathsf{partOf}, x)$
$r_2 : t(x, \mathsf{insertOn}, y), t(y, \mathsf{partOf}, z) \to t(x, \mathsf{insertOn}, z)$
$r_3 : t(x, \mathsf{partOf}, y), t(y, \mathsf{partOf}, z) \to t(x, \mathsf{partOf}, z)$

and, we exclude the presence of *indirect* recursion, in all cases where this involves *non-recursive rules*, like

$r_4 : t(x, \mathsf{contains}, y) \to t(x, \mathsf{partOf}, y)$
$r_5 : t(x, \mathsf{partOf}, y), t(y, \mathsf{partOf}, z) \to t(z, \mathsf{contains}, x)$

This mild restriction on recursion is of practical relevance, as it is enjoyed by the most relevant RDFS rules, like the mutually recursive ones for domain and range.

$r_{\mathsf{dom}} : t(x, \mathsf{domain}, z), t(y, x, y') \to t(y, \mathsf{type}, z)$
$r_{\mathsf{ran}} : t(x, \mathsf{range}, z'), t(y, x, y') \to t(y', \mathsf{type}, z')$

Datalog semantics is defined as the least fix-point of the immediate consequence operator (denoted by $\vdash_1$).

Definition 1 (Datalog Inference) *The single-step Datalog inference, denoted by* $D, R \vdash_1 D'$, *holds when* $D' = D \cup \{\mu(head(r)) \mid \mu(body(r)) \in D \text{ and } r \in R\}$, *with* μ *an homomorphism from variables to constants. Then, we write* $D, R \vdash D'$ *when there exists a positive integer* n *such that* $D_i, R \vdash_1 D_{i+1}$ *for all* $0 \leq i < n$, *with* $D = D_0$ *and* $D' \subseteq D_n$. *The triplestore* D *saturated with* R, *is defined as* $\mathrm{SAT}(D, R) = \{\mathrm{t} \in D' \mid D, R \vdash D'\}$.

We write $D, R \vdash p_{(u_0,u_n)}$ for the entailment of a path that holds if all path atoms are in $\mathrm{SAT}(D, R)$. Rule entailment, also referred as the immediate consequence operator for rules defines, by means of *semantic conditions*, when a Datalog rule r is entailed by a set R.

Definition 2 (Rule Entailment) *A rule* r *is entailed by a set* R, *denoted by* $R \vdash r$, *if for all triplestore* D *it holds that* $\mathrm{SAT}(D, r) \subseteq \mathrm{SAT}(D, R)$. *A set* R' *is entailed from* R, *denoted by* $R \vdash R'$ *when* $R \vdash r$ *for all* $r \in R'$.

A *deductive RDF triplestore* is a pair $\langle D, R\rangle$ where D is a triplestore and R is a finite set of (possibly recursive) rules. Triplestore entailment, denoted by $\langle D, R\rangle \vdash \langle D', R'\rangle$, holds when $D, R \vdash D'$ and $R \vdash R'$.

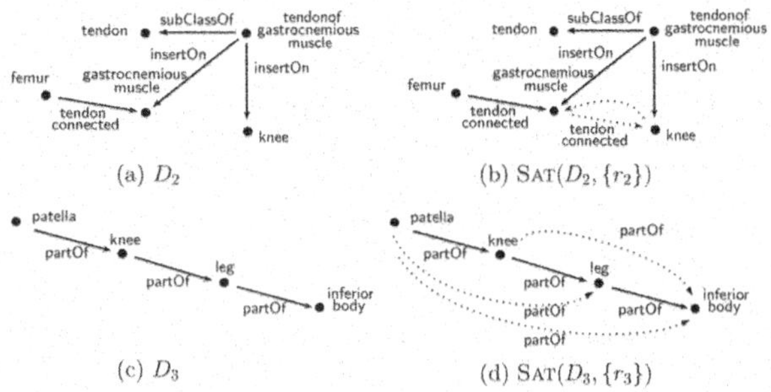

(a) D_2 (b) $\text{SAT}(D_2, \{r_2\})$ (c) D_3 (d) $\text{SAT}(D_3, \{r_3\})$

Figure 2: Triplestore examples

Bounded-level Modules

A module is declared by means of a signature Σ of the form $\Sigma = (\,\mathsf{p}_1, \ldots, \mathsf{p}_n\,)^k[\,\mathsf{a}\,]$ where the constants $\mathsf{p}_1, \ldots, \mathsf{p}_n$ represent the *properties of interest* of the module, the constant a represents an *object of interest* of the module, and k is a positive integer denoting the *level of detail* of the module. An example of module signature is $(\,\mathsf{partOf}\,)^3[\,\mathsf{eye}\,]$. Intuitively, a module M induced by a signature Σ on a reference system $\langle D, R\rangle$ is a deductive triplestore $M{=}\langle D_M, R_M\rangle$ which is logically entailed by $\langle D, R\rangle$ and conforming to Σ, in the sense that all data and rule atoms employ the properties $\mathsf{p}_1, \ldots, \mathsf{p}_n$ *only*. Furthermore, to control the module size, the facts in M are restricted to the *paths* rooted at the object of interest a, of length bounded by k.

We say that an atom conforms to Σ, denoted by $t(v_1, u, v_2) \mathrel{\vdots} \Sigma$, if u is a property of Σ or $u \in \text{VARS}$. A set of atoms Δ conforms to Σ if all of its atoms do. Then, $\langle D, R\rangle$ conforms to Σ if so do D and R. In Figure 2(c) it holds that $D_3 \mathrel{\vdots} (\,\mathsf{partOf}, \mathsf{subClassOf}\,)^2[\,\mathsf{knee}\,]$. However, it does not hold that $D_3 \mathrel{\vdots} (\,\mathsf{subClassOf}\,)^1[\,\mathsf{knee}\,]$.

Restricting the module paths is a way to effectively control the module size. Nevertheless, for the completeness of the module data, it is essential to guarantee that the module entails *all* of such bounded paths entailed by $\langle D, R\rangle$. In a deductive setting, adding new paths in the graph, defining properly D_M becomes challenging.

First, we observe that to avoid incomplete modules, the paths of D_M have to be drawn from $\text{SAT}(D, R)$. To see this, consider D_2 in Figure 2(a) and a rule inferring pairs of organs (y, z) physically connected by a tendon

$r_2 : t(x, \mathsf{insertOn}, y), t(x, \mathsf{insertOn}, z),$
$t(x, \mathsf{subClassOf}, \mathsf{tendon}) {\rightarrow} t(y, \mathsf{tendonConnected}, z)$

A user interested in the organs directly and indirectly connected to the femur of this triplestore can declare the module signature $\Sigma_2{=}(\,\mathsf{tendonConnected}\,)^2[\,\mathsf{femur}\,]$. By restricting the module data D_M to the paths in D_2 of length bounded by 2 that are rooted at femur and that use the property tendonConnected only, we get $D_M = \{t(\mathsf{femur}, \mathsf{tendonConnected}, \mathsf{gastroc.Muscle})\}$. This dataset has however to be considered incomplete.

As shown in Figure 2(b), the rule r_2 entails on D_2 also the fact $t(\mathsf{gastroc.Muscle}, \mathsf{tendonConnected}, \mathsf{knee})$. This forms a path of length two together with the original triple $t(\mathsf{femur}, \mathsf{tendonConnected}, \mathsf{gastroc.Muscle})$, that should be included in D_M. The example illustrates clearly that D_M depends from the rules in R.

However, taking into account *all* paths in $\text{SAT}(D, R)$ is not desirable for defining modules of bounded size. In some cases, the triples entailed by *recursive* rules may produce new edges in the data graph that behave like shortcuts between resources, thereby wasting the module parametricity. Consider D_3 in Figure 2(c) and the recursive rule r_3 defining the transitivity of partOf

$r_3 : t(x, \mathsf{partOf}, y), t(y, \mathsf{partOf}, z) \rightarrow t(x, \mathsf{partOf}, z)$

The saturated triplestore $\text{SAT}(D_3, r_3)$ is depicted in Figure 2(d). It contains $t(\mathsf{patella}, \mathsf{partOf}, \mathsf{knee})$ but also $t(\mathsf{patella}, \mathsf{partOf}, \mathsf{leg})$ and $t(\mathsf{patella}, \mathsf{partOf}, \mathsf{inferiorBody})$. More generally, it contains all triples of the form $\mathsf{t_b} = t(\mathsf{patella}, \mathsf{partOf}, \mathsf{b})$ entailed by the transitivity of partOf. This means that if we take into account the recursive rule r_3 for defining the module paths, then all triples $\mathsf{t_b}$ are likely to be part of the module induced by signature $(\,\mathsf{partOf}\,)^1[\,\mathsf{knee}\,]$. This undermines the module parametricity because it retrieves all resources connected with knee regardless of the level of detail k.

Our solution to both keep into account implicit triples and make parametricity effective, is to define the module data as a subgraph of a *partially-saturated* triplestore obtained by applying non-recursive rules only, while fully *delegating* to the module the recursive rules. This leads to the following novel definition of module.

Definition 3 (Module) *Let $\langle D, R\rangle$ be a deductive triplestore and $\Sigma = (\,\mathsf{p}_1, \ldots, \mathsf{p}_n\,)^k[\,\mathsf{a}\,]$ a signature. Then, $M{=}\langle D_M, R_M\rangle$ is a module for Σ on $\langle D, R\rangle$ if*

1. $\langle D_M, R_M\rangle \mathrel{\vdots} \Sigma$
2. $\langle D, R\rangle \vdash \langle D_M, R_M\rangle$
3. *if $p_{(\mathsf{a},\mathsf{b})} \mathrel{\vdots} \Sigma$ and $|p_{(\mathsf{a},\mathsf{b})}| \leq k$ then*
   (a) $D, R^{\mathsf{NonRec}} \vdash p_{(\mathsf{a},\mathsf{b})}$ *implies* $D_M, R_M \vdash p_{(\mathsf{a},\mathsf{b})}$
   (b) $D_M, R \vdash p_{(\mathsf{a},\mathsf{b})}$ *implies* $D_M, R_M \vdash p_{(\mathsf{a},\mathsf{b})}$

Point 1 and 2 of the definition state the well-formedness and the logical entailment of the modules, respectively. Point 3 is the crux of the definition. Property $3(a)$ says that every path rooted at a of k-bounded length and conforming to Σ, that is entailed by the *non-recursive* rules of the reference system R^{NonRec}, must also be inferable by M. Property $3(b)$ enforces that the module rules R_M infer the same paths conforming to Σ as the *whole set of rules* R, but only when applied to the module data D_M. In contrast with the spirit of previous approaches (e.g., (Grau et al. 2008)), our definition does not enforce that *every* fact in the signature entailed by the reference triplestore also belongs to the module. Relaxing the module conditions in this way allows to control the module size, and cope with recursive rules.

To illustrate the definition, consider the triplestore D_4 of Figure 3(a) equipped with the rules below.

$r_4 : t(x, \mathsf{hasFunction}, y) \rightarrow t(x, \mathsf{participatesTo}, y)$
$r'_4 : t(x, \mathsf{participatesTo}, y), t(y, \mathsf{subClassOf}, z) \rightarrow$
$t(x, \mathsf{participatesTo}, z)$

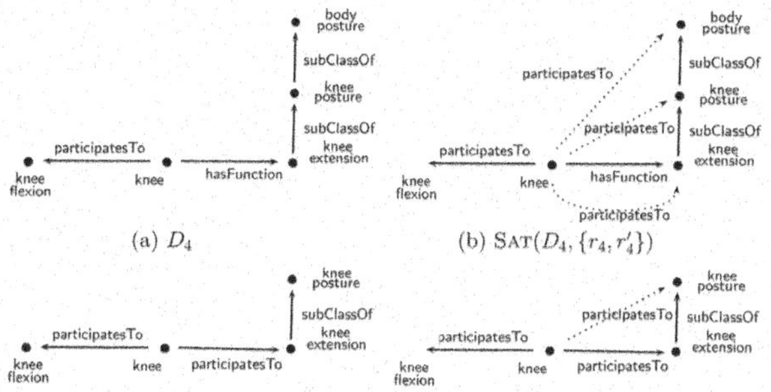

(a) D_4 (b) $\text{SAT}(D_4, \{r_4, r'_4\})$

(c) D_{M_4} for Σ_4 (d) $\text{SAT}(D_{M_4}, \{r'_4\})$

Figure 3: Triplestore and module examples

Figure 3(b) depicts $\text{SAT}(D_4, \{r_4, r'_4\})$. Consider now Σ_4=(participatesTo, subClassOf $)^2$[knee]. A module M_4 for Σ_4 contains all paths rooted at knee of length at most 2, employing participatesTo and subClassOf only.

Note that if the recursive rule r'_4 is considered, then the triple t_1=t(knee, participatesTo, bodyPosture) is included in the module dataset, which is not desirable. In contrast, $t_2 = t$(knee, participatesTo, kneePosture) is expected to be in a module for the signature Σ_4. A structure satisfying Definition 3 is $M_4 = \langle D_{M_4}, R_{M_4}\rangle$ with D_{M_4} depicted in Figure 3(c) and $R_{M_4} = \{r'_4\}$. Note that t_2 is not explicitly in the module dataset D_{M_4} but can be inferred by r'_4 as shown in Figure 3(d).

Next, we present two algorithms for extracting module data and rules compliant with this novel semantics.

Extracting Module Data

The extraction of the module dataset can be done by leveraging on the evaluation of Datalog queries and implemented on top of existing engines. Given a module signature Σ = ($p_1, \ldots, p_n$ $)^k$[a], the set of Datalog rules Π_Σ below computes all paths rooted at a, of length bounded by k, and built on the properties of interest of Σ. It does so, in the extension of the relation m, starting from a triplestore modeled with a single relation t.

$$\Pi_\Sigma = \begin{cases} m^1(\mathsf{a}, \mathsf{p}_i, x) & \leftarrow \quad t(\mathsf{a}, \mathsf{p}_i, x) \\ m^{j+1}(x, \mathsf{p}_i, y) & \leftarrow \quad m^j(x_1, y_1, x)\,, t(x, \mathsf{p}_i, y) \\ m(x, y, z) & \leftarrow \quad m^j(x, y, z) \end{cases}$$

An instance of the rules is included for each $i = 1..n$ and $j = 1..k$. Π_Σ is a non-recursive set of rules of size $O(nk)$ that can always be evaluated in at most k steps. Then, to infer all paths of bounded length entailed by non-recursive rules of a reference system, the set Π_Σ is evaluated together with R^{NonRec}. As a result, the union $\Pi_\Sigma \cup R^{\mathsf{NonRec}}$ gives a non-recursive set of rules that can be evaluated in LOGSPACE data-complexity. The completeness of module data extraction follows from the completeness of Datalog query evaluation. Below, we write $Q_m(D, \Pi_\Sigma \cup R^{\mathsf{NonRec}})$ for the answer set of the evaluation of the Datalog program $\Pi_\Sigma \cup R^{\mathsf{NonRec}}$ defining the relation m, on top of the dataset D. This constitutes the module data D_M.

Theorem 4 (Module Data Extraction) *For all path $\mathsf{p}_{(a,b)} \between \Sigma$ with $|\mathsf{p}_{(a,b)}| \le k$ we have $D, R^{\mathsf{NonRec}} \vdash \mathsf{p}_{(a,b)}$ if and only if $\mathsf{p}_{(a,b)} \in Q_m(D, \Pi_\Sigma \cup R^{\mathsf{NonRec}})$.*

Extracting Module Rules

We now present an algorithm for module rule extraction that, together with the dataset extracted in the previous section, yields a module compliant with our semantics.

By Definition 3, a module is constituted of rules *entailed* by that of the reference system, and built on the properties of interest *only*. As the properties of interest of a module may restrict those employed by a reference system, the module rules cannot be just a subset of the original ones. Rule extraction is thus performed by an *unfolding* algorithm, that proceeds by replacing the premises of a rule with that of another one, until obtaining a set conforming to the signature. To illustrate, consider Σ = (p, q $)^k$[a] and the rules below.

$r_1 : t(x, \mathsf{q}, y), t(y, \mathsf{partOf}, x) \rightarrow t(x, \mathsf{q}, y)$
$r_2 : t(x, \mathsf{p}, y) \rightarrow t(x, \mathsf{partOf}, y)$

Although the rule r_1 does not conform to Σ, it can be unfolded with r_2 so as to obtain a module rule. As the atom $t(y, \mathsf{partOf}, x)$ in the body of r_1 unifies with the conclusion of r_2, it can be replaced by $t(y, \mathsf{p}, x)$, so as to get the rule $\bar{r} = t(x, \mathsf{q}, y), t(y, \mathsf{p}, x) \rightarrow t(x, \mathsf{q}, y)$. Rule $\bar{r}$ is called an *unfolding* of r_1 with r_2.

In the above example, one unfolding step is enough to have a rule $\bar{r}$ that is conform to the module signature and that, by construction, is entailed by $\{r_1, r_2\}$. It is easy to see that this can be generalized, and that rules belonging to unfoldings of a set of rules R are entailed by R. However, in presence of recursive rules the set of unfoldings of a rule may be infinite, as illustrated below.

Example 5 *Consider Σ = (p, q $)^3$[a_1] and R with*

$r_1 : t(x, \mathsf{partOf}, y) \rightarrow t(x, \mathsf{q}, y)$
$r_2 : t(x, \mathsf{partOf}, y), t(y, \mathsf{partOf}, z) \rightarrow t(x, \mathsf{partOf}, z)$
$r_3 : t(x, \mathsf{p}, y) \rightarrow t(x, \mathsf{partOf}, y)$

Here, r_1 can be unfolded with r_2 and r_3, thus obtaining

$\bar{r} : t(x_1, \mathsf{p}, x_2), t(x_2, \mathsf{p}, x_3) \rightarrow t(x_1, \mathsf{q}, x_3)$

However, there exist infinitely many unfoldings of rule r_2 with itself that yield expressions of the form $t(x_1, \mathsf{p}, x_2), t(x_2, \mathsf{p}, x_3), t(x_3, \mathsf{p}, x_4) \rightarrow t(x_1, \mathsf{q}, x_4)$ that use any finite sequence of variables $x_1, \ldots, x_n$. This set of unfoldings cannot be strictly speaking a set of triplestore or module rules, because it is *infinite*.

To avoid ending up with infinite sets of module rules, we devised an unfolding algorithm based on a *breadth-first* strategy. Algorithm MRE performs Module Rules Extraction. It takes as input a set of rules to be unfolded N_{ToUnfold}, a set of rules to be used for the unfolding R_{ToApply}, and a signature Σ. Given a deductive triplestore $\langle D, R\rangle$ the first call to the algorithm is MRE($N_{\mathit{ToUnfold}}, R, \Sigma$). The set $N_{\mathit{ToUnfold}} \subseteq R$ is constituted of all rules $r \in R$ that conclude on a property of interest, that is $\mathit{head}(r) \between \Sigma$. Any rule belonging to N_{ToUnfold} (whose premises use properties that are not in Σ) is unfolded in a breadth-first fashion until no rule in R_{ToApply} can be applied. All rules in R are considered for

Algorithm 1: MRE($N_{ToUnfold}, R_{ToApply}, \Sigma$)

1 **forall the** $r_1 \in N_{ToUnfold}$ **do**
2   **if** $r_1 \,\mathring{:}\, \Sigma$ **then**
3     $R_M \leftarrow r_1$
4   remove r_1 from $R_{ToApply}$
5   **else**
6   **forall the** $r_2 \in R_{ToApply}$ *s.t.* $r_1 \neq r_2$ **do**
7   **forall the** $r \in RuleUnfolding(r_1, r_2)$ **do**
8   **if** $r \,\mathring{:}\, \Sigma$ **then**
9           $R_M \leftarrow r$
10         $R_M \leftarrow$ MRE($\{r\}, R_{ToApply} \backslash \{r, r_2\}, \Sigma$)
11 **return** R_M

unfolding ($R_{ToApply} = R$). Procedure *RuleUnfolding*(r_1, r_2) progressively unfolds each *subset* of atoms in the body of r_1 that unify with the conclusion of r_2. For example, the three breadth-first unfoldings of $r_1 : t(x, \mathsf{p}, y), t(x, \mathsf{p}, z) \rightarrow t(x, \mathsf{p}, y)$ with $r_2 : t(x, \mathsf{partOf}, y) \rightarrow t(x, \mathsf{p}, y)$ are

$\bar{r}_3 : t(x, \mathsf{p}, y), t(x, \mathsf{partOf}, z) \rightarrow t(x, \mathsf{p}, y)$
$\bar{r}_4 : t(x, \mathsf{partOf}, y), t(x, \mathsf{p}, z) \rightarrow t(x, \mathsf{p}, y)$
$\bar{r}_5 : t(x, \mathsf{partOf}, y), t(x, \mathsf{partOf}, z) \rightarrow t(x, \mathsf{p}, y)$

Note that a rule is never unfolded with itself by the algorithm (thus avoiding a depth-first fashion). The fact that r_2 used for the unfolding is discarded from $R_{ToApply}$ (line 10) ensures the termination of the extraction procedure, even in the presence of recursive rules.

Theorem 6 (Rule Extraction Algorithm) *Let R be a set of rules and Σ a module signature. Algorithm MRE always terminates in $O(2^{|R| \times |r|})$ and produces a set of rules R_M conforming to Σ such that for all $r \,\mathring{:}\, \Sigma$ it holds*

$$R_M \vdash r \quad \textit{implies} \quad R \vdash r \quad (\textsc{Soundness})$$

Furthermore, when $R^{\mathsf{Rec}} \,\mathring{:}\, \Sigma$ we also have

$$R \vdash r \quad \textit{implies} \quad R_M \vdash r \quad (\textsc{Completeness})$$

Algorithm MRE is sound, in the sense that it computes a set of rules entailed by R. Furthermore, for the case where all recursive rules in R conform to Σ, the algorithm is also complete, in the sense that it produces a set of rules R_M that entails all rules R can entail on the properties of Σ. As a consequence, any dataset D_M (computed as for Theorem 4) paired with R_M constitutes a module meeting Definition 3, and in particular the point 3(b). If this condition does not hold, module extraction may be incomplete. To see this, consider again $\langle D, R\rangle$ of Example 5 with $D = \{t(\mathsf{a}_1, \mathsf{p}, \mathsf{a}_2), t(\mathsf{a}_2, \mathsf{p}, \mathsf{a}_3), t(\mathsf{a}_3, \mathsf{p}, \mathsf{a}_4)\}$. Recall that $\Sigma = (\,\mathsf{p}, \mathsf{q}\,)^3[\,\mathsf{a}_1\,]$, and then notice that the recursive rule $r_2 \not\mathring{:} \Sigma$. Here, module data extraction yields $D_M = D$. Observe now that the atom $t(\mathsf{a}_1, \mathsf{q}, \mathsf{a}_4)$ belongs to $\textsc{Sat}(D_M, R)$. As MRE outputs the set $R_M = \{t(x, \mathsf{p}, y), t(y, \mathsf{p}, z) \rightarrow t(x, \mathsf{q}, z)\}$, the triple $t(\mathsf{a}_1, \mathsf{q}, \mathsf{a}_4)$ does not belong to $\textsc{Sat}(D_M, R_M)$, while it should. Hence, $\langle D_M, R_M\rangle$ does not satisfy Definition 3.

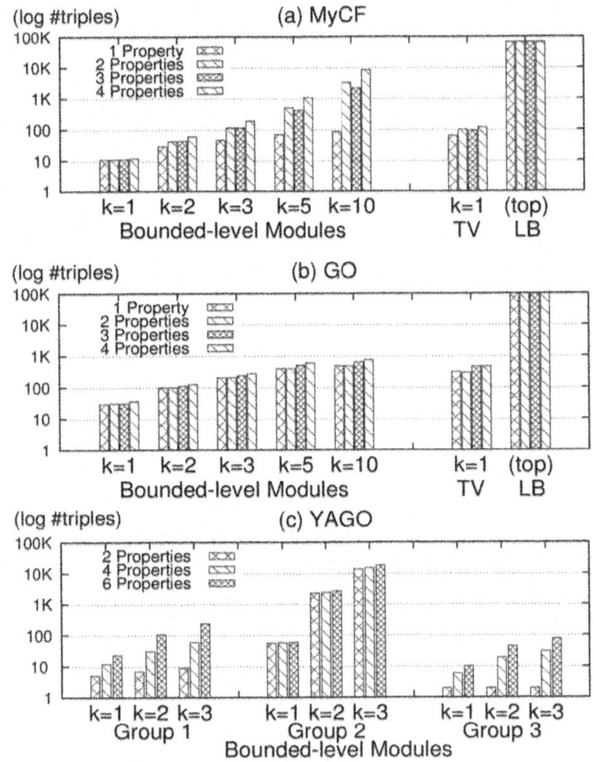

Figure 4: Size of Extracted Modules

Surprisingly enough, this case of incompleteness *is independent of algorithm MRE.* In fact, when R includes recursive rules that do not conform to Σ, it does not exist an algorithm that outputs a finite set of rules R_M such that $R \vdash r$ implies $R_M \vdash r$, for all $r \,\mathring{:}\, \Sigma$. As Example 5 illustrates, the extracted R_M must mimic an *infinite* set of rules of the form $t(x_1, \mathsf{p}, x_2), t(x_2, \mathsf{p}, x_3) \ldots t(x_{n-1}, \mathsf{p}, x_n) \rightarrow t(x_1, \mathsf{q}, x_n)$. One may think of capturing this infinite set by adding a recursive rule $r_{\mathsf{p}} : t(x, \mathsf{p}, y), t(y, \mathsf{p}, z) \rightarrow t(x, \mathsf{p}, z)$ together with $\bar{r} : t(x_1, \mathsf{p}, x_2), t(x_2, \mathsf{p}, x_3) \rightarrow t(x_1, \mathsf{q}, x_3)$. However, adding this recursive rule makes infer triples using p that are not entailed by the reference system, thereby violating point 2 of Definition 3. We can also ask whether this infinite set of rules can be reduced to a finite set that directly depends on k. Unfortunately, the answer is negative. Furthermore, it is unpractical for real systems to consider a specific module data D_M and bound by $O(|D_M|)$ the number of self-unfolding of a recursive rule during extraction, as this can output an unmanageable set of rules, that are (still) not robust to updates. Therefore, understanding when algorithm MRE is complete is key for module extraction.

This kind of unfolding issues have also been recognized and studied by earlier works on the optimization of recursive Datalog (Hillebrand et al. 1995).

Finally, note that Theorem 6 is actually stronger than what required by Definition 3, because (i) it is based on *semantic* conditions and therefore it holds for any rule r entailed by R (unfoldings are just a particular case) and (ii) it is independent from the module data, and thus suitable for other module semantics.

A characterization of the whole module extraction task follows as a corollary of Theorems 4 and 6.

Experiments

We implemented bounded-level module extraction on top of Jena 2.11.2 TDB, and compared it against two related approaches to show its benefits in terms of flexibility and succinctness of the extracted modules.

We considered the following three Semantic Web datasets.

MyCF	0.5M triples	11 domain-specific rules
GO	1M triples	15 domain-specific rules
Yago2*	14M triples	6 RDFS rules

Yago2* is the union of Yago2Taxonomy, Yago2Types and Yago2Facts datasets. We sampled classes and properties from these ontologies, and combined them to obtain a set of signatures used to run module extraction. We considered 2500 MyCF ontology classes combined with 20 subsets of its properties, of size 1-4. For the GO ontology (`www.geneontology.org`), we sampled 350 classes and 12 property sets (size 1-4). Since Yago knowledge is more diverse than a domain-specific ontology, to avoid empty modules we first selected three groups of properties that are frequently used together, and then subset them (size 2, 4, 6). We tested 100 Yago resources for each group. Finally, we made k ranging over $\{1, 2, 3, 5, 10\}$.

Closest competitor approaches Relevant methods to our work are Traversal Views (Noy and Musen 2004) and Locality-based modules (Grau et al. 2008). Traversal Views (TV) compute a bounded-level view of an RDF database, in the same spirit as our approach. This method does not support inference rules, and it does not give any guarantee about extracted modules. In practice, in the presence of rules, a traversal view may miss relevant triples. Locality-Based (LB) module extraction computes a conservative extension of an ontology by checking logical conditions on its schema. In contrast with our method, it cannot modularize untyped RDF data and, because it enforces strong logical guarantees on a module, it cannot control a priori its size.

Results of module data extraction Figure 4(a-b) reports on the size of bounded-level modules, compared with those of TV and LB. The graphs show the average number of triples, for modules grouped by the same number of properties and k value, in logarithmic scale. In Figure 4(c) we report the test on Yago2* with our approach, since LB does not support this RDF dataset.

As expected, the succinctness of bounded-level modules depends on k. The transitivity of the properties declared in the signature also has an impact. This is evident with Yago2* in Figure 4(c). Group 2 has properties inherently transitive (isLocatedIn, isConnectedWith) dominating for example (created, owns) in group 1 and (hasGender, isAffiliatedTo) in group 3. Hence, bounded-level modules can be very helpful to control the data succinctness with transitive properties.

Being TV unaware of rules, it may miss relevant data when implicit triples are not considered. We tested this claim, over the *non-saturated* MyCF ontology. Indeed, 42% (15072/35740) of the (non-empty) modules extracted by TV were missing relevant triples wrt our approach, as some subproperty rules were not evaluated. To overcome this limitation, we tested TV over the *saturated* MyCF. For concision, in Figure 4(a) we report only the minimal level of detail ($k = 1$). This already outlines a lower bound for the module size. As we can see, $k = 1$ already produces fairly larger modules than our approach. This is because of the MyCF rules for transitivity and property-chains. Increasing k gives modules of size in the order of the saturated triplestore. The same discussion holds for GO in Figure 4(b). Hence, by having modules made of *both* data and rules our approach allows to retain succinctness wrt TV.

LB extraction for *top-locality* modules has been tested thanks to the available prototype `www.cs.ox.ac.uk/isg/tools/ModuleExtractor/`. For MyCF and GO, it outputs almost the whole ontology (Figures 4(a-b)). This is due to ontology axioms that cannot be ignored for the logical completeness of the method.

To conclude, the experiments outline the advantages of bounded-level modules as i) flexibility, to accomodate diverse Semantic Web datasets, and ii) succinctness, when dealing with transitive properties and rules.

Related Work and Conclusion

Module extraction has been extensively studied for DL. Related works employ basically two approaches that consist in inferring a conservative extension of an ontology (Grau et al. 2008; Konev et al. 2008), and forgetting non-interesting relations of ontology schemas (Grau and Motik 2012). Approximations and heuristics have also been devised to mitigate the complexity costs (Nortje, Britz, and Meyer 2013), and have been validated by statistical analysis (Vescovo et al. 2013). Differently from our approach, all of these techniques focus exclusively on the ontology schema, and do not permit to modularize Semantic Web datasets starting also from ontology instances or RDF facts. The closest work to our, at least in spirit, is (Noy and Musen 2004). However, it does not consider inference, which makes module extraction challenging. Answering Datalog queries over RDF has been investigated in (Libkin, Reutter, and Vrgoc 2013) and (Bry et al. 2008).

We presented a novel approach for the extraction of bounded-level modules from deductive RDF triplestores, which provides new means to reuse of Linked-Data datasets, and favorizes the development of Semantic Web applications. The key contribution of the work is a novel module semantics allowing to bound their size, and compliant module extraction algorithms. As shown by our experiments, the resulting framework allows to efficiently extract expressive modules from Semantic Web ontologies and databases with formal guarantees, whilst effectively controlling their succinctness. Future works include the study of module robustness to updates (Goasdoue and Rousset 2013), the extension towards Datalog$\pm$ rules (Arenas, Gottlob, and Pieris 2014), and the connections between module extraction and recursive Datalog optimisation (Hillebrand et al. 1995).

Acknowledgements

This work has been partially supported by the project PAGODA (ANR-12-JS02-007-01) and by the LabEx PERSYVAL-Lab (ANR-11-LABX-0025-01).

References

Arenas, M.; Gottlob, G.; and Pieris, A. 2014. Expressive languages for querying the semantic web. In *Proceedings of the 33st Symposium on Principle of Database Systems (PODS-14)*.

Bry, F.; Furche, T.; Ley, C.; Linse, B.; and Marnette, B. 2008. RDFLog: Its like Datalog for RDF. In *Proceedings of the Workshop on (Constraint) Logic Programming (WLP-08)*.

Calì, A.; Gottlob, G.; and Pieris, A. 2011. New expressive languages for ontological query answering. In *Proceedings of the Twenty-Fifth AAAI Conference on Artificial Intelligence (AAAI-11)*.

De Giacomo, G.; Lenzerini, M.; and Rosati, R. 2011. Higher-order description logics for domain metamodeling. In *Proceedings of the Twenty-Fifth AAAI Conference on Artificial Intelligence (AAAI-11)*.

Goasdoue, F., and Rousset, M.-C. 2013. Robust module-based data management. *IEEE Transactions on Knowledge and Data Engineering (TKDE-13)*.

Grau, B. C., and Motik, B. 2012. Reasoning over ontologies with hidden content: The import-by-query approach. *Journal of Artificial Intelligence Research (JAIR-12)*.

Grau, B. C.; Horrocks, I.; Kazakov, Y.; and Sattler, U. 2008. Modular reuse of ontologies: Theory and practice. *Journal of Artificial Intelligence Research (JAIR-08)*.

Hillebrand, G. G.; Kanellakis, P. C.; Mairson, H. G.; and Vardi, M. Y. 1995. Undecidable boundedness problems for datalog programs. *Journal of Logic Programming (JLP-95)*.

Konev, B.; Lutz, C.; Walther, D.; and Wolter, F. 2008. Semantic modularity and module extraction in description logics. In *Proceedings of the European Conference on Artificial Intelligence (ECAI-08)*.

Libkin, L.; Reutter, J. L.; and Vrgoc, D. 2013. Trial for RDF: adapting graph query languages for RDF data. In *Proceedings of the 32st Symposium on Principles of Database Systems (PODS-13)*.

Nortje, R.; Britz, K.; and Meyer, T. 2013. Reachability modules for the description logic $\mathcal{SRIQ}$. In *Logic for Programming, Artificial Intelligence, and Reasoning*, Lecture Notes in Computer Science.

Noy, N. F., and Musen, M. A. 2004. Specifying ontology views by traversal. In *Proceedings of the International Semantic Web Conference (ISWC-04)*.

Palombi, O.; Ulliana, F.; Favier, V.; Léon, J.-C.; and Rousset, M.-C. 2014. My Corporis Fabrica: an ontology-based tool for reasoning and querying on complex anatomical models. *Journal of Biomedical Semantics (JBS-14)*.

Rousset, M.-C., and Ulliana, F. 2014. Extracting bounded-level modules from deductive RDF triplestores. Technical report. http://www.lirmm.fr/~ulliana/papers/aaai15-full.pdf.

Suchanek, F. M.; Kasneci, G.; and Weikum, G. 2007. Yago: A core of semantic knowledge. In *Proceedings of the World Wide Web Conference (WWW-07)*.

Vescovo, C. D.; Klinov, P.; Parsia, B.; Sattler, U.; Schneider, T.; and Tsarkov, D. 2013. Empirical study of logic-based modules: Cheap is cheerful. In *International Workshop on Description Logics (DL-03)*.

Proceedings of the Twenty-Ninth AAAI Conference on Artificial Intelligence

Question/Answer Matching for CQA System via Combining Lexical and Sequential Information

Yikang Shen[♯], Wenge Rong[†‡], Zhiwei Sun[†], Yuanxin Ouyang[†‡], Zhang Xiong[†‡]
[♯]Sino-French Engineer School, Beihang University, Beijing 100191, China
[†]School of Computer Science and Engineering, Beihang University, Beijing 100191, China
[‡]Research Institute of Beihang University in Shenzhen, Shenzhen 518057, China
{yikang.shen, w.rong, sunzhiwei, oyyx, xiongz}@buaa.edu.cn

Abstract

Community-based Question Answering (CQA) has become popular in knowledge sharing sites since it allows users to get answers to complex, detailed, and personal questions directly from other users. Large archives of historical questions and associated answers have been accumulated. Retrieving relevant historical answers that best match a question is an essential component of a CQA service. Most state of the art approaches are based on bag-of-words models, which have been proven successful in a range of text matching tasks, but are insufficient for capturing the important word sequence information in short text matching. In this paper, a new architecture is proposed to more effectively model the complicated matching relations between questions and answers. It utilises a similarity matrix which contains both lexical and sequential information. Afterwards the information is put into a deep architecture to find potentially suitable answers. The experimental study shows its potential in improving matching accuracy of question and answer.

Introduction

Community-based Question Answering (CQA) systems are Internet services which enable users to ask questions and receive answers. By using CQA systems, users can ask questions via sentences rather than issuing queries in the form of keywords to a Web search engine. CQA is proven success for knowledge sharing since it is easier for users to express their real information needs in natural language (Bilotti et al. 2010). Furthermore, using CQA is also easier to get answers to a personal nature, extremely specific questions, and even open-ended questions as in these cases it is difficult for a search engine to directly provide such complex and heterogeneous information (Chua and Banerjee 2013). CQA sites have become a kind of popular forum for people to seek information and share knowledge. Examples of such CQA sites include Yahoo! Answers and Baidu Zhidao.

Though CQA has shown its promising applicability, there still exists several challenges among which a notable one is the unanswered question rate. It is frequently observed that in spite of active participation in CQA sites, a significant portion of questions remain unanswered (Dror, Maarek, and Szpektor 2013). This phenomenon widely exists in CQA systems and is often referred as question starvation (Li and King 2010). Several efforts have been made to reduce the number of unanswered questions and one method has been attached much importance in the community, namely how to proactively seek knowledge from historical question/answer pairs.

Normally CQA sites have accumulated large archives of historical questions and associated answers. Retrieving relevant historical question/answer pairs which best match a user's new question or search query is an essential component of a CQA service. Additionally, when a user asks a new question in CQA service and good matches can be located, the lag time incurred by having to wait for a person to respond can be avoided, thus improving user satisfaction.

Question/answer pair retrieval has three major methods: 1) finding historical questions which are similar to the target question. For example, Carmel et al. tried to rank historical questions using both inter-question and question-answer similarity to respond to a newly posed question (Carmel, Shtalhaim, and Soffer 2000) (Figueroa and Neumann 2014); 2) identifying the most relevant answers to the target question within a collection of answers. A representative application was proposed by Surdeanu et al. (Surdeanu, Ciaramita, and Zaragoza 2008), who combine translation and similarity features to recommend historical answers by relevance to a given question, though it focuses only on *how to* questions; 3) combining question similarity and answer relevance. Shtok et al. proposed a two stage approach (Shtok et al. 2012), in the first stage historical questions similar to the new question are identified and ranked so as to produce a single resolved question candidate, in the second stage the best answer to the top candidate question is evaluated in order to verify whether it meets the underlying needs of the new question.

In this paper, we mainly focus on identifying the most relevant answers from a collection of answers by calculating the matching probability between the question q and each candidate answer d. The candidate answers are then ranked by their probability. Intuitively, many bag-of-words based models can be applied to solve this kind of problem, including vector space model (VSM) (Jeon, Croft, and Lee 2005a; 2005b; Duan et al. 2008), language model (LM) (Jeon, Croft, and Lee 2005b; Duan et al. 2008), and Okapi model (Okapi) (Jeon, Croft, and Lee 2005b). These early approaches are normally based purely on lexical matching techniques in the form of exact string matches for n-grams, as such they will fail to detect similar meaning which is conveyed by synonymous words. To overcome this problem, several approaches have been proposed: Wordnet-based and corpus-based semantic similarity measures, the translation model (TM) (Jeon, Croft, and Lee 2005b; Riezler et al. 2007; Xue, Jeon, and Croft 2008), and translation based language model (TRLM) (Cao et al. 2010).

These bag-of-words based schemas, although proven to be effective for tasks like information retrieval, are often incapable of modelling the matching between complicated and structured objects. Firstly, a text contains both syntactical and lexical information, however bag-of-words models normally put the structural information aside, e.g., the word sequence information. As a result, in some worst cases, though two phrases have the same bag-of-words representation, their real meaning is totally opposite (Socher et al. 2011b). Secondly, pre-defined functions cannot sufficiently take into account the complicated interaction between components within the texts (Lu and Li 2013), thereby making it more reasonable to use a trainable model.

In this research we try to make use of the most basic structural information, word sequence, to help improve the question and answer matching precision. Instead of simply disorganizing text into a set of words, we directly model sentences into an ordered list of vectors, where each unique vector represents a unique word. Both sequential and lexical information are stored in the ordered list of word vectors. Afterwards, the complex interaction between questions and answers is modelled into a similarity matrix (S-matrix). Finally, the pattern of the best matching QA pairs is recovered by a deep architecture. It is believed that this approach is able to explicitly capture the word sequence information and the lexical information in matching two structured objects. The experimental study conducted on a dataset from Baidu Zhidao shows promising results.

The rest of the paper is organised as follows. The proposed model will be illustrated in detail in Section 2. Section 3 covers the experimental study and also learned lessons. Section 4 will present related work in solving the CQA matching problem. Section 5 concludes the paper and highlights possible future research directions.

Methodology

In this paper, we aim to solve the problem of matching questions and answers in a CQA system by considering both lexical meaning and word sequence information. The basic architecture of the proposed model is depicted in Fig. 1, where three parts are included and summarised below:

S1 Questions and answers are represented as an ordered list of word vectors using the neural language model;

S2 The complex interaction between questions and answers is modelled into a two-dimensional matrix "S-matrix";

S3 A deep convolutional neural network is trained to give suitable answer probability.

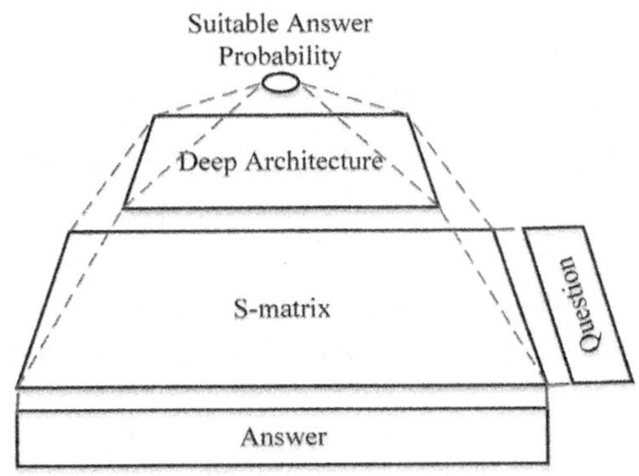

Figure 1: Architecture for Question and Answer Matching Approach

Question/Answer Sentences Representation

The first task of matching questions and answers is to properly present the sentences. In this research we employ the idea of neural language model (Bengio et al. 2006), which is able to jointly learn embedding of words into an n-dimensional vector space and then to use these vectors to predict how likely a word is given its context. One of the popular methods to calculate such embedding information is a model called skip-gram (Mikolov et al. 2013). When skip-gram networks are optimised via gradient ascent, the derivatives will modify the word embedding matrix $L \in R^{(n\times|V|)}$, where $|V|$ is the size of the vocabulary. The word vectors inside the embedding matrix will capture distributional syntactic and semantic information via the word co-occurrence statistics (Bengio et al. 2006; Collobert and Weston 2008; Mikolov et al. 2013).

Once this matrix is learned on an unlabelled corpus, it can be used for subsequent tasks by using each word's vector (a column in L) to represent that word. In the remainder of this paper, we represent a short text as an ordered list of these vectors $(x_1, ..., x_m)$. This representation contains more information than the bag-of-words representation. For example, the sentence "Why don't cat eat mice?" is transformed into a list of vector $(x_{why}, x_{don't}, x_{cat}, x_{eat}, x_{mice})$.

S-matrix

After the sentences in a question/answer pair are properly presented, the next step is to model the complex interaction between questions and answers. We calculate the cosine vector similarity between all words within the two sentences. These similarities fill a matrix as the one shown on the left side of Fig. 2. Consider a pair of question (represented as $(x_1^q, ..., x_n^q)$) and candidate answer (represented as $(x_1^d, ..., x_m^d)$) with the lengths n and m, respectively, it is able to map this pair into a matrix Σ of size $n \times m$, where σ_{ij} is defined as below:

$$\sigma_{ij} = cosine(x_i^q, x_j^d) \quad (1)$$

However, since the matrix dimensions vary according to the sentence lengths, we cannot simply feed the matrix into a standard neural network or classifier. As such in this paper,

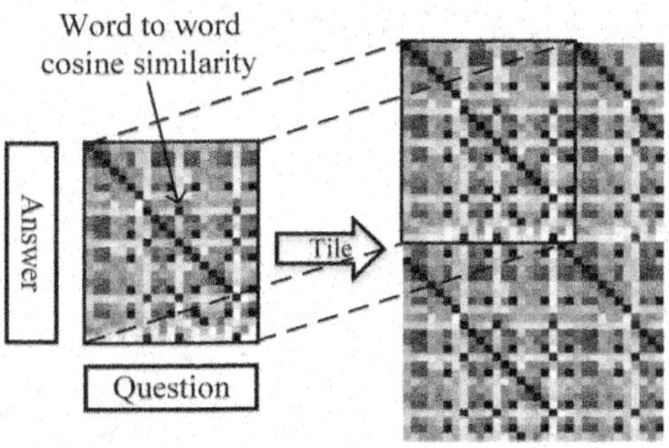

Figure 2: Example of Original Matrix and Tiled Matrix (darker pixel represent higher similarity).

we simply tile the matrix into a larger matrix of fixed size $n_f \times m_f$, as shown in right side of Fig. 2. As a result, it is able to keep all information stored in this matrix during the transformation. The matrix of fixed size is called an S-matrix, denoted by S. Although this approach limits us to deal with question and answer pairs with length smaller than n_f and m_f. In practice, most of the questions and answers in CQA sites are relatively short.

Suitable Answer Probability Estimation

Simply extracting the aggregate statistics of this matrix, such as the average similarity or a histogram of similarities, cannot accurately capture the global structure of the S-matrix. In order to utilise the information stored in the S-matrix to estimate whether the answer is suitable for the question, a deep convolution network (DCNN) (LeCun et al. 1998) is employed to create a function $f(S)$:

$$p_{d|q} = f(S) \tag{2}$$

where $p_{d|q}$ refers to the possibility of the answer d being suitable for the question q.

DCNN are variants of MLPs which are inspired from biology. From Hubel and Wiesel's early work on the cat's visual cortex (Hubel and Wiesel 1962), it is known that there exists a complex arrangement of cells within the visual cortex. These cells are sensitive to small sub-regions of the input space, called receptive fields, and are tiled in such a way as to cover the entire visual field. These filters are local in input space and are thus better suited to exploit the strong spatially local correlation present in natural images[1].

DCNN is employed in this research because the pattern, which signifies whether question and answer are matched, can be found in any part of the original S-matrix. Firstly, the original matrix is tiled into a bigger matrix, thus the same pattern can be repeated many times in the bigger matrix. Secondly, the question can be answered in different parts of the answer body, i.e., head, middle, or end.

The overall structure is illustrated in Fig. 3. The first convolution layer C1 is used to estimate phrase-level match score between the question and the answer. The input hidden units in C1 are connected to a local sub-matrix in the input S. If the k-th feature map at layer C1 is denoted as h^k, whose filters are determined by the weights W^k and bias b_k, x_{ij} denote a sub-matrix of S-matrix, then the feature map h^k is obtained as follows (for tanh non-linearity):

$$h_{ij}^k = tanh((W^k * x_{ij}) + b_k) \tag{3}$$

The matching score for each sub-matrix in S is calculated but only part of these sub-matrices contain useful information. The first max-pooling layer M1 is used to eliminate useless match scores. Max-pooling partitions the input matrix into a set of non-overlapping rectangles and for each such sub-region it outputs the maximum value. Layer C2 is used to estimate sentence-level match score and the input hidden units are connected to a local subset of units in M1. the second max-pooling layer M2 eliminates useless match scores in C2. Finally, a fully connected layer is used to estimate the final match score. Fig. 4 gives us some insights into layer C1 and M1. Convolutional layers C1 and C2 both contain multiple feature maps. Because similarity between phrases and sentences can be evaluated in variety of perspectives (Mikolov et al. 2013), our experiments will further confirm the usefulness of multiple feature maps.

We employ a discriminative training strategy with a large margin objective. Suppose that we are given the following triples (x, y^+, y^-) from the oracle, with x ($\in X$) matched with y^+ better than with y^- (both $\in Y$). We have the following ranking-based loss as objective:

$$L(W, D_{trn}) = \sum_{(x_i, y_i^+, y_i^-) \in D_{trn}} e_W(x_i, y_i^+, y_i^-) \tag{4}$$

where $e_W(x_i, y_i^+, y_i^-)$ is the error for triple (x_i, y_i^+, y_i^-), given by the following large margin form:

$$\begin{aligned} e_i &= e_W(x_i, y_i^+, y_i^-) \\ &= max(0, m_a + s(x_i, y_i^-) - s(x_i, y_i^+)) \end{aligned} \tag{5}$$

with $0 < m_a < 1$ controlling the margin in training.

Experimental Study

Dataset

For the purpose of evaluating and validating the proposed model, a dataset is installed by collecting data from Baidu Zhidao[2], the biggest Chinese CQA site. We randomly collected 438,078 questions throughout March 2013 from this CQA site. Among these questions, 303,588 (69.3%) questions have at least one answer, 196,879 (44.9%) questions have been solved (at least one answer has been marked as the best answer), while 134,490 (30.7%) questions have not received even one answer after 6 months since posting. This finding of question starvation is in accordance with previous report (Li and King 2010).

From this dataset, 196,879 solved questions are employed to create training data and testing data. Since S-matrix limits the maximum length of questions and answers to n_f and m_f, it is necessary to firstly select proper n_f and m_f values. Table 1 shows the number and proportion of questions

[1] http://deeplearning.net/tutorial/lenet.html

[2] http://zhidao.baidu.com/

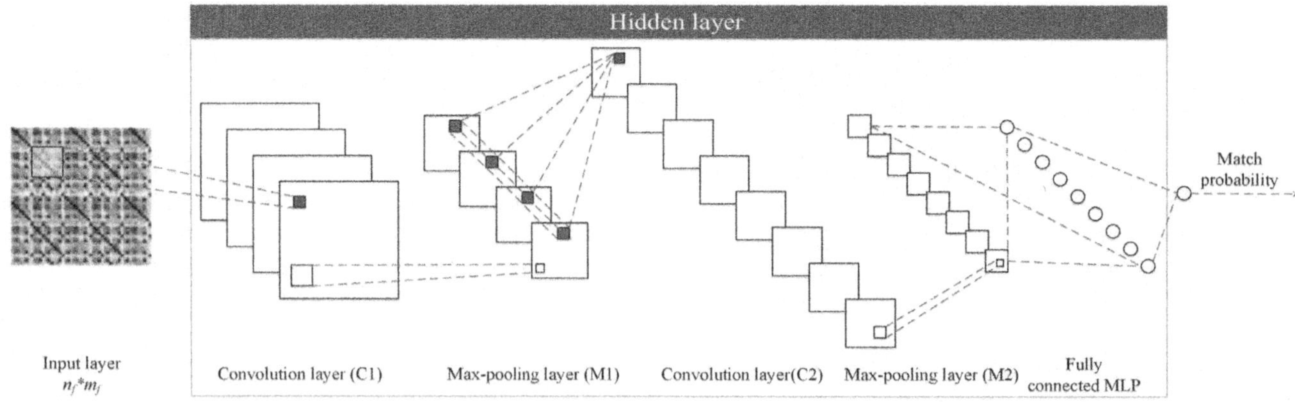

Figure 3: Architecture of Deep Convolutional Neural Network

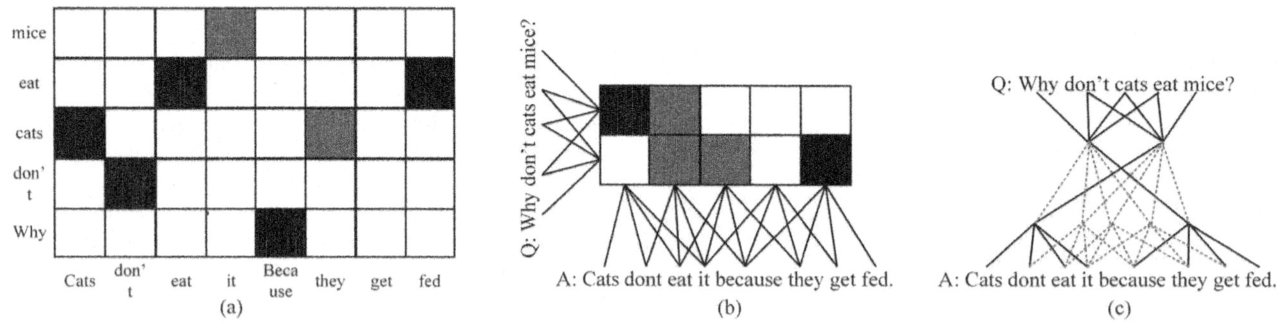

Figure 4: (a) is S-matrix(S) generated from question "Why don't cat eat mice?" and answer "Cats don't eat it because they get fed." (darker grid represents higher similarity or matching score) (b) is layer C1 result of S. In this example, units in C1 are connected to a $4 * 4$ local sub-matrix of S, weight W^k and bias b_k are trained on large QA archive. Layer M1 filters out low similarity grids, keeps high similarity dark grids. (c) emphasises the ability of matching question and answer at phrase level. With convolution layer, n-gram matching score is calculated. With pooling layer, important relation can be identified (solid line in (c)).

Table 1: Number and Coverage proportion of questions with different n_f and m_f

n_f	m_f	Question#	Coverage proportion
30	50	99,909	50.7%
40	60	115,666	58.7%

covered by different n_f and m_f. From the table it is observed that lengths of more than half of question and answer pairs are less than 30 and 50, respectively. Furthermore, if we gradually increase n_f and m_f from $(30, 50)$ to $(40, 60)$, the coverage only increases by 8.0%, but the cost of memory increases by 60%. Thus, it is reasonable to choose $n_f = 30$ and $m_f = 50$ in our experimental study. In real application, this model can be trained with high performance computing platform or parallel training method, n_f and m_f can be increased to several hundreds. As such, much more questions and answers can be covered.

To better evaluate the proposed method, several data subsets are utilised. Firstly, all 99,909 questions are randomly split into training and testing data. Training data contains 90,000 questions and 90,000 (x, y^+, y^-) triples are generated, where x is a solved question, y^+ is the best answer, and y^- is a randomly selected answer which belongs to a random category. Secondly, another 4 groups of 90,000 (x, y^+, y^-) triples are generated. They are noted as training data Tr_2, Tr_3, Tr_4, and Tr_5. Training data Tr_2 contains 18,000 different questions which belong to the category 'Computers & Internet'. Each pair of x and y^+ appear in 5 different triples with different y^-. Consequently, 90,000 different triples are generated. Training data Tr_3, Tr_4, and Tr_5 are produced with same method using questions in "Education & Science", "Games", and "Entertainment & Recreation". The remaining questions in these categories make up testing data Te_2, Te_3, Te_4, and Te_5. Each testing data contain at least 1,000 different questions. All models' parameters are learned from the training data. The hyper parameters are tuned on a validation set (as part of the training set).

Evaluation Metrics & Baseline

In order to evaluate the accuracy of matching questions and answers, a set of candidate answers is created with size 6 (one positive + five negative) for each question in the testing data. In Te_1 negative candidates usually belong to different categories to the questions, while in Te_{2-5} negative candidates always belong to the same category as the question. We compare the performance of our approach in ranking quality of the six candidate answers against that of others baselines. Discounted cumulative gain (DCG) (Järvelin and Kekäläinen 2000) is employed to evaluate the ranking quality. The premise of DCG is that highly relevant documents appearing lower in a ranking list should be penalised as the graded relevance value is reduced logarithmically proportional to the position of the result. DCG accumulated at a particular rank position p is defined as:

$$\text{DCG@p} = rel_1 + \sum_{i=2}^{p} \frac{rel_i}{\log_2(i)} \quad (6)$$

where best answer $rel = 1$, for other answers $rel = 0$. We choose DCG@1 to evaluate the precision of first rank result and DCG@6 to evaluate the quality of ranking, similar to the metrics introduced in (Lu and Li 2013).

We compare our S-matrix + DCNN approach against five popular retrieval models: Okapi model (Okapi) (Jeon, Croft, and Lee 2005b), Language model (LM) (Jeon, Croft, and Lee 2005b; Duan et al. 2008), Translation model (TM) (Jeon, Croft, and Lee 2005b; Riezler et al. 2007; Xue, Jeon, and Croft 2008), Translation based language model (TRLM) (Cao et al. 2010) and Random guess. The model parameters setup are same as in (Cao et al. 2010), but we use word vector cosine similarity for word translation probabilities in TM and TRLM model.

Experiment Settings

After the choice of n_f and m_f, each (x, y^+) and (x, y^-) pair becomes a 30×50 matrix and the training set is then transformed into 180,000 matrixes. Our goal is to train a classifier which can tell whether one matrix is formed by (x, y^+) or (x, y^-). In the following, convolution layers are labelled Cx, and max-pooling layers are labelled Px, where x is the layer index. Each unit in convolutional layer is connected to a 5×5 neighbourhood in the previous layer. Each unit in max-pooling layer Px is connected to a 2×2 neighbourhood in the corresponding feature map in Cx. Layer C1 is a convolutional layer with 20 feature maps. Layer M1 is a max-pooling layer with 20 feature maps. Layer C2 is a convolutional layer with 50 feature maps. Layer M2 is a max-pooling layer with 50 feature maps. Fully connected layer contains 500 units and is fully connected to M2. It has 900,000 trainable parameters in total.

Fig. 5 shows the evolution of nDCG@1 and nDCG@6 with different margin m_a. It is observed that 0.2 is the best choice of m_a. Table 2 shows that multiple feature maps in C1 and C2 achieve better precision than uni-feature map.

Result and Discussion

From Table 3, it is observed that S-matrix + DCNN, TRLM and TM perform better than the other methods on Te_1. This is because word embedding can capture more lexical information than traditional approaches. When comparing S-matrix + DCNN against the TRLM model, we are able to see that the improvement is due to extra structural information.

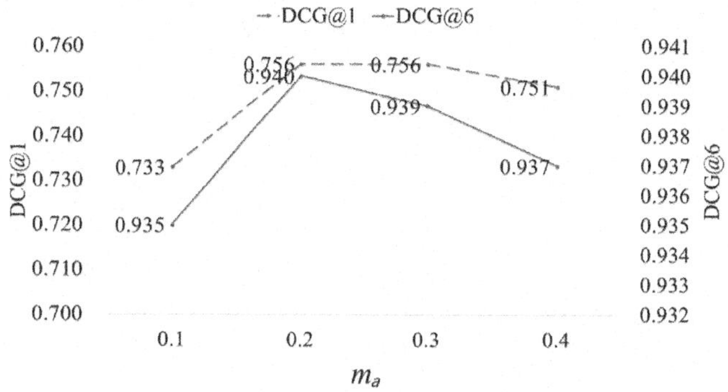

Figure 5: Evolution of DCG@1 and DCG@6 while m increasing

Table 2: Performance difference between uni-feature map and multiple feature map

Feature map in C1 & C2	1-1	20-50
DCG@1	0.691	**0.752**
DCG@6	0.927	**0.943**

Table 3: Performance of different approach on random category training data Te_1

Approach	DCG@1	DCG@6
S-matrix + DCNN (trained on Tr_1)	**0.752**	**0.943**
TRLM	0.696	0.924
TM	0.690	0.922
LM	0.634	0.819
Okapi	0.608	0.807
Random guess	0.167	0.550

From Table 4, it is observed that if the questions and answers are limited to a specific category, accuracy will decrease to some extent. This is because, within a single category, inappropriate answers are more similar to the best answer than random selected answers. In those cases, S-matrix + DCNN can still achieve better performance than traditional approaches. To further analyse the performance, we compared DCNN with Matrix sum (add all similarity together), Multilayer Perceptron (MLP) with a single hidden layer, and Logistic regression. Table 5 shows that DCNN can achieve a better performance than other methods. As such we conclude that DCNN has the ability to discover hidden information in S-matrix due to its ability to exploit the strong spatially local correlations.

Related work

Retrieving relevant historical answers in a large archive of questions and associated answers is an essential function of a CQA site. Most existing works employ bag-of-words based schema. However, in the question/answer matching process both syntactic and lexical information are important, but bag-of-words models remove the order of words. As a

Table 4: Performance of different approaches on mono-category training data Tr_{2-5}, S+DCNN (Tr_i) represents the training data belonging to the same category as the testing data

Approach	Te_2		Te_3		Te_4		Te_5	
	DCG@1	DCG@6	DCG@1	DCG@6	DCG@1	DCG@6	DCG@1	DCG@6
S+DCNN (Tr_i)	**0.658**	**0.912**	0.734	**0.939**	**0.619**	**0.894**	**0.543**	**0.866**
TRLM	0.601	0.885	0.698	0.924	0.562	0.865	0.492	0.843
TM	0.596	0.885	0.691	0.922	0.560	0.863	0.486	0.841
LM	0.624	0.830	**0.746**	0.881	0.544	0.765	0.488	0.740
Okapi	0.567	0.806	0.702	0.869	0.467	0.747	0.446	0.723
Random guess	0.167	0.550	0.167	0.550	0.167	0.550	0.167	0.550

Table 5: Performance of different approaches with the same S-matrix on Te_1

Approach	DCG@1	DCG@6
S-matrix + DCNN (trained on Tr_1)	**0.752**	**0.943**
S-matrix + Matrix sum	0.676	0.929
S-matrix + MLP	0.671	0.926
S-matrix + logistic	0.652	0.920
Random guess	0.167	0.550

result two irrelevant phrases could probably have the same bag-of-words representation (Socher et al. 2011b). To solve this problem, several approaches have been proposed. A solution in (Duan et al. 2008) considers the question structure for retrieval by building a structured tree for questions. Similarly, Bian et al. proposed an interesting learning framework for question retrieval (Bian et al. 2008). However, Wang et al. observed that current parsers are not well-trained for real-life questions, especially in informally stated questions (Wang, Ming, and Chua 2009). These proposed approaches need training data (that are difficult to get for general questions) and the experimental studies are conducted on factoid questions. Inspired by technologies in the image processing field, our work captures both lexical and sequential information in matching process. We focus on matching questions and answers, therefore a large scale of training data can be constructed based on the past question and answer pairs.

Our work is conceptually similar to the dynamic pooling algorithm for paraphrase identification, recently developed by Socher et al. (Socher et al. 2011a). Similar to our proposed model, their model constructs a neural network on the interaction space of two objects (sentences in their case), and outputs the measure of semantic similarity between them. The major differences are two-fold: 1) their model utilises parse trees to capture the structure information of sentences, and finds vector representations for each node of a parse tree using recursive autoencoders; 2) a dynamic pooling model is used to fit the similarity matrix into a fixed shape. Instead, our model employs two convolutional layers to capture the phrase and sentence level structural information, and tile the similarity matrix into a larger matrix: this is a process without loss of information.

Our work is in a sense related to that presented in (Lu and Li 2013). This work directly models object-object interactions with a deep architecture. This architecture is able to explicitly capture the natural non-linearity and the hierarchical structure in matching two structured objects. The main difference between their approach and our approach is that this model is also based on a bag-of-words schema. Their model represents each word with a single value. We use a 100-dimensional word embedding vector to represent words, and multiple senses of similarity between sentences are also considered through multiple feature maps.

Our work is also conceptually related to the convolutional neural network for modelling sentences (Kalchbrenner, Grefenstette, and Blunsom 2014). The idea of using DCNN to model phrase and sentence level property is similar. Different from our work, this work uses DCNN to model single sentence.

Conclusion and Future Works

In this research we presented a novel approach to meet the short text matching problems in CQA applications, inspired partially by the long thread of work on deep learning. The major contribution of this work consists of two parts. Firstly, questions and answers are modelled with an S-matrix by considering both lexical and structural interaction. Secondly, an effective approach of matching question and answer is realised by using a deep convolutional neural network. The experiments have shown the potential of the proposed method as compared against other popular methods. It is believed that this work might offer an insight for information seeking in CQA sites.

Our work opens several interesting new directions for future work. It is possible, for example, to try other word to word similarities, and the similarity between words can be also expressed as a vector as in (Mikolov et al. 2013). It is also interesting to explore the possibility of using this approach to solve other short text matching tasks (e.g., evaluation of machine translation, comment selection on a given tweet): this deserves further investigation in future work.

Acknowledgments

This work was partially supported by the National Natural Science Foundation of China (No. 61332018), the National High Technology Research and Development Program of China (No. 2013AA01A601), and the Fundamental Research Funds for the Central Universities. We are grateful to Shenzhen Key Laboratory of Data Vitalization (Smart City) for supporting this research.

References

Bengio, Y.; Schwenk, H.; Senécal, J.-S.; Morin, F.; and Gauvain, J.-L. 2006. Neural probabilistic language models. In *Innovations in Machine Learning*. Springer. 137–186.

Bian, J.; Liu, Y.; Agichtein, E.; and Zha, H. 2008. Finding the right facts in the crowd: factoid question answering over social media. In *Proceedings of the 17th International Conference on World Wide Web*, 467–476.

Bilotti, M. W.; Elsas, J. L.; Carbonell, J. G.; and Nyberg, E. 2010. Rank learning for factoid question answering with linguistic and semantic constraints. In *Proceedings of the 19th ACM Conference on Information and Knowledge Management*, 459–468.

Cao, X.; Cong, G.; Cui, B.; and Jensen, C. S. 2010. A generalized framework of exploring category information for question retrieval in community question answer archives. In *Proceedings of the 19th International Conference on World Wide Web*, 201–210.

Carmel, D.; Shtalhaim, M.; and Soffer, A. 2000. eresponder: Electronic question responder. In *Proceedings of the 7th International Conference on Cooperative Information Systems*, 150–161.

Chua, A. Y. K., and Banerjee, S. 2013. So fast so good: An analysis of answer quality and answer speed in community question-answering sites. *Journal of the American Society for Information Science and Technology* 64(10):2058–2068.

Collobert, R., and Weston, J. 2008. A unified architecture for natural language processing: deep neural networks with multitask learning. In *Proceedings of the 25th International Conference on Machine Learning*, 160–167.

Dror, G.; Maarek, Y.; and Szpektor, I. 2013. Will my question be answered? predicting "question answerability" in community question-answering sites. In *Proceedings of 2013 European Conference on Machine Learning and Principles and Practice of Knowledge Discovery in Databases, Part III*, 499–514.

Duan, H.; Cao, Y.; Lin, C.; and Yu, Y. 2008. Searching questions by identifying question topic and question focus. In *Proceedings of the 46th Annual Meeting of the Association for Computational Linguistics*, 156–164.

Figueroa, A., and Neumann, G. 2014. Category-specific models for ranking effective paraphrases in community question answering. *Expert Systems with Applications* 41(10):4730–4742.

Hubel, D. H., and Wiesel, T. N. 1962. Receptive fields, binocular interaction and functional architecture in the cat's visual cortex. *The Journal of physiology* 160(1):106–154.

Järvelin, K., and Kekäläinen, J. 2000. IR evaluation methods for retrieving highly relevant documents. In *Proceedings of the 23rd Annual International ACM SIGIR Conference on Research and Development in Information Retrieval*, 41–48.

Jeon, J.; Croft, W. B.; and Lee, J. H. 2005a. Finding semantically similar questions based on their answers. In *Proceedings of the 28th Annual International ACM SIGIR Conference on Research and Development in Information Retrieval*, 617–618.

Jeon, J.; Croft, W. B.; and Lee, J. H. 2005b. Finding similar questions in large question and answer archives. In *Proceedings of the 2005 ACM CIKM International Conference on Information and Knowledge Management*, 84–90.

Kalchbrenner, N.; Grefenstette, E.; and Blunsom, P. 2014. A convolutional neural network for modelling sentences. In *Proceedings of the 52nd Annual Meeting of the Association for Computational Linguistics*, 655–665.

LeCun, Y.; Bottou, L.; Bengio, Y.; and Haffner, P. 1998. Gradient-based learning applied to document recognition. *Proceedings of the IEEE* 86(11):2278–2324.

Li, B., and King, I. 2010. Routing questions to appropriate answerers in community question answering services. In *Proceedings of the 19th ACM Conference on Information and Knowledge Management*, 1585–1588.

Lu, Z., and Li, H. 2013. A deep architecture for matching short texts. In *Proceedings of the 27th Annual Conference on Neural Information Processing Systems*, 1367–1375.

Mikolov, T.; Chen, K.; Corrado, G.; and Dean, J. 2013. Efficient estimation of word representations in vector space. *CoRR* abs/1301.3781.

Riezler, S.; Vasserman, A.; Tsochantaridis, I.; Mittal, V. O.; and Liu, Y. 2007. Statistical machine translation for query expansion in answer retrieval. In *Proceedings of the 45th Annual Meeting of the Association for Computational Linguistics*.

Shtok, A.; Dror, G.; Maarek, Y.; and Szpektor, I. 2012. Learning from the past: answering new questions with past answers. In *Proceedings of the 21st International Conference on World Wide Web*, 759–768.

Socher, R.; Huang, E. H.; Pennington, J.; Ng, A. Y.; and Manning, C. D. 2011a. Dynamic pooling and unfolding recursive autoencoders for paraphrase detection. In *Proceedings of the 25th Annual Conference on Neural Information Processing Systems*, 801–809.

Socher, R.; Pennington, J.; Huang, E. H.; Ng, A. Y.; and Manning, C. D. 2011b. Semi-supervised recursive autoencoders for predicting sentiment distributions. In *Proceedings of the 2011 Conference on Empirical Methods in Natural Language Processing*, 151–161.

Surdeanu, M.; Ciaramita, M.; and Zaragoza, H. 2008. Learning to rank answers on large online QA collections. In *Proceedings of the 46th Annual Meeting of the Association for Computational Linguistics*, 719–727.

Wang, K.; Ming, Z.; and Chua, T. 2009. A syntactic tree matching approach to finding similar questions in community-based QA services. In *Proceedings of the 32nd Annual International ACM SIGIR Conference on Research and Development in Information Retrieval*, 187–194.

Xue, X.; Jeon, J.; and Croft, W. B. 2008. Retrieval models for question and answer archives. In *Proceedings of the 31st Annual International ACM SIGIR Conference on Research and Development in Information Retrieval*, 475–482.

Proceedings of the Twenty-Ninth AAAI Conference on Artificial Intelligence

A Hybrid Approach of Classifier and Clustering for Solving the Missing Node Problem

Sigal Sina
Bar-Ilan University, Israel
sinasi@macs.biu.ac.il

Avi Rosenfeld
Jerusalem College of Technology, Israel
rosenfa@jct.ac.il

Sarit Kraus
Bar-Ilan University, Israel
sarit@cs.biu.ac.il

Navot Akiva
Bar-Ilan University, Israel
navot.akiva@gmail.com

Abstract

An important area of social network research is identifying missing information which is not explicitly represented in the network or is not visible to all. In this paper, we propose a novel **H**ybrid **A**pproach of **C**lassifier and **C**lustering, which we refer to as **HACC**, to solve the *missing node identification* problem in social networks. HACC utilizes a classifier as a preprocessing step in order to integrate all known information into one similarity measure and then uses a clustering algorithm to identify missing nodes. Specifically, we used the information on the network structure, attributes about known users (nodes) and pictorial information to evaluate HACC and found that it performs significantly better than other missing node algorithms. We also argue that HACC is a general approach and domain independent and can be easily applied to other domains. We support this claim by evaluating HACC on a second *authorship identification* domain as well.

Introduction

Data clustering has been used for more than 50 years in order to find a natural grouping of a set of patterns, points, or objects based on similarity or dissimilarity measures (Jain 2010). The main challenge is to find the measures that can improve clustering accuracy. To achieve this goal, in this paper we propose **HACC**, a novel **H**ybrid **A**pproach of **C**lassifier and **C**lustering, for solving the *missing node identification* problem in social networks. Additionally, we argue that our approach is general and domain independent and can be easily applied to other domains. The novelty of HACC is its use of a small collection of labeled objects to tune and learn a classifier as a preprocessing step in order to integrate all known information into one similarity measure. The classifier learning is done only once and in advance, using labeled objects of different clusters than the clusters of the unlabeled data. Later, HACC can use this classifier to facilitate and improve the clustering result of different, large collections of unlabeled objects. To the best of our knowledge, HACC is the first algorithm to combine the use of supervised classifiers as a preprocessing step before activating the unsupervised clustering algorithm of objects of different clusters than the unlabeled ones.

Machine learning methods including clustering and classification are well-established and have been used in a variety of fields (Bishop 2006; Jain 2010). Several researchers have also suggested combining several methods of classification in order to yield better results (Kuncheva 2004). Examples of hybrid methods containing both clustering and classification classification were presented by Nguyen and Armitage, (Nguyen and Armitage 2008) and Shrot et al. (Shrot et al. 2014). However, these works used the clustering algorithm as a first step of unsupervised classification before a second, refinement step of supervised classification. Other work (Basu, Bilenko, and Mooney 2004) suggested a semi-supervised clustering framework, where the performance of unsupervised clustering algorithms can be improved with limited amounts of supervision in the form of labels on the data or constraints. They proposed a principled probabilistic framework based on Hidden Markov Random Fields (HMRFs) for semi-supervised clustering that combined the existing constraint-based and distance-based approaches in a unified model. However, their model assumed that part of objects needs to be clustered is labeled, while in HACC the classifier is learned in advance. Another difference is that the HACC classifier is based on a different set of labeled objects and clusters than the objects currently being processed.

To better understand HACC's novelty, consider the authorship identification domain. Existing works on authorship identification are unsupervised or supervised, where the author's model is learned based on the same author's previous publications (Stamatatos 2009). The generalization of the learned model is for new publications of the same authors, as the tagging of both sets is the same. In contrast, HACC learns models from one set of authors and generalizes its model to identify another set of authors. Here, the generalization is from one set of authors and their publications to identify a new set of authors and their new set of publications. As such, the tagging sets of the learned data and the testing data are different – not only the data points. The advantage of HACC's type of learning is that it facilitates a hybrid model that creates a classifier which is not used for categorization, but instead as input for a second learning model in HACC.

The main contribution of HACC is the way it utilizes a prelearned classifier as a preprocessing step. HACC creates one combined *affinity* measure between each object pair, which is the classifier's *confidence* score, that measures the probability that two objects needing to be clustered will be in the same cluster. We first demonstrate how HACC can be implemented in order to solve the *missing node identification* problem (Eyal, Rosenfeld, and Kraus 2011), which locates and identifies missing nodes within the network. For this domain, we conducted a thorough study which includes an intensive evaluation and analysis of 5 different types of classifiers and 12 different sets of domain features. We show that HACC performs significantly better than other missing node algorithms. To support the claim that HACC is domain independent and can be easily applied to other web domains, we also implemented HACC for an *authorship identification* task and again found that HACC performs significantly better than the baseline algorithm (Akiva and Koppel 2013).

HACC and Problem Definition

HACC proposes combining supervised classifiers as a preprocessing step before activating a clustering algorithm in order to effectively cluster a group of unlabeled objects. The goal of the clustering task is to discover the natural grouping of these unlabeled objects.

Problem Definition Suppose we have a set of data objects, D, which has an inherent clustering scheme and should be clustered into x clusters such that $C(D)$ represents all x clusters. For example, the data's clusters may represent nodes originating from a person within a social network or clusters of documents that an author wrote. D is divided into a set, O, of unlabeled data and a small additional collection of labeled objects $\hat{O}$ from D which is already labeled with its representative clusters. However, $\hat{O} << O$ and no overlap exists between the two sets (i.e. $\hat{O} \cap O = \emptyset$). Additionally, assuming $|C(O)|=K$ and $|C(\hat{O})|=\hat{K}$, then $x = K+\hat{K}$, meaning that the clusters from $\hat{O}$ do not appear within O such that $C(\hat{O}) \cap C(O)=\emptyset$. Our goal is to utilize $\hat{O}$ to help create the best possible division of O to K clusters.

The HACC Algorithm HACC is a two-staged algorithm, where its novelty is how it uses $\hat{O}$ to predict object pairs' *confidence* score in order to improve the clustering performance. The HACC algorithm is defined as follows:

1. Builds a classifier (Offline):
   (i) Inputs vectors of similarity features for all object pairs in $\hat{O}$ together with a label whether or not they belong to the same cluster or not;
   (ii) Returns a probabilistic *confidence* score whether they are in the same cluster.
2. Clusters objects in O (Online):
   (i) Calculates the similarity feature vectors, this time from all pairs of data objects in O, and inputs them into the classifier created at stage one to obtain the *confidence* score for each object pair;
   (ii) Uses the *confidence* scores as a combined *affinity* measure to create an *affinity* matrix for all pairs in O;
   (iii) Runs a clustering algorithm, such as K-means, that uses the *affinity* matrix as its input.

Note that the feature vectors of the classifier are similarity measures and thus are associated with each pair of objects and not with a single object.

The Evaluation Measure We used *purity* as our primary evaluation measure in order to gauge the effectiveness of clustering algorithms as it is an accepted measure of checking the quality and accuracy of clustering algorithms (Strehl and Ghosh 2003). The purity measure is calculated in the following two steps: Step one – each cluster is classified according to the true classification of the majority of samples in that cluster. Here, we classified each cluster according to the most frequent grouping label of the objects in that cluster; Step two – the number of correctly classified samples in all clusters are counted and divided by the number of samples. In our case, the number of samples that are classified is $|O|$. Formally, in our problem setting, where c_k is defined as the set of objects which were assigned to cluster k, and the objective truth for a sample $o \in O$ is denoted $t(o)$, purity is defined as: $purity(C) = \frac{1}{|O|} \sum_k max_{c \in C(O)} |c_k \cap \{o \in O \mid t(o) = c\}|$.

To demonstrate how HACC can be applied to two web domains, we now present a thorough study of the *missing node identification* problem as well as a brief study of the *authorship identification* problem.

The Missing Node Identification Problem

We begin with a background about the *missing node identification* problem. We then formally define the problem which we address, describe how HACC is implemented in this domain, and our experimental setup.

Overview and Background We focus on a specific variation of the missing nodes problem where the missing nodes requiring identification are "friends" of known nodes, as previously done with the MISC and SAMI based algorithms (Eyal, Rosenfeld, and Kraus 2011; Sina, Rosenfeld, and Kraus 2013). An unidentified friend is associated with a "placeholder" node to indicate the existence of the missing friend. Thus, a given missing node may be associated with several "placeholder" nodes, one for each friend of the missing node. Following this approach, the missing node challenge is to try to determine which of the "placeholder" nodes are associated with the same unidentified friend and thus to find the correct clustering of the "placeholder" nodes. To better understand this problem, consider the following example: A hypothetical company, Social News Inc., is running an online news service within LinkedIn. Many LinkedIn members are subscribers of this company's services, yet it would like to expand its customer base. Social News maintains a network of users, which is a subset of the group of LinkedIn users, and the links between these users. The users of LinkedIn who are not members of the service are not visible to their system. Social News Inc. would like to discover the LinkedIn nodes to lure them into joining their service. The company is thus faced with the missing nodes identification problem. By solving this problem, Social News Inc. could improve its advertising techniques and target users who have not yet subscribed to their service.

The *missing node identification* problem has recently generated research interest. Previously, Eyal et al. (Eyal, Rosenfeld, and Kraus 2011; Eyal et al. 2014) presented the MISC algorithm in order to solve this problem. MISC com-

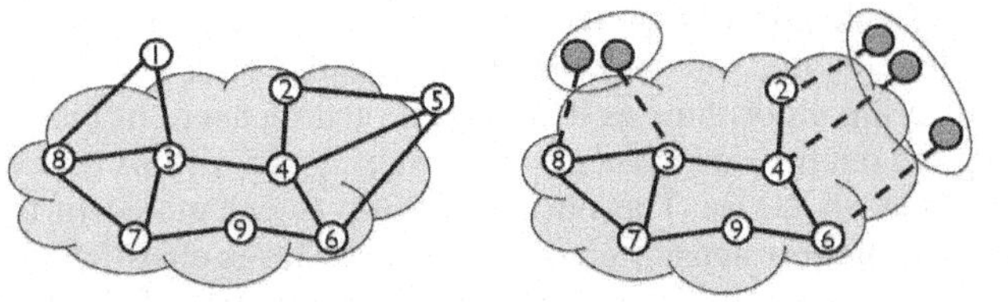

Figure 1: A full network, the known network and the visible network obtained (right) by adding the placeholders for the missing nodes 1 and 5, which need to be united into clusters.

bines spectral clustering algorithms (Ng, Jordan, and Weiss 2001) and metrics built for the missing link problem (Liben-Nowell and Kleinberg 2007). The main idea behind their work was to embed a set of data points, which should be clustered, in a graph structure representing the *affinity* between each pair of points based on the structure of the network. Kim and Leskovec (Kim and Leskovec 2011) tackled the *network completion* problem, which is a similar problem that deals with situations where only a part of the network is observed and the unobserved part must be inferred. They proposed the `KronEM` algorithm, which uses an Expectation Maximization approach and where the observed portion of the network is used to fit a Kronecker graph model of the full network structure. Sina et al. (Sina, Rosenfeld, and Kraus 2013) extended the *missing node identification* problem by considering how to incorporate information about the known nodes in the network in order to improve performance. They presented the `SAMI-A` and `SAMI-N` algorithms, which used different ways to integrate the additional attributes' information about the known nodes with the network structure's *affinity* measure. They showed that these algorithms, which leverage the additional information, achieve predictions with significantly better quality than both the `KronEM` and `MISC` algorithms, which only used information about the network's structure. However, none of these previous works considered how to generally incorporate information, including pictorial information which has become ubiquitous in many social networks, as we do in this work. The challenge in this type of data is that it requires a model that can handle missing features as many of the nodes have no pictures.

The idea of using information from specific nodes was previously considered in a variety of different problems. Several previous works (Gong et al. 2011; Yin et al. 2010) proposed a model to jointly infer missing links and missing node attributes by representing the social network as an augmented graph where the nodes' attributes are represented as special nodes in the network. Other approaches studied different ways of leveraging information about known nodes within the network in order to better solve the missing link or missing attribute problems. For example, Freno et al. (Freno, Garriga, and Keller 2011) proposed a supervised learning method which uses both the graph structure and node attributes to recommend missing links. Pictures in social networks are also considered in a variety of different problems. These problems include cascade prediction in the network (Cheng et al. 2014), placing images on the world map (Hauff and Houben 2012) and learning influence in the social network (Goyal, Bonchi, and Lakshmanan 2010). However, these works use the pictures' descriptions, tags and some properties, such as color histograms, but do not consider the relative similarity of pictures as in the PIC measure we propose.

Problem Definition We assume that there is a social network represented as an undirected graph G=(V, E), in which n=$|V|$ and e=$\langle v,u\rangle \in E$ represents an interaction between $v \in V$ and $u \in V$. In addition to the network structure, each node $v_i \in V$ is associated with an attribute vector $\vec{AV_i}$ of length l and a set of pictures IM_i of size l_2. We assume that each attribute in the attribute vectors is a binary value, i.e. each node has or does not have the attribute. Formally, we define a binary attribute matrix A of size nxl where $A_{i,j}$ indicates whether or not a node $v_i \in V$ has an attribute j. Some of the nodes in the network are missing and are not known to the system. We denote the set of missing nodes $V_m \subset V$, and assume that the number of missing nodes is given as K=$|V_m|$.

We denote the rest of the nodes as known, i.e., V_k=$V \setminus V_m$, and the set of known edges is $E_k = \{\langle v,u\rangle \mid v,u \in V_k \wedge \langle v,u\rangle \in E\}$. In order to identify the missing nodes, we focus on the visible part of the network that is available G_a=(V_a, E_a). In this network, each of the missing nodes is replaced by a set of placeholders. Formally, we define a set V_p for placeholders and a set E_p for the associated edges. For each missing node $v \in V_m$ and for each edge $\langle v,u\rangle \in E$, $u \in V_k$, a placeholder is created. That is, for each original edge $\langle v,u\rangle$ we assume that there is a placeholder v' for v in V_p and the placeholder is connected to the node u with a new edge $\langle v',u\rangle$, which belongs to E_p. When these components are considered together, V_a=$V_k \cup V_p$ and E_a=$E_k \cup E_p$. As for a given missing node v, there may be many placeholders in V_p. The missing node challenge is to try to determine which of the placeholders should be clustered together and associated with the original v, thus allowing us to reconstruct the original social network G.

To better understand this formalization, consider the following example: Assume we have a gamers' network where users may choose to register or remain anonymous before playing. An edge between two users indicates that these two users played a game together. We might have additional information regarding the registered users, such as pictures, origin, group membership and playing time. We consider the registered users to be the known nodes, while the anonymous users are the placeholders. We would like to identify which of the anonymous users are actually the same person.

Domain Features The success of a clustering algorithm depends on its *affinity* matrix - a calculated measure between each pair of nodes in the network, which is used to determine which of the placeholders are associated with the same source node. In `HACC`, we input vectors of similarity features for all node pairs to create the classifier model. This model returns as output a *confidence* score which is entered into a matrix and then used for the clustering algorithm. We considered as input a variety of known similarity measures as fields within the vectors. These include features based on network structure that were previously studied (Eyal, Rosenfeld, and Kraus 2011). Specifically, we used the two structure similarity measures that previously yielded the best results: the Relative Common Neighbors (RCN) measure (Liben-Nowell and Kleinberg 2007) and the Adamic/Adar (AA) measure (Adamic and Adar 2003), and a third structure similarity measure which is the combination of the two measures (RCN+AA), formally defined as $(RCN{+}AA)_{ij}{=}\frac{1}{2}(RCN_{ij}{+}AA_{ij})$. Additionally, we used two other similarity measures which are not based on the general structure of the network, but similarities between the attributes of a specific pair of nodes, v_i and v_j. The first measure is based on a previously developed measure of the common attributes between nodes (ATT) (Sina, Rosenfeld, and Kraus 2013) and a second measure based on picture similarity (PIC) is new to this work. We defined the picture similarity, PIC, as: $PIC_{ij}{=}MatchConf(i,j)$, where $MatchConf(i,j)$ represents the highest matching confidence between the pictures associated with nodes i and j, and zero if one of the nodes does not have any pictures. To calculate the matching confidence, we used a free web service for face detection and recognition http://betafaceapi.com/.

The MI-HACC Algorithm

Algorithm 1 (`MI-Alg`) presents the pseudocode for solving the *missing node identification* problem. The strength of the `HACC` approach is the novel way the *affinity* matrix is calculated in line 1. Our proposed algorithm, which we refer to as **`MIC`** (**M**issing node **I**dentification using a **C**lassifier) uses the `MI-Alg` algorithm as the basis of the implementation of the `HACC` approach. We implemented several variations of the `MIC` algorithm for different types of classifiers and different subsets of node features as input (defined above). First, and only once offline, we calculated the feature vectors which are composed of the similarity measures of structure, attributes and pictures for the *training* dataset, and used them to learn and store 5 types of classifiers: decision tree (tree), neural network (nnet), k-nearest-neighbors (kNN), AdaBoost and Bayes. During runtime for each one of the learned classifiers, we calculated the selected similarity measures for the *test* dataset, used it as the classifier's input and set the pairwise *affinity* according to the classifier *confidence* score for each pair of nodes. We created 4 data type variations for each one of the classifiers which contained a different subset of the similarity measures: the first was based on structure only (S), the second on structure and attributes (SA), the third on the structure and pictures (SP), and last on the structure, pictures and attributes (SAP). For example, we define the matrix of affinity measures for the decision tree classifier with the SAP variation $MC^{Tree\text{-}SAP-RCN}$ using the RCN measure as: $MC_{ij}^{Tree\text{-}SAP-RCN} = predict(tree, RCN_{ij}, PIC_{ij}, ATT_{ij})$. Overall there are 60 instances of the `MIC` algorithm: 5 classifier types (tree, nnet, kNN, AdaBoost and Bayes), 4 data types (S,SA,SP and SAP) and 3 structure similarity types (RCN,AA and RCN+AA).

Note that although `MI-Alg` is a generalization of the `MISC` algorithm (Eyal, Rosenfeld, and Kraus 2011), it also introduces a major change in addition to `HACC`'s novel calculation of the *affinity* matrix. In contrast to `MISC`, `MI-Alg` no longer processes the affinity measures of missing nodes through spectral clustering but instead exclusively uses the K-means clustering algorithm on the placeholders' affinity matrix. We chose to implement this change for two reasons: First, we wanted to improve the performance of the original `MISC` algorithm in large-scale networks. `MISC` applies spectral clustering to the affinity matrix of the entire network (of both known nodes and placeholders), while `MI-Alg` applies K-means only on the matrix of a small number of placeholder nodes; Second, we had to overcome a memory consumption challenge caused by the ATT measure calculation, which only yielded a partial solution in previous work (Sina, Rosenfeld, and Kraus 2013). Our preliminary tests show that this change improved the runtime and memory consumption without performance degradation.

Algorithm 1 MI-Alg (Missing node **I**dentification)

`Input`: $G_k{=}\langle V_k, E_k\rangle$ – the known part of the network
$G_a{=}\langle V_a, E_a\rangle$ – the available visible part of the network
K – the number of missing nodes
V_p – the placeholder nodes
$\alpha : G(V,E) \rightarrow \mathbb{R}^{|V_p|\times|V_p|}$ – a procedure for calculating the affinity matrix of placeholder nodes in a graph
`Output`: $C \in \mathbb{N}^{|V_a \setminus V_k|}$ - a vector indicating the cluster index of each placeholder node,
$\hat{G}{=}\left(\hat{V},\hat{E}\right)$ – prediction of the full network graph

1: $\mathbf{A} \leftarrow \alpha(G_a)$ – calculate the affinity matrix of the placeholder nodes in the graph
2: C $\leftarrow$ *k_means(***A***,N)* – cluster the rows which match the placeholder nodes to K clusters
3: $\hat{V} \leftarrow V_k$, $\hat{E} \leftarrow E_k$ – initialize the output graph to contain the known network
4: For each cluster $c \in C$ create a new node $v_c \in \hat{V}$
5: For each placeholder v in cluster c and edge $(u,v) \in E_a$, create an edge $(u,v_c) \in \hat{E}$
6: Return C, $\hat{G}{=}\left(\hat{V},\hat{E}\right)$

The Dataset and The Experimental Setup

We used a previously developed social network dataset, Steam (Becker et al. 2012) (http://steamcommunity.com), to empirically evaluate our work. The Steam community network is a large social network of players on the Steam gaming platform. The data we applied is from 2011 and contains 9 million nodes ("anonymous" users) and 82 million friendship edges. Each user had the following data: country (the origin of the user; 50% voluntarily provided their country), member since (the date when the user opened his Steam account), a list of game playing times and a list of group memberships. We chose three groups of attributes: country, playing time and player group association. These three groups formed a total of 60 attributes – one for the country, 20 attributes of different game playing times and 39 different official associations. We first crawled the social network and only selected nodes that had at least 2 games or groups. This crawling reduced the dataset size to 1.3 million nodes (users). We then extracted different network samples, using a Forest Fire (FF) walk (Leskovec and Faloutsos 2006). We crawled a 16K network from this reduced dataset, marked it as the *training* dataset and removed the nodes from the dataset. We then re-sampled the 16K node *training* dataset to extract several 2K *training* networks, which we used as $\hat{O}$ for learning the MIC classifiers and the parameters of the comparison algorithm MIWS (described below). Lastly we extracted several *test* networks O of different sizes from the remaining dataset. As the Steam dataset did not have pictures, we then added public pictures from Facebook's users who elected to make their Facebook profiles public. We crawled 100 sets of pictures from 100 randomly selected users from this directory and saved them anonymously. Each set contained 3-8 pictures from a specific profile. We used 50 sets for our *training* dataset and the other 50 sets for the test dataset. For each two pictures in each of the picture datasets (training/test), we calculated the matching confidence probability using Betafaceapi, a free web service for face detection and recognition package (http://betafaceapi.com/). Most of the pictures (80%) contained only 1 figure, while the others contained 2 or more figures. In this case, we used the highest calculated matching confidence probability.

Experimental Setup The experimental setup began by sampling a network from the dataset. This sampling was repeated 10 times, each starting from a different random node, in order to avoid randomization errors and biases, creating 10 different networks for each size. In the following step, K nodes were randomly selected as missing nodes. Each one of these nodes was then randomly associated with one of the picture sets. This was repeated 10 times from each one of the networks, resulting in different random instances of the problem setting for each combination of graph sizes and K. The randomly selected missing nodes were removed from each instance. Each missing node was replaced with a placeholder for each of its links to remaining nodes in the network. Each such placeholder was associated with one picture of the removed node. If the node had fewer pictures than numbers of links, some of the placeholders would not have an associated picture (on average only 54% of the placeholders had an attached picture). The resulting graph was inputted into the algorithm, which produced a clustering of the placeholders. By uniting the placeholders in each cluster into a new node and connecting the new node to the neighbors of the placeholders in the corresponding cluster, the algorithms created a predicted network. The goal of these algorithms was to predict a network that resembled the structure of the original network from which the random nodes were removed. The clustering produced by the algorithms was evaluated using the purity measure described above, and the average purity value achieved for all of the instances and/or for the instances of a specific K was reported. This result was also averaged over the different instances and/or for the instances of a specific K and was reported as well.

The Comparison Algorithm We compared our algorithm to a baseline, denoted **MIWS** (**M**issing node **I**dentification using a **W**eighted **S**um), which is a generalization of the previously published SAMI-A algorithm (Sina, Rosenfeld, and Kraus 2013)[1]. MIWS calculates an *affinity* measure based on a weighted sum between the 3 types of similarity measures: structure, attributes and pictures. Formally, we define the matrix of affinity measures MA^{RCN} using the RCN measure as: $MA^{RCN}_{ij} = (1-w_a-w_p)*RCN_{ij}+w_a*ATT_{ij}+w_p*PIC_{ij}$ where w_a is an input parameter that represents the relative weight of the attributes' similarity measure and w_p is an input parameter that represents the relative weight of the pictures' similarity measure. Similarly, we define MA^{AA}_{ij} for the AA measure and MA^{RCN+AA}_{ij} with the average of the RCN and AA measures. Here we also considered different subsets of similarity measures, thus overall there were 12 instances of the MIWS algorithm: 4 data types (S,SA,SP and SAP) and 3 structure similarity types (RCN,AA and RCN+AA).

Training the Algorithms

We used the training datasets to empirically learn the domain dependent classifiers for MIC and the domain optimal weights w_a and w_p for the comparison algorithm MIWS.

The Classifiers For the MIC algorithms, we used the *training* datasets to learn the 5 types of classifiers (tree, nnet, kNN, AdaBoost and Bayes) with the 4 data types (S,SA,SP and SAP) and 3 structure affinity types (RCN,AA and RCN+AA). Using the 2K *training* sample networks and the 50 *training* sets of pictures, we calculated the 5 affinity measures (RCN, AA, RCN+AA, ATT and PIC) for the 50 missing nodes configuration and saved the data as a list of rows as follows. For each two placeholders, i, j (i≠j), the row includes the affinity measures (RCN_{ij}, AA_{ij}, $RCN+AA_{ij}$,ATT_{ij}, PIC_{ij}) and an additional I_{ij} value of 1 or 0, which indicates whether or not the two placeholders originated from the same node. We repeated the run 10 times over the six training networks. As this data was unbalanced (only 2% of the data have an indicator I_{ij} of value 1), we undersampled the rows with an indicator I_{ij} of value 0, using a uniform probability of 5%. This undersampling produced data in which 28% of the rows had an indicator I_{ij} of value 1. We used this data to train and save the 60 variations of classifiers (using Matlab 2013). To evaluate these classifiers, we generated test data using an additional 2 runs over the six training networks. This time we did not undersample the data. We found that the average of the accuracy and precision (for class 0) measures were usually (all excluding kNN) high (over 95%), while the recall values (for class 1) were between 48%-65%.

The Weight Parameters In the MIWS algorithms, the weights w_a and w_p are used for the weighted sum between the structure affinity, the attributes affinity and the pictures affinity. We ran the MIWS algorithm with 3 data types (SA,SP and SAP) and 3 structure similarity types (RCN,AA and RCN+AA) using the 2K *training* sample networks, the same 5 missing node values (10, 20, 30,

[1]We chose not to compare MIC to the original MISC algorithm, which uses spectral clustering, nor to KronEM, another recently developed algorithm which only uses the network graph structure, as our preliminary tests showed that MIWS outperformed both of these algorithms.

40 and 50) and a range of weights between 0.2 and 0.8 with steps of 0.1. We repeated the run 10 times over the six training networks we had. Based on the *training* results, the best results for the SA and SP data types were achieved with w_a=0.5 for MIWS-SA-RCN and w_a=0.6 for both MIWS-SA-AA and MIWS-SA-RCN+AA, w_p=0.5 for both MIWS-SP-RCN and MIWS-SP-AA and w_p=0.4 for MIWS-SA-RCN+AA. For the SAP data type, the best results were achieved with w_a=0.3, w_a=0.3 for MIWS-SAP-RCN and w_a=0.5 and w_a=0.2 for both MIWS-SAP-AA and MIWS-SAP-RCN+AA.

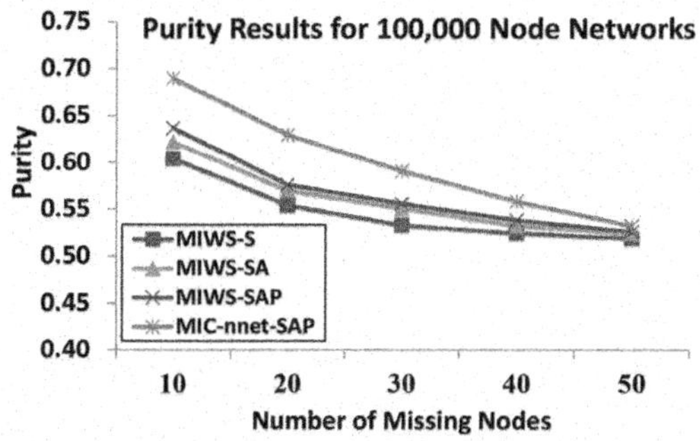

(a) Different missing nodes

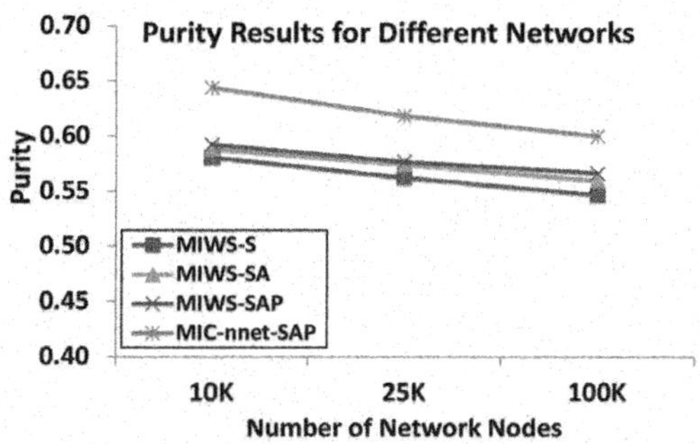

(b) Different network sizes

Figure 2: The purity results with the RCN+AA measure.

Evaluation and Results

We evaluated the two sets of configurations for the MIC and MIWS algorithms. We proceeded to compare the 10 networks of sizes 10K, 25K and 100K described above where we randomly removed sets of 10, 20, 30, 40, and 50 missing nodes. We repeated each configuration 10 times to obtain 100 results for each one of the missing nodes' values. Table 1 shows the average results for all missing node values for the different algorithm variations for the 10K, 25K and 100K node networks. MIC-nnet-SAP for all 3 variations of structure affinity (with no significant difference found between their results) outperformed MIWS and also all other MIC variations for all network sizes. For example, the result for the 100K node networks of RCN+AA MIC-nnet-SAP was found to be significantly better compared to RCN+AA MIWS-SAP (the ANOVA results at 0.05 is 4.75E-54). The results also confirm our claim that the additional pictorial information can improve the missing node identification compared to the previously known algorithms (MIWS-S and MIWS-SA) as depicted in Figure 2. This improvement is also true for MIC. For example, the results with the AA measure of MIC-nnet-SAP and MIC-nnet-SP were found to be significantly better than MIC-nnet-SA and MIC-nnet-S (the ANOVA results at the 0.05 level are p=4.49E-22, 2.78E-53, 0.16E-2 and 2.48E-22, respectively). Moreover, the results also show that HACC outperformed the previous algorithm even when a single, same feature such as the structure feature is exclusively considered. Table 1 shows that the MIC-nnet-S provided better results than MIWS-S for the 3 variations of structure affinity.

The Authorship Identification Problem

To demonstrate the generality of HACC, we chose to implement it on a second *authorship identification* task. Similar to the *missing node identification* problem, in this task there also were objects that needed to be identified as originating from a person. However, in this task instead of finding missing nodes, we needed to identify which anonymous documents originated from a given person.

Overview and Background Authorship analysis has a long history and the problem of clustering a set of anonymous documents according to authorship has been extensively explored (Stamatatos 2009). While the research originally started by focusing on literary works of disputed or unknown authorship, it also has been extended to web applications for purposes such as verifying the authorship of emails, blogs and web talkbacks (Cheng, Chandramouli, and Subbalakshmi 2011). Recent work (Layton, Watters, and Dazeley 2013) tried to cluster multiple documents, each of which written by a single author, while other work (Akiva and Koppel 2013) focused on a harder problem that aimed to segment a single unsegmented document according to authorship, with no guarantee that any unit longer than a single sentence was written by a single author. Other works also considered the problem of author identification or decomposing a document according to authorship, but their methods were supervised (Stamatatos 2007; Graham, Hirst, and Marthi 2005).

Problem Definition We studied the previously proposed author-clustering problem variation (Layton, Watters, and Dazeley 2013; Akiva and Koppel 2013). Briefly, given a collection of unlabeled texts taken from the works of multiple authors, our objective was to divide the texts of the respective authors into sets, given the number K of authors.

Domain Features We considered the M words that appear in the greatest number of different articles in the combined corpus as previously done (Akiva and Koppel 2013). We used two variations of this vector, one with a binary representation of a text and the other with its frequency. Accordingly, we calculated two similarity features for each pair of texts: one based on the binary vectors (Ratio) and the other based on the vectors with the word frequency (Cosine).

The AI-HACC Algorithm For the HACC implementation, we first found the M words that appeared in the greatest number of different articles and for each pair of texts we calculated the Ratio and the Cosine measures. We tuned the classifier in the same way we did for the *Missing Node Identification*, using a different *training* dataset (described next),

Table 1: The purity results for the 10K, 25K and 100K node networks.

	Data Type	S			SA			SP			SAP		
	Algorithm	RCN	AA	RCN+AA	RCN	AA	RCN+AA	RCN	AA	RCN+AA	RCN	AA	RCN+AA
10K	MIWS	0.5921	0.5666	0.5804	0.5986	0.5767	0.5879	0.5984	0.5729	0.5866	0.6029	0.5810	0.5921
	MIC-tree	0.5933	0.5887	0.5904	0.5922	0.5895	0.5900	0.6286	0.6203	0.6259	0.6279	0.6219	0.6278
	MIC-nnet	0.5956	0.5946	0.5950	0.6012	0.6017	0.5997	0.6397	0.6317	0.6409	0.6423	0.6412	0.6437
	MIC-kNN	0.5687	0.5672	0.5730	0.4880	0.4851	0.4921	0.4485	0.4495	0.4532	0.5139	0.5087	0.5139
	MIC-AdaBoost	0.5927	0.5864	0.5898	0.5933	0.5798	0.5912	0.5123	0.5087	0.5154	0.5186	0.5140	0.5193
	MIC-Bayes	0.5853	0.5412	0.5860	0.5835	0.5297	0.5851	0.5860	0.5448	0.5880	0.5837	0.5360	0.5861
25K	MIWS	0.5675	0.5497	0.5622	0.5762	0.5652	0.5743	0.5809	0.5570	0.5715	0.5812	0.5693	0.5765
	MIC-tree	0.5729	0.5739	0.5705	0.5723	0.5728	0.5702	0.5991	0.5967	0.5993	0.6009	0.6011	0.6008
	MIC-nnet	0.5773	0.5778	0.5774	0.5868	0.5868	0.5864	0.6149	0.6080	0.6139	0.6185	0.6174	0.6182
	MIC-kNN	0.5481	0.5541	0.5557	0.4617	0.4613	0.4628	0.4255	0.4274	0.4266	0.4815	0.4824	0.4817
	MIC-AdaBoost	0.5718	0.5692	0.5693	0.5700	0.5625	0.5692	0.4788	0.4798	0.4793	0.4883	0.4856	0.4878
	MIC-Bayes	0.5613	0.5044	0.5603	0.5588	0.5016	0.5601	0.5600	0.5074	0.5606	0.5600	0.5089	0.5610
100K	MIWS	0.5475	0.5369	0.5465	0.5545	0.5545	0.5597	0.5670	0.5520	0.5625	0.5601	0.5551	0.5662
	MIC-tree	0.5557	0.5581	0.5529	0.5543	0.5577	0.5537	0.5755	0.5760	0.5744	0.5795	0.5842	0.5791
	MIC-nnet	0.5616	0.5633	0.5607	0.5753	0.5794	0.5751	0.5927	0.5863	0.5909	0.5989	0.6010	0.5999
	MIC-kNN	0.5251	0.5359	0.5308	0.4340	0.4406	0.4343	0.3984	0.4040	0.4021	0.4461	0.4494	0.4472
	MIC-AdaBoost	0.5550	0.5543	0.5453	0.5470	0.5439	0.5488	0.4530	0.4563	0.4531	0.4635	0.4653	0.4632
	MIC-Bayes	0.5292	0.4640	0.5293	0.5287	0.4649	0.5290	0.5310	0.4677	0.5291	0.5296	0.4704	0.5299

and the classifier *confidence* score as the affinity measure for the K-means clustering algorithm.

The Dataset and the Experimental Setup For our experiments, we used texts on the same topic from the Reuters Corpus Volume 1 (RCV1). Specifically, we used the Reuter-50-50 dataset[2], which contains an online database with 5000 classified articles, 100 articles of 50 authors, divided into training and test sets for each author. One advantage of this dataset was its generality. It had been previously used in web classification tasks such as gender identification in e-mails, blogs and chatrooms (Cheng, Chandramouli, and Subbalakshmi 2011).

Our algorithm used 10 authors as a *training* dataset, $\hat{O}$, to learn the classifiers, and the other 40 authors as the *test* dataset, O, for comparison. The experimental setup began by choosing K authors randomly. It then chose 2-8 random texts for each of the K chosen authors. These selected texts were then delivered to the different algorithms. Finally we calculated the purity of the clustering results for each one of the algorithms according to their labels in the dataset.

The Comparison Algorithm We compared `HACC` to the algorithm presented in (Akiva and Koppel 2013) for the author-clustering problem. Their algorithm, which we denote `AkivaKoppel`, considers only the M words that appear in the greatest number of different articles in the combined corpus and uses only the binary vector representation of a text. Their algorithm takes the binary vectors as input, calculates the similarity measure between each pair of texts and delivers it to the n-cut clustering algorithm.

Evaluation and Results We repeated the experiment 40 times with K=10,20,30,40, which produced 160 different problem instances. We tested 3 configurations using the most common M words (M=500,1000,1500) that appear across the articles. For the `HACC` algorithm, we used a neural network classifier which previously provided the best results. Note that in the 1500 word configuration, the features calculation in `HACC` was done using all of the words. Table 2 shows the average purity results over all the runs with the different selection of the top words for the `AvikaKoppel` and `HACC-nnet`. Overall, `HACC-nnet` outperformed `AvikaKoppel` and demonstrated that the additional step of tuning a classifier in the *training* set can improve the authorship identification solution.

[2]Dataset creator and donator: Zhi Liu, liuzhi8673@gmail.com, National Engineering Research Center for E-Learning, China.

Table 2: Author identification purity results.

Algorithm	500	1000	1500*
AvikaKoppel	0.5058	0.5340	0.5418
HACC-nnet	0.5392	0.5617	0.5786

Conclusions and Future Work

This paper represents, to the best of our knowledge, the first work to combine supervised classifiers on clusters different than the clusters of the unlabeled objects as a preprocessing step before activating the clustering algorithm in order to divide a group of objects into K separate sets. The general `HACC` approach is particularly suitable when additional information is available which can be incorporated in a quick and efficient way. We believe that we also are the first to study the *missing node identification* problem by including information from pictures (which become more ubiquitous) together with the network structure and the attribute information of known nodes. Including pictorial data introduces a new research challenge as it requires a model that can handle missing features as many nodes have no pictures. The main key contributions of this paper are: (i) demonstration of how the novel `HACC` approach first utilizes a classifier as a preprocessing step in order to create one combined *affinity* component measure and (ii) showing that this general algorithm can be used to outperform known algorithms in web learning tasks such as the *missing node identification* problem and the *authorship identification* task. In the future, we would like to further explore the potential of our novel approach with other datasets, different domains and different similarity measures.

Acknowledgment

This research is based on work supported in part by MAFAT and ISRAEL SCIENCE FOUNDATION (grant #1488/14).

References

Adamic, L. A., and Adar, E. 2003. Friends and neighbors on the web. *Social Networks* 25(3):211–230.

Akiva, N., and Koppel, M. 2013. A generic unsupervised method for decomposing multi-author documents. *Journal of the American Society for Information Science and Technology* 64(11):2256–2264.

Basu, S.; Bilenko, M.; and Mooney, R. J. 2004. A probabilistic framework for semi-supervised clustering. In *Proceedings of the tenth ACM SIGKDD international conference on Knowledge discovery and data mining*, 59–68. ACM.

Becker, R.; Chernihov, Y.; Shavitt, Y.; and Zilberman, N. 2012. An analysis of the steam community network evolution. In *Electrical & Electronics Engineers in Israel (IEEEI), 2012 IEEE 27th Convention of*, 1–5. IEEE.

Bishop, C. M. 2006. *Pattern recognition and machine learning*, volume 1. Springer New York.

Cheng, J.; Adamic, L.; Dow, P. A.; Kleinberg, J. M.; and Leskovec, J. 2014. Can cascades be predicted? In *Proc of the 23rd international conference on WWW*, 925–936. International World Wide Web Conferences Steering Committee.

Cheng, N.; Chandramouli, R.; and Subbalakshmi, K. 2011. Author gender identification from text. *Digital Investigation* 8(1):78 – 88.

Eyal, R.; Rosenfeld, A.; Sina, S.; and Kraus, S. 2014. Predicting and identifying missing node information in social networks. *To Appear at ACM Transactions on Knowledge Discovery from Data (TKDD)*.

Eyal, R.; Rosenfeld, A.; and Kraus, S. 2011. Identifying missing node information in social networks. In *Twenty-Fifth AAAI Conference on Artificial Intelligence*.

Freno, A.; Garriga, C., G.; and Keller, M. 2011. Learning to Recommend Links using Graph Structure and Node Content. In *Neural Information Processing Systems Workshop on Choice Models and Preference Learning*.

Gong, N. Z.; Talwalkar, A.; Mackey, L. W.; Huang, L.; Shin, E. C. R.; Stefanov, E.; Shi, E.; and Song, D. 2011. Predicting links and inferring attributes using a social-attribute network (san). *CoRR*.

Goyal, A.; Bonchi, F.; and Lakshmanan, L. V. 2010. Learning influence probabilities in social networks. In *Proceedings of the third ACM international conference on Web search and data mining*, 241–250. ACM.

Graham, N.; Hirst, G.; and Marthi, B. 2005. Segmenting documents by stylistic character. *Natural Language Engineering* 11(04):397–415.

Hauff, C., and Houben, G.-J. 2012. Placing images on the world map: a microblog-based enrichment approach. In *Proc of the 35th international ACM SIGIR conference on Research and development in information retrieval*, 691–700. ACM.

Jain, A. K. 2010. Data clustering: 50 years beyond k-means. *Pattern Recognition Letters* 31(8):651–666.

Kim, M., and Leskovec, J. 2011. The network completion problem: Inferring missing nodes and edges in networks. *SIAM International Conference on Data Mining (SDM), 2011*.

Kuncheva, L. I. 2004. *Combining pattern classifiers: methods and algorithms*. John Wiley & Sons.

Layton, R.; Watters, P.; and Dazeley, R. 2013. Automated unsupervised authorship analysis using evidence accumulation clustering. *Natural Language Engineering* 19(01):95–120.

Leskovec, J., and Faloutsos, C. 2006. Sampling from large graphs. In *Proceedings of the 12th ACM SIGKDD international conference on Knowledge discovery and data mining*, 631–636. ACM.

Liben-Nowell, D., and Kleinberg, J. 2007. The link-prediction problem for social networks. *Journal of the American Society for Information Science and Technology* 58(7):1019–1031.

Ng, A. Y.; Jordan, M. I.; and Weiss, Y. 2001. On spectral clustering: Analysis and an algorithm. In *Advances in Neural Information Processing Systems 14*, 849–856. MIT Press.

Nguyen, T. T., and Armitage, G. 2008. A survey of techniques for internet traffic classification using machine learning. *Communications Surveys & Tutorials, IEEE* 10(4):56–76.

Shrot, T.; Rosenfeld, A.; Golbeck, J.; and Kraus, S. 2014. Crisp: an interruption management algorithm based on collaborative filtering. In *CHI*, 3035–3044.

Sina, S.; Rosenfeld, A.; and Kraus, S. 2013. Solving the missing node problem using structure and attribute information. In *Proceedings of the 2013 IEEE/ACM International Conference on Advances in Social Networks Analysis and Mining*, 744–751. ACM.

Stamatatos, E. 2007. Author identification using imbalanced and limited training texts. In *Database and Expert Systems Applications, 2007. DEXA'07. 18th International Workshop on*, 237–241. IEEE.

Stamatatos, E. 2009. A survey of modern authorship attribution methods. *Journal of the American Society for information Science and Technology* 60(3):538–556.

Strehl, A., and Ghosh, J. 2003. Cluster ensembles — a knowledge reuse framework for combining multiple partitions. *J. Mach. Learn. Res.* 3:583–617.

Yin, Z.; Gupta, M.; Weninger, T.; and Han, J. 2010. Linkrec: a unified framework for link recommendation with user attributes and graph structure. In *Proceedings of the 19th international conference on World wide web*, 1211–1212. ACM.

Proceedings of the Twenty-Ninth AAAI Conference on Artificial Intelligence

Recommending Positive Links in Signed Social Networks by Optimizing a Generalized AUC

Dongjin Song* **and David A. Meyer**†
*Department of Electrical and Computer Engineering,University of California, San Diego
La Jolla, USA, 92093-0409. Email: dosong@ucsd.edu
†Department of Mathematics,University of California, San Diego
La Jolla, USA, 92093-0112. Email: dmeyer@math.ucsd.edu

Abstract

With the rapid development of signed social networks in which the relationships between two nodes can be either positive (indicating relations such as like) or negative (indicating relations such as dislike), producing a personalized ranking list with positive links on the top and negative links at the bottom is becoming an increasingly important task. To accomplish it, we propose a generalized AUC (GAUC) to quantify the ranking performance of potential links (including positive, negative, and unknown status links) in partially observed signed social networks. In addition, we develop a novel link recommendation algorithm by directly optimizing the GAUC loss. We conduct experimental studies based upon Wikipedia, MovieLens, and Slashdot; our results demonstrate the effectiveness and the efficiency of the proposed approach.

Introduction

Signed social networks, in which the relationship between two nodes can be either positive (indicating relations such as trust) or negative (indicating relations such as distrust), are increasingly common in recent years. For instance, Slashdot (Lampe, Johnston, and Resnick 2007; Brzozowski, Hogg, and Szabo 2008; Kunegis, Lommatzsch, and Bauckhage 2009) is a social website of technology related news; in Slashdot Zoo, users can tag each other as friends (like) or foes (dislike) based upon their comments on different articles. Another example is Epinions (Guha et al. 2004), which is a product review website with an active user community. Users can express whether they trust or distrust other users based upon their reviews. Unlike traditional unsigned social networks which can be represented as binary adjacency matrices (with 1 indicating the existence of a link and 0 indicating the unknown status of a link), a signed network can be modeled as an adjacency matrix in which an entry is 1 (or -1) if the relationship is positive (or negative) and 0 if the relationship is unknown.

One fundamental problem in signed social networks is link recommendation. In unsigned social networks, link recommendation aims to suggest to each user a list of people (items) to whom the user probably will create new connections. In signed social networks, however, given a user, the aim could be to rank people (items) this user is interested in (i.e., positive links) on the top and people (items) this user is not interested in (i.e., negative links) at the bottom. To achieve this goal, it is important to quantify effectively how good such a ranking list is.

In the past few years, the area under the receiver operating characteristic (ROC) curve (AUC) (Hanley and Mcneil 1982) has shown its effectiveness for measuring the performance of binary classification or ranking. For instance, Cortes and Mohri (2004) showed that the average AUC is monotonically increasing as a function of the classification accuracy, while the standard deviation for uneven distributions and higher error rates was observed; Clauset et al. (2008) as well as Menon and Elkan (2011) used AUC to measure the effectiveness of link prediction; Rendle et al. (2009) utilized AUC to quantify personalized ranking performance within social networks.

The AUC, however, is not an appropriate way to quantify the ranking performance in signed networks because it only applies to the binary case, rather than to the triplet (positive, negative, and unknown) that we consider. In particular, given a signed social network, if AUC treats positive links as positive samples and the other links as negative samples, it will be impossible to quantify the ranking quality of negative links since unknown status links can either be positive or negative. Similarly, if AUC treats negative links as negative samples and the other links as positive samples, it will not measure the ranking performance of positive links correctly.

A plausible model for user behavior in signed social networks is that more extreme positive and negative relationships will be revealed before less extreme ones. Such a model implies that a personalized ranking list of potential links should place positive links at the top, negative links at the bottom, and unknown status links in the middle. Therefore, we propose a novel criterion—a generalized AUC (GAUC)—to quantify the ranking performance in signed social networks, and develop a new algorithm to perform link recommendation. The contributions of our work include:

- we propose a generalized AUC which will be maximized only if all positive links are ranked on top, all negative links are ranked at the bottom, and all unknown status links are in the middle.

- we develop a link recommendation approach by directly minimizing the loss of the proposed GAUC; the proposed model enjoys both low computational complexity and high memory efficiency.
- we conduct experimental studies based upon three real world datasets, i.e., Wikipedia, MovieLens, and Slashdot; the results demonstrate the effectiveness of the generalized AUC for quantifying link recommendation in signed social networks; the results also demonstrate the efficiency and the effectiveness of the proposed approach.

Related Work

In the past few years, various approaches (Heider 1946; Doreian and Mrvar 2009; Leskovec, Huttenlocher, and Kleinberg 2010a; 2010b; Dong et al. 2012; Yang et al. 2012; Ye et al. 2013; Song and Meyer 2014) have been developed to investigate signed social networks. Among these approaches, while most of them concentrate on edge sign prediction and community detection, few have focussed on link recommendation. Although the link recommendation problem in signed social networks is more difficult than in conventional unsigned social networks, we review related work in the conventional setting to motivate our proposed approach. In general, there are two types of link recommendation approaches in unsigned social networks. One uses network topology and another is model-based.

Network topological approaches recommend links based upon the network topological structure. For instance, Liben-Nowell and Kleinberg (2007) showed that common neighbors, Jaccard's coefficient, and Adamic/Adar (Adamic and Adar 2003) can be used for link prediction and recommendation; Katz (1953), which measures the ensemble of all paths, also demonstrated its effectiveness for link prediction and recommendation. These approaches, however, cannot perform link recommendation effectively when little network topological information is available, which often happens in real world sparse social networks.

To tackle this issue, model-based approaches have been developed. Specifically, there are two types of model-based methods. One is pointwise approaches, such as singular value decomposition (SVD), non-negative matrix factorization (NMF) (Lee and Seung 1999; Song, Meyer, and Min 2014), probabilistic matrix factorization (Salakhutdinov and Mnih 2007), and matrix factorization (MF) (Koren, Bell, and Volinsky 2009), which aim to reconstruct the network adjacency matrix with a low rank approximation. Another is pairwise approaches, such as maximum margin matrix factorization (Weimer, Karatzoglou, and Smola 2008) and Bayesian personalized ranking (BPR) (Rendle et al. 2009), which aim to provide a personalized ranking list based upon pairwise comparisons.

Although most of these approaches can be applied directly for link recommendation in signed social networks, they may not perform well because their objectives are inconsistent with that of link recommendation in signed networks. Therefore, we introduce a generalized AUC (GAUC) to quantify the personalized ranking performance in signed networks and develop a model to perform link recommendation by directly minimizing the loss of GAUC.

A Generalized AUC

In this section, we first introduce the area under the ROC curve (AUC) and then present a generalized AUC to measure the ranking performance in signed networks.

AUC

Given a binary classifier f and a training set $(a_i, b_i)_{i=1}^n$ with $a_i \in \mathbb{R}^d$ and $b_i \in \{-1, 1\}$, let $\mathcal{P} = \{a_i \mid b_i = 1\}$ be the set of positive samples and $\mathcal{N} = \{a_i \mid b_i = -1\}$ the set of negative samples. Then the AUC is defined by:

$$AUC = \frac{1}{|\mathcal{P}||\mathcal{N}|} \sum_{a_i \in \mathcal{P}} \sum_{a_j \in \mathcal{N}} I(f(a_i) > f(a_j)) \quad (1)$$

where $I(\cdot)$ is an indicator function which is 1 if the condition in the parenthesis is satisfied and 0 otherwise; $|\mathcal{P}|$ and $|\mathcal{N}|$ are the numbers of positive samples and negative samples, respectively. AUC is the value of the Wilcoxon-Mann-Whitney statistic (Hanley and Mcneil 1982) which is essentially the probability that a random element of one set $f(a_i)$ is larger than a random element of another $f(a_j)$. With an ideal ranking list, AUC should be 1 representing each positive sample is ranked higher than all the negative samples. For a random ranking, AUC will be 0.5.

A Generalized AUC

Given a signed social network which contains positive, negative, and unknown status links, an ideal personalized ranking list tends to rank positive links (indicating a relationship such as trust) on the top, negative links (indicating a relationship such as distrust) at the bottom, and unknown status links in the middle. Traditional AUC, however, cannot quantify such a ranking list appropriately because it considers only the binary case. For instance, if AUC treats positive links as positive examples and the other links as negative examples, it cannot quantify the ranking quality of negative links since unknown status links could be either positive or negative. Similarly, if AUC treats negative links as negative samples and the others as positive samples, it cannot measure the ranking quality of positive links.

Note that although mean average precision (MAP) and normalized discounted cumulative gain (NDCG) can be used to measure ranking performance in signed networks, they may not perform well because they tend to overestimate the positive links on the top and cannot quantify the negative links appropriately, because we aim to rank them at the bottom of the ranking list and there are much more unknown status links than negative links in real world applications.

To resolve these issues, we develop a novel criterion, named generalized AUC (GAUC), to measure the ranking performance in signed networks based upon the assumption that more extreme positive and negative relationships will be revealed before less extreme ones. Specifically, suppose we are given a classifier f and a training set $(a_i, b_i)_{i=1}^n$ with $a_i \in \mathbb{R}^d$ the ith sample, $b_i \in \{-1, 0, 1\}$ its label.

Let $\mathcal{P} = \{a_i \mid b_i = 1\}$ be the set of positive samples, $\mathcal{N} = \{a_i \mid b_i = -1\}$ be the set of negative samples, and $\mathcal{O} = \{a_i \mid b_i = 0\}$. Then GAUC can be defined as:

$$\begin{aligned} GAUC = & \frac{\eta}{|\mathcal{P}|(|\mathcal{O}| + |\mathcal{N}|)} \sum_{a_i \in \mathcal{P}} \sum_{a_s \in \mathcal{O} \bigcup \mathcal{N}} I(f(a_i) > f(a_s)) \\ & + \frac{1-\eta}{|\mathcal{N}|(|\mathcal{O}| + |\mathcal{P}|)} \sum_{a_t \in \mathcal{O} \bigcup \mathcal{P}} \sum_{a_j \in \mathcal{N}} I(f(a_j) < f(a_t)) \end{aligned} \tag{2}$$

where $|\mathcal{P}|$ denotes the number of positive samples, $|\mathcal{N}|$ represents the number of negative samples, and $|\mathcal{O}|$ is the number of unknown status samples. The first and second terms quantify the ranking performance of positive links and negative links, respectively. $0 \leq \eta \leq 1$ is a parameter which controls the tradeoff between these two terms. In this work, we set $\eta = \frac{|\mathcal{P}|}{|\mathcal{P}|+|\mathcal{N}|}$, i.e., the tradeoff is controlled by the relative fraction of the number of positive links and that of negative links. After substituting η in Eqn. (2), we can obtain

$$\begin{aligned} GAUC = & \frac{1}{(|\mathcal{P}| + |\mathcal{N}|)} \Big(\frac{1}{(|\mathcal{O}| + |\mathcal{N}|)} \sum_{a_i \in \mathcal{P}} \sum_{a_s \in \mathcal{O} \bigcup \mathcal{N}} I(f(a_i) \\ & > f(a_s)) + \frac{1}{(|\mathcal{O}| + |\mathcal{P}|)} \sum_{a_j \in \mathcal{N}} \sum_{a_t \in \mathcal{O} \bigcup \mathcal{P}} I(f(a_j) < f(a_t)) \Big). \end{aligned} \tag{3}$$

Like the AUC, GAUC will be 1 if we have a perfect ranking list and will be 0.5 if we have a random ranking list. The main difference between them is that GAUC can jointly quantify the ranking quality over positive links and negative links, in the presence of unknown links. We are aware that different variants of AUC (Nakas and Yiannoutsos 2004; Li 2009) have been developed in the past. GAUC differs from these variants by focusing on the head and tail of a ranking list.

Optimizing the Generalized AUC

In this section, we first state the problem we aim to study. Then, we propose a novel model for link recommendation by directly minimizing the loss of GAUC. Finally, we introduce an optimization procedure for our proposed approach.

Problem Statement

Suppose we are given a partially observed signed network $X \in \mathbb{R}^{n \times n}$ with $X_{ij} \in \{1, -1, 0, ?\}$, where 1 denotes a positive link, -1 represents a negative link, 0 is an unknown status link, and ? denotes a potential positive or negative link. In the training stage, we treat both 0 and ? as zero (i.e., potential links) and study the underlying mechanism for ranking observed positive links on the top and negative links at the bottom. In the test phase, we evaluate how these potential links are ranked based upon the relative positions of potential positive and negative links.

We aim to learn a mapping function f such that a ranking score for the link at i-th row and j-th column of X can be produced as

$$f(i, j, X) = \widehat{X_{ij}}. \tag{4}$$

Since many real world signed social networks are sparse graphs with low rank structure, a low rank model which is memory efficient can be employed to obtain the ranking score as follows:

$$f(i, j, U, V) = f(U_i, V_j) = U_i^T V_j \tag{5}$$

where $U_i \in \mathbb{R}^r$, $V_j \in \mathbb{R}^r$, and r is the rank ($r \ll n$).

Link Recommendation Model

Since GAUC is a reasonable way to quantify the ranking performance in signed social networks, an ideal link recommendation model would be expected to optimize GAUC directly. Based upon the low rank model in Eqn. (5), the loss of GAUC can be defined as:

$$\begin{aligned} & 1 - GAUC(U, V) = \\ & \frac{1}{(|\mathcal{P}| + |\mathcal{N}|)} \Big(\frac{1}{(|\mathcal{O}| + |\mathcal{N}|)} \sum_{X_{ij} \in \mathcal{P}} \sum_{X_{is} \in \mathcal{O} \bigcup \mathcal{N}} I(U_i^T V_j \\ & \leq U_i^T V_s) + \frac{1}{(|\mathcal{O}| + |\mathcal{P}|)} \sum_{X_{ij} \in \mathcal{N}} \sum_{X_{is} \in \mathcal{O} \bigcup \mathcal{P}} I(U_i^T V_j \geq U_i^T V_s) \Big). \end{aligned} \tag{6}$$

Since the indicator function $I(\cdot)$ is non-convex, hinge loss can be used as a convex surrogate in Eqn. (6). Therefore, an upper bound of GAUC loss can be derived based upon the following two inequalities (as shown in Figure 1):

$$I(U_i^T V_j \leq U_i^T V_s) \leq \max\Big(0, U_i^T(V_s - V_j) + 1\Big), \tag{7}$$

and

$$I(U_i^T V_j \geq U_i^T V_s) \leq \max\Big(0, U_i^T(V_j - V_s) + 1\Big). \tag{8}$$

Assuming $|\mathcal{O}| \gg |\mathcal{P}|$ and $|\mathcal{O}| \gg |\mathcal{N}|$ which holds for real world sparse signed graphs, the upper bound of GAUC loss can be written as the following objective:

$$\begin{aligned} \mathcal{Q}(U, V) = & \sum_{i=1}^{n} \sum_{j=1}^{n} \sum_{s=1}^{n} \max\Big(0, U_i^T(V_s - V_j) + 1\Big) \cdot \\ & I(X_{ij} = 1, X_{is} \neq 1) + \lambda_U \sum_i U_i^T U_i + \\ & \sum_{i=1}^{n} \sum_{j=1}^{n} \sum_{s=1}^{n} \max\Big(0, U_i^T(V_j - V_s) + 1\Big) \cdot \\ & I(X_{ij} = -1, X_{is} \neq -1) + \lambda_V \sum_j V_j^T V_j \end{aligned} \tag{9}$$

where the second and fourth terms are regularization terms used for preventing over-fitting. λ_U and λ_V are two hyperparameters for controlling the scale of regularization terms.

Optimization

Although $\mathcal{Q}(U, V)$ is non-convex and non-smooth with respect to U and V, a sub-gradient method can be employed to minimize the objective over U and V alternately. Specifically, the partial derivative of $\mathcal{Q}(U, V)$ given U_i is:

$$\frac{\partial \mathcal{Q}(U, V)}{\partial U_i} = \begin{cases} \sum_{j=1}^{n} \sum_{s=1}^{n} (V_s - V_j) + \lambda_U U_i, & \text{if } X_{ij} = 1, X_{is} \neq 1, \\ & \text{and } U_i^T(V_s - V_j) > -1; \\ \sum_{j=1}^{n} \sum_{s=1}^{n} (V_j - V_s) + \lambda_U U_i, & \text{if } X_{ij} = -1, X_{is} \neq -1, \\ & \text{and } U_i^T(V_j - V_s) > -1; \\ \lambda_U U_i, & \text{otherwise} \end{cases} \tag{10}$$

Algorithm 1 Optimization of $\mathcal{Q}(U, V)$

Input: X, U, V, α, number of batches b, number of iterations t, threshold ς, maximum iteration T.
Initialize: set $t = 0$, initialize U_0 and V_0 randomly
repeat
  $t = t + 1$;
  Calculate $\frac{\partial \mathcal{Q}(U_t, V_t)}{\partial U_t}$ based upon Eqn. (10);
  $U_{t+1} = U_t - \alpha \frac{\partial \mathcal{Q}(U_t, V_t)}{\partial U_t}$;
  Calculate $\frac{\partial \mathcal{Q}(U_t, V_t)}{\partial V_t}$ based upon Eqn. (11) and Eqn. (12);
  $V_{t+1} = V_t - \alpha \frac{\partial \mathcal{Q}(U_t, V_t)}{\partial V_t}$;
until $|\mathcal{Q}(U_{t+1}, V_{t+1}) - \mathcal{Q}(U_t, V_t)| < \varsigma$ or $t > T$

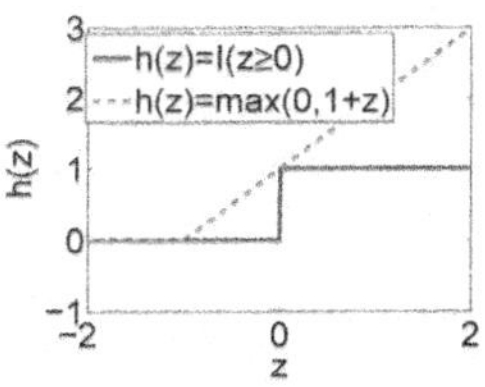

Figure 1: Convex surrogate loss of $I(z \geq 0)$.

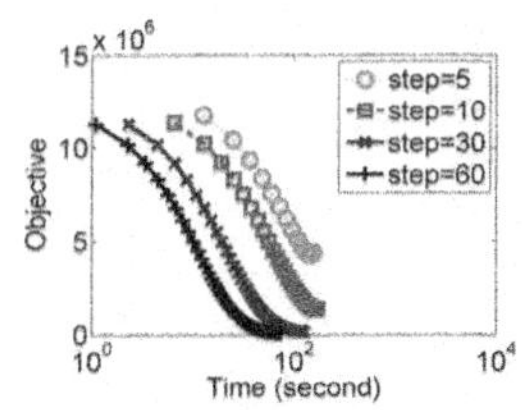

Figure 2: The efficiency of the proposed approach.

the partial derivative of $\mathcal{Q}(U, V)$ given V_j is:

$$\frac{\partial \mathcal{Q}(U, V)}{\partial V_j} = \begin{cases} -\sum_{i=1}^{n}\sum_{s=1}^{n} U_i + \lambda_V V_j, & \text{if } X_{ij} = 1, X_{is} \neq 1, \\ & \text{and } U_i^T(V_s - V_j) > -1; \\ \sum_{i=1}^{n}\sum_{s=1}^{n} U_i + \lambda_V V_j, & \text{if } X_{ij} = -1, X_{is} \neq -1, \\ & \text{and } U_i^T(V_j - V_s) > -1; \\ \lambda_V V_j, & \text{otherwise} \end{cases} \tag{11}$$

and the partial derivative of $\mathcal{Q}(U, V)$ given V_s is:

$$\frac{\partial \mathcal{Q}(U, V)}{\partial V_s} = \begin{cases} \sum_{i=1}^{n}\sum_{j=1}^{n} U_i + \lambda_V V_s, & \text{if } X_{ij} = 1, X_{is} \neq 1, \\ & \text{and } U_i^T(V_s - V_j) > -1; \\ -\sum_{i=1}^{n}\sum_{j=1}^{n} U_i + \lambda_V V_s, & \text{if } X_{ij} = -1, X_{is} \neq -1, \\ & \text{and } U_i^T(V_j - V_s) > -1; \\ \lambda_V V_s, & \text{otherwise.} \end{cases} \tag{12}$$

For practical applications, the size (or the number of the non-zero entries) of sparse signed networks maybe too large to handle. In this case, stochastic sub-gradient descent can be employed. In particular, assuming $|\mathcal{O}| \gg |\mathcal{P}|$ and $|\mathcal{O}| \gg |\mathcal{N}|$, let $q = |\mathcal{P}| + |\mathcal{N}|$ and b be the number of batches. The computational complexity of $\frac{\partial \mathcal{Q}(U,V)}{\partial U}$ (or $\frac{\partial \mathcal{Q}(U,V)}{\partial V}$) will be $O(\frac{n(q+r)}{b})$. The specific optimization procedure is shown in Algorithm 1.

Experiment

Datasets

We consider two well-known signed directed social networks, i.e., Wikipedia (Burke and Kraul 2008) and Slashdot (Lampe, Johnston, and Resnick 2007) [1]. The Wikipedia data comprise a voting network for promoting candidates to the role of admin. Slashdot is a social website focusing on technology related news. In Slashdot Zoo, users can tag each other as friends (like) or foes (dislike) based upon comments on articles.

Table 1: The statistics of two datasets.

Datasets	Wikipedia	MovieLens	Slashdot
Nodes	7,118	6040/3952	82,144
Edges	103,747	739,012	549,202
+edges	78.78%	77.84%	77.4%
−edges	21.21%	22.16%	22.6%
Density	0.0020	0.0309	0.000081

We also consider Movielens 1M dataset[2] which contains 6040 users as well as 3952 items. Although this dataset is mainly used for collaborative filtering, we preprocess it so that ratings of 4 and 5 are treated as positive links, ratings of 1 and 2 are treated as negative links, and other ones are treated as unknown status links.

The detailed statistics of these three datasets are provided in Table 1.

Evaluation Metrics

Given a fully observed signed social network $X \in \mathbb{R}^{n \times n}$ with $X_{ij} \in \{1, -1, 0\}$, we randomly remove a fraction (80%, 60% and 40%) of positive and negative links and use the rest to form a partially observed network for training (as X_{Train}). The zero entries in X_{Train} are called potential links because they could either be positive or negative in the future. The removed links form a test set X_{Test}.

To evaluate the effectiveness of the proposed model for link recommendation, we utilize GAUC (over 1, −1, and 0) in Eqn. (3), AUC (over 1 and −1) in Eqn. (1), and mean average precision (MAP) (over 1 and −1) to quantify the ranking performance over X_{Test}. To evaluate the effectiveness of top-k link recommendation, we also report its associated average Recall@k and average Precision@k for reference. Specifically, Recall@k is defined as:

$$\textit{Recall@k} = \frac{\#\textit{positive links in the top } k}{\#\textit{positive links}},$$

and Precision@k is given as

$$\textit{Precision@k} = \frac{\#\textit{positive links in the top } k}{\#\textit{positive links and negative links in the top } k}.$$

Parameter Setting

There are three hyper-parameters in our model, i.e., λ_U, λ_V, and k. We set $\lambda_U = \lambda_V$ for simplicity and search over the grid of $\{1, 5, 10, 20, 50, 100, 200\}$ to find the optimal setting for λ_U and λ_V. We also search over the grid of $\{10, 30, 50, 70, 90\}$ to find the optimal setting for k. Specifically, we conduct 5 fold cross-validation on X_{train} and

[1] These datasets are available online at `http://snap.stanford.edu/data/`.

[2] This dataset is available online at `http://grouplens.org/datasets/movielens/`.

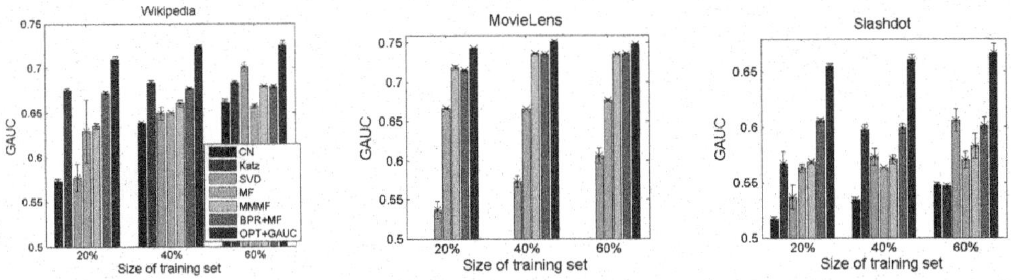

(a) GAUC on Wikipedia. (b) GAUC on MovieLens. (c) GAUC on Slashdot

Figure 3: GAUC on Wikipedia, MovieLens, and Slashdot. Error bars represent the standard deviations of uncertainty.

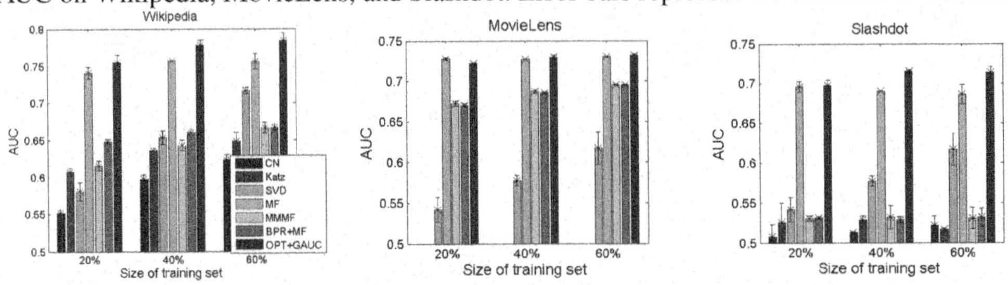

(a) AUC on Wikipedia. (b) AUC on MovieLens (c) AUC on Slashdot

Figure 4: AUC on Wikipedia, MovieLens, and Slashdot. Error bars represent the standard deviations of uncertainty.

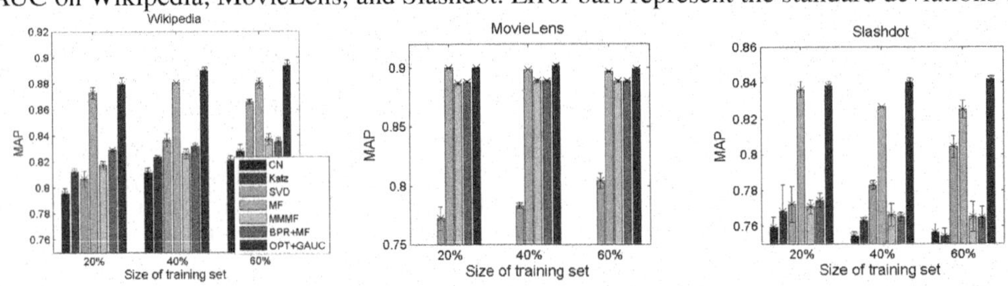

(a) MAP on Wikipedia. (b) MAP on MovieLens. (c) MAP on Slashdot

Figure 5: MAP on Wikipedia, MovieLens, and Slashdot. Error bars represent the standard deviations of uncertainty.

the parameter combination which achieves the best average GAUC is employed for test.

Results

Baslines: We compare the proposed approach (OPT+GAUC) with various baseline approaches to demonstrate its effectiveness. Among these baselines, common neighbor (CN) (Liben-Nowell and Kleinberg 2007) and Katz (Katz 1953) are obtained based upon the network topological structure; singular value decomposition (SVD) and matrix factorization (MF) (Koren, Bell, and Volinsky 2009) are two representative pointwise approaches for collaborative filtering; maximum margin matrix factorization (MMMF) (Weimer, Karatzoglou, and Smola 2008) and Bayesian personalized ranking based upon matrix factorization (BPR+MF) (Rendle et al. 2009) are two popular pairwise approaches for personalized ranking. For fair comparison, β in Katz is set as 0.005 because it achieves the best performance; we select the hyper-parameters of MF, MMMF, and BRP+MF in a similar way as we do for OPT+GAUC. To ensure our results are reliable, we conduct each experiment 5 times; the average GAUC/AUC/MAP/Recall@k/Precision@k and their associated standard deviations are reported for comparison.

Efficiency: We study the efficiency of the proposed approach by employing stochastic sub-gradient descent over 20% of the Wikipedia dataset. In particular, we partition X_{Train} into b batches and perform sub-gradient descent over U and V iteratively. Figure 2 shows the efficiency of the proposed approach with different numbers of batches ($b \in \{5, 10, 30, 60\}$). We observe that when b varies from 5 to 60, the objective function of our proposed approach converges faster. This is because the computational complexity of the sub-gradients linearly depends on b. Moreover, we observe that the GAUC/AUC/MAP does not decay very much while b is increasing.

Link recommendation: Figures 3, 4, and 5 show the GAUC/AUC/MAP and their associated standard deviations of various approaches on three datasets when the size of training set varies from 20% to 60%. We observe that CN is generally outperformed by other approaches because it only considers the neighborhood structure of the network; since Katz not only encodes neighborhood structure but also considers the high-order relationships, it can outperform CN in most cases. Note that CN and Katz cannot work on MovieLens because it is a bipartite network. For GAUC in Fig-

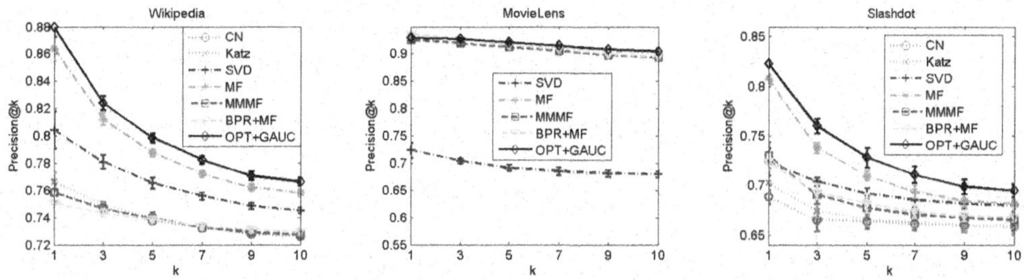

(a) Precision@k on Wikipedia. (b) Precision@k on MovieLens. (c) Precision@k on Slashdot

Figure 6: Precision@k for Wikipedia, MovieLens, and Slashdot. Error bars represent the standard deviations of uncertainty.

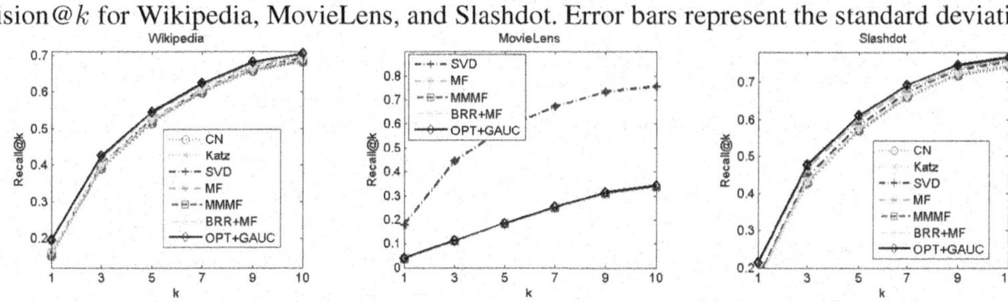

(a) Recall@k on Wikipedia. (b) Recall@k on MovieLens. (c) Recall@k on Slashdot

Figure 7: Recall@k for Wikipedia, MovieLens, and Slashdot. Error bars represent the standard deviations of uncertainty.

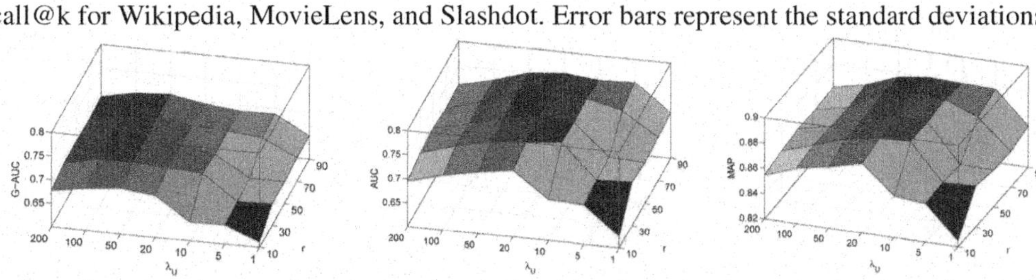

(a) GAUC on 20%Wikipedia. (b) AUC on 20%Wikipedia. (c) MAP on 20%Wikipedia.

Figure 8: Parameter sensitivity study for Wikipedia (20% training) with respect to GAUC, AUC, and MAP.

ure 3, we observe that, pairwise approaches, i.e., MMMF and BPR+MF, outperform pointwise approaches (i.e., SVD and MF) in most cases. This may be because SVD tends to over-fit the data and MF only reconstructs the partially observed network based upon observed positive as well as negative links (it neglects unknown status links). For AUC and MAP, SVD cannot perform as well as MF because SVD tends to over-fit the data (especially for smaller datasets); MMMF and BPR+MF are outperformed by MF as they do not directly model negative links. On the contrary, they treat both negative and unknown status links as 0. OPT+GAUC generally outperforms all baseline algorithms regarding GAUC/AUC/MAP, this is because OPT+GAUC models the triplet in signed networks more reasonably than other approaches.

Top-k link recommendation: We further investigate the effectiveness of the proposed approach by comparing its Precision@k and Recall@k with baseline methods (the size of training set is 40% for Wikipedia, MovieLens, and Slashdot) in Figure 6 and 7, respectively. We observe that while OPT+GAUC is among the best approaches for Recall@k (except in Figure 7(b)), it consistently achieves the best Precision@k in Figure 6(a) and 6(c). This indicates that modeling unknown status links helps to increase the performance of top-k link recommendation. We also observe that while SVD achieves the best Recall@k in Figure 7(b), it gets the worst Precision@k in Figure 6(b). This may be due to over-fitting. Note that all the other approaches except SVD achieve similar performance in Figure 6(b) and 7(b), this may be because MovieLens is a relatively dense graph and it contains sufficient observed links to estimate the ranking of potential links.

Parameter sensitivity: We study the sensitivity of OPT+GAUC with respect to the regularization parameters $\lambda_U \in \{1, 5, 10, 20, 50, 100, 200\}$ and $r \in \{10, 30, 50, 70, 90\}$. When we vary the value of λ_U or rank r, we keep the other parameters fixed. We plot the GAUC/AUC/MAP with respect to λ_U and r in Figure 8. We observe that OPT+GAUC is very stable as it achieves good GAUC/AUC/MAP when λ_U varies from 10 to 100 and k varies from 30 to 90. The results of other settings are similar and are omitted here due to space limitations.

Conclusions

In this paper, we proposed a generalized AUC (GAUC) to quantify the ranking performance in signed networks. Based upon the GAUC loss, we derived a link recommendation model by directly minimizing this loss and introduced an optimization procedure. We conducted experimental studies based upon three real world networks, i.e., Wikipedia,

MovieLens, and Slashdot. Our experiment results demonstrated the effectiveness and efficiency of the proposed approach.

Acknowledgement

This work was partially supported by the U.S. Department of Defenses Minerva Research Initiative under ARO grants W911NF-09-1-0081 and W911NF-12-1-0389.

References

Adamic, L. A., and Adar, E. 2003. Friends and neighbors on the web. *Social Networks* 25(3):211 – 230.

Brzozowski, M. J.; Hogg, T.; and Szabo, G. 2008. Friends and foes: ideological social networking. In *Proceedings of the SIGCHI Conference on Human Factors in Computing Systems*, 817–820.

Burke, M., and Kraul, R. 2008. Mopping up: Modeling wikipedia promotion decisions. In *Proceedings of the 2008 ACM Conference on Computer Supported Cooperative Work*, 27–36.

Clauset, A.; Moore, C.; and Newman, M. E. J. 2008. Hierarchical structure and the prediction of missing links in networks. *Nature* 453:98–101.

Cortes, C., and Mohri, M. 2004. Auc optimization vs. error rate minimization. In *Proceedings of Advances in Neural Information Processing Systems*, 537–546. MIT Press.

Dong, Y.; Tang, J.; Wu, S.; Tian, J.; Chawla, N. V.; Rao, J.; and Cao, H. 2012. Link prediction and recommendation across heterogeneous social networks. In *Proceedings of the IEEE 12th International Conference on Data Mining*, 181–190.

Doreian, P., and Mrvar, A. 2009. Partitioning signed social networks. *Social Networks* 1–11.

Guha, R. V.; Kumar, R.; Raghavan, P.; and Tomkin, A. 2004. Propogation of trust and distrust. In *Proceedings of the 13th International Conference on World Wide Web*, 403–412.

Hanley, J. A., and Mcneil, B. J. 1982. The meaning and use of the area under a receiver operating characteristic (roc) curve. *Radiology*.

Heider, F. 1946. Atitudes and cognitive organization. *Journal of Psychology* 21:107–112.

Katz, L. 1953. A new status index dervied from sociometric analysis. *Psychometrika* 18(1):39–43.

Koren, Y.; Bell, R.; and Volinsky, C. 2009. Matrix factorization techniques for recommender systems. *IEEE Computer* 42(8):30–37.

Kunegis, J.; Lommatzsch, A.; and Bauckhage, C. 2009. The slashdot zoo: Mining a social network with negative edges. In *Proceedings of the 19th International Conference on World Wide Web*, 541–570.

Lampe, C.; Johnston, E.; and Resnick, R. 2007. Follow the reader: filtering comments on slashdot. In *Proceedings of the SIGCHI Conference on Human Factors in Computing Systems*, 1253–1262.

Lee, D., and Seung, H. 1999. Learning the parts of objects by non-negative matrix factorization. *Nature* 401:788–799.

Leskovec, J.; Huttenlocher, D. P.; and Kleinberg, J. M. 2010a. Predicting positive and negative links in online social networks. In *Proceedings of the 20th International Conference on World Wide Web*, 641–650.

Leskovec, J.; Huttenlocher, D. P.; and Kleinberg, J. M. 2010b. Signed networks in social media. In *Proceedings of the SIGCHI Conference on Human Factors in Computing Systems*, 1361–1370.

Li, Y. 2009. A generalization of auc to an ordered multiclass diagnosis and application to longitudinal data analysis on intellectual outcome in pediatric brain-tumor patients. *Ph.D Thesis of Geogia State University*.

Liben-Nowell, D., and Kleinberg, J. 2007. The link prediction for social networks. *Journal of American Society for Information Science and Technology* 58(7):1019–1031.

Menon, A. K., and Elkan, C. 2011. Link prediction via matrix factorization. In *In Proceedings of the European Conference on Machine Learning, Part II, LNAI2912*, 437–452.

Nakas, C. T., and Yiannoutsos, C. T. 2004. Ordered multiple-class roc analysis with continuous measurements. *Statistics in Medicine* 23:3437–3449.

Rendle, S.; Freudenthaler, C.; Gantner, Z.; and Schmidt-Thieme, L. 2009. Bpr: Bayesian personalized ranking from implicit feedback. In *Proceedings of the 25th Conference on Uncertainty in Artificial Intelligence*, 452–461.

Salakhutdinov, R., and Mnih, A. 2007. Probabilistic matrix factorization. In *Proceedings of the Neural Information Processing Systems*.

Song, D., and Meyer, D. A. 2014. A model of consistent node types in signed directed social networks. In *Proceedings IEEE/ACM International Conference on Advances in Social Networks Analysis and Mining (ASONAM)*, 72–80.

Song, D.; Meyer, D. A.; and Min, M. R. 2014. Fast nonnegative matrix factorization with rank-one admm. In *NIPS 2014 Workshop on Optimization for Machine Learning (OPT2014)*.

Weimer, M.; Karatzoglou, A.; and Smola, A. 2008. Improving maximum margin matrix factorization. *Machine Leanring* 72(3):263–276.

Yang, S. H.; Smola, A. J.; Long, B.; Zha, H.; and Chang, Y. 2012. Friend or frenemy?: predicting signed ties in social networks. In *Proceedings of the 35th International ACM SIGIR Conference on Research and Development in Information Retrieval*.

Ye, J.; Cheng, H.; Zhu, Z.; and Chen, M. 2013. Predicting positive and negative links in signed social networks by transfer learning. In *Proceedings of the 23th International Conference on World Wide Web*.

Causal Inference via Sparse Additive Models with Application to Online Advertising

Wei Sun[1], Pengyuan Wang[2], Dawei Yin[2], Jian Yang[2], and Yi Chang[2]
[1]Purdue University, West Lafayette, IN,USA, sun244@purdue.edu
[2]Yahoo Labs, Sunnyvale, CA, USA, {pengyuan, daweiy, jianyang,yichang}@yahoo-inc.com

Abstract

Advertising effectiveness measurement is a fundamental problem in online advertising. Various causal inference methods have been employed to measure the causal effects of ad treatments. However, existing methods mainly focus on linear logistic regression for univariate and binary treatments and are not well suited for complex ad treatments of multi-dimensions, where each dimension could be discrete or continuous. In this paper we propose a novel two-stage causal inference framework for assessing the impact of complex ad treatments. In the first stage, we estimate the propensity parameter via a sparse additive model; in the second stage, a propensity-adjusted regression model is applied for measuring the treatment effect. Our approach is shown to provide an unbiased estimation of the ad effectiveness under regularity conditions. To demonstrate the efficacy of our approach, we apply it to a real online advertising campaign to evaluate the impact of three ad treatments: ad frequency, ad channel, and ad size. We show that the ad frequency usually has a treatment effect cap when ads are showing on mobile device. In addition, the strategies for choosing best ad size are completely different for mobile ads and online ads.

Introduction

In the current online advertising ecosystem, user are exposed to ads with diverse formats and channels, and user's behaviors are caused by complex ad treatments combining of various factors (Rosenkrans 2009). The complexity of ad treatments calls for an accurate and causal measurement of ad effectiveness, i.e., how the ad treatment *causes* the changes in outcomes. An outcome is the user's response in the ad campaigns, such as whether or not the user clicks a link, or searches for a brand. The gold standard of accurate ad effectiveness measurement is the experiment-based approach, such as A/B test, where different ad treatments are randomly assigned to users. However, the cost of fully randomized experiments is usually very high (Chan et al. 2010; Kohav and Longbotham 2010; Stitelman et al. 2011) and in some rich ad treatment circumstances, such fully randomized experiments are even infeasible (Bottou et al. 2013).

Hence it is critical and necessary to provide statistical approaches to estimate the ad effectiveness directly from observational data rather than experimental data. Previous studies based on observational data try to establish direct relationship between the ad treatment and a success action (Abraham 2008). However, in observational data, typically the user characteristics may affect both the exposed ad treatment and the success tendency. Ignoring such confounding effects of user characteristics may lead to a biased estimation of the treatment effect (Rosenbaum and Rubin 1984).

Causal inference aims to infer unbiased causality effect of the ad treatment from observational data, by eliminating the impact of the confounding factors such as user characteristics. The causal inference framework for a binary treatment was original proposed by Rosenbaum and Rubin (1983). They introduced the concept of propensity score and proposed to estimate it via a logistic regression. To expand the scope of causal inference from a binary treatment to a continuous/categorical treatment, a propensity function-based framework was proposed (Imai and van Dyk 2004), where Gaussian linear regression was applied to estimate the propensity function. Based on the estimated propensity score (or propensity function), an additional sub-classification procedure was usually performed to produce the final treatment effect estimation. Recently, machine learning algorithms, e.g. gradient boosted machine, bagged CART, and random forest, were employed to estimate the propensity score (Lee, Lessler, and Stuart 2010; Su et al. 2012). While these algorithms showed desirable performance, they mainly focused on the scenario with a univariate treatment and low dimensional user features. In online advertising, causal inference methods have been developed to estimate the causal effect (Chan et al. 2010; Dalessandro et al. 2012; Wang, Traskin, and Small 2013; Wang et al. 2014). Nevertheless, these works also mainly focused on the univariate and binary treatment and not well suited for measuring the effects of complex treatment (e.g., a two-dimensional treatment consists of ad exposure frequency and ad size), which are more realistic and in great demand.

Measuring complex ad treatment effectiveness is still facing four major challenges. First, the general ad treatment can be much more complex than binary treatment. It could be a discrete or continuous, uni- or multi-dimensional treatment.

Second, the widely enforced linearity condition on the relationship between ad treatment and user characteristics is too restricted. Third, the online dataset typically has high-dimensional user characteristics and it is generally believed that only a small number of features are truly informative while others are redundant. Forth, existing propensity-based sub-classification methods are sensitive to the choice of the number of sub-classes and the format of sub-classification.

To address above challenges, in this paper we propose a novel two-stage causal inference framework to tackle the general ad effectiveness measurement problem. In the first stage, we model the propensity parameter via a sparse additive model and in the second stage, we employ a propensity-adjusted regression model to measure the final treatment effect. The novelty and advantages of the proposed method can be summarized as follows:

- Our causal inference is fully general, where the treatment can be single- or multi-dimensional, and it can be binary, categorical, continuous, or a mixture of them. We prove that this framework offers an unbiased estimation of the treatment effect under standard assumptions.
- Our sparse additive model for propensity parameter estimation deals with high-dimensionality and non-linearity issues in online advertising data.
- The propensity-adjusted regression model in our second stage estimates the treatment effect directly and avoids the tuning in existing sub-classification methods.

We further apply our framework to an online advertising campaign and provide practical guideline to assess advertising strategy on mobile and online platforms. Our extensive experiments show that the ad frequency usually has a treatment effect cap on mobile devices and the choice of best ad size are completely different for ads shown on mobile and online. Hence it is important for the ad providers to make appropriate adjustment for the number of the ads and the format of the ads delivered to the users.

Background

We first review the basic concepts of causal inference, and then mention potential drawbacks of existing approaches.

Define a treatment as a random variable $\mathbf{T}$ and a potential outcome associated with a specific treatment $\mathbf{T} = \mathbf{t}$ as $Y(\mathbf{t})$. Since the treatment can be uni- or multi-dimensional, we use the boldface $\mathbf{T}$ and $\mathbf{t}$ to indicate a multivariate treatment variable and T and t to indicate a univariate treatment variable. In general, multivariate variable $\mathbf{T}$ could be of a mixture of categorical and continuous variables. For each user, indexed by $i = 1, 2, ..., N$, we observe a vector of pretreatment covariates (i.e., user characteristics) $\mathbf{X}_i$ of length p, a treatment $\mathbf{T}_i$, and an univariate outcome Y_i corresponding to the treatment received. Typically, one would like to evaluate the effect of a given treatment $\mathbf{t}$ on the outcome Y, removing the confounding effect of $\mathbf{X}$.

A primary interest of causal inference is the distribution $p(Y(\mathbf{t}))$ for each treatment $\mathbf{t}$. In order to unbiasedly evaluate this distribution, two standard assumptions are usually made in the literature (Rosenbaum and Rubin 1983).

Assumption 1: Stable unit treatment value assumption. The potential outcome for one unit should be unaffected by the particular assignment of treatments to the other units.

Assumption 2: Strong ignorability of treatment assignment. Given the covariates $\mathbf{X}$, the distribution of treatment $\mathbf{T}$ is independent of the potential outcome $Y(\mathbf{t})$ for all $\mathbf{t}$.

Assumption 1 allows us to model the outcome of one subject independent of another subject's treatment status, given the covariates. Assumption 2 enables the modeling of the treatment with respect to the covariates, independent of the outcome, i.e., all the features related to both the treatment assignment and the outcome have been included in the model. Under Assumption 2, Rosenbaum and Rubin (1983) showed that the distribution $p(Y(\mathbf{t}))$ can be computed as

$$p(Y(\mathbf{t})) = \int_{\mathbf{X}} p(Y(\mathbf{t})|\mathbf{T} = \mathbf{t}, \mathbf{X}) p(\mathbf{X}) d\mathbf{X}, \tag{1}$$

where $p(Y(\mathbf{t})|\mathbf{T} = \mathbf{t}, \mathbf{X})$ is the conditional distribution of $Y(\mathbf{t})$ given $\mathbf{t}$ and $\mathbf{X}$, and $p(\mathbf{X})$ is the distribution of $\mathbf{X}$. In order to compute (1), one can model $p(Y(\mathbf{t})|\mathbf{T} = \mathbf{t}, \mathbf{X})$ directly. But experience shows that the result can be strongly biased if the relationship between $\mathbf{T}$ and $\mathbf{X}$ is omitted or misspecified (Rosenbaum and Rubin 1983). When the observed covariates $\mathbf{X}$ is low-dimensional, one way to avoid this bias is to classify subjects according to $\mathbf{X}$ and estimate (1) via the weighted average over $\mathbf{X}$. However as the dimension of $\mathbf{X}$ increases, exact sub-classification according to covariates becomes computationally infeasible.

To address these issues, Rosenbaum and Rubin (1983) introduced the balancing score to summarize the information required to balance the distribution of covariates and proposed the propensity score method for the binary treatment problem. The balancing score is the random variable such that conditioned on it, the observed covariates and the treatment assignment are independent. Later on, Imai and van Dyk (2004) generalized propensity score to propensity function for a categorical or continuous treatment. Specifically, the propensity function $e(\mathbf{X})$ is defined as the conditional density of the treatment given the observed covariates, i.e., $e(\mathbf{X}) = p(\mathbf{T}|\mathbf{X})$. It was shown that this propensity function is a balancing score, that is, $p(\mathbf{T}|\mathbf{X}) = p(\mathbf{T}|e(\mathbf{X}))$. Hence we can obtain $p(Y(\mathbf{t}))$ in (1) as

$$p(Y(\mathbf{t})) = \int_{e(\mathbf{X})} p(Y(\mathbf{t})|\mathbf{T} = \mathbf{t}, e(\mathbf{X})) p(e(\mathbf{X})) de(\mathbf{X}). \tag{2}$$

To compute the integral in (2), Imai and van Dyk (2004) assumed that there existed a unique finite-dimensional propensity parameter $\boldsymbol{\theta}$ such that the propensity function $e(\mathbf{X})$ depended on $\mathbf{X}$ only through $\boldsymbol{\theta}(\mathbf{X})$. Here $\boldsymbol{\theta}$ is also a balancing score, and hence we can obtain $p(Y(\mathbf{t}))$ in (2) as

$$p(Y(\mathbf{t})) = \int_{\boldsymbol{\theta}} p(Y(\mathbf{t})|\mathbf{T} = \mathbf{t}, \boldsymbol{\theta}) p(\boldsymbol{\theta}) d\boldsymbol{\theta}. \tag{3}$$

Usually $\boldsymbol{\theta}$ has a much smaller dimension than X, hence this strategy tackles the high dimensionality issue of the covariates in (1).

In many advertising applications, $e(\mathbf{X})$ or $\boldsymbol{\theta}$ is unknown since the collected data are observational data. Although the ad publisher designs the advertising algorithm, the specific $e(\mathbf{X})$ may not be fully controlled due to the system complexity. More importantly, the probability of a specific user visiting an ad publisher is unknown, which is an important factor of $e(\mathbf{X})$. For example, some ads are only posted on given pages, and it is unknown whether a specific user visits this page or not. Therefore, in practice, we need to estimate $\boldsymbol{\theta}$ based on given samples.

To approximate (3), Imai and van Dyk (2004) suggested to estimate the propensity parameter $\boldsymbol{\theta}$ via Gaussian linear regression (for a continuous treatment) or linear logistic regression (for a binary treatment), classify samples into several sub-classes with similar value of the estimations of $\boldsymbol{\theta}$, estimate the treatment effect within each sub-class, and then average the estimators from each sub-class.

However, linear models for estimating $\boldsymbol{\theta}$ require restricted assumptions on functional form and distributions of variables. The violation of these assumptions may result in a biased treatment effect estimation (Lee, Lessler, and Stuart 2010). In addition, the final treatment effect estimation could be sensitive to the number of sub-classes and the strategy of sub-classification (Hullsiek and Louis 2002). Note that a larger number of sub-classes leads to a more accurate estimation of the integral in (3) but inevitably implies a less accurate estimation of the inner conditional distribution due to limited observations in each sub-class. Furthermore, although equal-frequency strategy is generally used to form the sub-classes (Rosenbaum and Rubin 1984; Imai and van Dyk 2004), experiments showed that this strategy often leads to highly unstable estimators for the extreme sub-classes (Hullsiek and Louis 2002). Therefore, it is necessary to introduce a new method which has a more flexible modeling strategy and can avoid the specifications of the number of sub-classes and the format of sub-classification.

Methodology

To address the above drawbacks, we propose a two-stage causal inference method for more realistic problem—complex ad effectiveness analysis. The method applies a more flexible modeling approach for estimating the propensity parameter and avoids specifying the number of sub-classes. The outline of our algorithm is shown in Table 1 and Figure 1. The detailed modeling approaches in Stages 1-2 are discussed in the following subsections.

Table 1: Our Two-stage Algorithm

Input:	$Y_i, \mathbf{X}_i, \mathbf{T}_i$ for $i = 1, 2, ...N$.
Output:	Estimated treatment effect for **t**.
Stage 1:	Obtain the estimated propensity parameter $\widehat{\boldsymbol{\theta}}(\mathbf{X}_i)$ by modeling $\mathbf{T}_i \vert \mathbf{X}_i$ via SAM.
Stage 2:	Calculate the final treatment effect by modeling $Y_i \vert \mathbf{T}_i, \widehat{\boldsymbol{\theta}}(\mathbf{X}_i)$ via GAM as in (10).

Stage 1: Propensity Parameter Estimation via SAM

We propose to estimate the propensity parameter via a sparse additive model (SAM) which relieves the restricted linear assumption in existing propensity parameter estimation approaches, and deals with the high-dimensionality issue of $\mathbf{X}$ where only a small number of them are truly informative. For a m-dimensional treatment $\mathbf{T} = (T_1, \ldots, T_m)$, we estimate the propensity parameter $\boldsymbol{\theta}_j$, $j = 1, \ldots, m$, by modeling each $T_j \vert \mathbf{X}$ via SAM. The final estimated propensity parameter for $\mathbf{T}$ is the combination of all the individually estimated propensity parameters, i.e., the tuple $(\boldsymbol{\theta}_1, \ldots, \boldsymbol{\theta}_m)$. In this sequel, we will discuss the modeling approach for a continuous treatment, a binary treatment, and a multi-class categorical treatment, separately. For ease of notation, we will suppress the dependence of T_j on the index j in this subsection and consider a generic modeling for $T \vert \mathbf{X}$ for a univariate treatment T.

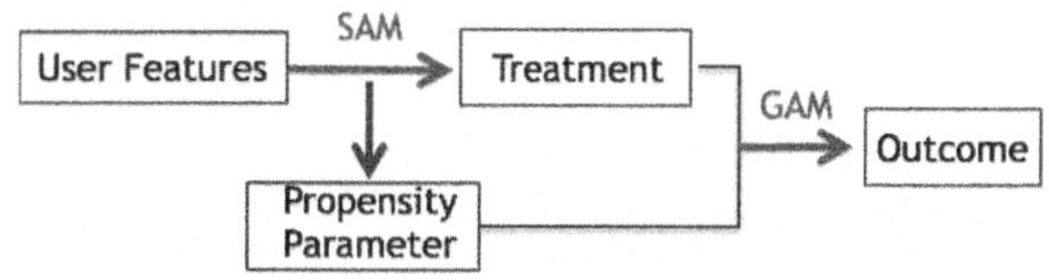

Figure 1: Outline of our algorithm. "SAM" and "GAM" refer to sparse additive model and generalized additive model, respectively.

Continuous treatment: For a continuous treatment T, Imai and van Dyk (2004) estimated the propensity parameter via a Gaussian linear regression $T = \mathbf{X}^T \beta + \epsilon$ with $\mathbf{X}$ the p-dimensional user features and ϵ a standard Gaussian. Despite of its simplicity, the linearity assumption is too restrictive. To relax this constraint, Woo et. al. (2008) applied the generalized additive model (GAM) (Hastie and Tibshirani 1990) to estimate the propensity parameter. For smooth functions $f_1, \ldots, f_p$, the additive model assumes $T = \sum_{j=1}^{p} f_j(X_j) + \epsilon$, which is more general than Gaussian linear regression, but only has good statistical and computational performance when p is relatively small.

In high-dimensional scenario, the sparsity constraint has been incorporated into the additive model for variable selection. The key idea of SAM (Ravikumar et al. 2009) is to scale each component function by a scalar β_j and then impose an l_1 penalty on the coefficient $\beta = (\beta_1, \ldots, \beta_p)^T$ to encourage the sparsity of the nonlinear components. Denote $\mathcal{H}_j$ as the Hilbert space of measurable functions $f_j(x_j)$ of the single variable x_j with $\mathbb{E}[f_j(X_j)] = 0$ and $\mathbb{E}[f_j^2(X_j)] < \infty$. The SAM solves

$$\min_{\beta \in \mathbb{R}^p, g_j \in \mathcal{H}_j} \quad \mathbb{E}\left(T - \sum_{j=1}^{p} \beta_j g_j(X_j)\right)^2 \tag{4}$$

$$\text{subject to} \quad \sum_{j=1}^{p} |\beta_j| \leq \lambda \tag{5}$$

$$\mathbb{E}(g_j) = 0, j = 1 \ldots, p \tag{6}$$

$$\mathbb{E}(g_j^2) = 1, j = 1 \ldots, p. \tag{7}$$

Similar to the lasso penalty (Tibshirani 1996) for Gaussian linear regression, the upper bound constraint in (5) encourages the sparsity, which results in a sparse additive function $\sum_{j=1}^{p} f_j(x_j) = \sum_{j=1}^{p} \beta_j g_j(x_j)$. Furthermore, the last two constraints (6) and (7) are used for identifiability. The above optimization problem can be solved efficiently by the coordinate descent algorithm (Ravikumar et al. 2009), where the tuning parameter λ can be tuned by BIC or stability-based criterion (Sun, Wang, and Fang 2013). After solving (4), we can estimate the propensity parameter $\boldsymbol{\theta}(\mathbf{X})$ using the vector of the fitted treatments $\widehat{T}$.

Binary treatment: The SAM in (4) can be extended to nonparametric logistic regression for estimating the propensity parameter $\boldsymbol{\theta}(\mathbf{X}) = \mathbb{P}(T = 1|\mathbf{X})$. Specifically, for a binary treatment $T \in \{0, 1\}$, the additive logistic model is

$$\mathbb{P}(T = 1|\mathbf{X}) = \frac{\exp\left(\sum_{j=1}^{p} f_j(X_j)\right)}{1 + \exp\left(\sum_{j=1}^{p} f_j(X_j)\right)}$$

with the population log-likelihood function $L(f) = \mathbb{E}[Tf(\mathbf{X}) - \log(1 + \exp(f(\mathbf{X})))]$. Then sparse additive logistic model can be solved by replacing the squared loss in (4) with the corresponding new log-likelihood $L(f)$. The propensity parameter $\boldsymbol{\theta}(\mathbf{X})$ for a binary treatment can then be estimated as the vector of fitted conditional probabilities $\widehat{\mathbb{P}}(T = 1|X_i)$ with $i = 1 \ldots, N$.

Multi-class treatment: When the treatment T is categorical with more than 2 classes, e.g., $T \in \{1, \ldots, K\}$, the one-vs.-rest multi-category strategy (Liu, Lafferty, and Wasserman 2008) can be employed. Specifically, the treatment T is expanded as a $K-1$ dimensional vector $(T^{(1)}, \ldots, T^{(K-1)})$ in which at most one element can be one and all others being zero. The multi-category additive logistic model is,

$$\mathbb{P}(T^{(k)} = 1|\mathbf{X}) = \frac{\exp\left(\sum_{j=1}^{p} f_j^{(k)}(X_j)\right)}{1 + \sum_{k'=1}^{K-1} \exp\left(\sum_{j=1}^{p} f_j^{(k')}(X_j)\right)},$$

for $k = 1, \ldots, K-1$ with the multinomial log-loss

$$l(f) = \sum_{k=1}^{K-1} T^{(k)} f^{(k)}(\mathbf{X}) - \log\left(1 + \sum_{k=1}^{K-1} \exp(f^{(k)}(\mathbf{X}))\right).$$

Finally, the propensity parameter for a K-class categorical treatment can be estimated as the $N \times (K-1)$ matrix whose (i, k)-th element is the estimated conditional probability $\widehat{\mathbb{P}}(T = k|X_i)$ for $k = 1, \ldots, K-1$ and $i = 1 \ldots, N$.

Stage 2: Propensity-adjusted Regression

With the propensity parameter $\boldsymbol{\theta}$, we now measure the treatment effect via the propensity-adjusted regression, which can more naturally estimate the treatment effect than the existing sub-classification methods. In short, we consider the propensity parameter as an additional feature and directly model the relationship between the outcome and the combination of treatment and propensity parameter via regression models. Specifically, given the propensity parameter $\boldsymbol{\theta}$ and the treatment $\mathbf{T}$, we model $Y|\mathbf{T}, \boldsymbol{\theta}$ as

$$Y = g(\mathbf{T}, \boldsymbol{\theta}) + \epsilon \tag{8}$$

with $g(\cdot)$ an unknown function and ϵ a standard Gaussian.

Next we show that the treatment effect estimator based on (8) is unbiased under some regularity conditions.

Theorem 1 *Under Assumptions 1-2, and assume true outcome model is* (8), *if there exists an unbiased functional estimator $\widehat{g}$ for g, i.e., $\mathbb{E}_{\mathcal{D}}[\widehat{g}] = g$ where the expectation is with respect to the samples $\mathcal{D}$, then the estimated treatment effect of $\mathbf{t}$ is unbiased. That is,*

$$\mathbb{E}_{\boldsymbol{\theta}}\left[\mathbb{E}_{\mathcal{D}}[\widehat{g}(\mathbf{t}, \boldsymbol{\theta})] - \mathbb{E}_{\mathcal{D}}[\widehat{g}(\mathbf{0}, \boldsymbol{\theta})]\right] = \mathbb{E}[Y(\mathbf{t}) - Y(\mathbf{0})].^{1} \tag{9}$$

Proof of Theorem 1: First, for any given treatment $\mathbf{t}$, we have $\mathbb{E}[Y(\mathbf{t})] = \mathbb{E}_{\boldsymbol{\theta}}\{\mathbb{E}[Y(\mathbf{t})|\boldsymbol{\theta}]\}$. Since the propensity parameter $\boldsymbol{\theta}$ is a balancing score, according to Theorem 3 in Rosenbaum and Rubin (1983) and Assumption 2, we have

$$(Y(\mathbf{t}), Y(\mathbf{0})) \perp\!\!\!\perp \mathbf{T}|\boldsymbol{\theta}.$$

Therefore, we have $\mathbb{E}[Y(\mathbf{t})|\boldsymbol{\theta}] = \mathbb{E}[Y(\mathbf{t})|\mathbf{T} = \mathbf{t}, \boldsymbol{\theta}]$ for any treatment $\mathbf{t}$. According to (8), we have $\mathbb{E}[Y(\mathbf{t})|\mathbf{T} = \mathbf{t}, \boldsymbol{\theta}] = g(\mathbf{t}, \boldsymbol{\theta})$ and $\mathbb{E}[Y(\mathbf{0})|\mathbf{T} = \mathbf{0}, \boldsymbol{\theta}] = g(\mathbf{0}, \boldsymbol{\theta})$. Combining these results with the unbiasedness of $\widehat{g}$ leads to (9). This ends the proof of Theorem 1. ■

We next discuss an estimation procedure of the treatment effect based on (8). Given the training samples $\{(Y_i, \mathbf{T}_i, \mathbf{X}_i,), i = 1, \ldots, n\}$, in Stage 1, we obtain the estimated propensity parameter $\widehat{\boldsymbol{\theta}}$ via SAM, and in Stage 2 we estimate the function $\widehat{g}(\cdot)$ in (8) via GAM, where GAM is applied since it offers flexible modeling and performs well when dimensions of $\mathbf{T}$ and $\boldsymbol{\theta}$ are low. Finally, the averaged treatment effect (ATE) of a treatment $\mathbf{t}$ can be estimated as

$$\widehat{\mathrm{ATE}(\mathbf{t})} = \frac{1}{N}\sum_{i=1}^{N}\left\{\widehat{g}(\mathbf{t}, \widehat{\boldsymbol{\theta}}(X_i)) - \widehat{g}(\mathbf{0}, \widehat{\boldsymbol{\theta}}(X_i))\right\}. \tag{10}$$

Simulations

This section evaluates the efficacy of our model via a simulated experiment. We first illustrate the performance of model fitting in Stage 1 by comparing our approach with up-to-date machine learning algorithms, and then demonstrate the superiority of our treatment effect estimation.

We set sample size $N = 1000$ and number of features $p = 200$. Define basis functions $f_1(x) = -2\sin(2x)$, $f_2(x) = x^2 - 1/3$, $f_3(x) = x - 0.5$, $f_4(x) = e^{-x} - e^{-1} - 1$, $f_5(x) = (x - 0.5)^2 + 2$, $f_6(x) = \mathbb{I}_{\{x>0\}}$, $f_7(x) = e^{-x}$, $f_8(x) = \cos(x)$, $f_9(x) = x^2$, and $f_{10}(x) = x$. We first generate the features $X_1, \ldots, X_p \overset{iid}{\sim} N(0, 1)$. The three dimensional treatment $\mathbf{T}$ and the outcome Y are produced as follows. We generate the continuous treatment $T_1|X \sim N(\sum_{j=1}^{4} f_j(X_j), 1)$, the binary treatment $T_2|X = 1$ if $\sum_{j=1}^{5} f_j(X_j) > 0$ and 0 otherwise, and the multi-class treatment $T_3|X \in \{1, 2, 3, 4\}$ based on 25%, 50%, 75%, and 100% quantiles of $\sum_{j=1}^{2} f_j(X_j)$, and generate the outcome model as $Y|X, \mathbf{T} \sim N(\sum_{j=1}^{5} f_{j+5}(X_j) + \alpha^T\mathbf{T}, 1)$ with $\alpha = (1, 1, 1)$.

In this example, the features $X_1, \ldots, X_5$ are informative variables and have confounding effects to both treatment and outcome, and the rest $X_6, \ldots, X_p$ are noisy variables to mimic the sparse data of online advertising. The true effects for three treatment T_1, T_2, or T_3 are all 1.

[1] We implicitly consider $\mathbf{t} = \mathbf{0}$ as the baseline treatment.

To evaluate the performance of model fitting in Stage 1, we independently generate a testing data with size 1000, and report the averaged prediction errors for fitting T_1 and the averaged misclassification errors for fitting T_2 over 100 replications. The results for fitting T_3 are similar and are omitted to save space. We compare SAM with gradient boosted machine (gbm), lasso, sparse logistic regression (slogit), bagged tree (bagging), and random forest (rf). As shown in Figure 2, SAM achieves smallest errors for both continuous and binary treatment model fittings and the advantages over other models are significant.

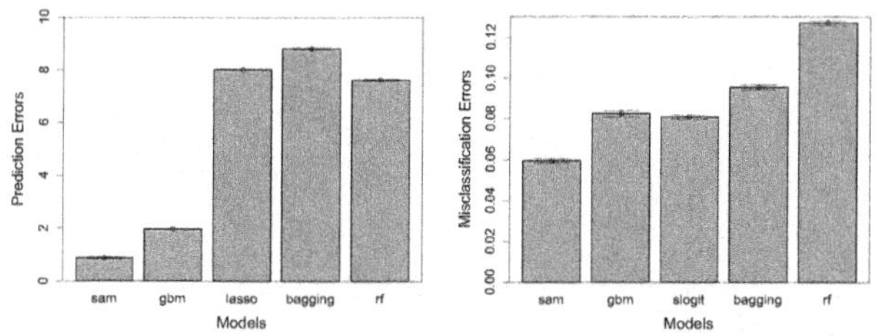

Figure 2: Errors of fitting T_1 (left plot) and T_2 (right plot). "sam" refers to sparse additive model, "gbm" refers to gradient boosted machine,"slogit" refers to sparse logistic regression, "bagging" refers to bagged tree, and "rf" refers to random forest. The one standard deviation bar is shown for each model.

The benefit of SAM is not at the cost of expensive computations. As shown in Figure 3, SAM is the second fastest algorithm when fitting the continuous treatment, which is only slightly slower than lasso, and its computational cost is comparable to gbm when fitting the binary treatment.

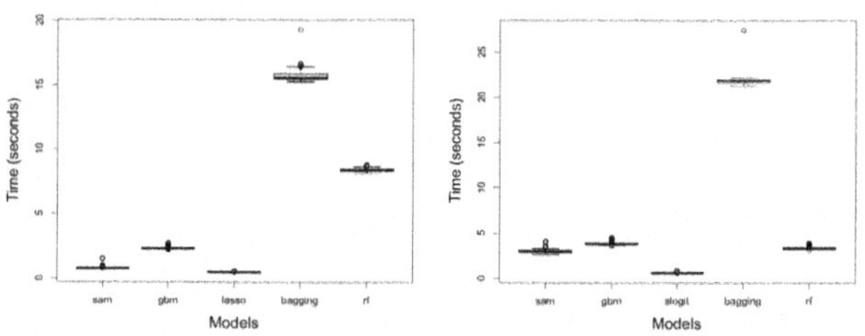

Figure 3: Computational time (in seconds) for fitting treatment T_1 (left plot) and treatment T_2 (right plot) from various models.

Secondly, we demonstrate the superior treatment effect estimation performance of our model. Specifically, we compute the absolute difference of the estimated treatment effects and their corresponding true treatment effects. We investigate the comparison among a direct treatment effect estimation method (Model 1), the existing propensity-adjusted methods (Models 2-3) as well as their sparse versions (Models 4-5), and the proposed two-stage models.

Model 1: a linear regression for $Y|(\mathbf{T}, \mathbf{X})$.

Model 2: fit a linear regression for $T_1|\mathbf{X}$, logistic regression for $T_2|\mathbf{X}$, multi-class logistic regression for $T_3|\mathbf{X}$ to obtain the propensity parameter matrix $\widehat{\boldsymbol{\theta}}$ and then fit a linear regression for $Y|\mathbf{T}, \widehat{\boldsymbol{\theta}}$.

Model 3: same as **Model 2** except that Stage 2 fits a GAM for $Y|\mathbf{T}, \widehat{\boldsymbol{\theta}}$.

Model 4: same as **Model 2** except that Stage 1 fits a linear sparse model for $T_j|\mathbf{X}$, $j = 1, 2, 3$.

Model 5: same as **Model 3** except that Stage 1 fits a linear sparse model for $T_j|\mathbf{X}$, $j = 1, 2, 3$.

Our Model 1: fit a SAM for $T_j|\mathbf{X}$, $j = 1, 2, 3$ to obtain $\widehat{\boldsymbol{\theta}}$ and fit a linear regression for $Y|\mathbf{T}, \widehat{\boldsymbol{\theta}}$.

Our Model 2: same as **Our Model 1** except that Stage 2 fits a GAM for $Y|\mathbf{T}, \widehat{\boldsymbol{\theta}}$.

In Figure 4, we report the sum of errors of all three treatment effect estimations over 100 replications. Clearly, our models achieve the smallest errors and their advantages are significant. For our two models, fitting a GAM in Stage 2 provides with more accuracy gain. Besides, comparing Model 2, Model 4, and our Model 1 reveals that the accuracy of treatment fitting in Stage 1 is extremely important for the final treatment effect estimation. Furthermore, the sparse models (Models 4-5) outperform their non-sparse counterparts (Models 2-3), which ensures the importance of feature selection in the high dimensional scenario.

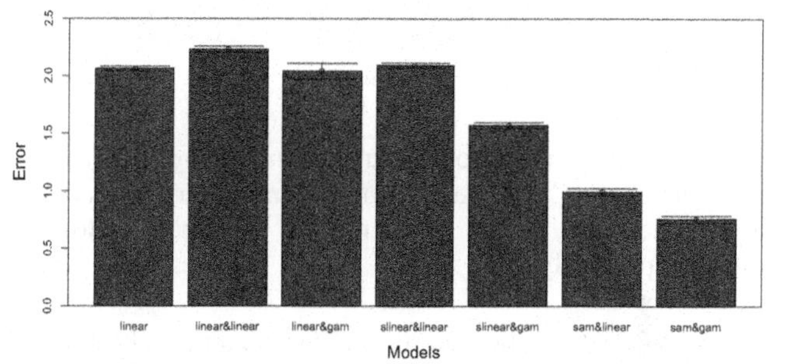

Figure 4: Errors of treatment effect estimations. "linear", "linear&linear", "linear&gam", "slinear&linear", "slinear&gam" refer to Models 1-5, and "sam&linear", "sam&gam" are our Models 1-2.

Experiments

We apply our model on a real advertising campaign for a major auto company from a premium internet media company. This campaign involves advertisements delivered via mobile devices (including iPhone, iPad, Android Phone, Android Tablet, Windows Phone and Windows Tablet) and personal computers (PCs). We aim to measure the exposure frequency impact and the size impact of the ads from both platforms.

The datasets contains about 5 millions of users, among which 1.6 thousand users perform success actions (online quotes) [2]. The advertising treatment $\mathbf{T}$ is a 3-dimensional

[2]The reported dataset and results are deliberately incomplete

vector: The first dimension is the ad frequency which can be treated as a continuous variable; the second dimension is the device indicator which is a binary variable with 1 referring to a mobile and 0 referring to a PC; and the third dimension is the ad size indicator which is a categorical variable with 3 classes: small, medium, and large. We consider ad frequency of values at most 10 which consists of 99% samples. In total, there are 2483 features, including the demographic information, personal interest, and online and TV activities. The personal interest includes high-dimensional and sparse features, and hence SAM is well suited for the modeling.

We first estimate the propensity parameter via SAM and compare it with estimators via gradient boosted machine and sparse linear model, where the latter two demonstrate good empirical performance in the simulations. The accuracy of the propensity parameter estimation is evaluated via the prediction errors by refitting the model for each treatment. The averaged prediction errors over all the treatments are summarized in Figure 5. Clearly, SAM achieves minimal errors and is significantly better than other two models.

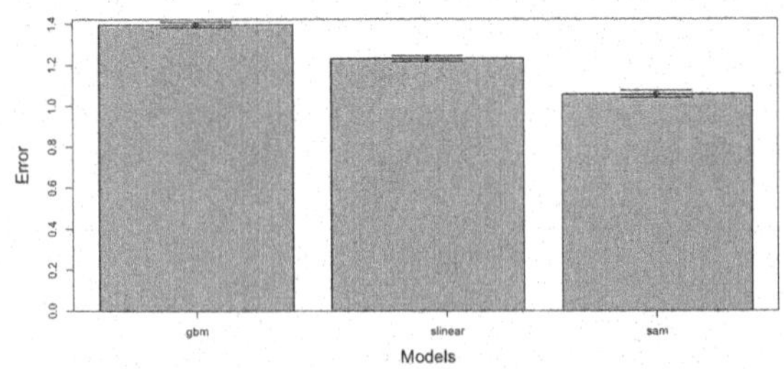

Figure 5: Prediction errors of treatment fitting in real example. The"gbm", "slinear", and "sam" refer to gradient boosted machine, sparse linear model, and sparse additive model, respectively.

We then illustrate the findings on mobile and desktop platforms from three perspectives: 1) the ad frequency impact ; 2) the ad size impact; and 3) the synthetic impact of ad frequency and ad size.

The ad frequency impact for both mobile devices and PCs. As shown in Figure 6, when the customers are exposed to ads via the mobile devices, the number of conversions monotonically increases as the ad exposure increases. When customers are exposed to ads via the PCs, the number of conversions increases at the beginning and then decreases, and the maximal number of conversions is obtained when the users are shown 7 ads via PCs. These results advise that 7 ads are sufficient to maximize the number of conversions for online advertisements and there is little demand for this auto company to deliver more than 7 ads to the eligible users; while they should continue to show ads to customers who are exposed to less than 10 mobile ads. In addition, Figure 6 delivers that the ad frequency effects on mobile devices are marginally much larger than that on PCs. Specifically, exposing the user to 5 ads via mobile, as opposed to 1 ad via mobile will lead to about 5 extra conversions; while exposing the user to 5 ads via PCs, as opposed to 1 ad via PCs will lead to only 1 extra conversion. This suggests that in this campaign users generally has a larger chance to convert when they are shown mobile ads, which is consistent with the observation in Butcher (2010) that mobile ad campaigns are generally more effective than online norms.

and subject to anonymization, and thus do not necessarily reflect the real portfolio at any particular time.

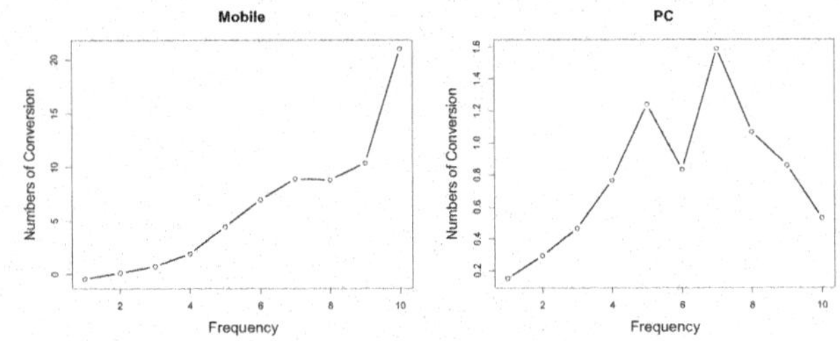

Figure 6: Fitted number of conversions versus the ad frequency for mobile devices (left) and PCs (right). The X axis is the ad frequency and Y axis is the fitted number of conversions based on our model.

The ad size impact for mobile devices and PCs from our causal inference estimation in Figure 7. A general trend is that, when the ads are shown via mobile devices, the smaller ad delivers more conversions than the larger ad. In contrast, when the ads are displayed on PCs, larger ad size triggers more conversions. This advises that on PCs it is more economic to split the large ads into several small ads to achieve more conversions.

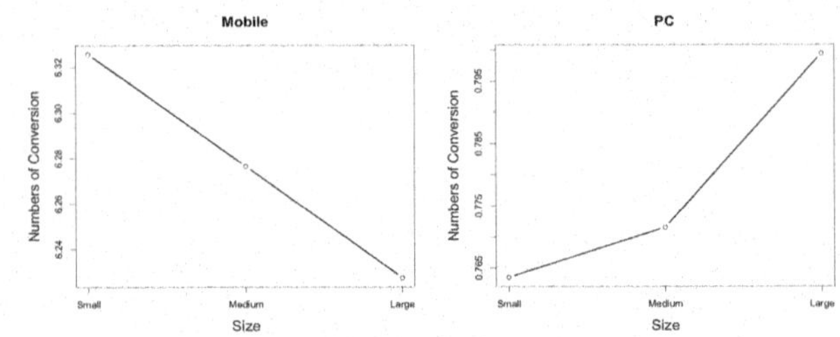

Figure 7: Fitted number of conversions versus the ad size for mobile devices (left) and PCs (right). The X axis is the ad size and Y axis is the fitted number of conversions based on our model.

The synthetic impact of ad frequency and ad size. We group ad frequencies as 1-2, 3-4, 5-6, 7-8, and 9-10 buckets for easy presentation. As illustrated in Figure 8, when the ads are shown on mobile devices, the largest conversion is obtained when the users are shown $9-10$ ads with small ad size; On the other hand, the largest conversion is obtained when the users are shown $7-8$ ads with large ad size via the PCs. Therefore, it is crucial for the ad providers to make appropriate adjustment based on the number and size of the ads the users have been exposed to.

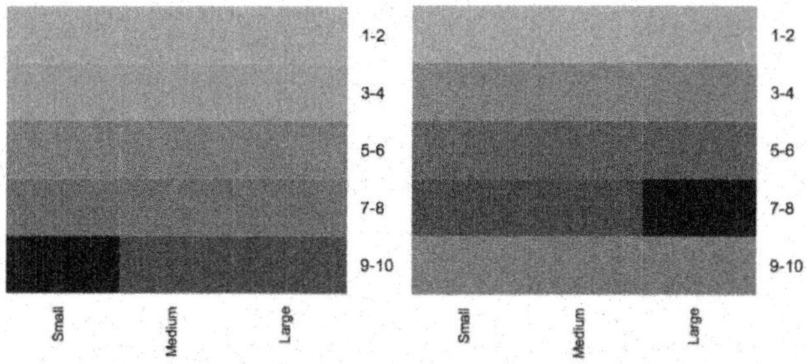

Figure 8: Heatmaps of fitted number of conversions for mobile devices (left plot) and PCs (right plot). The rows are the ad frequencies and the columns are the ad sizes.

Conclusion

In this paper we propose a novel two-stage causal inference framework for assessing the impact of complex advertising treatments. In Stage 1, we utilize SAM for propensity parameter estimation, which is essentially a non-parametric method which is more general and flexible than linear models and is suited for sparse advertising data with complex treatments. In Stage 2, we devise a propensity-adjusted regression to estimate treatment effect, which can more naturally estimate the treatment effect than the existing subclassification methods. Our model is theoretically unbiased and outperforms existing approaches in extensive experiments. Our approach is applied to a real campaign with both mobile and online ads to investigate the impact of ad frequency, ad size, and the synthetic impact across platforms. Our approach successfully draws meaningful insights from the complex dataset and provides practical guideline to the advertisers.

Note that our framework is not limited to online advertising, but is also applicable to other user engagement studies where causal impact of general treatments (e.g., UI design, content format, ad context) needs to be measured with observational data.

References

Abraham, M. 2008. The off-line impact of online ads. *Harvard Business Review* 86(4): 28.

Bottou, L.; Peters, J.; Quinonero-Candela, J.; Charles, D. X.; Chickering, D. M.; Portugaly, E.; Ray, D.; Simard, P.; and Snelson, E. 2013. Counterfactual reasoning and learning systems: The example of computational advertising. *The Journal of Machine Learning Research* 14:3207–3260.

Butcher, D. 2010. *Mobile ad campaigns 5 times more effective than online: InsightExpress study.* http://www.mobilemarketer.com.

Chan, D.; Ge, R.; Gershony, O.; Hesterberg, T.; and Lambert, D. 2010. Evaluating online ad campaigns in a pipeline: causal models at scale. In *Proceedings of SIGKDD*, 7–16. ACM.

Dalessandro, B.; Perlich, C.; Stitelman, O.; and Provost, F. 2012. Causally motivated attribution for online advertising. In *Proceedings of the Sixth International Workshop on Data Mining for Online Advertising and Internet Economy*, 7. ACM.

Hastie, T. J., and Tibshirani, R. J. 1990. *Generalized Additive Models*. Chapman and Hall/CRC.

Hullsiek, K., and Louis, T. 2002. Propensity score modeling strategies for the causal analysis of observational data. *Biostatistics* 2:179–193.

Imai, K., and van Dyk, D. A. 2004. Causal inference with general treatment regimes. *Journal of the American Statistical Association* 99:854–866.

Kohav, R., and Longbotham, R. 2010. Unexpected results in online controlled experiments. *SIGKDD Explorations* 12(2).

Lee, B.; Lessler, J.; and Stuart, E. 2010. Improving propensity score weighting using machine learning. *Statistics in Medicine* 29:337–346.

Liu, H.; Lafferty, J.; and Wasserman, L. 2008. Nonparametric regression and classification with joint sparsity constraints. In *Proceedings of NIPS*. ACM.

Ravikumar, P.; Lafferty, J.; Liu, H.; and Wasserman, L. 2009. Sparse additive models. *Journal of the Royal Statistical Society, Series B* 71:1009–1030.

Rosenbaum, P. R., and Rubin, D. B. 1983. The central role of the propensity score in observational studies for causal effects. *Biometrika* 70(1):41–55.

Rosenbaum, P. R., and Rubin, D. B. 1984. Reducing bias in observational studies using subclassification on the propensity score. *Journal of the American Statistical Association* 79(387):516–524.

Rosenkrans, G. 2009. The creativeness & effectiveness of online interactive rich media advertising. *Journal of Interactive Advertising* 9(2):18–31.

Stitelman, O.; Dalessandro, B.; Perlich, C.; and Provost, F. 2011. Estimating the effect of online display advertising on browser conversion. *Data Mining and Audience Intelligence for Advertising* 8.

Su, X.; Kang, J.; Fan, J.; Levine, R. A.; and Yan, X. 2012. Facilitating score and causal inference trees for large observational studies. *The Journal of Machine Learning Research* 13(1):2955–2994.

Sun, W.; Wang, J.; and Fang, Y. 2013. Consistent selection of tuning parameters via variable selection stability. *The Journal of Machine Learning Research* 14:3419–3440.

Tibshirani, R. 1996. Regression shrinkage and selection via the lasso. *Journal of the Royal Statistical Society. Series B (Methodological)* 267–288.

Wang, P.; Liu, Y.; Meytlis, M.; Tsao, H.-Y.; Yang, J.; and Huang, P. 2014. An efficient framework for online advertising effectiveness measurement and comparison. In *Proceedings of WSDM*. ACM.

Wang, P.; Traskin, M.; and Small, D. S. 2013. Robust inferences from a before-and-after study with multiple unaffected control groups. *Journal of Causal Inference* 1–26.

Woo, M.; Reiter, J.; and Karr, A. 2008. Estimation of propensity scores using generalized additive models. *Statistics in Medicine* 27:3805–3816.

Sampling Representative Users from Large Social Networks

Jie Tang[†♯], Chenhui Zhang[†♯], Keke Cai[‡], Li Zhang[‡], Zhong Su[‡]
[†]Department of Computer Science and Technology, Tsinghua University
[♯]Tsinghua National Laboratory for Information Science and Technology (TNList)
[‡]IBM, China Research Lab
jietang@tsinghua.edu.cn, zh.sherlock@gmail.com, {caikeke, lizhang, suzhong}@cn.ibm.com

Abstract

Finding a subset of users to statistically represent the original social network is a fundamental issue in Social Network Analysis (SNA). The problem has not been extensively studied in existing literature. In this paper, we present a formal definition of the problem of **sampling representative users** from social network. We propose two sampling models and theoretically prove their NP-hardness. To efficiently solve the two models, we present an efficient algorithm with provable approximation guarantees. Experimental results on two datasets show that the proposed models for sampling representative users significantly outperform (+6%-23% in terms of Precision@100) several alternative methods using authority or structure information only. The proposed algorithms are also effective in terms of time complexity. Only a few seconds are needed to sampling 300 representative users from a network of 100,000 users. All data and codes are publicly available.[1]

Introduction

In social networks, a small subset of users (e.g., opinion leaders) usually plays an important role in influencing the social dynamics (behavior and structure). For example, in HCI, for conducting surveys and collecting user feedbacks, selecting representative users is always a key issue (Landauer 1997). On the other hand, in a social network, users may have different *representative degrees* from different aspects (topics). For example, iPhone fans may have a high representative degree on some fashion products, while housewives have a high representative degree on cooking or children's products. One interesting question is: can we design an algorithm to automatically sampling representative users for different topics from large social networks?

Despite several relevant studies, such as those on social influence analysis (Anagnostopoulos, Kumar, and Mahdian 2008; Crandall et al. 2008; Singla and Richardson 2008; Tang et al. 2009), influence maximization (Kempe, Kleinberg, and Tardos 2003; Chen, Wang, and Yang 2009; Scripps, Tan, and Esfahanian 2009), and opinion leader finding (Goyal, Bonchi, and Lakshmanan 2008), there are few theoretical studies on the problem of sampling representative users (SRU). Unlike influence maximization, in which the goal is to find a set of nodes (users) in a social network who can maximize the spread of influence (Richardson and Domingos 2002; Kempe, Kleinberg, and Tardos 2003), the objective of sampling representative users is to identify a few "average" users who can *statistically* represent the characteristics of all users (Landauer 1997). Another type of related work is social influence analysis. Anagnostopoulos et al. (2008) and Singla and Richardson (2008) propose methods to qualitatively measure the existence of influence. Crandall et al. (2008) studies the correlation between social similarity and influence. Tang et al. (2009) presents a method for measuring the strength of such influence. The problem of sampling representative users from social networks is also relevant to graph sampling (Leskovec and Faloutsos 2006; Maiya and Berger-Wolf 2010; 2011; Ugander et al. 2013). However, most existing works focus on studying the network topology and ignore the topic information. Sun et al. (2013) aims to find representative users from the information spreading perspective and Ahmed et al. (2013) studies the network sampling problem in the dynamic environment. Papagelis et al. (2013) presents a sampling-based algorithm to efficiently explore a user's ego network respecting its structure and to quickly approximate quantities of interest. However, the problem itself is different from that sampling representative users for the whole network.

Problem and Our Solution. We use an example from a coauthor network to clearly demonstrate the motivation of this work. In Figure 1, the left figure shows a coauthor network and attributes (or interests) of each researcher. For example, George has a higher interest degree (0.9) on topic "database" than the degree (0.1) on "data mining". The right figure shows the output of topic-based representative users, highlighted with rectangles, where "Ada" and "Frank" are identified as the representative authors on topic "data mining" and "George" and "Eve" are representative users on the "database" topic. The weighted directed edge between the representative user and another user indicates how likely the selected user represents the other user. For example, on topic "data mining", "Ada" has a higher representative degree for "Eve" than "Bob". The problem of sampling representative users from large networks is fundamental for many social network mining tasks. For example, in existing literature,

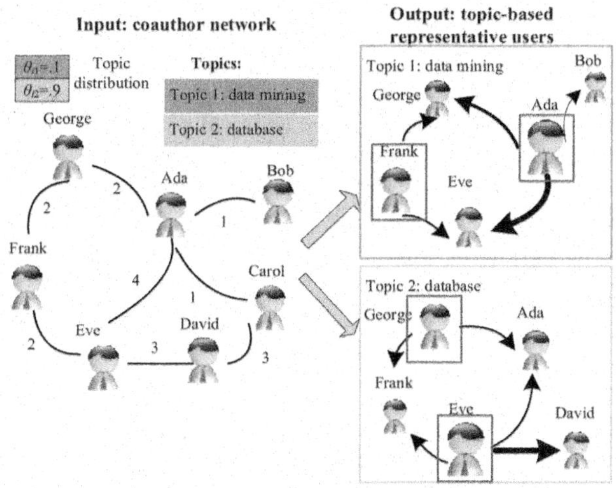

Figure 1: Example of sampling representative users from the coauthor network.

analytic/mining tasks were usually evaluated on a random sampled network. How reliable is the result? It is necessary to design a principled approach to solve the problem.

In this paper, we aim to systematically investigate the problem of sampling representative users from social networks. We formally define the and by linking it to the Dominating Set Problem, we prove that the problem is NP-hard (Cf. Section 3). We design a quality function Q to evaluate the set of sampled users and develop two instantiation models for estimating the Q function. To approximate the optimal solution, we present efficient algorithms to solve the two models with provable approximation guarantees. Finally, we conduct extensive experiments to demonstrate the effectiveness and efficiency of the proposed models on one coauthor dataset and another microblog dataset.

Problem Formulation

Consider a social network $G = (V, E)$, where V is the set of users and $E \subset V \times V$ is the set of directed/undirected links between users. Let $X_i = [x_{ik}]_{k=1\cdots d}$ denote a set of attributes (topics) associated with the user $v_i \in V$, where d is the number of attributes and x_{ik} records the value of the kth attribute of user v_i. For each edge $e_{ij} \in E$, we associate a weight w_{ij}.

Given this, we can define a function to indicate the representative degree of a subset of users T. More precisely, for any subset $T \subseteq V$ and a user $v_i \in V$, we define the *representative degree* of T for v_i on a specific attribute a_j to be $R(T, v_i, a_j)$ with a score ranging in $[0, 1]$. We say T perfectly represents v_i on attribute a_j if $R(T, v_i, a_j) = 1$. For $T = \emptyset$, we have $R(T, v_i, a_j) = 0$. If T contains only one user v, $R(T, v_i, a_j)$ is the degree that v represents v_i on attribute a_j. This score is determined by the input networking data and the way to compute the function R. This formulation is very flexible and can easily incorporate other information. For example, to incorporate the network information, a straightforward method is to treat each node in the network as an attribute and define a neighbor group for each node, i.e., T is equivalent to the set of neighbors for a given user v_i.

Without loss of generality, there are often two types of attributes. The first type is the numeric attribute. For example, in a coauthor network, an attribute can be the interest degree of a user on a topic. Those people with a higher value are more representative. The second type is the non-comparable attribute, for example, the job title. Intuitively, it is better to select users with different job titles (to cover all values of the attribute). To do this, one idea is to divide all people into different groups according to the attribute value. Then the problem is cast as selecting users to represent each group.

Based on this idea, we can define a group of people with attribute value a_{j_k} as $V_k \subseteq V$. We refer to such a group together with the corresponding attribute as an *attribute group*. We use t to denote the number of attribute groups and $\mathbf{G}$ to denote the set of all groups, thus

$$\mathbf{G} = \{(V_1, a_{j_1}), (V_2, a_{j_2}), \ldots, (V_t, a_{j_t})\}.$$

Now we give the definition of representative degree for each attribute group as follows.

Definition 1. ***Attribute group representative degree.*** *For an attribute group* (V_l, a_{j_l}) *(*$1 \leq l \leq t$*), let*

$$P(T, l) = \sum_{v_i \in V_l} R(T, v_i, a_{j_l})$$

be the representative degree of T *for attribute group* (V_l, a_{j_l})*. We say the attribute group* (V_l, a_{j_l}) *is represented if all people in* V_l *are perfectly represented on attribute* a_{j_l}*.*

In practice, it might be difficult to find a perfect representation. The representative degree $P(T, l)$ then quantifies how likely the subset T can represent all people in V_l on attribute a_{j_l}.

Our goal in this paper is to find the representative set T so that it has the highest representative degree $P(T, l)$ for all attributes. In general, given a social network G, the attributes distributions X, the attribute groups $\mathbf{G}$ and the representative set T, we can formally define the following problem:

Problem 1. ***Sampling Representative Users.*** *Given (1) a social network* $G = (V, E)$*, where* V *is the set of users and* E *is the set of directed edges, (2)* d *attributes associated with each user, a desirable number* k *of users to be selected, (3)* t *attribute groups to be represented, (4) a quality function* Q*, how to find the set* T *of* k *representative users with maximal quality? Formally, we have the following optimization problem:*

$$\arg\max_{T \subseteq V, |T| = k} Q(G, X, \mathbf{G}, T).$$

Proposed Models

In this section, we first perform a theoretical investigation of the problem of sampling representative users from a social network. We link this problem to the Dominating Set Problem and prove its NP-hardness. Then we develop two instantiation models for the problem.

Theoretical Basic

Given a predefined quality function $Q(G, X, \mathbf{G}, T)$, the problem of sampling the representative set with maximal quality is referred to as a *Q-evaluated Representative Users Sampling* Problem (shortly Q-SRU). For any specified Q, the Q-evaluated representative users sampling problem is a subproblem of the original representative users sampling problem. The following theorem shows the NP-hardness of this problem.

Theorem 1. *For any fixed Q, the Q-evaluated Representative Users Sampling problem is NP-hard.*

Proof. We prove the theorem by a reduction to the Dominating Set Problem (Garey and Johnson 1979; Karp 1972). We construct an instance of the Q-SRU problem as follows:

Consider in a network G, if there is only one attribute (i.e., a_1) and only one attribute group (V, a_1). For $v_i \neq v_{i'} \in V$, assign $R(\{v_{i'}\}, v_i, a_1) = 1$ if edge $e_{i,i'} \in E$; assign $R(\{v_{i'}\}, v_i, a_1) = 0$ otherwise. For every $v_i \in V$, we also assign $R(\{v_{i'}\}, v_i, a_1) = 1$. We can see that for a given subset of V, a person is perfectly represented if and only if the corresponding vertex is dominated. Therefore the Dominating Set Problem is equivalent to the problem of evaluating whether there exists a k-element representative set to represent all users perfectly.

Regarding the quality function, Q can be rewritten as a t-variable function f taking $P(T, l)$ $(1 \leq l \leq t)$ as parameters. When every $P(T, l)$ reaches its maximal value $|V_l|$, the value of f is maximized, and this must be the only maximal point of f (distinguishable). If we can find the maximal value of Q, we can accordingly determine whether f (equal to Q) reaches the maximal value, which allows us to further determine whether there exist a k-element dominating set. Based on this analysis, we can conclude that the Q-evaluated Representative Users Sampling problem is NP-hard. □

Two Sampling Models

In social science, two basic principles to select representative users are synecdoche (in which a specific instance stands for the general case) and metonymy (in which a specific concept stands for another related or broader concept) (Landauer 1997). In effect, we treat one user as being a synecdochic representative of all users, and we treat one measurement on that user as being a metonymic indicator of all of the relevant attributes of that user and all users. Based on the above principles, we can consider many different methods to choose the representative user, such as statistics (Landauer 1997), grounded theory (Strauss and Corbin 1990), political theory (Schuler and Namioka 1993), and design practice. Here, we develop two practical instantiation models: Statistical Stratified Sample (S^3) and Strategic Sampling for Diversity (SSD) models.

Model 1: Statistical Stratified Sample (S^3) Maximizing the representative degree of all attribute groups is infeasible in practice. Some trade-offs should be considered as we may need to choose some less representative users on some attributes in order to increase the global representative degree on all attributes groups.

For each attribute group $(V_l, a_{j_l}) \in \mathbf{G}$, we assign a score m_l $(m_l > 0)$ to indicate the "importance" of this group. Usually we can choose m_l to be related with the size of V_l. The groups with a higher m_l value should be better represented. We do not want to finally have an attribute group with only one single user. It is preferable to have some "bias" to select user who can represent large attribute groups. We use a value $\beta \in (0, 1]$ to denote this bias, and give the following quality function:

$$Q(G, X, \mathbf{G}, T) = \sum_{(V_l, a_{j_l}) \in \mathbf{G}} m_l \{P(T, l)\}^{\beta}. \quad (1)$$

To explain the "bias" clearly, we consider an extreme but intuitive case: The attribute groups have no intersection ($V_{l_1} \cap V_{l_2} = \emptyset$ for all l_1, l_2), and $R(T, v_i, a_j) = 1$ if $v_i \in T$, $R(T, v_i, a_j) = 0$ otherwise. Then for each group $1 \leq l \leq t$, the representative degree $P(T, l)$ is exactly the number of users in both T and V_l. Therefore the summation of all $P(T, l)$ is the fixed value $|T| = k$.

For $0 < \beta < 1$, by the concave property of function x^{β}, Q reaches the maximal value if and only if $P(T, l_1) : P(T, l_2) = m_{l_1}^{\frac{1}{1-\beta}} : m_{l_2}^{\frac{1}{1-\beta}}$ for any $1 \leq l, l' \leq t$. If we select $m_l = |V_l|^{1-\beta}$, the proportion of the selected users from each group tends to be the same. For $\beta \to 0$, the bias is linear in the sense that for every $1 \leq l \leq t$, the number of representative users for (V_l, a_{j_l}) is the same proportion of m_l. For $\beta = 1$, the bias tends to infinity in the sense that all the selected users represent the most important attribute group.

Model 2: Strategic Sampling for Diversity (SSD) In this model our goal is the diversification of delegates. When k is small, diversity means to find some users to cover (having a non-zero representative degree) as many groups as possible. We would ignore this case here, because the users to be selected are usually more than the number of attribute groups so that we can pick one user for each group to insure all groups are covered. Assume that there is a representative set T such that $P(T, l) > 0$ for every $1 \leq l \leq t$. "Diversity" here means that we want to sample users such that we have a balanced $P(T, l)$ for all attributes (by avoiding extremely large or small $P(T, l)$).

In practice, the size of attribute groups may vary significantly. For a large group V_l, $P(T, l)$ should be also relatively large. The objective is that all these values can be balanced. For example, an extreme case is that all the values are identical or the size of each group is the same. Simply requiring the distribution is not However, the practical case is much more complex. Consider the case that every attribute group has the same size and we want all $P(T, l)$ to be identical. In this case, any representative set is no better than the empty set, which represents every group with a same degree. This is not useful to solve the problem. We still require every attribute group to be well represented, thus we give the following quality function:

$$Q(G, X, \mathbf{G}, T) = \min_{(V_l, a_{j_l}) \in \mathbf{G}} \{\lambda_l \cdot P(T, l)\}, \quad (2)$$

```
Input: The set of users V; the set of attributes A; the attributes
       values X; the values R(T, v_i, a_j) for every |T| = 1
       and v_i ∈ V, a_j ∈ A; the number of users to find k.
Output: A set T of k representative users.
T = ∅;
while |T| < k do
    max = −1;
    foreach v_i ∉ T do
        foreach (V_l, a_{j_l}) ∈ G that v_i can contribute do
            foreach v_{i'} ∈ V_l that R({v_i}, v_{i'}, a_{j_l}) > 0 do
                Compute the increment of R(T, v_{i'}, a_{j_l});
            end
            Compute the total increment of P(T, l);
        end
        Compute the increment of quality by adding v_i;
        if increment > max then
            v = v_i;
            Update max;
        end
    end
    T = T ∪ {v};
    Update the values R(T, v_{i'}, a_j) and P(T, l);
end
return T;
```

Algorithm 1: Approximate algorithm for S^3 model.

where λ_l is a positive constant associated with the attribute group (V_l, a_{j_l}). Usually we choose $\lambda_l = |V_l|^{-1}$. We call the attribute group with smallest $\lambda_l \cdot P(T, l)$ the *poorest group*. The quality function depends on the performance of T for the poorest group.

Approximate Algorithms

In this section, we present efficient algorithms with provable approximation guarantee to solve the proposed models.

Approximate Algorithm for S^3 Model

We give a greedy heuristic algorithm. Each time we traverse all users and find the one that mostly increases the quality function Q. We use arrays to store how each user is represented on each attribute, and how each attribute group is represented. For the increase in quality achieved by adding a user $v_i \in V$, we only need to consider the attribute groups that v_i can contribute to (at most t) and v_i's neighbors (we say $v_{i'}$ is v_i's neighbor if $R(\{v_i\}, v_{i'}, a_j) > 0$ for some $a_j \in A$) in those attribute groups. The algorithm is summarized in Algorithm 1 and its complexity is $O(t \times k \times |E|)$.

Error Bound Analysis: We show that the algorithm can guarantee a $(1 - 1/e)$-approximate.

We first consider the submodular property of the quality function defined in Eq. 1. A function $f : V \to \mathbb{R}^+$ is submodular if for all sets $S \subseteq T \subseteq V$ and every element $v \in V$, it has

$$f(S \cup \{v\}) - f(S) \geq f(T \cup \{v\}) - f(T)$$

Function f is monotone increasing if for all sets $S \subseteq T \subseteq V$, there is

$$f(T) \geq f(S)$$

For a function f that is both monotonically increasing and submodular, we could add elements one-by-one into a set T. Suppose the elements are $v_1, v_2, \ldots, v_k$, and we use T_i to denote the set of i-th step $\{v_1, v_2, \ldots, v_i\}$ $(1 \leq i \leq k)$. We see that each time we add an element into T, there is an increment of $f(T)$. If some of the previous elements were not added, this increment becomes larger or stays the same. At each step, we choose to add an element $v \in V$ that maximizes $f(T \cup \{v\}) - f(T)$. In this way, we can use a greedy heuristic, that is each time we choose the element that increases $f(T)$ the most, i.e.,

$$f(T_2) - f(T_1) \geq f(T_3) - f(T_2) \geq \cdots \geq f(T_k) - f(T_{k-1})$$

Intuitively, the greedy algorithm can generate a good approximate solution for the problem of sampling a k-element set T that maximizes $f(T)$. Suppose the generated set is T and the optimal set is T^*. We consider the set $T \cup T^*$, whose function value is larger than (or worse case equal to) that of T^* according to the monotonic property of f. We can construct $T \cup T^*$ as follows: we first use greedy heuristic and add k elements of T into it, then we add elements in $T^* - T$ one-by-one. We see that for every element in $T^* - T$, the increment is not larger than the increment of any element in T. Since $l \leq k$ there must be $2 \cdot f(T) \geq f(T \cup T^*) \geq f(T^*)$. A tighter bound is reported in (Nemhauser, Wolsey, and Fisher 1978). For every monotonically increasing, submodular, non-negative function f on V, the set generated by the greedy heuristic is at least $(1 - 1/e)$ of the optimal solution.

Approximate Algorithm for SSD Model

For the SSD model, according to its definition of the quality function, intuitively we can design a greedy algorithm as follows: each time we choose the poorest group, and select a user to increase the representative degree of this group.

Similar to Algorithm 1, we use arrays to store the current values of $R(T, v_i, a_j)$ and $P(T, l)$ for every $v_i \in V$, $a_j \in A$ and $1 \leq l \leq t$. At the beginning of this algorithm, all groups are considered to be the poorest. Then we process with greedy heuristics as follows: We combine the procedure of finding the poorest group and the procedure of finding the user to improve this group together. We traverse every user v_i, and every group (V_l, a_{j_l}) to which v_i contributes. Then we compute the improvement of $P(V_l, l)$ by adding v_i (similar to Algorithm 1). If (V_l, l) is even poorer than the poorest ever seen, we mark v_i as the best candidate. If this group is as poor as the poorest group, we consider whether the improvement of $\lambda_l P(V_l, l)$ is larger than the previous poorest group. If so we mark v_i as the best candidate. Details of the algorithm and its error bound analysis is omitted for brevity.

Experimental Results

We conduct various experiments to evaluate the effectiveness of the proposed approach. All data sets, codes, and tools to visualize the mining results are publicly available. [1]

[1] http://arnetminer.org/repuser/

Experimental Setup

Datasets. We perform experiments on two different genres of datasets. The first type is author datasets: DB and DM. Each consists of authors and coauthor relationships extracted from major conferences in a specific domain, where the goal is to find who are representative authors in the corresponding domain. For the Database domain, we extract all authors from papers published on the three major conferences (SIGMOD, VLDB, ICDE) during 2007-2009. In total, we collect 8,027 authors and 23,770 coauthor relationships. For the Data Mining domain, we extract authors from papers published on the three major conferences (SIGKDD, ICDM, CIKM) during 2007-2009. In total, we collect 6,394 authors and 12,454 coauthor relationships.

As for the attributes of authors, we extract keywords from the papers in each dataset. For each author, we then define the value of an attribute as the number of times she/he uses the corresponding keyword in the authored papers. For each dataset, we first downcase all the keywords and then extract 200 most frequently used keywords. For evaluation, it is difficult to find a standard dataset with ground truth. Finally, we take program committee (PC) members of the conferences in each dataset during 2007-2009 as representative users. Typically, program committee members of a conference not only include top experts in a domain, but also include authors with expertise covering all subareas of the domain. Therefore, our goal is to predict who are representative users (PC members of the three major conferences) for the two research domains, respectively. Finally, we collect 291 representative users (by removing those who are not coauthors papers we collected) in the Database dataset and 373 representative users in the Data Mining dataset. Table 1 shows detailed statistics of the two datasets.

The second type of data is a mibroblog network. We crawled the messages from Weibo and classify them by keywords into 4 datasets, namely, program, food, student and public welfare. Then, we extracted the senders and the sender-follower relationships for each message. For program domain, we find 330 messages and collect 19,152 senders as well as 19,225 sender-follower relationships. There are 2,956 messages including 189176 senders and 204,863 sender-follower relationships in food domain. 859 messages with 79,052 senders and 76,559 sender-follower relationships are collected for student domain while 2,410 messages with 324,594 senders and 383,702 sender-follower relationships are collected for public welfare domain. We consider the basic information of each user as the attributes, including location, gender, registration date, verified type, status, description and the number of friends or followers. All the attributes are classified into several categories denoting by numbers and the value of an attribute is defined as those number. As there is no ground truth for the Weibo data, we mainly use this dataset for evaluating efficiency and qualitative evaluation.

Evaluation Measures, Baseline Methods. For comparison purposes, we define the following baseline methods:

- *InDegree*. It simply takes the number of links as the criteria to select the representative users who have the highest indegree scores.

Table 1: Statistics of the two datasets.

Dataset	Conf.	#authors	#coauthorships	#representatives
Database	SIGMOD	3,447	9,507	256
	VLDB	3,606	8,943	251
	ICDE	4,150	9,120	244
Sum	ALL	8,027	23,770	291
Data Mining	SIGKDD	2,494	4,898	243
	ICDM	2,121	3,452	211
	CIKM	2,942	4,921	205
Sum	ALL	6,394	12,454	373

- *HITS_h and HITS_a*. It applies the HITS algorithm (Kleinberg 1999) to the author networks to calculate two values for each node: *authority* representing a score of authority of the node, and *hub* value representing a score based on the node's out-links to other nodes, thus resulting in two baselines, HITS_h and HITS_a. The former selects nodes with the highest hub scores while the latter selects nodes with the highest authorities.
- *PageRank*. It employs the PageRank algorithm (Page et al. 1999) to estimate the importance of each node in a network via a random process. This method selects nodes with the highest PageRank scores as representative users.

In our method, we consider the network information by treating each node as an attribute. We implement all the algorithms C++. In all experiments, we conduct evaluations for all methods in terms of P@10, P@50, P@100, R@50, R@100, and F1-measure (Buckley and Voorhees 2004).

Results

We evaluate the performance of the proposed models for sampling representative users on the two datasets. Let f_l be the total frequency of the l-th keyword ($1 \leq l \leq 200$). We assign $m_l = f_l^{0.5}$ in the S^3 model and $\lambda_l = f_l^{-1}$ in the SSD model. The parameter β in the S^3 model is set to be $\beta = 0.7$, by tuning from 0.1 to 1 with interval 0.1. We also compare our approach to the baseline methods.

Table 2 and 3 list the results of the comparison methods on the two datasets with the following observations:

High Precision. The proposed models achieve the best performance on both datasets. In terms of P@10, P@50, and P@100, the S^3 model significantly outperforms the other methods (+18.0%-28.0% by P@50 for example) on the Database, and performs best as well on Data Mining in terms of P@10, P@50. On the Database the SSD model finally achieves the best accuracy by Precision, Recall, and F1-measure, while on Data Mining S^3 model achieves the best accuracy.

Precision-Recall Curve. Figure 2 illustrates the precision-recall curve of the different methods. It can be seen that on the Database dataset, our S^3 model clearly outperforms the baseline methods. The SSD underperforms the InDegree algorithm when the recall is small, but when increasing the recall, for example up to 40%, the SSD model performs the best, even better than the S^3 model. On the Data Mining dataset, the S^3 also model clearly performs best. The SSD model starts to perform better when increasing recall.

Table 2: Performance of different methods on the Database dataset (%). (In Model 1, we set $\beta = 0.6$.)

Methods	P@10	P@50	P@100	R@50	R@100	F1
InDegree	50.0	36.0	40.0	6.2	13.7	33.0
HITS_h	40.0	30.0	27.0	5.2	9.3	20.3
HITS_a	30.0	30.0	30.0	5.2	10.3	24.1
PageRank	40.0	26.0	27.0	4.5	9.3	24.7
S^3	70.0	46.0	46.0	7.9	15.8	41.9
SSD	10.0	36.0	39.0	6.2	13.4	32.6

Table 3: Performance of different methods on the Data Mining dataset (%). (In Model 1, we set $\beta = 0.6$.)

Methods	P@10	P@50	P@100	R@50	R@100	F1
InDegree	80.0	62.0	45.0	8.3	12.1	28.4
HITS_h	70.0	42.0	30.0	5.6	8.0	21.4
HITS_a	70.0	48.0	30.0	6.4	8.0	18.8
PageRank	50.0	38.0	30.0	5.1	8.0	24.9
S^3	80.0	64.0	53.0	8.6	14.2	36.7
SSD	20.0	32.0	22.0	4.3	5.9	22.5

Efficiency. We further compare the efficiency of the proposed methods with the baseline methods. Table 4 lists the CPU time required by the different methods to find representative users respectively from the coauthor datasets and the Weibo dataset. Our methods are found to be very efficient, for the SSD model only requires 0.54s for Database, 0.74s for Data Mining and 0.67s for Weibo in program domain, and is faster than the S^3 model.

Effect of Parameter β for S^3. On both datasets, the S^3 performs the best. We set the parameter β in the S^3 model as $\beta = 0.7$. We then analyze how the parameter affects the model performance. We test the performance of the S^3 model by with the parameter β varied. We found that the model is not very sensitive with β, although the performances of S^3 with different values for β are a bit different. Generally, S^3 achieves the best performance on Database at $\beta = 0.4$, and on Data Mining at $\beta = 0.7$. This confirms the effectiveness of our proposed methods.

Case Study. We demonstrate here the effectiveness of the two proposed models for representative user identification on the Database and Data Mining datasets.

Table 5 shows representative authors found by our methods and one baseline method (PageRank) from the two coauthor datasets. For each dataset, we list the top 10 representative authors found by the different methods (more details about the results is online available.). Compared with the authority-based baseline method (PageRank), our method has several distinct advantages: First, the baseline method can only measure the similarity between nodes, but does not consider the diversity of attributes, which is necessary for the statistical representation. Second, the baseline method cannot tell which users can be represented by a selected representative user on a specific attribute, while our methods have the capacity to do so.

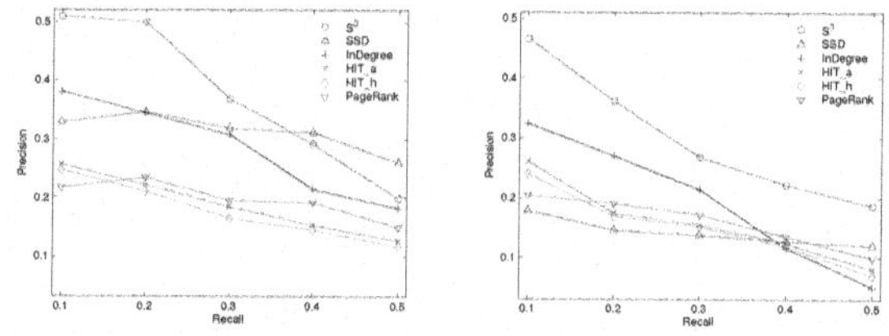

(a) Database (b) Data Mining

Figure 2: Precision-recall curves of the comparison methods on the Database and Data Mining datasets.

Table 4: Efficiency performance of different methods on the three datasets. The CPU time does not include the time of loading the network data. (Second)

Methods	Database (291)	Data Mining (373)	Weibo (200)	
			Program	Food
InDegree	0.10	0.16	0.01	0.02
HITS_h	2.44	1.58	0.99	45.66
HITS_a	2.44	1.58	0.95	45.60
PageRank	6.89	2.95	0.51	18.33
S^3	1.68	3.62	4.45	50.71
SSD	0.54	0.74	0.67	10.81

Conclusions

In this paper, we study a novel problem of sampling representative users from social networks, with the objective of finding a small subset of users to statistically represent all users in the original social network. We formally define this problem and perform a theoretical investigation of the problem, and prove its NP-hardness. Approximate algorithms for the two models have been developed to efficiently choose the set of representative users. Experimental results on two author datasets demonstrate the effectiveness and efficiency of the proposed models.

Acknowledgements

Jie Tang and Chenhui Zhang are supported by National 863 project (2014AA015103), National 973 projects (2014CB340506, 2012CB316006, 2011CB302302), NSFC

Table 5: Example of representative author sampling from the coauthor datasets. From each dataset, we list the top 10 representative users found by the two methods respectively.

S^3		PageRank	
Database	Data Mining	Database	Data Mining
Jiawei Han	Philip S. Yu	Serge Abiteboul	Philip S. Yu
Jeffrey F. Naughton	Jiawei Han	Rakesh Agrawal	Jiawei Han
Beng Chin Ooi	Christos Faloutsos	Michael J. Carey	Jian Pei
Samuel Madden	ChengXiang Zhai	Jiawei Han	Christos Faloutsos
Johannes Gehrke	Bing Liu	Michael Stonebraker	Ke Wang
Kian-Lee Tan	Vipin Kumar	Manish Bhide	Wei-Ying Ma
Surajit Chaudhuri	Jieping Ye	Ajay Gupta	Jianyong Wang
Elke A. Rundensteiner	Ming-Syan Chen	H. V. Jagadish	Jeffrey Xu Yu
Divyakant Agrawal	Padhraic Smyth	Surajit Chaudhuri	Haixun Wang
Wei Wang	C. Lee Giles	Warren Shen	Hongjun Lu

(61222212), and a research fund from IBM.

References

Ahmed, N. K.; Neville, J.; and Kompella, R. 2013. Network sampling: From static to streaming graphs. *ACM Trans. Knowl. Discov. Data* (8).

Anagnostopoulos, A.; Kumar, R.; and Mahdian, M. 2008. Influence and correlation in social networks. In *KDD'08*, 7–15.

Buckley, C., and Voorhees, E. M. 2004. Retrieval evaluation with incomplete information. In *SIGIR'2004*, 25–32.

Chen, W.; Wang, Y.; and Yang, S. 2009. Efficient influence maximization in social networks. In *KDD'09*, 199–207.

Crandall, D.; Cosley, D.; Huttenlocher, D.; Kleinberg, J.; and Suri, S. 2008. Feedback effects between similarity and social influence in online communities. In *KDD'08*, 160–168.

Garey, M. R., and Johnson, D. S. 1979. *Computers and Intractability: A Guide to the Theory of NP-Completeness.* W.H. Freeman and Company.

Goyal, A.; Bonchi, F.; and Lakshmanan, L. V. 2008. Discovering leaders from community actions. In *CIKM'2008*, 499–508.

Karp, R. M. 1972. *Reducibility Among Combinatorial Problems. In the book of Complexity of Computer Computations, R. E. Miller and J. W. Thatcher (editors).* New York, USA: Plenum.

Kempe, D.; Kleinberg, J.; and Tardos, E. 2003. Maximizing the spread of influence through a social network. In *KDD'03*, 137–146.

Kleinberg, J. 1999. Authoritative sources in a hyperlinked environment. *Journal of the ACM* 46(5):604–632.

Landauer, T. K. 1997. Behavioural research methods in human-computer interaction. *M. Helander, T.K. Landauer, and P. Prabhu, (Eds.), Handbook of Human-Computer Interaction.*

Leskovec, J., and Faloutsos, C. 2006. Sampling from large graphs. In *KDD'06*, 631–636.

Maiya, A. S., and Berger-Wolf, T. Y. 2010. Sampling community structure. In *WWW'10*, 701–710.

Maiya, A. S., and Berger-Wolf, T. Y. 2011. Benefits of bias: Towards better characterization of network sampling. In *KDD'11*, 105–113.

Nemhauser, G. L.; Wolsey, L. A.; and Fisher, M. L. 1978. An analysis of approximations for maximizing submodular set functions. *Mathematical Programming* 14(1):265–294.

Page, L.; Brin, S.; Motwani, R.; and Winograd, T. 1999. The pagerank citation ranking: Bringing order to the web. Technical Report SIDL-WP-1999-0120, Stanford University.

Papagelis, M.; Das, G.; and Koudas, N. 2013. Sampling online social networks. *IEEE TKDE* 25(3):662–676.

Richardson, M., and Domingos, P. 2002. Mining knowledge-sharing sites for viral marketing. In *KDD'02*, 61–70.

Schuler, D., and Namioka, A. 1993. *Participatory Design: Principles and Practices.* Hillsdale, NJ, USA: Erlbaum.

Scripps, J.; Tan, P.-N.; and Esfahanian, A.-H. 2009. Measuring the effects of preprocessing decisions and network forces in dynamic network analysis. In *KDD'2009*, 747–756.

Singla, P., and Richardson, M. 2008. Yes, there is a correlation: - from social networks to personal behavior on the web. In *WWW'08*, 655–664.

Strauss, A. L., and Corbin, J. M. 1990. *Basics of qualitative research : grounded theory procedures and techniques.* Newbury Park CA USA: Sage.

Sun, K.; Morrison, D.; Bruno, E.; and Marchand-Maillet, S. 2013. Learning representative nodes in social networks. In *PAKDD'13*, 25–36.

Tang, J.; Sun, J.; Wang, C.; and Yang, Z. 2009. Social influence analysis in large-scale networks. In *KDD'09*, 807–816.

Ugander, J.; Karrer, B.; Backstrom, L.; and Kleinberg, J. 2013. Graph cluster randomization: Network exposure to multiple universes. In *KDD'13*, 329–337.

Proceedings of the Twenty-Ninth AAAI Conference on Artificial Intelligence

Relating Romanized Comments to News Articles by Inferring Multi-*Glyphic* Topical Correspondence

Goutham Tholpadi, Mrinal Kanti Das, Trapit Bansal, Chiranjib Bhattacharyya
Indian Institute of Science
Bengaluru, INDIA 560004
{gtholpadi,mrinal,trapit,chiru}@csa.iisc.ernet.in

Abstract

Commenting is a popular facility provided by news sites. Analyzing such user-generated content has recently attracted research interest. However, in multilingual societies such as India, analyzing such user-generated content is hard due to several reasons: (1) There are more than 20 official languages but linguistic resources are available mainly for Hindi. It is observed that people frequently use romanized text as it is easy and quick using an English keyboard, resulting in multi-*glyphic* comments, where the texts are in the *same language* but in *different scripts*. Such romanized texts are almost unexplored in machine learning so far. (2) In many cases, comments are made on a specific part of the article rather than the topic of the entire article. Off-the-shelf methods such as correspondence LDA are insufficient to model such relationships between articles and comments. In this paper, we extend the notion of correspondence to model multi-lingual, multi-script, and inter-lingual topics in a unified probabilistic model called the Multi-glyphic Correspondence Topic Model (MCTM). Using several metrics, we verify our approach and show that it improves over the state-of-the-art.

1 Introduction

Analyzing comments on news articles can be cast as modeling correspondence between two sets of variables. Supervised methods do not scale due to unavailability of labeled datasets and rapid growth in unlabeled datasets. Unsupervised methods based on topic models are more appropriate, e.g. correspondence has been explored earlier for images–tags (Blei and Jordan 2003), and articles–comments (Das, Bansal, and Bhattacharyya 2014).

The motivation for this work stems from the problem of analyzing comments in multilingual environments such as in India. This is a hard problem due to several reasons:
(1) There are several nuances to the relationship between comments and articles. While many comments are related to the general topic of the article (*general* comments), some comments relate to a specific part of the article (*specific* comments). In many cases, comments talk about things unrelated to the article. Sometimes, the comment may seem close to topic of the article but was actually made with malicious intent to spam. We call such comments *irrelevant* comments.

(2) Several languages are simultaneously used in multilingual communities (e.g. there are more than 20 official languages in India (Wikipedia 2014)) but linguistic tools are available mainly for Hindi. Users comment in different languages, and even use different scripts for the *same* language. We call such comments as **multi-glyphic comments**. For example, in Dainik Jagran, a popular Hindi newspaper, we observe that around 19% of the comments are in English, 34% are in Hindi, and more than 46% are in romanized Hindi (*Rohin*).

Figure 1 shows examples of comments made on a Hindi news article, highlighting the topical nuances and the problem of romanized text. As far as we know, there are no freely available machine translation systems that can handle romanized texts for the languages considered in this work. Due to lack of labeled data, supervised methods are hard to apply. In the recent past, it has been observed that topic models can be useful for modeling correspondence between article and comments (Das, Bansal, and Bhattacharyya 2014). In this paper we explore a hierarchical Bayesian approach for modeling multi-glyphic correspondence.

Contributions. In this paper, we develop the notion of *multi-glyphic correspondence*, i.e. comments in multiple languages and multiple scripts relating to an article in a single language and single script. To model *specific* correspondence, we apply multiple topic vectors (MTV) with a stick-breaking prior (SBP) following Das, Bansal, and Bhattacharyya (2014). The challenge in modeling *topical* correspondence across languages/scripts is that the source of multi-linguality is only through comments which are small, and noisy. Existing models assume that the proportion over topics is the same for all comments on an article, which is hardly true and conflicts with the modeling choice of MTV. We address this issue for some languages by incorporating an additional multi-lingual comparable corpus. When such corpora are not available (e.g. for romanized text), we show that introducing model sparsity helps. To address irrelevant comments, we use two types of correspondence: *global correspondence* when comments relate to a global topic outside the article, and *null correspondence* when the comment is not related to any news article at all. Thus the complete model addresses multi-glyphic comment correspondence and topical correspondence in a unified man-

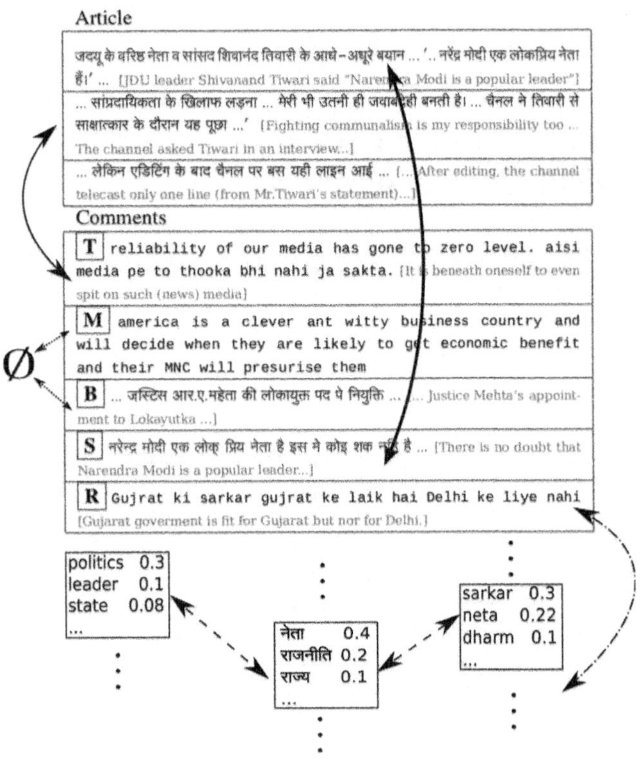

Figure 1: A Hindi article from Dainik Jagran with comments in English, Hindi, and *Rohin*. 5 types of comments are shown: topical (T), specific (S), corpus-topical (R), comment-topical (M), robotic (B). The first article segment, and the specific comment that discusses it, are marked in blue. English gloss for Hindi and *Rohin* text is shown next to it in gray. The different kinds of correspondence are shown using arrows: general (normal), specific (thick), global (dash-dotted), null (dotted), topical (dashed).

ner, where the two cooperate and reinforce the learning of each other. We name this model the **Multi-glyphic Correspondence Topic Model** (MCTM). We propose a collapsed Gibbs sampling inference procedure and evaluate the model on real-world data. We created manually annotated data sets for the comment classification task. The data and code have been released for public use (Tholpadi et al. 2014).

2 The Problem of Multi-glyphic Correspondence

We first discuss an empirical study on a real-life dataset. Then, we formally describe the problem objective.

Empirical Study

We performed an empirical study of comments for articles from two online sources—Dainik Jagran and Kendasampige[1]. Dainik Jagran (DJ) is India's highest–readership Hindi newspaper (MRUC 2013), while

[1]www.jagran.com, and www.kendasampige.com

Dainik Jagran	#comments	#comments per article	#words per comment
English	3017 (19.4%)	2.6 ± 3.1	36.3 ± 34.8
Hindi	5358 (34.5%)	4.7 ± 4.3	45.7 ± 29.1
Rohin	7164 (46.1%)	6.3 ± 7.3	38.7 ± 26.2
Kenda-sampige	#comments	#comments per article	#words per comment
English	9188 (24.2%)	3.2 ± 4.1	27.0 ± 35.0
Kannada	20169 (53.0%)	6.9 ± 7.3	32.2 ± 24.3
Rokan	8679 (22.8%)	3.0 ± 2.7	12.0 ± 15.3

Table 1: Comment statistics for the data sets. (Columns 3 and 4 are averages.)

Kendasampige (KS) is a very popular online Kannada magazine (TOI 2011).

On both sites, readers were found to comment in the vernacular language (Hindi or Kannada), in English, and in *romanized* vernacular[2]. The romanized vernacular text entered by these users follow none of the standard romanization rules/systems[3]. As far as we know, there is no way to convert them into meaningful vernacular text. We will refer to romanized Hindi and Kannada as ***Rohin*** and ***Rokan***. Note that there exist no machine translation systems for *Rohin* and *Rokan*, so that existing methods for article-comment analysis *cannot* be used in conjunction with machine translation. Some statistics for the data sets are shown in Table 1. We find that romanized text constitutes a significant portion of the comments (46.1% and 22.8%). This motivates the need for methods that can handle romanized comments.

We analyzed a total of 300 articles from both data sets (Section 5.4). We observed users commenting in different languages and using different scripts. We also found that not all comments were related to the article, but often referred to topics from other articles or even extraneous themes. Based on our analysis, we defined the following **topical categorization** of comments (the numbers in brackets indicate the percentage of comments of that type in the analyzed data):

- **Topical** (37%): discusses the topic of the article. Some of the topical comments (43%) are **specific** comments—relevant to a specific segment of the article.
- **Corpus-topical** (17%): discusses topics that occur in other articles in the corpus. Typically, this happens when a commenter raises other issues that she thinks are relevant to this article.
- **Comment-topical** (40%): discusses topics that do not occur in any article in the corpus, e.g. compliments, expletives, personal/extraneous information, URLs, etc.
- **Robotic** (6%): appear almost verbatim in many articles, irrespective of topicality to the article (suggesting that it may have been posted by a program such as a web robot).

Figure 1 shows an example for each of the above categories.

[2]A vernacular comment written using the Latin script.

[3]See http://en.wikipedia.org/wiki/Romanization.

Definitions.
Romanized text: Text in Roman script in a language usually written using another script.
Multi-glyphic comments: A set of comments where two comments using the same script may be in different languages, and two comments using different scripts may be in the same language.
Multi-glyphic correspondence: The topical relationship between a news article and its set of multi-glyphic comments.
Dialect: a script–language pair, e.g. Devanagari Hindi, romanized Hindi, and (romanized) English are three dialects.

Input. We formally represent the dataset as follows. We are given a set of articles $\{w_d\}_{d=1}^{D}$. Each article consists of segments (e.g. paragraphs) $\{w_{ds}\}_{s=1}^{S_d}$. Each segment consists of words $\{w_{dsn}\}_{n=1}^{N_{ds}}$. Each article has a set of multi-glyphic comments x_d. The comments are in L dialects, and we group the comments in dialect l in the set $x_{dl} = \{x_{dlc}\}_{c=1}^{C_{dl}}$ for $l = 1 \ldots L$. A single comment x_{dlc} consists of the words $\{x_{dlcm}\}_{m=1}^{M_{dlc}}$.

Objective. Our objective is to develop a hierarchical Bayesian model suitable for news articles and multi-glyphic comments. In the literature, this kind of model is called a *correspondence* model. Here, $\{w_d\}$ are independent variables and $\{x_d\}$ are dependent variables. The novelty in this problem is that the two variables can be in different spaces (dialects).

Related Work

As far as we know, all previous work on news and comments has focused on comments in the article dialect. Kant, Sengamedu, and Kumar (2012) detect spam in comments. Mahajan et al. (2012) use features based on Latent Dirichlet Allocation (LDA) (Blei, Ng, and Jordan 2003) to predict comment ratings. Ma et al. (2012) and Das, Bansal, and Bhattacharyya (2014) construct topic models for jointly modeling news and comments, similar to our work but in the monolingual setting. Sil, Sengamedu, and Bhattacharyya (2011) proposed a supervised approach to associate comments with segments. Our approach is unsupervised, and easier to adopt.

3 Modeling Multi-glyphic Correspondence

We first describe the basic model for correspondence and then propose our multi-glyphic correspondence topic model (MCTM).

Notation. We use the following notation in subsequent sections. Dir(), Categ(), Beta(), and Bern() represent the Dirichlet, Categorical, Beta, Bernoulli distributions, while SBP() represents a stick-breaking process (Ishwaran and James 2001). Unif(z) is a distribution assigning uniform probability to each component of z. We use $v \sim P$ to say that we sample a value for variable v from distribution P. $[N]$ is the set $\{1, \ldots, N\}$. V_l is the vocabulary size of dialect l. K and J are the number of article and comment topics, respectively. z and y denote the topic assignments for article and comment words, respectively. θ is the set of topic vectors for an article. ϕ denotes the word distributions for article topics.

Correspondence Topic Model. Correspondence LDA (CorrLDA) (Blei and Jordan 2003) can model correspondence between news articles and comments. Formally, the generative story is as follows.[4] First, sample the topics $\phi_k \sim \text{Dir}(\beta),\ k \in [K]$. Then, for each article w_d:

- Sample $\theta \sim \text{Dir}(\alpha)$.
- For each article word $w_n, n \in [N]$:
  - Sample $z_n \sim \text{Categ}(\theta)$.
  - Sample $w_n \sim \text{Categ}(\phi_{z_n})$.
- For each comment word $x_{cm}, c \in [C],\ m \in [M_c]$:
  - Sample $y_{cm} \sim \text{Unif}(z)$.
  - Sample $x_{cm} \sim \text{Categ}(\phi_{y_{cm}})$.

3.1 Multi-glyphic Correspondence Topic Model

CorrLDA works only for the monolingual case, and is not directly applicable to even multi-lingual comments. If machine translation is available for the dialect of the comment, then CorrLDA can be applied. We can also apply SCTM for modeling specific comments (Das, Bansal, and Bhattacharyya 2014). However, machine translation is not available for many languages and romanized texts. This makes the problem of multi-glyphic comments beyond the scope of the state-of-the-art.

Multi-glyphic Correspondence (MCTM-D). We use a set of topics $\{\{\phi_{lj}\}_{j=1}^{K}\}$ for each dialect l to generate words in dialect l. Additionally, we assume that each topic in dialect l has a corresponding topic in all other dialects. Let the comments x for an article w be divided into subsets based on dialect, so that $x = \{\{\{x_{lcm}\}_{m=1}^{M_{lc}}\}_{c=1}^{C_l}\}_{l=1}^{L}$. The generative story for comments is modified to sample each $x_{lcm} \sim \text{Categ}(\phi_{ly_{lcm}})$ where $\phi_{lk} \sim \text{Dir}(\beta)$ is a topic in dialect l. Note that the topics ϕ_{lk} and $\phi_{l'k}$ *correspond*, i.e. they represent what people are saying in different dialects on the same topic.

Applying Multiple Topic Vectors (MCTM-DS). Das, Bansal, and Bhattacharyya (2014) pointed out the unsuitability of CorrLDA for capturing specific correspondence and proposed the specific correspondence topic model (SCTM) for this purpose. Following SCTM, we use *multiple topic vectors* (MTV) per article, and a *stick-breaking prior* (SBP) for the distribution over the topic vectors to model specific correspondence. Let $\{\theta_t\}_{t=1}^{T}$ be the set of topic vectors. To generate each word, we first sample one of the topic vectors, then the topic, and finally the word. Due to MTV,

[4]For ease of exposition, we will reuse variables at different granularities. The meaning should be clear from the context.

topic proportions vary across segments in an article. Thus we are able to model a *Rohin* comment relating to a particular paragraph of a Hindi news article.

Incorporating Topic Correspondence across Dialects. One key assumption made earlier is that each topic in a dialect has a corresponding topic in every other dialect. This in turn assumes that the distribution over topics is the same for all the comments as well as the article. However, in MCTM-DS, we vary the topic distribution across segments in an article. Moreover, in practice, we find that comments are small, noisy and vary heavily in vocabulary. For example, if a Hindi article has no or few topical English comments, the English topic corresponding to the article's Hindi topic would be of low quality. Thus the notions of multi-glyphicity and MTV apparently conflict and pose a significant hurdle.

We address this issue (MCTM-DSC) by using additional multi-lingual *comparable* corpora, and modeling topic correspondence similar to the polylingual topic model (Mimno et al. 2009). The use of such corpora achieves two purposes simultaneously: (1) improving topic quality in each dialect, and (2) improving topic correspondence across dialects.

Modeling Non-article Correspondence. The model developed so far performs quite well for modeling multi-glyphic correspondence. However, we observe that there are many *irrelevant* comments in the data—comments that do not correspond to the article. We make the following modeling choices for non-article correspondence.

Global correspondence (MCTM-DSG). To model the topicality of comments to other news articles in the corpus, we relax the constraint that the article is the source of all the topics in a comment, and allow the *article corpus* (the set of all articles in the corpus) to be a secondary source of topics. We introduce a *topic source distribution* p_{lc} for each comment, and a *topic source variable* q_{lcm} for each comment word. Each comment x_{lc} is now generated as follows.

- Sample $p_{lc} \sim$ Dir(λ).
- Sample $\rho_{lc} \sim$ Dir(δ).
- Sample $\epsilon_{lc} \sim$ Dir(η).
- For each word x_{lcm}, $m \in [M_{lc}]$:
  - Sample $q_{lcm} \sim$ Categ(p_{lc}).
  - If $q_{lcm} = 1$:
    - Sample $b_{lcm} \sim$ Categ(ρ_{lc}).
    - Sample $y_{lcm} \sim$ Unif($z_{b_{lcm}}$).
  - Else If $q_{lcm} = 2$: Sample $y_{lcm} \sim$ Categ(ϵ_{lc}).
  - Sample $x_{lcm} \sim$ Categ($\phi_{ly_{lcm}}$).

Null correspondence (MCTM-DSGN). To model topics that occur in comments but not in the articles, we extend MCTM to incorporate the *comment corpus* (the set of all comments) as another topic source. We introduce a secondary set of topics ψ_{lj}, $l \in [L], j \in [J]$ that we call *comment topics*. These word distributions are used only for generating comments. We add a component to p_{lc} where p_{lc3}=Pr[comment corpus is a topic source for a comment word], and use a *comment corpus topic vector* χ_{lc}, a distribution over comment topics. The generative story is similar to MCTM-DSG, with the following differences: (1) For each comment, we also sample $\chi_{lc} \sim$ Dir(ξ). (2) If $q_{lcm} = 3$, we sample $y_{lcm} \sim$ Categ(χ_{lc}), and $x_{lcm} \sim$ Categ($\psi_{ly_{lcm}}$).

Roboticity. Interestingly, the model associates robotic comments with comment topics, even when there are articles in the corpus that may seem topically related to these comments. This is because each robotic comment occurs many times in the corpus, and thus the probability of generating them from comment topics is generally greater. Thus the MCTM-DSGN model captures both comment-topical and robotic comments (but fails to distinguish between the two).

Incorporating Sparsity. We describe two kinds of sparsity and propose a joint sparsity model.

Topic sparsity. Wang and Blei (2009) force each topic to be a distribution over a small subset of the vocabulary to get sparse topics without sacrificing smoothness. For this, we define *topic sparsity parameters* κ_{lk}=fraction of the vocabulary included in topic ϕ_{lk}, and binary *sparsity variables* $a_{lkv} = 1$ if $v \in \phi_{lk}$, and 0 otherwise. The generative story for each topic ϕ_{lk}, $l \in [L], k \in [K]$ becomes:

- Sample $\kappa_{lk} \sim$ Beta(ν).
- For each word $v \in [V_l]$: Sample $a_{lkv} \sim$ Bern(κ_{lk}).
- Sample $\phi_{lk} \sim$ Dir(βa_{lk}).

Here, Dir(βa_{lk}) is a distribution over the subset of the vocabulary defined by a_{lk}.

Word sparsity. Das, Bansal, and Bhattacharyya (2014) introduce *word sparsity* (they call it "topic diversity") by forcing each word to belong to a small subset of the topics. For this, we define *word sparsity parameters* σ_{lv}=fraction of the K topics that word v may belong to. Using a_{lkv} as before, the generative story changes to:

- For each dialect $l \in [L]$, for each word $v \in [V_l]$: Sample $\sigma_{lv} \sim$ Beta(μ).
- For each topic ϕ_{lk}, $l \in [L], k \in [K]$:
  - For each word $v \in [V_l]$: Sample $a_{lkv} \sim$ Bern(σ_{lv}).
  - Sample $\phi_{lk} \sim$ Dir(βa_{lk}).

Joint topic-word sparsity (MCTM-DSGNP). We combine the benefits of both schemes by using a **joint topic-word sparsity** scheme. The steps of both generative stories are combined, but with one modification—we now sample $a_{lkv} \sim$ Bern($\kappa_{lk}\sigma_{lv}$). However, this causes coupling between κ_{lk} and σ_{lv}, making it difficult to integrate them out for doing collapsed Gibbs sampling. To decouple κ_{lk} and σ_{lv}, we introduce auxiliary *topic sparsity variables* e_{lkv} and *word sparsity variables* f_{lkv}, and define $a_{lkv} = e_{lkv} f_{lkv}$.

For the complete plate diagram and generative process, see the supplementary material (Tholpadi et al. 2014).

4 Collapsed-Blocked Gibbs Sampling

We use Gibbs sampling for estimating the MCTM model. We want to **collapse** all real-valued variables and preserve only categorical variables so that we can converge faster,

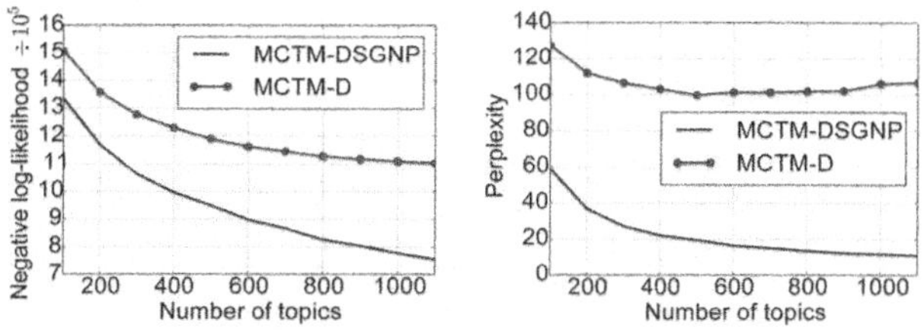

(a) Training data fit (b) Held-out data perplexity

Figure 2: Model fit for the DJ corpus (lower is better).

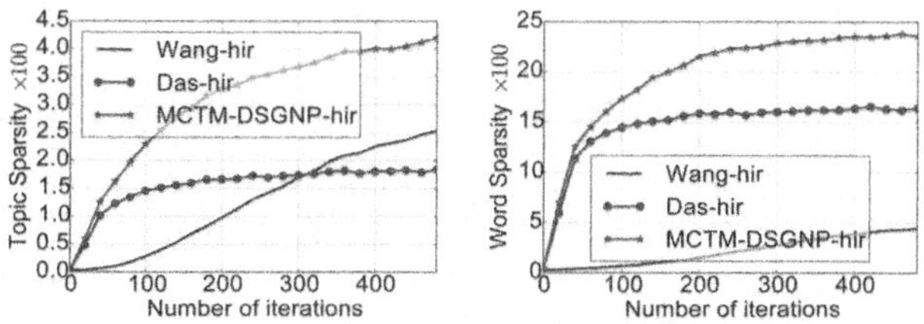

(a) Topic sparsity (b) Word sparsity

Figure 3: Sparsity levels achieved by different models on the DJ corpus for *Rohin* (higher is better).

and also to avoid round-off errors. The main challenges that make the inference non-standard are:

- Coupling between κ and σ—we solve this by introducing auxiliary variables e and f.
- Sampling r (due to the SBP prior)—we use the equivalence of the SBP to the Generalized Dirichlet (GD) distribution (Connor and Mosimann 1969) and derive the sampling update.
- Interdependence between q, b, y, and between a, e, f—we handle this issue by doing **blocked** Gibbs sampling.

The details of the inference procedure are given in the supplementary material (Tholpadi et al. 2014).

5 Experiments

We evaluated the MCTM model on two data sets crawled from the web. Since previous work are not applicable to our setting, we used the MCTM-D model as the closest extension to existing methods and compare it with all model variants. We approached the evaluation from three angles:

- Is the model a good fit for the data?
- How does sparsity affect topic quality?
- Can the model detect comment categories?

5.1 Data and Preprocessing

We gathered articles with comments from a Hindi newspaper Dainik Jagran (DJ) (5699 articles) and from a Kannada magazine Kendasampige (KS) (5329 articles). For each article, we extracted segments that approximately corresponded to paragraphs. We identified the language of the comments using the Unicode code block or, in the case of *Rohin*/*Rokan*, a language detection library (Shuyo 2010). We selected articles with at least 5 comments and constructed 2 data sets with 1142 (DJ) and 2905 (KS) articles. Section 2 discusses some statistics of the data sets. The vernacular text was stemmed (Reddy and Sharoff 2011) and normalized to map variant Unicode sequences of a word to a unique sequence. We also hand-crafted stop word lists for each of the 5 dialects (totalling 4368 words).

Language	English	Hindi	Kannada	*Rohin*	*Rokan*
# stop words	627	1118	595	1000	1028
V_l	~6K	~10K	~15K	~6K	~2.5K

For the specific comment detection task, we used a multilingual comparable corpus of 1000 document pairs extracted from the English and Kannada Wikipedias.

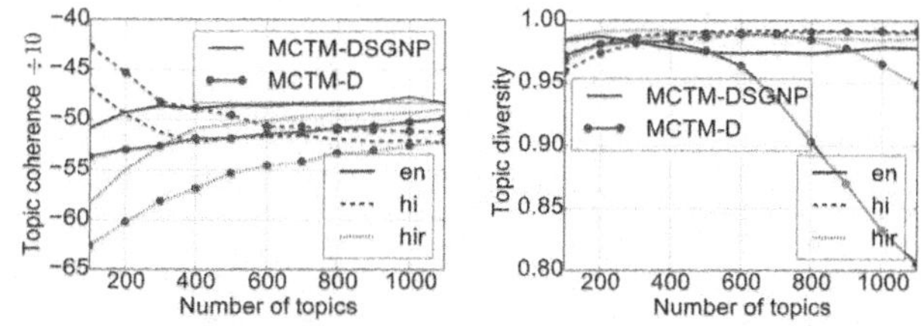

(a) Topic coherence (b) Topic diversity

Figure 4: Topic quality (for the top 20 words) achieved on the DJ corpus (higher is better).

5.2 MCTM-DSGNP is a Better Fit for Data

We want to evaluate whether the model is able to learn well, and whether it is a good fit for the data. We ran the model on the DJ corpus with the following configuration: $T{=}\frac{S_{dl}}{2}$, K=500, J=4, α=.01, β=.01, ω=.01, γ=[.05,.1], $\delta \propto (N_{dls})_{s=1}^{S_{dl}}$, η=.01, ξ=.01, $\lambda \propto [.72,.18,.1] \times M_{dll'c}$. We did a grid search for K and J and chose values that gave the best human-readable topics. T was set such that there was one topic vector for every two segments. δ was set so that larger segments were more likely to generate comments. The λ used captures our rough guess that around 10% of the comments are comment-topical or robotic, less than 20% are corpus-topical, and the remaining are relevant to the article. The other parameters were chosen to encourage peaked distributions for topics and words (Heinrich 2009).

We found that both MCTM-D and MCTM-DSGNP have good convergence, and the training data likelihood stabilizes at around 500 iterations. We evaluated how well the model fits the training data and held-out test data. Figure 2(a) shows the training data negative log-likelihood for different values of K for both models. MCTM-DSGNP clearly outperforms the baseline, and does even better at higher K. To make sure the model does not overfit, we computed the perplexity on held-out data (Figure 2(b)), and found that MCTM-DSGNP can handle unseen data better than MCTM-D.

5.3 Good Topic Quality with High Sparsity

Wang and Blei (2009) define the *complexity* of a topic ϕ_{lk} as the number of words that belong to the topic, i.e.

Kendasampige	Specific (S)		
Model	P	R	F1
MCTM-D	.188	.875	.401
MCTM-DS	.186	**.890**	.400
MCTM-DSG	.189	.874	.402
MCTM-DSGN	.193	.835	.405
MCTM-DSGNP	.197	.768	.395
MCTM-DSGNPC	**.217**	.706	**.405**

Dainik Jagran	Corpus+Comment +Robotic (RMB)			Comment+ Robotic (MB)			Robotic (B)		
Model	P	R	F1	P	R	F1	P	R	F1
MCTM-D	.738	.303	.414	.584	.343	.418	.051	.116	.122
MCTM-DS	.765	.314	.430	.617	**.351**	.438	.123	.420	.353
MCTM-DSG	.759	.306	.420	.614	.335	.425	.137	.393	.367
MCTM-DSGN	**.825**	.413	.538	.788	.262	.480	.325	**.879**	.828
MCTM-DSGNP	.762	**.515**	**.586**	**.776**	.204	**.485**	**.438**	.862	**.841**

Correspondence types: **D** multi-glyphic, **S** specific, **G** global, **N** null, **P** sparsity, **C** comparable corpora

Table 2: Precision (P), recall (R) and F1-score (F1) for identifying different kinds of comments.

$\text{complexity}_{lk} = \sum_v a_{lkv}$. Since we defined the model objectives in terms of sparsity, we defined two *sparsity* metrics to measure the performance of the sparsity schemes:

$$\text{topic sparsity}_{lk} = \frac{1}{\sum_v a_{lkv}}, \ \text{word sparsity}_{lv} = \frac{1}{\sum_k a_{lkv}}.$$

Figure 3 shows the average sparsity (over all topics/words) for *Rohin* on the DJ corpus (the results were similar for other dialects). We compare the topic, word, and joint sparsity schemes. We see that our scheme achieves sparsity very early, and leads to higher sparsity.

A natural question to ask is: Does the high topic sparsity affect topic quality? To check this, we plot topic coherence (Mimno et al. 2011) and topic diversity (Das, Bansal, and Bhattacharyya 2014) for the different dialects and compare it with MCTM-D which used no sparsity schemes (Figure 4). We see that there is no loss in topic quality or diversity in spite of the high sparsity. The comment topics discovered were especially interesting, since we found that they could be categorized into different classes such as "compliments", "foreign words", "commenter names", "expletives", etc. (Tholpadi et al. 2014).

5.4 Comment Category Detection Task

We apply the different model variants to the task of detecting different kinds of comments in articles. For the purpose of evaluation, we created two gold standard data sets by manual annotation.

Specific correspondence Data Set. We annotated 202 articles in the KS corpus, together containing 6192 comments, of which 3075 were in *concomitant* dialects, i.e. comment dialects other than the article language. For each article, we asked an annotator to read the article body, and then annotate each *concomitant dialect* comment[5] as 'Non-Topical', 'Topical, but not specific', or 'Topical, and specific to segments $s_1, s_2, \ldots$', where s_i is a segment index.

Topical Correspondence Data Set. We annotated 102 articles in the DJ corpus, together containing 1379 comments, of which 855 were in concomitant dialects. Each comment was marked as 'Topical', 'Corpus-topical', 'Comment-topical', or 'Robotic'.

Algorithms for Comment Detection. As far as we know, there are no freely available translation/transliteration systems or parallel/comparable corpora in *Rohin*/*Rokan*. Hence, none of the existing cross-language methods for classification can be used as baselines for our data sets. Given this constraint, we came up with the best possible baseline for our setting, viz. the MCTM-D model.

For the MCTM-DSGNP model, we used a combination of the topic sources for a comment ($b_{dll'c}$) and the topic vector to determine the category of the comment. For the MCTM-D model, we constructed topic vectors for each comment and segment, and used cosine similarity with tuned thresholds to determine the comment category. The details of the algorithms are given in the supplementary material (Tholpadi et al. 2014).

Results. The results of the evaluation on Kendasampige and Dainik Jagran are shown in Table 2. For the specific comment detection task, we see a steady improvement in precision (up to 15%), especially by using comparable corpora (MCTM-DSGNPC). Also note that the MCTM-D method requires tuning thresholds to achieve the best performance, while the MCTM-DSGNPC method requires no tuning, which is useful when labeled data is not available.

For detecting irrelevant comments (**RMB** and **MB**), MCTM-DSGN gives huge gains over the simpler models (up to **42%**). This is expected since this model explicitly captures global and null correspondence. In particular, we see massive improvement (up to **589%**) on the robotic comment detection task. Also observe that introducing sparsity (MCTM-DSGNP) almost always helps improve performance on all tasks.

6 Conclusion

In this paper, we studied the phenomenon of multi-glyphic comments to online news, especially the presence of *romanized* text, and identified challenges in learning different kinds of topical correspondence. We developed the MCTM model to address the challenges using a hierarchical Bayesian approach. Evaluation on real-world data sets show the efficacy of the model, and potential for various applications. To facilitate further research in this new area, we have released the annotated data sets and code for public use.

Acknowledgments

We thank Adway Mitra for useful discussions, and Chaitra Shankar for help with the annotation. This work is supported by the Dept. of Science and Technology, Govt. of India.

[5]Analyzing comments in the article dialect has been addressed in previous work; we focus on concomitant dialects in this work.

References

Blei, D. M., and Jordan, M. I. 2003. Modeling annotated data. In *Proceedings of the 26th annual international ACM SIGIR conference on Research and development in informaion retrieval*, 127–134. ACM.

Blei, D. M.; Ng, A. Y.; and Jordan, M. I. 2003. Latent dirichlet allocation. *The Journal of Machine Learning Research* 3:993–1022.

Connor, R. J., and Mosimann, J. E. 1969. Concepts of independence for proportions with a generalization of the dirichlet distribution. *Journal of the American Statistical Association* 64(325):194–206.

Das, M. K.; Bansal, T.; and Bhattacharyya, C. 2014. Going beyond corr-lda for detecting specific comments on news & blogs. In *Proceedings of the 7th ACM international conference on Web search and data mining*, 483–492. ACM.

Heinrich, G. 2009. Parameter estimation for text analysis. Technical report.

Ishwaran, H., and James, L. F. 2001. Gibbs sampling methods for stick-breaking priors. *JASA* 96(453).

Kant, R.; Sengamedu, S. H.; and Kumar, K. S. 2012. Comment spam detection by sequence mining. In *Proceedings of the fifth ACM international conference on Web search and data mining*, 183–192. ACM.

Ma, Z.; Sun, A.; Yuan, Q.; and Cong, G. 2012. Topic-driven reader comments summarization. In *Proceedings of the 21st ACM international conference on Information and knowledge management*, 265–274. ACM.

Mahajan, D. K.; Rastogi, R.; Tiwari, C.; and Mitra, A. 2012. Logucb: an explore-exploit algorithm for comments recommendation. In *Proceedings of the 21st ACM international conference on Information and knowledge management*, 6–15. ACM.

Mimno, D.; Wallach, H. M.; Naradowsky, J.; Smith, D. A.; and McCallum, A. 2009. Polylingual topic models. In *Proceedings of the 2009 Conference on Empirical Methods in Natural Language Processing: Volume 2-Volume 2*, 880–889. Association for Computational Linguistics.

Mimno, D.; Wallach, H. M.; Talley, E.; Leenders, M.; and McCallum, A. 2011. Optimizing semantic coherence in topic models. In *Proceedings of the Conference on Empirical Methods in Natural Language Processing*, 262–272. Association for Computational Linguistics.

MRUC. 2013. Indian Readership Survey. http://mruc.net/sites/default/files/irs_2013_topline_findings.pdf. [Online; accessed 12-Nov-2014].

Reddy, S., and Sharoff, S. 2011. Cross language pos taggers (and other tools) for indian languages: An experiment with kannada using telugu resources. In *Proceedings of the Fifth International Workshop On Cross Lingual Information Access*, 11–19. Chiang Mai, Thailand: Asian Federation of Natural Language Processing.

Shuyo, N. 2010. Language detection library for java.

Sil, D. K.; Sengamedu, S. H.; and Bhattacharyya, C. 2011. Supervised matching of comments with news article segments. In *Proceedings of the 20th ACM international conference on Information and knowledge management*, 2125–2128. ACM.

Tholpadi, G.; Das, M.; Bansal, T.; and Bhattacharyya, C. 2014. Supplementary material to Relating Romanized Comments to News Articles by Inferring Multi-glyphic Topical Correspondence. http://mllab.csa.iisc.ernet.in/mctm. [Online; accessed 12-Nov-2014].

TOI. 2011. Kannada Sahitya Sammelana: Kannada blogs, sites give the write connect. http://timesofindia.indiatimes.com/articleshow/7434091.cms. [Online; accessed 12-Nov-2014].

Wang, C., and Blei, D. M. 2009. Decoupling sparsity and smoothness in the discrete hierarchical dirichlet process. In *Advances in neural information processing systems*, 1982–1989.

Wikipedia. 2014. Languages of India (Official languages). http://en.wikipedia.org/wiki/Languages_of_India#Official_languages. [Online; accessed 18-Nov-2014].

Proceedings of the Twenty-Ninth AAAI Conference on Artificial Intelligence

Mining User Intents in Twitter: A Semi-Supervised Approach to Inferring Intent Categories for Tweets

Jinpeng Wang[1], Gao Cong[2], Wayne Xin Zhao[3], Xiaoming Li[1]
[1]Department of Computer Science and Technology, Peking University, China,
[2]School of Computer Engineering, Nanyang Technological University, Singapore
[3]School of Information, Renmin University of China, China
JooPoo@pku.edu.cn, gaocong@ntu.edu.sg, batmanfly@gmail.com, lxm@pku.edu.cn

Abstract

In this paper, we propose to study the problem of identifying and classifying tweets into intent categories. For example, a tweet "I wanna buy a new car" indicates the user's intent for buying a car. Identifying such intent tweets will have great commercial value among others. In particular, it is important that we can distinguish different types of intent tweets. We propose to classify intent tweets into six categories, namely Food & Drink, Travel, Career & Education, Goods & Services, Event & Activities and Trifle. We propose a semi-supervised learning approach to categorizing intent tweets into the six categories. We construct a test collection by using a bootstrap method. Our experimental results show that our approach is effective in inferring intent categories for tweets.

Introduction

Posting short messages (i.e., tweets) through microblogging services (e.g., Twitter) has become an indispensable part of the daily life for many users. Users heavily express their needs and desires on Twitter, and tweets have been considered as an important source for mining user intents (Hollerit, Kröll, and Strohmaier 2013; Zhao et al. 2014). For example, the intent tweet "I am planning to travel to New York" explicitly indicates the user's intent. Such intent tweets can be exploited by interested parties, e.g., companies, government, public organizations, etc. For the example intent tweet, it will be more interesting if we categorize it to the *travel* category for marketing services.

In this paper, we study the task of identifying and inferring intent categories for tweets, which will benefit many commercial applications. Based on our analysis on a tweet corpora and the taxonomy of Groupon website, we propose to divide the intent tweets into six categories namely *Food & Drink*, *Travel*, *Career & Education*, *Goods & Services*, *Event & Activities* and *Trifle*. An example intent tweet of *Goods & Services* category is "I want to have a new car" and an example intent tweet of *Event & Activities* category is "I plan to go to swimming". With the inferred intent categories, one can potentially employ Twitter as a market or auction place, where we can find people with particular intents or desires through their tweets.

To the best of our knowledge, there exists no reported study of inferring intent categories for tweets in the context of commerce marketing. Tweets often contain sentences and user intent is often explicitly expressed in tweets. Moreover, tweets often contain more information than queries, e.g., friendship and context. It is reported in (Morris, Teevan, and Panovich 2010) that users prefer social sites over search engines when talking about opinions and recommendations. Note that although only a small portion of tweets (7% in our corpus by randomly sampling tweets) are sent with specific meanings or contain explicit intents, the number of intent tweets is still very huge since the number of tweets is enormous[1]. Nevertheless, the problem of inferring the intent categories of tweets is still challenging. Tweets are very noisy and often contain slang, misspellings, emotions and hashtags. In addition, it is very time-consuming to generate labeled data if we adopt the supervised approach.

To address the challenge, we formulate the problem as a classification problem and propose a graph-based semi-supervised approach to inferring intent categories for tweets. Our approach has two significant merits. (1) *Noise resistant:* to reduce noise in tweets, we propose to use intent-keywords instead of all the words as basic information units which are derived from a unsupervised bootstrap based method. (2) *Weak supervision:* we propose an optimization model which is built on the intent graph with tweets and intent-keywords as nodes. An edge in the intent graph can be established to model the association between two tweets, two intent-keywords, or a tweet and an intent-keyword. With effective information propagation via graph regularization, only a small set of tweets with category labels is needed as the supervised information.

We conduct experiments on a tweet dataset generated by a bootstrap based method. Our experimental results show that the proposed method outperforms several competitive baselines in inferring the categories of intent tweets.

Related Work

Query intent classification The existing work on query intent classification can be roughly divided into two types based on the classification taxonomy employed. The first

[1]Statistics from Twitter show that approximately 500 million tweets are sent every day: http://goo.gl/407UDX.

type is classifying queries according to the query type, such as informational or navigational or transactional (Cao et al. 2009; Kang and Kim 2003); and the other type is classifying queries according to the user intent, such as "jobs" or "travel" (Hu et al. 2009; Shen et al. 2006; Beitzel et al. 2007; Li, Wang, and Acero 2008). The latter task is related to our work, but it differs in several aspects. User intent deduction from queries suffers from the lack of sufficient words due to the lengths of queries. The existing work on query intent classification focuses on expanding features of queries by including external knowledge, such as search snippets from search engine, click-through (Li, Wang, and Acero 2008) and facets from Wikipedia (Hu et al. 2009). In addition, the intents of queries are typically implicit. For example, a keyword query like "xbox" does not explicitly express user intents. In contrast, tweets often contain sentences that explicitly express the user intent. For example, tweets like "I want to buy an xbox." explicitly express the user intent. Our focus in this paper is to identify intent tweets that explicitly express user intents, which is different from query intent classification.

Online commercial intention identification This task is to identify online commercial intention from queries, documents or tweets. Most studies focus on capturing commercial intent by analyzing search queries (Dai et al. 2006; Strohmaier and Kröll 2012) or click-through (Ashkan and Clarke 2009). Chen et al. (2013) aims at identifying intents expressed in posts of forums. Posts differs from tweets in several aspects. First, posts are longer and thus contain more information than tweets. Second, posts in the same forum have similar topics, and this can be exploited for identifying intent posts. Third, the portion of user intention is much larger than that of tweet, e.g., there are many posts that express the intent to buy phones on a digital forum. The most related is the work (Hollerit, Kröll, and Strohmaier 2013), which attempts to detect commercial intent tweets, but does not consider other types of intent tweets as we do in our work. The method by Hollerit, Kröll, and Strohmaier employs traditional classification models like SVM, and uses n-gram and part-of-speech tags as features. This method can be used to detect other types of intent tweets although the work (Hollerit, Kröll, and Strohmaier 2013) focuses on commercial intent tweets. This work can be treated as one of our subtasks, i.e., identifying *Goods & Services* intent.

Problem Statement

Intent Tweet: Inspired by the definition on intent post in discussion forums (Chen et al. 2013), and the definition on commercial intent tweets (Hollerit, Kröll, and Strohmaier 2013), we define a tweet as an *intent tweet* if (1) it contains at least one verb and (2) explicitly describes the user's intent to perform an activity (3) in a recognizable way.

Example 1: Tweet "I want to buy an xbox, if get A in this examination. Bless me!!!" is an intent tweet and it satisfies all the three conditions in the definition. □

In the first part of the definition, the verb is important in exhibiting user intent (Hollerit, Kröll, and Strohmaier 2013), e.g., the verb "want" in Example 1. In the second part, we require that the intent is explicitly described as it is required in previous work (Chen et al. 2013). This is in contrast with implicit intents that need inference or deduction. An example of tweet with an implicit intent is "Anyone knows the battery life of HTC one" and it is difficult to know whether the author was thinking about buying a HTC one. *Recognizable* (Kirsh 1990) here refers to "the ability to make a decision in constant time" and is also used for defining commercial intent (Hollerit, Kröll, and Strohmaier 2013). Note that with this definition, it would make less ambiguity for both annotating and identifying intent tweets.

We further define *intent-indicator* and *intent-phrase*, which are the key elements in our proposed approach.

Intent-Indicator: It comprises a group of terms that are used by users to express their intents. It is a verb or infinitive phrase that immediately follows a subject word, e.g., "I". For example, in tweet "I want to buy an xbox", "want to" is an intent-indicator, indicating the tweet is likely to be an intent tweet. For Part-of-Speech Tagging, we use Tweet NLP [2].

Intent-Keyword: It is a noun, verb, multi-word verb or compound noun (consisting of several nouns) contained in a verb or noun phrase which immediately follows an intent-indictor, e.g., in Example 1, "buy and "xbox which are contained in the phrase "buy an xbox" are intent-keywords. If one intent-keyword contains another intent-keyword, we keep the longer one. Furthermore, a phrase that immediately follows an intent-indicator is referred to as an *intent-phrase*.

Categories of Intent Tweets

Users' intents exhibited in tweets may belong to different categories, and different categories of intents may be of interest to different applications. However, no existing work has attempted to establish the categories for intent tweets.

To establish taxonomy for intent tweets, we have reviewed a large number of tweets and studied the taxonomy of Groupon[3]. The reasons that we refer to the taxonomy of Groupon are: 1) The intent expressed in tweets by Twitter users are usually related to daily life; and 2) Groupon offers deals that cover a wide range of daily life. Finally, we define six types of intent[4]:

- **Food & Drink**: the tweet authors plan to have some food or drink. It corresponds to the *Food & Drink* category of Groupon.
- **Travel intent**: the tweet authors are interested in visiting some specific points of interests or places. This category corresponds to the *Getaways* category of Groupon.
- **Career & Education intent**: the tweet authors want to get a job, get a degree or do something for self-realization. This category is not in Groupon, but we find that a good portion of intent tweets can be categorized into *Career & Education*. This category also appears in Twellow[5] that organizes twitter users into a taxonomy.
- **Goods & Services intent**: the tweet authors are interested in or want to have some non-food/non-drink goods (e.g., car) or

[2]http://www.ark.cs.cmu.edu/TweetNLP/

[3]http://www.groupon.com

[4]Groupon has 8 first-level categories: *Food & Drink*, *Event & Activities*, *Beauty & Spas*, *Health & Fitness*, *Automotive*, *Shopping*, *Apparel* and *Gateways*.

[5]http://www.twellow.com

services (e.g., haircut). This category corresponds to the combination of four categories in Groupon, namely *Beauty & Spas*, *Health & Fitness*, *Automotive*, *Shopping* and *Apparel*. They are combined because they all belong to *Goods & Services* and each of these categories takes only a very small proportion on Twitter.

- **Event & Activities**: the tweet authors want to participate in some activities which do not belong to the aforementioned categories (e.g., concert). This category corresponds to the *Event & Activities* category of Groupon.
- **Trifle intent**: This category of intent tweets talks about daily routine, or some mood trifles (Java et al. 2007).

Data Preparation

Since the proportion of intent tweets is small, we will obtain few intent tweets by sampling the tweets. We do not want to construct an unbalanced test collection with an overwhelming number of non-intent tweets for intent classification. Based on the definitions of intent-indicator and intent-keyword, we propose a novel method to construct the test collection. The idea is that a tweet is more likely to be an intent tweet if it contains an intent-indicator. We adopt the bootstrapping based method (Riloff, Wiebe, and Wilson 2003; Zhao et al. 2014) to retrieve intent tweets.

Specifically, given a seed set of intent-indicators, (e.g., "want to"), (1) we extract the intent-phrases (e.g., "buy an xbox") that frequently co-occur with intent-indicators, and (2) we use the extracted intent-phrases to extract more intent-indicators. For instance, we extract intent-phrase "buy an xbox" by using intent-indicator "want to" if their co-occurrence frequency is above a certain threshold, and we further use this intent-phrase to extract more intent-indicators like "wanna to". We repeat these steps until we cannot extract more intent-indicators and intent-phrases. Finally (3) tweets which contain these extracted intent-indicators are kept in our test collection for manual annotation. In this paper, we focus on the intents of the tweet authors. We also discard tweets that express the negative intents by filtering out those that contain negative words (e.g., "don't wanna").

We use the Twitter data (Kwak et al. 2010), which spanned the second half of 2009. We first identify potential intent tweets by using the above bootstrapping based method. We randomly sample 3,000 potential intent tweets, and two annotators with experiences of using Twitter are employed to annotate the category label[6]. For each tweet, each annotator first determines whether it is an intent tweet according to our definition above. If yes, the annotator further labels its intent category according to the description on the six intent categories above. Finally, we get 1,599 intent tweets and 531 non-intent tweets with the same label by the two annotators. In other words, we discard 870 tweets with inconsistent annotations. The Cohen's Kappa coefficient between the two annotators is 65.35%, which is still a high value. We summarize the statistics of this dataset in Table 1. Note that 75.08% of these tweets identified by the bootstrap method are intent tweets, which indicates that the bootstrap based method is indeed an effective unsupervised approach to retrieving intent tweets.

[6]The annotated data set is available at http://joopoo.github.io

Table 1: Statistics and examples of intent categories in our test collection.

Category	# (%)	Example
Food & Drink	245 (11.50%)	hungry...i need a salad......four more days to the BEYONCE CONCERT...
Travel	187 (8.78%)	I need a vacation really bad. I need a trip to Disneyland!
Career & Education	159 (7.46%)	this makes me want to be a lawyer RT @someuser new favorite line from an ...
Goods & Services	251 (11.78%)	mhmmm, i wannna a new phoneeee. ... i have to go to the hospital. ...
Event & Activities	321 (15.07%)	on my way to go swimming with the twoon @someuser; i love her so muchhhhh!
Trifle	436 (20.47%)	I'm so happy that I get to take a shower with myself. :D
Non-intent	531 (24.92%)	So sad that Ronaldo will be leaving these shores...http://URL

Our methods are built on *intent-keywords* as the information units. Thus, each tweet in the test collection is kept with the annotations of intent-keywords identified by the unsupervised bootstrap method.

Inferring Intent Categories

Given a set of intent tweets and a set of intent-keywords, and a small number of labeled tweets as the input, this task is to infer the intent categories for each tweet in the set of intent tweets. We first construct an intent-graph. The intent-graph models associations between intent tweets and their intent-keywords. Based on the intent-graph, we formulate the problem of inferring intent categories from a small number of labeled tweets as an optimization problem. Note that our approach derives intent-keywords using the unsupervised bootstrap method without relying on any dictionary for intent-keywords. This is desirable since tweets are often written in informal language and a dictionary of intent-keywords is not available.

Intent-graph

We construct an intent-graph as illustrated in Figure 1 from the input data to characterize the relations among tweets and intent-keywords. In Figure 1, there are two types of nodes, namely intent tweet nodes and intent-keyword nodes. The tweet nodes associated with labels (e.g., "food") are labeled intent tweets, and the tweet nodes associated with "?" are unlabeled intent tweets. There are three types of edges in the intent-graph, i.e., edges between tweets and keywords (black edges), edges between tweets (green edges), and edges between keywords (blue edges). Specifically, we establish an edge between a tweet node and a keyword node if the keyword is contained in the tweet; we establish an edge between two keyword nodes if they co-occur in the same tweet; we establish an edge between two tweet nodes if their intent-keywords share common words. We will present how to compute weight for each edge in the following.

Formulation

We introduce the notations to be used and formally define our task. We denote by $\mathcal{X} = \{x_1, \cdots, x_{|\mathcal{T}|}, \cdots, x_{|\mathcal{T}|+|\mathcal{W}|}\}$

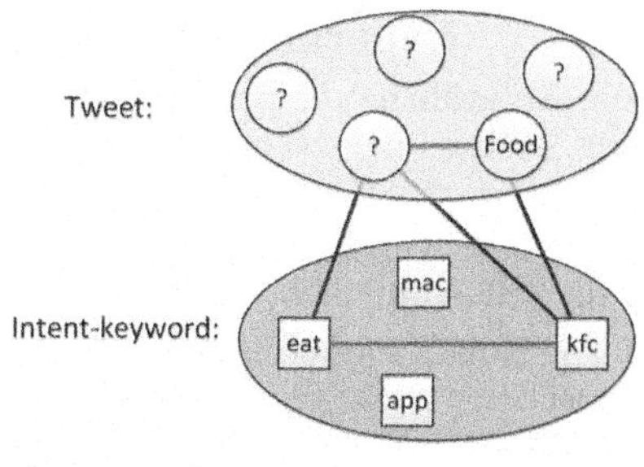

Figure 1: Example intent graph.

the set of nodes in intent-graph, where the first $|\mathcal{T}|$ nodes represent intent tweets and last $|\mathcal{W}|$ nodes are intent-keywords. We assume that these input tweets have been preprocessed in order to obtain a relatively balanced distribution of intent tweets and non-intent tweets. Let the first l nodes $\mathcal{X}^l = \{x_1, ..., x_l\}$ be the labeled intent tweets w.l.o.g., and the remaining nodes $(\mathcal{X} \setminus \mathcal{X}^l)$ are either unlabeled tweet nodes or intent-keyword nodes. In our problem setting, there are only a few labeled instances but many unlabeled instances, i.e. $l \ll |\mathcal{T}|$. Let $\mathcal{C}$ be the set of intent categories (six intent categories in our case). Each labeled tweet node x_i is associated with a vector of $|\mathcal{C}|$ elements, which represent the ground truth category of the tweet. Each element $\acute{y}_i^c$ in the vector represents whether x_i belongs to category c: If x_i has label c, then $\acute{y}_i^c = 1$; otherwise, $\acute{y}_i^c = 0$. Similarly, each node x_i in $\mathcal{X}$ is associated with a vector of $|\mathcal{C}|$ elements, which represent the estimated confidence scores that x_i belongs to each category c in $\mathcal{C}$. Each element f_i^c in the vector represents the confidence score of node x_i belonging to category c estimated by our proposed method.

The problem of inferring categories for unlabeled intent tweets is transformed into estimating f_i^c for each $c \in \mathcal{C}$ and each unlabeled intent tweet t_i. Then the category with the highest intent score for each unlabeled tweet node t_i is chosen as the inferred category, i.e., $\hat{c} = \text{argmax}_{c \in \mathcal{C}} f_i^c$.

The above formulation assumes that the input tweet itself is an intent tweet, which can be classified into one of the six intent categories in Table 1. Not all the tweets are intent tweets, we take a relatively simple but effective method to identify non-intent tweets: if the values for all these elements in the vector f_i^c are smaller than a predefined threshold η, which is set by cross-validation.

Optimization Model

Since we have only a few labeled data, it will be infeasible to train reliable models by only using these labeled data. Our idea is to leverage the association between nodes and propagate the evidence of intent categories via the intent graph. Intuitively, a node should have a similar category label with its neighboring nodes according to the manifold assumption proposed in (Belkin, Matveeva, and Niyogi 2004; Zhu et al. 2003; Wang and Zhang 2006). Besides, we can incorporate the available label information as the supervised information. We adopt the regularization based method to model the association between nodes and incorporate the supervised information. Specially, in our regulation function, we model three types of associations and one penalty function.

Association between tweets and intent-keywords: On the intent graph, an undirected edge (i, j) exists if the ith tweet contains the jth intent-keyword. If tweet t contains intent-keyword w, the confidence scores of t and w should be similar with each other on every category. Note that for each intent-keyword node w, we also model its confidence score of belonging to each category. We model this as follows [7],

$$R_1 = \sum_{t \in \mathcal{T}} \sum_{w \in \mathcal{W}} s(t, w)(f_t^c - f_w^c)^2, \tag{1}$$

where $s(t, w)$ is the similarity between tweet t and intent-keyword w and $s(t, w)$ is computed by $s(t, w) = \frac{n_{t,w}}{n_t} \times \log \frac{n_w}{|\mathcal{T}|}$, where $n_{t,w}$ is the frequency of word w in tweet t, n_t is the number of intent-keywords in t, n_w is the number of intent tweets that contain intent-keyword w. In the second factor $\log \frac{n_w}{|\mathcal{T}|}$, w is an intent-keyword, which is useful for determining the category of an intent tweet. Unlike the idea of *idf* in information retrieval, we assume a more frequent intent-keyword should be assigned with a larger weight.

Association between two tweets: If tweet t_1 is similar to tweet t_2, the confidence scores of these two tweets should be similar on every category. We model this as follows,

$$R_2 = \sum_{t_1 \in \mathcal{T}} \sum_{t_2 \in \mathcal{T}} s(t_1, t_2)(f_{t_1}^c - f_{t_2}^c)^2, \tag{2}$$

where $s(t_1, t_2)$ is the similarity between t_1 and t_2. Each tweet is represented as a vector where each of its elements corresponds to a distinct intent-keyword. We use the cosine similarity to compute the similarity of two tweets. $s(t_1, t_2) = \sum_{w \in \mathcal{W}} \frac{n_{t_1,w} n_{t_2,w}}{\sqrt{(\sum_{w'} n_{t_1,w'}^2)(\sum_{w'} n_{t_2,w'}^2)}}$ where $n_{t_1,w}$ and $n_{t_2,w}$ denote the frequencies of word w in t_1 and t_2, respectively.

Association between two intent-keywords: If intent-keyword w_1 is used in a similar way as is intent-keyword w_2, i.e., they co-occur in many tweets, then their confidence scores on every category should be similar. We model this as follows,

$$R_3 = \sum_{w_1 \in \mathcal{W}} \sum_{w_2 \in \mathcal{W}} s(w_1, w_2)(f_{w_1}^c - f_{w_2}^c)^2, \tag{3}$$

where $s(w_1, w_2)$ is the similarity between w_1 and w_2. We represent each word as a vector where each of its elements corresponds to an intent tweet, and then we use the cosine similarity to compute their similarity $s(w_1, w_2) = \sum_{t \in \mathcal{T}} \frac{n_{t,w_1} n_{t,w_2}}{\sqrt{(\sum_{t'} n_{t',w_1}^2)(\sum_{t'} n_{t',w_2}^2)}}$, where n_{t,w_1} and n_{t,w_2} denote the frequencies of word w_1 and w_2 in t, respectively.

Penalty Function - Integrating Labeled Data: We have a small number of labeled intent tweets, which are the supervised information. We incorporate the supervised information in our optimization model as follows,

[7] For the convenience of parameter estimation, we use the squared difference to measure the difference between two probability distributions.

$$R_4 = \sum_{t \in \mathcal{X}^l} (f_t^c - \acute{y}_t^c)^2, \quad (4)$$

where $\acute{y}_t^c$ is the label of the intent tweet t on category c.

Final Model The regularization factors and penalty function can be enforced through the terms of the objective function in the following minimization problem where $\mathbf{f}^c = [f_1^c, ..., f_{|\mathcal{X}|}^c]^\top$,

$$\begin{aligned}
\hat{\mathbf{f}}^c &= \underset{\mathbf{f}^c}{\operatorname{argmin}} \sum_{t \in \mathcal{X}^l} (f_t^c - \acute{y}_t^c)^2 \\
&+ \gamma\Big(\lambda_1 \sum_{t \in \mathcal{T}} \sum_{w \in \mathcal{W}} s(t,w)(f_t^c - f_w^c)^2 \\
&+ \lambda_2 \sum_{t_1 \in \mathcal{T}} \sum_{t_2 \in \mathcal{T}} s(t_1,t_2)(f_{t_1}^c - f_{t_2}^c)^2 \\
&+ \lambda_3 \sum_{w_1 \in \mathcal{W}} \sum_{w_2 \in \mathcal{W}} s(w_1,w_2)(f_{w_1}^c - f_{w_2}^c)^2\Big) \quad (5)
\end{aligned}$$

where $\lambda_1, \lambda_2, \lambda_3 > 0$, and $\lambda_1 + \lambda_2 + \lambda_3 = 1$; the three parameters control the effect of different kinds of edge. The parameter $\gamma \geq 0$ represents the influence of each source of learning (adjacent nodes vs. labeled nodes) on the intent score of f_i^c. Equation 5 can be rewritten as follows,

$$\hat{\mathbf{f}}^c = \underset{\mathbf{f}^c}{\operatorname{argmin}} (\mathbf{f}^c - \acute{\mathbf{y}}^c)^\top \mathbf{I}_l (\mathbf{f}^c - \acute{\mathbf{y}}^c) + \gamma (\mathbf{f}^c)^\top \mathbf{\Delta} \mathbf{f}^c \quad (6)$$

where $\mathbf{I}_l$ is a diagonal matrix which the first l diagonal elements (corresponding to the first l labeled tweets) are all 1 and other diagonal elements are all 0, $\acute{\mathbf{y}}^c = [y_1^c..., y_{|\mathcal{X}|}^c]^\top$, and $\mathbf{\Delta}$ is the graph Laplacian matrix. Here the first $|\mathcal{X}^l|$ elements of $\acute{\mathbf{y}}^c$ are defined earlier, which represent the ground truth categories of labeled tweets; the remaining elements of $\acute{\mathbf{y}}^c$ are set as 0. We have $\mathbf{\Delta} = \mathbf{A} - \mathbf{S}$, where $\mathbf{S}$ is a $|\mathcal{X}| \times |\mathcal{X}|$ matrix of weighted "edge" weights (i.e., similarities) and

$$S_{ij} = \begin{cases} \lambda_1 \cdot \gamma \cdot s(t_i, w_j), & i \in \mathcal{T}, j \in \mathcal{W} \\ \lambda_1 \cdot \gamma \cdot s(w_i, t_j), & i \in \mathcal{W}, j \in \mathcal{T} \\ 2 \cdot \lambda_2 \cdot \gamma \cdot s(t_i, t_j), & i \in \mathcal{T}, j \in \mathcal{T} \\ 2 \cdot \lambda_3 \cdot \gamma \cdot s(w_i, w_j), & i \in \mathcal{W}, j \in \mathcal{W}. \end{cases}$$

$\mathbf{A}$ is a $|\mathcal{X}| \times |\mathcal{X}|$ diagonal matrix derived from $\mathbf{S}$ as $\mathbf{A}_{ii} = \sum_{j=1}^{|\mathcal{X}|} \mathbf{S}_{ij}$. Then the solution of Eq. 6 can be obtained as follows (see (Belkin, Matveeva, and Niyogi 2004) for details),

$$\hat{\mathbf{f}}^c = (\mathbf{I}_l + \gamma \mathbf{\Delta})^{-1} \mathbf{I}_l \acute{\mathbf{y}}^c \quad (7)$$

Because $(\mathbf{f}^c)^\top \mathbf{\Delta} \mathbf{f}^c > 0$, $\mathbf{\Delta}$ is a symmetric and positive semi-definite matrix. Consequently the above solution is the unique answer to our optimization problem. The solution can be obtained by an efficient power iterative method[8]. With very large amount of tweets, we can consider splitting tweets into small clusters and build intent-graph independently for each cluster.

[8]http://goo.gl/rj7rKf

Experiments

In this section, we evaluate the performance of intent category inference. We used the test collection in Table 1.

Methods

We compare the following methods in our experiments:

- **SVM-Multi**: It is the "one-versus-all" SVM, where a single classifier is trained per class to distinguish that class from all the other classes. We use each binary SVM classifier to predict, and choose the prediction with the highest confidence score. We use bag-of-words of tweets as the features for building classifiers.
- **Hollerit's Method**: It uses the same classifier as does SVM-Multi (Hollerit, Kröll, and Strohmaier 2013). But it uses n-grams and part-of-speech as features.
- **Velikovich's Method**: It is a graph propagation algorithm which is proposed in (Velikovich et al. 2010). The confidence score of a tweet belonging to a category is computed as the sum over the maximum weighted path from every labeled node of the category to the tweet.
- **Hassan's Method**: It is a graph propagation algorithm proposed in (Hassan and Radev 2010). The confidence score of a tweet belonging to a category is computed as the excepted number of steps from the tweet node to the labeled nodes.
- **Ours**: Our semi-supervised approach.

To tune the parameters in the various methods, we first randomly sample 50 instances for each category from all the labeled data, denoted as $\mathcal{D}_A$, and the rest labeled data is denoted as $\mathcal{D}_B$. Then we use $\mathcal{D}_A$ for parameter tuning with five-fold cross-validation. For the rest experiments, each method uses the corresponding optimal parameters derived by cross-validation. Then, we randomly sample 10 labeled instances for each category from $\mathcal{D}_A$ as training data, and use $\mathcal{D}_B$ as test data. Such experiments were performed ten runs, and the average of ten runs is reported.

Metrics

To measure the average performance of a classifier over multiple categories, the macro-average and the micro-average are widely used. The macro-average weights equally all the categories. The micro-average weights equally individual tweets, thus favoring the performance of larger classes.

Overall Performance

In this set of experiments, we set the number of labeled instances at ten for each of the six categories, and the rest of labeled instances are used for testing. Our method and two graph propagation baselines rely on graphs built with textual similarities between tweets, between words, or between a word and a tweet.

Table 2 present the F1 results of individual categories, as well as Macro-F1 and Micro-F1 over the six categories. We can see that our method performs much better than the four baselines in terms of both Macro-F1 and Micro-F1. In particular, it yields large improvements over the best baseline (i.e., *Velikovich's* method), by 20.30% and 25.25%, respectively, for Macro-F1 and Micro-F1. For individual categories, our method achieves the best performance in all categories except *Trifle*. Inferring tweets for this category is difficult, because some tweets in *Trifle* are similar to tweets in

Table 2: The F1 scores on all categories (with 10 labeled instances per category as training data).

Category	Food	Travel	Self	Goods	Event	Trifle	Non-intent	Marco-F1	Micro-F1
SVM-Multi	38.89%	52.70%	37.74%	28.66%	16.75%	20.16%	32.53%	32.49%	33.11%
Hollerit's	45.35%	50.62%	34.78%	30.70%	23.25%	**21.48%**	14.21%	31.48%	31.37%
Velikovich's	44.89%	49.56%	45.21%	29.72%	26.36%	19.79%	21.38%	33.84%	33.70%
Hassan's	28.40%	18.05%	43.07%	24.27%	20.10%	16.05%	31.74%	25.96%	26.46%
Ours	**54.63%**	**58.64%**	**45.73%**	**43.25%**	**27.13%**	20.04%	**35.56%**	**40.71%**	**42.21%**

Travel and *Event & Activities*. All methods perform poorly on this category. For the *non-intent* category, our method also performs best by using the effective threshold filtering method described in the section of Formulation.

We next compare the performance of four baselines. We can see that *SVM-Multi* is a robust method, which achieves better results than *Hollerit's* method. For the two graph propagation algorithms, *Velikovich's* method performs the best while *Hassan's* method is the worst among these four baselines. Their main difference is that they adopt different evaluation methods to estimate the relationship between unlabeled tweets and labeled nodes—*Velikovich's* method uses weighted path while *Hassan's* method uses excepted steps. The excepted steps may be too coarse to estimate the relationship between unlabeled tweets and labeled nodes.

Varying the Number of Labeled Instances

This set of experiments is to study how the number of labeled instances affects the classification accuracy. We vary the number of labeled instances in a category from 5 to 50. Figure 2 shows the performance of all methods in terms of Macro-F1, and our method is consistently better than other baselines with different numbers of labeled instances.

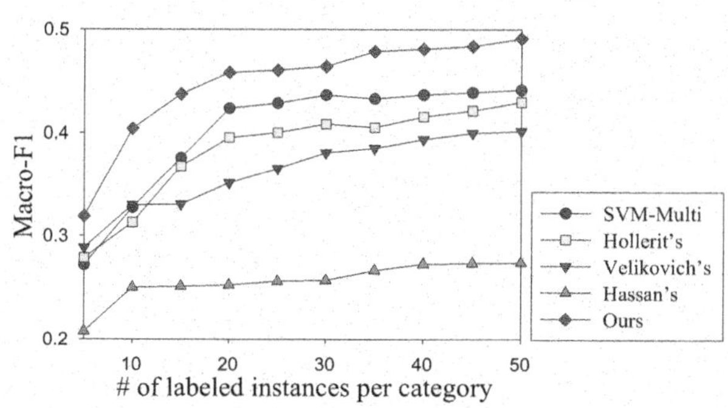

Figure 2: The overall performance of intent category inference in terms of Macro-F1.

Table 3: Performance comparison with different types of words in terms of Macro-F1.

Method	Velikovich's	Hassan's	Ours
All words	20.16%	18.06%	30.32%
Intent-keywords	**33.84%**	**25.96%**	**40.71%**

Table 4: Top five intent-keywords for every intent category.

Food.	Travel	Career.	Goods.	Event.	Trifle
snack	quay	hire	pen	movie	space
nestea	travel	student	kitten	soccer	sex
eat	train	lawyer	t-shirts	songs	texting
pudding	august	incomes	shelf	bruno	buddies
corn	houston	fighter	print	television	tweet

Intent-keywords or Bag-of-words?

In our earlier experiments, we only consider intent-keywords for computing textual similarities but not all the words. This set of experiments is to evaluate whether intent-keywords can better capture intent-oriented associativity between textual units (e.g., a tweet or a word) than all the words. Thus, we use our method and two graph propagation baselines as testing methods as they compute the textual similarity. We consider two ways to compute the tweet-tweet similarity and tweet-word similarity: either using all the words or using only intent-keywords.

As shown in Table 3, the performance of using intent-keywords is consistently better than that of using all words for these three methods. This is because tweets are usually noisy and not all the tokens in a tweet are related to intents. In contrast, intent-keywords are more discriminative features to infer intent categories. Having observed the effectiveness of intent-keywords, we present top intent-keywords for every intent category in Table 4, where are meaningful.

Parameter Analysis

The first parameter that requires tuning for our model is the trade-off coefficient γ in Eq. 5. We examine F1 scores of our model by varying γ from 0.1 to 2.0 with a gap of 0.1. We found that $\gamma = 0.7$ gives the best performance in terms of Macro-F1 and Micro-F1. For $\lambda_1, \lambda_2, \lambda_3$ in Eq. 5, we did a line search to find an optimal set of parameters and our results reveal that simply setting $\lambda_1 = \lambda_2 = \lambda_3 = \frac{1}{3}$ gives good performance which is only slightly worse than what can be obtained by the optimal parameters. Hence, for simplicity, we set all λs to be 1/3 in our experiments.

Conclusions

In this paper, we propose to study the problem of inferring intent categories for tweets. We formulate the problem as a classification problem, and propose a graph-based semi-supervised approach to solve this problem. Our experimental results on a tweet dataset demonstrate the effectiveness of the proposed approach in labeling the categories of intent tweets.

Acknowledgments

This research was carried out at the Rapid-Rich Object Search (ROSE) Lab at the Nanyang Technological University, Singapore. The ROSE Lab is supported by the National Research Foundation, Prime Minister's Office, Singapore, under its IDM Futures Funding Initiative and administered by the Interactive and Digital Media Programme Office. This research was also supported by the National Key Basic Research Program (973 Program) of China under grant No. 2014CB340400, NSFC Grant 61272340 and 61472013. Xin Zhao was partially supported by the pilot project under Baidu open cloud service platform on the special topic "mining users' commercial intents from online social media data".

References

Ashkan, A., and Clarke, C. L. 2009. Term-based commercial intent analysis. In *SIGIR*, 800–801.

Beitzel, S. M.; Jensen, E. C.; Lewis, D. D.; Chowdhury, A.; and Frieder, O. 2007. Automatic classification of web queries using very large unlabeled query logs. *ACM Trans. Inf. Syst.* 25(2).

Belkin, M.; Matveeva, I.; and Niyogi, P. 2004. Regularization and semi-supervised learning on large graphs. In *In COLT*, 624–638.

Cao, H.; Hu, D. H.; Shen, D.; Jiang, D.; Sun, J.-T.; Chen, E.; and Yang, Q. 2009. Context-aware query classification. In *SIGIR*, 3–10.

Chen, Z.; Liu, B.; Hsu, M.; Castellanos, M.; and Ghosh, R. 2013. Identifying intention posts in discussion forums. In *NAACL-HLT*, 1041–1050.

Dai, H. K.; Zhao, L.; Nie, Z.; Wen, J.-R.; Wang, L.; and Li, Y. 2006. Detecting online commercial intention (oci). In *WWW*, 829–837.

Hassan, A., and Radev, D. 2010. Identifying text polarity using random walks. In *ACL*, 395–403.

Hollerit, B.; Kröll, M.; and Strohmaier, M. 2013. Towards linking buyers and sellers: Detecting commercial intent on twitter. In *WWW*, 629–632.

Hu, J.; Wang, G.; Lochovsky, F.; Sun, J.-t.; and Chen, Z. 2009. Understanding user's query intent with wikipedia. In *WWW*, 471–480.

Java, A.; Song, X.; Finin, T.; and Tseng, B. 2007. Why we twitter: Understanding microblogging usage and communities. In *WebKDD/SNA-KDD*, 56–65.

Kang, I.-H., and Kim, G. 2003. Query type classification for web document retrieval. In *SIGIR*, 64–71.

Kirsh, D. 1990. When is information explicitly represented. *The Vancouver studies in cognitive science* 340–365.

Kwak, H.; Lee, C.; Park, H.; and Moon, S. 2010. What is twitter, a social network or a news media? In *WWW*, 591–600.

Li, X.; Wang, Y.-Y.; and Acero, A. 2008. Learning query intent from regularized click graphs. In *SIGIR*, 339–346.

Morris, M. R.; Teevan, J.; and Panovich, K. 2010. What do people ask their social networks, and why?: A survey study of status message q&a behavior. In *CHI*, 1739–1748.

Riloff, E.; Wiebe, J.; and Wilson, T. 2003. Learning subjective nouns using extraction pattern bootstrapping. CONLL, 25–32.

Shen, D.; Sun, J.-T.; Yang, Q.; and Chen, Z. 2006. Building bridges for web query classification. In *SIGIR*, 131–138.

Strohmaier, M., and Kröll, M. 2012. Acquiring knowledge about human goals from search query logs. *IP&M* 48(1):63–82.

Velikovich, L.; Blair-Goldensohn, S.; Hannan, K.; and McDonald, R. 2010. The viability of web-derived polarity lexicons. In *ACL*, 777–785.

Wang, F., and Zhang, C. 2006. Label propagation through linear neighborhoods. In *ICML*, 985–992.

Zhao, X. W.; Guo, Y.; He, Y.; Jiang, H.; Wu, Y.; and Li, X. 2014. We know what you want to buy: A demographic-based system for product recommendation on microblogs. In *KDD*, 1935–1944.

Zhu, X.; Ghahramani, Z.; Lafferty, J.; et al. 2003. Semi-supervised learning using gaussian fields and harmonic functions. In *ICML*, volume 3, 912–919.

Burst Time Prediction in Cascades

Senzhang Wang⋆, Zhao Yan⋆, Xia Hu†, Philip S. Yu‡, Zhoujun Li⋆
⋆ State Key Laboratory of Software Development Environment,
Beihang University, Beijing, 100191, China
† Arizona State University, Tempe, AZ 85287, USA
‡ University of Illinois at Chicago, Chicago, IL 60607, USA
{szwang, yanzhao, lizj}@buaa.edu.cn, psyu@uic.edu, xia.hu@asu.edu

Abstract

Studying the bursty nature of cascades in social media is practically important in many applications such as product sales prediction, disaster relief, and stock market prediction. Although the cascade volume prediction has been extensively studied, how to predict when a burst will come remains an open problem. It is challenging to predict the time of the burst due to the "quick rise and fall" pattern and the diverse time spans of the cascades. To this end, this paper proposes a classification based approach for burst time prediction by utilizing and modeling rich knowledge in information diffusion. Particularly, we first propose a time window based approach to predict in which time window the burst will appear. This paves the way to transform the time prediction task to a classification problem. To address the challenge that the original time series data of the cascade popularity only are not sufficient for predicting cascades with diverse magnitudes and time spans, we explore rich information diffusion related knowledge and model them in a scale-independent manner. Extensive experiments on a Sina Weibo reposting dataset demonstrate the superior performance of the proposed approach in accurately predicting the burst time of posts.

Introduction

Burst, defined as "a brief period of intensive activity followed by long period of nothingness" (Barabási 2011), is a common phenomenon in human activities. The bursty nature of human behavior is observed and studied extensively in many domains, such as electronic communication (Barabási 2005), library visiting (Vazquez et al. 2006), stock trading (Zhu and Shasha 2003), as well as cascades spreading in social media (Matsubara et al. 2012).

With the bursty nature of the cascades and the challenge of information overload in social media, an interesting problem arises: *Can we predict the burst time during cascade spreading?* Predicting the burst time of cascades is of outstanding interest for many applications in various domains, such as product sales prediction (Gruhl et al. 2005; Chen et al. 2013), disaster relief (Sakaki, Okazaki, and Matsuo 2010), and stock market prediction (Pinsen 2012). Yahoo! Finance reported that, Didier Sornette, a former physicist has developed a statistical model with the help of social media data to predict when a financial bubble will burst (Pinsen 2012). As said in the report: " the Sornette model is now predicting a stock market crash as early as next year."

Existing related works on cascades prediction mainly focus on predicting their future volume, ranging from the future popularity prediction (Szabo and Huberman 2008; Hong, Dan, and Davison 2011) to the aggregate size prediction (Petrovic, Osborne, and Lavrenko 2011; Cheng et al. 2014). Recently, some efforts have also been devoted to modeling the burst patterns and using the burst patterns to cluster the cascades(Crane and Sornette 2008; Yang and Leskovec 2011; Matsubara et al. 2012). Another related area is burst detection (Kleinberg 2002; Zhu and Shasha 2003; Parikh and Sundaresan 2008). Burst detection focuses on detecting instead of predicting the burst. How to predict the burst time of cascades still remains an open problem.

Predicting the burst time of the cascades is a non-trivial task due to the following two major challenges. First, existing prediction approaches cannot be directly applied to predict burst time due to the "quick rise-and-fall" pattern of the bursts. For example, traditionally, regression is widely used for predicting and forecasting (Mill 1990; Li et al. 2011) by learning relationships among features based on historical data. With the "quick rise-and-fall" property (Matsubara et al. 2012) of bursts in cascades, the correlation between historical data and future data becomes difficult to be captured by regression-based methods. This motivates us to investigate: are there any other knowledge could be helpful and how to model them? The second challenge is the significantly distinct life spans of different cascades. The vast difference in magnitude and time span of the cascades makes extracting comparable features difficult, and results in building predictive models challenging. For example, given two cascades with the time spans of 10 days and 10 hours respectively, it is more meaningful to predict the formal one on the daily basis and the latter one on the hourly basis. Therefore, instead of simply modeling all the cascades in the original time scale without distinguishing their diverse time spans, a more general and time-independent model is necessary.

In this paper, we propose to formulate the burst time prediction task as a classification problem by time window based transformation. Instead of predicting the exact occurring time of the burst, we predict in which time window the burst will appear. Since we conduct the prediction in the time window granularity, cascades with diverse time spans can be handled in a unified way. Motivated by previous studies on utilizing social theories to analyze and predict information diffusion in social media (Oh, Susarla, and Tan 2008; Hu et al. 2013; Wang et al. 2014a; Hu et al. 2009), we explore rich social knowledge available during cascades spreading such as knowledge on user profile and social relation to help this task. To utilize rich knowledge in a unified way and eliminate the difference of cascades in magnitude and time span, we model them in a scale-independent manner by deriving scale-independent features. We evaluate the proposed approach on a Sina Weibo reposting dataset that contains 300,000 posts and each post is reposted for 80 times on average. The results show the effectiveness of the proposed approach in accurately predicting the burst time of the posts.

Problem Statement

We will start with some definitions, and then will give two problems need to solve for the burst time prediction task. There is no clear definition of the "burst time" of a cascade, because it is hard to exactly say at what time a burst begins or in which time interval a burst exists. Alternatively, we consider the time of the *global spike* of the cascade defined as follows as its burst time we need to predict.

Definition 1 ***Global Spike.*** *Suppose 1) the time span T^c of the cascade c can be equally divided into K time windows, that is $T^c = \{(n_1^c, 1), (n_2^c, 2), ...(n_K^c, K)\}$, where $n_j^c(j = 1, 2..., K)$ is the number of reposts in the j_{th} time window, and 2) the number of reposts n_k^c is a function of the time window k: $n_k^c = f_c(k)$. The global spike of c is the $f_c(k_{max})$ that satisfies $\forall 1 \leq k \leq K, f_c(k_{max}) \geq f_c(k)$, and k_{max} is the time window of the global spike.*

The time series of the cascades may also have some local peaks where the values are larger than their neighbors. Such values can be considered as *local spikes* of the cascade.

Definition 2 ***Local Spike.*** *Given the time window related function $n_k^c = f_c(k)$ of cascade c and the divided time windows $T^c = \{(n_1^c, 1), (n_2^c, 2), ...(n_K^c, K)\}$ in Definition 1, $f_c(k_{lmax})$ is a local spike of cascade c if the following condition is satisfied: $\forall -s \leq i \leq +s, f_c(k_{lmax}) \geq f_c(k_{lmax} + i)$, where s is a predefined threshold.*

Previous studies showed that most cascades usually have one notable global spike with several less remarkable local spikes (Crane and Sornette 2008; Yang and Leskovec 2011; Matsubara et al. 2012). Therefore, it makes sense to use the time of global spike as the burst time of the cascade c.

To address the challenge that the time spans of cascades may differ significantly, we propose a time window based approach to eliminate the difference of time spans for various cascades. Specifically, we first divide the time spans of all the cascades into K time windows, and then try to predict the bursts of the cascades appearing in which future time window. Before stating the problem, we first define the μ_{th} future time window of a cascade as follow.

Definition 3 ***The μ_{th} future time window.*** *Given constant K, μ and the cascade c with an observed spreading time interval $[t_0^c, t_{current}^c]$, where t_0^c is the starting time of the cascade c and $t_{current}^c$ is the current time, the μ_{th} future time window of c is defined as such a time interval $[t_{current}^c + \frac{\mu-1}{K} \times (t_{current}^c - t_0^c), t_{current}^c + \frac{\mu}{K} \times (t_{current}^c - t_0^c)]$.*

Based on the above definitions, we next introduce how to address the burst time prediction task by answering the following two questions.

I. Given a new cascade c with an early stage of observed diffusion process, how could we predict whether a burst will occur in its μ_{th} future time window?

II. How could we further predict in which future time window the burst will appear?

Question **I** can be considered as a binary classification problem and solved by a general classification method, such as SVM or decision tree. If we can accurately answer Question **I**, Question **II** can be solved based on the solution of Question **I**. A straightforward approach is to consider Question **II** as a multi-classification problem. However, our later experiment results will show that this attempt usually cannot get desirable results due to the fact that the classification performance with different μ may be significantly distinct. In the next section, we will introduce an effective approach to answer question **II** by recursively solving question **I**.

CPB: Classification based Framework for Burst Time Prediction

In this section, we first describe how we transform the time prediction task to a classification problem. Then we introduce what knowledge we exploit and how to model them in a scale-independent manner to help the classification task.

The intuition is that though the magnitudes and time spans of the cascades may be significantly different, the shapes of their time series curves may be similar. Motivated by this, we propose the ***time window based transformation*** which equally divides the time spans of all the cascades into the same number of time windows. Then instead of predicting at which exact time point the burst will appear, we predict in which time window it occurs.

The general methodology would be to represent a cascade with a set of features extracted from rich information diffusion related knowledge, and then we use **C**lassifiers to **P**redict the **B**urst will occur in which future time window (CPB). As an illustration, Figure 1 shows how we construct the classifier to predict whether a burst will occur in the 1_{st} future time window based on two cascades with significantly different time spans and popularities. The upper part illustrates how we extract the positive and negative samples from the raw times series data of the cascades. Horizontal axis is time and vertical axis is the reposting count. Given a cascade c with observed spreading process in the time interval $[t_0^c, t_{current}^c]$ (the green vertical line represents $t_{current}^c$), we first equally divide $[t_0^c, t_{current}^c]$ into K time windows. If a burst appears in the following future time window, the partial data between $[t_0^c, t_{current}^c]$ is considered as a positive sample; otherwise, it is a negative sample. We will introduce

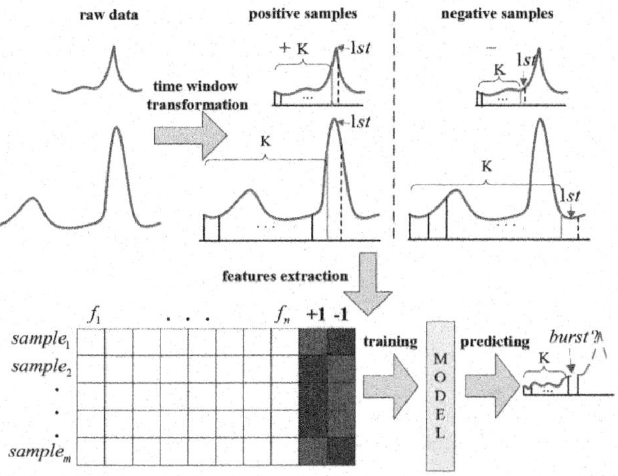

Figure 1: Illustration of the classifier construction to predict whether a burst will occur in the 1_{st} future time window.

how to extract these training samples in details later. Next we construct the classifier based on the extracted samples. Since the popularity information is insufficient, we will later elaborate what knowledge we will use and how to extract features from them. One can see that the proposed framework enables us to handle cascades with various time spans and popularities uniformly. Finally, when a new cascade comes, we use the trained model to predict whether a burst will appear in its next time window.

Time Window based Transformation to Construct Classifiers

To answer question **I** in Section 2, we first introduce how to extract training samples based on the time window based transformation and how to use these samples to construct classifiers. We next present how to answer question **II** by recursively solving question **I**.

Classifier Construction for Question I. For each cascade c, we construct classifiers for predicting whether the burst will appear in its 1_{st}, 2_{nd},... μ_{th} future time windows respectively, and extract corresponding training samples. For brevity, we only introduce how to construct the 1_{st} future time window classifier as an example, and all the other classifiers can be constructed in the similar way.

To construct positive samples for the 1_{st} future window classifier, we first identify the time of the global spike t^c_{max} for cascade c, and then we equally divide the time interval $[t^c_0, t^c_{max}]$ into $K+1$ time windows $\{[t^c_0, t^c_1], (t^c_1, t^c_2]...(t^c_K, t^c_{max}]\}$. The time of the burst t^c_{max} can be considered to be in the last time window. If the current time is t^c_K and we can only observe the reposting data of c before t^c_K, the burst will occur in the next time window, namely the 1_{st} future time window. Therefore, cascade c with observed time interval $[t^c_0, t^c_K]$ can be considered as a positive sample of the 1_{st} future time window classifier. For the negative samples, we first randomly select a time point $\bar{t}^c_K$ such that the burst will not appear in the next time window. To do this, we equally divide the time interval $[t^c_0, t^c_{max}]$ into $K+l+1$ time windows $\{[t^c_0, \bar{t}^c_1], ...(\bar{t}^c_{K-1}, \bar{t}^c_K]..., (\bar{t}^c_{K+l}, t^c_{max}]\}$, where l is a random positive or negative integer. A positive l means the burst does not occur before the K_{th} window; while a negative l means the burst occurs before the K_{th} window. Cascade c with observed time interval $[t^c_0, \bar{t}^c_K]$ can be considered as a negative sample of the 1_{st} future time window classifier. For a testing sample, assuming the start time is t_0 and the current time is $t_{current}$, we also divide $[t_0, t_{current}]$ into K time windows.

Answering Question II. To answer question **II**, we start with predicting whether the burst will appear in the 1_{st} future time window using the 1_{st} future time window classifier. If the answer is *YES*, the process stops and outputs the result; otherwise, we use the 2_{nd} future time window classifier to predict whether it will appear in the 2_{nd} future time window. The above process continues recursively until some classifier gives a positive prediction. If all the classifiers give the negative answer, we predict the burst appears in the last time window.

The reason why we conduct the prediction in this way is that, as shown in later experiment, the classification performance decreases with the increase of the parameter μ. Intuitively, bursts occurring in the near future time windows are easier to predict than those in farther future time windows. If two classifiers, for example the 1_{st} and 2_{nd} future time window classifiers both give positive predictions, we think the burst is more likely to appear in the 1_{st} future time window because the former classifier is more accurate.

Model Information Diffusion Related Knowledge in a Scale-Independent Manner

Besides the repost count, the cascades are also associated with a lot of other information, such as user profile and social relation. Oh et al.'s study showed that there are a number of mechanisms by which social influence is transmitted such as networked structure and conformity (Oh, Susarla, and Tan 2008). Cheng et al. also found that the network structure information are helpful to predict cascades (Cheng et al. 2014). Motivated by these works, we explore rich knowledge in information diffusion and roughly categorize them into four types: general time series based knowledge, fluctuation knowledge, user profile knowledge, and social relation knowledge. For each type of knowledge, we extract corresponding scale-independent features.

General Time Series based Knowledge The popularity of a cascade in each time window can be considered as general time series data (Wang et al. 2014b). We extract the following scale-independent features from the general time series based knowledge.

Average one-step increase rate (AIR_{+1}): Given the number of reposts n^c_k and n^c_{k+1} in the k_{th} and $(k+1)_{th}$ time windows respectively, the average one-step increase rate between two successive windows is defined as

$$AIR^c_{+1} = \frac{1}{K-1} \sum_{i=1}^{K-1} \frac{n^c_{k+1} - n^c_k}{n^c_k} \quad (1)$$

Average two-step increase rate (AIR_{+2}): Similar to

AIR_{+1}, we extract the average increase rate between every other time window (n_k^c, t_k^c) and (n_{k+2}^c, t_{k+2}^c) as the AIR_{+2}.

Recent data may be more useful to predict the future trend of the cascade; hence we also extract some features that are only related to the latest data.

Average spreading speed in the latest l time windows (ASS_l). The average spreading speed in the latest l windows can be defined as

$$ASS_l^c = \frac{1}{l}\sum_{i=1}^{l}\frac{n_{K-i}^c}{t^c} \tag{2}$$

where t^c is the length of the time window in cascade c.

Average one-step increase rate in the latest l time windows (AIR_l_{+1}). The average one-step increase rate in the latest l time windows of cascade c is defined as

$$AIR\_l_{+1}^c = \frac{1}{l-1}\sum_{i=0}^{l-1}\frac{n_{K-i}^c - n_{K-i-1}^c}{n_{K-i-1}^c} \tag{3}$$

Average two-step increase rate in the latest l time windows(AIR_l_{+2}). We extract two-step increase rate between every other time windows in the latest l time windows.

Fluctuation Knowledge The spreading process of cascades is rather dynamic and fluctuates over time (Petrovic, Osborne, and Lavrenko 2011; Myers and Leskovec 2014). An important reason causing the temporal dynamic is that users' behavior is highly related to the time. Myers et al. (Myers and Leskovec 2014) and Sakaki et al. (Sakaki, Okazaki, and Matsuo 2010) discovered that the fluctuation property of cascade spreading is helpful to predict the future popularity of photo reshare cascades and tweets. Therefore, we also explore the fluctuation knowledge of cascades and extract fluctuation features.

Hour (H). We use the hour of current time as a feature with 24 values from 0 to 23.

Day (D). The day of the week is selected as the second time related feature with 7 values from 0 to 6.

Number of local spikes N_l. Given a cascade c and the current time $t_{current}$, we identify all the local spikes before $t_{current}$ and use the number of local spikes as a feature.

Average normalized distance between two successive local spikes (ADLL). Assuming k_{lmax_m} and $k_{lmax\_(m+1)}$ are two time windows in which two successive local spikes occurs, the normalized distance between two successive local spikes is defined as $d^c(m, m+1) = k_{lmax\_(m+1)} - k_{lmax\_m}$. The average normalized distance between two successive spikes can be computed by

$$ADLL^c = \frac{1}{M}\sum_{i=1}^{M} d^c(i, i+1) \tag{4}$$

where m is the number of local spikes.

The normalized distance between the latest local spike and the current time (DLC). Assuming k_{lmax_l} is the time window of the latest local spike and $k_{current}$ is the current time window, the normalized distance between the latest local spike and current time can be defined as

$$DLC^c = k_{current} - k_{lmax\_l} \tag{5}$$

One-step consistency (F_{+1}^c). The one-step consistency between time windows k and $k+1$ is defined as

$$f_{+1}^c(k, k+1) = \begin{cases} 0 \; if \; n_k^c \geq n_{k+1}^c \\ 1 \; if \; n_k^c < n_{k+1}^c \end{cases} \tag{6}$$

The one-step consistency of c is the sum of the one-step consistency between all the successive two time windows

$$F_{+1}^c = \sum_{k=1}^{K-1} f_{+1}^c(k, k+1) \tag{7}$$

Two-step consistency (F_{+2}^c). We also extract the two-step consistency between every other time windows k and $k+2$.

User Profile Knowledge Different from traditional time series data, the cascades are triggered and driven by users. The posts originating from different users may have significantly different impact on the spreading of the cascades (Kupavskii et al. 2013). Hence we also use the user profile knowledge and categorize them into two types: profile based knowledge and authority based knowledge. The profile based knowledge includes **gender**, **location**, and **number of posts**. The authority based knowledge includes **number of followers**, **number of followees**, whether the user is a **verified** user, **PageRank score**, and **HITS score** of the user. The PageRank and HITS scores are computed based on the following relationship graph of all the users. For each type of knowledge, we first obtain the corresponding data in each time window, and then derive scale-independent features based on the time series data in all the time windows. Due to space limitation, we only take the gender as an example to illustrate how we extract scale-independent features from the gender knowledge.

In each time window (n_k^c, t_k^c), assuming the numbers of male and female users reposting post c are $n_{k\_m}^c$ and $n_{k\_f}^c$ respectively, we compute the ratio $g_k^c = \frac{n_{k\_m}^c}{n_{k\_f}^c}$. By calculating the ratios in all the time windows, we obtain such a gender related time series $G^c = \{g_1^c, g_2^c, ..., g_K^c\}$. Based on G^c, we can finally derive some scale-independent features such as average one-step increase rate, average two-step increase rate, the latest one-step gender ratio, and the latest two-step gender ratio. As the calculation of above derived features is similar to that of the general time series features, we omit the mathematical equations for brevity. For other user profile knowledge, we also extract scale-independent features in the similar way.

Social Relation Knowledge The social relations among users and the spreading paths of the cascades may also be helpful. Cheng et al. studied whether the cascade is spreading primarily within a community or across many to predict the future popularity of the cascade (Cheng et al. 2014). Ma et al. also studied that the total number of exposed users is an important feature in predicting Twitter hashtag popularity (Ma, Sun, and Cong 2013). To examine whether the social relation knowledge is helpful to predict burst time of cascades, we explore some structure knowledge based on users' social relations in cascade diffusion, and derive corresponding scale-independent features.

Table 1: Classification result for various learning algorithms.

Algorithm	F1-measure	AUC	Accuracy
Logistic Regression	0.826	0.895	82.8%
Multilayer Perceptron	0.899	0.915	90.2%
Adaboost	0.854	0.929	85.4%
Random Forest	0.892	0.904	89.2%
J48 Decision Tree	**0.928**	0.922	92.2%
Random Tree	0.904	**0.934**	**92.4%**
LibSVM	0.824	0.828	82.8%

We use five network structure measures to represent the social relation knowledge: **Wiener index** (Goel et al. 2013), **graph edit distance** (Papadimitriou, Dasdan, and Garcia-Molina 2008), **vertex and edge overlap** (VEO) (Papadimitriou, Dasdan, and Garcia-Molina 2008), **graph density** (Cheng et al. 2014), and **Entropy of degree distribution** (Kong et al. 2014). Wiener index is a measure of the structure vitality of a cascade. Graph edit distance and VEO are both used to measure the similarity of two graphs. Graph density is to measure how closely the nodes are connected in a graph. Entropy of degree distribution is a measure to describe the degree distribution of a graph.

We take the graph edit distance as an example to show how we model the social relation knowledge and extract features. All the other measures can be modeled in the similar way. For each time window k, we first extract a graph G_k^c based on the nodes involved in cascade c before the current time window and the following relationships among these nodes. Then we can obtain a set of graphs $\mathcal{G}^c = \{G_1^c, G_2^c...., G_K^c\}$. Based on $\mathcal{G}^c$ we can compute the graph edit distance $d_{k,k+1}$ between two successive graphs G_k^c and G_{k+1}^c. Then we can further obtain the time series data of the graph edit distance $D = \{d_{1,2}, d_{2,3}..., d_{K-1,K}\}$. Using the time series data of D, we derive some scale-independent features similar to the general time series features.

Evaluations

We use the public available Sina Weibo reposting dataset[1] (Zhang et al. 2013) to evaluate the proposed approach. This dataset contains 1,776,950 users, 308,489,739 following relationships, 300,000 popular microblog diffusion episodes with the original microblog and all its reposts. On average each microblog has been reposted for about 80 times. First, we verify whether the proposed approach can learn an accurate classifier by examining the classification performance with various learning algorithms. Then we study the effect of parameters on the classification performance. Next we conduct the feature importance analysis to verify the importance of different knowledge in the studied task. Finally, we quantitively evaluate how accurate CPB can predict the burst time of the cascades by comparing it against baselines.

Performance Analysis. We first exam the classification performance of various learning algorithms. We use 10-fold cross validation to evaluate on three metrics: F1-measure, AUC (Area Under ROC Curve) and classification accuracy. In this experiment, we divide the time spans of all the cascades into 10 time windows and predict whether the burst occurs in the first future time window. The result is given in Table 1. As shown in the table, the classification accuracy of all the used classification techniques are over 80%. The performance of Multilayer Perceptron, Random Forest, and J48 Decision Tree are not significantly different: the accuracy is around 90%. It implies that when sufficient features are available, this prediction task is not much sensitive to the choice of the learning algorithms. In our experiment, Random Tree is shown to be the most accurate algorithm with a classification accuracy of 92.4% and AUC value of 0.934. Hence, in the following experiments we use Random Tree as our classification method.

[1]http://arnetminer.org/Influencelocality#b2354

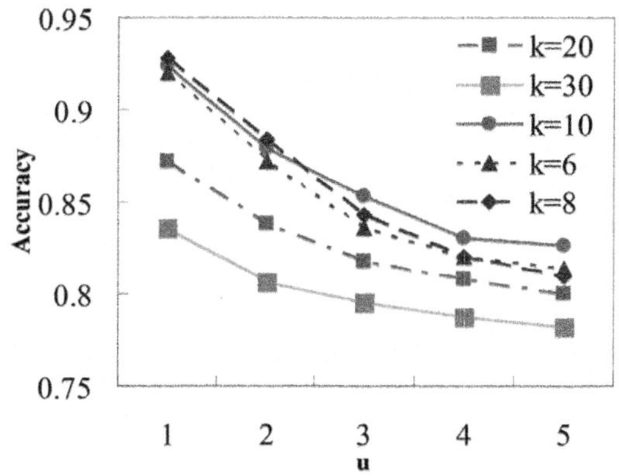

Figure 2: Classification accuracy with various K and μ.

Effect of Parameters. To study the effect of parameters K and μ on the classification performance, we conduct experiment with various K over different μ. Here K is the number of divided time windows and μ is the future time window in which we predict whether the burst occurs. Note that given a cascade c, the burst time window μ may change if K changes. The results are given in Figure 2. The x-axis is the future time window with μ from 1 to 5 and the y-axis shows the classification accuracy. We first set K to a set of relatively small numbers: $K = 6$, $K = 8$, and $K = 10$. Ones can observe a monotonically decrease trend in classification accuracy with the increase of the parameter μ. It means the burst occurring in a farther away future time window is harder to predict than that occurring in a time window which is closer to the current time. Ones also can see the classification performance does not show significant difference when the K values are relatively small.

To further verify whether larger K can impact the classification performance, we set K to two larger values: $K = 20$ and $K = 30$. Ones can see that the classification performance drops remarkably if K is set to a relatively large value. The result is not surprising as larger K means smaller time window and more fine-grained prediction. Smaller time window makes the difference between the data in two successive time windows smaller and thus harder to distinguish.

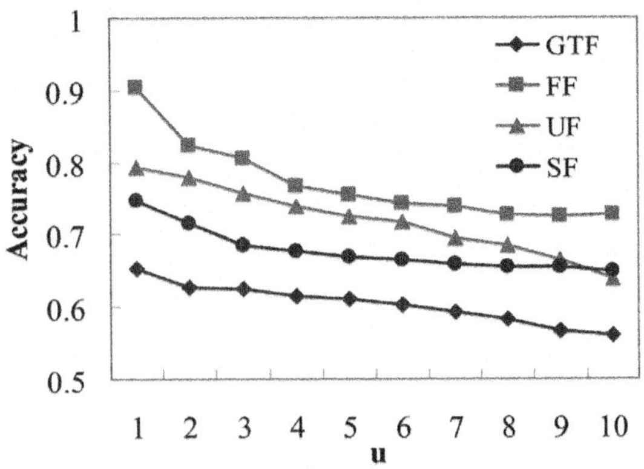

Figure 3: The classification accuracy by using general time series features (GTF), fluctuation features (FF), user profile features (UF), and social relation features (SF) separately.

Feature Importance Analysis We study the importance of the features derived from different types of knowledge. Figure 3 shows the classification accuracy achieved by the classifiers trained on each group of features separately. We summarize the results by the following observations:

- *General time series related features are surprisingly not very useful.* Figure 3 shows that the classification accuracy is less that 66% if we only use the general time series features. It implies that it is hard to predict the burst time by only using the time series of the cascade popularity.
- *Fluctuation features are most important.* With the fluctuation features, the classification accuracy on the 1_{st} future time window is near 90%, which is the highest in the four groups of features.
- *The user profile features and social relation features are helpful.* Surprisingly, user profile and social relation features both perform better than general time series features. Only using the user features, the accuracy is around 80% for the 1_{st} future time window prediction, and the figure is 75% for the social relation features only.

Quantitive Comparison with Baselines To quantitively evaluate how accurate CPB can predict the burst time of cascades, we compare it with the following four baselines.

- **Random**. We randomly select a future time window as the time window in which the burst occurs.
- **Multi-Classification (Multi_C)**. We consider the problem of predicting the time window in which the burst occurs as a multi-classification problem.
- **SPIKEM**. SPIKEM (Matsubara et al. 2012) is designed to capture the diffusion patterns of cascades. To make it comparable, we first use SPIKEM to forecast the future volume of a cascade based on its early data, and then identify the burst time window based on the predicted future volume in each future time window.
- **CPB Only Using Time Series Features of the Cascades Popularity (CPB_CP).** To study whether the rich knowledge can improve the prediction performance, we also use CPB with only the time series features of the cascades popularity as a baseline.

Table 2: Quantitive comparison against four baselines.

μ	Random	Multi_C	CPB_CP	SPIKEM	CPB
2	0.250	0.060	0.056	0.108	**0.042**
3	0.296	0.132	0.125	0.224	**0.065**
4	0.312	0.135	0.158	0.227	**0.102**
5	0.320	0.172	0.186	0.246	**0.142**
6	0.325	0.178	0.182	0.222	**0.144**
7	0.330	0.176	0.184	0.254	**0.146**
8	0.336	0.188	0.192	0.267	**0.152**

We use the Mean Absolute Error (MAE) computed by $MAE = E(\frac{|I^c - \hat{I}^c|}{l})$ as the evaluation metric. Here I^c denotes the true future time window in which the burst occurs, $\hat{I}^c$ is the predicted time window, and l is the number of future time windows. For ease of comparison, we first fix the number of future time windows l. Then we select the testing samples whose bursts occur in one of the l future time windows. Table 2 gives the results with l from 2 to 8. The figures in bold show the best results. Ones can see CPB performs significantly better than the four baselines in terms of MAE in all the cases. The MAE increases with the increase of l, which implies bursts in a farther away time window is harder to predict. Ones can also see although Multi-Classification approach is significantly better than random method, it is less effective than CPB. The performance of SPIKEM is not desirable: even inferior to Multi-Classification method. This is mainly because SPIKEM only utilizes the time series data of the cascade popularity, but cannot capture and handle various knowledge we study. Compared to CPB_CP, the MAE value achieved by CPB decreases by an average of about 30%. It implies that the rich knowledge in information diffusion does help our task.

Conclusion

In this paper, we studied the problem of burst time prediction in cascades and proposed a novel classification based framework CPB by exploring rich knowledge associated to information diffusion. Our solution allows us to predict the cascades with diverse magnitudes and time spans in a unified manner, since we conduct the prediction in the time window granularity by a novel time window based transformation. Extensive evaluations on a real social network dataset demonstrate the effectiveness of CPB.

Acknowledgments

This work is supported in part by NSFC (Nos. 61170189, 61370126, 61202239), the Fund of the State Key Laboratory of Software Development Environment (No. SKLSDE-2013ZX-19), the Innovation Foundation of BUAA for PhD Graduates (No. YWF-14-YJSY-021), Microsoft Research Asia Fund (No. FY14-RES-OPP-105), NSF through grants CNS-1115234, and OISE-1129076, and the Pinnacle Lab at Singapore Management University.

References

Barabási, A.-L. 2005. The origin of bursts and heavy tails in human dynamics. *Nature* 435:207–211.

Barabási, A.-L. 2011. *BURSTS: The Hidden Pattern Behind Everything We Do*. Plume, reprint edition.

Chen, Y.; Amiri, H.; Li, Z.; and Chua, T.-S. 2013. Emerging topic detection for organizations from microblogs. In *Proceedings of the 36th international ACM SIGIR conference on Research and development in information retrieval.*

Cheng, J.; Adamic, L. A.; Dow, P. A.; Kleinberg, J.; and Leskovec, J. 2014. Can cascades be predicted? In *Proceedings of the 23rd Internatioanl World Wide Web Conference.*

Crane, R., and Sornette, D. 2008. Robust dynamic classes revealed by measuring the response function of a social system. *Proceedings of the National Academy of Sciences of the United States of America* 105(41):15649–15663.

Goel, S.; Anderson, A.; Hofman, J.; and Watts, D. 2013. The structure virality of online diffusion. In *Preprint*.

Gruhl, D.; Guha, R.; Novak, R. K. J.; and Tomkins, A. 2005. The predictive power of online chatter. In *Proceedings of the 11th ACM SIGKDD Conference on Knowledge Discovery and Data Mining.*

Hong, L.; Dan, O.; and Davison, B. D. 2011. Predicting popular messages in twitter. In *Proceedings of the 20th Internatioanl World Wide Web Conference.*

Hu, X.; Sun, N.; Zhang, C.; and Chua, T.-S. 2009. Exploiting internal and external semantics for the clustering of short texts using world knowledge. In *Proceedings of the 18th ACM conference on Information and knowledge management.*

Hu, X.; Tang, L.; Tang, J.; and Liu, H. 2013. Exploiting social relations for sentiment analysis in microblogging. In *Proceedings of the sixth ACM International Conference on Web Search and Data Mining.*

Kleinberg, J. 2002. Bursty and hierarchical structure in streams. In *Proceedings of the 8th ACM SIGKDD Conference on Knowledge Discovery and Data Mining.*

Kong, S.; Mei, Q.; Feng, L.; Zhao, Z.; and Ye, F. 2014. On the real-time prediction problem of bursting hashtags in twitter. *CoRR abs/1401.2018.*

Kupavskii, A.; Umnov, A.; Gusev, G.; and Serdyukov, P. 2013. Predicting the audience size of a tweet. In *Proceedings of the Seventh International AAAI Conference on Weblogs and Social Media.*

Li, L.; Liang, C.-J. M.; Liu, J.; Nath, S.; Terzis, A.; and Faloutsos, C. 2011. Thermocast: A cyber-physical forcasting model for data centers. In *Proceedings of the 17th ACM SIGKDD Conference on Knowledge Discovery and Data Mining.*

Ma, Z.; Sun, A.; and Cong, G. 2013. On predicting the popularity of newly emerging hashtags in twitter. *Journal of the American Society for Information Science and Technolody* 64(7):1399–1410.

Matsubara, Y.; Sakurai, Y.; Prakash, B. A.; Li, L.; and Faloutsos, C. 2012. Rise and fall patterns of information diffusion: Model and implications. In *Proceedings of the 18th ACM SIGKDD Conference on Knowledge Discovery and Data Mining.*

Mill, T. C. 1990. *Time Series Techniques for Economists.* Cambridge University Press.

Myers, S., and Leskovec, J. 2014. The bursty dynamics of the twitter information network. In *Proceedings of the 23th Internatioanl World Wide Web Conference.*

Oh, J.; Susarla, A.; and Tan, Y. 2008. Examining the diffusion of user-generated content in online social networks. *Social Science Research Network.*

Papadimitriou, P.; Dasdan, A.; and Garcia-Molina, H. 2008. Web graph similarity for anomaly detection. In *Proceedings of the 17th Internatioanl World Wide Web Conference.*

Parikh, N., and Sundaresan, N. 2008. Scalable and near real-time burst detection from ecommerce queries. In *Proceedings of the 14th ACM SIGKDD Conference on Knowledge Discovery and Data Mining.*

Petrovic, S.; Osborne, M.; and Lavrenko, V. 2011. Rt to win! predicting message propagation in twitter. In *Proceedings of the Fifth International AAAI Conference on Weblogs and Social Media.*

Pinsen, D. 2012. Predicting the bursting of a market bubble. In *http://finance.yahoo.com/news/predictingbursting-market-bubble-171432469.html.*

Sakaki, T.; Okazaki, M.; and Matsuo, Y. 2010. Earthquake shakes twitter users: real-time event detection by social sensors. In *Proceedings of the 19th Internatioanl World Wide Web Conference.*

Szabo, G., and Huberman, B. A. 2008. Predicting the popularity of online content. *ArXiv e-prints.*

Vazquez, A.; Oliveira, J. G.; Dezso, Z.; Goh, K.-I.; Kondor, I.; and Barabasi, A.-L. 2006. Modeling bursts and heavy tails in human dynamics. *Physical Review* E(73).

Wang, S.; Hu, X.; Yu, P. S.; and Li, Z. 2014a. Mmrate: Inferring multi-aspect diffusion networks with multi-pattern cascades. In *Proceedings of the 20th ACM SIGKDD Conference on Knowledge Discovery and Data Mining.*

Wang, S.; Xie, S.; Zhang, X.; Li, Z.; Yu, P. S.; and Shu, X. 2014b. Future influence ranking of scientific literature. In *Proceedings of the 2014 SIAM International Conference on Data Mining.*

Yang, J., and Leskovec, J. 2011. Patterns of temporal variation in online media. In *Proceedings of the fourth ACM International Conference on Web Search and Data Mining.*

Zhang, J.; Liu, B.; Tang, J.; Chen, T.; and Li, J. 2013. Social influence locality for modeling retweeting behaviors. In *Proceedings of the 23rd International Joint Conference on Artificial Intelligence.*

Zhu, Y., and Shasha, D. 2003. Efficient elastic burst detection in data streams. In *Proceedings of the 9th ACM SIGKDD Conference on Knowledge Discovery and Data Mining.*

Clustering-Based Collaborative Filtering for Link Prediction *

Xiangyu Wang, Dayu He, Danyang Chen, Jinhui Xu
Department of Computer Science and Engineering
State University of New York at Buffalo
{xiangyuw,dayuhe,danyangc,jinhui}@buffalo.edu

Abstract

In this paper, we propose a novel collaborative filtering approach for predicting the unobserved links in a network (or graph) with both topological and node features. Our approach improves the well-known compressed sensing based matrix completion method by introducing a new multiple-independent-Bernoulli-distribution model as the data sampling mask. It makes better link predictions since the model is more general and better matches the data distributions in many real-world networks, such as social networks like Facebook. As a result, a satisfying stability of the prediction can be guaranteed. To obtain an accurate multiple-independent-Bernoulli-distribution model of the topological feature space, our approach adjusts the sampling of the adjacency matrix of the network (or graph) using the clustering information in the node feature space. This yields a better performance than those methods which simply combine the two types of features. Experimental results on several benchmark datasets suggest that our approach outperforms the best existing link prediction methods.

1 Introduction

Over the last few years, there is a rapidly growing interest in predicting the potential or absent links between nodes in large, complex networks. The link information represents the interactions, relationships, or influences between different nodes. Thus, predicting the likelihood of the unknown links is essential to forecasting the future or determining the hidden relationships between the nodes. For instance, with the surge of social networks in our daily life, link prediction has been widely applied in friendship recommendation and social network marketing (Liben-Nowell and Kleinberg 2003). In this paper, we focus on predicting unknown links in a partially observed network. The observed information can be classified into two categories. One is the set of topological features, such as edges or links, and the other is the set of node features, such as a user's name, gender, location, school, and other profile elements in some networks like Facebook.

*The research of this work was supported in part by NSF under grants IIS-1115220, IIS-1422591, and CCF-1422324.

1.1 Previous Work

A number of methods have been developed to predict the absent links, using either one or both types of features. A straightforward way of link prediction is to first compute the similarity between each pair of nodes and then use it to determine the likelihood of their possible link. Two types of similarity between a pair of nodes are frequently used. One is based on node attributes such as the number of common features shared by them (Lin 1998), and the other is based on graph-topological features such as the paths or neighbors connecting them (Leicht, Holme, and Newman 2006; Lü, Jin, and Zhou 2009). A major challenge encountered by such methods is that the node features are often treated independently of the topological features, and therefore it lacks a consistent and appropriate way to define similarity using the two types of correlated features. As a result, the performance of such methods could vary significantly among different types of similarities. To overcome this obstacle, several Bayesian probabilistic models have been proposed to make predictions by learning a link probability distribution model from the observed network (Wang, Satuluri, and Parthasarathy 2007; Miller, Griffiths, and Jordan 2009; Sarkar, Chakrabarti, and Jordan 2012). In such models, the node features and topological features are represented as random variables, and their relations are estimated via some assumed latent structure from the Bayesian method.

Another approach for link prediction is to formulate it as an adjacency matrix recovery problem, and use some sparse matrix recovery methods or collaborative filtering methods to solve it (Menon and Elkan 2011; Koren, Bell, and Volinsky 2009; Singh and Gordon 2008; Agrawal, Garg, and Narayanam 2013; Ye et al. 2013). Comparing to the statistical models, the matrix recovery approach has a prominent advantage, that is, its stability and accuracy of solutions can be theoretically ensured by the well-developed sparse recovery theory (Zhou et al. 2010; Candès and Plan 2009; Wang and Xu 2012). However, it also suffers from two limitations. One limitation is that the matrix recovery approach uses matrix norm as its measure and thus mainly focuses on the topological features. The other limitation is that the matrix recovery approach searches the missing links along the norm-minimizing direction (Menon and Elkan 2011; Chen 2008) (*e.g.,* similar to the least square problem), and the resulting matrix may not always reflect the real structure of the network.

Thus it is desirable to combine the advantages of the two approaches, and avoid their respective limitations. This motivates us to propose a new model to predict links by learning the original structure from both node and topological features and guarantee the stability of the solutions.

1.2 Main Ideas

A key assumption of our approach is that the two types of features are correlated and the topological feature is a reflection of some correlated node features. Thus, our approach tries to make use of the node features to help determining the unknown topological features. Particularly, our approach adopts the following main ideas.

Firstly, to ensure stability of predication, our approach adopts the framework of the reliable matrix completion approach. The predication can be treated as recovering the (partially unknown) original link matrix from the observed (*i.e.,* sampled) matrix M with $M_{ij} = 1$ indicating a link between nodes N_i and N_j. An effective strategy of sampling is proposed, in this paper, to guarantee the recovered matrix obeying the real structure of the original network (*i.e.,* the network containing both the observed and unknown links). The newly recovered links are the predications.

Secondly, for each node N_j, our approach views its observed neighbors as a cluster in the node feature space. A node N_i has a link to N_j if it belongs to the cluster of N_j in the node feature space. Thus, the j-th column M_j of the link matrix can be viewed as a vector generated by a Bernoulli distribution model in which the probability P_j is calculated by N_j's cluster. That is, we have $M_{ij} = 1$ with probability P_j (if N_i is inside the cluster of N_j) and $M_{ij} = 0$ with probability $1 - P_j$ (if N_i is outside the cluster). A major advantage of such a model is that it allows us to extend the well-known matrix completion framework (Candès and Tao 2005; Candès and Recht 2009; Zhou et al. 2010; Gross 2011) and prove the stability of our approach. In the original matrix completion framework, the stability is shown based on the assumption that every entry of the matrix is sampled by the same Bernoulli distribution. In our approach, the stability is analyzed under a more practical model in which the columns of the matrix are generated by multiple independent Bernoulli distributions and the probability of each entry depends on the actual relations between the corresponding node and its neighbors. There are also some existing non-uniform sampling models. A representative one is the local coherences model introduced by Chen *et al.* (Chen et al. 2014), in which each entry is sampled based on its own row and column coherence coefficient. Comparing to our model, these methods still depend only on the topological features (*i.e.,* without using the node feature information). Furthermore, computing the local coherences could be quite expensive, which needs to perform Singular Value Decomposition on a large-scale adjacency matrix.

Thirdly, our approach adopts an adaptive calibration strategy to obtain the Bernoulli model generating each column M_j. Hence the partially unknown network structure can be more accurately estimated. It consists of two calibration phases. In the first phase, our approach calculates a unique weight vector for each node N_j. This gives us the tightest cluster after filtering out those node features irrelevant to the cluster. In the second phase, the sampling probability of each column is adjusted based on the obtained clustering information, which serves as a bridge between the node feature space and the topological feature space. This allows us to use the relevant node features to help predicting the topological features.

1.3 Our Contributions

Our proposed approach has the following main contributions.

(1) *A matrix completion model based on multiple independent Bernoulli distributions*: We extend the original matrix completion model for the reconstruction of a partially observed network by using a new data distribution model. A theoretical analysis on the stability is provided to ensure the performance of this model.

(2) *An adaptive calibration strategy based on feature subspace*: We introduce a new way to bridge the node feature space and the topological feature space, which allows us to use relevant node features to predict topological features.

The rest of the paper is organized as follows. In the second section, we present our new model for link prediction. A stability analysis of this model is given in the third section. Experimental results are shown in the fourth section. Conclusion remarks are given in the last section.

2 Proposed Model for Link Prediction

Let $\mathbb{G}$ be a directed graph representing the considered network, and N be the set of n nodes of $\mathbb{G}$ with N_i being the i-th node of $\mathbb{G}$. Let $M \in \mathbb{R}^{n\times n}$ be the observed adjacency matrix of the network, and M_j be its j-th column. $M_{ij} = 1$ if a link from N_i to N_j is observed, and $M_{ij} = 0$ otherwise. Denote Ω the set of indices of all non-zero entries in M. Then predicting unknown links is equivalent to recover the unobserved links in M based on Ω. Let $\tilde{M}$ be the resulting (or recovered) adjacency matrix. The predicted links are stored in $\tilde{M} - M$.

2.1 Problem Description and Preliminary

We now formulate the link prediction problem in the matrix completion framework (Candès and Recht 2009) as follows.

$$\begin{aligned} &\min \; ||\tilde{M}||_* \\ &\text{subject to } \mathcal{P}_\Omega(\tilde{M}) = \mathcal{P}_\Omega(M), \end{aligned} \tag{1}$$

where $||\tilde{M}||_*$ denotes the nuclear norm of $\tilde{M}$, which is a good convex relaxation of *matrix rank*, and $\mathcal{P}_\Omega$ is the sampling projector determined by our multiple independent Bernoulli distribution model. The definition of $\mathcal{P}_\Omega$ will be introduced later. The observed links in M are treated as the links sampled from the unknown original adjacency matrix of $\mathbb{G}$ by $\mathcal{P}_\Omega$. In matrix completion theory, the quality of recovery depends on sampling. Hence, our model focuses on constructing $\mathcal{P}_\Omega(M)$ so that it closely reflects the structure of $\mathbb{G}$. In the following subsections, we explain how to achieve this.

To be consistent with the framework in (Candès and Recht 2009; Gross 2011), below we introduce some necessary definitions and assumptions required by the matrix completion framework.

Let $M = \sum_{k=1}^{r} \delta_k u_k v_k^\top$ be the SVD form of $M$and r be the rank of M. Let U and V be the spaces spanned by $\{u_k\}_{k=1}^{r}$ and $\{v_k\}_{k=1}^{r}$, respectively. Assume that M has low rank and satisfies the following coherence condition introduced in (Gross 2011).

Definition 1 *The $n \times n$ matrix M has the coherence μ with respect to basis $\{\omega_{ij}\}_{ij}^{n^2}$ if*

$$\max_{ij} ||\mathcal{P}_T(\omega_{ij})||_F^2 \leq \frac{\mu r}{n}, \tag{2}$$

$$\max_{ij} \langle \omega_{ij}, sgn(UV^\top) \rangle \leq \frac{\mu r}{n^2}, \tag{3}$$

where $\text{sgn}(UV^\top)$ is the sign function of $UV^\top$ (denoted by sgn). Let $||M||_2$ be the spectral norm of a matrix M, and $||M||_F$ be its Frobenius norm.

Below we discuss our model.

2.2 Node Clusters

A key assumption used in the original matrix completion framework is that elements in $\mathcal{P}_\Omega(M)$ are generated by a sequence of independent identically distributed $0/1$ Bernoulli random variables. Below, we introduce a new probabilistic model for $\mathcal{P}_\Omega$ based on the correlation between the topological features M and the node features F.

For each node, we assume that all its possible linking nodes aggregate as a cluster. Let $\{M_{ij}\}_{i=1}^{k}$ be the set of nonzero entries of vector M_j, and $\{N_i\}_{i=1}^{k}$ be the corresponding nodes which have a link to node N_j in M. $\{N_i\}_{i=1}^{k}$ forms a neighborhood of N_j (this is based on a commonly used belief that two nodes sharing a link have certain similarity). By our assumption that topological features are reflections of node features, this means that $\{N_i\}_{i=1}^{k}$ aggregates in the f-dimensional node feature space or its subspace, where f is the number of node features in the network. To measure the quality of the aggregation, we can find a weight vector $W_j \in \mathbb{R}^f$ to make $\{N_i\}_{i=1}^{k}$ become the smallest weighted cluster of N_j. More specifically, let $F \in \mathbb{R}^{f\times k}$ denote the feature matrix of the k nodes with the i-th column F_i being the feature vector of N_i; the cluster of N_j is estimated by the following

$$\delta_j = \min_{W_j} \frac{1}{k} \sum_{i=1}^{k} ||W_j \otimes F_i - F_j||, \tag{4}$$

where δ_j is the radius of cluster of each N_j, and $\otimes$ is an element-by-element multiplication.[1] Using W_j and δ_j, we can determine whether any other node N_i is inside the cluster.

[1]That is, the result of $W_j \otimes F_i$ is still a f dimensional vector with its q-th entry equaling to the product of the two q-th entries in W_j and F_i respectively.

2.3 Multiple Independent Bernoulli Distribution Model

With the above ideas, we can define the *multiple independent Bernoulli distribution model* in the following way. Let $\{m_{ij}\}_{1\leq i\leq n, 1\leq j\leq n}$ be a sequence of random variables independently sampled from $0/1$ Bernoulli's distribution with

$$m_{ij} = \begin{cases} 1 & \text{if } N_i \text{ is inside } N_j\text{'s cluster} \\ 0 & \text{if } N_i \text{ is outside } N_j\text{'s cluster} \end{cases} \tag{5}$$

with the probability

$$\mathbb{P}(m_{ij} = 1) = P_j, \tag{6}$$

where P_j is decided only by the cluster of N_j (*i.e.* W_j and δ_j). Then the operator $\mathcal{P}_\Omega$ in Eq(1) is defined as

$$\mathcal{P}_\Omega(M) = \sum_{i,j\in\Omega} \frac{1}{P_j} \omega_{ij} \langle \omega_{ij}, M \rangle, \tag{7}$$

where $\omega_{ij} = \{e_i e_j\}_{i,j}^{n}$ and $\{e_i\}_{i=1}^{n}$ is the standard basis; $\langle , \rangle$ is the matrix inner product defined as $\langle M_1, M_2 \rangle = tr(M_1^\top M_2)$ for two matrices M_1 and M_2. After defining $\mathcal{P}_\Omega$, we now need to calculate the probability P_j.

2.4 Adaptive Calibration

To obtain the sampling probability P_j for the jth column, we use a two-phase adaptive calibration strategy.

The first phase is only for the purpose of estimating the structure of the original network. In this phase, we use a uniform Bernoulli distribution to sample at least $O(\mu n r \log n)$ entries in Ω, which means that for each column we can sample at least $O(\mu r \log n)$ entries. Then, for each j, we obtain the radius δ_j and the feature weight W_j using Eq(4). With these, we can calculate the distances between node N_j and each of its neighbors N_k by the following equation.

$$\delta_{kj} = ||W_j \otimes F_k - F_j||. \tag{8}$$

Note that we only need the feature information of each node, which is already available.

In the second phase, we first set the sampling probability P_j using the clustering information computed in the first phase, and then calculate $\mathcal{P}_\Omega(M)$ by Eq(7). More specifically, we first compare δ_{kj} with δ_j to obtain the total number D_j of nodes inside the cluster of N_j, and then set the sampling probability of the jth column as

$$P_j = \max\left(\frac{D_j}{n}, \frac{\mu r \log n}{n}\right). \tag{9}$$

With this calibration, the stability of the recovery only depends on P_j. As a result, it guarantees that our recovery can preserve the main structure of the original network structure. We analyze the recovery stability in the next section.

3 Stability Analysis

In this section, we show stability of our prediction approach by analyzing the stability of the equivalent matrix completion approach under the multiple independent Bernoulli distribution model.

Theorem 1 *Let M be an $n \times n$ matrix of rank r sampled from the multiple independent Bernoulli distributions. If Ω is generated by a sequence of independent $0/1$ Bernoulli random variables $\{m_{ij}\}$ with probability $\mathbb{P}(m_{ij} = 1) = P_j \geq \frac{\mu r \log n}{n}$, then there exist numerical constants C_0 and β, such that the minimizer to the problem (1) is unique and equal to M with probability at least $1 - C_0 n^{-\beta}$.*

To prove this theorem, we first recall how stability is shown in the original matrix completion model (Candès and Recht 2009; Gross 2011). Let T be the linear space spanned by both $\{u_k\}_{k=1}^r$ and $\{v_k\}_{k=1}^r$. Define the orthogonal projector $\mathcal{P}_T$ onto T as

$$\mathcal{P}_T(M) = \mathcal{P}_U M + \mathcal{P}_V M - \mathcal{P}_U M \mathcal{P}_V. \tag{10}$$

Denote by $\mathcal{P}_{T^c}$ the orthogonal projector onto the orthogonal compliment subspace of T.

Our proof strategy follows the architecture of (Candès and Recht 2009; Gross 2011), that is, we need to construct a dual certificate matrix $Y \in \text{range}(\mathcal{P}_\Omega)$ satisfying the following Lemma.

Lemma 1 *There exists a matrix M of rank r which is the solution of the problem (1), if the following two conditions hold:*

1. *$\mathcal{P}_\Omega$ restricted to elements in T is injective.*
2. *There exists a dual certificate $Y \in$ range$(\mathcal{P}_\Omega)$ obeys*

$$||\mathcal{P}_T(Y) - sgn||_F \leq \frac{1}{C_R n^3}, \ C_R > 1. \tag{11}$$

$$||\mathcal{P}_{T^c}(Y)||_2 < 1. \tag{12}$$

Below we show that the two conditions indeed hold.

3.1 The Injectivity

To prove the injectivity, a key step is to show the operator $\mathcal{P}_T \mathcal{P}_\Omega \mathcal{P}_T$ has a small spectral norm with a large probability.

Lemma 2 *Let Ω be the set of indices sampled using the multiple independent Bernoulli distribution model, there exists a numerical constants C_1 such that for all $t < 1$,*

$$||\mathcal{P}_T \mathcal{P}_\Omega \mathcal{P}_T - \mathcal{P}_T||_2 \leq t \tag{13}$$

with probability at least $1 - 2n^{-C_1 t^2}$, if $\min P_j \geq \frac{\mu r \log n}{n}$.

Proof: Firstly, for any matrix X, we have

$$\begin{aligned} & [\mathcal{P}_T \mathcal{P}_\Omega \mathcal{P}_T - \mathcal{P}_T](X) \\ = \ & \sum_j \left[\sum_i \left(\frac{m_{ij}}{P_j} - 1\right) \langle \omega_{ij}, \mathcal{P}_T(X) \rangle \mathcal{P}_T(\omega_{ij}) \right]. \end{aligned} \tag{14}$$

Define a new family of operators as $Z_{ij}(X) = (\frac{m_{ij}}{P_j} - 1)\langle \omega_{ij}, \mathcal{P}_T(X) \rangle \mathcal{P}_T(\omega_{ij})$. Then

$$\begin{aligned} & ||\sum_{ij} E Z_{ij}(X)^2||_2 \\ = \ & ||\sum_{ij} \left(\frac{m_{ij}}{P_j} - 1\right) \langle \omega_{ij}, \mathcal{P}_T(\omega_{ij}) \rangle Z_{ij}(X)||_2 \\ \leq \ & \left(\frac{1}{\min P_j} - 1\right) ||\mathcal{P}_T(\omega_{ij})||_F^2 ||\sum_{ij} E Z_{ij}(X)||_F \\ \leq \ & \frac{1 - \min P_j}{\min P_j} ||\mathcal{P}_T(\omega_{ij})||_F^2 ||\sum_{ij} E \mathcal{P}_T \mathcal{P}_{\Omega_{ij}} \mathcal{P}_T(X)||_F \\ \leq \ & \left(\frac{1}{\min P_j} - 1\right) ||\mathcal{P}_T(\omega_{ij})||_F^2 ||\mathcal{P}_T(X)||_F, \end{aligned} \tag{15}$$

where $\langle \omega_{ij}, \mathcal{P}_T(\omega_{ij}) \rangle = ||\mathcal{P}_T(\omega_{ij})||_F^2$. Then, based on Eq(2), we have

$$||\sum_{ij} E Z_{ij}^2||_2 \leq \left(\frac{1}{\min P_j} - 1\right) \frac{\mu r}{n}. \tag{16}$$

Next, we have

$$\begin{aligned} ||Z_{ij}||_2 & \leq \frac{1}{P_j} ||\mathcal{P}_T \mathcal{P}_{\Omega_{ij}} \mathcal{P}_T||_2 \\ & \leq \frac{1}{\min P_j} ||\mathcal{P}_T(\omega_{ij})||_F^2 \\ & \leq \frac{\mu r}{(\min P_j) n}. \end{aligned} \tag{17}$$

Since $EZ_{ij} = 0$, by the *Matrix Berstein Inequality* (Tropp 2012) (*i.e.,* Theorem 2), we have the following inequality for any $t \leq 1/2$

$$\Pr(||\mathcal{P}_T \mathcal{P}_\Omega \mathcal{P}_T - \mathcal{P}_T||_2 \geq t) \leq 2n^{-C_1 t^2} \tag{18}$$

if $\min P_j \geq \frac{\mu r \log n}{n}$, where $C_1 > 0$ is a constant coefficient. □

3.2 The Dual Certificate

To construct the dual certificate Y, we use the strategy of golfing scheme (Gross 2011) introdued by Gross. The golfing scheme first partitions Ω into l non-overlapping groups, *i.e.,* $\Omega = \bigcup_{1 \leq k \leq l} \Omega_k$, then set $Y_0 = 0$ and

$$Y_k = Y_{k-1} + \mathcal{P}_{\Omega_k} \mathcal{P}_T(\text{sgn} - Y_{k-1}), \tag{19}$$

where $\mathcal{P}_{\Omega_k}$ has a parameter $Pr(m_{ij}^{(k)} = 1) = P_j^{(k)}$, and sgn stands for the sign function of M. This series $\{Y_k\}_{k=1}^l$ will converge to the expected dual certificate Y_l.

Let $Z_0 = \text{sgn}$. Then we have

$$Z_k = \mathcal{P}_T(\text{sgn} - Y_{k-1}), \tag{20}$$

$$Y_k = \sum_{i=1}^k \mathcal{P}_{\Omega_i} Z_{i-1}. \tag{21}$$

The following two lemmas are key components for proving the conditions (*i.e.,* Eq(11) and Eq(12)) for the dual certificate Y in Lemma 1.

Lemma 3 *Suppose $Z \in T$, then*

$$Pr(||(\mathbf{1} - \mathcal{P}_T\mathcal{P}_{\Omega'}\mathcal{P}_T)Z||_\infty > \alpha||Z||_\infty) \leq 2n^{-C_2\alpha^2}, \quad (22)$$

with $\alpha, C_2 > 0$, if $\min P'_j \geq \frac{r\mu \log n}{n}$.

The proof is shown below. By a similar argument given in (Gross 2011), we also know that the series $\{Y_k\}_{k=1}^l$ converges to the expected dual certificate Y_l from this lemma.

Proof: For any $Z \in T$, we have $\mathcal{P}_T\mathcal{P}_{\Omega'}\mathcal{P}_T Z = \mathcal{P}_T\mathcal{P}_{\Omega'}Z$. Then we know that

$$Z - \mathcal{P}_T\mathcal{P}_{\Omega'}\mathcal{P}_T Z = \sum_i\sum_j(1 - \frac{m'_{ij}}{P'_j})\langle\omega_{ij}, Z\rangle\mathcal{P}_T\omega_{ij}. \quad (23)$$

For any pair of $\{i', j'\} \in \Omega'$, let

$$\begin{aligned} X_{ij} &= \langle(1 - \frac{m'_{ij}}{P'_j})\langle\omega_{ij}, Z\rangle\mathcal{P}_T\omega_{ij}, \omega_{i'j'}\rangle \\ &= (1 - \frac{m'_{ij}}{P'_j})\langle\omega_{ij}, Z\rangle\langle\mathcal{P}_T\omega_{ij}, \omega_{i'j'}\rangle. \end{aligned} \quad (24)$$

Then, we have $|Z - \mathcal{P}_T\mathcal{P}_{\Omega'}\mathcal{P}_T Z|_{i'j'} = \sum_{ij} X_{ij}$ and

$$\begin{aligned} &\sum_{ij} EX_{ij}^2 \\ &\leq (\frac{1}{\min P'_j} - 1)\sum_{ij}|\langle\omega_{ij}, Z\rangle|^2|\langle\mathcal{P}_T\omega_{ij}, \omega_{i'j'}\rangle|^2 \\ &\leq (\frac{1}{\min P'_j} - 1)||Z||_\infty^2||\mathcal{P}_T\omega_{i'j'}||_F^2 \\ &\leq (\frac{1}{\min P'_j} - 1)\frac{\mu r}{n}||Z||_\infty^2. \end{aligned} \quad (25)$$

Also, we know that

$$\begin{aligned} |X_{ij}| &\leq (\frac{1}{\min P'_j} - 1)||Z||_\infty|\langle\mathcal{P}_T\omega_{ij}, \omega_{i'j'}\rangle| \\ &\leq (\frac{1}{\min P'_j} - 1)\frac{\mu r}{n}||Z||_\infty. \end{aligned} \quad (26)$$

Thus, if $\min P'_j \geq \frac{r\mu\log n}{n}$, by Bernstein's inequality, we know that there exists a constant $C_2 > 0$ such that

$$\begin{aligned} &\Pr(||(\mathbf{1} - \mathcal{P}_T\mathcal{P}_{\Omega'}\mathcal{P}_T)Z||_\infty > \alpha||Z||_\infty) \\ &\leq 2\exp\left(-C_2\frac{\alpha^2 n \min P'_j}{\mu r}\right). \end{aligned} \quad (27)$$

This completes the proof of the lemma. □

Next lemma is similar to Lemma 9 of (Gross 2011), it states as follows.

Lemma 4 *Suppose $Z \in T$, then*

$$Pr(||\mathcal{P}_{T^c}\mathcal{P}_\Omega Z||_2 > t) \leq 2\exp\left(-\frac{t^2 n \min P_j}{C_3 \max||Z||_2^2\mu}\right), \quad (28)$$

for $t \leq \frac{\max||Z||_2}{4\sqrt{r}}$

Proof: Let $X_{ij} = \mathcal{P}_{T^c}\frac{m_{ij}}{P_j}\langle\omega_{ij}, Z\rangle\omega_{ij}$. Then $\mathcal{P}_{T^c}\mathcal{P}_\Omega Z = \sum_{ij} X_{ij}$ and $EX_{ij} = 0$.

By the fact that

$$||\mathcal{P}_{T^c}\omega_{ij}||_F^2 = \sup_{\psi\in T^c\ ||\psi||_2=1}\langle\omega_{ij}, \psi\rangle, \quad (29)$$

and Lemma 8 of (Gross 2011), we have

$$\begin{aligned} \sum_{ij}\mathrm{Var}(X_{ij}) &\leq \sum_{ij}\frac{1}{\min P_j}|\langle\omega_{ij}, Z\rangle|^2||\mathcal{P}_{T^c}\omega_{ij}||_F^2 \\ &\leq \frac{1}{\min P_j}\sup_\psi\sum_{ij}|\langle\omega_{ij}, Z\rangle|^2\langle\psi, \omega_{ij}^2\psi\rangle \\ &\leq \frac{\mu\max||Z||_2^2}{n\min P_j}. \end{aligned} \quad (30)$$

Also, we know that

$$|X_{ij}| \leq \frac{1}{\min P_j}|\langle\omega_{ij}, Z\rangle|||\mathcal{P}_{T^c}\omega_{ij}||_F \leq \frac{\mu\max||Z||_2}{n\min P_j}. \quad (31)$$

By Bernstein's inequality, the lemma follows. □

3.3 Matrix Berstein Inequality

Theorem 2 *(Matrix Berstein Inequality (Tropp 2012)) Let $(Y_k)_{k\geq 1}$ be independent matrices in $\mathbb{R}^{m\times n}$ satisfying*

$$EY_k = 0 \text{ and } ||Y_k||_2 \leq R. \quad (32)$$

Define the variance parameter δ as

$$\delta^2 = \max(||\sum_k EY_kY_k^\top||_2, ||\sum_k EY_k^\top Y_k||_2). \quad (33)$$

Then, for all $t \geq 0$

$$Pr(||\sum_k Y_k||_2 \geq t) \leq (m+n)\exp\left(\frac{-t^2}{3\delta^2 + 2Rt}\right). \quad (34)$$

3.4 Proof of Lemma 1

Now we show that the constructed dual certificate Y_l satisfies the two conditions Eq(11) and Eq(12) in Lemma 1.

Proof: *(a)* Let $Z_k = (\mathbf{1} - \mathcal{P}_T\mathcal{P}_{\Omega'}\mathcal{P}_T)Z_{k-1}$, then by Lemma 3, we have

$$||Z_k||_\infty \leq \alpha||Z_{k-1}||_\infty, \quad (35)$$

with large probability.

Then we have

$$||Z_k||_\infty \leq \alpha^k||\mathrm{sgn}||_\infty. \quad (36)$$

It follows that

$$||Z_k||_F \leq \alpha^k||\mathrm{sgn}||_F = \alpha^k\sqrt{r}. \quad (37)$$

Set $\alpha = 1/2$ and $l = \lceil\log_2(2n^3\sqrt{r})\rceil$, we get

$$||\mathcal{P}_T(Y_l) - \mathrm{sgn}||_F = \sum_{k=1}^l(\frac{1}{2})^{k-1} \leq \frac{1}{C_R n^3}, \quad (38)$$

with $C_R > 1$.

(b) By Lemma 4, and setting $\max ||Z_k||_2 = \frac{\sqrt{r}}{2^k}$ (by Eq(37)), we have

$$||\mathcal{P}_{T^c}\mathcal{P}_\Omega Z_k||_2 \le \frac{1}{4}2^{-k}. \tag{39}$$

It follows that

$$||\mathcal{P}_{T^c}\mathcal{P}_\Omega Y_l||_2 \le \frac{1}{4}\sum_{k=1}^{l}(\frac{1}{2})^{k-1} < \frac{1}{2}. \tag{40}$$

This means that Y_l satisfies both conditions. □

Now with $\max ||Z_k||_2 = \frac{\sqrt{r}}{2^k}$ as above and $\min P_j \ge \frac{\mu r \log n}{n}$, we can bound the probabilities in Lemmas 2,3,4 by

$$1 - C_0 n^{-\beta}, \tag{41}$$

where $C_0, \beta > 0$ are some constant coefficients. Thus Theorem 1 follows. This indicates that our prediction model has guaranteed performance with $|\Omega| \ge O(\mu r n \log^2 n)$.

4 Experiments

To evaluate the performance of our proposed approach, we implement our clustering-based collaborative filtering method (CBCF) and compare it with some existing link prediction methods. Experimental results are reported as the area under the ROC curve (AUC). The regularization parameters of our model are selected following the same rules in (Goldfarb and Ma 2011). In our experiments, we use the proximal gradient algorithm (APG) in (Cai, Candès, and Shen 2010; Shen, Toh, and Yun 2011; Goldfarb and Ma 2011) as the numerical solver. As for the running time, the first phase of the adaptive calibration procedure takes $O(f\mu r n \log n)$ time, and the second phase takes $O(fn^2)$ time, where f is the number of node features and is in general much smaller than n. Since APG needs to perform SVD on matrix M, which will dominate the time of the adaptive calibration, our model thus has asymptotically the same time complexity as APG. The readers are referred to the reference of APG for more details.

Firstly, we compare our method with a matrix factorization and bilinear regression model (FactBLR) proposed by (Menon and Elkan 2011). The FactBLR extracts edge information using matrix factorization and makes use of explicit node information through bilinear regression. Its prediction is made based on the linear combination of both types of information. Thus, it outperforms the popular link prediction methods which used only one type of information. As comparisons with our approach, we perform these methods on two datasets: the protein interaction dataset (Protein) from (Tsuda and Noble 2004) and the metabolic pathway interaction dataset (Metabolic) from (Yamanishi, Vert, and Kanehisa 2005). Protein dataset contains 2617 proteins and each protein has a 76 dimensional feature. Metabolic dataset contains 668 nodes and each node has a 325 dimensional feature. To be consistent with FactBLR experiments in (Menon and Elkan 2011), we uniformly select 10% of the interactions as training set for each dataset and repeat the whole evaluation process 10 times. We use the popular unsupervised scoring methods Katz and Shortest-Path (ShP) as the standard baseline (Menon and Elkan 2011). Results are reported in Table 1. From the table, it is clear that (1) CBCF significantly outperforms the methods which use only the topological features or only the node features, since CBCF scores a link depending on more information; (2) CBCF still shows advantages compared to FactBLR, which linearly combines the topological feature and node feature. This is reasonable, since there could be different data types and value systems between the topological feature space and the node feature space. For example, the value of topological feature is usually 1 or 0, but the value of node feature could be either a very large number or a very small number. Thus a score generated from a linear combination of these two feature spaces could be weighted unnecessarily more for one feature.

Table 1: Mean AUC scores for Katz, Shortest Path, FactBLR and CBCF

DATASET	KATZ	SHP	FACTBLR	CBCF
PROTEIN	0.727	0.726	0.813	0.831
METABOLIC	0.608	0.626	0.763	0.776

Table 2: Mean AUC scores for Katz, SPLR and CBCF with different corruption fraction δ

δ	KATZ	SPLR	CBCF
5%	0.9298	0.9293	0.9453
10%	0.9189	0.9221	0.9411
20%	0.8941	0.8997	0.9248

Secondly, we compare CBCF with the sparse and low rank matrices recovery method (SPLR) proposed by (Savalle, Richard, and Vayatis 2012). Low rank and sparseness are usually the characters of the social network dataset, especially when the whole dataset is obtained by sampling. SPLR has demonstrated its ability in processing such type of datasets. SPLR is based on the original matrix completion model which assumes that the observed data is sampled from identical independent Bernoulli distributions. Following the experiments of (Savalle, Richard, and Vayatis 2012), we use the Facebook100 dataset proposed by (Traud, Mucha, and Porter 2011), which contains the Facebook friendship relations between students in one hundred universities. We choose the same university dataset, which has 41554 users and each user has a 7 dimensional feature. For consistency, we first filter the data to retain only 10% of nodes which have the highest number of friends. Then uniformly corrupt the entries of the adjacency matrix with a fixed fraction δ. Also Katz method is used as the baseline. Results are reported in Table 2.The related ROC graph is shown in Figure1. From this table, we can make two remarks. (1) This comparison shows that our new matrix model performs better than the original matrix completion model, which seems to suggest that the multiple independent Bernoulli distribution model is more suitable for social network data. (2) This experiment shows that our approach can also be applied to low rank and sparse datasets.

5 Conclusion

In this paper we proposed a link prediction approach based on a new multiple independent Bernoulli matrix completion

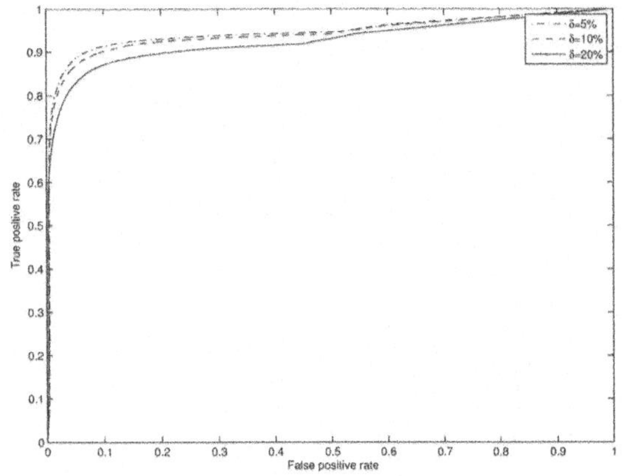

Figure 1: ROC graph for CBCF with different δ.

model. Our approach has a few advantages over the existing ones. Firstly, it is more general and a better fit for predicting unobserved links in many real-world networks such as social networks. This is because in such networks, each node often selects its linked nodes independently and follows only its own interest. Secondly, it allows us to ensure the stability of the solutions, which is given in the third section. Thirdly, it builds a bridge between the topological feature space and the node feature space through clustering, which allows us to collaboratively achieve better solutions by utilizing the two types of features and can deal with networks with insufficient node features.

Experimental results on several benchmark datasets suggest that our approach outperforms the original matrix completion model as well as the matrix factorization and bilinear regression method.

References

Agrawal, P.; Garg, V. K.; and Narayanam, R. 2013. Link label prediction in signed social networks. In *IJCAI*.

Cai, J.-F.; Candès, E. J.; and Shen, Z. 2010. A singular value thresholding algorithm for matrix completion. *SIAM Journal on Optimization* 20(4):1956–1982.

Candès, E. J., and Plan, Y. 2009. Matrix completion with noise. *CoRR* abs/0903.3131.

Candès, E. J., and Recht, B. 2009. Exact matrix completion via convex optimization. *Foundations of Computational Mathematics* 9(6):717–772.

Candès, E. J., and Tao, T. 2005. Decoding by linear programming. *CoRR* abs/math/0502327.

Chen, Y.; Bhojanapalli, S.; Sanghavi, S.; and Ward, R. 2014. Coherent matrix completion. In *ICML*, 674–682.

Chen, P. 2008. Optimization algorithms on subspaces: Revisiting missing data problem in low-rank matrix. *International Journal of Computer Vision* 80(1):125–142.

Goldfarb, D., and Ma, S. 2011. Convergence of fixed-point continuation algorithms for matrix rank minimization. *Foundations of Computational Mathematics* 11(2):183–210.

Gross, D. 2011. Recovering low-rank matrices from few coefficients in any basis. *IEEE Transactions on Information Theory* 57(3):1548–1566.

Koren, Y.; Bell, R. M.; and Volinsky, C. 2009. Matrix factorization techniques for recommender systems. *IEEE Computer* 42(8):30–37.

Leicht, E. A.; Holme, P.; and Newman, M. E. J. 2006. Vertex similarity in networks. *Physical Review E* 73.

Liben-Nowell, D., and Kleinberg, J. M. 2003. The link prediction problem for social networks. In *CIKM*, 556–559.

Lin, D. 1998. An information-theoretic definition of similarity. In *ICML*, 296–304.

Lü, L.; Jin, C.-H.; and Zhou, T. 2009. Similarity index based on local paths for link prediction of complex networks. *Physical Review E* 80:046122.

Menon, A. K., and Elkan, C. 2011. Link prediction via matrix factorization. In *ECML/PKDD (2)*, 437–452.

Miller, K.; Griffiths, T.; and Jordan, M. 2009. Nonparametric latent feature models for link prediction. In *Advances in Neural Information Processing Systems 22*, 1276–1284.

Sarkar, P.; Chakrabarti, D.; and Jordan, M. I. 2012. Nonparametric link prediction in dynamic networks. In *ICML*.

Savalle, P.-A.; Richard, E.; and Vayatis, N. 2012. Estimation of simultaneously sparse and low rank matrices. In *ICML*.

Shen, Z.; Toh, K.-C.; and Yun, S. 2011. An accelerated proximal gradient algorithm for frame-based image restoration via the balanced approach. *SIAM J. Imaging Sciences* 4(2):573–596.

Singh, A. P., and Gordon, G. J. 2008. A unified view of matrix factorization models. In *Proceedings of the European conference on Machine Learning and Knowledge Discovery in Databases - Part II*, number 16 in ECML PKDD '08, 358–373. Springer-Verlag.

Traud, A. L.; Mucha, P. J.; and Porter, M. A. 2011. Social structure of facebook networks. *CoRR* abs/1102.2166.

Tropp, J. 2012. User-friendly tail bounds for sums of random matrices. *Foundations of Computational Mathematics* 12(4):389–434.

Tsuda, K., and Noble, W. S. 2004. Learning kernels from biological networks by maximizing entropy. In *ISMB/ECCB (Supplement of Bioinformatics)*, 326–333.

Wang, Y.-X., and Xu, H. 2012. Stability of matrix factorization for collaborative filtering. In *ICML*.

Wang, C.; Satuluri, V.; and Parthasarathy, S. 2007. Local probabilistic models for link prediction. In *ICDM '07*, 322–331.

Yamanishi, Y.; Vert, J.-P.; and Kanehisa, M. 2005. Supervised enzyme network inference from the integration of genomic data and chemical information. In *ISMB (Supplement of Bioinformatics)*, 468–477.

Ye, J.; Cheng, H.; Zhu, Z.; and Chen, M. 2013. Predicting positive and negative links in signed social networks by transfer learning. In *WWW*, 1477–1488.

Zhou, Z.; Li, X.; Wright, J.; Candès, E. J.; and Ma, Y. 2010. Stable principal component pursuit. *CoRR* abs/1001.2363.

Proceedings of the Twenty-Ninth AAAI Conference on Artificial Intelligence

Mining Query Subtopics from Questions in Community Question Answering

Yu Wu,[†*] **Wei Wu,**[‡] **Zhoujun Li,**[†] **Ming Zhou**[‡]
[†]State Key Lab of Software Development Environment, Beihang University, Beijing, China
[‡]Microsoft Research, Beijing, China
{wuyu,lizj}@buaa.edu.cn {wuwei,mingzhou}@microsoft.com

Abstract

This paper proposes mining query subtopics from questions in community question answering (CQA). The subtopics are represented as a number of clusters of questions with keywords summarizing the clusters. The task is unique in that the subtopics from questions can not only facilitate user browsing in CQA search, but also describe aspects of queries from a question-answering perspective. The challenges of the task include how to group semantically similar questions and how to find keywords capable of summarizing the clusters. We formulate the subtopic mining task as a non-negative matrix factorization (NMF) problem and further extend the model of NMF to incorporate question similarity estimated from metadata of CQA into learning. Compared with existing methods, our method can jointly optimize question clustering and keyword extraction and encourage the former task to enhance the latter. Experimental results on large scale real world CQA datasets show that the proposed method significantly outperforms the existing methods in terms of keyword extraction, while achieving a comparable performance to the state-of-the-art methods for question clustering.

Introduction

Community question answering (CQA) has become a popular platform for people to share their knowledge and learn from each other. Large CQA portals like Yahoo! Answers and Baidu Knows have integrated the functions of search engines and social media. They not only allow their users to search and browse existing content, but also encourage them to share and interact with others. Recently, Quora and Zhihu have emerged as a new type of CQA service. These web sites further enhance the social features of Yahoo! Answers and Baidu Knows with social links between users.

With the flourishing of CQA service, researchers have studied how to leverage the content in CQA to fulfill users' information needs. A typical way is to let users search existing questions. A lot of work has been done along this line (Jeon, Croft, and Lee 2005; Xue, Jeon, and Croft 2008; Cao et al. 2009). Although existing work mainly focuses on handling long question queries, recently, it was reported that many users are still used to issuing short queries on CQA portals. For example, in a one-day search log of Yahoo! Answers, 24% of queries were shorter than 4 words and were incomplete sentences (Wu et al. 2014). In contrast to long question queries, short queries are usually ambiguous and multi-faceted. Users who issue short queries may either have difficulty in formulating a full-fledged question or just want to browse some relevant questions and learn related knowledge. Therefore, for these queries, rather than throwing a bulk of questions with mixed topics to users, it is better to organize the returned questions into different clusters and summarize each cluster with one or several keywords. The clusters and keywords represent subtopics of a short query and can quickly guide users to what they are looking for.

In addition to facilitating browsing in question search, subtopics from questions also reflect users' informational intent and thus describe queries from a question-answer perspective. The information is particularly useful for navigational queries and transactional queries in web search. For example, "twitter" is a navigational query, and the top subtopics mined from query logs and top search results are "twitter.com," "login," "news," etc. However, even for these queries, people sometimes still want to seek useful information and learn knowledge about a specific aspect of the queries. Currently, they usually post questions in CQA portals and wait for others' help. Therefore, CQA is a valuable resource for capturing users' informational intent. From questions in Yahoo! Answers, we clearly observed subtopics for query "twitter" such as "technology," "celebrities," and "search." These subtopics clarify the aspects people would like to ask concerning "twitter" and are valuable for query suggestion and question recommendation in CQA search. Table 1 gives more examples for comparing subtopics mined from CQA, query logs, and top search results.

We propose mining query subtopics from questions in community question answering (CQA). The subtopics are represented as a number of clusters of questions with keywords summarizing the clusters. As far as we know, we are the first to study the problem of query subtopic mining in CQA. The task of subtopic mining consists of three subtasks: question retrieval, question clustering, and keyword extraction. For question retrieval, we employ the method proposed by Wu et al. (2014), which represents the state-of-the-art method in question retrieval for short queries.

*The work was done when the first author was an intern in Microsoft Research Asia.

Query: **Math**
CQA: Algorithm, Algebra, Probability
Query log: Game, Play ground, definition
Web Result: Online, Games, practice
Query: **New York**
CQA: Football, Restruant, Shopping
Query log: city, news, company
Web Result: City, News, hotel
Query: **Twitter**
CQA: Technology, Celebrities, Twitter Search
Query log: twitter.com, api, widget
Web Result: login, account, news
Query: **Steve Jobs**
CQA: Design, ipad, Leadership
Query log: Cancer, Biography, Quotes
Web Result: Biography, News, Ceo

Table 1: Subtopics from different sources

The challenges include how to group semantically similar questions and how to find keywords capable of summarizing the clusters. Existing methods for subtopic mining from query log and search results usually conduct clustering and keyword extraction in separate steps (Zeng et al. 2004; Wang et al. 2013). We propose formulating query subtopic mining as a non-negative matrix factorization (NMF) problem and further extend the model of NMF to incorporate question similarity into learning. Thus, question clustering and keyword extraction are conducted in a unified framework by simultaneously factorizing a tf-idf matrix and a question similarity matrix. Compared with existing methods, our method jointly optimizes question clustering and keyword extraction. The good clustering performance can enhance the performance of keyword extraction. We derive a projected gradient descent based algorithm that can efficiently solve the optimization problem and propose a heuristic but effective method that can estimate the number of subtopics from data for practical application.

We implemented our method with question similarity estimated using answers and categories in CQA and tested its performance on Quora and Zhihu data. We set up experiments on Quora and Zhihu because questions have rich topics annotated by users and thus we can easily build up large scale evaluation data sets without expensive and exhausting human annotation. We evaluated different subtopic mining methods on both question clustering and keyword extraction. The experimental results show that our method can significantly outperform existing methods for keyword extraction, while achieving a comparable performance with the state-of-the-art methods of question clustering.

Our contributions in this paper are three-fold: 1) proposal of mining query subtopics from questions in CQA; 2) formulation of the task as an NMF optimization problem, derivation of an efficient algorithm, and implementation with metadata in CQA; 3) empirical verification of the efficacy of the method on large scale CQA data.

Related Work

Existing research on identifying query subtopics can be categorized into two groups: mining from query logs (Beeferman and Berger 2000; Wen, Nie, and Zhang 2001; Craswell and Szummer 2007; Hu et al. 2012), and mining from top web search results (Zeng et al. 2004; Wang and Zhai 2007; Wang et al. 2013). In the former group, a lot of methods perform query clustering on a click-through bipartite graph and the clusters represent aspects of queries. For example, Hu et al. (2012) proposed clustering URLs and keywords that are either the prefix or suffix of a query. The clustering was conducted with similarity extracted from a click-through bipartite graph. The keywords together with the URLs in a cluster were taken as subtopics of a query. Instead of analyzing query logs, the latter group extracts aspects of queries from plain text. For example, Zeng et al. (2004) formalized search result clustering as a salient phrase ranking problem. Documents that share the same salient phrase were grouped together. The salient phrases associated with documents represent subtopics of a query. Recently, Wang et al. (2013) proposed clustering top search results and then extracting key phrases in the clusters as subtopics of queries. Our method is unique in that 1) it extracts subtopics from questions, and thus explains queries from a question-answering perspective; 2) it studies how to leverage the metadata of CQA to enhance clustering and keyword extraction of questions.

In this paper, we have formulated the query subtopic mining task as a non-negative matrix factorization (NMF) problem. The model of NMF, due to its good interpretability and superior performance, has been applied to many tasks like document clustering (Xu, Liu, and Gong 2003), document classification (Zhu et al. 2007), multi-document summarization (Wang et al. 2008), and subgroup identification (Mandayam-Comar, Tan, and Jain 2010). Various extensions such as GNMF (Cai et al. 2011) and symmetric NMF (Kuang, Park, and Ding 2012) were also developed and have proven to be effective in document clustering. As far as we know, our method is the first application of NMF to the subtopic mining task. By doing so, we jointly optimize question clustering and keyword extraction. To leverage metadata in CQA portals, we also extend the traditional NMF by simultaneously factorizing a tf-idf matrix and a question similarity matrix. Our model is similar to the one proposed by Zhu et al. (2007). The difference is that they perform classification and NMF is only used to learn document feature vectors for a classifier. We perform query subtopic mining, and both document representation and word representation are learnt through NMF and evaluated in question clustering and keyword extraction.

A Matrix Factorization Approach for Query Subtopic Mining

In this section, we elaborate our approach for mining query subtopics from questions in CQA. The task includes three subtasks: question retrieval for short queries, question clustering, and keyword extraction. For the first subtask, we employ the method proposed by Wu et al. (2014) as it represents the state-of-the-art method for short query question search. For the other two subtasks, one solution is to follow an existing method for subtopic mining from search results, and conduct question clustering and keyword extraction in separate steps. The problem is that the correlation between the two subtasks is ignored. Intuitively, question clustering and keyword extraction should be coupled, and good clustering can enhance the performance of keyword extraction.

We have considered modeling question clustering and keyword extraction in a unified framework. Specifically, we formulate the two subtasks as a non-negative matrix factorization problem. The method simultaneously embeds questions and words into a vector space, and elements of the vectors indicate groups of questions and representative words of the groups. In this way, question clustering and keyword extraction are jointly optimized and the two subtasks interact with each other in the learning process. To leverage the meta data in CQA, we further extend the basic NMF model and incorporate question similarity estimated from the metadata into learning. Then, vectors of questions and vectors of words are learnt by simultaneously factorizing a tf-idf matrix and a question similarity matrix.

We first introduce the formulation of our method, then we derive an efficient algorithm based on projected gradient descent (Lin 2007) to solve the optimization problem.

Problem Formulation

Suppose that we have a question set $\mathbb{Q}$ that is a subset of a CQA web site. Given a query q, we have some questions $\mathcal{Q} = \{Q_1, Q_2, \ldots, Q_n\}$ returned by the retrieval model. Suppose that there are k subtopics of q implied by $\mathcal{Q}$. Our goal is to recover the subtopics by a partition $\mathcal{C} = \{C_1, C_2, \ldots, C_k\}$ of $\mathcal{Q}$. Each C_i is a cluster of questions and we summarize C_i by keyword w_i. The cluster-keyword pair (C_i, w_i) represents the i-th subtopic of q. Note that in this work, we assume that each question only belongs to one subtopic and only consider using one keyword to summarize each cluster. It is easy to extend this work to involve cases that involve one question with multiple subtopics and one cluster with multiple keywords. We leave these cases for future investigations. Let $\mathcal{W} = \{w_1, w_2, \ldots, w_m\}$ denote words appearing in $\mathcal{Q}$. We assume that the subtopics correspond to a subspace of $\mathbb{R}^k$, where $k \ll \min(m, n)$, and consider learning a vector $v_i = (v_{i1}, v_{i2}, \ldots, v_{ik})$ and a vector $u_i = (u_{i1}, u_{i2}, \ldots, u_{ik})$ in $\mathbb{R}^k$ to represent question Q_i and word w_i, respectively. Thus, $\mathcal{Q}$ and $\mathcal{W}$ can be represented as $V = (v_1^\top, v_2^\top, \ldots, v_n^\top)^\top$ and $U = (u_1^\top, u_2^\top, \ldots, u_m^\top)^\top$, respectively. Each element of U and V reveals the intensity of a question and a word in a subtopic and therefore we require U and V to be non-negative. The cluster-word pair (C_j, w_j) is defined as $C_j = \{q_i \mid \max_{1 \leqslant s \leqslant k} v_{is} = j\}$ and $w_j = p_s$ where $s = \arg\max_{1 \leqslant r \leqslant m} u_{rj}, \forall\, 1 \leqslant j \leqslant k$.

We aim to learn U and V in a unified framework. To this end, we further assume that there is an $m \times n$ matrix X measuring the similarity of words and questions, and an $n \times n$ matrix D measuring the similarity of questions. A common setup of X is using tf-idf as weights. We consider recovering U and V from X and D, and expect similar question-word pairs and question-question pairs are still similar in $\mathbb{R}^k$. This leads to the following optimization problem:

Algorithm 1: Optimization Algorithm for Problem (1)

Input: $\alpha \geqslant 0, \gamma_0 = 1, 0.1 < \beta < 0.5, 0 < \epsilon \ll 1,$
$0 < \sigma < 1, t = 1, T$ = max iteration count
Initialize $U = U_1 \geqslant 0, V = V_1 \geqslant 0$
repeat
  $\gamma_t = 1; U' = [U_t - \gamma_t[\frac{\partial O}{\partial U}]_t]_+;$
  if $O(U', V_t) - O(U_t, V_t) > \sigma \cdot trace[[\frac{\partial O}{\partial U}]_t^\top \cdot (U' - U_t)]$
  then
    repeat
      $\gamma_t = \gamma_t \cdot \beta; U' = [U_t - \gamma_t[\frac{\partial O}{\partial U}]_t]_+;$
    until
    $O(U', V_t) - O(U_t, V_t) \leqslant \sigma \cdot trace[[\frac{\partial O}{\partial U}]_t^\top \cdot (U' - U_t)]$
    or $U' = U_t$;
  end
  $U_{t+1} = [U_t - \gamma_t[\frac{\partial O}{\partial U}]_t]_+, V' = [V_t - \gamma_t[\frac{\partial O}{\partial V}]_t]_+$
  if
  $O(U_{t+1}, V') - O(U_{t+1}, V_t) > \sigma \cdot trace[[\frac{\partial O}{\partial V}]_t^\top \cdot (V' - V_t)]$
  then
    repeat
      $\gamma_t = \gamma_t \cdot \beta; V' = [V_t - \gamma_t[\frac{\partial O}{\partial V}]_t]_+;$
    until $O(U_{t+1}, V') - O(U_{t+1}, V_t) \leqslant$
    $\sigma \cdot trace[[\frac{\partial O}{\partial V}]_t^\top \cdot (V' - V_t)]$ ***or*** $V' = V$;
  end
  $V_{t+1} = [V_t - \gamma_t[\frac{\partial O}{\partial V}]_t]_+, t = t + 1;$
until $t > T$ ***or*** $(||[\frac{\partial O}{\partial U}]_t||_F < \epsilon \cdot ||[\frac{\partial O}{\partial U}]_1||_F$ ***and***
$||[\frac{\partial O}{\partial V}]_t||_F < \epsilon \cdot ||[\frac{\partial O}{\partial V}]_1||_F)$;
Output: U_t, V_t

$$\begin{aligned} \arg\min_{U,V} \quad & ||X - UV^\top||_F^2 + \alpha||D - VV^T||_F^2, \quad (1) \\ \text{s.t.} \quad & U \geqslant 0,\ V \geqslant 0, \end{aligned}$$

where $||\cdot||_F$ is the Frobenius norm of a matrix, and $\alpha \geqslant 0$ acts as a trade-off between the two factorization items.

In Problem (1), question clustering and keyword extraction are performed in a unified framework by simultaneously learning V and U. Ideally, we expect to learn a good representation of questions from D and X and let the representation of questions enhance the learning of word representation by the minimization of $||X - UV^\top||_F^2$. This idea is verified in our experiments.

Problem (1) is a natural extension of the existing non-negative matrix factorization (NMF) approaches. Specifically, when $\alpha = 0$, our method degenerates to the standard NMF method (Xu, Liu, and Gong 2003), while when α goes to $+\infty$, it becomes the symmetric NMF method recently proposed by Kuang et al. (2012). Therefore, we actually apply the idea of NMF to subtopic mining and, to the best of our knowledge, we are the first to formulate the problem of subtopic mining as a matrix factorization problem.

Algorithm

The object function (1) is non-convex with respect to both V and U. Therefore, it is difficult to find a global minimum. To solve this problem, we derive an efficient algorithm based on the projected gradient descent framework in (Lin 2007). The details are described in Algorithm 1.

In Algorithm 1, we denote the objective function of (1) as $O(U, V)$, and the gradients of U and V in the t-th iteration are given by

$$[\frac{\partial O}{\partial U}]_t = -2XV_t + 2U_tV_t^\top V_t$$

$$[\frac{\partial O}{\partial V}]_t = -2X^\top U_{t+1} + 2V_tU_{t+1}^\top U_{t+1} - 4\alpha DV_t + 4\alpha V_tV_t^\top V_t,$$

where U_t and U_{t+1} represent matrix U in the t-th and $t+1$-th iteration, and V_t represents V in the t-th iteration. $[\cdot]_+$ is a projection function that forces the entries of U and V to be non-negative by shrinking the negative ones to zero.

The algorithm iteratively optimizes U and V by stepping toward the negative of the gradients and projecting the updates to the non-negative cone. Since k is the number of subtopics and much smaller than the number of words m and the number of questions n, the time complexity is $O(nkm)$ for updating U, and $O(nkm + n^2k)$ for updating V. Thus, the overall time complexity of Algorithm 1 is no more than $O(\max(m, n)^2k)$.

Experiment

We conducted experiments to test the proposed method on question clustering and keyword extraction.

Data Sets

To avoid expensive and exhausting human annotation, we propose automatically generating evaluation data from questions with topics edited by users in CQA portals. Specifically, we have considered Quora [1] and Zhihu [2], because questions on these sites have key phrases as topics edited by users. We first crawled $600,000$ questions from Quora and $60,000$ questions from Zhihu, and separately indexed the two data sets. Then, we collected 2000 English queries and 1000 Chinese queries from query logs of a commercial search engine, and employed the model proposed in (Wu et al. 2014) to get the top 1000 questions for each query. After that, we collected all the topics in the returned results and organized questions into the topics. For the questions with multiple topics, we randomly picked one topic. In this manner, we obtained several question groups so that each group has a topic. The question groups associated with the topics represent subtopics of the queries. Since all baseline methods, including our method, can only learn subtopics from question texts, we removed the groups in which none of the words in the topic appear in the questions. To further filter noise in the topics, we removed groups with less than 5 questions for Quora data and groups with less than 3 questions for Zhihu data. Queries with less than 3 groups of questions were also removed. After pre-processing, we obtained 1287 queries for Quora data and 713 queries for Zhihu data. On average, each query in Quora had 7.01 topics, and each topic had 16.49 questions. The numbers for Zhihu data were 7.00 and 6.52, respectively. 64% topics in Quora and 68% topics in Zhihu consisted of a single word or a single word plus the query. Therefore, we only considered extracting keywords as subtopics. If a topic consisted of more than one word (except the query), we checked if the extracted keyword was contained by the topic. This can reduce the complexity of the experiments and ensures that the comparisons are fair for all the methods. For Quora data, after stemming and removing stop words, on average there were 431.38 words for each query, while for Zhihu data, after conducting Chinese word segmentation, on average there were 276.19 words for each query.

[1]https://www.quora.com/

[2]http://www.zhihu.com/

Implementation of Question Similarity

To implement our method, we need to specify matrices X and D in (1). We set X a matrix with word tf-idf as weights, and normalized each column of X to norm 1. For question similarity, we considered three features: 1) cosine of tf-idf vectors of questions. This might generate some overlap between X and D, but has been proven effective in the experiments; 2) Question-answer topic model proposed in (Ji et al. 2012). We trained the topic models using 1 million question-answer pairs collected from Yahoo! Answers and Baidu Knows, and calculated question-question similarity in a topic space; 3) Explicit semantic analysis (ESA) proposed in (Gabrilovich and Markovitch 2007). In ESA, texts are explicitly represented as weighted vectors of predetermined concepts from Wikipedia and the cosine of the vectors is calculated as the similarity of text fragments. Inspired by ESA, we leveraged the predefined categories of CQA sites to calculate question similarity in Quora and Zhihu. In fact, many CQA sites have category systems (e.g., Yahoo! Answers, see https://answers.yahoo.com/dir/index) with categories that are similar to the concepts of Wikipedia. We took the root categories of Yahoo! Answers for Quora data and root categories of Baidu Knows for Zhihu data as concepts, and trained naive Bayes classifiers to obtain the vector representations of questions. We considered the category systems of Yahoo! Answers and Baidu Knows, because they are the largest English and Chinese CQA sites, respectively. Question similarity then was calculated as the cosine of the vectors of categories. The three features were linearly combined by learning a Ranking SVM model (Herbrich, Graepel, and Obermayer 1999) from extra training data created using another 2000 English queries and 1000 Chinese queries. Questions in the training data were grouped in the same way as the evaluation data, and those in the same group were regarded as being similar.

We created D by combining the three features. By doing so, we actually incorporated the information of answers and categories in CQA into learning. We also observed that D is dense but most of its elements have small values. Therefore, to filter noise and enhance efficiency, we further shrank the elements of D by considering their nearest neighbors. Formally, D was defined as

$$D_{ij} = \begin{cases} 1 & \text{if } q_i \in NN_p(q_j) \text{ or } q_j \in NN_p(q_i) \\ 0 & \text{other,} \end{cases} \quad (2)$$

where D_{ij} is the element of D in the i-th row and j-th column, and $NN_p(q_i)$ means the p nearest neighbors of question q_i found by the similarity function. p is a parameter that needs tuning.

Evaluation Metrics

For question clustering, we followed the example of most document clustering methods and employed accuracy (AC) as an evaluation measure. Given a question q_i, suppose that the cluster label in the evaluation data is a_i, and the predicted cluster label by the algorithm is l_i, then AC is calculated as follows:

$$AC = \frac{\sum_{i=1}^{n} \sigma(a_i, map(l_i))}{n}, \quad (3)$$

where n is the total number of questions under a query. $\sigma(x, y) = 1$ if $x = y$, otherwise it is equal to 0. $map(l_i)$ is a function that maps every predicted label l_i to an optimal label in the evaluation data by the best match theory (Plummer and Lovász 1986).

For keyword extraction, if the extracted keyword exactly matched the topic or it was contained by the topic (words in queries and stop words were excluded), we judged the extraction correct. Then, we calculated the ratio of correct extractions and averaged it over queries to evaluate keyword extraction methods.

Baselines

We considered two groups of baselines: 1) first conducting question clustering, and then extracting a keyword for each cluster; An example is the method proposed by Wang et al. (2013); 2) first extracting keywords from the whole question set, and then organizing questions into clusters based on the keywords. A representative is the method proposed by Zeng et al. (2004).

First clustering, and then keyword extraction: In addition to the hierarchical agglomerative clustering (HAC) method in (Wang et al. 2013), we also implemented kernel k-means (Dhillon, Guan, and Kulis 2004), spectral clustering (Ng, Jordan, and Weiss 2001), NMF (Xu, Liu, and Gong 2003), GNMF (Cai et al. 2011), and symmetric NMF (SymNMF) (Kuang, Park, and Ding 2012) as clustering methods. Based on the clustering results, we implemented typical keyword extraction methods, including TFIDF, TextRank (Mihalcea and Tarau 2004) with window size 2, and the recently proposed topical PageRank (TPR) (Liu et al. 2010). In TPR, we used the question-answer topic model trained from the 1 million CQA dataset to estimate the topic distributions of words.

First keyword extraction, and then clustering: we implemented the method proposed by Zeng et al. (2004). In our experiments, we trained a keyword ranker using the data with which we learned the question similarity. To make a fair comparison, we further clustered the questions that could not be grouped by the method of Zeng et al. by calculating the similarity of the questions with the centroid of each cluster and assigning the questions to the most similar cluster.

Evaluation Results

With both Quora and Zhihu data, we randomly set initializations for kernel k-means, spectral clustering, NMF, GNMF, SymNMF, and our method 5 times, and reported the average results of the 5 runs. For our method, we followed existing methods (Cai et al. 2011; Kuang, Park, and Ding 2012) and implemented Algorithm 1 with $\beta = 0.1$, $\sigma = 0.01$, $\epsilon = 10^{-4}$, and $T = 200$. α in Equation (1) and the number of nearest neighbors p for D needed tuning. Therefore, we randomly split the evaluation data into a validation set and a test set with a ratio of $1 : 3$, and selected α from $\{0.1, 1, 10, 100\}$ and p from 1-10 of the validation set. The best choice for α was 100 with both the Quora and Zhihu data, while with the Quora data the best p was 7, and with the Zhihu data the best p was 4. With these settings, we compared different methods on the test set.

	Quora	Zhihu
The method of Zeng et al. (2004)	0.383	0.410
Kernel k-means	0.516	0.410
HAC	0.434	0.488
Spectral clustering	**0.602**	**0.586**
NMF	0.520	0.519
GNMF	0.579	0.564
SymNMF	**0.606**	**0.592**
Our method	**0.607**	**0.594**

Table 2: Evaluation on question clustering

	Quora	Zhihu
SymNMF+TFIDF	0.369	0.305
SymNMF+TextRank	0.312	0.257
SymNMF+TPR	0.229	0.162
Our method+TFIDF	0.370	0.307
Our method+TextRank	0.311	0.257
Our method+TPR	0.232	0.167
The method of Zeng et al. (2004)	0.380	0.279
Our method	**0.398**	**0.318**

Table 3: Evaluation on keyword extraction

Table 2 shows the evaluation results of question clustering. Our method, SymNMF, and spectral clustering performed comparably well on both data sets, and the three methods significantly outperformed the other clustering methods (t-test with p value < 0.01). It is not surprising that the proposed method is comparable with SymNMF, as they leverage the same information in a similar way for clustering. The difference is that our method can also leverage the good performance of clustering to enhance the recognition of keywords, as will be seen later. The method from Zeng et al. (2004) organized questions based on the common keywords they share. In practice, however, questions under the same subtopic do not necessarily share common words. That is why the method performs badly on question clustering, even though we have conducted post-processing as a remedy.

We took SymNMF as the best performing clustering method and combined it with different keyword extraction methods. Table 3 shows the evaluation results on keyword extraction. We conducted a statistical test (t-test), and the results show that our method significantly outperformed all other methods (p value < 0.01). In the first group of baselines, although SymNMF is powerful at grouping questions, question clustering and keyword extraction have to be optimized separately. The power of SymNMF only weakly influenced keyword extraction. On the other hand, we checked the learnt U and V in (1), and found that our method not only grouped semantically similar questions together through V, but also weighted the questions in the group according to their topic concentration. The questions that are more topically concentrated had larger weights, and these questions further highlighted the salient words they contain. This explains why our method performs significantly better on keyword extraction than SymNMF plus a bunch of state-of-the-art keyword extraction methods, even though they achieved comparable performance on clustering. The advantage of joint optimization of question clustering and keyword extraction was further verified by the performance drop when only treating our method as a clustering method and combining it with other keyword extraction methods. Topical PageRank performs worse than TFIDF and the TextRank. This may stem from the noise in CQA data for learning the topic space. The method proposed by Zeng et al. (2004) learns a supervised ranker for keyword extraction, but ignores the useful local information from clusters. Therefore, it is worse than our method.

Discussions

Besides the comparison with existing methods, there are some other problems worth investigation. First, in addition to performing clustering, NMF and GNMF can also jointly optimize question clustering and keyword extraction. Therefore, it is interesting to check if our method can outperform these two models when all of them perform joint optimization. Second, to filter noise, we shrank the values of D and used a sparse matrix in the experiments. The preprocessing can enhance efficiency, but we do not know if the sparse D is better than the original dense D in terms of performance. Finally, we leveraged three features to construct D. A natural question is how these features contributed to the final results. Table 4 reports some of the comparison results, which is an attempt to answer the questions above. From the fourth row, the results represent the comparison of the proposed method with D using partial features and all features. Note that to highlight the differences, we reported the percent deviation of different methods from our method on the two tasks. From the table, you can see 1) our extension to NMF brought performance improvement on both question clustering and keyword extraction. This demonstrates that D is useful for both question clustering and keyword extraction. Moreover, although GNMF and our method (1) leveraged the same information, the performance difference verified that our extension is more effective for the task of subtopic mining. 2) the decrease in D with nearest neighbors can really make the learning method robust to noise. 3) with the similarity estimated from the answers and categories of CQA, the performance on clustering improved. This is reasonable since the two features can capture the semantic similarity of questions, and can group the questions from the same topic but that share few common words.

	clustering		keyword	
	Quora	Zhihu	Quora	Zhihu
NMF	-8.7	-7.5	-3.6	-4.7
GNMF	-2.8	-2.7	-1.5	-2.9
Dense D	-4.0	-3.7	-3.4	-4.5
TFIDF	-3.2	-2.9	+1.3	+1.1
TFIDF+Topic Model	-1.2	-1.4	+0.5	+0.5
TFIDF+Category	-0.9	-1.2	+0.6	+0.4

Table 4: Discussions on the implementation of our method

Algorithm 2: A heuristic method for selecting k

```
Input: k_0 = 1, k_1 = sqrt(n/2), t, i = 1
d_0 = InnerDis(k_0); d_1 = InnerDis(k_1);
if d_0/d_1 < t then
    repeat
    |  i = i + 1; k_i = k_{i-1} + 1; d_i = Inner(k_i);
    until d_0/d_i > t;
end
else
    repeat
    |  i = i + 1; k_i = k_{i-1} - 1; d_i = Inner(k_i)
    until d_0/d_i < t;
end
Output: k = k_i
```

On the other hand, with these questions, noise for keyword recognition was also introduced, which is why the more features we used for constructing D, the worse results we got for keyword extraction.

In practice, unlike the experiments, the number of subtopics k is usually unknown. To make our method applicable, we propose a heuristic method to estimate k. Formally, we define the distance between two questions Q_i and Q_j as $Distance(i,j) = 1 - Sim(i,j)$, where $Sim(i,j)$ is the similarity of Q_i and Q_j calculated using the linear combination of the three features. Then, suppose that there are k groups of questions, we define the inner group distance as $InnerDis(k) = \frac{1}{k}\sum_{1 \leqslant l \leqslant k} \frac{1}{n_c^2} \sum_{Q_i, Q_j \in C_l} Distance(i,j)$, where C_l is the l-th group and n_c denotes the number of questions in C_l. We propose an iterative method to obtain the optimal k. Specifically, for each query, we suppose that $k_0 = 1$ at the beginning. In other words, all questions belong to one cluster. We select a k by making $InnerDis(k_0)/InnerDis(k)$ close to a threshold t. If the ratio is too large, then we reduce k, otherwise we enlarge k. The threshold can be obtained by asking human labelers to manually group questions for a small query set and averaging $InnerDis(k_0)/InnerDis(k_q)$ over queries, where k_q is the number of question groups for query q decided by humans. Algorithm 2 summarizes the method.

To test our idea, we estimated the threshold t using the validation set (it is 1.15) and checked how the automatically selected k is different from the one obtained based on human annotated topics on the test set. Table 5 reports the results, in which Avg is the average of absolute deviation of k over

v''s posting (one week in our dataset from Section 6). Individual conformity represents how strongly v's posting behavior conforms to that of her friends. In our dataset, we discover that nearly 30% of users have a conformity > 0.6. We divided the users into three groups according to their conformity values and randomly selected 100 users from each group to calculate the distribution of the times a posting had been reposted before they forwarded it. Our analysis revealed that users with high conformity either repost very popular postings or brand new ones posted by their close friends, often related to their personal offline life. Low conformity users, in contrast, do not seem to show any clear pattern. Therefore, we model herd behavior at different intensities for different conformity levels. Given a conformity vector for all nodes, we define a CTMC as follows.

module "herd behavior"
  $n : [0..|V|]$ init by $|I|$;
  /* conformity $\geq 60\%$ */
  $[CH]\ n > 0 \rightarrow 1 + \psi(n) * \text{conformity}_{\text{high}} : (n' = n + 1);$
  /* $60\% >$ conformity $\geq 30\%$ */
  $[CM]\ n > 0 \rightarrow 1 + \psi(n) * \text{conformity}_{\text{middle}} : (n' = n + 1);$
  /* conformity $< 30\%$ */
  $[CL]\ n > 0 \rightarrow 1 + \psi(n) * \text{conformity}_{\text{low}} : (n' = n + 1);$
end module

The module definition syntax used here is based on the Reactive Modules formalism (Alur and Henzinger 1999), with local variables and transition commands that reflect the operational behavior of the module, i.e., state transitions of the CTMC. Here, the local variable n (with range from 0 to $|V|$) represents the current number of influenced nodes, which is initialized as $|I|$. The form of each transition command is [action label] guard condition $\rightarrow$ rate : updates. Updates can be performed if and only if the current state of the CTMC meets the guard condition. We label each node's incoming edge by its conformity level in the CTMC for the inferred diffusion network, with $[CH]$ for high, $[CM]$ for medium, and $[CL]$ for low conformity. For each level i, conformity_i is the average value for all nodes at this level. The transition rate function $\Phi(n) = 1 + \psi(n) \cdot \text{conformity}_i$ models the changing trend of the rate as the number of influenced users increases. We define $\psi(n) = \gamma\left(1 + e^{-\delta\left(\frac{n}{|V|} - \mathrm{b}\right)}\right)^{-1}$ for $\gamma > 0$, as this mirrors the spread process for popular events in a network, first increasing gradually at an increasing rate and then stabilizing. The range of $\psi(n)$ is determined by γ, the curve's slope by δ, and b is the rate's breakpoint. In our experiments, we study how these variables affect the initial set selection for influence maximization.

Activeness of Actors. Studies (Lang and Wu 2011; Viswanath et al. 2009) show that social actors exhibit different levels of activeness. In particular, highly active ones contribute more towards the interaction, e.g. by reposting messages and posting new stories. Although there are many other factors, such as user interests, beliefs, and topics, much of their effects can be attributed to a user's activeness.

From our real diffusion dataset (cf. Section 6), we first measure the activeness of every node $v \in V$ as $\text{activeness}(v) = |v_p|$, i.e., the total number of messages

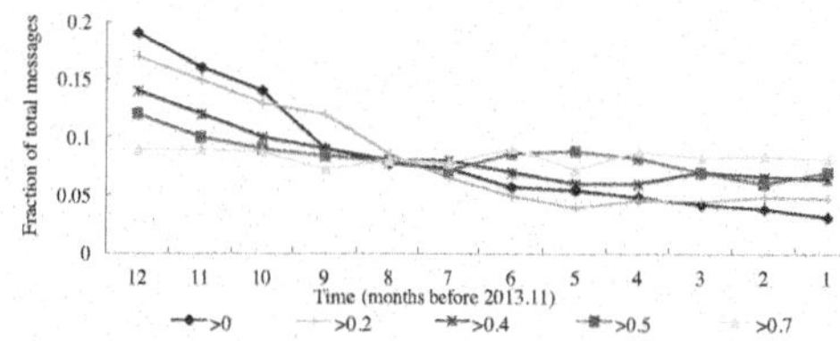

Figure 2: Fraction of interactions over time for one year.

the user has posted or reposted (during a one week period in our experiments). For analysis purposes, we divided the users into groups according to their activeness values and randomly selected 10% of users in each group to calculate the average interaction levels based on one year of historic data. Figure 2 illustrates that highly active users display a relatively more even distribution of posting messages over time, compared to other groups. On the contrary, less active users post less and less over time. The trends are different for different groups. To capture this, we thus divide the user base into two parts using a threshold on their activeness. For active nodes (whose activeness is larger than the threshold), we assume stable transition rates for all of their incoming edges during the diffusion process. On the contrary, the incoming edges' transition rates for inactive nodes (low level activeness) will stochastically decrease over time, following an exponential distribution with expectation decreaseRate. Given a classification threshold γ, the function Φ of this dynamic module can be expressed as

$$\Phi = \begin{cases} \text{decreaseDelta}^{\text{step}} & \text{activeness} < \gamma \\ 1 & \text{otherwise} \end{cases}$$

Then, given an activeness vector of all nodes, we define the activeness module using a label AL for low activeness and a parameter decreaseRate to control the evolution.

module "Activeness"
  $\text{const float decreaseRate};$
  $\text{const float decreaseDelta};$
  $\text{step} : [0..\text{IntMax}]$ init by 0;
  $[\,]\ \text{step} \geq 0 \rightarrow \text{decreaseRate} : (\text{step}' = \text{step} + 1);$
  $[AL]\ \text{step} > 0 \rightarrow \text{decreaseDelta}^{\text{step}} : (\text{step}' = \text{step});$
end module

5 Influence Analysis and Maximization

We now define the influence function for the DYNADIFFUSE model and apply our novel stochastic model checking approach to predict the influence spread.

5.1 Spread Analysis

Definition 5. *The **influence spread** $\sigma_T(I)$ of an initial set I until time T in a* DYNADIFFUSE *model M_I is defined as the expected number of nodes influenced until T:*

$$\sigma_T(I) = \mathbb{E}N_T(I) = \sum_{i=1}^{|V|} P(t_i \leq T | M_I),$$

where t_i denotes the time when node i is influenced.

To estimate the influence spread of a given initial set I, we rely on stochastic model checking (Kwiatkowska, Norman, and Parker 2007), a method for computing possible behaviors of a stochastic system. Given a model description and a formula in temporal logic, stochastic model checking provides the likelihood of the model satisfying the formula as well as a wider range of quantitative measures relating to model behavior. For example, one can use stochastic model checking to determine the expected running time or expected number of lost messages of a system.

Transitions (except self-loops) of the DYNADIFFUSE model correspond to non-influenced nodes becoming influenced. To calculate $\mathbb{E}N_T(I)$, we tie a reward to every such transition, and accumulate all rewards in the diffusion process to estimate the number of influenced nodes. Given a DYNADIFFUSE model M, we denote the instantaneous reward associated with the transition from state i to state j as reward_{ij}. The reward Markov process associated with M is then $(M, \mathbb{RE}_M)$, where the reward accumulated in the time interval $(0, t]$ is $\mathbb{RE}_M = \int_0^t \text{reward}_{M(u-),M(u)} dN_M(t)$, where $N_M(t)$ is the number of state transitions of M in the time interval $(0, t]$. Assume $\text{reward}_{ij} = 1$ for all transitions. Then $\mathbb{RE}_M = \int_0^t dN_M(t) = \sum_{i=1}^{|V|} P(t_i \leq T|M_I)$. This can be determined using a Uniformisation based Stochastic Model Checking approach (Kwiatkowska, Norman, and Parker 2007). It allows us to either get an exact result by verification, or to estimate the result using a faster simulation approach. In our study, we used the PRISM system (Kwiatkowska, Norman, and Parker 2011) for this.

5.2 Scalable Influence Maximization

Complexity, Monotonicity, and Submodularity.

Theorem 1. *Continuous time constrained influence maximization on a* DYNADIFFUSE *model is* NP-hard.

Proof. With dynamic modules $D = \emptyset$ and $T \to \infty$, our DYNADIFFUSE model turns out to be an instance of the independent cascade model. Hence, the latter is a special case of DYNADIFFUSE. As the traditional influence maximization problem is known to be NP-hard (Kempe, Kleinberg, and Tardos 2003), this new problem is also NP-hard. □

Theorem 2. *The influence function $\sigma_T(I)$ for* DYNADIFFUSE *is monotonous.*

Proof. If initial nodes are influenced at $t = 0$, each transition (except self-loops) of a DYNADIFFUSE model means there will be a new influenced node. The time delay is determined by an exponential distribution with a step-varied expectation value. Consider the possible distributions of all possible time differences between each pair of states in the model. There will be a series of different state graphs χ. For a given $\Delta x \in \chi$, we define $\sigma_{T,\Delta x}(I)$ as equal to the number of nodes reachable from I by at least one path with length no larger than T. It is very natural to discover that $\sigma_{T,\Delta x}(S) \leq \sigma_{T,\Delta x}(S \cup v)$ (for $S \subset V$). Therefore, $\sigma_{T,\Delta x}(I)$ is monotonous. As $\sigma_T(I) = (\sum_{x \in \chi} \sigma_{T,\Delta x}(I))/|\chi|$, we obtain that $\sigma_T(I)$ is monotonous as well. □

Theorem 3. *The influence function $\sigma_T(I)$ for* DYNADIFFUSE *is submodular.*

Proof. Consider any set of nodes $V_1 \subseteq V_2 \subseteq V$, and a node $v_0 \in V \setminus V_2$ (if $V_2 = V$, then trivially $V_{01,T} = V_{02,T}$ below). We again use $\Delta x \in \chi$, as in the proof of Theorem 2. We assume $\Delta V_{0i,T}$ is the set of nodes that can be reached from v_0, but cannot be reached by V_i $(i = 1, 2)$ within the T bound in the Δx graph. Since $V_1 \subseteq V_2$, we obtain $\Delta V_{01,T} \geq \Delta V_{02,T}$. We see that $\sigma_{T,\Delta x}(V_1 \cup \{v_0\}) - \sigma_{T,\Delta x}(V_1) = \Delta V_{01,T} \geq \Delta V_{02,T} = \sigma_{T,\Delta x}(V_2 \cup \{v_0\}) - \sigma_{T,\Delta x}(V_2)$ and thus $\sigma_{T,\Delta x}(I)$ is submodular. From this it follows that $\sigma_T(I)$ is submodular, concluding the proof. □

FASTMARGIN Greedy Algorithm. The standard greedy algorithm for maximizing monotonic and submodular functions has a provable lower bound ratio of $1 - 1/e$. However, for genuine scalability, we propose a faster marginal influence spread estimation algorithm for the continuous time diffusion model. Our algorithm (Algorithm 2) first predicts a relatively precise influence spread using stochastic model checking on the CTMC Parallel Composition. Then, we predict the increased marginal influence spread $(\sigma_T(I \cup \{v\}) - \sigma_T(I))$ of adding each $v \in V \setminus I$ when selecting an additional node to be added to the current initial set. To improve the efficiency, we estimate this marginal influence spread using a faster discounted formula for $\sigma_T(\{v\})$ in Line 12, instead of determining a precise value with stochastic model checking.

Algorithm 2 FASTMARGIN Greedy algorithm

Require: a DYNADIFFUSE for a graph $G = (V, E)$, the size k of the desired initial set, a time constraint T

1: $I \leftarrow \emptyset$;
2: **for** each $v \in V$ **do**
3: predict accurate $\sigma_T(\{v\})$ using stochastic model checking
4: $u \leftarrow \text{argmax}_v(\sigma_T(\{v\}))$
5: $I \leftarrow \{u\}$
6: **for** $i \leftarrow 2$ to k **do**
7: **for** each $v \in V \setminus I$ **do**
8: **if** $(v, u) \in E$ **and** $u \in N(I)$ **then**
9: $P_{I,u} \leftarrow 1 - \Pi_{(w,u) \in E, w \in I}(1 - e^{-r_{u,w}(T)})$
10: **else**
11: $P_{I,u} \leftarrow 0$
12: $\Delta\sigma_T(\{v\}) \leftarrow \sigma_T(I \cup \{v\}) - \sigma_T(I)$ $\approx \sigma_T(\{v\}) \frac{\Sigma_{(v,u) \in E}(1-e^{-r_{v,u}(T)})(1-P_{I,u})\sigma_T(\{u\})}{\Sigma_{(v,u) \in E}(1-e^{-r_{v,u}(T)})\sigma_T(\{u\})}$
13: $u \leftarrow \text{argmax}_v(\Delta\sigma_T(\{v\}))$ # using CELF
14: $I \leftarrow I \cup \{u\}$
15: **return** I # best set I

Here, $N(I)$ is the set of directed successors of I, and $P_{I,u}$ is the probability that u is influenced immediately by current initial nodes. We estimate the probability with an exponential distribution for the whole diffusion period. The discount is to subtract the influence spread that may be obtained by I from $\sigma_T(\{v\})$. The higher the probability that v's neighbors are already influenced by I, the larger the discount that should be applied to $\sigma_T(\{v\})$. For scalability to large networks, we also adopt the CELF lazy evaluation approach

(Leskovec et al. 2007), which dramatically reduces the number of evaluations of $\text{argmax}_v(\sigma_T(I \cup \{v\}) - \sigma_T(I))$. We call this algorithm FASTMARGIN. This algorithm can flexibly be used in any continuous-time constrained diffusion model that assumes that the diffusion rate follows the exponential distribution.

Time and space complexities. Let $d_{\max}$ be the maximum degree of all nodes, and S and R be the states and transition matrix of a DYNADIFFUSE instance, respectively. In Algorithm 2, the first for loop requires $O(|V||S|^2)$ time for uniformisation. The second for loop will cost $O((k-1)|V|d_{\max})$. So the total runtime complexity is $O(|V||S|^2 + (k-1)|V|d_{max})$. However, the standard greedy algorithm's time complexity is $O(k|V||S|^2)$. Thus, they have the same running time when $k = 1$, and Algorithm 2 is faster for $k > 1$. The space complexity is $O(|V|(|S| + |R|))$, dominated by stochastic model checking in line 3.

6 Experimental Evaluation

Dataset. We evaluate our model and algorithm on a microblog diffusion dataset from Sina Weibo, a major Chinese microblogging platform. The data covers $96,700$ users and $373,412$ microblog postings ($211,052$ original and $162,360$ reposted) from the time period of November 2–8, 2013. For each of these postings, it contains a set of time-stamped reposting logs with user ID, reposting time, and reposting contents, in total nearly $4,000,000$ entries. From this data, we inferred an underlying diffusion network with $6,000$ top nodes and the $30,000$ fastest edges using the algorithm from Gomez-Rodriguez, Balduzzi, and Schölkopf (2011), and calculated the conformity and activeness vectors.

Comparing Models. Figure 3a shows that the seeds' influence spread obtained by DYNADIFFUSE (i.e., FastMargin-Dynamic, CELF-Dynamic) is consistently superior to that of the *static* continuous time diffusion model (Gomez-Rodriguez and Schölkopf 2012) (i.e., FastMargin–Static, CELF–Static), as well as the IC model (Kempe, Kleinberg, and Tardos 2003) (i.e., CELF-IC). The FASTMARGIN algorithm is slightly less precise than the pure CELF algorithm because of its heuristics, but the gap is not large. We additionally compare the DYNADIFFUSE-estimated influence spread with the *real influence spread* in the social network. To assess the real diffusion, we first crawled all original microblogs published on November 9, 2013 for every user in the obtained initial set and then calculated the average total number of repostings in the following week ($T = 1$ to 7). We regard the average total number of repostings as the influence spread for each user. We only calculate the reposting numbers within our data set (96,700 users) and minus the overlap. Figure 3b illustrates that the estimated results of our dynamic model, i.e., FastMargin–Dynamic (Slow, Quick), are closer to the real situation than those of the static diffusion model, FastMargin–Static. Moreover, the evolution speed parameters in our model influence the precision of the estimated results. To get even more precise results, we could easily tune them with collected historic data. Note that DYNADIFFUSE consistently outperforms existing models across different values of these parameters.

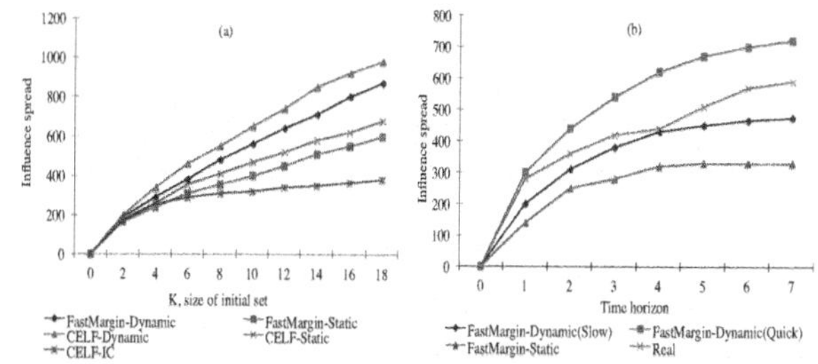

Figure 3: (a) Diffusion models comparison by DYNADIFFUSE with $T = 3$ days. Herd behavior module: $\delta = 30$, $b = 0.05$, activeness module: decreaseDelta $= 0.9$, decreaseRate $= 0.2$. (b) Comparison by the real influence spread with $K = 6$. Slow evolution: $\delta = 30$, $b = 0.05$, decreaseDelta $= 0.9$, decreaseRate $= 0.2$. Quick evolution: $\delta = 100$, $b = 0.01$, decreaseDelta $= 0.9$, decreaseRate $= 0.4$. Legend: greedy algorithm–diffusion model

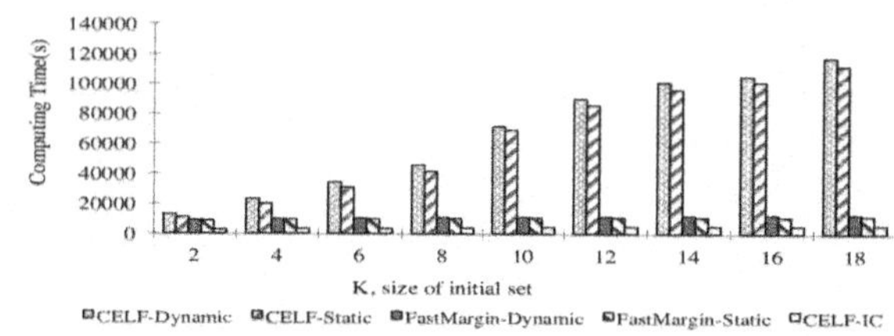

Figure 4: Running time of algorithms ($T = 6$ days)

Comparing Algorithms. We then evaluated the efficiency and scalability of DYNADIFFUSE and the FASTMARGIN algorithm. Figure 4 shows running time on a workstation (2.5GHz Dual core, 4GB RAM). FastMargin–Dynamic and FastMargin–Static are significantly faster than CELF (CELF–Dynamic and CELF–Static) and are more scalable as K grows. Interestingly, the time gap between DYNADIFFUSE (i.e., CELF–Dynamic, FastMargin–Dynamic) and the static model (i.e., CELF–Static, FastMargin–Static) is very small. The analysis for DYNADIFFUSE with FASTMARGIN is thus just slightly more costly than for the IC model, yet produces an initial set of significantly higher quality. Note that FASTMARGIN's running time remains almost constant as k increases. CELF-IC has similar behavior, but with worse output quality, as we have seen earlier.

7 Conclusion and Future Work

We have presented the novel continuous constrained influence maximization problem for dynamic networks, and introduced a novel diffusion model called DYNADIFFUSE for it. Under DYNADIFFUSE, we employ an innovative stochastic model checking approach to considering dynamic effects and estimating the influence spread of a set of nodes within a given time frame. Our experiments show that network dynamics indeed have strong effects on the solution's quality. In the future, we will investigate how to learn dynamic behavior from data. Additionally, we believe that our novel approach of relying on stochastic model checking can serve as an important new framework for many new forms of social network analysis.

Acknowledgments

This work is supported by the National Natural Science Foundation of China under grants 91318301, 91218302, 61432001, 61303163.

References

Alur, R., and Henzinger, T. A. 1999. Reactive modules. *Formal Methods in System Design* 15(1):7–48.

Chen, W.; Lu, W.; and Zhang, N. 2012. Time-critical influence maximization in social networks with time-delayed diffusion process. In *Proc. AAAI*, 592–598.

Chen, W.; Wang, Y.; and Yang, S. 2009. Efficient influence maximization in social networks. In *Proc. SIGKDD*, 199–208.

Cohen, E.; Delling, D.; Pajor, T.; and Werneck, R. F. 2014. Sketch-based influence maximization and computation: Scaling up with guarantees. In *Proc. CIKM*, 629–638.

Domingos, P., and Richardson, M. 2001. Mining the network value of customers. In *Proc. SIGKDD*, 57–66.

Gomez-Rodriguez, M., and Schölkopf, B. 2012. Influence maximization in continuous time diffusion networks. In *Proc. ICML*, 313–320.

Gomez-Rodriguez, M.; Balduzzi, D.; and Schölkopf, B. 2011. Uncovering the temporal dynamics of diffusion networks. In *Proc. ICML*, 561–568.

Gomez-Rodriguez, M.; Leskovec, J.; and Schölkopf, B. 2013. Structure and dynamics of information pathways in online media. In *Proc. WSDM*, 23–32.

Guille, A.; Hacid, H.; Favre, C.; and Zighed, D. A. 2013. Information diffusion in online social networks: a survey. *SIGMOD Rec.* 42(1):17–28.

Kempe, D.; Kleinberg, J.; and Tardos, E. 2003. Maximizing the spread of influence through a social network. In *Proc. SIGKDD*, 137–146.

Kimura, M., and Saito, K. 2006. Tractable models for information diffusion in social networks. In *Proc. PKDD*, 259–271.

Kossinets, G.; Kleinberg, J.; and Watts, D. 2008. The structure of information pathways in a social communication network. In *Proc. SIGKDD*, 435–443.

Kwiatkowska, M.; Norman, G.; and Parker, D. 2007. Stochastic model checking. In *Proc. SFM*, 220–270.

Kwiatkowska, M.; Norman, G.; and Parker, D. 2011. PRISM 4.0: Verification of probabilistic real-time systems. In *Proc. CAV*, 585–591.

Lang, J., and Wu, S. 2011. Social network user lifetime. In *Proc. ASNAM*, 289–296.

Leskovec, J.; Krause, A.; Guestrin, C.; Faloutsos, C.; Van-Briesen, J.; and Glance, N. 2007. Cost-effective outbreak detection in networks. In *Proc. SIGKDD*, 420–429.

Li, H.; Bhowmick, S. S.; and Sun, A. 2011. Casino: towards conformity-aware social influence analysis in online social networks. In *Proc. CIKM*, 1007–1012.

Liu, B.; Cong, G.; Xu, D.; and Zeng, Y. 2012. Time constrained influence maximization in social networks. In *Proc. ICDM*, 439 –448.

Liu, B.; Cong, G.; Zeng, Y.; Xu, D.; and Chee, Y. M. 2014. Influence spreading path and its application to the time constrained social influence maximization problem and beyond. *TKDE* 26(8):1904–1917.

Matsubara, Y.; Sakurai, Y.; Prakash, B. A.; Li, L.; and Faloutsos, C. 2012. Rise and fall patterns of information diffusion: model and implications. In *Proc. SIGKDD*, 6–14.

Mislove, A.; Koppula, H. S.; Gummadi, K. P.; Druschel, P.; and Bhattacharjee, B. 2008. Growth of the flickr social network. In *Proc. WOSN*, 25–30.

Raafat, R. M.; Chater, N.; and Frith, C. 2009. Herding in humans. *Trends in cognitive sciences* 13(10):420–428.

Tang, J.; Musolesi, M.; Mascolo, C.; and Latora, V. 2010. Characterising temporal distance and reachability in mobile and online social networks. *SIGCOMM Comput. Commun. Rev.* 40(1):118–124.

Tang, J.; Wu, S.; and Sun, J. 2013. Confluence: Conformity influence in large social networks. In *Proc. SIGKDD*, 347–355.

Tang, Y.; Xiao, X.; and Shi, Y. 2014. Influence maximization: Near-optimal time complexity meets practical efficiency. In *Proc. SIGMOD*, 75–86.

Viswanath, B.; Mislove, A.; Cha, M.; and Gummadi, K. P. 2009. On the evolution of user interaction in facebook. In *Proc. WOSN*, 37–42.

A Probabilistic Model for Bursty Topic Discovery in Microblogs

Xiaohui Yan, Jiafeng Guo, Yanyan Lan, Jun Xu, Xueqi Cheng
Institute of Computing Technology, Chinese Academy of Science
No.6 Kexueyuan South Road, Haidian District
Beijing, China 100190

Abstract

Bursty topics discovery in microblogs is important for people to grasp essential and valuable information. However, the task is challenging since microblog posts are particularly short and noisy. This work develops a novel probabilistic model, namely Bursty Biterm Topic Model (BBTM), to deal with the task. BBTM extends the Biterm Topic Model (BTM) by incorporating the burstiness of biterms as prior knowledge for bursty topic modeling, which enjoys the following merits: 1) It can well solve the data sparsity problem in topic modeling over short texts as the same as BTM; 2) It can automatical discover high quality bursty topics in microblogs in a principled and efficient way. Extensive experiments on a standard Twitter dataset show that our approach outperforms the state-of-the-art baselines significantly.

Introduction

Nowadays microblog services have become an important platform for people to share and access information. In Twitter, about 58 million posts are produced every day, involving various topics such as daily chatting, business promotions, and news stories. Among them, there are always many novel topics emerging and attracting wide interest, referred as bursty topics. These topics are often related to some important events or issues in either cyber or physical space. Thus discovering bursty topics can provide people essential and valuable information, and consequently benefit many related applications such as public opinion analysis, business intelligence, and news clues tracking.

However, bursty topic discovery in microblogs is challenging. First, the posts in microblogs are particularly short. How to distill high quality topics from short texts is a nontrivial problem. Second, posts are particularly diverse and noisy, with a large proportion of common and meaningless subjects such as pointless babbles and daily chatting (Analytics 2009). These posts overwhelm in microblogs, making it difficult to distinguish bursty topics from non-bursty content.

In previous studies, a typical way for this task is to detect bursty features (e.g., words or phrases) and then cluster them (Mathioudakis and Koudas 2010; Cataldi, Di Caro, and Schifanella 2010; Li, Sun, and Datta 2012). However, there are two drawbacks within these methods. First, they require cumbersome and complicated heuristic tuning and post-processing, since the bursty features detected are noisy and ambiguous, which are not easy to cluster. Second, representing the topics only by bursty features will lose much information, making them difficult to read and understand.

Another attempt is to discover bursty topics via topic models, a widely used tool for topic discovery in text collections (Hofmann 1999; Blei, Ng, and Jordan 2003). However, conventional topic models are designed to reveal the main topics in a collection (Blei 2012), not directly applicable for bursty topic discovery in microblogs. Although some post-processing techniques can be used to detect bursty topics from the learned topics of conventional topic models (Lau, Collier, and Baldwin 2012), it is not economical since most of the discovered topics might not be bursty. To amend this problem, some researchers tried to introduce the temporal information into topic models (Diao et al. 2012; Yin et al. 2013). Unfortunately, they still rely on post-processing steps or heuristic techniques to distill bursty topics. Furthermore, all of these above methods use topic models designed for normal texts (e.g., LDA), which have been shown not effective for short texts such as microblog posts (Hong and Davison 2010; Yan et al. 2013).

In this paper, we focus on the problem of discovering bursty topics in a microblog stream divided by certain time slices (e.g., day). Formally, a topic is considered to be bursty in a time slice if it is heavily discussed in that time slice, but not in most of other time slices. We propose to discover such bursty topics in a principled way via a novel probabilistic model, namely Bursty Biterm Topic Model (BBTM). Our work is based on a recently introduced Biterm Topic Model (BTM) (Yan et al. 2013), which models biterms (i.e., word pairs) rather than words for effective topic modeling in short texts. The key idea of our approach is to exploit the burstiness of biterms as prior knowledge to incorporate into BTM for bursty topic modeling. BBTM enjoys two substantial merits over the previous methods. First, it well solves the data sparsity problem in topic modeling over short texts, as compared with those methods based on conventional topic models. Second, it can learn bursty topics in a principled and efficient way without any heuristic post-processing steps.

We have conducted extensive experiments over a standard Twitter dataset. The experimental results demonstrate that our approach achieves substantial improvement over the state-of-the-art methods.

Biterm Topic Model

For completeness, we first briefly review the biterm topic model (i.e., BTM) (Yan et al. 2013; Cheng et al. 2014), a recently proposed probabilistic topic model for short texts. Before BTM, most conventional topic models, such as PLSA (Hofmann 1999) and LDA (Blei, Ng, and Jordan 2003), model each document as a mixture of topics, and thus suffer from the data sparsity problem when documents are extremely short (Hong and Davison 2010; Tang et al. 2014). Instead, BTM learns topics by modeling the generation of biterms (i.e., unordered co-occurring word pairs) in the collection, whose effectiveness are not affected by the length of documents, making it more appropriate for short texts.

The intuition of BTM is that if two words co-occur more frequently, they are more likely to belong to a same topic. Based on this idea, BTM models each biterm as two words draw from a same topic, while a topic is drawn from a mixture of topics over the whole collection. Specifically, given a short text collection, suppose it contains N_B biterms $\mathbb{B}=\{b_1, ..., b_{N_B}\}$ where $b_i=(w_{i,1}, w_{i,2})$, and K topics expressed over W unique words, the generative process described by BTM is as follows:

1. For the collection,
   - draw a topic distribution $\boldsymbol{\theta} \sim \mathrm{Dir}(\boldsymbol{\alpha})$
2. For each topic z,
   - draw a word distribution $\boldsymbol{\phi}_z \sim \mathrm{Dir}(\boldsymbol{\beta})$
3. For each biterm $b_i \in \mathbb{B}$,
   - draw a topic assignment $z \sim \mathrm{Multi}(\boldsymbol{\theta})$
   - draw two words $w_{i,1}, w_{i,2} \sim \mathrm{Mulit}(\boldsymbol{\phi}_z)$

where $\boldsymbol{\theta}$ defines a K-dimensional multinomial distribution over topics, and $\boldsymbol{\phi}_z$ defines a W-dimensional multinomial distribution over words. The graphical representation of BTM is illustrated in Figure 1 (a).

Bursty Topic Modeling

BTM is an effective topic model over short texts but not designed for bursty topic discovery. In other words, each biterm occurrence contributes equally in BTM, but in microblogs a large proportion of biterms in microblogs are about common topics such as daily life and chatting. Consequently, BTM tends to discover common topics in microblogs.

To discover bursty topics through BTM, it is important to emphasize those biterms relevant to bursty topics and make the model focus on these observations. Therefore, we introduce and quantify the burstiness of biterms and incorporate it as prior knowledge into BTM for bursty topic discovery.

Bursty Probability of Biterm

Intuitively, when a bursty topic breaks out, relevant biterms can be observed more frequently than usual. For instance, the biterms such as "world cup", "football brazil" became much more popular than usual in Twitter when World Cup 2014 took place. Such biterms provide us crucial clues for bursty topic discovery. Based on the above observation, we introduce a probability measurement, called *bursty probability*, to quantify the burstiness of biterms, which can be estimated from the temporal frequencies of the biterms.

Suppose a biterm b occurred $n_b^{(t)}$ times in the posts published in time slice t. Since a biterm might be observed either in normal usage (e.g., daily chatting) or in some bursty topic, we decompose $n_b^{(t)}$ into two parts: $n_{b,0}^{(t)}$ is the count of biterm b occurred in normal usage, while $n_{b,1}^{(t)}$ is the count of b occurred in bursty topics, with $n_{b,0}^{(t)}+n_{b,1}^{(t)}=n_b^{(t)}$. Note that both $n_{b,0}^{(t)}$ and $n_{b,1}^{(t)}$ are not observed, however, we can determine their value approximately based on the temporal frequencies of b.

Specifically, for a large collection it is reasonable to assume that the normal usage of a biterm is stable during a period of time. In other words, $n_{b,0}^{(t)}$ is supposed to almost be constant over time. Conversely, $n_{b,1}^{(t)}$ may change significantly across different time slices. When some bursty topic relevant to b_i breaks out, $n_{b,1}^{(t)}$ might rise steeply. while in most other time slices, there is no such bursty topic taking place, $n_{b,1}^{(t)}$ will be close to 0. Based on the above analysis, we estimate $n_{b,0}^{(t)}$ by the mean of $n_b^{(t)}$ in the last S time slices, i.e., $\bar{n}_b^{(t)}=\frac{1}{S}\sum_{s=1}^{S} n_b^{(t-s)}$. Consequently, we can obtain $\hat{n}_{b,1}^{(t)}=(n_b^{(t)}-\bar{n}_b^{(t)})_+$, where $(x)_+=\max(x,\epsilon)$, and ϵ is a small positive number to avoid zero probability. In our experiments, we set $S=10$, $\epsilon=0.01$ after some preliminary experiments.

With $n_b^{(t)}$ and $\hat{n}_{b,1}^{(t)}$ in hand, it is straightforward to measure the possibility of b generated from a bursty topic in time slice t as:

$$\eta_b^{(t)} = \frac{(n_b^{(t)}-\bar{n}_b^{(t)})_+}{n_b^{(t)}}. \tag{1}$$

We refer $\eta_b^{(t)}$ as the bursty probability of biterm b in time slice t. The calculation of $\eta_b^{(t)}$ implies that a biterm occurred much more frequently in a time slice than other time slices will be more likely to be generated from bursty topics [1].

Bursty Biterm Topic Models

We now describe our approach for bursty topic modeling in microblogs, i.e., Bursty Biterm Topic Model (BBTM). In the following, since we focus on data in a single time slice, we

[1]In our experiments, we found $\eta_b^{(t)}$ in Eq. (1) might be overestimated for rare biterms whose $\bar{n}_b^{(t)} issmall$. Since the rare biterms are more likely to be generated by random factors rather than bursty topics, we set $\eta_b^{(t)}$ to $\epsilon/n_b^{(t)}$ if $\bar{n}_b^{(t)} < 5$.

Figure 1: Graphical representation of (a) the biterm topic model, and (b) the bursty biterm topic model.

will not specify the time slice in the notations. For instance, we write $\eta_b^{(t)}$ as η_b for simplification.

As we suppose that a biterm might be observed either in normal usage or in some bursty topic, the basic idea of BBTM is to distinguish the occurrences of biterms from the two parts to learn bursty topics. Specifically, we define a binary variable e_i to denote the source of an occurrence of biterm b_i. $e_i = 0$ indicates b_i is generated by normal usage, while $e_i = 1$ indicates b_i is generated from some bursty topic. Recall that the bursty probability of a biterm encodes our prior knowledge of how likely the biterm is generated from a bursty topic, we thus define a Bernoulli distribution with parameter η_{b_i} as the prior distribution of e_i. Moreover, we introduce K multinomial distributions over the words (i.e., $\{\boldsymbol{\phi}_k | k \in [1, K]\}$) to denote the bursty topics in the collection, and a background word distribution $\boldsymbol{\phi}_0$ to denote the normal usage. The generative process of the biterm set $\mathbb{B}$ in the time slice in BBTM is then defined as follows:

1. For the collection,
   - draw a bursty topic distribution $\boldsymbol{\theta} \sim \text{Dir}(\alpha)$
   - draw a background word distribution $\boldsymbol{\phi}_0 \sim \text{Dir}(\beta)$
2. For each bursty topic $k \in [1, K]$,
   - draw a word distribution $\boldsymbol{\phi}_k \sim \text{Dir}(\beta)$
3. For each biterm $b_i \in \mathbb{B}$
   - draw $e_i \sim \text{Bern}(\eta_{b_i})$
   - If $e_i = 0$,
     - draw two words $w_{i,1}, w_{i,2} \sim \text{Multi}(\boldsymbol{\phi}_0)$
   - If $e_i = 1$,
     - draw a bursty topic $z \sim \text{Multi}(\boldsymbol{\theta})$
     - draw two words $w_{i,1}, w_{i,2} \sim \text{Multi}(\boldsymbol{\phi}_z)$

Its graphical representation is shown in Figure 1 (b), where B denotes the number of distinct biterms in $\mathbb{B}$.

Discussion

In BBTM, the prior distribution η_b indicates how likely a biterm b is generated by bursty topics, which plays a key role in guiding the model to distinguish whether a biterm b is generated from burst topics or not. Previous work measuring word burstiness with statistical testing (Swan and Allan 1999; Lijffijt 2013) or sigmoid mapping of the variance of temporal frequencies of words (Fung et al. 2005; Li, Sun, and Datta 2012) can only determine whether a biterm is bursty or not, rather than the probability of a biterm generated from bursty topics. Therefore, using them as the prior will lead to inferior results, as shown in our preliminary experiments.

The background word distribution introduced by BBTM is used to filter out biterms not related to bursty topics. In (Mei and Zhai 2005), a background word distribution is also introduced into a topic model to distill temporal themes from a text stream. However, the background word distribution is simply set to the empirical word distribution that contributes equally on the generation of each word. In BBTM, the background word distribution is learned from the data. Its impact on the generation of biterms is different due to the biterm-wise prior η_b.

Parameter Estimation

In BBTM, the parameter set need to estimate is $\boldsymbol{\Theta} = \{\boldsymbol{\theta}, \boldsymbol{\phi}_0, ..., \boldsymbol{\phi}_K\}$, if given the hyperparameters α and β. It is not hard to write out the likelihood of the biterm set $\mathbb{B}$:

$$
\begin{aligned}
P(\mathbb{B}) \;=\; & \prod_{i=1}^{N_B} \int \Big(\phi_{0,w_{i,1}} \phi_{0,w_{i,2}} (1 - \eta_{b_i}) + \\
& \sum_{k=1}^{K} \theta_k \phi_{k,w_{i,1}} \phi_{k,w_{i,2}} \eta_{b_i} \Big) \mathrm{d}\boldsymbol{\Theta}. \qquad (2)
\end{aligned}
$$

Since the parameters in $\boldsymbol{\Theta}$ are coupled in Eq. (2), it is intractable to determine them exactly. Following (Griffiths and Steyvers 2004), we use the collapsed Gibbs sampling algorithm for approximate estimation.

The basic idea is to estimate the parameters alternatively using samples drawn from the posterior distributions of latent variables sequentially conditioned on the current values of all other variables and the data. In BBTM, there are two types of latent variables, i.e., e_i and z_i. We draw them jointly according to the following conditional distribution

Algorithm 1: Gibbs sampling algorithm for BBTM

Input: $K, \alpha, \beta, \mathbb{B}$
Output: $\{\phi_k\}_{k=0}^{K}, \boldsymbol{\theta}$
Randomly initialize $\mathbf{e}$ and $\mathbf{z}$
for $iter$ = 1 *to* N_{iter} **do**
  foreach $b_i = (w_{i,1}, w_{i,2}) \in \mathbb{B}$ **do**
    Draw e_i, k from Eqs.(3-4)
    if $e_i = 0$ **then**
      Update the counts $n_{0,w_{i,1}}, n_{0,w_{i,2}}$
    else
      Update the counts $n_k, n_{k,w_{i,1}}, n_{k,w_{i,2}}$
Compute the parameters by Eqs. (5-6)

(the derivation is provided in the supplemental material):

$$P(e_i = 0|\mathbf{e}^{\neg i}, \mathbf{z}^{\neg i}, \mathbb{B}, \alpha, \beta, \boldsymbol{\eta}) \propto$$

$$(1 - \eta_{b_i}) \cdot \frac{(n_{0,w_{i,1}}^{\neg i} + \beta)(n_{0,w_{i,2}}^{\neg i} + \beta)}{(n_{0,\cdot}^{\neg i} + W\beta)(n_{0,\cdot}^{\neg i} + 1 + W\beta)}, \quad (3)$$

$$P(e_i = 1, z_i = k|\mathbf{e}^{\neg i}, \mathbf{z}^{\neg i}, \mathbb{B}, \alpha, \beta, \boldsymbol{\eta}) \propto$$

$$\eta_{b_i} \cdot \frac{(n_k^{\neg i} + \alpha)}{(n_{\cdot}^{\neg i} + K\alpha)} \cdot \frac{(n_{k,w_{i,1}}^{\neg i} + \beta)(n_{k,w_{i,2}}^{\neg i} + \beta)}{(n_{k,\cdot}^{\neg i} + W\beta)(n_{k,\cdot}^{\neg i} + 1 + W\beta)}, \quad (4)$$

where $\mathbf{e} = \{e_i\}_{i=0}^{N_B}$, $\mathbf{z} = \{z_i\}_{i=0}^{N_B}$, $\boldsymbol{\eta} = \{\eta_b\}_{b=0}^{B}$, $n_{0,w}$ is the number of times that word w is assigned to the background word distribution, $n_{0,\cdot} = \sum_{w=1}^{W} n_{0,w}$ is the total number of words assigned to the background word distribution, n_k is the number of biterms assigned to bursty topic k, $n_{\cdot} = \sum_{k=1}^{K} n_k$ is the total number of biterms assigned to bursty topics, $n_{k,w}$ is the number of times that word w is assigned to bursty topic k, $n_{k,\cdot} = \sum_{w=1}^{W} n_{k,w}$ is the total number of words assigned to bursty topic k, and $\neg i$ means ignoring biterm b_i.

The Gibbs sampling algorithm of BBTM is outlined in Algorithm 1. First, we randomly initialize the latent variables. Then, we iteratively draw samples of the latent variables for each biterm according to Eqs. (3-4). After a sufficient number of iterations, we collect the counts n_k and $n_{k,w}$ to estimate the parameters by:

$$\hat{\phi}_{k,w} = \frac{n_{k,w} + \beta}{n_{k,\cdot} + W\beta}, \quad (5)$$

$$\hat{\theta}_k = \frac{n_k + \alpha}{n_{\cdot} + K\alpha}. \quad (6)$$

Runtime Analysis. Recall that the time complexity of BTM is $O(N_{iter} K N_B)$ and the memory complexity is $K(1+W)+N_B$ (Yan et al. 2013), where N_B is the number of biterms in $\mathbb{B}$. Compared with BTM, BBTM introduces an additional topic, namely the background word distribution, thus its time complexity is $O(N_{iter}(K+1)N_B)$. Moreover, it need to maintain $\boldsymbol{\eta}$ in memory, so its memory complexity is $(K+1)(1+W)+N_B+B$.

Experiments

In this section, we empirically verify the performance of BBTM on bursty topic discovery in microblogs both quantitatively and qualitatively.

Experimental Settings

Dataset. We use a standard microblog dataset, i.e., the Tweets2011 collection published in TREC 2011 microblog track[2]. The dataset contains approximately 16 million tweets sampled in 17 days from Jan. 23 to Feb. 8, 2011. We preprocessed the raw data in the same way as (Yan et al. 2013). Furthermore, we filtered biterms occurred only one time in the collection to save computational cost since most of them are meaningless.

Baseline Methods. We compare our approach against the following baseline methods: 1) **Twevent** (Li, Sun, and Datta 2012) first detects bursty tweet segments and then clustering them to obtain bursty topics. To make a fair comparison, we simply used individual words as segments, and did not exploit Wikipedia to filter the final clusters. 2) **OLDA** (Lau, Collier, and Baldwin 2012) uses online LDA (AlSumait, Barbará, and Domeniconi 2008) to learn topics in each time slice, and then detects bursty topics by measuring the Jensen-Shannon divergence between the words distribution before and after an update of the topics. 3) **UTM** (User-Temporal Mixture model) (Yin et al. 2013) supposes the temporal topics follow a time-dependent topic distribution, and the non-bursty topics follow a user-dependent topic distribution. To ensure the temporal topics discovered to be bursty, the authors heuristically boosted the probability of bursty words in the temporal topics. 4) **IBTM** trains individual BTM (Yan et al. 2013) for each time slice. To distinguish between bursty topics and non-bursty topics, we first greedily matched the topics in two adjacent time slices according their cosine similarity, and then used the post-processing step in OLDA to detect bursty topics. 5) **BBTM-S** is a simplified version BBTM. In BBTM-S, for each occurrence of biterm b_i, we directly draw e_i from a Bernoulli distribution with parameter η_{b_i}, rather than take it as a latent variable. If $e_i = 1$, b_i is selected into the training set, otherwise it is discarded. Finally, we simply train a BTM over the selected biterms to learn the bursty topics.

Parameter Setting. In our experiments, the length of a time slice is set to a day, a typical setting in the literature (Lau, Collier, and Baldwin 2012; Li, Sun, and Datta 2012). Following the convention in BTM (Yan et al. 2013), we set $\alpha = 50/K$ and $\beta = 0.01$ in BBTM. The number of bursty topics K are varied from 10 to 50. The other parameters of the baseline methods are set by their default values in their papers.

Accuracy of Bursty Topics Discovered

First of all, we evaluate the accuracy of the bursty topics discovered by different methods. We asked 5 volunteers to manually label the bursty topics discovered by all of these methods. To ensure unbiased judgment, all the topics generated are randomly mixed before labeling. For each bursty topic, we provided the volunteers its 50 most probable words and time slice information, and external tools, such as Google and Twitter search, to help their judgement.

[2]http://trec.nist.gov/data/tweets/

Method	P@10	P@30	P@50
Twevent	0.592	0.681	0.636
UTM	0.565	0.488	0.453
OLDA	0.231	0.217	0.185
IBTM	0.300	0.325	0.297
BBTM-S	0.785	0.832	0.790
BBTM	**0.810**	**0.865**	**0.842**

Table 1: Accuracy of the bursty topics discovered (measured by Precision@K).

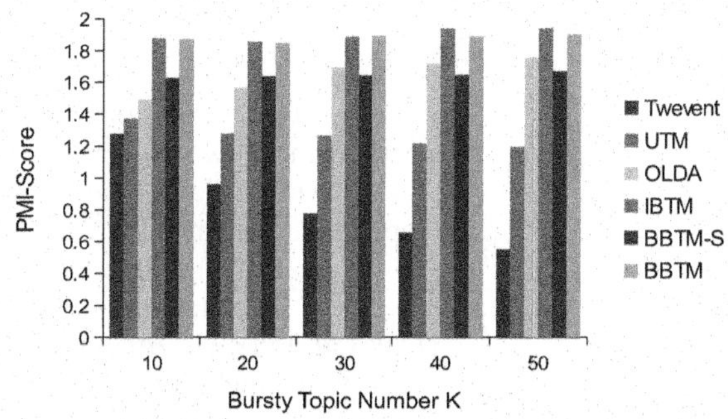

Figure 2: Coherence of the bursty topics discovered (measured by PMI-Score).

If the bursty topic presented is both meaningful and bursty in its time slice, it gets 1 point; Otherwise, it gets 0 point. A bursty topic is correctly detected if more than half of judges assigned 1 point to it. The comparison of different methods are then based on the average precision at K ($P@K$), i.e., the proportion of correctly detected busty topics among the learned K bursty topics.

Table 1 lists the precisions of all the methods with different settings of bursty topic number K. We find that 1) BBTM always achieves a high precision over 0.8, which is substantially better than other methods. 2) The simplified version of BBTM, i.e., BBTM-S, falls behind BBTM but works much better than other baselines. We analyze the reason why BBTM-S is worse than BBTM. We find that the biterm sampling process simply using the prior distribution may throw away some potential bursty biterms with moderate busty probability. Meanwhile, from Eq. (4) we can see that the topic assignment of b_i is actually affected by two factors simultaneously. One is the prior knowledge encoded by bursty probability, and the other is co-occurrence patterns with other biterms in the time slice. By preserving all the biterms and modeling the two parts jointly, BBTM thus can better capture the bursty topics. 3) Twevent outperforms other baseline methods that based on topic models (i.e., OLDA, UTM and IBTM). Further examination shows that many topics discovered by these topic model based methods are still about common subjects such as sentiment and life. 4) Moveover, we also find that IBTM outperforms OLDA though they use the same post-processing step, indicating that BTM can better model topics over short texts than LDA.

For qualitative analysis, in Table 2 we show 5 bursty topics (represented by the most probable words) discovered by BBTM along with the corresponding topic probability, i.e., $\hat{\theta}_k$. To help us better understand the results, we also present a news title for each topic obtained by searching its keywords and date in Google. We can see that the 5 bursty topics coincide well with the real-world events reported by the news titles, suggesting the good detection accuracy and potential value of our approach on event detection and summarization.

Coherence of Bursty Topics Discovered

Next, we evaluate the interpretability of the learned bursty topics based on the coherence measure. One popular metric is the PMI-Score (Newman et al. 2010), which calculates the average Pointwise Mutual Information (PMI) between the most probable words in each topic using the large-scale Wikipedia data. A larger PMI-Score indicates the topic is more coherent.

The result is shown in Figure 2. We have the following observations. 1) The PMI-Score of BBTM is comparable to IBTM and almost always the highest, indicating good coherence of the learned bursty topics from microblogs. 2) BBTM-S achieves a comparable PMI-Score with OLDA which is substantially higher than UTM and Twevent. However, BBTM-S is lower than BBTM, since it loses a large part of useful word co-occurrence information by filtering the biterms. 3) The PMI-Score of Twevent is always the lowest, indicating that topics obtained by simply clustering the bursty words might be noisy and less coherent. 4) The PMI-Score of UTM is lower than the other topic model based methods. An explanation is that UTM heuristically boosts the probability of bursty words in the temporal topics, which might disturb the topic learning process and degrade the quality of the learned topics.

For qualitative analysis, we chose a hot bursty topic by selecting a hashtag with high bursty probability estimated by Eq.(1). The hashtag is "#ntas" occurred in Jan. 26, 2011, which denotes NTA (National Television Awards), a prominent ceremony in British held on that day. For comparison, we first calculate the empirical word distribution in the tweets containing the hashtag. Then for each method, we select the bursty topic closest to the empirical word distribution of the hashtag under the cosine similarity, and list the results in Table 3.

From Table 3, we can see that: 1) The bursty topics discovered by BBTM is the closest to NTA, and even better explains NTA than the empirical word distribution by ranking some common words such as "morning" and "doctor" in lower position. 2) The bursty discovered BBTM-S is also clearly about NTA, but slightly less readable than BBTM. 3) The bursty topic discovered by Twevent is not well readable, though the words are bursty in the data. UTM seems to have the same problem of Twevent, since it boosts the probability of burst words in each topic in a heuristic way. 4) The topics discovered by OLDA and BTM are relevant to NTA, but they contain many common words such as "year" and "good", suggesting that it is a common issue of the standard topic models.

k	The 10 most probable words	$\hat{\theta}_k$
2	police officers shot shooting detroit twitter adam suspect year revenue (Two St. Petersburg police officers were shot and killed)	0.036
11	airport moscow police news killed people dead blast suicide explosion (Deadly suicide bombing hits Moscow's Domodedovo airport)	0.057
15	open #ausopen nadal australian murray mike tomlin cloud #cloud avril (Australian Open Tennis Championships 2011)	0.015
25	jack lalanne fitness 96 dies guru rip died age dead (Jack LaLanne: US fitness guru who last ate dessert in 1929 dies aged 96)	0.044
26	court emanuel rahm chicago ballot mayor mayoral run appellate rules (Court tosses Emanuel off Chicago mayoral ballot)	0.024

Table 2: Bursty topics discovered by BBTM on Jan. 24, 2011. The sentences in parenthesis are news titles corresponding to these topics obtained by querying the most probable words and its date in Google.

Empirical	Twevent	UTM	OLDA	IBTM	BBTM-S	BBTM
#ntas	#thegame	#thegame	amazing	award	award	#ntas
win	malik	malik	vote	shorty	win	award
love	ant	sitting	award	nominate	bell	awards
award	melanie	standing	movie	oscar	taco	win
matt	eastenders	cut	year	awards	high	#nta
morning	derwin	empty	listen	#ntas	shortly	national
watching	#ntas	pres	awesome	film	speed	love
doctor	tosh	reform	film	win	nominate	tv
lacey	nta	remind	king	love	#ntas	television
cardle	corrie	ai	music	good	rail	nta

Table 3: The bursty topic discovered by each method mostly relates to "#ntas" on Jan.26, 2011. The first column list the most frequent words in the tweets with hashtag "#ntas".

Novelty of Bursty Topics Discovered

In microblogs, we know that the content of bursty topics change continually. We would like to compare the sensitivity of these methods on discovering novel bursty topics by evaluating the novelty of the learned bursty topics across different time slice [3]. Specifically, given a topic set sequence $\{\mathbb{Z}^{(0)}, ..., \mathbb{Z}^{(t)}\}$, we collect the T most probable words of each topic in $\mathbb{Z}^{(t)}$ to construct a *topical word set* $\mathbb{W}^{(t)}$ for each time slice. Then, we define the novelty of $\mathbb{Z}^{(t)}$ as the ratio of novel words in the topical word set, compared to the last time slice. Formally:

$$\text{Novelty}(\mathbb{Z}^{(t)}) = \frac{|\mathbb{W}^{(t)}| - |\mathbb{W}^{(t)} \cap \mathbb{W}^{(t-1)}|}{T * K},$$

where $|\cdot|$ denotes the number of elements of a set. In our experiments, we chose $T = 10$.

In Figures 3, we plot the change of the novelty of the bursty topics as a function of the bursty topic number K. We observe that 1) Both BBTM and BBTM-S significantly outperform OLDA and IBTM, especially when K is large, implying these two bursty oriented methods are more sensitive to bursty topics in microblogs than the temporal topic models. 2) Twevent obtains a very high novelty when K is small, since it summarizes burst topics only with bursty words. However, the novelty decreases fast with the increase of topic number K. Further investigation found that the reason is that many small-sized clusters (e.g., with 2 or 3 words) are discovered by Twevent.

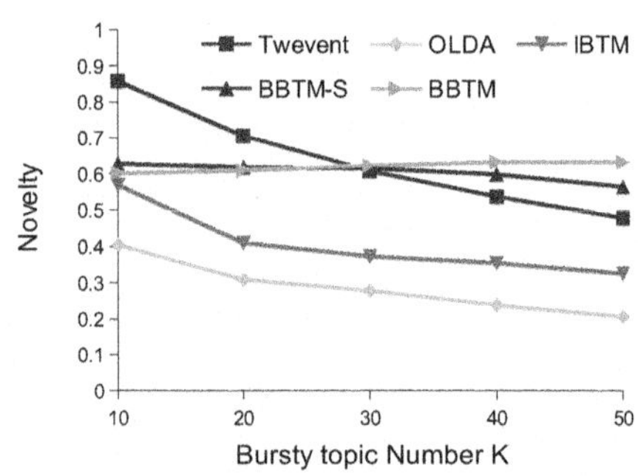

Figure 3: Novelty of the bursty topic discovered.

Efficiency Comparison

Finally, we compare the training time of the methods based on topic models. The experiments are conducted on a personal computer with two Dual-core 2.6GHz Intel processors and 4 GB of RAM, and all the codes are implemented in C++. We summarize the average runtime of per iteration over microblog posts in a single day in Table 4. It is not

[3]Since UTM is a retrospective topic detection model that models topics as static over time, we do not compare it here.

K	UTM	OLDA	IBTM	BBTM-S	BBTM
10	4.24	1.84	4.66	**0.03**	1.57
20	6.02	2.61	5.97	**0.06**	2.89
30	7.84	3.28	7.24	**0.09**	4.40
40	9.79	4.02	8.54	**0.13**	5.71
50	11.63	4.83	9.99	**0.17**	7.24

Table 4: Time cost (second) per iteration.

surprising that BBTM-S costs much less time than other methods, since it only used a subset of biterms for training. We also find that BBTM is much efficient than IBTM and UTM, since it focuses on learning busty topics and spends much less time on learning non-bursty topics. Note that both BBTM and BBTM-S do not require any post-processing steps as OLDA and IBTM, which will cost additional time.

Conclusions & Future Work

We study the problem of bursty topics discovery in microblogs, which is challenging due to the microblog posts are particularly short and noisy. To tackle this problem, we develop a novel bursty biterm topic model (i.e., BBTM) based on the recently introduced short text topic model (i.e., BTM). The key idea is to exploit the burstiness of biterms as the prior knowledge and incorporate it into BTM in a principled way for bursty topic modeling. Our approach can not only well solve the data sparsity problem in topic modeling over short texts, but also automatically learn bursty topics in a efficient way. Experimental results demonstrate the substantial superiority of our approach over the state-of-the-art methods.

For the future work, we would like to further improve the estimation of bursty probability by including more information of the biterms. It would also be interesting to investigate how to model the microblog streams together with other streaming data, like news streams, to better detect and represent bursty topics.

Acknowledgements

This work is funded by the National Basic Research Program of China under Grants No. 2014CB340401, No. 2012CB316303, National High Technology Research and Development Program of China under Grant No. 2012AA011003, No. 2014AA015103, National Natural Science Foundation of China under Grant No. 61232010, 61472401, and National Key Technology R&D Program under Grant No. 2012BAH39B04. We would like to thank the anonymous reviewers for their valuable comments.

References

AlSumait, L.; Barbará, D.; and Domeniconi, C. 2008. Online LDA: Adaptive topic models for mining text streams with applications to topic detection and tracking. In *ICDM*, 3–12. IEEE.

Analytics, P. 2009. Twitter study–august 2009. *San Antonio, TX: Pear Analytics.*

Blei, D.; Ng, A.; and Jordan, M. 2003. Latent Dirichlet allocation. *JMLR* 3:993–1022.

Blei, D. M. 2012. Probabilistic topic models. *Communications of the ACM* 55(4):77–84.

Cataldi, M.; Di Caro, L.; and Schifanella, C. 2010. Emerging topic detection on twitter based on temporal and social terms evaluation. In *MDMKDD*, 4. ACM.

Cheng, X.; Yan, X.; Lan, Y.; and Guo, J. 2014. BTM: Topic modeling over short texts. *IEEE Transactions on Knowledge and Data Engineering*.

Diao, Q.; Jiang, J.; Zhu, F.; and Lim, E.-P. 2012. Finding bursty topics from microblogs. In *ACL*, 536–544.

Fung, G. P. C.; Yu, J. X.; Yu, P. S.; and Lu, H. 2005. Parameter free bursty events detection in text streams. In *Proceedings of the 31st international conference on Very large data bases*, 181–192. VLDB Endowment.

Griffiths, T. L., and Steyvers, M. 2004. Finding scientific topics. *PNAS* 101(Suppl 1):5228–5235.

Hofmann, T. 1999. Probabilistic latent semantic analysis. *UAI*.

Hong, L., and Davison, B. 2010. Empirical study of topic modeling in Twitter. In *Proceedings of the First Workshop on Social Media Analytics*, 80–88. ACM.

Lau, J. H.; Collier, N.; and Baldwin, T. 2012. On-line trend analysis with topic models:#twitter trends detection topic model online. In *COLING*, 1519–1534.

Li, C.; Sun, A.; and Datta, A. 2012. Twevent: segment-based event detection from tweets. In *CIKM*, 155–164. ACM.

Lijffijt, J. 2013. A fast and simple method for mining subsequences with surprising event counts. In *ECML PKDD 2013, Prague, Czech Republic, Proceedings, Part I*, 385–400.

Mathioudakis, M., and Koudas, N. 2010. Twittermonitor: Trend detection over the twitter stream. In *SIGMOD*, 1155–1158. New York, NY, USA: ACM.

Mei, Q., and Zhai, C. 2005. Discovering evolutionary theme patterns from text: an exploration of temporal text mining. In *Proceedings of the eleventh ACM SIGKDD international conference on Knowledge discovery in data mining*, 198–207. ACM.

Newman, D.; Lau, J. H.; Grieser, K.; and Baldwin, T. 2010. Automatic evaluation of topic coherence. In *NAACL HLT*, 100–108.

Swan, R., and Allan, J. 1999. Extracting significant time varying features from text. In *Proceedings of the eighth international conference on Information and knowledge management*, 38–45. ACM.

Tang, J.; Meng, Z.; Nguyen, X.; Mei, Q.; and Zhang, M. 2014. Understanding the limiting factors of topic modeling via posterior contraction analysis. In *ICML*, 190–198.

Yan, X.; Guo, J.; Lan, Y.; and Cheng, X. 2013. A biterm topic model for short texts. In *WWW*, 1445–1456.

Yin, H.; Cui, B.; Lu, H.; Huang, Y.; and Yao, J. 2013. A unified model for stable and temporal topic detection from social media data. In *ICDE*, 661–672. IEEE.

On the Scalable Learning of Stochastic Blockmodel

Bo Yang and **Xuehua Zhao**
School of Computer Science and Technology, Jilin University, Changchun, China
Key Laboratory of Symbolic Computation and Knowledge Engineering of Ministry of Education, China
ybo@jlu.edu.cn

Abstract

Stochastic blockmodel (SBM) enables us to decompose and analyze an exploratory network without a priori knowledge about its intrinsic structure. However, the task of effectively and efficiently learning a SBM from a large-scale network is still challenging due to the high computational cost of its model selection and parameter estimation. To address this issue, we present a novel SBM learning algorithm referred to as BLOS (BLOck-wise Sbm learning). Distinct from the literature, the model selection and parameter estimation of SBM are concurrently, rather than alternately, executed in BLOS by embedding the minimum message length criterion into a block-wise EM algorithm, which greatly reduces the time complexity of SBM learning without losing learning accuracy and modeling flexibility. Its effectiveness and efficiency have been tested through rigorous comparisons with the state-of-the-art methods on both synthetic and real-world networks.

Introduction

Formally, a standard SBM is defined as a triple (K, Π, Ω). K is the number of blocks. Π is a $K \times K$ matrix, in which π_{ql} denotes the probability that a link from one node in block q connects to another node in block l. Ω is a K-dimension vector, in which ω_k denotes the probability that a randomly chosen node falls in block k.

SBM is often used as a generative model to decompose real-world networks or synthesize artificial networks, which contain either assortative communities, disassortative multi-partites, or arbitrary mixtures of them. Moreover, SBM can be used as a prediction model for link prediction. Being a powerful tool of network analysis, SBM has attracted more and more attentions (Newman and Leicht 2007; Airoldi et al. 2009; Latouche et al. 2011; Karrer and Newman 2011; Yang et al. 2011; Yang, Liu, and Liu 2012) since it was originally proposed (Holland and Leinhardt 1981).

Although SBM has superiority in structure analysis, however, SBM learning is computationally intractable, which limits it to a narrow range of applications just involving very small networks. For the current algorithms, given the number of blocks K, i.e. we do not consider model selection, the time of learning is at least $O(K^2n^2)$. Otherwise, it quickly goes up to $O(n^5)$ in that the process of determining "true" block numbers is very time-consuming. In another word, if we use a conventional PC to run current algorithms, the networks we can efficiently handle contain at most hundreds of nodes, far from the scales faced in practice.

The learning of SBM consists of two main sub-tasks: to determine block number K and to estimate parameter Π and Ω, corresponding to model selection and parameter estimation, respectively. Model selection aims at selecting a model having a good tradeoff between data fitting and model complexity, in obtaining a better generalization ability. Since the tradeoff can be measured by the quantity of its parameters, to select a "good" model for SBM means to determine a reasonable value of K in the sense that the parameter number of SBM is actually a function of K. For example, the parameter number of a standard SBM is equal to $K^2 + K + 1$. Formally, for a given network N, the objective of SBM learning can be stated as: $\arg\min_{K,h} C(N, K, h)$, where h denotes model parameters (i.e. Π and Ω), C denotes the cost function evaluating the tradeoff of parameterized model (K, h). A widely used cost function is: $C(N, K, h) = -\log L(N|K, h) + p(K, h)$, where $\log L(N|K, h)$ indicates the data fitting in terms of the maximum log-likelihood of N given a model and its parameters, and $p(K, h)$ is a regularization item that penalizes models with high complexity.

In the literature, MCMC (Snijders and Nowicki 1997; Yang et al. 2011; McDaid et al. 2013), EM (Newman and Leicht 2007), variational EM (Latouche, Birmele, and Ambroise 2012), and variational Bayes EM (Airoldi et al. 2009; Latouche, Birmele, and Ambroise 2012; Gopalan et al. 2012) have been adopted to estimate the parameters of SBM. Currently, the model selection methods used by SBM learning are either cross validation (Airoldi et al. 2009), or MDL (Yang, Liu, and Liu 2012), or different approximations of Bayesian model evidence, mainly including BIC (Airoldi et al. 2009), ICL(Daudin, Picard, and Robin 2008), and Variation based approximate evidence (Hofman and Wiggins 2008; Latouche, Birmele, and Ambroise 2012).

Current SBM learning algorithms adopt a model-wise learning mechanism to integrate the aforementioned methods of parameter estimation and model selection. That is, they parameterize and then evaluate all candidates in a model space one by one. Finally, the parameterized model

where $\gamma_{ik} = E[z_{ik}; h^{(t-1)}]$ denotes the posteriori probability of node i belonging to block k given $h^{(t-1)}$. We have:

$$\gamma_{ik} = \frac{\omega_k^{(t-1)} \prod_{j=1}^{n} f(\theta_{kj}^{(t-1)}, a_{ij})}{\sum_{k=1}^{K} \omega_k^{(t-1)} \prod_{j=1}^{n} f(\theta_{kj}^{(t-1)}, a_{ij})} \tag{8}$$

M-step: To maximize $Q(h, h^{(t-1)}) + \log p(h)$, where $\log p(h) = -\frac{1}{2} \sum_{\omega_q > 0} \sum_{\omega_l > 0} \log \omega_q \omega_l - \frac{2K_g^2 + K_g}{2} \log n - \frac{K_g^2 + K_g}{2}(1 + \log \kappa_d)$. By solving this optimization with a constraint $\sum_{k=1}^{K} \omega_k = 1$, we have:

$$\begin{cases} \omega_k^{(t)} = \dfrac{\max\{0, \sum_{i=1}^{n} \gamma_{ik} - K_g\}}{\sum_{j=1}^{K} \max\{0, \sum_{i=1}^{n} \gamma_{ij} - K_g\}} \\ \theta_{kj}^{(t)} = \dfrac{\sum_{i=1}^{n} a_{ij} \gamma_{ik}}{\sum_{i=1}^{n} \gamma_{ik}} \end{cases} \tag{9}$$

Note that, the parameter Π of standard SBM can also be iteratively computed in terms of γ, as follows:

$$\pi_{pl} = \frac{\sum_i \sum_j \gamma_{ip} \gamma_{jl} a_{ij}}{\sum_i \sum_j \gamma_{ip} \gamma_{jl}} \tag{10}$$

It is easy to verify, the complexity of calculating Θ of fg-SBM according to Eq.9 is $O(Kn^2)$, yet the time of calculating Π according to Eq.10 is $O(K^2 n^2)$.

Since the prior of block assignment Ω characterizes the normalized distribution of block size, the calculation of ω_k in Eq.9 partially reflect the process of block-wise model selection, in which blocks being not sufficiently supported by data will be annihilated timely. More specifically, for each individual block k, ω_k will become and thereafter keep zero if its expectation size at present, i.e. $\sum_{i=1}^{n} \gamma_{ik}$, is less than the number of existing blocks.

If one considers such a model selection as a voting game, Eq.9 actually implies a new mechanism design particularly for SBM learning according to MML, in which candidates will be disqualified and then timely excluded from the current playoff of the game if the votes they have won from all nodes are less than the total number of existing candidate blocks. Note that, the threshold for qualifying individual blocks, i.e. K_g, is not fixed but self-adjusted during whole learning process. That is to say, the regulations of threshold at different stages will be self-adaptive to the block parameterization (in terms of the calculation of Θ and Γ) and block evaluation (in terms of the calculation of Ω) of both previous and current playoffs. The self-adaption of evaluating criterion is one of main features of block-wise SBM learning. In addition, the criterions at different stages will be evolving from strict to loose with the gradual reduction of candidates during playoffs, implying many trivial blocks will be removed as early as possible and thereby considerable computational cost of corresponding parameterization will be saved in this way.

The mechanism of block-wise SBM learning Based on the above analysis, Table 1 summarizes the detailed mechanism of block-wise SBM learning. Corresponding to the aforementioned framework, the evaluation, selection, parameterization and annihilation of blocks are performed in a block-wise mode within a FOR-loop.

Table 1: The implementation of block-wise SBM learning

	Algorithm BLOS
	Input: N, K_{min}, K_{max}
	Output: X and Z
01	Initial: $B = \{b_1, \ldots, b_{K_{max}}\}; t \leftarrow 0; K_g \leftarrow K_{max}; \varepsilon; \Theta^{(0)}$;
02	$\Omega^{(0)}; u_{ik}^{(0)} \leftarrow \prod_{j=1}^{n} f(\theta_{kj}^{(0)}, a_{ij})$, for $i = 1, \ldots, n$ and $\forall b_k \in B$;
03	REPEAT
04	$t \leftarrow t + 1$;
05	FOR $\forall b_k \in B$ DO
06	$\gamma_{ik}^{(t)} \leftarrow \frac{\omega_k^{(t-1)} u_{ik}^{(t-1)}}{\sum_{b_j \in B} \omega_j^{(t-1)} u_{ij}^{(t-1)}}$, for $i = 1, \ldots, n$;
07	$\omega_k^{(t)} \leftarrow \frac{\max\{0, \sum_{i=1}^{n} \gamma_{ik}^{(t)} - K_g\}}{\sum_{b_j \in B} \max\{0, \sum_{i=1}^{n} \gamma_{ij}^{(t)} - K_g\}}$;
08	$S \leftarrow \sum_{b_j \in B} \omega_j^{(t)}$;
09	$\omega_j^{(t)} \leftarrow \omega_j^{(t)} S^{-1}, \forall b_j \in B$;
10	IF $\omega_k^{(t)} > 0$ THEN
11	$\theta_{ki}^{(t)} \leftarrow \frac{\sum_{i=1}^{n} a_{ij} \gamma_{ik}^{(t)}}{\sum_{i=1}^{n} \gamma_{ik}^{(t)}}$, for $i = 1, \ldots, n$;
12	$u_{ik}^{(t)} \leftarrow \prod_{j=1}^{n} f(\theta_{kj}^{(t)}, a_{ij})$, for $i = 1, \ldots, n$;
13	ELSE
14	$K_g \leftarrow K_g - 1$;
15	$B \leftarrow B - \{b_k\}$;
16	ENDIF
17	ENDFOR
18	$X^{(t)} \leftarrow \{K_g, \Theta^{(t)}, \Omega^{(t)}\}$;
19	compute $C(N, X^{(t)})$ by Eq. 6;
20	UNTIL $\lvert C(N, X^{(t-1)}) - C(N, X^{(t)}) \rvert < \varepsilon$ or $K_g < K_{min}$;
21	$X \leftarrow X^{(t)}$;

Time complexity analysis The nested REPEAT and FOR loops are the most time-consuming in BLOS, which dominate the whole time of learning. In the body of FOR-loop, it takes $O(nK_g)$ time to calculate $\gamma_{\cdot k}$ in line 06 and ω_k in line 07, respectively, and takes $O(n^2)$ time to calculate $\theta_{k\cdot}$ in line 11 and $u_{\cdot k}$ in line 12, respectively. Accordingly, the FOR-loop takes $O(nK_g^{(t)} K_g^{(t)} + n^2 K_g^{(t+1)})$ time, where $K_g^{(t)}$ denotes the size of set B at the t-th iteration of REPEAT-loop. Cost computation in line 19 takes $O(n^2 K_g^{(t+1)} + (K_g^{(t+1)})^2)$ time. So, it will take $O(nK_g^{(t)} K_g^{(t)} + n^2 K_g^{(t+1)} + (K_g^{(t+1)})^2) < O(n^2 K_g^{(t)})$ time to perform the t-th REPEAT-loop. Thus, the complexity of REPEAT-loop is $O(\sum_{t=1}^{T} n^2 K_g^{(t)})$, where T is number of total iterations. Note that, the initialization of all $u_{ik}^{(0)}$ takes $O(n^2 K_{max})$ time, so the total time complexity of BLOS is $O(\sum_{t=1}^{T} n^2 K_g^{(t)} + n^2 K_{max})$. Since $K_g^{(t)} \leq K_{max}$, in the worst case, the time of BLOS is bounded by $O(Tn^2 K_{max})$. If the real number of blocks (say K) is known, the worst time of BLOS is $O(Tn^2 K)$ by initializing $K_{max} = K$. Otherwise, it will be $O(Tn^3)$ by initializing $K_{max} = O(n)$.

Validations

Next, we design experiments oriented toward evaluating the accuracy, the scalability, and the tradeoff between accuracy and scalability of BLOS. In order to sufficiently demonstrate the superiority of BLOS, Four state-of-the-art SBM learning methods, VBMOD (Hofman and Wiggins 2008), GSMDL

(Yang, Liu, and Liu 2012), SICL (Daudin, Picard, and Robin 2008) and SILvb (Latouche, Birmele, and Ambroise 2012), are selected as comparative methods, whose rationale and time complexity are summarized in Table 2. All experiments are performed on a conventional personal computer with a 2GH CPU and a 4GB RAM.

Table 2: Time complexity of SBM learning algorithms

Algorithm	Parameter estimation	Model selection	Learning strategy	K	N/K
BLOS	BEM	MML	B	$O(TKn^2)$	$O(Tn^3)$
VBMOD	VBEM	VAE	M	$O(TKn^2)$	$O(Tn^4)$
GSMDL	EM	MDL	M	$O(TK^2n^2)$	$O(Tn^5)$
SICL	VEM	ICL	M	$O(TK^2n^2)$	$O(Tn^5)$
SILvb	VBEM	VAE	M	$O(TK^2n^2)$	$O(Tn^5)$

In Table 2, K is the real number of blocks and T is the required iterations. "BEM", "VBEM", "VEM" mean "block-wise EM", "variational Bayes EM", "variational EM", respectively. "B" and "M" mean "block-wise" and "model-wise", respectively. "VAE" is the abbreviation of variational based approximate evidence. "K" and "N/K" indicate "K is known " and "K is unknown", respectively. In both cases, we list the worst time complexity of respective algorithms.

Validation on accuracy We first generate three types of synthetic networks according to specific SBMs, which respectively contain a community structure, a hub structure, and a hybrid structure of community and multipartite. Each type of networks is further divided into five groups according to the true block number they contain, i.e., $K_{true} = 3$, 4, 5, 6 or 7. Each group has 100 networks and each network contains 50 nodes. The parameters of three types of SBMs are given as follows:

Type I, containing a community structure: $\pi_{ij} = 0.9 \times I(i = j) + 0.1 \times I(i \neq j)$ and $\forall k : \omega_k = 1/K_{true}$.

Type II, containing a hub structure: $\pi_{ij} = 0.9 \times I(i = j$ or $i = 1$ or $j = 1) + 0.1 \times I(i \neq j$ and $i, j \neq 1)$ and $\forall k : \omega_k = 1/K_{true}$.

Type III, containing a hybrid structure of community and multipartite: $\forall k, \omega_k = 1/K_{true}$ and block matrix Π takes following form:

$$\Pi = \begin{bmatrix} p_1 & & p_2 & \cdot & & & \\ & \ddots & & \cdot & & p_2 & \\ p_2 & & p_1 & \cdot & & & \\ \cdot & \cdot & \cdot & \cdot & \cdot & \cdot & \cdot \\ & & & \cdot & p_2 & & p_1 \\ & p_2 & & \cdot & & \ddots & \\ & & & \cdot & p_1 & & p_2 \end{bmatrix} \begin{matrix} \left.\vphantom{\begin{matrix}a\\a\\a\end{matrix}}\right\} k_1 \\ \\ \left.\vphantom{\begin{matrix}a\\a\\a\end{matrix}}\right\} k_2 \end{matrix}$$

where k_1 and k_2 denote the number of communities and multipartite components, respectively. We have $k_1 + k_2 = K_{true}$. When K_{true} takes 3, 4, 5, 6 and 7 in turn, k_1 takes 1, 2, 3, 3 and 3, accordingly. In this experiment, we set $p_1 = 0.9$ and $p_2 = 0.1$.

For each type of block structure, we calculate the average NMI(normalized mutual information) over 100 synthetic networks for each algorithm; results are given in Table 3, in which the numbers in brackets on the right hand side show the ranks in terms of decreasing average NMI, indicating the accuracy rank of tested algorithms on average. For networks of Type I, SILvb and VBMOD perform slightly better than other algorithms. For networks of Type II and III, SILvb and BLOS perform better than others. VBMOD is stable for community detection, but it fails to handle networks containing beyond community structures.

Validation on computational scalability Next, we use synthetic networks with various scales to test the computing cost of different algorithms. Here, synthetic networks to be used are also generated according to the SBM of Type III. Specifically, its parameters are: $K_{true} = 8$, $k_1 = 3$, $k_2 = 5$ and $\forall k : \omega_k = 0.125$. n alternatively takes 200, 400, 600, 800, 1000, 2000, 5000, 10000, and 15000. In the case of $n < 5000$, we set $p_1 = 0.5$ and $p_2 = 0.01$. Otherwise, we set $p_1 = 0.1$ and $p_2 = 0.0001$. Correspondingly, we generate nine groups of networks with different scales and each group contains 50 randomly generated networks.

For all five algorithms, we set the same model space to search and the same convergence threshold, i.e., $K_{min} = 1$, $K_{max} = 20$ and $\varepsilon = 10^{-4}$. Fig. 1 shows the actual running time on average of five algorithms. Table 4 shows the NMI of detected block structures for these networks, in which "–" denotes "not available due to out of memory".

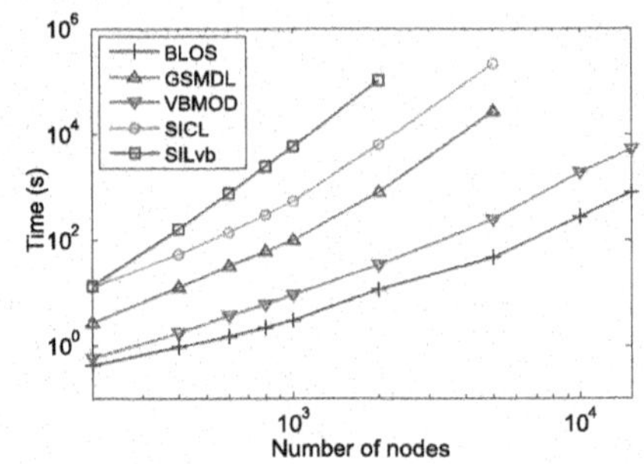

Figure 1: Running time in terms of network scale.

Overall, we have following observations: 1) BLOS runs the most efficient and its actual running time is significantly fewer than its competitors. 2) It is computationally intractable for model-wise methods such as SILvb and SICL to process large networks. Note that, SILvb needs to take 5834 seconds to handle 1000 nodes, and the time will sharply increase to 100,788 seconds (28 hours) when handling 2000 nodes. Comparatively, BLOS runs much faster and is able to handle 2000 nodes within 12 seconds, gaining a 8400-fold speedup of SILvb. SICL spends 216,893 seconds (60 hours) to handle 5000 nodes; BLOS only takes 46 seconds to handle the same network, gaining a 4700-fold speedup. 3) VBMOD adopts a model-wise scheme to learn SBM as well, while it runs much faster than SILvb, SICL and GSMDL. But VBMOD achieves its scalability by greatly simplifying SBM to be learned, i.e. compressing original $K \times K$ matrix Π into two scalar variables, at the price of losing the flexibility of modeling heterogeneous structures. 4) From Fig. 1 and Table 4, one can observe the best tradeoff between accuracy

Table 3: Accuracy of detected block structures in three types of networks

Methods	Networks of Type I K_{true} 3	4	5	6	7	Average	Networks of Type II K_{true} 3	4	5	6	7	Average	Networks of Type III K_{true} 3	4	5	6	7	Average
BLOS	1	1	1	0.951	0.877	0.966(3)	0.997	1	1	0.950	0.868	0.963(2)	1	1	1	0.978	0.878	0.971(2)
GSMDL	0.998	1	1	0.894	0.783	0.935(5)	0.985	0.994	1	0.889	0.788	0.931(4)	0.989	1	1	0.946	0.851	0.957(4)
VBMOD	1	1	1	1	0.861	0.972(2)	0.592	0.771	0.851	0.850	0.837	0.780(5)	0.764	0.863	0.742	0.811	0.780	0.792(5)
SICL	1	1	1	0.940	0.837	0.955(4)	1	1	1	0.944	0.855	0.960(3)	1	1	1	0.981	0.850	0.966(3)
SILvb	1	1	1	0.999	0.947	0.989(1)	1	1	1	0.999	0.951	0.990(1)	1	1	1	1	0.941	0.988(1)

and scalability demonstrated by BLOS. That is, compared with state-of-the-art algorithms, BLOS is able to effectively and efficiently handle much larger networks while preserving rather good learning precision.

Table 4: NMI of detections by five algorithms

Number of nodes	BLOS	GSMDL	VBMOD	SICL	SILvb
200	1	0.996	0.890	1	1
400	1	0.989	0.890	1	1
600	1	0.937	0.890	1	1
800	1	0.933	0.890	1	1
1000	1	0.924	0.890	1	1
2000	1	0.913	0.890	1	1
5000	1	0.890	0.890	1	–
10000	0.955	–	0.890	–	–
15000	0.940	–	0.890	–	–

Validation on real-world networks Now we test the performance of algorithms with real-world networks. Total 9 real-world networks are selected, which are widely used as benchmarks to validate the performance of block structure detection or scalability. The structural features of these networks are summarized in Table 5. Some have ground truth block structures. "–" means ground truth is not available.

Table 5: Structural features of 12 real-world networks

Network	Type	# of node	# of edge	Clustering coefficient	Average degree	Structure
Karate	Undirected	34	78	0.57	4.59	community
Dolphins	Undirected	62	159	0.26	5.13	community
Foodweb	Undirected	75	113	0.33	3.01	hybrid
Polbooks	Undirected	105	441	0.49	8.40	community
Adjnoun	Undirected	112	425	0.17	7.59	bipartite
Football	Undirected	115	613	0.40	10.7	community
Email	Undirected	1133	5451	0.22	9.62	–
Polblogs	Directed	1222	16714	0.32	27.4	–
Yeast	Undirected	2224	6609	0.13	5.94	–

For each algorithm, we fix $K_{min} = 1$ and set K_{max} according to Table 6. One can see the running time of BLOS is significantly lower than others, particularly for larger networks. For networks having ground truth, the true block numbers are listed below "K_{true}" in Table 7, and the detected numbers by algorithms are listed behind "/". We adopt NMI to measure the distance between ground truth and detections of algorithms. The last line gives the ranks of respective algorithms in terms of average NMI. BLOS performs the best when processing such real-world networks.

Table 6: Actual running time in real-world networks (s)

Networks	K_{max}	BLOS	GSMDL	VBMOD	SICL	SILvb
Karate	$n/2$	**0.13**	0.23	0.19	0.34	0.42
Dolphins	$n/2$	**0.32**	1.55	0.45	4.08	2.03
Foodweb	$n/2$	**0.33**	1.60	0.53	4.92	2.31
Polbooks	$n/2$	**0.96**	8.06	2.02	36.80	12.76
Adjnoun	$n/2$	**1.10**	8.09	2.12	40.08	16.34
Football	$n/2$	**1.20**	8.11	2.20	42.14	18.11
Email	100	**41.09**	18575	389	35288	78597
Polblogs	100	**43.82**	26031	618	44834	106034
Yeast	100	**104**	>48h	1677	>48h	>48h

Table 7: NMI of detections by five algorithms

Networks	K_{true}	BLOS	GSMDL	VBMOD	SICL	SILvb
Karate	2	**0.839**/3	0.754/4	0.837/2	0.792/4	0.770/4
Dolphins	2	**0.660**/3	0.551/4	0.628/4	0.368/3	0.387/3
Foodweb	5	**0.269**/4	0.185/5	0.023/2	0.199/2	0.201/2
Polbooks	3	**0.585**/4	0.469/6	0.512/6	0.458/5	0.455/5
Adjnoun	2	**0.206**/5	0.193/8	0.020/5	0.040/3	0.046/3
Football	12	0.884/10	0.824/10	0.862/9	**0.910**/10	**0.910**/10
avg(rank)		**0.574**(1)	0.496(2)	0.480(3)	0.461(5)	0.461(4)

Conclusion

Current SBMs face two main difficulties, which jointly make their learning processes not scalable. (1) Some parameters like Π cannot be estimated in an efficient way; (2) the posterior of Z cannot be explicitly derived due to the dependency of its components. Therefore, one has to assume an approximate distribution of Z and then turn to variational techniques. While, it is difficult to integrate variational methods with current model evaluation criteria to analytically derive a block-wise learning mechanism, enabling to perform parameter estimation and model selection concurrently. In view of this, we raised a reparameterized SBM and then theoretically derived a bock-wise learning algorithm, in which parameter estimation and model selection are executed concurrently in the scale of blocks. Validations show that BLOS achieves the best tradeoff between effectiveness and efficiency. Particularly, compared to SILvb, a recently proposed method with an excellent learning accuracy, BLOS achieves a n^2-fold speedup, reducing learning time from $O(n^5)$ to $O(n^3)$, while preserving competitive enough learning accuracy.

Acknowledgements

This work was funded by the Program for New Century Excellent Talents in University under Grant NCET-11-0204, and the National Science Foundation of China under Grants 61133011, 61373053, and 61300146.

References

Airoldi, E. M.; Blei, D. M.; Fienberg, S. E.; and Xing, E. P. 2009. Mixed membership stochastic blockmodels. In *Advances in Neural Information Processing Systems*, 33–40.

Daudin, J.-J.; Picard, F.; and Robin, S. 2008. A mixture model for random graphs. *Statistics and computing* 18(2):173–183.

Figueiredo, M. A., and Jain, A. K. 2002. Unsupervised learning of finite mixture models. *Pattern Analysis and Machine Intelligence, IEEE Transactions on* 24(3):381–396.

Gopalan, P.; Gerrish, S.; Freedman, M.; Blei, D. M.; and Mimno, D. M. 2012. Scalable inference of overlapping communities. In *Advances in Neural Information Processing Systems*, 2249–2257.

Hofman, J. M., and Wiggins, C. H. 2008. Bayesian approach to network modularity. *Physical review letters* 100(25):258701.

Holland, P. W., and Leinhardt, S. 1981. An exponential family of probability distributions for directed graphs. *Journal of the american Statistical association* 76(373):33–50.

Karrer, B., and Newman, M. E. 2011. Stochastic blockmodels and community structure in networks. *Physical Review E* 83(1):016107.

Lanterman, A. D. 2001. Schwarz, wallace, and rissanen: Intertwining themes in theories of model selection. *International Statistical Review* 69(2):185–212.

Latouche, P.; Birmelé, E.; Ambroise, C.; et al. 2011. Overlapping stochastic block models with application to the french political blogosphere. *The Annals of Applied Statistics* 5(1):309–336.

Latouche, P.; Birmele, E.; and Ambroise, C. 2012. Variational bayesian inference and complexity control for stochastic block models. *Statistical Modelling* 12(1):93–115.

McDaid, A. F.; Murphy, T. B.; Friel, N.; and Hurley, N. J. 2013. Improved bayesian inference for the stochastic block model with application to large networks. *Computational Statistics & Data Analysis* 60:12–31.

Newman, M. E., and Leicht, E. A. 2007. Mixture models and exploratory analysis in networks. *Proceedings of the National Academy of Sciences* 104(23):9564–9569.

Snijders, T. A., and Nowicki, K. 1997. Estimation and prediction for stochastic blockmodels for graphs with latent block structure. *Journal of classification* 14(1):75–100.

Titterington, D. M.; Smith, A. F.; Makov, U. E.; et al. 1985. *Statistical analysis of finite mixture distributions*, volume 7. Wiley New York.

Yang, T.; Chi, Y.; Zhu, S.; Gong, Y.; and Jin, R. 2011. Detecting communities and their evolutions in dynamic social networksa bayesian approach. *Machine learning* 82(2):157–189.

Yang, B.; Liu, J.; and Liu, D. 2012. Characterizing and extracting multiplex patterns in complex networks. *Systems, Man, and Cybernetics, Part B: Cybernetics, IEEE Transactions on* 42(2):469–481.

RAIN: Social Role-Aware Information Diffusion

Yang Yang[†♯], Jie Tang[†♯], Cane Wing-ki Leung[‡],
Yizhou Sun[⋆], Qicong Chen[†], Juanzi Li[†], Qiang Yang[‡]
[†]Department of Computer Science and Technology, Tsinghua University, China
[♯]Tsinghua National Laboratory for Information Science and Technology (TNList), China
[‡]Huawei Noah's Ark Lab, Hong Kong
[⋆]College of Computer and Information Science, Northeastern University, USA
{sherlockbourne, cane.leung}@gmail.com, ljz@keg.tsinghua.edu.cn,
jietang@tsinghua.edu.cn, yzsun@ccs.neu.edu, qyang@cse.ust.hk

Abstract

Information diffusion, which studies how information is propagated in social networks, has attracted considerable research effort recently. However, most existing approaches do not distinguish social roles that nodes may play in the diffusion process. In this paper, we study the interplay between users' social roles and their influence on information diffusion. We propose a Role-Aware INformation diffusion model (**RAIN**) that integrates social role recognition and diffusion modeling into a unified framework. We develop a Gibbs-sampling based algorithm to learn the proposed model using historical diffusion data. The proposed model can be applied to different scenarios. For instance, at the micro-level, the proposed model can be used to predict whether an individual user will repost a specific message; while at the macro-level, we can use the model to predict the scale and the duration of a diffusion process. We evaluate the proposed model on a real social media data set. Our model performs much better in both micro- and macro-level prediction than several alternative methods.

Introduction

Information diffusion, also known as *diffusion of innovations*, is the study of how information propagates in or between networks (Rogers 2010). Central to information diffusion is the *influence* of individual nodes (or users in online social networks). In representative information diffusion models, such as the Linear Threshold (LT) model (Granovetter 1978) and the Independent Cascade (IC) model (Goldenberg, Libai, and Muller 2001), every directed link from a user v to another user u in a given network is associated with a non-negative weight, to reflect how much influence user v has on user u in information diffusion.

In reality, the information diffusion process is complex, as is the influence of one user on another. How information may diffuse in a network is affected by the structure of the network, in which users' structural properties reflect their *social roles* in different communities (Wasserman and Faust 1994). Users' social roles in turn affect the influence they may have on other users, and hence the information diffusion process. Based on Twitter where a tweet corresponds to a piece of information and retweeting corresponds to information diffusion, a study reveals that 25% of information diffusion is controlled by 1% of users serving the role of *structural hole spanners*, who are bridges between otherwise disconnected communities in a network (Lou and Tang 2013). Another study shows that 50% of URLs on Twitter are posted by less than 1% of users who act as *opinion leaders*, who are people taking central positions in a community (Wu et al. 2011). Compared with posts originated from ordinary users, those from opinion leaders not only attracted much more retweets (larger diffusion scales), but also have longer lifespans (longer diffusion lengths). All these findings suggest that it is crucial to consider users' social roles in information diffusion modeling.

Social roles and diffusion are not independent of each other in nature. To further motivate our study on social role aware information diffusion, we present an exploratory analysis on a large social network with 200 million users and 174 million microblog messages. Each post (message) in this network is considered a piece of information, while reposting (or retweeting in Twitter) corresponds to the diffusion of information. We analyze how users taking three roles, namely opinion leaders, structural hole spanners and ordinary users, influence other users' probability of reposting a message.

Figure 1 provides the results. When an opinion leader reposts a message, the probability that her follower v will subsequently repost the message is 12 times higher than the case where the message is reposted by an ordinary user in the first place (corresponding to two-step flow theory (Lazarsfeld, Berelson, and Gaudet 1944)). More interestingly, if the number of reposting opinion leaders, all followed by v, reaches 3, the probability that v will subsequently repost decreases significantly, but keeps increasing after that. Regarding this finding, we conjecture that 2-3 opinion leaders are sufficient to spread a piece of information throughout a community, making their followers unwilling to repost a message that

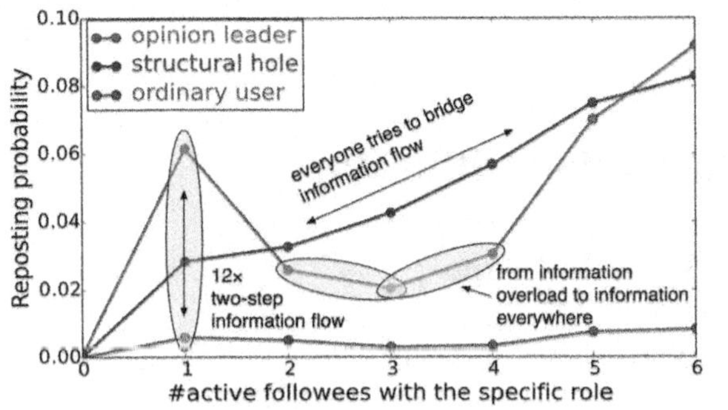

Figure 1: Diffusion influence analysis. We study how users with different roles affect other users' probability of reposting a certain message. In the figure, y-axis denotes the probability that a user v will repost a certain message. X-axis denotes the number of v's followees who reposted the message before v did.

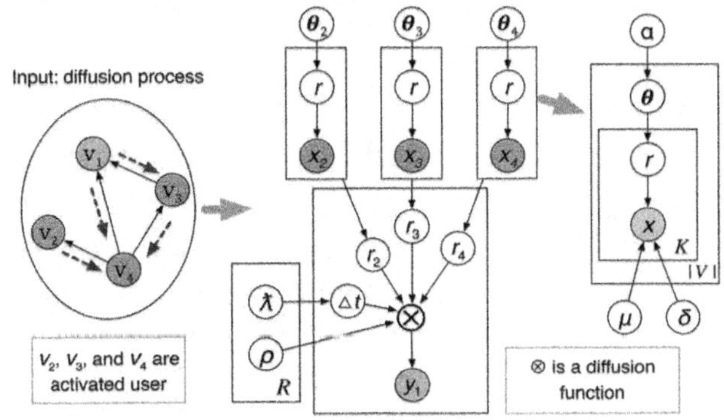

Figure 2: Illustration of RAIN. Notice that r_2 is the social role that v_2 plays when she tries to activate v_1; an r with no subscript indicates the role sampled for generating a user's social attributes.

most of her friends would have known already. However, when a message attracts the attention of more than 3 opinion leaders in a community, it may have become so influential and popular that reposting the message becomes a social norm that other users might want to adopt, which leads information overload to information everywhere. Results on structural hole spanners show a different story. The probability for v to repost a post keeps increasing with the number of her reposting followees who are structural hole spanners. As structural hole spanners are those who bridge different otherwise disconnected communities, they tend to bring information that a certain community is rarely exposed to, thus may be able to interest v more easily (Burt 2001). This result also suggests that most users tires to bridge information flow between different groups. To summarize, the probability that a user will repost a message depends strongly on the roles of her followees who reposted the message. It is therefore crucial to capture users' social roles when modeling the information diffusion process.

Intuitively, a user may play multiple roles with respect to different communities or social circles, thus exhibiting different influential strengths in different diffusion processes. For instance, one may act as an opinion leader when speaking on her area of expertise, and a structural hole spanner when forwarding a piece of news from her colleagues to her family members. How to effectively uncover the social roles users play in information diffusion processes remains an open problem. In this paper, we approach this problem through a *role-aware information diffusion model*. There are two intuitions behind our model. Firstly, a user may play multiple social roles in a network as noted. We therefore propose to learn a probability distribution over social roles for each user, allowing a user to play different roles in different diffusion processes. Secondly, as social roles and diffusion process are interrelated, we can exploit the observed diffusion in a network to help infer the unobserved roles of users and the influence of each role. As such, our model takes as input a social network and its information diffusion traces. It then jointly learns the social role distributions of users and the influence of each role by utilizing both users' structural properties and their behaviors as observed in the diffusion traces. We summarize our technical contributions as follows:

- We propose the problem of role-aware information diffusion modeling in online social networks.
- We formulate a generative model and devise a Gibbs sampler that integrates social roles learning and diffusion modeling into a unified probabilistic framework.
- Employing a large real-world network as experimental data, we conduct extensive experiments to validate the proposed model over several baselines.

Social Role-Aware Diffusion Model

Formulation

Let $G = (V, E, X)$ be a social network, where V is a set of users, $E \subseteq V \times V$ is a set of links between users, $e_{vu} \in E$, denotes a directed (follow) link from user v to u ($v, u \in V$), and X is a $|V| \times K$ social attribute matrix, with each row $\mathbf{x}_v = \{x_1, \ldots, x_K | x_i \in \mathbb{R}\}$ representing K *social attributes* of the user v. The K social attributes to use can be defined based on application-specific needs. Examples include PageRank score (Page et al. 1999), network constraint score (Burt 2009; Lou and Tang 2013), node degree, etc. For each node $v \in V$, we use $B(v) = \{u | u \in V, e_{vu} \in E\}$ to denote the set of followees of v.

Different pieces of messages will be propagated over G. When a user v posts or reposts a specific message i at time t, we say that the user v is activated with respect to i at t (and will stay active after t).

To model the intuition that a user may take different social roles in different diffusion processes, we associate each user with a *social role distribution*:

Definition 1. **Social Role Distribution.** The social role distribution of user $v \in V$ is denoted by θ_v, which is a R-dimensional vector and satisfies $\sum_r \theta_{vr} = 1$. θ_{vr} is the probability that v plays role r when diffusing a message.

Model Description

We propose a social Role-Aware INformation diffusion model (RAIN) for learning users' social roles and modeling information diffusion simultaneously. Figure 2 illus-

Table 1: Notations in the proposed model.

SYMBOL	DESCRIPTION
R	number of latent roles
K	total number of social attributes of users
T	the largest timestamp in the given diffusion trees
Δt	diffusion time delay
t_{iu}	the time when u becomes active to diffuse i
y_{itu}	a binary variable denoting whether user u is activated for message i at time t
r_u	a latent variable denoting the social role of user u
z_{iuv}^t	a latent variable indicating whether user u successfully activates user v to diffuse i at time t
θ_v	social role distribution of user v
ρ_r	Bernoulli distribution over z_{iuv} associated with r
λ_r	geometric distribution over Δt associated with r
μ_{rk}, δ_{rk}	mean and precision of the Gaussian distribution used to sample the k-th attribute of users with r

trates our model. RAIN determines social role distribution of each user according to both her structural attributes and her behavior in diffusion process. Inspired by the work in (Lou and Tang 2013), we consider three social roles in this paper, namely *opinion leaders*, *structural hole spanners*, and *ordinary users*. Existing work detects social roles of users only based on their social attributes. For example, Burt (Burt 2009) treats users with small network constraint scores as structural hole spanners, while users with high pagerank scores are often considered opinion leaders (Page et al. 1999). However, using these methods alone to identify the roles of users fall short in detecting the different roles that a certain user may take in different diffusion processes. In RAIN, the social role distribution of each user is determined not only by her social attributes but also by her information diffusion behaviors. Overall, our generative model contains two parts: users' social attributes generation and information diffusion process generation.

Generative process. We first introduce the diffusion process generation. Inspired by our exploratory analysis, which reveals that the social role of a user affects her influential strength and diffusion delay, we introduce per-role parameters ρ_r and λ_r as the probability that users playing role r will activate another user successfully and will cause a 1-timestamp diffusion delay respectively. We then use a diffusion function (e.g., a threshold function or a cascade function) parametrized by ρ_r and λ_r to determine whether a user will become active. In this paper, to make things concrete, we focus on the Independent Cascade model.

More specifically, we first generate the influential strength and diffusion delay with respect to each social role r: $\rho_r \sim \text{Beta}(\beta)$, $\lambda_r \sim \text{Beta}(\gamma)$. Consider message i which is first posted by user u at time t, u will have a chance to activate each inactive follower v: first, we sample the role r, which user u is playing when she tries to activate v: $r \sim \text{Mult}(\theta_u)$. Next, we generate a diffusion delay Δt according to the geometric distribution $P(\Delta t|\lambda_r)$. At time $t' = t + \Delta t + 1$, we toss a coin: $z_{iuv}^{t'} \sim \text{Bernoulli}(\rho_r)$, to determine whether u will succeed in activating v. At anytime, user v will become active if at least one of her followees activate her successfully. Notice that multiple activation attempts are sequenced in an arbitrary order. After v becomes active, she will then execute the diffusion process we just described to try to activate her inactive followers. The process terminates when no more activation is possible.

For the social attribute generation process, we assume that each attribute of a user v is sampled according to a Gaussian distribution. Users with the same social roles have similar social attributes and share the same Gaussian distribution. Thus, we first generate each user v's social role distribution: $\theta_v \sim \text{Dir}(\alpha)$. Then, for each role r, we generate K Gaussian parameters: $(\mu_{rk}, \delta_{rk}) \sim \text{NG}(\tau)$, for $k = 1, ..., K$. Next, for the k-th attribute of user v, we generate a latent variable: $r \sim \text{Mult}(\theta_v)$. Finally, we generate that attribute: $x_{vk} \sim \text{N}(\mu_{rk}, \delta_{rk}^{-1})$. Table 1 summarizes major notations used in RAIN.

Likelihood function. For each message i, we define A_{it} as the set of users who become active at time t, $D_{it} = A_{i0} \cup \cdots \cup A_{it}$ as the set of users who are active by time t, and the binary variable y_{itu} to denote whether user u is activated ($y_{itu} = 1$) or not ($y_{itu} = 0$) with respect to message i at time t. For user v, $\mathbf{z}_{i*v}^t = (z_{iuv}^t)_{u \in B(v) \cap D_{it-1}}$ is an indicator vector. $z_{iuv}^t = 1$ if user u succeeds in activating user v at time t to diffuse message i, and $z_{iuv}^t = 0$ if user u fails to activate v within time $[t_{iu}+1, t]$, where t_{iu} indicates the time u was activated to diffuse message i.

We consider the probability that user u will succeed in activating one of her followers v at time t ($z_{iuv}^t = 1$), by considering u's social role information:

$$\varphi_{iuv}^t = \sum_r \rho_r \lambda_r (1-\lambda_r)^{t-t_{iu}-1} \theta_{ur} \tag{1}$$

We define D_{it} as the set of users who are active by time t. If user v is not activated by user $u \in B(v) \cap D_{it-1}$ within the time period $[t_{iu}+1, t]$, then $z_{iuv}^t = 0$ with probability:

$$\varepsilon_{iuv}^t = \sum_r \theta_{ur} [\rho_r (1-\lambda_r)^{t-t_{iu}} + 1 - \rho_r] \tag{2}$$

Based on Eqs. (1) and (2), the probability that user v is active at time t can be expressed as:

$$P(v \in A_{it}) = \prod_{u \in B(v) \cap D_{it-1}} (\varphi_{iuv}^t + \varepsilon_{iuv}^t) - \prod_{u \in B(v) \cap D_{it-1}} \varepsilon_{iuv}^t \tag{3}$$

Further, the probability that user v is never activated by the last timestamp T can be written as:

$$P(v \notin D_{iT}) = \prod_{u \in B(v) \cap D_{iT}} \sum_r (1-\rho_r)\theta_{ur} \tag{4}$$

For the social attribute generation part, we have:

$$P(x_{uk}) = \sum_r \sqrt{\frac{\delta_{rk}}{2\pi}} \exp\{-\frac{\delta_{rk}(x_{uk}-\mu_{rk})^2}{2}\}\theta_{ur} \tag{5}$$

Based on Eqs. (3) to (5), we obtain the following likelihood function:

$$L = \prod_{i=1}^{I}\prod_{t=1}^{T}\prod_{v\in A_{it}} P(v\in A_{it}) \times \prod_{i=1}^{I}\prod_{v\notin D_{iT}} P(v\notin D_{iT})$$
$$\times \prod_{u\in V}\prod_{k=1}^{K} P(x_{uk}) \times \prod_{u\in V}\prod_{r=1}^{R} P(\theta_{ur}|\alpha) \quad (6)$$
$$\times \prod_{r=1}^{R}\{P(\rho_r|\beta)+P(\lambda_r|\gamma)\} \times \prod_{r=1}^{R}\prod_{k=1}^{K} P(\mu_{rk},\delta_{rk}|\tau)$$

Model learning

We employ Gibbs sampling (Resnik and Hardisty 2010), (Yang et al. 2014) to estimate the unknown parameters in the proposed model. Specifically, we begin with the posterior for sampling the latent variable r for each social attribute of a user u:

$$P(r_{uk}|\mathbf{r}_{\neg uk},\mathbf{x}) = \frac{n_{ur_{uk}}^{\neg uk}+\alpha}{\sum_r(n_{ur}^{\neg uk}+\alpha)} \frac{\Gamma(\tau_2+\frac{n_{r_{uk}k}}{2})}{\Gamma(\tau_2+\frac{n_{r_{uk}k}^{\neg uk}}{2})} \times \frac{\sqrt{(\tau_1+n_{r_{uk}k}^{\neg uk})}\eta(n_{r_{uk}k}^{\neg uk},\bar{x}_{r_{uk}k}^{\neg uk},s_{r_{uk}}^{\neg uk})}{\sqrt{(\tau_1+n_{r_{uk}k})}\eta(n_{r_{uk}k},\bar{x}_{r_{uk}k},s_{r_{uk}})} \quad (7)$$

where the counter n_{ur} (resp. n_{rk}) denotes the number of times r being sampled with (resp. the k-th social attribute of) user u; $\bar{x}_{rk}$ and s_{rk} are respectively the mean and variance of the k-th social attribute associated with role r; The superscript $\neg uk$ on the counters indicates exclusion of the current observation (resp. the k-th structural attribute of user u) from the counts. One challenge in Eq. (7) is the calculation of Gamma functions, which we approximated in this work using Stirling's formula (Abramowitz and Stegun 1970). The function $\eta(\cdot)$ is used to simplify the presentation of Eq. (7) and is defined as:

$$\eta(\cdot) = [\tau_3+\frac{1}{2}(n_{r_{uk}k}s_{r_{uk}k}+\frac{\tau_1 n_{r_{uk}k}(\bar{x}_{r_{uk}k}-\tau_0)^2}{\tau_1+n_{r_{uk}k}})]^{(\tau_2+\frac{n_{r_{uk}k}}{2})} \quad (8)$$

In Eqs. (7) and (8), τ is the parameter of normal-gamma prior. Similarly, we evaluate the posterior for sampling the latent variables $(\mathbf{t},\mathbf{r},\mathbf{z})$ for each diffusion process:

$$P(r_{iuv},\Delta t_{iuv},z_{iuv}|\mathbf{r}_{\neg iuv},\Delta\mathbf{t}_{\neg iuv},\mathbf{z}_{\neg iuv},\mathbf{y})$$
$$= \frac{n_{ur_{iuv}}^{\neg iuv}+\alpha}{\sum_r(n_{ur}^{\neg iuv}+\alpha)} \times \frac{n_{z_{iuv}r_{iuv}}^{\neg iuv}+\beta_1^{z_{iuv}}\beta_0^{1-z_{iuv}}}{n_{1r_{iuv}}^{\neg iuv}+\beta_1+n_{0r_{iuv}}^{\neg iuv}+\beta_0} \quad (9)$$
$$\times \frac{(n_{r_{iuv}}^{\neg iuv}+\gamma_1)\prod_{t=0}^{\Delta t-2}(s_{r_{iuv}}^{\neg iuv}-n_{r_{iuv}}^{\neg iuv}+\gamma_0+t)}{\prod_{t=0}^{\Delta t-1}(\gamma_1+s_{r_{iuv}}^{\neg iuv}+\gamma_0+t)} \times \Phi$$

where n_r (resp. n_{zr}) denotes the number of times r sampled (resp. with z); s_r denotes the sum of Δt that has been sampled with r. We use Φ to indicate $\frac{P(\mathbf{y}|\mathbf{z},\Delta\mathbf{t})}{P(\mathbf{y}_{\neg iuv}|\mathbf{z}_{\neg iuv},\Delta\mathbf{t}_{\neg iuv})}$ for brevity. Intuitively, Φ is used to handle contradictions arise during the sampling process. Please refer to more details about Φ and other implementation notes here[1].

We now estimate model parameters by the sampling results. The updating rules for θ, λ, and ρ can be deduced as:

$$\theta_{ur} = P(\tilde{r}=r|\mathbf{r},\Delta\mathbf{t},\mathbf{z},\mathbf{y}) = \frac{n_{ur}+\alpha}{\sum_r(n_{ur}+\alpha)}$$
$$\lambda_r = P(\Delta\tilde{t}=1|\tilde{r}=r,\mathbf{r},\Delta\mathbf{t},\mathbf{z},\mathbf{y}) = \frac{n_r+\gamma_1}{\gamma_1+s_r+\gamma_0} \quad (10)$$
$$\rho_r = P(\tilde{z}=1|\tilde{r}=r,\mathbf{r},\Delta\mathbf{t},\mathbf{z},\mathbf{y}) = \frac{n_{(z=1)r}+\beta_1}{n_{1r}+\beta_1+n_{0r}+\beta_0}$$

where $\tilde{r}$, $\Delta\tilde{t}$ and $\tilde{z}$ respectively represent a new observation of r, Δt and z. Note that the updating rules of both μ_{rk} and δ_{rk} involve an integration that is intractable. Hence, we approximate μ_{rk} and δ_{rk} as $E(\mu_{rk})$ and $E(\delta_{rk})$ respectively according to (Bernardo and Smith 2009):

$$\mu_{rk} \approx E(\mu_{rk}) = \frac{\tau_0\tau_1+n_{rk}\bar{x}_{rk}}{\tau_1+n_{rk}},$$
$$\delta_{rk} \approx E(\delta_{rk}) = \frac{2\tau_2+n_{rk}}{2\tau_3+n_{rk}s_{rk}+\frac{\tau_1 n_{rk}(\bar{x}_{rk}-\tau_0)^2}{\tau_1+n_{rk}}} \quad (11)$$

Experimental Results

All data and codes used here are publicly available[1].

Experimental Setup

Data set. We conduct experiments on real data from Tencent Weibo[2], a popular Twitter-like microblogging service in China. The complete data set contains the directed following networks and tweets (posting logs) of over 200 million users. If there exists a following link from a user v to another user u, we say that v is a follower of u, and that u is a followee of v. Similar to Twitter, there are two types of posts in Tencent Weibo, namely original posts (tweets) and reposts (or retweets). The reposting log of an original post essentially represents an information diffusion process. We extracted the complete following relationships between users and all posting logs of November 1st, 2011 as the training set, and those of November 2nd, 2011 as the test set to evaluate the proposed model. In total, we have 184,491 users, and 4,588,559 original posts. We removed from both the training and test sets original posts that were reposted by fewer than 5 users, and use the remaining 242,831 original posts for experiments.

We further categorize posts in our data set based on their topics, as existing work has discovered that information diffusion behavior of users is dependent on the topic of the information (Yang and Leskovec 2010). Specifically, we first use LDA (Blei, Ng, and Jordan 2003) to extract latent topics from all the posts in our data set, and assign each post to the topic to which it is most relevant. Due to the space limitation, we only present the results on the 4 most popular topics: campus, horoscope, movie, and history.

[1] http://arnetminer.org/rain/
[2] http://t.qq.com/

Tasks. We evaluate the proposed model, RAIN, based on the following two tasks. (1) At the **micro-level**, how accurate is RAIN in predicting whether a user will repost a given message? (2) At the **macro-level**, how well does RAIN predict the scale and duration of a diffusion process?

Micro-Level Evaluation

Evaluation setting. Given an original post (message) on a particular topic, we aim to identify users who will most likely repost this message. Specifically, for each original post in the test set, we rank all users according to their probability of reposting the given message as predicted by RAIN and several baseline methods (described below). Note that on average, each original message in our data set was only reposted by 0.008% of users. We consider the following baselines in our experiments:

Count. Given an original post i, this method ranks users, in descending order, by the number of followees who have reposted i. This method assumes that a user's reposting decision only depends on her followees' decisions.

SVM. This method predicts whether user v will repost message i based on three features: the number of v's followers who have reposted i, the number of v's followees who have reposted i, and the number of times v reposted a message posted by the author of i before. Similar features have been utilized in (Zhang et al. 2013). This method then trains a Ranking SVM (Joachims 2002; 2006) to predict v's probability of reposting i. For Ranking SVM, we use TreeRankSVM (Airola, Pahikkala, and Salakoski 2011) to handle our large-scale data.

IC Model. This method employs the traditional Independent Cascade (IC) model (Goldenberg, Libai, and Muller 2001; Kempe, Kleinberg, and Tardos 2003). We estimate the parameters of the IC model from the training set by the learning algorithm proposed in (Kimura et al. 2011).

RAIN. This is the proposed social role-aware diffusion model. For each message i, both this method and IC model use simulation to estimate the probability of a user being activated and rank all users by that. We empirically set the model parameters as: $R = 10$, $\alpha = 0.1$, $\beta = (1, 1)$, and $\gamma = (1, 1)$.

Performance comparison. Table 2 shows the performance of RAIN and baselines in the micro-level prediction task. Overall, all models perform unsatisfactorily, which is not surprising due to the small percentage of positive instances in the data set (around 0.008%). RAIN outperforms baselines by 32.6% in terms of MAP (mean average precision on all instances). Due to the lack of supervised information, Count performs worst on all topics. SVM generates mixed performance. It performs well on "local" topics (e.g., "horoscope", as people tend to be interested in posts about their own constellations), but falls short on more "global" topics (e.g., "movie"). This can be explained by the fact that SVM optimizes the reposting probability of each user independently by considering only her local diffusion features, while neglecting the overall mechanism behind the whole diffusion process. For IC, its performance is hindered by the over-fitting problem resulting from its large number of unknown parameters to learn. RAIN addresses such a problem by allowing users with the same social role to share the same diffusion patterns, thus greatly reduces the number of model parameters.

Table 2: Performance of repost prediction on several topics.

Topic	Method	P@10	P@50	P@100	MAP
Campus	Count	0.028	0.010	0.006	0.068
	SVM	0.098	0.045	0.032	0.127
	IC Model	**0.231**	0.142	0.102	0.259
	RAIN	0.228	**0.145**	**0.106**	**0.263**
Horoscope	Count	0.019	0.010	0.006	0.005
	SVM	0.124	**0.162**	0.088	**0.263**
	IC Model	0.149	0.111	0.098	0.125
	RAIN	**0.171**	0.121	**0.102**	0.130
Movie	Count	0.015	0.007	0.004	0.009
	SVM	0.094	0.111	0.060	0.199
	IC Model	0.227	0.147	**0.147**	0.236
	RAIN	**0.229**	**0.173**	0.144	**0.238**
History	Count	0.191	0.056	0.033	0.096
	SVM	0.154	0.051	0.030	0.221
	IC Model	0.206	0.134	**0.135**	0.230
	RAIN	**0.225**	**0.171**	0.134	**0.262**

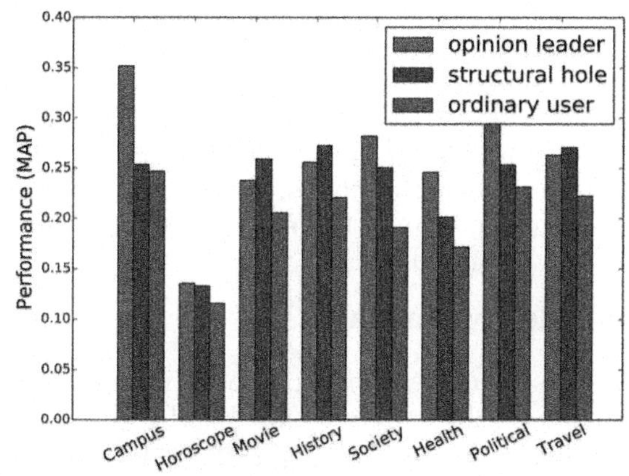

Figure 3: Social role analysis.

Social role analysis. We further study how social roles influence the diffusion process of messages with different topics. To conduct this experiment, we first analyze the estimated Gaussian parameters of the RAIN, which summarize the structural properties of users taking a certain role, to uncover the meaning of the latent roles learned by RAIN. For instance, a latent role with high PageRank score is considered to be representing the opinion leader role. Next, we group users into opinion leaders, structural hole spanners, and ordinary users. Finally, we use RAIN to perform per-group predictions and analyze the results. We present four more topics in this experiment: society, health, political, and travel. As Figure 3 shows, RAIN can better predict the diffusion behavior of opinion leaders and structural hole spanners, as ordinary users tend to behave more randomly. Fur-

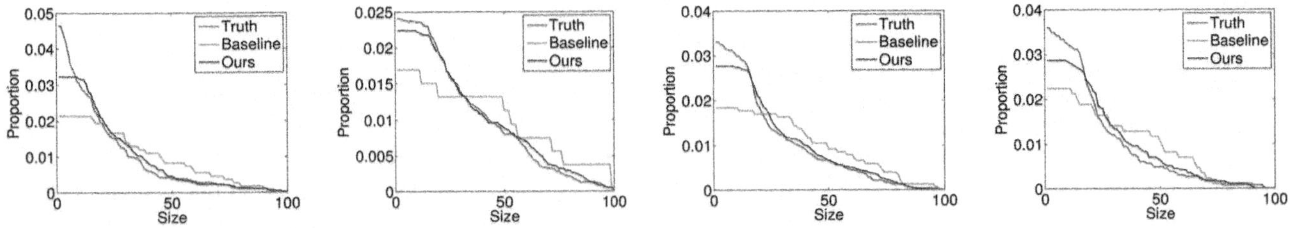

(a) Campus (b) Horoscope (c) Movie (d) History

Figure 4: Diffusion scale distributions of the different topics in the test set.

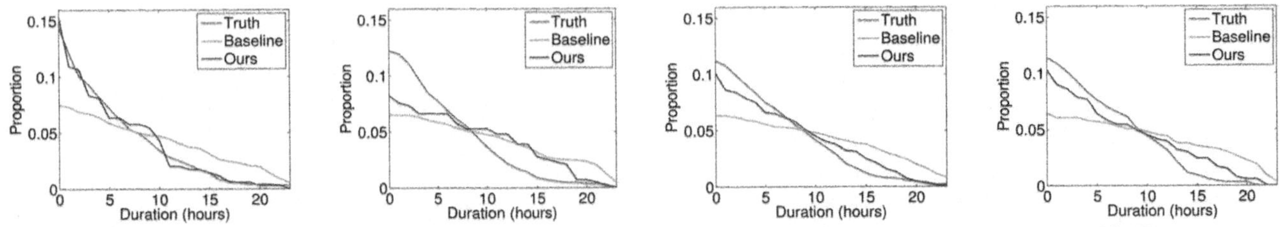

(a) Campus (b) Horoscope (c) Movie (d) History

Figure 5: Diffusion duration distributions of the different topics in the test set.

thermore, opinion leaders can be better predicted on more regional and specialized topics (e.g., "campus", "society" and "political"), while structural hole spanners can be better predicted on more general topics, which tend to propagate from one community to another more easily (e.g., "movie", "history", and "travel").

Macro-Level Evaluation

Evaluation setting. At the macro-level, we use the fitted model to predict the *scale* and *duration* of a diffusion process. Specifically, we first trace the diffusion process of each topic by selecting all original posts relevant to that topic. Then, we evaluate how accurate RAIN can predict for each topic its diffusion scale, defined as the number of reposts of the original posts under that topic, and the diffusion duration, defined as the last reposting time of these posts. We use the IC model as the baseline for comparison.

Scale and duration prediction. Figs. 4(a)-(d) show the diffusion scale prediction results for the 8 different topics. The x-axis in each sub-figure denotes the number of reposts, and the y-axis denotes the proportion of original posts with a particular number of reposts. Overall, RAIN performs better, while the baseline method tends to overestimate diffusion scale. Figs. 5(a)-(d) show the diffusion duration prediction results of the two models. The x-axis in each sub-figure denotes the time interval between the posting time of an original post and the latest repost time of it, while the y-axis shows the proportion of the original posts with a particular diffusion duration.

Related Work

Recent years have seen extensive modeling efforts on the information diffusion (Lerman and Ghosh 2010; Gomez Rodriguez, Leskovec, and Krause 2010; Leskovec et al. 2007; Sadikov et al. 2011), with the two types of fundamental models being Linear Threshold (LT) models (Granovetter 1978) and Independent Cascade (IC) models (Goldenberg, Libai, and Muller 2001). Both types of models assume that the tendency of an inactive user to become active increases monotonically with the number of her active neighbors. However, according to the experiments conducted in this paper, we show that the probability of a user become active is not a simple monotonic function of the number of her active neighbors, but is relevant to the social roles of her followees.

Social influence and conformity is another related topic. Barbieri et al. (2013) studied social influence from a topic modeling perspective. Myers et al. (2012) considered external influence in information diffusion. In their model, information can be diffused to a node through links in the given network or through influence of external sources. Tang et al. (2009) studied the problem of learning influence probabilities between users in social networks. Tang et al. (2013) further investigate how conformity influence users' behaviors and Zhang et al. (2014) extended the problem with awareness of social roles. Rodriguez et al. (2013) applied the survival theory to generalize some existing diffusion models into a multiplicative model. In contrast to our work, these studies focus only on the diffusion process without considering how different types of users may influence such process.

Conclusion

In this paper, we study a novel problem of social role-aware information diffusion, with an emphasis on understanding the interplay between users' social roles and their influence on information diffusion. We propose a social role-aware information diffusion (RAIN) model, which integrates social role extraction and diffusion modeling into a unified framework. We evaluate the proposed model on a real social media data set at both micro- and macro-levels. Compared with several alternative methods, our model shows better performance.

Acknowledgements

Yang Yang and Jie Tang are supported by National 863 project (No. 2014AA015103), National 973 projects (No. 2014CB340506, No. 2012CB316006, No. 2011CB302302), NSFC (No. 61222212), and a research fund from Huawei Inc. Qiang Yang and Cane Leung have been supported in part by National 973 project 2014CB340304 and Hong Kong RGC Projects 621013, 620812, and 621211. Yizhou Sun is supported by Yahoo! ACE Award and NEU TIER 1 Grant.

References

Abramowitz, M., and Stegun, I. 1970. *Handbook of mathematical functions*. Dover Publishing Inc. New York.

Airola, A.; Pahikkala, T.; and Salakoski, T. 2011. An improved training algorithm for the linear ranking support vector machine. In *ICANN 2011*, 134–141.

Barbieri, N.; Bonchi, F.; and Manco, G. 2013. Topic-aware social influence propagation models. *Knowledge and information systems* 37(3):555–584.

Bernardo, J. M., and Smith, A. F. 2009. *Bayesian theory*, volume 405. Wiley. com.

Blei, D. M.; Ng, A. Y.; and Jordan, M. I. 2003. Latent dirichlet allocation. *JMLR* 3:993–1022.

Burt, R. S. 2001. Structural holes versus network closure as social capital. *Social capital: Theory and research* 31–56.

Burt, R. S. 2009. *Structural holes: The social structure of competition*. Harvard University Press.

Goldenberg, J.; Libai, B.; and Muller, E. 2001. Talk of the network: A complex systems look at the underlying process of word-of-mouth. *Marketing letters* 12(3):211–223.

Gomez Rodriguez, M.; Leskovec, J.; and Krause, A. 2010. Inferring networks of diffusion and influence. In *KDD'10*, 1019–1028.

Granovetter, M. 1978. Threshold models of collective behavior. *American journal of sociology* 83(6):1420.

Joachims, T. 2002. Optimizing search engines using clickthrough data. In *KDD'02*, 133–142.

Joachims, T. 2006. Training linear svms in linear time. In *KDD'06*, 217–226.

Kempe, D.; Kleinberg, J.; and Tardos, É. 2003. Maximizing the spread of influence through a social network. In *KDD'03*, 137–146.

Kimura, M.; Saito, K.; Ohara, K.; and Motoda, H. 2011. Learning information diffusion model in a social network for predicting influence of nodes. *Intelligent Data Analysis* 15(4):633–652.

Lazarsfeld, P. F.; Berelson, B.; and Gaudet, H. 1944. The peoples choice: How the voter makes up his mind in a presidential election. *New York: Duell, Sloan and Pearce*.

Lerman, K., and Ghosh, R. 2010. Information contagion: An empirical study of the spread of news on digg and twitter social networks. In *ICWSM'10*, 90–97.

Leskovec, J.; McGlohon, M.; Faloutsos, C.; Glance, N. S.; and Hurst, M. 2007. Patterns of cascading behavior in large blog graphs. In *SDM'07*, 551–556.

Lou, T., and Tang, J. 2013. Mining structural hole spanners through information diffusion in social networks. In *WWW'13*, 825–836.

Myers, S. A.; Zhu, C.; and Leskovec, J. 2012. Information diffusion and external influence in networks. In *KDD'12*, 33–41.

Page, L.; Brin, S.; Motwani, R.; and Winograd, T. 1999. The pagerank citation ranking: Bringing order to the web. Technical Report SIDL-WP-1999-0120, Stanford University.

Resnik, P., and Hardisty, E. 2010. Gibbs sampling for the uninitiated. Technical report, DTIC Document.

Rodriguez, M. G.; Leskovec, J.; and Schölkopf, B. 2013. Modeling information propagation with survival theory. *ICML'13* 666–674.

Rogers, E. M. 2010. *Diffusion of innovations*. Simon and Schuster.

Sadikov, E.; Medina, M.; Leskovec, J.; and Garcia-Molina, H. 2011. Correcting for missing data in information cascades. In *WSDM'11*, 55–64.

Tang, J.; Sun, J.; Wang, C.; and Yang, Z. 2009. Social influence analysis in large-scale networks. In *KDD'09*, 807–816.

Tang, J.; Wu, S.; and Sun, J. 2013. Confluence: Conformity influence in large social networks. In *KDD'13*, 347–355.

Wasserman, S., and Faust, K. 1994. *Social Network Analysis: Methods and Applications*. Cambridge University Press. chapter 9.

Wu, S.; Hofman, J. M.; Mason, W. A.; and Watts, D. J. 2011. Who says what to whom on twitter. In *WWW'11*, 705–714.

Yang, J., and Leskovec, J. 2010. Modeling information diffusion in implicit networks. In *ICDM'10*, 599–608.

Yang, Y.; Jia, J.; Zhang, S.; Wu, B.; Li, J.; and Tang, J. 2014. How do your friends on social media disclose your emotions? In *AAAI'14*, 1–7.

Zhang, J.; Liu, B.; Tang, J.; Chen, T.; and Li, J. 2013. Social influence locality for modeling retweeting behaviors. In *AAAI'13*, 2761–2767.

Zhang, J.; Tang, J.; Zhuang, H.; Leung, C. W.-K.; and Li, J. 2014. Role-aware conformity influence modeling and analysis in social networks. In *AAAI'14*, 958–965.

Proceedings of the Twenty-Ninth AAAI Conference on Artificial Intelligence

Collaborative Topic Ranking: Leveraging Item Meta-Data for Sparsity Reduction

Weilong Yao* [1,3], Jing He[2], Hua Wang[2], Yanchun Zhang[2,3], Jie Cao[4]
[1]University of Chinese Academy of Sciences, Beijing, China
[2]Centre for Applied Informatics, College of Engineering & Science, Victoria University, Australia
[3]Fudan University, Shanghai, China
[4] Nanjing University of Finance and Economics, Nanjing, China
yaoweilong12@mails.ucas.ac.cn
{Jing.He,Hua.Wang,Yanchun.Zhang}@vu.edu.au, tcaojie690929@163.com

Abstract

Pair-wise ranking methods have been widely used in recommender systems to deal with implicit feedback. They attempt to discriminate between a handful of observed items and the large set of unobserved items. In these approaches, however, user preferences and item characteristics cannot be estimated reliably due to overfitting given highly sparse data. To alleviate this problem, in this paper, we propose a novel hierarchical Bayesian framework which incorporates "bag-of-words" type meta-data on items into pair-wise ranking models for one-class collaborative filtering. The main idea of our method lies in extending the pair-wise ranking with a probabilistic topic modeling. Instead of regularizing item factors through a zero-mean Gaussian prior, our method introduces item-specific topic proportions as priors for item factors. As a by-product, interpretable latent factors for users and items may help explain recommendations in some applications. We conduct an experimental study on a real and publicly available dataset, and the results show that our algorithm is effective in providing accurate recommendation and interpreting user factors and item factors.

Introduction

Recommender systems, as a subclass of information filtering systems, attempt to model user preferences by analysing user feedback. Explicit user feedback, e.g., numeric rating has been well studied in the literature (Koren 2008; Rendle 2010). In most applications, however, the collected data of user behaviors, e.g., assigning tags (Pan and Chen 2013b), purchasing products (Rendle et al. 2009) and watching videos (Rendle and Freudenthaler 2014), are usually implicit. Collaborative Filtering (CF) with implicit feedback is referred as One-Class Collaborative Filtering (OCCF) (Pan et al. 2008).

Existing approaches to OCCF can be classified into two categories: (1) point-wise preferences methods and (2) pair-wise preferences methods. The main idea of these methods is to learn user factors and item factors for modeling user preferences and item characteristics, respectively. Point-wise methods assume that observed feedback denotes "like" and unobserved feedback denotes "dislike", and propose to train a recommendation model by approximating the absolute rating scores (Hu, Koren, and Volinsky 2008; Wang and Blei 2011), while pair-wise methods assume that a user prefers an observed item to an unobserved item, and convert the problem to a pair-wise ranking problem (Rendle et al. 2009; Takács and Tikk 2012). Empirically, the latter assumption of pair-wise preferences over two items yields better recommendation accuracy than the point-wise assumption (Lee et al. 2014).

However, the data sparsity problem has become a major bottleneck for pair-wise ranking methods. In real world scenarios, a user typically interacts with a limited number of items out of possibly thousands or millions of items, which leads to extremely sparse user implicit feedback. These latent factors based methods are too flexible and are very likely to suffer from overfitting given sparse data, even for small dimensionality of latent factors. That is, the amount of information for learning user factors and item factors is far from enough.

In many practical situations, though, we have more information than the simple implicit feedback. Typically the item in a recommender system is equipped with "bag-of-words" type meta-data. Please note that "word" in this context is a general term used to denote elements like *phrases*, *tags* and *movie actors* in the applications of article recommendation, tag-based picture recommendation, and movie recommendation, respectively. The meta-data is highly informative in terms of identifying item characteristics to differentiate the item from others. This is especially crucial for addressing the OCCF problem, as we are mostly interested in distinguishing those items which are of potential interest to users from others. For example, given a user who likes "machine learning" articles and two articles j_1 and j_2, we would recommend him/her the article j_1 rather than j_2 if we have the prior knowledge that j_1 is about "machine learning" while j_2 is not. Thus, it is natural to consider item meta-data for alleviating data sparsity. Nevertheless, existing pair-wise ranking approaches fail to provide a natural way to consider such

*This work was done when the first author was visiting Victoria University, Australia.

meta-data available as free-form text.

In this paper, we propose a novel hierarchical Bayesian framework, called Collaborative Topic Ranking (CTRank), which incorporates meta-data on items and implicit feedback simultaneously for collaborative filtering with highly sparse implicit feedback. By extending pair-wise ranking models with probabilistic topic models, CTRank can utilize item meta-data to tackle the data sparsity problem and further to enhance recommendation accuracy. In CTRank, topic models serve to identify topic proportions from item meta-data, while pair-wise ranking models are to fit a ranked list of items.

We also note that, by discovering the latent topics behind both users and items, CTRank can reveal how an item relates to a user's preferences. The topic representation provides interpretability and may help in explaining recommendations to users. Specifically, the entities of user factors reveal his/her preferences towards the specific topics, while the entities of item factors represent its affinity to the topics. With topics serving as a bridge between users and items, there could be many ways to construct effective explanations for recommendations, e.g., word clouds (Vig, Sen, and Riedl 2009).

To summarize, the contributions of this paper are as follows: (1) We propose a hierarchical Bayesian framework, CTRank, which leverages item meta-data to remedy the data sparsity for OCCF problem by bridging the gap between pair-wise ranking and probabilistic topic modeling. Further, in the proposed framework, two alternative models are developed based on different assumptions. (2) We develop an efficient EM-style algorithm to learn the parameters in CTRank. (3) We conduct an experimental study on a large and real-world dataset. The results empirically show that CTRank outperforms other recommendation methods, in terms of prediction accuracy. Our method is also able to interpret user factors and item factors.

Preliminaries

We start with formulating the problem discussed in this paper, and then review some related works on point-/pair-wise methods for OCCF, Latent Dirichlet Allocation (LDA) (Blei, Ng, and Jordan 2003) and sparsity reduction.

Problem Definition Let $\mathcal{U}$ and $\mathcal{I}$ denote sets of users and items, respectively. The set of observed implicit feedback $\mathcal{R}^+ = \{(i,j) : r_{ij} = 1, i \in \mathcal{U}, j \in \mathcal{I}\}$ from n users and m items is available, where r_{ij} denotes the preferences from user i for item j. The item meta-data $\mathbf{w}_j$ is in the form of "bag-of-words" representation. Needless to say, this is pervasive in web applications.

Let $u_i, v_j \in \mathbb{R}^K$ be user i's factor vector and item j's factor vector respectively, where K is the dimensionality of latent space. We also have the corresponding representation in matrix form, i.e.,$\mathbf{U} = u_{1:n}$ and $\mathbf{V} = v_{1:m}$. The goal is to learn user factors $\mathbf{U}$ and item factors $\mathbf{V}$ from implicit feedback and to generate a personalized ranked list of items for each user i.

Point-wise Ranking for OCCF Point-wise approaches (Hu, Koren, and Volinsky 2008; Pan et al. 2008; Wang and Blei 2011) assume unobserved feedback as a rating 0 and learn latent factors by solving the following regression problem:

$$r_{ij} = 1, r_{ik} = 0, j \in \mathcal{I}_i^+, k \in \mathcal{I} \backslash \mathcal{I}_i^+, \quad (1)$$

where $\mathcal{I}_i^+ = \{j : (i,j) \in \mathcal{R}^+\}$.

Pair-wise Ranking for OCCF Pair-wise ranking approaches capture the pair-wise preferences over two items. Specifically, it is assumed that item j is preferred over item k for a given user i, if and only if j but not k is observed:

$$r_{ij} \succ r_{ik}, j \in \mathcal{I}_i^+, k \in \mathcal{I} \backslash \mathcal{I}_i^+ \quad (2)$$

where $\succ$ denotes a total order regarding user preferences. Our model falls into this category.

The foremost of pair-wise ranking models is Bayesian Personalized Ranking (BPR) (Rendle et al. 2009) which maximizes the likelihood of pair-wise preferences over observed items and unobserved items. More works that extend BPR are detailed in (Krohn-Grimberghe et al. 2012; Pan and Chen 2013a; 2013b). Given sparse data, such latent factor models are too flexible and would overfit if they are not regularized appropriately. Also, all of the above pair-wise methods ignore additional item meta-data while generating recommendations.

Based on pair-wise learning to rank techniques (Liu 2009), several approaches have been proposed to consider additional textual information in some applications (Chen et al. 2012; Qiang, Liang, and Yang 2013). However, directly adopting these ranking approaches is not suitable for OCCF due to that they only learn a single ranking function, i.e., they are non-personalized. The other key difference between those works and ours is how to use textual information. Specifically, previous models utilize textual information to manually craft application-oriented features while we focus on leveraging meta-data, e.g., textual information, for the purpose of automatic feature learning.

LDA for CF In this work, we use LDA (Blei, Ng, and Jordan 2003) to discover topics from meta-data available as free form text. For LDA and Matrix Factorization (MF) techniques, both of which are methods to reduce original data into latent space, it is natural to combine them together. Typical works include (Agarwal and Chen 2010; Shan and Banerjee 2010; Wang and Blei 2011; McAuley and Leskovec 2013). With point-wise preference assumption, these methods focus on squared error minimization and are suitable for rating prediction. However, it is the relevancy of the top items on the list that is crucial to the success of recommender systems, which just has been ignored by point-wise approaches. To overcome this limitation, we propose to directly approximate the order of items. In the experimental study, we use CTR (Wang and Blei 2011) as our major comparison method.

Sparsity Reduction for CF Recently, several research works have been conducted on sparsity reduction. In (Li, Yang, and Xue 2009; Pan et al. 2010), transfer learning techniques are used to transfer knowledge from auxiliary domain to the target domain for sparsity reduction while in practice an auxiliary domain is difficult to identify. Our work

Table 1: Some notations used in this paper.

Notation	Description
K	the number of topics
α	Dirichlet prior
I_K	K-dimensional identity matrix
w_{jt}	the t-th word in item j
$\mathbf{w}_j$	item j's word vector (meta-data)
$\mathbf{W} = \mathbf{w}_{1:m}$	item-word matrix
z_{jt}	the topic assigned to word w_{jt}
θ_j	item j's topic proportions
β_k	topic k's distribution over words
δ_{ijk}	response variable
$\boldsymbol{\delta} = (\delta_{ijk})_{i=1,j=1,k=1}^{n \times m \times m}$	response variable matrix
$\mathcal{P}_i = \{(j,k) : r_{ij} \succ r_{ik}\}$	user i's pair-wise preferences
T_j	number of words in item j
λ_u, λ_v	precision parameter
c_{ijk}	confidence parameter

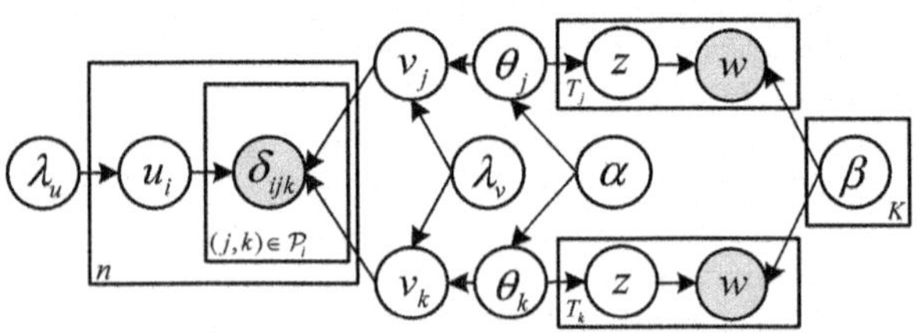

Figure 1: The CTRank model in plate notation.

is also related to hybrid recommendation approaches which combines content-based models with CF models in different ways (Kim et al. 2006; Gunawardana and Meek 2009; Tang and Zhou 2013). However, these methods are devised for explicit feedback while we focus on implicit feedback.

Collaborative Topic Ranking

In this section, we present the proposed model, CTRank, which integrates pair-wise ranking models with LDA into a unified generative model for collaborative filtering with highly sparse implicit feedback.

Model Description

Overview Fig. 1 shows the graphical representation of CTRank, with the notations described in Table 1. The basic idea here is to use two correlated generative processes to model item meta-data and pair-wise preferences together. The first process is to model words associated with items and to specify the relationship between item factors and item topic proportions. Consequently, meta-data is introduced into our generative model. Specifically, we follow the same process as in LDA to generate words (meta-data), and we regularize item factors v_j through the item's topic proportions θ_j. This is a key difference between CTRank and existing pair-wise models that attach latent factors with zero-mean Gaussian priors to each item. The second process models the interaction among user i, observed item j and unobserved item k. In particular, δ_{ijk} is observed response variable which denotes the response from user i for item j over k. With different assumptions on δ_{ijk}, we develop two alternative models for capturing the relative order of pair-wise items.

Bernoulli Assumption First, a natural choice is to directly model the order of the pair-wise items. Specifically, we assume δ_{ijk} follows Bernoulli distribution, then the generative process of CTRank is as follows:

1. For each item j,
   (a) Draw topic proportions $\theta_j \sim$ Dirichlet(α).
   (b) Draw item factor vector $v_j \sim \mathcal{N}(\theta_j, \lambda_v^{-1} I_K)$.
   (c) For each word w_{jt} in $\mathbf{w}_j$,
      i. Draw a topic $z_{jt} \sim$ Mult(θ_j).
      ii. Draw word $w_{jt} \sim$ Mult($\beta_{z_{jt}}$).
2. For each user i,
   (a) Draw user factor vector $u_i \sim \mathcal{N}(0, \lambda_u^{-1} I_K)$.
   (b) For each pair-wise preferences $(j,k) \in \mathcal{P}_i$, draw the response variable $\delta_{ijk} = 1 \sim$ Bernoulli($\rho_{ijk}^{c_{ijk}}$),

where ρ_{ijk} is the individual probability that user i really prefers item j over k, and is given by:

$$\begin{aligned} \rho_{ijk} &= P(r_{ij} \succ r_{ik} | u_i, v_j, v_k, ...) \\ &= P(\delta_{ijk} = 1 | u_i, v_j, v_k, ...) \\ &= \left(1 + exp^{-(u_i^{\mathrm{T}} v_j - u_i^{\mathrm{T}} v_k)}\right)^{-1}. \end{aligned} \tag{3}$$

c_{ijk} is the confidence parameter for user i's preferences for item j over k. For simplicy, we set $c_{ijk} = 1$ in our experiments. For $(j,k) \in \mathcal{P}_i$, j is an observed item and k is an unobserved item which is sampled from user i's unobserved items using bootstrap sampling (Rendle et al. 2009).

Based on the generative process above, we have the following conditional probability: $P(\boldsymbol{\delta}|\mathbf{U},\mathbf{V}) = \prod_{i=1}^{n} \prod_{(j,k)\in\mathcal{P}_i} P(\delta_{ijk} = 1|\mathbf{U},\mathbf{V})^{c_{ijk}}$. User factor matrix and item factor matrix are given by $P(\mathbf{U}|\lambda_u) = \prod_{i=1}^{n} \mathcal{N}(u_i|0, \lambda_u^{-1} I_k)$ and $P(\mathbf{V}|\theta,\lambda_v) = \prod_{j=1}^{m} \mathcal{N}(v_i|\theta_j, \lambda_v^{-1} I_k)$, respectively. As in LDA (Blei, Ng, and Jordan 2003), the likelihood of the meta-data under the topic model is a product of likelihood of each $\mathbf{w}_j$, $P(\mathbf{W},\theta|\alpha,\beta) = \prod_{j=1}^{m} \prod_{t=1}^{T_j} \sum_{k=1}^{K} \theta_{jk}\beta_{k,w_{jt}}$. Here we fix the hyperparameter $\alpha = 1$ to keep the computation simple.

Parameters can be learned by using the maximum a posteriori probability (MAP) estimator. Through Bayesian inference, we have the following posteriori probability of $\mathbf{U}$, $\mathbf{V}$ and θ given the model parameters:

$$\begin{aligned} &P(\mathbf{U},\mathbf{V},\theta|\boldsymbol{\delta},\mathbf{W},\beta,\alpha,\lambda_u,\lambda_v) \propto \\ &P(\mathbf{U}|\lambda_u)P(\mathbf{V}|\theta,\lambda_v)P(\boldsymbol{\delta}|\mathbf{U},\mathbf{V})P(\mathbf{W},\theta|\alpha,\beta). \end{aligned} \tag{4}$$

That is, in our model, it is equivalent to maximize the following log-likelihood:

$$\begin{aligned} \mathcal{L}_1 = &- \sum_{ijk} c_{ijk} \log\left(1 + exp^{-(u_i^{\mathrm{T}} v_j - u_i^{\mathrm{T}} v_k)}\right) - \frac{\lambda_u}{2} \sum_i u_i^{\mathrm{T}} u_i \\ &- \frac{\lambda_v}{2} \sum_j (v_j - \theta_j)^{\mathrm{T}} (v_j - \theta_j) + \sum_{jt} \log\left(\sum_k \theta_{jk}\beta_{k,w_{jt}}\right) \\ &+ \mathcal{C}, \end{aligned} \tag{5}$$

where $\mathcal{C}$ is a constant and can be omitted.

Gaussian Assumption Unlike in the first model, we use δ_{ijk} to model the preference difference between a pair of items, i.e., $\delta_{ijk} = r_{ij} - r_{ik}$: when $\delta_{ijk} > 0$, item j ranks higher than k, otherwise lower. Specifically, we draw the response variable as follows:

$$\delta_{ijk} \sim \mathcal{N}(u_i^{\mathrm{T}} v_j - u_i^{\mathrm{T}} v_k, c_{ijk}^{-1}). \tag{6}$$

The complete log-likelihood is denoted as $\mathcal{L}_2$:

$$\mathcal{L}_2 = -\sum_{ijk} \frac{c_{ijk}}{2}(\delta_{ijk} - (u_i^{\mathrm{T}} v_j - u_i^{\mathrm{T}} v_k))^2 - \frac{\lambda_u}{2}\sum_i u_i^{\mathrm{T}} u_i - \frac{\lambda_v}{2}\sum_j (v_j - \theta_j)^{\mathrm{T}}(v_j - \theta_j) + \sum_{jt} \log (\sum_k \theta_{jk}\beta_{k,w_{jt}}) \tag{7}$$

Discussion By defining $\Delta_{ijk} = u_i^{\mathrm{T}} v_j - u_i^{\mathrm{T}} v_k$ as predicted preference difference, we derive a general framework by rewriting $\mathcal{L}_1$ and $\mathcal{L}_2$ as follows:

$$\mathcal{L} = -\sum_{ijk} c_{ijk}\ell(\delta_{ijk}, \Delta_{ijk}) - \frac{\lambda_u}{2}\sum_i u_i^{\mathrm{T}} u_i - \frac{\lambda_v}{2}\sum_j (v_j - \theta_j)^{\mathrm{T}}(v_j - \theta_j) + \sum_{jt} \log (\sum_k \theta_{jk}\beta_{k,w_{jt}}), \tag{8}$$

where $\ell(\delta_{ijk}, \Delta_{ijk})$ is pair-wise loss function, such as log-loss in $\mathcal{L}_1$, and squared loss in $\mathcal{L}_2$. With this framework, more pair-wise loss functions can be adapted for collaborative topic ranking, such as hinge loss (Joachims 2002) and exponential loss (Freund et al. 2003). From this point of view, we refer the first model as CTRank-log and the second model CTRank-squared.

As Eq. 8 shows, the framework CTRank mainly consists of two key components: a ranking modeling component and a meta-data modeling component, between which a topic regularization term $\sum_j (v_j - \theta_j)^{\mathrm{T}}(v_j - \theta_j)$ serves as a bridge. In CTRank, topic proportions guide the learning of latent factors for ranking while the latent factors further improve the meta-data modeling. As with previous pair-wise ranking approaches, the ranking component is too flexible and needs to be regularized appropriately. In our model, topic proportions θ_j are used as priors to specific constraints on item factors v_j, reducing the effective degrees of freedom and yielding good performance. The parameter λ_v controls the extent of topic regularization, and thus plays a vital role in our model. In the extreme case, if we use a very small value of λ_v, we almost lose the effect from topic information, then CTRank reduces to a general pair-wise ranking approach. On the other side, if we employ a very large value of λ_v, topic proportions θ_j will dominate the learning process, and then CTRank benefits little from the ranking component.

Taking a deep insight into Eq. 8, we find that maximizing $-\sum_j (v_j - \theta_j)^{\mathrm{T}}(v_j - \theta_j)$ will make v_j close to its topic proportions parameter θ_j. If items j and k are similar in terms of topic distributions, we are actually minimizing the distance between item factors v_j and v_k. That is, knowledge can be transferred from items with sufficient feedback to items with little feedback. Consequently, we can still learn an accurate representation for items even though the data is extremely sparse.

Parameter Learning

Since the two proposed models can be optimized in a similar way, we only demonstrate how parameters of CTRank-squared are learned in this subsection. We optimize the objective function $\mathcal{L}_2$ using coordinate ascent which alternatively optimizes latent factor variables u_i, v_j and topic proportions θ_j.

We first fix θ_j and update u_i, v_j and v_k using the following stochastic Newton-Raphson rules:

$$u_i = u_i - \eta \frac{\lambda_u u_i - c_{ijk}\mathcal{E}_{ijk}(v_j - v_k)}{\lambda_u + c_{ijk}(v_j - v_k)^{\mathrm{T}}(v_j - v_k)}, \tag{9}$$

$$v_j = v_j - \eta \frac{\lambda_v (v_j - \theta_j) - c_{ijk}\mathcal{E}_{ijk} u_i}{\lambda_v + c_{ijk} u_i^{\mathrm{T}} u_i}, \tag{10}$$

$$v_k = v_k - \eta \frac{\lambda_v (v_k - \theta_k) + c_{ijk}\mathcal{E}_{ijk} u_i}{\lambda_v + c_{ijk} u_i^{\mathrm{T}} u_i}, \tag{11}$$

where η is learning rate, and $\mathcal{E}_{ijk} = \delta_{ijk} - (u_i^{\mathrm{T}} v_j - u_i^{\mathrm{T}} v_k)$.

Given updated $\mathbf{U}$ and $\mathbf{V}$, we now optimize topic proportions θ_j. We define $q(z_{jt} = k) = \phi_{jtk}$, where $\phi_j = (\phi_{jtk})_{t=1,k=1}^{T \times K}$. We then separate the terms that contain θ_j and apply Jensen's inequality to obtain a tight lower bound of $\mathcal{L}_2(\theta_j)$:

$$\mathcal{L}_2(\theta_j) \geq \sum_t \sum_k \phi_{jit}(\log \theta_{jk}\beta_{k,w_{jt}} - \log \phi_{jtk}) - \frac{\lambda_v}{2}(v_j - \theta_j)^{\mathrm{T}}(v_j - \theta_j) = \mathcal{L}_2(\theta_j, \phi_j). \tag{12}$$

The optimal ϕ_{jtk} satisfies $\phi_{jtk} \propto \theta_{jk}\beta_{k,w_{jt}}$. Thus, projection gradient (Bertsekas 1999) can be applied to update θ_j.

For the parameter β, we follow the same M-step update as in LDA (Blei, Ng, and Jordan 2003), i.e.,

$$\beta_{kt'} \propto \sum_j \sum_t \phi_{jtk} \mathbb{1}(w_{jt} = t'), \tag{13}$$

where $\mathbb{1}(x)$ is an indicator function that is equal to 1, if x is true, otherwise 0.

In practice, we iteratively update the parameters until the likelihood does not increase (by 0.01%) or the maximum iteration limit, say 100, is reached.

Top-N Recommendation

After we learn the optimal parameters $\mathbf{U}$, $\mathbf{V}$, and θ, we predict r_{ij} from its expectation, based on which a ranked list of N items is generated, as follows:

$$\mathbb{E}(r_{ij}|u_i, v_j, \theta, ...) = u_i^{\mathrm{T}} v_j. \tag{14}$$

Complexity Analysis

The complexity for updating $\mathbf{U}$ and $\mathbf{V}$ is in the order of $O(n\bar{n}K)$, where $\bar{n}$ is the average number of items a user likes. Optimizing θ requires time $O(m(\bar{T}K + \tilde{i}K))$, where $\bar{T}$ is the average number of words in an item and $\tilde{i}$ is the number of iterations for projection gradient algorithm. The final complexity for one full iteration of CTRank is $O(n\bar{n}K + m(\bar{T}K + \tilde{i}K))$ which is much lower than that of CTR, our major counterpart, $O(2n\bar{n}K^2 + (n+m)K^3 + m(\bar{T}K + \tilde{i}K))$.

Experiments

Experiment Settings

Dataset CiteULike[1] is an academic social network, which allows users to create individual reference libraries for the articles they like. In this work, we use a large dataset collected by Wang (Wang and Blei 2011) from CiteULike.

Articles in a user's reference library are considered as observed items. In this dataset, 5551 users expressed 204,986 observed ratings for 16,980 items (articles) with a high sparseness of 99.78%. On average, each user has 37 articles in the library, ranging from 1 to 321, and each article appears in 12 users' libraries, ranging from 1 to 321. By randomly removing observed feedback, we obtain 4 datasets with different sparsity levels of 99.80%, 99.85%, 99.90% and 99.95% correspondingly. For each article, its title and abstract are abstracted to form the bag-of-word representation of metedata. Removing stop words and choosing top words based on tf-idf (Manning, Raghavan, and Schütze 2008) construct a corpus with 1.6M terms from a vocabulary of size 8000.

Evaluation Following one-class CF literature (Rendle et al. 2009; Hariri, Mobasher, and Burke 2012; Paquet and Koenigstein 2013), we adopt the popular 10-fold leave-one-out cross validation to evaluate the performance of recommendation models. That is, we randomly remove one example from CiteULike dataset $\mathcal{R}^+$ to form test set $\mathcal{R}_{test}$, and the remaining constitutes the training set $\mathcal{R}_{train}$. The models are learned on $\mathcal{R}_{train}$ and their predicted ranking is evaluated on $\mathcal{R}_{test}$ by averaging HitRatio@N, the probability that the removed article is recommended as part of the top-N recommendations:

$$HitRatio@N = \frac{1}{|\mathcal{R}_{test}|} \sum_{(i,j)\in\mathcal{R}_{test}} \mathbb{I}(rank_{ij} < N),$$

where $rank_{ij}$ denotes the rank position of item j in user i's recommendation list. We repeat this process 10 times and report the average results. As the definition shows, a higher value of HitRatio@N indicates a better performance.

Parameter Effect on CTRank

We vary the dimensionality of latent space K in CTRank models in the range $\{100, 150, 200, 250\}$, and the precision parameter λ_v in the range $\{0.0025, 0.025, 0.25, 2.5\}$ with fixed $\lambda_u = 0.0025$. How proposed models behave with different combinations of parameters are shown in Fig. 2.

Effect of Dimensionality In Fig. 2(a), we investigate the effect of K on the performance of CTRank, measured by HitRatio@10. As expected, HitRatio@10 increases monotonically with the growing number of iterations. When the dimensionality grows from 100 to 200, CTRank achieves higher HitRatio@10. We also notice that CTRank with $K = 250$ yields slightly lower HitRatio@10 than $K = 200$ even though the former is the quickest approach leading to convergence.

[1]http://www.citeulike.org

Effect of Parameter λ_v In Fig. 2(b), we observe that the value of λ_v affects the recommendation performance significantly, which demonstrates that exploiting topic information can greatly improve recommendation accuracy. It is also observed that, as λ_v decreases, the HitRatio@10 value increases at first, but when λ_v goes beyond a certain threshold like 0.025, the HitRatio@10 value drops with further decrease of λ_v. This shows that purely using implicit feedback or purely using topic information cannot generate better performance than appropriately fusing these two sources together.

Effect of Loss Function The loss function determines how the ranking component impacts latent factors. As shown in Fig. 2(c), CTRank-log converges very early but only converges to a low value of HitRatio@10, whereas CTRank-squared obtains increasing HitRatio@10 as the growth of the number of iteration. The poor performance of CTRank-log arises from the limitation that the approaches minimizing log-loss function focus on incorrectly ordered pairs, and benefit little from pairs that are currently correctly ordered. In the scenarios where the majority of items are irrelevant, a sampled unobserved example is likely to be ranked correctly below an observed item, and thus these models do not benefit from the training examples, i.e., the gradient vanishes.

Performance Comparison

To evaluate the proposed model, we compare it with other models in datasets with varying sparsity levels.

Comparison Methods To study the effect of topic information discovered from meta-data, we consider the following general pair-wise ranking approaches which do not consider topic information.

BPR: Bayesian Personalized Ranking optimization for MF (Rendle et al. 2009), which is the state-of-the-art approach for implicit feedback data. It can be absorbed as a special case of CTRank-log without considering topic information.

PALS: Pair-wise Alternating Least Squares, a variant of CTRank-squared without considering topic information.

To investigate the advantage of pair-wise methods over point-wise approaches, we compare CTRank with **CTR** (Wang and Blei 2011), a point-wise model, which links MF and LDA together.

Parameter Settings For all comparison methods, we set respective optimal parameters either according to corresponding references or based on our validation experiments. Specifically, we randomly select one test example per user from training set and use these examples as validation set to determine the trade-off parameters $\{K, \lambda_v, \lambda_u\}$. For all these latent factor based methods, we set the dimensionality of latent space $K = 200$ and the learning rate $\eta = 0.005$. For BPR, parameters λ_u and λ_v are 0.0025. For PALS $\lambda_v = \lambda_u = 0.0025$. For CTR, λ_u and λ_v are set to 0.01 and 100, respectively. For CTRank models, $\lambda_v = 0.025$, $\lambda_u = 0.0025$.

Comparison Results We report the comparison results in Table 2. The key conclusions are summarized as follows: (1)

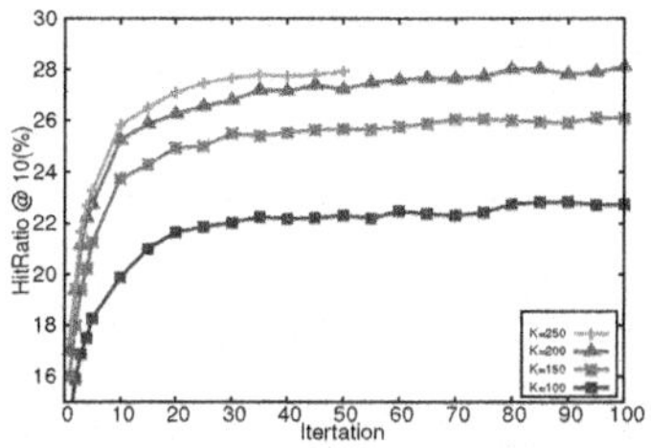

(a) Effect of the dimensionality K.

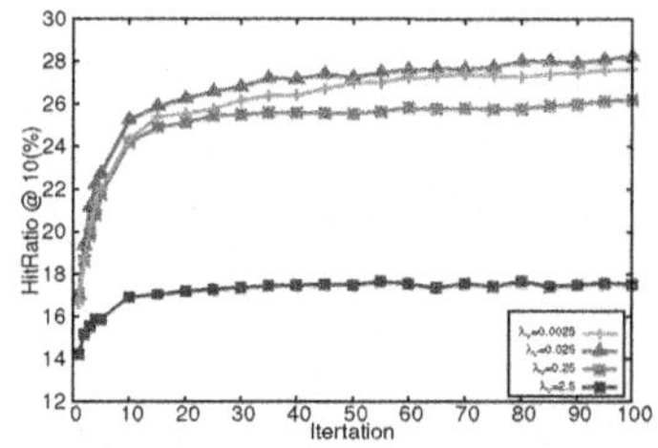

(b) Effect of the parameter λ_v.

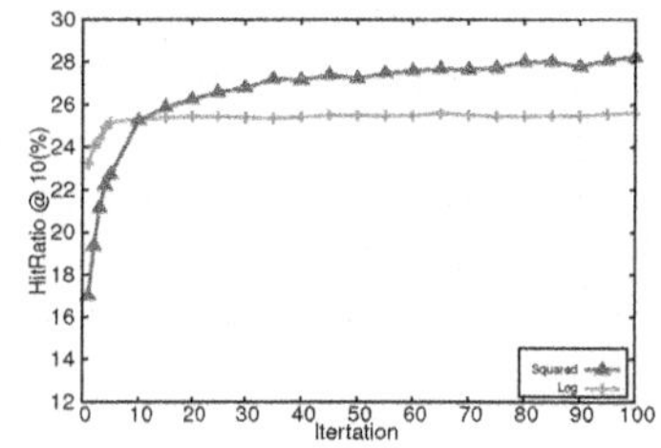

(c) Effect of the loss function.

Figure 2: Effect of parameters on the performance of CTRank. The sparsity level of the dataset used is 99.80%. Parameter settings: (a) $\lambda_v = 0.025$, $\lambda_u = 0.0025$ and squared loss is used. (b) $\lambda_u = 0.0025$, $K = 200$ and squared loss is used. (c) $\lambda_v = 0.025$, $\lambda_u = 0.0025$, $K = 200$.

Table 2: HitRatio (%) comparison over datasets with different sparsity levels. Numbers in boldface (e.g., **21.13**) and in Italic (e.g., *18.27*) are the best and second best results among all methods, respectively. N is the number of recommended items.

Methods	Sparsity											
	99.80%			99.85%			99.90%			99.95%		
	N=5	N=10	N=15	N=5	N=10	N=15	N=5	N=10	N=15	N=5	N=10	N=15
BPR	16.59	22.75	27.49	10.37	16.33	20.55	5.40	9.71	13.64	4.77	7.94	10.59
PALS	18.04	25.62	29.94	11.69	17.29	21.17	6.70	10.61	13.80	3.31	5.56	7.44
CTR	17.51	24.84	*30.23*	12.43	*19.04*	23.01	6.12	10.23	13.13	4.99	9.01	12.47
CTRank-log	*18.27*	*25.65*	29.43	*13.01*	18.84	*23.61*	*7.30*	*11.71*	*15.18*	*6.10*	*9.76*	*12.56*
CTRank-squared	**21.13**	**28.33**	**32.73**	**14.80**	**20.52**	**25.40**	**8.90**	**14.39**	**18.52**	**6.11**	**9.97**	**12.83**

The proposed CTRank-squared outperforms all other baselines at all sparsity levels while CTRank-log achieves the second best results in most cases. (2) The improvement from CTRank-squared over PALS and that from CTRank-log over BPR coincide with our assumption that meta-data can be used to differentiate the relevant items from the irrelevant ones. In particular, the relative improvement is more significant when the data is more sparse, which confirms the effectiveness of CTRank in alleviating data sparsity. (3) The pair-wise approaches directly optimizing ranking loss yields better performance than point-wise approaches, as revealed by CTRank and CTR.

Table 3: An example user from CiteULike dataset. We show some typical articles he/she likes, top 3 topics in u_i and top 5 recommended articles. $\surd$ means the target article.

Articles in his/her library	1. Parallel human genome analysis microarray based expression monitoring of genes 2. Gene expression data analysis 3. Experimental design for gene expression microarrays 4. The nature of statistical learning theory 5. On the convergence properties of the em algorithm 6. A tutorial on support vector machines for pattern recognition ...	
	CTRank	
Top 3 topics	1. gene-expression-microarray-expressed-profiling-... 2. algorithms-class-optimization-output-binary-... 3. learning-classification-machine training-vector-...	
Top 5 Articles	1. Distinct types of diffuse large bcell lymphoma identified by gene expression profiling	$\surd$
	2. An introduction to support vector machines and other kernelbased learning methods	
	3. Interpreting patterns of gene expression with selforganizing maps	
	4. The elements of statistical learning	
	5. Computational cluster validation in postgenomic data analysis	

Interpretability

Besides promising recommendation performance, an important advantage of our model is that it can interpret fine-grained levels of latent spaces: (1) user preferences space (u_i) and (2) item characteristics space (v_j) using the topics identified by CTRank. In Table 3, we show an example user from CiteULike dataset. From the user's library, we may observe that he/she is interested in the topics "gene expression" and "machine learning". We also list the user's top-3 topics (found by $k = \arg\max_k u_{ik}$) along with top-5 articles recommended by CTRank. It is obvious that user preferences can be well explained by the learned topics, and the recommended articles are closely linked to these topics. Likewise, we can also interpret item characteristics using top topics discovered by CTRank. And the overlapping topics between users and items may serve to generate explanations for recommendations.

Conclusion

In this paper, we propose a novel hierarchical Bayesian framework CTRank that incorporates "bag-of-words" type meta-data on items into pair-wise ranking models for alleviating the data sparsity problem. By regularizing item factors through item topic proportions, CTRank extends pair-wise ranking models with topic models. This design allows to learn expressive latent factors for users and items from extremely sparse implicit feedback. As an additional benefit, CTRank is able to provide interpretable user factors and item factors. This property may help in generating explanations for recommendations in some applications.

Acknowledgment

This work is partially supported by the National Natural Science Foundation of China (Grant No. 61272480, 61332013 and 71372188) and National Center for International Joint Research on E-Business Information Processing under Grant 2013B01035.

References

Agarwal, D., and Chen, B.-C. 2010. flda: matrix factorization through latent dirichlet allocation. In *WSDM'10*, 91–100. ACM.

Bertsekas, D. P. 1999. Nonlinear programming.

Blei, D. M.; Ng, A. Y.; and Jordan, M. I. 2003. Latent dirichlet allocation. *JMLR* 3:993–1022.

Chen, K.; Chen, T.; Zheng, G.; Jin, O.; Yao, E.; and Yu, Y. 2012. Collaborative personalized tweet recommendation. In *SIGIR'12*, 661–670. ACM.

Freund, Y.; Iyer, R.; Schapire, R. E.; and Singer, Y. 2003. An efficient boosting algorithm for combining preferences. *JMLR* 4:933–969.

Gunawardana, A., and Meek, C. 2009. A unified approach to building hybrid recommender systems. In *RecSys'09*, 117–124. ACM.

Hariri, N.; Mobasher, B.; and Burke, R. 2012. Context-aware music recommendation based on latenttopic sequential patterns. In *RecSys'12*, 131–138. ACM.

Hu, Y.; Koren, Y.; and Volinsky, C. 2008. Collaborative filtering for implicit feedback datasets. In *ICDM'08*, 263–272. IEEE.

Joachims, T. 2002. Optimizing search engines using clickthrough data. In *KDD'02*, 133–142. ACM.

Kim, B. M.; Li, Q.; Park, C. S.; Kim, S. G.; and Kim, J. Y. 2006. A new approach for combining content-based and collaborative filters. *Journal of Intelligent Information Systems* 27(1):79–91.

Koren, Y. 2008. Factorization meets the neighborhood: a multifaceted collaborative filtering model. In *KDD'08*, 426–434. ACM.

Krohn-Grimberghe, A.; Drumond, L.; Freudenthaler, C.; and Schmidt-Thieme, L. 2012. Multi-relational matrix factorization using bayesian personalized ranking for social network data. In *WSDM'12*, 173–182. ACM.

Lee, J.; Bengio, S.; Kim, S.; Lebanon, G.; and Singer, Y. 2014. Local collaborative ranking. In *WWW'14*, 85–96. International World Wide Web Conferences Steering Committee.

Li, B.; Yang, Q.; and Xue, X. 2009. Can movies and books collaborate? cross-domain collaborative filtering for sparsity reduction. In *IJCAI'09*, volume 9, 2052–2057.

Liu, T.-Y. 2009. Learning to rank for information retrieval. *Foundations and Trends in Information Retrieval* 3(3):225–331.

Manning, C. D.; Raghavan, P.; and Schütze, H. 2008. *Introduction to information retrieval*, volume 1. Cambridge university press Cambridge.

McAuley, J., and Leskovec, J. 2013. Hidden factors and hidden topics: understanding rating dimensions with review text. In *RecSys'13*, 165–172. ACM.

Pan, W., and Chen, L. 2013a. Cofiset: Collaborative filtering via learning pairwise preferences over item-sets. In *ICDM'13*, 180–188. SIAM.

Pan, W., and Chen, L. 2013b. Gbpr: group preference based bayesian personalized ranking for one-class collaborative filtering. In *IJCAI'13*, 2691–2697. AAAI Press.

Pan, R.; Zhou, Y.; Cao, B.; Liu, N. N.; Lukose, R.; Scholz, M.; and Yang, Q. 2008. One-class collaborative filtering. In *ICDM'08*, 502–511. IEEE.

Pan, W.; Xiang, E. W.; Liu, N. N.; and Yang, Q. 2010. Transfer learning in collaborative filtering for sparsity reduction. In *AAAI'10*, volume 10, 230–235.

Paquet, U., and Koenigstein, N. 2013. One-class collaborative filtering with random graphs. In *WWW'13*, 999–1008. International World Wide Web Conferences Steering Committee.

Qiang, R.; Liang, F.; and Yang, J. 2013. Exploiting ranking factorization machines for microblog retrieval. In *CIKM'13*, CIKM '13, 1783–1788. New York, NY, USA: ACM.

Rendle, S., and Freudenthaler, C. 2014. Improving pairwise learning for item recommendation from implicit feedback. In *WSDM'14*, 273–282. ACM.

Rendle, S.; Freudenthaler, C.; Gantner, Z.; and Schmidt-Thieme, L. 2009. Bpr: Bayesian personalized ranking from implicit feedback. In *UAI'09*, 452–461. AUAI Press.

Rendle, S. 2010. Factorization machines. In *ICDM'10*, 995–1000. IEEE.

Shan, H., and Banerjee, A. 2010. Generalized probabilistic matrix factorizations for collaborative filtering. In *ICDM'10*, 1025–1030. IEEE.

Takács, G., and Tikk, D. 2012. Alternating least squares for personalized ranking. In *RecSys'12*, 83–90. ACM.

Tang, X., and Zhou, J. 2013. Dynamic personalized recommendation on sparse data. *IEEE Transactions on Knowledge and Data Engineering* 25(12):2895–2899.

Vig, J.; Sen, S.; and Riedl, J. 2009. Tagsplanations: explaining recommendations using tags. In *IUI'09*, 47–56. ACM.

Wang, C., and Blei, D. M. 2011. Collaborative topic modeling for recommending scientific articles. In *KDD'11*, 448–456. ACM.

Proceedings of the Twenty-Ninth AAAI Conference on Artificial Intelligence

Robust Image Sentiment Analysis Using Progressively Trained and Domain Transferred Deep Networks

Quanzeng You and **Jiebo Luo**
Department of Computer Science
University of Rochester
Rochester, NY 14623
{qyou, jluo}@cs.rochester.edu

Hailin Jin and **Jianchao Yang**
Adobe Research
345 Park Avenue
San Jose, CA 95110
{hljin, jiayang}@adobe.com

Abstract

Sentiment analysis of online user generated content is important for many social media analytics tasks. Researchers have largely relied on textual sentiment analysis to develop systems to predict political elections, measure economic indicators, and so on. Recently, social media users are increasingly using images and videos to express their opinions and share their experiences. Sentiment analysis of such large scale visual content can help better extract user sentiments toward events or topics, such as those in image tweets, so that prediction of sentiment from visual content is complementary to textual sentiment analysis. Motivated by the needs in leveraging large scale yet noisy training data to solve the extremely challenging problem of image sentiment analysis, we employ Convolutional Neural Networks (CNN). We first design a suitable CNN architecture for image sentiment analysis. We obtain half a million training samples by using a baseline sentiment algorithm to label Flickr images. To make use of such noisy machine labeled data, we employ a progressive strategy to fine-tune the deep network. Furthermore, we improve the performance on Twitter images by inducing domain transfer with a small number of manually labeled Twitter images. We have conducted extensive experiments on manually labeled Twitter images. The results show that the proposed CNN can achieve better performance in image sentiment analysis than competing algorithms.

Introduction

Online social networks are providing more and more convenient services to their users. Today, social networks have grown to be one of the most important sources for people to acquire information on all aspects of their lives. Meanwhile, every online social network user is a contributor to such large amounts of information. Online users love to share their experiences and to express their opinions on virtually all events and subjects.

Among the large amount of online user generated data, we are particularly interested in people's opinions or sentiments towards specific topics and events. There have been many works on using online users' sentiments to predict box-office revenues for movies (Asur and Huberman 2010), political elections (O'Connor et al. 2010; Tumasjan et al. 2010) and economic indicators (Bollen, Mao, and Zeng 2011; Zhang, Fuehres, and Gloor 2011). These works have suggested that online users' opinions or sentiments are closely correlated with our real-world activities. All of these results hinge on accurate estimation of people's sentiments according to their online generated content. Currently all of these works only rely on sentiment analysis from textual content. However, multimedia content, including images and videos, has become prevalent over all online social networks. Indeed, online social network providers are competing with each other by providing easier access to their increasingly powerful and diverse services. Figure 1 shows example images related to the 2012 United States presidential election. Clearly, images in the top and bottom rows convey opposite sentiments towards the two candidates.

Figure 1: Examples of Flickr images related to the 2012 United States presidential election.

A picture is worth a thousand words. People with different backgrounds can easily understand the main content of an image or video. Apart from the large amount of easily available visual content, today's computational infrastructure is also much cheaper and more powerful to make the analysis of computationally intensive visual content analysis feasible. In this era of big data, it has been shown that the integration of visual content can provide us more reliable or complementary online social signals (Jin et al. 2010; Yuan et al. 2013).

To the best of our knowledge, little attention has been paid to the sentiment analysis of visual content. Only a few recent works attempted to predict visual sentiment using features from images (Siersdorfer et al. 2010; Borth et al. 2013b; 2013a; Yuan et al. 2013) and videos (Morency, Mihalcea, and Doshi 2011). Visual sentiment analysis is extremely challenging. First, image sentiment analysis is inherently more challenging than object recognition as the latter is usually well defined. Image sentiment involves a much higher level of abstraction and subjectivity in the human recognition process (Joshi et al. 2011), on top of a wide variety of visual recognition tasks including object, scene, action and event recognition. In order to use supervised learning, it is imperative to collect a large and diverse labeled training set perhaps on the order of millions of images. This is an almost insurmountable hurdle due to the tremendous labor required for image labeling. Second, the learning schemes need to have high generalizability to cover more different domains. However, the existing works use either pixel-level features or a limited number of predefined attribute features, which is difficult to adapt the trained models to images from a different domain.

The deep learning framework enables robust and accurate feature learning, which in turn produces the state-of-the-art performance on digit recognition (LeCun et al. 1989; Hinton, Osindero, and Teh 2006), image classification (Cireşan et al. 2011; Krizhevsky, Sutskever, and Hinton 2012), musical signal processing (Hamel and Eck 2010) and natural language processing (Maas et al. 2011). Both the academia and industry have invested a huge amount of effort in building powerful neural networks. These works suggested that deep learning is very effective in learning robust features in a supervised or unsupervised fashion. Even though deep neural networks may be trapped in local optima (Hinton 2010; Bengio 2012), using different optimization techniques, one can achieve the state-of-the-art performance on many challenging tasks mentioned above.

Inspired by the recent successes of deep learning, we are interested in solving the challenging visual sentiment analysis task using deep learning algorithms. For images related tasks, Convolutional Neural Network (CNN) are widely used due to the usage of convolutional layers. It takes into consideration the locations and neighbors of image pixels, which are important to capture useful features for visual tasks. Convolutional Neural Networks (LeCun et al. 1998; Cireşan et al. 2011; Krizhevsky, Sutskever, and Hinton 2012) have been proved very powerful in solving computer vision related tasks. We intend to find out whether applying CNN to visual sentiment analysis provides advantages over using a predefined collection of low-level visual features or visual attributes, which have been done in prior works.

To that end, we address in this work two major challenges: 1) how to learn with large scale weakly labeled training data, and 2) how to generalize and extend the learned model across domains. In particular, we make the following contributions.

- We develop an effective deep convolutional network architecture for visual sentiment analysis. Our architecture employs two convolutional layers and several fully connected layers for the prediction of visual sentiment labels.
- Our model attempts to address the weakly labeled nature of the training image data, where such labels are machine generated, by leveraging a progressive training strategy and a domain transfer strategy to fine-tune the neural network. Our evaluation results suggest that this strategy is effective for improving the performance of neural network in terms of generalizability.
- In order to evaluate our model as well as competing algorithms, we build a large manually labeled visual sentiment dataset using Amazon Mechanical Turk. This dataset will be released to the research community to promote further investigations on visual sentiment.

Related Work

In this section, we review literature closely related to our study on visual sentiment analysis, particularly in sentiment analysis and Convolutional Neural Networks.

Sentiment Analysis

Sentiment analysis is a very challenging task (Liu et al. 2003; Li et al. 2010). Researchers from natural language processing and information retrieval have developed different approaches to solve this problem, achieving promising or satisfying results (Pang and Lee 2008). In the context of social media, there are several additional unique challenges. First, there are huge amounts of data available. Second, messages on social networks are by nature informal and short. Third, people use not only textual messages, but also images and videos to express themselves.

Tumasjan et al. (2010) and Bollen et al. (2011) employed pre-defined dictionaries for measuring the sentiment level of Tweets. The volume or percentage of sentiment-bearing words can produce an estimate of the sentiment of one particular tweet. Davidov et al. (2010) used the weak labels from a large amount of Tweets. In contrast, they manually selected hashtags with strong positive and negative sentiments and ASCII smileys are also utilized to label the sentiments of tweets. Furthermore, Hu et al. (2013) incorporated social signals into their unsupervised sentiment analysis framework. They defined and integrated both emotion indication and correlation into a framework to learn parameters for their sentiment classifier.

There are also several recent works on visual sentiment analysis. Siersdorfer et al. (2010) proposes a machine learning algorithm to predict the sentiment of images using pixel-level features. Motivated by the fact that sentiment involves high-level abstraction, which may be easier to explain by objects or attributes in images, both (Borth et al. 2013a) and (Yuan et al. 2013) propose to employ visual entities or attributes as features for visual sentiment analysis. In (Borth et al. 2013a), 1200 adjective noun pairs (ANP), which may correspond to different levels of different emotions, are extracted. These ANPs are used as queries to crawl images from Flickr. Next, pixel-level features of images in each ANP are employed to train 1200 ANP detectors. The responses of these 1200 classifiers can then be considered as mid-level features for visual sentiment analysis. The work in (Yuan et al. 2013) employed a similar mechanism. The main difference is that 102 scene attributes are used instead.

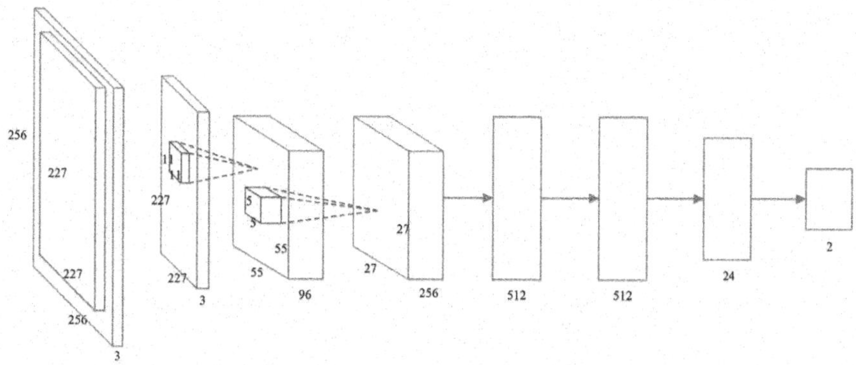

Figure 2: Convolutional Neural Network for Visual Sentiment Analysis.

Convolutional Neural Networks

Convolutional Neural Networks (CNN) have been very successful in document recognition (LeCun et al. 1998). CNN typically consists of several convolutional layers and several fully connected layers. Between the convolutional layers, there may also be pooling layers and normalization layers. CNN is a supervised learning algorithm, where parameters of different layers are learned through back-propagation. Due to the computational complexity of CNN, it has only be applied to relatively small images in the literature. Recently, thanks to the increasing computational power of GPU, it is now possible to train a deep convolutional neural network on a large scale image dataset (Krizhevsky, Sutskever, and Hinton 2012). Indeed, in the past several years, CNN has been successfully applied to scene parsing (Grangier, Bottou, and Collobert 2009), feature learning (LeCun, Kavukcuoglu, and Farabet 2010), visual recognition (Kavukcuoglu et al. 2010) and image classification (Krizhevsky, Sutskever, and Hinton 2012). In our work, we intend to use CNN to learn features which are useful for visual sentiment analysis.

Visual Sentiment Analysis

We propose to develop a suitable convolutional neural network architecture for visual sentiment analysis. Moreover, we employ a progressive training strategy that leverages the training results of convolutional neural network to further filter out (noisy) training data. The details of the proposed framework will be described in the following sections.

Visual Sentiment Analysis with regular CNN

CNN has been proven to be effective in image classification tasks, e.g., achieving the state-of-the-art performance in ImageNet Challenge (Krizhevsky, Sutskever, and Hinton 2012). Visual sentiment analysis can also be treated as an image classification problem. It may seem to be a much easier problem than image classification from ImageNet (2 classes vs. 1000 classes in ImageNet). However, visual sentiment analysis is quite challenging because sentiments or opinions correspond to high level abstractions from a given image. This type of high level abstraction may require viewer's knowledge beyond the image content itself. Meanwhile, images in the same class of ImageNet mainly contain the same type of object. In sentiment analysis, each class contains much more diverse images. It is therefore extremely challenging to discover features which can distinguish much more diverse classes from each other. In addition, people may have totally different sentiments over the same image. This adds difficulties to not only our classification task, but also the acquisition of labeled images. In other words, it is nontrivial to obtain highly reliable labeled instances, let alone a large number of them. Therefore, we need a supervised learning engine that is able to tolerate a significant level of noise in the training dataset.

The architecture of the CNN we employ for sentiment analysis is shown in Figure 2. Each image is resized to 256×256 (if needed, we employ center crop, which first resizes the shorter dimension to 256 and then crops the middle section of the resized image). The resized images are processed by two convolutional layers. Each convolutional layer is also followed by max-pooling layers and normalization layers. The first convolutional layer has 96 kernels of size $11 \times 11 \times 3$ with a stride of 4 pixels. The second convolutional layer has 256 kernels of size 5×5 with a stride of 2 pixels. Furthermore, we have four fully connected layers. Inspired by (Çaglar Gülçehre et al. 2013), we constrain the second to last fully connected layer to have 24 neurons. According to the Plutchik's wheel of emotions (Plutchik 1984), there are a total of 24 emotions belonging to two categories: positive emotions and negative emotions. Intuitively, we hope these 24 nodes may help the network to learn the 24 emotions from a given image and then classify each image into positive or negative class according to the responses of these 24 emotions.

The last layer is designed to learn the parameter w by maximizing the following conditional log likelihood function (x_i and y_i are the feature vector and label for the i-th instance respectively):

$$l(w) = \sum_{i=1}^{n} \ln p(y_i = 1|x_i, w) + (1 - y_i) \ln p(y_i = 0|x_i, w) \tag{1}$$

where

$$p(y_i|x_i, w) = \frac{\exp(w_0 + \sum_{j=1}^{k} w_j x_{ij})^{y_i}}{1 + \exp(w_0 + \sum_{j=1}^{k} w_j x_{ij})^{y_i}} \tag{2}$$

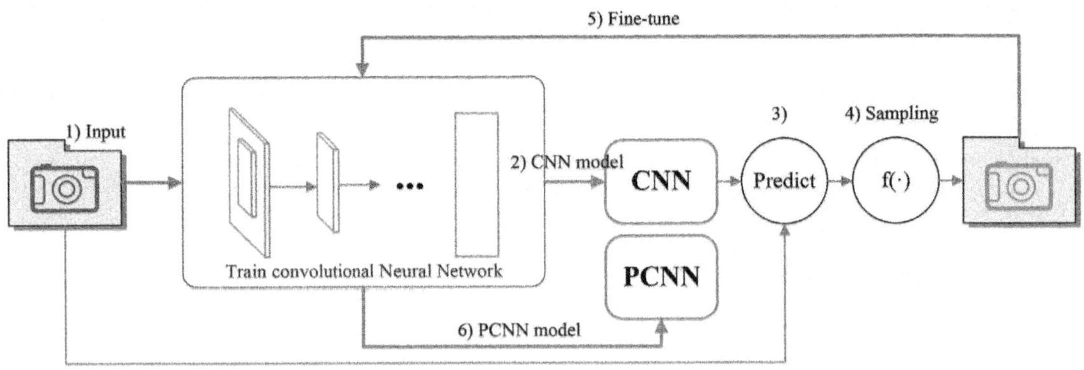

Figure 3: Progressive CNN (PCNN) for visual sentiment analysis.

Visual Sentiment Analysis with Progressive CNN

Since the images are weakly labeled, it is possible that the neural network can get stuck in a bad local optimum. This may lead to poor generalizability of the trained neural network. On the other hand, we found that the neural network is still able to correctly classify a large proportion of the training instances. In other words, the neural network has learned knowledge to distinguish the training instances with relatively distinct sentiment labels. Therefore, we propose to progressively select a subset of the training instances to reduce the impact of noisy training instances. Figure 3 shows the overall flow of the proposed progressive CNN (PCNN). We first train a CNN on Flickr images. Next, we select training samples according to the prediction score of the trained model on the training data itself. Instead of training from the beginning, we further fine-tune the trained model using these newly selected, and potentially cleaner training instances. This fine-tuned model will be our final model for visual sentiment analysis.

Algorithm 1 Progressive CNN training for Visual Sentiment Analysis

Input: $X = \{x_1, x_2, \dots, x_n\}$ a set of images of size 256×256
$Y = \{y_1, y_2, \dots, y_n\}$ sentiment labels of X

```
Train convolutional neural network CNN with input X and Y
Let S ∈ R^{n×2} be the sentiment scores of X predicted using CNN
for s_i ∈ S do
    Delete x_i from X with probability p_i (Eqn.(3))
end for
Let X' ⊂ X be the remaining training images, Y' be their sentiment labels
Fine-tune CNN with input X' and Y' to get PCNN
return PCNN
```

In particular, we employ a probabilistic sampling algorithm to select the new training subset. The intuition is that we want to keep instances with distinct sentiment scores between the two classes with a high probability, and conversely remove instances with similar sentiment scores for both classes with a high probability. Let $s_i = (s_{i1}, s_{i2})$ be the prediction sentiment scores for the two classes of instance i. We choose to remove the training instance i with probability p_i given by Eqn.(3). Algorithm 1 summarizes the steps of the proposed framework.

$$p_i = \max(0, 2 - \exp(|s_{i1} - s_{i2}|)) \quad (3)$$

When the difference between the predicted sentiment scores of one training instance are large enough, this training instance will be kept in the training set. Otherwise, the smaller the difference between the predicted sentiment scores become, the larger the probability of this instance being removed from the training set.

Experiments

We choose to use the same half million Flickr images from SentiBank[1] to train our Convolutional Neural Network. These images are only weakly labeled since each image belongs to one adjective noun pair (ANP). There are a total of 1200 ANPs. According to the Plutchik's Wheel of Emotions (Plutchik 1984), each ANP is generated by the combination of adjectives with strong sentiment values and nouns from tags of images and videos (Borth et al. 2013b). These ANPs are then used as queries to collect related images for each ANP. The released SentiBank contains 1200 ANPs with about half million Flickr images. We train our convolutional neural network mainly on this image dataset. We implement the proposed architecture of CNN on the publicly available implementation Caffe (Jia 2013). All of our experiments are evaluated on a Linux X86_64 machine with 32G RAM and two NVIDIA GTX Titan GPUs.

Comparisons of different CNN architectures

The architecture of our model is shown in Figure 2. However, we also evaluate other architectures for the visual sentiment analysis task. Table 1 summarizes the performance of different architectures on a randomly chosen Flickr testing dataset. In Table 1, iCONV-jFC indicates that there are

[1] http://visual-sentiment-ontology.appspot.com/

i convolutional layers and *j* fully connected layers in the architecture. The model in Figure 2 shows slightly better performance than other models in terms of F1 and accuracy. In the following experiments, we mainly focus on the evaluation of CNN using the architecture in Figure 2.

Table 1: Summary of performance of different architectures on randomly chosen testing data.

Architecture	Precision	Recall	F1	Accuracy
3CONV-4FC	0.679	0.845	0.753	0.644
3CONV-2FC	0.69	0.847	0.76	0.657
2CONV-3FC	0.679	0.874	0.765	0.654
2CONV-4FC	0.688	0.875	0.77	0.665

Baselines

We compare the performance of PCNN with three other baselines or competing algorithms for image sentiment classification.

Low-level Feature-based Siersdorfer et al. (2010) defined both global and local visual features. Specifically, the global color histograms (**GCH**) features consist of 64-bin RGB histogram. The local color histogram features (**LCH**) first divided the image into 16 blocks and used the 64-bin RGB histogram for each block. They also employed SIFT features to learn a visual word dictionary. Next, they defined bag of visual word features (**BoW**) for each image.

Mid-level Feature-based Damian et al. (2013a; 2013b) proposed a framework to build visual sentiment ontology and **SentiBank** according to the previously discussed 1200 ANPs. With the trained 1200 ANP detectors, they are able to generate 1200 responses for any given test image using these pre-trained 1200 ANP detectors. A sentiment classifier is built on top of these mid-level features according to the sentiment label of training images. **Sentribute** (Yuan et al. 2013) also employed mid-level features for sentiment prediction. However, instead of using adjective noun pairs, they employed scene-based attributes (Patterson and Hays 2012) to define the mid-level features.

Deep Learning on Flickr Dataset

We randomly choose 90% images from the half million Flickr images as our training dataset. The remaining 10% images are our testing dataset. We train the convolutional neural network with 300,000 iterations of mini-batches (each mini-batch contains 256 images). We employ the sampling probability in Eqn.(3) to filter the training images according to the prediction score of CNN on its training data. In the fine-tuning stage of PCNN, we run another 100,000 iterations of mini-batches using the filtered training dataset. Table 2 gives a summary of the number of data instances in our experiments. Figure 4 shows the filters learned in the first convolutional layer of CNN and PCNN, respectively. There are some differences between 4(a) and 4(b). While it is somewhat inconclusive that the neural networks have reached a better local optimum, at least we can conclude that the fine-tuning stage using a progressively cleaner training dataset has prompted the neural networks to learn different knowledge. Indeed, the evaluation results suggest that this fine-tuning leads to the improvement of performance.

Table 2: Statistics of the number of Flickr image dataset.

Models	training	testing	# of iterations
CNN	401,739	44,637	300,000
PCNN	369,828	44,637	100,000

Table 3: Performance on the Testing Dataset by CNN and PCNN.

Algorithm	Precision	Recall	F1	Accuracy
CNN	0.714	0.729	0.722	0.718
PCNN	**0.759**	**0.826**	**0.791**	**0.781**

Table 3 shows the performance of both CNN and PCNN on the 10% randomly chosen testing data. PCNN outperformed CNN in terms of *Precision*, *Recall*, *F1* and *Accuracy*. The results in Table 3 and the filters from Figure 4 shows that the fine-tuning stage of PCNN can help the neural network to search for a better local optimum.

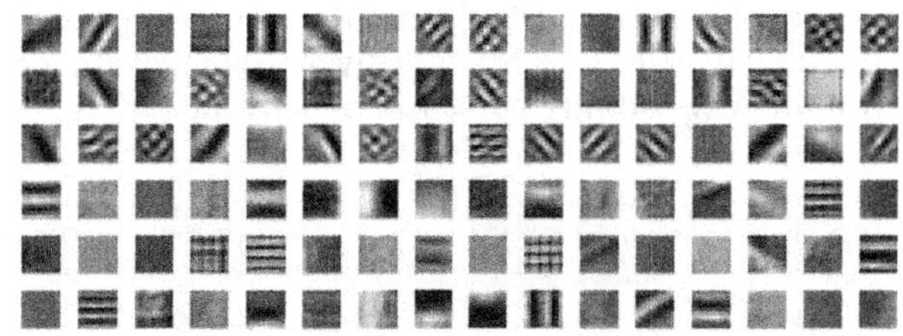

(a) Filters learned from CNN

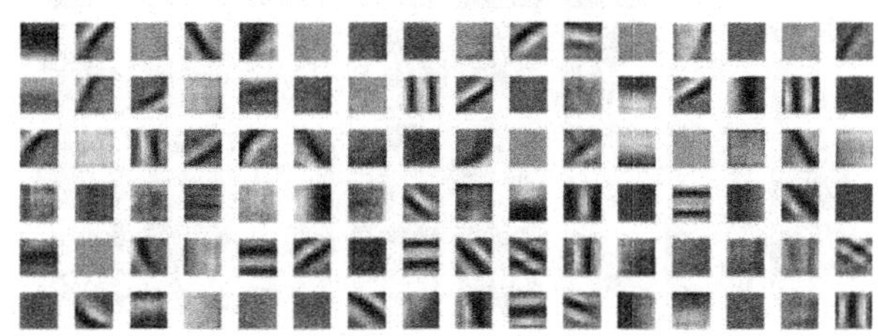

(b) Filters learned from PCNN

Figure 4: Filters of the first convolutional layer.

Twitter Testing Dataset

We also built a new image dataset from image tweets. Image tweets refer to those tweets that contain images. We built a total of 1269 images as our candidate testing images. We employed crowd intelligence, Amazon Mechanical Turk (AMT), to generate sentiment labels for these testing images, in a similar fashion to (Borth et al. 2013b). We recruited 5 AMT workers for each of the candidate image. Table 4 shows the statistics of the labeling results from the Amazon Mechanical Turk. In the table, "five agree" indicates that all the 5 AMT workers gave the same sentiment label for a given image. Only a small portion of the images, 153 out of 1269, had significant disagreements between the 5 workers (3 vs. 2). We evaluate the performance of Con-

Table 5: Performance of different algorithms on the Twitter image dataset (Acc stands for Accuracy).

Algorithms	Five Agree				At Least Four Agree				At Least Three Agree			
	Precision	Recall	F1	Acc	Precision	Recall	F1	Acc	Precision	Recall	F1	Acc
CNN	0.749	0.869	0.805	0.722	0.707	0.839	0.768	0.686	0.691	**0.814**	0.747	0.667
PCNN	**0.77**	**0.878**	**0.821**	**0.747**	**0.733**	**0.845**	**0.785**	**0.714**	**0.714**	0.806	**0.757**	**0.687**

Table 4: Summary of AMT labeled results for the Twitter testing dataset.

Sentiment	Five Agree	At Least Four Agree	At Least Three Agree
Positive	581	689	769
Negative	301	427	500
Sum	882	1116	1269

volutional Neural Networks on this manually labeled image dataset according to the model trained on Flickr images. Table 5 shows the performance of the two frameworks. Not surprisingly, both models perform better on the less ambiguous image set ("five agree" by AMT). Meanwhile, PCNN shows better performance than CNN on all the three labeling sets in terms of both F1 and accuracy. This suggests that the fine-tuning stage of CNN effectively improves the generalizability extensibility of the neural networks.

Figure 5: Positive (top block) and Negative (bottom block) examples. Each column shows the negative example images for each algorithm (PCNN, CNN, Sentribute, Sentibank, GCH, LCH, GCH+BoW, LCH+BoW). The images are ranked by the prediction score from top to bottom in a decreasing order.

Transfer Learning

Half million Flickr images are used in our CNN training. The features learned are generic features on these half million images. Table 5 shows that these generic features also have the ability to predict visual sentiment of images from other domains. The question we ask is whether we can further improve the performance of visual sentiment analysis on Twitter images by inducing transfer learning. In this section, we conduct experiments to answer this question.

The users of Flickr are more likely to spend more time on taking high quality pictures. Twitter users are likely to share the moment with the world. Thus, most of the Twitter images are casually taken snapshots. Meanwhile, most of the images are related to current trending topics and personal experiences, making the images on Twitter much diverse in content as well as quality.

In this experiment, we fine-tune the pre-trained neural network model in the following way to achieve transfer learning. We randomly divide the Twitter images into 5 equal partitions. Every time, we use 4 of the 5 partitions to fine-tune our pre-trained model from the half million Flickr images and evaluate the new model on the remaining partition. The averaged evaluation results are reported. The algorithm is detailed in Algorithm 2.

Algorithm 2 Transfer Learning to fine-tune CNN

Input: $X = \{x_1, x_2, \ldots, x_n\}$ a set of images of size 256×256
$Y = \{y_1, y_2, \ldots, y_n\}$ sentiment labels of X
Pre-trained CNN model M

Randomly partition X and Y into 5 equal groups $\{(X_1, Y_1), \ldots, (X_5, Y_5)\}$.
for i from 1 to 5 **do**
  Let $(X', Y') = (X, Y) - (X_i, Y_i)$
  Fine-tune M with input (X', Y') to obtain model M_i
  Evaluate the performance of M_i on (X_i, Y_i)
end for
return The averaged performance of M_i on (X_i, Y_i) (i from 1 to 5)

Similar to (Borth et al. 2013b), we also employ 5-fold cross-validation to evaluate the performance of all the baseline algorithms. Table 6 summarizes the averaged performance results of different baseline algorithms and our two CNN models. Overall, both CNN models outperform the baseline algorithms. In the baseline algorithms, Sentribute gives slightly better results than the other two baseline algorithms. Interestingly, even the combination of using low-level features local color histogram (LCH) and bag of visual words (BoW) shows better results than SentiBank on our

Table 6: 5-Fold Cross-Validation Performance of different algorithms on the Twitter image dataset. Note that compared with Table 5, both fine-tuned CNN models have been improved due to domain transfer learning (Acc stands for Accuracy).

Algorithms	Five Agree				At Least Four Agree				At Least Three Agree			
	Precision	Recall	F1	Acc	Precision	Recall	F1	Acc	Precision	Recall	F1	Acc
GCH	0.708	0.888	0.787	0.684	0.687	0.84	0.756	0.665	0.678	**0.836**	0.749	0.66
LCH	0.764	0.809	0.786	0.71	0.725	0.753	0.739	0.671	0.716	0.737	0.726	0.664
GCH + BoW	0.724	0.904	0.804	0.71	0.703	0.849	0.769	0.685	0.683	**0.835**	0.751	0.665
LCH + BoW	0.771	0.811	0.79	0.717	0.751	0.762	0.756	0.697	0.722	0.726	0.723	0.664
SentiBank	0.785	0.768	0.776	0.709	0.742	0.727	0.734	0.675	0.720	0.723	0.721	0.662
Sentribute	0.789	0.823	0.805	0.738	0.75	0.792	0.771	0.709	0.733	0.783	0.757	0.696
CNN	**0.795**	**0.905**	**0.846**	**0.783**	**0.773**	**0.855**	**0.811**	**0.755**	**0.734**	**0.832**	**0.779**	**0.715**
PCNN	**0.797**	**0.881**	**0.836**	**0.773**	**0.786**	**0.842**	**0.811**	**0.759**	**0.755**	**0.805**	**0.778**	**0.723**

Twitter dataset. Both fine-tuned CNN models have been improved. This improvement is significant given that we only use four fifth of the 1269 images for domain adaptation. Both neural network models have similar performance on all the three sets of the Twitter testing data. This suggests that the fine-tuning stage helps both models to find a better local minimum. In particular, the knowledge from the Twitter images starts to determine the performance of both neural networks. The previously trained model only determines the start position of the fine-tuned model.

Meanwhile, for each model, we respectively select the top 5 positive and top 5 negative examples from the 1269 Twitter images according to the evaluation scores. Figure show those examples for each model. In both figures, each column contains the images for one model. A green solid box means the prediction label of the image agrees with the human label. Otherwise, we use a red dashed box. The labels of top ranked images in both neural network models are all correctly predicted. However, the images are not all the same. This on the other hand suggests that even though the two models achieve similar results after fine-tuning, they may have arrived at somewhat different local optima due to the different starting positions, as well as the transfer learning process. For all the baseline models, it is difficult to say which kind of images are more likely to be correctly classified according to these images. However, we observe that there are several mistakenly classified images in common among the models using low-level features (the four rightmost columns in Figure). Similarly, for Sentibank and Sentribute, several of the same images are also in the top ranked samples. This indicates that there are some common learned knowledge in the low-level feature models and mid-level feature models.

Conclusions

Visual sentiment analysis is a challenging and interesting problem. In this paper, we adopt the recent developed convolutional neural networks to solve this problem. We have designed a new architecture, as well as new training strategies to overcome the noisy nature of the large-scale training samples. Both progressive training and transfer learning inducted by a small number of confidently labeled images from the target domain have yielded notable improvements. The experimental results suggest that convolutional neural networks that are properly trained can outperform both classifiers that use predefined low-level features or mid-level visual attributes for the highly challenging problem of visual sentiment analysis. Meanwhile, the main advantage of using convolutional neural networks is that we can transfer the knowledge to other domains using a much simpler fine-tuning technique than those in the literature e.g., (Duan et al. 2012).

It is important to reiterate the significance of this work over the state-of-the-art (Siersdorfer et al. 2010; Borth et al. 2013b; Yuan et al. 2013). We are able to directly leverage a much larger weakly labeled data set for training, as well as a larger manually labeled dataset for testing. The larger data sets, along with the proposed deep CNN and its training strategies, give rise to better generalizability of the trained model and higher confidence of such generalizability. In the future, we plan to develop robust multimodality models that employ both the textual and visual content for social media sentiment analysis. We also hope our sentiment analysis results can encourage further research on online user generated content.

We believe that sentiment analysis on large scale online user generated content is quite useful since it can provide more robust signals and information for many data analytics tasks, such as using social media for prediction and forecasting. In the future, we plan to develop robust multimodality models that employ both the textual and visual content for social media sentiment analysis. We also hope our sentiment analysis results can encourage further research on online user generated content.

Acknowledgments

This work was generously supported in part by Adobe Research. We would like to thank Digital Video and Multimedia (DVMM) Lab at Columbia University for providing the half million Flickr images and their machine-generated labels.

References

Asur, S., and Huberman, B. A. 2010. Predicting the future with social media. In *WI-IAT*, volume 1, 492–499. IEEE.

Bengio, Y. 2012. Practical recommendations for gradient-based training of deep architectures. In *Neural Networks: Tricks of the Trade*. Springer. 437–478.

Bollen, J.; Mao, H.; and Pepe, A. 2011. Modeling public mood and emotion: Twitter sentiment and socio-economic phenomena. In *ICWSM*.

Bollen, J.; Mao, H.; and Zeng, X. 2011. Twitter mood predicts the stock market. *Journal of Computational Science* 2(1):1–8.

Borth, D.; Chen, T.; Ji, R.; and Chang, S.-F. 2013a. Sentibank: large-scale ontology and classifiers for detecting sentiment and emotions in visual content. In *ACM MM*, 459–460. ACM.

Borth, D.; Ji, R.; Chen, T.; Breuel, T.; and Chang, S.-F. 2013b. Large-scale visual sentiment ontology and detectors using adjective noun pairs. In *ACM MM*, 223–232. ACM.

Çaglar Gülçehre; Cho, K.; Pascanu, R.; and Bengio, Y. 2013. Learned-norm pooling for deep neural networks. *CoRR* abs/1311.1780.

Cireşan, D. C.; Meier, U.; Masci, J.; Gambardella, L. M.; and Schmidhuber, J. 2011. Flexible, high performance convolutional neural networks for image classification. In *IJ-CAI*, 1237–1242. AAAI Press.

Davidov, D.; Tsur, O.; and Rappoport, A. 2010. Enhanced sentiment learning using twitter hashtags and smileys. In *ICL*, 241–249. Association for Computational Linguistics.

Duan, L.; Xu, D.; Tsang, I.-H.; and Luo, J. 2012. Visual event recognition in videos by learning from web data. *IEEE PAMI* 34(9):1667–1680.

Grangier, D.; Bottou, L.; and Collobert, R. 2009. Deep convolutional networks for scene parsing. In *ICML 2009 Deep Learning Workshop*, volume 3. Citeseer.

Hamel, P., and Eck, D. 2010. Learning features from music audio with deep belief networks. In *ISMIR*, 339–344.

Hinton, G. E.; Osindero, S.; and Teh, Y.-W. 2006. A fast learning algorithm for deep belief nets. *Neural computation* 18(7):1527–1554.

Hinton, G. 2010. A practical guide to training restricted boltzmann machines. *Momentum* 9(1):926.

Hu, X.; Tang, J.; Gao, H.; and Liu, H. 2013. Unsupervised sentiment analysis with emotional signals. In *WWW*, 607–618. International World Wide Web Conferences Steering Committee.

Jia, Y. 2013. Caffe: An open source convolutional architecture for fast feature embedding. http://caffe.berkeleyvision.org/.

Jin, X.; Gallagher, A.; Cao, L.; Luo, J.; and Han, J. 2010. The wisdom of social multimedia: using flickr for prediction and forecast. In *ACM MM*, 1235–1244. ACM.

Joshi, D.; Datta, R.; Fedorovskaya, E.; Luong, Q.-T.; Wang, J. Z.; Li, J.; and Luo, J. 2011. Aesthetics and emotions in images. *IEEE Signal Processing Magazine* 28(5):94–115.

Kavukcuoglu, K.; Sermanet, P.; Boureau, Y.-L.; Gregor, K.; Mathieu, M.; and LeCun, Y. 2010. Learning convolutional feature hierarchies for visual recognition. In *NIPS*, 5.

Krizhevsky, A.; Sutskever, I.; and Hinton, G. E. 2012. Imagenet classification with deep convolutional neural networks. In *NIPS*, 4.

LeCun, Y.; Boser, B.; Denker, J. S.; Henderson, D.; Howard, R. E.; Hubbard, W.; and Jackel, L. D. 1989. Backpropagation applied to handwritten zip code recognition. *Neural computation* 1(4):541–551.

LeCun, Y.; Bottou, L.; Bengio, Y.; and Haffner, P. 1998. Gradient-based learning applied to document recognition. *Proceedings of the IEEE* 86(11):2278–2324.

LeCun, Y.; Kavukcuoglu, K.; and Farabet, C. 2010. Convolutional networks and applications in vision. In *ISCAS*, 253–256. IEEE.

Li, G.; Hoi, S. C.; Chang, K.; and Jain, R. 2010. Microblogging sentiment detection by collaborative online learning. In *ICDM*, 893–898. IEEE.

Liu, B.; Dai, Y.; Li, X.; Lee, W. S.; and Yu, P. S. 2003. Building text classifiers using positive and unlabeled examples. In *ICDM*, 179–186. IEEE.

Maas, A. L.; Daly, R. E.; Pham, P. T.; Huang, D.; Ng, A. Y.; and Potts, C. 2011. Learning word vectors for sentiment analysis. In *ACL*, 142–150.

Morency, L.-P.; Mihalcea, R.; and Doshi, P. 2011. Towards multimodal sentiment analysis: Harvesting opinions from the web. In *ICMI*, 169–176. New York, NY, USA: ACM.

O'Connor, B.; Balasubramanyan, R.; Routledge, B. R.; and Smith, N. A. 2010. From tweets to polls: Linking text sentiment to public opinion time series. *ICWSM* 11:122–129.

Pang, B., and Lee, L. 2008. Opinion mining and sentiment analysis. *Foundations and trends in information retrieval* 2(1-2):1–135.

Patterson, G., and Hays, J. 2012. Sun attribute database: Discovering, annotating, and recognizing scene attributes. In *CVPR*.

Plutchik, R. 1984. Emotions: A general psychoevolutionary theory. *Approaches to emotion* 1984:197–219.

Siersdorfer, S.; Minack, E.; Deng, F.; and Hare, J. 2010. Analyzing and predicting sentiment of images on the social web. In *ACM MM*, 715–718. ACM.

Tumasjan, A.; Sprenger, T. O.; Sandner, P. G.; and Welpe, I. M. 2010. Predicting elections with twitter: What 140 characters reveal about political sentiment. *ICWSM* 178–185.

Yuan, J.; Mcdonough, S.; You, Q.; and Luo, J. 2013. Sentribute: image sentiment analysis from a mid-level perspective. In *Proceedings of the Second International Workshop on Issues of Sentiment Discovery and Opinion Mining*, 10. ACM.

Zhang, X.; Fuehres, H.; and Gloor, P. A. 2011. Predicting stock market indicators through twitter i hope it is not as bad as i fear. *Procedia-Social and Behavioral Sciences* 26:55–62.

Are Features Equally Representative? A Feature-Centric Recommendation

Chenyi Zhang[1,2], Ke Wang[2*], Ee-peng Lim[3], Qinneng Xu[4], Jianling Sun[1] and Hongkun Yu[5]
[1]College of Computer Science, Zhejiang University
[2]School of Computing Science, Simon Fraser University
[3]School of Information Systems, Singapore Management University
[4]Department of Systems Engineering and Engineering Management, City University of Hong kong
[5]Department of Computer Science, University of Illinois at Urbana-Champaign
{chenyiz,wangk}@sfu.ca, eplim@smu.edu.sg, qinnengxu3-c@my.cityu.edu.hk, sunjl@zju.edu.cn, hyu50@illinois.edu

Abstract

Typically a user prefers an item (e.g., a movie) because she likes certain features of the item (e.g., director, genre, producer). This observation motivates us to consider a *feature-centric recommendation* approach to item recommendation: instead of directly predicting the rating on items, we predict the rating on the features of items, and use such ratings to derive the rating on an item. This approach offers several advantages over the traditional item-centric approach: it incorporates more information about why a user chooses an item, it generalizes better due to the denser feature rating data, it explains the prediction of item ratings through the predicted feature ratings. Another contribution is turning a principled item-centric solution into a feature-centric solution, instead of inventing a new algorithm that is feature-centric. This approach maximally leverages previous research. We demonstrate this approach by turning the traditional item-centric latent factor model into a feature-centric solution and demonstrate its superiority over item-centric approaches.

1 Introduction

The objective of recommender systems is to predict user preferences on items based on preferences observed on other items in the past. Two basic approaches are content-based filtering and collaborative filtering:

Content-based filtering: In this approach, keywords or features are used to describe the items and a user profile is built using the past item ratings to summarize the types of items this user likes. This approach follows the design principle that **liking a feature in the past leads to liking the feature in future**. A drawback is that if a user A has not liked any feature of an item X in the past, X will not be recommended to the user, even though many users with the same profile as A like X.

Collaborative filtering: This approach addresses the above problem by collaborative learning: if a user A liked some items that were also liked by user B, A is likely to share the same preference with B on another item. The design principle of this approach is that **liking same items (as other users) leads to liking more same items**.

Hybrid approaches combine content-based filtering and collaborative filtering. Despite their differences, all these approaches are *item-centric* in that major activities such as rating collection, model building, and rating prediction are centered around items. In this work, we consider another design principle: **liking same features (as other users) leads to liking more same features**, which leads to a new approach called *feature-centric recommendation*. Let us motivate this design principle and our approach.

1.1 Motivation

A user likes an item because of some *specific features* of the item. When a user likes an item, she may like some features of the item but is not impressed with other features; consequently, two users may like the same item for different reasons. For example, a user may like the rate of a hotel but not its service, while another user may like the cleanliness of the hotel but nothing else. If the above observation holds, the design principle "liking same items (as other users) leads to liking more same items" practised by the standard collaborative filtering may not work.

To explain our point, let us consider the toy example with four items W={anti-allergy, rose}, X={anti-allergy, rose}, Y={anti-allergy, orange}, and Z={sun proof, rose} where {} contains the features for the item. In the history, suppose that user A loves W and X due to "anti-allergy" and user B loves W, X, and Z due to "rose". In traditional collaborative filtering, it will recommend Z to user A since A and B both like W and X whereas A would rather love Y. On the other hand, for content-based filtering, Y has the feature "anti-allergy" and Z has the feature "rose" as in W and X. Therefore, the score is the same, but it is obvious that A will love Y more than Z from the view of feature level.

User's preferences on features are available in many real life rating systems. For example, in the hotel rating systems a user can rate specific features (cleanliness, service, etc.)

*Work done while visiting the Living Analytics Research Centre, Singapore Management University of a hotel. Other systems (Sen, Vig, and Riedl 2009) allow users to explicitly express preferences on features by attaching personal tags to an item. The ratings of features (e.g., director, actor) can also be implicitly inherited from the features of items (e.g., movie). Such information manifests the user's reasons for rating the item, led by different preferences on features.

1.2 Our Approach

Our approach is motivated by the above discussion, therefore, if we can predict user's preference on features, we are able to predict user's preference on an item; if we can express observed preference on features in the same format as observed preference on items, any principled collaborative filtering algorithm for items can be applied to predict user's preference on features. This thinking leads to a *feature-centric recommendation* approach in which features of items are the "King": given the usual user-item rating matrix R, we first convert item ratings into feature ratings and obtain a user-feature rating matrix R'. We directly perform collaborative filtering on R', which practices our design principle "liking same features (as other users) leads to liking more same features". The output is a model for predicting a user's rating on a feature.

To predict a user's rating on an unrated item, we need to integrate the predicted feature ratings to derive the rating for the item. While sum and average are obvious choices, features are not equally representative, e.g., the feature "anti-allergy" clearly has a more significance than the other features for user A. So we present two novel integration approaches, one is heuristic based and one is regression based, to give different significance for feature preferences.

The key innovation is that our approach transforms the item ratings into feature ratings and later the modeling is fully at the feature level. To this end, our approach takes the advantages of collaborative filtering and content-based filtering, e.g., even if items are not shared among users, features of items may still be shared, which helps address the cold start problem of a new item. As the final prediction on the item rating is an integration of a set of feature ratings, our modeling actually involves no "items", which is fundamentally different to the modeling of the existing feature based recommendations (Chen et al. 2012; Han and Karypis 2005). Their modelings all have "items" (e.g., latent item vectors) which directly affect the final prediction while features are used as a finer description to regularize the item ratings. However, we fully rely on the feature ratings and may avoid the side effects introduced by items.

The rest of the paper is organized as follows: Section 2 discusses related works. Section 3 introduces our model. Section 4 presents our experimental studies. Finally we conclude the paper.

2 Related Work

2.1 Item-Centric Approaches

Many content-based filtering, collaborative filtering and hybrid approaches (Adomavicius and Tuzhilin 2005) are item-centric in that rating, model building, similarity, and filtering are centered around items, and feature information is only used to measure similarity of items (for content-based filtering). (Han and Karypis 2005) proposed that "user who bought products with features also bought a product with the same features", but still treated items as central roles and features as side information. Our approach is feature-centric: it captures the preference of features at the rating time, which is different from learning the user profile as the outcome of content-based filtering, and it performs collaborative filtering on feature ratings and predicts the rating of features. The prediction of item ratings is performed only at the final step by integrating the predicted ratings of features.

2.2 Latent Factor Models

Recent works use the latent factor model to extract low-dimensional latent user and item vectors for predicting the rating of items (Salakhutdinov and Mnih 2008a; 2008b; Zhang et al. 2014a), and several works (Zhang et al. 2014b; Wang and Blei 2011) extend items with content in this model. The regression-based latent factor model (Agarwal and Chen 2009) incorporated features and past interactions to regress the latent vectors. Items with similar features tend to have similar latent vectors, so features have indirect impact on the final ratings. (Agarwal, Chen, and Pang 2011) further extended (Agarwal and Chen 2009) by modeling user-generated opinionated texts. In (Gantner et al. 2010), the features of users and items are used to predict the latent factors of new users and new items; existing users and items do not benefit from the available feature information. The collaborative topic regression (CTR) (Wang and Blei 2011) studies the recommendation for scientific articles with each article being modeled by topic modeling on the text content of the article. The factorization machine (FM) (Rendle 2012) models multidimensional variable interactions (user, item, feature, etc.) through latent vectors. The tensor factorization (Karatzoglou et al. 2010) generalizes the rating matrix with additional context information. The co-factorization machine (Hong, Doumith, and Davison 2013) couples the learning of two FMs to study two aspects of tweeter data. All these methods treat the features of an item equally as side information and no preference is captured on features.

2.3 Tag-Aware Recommendation

(Sen, Vig, and Riedl 2009) predicts users' ratings for items based on inferred preferences for tags, but the preferences are global for all items, that is, a tag is either liked or disliked for all items. The work in (Gedikli and Jannach 2010; 2013) improves upon this by predicting tag preferences in the context of an item. All these methods infer the preferences for the user's own tags; if an unrated item is attached with tags that the user has never used before, no prediction can be made for the item. Our method does not have this problem because it employs collaborative filtering on feature ratings, which can predict a rating for any pair of user and feature. The tag-aware recommendation in (Tso-Sutter, Marinho, and Schmidt-Thieme 2008) models a 3-way relation $< user, item, tag >$ by 2-way relations $< user, tag >$, $< item, tag >$, and $< user, item >$, which cannot express the 3-way information that a user i tags an item j using a tag t. There is a similar problem with (Zhou et al. 2009). In (Zhen, Li, and Yeung 2009), the tag information acts as a new regularization term in matrix factorization to constrain the latent vectors between users who used similar tags. Features play a more central role in our model in that we learn latent vectors for features and predict the rating of features. If a user prefers an item because of specific features of the item, our feature-centric approach is more sensitive to user preferences.

3 Feature-Centric Recommendation

We present a feature-centric recommendation approach to utilize user's feature preferences to improve recommendation of items. This approach is shown in Figure 1 where the dashed box encompasses a standard collaborative filtering method. We consider the latent factor model for this box, but it could be replaced with any other collaborative filtering methods. We discuss the key steps of extracting an observed feature rating matrix and predicting item ratings from feature ratings in the following sections.

3.1 Extracting User-Feature Rating Matrix

We assume there are I users, J items, T features. Each item j is associated with a bag of features, denoted by B_j. For a feature t, S_t denotes the set of items j such that $t \in B_j$. The original rating data can be represented by an $I \times J$ user-item rating matrix R in which each element r_{ij} indicates user i's rating value to item j.

In addition, when the user i rates the item j, the user may optionally rate or select (such as tagging) some features t of item j. If the user rates the feature t for item j, $h_{it}(j)$ denotes this rating. If the user i selects the feature t but does not rate t, $h_{it}(j) = r_{ij}$, which is user i's rating on item j. If the user i does not select any feature at all when rating the item j, $h_{it}(j) = r_{ij}$ for all features t of item j as we believe that the user implicitly selects all features. In all other cases, $h_{it}(j)$ is undefined.

User-feature rating matrix. For user i and feature t, $\{h_{it}(j)\}$ denotes the bag of defined ratings $h_{it}(j)$ for all items $j \in S_t$. We extract an $I \times T$ *user-feature rating matrix* denoted by R', there is one row for each user i, one column for each feature t, and the entry for (i, t) is equal to $\{h_{it}(j)\}$. As the toy example in Section 1.1, if user A rates the item W with the rating 4 and the item X with the rating 4, and selects the feature "anti-allergy" for both, so $h_{A,anti-allergy}(W) = 4$ and $h_{A,anti-allergy}(X) = 4$, and the entry for ($A$,"anti-allergy") is $\{4, 4\}$.

We adopt latent factor model (Salakhutdinov and Mnih 2008b) on R' to produce the latent user vector u_i for each user i and the latent feature vector f_t for each feature t, and the objective is to minimize $\sum_{j\in S_t} \varepsilon_{ijt}(h_{it}(j) - u_i^T f_t)^2$ where ε_{ijt} is equal to 1 if $h_{it}(j)$ is defined, and is equal to 0 otherwise. User i's predicated rating on feature t is given by $u_i^T f_t$. This part is the standard method for the latent factor model except that items are substituted by features. The interested reader please refer to (Salakhutdinov and Mnih 2008b) for the detailed inference.

3.2 Predicting Item Ratings by Heuristic

We present two heuristic strategies for integrating the predicted feature ratings to derive the predicted item rating for a user in this section. One strategy is using the average of feature ratings to predict the rating $\hat{r}_{ij}$ for item j, that is,

$$\hat{r}_{ij} = \frac{1}{|B_j|} \sum_{t \in B_j} u_i^T f_t \tag{1}$$

This prediction treats all features in B_j equally because each $u_i^T f_t$ has the weight $1/|B_j|$. It does not take into account, for example, whether the user occasionally selects the feature t by chance or consistently selects the feature. Below, we present another strategy that consider such differences.

The second strategy is to introduce a weighting scheme specific to individual users. If a user i selects a feature t frequently, the user is more interested in t. Besides relative frequency of selection, the absolute number of selection also matters. For example, selecting a feature twice out of 3 ratings has the same frequency as selecting a feature 20 times out of 30 ratings, but the latter has more statistical significance. This strategy suggests that features are not equally representative.

We propose a single weighting scheme to account for both relative frequency and statistical significance. Suppose that a user i has rated N items, among them, the feature t was selected s times. We can regard this as one sample where the event t was observed s times in N trials, where $\hat{p} = \frac{s}{N}$ is the *observed proportion*. We want to bound the *true proportion* that the user selects the feature t. Let $CI(s, N)$ denote the confidence interval for user i selecting feature t. We adopt the following Wilson score (Wilson 1927) interval since it is an improvement over the usual normal approximation.

$$CI(s, N) = [c - \sigma, c + \sigma] \tag{2}$$

where

$$c = \frac{1}{1 + \frac{1}{N} z^2} (\hat{p} + \frac{1}{2N} z^2)$$

$$\sigma = \frac{1}{1 + \frac{1}{N} z^2} z \sqrt{\frac{1}{N} \hat{p}(1 - \hat{p}) + \frac{1}{4N^2} z^2}$$

z is the $1 - \frac{1}{2}\alpha$ percentile of a standard normal distribution and α is the error percentile. For a 95% confidence level the error α is 5%, so $1 - \frac{1}{2}\alpha = 0.975$ and $z = 1.96$.

A larger c and a smaller interval size σ represent a more significant selection of t. Therefore, we use the mid-point of the lower bound $c - \sigma$ and the interval center c to measure the weight of selecting t by user i: $l_{it} = \dfrac{1}{2}(c - \sigma + c) = c - \dfrac{1}{2}\sigma$. The predicted rating $\hat{r}_{ij}$ of item j by user i is then defined as

$$\hat{r}_{ij} = \frac{1}{L_j} \sum_{t \in B_j} l_{it} u_i^T f_t \tag{3}$$

where $L_j = \sum_{t \in B_j} l_{it}$. Note that this weighting scheme is unique to features, not items, because only a feature can be selected by a user multiple times.

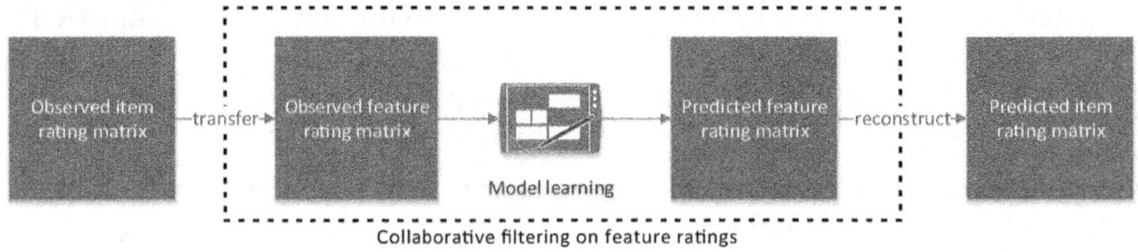

Figure 1: The feature-centric recommendation approach

3.3 Predicting Item Ratings through Regression

In the previous section, the weighting schemes are computed by heuristic, which may not capture the essential by model fitting. In this section, we propose a regression model to automatically learn the global weighting for features. We assume that there exists a weighting vector $\mathbf{w}$, with $w_t \in \mathbf{w}$ representing the importance for each feature t. The training set contains historic ratings, where $\mathbf{x}_k$ is the kth input data and y_k is the kth output data, in particular, if this rating is made by user i, $y_k = r_{ij}$, $\mathbf{x}_k(t) = u_i f_t$ if $t \in B_j$ and $\mathbf{x}_k(t) = 0$ otherwise. The regression model is trained by the relationship between input and output data: $y_k = \mathbf{w}^T\mathbf{x}_k + b_i$. Following support vector regression (Smola and Scholkopf 2004), our goal is to find optimal weighting $\mathbf{w}$ and user specific bias b_i that fit the model best. The optimization problem becomes,

$$\min_{\mathbf{w},\xi,\xi^*} \frac{1}{2}\|\mathbf{w}\|^2 + \frac{C}{2}\sum_k(\xi_k^2 + \hat{\xi}_k^2) \quad (4)$$

$$s.t. \quad |\mathbf{w}^T\mathbf{x}_k + b_i - y_k| \le \varepsilon + \xi_k; \quad (5)$$

$$\xi_k, \hat{\xi}_k \ge 0; \forall k. \quad (6)$$

where $\xi_k, \hat{\xi}_k$ are slack variables and C is a constant.

The primal Lagrangian is,

$$\mathcal{L}_P = \frac{1}{2}\|\mathbf{w}\|^2 + \sum_k \alpha_k(\mathbf{w}^T\mathbf{x}_k + b_i - y_k - \varepsilon - \xi_k) + \sum_k \hat{\alpha}_k(y_k - \mathbf{w}^T\mathbf{x}_k - b_i - \varepsilon - \hat{\xi}_k) + \frac{C}{2}\sum_k(\xi_k^2 + \hat{\xi}_k^2) \quad (7)$$

where $\alpha_k, \hat{\alpha}_k$ are Lagrange multipliers. We take the derivatives with respect to $\mathbf{w}, b_i, \xi_k, \hat{\xi}_k$, leading to the KKT conditions (Kuhn and Tucker 1951) as follows:

$$\mathbf{w} = \sum_i(\alpha_k - \hat{\alpha}_k)x_k, \quad \xi_k = \alpha_k/C, \quad \hat{\xi}_k = \hat{\alpha}_k/C \quad (8)$$

We skip the comprehensive inference as SVR is a principled method. More details refer to (Smola and Scholkopf 2004). Once the optimal weighting vector $\mathbf{w}$ and the bias term b_i are found, the predicted rating for specific item j is given by:

$$\hat{r}_{ij} = \sum_{t \in B_j} w_t u_i^T f_t + b_i \quad (9)$$

Feature selection. We conduct a 2-step feature selection that aims at the representative features. (1) we calculate the cosine similarity to quantify correlations between various predictors (feature ratings) and the item ratings to identify the best predictors. According to the result, we remove features with relatively low similarity by a threshold. (2) we fit the model with the remaining features. If the model performance is close to the original one, we believe that the removed features are less representative. This procedure is optional but helps the prediction accuracy.

Table 1: Statistics of data sets

	Delicious	Lastfm	DBLP	Movielens
User	1867	2100	6815	1857
Item	69223	18744	78745	4721
Feature	40897	12647	81901	8288
Item ratings	104799	71064	436704	20607
Feature ratings	437593	186479	2554597	36885
Density (item)	8.1×10^{-4}	1.8×10^{-3}	8.1×10^{-4}	2.3×10^{-3}

4 Experimental Evaluation

We report our findings on the evaluation of the proposed feature-centric recommendation against well known baselines using real life data sets. We first introduce data sets, baseline methods, and evaluation metrics.

4.1 Data Sets

We employed four data sets: *Delicious*, *Lastfm*, *DBLP*, and *Movielens*. The first two data sets were recommended as benchmark data sets for studying recommender systems by the 2011 HetRec conference[1]. These data sets contain user's tagging information on bookmarks and music songs, which expresses user's ratings or preferences on items. We treat tags as the features of an item. Delicious contains 1867 users' ratings on 69223 items with 40897 unique features. Lastfm contains 2100 users' ratings on 18744 items with 12647 unique features. The third data set *DBLP* contains authors, papers and citation information from an academic network. We treated authors as users, papers as items, each publishing/citation of a paper as user's rating on the paper, and treated the venues and authors of a paper as the features of the paper. After removing the users with fewer than 10 papers from the original DBLP data set[2], the final data set contains 6815 users' ratings on 78475 items with 81858 unique features. All the above data sets have binary ratings. The fourth data set *Movielens*, also recommended by the 2011

[1]http://www.grouplens.org/data sets/hetrec-2011/

[2]http://arnetminer.org/citation

HetRec conference, was collected from a movie review system. This data set has the ratings ranged from 1 to 5. We removed those movies without any ratings. The resulting data set has 1857 users' ratings on 4721 items with 8288 unique features (i.e., tags). The statistics of these data sets are found in Table 1. We conducted 10-fold cross validation for all data sets.

4.2 Evaluated Methods

The first baseline is the probabilistic matrix factorization that ignores features of items:

Probabilistic matrix factorization (denoted PMF): This method adopts matrix factorization on the user-item rating matrix (Salakhutdinov and Mnih 2008b). Following (Salakhutdinov and Mnih 2008b), we set the parameters $\lambda_u = \lambda_v = 0.01$.

The next four baselines consider features of an item. All the baselines were previously proposed in the literature.

Collaborative topic regression (denoted CTR): This is matrix factorization with topic modeling applied to features of items (Wang and Blei 2011). Following (Wang and Blei 2011), we set the parameters $\lambda_u = \lambda_v = 0.01, \alpha = 50/D$ and $\beta = 0.01$.

Factorization machine (denoted FM): This is the factorization machine approach in (Rendle 2012). FM takes selected features into consideration equally while our model gives more importance to representative features. We run the code of (Rendle 2012) with the default settings. Note that we need not compare with (Chen et al. 2012) since it can be modeled by FM as indicated in (Rendle 2012).

Regression latent factor model (denoted RLFM): This is the regression based latent factor model in (Agarwal and Chen 2009). RLFM incorporated features as side information to regress the latent vectors so as to improve the performance. We run the code of (Agarwal and Chen 2009) with the default settings.

Similarity based method (denoted SIM): This is a content-based filtering approach that uses the SVM regression (Gedikli and Jannach 2013) to predict the user's ratings on items according to inferred feature preferences. Note that the computation of SIM is not in the latent space.

The next method is the feature-centric approach proposed in this work:

Feature-centric recommendation (denoted FCR): This is the feature-centric solution proposed in Section 3. We denote FCR-a, FCR-u and FCR-r for different integration strategies, i.e., averaged heuristic, user-specific heuristic and regression model. FCR-a is computed by Eq. (1), FCR-u is computed by Eq. (3), and FCR-r is computed by Eq. (9).

For all methods except for SIM, we adopt the dimensionality of $D = 20$ for latent vectors and the learning rate of $\eta = 0.0001$.

4.3 Evaluation Metrics

RMSE (root mean squared error) and **MAE** (mean absolute error) quantify the difference between the rating values predicted by a recommender and the true values in the testing set. These two metric are defined as follows: $RMSE = \sqrt{\frac{1}{n}\sum_{i,j}(r_{ij} - \hat{r}_{ij})^2}$, $MAE = \frac{1}{n}\sum_{i,j}|r_{ij} - \hat{r}_{ij}|$, where r_{ij} is the true rating value, $\hat{r}_{ij}$ is the predicted rating value, and n is the number of ratings in the testing set. The smaller these values are, the better the result is. As pointed out in (Koren 2009), achievable RMSE values lie in a quite compressed range and small improvements in RMSE terms can have a significant impact on the quality of the top few presented recommendations.

4.4 Experimental Results

Table 2 shows RMSE and MAE with standard errors for different methods. Among them, FM and RLFM are recent developed models which can incorporate features for better predications. The best performers for each data set are highlighted in bold face. All reported RMSE and MAE are the average of the 10 runs in the 10-fold cross-validation.

First, PMF performs poorly on all data sets since it only considers the item ratings and ignores the feature information. When this matrix is sparse, the ratings as only the similarity information among users are hardly enough to make accurate recommendation. CTR slightly improve the performance over PMF by using features as the side information to regularize the original matrix. The improvement is not significant since the role of features is limited to regularization; there is no direct participation in rating prediction. On Lastfm, their performances are even worse than PMF. The next three baselines, FM, RLFM, SIM, further improves the performance with similar improvement. FAR has a similar performance to CTR as both methods use features as side information to regularize the original matrix.

FCR-a is our proposed feature-centric method with averaged heuristic and performs close to FM because these methods involve features in matrix factorization and infer latent feature vectors for prediction. However, FM involves the pairwise interactions between latent item vectors and latent feature vectors, which may be complex and improper in real-life applications; on the contrary, our model provides a simple and clean solution.

By incorporating the user-specific heuristic, FCR-u achieves significant improvements over FCR-a. This weighting scheme gives more trust to features that are more frequently selected by users. Through a regression model, FCR-r finds proper weighting for features and achieves better results compared to FCR-u.

Overall, FCR is the the best performing method for all data sets, which verifies the effectiveness of the proposed feature-centric approach. Among the three integration strategies, FCR-r performs the best on Delicious and Lastfm, which suggests that the regression model yields better weighting for features. For example, the rating density is very sparse for DBLP and Delicious and matrix factorization on traditional user-item rating matrix works poorly. In the feature-centric FCR, this problem does not occur because the features of items act as a media for collaborative learning between users. For the DBLP data set, the users working in AI areas may focus on AAAI, IJCAI, ICML conferences (which are features of papers), so even the citation/publishing data is sparse, the interests of users are

Table 2: $RMSE$ and MAE of four data sets

Methods	Delicious RMSE	Delicious MAE	Lastfm RMSE	Lastfm MAE	DBLP RMSE	DBLP MAE	Movielens RMSE	Movielens MAE
Baselines								
PMF	0.8907 ± 0.0046	0.8081 ± 0.0048	0.4449 ± 0.0040	0.3179 ± 0.0022	0.5060 ± 0.0021	0.3800 ± 0.0020	1.1271 ± 0.0247	0.8622 ± 0.0197
CTR	0.7844 ± 0.0004	0.7431 ± 0.0005	0.5078 ± 0.0025	0.4084 ± 0.0025	0.4943 ± 0.0021	0.3653 ± 0.0018	1.0880 ± 0.0191	0.8315 ± 0.0156
FM	0.3551 ± 0.0017	0.2906 ± 0.0020	0.3239 ± 0.0022	0.2534 ± 0.0030	0.1821 ± 0.0023	0.1167 ± 0.0020	1.2049 ± 0.0229	0.9467 ± 0.0194
RLFM	0.4182 ± 0.0010	0.3978 ± 0.0010	0.3208 ± 0.0014	0.2235 ± 0.0015	0.2297 ± 0.0007	0.1930 ± 0.0007	1.0662 ± 0.0215	0.8056 ± 0.0145
SIM	0.4001 ± 0.0008	0.3872 ± 0.0011	0.3269 ± 0.0013	0.2941 ± 0.0013	0.3064 ± 0.0003	0.3032 ± 0.0003	1.0137 ± 0.0190	0.7616 ± 0.0123
Proposed Methods								
FCR-a	0.3169 ± 0.0020	0.2396 ± 0.0016	0.3790 ± 0.0023	0.3062 ± 0.0022	0.2043 ± 0.0016	0.1393 ± 0.0017	0.9966 ± 0.0148	0.7770 ± 0.0105
FCR-u	0.2572 ± 0.0023	0.1645 ± 0.0014	0.2455 ± 0.0032	0.1468 ± 0.0020	0.1204 ± 0.0010	$\mathbf{0.0739} \pm 0.0006$	$\mathbf{0.9515} \pm 0.0150$	0.7306 ± 0.0092
FCR-r	$\mathbf{0.2176} \pm 0.0011$	$\mathbf{0.1513} \pm 0.0009$	$\mathbf{0.1868} \pm 0.0020$	$\mathbf{0.1066} \pm 0.0016$	$\mathbf{0.1064} \pm 0.0004$	0.0841 ± 0.0003	0.9724 ± 0.0201	$\mathbf{0.7208} \pm 0.0125$

Table 3: Paired t-Test(2-tail) of FCR-a and FCR-r

t-Test	Delicious	Lastfm	DBLP	Movielens
RMSE	2.4×10^{-15}	1.5×10^{-16}	5.1×10^{-16}	1.4×10^{-4}
MAE	2.2×10^{-15}	1.6×10^{-17}	8.1×10^{-15}	1.3×10^{-7}

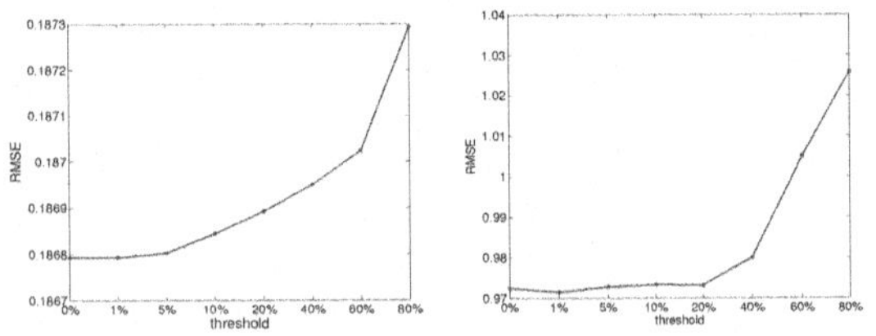

Figure 2: Feature selection for FCR-r on Lastfm (left) and MovieLens (right). y-axis represents RMSE and x-axis represents the percentage of the features with lower correlations removed

Figure 3: Representative features on Lastfm

closely related through similar publishing venues. For the Movielens data set, the improvement is least mainly because user's interests are more diverse on movies, leading to less collaborative learning effect through features.

t-Test. To further verify the statistical significance of the improvement introduced by the regression model, we conducted the paired t-Test (2-tail) on FCR-a and FCR-r over 10 folds. As shown in Table 3, the t-Test results (p-values) are less than 0.01, which suggests that the improvement of FCR-r over FCR-a is statistically significant.

Representative features. We perform the 2-step feature selection for FCR-r and study the representative features. Figure 2 presents the RMSE results on Lastfm and MovieLens when removing those features with lower correlations. We observe that the lowest 1% features have no contributions to the model since the RMSE is slightly improved without them. With more features removed, the RMSE is steady at first, indicating those features are less representative, i.e., lowest 5% on Lastfm and lowest 20% on Movielens. Then the RMSE goes up steeply when removing those features with higher correlations. Note that the results are still better than most baselines even if the lowest 80% of the features are removed. This also coincides with our thinking that the features with higher correlations are more representative. Figure 3 demonstrates the representative features on Lastfm with visualization tools.

Discussions. In summary, the proposed feature-centric approach demonstrates superiority over item-centric approaches. This superiority is especially obvious for a sparse rating matrix in which case collaborative filtering on features is a much better option than collaborative filtering on items because feature ratings are denser than item ratings. Content-based filtering, i.e., SIM, extends items with content/features, and more recently, several works extend collaborative filtering (i.e., the latent factor model) to items with content and features, i.e., CTR and RLFM. The improvement is limited because features are used as auxiliary information such as a new regularization term in matrix factorization. Our feature-centric approach acknowledges the upmost importance of features in item preferences by allowing the features to play a central role from rating capturing to model building to rating prediction, which yields significant improvements. The studies also suggested that a model based regression is a viable weighting strategy for integrating feature ratings and finding representative features. Those representative features should be highly considered in real-life recommendations.

5 Conclusion

Traditional recommender systems are item-centric in that all steps are centered around items: rating collection, model extraction, and rating prediction. Even if features of items are considered, they serve only the description of items in order to enhance the similarity comparison between items and users. This work is based on a simple observation: a user prefers an item because she likes certain features of the item; therefore, a good prediction on features would lead to a good prediction on items. This observation motivates a feature-centric approach that aims to predict feature ratings in order to predict item ratings. Our contribution is to reformulate the item prediction problem into the feature prediction problem and turn the solution into a solution for item prediction. Two clear benefits of this approach are: it enables a principled item prediction (e.g., latent factor model) on feature prediction with little changes, and it enables collaborative filtering on the denser feature ratings, therefore, maximizes the effect of collaborative filtering and addresses the well known sparsity of rating data.

Acknowledgements

This work is partially supported by China Knowledge Centre for Engineering Sciences and Technology (No. CKCEST-2014-1-5), partially supported by a Discovery Grant from Natural Sciences and Engineering Research Council of Canada, and partially supported by the Singapore National Research Foundation under its International Research Centre@ Singapore Funding Initiative and administered by the IDM Programme Office, Media Development Authority (MDA). Ke Wang's work is partially done when he visited SA Center for Big Data Research hosted in Renmin University of China. This Center is partially funded by a Chinese National 111 Project Attracting International Talents in Data Engineering and Knowledge Engineering Research.

References

Adomavicius, G., and Tuzhilin, A. 2005. Toward the next generation of recommender systems: A survey of the state-of-the-art and possible extensions. *IEEE Transcation on Knowledge and Data Engineering (TKDE)* 17(6):734–749.

Agarwal, D., and Chen, B.-C. 2009. Regression-based latent factor models. In *KDD*, 19–28. ACM.

Agarwal, D.; Chen, B.-C.; and Pang, B. 2011. Personalized recommendation of user comments via factor models. In *EMNLP*, 571–582. Association for Computational Linguistics.

Chen, T.; Zhang, W.; Lu, Q.; Chen, K.; Zheng, Z.; and Yu, Y. 2012. Svdfeature: a toolkit for feature-based collaborative filtering. *The Journal of Machine Learning Research* 13(1):3619–3622.

Gantner, Z.; Drumond, L.; Freudenthaler, C.; Rendle, S.; and Schmidt-Thieme, L. 2010. Learning attribute-to-feature mappings for cold-start recommendations. In *ICDM*, 176–185. IEEE.

Gedikli, F., and Jannach, D. 2010. Rating items by rating tags. In *Proceedings of the 2010 Workshop on Recommender Systems and the Social Web at ACM RecSys*, 25–32.

Gedikli, F., and Jannach, D. 2013. Improving recommendation accuracy based on item-specific tag preferences. *ACM Transactions on Intelligent Systems and Technology (TIST)* 11:1–11:19.

Han, E.-H. S., and Karypis, G. 2005. Feature-based recommendation system. In *CIKM*, 446–452. ACM.

Hong, L.; Doumith, A. S.; and Davison, B. D. 2013. Co-factorization machines: modeling user interests and predicting individual decisions in twitter. In *WSDM*, 557–566. ACM.

Karatzoglou, A.; Amatriain, X.; Baltrunas, L.; and Oliver, N. 2010. Multiverse recommendation: n-dimensional tensor factorization for context-aware collaborative filtering. In *Recsys*, 79–86. ACM.

Koren, Y. 2009. Collaborative filtering with temporal dynamics. In *KDD*, 447–456. New York, NY, USA: ACM.

Kuhn, H. W., and Tucker, A. W. 1951. Nonlinear programming. In *Proceedings of the Second Berkeley Symposium on Mathematical Statistics and Probability*, 481–492. University of California Press.

Rendle, S. 2012. Factorization machines with libfm. *ACM Transactions on Intelligent Systems and Technology (TIST)* 3(3):57:1–57:22.

Salakhutdinov, R., and Mnih, A. 2008a. Bayesian probabilistic matrix factorization using markov chain monte carlo. In *ICML*, 880–887. ACM.

Salakhutdinov, R., and Mnih, A. 2008b. Probabilistic matrix factorization. In *NIPS*, 1257–1264.

Sen, S.; Vig, J.; and Riedl, J. 2009. Tagommenders: connecting users to items through tags. In *WWW*, 671–680. ACM.

Smola, A. J., and Scholkopf, B. 2004. A tutorial on support vector regression. *Statistics and computing* 14(3):199–222.

Tso-Sutter, K. H.; Marinho, L. B.; and Schmidt-Thieme, L. 2008. Tag-aware recommender systems by fusion of collaborative filtering algorithms. In *Proceedings of the 2008 ACM symposium on Applied computing*, 1995–1999. ACM.

Wang, C., and Blei, D. M. 2011. Collaborative topic modeling for recommending scientific articles. In *KDD*, 448–456. ACM.

Wilson, E. B. 1927. Probable inference, the law of succession, and statistical inference. *Journal of the American Statistical Association* 22(158):209–212.

Zhang, C.; Wang, K.; Yu, H.; Sun, J.; and Lim, E.-p. 2014a. Latent factor transition for dynamic collaborative filtering. In *SDM*, 452–460.

Zhang, C.; Zhao, X.; Wang, K.; and Sun, J. 2014b. Content+ attributes: A latent factor model for recommending scientific papers in heterogeneous academic networks. In *ECIR*, 39–50.

Zhen, Y.; Li, W.-J.; and Yeung, D.-Y. 2009. Tagicofi: tag informed collaborative filtering. In *Recsys*, 69–76. ACM.

Zhou, T. C.; Ma, H.; King, I.; and Lyu, M. R. 2009. Tagrec: Leveraging tagging wisdom for recommendation. In *International Conference on Computational Science and Engineering*, volume 4, 194–199. IEEE.

Incorporating Implicit Link Preference Into Overlapping Community Detection

Hongyi Zhang[1,2], **Irwin King**[1,2], **Michael R. Lyu**[1,2]
[1]Shenzhen Key Laboratory of Rich Media Big Data Analytics and Applications, Shenzhen Research Institute, The Chinese University of Hong Kong, Shenzhen, China
[2]Department of Computer Science and Engineering, The Chinese University of Hong Kong, Shatin, N.T., Hong Kong
{hyzhang, king, lyu}@cse.cuhk.edu.hk

Abstract

Community detection is an important technique to understand structures and patterns in complex networks. Recently, overlapping community detection becomes a trend due to the ubiquity of overlapping and nested communities in real world. However, existing approaches have ignored the use of implicit link preference information, i.e., links can reflect a node's preference on the targets of connections it wants to build. This information has strong impact on community detection since a node prefers to build links with nodes inside its community than those outside its community. In this paper, we propose a preference-based nonnegative matrix factorization (PNMF) model to incorporate implicit link preference information. Unlike conventional matrix factorization approaches, which simply approximate the original adjacency matrix in value, our model maximizes the likelihood of the preference order for each node by following the intuition that a node prefers its neighbors than other nodes. Our model overcomes the indiscriminate penalty problem in which non-linked pairs inside one community are equally penalized in objective functions as those across two communities. We propose a learning algorithm which can learn a node-community membership matrix via stochastic gradient descent with bootstrap sampling. We evaluate our PNMF model on several real-world networks. Experimental results show that our model outperforms state-of-the-art approaches and can be applied to large datasets.

1 Introduction

Discovering the community structure in complex networks has been extensively investigated in the past decade (Fortunato 2010). A community is intuitively regarded as a group of nodes with more links inside the group than between its member and outside the group (Girvan and Newman 2002). In real world, communities can be social circles manually categorized by users in ego networks (McAuley and Leskovec 2012), authors from the same institution in collaboration networks (Newman 2001), proteins with the same functionality in biochemical networks (Gavin et al. 2002), etc. The research issue of finding such groups is known as the *community detection* problem.

Classic methods in community detection assume that one node belongs to exactly one community. However, many complex networks we encounter in daily life allow multiple memberships. For example, two colleagues in the same department are also in the same company (nested), one can join in several discussion groups in an online forum (overlapping), etc. Thus, the topic of overlapping community detection has attracted major attention recently (Xie, Kelley, and Szymanski 2013).

Existing overlapping community detection approaches can be categorized into two classes: one is based on dense subgraph extraction (Ahn, Bagrow, and Lehmann 2010; Palla et al. 2005; Kumpula et al. 2008), which uses certain criteria to find overlapping dense subgraphs or clusters in the network to be communities; the other is based on community affiliation model (Psorakis et al. 2011; Wang et al. 2011; Yang and Leskovec 2013; Zhang and Yeung 2012), which determines the number of communities in advance and assigns each node to multiple communities according to some optimization function. However, both classes of approaches only focus on links themselves but ignore the implicit preference information in links. In fact, a link can reflect the preferences of both sides to some extent. For example, in a social network, if user A wants to make friend with user B, a typical way for A is to send a friend invitation to B and wait for him to accept it. They cannot be friends if either step goes wrong. Thus, when we see the fact that A and B are friends, it is reasonable to argue that A prefers B than other strangers to be his friend. Assuming B also receives other people's invitations and only accepts a few of them (this is very likely to happen in real world), we can also argue that B prefers A than others who are still strangers to him. Following the intuition that a node are more likely to build links with other nodes in the same community than those outside its community, the implicit preference information can be helpful for community detection.

For the second class of approaches, i.e., community affiliation based approaches, nonnegative matrix factorization (NMF) has been applied as a standard technique. The basic idea of NMF technique is to find a node-community membership matrix F ($F_{u,c}$ represents the weight of node u in community c) and approximate the adjacency matrix G via

FF^T. Existing approaches use either the conventional least squares error or the generalized KL divergence as objective function (Lee and Seung 2001). However, both objective functions try to approximate the adjacency matrix G in value, which are inevitable to cause the indiscriminate penalty problem. Let us assume that there are two non-linked pairs (i, j) and (i, k), where i, j belong to the same community while i, k do not. Since i, j both have positive weights in some community c, $F_i F_j^T$ is positive. However, existing NMF based approaches will penalize $F_i F_j^T$ for being positive since $G_{i,j} = 0$. Thus, there is no difference between j and k with respect to i, which is against the intuition that for node i, node j in the same community is more preferable than node k outside i's community. In fact, it is reasonable that $F_i F_j^T$ is higher than $F_i F_k^T$, and indiscriminately penalizing the two pairs are problematic.

In this paper, we present a preference-based nonnegative matrix factorization (PNMF) model that not only fixes the indiscriminate penalty problem of previous NMF based models, but also incorporates the implicit link preference information into model formulation. Our model uses a new objective function, which maximizes the likelihood of a pairwise preference order for each node. In other words, from a node's perspective, we manage to ensure that the preference of any of its friends is higher than any of other nodes. When factorizing the adjacency matrix with node-community relationship matrix, our model gives no penalty to a non-zero value appearing in the position of a non-linked pair, as long as all the pair-wise preferences are preserved. Thus, this objective function can be regarded as a relaxation of previous approaches. We exploit stochastic gradient descent with bootstrap sampling to solve the optimization problem. We conduct experiments in several real world datasets including some with ground-truth communities. By comparing our model with several state-of-art approaches, we show that our model can detect overlapping communities with higher quality on widely-used metrics in community detection. It can also be applied to large datasets.

The remainder of this paper is organized as follows. Section 2 provides an overview of overlapping community detection and other works related to our model. Section 3 presents our PNMF model in mathematical form and propose a stochastic gradient descent method to learn model parameters, i.e., community weights for each node. Experimental results are shown in Section 4, followed by conclusions in Section 5.

2 Related Work

Traditional community detection methods are based on graph clustering/partitioning (Fortunato 2010; Newman 2004). To measure the quality of a particular partition, different functions are created. Among them, modularity is the most popular one (Newman 2006). However, the most severe drawback of these methods is that each node can only be assigned to a single community, which is against the nature of the real world. Thus, overlapping community detection has attracted lots of attention recently due to its practical assumption (Xie, Kelley, and Szymanski 2013).

Almost all the early work in overlapping community detection are based on dense subgraph extraction. Clique Percolation method (CPM) (Palla et al. 2005), which is still one of the most popular methods now, finds all the k-cliques at first and then combines cliques with $k - 1$ common nodes to be a community. Kumpula et al. propose a sequential alternative of CPM, which significantly reduces the time of finding cliques (Kumpula et al. 2008). Link clustering (Ahn, Bagrow, and Lehmann 2010) uses links instead of nodes for clustering and consequently generates overlapping communities.

Community affiliation based approaches solve overlapping community detection from the perspective of communities. They determine the number of communities in advance, then assign nodes to each community based on some criterion. Some approaches apply *Markov Chain Monte Carlo (MCMC)* to iteratively change node membership until a local optimal is reached (Karrer and Newman 2011; Yang and Leskovec 2012). However, the performance is not good enough and they suffer from convergence problems. Recently, *nonnegative matrix factorization (NMF)* has become a standard technique since the latent factor can be naturally regarded as communities and it automatically generates overlapping communities. Psorakis et al. employ a Baysian generative model, which puts a half-normal prior β_i over each community and then maximizes the log-likelihood of generating original graph (Psorakis et al. 2011). Want et al. apply a multiplicative update rule to minimize $||G - FF^T||_F^2$, where G is the adjacency matrix and F is the targeted node-community membership matrix (Wang et al. 2011). Zhang and Yeung incorporate a community interaction matrix B, which represents the relations between communities and approximate G by a nonnegative matrix tri-factorization FBF^T with bounds in F (Zhang and Yeung 2012). Yang and Leskovec develop a scalable model, which relaxes the graph fitting problem into a continuous optimization problem (Yang and Leskovec 2013). Though different objective functions have been engaged, the idea of these NMF-based methods is always to approximate the original adjacency matrix in value.

Baysian Personalized Ranking (BPR) (Rendle et al. 2009b) is proposed to rank items for a specific user in recommender systems while only implicit feedback (e.g. clicks) is available. The basic assumption is that a user prefers labeled items than unlabeled ones. While traditional methods replace missing values with zeros or negative ones, BPR uses pairwise preference as training data to learn the model parameters. Technically, it maximizes a posterior probability $p(\Theta| >_u)$ where Θ is the parameter and $>_u$ is the latent preference structure for user u. We adopt this idea into our overlapping community detection task for a different learning goal of maximizing the probability $p(>_u |F)$, where F is a nonnegative matrix representing the latent node-community membership. BPR has become a classical model in one-class collaborative filtering and there are many further work on top of it. For example, Rendle et al. extend the original matrix factorization to a tensor factorization to recommend personalized tags for a user given an item (Rendle et al. 2009a). Zhao et al. leverage social connections to improve item recommendations by building a new preference system (Zhao, McAuley, and King 2014).

3 Community Detection via PNMF

In this section, we present our PNMF model in the context of overlapping community detection and propose a stochastic gradient descent method with bootstrap sampling to learn model parameters.

Preliminaries

Given an unweighted and undirected network $N(V, E)$, where V is the set of n nodes and E is the set of m edges, we can obtain its adjacency matrix $G \in \{0,1\}^{n\times n}$ whose (i,j) entry $g_{i,j}$ is an indicator of whether node i and node j are connected. Since the network is undirected, G is a symmetric matrix.

We denote the set of communities by C and the number of communities by p. We use a nonnegative matrix $F \in \mathbb{R}_+^{n\times p}$ to denote the node-community membership for all the nodes. Each entry $F_{u,c}$ represents the weight between node $u \in V$ and community $c \in C$. The larger $F_{u,c}$ is, the more possible that u belongs to c. On the other hand, if $F_{u,c}$ is 0, u does not belong to c.

Given the information above, the objective is to recover G with some properties preserved by a nonnegative matrix factorization FF^T, i.e.,

$$G \approx FF^T. \tag{1}$$

Previous approaches simply approximate G in value. They expect $F_u F_v^t$ to be close to 1 if u, v are linked and to be 0 otherwise. In our model, we preserve the preference orders observed in G for all the nodes. We will discuss the details later.

The set of i's neighbors is denoted by $N^+(i)$. In addition, we define $N^-(i) := N^+(i)^c \backslash \{i\}$ to be "non-neighbors" of i, where $N^+(i)^c$ denotes the complement set of $N^+(i)$. By definition, $V = N^+(i) \cup N^-(i) \cup \{i\}$ for every i. Moreover, we define a learning set $S : V \times V \times V$ by

$$S = \{(i,j,k) | i \in V, j \in N^+(i), k \in N^-(i)\},$$

which consists of all the triples (i, j, k), where j is a neighbor of i while k is not.

In the end, we list three basic assumptions on implicit link preference in order to make model formulation clearer.

1. **Node independence**. Each node determines its preferences independently. The network can be regarded as a result after all the nodes make their decisions. Specifically, a link will be built between u and v if and only if u has a high preference on v and symmetrically v has a high preference on u.
2. **Higher preference on neighbors**. Let $u >_i v$ denote that node i prefers node u than node v. For a fixed node i, we have $j >_i k$ if $j \in N^+(i)$ and $k \in N^-(i)$, but no preference information between j and k is indicated if $j, k \in N^+(i)$ or $j, k \in N^-(i)$. Thus, the use of the learning set S is to record all the single triples (i, j, k) satisfying that i prefers to build a link with j than k.
3. **Pair independence**. For a fixed node i, its preference on j and k is independent with its preference on u and v when $j, u \in N^+(i)$ and $k, v \in N^-(i)$.

Model Formulation

Based on our motivation, we aim to find the node-community membership matrix, which maximizes the likelihood of observed preference order for all the nodes. According to the "node independence" assumption, the overall likelihood can be denoted as a product of likelihood of each node. Thus, our objective function can be written as

$$\max_{F\in\mathbb{R}_+^{n\times p}} \prod_{i\in V} p(>_i | F), \tag{2}$$

where $>_i$ denotes the observed preferences for node i and F is the node-community membership matrix.

According to the "high preference on neighbors" assumption and the "pair independence" assumption, the probability of preference order for a single node i can be written as

$$\begin{aligned} p(>_i | F) &= \prod_{(j,k)\in V\times V} p(j >_i k|F)^{\delta(j\in N^+(i))\delta(k\in N^-(i))} \\ &\quad \cdot (1 - p(j >_i k|F))^{1-\delta(j\in N^+(i))\delta(k\in N^-(i))} \\ &= \prod_{(j,k)\in V\times V} p(j >_i k|F)^{\delta((i,j,k)\in S)} \\ &\quad \cdot (1 - p(j >_i k|F))^{\delta((i,j,k)\notin S)}, \end{aligned} \tag{3}$$

where S is the learning set mentioned in preliminaries and δ is the indicator function

$$\delta(a) = \begin{cases} 1 & \text{if } a \text{ is true,} \\ 0 & \text{else} \end{cases}.$$

For a triple (i, j, k), if $(i, j, k) \in S$, then $(i, k, j) \notin S$. Given $p(j >_i k|F) + p(k >_i j|F) = 1$, it is easy to see that $p(j >_i k|F)^{\delta((i,j,k)\in S)} = (1 - p(k >_i j|F)^{\delta((i,k,j)\notin S)}$. Applying this to Equation (3), maximizing $p(>_i |F)$ is equivalent to

$$\max_{F\in\mathbb{R}_+^{n\times p}} \prod_{(j,k)\in V\times V} p(j >_i k|F)^{\delta((i,j,k)\in S)}. \tag{4}$$

Combining Equation (2) and (4), our objective function can be rewritten as

$$\max_{F\in\mathbb{R}_+^{n\times p}} \prod_{(i,j,k)\in S} p(j >_i k|F). \tag{5}$$

Based on the intuition that two nodes have a higher probability to be linked if they share more communities, we define the probability that i prefers j than k given the node-community membership matrix as

$$p(j >_i k|F) = \sigma(F_i \cdot F_j^T - F_i \cdot F_k^T), \tag{6}$$

where σ is the sigmoid function $\sigma(x) := \frac{1}{1+e^{-x}}$.

The sigmoid function can map any real number into $(0, 1)$. We can see that the probability i prefers j than k is 0.5 when $F_i F_j^T = F_i F_k^T$. Also, this probability is close to

0 when $F_i F_j^T \ll F_i F_k^T$ and is close to 1 when $F_i F_j^T \gg F_i F_k^T$. These properties precisely characterize the requirements of our model.

For simplicity, we define $\hat{x}(i,j) := F_i \cdot F_j^T$. Equation (6) can be rewritten as

$$p(j >_i k|F) = \sigma(\hat{x}(i,j) - \hat{x}(i,k)). \tag{7}$$

Now combining Equation (5), (6), and (7), the final objective function of our PNMF model is

$$\begin{aligned} l(F) &:= \max_{F \in \mathbb{R}_+^{n \times p}} \ln \prod_{(i,j,k) \in S} p(j >_i k|F) - \lambda \cdot reg(F) \\ &= \max_{F \in \mathbb{R}_+^{n \times p}} \sum_{(i,j,k) \in S} \ln p(j >_i k|F) - \lambda \cdot reg(F) \\ &= \max_{F \in \mathbb{R}_+^{n \times p}} \sum_{(i,j,k) \in S} \ln \sigma(\hat{x}(i,j) - \hat{x}(i,k)) - \lambda \cdot reg(F), \end{aligned} \tag{8}$$

where $reg(F)$ is the regularization term we add to avoid overfitting and λ is the regularization parameter. We choose Frobenius norm as the regularization term, i.e., we set $reg(F) = ||F||_F^2$, since it is differentiable and fits our parameter learning process.

Parameter Learning

To make our model applicable to large datasets, we employ the widely used stochastic gradient descent (SGD) as our learning approach. In each update step, SGD randomly selects a triple in learning set S and updates the corresponding model parameters Θ by walking along the gradient direction,

$$\Theta^{t+1} = \Theta^t + \alpha \frac{\partial l}{\partial \Theta}, \tag{9}$$

where α is the learning rate. Specifically, the derivative of Equation (9) is calculated by

$$\begin{aligned} \frac{\partial l}{\partial \Theta} &= \frac{\partial}{\partial \Theta} \ln \sigma(\hat{x}(i,j) - \hat{x}(i,k)) - \lambda \frac{\partial}{\partial \Theta} reg(F) \\ &= \frac{-e^{\hat{x}(i,k) - \hat{x}(i,j)}}{1 + e^{\hat{x}(i,k) - \hat{x}(i,j)}} \cdot \frac{\partial}{\partial \Theta}(\hat{x}(i,j) - \hat{x}(i,k)) - \lambda \Theta \end{aligned} \tag{10}$$

and

$$\frac{\partial}{\partial \Theta}(\hat{x}(i,j) - \hat{x}(i,k)) = \begin{cases} F_{j,t} - F_{k,t} & \text{if } \Theta = F_{i,t} \\ F_{i,t} & \text{if } \Theta = F_{j,t} \\ -F_{i,t} & \text{if } \Theta = F_{k,t} \\ 0 & \text{else} \end{cases}, \tag{11}$$

where λ is the regularization parameter. Regarding the nonnegative constraints, we exploit the idea of projected gradient methods for NMF (Lin 2007), which maps the value of a parameter back to nonnegativity.

The whole process of parameter learning is described in Algorithm 1. As we can see, the time complexity of each iteration is $O(mp)$, where m is the number of links, and p is the number of community. The space complexity is $O(np)$, where n is the number of node, since we need to save the node-community membership matrix into memory.

Algorithm 1 Community detection using PNMF

Input: G, the adjacency matrix of original graph
Output: F, the node-community membership matrix

initialize F
compute initial loss
repeat
  for *num_samples* $= 1$ to $|E|$ **do**
    sample node i from V uniformly at random
    sample node j from $N^+(i)$ uniformly at random
    sample node k from $N^-(i)$ uniformly at random
    for each entry Θ in F_i, F_j and F_k **do**
      update Θ according to Equation (9), (10), (11)
      $\Theta \leftarrow \max(\Theta, 0)$
    end for
  end for
  compute loss
until convergence or *max_iter* is reached

Other Issues

Choosing the number of communities. Before learning the parameters, we need to set the number of communities p in advance. However, we have no prior knowledge about it. Here we adopt the approach in (Airoldi et al. 2008). We first reserve 10% of links as validation set. Then we vary p and learn model parameters with the remaining 90% of links for each p. After that, we use the node-community membership matrix F to generate the adjacency matrix G and use G to predict the links in validation set according to our motivation that linked pairs have higher value than non-linked pairs in G. Finally, we pick the p with the best prediction score as our pre-assigned number of communities.

Setting membership threshold. After we learn F, we need to set a threshold δ in order to determine whether a node belongs to a community or not. If $F_{u,c} \geq \delta$, we say that node u belongs to community c. According to Equation (6), we need $p(j >_i k|F)$ to be closer to 1 than 0 if i prefer j than k. We assume that i, j share exactly one community and i, k do not share any communities. Thus $F_i F_k^T = 0$. Due to the symmetry of i and j, we have

$$\sigma(F_i F_j^T - F_i F_k^T) = \sigma(\delta^2 - 0) = \frac{1}{1 + e^{-\delta^2}} = \beta,$$

where β is in the range of $(0.5, 1)$. When β is given, we can compute δ by

$$\delta = \sqrt{-\ln(\frac{1}{\beta} - 1)}. \tag{12}$$

4 Experiments

In this section, we conduct several experiments to compare our PNMF model with other state-of-the-art overlapping community detection approaches in terms of community quality and scalability.

Datasets

We examine our model with several benchmark datasets available on the Internet. We separate them into two categories, one without ground-truth communities and the

Dataset	GT	V	E
Dolphins	N	62	159
Les Misérables	N	77	254
Books about US politics	N	105	441
Word adjacencies	N	112	425
American college football	N	115	613
Jazz musicians	N	198	2,742
Network science	N	1,589	2,742
Power grid	N	4,941	6,594
High-energy theory	N	8,361	15,751
DBLP	Y	317,080	1,049,866
Amazon	Y	334,863	925,872
YouTube	Y	1,134,890	2,987,624

Table 1: **Statistics of twelve datasets (nine without ground-truth and three with ground-truth). GT: whether has ground-truth communities or not, V: number of nodes, E: number of links.**

other with ground-truth communities. For the first category, we choose nine undirected networks collected by Newman[1] as our datasets. For the second category, three large datasets from SNAP[2] are used. Among them, *DBLP* is a coauthorship network in computer science, *Amazon* is a product co-purchase network, *YouTube* is an online social network with communities of various video interests. Simple statistics for all the datasets can be found in Table 1.

Baseline methods

We select five state-of-the-art algorithms to be our baseline methods. The latter three are nonnegative matrix factorization based models, thus are highly comparable with our PNMF model.

SCP (Sequential Clique Percolation) (Kumpula et al. 2008). Since the original Clique Percolation method (Palla et al. 2005) is slow when dealing with large datasets, we choose a sequential alternative, which obtains the same performance but is much faster. For the choice of k-clique, we set k to be 4 or 5.

LC (Link Clustering) (Ahn, Bagrow, and Lehmann 2010). We do not manually set the threshold at which the dendrogram is cut. The algorithm automatically chooses the threshold where the maximum partition density is found. Among the detected communities, we get rid of all the communities whose size is smaller than 3 since these communities make no sense.

BNMF (Baysian NMF) (Psorakis et al. 2011). We use the classic squared loss $||G - WH^T||_F^2$ as the loss function, where G is the adjacency matrix, W and H are the results of nonnegative matrix factorization.

BNMTF (Bounded NM Tri-Factorization) (Zhang and Yeung 2012). To be consistent with BNMF, we also use squared loss $||G - FBF^T||_F^2$ as our loss function, where F and B are the results of nonnegative matrix tri-factorization.

BigCLAM (Yang and Leskovec 2013). For the number of communities, we set a minimum value and a maximum value and let the algorithm find the best choice between these two numbers based on cross-validation.

Metrics

We choose two well-known metrics to measure the performance of our model. The choice of metric depends on whether the specific dataset has ground-truth communities.

Modularity. We employ the most widely used modularity (Newman 2006) as our measure for datasets without ground-truth communities. Since communities are overlapping in our case, we need to modify the original definition of modularity a bit. The new modularity Q is defined as

$$Q = \frac{1}{2m} \sum_{u,v \in V} (g_{u,v} - \frac{d(u)d(v)}{2m}) |C_u \cup C_v|,$$

where m denotes the number of links, V denotes the set of nodes, $g_{i,j}$ denotes the (i,j) entry of adjacency matrix G, $d(i)$ denotes the degree of node i, and C_u denotes the set of communities including u.

As we mentioned, two nodes are more possible to link each other if they have more common communities. Modularity matches our intuition very well in the way that more common communities two nodes have, more penalty they will receive if they do not build a link between them. $\frac{d(u)d(v)}{2m}$ can be regarded as the link probability between u and v.

$\mathbf{F_1}$ score. For datasets with ground-truth communities, we employ another criterion F_1 score to measure the quality of detected communities. We denote the set of ground-truth communities as C and the set of detected communities as $\hat{C}$. C_i represents the i-th community in C and $\hat{C}_i$ represents the i-th community in $\hat{C}$. We define F_1 score to be the average of the F_1 score of the best-matching ground-truth community to each detected community, i.e,

$$F_1 = \frac{1}{|\hat{C}|} \sum_{\hat{C}_i \in \hat{C}} F_1(C_{b(i)}, \hat{C}_i),$$

where the best matching function $b(i)$ is defined as

$$b(i) = \arg\max_j F_1(C_j, \hat{C}_i),$$

and $F_1(\cdot,\cdot)$ is the harmonic mean of precision and recall.

Results

We compare our PNMF model with all the baseline methods listed above and show the results in Table 2. For the first nine datasets without ground-truth communities, we use modularity as our measurement. The results show that our model performs best on seven out of nine datasets. Especially, our model dominates other nonnegative matrix factorization based models (BNMF, BNMTF, BigCLAM) on all the datasets except "Jazz musicians".

For the last three datasets with ground-truth communities, we use F_1 score as our measurement. We can see that our model significantly outperforms LC and is comparable with the other two methods with a fair overall advantage. Another advantage of our model is scalability. Some results are

[1] http://www-personal.umich.edu/mejn/netdata

[2] http://http://snap.stanford.edu/data/

Dataset	Metric	SCP	LC	BNMF	BNMTF	BigCLAM	PNMF
Dolphins	M	0.3049	0.6538	0.5067	0.5067	0.4226	**0.9787**
Les Misérables	M	0.3066	0.7730	0.1247	0.1031	0.5395	**1.1028**
Books about US politics	M	0.4955	0.8507	0.4613	0.4924	0.5290	**0.8640**
Word adjacencies	M	0.0707	0.2705	0.2539	0.2677	0.2312	**0.6680**
American college football	M	0.6050	0.8907	0.5584	0.5733	0.5175	**1.0492**
Jazz musicians	M	0.0114	1.1424	0.1133	0.1118	**1.1438**	0.9357
Network science	M	0.7286	0.9558	0.6607	0.7413	0.5026	**1.6570**
Power grid	M	0.0439	0.3713	0.3417	0.3682	1.0097	**1.1051**
High-energy theory	M	0.5427	**0.9965**	0.5648	0.6004	0.9636	0.9725
DBLP	F_1	0.0967	0.0402	-	-	0.0390	**0.0985**
Amazon	F_1	0.0315	0.0070	-	-	**0.0441**	0.0419
YouTube	F_1	0.0445	-	-	-	0.0194	**0.0605**

Table 2: **Experimental results in terms of modularity (M) and $\mathbf{F_1}$ score (F_1).**

not shown because the corresponding baseline methods cannot scale to networks with such size. Only SCP, BigCLAM and our PNMF model can deal with the largest dataset, i.e. "YouTube", which consists of more than one million nodes.

For the choice of membership threshold β, we examine different values from 0.5 to 1 to find a reasonable range. It is clear that a community will contain less nodes if we set a higher value to β. According to our experiments, $[0.7, 0.8]$ appears to be a suitable range for candidates since a community may contain nearly half of the nodes when β is less than 0.7, while many nodes may not belong to any communities when β is larger than 0.8. To determine the final value of β, we again use the cross-validation paradigm with several candidates in this range and pick the one with the best performance on validation data.

Convergence Issues

Since our PNMF model applies stochastic gradient descent as learning technique, we also observe convergence rate and convergence speed while conducting experiments. For convergence rate, as long as the learning rate and the regularization parameter are appropriate, all the datasets can converge before reaching maximum number of iteration. For convergence speed, Figure 1(a) show the results on five UMich datasets and Figure 1(b) show the results of three SNAP datasets. Here the y-axis represents the ratio of current loss to initial loss. From both figures we can see that loss drops quickly in the beginning and starts to slow down significantly after it reaches 20% of initial loss. Comparing these two figures, we can also find that, although SNAP datasets need more time for one iteration than UMich datasets, the total number of iteration is smaller, which proves the scalability of our model from another perspective.

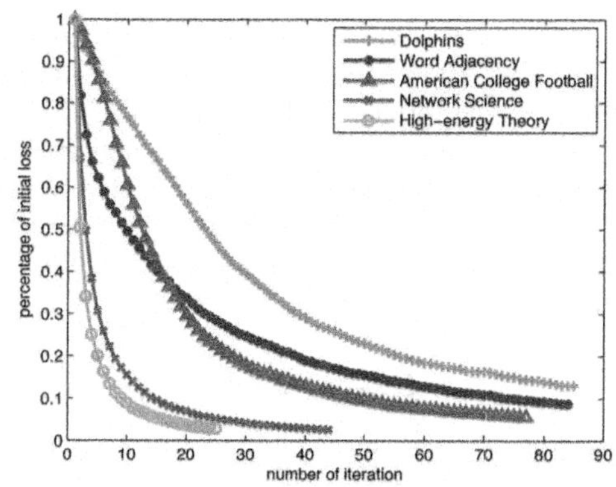

(a) **UMich datasets**

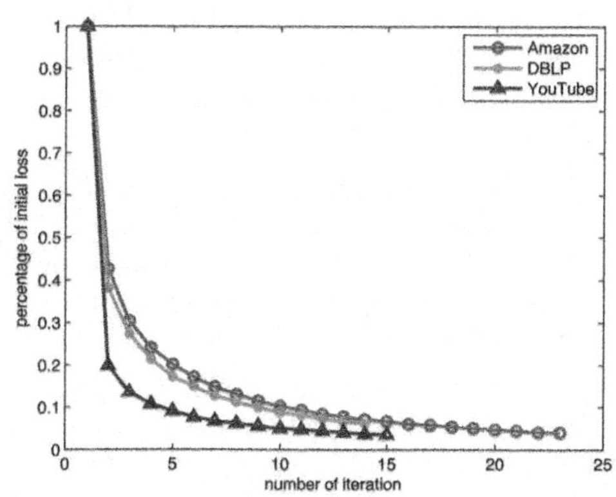

(b) **SNAP datasets**

Figure 1: **Convergence speed of learning algorithm**

5 Conclusion and Future Work

In this paper, we have presented a preference-based nonnegative matrix factorization (PNMF) model for overlapping community detection. The most important contribution of our model is to incorporate implicit link preference information into model formulation. By following the intuition that a node prefers any of its neighbors than any of its "non-neighbors", we maximize the likelihood of a preference order for each node instead of simply approximating the original adjacency matrix in value. Our model can eliminate the unreasonable indiscriminate penalty on pairs inside and between communities. In the learning process, we choose stochastic gradient descent with bootstrap sampling to learn the parameters of node-community membership matrix. We apply our PNMF model on several real-world datasets both with and without ground-truth communities. Our results show that our PNMF model outperforms state-of-art approaches in two metrics, namely modularity and F_1 score, and is scalable for large datasets.

Our current work only focuses on the difference between neighbors and "non-neighbors". We assume that all the "non-neighbors" have the same preference. However, this assumption may not hold in real-world networks. Considering two nodes A and B with no link between them, if there are other nodes which are neighbors of both A and B, from the perspective of A it is reasonable to assign higher preference on B than nodes which have no common neighbors with A. We plan to employ the concept of common neighbors to enhance our preference system in our future work.

Acknowledgement

The work described in this paper was fully supported by the National Grand Fundamental Research 973 Program of China (No. 2014CB340401 and No. 2014CB340405), the Research Grants Council of the Hong Kong Special Administrative Region, China (Project No. CUHK 413212 and CUHK 415113), and Microsoft Research Asia Regional Seed Fund in Big Data Research (Grant No. FY13-RES-SPONSOR-036).

References

Ahn, Y.-Y.; Bagrow, J. P.; and Lehmann, S. 2010. Link communities reveal multiscale complexity in networks. *Nature* 466(7307):761–764.

Airoldi, E. M.; Blei, D. M.; Fienberg, S. E.; and Xing, E. P. 2008. Mixed membership stochastic blockmodels. *Journal of Machine Learning Research* 9(1981-2014):3.

Fortunato, S. 2010. Community detection in graphs. *Physics Reports* 486(3):75–174.

Gavin, A.-C.; Bösche, M.; Krause, R.; Grandi, P.; Marzioch, M.; Bauer, A.; Schultz, J.; Rick, J. M.; Michon, A.-M.; Cruciat, C.-M.; et al. 2002. Functional organization of the yeast proteome by systematic analysis of protein complexes. *Nature* 415(6868):141–147.

Girvan, M., and Newman, M. E. 2002. Community structure in social and biological networks. *Proceedings of the National Academy of Sciences* 99(12):7821–7826.

Karrer, B., and Newman, M. E. 2011. Stochastic blockmodels and community structure in networks. *Physical Review E* 83(1):016107.

Kumpula, J. M.; Kivelä, M.; Kaski, K.; and Saramäki, J. 2008. Sequential algorithm for fast clique percolation. *Physical Review E* 78(2):026109.

Lee, D. D., and Seung, H. S. 2001. Algorithms for non-negative matrix factorization. In *Advances in neural information processing systems*, 556–562.

Lin, C.-J. 2007. Projected gradient methods for nonnegative matrix factorization. *Neural computation* 19(10):2756–2779.

McAuley, J., and Leskovec, J. 2012. Learning to discover social circles in ego networks. In *NIPS*, volume 272, 548–556.

Newman, M. E. 2001. The structure of scientific collaboration networks. *Proceedings of the National Academy of Sciences* 98(2):404–409.

Newman, M. E. 2004. Detecting community structure in networks. *The European Physical Journal B-Condensed Matter and Complex Systems* 38(2):321–330.

Newman, M. E. 2006. Modularity and community structure in networks. *Proceedings of the National Academy of Sciences* 103(23):8577–8582.

Palla, G.; Derényi, I.; Farkas, I.; and Vicsek, T. 2005. Uncovering the overlapping community structure of complex networks in nature and society. *Nature* 435(7043):814–818.

Psorakis, I.; Roberts, S.; Ebden, M.; and Sheldon, B. 2011. Overlapping community detection using bayesian non-negative matrix factorization. *Physical Review E* 83(6):066114.

Rendle, S.; Balby Marinho, L.; Nanopoulos, A.; and Schmidt-Thieme, L. 2009a. Learning optimal ranking with tensor factorization for tag recommendation. In *Proceedings of the 15th ACM SIGKDD international conference on Knowledge discovery and data mining*, 727–736. ACM.

Rendle, S.; Freudenthaler, C.; Gantner, Z.; and Schmidt-Thieme, L. 2009b. Bpr: Bayesian personalized ranking from implicit feedback. In *Proceedings of the Twenty-Fifth Conference on Uncertainty in Artificial Intelligence*, 452–461. AUAI Press.

Wang, F.; Li, T.; Wang, X.; Zhu, S.; and Ding, C. 2011. Community discovery using nonnegative matrix factorization. *Data Mining and Knowledge Discovery* 22(3):493–521.

Xie, J.; Kelley, S.; and Szymanski, B. K. 2013. Overlapping community detection in networks: The state-of-the-art and comparative study. *ACM Computing Surveys (CSUR)* 45(4):43.

Yang, J., and Leskovec, J. 2012. Community-affiliation graph model for overlapping network community detection. In *Data Mining (ICDM), 2012 IEEE 12th International Conference on*, 1170–1175. IEEE.

Yang, J., and Leskovec, J. 2013. Overlapping community detection at scale: a nonnegative matrix factorization approach. In *Proceedings of the sixth ACM international conference on Web search and data mining*, 587–596. ACM.

Zhang, Y., and Yeung, D.-Y. 2012. Overlapping community detection via bounded nonnegative matrix tri-factorization. In *Proceedings of the 18th ACM SIGKDD international conference on Knowledge discovery and data mining*, 606–614. ACM.

Zhao, T.; McAuley, J.; and King, I. 2014. Leveraging social connections to improve personalized ranking for collaborative filtering. In *Proceedings of the 23rd ACM International Conference on Conference on Information and Knowledge Management*, 261–270. ACM.

Retweet Behavior Prediction Using Hierarchical Dirichlet Process

Qi Zhang, Yeyun Gong, Ya Guo, Xuanjing Huang
Shanghai Key Laboratory of Intelligent Information Processing
School of Computer Science, Fudan University
825 Zhangheng Road, Shanghai, P.R.China
{qz, 12110240006, 13210240002, xjhuang}@fudan.edu.cn

Abstract

The task of predicting retweet behavior is an important and essential step for various social network applications, such as business intelligence, popular event prediction, and so on. Due to the increasing requirements, in recent years, the task has attracted extensive attentions. In this work, we propose a novel method using non-parametric statistical models to combine structural, textual, and temporal information together to predict retweet behavior. To evaluate the proposed method, we collect a large number of microblogs and their corresponding social networks from a real microblog service. Experimental results on the constructed dataset demonstrate that the proposed method can achieve better performance than state-of-the-art methods. The relative improvement of the the proposed over the method using only textual information is more than 38.5% in terms of F1-Score.

Introduction

Social media are rapidly growing, with thousands of millions of users participating in them every day. According to the social media report done by Nielsen[1], U.S. audiences spent more than 121.1B minutes in social media in a month. Microblog services usually provide a function, retweet, for users to re-post someone else's microblogs. Through this feature, users can quickly share the microblogs that they view as valuable and important with all of their followers. This causes content to spread from one community to another. Moreover, because microblog services also provide applications for users to share and consume content on mobile devices, information can rapidly spread much faster than any other infectious method. Retweet is usually considered to be the main essence of the viral aspect of content spreading in social media (Rodrigues et al. 2011). Hence, the task of predicting retweet behaviors has been used in various social network applications such as business intelligence (Castellanos et al. 2011; Hoffman and Fodor 2010), microblog retrieval (Chang and Kim 2012), popular event prediction (Hong, Dan, and Davison 2011; Gupta et al. 2012), and so on.

[1]http://www.nielsen.com/us/en/reports/2012/state-of-the-media-the-social-media-report-2012.html

Due to the increasing requirements of predicting retweet behaviors in recent years, the task of how to model retweet behaviors has received considerable attention. Various methods have been proposed from different perspectives, including social influence (Liu et al. 2010; Zhang et al. 2013), textual features (Naveed et al. 2011), social features (Zaman et al. 2010; Petrovic, Osborne, and Lavrenko 2011; Luo et al. 2013), history information (Feng and Wang 2013), visual features (Can, Oktay, and Manmatha 2013), and combinations of different features (Suh et al. 2010). There are also a variety of works studying different models to achieve the task, including Matchbox (Stern, Herbrich, and Graepel 2009; Zaman et al. 2010), multiple additive regression-trees (MART) (Wu et al. 2008), maximum entropy classifier (Artzi, Pantel, and Gamon 2012), autoregressive-moving-average (ARMA) (Luo, Wang, and Wu 2012), factor graph model (Yang et al. 2010), conditional random fields (Peng et al. 2011) et al.

Through analyzing retweet microblogs, we find that even though several microblogs have the same content posted or retweeted by several followers of a user, the user may only retweet one of them. Who post the microblog and other factors may also impact a user's decision. In this paper, we argue that whether a user will retweet a microblog or not is based on the following three main factors: 1) social information (e.g. who post or re-post the microblog); 2) content information (e.g. the topics of the microblog); 3) user properties (e.g. the interests of the user). However, because most existing methods only consider either structural or textual information, it is difficult to effectively process this type of issue.

In this paper, we propose a novel model based on non-parametric statistical methods to incorporate textual, structural, and temporal information to model retweet behavior. For analyzing the retweet phenomenon and evaluating the proposed method, we collected a large dataset from a real online microblog service. We crawled not only the microblog posts itself but also the social networks of the corresponding users. From the constructed dataset, we observe that the retweet behavior is influenced by not only the content itself, but also structural and temporal information. Based on these observations, we adapted the hierarchical Dirichlet process (HDP) (Teh et al. 2006) to define a novel nonparametric method to model retweet behaviors. The retweet prediction algorithm uses the estimated model and several simple steps to achieve the task. The experimental results on the constructed dataset demonstrated that the proposed method could achieve significantly better performance than state-of-the-art methods. Moreover, in a comparison of the performances of the methods without incorporating all these factors, we also observed that combining all these factors could significantly improve the effectiveness of prediction. The main contributions of this work can be summarized as follows:

- We propose a novel nonparametric Bayesian model adapted from the hierarchical Dirichlet process to combine textual, structural, and temporal information for predicting retweet behaviors.
- We construct a large collection of microblogs from a real microblogging service. It contains both microblog content and the social network information of related users.
- Experimental results demonstrate that the proposed method can achieve better performance than state-of-the-art methods.

The Proposed Method

The Problem Statement

Given a microblog m and a user u, the retweet prediction task is to decide whether the user u will retweet the microblog or not. In Twitter-like services, a user u_A can follow other users. If u_A follows u_B, the activities (e.g. tweet, retweet) of u_B are visible to u_A. User u_A is called the *follower* of u_B and u_B is called the *followee* of u_A. Hence, to model the retweet prediction behavior of a user u, we can restore the browsing history of user u through collecting microblogs posted by the followees of u. Let D_u to represent all the microblogs which are posted by the followees of the user u. The dth microblog in D_u consists of a sequence of words $w_d = \{w_{dn}\}_{n=1}^{N_d}$, where N_d is the number of words in the dth microblog, and w_{dn} is one of the word belonging the vocabulary W. a_d denotes the author of the dth microblog. In this work, we only consider the microblogs posted or retweeted by the followees of a user.

Data Analyses

To analyze the retweet behavior and construct evaluation data set, we crawled a large number of microblogs based on the properties of microblog service. According to the design of Twitter-like microblog services (e.g. Twitter, Sina Weibo, et al.), only the microblogs posted by the followees of the user will be shown up for him to read. Hence, for evaluation and analysis, we collected the data set from Sina Weibo[2] with the following ways. Firstly, we randomly select 200 users as the *central users* we studied in this work. To restore what they have seen from the microblog services, we firstly collected the 2-ego network for all the central users based on their follower-followee relationships. Through this step, we constructed a social network which

Table 1: Statistics of the data set

# Users	2,073,121
# Following-Relationships	299,602,693
# Microblogs	84,768,859
# Retweets w/o reply	34,024,561
# Retweets with reply	16,974,326

contains 2.07 million users and 299.6 million following relationships among them. Since existing methods have demonstrated that users' profiles are useful for this task and some of works are based on the features extracted from it, we also crawled the following profiles of users: name, gender, residence, birthday, verification status, #followers, #followees, #microblogs, et al. Finally, we crawled the latest 2,000 microblogs (including tweets and retweets) posted by the followees of all central users. Through this step, about 84.8 million microblogs were collected.

Table 1 shows the statistics of the collected data set. We split the retweets into two categories based on whether they contain reply or not. From the table, we can observe that about 60.2% microblogs are retweets. The percentages of retweets in the data set are much higher comparing to the statistics reported in (Boyd, Golder, and Lotan 2010). Among all the retweets, about 33.3% of them contain not only the original microblog but also replies. In (Yu, Asur, and Huberman 2012), Yu et al. reported the similar statistical result as us. We think that these statistics reflect the practices of social medias in different cultures.

For analyzing the retweet behaviors, we firstly restored the *browsing history* for all 200 central users based on the microblogs posted by their followees. The 1-ego networks of these users can be directly extracted from the crawled social networks. A user's browsing history contains the microblogs which were posted by the followees of the user and were sorted by their posting times from near to far. Through the recovered browsing histories of users and the microblogs posted by themselves we can get the following observations:

- The 1-ego network of all 200 central users contain 82,311 nodes in total. It means that the total number of followees of them are 82,311 users. From analyzing the microblogs reposted by the central users, we can only find 52,177 users. It only covers 63.3% of all the followees. Further more, among these users, less than 17.8% users have more than one microblogs reposted by the central users. The frequencies of them almost follow the power law. Moreover, for different central users, the percentages of users involved in the retweet actions vary greatly from less than 5% to more than 90%. From these statistics, we can observe that the authors of microblogs would impact the retweet behavior.
- Among all the microblogs reposted by the central users, 42.1% of them occur more than one times in their browsing history. It means that more than one followees posted or reposted the same microblog. However, users may not retweet the first one he saw from their browsing

[2]It is one of the most popular website providing microblogging service in China. http://www.weibo.com

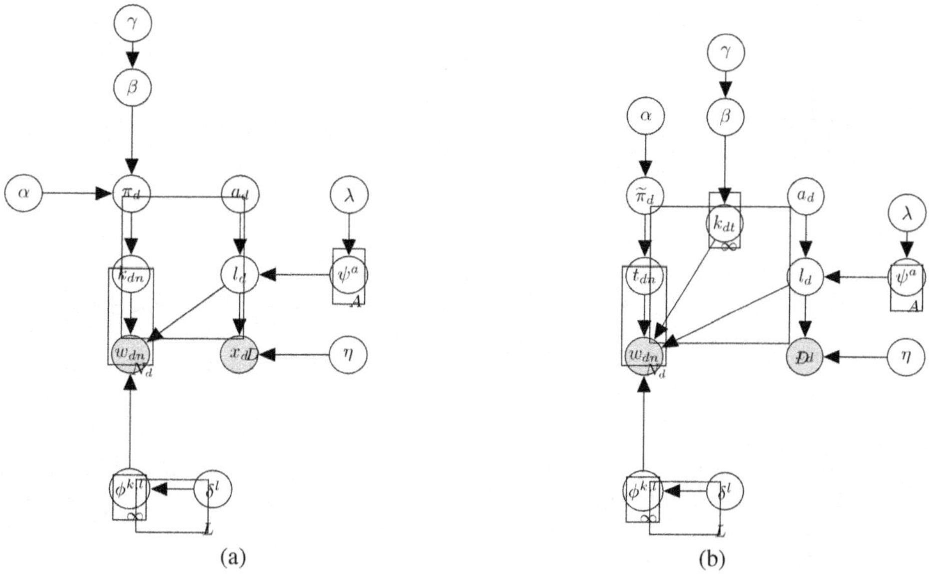

Figure 1: The graphical representation of the proposed models. (a) The original representation. (b) Chinese restaurant franchise construction.

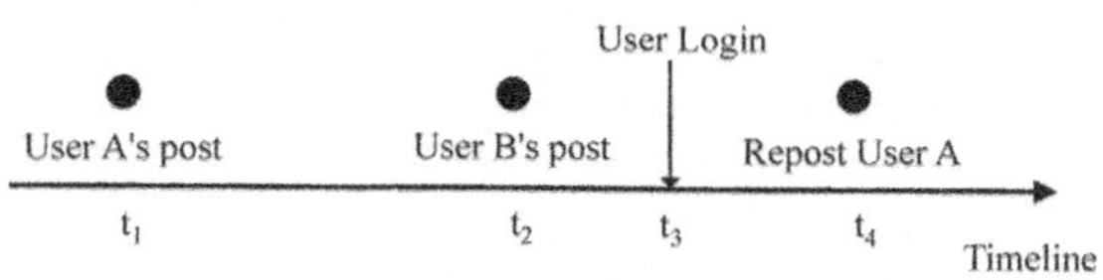

Figure 2: An example of retweet behavior.

history. Figure 2 illustrates this kind of issue. User A and B posted/reposted the same microblog at time t_1 and t_2 respectively. Since the user login at the time t_3, the microblog posted by user B should be shown to the user before user A's. However, the user reposted the microblog posted by user A. According to the statistics, about 37.4% retweet behaviors belong to this type. It can also demonstrate in a manner that retweet behaviors are impacted by not only the content but also who posted it.

- To understand the topics user concentrated on vary over time, we aggregate the microblog posts published in a month together as a document. Then we use HDP to estimate topics of them. From the results, we find that topics user concentrated on are time dependent. For different users, the number of estimated topics varies greatly from less than ten to more than fifty.

The Generation Process

Through descriptions given by the previous sections, we can observe that the retweet behaviors may be impacted by textual, structural and temporal information. Inspired by these observations, in this work, we assume that whether a user retweets a microblog is influenced by:

1. Who posted the microblog.
2. How many followees of the user have posted or retweeted the microblog.
3. The content of the microblog.
4. The time-dependent interests of the user.

Based on these observations, we propose to extend HDP to model the author, structure, and content information. The temporal information is incorporated into the predication stage.

Author Influence. According to the statistics described in the previous section, we can see that users may only retweet microblogs posted by several specific followees of them. Therefore, for user u, we assume that the probability of retweeting microblogs posted by p_{fe_i} for each followee fe_i subject to binomial distribution with Beta prior.

Structure Influence. From data analyses, we also know that the retweet behavior is influenced by their neighbours. Some users prefer to retweet the microblogs which have been retweeted by many their followees, while someone won't like to retweet this kind microblogs. Therefore, we assume that each user corresponds to a distribution. We firstly normalize the retweet times of the microblogs to range from 0 to 1, we use x_d to represent the normalized result. Then, each retweet label is associated with a continuous distribution over x_d. All the results, in this paper, we employ the Beta distribution which can behave versatile shapes.

Content Influence. The content influence is modeled by hidden topics. Since the actual number of topics is an unknown priori, we adopt HDP-based topic model to achieve the task. We use t to represent the cluster contained in the microblog, and k represents the topic for each cluster. We can use a Gibbs sampler to get latent variables, and then the generate probabilities of the microblog d can be calculated for each label respectively as follows:

$$p_c(w_d|\mathbf{t},\mathbf{k},\mathbf{l}) = \prod_{n=1}^{N_d} f^{k_{dt_{dn}},l_d}(w_{dn}), \tag{1}$$

where w_d are the words in microblog d, N_d is the number of words in microblog d, w_{dn} is the nth word in microblog d, $k_{dt_{dn}}$ is the topic for cluster t_{dn} in microblog d, l_d is the retweeted label for microblog d, $f^{k_{dt_{dn}},l_d}(w_{dn})$ is the likelihood of generating w_{dn} for topic $k_{dt_{dn}}$ and retweet label l_d.

Incorporate author, structure, and content information into hierarchical Dirichlet process, we propose the model ASC-HDP. A represents author, S represents structure, and C represents content. Let A_u to represent the number of followees of user u, and D_a to represent the number of microblogs of user a. $m_{.k}$ represents the number of clusters previously assigned with topic k. n_{dt} is the number of words of cluster t in microblog d. We use $p(w_{dn} = w|t_{dn}, l_d, k_{dt_{dn}})$ to represent the generative probability of word w_{dn} given cluster t_{dn}, retweeted label l_d and the topic $k_{dt_{dn}}$ for the cluster t_{dn}. We can get the generation process of our model as follows:

For each followee of the user u. $a = 1, 2, ..., A_u$

1. Draw $\psi_a \sim Beta(\lambda)$
2. For each microblog of followee a. $d = 1, 2, ..., D_a$.
   - a. Draw a retweet label $l_d \sim Binomial(\psi^a)$
   - b. Draw a normalized retweet times $x_d \sim Beta(\eta_{l_d})$
   - c. For each word $n = 1, ..., N_d$
     - i. Choose an exist cluster $t_{dn} = t \propto n_{dt}$
     - ii. Choose a new cluster $t_{dn} = t^{new} \propto \alpha$
     - iii. If choose an existing cluster then Draw a word $w_{dn} = w$ according to probability $p(w_{dn} = w|t_{dn}, l_d, k_{dt_{dn}})$
     - iv. If choose a new cluster then
       - i) Choose an existing topic $k_{dt_{dn}^{new}} = k \propto m_{.k}$
       - ii)Choose a new topic $k_{dt_{dn}^{new}} = k^{new} \propto \gamma$
       - iii) Draw a word $w_{dn} = w$ according to probability $p(w_{dn} = w|t_{dn}, l_d, k_{dt_{dn}^{new}})$

Fig. 1 shows the graphical representation of the generation process.

Learning and inference

To learn the parameters of ASC-HDP, we use Gibbs sampler to sample cluster assignments $\mathbf{t}$ and topic assignments $\mathbf{k}$ for the training data. For the test data, we also need to sample the retweet label $\mathbf{l}$. Adding a superscript $\neg i$ to a variable, indicate the same quantity it is added to without the contribution of object i. For example, $n_{dt}^{\neg dn}$ represents the number of words of cluster t in microblog d without the contribution of word w_{dn}.

Sampling t. To resample cluster t_{dn} for the nth word in microblog d, we make use of exchangeability and imagine word n being the last word in microblog d. We obtain the conditional posterior for t_{dn} by combining the conditional prior distribution for t_{dn} with the likelihood of generating w_{dn}. For the previously used cluster t, the conditional probability of $t_{dn} = t$ is as follows:

$$p(t_{dn} = t|\mathbf{t}_{\neg dn}, \mathbf{k}, \mathbf{l}) \propto \frac{n_{dt}^{\neg dn}}{n_{..}^{\neg dn} + \alpha} f_{\neg w_{dn}}^{k_{dt},l}(w_{dn}), \tag{2}$$

For a new cluster t^{new}, the conditional probability of $t_{dn} = t^{new}$ is as follows:

$$\begin{aligned} &p(t_{dn} = t^{new}|\mathbf{t}_{\neg dn}, \mathbf{k}, \mathbf{l}) \\ &\propto \frac{\alpha}{n_{..}^{\neg dn} + \alpha} p(w_{dn}|\mathbf{t}_{\neg dn}, t_{dn} = t^{new}, \mathbf{k}, \mathbf{l}), \end{aligned} \tag{3}$$

where $\frac{\alpha}{n_{..}^{\neg dn}+\alpha}$ is the prior probability that t_{dn} takes at a new cluster t^{new}. $p(w_{dn}|\mathbf{t}_{\neg dn}, t_{dn} = t^{new}, \mathbf{k}, \mathbf{l})$ is the likelihood due to w_{dn} for $t_{dn} = t^{new}$, which can be calculated by integrating out the possible values of $k_{dt^{new}}$ as follows:

$$\begin{aligned} &p(w_{dn}|\mathbf{t}_{\neg dn}, t_{dn} = t^{new}, \mathbf{k}, \mathbf{l}) \\ &= \sum_{k=1}^{K} \frac{m_{.k}}{m_{..} + \gamma} f_{\neg w_{dn}}^{k,l}(w_{dn}) + \frac{\gamma}{m_{..} + \gamma} f_{\neg w_{dn}}^{k^{new},l}(w_{dn}), \end{aligned} \tag{4}$$

where $m_{..}$ is the total number of clusters assigned to any topic. $\frac{\gamma}{m_{..}+\gamma}$ is the prior probability that assigned to a new topic k^{new}. $f_{\neg w_{dn}}^{k^{new},l}(w_{dn})$ is the prior density of w_{dn}.

If $t_{dn} = t^{new}$, the probability of exist topic k for this table is calculated by the following equation:

$$p(k_{dt^{new}} = k|\mathbf{t}, \mathbf{k}^{\neg dt}, l_d) \propto \frac{m_{.k}}{m_{..} + \gamma} f_{\neg w_{dn}}^{k,l_d}(w_{dn}), \tag{5}$$

and the probability of new topic k^{new} can be calculated by the following equation:

$$p(k_{dt^{new}} = k^{new}|\mathbf{t}, \mathbf{k}^{\neg dt}, l_d) \propto \frac{\gamma}{m_{..} + \gamma} f_{\neg w_{dn}}^{k^{new},l_d}(w_{dn}), \tag{6}$$

Sampling k. Since changing k_{dt} actually changes the component membership of all data items in the cluster t, so that the conditional probability for exist topic k is

$$p(k_{dt} = k|\mathbf{t}, \mathbf{k}^{\neg dt}, l) \propto \frac{m_{.k}^{\neg dt}}{m_{..} + \gamma} f_{\neg \mathbf{w}_{dt}}^{k,l_d}(\mathbf{w}_{dt}) \tag{7}$$

and for a new topic k^{new} is

$$p(k_{dt} = k^{new}|\mathbf{t}, \mathbf{k}^{\neg dt}, l) \propto \frac{\gamma}{m_{..} + \gamma} f_{\neg \mathbf{w}_{dt}}^{k^{new},l_d}(\mathbf{w}_{dt}), \tag{8}$$

where $\mathbf{w}_{dt}$ is the words of cluster t in microblog d.

Sampling l. The component membership of all the data items in microblog d will change when l_d changes, so

$$\begin{aligned} &p(l_d = l|\mathbf{t}, \mathbf{k}, w_d, \mathbf{l}_{\neg d}, x_d) \propto \frac{N_a^l + \lambda_1}{N_a + \lambda_1 + \lambda_2} \\ &\cdot \frac{(1 - x_d)^{\eta_{l1}-1} x_d^{\eta_{l2}-1}}{B(\eta_{l1}, \eta_{l2})} \cdot \prod_{n=1}^{N_d} f(w_{dn}|\phi^{k_{dt_{dn}},l}), \end{aligned} \tag{9}$$

where N_a is the number of microblogs of user a saw by user u. N_a^l is the times of user u retweet from user a.

For simplicity, we update η after each sample by the method of moments, detailed as follows:

$$\eta_{l1} = \overline{x}_d^l(\frac{\overline{x}_d^l(1-\overline{x}_d^l)}{\delta_l^2} - 1)$$
$$\eta_{l2} = (1-\overline{x}_d^l)(\frac{\overline{x}_d^l(1-\overline{x}_d^l)}{\delta_l^2} - 1), \quad (10)$$

where $\overline{x}_d^l$ is the sample mean and δ_l^2 is the biased sampled variance of the retweet times belonging to retweet label l. Sparsity is a serious problem for parameter estimation of η, so when the user have retweeted less than twenty times we set $\eta_{l1} = \eta_{l2} = 0.5$ to avoid the error caused by estimation error.

Retweet Predication

Given the unlabeled microblogs a user saw, we firstly do sampling. After the hidden variables of words become stable, we can estimate the topic distribution of the cluster in the microblog d through Eq.(7) and Eq.(8). Besides that, as described in the previous sections, the topics user interested in may vary over time. Hence, we propose to increase the weights for the hot topics in recent month by $p(k|c_d)$, which is the probability of topic k in the current month. If the topic k is not appear in the current month, $p(k|c_d)$ will be 0. We propose to use the following equation:

$$p^*(k_{dt}|\mathbf{t}, \mathbf{k}_{\neg dt}, l) = p(k_{dt}|\mathbf{t}, \mathbf{k}_{\neg dt}, l)(p(k_{dt}|c_d) + 1). \quad (11)$$

Based on these steps, we can calculate the the probability of retweeting as follows:

$$p(l_d = l|\mathbf{t}, \mathbf{k}_{\neg dt}, w_d, \mathbf{l}_{\neg d}, x_d) \quad (12)$$
$$\propto \frac{N_a^l + \lambda_1}{N_a + \lambda_1 + \lambda_2} \frac{(1-x_d)^{\eta_{l1}-1} x_d^{\eta_{l2}-1}}{B(\eta_{l1}, \eta_{l2})}$$
$$\sum_{k=1}^{K} p^*(k_{dt_{dn}}|\mathbf{t}, \mathbf{k}_{\neg dt}, l) \prod_{n=1}^{N_d} f(w_{dn}|\phi^{k_{dt_{dn}}, l}) p(w_{dn}|w_d),$$

where $p(w_{dn}|w_d)$ is the weight of the word in the microblog d, which can be estimated by the TF·IDF score of word w_{dn}.

Experiments

Experiment Configurations

For each user, we randomly selected about 70% of all microblogs in their browsing history as training data and 10% as development data. The other 20% are used as the test data. For evaluation metrics, we use precision (P), recall (R), and F1-score (F_1) to evaluate the performance. Precision is calculated based on the percentage of "retweets truly identified" among "retweets labeled by system". Recall is calculated based on the "retweets truly identified" among "golden standard retweets". F1-score is the harmonic mean of precision and recall. We ran our model with 500 iterations of Gibbs sampling. In the HDP-based model, we used $\gamma \sim Gamma(1, 1)$ and $\alpha \sim Gamma(1, 1)$ as prior distributions for the concentration parameters. The base measure H for both retweet labels used is a symmetric Dirichlet distribution with parameters of 0.5. In the LDA-based model, we use $\alpha = 50.0/K$ and $\delta = 0.1$ for both retweet labels, after trying a few different numbers of topics, we empirically set the number of topics to 20. In both of the two model we set parameter $\lambda_1 = \lambda_2 = 0.1$.

Table 2: The performances of different methods in the test dataset.

Method	Precision	Recall	F1-Score
Naive Bayes	0.362	0.617	0.456
SVM^{Rank}	0.485	0.450	0.467
LRC-BQ	0.547	0.638	0.589
C-LDA	0.474	0.507	0.490
AC-LDA	0.752	0.545	0.632
SC-LDA	0.446	0.650	0.529
ASC-LDA w/o t	0.680	0.624	0.650
ASC-LDA	0.694	0.636	0.664
C-HDP	0.514	0.541	0.527
AC-HDP	**0.809**	0.533	0.643
SC-HDP	0.456	**0.727**	0.561
ASC-HDP w/o t	0.686	0.695	0.691
ASC-HDP	0.746	0.715	**0.730**

For comparison with the proposed model, we also evaluated the following methods on the constructed dataset:

- **Naive Bayes**: The retweet predication task can be formalized as a binary classification task, where each microblog is assigned either positive or negative label to represent whether it will be retweeted or not. Hence, we applied Naive Bayes to model the posterior probability of labels given a microblog.
- **SVM^{Rank}**: We implemented the method proposed in (Luo et al. 2013), where microblog content, retweet history, followers status, followers active time and followers interests are incorporated under the learning-to-rank framework, to achieve the task.
- **LRC-BQ**: It combines the influence locality function and additional features (including personal attributes, instantaneity topic propensity, et al.) (Zhang et al. 2013). Based on their description, we also collected the properties of users needed and implemented this method.
- **C-HDP**: It represents the model only taking the content information into consideration.
- **SC-HDP**: It omits the influence of the author of microblog. Given a microblog, we assume that whether a user u retweet a microblog subject to binomial distribution, which is not relate to its author.
- **AC-HDP**: It denotes the model which does not consider the influence of actions of social network of this microblog.
- **ASC-HDP w/o t**: In this model, we don't use Eq.(11) in the predication stage of the model ASC-HDP.
- **ASC-LDA**: The proposed methods can also be adopted based on Latent Dirichlet Allocation (LDA) model, where each document is viewed as a mixture of topics. We regard microblogs as general documents and learn an LDA-based model from microblogs.

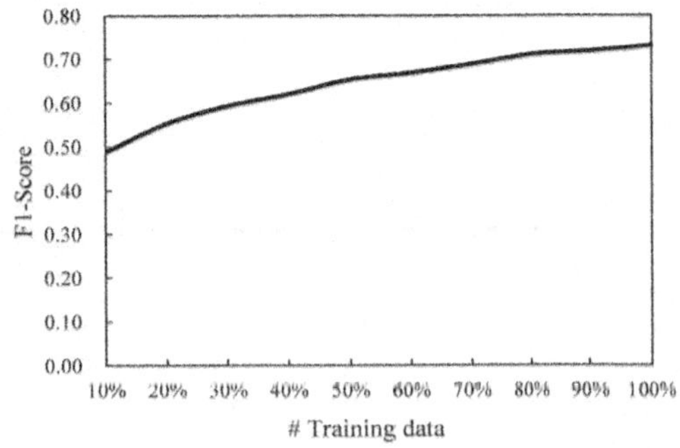

Figure 3: The influence of the number of training data for ASC-HDP.

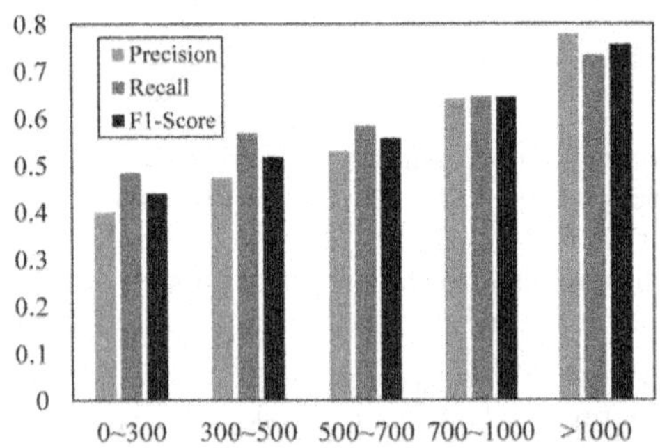

Figure 4: The influence of the number of microblogs posted by users.

Experimental Results

Table 2 shows the comparisons of the proposed method ASC-HDP with the state-of-the-art discriminative and generative methods on the constructed evaluation dataset. From the results, we can observe that the proposed method is significantly better than the other methods. Through comparing the results between ASC-HDP and C-HDP, AC-HDP, SC-HDP, and ASC-HDP w/o t, we can see the ASC-HDP achieves the significantly better F1-score than other the methods. The results demonstrate that all the factors which we proposed in the previous section can impact the performance of the prediction. From the results of AC-HDP and SC-HDP, we can observe that the author information and neighbourhood information can only benefit the precision and recall aspects respectively. Comparing F1-score of C-HDP with ASC-HDP's, we can see the temporal, structural and author information together bring about 38.5% relative improvement. For LDA based models, we can also observe that the author and social information can also benefit a lot. The performances of LRC-BQ in the constructed dataset is lower the performances reported in (Zhang et al. 2013). This is due to the reason that we do not limit the popularity of the retweets. The topics and content are much more diverse. The results also show that discriminative methods achieve worse results than generative methods. We think that the noisy and varieties content is one of the main reasons of the low performances.

Figure 3 shows the inference of the number of training data. From the results, we can observe that the proposed method ASC-HDP can achieve better performance than other methods with only 30% training data. The results also suggests that the performances of ASC-HDP can further increase with more training data. We have the intuition that if user have posted a large number microblogs, we can accurately estimate their behaviors. To investigate this intuition, we split the users into five groups based on the number of microblogs posted by them. Figure 4 shows the results. We can see that the more microblogs posted by users, the more accuracy we can get.

From the description of the LDA based model, we can know that there are several hyperparameters in ASC-LDA. Among them the number of topics is one the most important factors. Table 3 shows the influence of the number of topics. From the table, we can observe that the proposed model obtains the best performance when the number of topics is set to 20. While, when the number of topics is set to 10 and 30, the performances can compare with it. From analyzing the estimated topics of HDP, we find that the number of topics for most of the users are also in this range. However, the number of topics of different users vary greatly. Hence, HDP-based methods are more suitable for this task. The experimental results also demonstrate it.

Table 3: The inferences of different number of topics for ASC-LDA.

# Topics	Precision	Recall	F1-Score
10	0.681	0.625	0.651
20	**0.694**	**0.636**	**0.664**
30	0.692	0.629	0.659
50	0.659	0.608	0.633
70	0.645	0.593	0.618

Conclusions

In this paper, we proposed a novel method, which is based on hierarchical Dirichlet process, to combine structural, textual, and temporal information to predict retweet behavior. For evaluating the proposed method, we collected a large number of microblogs and their corresponding social networks from a microblog service. Experimental results demonstrate that the proposed method can achieve better performance than state-of-the-art methods. The relative improvement of the the proposed ASC-HDP over C-HDP is more than 38.5% in terms of F1-Score.

Acknowledgement

The authors wish to thank the anonymous reviewers for their helpful comments. This work was partially funded by National Natural Science Foundation of China (No. 61473092 and 61472088), Shanghai Leading Academic Discipline Project (B114).

References

Artzi, Y.; Pantel, P.; and Gamon, M. 2012. Predicting responses to microblog posts. In *Proceedings of NAACL-HLT '12.*

Boyd, D.; Golder, S.; and Lotan, G. 2010. Tweet, tweet, retweet: Conversational aspects of retweeting on twitter. In *Proceedings of HICSS '10.*

Can, E. F.; Oktay, H.; and Manmatha, R. 2013. Predicting retweet count using visual cues. In *Proceedings of CIKM '13.*

Castellanos, M.; Dayal, U.; Hsu, M.; Ghosh, R.; Dekhil, M.; Lu, Y.; Zhang, L.; and Schreiman, M. 2011. Lci: a social channel analysis platform for live customer intelligence. In *Proceedings of SIGMOD '11.*

Chang, J., and Kim, H.-j. 2012. Twitter search methods using retweet information. In *Proceedings of BUSTECH '12*, 67–71.

Feng, W., and Wang, J. 2013. Retweet or not?: personalized tweet re-ranking. In *Proceedings of WSDM.*

Gupta, M.; Gao, J.; Zhai, C.; and Han, J. 2012. Predicting future popularity trend of events in microblogging platforms. *Proceedings of ASIS&T.*

Hoffman, D. L., and Fodor, M. 2010. Can you measure the roi of your social media marketing. *MIT Sloan Management Review* 52(1):41–49.

Hong, L.; Dan, O.; and Davison, B. D. 2011. Predicting popular messages in twitter. In *Proceedings of WWW '11.*

Liu, L.; Tang, J.; Han, J.; Jiang, M.; and Yang, S. 2010. Mining topic-level influence in heterogeneous networks. In *Proceedings of CIKM '10.*

Luo, Z.; Osborne, M.; Tang, J.; and Wang, T. 2013. Who will retweet me?: Finding retweeters in twitter. In *Proceedings of SIGIR '13.*

Luo, Z.; Wang, Y.; and Wu, X. 2012. Predicting retweeting behavior based on autoregressive moving average model. In *Web Information Systems Engineering-WISE 2012.* 777–782.

Naveed, N.; Gottron, T.; Kunegis, J.; and Alhadi, A. C. 2011. Bad news travel fast: A content-based analysis of interestingness on twitter. In *Proceedings of the 3rd International Web Science Conference*, 8. ACM.

Peng, H.-K.; Zhu, J.; Piao, D.; Yan, R.; and Zhang, Y. 2011. Retweet modeling using conditional random fields. In *Proceedings of ICDMW '11.*

Petrovic, S.; Osborne, M.; and Lavrenko, V. 2011. Rt to win! predicting message propagation in twitter. In *Proceedings of the Fifth International AAAI Conference on Weblogs and Social Media.*

Rodrigues, T.; Benevenuto, F.; Cha, M.; Gummadi, K.; and Almeida, V. 2011. On word-of-mouth based discovery of the web. In *Proceedings of SIGCOMM '11.*

Stern, D. H.; Herbrich, R.; and Graepel, T. 2009. Matchbox: large scale online bayesian recommendations. In *Proceedings of WWW '09.*

Suh, B.; Hong, L.; Pirolli, P.; and Chi, E. H. 2010. Want to be retweeted? large scale analytics on factors impacting retweet in twitter network. In *Proceedings of SocialCom '10.*

Teh, Y. W.; Jordan, M. I.; Beal, M. J.; and Blei, D. M. 2006. Hierarchical dirichlet processes. *Journal of the american statistical association* 101(476).

Wu, Q.; Burges, C. J.; Svore, K. M.; and Gao, J. 2008. Ranking, boosting, and model adaptation. *Tecnical Report, MSR-TR-2008-109.*

Yang, Z.; Guo, J.; Cai, K.; Tang, J.; Li, J.; Zhang, L.; and Su, Z. 2010. Understanding retweeting behaviors in social networks. In *Proceedings of CIKM '10.*

Yu, L. L.; Asur, S.; and Huberman, B. A. 2012. Artificial inflation: The real story of trends and trend-setters in sina weibo. In *Processings of SocialCom-PASSAT '12.*

Zaman, T. R.; Herbrich, R.; Van Gael, J.; and Stern, D. 2010. Predicting information spreading in twitter. In *Workshop on Computational Social Science and the Wisdom of Crowds, NIPS.*

Zhang, J.; Liu, B.; Tang, J.; Chen, T.; and Li, J. 2013. Social influence locality for modeling retweeting behaviors. In *Proceedings of IJCAI'13.*

Exploring Key Concept Paraphrasing based on Pivot Language Translation for Question Retrieval

Wei-Nan Zhang[1], Zhao-Yan Ming[2*], Yu Zhang[1], Ting Liu[1], Tat-Seng Chua[3]
1 Research Center for Social Computing and Information Retrieval, Harbin Institute of Technology
2 Department of Computer Science, Digipen Institute of Technology
3 School of Computing, National University of Singapore

Abstract

Question retrieval in current community-based question answering (CQA) services does not, in general, work well for long and complex queries. One of the main difficulties lies in the word mismatch between queries and candidate questions. Existing solutions try to expand the queries at word level, but they usually fail to consider concept level enrichment. In this paper, we explore a pivot language translation based approach to derive the paraphrases of key concepts. We further propose a unified question retrieval model which integrates the key concepts and their paraphrases for the query question. Experimental results demonstrate that the paraphrase enhanced retrieval model significantly outperforms the state-of-the-art models in question retrieval.

Introduction

Question retrieval[1] in community based question answering (CQA) is different from general Web search (Xue, Jeon, and Croft 2008). Unlike the Web search engines that return a long list of ranked documents, question retrieval returns several relevant questions with possible answers directly. While in traditional question answering (QA), the main tasks are answer extraction (Kwok, Etzioni, and Weld 2001; Moldovan et al. 2003), answer matching (Cui, Kan, and Chua 2007) and answer ranking (Ko et al. 2010), with CQA, the main task is to search for relevant questions with good ready answers (Cao et al. 2012).

One of the major challenges for question retrieval is the **word mismatch** between queries and candidate questions. For example, in Table 1, the query and question are relevant to each other, but the same meaning is expressed with different word forms, such as *"get colds"* and *"catch a cold"*, *"lower temperature"* and *"winter months"*. These make it non-trivial for semantic level question matching.

To tackle the word mismatch problem, previous work mainly resorts to query expansion. (Xu and Croft 1996) explored local and global features to expand single terms in queries. (Collins-Thompson and Callan 2005) used synonyms, cue words, co-occurrence and background smoothing to determine query associations. However, the former approach fails to assign explicit weights to the expanded aspects and the later approach overlooks phrase level evidences for query expansion. Meanwhile, pseudo relevance feedback (Baeza-Yates and Ribeiro-Neto 2011) and blending (Belkin et al. 1993) are also two effective approaches to tackle the word mismatch between queries and the candidate documents in the term level. (Zhou et al. 2013) utilized the Wikipedia as an external knowledge base to enhance the performance of question retrieval. Despite their success, literature that considers the concept level expansion by exploiting multiple external knowledge sources is still sparse.

In this paper, we take three major actions to solve the word mismatch problem in question retrieval from CQA archives as illustrated in Figure 1. First, we utilize a pivot language translation approach (Callison-Burch 2008) to explore key concept paraphrases in the queries from bilingual parallel corpora[2]. Figure 2 presents an example of pivot language translation for concept paraphrasing. We put the original concept "get colds" on the left column. The arrow directions represent the translation from source to target. English concepts on right column indicate the candidate paraphrases. Pivot languages are on the intermediate columns, German and Chinese for (a) and (b) respectively. Both of the translations in two directions are obtained by using the method of (Koehn, Och, and Marcu 2003).

Second, we estimate the importance of the generated paraphrases for the original query under two considerations. One

Table 1: An example for illustrating the word mismatch between a query and a relevant question.

Query
Q1: Why do people *get colds* more often in *lower temperature*?
Relevant Question:
Q2:Why are you less likely to *catch a cold* or flu in spring summer and autumn than *winter months*?

[*]corresponding author

[1]Here we define question retrieval in CQA services as a task that new questions are used as queries to find relevant questions with ready answers. For simplicity and consistency, we use the term "query" to denote new questions posed by users and "question" to denote those answered questions available in the CQA archives.

[2]Bilingual corpora have been verified to be the effective resource in many subjects of information retrieval (Mehdad, Negri, and Federico 2011).

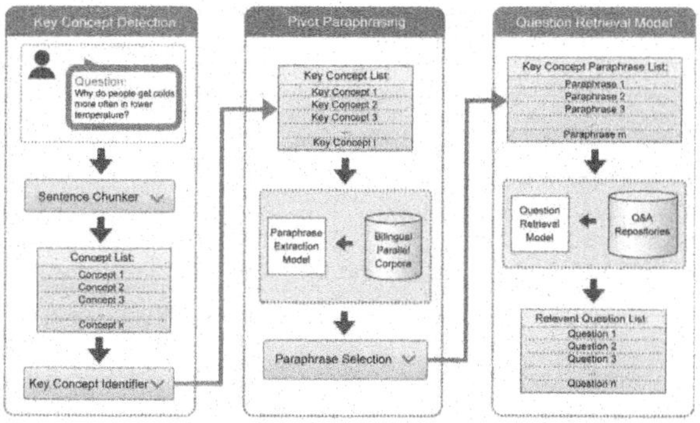

Figure 1: The framework of key concept paraphrase based question retrieval.

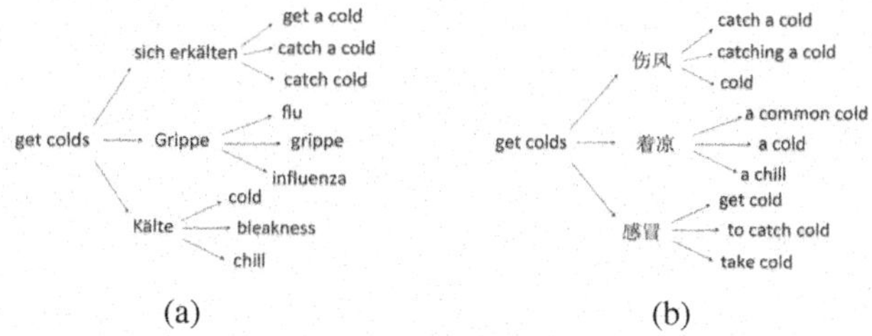

Figure 2: An example of pivot language translation approach to explore concept paraphrases.

is based on the paraphrase generation probabilities obtained from a pivot language translation approach. The other is based on the statistical distribution of paraphrases in the Q&A repository, which reflects the importance of the given concept paraphrases over the whole data set.

Finally, we propose a novel probabilistic retrieval model which integrates the state-of-the-art probabilistic retrieval model, key concept model, and key concept paraphrase model. The contributions of this work are twofold:

- To the best of our knowledge, this is the first attempt at using a pivot translation approach with multiple languages to explore concept level paraphrases as a semantic expansion of queries for question retrieval.
- Second, towards question retrieval task, we propose a question retrieval model using key concepts and their paraphrases which can be seamlessly integrated with the state-of-the-art question retrieval frameworks.

Key Concept Paraphrase based Question Retrieval

In this section, we will detail the proposed scheme that uses the key concept paraphrase as the expansions of queries for question retrieval. We will present the framework of the scheme, which consists of three components as shown in Figure 1. It can be decomposed into the following parts.

Key Concept Detection

According to (Bentivogli and Pianta 2003), single words, idioms, restricted collocations or free combination of words can be used to express concepts. Prevalent work (Bendersky and Croft 2008; Bendersky, Metzler, and Croft 2010) used the noun phrases as concepts in verbose queries for web search. Noun phrases have been verified to be reliable in the key concept detection in information retrieval (Bendersky and Croft 2008; Xu and Croft 1996) and natural language processing (Hulth 2003). Moreover, as verb phrases that usually represent events or relations between entities, are important information carriers, we also consider verb phrases as concepts.

In this study, we implement and extend the state-of-the-art key concept detection approach (Bendersky, Metzler, and Croft 2010). Our proposed features include statistical, syntactic and semantic linking information. The summary of these features are presented in Table 2.

Inspired by (Bendersky and Croft 2008), we assume that each concept c_i can be classified into one of the mutually exclusive classes: KC (key concept class) or NKC (non-key concept class). Meanwhile, we directly estimate the $p(c_i|q) = \frac{p_k(c_i)}{\sum_{c_i \in q} p_k(c_i)}$. Here, given the manually ranked concepts as the training set, we aim to learn a pair-wise ranking function of the form $p_k : X \rightarrow \mathbb{R}$, such that $p_k(c_i) > p_k(c_j)$ indicates that concept c_i has a higher probability than concept c_j of belonging to class KC. Meanwhile, we also notice that the named entities are usually stable in form. [3]

Pivot Language Translation Approach to Key Concept Paraphrasing

To overcome the surface word mismatching between semantic similar questions, we propose to use a pivot language to bridge the semantic gap. Basically, the pivot language translation approach translates a concept in the target language into an auxiliary (or pivot) language, such that the concepts in the auxiliary language carry the meaning of the target concept, but strip off the original word form. It then translates the concepts in the auxiliary language back into the target language. In this way, the target concept is expanded into other forms in its own language, with the aid of another language. The pivot language translation approach is formally proposed and extended by (Callison-Burch 2008). In the following, we will describe our approach of using pivot language translation to expand the key concepts for question retrieval.

Candidate Paraphrases Generation Given concept c_i in one language, English for example, we aim to find a plurality of English concepts $\mathbb{c}_j$ with the probability $p(\mathbb{c}_j|c_i) > \tau$, where τ is a threshold for initially filtering out those candidate paraphrases with low quality. The probability that $\mathbb{c}_j$ is the paraphrase of c_i is implemented as a conditional probability $p(\mathbb{c}_j|c_i)$, in terms of the translation probability $p(f|c_i)$ that English concept c_i translates as a particular concept f

[3] The named entities and the concepts are recognized by using the Stanford core-nlp toolkit (http://nlp.stanford.edu/software/corenlp.shtml) and the openNLP (http://opennlp.apache.org/) toolkit.

Table 2: A summary of features used in the key concept detection task.

Feature Name	Feature Description
$df(c_i)$	Concept document frequency in the corpus.
$ngram\_tf(c_i)$	Concept term frequency counted from Google n-grams data (Brants and Franz 2006).
$dep\_subj(c_i)$	Whether one of the words in the concept has the syntactic role of $nsubj$.
$dep\_obj(c_i)$	Whether one of the words in the concept has the syntactic role of $dobj$.
$ne(c_i)$	Whether part of the concept or the concept itself is a named entity.
$wiki\_link(c_i)$	The proportion of the concept occurring as anchor texts in the Wikipedia articles (Odijk, Meij, and de Rijke).

in the pivot language, and $p(\mathbb{c}_j|f)$ that the pivot language concept f translates as the candidate concept paraphrase $\mathbb{c}_j$.

Meanwhile, we also adopt three strategies which are proposed by (Callison-Burch 2008), to improve the performance of the accuracy of paraphrase generation. They are language model for paraphrase re-ranking, multiple parallel corpora and syntactic constraint. We then obtain the paraphrase probability as follows:

$$p(\mathbb{c}_j|c_i) = p(\mathbb{c}_j|c_i, s(c_i)) \approx \sum_{l \in L} \frac{\sum_f p(f|c_i, s(c_i))p(\mathbb{c}_j|f, s(c_i))}{|L|} \tag{1}$$

where $p(f|c_i, s(c_i)) = \frac{\text{count}(f, c_i, s(c_i))}{\sum_f \text{count}(f, c_i, s(c_i))}$, L and $s(c_i)$ represent the set of multiple languages and the syntactic role of c_i respectively. $\text{count}(f, c_i, s(c_i))$ equals to the co-occurrence times of f and c_i with the same syntactic constraint. $p(\mathbb{c}_j|f, s(c_i))$ can be estimated in a similar way.

Paraphrase Selection To select the generated paraphrases for the question retrieval model, we introduce two schemes for allocating the weights for each candidate paraphrase $\mathbb{c}_j$ of concept c_i, by considering their generating probabilities and the statistical distributions in the whole corpora.

Paraphrase probability based weighting scheme
As not all the generated paraphrases are considered to be integrated into the retrieval model, we need to normalize the paraphrase generation probabilities to help distinguish the important paraphrases by using the following equation:

$$w_{pp}(\mathbb{c}_j) = 1 - \frac{\log p(\mathbb{c}_j|c_i)}{\sum_{\mathbb{c}_j} \log p(\mathbb{c}_j|c_i)} \tag{2}$$

where $p(\mathbb{c}_j|c_i)$ is computed by Equation (1).

In this weighting scheme, we obtain the final weights of the paraphrases as $w_{pp}(\mathbb{c}_j)$. Here, we assume the higher the paraphrase probability, the more important the paraphrase is. As the value of $\log p(\mathbb{c}_j|c_i)$ is negative, the normalization item is in inverse ratio of the paraphrase weight.

Statistical distribution based weighting scheme
The statistical distributions of candidate paraphrase $\mathbb{c}_j$ reflects the importance of candidate paraphrases in the whole Q&A repository. Here, we introduce the *entropy* of the candidate paraphrase $\mathbb{c}_j$ to represent its weight, as *entropy* is defined to describe the importance of particular sample in the whole data set. Hence, the weights of $\mathbb{c}_j$ can also be formulated as follows.

$$w_{sd}(\mathbb{c}_j) = \frac{p(\mathbb{c}_j) \log p(\mathbb{c}_j)}{\sum_{\mathbb{c}_j} p(\mathbb{c}_j) \log p(\mathbb{c}_j)} \tag{3}$$

Here, we use the maximum likelihood estimation $p(\mathbb{c}_j) = \frac{df(\mathbb{c}_j)}{\sum_{\mathbb{c}_j} df(\mathbb{c}_j)}$ ($df(\mathbb{c}_j)$ represents the document frequency of $\mathbb{c}_j$.) by counting how often the candidate paraphrase $\mathbb{c}_j$ occurred in the whole data set.

Finally, we use a linear integration to combine the proposed weighting scheme w_{pp} and w_{sd} as follow:

$$\hat{p}(\mathbb{c}_j|c_i) = \frac{\delta w_{pp}(\mathbb{c}_j) + (1-\delta) w_{sd}(\mathbb{c}_j)}{\sum_{\mathbb{c}_j} (\delta w_{pp}(\mathbb{c}_j) + (1-\delta) w_{sd}(\mathbb{c}_j))} \tag{4}$$

where δ, which is a free parameter in $[0, 1]$ to balance the two weighting schemes.

Key Concept Paraphrasing based Question Retrieval Model

In this section, we will derive the novel question retrieval model that integrates the key concept and paraphrase model from a general key concept model step by step.

Key Concept based Retrieval Model We start by ranking a question q^* in response to a query q by estimating the ranking score of q^* as in standard language model (Ponte and Croft 1998). Then inspired by (Bendersky and Croft 2008), we obtain the key concept model for question retrieval as:

$$rankScore(q^*) = \sum_i p(q|q^*, c_i)p(c_i|q^*) \tag{5}$$

To estimate the joint conditional probability, we use a linear interpolation of the individual probabilities following (Bendersky and Croft 2008; Wei and Croft 2006).

$$rankScore(q^*) = \lambda' p(q|q^*) + (1-\lambda') \sum_i p(q|c_i)p(c_i|q^*) \tag{6}$$

We assume a uniform distribution for $p(q)$ and $p(c_i)$, then $\frac{p(q)}{p(c_i)}$ equals to a constant C. By using a normalized parameter $\lambda = \frac{\lambda'}{\lambda' + (1-\lambda')C}$ ($\lambda \in [0, 1]$), we obtain the ranking function as:

$$rankScore(q^*) \propto \lambda p(q|q^*) + (1-\lambda) \sum_i p(c_i|q)p(c_i|q^*) \tag{7}$$

Concept Paraphrase based Retrieval Model For the concept c_i in query q, we use $\mathbb{c}_j$ to represent the corresponding paraphrase of c_i in the candidate question q^*. First, we want to explore the paraphrases potentially generated the actual concepts in query q. And then we get Equation (8).

$$\begin{aligned} rankScore(q^*) \propto & \lambda p(q|q^*) \\ & + (1-\lambda) \sum_i \sum_j p(c_i|q)p(c_i|q^*, \mathbb{c}_j)p(\mathbb{c}_j|q^*) \end{aligned} \tag{8}$$

Here, we use an interpolation of $p(c_i|q^*)$ and $p(\mathbb{c}_j|c_i)$ to estimate $\sum_j p(c_i|q^*, \mathbb{c}_j)p(\mathbb{c}_j|q^*)$ as $\theta p(c_i|q^*) + (1 - \theta)\sum_j p(c_i|\mathbb{c}_j)p(\mathbb{c}_j|q^*)$.

For implementation, we may only consider the explicit concepts and their corresponding paraphrases, i.e., the concepts and the paraphrases that appear in the actual query q and candidate question q^* respectively. We then obtain the new question retrieval model which integrates the key concept model and paraphrase model as in Equation (9).

$$rankScore(q^*) \propto \alpha p(q|q^*) + \beta \sum_{c_i \in q} p(c_i|q)p(c_i|q^*) + \gamma \sum_{c_i \in q} p(c_i|q) \sum_{\mathbb{c}_j \in q^*} p(\mathbb{c}_j|c_i)p(\mathbb{c}_j|q^*) \quad (9)$$

where $\alpha = \frac{\lambda}{Z}$, $\beta = \frac{(1-\lambda)\theta}{Z}$, $\gamma = \frac{(1-\lambda)(1-\theta)C'}{Z}$. $Z = \lambda + (1-\lambda)\theta + (1-\lambda)(1-\theta)C'$, α, β and γ are three free parameters in $[0, 1]$ to balance the three parts of the model and $\alpha + \beta + \gamma = 1$. $p(c_i|q)$ and $p(\mathbb{c}_j|c_i)$ can be estimated by the maximum likelihood estimation and Equation (4) respectively. $p(c_i|q^*)$ and $p(\mathbb{c}_j|q^*)$ can be estimated by the maximum likelihood. We assume a uniform distribution for $p(\mathbb{c}_j)$ and $p(c_i)$, and thus $\frac{p(c_i)}{p(\mathbb{c}_j)}$ equals to a constant C'. It is worth noticing that the former model $p(q|q^*)$ can be implemented in any one of the existing probabilistic ranking models. In this paper, we choose the state-of-the-art question retrieval model, namely, translation based language model (TLM) which is proposed by Xue et al., (2008) (Xue, Jeon, and Croft 2008).

Experiment Results

Evaluation on Key Concept Detection

For key concept detection, we randomly selected 1,000 questions from the 1 million plus question data. They had no overlapping concepts with the searching queries. After question chunking, we obtained a total of 3,685 concepts. For a given concept, two annotators manually labeled it as KC or NKC. When conflicts occurred, another annotator was involved to make the final decision.

For comparison, we implemented the state-of-the-art key concept detection approach (Bendersky, Metzler, and Croft 2010) as our baseline. Precision at position one ($p@1$) and mean reciprocal rank (MRR) are adopted as our evaluation metrics. And the MRR calculated on the returned top 5 concepts. We use 5-fold cross validation on the 3,685 concepts of the 1,000 questions for the key concept detection experiment. Table 3 shows the experiment results of key concept detection. From Table 2, we can see that the baseline can be enhanced by the features proposed in our approach. The reason is that we not only capture the statistical information, such as the document frequency and Google *n-gram*, but also obtain the advantages of linguistic analysis, such as dependency parsing and named entity recognition, and external knowledge base, such as Wikipedia. We notice that the performance of the baseline in this paper is lower than that in the original paper. This is due to the difference of data set.

Table 3: Experimental results on key concept detection. $\mathscr{F}$ denotes the use of our proposed features. $*$ indicates the statistical significance over the baseline (within 0.95 confidence interval using the t-test)

	Bendersky et al.2010	Bendersky et al.2010($\mathscr{F}$)
MRR	82.14	**84.57***
$p@1$	68.57	**71.42***

Table 4: Experiment results of key concept paraphrase generation on the percentage of correct meaning. $\star$ indicates the statistical significance over the baseline (within 0.95 confidence interval using the t-test)

	MonolingTrans	BilingPivot
Average Accuracy	55.47%	**59.29%***

Evaluation on Paraphrase Generation

Paraphrase Generation Results For paraphrase generation, we used the Europarl (Koehn 2005) which contains ten parallel corpora between English and (each of) Danish, Dutch, Finnish, French, German, Greek, Italian, Portuguese, Spanish, and Swedish. With approximate 30 million words per language, we obtained a total of 315 million English words. We used Giza++ (Och and Ney 2003) to create automatic word alignments. A trigram language model was trained on the English sentences using the SRI language modeling toolkit (Stolcke 2002).

As the bilingual parallel corpora are used for paraphrase generation in our proposed approach, we call it "**BilingPivot**" for short. Meanwhile, paraphrase generation can also be done from monolingual parallel corpora by using monolingual translation model (Quirk, Brockett, and Dolan 2004; Ibrahim, Katz, and Lin 2003; Dolan, Quirk, and Brockett 2004; Marton, Callison-Burch, and Resnik 2009). For comparison, we implemented the method of paraphrase generation from monolingual parallel corpora in (Marton, Callison-Burch, and Resnik 2009), which is the state-of-the-art model, and use it as our baseline. We call it "**MonolingTrans**" for short. For training, we used the similar question pairs in (Bernhard and Gurevych 2009) and Microsoft parallel corpus in (Quirk, Brockett, and Dolan 2004; Dolan, Quirk, and Brockett 2004) as the monolingual parallel corpora.

For evaluation, we invited two native English speakers to provide their judgments on whether the generated concepts have the same meaning as the original concepts. As the experimental results were evaluated by two annotators, 20% of their annotated data are overlapped data for computing the annotation agreements. For the paraphrase generation task, the Cohen's *kappa* (Cohen and others 1960) coefficient equals to 0.617, which is interpreted as "good" agreement.

The experimental results are presented in Table 4 with the evaluation of *average accuracy*. From Table 4, we can see that BilingPivot outperforms MonolingTrans on the correct meaning. It is because monolingual method uses the translation model to capture the similarity between each term pair in monolingual parallel sentences. In this case, the similarity is calculated by the statistical co-occurrence between two terms in the same language. Hence, it may cause error in paraphrase generation as the most co-occurrent phrases are not always paraphrases.

Pivot Languages Analysis To study the performances of different pivot languages on generating paraphrases, we remove one language at a time and use the remaining 9 pivot languages for paraphrase generation. Table 5 shows the experimental results of pivot language analysis. We randomly select 110 concepts paraphrases for analysis.

From Table 5, we observe that German language contributes the most and Danish the least in terms of the accuracy of paraphrase generation. The statistics on our Q&A repository show that NP (Noun Phrase) is the majority type of concept (44.02%). Hence, we further check the part-of-speech (pos) distributions on the generated paraphrases for each language resource. Table 6 shows the pos distributions of the generated paraphrases on percentage.

From Table 6, we found that German and Danish corpora contain the most and least percentage of NPs for generating noun phrase (NP) respectively. It suggests that the pivot languages which are suitable for NP paraphrasing are more likely to perform better on generating accurate paraphrases than other pivot languages. Hence, it may explain the reason of the accuracy changes by removing of the German and Danish corpora respectively.

Second, according to the analysis of the Europarl corpora on machine translation (Koehn 2005), the author had revealed that an apparent reason for the differences of the translations between two languages is the variance of morphological richness. Noun phrases in German are marked with cases, which manifests themselves as different word endings at nouns, determiners etc. Hence, The richness of German may explain the highest contributions of it on the paraphrasing performance by using it as the pivot language.

Moreover, when Danish language is removed, we obtain the smallest number of generated paraphrases. Although each of the language resource is about the same scale in terms of sentence number, the sparsity of the vocabularies on each pivot approach are different, which may lead to the different performance on paraphrasing. According to the s-tatistics by (Koehn 2005), the Finnish vocabulary is about five times as big as English, due to the morphology. Checking the number of unique words on each language resource. We find that the Danish and Swedish corpora have the largest and smallest numbers of unique words respectively. Hence, we can deduce that the differences on the quantities of generating paraphrases may be cause by the different scales of vocabularies of each corpus.

Question Retrieval Results

Question Retrieval Data Set We collected a total number of 1, 123, 034 questions as the retrieval corpus, which covers a range of popular topics, including health, internet, etc. For question retrieval experiment, we randomly selected 140 questions as searching queries and 28 as development set to tune all the involved parameters. Table 7 details the statistics of our data set.

Table 7: Statistics of question retrieval data set.

# of queries	140
# of total questions	1,123,034
# of relevant questions	1028
# of development queries	28

To obtain the relevance ground truth of each question query, we pooled the top 20 results from various methods, namely, the vector space model, okapi BM25 model, language model and our proposed methods. We then asked t-wo annotators, who were not involved in the design of the proposed methods, to independently annotate whether the candidate question is relevant with the query or not. When conflicts occurred, another annotator was involved to make the final decision.

State-of-the-Art Methods To verify the effectiveness of our proposed key concept paraphrase based question retrieval model, we comparatively evaluate the following question retrieval models.

- **TLM**: The translation based language model proposed by (Xue, Jeon, and Croft 2008) is involved as a baseline.
- **STM**: We run the syntactic tree matching model (Wang, Ming, and Chua 2009) as a baseline. It is a structure based approach, which uses the tree kernel function to measure the similarity between query and candidate question.
- **REL**: We choose the pseudo relevance feedback (PRF) on language model (Cao et al. 2008) as a baseline.
- **WKM**: We implement the world knowledge (WK) based question retrieval model Zhou et al. (Zhou et al. 2013) as another state-of-the-art model. The world knowledge can be seen as an external source for query expansion.
- **KCM**: We present the key concept based retrieval model proposed by (Bendersky, Metzler, and Croft 2010) as a baseline.
- ***Mono*KCM**: We employ the *Mono*KCM as a baseline. It utilizes the phrase based statistical machine translation model to obtain the translation probabilities.
- ***Para*KCM**: Our proposed pivot language translation based key concept paraphrase model.

Question Retrieval Results For evaluation, we use precision at position 1 ($p@1$) and 10 ($p@10$) and mean average precision (MAP) (Baeza-Yates and Ribeiro-Neto 2011). The experimental results are presented in Table 8.

Table 8 shows that first, KCM model outperforms TLM model in the question retrieval, which reveals that the key concept based query refinement scheme is more effective in question retrieval task. The reason is that TLM model employs IBM translation model 1 to capture the word translation probabilities. However, questions in CQA repositories are usually verbose and some of the words are noise for question matching. Hence, the quality of word alignment is poorer. Moreover, it will influence the translation accuracy.

Second, STM model captures the structure similarities between queries and questions. It can improve the performance of string matching in question retrieval. However the semantic similarity in STM is measured by WordNet and a rule-

Table 5: Pivot language analysis. %chg of accuracy represents the changes of accuracy on both correct meaning and grammar when a single pivot language is removed. Negative value for a pivot language indicates that the accuracy has decreased after the pivot language is removed.

	Danish	German	Greek	Spanish	Finnish
% accuracy change	−11.57	**-33.02**	−22.88	−18.91	−18.71
# of paraphrases	**1,928**	2,027	3,074	4,019	5,109
	French	Italian	Dutch	Portuguese	Swedish
% accuracy change	−17.05	−20.18	−21.11	−20.5	−20.31
# of paraphrases	5,446	6,333	6,739	7,099	7,487

Table 6: The *pos* distributions of paraphrases on each pivot language. The values represent the percentages of *pos* of the generated paraphrases when only used a single pivot language for paraphrasing. Here, "ADJP", "JJ", "NP", "PP" and "VP" represent adjective phrase, adjective word, noun phrase, preposition phrase and verb phrase respectively.

	Danish	German	Greek	Spanish	Finnish	French	Italian	Dutch	Portuguese	Swedish
ADJP	**6.80**	4.94	5.75	3.14	3.07	3.31	3.09	2.99	3.71	3.50
JJ	4.08	**6.17**	3.45	2.35	1.84	1.65	1.55	1.49	1.39	1.31
NP	41.50	**48.15**	44.25	47.06	42.94	42.70	43.56	44.03	42.92	43.11
PP	8.16	8.64	9.20	10.59	9.82	10.19	10.82	10.70	11.37	**11.38**
VP	37.41	32.10	35.63	34.12	**39.26**	37.47	29.90	35.32	33.87	34.14
Others	2.04	0.00	1.72	2.75	3.07	4.68	5.93	5.47	**6.73**	6.56

Table 8: Experimental results among different question retrieval models. The † and ‡ indicate that the results of *Para*KCM and *Mono*KCM are statistical significant over all baselines and the TLM, STM, REL, WKM and KCM models (within 0.95 confidence interval using the t-test) respectively. % changes denote the improved performance in percentage. The results of our approach are in bold.

Models	$p@1$	$p@10$	MAP
TLM	0.1928	0.1759	0.2889
STM	0.2071	0.1864	0.2973
REL	0.2143	0.2015	0.3124
WKM	0.2071	0.1981	0.3203
KCM	0.2143	0.2067	0.3237
*Mono*KCM	$0.2214^{\ddagger}$	$0.2179^{\ddagger}$	$0.3554^{\ddagger}$
***Para*KCM**	$\mathbf{0.2357}^{\dagger}$	$\mathbf{0.2280}^{\dagger}$	$\mathbf{0.3910}^{\dagger}$

based approach, which has the limitation of data sparseness on UGC query expansion.

Third, WKM model generalizes the concepts in queries by exploiting their synonyms, hypernyms, associative concepts etc., through Wikipedia thesaurus. These synonyms and associative concepts can be seen as an expansion for query and perform better than traditional bag-of-word (BoW) models. However, the number of synonyms extracted by only using the Wikipedia concepts is quite sparse. Meanwhile, the associative concepts may introduce more relevant terms rather than similar terms.

Fourth, *Mono*KCM model outperforms the KCM model. It shows that the concept paraphrase resources can further improve the performance of concept based question retrieval model. It verifies that both query refinement and expansion are important to question retrieval. Meanwhile, we can see that *Mono*KCM model outperforms the TLM model by a large margin. It shows that the phrase based translation model can better capture the similarities between query and candidate questions than the word level translation model.

Fifth, the results of *Para*KCM model indicate that question retrieval model can be benefited from concept based query refinement and concept paraphrase based query expansion. Moreover, our proposed *Para*KCM model outperforms *Mono*KCM model, which shows that paraphrases generated from bilingual parallel corpora can enhance the performance of retrieval model more than that from the monolingual parallel corpus. This may be caused by the difference between the above two approaches of the accuracy of paraphrase generation .

Sixth, the proposed *Para*KCM model outperforms the REL model. It illustrates that our proposed model is more effective than the REL model on query expansion for the question retrieval task. This is because the proposed approach capture not only the term importance, but also the concept importance. Hence, it can be seen as the adopting of the term context information, which can overcome the shortage of REL model. Moreover, as the questions are extremely short than the documents, the number of expansion terms obtained by REL model is very limited.

Conclusion

In this paper, we proposed a pivot language translation approach to paraphrase key concept. Further, we expanded queries with the generated paraphrases for question retrieval. The experimental results showed that the key concept paraphrase based question retrieval model outperformed the state-of-the-art models in the question retrieval task. In the future, we plan to generate the concept paraphrases by considering to jointly estimate their probabilities on the multiple linguistic resources.

Acknowledgments

We would like to acknowledge the reviewers for their insight reviews. We thank Yiming Li for his help on the proofreading of the camera-ready version. This paper is supported by the 973 Program (Grant No. 2014CB340503), National Natural Science Foundation (Grant No. 61133012, 61472105).

References

Baeza-Yates, R. A., and Ribeiro-Neto, B. A. 2011. *Modern Information Retrieval - the concepts and technology behind search, Second edition*. Pearson Education Ltd., Harlow, England.

Belkin, N. J.; Cool, C.; Croft, W. B.; and Callan, J. P. 1993. The effect multiple query representations on information retrieval system performance. In *ACM SIGIR conference on Research and development in information retrieval*, SIGIR '93, 339–346.

Bendersky, M., and Croft, W. B. 2008. Discovering key concepts in verbose queries. In *ACM SIGIR conference on Research and development in information retrieval*, SIGIR '08, 491–498.

Bendersky, M.; Metzler, D.; and Croft, W. B. 2010. Learning concept importance using a weighted dependence model. In *WSDM*, 31–40.

Bentivogli, L., and Pianta, E. 2003. Beyond lexical units: enriching wordnets with phrasets. In *European chapter of the Association for Computational Linguistics - Volume 2*, EACL '03, 67–70.

Bernhard, D., and Gurevych, I. 2009. Combining lexical semantic resources with question & answer archives for translation based answer finding. In *ACL-IJCNLP*, ACL '09, 728–736.

Brants, T., and Franz, A. 2006. Web 1t 5-gram version 1.

Callison-Burch, C. 2008. Syntactic constraints on paraphrases extracted from parallel corpora. In *Empirical Methods in Natural Language Processing*, EMNLP '08, 196–205.

Cao, G.; Nie, J.-Y.; Gao, J.; and Robertson, S. 2008. Selecting good expansion terms for pseudo-relevance feedback. In *ACM SIGIR conference on Research and development in information retrieval*, SIGIR '08, 243–250. New York, NY, USA: ACM.

Cao, X.; Cong, G.; Cui, B.; Jensen, C. S.; and Yuan, Q. 2012. Approaches to exploring category information for question retrieval in community question-answer archives. *ACM Trans. Inf. Syst.* 30(2):7.

Cohen, J., et al. 1960. A coefficient of agreement for nominal scales. *Educational and psychological measurement* 20(1):37–46.

Collins-Thompson, K., and Callan, J. 2005. Query expansion using random walk models. In *Proceedings of the 14th ACM international conference on Information and knowledge management*, CIKM '05, 704–711.

Cui, H.; Kan, M.-Y.; and Chua, T.-S. 2007. Soft pattern matching models for definitional question answering. *ACM Trans. Inf. Syst.* 25(2).

Dolan, B.; Quirk, C.; and Brockett, C. 2004. Unsupervised construction of large paraphrase corpora: exploiting massively parallel news sources. In *Proceedings of the 20th international conference on Computational Linguistics*, COLING '04.

Hulth, A. 2003. Improved automatic keyword extraction given more linguistic knowledge. In *Empirical methods in natural language processing*, EMNLP '03, 216–223.

Ibrahim, A.; Katz, B.; and Lin, J. 2003. Extracting structural paraphrases from aligned monolingual corpora. In *Proceedings of the second international workshop on Paraphrasing - Volume 16*, PARAPHRASE '03, 57–64.

Ko, J.; Si, L.; Nyberg, E.; and Mitamura, T. 2010. Probabilistic models for answer-ranking in multilingual question-answering. *ACM Trans. Inf. Syst.* 28(3):16:1–16:37.

Koehn, P.; Och, F. J.; and Marcu, D. 2003. Statistical phrase-based translation. In *North American Chapter of the Association for Computational Linguistics on Human Language Technology - Volume 1*, NAACL '03, 48–54.

Koehn, P. 2005. Europarl: A parallel corpus for statistical machine translation. In *MT summit*, volume 5.

Kwok, C.; Etzioni, O.; and Weld, D. S. 2001. Scaling question answering to the web. *ACM Trans. Inf. Syst.* 19(3):242–262.

Marton, Y.; Callison-Burch, C.; and Resnik, P. 2009. Improved statistical machine translation using monolingually-derived paraphrases. In *Empirical Methods in Natural Language Processing: Volume 1 - Volume 1*, EMNLP '09, 381–390.

Mehdad, Y.; Negri, M.; and Federico, M. 2011. Using bilingual parallel corpora for cross-lingual textual entailment. In *Annual Meeting of the Association for Computational Linguistics: Human Language Technologies-Volume 1*, 1336–1345. Association for Computational Linguistics.

Moldovan, D.; Paşca, M.; Harabagiu, S.; and Surdeanu, M. 2003. Performance issues and error analysis in an open-domain question answering system. *ACM Trans. Inf. Syst.* 21(2):133–154.

Och, F. J., and Ney, H. 2003. A systematic comparison of various statistical alignment models. *Comput. Linguist.* 29(1):19–51.

Odijk, D.; Meij, E.; and de Rijke, M. In *Proceedings of the 10th Conference on Open Research Areas in Information Retrieval*, 9–16.

Ponte, J. M., and Croft, W. B. 1998. A language modeling approach to information retrieval. In *Proceedings of the 21st annual international ACM SIGIR conference on Research and development in information retrieval*, SIGIR '98, 275–281.

Quirk, C.; Brockett, C.; and Dolan, W. B. 2004. Monolingual machine translation for paraphrase generation. In *EMNLP*, 142–149.

Stolcke, A. 2002. Srilm - an extensible language modeling toolkit. In *INTERSPEECH*.

Wang, K.; Ming, Z.; and Chua, T.-S. 2009. A syntactic tree matching approach to finding similar questions in community-based qa services. In *SIGIR*, 187–194.

Wei, X., and Croft, W. B. 2006. Lda-based document models for ad-hoc retrieval. In *Proceedings of the 29th annual international ACM SIGIR conference on Research and development in information retrieval*, SIGIR '06, 178–185. New York, NY, USA: ACM.

Xu, J., and Croft, W. B. 1996. Query expansion using local and global document analysis. In *Proceedings of the 19th annual international ACM SIGIR conference on Research and development in information retrieval*, SIGIR '96, 4–11.

Xue, X.; Jeon, J.; and Croft, W. B. 2008. Retrieval models for question and answer archives. In *Proceedings of the 31st annual international ACM SIGIR conference on Research and development in information retrieval*, SIGIR '08, 475–482.

Zhou, G.; Liu, Y.; Liu, F.; Zeng, D.; and Zhao, J. 2013. Improving question retrieval in community question answering using world knowledge. In *IJCAI*, 2239–2245. AAAI Press.

Representation Learning for Aspect Category Detection in Online Reviews

Xinjie Zhou, Xiaojun Wan* and **Jianguo Xiao**
Institute of Computer Science and Technology, Peking University, Beijing 100871, China
The MOE Key Laboratory of Computational Linguistics, Peking University, Beijing 100871, China
{zhouxinjie, wanxiaojun, xiaojianguo}@pku.edu.cn

Abstract

User-generated reviews are valuable resources for decision making. Identifying the aspect categories discussed in a given review sentence (e.g., "food" and "service" in restaurant reviews) is an important task of sentiment analysis and opinion mining. Given a predefined aspect category set, most previous researches leverage hand-crafted features and a classification algorithm to accomplish the task. The crucial step to achieve better performance is feature engineering which consumes much human effort and may be unstable when the product domain changes. In this paper, we propose a representation learning approach to automatically learn useful features for aspect category detection. Specifically, a semi-supervised word embedding algorithm is first proposed to obtain continuous word representations on a large set of reviews with noisy labels. Afterwards, we propose to generate deeper and hybrid features through neural networks stacked on the word vectors. A logistic regression classifier is finally trained with the hybrid features to predict the aspect category. The experiments are carried out on a benchmark dataset released by SemEval-2014. Our approach achieves the state-of-the-art performance and outperforms the best participating team as well as a few strong baselines.

Introduction

User-generated reviews play an important role in each individual's decision making process. Opinion mining and sentiment analysis for online reviews has become a trending research topic in both academic and industrial fields since early 2000 (Turney, 2002; Pang et al., 2002). Aspect category detection is one of the opinion mining tasks which aims to identify the aspect categories discussed in a review sentence. A set of aspect categories are usually predefined which makes the task become a multi-label classification problem. For example, in SemEval-2014, {"service", "food", "price", "ambience", "anecdote /miscellaneous"} is defined as the aspect category set for restaurant reviews. In the sentence "*Service is top notch.*", "service" should be detected as the aspect category. Opinion without knowing the target is of limited use (Liu, 2011). Identifying the aspect category helps to get target-dependent sentiment and contributes to aspect-specific opinion summarization.

Previous researches have proposed several models to address this task and SVM classification is one of the most popular ones (Ganu et al.,2009; Kiritchenko et al 2014). These existing methods have shown the significance of lexical information in aspect category detection. However, the unigram or n-gram based features usually use one-hot representations and fail to capture semantic relations between different words. Words that appear in the training data cannot provide any information if it does not appear in the test data. Associations between different words cannot be quantitatively measured via the one-hot vectors. To overcome the shortcomings of the existing studies, we propose a representation learning approach for aspect category detection.

Firstly, we propose a semi-supervised word embedding algorithm. It captures semantic relations between words, relations between words and aspects, and relations between sentiment words and aspects. After obtaining the word vectors, we average all the word vectors in a sentence as its continuous representation (Huang et al., 2012). Different from existing works that directly learn supervised classifiers based on the sentence vectors (Tang et al., 2014b), we propose to generate deeper and hybrid features which help to boost the performance. Two different kinds of neural networks are used for learning shared features and aspect-specific features respectively. We get the hybrid features by concatenating them together. The logistic regression classifier trained on the hybrid features achieves the state-of-the-art performance on the benchmark dataset

* Xiaojun Wan is the corresponding author.

released by SemEval-2014[1]. The performance is higher than that of the best participating team as well as a few strong baselines.

The main contributions of the study are summarized as follows, 1) we propose a representation learning approach for aspect category detection which achieves the state-of-the-art performance on a benchmark dataset. 2) We propose a semi-supervised word embedding algorithm which captures semantic relations between words, relations between words and aspects, and relations between sentiment words and aspects in a unified framework. 3) We generate deeper and hybrid features by using two different kinds of neural networks. It shows better performance than either the shared features or the aspect-specific features.

Problem Definition

Aspect category detection is a major evaluation task of SemEval-2014 (Semantic Evaluation), which attracted 18 teams global wide to participate in. Aspect category detection aims to identify the aspect categories discussed in a given review sentence. Formally, an aspect category set $A = \{a_1, a_2, a_3 \ldots a_N\}$ which contains N categories is predefined for a product domain. For a review dataset $D = \{s_1, s_2, s_3 \ldots s_K\}$ which contains K sentences, we need to predict a binary label vector $y_i \in R^{N\times 1}$ $(1 \le i \le K)$ for each sentence. Each value in y_i indicates whether the sentence s_i is discussing an aspect category or not. Specifically, $y_i^m = 1$ $(1 \le i \le K, 1 \le m \le N)$ means that sentence s_i contains the aspect category a_m and $y_i^m = 0$ otherwise. In SemEval-2014, the restaurant review dataset is used for evaluation. Five aspect categories are predefined for the domain, i.e. A = {"food", "service", "price", "ambience", "anecdote /miscellaneous" ("a/m" for short)}.

Aspect category is sometimes the hypernym of the aspects in a sentence. For example, in the review "the steak was mouthwatering!", the aspect category "food" is the hypernym of the aspect "steak". Meanwhile, some review sentences do not contain any aspect but are still expressing an opinion towards a target, such as the following one "Everything is tasty and well-portioned." Aspect category detection can solve such implicit aspect extraction problem (Hai, Chang, and Kim, 2011) elegantly by regarding it as a classification task. The implicit aspect can be detected if it is included in the aspect category set.

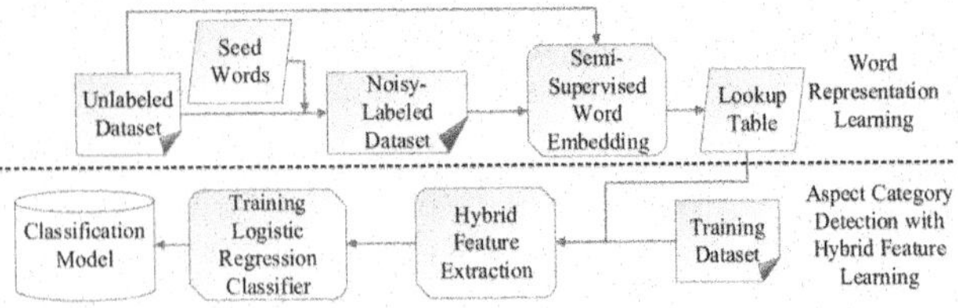

Figure 1. The framework of our proposed approach

[1] http://alt.qcri.org/semeval2014/task4/

Our Proposed Approach

In this section, we describe our representation learning approach for aspect category detection. We first propose a semi-supervised word embedding algorithm to obtain word vectors. Secondly, we acquire deeper and hybrid features through neural networks for supervised prediction. The general framework of our approach is shown in Figure 1.

Word Representation Learning

As shown in Figure 1, the word representation learning method leverages a large unlabeled review dataset. We use several seed words to assign category labels. The noisy-labeled data help our algorithm to obtain aspect-specific word embedding. The rest of the dataset remains as unlabeled. It helps to capture semantic relations between different words. We also extract sentiment word and aspect word pairs though dependency patterns. They enable our algorithm to learn relations between sentiment words and aspects.

To capture the semantic associations, we follow the strategy of word2vec. The skip-gram model of word2vec tries to maximize the probability of predicting a context word from a center word (Mikolov et al, 2013),

$$p(w_O|w_I) = \frac{\exp({v'_{w_O}}^{\mathrm{T}} v_{w_I})}{\sum_{w=1}^{W} \exp({v'_w}^{\mathrm{T}} v_{w_I})}$$

where w_O and w_I are the input (word) and output (context word); v_* and v'_* denotes the vectors associated with a word and a context word, respectively. The formulation forces words with similar contexts to get similar vector representations. However, it is impractical because the partition function grows linearly with the vocabulary size which could be hundreds of thousands.

A computationally efficient approximation for the above equation is negative sampling which has been used in Gutmann and Hyvarinen (2012) and Mnih and Teh (2012). A log-bilinear model is used to predict whether two words are in the same context and the loss function becomes,

$$L_1 = -\log \sigma({v'_{w_O}}^{\mathrm{T}} v_{w_I}) - \sum_{i=1}^{n} E_{w_i \sim P_n(w)}[\log \sigma(-{v'_{w_i}}^{\mathrm{T}} v_{w_I})]$$

where $\sigma(\cdot)$ is the sigmoid function, w_O is the actual context word and w_i is the negative sample from the noise distribution $P_n(w)$. Mikolov et al. (2013) set $P_n(w)$ as the 3/4rd power of the unigram distribution which outperforms the unigram and the uniform distribution significantly.

Since the skip-gram model only captures word semantic relations, we hope that words associated with different aspects fall into different positions in the vector space. A straight-forward strategy is adding supervision to the learning algorithm. While manual annotation can be time-consuming and expensive, we use distant supervision instead. Several seed words are selected to assign category labels to sentences which contain these seed words. For minimizing the human interaction, we only use the category names as the seed words to get noisy labels. For example, all the review sentences which contain "food" are regarded to fall into the "food" category. We do not collect any labeled data for "a/m" because this category is quite ambiguous and may involve any aspect aside from the other four categories. The labeled sentences are further sampled to balance the amounts of sentences in different categories.

For each sentence s_i with a noisy label vector y_i, we use logistic regression to classify the aspect category and adopt the cross entropy loss function,

$$L_2 = \sum_{1 \le m \le N} -y_i^m \log \sigma\left(x_m{}^{\mathrm{T}} V_i + b_m\right) - \left(1 - y_i^m\right) \log \sigma\left(-x_m{}^{\mathrm{T}} V_i - b_m\right)$$

where x_m is the weight vector for the features, b_m is the bias and V_i is the sentence vector for s_i. We simply average all the word vectors v_w $(w \in s_i)$ to get the sentence vector.

Apart from the word-aspect association, capturing the relation between sentiment words and aspects can also be useful for aspect category detection (McAuley et al., 2012). Many sentiment words such as "delicious" and "tasty" are aspect-specific because they can only describe "food". For each sentiment word – aspect word pair, we hope that the embedding algorithm can make them fall into the same side of a classification hyperplane defined by x_m and b_m (the same classification hyperplane for the sentences). We use dependency patterns to extract word pairs such as "food" and "delicious" from the phrase "food is delicious". The pattern is defined as "Noun → SBJ → W ← PRD ← Adjective" where "Noun" and "Adjective" represent the part-of-speech tags, "SBJ" and "PRB" are dependency relations, "W" can be any word. The noun word and the adjective word together are treated as a word pair. For each word pair (w_1, w_2), their probabilities of falling into an aspect category should be similar which brings the following loss function,

$$L_3 = \left[\sigma\left(x_m{}^{\mathrm{T}} v_{w_2} + b_m\right) - \sigma\left(x_m{}^{\mathrm{T}} v_{w_1} + b_m\right)\right]^2$$

The above equation tends to narrow the distance between $\sigma\left(x_m{}^{\mathrm{T}} v_{w_2} + b_m\right)$ and $\sigma\left(x_m{}^{\mathrm{T}} v_{w_1} + b_m\right)$.

Finally, we learn the word vectors by aggregating all the above loss functions,

$$minimize\ L = L_1 + L_2 + L_3$$

The parameters are learned through stochastic gradient descent. We omit the details due to limited space.

Aspect Category Detection with Hybrid Feature Learning

We simply average all the word vectors to obtain the sentence vector. Different from most of the previous researches that directly learn supervised classifiers on the sentence vector, we choose to get deeper and hybrid features through different two-layer feed-forward neural networks.

The input of a neural network is a sentence vector V_i which represents the sentence s_i in the training dataset. We adopt sigmoid as the activation function and get the hidden units H_i as

$$H_i = \sigma(W_1 V_i + B_1)$$

and the output layer O_i as

$$O_i = \sigma(W_2 H_i + B_2)$$

where W_1 and B_1 are the parameters of the first layer, W_2 and B_2 are the parameters of the second layer.

We introduce two different settings of the neural network to obtain the shared and aspect-specific features, respectively. In the first setting, a two-layer neural network is trained to fit all the aspect categories simultaneously as shown in Figure 2.a. The neural network outputs five binary variables to represent five aspect categories. The output O_i represents the label vector y_i for the sentence s_i. We use back-propagation to learn the parameters. In this setting, the model learns the same features (i.e. the hidden layer) to predict all the aspect categories. Therefore, we describe the hidden layer as shared features.

In the second setting, we use five different two-layer neural networks to predict each of the five aspect

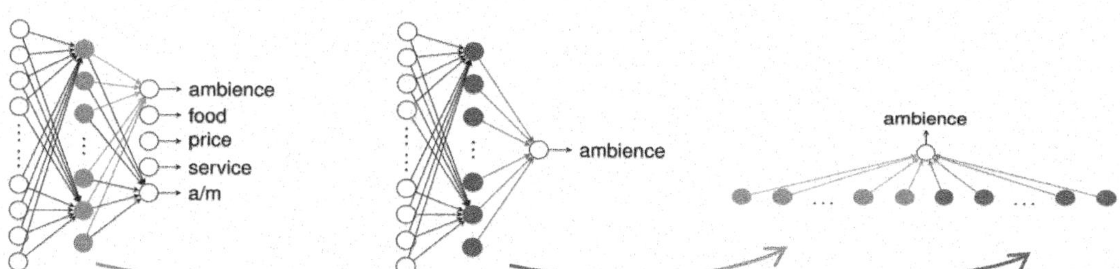

(a) Learning shared features (b) Learning aspect-specific features (c) Hybrid features and weight initialization
Figure 2. Learning Deeper and Hybrid Features

categories. In this setting, the output O_i corresponds to one of the five values in y_i. The hidden layer for each aspect is different from each other because they are trained separately (Figure 2.b). The features only need to adapt to one of the aspect category. Therefore, we describe the hidden layer as aspect-specific features.

Finally, we concatenate the shared and aspect-specific features to form our hybrid features. A 2-class logistic regression classifier is trained on the hybrid features for each of the aspect (Figure 2.c). We use the weights learned from the neural networks to initialize the weights here. Afterwards, the weights are fine-tuned through stochastic gradient descent. The weight initialization step helps the training procedure converge much faster.

Experiments

Dataset

We used the restaurant review dataset released by SemEval-2014 which modified and extended the dataset of Ganu et al. (2009). The training dataset contains 3,041 sentences and the test dataset contains 800 sentences. We show the number of sentences in each category in Table 1.

Category	# of sentences	
	Training	Test
food	1232	418
price	321	83
service	597	172
ambience	431	118
a/m	1132	234

Table 1. Statistics of the SemEval-2014 Restaurant Review Dataset

Additionally, we collected an Extended Restaurant Review Dataset to learn the word representations. Part of the dataset is provided by Yelp Dataset Challenge[2]. The rest of the dataset is crawled from Citysearch[3]. We use the category names "food", "price", "service" and "ambience/ambiance" as seed words to obtain lots of noisy-labeled sentences (Purver and Battersby, 2012). Mate-tools (Bohnet, 2010) is used to parse the dataset and get adjective-noun word pairs via the dependency pattern. Note that the Extended Restaurant Review Dataset is only used for learning better word representations. The final classification model is trained on the SemEval-2014 Restaurant Review Dataset. The detailed statistics of the dataset are shown in Table 2.

[2] http://www.yelp.com/dataset_challenge

[3] http://www.citysearch.com/

# of unlabeled sentences	# of noisy-labeled sentences	# of word pairs
8,324,813	1,214,762	1,790,421

Table 2. Statistics of the Extended Restaurant Review Dataset

Experiment Setup

In word representation learning, we set the vector size as 500 and the context windows as 5. The learning rate is set to 0.025 following word2vec and it declines with the training procedure. All the word vectors (v_i) and the classification weights (x_m and b_m) are initialized randomly between -0.5 and 0.5.

For learning the hybrid features, we use two 2-layer neural networks, both of which contain 50 hidden units. We use the labeled dataset (not the noisy-labeled dataset) to train them through back-propagation. The mini-batch stochastic gradient descent is used to update the parameters. The batch size is set to 50. The training procedure is run for 500 epochs when the training error becomes steady.

Results and Analysis

Baseline Methods

Firstly, we compare our method with several traditional classification algorithms.

KNN: This is the baseline provided by SemEval-2014 (Pontiki et al., 2014). For each test sentence s_i, k most similar training sentences are first found. The Dice coefficient is used to measure the sentence similarity. Then, s_i is assigned the m most frequent aspect category labels of the k retrieved sentences; m is the most frequent number of aspect category labels per sentence among the k sentences.

NB, LR and **SVM**: We use Naïve Bayes, Logistic Regression and Support Vector Machine as the classification algorithms with unigram and bigram features.

SVM-DS: We incorporate distant supervision into the SVM model. Both manually labeled data and the noisy-labeled data are used for training.

NRC: This is the best system in the evaluation (Kiritchenko et al., 2014). They also adopt SVM as the classification algorithm. The features include n-grams, stemmed n-grams, character n-grams, non-contiguous n-grams, word cluster n-grams and lexicon features. **NRC-Lexicon** is the result without the lexicon features.

SemEval-Avg: The average result of all the systems in SemEval-2014.

We also compare our method with existing word embedding algorithms including **C&W** (Collobert and Weston, 2008), **word2vec** (Mikolov et al, 2013), **HLBL** (Mnih and Hinton, 2008) and **GloVe** (Pennington et al. 2014). Pre-trained word vectors are publicly available on

Proceedings of the Twenty-Ninth AAAI Conference on Artificial Intelligence

Person Identification Using Anthropometric and Gait Data from Kinect Sensor

Virginia O. Andersson and **Ricardo M. Araujo**
PPGC - Federal University of Pelotas
Rua Gomes Carneiro, 1, Pelotas, RS, Brazil - 96010-610
vandersson@inf.ufpel.edu.br, ricardo@inf.ufpel.edu.br

Abstract

Uniquely identifying individuals using anthropometric and gait data allows for passive biometric systems, where cooperation from the subjects being identified is not required. In this paper, we report on experiments using a novel data set composed of 140 individuals walking in front of a Microsoft Kinect sensor. We provide a methodology to extract anthropometric and gait features from this data and show results of applying different machine learning algorithms on subject identification tasks. Focusing on KNN classifiers, we discuss how accuracy varies in different settings, including number of individuals in a gallery, types of attributes used and number of considered neighbors. Finally, we compare the obtained results with other results in the literature, showing that our approach has comparable accuracy for large galleries.

Introduction

Biometric systems is an important application area for artificial intelligence in general and machine learning in particular. As these systems become more popular, with applications ranging from surveillance to entertainment (Wang 2012), a better handling of lower-quality data from cheaper sensors becomes necessary.

A relatively recent trend in biometrics is performing person recognition using full-body characteristics, including anthropometric measurements of body parts and dynamic gait features from walking patterns. This is often performed with the use of video cameras and complex feature-extraction algorithms from video footages.

The Microsoft Kinect device is a set of sensors with an accompanying Software Development Kit (SDK) that is able to track movements from users by using a skeleton mapping algorithm. The first version of the device is able to track 48 skeletal points at 30 frames per second and is used in the X-Box 360 video-game console as an input for a gesture-based interface.

While this device is primarily aimed at tracking users that are standing in the same place, it has been used to track walking subjects in order to extract gait information (Araujo, Graña, and Andersson 2013). This use provides a cheaper, off-the-shelf, alternative to complex multi-part video setups.

However, several limitations, including range, lighting and occlusions degrade the accuracy of the data provided by the device and impose significant challenges to its use in a biometric system. Hence, while using the Kinect device greatly simplifies the data capturing stage, it may require improved techniques to handle these limitations.

In this paper, we provide a comparison of machine learning algorithms applied to a large data set comprised of walking subjects captured using the 2010 version of the Kinect device, aiming at person recognition. We focus on the K-Nearest Neighbors algorithm that is widely used in the literature, but also provide comparisons with Multi-Layer Perceptrons and Support Vector Machines.

Related Work

The use of body measurements aiming at subject identification can be traced back to mid-XIX century in the France police (Harrap 1956). (Godil, Grother, and Ressler 2003) performed an extensive analysis of the effectiveness of using body measurements and shape for identification purposes, using the CAESAR database, which collects accurate static anthropometric data using markers.

The use of joint positions collected using a Kinect device appears in (Munsell et al. 2012) as part of a broader set of features that included motion patterns; a SVM was used for classification along with a statistical model. In (Araujo, Graña, and Andersson 2013) body segment lengths derived from joint positions were used exclusively to train a KNN classifier. Both cases used only a very limited data set with the former using 20 individuals and the latter 8.

Using human gait as a biometric feature was motivated by evidences that individuals describe unique patterns during their gait cycles (Murray, Drought, and Kory 1964). Approaches used to extract and analyze human gait can be classified as (i) model-based, where the human gait is described by gait theory fundamentals and is reconstructed through a model, e.g. "stick figure", that fits the person in every gait sequence frame; the spatiotemporal and kinematic parameters, then, are extracted from the model during gait cycle; and (ii) model-free, where features such as silhouette or enclosing boxes are used as attributes, without explicitly considering human gait fundamentals (Ng et al. 2011).

Recent model-based approaches include (Cunado, Nixon, and Carter 2003), where gait analysis was restricted to the use of sagital rotations of hips, knees, and ankles and a KNN classifier was used to perform person identification. KNN is also used in (Yoo and Nixon 2011), where a detailed method to extract simplified skeleton figures from videos is presented and gait features are extracted from these figures.

Model-free approaches include the concept of Gait Energy Images (Han and Bhanu 2006). In (Sivapalan et al. 2011), Gait Energy Volumes are proposed as an extension and a database containing depth information on 15 subjects walking towards a Kinect sensor is used to test the methodology, using an KNN-based approach.

In (Hofmann and Bachmann 2012), the authors proposed the use of Depth Gradient Histogram Energy Image to improve identification when many more subjects are being identified, reporting high accuracy (81%-92%) over a data set created using a Kinect sensor; however, the database used contains only very few gait cycles due to a fixed sensor placement and only depth and regular video data is used. Therefore this approach focused on generic object-motion characteristics, without considering gait signature information. Again, a KNN classifier is used.

Compared to previous approaches, the present paper makes use of a comprehensive (140 subjects) data set captured using a Kinect sensor, extends the attributes to include both body measurements and model-based gait information and provides more in-depth experiments using the data, including insights on the used machine learning classifiers.

Methodology

The Kinect Sensor

The Kinect device used in our experiments was the 2010 model for the X-Box 360 video-game console, connected through an adapter cable to a PC running the SDK version 1.0. This device is equipped with a RGB camera and a depth sensor composed of an infrared light emitter and a infrared-sensitive camera.

A software library, called NUI API (Natural User Application Programming Interface), retrieves and process data from the sensors. This API is responsible for providing detailed information about the location, position and orientation of individuals located in front of the sensor. This information is provided to the application as a set of 48 three-dimensional points called "skeleton points". These points approximate the main joints of human body and the actual position of the individual in front of the sensor.

The API provides data in the form of frames at the rate of 30 frames per second. Each frame contains an array containing all the extracted points at the moment of the capture.

Capturing Methodology

Volunteers walked in front of the sensor in a semi-circular trajectory while data was being recorded. A spinning dish was used to help move the Kinect sensor to follow the person during the walk. This combination of trajectory and Kinect's pan camera movement allows several gait cycles to be captured per individual without distortions caused by subjects moving in or out of the sensor's field of view. Each subject executed five round trip free cadence walk, starting on the left of the sensor, walking clockwise to the right of the sensor and then back.

The volunteers were recruited for the experiment at a university campus. The majority of subjects were college students, with ages between 17 and 35 years old. Each of the subjects that accepted to participate in the experiment provided gender, height and weight information. They were wearing light clothing, since the captures were conducted during summer. The captures were conducted in an empty classroom at day time with mostly artificial lighting. A total of 140 individuals were captured using the proposed methodology (95 men and 45 women). In most cases, each individual generated about 500 to 600 frames and completed between 6 and 12 gait cycles per walk.

Raw skeleton data often presents noise in the joint positions due to errors in the tracking process. In order to reduce this noise we applied an Auto Regressive Moving Average (ARMA) filter (Azimi 2012) with a window of size 8, set in an ad hoc fashion by observing a visual reconstruction of walks before and after the filter. This filter was applied to all walk samples before being used.

From the captured raw data, attributes were extracted for each walk, composing labeled examples where the label is an anonymized identifier of an individual. The attributes are divided in two sets: *gait attributes* and *anthropometric attributes*. In what follows we describe how each attribute is defined. The full data set is available at http://ricardoaraujo.net/kinect.

Gait Attributes Model-based gait analysis considers the human gait theory to help extract parameters from human walk. The angles described by the joints of the hips, knees and ankles, known as kinematic parameters, were calculated for each frame captured, using the pendulum model proposed in (Cunado, Nixon, and Carter 2003) and depicted in Figure 1 (b). Furthermore, we calculate the foot angle, described in (Murray, Drought, and Kory 1964), depicted in Figure 1 (c) and the spatiotemporal parameters described in (Yoo and Nixon 2011): the step length, stride length (or "gait cycle size"), cycle time and velocity.

As shown in Figure 1 (b), the angle θ is formed during a gait cycle between the segments of the thigh and a projection of the hip. Between the leg and the knee projection the angle γ is defined; α is the angle of the ankle rotation formed by the foot segment and the ankle projection and the foot angle β is formed by the opening of the foot in relation to the axis of the heel. These angles describe periodic curves during a walk, which can have useful characteristics for biometric recognition (Harrap 1956).

The periodic curves generated by the lower joint angles are composed by flexion and extension phases, visually noticed by peaks (flexion) and valleys (extension) (Murray, Drought, and Kory 1964). The arithmetic average and standard deviation were computed for the flexion peaks and extension valleys in order to characterize the curves of each individual. Lower and higher flexion peaks and extension valleys were treated separately, generating an arithmetic average and standard deviation for each high and low phase. Each lower joint was considered independent of the others,

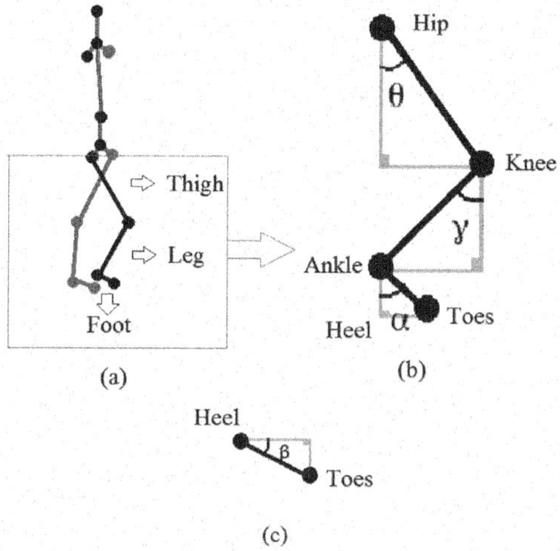

Figure 1: Angles tracked to compose gait attributes.

generating attributes equally independent.

Spatiotemporal parameters were calculated based on the step length and frame rate of the Kinect sensor. The step length was obtained by averaging the highest values of the difference between the right and left heels. In addition, we use as attributes the stride length (Eq. 1), average stride length over all n strides (Eq. 2), cycle time (Eq. 3) and velocity (Eq. 4). A total of 60 gait attributes were defined.

$$strideLength = 2 * stepLength \quad (1)$$

$$avgStrideLength = \sum_{i=1}^{n} \frac{strideLength}{n} \quad (2)$$

$$cycleTime = \frac{avgCyclePeriod}{30} \quad (3)$$

$$velocity = \frac{avgStrideLength}{cycleTime} \quad (4)$$

Anthropometric Attributes For each frame captured the measurements of several body segments, shown in Figure 2, were calculated using the Euclidean distance between joints, in a similar fashion to the methodology employed in (Araujo, Graña, and Andersson 2013). The subject's height was defined as the sum of the neck length, upper and lower spine length and the averages lengths of the left and right hips, thighs and lower legs.

The mean and standard deviation of each body segment and height over all frames of a walk were calculated. Measurements beyond two standard deviations from the mean were discarded and attributed to noise. The recalculated means for each part were used as attributes, totaling 20 anthropometric attributes.

Classifiers

From our literature review, K-Nearest Neighbor (KNN) classifier is the most commonly used model in full-body biometrics, followed by Support Vector Machines (SVM). In this section, we compare these two models applied to our data set and, in addition, also Multi-Layer Perceptron (MLP).

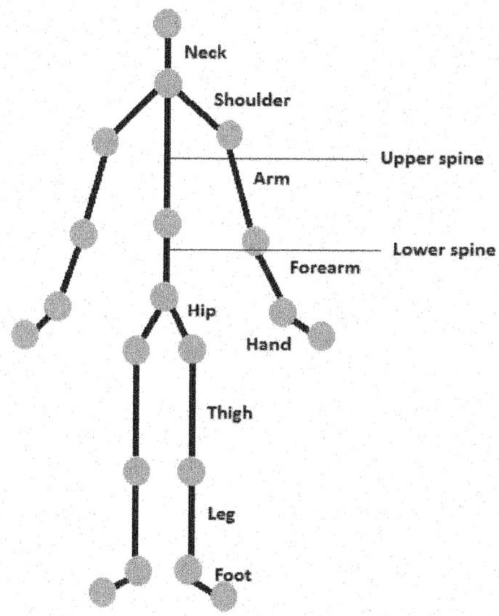

Figure 2: Tracked joints (circles) and body segments used as attributes.

Parameters for each algorithm were set by varying their values while trying to maximize the resulting accuracy using a 10-fold cross-validation (Mitchell 1997) over a smaller random validation subset composed of 20 users. The same number of evaluations was performed for each classifier. All attributes were normalized before use by mapping their values to the range $\{-1, 1\}$.

KNN was set to $K = 5$, Manhattan distance as the distance metric and distance weighting of $1/d$. For the MLP, we only considered networks with a single hidden layer and the number of hidden units was set to 40. Training was performed using the Backpropagation (Haykin 2008) algorithm with momentum set to 0.2, learning rate to 0.3 and 1000 maximum epochs. The SVM was trained using the Sequential Minimal Optimization (SMO) algorithm (Platt 1999), using a polynomial kernel and $C = 100.0$.

We use 10-fold cross-validation to validate the models with the above parameters i.e. the data set was randomly partitioned in 10 subsets and training was performed ten times, each time leaving one partition out of the training process, which was used for testing; the reported accuracies are the averages of these ten executions. When required, statistical significance tests are performed using a Wilcoxon signed-rank test (Wilcoxon 1945).

Results

Classifiers Accuracy

Figure 3 plots accuracy data over the 10 validation folds for each algorithm and data set. Table 1 shows the mean values for each case.

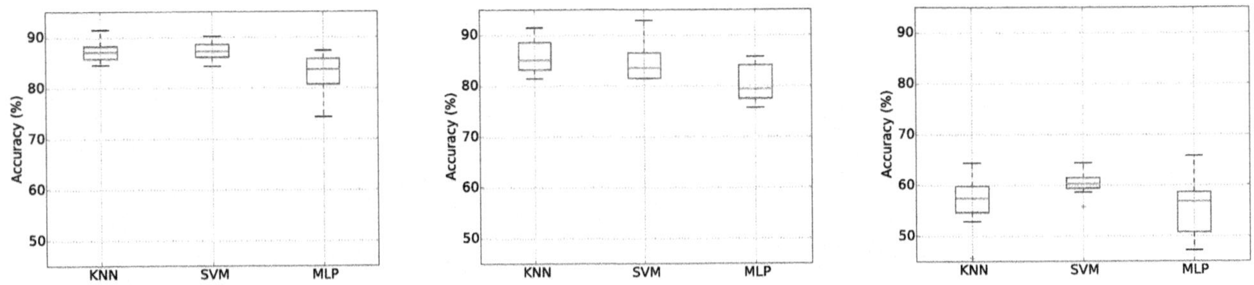

(a) All attributes. (b) Anthropometric attributes. (c) Gait attributes.

Figure 3: Accuracy boxplots for each classifier and different attributes.

Overall, we can observe that only using gait attributes leads to a poor performance, much worse than using only anthropometric attributes. Nonetheless, combining the two subsets allows for higher accuracy.

In all cases MLP performed consistently worse than KNN and SVM. When using all attributes, KNN and SVM performed about the same; the difference in the means is not statistically significant ($p = 0.991$).

When considering only anthropometric attributes, KNN displayed slightly better mean, but not very statistically significant ($p = 0.248$). The results for KNN are, however, more consistent, with smaller standard deviation and a higher median.

For gait attributes SVM has a small, but statistically significant ($p = 0.032$), lead over KNN. It is also more consistent and has a higher median. While MLP still performs poorly over gait attributes, the difference is not as accentuated as for the other cases.

These results lead to the conclusion that KNN and SVM perform about equally well on the problem, but the chosen MLP performs considerably and consistently worse. This is consistent with the literature, where KNN and SVM are often used. The preference for KNN may be due to it being easy and fast to train, allowing for quicker experimentation.

The comparatively small increase in accuracy when combining both types of attributes shows that gait attributes do not provide much value beyond anthropometric attributes, an evidence that the two are somewhat correlated. It is clear that the latter is responsible for most of the response, with gait attributes contributing only an average of 3.3 percentage points. Nonetheless, gait attributes do show a measurable contribution and by themselves are reasonably useful (much better than random) for person identification.

Table 1: Classifiers' mean accuracy using different attributes. Bold text highlights the best values for each column.

Classifier	Gait	Anthropometric	All
SVM	**62.9%**	84.7%	86.3%
KNN	59.5%	**85.4%**	**87.7%**
MLP	59.2%	79.7%	84.7%

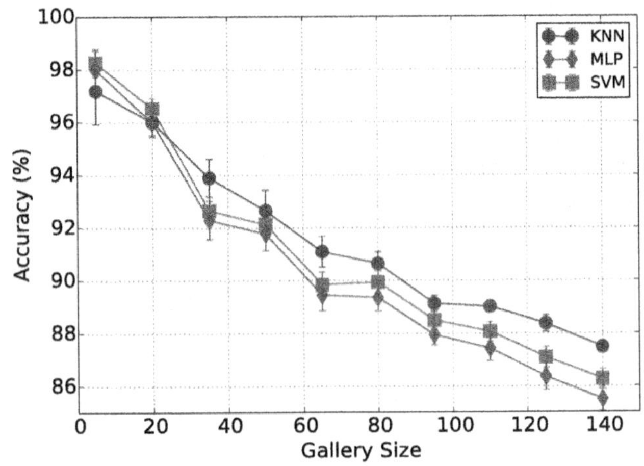

Figure 4: Classifiers' average accuracy for different gallery sizes using all attributes. Error bars are 95% confidence intervals.

Gallery Size

While the results in Table 1 are reasonable and useful for a number of application (possibly excluding strict authentication), they may seem worse than results presented in similar previous works - e.g. (Araujo, Graña, and Andersson 2013) where upwards of 98% accuracy was reported, but for only 9 subjects. One key missing aspect of these previous work is an account for how accuracy varies with the size of the gallery being identified.

Figure 4 shows how accuracy evolves when subjects in increasingly large galleries must be identified. Each point (except for 140) is the average over 10 galleries with the same size and randomly drawn from the complete data set. For very small galleries, accuracies are close to 98%, steadily converging to the results seen in Table 1.

Additionally, we can observe that KNN actually performs worse for small galleries, only becoming better than SVM and MLP when considering more than 20 individuals.

Figure 5 shows how accuracy vary for different gallery sizes and when using different attribute sets. Again we can observe that gait attributes are overall far less useful for the task than anthropometric attributes. Nonetheless, for very small galleries ($N = 5$ in the figure), using only gait attributes provides reasonable performance.

Accuracy using gait attributes degrades much faster when increasing gallery size. Nonetheless, it is for large galleries that using gait information in addition to anthropometric attributes is useful. For galleries of size 105 or less there are no statistically significant differences in accuracy between using gait information or not (assuming significance level of 0.05) but there are significant, if rather small, differences for larger galleries.

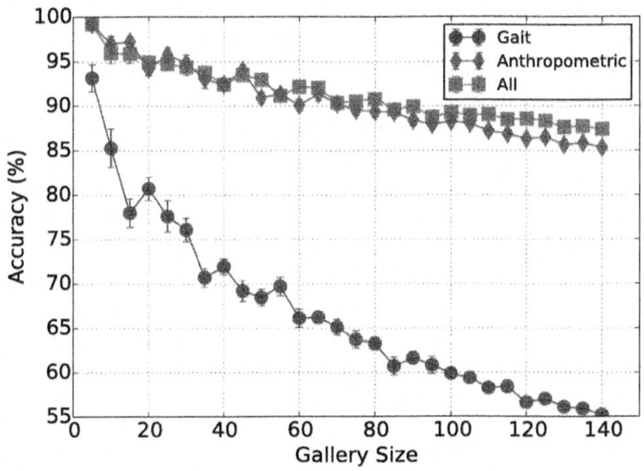

Figure 5: Average KNN accuracy for different gallery sizes and different attribute sets. Error bars represent 95% confidence intervals.

Number of Neighbors

While we used the same value of K for all gallery sizes when using KNN classifier, one may consider how this parameter affects overall performance. In order to provide an answer, for each gallery size we varied the value of K from 1 to 101 (or the maximum number of individuals in the gallery; odd values only were considered) and measured the resulting performance for each K, again as an average over 10 folds using cross-validation.

Figure 6 shows the best K for each gallery size, along with the accuracy obtained when using the best K. While the data is noisy, the general trend is clear: larger galleries benefit from larger values of K but these values do not vary considerably. Going from a gallery of 10 individuals to 140 individuals only increases the value of K from 1 to 5, a two-step change. The average improvement over a fixed $K = 5$ was of 0.6 percentage point.

Even though the best K varies little with gallery size, this parameter does have a strong effect in accuracy. Figure 7 shows how accuracy varies with K for different gallery sizes. Increasing K beyond the optimal value leads to an almost linear decrease in accuracy. This shows that accuracy is quite sensitive to K, even though the differences in optimal values for different gallery sizes do not vary significantly; hence, knowing the optimal value for some sizes allows for a quick search for optimal values for other sizes, since there seems to be no need for an exhaustive search over a wide range of values. A gradient search should suffice in finding this parameter.

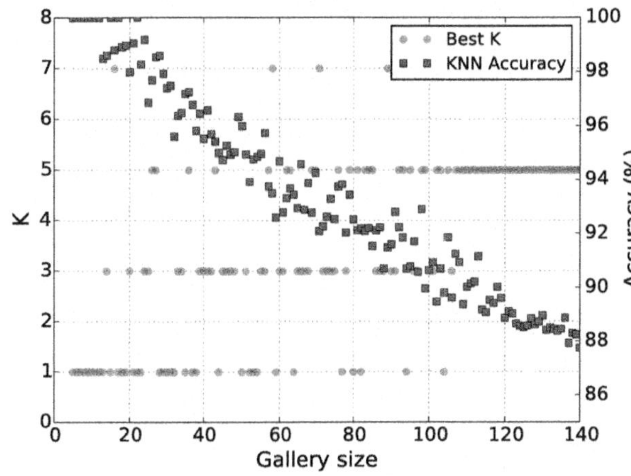

Figure 6: Best found K and KNN accuracy with best K for different gallery sizes.

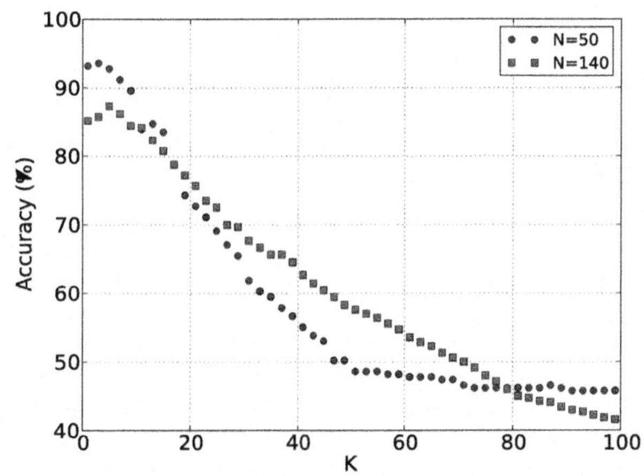

Figure 7: KNN accuracy for different values of K and two gallery sizes.

Comparison to Other Approaches

Figure 6 allows for a rough comparison with previous similar works. For instance, (Yoo and Nixon 2011), using regular video cameras to extract 2D stick-figures information from individuals, reports an accuracy of 84.0% using KNN to classify 100 individuals, against 89.4% using our methodology and data set. However, they also report a 96.7% accuracy using 30 individuals, while ours is of 94.0%, an evidence that the adequacy of a methodology, including the chosen classifier and attributes, is conditional on the number of individuals being identified.

In (Hofmann and Bachmann 2012), only images' energies are used for identification - i.e. it does not try to reconstruct a

Table 2: Attributes selected from a Correlation-based Feature Subset Selection and how much removing each of the set affects KNN accuracy, in percentage points.

Attribute	Average Accuracy Change
Stride Length (gait)	-4.4%
Right Foot	-3.2%
Right Hand	-2.9%
Neck	-2.6%
Upper Spine	-1.9%
Right Shoulder	-1.7%
Left Hip	-1.7%
Height	-1.4%
Right Leg	-1.3%
Left Angle Peaks (gait)	-0.7%
Left Forearm	-0.6%
Right Thigh	-0.6%
Left Thigh	0.0%
Left Leg	0.0%

skeleton model from video images - and an 81.0% accuracy is reported for 176 individuals. While a more direct comparison is not possible given our more limited data set, fitting an exponential function to Figure 6, yields a projection of 84.5% for this same gallery size.

Relevant Attributes

The complete data set contains a total 80 attributes. In the provided experiments, all were used, but such large number of attributes lead to high computational requirements and may reduce accuracy if many attributes are irrelevant.

In order to better understand the role each attribute has in the obtained results, we applied a correlation-based feature subset selection (Hall 1998) to the data. The resulting subset contains only 14 attributes, shown in Table 2. While using this subset does not improve accuracy, it only performs an average of 0.1 percentage point worse when compared to the case where all attributes are provided.

It is also possible to observe that 12 of the 14 selected attributes are anthropometric and only 2 are related to gait. This reinforces our previous observation that gait features are largely correlated to anthropometric features but less reliable for identification. Nonetheless, Step Length, a gait attribute, provides the largest drop in accuracy when individually removed from this set.

Conclusions

We reported on the ability of different classifiers to discriminate walking individuals tracked by a Microsoft Kinect device, aiming at composing a full-body person identification system. In order to do so, we detailed how attributes could be extracted from the raw data and categorized these attributes as based on static body measurements (anthropometric) or motion patterns (gait). A data set composed of 140 subjects was used and three classifiers were tested (KNN,MLP and SVM).

The main contribution of this paper was to provide a set of simulations that allowed for the comparison between commonly used classifiers applied to a novel biometric data set. The experiments considered several different conditions, notably different gallery sizes and different combinations of attributes.

Our results showed that the defined gait attributes are less useful than anthropometric attributes when each is used separately; accuracies using only gait also fall faster as gallery size is increased. However, combining the two attribute types allows for higher accuracies when the number of subjects is large enough. By reducing the dimensionality of the data, we showed evidences that a very compact set of attributes is enough to ensure high accuracy and that in this smaller set, gait information is very relevant.

When comparing the classifiers, our results showed evidences that KNN and SVM display similar accuracies, while MLP perform considerably worse for all tested variations of attributes, with the exception of very small galleries. Focusing on KNN, we showed that the number of neighbors (K) does not vary considerably when very different gallery sizes are used. In addition, our best results are generally comparable to accuracies reported in the literature, but the comparison methodology does not allow for stronger claims.

In conclusion, a full-body person identification system was shown to be viable using data from a Kinect device and the proposed methodology, but the observed accuracies are not high enough for critical applications, suggesting that this approach should be used as a complement to other techniques (e.g. face recognition).

Future work include finding and testing better gait-based attributes that can be easily inferred from Kinect data and testing the trained classifiers in real-world uncontrolled scenarios.

Acknowledgments

This work is supported by CNPq (Brazilian National Research Council) through grant number 477937/2012-8.

References

Araujo, R. M.; Graña, G.; and Andersson, V. 2013. Towards skeleton biometric identification using the microsoft kinect sensor. In *the 28th Annual ACM Symposium*, 21–26. New York, New York, USA: ACM Press.

Azimi, M. 2012. Skeleton joint smoothing white paper. Technical report, Microsoft Inc.

Cunado, D.; Nixon, M. S.; and Carter, J. N. 2003. Automatic extraction and description of human gait models for recognition purposes. *Computer Vision and Image Understanding* 90(1):1–41.

Godil, A.; Grother, P.; and Ressler, S. 2003. Human identification from body shape. In *Proceedings of the 4th International Conference on 3D Digital Imaging and Modeling*, 1–7. IEEE Computer Society Press.

Hall, M. A. 1998. *Correlation-based Feature Subset Selection for Machine Learning*. Ph.D. Dissertation, University of Waikato, Hamilton, New Zealand.

Han, J., and Bhanu, B. 2006. Individual recognition using gait energy image. *IEEE Transactions on Pattern Analysis and Machine Intelligence* 28(2):316–322.

Harrap, G. G. 1956. *Alphonse Bertillon: Father of scientific detection*. New York: Abelard-Schuman.

Haykin, S. 2008. *Neural Networks and Learning Machines (3rd Edition)*. Prentice Hall, 3 edition.

Hofmann, M., and Bachmann, S. 2012. 2.5d gait biometrics using the depth gradient histogram energy image. In *Proceedings of the IEEE Fifth International Conference on Biometrics: Theory, Applications and Systems (BTAS)*, 399 – 403.

Mitchell, T. 1997. *Machine Learning*. New York, NY, USA: McGraw-Hill, Inc., 1 edition.

Munsell, B. C.; Temlyakov, A.; Qu, C.; and Wang, S. 2012. Person identification using full-body motion and anthropometric biometrics from kinect videos. In Fusiello, A.; Murino, V.; and Cucchiara, R., eds., *ECCV Workshops (3)*, volume 7585 of *Lecture Notes in Computer Science*, 91–100. Springer.

Murray, M. P.; Drought, A. B.; and Kory, R. C. 1964. Walking patterns of normal men. *The Journal of Bone Joint Surgery* 46:335–360.

Ng, H.; Tong, H.-L.; Tan, W. H.; and Abdullah, J. 2011. Improved gait classification with different smoothing techniques. *International Journal on Advanced Science, Engineering and Information Technology* 1(3):242–247.

Platt, J. C. 1999. Advances in kernel methods. Cambridge, MA, USA: MIT Press. chapter Fast Training of Support Vector Machines Using Sequential Minimal Optimization, 185–208.

Sivapalan, S.; Chen, D.; Denman, S.; Sridharan, S.; and Fookes, C. 2011. Gait energy volumes and frontal gait recognition using depth images. In Jain, A. K.; Ross, A.; Prabhakar, S.; and Kim, J., eds., *IJCB*, 1–6. IEEE.

Wang, L. 2012. Some issues of biometrics: technology intelligence, progress and challenges. *International Journal of Information Technology and Management* 11(1/2):72.

Wilcoxon, F. 1945. Individual comparisons by ranking methods. *Biometrics Bulletin* 1(6):80–83.

Yoo, J.-H., and Nixon, M. S. 2011. Automated markerless analysis of human gait motion for recognition and classification. *ETRI Journal* 33(2):259–266.

Proceedings of the Twenty-Ninth AAAI Conference on Artificial Intelligence

R1SVM: A Randomised Nonlinear Approach to Large-Scale Anomaly Detection

Sarah M. Erfani[*†], **Mahsa Baktashmotlagh**[†], **Sutharshan Rajasegarar**[†]
Shanika Karunasekera[*†], **Chris Leckie**[*†]
[†]NICTA Victoria Research Laboratory
[*]Department of Computing and Information Systems,
The University of Melbourne, Australia

Abstract

The problem of unsupervised anomaly detection arises in a wide variety of practical applications. While one-class support vector machines have demonstrated their effectiveness as an anomaly detection technique, their ability to model large datasets is limited due to their memory and time complexity for training. To address this issue for supervised learning of kernel machines, there has been growing interest in random projection methods as an alternative to the computationally expensive problems of kernel matrix construction and support vector optimisation. In this paper we leverage the theory of nonlinear random projections and propose the *Randomised One-class SVM (R1SVM)*, which is an efficient and scalable anomaly detection technique that can be trained on large-scale datasets. Our empirical analysis on several real-life and synthetic datasets shows that our randomised 1SVM algorithm achieves comparable or better accuracy to deep autoencoder and traditional kernelised approaches for anomaly detection, while being approximately 100 times faster in training and testing.

Introduction

Unsupervised anomaly detection (also known as outlier detection) plays a significant role in a variety of applications, such as fraud detection, network intrusion detection and fault diagnosis. One-class Support Vector Machines (1SVMs) (Schölkopf et al. 2001; Tax and Duin 2004) have proven to be a very effective unsupervised learning method to construct highly accurate classifiers for anomaly detection. However, 1SVMs are often impractical for use on very large datasets due to the computational and memory complexity of their underlying optimisation problem during training (Vapnik 1998; Vishwanathan, Smola, and Murty 2003; Bengio and LeCun 2007). Recently, there has been growing interest in randomised approaches to improve the efficiency of kernel methods for supervised learning of SVMs (Rahimi and Recht 2007; 2009). In this paper, we build on the theory of nonlinear random projections in order to accelerate the training of 1SVMs, and propose a new form of anomaly detector called *Randomised One-class SVM* (R1SVM). We show that R1SVM can achieve comparable or better accuracy than an existing 1SVM method, while reducing training and testing time by up to two orders of magnitude.

A key challenge in anomaly detection is how to characterise the distribution of "normal" (i.e., non-anomalous) data. This is particularly challenging when the process that generated the normal data has an unknown, potentially complex underlying distribution. 1SVM approaches have had considerable success in addressing this modelling task by using a kernel function to implicitly map the data from the input space to a higher dimensional feature space, in which a relatively simple model such as a hyperplane (Schölkopf et al. 2001), hypersphere (Tax and Duin 2004) or hyperellipsoid (Wang, Yeung, and Tsang 2006; Rajasegarar et al. 2010) can be used to characterise normal observations.

A practical limitation of 1SVM approaches is their computational and memory complexity for training. In a dataset with n records, each with d dimensions, training using a nonlinear kernel requires $O(dn^2)$ computational complexity, as well as $O(dn^2)$ memory complexity for the kernel matrix (Tax and Duin 2004). This limits the utility of 1SVM in applications involving large datasets. While training can be performed on a smaller sample of the training data, this can reduce the accuracy of the 1SVM due to the sparse sampling of the underlying distribution, particularly in applications that involve high dimensional input spaces.

Recently, there has been significant progress in using randomised features in conjunction with linear algorithms to reveal nonlinear patterns in data. In particular, a nonlinear, randomised variant of component analysis methods such as Principal Component Analysis (RPCA) and Canonical Correlation Analysis (RCCA) has been proposed (Lopez-Paz et al. 2014). These randomised variants have been applied to the tasks of regression and classification of large datasets, and exhibited significant savings in computation time while incurring little or no loss in accuracy.

In this paper, we propose a novel application of randomised methods by deriving a highly scalable algorithm for anomaly detection based on training a linear one-class SVM using randomised, nonlinear features. By using randomised features rather than finding a set of optimised support vectors, we can substantially reduce the cost of training our one-class SVM. We provide extensive empirical testing to show that our randomised 1SVM method achieves substantial improvement in both computational complexity and accuracy over exact kernel methods.

To the best of our knowledge this is the first attempt to exploit nonlinear random features in kernel-based methods for anomaly detection. In addition to significantly reducing computational complexity, we show that our randomised 1SVM algorithm achieves comparable or better accuracy compared to autoencoder and kernelised approaches to anomaly detection. We postulate that this improvement in accuracy is due to the implicit regularisation induced by randomness, as well as an improvement in the separation between normal and anomalous data points when compared in the nonlinear feature space. By improving the efficiency of training 1SVMs in this way, we believe it will be possible to apply anomaly detection to data-intensive applications in resource constrained environments, such as wireless sensor networks.

Related Work and Background

While numerous 1SVM formulations using nonlinear kernel have been proposed in the literature (Schölkopf et al. 2001; Tax and Duin 2004; Bottou and Lin 2007), a common feature of many formulations is the solution of a quadratic programming (QP) problem. In particular, these kernel-based methods rely on the calculation of a kernel matrix over all pairs of data points, which limits the scalability of training 1SVMs on large datasets. This can also limit the effectiveness of 1SVMs on high dimensional input spaces, given the need to have a sufficiently large training dataset that spans the variation in the high dimensional space.

Existing approaches to address the scalability problems of SVMs can be classified into two general categories. One category comprises hybrid and complimentary methods for SVMs, which are used to preprocess the data prior to processing by the SVM. For example, clustering (Sun et al. 2004), dimension reduction techniques such as PCA or KPCA (Cao et al. 2003; Subasi and Ismail Gursoy 2010), and deep belief networks (Bengio and LeCun 2007) are some of the most well-known approaches. Although these approaches play an important role in building the model, they do not directly address the scalability of the SVM itself. The second category includes methods that aim to alleviate the QP problem of kernel machines. A more heuristic approach is to reduce the size of the QP problem by breaking it into smaller pieces, for example by using chunking (Vapnik 1998; Sonnenburg et al. 2006), decomposition (Vishwanathan, Smola, and Murty 2003; Joachims 1999), or Sequential Minimal Optimisation (SMO) (Platt 1999). An alternative to enhance the computational efficiency of SVMs is to instead use an approximation of QP (Fung and Mangasarian 2001). A more radical approach is to totally avoid the QP problem, and obtain the solution through a fast iterative scheme (Fung and Mangasarian 2003; Yang, Duraiswami, and Davis 2005).

To reduce the memory and computational complexity, a popular approach is to obtain a low-rank approximation of the kernel matrix. Selective sampling (or active learning) methods iterate through the training data and sample a small subset of the records that are near the boundary in the feature space with higher probabilities, e.g., (Tong and Koller 2002), or see (Settles 2010) for a survey. To avoid the computational cost of processing the whole dataset, Lee and Mangasarian (2001) propose the use of random sampling to obtain a result that is close to the original SVM.

A more recent trend explores the use of randomisation, such as linear random projection (Blum 2006) as a substitute for the computationally expensive cost of kernel matrix construction. An early example is the work of Achlioptas, McSherry, and Schölkopf (2002), which replaces the kernel function by a randomised kernel to speedup KPCA. The work of Rahimi and Recht (2007; 2009) made a breakthrough in this approach. They replicated an RBF kernel by randomly projecting the data to a lower dimensional space and then used linear algorithms. Random projection avoids the computational complexity of traditional optimisation methods needed for nonlinear kernels. More recently, Kar and Karnick (2012), and Hamid et al. (2014) have extended the method of Rahimi and Recht to other types of kernels, e.g., dot-product and polynomial kernels.

In this paper, we build on the work of Rahimi and Recht by developing a model for using randomised projection in the context of unsupervised learning of a 1SVM. In the next section we describe our proposed randomised 1SVM scheme.

Proposed Approach — R1SVM

In this section we present our Randomised 1SVM (R1SVM) model for anomaly detection. We begin by recalling a few key aspects of one-class SVMs, and then introduce the use of nonlinear random projections for detecting anomalies in large-scale data. Random projections have been utilised mainly in distance-based classification or data reconstruction schemes to speedup the search, as it approximately preserves L_2 distances among a set of points. Thus instead of performing the search in a high-dimensional space, the search is conducted in a space of reduced dimension but on a larger neighbourhood. Note that in our context, ultimately, our goal is anomaly detection. Therefore, we are not necessarily interested in deriving a representation that allows for the best classification or reconstruction of the data, but we rather seek to find a model of the underlying distribution of the data which can then be used to detect anomalies.

One-class SVM (1SVM)

Let $\boldsymbol{X} = [\boldsymbol{x}_1, \cdots, \boldsymbol{x}_n]$ be the $d \times n$ matrix containing n training points $\boldsymbol{x}_i \in \mathbb{R}^d$ of one specific class, and let ϕ be a feature map $\boldsymbol{X} \rightarrow \mathcal{H}$ such that the dot product in $\mathcal{H}$ can be computed using some kernel $k(\boldsymbol{x}, \boldsymbol{x}') =< \phi(\boldsymbol{x}), \phi(\boldsymbol{x}') >_{\mathcal{H}}$.

A One-class Support Vector Machine (1SVM) (Schölkopf et al. 2001; Manevitz and Yousef 2002) finds anomalies by first projecting the data to the feature space $\mathcal{H}$, and then finding a hyperplane that best separates the data from the origin. In other words, the decision function in the 1SVM returns +1 in a region where most of the data points occur (i.e., where the probability density is high), and returns -1 elsewhere.

Defining a family of sets $C_{\boldsymbol{s},\rho} = \{\boldsymbol{x} | f_{\boldsymbol{s},\rho}(\boldsymbol{x}) > 0\}$, the 1SVM estimates a function $f_{\boldsymbol{s},\rho}(\boldsymbol{x}) = \text{sgn}(\boldsymbol{s}.\phi(\boldsymbol{x}) - \rho)$ that maximises the distance of all the data points (in the feature space $\mathcal{F}$) from the hyperplane to the origin, parameterised by a weight vector $\boldsymbol{s}$ and an offset ρ.

Thus, the resulting binary function $f_{\boldsymbol{s},\rho}(\boldsymbol{x})$ can be estimated by minimising the regularised risk:

$$R^{reg}[f_{\boldsymbol{s},\rho}(\boldsymbol{x})] = R^{emp}[f_{\boldsymbol{s},\rho}(\boldsymbol{x})] + \frac{1}{2}\|f_{\boldsymbol{s},\rho}(\boldsymbol{x})\|^2_{\mathcal{H}} \quad (1)$$

where $R^{emp}(.)$ is the empirical risk and $\frac{1}{2}\|f_{\boldsymbol{s},\rho}(\boldsymbol{x})\|^2_{\mathcal{H}}$ is the regulariser. The empirical risk is the average loss and can be written as

$$R^{emp}[f_{\boldsymbol{s},\rho}(\boldsymbol{x})] \equiv \frac{1}{n}\sum_{i=1}^{n} c(f_{\boldsymbol{s},\rho}(\boldsymbol{x}_i), y_i) \quad (2)$$

where $c(f_{\boldsymbol{s},\rho}(\boldsymbol{x}_i), y_i)$ is the loss function that penalises the deviation between the prediction $f_{\boldsymbol{s},\rho}(.)$ and the label y, i.e., this captures the cost of the errors caused when $f_{\boldsymbol{s},\rho}(.)$ is negative on training vectors.

Replacing $\|f_{\boldsymbol{s},\rho}(.)\|^2_{\mathcal{H}}$ with a *maximum margin* regulariser $\|\boldsymbol{s}\|^2$ to penalise complex regions, we can setup the following quadratic program for 1SVM:

$$\begin{aligned} \min_{\boldsymbol{s},\xi_i,\rho} \quad & \tfrac{1}{2}\|\boldsymbol{s}\|^2 + \tfrac{1}{\nu n}\textstyle\sum_{i=1}^{n}\xi_i - \rho \\ s.t. \quad & (\boldsymbol{s}.\boldsymbol{\phi}(\boldsymbol{x}_i)) \geq \rho - \xi_i, \\ & \xi_i \geq 0 \end{aligned} \quad (3)$$

where $\nu \in (0, 1]$ is a regularisation parameter that controls the fraction of anomalies and the fraction of support vectors, and ξ_i are the slack variables that allow some of the data vectors to lie on the wrong side of the hyperplane. By introducing the Lagrange multipliers, we arrive at the following quadratic program, which is the dual of the primal program in (3):

$$\begin{aligned} \min_{\alpha} \quad & \tfrac{1}{2}\textstyle\sum_{ij}\alpha_i\alpha_j k(\boldsymbol{x}_i, \boldsymbol{x}_j) \\ s.t. \quad & 0 \leq \alpha_i \leq \tfrac{1}{\nu n}, \\ & \textstyle\sum_1^n \alpha_i = 1 \end{aligned} \quad (4)$$

where α_i are the Lagrange multipliers. Further, $\boldsymbol{s} = \sum_i \alpha_i \boldsymbol{\phi}(\boldsymbol{x}_i)$. Using the Karush-Kuhn-Tucker optimality conditions (KKT conditions) the data vectors can be characterised in terms of whether they fall below, above, or on the hyperplane boundary in the feature space depending on the corresponding α_i values. Data vectors with positive α_i values are the support vectors. Further, for $0 < \alpha_i < 1/\nu n$, the data vectors fall on the hyperplane and hence ρ can be recovered using these vectors, vis-a-vis $\rho =< \boldsymbol{s}, \boldsymbol{\phi}(\boldsymbol{x}_i) >= \sum_j \alpha_j k(\boldsymbol{x}_j, \boldsymbol{x}_i)$. Therefore, the decision function can now be written as

$$\begin{aligned} f_{\boldsymbol{s},\rho}(\boldsymbol{x}) &= \operatorname{sgn}(\boldsymbol{s}.\boldsymbol{\phi}(\boldsymbol{x}) - \rho) \\ &= \operatorname{sgn}(\alpha_i k(\boldsymbol{x}_i, \boldsymbol{x}) - \rho) \end{aligned} \quad (5)$$

The solution to the quadratic program in (4) is characterised by the parameter $\nu \in (0, 1]$, which sets an upper bound on the fraction of anomalies (training examples regarded as out-of-class) and a lower bound on the number of training examples used as support vectors.

The computational complexity of 1SVM using an SMO solver is approximately $O(dn^2)$ for the RBF kernel (Vempati et al. 2010), and $O(dn)$ for a linear kernel with n being the number of samples and d the number of dimensions in feature space. However, it has been noted that when 1SVM is used with a linear kernel, it introduces a bias to the origin. This problem can be removed by using an RBF kernel, which has a higher computational complexity associated with the higher dimensional kernels, thus making it cumbersome for processing with large scale data.

In order to overcome this limitation, in the next section, we propose to exploit nonlinear random projections inside a linear 1SVM, which serves as a good approximation of a nonlinear 1SVM.

Randomised 1SVM

We propose R1SVM, a nonlinear randomised variant of 1SVM, which applies the original linear 1SVM method on a randomised nonlinear projection of the data. We first discuss how to generate the nonlinear random features from the original data, and then we show how to employ these features to detect anomalies using a linear 1SVM. This approach eliminates the need to deal with large kernel matrices for large datasets, consequently reducing the computational complexity while achieving comparable or better anomaly detection performance than a traditional 1SVM (as shown in the Evaluation section).

Generating Nonlinear Random Features Consider the problem of fitting a function f (note that the subscripts s and ρ in $f_{s,\rho}$ are omitted for brevity) to the data set $\{\boldsymbol{x}_i, y_i\}$, where y_i values are always set to 1 for the one-class problem. This fitting problem consists of finding f that minimises the empirical risk in equation (2). For the 1SVM problem, the loss function $c(y, y')$ is of the form $c(y, y') = max(0, 1 - yy')$. Using the kernel function, the function $f(\boldsymbol{x}) = sgn(\boldsymbol{s}.\boldsymbol{\phi}(\boldsymbol{x}) - \rho)$ becomes $f(\boldsymbol{x}) = \sum_i^n \alpha_i k(\boldsymbol{x}, \boldsymbol{x}_i)$. Therefore, in the general form, the function $f(\boldsymbol{x})$ can be written as $f(\boldsymbol{x}) = \sum_{i=1}^{\infty} \alpha(\boldsymbol{s}_i)\boldsymbol{\phi}(\boldsymbol{x}; \boldsymbol{s}_i)$, where $\boldsymbol{\phi}$ are parameterised by vector $\boldsymbol{s}$ and weighted by α_i. By jointly optimising over $\boldsymbol{s}$ and α_i, in a greedy manner, the solution can be found (Rahimi and Recht 2007). However, this is computationally intensive. Rahimi and Recht (2009) have proved that this nonlinear optimisation problem over $(\boldsymbol{\alpha}, \boldsymbol{s}_1, \cdots, \boldsymbol{s}_n)$ in f, can be solved by randomly sampling the $\boldsymbol{s}_i \in \mathbb{R}^d$ from a data-independent distribution $p(\boldsymbol{s})$ and creating k-dimensional random features $\boldsymbol{z}(\boldsymbol{X}) = [\boldsymbol{z}_1 \cdots \boldsymbol{z}_k]$, where $\boldsymbol{z}_i = [\cos(\boldsymbol{s}_i^T \boldsymbol{x}_1 + b_i), \cdots, \cos(\boldsymbol{s}_i^T \boldsymbol{x}_n + b_i)]$ are Fourier based random features. For more details refer to (Rahimi and Recht 2007). Thus, we arrive at the following simplified optimisation problem:

$$\begin{aligned} \min_{\boldsymbol{\alpha}\in\mathbb{R}^k} \quad & \tfrac{1}{n}\textstyle\sum_i c(\boldsymbol{\alpha}^T \boldsymbol{z}_i, y_i) \\ s.t. \quad & \|\boldsymbol{\alpha}\|_\infty \leq B \end{aligned} \quad (6)$$

where B is a regularisation constant. Furthermore, it is shown by Rahimi and Recht (2009) that using randomly selected features in nonlinear spaces causes only *bounded* error compared to using optimised features:

Theorem 1. *Let p be a distribution on Ω and $|\phi(\boldsymbol{x};\boldsymbol{s})| \leq 1$. Let $\mathcal{F} = \{f(\boldsymbol{x}) = \int_{\delta} \alpha(\boldsymbol{s})\phi(\boldsymbol{x};\boldsymbol{s})d\boldsymbol{s} \mid |\alpha(\boldsymbol{s})| \leq Bp(\boldsymbol{s})\}$. Draw $\boldsymbol{s}_1, \cdots, \boldsymbol{s}_k$ iid from p. Further let $\lambda > 0$, and c be some L-Lipschitz loss function, then the function $f_k(\boldsymbol{x}) = \sum_{i=1}^{k} \alpha_i \phi(\boldsymbol{x};\boldsymbol{s}_i)$ minimises the empirical risk $c(f_k(\boldsymbol{x}), y)$ has a distance from the c-optimal estimator in F bounded by*

$$E_p[c(f_k(\boldsymbol{x}), y)] - \min_{f \in \mathcal{F}} E_p[c(f(\boldsymbol{x}), y)] \leq O\left(\frac{LB}{\sqrt{n}} + \frac{1}{\sqrt{k}} LB \sqrt{\log \frac{1}{\delta}}\right) \tag{7}$$

with a probability of at least $1 - 2\delta$.

The convergence rate of our randomised R1SVM to its original kernel 1SVM version can be expressed by the following theorem (Lopez-Paz et al. 2014):

Theorem 2. *Given the data $\boldsymbol{X} \in \mathbb{R}^{n \times d}$, a shift invariant kernel k, a kernel matrix $\boldsymbol{K}_{ij} = k(\boldsymbol{x}_i, \boldsymbol{x}_j)$ and its approximation $\hat{\boldsymbol{K}}$ using k random features, it can be proven that*

$$\mathbb{E}\|\hat{\boldsymbol{K}} - \boldsymbol{K}\| \leq \sqrt{\frac{3n^2 \log n}{k}} + \frac{2n \log n}{k}. \tag{8}$$

The proof to this theorem can be found in (Lopez-Paz et al. 2014).

Evaluation and Discussion

In this section, we evaluate the effectiveness of our R1SVM method for anomaly detection by conducting the following two experiments. First, we empirically explore the impact of random projections on the separability of normal data records from anomalous records. Then we compare the performance of R1SVM in terms of accuracy, training and testing time, with a 1SVM scheme called Support Vector Data Decomposition (SVDD), and a deep autoencoder (AE).

Experimental setup: For visualisation purposes, in the first experiment, we used a tool called *improved Visual Assessment of cluster Tendency* (iVAT) (Wang et al. 2010), which helps visualise the possible number of clusters in, or the cluster tendency of, a set of objects. iVAT reorders the dissimilarity matrix of the given set of objects so that it can display any clusters as dark blocks along the diagonal of the image.

In the second experiment we used the `svdd` implementation from Dd-tools (Tax 2013) as the one-class SVM method. Note that the hypersphere-based SVDD model using an RBF kernel is equivalent to a hyperplane-based 1SVM model. In the case of the autoencoder, we implemented a basic autoencoder including five-layers with tied weights and a sigmoid activation function for both the encoder and decoder. The training is conducted in mini-batches of $q = 100$ records. Initially the autoencoder was trained based on greedy layer-wise pre-training (i.e., training one layer at a time) to extract features, and then using these features to train the next layer. Training a network implies finding parameters (network weight and bias) that minimise the reconstruction error between the inputs $\boldsymbol{x}$ and the reconstruction of $\boldsymbol{x}$ at the output $\bar{\boldsymbol{x}}$, $l(\boldsymbol{x}, \bar{\boldsymbol{x}}) = \| \boldsymbol{x} - \bar{\boldsymbol{x}} \|^2$.

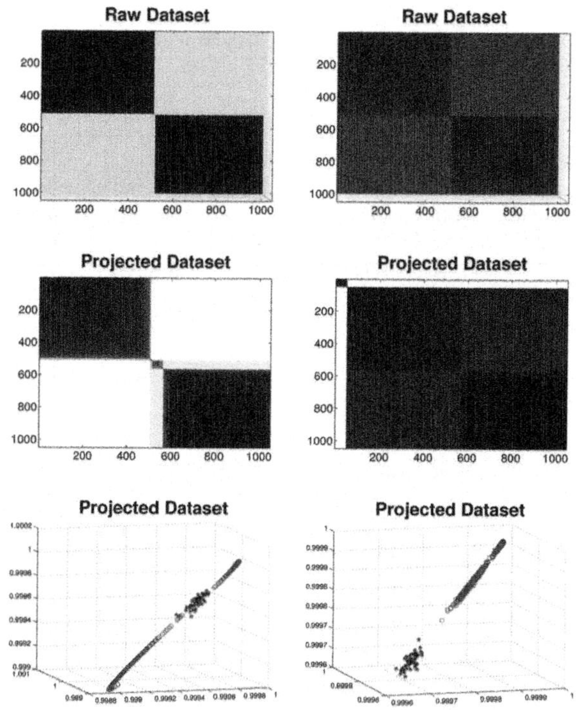

a) Banana dataset b) HAR dataset

Figure 1: Demonstration of the effect of nonlinear projection on normal and anomalous records.

Once the network was trained, the learned parameter values were used as initialisation values of a multilayer perceptron (MLP) with the same number of inputs and outputs. Then the network was fine-tuned by gradient descent to adjust the parameters. The whole process of pre-training and fine-tuning was performed in an unsupervised manner for anomaly detection. Anomalies then can be identified by the autoencoder based on the history of the squared error between the inputs and outputs for the training records. Let e be the reconstruction error of $\boldsymbol{x}_i \in \mathbf{X}$, where $i = 1, \ldots, n$. If the reconstruction error for a test sample is larger than the threshold $\tau = \mu(\mathsf{e}) + 3\sigma(\mathsf{e})$, the record is identified as anomalous, otherwise it is identified as normal.

Datasets: The experiments are conducted on six real-life datasets from the UCI Machine Learning Repository: (i) Forest (ii) Adult (iii) Gas Sensor Array Drift (Gas), (iv) Opportunity Activity Recognition (OAR), (v) Daily and Sport Activity (DSA), and (vi) Human Activity Recognition using Smartphones (HAR), with dimensionalities of 54, 123,128, 242, 315[1] and 561 features, respectively. We also use two synthetic datasets. One is a "Smiley" dataset, generated from a mixture of two compact Gaussians and an arc shaped distribution. The dataset contains 20 dimensions and in any two dimensions the components of the face are ran-

[1]DSA is a large dataset comprising the time series measurements from 45 wearable sensors for 19 activities. We select a portion of the time series for each of the first 7 activities, yielding a total of 315 concatenated time series features.

Table 1: Comparison of AUC, train and test time of R1SVM with SVDD and autoencoder (AE).

		SVDD			*AE*			*R1SVM*		
Dataset	Features	AUC	Train time	Test time	AUC	Train Time	Test time	AUC	Train time	Test time
Smiley	20	0.85	1.58	2.3×10^{-2}	**0.98**	0.61	1.1×10^{-3}	**0.98**	$\mathbf{7.8 \times 10^{-3}}$	$\mathbf{1.0 \times 10^{-5}}$
Forest	54	0.97	2.12	2.2×10^{-2}	**0.99**	0.47	1.5×10^{-3}	**0.99**	$\mathbf{5.3 \times 10^{-3}}$	$\mathbf{1.2 \times 10^{-5}}$
Banana	100	0.92	2.75	2.4×10^{-2}	**0.99**	0.79	2.6×10^{-3}	**0.99**	$\mathbf{5.3 \times 10^{-3}}$	$\mathbf{1.2 \times 10^{-5}}$
Adult	123	0.87	2.83	2.7×10^{-2}	**0.99**	0.65	2.6×10^{-3}	**0.99**	$\mathbf{5.3 \times 10^{-3}}$	$\mathbf{1.3 \times 10^{-5}}$
Gas	128	0.91	1.06	2.6×10^{-2}	**0.98**	0.99	2.2×10^{-3}	**0.98**	$\mathbf{2.0 \times 10^{-3}}$	$\mathbf{1.0 \times 10^{-5}}$
OAR	242	0.91	1.08	2.5×10^{-2}	**0.97**	0.67	5.8×10^{-3}	**0.97**	$\mathbf{2.3 \times 10^{-3}}$	$\mathbf{1.1 \times 10^{-5}}$
DSA	315	0.84	1.13	3.4×10^{-2}	**0.98**	0.63	5.5×10^{-3}	**0.98**	$\mathbf{5.0 \times 10^{-3}}$	$\mathbf{1.5 \times 10^{-5}}$
HAR	561	0.88	2.11	4.2×10^{-2}	**0.99**	1.02	1.4×10^{-2}	**0.99**	$\mathbf{8.4 \times 10^{-3}}$	$\mathbf{1.4 \times 10^{-5}}$

*Note: The reported time is in seconds.

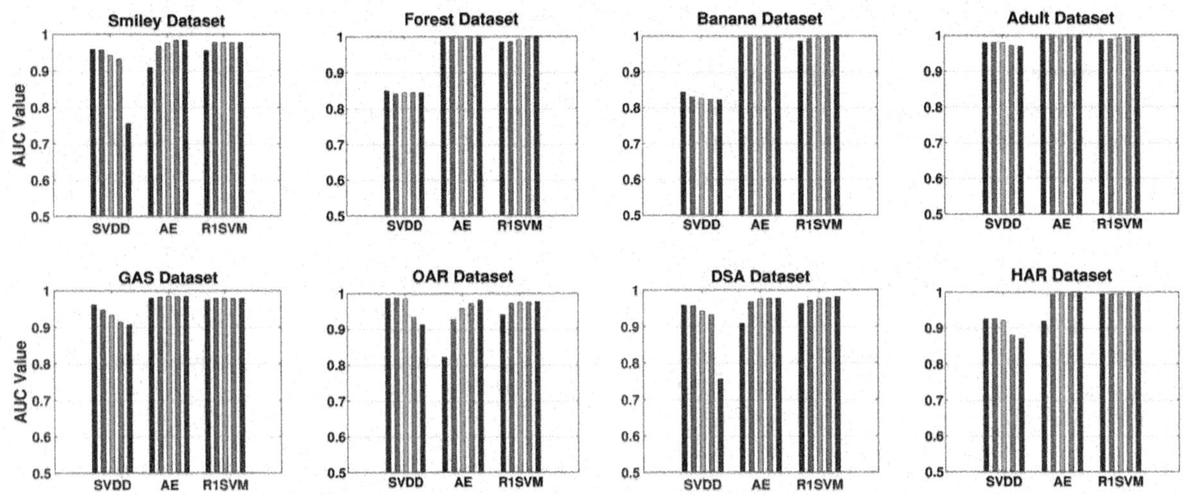

Figure 2: Comparison of accuracy of anomaly detection methods as the number of training records is varied.

domly moved. The other is the "Banana" dataset that is a mixture of two banana shaped distributions, which are randomly moved in 100 dimensions. All the records in each dataset are normalised between [0,1].

Although R1SVM is designed to overcome the challenges that arise for anomaly detection in large datasets, we conducted our experiments on datasets with varying numbers of dimensions and records, from 200 to 40,000 records, to assess the effect of data size on its performance. In each experiment, 80% of records are randomly selected for training and 20% for testing, and then, respectively, mixed with 5% and 20% anomalous records, randomly drawn from $U(0, 1)$. Note that training is performed in an unsupervised way, and labels are only used for testing.

Accuracy Metric: We use the Receiver Operating Characteristic (ROC) curve and the corresponding Area Under the Curve (AUC) to measure the performance of all the methods. The reported training/testing times are in seconds based on experiments run on a machine with an Intel Core i7 CPU at 3.40 GHz and 8 GB RAM. The stated AUC values and training/testing times are the average of 1000 iterations for each experiment.

Experiment 1: Interpretation of Basis for Anomaly Detection with R1SVM

Fig. 1 demonstrates the benefits of using random nonlinear features for anomaly detection on two datasets, Banana and HAR (due to the shortage of space images of the other datasets are not shown). The interpretation of the subfigures, from the top is as follows: iVAT image of the raw datasets, the iVAT image of the projected datasets, and the scatter plot of the projected datasets (projected to $\mathbb{R}^3$). As can be seen in the image of the raw datasets, normal records (first 1000 records) appear in dense blocks, while the anomalous records (last 50 records) are shown in gray shadow (since they are distributed across the dataset). When the data are projected to a lower space, a clearer separation appears between the normal records and anomalies, as reflected in the improved clarity and contrast in the block structure. This is also reflected in the corresponding scatter plots, which show the effect of projection on normal records (shown in blue) and anomalies (shown in black). We postulate that the explanation of this effect is the concentration of the data around its mean as a result of the random projection (Dasgupta 2000; Zimek, Schubert, and Kriegel 2012)

Table 2: Comparing computational and memory complexity of SVDD, AE and R1SVM

Technique	SVDD	AE	R1SVM
Training	$O(dn^2)$	$O(dmn)$	$O(kn)$
Testing	$O(dn)$	$O(dmn)$	$O(k+d)$
Memory	$O(dn^2)$	$O(dq)$	$O(kn)$

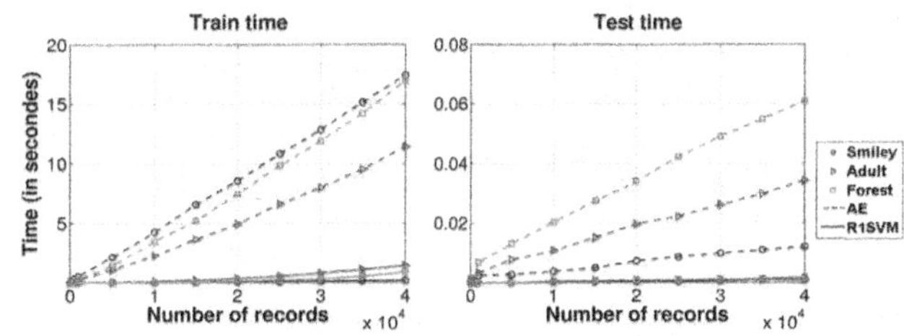

Figure 3: Comparison of the training and testing time of AE and R1SVM on large datasets.

Experiment 2: Empirical Performance of R1SVM

Table 1 compares the AUC results, training and testing time of R1SVM with SVDD and AE for several medium size (2000 records) datasets — a limit of 2000 records was chosen because the performance of SVDD significantly degrades on larger datasets. As shown in the table, our proposed approach delivers a comparable AUC to the state-of-the-art AE. However, the AUC of SVDD is significantly lower — e.g., up to 14% for DSA and 13% for Smiley datasets. A more significant advantage of R1SVM is its reduction in training/testing time. R1SVM reduces theses measures by factor of approximately 100 and 1000 times compared to AE and SVDD, respectively.

When selecting an anomaly detection technique, the size of the training dataset is an immediate concern. Some techniques, such as kernel machines, can perform best with small datasets, i.e., their performance decays as the number of records grows. In contrast, methods like AE can be inaccurate if trained with small numbers of records (Bengio and LeCun 2007). Additionally, the training time for some techniques is prohibitive for large numbers of records, e.g., the time complexity of kernel-based methods can grow at least quadratically in the number of data records. Fig. 2 and Fig. 3 show how the AUC and training/testing time vary with the number of training records.

Fig. 2 shows the impact of larger-scale training and high-dimensional data on the accuracy of the studied approaches. We observe that the accuracy of SVDD decreases as the number of training records increases. In some cases, e.g., Smiley, OAR and DSA datasets, SVDD experiences a substantial decrease in AUC when the number of training records reaches 5000. In contrast, the accuracy of AE can initially be low but increases as the data size grows. Overall, only R1SVM delivers more consistent results across various ranges of data sizes.

An attractive property of autoencoders is their efficiency in training/testing time, which scales linearly with the number of records. Therefore, we compared the training and testing time of AE and R1SVM for large datasets. The results in Fig. 3 suggest that although both measures grow linearly for the two techniques, the training/testing time of AE grow at a much faster rate. The AUC values for this experiment are not included, since they were more or less consistant. Table 2 summarises the computational and memory complexity of these techniques, where m and q are the size of the bottleneck layer and batch in the AE.

In summary, the above experiments demonstrate that R1SVM is as accurate as a deep autoencoder, but approximately 100 times faster in terms of training/testing time. It is also important to note that the training algorithm of R1SVM requires only one parameter, k, to be set. Since we are interested in anomaly detection, modelling the underlying distribution is more important than preserving distances among classes, therefore the data can be projected to very low dimensions. In our empirical analysis we have also tested the sensitivity of R1SVM to the choice of the parameter k. Overall, the value of k has little effect on accuracy, while larger values of the k increase the training time. Hence, smaller values of k are most effective.

Conclusion and Future Work

We presented R1SVM, an unsupervised anomaly detection technique that approximates a nonlinear 1SVM through applying the original linear 1SVM method on a randomised nonlinear projection of the data. Using a simple but effective random projection overcomes the scalability issues of 1SVM methods while enhancing the accuracy of anomaly detection. Our empirical analysis on several benchmark datasets shows that R1SVM not only delivers significant improvements over a conventional nonlinear 1SVM, but it matches the performance of a state-of-the-art deep autoencoder — while reducing its training and testing time by up to two orders of magnitude. These savings in time and space enable R1SVM to execute anomaly detection on large datasets more efficiently, in real-time applications or memory constrained devices, such as smart phones and wireless sensor networks. In addition to large-scale training, the other major advantage of R1SVM is that it is also shown to be effective at maintaining its accuracy on small datasets when training data is limited.

In future work, we will also explore the changes in the eigen-spectrum of the kernel matrix and generalisation error bound when using the Nyström method. Unlike random Fourier features, the basis functions in the Nyström method are data dependent and randomly sampled from the training data.

Acknowledgment

NICTA is funded by the Australian Government as represented by the Department of Broadband, Communications and the Digital Economy and the Australian Research Council through the ICT Centre of Excellence program.

References

Achlioptas, D.; McSherry, F.; and Schölkopf, B. 2002. Sampling techniques for kernel methods. In *Proceedings of Advances in Neural Information Processing Systems (NIPS)*, volume 1, 335.

Bengio, Y., and LeCun, Y. 2007. Scaling learning algorithms towards AI. *Large-Scale Kernel Machines* 34.

Blum, A. 2006. Random projection, margins, kernels, and feature-selection. In *Subspace, Latent Structure and Feature Selection*. 52–68.

Bottou, L., and Lin, C.-J. 2007. Support vector machine solvers. *Large scale kernel machines* 301–320.

Cao, L. J.; Chua, K. S.; Chong, W. K.; Lee, H. P.; and Gu, Q. M. 2003. A comparison of PCA, KPCA and ICA for dimensionality reduction in support vector machine. *Neurocomputing* 55(1):321–336.

Dasgupta, S. 2000. Experiments with random projection. In *Proceedings of the 16th Conference on Uncertainty in Artificial Intelligence (UAI)*, 143–151.

Fung, G., and Mangasarian, O. L. 2001. Proximal support vector machine classifiers. In *Proceedings of the 7th ACM SIGKDD International Conference on Knowledge Discovery and Data Mining*, 77–86.

Fung, G., and Mangasarian, O. L. 2003. Finite Newton method for Lagrangian Support Vector Machine classification. *Neurocomputing* 55(1):39–55.

Hamid, R.; Xiao, Y.; Gittens, A.; and DeCoste, D. 2014. Compact random feature maps. In *Proceedings of 31st International Conference on Machine Learning (ICML)*.

Joachims, T. 1999. Making large scale SVM learning practical. *Advances in Kernel Methods - Support Vector Learning*.

Kar, P., and Karnick, H. 2012. Random feature maps for dot product kernels. In *Proceedings of the 15th International Conference on Artificial Intelligence and Statistics (AISTATS)*, 583–591.

Lee, Y.-J., and Mangasarian, O. L. 2001. RSVM: Reduced Support Vector Machines. In *Proceedings of the SIAM International Conference on Data Mining (SDM)*, volume 1, 325–361.

Lopez-Paz, D.; Sra, S.; Smola, A.; Ghahramani, Z.; and Schölkopf, B. 2014. Randomized nonlinear component analysis. In *Proceedings of the 28th International Conference on Machine Learning (ICML)*.

Manevitz, L. M., and Yousef, M. 2002. One-class SVMs for document classification. *Journal of Machine Learning Research (JMLR)* 2:139–154.

Platt, J. C. 1999. Fast training of support vector machines using sequential minimal optimization. In *Advances in Kernel Methods*, 185–208.

Rahimi, A., and Recht, B. 2007. Random features for large-scale kernel machines. In *Advances in Neural Information Processing Systems (NIPS)*, 1177–1184.

Rahimi, A., and Recht, B. 2009. Weighted sums of random kitchen sinks: Replacing minimization with randomization in learning. In *Advances in Neural Information Processing Systems (NIPS)*, 1313–1320.

Rajasegarar, S.; Leckie, C.; Bezdek, J. C.; and Palaniswami, M. 2010. Centered hyperspherical and hyperellipsoidal one-class support vector machines for anomaly detection in sensor networks. *IEEE Transactions on Information Forensics and Security (IEEE IFS)* 5(3):518–533.

Schölkopf, B.; Platt, J. C.; Shawe-Taylor, J.; Smola, A. J.; and Williamson, R. C. 2001. Estimating the support of a high-dimensional distribution. *Neural computation* 13(7):1443–1471.

Settles, B. 2010. Active learning literature survey. *University of Wisconsin, Madison* 52:55–66.

Sonnenburg, S.; Rätsch, G.; Schäfer, C.; and Schölkopf, B. 2006. Large scale multiple kernel learning. *Journal of Machine Learning Research (JMLR)* 7:1531–1565.

Subasi, A., and Ismail Gursoy, M. 2010. EEG signal classification using PCA, ICA, LDA and support vector machines. *Expert Systems with Applications* 37(12):8659–8666.

Sun, S.-Y.; Tseng, C.-L.; Chen, Y.; Chuang, S.; and Fu, H. 2004. Cluster-based support vector machines in text-independent speaker identification. In *Proceedings of the IEEE International Joint Conference on Neural Networks (IJCNN)*, volume 1.

Tax, D. M., and Duin, R. P. 2004. Support Vector Data Description. *Machine Learning* 54:45–66.

Tax, D. 2013. DDtools, the Data Description toolbox for Matlab. Version 2.0.2.

Tong, S., and Koller, D. 2002. Support vector machine active learning with applications to text classification. *Journal of Machine Learning Research (JMLR)* 2:45–66.

Vapnik, V. N. 1998. Statistical learning theory.

Vempati, S.; Vedaldi, A.; Zisserman, A.; and Jawahar, C. 2010. Generalized RBF feature maps for Efficient Detection. In *Proceedings of the 21st British Machine Vision Conference*, 1–11.

Vishwanathan, S.; Smola, A. J.; and Murty, M. N. 2003. Simplesvm. In *Proceedings of the International Conference on Machine Learning (ICML)*, 760–767.

Wang, L.; Nguyen, U. T.; Bezdek, J. C.; Leckie, C.; and Ramamohanarao, K. 2010. iVAT and aVAT: enhanced visual analysis for cluster tendency assessment. In *Advances in Knowledge Discovery and Data Mining*. 16–27.

Wang, D.; Yeung, D. S.; and Tsang, E. C. 2006. Structured one-class classification. *IEEE Transactions on Systems, Man, and Cybernetics, Part B: Cybernetics,* 36(6):1283–1295.

Yang, C.; Duraiswami, R.; and Davis, L. S. 2005. Efficient kernel machines using the improved fast Gauss transform. In *Advances in Neural Information Processing Systems*, 1561–1568.

Zimek, A.; Schubert, E.; and Kriegel, H.-P. 2012. A survey on unsupervised outlier detection in high-dimensional numerical data. *Statistical Analysis and Data Mining* 5(5):363–387.

Personalized Tag Recommendation through Nonlinear Tensor Factorization Using Gaussian Kernel

Xiaomin Fang and **Rong Pan***
Department of Computer Science
Sun Yat-sen University
Guangzhou, China
{fangxmin@mail2, panr@}.sysu.edu.cn

Guoxiang Cao, Xiuqiang He and **Wenyuan Dai**
Huawei Technologies Co., Ltd.
Bantian, Longgang District
Shenzhen, China
{benjamin.cao, hexiuqiang, dai.wenyuan}@huawei.com

Abstract

Personalized tag recommendation systems recommend a list of tags to a user when he is about to annotate an item. It exploits the individual preference and the characteristic of the items. Tensor factorization techniques have been applied to many applications, such as tag recommendation. Models based on Tucker Decomposition can achieve good performance but require a lot of computation power. On the other hand, models based on Canonical Decomposition can run in linear time and are more feasible for online recommendation. In this paper, we propose a novel method for personalized tag recommendation, which can be considered as a nonlinear extension of Canonical Decomposition. Different from linear tensor factorization, we exploit Gaussian radial basis function to increase the model's capacity. The experimental results show that our proposed method outperforms the state-of-the-art methods for tag recommendation on real datasets and perform well even with a small number of features, which verifies that our models can make better use of features.

Introduction

Nowadays, a great amount of information springs up in the Internet and users struggle to find the items they are really interested in. To tackle this problem, recommendation systems are designed to recommend appropriate items to the users according to their habits. Collaborative tagging systems like *Delicious*, *Last.fm* and *Movielens* allow users to upload resources and annotate them. The activity that users annotate items, such as movies, songs and pictures with some keywords, is called tagging. A tag can be viewed as an implicit rating and be used to identify not only the features of the items, but also the users' personality. Tag recommendation is a task to suggest tags to a user when he is about to annotate an item. Given an item, different users may use different tags to annotate it. Personalized tag recommender systems utilize users' past tagging behaviors to predict their future behaviors. For example, if two users annotated an item with the same tag before, it is likely that they will annotate another item with the same tag in the future.

*Corresponding author

Some tag recommender systems rank tags by means of tensor factorization techniques. Tensor factorization is a high-order extension of matrix factorization. Tensor factorization-based models decompose the user-item-tag tensor into three matrices to learn the latent features of the users, items and tags. Higher Order Singular Vector Decomposition (HOSVD) (Symeonidis, Nanopoulos, and Manolopoulos 2008), Multiverse (Karatzoglou et al. 2010) and RTF (Rendle et al. 2009) are based on Tucker Decomposition (TD), which can improve the state-of-the-art recommenders in prediction quality, but require too much computation power. In contrast, pairwise interaction tensor factorization (PITF) (Rendle and Schmidt-Thieme 2010) is based on another factorization approach, Canonical Decomposition (CD). It is linear both in the dataset size and the feature dimensionality. In this paper, we present a novel approach based on Canonical Decomposition and can be considered as a nonlinear generalization of CD. We use Gaussian radial basis function to capture the complex relations between the users, items and tags. We will analyze why exploiting Gaussian can make better use of the latent features and its relation to the traditional linear tensor factorization techniques. Our experimental results show that our proposed model outperforms other competitive methods and can achieve good performance with only a small number of latent features.

The contributions of our work are summarized as follows.

- We propose a novel nonlinear approach based on Canonical Decomposition, which employs Gaussian radial basis function. The time performance is comparable to PITF and runs in linear time.
- We compare our nonlinear approach to the traditional linear methods and analyze the reasons why the Gaussian-based method can make better use of the latent features.
- The experimental results demonstrate that our method outperforms other methods on real datasets and performs well even with only a small number of latent features.

Related Work

Tag Recommendation Techniques

There is a lot of previous work on tag recommendation. Work by Krestel, Fankhauser, and Nejdl proposed an approach based on Latent Dirichlet Allocation(LDA). Given a document, the top terms composing its latent topics are recommended to the users. By this way, the terms in the same topic but showed in the other documents have the opportunity to be presented. Lipczak et al. employed probabilistic latent topic model for tag recommendation as well. They added a variable of tag to LDA, so as to link the tags to the topics of the document. Liu et al. ranked the tags for images by using random walks. However, the systems mentioned above are impersonalized. Different users may prefer different tags for the same item. Work by Guan et al. ranked tags by a graph-based ranking algorithm. It takes personalized tag recommendation as a "query and ranking" problem. The query consists of two parts, the user and the item. The tags are related to the item and the user. Besides, Durao and Dolog introduced a hybrid approach. It makes use of several factors, including tag similarity, tag popularity, tag representativeness and affinity between user and tag to provide appropriate tags.

Tensor Factorization Techniques

Tucker Decomposition and Canonical Decomposition are the high-order extension of Singular Value Decomposition (SVD). Nickel, Tresp, and Kriegel applied tensor factorization to collective entity resolution. Some studies (Dunlavy, Kolda, and Acar 2011; Ermiş, Acar, and Cemgil 2012; Spiegel et al. 2012) proposed tensor-based models to solve the problem of link prediction by incorporating time information. Moreover, tensor factorization is applied to personalized recommendation, including personalized web search (Sun et al. 2005), hyperlink recommendation (Gao et al. 2012) and personalized tag recommendation (Rendle and Schmidt-Thieme 2010; Symeonidis, Nanopoulos, and Manolopoulos 2008; 2010; Rendle et al. 2009; Chi and Zhu 2010). With respect to personalized tag recommendation, Higher Order Singular Vector Decomposition (HOSVD) (Symeonidis, Nanopoulos, and Manolopoulos 2008) and RTF (Rendle et al. 2009) are based on Tucker Decomposition (TD), while PITF (Rendle and Schmidt-Thieme 2010) is based on Canonical Decomposition (CD). HOSVD can not deal with missing values and it fills the unknown entries with 0. RTF handles the missing values by adding pairwise ranking constraint. Although TD-based methods outperform other state-of-the-art tag recommendation approaches, they require a lot of computation power. Therefore, they are not feasible for online recommendation. Compared with TD-based methods, CD-based methods have a huge advantage in running time, because they can be trained in linear time. PITF, an extension of CD, splits the ternary relation of users, items and tags into two relations, user-tag and item-tag and its quality is comparable to RTF.

Notations and Preliminaries

Tensor Factorization

A tensor is a multidimensional or multi-way array and the order of a tensor is the number of the dimensions.

Tucker Decomposition (TD) (Tucker 1966) and Canonical Decomposition (CD) (Carroll and Chang 1970; Harshman 1970) can be seen as higher-order extension of the matrix factorization, Singular Value Decomposition (SVD).

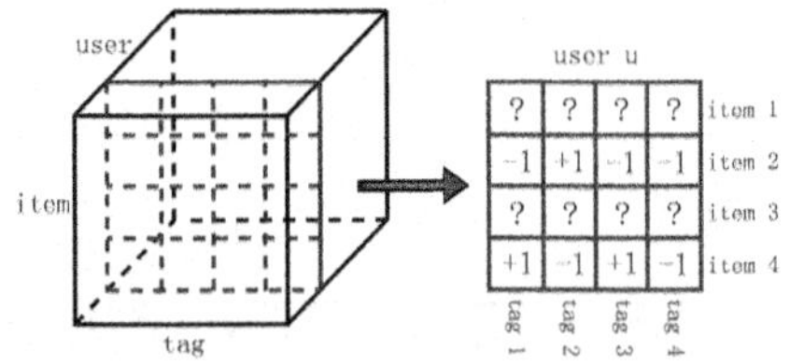

Figure 1: Tensor construction and post-based ranking interpretation for personalized tag recommendation

Tucker Decomposition (TD) decomposes a tensor into a core tensor multiplied by a matrix along each mode. Take a three-order tensor $\mathbf{A} \in \mathbb{R}^{I\times J\times K}$ for example and it can be written as

$$\mathbf{A}_{i,j,k} = \sum_{r_1=1}^{R_1}\sum_{r_2=1}^{R_2}\sum_{r_3=1}^{R_3} \mathbf{C}_{r_1,r_2,r_3}\cdot \mathbf{X}_{i,r_1}\cdot \mathbf{Y}_{j,r_2}\cdot \mathbf{Z}_{k,r_3}, \tag{1}$$

where $\mathbf{X} \in \mathbb{R}^{I\times R_1}$, $\mathbf{Y} \in \mathbb{R}^{J\times R_2}$, $\mathbf{Z} \in \mathbb{R}^{K\times R_3}$ and $\mathbf{C} \in \mathbb{R}^{R_1\times R_2\times R_3}$ is a core tensor. R_1, R_2 and R_3 are the number of latent features.

Canonical Decomposition (CD) decomposes a tensor into a sum of component rank-one tensors. Let $\mathbf{A} \in \mathbb{R}^{I\times J\times K}$ be a tensor and it can be written as

$$\mathbf{A}_{i,j,k} = \sum_{r=1}^{R} \mathbf{X}_{i,r}\cdot \mathbf{Y}_{j,r}\cdot \mathbf{Z}_{k,r}, \tag{2}$$

where $\mathbf{X} \in \mathbb{R}^{I\times R}$, $\mathbf{Y} \in \mathbb{R}^{J\times R}$, $\mathbf{Z} \in \mathbb{R}^{K\times R}$ and R is the number of latent features.

$\mathbf{X}$, $\mathbf{Y}$, $\mathbf{Z}$ in Eqs. (1) and (2) are in analogy with the factor matrices in Singular Value Decomposition (SVD) and values in core tensor $\mathbf{C}$ is in analogy with eigenvalues. Besides, if we compare the running time of TD in Eq. (1) and CD in Eq. (2), we can find that CD is linear in feature dimensionality but the time complexity of TD is much higher.

Personalized Tag Recommendation

Tagging is a process that a user associates an item with its keywords, which are called tags. We use the similar notation of (Rendle et al. 2009; Rendle and Schmidt-Thieme 2010) for the formulation of personalized tag recommendation. Let U be the set of users, I be the set of items, and T be the set of tags. The process that user u annotate item i with tag t is symbolized by a triple (u, i, t). Let $S \in U \times I \times T$ denote the set of tagging history. If a triple $(u, i, t) \in S$, it means a particular user u has annotated a specific item i with tag t. The relation between the users, items and tags for personalized tag recommendation can represented by a three-order tensor, which is depicted in Figure 1.

Rendle et al. introduced post-based ranking interpretation scheme for personalized tag recommendation and we employ the schema in this paper. Let P_S represent the set of all of the user-item pairs (u, i) in S and it can be written as

$$P_S = \{(u,i) | \exists (u,i,t) \in S\}.$$

Post-based schema generates positive examples and negative examples only from the observed posts $(u, i) \in P_S$. Given a post $(u, i) \in P_S$, all of the triples $(u, i, t) \in S$ are taken as positive examples and the triples $(u, i, t) \notin S$ are taken as negative examples. If $(u, i) \notin P_S$, we do not know that user's preference for that item. Thus, all the entries for the unobserved posts are taken as missing values. We formulate the relevance of (u, i, t) with $f(u, i, t)$. Given a post (u, i), if user u has annotated item i with tag t^{pos} rather than tag t^{neg}, it implies that user u prefers tag t^{pos} to tag t^{neg} for that post. In other words, $f(u, i, t^{pos}) > f(u, i, t^{neg})$, iff triple $(u, i, t^{pos}) \in S$ and triple $(u, i, t^{neg}) \notin S$. Thus, in this paper, we use notation t^{pos} for "positive tags", and notation t^{neg} for "negative tags". As a result, the pairwise ranking constraints D_S from S is defined as

$$D_S = \{(u, i, t^{pos}, t^{neg}) | (u, i, t^{pos}) \in S \wedge (u, i, t^{neg}) \notin S\}.$$

The elements in D_S are used as training examples for tag recommendation. Figure 1 shows the tensor construction and a toy example of post-based ranking interpretation for personalized tag recommendation. User u has labeled item 4 with tag 1 and tag 3. Thus, we assume user u prefers tag 1 and tag 3 to tag 2 and tag 4. Besides, since user u has not labeled item 1 and item 4, the values of all the entries in the first row and the third row are missing.

Nonlinear Tensor Factorization using Gaussian Kernal for Tag Recommendation

Nonlinear Tensor Factorization using Gaussian

In this paper, we introduce a nonlinear way for tensor decomposition, and we refer to it as Nonlinear Tensor Factorization (NLTF). The ternary relation between users, items and tags is represented by a three-order tensor with $|U|$ users, $|I|$ items and $|T|$ tags. The tensor can be decomposed into three components, a user matrix $\mathbf{U} \in \mathbb{R}^{|U| \times R}$, an item matrix $\mathbf{I} \in \mathbb{R}^{|I| \times R}$ and a tag matrix $\mathbf{T} \in \mathbb{R}^{|T| \times R}$, where R is the number of features. The entries in the i-th row of matrix $\mathbf{U}$, matrix $\mathbf{I}$ and matrix $\mathbf{T}$ indicate the latent features of i-th user, i-th item and i-th tag, respectively. Each column of matrices $\mathbf{U}$, $\mathbf{I}$ and $\mathbf{T}$ can be considered as a latent topic.

Analogous to the previous work (Rendle and Schmidt-Thieme 2010), we model three pairwise relations user-item, user-tag and item-tag rather than directly model ternary relation use-item-tag. As we have mentioned, an entry in a feature vector stands for a latent topic. Without loss of generality, we take relation item-tag for example. We first make an assumption that the latent topics are independent to each other. Fox example, if the items are movies, the first latent topic might be comedy and the second latent topic might be action. If tag t is intimately related to item i with respect to the first topic, the value of the first latent feature of tag t should be close to the value of the first latent feature of item i. Taking consideration of it, we assume if item i and tag t are relevant with the k-th topic, then $\mathbf{T}_{t,k}$ obeys the Gaussian distribution $N(\mathbf{I}_{i,k}, \sigma^2)$ and vice versa, where $\mathbf{T}_{t,k}$ represents the k-th feature of tag t and $\mathbf{I}_{i,k}$ represents the k-th feature of item i. In other words, the distance between the value of the k-th feature of tag t and the k-th feature of item i obeys Gaussian distribution. The smaller the distance is, the more relevant are item i and tag t. It can be written as

$$||\mathbf{I}_{i,k} - \mathbf{T}_{t,k}|| \sim N(0, \sigma^2),$$

where σ is the standard deviation of the Gaussian distribution. The situations of user-tag and user-item relations are in analogy to that of the item-tag relation. However, the distributions of the latent topics of user-item, user-tag and item-tag relationships might be different. Thus, we define two sets of the features for the users, items and tags, respectively, and we have

$$\begin{aligned} ||\mathbf{U}^I_{u,k} - \mathbf{I}^U_{i,k}|| &\sim N(0, \sigma^2), \\ ||\mathbf{U}^T_{u,k} - \mathbf{T}^U_{t,k}|| &\sim N(0, \sigma^2), \\ \text{and } ||\mathbf{I}^T_{i,k} - \mathbf{T}^I_{t,k}|| &\sim N(0, \sigma^2), \end{aligned}$$

where $\mathbf{U}^T, \mathbf{U}^I \in \mathbb{R}^{|U| \times R}$, $\mathbf{I}^U, \mathbf{I}^T \in \mathbb{R}^{|I| \times R}$, $\mathbf{T}^U$, and $\mathbf{T}^I \in \mathbb{R}^{|T| \times R}$.

With the assumptions made, given a particular triple (u, i, t), we define its relevant score $f(u, i, t)$ as

$$\begin{aligned} f(u,i,t) = &\sum_k \zeta_k^{UI} \cdot exp(-\frac{1}{2}\beta||\mathbf{U}^I_{u,k} - \mathbf{I}^U_{i,k}||^2) \\ &+ \sum_k \zeta_k^{UT} \cdot exp(-\frac{1}{2}\beta||\mathbf{U}^T_{u,k} - \mathbf{T}^U_{t,k}||^2) \\ &+ \sum_k \zeta_k^{IT} \cdot exp(-\frac{1}{2}\beta||\mathbf{I}^T_{i,k} - \mathbf{T}^I_{t,k}||^2), \end{aligned} \quad (3)$$

where $\beta = 1/\sigma^2$. ζ_k^{UI} is the weight or the importance of the k-th topic for relation user-item. Similarly, ζ_k^{UT} and ζ_k^{IT} are the importance of the k-th topic for relations user-tag and item-tag, respectively.

In fact, the NLTF model can be represented by a neural network with a specific activation function and a three-layer networks structure. The framework of the neural network is depicted in Figure 2. The neural network contains three layers, input layer, hidden layer and output layer. The input layer of the neural network is composed of six blocks and the hidden layer is composed of three blocks. The first two block of the input layer and the first block of hidden layer corresponds to relation user-item. The representation of relations user-tag and item-tag are in analogy with relation user-item. For the input representation, one-of-n encoding schema is used. Given a triple (u, i, t), the u-th unit in the first block is set to be 1 and all the other units in the first block are set to be 0. The settings for the other input blocks are similar. For the hidden layer, we use $exp(-\frac{1}{2}\beta||p-q||^2)$ as the activation function, where p and q are the weights of the nonzero input units. Take relation user-item for example. p and q correspond to $\mathbf{U}^I_{u,k}$ and $\mathbf{I}^U_{i,k}$ in Eq. (3), respectively. ζ_k^{UI} in Eq. (3) corresponds to the weight of the k-th unit in the first block of the hidden layer.

For a single training example $(u, i, t^{pos}, t^{neg}) \in D_S$, we define the objective function for personalized tag recommendation with respect to that single example as follows.

$$J(u, i, t^{pos}, t^{neg}) = sigmoid(f(u, i, t^{pos}) - f(u, i, t^{neg})), \quad (4)$$

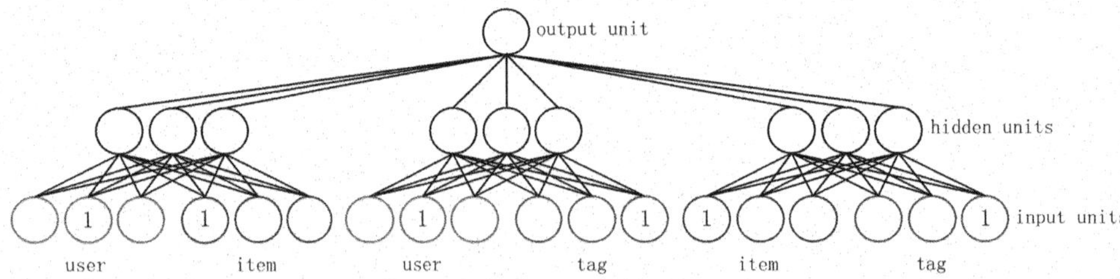

Figure 2: Neural network representation for NLTF

where $sigmoid(x) = \frac{1}{1+exp(-x)}$. It is clear that the sigmoid function, $sigmoid(x)$, is a monotonically increasing function. If a particular user u has annotated item i with tag t^{pos}, but not tag t^{neg}, it indicates that he prefers tag t^{pos} to tag t^{neg}. Thus, the difference of the relevant scores between (u, i, t^{pos}) and (u, i, t^{neg}) should be large and we use sigmoid function to model it.

Given a training set D_S, the overall objective function is defined as

$$J(D_S) = \sum_{(u,i,t^{pos},t^{neg}) \in D_S} J(u, i, t^{pos}, t^{neg}). \quad (5)$$

The parameters estimation for the tag recommendation task can be formulated as the optimization problem of maximizing $J(D_S)$.

Note that, given an example (u, i, t^{pos}, t^{neg}), the first component in $f(u, i, t)$ is eliminated when calculate $f(u, i, t^{pos}) - f(u, i, t^{neg})$ in Eq. (4). Thus, we drop it from $f(u, i, t)$. Besides, when maximizing the objective function, the scale of ζ_k^{UI}, ζ_k^{UT} and ζ_k^{IT} will get large, which leads to overfitting. To address this issue, we simply set the values of ζ_k^{UI}, ζ_k^{UT} and ζ_k^{IT} to 1. Therefore, given a triple (u, i, t), the relevant score $f(u, i, t)$ is simplified as

$$f(u,i,t) = \sum_k exp(-\frac{1}{2}\beta||\mathbf{U}_{u,k}^T - \mathbf{T}_{t,k}^U||^2) + \sum_k exp(-\frac{1}{2}\beta||\mathbf{I}_{i,k}^T - \mathbf{T}_{t,k}^I||^2). \quad (6)$$

Parameters Learning

We use stochastic gradient descent, a widely used technique, to optimize the objective function $J(D_S)$. We randomly select a training example (u, i, t^{pos}, t^{neg}) from D_S and perform an update for that example. This process repeats until convergence. The gradients for the nonlinear tensor factorization model are

$$\frac{\partial f_{u,i,t}}{\partial \mathbf{U}_{u,k}^T} = -\beta \cdot exp(-\frac{1}{2}\beta||\mathbf{U}_{u,k}^T - \mathbf{T}_{t,k}^I||^2)(\mathbf{U}_{u,k}^T - \mathbf{T}_{t,k}^U),$$

$$\frac{\partial f_{u,i,t}}{\partial \mathbf{I}_{i,k}^T} = -\beta \cdot exp(-\frac{1}{2}\beta||\mathbf{I}_{i,k}^T - \mathbf{T}_{t,k}^I||^2)(\mathbf{I}_{i,k}^T - \mathbf{T}_{t,k}^I),$$

$$\frac{\partial f_{u,i,t}}{\partial \mathbf{T}_{t,k}^U} = \beta \cdot exp(-\frac{1}{2}\beta||\mathbf{U}_{u,k}^T - \mathbf{T}_{t,k}^I||^2)(\mathbf{U}_{u,k}^T - \mathbf{T}_{t,k}^U),$$

and $$\frac{\partial f_{u,i,t}}{\partial \mathbf{T}_{t,k}^I} = \beta \cdot exp(-\frac{1}{2}\beta||\mathbf{I}_{i,k}^T - \mathbf{T}_{t,k}^I||^2)(\mathbf{I}_{i,k}^T - \mathbf{T}_{t,k}^I).$$

With the gradients, we can update the parameters of our model. We first initialize all of the parameters and then learn the parameters until convergence.

Comparison with Other Tensor Factorization Models

HOSVD (Karatzoglou et al. 2010), RTF (Rendle et al. 2009) and PITF (Rendle and Schmidt-Thieme 2010) are models based on linear tensor factorization. In particular, HOSVD and RTF are TD-based and PITF is CD-based. Our proposed model NLTF can be seen as a nonlinear extension of the CD-based models. We use Gaussian radial basis function rather than employing dot product used in PITF.

Let's assume the number of features of users, items and tags are the same for TD-based models, which is R. If we exploit stochastic gradient descent (SGD) to learn the parameters for all models, given a training example, TD-based models take $O(R^3)$ to update the parameters, while CD-based models take $O(R)$, where R is the number of features. For prediction, given a post $(user, item)$, TD-based models take $O(|T| \cdot R + R^3)$ to rank the tags, while CD-based models take $O(|T| \cdot R)$. Therefore, CD-based models outperform TD-based models in terms of the running time and are more feasible for online tag recommendation.

On the other hand, our model that exploits Gaussian radial basis function to calculate the similarity is better than models exploiting dot product. Models employing dot product can be viewed as two-class classifiers, while models employing Gaussian radial basis function can be seen as multi-class classifiers. For example, we want to provide a set of tags to user u who has just watched movie i. Let's assume there is only one latent feature $\mathbf{I_{i,1}}$. For dot product, if the value of $\mathbf{I}_{i,1}$ is positive, it may indicate the movie is a comedy; otherwise, the movie is not. Thus, if the value of $\mathbf{I}_{i,1}$ is positive and tag t is related to comedies, the value of $\mathbf{T}_{t,1}$ should be positive so as to make the dot product of $\mathbf{I}_{i,1}$ and $\mathbf{T}_{t,1}$ large, so that tag t can rank high given post (u, i). For Gaussian-based models, a toy example is depicted in Figure 3. The horizontal axis represents the value of $\mathbf{I_{i,1}}$.If $\mathbf{I}_{i,1} \in (-3, 3)$, the movie is probably an action; if $\mathbf{I}_{i,1} \in (-9, -5)$, the movie is probably an romantic; if $\mathbf{I}_{i,1} \in (5, 9)$, the movie is probably an drama; if $\mathbf{I}_{i,1} \in (-\infty, 20) \bigcup (20, \infty)$, it does not belong to any of the categories in Figure 3. For instance, tag t is "comedy" and movie i_1 and movie i_2 are annotated with tag t. As we assume, if an item and a tag are related, the distance between the feature of that item and the feature of that tag obeys

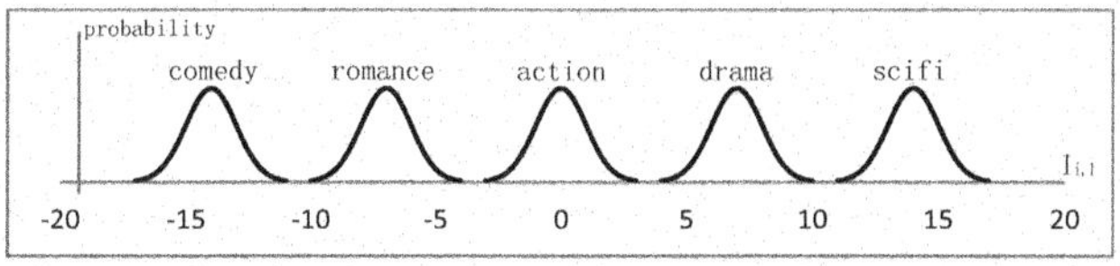

Figure 3: A toy example of nonlinear tensor factorization using Gaussian radial basis function

Gaussian distribution. That means the distance between the feature of tag t and the feature of movie i_1 is likely to be small and the distance between the feature of tag t and the feature of movie i_2 is likely to be small as well. Thus, the feature of i_1 is likely to be close to the feature of i_2. In other words, the features of the movies that belong to the same categories are likely to be close to each other and obey Gaussian distribution. We can distinguish several categories by using only one feature, because different categories fall into different part of the coordinate axis. In conclusion, Gaussian-based models can deal with more than two classes with only one feature, but dot product can handle only two classes. Thus, exploiting Gaussian function on radial basis distance can make better use of the latent features than dot product. The experimental results on real datasets in the next section demonstrate this point.

Experimental Results

Experimental Setup

We use four datasets to evaluate the performance of our proposed model, including *Delicoius-small*[1], *Last.fm*[2], *Movielens*[3] and *Delicious-large*[4] (Wetzker, Zimmermann, and Bauckhage 2008). Three smaller datasets *Delicious-small*, *Last.fm* and *Movielens* come from the 2-nd International Workshop on Information Heterogeneity and Fusion in Recommender Systems (HetRec 2011). The larger dataset *Delicious-large* (Wetzker, Zimmermann, and Bauckhage 2008) contains the complete bookmarking activity for almost 2 million users from the launch of the social bookmarking website in 2003 to the end of March 2011. For each dataset, we removed the infrequent users, items occurred in less than 5 posts and tags occurred in less than 5 triplets. The statistics of datasets after removal are described in Table 2. To avoid randomness of the results, we perform 10-fold cross-validation for the three smaller datasets, *Delicious-small*, *Last.fm* and *Movielens*. For larger dataset *Delicious-large*, we randomly sample about 40 thousand posts for test and the remaining data is used for training.

To evaluate our method, we introduce two baseline functions $N_{UT}(u,t)$ and $N_{IT}(i,t)$. Given user u and tag t, we define $N_{UT}(u,t)$ as

$$N_{UT}(u,t) = |\{i|(u,i,t) \in S\}|.$$

[1]http://www.delicious.com

[2]http://www.lastfm.com

[3]http://www.grouplens.org

[4]http://www.zubiaga.org/resources/socialbm0311

Table 2: Data statistics

Dataset	Users	Items	Tags	Posts	Triples
Delicious-small	1.8K	35.9K	9.3K	66.7K	312.0K
Last.fm	1.6K	7.3K	2.3K	61.1K	164.5K
Movielens	0.7K	2.6K	1.6K	17.8K	30.8K
Delicious-large	1.5M	7.5M	2.6M	198.9M	675.0M

Besides, given item i and tag t, we define $N_{IT}(i,t)$ as

$$N_{IT}(i,t) = |\{u|(u,i,t) \in S\}|.$$

We compare our proposed model NLTF with several baselines, including PITF, SVD, Top-UT, Top-IT and Top-UT+IT, where SVD only employs two-dimension relation item-tag, Top-UT ranks tags based on $N_{UT}(u,t)$, Top-IT ranks tags based on $N_{IT}(i,t)$ and Top-UT+IT ranks tags based on $N_{UT}(u,t) + N_{IT}(i,t)$. Here, Top-UT represents the affinity between users and tags, Top-IT represents the tag popularity and Top-UT+IT can be seen as a simple ensemble of Top-UT and Top-IT. We do not compare NLTF with TD-based models like HOSVD and RTF, because the computation time is unacceptable in practice, especially for larger dataset *Delicious-large*. Besides, the experimental results in (Rendle and Schmidt-Thieme 2010) show that the performance of PITF is comparable to TD-based models. For each dataset. we tuned the hyper-parameters of all models by grid search to achieve the best results.

Evaluation Methodology

We treat personalized tag recommendation as a information retrieval problem and employ Normalized Discounted Cumulative Gain (NDCG) as our metrics to evaluate the performance of the models. NDCG is widely used in information retrieval and it makes the assumption that relevant tags are more valuable if it appears earlier in the recommendation list.

Discounted Cumulative Gain (DCG) evaluates the gain of a tag based on its position in the ranked sequence returned by the model. The DCG accumulated at a particular position p is defined as

$$DCG@p = rel(1) + \sum\nolimits_{k=1}^{p} \frac{rel(k)}{\log_2(k)}, \tag{7}$$

where $rel(k)$ is 1 if the tag at position k is relevant or 0 otherwise. In order to normalize the metric, Ideal Discounted Cumulative Gain (IDCG) is introduced, which is the DCG of the ideal ranked sequence. Normalized Discounted Cumulative Gain (NDCG) is defined as

$$NDCG@p = \frac{DCG@p}{IDCG@p}. \tag{8}$$

Performance on Smaller Datasets

Comparisons with Baselines Table 3 shows the performance of different methods on three smaller datasets *Delicious-small*, *Last.fm* and *Movielens*. For NLTF and PITF, the number of features $R = 64$, and for SVD, $R =$

Figure 4: Tag distribution on dataset *Movielens* with the number of features $R = 1$

Table 1: Description of tags on dataset *Movielens* with the number of features $R = 1$

Oscar and AFI	Movie Categories	Movie Content	Adjective	Others
afi 100	scifi	war	atmospheric	erlends dvds
oscar (best directing)	fantasy	world war ii	disturbing	my movies
oscar (best cinematography)	comedy	surreal	deliberate	johnny depp
oscar (best supporting actor)	action	serial killer	quirky	boring
afi 100 (thrills)	anime	time travel	reflective	based on a book
oscar (best actor)	classic	true story	visceral	franchise

256 because NLTF and PITF saturate at 64 features and SVD saturates at 256 features. It can be seen from Table 3 that NLTF outperforms other competitive methods on *Delicious-small* and *Last.fm*, but PITF performs a little bit better than our method on *Movielens*. Since the data in *Delicious-small* and *Last.fm* is relatively sparser than the data in *Movielens*, it should be the case that our method has some advantages when the data is sparser. Moreover, our method beats Top-UT+IT on all the datasets, which integrates tag popularity and affinity between users and tags, but PITF works worse than Top-UT-IT on *Delicious-small*.

Table 3: NDCG@5 of different methods on three smaller datasets

	Delicious-small	Last.fm	Movielens
PITF-64	0.2518	0.6715	0.6466
NLTF-64	0.2718	0.6986	0.6309
SVD-256	0.1089	0.3633	0.1673
Top-UT	0.2416	0.3811	0.4082
Top-IT	0.1110	0.4683	0.2851
Top-UT+IT	0.2607	0.4588	0.4909

Impact of Number of Features The performances of the NLTF and PITF depend on the number of features. Table 4 shows the impact of the number of features on the three datasets *Delicious-small*, *Last.fm* and *Movielens*. As expected, the performances of NLTF and PLTF increase when we increase the number of features. Their performances saturate at 64 features on all three datasets. Besides, the performance of NLTF is much better than PITF when the number of feature is small, because models exploiting Gaussian like NLTF can make better use of the latent features than models exploiting dot product like PITF, just as we analyze in Section and the effect is more significant when only a smaller number of features are used.

Besides, in order to verify the point that using Gaussian can make better use of features than using dot product, we carry out another experiment. We train our proposed model NLTF by using only one feature on *Movielens*, so as to observe whether the tag distribution is corresponding to the toy example in Figure 3. In order to get better observation, the unpopular tags are removed. The tag distribution on dataset *Movielens* with the number of features $R = 1$ is depicted in Figure 4 and the description of which is showed in Table 1. As we can see, NLTF divides the tags into four groups automatically, including *Oscar and AFI*, *movie categories*, *movie content* and *adjective*. Tags in the same group are close to each other and some of their labels overlapped. Tags in *others* do not belong to any groups, thus they might do little help to personalized tag recommendation.

Table 4: NDCG@5 for different number of features on three smaller datasets

	feature	4	8	16	32	64
Delicious -small	PITF	0.068	0.100	0.157	0.231	0.252
	NLTF	0.075	0.126	0.188	0.247	0.272
Last.fm	PITF	0.369	0.502	0.601	0.654	0.672
	NLTF	0.445	0.562	0.652	0.692	0.699
Movielens	PITF	0.321	0.468	0.576	0.629	0.647
	NLTF	0.479	0.564	0.606	0.624	0.631

Performance on Large-Scale Dataset

In addition, we compare our method NLTF with PITF on a large-scale dataset *Delicious-large*, which contains more than 0.6 billion triples and about 0.2 billion posts. There is no previous work has conducted experiments for personalized tag recommendation on such a large-scale dataset before to our best knowledge. We conduct experiments on a computer with a 6-core intel i7 CPU and the performance after 30 iterations is showed in Table 5. From the figure, we can see that our method greatly outperforms PITF even on large scale dataset.

Table 5: Comparison of NLTF and PITF on larger dataset

	NDCG@1	NDCG@3	NDCG@5	NDCG@10
NLTF	0.3143	0.3053	0.3214	0.3579
PITF	0.2845	0.2758	0.2907	0.3247

Conclusion and Future Work

We introduce a nonlinear tensor factorization method based on Canonical Decomposition in this paper. Our proposed method exploits Gaussian radial basis function and can make better use of features than dot product. The models exploiting Gaussian can be considered as a multi-class classifiers, while the models exploiting dot product can be considered as a two-class classifiers. Additionally, our experimental results show that our method outperforms the baseline methods and can achieve very good performance with only a small number of features.

For future work, we plan to leverage the profile of users, the content of the items and tags to make better predictions for tag recommendation.

Acknowledgements

We would like to thank the many referees of the previous version of this paper for their extremely useful suggestions and comments. This work was supported by Huawei Innovation Research Program (HIRP) and National Science Foundation of China (61033010).

References

Carroll, J., and Chang, J. 1970. Analysis of individual differences in multidimensional scaling via an n-way generalization of "eckart-young" decomposition. *Psychometrika* 35(3):283–319.

Chi, Y., and Zhu, S. 2010. Facetcube: a framework of incorporating prior knowledge into non-negative tensor factorization. In *Proceedings of the 19th ACM international conference on Information and knowledge management*, 569–578. ACM.

Dunlavy, D. M.; Kolda, T. G.; and Acar, E. 2011. Temporal link prediction using matrix and tensor factorizations. *ACM Transactions on Knowledge Discovery from Data (TKDD)* 5(2):10.

Durao, F., and Dolog, P. 2010. Extending a hybrid tag-based recommender system with personalization. In *Proceedings of the 2010 ACM Symposium on Applied Computing*, 1723–1727. ACM.

Ermiş, B.; Acar, E.; and Cemgil, A. T. 2012. Link prediction via generalized coupled tensor factorisation. *arXiv preprint arXiv:1208.6231*.

Gao, D.; Zhang, R.; Li, W.; and Hou, Y. 2012. Twitter hyperlink recommendation with user-tweet-hyperlink three-way clustering. In *Proceedings of the 21st ACM international conference on Information and knowledge management*, 2535–2538. ACM.

Guan, Z.; Bu, J.; Mei, Q.; Chen, C.; and Wang, C. 2009. Personalized tag recommendation using graph-based ranking on multi-type interrelated objects. In *Proceedings of the 32nd international ACM SIGIR conference on Research and development in information retrieval*, 540–547. ACM.

Harshman, R. A. 1970. Foundations of the PARAFAC procedure: Models and conditions for an "explanatory" multimodal factor analysis. *UCLA working papers in phonetics* 16:1.

Karatzoglou, A.; Amatriain, X.; Baltrunas, L.; and Oliver, N. 2010. Multiverse recommendation: n-dimensional tensor factorization for context-aware collaborative filtering. In *Proceedings of the fourth ACM conference on Recommender systems*, 79–86. ACM.

Krestel, R.; Fankhauser, P.; and Nejdl, W. 2009. Latent dirichlet allocation for tag recommendation. In *Proceedings of the third ACM conference on Recommender systems*, 61–68. ACM.

Lipczak, M.; Hu, Y.; Kollet, Y.; and Milios, E. 2009. Tag sources for recommendation in collaborative tagging systems. *ECML PKDD discovery challenge* 157–172.

Liu, D.; Hua, X.-S.; Yang, L.; Wang, M.; and Zhang, H.-J. 2009. Tag ranking. In *Proceedings of the 18th international conference on World wide web*, 351–360. ACM.

Nickel, M.; Tresp, V.; and Kriegel, H.-P. 2011. A three-way model for collective learning on multi-relational data. In *Proceedings of the 28th international conference on machine learning (ICML-11)*, 809–816.

Rendle, S., and Schmidt-Thieme, L. 2010. Pairwise interaction tensor factorization for personalized tag recommendation. In *Proceedings of the third ACM international conference on Web search and data mining*, 81–90. ACM.

Rendle, S.; Balby Marinho, L.; Nanopoulos, A.; and Schmidt-Thieme, L. 2009. Learning optimal ranking with tensor factorization for tag recommendation. In *Proceedings of the 15th ACM SIGKDD international conference on Knowledge discovery and data mining*, 727–736. ACM.

Spiegel, S.; Clausen, J.; Albayrak, S.; and Kunegis, J. 2012. Link prediction on evolving data using tensor factorization. In *New Frontiers in Applied Data Mining*. Springer. 100–110.

Sun, J.-T.; Zeng, H.-J.; Liu, H.; Lu, Y.; and Chen, Z. 2005. Cubesvd: a novel approach to personalized web search. In *Proceedings of the 14th international conference on World Wide Web*, 382–390. ACM.

Symeonidis, P.; Nanopoulos, A.; and Manolopoulos, Y. 2008. Tag recommendations based on tensor dimensionality reduction. In *Proceedings of the 2008 ACM conference on Recommender systems*, 43–50. ACM.

Symeonidis, P.; Nanopoulos, A.; and Manolopoulos, Y. 2010. A unified framework for providing recommendations in social tagging systems based on ternary semantic analysis. *Knowledge and Data Engineering, IEEE Transactions on* 22(2):179–192.

Tucker, L. R. 1966. Some mathematical notes on three-mode factor analysis. *Psychometrika* 31:279–311.

Wetzker, R.; Zimmermann, C.; and Bauckhage, C. 2008. Analyzing social bookmarking systems: A del.icio.us cookbook. In *Mining Social Data (MSoDa) Workshop Proceedings*, 26–30.

A Multivariate Timeseries Modeling Approach to Severity of Illness Assessment and Forecasting in ICU with Sparse, Heterogeneous Clinical Data

Marzyeh Ghassemi
Computer Science
MIT
Cambridge, MA 02139 USA
mghassem@mit.edu

Marco A.F. Pimentel *
Engineering Science
University of Oxford
Oxford, UK
marco.pimentel@eng.ox.ac.uk

Tristan Naumann
Computer Science
MIT
Cambridge, MA
tjn@mit.edu

Thomas Brennan
Health Science Technology
MIT
Cambridge, MA
tpb@mit.edu

David A. Clifton
Engineering Science
University of Oxford
Oxford, UK
davidc@robots.ox.ac.uk

Peter Szolovits
Computer Science
MIT
Cambridge, MA
psz@mit.edu

Mengling Feng †
Health Science Technology
MIT
Cambridge, MA
mfeng@mit.edu

Abstract

The ability to determine patient acuity (or severity of illness) has immediate practical use for clinicians. We evaluate the use of multivariate timeseries modeling with the multi-task Gaussian process (GP) models using noisy, incomplete, sparse, heterogeneous and unevenly-sampled clinical data, including both physiological signals and clinical notes. The learned multi-task GP (MTGP) hyperparameters are then used to assess and forecast patient acuity. Experiments were conducted with two real clinical data sets acquired from ICU patients: firstly, estimating cerebrovascular pressure reactivity, an important indicator of secondary damage for traumatic brain injury patients, by learning the interactions between intracranial pressure and mean arterial blood pressure signals, and secondly, mortality prediction using clinical progress notes. In both cases, MTGPs provided improved results: an MTGP model provided better results than single-task GP models for signal interpolation and forecasting (0.91 vs 0.69 RMSE), and the use of MTGP hyperparameters obtained improved results when used as additional classification features (0.812 vs 0.788 AUC).

1 Introduction

Motivation Decisions in the intensive care unit (ICU) are frequently made in settings with a high degree of uncertainty based on a wide variety of data sources, such as vital signs, clinical notes, fluids, medications, etc. Clinical data collection is rapidly expanding, but these data are often sparse and irregularly sampled, and contaminated by a variety of noise interference and human error. The ICU is playing an expanding role in acute hospital care (Vincent 2013), and in such data-heavy settings, a more concise representation of patient records would help clinical staff to quickly assess patient state and plan care.

*The first two authors contributed equally on this work.

†Corresponding author.

Goal High quality clinical care depends on the ability to combine heterogeneous clinical data to understand the severity of illness (acuity) in patients. Clinical research often uses risk of mortality as a surrogate for patient acuity, often evaluated at a single end point, such as after 28-days post-discharge. Most acuity scores rely on static snapshots of a patient and do not incorporate evolving clinical information such as new notes, lab values, etc. Our goal is to provide a concise representation of these multiple related timeseries so that they can be compared and assessed.

Challenge The general issue of comparing signals that are not aligned and irregularly sampled has been considered before (see 2.2). Establishing similarity metrics among timeseries data is an important part of many learning tasks and often is achieved using a variety of summarization methods. However, many modeling methods fail when applied to irregularly sampled data unless strong assumptions are made about the functional form present in the underlying data source. Furthermore, in cases where such methods work, data imputation is often necessary, which can introduce additional sources of error and bias. Finally, many methods work on a single timeseries, but fail to generalize to (or take advantage of) other related time-series data. In the remainder of this paper, we refer to noisy, sparse, heterogeneous, irregularly sampled data as "irregularly-sampled" data.

Solution Our proposed technique transforms a variety of irregularly-sampled clinical data into a new latent space using the hyperparameters of multi-task GP (MTGP) models. Patients are compared based on their similarity in the new hyperparameter space. Our work differs from other work in that it: 1) uses the correlation between and within multiple time-series to estimate parameters instead of considering each timeseries separately; 2) infers a compact latent representation of the source data, rather than finding patterns that are common within different timeseries; and 3) leverages the information contained in the inferred model hyperparameters for supervised learning, whereas others use the predicted mean function of the GP as a pre-processing or smoothing step (see 2.3).

Contributions This paper makes the following contributions:

- We propose a method using MTGP for forecasting patient acuity based on irregularly sampled heterogeneous clinical data.
- We propose a new latent space for representing multi-dimensional timeseries using inferred MTGP hyperparameters.
- We evaluate our approach in two ways: 1) estimating and forecasting a cerebrovascular autoregulation index from noisy physiological time-series data in patients who suffered a traumatic brain injury and 2) transforming irregular ICU patient clinical notes into timeseries, and using MTGP hyperparameters from these timeseries as features to predict mortality probability.

2 Related Work

2.1 Clinical Assessment

In the clinical world, there are practical examples of data being used to infer patient acuity in the form of ICU scoring systems. ICU scoring systems such as SAPS (simplified acute physiology score) use physiologic and other clinical data for acuity assessment. However, in 2012 scoring systems were used in only 10% to 15% of US ICUs (Breslow and Badawi 2012). Recent work has focused on feature engineering for mortality prediction. This is usually accomplished by windowing or aggregating the structured numerical data so that a single feature matrix can be fed into a structured deterministic classifier (Hug and Szolovits 2009; Lehman et al. 2012; Joshi and Szolovits 2012; Ghassemi et al. 2014).

2.2 Timeseries Abstraction

The timeseries abstraction/summarization literature deals more directly with the time-varying nature of data. Dynamic time warping measures similarity between two temporal sequences that may vary in time or speed (Li and Clifford 2012). Another approach is time-series symbolization, which involves discretizing timeseries into sequences of symbols and attaching meaning to the groupings of the symbols (Lin et al. 2007; Saeed and Mark 2006; Syed and Guttag 2011). These approaches rely on some known regularity underlying a signal (e.g. ECG signals), and are often unsuitable for irregularly sampled timeseries. Full latent variable models have been applied to abstracting signals into higher level representations. For example, Fox et al. used beta processes to model multiple related timeseries (Fox et al. 2011), and Marlin et al. used Gaussian mixture models on the first 24 hours of monitor-signals data with hourly-discretization (Marlin et al. 2012). Nevertheless, latent variable approaches are unable to cope with missing and unevenly-sampled data as is, and require either strong assumptions about observations when they change asynchronously, or the computationally expensive approach of modeling time between observations directly as another latent variable.

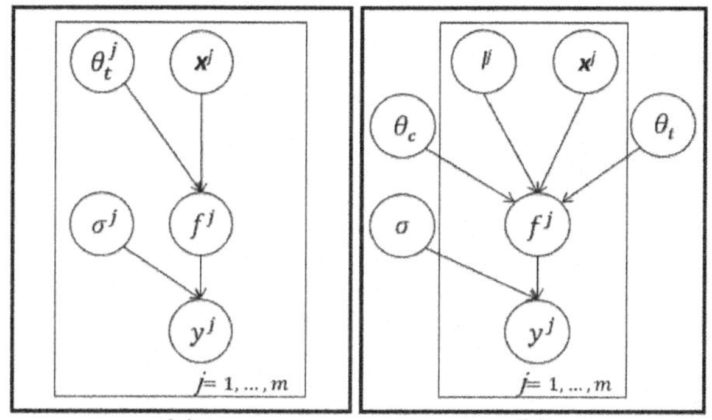

Figure 1: Graphical model for **(a)** m single-task Gaussian processes with m sets of: inputs X^i, temporal covariance hyperparameters θ_t^i, estimated functions f^i, noise terms σ^i, and outcomes y^i; and **(b)** a multi-task Gaussian process which relates m tasks through all prior variables, with the tasks' labels l and similarity matrix θ_c.

2.3 Gaussian Processes

Gaussian processes (GP) form the basis for a Bayesian modeling technique that has been used for various machine learning tasks (Rasmussen and Williams 2006). Most commonly, GPs are used to predict a single output (denoted here as "task") based on one or more input timeseries. We refer to this model as a single-task GP (STGP). Lasko et al. attempted to use Gaussian process regression as a smoothing function of irregularly-sampled signals (Lasko, Denny, and Levy 2013). This is a common usage model for GPs on clinical timeseries: GPs are used to model observed data through the predicted mean function of the timeseries. Clifton et al. used GPs as a framework for coping with data artifacts and incompleteness in mobile sensor data (Clifton et al. 2013b). In a related work (Clifton et al. 2013a), a functional version of extreme value statistics was proposed for physiological data in order to compare different timeseries. Similarly, GPs were used for robust regression of noisy heart rate data (Stegle et al. 2008). The remainder of the related work has used STGP models to predict a single output based on one or more input variables.

3 Methods

In the present study, we explore the potential of a novel approach using MTGP models (Bonilla, Chai, and Williams 2007) to learn the correlation between and within timeseries, and obtain a concise representation of time-varying physiological and clinical data based on the inferred hyperparameters.

Here, we motivate the use of MTGPs and describe the method (source code is available on-line[1]) that we have adapted for hyperparameter construction (Durichen et al. 2014).

[1]http://www.robots.ox.ac.uk/ davidc/publications_MTGP.php

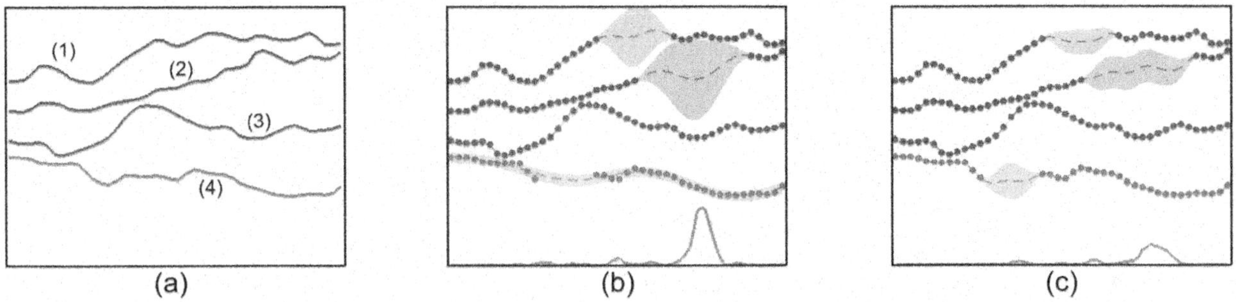

Figure 2: (a) A sample function with 4 tasks; (b) Single-task GP (STGP) and (c) multi-task GP (MTGP) predictions on all tasks. The dots represent observations, while dashed lines and colored areas represent the predictive mean and 95% confidence interval, respectively. The line on the bottom represents the mean absolute error (over the 4 tasks) between the predictions and the correspondent reference values. We observe that the overall error obtained in (c) is lower than that in (b), which suggests that the use of MTGP yielded better predictions by taking into account the correlation between the different tasks.

3.1 Multi-Task Gaussian Process Models

The general STGP framework may be extended to the problem of modeling m tasks simultaneously where each model uses the same index set $\mathbf{x}$ (e.g., physiological or clinical timeseries). A naïve approach is to train a STGP model independently for each task, as illustrated in Figure 1(a). We introduce instead an extension to multi-task GP models proposed in (Bonilla, Chai, and Williams 2007), which makes use of the covariance in related tasks to reduce uncertainty in the inferred signal.

Let $\mathbf{X_n} = \{x_i^j \mid j = 1,...,m, i = 1,...,n_j\}$ and $\mathbf{Y_n} = \{y_i^j \mid j = 1,...,m, i = 1,...,n_j,\}$ be the training indices and observations for the m tasks, where task j has n_j number of training data. We consider the regression model $\vec{y}_n = g(\vec{x}_n) + \epsilon$, in which $g(x)$ represents the latent function and $\epsilon \sim \mathcal{N}(0, \sigma_n^2)$ is a noise term. GP models assume that the function $g(\vec{x}_n)$ can be interpreted as a probability distribution over functions such that $\tilde{\mathbf{y}}_\mathbf{n} = g(\vec{x}_n) \sim \mathcal{GP}\Big(m(\vec{x}_n), k(\vec{x}_n, \vec{x}_n')\Big)$, where $m(\vec{x}_n)$ is the mean function of the process (assumed $=$ 0) and $k(\vec{x}_n, \vec{x}_n')$ is a covariance function describing the coupling among the independent variables $\vec{x}_n$ as a function of their kernel distance. To specify the affiliation of index x_i^j and observation y_i^j to task j, a label $l^j = j$ is added as an additional input to the model, as shown in Figure 1(b). To model the correlation between tasks as well as the temporal behaviour of the tasks within a unified GP model, two independent covariance functions are assumed, and the covariance matrix $\mathbf{K}_{MT}$ for all m tasks can be written

$$\mathbf{K}_{MT}(\mathbf{X}_n, \mathbf{l}, \boldsymbol{\theta}_c, \boldsymbol{\theta}_t) = \mathbf{K}_c(\mathbf{l}, \boldsymbol{\theta}_c) \otimes \mathbf{K}_t(\mathbf{X}_n, \boldsymbol{\theta}_t) \quad (1)$$

where $\otimes$ is the Kronecker product, $\mathbf{l} = \{j \mid j = 1,...,m\}$, $\mathbf{K}_c$ and $\mathbf{K}_t$ represent the correlation and temporal covariance functions, and $\boldsymbol{\theta}_c$ and $\boldsymbol{\theta}_t$ are vectors containing hyperparameters for $\mathbf{K}_c$ and $\mathbf{K}_t$, respectively. Within geostatistics, this approach is also known as the *intrinsic correlation model* (Wackernagel 2003).

By modifying the temporal covariance function we can encode our prior knowledge concerning the functional behavior of the tasks that we wish to model. The most frequently-used example is the squared-exponential covariance function (Rasmussen and Williams 2006):

$$\mathbf{K}_t = \theta_A^2 \exp\left\{-\frac{\| x - x' \|^2}{2\theta_L^2}\right\}, \quad (2)$$

where $\boldsymbol{\theta}_t = \{\theta_A, \theta_L\}$, and θ_A and θ_L are hyperparameters modeling the y-scaling and x-scaling (or time-scale if the data are timeseries) of the covariance function, respectively.

To construct a valid positive semidefinite correlation covariance function $\mathbf{K}_c$, we used the Cholesky decomposition and the "free-form" parameterization of the elements of the lower triangular matrix $\mathbf{L}$ proposed in (Bonilla, Chai, and Williams 2007), such as

$$\mathbf{K}_c = \mathbf{L}\mathbf{L}^\top, \quad \mathbf{L} = \begin{bmatrix} \theta_{c,1} & 0 & \dots & 0 \\ \theta_{c,2} & \theta_{c,3} & & 0 \\ \vdots & & \ddots & \vdots \\ \theta_{c,k-m+2} & \theta_{c,k-m+2} & \dots & \theta_{c,k} \end{bmatrix} \quad (3)$$

where $k = \sum_{i=1}^m i$ is the number of correlation hyperparameters.

Identically to STGPs, the hyperparameters $\boldsymbol{\theta}$ for a MTGP may be optimized by minimizing the negative log marginal likelihood via gradient descent (Rasmussen and Williams 2006), and predictions for test indices $\{\mathbf{x}_p^*, \mathbf{l}_p^*\}$ can be made by computing the conditional probability $p(\mathbf{y}_p^* | \mathbf{x}_p^*, \mathbf{l}_p, \mathbf{x}_n, \mathbf{l}_n, \mathbf{y}_n)$.

Figure 2 shows an example of STGPs and an MTGP applied to a simple synthetic dataset with 4 sample tasks. Tasks 1 and 2 were correlated, task 1 and task 2 were both anti-correlated with task 4, and task 3 was uncorrelated with all other tasks. For this, 4 tasks were sampled from a MTGP model with the following hyperparameters: $\theta_L = \theta_A = \theta_{c,1} = \theta_{c,2} = \theta_{c,3} = \theta_{c,6} = \theta_{c,10} = 1$, $\theta_{c,4} = \theta_{c,5} = \theta_{c,0} = 0$, and $\theta_{c,7} = \theta_{c,8} = -1$. Artificial gaps were then randomly created in different tasks at different time points and with different durations. The STGP

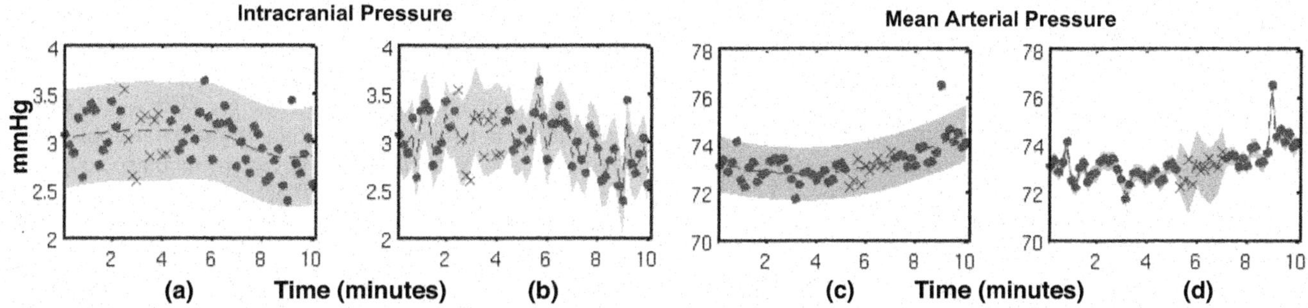

Figure 3: An example of a single-task GP (STGP) and multi-task GP (MTGP) applied to intracranial pressure (ICP) and mean arterial blood pressure (ABP) signals from a traumatic brain injury patient. (a) and (c) show the performance of STGP, whereas (b) and (d) show the improved performance of MTGP, which takes into account the correlation between ICP and ABP. Dots represent observations, crosses represent missing observations (test observations), the dotted line shows the function mean and the shaded area show the 95% confidence interval. We note that the timescale parameter "selected" by the MTGP, which takes into account the correlation between the tasks, is shorter than the one selected by the STGP, which yields to higher likelihood of the test observations (crosses).

(Figure 2(b)), applied to each task independently, fails to adequately represent the functions, particularly where data are not available. Figure 2(c) shows that the MTGP improves the predictions in all 4 tasks by capturing the relationships between them.

The MTGP has several useful properties as compared to the traditional GP:

- We can allow task-specific training indices n_j; i.e., training data may be observed at different times for different tasks (Figure 2);
- The correlations within and between tasks are automatically learned from the data by fitting the covariance function in Equation 1; and
- The framework assumes that the tasks have similar temporal characteristics and hyperparameters θ_t.

A limitation of the MTGP is computational cost: $\mathcal{O}(m^3n^3)$ compared with $m \times \mathcal{O}(n^3)$ for STGPs. This limitation is not as relevant for our application, given that we are not dealing with densely-sampled time-series data, but data which is sparse and irregular. Another limitation of the MTGP is that the number of hyperparameters can increase rapidly for an increasing number of tasks, which can lead to a multi-modal parameter space.

3.2 Signal Representation via Hyperparameters

We propose using the inferred MTGP hyperparameters $\boldsymbol{\theta}$ that describe the temporal correlation within and between tasks as features that represent our set of observations: θ_A and θ_L which respectively govern each output scale of our functions and the input, or time, scale, and $\theta_{c,i}$ that correspond to the correlation between the different tasks (outputs) modelled. In effect, $\boldsymbol{\theta}$ provides a new latent search space to examine and evaluate the similarity of any two given multidimensional functions. Importantly, these parameters are:

1. a means of representing the functional behavior a set of observations $\{\vec{y}_n, \vec{x}_n\}$;
2. learned directly from data; and
3. generalizable to any type of longitudinal data, including categorical and numerical types.

4 Experiment 1: From Multiple Noisy Time-Series Data to Acuity Assessment

In this experiment, we use physiological signals from Traumatic Brain Injury (TBI) patients to test the MTGP's ability to assess and forecast multiple related signals. We examine two noisy timeseries: the intracranial pressure (ICP) and mean arterial blood pressure (ABP). Continuous monitoring of ICP and ABP has become a standard in neurological ICUs. Cerebrovascular autoregulation is an important mechanism to sustain adequate cerebral blood flow (Werner and Engelhard 2007), and impairment of this mechanism indicates an increased risk to secondary brain damage and mortality (Hlatky, Valadka, and Robertson 2005).

Cerebrovascular autoregulation is most commonly assessed based on the Pressure-Reactivity Index (PRx), which is defined as a sliding window Pearson's correlation between the ICP and ABP (Czosnyka et al. 1997). However, the ICP and ABP timeseries are often contaminated by artifacts and missing data, and PRx can no longer be calculated in these situations. Although methods have been proposed to detect and remove artifacts (Feng et al. 2011), the artifact removal process still creates gaps of missing data in the timeseries.

In this experiment, we demonstrate how the proposed MTGP model can be applied to interpolate the incomplete data in ICP and ABP signals and, more importantly, to accurately estimate PRx.

4.1 Data

The ICP and ABP data were collected from 35 TBI patients who were monitored for more than 24-hours in a Neuro-ICU of a tertiary care hospital between January 2009 and December 2010. The continuously monitored physiological readings were sampled and recorded every 10 seconds. For experimental evaluation, we selected 30 ten-minute windows from each patient recording, where ICP and ABP signals were free from artifacts and missing values. We then randomly introduced artificial gaps in both signals as shown in Figure 3. We evaluated the PRx estimation accuracy, and we further compared the performance of MTGP to that of STGP, which models each signal independently. For implementation, priors over the hyperparameters were selected after 100 random initializations for each case.

4.2 Results

The quality of predictions are evaluated using the squared error loss, where we compute the squared residual $(y^* - \hat{y}^*)^2$ between the mean prediction $(\hat{y}^*)$ and the target (y^*) at each test point, and the squared root of the average over the test set to produce the root mean squared error (RMSE). As the RMSE is sensitive to the overall scale of the target values, we additionally evaluate the negative log probability of the target under the model, by defining the mean standardized log loss (MSLL) as

$$\text{MSLL}(\hat{\mathbf{y}}^*, \mathbf{y}^*) = \frac{1}{p}\sum_{i=1}^{p}\Big(- \log p(\hat{y}_i^* | f, x_i^*) + \log p(\hat{y}_i^* | m(\mathbf{y}_n), \text{var}(\mathbf{y}_n), x_i^*\Big),$$

where the first term is the log likelihood of $\hat{y}_i^*$ given our latent function f and the test index x_i^*. This probability is normalized by the second term, the log likelihood of $\hat{y}_i^*$ under a trivial model that predicts using a Gaussian with mean $m(\mathbf{y}_n)$ and variance $\text{var}(\mathbf{y}_n)$ of the training labels.

Signal	Measure	STGP	MTGP
ICP	RMSE	0.91	0.69
	MSLL	0.6	0.45
ABP	RMSE	2.77	1.98
	MSLL	0.65	0.55
PRx-PRx*	RMSE	-	0.09

Table 1: Performance of single-task GP (STGP) and multi-task GP (MTGP). PRx-PRx* refers to the difference between the reference PRx (Pearson correlation coefficient of ICP and ABP for a given window) and PRx*, the estimated PRx index (posterior MTGP hyperparameter that measures the interaction between the two tasks).

Table 1 shows the overall performance of our approach. We note that the MTGP was able to estimate the correlation between the ICP and ABP signals – PRx – accurately even with incomplete data. The average RMSE between the true correlation coefficients and the MTGP estimated ones with the incomplete data was 0.09 (Table 1). This suggests that the posterior hyperparameter of MTGP, which measures the interactions between ICP and ABP, may be used as an index to model the cerebrovascular autoregulation mechanism and thus the risk of secondary brain injury.

We note that the scale of ICP values is normally between 1 to 20 mmHg, and the specific ICP value determines whether the achieved reduction in RMSE is clinically significant. If the ICP has already elevated to somewhere near 20 mmHg, any slight increase in ICP may result in secondary damage to the brain. In this case, even small reductions to RMSE are more desirable to guide the medical interventions.

We also observe that the MTGP provides a significant improvement in interpolating values for both signals, as the correlation between the two physiological variables is taken into account. Particularly, in periods of incomplete data (see Figure 3), the predictions are much more accurate compared to STGP. This shows that the proposed MTGP model can also be used for accurate interpolation and forecasting of ICP and ABP timeseries in the applications of advanced alarming and physiological trajectory analysis.

5 Experiment 2: From Heterogenous Clinical Data to ICU Acuity Forecasting

To demonstrate the effectiveness of the proposed MTGP model on features inferred from sparse, irregularly sampled timeseries, we applied MTGPs to clinical notes from the ICU for mortality prediction as summarized in Figure 4. Gold-standard clinical models typically use population-based acuity scores, such as SAPS-I (Le Gall et al. 1984), based on snapshots of the patient's status during their stay in the ICU. These scores are inherently limited because patient state (or severity of illness) constantly evolves.

5.1 Data

We used 2001–2006 ICU data from the open-access MIMIC II 2.6 database (Saeed et al. 2011), which includes electronic medical records (EMRs) for $26,870$ ICU patients at the Beth Israel Deaconess Medical Center (BIDMC).

For each patient we extracted the SAPS-I score, calculated from clinical variables over a patient's first 24-hours in the ICU. We used all notes from nursing, physicians, labs, and radiology recorded prior to the patient's first discharge from ICU. Discharge summaries were excluded because they typically state the patient's outcome explicitly. Patients were excluded if their notes had fewer than 100 words, fewer than 6 total notes in their record, or were under the age of 18. Patient mortality outcomes were measured at hospital discharge and 1 year post-discharge.

The final cohort consisted of 10,202 patients with 313,461 notes. A random 30% of the patients (3,040) were held back as a test set. The remaining 70% of patients (7,162) were used to train topic models and mortality predictors. The test set contained 93,411 notes, and the training set had 220,005.

5.2 Clinical Note Decomposition to Timeseries

Beginning from sparse, irregularly sampled clinical notes, we first performed topic modeling as a form of dimensionality reduction as described in (Ghassemi et al. 2014). Topics inference was performed on notes using $T = 50$ topics over the words (W) in our vocabulary (Blei, Ng, and Jordan 2003; Griffiths and Steyvers 2004). We normalized hyperparameters on the Dirichlet priors for the topic distributions (α) and the topic-word distributions (β) as $\alpha = \frac{50}{T}$, and $\beta = \frac{200}{W}$.

The topic inference resulted in a 50-dimensional vector of topic proportions for *each note* in every patient's record. We concatenated topic vectors into a matrix q where the element q_{nk} was the proportion of topic k in the nth note.

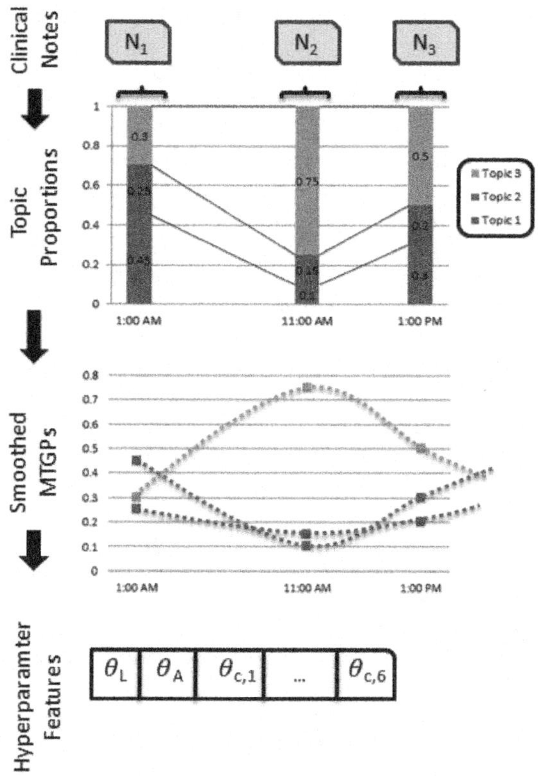

Figure 4: 1) We perform a pre-projection step where clinical notes are transformed into timeseries using Latent Dirichlet Allocation; 2) the new set of topic proportion timeseries are fitted using the MTGPs; 3) inferred hyperparameters $\theta_L, \theta_A, \theta_{c,1}, \ldots, \theta_{c,6}$ are derived, projecting into the new latent space; 4) latent features (hyperparameters) are used as features in combination with topic proportions and the SAPS acuity score to 5) forecast patient mortality.

5.3 Hyperparameter Construction

Once notes were transformed into multi-dimensional numeric vectors, we used the MTGPs to model the per-note change in topic membership over a patient's stay. This is critical for comparing two patients' records given that patients have different lengths of stay and note taking intervals depend on staff, clinical condition, and other factors.

From the topic enrichment measure (ϕ), we chose the topics with a posterior likelihood above or below 5% of the population baseline likelihood across topics. This yielded nine topics (see Table 5.3 for a summary of the chosen topics, and the Appendix for more details). We employed MTGP to learn the temporal correlation between the nine topics and the overall temporal variability of the multiple timeseries.

From the available data sources, we formed a set of three feature matrices: (1) the admitting SAPS-I score for every patient, (2) the average topic membership for the nine identified topics (matrix q), and (3) the inferred MTGP hyperparameters across the nine topic vectors from q. Importantly, the admitting SAPS-I score and mean topic members (1 and 2) are both *static measures*. SAPS-I collapses data from the first 24 hours of the record, while the average topic membership collapses the entire per-note timeseries for each patient's record into an aggregate measure. Our proposed MTGP hyperparameters (3) complement these measures with information about the per-note timeseries.

	Top Five Words	Possible Topic
In-hospital Mortality	liver, renal, hepatic, ascites, dialysis	Renal Failure
	thick, secretions, vent, trach, resp	Respiratory infection
	remains, family, gtt, line, map	Systematic organ failure
	increased, temp, hr, pt, cc	Multiple physiological changes
	intubated, vent, ett, secretions, propofol	Respiratory failure
	name, family, neuro, care, noted	Discussion of end-of-life care
Survival	cabg, pain, ct, artery, coronary	Cardio-vascular surgery
	chest, pneumothorax, tube, reason, clip	
	pain, co, denies, oriented, neuro	Responsive patient

Table 2: Top five words in chosen topics (enriched for in-hospital mortality/survival).

5.4 Outcome Classification

We considered five feature prediction regimes that combined subsets of the feature matrices 1, 2, and 3 as an aggregate feature matrix. We trained two supervised classifiers that were identical in the five feature sets used, but provided different objective functions for optimization: Lasso logistic regression and L2 linear kernel SVM.

Classifiers were trained to create classification boundaries for two clinical outcomes: in-hospital mortality and 1-year post-discharge mortality. All outcomes had large class-imbalance (e.g., in-hospital mortality rates of 10.9%). To address this issue, we randomly sub-sampled the negative class in the training set to produce a minimum 70%/30% ratio between the negative and positive classes. Test set distributions were not modified, and reported performance reflects those distributions. Due to space constraints, we only reported results on a completely held out test set. We performed 5-fold cross-validation on the remaining data, and cross-validation results were similar to those obtained on the completely held-out test set.

We evaluated the performance of all classifiers using the area under the Receiver Operating Characteristic curve (AUC) on the held-out test set. Table 3 reports results from the Lasso model. Results obtained using the L2 linear kernel SVM were not statistically different.

Features	Hospital Mortality	1-Year Mortality
SAPS-I	0.702	0.500
Ave. Topics	0.759	0.653
SAPS-I + MTGP	0.775	0.624
Ave. Topics + MTGP	0.788	0.673
SAPS-I + Ave. Topics + MTGP	0.812	0.686

Table 3: Prediction results of hospital and 1-year mortality, AUC for various feature combinations.

5.5 Results

SAPS-I had the poorest predictive power, which is understandable given that it is only an initial snapshot (24 hours) of the severity of illness. We used the static SAPS-I score due to its status as the gold-standard in clinical scoring, and our argument in the second experiment is that the MTGP hyper-parameter space complements this clinical score, rather than competes with it. The average value of the most significant topics significantly improved upon that predictive power. The performance of MTGP Hyperparameters on their own was similar to that of the Topics: AUC of 0.749 and 0.624 for in-hospital and 1 year mortality, respectively.

Given that the hyperparameters were optimized from per-note topic features (that are themselves the output of an unstructured learning problem), it is most sensible that the topics information should be used in combination with the MTGP hyperparameters to describe patient state. We obtained improved predictive performance for both mortality outcomes when combining both MTGP hyperparameters with SAPS-I and the significant topics. This is likely because the hyperparameters provide complementary information to both SAPS-I and the significant topics. Both SAPS-I and the topic features capture a single aggregate measure of membership in certain latent dimensions related to outcome, while the MTGP hyperparameters capture movement over the course of a hospital stay within those dimensions. The best predictive performance occurred when all features were combined, e.g. SAPS-I + significant topics + MTGP hyperparameters.

6 Conclusion

The ability to determine on-going patient acuity has immediate clinical use. But clinical data are often noisy, sparse and irregularly sampled. The secondary nature of medical data is also true in other domains of application such as social media, online retailers, and online content distributors (e.g., Yelp reviews, Twitter tweets, Amazon product reviews and ratings). In all these cases, data are likely to suffer from the same problems mentioned above, but there is still a need to understand how sets of information are related. A key to analyzing such data is representing the time-series data in a manner that allows for effective discrimination between two or more patterns.

The goal of this work was to transform multiple clinical data sources (e.g., notes, acuity scores) into a new latent space where the information could be viewed as timeseries data, and abstracted features represent the series dynamics. We demonstrated our method's applicability to physiological and clinical data using two different experiments.

MTGPs were able to estimate the cerebrovascular autoregulation index in TBI patients. The biggest advantage of MTGP over STGP is the ability to estimate the correlations between ICP and MAP, even in the presence of missing data. This allows continuous assessment of the cerebral autoregulation mechanism, which is an important indicator of secondary brain damage and mortality.

Inferred MTGP hyperparameters were also able to increase classification performance on mortality prediction of ICU patients. The use of temporal information in clinical care is fundamental, and the large number of independent devices used in a modern ICU provides heterogeneous data. Using our method to summarize heterogenous clinical patient data into a more concise form, clinicians can leverage the collective knowledge of patient trajectories and outcomes. Concise representations of clinical notes are easier for clinicians to use, because they aggregate multi-author notes over time into topic timeseries that are more easily labeled (e.g. by viewing the top words) and tracked over a patient's record.

The main limitation in using this approach to characterize timeseries is computational cost. We conducted an exhaustive grid search over the constrained hyperparameter space. Computational costs may be addressed using a recently proposed Bayesian optimization for automatically tuning the MTGP hyperparameters (Swersky, Snoek, and Adams 2013) in large datasets. In a "real-time" setting, the computational cost for m tasks is $O(m^3, n^3)$. An overview of sparse GP methods is presented in (Quionero-Candela and Rasmussen 2005), which aims to find a smaller set of pseudo-inputs n' to reduce computational complexity. Further improvement is possible by 1) exploiting the Kronecker product (Stegle et al. 2011), 2) limiting the training data to the same time instances of each dimension of the data (Evgeniou, Micchelli, and Pontil 2005), or 3) by using recursive algorithms (Pillonetto, Dinuzzo, and De Nicolao 2010). Applications that require close-to-real-time retraining (e.g. Experiment 2), would benefit from these techniques, while operating over longer time-scales would be less sensitive.

7 Acknowledgements

This research was funded in part by the Intel Science and Technology Center for Big Data, the National Library of Medicine Biomedical Informatics Research Training grant (NIH/NLM 2T15 LM007092-22), and the R01 grant EB001659 from the National Institute of Biomedical Imaging and Bioengineering (NIBIB) of the National Institutes of Health (NIH). MAFP was supported by the RCUK Digital Economy Programme and FCT, Portugal. DAC was supported by a Royal Academy of Engineering Research Fellowship and by the Wellcome Trust and EPSRC. MF was supported by the A*STAR Graduate Scholarship.

Appendix

Supplementary material at http://mghassem.mit.edu/wp-content/uploads/2014/11/suppGhassemiAAAI2015.pdf.

References

Blei, D.; Ng, A.; and Jordan, M. 2003. Latent dirichlet allocation. *JMLR* 3(5):993–1022.

Bonilla, E. V.; Chai, K. M. A.; and Williams, C. K. 2007. Multi-task gaussian process prediction. In *Advances in Neural Information Processing Systems*, 153–160.

Breslow, M. J., and Badawi, O. 2012. Severity scoring in the critically ill: Part 1interpretation and accuracy of outcome prediction scoring systems. *CHEST Journal* 141(1):245–252.

Clifton, D.; Clifton, L.; Hugueny, S.; Wong, D.; and Tarassenko, L. 2013a. An extreme function theory for novelty detection. *Selected Topics in Signal Processing, IEEE Journal of* 7(1):28–37.

Clifton, L.; Clifton, D.; Pimentel, M.; Watkinson, P.; and Tarassenko, L. 2013b. Gaussian processes for personalized e-health monitoring with wearable sensors. *Biomedical Engineering, IEEE Transactions on* 60(1):193–197.

Czosnyka, M.; Smielewski, P.; Kirkpatrick, P.; Laing, R.; Menon, D.; and Pickard, J. 1997. Continuous assessment of the cerebral vasomotor reactivity in head injury. *Neurosurgery* 41(1):11–17.

Durichen, R.; Pimentel, M.; Clifton, L.; Schweikard, A.; and Clifton, D. 2014. Multi-task gaussian processes for multivariate physiological time-series analysis.

Evgeniou, T.; Micchelli, C. A.; and Pontil, M. 2005. Learning multiple tasks with kernel methods. In *Journal of Machine Learning Research*, 615637. 00441.

Feng, M.; Loy, L.; Zhang, F.; and Guan, C. 2011. Artifact removal for intracranial pressure monitoring signals: a robust solution with signal decomposition. In *Conf Proc IEEE Eng Med Biol Soc*, 797–801. American Medical Informatics Association.

Fox, E. B.; Sudderth, E. B.; Jordan, M. I.; and Willsky, A. S. 2011. Joint modeling of multiple related time series via the beta process. *arXiv preprint arXiv:1111.4226*.

Ghassemi, M.; Naumann, T.; Doshi-Velez, F.; Brimmer, N.; Joshi, R.; Rumshisky, A.; and Szolovits, P. 2014. Unfolding physiological state: Mortality modelling in intensive care units. 75–84.

Griffiths, T., and Steyvers, M. 2004. Finding scientific topics. In *PNAS*, volume 101, 5228–5235.

Hlatky, R.; Valadka, A. B.; and Robertson, C. S. 2005. Intracranial pressure response to induced hypertension: role of dynamic pressure autoregulation. *Neurosurgery* 57(5):917–923.

Hug, C. W., and Szolovits, P. 2009. Icu acuity: real-time models versus daily models. In *AMIA Annual Symposium Proceedings*, volume 2009, 260. American Medical Informatics Association.

Joshi, R., and Szolovits, P. 2012. Prognostic physiology: Modeling patient severity in intensive care units using radial domain folding. In *AMIA Annual Symposium Proceedings*, volume 2012, 1276. American Medical Informatics Association.

Lasko, T. A.; Denny, J. C.; and Levy, M. A. 2013. Computational phenotype discovery using unsupervised feature learning over noisy, sparse, and irregular clinical data. *PloS one* 8(6):e66341.

Le Gall, J.-R.; Loirat, P.; Alperovitch, A.; Glaser, P.; Granthil, C.; Mathieu, D.; Mercier, P.; Thomas, R.; and Villers, D. 1984. A simplified acute physiology score for icu patients. *Critical care medicine* 12(11):975–977.

Lehman, L.-w.; Saeed, M.; Long, W.; Lee, J.; and Mark, R. 2012. Risk stratification of icu patients using topic models inferred from unstructured progress notes. In *AMIA Annual Symposium Proceedings*, volume 2012, 505. American Medical Informatics Association.

Li, Q., and Clifford, G. 2012. Dynamic time warping and machine learning for signal quality assessment of pulsatile signals. *Physiological Measurement* 33(9):1491.

Lin, J.; Keogh, E.; Wei, L.; and Lonardi, S. 2007. Experiencing sax: a novel symbolic representation of time series. *Data Mining and Knowledge Discovery* 15(2):107–144.

Marlin, B. M.; Kale, D. C.; Khemani, R. G.; and Wetzel, R. C. 2012. Unsupervised pattern discovery in electronic health care data using probabilistic clustering models. In *Proceedings of the 2nd ACM SIGHIT International Health Informatics Symposium*, 389–398. ACM.

Pillonetto, G.; Dinuzzo, F.; and De Nicolao, G. 2010. Bayesian online multitask learning of gaussian processes. *Pattern Analysis and Machine Intelligence, IEEE Transactions on* 32(2):193205. 00025.

Quionero-Candela, J., and Rasmussen, C. E. 2005. A unifying view of sparse approximate gaussian process regression. *J. Mach. Learn. Res.* 6:19391959.

Rasmussen, C. E., and Williams, C. K. I. 2006. *Gaussian Processes for Machine Learning (Adaptive Computation and Machine Learning)*. The MIT Press.

Saeed, M., and Mark, R. 2006. A novel method for the efficient retrieval of similar multiparameter physiologic time series using wavelet-based symbolic representations. In *AMIA Annual Symposium Proceedings*, volume 2006, 679. American Medical Informatics Association.

Saeed, M.; Villarroel, M.; Reisner, A. T.; Clifford, G.; Lehman, L.-W.; Moody, G.; Heldt, T.; Kyaw, T. H.; Moody, B.; and Mark, R. G. 2011. Multiparameter intelligent monitoring in intensive care ii (mimic-ii): a public-access intensive care unit database. *Critical care medicine* 39(5):952.

Stegle, O.; Fallert, S.; MacKay, D. J. C.; and Brage, S. 2008. Gaussian process robust regression for noisy heart rate data. *Biomedical Engineering, IEEE Transactions on* 55(9):2143–2151.

Stegle, O.; Lippert, C.; Mooij, J. M.; Lawrence, N. D.; and Borgwardt, K. M. 2011. Efficient inference in matrix-variate gaussian models with$\backslash$ iid observation noise. In *Advances in Neural Information Processing Systems*, 630638.

Swersky, K.; Snoek, J.; and Adams, R. P. 2013. Multi-task bayesian optimization. In *Advances in Neural Information Processing Systems*, 2004–2012.

Syed, Z., and Guttag, J. V. 2011. Unsupervised similarity-based risk stratification for cardiovascular events using long-term time-series data. *Journal of Machine Learning Research* 12:999–1024.

Vincent, J.-L. 2013. Critical care-where have we been and where are we going? *Critical Care* 17(Suppl 1):S2.

Wackernagel, H. 2003. *Multivariate Geostatistics*. Springer.

Werner, C., and Engelhard, K. 2007. Pathophysiology of traumatic brain injury. *Br. J. Anaesth* 99(1):4–9.

Proceedings of the Twenty-Ninth AAAI Conference on Artificial Intelligence

Probabilistic Graphical Models for Boosting Cardinal and Ordinal Peer Grading in MOOCs

Fei Mi, Dit-Yan Yeung
Department of Computer Science and Engineering
Hong Kong University of Science and Technology
Hong Kong
fmi@cse.ust.hk, dyyeung@cse.ust.hk

Abstract

With the enormous scale of massive open online courses (MOOCs), peer grading is vital for addressing the assessment challenge for open-ended assignments or exams while at the same time providing students with an effective learning experience through involvement in the grading process. Most existing MOOC platforms use simple schemes for aggregating peer grades, e.g., taking the median or mean. To enhance these schemes, some recent research attempts have developed machine learning methods under either the cardinal setting (for absolute judgment) or the ordinal setting (for relative judgment). In this paper, we seek to study both cardinal and ordinal aspects of peer grading within a common framework. First, we propose novel extensions to some existing probabilistic graphical models for cardinal peer grading. Not only do these extensions give superior performance in cardinal evaluation, but they also outperform conventional ordinal models in ordinal evaluation. Next, we combine cardinal and ordinal models by augmenting ordinal models with cardinal predictions as prior. Such combination can achieve further performance boosts in both cardinal and ordinal evaluations, suggesting a new research direction to pursue for peer grading on MOOCs. Extensive experiments have been conducted using real peer grading data from a course called "Science, Technology, and Society in China I" offered by HKUST on the Coursera platform.

Introduction

Massive open online courses (MOOCs) are drawing increased attention lately because they can go well beyond the boundaries of traditional classrooms and audiences. While each offering of a traditional course delivered by a famous professor from a top university can typically benefit at most hundreds of students, and only students, an online version can easily scale it up by several orders of magnitude and make it available to people from all walks of life around the globe. However, the massive scale of MOOCs poses great challenges to student assessment. While most existing MOOCs simply give multiple-choice assignment or exam questions which can be graded automatically, open-ended and free-response exercises or essays are arguably vital for assessing learning outcomes of many courses (Paré and Joordens 2008). Unfortunately, satisfactory automatic grading of such assessment forms is beyond the current state of the art. A practical approach to tackle this problem is *peer grading* or *peer assessment* (Godlee et al. 2003; Sadler and Good 2006), in which students also play the role of graders in grading a small number of assignments submitted by other students according to the rubrics or benchmarks provided by the course instructor. The final score assigned to a submission is usually some aggregate, such as the median or mean, of the peer grades given by the graders. Due to the great diversity in student background, purpose and engagement, applying peer grading to give students a fair judgment of their learning efforts and achievements is hardly a trivial task. For example, by monitoring the registration information and accessing IP addresses of the students in one of the MOOCs offered by our university on the Coursera platform, we found the students were from around 160 different countries. Also, a recent study (Anderson et al. 2014) showed that students in a MOOC often exhibit different engagement styles probably corresponding to different purposes.

There are generally two basic rationales behind peer grading research, namely, cardinal and ordinal. In cardinal peer grading or absolute judgment (Barnett 2003; Paré and Joordens 2008), the peer evaluations for assignments are in the form of explicit numerical scores. This cardinal setting is currently the most common choice for MOOCs. Its goal is usually to minimize the absolute prediction deviation from some ground truth. However, (Shah et al. 2013; 2014) argued that it is sometimes easier for non-expert peer graders to make comparison than to give absolute scores and hence ordinal evaluation can sometimes be more effective than cardinal evaluation. As demonstrated by (Stewart, Brown, and Chater 2005; Carterette et al. 2008; Shah et al. 2014), on specific tasks, relative judgment or ordinal evaluation is more accurate than absolute judgment or cardinal evaluation. In ordinal peer grading, peer graders perform ordinal comparisons by ranking different assignments in terms of quality. A special case is pairwise comparison in which two assignments are compared at a time. The goal of ordinal peer grading is to predict the relative ranking correctly. We note that curved grading is used by many courses. As such, even absolute scores have to be converted into percentiles before the final grades are assigned. Thus we believe that both the cardinal and ordinal aspects have important roles to play in peer grading.

Before we proceed to focus on peer grading for MOOCs, we note that reviewing or ranking items is a broad topic. Some examples include ranking search results (Aslam and Montague 2001; Joachims 2002), reviewing conference or journal papers (Peters and Ceci 1982; Harnad 2000; Rowland 2002), admitting college students, as well as voting for candidates as a social choice problem (Coughlin 1992; Arrow 2012). Without going into a detailed comparison due to page constraints, we just emphasize that peer grading for MOOCs is somewhat unique in that the peer grades are often very sparse and a total order of all the items is needed to evaluate all students. Peer grading is also related to a rapidly growing area called crowdscourcing (Surowiecki 2005; Howe 2006) which seeks to take advantage of the wisdom of the crowd. A crucial research issue in crowdsourcing is how to aggregate the results provided by individual workers to give better-quality results.

The main contribution of this paper is twofold:

- We propose novel extensions to some state-of-the-art probabilistic graphical models for cardinal peer grading (Piech et al. 2013). Based on both average-case and worst-case performance criteria, our models show improvement in cardinal evaluation. Moreover, our extensions also outperform conventional ordinal models significantly in ordinal evaluation.
- We combine cardinal and ordinal models by augmenting ordinal models with the cardinal predictions as prior. Such combination can achieve further performance boosts in both cardinal and ordinal evaluations.

To our knowledge, this is the first research work which studies both the cardinal and ordinal aspects of peer grading within a common framework.

Related Work

We first review some existing methods for peer grading under the cardinal setting for predicting scores and the ordinal setting for predicting ranking or pairwise preferences.

The Vancouver algorithm (de Alfaro and Shavlovsky 2014) measures each student's grading accuracy by comparing the grades assigned by the student with the grades given to the same submissions by other students. Specifically, the grading accuracy is determined by the grading variance and higher weights are assigned to graders with higher grading accuracy. It iteratively updates the grading variance of each user from the consensus grades and computes more precise consensus grades from the updated grader variance. Inspired by the PageRank algorithm (Page et al. 1999) which was first used by the Google search engine, the PeerRank algorithm (Walsh 2014) was proposed as another iterative consensus algorithm. It relates a grader's grading ability to her performance in the course because the peer graders are also students. In (Patricia, Nardine, and Carles 2014), a trust graph is built over the referees and is used to compute the weights for assessment aggregation. Incorporated in the trust network are staff grades that are used for performance evaluation. Most related to our research is the work reported in (Piech et al. 2013) which proposed probabilistic models that model the relationships between the grader's bias and reliability, the true score of each submission, and the observed peer grades. Their PG_3 model assumes that high-scoring students tend to be more reliable as graders. The realization of this idea is extended in our proposed models to be described in the next section.

For ordinal methods, the Bradley-Terry model is used in (Shah et al. 2013) to learn the latent ability of the students from ordinal peer comparisons and perform cross-validation experiments to predict peer preferences. In (Raman and Joachims 2014), several statistical models for ordinal comparison, including the Bradley-Terry Model, Mallows Model, Thurstone Model, and Plackett-Luce Model, are applied to peer grading tasks. Performance evaluation is based on data collected from the real peer grading process of a (traditional) class consisting of 170 students.

An observation from these previous studies is worth mentioning. Not surprisingly, having more peer evaluations per submission improves the estimation accuracy for both the cardinal and ordinal settings. However, if a student is given too many assignments to grade, she may just complete the task randomly, defeating the purposes of improving the estimation accuracy and benefiting the students through the peer review process as a learning experience. Consequently, data sparsity is more of the norm than the exception and hence is a key issue to address.

Cardinal Peer Grading

We first study cardinal peer grading in this section. Our models are extensions of the probabilistic models proposed in (Piech et al. 2013). Like the models (named PG_1 to PG_3) in (Piech et al. 2013), we explicitly model the bias and reliability of each grader. While the bias corresponds to a constant grade inflation or deflation, the reliability measures how close on average is the assessment by a grader from the latent true score of the submission after eliminating the bias. Concretely, the reliability is defined as the inverse variance (or precision) of a Gaussian distribution. The experiments in (Piech et al. 2013) show that PG_3, which uses a linear relationship to relate the reliability and true score of a grader in a deterministic fashion, outperforms PG_1 which is a simpler model. We note that the idea of assigning grades by also capturing the grader's effort and grading accuracy has been exploited by other researchers, e.g., (Shah et al. 2013; Walsh 2014).

Although dependency exists between a grader's reliability and her true score, we believe that a linear deterministic relationship is overly rigid and may not provide a good enough model for many graders. Here we propose to relax it by using a probabilistic relationship instead, resulting in two models referred to as PG_4 and PG_5 in the sequel. Besides modeling the effect of the grader's true score on her reliability, we have also considered some other features such as the course forum reputation score, performance in in-video quizzes, and number of course forum views. However, none of them turns out to be more effective than the grader's true score. This is at least true for the course considered in this study. As such, we will only focus on the influence of a grader's true score on her grading reliability in this paper.

Notations

Let v denote an arbitrary grader and V the collection of all graders. Similarly, let u denote an arbitrary student (a.k.a. gradee) whose submissions are graded and U the collection of all students. Table 1 shows the variables used in the graphical model. We note that the only observed variable z_u^v represents the score or peer assessment assigned to a submission of student u by grader v.

Notation	Description
τ_v	Reliability of grader v
b_v	Bias of grader v
s_u	True score for a submission of student u
z_u^v	Score assigned to a submission of u by v

Table 1: Notations used in our models

Graphical Model

As depicted in Figure 1, the plate notation is used to represent separately the gradee and grader roles for clarity. For the peer grading setting, however, the gradees and graders actually correspond to (roughly) the same group of students. The first three variables in Table 1 are latent variables in the graphical model for the reliability, bias, and true score of a student, and the last one is the only observed variable involving both a gradee and a grader. The hyperparameters $\mu_0, \gamma_0, \beta_0, \eta_0$ are used for specifying the probability distributions of the latent variables. A major difference between this model and the model in (Piech et al. 2013) is the way in which the relationship between the reliability and true score of a grader is modeled. Here we impose a probabilistic relationship between them. Moreover, unlike PG_3, we represent the reliability explicitly as a random variable in the graphical model to make it easier for future extension to incorporate other factors that can influence the reliability.

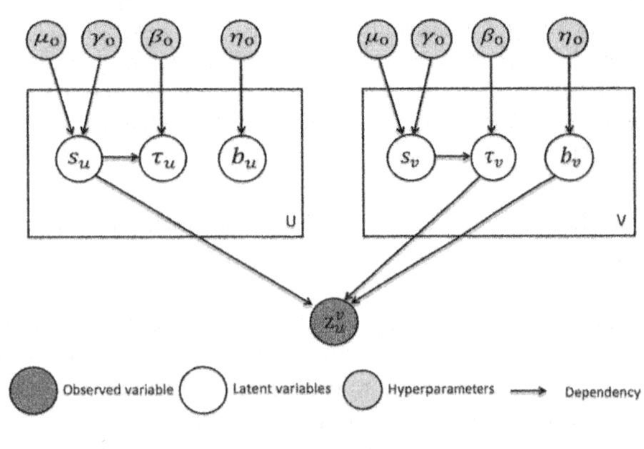

Figure 1: Graphical model

Two Model Variants: PG_4 and PG_5

PG_4 *Model*	PG_5 *Model*
$\tau_v \sim \mathcal{G}(s_v, \beta_0)$	$\tau_v \sim \mathcal{N}(s_v, \frac{1}{\beta_0})$
$b_v \sim \mathcal{N}(0, \frac{1}{\eta_0})$	$b_v \sim \mathcal{N}(0, \frac{1}{\eta_0})$
$s_u \sim \mathcal{N}(\mu_0, \frac{1}{\gamma_0})$	$s_u \sim \mathcal{N}(\mu_0, \frac{1}{\gamma_0})$
$z_u^v \sim \mathcal{N}(s_u + b_v, \frac{1}{\tau_v})$	$z_u^v \sim \mathcal{N}(s_u + b_v, \frac{\lambda}{\tau_v})$

To realize the graphical model formulation in Figure 1, we propose two model variants called PG_4 and PG_5. In PG_4, a grader's reliability τ_v follows the gamma distribution with rate parameter β_0 and the grader's true score s_v as the shape parameter. Consequently, as desired, the mean reliability of a grader is s_v/β_0, which increases with her latent true score.

On the other hand, PG_5 assumes that τ_v follows the Gaussian distribution with s_v as the mean and $1/\beta_0$ as the variance. We note that the β_0 parameter in PG_5 is different from that in PG_4, but we want to describe both PG_4 and PG_5 using the same graphical model in Figure 1. For both PG_4 and PG_5, the mean reliability of grader v is positively correlated with her true score s_v and both the bias and true score follow the Gaussian distributions. The mean bias across all graders is assumed to be zero and the mean true score μ_0 is set to the average score of all the submissions. The observed score z_u^v follows the Gaussian distribution with the mean equal to the true score plus the grader's bias and the variance inversely related to the grader's reliability. In this sense, the hyperparameter β_0 in PG_4 plays an important role in scaling τ_v to a proper range before plugging into the variance of the Gaussian density. In PG_5, the scale of τ_v depends on s_v or the grading scheme for a specific grading task, so we have a hyperparameter λ, similar to the role of β_0 in PG_4, to scale the variance of the Gaussian density. Due to page constraints, details of the model inference procedures for PG_4 and PG_5 are described in the appendix. They are mostly based on Gibbs sampling by running for 300 iterations with the first 60 burn-in samples eliminated. For the latent variables s_u in PG_4 and τ_v in PG_5, however, closed-form distributions are not available for performing Gibbs sampling and hence discrete approximation is applied with fine separating intervals. Moreover, for a small group of graders with no submission and hence no score for an assignment, we assume that they have the lowest scores and relatively low reliability among all graders for a particular assignment.

Dataset

The peer grading dataset used in our experiments is from a course called "Science, Technology, and Society in China I" offered by our university on the Coursera platform. Table 2 gives summary statistics of the three assignments involving peer grading. The peer grading method adopted by the course is detailed below:

- There are three assignments, each of which asks the students to write a short essay with suggested word limit (250 for the first and 500 each for the second and third ones).

- For each assignment, each student was asked to evaluate three other submissions although some ended up evaluating more and some less. A few even evaluated more than 10. Grader assignment was done automatically and randomly by the system with the goal of maintaining a similar number of graders for each submission.
- Grading was based on three rubrics provided: 0-7, 0-7, 0-7 for assignment 1 and 0-7, 0-7, 0-11 for assignments 2 and 3. The median of the peer grades for each rubric was used to compute the assignment score for each submission.

For each assignment, as in Table 2, around 20 submissions were graded by the course instructor, and on average, there are 4 peer graders per staff-graded assignment. We treat these staff grades as ground truth for those submissions involved. This is a versatile dataset for peer grading research. Not only is it reasonably large with 7546 peer grades, but it also contains more submissions with staff grades than some other related datasets, e.g., 3 to 5 staff-graded submissions per assignment in (Piech et al. 2013). As such, both cardinal and ordinal evaluations using ground-truth data can be conducted.

	Assignment 1	Assignment 2	Assignment 3
# finished students	1202	845	724
# peer grades	3201	2261	2084
# staff grades	23	19	23
Full score	21	25	25
Mean score	14.8 (70%)	17.2 (69%)	16.5 (58%)

Table 2: Summary statistics of assignments for peer grading

Results for Cardinal Experiments

Table 3, Table 4, and Figure 2 show experimental results for cardinal evaluation on the three assignments with the staff grades acting as ground truth for the instructor-graded submissions. From the probabilistic models, we can see that the precision parameter of the Gaussian distribution for the observed score is determined by the grader's reliability. So in PG_4, we mainly tune the rate parameter β_0 which is the rate parameter in the gamma distribution for the grader's reliability. For PG_5, we mainly tune λ in the density function for the observed score. During experiments, we found that PG_3 is more sensitive to hyperparameters due to their linearity assumption, compared with β_0 in PG_4 and λ in PG_5. Moreover, the hyperparameters η_0 and γ_0 in PG_4 and PG_5, which control the variance of the grader's bias and that of the true score respectively, need to be tuned slightly. During the parameter tuning process, we try multiple combinations of η_0 and γ_0 in the range $[0.04, 0.2]$. For each combination, we perform line search within a certain range on β_0 for PG_4 and on λ for PG_5. The search range is $[100, 600]$ with a fixed interval of 50. For completeness, sensitivity analysis of the hyperparameters is provided in the appendix.

Average-Case Performance Here we use the root-mean-square error (RMSE) as an average measure for the difference between the score predicted by a model and that assigned by the instructor. Table 3 reports the best results, averaged over 10 runs, among hyperparameter settings in the range considered. Both the mean and standard deviation over 10 runs are shown for each assignment. We can see that PG_3, PG_4, and PG_5 have lower RMSE than the Median baseline and PG_1, showing that coupling a grader's reliability and true score is effective. Moreover, compared with PG_3, PG_4 and PG_5 can achieve quite significant RMSE improvement for assignments 2 and 3 although they are slightly worse than PG_3 for assignment 1. On average, PG_5 gives the best performance with 33% improvement for assignments 1 and 3 and 15% improvement for assignment 2 over the Median baseline which is used by Coursera as the default scheme. Relatively speaking, PG_4 performs slightly worse than PG_5 but it still outperforms PG_3 on average. Although PG_3 performs the best for assignment 1, its performance for assignments 2 and 3 is much worse than PG_4 and PG_5. We believe the probabilistic dependency between a grader's reliability and true score as adopted by PG_4 and PG_5 plays a crucial role in achieving the performance boost.

	Assignment 1		Assignment 2		Assignment 3	
	Mean	*Std*	*Mean*	*Std*	*Mean*	*Std*
Median	4.94		5.54		4.12	
PG_1	3.77 (23%)	0.02	4.93 (11%)	0.03	3.66 (11%)	0.01
PG_3	**3.22 (35%)**	0.02	5.24 (5%)	0.04	3.15 (23%)	0.02
PG_4	3.35 (32%)	0.05	4.75 (14%)	0.06	2.83 (31%)	0.09
PG_5	3.31 (33%)	0.05	**4.69** (15%)	0.05	**2.76 (33%)**	0.09

Table 3: Experimental results for cardinal models. Median represents taking the medium of the peer grades. PG_1 and PG_3 are models proposed in (Piech et al. 2013) and PG_4 and PG_5 are our models described above.

Worst-Case Performance and Model Sensitivity We also assess the worst-case performance of each method by measuring the maximum prediction deviation from the instructor's score. Table 4 shows that PG_4 and PG_5 have lower worst-case prediction errors than PG_3 for all three assignments, with PG_5 being the better. Moreover, from Figure 2 in which the submissions are sorted according to the instructor's grades, we can see that the predicted scores of PG_4 and PG_5 fluctuate less from the instructor's grades compared with PG_3. For some submissions with similar instructor's grades, the predicted scores by PG_3 differ quite significantly. For example, the 7th and 8th submissions of assignment 1 have the same score from the instructor but the predicted scores by PG_3 differ by around 8 points. Too much fluctuation is undesirable and can flag concerns about grading fairness as the ranking of the submissions according to the scores will be affected more seriously.

	Assignment 1	Assignment 2	Assignment 3
PG_3	6.52	11.10	6.77
PG_4	5.84	9.86	6.70
PG_5	**5.81**	**9.85**	**5.79**

Table 4: Maximum prediction deviation from the ground truth for the optimal settings in Table 3.

Although Table 3 shows that PG_3 performs the best for assignment 1 under an average-case performance measure, considering also its worst-case performance and the fairness concern does not favor PG_3 as the preferred choice. In PG_3, the latent true score of a student is inferred directly from both the observed score when she plays the role of a gradee and the observed scores when she plays the role of a grader. However, in PG_4 and PG_5, the observed scores by a grader only infer her reliability, which then indirectly infers her true score. Consequently, the student's score in PG_4 and PG_5 is less sensitive to her own performance as a grader than PG_3. Considering various factors related to both average-case and worst-case performance assessment, it is fair to conclude that PG_4 and PG_5 outperform PG_3 under cardinal evaluation.

Ordinal Peer Grading

We now study the other aspect of peer grading, ordinal peer grading, and propose a novel approach to combining cardinal and ordinal models for enhanced performance. An ordinal peer grading task could be formulated as a rank aggregation problem (Dwork et al. 2001) or a preference learning problem (Chu and Ghahramani 2005; Fürnkranz and Hüllermeier 2010). In this paper, we consider a specific form of ordinal peer grading in terms of pairwise preferences (Fürnkranz and Hüllermeier 2003). In pairwise preference learning, a classical model is the Bradley-Terry model (Bradley and Terry 1952) which was recently applied to peer grading (Shah et al. 2013; Raman and Joachims 2014). Specifically, pairwise ordinal peer grading takes as training data examples with partial and possibly inconsistent pairwise preferences. The learning task is to predict from the data a total order or ranking of all the submissions.

Our proposition is to augment ordinal models, e.g., the Bradley-Terry model, with prior information from predictions of cardinal models studied in the previous section. For the sake of referencing, we refer to this extension as "Cardinal + Ordinal" models in the sequel. To gain a deeper understanding of this approach, we consider several combinations of cardinal and ordinal models in our experiments.

Combining Cardinal and Ordinal Models

We first briefly review the Bradley-Terry model which is referred to as BTL in (Shah et al. 2013) and BT in (Raman and Joachims 2014). In the ordinal setting, $u_i \succ_{\rho(v)} u_j$ indicates that grader v prefers u_i over u_j. The probability of observing $u_i \succ_{\rho(v)} u_j$ is defined using a logistic function with parameter $s_{u_i} - s_{u_j}$, where s_{u_i} and s_{u_j} are the latent true scores of submissions by u_i and u_j respectively:

$$\text{hypothesis} = P(u_i \succ_{\rho(v)} u_j) = \frac{1}{1+\exp(-(u_i - u_j))}$$

Besides using the Bradley-Terry model, some recent attempts such as RBTL (Shah et al. 2013) and BT+G (Raman and Joachims 2014) incorporate the grader's reliability to boost the performance of ordinal peer grading. The rationale for incorporating the grader's reliability in RBTL is similar to PG_3 while that for BT+G is similar to PG_1. If we assume a Gaussian prior on the latent true scores of all students with mean μ and variance σ^2, the cost function of the Bradley-Terry model is defined as follows:

$$\mathcal{L} = \frac{\lambda}{2\sigma^2} \sum_{u \in U} (s_u - \mu)^2 - \sum_{v \in V} \sum_{u_i \succ_{\rho(v)} u_j} \log(\text{hypothesis})$$

where the first term is a regularization term to avoid overfitting and the second term is the data likelihood term. Since the cost function above is jointly convex with respect to all the latent variables, stochastic gradient descent (SGD) can be used for solving the optimization problem.

Due to the data sparsity issue as discussed before, maximizing the data likelihood alone may lead to inconsistent and bad estimations. The regularization term defined based on the prior latent score distribution thus plays an important role. The original ordinal peer grading models (Shah et al. 2013; Raman and Joachims 2014) assume that all students have the same prior score distribution. Here, we propose to augment the ordinal models with the prior given by the predictions of the cardinal models. Alternatively, we may also interpret it as tuning the predictions of the cardinal models with the ordinal peer preferences. So the parameter μ in previous cost function is changed to the predicted score μ_u for submission u obtained from a cardinal model, with the modified cost function given by:

$$\mathcal{L} = \frac{\lambda}{2\sigma^2} \sum_{u \in U} (s_u - \mu_u)^2 - \sum_{v \in V} \sum_{s_{u_i} \succ_{\rho(v)} s_{u_j}} \log(\text{hypothesis})$$

This formulation offers a principled approach to combining both cardinal and ordinal evaluations.

Results for Ordinal Experiments

We first generate pairwise preferences from the cardinal evaluations of each peer grader to form the training data. Ties are excluded as they indicate lack of preference. Our underlying assumption is that the absolute evaluations of a grader on a set of assignments also reflect her ordinal preferences. Table 5 shows the results based on an accuracy measure that reflects the percentage of correctly evaluated pairs, which is similar to Kendall's tau rank correlation coefficient (Litchfield Jr and Wilcoxon 1955), except that we exclude ties and discordant pairs from consideration. For example, if there are 100 pairwise preferences based on the instructor's grading (with ties ignored) and a model correctly predicts 75 of them, then its accuracy is 0.75. The results in Table 5 are for the best hyperparameter settings averaged over 10 runs. For the "Cardinal + Ordinal" models, the best results also consider different cardinal priors corresponding to different hyperparameter settings explored by the cardinal models. Since preliminary investigation showed that the accuracy during testing converged fast, so we only report the average accuracy at iteration 30 for simplicity. We also report the results in Table 6 using the evaluation metric in Table 3 for cardinal evaluation.

We first note that two minor results about the pure ordinal models are consistent with those reported previously (Shah et al. 2013; Raman and Joachims 2014). First, the pure ordinal models have accuracy comparable with the Median baseline even though converting numerical scores to pairwise preferences incurs information loss. Second, modeling grader reliability in pure ordinal models (RBTL, BT+G) can slightly improve the performance of BT. Besides, we have found that simply maximizing the data likelihood as in BT Same Initial or BT Random Initial does not perform well,

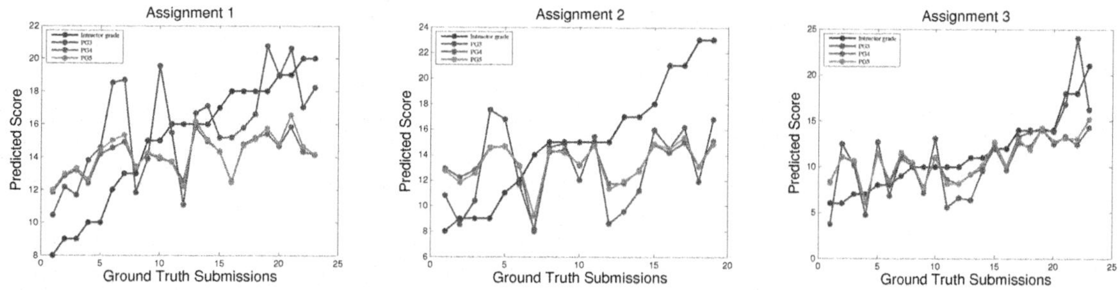

Figure 2: For the results in Table 3, the figures above show the exact predicted scores of PG_3, PG_4 and PG_5 compared with the instructor grades for the optimal settings reported in Table 3, with instructor grades sorted in ascending order.

showing that peer preferences alone have drawbacks in preference prediction.

On the other hand, our extensive experiments show two major results:

- Cardinal models can perform much better than pure ordinal models even for ordinal evaluation;
- Combining cardinal and ordinal models can further boost the accuracy in both cardinal and ordinal evaluations.

From results in Table 5, cardinal models outperform pure ordinal ones because they use fine-grained numerical information rather than binary comparisons (better or worse) in the ordinal setting. For example, with absolute evaluations, we can interpret the numerical scores as degree of preferences, and we could also model grader's bias from numerical evaluations. With the help of prior from cardinal models, combining cardinal and ordinal models ("Cardinal + Ordinal") gives the best ordinal accuracy for all three assignments among all the models. As it may be interpreted as tuning the cardinal predictions as well, we also evaluate the combined models in a cardinal way in Table 6, which shows consistent cardinal performance boost against all corresponding pure cardinal models for all three assignments in Table 3. For now, the ordinal comparisons are generated from cardinal evaluations. If ordinal data are generated directly, combining cardinal and ordinal models may be used to further tune and reinforce each other so that further improvement may be possible.

From another perspective, the technique to combine cardinal and ordinal models may be used to alleviate the data sparsity problem in peer grading as well. In other words, with cardinal evaluations, we can generate ordinal comparisons and combine the models using two types of input to boost accuracy. If we are forced to make only one choice, our recommendation would be a cardinal peer grading method which can obtain more accurate grade prediction as demonstrated above. In addition, from (Shah et al. 2013), ordinal models need more comparisons per grader to get a reasonable accuracy. For typical peer grading task with open-ended exercises of several hundred words, it is hard for peer graders to compare submissions in detail. At last, we maintain that it is easier for students to perform cardinal grading for typical peer grading tasks because the instructor's detailed cardinal rubrics can clarify students' thoughts, while quantizing the subjective and vague evaluation standard when making ordinal comparisons.

	Assignment 1	**Assignment 2**	**Assignment 3**
Cardinal Models			
PG_3	0.7526	0.6155	0.7775
PG_4	0.6928	0.6552	0.7854
PG_5	0.6979	0.6616	0.7889
"Cardinal + Ordinal" Models			
PG_3+BT	0.7577	0.6110	0.7892
PG_4+BT	0.7221	0.6484	0.7931
PG_5+BT	0.7191	0.6646	0.8000
PG_3+BT+G	0.7645	0.6587	0.7879
PG_4+BT+G	0.7145	0.7032	0.7896
PG_5+BT+G	0.7170	**0.7065**	**0.8013**
PG_3+RBTL	**0.7660**	0.6494	0.7979
PG_4+RBTL	0.7064	0.6745	0.7835
PG_5+RBTL	0.7201	0.6845	0.8009
Pure Ordinal Models			
BT (or BTL)	0.6536	0.6329	0.6896
RBTL	0.6583	0.6432	0.6996
BT+G	0.6547	0.6535	0.7009
BT Same Initial	0.6387	0.6194	0.6407
BT Random Initial	0.6381	0.6416	0.6667
Baseline Method			
Median	0.6043	0.6610	0.6753

Table 5: Ordinal evaluation results for different models. Cardinal models: described above but evaluated differently here. "Cardinal + Ordinal" models: ordinal models with predictions from different cardinal models as prior. Pure ordinal models: BTL and RBTL from (Shah et al. 2013), BT and BT+G from (Raman and Joachims 2014); BT Same Initial or BT Random Initial, similar to BT (or BTL), has no prior on the student scores for regularization with the same or random scores initially for all students. Median: baseline that takes the median of the peer grades.

Conclusion

In this paper, we have proposed a new probabilistic model for peer grading and a novel mechanism for combining cardinal and ordinal models. Extensive experiments on both cardinal and ordinal evaluations show promising results.

Acknowledgments

This research has been supported by *General Research Fund 621310* from the Research Grants Council of Hong Kong. We would also like to thank the instructor of the Coursera course, Naubahar Sharif, for letting us use the course data for our research and the Coursera support team in our uni-

	Assignment 1	Assignment 2	Assignment 3
PG_3+BT	3.04	5.30	3.18
PG_3+BT+G	3.01	**4.95**	**3.10**
PG_3+RBTL	**3.00**	5.04	3.15
PG_4+BT	3.47	4.87	3.03
PG_4+BT+G	**3.31**	**4.52**	2.91
PG_4+RBTL	3.44	4.70	**2.77**
PG_5+BT	3.30	4.77	2.93
PG_5+BT+G	3.35	**4.50**	2.74
PG_5+RBTL	**3.24**	4.62	**2.70**

Table 6: Cardinal evaluation (RMSE) results for "Cardinal+Ordinal" models

versity, particularly Tony Fung, for their help in accessing and processing the data.

References

Anderson, A.; Huttenlocher, D.; Kleinberg, J.; and Leskovec, J. 2014. Engaging with massive online courses. In *Proceedings of the 23rd International Conference on World Wide Web*, 687–698.

Arrow, K. J. 2012. *Social Choice and Individual Values*, volume 12. Yale University Press.

Aslam, J. A., and Montague, M. 2001. Models for metasearch. In *Proceedings of the 24th Annual International ACM SIGIR Conference on Research and Development in Information Retrieval*, 276–284.

Barnett, W. 2003. The modern theory of consumer behavior: Ordinal or cardinal? *The Quarterly Journal of Austrian Economics* 6(1):41–65.

Bradley, R. A., and Terry, M. E. 1952. Rank analysis of incomplete block designs: I. the method of paired comparisons. *Biometrika* 39(3/4):324–345.

Carterette, B.; Bennett, P. N.; Chickering, D. M.; and Dumais, S. T. 2008. Here or there. In *Advances in Information Retrieval*, 16–27.

Chu, W., and Ghahramani, Z. 2005. Preference learning with Gaussian processes. In *Proceedings of the 22nd International Conference on Machine learning*, 137–144.

Coughlin, P. J. 1992. *Probabilistic Voting Theory*. Cambridge University Press.

de Alfaro, L., and Shavlovsky, M. 2014. Crowdgrader: Crowdsourcing the evaluation of homework assignments. In *Proceedings of the 45th ACM Technical Symposium on Computer Science Education*, 415–420.

Dwork, C.; Kumar, R.; Naor, M.; and Sivakumar, D. 2001. Rank aggregation methods for the web. In *Proceedings of the 10th International Conference on World Wide Web*, 613–622.

Fürnkranz, J., and Hüllermeier, E. 2003. Pairwise preference learning and ranking. In *Proceedings of the 14th European Conference on Machine Learning*, 145–156.

Fürnkranz, J., and Hüllermeier, E. 2010. *Preference Learning*. Springer.

Godlee, F.; Jefferson, T.; Callaham, M.; Clarke, J.; Altman, D.; Bastian, H.; Bingham, C.; and Deeks, J. 2003. *Peer Review In Health Sciences*. BMJ Books London.

Harnad, S. 2000. The invisible hand of peer review. *Exploit Interactive* 5(April).

Howe, J. 2006. The rise of crowdsourcing. *Wired Magazine* 14(6):1–4.

Joachims, T. 2002. Optimizing search engines using clickthrough data. In *Proceedings of the 8th ACM SIGKDD International Conference on Knowledge Discovery and Data Mining*, 133–142.

Litchfield Jr, J. T., and Wilcoxon, F. 1955. Rank correlation method. *Analytical Chemistry* 27(2):299–300.

Page, L.; Brin, S.; Motwani, R.; and Winograd, T. 1999. The PageRank citation ranking: Bringing order to the web. Technical Report 1999-66, Stanford InfoLab.

Paré, D. E., and Joordens, S. 2008. Peering into large lectures: examining peer and expert mark agreement using peerScholar, an online peer assessment tool. *Journal of Computer Assisted Learning* 24(6):526–540.

Patricia, G.; Nardine, O.; and Carles, S. 2014. Collaborative assessment. In *Extended Proceedings of the 7th International Conference on Educational Data Mining (EDM 2014)*.

Peters, D. P., and Ceci, S. J. 1982. Peer-review practices of psychological journals: The fate of published articles, submitted again. *Behavioral and Brain Sciences* 5(02):187–195.

Piech, C.; Huang, J.; Chen, Z.; Do, C.; Ng, A.; and Koller, D. 2013. Tuned models of peer assessment in MOOCs. In *Proceedings for the 6th International Conference on Educational Data Mining.*, 153–160.

Raman, K., and Joachims, T. 2014. Methods for ordinal peer grading. In *Proceedings of the 20th ACM SIGKDD International Conference on Knowledge Discovery and Data mining*.

Rowland, F. 2002. The peer-review process. *Learned Publishing* 15(4):247–258.

Sadler, P. M., and Good, E. 2006. The impact of self- and peer-grading on student learning. *Educational Assessment* 11(1):1–31.

Shah, N. B.; Bradley, J. K.; Parekh, A.; Wainwright, M.; and Ramchandran, K. 2013. A case for ordinal peer-evaluation in moocs. In *NIPS Workshop on Data Driven Education*.

Shah, N. B.; Balakrishnan, S.; Bradley, J.; Parekh, A.; Ramchandran, K.; and Wainwright, M. 2014. When is it better to compare than to score? *arXiv preprint arXiv:1406.6618*.

Stewart, N.; Brown, G. D.; and Chater, N. 2005. Absolute identification by relative judgment. *Psychological Review* 112(4):881–911.

Surowiecki, J. 2005. *The Wisdom of Crowds*. Random House LLC.

Walsh, T. 2014. The peerrank method for peer assessment. In *Proceedings of the 21th European Conference on Artificial Intelligence*.

Efficient Computation of Semivalues for Game-Theoretic Network Centrality

Piotr L. Szczepański*
Warsaw University of Technology, Poland

Mateusz K. Tarkowski*
University of Oxford, United Kingdom

Tomasz P. Michalak[1,2] and **Paul Harrenstein**[1] and **Michael Wooldridge**[1]
[1]University of Oxford, United Kingdom
[2]University of Warsaw, Poland

Abstract

Solution concepts from cooperative game theory, such as the Shapley value or the Banzhaf index, have recently been advocated as interesting extensions of standard measures of node centrality in networks. While this direction of research is promising, the computation of game-theoretic centrality can be challenging. In an attempt to address the computational issues of game-theoretic network centrality, we present a generic framework for constructing game-theoretic network centralities. We prove that all extensions that can be expressed in this framework are computable in polynomial time. Using our framework, we present the first game-theoretic extensions of weighted and normalized degree centralities, impact factor centrality, distance-scaled and normalized betweenness centrality, and closeness and normalized closeness centralities.

Introduction

Determining whether a given node or edge in a network is more significant (or *central*) than another is an important research topic, studied in fields like social network analysis, biology, and computer science. To this end, researchers have proposed a range of *centrality measures* that aim to numerically characterise the centrality of a node or edge. Among the numerous centrality measures proposed in the literature, the four most fundamental and prominent are *degree centrality*, *closeness centrality*, *betweenness centrality* (Freeman 1979), and *eigenvector centrality* (Bonacich 1972).

Recently, solution concepts from the field of cooperative game theory (e.g., the Shapley value (Shapley 1953), the Banzhaf power index (Banzhaf 1965), and, more generally, semivalues (Dubey, Neyman, and Weber 1981)) have been advocated as measures of network centrality extending standard centrality measures (Gómez et al. 2003; Amer, Giménez, and Magaña 2012). The basic idea behind game-theoretic network centrality is to consider network nodes as players in a cooperative game (where players form coalitions and divide between them the payoff from cooperation). In this setting, game-theoretic solution concepts of payoff division become metrics for network analysis. We refer the reader to Tarkowski et al. (2014) for an overview on the topic. This approach has been considered for a variety of applications, such as social and organisational network analysis (Suri and Narahari 2010), biological networks (Kotter et al. 2007), and covert networks (Michalak et al. 2013a).

Many studies of the complexity of game-theoretic solution concepts have been carried out over the past decade (see Chalkiadakis, Elkind, and Wooldridge (2012)). Unfortunately, for many representations of games, the solution concepts of most interest are computationally intractable (typically, $\#P$-complete). However, only a few studies to date have investigated whether negative complexity results carry over when these solution concepts are applied to network centrality. Among those, Michalak et al. (2013a) established that computing the Shapley value-based centrality measure for connectivity games on graphs is $\#P$-complete. It is also known that various other cooperative games on graphs that could be used as centrality measures are challenging (Nebel 2011; Aziz and de Keijzer 2014). [1]

Fortunately, positive results have also been established. In particular, it is possible to compute in polynomial time various Shapley value-based centrality measures that extend standard degree and closeness centrality (Michalak et al. 2013b). A similar positive result was obtained for the standard betweenness centrality (Szczepański, Michalak, and Rahwan 2012). However, many other centrality measures have not been extended to game-theoretic centrality, nor is the computational complexity of such extensions known.

In this paper, we address this issue. We present a general framework in which it is possible to construct a variety of game-theoretic network centralities (and, in particular, extensions of standard centrality measures) such that they can be computed in polynomial time. Using this key result, we are able to present game-theoretic extensions of weighted and normalized degree centralities, impact factor centrality, distance-scaled and normalized betweenness centrality, and closeness and normalized closeness centralities. As a corollary of our general result, all of these centrality measures can be computed in polynomial time.

*Both first authors contributed equally to the paper.

[1]In principle, any cooperative game described on a graph and an associated solution concept can be considered as a game-theoretic centrality measure.

Preliminaries

A *network* is a graph $G = (V, E)$, where V is a set of nodes and E a subset of unordered pairs (v, u) of nodes in V. A *path* π_{st} from node s to node t in a graph G is an ordered set $(v_0, v_1, \ldots, v_n)$ such that $v_0 = s$ and $v_n = t$ and $(v_i, v_{i+1}) \in E$ for all i with $1 \leq i < n$. We define the set of *neighbours* of a node v and a subset C of nodes by $E(i) = \{j : (i, j) \in E\}$ and $E(C) = \bigcup_{i \in C} E(i) \setminus C$, respectively. We refer to the *degree* of a node v by $deg(v) = |E(v)|$. The *distance* from a node s to a node t is denoted by $dist(s, t)$ and is defined as the size of the shortest path between s and t. The distance between a node v and a subset of nodes $C \subseteq V$ is denoted by $dist(C, v) = \min_{u \in C} dist(u, v)$. Paths, neighbours, and distances are prominent in definitions of *network centrality measures*, i.e., functions that associate with each node a real value that represents its centrality, and we will refer to them as *(graph) items*.

A cooperative game consists of a set $N = \{1, 2, \ldots, n\}$ of *players* and a *characteristic function* $\nu : 2^N \to \mathbb{R}$, which assigns to each *coalition* $C \subseteq N$ of players a real value (or payoff) indicating its performance, where $\nu(\emptyset) = 0$. A *cooperative game in characteristic function form* is a pair (N, ν), but we will refer to it simply by ν. In our network setting we will always consider the set of players as the set of nodes V in a graph G. The *grand coalition* is the set N of all players.

A basic research problem in cooperative game theory is how to divide the payoff from cooperation (usually the value of the grand coalition) among the players. *Semivalues* (Dubey, Neyman, and Weber 1981) represent an important class of solutions to this problem. To define semivalues, let us denote by $\mathrm{MC}(C, i)$ the marginal contribution of the player i to the coalition C, i.e., $\mathrm{MC}(C, i) = \nu(C \cup \{i\}) - \nu(C)$. Let $\beta : \{0, 1, \ldots, |N| - 1\} \to [0, 1]$ be a function such that $\sum_{k=0}^{|N|-1} \beta(k) = 1$. Intuitively, when we calculate the expected marginal contribution of a node, $\beta(k)$ will be the probability that a coalition of size k is chosen for this node to join. This is why $\beta(k)$ is defined on values ranging from 0 to $|N| - 1$. Since a node i cannot join a coalition that it is already in, we only need to look at coalitions not containing i. Given β, the semivalue $\phi_i(\nu)$ for a player i in cooperative game ν is:

$$\phi_i(\nu) = \sum_{0 \leq k < |V|} \beta(k) \mathbb{E}_{C_k}[\mathrm{MC}(C_k, i)], \qquad (1)$$

where C_k is the random variable of all possible coalitions of size k drawn with uniform probability form the set $N \setminus \{i\}$, and $\mathbb{E}_{C_k}[\cdot]$ is the expected value operator for the random variable C_k.

The Shapley value (Shapley 1953) and the *Banzhaf index* of power (Banzhaf 1965) are two prominent and well-known examples of semivalues. They are defined by β-functions $\beta^{Shapley}$ and $\beta^{Banzhaf}$, respectively:

$$\beta^{Shapley}(i) = \frac{1}{|N|} \quad \text{and} \quad \beta^{Banzhaf}(i) = \frac{\binom{|N|-1}{i}}{2^{|N|-1}}.$$

For the purposes of defining a cooperative game on any network, we will systematically associate characteristic functions with graphs through *representation functions*.

Definition 1 (Representation function) *A* representation function *is a function ψ that maps every graph $G = (V, E)$ onto a cooperative game (N, ν_G) with $N = V$.*

Now, solution concepts like semivalues can be used in the network setting by applying them to the characteristic function that a network represents.

Definition 2 (Game-theoretic centrality measure) *Formally, we define a game-theoretic centrality measure as a pair (ψ, ϕ) consisting of a representation function ψ and a solution concept ϕ.*

Example 1 *Let us consider a game-theoretic centrality measure $(\psi_R, \phi^{Shapley})$. We say that ψ_R is a representation function since it associates a coalitional game with any graph $G = (V, E)$, i.e. every graph represents a cooperative game. We have $\psi_R(G) = (V, \nu_G)$, where V is the set of nodes and $\nu_G : 2^V \to \mathbb{R}$ is the characteristic function. Let ν_G be the ranking of groups of nodes in G based on classical group betweenness centrality. In other words, ψ_R is simply the group betweenness centrality for any graph. For a specific graph G, the importance of each node $u \in V$ according to $(\psi_R, \phi^{Shapley})$ is evaluated by the Shapley value of the game $\psi_R(G)$, i.e. $\phi_u^{Shapley}(\nu_G)$. Since we started off with a standard centrality measure (betweenness centrality) and applied a game-theoretic solution concept to it (the Shapley value), we call the resulting centrality measure a game-theoretic extension of betweenness centrality.*

A Motivation for Game-Theoretic Centrality

In this section, we provide a brief motivation for game-theoretic network centrality. To this end, we list a number of applications of this approach, discuss how game theory accounts for synergies within networks, and conclude with a brief motivating example.

First, let us begin with real-world applications for which game-theoretic centrality has been advocated. Suri and Narahari (2010) applied a variant of Shapley-value degree centrality to study a co-authorship network of 8361 researchers from the field of high-energy Physics. They show that their centrality measure achieves better results than maximum degree heuristics—a well-known heuristic in the literature for the top-k node problem for information diffusion. Szczepański, Michalak, and Wooldridge (2014) use their game-theoretic centrality in order to analyse a citation network of 2084055 publications, 2244018 citation relationships and 22954 communities (that represent journals, conference proceedings, etc.). This innovative approach not only considers the importance of individual authors, but also that of the communities to which they belong. Lindelauf, Hamers, and Husslage (2013), Skibski et al. (2014) and Michalak et al. (2013a) use game-theoretic centrality in order to study key nodes in terrorist networks. This type of analysis is imperative to understanding the hierarchy of such organisations and for the efficient deployment of investigation resources.

The main motivation for applying cooperative game-theory to the field of network centrality is that it considers the functioning of nodes *jointly*, rather than in separation.

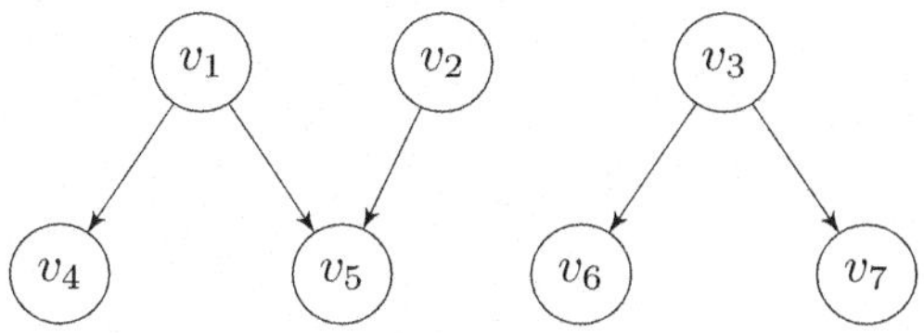

Figure 1: A graph presenting domination within a network. An edge (s,t) indicates that node s dominates node t. Which nodes should be considered most dominant?

Even if some nodes are relatively unimportant to the network individually, the synergy that results from their joint work may make them very important. By the same token, if we consider the contribution of some graph entities (e.g., paths within the network) made by a node to be relatively large, if many other nodes contribute these same entities, then then the contribution of this node is not as important as we originally surmised.

Example 2 *As an example, we will consider the β-measure (Brink and Gilles 2000) and how it handles synergies. Consider the context of ranking nodes in a directed network, $D = (V, E)$, according to their domination (control power) over other nodes. We say that a node s controls the node t if $(s,t) \in E$. In this context, a natural centrality measure (referred to in the literature as the score measure) of the node s is its outdegree, i.e., $\sigma_D(s) = |\{t \in V : (s,t) \in E\}|$. Similarly, we can consider the centrality of a group, C, as the number of nodes that this group controls, i.e., $\sigma_D(C) = |\{t \in V : \exists_s (s,t) \in E\}|$. However, if we consider coalitions of nodes, then if there is a crossover between the nodes controlled by members of the coalition, then we have negative synergy. In other words, the members together control fewer nodes than the simple sum of their individual centralities.*

Consider now the representation function $\psi(D) = \sigma_D$ and the centrality measure $(\psi, \phi^{Shapley})$. Brink and Gilles show that this centrality measure is equal to $\beta_D(s) = \sum_{t \in E(s)} \frac{1}{|E(t)|}$, where $E(v)$ is the neighbourhood of the node v. As compared to σ_D, we see that this centrality measure divides the resulting reward (i.e., raise in centrality) from controlling a node evenly between all nodes that dominate it.

If we look at Figure 1, then which nodes in this network should we consider to be most dominant (i.e., central)? According to the score measure, both v_1 and v_3 are equally dominant. However, we see that node v_4 is dominated by two nodes rather than one. This—depending on the application—could indicate one of a number of things:

- *v_4 is easy to dominate, and thereby does not contribute as much to the "domination power" of a node;*
- *The utility from dominating an already dominated node can be smaller; or*
- *Only one node can control any other node, and in the case of multiple dominators there is some probability distribution over which node is actually in control.*

The β-measure has the correct approach, ranking v_3 as the most dominant node, v_1 as second, followed by v_2 and then by the rest of the nodes. The gain in rank from dominating v_5 is equal to $\frac{1}{2}$ for both v_1 and v_2. In other words, each node—in expectation—dominates half of v_5.

The Class $\mathscr{M}$ of Representation Functions

In this section, we define a class $\mathscr{M}$ of representation functions. It will later be central in identifying which game-theoretic centralities are polynomially computable. Let us assume that the characteristic function ν_G represented by graph $G = (V, E)$ (as given by a representation function $\psi(G) = \nu_G$) can be computed by counting certain types of graph entities. These entities can be, for instance, nodes, paths, or shortest paths. For the purposes of this paper, we will call them *items* and denote them by ϑ. The set of all items in the particular graph G is denoted by Θ_G. We will also partition Θ_G into pairwise disjoint *groups*: $\Theta_1, \Theta_2 \ldots, \Theta_l, \ldots, \Theta_{h(G)}$. The number of these groups depends on the graph in question, and we will denote it by $h(G)$.

Example 3 *Let us consider a graph $G = (V, E)$ and a characteristic function ν_G, where the value of any subset of nodes is proportional to the number of shortest paths that pass through it. Let us denote the set of all shortest paths in G by $SP(G)$. There can be many different shortest paths between each pair of nodes $s, t \in V$. We can therefore partition $SP(G)$ into groups that contain all the shortest paths between the same pair of nodes. Thus, in this setting, we have the set of items $\Theta_G = SP(G)$, $h(G) = V^2$ disjoint groups that we denote by Θ_{st} and index by pairs of nodes.*

In the class $\mathscr{M}$, the value $\nu_G(C)$ of the coalition $C \subseteq V$ depends on the graph items associated with it. We will distinguish *positive*, *negative*, or *neutral association relations* between nodes and items, and we will denote them by R, $\widetilde{R}$, and N, respectively. Formally, $R, \widetilde{R}, N \subseteq V \times \Theta_G$. For instance, a shortest path π_{st} can be negatively related to the nodes s and t, positively related to all other nodes that it visits and neutrally related with all nodes that it does not visit.

We will denote by $\widetilde{R}(u, \vartheta)$ the fact that item $\vartheta \in \Theta_G$ is *negatively* related with node $u \in V$. By this we mean that when u joins a coalition C it takes away the value of ϑ, provided it has been previously contributed by any of the nodes in C. Similarly, by $R(u, \vartheta)$ we denote that ϑ is *positively* related with u. Whenever u joins a coalition C, it contributes the value of ϑ to this coalition (provided that ϑ is not already positively or negatively related to some node in C). Finally, $N(u, \vartheta)$ conveys the property that u neither contributes nor takes away the value of ϑ. We have $N(u, \vartheta)$ if and only if neither $\widetilde{R}(u, \vartheta)$ nor $R(u, \vartheta)$.

By now we have introduced relations between nodes and items. These definitions can be naturally extended to sets of nodes. In particular, for each coalition C and item ϑ, we have three mutually exclusive and exhaustive possibilities:

$$\widetilde{R}(C, \vartheta) \text{ if and only if } \exists_{v \in C} \widetilde{R}(v, \vartheta),$$
$$R(C, \vartheta) \text{ if and only if } \exists_{v \in C} R(v, \vartheta) \text{ and } \neg \exists_{u \in C} \widetilde{R}(u, \vartheta),$$
$$N(C, \vartheta) \text{ if and only if } \forall_{v \in C} N(v, \vartheta).$$

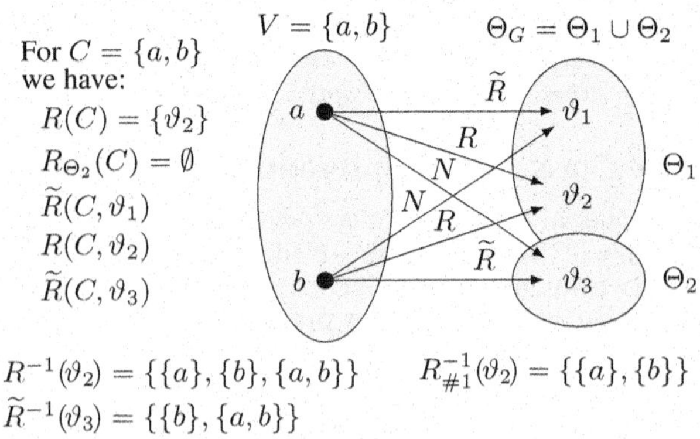

Figure 2: An example of notation used to describe relations between nodes and items.

For clarity, we will use the following notation for the relation R (and similarly for $\widetilde{R}$ and N),

$$\begin{aligned} R(C) &= \{\vartheta \in \Theta_G : R(C, \vartheta)\}, \\ R_{\Theta_l}(C) &= \{\vartheta \in \Theta_l : R(C, \vartheta)\}, \\ R^{-1}(\vartheta) &= \{C \subseteq V : R(C, \vartheta)\}, \\ R^{-1}_{\#k}(\vartheta) &= \{C \subseteq V : R(C, \vartheta) \text{ and } |C| = k\}. \end{aligned}$$

Thus, $R(C)$ denotes the set of items assigned to coalition C, $R_{\Theta_l}(C)$ the set of items in group Θ_l that is assigned to C, $R^{-1}(\vartheta)$ the set of coalitions to which item ϑ is assigned, and $R^{-1}_{\#k}(\vartheta)$ the set of coalitions of size k to which ϑ is assigned. Note that in the case of a singleton coalition we write $R(u)$ instead of $R(u)$ to avoid clutter.

Given the above framework, we will now present the class of characteristic functions that can be expressed in terms of graph items. For a characteristic function ν in this class, we will say that a set of items, relations and functions *models* ν.

Definition 3 (Model of a characteristic function) *Given a graph G, a* model *of a characteristic function ν_G is a tuple*

$$M_G = (\Theta_1, \ldots, \Theta_{h(G)}, R, \widetilde{R}, f, g),$$

where $\Theta_1, \ldots, \Theta_{h(G)}$ is a partition of a set Θ_G of items; R, $\widetilde{R}$ and $N = \neg R \wedge \neg\widetilde{R}$ are positive, negative and neutral association relations, respectively; and $f : \Theta_G \to \mathbb{R}$ and $g : \mathbb{N} \to \mathbb{R}$ are functions, such that the following properties hold:

$(M1)$ $\nu_G(C) = g(|C|) \sum_{\vartheta \in R(C)} f(\vartheta)$;

$(M2)$ $\forall_{1 \le l \le h(G)} \forall_{\vartheta_i, \vartheta_j \in \Theta_l}\ f(\vartheta_i) = f(\vartheta_j)$;

$(M3)$ $\forall_{1 \le l \le h(G)} \forall_{\vartheta_i, \vartheta_j \in \Theta_l}\ |N^{-1}_{\#k}(\vartheta_i)| = |N^{-1}_{\#k}(\vartheta_j)|$;

$(M4)$ $\forall_{1 \le l \le h(G)} \forall_{\vartheta_i, \vartheta_j \in \Theta_l}\ |R^{-1}_{\#k}(\vartheta_i)| = |R^{-1}_{\#k}(\vartheta_j)|$.

If properties $(M2)$, $(M3)$, and $(M4)$ hold, then for all $\vartheta \in \Theta_l$ we use the following notation:

$$f(\Theta_l) = f(\vartheta), \ |N^{-1}_{\#k}(\Theta_l)| = |N^{-1}_{\#k}(\vartheta)|, \ |R^{-1}_{\#k}(\Theta_l)| = |R^{-1}_{\#k}(\vartheta)|.$$

Also note that Properties $(M3)$ and $(M4)$ imply that $|\widetilde{R}^{-1}_{\#k}(\vartheta_i)| = |\widetilde{R}^{-1}_{\#k}(\vartheta_j)|$ and we also abuse notation by writing $|\widetilde{R}^{-1}_{\#k}(\Theta_l)|$.

In short, the above definition ensures that the relations R, $\widetilde{R}$ (and implicitly N) in the model $M_G = (\Theta_1, \ldots, \Theta_{h(G)}, R, \widetilde{R}, f, g)$ (of the characteristic function ν_G) indeed satisfy the negative, positive and neutral properties discussed at the beginning of this section. In particular, Property $(M1)$ states that the value of a coalition is the product of a function of its size and the sum of the contributions of its members over all positively related items. The rest of the properties state that groups must group together similar items. Specifically, Property $(M2)$ states that the value of every item in a group must be the same. Moreover, Properties $(M3)$ and $(M4)$ state that the set of coalitions of size k to which any item is related (by relation R, N, and consequently by $\widetilde{R}$) is the same for items in the same group.

Now, we are ready to formally define the class $\mathscr{M}$ of representation functions:

Definition 4 (The class $\mathscr{M}$) *$\mathscr{M}$ is the class of representation functions such that for all $\psi \in \mathscr{M}$, and for every graph G, there exists a model M_G of $\psi(G)$.*

Example 4 *Let us consider Figure 2. We want to find an $M_G = (\Theta_1, \Theta_2, R, \widetilde{R}, f, g)$ such that it models $\nu_G(\{a\}) = 1, \nu_G(\{b\}) = 1, \nu_G(\{a, b\}) = 2$. We define $f(\vartheta_1) = f(\vartheta_2) = 1$, $f(\vartheta_3) = 2$ (satisfying $(M2)$) and $g(k) = k$. Property $(M1)$ holds, since $\nu_G(\{a\}) = \nu_G(\{b\}) = g(1)f(\vartheta_2)$ and $\nu_G(\{a, b\}) = g(2)f(\vartheta_2)$. However, property $(M3)$ is not satisfied since $|N^{-1}_{\#1}(\vartheta_1)| \neq |N^{-1}_{\#1}(\vartheta_2)|$. This can be fixed by defining three groups of singletons instead. In fact, a partition of singletons will always satisfy properties $(M2)$, $(M3)$ and $(M4)$. The motivating for groups will become apparent in the next chapter. We will show how restricting the number of groups (without restricting the number of items) will yield polynomial computation.*

Computing Semivalue-based Centralities

For each representation function ψ and semivalue ϕ, we define the computational problem SEMIVALUE(ψ, ϕ):

SEMIVALUE(ψ, ϕ)
Given: Graph $G = (V, E)$, node $u \in V$
Problem: Compute $\phi_u(\psi(G))$

In general, this problem is intractable and it is not immediately obvious what restrictions would yield polynomial computations. Even if we restrict ourselves to the class of representation functions $\mathscr{M}$, there are still functions in this class for which SEMIVALUE(ψ, ϕ) is intractable (for example, if $h(G)$ is exponential in the size of $|V|$). However, we will define a subclass $\mathscr{M}^*$ of $\mathscr{M}$ such that SEMIVALUE(ψ, ϕ) can be computed in polynomial time for all $\psi \in \mathscr{M}^*$.

Definition 5 (The subclass $\mathscr{M}^*$ of $\mathscr{M}$) *$\mathscr{M}^*$ is the subclass of representation functions in $\mathscr{M}$ for which additionally the following properties hold:*

$(M1^*)$ *$\exists_{n \in \mathbb{N}} \forall_G \exists_{M_G}$ M_G models $\psi(G)$ and $h(G) \le O(|V|^n)$;*

$(M2^*)$ *f and g can be computed in time polynomial in $|V|$;*

$(M3^*)$ *If $\psi(G)$ is modelled by $(\Theta_1, \ldots, \Theta_{h(G)}, R, \widetilde{R}, f, g)$, then the function that for each G returns*

$(f, g, |R_{\Theta_l}(u)|, |\widetilde{R}_{\Theta_l}(u)|, |N^{-1}_{\#k}(\Theta_l)|, |R^{-1}_{\#k}(\Theta_l)|)$ *is computable in time polynomial in* $|V|$.

Below, we show that the class $\mathscr{M}^*$ is sufficiently broad to capture all fundamental network centrality measures and their variants known in the literature. Furthermore, the properties $(M1^*)$ through $(M3^*)$ allow us to compute the expected marginal contributions of a node by iterating over a polynomial number of groups of items (Θ_l) and sizes of coalitions ($|C|$) rather than all items ($\vartheta \in \Theta_G$) and all coalitions ($C \subseteq V$). Our key result is as follows:

Theorem 1 *For all* $\psi \in \mathscr{M}^*$ *and all semivalues* ϕ, SEMIVALUE(ψ, ϕ) *can be solved in polynomial time.*

Proof: In order to solve SEMIVALUE(ψ, ϕ) in polynomial time, we will use equation (1) and show how to compute $\mathbb{E}_{C_k}[\text{MC}(C_k, u)]$ in polynomial time for all k. To this end, we need to consider the contributions of the node u to C_k through the various items that u is in relation with (as defined by $R(u)$, $\widetilde{R}(u)$ and $N(u)$).

We will denote by $\text{MC}(C, u, \vartheta)$ the marginal contribution of node u to C through the item ϑ (which we will define below). In effect, we have

$$\text{MC}(C, u) = \sum_{\vartheta \in \Theta_G} \text{MC}(C, u, \vartheta).$$

Two computational issues arise. First, we cannot immediately use this result, as it would require iteration over all coalitions. Second, iterating over a possibly exponential number of items within this sum is quite troubling. To address the first issue, we will denote by $\text{MC}(k, u, \vartheta)$ the sum of contributions of u through ϑ to all coalitions of size k. To address the second, for all groups Θ_l we will consider instead $\text{MC}(k, u, \Theta_l) = \sum_{\vartheta \in \Theta_l} \text{MC}(k, u, \vartheta)$. We get:

$$\begin{aligned}\mathbb{E}_{C_k}[\text{MC}(C_k, u)] &= \sum_{1 \le l \le h(G)} \mathbb{E}_{C_k}[\text{MC}(C_k, u, \Theta_l)] \\ &= \sum_{1 \le l \le h(G)} \frac{\text{MC}(k, u, \Theta_l)}{\binom{|V|-1}{k}}. \qquad (2)\end{aligned}$$

The remainder of the proof will focus on defining $\text{MC}(C, u, \vartheta)$ and computing $\text{MC}(k, u, \vartheta)$. Polynomial computation of $\text{MC}(k, u, \Theta_l)$ will follow. A node u can contribute (possibly negative) value to a coalition C through $\vartheta \in \Theta_l$ in one of three mutually exclusive ways. These are:

[1] $R(u, \vartheta)$ and $N(C, \vartheta)$,

[2] $\widetilde{R}(u, \vartheta)$ and $R(C, \vartheta)$, and

[3] $R(u, \vartheta)$ or $N(u, \vartheta)$, and $R(C, \vartheta)$.

For all other cases $\text{MC}(C, u, \vartheta) = 0$. Since the remainder of the proof hinges on the understanding of these cases, let us illustrate them on our running example from Figure 2.

Example 5 *Let* $S = \{a\}$. *We will compute the contribution of node b to coalition S. We have* $MC(S, b, \vartheta_1) = 0$, *since* $\widetilde{R}(S, \vartheta_1)$ *(meaning there is nothing to take away). Evidently, none of the cases* [1], [2], [3] *are satisfied. We also have* $\widetilde{R}(b, \vartheta_3)$ *and* $N(S, \vartheta_3)$, *which implies* $MC(S, b, \vartheta_3) = 0$. *A contribution can only be made through the item* ϑ_2. *We have:* $R(b, \vartheta_2)$ *and* $R(S, \vartheta_2)$, *which satisfies condition* [3]. *It is not immediately obvious why a contribution is made, since* ϑ_2 *is already positively related with S. However, it is necessary to keep in mind that the size of the coalition will change. Due to the function g, this means that the value added by item* ϑ_2 *will now be* $g(k+1)f(\vartheta_2)$ *instead of* $g(k)f(\vartheta_2)$. *We say, then, that b contributes the value* $g(k+1)f(\vartheta_2) - g(k)f(\vartheta_2)$ *through the item* ϑ_2 *to coalition S.*

We compute $\text{MC}(k, u, \vartheta)$ in these three cases. In equations (3), (4) and (5) we will use properties $(M2)$ and $(M3)$ to give a closed formula that depends just on Θ_l and the size of the coalition, but not on ϑ itself. These formulas can be computed in polynomial time due to $(M3^*)$.

For the first case, $\text{MC}(C, u, \vartheta) = g(k+1)f(\vartheta)$. There are $|N^{-1}_{\#k}(\vartheta)|$ coalitions of size k such that $N(C, \vartheta)$. Thus, for $\vartheta \in \Theta_l$ we have:

$$\begin{aligned}\text{MC}^{[1]}(k, u, \vartheta) &= g(k+1)f(\vartheta)|N^{-1}_{\#k}(\vartheta)| \\ &= g(k+1)f(\Theta_l)|N^{-1}_{\#k}(\Theta_l)|. \qquad (3)\end{aligned}$$

For the second case, $\text{MC}(C, u, \vartheta) = -g(k)f(\vartheta)$. There are $|R^{-1}_{\#k}(\vartheta)|$ coalitions of size k such that $R(C, \vartheta)$. We have:

$$\begin{aligned}\text{MC}^{[2]}(k, u, \vartheta) &= -g(k)f(\vartheta)|R^{-1}_{\#k}(\vartheta)| \\ &= -g(k)f(\Theta_l)|R^{-1}_{\#k}(\Theta_l)|. \qquad (4)\end{aligned}$$

For the third case, $\text{MC}^{[3]}(C, u, \vartheta) = \Delta^k f(\vartheta)$, where $\Delta^k = g(k+1) - g(k)$. There are exactly $|R^{-1}_{\#k}(\vartheta)|$ coalitions of size k such that $R(C, \vartheta)$. We therefore have:

$$\text{MC}^{[3]}(k, u, \vartheta) = \Delta^k f(\vartheta)|R^{-1}_{\#k}(\vartheta)| = \Delta^k f(\Theta_l)|R^{-1}_{\#k}(\Theta_l)|. \quad (5)$$

Since $\text{MC}^{[i]}(k, u, \vartheta)$ depends on the group Θ_l such that $\vartheta \in \Theta_l$, equivalently we write $\text{MC}^{[i]}(k, u, \Theta_l)$. Using equations (3), (4) and (5), we find that $\text{MC}(k, u, \Theta_l)$ equals

$$\begin{aligned}\text{MC}(k, u, \Theta_l) = &\sum_{\vartheta \in R_{\Theta_l}(u)} \text{MC}^{[1]}(k, u, \vartheta) \\ + &\sum_{\vartheta \in \widetilde{R}_{\Theta_l}(u)} \text{MC}^{[2]}(k, u, \vartheta) + \sum_{\vartheta \in R_{\Theta_l}(u) \cup N_{\Theta_l}(u)} \text{MC}^{[3]}(k, u, \vartheta).\end{aligned}$$

Using equations (3), (4) and (5) this term can be rewritten as

$$\begin{aligned}\text{MC}(k, u, \Theta_l) &= |R_{\Theta_l}(u)|\text{MC}^{[1]}(k, u, \Theta_l) \\ &+ |\widetilde{R}_{\Theta_l}(u)|\text{MC}^{[2]}(k, u, \Theta_l) \\ &+ \big(|R_{\Theta_l}(u)| + |N_{\Theta_l}(u)|\big)\text{MC}^{[3]}(k, u, \Theta_l). \qquad (6)\end{aligned}$$

Observe that the summations over the potentially exponentially growing sets $R_{\Theta_l}(u)$, $\widetilde{R}_{\Theta_l}(u)$, and $N_{\Theta_l}(u)$ fall out of the equation. Moreover, in virtue of property $(M3^*)$, this term can be computed in polynomial time.

Finally, equations (6), (2) and (1) yield the following closed formula for the semivalue of node v, which also furnishes us with a polynomial algorithm:

$$\phi_v(\nu) = \sum_{0 \le k < |V|} \beta(k) \sum_{1 \le l \le h(G)} \frac{\text{MC}(k, u, \Theta_l)}{\binom{|V|-1}{k}}. \qquad (7)$$

This concludes the proof. □

Corollary 1 *If $\psi \in \mathscr{M}^*$, then there exist m_1, m_2, and m_3 such that f can be computed in time $O(|V|^{m_1})$; g in time $O(|V|^{m_2})$; and $|N^{-1}_{\#k}(\Theta_l)|$, $|R^{-1}_{\#k}(\Theta_l)|$, $|R_{\Theta_l}(u)|$ and $|\widetilde{R}_{\Theta_l}(u)|$ can be computed in time $O(|V|^{m_3})$. We can solve* SEMIVALUE(ψ,ϕ) *in time $O\big(h(G)|V|^{m_1} + |V|^{m_2+1} + h(G)|V|^{m_3+1}\big)$.*

Corollary 2 *For all $\psi \in \mathscr{M}^*$ we can compute the Shapley value-based and Banzhaf centralities in polynomial time.*

An Algorithm for Semivalue-based Centrality

The Algorithm 1 (SEMI) is a direct implementation of equation (7). In lines 5-7, 8-10 and 11-12, it computes the contribution of v to C_k associated with the expressions $\mathrm{MC}^{[1]}(k,v,\Theta_l)$, $\mathrm{MC}^{[2]}(k,v,\Theta_l)$ and $\mathrm{MC}^{[3]}(k,v,\Theta_l)$, respectively.

Algorithm 1: (SEMI) The semivalue-based centrality

Input: Graph $G=(V,E)$, node $v \in V$, model $M_G = (\{\Theta_i\}_1^{h(G)}, R, \widetilde{R}, f, g)$, function β, functions c^N_G and c^R_G, precomputed vectors $\{|R_{\Theta_l}(\{v\})| : 1 \le l \le h(G) \wedge v \in V\}$, and $\{|\widetilde{R}_{\Theta_l}(\{v\})| : 1 \le l \le h(G) \wedge v \in V\}$

Output: semivalue, $\phi_v(\Psi(G))$, for the node v

1 $\phi_v \leftarrow 0$;
2 **for** $k \leftarrow 0$ **to** $|V|-1$ **do**
3 $\quad \mathrm{MC}_k \leftarrow 0$;
4 $\quad$ **for** $l \leftarrow 1$ **to** $h(G)$ **do**
$\quad\quad$ // ************[$R(v,\vartheta)$ and $N(C,\vartheta)$]**********
5 $\quad\quad |N^{-1}_{\#k}(\Theta_l)| \leftarrow c^N_G(\vartheta \in \Theta_l, k)$;
6 $\quad\quad \mathrm{MC}^{[1]} \leftarrow g(k+1) f(\Theta_l) |N^{-1}_{\#k}(\Theta_l)|$;
7 $\quad\quad \mathrm{MC}_k \leftarrow \mathrm{MC}_k + |R_{\Theta_l}(\{v\})| \mathrm{MC}^{[1]}$;
$\quad\quad$ // ************[$\widetilde{R}(v,\vartheta)$ and $R(C,\vartheta)$]***********
8 $\quad\quad |R^{-1}_{\#k}(\Theta_l)| \leftarrow c^R_G(\vartheta \in \Theta_l, k)$;
9 $\quad\quad \mathrm{MC}^{[2]} \leftarrow g(k) f(\Theta_l) |R^{-1}_{\#k}(\Theta_l)|$;
10 $\quad\quad \mathrm{MC}_k \leftarrow \mathrm{MC}_k - |\widetilde{R}_{\Theta_l}(\{v\})| \mathrm{MC}^{[2]}$;
$\quad\quad$ // ******[$R(v,\vartheta)$ or $N(v,\vartheta)$, and $R(C,\vartheta)$]******
11 $\quad\quad \mathrm{MC}^{[3]} \leftarrow \big(g(k+1) - g(k)\big) f(\Theta_l) |R^{-1}_{\#k}(\Theta_l)|$;
12 $\quad\quad \mathrm{MC}_k \leftarrow \mathrm{MC}_k + |R_{\Theta_l}(\{v\}) \cup N_{\Theta_l}(\{v\})| \mathrm{MC}^{[3]}$;
13 $\quad \mathrm{MC}_k \leftarrow \frac{\beta(k)}{\binom{|V|-1}{k}} \mathrm{MC}_k$;
14 $\quad \phi_v \leftarrow \phi_v + \mathrm{MC}_k$;

Recall that polynomial computation of $|N^{-1}_{\#k}(\Theta_l)|$ and $|R^{-1}_{\#k}(\Theta_l)|$ was one of our assumptions in $\mathscr{M}^*$. The functions for calculating these values are represented in the pseudocode by c^N_G and c^R_G and must be provided in the input. The values $|R_{\Theta_l}(\{v\})|$ and $|\widetilde{R}_{\Theta_l}(\{v\})|$ must be precomputed for all $1 \le l \le h(G)$ and $v \in V$. Given those precomputations, $|N_{\Theta_l}(\{v\})|$ can also be computed in constant time. Due to Corollary 1, the time complexity of this algorithm is $O\big(h(G)|V|^{m_1} + |V|^{m_2+1} + h(G)|V|^{m_3+1}\big)$.

Centrality measure	$f(v)$	$g(\lvert C \rvert)$	Complexity
degree$^{(*)}$ (Everett and Borgatti 1999)	1	1	$O(\lvert V \rvert^2)$
weighted degree (Newman 2004)	$\frac{1}{deg(v)}$	1	$O(\lvert V \rvert^2)$
impact factor (Bollen et al. 2005)	1	$\frac{1}{\lvert C \rvert}$	$O(\lvert V \rvert^2)$
normalized degree (Everett and Borgatti 1999)	1	$\frac{1}{\lvert V \rvert - \lvert C \rvert}$	$O(\lvert V \rvert^2)$

$^{(*)}$(Michalak et al. 2013b) presented an algorithm for the Shapley Value-based degree centrality. Our algorithm applies to all semivalues.

Table 1: The f and g functions for various degree centralities

Computing Semivalues for Classic Centrality

In this section, we show that our framework has strong practical applications. It identifies efficiently computable game-theoretic extensions of such fundamental centrality measures as degree, betweenness, and closeness. Moreover, it provides a general and ready-to-use procedure to construct polynomial-time algorithms. Since our approach is general, it does not always yield optimal algorithms.[3] However, it constitutes a starting point for investigating them.

Parameterised degree centrality

In this section, we define in our framework the class of cooperative games, where a node's value is based on its degree. We consider the general parameterised group degree centrality of a coalition C in graph G, which is defined by:

$$\psi^D(G)(C) = \nu^D_G(C) = g(|C|) \sum_{v \in E(C)} f(v),$$

where $E(C)$ is the set of neighbours of C, and f and g are polynomially computable parameters such that $deg(u) = deg(v)$ implies $f(u) = f(v)$ for all $u, v \in V$. Using this characteristic function, we build game-theoretic extensions of degree, weighted degree, impact factor and normalized degree centralities (Table 1).

Proposition 1 *The parameterised representation function ψ^D (for polynomially computable parameters f and g) belongs to $\mathscr{M}^*$. Consequently,* SEMIVALUE(ψ^D,ϕ) *can be solved in polynomial time and the corresponding semivalue-based centrality can be computed in time $O(|V|^2 + |V|^{m_1+1} + |V|^{m_2+1})$.*

Proof: We will prove that for every ν^D_G we can find an $M_G = (\{\Theta_i\}_1^{h(G)}, R, \widetilde{R}, N, f, g)$ that models it, proving $\psi^D(G)$ is in the class $\mathscr{M}$. Next, we will show that all properties necessary for $\mathscr{M}^*$ are also satisfied. To this end, for all graphs G we define the set of items $\Theta_G = V$. The two relations, $R, \widetilde{R} \subseteq V \times V$, will be as follows:

$$R(v,u) \text{ if and only if } \exists_{(v,u)\in E}\ v \neq u$$
$$\widetilde{R}(v,u) \text{ if and only if } v = u.$$

And we define the partitions of Θ_G by $\Theta_i = \{v \in V : deg(v) = i\}$. Hence, we can rewrite $\nu_G^D(C) = g(|C|)\sum_{\vartheta \in R(C)} f(\vartheta)$, satisfying property $(M1)$. $(M2)$ is satisfied due to our assumption on f and all the examples in Table 1 satisfy it as well. Next, we consider the relations with respect to coalition sizes k and for $v \in \Theta_G$ we have:

$$|N^{-1}_{\#k}(v)| = \begin{cases} 0 & \text{if } |V|-1-deg(v) < k \\ \binom{|V|-1-deg(v)}{k} & \text{otherwise.} \end{cases}$$

$$|R^{-1}_{\#k}(v)| = \begin{cases} 0 & \text{if } |V| = k \\ \binom{|V|}{k} - |N^{-1}_{\#k}(v)| - \binom{|V|-1}{k-1} & \text{otherwise.} \end{cases}$$

Note that for all Θ_l and all $\vartheta_i, \vartheta_j \in \Theta_l$ we have that $|N^{-1}_{\#k}(\vartheta_i)| = |N^{-1}_{\#k}(\vartheta_j)|$ and $|R^{-1}_{\#k}(\vartheta_i)| = |R^{-1}_{\#k}(\vartheta_j)|$, satisfying $(M3)$ and $(M4)$. Hence, $\psi \in \mathscr{M}$.

Regarding $\mathscr{M}^*$, property $(M1^*)$ holds trivially, since clearly $h(G) \leq |V|$ and from the definition of $\psi^D(G)(C)$ property $(M2^*)$ holds trivially as well. For each $v \in V$ and $1 \leq l \leq h(G)$ it is easy to compute $|R_{\Theta_l}(\{v\})|$ and $|\widetilde{R}_{\Theta_l}(\{v\}|$, which satisfies $(M3^*)$. Finally, $|N^{-1}_{\#k}(\vartheta)|$ and $|R^{-1}_{\#k}(\vartheta)|$ can be computed in polynomial time simply from their definitions shown above, satisfying property $(M3^*)$.

Due to Theorem 1, we can compute semivalue-based centralities based on v_G^D in polynomial time. Due to Corollary 1, we can compute $\phi_v(\nu_G^D)$ in time $O(|V|^2 + |V|^{m_1+1} + |V|^{m_2+1})$. □

Parameterised betweenness centrality

In this subsection, we show that it is possible to express in our framework the class of cooperative games, where a node's value is based on its betweenness centrality. To this end, we will denote the set of paths between s and t by $\Pi_{s,t}$ and the set of all shortest paths in G by $\mathrm{SP}(G)$. Also, we will denote by σ_{st} the number of shortest paths between s and t (if $s = t$ then $\sigma_{st} = 1$) and by $\sigma_{st}(C)$ the number of shortest paths between s and t that pass through some node $v \in C$.

The general parameterised group betweenness centrality of a coalition C in graph G is defined by:

$$\psi^B(G)(C) = \nu_G^B(C) = g(|C|)\sum_{s,t \notin C} \sigma_{st}(C) f(s,t),$$

where f and g polynomially computable parameters.[2] Using this characteristic function, we build game-theoretic extensions of stress, betweenness, distance-scaled betweenness and normalized betweenness centralities (Table 2).

Proposition 2 *The parameterised representation function ψ^B (for polynomially computable parameters f and g) belongs to $\mathscr{M}^*$. Consequently,* SEMIVALUE(ψ^B, ϕ) *can be solved in polynomial time and the corresponding semivalue-based centrality can be computed in time* $O(|V|^3 + |V|^{m_1+2} + |V|^{m_2+1})$.

[2] If $\sigma_{xy}(C') = 0$, we postulate $\frac{0}{0} = 0$.

Centrality measure	$f(s,t)$	$g(\|C\|)$	Complexity
stress$^{(*)}$ (Szczepański et al. 2012)	1	1	$O(\|V\|^3)$
betweenness$^{(*)}$ (Everett and Borgatti 1999)	$\frac{1}{\sigma_{st}}$	1	$O(\|V\|^3)$
distance-scaled betw. (Brandes 2008)	$\frac{1}{\sigma_{st} dist(s,t)}$	1	$O(\|V\|^3)$
normalized betw. (Everett and Borgatti 1999)	$\frac{1}{\sigma_{st}}$	$\frac{2}{(\|V\|-\|C\|)(\|V\|-\|C\|-1)}$	$O(\|V\|^3)$

$^{(*)}$Szczepański et al. 2012 presented the algorithms for the Shapley Value-based betweenness and stress centralities. Our algorithm applies to all semivalues.

Table 2: f and g for various betweenness centralities

Centrality measure	$f(d)$	$g(\|C\|)$	Algorithm
closeness (Everett and Borgatti 1999)	1	1	$O(\|V\|^4)$
harmonic$^{(*)}$ (Boldi and Vigna 2013)	$\frac{1}{d}$	1	$O(\|V\|^4)$
influence game$^{(*)}$ (Michalak et al. 2013b)	positive value decreasing	1	$O(\|V\|^4)$
normalized closeness (Everett and Borgatti 1999)	$\frac{1}{\sigma_{st}}$	$\frac{1}{(\|V\|-\|C\|)}$	$O(\|V\|^4)$

$^{(*)}$Michalak et al. 2013b presented for these functions an algorithm for the Shapley Value. Our algorithm applies to all semivalues.

Table 3: f and g for various closeness centralities

Sketch of proof: We will show how to define for every ν_G^B the model M_G satisfying the conditions $(M1)$ and $(M2)$ for class $\mathscr{M}$. To this end, we define $\Theta_G = SP(G)$. Also, we define the two relations, $R, \widetilde{R} \subseteq V \times SP(G)$, as follows:

$$R(v, \pi_{st}) \text{ if and only if } v \in \pi_{st} \text{ and } v \neq s \text{ and } v \neq t$$
$$\widetilde{R}(v, \pi_{st}) \text{ if and only if } v = s \text{ or } v = t.$$

and we define the of partitions of Θ_G as $\Theta_{st} = \{\pi_{st} \in SP(G) : \pi_{st} \in \Pi_{st}\}$. Thus $\nu_G^B(C) = g(|C|)\sum_{\vartheta \in R(C)} f(\vartheta)$, satisfying $(M1)$ and $(M2)$. □

Parameterised closeness centrality

The last class of characteristic functions that we will define in our framework assigns value to a node based on its distance to other nodes. The parameterised closeness centrality is defined as follows:

$$\psi^{CL}(G)(C) = \nu_G^{CL}(C) = g(|C|)\sum_{v \in V} f(dist(C, v)),$$

where f and g are polynomially computable parameters. Using this characteristic function, we build game-theoretic extensions of closeness, harmonic, influence game and normalized closeness centralities (Table 3).

Proposition 3 *The parameterised representation function ψ^{CL} (for polynomially computable parameters f and g) belongs to $\mathscr{M}^*$. Consequently,* SEMIVALUE(ψ^{CL}, ϕ) *can be solved in polynomial time and the corresponding semivalue-based centrality can be computed in time* $O(|V|^4 + |V|^{m_1+2} + |V|^{m_2+1})$.

Sketch of proof: We will show how to define a model M_G for every ν_G^{CL}. To this end, we will define items as pairs of the form $\langle u, l\rangle \subseteq V \times \{0, .., |V|-1\}$. They will represent nodes and all possible distances between them. We define $\Theta_G = \{\langle u, l\rangle \in V \times \mathbb{N} : \exists_{v\in V} dist(u, v) = l\}$ and the partition $\{\{\vartheta\}|\vartheta \in \Theta_G\}$ of singletons. Next, we define the two relations, $R, \widetilde{R} \subseteq V \times V \times \{0, \ldots, |V|-1\}$, as follows:

$$R(v, \langle u, l\rangle) \text{ if and only if } dist(v, u) = l$$
$$\widetilde{R}(v, \langle u, l\rangle) \text{ if and only if } dist(v, u) < l.$$

Thus $\nu_G^{CL}(C) = g(|C|) \sum_{\vartheta\in R(C)} f(\vartheta)$, satisfying $(M1)$.[3] $(M2)$ holds for all entries in Table 3. $(M3)$ and $(M4)$ hold since item groups are singletons. Hence $\psi^{CL} \in \mathscr{M}$. □

Related Work

Grofman and Owen (1982) were the first to apply a game-theoretic solution concept—the Banzhaf index—as a centrality measure. Gómez et al. (2003) proposed a centrality measure based on the Shapley value and Myerson value for graph-restricted games Myerson (1977). Amer and Giménez (2004) proposed to use semivalues as a measure of the importance of nodes, and Amer, Giménez, and Magaña (2012) followed for directed networks. Recently, Szczepański, Michalak, and Wooldridge (2014) developed the first game-theoretic measure of centrality based on the Owen value (Owen 1977) that takes into account the *community structure* of the underlying network. We also mention some works on the computational aspects of cooperative games on graphs (Bachrach and Rosenschein 2009; Greco et al. 2011).

Works on the computational characteristics of game-theoretic centrality include Michalak et al. (2013b), who proposed, inter alia, polynomial algorithms for Shapley value-based degree and closeness centralities, and Szczepański, Michalak, and Rahwan (2012), who proposed polynomial algorithms for Shapley value-based betweenness and stress centralities. Michalak et al. (2013a) proposed fast algorithms for connectivity games.

Game-theoretic centralities were first used by Suri and Narahari (2010) in the interesting application of influence propagation in networks. In particular, the authors used the Shapley value to approximate the solution to the top k-node problem, i.e., the problem of identifying the k most influential nodes in a network. Solution concepts from cooperative game theory have been applied to many other graph-related problems, such as studies of the synergies between agents (Procaccia, Shah, and Tucker 2014), wire-tapping communication networks (Aziz et al. 2009).

Our paper also contributes to the line of research on modelling characteristic functions using specific combinatorial structures such as graphs. This includes works by Deng and Papadimitriou (1994), Greco et al. (2009), and Wooldridge and Dunne (2006). Such representations are guaranteed to be concise, however they are not fully expressive.

[3]In our examples f ignores the first parameter of ϑ and is simply a function of distance.

Future Work

A few future research directions stem from this work. First, it may be possible to broaden the scope of the class of game-theoretic network centralities presented in this paper or to find new classes altogether. For example, perhaps it would be possible to extend our model to *coalitional semivalues* (Szczepański, Michalak, and Wooldridge 2014): the family of solution concepts for cooperative games with *a priori*-given unions. Second, we have presented generalised degree, betweenness and closeness centralities, but many more cooperative games and their semivalues can be used to analyse networks. Finally, it would be interesting to perform an experimental analysis of the suitability of different semivalues for particular applications. The algorithms presented in this paper aim to facilitate the tractable computations that are necessary for such studies.

Acknowledgements

Paul Harrenstein, Tomasz Michalak and Michael Wooldridge were supported by the European Research Council under Advanced Grant 291528 ("RACE"). Piotr Szczepański, Mateusz Tarkowski and Tomasz Michalak were supported by the Polish National Science grant DEC-2013/09/D/ST6/03920.

References

Amer, R., and Giménez, J. M. 2004. A connectivity game for graphs. *Mathematical Methods of Operations Research* 60(3):453–470.

Amer, R.; Giménez, J.; and Magaña, A. 2012. Accessibility measures to nodes of directed graphs using solutions for generalized cooperative games. *Mathematical Methods of Operations Research* 75(1):105–134.

Aziz, H., and de Keijzer, B. 2014. Shapley meets Shapley. In Mayr, E. W., and Portier, N., eds., *31st International Symposium on Theoretical Aspects of Computer Science (STACS 2014)*, volume 25, 99–111.

Aziz, H.; Lachish, O.; Paterson, M.; and Savani, R. 2009. Wiretapping a hidden network. In *Proceedings of the the 5th Workshop on Internet & Network Economics (WINE '09)*, 438–446.

Bachrach, Y., and Rosenschein, J. S. 2009. Power in threshold network flow games. *Autonomous Agents and Multi-Agent Systems* 18(1):106–132.

Banzhaf, J. F. 1965. Weighted Voting Doesn't Work: A Mathematical Analysis. *Rutgers Law Review* 19:317–343.

Boldi, P., and Vigna, S. 2013. Axioms for centrality. *CoRR* abs/1308.2140.

Bollen, J.; Sompel, H. V.; Smith, J. A.; and Luce, R. 2005. Toward alternative metrics of journal impact: A comparison of download and citation data. *Information Processing and Management* 41(6):1419–1440.

Bonacich, P. 1972. Factoring and weighting approaches to status scores and clique identification. *Journal of Mathematical Sociology* 2(1):113–120.

Brandes, U. 2008. On variants of shortest-path betweenness centrality and their generic computation. *Social Networks* 30(2):136–145.

Brink, R., and Gilles, R. P. 2000. Measuring domination in directed networks. *Social Networks* 22(2):141 – 157.

Chalkiadakis, G.; Elkind, E.; and Wooldridge, M. 2012. *Computational Aspects of Cooperative Game Theory*. Synthesis Lectures on Artificial Intelligence and Machine Learning. Morgan & Claypool.

Deng, X., and Papadimitriou, C. 1994. On the complexity of cooperative solution concepts. *Mathematics of Operations Research* 19(2):257–266.

Dubey, P.; Neyman, A.; and Weber, R. J. 1981. Value theory without efficiency. *Mathematics of Operations Research* 6(1):122–128.

Everett, M. G., and Borgatti, S. P. 1999. The centrality of groups and classes. *Journal of Mathematical Sociology* 23(3):181–201.

Freeman, L. 1979. Centrality in social networks: Conceptual clarification. *Social Networks* 1(3):215–239.

Gómez, D.; González-Arangüena, E.; Manuel, C.; Owen, G.; Del Pozo, M.; and Tejada, J. 2003. Centrality and power in social networks: A game theoretic approach. *Mathematical Social Sciences* 46(1):27–54.

Greco, G.; Malizia, E.; Palopoli, L.; and Scarcello, F. 2009. On the complexity of compact coalitional games. In Boutilier, C., ed., *Proceedings of the Twenty First International Joint Conference on Artifical Intelligence (IJCAI '09)*, 147–152.

Greco, G.; Malizia, E.; Palopoli, L.; and Scarcello, F. 2011. On the complexity of the core over coalition structures. In Walsh, T., ed., *Proceedings of the Twenty-Second International Joint Conference on Artificial Intelligence (IJCAI'11)*, 216–221. Morgan Kaufmann.

Grofman, B., and Owen, G. 1982. A game-theoretic approach to measuring centrality in social networks. *Social Networks* 4:213–224.

Kotter, R.; Reid, A. T.; Krumnack, A.; Wanke, E.; and Sporns, O. 2007. Shapley ratings in brain networks. *Front Neuroinform* 1:2.

Lindelauf, R.; Hamers, H.; and Husslage, B. 2013. Cooperative game theoretic centrality analysis of terrorist networks: The cases of jemaah islamiyah and Al Qaeda. *European Journal of Operational Research* 229(1):230–238.

Michalak, T. P.; Rahwan, T.; Szczepański, P. L.; Skibski, O.; Narayanam, R.; Wooldridge, M. J.; and Jennings, N. R. 2013a. Computational analysis of connectivity games with applications to the investigation of terrorist networks. In Rossi, F., ed., *Proceedings of the Twenty-Third international joint conference on Artificial Intelligence (IJCAI'13)*, 293–301. AAAI Press.

Michalak, T. P.; Aadithya, K. V.; Szczepanski, P. L.; Ravindran, B.; and Jennings, N. R. 2013b. Efficient computation of the Shapley value for game-theoretic network centrality. *Journal of Artificial Intelligence Research (JAIR)* 46:607–650.

Myerson, R. 1977. Graphs and cooperation in games. *Mathematics of Operations Research* 2(3):225–229.

Nebel, F. 2011. Graph-based coalitional games: An analysis via characteristics. In *Proceedings of the 5th International ICST Conference on Performance Evaluation Methodologies and Tools (VALUETOOLS '11)*, 476–485. ICST (Institute for Computer Sciences, Social-Informatics and Telecommunications Engineering), Brussels, Belgium.

Newman, M. E. J. 2004. Analysis of weighted networks. *Physical Review E* 70(5):056131.

Owen, G. 1977. Values of games with a priori unions. In *Mathematical economics and game theory: Essays in honor of Oskar Morgenstern*, volume 141 of *Lecture Notes in Economics and Mathematical Systems*. Springer. 76–88.

Procaccia, A. D.; Shah, N.; and Tucker, M. L. 2014. On the structure of synergies in cooperative games. In Brodley, C. E., and Stone, P., eds., *Proceedings of the Twenty-Eighth AAAI Conference on Artificial Intelligence (AAAI 2014)*, 763–769. AAAI Press.

Shapley, L. S. 1953. A value for n-person games. In Kuhn, H., and Tucker, A., eds., *Contributions to the Theory of Games II*, volume 28 of *Annals of Mathematical Studies*. Princeton University Press. 307–317.

Skibski, O.; Michalak, T.; Rahwan, T.; and Wooldridge, M. 2014. Algorithms for the Shapley and Myerson values in graph-restricted games. In Lomuscio, A.; Scerri, P.; Bazzan, A.; and Huhns, M., eds., *Proceedings of the 13th International Conference on Autonomous Agents and Multiagent Systems (AAMAS 2014*, 197–204. IFAAMAS.

Suri, N., and Narahari, Y. 2010. A Shapley Value based approach to discover influential nodes in social networks. *IEEE Transactions on Automation Science and Engineering* 99:1–18.

Szczepański, P. L.; Michalak, T.; and Rahwan, T. 2012. A new approach to betweenness centrality based on the Shapley value. In Conitzer, V., and Winikoff, M., eds., *Proceedings of the 11th International Joint Conference on Autonomous Agents and Multi-Agent Systems (AAMAS 2012)*, 239–246. IFAAMAS.

Szczepański, P.; Michalak, T.; and Wooldridge, M. 2014. A centrality measure for networks with community structure based on a generalization of the Owen value. In Schaub, T.; Friedrich, G.; and O'Sullivan, B., eds., *Proceedings of the 21st European Conference on Artificial Intelligence (ECAI'14)*, 867–872.

Tarkowski, M.; Michalak, T.; Rahwan, T.; Elkind, E.; and Wooldridge, M. 2014. Game-theoretic network centrality measures—a critical survey. *mimeo*, University of Oxford.

Wooldridge, M., and Dunne, P. 2006. On the computational complexity of coalitional resource games. *Artificial Intelligence* 170(10):835–871.

Proceedings of the Twenty-Ninth AAAI Conference on Artificial Intelligence

Embedded Unsupervised Feature Selection

Suhang Wang, Jiliang Tang, Huan Liu
School of Computing, Informatics, and Decision Systems Engineering
Arizona State University, USA
{suhang.wang, jiliang.tang, huan.liu}@asu.edu

Abstract

Sparse learning has been proven to be a powerful technique in supervised feature selection, which allows to embed feature selection into the classification (or regression) problem. In recent years, increasing attention has been on applying spare learning in unsupervised feature selection. Due to the lack of label information, the vast majority of these algorithms usually generate cluster labels via clustering algorithms and then formulate unsupervised feature selection as sparse learning based supervised feature selection with these generated cluster labels. In this paper, we propose a novel unsupervised feature selection algorithm EUFS, which directly embeds feature selection into a clustering algorithm via sparse learning without the transformation. The Alternating Direction Method of Multipliers is used to address the optimization problem of EUFS. Experimental results on various benchmark datasets demonstrate the effectiveness of the proposed framework EUFS.

Introduction

In many real-world applications such as data mining and machine learning, one is often faced with high-dimensional data (Jain and Zongker 1997; Guyon and Elisseeff 2003). Data with high dimensionality not only significantly increases the time and memory requirements of the algorithms, but also degenerates many algorithms' performance due to the curse of dimensionality and the existence of irrelevant, redundant and noisy dimensions(Liu and Motoda 2007). Feature selection, which reduces the dimensionality by selecting a subset of most relevant features, has been proven to be an effective and efficient way to handle high-dimensional data (John *et al.* 1994; Liu and Motoda 2007).

In terms of the label availability, feature selection methods can be broadly classified into supervised methods and unsupervised methods. The availability of the class label allows supervised feature selection algorithms (Duda *et al.* 2001; Nie *et al.* 2008; Zhao *et al.* 2010; Tang *et al.* 2014) to effectively select discriminative features to distinguish samples from different classes. Sparse learning has been proven to be a powerful technique in supervised feature selection (Nie *et al.* 2010; Gu and Han 2011; Tang and Liu 2012a), which enables feature selection to be embedded in the classification (or regression) problem. As most data is unlabeled and it is very expensive to label the data, unsupervised feature selection attracts more and more attentions in recent years (Wolf and Shashua 2005; He *et al.* 2005; Boutsidis *et al.* 2009; Yang *et al.* 2011; Qian and Zhai 2013; Alelyani *et al.* 2013).

Without label information to define feature relevance, a number of alternative criteria have been proposed for unsupervised feature selection. One commonly used criterion is to select features that can preserve the data similarity or manifold structure constructed from the whole feature space (He *et al.* 2005; Zhao and Liu 2007). In recent years, applying sparse learning in unsupervised feature selection has attracted increasing attention. These methods usually generate cluster labels via clustering algorithms and then transform unsupervised feature selection into sparse learning based supervised feature selection with these generated cluster labels such as Multi-cluster feature selection (MCFS) (Cai *et al.* 2010), Nonnegative Discriminative Feature Selection (NDFS) (Li *et al.* 2012), and Robust Unsupervised Feature Selection (RUFS) (Qian and Zhai 2013).

In this paper, we propose a novel unsupervised feature selection algorithm, i.e., Embedded Unsupervised Feature Selection (EUFS). Unlike existing unsupervised feature selection methods such as MCFS, NDFS or RUFS, which transform unsupervised feature selection into sparse learning based supervised feature selection with cluster labels generated by clustering algorithms, we directly embed feature selection into a clustering algorithm via sparse learning without the transformation (see Figure 1). This work theoretically extends the current state-of-the-art unsupervised feature selection, algorithmically expands the capability of unsupervised feature selection, and empirically demonstrates the efficacy of the new algorithm. The major contributions of this paper are summarized next.

- Providing a way to directly embed unsupervised feature selection algorithm into a clustering algorithm via sparse learning instead of transforming it into sparse learning based supervised feature selection with cluster labels;
- Proposing an embedded feature selection framework EUFS, which selects features in unsupervised scenarios with sparse learning; and

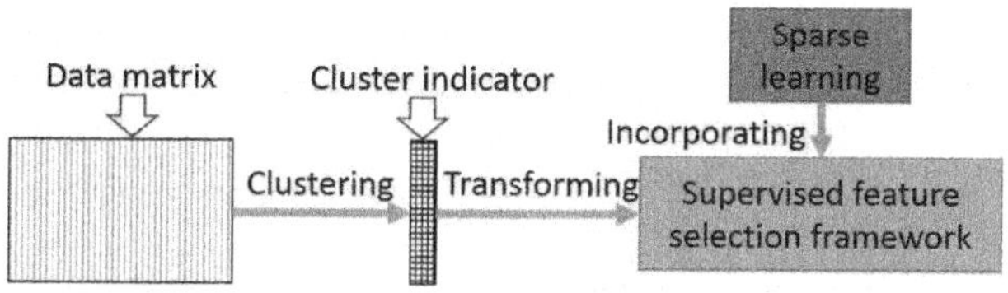

(a) Existing sparse learning based unsupervised feature selection method

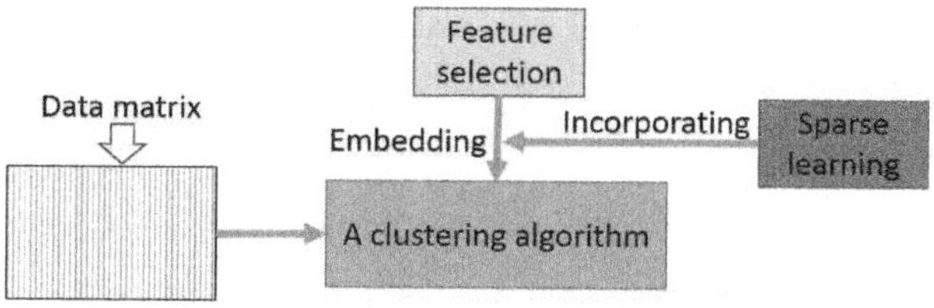

(b) Embedded unsupervised feature selection

Figure 1: Differences between the existing sparse learning based unsupervesd feature selection methods and the proposed embedded unsupervised feature selection

- Conducting experiments on various datasets to demonstrate the effectiveness of the proposed framework EUFS.

The rest of this paper is organized as follows. In Section 2, we give details about the embedded unsupervised feature selection framework EUFS. In Section 3, we introduce a method to solve the optimization problem of the proposed framework. In Section 4, we show empirical evaluation with discussion. In section 5, we present the conclusion with future work.

Embedded Unsupervised Feature Selection

Throughout this paper, matrices are written as boldface capital letters and vectors are denoted as boldface lowercase letters. For an arbitrary matrix $\mathbf{M} \in \mathbb{R}^{m \times n}$, $\mathbf{M}_{ij}$ denotes the (i, j)-th entry of $\mathbf{M}$ while $\mathbf{m}_i$ and $\mathbf{m}^j$ mean the i-th row and j-th column of $\mathbf{M}$ respectively. $||\mathbf{M}||_F$ is the Frobenius norm of $\mathbf{M}$ and Tr($\mathbf{M}$) is the trace of $\mathbf{M}$ if $\mathbf{M}$ is square. $\langle \mathbf{A}, \mathbf{B} \rangle$ equals Tr($\mathbf{A}^T\mathbf{B}$), which is the standard inner product between two matrices. $\mathbf{I}$ is the identity matrix and $\mathbf{1}$ is a vector whose elements are all 1. The $l_{2,1}$-norm is defined as $||\mathbf{M}||_{2,1} = \sum_{i=1}^{m} ||\mathbf{m}_i|| = \sum_{i=1}^{m} \sqrt{\sum_{j=1}^{n} \mathbf{M}_{ij}^2})$.

Let $\mathbf{X} \in \mathbb{R}^{N \times d}$ be the data matrix with each row $\mathbf{x}_i \in \mathbb{R}^{1 \times d}$ being a data instance. We use $\mathcal{F} = \{f_1, \dots, f_d\}$ to denote the d features and $\mathbf{f}_1, \dots, \mathbf{f}_d$ are the corresponding feature vectors. Assume that each feature has been normalized, i.e., $||\mathbf{f}_j||_2 = 1$ for $j = 1, \dots, d$. Suppose that we want to cluster $\mathbf{X}$ into k clusters $(C_1, C_2, \dots, C_k)$ under the matrix factorization framework as:

$$\begin{aligned} &\min_{\mathbf{U},\mathbf{V}} \ ||\mathbf{X} - \mathbf{U}\mathbf{V}^T||_F^2 \\ &s.t.\ \mathbf{U} \in \{0, 1\}^{N \times k}, \mathbf{U}^T\mathbf{1} = \mathbf{1} \end{aligned} \tag{1}$$

where $\mathbf{U} \in \mathbb{R}^{N \times k}$ is the cluster indicator and $\mathbf{V} \in \mathbb{R}^{d \times k}$ is the latent feature matrix. The problem in Eq.(1) is difficult to solve due to the constraint on $\mathbf{U}$. Following the common relaxation for label indicator matrix (Von Luxburg 2007; Tang and Liu 2012b), the constraint on $\mathbf{U}$ is relaxed to orthogonality, i.e., $\mathbf{U}^T\mathbf{U} = \mathbf{I}$, $\mathbf{U} \geq \mathbf{0}$. After the relaxation, Eq.(1) can be rewritten as:

$$\begin{aligned} &\min_{\mathbf{U},\mathbf{V}} \ ||\mathbf{X} - \mathbf{U}\mathbf{V}^T||_F^2 \\ &s.t.\ \mathbf{U}^T\mathbf{U} = \mathbf{I}, \mathbf{U} \geq \mathbf{0} \end{aligned} \tag{2}$$

Another significance of the orthogonality constraint on $\mathbf{U}$ is to allow us to perform feature selection via $\mathbf{V}$, which can be stated by the follow theorem:

Theorem 1. *Let $\mathbf{X} = [\mathbf{f}_1, \mathbf{f}_2, \dots, \mathbf{f}_d]$, and $||\mathbf{f}_i|| = 1$ for $i = 1, \dots, d$. We use $\mathbf{U}\mathbf{V}^T$ to reconstruct $\mathbf{X}$, i.e., $\hat{\mathbf{X}} = \mathbf{U}\mathbf{V}^T$. If $\mathbf{U}$ is orthogonal, then we can perform feature selection via $\mathbf{V}$.*

Proof. Since $\hat{\mathbf{X}} = \mathbf{U}\mathbf{V}^T$, we have $\hat{\mathbf{f}}_i = \mathbf{U}\mathbf{v}_i^T$. Then

$$||\hat{\mathbf{f}}_i||_2 = ||\mathbf{U}\mathbf{v}_i^T||_2 = \left(\mathbf{v}_i\mathbf{U}^T\mathbf{U}\mathbf{v}_i\right)^{1/2} = ||\mathbf{v}_i||_2 \tag{3}$$

Consider the case that $||\mathbf{v}_i||_2$ is close to 0, which indicates that the reconstructed feature representation $||\hat{\mathbf{f}}_i||_2$ is close to 0. $||\mathbf{f}_i|| = 1$ means $\mathbf{f}_i$ is not well reconstructed via $\hat{\mathbf{f}}_i$, which suggests that this corresponding feature could be not representative and we should exclude such features to have a better reconstruction. One way to do this is to add a selection matrix diag($\mathbf{p}$) to $\mathbf{X}$ and $\mathbf{V}$ as,

$$||\mathbf{X}\text{diag}(\mathbf{p}) - \mathbf{U}(\text{diag}(\mathbf{p})\mathbf{V})^T||_F^2 \tag{4}$$

where $\mathbf{p} = \{0, 1\}^d$ with $p_i = 1$ if the i-th feature is selected and otherwise $p_i = 0$, which completes the proof. □

With Theorem 1, if we want to select m features for the clustering algorithm in Eq.(2), we can rewrite it as:

$$\begin{aligned} &\min_{\mathbf{U},\mathbf{V}} \ ||\mathbf{X}\text{diag}(\mathbf{p}) - \mathbf{U}(\text{diag}(\mathbf{p})\mathbf{V})^T||_F^2 \\ &s.t.\ \mathbf{U}^T\mathbf{U} = \mathbf{I}, \mathbf{U} \geq \mathbf{0} \\ &\mathbf{p} \in \{0, 1\}^d, \mathbf{p}^T\mathbf{1} = m \end{aligned} \tag{5}$$

The constraint on $\mathbf{p}$ makes Eq.(5) mixed integer programming (Boyd and Vandenberghe 2004), which is difficult to solve. We relax the problem in the following way. First, the following theorem suggests that we can ignore the selection matrix on $\mathbf{X}$ as

$$\begin{aligned} &\min_{\mathbf{U},\mathbf{V}} \ ||\mathbf{X} - \mathbf{U}(\text{diag}(\mathbf{p})\mathbf{V})^T||_F^2 \\ &s.t.\ \mathbf{U}^T\mathbf{U} = \mathbf{I}, \mathbf{U} \geq \mathbf{0} \\ &\mathbf{p} \in \{0, 1\}^d, \mathbf{p}^T\mathbf{1} = m \end{aligned} \tag{6}$$

Theorem 2. *The optimization problems in Eq.(5) and Eq.(6) are equivalent.*

Proof. One way to prove Theorem 2 is to show that the objective functions in Eq.(5) and Eq.(6) are equivalent. For Eq.(5), we have

$$\begin{aligned} &||\mathbf{X}\text{diag}(\mathbf{p}) - \mathbf{U}(\text{diag}(\mathbf{p})\mathbf{V})^T||_F^2 \\ &= \sum_{i=1}^{d} ||p_i\mathbf{f}_i - p_i\mathbf{U}\mathbf{v}_i^T||_F^2 \\ &= \sum_{i:p_i=1} ||\mathbf{f}_i - \mathbf{U}\mathbf{v}_i^T||_F^2 \end{aligned} \tag{7}$$

And for Eq.(6), we have

$$\begin{aligned}
&||\mathbf{X} - \mathbf{U}(\text{diag}(\mathbf{p})\mathbf{V})^T||_F^2 \\
&= \sum_{i=1}^{d} ||\mathbf{f}_i - p_i \mathbf{U}\mathbf{v}_i^T||_F^2 \\
&= \sum_{i:p_i=1} ||\mathbf{f}_i - \mathbf{U}\mathbf{v}_i^T||_F^2 + (N - m)
\end{aligned} \tag{8}$$

which complete the proof. □

We observe that diag(p) and $\mathbf{V}$ is as the form of diag(p)$\mathbf{V}$ in Eq.(6). Since $\mathbf{p}$ is a binary vector and $N - m$ rows of the diag(p) are all zeros, diag(p)$\mathbf{V}$ is a matrix where elements of many rows are all zeros. This motivates us to absorb the diag(p) into $\mathbf{V}$, i.e., $\mathbf{V}$ = diag(p)$\mathbf{V}$, and add $l_{2,1}$ norm on $\mathbf{V}$ to achieve feature selection as

$$\begin{aligned}
&\arg\min_{\mathbf{U},\mathbf{V}} ||\mathbf{X} - \mathbf{U}\mathbf{V}^T||_F^2 + \alpha||\mathbf{V}||_{2,1} \\
&s.t.\ \mathbf{U}^T\mathbf{U} = \mathbf{I}, \mathbf{U} \geq \mathbf{0}
\end{aligned} \tag{9}$$

Since we forces some rows of $\mathbf{V}$ close to 0, $\mathbf{U}$ and $\mathbf{V}$ may poorly reconstruct some data instances. Reconstructing errors from these instances may easily dominate the objective function because of the squared errors. To make the model robust to these instances, we adopt robust analysis, i.e., replace the loss function by $l_{2,1}$-norm, as follows

$$\begin{aligned}
&\arg\min_{\mathbf{U},\mathbf{V}} ||\mathbf{X} - \mathbf{U}\mathbf{V}^T||_{2,1} + \alpha||\mathbf{V}||_{2,1} \\
&s.t.\ \mathbf{U}^T\mathbf{U} = \mathbf{I}, \mathbf{U} \geq \mathbf{0}
\end{aligned} \tag{10}$$

To take advantage of information from attribute-value part, i.e, $\mathbf{X}$, similar data instances should have similar labels, according to the spectral analysis (Von Luxburg 2007), we further add the following term to force similar instances with similar labels as:

$$\min \text{Tr}(\mathbf{U}^T\mathbf{L}\mathbf{U}) \tag{11}$$

where $\mathbf{L} = \mathbf{D} - \mathbf{S}$ is the Laplacian matrix and $\mathbf{D}$ is a diagonal matrix with its elements defined as $D_{ii} = \sum_{j=1}^{n} S_{ij}$. $\mathbf{S} \in \mathbb{R}^{N \times N}$ denotes the similarity matrix based on $\mathbf{X}$, which is obtained through RBF kernel as

$$S_{ij} = e^{-\frac{||\mathbf{x}_i - \mathbf{x}_j||^2}{\sigma^2}} \tag{12}$$

Putting Eq.(10) and Eq.(11) together, the proposed framework EUFS is to solve the following optimization problem:

$$\begin{aligned}
&\arg\min_{\mathbf{U},\mathbf{V}} ||\mathbf{X} - \mathbf{U}\mathbf{V}^T||_{2,1} + \alpha||\mathbf{V}||_{2,1} + \beta\text{Tr}(\mathbf{U}^T\mathbf{L}\mathbf{U}) \\
&s.t.\ \mathbf{U}^T\mathbf{U} = \mathbf{I}, \mathbf{U} \geq \mathbf{0}
\end{aligned} \tag{13}$$

Optimization Algorithm

The objective function in Eq.(13) is not convex in both $\mathbf{U}$ and $\mathbf{V}$ but is convex if we update the two variables alternatively. Following (Huang *et al.* 2014), we use Alternating Direction Method of Multiplier (ADMM) (Boyd *et al.* 2011) to optimize the objective function. By introducing two auxiliary variables $\mathbf{E} = \mathbf{X} - \mathbf{U}\mathbf{V}^T$ and $\mathbf{Z} = \mathbf{U}$, we can convert Eq.(13) into the following equivalent problem,

$$\begin{aligned}
&\arg\min_{\mathbf{U},\mathbf{V},\mathbf{E},\mathbf{Z}} ||\mathbf{E}||_{2,1} + \alpha||\mathbf{V}||_{2,1} + \beta\text{Tr}(\mathbf{Z}^T\mathbf{L}\mathbf{U}) \\
&s.t.\quad \mathbf{E} = \mathbf{X} - \mathbf{U}\mathbf{V}^T, \mathbf{Z} = \mathbf{U}, \mathbf{U}^T\mathbf{U} = \mathbf{I}, \mathbf{Z} \geq \mathbf{0}
\end{aligned} \tag{14}$$

which can be solved by the following ADMM problem

$$\begin{aligned}
\min_{\mathbf{U},\mathbf{V},\mathbf{E},\mathbf{Z},\mathbf{Y}_1,\mathbf{Y}_2,\mu} &||\mathbf{E}||_{2,1} + \alpha||\mathbf{V}||_{2,1} + \beta\text{Tr}(\mathbf{Z}^T\mathbf{L}\mathbf{U}) \\
&+ \langle \mathbf{Y}_1, \mathbf{Z} - \mathbf{U} \rangle + \left\langle \mathbf{Y}_2, \mathbf{X} - \mathbf{U}\mathbf{V}^T - \mathbf{E} \right\rangle \\
&+ \frac{\mu}{2}(||\mathbf{Z} - \mathbf{U}||_F^2 + ||\mathbf{X} - \mathbf{U}\mathbf{V}^T - \mathbf{E}||_F^2) \\
s.t.\quad &\mathbf{U}^T\mathbf{U} = \mathbf{I}, \mathbf{Z} \geq \mathbf{0}
\end{aligned} \tag{15}$$

where $\mathbf{Y}_1, \mathbf{Y}_2$ are two Lagrangian multipliers and μ is a scalar to control the penalty for the violation of equality constraints $\mathbf{E} = \mathbf{X} - \mathbf{U}\mathbf{V}^T$ and $\mathbf{Z} = \mathbf{U}$.

Update E

To update $\mathbf{E}$, we fix the other variables except $\mathbf{E}$ and remove terms that are irrelevant to $\mathbf{E}$. Then Eq.(15) becomes

$$\min_{\mathbf{E}} \frac{1}{2}||\mathbf{E} - (\mathbf{X} - \mathbf{U}\mathbf{V}^T + \frac{1}{\mu}\mathbf{Y}_2)||_F^2 + \frac{1}{\mu}||\mathbf{E}||_{2,1} \tag{16}$$

The equation has a closed form solution by the following Lemma (Liu *et al.* 2009)

Lemma 3. *Let* $\mathbf{Q} = [\mathbf{q}_1; \mathbf{q}_2; ...; \mathbf{q}_m]$ *be a given matrix and* λ *a positive scalar. If the the optimal solution of*

$$\min_{\mathbf{W}} \frac{1}{2}||\mathbf{W} - \mathbf{Q}||_F^2 + \lambda||\mathbf{W}||_{2,1} \tag{17}$$

is $\mathbf{W}^*$, *then the* i*-th row of* $\mathbf{W}^*$ *is*

$$\mathbf{w}_i^* = \begin{cases} (1 - \frac{\lambda}{||\mathbf{q}_i||})\mathbf{q}_i, & \text{if } ||\mathbf{q}_i|| > \lambda \\ \mathbf{0}, & \text{otherwise} \end{cases} \tag{18}$$

Apparently, if we let $\mathbf{Q} = \mathbf{X} - \mathbf{U}\mathbf{V}^T + \frac{1}{\mu}\mathbf{Y}_2$, then using Lemma 3, $\mathbf{E}$ can be updated as

$$\mathbf{e}_i = \begin{cases} (1 - \frac{1}{\mu||\mathbf{q}_i||})\mathbf{q}_i, & \text{if } ||\mathbf{q}_i|| > \frac{1}{\mu} \\ \mathbf{0}, & \text{otherwise} \end{cases} \tag{19}$$

Update V

To update $\mathbf{V}$, we fix the other variables except $\mathbf{V}$ and remove terms that are irrelevant to $\mathbf{V}$, then Eq.(15) becomes

$$\min_{\mathbf{V},\mathbf{U}^T\mathbf{U}=\mathbf{I}} \frac{\mu}{2}||\mathbf{X} - \mathbf{U}\mathbf{V}^T - \mathbf{E} + \frac{1}{\mu}\mathbf{Y}_2||_F^2 + \alpha||\mathbf{V}||_{2,1} \tag{20}$$

Using the fact that $\mathbf{U}^T\mathbf{U} = \mathbf{I}$, we can reformulate Eq.(20) as

$$\min_{\mathbf{V}} \frac{1}{2}||\mathbf{V} - (\mathbf{X} - \mathbf{E} + \frac{1}{\mu}\mathbf{Y}_2)^T\mathbf{U}||_F^2 + \frac{\alpha}{\mu}||\mathbf{V}||_{2,1} \tag{21}$$

Again, the above equation has a closed form solution according to Lemma 3. Let $\mathbf{K} = (\mathbf{X} - \mathbf{E} + \frac{1}{\mu}\mathbf{Y}_2)^T\mathbf{U}$, then

$$\mathbf{v}_i = \begin{cases} (1 - \frac{\alpha}{\mu||\mathbf{k}_i||})\mathbf{k}_i, & \text{if } ||\mathbf{k}_i|| > \frac{\alpha}{\mu} \\ \mathbf{0}, & \text{otherwise} \end{cases} \tag{22}$$

Update Z

Similarly, to update $\mathbf{Z}$, we fix $\mathbf{U}, \mathbf{V}, \mathbf{E}, \mathbf{Y}_1, \mathbf{Y}_2, \mu$ and remove terms irrelevant to $\mathbf{Z}$, then Eq.(15) becomes

$$\min_{\mathbf{Z}\geq\mathbf{0}} \frac{\mu}{2}||\mathbf{Z}-\mathbf{U}||_F^2 + \beta\text{Tr}(\mathbf{Z}^T\mathbf{L}\mathbf{U}) + \langle\mathbf{Y}_1, \mathbf{Z}-\mathbf{U}\rangle \quad (23)$$

We can rewrite Eq.(23) by putting the second and third terms to the quadratic term and get a compact form

$$\min_{\mathbf{Z}\geq\mathbf{0}} ||\mathbf{Z}-\mathbf{T}||_F^2 \quad (24)$$

where $\mathbf{T}$ is defined as

$$\mathbf{T} = (\mathbf{U} - \frac{1}{\mu}\mathbf{Y}_1 - \frac{\beta}{\mu}\mathbf{L}\mathbf{U}) \quad (25)$$

Eq.(24) can be further decomposed to element-wise optimization problems as

$$\min_{Z_{ij}\geq 0} (Z_{ij} - T_{ij})^2 \quad (26)$$

Clearly, the optimal solution of the above problem is

$$Z_{ij} = \max(T_{ij}, 0) \quad (27)$$

Update U

Optimizing Eq.(15) with respect to $\mathbf{U}$ yields the equation

$$\min_{\mathbf{U}^T\mathbf{U}=\mathbf{I}} \langle\mathbf{Y}_1, \mathbf{Z}-\mathbf{U}\rangle + \left\langle\mathbf{Y}_2, \mathbf{X}-\mathbf{U}\mathbf{V}^T-\mathbf{E}\right\rangle + \frac{\mu}{2}(||\mathbf{Z}-\mathbf{U}||_F^2 + ||\mathbf{X}-\mathbf{U}\mathbf{V}^T-\mathbf{E}||_F^2) + \beta\text{Tr}(\mathbf{Z}^T\mathbf{L}\mathbf{U}) \quad (28)$$

By expanding Eq.(28) and dropping terms that are independent of $\mathbf{U}$, we arrive at

$$\min_{\mathbf{U}^T\mathbf{U}=\mathbf{I}} \frac{\mu}{2}||\mathbf{U}||_F^2 - \mu\langle\mathbf{N}, \mathbf{U}\rangle \quad (29)$$

where $\mathbf{N}$ is defined as

$$\mathbf{N} = \frac{1}{\mu}\mathbf{Y}_1 + \mathbf{Z} - \beta\mathbf{L}\mathbf{Z} + (\mathbf{X} - \mathbf{E} + \frac{1}{\mu}\mathbf{Y}_2)\mathbf{V} \quad (30)$$

We can further write the above equation into a more compact form as

$$\min_{\mathbf{U}^T\mathbf{U}=\mathbf{I}} ||\mathbf{U}-\mathbf{N}||_F^2 \quad (31)$$

And now we have converted the objective function of updating $\mathbf{U}$ to the classical Orthogonal Procrutes problem (Schönemann 1966) and can be solved using the following lemma (Huang *et al.* 2014)

Lemma 4. *Given the objective in Eq.(31), the optimal* $\mathbf{U}$ *is defined as*

$$\mathbf{U} = \mathbf{P}\mathbf{Q}^T \quad (32)$$

where $\mathbf{P}$ *and* $\mathbf{Q}$ *are the left and right singular vectors of the economic singular value decomposition (SVD) of* $\mathbf{N}$.

Update $\mathbf{Y}_1$, $\mathbf{Y}_2$ and μ

After updating the variables, we now need to update the ADMM parameters. According to (Boyd *et al.* 2011), they are updated as follows

$$\mathbf{Y}_1 = \mathbf{Y}_1 + \mu(\mathbf{Z}-\mathbf{U}) \quad (33)$$

$$\mathbf{Y}_2 = \mathbf{Y}_2 + \mu(\mathbf{X}-\mathbf{U}\mathbf{V}^T-\mathbf{E}) \quad (34)$$

$$\mu = \max(\rho\mu, \mu_{max}) \quad (35)$$

Here, $\rho > 1$ is a parameter to control the convergence speed and μ_{max} is a larger number to prevent μ becomes too large.

With these updating rules, EUFS algorithm is summarized in Algorithm 1.

Algorithm 1 Embedded Unsupervised Feature Selection

Input: $\mathbf{X} \in \mathbf{R}^{N\times d}, \alpha, \beta, n$, latent dimensional k

Output: n features for the dataset

Initialize $\mu = 10^{-3}, \rho = 1.1, \mu_{max} = 10^{10}$, $\mathbf{U} = \mathbf{0}, \mathbf{V} = \mathbf{0}$ (or initialized using K-means)

repeat

Calculate $\mathbf{Q} = \mathbf{X} - \mathbf{U}\mathbf{V}^T + \frac{1}{\mu}\mathbf{Y}_2$

Update $\mathbf{E}$

$$\mathbf{e}_i = \begin{cases} (1 - \frac{1}{\mu||\mathbf{q}_i||})\mathbf{q}_i, & \text{if } ||\mathbf{q}_i|| > \frac{1}{\mu} \\ \mathbf{0}, & \text{otherwise} \end{cases} \quad (36)$$

Calculate $\mathbf{K} = (\mathbf{X} - \mathbf{E} + \frac{1}{\mu}\mathbf{Y}_2)^T\mathbf{U}$

Update $\mathbf{V}$

$$\mathbf{v}_i = \begin{cases} (1 - \frac{\alpha}{\mu||\mathbf{k}_i||})\mathbf{k}_i, & \text{if } ||\mathbf{k}_i|| > \frac{\alpha}{\mu} \\ \mathbf{0}, & \text{otherwise} \end{cases} \quad (37)$$

Calculate $\mathbf{T}$ using Eq.(25)

Update $\mathbf{Z}$ using Eq.(27)

Calculate $\mathbf{N}$ according to Eq.(30)

Update $\mathbf{U}$ by Lemma 4

Update $\mathbf{Y}_1, \mathbf{Y}_2, \mu$

until convergence

Sort each feature of $\mathbf{X}$ according to $||\mathbf{v}_i||_2$ in descending order and select the top-n ranked ones

Parameter Initialization

One way to initialize $\mathbf{U}$ and $\mathbf{V}$ is to simply set them to be $\mathbf{0}$. As the algorithm runs, the objective function will gradually converge to the optimal value. To accelerate the convergence speed, following the common way of initializing NMF, we can use k-means to initialize $\mathbf{U}$ and $\mathbf{V}$. To be specific, we apply k-means to cluster rows of $\mathbf{X}$ and get the soft cluster indicator $\mathbf{U}$. $\mathbf{V}$ is simply set as $\mathbf{X}^T\mathbf{U}$. μ is typically set in the range of 10^{-6} to 10^{-3} initially depending on the datasets and is updated in each iteration. μ_{max} is set to be a large value such as 10^{10} to give μ freedom to increase but prevent it from being too large. ρ is empirically set to 1.1 in our algorithm. The larger ρ is , the faster μ becomes larger and the more we penalize the deviation of the equality constraint, which makes it converges faster. However, we may sacrifice some precision of the final objective function with large ρ.

Convergence Analysis

The convergence of our algorithm depends on the convergence of the ADMM. The detailed convergence proof of ADMM can be found in (Goldstein *et al.* 2012; Boyd *et al.* 2011). The convergence criteria can be set as $\frac{|\mathbf{J}_{t+1}-\mathbf{J}_t|}{\mathbf{J}_t} < \epsilon$, where $\mathbf{J}_t$ is the objective function value in Eq.(14) and ϵ is some tolerance value. In practice, we can control the number of iterations by setting a maximum iteration value. Our experiments find that our algorithm converges within 110 iterations for all the datasets we used.

Time Complexity Analysis

The computation cost for $\mathbf{E}$ depends on the computation of $\mathbf{Q} = \mathbf{X} - \mathbf{U}\mathbf{V}^T + \frac{1}{\mu}\mathbf{Y}_2$ and update of $\mathbf{E}$. Since $\mathbf{U}$ is sparse, i.e., each row of $\mathbf{U}$ only has one nonzero element, then the computation cost is O(Nd) and O(Nd), respectively.

Similarly, the computation cost for $\mathbf{V}$ involves the computation of $\mathbf{K} = (\mathbf{X} - \mathbf{E} + \frac{1}{\mu}\mathbf{Y}_2)^T\mathbf{U}$ and update of $\mathbf{V}$, which is O(Nd) again due to the sparsity of $\mathbf{U}$.

The main computation cost for $\mathbf{Z}$ is the computation of $\mathbf{T} = (\mathbf{U} - \frac{1}{\mu}\mathbf{Y}_1^T - \frac{\beta}{\mu}\mathbf{L}\mathbf{U})$, which is O($k^2$) due to the sparsity of both $\mathbf{U}$ and $\mathbf{L}$.

The main computation cost of $\mathbf{U}$ involves the computation of $\mathbf{N}$ and its SVD decomposition, which is O(Ndk) and O(Nk^2). The computational cost for $\mathbf{Y_1}$ and $\mathbf{Y_2}$ are both O(Nd). Therefore, the overall time complexity is O($Ndk + Nk^2$). Since $d \gg k$, the final computation cost if O(Ndk) for each iteration.

Experimental Analysis

In this section, we conduct experiments to evaluate the effectiveness of EUFS [1]. After introducing datasets and experimental settings, we compare EUFS with the state-of-the-art unsupervised feature selection methods. Further experiments are conducted to investigate the effects of important parameters on EUFS.

Datasets

The experiments are conducted on 6 publicly available benchmark datasets, including one Mass Spectrometry (MS) dataset ALLAML (Fodor 1997), two microarray datasets, i.e., Prostate Cancer gene expression (Prostate-GE) [2] (Singh *et al.* 2002) and TOX-171, two face image datasets, i.e., PIX10P and PIE10P[3] and one object image dataset COIL20[4] (Nene *et al.* 1996). The statistics of the datasets used in the experiments are summarized in Table 1.

[1]The implementation of EUFS can be found from http://www.public.asu.edu/ swang187/

[2]ALLAML and Prostate-GE are publicly available from https://sites.google.com/site/feipingnie/file

[3]TOX-171, PIX10P and PIE10P are publicly available from http://featureselection.asu.edu/datasets.php

[4]COIL20 is publicly available from http://www.cad.zju.edu.cn/home/dengcai/Data/MLData.html

Table 1: Statistics of the Dataset

Dataset	# of Samples	# of Features	# of Classes
ALLAML	72	7192	2
COIL20	1440	1024	20
PIE10P	210	1024	10
TOX-171	171	5748	4
PIX10P	100	10000	10
Prostate-GE	102	5996	2

Experimental Settings

Following the common way to evaluate unsupervised feature selection algorithms, we assess EUFS in terms of clustering performance (Zhao and Liu 2007; Li *et al.* 2012). We compare EUFS with the following representative unsupervised feature selection algorithms:

- **All Features**: All original features are adopted
- **LS**: Laplacian Score (He *et al.* 2005) which evaluates the importance of a feature through its power of locality preservation
- **MCFS**: Multi-Cluster Feature Selection (Cai *et al.* 2010) which selects features using spectral regression with l_1-norm regularization
- **NDFS**: Nonnegative Discriminative Feature Selection (Li *et al.* 2012) which selects features by a joint feamewrok of nonnegative spectral analysis and $l_{2,1}$ regularized regression
- **RUFS**: Robust Unsupervised Feature Selection (Qian and Zhai 2013) which jointly performs robust label learning via local learning regularized robust orthogonal nonnegative matrix factorization and robust feature learning via joint $l_{2,1}$-norms minimization.

Two widely used evaluation metrics, *accuracy* (ACC) and *normalized mutual information* (NMI), are employed to evaluate the quality of clusters. The larger ACC and NMI are, the better performance is.

There are some parameters to be set. Following (Qian and Zhai 2013), for LS, MCFS, NDFS, RUFS and EUFS, we fix the neighborhood size to be 5 for all the datasets. To fairly compare different unsupervised feature selection methods, we tune the parameters for all methods by a "grid-search" strategy from $\{10^{-6}, 10^{-4}, \ldots, 10^4, 10^6\}$. For EUFS, we set the latent dimension as the number of clusters. How to determine the optimal number of selected features is still an open problem (Tang and Liu 2012a), we set the number of selected features as {50, 100, 150, ..., 300} for all datasets. Best clustering results from the optimal parameters are reported for all the algorithms. In the evaluation , we use K-means to cluster samples based on the selected features. Since K-means depends on initialization, following previous work, we repeat the experiments 20 times and the average results with standard deviation are reported.

Experimental Results

The experimental results of different methods on the datasets are summarized in Table 2 and Table 3. We make the follow-

Table 2: Clustering results(ACC%±std) of different feature selection algorithms on different datasets. The best results are highlighted in bold. The number in parentheses is the number of features when the performance is achieved

Dataset	ALL Features	Laplacian Score	MCFS	NDFS	RUFS	EUFS
ALLAML	67.3±6.72	73.2±5.52(150)	68.4±10.4(100)	69.4±0.00(100)	72.2±0.00(150)	**73.6±0.00**(100)
COIL20	53.6±3.83	55.2±2.84(250)	59.7±4.03(250)	60.1±4.26(300)	62.7±3.51(150)	**63.4±5.47**(100)
PIE10P	30.8±2.29	36.0±2.95(100)	44.3±3.20(50)	40.5±4.51(100)	42.6±4.61(50)	**46.4±2.69**(50)
TOX-171	41.5±3.88	47.5±3.33(200)	42.5±5.15(100)	46.1±2.55(100)	47.8±3.78(300)	**49.5±2.57**(100)
PIX10P	74.3±12.1	76.6±8.10(150)	75.9±8.59(200)	76.7±8.52(200)	73.2±9.40(300)	**76.8±5.88**(150)
Prostate-GE	58.1±0.44	57.5±0.49(300)	57.3±0.50(300)	58.3±0.50(100)	59.8±0.00(50)	**60.4±0.80**(100)

Table 3: Clustering results(NMI%±std) of different feature selection algorithms on different datasets. The best results are highlighted in bold. The number in parentheses is the number of features when the performance is achieved

Dataset	ALL Features	Laplacian Score	MCFS	NDFS	RUFS	EUFS
ALLAML	8.55±5.62	15.0±1.34(100)	11.7±12.2(50)	7.20±0.30(300)	12.0±0.00(150)	**15.1±0.00**(100)
COIL20	70.6±1.95	70.3±1.73(300)	72.4±1.90(150)	72.1±1.75(300)	73.1±1.69(150)	**77.2±2.75**(100)
PIE10P	32.2±3.47	38.5±1.44(50)	**54.3±3.39**(50)	46.0±3.14(100)	49.6±5.15(50)	49.8±3.10(150)
TOX-171	17.8±5.20	**30.5±2.70**(150)	17.7±6.88(100)	22.3±2.41(300)	28.8±2.71(300)	26.0±2.41(100)
PIX10P	82.8±6.48	84.3±4.63(150)	85.0±4.95(200)	84.8±4.76(200)	81.1±6.23(300)	**85.1±4.30**(50)
Prostate-GE	1.95±0.27	1.59±0.21(300)	1.53±0.21(300)	2.02±0.25(100)	2.86±0.00(50)	**3.36±0.48**(100)

ing observations:

- Feature selection is necessary and effective. The selected subset of the features can not only reduce the computation cost, but also improve the clustering performance;
- Robust analysis is also important for unsupervised feature selection, which helps us select more relevant features and improve the performance;
- EUFS tends to achieve better performance with usually fewer selected features such as 50 or 100; and
- Most of the time, the proposed framework EUFS outperforms baseline methods, which demonstrates the effectiveness of the proposed algorithm. There are two major reasons. First, we directly embed feature selection in the process of clustering using sparse learning and the norm of the latent feature reflects the quality of the reconstruction and thus the importance of the original feature. Second, the graph regularize helps to learn better cluster indicators that fits the existing manifold structure, which leads to a better latent feature matrix. Finally, we introduce robust analysis to ensure that these poorly reconstructed instances have less effect on feature selection.

We also perform parameter analysis for some important parameters of EUFS. Due to space limit, we only report the results on COIL20 in Figure2. The experimental results show that our method is not very sensitive to α and β. However, the performance is relatively sensitive to the number of selected features, which is a common problem for many unsupervised feature selection methods.

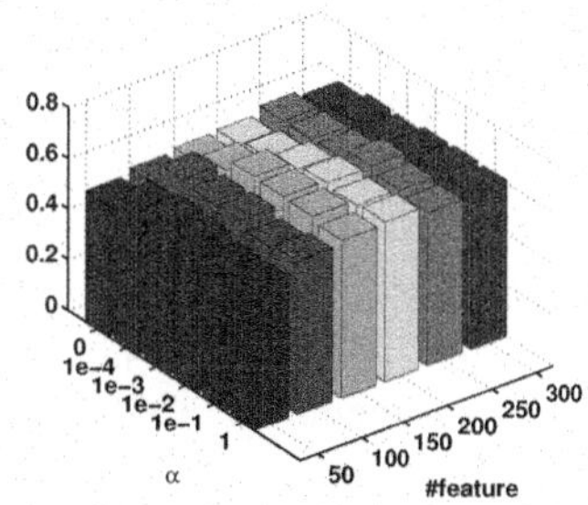

(a) ACC for COIL20 ($\beta = 0.1$)

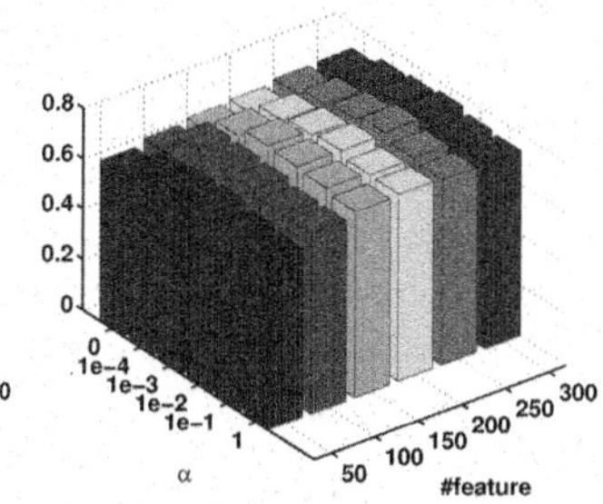

(b) NMI for COIL20 ($\beta = 0.1$)

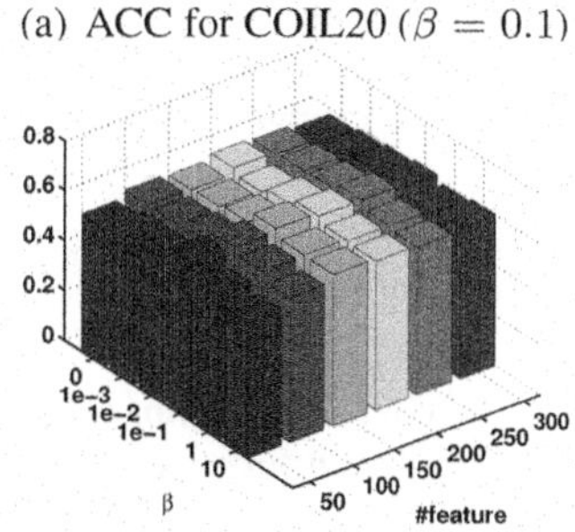

(c) ACC for COIL20 ($\alpha = 0.1$)

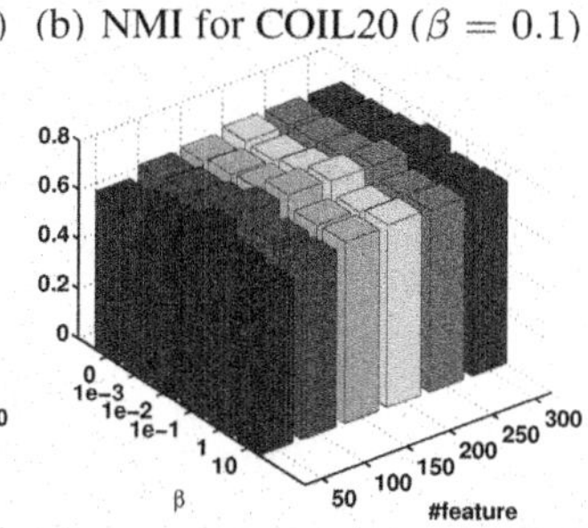

(d) NMI for COIL20 ($\alpha = 0.1$)

Figure 2: ACC and NMI of EUFS with different α, β and feature numbers on datasets COIL20

Conclusion

We propose a new unsupervised feature selection approach, EUFS, which directly embeds feature selection into a clustering algorithm via sparse learning. It eliminates the need for transforming unsupervised feature selection into the sparse learning based supervised feature selection with pseudo labels. Nonnegative orthogonality is applied on the cluster indicator to make the problem tractable and ensure that feature selection on latent features has similar effects as on original features. $l_{2,1}$-norm is applied on the cost function to reduce the effects of the noise introduced by the reconstruction of $\mathbf{X}$ and feature selection on $\mathbf{V}$. Experimental results on 6 different real world datasets validate the unique contributions of EUFS. Future work is to investigate if EUFS can be extended to dimensionality reduction algorithms.

Acknowledgments

This material is based upon work supported by, or in part by, the National Science Foundation (NSF) under grant number

IIS-1217466.

References

Salem Alelyani, Jiliang Tang, and Huan Liu. Feature selection for clustering: A review. In *Data Clustering: Algorithms and Applications*, pages 29–60. CRC Press, 2013.

Christos Boutsidis, Petros Drineas, and Michael W Mahoney. Unsupervised feature selection for the k-means clustering problem. In *Advances in Neural Information Processing Systems*, pages 153–161, 2009.

Stephen Boyd and Lieven Vandenberghe. *Convex optimization*. Cambridge university press, 2004.

Stephen Boyd, Neal Parikh, Eric Chu, Borja Peleato, and Jonathan Eckstein. Distributed optimization and statistical learning via the alternating direction method of multipliers. *Foundations and Trends® in Machine Learning*, 3(1):1–122, 2011.

Deng Cai, Chiyuan Zhang, and Xiaofei He. Unsupervised feature selection for multi-cluster data. In *Proceedings of the 16th ACM SIGKDD international conference on Knowledge discovery and data mining*, pages 333–342. ACM, 2010.

Richard O Duda, Peter E Hart, and David G Stork. Pattern classification. 2nd. *Edition. New York*, 2001.

Stephen P. A. Fodor. Dna sequencing: Massively parallel genomics. 277(5324):393–395, 1997.

Tom Goldstein, Brendan ODonoghue, and Simon Setzer. Fast alternating direction optimization methods. *CAM report*, pages 12–35, 2012.

Quanquan Gu and Jiawei Han. Towards feature selection in network. In *Proceedings of the 20th ACM international conference on Information and knowledge management*, pages 1175–1184. ACM, 2011.

Isabelle Guyon and André Elisseeff. An introduction to variable and feature selection. *The Journal of Machine Learning Research*, 3:1157–1182, 2003.

Xiaofei He, Deng Cai, and Partha Niyogi. Laplacian score for feature selection. In *Advances in neural information processing systems*, pages 507–514, 2005.

Jin Huang, Feiping Nie, Heng Huang, and Chris Ding. Robust manifold nonnegative matrix factorization. *ACM Transactions on Knowledge Discovery from Data (TKDD)*, 8(3):11, 2014.

Anil Jain and Douglas Zongker. Feature selection: Evaluation, application, and small sample performance, 1997.

George H John, Ron Kohavi, Karl Pfleger, et al. Irrelevant features and the subset selection problem. In *ICML*, volume 94, pages 121–129, 1994.

Zechao Li, Yi Yang, Jing Liu, Xiaofang Zhou, and Hanqing Lu. Unsupervised feature selection using nonnegative spectral analysis. In *Proceedings of the Twenty-Sixth AAAI Conference on Artificial Intelligence, July 22-26, 2012, Toronto, Ontario, Canada.*, 2012.

Huan Liu and Hiroshi Motoda. *Computational methods of feature selection*. CRC Press, 2007.

Jun Liu, Shuiwang Ji, and Jieping Ye. Multi-task feature learning via efficient l 2, 1-norm minimization. In *Proceedings of the Twenty-Fifth Conference on Uncertainty in Artificial Intelligence*, pages 339–348. AUAI Press, 2009.

Sameer A Nene, Shree K Nayar, Hiroshi Murase, et al. Columbia object image library (coil-20). Technical report, Technical Report CUCS-005-96, 1996.

Feiping Nie, Shiming Xiang, Yangqing Jia, Changshui Zhang, and Shuicheng Yan. Trace ratio criterion for feature selection. In *AAAI*, volume 2, pages 671–676, 2008.

Feiping Nie, Heng Huang, Xiao Cai, and Chris H Ding. Efficient and robust feature selection via joint ?2, 1-norms minimization. In *Advances in Neural Information Processing Systems*, pages 1813–1821, 2010.

Mingjie Qian and Chengxiang Zhai. Robust unsupervised feature selection. In *Proceedings of the Twenty-Third international joint conference on Artificial Intelligence*, pages 1621–1627. AAAI Press, 2013.

Peter H Schönemann. A generalized solution of the orthogonal procrustes problem. *Psychometrika*, 31(1):1–10, 1966.

Dinesh Singh, Phillip G Febbo, Kenneth Ross, Donald G Jackson, Judith Manola, Christine Ladd, Pablo Tamayo, Andrew A Renshaw, Anthony V D'Amico, Jerome P Richie, et al. Gene expression correlates of clinical prostate cancer behavior. *Cancer cell*, 1(2):203–209, 2002.

Jiliang Tang and Huan Liu. Feature selection with linked data in social media. In *Proceedings of the Twelfth SIAM International Conference on Data Mining, Anaheim, California, USA, April 26-28, 2012.*, pages 118–128, 2012.

Jiliang Tang and Huan Liu. Unsupervised feature selection for linked social media data. In *Proceedings of the 18th ACM SIGKDD international conference on Knowledge discovery and data mining*, pages 904–912. ACM, 2012.

Jiliang Tang, Salem Alelyani, and Huan Liu. Feature selection for classification: A review. In *Data Classification: Algorithms and Applications*. 2014.

Ulrike Von Luxburg. A tutorial on spectral clustering. *Statistics and computing*, 17(4):395–416, 2007.

Lior Wolf and Amnon Shashua. Feature selection for unsupervised and supervised inference: The emergence of sparsity in a weight-based approach. *The Journal of Machine Learning Research*, 6:1855–1887, 2005.

Yi Yang, Heng Tao Shen, Zhigang Ma, Zi Huang, and Xiaofang Zhou. l2, 1-norm regularized discriminative feature selection for unsupervised learning. In *IJCAI Proceedings-International Joint Conference on Artificial Intelligence*, volume 22, page 1589, 2011.

Zheng Zhao and Huan Liu. Spectral feature selection for supervised and unsupervised learning. In *Proceedings of the 24th international conference on Machine learning*, pages 1151–1157. ACM, 2007.

Zheng Zhao, Lei Wang, and Huan Liu. Efficient spectral feature selection with minimum redundancy. In *Proceedings of the Twenty-Fourth AAAI Conference on Artificial Intelligence, AAAI 2010, Atlanta, Georgia, USA, July 11-15, 2010*, 2010.

Proceedings of the Twenty-Ninth AAAI Conference on Artificial Intelligence

Learning User-Specific Latent Influence and Susceptibility from Information Cascades

Yongqing Wang*, Huawei Shen†, Shenghua Liu† and Xueqi Cheng†
CAS Key Laboratory of Network Data Science and Technology,
Institute of Computing Technology, Chinese Academy of Sciences, Beijing 100190, China
*wangyongqing@software.ict.ac.cn, †{shenhuawei,liushenghua,cxq}@ict.ac.cn

Abstract

Predicting cascade dynamics has important implications for understanding information propagation and launching viral marketing. Previous works mainly adopt a pair-wise manner, modeling the propagation probability between pairs of users using n^2 independent parameters for n users. Consequently, these models suffer from severe overfitting problem, especially for pairs of users without direct interactions, limiting their prediction accuracy. Here we propose to model the cascade dynamics by learning two low-dimensional user-specific vectors from observed cascades, capturing their influence and susceptibility respectively. This model requires much less parameters and thus could combat overfitting problem. Moreover, this model could naturally model context-dependent factors like cumulative effect in information propagation. Extensive experiments on synthetic dataset and a large-scale microblogging dataset demonstrate that this model outperforms the existing pair-wise models at predicting cascade dynamics, cascade size, and "who will be retweeted".

Introduction

Social media is revolutionizing the dissemination of information via its great ease in information delivery, accessing and filtering. In social media, users could post original messages or forward messages that they see from other users. Information propagation proceeds along social relationships between users, explicit or implicit, forming cascade dynamics. Modeling and predicting the cascade dynamics has important implications to understanding information propagation and launching viral marketing in social media. The key for this problem is inferring the interpersonal influence between users or estimating the probability that information propagates between them, fundamental to influence maximization (Kempe, Kleinberg, and Tardos 2003; Chen, Wang, and Yang 2009; Cheng et al. 2013), social recommendation (Huang et al. 2012; Ma, King, and Lyu 2009), and viral marketing (Richardson and Domingos 2002; Leskovec, Adamic, and Huberman 2007).

Existing studies mainly aim to determine the propagation probability of information between all pairs of users, based on structure of social network, the record of information cascade, and demographic/content characteristics of users. Kempe et al. (Kempe, Kleinberg, and Tardos 2003) implemented the independent cascade model for information propagation, assuming a uniform propagation probability or a degree-modulated propagation probability. Goyal et al. (Goyal, Bonchi, and Lakshmanan 2010) provided two static models in terms of Bernoulli distribution and Jaccard index, and learned temporal factors to maximize likelihood of cascades. Saito et al. (Saito, Nakano, and Kimura 2008) learned the propagation probability for independent cascade model in terms of expectation maximization of cascades. Artzi et al. (Artzi, Pantel, and Gamon 2012) estimated the propagation probability by exploiting demographic and content characteristics. These methods all adopt a pair-wise manner, modeling the propagation probability between pairs of users using n^2 independent parameters for n users. Consequently, these models suffer from severe overfitting problem, limiting their prediction accuracy. For example, for a pair of users without observed interactions, these methods take the propagation probability between them as zero, indicating that it is never happened to propagate information between the two users in the future. To the best of our knowledge, we lack a model that could concisely model the interpersonal influence and accurately predict the cascade dynamics in large-scale social networks.

In this paper, we propose to model the cascade dynamics by learning two low-dimensional latent vectors for each user from observed cascades, capturing her influence and susceptibility respectively. In this latent influence and susceptibility (LIS) model, the propagation probability that one user forwards a piece of information is determined by the product of her activated neighbors' influence vectors and her own susceptibility vector. The benefits of this model are three-fold: (1) It directly models user-specific influence and susceptibility, instead of the interpersonal influence between all pairs of users. Thus it requires much less parameters, and pairs of users are no longer independent, effectively combating the overfitting problem for pairs of users without direct interactions; (2) It could naturally capture context-dependent factors like cumulative effect in information propagation. For a target user, context means her previous exposures to the same message. In this model, one user's previous exposures to a message improve the probability that she propagates the message, flexibly combining the benefits of both cascade model and threshold model; (3) It is applicable to scenarios with explicit or implicit social networks, since it learns user-specific influence and susceptibility from the observed information cascades rather than the underlying social networks like many existing methods.

We evaluate the proposed LIS model by extensive experiments on synthetic dataset and a large-scale microblogging dataset from Sina Weibo, the largest social media in China. Compared with several widely-used methods that work in pair-wise manner, LIS model consistently outperforms them at predicting the dynamics of cascades. Moreover, the learned user-specific influence and susceptibility vectors provide us a quantitative way to understand topic-related interpersonal influence in information propagation.

Problem formulation

In this paper, we focus on the problem of inferring users' influence and susceptibility from detailed records of message cascades. Before diving into the details of the proposed model, we first clarify the two main motivations underlying our model.

First, existing models suffer from severe overfitting problem, especially for the pair of users without direct interactions. As shown in Fig. 1(a), when messages are forwarded by users along social links among them, not all social links matter in these message cascades. For example, no forwarding behavior occurs between users u_1 and u_4, although they have direct social link. In this case, existing models take the propagation probability between them as zero, implying that it is never happened to propagate information between the two users in the future. This overfitting problem is actually caused by the hypothesis of existing models: *interpersonal influence between different pairs of users is independent of each other*. This motivates us to adopt a user-specific manner for modeling interpersonal influence among users, whose existence has been proved in (Aral and Walker 2012; Aral, Muchnik, and Sundararajan 2009). Specifically, each user u is modeled by two non-negative d-dimensional vectors: an influence vector I_u and a susceptibility vector S_u, characterizing the influence and susceptibility of user u over d latent topics. For a pair of user (u, v), the interpersonal influence of u on v could be simply computed by the scalar product of I_u and S_v. This concise representation requires only $2nd$ ($\ll n^2$) parameters for n users.

Second, the role of context in information propagation is rarely captured. Existing models mostly assume that users are *memoryless*, i.e., whether a user forwards one message is not affected by her previous exposures to the message. Indeed, this assumption is not supported by empirical observations from real cascades of messages. Fig. 1(b) depicts the relationship between the number of times k that one user is exposed to a message and the probability that the user will forward the message when she is exposed to the message for the k-th time. As the number of exposures increases, the forwarding probability increases accordingly: from 0.008 when the number of exposures is 1 to 0.261 when the number of exposures is 5. This observation clearly demonstrates that cumulative effect does exist in information propagation, an effect also observed in many other scenarios (Bao et al.

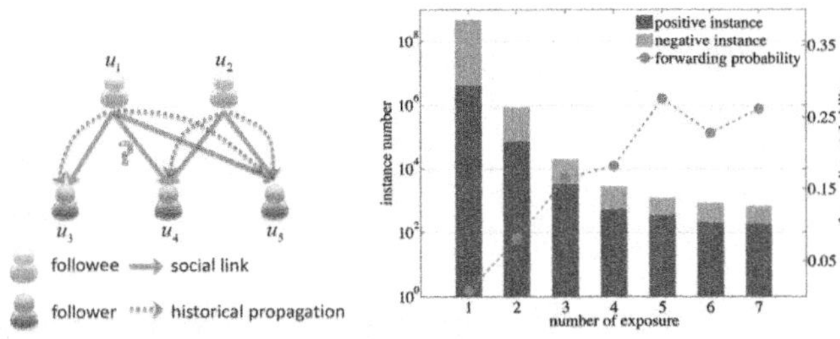

(a) (b)

Figure 1: Motivations underlying our model. (a) Example of cascades to illustrate the overfitting problem suffered by pair-wise models; (b) Relationship between forwarding probability and number of exposures (observed from Sina Weibo, Jan. 1-15, 2011).

2013a; Leskovec, Adamic, and Huberman 2007). This motivates us to adopt a context-dependent way to model the cumulative effect.

Given a message m, we denote its cascade C^m with a chronological list of activated users $(a_1^m, \ldots, a_N^m)$, where users are ranked in the ascending order of the time they forward the message m. Whenever one user is activated (i.e., she posts or forwards the message), she has one chance to attempt to activate other users. Whether her attempt succeeds depends on the *cascade context* at that time.

Cascade context: When one user a_i^m $(i = 1, \ldots, N)$ becomes activated and she attempts to activate a user v, the cascade context for this attempt is defined as

$$\mathcal{D}_{v,i}^m = \{a_j^m | j \leq i, \delta(a_j^m, v) = 1\}, \tag{1}$$

where the indicator function $\delta(u, v)$ means whether v could be exposed to the message from u. In other words, cascade context means v's previous exposures to the message from other users.

In practice, it is difficult to exactly determine $\delta(u, v)$ since there is no reliable mechanism to know whether user v is exposed to a message forwarded by user u, even when direct social link exists between them. In this paper, we circumvent this problem using a delegate of the function δ, i.e., the aggregate diffusion network of historical cascades of messages. Detailed discussions about diffusion network are given in experiments on real dataset. Diffusion network characterizes the actual flow of information between users in the past, providing us a good approximation for potential information propagation in the future. More importantly, diffusion network is always embedded in the collection of message cascades while social network is not explicitly available in many scenarios. Therefore, the proposed model is generally applicable to the scenarios with or without explicit social network.

With the above notations, we now model cascade dynamics of messages. For a message m with the cascade $(a_1^m, \ldots, a_N^m)$, each user could be denoted by an N-dimensional status vector $\mathbf{z}_v^m$, with its element $z_{v,j}^m$ indicating whether the user v is in activated status right after she is exposed to the message m from user a_j^m. If user v becomes activated when she is exposed to the message m from

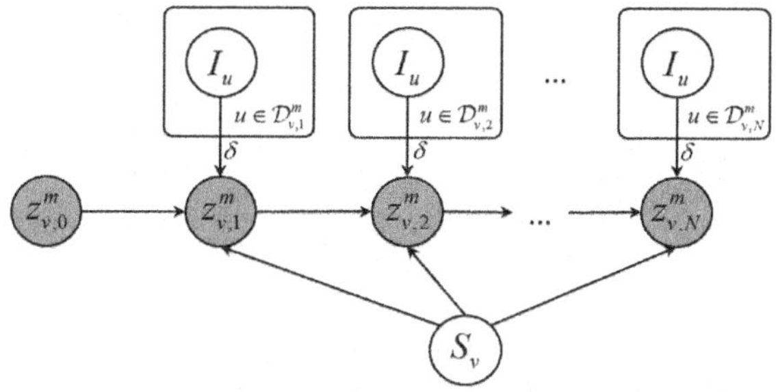

Figure 2: Graphical representation of the proposed model.

user a^m_j, we have $z^m_{v,i} = 0$ $(1 \le i < j)$ and $z^m_{v,i} = 1$ $(j \le i \le N)$. If v keeps inactivated during the cascade dynamics of message m, $z^m_{v,i} = 0$ for any i.

The likelihood of $\mathbf{z}^m_v$ is written as

$$P(\mathbf{z}^m_v|\delta) = p\left(z^m_{v,0}\right) \prod_{i=1}^{N} p\left(z^m_{v,i}|z^m_{v,i-1}, \mathcal{D}^m_{v,i}, \delta\right), \quad (2)$$

where $z^m_{v,0}$ is introduced only for simplifying the notation. Here the first term depicts whether v is the source of message m, defined as

$$p\left(z^m_{v,0} = 1\right) = \begin{cases} 1, v \text{ is the source} \\ 0, \text{otherwise} \end{cases}. \quad (3)$$

The second term characterizes the transition of user's status, formally defined as

$$\begin{aligned} &p\left(z^m_{v,i} = 1|z^m_{v,i-1} = 1, \mathcal{D}^m_{v,i}, \delta\right) = 1, \\ &p\left(z^m_{v,i} = 1|z^m_{v,i-1} = 0, \mathcal{D}^m_{v,i}, \delta\right) = \\ &\qquad 1 - \exp\left(-\lambda\delta(a^m_i, v) \textstyle\sum_{u \in \mathcal{D}^m_{v,i}} I^T_u S_v\right), \quad (4) \\ &p\left(z^m_{v,i} = 0|z^m_{v,i-1} = 0, \mathcal{D}^m_{v,i}, \delta\right) = \\ &\qquad 1 - p\left(z^m_{v,i} = 1|z^m_{v,i-1} = 0, \mathcal{D}^m_{v,i}, \delta\right), \end{aligned}$$

where λ is a scaling factor, modulating the effect of cascade context. The first equation implies that a user cannot become inactivated as long as she is activated. The other two equations model how the transition probability is influenced by cascade context, reflected by a cumulative manner of interpersonal influence. The factor $\delta(a^m_i, v)$ determines whether the user v could be exposed to the message m from user a^m_i. For clarity, we give a graphical model representation in Fig. 2 to illustrate the process that user v's status changes with the dynamics of message m.

Assuming independent cascades, the likelihood of all cascades $\mathbf{C}$ is a product of the likelihoods given by Eq. (2)

$$L(\mathbf{C}) = \prod_{m=1}^{|\mathbf{C}|} \prod_{v \in V} P\left(\mathbf{z}^m_v|\delta\right). \quad (5)$$

The parameters of the model are learned by minimizing the negative logarithmic likelihood, namely loss function, of all the collection of cascades as the following objective function

$$\mathcal{L}(\mathbf{C}) = -\sum_{m=1}^{|\mathbf{C}|} \sum_{v \in V} \sum_{i=1}^{N} \log p\left(z^m_{v,i}|z^m_{v,i-1}, \mathcal{D}^m_{v,i}, \delta\right). \quad (6)$$

Algorithm 1 Parameter estimation

Input: Collection of cascades observed in a given time period, the maximum epoch M, and regularization parameters γ_I and γ_S
Output: User-specific influence and susceptibility I, S

Construct diffusion network δ from cascades
Initialize parameters with random values, including I, S
repeat
  for $i = 1$ to n **do**
    Calculate gradients $\partial\hat{\mathcal{L}}/\partial I_u$ and $\partial\hat{\mathcal{L}}/\partial S_v$
  end for
  Update I and S with PG method
until maximum epoch M is reached or gradients vanish

Note that $p\left(z^m_{v,0}\right)$ is always 1, hence omitted in Eq. (6).

Parameter estimation

In this section, we develop algorithm to estimate the parameters of the proposed model. Generally speaking, parameter estimation could be completed via directly minimizing Eq. (6) with respect to I and S. However, the huge number of possible configurations of cascade contexts in Eq. (6) results in high computational cost. Indeed, *one* cascade context could repeatedly occur in many cascades, causing huge duplicated computation of Eq. (4).

Here we propose to reduce the duplicated computation by taking advantage of overlapped cascade contexts among multiple cascades. Firstly, we introduce some symbols to simplify the optimization. Let $\mathcal{P}(v)$ be the set of possible configurations of cascade contexts pertaining to v, occurred in all cascades. For example, as shown in Fig. 1(a), $\{u_1\}$, $\{u_2\}$ and $\{u_1, u_2\}$ are all the cascade contexts for user u_5. We group cascade contexts in terms of users and re-organize the logarithmic likelihood in Eq. (6) as

$$\mathcal{L}(\mathbf{C}) = -\sum_{v \in V} \sum_{\substack{\mathcal{D}_{v,i} \in \\ \mathcal{P}(v)}} \left(n_{z_{v,i},\mathcal{D}_{v,i}} \log p\left(z_{v,i}|z_{v,i-1}, \mathcal{D}_{v,i}, \delta\right)\right), \quad (7)$$

where $\mathcal{D}_{v,i}$ refers to one configuration of cascade context for user v, independent of specific cascade, and $n_{z_{v,i},\mathcal{D}_{v,i}}$ counts the frequency of the configuration $\mathcal{D}_{v,i}$ emerged in all cascades, relative to user v's status $z_{v,i}$.

Parameters estimated by directly minimizing the logarithmic likelihood in Eq. (7) may suffer from overfitting problem, a common problem in likelihood maximization estimation. To combat this problem, we regularize the parameter vectors I and S and obtain the final objective function for parameter estimation

$$\begin{aligned} \hat{\mathcal{L}}(\mathbf{C}) = &-\sum_{v \in V} \sum_{\substack{\mathcal{D}_{v,i} \in \\ \mathcal{P}(v)}} \left(n_{z_{v,i},\mathcal{D}_{v,i}} \log p\left(z_{v,i}|z_{v,i-1}, \mathcal{D}_{v,i}, \delta\right)\right) \\ &+ \gamma_I\|I\|^2_F + \gamma_S\|S\|^2_F, \\ &s.t.\ I_{ij} \ge 0, S_{ij} \ge 0, \forall i, j, \end{aligned} \quad (8)$$

where γ_I and γ_S are regularization parameters, and $\|\cdot\|_F$ is Frobenius norm.

Finally, using *Projected Gradient* (PG) method (Lin 2007), we develop an iterative algorithm for parameter estimation, leveraging the gradients with respect to I and S

as

$$
\begin{aligned}
\frac{\partial \hat{\mathcal{L}}}{\partial I_u} =& -\lambda \sum_{v \in V} S_v \sum_{\substack{\mathcal{D}_{v,i} \in \\ \mathcal{P}(v)}} \mathcal{I}_{u \in \mathcal{D}_{v,i}} \Big(n_{z_{v,i}=1,\mathcal{D}_{v,i}} \frac{1 - p_{v,\mathcal{D}_{v,i}}}{p_{v,\mathcal{D}_{v,i}}} \\
& - n_{z_{v,i}=0,\mathcal{D}_i(v)} \Big) + \gamma_I I_u, \\
\frac{\partial \hat{\mathcal{L}}}{\partial S_v} =& -\lambda \sum_{\substack{\mathcal{D}_{v,i} \in \\ \mathcal{P}(v)}} \sum_{u \in \mathcal{D}_{v,i}} I_u \Big(n_{z_{v,u}=1,\mathcal{D}_{v,u}} \frac{1 - p_{v,\mathcal{D}_{v,u}}}{p_{v,\mathcal{D}_{v,u}}} \\
& - n_{z_{v,u}=0,\mathcal{D}_{v,u}} \Big) + \gamma_S S_v,
\end{aligned} \tag{9}
$$

where $\mathcal{I}$ is an indicator function, and $p_{v,\mathcal{D}_{v,i}}$ is a concise form of $p(z_{v,i} = 1 | z_{v,i-1}, \mathcal{D}_{v,i}, \delta)$. The algorithm for parameter estimation is described in Algorithm 1.

Experiments

We evaluate LIS model on both synthetic data and real world data, i.e. microblogging data from Sina Weibo. Here we only choose scalable modeling methods as baselines, i.e., expectation maximization estimation (EM) (Saito, Nakano, and Kimura 2008), static Bernoulli model (SB), and static Jaccard model (SJ) (Goyal, Bonchi, and Lakshmanan 2010). To reduce the overfitting problem suffered from these models, we apply *matrix factorization* (MF) method (Salakhutdinov and Mnih 2008) as a post-processing improvement, forming a stronger baseline. We demonstrate the benefit of the LIS model at predicting the cascade dynamics, cascade size, and "who will be retweeted". Finally, we analyze the topics associated with the learned user-specific latent influence and susceptibility.

Experiments on synthetic data

To validate whether the proposed algorithm could obtain good estimation of user-specific influence and susceptibility, we first conduct tests on synthetic data, where cascades are generated according to parameters known a prior. These tests also offer us some intuitions about difficulties at predicting cascade dynamics.

Experimental setup. We first generate two synthetic diffusion networks: one is constructed using Barabási-Albert (BA) model (Barabási and Albert 1999), denoted as original network; the other is generated by shuffling the original network (Molloy and Reed 1995), denoted as shuffle network. We set the dimensionality of user's influence I_u and susceptibility S_u as 5, and sample I_u and S_u from $f(\mathbf{x}) = 1/2\sqrt{\mathbf{x}}, \mathbf{x} \sim U(0,1)^5$, where $U(0,1)$ refers to a uniform distribution. We then generate cascades over the two networks according to our LIS model with $\lambda = 0.01$. We take 80% of the cascades generated from original network as training dataset, and the rest of cascades generated from the original network and the cascades from the shuffle network as test dataset. The two test datasets have equal size, offering a fair comparison.

Predicting cascade dynamics. We deal with this problem as a set of binary classification problem, predicting whether one user will be activated under specific cascade context. Thus we use AUC (the area of under the ROC curve) as the evaluation metric (Fawcett 2006). As a reference for the performance comparison, we offer an upper bound of our LIS model (denoted as UB): predicting cascade dynamics according to the parameters I and S that are used to generate cascades in test data.

Table 1: Cascade dynamics prediction on synthetic data

network	UB	LIS	SB	SJ	EM
original	0.659	0.654	0.607	0.618	0.561
shuffle	0.659	0.608	0.509	0.525	0.507

Table 2: Dataset statistics

	training data			test data	
	cascades	period		cascades	period
D1	395,852	01/01-01/15	T1	160,868	01/16-01/31
D2	453,356	01/16-01/31	T2	122,509	02/01-02/05
D3	386,152	02/01-02/15	T3	145,143	02/16-02/20

Results are listed in Table 1. It is seen that LIS model consistently outperforms baselines, and its AUC value is very close to UB, when predicting on original network. Particularly, the performance of LIS model is stable on both original and shuffle networks, while baseline methods suffer from much performance reduction (some even close to 0.5, equal to random guess approach), resulted from the overfitting problem of pair-wise models.

Experiments on Microblog

Dataset. The Microblog data from Sina Weibo website is published by WISE 2012 Challenge[1], spanning from January 1, 2011 to Feburary 15, 2011. We extract the cascade records posted between January 1, 2011 and February 15, 2011, and split the extracted records into three training datasets, i.e., D1, D2, D3, each persisting a period of half a month. Furthermore, for each training dataset, we extract the cascade records in the following 5 days as test, i.e., T1, T2 and T3. We only consider the users who appear in all the three training datasets, obtaining 199,408 users. Dataset statistics are depicted in Table 2. We conduct an empirical study to demonstrate the severity of overfitting problem. Over 70% of *forwarding traces*—historical paths for information flows—in test data are never observed in training data, posing a big challenge to previous pair-wise models, when applied in real data.

Diffusion network. Exact diffusion network is hard to obtain, since there is no clear clues indicating whether a user is exposed to a message forwarded by her followee. Previous works focus on directly inferring diffusion networks, which is not applicable to large-scale scenarios (Gomez-Rodriguez, Leskovec, and Krause 2010; Gomez-Rodriguez, Leskovec, and Schölkopf 2013; Du et al. 2012; Kurashima et al. 2014). Here we estimate diffusion network according to a large collection of historical cascades: one cascade has a collection of forwarding traces over the period of observation, forming a directed graph. We aggregate these graphs of all cascades into a diffusion network, providing us a good approximation for potential information propagation in the

[1] http://www.wise2012.cs.ucy.ac.cy/challenge.html

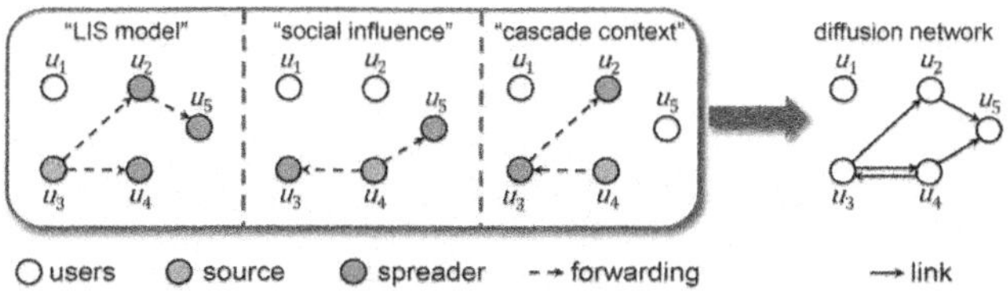

Figure 3: Illustration of constructing diffusion network. The left box contains three observed cascades, and the right is their aggregated diffusion network.

future. Figure 3 gives an example to illustrate the construction of diffusion network.

Predicting cascade dynamics. We introduce the length of cascade context l to capture user's context-dependent level for exploring context-dependent factors like cumulative effects in information propagation. When a user decides whether or not to forward a message, only the recent l exposures take effects in cascade context. The case $l = 0$ implies that users are memoryless, i.e., without cumulative effect, reproducing the independent assumption (Kempe, Kleinberg, and Tardos 2003). To illustrate the difference of prediction performance at combating overfitting problem, we additionally evaluate the prediction only over observed forwarding traces. The experimental results are presented in Fig. 4. Despite that baselines can better handle prediction instances over observed forwarding traces, the AUCs decrease dramatically when applied to the prediction over all forwarding traces in test data. It means that pair-wise models, even with an improvement using matrix factorization, still suffer from overfitting problem when a large proportion of forwarding traces in test data are unobserved. LIS model shows stable performance, indicating that it works consistently better than baseline models, no matter whether the forwarding traces are happened in history. Furthermore, we explore the effects of different length of cascade context l in LIS model. With different settings of l, LIS model performs better as the increase of l, shown in both two types of AUCs. It agrees with the empirical observation on cumulative effect of information propagation (Ugander et al. 2012; Bao et al. 2013a; Leskovec, Adamic, and Huberman 2007), and LIS model can effectively capture the effects.

Cascade size prediction. Cascade size prediction, as a key part of influence maximization and viral marketing, is one of the most important applications based on modeling cascade dynamics (Bao et al. 2013b; Shen et al. 2014). To guarantee that all cascades propagate sufficiently from their message sources, we only choose such cascades that are initially posted at the first day in each test data for cascade size prediction. Starting from the true sources of cascades in training dataset, we simulate cascade dynamics using the learned LIS model as a prediction. We group simulated cascades into bins according to their cascade size. By counting the number of cascades in each bin, we get a vector of counts indexed by cascade sizes. In the same way, we also get the vector of counts from the real cascades in test data as the ground truth, and we smooth out those size bins containing few cascades for statistical significance. Thus the cascade

Table 4: Accuracies and MRRs of prediction of "who will be retweeted"

		LIS ($l = 5$)	SB	SJ	EM
Acc(%)	T1	58.48	57.02	49.99	53.48
	T2	57.61	55.05	49.65	52.23
	T3	59.58	55.38	50.85	55.41
MRR	T1	0.791	0.784	0.748	0.766
	T2	0.786	0.773	0.745	0.758
	T3	0.797	0.775	0.752	0.775

size prediction can be evaluated by *mean absolute percentage error* (MAPE), where a smaller value indicates a better prediction. Since the cascades are generated by simulations, we repeat the prediction, recording the average values and standard deviations of MAPE in Table 3. It is seen that all LIS models with different settings of l achieve better MAPE values than baselines on test data, indicating LIS model can estimate completed cascades propagation more efficiently than pair-wise models. Particularly, the MAPEs in test data T2 are much larger than the values in the other two test data. One possible explanation is that these cascades in test data T2 span Chinese New Year (from Jan. 2 to Jan. 8, 2011) when users were dominated by offline social activities. Thus, it is hardly to observe completed cascades in the short period, resulting in unexpected performance by simulating complete cascades without accounting these factors.

Prediction of "who will be retweeted". The problem "who will be retweeted" is a way to examine interpersonal influence under quantitative understanding. In the scene of multi-exposures, high interpersonal influence will have high probability to be forwarded. LIS model provides a direct quantitative metric for interpersonal influence by the scalar product of I_i and S_j between user i and j. Propagation probability is another metric of interpersonal influence for traditional pair-wise models. We therefore deal with the prediction task as a ranking problem of interpersonal influence. The user with higher rank is more probable to be retweeted. We evaluate the prediction performance by metrics of average *Accuracy* (Acc) of top-1 prediction and *Mean Reciprocal Rank* (MRR) (Voorhees 1999). The larger values of Acc and MRR indicate better predictions. The results are given in Table 4. It is seen that LIS model achieves a much better Acc and MRR than the baselines, which indicates that LIS model provides a more efficient perspective to inspect interpersonal influence in information cascades.

Topic allocation in latent features To explore topic allocation in LIS model, we select top 10,000 users for each dimension of latent influence and susceptibility features, according to their influence and susceptibility respectively. We use hashtags as the topic of these messages posted by the selected users. Messages without hashtags are discarded. We keep 8 hashtags with statistical significance in terms of message number. Then we calculate the distribution of each remained hashtags in latent features according to the frequency used by users. Next, we rank hashtags by the results of distribution in latent features and utilize kendall-τ rank correlation coefficient (Kendall 1938) to analyze the difference between pairs of features. Figure 5 shows the heat map

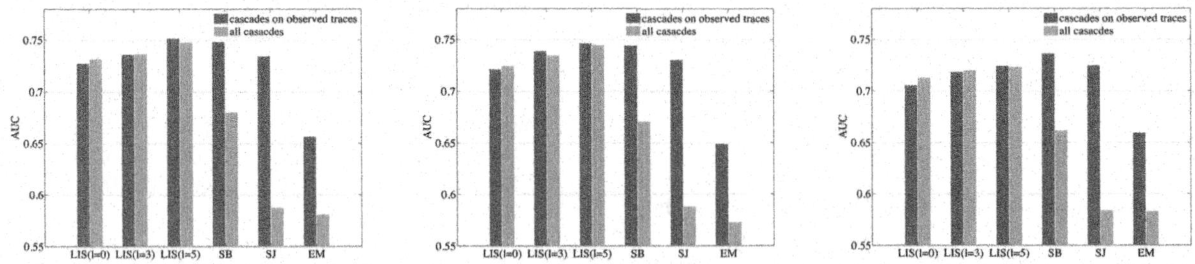

(a) T1 (b) T2 (c) T3

Figure 4: AUCs of cascade dynamics prediction on microblog.

Table 3: MAPEs of cascade size prediction

	LIS ($l = 0$)	LIS ($l = 3$)	LIS ($l = 5$)	SB	SJ	EM
T1	0.163±0.0133	0.140±0.0155	0.141±0.0217	0.191±0.0190	0.524±0.0046	0.258±0.0160
T2	0.287±0.0093	0.280±0.0080	0.286±0.0065	0.333±0.0099	0.621±0.0048	0.338±0.0387
T3	0.095±0.0150	0.094±0.0150	0.097±0.0093	0.171±0.0388	0.505±0.0450	0.189±0.0112

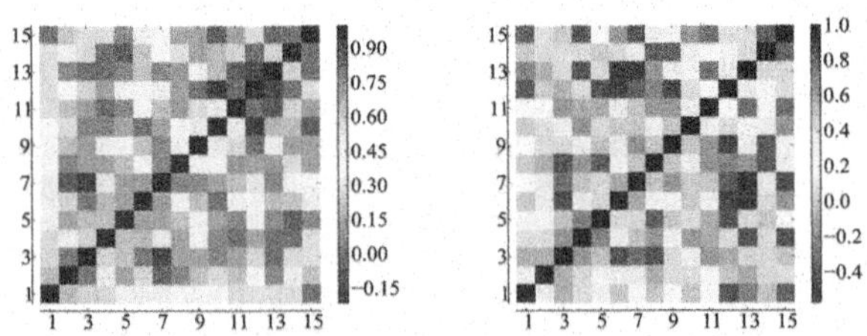

(a) influence (b) susceptibility

Figure 5: Kendall-τ rank correlation coefficient.

of difference between pairs of features. Every grid represents the correlation between two features. The coefficient values close to 1 or -1 refer to positive and negative correlation between two features, depicted in deep blue or deep red respectively. If two features are independent, the coefficient value approaches to 0, colored by yellow. As shown in Fig. 5, most pairs of features are approximatively independent in both influence and susceptibility, indicating that the learned features are highly discriminative in topic level. Furthermore, we illustrate the top 3 hashtags in latent features shown in Table 5, containing four pairs of features and their hashtags. The influence features 3 and 7 are coherent well with high kendall-τ coefficients 0.93, as hashtag "Xiaomi release" is on the top of both. Those influence and susceptibility features with lower or zero kendall-τ coefficients have distinguished hashtags.

Table 5: Topic allocation in features

(a) two pairs of features in influence

kendall-τ coefficients	feature index	ranked hash tags
0.93	3	1. Xiaomi release; 2. Tang Jun education qualification fake; 3. House prices
	7	1. Xiaomi release; 2. Qian Yunhui; 3. House prices
0	2	1. Yao Ming retire; 2. Case of running fast car in Heibei University; 3. Xiaomi release
	14	1. Xiaomi release; 2. Qian Yunhui; 3. House prices

(b) two pairs of features in susceptibility

kendall-τ coefficients	feature index	ranked hash tags
0.43	6	1. Incident of self-burning at Yancheng, Jiangsu; 2. Tang Jun education qualification fake; 3. Yao Ming retire
	11	1. Xiaomi release; 2. Qian Yunhui; 3. House prices
0	4	1. Incident of self-burning at Yancheng, Jiangsu; 2. Tang Jun education qualification fake; 3. Case of running fast car in Heibei University
	7	1. Qian Yunhui; 2. Incident of self-burning at Yancheng, Jiangsu; 3. House prices

Conclusions

In this paper, we proposed a concise probabilistic model for the information propagation on social network, explicitly characterizing the influence and susceptibility of each user with two low-dimensional vectors respectively. The proposed model distinguishes itself from previous models at its capability of modeling both the interpersonal influence between any pair of users and the cumulative effect in information propagation. We also designed effective algorithms to train the model based on maximizing logarithmic likelihood of information cascades. Our model does not require the knowledge of social network structure, hence having wide applicability to the scenarios with or without explicit social networks. We evaluated the effectiveness of our model on synthetic dataset and a large-scale microblogging dataset from Sina Weibo, the largest social media in China. Experimental results demonstrate that our model consistently outperforms existing methods at predicting cascade dynamics, cascade size, and "who will be retweeted". Moreover, the learned user-specific influence and susceptibility vectors provide us a quantitative way to understand topic-related interpersonal influence in information propagation.

Acknowledgments

This work was funded by the National Basic Research Program of China under grant number 2012CB316303, the National High-tech R&D Program of China under grant number 2014AA015103, and the National Natural Science Foundation of China with Nos 61232010, 61472400, 61202213, 61272536. This work is also partly funded by the Beijing Natural Scientific Foundation of China under grant number 4122077. The authors thank to the members of NASC research group (www.groupnasc.org) for valuable discussions and suggestions.

References

Aral, S., and Walker, D. 2012. Identifying influential and susceptible members of social networks. *Science* 337(6092):337–341.

Aral, S.; Muchnik, L.; and Sundararajan, A. 2009. Distinguishing influence-based contagion from homophily-driven diffusion in dynamic networks. *Proceedings of the National Academy of Sciences* 106(51):21544–21549.

Artzi, Y.; Pantel, P.; and Gamon, M. 2012. Predicting responses to microblog posts. In *Proceedings of the 2012 Conference of the North American Chapter of the Association for Computational Linguistics*, 602–606.

Bao, P.; Shen, H.; Chen, W.; and Cheng, X. 2013a. Cumulative effect in information diffusion: Empirical study on a microblogging network. *PLoS ONE* 8(10):e76027.

Bao, P.; Shen, H.; Huang, J.; and Cheng, X. 2013b. Popularity prediction in microblogging network: a case study on sina weibo. In *Proceedings of the 22nd International Conference on World Wide Web Companion*, 177–178.

Barabási, A., and Albert, R. 1999. Emergence of scaling in random networks. *Science* 286(5439):509–512.

Chen, W.; Wang, Y.; and Yang, S. 2009. Efficient influence maximization in social networks. In *Proceedings of the 15th ACM SIGKDD International Conference on Knowledge Discovery and Data Mining*, 199–208.

Cheng, S.; Shen, H.; Huang, J.; Zhang, G.; and Cheng, X. 2013. Staticgreedy: Solving the scalability-accuracy dilemma in influence maximization. In *Proceedings of the 22nd ACM International Conference on Conference on Information & Knowledge Management*, 509–518.

Du, N.; Song, L.; Smola, A. J.; and Yuan, M. 2012. Learning networks of heterogeneous influence. In *Advances in Neural Information Processing Systems*, 2789–2797.

Fawcett, T. 2006. An introduction to roc analysis. *Pattern Recognition Letters* 27:861–874.

Gomez-Rodriguez, M.; Leskovec, J.; and Krause, A. 2010. Inferring networks of diffusion and influence. In *Proceedings of the 16th ACM SIGKDD International Conference on Knowledge Discovery and Data Mining*, 1019–1028.

Gomez-Rodriguez, M.; Leskovec, J.; and Schölkopf, B. 2013. Modeling information propagation with survival theory. In *Proceedings of the 30th International Conference on Machine Learning*, 666–674.

Goyal, A.; Bonchi, F.; and Lakshmanan, L. V. 2010. Learning influence probabilities in social networks. In *Proceedings of the 3rd ACM International Conference on Web Search and Data Mining*, 241–250.

Huang, J.; Cheng, X.; Shen, H.; Zhou, T.; and Jin, X. 2012. Exploring social influence via posterior effect of word-of-mouth recommendations. In *Proceedings of the 5th ACM International Conference on Web Search and Data Mining*, 573–582.

Kempe, D.; Kleinberg, J.; and Tardos, É. 2003. Maximizing the spread of influence through a social network. In *Proceedings of the 9th ACM SIGKDD International Conference on Knowledge Discovery and Data Mining*, 137–146.

Kendall, M. G. 1938. A new measure of rank correlation. *Biometrika* 81–93.

Kurashima, T.; Iwata, T.; Takaya, N.; and Sawada, H. 2014. Probabilistic latent network visualization: Inferring and embedding diffusion networks. In *Proceedings of the 20th ACM SIGKDD International Conference on Knowledge Discovery and Data Mining*, 1236–1245.

Leskovec, J.; Adamic, L. A.; and Huberman, B. A. 2007. The dynamics of viral marketing. *ACM Transactions on the Web* 1(1).

Lin, C. J. 2007. Projected gradient methods for nonnegative matrix factorization. *Neural Computation* 19(10):2756–2779.

Ma, H.; King, I.; and Lyu, M. R. 2009. Learning to recommend with social trust ensemble. In *Proceedings of the 32nd International ACM SIGIR Conference on Research and Development in Information Retrieval*, 203–210. ACM.

Molloy, M., and Reed, B. 1995. A critical point for random graphs with a given degree sequence. *Random Structures & Algorithms* 6(2-3):161–180.

Richardson, M., and Domingos, P. 2002. Mining knowledge-sharing sites for viral marketing. In *Proceedings of the 8th ACM SIGKDD International Conference on Knowledge Discovery and Data Mining*, 61–70.

Saito, K.; Nakano, R.; and Kimura, M. 2008. Prediction of information diffusion probabilities for independent cascade model. In *Knowledge-Based Intelligent Information and Engineering Systems*, 67–75.

Salakhutdinov, R., and Mnih, A. 2008. Probabilistic matrix factorization. *Advances in Neural Information Processing Systems* 20:1257–1264.

Shen, H.; Wang, D.; Song, C.; and Barabási, A. 2014. Modeling and predicting popularity dynamics via reinforced poisson processes. In *Proceedings of the 28th AAAI Conference on Artificial Intelligence*, 291–297.

Ugander, J.; Backstrom, L.; Marlow, C.; and Kleinberg, J. 2012. Structural diversity in social contagion. *Proceedings of the National Academy of Sciences* 109(16):5962–5966.

Voorhees, E. M. 1999. The TREC8 Question Answering Track Report. In *Text REtrieval Conference*.

Cognitive Modeling

Proceedings of the Twenty-Ninth AAAI Conference on Artificial Intelligence

Kickback Cuts Backprop's Red-Tape: Biologically Plausible Credit Assignment in Neural Networks

David Balduzzi
david.balduzzi@vuw.ac.nz
Victoria University of Wellington

Hastagiri Vanchinathan
hastagiri@inf.ethz.ch
ETH Zurich

Joachim Buhmann
jbuhmann@inf.ethz.ch
ETH Zurich

Abstract

Error backpropagation is an extremely effective algorithm for assigning credit in artificial neural networks. However, weight updates under Backprop depend on lengthy recursive computations and require separate output and error messages – features not shared by biological neurons, that are perhaps unnecessary. In this paper, we revisit Backprop and the credit assignment problem.

We first decompose Backprop into a collection of interacting learning algorithms; provide regret bounds on the performance of these sub-algorithms; and factorize Backprop's error signals. Using these results, we derive a new credit assignment algorithm for nonparametric regression, Kickback, that is significantly simpler than Backprop. Finally, we provide a sufficient condition for Kickback to follow error gradients, and show that Kickback matches Backprop's performance on real-world regression benchmarks.

Introduction

The discovery of error backpropagation was hailed as a breakthrough because it solved the main problem of distributed learning – the spatial credit assignment problem (Werbos 1974; Rumelhart, Hinton, and Williams 1986). Decades later, Backprop is the workhorse underlying most deep learning algorithms, and a major component of the state-of-the-art in supervised learning.

Since Backprop's introduction, there has been tremendous progress improving the performance of neural networks. An enormous amount of effort has been expended exploring the effects of: the activation functions of nodes; network architectures (e.g. number of layers and number of nodes); regularizers such as dropout (Srivastava et al. 2014); modifications to accelerate gradient descent; and unsupervised methods for pre-training to find better local optima.

However, it was known from the start that Backprop is not biologically plausible (Crick 1989). Implementing Backprop requires that neurons produce two distinct signals – outputs and errors – whereas only one has been observed in cortex (Lamme and Roelfsema 2000; Roelfsema and van Ooyen 2005).

It is therefore remarkable that almost no attempts have been made to rethink the core algorithm – backpropagation – and the problem that it solves – credit assignment. This paper revisits the credit assignment problem and takes a fresh look at the signaling architecture that underlies Backprop.

Outline. Our starting point is to decompose Backprop into local learning algorithms, Theorem 1. Nodes under Backprop are modeled as agents that minimize their losses. Backprop ensures that nodes cooperate, towards the shared goal of minimizing the output layer's error, by gluing together their loss functions using recursively computed error signals.

Reformulating Backprop as local learners immediately suggests modifying the signaling architecture (the glue) whilst keeping the learners. In this paper, we aim to simplify Backprop's error signals.

Theorem 2 lays the groundwork, by providing a regret bound for local learners that holds for any scalar feedback – and not just the error signals used by Backprop.

The next step is to show that, when a neural network has 1-dimensional outputs (e.g. nonparametric regression), Backprop's error signals factorize into two components, Theorem 3. The first component is a scalar error computed at the output layer that is analogous to a neuromodulatory signal; the second is a complicated sum over paths to the output layer that has no biological analog.

Our proposed algorithm, *Kickback*, modifies Backprop by truncating the second component. Kickback is *not* gradient descent on the output error. Nevertheless, Theorem 4 provides a simple sufficient condition, coherence, for Kickback to follow the error gradient.

It turns out that many of the components of Kickback have close neurophysiological analogs. We discuss Kickback's biological significance by relating it to a recently developed, discrete-time model neuron (Balduzzi and Besserve 2012).

Finally, we present experiments demonstrating that Kickback matches Backprop's performance on standard benchmark datasets.

Synopsis. Our contribution is twofold. Firstly, we provide a series of simple, fundamental theorems on Backprop, one of the most heavily used learning algorithms. In particular, Theorem 1 suggests that ideas from multi-agent learning and mechanism design have a role to play in deep learning.

Secondly, we propose Kickback, a stripped-down variant of Backprop that simultaneously performs well and ties in nicely with the signaling architecture of cortical neurons.

Related work. The idea of building learning algorithms out of individual learning agents dates back to at least (Selfridge 1958). More recent approaches include REINFORCE (Williams 1992), the hedonistic neurons in (Seung 2003), and the neurons modeled using online learning in (Hu et al. 2013). None of these approaches have led to algorithms that are competitive on benchmarks.

The algorithm closest to Kickback is attention-gated reinforcement learning (AGREL), which also eliminates the error signals from Backprop (Roelfsema and van Ooyen 2005). AGREL and Kickback are analogous at a high level, however the details differ markedly. In terms of results, the main differences are as follows. Firstly, we implement Kickback for networks with 2 and 3 hidden layers; whereas AGREL was only implemented for 1 hidden layer. Indeed, as discussed in (Roelfsema and van Ooyen 2005), extending AGREL to multiple hidden layers is problematic. Secondly, AGREL achieved comparable performance to Backprop on toy datasets: XOR, counting, and a mine detection dataset containing ± 200 inputs; whereas Kickback matches Backprop on much larger, real-world nonparametric regression problems. Finally, AGREL converges 1.5 to 10 times slower than Backprop, whereas Kickback's convergence is essentially identical to Backprop.

Error Backpropagation

Recent work has shown that using rectilinear functions instead of sigmoids can significantly improve the performance of neural networks. We restrict to rectifiers because they perform well empirically (Jarrett et al. 2009; Nair and Hinton 2010; Glorot, Bordes, and Bengio 2011; Krizhevsky, Sutskever, and Hinton 2012; Zeiler et al. 2013; Dahl, Sainath, and Hinton 2013; Maas, Hannun, and Ng 2013), are more realistic models of cortical neurons than sigmoid units (Glorot, Bordes, and Bengio 2011), and are universal function approximators (Leshno et al. 1993).

Denote the positive and negative rectifiers by $P(a) := \max(0, a)$ and $N(a) := -\max(0, a)$ respectively. Rectifiers are continuous everywhere and differentiable everywhere except at 0. The subgradients are:

$$\nabla P(a) := \begin{cases} 1 & a > 0 \\ 0 & \text{else} \end{cases} \qquad \nabla N(a) := \begin{cases} -1 & a > 0 \\ 0 & \text{else.} \end{cases}$$

Let $S(a)$ denote either $P(a)$ or $N(a)$; the notation is useful when discussing positive and negative rectifiers simultaneously. Similarly, let $\mathbb{1}$ denote either subgradient. The subgradient $\mathbb{1}$ acts as a *signed* indicator function.

The output of node j is $S_{\mathbf{w}_j}(\mathbf{x}) := S(\langle \mathbf{w}_j, \mathbf{x} \rangle)$. We say that node j fires if $\langle \mathbf{w}_j, \mathbf{x} \rangle > 0$; the firing rate is $|S_{\mathbf{w}_j}(\mathbf{x})|$.

From global to local learning. Under Backprop the entire neural network optimizes a single objective function using gradient descent on the network's error. The partial derivatives with respect to weights are computed via the chain rule.

In more detail, suppose a neural network has error function $E(\mathbf{x}, y)$ that depends on the output layer $\mathbf{x}_o$ and labels y. Backprop recursively updates weight vectors using the chain rule. For nodes in the output layer, $\delta_o := \frac{\partial E}{\partial x_o}$. For hidden node j, the error signal is derived via

$$\delta_j := \sum_{\{k \mid j \to k\}} w_{jk} \mathbb{1}_k \delta_k. \tag{1}$$

Our first result is that, when the hidden nodes are rectilinear, Backprop decomposes into many interacting learning algorithms that maximize local objective functions.

Consider the following setup.

Definition 1 (rectilinear loss). *A node with a rectilinear activation function $S_{\mathbf{w}}(\bullet)$ receives input $\mathbf{x}$ and incurs **rectilinear loss***

$$\ell_{RL}(\mathbf{w}, \mathbf{x}, \varphi) := \varphi \cdot S_{\mathbf{w}}(\mathbf{x}) = \begin{cases} \pm\varphi \cdot \langle \mathbf{w}, \mathbf{x} \rangle & \textit{if } \langle \mathbf{w}, \mathbf{x} \rangle > 0 \\ 0 & \textit{else} \end{cases}$$

that depends on an externally provided scalar φ.

If the node fires then the rectilinear loss is the linear loss $\ell_L(\mathbf{w}, \varphi \cdot \mathbf{x}) := \langle \mathbf{w}, \varphi \cdot \mathbf{x} \rangle$, which has been extensively analyzed in online learning (Cesa-Bianchi and Lugosi 2006). If the node does not fire then the rectilinear loss is zero.

Theorem 1 (Backprop decomposes into local learners). *The weight updates induced by Backprop on rectilinear hidden node j are the same as gradient descent on the rectilinear loss:*

$$\nabla_{\mathbf{w}_j} \ell_{RL}(\mathbf{w}_j, \mathbf{x}, \delta_j) = \nabla_{\mathbf{w}_j} E(\mathbf{x}_o, y).$$

The rectilinear loss resembles the hinge loss. However, it is not convex since, even if the node has a positive rectifier, φ is not necessarily positive.

Proof Sketch. Let $a_j = \langle \mathbf{w}_j, \mathbf{x} \rangle$ and $x_j = S(a_j)$. Weight updates under Backprop are

$$\Delta w_{ij} \propto -\frac{\partial E}{\partial w_{ij}} = -\frac{\partial E}{\partial a_j} \frac{\partial a_j}{\partial w_{ij}} = -\delta_j \cdot x_i \cdot \mathbb{1}_j.$$

Weight updates for gradient descent on the rectilinear loss are

$$\Delta w_{ij} \propto -\frac{\partial \ell_{RL}}{\partial w_{ij}} = -\varphi \cdot x_i \cdot \mathbb{1}_j. \tag{2}$$

Substituting $\varphi \leftarrow \delta_j$ yields the theorem. □

Backprop is thus a collection of local optimizations glued together by the recursively computed error signals.

A regret bound. Since the rectilinear loss has not been previously studied, our second result is a guarantee on the predictive performance of the local learners.

Theorem 2 (regret bound for local learners). *Suppose that weights are projected into a compact convex set $\mathcal{K}$ at each time step. Let $F := \{t \mid S_{\mathbf{w}^t}(\mathbf{x}^t) > 0\}$ denote the timepoints when the node fired.*

The following guarantee holds for any sequence of inputs and scalar feedback when $|F| \geq 1$:

$$\frac{1}{|F|}\left[\sum_{t\in F}\ell_{RL}(\mathbf{w}^t,\mathbf{x}^t,\varphi^t) - \inf_{\mathbf{w}\in\mathcal{K}}\sum_{t\in F}\ell_{RL}(\mathbf{w},\mathbf{x}^t,\varphi^t)\right] \leq \sqrt{\frac{8DE}{|F|}}$$

where $D = \max_{t\in F}\left\{\|\varphi^t\cdot\mathbf{x}^t\|_2^2\right\}$ *and* $E = \max_{\mathbf{w}\in\mathcal{K}}\|\mathbf{w}\|_2^2 - \|\mathbf{w}_1\|_2^2$.

Theorem 2 shows that the loss incurred by rectifiers on *the inputs that cause them to fire* converges towards the loss of the best weight-vector in hindsight. The theorem is shown for hard constraints (i.e. projecting into $\mathcal{K}$); similar results hold for convex regularizers.

The result holds for arbitrary sequences of inputs and feedbacks, including adversarial. It is therefore more realistic than the standard *i.i.d.* assumption. Indeed, even if a network's inputs are *i.i.d.*, the inputs to nodes in deeper layers are not – due to weight-updates within the network.

Proof Sketch. Standard results on online learning do not directly apply, since the rectilinear loss is not convex. To adapt these results, observe that, by (2), nodes only learn from the inputs that cause them to fire.

Clearly, $S_{\mathbf{w}^t}(\mathbf{x}^t) = \langle\mathbf{w}^t,\mathbf{x}^t\rangle$ for all $t \in F$. That is, a node's output is linear on the inputs for which it fires. Further, the rectilinear loss is linear on F. The theorem follows from a well-known result on gradient descent for the linear loss, see (Hazan 2012). □

Theorem 2 is not restricted to Backprop's error signals; it holds for any sequence of scalars $\{\varphi^t\}$. This suggests exploring alternate ways of gluing together local learners.

Kickback: truncated error backpropagation

Backprop has two unfortunate properties. Firstly, the error signals δ_j are computationally expensive: they depend on the activity and weights of all downstream nodes in the network. Secondly, nodes produce two distinct signals: outputs that are fed forward and errors that are fed back. In contrast, cortical neurons communicate with only one signal type, spikes, which are sent in all directions. This suggests that it may be possible to make do with less.

Viewed from a distance, Backprop is a single distributed optimization, performing gradient descent on the network's error. Zooming in, via Theorem 1, reveals that Backprop is a collection of local learners *glued together* by recursively computed error signals. We thus have a framework for experimenting with alternate feedback signals (Balduzzi 2014).

Kickback takes the same local learners as Backprop but weakens the glue that binds them, thereby reducing communication complexity and increasing biological plausibility.

Factorizing Backprop's error signals. It is necessary to distinguish between global and local error signals. Local errors signals are the recursively computed signals δ_j. The global error is the derivative of the network's error function with respect to the activity of the output layer.

Definition 2 (influence). *The influence of node j on node k is $\tau_{jk} := w_{jk}\mathbb{1}_k$. The **influence** of node j on the next layer is $\tau_j := \sum_{\{k|j\to k\}}\tau_{jk}$. The **total influence** of node j on downstream nodes is*

$$\pi_j := \left(\sum_{\{k|j\to k\}}\tau_{jk}\left(\sum_{\{l|k\to l\}}\tau_{kl}\left(\sum_{\{m|l\to m\}}\cdots\right)\right)\right), \tag{3}$$

the sum over all paths from j to the output layer.

Our third result is that Backprop's error signals factorize whenever a neural network has 1-dimensional outputs.

Theorem 3 (error signal factorization). *Suppose neural network N has scalar output and let $\beta = \frac{\partial E}{\partial x_o}$ be the global error. Then, the error signal of a hidden node j factorizes as*

$$\delta_j = \beta\cdot\pi_j = \big(\textit{global error}\big)\cdot\big(\textit{total influence}_j\big). \tag{4}$$

The theorem holds in the setting of nonparametric regression. Multi-label classification is excluded.

Proof Sketch. Backprop recursively updates weight vectors using the chain rule, recall (1). When the output is one-dimensional, x_o contributes β to the recursive computation of π_j over hidden nodes. □

Kickback. We are now ready to introduce Kickback.

Algorithm 1 (Kickback). *The **truncated feedback** ϵ_j at node j is*

$$\epsilon_j := \beta\cdot\tau_j = \big(\textit{global error}\big)\cdot\big(\textit{influence}_j\big). \tag{5}$$

*Under **Kickback**, hidden nodes perform gradient descent on the rectilinear loss with truncated feedback:*

$$\Delta w_{ij} \propto -\nabla_{w_{ij}}\ell_{RL}(\mathbf{w}_j,\mathbf{x},\epsilon_j) = -\beta\cdot\tau_j\cdot x_i\cdot\mathbb{1}_j. \tag{6}$$

Kickback and Backprop are contrasted in Figure 1 and in equations (4) versus (5). Importantly, Kickback eliminates the need for nodes to communicate error signals – as distinct from their outputs.

Kickback as time-averaged Backprop. Truncating the feedback signal, from (4) to (5), preserves more information than appears at first glance. The truncated signal received by node j *explicitly* depends on j's influence on the next layer. However, Kickback *implicitly* incorporates information about the influence of multiple layers.

For simplicity, suppose there is no regularizer and that the learning rate η is constant. Then, summing over the updates in (2), a weight at time T is $w_{ij}^T = \eta\sum_{t\in F_j}\varphi_j^t x_i^t$. In the specific case of Kickback, the weight is

$$w_{ij}^T = \eta\sum_{t\in F_j}\left(\beta^t x_i^t\tau_j^t\right) = \eta\sum_{t\in F_j}\left(\beta^t x_i^t\sum_{\{k|j\to k\}}w_{jk}^t\mathbb{1}_k\right).$$

The weight w_{ij}^T thus implicitly incorporates the effect of interactions $\tau_{jk}^t = w_{jk}^t\mathbb{1}_k^t$ in the next layer down, and so on recursively.

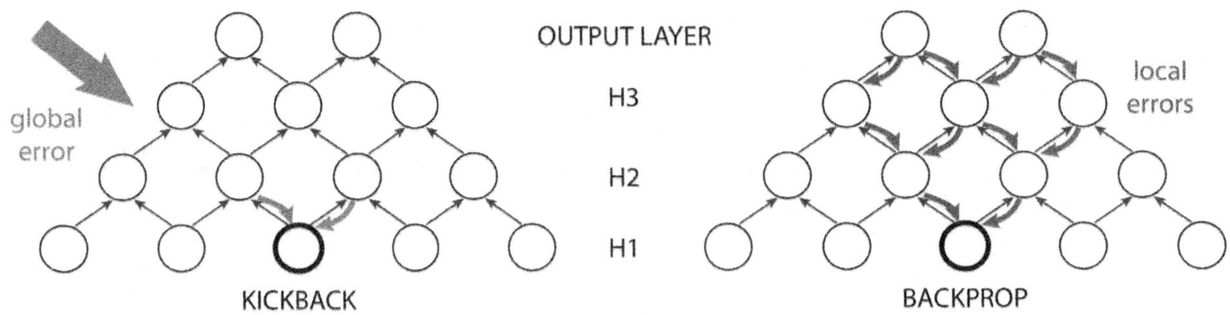

Figure 1: **Schematic comparison of Kickback and Backprop.** Black arrows represent feedforward conenctivity. Colored arrows depict paths used to compute the bold node's feedback under each algorithm.

Coherence. With a small enough learning rate, gradient descent will tend towards a local minimum. Kickback does not perform gradient descent on the error function since it uses modified feedback signals. Thus, without further assumptions, it is not guaranteed to improve performance. Our fourth result is to provide a sufficient condition.

Definition 3 (coherence). *Node j is **coherent** when $\tau_j > 0$. A network is coherent when all its nodes are coherent.*

Example 1 (signed coherence). *An easy way to guarantee coherence for every node is to impose the purely* local *condition that all connections targeting positive nodes have positive weights, and similarly that all connections targeting negative nodes have negative weights.*

If a network is coherent, then increasing a positive node's firing rate increases the average (signed) activity in the next layer and *all downstream layers*. Increasing the activity of negative nodes has the opposite effect.

On the other hand, if a network is not coherent, then nothing can be said in general about how the activity of nodes in one layer affects other layers.

Coherence thus enforces *interpretability*: it ensures that a node's influence on the next layer is indicative of its *total* influence on all downstream layers.

Theorem 4 (coherence $\implies$ Kickback reduces error). *If a network is coherent then weight updates under Kickback, with a sufficiently small learning rate, improve performance.*

Proof Sketch. It suffices to show that the feedback has the same sign under Backprop, $\delta_j = \beta \cdot \pi_j$, and Kickback, $\epsilon_j = \beta \cdot \tau_j$ for an arbitrary hidden node j.

If j is coherent then $\tau_j > 0$. If, furthermore, all downstream nodes are coherent, then unraveling (3) obtains that $\pi_j > 0$. The result follows. □

Under Backprop, each node's total influence is computed explicitly. Kickback makes do with less information: a node "knows" its influence on the next layer, but does not "know" its total influence.

Biological relevance

There is a direct link from Kickback to neurobiology provided by the *selectron*: a simplified model neuron (Balduzzi and Besserve 2012). The selectron is derived from standard models of neural dynamics and learning – the Spike Response Model (SRM) and Spike-Timing Dependent Plasticity (STDP) – by taking the so-called "fast-time constant limit" to go from continuous to discrete time.

Theorem 5 (selectron). *The fast time-constant limit of the SRM (Gerstner and Kistler 2002) is a node that outputs 1 if $\langle \mathbf{w}, \mathbf{x}\rangle > 0$ and 0 otherwise.*

Weight updates in the fast time-constant limit of neuromodulated STDP (Song, Miller, and Abbott 2000) are

$$\Delta w_{ij} \propto \nu \cdot x_i \cdot \mathbb{1}_j = \begin{cases} \nu \cdot x_i & \text{if } \langle \mathbf{w}_j, \mathbf{x}\rangle > 0 \\ 0 & \text{else,} \end{cases} \tag{7}$$

where ν is a global, scalar-valued neuromodulatory signal.

The weight updates in (7) *are gradient* ascent *on*

$$\textit{Reward}(\mathbf{w}, \mathbf{x}, \nu) := \nu \cdot P_{\mathbf{w}}(\mathbf{x}) = \begin{cases} \nu\langle \mathbf{w}, \mathbf{x}\rangle & \text{if } \langle \mathbf{w}_j, \mathbf{x}\rangle > 0 \\ 0 & \text{else.} \end{cases}$$

Setting $\varphi := -\nu$ in *Reward*$(\mathbf{w}, \mathbf{x}, \nu)$ recovers the rectilinear loss in Definition 1. The selectron thus maximizes a *rectilinear reward* via the same weight updates used to minimize the rectilinear loss. The difference between the two models is that the selectron has 0/1-valued outputs (spikes), whereas nodes have real-valued outputs (firing rates).

Proof. (Balduzzi and Besserve 2012). □

Kickback's weight updates are $\Delta w_{ij} \propto -\beta \cdot \tau_j \cdot x_i \cdot \mathbb{1}_j$. Each factor has a biological analog. The global error, β, corresponds to neuromodulators, such as dopamine, that have been experimentally observed to signal prediction errors for future rewards (Schultz, Dayan, and Montague 1997). The *kickback* term, τ_j, corresponds to NMDA backconnections that have a multiplicative effect on synaptic updates, proportional to the weighted sum of downstream activity (Vargas-Caballero and Robinson 2003; Roelfsema and van Ooyen 2005). The feedforward term, x_i, corresponds to presynaptic spiking activity (Song, Miller, and Abbott 2000). Finally, the signed indicator function $\mathbb{1}_j$, ensures that only active nodes update their weights – thereby playing the role of post-synaptic activity in STDP.

The regret bound in Theorem 2 is also biologically significant. Synapses incur a significant metabolic cost (Tononi and Cirelli 2014). Regularizing synaptic weights provides a way to quantify metabolic costs. Indeed, limits on the physical size and metabolic budget of synapses suggest that synaptic weights may be constrained to an ℓ_1-ball (Balduzzi and Besserve 2012).

To the best of our knowledge, Theorem 2 is the first *adversarial* generalization bound for a biologically derived model. The generalization bound for the selectron in (Balduzzi and Besserve 2012) assumes that inputs are *i.i.d.* Moving beyond the *i.i.d.* assumption is important because biological organisms face adversarial environments.

The final ingredient is coherence. Investigating biologically plausible mechanisms that ensure coherence (or some other sufficient condition) is deferred to future work.

Experiments

Goals. Our primary aim is to compare Kickback's performance to Backprop. We present results on two robotics datasets, SARCOS[1] and Barrett WAM[2]. Kickback's performance across multiple hidden layers is of particular interest, since it truncates errors. Results for 3 hidden layers are reported; results for 1 and 2 hidden layers were similar.[3] A secondary aim is to investigate the effect of coherence.

Competing on the datasets tackled by deep learning algorithms is not yet feasible. Further work is required to adapt Kickback to multiclass learning.

Architecture. Experiments were performed on a 5-layer network with 2 output nodes, 10, 100 and 200 nodes in three hidden layers, and with the input layer directly drawn from the data. Experiments were implemented in Theano (Bergstra et al. 2010). All nodes are rectifiers. We set half of nodes as positive and half as negative. Output nodes perform rectilinear regression, see below, whereas hidden nodes minimize the rectilinear loss on feedback implementing either Kickback or Backprop.

Training was performed in batch sizes of 20. Lower batch-sizes yield better performance at the cost of longer training times. We chose 20 as a reasonable compromise.

Rectilinear regression. Recently, (Glorot, Bordes, and Bengio 2011) introduced an ℓ_1 penalty on firing rates, which encourages sparsity and can improve performance. Here, we consider an ℓ_2-penalty: $\boldsymbol{\ell}_{RL}(\mathbf{w},\mathbf{x},\varphi) - \frac{1}{2}S_{\mathbf{w}}(\mathbf{x})^2$. Weight updates under gradient descent are

$$\Delta\mathbf{w} \propto \begin{cases}(\varphi - \langle\mathbf{w},\mathbf{x}\rangle)\mathbf{x} & \text{if } \langle\mathbf{w},\mathbf{x}\rangle > 0\\ 0 & \text{else.}\end{cases} \tag{8}$$

Notice that the penalty $\langle\mathbf{w},\mathbf{x}\rangle$ in (8) is the firing rate. Comparing with the gradient $(\varphi - \langle\mathbf{w},\mathbf{x}\rangle)\mathbf{x}$ of the mean-squared error $\frac{1}{2}(\varphi - \langle\mathbf{w},\mathbf{x}\rangle)^2$ shows that the ℓ_2-activation penalty leads nodes to *perform linear regression on the inputs that cause them to fire* (Balduzzi 2013). A regret bound analogous to Theorem 2 holds for rectilinear regression, with a faster convergence rate of $O(\frac{\log|F|}{|F|})$.

Training error is the MSE of the output node with the correct sign[4]; test error is the sum of the output nodes' MSEs.

Initialization and coherence. No pretraining was used. We consider two network initializations. The first is **uniform**: draw weights uniformly at random from an interval symmetric about 0, without regard to coherence. The second initialization, **signed** is taken from Example 1: draw weights uniformly, then change their signs so that connections targeting positive nodes have positive weights and conversely for negative nodes. **Signed** guarantees coherence at initialization. Although it is possible to impose coherence during training, we found that doing so was unnecessary in practice.

Results are plotted under both initializations for Kickback – excepting Panel (e), where **uniform** failed to converge. For Backprop, the initialization that yielded the *better* performance is reported.

Results. We report normalized mean-squared errors. To directly compare the behavior of the algorithms, we report individual runs. Performance was robust to significant changes in tuning parameters: e.g. changing parameters by $2\times$ increased the MSE on SARCOS 3 from .6% to .8%.

Each SARCOS dataset consists of 44,484 training and 4,449 test points; Barrett split as 12,000 and 3,000. Parameters were tuned via grid-search with 5-fold cross-validation. Backprop's only parameter is the learning rate. Kickback was implemented with a learning rate tuned for Backprop. Kickback has two additional parameters that rescale the feedback to hidden layers 1 & 2. We observed that tuning via cross-validation typically set the rescaling factors such that the truncated errors are rescaled to about same magnitude, on average, as Backprop's feedback.

Kickback and Backprop are competitive with non-parametric methods such as kernel regression, e.g. (Kpotufe and Boularias 2013). Kickback performs best with **signed** initialization, as expected from Theorem 4. With **signed** initialization, Kickback almost exactly matches Backprop in all 6 datasets. Importantly, Kickback continues to reduce the MSE after 100s of epochs; following the correct gradient even when the error is small.

The comparison between Backprop and Kickback is not completely fair: Kickback's additional parameters cause it to outperform Backprop in panel (b). We have endeavored to keep the comparison as level as possible.

The effect of coherence. Kickback's performance was better than expected: coherence was not imposed after initialization under **signed**; and no guarantees are applicable to **uniform**. A possible explanation is that Kickback preserves or increases coherence.

[1]Taken from www.gaussianprocess.org/gpml/data/.

[2]Taken from http://www.ias.tu-darmstadt.de/\\Miscellaneous/Miscellaneous.

[3]In short: the performance of both Kickback and Backprop is worse, but still comparable, with fewer layers.

[4]Recall there is one positive and one negative output rectifier.

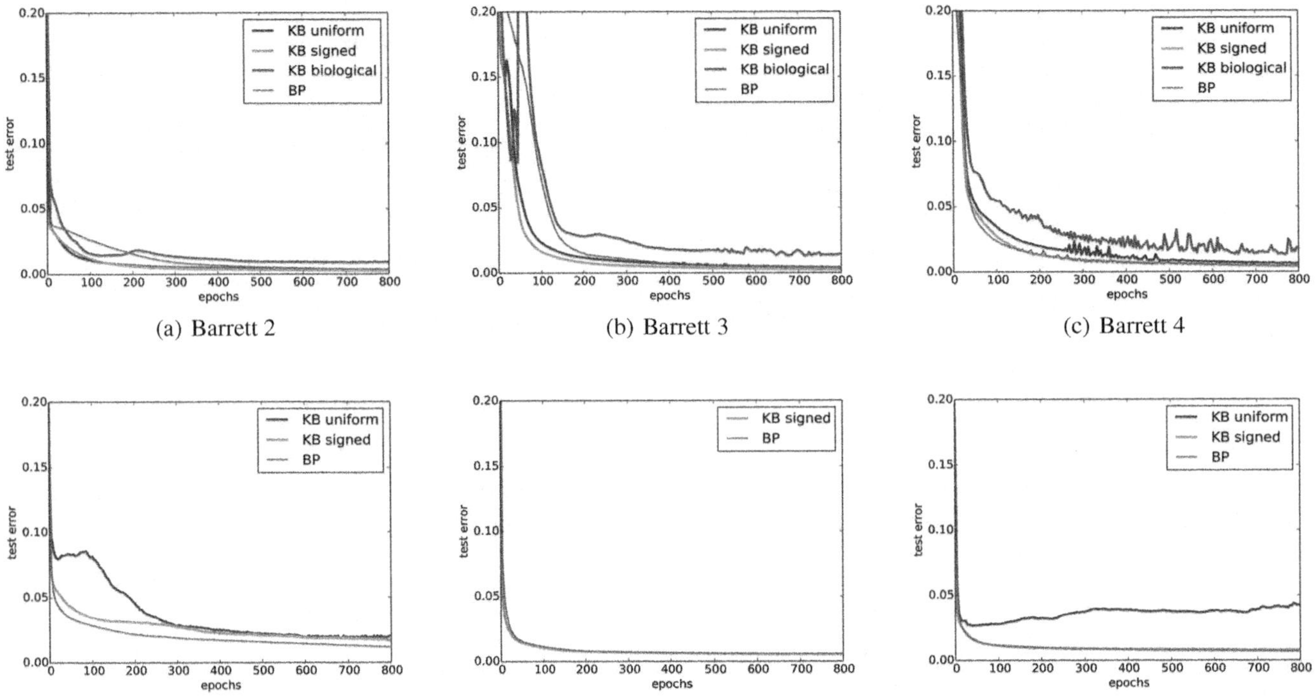

(a) Barrett 2 (b) Barrett 3 (c) Barrett 4

(d) SARCOS 1 (e) SARCOS 3 (f) SARCOS 7

Figure 2: **Mean-squared test error per epoch for Kickback and Backprop.**

To test this hypothesis, we quantified the coherence of layer α as $\text{coh}(L_\alpha) = \frac{\sum_{j\in L_\alpha} \tau_j}{\sum_{j\in L_\alpha}|\tau_j|}$, which lies in $[-1, 1]$. With **signed** initialization, coherence consistently remained above 0.9 under Kickback; but exhibited considerable variability under Backprop. With **uniform** initialization, Kickback increased the coherence of hidden layers 2 & 3, from 0 to > 0.5, with the exception of panel (c). Backprop did not alter coherence in any consistent way.

Barrett 4 is the only dataset where nodes become incoherent (coh < 0) on average. The oscillations in Panel (c) for **uniform** arise because Kickback is not guaranteed to follow the training error gradient in the absence of coherence. It is surprising the network learns at all. Note that oscillations do not occur when networks are given a **signed** initialization.

Conclusion

A necessary step towards understanding how the brain assigns credit is to develop a minimal working model that fits basic constraints.

Backprop solves the credit assignment problem. It is one of the simplest and most effective methods for learning representations. In combination with various tricks and optimizations, it continues to yield state-of-the-art performance. However, it flouts a basic constraint imposed by neurobiology: it requires that nodes produce error signals that are distinct from their outputs.

Kickback is a stripped-down version of Backprop motivated by theoretical (Theorems 1–4) and biological (Fig. 1 and Theorem 5) considerations. Under Kickback, nodes perform gradient descent, or ascent, on the representation – that is, the kicked back activity – produced by the next layer. The sign of the global error determines whether nodes follow the gradient downwards, or upwards.

Kickback is the first competitive algorithm with biologically plausible credit-assignment. Earlier proposals were not competitive and only worked for one hidden-layer (Kickback works well for ≤ 3 hidden-layers; we have not tested ≥ 4). Kickback's simplified signaling is suited to hardware implementations (Indiveri et al. 2011; Nere et al. 2012).

An important outcome of the paper is a new formulation of Backprop in terms of interacting local learners, that may connect deep learning to recent developments in multi-agent systems (Seuken and Zilberstein 2008; Sutton et al. 2011) and mechanism design (Balduzzi 2014).

Kickback's rescaling factors (1 per hidden layer) are a loose-end that require addressing in future work.

Perhaps the most important direction is to extend Kickback to multiclass learning. For this, it is necessary to consider multidimensional outputs, in which case the derivative of the energy function with respect to the output layer is not a scalar. A natural approach to tackle this setting is to use more sophisticated global error signals. Indeed, modeling the neuromodulatory system as producing scalar outputs is a vast oversimplification (Dayan 2012).

Finally, reinforcement learning is a better model of how an agent adapts to its environment than supervised learning (Veness et al. 2010). A natural avenue to explore is how Kickback, suitably modified, performs in this setting.

Acknowledgements. We thank Jacob Abernethy and Satinder Singh for useful conversations. This research was supported in part by SNSF grant 200021_137971.

References

Balduzzi, D., and Besserve, M. 2012. Towards a learning-theoretic analysis of spike-timing dependent plasticity. In *Advances in Neural Information Processing Systems (NIPS)*.

Balduzzi, D. 2013. Randomized co-training: from cortical neurons to machine learning and back again. *Randomized Methods for Machine Learning Workshop, Neural Inf Proc Systems (NIPS)*.

Balduzzi, D. 2014. Cortical prediction markets. In *Proc. 13th Int Conf on Autonomous Agents and Multiagent Systems (AAMAS)*.

Bergstra, J.; Breuleux, O.; Bastien, F.; Lamblin, P.; Pascanu, R.; Desjardins, G.; Turian, J.; Warde-Farley, D.; and Bengio, Y. 2010. Theano: A CPU and GPU Math Expression Compiler. In *Proc. Python for Scientific Comp. Conf. (SciPy)*.

Cesa-Bianchi, N., and Lugosi, G. 2006. *Prediction, Learning and Games*. Cambridge University Press.

Crick, F. 1989. The recent excitement about neural networks. *Nature* 337(12):129–132.

Dahl, G. E.; Sainath, T. N.; and Hinton, G. 2013. Improving deep neural networks for LVCSR using rectified linear units and dropout. In *IEEE International Conference on Acoustics, Speech and Signal Processing (ICASSP)*.

Dayan, P. 2012. Twenty-Five Lessons from Computational Neuromodulation. *Neuron* 76:240–256.

Gerstner, W., and Kistler, W. 2002. *Spiking Neuron Models*. Cambridge University Press.

Glorot, X.; Bordes, A.; and Bengio, Y. 2011. Deep Sparse Rectifier Neural Networks. In *Proc. 14th International Conference on Artificial Intelligence and Statistics (AISTATS)*.

Hazan, E. 2012. The convex optimization approach to regret minimization. In Sra, S.; Nowozin, S.; and Wright, S. J., eds., *Optimization for machine learning*. MIT Press.

Hu, T.; Towfic, Z. J.; Pehlevan, C.; Genkin, A.; and Chklovskii, D. B. 2013. A Neuron as a Signal Processing Device. In *Asilomar Conference on Signals, Systems and Computers*.

Indiveri, G.; Linares-Barranco, B.; Hamilton, T. J.; van Schaik, A.; Etienne-Cummings, R.; Delbruck, T.; Liu, S.-C.; Dudek, P.; Häfliger, P.; and *et al.* 2011. Neuromorphic silicon neuron circuits. *Front. Neurosci* 5(73).

Jarrett, K.; Kavukcuoglu, K.; Ranzato, M.; and LeCun, Y. 2009. What is the Best Multi-Stage Architecture for Object Recognition? In *Proc. International Conference on Computer Vision (ICCV)*.

Kpotufe, S., and Boularias, A. 2013. Gradient Weights help Nonparametric Regressors. In *Advances in Neural Information Processing Systems (NIPS)*.

Krizhevsky, A.; Sutskever, I.; and Hinton, G. E. 2012. Imagenet classification with deep convolutional neural networks. In *Advances in Neural Information Processing Systems (NIPS)*.

Lamme, V., and Roelfsema, P. 2000. The distinct modes of vision offered by feedforward and recurrent processing. *Trends in Neurosci.* 23(11):571–579.

Leshno, M.; Lin, V. Y.; Pinkus, A.; and Schocken, S. 1993. Multilayer Feedforward Networks With a Nonpolynomial Activation Function Can Approximate Any Function. *Neural Networks* 6:861–867.

Maas, A. L.; Hannun, A. Y.; and Ng, A. 2013. Rectifier Nonlinearities Improve Neural Network Acoustic Models. In *Proceedings of the 30th International Conference on Machine Learning (ICML)*.

Nair, V., and Hinton, G. 2010. Rectified Linear Units Improve Restricted Boltzmann Machines. In *Proceedings of the 27th International Conference on Machine Learning (ICML)*.

Nere, A.; Olcese, U.; Balduzzi, D.; and Tononi, G. 2012. A neuromorphic architecture for object recognition and motion anticipation using burst-STDP. *PLoS One* 7(5):e36958.

Roelfsema, P. R., and van Ooyen, A. 2005. Attention-gated reinforcement learning of internal representations for classification. *Neural Comput* 17(10):2176–2214.

Rumelhart, D. E.; Hinton, G. E.; and Williams, R. J. 1986. Learning representations by back-propagating errors. *Nature* 323:533–536.

Schultz, W.; Dayan, P.; and Montague, P. 1997. A neural substrate of prediction and reward. *Science* 275(1593-1599).

Selfridge, O. G. 1958. Pandemonium: a paradigm for learning. In *Mechanisation of Thought Processes: Proceedings of a Symposium Held at the National Physics Laboratory*.

Seuken, S., and Zilberstein, S. 2008. Formal models and algorithms for decentralized decision making under uncertainty. *Auton Agent Multi-Agent Syst* 17(2):190–250.

Seung, H. S. 2003. Learning in Spiking Neural Networks by Reinforcement of Stochastic Synaptic Transmission. *Neuron* 40(1063-1073).

Song, S.; Miller, K. D.; and Abbott, L. F. 2000. Competitive Hebbian learning through spike-timing-dependent synaptic plasticity. *Nat Neurosci* 3(9).

Srivastava, N.; Hinton, G.; Krizhevsky, A.; Sutskever, I.; and Salakhutdinov, R. 2014. Dropout: A Simple Way to Prevent Neural Networks from Overfitting. *JMLR* 15:1929–1958.

Sutton, R.; Modayil, J.; Delp, M.; Degris, T.; Pilarski, P. M.; White, A.; and Precup, D. 2011. Horde: A Scalable Real-time Architecture for Learning Knowledge from Unsupervised Motor Interaction. In *Proc. 10th Int. Conf. on Autonomous Agents and Multiagent Systems (AAMAS)*.

Tononi, G., and Cirelli, C. 2014. Sleep and the Price of Plasticity: From Synaptic and Cellular Homeostasis to Memory Consolidation and Integration. *Neuron* 81(1):12–34.

Vargas-Caballero, M., and Robinson, H. P. 2003. A slow fraction of Mg2+ unblock of NMDA receptors limits their contribution to spike generation in cortical pyramidal neurons. *J Neurophysiol* 89(5):2778–83.

Veness, J.; Ng, K. S.; Hutter, M.; and Silver, D. 2010. Reinforcement Learning via AIXI Approximation. In *Proc. 24th AAAI Conference on Artificial Intelligence (AAAI)*.

Werbos, P. J. 1974. *Beyond Regression: New Tools for Prediction and Analysis in the Behavioral Sciences*. Ph.D. Dissertation, Harvard.

Williams, R. J. 1992. Simple Statistical Gradient-Following Algorithms for Connectionist Reinforcement Learning. *Machine Learning* 8:229–256.

Zeiler, M. D.; Ranzato, M.; Monga, R.; Mao, M.; Yang, K.; Le, Q. V.; Nguyen, P.; Senior, A.; Vanhoucke, V.; Dean, J.; and Hinton, G. 2013. On Rectified Linear Units for Speech Processing. In *IEEE Int Conf on Acoustics, Speech and Signal Proc (ICASSP)*.

Proceedings of the Twenty-Ninth AAAI Conference on Artificial Intelligence

An Agent-Based Model of the Emergence and Transmission of a Language System for the Expression of Logical Combinations

Josefina Sierra-Santibáñez
Technical University of Catalonia, Campus Nord, Ed. Omega
c/ Jordi Girona Salgado 1-3, Barcelona 08034 Spain
E-mail: Maria.Josefina.Sierra@upc.edu

Abstract

This paper presents an agent-based model of the emergence and transmission of a language system for the expression of logical combinations of propositions. The model assumes the agents have some cognitive capacities for invention, adoption, repair, induction and adaptation, a common vocabulary for basic categories, and the ability to construct complex concepts using recursive combinations of basic categories and logical categories. It also supposes the agents initially do not have a vocabulary for logical categories (i.e. logical connectives), nor grammatical constructions for expressing logical combinations of basic categories through language. The results of the experiments we have performed show that a language system for the expression of logical combinations emerges as a result of a process of self-organisation of the agents' linguistic interactions. Such a language system is concise, because it only uses words and grammatical constructions for three logical categories (i.e. and, or, not). It is also expressive, since it allows the communication of logical combinations of categories of the same complexity as propositional logic formulas, using linguistic devices such as syntactic categories, word order and auxiliary words. Furthermore, it is easy to learn and reliably transmitted across generations, according to the results of our experiments.

1 Introduction

The question of the *origins and evolution of language* has received much interest in the last two decades. It has been approached from different disciplines such as anthropology, historical linguistics, evolutionary biology or artificial intelligence. In particular in artificial intelligence *agent-based models*, implemented and tested in computer simulations, have been used to study the emergence and evolution of language (Hurford, Studdert-Kennedy, and Kight 1998; Briscoe 2002; Lyon, Nehaniv, and Cangelosi 2007; Cartmill et al. 2014). Depending on whether these models emphasise the role of biological evolution or the role of cultural evolution, agent-based models are classified into two areas: *Biolinguistics*, which assumes that the structure of language is determined to a large extent by biological factors (Di Sciullo and Boeckx 2011); and *Evolutionary Linguistics*, which supposes language is primarily shaped by cultural forces (Minett and Wang 2005; Steels 2012).

The agent-based model proposed in this paper follows the evolutionary linguistics approach: It involves a population of autonomous software agents that interact with each other playing language games. A language game (Wittgenstein 1953) is typically an interaction between two agents, a speaker and a hearer. The speaker has a communicative goal, conceptualises the world for language, transforms this conceptualisation into an utterance, and communicates that utterance to the hearer. The hearer tries to parse the utterance, reconstruct its meaning and map it onto its own internal representation of the world. Speaker and hearer normally use extralinguistic means to determine the outcome of a language game and, depending on that outcome, employ different strategies to expand and adapt their internal languages in order to be more successful in future language games.

The agents in these models are initially endowed with a set of cognitive abilities that are assumed to be necessary for seeing the emergence of possible language systems that allow them to be successful in a language game (e.g. the ability to construct complex concepts, or to use and detect linguistic devices such as word order, syntactic categories or case markers). Then, they are made to play a series of language games, where they configure possible language systems and try them out. The goal of the experiments is to find out whether the population as a whole succeeds in the language game, i.e. communicates effectively, and to observe the conceptualisations and linguistic constructions that emerge in the population as a result of the processes of collective invention and negotiation, as well as the evolution over time of various macroscopic features of these language systems, such as the average size of the agents' grammars, or the similarity of their grammatical constructions.

Theories of language evolution study language change at two levels: that of language systems and that of language strategies. *Language systems* capture the regularity observed in some part of the vocabulary or the grammar of a language, for example, a system of colour terms, cases, tense-aspect distinctions or logical combinations. Language systems group a set of paradigmatic choices both on the side of meaning (the conceptual system) and on the side of form (the linguistic system). The *conceptual system* contains the semantic distinctions that are expressible in the language system and can therefore be used as building blocks for conceptualisation. The *linguistic system* includes the syntactic categories and grammatical constructions necessary to turn a conceptualisation into a concrete utterance (Steels 2011). Linguists call the approach underlying a language system a *language strategy*. A given language comprises many different language systems, which are closely integrated.

Agent-based experiments in evolutionary linguistics aim to explain how particular language systems and strategies may emerge and evolve. Examples of language systems that have been studied using agent-based models are: (1) *case systems* to express the role of participants in events (Steels 1998; Batali 1998); (2) *tense-aspect distinctions* (Gerasymova, Spranger, and Beuls 2012); (3) *agreement markers* to group words together (Beuls and Steels 2013); (4) *vocabularies* in co-evolution with *semantic categories* (Steels and Belpaeme 2005; Lara and Alfonseca 2000; 2002).

The rest of this paper is organised as follows. Firstly, we explain what we mean by a language system for the expression of logical combinations and specify the set of meanings that constitute its conceptual system. Secondly, we introduce the formalism the agents use to represent their grammars and the linguistic devices they may use to express the relation between each connective and its arguments in a sentence. Then, we describe the particular type of linguistic interaction that allows the agents to construct a common lexicon and a grammar, paying special attention to cognitive abilities for invention, adoption, repair, induction and adaptation. Next, we present the results of some experiments which study the emergence of a language system for the expression of logical combinations and its transmission across generations. Finally, we summarise the main contributions of the paper.

2 Conceptual System

We consider a scenario in which a group of agents try to communicate about *subsets of objects* of the set of all the objects in their particular context. We assume the agents have already developed a set of basic categories and a set of logical categories which allow them to build internal representations of the subset of objects that constitutes the topic of the language game they participate in at a given moment. In the agents' memories, basic categories are represented by propositional logic symbols such as `up` or `le`, which denote the propositions 'I am referring to the objects which are up' and 'I am referring to the objects which are to the left' respectively. Logical categories allow the agents to construct logical combinations of basic categories, which they represent internally by propositional logic formulas.

We also suppose that, at the beginning of a simulation run, the agents have a common vocabulary for referring to basic categories, but that they cannot express logical categories nor the logical formulas they can construct with them in their common language. This means that the agents are able to construct complex meanings such as 'I am referring to the objects which are either up or to the left, but not both', but they do not know how to communicate them. They should learn to express such meanings during the simulations.

The particular set of logical categories the agents can use to construct logical combinations of basic categories is the set of propositional logic connectives $\{\neg, \wedge, \vee\}$. The rest of the standard connectives of propositional logic (i.e. $\rightarrow$ and $\leftrightarrow$) can be expressed using formulas which recursively combine $\wedge, \vee$ and $\neg$ as follows: $A \rightarrow B \equiv \neg A \vee B$ and $A \leftrightarrow B \equiv (A \wedge B) \vee (\neg A \wedge \neg B)$. In fact, every propositional logic formula is logically equivalent to another formula which uses only the connectives $\wedge$, $\vee$ and $\neg$.

The assumption that the agents initially have a set of basic categories, three logical categories, and a common vocabulary for basic categories is based on results from studies on the emergence of vocabularies for spatial concepts, colours or logical categories, in co-evolution with the semantic categories associated with these concepts, (Steels 1995; Steels and Belpaeme 2005; Sierra-Santibáñez 2002).

Previous works have also used experiments in which the topic of the language game is a subset of objects. However, the agents in (Beuls and Steels 2013) conceptualise the topic using a set of distinctive properties in which each property refers to a single object of the topic, and the role of agreement markers is to indicate which properties of the distinctive set refer to the same object. Consequently, the agents in (Beuls and Steels 2013) can only construct internal representations which are conjunctions of basic properties. The agents in (Sierra-Santibáñez 2014) conceptualise the topic using a propositional logic formula which combines basic categories and a Boolean function. This allows them to build a wider range of internal representations: negations, disjunctions, implications or any other type of logical formula that can be constructed using a single Boolean function of one or two arguments. But they are not able to construct logical formulas which contain more than one Boolean function. That is, their conceptual system does not include any recursive logical formulas. The conceptual system used in the present paper, in contrast, contains every propositional logic formula. Because in the present paper we precisely address the problem of the linguistic expression of recursive logical formulas combining basic categories and $\neg, \vee, \wedge$.

3 Linguistic System

Prolog Grammar Rules (Colmerauer et al. 1973; Pereira and Warren 1980) are used to represent the grammars constructed by the individual agents. The head of such rules is an atomic formula whose predicate symbol denotes a syntactic category (e.g. s for sentence) and whose arguments specify a number of aspects of the phrase described by that rule. In this paper the first argument conveys semantic information and the second one a score in the interval [0,1] that estimates the usefulness of the rule in previous communication. Semantic information can be a proposition, a logical connective of the form `or`, `and` or `not`, or a propositional logic formula constructed from the others. Logical formulas are represented using Lisp-like (McCarthy 1960) notation.

The following grammar uses *syntactic categories* and *word order* to express the relation between a connective and its arguments in a sentence. The number appearing in first place on the right hand side of grammar rules 3 and 6 indicates the position (i.e. first 1, second 2 or third 3) of the word associated with the main connective of the formula in the sentence with respect to the positions of the expressions associated with its arguments. This convention is necessary, because left recursive grammar rules cannot be used in Prolog. So the actual sentence generated by this grammar to express `[and,le,up]` is '2yizqarr', which can be parsed into 'izqyarr', where the word 'y' associated with the connective (`and`) is in the second position of the sentence.

$$s(\text{up}, S) \rightarrow \text{arr}, \{S\ is\ 0.7\} \quad (1)$$

$$s(\text{le}, S) \rightarrow \text{izq}, \{S\ is\ 0.25\} \quad (2)$$

$$s([P,Q,R], S) \rightarrow 2,\ c2(P,S_1), s(Q,S_2), s(R,S_3), \{S\ is\ S_1{\cdot}S_2{\cdot}S_3{\cdot}0.1\} \quad (3)$$

$$c2(\text{and}, S) \rightarrow \text{y}, \{S\ is\ 0.5\} \quad (4)$$

$$c2(\text{or}, S) \rightarrow \text{o}, \{S\ is\ 0.5\} \quad (5)$$

$$s([P,Q],S) \rightarrow 1, c1(P,S_1), s(Q,S_2)\{S\ is\ S_1{\cdot}S_2{\cdot}0.6\} \quad (6)$$

$$c1(\text{not}, S) \rightarrow \text{no}, \{S\ is\ 0.5\} \quad (7)$$

This grammar, however, does not allow the agents in the present paper to unambiguosly communicate certain meanings. For example, it generates the same sentence, *'noarryizq',* to express formulas `[not,[and,up,le]]` and `[and,[not,up],le]`. Natural language, on the other hand, provides means to mark the difference between both meanings: `[not,[and,up,le]]` can be expressed as the English sentence *I'm referring to the objects which are not both up and to the left*, and `[and,[not,up],le]` as the sentence *I'm referring to the objects which are not up and which are to the left.* English does so by introducing an auxiliary word (i.e. *'both'*) to distinguish between both formulas, instead of new connectives (different from `and,or,not`) with their associated words and constructions. The auxiliary word *'both'* indicates that the conjunction following it forms an indivisible group and, therefore, that `not` (i.e. the negation) applies to the entire conjunction rather than just to the first element of such a conjunction. Thus a refined version of the grammar above would use sentence *'nogrouparryizq'* to express formula `[not,[and,up,le]]` and sentence *'noarryizq'* to mean `[and,[not,up],le]`, where *'group'* is an auxiliary word, invented by an agent, which plays the same role as *'both'* or *'either'* in English.

A similar problem comes up if we try to use the grammar above (extended by rule $s(\text{do}, S) \rightarrow \text{aba}, \{S\ is\ 0.1\}$) to express formula `[or,up,[and,do,le]]`, which can be paraphrased in English as *'the objects which are up, or down and to the left'*. It generates sentence *'arroabayizq'*, which is ambiguous with respect to the scope of words *'y'* and *'o'* in that sentence. For example, *'y'* could join expressions *'arroaba'* and *'izq'*, or expressions *'aba'* and *'izq'*. In the English sentence, a 'comma' is used to delimit the two main parts of the sentence. In speech the disambiguating role of punctuation marks is played by pauses, and in this work we will treat pauses as auxiliary words which indicate that the sentence following them forms an indivisible group and that the connectives in that group are within the scope of another connective. Thus a refined version of the grammar above would express `[or,up,[and,do,le]]` using sentence *'arropauseabayizq'*, where *'pause'* is also an auxiliary word invented or adopted by an agent.

The linguistic system constructed by the agents in the experiments described in this paper therefore uses three types of linguistic devices to express the relation between each connective and its arguments in a sentence: *syntactic categories, word order* and *auxiliary words.* Whereas the linguistic systems in (Steels 1998; Kirby 2002; Garcia and Steels 2014; Sierra-Santibáñez 2014) use only *syntactic categories* and *word order;* and those in (Gerasymova, Spranger, and Beuls 2012; Beuls and Steels 2013) use only tense-aspect or agreement markers[1]. The added difficulty of parsing and producing sentences with auxiliary words is, however, offset by the higher expressiveness of the present linguistic system, which allows the unambiguous communication of every propositional logic formula (see appendix A), and by the simplicity of its set of logical categories, which only contains logical connectives `and`, `or` and `not`.

4 Language Game

The main steps of the language game used in this paper, which is played by two agents randomly chosen from the population, are as follows:

1. The speaker chooses a logical formula (i.e. a meaning) from its set of conceptualisations of the subset of objects that constitutes the topic of the language game, generates or invents a sentence that expresses this formula, and communicates that sentence to the hearer.
2. The hearer tries to interpret the sentence communicated by the speaker. If it can parse it using its own grammar, it extracts a meaning (i.e. a logical formula); otherwise, the speaker communicates the formula it had in mind to the hearer, and the hearer adopts an association between that formula and the sentence used by the speaker.
3. Depending on the outcome of the language game speaker and hearer expand or adapt their grammars to be more successful in future language games.

A language game *succeeds* if the hearer can parse the sentence communicated by the speaker and if its interpretation of that sentence is logically equivalent to the formula the speaker had in mind; otherwise, the language game *fails*.

4.1 Generation, Invention and Repair

At the early stages of a simulation run the agents cannot use their own grammars to generate sentences for most meanings, because they all begin with a common lexicon for basic categories, but no lexicon for logical categories nor grammar rules. In order to let language get off the ground, the agents are allowed to invent new sentences for those meanings they cannot express using their grammars. A new sentence E for a propositional logic formula F of the form `[not,A]` or `[⊗,A,B]` is invented as follows[2]: a new word is invented for its main connective (`not` or $\otimes$), an expression is generated for each argument (`A` and `B`), and the two or three expressions generated (depending on the type of formula) are concatenated in random order.

[1] Represented by affixes (groups of letters attached to words).

[2] If F is atomic, invention is not necessary because there exists a word in the common lexicon that expresses F. New words are sequences of three to six letters randomly chosen from the alphabet.

Once an agent can generate a sentence for a particular meaning using its grammar, it does not keep inventing new sentences for that meaning. It selects the sentence with the highest score from the set of all the sentences it can generate for that meaning. The *score of a sentence* (or a *meaning*) generated by a grammar rule is computed using the arithmetic expression on the right hand side of that rule, e.g. the score of sentence *'izqyarr'* –generated by rule 3 to express `[and,le,up]`– is computed multiplying the score of that rule (0.1) by the scores of rules 1, 2 and 4 (0.7, 0.25 and 0.5 respectively), which generate the words *'arr'*, *'izq'* and *'y'* associated with the constituents of that formula. The *score of a grammar rule* is the last number in the arithmetic expression that appears on the right hand side of that rule.

However, if an agent realises that the sentence generated by a grammar rule is ambiguous (e.g. sentence *'noarryizq'*, generated by rule 6, can be parsed as `[not,[and,up,le]]` or as `[and,[not,up],le]`), it applies a *repair operator* to that rule, replacing it with a set of rules (e.g. rules 8 and 9) that use additional checks and an auxiliary word invented or adopted by the agent to distinguish between the possible meanings of that sentence. For example, rule 8 refines rule 6 by adding check Q\=[_,_,_], which ensures rule 8 is not applied to negations of conjunctions or disjunctions; and rule 9 introduces an auxiliary word (e.g. *'group'*) which indicates that the scope of *not* is the conjunction or disjunction following that auxiliary word.

$$s([P,Q],S)\rightarrow 1, c1(P,S_1), s(Q,S_2), \{Q \backslash = [\_,\_,\_], \; S \; is \; S_1 \cdot S_2 \cdot 0.1\} \quad (8)$$

$$s([P,[Q,R,T]],S)\rightarrow 1, c1(P,S_1), \text{group}, s([Q,R,T],S_2), \{S \; is \; S_1 \cdot S_2 \cdot 0.1\} \quad (9)$$

Repair operations are also applied to grammar rules which generate ambiguous sentences to express conjunctions or disjunctions. For example, a *repair operator* may replace grammar rule 3 with rules 10, 11, 12 and 13. Rule 10 adds checks Q\=[_,_,_] and R\=[_,_,_] to ensure that the grammatical construction represented by rule 3 is not applied to conjunctions or disjunctions of other conjunctions or disjunctions. Rules 11, 12 and 13 introduce an auxiliary word invented or adopted by the agent (e.g. *'pause'*,) to indicate that the conjunction or disjunction following that word is within the scope of the main connective of the sentence.

$$s([P,Q,R],S) \rightarrow 2, c2(P,S_1), s(Q,S_2), s(R,S_3), \{Q \backslash = [\_,\_,\_], R \backslash = [\_,\_,\_], S \; is \; S_1 \cdot S_2 \cdot S_3 \cdot 0.1\} \quad (10)$$

$$s([P,[Q_1,Q_2,Q_3],R],S) \rightarrow 2, c2(P,S_1), \text{pause}, s([Q_1,Q_2,Q_3],S_2), s(R,S_3), \{R \backslash = [\_,\_,\_], S \; is \; S_1 \cdot S_2 \cdot S_3 \cdot 0.1\} \quad (11)$$

$$s([P,Q,[R_1,R_2,R_3]],S) \rightarrow 2, c2(P,S_1), s(Q,S_2), \text{pause}, s([R_1,R_2,R_3],S_3), \{Q \backslash = [\_,\_,\_], S \; is \; S_1 \cdot S_2 \cdot S_3 \cdot 0.1\} \quad (12)$$

$$s([P,[Q_1,Q_2,Q_3],[R_1,R_2,R_3]],S) \rightarrow 2, c2(P,S_1), \text{pause}, s([Q_1,Q_2,Q_3],S_2), \text{pause}, s([R_1,R_2,R_3],S_3), \{S \; is \; S_1 \cdot S_2 \cdot S_3 \cdot 0.1\} \quad (13)$$

4.2 Interpretation and Adoption

In a language game the hearer tries to interpret the sentence communicated by the speaker using its own grammar. However, at the early stages of a simulation run the agents cannot parse most of the sentences communicated by speakers, because they begin with a common lexicon for basic categories but no grammar rules, except those that generate the words associated with basic categories. When this happens, the speaker communicates the formula F it had in mind to the hearer, and the hearer adopts an association between F and the sentence E used by the speaker, adding a new rule of the form $s(F,S)\rightarrow E,\{S \; is \; 0.1\}$ to its grammar. The initial score of the rules invented or adopted by the agents is 0.1.

Although in real life speakers do not communicate the exact meaning they have in mind to hearers, they usually provide some form of contextual or gestural feedback. Actually, some capacity for *intention-reading* seems to be necessary for language acquisition (Tomasello 2003). Most studies on grammar emergence and evolution also use language games in which the meaning intended by the speaker is communicated to the hearer (Beuls and Steels 2013; Gerasymova, Spranger, and Beuls 2012; Kirby 2002; Batali 1998; Sierra-Santibáñez 2014). The difficulty of studying language evolution in its full complexity leads researchers to focus on particular aspects of it, assuming results from research works addressing issues such as vocabulary and concept formation (Steels 1995; Lara and Alfonseca 2000; Sierra-Santibáñez 2001; Steels and Belpaeme 2005), or speech evolution (de Boer 2001; Zuidema and de Boer 2010).

Once an agent can parse a sentence using its grammar, it selects the meaning with the highest score from the set of all the meanings it can obtain for that sentence. However, if the meaning chosen by the hearer is not logically equivalent to the meaning the speaker had in mind, the speaker communicates the meaning it had in mind to the hearer and the hearer adopts an association between that meaning and the sentence used by the speaker.

4.3 Induction

Invention and adoption allow the agents to construct and learn associations between sentences and meanings. From these associations they induce grammatical constructions and lexical entries they incorporate to their grammars and use in subsequent language games to generate and interpret other sentences. Induction is performed applying three operations, which adapt the rules *simplification* and *chunk* in (Kirby 2002) to the type of grammars built by our agents. Let us see how these operations work with some examples. Suppose an agent adds rule 14 to its grammar.

$$\text{s([and,le,up],S)} \rightarrow izqyarr, \{S \; is \; 0.7\} \quad (14)$$

Simplification of rules 1 and 14 allows replacing rule 14 with 15, which is more general because it can express meanings of the form `[and,le,R]`, where R is a variable.

$$\text{s([and,le,R],S)} \rightarrow izqy, s(R,S_R), \{S \; is \; S_R \cdot 0.1\} \quad (15)$$

A second application of simplification to rules 15 and 2 allows replacing 15 with 16, where R and Q represent any meaning that can be expressed by a sentence, i.e. by an expression of syntactic category s.

$$\text{s([and,Q,R],S)}\rightarrow 2,y,s(Q,S_Q),s(R,S_R),\{S\ is\ S_Q{\cdot}S_R{\cdot}0.1\} \quad (16)$$

If the agent's grammar contained rule 17, *chunk I* would allow the agent to generalise rules 16 and 17 as follows.

$$\text{s([or,Q,R],S)}\rightarrow 2,o,s(Q,S_Q),s(R,S_R),\{S\ is\ S_Q{\cdot}S_R{\cdot}0.6\} \quad (17)$$

Chunk I creates a new syntactic category $c2$, and replaces rules 16 and 17 with rules 18, 19 and 20. Rule 18 generalises 16 and 17, because it can express meanings of the form `[P,Q,R]`, where `P` is any logical category that can be expressed by a word of syntactic category $c2$. Rules 19,20 state that words *'y'* and *'o'* belong to syntactic category $c2$.

$$\text{s([P,Q,R],S)}\rightarrow 2,c2(P,S_1),s(Q,S_2),s(R,S_3),\{S\ is\ S_1{\cdot}S_2{\cdot}S_3{\cdot}0.1\} \quad (18)$$

$$\text{c2(and,S)}\rightarrow y,\{S\ is\ 0.1\} \quad (19)$$

$$\text{c2(or,S)}\rightarrow o,\{S\ is\ 0.1\} \quad (20)$$

Chunk II allows adding words to syntactic categories created by chunk I. Chunk II replaces a grammar rule for a specific connective (e.g. 21) with a new word of a syntactic category created by chunk I, if the rules for the connective and the syntactic category (e.g. 18) are sufficiently similar. Suppose again the agent added rule 21 to its grammar.

$$\text{s([if,Q,R],S)}\rightarrow 2,si,s(Q,S_Q),s(R,S_R),\{S\ is\ S_Q{\cdot}S_R{\cdot}0.1\} \quad (21)$$

Chunk II, applied to 21 and 18, would replace 21 with 22.

$$\text{c2(if,S)}\rightarrow \text{si},\ \{\text{S is } 0.1\} \quad (22)$$

Although both induction and repair operations manipulate the set of rules in an agent's grammar, there are important differences between them. The former are applied whenever a new association is added to an agent's grammar. They replace a single rule or a pair of them with a grammar rule that is more general, i.e. that can be used to express more meanings. The repair operations used in the agent-based model proposed in this paper, on the other hand, do not generalise existing rules, as induction operations do. Instead, they specialise grammar rules which are too general and can generate ambiguous sentences. Induction rules operationalise the *pattern-finding* ability children develop according to *the usage-based theory of language acquisition* (Tomasello 2003). Whereas repair operations implement cognitive processes associated with a particular type of grammar invention and overgeneralisation examples reported in studies of children language acquisition (Tomasello 2006).

4.4 Adaptation

Coordination of the agents' grammars is necessary, because different agents can invent different words to refer to the same connective and they may concatenate the expressions associated with the components of a formula in different orders when they try to express it as a sentence. Although (Steels 1998; Kirby 2002) also study the acquisition of word-order based grammar, they do not address the issue of coordination. Because the populations in these works consist only of two agents, which necessarily share the same history of linguistic interactions. In the experiments discussed in the present paper coordination is achieved through a process of self-organisation of the agents' linguistic interactions, which takes place when these agents adapt their preferences for vocabulary and grammatical constructions to those they observe are used more often by other agents.

The agents adapt the scores of their grammar rules (i.e. their preferences for vocabulary and grammatical constructions) at the last step of a language game, when the speaker communicates the meaning it had in mind to the hearer, and only in the case in which the speaker can generate at least one sentence for the meaning it is trying to communicate using its grammar and the hearer can parse the sentence communicated by the speaker. If an agent can generate several sentences for expressing a given meaning, it chooses the sentence with the highest score, and temporarily stores the other sentences in a set called *competing sentences*; similarly, if it can obtain several meanings for a sentence, it selects the meaning with the highest score and stores the other meanings in a set called *competing meanings*. In a language game only the agent playing the role of hearer adapts the scores of its grammar rules. However, as all the agents in the population play both the role of speaker and that of hearer in different language games, all of them have ample opportunity to adapt the scores of their grammar rules during a simulation.

If the meaning interpreted by the hearer is logically equivalent to the meaning the speaker had in mind, the hearer adjusts the scores of its grammar rules both at the level of interpretation and at that of generation: 1) It increases the scores of the rules it used for obtaining the meaning the speaker had in mind and decreases the scores of the rules it used for obtaining competing meanings. 2) It tries to simulate what it would have said if it had been in the speaker's place, i.e. it tries to express the meaning the speaker had in mind using its own grammar; and it increases the scores of the rules that generate the sentence used by the speaker and decreases the scores of the rules that generate competing sentences.

If the meaning interpreted by the hearer is not logically equivalent to the meaning the speaker had in mind, the hearer decreases the scores of the rules it used for obtaining its interpretation of the sentence used by the speaker, and adopts an association between the sentence and the meaning used by the speaker if it cannot obtain such an association using its own grammar.

5 Experiments

The agent-based model proposed in this paper has been implemented in Prolog (Bueno et al. 1997) and tested on a series of experiments which study both the emergence of a language system for the expression of logical combinations and its transmission across generations.

In the first experiment, which studies language emergence, the agents begin with a common lexicon for basic categories[3] but no grammar rules. Then they play 6060 language games about propositional logic formulas constructed

[3](Gerasymova, Spranger, and Beuls 2012; Beuls and Steels 2013) also use simulations with software agents and initialise the agents with a common vocabulary for basic categories.

Proceedings of the Twenty-Ninth AAAI Conference on Artificial Intelligence

Moral Decision-Making by Analogy: Generalizations versus Exemplars

Joseph A. Blass, Kenneth D. Forbus
Qualitative Reasoning Group, Northwestern University
2133 Sheridan Road, Evanston, IL 60208 USA
Contact: joeblass@u.northwestern.edu

Abstract

Moral reasoning is important to model accurately as AI systems become ever more integrated into our lives. Moral reasoning is rapid and unconscious; analogical reasoning, which can be unconscious, is a promising approach to model moral reasoning. This paper explores the use of analogical generalizations to improve moral reasoning. Analogical reasoning has already been used successfully to model moral reasoning in the MoralDM model, but it exhaustively matches across all known cases, which is computationally intractable and cognitively implausible for human-scale knowledge bases. We investigate the performance of an extension of MoralDM to use the MAC/FAC model of analogical retrieval over three conditions, across a set of highly confusable moral scenarios.

Introduction

Research on moral reasoning and decision-making in humans has revealed that certain moral decisions are based on moral rules rather than utilitarian considerations. These rules are concerned with the morality of actions rather than their outcomes (Baron and Spranca 1997). Furthermore, people are sensitive to structural differences, leading us to make different judgments even when considering cases that seem similar on the surface. Consider these two scenarios (from Waldmann and Dietrich 2007) below:

> Bomb 1: "In a restaurant, a bomb threatens to kill 9 guests. The bomb could be thrown onto the patio, where 1 guest would be killed [but the 9 would be spared]."

> Bomb 2: "In a restaurant, a bomb threatens to kill 9 guests. One [separate] guest could be thrown on the bomb, which would kill this one guest [but the 9 would be spared]."

Despite the two scenarios having strong surface and structural similarities as well as identical utilitarian considerations, participants in this study generally said that taking the proposed action was morally acceptable in the first scenario but not in the second scenario.

In addition to making non-utilitarian moral decisions, humans tend to be able to judge the moral value of actions and situations quickly and with little conscious reasoning; in fact, there is evidence that justifications for moral judgments come after the judgment has been made (Haidt 2001). Furthermore, research suggests that our moral rules are not innate or learned by rote, but are acquired culturally from exposure to moral narratives (Darley and Shultz 1990). These features suggest that purely first-principles, rule-based reasoning is not sufficient to account for moral reasoning.

Analogical reasoning involves comparing structured cases. Analogical reasoning can be unconscious (Day and Gentner 2003), and is therefore an intriguing approach for modeling moral decision-making. However, analogical retrieval often results in a match with strong surface similarities, rather than structural or relational similarities, although experts do not show this pattern (Novick 1988). This poses a problem for cases such as the two bomb scenarios, since each scenario is most surface-similar to the other, and therefore the likely target of a match for someone who knows one scenario and is evaluating the other.

A potential solution is to use analogical generalizations, built from similar-enough exemplars, which emphasize what is common between them while deprecating facts unique to individual exemplars. If presented in an order conducive to assimilation, generalizations will be formed on the basis of higher-order relations shared across cases (Kuehne et al. 2000); as the generalizations grow, these facts become more important than facts unique to cases. The Sequential Analogical Generalization Engine (SAGE), has been shown to facilitate analogical reasoning (McLure, Friedman, and Forbus 2010; Chang and Forbus 2013).

This paper shows how reasoning by analogy using generalizations of solved moral scenarios, rather than across those individual cases, leads to better performance as the size of the training case-library grows. Forming these generalizations is important as it may better represent the way we learn and reason about moral dilemmas. It will eventually be important for autonomous moral reasoning systems to *learn* moral rules, not just be told them. Firm rules can be brittle and contradict each other (Iliev et al. 2009), yet humans do not stop making consistent moral decisions; our systems need to learn and reason the same way we do in moral domains if we are ever to trust them to make the right decision in high-stakes environments, such as driving a car on the highway.

This work is a continuation of research done on MoralDM, a model of moral judgment (Dehghani et al. 2008a, Dehghani et al. 2008b). We begin by reviewing the relevant psychological background and findings on moral decision-making and analogical reasoning. Next we briefly describe previous work on MoralDM. Then we show how an analogy-only adaptation of that system performs using four analogy-based conditions across different sizes of case libraries. Finally, we discuss future work.

The Psychology of Moral Decision-Making

The four findings most relevant to the present study are:

1) Protected Values

To account for the non-utilitarian choices people often seem to prefer when making moral judgments, researchers have proposed the existence of *Protected Values* (PVs), or *Sacred Values* (Baron and Spranca 1997; Tetlock 2000). These PVs concern actions rather than outcomes. Most people seem to have a PV "it is wrong to kill a person"; it is the act of killing itself, rather than the consequence of a person being dead, that violates the PV, and is therefore morally forbidden.

2) Principle of Double Effect

The first bomb scenario above seems to contradict the idea of PVs, since throwing the bomb onto the patio is taking an action that violates a PV. Tossing the bomb is acceptable because of the Principle of Double Effect (PDE). PDE (Foot 1967; Thomson 1985) states that harm caused as a side effect of preventing a greater harm is permissible, but harm caused *in order* to prevent a greater harm is forbidden. If you decide to throw the bomb on the patio, you are not trying to kill the person on the patio, only trying to get the bomb away from the nine people inside. The death of the one person outside is an unfortunate side effect. If, however, you throw the person on the bomb, then the death of the one is causally necessary to the saving of the nine: the harm caused is used as the *means* to avoid the harm prevented. PDE has recently been criticized in light of findings that seem to contradict its formulation of harm as means vs. side effect (e.g., Greene et al. 2009). However, for the current study PDE provides the simplest and most comprehensive account of the results we simulate.

3) Moral Rules Are Acquired From Culture

There is scientific consensus that we acquire our moral rules and senses of right and wrong from culture (Prasad 2007; Dehghani et al. 2009) and in stages (Kohlberg 1973). The particular rules vary with culture: for example, many Americans see desecrating the U.S. flag as a moral violation; non-US citizens do not. The cultural acquisition of moral rules is important for AI because it gives us a model of learning to apply in order to learn moral rules. Certainly children are told "killing is wrong", but they are also told why it is wrong; we learn right from wrong by examining the similarities and differences among the many cultural narratives we are exposed to that concern moral rules (Gentner and Medina 1998). It is from these cultural narratives that the rules arise; if we are to build an effective cognitive simulation of moral decision-making, such a model would need not only to be able to make decisions like those of different people based on the PVs they hold, but to extract those PVs from the cultural narratives those people learned them from. The present study takes an important step in that direction.

4) Moral Decisions Are Fast and May Be Subconscious

People are able to make moral decisions extremely quickly (Haidt 2001). When presented with a choice we can often say almost instantly whether it is morally permissible. Non-utilitarian moral judgments stay fast under cognitive load (Greene et al. 2008), and justifications for the morality of an action often come after the judgment has been made (Haidt 2001). The speed and subconscious nature of these judgments suggests analogical, rather than first-principles, reasoning. Analogical reasoning has previously been used to successfully model automatic and rapid reactions (e.g., Wilson, Forbus, and McLure 2013).

Analogy and Decision-Making

Analogy has been demonstrated to be an important tool in reasoning and decision-making; we use our past experiences and draw inferences from previous choices in choosing what to do (Markman and Medin 2002). One of the primary models of analogical reasoning and inference in humans, structure mapping theory (Gentner 1983), involves finding an alignment, or shared relational structures, between two descriptions. Items present in one description and not in the other are postulated as *candidate inferences*. Analogical decision-making involves identifying the decision from the retrieved case and making the analogous decision in the new case.

We have a huge amount of experience; how do we decide what, from our long-term-memory, is the proper case to reason from analogically? Research has demonstrated that *surface* similarity between a case in long-term-memory and the target case being evaluated increases the likelihood of it being retrieved; on the other hand, *structural* similarity between those cases retrieved and the target case is the best predictor for inference (Forbus, Gentner, and Law 1994; Gentner, Rattermann, and Forbus 1993). That is, surface similarity defines what stories we retrieve from memory, but structural similarity defines which of those stories we reason from. Next, the analogical models used here are described.

The Structure Mapping Engine

SME, the Structure Mapping Engine (Falkenhainer, Forbus, and Gentner 1989), is a computational model of analogy and similarity based on Gentner's (1983) structure mapping theory. SME takes in two structured, relational cases, a *base* and a *target*, and computes up to three *mappings* between them. Mappings include the *correspondences* between expressions and entities in the two cases, *candidate inferences* suggested by the mapping, and a *similarity score*. The similarity score is normalized by dividing it by the score of the mapping from the target to itself.

MAC/FAC

Running SME across every case in memory would be prohibitively expensive and cognitively impossible for human-scale memories. MAC/FAC (Forbus, Gentner, and Law 1994) takes in a *probe* case like those used by SME as well as a case library of other such cases. MAC/FAC efficiently generates *remindings*, which are SME mappings, for the probe case with the most similar from the case library. MAC/FAC proceeds in two stages. In the first stage, it computes dot products between content vectors of the probe and each case in the case library. This process is fast, coarse, and serves as a model of retrieval based on similarity. Up to the three most similar cases from the first stage are passed on to the second stage (fewer than three are passed on if scores are not close enough to the best match). In the second stage, SME calculates mappings between each retrieved case and the probe. The three best mappings are returned as MAC/FAC's output. Fewer than three are returned if not close to the score of the best mapping.

The Sequential Analogical Generalization Engine

The Sequential Analogical Generalization Engine (SAGE) is a computational model of analogical generalization. SAGE is a descendent of SEQL (Kuehne et al. 2000), extended with probabilities (Halstead and Forbus 2005). Within a particular *generalization context*, which is a case library composed of generalizations and ungeneralized exemplars, cases are either assimilated based on similarity into generalizations, or left ungeneralized if they are too dissimilar to the rest.

When a case arrives, SAGE uses MAC/FAC to retrieve remindings from the generalization context using the new case as a probe. If the similarity score from the top reminding is above the *similarity threshold*, the case is assimilated into the retrieved generalization. If not, it is left as an ungeneralized exemplar, but future cases may merge with it to form new generalizations.

SAGE creates generalizations from cases that include all the facts across all those cases, with non-identical corresponding entities replaced by abstract entities, and assigns to each fact a probability that reflects the frequency with which it was present in the assimilated cases. A fact with probability 1/n indicates that it is only true in 1/n of the cases. When a new case is assimilated the probabilities are updated. In creating SME mappings between cases and generalizations, only facts above a predetermined probability cutoff are used. This means that facts specific to only a few cases end up being unimportant when doing analogical reasoning against that generalization, and that as the number of assimilated exemplars grows, the generalization becomes more representative of the shared structures of its constituent cases.

MoralDM

MoralDM (Dehghani et al. 2008a,b) solved moral dilemmas using two reasoning systems: first-principles reasoning, based on established psychological moral reasoning principles including PVs and PDE, and analogical reasoning against solved cases. The solutions to moral dilemmas depend on the particular moral norms of the person making the decision and are therefore inherently subjective, yet within particular cultures and groups overall trends do emerge; we take the majority decision of participants in the original study as being correct.

MoralDM used a combination of first-principles rules and analogical reasoning to detect PVs. It compared a new dilemma with all known cases using SME, before any first-principles reasoning was done, and picked the choice suggested by the most cases (or the most similar, in case of a tie). While guaranteeing the best precedent will be found, this approach would not scale to human-sized memories. If only first-principles reasoning or analogical reasoning suggested a choice, that choice was the output. If the two systems disagreed, first-principles reasoning was chosen over analogy. Our extension starts with some first-principles reasoning to establish PVs and other facts to prime comparisons, then uses analogy. It extends MoralDM by using MAC/FAC to retrieve cases, and SAGE to construct generalizations from cases. It also adds a stronger, domain-independent consistency check. That is, it tests to see if a candidate inference is already known to be false in the target, and if so, ignores the match. Dehghani's original MoralDM used a comparison between qualitative order of magnitude estimates as a domain-specific test for candidate inferences.

Experiment

For MoralDM to have relevant facts to compare, it has to do a small amount of explicit reasoning. It uses rules to determine whether a choice involves a PV, and ascertains the number of individuals affected by each choice. It checks whether the choice is an action or omission: consequences being equally bad, humans prefer inaction to action (Ritov and Baron 1999). Finally, it checks whether the action prevents some alternative negative outcome, and if so, whether the action directly prevents the negative outcome (i.e., as a means or side effect, which is relevant to PDE). Ultimately these facts, too, might be learned via analogical generalization, but that is future work.

We compared the performance of four conditions: (1) MAC/FAC over SAGE generalizations, (2) MAC/FAC over the union of generalizations and cases, (3) MAC/FAC over cases alone; and (4) Best SME match. For brevity, we refer to these as M+G, M+GC, M+C, and BestSME, respectively. BestSME serves as a baseline: since it is exhaustive, it should always provide the most accurate match. The training and test sets were drawn from eight trolley-like problems from Waldmann and Dieterich's (2007) study, which were converted from simplified text to formal representations using EA NLU (Tomai 2009), and were slightly modified by hand (to indicate, for example, that when a trolley hits a bus, the bus' passengers die). The training cases are identical to those we test, with two extra facts: one indicating the correct choice, and one justifying that choice. Here is an example:

```
(implies
  (and
    (protectedValueChoice throw18421)
    (protectedValueChoice Inaction18657)
    (uninferredSentence
      (affectsSigLargerGroup throw18421))
    (uninferredSentence
      (affectsSigLargerGroup Inaction18657))
    (directlyResponsible you18016 throw18421)
    (uninferredSentence
      (directlyResponsible you18016
                           Inaction18657))
    (preventsAlternativeNegativeOutcome
                           throw18421)
    (uninferredSentence
      (usedAsMeansToPreventNegOutcome
                           throw18421)))
  (rightChoice throw18421))

(makeDecision you18016 throw18421))
```

The antecedents of the implication are derived during the precomputing phase, whereas the `makeDecision` fact is what is being inferred analogically. Note that the extra facts we provided our model in the solutions were not so differentiated as to provide the system with categories. For example, in the second bomb scenario, the added implication fact is structurally identical to first, except the final fact is not wrapped in "uninferredSentence" (indicating that the final fact is true in the second bomb scenario but not the first). Additional information can be found in the on-line supplemental material[1].

We have other cases than the eight we tested but restricted ourselves to these for two reasons. First, the other dilemmas (all drawn from psychological experiments) always have as the right answer "do nothing", which means a system could perform well by chance. Second, these eight cases consist of four matched pairs of cases which are highly confusable, sharing both surface and structural features. One case from each pair is an instance of PDE acceptability (like the first bomb scenario); the other is not. Each scenario therefore has three matches and four confounds, including one direct confound (i.e., the two bomb scenarios are each other's direct confounds), making analogical reasoning tougher.

Methods

For each case we constructed training sets composed of all subsets of the other seven cases. The order of cases within training sets was randomized, as was the order of training sets (results are averaged by training set size, so order does not matter). For each trial, the model constructs generalizations using SAGE over the training set. The model performs MAC/FAC over these generalizations (M+G), over the ungeneralized cases (M+C), and over the union of generalizations and cases (M+GC), using the test case as a probe. After retrieval it performs a consistency check on the reminding: if a candidate inference hypothesizes something known to be false, then the mapping is rejected and the model moves to the next best. If it runs through all remindings it performs one additional retrieval over the case library without the rejected cases. If a candidate inference from the best consistent mapping is of the form `(makeDecision ?actor ?action)`, it is treated as the solution to the dilemma. The model keeps track of both the answer and the number of consistency checks performed.

As a baseline, in the BestSME condition the model exhaustively performs SME matches between the test case and all cases in the library, using the highest match that passes the consistency check. We assume that this technique will return the most accurate outcome possible, as it guarantees the best consistent match. However, it is computationally intractable and cognitively implausible to match a case against every single case stored in memory for human-scale memories. We compared the BestSME match results to Dehghani et al.'s (2008a, experiment 3) findings across the same eight test cases. Note that, because of the

[1] http://www.qrg.northwestern.edu/papers/aaai15/moraldm-extras.html

nature of our consistency check, our four experimental techniques are unable to get the wrong answer (i.e., postulate a fact known to be false). These modules could either get the right answer, or no answer at all; our measure is therefore proportion correct.

We had the following hypotheses: (H1) Since moral rules concern underlying structures rather than surface features, M+G or M+GC will lead to better moral judgments as the size of the training case library increases. (H1a) All techniques will improve as the number of matching cases in the training set increases. (H1b) All techniques will worsen as the number of conflicting cases in the training set increases. (H2) With small case libraries M+G, M+C, and M+GC will perform equally well. As training sets increase in size, M+G will outperform M+GC, which will outperform M+C. (H3) M+G will get the right answer earlier than M+C or M+GC, i.e. requiring fewer consistency checks and performing fewer additional retrievals. (H4) BestSME will outperform Dehghani et al's (2008a) version, due to its enhanced consistency check and initial reasoning.

Results

Across all trials, M+G performed as well as BestSME, with identical statistics. (Please consult the supplementary materials for details.) Since BestSME is exhaustive, this indictates that M+G performs at ceiling.

We performed a logistic regression to determine the effects of experimental technique, case library size, and technique given case library size. Case library size was a significant predictor of accuracy (Wald's chi-square (χ^2) = 68.674, $p<10^{-4}$, odds ratio (OR) = 3.6) and we found a marginal effect of experimental technique ($\chi^2 = 3.69$, $p = 0.055$, OR = 1.4), as well as a significant interaction between experimental technique given number of training cases ($\chi^2 = 5.67$, $p<0.05$, OR = 2.6. Consistent with H1, there was a significant improvement in performance as training size increased across all conditions (M+G: r=0.4, $p<10^{-4}$; M+C: r=0.32, $p<10^{-4}$; M+GC: r=0.295, $p<10^{-4}$) (Figure 1). Because BestSME and M+G performed identically, their lines on Figure 1 overlap perfectly. Dehghani and colleagues (2008a) found similar improvement with number of training cases for BestSME (r=0.97, $p<10^{-4}$) using their consistency check, although BestSME was at most 75% accurate in that study. Our correlations were all significantly different from each other ($p<0.05$, using the Fisher r-to-z transformation), except for M+G vs. M+GC. In accordance with H1a, performance improved as the number of matching cases in the training set increased (M+G: r=0.64, $p<10^{-4}$; M+C: r=0.61, $p<10^{-4}$; M+GC: r=0.57, $p<10^{-4}$). Consistent with H1b, M+C and M+GC worsened with number of confounds (both r=-0.11, $p>0.001$) but contrary to H1b M+G and BestSME did not worsen ($p = 0.08$).

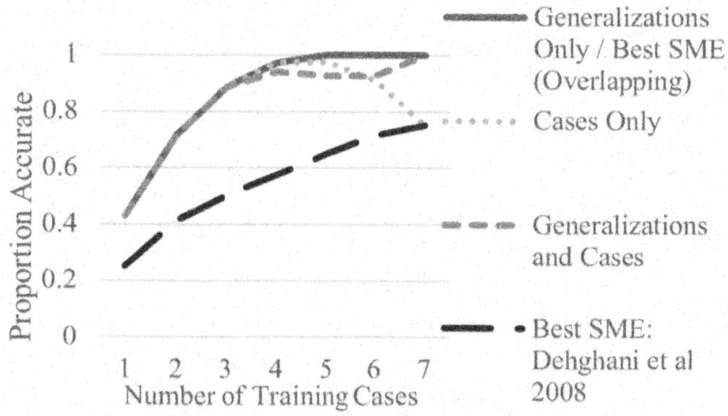

Figure 1: Accuracy by Number of Training Cases

Given that in our logistic regression we found a marginal main effect of condition and a significant interaction between condition and number of training cases, we decided to evaluate H2 by performing logistic regressions separately over trials using large (5-7 cases) and small (1-4 cases) case libraries. In accordance with H2, condition did not predict performance with case libraries of up to size 4, although there was still an effect of case library size ($\chi^2 = 278.29$, $p < 10^{-4}$, odds ratio = 3.2). For case libraries of sizes 5-7, however, there was a significant relationship between condition and performance (χ^2= 6.55, $p < 0.05$, odds ratio 0.5)[2], and no effect of case library size. We performed t-tests to determine the relative performance of each condition and found that BestSME and M+G outperformed both M+GC and M+C ($p<0.0167$). Note that with a case library of size seven, BestSME, M+G, and M+GC all performed perfectly. Contrary to H2, M+GC did not significantly outperform M+C with large training case libraries.

As predicted in H3, M+G required significantly fewer consistency checks than M+C or M+GC; M+C required significantly fewer checks than M+GC (all $p<10^{-4}$) (Figure 2). Being exhaustive, BestSME with the new consistency check, as well as with Dehghani et al.'s (2008a) consistency check, always performed as many consistency checks as there were training cases. These data are not displayed in Figure 2. There was a significant increase in consistency checks as the training set increased in size for M+GC (r=0.12, $p<10^{-4}$), and M+C (r=0.25, $p<10^{-4}$), but not M+G. Additionally, M+G and M+GC required an additional retrieval 25% of the time; M+C required an additional retrieval 35% of the time (a significant difference, $p<10^{-4}$).

Finally, as predicted in H4, our new consistency check led BestSME to outperform the original MoralDM. With case libraries of size 1-6, our technique significantly outperformed the previous technique (all $p<10^{-4}$); with case

[2] Condition is not a continuous variable; the coding we used for the purpose of analysis is 1 = M+G, 2 = M+GC, 3 = M+C.

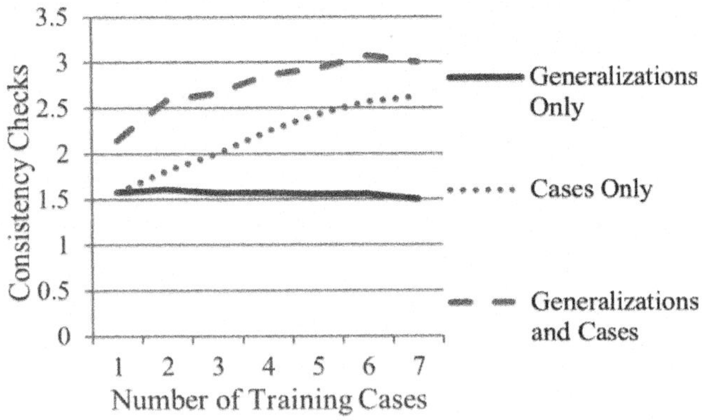

Figure 2: Consistency Checks by Number of Training Cases

library size 7 the result was not significant (p=0.07). We believe that this is because there are only eight cases with training size 7, since each such case requires all other cases to be in the training set, and that if the sample size were increased the difference would become statistically significant. For further information on our statistical analyses as well as an exploration of why performance of M+C improves with medium case library size and worsens with larger case libraries, consult our supplementary materials.

Discussion and Future Work

With only eight test cases and a maximum case library size of seven, all of which concern PDE, this experiment was performed on a highly restricted domain. We consider our results preliminary, but they suggest that analogical reasoning across generalizations of solved moral dilemmas is a more faithful model of human moral reasoning than analogical reasoning over ungeneralized cases, given its high accuracy and that it consistently got the correct answer on the first or second retrieval. This is consistent with the psychological finding that moral judgments develop over time from the acquisition of cultural narratives. Of course, human moral capacities develop over a longer period of time and with exposure to many more than seven stories; our system performs well with a small case library due to the simplicity of its representations, concentrated experience, restriction to PDE, and pre-defined PV rules. As with humans, many of whom cannot articulate PDE but nonetheless abide by it, our system followed the rule of PDE without being given it explicitly. Rather, SAGE was able to recognize which scenarios were acceptable PDE or not, and when a new scenario came in, effectively make inferences based on the relational structure, rather than surface features.

We believe analogical reasoning across generalizations (M+G) eventually outperformed reasoning across cases (M+C) because irrelevant surface features (such as the mechanism of action being a bomb instead of a trolley) fell away, leaving overall structural similarities and justifications. When reasoning using generalizations, there were fewer surface features to mislead MAC/FAC into making a faulty match. These findings seem consistent with humans, who might hear several different stories illustrating the same moral principle and eventually view them as instances of that principle, not only exemplars. The principles at work and justification for the outcome then become more important than the details of the story, and lead to better moral judgments. As in Winston (1981), SAGE generalizations behave as pseudo-rules; in contrast to that work, however, generalizations do not have to be extracted into an explicit "if-then" formulation, nor did SAGE need to be explicitly told what to use as a precedent in analogical reasoning, for a match to happen properly and produce the appropriate conclusion.

Reasoning by analogy to generalizations performed as well as the BestSME match across all cases (the best possible performance). Reasoning by analogy to the union of generalizations and cases was also highly accurate, although it required a large number of consistency checks which increased with case library size. Given the high accuracy of these techniques and the computational intractability of exhaustively matching across all cases in human-scale memory, we conclude that reasoning by analogy to generalizations is potentially an excellent technique for solving moral dilemmas by analogy.

Finally, our pump-priming reasoning and consistency check made Best SME more accurate than Dehghani et al.'s (2008a) findings across the same dataset. Furthermore, the updated consistency check is applicable to any analogical retrieval, whereas Dehghani et al.'s (2008a), was specific to the moral domain.

As the corpus of findings and moral narratives grows, it will be important to see how well this model scales. We plan to expand the pool of training cases, ideally beyond psychology-study-style moral dilemmas and into cultural narratives such as Aesop's fables. We also plan to expand upon Dehghani et al.'s (2009) work, to simulate how different cultural narratives lead to different moral decisions. Recently psychologists have shown how taking on different roles, each with their own associated narratives and duties, leads to different moral judgments (Sachdeva, Singh, and Medin 2011), which is also worth exploring computationally.

Acknowledgements

We thank Linsey Smith, Dedre Gentner, and Tom Hinrichs for their help with statistics and programming, and Morteza Dehghani for creating MoralDM and providing helpful advice. This research was sponsored by the Socio-Cognitive

Architectures Program of the Office of Naval Research, N00014-13-1-0470.

References

Baron, J., and Spranca, M. 1997. Protected Values. *Organizational Behavior and Human Decision Processes*, 70(1), 1-16.

Chang, M. D. and Forbus, K. D. 2013. Clustering Hand-Drawn Sketches via Analogical Generalization. *Proceedings of the Twenty-Fifth Innovative Applications of Artificial Intelligence (IAAI-13),* 1507-1512. Bellevue, Washington.

Darley, J.M., and Shultz, T.R. 1990. Moral Rules: Their Content and Acquisition. *Annual Review of Psychology*, 41(1), 525-556.

Day, S.B., and Gentner, D. 2003. Analogical Inference in Automatic Interpretation. *Proceedings of the Twenty-Fifth Annual Meeting of the Cognitive Science Society*. Boston, MA.

Dehghani, M., Tomai, E., Forbus, K., Klenk, M. 2008a. An Integrated Reasoning Approach to Moral Decision-Making. *Proceedings of the Twenty-Third AAAI Conference on Artificial Intelligence (AAAI).* 1280-1286. Chicago, IL.

Dehghani, M., Tomai, E., Forbus, K., Iliev, R., Klenk, M. 2008b. MoralDM: A Computational Modal of Moral Decision-Making. *Proceedings of the 30th Annual Conference of the Cognitive Science Society (CogSci).* Washington, D.C.

Dehghani, M., Sachdeva, S., Ekhtiari, H., Gentner, D., and Forbus, K. 2009. The role of cultural narratives in moral decision making. In *Proceedings of the 31th Annual Conference of the Cognitive Science Society*, 1912-1917.

Falkenhainer, B., Forbus, K. and Gentner, D. 1989. The Structure Mapping Engine: Algorithm and examples. *Artificial Intelligence*, 41(1), 1-63

Foot, P. 1967. The problem of abortion and the doctrine of the double effect. *Oxford Review*, 5, 5–15.

Forbus, K., Gentner, D., and Law, K. 1994. MAC/FAC: A model of similarity-based retrieval. *Cognitive Science*, 19(2), 141-205.

Gentner, D. 1983. Structure-Mapping: A Theoretical Framework for Analogy. *Cognitive Science* 7(2), 155-170.

Gentner, D., and Medina, J. 1998. Similarity and the development of rules. *Cognition*, 65(2), 263-297.

Gentner, D., and Rattermann, M.J., and Forbus, K. 1993. The roles of similarity in transfer: Separating retrievability and inferential soundness. *Cognitive Psychology*, 25(4), 524-575

Greene, J. D., Morelli, S. A., Lowenberg, K., Nystrom, L. E., and Cohen, J. D. 2008. Cognitive load selectively interferes with utilitarian moral judgment. *Cognition*, 107(3), 1144-1154.

Greene, J. D., Cushman, F. A., Stewart, L. E., Lowenberg, K., Nystrom, L. E., and Cohen, J. D. 2009. Pushing moral buttons: The interaction between personal force and intention in moral judgment. *Cognition*, 111(3), 364-371.

Haidt, J. 2001. The emotional dog and its rational tail: A social intuitionist approach to moral judgment. *Psychological Review*, 108(4), 814-834.

Halstead, D. T., and Forbus, K. D. 2005. Transforming between propositions and features: Bridging the gap. In *Proceedings of the National Conference on Artificial Intelligence*, 777-782. Pittsburgh, PA.

Iliev, R., Sachdeva, S., Bartels, D.M. Joseph, C.M., Suzuki, S., and Medin, D.L. 2009. Attending to Moral Values. In Daniel M. Bartels, Christopher W. Bauman, Linda J. Skitka, and Douglas L. Medin (Eds.) *Moral Judgment and Decision Making: The Psychology of Learning and Motivation*, Vol 50. 169-190. San Diego: Elsevier

Kuehne, S., Forbus, K., Gentner, D., and Quinn, B. 2000. SEQL: Category Learning as Progressive Abstraction Using Structure Mapping. In *Proceedings of the 22nd Annual Meeting of the Cognitive Science Society*, 770-775.

Markman, A and Medin, D.L. 2002. Decision Making. In Pashler, H. and Medin, D. (Eds). *Stevens Handbook of Experimental Psychology, 3rd edition: Volume 2, Memory and Cognitive Processes*. New York: Wiley.

McLure, M., Friedman, S.E., and Forbus, K.D. 2010. Learning concepts from sketches via analogical generalization and near-misses. *Proceedings of the 32nd Annual Conference of the Cognitive Science Society (CogSci).* Portland, OR.

Novick, L.R. 1988. Analogical Transfer, Problem Similarity, and Expertise. *Journal of Experimental Psychology: Learning, Memory, and Cognition*. 14(3), 510-520.

Prasad, L. 2007. *Poetics of Conduct*. Columbia University Press, New York.

Ritov, I., and Baron, J. 1999. Protected Values and Omission Bias. *Organizational Behavior and Human Decision Processes*, 79(2), 79-94.

Sachdeva, S., Singh, P., and Medin, D. 2011. Culture and the Quest for Universal Principles in Moral Reasoning. *International Journal of Psychology*, 46(3), 161-176.

Tetlock, P. E. 2000. Cognitive biases and organizational correctives: Do both disease and cure depend on the ideological beholder? *Administrative Science Quarterly*, 45(2), 293-326

Thomson, J.J. 1985. The trolley problem. *Yale Law Journal*, 94, 1395–1415.

Tomai, E., 2009. A Pragmatic Approach to Computational Narrative Understanding. Ph.D. Dissertation, Department of Electrical Engineering and Computer Science, Northwestern University, Evanston, IL.

Wilson, J. R., Forbus, K. D., and McLure, M. D. (2013). Am I Really Scared? A Multi-phase Computational Model of Emotions. In *Proceedings of the Second Annual Conference on Advances in Cognitive Systems ACS.* 289-304.

Winston, P.H. 1982. Learning new principles from precedents and exercises. *Artificial Intelligence*, 19, 321-350.

Proceedings of the Twenty-Ninth AAAI Conference on Artificial Intelligence

AffectiveSpace 2: Enabling Affective Intuition for Concept-Level Sentiment Analysis

Erik Cambria
School of Computer Engineering
NTU, Singapore
cambria@ntu.edu.sg

Jie Fu
School of Computing
NUS, Singapore
jie.fu@comp.nus.edu.sg

Federica Bisio
DITEN
University of Genoa, Italy
federica.bisio@edu.unige.it

Soujanya Poria
School of Computer Engineering
NTU, Singapore
sporia@ntu.edu.sg

Abstract

Predicting the affective valence of unknown multi-word expressions is key for concept-level sentiment analysis. AffectiveSpace 2 is a vector space model, built by means of random projection, that allows for reasoning by analogy on natural language concepts. By reducing the dimensionality of affective common-sense knowledge, the model allows semantic features associated with concepts to be generalized and, hence, allows concepts to be intuitively clustered according to their semantic and affective relatedness. Such an affective intuition (so called because it does not rely on explicit features, but rather on implicit analogies) enables the inference of emotions and polarity conveyed by multi-word expressions, thus achieving efficient concept-level sentiment analysis.

Introduction

Concept-level sentiment analysis focuses on a semantic analysis of text through the use of web ontologies or semantic networks, which allow the aggregation of conceptual and affective information associated with natural language opinions. By relying on large semantic knowledge bases, such approaches step away from blind use of keywords and word co-occurrence count, but rather rely on the implicit features associated with natural language concepts.

Unlike purely syntactical techniques, concept-based approaches are able to detect also sentiments that are expressed in a subtle manner, e.g., through the analysis of concepts that do not explicitly convey any emotion, but which are implicitly linked to other concepts that do so. The bag-of-concepts model can represent semantics associated with natural language much better than bags of words. In the bag-of-words model, in fact, a concept such as `cloud computing` would be split into two separate words, disrupting the semantics of the input sentence (in which, for example, the word `cloud` could wrongly activate concepts related to `weather`).

The analysis at concept-level allows for the inference of semantic and affective information associated with natural language opinions and, hence, enables a comparative fine-grained feature-based sentiment analysis. Rather than gathering isolated opinions about a whole item (e.g., iPhone6), users are generally more interested in comparing different products according to their specific features (e.g., iPhone6's vs GalaxyS6's touchscreen), or even sub-features (e.g., fragility of iPhone6's vs GalaxyS6's touchscreen).

In this context, common-sense knowledge is key for properly deconstructing natural language text into sentiments – for example, to appraise the concept `small room` as negative for a hotel review and `small queue` as positive in a patient opinion, or the concept `go read the book` as positive for a book review but negative for a movie review. The inference of emotions and polarity from natural language concepts, however, is a formidable task as it requires advanced reasoning capabilities such as common-sense, analogical, and affective reasoning.

In this work, we present AffectiveSpace 2, a novel vector space model for concept-level sentiment analysis that allows for reasoning by analogy on natural language concepts, even when these are represented by highly dimensional semantic features. In this sense, AffectiveSpace 2 can be seen as a powerful tool to address the emerging issue of "Big Dimensionality" (Zhai, Ong, and Tsang 2014) in the context of natural language processing (NLP) and sentiment analysis. The proposed model, however, should not be considered solely as a NLP tool, but rather as a framework for analogical reasoning that can be embedded in potentially any cognitive system dealing with real-world semantics, e.g., concepts associated with images (Cambria and Hussain 2012a), audio (Principi et al. 2015), handwriting (Wang et al. 2013), and multimodal data (Poria et al. 2015).

The rest of the paper is organized as follows: the first section presents related work in the field of concept-level sentiment analysis; the following two sections describe in detail how AffectiveSpace 2 is built and clustered, respectively; an evaluation section proposes experimental results for an opinion mining task; finally, the last section provides some concluding remarks.

Related Work

Concept-level sentiment analysis is a NLP task that has recently raised growing interest both within the scientific community, leading to many exciting open challenges, as well as in the business world, due to the remarkable benefits to be had from marketing and financial market prediction.

The potential applications of concept-level sentiment analysis, in fact, are countless and span interdisciplinary areas such as stock market prediction, political forecasting, social network analysis, social stream mining, and human-robot interaction.

For example, Li et al. (Li et al. 2014) implemented a generic stock price prediction framework and plugged in six different models with different analyzing approaches. They used Harvard psychological dictionary and Loughran-McDonald financial sentiment dictionary to construct a sentiment space. Textual news articles were then quantitatively measured and projected onto such a sentiment space. The models' prediction accuracy was evaluated on five years historical Hong Kong Stock Exchange prices and news articles and their performance was compared empirically at different market classification levels.

Rill et al. (Rill et al. 2014) proposed a system designed to detect emerging political topics in Twitter sooner than other standard information channels. For the analysis, authors collected about 4 million tweets before and during the parliamentary election 2013 in Germany, from April until September 2013. It was found that new topics appearing in Twitter can be detected right after their occurrence. Moreover, authors compared their results to Google Trends, observing that the topics emerged earlier in Twitter than in Google Trends.

Jung and Segev (Jung and Segev 2014) analyzed how communities change over time in the citation network graph without additional external information and based on node and link prediction and community detection. The identified communities were classified using key term labeling. Experiments showed that the proposed methods can identify the changes in citation communities multiple years in the future with performance differing according to the analyzed time span.

Montejo-Raez et al. (Montejo-Raez et al. 2014) introduced an approach for sentiment analysis in social media environments. Similar to explicit semantic analysis, microblog posts were indexed by a predefined collection of documents. In the proposed approach, performed by means of latent semantic analysis, these documents were built up from common emotional expressions in social streams.

Bell et al. (Bell et al. 2014) proposed a novel approach to social data analysis, exploring the use of microblogging to manage interaction between humans and robots, and evaluating an architecture that extends the use of social networks to connect humans and devices. The approach used NLP techniques to extract features of interest from textual data retrieved from a microblogging platform in real-time and, hence, to generate appropriate executable code for the robot. The simple rule-based solution exploited some of the 'natural' constraints imposed by microblogging platforms to manage the potential complexity of the interactions and to create bi-directional communication.

Building AffectiveSpace 2

The best way to solve a problem is to already know a solution for it. But, if we have to face a problem we have never met before, we need to use our intuition. Intuition can be explained as the process of making analogies between the current problem and the ones solved in the past to find a suitable solution. This kind of thinking is maybe the essence of human intelligence since in everyday life no two situations are ever the same and we have to continuously perform analogical reasoning for problem solving and decision making.

The human mind constructs intelligible meanings by continuously compressing over vital relations (Fauconnier and Turner 2003). The compression principles aim to transform diffuse and distended conceptual structures to more focused versions so as to become more congenial for human understanding. In order to emulate such a process, principal component analysis (PCA) was previously applied on the matrix representation of AffectNet (Cambria and Hussain 2012b), a semantic network in which common-sense concepts were linked to semantic and affective features (Table 1). The result was AffectiveSpace.

PCA is most widely used as a data-aware method of dimensionality reduction (Jolliffe 2005). PCA is closely related to the low-rank approximation method, singular value decomposition (SVD), in the sense that PCA works on a transformed version of the data matrix (Menon and Elkan 2011). SVD seeks to decompose the AffectNet matrix $A \in \mathbb{R}^{n \times d}$ into three components,

$$A = USV^T, \qquad (1)$$

where U and V are unitary matrices, and S is an rectangular diagonal matrix with nonnegative real numbers on the diagonal.

SVD has been proved to be optimal in preserving any unitarily invariant norm[1] $\| \cdot \|_M$ (Menon and Elkan 2011):

$$\| A - A_k \|_M = \min_{\mathrm{rank(B)=k}} \| \mathrm{A} - \mathrm{B} \|_{\mathrm{M}}, \qquad (2)$$

where A_k, i.e., AffectiveSpace, is formed by only containing the top k singular values in S. Hence, in AffectiveSpace, common-sense concepts and emotions are represented by vectors of k coordinates. These coordinates can be seen as describing concepts in terms of 'eigenmoods' that form the axes of AffectiveSpace, i.e., the basis e_0,...,e_{k-1} of the vector space. For example, the most significant eigenmood, e_0, represents concepts with positive affective valence. That

[1]A norm $\|\cdot\|_M$ is unitarily invariant if $\|UAV\|_M = \|A\|_M$ for all A and all unitary U, V.

Table 1: A snippet of the AffectNet matrix

AffectNet	*IsA-pet*	*KindOf-food*	*Arises-joy*	...
dog	0.981	0	0.789	...
cupcake	0	0.922	0.910	...
songbird	0.672	0	0.862	...
gift	0	0	0.899	...
sandwich	0	0.853	0.768	...
rotten fish	0	0.459	0	...
win lottery	0	0	0.991	...
bunny	0.611	0.892	0.594	...
police man	0	0	0	...
cat	0.913	0	0.699	...
rattlesnake	0.432	0.235	0	...
...	...	...	...	...

is, the larger a concept's component in the e_0 direction is, the more affectively positive it is likely to be. Concepts with negative e_0 components, then, are likely to have negative affective valence.

Thus, by exploiting the information sharing property of SVD, concepts with the same affective valence are likely to have similar features – that is, concepts conveying the same emotion tend to fall near each other in AffectiveSpace. Concept similarity does not depend on their absolute positions in the vector space, but rather on the angle they make with the origin. For example, concepts such as `beautiful day`, `birthday party`, and `make someone happy` are found very close in direction in the vector space, while concepts like `feel guilty`, `be laid off`, and `shed tear` are found in a completely different direction (nearly opposite with respect to the centre of the space).

The problem with this kind of representation is that it is not scalable: when the number of concepts and of semantic features grows, the AffectNet matrix becomes too high-dimensional and too sparse for SVD to be computed (Balduzzi 2013). Although there has been a body of research on seeking for fast approximations of the SVD, the approximate methods are at most ≈ 5 times faster than the standard one (Menon and Elkan 2011), making it not attractive for real-world big data applications.

It has been conjectured that there might be simple but powerful meta-algorithms underlying neuronal learning (Lee et al. 2011). These meta-algorithms should be fast, scalable, effective, with few-to-no specific assumptions, and biologically plausible (Balduzzi 2013). Optimizing all the $\approx 10^{15}$connections through the last few million years' evolution is very unlikely (Balduzzi 2013). Alternatively, nature probably only optimizes the global connectivity (mainly the white matter), but leaves the other details to randomness (Balduzzi 2013). In order to cope with the ever-growing number of concepts and semantic features, thus, we replace SVD with random projection (RP) (Bingham and Mannila 2001), a data-oblivious method, to map the original high-dimensional data-set into a much lower-dimensional subspace by using a Gaussian $\mathrm{N}(0, 1)$ matrix, while preserving the pair-wise distances with high probability. This theoretically solid and empirically verified statement follows Johnson and Lindenstrauss's (JL) Lemma (Balduzzi 2013). The JL Lemma states that with high probability, for all pairs of points $\mathrm{x}, \mathrm{y} \in \mathrm{X}$ simultaneously,

$$\sqrt{\frac{m}{d}} \parallel x - y \parallel_2 (1-\varepsilon) \leq \parallel \Phi x - \Phi y \parallel_2 \leq \tag{3}$$

$$\leq \sqrt{\frac{m}{d}} \parallel x - y \parallel_2 (1+\varepsilon), \tag{4}$$

where X is a set of vectors in Euclidean space, d is the original dimension of this Euclidean space, m is the dimension of the space we wish to reduce the data points to, ε is a tolerance parameter measuring to what extent is the maximum allowed distortion rate of the metric space, and Φ is a random matrix.

Structured random projection for making matrix multiplication much faster was introduced in (Sarlos 2006). Achlioptas (Achlioptas 2003) proposed *sparse random projection* to replace the Gaussian matrix with i.i.d. entries in

$$\phi_{ji} = \sqrt{s} \begin{cases} 1 & \text{with prob. } \frac{1}{2s} \\ 0 & \text{with prob.} 1 - \frac{1}{s} \\ -1 & \text{with prob.} \frac{1}{2s} \end{cases}, \tag{5}$$

where one can achieve a $\times 3$ speedup by setting $s = 3$, since only $\frac{1}{3}$ of the data need to be processed. However, since our input matrix is already too sparse, we avoid using sparse random projection.

When the number of features is much larger than the number of training samples ($d \gg n$), subsampled randomized Hadamard transform (SRHT) is preferred, as it behaves very much like Gaussian random matrices but accelerates the process from $\mathcal{O}(n\, d)$ to $\mathcal{O}(n \log d)$ time (Lu et al. 2013). Following (Tropp 2011) (Lu et al. 2013), for $d = 2^p$ where p is any positive integer, a SRHT can be defined as:

$$\Phi = \sqrt{\frac{d}{m}} \mathrm{RHD} \tag{6}$$

where

- m is the number we want to subsample from d features randomly.
- R is a random $m \times d$ matrix. The rows of R are m uniform samples (without replacement) from the standard basis of $\mathbb{R}^d$.
- H$\in \mathbb{R}^{d \times d}$ is a normalized Walsh-Hadamard matrix, which is defined recursively: $H_d = \begin{bmatrix} H_{d/2} & H_{d/2} \\ H_{d/2} & H_{d/2} \end{bmatrix}$ with $H_2 = \begin{bmatrix} +1 & +1 \\ +1 & -1 \end{bmatrix}$.
- D is a $d \times d$ diagonal matrix and the diagonal elements are i.i.d. Rademacher random variables.

Our subsequent analysis only relies on the distances and angles between pairs of vectors (i.e. the Euclidean geometry information), and it is sufficient to set the projected space to be logarithmic in the size of the data (Ailon and Chazelle 2010) and apply SRHT. The result is a new vector space model, AffectiveSpace 2 (Fig. 1), which preserves the semantic and affective relatedness of common-sense concepts while being highly scalable.

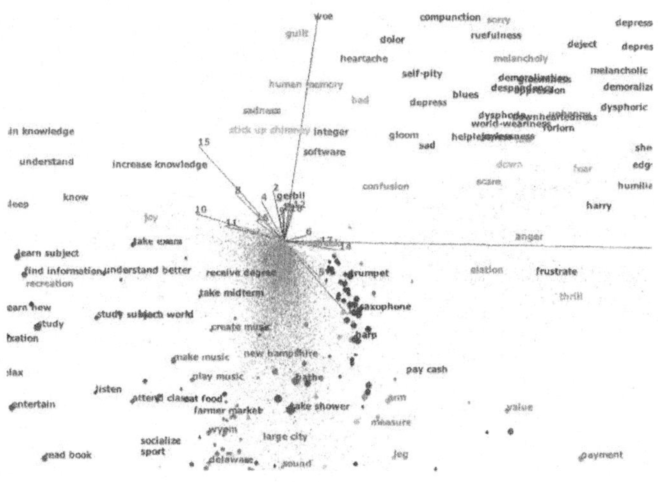

Figure 1: AffectiveSpace 2

Clustering AffectiveSpace 2

To reason on the disposition of concepts in AffectiveSpace 2, we use the Hourglass of Emotions (Fig. 2), an affective categorization model developed starting from Plutchik's studies on human emotions (Plutchik 2001). In the model, sentiments are re-organized around four independent dimensions whose different levels of activation make up the total emotional state of the mind. The Hourglass of Emotions, in fact, is based on the idea that the mind is made of different independent resources and that emotional states result from turning some set of these resources on and turning another set of them off (Minsky 2006).

In the model, affective states are not classified, as often happens in the field of emotion analysis, into basic emotional categories, but rather into four concomitant but independent dimensions, characterized by six levels of activation, which determine the intensity of the expressed/perceived emotion as a $float \in$ [-1,+1]. Such levels are also labeled as a set of 24 basic emotions (six for each of the affective dimensions) in a way that allows the model to specify the affective information associated with text both in a dimensional and in a discrete form.

Such basic emotions are used as initial centroids in AffectiveSpace 2 for clustering the vector space by means of sentic medoids (Cambria et al. 2011). Unlike the k-means algorithm (which does not pose constraints on centroids), sentic medoids do assume that centroids must coincide with k observed points, which allows to better cluster a vector space of common-sense knowledge. The sentic medoids approach is similar to the partitioning around medoids (PAM) algorithm, which determines a medoid for each cluster selecting the most centrally located centroid within that cluster. Unlike other PAM techniques, however, the sentic medoids algorithm runs similarly to k-means and, hence, requires a significantly reduced computational time. Generally, the initialization of clusters for clustering algorithms is a problematic task as the process often risks getting trapped in local optimum points, depending on the initial choice of centroids.

For this study, however, the set of 24 basic emotions of the Hourglass model are used as initial centroids. For this reason, what is usually seen as a limitation of the algorithm can be seen as advantage for this study, since what is being sought is not the k centroids leading to the best k clusters, but indeed the k centroids identifying the emotions we are interested in. Therefore, given that the distance between two points in the space is defined as $D(e_i, e_j) = \sqrt{\sum_{s=1}^{d'} \left(e_i^{(s)} - e_j^{(s)}\right)^2}$, the adopted algorithm can be summarized as follows:

1. Each centroid $\bar{e}_i \in \mathbb{R}^{d'}$ $(i = 1, 2, ..., k)$ is set as one of the 24 basic emotions of the Hourglass model;
2. Assign each instance e_j to a cluster $\bar{e}_i$ if $D(e_j, \bar{e}_i) \leq D(e_j, \bar{e}_{i'})$ where $i(i') = 1, 2, ..., k$;
3. Find a new centroid $\bar{e}_i$ for each cluster c so that $\sum_{j \in Cluster\ c} D(e_j, \bar{e}_i) \leq \sum_{j \in Cluster\ c} D(e_j, \bar{e}_{i'})$;
4. Repeat step 2 and 3 until no changes on centroids are observed.

Experimental Results

In order to evaluate the new analogical reasoning model, a comparison between AffectiveSpace and AffectiveSpace 2 has been performed both over a benchmark for affective common-sense knowledge (BACK) (Cambria and Hussain 2012b), for directly testing the affective analogical reasoning capabilities of the two models, and over a dataset of natural language opinions, for comparing how the two different configurations of AffectiveSpace (SVD-built versus RP-built) perform within the more practical task of concept-level opinion mining. Both vector space models were built upon the new 50k×120k AffectNet matrix.

Mood-Tag Evaluation

We compared AffectiveSpace and AffectiveSpace 2 on BACK, a benchmark for affective common-sense knowledge built by applying concept frequency - inverse opinion frequency (CF-IOF) (Cambria et al. 2010) on a 5,000-blogpost database extracted from LiveJournal[2], a virtual community of users who keep a blog, journal, or diary.

An interesting feature of this website is that bloggers are allowed to label their posts with both a category and a mood tag, by choosing from predefined categories and mood themes or by creating new ones. Since the indication of mood tags is optional, posts are likely to reflect the true mood of the authors.

CF-IOF weighting was exploited to filter out common concepts in the LiveJournal corpus and detect relevant mood-dependent semantics for each of the Hourglass sentic levels. The result was a benchmark of 2,000 affective concepts that were screened by 21 English-speaking students who were asked to evaluate the level b associated to each concept $b \in \Theta = \{\theta \in \mathbb{Z} \mid -1 \leq \theta \leq 1\}$ for each of the four affective dimensions. BACK's concepts were compared

[2]http://livejournal.com

with the classification results obtained by applying AffectiveSpace and AffectiveSpace 2, showing a consistent boost in classification performance (Table 2).

Sentic Computing Engine

The sentic computing engine (Cambria and Hussain 2012b) consists of four main components: a pre-processing module, which performs a first skim of text; a semantic parser, to deconstruct text into concepts; the IsaCore module, for aspect extraction; and the AffectiveSpace module, for polarity detection (Fig. 3).

Although similar in their structure, the last two modules are intrinsically different for the kind of knowledge they leverage on and for the task they fulfill. IsaCore (Cambria et al. 2014) is a semantic network of common knowledge (vocabulary knowledge collected from the Web), which focuses on the IsA relationship (e.g., Pablo Picasso-IsA-artist). AffectiveSpace is a vector space of affective common-sense knowledge (trivial knowledge that would not normally be found on the Web) leveraging on multiple relationships (e.g., LocatedAt, IsUsedFor, Arises, etc.). Hence, while the former exploits semantics to perform the task of aspect extraction, the latter uses sentics (i.e., affective information) to infer the polarity of natural language concepts.

Hourglass Interval	Sentic Level	AffSpace Accuracy	AffSpace 2 Accuracy
[G(1),G(2/3))	ecstasy	77.3%	84.5%
[G(2/3), G(1/3))	joy	83.9%	90.1%
[G(1/3),G(0))	serenity	68.8%	76.3%
(G(0), –G(1/3)]	pensive-ness	74.5%	79.0%
(–G(1/3), –G(2/3)]	sadness	81.2%	89.6%
(–G(2/3), –G(1)]	grief	79.5%	87.4%

Table 2: Comparative evaluation of AffectiveSpace and AffectiveSpace 2 over the classification of Pleasantness sentic levels.

The engine does not aim to deeply understand natural language text, but rather to simply infer the denotative and connotative information associated with relevant concepts. In order to infer the polarity of a sentence, in fact, the sentic computing engine only needs to extract the features or aspects of the discussed service or product, e.g., size or weight of a phone, and the sentiments associated with each of these, e.g., positive or negative, so that the output of a sentence such as "I love the phone's touchscreen but its battery life is too short" would be something like <touchscreen: +> and <battery: –>.

The pre-processing module firstly exploits linguistic dictionaries to interpret all the affective valence indicators usually contained in opinionated text, e.g., special punctuation, complete upper-case words, cross-linguistic onomatopoeias, exclamation words, degree adverbs, and emoticons. Secondly, the module detects negation and spreads it in a way

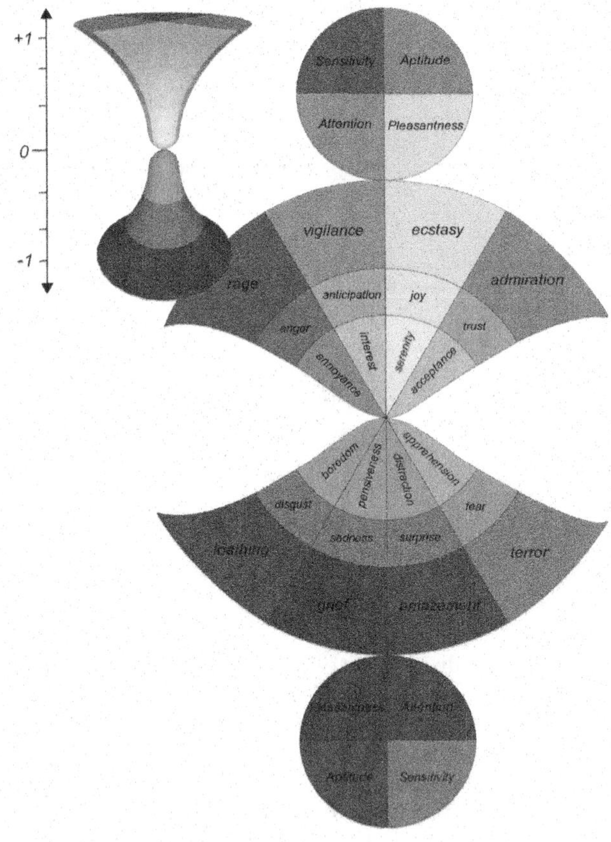

Figure 2: The Hourglass model

that it can be accordingly associated to concepts during the parsing phase. Such task is not trivial as not all appearances of explicit negation terms reverse the polarity of the enclosing sentence and that negation can often be expressed in rather subtle ways. Lastly, the module converts text to lower-case and, after lemmatizing it, splits the opinion into single clauses according to grammatical conjunctions.

For parsing text, the sentic parser is exploited for identifying concepts without requiring time-consuming phrase structure analysis. The parser uses knowledge about the lexical items found in text to choose the best possible construction for each span of text. Specifically, it looks each lexical item up in AffectNet and IsaCore, obtaining information about the basic category membership of that word. It then efficiently compares these potential memberships with the categories specified for each construction in the corpus, finding the best matches so that, for example, a concept like `buy christmas present` can be extracted from sentences such as "today I bought a lot of very nice Christmas gifts". Additionally, the sentic parser provides, for each retrieved concept, its relative frequency, valence, and status, i.e., the concept's occurrence in the text, its positive or negative connotation, and the degree of intensity with which the concept is expressed, respectively.

For each clause, the module outputs a small bag of concepts (SBoC), which is later on analyzed separately by the

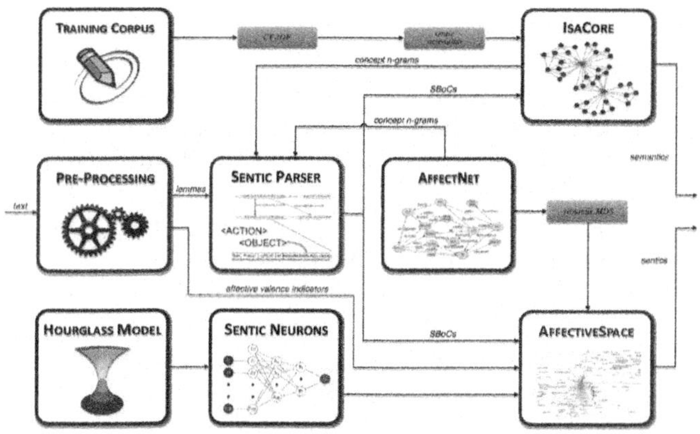

Figure 3: Block diagram of the sentic computing engine

IsaCore and AffectiveSpace modules. While the former exploits the graph representation of the common and common-sense knowledge base to detect semantics, the latter exploits the vector space representation of AffectNet to infer sentics. In particular, the IsaCore module applies spectral association for assigning activation to key nodes of the semantic network, which are used as seeds or centroids for classification. Such seeds can simply be the concepts corresponding to the class labels of interest or can be found by applying CF-IOF on a training corpus.

After seed concepts are identified, the module spreads their values across the IsaCore graph. This operation, an approximation of many steps of spreading activation, transfers the most activation to concepts that are connected to the seed concepts by short paths or many different paths in affective common-sense knowledge. Therefore, the concepts of each SBoC provided by the sentic parser are projected on the matrix resulting from spectral association in order to calculate their semantic relatedness to each seed concept and, hence, their degree of belonging to each different class. Such classification measure is directly proportional to the degree of connectivity between the nodes representing the retrieved concepts and the seed concepts in the IsaCore graph. The concepts retrieved by the sentic parser are also given as input to the AffectiveSpace module, which, in turn, exploits dimensionality reduction to infer the affective information associated with them. To this end, the concepts of each SBoC are projected into AffectiveSpace and, according to their position in the vector space, they are assigned to an affective class specified by the Hourglass model. In order to test the performance of the proposed model, such an operation is performed both with the SVD-built AffectiveSpace and with AffectiveSpace 2.

These are embedded in the sentic computing engine and evaluated against a dataset obtained from PatientOpinion[3], a social enterprise pioneering an online feedback service for users of the UK national health service. It is a manually tagged dataset of 2,000 patient opinions that associates to each post a category (namely, clinical service, communication, food, parking, staff, and timeliness) and a positive or negative polarity.

[3]http://patientopinion.org.uk

The dataset is hereby used to test the combined detection of opinion targets and the polarity associated with these. Results show that AffectiveSpace 2 generally outperforms standard AffectiveSpace, especially for categories where polarity is more difficult to detect in which affect is usually conveyed more implicitly, e.g., 'communication' and 'timeliness' (Table 3).

	AffSpace Accuracy	**AffSpace 2 Accuracy**
clinical service	75.2%	80.8%
communication	74.5%	85.1%
food	82.0%	83.7%
parking	74.0%	74.0%
staff	81.1%	83.2%
timeliness	73.4%	84.6%

Table 3: F-measure values relative to PatientOpinion evaluation.

Conclusions and Future Work

In a world in which millions of people express their opinions about commercial products and services everywhere on the Web, the distillation of knowledge from this huge amount of unstructured information is a key factor for tasks such as social media marketing, product positioning, and financial market prediction.

Common-sense reasoning is a good solution to the problem of concept-level sentiment analysis but scalability is a major factor in jeopardizing the efficiency of analogical reasoning in a multi-dimensional vector space of concepts.

In this work, we presented AffectiveSpace 2, a language visualization and analysis system that allows for reasoning by analogy on natural language concepts, even when these are represented by highly dimensional semantic features.

In this sense, AffectiveSpace 2 can be seen as a powerful tool for tackling the emerging issue of "Big Dimensionality" in the context of NLP, but also as a general framework for analogical reasoning that can be embedded in potentially any cognitive system dealing with real-world semantics.

References

Achlioptas, D. 2003. Database-friendly random projections: Johnson-lindenstrauss with binary coins. *Journal of computer and System Sciences* 66(4):671–687.

Ailon, N., and Chazelle, B. 2010. Faster dimension reduction. *Communications of the ACM* 53(2):97–104.

Balduzzi, D. 2013. Randomized co-training: from cortical neurons to machine learning and back again. *arXiv preprint arXiv:1310.6536*.

Bell, D.; Koulouri, T.; Lauria, S.; Macredie, R.; and Sutton, J. 2014. Microblogging as a mechanism for human-robot interaction. *Knowledge-Based Systems* 69:64–77.

Bingham, E., and Mannila, H. 2001. Random projection in dimensionality reduction: applications to image and text data. In *Proceedings of the seventh ACM SIGKDD international conference on Knowledge discovery and data mining*, 245–250. ACM.

Cambria, E., and Hussain, A. 2012a. Sentic album: Content-, concept-, and context-based online personal photo management system. *Cognitive Computation* 4(4):477–496.

Cambria, E., and Hussain, A. 2012b. *Sentic Computing: Techniques, Tools, and Applications*. Dordrecht, Netherlands: Springer.

Cambria, E.; Hussain, A.; Durrani, T.; Havasi, C.; Eckl, C.; and Munro, J. 2010. Sentic computing for patient centered application. In *IEEE ICSP*, 1279–1282.

Cambria, E.; Mazzocco, T.; Hussain, A.; and Eckl, C. 2011. Sentic medoids: Organizing affective common sense knowledge in a multi-dimensional vector space. In Liu, D.; Zhang, H.; Polycarpou, M.; Alippi, C.; and He, H., eds., *Advances in Neural Networks*, volume 6677 of *Lecture Notes in Computer Science*, 601–610. Berlin: Springer-Verlag.

Cambria, E.; Song, Y.; Wang, H.; and Howard, N. 2014. Semantic multi-dimensional scaling for open-domain sentiment analysis. *IEEE Intelligent Systems* 29(2):44–51.

Fauconnier, G., and Turner, M. 2003. *The Way We Think: Conceptual Blending and the Mind's Hidden Complexities*. Basic Books.

Jolliffe, I. 2005. *Principal component analysis*. Wiley Online Library.

Jung, S., and Segev, A. 2014. Analyzing future communities in growing citation networks. *Knowledge-Based Systems* 69:34–44.

Lee, H.; Grosse, R.; Ranganath, R.; and Ng, A. Y. 2011. Unsupervised learning of hierarchical representations with convolutional deep belief networks. *Communications of the ACM* 54(10):95–103.

Li, X.; Xie, H.; Chen, L.; Wang, J.; and Deng, X. 2014. News impact on stock price return via sentiment analysis. *Knowledge-Based Systems* 69:14–23.

Lu, Y.; Dhillon, P.; Foster, D. P.; and Ungar, L. 2013. Faster ridge regression via the subsampled randomized hadamard transform. In *Advances in Neural Information Processing Systems*, 369–377.

Menon, A. K., and Elkan, C. 2011. Fast algorithms for approximating the singular value decomposition. *ACM Transactions on Knowledge Discovery from Data (TKDD)* 5(2):13.

Minsky, M. 2006. *The Emotion Machine: Commonsense Thinking, Artificial Intelligence, and the Future of the Human Mind*. New York: Simon & Schuster.

Montejo-Raez, A.; Diaz-Galiano, M.; Martinez-Santiago, F.; and Urena-Lopez, A. 2014. Crowd explicit sentiment analysis. *Knowledge-Based Systems* 69:134–139.

Plutchik, R. 2001. The nature of emotions. *American Scientist* 89(4):344–350.

Poria, S.; Cambria, E.; Hussain, A.; and Huang, G.-B. 2015. Towards an intelligent framework for multimodal affective data analysis. *Neural Networks, DOI:10.1016/j.neunet.2014.10.005*.

Principi, E.; Squartini, S.; Cambria, E.; and Piazza, F. 2015. Acoustic template-matching for automatic emergency state detection: An elm based algorithm. *Neurocomputing* 149:426–434.

Rill, S.; Reinel, D.; Scheidt, J.; and Zicari, R. 2014. Politwi: Early detection of emerging political topics on twitter and the impact on concept-level sentiment analysis. *Knowledge-Based Systems* 69:14–23.

Sarlos, T. 2006. Improved approximation algorithms for large matrices via random projections. In *Foundations of Computer Science, 2006. FOCS'06. 47th Annual IEEE Symposium on*, 143–152. IEEE.

Tropp, J. A. 2011. Improved analysis of the subsampled randomized hadamard transform. *Advances in Adaptive Data Analysis* 3(01n02):115–126.

Wang, Q.; Cambria, E.; Liu, C.; and Hussain, A. 2013. Common sense knowledge for handwritten chinese recognition. *Cognitive Computation* 5(2):234–242.

Zhai, Y.; Ong, Y.-S.; and Tsang, I. 2014. The emerging "big dimensionality". *IEEE Computational Intelligence Magazine* 9(3):14–26.

Proceedings of the Twenty-Ninth AAAI Conference on Artificial Intelligence

Dialogue Understanding in a Logic of Action and Belief

Alfredo Gabaldon* and **Pat Langley**
Silicon Valley Campus
Carnegie Mellon University
Moffett Field, CA 94035 USA
alfredo.gabaldon@sv.cmu.edu
patrick.w.langley@gmail.com

Abstract

In recent work, Langley et al. (2014) introduced UMBRA, a system for plan and dialogue understanding. The program applies a form of abductive inference to generate explanations incrementally from relational descriptions of observed behavior and knowledge in the form of rules. Although UMBRA's creators described the system architecture, knowledge, and inferences, along with experimental studies of its operation, they did not provide a formalization of its structures or processes. In this paper, we analyze both aspects of the architecture in terms of the Situation Calculus—a classical logic for reasoning about dynamical systems—and give a specification of the inference task the system performs. After this, we state some properties of this formalization that are desirable for the task of incremental dialogue understanding. We conclude by discussing related work and describing our plans for additional research.

Introduction

Humans and other agents who engage in dialogue with others must build a model of other agents' mental states and update their own beliefs and goals as the dialogue progresses. This is particularly important when the purpose of communication is the joint execution of a task. We refer to this mental ascription problem as *dialogue understanding*. This problem is particularly challenging for agents who engage in realistic dialogues, where much is left unsaid by participants who assume substantial background knowledge and ability to infer implicit content.

In this paper, we present a formalization of dialogue understanding in the situation calculus (McCarthy and Hayes 1969)—a logical language for representing and reasoning about dynamic domains—extended with belief and goal modalities. The analysis is inspired by UMBRA, a system for plan and dialogue understanding (Langley et al. 2014; Meadows, Langley, and Emery 2013), and it adopts the same types of knowledge. Our formalization is novel and of independent interest, but it also contributes by providing a formal representation of UMBRA's knowledge structures and a specification of the dialogue understanding problem it addresses. Our specification is only an approximate description, in that we do not attempt to capture why UMBRA favors one explanation over another. The next section provides a brief overview of this system.

After we present our formalization of dialogue understanding, we show three types of desirable properties that follow from it. First, we demonstrate that the formal framework correctly incorporates UMBRA's knowledge structures. Second, we clarify a relationship between two different specifications of dialogue understanding. Finally, we reveal a property of dialogues and their explanations in terms of *common ground* (Clark 1996). We close with a discussion of related research and plans for future work.

A Dialogue Understanding Architecture

Langley et al. (2014) describe UMBRA, a system that incrementally processes observed activities, including dialogues, by computing explanations using a form of abduction. One of our goals is to develop a logical formalization of the knowledge used in UMBRA and the understanding problem it addresses. We make some simplifying assumptions, but we believe our specification is close enough to be valuable and can be extended to capture more of UMBRA's current functionality. Moreover, future development of UMBRA may proceed alongside the formal specification.

UMBRA incorporates three key theoretical assumptions: (a) that dialogue understanding relies on inference about the mental states of participants, (b) that it is an inherently abductive task, and (c) that it proceeds incrementally, which is both realistic and computationally tractable.

The system assumes a *working memory* that stores the mental states of dialogue participants at a given moment. These states are described in terms of *beliefs* and *goals* about the physical world and about other agents. UMBRA uses a declarative representation similar to predicate logic. Examples of working memory elements are *belief(medic, has-injury(p1, i1))* and *goal(expert, stable(p1))*. Beliefs and goals can be nested and have two temporal arguments that encode an interval during which a given literal holds. Additional elements express linear constraints on time points. We omit these temporal arguments, constraints, and the reasoning needed to enforce them. Our logic uses a form of temporal ordering on events, but not one based on time points.

*Current affiliation: GE Global Research, One Research Circle, Niskayuna, NY 12309

The content of nonnested beliefs and goals is literals, such as *has-injury(p1)*, that represent domain information. Since the aim is to understand dialogues, UMBRA also incorporates a notation for six types for speech acts (Austin 1962; Searle 1969): inform, acknowledge, question, propose, accept, reject. The system also expresses these in a predicate-like notation, such as *inform(speaker, listener, content)*, that it can embed in beliefs within working memory.

UMBRA also incorporates a *knowledge* store – essentially a set of rules that encode different types of domain-specific and domain-independent knowledge. Unlike the contents of working memory, such knowledge is stable and changes rarely. The system utilizes four types of knowledge:

- *Speech act rules*, one for each speech act type, that describe the conditions and effects of a speech act on the mental state of agents in a domain-independent manner.
- *Conceptual rules* that define complex predicates in terms of simpler ones, forming a concept hierarchy.
- *Goal-generating rules* that encode conditions which give rise to new goals.
- *Dialogue grammar rules* that specify the patterns of speech acts that constitute a well-formed dialogue.

We will describe these rules in more detail and provide examples when we formalize them later in the paper.

In terms of computational mechanisms, UMBRA processes dialogues in an on-line manner, receiving beliefs about the occurrence of speech acts and attempting to explain them as they arrive. An explanation takes the form of a directed graph, similar to a proof tree, with the nodes being elements in working memory. UMBRA builds such an explanation incrementally, applying a form of abductive inference that extends the explanation, making default assumptions as it attempts to show the observed speech acts combine into a well-formed dialogue.

Formal Preliminaries

In this section, we give an overview of the logical framework on which we base our formalization: the situation calculus (McCarthy and Hayes 1969). In particular, we use an axiomatization that includes Reiter's (1991) solution to the Frame Problem and its extension with modalities for *knowledge* (Scherl and Levesque 2003) and *goals* (Shapiro, Lesperance, and Levesque 1998; 2005).

The situation calculus is a predicate logic language for representing dynamic domains. Its ontology includes *actions* that cause the change, *situations* that represent possible states of the domain, and domain *objects* that include a set of agents. The (actual) initial situation of the domain is encoded by the constant S_0, and the set of situations an agent may believe possible is denoted by the predicate *Init(s)*. The situation that results from executing an action a in a situation s is specified by the function $do(a, s)$. A set of domain-independent axioms ensures that $do(a, s)$ is a unique situation, creating tree-like structures for situations with initial situations as the roots. By nesting the function do, one can create sequences of actions $do(a_n, do(a_{n-1}, \ldots, do(a_1, s)\ldots))$. We will use the notation $do([a_1, \ldots, a_n], s)$ as shorthand for such a situation.

A relation $s \sqsubseteq s'$ represents the existence of a path from s to s'. The domain properties that change when actions are executed are called *fluents* and are represented by predicates with a situation argument. For example, $critical(p, s)$ may specify that a patient p is in critical condition in s. The effect of actions on fluents is defined by a set of *successor state axioms*, which capture succinctly the effect of actions on fluents and incorporate a solution to the frame problem (Reiter 1991). We will not be concerned here with actions that affect the physical world, so the only successor state axioms we show are those for two special fluents, $B(ag, s'.s)$ and $G(ag, s', s)$. We use these to model a possible-world semantics for beliefs and goals in the situation calculus. This approach to beliefs and goals is based on the work of Moore (1985) and the extensions of this work cited above.

The fluent $B(ag, s', s)$ means intuitively that, in situation s, agent ag believes s' may be the actual situation.[1] Similarly, $G(ag, s', s)$ states that, in situation s, ag considers s' to be consistent with what it wants to achieve. In order to make B and G behave as intended, one includes a number of axioms that constrain these relations to be transitive and Euclidean, and that all situations B-related to an initial situation are also initial. We defer to the cited work for details.

We can then define the belief and goal modalities $belief(ag, \phi, s)$ and $goal(ag, \phi, s)$ as macros in terms of B and G:

- An agent believes formula ϕ holds in a situation s if it holds in all B-accessible situations s':

$$belief(ag, \phi, s) \stackrel{\text{def}}{=} (\forall s')(B(ag, s', s) \supset \phi[s'])$$

- An agent has goal ϕ in situation s if ϕ holds in all situations s' that are G-accessible and there is a path from a current possible (B-accessible) situation to s':[2]

$$goal(ag, \phi, s) \stackrel{\text{def}}{=} (\forall s', s'')(G(ag, s', s) \land B(ag, s'', s) \land s'' \sqsubseteq s' \supset \phi[s'])$$

Note that these definitions use formulae ϕ in reified form. We also use the notation $\phi[s]$, where ϕ denotes a formula in which the situation argument in fluents is replaced by a placeholder. Then $\phi[s]$ denotes the formula obtained by replacing variable s for the placeholder. We use this notation with macros as well. For more details on this encoding of formulae, we refer the reader to (De Giacomo, Lesperance, and Levesque 2000).

Finally, we use a reserved predicate $Poss(a, s)$ and a set of *action precondition axioms* to specify the conditions that make it possible to execute an action in a given situation. Later we will use these axioms to formalize the preconditions of speech acts.

[1] Scherl and Levesque (2003; 2003) and Scherl, Lesperance, and Levesque (1998; 1998; 2005) instead use the predicate $K(ag, s', s)$ and focus on knowledge rather than belief.

[2] The definition used by Shapiro et al. differs slightly by allowing maintenance goals in addition to achievement goals.

Representational Assumptions

We assume a situation calculus language that includes predicate and function symbols to represent the domain of interest. We also include action functions to represent speech acts in an almost identical form as UMBRA, such as $\mathit{inform}(ag_s, ag_l, \ell)$. However, recall that these are action terms and ℓ is a situation calculus formula with situation variables replaced by a placeholder.

The initial mental state of the agents is given by a set of ground facts

$$\mathit{belief}(Ag, L, S_0)$$

that correspond to the initial contents of working memory before any speech acts occur. As in UMBRA, we assume that L is a ground *literal* (an atomic formula or its negation).

Speech Act Rules

UMBRA specifies the preconditions and effects of a speech act in a speech act rule. Consider the simplified rule for the *inform* speech act:

$$\begin{aligned}&\mathit{inform}(S, L, C, T_1) \leftarrow\\&\quad \mathit{belief}(S, C, T_1),\\&\quad \mathit{goal}(S, \mathit{belief}(L, C, T_2), T_1),\\&\quad \mathit{belief}(S, \mathit{belief}(L, C, T_2), T_2),\\&\quad \mathit{belief}(L, \mathit{goal}(S, \mathit{belief}(L, C, T_2), T_2), T_2),\\&\quad \mathit{belief}(L, \mathit{belief}(S, C, T_1), T_2),\\&\quad \mathit{belief}(L, C, T_2),\\&\quad T_1 < T_2.\end{aligned}$$

UMBRA uses a temporal argument to distinguish preconditions from effects. The first two literals in the body, with temporal argument T_1, of this rule are the conditions. The other literals, except for the temporal constraint, are effects.

From the preconditions specified by the inform speech act, we obtain a precondition axiom for inform:[3]

$$\begin{aligned}Poss(\mathit{inform}(a_s, a_l, \ell), s) \equiv&\\&\mathit{belief}(a_s, \ell, s) \wedge\\&\mathit{goal}(a_s, \mathit{belief}(a_l, \ell), s) \ .\end{aligned}$$

As mentioned earlier, speech acts only affect the B and G accessibility relations, so their effects are captured in the successor state axioms for these relations. The successor state axiom for B has the form

$$\begin{aligned}&B(ag, s'', do(a, s)) \equiv\\&(\exists s')[B(ag, s', s) \wedge s'' = do(a, s') \wedge Poss(a, s') \wedge\\&(\forall ag_s, ag_l, \ell)(a = \mathit{inform}(ag_s, ag_l, \ell) \supset \Phi_{inf} \wedge\\&\quad a = \mathit{acknowledge}(ag_s, ag_l, \ell) \supset \Phi_{ack} \wedge\\&\quad a = \ldots)]\end{aligned} \quad (1)$$

where Φ_{inf} stands for

$$\begin{aligned}&ag = ag_s \supset \mathit{belief}(ag_l, \ell, s') \wedge\\&ag = ag_l \supset (\mathit{goal}(ag_s, \mathit{belief}(a_l, \ell), s') \ \wedge\ \ell[s']) \ \wedge\\&ag \neq ag_s \wedge ag \neq ag_l \supset\\&\qquad \{\mathit{belief}(ag_s, \mathit{belief}(ag_l, \ell), s'') \wedge\\&\qquad\quad \mathit{belief}(ag_l, \mathit{goal}(ag_s, \mathit{belief}(ag_l, \ell)), s'') \wedge\\&\qquad\quad \mathit{belief}(ag_l, \mathit{belief}(ag_s, \ell), s') \wedge\\&\qquad\quad \mathit{belief}(ag_l, \ell, s')\}\end{aligned}$$

and Φ_{sp} for other speech acts sp are similar in their structure.

The successor state axiom for G is analogous but simpler, since the only speech act that affects it directly is *accept*:

$$\begin{aligned}&G(ag, s', do(a, s)) \equiv\\&G(ag, s', s) \wedge (\exists s'')(B(ag, s'', s) \wedge do(a, s'') \sqsubseteq s') \wedge\\&\quad (\forall ag_l, \ell)(a = \mathit{accept}(ag, ag_l, \ell) \supset \ell[s'])].\end{aligned} \quad (2)$$

This axiom accounts for achievement goals and the one speech act, *accept*, that has an effect on relation G. As Shapiro et al. (2005) have shown, it can be generalized to handle *maintenance goals* (i.e., goals for something to hold over a period of time) and to handle events that cancel an existing goal, such as a *cancel_propose* speech act.

Conceptual Rules

Consider now the knowledge that UMBRA encodes in its conceptual rules, which define complex concepts in terms of simpler ones. As part of a theory of actions, these rules can be cast as *state constraints* on situations, which are also called *static laws*. Dealing with state constraints is a challenging task known in AI as the *ramification problem*, especially when the constraints include cycles. Fortunately, due to the hierarchical nature of the concept definitions, conceptual rules are acyclic and therefore simpler to handle.

However, before we can incorporate concept definitions, we must first express the conceptual rules' knowledge in our logical language. A simple example of such a rule is: "A patient is in critical condition if she has an artery bleeding," which we may encode as the implication

$$\begin{aligned}(\mathit{body\_part}(p, b, s) \wedge \mathit{artery}(b, s) \wedge \mathit{bleeding}(b, s))&\\ \supset \mathit{critical}(p, s) \ .&\end{aligned}$$

The fact that all literals in this formula have the same situation argument s indicates that it is indeed a state constraint. In general, conceptual rules can be encoded as formulae of the form

$$F(\vec{y}, s) \supset p(\vec{x}, s) \ , \quad (3)$$

where the only free variables in formula $F(\vec{y}, s)$ are $\vec{y}$ and s, the only situation term that appears in it is s, and p is a fluent predicate.

If an agent is informed that $\mathit{critical}(P_1)$, UMBRA's explanation mechanism would infer, assuming the above rule is the only one with *critical* in the head, that P_1 is bleeding from an artery. In other words, the system makes an implicit assumption that, for a concept p, the set of all conceptual rules with head p constitute a complete definition of that concept. In order to capture this behavior in our formalization, we must gather, for each high-level concept, all the conceptual rules that define it and put their encoding into the form of an equivalence,

$$\mathbf{F}(\vec{y}, s) \equiv p(\vec{x}, s) \ , \quad (4)$$

where $\mathbf{F}(\vec{y}, s)$ stands for the formula $F_1(\vec{y}_1, s) \vee \ldots \vee F_n(\vec{y}_n, s)$ such that each disjunct corresponds to the antecedent of a conceptual rule for p.

Assuming that all agents utilize their conceptual rules, incorporating them into the formalization means that all the worlds considered possible by an agent should satisfy the

[3]Throughout the paper, we assume variables that appear free in formulae are implicitly universally quantified with widest scope.

rules. Thus we must add them as conditions that are satisfied by situation s'' in the successor state axiom (1) for B. For each concept p defined by the conceptual rules, we would add the conjunct

$$\mathbf{F}(\vec{y}, s') \equiv p(\vec{x}, s') \ . \qquad (5)$$

For the example rule above, we would add the condition

$$(\mathit{body\_part}(p, b, s') \wedge \ldots) \equiv \mathit{critical}(p, s') \ .$$

This means that, if an agent is informed that $\mathit{critical}(P_1)$, not only will this hold in all the resulting situations believed possible, but so will $\mathit{body\_part}(P_1, B_1)$, $\mathit{artery}(B_1)$, and $\mathit{bleeding}(B_1)$ for some object B_1. In other words, the agent will come to believe these literals.

Goal-Generating Rules

Another form of knowledge describes situations in which new goals arise. UMBRA encodes this content in terms of *goal-generating rules*, which are similar to conceptual rules except that their heads are literals that become goals when the rule applies. If a rule's body is satisfied by the current contents of working memory, then the system adds the instantiated head to memory as a new goal. An example is a rule that states: "If an agent believes that a patient is in critical condition, then it has the goal of getting the patient in stable condition."

We can express goal-generating rules in our logic as formulae of the form

$$\begin{array}{c} \mathit{belief}(ag, f_1(\vec{y}_1), s) \wedge \ldots \wedge \mathit{belief}(ag, f_n(\vec{y}_n), s) \\ \supset \mathit{goal}(ag, p(\vec{x}), s) \end{array} \qquad (6)$$

with one example being

$$\mathit{belief}(ag, \mathit{critical}(p), s) \supset \mathit{goal}(ag, \mathit{stable}(p), s) \ .$$

As with conceptual rules, the presence of formulae like (6) in our formalization means that we have another instance of the ramification problem, but this time for goals. Like conceptual rules, these are stratified, but this involves only two strata, since the antecedents are expressed in terms of belief, while the consequents are instead stated in terms of the goal modality.

We can then incorporate formulae (6) from goal generating rules as additional conditions in the successor state axiom (2) of relation G. We add these conditions as conjuncts of the form:

$$\bigwedge_{i=1,\ldots,n} \mathit{belief}(ag, f_i(\vec{y}_i), do(a, s)) \supset p(\vec{x}, s') \ .$$

Dialogue Grammar Rules

We have described our formalization of the direct and indirect effects of speech acts on agents' mental states as encoded by the B and G relations. We need one last form of knowledge before we can specify the dialogue understanding problem, namely, knowledge about what counts as a well-formed dialogue. UMBRA stores this knowledge in a "dialogue grammar" that it also encodes as rules. Intuitively, this grammar specifies what sequences of speech acts are acceptable dialogues. The grammar imposes conditions on the types, the agents, and the content of the speech acts that may appear in a legitimate conversation.

In our analysis, we will use formulae with a similar but slightly simpler grammar-like structure. We will define a dialogue as a sequence of *adjacency pairs* (Sacks, Schegloff, and Jefferson 1974) and generalizations of this idea: *inform-acknowledge, question-inform-acknowledge, propose-accept* and *propose-reject-inform-acknowledge.* We refer to these short sequences of speech acts as *exchanges* and define them by means of macros:

- An *inform-acknowledge* exchange is a corresponding pair of speech acts with matching speaker, listener and content arguments:

$$\begin{array}{l} \mathit{inform\_ack}(a_1, a_2, s) \stackrel{\text{def}}{=} (\exists ag_s, ag_l, \ell) \\ \quad a_1 = \mathit{inform}(ag_s, ag_l, \ell) \wedge \\ \quad a_2 = \mathit{acknowledge}(ag_l, ag_s, \ell). \end{array}$$

- The *question-inform-acknowledge* exchange, in addition to the right pattern of arguments, requires that the content of the inform act be relevant to the content of the question. We do not define *relevant* here, but its intended purpose is to capture whether the content of the inform following a question can be considered an answer.

$$\begin{array}{l} \mathit{question\_inform\_ack}(a_1, a_2, a_3, s) \stackrel{\text{def}}{=} (\exists ag_s, ag_l, \ell, \ell') \\ \quad a_1 = \mathit{question}(ag_s, ag_l, \ell) \wedge \\ \quad a_2 = \mathit{inform}(ag_l, ag_s, \ell') \wedge \\ \quad a_3 = \mathit{acknowledge}(ag_s, ag_l, \ell') \wedge \\ \quad \mathit{relevant}(\ell, \ell', s). \end{array}$$

  The *propose-accept* exchange is similar to *inform-acknowledge* and we omit it.

- In a *propose-reject-inform-ack* exchange, an agent rejects a proposal and informs the other agent of its reason for rejecting it:

$$\begin{array}{l} \mathit{propose\_reject\_inform\_ack}(a_1, a_2, a_3, a_4, s) \stackrel{\text{def}}{=} \\ (\exists ag_s, ag_l, \ell, \ell') a_1 = \mathit{propose}(ag_s, ag_l, \ell) \wedge \\ \quad a_2 = \mathit{reject}(ag_l, ag_s, \ell) \wedge \\ \quad a_3 = \mathit{inform}(ag_l, ag_s, \ell') \wedge \\ \quad a_4 = \mathit{acknowledge}(ag_s, ag_l, \ell') \wedge \\ \quad \mathit{relevant}(\ell, \ell', s). \end{array}$$

In addition, we introduce a macro for situations that correspond to a sequence of actions that ends in one of the above exchanges. Intuitively, $\mathit{exchange}(s', s)$ means that executing one of the exchanges in situation s' results in situation s:

$$\begin{array}{l} \mathit{exchange}(s', s) \stackrel{\text{def}}{=} (\exists a_1, a_2, a_3, a_4) \\ s = do(a_1, do(a_2, s')) \wedge \mathit{inform\_ack}(a_2, a_1, s') \vee \\ s = do(a_1, do(a_2, do(a_3, s'))) \wedge \\ \qquad \mathit{question\_inform\_ack}(a_3, a_2, a_1, s') \vee \\ s = do(a_1, do(a_2, s')) \wedge \mathit{propose\_accept}(a_2, a_1, s') \vee \\ s = do(a_1, do(a_2, do(a_3, do(a_4, s')))) \wedge \\ \qquad \mathit{propose\_reject\_inform\_ack}(a_4, a_3, a_2, a_1, s'). \end{array}$$

Finally, we define $\mathit{dialogue}(s)$ to denote a (possibly empty) dialogue has led to situation s. This holds if s is an initial situation or a dialogue followed by an exchange leads to s:

$$\mathit{dialogue}(s) \equiv s = S_0 \vee (\exists s') \mathit{exchange}(s', s) \wedge \mathit{dialogue}(s').$$

Dialogue Understanding

We can now state the problem of *dialogue understanding*. Given a sequence of observed speech acts, the task is to find (a) a set of belief and goal facts and (b) implicit speech acts such that a background theory together with the facts entails that the sequence of speech acts is a well-formed dialogue.

We will consider two versions of this task. The first is a *global* dialogue understanding problem in which the observed speech acts are given at once. The second task is an *incremental* version in which the observations are given sequentially and the explanation is obtained in an iterative fashion. The latter comes closer to the way that humans and UMBRA interpret dialogues.

To continue, we must introduce a few concepts and notation. *Belief facts* and *goal facts* are ground atomic formulae of the form $belief(Ag, \ell, S)$, respectively, $goal(Ag, \ell, S)$. By *fact* we mean a belief or a goal fact. We say a fact is *relative to situation* S if S is its situation argument. Let T be a theory comprised of four sets:

- T_{sc}, the foundational situation calculus axioms;
- T_{sa}, a speech act theory including the axioms for modalities B and G;
- T_g, the dialogue grammar axioms; and
- T_{S_0}, the initial mental state.

We say a *dialogue* is a situation term $do([Sp_1, \ldots, Sp_n], S_0)$ where each Sp_i is a ground speech act term. Let $\widehat{D}$, which is called an *extension* of $D = do([Sp_1, \ldots, Sp_n], S_0)$, be a term of the form $do([Sp'_1, \ldots, Sp'_m], S_0)$, such that $n \leq m$ and there is an injective function $f : \{1, \ldots, n\} \mapsto \{1, \ldots, m\}$, $f(i) < f(j)$ if $i < j$, and $Sp_i = Sp'_{f(i)}$.

In other words, all speech acts of D appear in $\widehat{D}$ with their order preserved. We also need a macro $executable(s)$, which means that each action in a sequence is possible:

$$executable(s) \stackrel{\text{def}}{=} (\forall a, s').do(a, s') \sqsubseteq s \supset Poss(a, s')$$

and the notion of a *global hypothesis for dialogue D*, which is a set $GH_{\widehat{D}}$ of facts each relative to a situation subterm of $do(\widehat{D}, S_0)$, where $\widehat{D}$ is equal to or an extension of D.

Definition 1 (Global Explanation) *The global hypothesis $GH_{\widehat{D}}$ of D is a* global explanation *of a dialogue D if*

- *$T \cup GH_{\widehat{D}}$ is consistent and*
- *$T \cup GH_{\widehat{D}} \models executable(do(\widehat{D}, S_0)) \wedge dialogue(do(\widehat{D}, S_0))$.*

It is clear that this problem involves a form of abductive inference. Indeed, the above definition is rather close in form to the standard definition of logic-based abduction (e.g., see Eiter and Gottlob 1995). One glaring omission is the absence of any preference, such as minimality, on explanations. We leave this aspect underspecified and assume that some criterion is used uniformly.

In the incremental form of the problem, in addition to an observed partial dialogue, we are also given the explanation obtained in the preceding iteration. This leads to the concept of a *local hypothesis* for a dialogue D, which is a set LH_D of facts all relative to $do(D, S_0)$.

Let D' be a dialogue, E' be a set of facts each relative to a subterm of $do(D', S_0)$, and Sp be a ground speech act term. Intuitively, D' and E' are the current dialogue and its explanation prior to the most recent observation Sp.

Definition 2 (Incremental Explanation) *Let D',E' and Sp be as above and $D = do(\widehat{Sp}, do(D', S_0))$. A local hypothesis LH_D of dialogue D is a* local explanation *of Sp with respect to D' and E' if*

- *$T \cup E' \cup LH_D$ is consistent and*
- *$T \cup E' \cup LH_D \models executable(do(\widehat{Sp}, do(D', S_0))) \wedge dialogue(do(\widehat{Sp}, do(D', S_0)))$.*

Notice that, according to this definition, the prior dialogue D' is not expanded as part of the explanation. The prior explanation E' is also preserved, since the incremental nature of the process is intended to make only "local" decisions and assumptions. We only expand the singleton sequence Sp and the hypothesis contains only facts relative to D.

Building dialogue explanations incrementally by making local assumptions makes the computational problem more tractable, but obviously there is a price to pay. The process may fail to find a local explanation even if a global explanation exists. In the next section we show that, if local explanations are found for a complete dialogue, then their union coincides with a global explanation.

Relevant Properties

With our formal framework in place and our specification of the dialogue understanding task, we can now formulate a number of properties. We consider properties about the framework, about the dialogue understanding formulations, and about the dialogues themselves.

In terms of framework properties, we can show that the successor state axioms of the modalities B and G capture the effects of the speech acts as intended. For instance, for *inform*, we have:

Proposition 1 *Let A, B be agents, S a ground situation term and ℓ a formula. The logical consequences of a theory T include:*

- *$belief(A, belief(B, \ell), do(inform(A, B, \ell), S))$;*
- *$belief(B, belief(A, \ell), do(inform(A, B, \ell), S))$;*
- *$belief(B, goal(A, belief(B, \ell)), do(inform(A, B, \ell), S))$;*
- *$belief(B, \ell, do(inform(A, B, \ell), S))$.*

We can also verify that the framework correctly incorporates knowledge about conceptual inference and goal generation. Suppose that a formula $F(\vec{y}, s) \equiv p(\vec{x}, s)$, corresponding to conceptual rules for predicate p, has been included in a theory T as described above. Then we have:

Proposition 2

$$T \models belief(ag, F(\vec{y}), s) \supset belief(ag, p(\vec{x}), s).$$

For example, if we have $belief(A, body\_part(P_1, B_1), S)$ and $belief(A, artery(B_1), S)$ hold, then we will also have $belief(A, critical(P_1), do(inform(B, A, bleeding(P_1)), S))$.

A similar result holds regarding goal-generating knowledge. After incorporating a formula (6), we have:

Proposition 3

$$T \models \bigwedge_{i=1,\ldots,n} belief(ag, f_i(\vec{y}_i), s) \supset goal(ag, p(\vec{x}), s).$$

Consider next our two notions of explanation. One question we raised earlier was whether incremental processing of a dialogue will eventually arrive at a global explanation. The next proposition establishes this property.

Proposition 4 *Suppose that a sequence of observed speech acts $Sp_1, \ldots, Sp_n$ results in a sequence of local explanations $E_1, \ldots, E_n$ and an expanded dialogue $\widehat{D}$ of $D = do([Sp_1, \ldots, Sp_n], S_0)$. Then $E_1 \cup \ldots \cup E_n$ is a global explanation of D.*

As mentioned earlier, even if the converse of this proposition holds and a global explanation exists, incremental dialogue processing may fail to find a sequence of local explanations for the complete conversation. One alternative would be to incorporate backtracking into the explanation process. However, the computational advantage of incremental processing would then be largely lost. We will explore other options in future work.

Finally, an interesting property of dialogues and their explanations involves the important notion of *common ground* (Clark 1996). For a pair of agents engaged in a dialogue, we can define the common ground as the set of literals ℓ mutually believed by both agents in a given situation:[4]

$$\begin{array}{l} cg(ag_1, ag_2, \ell, s) \stackrel{\text{def}}{=} \\ belief(ag_1, \ell, s) \wedge belief(ag_2, \ell, s) \wedge \\ belief(ag_1, belief(ag_2, \ell), s) \wedge \\ belief(ag_2, belief(ag_1, \ell), s) \wedge \\ belief(ag_1, belief(ag_2, belief(ag_1, \ell)), s) \wedge \\ belief(ag_2, belief(ag_1, belief(ag_2, \ell)), s). \end{array}$$

We can then state the property that, as a dialogue progresses and is incrementally explained, the common ground between the agents is nondecreasing. Let D be a dialogue with local explanations $E_1, \ldots, E_n$ and expanded dialogue $\widehat{D}$. Let D_i be the prefix of D that consists of the first i speech acts and $\widehat{D}_i$ be the expanded dialogue that corresponds to local explanation E_i.

Proposition 5 *Let T, $E_1, \ldots, E_n$, D, $\widehat{D}$ be as defined above and $S_k = do(\widehat{D}_k, S_0)$ for any k. If $1 \leq i \leq j \leq n$, then*

$$T \bigcup_{l=1,\ldots,n} E_l \models cg(ag_1, ag_2, \ell, S_i) \supset cg(ag_1, ag_2, \ell, S_j).$$

Related Research

The problem of dialogue understanding has received some attention in the literature. Our formalization builds substantially on earlier work on theories of action, speech act theory, possible worlds approaches to belief, and others analyses.

Our situation calculus framework is based on the work of Scherl and Levesque (2003) and Shapiro, Lesperance, and Levesque (1998; 2005). Our formalization uses their successor state axioms for relations B and G but modifies them to incorporate conceptual and goal-generating knowledge. Other formalisms for belief and goals, based on different logics, include (Herzig and Longin 2000; Martin, Narasamdya, and Thielscher 2004; van Benthem, van Eijck, and Kooi 2006; Baral et al. 2010). Earlier work on speech acts, especially analyses of speech acts' conditions and effects in terms of mental states (Perrault and Allen 1980; Allen and Perrault 1980), has also influenced our formalization in substantial ways.

Above the utterance level, Carberry and Lambert (1999) report a dialogue interpretation system that is also based on speech acts. Their system can recognize subdialogues used by an agent who is convincing another of some proposition, which we have not addressed. Although they described their interpretation mechanism in pseudo-code, rather than declaratively, their "discourse recipes" specify speech acts in terms of agents' beliefs.

We have formalized the dialogue understanding problem in terms of logical abduction, and some earlier work has taken a similar approach. For instance, Litman and Allen (1985; 1987) present an abductive approach to dialogue processing, as does work reported by McRoy and Hirst (1995) that includes mechanisms for recovering from misunderstandings. Hobbs et al. (1993) have also used abductive inference for understanding, but only for processing at the sentence level.

Finally, we should mention important prior research on formalizations of discourse structure, such as that arising in dialogue. This includes the comprehensive work of Asher and Lascarides (2003), which extends Discourse Representation Theory (Kamp and Reyle 1993), and Rhetorical Structure Theory (Mann and Thompson 1987), among other prominent contributions.

Conclusions

In this paper, we have presented a formalization of dialogue understanding in an extended situation calculus that includes modalities for belief and goals. Our framework builds on speech act theory and encodes both their direct effects on agents' mental states and their indirect effects due to inferences by conceptual and goal-generating knowledge. We provided two specifications of the dialogue interpretation task, and we showed a number of desirable properties about the formalization, the two variants of dialogue understanding, and the evolution of common ground, in terms of shared beliefs and goals, as a conversation progresses.

We believe that our framework for dialogue understanding is valuable both in its own right and as a formal specification for UMBRA, a system that interprets high-level dialogues through a process of incremental abduction. In future research, we intend to elaborate the framework to support a broader set of speech acts, additional forms of belief and goal revision, and forms of limited belief. We also hope to analyze more subtle aspects of conversation, such as whether a speaker's utterances are considerate of the listener's mental state and general sensibilities.

[4]Clearly, what we really need here is a mutual belief modality, but we can still state a useful property without it.

Acknowledgments

This research was supported in part by Grant N00014-09-1-1029 from the Office of Naval Research. We thank Paul Bello, Will Bridewell, and Ben Meadows for useful discussions and the reviewers for valuable comments.

References

Allen, J., and Perrault, C. 1980. Analyzing intention in utterances. *Artificial Intelligence* 15:143–178.

Asher, N., and Lascarides, A. 2003. *Logics of conversation.* Cambridge University Press.

Austin, J. L. 1962. *How to do things with words.* Cambridge, MA: Harvard University Press.

Baral, C.; Gelfond, G.; Son, T. C.; and Pontelli, E. 2010. Using answer set programming to model multi-agent scenarios involving agents' knowledge about other's knowledge. In *Proceedings of the Ninth International Conference on Autonomous Agents and Multiagent Systems*, 259–266.

Carberry, S., and Lambert, L. 1999. A process model for recognizing communicative acts and modeling negotiation subdialogues. *Computational Linguistics* 25:1–53.

Clark, H. H. 1996. *Using language.* Cambridge, UK: Cambridge University Press.

De Giacomo, G.; Lesperance, Y.; and Levesque, H. 2000. ConGolog, a concurrent programming language based on the situation calculus. *Artificial Intelligence* 121:109–169.

Eiter, T., and Gottlob, G. 1995. The complexity of logic-based abduction. *Journal of the ACM* 42:3–42.

Herzig, A., and Longin, D. 2000. Belief dynamics in cooperative dialogues. *Journal of Semantics* 17:91–115.

Hobbs, J. R.; Stickel, M. E.; Appelt, D. E.; and Martin, P. 1993. Interpretation as abduction. *Artificial Intelligence* 63:69–142.

Kamp, H., and Reyle, U. 1993. *From discourse to logic.* Dordrecht, The Netherlands: Kluwer Academic Publishers.

Langley, P.; Meadows, B.; Gabaldon, A.; and Heald, R. 2014. Abductive understanding of dialogues about joint activities. *Interaction Studies*, 15:426–453.

Litman, D. J., and Allen, J. F. 1987. A plan recognition model for subdialogues in conversations. *Cognitive Science* 11:163–200.

Litman, D. 1985. Plan recognition and discourse analysis: An integrated approach for understanding dialogues. PhD Thesis, Technical Report 170, Department of Computer Science, Univ. of Rochester.

Mann, W. C., and Thompson, S. A. 1987. *Rhetorical structure theory: Description and construction of text structures.* Springer.

Martin, Y.; Narasamdya, I.; and Thielscher, M. 2004. Knowledge of other agents and communicative actions in the fluent calculus. In *Proceedings of the Ninth International Conference on Principles of Knowledge Representation and Reasoning*, 623–633.

McCarthy, J., and Hayes, P. 1969. Some philosophical problems from the standpoint of artificial intelligence. In Meltzer, B., and Michie, D., eds., *Machine intelligence 4.* Edinburgh University Press. 463–502.

McRoy, S., and Hirst, G. 1995. The repair of speech act misunderstandings by abductive inference. *Computational Linguistics* 21:435–478.

Meadows, B.; Langley, P.; and Emery, M. 2013. Understanding social interactions using incremental abductive inference. In *Proceedings of the Second Annual Conference on Advances in Cognitive Systems*, 39–56.

Moore, R. C. 1985. A formal theory of knowledge and action. In Hobbs, J. R., and Moore, R. C., eds., *Formal theories of the common sense world.* Norwood, NJ: Ablex Publishing. 319–358.

Perrault, C. R., and Allen, J. F. 1980. A plan-based analysis of indirect speech acts. *Computational Linguistics* 6:167–182.

Reiter, R. 1991. The frame problem in the situation calculus: A simple solution (sometimes) and a completeness result for goal regression. In Lifschitz, V., ed., *Artificial intelligence and mathematical theory of computation.* New York: Academic Press. 359–380.

Sacks, H.; Schegloff, E. A.; and Jefferson, G. 1974. A simplest systematics for the organization of turn-taking for conversation. *Language* 50:696–735.

Scherl, R. B., and Levesque, H. J. 2003. Knowledge, action, and the frame problem. *Artificial Intelligence* 144:1–39.

Searle, J. 1969. *Speech Acts: An essay in the philosophy of language.* New York: Cambridge University Press.

Shapiro, S.; Lesperance, Y.; and Levesque, H. J. 1998. Specifying communicative multi-agent systems. In *Agents and Multi-Agent Systems Formalisms, Methodologies, and Applications.* Springer. 1–14.

Shapiro, S.; Lesperance, Y.; and Levesque, H. J. 2005. Goal change. In *Proceedings of the 19th International Joint Conference on Artificial Intelligence*, 582–588.

van Benthem, J.; van Eijck, J.; and Kooi, B. 2006. Logics of communication and change. *Information and Computation* 204:1620–1662.

Automated Construction of Visual-Linguistic Knowledge via Concept Learning from Cartoon Videos

Jung-Woo Ha, Kyung-Min Kim, and Byoung-Tak Zhang

School of Computer Science and Engineering & Institute for Cognitive Science
Seoul National University, Seoul 151-744, Korea
{jwha, kmkim, btzhang}@bi.snu.ac.kr

Abstract

Learning mutually-grounded vision-language knowledge is a foundational task for cognitive systems and human-level artificial intelligence. Most of knowledge-learning techniques are focused on single modal representations in a static environment with a fixed set of data. Here, we explore an ecologically more-plausible setting by using a stream of cartoon videos to build vision-language concept hierarchies continuously. This approach is motivated by the literature on cognitive development in early childhood. We present the model of deep concept hierarchy (DCH) that enables the progressive abstraction of concept knowledge in multiple levels. We develop a stochastic method for graph construction, i.e. a graph Monte Carlo algorithm, to search efficiently the huge compositional space of the vision-language concepts. The concept hierarchies are built incrementally and can handle concept drift, allowing for being deployed in lifelong learning environments. Using a series of approximately 200 episodes of educational cartoon videos we demonstrate the emergence and evolution of the concept hierarchies as the video stories unfold. We also present the application of the deep concept hierarchies for context-dependent translation between vision and language, i.e. the transcription of a visual scene into text and the generation of visual imagery from text.

Introduction

Recent explosion of data enhances the importance of automatic knowledge acquisition and representation from big data. Linguistically-oriented representation formalisms such as semantic networks (Steyvers and Tenenbaum 2005) and WordNet (Fellbaum 2010) are popular and extremely useful. However, mutually-grounded vision-language concepts are more foundational for cognitive systems that work in perception-action cycles. Existing text-oriented representations are inefficient for learning multimodal concepts from large-scale data, such as videos. Continuous knowledge construction from multimodal data streams is essential for achieving human-level artificial intelligence based on lifelong learning (Muggleton 2014, Zhang 2013).

The task of vision-language learning is to automatically build the relationships between vision and language from multimodal sources of data. Previous works on multimodal learning have focused on either cognitive theory or practical applications. On the practical side, the latent Dirichlet allocation (LDA) models were applied to image annotation (Blei and Jordan 2003) and video object detection (Zhao et al. 2013). Recently, deep learning models were also used for image annotation (Srivastava and Salakutdinov 2012) and descriptive sentence generation (Kiros et al. 2014). However, they mainly focused on automatic annotation rather than constructing semantic knowledge at a higher level. Furthermore, the techniques mostly have concentrated on efficient learning from a static large-scale dataset (Ordornez et al. 2011, Deng et al. 2009) but seldom considered the dynamic change of the contents, i.e. concept drift. Some recent proposals have addressed hierarchical representations (Jia et al. 2013, Lewis and Frank 2013, Abbott et al. 2012), but they are biased to one modality or a static database.

Here we propose a hierarchical model of automatically constructing visual-linguistic knowledge by dynamically learning concepts represented with vision and language from videos, i.e., a deep concept hierarchy (DCH). DCH consists of two or more concept layers and one layer of multiple modalities. The concepts at the higher levels represent more abstract concepts than at the lower layers. The modality layer contains the populations of many microcodes encoding the higher-order relationships among two or more visual and textual variables (Zhang et al. 2012). Each concept layer is represented by a hypergraph (Zhou et al. 2007). This structure coincides with the grounded theory of the human cognition system where a concept is grounded in the modality-specific regions (Kiefer and Barsalou 2013). The structure enables the multiple levels of concepts to be represented by the probability distribution of the visual-textual variables.

The concept construction of DCH from videos involves two technical issues. One is to search a huge space of DCH represented by hypergraphs. The other is to deal with concept drift contained in the video data. For handling these two issues, DCH uses a method based on a Monte Carlo simulation for efficiently exploring the search space, i.e., a graph Monte Carlo (graph MC). The graph MC is a stochastic method for efficiently finding desired graph structures by the repetition of probabilistically generating connections among nodes using observed data instead of sampling. The model structure flexibly grows and shrinks by the graph MC, in contrast to other deep learning models. DCH incrementally learns the concepts by the graph MC and the weight update process while observing new videos, thus robustly tracing concept drift and continuously accumulating new conceptual knowledge. This process is formalized as a sequential Bayesian inference. The learning mechanism is inspired by the cognitive developmental process of children constructing the visually grounded concepts from multimodal stimuli (Meltzoff 1990).

For evaluation, we used the collection of cartoon videos for children, entitled "Pororo", consisting of 183 episodes with 1,232 minutes of playing time. Experimental results show DCH faithfully captures visual-linguistic concepts at multiple abstraction levels, reflecting the concept drift in the progress of the stories. Technically, we investigate the effective combinations of hierarchy architectures and graph MC variants to construct the DCH fast, flexibly, and robustly based on sequentially observed data over an extended period of time. We also present the application of the concept hierarchies for story- and context-aware conversion between the video scenes and the text subtitles.

Visual-Linguistic Concept Representation

To be concrete, we start with the video data from which we extract the vision-language concepts. The whole data set consists of episodes, which are preprocessed into sequences of sentence-image pairs by capturing a scene whenever a subtitle appears. This data generation imitates the process of how a child remembers what the characters say in a scene while observing videos. The vocabulary for the visual words is defined by the set of patches extracted by maximally stable external regions (MSER). Each patch is represented by the vector of SIFT and RGB features. If we represent a textual word as w_i and a visual word as r_i, the utterance-scene is represented as a vector of the form:

$$\mathbf{x}^{(t)} = (\mathbf{w}^{(t)}, \mathbf{r}^{(t)}) = (w_1, ..., w_M, r_1, ..., r_N), \quad (1)$$

$$D_N = \{(\mathbf{w}^{(t)}, \mathbf{r}^{(t)}) \mid t = 1, ..., T\}, \quad (2)$$

where M and N are the sizes of the textual and visual vocabularies.

Figure 1 shows three instances of the concepts learned from utterance-scene pairs. The objective is to construct a knowledge representation from the data that keeps main conceptual information.

Sparse Population Coding

Sparse population coding (SPC) is a principle to encode data of n variables compactly using multiple subsets of size k. The subset is called a microcode and, typically, its size is small, i.e. $k << n$, and thus sparse. The population of microcodes characterizes the empirical distribution of the data in the form of a finite mixture. Previous work shows that SPC is useful for dynamically learning concepts from video data by defining a microcode as a subset of image patches and textual words (Zhang et al. 2012). Formally, the empirical distribution of the observed video data consisting of continuous T scene-utterance pairs can be represented by the population code:

$$P(D \mid \theta) = \prod_{t=1}^{T} P(\mathbf{x}^{(t)} \mid \theta) = \prod_{t=1}^{T} \sum_{i=1}^{M} \alpha_i f_i(\mathbf{w}^{(t)}, \mathbf{r}^{(t)} \mid e_i). \quad (3)$$

where e_i and α_i denote a microcode and its weight, and $f_i(\mathbf{x} \mid e_i)$ is a density function. Also, α_i is a nonnegative value less than 1, summed to be 1. In above equation, a model parameter θ is defined as $\theta = (\boldsymbol{\alpha}, \mathbf{e})$, where $\mathbf{e}$ and $\boldsymbol{\alpha}$

	1~13 episodes (1 DVD)			1~183 episodes (14 DVDs)		
Concepts	Visual nodes	# of nodes (V/L)	Top 15 linguistic nodes	Visual nodes	# of nodes (V/L)	Top 15 linguistic nodes
Pororo	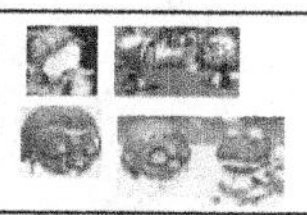	986/230	crong, you, clean, over, draw, huh, to, it, I, up, said, the, moving, is, pororo		12870/1031	crong, you, snowboarding, transforming, rescuing, pororo, the, lamp, seven, are, quack, yellow, not, lollipop, cake,
Eddy		644/198	I, ear, art, midget, game, nothing, say, early, diving, lost, middle, lesson, case, because, snowballs		9008/860	transforming, I, hand, careful, throw, art, suit, midget, farted, reverse, stage, luggage, gorilla, pole, cannon
Tongtong	-	0/0	-	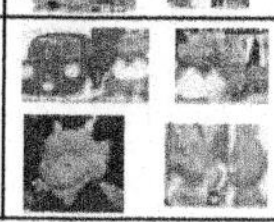	1812/429	kurikuri, doodle, doo, avoid, airplane, crystal, puts, branch, bland, finding, pine, circle, kurikuritongtong, bees, talent

Figure 1: Visual-linguistic representation and development of three character concepts of video contents. A scene-utterance pair is represented by the sets of image patches and words and the concepts of the video stories are represented by these patches and words. *Tongtong* is not seen in episodes 1~13 and appears in episode 56 for the first time.

are the sets of M microcodes and their weights.

Deep Concept Hierarchies

SPC can be considered as a hypergraph, where the hyperedges represent the microcodes. An equivalent representation is a two-layer network where the upper-layer nodes indicate microcodes (hyperedges) and the lower-layer nodes indicate the data variables. Though the representation power is large, the number of upper-layer nodes may grow fast with the growing number of input units, i.e. the visual and textual vocabulary sizes in our video data. To resolve this problem, we introduce additional layers, resulting in a deep concept hierarchy (DCH) shown in Figure 2. A DCH model has explicit concept layers for representing abstract concepts. The connections between layers are sparse, which is contrasted to the deep neural networks that have full connectivity between layers. Also, the number of nodes in each layer flexibly changes for dynamically constructing knowledge as the learning proceeds, which is also contrasted to other deep learning models. This sparse and hierarchical structure reduces the model complexity and DCH pursues a parse modular hierarchical structure, as found in human brains (Quiroga 2012).

Mathematically, DCH represents the empirical distribution of data using a multiple layers of microcodes or concepts. Consider a DCH model with two concept layers in this study. Assume that a node of the top concept layer denotes a character appearing in the video. Let $\mathbf{c}^1=(c_1^1,...,c_{K_1}^1)$ and $\mathbf{c}^2=(c_1^2,...,c_{K_2}^2)$ denote the binary vectors representing the presence of concrete and abstract concepts, where K_1 and K_2 are the sizes of the two vectors. In addition, the sizes of the observable variables, which are M and N in (1), increase whenever observing new words and patches. The probability density of a scene-text pair ($\mathbf{r}$, $\mathbf{w}$) for a given $\mathbf{h}$=($\mathbf{e}$, $\boldsymbol{\alpha}$), $\mathbf{c}^1$, and $\mathbf{c}^2$ can be formulated as

$$P(\mathbf{r},\mathbf{w}\,|\,\mathbf{c}^1,\mathbf{c}^2)=\sum\nolimits_{\mathbf{h}} P(\mathbf{r},\mathbf{w}\,|\,\mathbf{h},\mathbf{c}^1,\mathbf{c}^2)P(\mathbf{h}\,|\,\mathbf{c}^1,\mathbf{c}^2), \quad (4)$$

where $\mathbf{e}$ and $\boldsymbol{\alpha}$ denote the population of microcodes and their weights. Each microcode e is defined as two sparse binary vectors whose size is M and N at the time when the scene is observed, respectively. Therefore, DCH can model the concepts as probabilistic associations among words and images. Figure 2 (b) shows an instance of DCH with two concept layers learning concepts from videos.

DCH is basically a hierarchy of hypergraphs. That is, each layer of DCH can be equivalently transformed into a hypergraph by denoting a variable value and a higher-order association as a vertex and a hyperedge, as shown in Figure 2 (c). Now the problem is, the number of possible hyperedges exponentially increases proportional to the number of vertices in a hypergraph. For a k-hypergraph, a hypergraph consisting of hyperedges with k vertices (k-hyperedge) only, the number of possible hypergraphs are $|\Omega|=2^{C(n,k)}$, where $n = |V|$ and $C(n, k)$ denote the number of cases to choose k items from a set with n elements. Ω is denoted as the set of all the hypergraphs. Therefore, the problem space of a DCH model represented by (0, n)-hypergraphs becomes $|\Omega|=2^{2^{|\mathbf{x}|}}$, where $|\mathbf{x}|$ denotes the size of the observable variable set. It is infeasible to explore this huge combinatorial search space with an exhaustive approach.

Learning of Deep Concept Hierarchies

Graph Monte Carlo

We propose a method for efficiently constructing hypergraphs incrementally from incoming data. The idea is to use Monte Carlo search on the hypergraph space. The resulting graph Monte Carlo method (graph MC) assumes two conditions:

i) The graph structure in the t-th iteration is determined by that of the t-1 the iteration.
ii) Estimating the empirical distribution asymptotically converges to exploring all theoretical spaces when data are large enough.

Formally, for a given dataset D, an optimal hypergraph

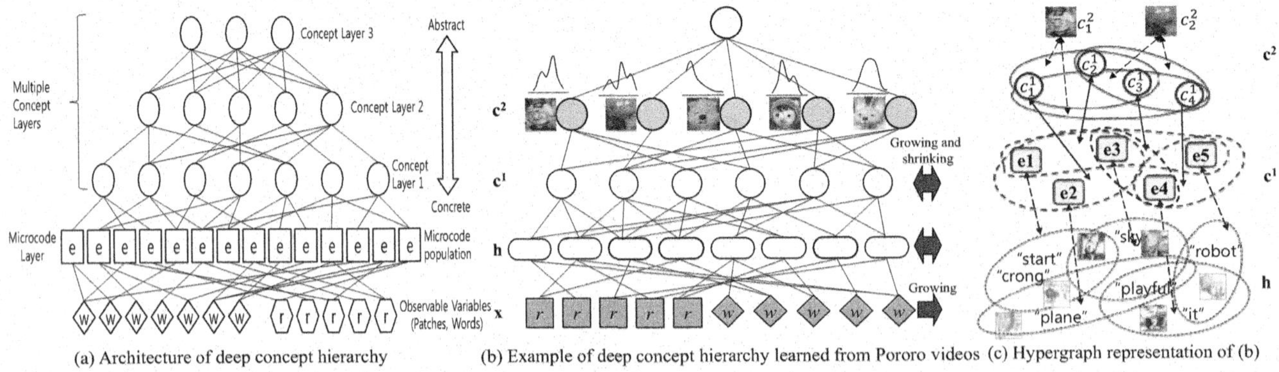

Figure 2: Examples of deep concept hierarchies. (a) presents an architecture of deep concept hierarchy and (b) is an instance of a DCH model with two concept layers learning concepts from Pororo. (c) is the hypergraph representation of (b). Gray boxes in (b) denote observable variables.

G^* corresponding to a model is formulated with Bayes rule:

$$G^* = \arg\max_{G_t} P(G_t \mid D) = \arg\max_{G_t} P(D \mid G_t) P(G_{t-1}), \quad (5)$$

where G_t is a k-hypergraph in the t-th time step. G is constructed to maximize $P(G_t|D)$ by the repetition of replacing hyperedges whenever observing the data:

$$\Delta G = \Delta G \cup \{e\} \text{ and } e = \bigcup_{m=1}^{k} v(x), \quad (6)$$

$$P(e) = \prod_{v \in e} P(v(x)), \quad (7)$$

where ΔG is a new hyperedge set, and e and $v(x)$ denote a generated hyperedge and the vertex corresponding to a variable x. Both the initial values of ΔG and e are empty. $P(e)$ denotes the probability with which e is generated. $P(v(x))$ denotes the probability of which vertices are connected as hyperedges. The graph MC is addressed in terms of the Metropolis-Hastings algorithm under two conditions:

i) A hypergraph G is factorized by its hyperedges to represent a probability distribution (Besag 1974).
ii) ΔG is generated to equivalently represent a sampling instance $\mathbf{x}$.

Then, G^* representing the empirical distribution of the observed data can be constructed by the graph MC. $P(v(x))$ in (7) determines the property of the constructed graph structures, thus playing a role of the learning strategy of the graph MC. Note that $P(v(x))$ is computed from the currently observed data instance according to assumption ii). We define $P(v(x))$ based on three different approaches.

Uniform Graph Monte Carlo

Uniform graph Monte Carlo (UGMC) uses the same probability as $P(v(x))$ for all the variables with the positive value of the data. Then, the probability is defined as follows:

$$P(v(x)) = \left|\{x \mid x \in \mathbf{x}_{+}^{(n)}\}\right|^{-1} \text{ and } P(e) = C(k, |\mathbf{x}_{+}^{(n)}|)^{-1}, \quad (8)$$

where $\mathbf{x}_{+}^{(n)}$ denotes the set of variables with the positive value of the n-th data instance. Then, all the possible hyperedges for a given instance are generated with the same probability.

Poorer-Richer Graph Monte Carlo

The $P(e)$ of each possible hyperedge for a given instance is different from each other in poorer-richer graph Monte Carlo (PRGMC). In PRGMC, a vertex more included in a hypergraph has higher probability. The $P(v(x))$ of PRGMC is defined as follows:

$$P(v(x)) = \frac{R^{+}\{d(v(x))\}}{|\mathbf{x}|}, \; d(v(x)) = \sum_{e_i \in G_t} \alpha_i h(v(x), e_i), \quad (9)$$

where $R^{+}(.)$ is a rank function in ascending order, $d(v)$ is the degree of vertex of v, and $h(v, e)$ denotes an indicator function which are 1 when e includes v. For enabling new variables not existing in G_{t-1} to be selected, their $d(v)$ is set to a small value. This approach makes a hypergraph contain the patterns which frequently appear in the training data. Therefore, PRGMC constructs a smaller and denser hypergraph, compared to that built by UGMC.

Fair Graph Monte Carlo

Fair graph Monte Carlo (FGMC) prefers the subpatterns less frequently appearing in the training data, contrary to PRGMC. The $P(v(x))$ is defined as:

$$P(v(x)) = R^{-}\{d(v(x))\} / |\mathbf{x}|, \quad (10)$$

where $R^{-}(.)$ is a rank function in descending order. Therefore, a larger and sparser graph is constructed by FGMC and the concepts are represented with much more diverse words and patches.

Learning of Concept Layers

To learning the concept layers we should address three issues: i) determining the number of the nodes of the concrete concept layer $\mathbf{c}^1$ ($\mathbf{c}^1$-nodes), ii) associating between $\mathbf{c}^1$-nodes and modality layer $\mathbf{h}$, and iii) associating between $\mathbf{c}^1$-nodes and the abstract concept nodes ($\mathbf{c}^2$-nodes). The idea is to split the hyperedge set in $\mathbf{h}$ into multiple subgraph clusters, which correspond to the nodes of the $\mathbf{c}^1$ layer. The number of the $\mathbf{c}^1$-nodes are determined based on the distribution of the mean similarities among the hyperedges of a subgraph on all the clusters:

$$Sim(\mathbf{h}^m) = Dist(\mathbf{h}^m) / |\mathbf{h}^m|, \quad (11)$$

where $\mathbf{h}^m$ denotes the subgraph associated with the m-th $\mathbf{c}^1$-node and $Dist(\mathbf{h}^m)$ is the sum of the distance between all the hyperedges of $\mathbf{h}^m$. Then, the distance is estimated by converting the words into the real-value vectors by word2vec (Mikolov et al. 2013). Considering the story-specific semantics of words, we used the corpus of cartoon video subtitles instead of conventional text corpora. If $Sim(\mathbf{h}^m) > \theta_{max}$, $\mathbf{h}^m$ is split into two subgraphs and a new $\mathbf{c}^1$-node is added into the $\mathbf{c}^1$ layer and associated with one of the split subgraph. On the other hand, if all the mean similarities are smaller than θ_{min}, the number is reduced and the associations are conducted again. θ_{max} and θ_{min} are adaptively determined from the mean and the variance of the similarity. $\mathbf{c}^2$-nodes are associated with a $\mathbf{c}^1$-node when the characters corresponding to the $\mathbf{c}^2$-nodes appear in the hyperedges of the subgraph associated with the $\mathbf{c}^1$-node.

Incremental Concept Construction

DCH learns incrementally, i.e. builds the visual-linguistic concepts dynamically while sequentially observing scene-text pairs. We use all the scene-text pairs of one episode as a mini corpus. On sequential observation of the episodes, DCH predicts the concepts from the population and updates the population from the observed data and characters. Formally, this implements a sequential Bayesian estimation:

$$P_t(\mathbf{h},\mathbf{c}^1 \mid \mathbf{r},\mathbf{w},\mathbf{c}^2) = \frac{P(\mathbf{r},\mathbf{w} \mid \mathbf{h},\mathbf{c}^1,\mathbf{c}^2)P(\mathbf{c}^2 \mid \mathbf{c}^1,\mathbf{h})P_{t-1}(\mathbf{h},\mathbf{c}^1)}{P(\mathbf{r},\mathbf{w},\mathbf{c}^2)}, \quad (12)$$

where P_t is a probability distribution at the t-th episode. When observing the t-th episode, the prior distribution $P_{t-1}(\mathbf{h})$ is updated to the posterior distribution by calculating the likelihood and normalizing. Then, the posterior is used as the prior for learning from the next episode. Note that the $P(\mathbf{r},\mathbf{w},\mathbf{c}^2)$ is independent on the model because ($\mathbf{r}$, $\mathbf{w}$) and $\mathbf{c}^2$ are given from the observed data. Therefore, (12) is reformulated when the empirical distributions are used:

$$P_t(\mathbf{h},\mathbf{c}^1 \mid \mathbf{r},\mathbf{w},\mathbf{c}^2) \propto \prod_{d=1}^{D_t}\left\{P(\mathbf{r}^{(d)},\mathbf{w}^{(d)} \mid \mathbf{h},\mathbf{c}^1,\mathbf{c}^2)P(\mathbf{c}^2 \mid \mathbf{c}^1)P(\mathbf{c}^1 \mid \mathbf{h})P_{t-1}(\mathbf{h})\right\}, \quad (13)$$

The data generation term is divided into textual and visual features:

$$\log P(\mathbf{r}^{(d)},\mathbf{w}^{(d)} \mid \mathbf{c}^2,\mathbf{c}^1,\mathbf{h}) = \sum_{n=1}^{N}\log P(r_n^{(d)} \mid \mathbf{c}^2,\mathbf{c}^1,\mathbf{h}) + \sum_{m=1}^{M}\log P(w_m^{(d)} \mid \mathbf{c}^2,\mathbf{c}^1,\mathbf{h}). \quad (14)$$

Then the probability that the m-th element of the word vector is 1 is defined as follows:

$$P(w_m^{(d)}=1 \mid \mathbf{c}^2,\mathbf{c}^1,\mathbf{h})=\exp\left(s_m^{\mathbf{w}}-\sum_{i=1}^{|\mathbf{h}^{\mathbf{c}}|}\alpha_i\right),\ \mathbf{s}^{\mathbf{w}}=\sum_{i=1}^{|\mathbf{e}^{\mathbf{c}}|}\alpha_i e_i^{\mathbf{w}}, \quad (15)$$

where s_m is the m-th value of $\mathbf{s}$ and $\mathbf{e}^{\mathbf{c}}$ denotes the subpopulation of microcodes associated with $\mathbf{c}^1$. $e_i^{\mathbf{w}}$ denotes the textual and visual vectors of the i-th microcode. The probability of the image patches can be computed by the same way. The second term of (13) is related to predicting the characters from the mixtures of concrete concepts. It is defined to prefer more distinct concrete concepts for each character variable. The third term reflects the similarities of the subpopulation for each concrete concept node. The last term is determined from the used strategy of the graph MC. The weight of the microcodes is defined as a function of how frequently the words and patches of the microcode occur in the observed data. Whenever observing a new episode, the weight is updated:

$$\alpha_i^t=\lambda\alpha_i+(1-\lambda)\alpha_i^{t-1}, \quad (16)$$

where λ is a constant for moderating the ratio of the new observed episode and the previous episodes. In this study, we set λ to 0.9.

Vision-Language Conversion

The constructed visual-linguistic knowledge is used to convert scenes to text and vice versa, considering observed video stories. We view a vision-language conversion as a machine translation problem. Then, when source and target languages are substituted with scenes and subtitles, the vision-language translation is formulated:

$$\mathbf{w}^* = \arg\max_{\mathbf{w}} P(\mathbf{w} \mid \mathbf{r},\theta) = \arg\max_{\mathbf{w}} P(\mathbf{r} \mid \mathbf{w},\theta)P(\mathbf{w},\theta), \quad (17)$$

where $\mathbf{w}^*$ are the best subtitles generated from the constructed concept knowledge, and θ is a DCH model. $\mathbf{r}^*$ can also be defined in the same way. Here $\mathbf{w}^*$ is aligned to be a sentence by concatenating the words based on n-gram until a period appears and $\mathbf{r}^*$ is synthesized to be a combination of the patches.

Experimental Results

Video Data Description and Parameter Setup

We use cartoon videos, called "*Pororo*", of 14 DVD titles with 183 episodes and 1,232 minutes of playing time. Pororo is a famous cartoon video appearing. By preprocessing, each scene is captured whenever a subtitle appears, transforming all the videos into the set of 16,000 scene-subtitle pairs. A scene image is represented by a bag of image patches extracted by maximally stable external regions (MSER), and each patch is defined as a feature vector by using SIFT and quantizing RGB pixel values.

We used a DCH model with two concept layers. A microcode consists of two image patches and a phrase with three consecutive words. The image patches are selected by UGMC and a phrase is selected with the maximum value of $P(v(x))$ of the words in the phrase. The initial number of $\mathbf{c}^1$-nodes starts at 10 and θ_{max} and θ_{min} are defined as follows:

$$\theta_{\max}^t = \begin{cases} \mu^t+\eta\cdot(\mu^t-\mu^{10})\cdot\sigma^t,\ t>10 \\ \mu^t+\eta\cdot\sigma^t,\ t\le 10 \end{cases},\ \theta_{\min}^t=0, \quad (18)$$

where μ^t and σ^t denote the mean and the standard deviation of the subgraph similarities after observing the t-th episode, and η is a constant for moderating the increasing speed of the $\mathbf{c}^1$ layer size. In this study, we set it to 0.75.

Concept Representation and Development

To demonstrate the evolution of concepts in DCH, we have examined how the characters, such as "*Pororo*", "*Eddy*", and "*Tongtong*", are differently described as the story unfolds. Figure 1 compares the descriptions after learning up to episode 13 (DVD 1) and 183 (DVD 14). Considering the fact that *Pororo* is a brother of *Crong*, *Tongtong* casts "*Kurikuri*" for magic, and *Eddy* is an engineer, the descriptive words for each character are suitable. We observe that the number of visual and linguistic nodes tends to increase. This is because the concepts continuously develop while observing the videos. The character concepts can be visualized as a multimodal

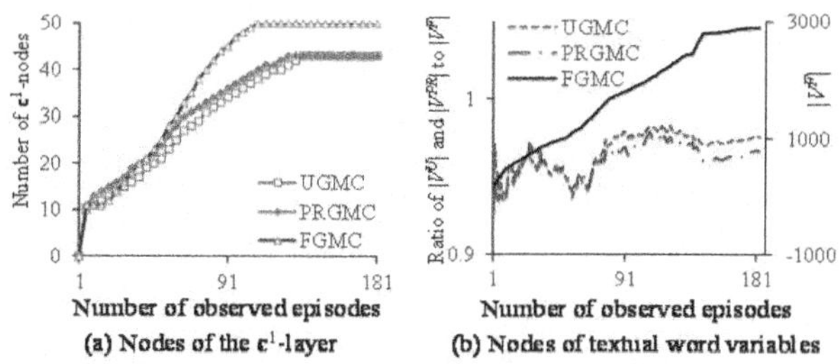

Figure 3: Changes of model complexity according to the learning strategies of the graph MC. In (b), V^U, V^{PR}, and V^F denote the vertex sets of the model constructed by UGMC, PRGMC, and FGMC.

concept map, which is used for knowledge representation as shown in Figure S1 in supplementary material. Specifically, we observed that the number of $\mathbf{c}^1$-nodes increases in early stages and then saturates (Figure 3). This indicates that new concrete concepts are learned rather earlier and, as time goes on, familiar concepts reappear. Figure 3(a) compares the complexity growth curves of DCH by three learning methods. FGMC is the most fast-growing strategy employing more $\mathbf{c}^1$-nodes because it tends to select diverse words and patches, as compared to UGMC and PRGMC. This is verified by Figure 3(b) which shows more vertices are included in the models constructed by FGMC. To see if DCH correctly learned the distinguishable concepts, we have analyzed the $\mathbf{c}^1$-nodes by PCA. Figure 4 shows that different characters are well discriminated by the learned microcodes (the first component ratio = 0.70 in (a)).

Vision-Language Translation Results

The constructed DCH was evaluated by using it for "story-aware" vision-language translation. Table 1 shows the performance of the sentence generation from the images. The test data consist of 183 images from randomly selecting one image per episode, and they are not used in training the models. The results are averaged over 10 experiments. The performances were estimated by how many words in the generated sentences and the original

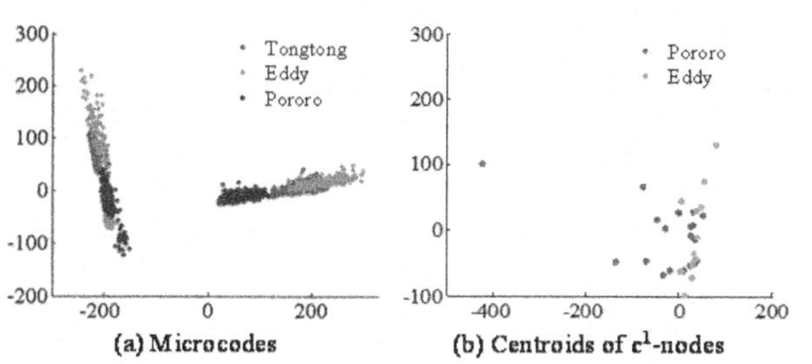

Figure 4: PCA plot of microcodes associated with the concrete concept nodes (**c1**-nodes) and their centroids of the models learned from 183 episodes by UGMC.

	Measure	PRGMC	UGMC	FGMC	SPC
Ep 1	Precision	**0.196**	0.077	0.167	0.195
	Recall	0.117	0.285	0.151	**0.302**
	F-score	0.146	0.122	0.158	**0.237**
Ep 1~9	Precision	0.225	0.221	**0.230**	0.175
	Recall	0.268	0.283	**0.303**	0.278
	F-score	0.245	0.248	**0.261**	0.215
Ep 1~18	Precision	0.240	0.247	**0.253**	0.239
	Recall	0.293	0.293	**0.378**	0.283
	F-score	0.264	0.268	**0.303**	0.259
Ep 1~36	Precision	0.267	0.251	**0.268**	0.242
	Recall	0.315	0.284	**0.376**	0.291
	F-score	0.289	0.266	**0.313**	0.264

Table 1: Performance of scene-to-sentence generation as the increase of the observed videos.

subtitles are matched. We examined how the different graph MC algorithms effect on the results. The precision of PRGMC increases faster in early videos but slower in late ones than that of FGMC. PRGMC is good at fast memorizing of main information but loses details. On the contrary, FGMC requires a more complex structure to memorize more information but shows higher accuracy. This is consistent with the results in Figure 3. In addition, the result shows that the introduction of concept layers improves the accuracy of the constructed knowledge. More examples of generated sentences and scene images are provided as supplementary material in Figures S2 and S3. It is interesting to note that the recall images are like mental imagery as demonstrated in movie recall in humans (Nishimoto et al. 2011). Overall, the results in Figure S2 and S3 demonstrate that the more episodes the DCH learned, the more diversity are generated in sentences and images. It should be noted that this is not for free; Observing more episodes requires heavier computational costs. The tradeoff should be made by the controlling the greediness of the graph MC algorithms as examined above.

Concluding Remarks

We have presented a deep concept hierarchy (DCH) for automated knowledge construction by learning visual-linguistic concepts from cartoon videos. DCH represents mutually-grounded vision-language concepts by building multiple layers of hypergraph structures. Technically, the main difficulty is how to efficiently learn the complex hierarchical structures of DCH in online situations like videos. Our main idea was to use a Monte Carlo method. We have developed a graph MC method that essentially searches "stochastically" and "constructively" for a hierarchical hypergraph that best matches the empirical distribution of the observed data. Unlike other deep learning models, the DCH structure can be incrementally reorganized. This flexibility enables the model to handle concept drifts in stream data, as we have demonstrated in the experiments on a series of cartoon videos of 183 episodes.

We have analyzed and compared three strategies for the graph MC: uniform graph Monte Carlo (UGMC), poorer-richer graph Monte Carlo (PRGMC), and fair graph Monte Carlo (FGMC) depending on the probability of selecting vertices. The use of hierarchy improved the generalization performance while paying slight prices in computational cost. Among the variants of the Monte Carlo algorithms, we found that the PRGMC and the FGMC work better in earlier and later stages of video observation in the visual-language translation task. Overall, our experimental results demonstrate that DCH combined with the graph MC algorithms captures the mixed visual-linguistic concepts at multiple abstraction levels by sequentially estimating the probability distributions of visual and textual variables extracted from the video data. In future work, it would be interesting to see how the methods scale up on a much larger dataset with more complex story structures than the educational cartoon videos for children.

Acknowledgments

This work was supported by the National Research Foundation of Korea grant (NRF-2010-0017734). In addition, this work was supported in part by ICT R&D program of MSIP/IITP (10035348, 14-824-09-014, 10044009), the US Air Force Research Laboratory (AFOSR 124087), and Samsung Electronics Co., Ltd.

References

Abbott, J. T., Austerweil, J. L., and Griffiths, T. L. 2012. Constructing a Hypothesis Space from the Web for Large-scale Bayesian Word Learning. In *Proceedings of the 34th Annual Conference of the Cognitive Science Society* (*Cogsci 2012*). 54-59.

Besag, J. 1974. Spatial Interaction and the Statistical Analysis of Lattice Systems. *Journal of the Royal Statistical Society*, *Series B*, 36(2):192-236.

Blei, D, M. and Jordan, M. 2003. Modeling Annotated Data. In *Proceedings of the 26th annual ACM SIGIR Conference on Research and Development in Information Retrieval* (*SIGIR 2003*). 127-134.

Deng, J., Dong, W., Socher, R., Li, L.-J., Li, K., and L. Fei-Fei. 2009. ImageNet: A Large-scale Hierarchical Image Database. In *Proceedings of IEEE Conference on Computer Vision and Pattern Recognition 2009* (*CVPR 2009*). 248-255.

Fellbaum, C. 2010. WordNet, In R. Poli et al. (eds), *Theory and Applications of Ontology Applications*, pp. 231-243, Springer Science+Business Media.

Jia, Y., Abbott, J., Austerweil, J. L., Griffiths, T. L., and Darrell, T. 2013. Visual Concept Learning: Combining Machine Vision and Bayesian Generalization on Concept Hierarchies. *Advances in Neural Information Processing Systems 26* (*NIPS 2013*).

Kiefer, M. and Barsalou, L. W. 2013. Grounding the Human Conceptual System in Perception, Action, and Internal States, *Action Science: Foundation of an Emerging Discipline*, W. Prinz, M. Belsert, and A. Herwig (Ed.), MIT Press Scholarship Online.

Kiros, R., Salakutdinov, R., and Zemel, R. 2014. Multimodal Neural Language Models, In *Proceedings of the 31st International Conference on Machine Learning* (*ICML* 2014).

Lewis, M. and Frank, M. C. 2013. An Integrated Model of Concept Learning and Word-Concept Mapping. In *Proceedings of the 35th Annual Conference of the Cognitive Science Society* (*Cogsci 2013*).

Meltzoff, A. N. 1990. Toward a Developmental Cognitive Science: The Implications of Cross-modal Matching and Imitation for Development of Representation and Memory in Infancy, *Annual New York Academy Science* 608:1-31.

Mikolov, T. Sutskever, I. Chen, K., Corrado, G., and Dean, J. Distributed Representation of Words and Phrases and Their Compositionality, In *Proceedings of Advances in Neural Information Processing Systems* (*NIPS 2013*). 3111-3119.

Muggleton, S. 2014. Alan Turing and the Development of Artificial Intelligence. *AI Communications*, 27:3-10.

Nishimoto, S., Vu, A. T., Naselaris, T., Benjamini, Y., Yu, B., and Gallant, L. 2011. Reconstructing Visual Experiences from Brain Activity Evoked by Natural Movies, *Current Biology* 21:1641-1646.

Ordonez, V., Kulkarni, G., and Berg, T. 2011. Im2text: Describing Images using 1 Million Captioned Photographs. In *Proceedings of Advances in Neural Information Processing Systems* (*NIPS* 2011), 1143–1151.

Quiroga, R. Q. 2012. Concept Cells: The Building Blocks of Declarative Memory Functions. *Nature Reviews Neuroscience* 13:587-597.

Socher, R., Ganjoo, M., Manning, C. D. and Ng, A. 2013. Zero-Shot Learning through Cross-modal Transfer. In *Proceedings of Advances in Neural Information Processing Systems* (*NIPS* 2013), 935–943.

Srivastava, N. and Salakutdinov, R. 2012. Multimodal Learning with Deep Boltzmann Machines. *Advances in Neural Information Processing Systems 2012* (*NIPS 2012*). 2222-2230.

Steyvers, M. and J. B. Tenenbaum. 2005. The Large-scale Structure of Semantic Networks: Statistical Analyses and a Model of Semantic Growth. *Cognitive Science*, 29:41-78.

Zhang, B.-T. 2013. Information-Theoretic Objective Functions for Lifelong Learning. *AAAI 2013 Spring Symposium on Lifelong Machine Learning*. 62-69.

Zhang, B.-T., Ha, J.-W., and Kang, M. 2012. Sparse Population Code Models of Word Learning in Concept Drift. In *Proceedings of the 34th Annual Conference of Cogitive Science Society* (*Cogsci* 2012). 1221-1226.

Zhao, G., Yuan, J., and Hua, G. 2013. Topical Video Object Discovery from Key Frames by Modeling Word Co-occurrence Prior. In *Proceedings of IEEE Conference on Computer Vision and Pattern Recognition* 2013 (*CVPR 2013*). 1602-1609.

Zhou, D., Huang, J., and Schoelkopf, B. 2007. Learning with Hypergraphs: Clustering, Classification, and Embedding. In *Proceedings of Advances in Neural Information Processing Systems 2006* (*NIPS 2006*). 1601-1608.

Bayesian Affect Control Theory of Self

Jesse Hoey
David R. Cheriton School of Computer Science
University of Waterloo, 200 University Ave. West,
Waterloo, Ontario, N2L3G1, Canada
jhoey@cs.uwaterloo.ca

Tobias Schröder
Potsdam University of Applied Sciences,
Kiepenheuerallee 5,
14469 Potsdam, Germany
post@tobiasschroeder.de

Abstract

Notions of *identity* and of the *self* have long been studied in social psychology and sociology as key guiding elements of social interaction and coordination. In the AI of the future, these notions will also play a role in producing natural, socially appropriate artificially intelligent agents that encompass subtle and complex human social and affective skills. We propose here a Bayesian generalization of the sociological *affect control theory of self* as a theoretical foundation for socio-affectively skilled artificial agents. This theory posits that each human maintains an internal model of his or her deep sense of "self" that captures their emotional, psychological, and socio-cultural sense of being in the world. The "self" is then externalised as an identity within any given interpersonal and institutional situation, and this situational identity is the person's local (in space and time) representation of the self. Situational identities govern the actions of humans according to affect control theory. Humans will seek situations that allow them to enact identities consistent with their sense of self. This consistency is cumulative over time: if some parts of a person's self are not actualized regularly, the person will have a growing feeling of inauthenticity that they will seek to resolve. In our present generalisation, the self is represented as a probability distribution, allowing it to be multi-modal (a person can maintain multiple different identities), uncertain (a person can be unsure about who they really are), and learnable (agents can learn the identities and selves of other agents). We show how the Bayesian affect control theory of self can underpin artificial agents that are socially intelligent.

Introduction

Designers of intelligent agents are increasingly looking towards the social sciences for ideas on how to create more natural and aligned social interactions. This endeavour requires mathematical models of cognition, but also of emotion or affect, in ways that capture the subtle cultural rules underlying human coordination and cooperation. Affect control theory (ACT) (Heise 2007) is a mathematically formalized sociological theory of the interplays between cultural representations, interactants' identities[1], and affective experience (Heise 2007). ACT posits that humans will strive to achieve consistency in shared affective cultural sentiments about events, and will seek to increase *alignment* with other agents (including artificial ones).

While ACT models interactions of agents specific to given situations, the affect control theory of self (ACT-S) was developed to include more dispositional, cross-situational knowledge about agents (MacKinnon and Heise 2010). ACT-S describes the *self* as the totality of a person's sense of themselves, and may include many identities that a person can enact in different social situations. ACT-S describes how a person will select an identity to enact in a given situation as the one that will best lead to an interaction (according to ACT) that confirms their true sense of themselves (their *self*). This interaction makes the person feel *authentic*, but others may lead to feelings of inauthenticity, and to further pressure to seek self-confirming interactions.

Recently, a probabilistic and decision theoretic generalisation of ACT, called *BayesAct*, has been shown to be a suitable framework for developing socially and emotionally intelligent agents (Hoey, Schröder, and Alhothali 2013b; Lin et al. 2014). *BayesAct* is a partially-observable Markov decision process (POMDP) model, and thus generalises ACT by modeling affective states as probability distributions, and allowing decision-theoretic reasoning about affect and other application-specific "cognitive" aspects. In this paper, we present a similar generalisation for the affect control theory of self, called *BayesAct-S*. The introduction of probability distributions to ACT-S resolves some key problems with the sociological theory that we expose in this paper.

Background

Affect Control Theory

Affect Control Theory (ACT) arises from work on the psychology of human social interaction (Heise 2007). ACT proposes that social perceptions, behaviours, and emotions are guided by a psychological need to minimize the differences between culturally shared fundamental affective sentiments

[1]The meaning of the term *identity* differs considerably across scientific disciplines. Here, we adhere to the tradition in sociology where it essentially denotes a kind of person in a social situation.

about social situations and the transient impressions resulting from the interactions between elements within those situations. Fundamental sentiments, $\mathbf{f}$, are representations of social objects, such as interactants' identities and behaviours, as vectors in a 3D affective space, hypothesised to be a universal organising principle of human socio-affective experience (Osgood, May, and Miron 1975). The basis vectors of affective space are called Evaluation/valence, Potency/control, and Activity/arousal (EPA). EPA profiles of concepts can be measured with the *semantic differential*, a survey technique where respondents rate affective meanings of concepts on numerical scales with opposing adjectives at each end (e.g., good, nice vs. bad, awful for E, weak, little vs. strong, big for P, and calm, passive vs. exciting, active for A). Affect control theorists have compiled lexicons of a few thousand words along with average EPA ratings obtained from survey participants who are knowledgeable about their culture (Heise 2010). For example, most English speakers agree that professors are about as nice as students (E), more powerful (P) and less active (A). The corresponding EPAs are $[1.7, 1.8, 0.5]$ for professor and $[1.8, 0.7, 1.2]$ for student[2]. In Japan, professor has the same P (1.8) but students are seen as much less powerful (-0.2). As the EPA structure of social concepts has been shown to be highly consensual within cultures, affective lexicons can be regarded as rudimentary collective representations of human sociality (Ambrasat et al. 2014).

Social events can cause transient impressions, $\boldsymbol{\tau}$ (also three dimensional in EPA space) of identities and behaviours that may deviate from their corresponding fundamental sentiments, $\mathbf{f}$. ACT models this formation of impressions from events with a grammar of the form actor-behaviour-object. Consider for example a professor (actor) who yells (behaviour) at a student (object). Most would agree that this professor appears considerably less nice (E), a bit less potent (P), and certainly more aroused (A) than the cultural average of a professor. Such transient shifts in affective meaning caused by specific events are described with models of the form $\boldsymbol{\tau}' = M\mathscr{G}(\mathbf{f}', \boldsymbol{\tau})$, where M is a matrix of statistically estimated prediction coefficients from empirical impression-formation studies and $\mathscr{G}$ is a vector of polynomial features in $\mathbf{f}'$ and $\boldsymbol{\tau}$. In ACT, the weighted sum of squared Euclidean distances between fundamental sentiments and transient impressions is called *deflection*, and is hypothesised to correspond to an aversive state of mind that humans seek to avoid. This *affect control principle* allows ACT to compute *normative* actions for humans: those that minimize the deflection. Normative predictions of ACT have been shown to be highly accurate in explaining verbal behaviours of mock leaders in a computer-simulated business (Schröder and Scholl 2009), non-verbal displays in dyadic interactions (Schröder et al. 2013), and group dynamics (Heise 2013), among others (MacKinnnon and Robinson 2014).

[2]Values range by convention from -4.3 to $+4.3$ (Heise 2010). This range has historical roots in Osgood's massive cross-cultural studies of affective sentiments (Osgood, May, and Miron 1975). The Bayesian version (*BayesAct*) operates on a real-valued scale and so is not restricted to only consider vectors within that range.

Partially Observable Markov Decision Processes

A partially observable Markov decision process (POMDP) (Åström 1965) is a stochastic control model that consists of a finite set $\mathcal{X}$ of states; a finite set $\mathcal{A}$ of actions; a stochastic transition model $\Pr : X \times A \to \Delta(X)$, with $\Pr(x'|x, a)$ denoting the probability of moving from state x to x' when action a is taken, and $\Delta(X)$ is a distribution over $\mathcal{X}$; a finite observation set $\boldsymbol{\Omega_x}$; a stochastic observation model, $\Pr(\omega_x|x)$, denoting the probability of making observation $\omega_x \in \boldsymbol{\Omega_x}$ while the system is in state x; and a reward $R(a, x')$ for a transition to x' induced by action a.

A *policy* maps *belief states* (i.e., distributions over $\mathcal{X}$) into choices of actions, such that the expected discounted sum of rewards is (approximately) maximised.

In this paper, we will be dealing with *factored* POMDPs in which the state is represented by the cross-product of a set of variables or features. POMDPs have been used as models for many human-interactive domains, including intelligent tutoring systems (Folsom-Kovarik, Sukthankar, and Schatz 2013), spoken dialogue systems (Williams and Young 2006), and assistive technologies (Hoey et al. 2012).

BayesAct

Recently, ACT was generalised and formulated as a POMDP (Hoey, Schröder, and Alhothali 2013b) for human-interactive artificially intelligent systems. This new model, called *BayesAct*, generalises the original theory in three ways. First, sentiments are viewed as probability distributions over latent variables rather than points in the EPA space, allowing for multimodal, uncertain and dynamic sentiments to be modeled and learned. Second, affective interactions are augmented with *propositional* state (e.g. the usual state space considered in typical AI applications). Third, an explicit reward function allows for goals that go beyond simple deflection minimization.

A *BayesAct* POMDP models an interaction between two agents (human or machine) denoted *agent* and *client*. The state is the product of six 3-dimensional continuous random variables corresponding to fundamental and transient sentiments about the *agent*'s identity ($\mathbf{F}_a, \mathbf{T}_a$), behaviour ($\mathbf{F}_b, \mathbf{T}_b$) and *client*'s identity ($\mathbf{F}_c, \mathbf{T}_c$). We use $\mathbf{F} = \{\mathbf{F}_a, \mathbf{F}_b, \mathbf{F}_c\}$ and $\mathbf{T} = \{\mathbf{T}_a, \mathbf{T}_b, \mathbf{T}_c\}$. Actions in the *BayesAct* POMDP are factored in two parts: $\mathbf{b_a}$ denotes the *affective* component or interpretation, and a represents the *propositional* part. For example, if a tutor gives a hard exercise to do, the manner in which it is presented, and the difficulty of the exercise, combine to form an affective impression $\mathbf{b_a}$ that is communicated. The actual exercise itself (content, difficulty level, etc) is the *propositional* part of the action, a. The fundamental behaviour, $\mathbf{F}_b$, denotes either observed *client* or taken *agent* affective action. That is, when *agent* acts, there is a deterministic mapping from the affective component of his action (denoted $\mathbf{b_a}$ in *BayesAct*) to the *agent*'s behaviour $\mathbf{F}_b$. When *client* acts, *agent* observes evidence of $\mathbf{F}_b$ (as the affective behaviour of the other agent).

The transient impressions, $\mathbf{T}$, evolve according to the deterministic impression-formation operator in ACT ($M\mathscr{G}$). Fundamental sentiments are expected to stay approximately constant over time, but are subject to random drift (with noise Σ_f) and are expected to also remain close to the transient impressions because of the *affect control principle*. Thus, the dynamics of $\mathbf{F}$ can be written as:

$$Pr(\mathbf{f}'|\mathbf{f},\boldsymbol{\tau}) \propto e^{-\psi(\mathbf{f}',\boldsymbol{\tau})-\xi(\mathbf{f}',\mathbf{f})} \quad (1)$$

where $\psi \equiv (\mathbf{f}' - \boldsymbol{M}\mathscr{G}(\mathbf{f}',\boldsymbol{\tau}))^T\boldsymbol{\Sigma}^{-1}(\mathbf{f}' - \boldsymbol{M}\mathscr{G}(\mathbf{f}',\boldsymbol{\tau}))$ combines the *affect control principle* with the impression formation equations and $\xi \equiv (\mathbf{f}' - \mathbf{f})^T\boldsymbol{\Sigma}_f^{-1}(\mathbf{f}' - \mathbf{f})$ represents the inertia of fundamental sentiments. The two terms can be combined into a single Gaussian that is non-linearly dependent (due to the polynomial features in $\mathscr{G}(\tau,\mathbf{x})$) on the previous state. *BayesAct* thus uses sample-based representation for beliefs, and a *bootstrap filter* for belief updates.

The probability distribution in (1) gives the normative (expected) action as one of the components of $\mathbf{f}'$: $\mathbf{f}_b'$. Thus, by integrating over $\mathbf{f}_a$ and $\mathbf{f}_c$ and the previous state, we obtain a distribution over $\mathbf{f}_b$ that acts as a *normative action prediction*: it tells the agent what to expect from other agents, and what action is expected from it.

BayesAct includes an application-specific set of random variables $\mathbf{X}$ that are interpreted as the *non-affective* elements of the domain (e.g. whose turn it is, behaviours of other agents, game states, student knowledge representations for intelligent tutors, or plan-steps representing progress through a task). The dynamics of $\mathbf{X}$ are application specific, but depend in general on the *deflection*, and on the propositional component of the action, a (which complements the affective component, $\mathbf{b_a}$). Thus, we require a definition for $Pr(\mathbf{x}'|\mathbf{f},\boldsymbol{\tau},\mathbf{x},a)$. We refer to this distribution as the *social coordination* rule: it defines what agents are expected to do in a situation with sentiments $\mathbf{f}$ and $\boldsymbol{\tau}$. For example, we would expect faster learning from a student if deflection is low, as they do not have to use valuable cognitive resources to deal with any mis-alignment with the tutor. $\mathbf{X}$ also may condition the affective dynamics of $\mathbf{F}$ and $\mathbf{T}$ (e.g. a professor will act differently with students of differing skill levels).

The *BayesAct* POMDP assumes that the state is not observable, but that observations are obtained for some (possibly empty) subset of $\mathbf{X}$ and for the affective behaviour $\mathbf{F}_b$. As affective identities are latent variables, they are learned (as inference) in the POMDP. Thus, if behaving normatively, an agent will perform affective actions ($\mathbf{F}_b$) that allow other agents to infer what his (true) identity is. The normative action is thought to be used by humans as an emotional "fast thinking" heuristic: roughly corresponding to "System 1" thinking (Kahneman 2011). If agents are fully cooperative and aligned, then no further planning is required to ensure goal achievement. Agents do what is expected of them (which may involve planning over $\mathbf{X}$, but not over $\mathbf{F}$ and $\mathbf{T}$), and expect others to do so as well. However, when alignment breaks down, or in non-cooperative situations, then slower, more deliberative "System 2" thinking is required.

To accomplish this deliberative thinking, *BayesAct* uses a Monte-Carlo tree search (MCTS) method called POMCP-C (Asghar and Hoey 2014). This method builds a search tree by sampling trajectories from the POMDP as a simulator. It requires an *action bias* from which samples are drawn in the action space, which here is the normative action prediction as above.

Affect Control Theory of Self

The affect control theory of self (ACT-S) describes a higher-order level of socio-affective control than ACT (MacKinnon and Heise 2010). ACT governs the choice of behaviours in a given situation given an identity. In contrast, ACT-S is used to select identities to enact in a particular setting and institution, respecting situational and dispositional constraints simultaneously. ACT-S describes a person's sense of *self* using the *fundamental self-sentiment*, an EPA vector that describes a composite feeling for the overall self. The fundamental self sentiment is thought to be relatively stable over time, providing a sense of consistency and giving protection against disruptive events. However, it can change drastically in short periods in exceptional circumstances.

ACT-S describes the recent history of self-feelings with a *situational self-sentiment* (again, an EPA vector). The situational self-sentiment is the ephemeral feeling about the *self* that a person has within a given setting. This feeling is a combination of the recently experienced interactions with others, with the situation, and with the institution in which the experiences occurred. The affect control principle's primary proposition is that *people construct situational self-sentiments that are consistent with their fundamental self-sentiment*. The difference between these two is called the *inauthenticity*: if one cannot enact a series of identities that create a situational self-sentiment that is consistent with one's fundamental self-sentiment, one feels a sense of *inauthenticity* in the situation (MacKinnon and Heise 2010).

We will denote the fundamental self sentiment as $\mathbf{S_f} = \{\mathrm{S_{f}}_j\}$ and the situational self-sentiment as $\mathbf{S_s} = \{\mathrm{S_{s}}_j\}$ where $j \in \{e,p,a\}$ and both are three-dimensional vectors. The *inauthenticity* is a three dimensional vector $\mathbf{I} = \{\mathrm{I}_j\}$, and is computed as $\mathbf{I} = \mathbf{F}_a - \mathbf{S_f}$ (a 3-vector difference): it gives the difference between the currently felt identity $\mathbf{F}_a$ and the fundamental self sentiment, $\mathbf{S_f}$.

The situational self-sentiment is defined as a weighted accumulation of identities enacted over time (Heise 2007):

$$\mathbf{s_s}^T = \sum_{t=0}^{T} w(t,T)\mathbf{f}_a^t \quad (2)$$

where superscripts denote time indices and $w(t,T)$ is a decay function, e.g. $w(t,T) = \eta^{T-t}$, with $0 < \eta \leq 1$ being a decay constant. The inauthenticity also accumulates over time, such that, at time T we have the accumulated inauthenticity, $\mathbf{I_a}$:

$$\mathbf{i_a}^T = \sum_{t=0}^{T} w(t,T)\left(\mathbf{f}_a^t - \mathbf{s_f}^t\right) = \mathbf{s_s}^T - \sum_{t=0}^{T} w(t,T)\mathbf{s_f}^t \quad (3)$$

We can make the further assumption that the fundamental self sentiment does not change very quickly, so that $\mathbf{s_f}^t = \mathbf{s_f}$, and we understand that $\mathbf{s_f}$ means the fundamental self-sentiment at the current time, T. Thus, we can write:

$$\mathbf{i_a}^T = \mathbf{s_s}^T - \mathbf{s_f}\sum_{t=0}^{T} w(t,T)$$

which, if we use the geometric decay constant η as above, and let $T \to \infty$, becomes

$$\mathbf{i_a} = \mathbf{s_s} - \mathbf{s_f}\frac{1}{1-\eta} \tag{4}$$

Where $\mathbf{i_a}$, $\mathbf{s_s}$ and $\mathbf{s_f}$ represent the accumulated inauthenticity, situational self-sentiment, and fundamental self sentiment at the current time.

We can see from Equation 2 that the enacted identities are summed to create the situational self sentiment. What this implies is that a person can create a situational self-sentiment that is neutral by acting very positively (E), and then acting negatively to offset the positivity. For example, one could enact the identity of a *saint* ($E = 2.81$), followed by the identity of a *sinner* ($E = -1.68$), and if $w = 0.6$, the resulting self sentiment would be close to $E = 0$, and the actor would feel very neutral. As a more realistic example, consider the fictional case of Sara Sim, the CEO of a large and prosperous technology firm. Sara has both the *female* identity $EPA = \{1.60, 0.22, 0.42\}$, and the *executive* identity $EPA = \{1.26, 1.93, 1.44\}$. These two identities are substantially different on the potency and activity axes. If we assume that Sara primarily enacts her *executive* identity during the day while at work (call this $t = 2-5$), and her *female* identity in the evenings ($t = 6-7$) and mornings ($t = 0-1$) while at home with her family, then, taking $\eta = 0.8$, we have that her self sentiment at the end of the day according to Equation 2 would be $\{6.02, 4.15, 3.68\}$, which if rescaled by $1-\eta$ according to Equation 4, gives $\{1.20, 0.83, 0.74\}$, with a closest label of *businesswoman* in EPA lexicons.

Bayesian Affect Control Theory of Self

In *BayesAct*, identities are no longer points in the EPA space, but probability distributions. Here, we hypothesise that both fundamental self-sentiments and situational self-sentiments are also probability distributions. The idea of treating sentiments as distributions removes a drawback of affect control theory, that a single identity must be selected at each time, and that each behaviour can only correspond with a single sentiment. One frequently encounters situations where multiple identities may be mixed, and multiple sentiments may occur simultaneously (Smith-Lovin 2007).

If we follow (Heise 2007), we would model the situational self-sentiment is as a sum of random variables given by Equation 2. We describe this model in the next section. Alternatively, in the subsequent section, we consider the situational self sentiment as a random variable that evolves as a function of the current enacted identity and the previous situational self-sentiment in a probabilistic mixture or "noisy-or" model.

Situational Self Sentiment: Summed Identities

Assume $w(T,T) = 1$ and re-write Equation 2 as:

$$\mathbf{s_s}^T = \mathbf{f}_a^T + \eta\sum_{t=0}^{T-1} w(t, T-1)\mathbf{f}_a^t = \mathbf{f}_a^T + \eta\mathbf{s_s}^{T-1}$$

or, alternatively:

$$\mathbf{s_s}' = \eta\mathbf{s_s} + \mathbf{f}_a \tag{5}$$

and thus, to compute $Pr(\mathbf{S_s}^T)$, we will need the convolution

$$Pr(\mathbf{s_s}^T) = Pr(\mathbf{f}_a^T) * Pr(\eta\mathbf{s_s}^{T-1}) \tag{6}$$

This convolution is not obvious to compute given distributions as sample sets of three dimensional vectors.

Situational Self Sentiment: Mixed Distributions

Rather than computing a probability distribution over the sum of fundamentals, we can sum the probability distributions by considering them as a probabilistic mixture model. The idea is that the situational self-sentiment at the current time step, $\mathbf{S_s}'$, is *caused* by *either* the previous situational self-sentiment, $\mathbf{S_s}$ *or* the current fundamental identity, $\mathbf{F}'_a$. However, the person is *uncertain* about which of these elements is the true cause of current situational self sentiment. As we are representing the person's subjective belief, the situational self-sentiment is really a probabilistic mixture of both. The person knows they used to feel one way, and knows they have just felt another way (which may be consistent), and knows that the way they feel is something of a combination of both of these feelings.

Mathematically, we consider that there is a binary random variable C that is drawn from a Bernoulli distribution with parameter η (i.e. a weighted coin flip with probability η of turning up heads), and that $C = c$ ("true") means that $\mathbf{S_s}'$ is caused by $\mathbf{S_s}$, and $C = \overline{c}$ ("false") means that it is caused by $\mathbf{F}'_a$. Thus:

$$c \sim Bernoulli(\eta, 1-\eta) \tag{7}$$

$$\mathbf{s_s}' = c\mathbf{s_s} + (1-c)\mathbf{f}'_a \tag{8}$$

This means that to compute $Pr(\mathbf{S_s}')$ we can sum over $C, \mathbf{F}'_a, \mathbf{S_s}$:

$$\begin{aligned}
Pr(\mathbf{s_s}') =& \int_{\mathbf{s_s},\mathbf{f}'_a}\big[Pr(\mathbf{s_s}', c|\mathbf{s_s}, \mathbf{f}'_a) + \\
&\quad Pr(\mathbf{s_s}', \overline{c}|\mathbf{s_s}, \mathbf{f}'_a)\big]Pr(\mathbf{s_s}, \mathbf{f}'_a)d\mathbf{s_s}d\mathbf{f}'_a \\
=& \int_{\mathbf{s_s},\mathbf{f}'_a}\big[Pr(\mathbf{s_s}'|c, \mathbf{s_s})Pr(c)Pr(\mathbf{s_s}, \mathbf{f}'_a) + \\
&\quad Pr(\mathbf{s_s}'|\overline{c}, \mathbf{f}'_a)Pr(\overline{c})Pr(\mathbf{s_s}, \mathbf{f}'_a)\big]\, d\mathbf{s_s}d\mathbf{f}'_a \\
=& Pr(c)Pr(\mathbf{s_s}) + Pr(\overline{c})Pr(\mathbf{f}_a) \\
=& \eta Pr(\mathbf{s_s}) + (1-\eta)Pr(\mathbf{f}_a)
\end{aligned} \tag{9}$$

We may also want C to be conditioned on other elements of the state, such as the institution (part of $\mathbf{X}$ in *BayesAct*), in which case we work with $Pr(C|\mathbf{X})$, or we could write the parameter as a function of the state, $\eta(\mathbf{x})$. We also may consider that some additional noise is added at each time step, so that

$$\mathbf{s_s}' = c\mathbf{s_s} + (1-c)\mathbf{f}'_a + \rho \tag{10}$$

where $\rho \sim \mathcal{N}(\mathbf{s_s}; 0, \mathbf{\Sigma_s})$ is normally distributed random noise (may be different noises for c and $\overline{c}$). In this case, we have

$$\begin{aligned}
Pr(\mathbf{s_s}') =& \eta\int_{\mathbf{s_s}} \mathcal{N}(\mathbf{s_s}'; \mathbf{s_s}, \mathbf{\Sigma_s})Pr(\mathbf{s_s}) + \\
&(1-\eta)\int_{\mathbf{f}'_a} \mathcal{N}(\mathbf{s_s}'; \mathbf{f}'_a, \mathbf{\Sigma_s})Pr(\mathbf{f}'_a)
\end{aligned} \tag{11}$$

As we are representing these distributions with sample sets, it is easy to apply Equation 9 in practice, by choosing a random sample of ηN samples from $Pr(\mathbf{s_s}^{T-1})$ and $(1-\eta)N$ samples from $Pr(\mathbf{f}_a)$. Equation 11 is also straightforward, as we simply do the same but add some random normally distributed noise to each sample.

Differences between the two representations

The two representations of the situational self-sentiment described in the last two sections are fundamentally different ways of looking at how the self-sentiments are updated sequentially. In the first case, identities are summed over time as vectors, thus averaging out to create the situational self-sentiment. In the following, we refer to this as "averaging". In the second case, identities are mixed over time. We will refer to this as "noisy-or".

Consider again the case of Sara Sim. If using averaging, Sara's situational self-sentiment will be a unimodal distribution centered around "businesswoman" (EPA=$\{1.4, 1.1, 0.9\}$). If using noisy-or, the situational self-sentiment will be bimodal, with one mode at "female" and the other at "executive". Now, which of these two self-sentiments match her fundamental self-sentiment better? If she could enact the identity of "businesswoman" exactly at home and at work, would she feel more or less authentic? If the former, then we should consider the averaging model as more accurate. If the latter, it would be the noisy-or model. We believe the latter is more accurate: Sara wants to feel like a female when out on a romantic dinner with her partner, not like a businesswoman. She wants to feel like a powerful executive while at work, not a menial businesswoman. If one were to ask Sara at the end of her day how she felt using a single word, she might average and report *businesswoman*. On the other hand, if given more flexibilty in her answer, she might report that she feels a bit of both *female* and *executive*.

Females in powerful roles will often be assigned the less powerful of the two identities by others, especially if there are no direct personal or institutional indications of the more powerful roles. For example, consider the case of Merribel G. Krosby, a female professor with a feminine and youthful outward appearance. The identity of professor has an EPA of $\{1.61, 1.58, 0.35\}$, while female is as before $\{1.6, 0.22, 0.42\}$. The average identity for Merribel is $EPA = \{1.6, 0.86, 0.36\}$, and is closest to that of a "graduate student" ($EPA = \{1.6, 1.58, 0.35\}$) if considering the academic setting. People across the academic setting, from directors and deans to undergraduate students, often treat Merribel as a grad student, or simply a student ($EPA = \{1.49, 0.31, 0.75\}$), or as a female, because there is no direct visual evidence when meeting her that she is a professor. However, this assignment of role is not satisfying to Merribel, as it minimises her self-sentiments of powerfulness within the academic setting. In contrast, if she is going out with a romantic interest who treats her only as a professor, she may feel frustrated as she wishes to be seen outside of that role. In these situations, Merribel will feel like she has to play the role assigned to her by the other person, as not doing so will create significant deflection that is difficult to avoid. Merribel's feelings of inauthenticity when treated as the average of her two identities seems to be a good indication that the noisy-or model may be a more accurate representation of what is happening in this situation at least[3].

Comparing Situational and Fundamental Selves

Once we have the distribution $Pr(\mathbf{s_s})$, we want to compare to an existing distribution describing the fundamental self-sentiment, $Pr(\mathbf{s_f})$ in order to compute the accumulated inauthenticity. Although it may seem intuitive to use Equation 4, when considering distributions, the resulting probabilistic difference will be incorrect [4]. Instead, we want to measure inauthenticity as a function over the sentiment space which is a ratio of the two:

$$\mathbf{i_a}(\mathbf{s}) = ln\left(\frac{Pr(\mathbf{s_s})}{Pr(\mathbf{s_f})}\right) \tag{12}$$

Equation 12 can be used to compute the expected inauthenticity as the integral over the EPA space, s:

$$\mathbb{E}[\mathbf{i_a}] = \int_{\mathbf{s}} \mathbf{i_a}(\mathbf{s})Pr(\mathbf{s_s})d\mathbf{s} \tag{13}$$

We recognize this as the Kullback-Leibler (KL) divergence between $\mathbf{s_f}$ and $\mathbf{s_s}$. This can be used to select an person to interact with in the following way. Suppose our agent already interacted with M different persons, and had learned a situational self-sentiment, $\mathbf{s_s}_j$ for each $j \in \{1 \dots M\}$. Assuming the agent has a fixed fundamental self sentiment, $\mathbf{s_f}$, it would select j^* as the next person to interact with, where

$$j^* = \arg\min_j \left(\int_{\mathbf{s}} ln\left(\frac{Pr(\mathbf{s_s}_j)}{Pr(\mathbf{s_f})}\right) Pr(\mathbf{s_s}_j)d\mathbf{s}\right) \tag{14}$$

Updating fundamental self-sentiments

Finally, we may want to be able to update the fundamental self-sentiment as a function of the history of situational self-sentiments. This would enable agents to learn through social interaction about other agents' more enduring sense of self or personality. We can do this using the following analogue of Equation 8:

$$c_f \sim Bernoulli(\eta_f, 1-\eta_f) \tag{15}$$

$$\mathbf{s_f}' = c_f\mathbf{s_f} + (1-c_f)\mathbf{s_s}' \tag{16}$$

As we expect fundamental self-sentiments to change slowly, we would expect that $\eta_f > \eta$ and is very close to 1.0.

We may find some parts of an individual's self-sentiment decaying faster than others, and this may have a profound impact on interpersonal relations. Take for example, a father-daughter relationship which supports the self-sentiment of

[3]While we have received significant support in personal communication from sociologists for the "noisy-or" model, a social-psychological experiment will need to be carried out to test these models. For example, people could be queried for sentiments of different pairs of identities, and then for the average.

[4]e.g. consider a convolution of two identical distributions, which gives a third distribution with all possible ways of subtracting elements from each.

father for the father and *daughter* for the daughter. Upon leaving home, the daughter's *daughter* identity rapidly diminishes as she engages in fewer interactions with her father, and she has a small η_f value (perhaps brought on by her change of situation). The father's η_f value remains the same though, so his self-sentiment of *father* decreases much less quickly. Thus, a discrepancy is created. The father attempts to resolve the discrepancy (the daughter is not communicating with him enough to support his sense of *father*) by attempting to interact with his daughter. This creates inauthenticity for both people, due to a difference in η_f values.

Simulations

To implement *BayesAct-S* in practice, we make use of the *BayesAct* function $\texttt{SIMULATE}(\mathbf{f}_a, \mathbf{f}_c) \rightarrow (\mathbf{f}_a', \mathbf{f}_c')$[5]. This function is used to map a distribution over agent and client identities, $\mathbf{f}_a$ and $\mathbf{f}_c$, respectively, to another such distribution after a single interaction (agent acts, client acts). There are two cases to be considered: known or unknown *client* identity. If the client identity is known, SIMULATE creates two *BayesAct* Agent instances, one for *agent* and one for the known *client* identity. Two updates then occur: one to update an *agent* simulator, and one to update a (known) *client* simulator. In the second case, the client identity is unknown (a stranger, so $\mathbf{f}_c$ is set to $\mathbf{s}_o$, e.g. the mean of all identities in the lexicon). In this case, SIMULATE only create a single *BayesAct* Agent instance for *agent*, and does a *BayesAct* simulation where the observations on *client* turn are null, so the weights computed are the same for all samples. This is the same as assuming the *client* does the deflection minimizing predictions of the *agent* (with added noise).

A simulation proceeds for T steps, starting with a situational self-sentiment $\mathbf{s_s}$ equal to the fundamental self-sentiment, $\mathbf{s_f}$. After each call to SIMULATE, we update the situational self-sentiment using the resulting $\mathbf{f}_a$ as $\mathbf{s_s}' \leftarrow \eta\mathbf{s_s} + (1-\eta)\mathbf{f}_a$. This is shorthand to mean that $\mathbf{s_s}'$ is distributed according to a probabilistic mixture of $\mathbf{s_s}$ and $\mathbf{f}_a$, with probabilities η and $1-\eta$. In practice, we accomplish this by drawing ηN samples from $Pr(\mathbf{s_s})$ and $(1-\eta)N$ samples from $Pr(\mathbf{f_a})$ to create the distribution $Pr(\mathbf{s_s}')$ represented with N samples. At the end of T steps, we can then look at the situational self-sentiment and see how this has changed based on the interaction.

We will consider the case of a female *agent* with a mixture of two identities, *daughter* (EPA=$[2.73, 1.13, 1.28]$) and *employer* (EPA=$[1.48, 1.93, 0.74]$), with equal proportions (0.5). There are two known client identities: *mother* (EPA=$[3.12, 2.98, 1.44]$ from female or agent perspective) and *employee* (a female, with EPA=$[1.88, 0.05, 0.84]$). We will expect that, when interacting with the *mother*, the *female/employer agent* will end up with a self sentiment focused on *daughter*. In contrast, when interacting with the *employee*, the *female/employer agent* will end up with a self-sentiment focused on *employer*.

Figure 1 shows the results of a simulation with $T = 20$, $\eta = 0.95$, $\eta_f = 1.0$ and with $N = 2000$ samples for the identities in *BayesAct*. The *BayesAct* parameters are: Σ is diagonal with elements 0.1, and Σ_f is diagonal with elements 0.001 for client identity, and 0.01 for agent identity. Thus, we have made the *agent* more *susceptible* to the actions of the *client* than the other way around. The initial variances on agent and client identities are 0.01.

The simulated *client* in SIMULATE uses the heuristic policy of *BayesAct*, since this will be approximately correct for it in any case. This heuristic policy does a one-step lookahead using the normative predictions of the affect control principle (see (Hoey, Schröder, and Alhothali 2013a) for details). The simulated *agent*, on the other hand, *must* use the POMCP-C policy, as the heuristic policy uses an *average* identity to compute the best behaviour. For a person with multiple, simultaneous identities, this will cause problems as the reactions will be for neither one or the other identity.

We see in Figure 1 that interactions with a *mother* identity accentuates the *daughter* self-sentiment, while interactions with a *employee* identity accentuates the *employer* self-sentiment. Interactions with a stranger (unknown identity)creates a sort of middle ground identity.

We can now investigate how the *agent* selects a new in-

[5] *BayesAct* code and videos of simulations are available at bayesact.ca.

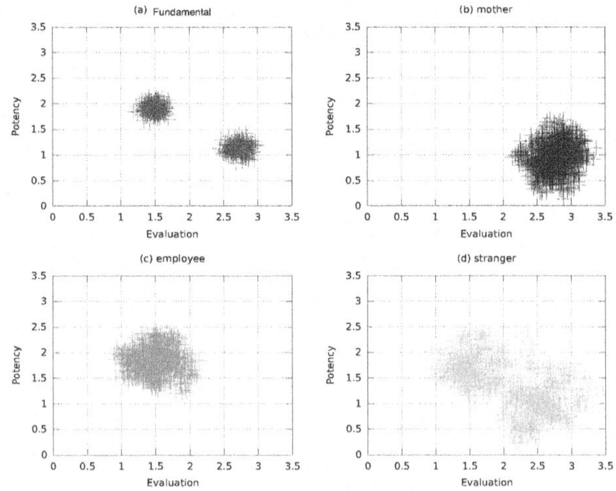

Figure 1: *agent* final self-sentiment after interacting with different *clients*. *agent* starts with the self-sentiment that is mixed between *daughter* (P=1.13) and *employer* (P=1.93). After $T = 20$: (a) fundamental self-sentiment; and after interacting with (b) *mother*; (c) *employee*; (d) a stranger.

	employee	stranger	mother
employee	3.09	2.46	**2.17**
stranger	2.37	2.96	**2.27**
mother	**2.18**	2.38	2.80

Table 1: KL-divergences after $T = 20$ steps. If the daughter/employer *agent* has interacted for 20 steps with the (row) identity, then interacting with the (column) identity will cause the divergence between situational self-sentiments and fundamental self-sentiments as shown. Smaller divergences means the identity is a preferable interactant.

teractant based on the divergence between the situational and fundamental self-sentiments. Given the situational self-sentiment $\mathbf{s_s}$ for each interactant (e.g. as shown in Figure 1), we create a *predicted* situational self-sentiment (that will be achieved by future interactions) by simply creating a mixture of every pair of situational self-sentiments. We then compute the divergence from the fundamental self-sentiment of this mixture, using Equation 14. To compare two belief distributions in practice, we use a nearest-neighbours approach (Perez-Cruz 2008). Table 1 shows the KL-divergences (closer to zero means a more compatible interactant, shown in **boldface**). We see that, after interacting with the *employee* for 20 steps (first row), the *mother* is the most likely interactant. After interacting with a *mother*, however, the best interactant is *employee*. After interacting with a *stranger*, the *agent* will prefer interacting with either *mother* or *employee*, with slight preference for *mother*.

Discussion

The socio-affective model described in this paper is used for fast, heuristic, everyday human interaction: it is what agents can use to "get along" with other agents or humans in a social world. While *BayesAct* (Hoey, Schröder, and Alhothali 2013b; 2013a) integrates this heuristic into a cognitive reasoning engine (a POMDP), *BayesAct-S* (this paper) expands this notion to a societal level, giving agents an intrinsic guide to selecting goals, settings, institutions, and individuals to engage with. In this hierarchy, the high level is reasoning about the self and longer-term goals, while the lower level is considering individual interactions with other agents, guided in part by the affect control principle. Although this could be formalised as a hierarchical POMDP (Theocharous, Rohanimanesh, and Mahadevan 2001), here the higher level simply uses a heuristic policy based on the inauthenticity.

Thus, *BayesAct-S* agents use a novel unification of cognitive (individual) and affective (social) reasoning, but are free to use the cognitive component to model other agents at any level of detail, including as full POMDPs (Doshi and Gmytrasiewicz 2009). Linking the social and individual has relatively recently come into focus in AI research (Castelfranchi 1998), and recent work has looked at unifying appraisal theories of emotions with cognitive reasoning and reinforcement learning. For example, (Hogewoning et al. 2007) links valence with an exploration bonus, and in (Marinier III and Laird 2008), the SOAR cognitive architecture is augmented with a reinforcement learning agent that uses emotional appraisals as intrinsic reward signals.

BayesAct-S is defined with observations and actions in the 3-D EPA space. Therefore, to implement a *BayesAct-S* agent, we require the definition of input and output mappings to translate EPA vectors ($\mathbf{b_a}$) into physical actions and to translate observations of the world into EPA vectors ($\mathbf{F}_b$). These I/O mappings are application dependent. For example, in text-based applications such as the tutoring system in (Hoey, Schröder, and Alhothali 2013b), one may use a semantic analysis of the messages (Pang and Lee 2008). In an embodied agent, one might use facial expressions, gestures or body language measures (Schröder et al. 2013; Lin et al. 2014).

As discussed in (Rogers, Schröder, and von Scheve 2014), affect control theory is conceptually compatible with both dimensional (Russell and Mehrabian 1977) and appraisal (Scherer, Banziger, and Roesch 2010) theories of emotions. The EPA dimensions of affective space can be understood as very basic appraisal rules related to the goal congruence of an event (E), the agent's competence/coping potential (P), and the urgency implied by the situation (A) (Rogers, Schröder, and von Scheve 2014; Rogers, Schröder, and Scholl 2013; Scherer, Dan, and Flykt 2006). However, ACT is also more general and more parsimonious than many appraisal theories, since deflection minimisation is the only prescribed mechanism, while the more specific goals tied to types of agents and situations are assumed to emerge from the semantic knowledge base of the model. Although it is clear that a 3-D vector cannot explain *all* the facets of emotions and identities, this simple scheme has been repeatedly shown to explain roughly 50% of the semantic variability in word association data (Osgood, Suci, and Tannenbaum 1957; Osgood, May, and Miron 1975). The EPA dimensions are also thought to be related directly to intrinsic reward (Fennell and Baddeley 2013). That is, reward is assessed by humans along the same three dimensions: Evaluation roughly corresponds with expected value, Potency with risk (e.g. powerful things are more risky to deal with, because they do what they want (Scholl 2013)), and Activity corresponds roughly with uncertainty, increased risk, and decreased values (e.g. faster more exited things are more risky and less likely to result in reward).

ACT has intellectual origins in symbolic interactionism, a paradigm that emphasizes the importance of semiotic references for the regulation of social interaction (MacKinnon 1994). Recent work has pointed out how the statistical EPA model is compatible with symbolic approaches to social cognition at the societal level as well as notions of embodied "deep meanings" at the level of individual brains. In many ways, the EPA model can be regarded as a "translation" between societal symbols and signals of the body (Schröder and Thagard 2013; Thagard and Schröder 2014).

Conclusion

We have described a probabilistic and decision theoretic generalisation of the *affect control theory of self*, a coherent and well-grounded sociological theory of human social interactions that uses affective descriptions of identities, selves and behaviours. We have shown how this theory can be used to construct socially and emotionally aware agents that can reason about the affective identities of others and use this reasoning to guide their choices of whom to interact with and what to do in each interaction. In future, we plan to apply these concepts in social networking applications, assistive technologies, and to further investigate the usage of external rewards in guiding agent behaviours. We plan to investigate large-scale social simulations based on these concepts. *BayesAct-S* could also substantiate recent developments of a "social physics" (Pentland 2014) by enhancing it with a well-grounded theory of the behaviours of individuals.

Acknowledgments

Thanks to Neil J. MacKinnon, Lynn Smith-Lovin, David R. Heise, and Kimberly B. Rogers for helpful discussions. This work was funded in part by a grant from the Natural Sciences and Engineering Research Council of Canada.

References

Åström, K. J. 1965. Optimal control of Markov decision processes with incomplete state estimation. *J. Math. Anal. App.* 10:174–205.

Ambrasat, J.; von Scheve, C.; Conrad, M.; Schauenburg, G.; and Schröder, T. 2014. Consensus and stratification in the affective meaning of human sociality. *Proceedings of the National Academy of Sciences* 111(22):8001–8006.

Asghar, N., and Hoey, J. 2014. Monte-carlo planning for socially aligned agents using Bayesian affect control theory. Tech. Rep. CS-2014-21, U. of Waterloo School of Computer Science.

Castelfranchi, C. 1998. Modeling social action for AI agents. *Artificial Intelligence* 103:157–182.

Doshi, P., and Gmytrasiewicz, P. 2009. Monte-Carlo sampling methods for approximating interactive POMDPs. *Journal of Artificial Intelligence Research* 34:297–337.

Fennell, J. G., and Baddeley, R. J. 2013. Reward is assessed in three dimensions that correspond to the semantic differential. *PLoS One* 8(2: e55588).

Folsom-Kovarik, J. T.; Sukthankar, G.; and Schatz, S. 2013. Tractable POMDP representations for intelligent tutoring systems. *ACM Trans. Intell. Syst. Technol.* 4(2):29:1–29:22.

Heise, D. R. 2007. *Expressive Order: Confirming Sentiments in Social Actions*. Springer.

Heise, D. R. 2010. *Surveying Cultures: Discovering Shared Conceptions and Sentiments*. Wiley.

Heise, D. R. 2013. Modeling interactions in small groups. *Social Psychology Quarterly* 76:52–72.

Hoey, J.; Boutilier, C.; Poupart, P.; Olivier, P.; Monk, A.; and Mihailidis, A. 2012. People, sensors, decisions: Customizable and adaptive technologies for assistance in healthcare. *ACM Trans. Interact. Intell. Syst.* 2(4):20:1–20:36.

Hoey, J.; Schröder, T.; and Alhothali, A. 2013a. Affect control processes: Intelligent affective interaction using a partially observable Markov decision process. http://arxiv.org/abs/1306.5279.

Hoey, J.; Schröder, T.; and Alhothali, A. 2013b. Bayesian affect control theory. In *Proc. of Intl. Conf. on Affective Computing and Intelligent Interaction*.

Hogewoning, E.; Broekens, J.; Eggermont, J.; ; and Bovenkamp, E. G. 2007. Strategies for affect-controlled action-selection in SOAR-RL. In Mira, J., and Àlvarez, J., eds., *IWINAC*, volume 4528 Part II of *LNCS*, 501–510.

Kahneman, D. 2011. *Thinking, Fast and Slow*. Doubleday.

Lin, L.; Czarnuch, S.; Malhotra, A.; Yu, L.; Schröder, T.; and Hoey, J. 2014. Affectively aligned cognitive assistance using Bayesian affect control theory. In *Proc. of IWAAL*.

MacKinnnon, N. J., and Robinson, D. T. 2014. 25 years of research in affect control theory. *Adv. in Group Processing* 31.

MacKinnon, N. J., and Heise, D. R. 2010. *Self, identity and social institutions*. New York, NY: Palgrave and Macmillan.

MacKinnon, N. J. 1994. *Symbolic Interactionism as Affect Control*. Albany: State University of New York Press.

Marinier III, R. P., and Laird, J. E. 2008. Emotion-driven reinforcement learning. In *Proc. of 30th Annual Meeting of the Cognitive Science Society*, 115–120.

Osgood, C. E.; May, W. H.; and Miron, M. S. 1975. *Cross-Cultural Universals of Affective Meaning*. U. of Illinois Press.

Osgood, C. E.; Suci, G. J.; and Tannenbaum, P. H. 1957. *The Measurement of Meaning*. Urbana: University of Illinois Press.

Pang, B., and Lee, L. 2008. Opinion mining and sentiment analysis. *Foundations and trends in information retrieval* 2.1(2):1–135.

Pentland, A. 2014. *Social Physics*. Penguin Press.

Perez-Cruz, F. 2008. Kullback-Leibler divergence estimation of continuous distributions. In *IEEE International Symposium on Information Theory (ISIT)*, 1666–1670.

Rogers, K. B.; Schröder, T.; and Scholl, W. 2013. The affective structure of stereotype content: Behavior and emotion in intergroup context. *Social Psychology Quarterly* 76:125–150.

Rogers, K. B.; Schröder, T.; and von Scheve, C. 2014. Dissecting the sociality of emotion: A multi-level approach. *Emotion Review* 6(2):124–133.

Russell, J. A., and Mehrabian, A. 1977. Evidence for a three-factor theory of emotions. *Journal of research in Personality* 11(3):273–294.

Scherer, K. R.; Banziger, T.; and Roesch, E. 2010. *A Blueprint for Affective Computing*. Oxford University Press.

Scherer, K. R.; Dan, E. S.; and Flykt, A. 2006. What determines a feeling's position in affective space: A case for appraisal. *Cognition and Emotion* 20(1):92–113.

Scholl, W. 2013. The socio-emotional basis of human interaction and communication: How we construct our social world. *Social Science Information* 52:3 – 33.

Schröder, T., and Scholl, W. 2009. Affective dynamics of leadership: An experimental test of affect control theory. *Social Psychology Quarterly* 72:180–197.

Schröder, T., and Thagard, P. 2013. The affective meanings of automatic social behaviors: Three mechanisms that explain priming. *Psychological Review* 120:255–280.

Schröder, T.; Netzel, J.; Schermuly, C.; and Scholl, W. 2013. Culture-constrained affective consistency of interpersonal behavior: A test of affect control theory with nonverbal expressions. *Social Psychology* 44:47–58.

Smith-Lovin, L. 2007. The strength of weak identities: Social structural sources of self, situation and emotional experience. *Social Psychology Quarterly* 70(2):106–124.

Thagard, P., and Schröder, T. 2014. Emotions as semantic pointers: Constructive neural mechanisms. In Barrett, L. F., and Russell, J., eds., *The psychological construction of emotion*. New York: Guilford.

Theocharous, G.; Rohanimanesh, K.; and Mahadevan, S. 2001. Learning hierarchical partially observed Markov decision process models for robot navigation. In *IEEE Intl. Conf. on Robotics and Automation*.

Williams, J. D., and Young, S. 2006. Partially observable Markov decision processes for spoken dialog systems. *Computer Speech and Language* 21(2):393–422.

Heuristic Induction of Rate-Based Process Models

Pat Langley and **Adam Arvay**
Department of Computer Science, University of Auckland,
Private Bag 92019, Auckland 1142, New Zealand

Abstract

This paper presents a novel approach to inductive process modeling, the task of constructing a quantitative account of dynamical behavior from time-series data and background knowledge. We review earlier work on this topic, noting its reliance on methods that evaluate entire model structures and use repeated simulation to estimate parameters, which together make severe computational demands. In response, we present an alternative method for process model induction that assumes each process has a rate, that this rate is determined by an algebraic expression, and that changes due to a process are directly proportional to its rate. We describe RPM, an implemented system that incorporates these ideas, and we report analyses and experiments that suggest it scales well to complex domains and data sets. In closing, we discuss related research and outline ways to extend the framework.

1 Background and Motivation

Reasoning about scientific domains is a high-level cognitive task that is widely viewed as requiring considerable intelligence. Over the past three decades, research on computational scientific discovery (Shrager and Langley 1990; Džeroski and Todorovski 2007) has addressed a variety of tasks that arise in the pursuit of knowledge. Efforts in this paradigm are distinguished from mainstream work in data mining and machine learning by producing content stated in established scientific formalisms, ranging from componential models in particle physics to causal diagrams in genetics and to reaction pathways in biochemistry.

Much of the research in this area has focused on equation discovery, which has played a key role in the history of science and which has clear applications in many different disciplines. However, this task often arises in the early stages of a field's development, before theoretical knowledge supports the creation of explanatory models that account for observations in deeper terms. The task of explanatory model construction has received less attention from computational researchers, but there has been some progress on this topic.

One important form of such tasks, known as *inductive process modeling* (Langley et al. 2002), accepts generic knowledge about processes that can occur in a domain and time-series data for a number of variables. The aim is to find a concrete model, including numeric parameters, that reproduces their trajectories over time and makes accurate predictions for new values. One can compile this model into a set of differential equations, but it also explains observations in terms of underlying processes. This distinguishes the paradigm from other work on modeling time series, including alternative methods for finding differential equations.

In the sections that follow, we review drawbacks of previous efforts on inductive process modeling, focusing on their computational expense and problems with parameter estimation. In response, we present a new approach to process model induction that adopts representational assumptions which let it carry out heuristic rather than exhaustive search through the space of model structures, making it both more efficient and more reliable. We also describe an implemented system that incorporates these ideas, and we report experimental studies that demonstrate its ability to identify relevant processes, handle noisy observations, and construct accurate models that relate many variables. We conclude by discussing our framework's relation to earlier work and proposing responses to its limitations.

2 Critique of Process Modeling Research

Research on inductive process modeling has made continual progress since its first appearance over a decade ago (Langley et al. 2002). Advances have included adding the ability to incorporate hierarchical knowledge (Todorovski et al. 2005), handle missing values (Bridewell et al. 2006), combine models without losing interpretability (Bridewell et al. 2005), incorporate constraints to reduce search (Bridewell and Langley 2010), and even learn such constraints from sample models (Bridewell and Todorovski 2007). The framework has been applied to model construction in ecology (Asgharbeygi et al. 2006), hydrology (Bridewell et al. 2008), and biochemistry (Langley et al. 2006). Despite this progress, research has been hampered by three key features of the induction algorithms used to date.

The first characteristic is that, even though process models are compositional in nature, current algorithms evaluate only complete model structures. This evaluation involves comparing a parameterized model's predictions with observed time series. Existing systems generate many model structures up to a given complexity level, then parameterize and evaluate each candidate in turn. This approach does not support heuristic search through the space of model structures. Runs on domains that involve small sets of variables and generic processes have produced a few thousand model structures, which is computationally tractable. But the number of structures grows exponentially with the number of variables and generic processes, even with constraints, which means the standard approach will not scale.

Another drawback is that existing algorithms rely on repeated simulation to estimate parameters for each model structure. They start with values selected randomly within a given range for each parameter, simulate the parameterized model, and calculate error with respect to observed values. These methods use the error gradient to revise parameters, simulate the new model, and continue until improvements cease, indicating they have reached a local optimum. Hundreds of iterations are not uncommon, so that repeated simulations to guide search through parameter space dominate processing. In most runs, 99.99 percent of the CPU time is taken by running simulations for parameter estimation.

Finally, even with this expensive iteration for parameter estimation, the local optima found by traditional techniques may not fit the observed time series very well. To ensure arrival at reasonable parameters, they have resorted to repeated restarts from different random values. For some parameter spaces, ten restarts suffices to produce reasonable results, but informal experiments suggest that, in some cases, more than a hundred restarts are needed for reliable estimation. This further adds to the computational burden and, again, it must be borne separately for each distinct model structure.

Taken together, these features have made previous approaches to process model induction computationally expensive in the extreme, effectively limiting both the complexity of the models and the size of the data sets they can address. Moreover, even with extensive computation, problems with local optima mean that existing methods are not as reliable as one would desire. This suggests the need for a new approach to finding process models that is more tractable and reliable than existing alternatives.

3 Heuristic Induction of Process Models

To address these issues, we have developed a new approach to inducing process models that, we maintain, should be far more efficient and robust than its predecessors. In this section, we present some assumptions that constrain the induction task substantially. After this, we describe RPM, an implemented system that takes advantage of these assumptions in its operation. Finally, we make some high-level theoretical claims about the framework.

3.1 Simplifying Assumptions

To make the model induction task more tractable, we first restrict our notation, assuming that all processes concern changes over time and that they effect these changes at a specific *rate*. Chemical reactions are one obvious example of this idea; a given reaction involves the same substances, but its rate of operation can vary over time. Earlier work on inductive process modeling has included purely algebraic processes that describe instantaneous relations, which we hold are contrary to the notion of a process.

Second, we assume that each process has one or more associated derivatives and, moreover, that these are directly proportional to its rate. For instance, a chemical reaction that combines two substances, C_1 and C_2, to produce a third, C_3, has three derivative expressions of the form $dC_i/dt = k \times R$, where R is the rate and k is a constant parameter. We can distinguish between variables that are *inputs* to a process, which it consumes and thus have negative coefficients in their expressions, and variables that are *outputs*, which a process produces and thus have positive coefficients. This does not mean these variables always increase or decrease over time, since other processes may also influence them.

Third, we assume that the rate of each process is determined by a parameter-free algebraic expression. In some chemical reactions, this expression is the product of the concentrations of the input substances. For instance, the rate at which two substances react, given concentrations C_1 and C_2, might be $C_1 \times C_2$, whereas one in which three substances react might be $C_1 \times C_2 \times C_3$. We assume that rates are always positive and inherently unobservable, so we can adopt any measurement scale we like, avoiding the need for coefficients. Some rate equations, like the 'monod' expression $X/(k+X)$ in biochemical models, include parameters. For now, we will exclude these from our framework, but we will return to them when discussing future research.

Fourth, we assume that, if a variable appears in the rate expression for a process, then it must also appear in a derivative expression associated with that process. For instance, if the rate equation for a process is $X \times Y$, this means it must include derivative expressions for both X and Y, possibly along with ones for other variables. This rules out 'gratuitous' processes with terms that influence rates but are not affected in turn. At first glance, this appears to cause difficulty for chemical reactions that involve catalysts, but we can treat them as special cases in which the proportionality coefficient for derivative equations are near zero.

The simple model for a predator-prey ecosystem in Table 1 illustrates these ideas. Each process has an associated rate expression, one specifying that the rate equals the product of two variables and the others stating that it equals a single variable. Each process also has one or more associated derivatives that are directly proportional to the rate, with parameters detailing this dependence. Finally, every term that appears in the rate expression for a process also appears in some derivative expression. Generic processes take a similar form but utilize typed variables. These assumptions constrain considerably the process models that are possible, although one can still state a large number of such structures.

Our notation borrows heavily from Forbus' (1984) Qualitative Process theory. Rates also played a key role in his framework, with an algebraic rate expression corresponding to a set of indirect influences in a qualitative process. Moreover, each equation that relates a derivative to a rate maps onto a direct influence in a qualitative process. Forbus' framework could have multiple rates per process and ours allows only one, but otherwise they are very similar.

A final issue concerns not the structure of process models but the data available to induce them. For reasons that will become apparent shortly, we assume that observations

Table 1: A three-process model for a system involving the predator *Nasutum* and the prey *Aurelia* that illustrates our framework's assumptions. Each process has a rate determined by an algebraic expression and includes one or more derivatives that are proportional to this rate.

```
exponential_change[aurelia]
  rate          r = aurelia
  parameters    A = 0.75
  equations     d[aurelia] = A × r
exponential_change[nasutum]
  rate          r = nasutum
  parameters    B = -0.57
  equations     d[nasutum] = B × r
holling_predation[nasutum, aurelia]
  rate          r = nasutum × aurelia
  parameters    C = 0.0024
                D = -0.011
  equations     d[nasutum] = C × r
                d[aurelia] = D × r
```

are given for all variables to be included in candidate models. Some early work in the paradigm (e.g., Langley et al. 2002) took the same position, but many recent efforts (e.g., Bridewell et al. 2008) explicitly attempt to handle unobserved terms. This is one reason they require simulation of full models to estimate parameters, as it lets them calculate values for such terms. This makes our approach more limited, but early work on induction of decision trees and Bayesian networks relied on analogous simplifications, and we discuss ways to move beyond it later in the paper.

3.2 A Regression-Guided Process Modeler

We have incorporated these ideas into RPM, a new system for inductive process modeling that uses the assumptions to constrain search and make the discovery task tractable. The system inputs a set of typed variables,[1] a subset of these variables to be predicted, a set of generic processes in the form just described, and an observed time series for each variable. The program returns a model stated as a set of differential equations, one for each dependent variable, that predicts the corresponding derivative as a linear combination of process rates. If it cannot find acceptable equations for some variables, it returns a partial model.

Before it begins to search, RPM takes a number of initialization steps. First it uses the task variables to instantiate the generic processes in all ways that are consistent with the latters' type constraints. For instance, suppose the modeling task involves three variables, A, B, and C, where A has type prey, B has type prey or predator, and C has type predator. Further suppose that the generic process *holling_predation* includes two generic variables, X and Y, where the first has type *prey* and the second *predator*. In this case, RPM would generate three instances of *holling_predation*, one with X bound to A and Y bound to B, one with X bound to A and Y bound to C, and one with X bound to B and Y bound to C. The result is a set of process instances, each with an instantiated rate expression and derivative terms.

Next, the system estimates the derivatives for each dependent variable on each time step. For this purpose, it uses the 'center difference' method, which calculates the derivative for variable X at time t as the average of $X(t) - X(t-1)$ and $X(t+1) - X(t)$. This produces a trajectory, over time, of estimated derivatives for each dependent variable. RPM also uses the observed time series to calculate rates for each such process instance. If the third process instance just discussed has the rate expression $B \times C$, then RPM would multiply B by C at each time to obtain the associated process rate. The assumption that rates are parameter-free algebraic functions of observed variables lets it make this calculation for each candidate process instance. The result is a trajectory, over time, of the rate for each instantiated process.

RPM then iterates through the dependent variables, attempting to find a differential equation for each one that predicts its observed changes as a function of process rates. For each variable D, it considers only those process instances P that include D as a dependent term, as others would not make appropriate predictors. The system then examines, in turn, each linear equation of the form $D = a \times P$, using linear regression to calculate the parameter a. If the r^2 for any of these equations exceeds a user-specified threshold, then RPM adds the best candidate to its model and examines the next dependent variable. If not, then it considers all pairs of process instances, P_1 and P_2, in which D is a dependent term and considers each linear equation of the form $D = a \times P_1 + b \times P_2$. For this it uses multiple linear regression to estimate the parameters a and b. Again, if some equation's r^2 exceeds the threshold, the system adds the best to the model. Otherwise, it examines triples of processes, and so on, continuing until reaching a user-specified maximum.

In summary, RPM carries out a sequential form of greedy search through the space of process models, in that once it selects an equation for one variable, it cannot change its mind. This means that, if more than one equation produces acceptable r^2 values, the system may make an incorrect choice that will cause it difficulty later. Nevertheless, greedy search is highly efficient when its heuristics guide search down useful paths, and more efficient induction of process models is one of our primary concerns.

Knowledge about processes modulates search for individual equations in four complementary ways. First, RPM groups generic processes into types, such as *predation* and *organism loss*. Different processes in the same class relate the same number and types of variables but differ in their algebraic rate expressions. RPM only considers models that contain at most one process instance of each type with the same arguments. Suppose we have two generic predation processes that relate a predator population X with a prey population Y, one with rate $X \times Y$ and another with X/Y. Suppose we have two variables, A and B, the first a predator and the second a prey. This gives two process instances – $predation(A, B)$ with rate $A \times B$ and $predation(A, B)$ with rate A/B – which RPM treats as mutually exclusive, ensuring no model structure contains more than one.

[1]Type constraints are disjunctive, in that a given variable may have more than one possible type, say either predator or prey.

Second, generic processes may include numeric constraints on the parameters that appear in proportionality equations. For instance, predation processes specify that the predator's coefficient must be positive, whereas that for the prey must be negative, indicating predation causes the predator's population to increase and the prey's to decrease. Once RPM finds an equation for a variable with an acceptable fit, it checks the equation's parameters to see if they satisfy its associated processes' constraints. If not, then it abandons the equation and continues to look for other candidates. In cases where an organism may be either a predator or a prey, the system will find two equations that fit the data equally well, but only one will have parameters with the correct signs.

Third, if RPM incorporates a process P into the equation for one dependent variable, say D_1, that includes another variable, say D_2, then it must include P in all equations that it later considers for predicting D_2. These constraints reduce the number of process combinations RPM considers when searching for later equations. In some cases, given the user-specified limit on the number of processes allowed, it fully determines an equation's form, eliminating search entirely.

Finally, to make such constraints more effective, the system utilizes information about earlier equations to decide which variable to focus on next. For each variable not yet incorporated into the model, it calculates the number of processes in which it already appears. RPM then selects the one that takes part in the most processes (breaking ties at random), as it will have more terms in its equation determined. This is similar to selection of the most constrained variable in work on constraint satisfaction. Unless the data set can be partitioned into subsets of variables that do not interact, this heuristic further reduces the search needed to find equations.

Together, these techniques limit greatly the number of model structures that RPM entertains during its discovery efforts. They make the difference between tractable heuristic search and the intractable methods used in previous systems.

3.3 Theoretical Claims

Based on our earlier observations, we can make a number of theoretical claims about the new approach to process model induction and our implementation of its ideas.

- RPM should duplicate previous methods' abilities to identify the structure of process models and distinguish irrelevant processes from ones that, taken together, account for the observed trajectories.
- Because the system estimates parameters for each equation separately, and without relying on repeated simulation of complete models, it should be far more efficient computationally.
- RPM's reliance on multiple linear regression, a statistical technique with an ability to tolerate noise and low variance, should let it avoid local optima at the equation level and find parameters that fit the data well.
- Heuristic search through the structure space should let the system scale well to models of high complexity, providing they are sparsely connected in that each variable is influenced by only a few processes.

If these claims hold true, then RPM should be far more effective at inducing process models than systems that have previously addressed this challenging class of problems.

4 Evaluation of the Approach

A complexity analysis of the new approach is encouraging even in the worst case. Let V be the number of variables, P the number of generic processes, S the number of samples, k the maximum number of variables in a process, and j the maximum number of processes in an equation. The total number of process instances $I = P \times V!/(V-K)!$, but RPM only considers process instances in which a given variable appears, meaning the number in play for each equation is at most $I' = P \times (V!/(V-K)! - (V-1)!/(V-K-1)!)$. This gives $J' = I'!/(J! \times (I'-J)!)$ as the maximum number of equations considered for each variable, leading to $S \times V \times J'$ as the total time complexity. Assuming $k = 3$ and $j = 3$, which are reasonable values, J' is approximated by $P^3 \times V^{7.4}$, giving an effective complexity of $S \times P^3 \times V^{8.4}$. However, this analysis ignores our heuristics' role in guiding the selection of variables and search for equations, so we have also studied our method's empirical behavior.

4.1 Empirical Behavior on Natural Data

To demonstrate RPM's relevance to natural science, our initial runs focused on published data about a simple predator-prey ecosystem (Veilleux 1979). These involve 26 samples of two protozoa – *Nasutum* and *Aurelia* – with the former preying on the latter, as their populations vary over time. Earlier methods for inductive process modeling have reported reasonable results on these time-series data (Bridewell et al. 2008). Our purpose here was not to claim superiority, but simply to show that our new mechanism for constructing process models produces accurate and plausible explanations for actual scientific data.

When provided with these data and two generic processes, one for predation and another for exponential loss/growth, RPM induces the model shown earlier in Table 1. This maps onto the equation $d[aurelia] = 0.75 \times aurelia + -0.011 \times nasutum \times aurelia$, for which r^2 is 0.84, and $d[nasutum] = 0.0024 \times nasutum \times aurelia + -0.57 \times nasutum$, for which r^2 is 0.71. Figure 1 plots the observed trajectories and the simulated ones produced when we provided these equations to a differential equation solver. The model does not reproduce the observed trajectories perfectly, but it does capture the peaks and troughs, offset slightly. This result is encouraging, as RPM evaluates equations based on prediction of observed derivatives, not on the trajectories themselves, as did its predecessors. If reproducing trajectories is important, one could use gradient descent through parameter space with estimated coefficients as starting points.

4.2 Induction with Irrelevant Processes

We also desire to demonstrate that RPM does not confuse relevant process instances with irrelevant ones when searching the space of model structures. To this end, we provided the system with eight additional generic processes for the predator-prey domain. These differed from the original ones in the algebraic expression that determines each process rate.

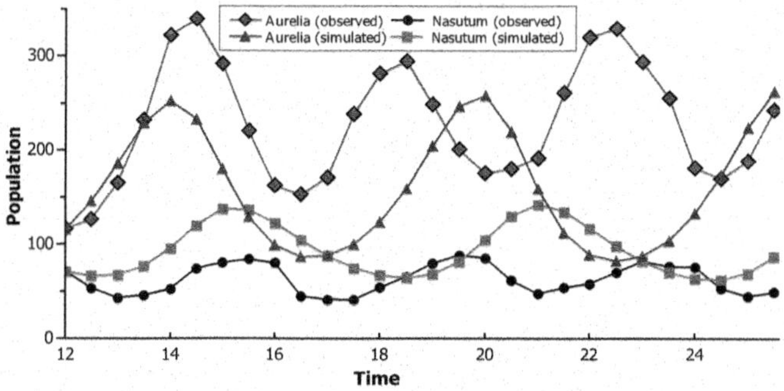

Figure 1: Observed and simulated trajectories for a predator-prey system involving the protozoa *Nasutum* and *Aurelia*.

We included four alternative algebraic forms for individual loss/growth of an organism and another four alternative forms for predation. On runs with the natural data for *Nasutum* and *Aurelia*, as well as on synthetic data generated using the X and $X \times Y$ rate terms, RPM found the same process models as before. This suggests the system can distinguish relevant processes from irrelevant ones effectively.

Because we are centrally concerned with efficient induction, we also measured RPM's run time when presented with different numbers of irrelevant processes. Figure 2 plots the CPU seconds required as a function of the number of generic processes, starting with two relevant ones and adding two irrelevant ones on each increment. The growth in computation time appears to be greater than linear, but the overall behavior still scales reasonably well with the number of irrelevant processes and much better than our worst-case analysis.

4.3 Handling Noise and Complex Models

In addition, we examined RPM's ability to handle noisy observations. This is especially important given the system's focus on finding equations that predict estimated derivatives, as taking differences between succssive observed values can magnify noise substantially. For instance, when we added five percent noise to synthetic data for the five predator-prey system, 0.28 was the highest r^2 value found for any derivative, and RPM could distinguish only some of the target equations from alternative forms. However, when we smoothed the observed values using locally weighted regression (Cleveland 1979), the system found all target equations without difficulty, even when the noise level was ten percent and we provided the irrelevant processes described above. This suggests that preprocessing with simple and inexpensive smoothing techniques will suffice for the approach to handle substantial amounts of observational noise.

Moreover, because we wanted to demonstrate that our approach can induce process models that involve many variables, we ran RPM on a synthetic predator-prey data set with 20 organisms. The target model corresponded to a linear food chain in which organism 20 preys on organism 19, which in turn preys on organism 18, and so forth, with organism 1 at the bottom. The model augmented these 19 predation processes with an exponential growth process for organism 1 and an exponential loss process for organism 20.

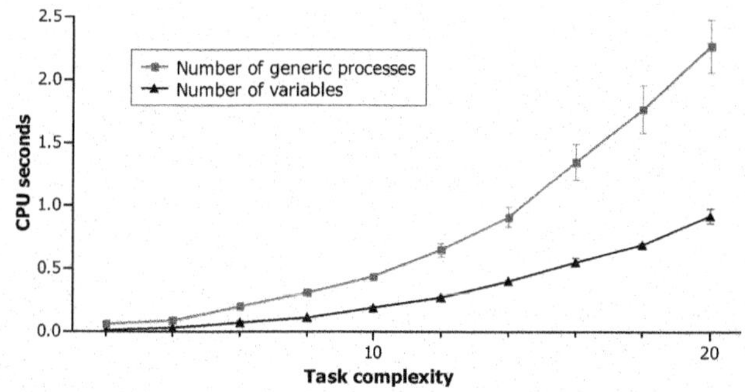

Figure 2: RPM's processing time as a function of the number of generic processes, given five variables, and as a function of the number of variables, given two generic processes.

RPM identifies correctly the structure of the target model from noise-free data involving 236 samples. The system generates 400 process instances, but it considers only 1,483 equation structures during search because those found for early variables constrain both which processes to incorporate and which variables to examine next. Earlier systems that carry out nonheuristic search through the structure space would have great difficulty finding models of this complexity. We also systematically varied the number of variables and recorded CPU time. Figure 2 shows this grows at a reasonable rate, indicating the heuristics provide average-case behavior far better than our worst-case analysis.

4.4 Comparison to SC-IPM

Finally, we ran a comparison between RPM and SC-IPM (Bridewell and Langley 2010), an earlier system for inducing process models from time series, on synthetic data generated from a known target. The target model involved three organisms that interact through two predation processes in a single food chain, with one process for growth and another for loss at either end. We provided both systems with 100 observations for each of these simulated variables and analogous background knowledge about generic processes.

SC-IPM has two parameters that RPM lacks: the number of model structures it considers and the number of times it restarts gradient descent during parameter estimation. Higher values improve the system's chances of finding a good model but also increase its processing time. We held the first parameter constant at 600, which seemed sufficient to ensure SC-IPM examines the target structure, and varied the second from 10 to 150 restarts. In each case, we recorded run time and mean squared error on the training data.

Figure 3 plots SC-IPM's performance on these dimensions, along with the time and error for ten RPM runs. The results are umambiguous. RPM finds very accurate models reliably, whereas SC-IPM induces ones with comparable accuracy rarely even on its most expensive runs. Moreover, although both are written in Lisp, RPM finds these models more than *83,000 times faster* than even the most rapid SC-IPM runs. Rather than examining 600 model structures, RPM considered only 21 equations, each of which it fit using multiple linear regression rather than gradient descent.

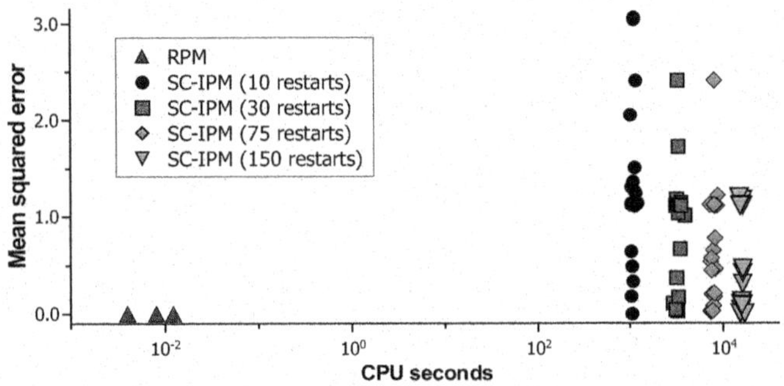

Figure 3: Processing time vs. error for RPM and SC-IPM with different number of restarts for gradient descent search.

These experimental results, taken together, offer support for our claims that the new approach induces accurate process models in a computationally tractable manner. The system responds well to irrelevant processes, noisy observations, and substantial model complexity, and it compares very favorably to a representative earlier system in both reliability and processing time.

5 Related Research

The approach to inductive process modeling we have reported here incorporates ideas from earlier efforts, but it also introduces novel features that distinguish it from predecessors. The framework draws directly from Forbus' (1984) early work on qualitative process theory, which also encodes scientific accounts as sets of interacting processes. Our reliance on quantitative processes is not unique; the representational innovation lies in reformulating processes in terms of algebraic expressions that determine rates and in terms of derivatives that are proportional to these rates. The resulting class of models still have broad coverage, but they are far more amenable to computational discovery.

We have already discussed earlier work on inductive process modeling, but not related research on discovering differential equation models from time series. We will not review traditional work on system identification, which assumes functional forms and focuses on parameter estimation. However, Džeroski and Todorovski's (1995) LaGrange system searches the space of functional forms, and the closely related LaGramge (Todorovski and Džeroski 1995) uses grammatical knowledge to inform this search. Bradley et al.'s (2001) PRET addresses the same task, analyzing qualitative regularities in data to limit the structures it considers. Genetic programming methods (e.g., Koza et al., 2001; Schmidt & Lipson, 2009) use evolutionary search techniques, with more recent systems sampling data to avoid overfitting, but they search a larger space of differential equations, making them less scalable and more likely to produce uninterpretable models. LaGrange comes closest to our approach, constructing equations for each derivative as linear functions of algebraic expressions, but, like other systems, does not incorporate processes to constrain search.

We should also note that Srividhya et al. (2007) report a related approach to inducing differential-equation models for biochemical pathways, which we discovered only after developing RPM. This uses knowledge about types of reactions to generate candidate equation structures, which it then fits to estimated derivatives of chemical concentrations. Their method also invokes multiple linear regression to find coefficients and pursues greedy search for model structures. Their system also favors equations with fewer terms, but it does not use heuristics to order variables or require that later equations be consistent with earlier ones. It also relies on chemical constraints about numbers of molecules in reactions, making it less general than our framework.

6 Limitations and Future Work

Our experimental results suggest that the new approach to process model induction can find accurate and plausible models in reasonable amounts of time. However, this behavior relies on some assumptions that we should aim to relax in our future analyses and implementations.

The framework's requirement that processes comprise an algebraic rate expression and derivatives proportional to this rate is useful but not very limiting. However, the assumption that rate expressions be parameter-free, which it uses to calculate rates from variables, means it cannot encode some models that earlier systems considered. In future work, we plan to weaken this restriction by allowing one parameter per rate equation and using the reliable LMS algorithm to estimate their values. One parameter per process means each linear differential equation has at most one free parameter per term. For a given equation, the extended RPM could make an initial guess about these parameter values, then use the LMS method to iteratively revise them, using r^2 as an error metric. This should let us handle many parameterized rate expressions, including the monod function that is used widely in ecology and biochemistry.

We should also explore replacing the greedy search method through the space of model structures with beam search. Experience with RPM suggests that, when observed trajectories are reasonably flat, multiple equations have similar r^2 scores. Beam search would let the system retain multiple equations for each variable, delaying decisions about which to retain until it has acquired information about equations for other variables. This should also reduce reliance on the r^2 threshold, which we currently tune manually to a level appropriate for the data set being analyzed.

We have seen that RPM's adoption of heuristic search lets it induce reasonably complex models, but it still uses an exhaustive method to find individual equations, at least in its early stages. True scalability to hundreds or thousands of equations will also require heuristic construction of differential equations for each dependent variable. The natural response is to adapt greedy forward-search techniques for feature selection (Blum and Langley 1997), but relations among process rates, which can share variables, make r^2 an unreliable metric for the usefulness of individual terms. We must identify more informative guides to support effective heuristic search through the space of component equations.

Finally, we must extend the framework to induce process models even when some variables remain unobserved. We assumed fully observable domains because, combined with parameter-free rate expressions, it let our mechanism use linear regression to find each equation in a model separately from others. This was the key source of RPM's scalability to complex models, but in future work we should move beyond this restriction. Following Bridewell et al. (2006), we can handle occasional missing values using an iterative-optimization scheme, but the more challenging case concerns entirely unobserved variables. Our assumption that derivatives depend on linear combinations of process rates should let us extend that approach to such cases, but whether it retains good convergence properties is an open question.

7 Concluding Remarks

In this paper, we critiqued earlier research on inductive process modeling, which involves constructing differential equation accounts of time series from knowledge about generic processes. We also presented a new approach to this task, and its implementation in the RPM system, that builds on some important assumptions. These included associating with each process a rate that is determined by a parameter-free algebraic equation, along with one or more derivatives that are directly proportional to this rate. We argued that this constrained framework should be more tractable computationally and more robust on parameter estimation.

We presented a complexity analysis that shows the new approach should scale reasonably to induction tasks that involve irrelevant processes and target models with many variables. More important, we showed encouraging experimental results on both natural and synthetic data. In the latter case, we demonstrated that RPM can ignore irrelevant processes, handle noisy data when aided by standard smoothing techniques, and scale well enough to induce process models with 20 variables. In addition to these promising findings, we outlined steps to overcome our simpliying assumptions that should broaden the coverage and applicability of the modeling framework's future implementations.

Acknowledgements

This research reported here was supported in part by ONR Grant N00014-11-1-0107. We thank Will Bridewell, Sašo Džeroski, Rich Morin, Son To, and Ljupčo Todorovski for discussions that led to the approach we have described.

References

Asgharbeygi, N.; Langley, P.; Bay, S.; and Arrigo, K. 2006. Inductive revision of quantitative process models. *Ecological Modelling* 194:70–79.

Blum, A.; and Langley, P. 1997. Selection of relevant features and examples in machine learning. *Artificial Intelligence* 97:245–271.

Bradley, E.; Easley, M.; and Stolle, R. 2001. Reasoning about nonlinear system identification. *Artificial Intelligence* 133:139–188.

Bridewell, W.; Bani Asadi, N.; Langley, P.; and Todorovski, L. 2005. Reducing overfitting in process model induction. In *Proceedings of the Twenty-Second International Conference on Machine Learning*, 81–88. Bonn, Germany.

Bridewell, W.; Langley P.; Racunas, S.; and Borrett, S. R. 2006. Learning process models with missing data. In *Proceedings of the Seventeenth European Conference on Machine Learning*, 557–565. Berlin:Springer.

Bridewell, W.; and Langley, P. 2010. Two kinds of knowledge in scientific discovery. *Topics in Cognitive Science* 2:36–52.

Bridewell, W.; Langley, P.; Todorovski, L.; and Džeroski, S. 2008. Inductive process modeling. *Machine Learning* 71:1–32.

Bridewell, W.; and Todorovski, L. 2007. Learning declarative bias. In *Proceedings of the Seventeenth Annual International Conference on Inductive Logic Programming*, 63–77. Corvallis, OR:Springer.

Cleveland, W. S. 1979. Robust locally weighted regression and smoothing scatterplots. *Journal of the American Statistical Association* 74:829-836.

Džeroski, S.; and Todorovski, L. (Eds.) 2007. *Computational discovery of communicable scientific knowledge*. Berlin: Springer.

Džeroski, S.; and Todorovski, L. 1995. Discovering dynamics: From inductive logic programming to machine discovery. *Journal of Intelligent Information Systems* 4:89-108.

Forbus, K. D. (1984). Qualitative process theory. *Artificial Intelligence, 24*, 85–168.

Koza, J. R.; Mydlowec, W.; Lanza, G.; Yu, J.; and Keane, M. A. 2001. Reverse engineering of metabolic pathways from observed data using genetic programming. *Pacific Symposium on Biocomputing* 6:434–445.

Langley, P.; Sánchez, J.; Todorovski, L.; and Džeroski, S. 2002. Inducing process models from continuous data. In *Proceedings of the Nineteenth International Conference on Machine Learning*, 347–354. San Francisco: Morgan Kaufmann.

Langley, P.; Shiran, O.; Shrager, J.; Todorovski, L.; and Pohorille, A. 2006. Constructing explanatory process models from biological data and knowledge. *Artificial Intelligence in Medicine* 37:191–201.

Schmidt, M.; and Lipson, H. 2009. Distilling free-form natural laws from experimental data. *Science* 324:81–85.

Shrager, J.; and Langley, P. (Eds.) 1990. *Computational models of scientific discovery and theory formation*. San Mateo, CA: Morgan Kaufmann.

Srividhya, J.; Crampin, E. J.; McSharry, P. E.; and Schnell, S. 2007. Reconstructing biochemical pathways from time course data. *Proteomics* 7:828–838.

Todorovski, L.; Bridewell, W.; Shiran, O.; and Langley, P. 2005. Inducing hierarchical process models in dynamic domains. In *Proceedings of the Twentieth National Conference on Artificial Intelligence*, 892–897. Pittsburgh: AAAI Press.

Todorovski, L.; and Džeroski, S. 1997. Declarative bias in equation discovery. In *Proceedings of the Fourteenth International Conference on Machine Learning*, 376–384. Nashville, TN: Morgan Kaufmann.

Veilleux, B. G. 1979. An analysis of predatory interaction between paramecium and didinium. *Journal of Animal Ecology* 48:787-803.

Spontaneous Retrieval from Long-Term Memory for a Cognitive Architecture

Justin Li and **John Laird**
University of Michigan
2260 Hayward Street
Ann Arbor, MI 48109-2121
{justinnh, laird}@umich.edu

Abstract

This paper presents the first functional evaluation of spontaneous, uncued retrieval from long-term memory in a cognitive architecture. The key insight is that current deliberate cued retrieval mechanisms require the agent to have knowledge of when and what to retrieve — knowledge that may be missing or incorrect. Spontaneous uncued retrieval eliminates these requirements through automatic retrievals that use the agent's problem solving context as a heuristic for relevance, thus supplementing deliberate cued retrieval. Using constraints derived from this insight, we sketch the space of spontaneous retrieval mechanisms and describe an implementation of spontaneous retrieval in Soar together with an agent that takes advantage of that mechanism. Empirical evidence is provided in the Missing Link word-puzzle domain, where agents using spontaneous retrieval out-perform agents without that capability, leading us to conclude that spontaneous retrieval can be a useful mechanism and is worth further exploration.

Introduction

In almost every cognitive architecture, there is a distinction between short-term (working) memory and long-term declarative memory, and the mechanisms that transfer knowledge between the two have been a topic of study since cognitive architectures existed (Raaijmakers and Shiffrin 1981). Although many long-term memory mechanisms have been explored, one remains curiously unexamined: that of a mechanism which automatically (*spontaneously*) retrieves knowledge from long-term memory to short-term memory.

This is surprising, as human involuntary memory has been recognized since the first systematic studies of memory (Ebbinghaus 1913), and has continued to receive attention up to the present day (Kvavilashvili and Mandler 2004; Hintzman 2011). Its utility for artificial agents, however, has not been evaluated. This is likely due to the success of deliberate retrievals, and agent designers' preference for mechanisms whose behavior they can specify precisely. The inherent unpredictability of spontaneous retrievals, both in when the retrieval occurs and in what memory is returned, may make it difficult to design agents that can effectively use such a mechanism without compromising task performance. Furthermore, it is difficult to imagine the circumstances under which spontaneous retrieval would out-perform an agent with top-down control of its memory.

This paper takes the first step in exploring how spontaneous retrieval can be effectively used in artificial agents. The key insight is that deliberate retrieval has certain knowledge requirements — namely the knowledge of when to search memory and what to search for — that spontaneous retrieval does not. We therefore hypothesize that spontaneous retrieval could be well-suited for agents in domains where this knowledge is unavailable or otherwise incorrect. This insight is crucial in defining a space of possible spontaneous retrieval mechanisms, as well as in deriving the design principles necessary for an agent to take advantage of these retrievals. Results from the Missing Link word puzzle support our hypothesis, and further hint at the conditions under which spontaneous retrieval can be beneficial.

Background: Memory Mechanisms in Cognitive Architectures

The goal of cognitive architecture research is to explore and understand the computational mechanisms that support general intelligence. Although there are a number of cognitive architectures in use, the majority share a similar core design; here the focus is on ACT-R (Anderson 2007) and Soar (Laird 2012), two widely used architectures.

All knowledge is represented as an edge-labeled directed graph in ACT-R and Soar. *Working memory* holds the knowledge that is immediately relevant to the agent's current situation, while *long-term memory* contains other general knowledge about the world; a single piece of knowledge in either memory is called a *memory element*. Working memory has specialized *buffers* that contain information about the agent's perception and motor output; an input-processing-output step is called a *decision cycle*. These buffers may be changed by *procedural rules*, which match on and modify working memory.

In addition to input and output buffers, there are also buffers for long-term memory access, where rules can initiate *retrievals*. Such retrievals require that the agent create *cues* that describe the desired features; long-term memory then finds all memory elements that match the cue, and returns a single element (a graph vertex together with all of its outgoing edges) as determined by some *bias*. In ACT-R and

Soar, this bias is called *activation*, and is the sum of several factors. One factor is an element's *base-level activation*, which decreases (*decays*) over time but increases (*is boosted*) with every access (every retrieval or storage of the element). Another factor is activation that has *spread* from neighboring elements, allowing the bias to take the current context of the agent into account. The higher the total activation, the more likely an element is selected for retrieval (assuming it matches the cue); the element is recreated in the long-term memory buffer, where it can be matched on and modified by rules. Similarly, the agent can also *store* a working memory element into long-term memory through this buffer.

Long-term memory retrieval must be *deliberately* initiated: the retrieval buffer never changes without some rule firing. In contrast, a retrieval that is spontaneous would change the buffer without action on the part of the agent; this is known as *buffer stuffing* by the ACT-R community. One such mechanism has been implemented in ACT-R's declarative memory, but has never been used. This is partially due to the lack of documentation in the manual, and partially because it is easier to create cognitive models that have top-down control of memory retrievals (Lebiere 2014).

Outside of cognitive architecture research, the case-based reasoning (CBR) community has also considered the problem of when to search for relevant cases (Riesbeck and Schank 1989). The focus of that work, however, remains on a useful definition of relevance, while ignoring when relevant cases should be searched for; in fact, most CBR agents begin by being given a case, for which spontaneity has no role (Aamodt and Plaza 1994). Our work has similarities with work on spontaneous analogies (Pickett and Aha 2013), although "spontaneity" in that work is only vaguely defined and focuses more on perceptual features. As a result, the work reported here is the first application of a spontaneous retrieval mechanism that we know of.

Theoretical Benefits of Spontaneous Retrieval

To design a spontaneous retrieval mechanism, it is necessary to first consider the role it plays in an intelligent agent. The goal of all long-term memory retrievals, deliberate or spontaneous, is to find knowledge that is relevant to the agent's current task; in other words, it is a mechanism for *knowledge search* (Newell 1990). This search is necessary because knowledge in long-term memory may not always be well organized and immediately accessible. This is especially true for a long-lived agent that acquires knowledge during its lifetime and must use that knowledge for multiple goals. In this context, the cues created by the agent in a deliberate retrieval provide heuristic guidance for what knowledge might be relevant. Since the search is deliberate, however, the agent's rules dictate not only what to search for, but also *when* to perform this search. This raises the question of how the agent copes when it lacks this search-guidance knowledge, or when the heuristics are incorrect. It would be beneficial to have a mechanism that provides a more general heuristic that is robust to the agent's lack of search knowledge, even if it is not as accurate as is possible with a deliberate cue.

Consider an agent in the real world, where it perceives an abundance of objects every perceptual cycle. The agent may have additional knowledge about many of these objects, but for the majority of objects, this knowledge does not immediately benefit the agent. Moreover, the agent may not know which objects are important, and therefore cannot focus its search on these objects, if any of the objects are important at all. Without this search-guidance knowledge and with only deliberate retrieval, the agent could only retrieve additional information by brute force. Spontaneous retrieval could help in this situation by using subsymbolic information in the agent to heuristically provide it with knowledge.

This analysis has several implications for the design of the mechanism. These implications are further discussed in the next section, but the most important one is that the mechanism cannot depend on the agent's procedural knowledge to initiate the search nor to provide a cue to guide search, since it must be robust to the agent's lack of knowledge of both when to search and what to search for. The mechanism must therefore be automatic or *spontaneous* and *uncued* — hence the focus of this paper on spontaneous retrieval. In particular, we claim that spontaneous retrieval can, under the right circumstances, allow an agent to overcome its lack of knowledge of:

- C1 *when* to search long-term memory
- C2 what to search for in long-term memory, if the *cue* is unknown
- C3 what to search for in long-term memory, if the *relation* of the cue to the desired knowledge is unknown

The Space of Spontaneous Retrieval Mechanisms

The problem of missing or incorrect heuristics for knowledge search presents additional constraints on spontaneous retrieval beyond the need for it to be automatic and uncued. Within these constraints and guided by the theoretical benefits, there is a space for variations in implementation.

The first consideration is the conditions under which a spontaneous retrieval should occur, which must take into account its interaction with deliberate retrieval. The simplest choice is to provide an additional buffer into which spontaneously retrieved elements can be placed, so that deliberate retrievals are not overwritten. This requires the agent to decide which of the two retrievals are more important, or otherwise integrate these two sources of information. On the other hand, having a single buffer for both retrievals better reflects how both mechanisms serve the same purpose in knowledge search, allowing the agent to be agnostic as to the source of the retrieval. In such an approach, spontaneous retrievals occur only when no other retrievals are deliberately initiated by the agent.

A different consideration is that the retrieved element should be relevant to the agent's current situation. This is a requirement shared with deliberate retrieval, and if activation is used as a proxy for relevance, the solution of spreading activation also applies to spontaneous retrieval. There is, however, no standard algorithm for spreading activation; in particular, the *source* of the spread may be different. In ACT-R, spreading activation originates from elements in working memory, increasing the likelihood that its immediate neighbors will be retrieved. Note that the activation due to spreading is separate from the activation due to base-level, so the resulting retrieval bias may lack the historical context of previous retrievals. A different spreading mechanism could directly affect base-level, by treating the event as another retrieval or storage. More nuanced spreading mechanisms are also possible, where there is a limit to the distance to which activation spreads, or where the change in retrieval bias decreases as the affected element is further away from the source. Finally, if the knowledge graph includes cycles, there may be differences in whether spreading affects the same element multiple times; in this case, mechanisms like inhibition may be necessary to prevent runaway positive feedback loops (Lebiere and Best 2009).

Although non-activation-based mechanisms are also possible — one can cast spontaneous retrieval as learning a mapping from agent state to a single long-term memory element — they are not well studied in literature.

A related but separate design decision is the selection of the element to be retrieved. Several possibilities exist, drawing inspiration from action selection in reinforcement learning: to always select the most highly activated element; to be epsilon-greedy, where the most highly activated element is selected except for some small probability of a random selection; or to use a softmax function where the probability of an element being retrieved is proportional to its activation value. Again, these options also exist for deliberate cued retrieval, except that with spontaneous retrieval, there is no hard constraint for the element to match a cue; in fact, uncued retrievals are a natural extension of partial matching mechanisms that are available in ACT-R and in Soar's episodic memory.

Implementation In Soar

For our implementation of spontaneous retrieval in Soar, we chose to maximize the similarities between deliberate and spontaneous retrieval, and to highlight the unique aspects of spontaneous retrieval. Spontaneous retrieval therefore selects the most highly activated element and uses the same buffer as deliberate retrieval, and only occurs when no deliberate retrievals are in progress. Spreading activation occurs whenever an element is stored or retrieved, and is treated as another access to the affected elements. Specifically, both the parents and the children of the source node, and the parents and children of those neighbors, and so on, are all affected, up to some parameterized distance d.

There are three constraints on spontaneous retrieval to prevent positive feedback loops. First, activation is not allowed to spread in a cycle, so each element could only be activated once per spread. Second, spontaneous retrieval can only return elements that are not already in working memory, with the exception that, if the element that was previously spontaneously retrieved remains the most highly activated one, it is kept in working memory and no other element replaces it. Finally, spontaneously retrieved elements do not receive a boost in base-level activation; this prevents the element from continually having the highest activation.

In terms of computational efficiency, calculating the effects of spreading activation is expensive, and has been an ongoing research problem for the cognitive architecture community (Douglass and Myers 2010; Chen, Petrovic, and Clark 2014). The goal of this research is to investigate the functionality that spontaneous retrieval affords, so our implementation of spreading activation is straightforward and unoptimized. The functionality of our implementation of spontaneous retrieval does not depend on the underlying implementation details of spreading activation. Specifically, Soar's long-term memory is implemented as a SQLite database, which uses indices to allow efficient queries; in particular, all long-term memory elements are indexed by their activation value for fast deliberate retrieval (Derbinsky, Laird, and Smith 2010). For spontaneous retrieval, an element is selected by iterating through the index until an element is found that is not already in working memory. This allows spontaneous retrieval to take advantage of any efficiency improvements for spreading activation, and data are presented below to show the costs of these two processes separately.

Evaluation in the Missing Link Domain

In order to evaluate the benefits of spontaneous retrieval, we use the Missing Link word puzzle as a domain. In this puzzle, the agent is given three words (*stems*) as the clue (for example, `fall`, `fort`, and `time`), and must provide a fourth word (the *link*; in this case, `night`) that forms compound words or phrases with all three stems (`nightfall`, `fortnight`, `nighttime`). The puzzles used in this evaluation are gathered from the Unix word list, using compound words that can be completely divided into two shorter words; a total of 550 compound words formed by 195 stems are used, with each stem being used in an average of 2.8 compound words. In the single-link representation (explained below), the compound words and stems form a connected bipartite graph of diameter 12.

It should be noted that this puzzle is the same one used in the Remote Associates Test (Mednick 1962), and it was chosen for some of the same reasons. In addition to the large amount of search necessary to find the solution, the puzzle also allows the agent's knowledge and the important features of the environment to be transparently manipulated. Search guidance in this domain depends on the connections between the stems and their compound words, which in turn depends on the source of knowledge. A generic dictionary may provide only the component stems of a compound word, while a knowledge base optimized for the Missing Link puzzle would have connections directly between the stems. While the existence of the latter connections may make the puzzle trivial, spontaneous retrieval may help with less specialized representations. To model this variation in knowledge, three different representations are tested in the basic domain (they are also depicted in Figure 1):

- The *single*-link representation only has links from the compound words to its prefixes and suffixes.
- The *double*-link representation also has links from the stems to all their compound words.
- The *direct*-link representation also has links between the prefixes and suffixes of any compound word.

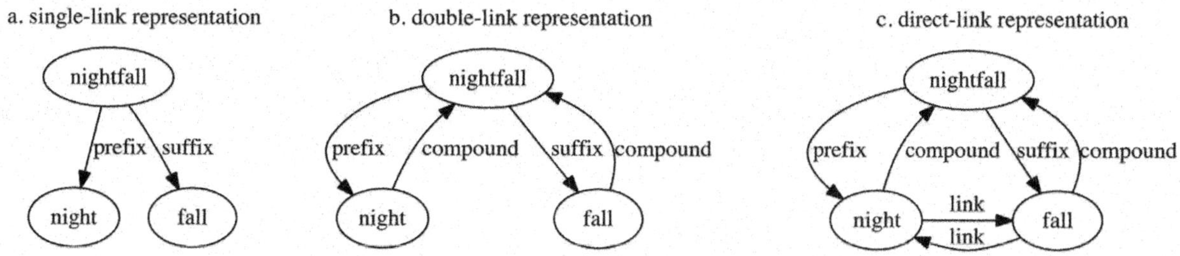

Figure 1: Different representations of knowledge in the Missing Link domain. The nodes are labeled for convenience only; in reality, the string that represents the word (eg. `night`) is a child of the node. For simplicity, other compound words that also use these stems are not shown.

Two additional variations of the Missing Link domain are used. In the first variation, Subset Missing Link, the agent is additionally presented with *distractors*, other words that do not form compound words with the missing link. In the above example, the additional words `foot` and `man` might also be presented to the agent. The addition of distractors models how only a subset of features in the environment may be relevant to the agent's goals.

The second variation modifies the Missing Link domain on a multi-puzzle level. In this Probabilistic Missing Link domain, each puzzle has only some probability of being solvable (that is, that a link exists between the three stems). As with the first variation, this models how only a subset of features are relevant, except in the temporal dimension.

These three domain variations correspond to three cases where spontaneous retrieval is likely to be beneficial. In the Missing Link domain with the single-link representation, the agent does not know the relation of the stem to its compound word (ie. whether it's a prefix or a suffix), and must therefore search memory with both (C3). For Subset Missing Link, the agent does not know which portion of its percepts are important and should be used as the cue to search memory (C2), while for Probabilistic Missing Link, the agent does not have knowledge of whether searching at this time will be beneficial, or if it will just consume resources (C1).

Since the agent can always use brute-force search to find the solution, the metric for this evaluation is not the number of puzzles that the agent solves, but the amount of computation needed to do so, in both decision cycles and real time.

Agent Design

In each puzzle, the domain presents the stems as strings. Both agents with and without spontaneous retrieval must first retrieve the long-term memory representations of the stems. To correctly solve a Missing Link puzzle, an agent without spontaneous retrieval must retrieve all compound words that contain each stem, as well as the other stem that forms those compound words, before finally checking if a missing link exists that is shared by the compound words of all three stems. The differences in representation only determine how quickly this can be done. With the single-link representation, the agent must do all of these steps. With the double-link representation, the agent does not need to retrieve the compound words. With the direct-link representation, the agent can directly check for a missing link. This is true in the two domain variations as well: the stems must be expanded to detect which three have a missing link, just as they must be expanded to determine whether a solution exists for any three stems.

A different search process is possible with spontaneous retrieval. When the memory element representing each stem is retrieved, activation spreads to its compound words and to the other prefix/suffix. Since the missing link is the only word which receives three activation boosts, it has the highest activation and is the first element to be spontaneously retrieved. The agent can then verify that the spontaneously retrieved word forms compound words with all three stems. The benefit of spontaneous retrieval is therefore that the stem–compound-word–stem connections do not need to be deliberately explored. Alternately, spontaneous retrieval can be thought of as using spreading activation to specify a search criteria based on the *graph topology* around the cue elements, one that is not constrained to return elements that must be direct neighbors of the cue.

Deliberate and spontaneous retrievals should not be thought of as separate strategies, however, but as two mechanisms working towards the same goal. Spontaneous retrieval is returning elements that the agent could deliberately retrieve, given the correct sequence of retrievals with the correct cues — since in this domain deliberate retrieval is only used for brute-force search, spontaneous retrieval allows the agent to skip ahead in its reasoning. However, there are also cases where spontaneous retrieval may mislead the agent; for the Subset Missing Link domain in particular, the retrieval of the distractors could be interleaved with the retrieval of the real stems, allowing time for the activation of the missing link to decay. This may cause a more-recently-boosted element to be returned by spontaneous retrieval instead, which would fail the verification. In this case, the agent must resort to the deliberate strategy, at least until a different element is spontaneous retrieved.

It should be noted that the spontaneity of spontaneous retrieval is not strictly necessary for this domain. Since the puzzles are episodic, one can imagine the agent deliberately retrieving the solution when a new puzzle is presented, but using a mechanism that returns that most highly activated element. This agent would do better than a spontaneous retrieval agent, since it is taking advantage of the episodic nature of the environment. To demonstrate the benefits of spontaneous retrieval, however, the agent uses the deliberate, brute-force search, but takes advantage of any spontaneously retrieved knowledge; that is, spontaneous retrieval provides usable knowledge without being asked to do so. The focus is on spontaneous retrieval complementing deliberate retrieval, especially when brute force becomes more expensive in the Subset and Probabilistic Missing Link variations.

For this reason, agents must be designed so that they can move from deliberate retrievals to spontaneous retrievals and back, and be able to integrate information from both. This can be achieved by conditioning the processing of retrieved memory elements not by the mechanism that retrieved it, but by the information that it represents. For example, in the Missing Link domain, if the retrieved element is a compound word that contains a stem, it should be stored so that the other prefix/suffix can be retrieved later; on the other hand, if the retrieved element is not connected to the stems, it may be the missing link, and it should be verified as the answer. The key is that these behaviors depend only on the agent state and how the retrieval should be used, but not on whether the retrieval was deliberate or spontaneous. Rules that process retrievals only match on the features of the retrieved element, and not on which mechanism retrieved the element or why it is retrieved; in fact, neither mechanism provides the latter. By separating the processing of information from the its source, the agent can effectively use both the knowledge that it knows it needs as well as any spontaneously retrieved shortcuts.

Results

All results in this section are averaged over 100 puzzles. Since each puzzle is independent, the agent is reset between puzzles to negate any recency and frequency effects of activation. The knowledge of compound words and their stems is loaded into the agent's long-term memory before each puzzle. Spreading activation is limited to a distance of two, the distance necessary to reach the solution word (from a stem to its compound words, then from the compound words to the missing link); we briefly discuss the effects of alternate settings of this parameter in the conclusion. All agents are written as deliberate agents, with the processing of retrieved elements then modified to be agnostic to the retrieval mechanism. In fact, the "deliberate" and "spontaneous" agents have the exact same rules, with the only difference being that the architecture provides spontaneous retrievals for the "spontaneous" agent. No effort was made to space deliberate retrievals so that spontaneous retrievals could occur.

Efficiency of Spontaneous Retrieval

To evaluate the efficiency of spontaneous retrieval, we instrumented Soar to measure the amount of time spent calculating the effects of spreading activation, versus that of selecting the most highly activated element in long-term memory. Averaged over 100 puzzles, an agent with the single-link representation takes an average of 350.7 milliseconds to solve a puzzle, of which 335.2 milliseconds is spent updating activation values, and only 0.85 milliseconds for spontaneous retrieval; this sub-millisecond cost over multiple decision cycles is inconsequential given that cognitive architectures limit each individual decision cycle to 50 milliseconds.

Since spreading activation also affects the outcome of deliberate retrievals, it is included in the results below for both the deliberate and spontaneous agents.

Missing Link

The purpose of this experiment is to demonstrate that spontaneous retrieval can overcome a lack of knowledge of how percepts relate to the desired knowledge. A brute-force search would require the agent to iterate through all possible relations in the worst case, although there are only two possible relations (ie. prefix or suffix) in this domain. The average number of decision cycles and amount of real time needed to solve a puzzle by different agents are shown in the table below.

Knowledge	**Decision Cycles**		**Real Time (msec)**	
Rep.	Delib.	Spon.	Delib.	Spon.
Single	56.1	24.5	2631.6	350.7
Double	60.9	60.9	1167.7	1173.1
Direct	12.0	12.0	267.8	268.3

For the single-link representation, the spontaneous retrieval agent takes half the number of decisions to complete the task, and an even smaller proportion of real time. As hypothesized during the discussion of agent design, this is because activation spreads to the missing link, which spontaneous retrieval then puts into working memory. This eliminates many decision cycles during which the deliberate approach is exhaustively expanding the stems and the compound words. The difference in real time is more dramatic because of the cost of spreading activation — since there are fewer retrievals, there are fewer boosts to base-level activation and therefore fewer spreads. This difference would be smaller with a more efficient spreading activation algorithm.

Spontaneous retrieval has little effect on either metric for the other two representations, although the source of this lack of differentiation is different. For the direct-link representation, the missing link could be immediately determined after the stem elements are retrieved, removing the need to search long-term memory. For the double-link representation, the majority of agent processing is from retrieving the other prefix/suffix of the compound words; there are no gaps between these uses of long-term memory, leaving no opportunity for spontaneous retrievals to occur. This raises questions about balancing deliberate and spontaneous retrievals, as well as whether spontaneous retrievals should be placed in a different buffer; these issues are addressed in the conclusion. Regardless, although spontaneous retrievals has no benefits when these knowledge representations are used, it also incurs minimal cost.

The results across all three knowledge representations agree with the original insight that spontaneous retrieval supplements deliberate retrieval when the agent lacks search-guidance knowledge. The more optimized the knowledge base for a task — as more connections are added between

Proceedings of the Twenty-Ninth AAAI Conference on Artificial Intelligence

Learning Plausible Inferences from Semantic Web Knowledge by Combining Analogical Generalization with Structured Logistic Regression

Chen Liang & Kenneth D. Forbus
Qualitative Reasoning Group, Northwestern University
2133 Sheridan Road, Evanston, IL, 60208 USA
contact: chenliang2013@u.northwestern.edu

Abstract

Fast and efficient learning over large bodies of commonsense knowledge is a key requirement for cognitive systems. Semantic web knowledge bases provide an important new resource of ground facts from which plausible inferences can be learned. This paper applies structured logistic regression with analogical generalization (SLogAn) to make use of structural as well as statistical information to achieve rapid and robust learning. SLogAn achieves state-of-the-art performance in a standard triplet classification task on two data sets and, in addition, can provide understandable explanations for its answers.

Introduction

Learning is a key part of cognitive systems. Humans are fast, efficient learners: with a few observations, we can acquire new knowledge to reason and make predictions. Moreover, we can also explain our reasoning to others to convince or persuade them. These two abilities are the focus of this work. Analogical learning has proven to be a promising model for human learning. It has been used to learn spatial prepositions (Lockwood et al. 2008), learn sketched concepts (McLure et al 2015), and construct hierarchical concepts (Liang & Forbus, 2014). Computational models of structural alignment and structure mapping have demonstrated the ability to learn linguistic patterns at a similar pace to human infants. (Kuehne et al. 2000). SAGE, which implements analogical generalization, is used as a learning module for the Companion cognitive architecture (Forbus et al. 2009).

Like humans, cognitive systems need knowledge and the ability to reason with it. Hand-coding knowledge and inference rules is not a scalable solution. Semantic web knowledge bases are a potential resource for cognitive systems to automatically acquire common sense knowledge and learn plausible inferences. Semantic web KBs like Freebase, WordNet, and YAGO have accumulated considerable structured data, which is already used to support AI tasks like question answering and information retrieval. These KBs continue to grow rapidly.

Using semantic web KBs brings up two concerns. First, because they can be extracted from text or collected by crowd-sourcing, they are often incomplete and noisy. Traditional logical inference may not be sufficiently robust to reason over them. Second, unlike images, auditory data or raw text, semantic web data is inherently structured. Although statistical methods can handle uncertainty well, most such methods are designed to work over feature vectors, and are not able to operate over structures.

Statistical relational learning focuses on extending statistical machine learning methods from feature vectors to relational data. For example, Markov logic networks (Richardson & Domingos, 2006) combine first-order logic with Markov networks, providing the representation power of the former and the statistical power of the latter. But it suffers from scalability problems. Other models, like neural networks or bilinear models, work on vector embedding of entities (Socher et al. 2013, Wang et al. 2014). They can achieve high prediction accuracy efficiently, but the opacity of the models makes it hard for users to interpret and understand their answers.

This paper describes how structured logistic regression with analogical generalization (SLogAn) can be used to learn plausible inferences from semantic web knowledge. We start by summarizing the models we build upon, and then describe our new method, covering case construction, learning, prediction, and explanation generation. We compare it to state-of-the-art methods on a standard triplet classification task with two datasets, showing that it has competitive performance, and, at the same time, can provide understandable explanations for its answers.

Background

We assume Gentner's (1983) structure-mapping theory. Our model is built upon the Sequential Analogical Generalization Engine (SAGE; McLure et al. 2010), which in turn uses the Structure-Mapping Engine (Falkenhainer et al. 1989) for analogical comparison and MAC/FAC (Forbus et al. 1995) for analogical retrieval. We start with SME since it is the most fundamental. SME takes as input two structured representations, a *base* and *target*, and produces one or more mappings. Each mapping provides a set of correspondences (i.e. what goes with what), a structural evaluation score which provides an overall estimate of match quality, and candidate inferences. We refer to the similarity score of a mapping as NSIM(base,target), which is normalized to [0,1] by dividing the raw score by the mean of the self-scores of the base and target[1]. Forward candidate inferences go from base to target, reverse candidate inferences go from target to base. MAC/FAC takes as input a case library, which is a set of structured descriptions, and a probe, which is a structured description. It returns one or more approximations to the most similar case in the case library, using a two-stage process that enables it to scale to large case libraries. The first stage uses a flattened version of the relational structure of cases, called *content vectors*, whose dimensions are proportional to the weighted number of occurrences of each predicate in a description. The dot product of two content vectors is an estimate of SME's structural evaluation score for the structured representations, making it a useful coarse filter. Both SME and MAC/FAC have been used to model a variety of psychological phenomena.

SAGE maintains, for each concept, a *generalization context*. A generalization context has a trigger, which is used to test whether or not an incoming example should be added to it. (An incoming example might satisfy multiple triggers, and hence be processed by several generalization contexts.) Each generalization context maintains a set of *generalizations* and a set of *unassimilated examples*. (Either of these sets might be empty, and both are initially.) Generalizations are also structured representations, but associated with their statements are probabilities, based on the number of times facts that align with them are found in examples that are part of that generalization.

Every time a new example is added, SAGE uses MAC/FAC to retrieve up to three examples or generalizations, based on whatever is the most similar to the new example. If nothing is retrieved, or the similarity to the returned item is less than an *assimilation threshold*, the new example is stored as is. Otherwise, if the returned item is a generalization, the new example is assimilated into it. If the returned item is a previously unassimilated example, then the two are combined into a new generalization.

The assimilation process increments frequency counts associated with each statement, based on whether or not something in the example aligned with it. For a new generalization, such facts are always either 1.0 (in both) or 0.5. If, for example, one black cat and two grey cats had been seen, then P[(primaryObjectColor <*GenEnt*> Black)] = 1/3. Facts whose probabilities drop too low are pruned, for efficiency. Importantly, these generalizations do not have logical variables: When non-identical entities are aligned, as in the cats example, a new arbitrary individual (called <*GenEnt*> above) is constructed to stand for the aligned individuals, with its characteristics being determined by the set of statements in the generalization that constrain it.

In most semantic web KBs, knowledge is stored in the triplet format: "entity relation entity". Since there are only binary relations, it can be seen as a labeled, directed graph. Each entity is a node, and each triplet between two entities is an edge labeled with the relation. Semantic web KBs have been used in a variety of tasks, including triplet classification. Given triplets extracted from a KB, the system should learn to distinguish correct triplets like "Obama nationality USA" from incorrect ones like "Obama nationality Kenya". Then, the learned model is tested on a holdout test set, with performance measured by classification accuracy.

Method

We extend analogical generalization with structured logistic regression to make use of the structural as well as the statistical information in the semantic web KB. The goal is to learn what kinds of inferences are plausible. For example, when learning about relation "nationality", we are not learning what people from different countries look like. Instead, we are learning about how to infer a person's nationality. One possible inference might be "this person comes from Chicago, and I know several people from Chicago. What are their nationalities?"

Case construction by path-finding

The first step is to prepare the input data. Analogical comparison and generalization work on cases. For this task, cases contain structured information about particular triplets. The idea is to include enough information to enable the

[1]The mapped representations are subsets of both base and target, so its score is lower than either of their self-scores.

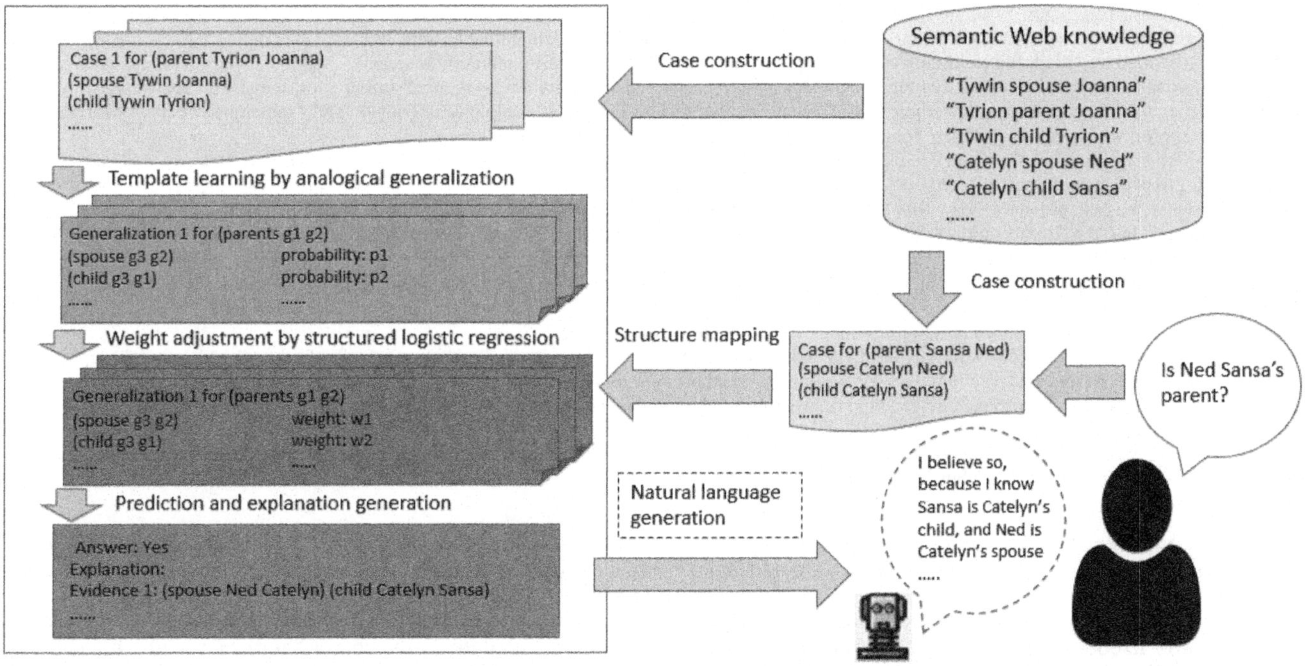

Figure 1: Intended workflow for SLogAn. The learning system gets input from semantic web knowledge base, does template learning and weight adjustment with the data. Using the learned generalizations, it provides answers, with explanations, for the user's queries. Natural language generation (dashed lines) is not yet implemented.

system to distinguish correct from incorrect triplets, while limiting the size of the cases for the sake of efficiency and to reduce the number of irrelevant matches.

As discussed above, a semantic web KB can be viewed as a graph. We use path-finding as a heuristic to pick relevant facts for case construction. For example, when we want to create a case for a triplet with A and B as head and tail entities, we use depth-first-search to find paths between them and put all the facts along the paths found into the case. In a large scale and highly connected knowledge base, an exhaustive search will be prohibitive, so we use limits on branching factor and search depth to randomly select parts of the search tree to explore.

These two thresholds control the tradeoff between information and efficiency. The larger the branching factor, the more information is in the case, and the larger the search depth, the more distant are the relationships between the two entities that can be found. The bound on branching factor is applied to each type of relation separately. For example, if we hit the entity "Chicago" in the search, and it has a "location" relation with 100 people and a "place_of_birth" relation with 10 people and the upper limit is 20, we randomly select 20 of the 100 Chicagoans to explore, and use all of the 10 people born in Chicago to explore, because the number is less than 20.

The intuition is that the facts we use to infer a relation will be represented by a small number of fixed paths between the entities in the case. In other words, if some relation holds between two entities, they are likely to be indirectly related to each other in some other ways.

Since there are only positive examples in the original dataset, we corrupt the correct triplets by changing their tail entities to wrong ones to get negative examples, just like Socher et al. (2013) did. We treat the training set as our knowledge base, and create cases from it. With just a few cases, SLogAn is able to learn plausible inferences. For the triplet classification task, we used only 10 positive and 10 negative examples for each relation.

Analogical generalization: structural alignment for template learning

The second step is to decide what to include in the inference, i.e., learning a template for the inference. This is done by SAGE. As outlined above, SAGE can create generalizations by comparing examples and compressing them into one prototype. A generalization works as a template for an inference. It is trivial to compare feature vectors because they all share the same dimensions, but it takes some effort to find the best way to align structured representations of examples and compress them into one structurally consistent template that summarizes the facts. SME does this job by finding the best structural alignment with systematicity as main criterion and several constraints to ensure structural consistency. We also require the head entity and tail entity of one triplet to be respectively matched to those of the other triplet in the mapping to make sure they are the focus of the template. Note that, unlike the way

Explanation for (taufaahau_tupou_iv ethnicity tongans):
Evidence 1: (taufaahau_tupou_iv parents viliami_tungi_mailefihi) (viliami_tungi_mailefihi ethnicity tongans)
Evidence 2: (viliami_tungi_mailefihi children taufaahau_tupou_iv) (viliami_tungi_mailefihi ethnicity tongans)
Evidence 3: (taufaahau_tupou_iv nationality tonga) (george_tupou_i_of_tonga nationality tonga) (george_tupou_i_of_tonga ethnicity tongans)
comment: I believe Taufa'ahau Tupou IV's ethnicity is Tongan, because I know his parent's ethnicity is Tongan, and I remember a person from the same country as him, whose ethnicity is also Tongan.

Explanation for (qusay_hussein parents saddam_hussein):
Evidence 1: (qusay_hussein parents sajida_talfah) (uday_hussein parents sajida_talfah) (uday_hussein parents saddam_hussein)
Evidence 2: (qusay_hussein parents sajida_talfah) (uday_hussein parents sajida_talfah) (saddam_hussein children uday_hussein)
Evidence 3: (qusay_hussein parents sajida_talfah) (saddam_hussein spouse sajida_talfah)
comment: I believe Saddam is Qusay's parent, because I know Saddam is Qusay's sibling Uday's parent and Qusay's parent Sajida's spouse.

Explanation for (vuk_stefanovic_karadzic religion serbian_orthodox_church):
Evidence 1: (vuk_stefanovic_karadzic ethnicity serbs) (gavrilo_princip ethnicity serbs) (gavrilo_princip religion serbian_orthodox_church)
Evidence 2: (vuk_stefanovic_karadzic ethnicity serbs) (zoran_in_ic ethnicity serbs) (zoran_in_ic religion serbian_orthodox_church)
Evidence 3: (vuk_stefanovic_karadzic ethnicity serbs) (alexander_i_of_yugoslavia ethnicity serbs) (alexander_i_of_yugoslavia religion serbian_orthodox_church)
comment: I believe Vuk Stefanovic Karadzic's religion is the Serbian orthodox church, because I can recall several persons with the same ethnicity, whose religion is the Serbian orthodox church.

Figure 2: Examples of explanations and comments: with only ground facts and no prior knowledge about the relations, the system learns to make inference about them with high accuracy and provide the explanations for its answers. The comments are generated manually.

SAGE is usually used, we first created generalizations with positive examples only, and then add negative examples to these generalizations so that they contain facts from positive as well as negative examples. In this way, some facts could contribute negatively to the target relation. For example, if I know that B is A's parent, then A cannot be B's parent. Although that fact never appears in a positive example, it is still a critical fact to consider in the inference.

Using multiple generalizations together as one template has strong expressive power. Learning plausible inferences is similar to learning the concept of the target relation. A concept can be represented by several generalizations in a generalization context, which is analogous to a disjunctive normal form. Each generalization can be seen as a conjunction of facts inside it. Facts with negative weights play the role of negations. Combining multiple generalizations forms a disjunctive representation of the concept. If we also combine the generalizations with structured logistic regression, the model can be seen as a structured 2-layer neural network. Each generalization plays the role of a logistic unit, but the weight vector of the unit in standard neural network is changed to a structured template with associated weights to handle structured input instead of feature vectors. Correspondingly, the dot-product operation to activate a unit in standard neural network is replaced with a structure mapping process. In this triplet classification task, although multiple generalizations can help in accuracy, we did not use them for the sake of efficiency.

Structured logistic regression: structure mapping and gradient descent for weight adjustment

The third step is to learn how much each fact in the template supports or contradicts the target relation. Each expression in the template is associated with a weight measuring its positive support. So if a fact contradicts the target relation, it gets a negative score. We use the probability of each fact as an initial value for its weight. To further adjust the weights, we propose *structured logistic regression*, which is an extension of logistic regression from feature vectors to structured cases by combining it with structure mapping.

Structured logistic regression works as follows. Given an example, we compare it to the generalization with SME. With the resulting mapping, we compute the prediction score of the example being a positive example with

$$p = \frac{1}{1 + e^{-s}}$$

where s is the similarity score computed by SME. Then, we use cross entropy to define the prediction error and L1 regularization to promote sparsity in weights for better explanation generation:

$$J = -\sum_{i=0}^{n} [(1 - y_i)\log(1 - p_i) + y_i \log(p_i)] + \alpha \sum_{j=1}^{m} |w_j|$$

n and m are the number of examples and facts in the generalizations respectively. y_i and p_i are the label (1 for positive, 0 for negative) and prediction score of the ith example. α controls the strength of the regularization. Since this error depends on similarity score and similarity score depends on the weights, we can calculate the derivate of the error with respect to the weights and do gradient descent on them. The prediction error on the validation set is used to decide when to stop the weight adjustment.

Prediction and explanation generation by finding most weighted paths

After training, the model has learned to assign high scores to the positive examples and low scores to the negative examples. We use the validation set to decide the criterion c. When the score is larger than c, the model predicts true, otherwise it predicts false.

Explanations are representations of one's own reasoning which can be understood by others. Since SLogAn uses the structured representation directly, it is more interpretable for the user. By finding the highest weighted paths, we could provide understandable explanations. The intuition here is that each path between two entities represents one inference chain. From the weights, we can know whether a given inference chain supports or contradicts the target relation, and how important it is. Given a path between the two entities in the query triplet, we use the average weight of the facts along this path as its weight. Then, we rank the paths with the absolute value of their weights. Finally, we pick several paths on the top as the explanation for the answer. To make the explanation clearer to the user, we use L1 regularization to induce sparsity in the weight adjustment, so that it prefers a few high weights rather than many low weights, in other words, it provides a few strong pieces of evidence rather than many weak pieces of evidence.

Experiment

To test it, we compare SLogAn's performance to state-of-the-art performance on the triplet classification task. The datasets were collected by Socher et al. (2013). One dataset contains triplets from Freebase consisting of 13 relations and 38,696 entities, the other dataset, from WordNet, consisting of 11 relations and 75,043 entities. More information about the number of triplets in training, validation and test sets is shown in Table 1.

Datasets	#Relations	#Entities	#Train	#Validation	#Test
WN11	11	38,696	112,581	2,609	10,544
FB13	13	75,043	316,232	5,908	23,733

Table 1: Statistics of WordNet and Freebase datasets

As for the hyperparameters, the limit on branching factor is 20 and the search depth is 3 for FB13 and 5 for WN11, which is chosen based on run time limit. (On average, one entity in FB13 has $316232/75043 \approx 4.2$ outgoing triplets, while the same number is $112581/38696 \approx 2.9$ in WN11, so the search depth is lower on FB13.) For each relation, we randomly select 10 triplets as positive examples, and create their corresponding negative examples as training data. The regularization parameter α is set to 0.01, which is decided by prediction error on validation set.

Other methods have been tested on exactly the same datasets, making the results useful for comparison. Table 2 shows accuracy performances from Wang et al (2014). SLogAn is 2nd on WN11 and FB13, and no method consistently outperforms it on both datasets. Thus our method performs at a level that is competitive with the state-of-the-art. Other approaches have not provided information concerning statistical significance, so we will not be able to compare that against them. The difference between SLogAn and chance is statistically significant with $p < 0.001$. Prediction accuracies of different relations are shown in Table 3. SLogAn learns from the data collected by path-finding during case construction, so its performance drops on relations like "similar to" because it is hard to find a path in the KB between entities like "adamant_1" and "physiologist_1", although they are "similar to" each other.

Model	WordNet11	Freebase13
Distance Model	53.0	75.2
Hadamard Model	70.0	63.7
Single Layer Model	69.9	85.3
Bilinear Model	73.8	84.3
Neural Tensor Network	70.4	87.1
TransH	78.8	83.3
SLogAn	75.3	85.3

Table 2: Triplet classification accuracy (%) of different models

The results provided by other methods are opaque to users. Since they are based on vector embedding, they cannot easily explain why they make certain predictions. In contrast, we work on the structured data directly. From the explanation the model provides, the user is able to see how its reasoning works. Examples of explanations are shown in Figure 2. Note that unfamiliar examples are intentionally chosen to show how explanations help with human

WordNet11	accuracy	Freebase13	accuracy
has instance	74.5	gender	85.9
type of	76.9	nationality	94.6
member meronym	75.8	profession	81.4
member holonym	74.2	institution	79.4
part of	72.0	cause of death	76.9
has part	73.5	religion	82.2
subordinate instance of	81.7	ethnicity	87.9
domain region	69.9		
synset domain topic	76.0		
similar to	50.0		
domain topic	69.0		

Table 3: Triplet classification accuracy (%) of different relations

validation of the results and increase trust in prediction: even without explanations, familiar examples are easy for people to validate. We used the top 3 most weighted paths as the explanation for each example.

Discussion

SLogAn learned plausible inferences from semantic web knowledge to achieve competitive performance to state-of-the-art methods on the triplet classification task, and, moreover, provides understandable explanations. These two abilities would make a cognitive system more autonomous and independent because it does not need to be told about everything it will be asked for, and more trustworthy and helpful because it can explain its answer to the user.

For example, when asked about "is Taufa'ahau Tupou IV's ethnicity Tongan?", even though the system is not told about this fact or how to infer one's ethnicity, it can learn it from several examples it knows of the relation "ethnicity" and makes a prediction based on its knowledge of Taufa'ahau Tupou IV and Tongan with reasonable accuracy. If the users are only provided with the answer, they have to decide whether to believe it or not based on their trust of the system. However, if the system could say, "I believe Taufa'ahau Tupou IV's ethnicity is Tongan, because I know his parent's ethnicity is Tongan, and I remember a person with the same nationality whose ethnicity is also Tongan", it is easier to convince the users when the system is correct, and alert them when the system is wrong. It would make cooperation more efficient and natural, by reducing the labor of human validation.

Related work

Many vector embedding based methods have been tested on the triplet classification tasks. Socher et al. (2013) and Wang et al. (2014) are the most recent and have the best performance. Their models are quite different from ours. They learn vector representations for the entities and parameterization (translation or tensor) for each relation that implicitly encode the knowledge about them. During training, they created negative examples for every triplet in the training set and train on all of them. In contrast, SLogAn only randomly selects a few triplets and creates cases and corresponding negative examples for them. Instead of implicit encoding of knowledge with vector embedding, we use the structured knowledge directly and learn generalizations that explicitly encode valid inferences. This gives our model interpretability. Moreover, SLogAn can learn each relation separately, while theirs have to learn all the relations together.

Several previous efforts have used path-finding for relational learning. Sharma & Forbus (2010) used higher-order knowledge about relations and reinforcement learning to construct plausible inference patterns, whereas SLogAn is learning from purely ground facts. Integrating these methods could prove valuable. Richards & Mooney (1992) uses path-finding to find candidate clauses for learning first-order rules, but it was computationally expensive. Lao et al. (2011) used limited-length path-finding in NELL knowledge base to create features and do logistic regression with them. As is discussed above, SLogAn can use multiple generalizations to handle disjunctive concepts, and thus has more expressive power. Also note that SLogAn can potentially work with other case construction methods as long as they provide structured representations of relevant information.

Structural logistic regression (Popescul & Ungar, 2003) generates features by propositionalizing first-order rules learned by inductive logic programming, and uses logistic regression with these features for classification. Relational logistic regression (Kazemi et al. 2014) uses logistic regression to learn weights for first-order formulae in defining the conditional probability of a new relation given those formulae. Their ways of adding the counts of certain facts as features are possible improvements for the current model. Although the triplet classification task only deals with binary relations, SLogAn has the ability to deal with higher arity and high-order relations because it builds on SME and SAGE, which can handle them. Halstead & Forbus (2005) takes a similar approach to this work. They used SAGE to generate probabilistic generalizations to turn structured cases into features and built a Bayesian network on top of them to make predictions.

Deductive systems like Cyc and SHAKEN (Clark et al. 2001) can also provide explanations, but those explanations tend to be narrow and deeply nested, whereas the explanations produced by our current system are broad and shallow, more akin to explanations found in evidential reasoning arenas (e.g. intelligence analysis). Extensions to handle deeper nested inference by adding more levels to the current system are interesting, and will be crucial for learning more complex yet still interpretable models for prediction.

Conclusion and future work

This work shows that analogical generalization and structure mapping can be combined with statistical machine learning methods to achieve state-of-the-art performance on a standard task, while preserving interpretability. It enables cognitive systems to learn from structured data, e.g. semantic web resources, to do reasoning with what they have learned, and to explain their reasoning to the user.

We plan to explore several future directions. First, semantic web knowledge typically contains only binary relations involving entities. However, SME and SAGE are designed to work on cases that also include high-order relations that express arguments and explanations. We plan to test this method with representations produced via learning by reading systems (Forbus et al. 2007) and sketch understanding systems (Forbus et al. 2011). Second, we plan to compare its performance to other SRL methods on other tasks, such as link prediction. Third, unsupervised learning of high-level representations to disentangle independent factors and discover patterns has recently drawn a lot of attention (Lee et al. 2011, Bengio, 2009). The learned representations can be used to represent the input more compactly and help supervised learning to achieve better performance. Extending the current model to learn high-level representations for structured examples that are understandable, more compact and useful for supervised learning is a promising direction. Fourth, we plan to integrate it into our Companion cognitive architecture, to provide a new learning capability and exploit Companion's interaction capabilities to implement the full workflow of Figure 1.

Acknowledgements

This research was sponsored by the Socio-Cognitive Architectures Program of the Office of Naval Research, N00014-13-1-0470.

References

Bengio, Y. (2009). Learning Deep Architectures for AI. *Found. Trends Mach. Learn.*, 2(1), 1-127. doi: 10.1561/2200000006

Clark, P. et al. (2001). Knowledge entry as the graphical assembly of components. *Proceedings of the 1st international conference on Knowledge capture* (pp. 22-29). ACM.

Falkenhainer, B., Forbus, K. D., & Gentner, D. (1989). The structure-mapping engine: Algorithm and examples. *Artificial intelligence*, 41(1), 1-63.

Forbus, K., Riesbeck, C., Birnbaum, L., Livingston, K., Sharma, A., & Ureel, L. (2007). Integrating Natural Language, Knowledge Representation and Reasoning, and Analogical Processing to Learn by Reading. *Proceedings of AAAI-07*.

Forbus, K., Usher, J., Lovett, A., Lockwood, K., & Wetzel, J. (2011). CogSketch: Sketch Understanding for Cognitive Science Research and for Education. *Topics in Cognitive Science*, 3(4), 648-666. doi: 10.1111/j.1756-8765.2011.01149.x

Forbus, K. D., Gentner, D., & Law, K. (1995). MAC/FAC: A Model of Similarity-Based Retrieval. *Cognitive Science*, 19(2), 141-205.

Forbus, K. D., Klenk, M., & Hinrichs, T. (2009). Companion cognitive systems: Design goals and lessons learned so far. *IEEE Intelligent systems*, 24(4), 36-46.

Gentner, D. (1983). Structure-Mapping: A Theoretical Framework for Analogy. *Cognitive Science*, 7(2), 155-170.

Halstead, D. and Forbus, K. (2005). Transforming between Propositions and Features: Bridging the Gap. *Proceedings of AAAI-2005*. Pittsburgh, PA.

Kazemi, S. M., Buchman, D., Kersting, K., Natarajan, S., & Poole, D. (2014). Relational logistic regression. *Proc. 14th International Conference on Principles of Knowledge Representation and Reasoning (KR-2014)*.

Kuehne, S., Gentner, D. and Forbus, K. (2000). Modeling infant learning via symbolic structural alignment. *Proceedings of CogSci 2000, August*.

Lao, N., Mitchell, T., & Cohen, W. W. (2011). Random walk inference and learning in a large scale knowledge base. *Proceedings of the Conference on Empirical Methods in Natural Language Processing*, Edinburgh, United Kingdom.

Lee, H., Grosse, R., Ranganath, R., & Ng, A. Y. (2011). Unsupervised learning of hierarchical representations with convolutional deep belief networks. *Communications of the ACM*, 54(10), 95-103.

Liang, C. and Forbus, K. (2014). Constructing Hierarchical Concepts via Analogical Generalization. *Proceedings of the Cognitive Science Society*.

Lockwood, K., Lovett, A., & Forbus, K. (2008). Automatic classification of containment and support spatial relations in English and Dutch. In *Spatial Cognition VI. Learning, Reasoning, and Talking about Space* (pp. 283-294). Springer Berlin Heidelberg.

McLure, M., Friedman, S., & Forbus, K. (2015). Extending Analogical Generalization with Near-Misses. *Proceedings of AAAI-2015*.

McLure, M., Friedman, S., & Forbus, K. (2010). Learning concepts from sketches via analogical generalization and near-misses. *Proceedings of the 32nd Annual Conference of the Cognitive Science Society (CogSci)*, Portland, OR.

Popescul, A., & Ungar, L. H. (2003). Structural logistic regression for link analysis. Departmental Papers (CIS), 133.

Richards, B. L., & Mooney, R. J. (1992). Learning relations by pathfinding. *Proceedings of the tenth national conference on Artificial intelligence*.

Richardson, M., & Domingos, P. (2006). Markov logic networks. *Machine learning*, 62(1-2), 107-136.

Sharma, A. and Forbus, K.D. (2013). Graph Traversal Methods for Reasoning in Large Knowledge-Based Systems. *Proceedings of the Twenty-Seventh AAAI Conference on Artificial Intelligence (AAAI-13)*, Bellevue, Washington.

Socher, R., Chen, D., Manning, C. D., & Ng, A. (2013). Reasoning With Neural Tensor Networks for Knowledge Base Completion. *Proceedings of Advances in neural information processing systems*.

Wang, Z., Zhang, J., Feng, J., & Chen, Z. (2014). Knowledge Graph Embedding by Translating on Hyperplanes. *Proceedings of Twenty-Eighth AAAI Conference on Artificial Intelligence*.

Ontology-Based Information Extraction with a Cognitive Agent

Peter Lindes, Deryle W. Lonsdale, David W. Embley
Brigham Young University
Provo, Utah 84602

Abstract

Machine reading is a relatively new field that features computer programs designed to read flowing text and extract fact assertions expressed by the narrative content. This task involves two core technologies: natural language processing (NLP) and information extraction (IE). In this paper we describe a machine reading system that we have developed within a cognitive architecture. We show how we have integrated into the framework several levels of knowledge for a particular domain, ideas from cognitive semantics and construction grammar, plus tools from prior NLP and IE research. The result is a system that is capable of reading and interpreting complex and fairly idiosyncratic texts in the family history domain. We describe the architecture and performance of the system. After presenting the results from several evaluations that we have carried out, we summarize possible future directions.

Introduction

Much Web traffic involves people searching for genealogical data that might inform them about their family history. A great online supply of historical documents containing such data exists, but most were generated long before modern digital technology was available. In this paper we discuss one way of extracting information from historical documents in a digital form so it can be searchable.

Various approaches are possible depending upon the type of document involved. Census records are highly structured but are largely handwritten. Involving vast pools of human annotators to hand-index entries has proven useful in this case, as was shown recently for the 1940 U.S. census.

A large corpus of family history books written before the digital age is now also becoming available online. Figure 1 shows a short example of text from p. 419 of one such book (Vanderpoel 1902). Many parts of this book have information in a fairly structured form, as can be seen in the list of children. However, much of the rest of the text follows a greatly abbreviated and highly formulaic style of English lexis and grammar. Typically these books were digitized by scanning them into PDF files and using optical character recognition (OCR) algorithms to extract the raw text. Of

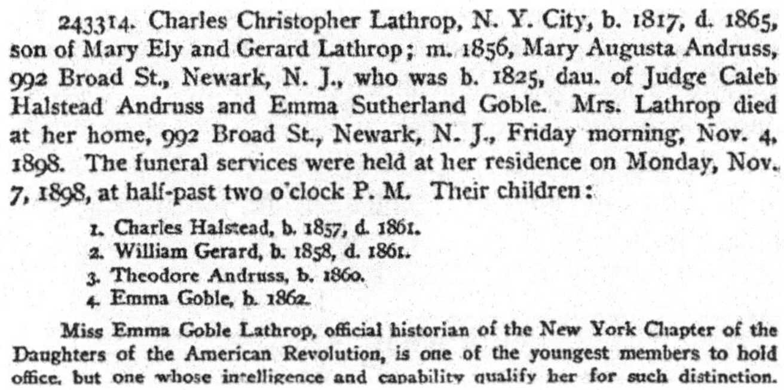
243314. Charles Christopher Lathrop, N. Y. City, b. 1817, d. 1865, son of Mary Ely and Gerard Lathrop; m. 1856, Mary Augusta Andruss, 992 Broad St., Newark, N. J., who was b. 1825, dau. of Judge Caleb Halstead Andruss and Emma Sutherland Goble. Mrs. Lathrop died at her home, 992 Broad St., Newark, N. J., Friday morning, Nov. 4, 1898. The funeral services were held at her residence on Monday, Nov. 7, 1898, at half-past two o'clock P. M. Their children:

1. Charles Halstead, b. 1857, d. 1861.
2. William Gerard, b. 1858, d. 1861.
3. Theodore Andruss, b. 1860.
4. Emma Goble, b. 1862.

Miss Emma Goble Lathrop, official historian of the New York Chapter of the Daughters of the American Revolution, is one of the youngest members to hold office, but one whose intelligence and capability qualify her for such distinction.

Figure 1: Sample of domain text (Vanderpoel 1902).

course the OCR process introduces a sizable number of errors. Once a book has been digitized, manual annotation and indexation can be performed to identify interesting facts using existing tools. However, the task is enormous, challenging, and complicated.

Another solution is to automatically extract information from the textual content. This requires integrating several types and levels of knowledge: lexical, syntactic, semantic, and pragmatic. In this paper we describe a system called OntoSoar that is designed to apply all these levels of knowledge to the problem of extracting information from genealogy books in an automatic fashion. Built within a cognitive architecture framework and targeting information specified by a user-supplied ontology, its advanced text processing and information extraction functions integrate seamlessly. We discuss performance of the system and evaluate it against a gold-standard corpus of human annotations.

Related work

Our work derives from several principal threads of ongoing research: natural language processing (NLP), information extraction, cognitive grammar, and deep reading.

The task is largely linguistic since we are processing running text. However, as mentioned above, the text departs from normal expectations of "grammatical" English; this complicates the syntactic processing—or parsing—stage.

We (Lonsdale et al. 2007) and others (Akbik and Bross 2009) have successfully used the link grammar (LG) parser to parse text that, like ours, is linguistically idiosyncratic and varies from book to book. The LG parser is an open-source parsing tool that is both robust and flexible (Sleator and Temperley 1993). It looks for pairwise associations (linkages) between words and annotates the linkages with labels and (optionally) scores.

Our text processing, though, must go beyond mere syntactic parsing: we require further semantic treatment to recognize the concepts and relationships of interest. Some (but not all) work in semantic formalisms has sought to account for human language processing and the deep structures needed to understand literal and non-literal meaning (Jackendoff 1990; 1996; 2002; 2003; Lakoff and Johnson 1980) including grounding it in direct perceptual experience, agency, and embodiment (Johnson 1987). This area of cognitive linguistics is finding increasing application in systems for understanding human language.

One thread of cognitive semantic systems research has resulted in a concrete language processing system (Feldman 2006; Bryant 2008; Chang 2008). A central component of this research is a grammatical theory called Embodied Construction Grammar (Bergen and Chang 2013). Hoffman and Trousdale (2013) survey common construction grammar tenets shared across approaches, which are directly relevant to our current implementation.

Another branch of computer science has tried to build functioning models of human cognition, called cognitive architectures. These theories and the associated implementations draw heavily on experimental evidence from psychology and measurements of how the brain processes information. Anderson (2007) gives a good introduction to this field. Soar is a mature and versatile cognitive architecture (Newell 1990; Laird 2012) that has been applied to many application areas. We use Soar as our framework for representing meaning and performing reasoning on it across several complex knowledge structures. Cognitive modeling of language use in Soar was pioneered by the NL-Soar system (Lewis 1993), which parses sentences using methods inspired by psycholinguistic research on human sentence processing.

We have built on the core Soar cognitive architecture, finding it to be a good candidate to act as an agent for language understanding. LG-Soar is a Soar-based language processing system that uses the LG parser discussed above, along with a semantic interpreter developed inside Soar to extract meaning from input sentences. LG-Soar has been used for information extraction applications (Lonsdale et al. 2008) and in a robotics system that can learn new linguistic constructions (Mohan et al. 2012). The present work derives from this approach, but with an innovative form of semantic analyzer. Soar's use in this project derives in part from the fact that Soar is intended to model human cognition (Newell 1990) and by the importance of agency in understanding language (Melby and Warner 1995).

Several and varied methods exist for extracting useful information from the wide range of existing text types. Sarawagi (2007) reviews the whole field of information extraction. Buitelaar et al. (2009) present an approach to linguistic grounding of ontologies. They argue that "currently available data-models are not sufficient ... without linguistic grounding or structure". Notably absent from these discussions is consideration of a deep understanding of language.

Another approach called "machine reading" is discussed in depth by (Hruschka 2013). He reviews three systems for building knowledge bases by machine reading the web: YAGO, KnowItAll, and NELL. Each system starts with some seed knowledge and uses various techniques to make both the accumulated set of fact assertions and the underlying ontology grow by reading large amounts of knowledge from the web. However, these systems still have fairly low accuracy in extracting individual facts and are not tuned to the special sublanguages of English such as those used in many family history books.

One of the features of OntoSoar is its ability to take extracted information in its internal representation of the meaning of input text and transform that information to populate an ontology[1] provided by the user. This amounts to a special case of the general problem of ontology matching, for which there is also a large literature.

An overview and survey of this field is given by Euzenat and Schvaiko (2007) . Bleiholder and Naumann (2008) and Mitra, Noy, and Jaizwal (2004), as well as many others, discuss specific approaches in more detail. Most of this literature deals with how to map information from one web site to another, or onto some pre-defined ontology. Fortunately for us our ontology mapping problem is much simpler since we are working within a well understood domain.

Our work unites these various streams of computational research and illustrates how the result can process certain types of data-rich text. Since our system uses both ontology-based and Soar-based processing, we call it OntoSoar. The innovative semantic analyzer described here is based on a number of ideas derived from the literature on cognitive semantics, construction grammar, and cognitive architectures.

For ontology specification we use the OntoES data extraction approach (Embley, Liddle, and Lonsdale 2011) and conceptual modeling system (Embley, Kurtz, and Woodfield 1992). In part OntoES draws on a large body of literature on conceptual modeling to produce a framework called OSM capable of representing a wide variety of conceptual models and populating them with data.

Figure 2 shows a sample user ontology. The ontology object and relationship sets are based on simple English sentences and phrases. Reading via arrow direction yields full names for relationship sets: e.g. "Person born on BirthDate", "Person died on DeathDate", "Person married Spouse on MarriageDate", "Son of Person", "Daughter of Person". OntoSoar uses these names for matching Soar conceptualizations with ontology conceptualizations.

OSM is a logic-based representation: the object sets are 1-place predicates, the n-ary relations are n-place predicates, and the constraints are representable as well-formed formulas. Whereas the figure presents the ontology in its graphical illustration form, its contents could also be listed entirely in the predicate logic formulation. Our OntoES system can translate extracted information directly into RDF and OWL.

[1]We use the term "ontology" as usually found in information extraction literature: a computerized conceptual model that can be populated with facts (Gruber 1993).

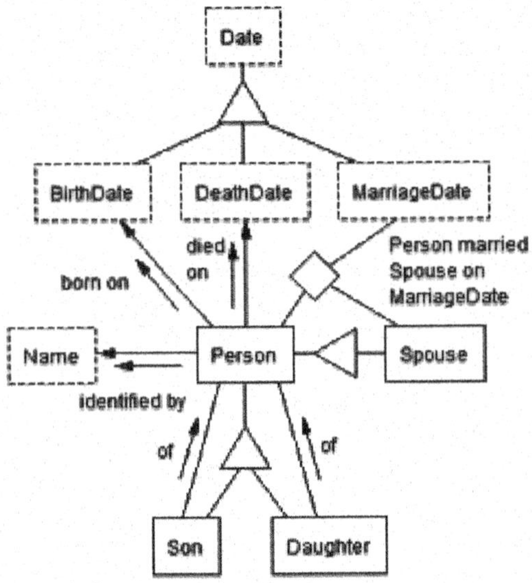

Figure 2: Sample ontology.

OntoSoar fits into this overall OntoES system by reading in a user ontology in OSMX[2] form and outputting a modified OSMX file which contains the fact assertions it found in a given input text. In addition, OntoSoar can be evaluated by using the OntoES tools to compare the fact assertions found by OntoSoar with those found by a human annotator in the same text.

OntoSoar processing

In this section we sketch how we use lexical, syntactic, and semantic analysis tools to extract information from data-rich texts and match that data to a conceptual model of the family history domain provided by a user, populating that model with fact assertions found in the text. Several levels of knowledge interact in our system: lexical, syntactic, semantic, and pragmatic.

OntoSoar is built using Java components, some Java libraries, some custom Java components, the LG parser, the Soar system, and Soar code that implements all the semantic components. Figure 3 shows a basic overview of the processing pipeline, with the superordinate arrow labeled "Soar" indicating the cognitive agent framework.

To summarize, each book is digitized via camera capture, and the images undergo optical character recognition (OCR) analysis. The resulting PDF files serve as input to OntoSoar, along with an OSMX target ontology that specifies the targeted content. OntoSoar divides the raw input text into sentence-like segments, then processes the pages one segment at a time, parsing each segment and performing semantic interpretation on the result. A mapping component takes a conceptual model in the form of an OSMX file, populates it with fact assertions derived from the semantic structures, and outputs the populated ontology as a new OSMX file. This output file can then be viewed, evaluated, or imported into a database by tools from the OntoES tool set.

Linguistic processing

OntoSoar first divides the raw input text into segments corresponding to short sentences. Tokenization includes word-level corrections to reduce OCR errors and relexing tokens acting as abbreviations in the domain: born for b., died for d., daughter for dau., and so on. Often, to avoid repetition, pronouns (he, she, they, etc.) are elided from genealogical text; in such cases we insert a temporary placeholder token GP (Generic Pronoun).

The next step involves parsing the incoming segment with the link grammar (LG) parser. Consider this partial example linkage produced for the sample text:

```
2: Charles Christopher Lathrop, N. Y. City, born 1817, died 1865,
   son of Mary Ely and Gerard Lathrop ;  ';'

                       +-----------------Ss--------------
                       +------MX------+-------Xc-------+
                       |    +----Xd---+--MX*p-+---Xca--+
   +----G----+----G----+    | +-G+-G-+ +-Xd-+--IN-+  |
   |         |         |    | |  |   | |    |     |  |
Charles Christopher Lathrop , N. Y. City , born.v 1817 ,
```

G links build proper nouns, and the Ss link connects the subject with the verb (not illustrated). Careful inspection shows two incorrect MX (i.e. appositive) links, indicating that the LG parser thinks that "Charles Christopher Lathrop" is "N. Y. City" and that the latter was born in 1817. However, this is corrected downstream by the semantic processor.

The Meaning Builder is a component based on Embodied Construction Grammar (ECG) (Bergen and Chang 2013; Bryant 2008; Chang 2008), though we depart from the core theory in two fundamental ways. First, construction grammar in general and ECG in particular build constructions directly from input text. However, OntoSoar builds constructions from the LG parser linkages, allowing OntoSoar to act on information about words and their relationships.

(Bryant 2008) uses a compiler for converting a formal grammar written in this ECG language into an internal form; we instead hand-coded ECG rules as Soar productions. Some of these are declarative, building static data structures. Other productions fire as the semantic analysis is proceeding and thus enact procedural knowledge. In the future we may be able to build a compiler to convert ECG grammar rules directly into Soar code.

Figure 4 shows part of the LG linkage for our sample segment and a set of overarching rectangles and arrows that represent the constructions recognized from this segment. The lower level rectangles have arrows pointing to the words that make up the form pole (i.e. anchors) of each of those constructions. Though not shown, each construction builds on words that it contains and on the leftward links from each word. The ovals represent meaning structures built from the constructions.

LifeEvent structures form the root of meaning networks. Each meaning structure has a number of internal slots—called roles—(not shown) that store values of properties or references to other meaning structures. For example,

[2]OSMX is the XML file format we use for storing conceptual ontologies and their content in the Object-oriented Systems Modeling (OSM) conceptual modeling language.

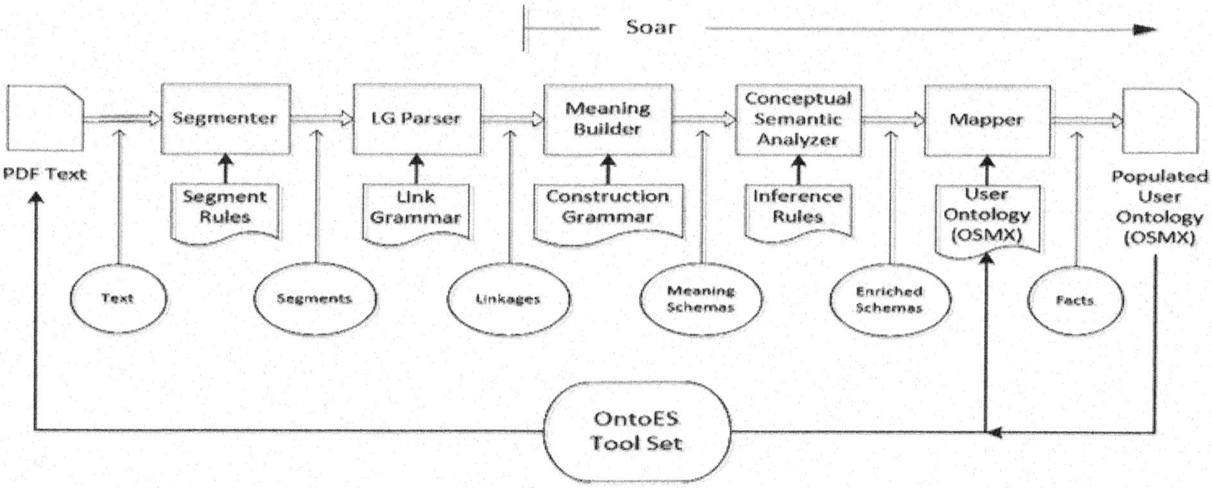

Figure 3: OntoSoar system architecture

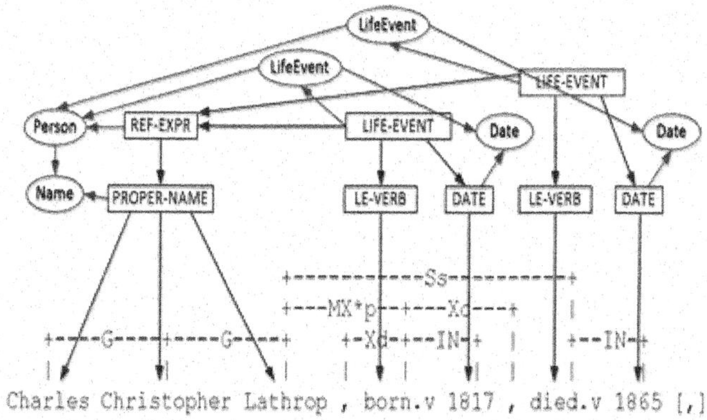

Figure 4: Example of construction with meanings

a LifeEvent has a subject role requiring a Person and a date role requiring a Date. A Person's name role takes a Name, but it also has birth and death roles which point to LifeEvents, if filled.

For each input word OntoSoar executes a comprehend-word operator that in turn invokes a build-meaning operator. Other operators such as lexical-construction and proper-name perform specialized word-based mappings for building these semantic structures.

The Meaning Builder expects arguments of type Person for predicates such as "was born" or "son of", hence a proper name refers to a Person if it is an argument of such a predicate. In this way the Meaning Builder constructs a network of meaning structures with their roles, many of which are not yet filled. This network provides the basis for further semantic analysis.

The Conceptual Semantic Analyzer takes the meaning structures supplied by the Meaning Builder and expands and enhances them using inference rules implemented as Soar productions. For example, the presence of a phrase like "is not living" in the text triggers search for a death event for the subject person, and also a Date schema with its value set to UNKNOWN; when a death date is reported, its value is set explicitly. Similarly, when the text mentions that someone "is married" without further comment, the system will infer the existence of a second person whose name is UNKNOWN. Another example of inference involves reference resolution, where pronouns and GP tokens are associated by backward search for the Person they refer to. This is implemented with the resolve-reference operator, which performs basic search but does not yet take advantage of gender and number agreement or the specific meanings of nouns like "widow".

In OntoSoar the meaning schemas are modeled on image schemas (Johnson 1987), though they are not connected to perception in any direct way. Nevertheless the matching of one schema with roles that connect to other schemas in a network provides declarative knowledge that enables adding the procedural knowledge for inferencing.

Matching target ontologies

The information OntoSoar targets is subject to some simplification: while identifying unique individuals and associated names, gender, important dates, and family relationships, we exclude for now geographical locations plus other facts like employment or religion. We also adopt simplifying assumptions about family relationships, namely that a marriage is between a man and a woman, and that parent/child relationships are only for biological parents. These limitations and assumptions can be relaxed in future work.

Once we have analyzed an input segment to build our internal meaning structures, the final step is to project those meanings onto the ontology provided by the user. This work is done in two steps. Since both the internal meaning schemas of ECG and the user ontology are static, we can find object and relationship sets in the ontology that match parts of our schemas statically before we have seen any input data. Then when a segment has been completely analyzed, we can use these matches to map the specific meanings found in the segment onto fact assertions in the ontology.

OntoSoar's find-matches operator executes the matching procedure, along with various other operators that match keywords from the internal schemas with words taken from the names of the sets in the ontology:

- A lexical schema matches against any lexical object set (i.e. boxes in Figure 2 with dashed borders) that has a word in its name[3] matching one of the schema keywords.
- The Person schema matches to any object set regardless of its name as long as it has a relationship set connecting to a lexical object set that matches ProperName.
- The Couple schema matches against a pattern with a relationship set with three or more arguments connecting the object set that matches Person with one of its specializations (pointed to by the triangle in Figure 2) and a third argument that matches Date if that relationship set also has married in its name.
- The FamilyRelationship schema has a matching algorithm that looks for specializations of the object set which matches Person whose names contain the keywords son, daughter, or child.
- The LifeEvent schema looks for matches to relationship sets where the name of the relationship set has a word that matches one of the verbs that can generate a LifeEvent (e.g. "born" or "died"). These matches are recorded according to the verb that matches, so that the general LifeEvent schema will match several relationship sets, with the correct match being chosen later on according to the specific verb present. This matching also connects to the correct specialization of Person.

When the semantic analysis of a given segment has been completed, the OntoSoar extract-facts operator projects as many fact assertions as possible from the meanings found for the segment into the user ontology. Separate sub-operators extract assertions according to the various types of matches found previously. This assertion extraction process is fairly straightforward since we have already done the hard part in the matching.

Evaluation and Results

So far we have run several evaluations of OntoSoar's performance, across different documents and while using different user ontologies. First, we processed the sample text page, plus another page relatively similar to it from another book, using the ontology in Figure 2. For each sample text an output OSMX file was produced which contained fact assertions populating the ontology with persons identified by names, birth and death dates, and marriages.

Table 1 shows combined precision, recall, and F-measure result set for Samples 1 and 2 when compared to human annotations. Overall the precision is quite high, but the recall is lower. The primary reason for the recall errors is the lack of understanding of all the linguistic constructions used in the text.

[3]Ontology names are in camel-case and are split by OntoSoar.

Category	Exist	Found	Good	P %	R %	F %
Persons	31	26	25	96.2	80.6	87.7
Births	14	14	13	92.9	92.9	92.9
Deaths	9	7	7	100.0	77.8	87.5
Marriages	7	7	5	71.4	71.4	71.4
Children	16	2	2	100.0	12.5	22.2
Tot./Avg.	77	56	52	92.9	67.5	78.2

Table 1: Combined accuracy measures for Samples 1 and 2

Persons: The system has an ontological committment for creating a Person: there must be a proper name, and that name must be the grammatical subject or object of a predicate which applies to people, such as "born", "married", or "son of".

For the two sample text pages, OntoSoar missed finding six people. One was missed in the first sample text because the last sentence contained no identifiable predicates associated with her mention. In another case in the second text page, a person was incorrectly identified because of a segmentation ambiguity. Another was missed because of OntoSoar's current inability to unpack the dense semantics in the expression "...by whom she had one son...". Other reference resolution problems explain the other missing Persons.

Births and Deaths: OntoSoar finds every birth event, but in one case it is assigned to the wrong person due to unclear reference. Some dates are marked as UNKNOWN when the English text states that a person died (e.g. with the phrase "... is not living") but does not specify the date.

Marriages: OntoSoar finds all mentioned marriages (one in the first sample page, and six in the second), but in two cases from the latter it attaches the wrong subject to them.

Sons and Daughters: Many of the parent-child relationships in these sample texts, and in many other texts as well, are represented as enumerated lists of children. OntoSoar does not yet implement any list processing. This caused a total of 12 recall errors.

Beyond the two sample pages mentioned above, we also evaluated OntoSoar performance on a larger sampling of texts from family history books. We have access to a private repository of over a hundred thousand such books. We selected 200 books at random from this collection, and then randomly chose a sequence of three consecutive and data-rich pages from each of these books. We then arbitrarily chose twelve books' three-page ranges and ran them through OntoSoar. With minor adaptations to the input process, all twelve of the text files ran successfully through OntoSoar.

Performing a complete measure of the precision and recall of OntoSoar on this data would require manually annotating all the texts for all the relations of interest, which was beyond the scope of the available resources. However, we have looked through all the output files to examine the fact assertions that OntoSoar claims to have found and evaluated each as correct or not. The results are summarized in Table 2; the "Ely" and "Myra" files are the two sample pages discussed above.

In evaluating the matches, persons were considered correct if OntoSoar found at least a subset of the name given in the text with no extraneous material. Births and deaths were

File	Segs	Persons Found	Persons Correct	Births & Deaths Found	Births & Deaths Correct	Marriages Found	Marriages Correct	Children Found	Children Correct	Run Time Secs	Run Time Segs/Sec
Ely	15	11	100.00%	10	100.00%	1	100.00%	2	100.00%	15	1.000
Myra	23	15	93.33%	11	100.00%	6	66.67%	0	0.00%	10	2.300
Other documents	1547	328	73.48%	176	40.34%	78	51.28%	31	77.42%	1489	1.039

Table 2: Precision results for additional texts

considered correct if they were attached to a legitimate person and the date was complete. A marriage was considered correct if it connected the two correct people, even if the date was not found or incomplete. A child was considered correct if a person of the right gender was connected as a son or daughter to at least one of the correct parents.

The table only gives an estimate of precision; no attempt was made to measure either recall or F-measure. Unsurprisingly, the overall recall for these twelve files is rather low. If no facts were found in a particular case, the precision is marked as N/A. Overall OntoSoar processing time is consistent, at about one second per segment.

Many issues contribute to both recall and precision being much lower than for our original two samples. Some, such as OCR errors, are mostly beyond the reach of OntoSoar to solve. Other types of errors, however, could be reduced substantially by further improvements to OntoSoar within the scope of its existing architecture. For example, OntoSoar currently misses the many instances of dates formatted like "25 June 1823" or "6/25/1823" or even "Private" (indicating a person alive at time of publication). Nor can OntoSoar correctly unpack combined personal name constructions like "John Phillip and Alice Adel (Billeter) Harris", a common structure in this domain. Extending OntoSoar's capabilities in such areas will be straightforward.

Our work is preliminary, so we include a few notes about portability. We have directed very little effort at this specific text type: only the semantic interpretation rules that the agent executes were hand-crafted for the specific text type of this domain. Other text domains would require more semantic rules, but their integration into the system would be straightforward.

OntoSoar's conceptual-model-based ontologies are built by end-users, so presumably they may have different ways of conceptualizing or expressing the desired relationships than in the ontology depicted in Figure 2. We tested OntoSoar performance on two other ontologies representing largely the same information but structured differently. OntoSoar did well in finding Persons, Births, Deaths, and Marriages. However, the second ontology only specified Parent-Child relations, but not with specializations of Child for Son and Daughter, so OntoSoar was not able to distinguish these when using that ontology. The third ontology did not have any object sets for Child, so none of these were recognized. With more inference rules for reasoning about all possible arrangements of family relationships, these connections should be made.

Finally, we ran the system on all 830 pages of the book mentioned earlier (Vanderpoel 1902), which contains the partial page shown in Figure 1. Processing took about 8 hours on a typical PC desktop. The collection of assertions extracted consists of:

Persons	16,848
Births	8,609
Deaths	2,406
Genders	1,674
Couples	3,343
Children	3,049
Total	35,929

Conclusions and Future Work

From our work—preliminary though it is at this point— we are already able to draw several conclusions:

- Our linguistic analysis components are capable of extracting fact assertions from complex genealogical texts. In particular, an agent-based cognitive construction grammar framework provides a viable semantic representation.
- Meaning structures can be mapped onto ontologies to populate a user-specified conceptual model.
- The Soar cognitive architecture supports the above processes and provides a basis for more extensive inferencing for higher-level linguistic issues.

This work also represents a sizable increase in the quantity of running text that any Soar-based system has processed; treating a whole book of hundreds of pages with Soar is unprecedented.

Incremental improvement to OntoSoar is possible by adding or modifying rules in several parts of the system: the Segmenter can be made to recognize and expand new abbreviations such as "b", "dau", and "Bapt."; the grammar of the LG Parser can be augmented to understand different date formats; and the constructions in the Semantic Analyzer can be expanded to recognize common phrases like "his widow" and "they had one son".

Previous work has demonstrated incremental word-by-word language modeling in Soar with parsers other than the LG parser (Rytting and Lonsdale 2006); this permits interleaving syntactic and semantic processing at the word level. The basic pipeline described in this paper could be improved to allow for more interaction between semantics and the parser, the syntax, or even the segmenter.

Several Soar systems have learned tasks by observing humans doing the tasks. We anticipate being able to integrate this ability into our work, since the OntoES Annotator already provides a framework for human annotators doing the same task as OntoSoar. As the system scales up to handle more books of wider coverage, this type of human input would be helpful in the initial stages of processing each new book to adapt to its linguistic style.

References

Akbik, A., and Bross, J. 2009. Wanderlust: Extracting semantic relations from natural language text using dependency grammar patterns. In *Proceedings of the World Wide Web Conference (WWW2009) Semantic Search 2009 Workshop (SemSearch09)*.

Anderson, J. R. 2007. *How Can the Human Mind Occur in the Physical Universe?* Oxford and New York: Oxford University Press.

Bergen, B., and Chang, N. 2013. Embodied construction grammar. In Hoffman, T., and Trousdale, G., eds., *The Oxford Handbook of Construction Grammar*. New York: Oxford University Press. 168–190.

Bleiholder, J., and Naumann, F. 2008. Data fusion. *ACM Computing Surveys* 41(1):1–41.

Bryant, J. E. 2008. *Best-Fit Constructional Analysis*. Ph.D. Dissertation, University of California at Berkeley.

Buitelaar, P.; Cimiano, P.; Haase, P.; and Sintek, M. 2009. Towards linguistically grounded ontologies. In *Proceedings of the 6th European Semantic Web Conference (ESWC'09)*.

Chang, N. C.-L. 2008. *Constructing grammar: A computational model of the emergence of early constructions*. Ph.D. Dissertation, University of California at Berkeley.

Embley, D. W.; Kurtz, B. D.; and Woodfield, S. N. 1992. *Object-Oriented Systems Analysis: A Model-Driven Approach*. Englewood Cliffs, NJ: Yourdon Press.

Embley, D. W.; Liddle, S. W.; and Lonsdale, D. W. 2011. Conceptual modeling foundations for a web of knowledge. In Embley, D. W., and Thalheim, B., eds., *Handbook of Conceptual Modeling*. Springer. chapter 15.

Euzenat, J., and Schvaiko, P. 2007. *Ontology Matching*. Berlin: Springer.

Feldman, J. A. 2006. *From Molecule to Metaphor: A Neural Theory of Language*. Cambridge, MA: MIT Press.

Gruber, T. R. 1993. A translation approach to portable ontology specifications. *Knowledge Acquisition* 5(2):199–220.

Hoffman, T., and Trousdale, G., eds. 2013. *The Oxford Handbook of Construction Grammar*. New York: Oxford University Press.

Hruschka, E. R. J. 2013. Machine reading the web. Tutorial given at the 22nd International World Wide Web Conference, Rio de Janeiro, Brazil, 13-17 May, 2013.

Jackendoff, R. 1990. *Semantic Structures*. The MIT Press.

Jackendoff, R. 1996. Semantics and cognition. In Lappin, S., ed., *The Handbook of Contemporary Semantic Theory*. Blackwell.

Jackendoff, R. 2002. *Foundations of Language: Brain, Meaning, Grammar, Evolution*. Oxford University Press.

Jackendoff, R. 2003. Précis of foundations of language: Brain, meaning, grammar, evolution. *Behavioral and Brain Sciences* 26:651–707.

Johnson, M. 1987. *The Body in the Mind: The Bodily Basis of Meaning, Imagination, and Reason*. Chicago: The University of Chicago Press.

Laird, J. E. 2012. *The Soar Cognitive Architecture*. Cambridge, MA: The MIT Press.

Lakoff, G., and Johnson, M. 1980. The metaphorical structure of the human conceptual system. *Cognitive Science* 4:195–208.

Lewis, R. L. 1993. *An Architecturally-based Theory of Human Sentence Comprehension*. Ph.D. Dissertation, Carnegie Mellon University.

Lonsdale, D.; Hutchison, M.; Richards, T.; and Taysom, W. 2007. An NLP System for Extracting and Representing Knowledge from Abbreviated Text. In *Selected Proceedings of the Deseret Language and Linguistics Society Symposium*, 37–44. Brigham Young University.

Lonsdale, D.; Tustison, C.; Parker, C.; and Embley, D. 2008. Assessing clinical trial eligibility with logic expression queries. *Data & Knowledge Engineering* 66(1):3–17.

Melby, A. K., and Warner, C. T. 1995. *The Possibility of Language: A Discussion of the Nature of Language, with Implications for Human and Machine Translation*. Benjamin Translation Series. John Benjamins.

Mitra, P.; Noy, N. F.; and Jaizwal, A. R. 2004. Omen: A probabilistic ontology mapping tool. In *Proceedings of the Meaning Coordination and Negotiation workshop at the International Semantic Web Conference (ISwC)*, 537–547.

Mohan, S.; Mininger, A. H.; Kirk, J. R.; and Laird, J. E. 2012. Acquiring grounded representations of words with situated interactive instruction. *Advances in Cognitive Systems* 2:113–130.

Newell, A. 1990. *Unified Theories of Cognition*. Cambridge, MA: Harvard University Press.

Rytting, A., and Lonsdale, D. 2006. An operator-based account of semantic processing. In Lenci, A.; Montemagni, S.; and Pirrelli, V., eds., *Acquisition and representation of word meaning: theoretical and computational perspectives*. Pita/Rome: Istituti Editorialie Poligraphici Internazionali. 117–137.

Sarawagi, S. 2007. Information extraction. *Foundations and Trends in Databases* 1(3):261–377.

Sleator, D. D., and Temperley, D. 1993. Parsing English with a Link Grammar. In *Proceedings of the Third International Workshop on Parsing Technologies (IWPT)*.

Vanderpoel, G. B. 1902. *The Ely Ancestry: Lineage of Richard Ely of Plymouth England, who came to Boston, Mass., about 1655, & settled at Lyme, Conn, in 1660*. New York: The Calumet Press.

Proceedings of the Twenty-Ninth AAAI Conference on Artificial Intelligence

Extending Analogical Generalization with Near-Misses

Matthew D. McLure
Qualitative Reasoning Group
Northwestern University
2133 Sheridan Road
Evanston, IL, 60208, USA
mclure@u.northwestern.edu

Scott E. Friedman
Smart Information Flow Technologies (SIFT)
Minneapolis, MN, USA
friedman@sift.net

Kenneth D. Forbus
Qualitative Reasoning Group
Northwestern University
2133 Sheridan Road
Evanston, IL, 60208, USA
forbus@northwestern.edu

Abstract

Concept learning is a central problem for cognitive systems. Generalization techniques can help organize examples by their commonalities, but comparisons with non-examples, *near-misses,* can provide discrimination. Early work on near-misses required hand-selected examples by a teacher who understood the learner's internal representations. This paper introduces Analogical Learning by Integrating Generalization and Near-misses (ALIGN) and describes three key advances. First, domain-general cognitive models of analogical processes are used to handle a wider range of examples. Second, ALIGN's analogical generalization process constructs multiple probabilistic representations per concept via clustering, and hence can learn disjunctive concepts. Finally, ALIGN uses unsupervised analogical retrieval to find its own near-miss examples. We show that ALIGN out-performs analogical generalization on two perceptual data sets: (1) hand-drawn sketches; and (2) geospatial concepts from strategy-game maps.

Introduction

Learning concepts from examples is a core capability for cognitive systems. While many approaches learn over feature vectors, this work involves learning from more expressive relational representations, similar to inductive logic programming (Muggleton and De Raedt 1994; Cleuziou, Martin, and Vrain 2003). We focus here on similarity-based supervised learning, where labeled examples are available. Winston (1970) introduced the idea of a near-miss, a negative example that is very similar to a positive example. The small number of differences – ideally one – simplified the learner's search for necessary conditions for category membership. Winston's system used analogical matching to compare the structured representations of the positive and negative examples in order to find the difference(s). Winston's system had some important limitations: it used a domain-specific analogical matcher; it required the teacher to know the internal representations of the concept; it required the teacher to label near-misses; it learned one representation per concept and thus could not handle disjunctive concepts; and it was only tested on blocks-world scenes.

Since that time, the state of the art in knowledge representation and analogical reasoning has improved to the point where a more general model capable of using near-misses can be formulated over more general representations. This paper describes Analogical Learning by Integrating Generalization and Near-misses (ALIGN), which is built on Gentner's (1983) structure-mapping theory of analogy and similarity. Computational models of human analogical matching, retrieval, and generalization (summarized below) are combined and extended to yield three important advantages: (1) ALIGN learns both characteristic properties (i.e., descriptions generalized over positive examples) and discriminative properties (i.e., strict membership criteria) of categories; (2) ALIGN can learn disjunctive categories; and (3) ALIGN automatically identifies near-misses via analogical retrieval, so the teacher does not need to provide them or know the underlying knowledge representations.

We provide empirical results to support these claims, using ALIGN to learn spatial concepts from hand-sketched examples in a sketch understanding system. We use sketched materials for two reasons. First, visual and spatial information is of great importance in domains such as science, engineering, and art, and typically involves rich, relational representations. Second, encoding spatial representations automatically from raw ink reduces tailorability, as opposed to hand-generated representations.

We start by summarizing the analogical processing models that ALIGN uses, and the sketch understanding system we used to automatically encode examples for the experiments. We then describe ALIGN and two experimental analyses: (1) ALIGN learns concepts from sketches of everyday objects; and (2) ALIGN learns geospatial concepts from circled examples on a strategy-game map. We close with related and future work.

Background

Computational models of Structure-Mapping

Structure-Mapping is a psychological theory of analogy and similarity that has been used to explain how people compare visual stimuli (Markman and Gentner 1996; Sagi, Gentner, and Lovett 2012), learn abstract categories (Gentner and Namy 1999), and learn contrastive categories via difference detection (Smith and Gentner 2014). It defines analogical comparison as a process of aligning two structured representations, a base and a target, guided by mapping constraints. The matching process produces *correspondences* that specify which elements (i.e., entities and expressions) in the base go with which elements in the target. Structure-mapping also generates *candidate inferences* that project unshared structure (i.e., non-corresponding expressions) from base to target or vice-versa.

The Structure-Mapping Engine (SME)

The Structure-Mapping Engine (Falkenhainer, Forbus, and Gentner 1989) is a computational model of structure-mapping theory. SME operates via a local-to-global process, initially constructing local match hypotheses in parallel, followed by a serial phase that greedily coalesces islands of matches into globally consistent mappings, guided by a scoring process based on structure-mapping principles. Each mapping contains a set of correspondences and a *similarity score* that captures the overall similarity. The similarity score is normalized to the closed interval [0, 1] by dividing by the mean of the scores of the self-matches of base and target. Each mapping can contain candidate inferences, from base to target, and reverse candidate inferences, from target to base. Candidate inferences can include *analogy skolems*, which are entities hypothesized via projection because they lack a correspondent in the other case.

MAC/FAC

MAC/FAC (Forbus, Gentner, and Law 1995) is a model of similarity-based retrieval built on SME. The inputs are (1) a *probe* case and (2) a set of cases from which to retrieve, called a *case library*. MAC/FAC retrieves up to three similar cases from the case library based on similarity to the probe. The algorithm has two stages. The first stage (MAC) computes in parallel coarse similarity estimates between the probe and every case in the case library using content vectors, a redundant non-structured representation computed from the cases. Each dimension in a content vector is proportional to the number of statements using that predicate in the original case, thus the dot product estimates the number of local matches that SME will find between the probe and each case. This scales well to large case libraries. The cases with the highest dot product with the probe are passed to the second stage, FAC. FAC uses SME to compare the probe to each MAC result, in parallel. The case with highest SME similarity score, plus up to two more if very close to the top scorer, are returned as the reminding(s).

Sequential Analogical Generalization Engine (SAGE)

The Sequential Analogical Generalization Engine (SAGE) is a model of analogical generalization built on SME, and the successor to SEQL (Kuehne et al. 2000). SAGE maintains a *generalization context* for each concept, where incoming training examples are incrementally clustered to form *generalizations* (two or more analogically mapped examples) and *unassimilated examples* (clusters of size one). SAGE generalizations are themselves cases, but each expression in a generalization is assigned a probability based on the frequency with which it corresponded to expressions in co-clustered examples.

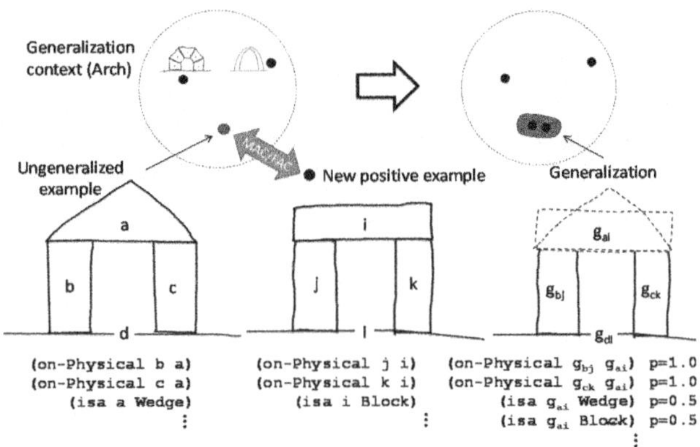

Figure 1: An example is added to the "Arch" generalization context and generalized with a previously unassimilated example.

The SAGE algorithm consists of two stages: (1) *select* at most one existing cluster that is sufficiently similar to the incoming example, and (2) *merge* the incoming example into the cluster, if sufficiently similar. The select process uses MAC/FAC, with the new example as the probe and the generalization context as the case library. If the normalized similarity score of the best reminding is greater than the *assimilation threshold* of the generalization context, SAGE merges the example; otherwise, the new example is added as an unassimilated example.

The merge process uses the correspondences in the SME mapping to (1) update the probabilities associated with each existing expression in the generalization, and (2) add new expressions from the example to the generalization. When non-identical entities correspond in the mapping, SAGE replaces them with *generalized entities* (i.e., symbols that represent multiple symbols from examples). A merge is illustrated in Figure 1, where corresponding expressions in the resulting generalization have p = 1.0, and non-corresponding expressions have a p = 0.5. SME uses these probabilities to bias the local scores on match

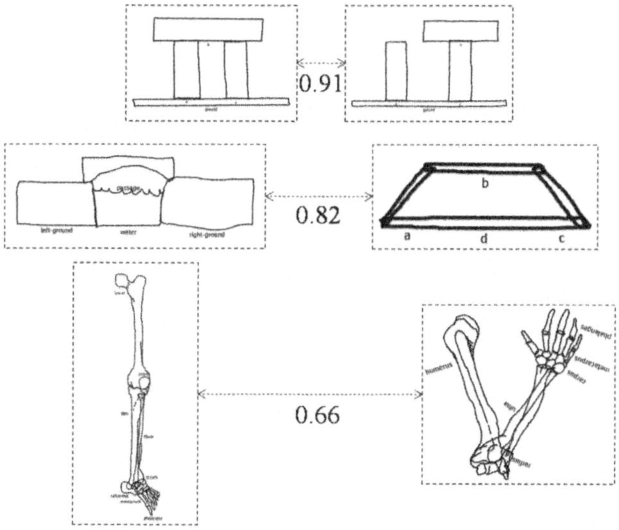

Figure 2: Three pairs of sketched objects with decreasing normalized similarity scores, from top to bottom. All three pairs are potential near-misses because their labels differ.

hypotheses. As SAGE assimilates more examples into a generalization, some expressions will retain high probability, while others will diminish. Consequently, generalizations in SAGE express a probability distribution over their expressions, separating characteristic (high probability) structure from incidental (low-probability) structure. SAGE uses a *probability threshold* to prune low-probability expressions from the generalization and maintain tractability.

SAGE has been used to learn and classify musical genres (Dehghani and Lovett 2006), spatial prepositions (Lockwood, Lovett, and Forbus 2008), and sketched every-day objects (Lovett, Dehghani, and Forbus 2007; McLure, Friedman, and Forbus 2012), suggesting that it provides a domain-general foundation for ALIGN.

CogSketch

Sketching is a powerful way to express visual and spatial ideas. CogSketch (Forbus et al. 2011) is an open-domain sketch understanding system. Users draw digital ink, which they segment into visual entities (glyphs) and label with concepts drawn from a large (OpenCyc-derived) knowledge base.[1] Conceptual labeling is a practical vehicle for information that is often conveyed with language during human-to-human sketching (e.g., "this is a block"). CogSketch constructs visual representations from what is drawn (e.g., that two glyphs have intersecting edges) and spatial representations from both the visual and conceptual information (e.g., that the objects depicted by the glyphs are touching). Figure 2 shows six examples. CogSketch's extensive vocabulary of representations is motivated by human spatial cognition, including relations

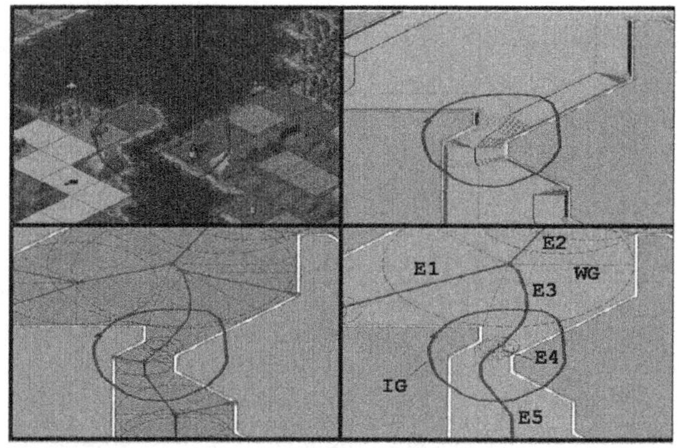


```
(isa SG SelectionGlyph)   (isa E4 StraightEdge)
(isa WG WaterGlyph)       (narrowRadius E4)
(bisects WG SG)           (lengthShort E4)
(medialAxisEdge WG E4)    (clockwiseNeighborAtJct E1 E2)
(contains SG E4)          (sourceJct (elementsConnected E1 E2))
(intersectsInk SG E3)     (obtuseJct (elementsConnected E1 E2))
(isa E4 SinkEdge)         (straightJct (directedConnection E3 E4))
                 ⋮
```

Figure 3: A water glyph (top-left) is decomposed into its skeleton edges (bottom right) by using a grassfire algorithm (top-right) to compute a medial-axis transform, which is pruned and segmented according to its radius function.

for adjacency, relative position and size, and topological relationships. It is capable of analyzing the same sketch at multiple levels of description (i.e., edges, objects, and groups).

CogSketch interacts with the strategy game Freeciv to encode qualitative structured representations for regions on the map. CogSketch renders the map and creates glyphs for units, cities, and *terrain blobs* (i.e., polygons that outline groups of tiles that share some property). The user selects a region by drawing a glyph on the map (e.g., the red circle in Figure 3). When the user assigns a conceptual label to the selection glyph, CogSketch automatically encodes a case. The encoding scheme used in our geospatial classification task (illustrated in Figure 3) begins by detecting and recording topological relationships between the selection glyph and overlapping land or water terrain blobs. Any blob glyph that overlaps the selection glyph is decomposed into a skeleton based on the Medial Axis Transform (MAT). Each skeleton is further segmented at points corresponding to qualitative changes in the radius function (i.e., the distance from each point to its closest points on the exterior) – a strategy inspired by shock graphs (Siddiqi et al. 1999). The result for each blob glyph is a network of edges directed from its wider sections to its narrower sections. The scheme encodes qualitative properties over these edges including length, radius function, curvature, and various aspects of connectivity. Finally, topological relationships between each edge and the selection glyph are encoded.

CogSketch has been used to model visual problem solving (Lovett, Forbus, and Usher 2010), including

[1] www.cyc.com/platform/opencyc

cultural differences (Lovett and Forbus 2011). It has also been used as a platform for sketch-based educational software (Yin et al. 2010). These experiments suggest that the representations it produces are both realistic and useful.

ALIGN

Similarity can be deceptive. Isthmuses are similar to straits, bays are similar to peninsulas, and bridges are similar to arches. In this section, we describe how ALIGN leverages these deceptive similarities as opportunities to learn and represent category boundaries. We begin by discussing how ALIGN detects and exploits deceptive similarities, then we describe how it represents and revises its hypotheses, and finally we describe how it classifies examples with a mix of similarity and hypothesis-testing.

Detecting & Exploiting Near-Misses with Analogy

Given a labeled training example (e.g., of an *arch*), ALIGN uses MAC/FAC to retrieve similar training examples with *different* labels (e.g., *bridge*) or a *null* label.[2] High-similarity pairs of examples with different labels above a *similarity threshold* (equal to SAGE's assimilation threshold) are *near-misses*. Using the best SME mapping between the positive (*arch*) and negative (*bridge* or *null*) example, ALIGN uses the candidate inferences (i.e., projected expressions across cases) to produce hypotheses about category boundaries.

ALIGN distinguishes between two types of candidate inferences (CIs) that produce different hypotheses:

1. *Positive-to-negative CIs* (PNCIs) project relations from the positive example in terms of the negative example's entities. ALIGN converts these to *inclusion hypotheses*: necessary criteria for asserting category membership.

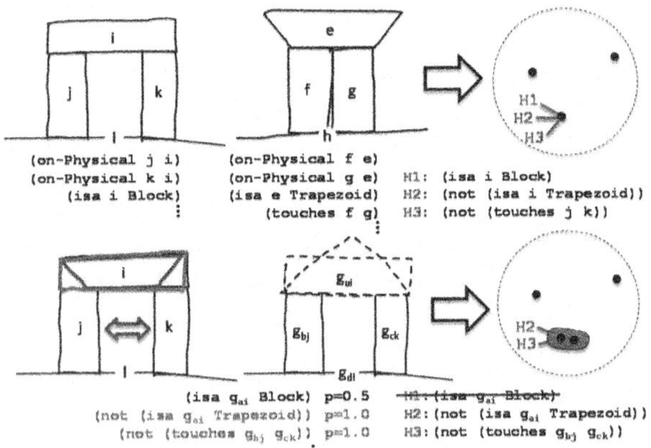

Figure 4: A near-miss pair and hypothesis revision

2. *Negative-to-positive CIs* (NPCIs) project relations from the negative example, in terms of the positive example's entities. ALIGN converts these to *exclusion hypotheses*: sufficient criteria for blocking category membership.

ALIGN associates hypotheses with the positive example, and represents hypotheses in terms of the positive example's entities. For PNCIs, this requires a translation step that replaces the entities mentioned (from the negative side) with their corresponding (positive) entities. In Figure 4 (top), H1 is an inclusion hypothesis for the category *arch* resulting from the PNCI `(isa e Block)`, and H3 is an exclusion hypothesis resulting from the NPCI `(touches f g)`.

ALIGN also represents skolems in its hypotheses. A skolem in a PNCI is replaced with the positive entity from which it was projected, e.g. `(AnalogySkolemFn m)` translates to `m`. In contrast, NPCIs with skolems result in more complex exclusion hypotheses, because they need to

```
CL = {} ;; a case library for training examples
;; S = similarity threshold, M_YX = reverse mapping of M_XY
TrainOn(example P, label L_P) ;; label may be null
  if L_P
    GC_P = Label→GeneralizationContext (L_P)
    {G_P, M_GP} = SageAdd (P, GC_P, S) ;; if unassimilated,
                                      ;; G_P=P & M_GP=null
  for each {N, M_NP} in MacFacRetrieve(P,CL)
    L_N = Example→Label(N)
    {G_N, M_GN} = Example→Generalization (N)
    if L_P ≠ L_N and NormScore(M_NP) > S ;; a near-miss
      GenerateNewCriteria(L_P, G_P, P, N, M_NP, M_PG)
      GenerateNewCriteria(L_N, G_N, N, P, M_PN, M_NG)
  CL = CL + P

GenerateNewCriteria(label L, gen G, pos P, neg N,
                    mapping M_NP, mapping M_PG)
  if L and not BlockedByCriteria(N, G, M_GP, M_PN)
    H_PL = ExtractCriteria(P, L, M_NP)
    AddCriteria(G, GeneralizeCriteria(H_PL, M_PG))

TestOn(unlabeled example U)
  D = {} ;; discarded remindings
  for 1 to 3
    R = MacFacRetrieve(U, (CL – D))
    for each {E, M_EU} in SortByGenSimilarity(R, U)
      L_E = Example→Label(E)
      {G_E, M_GE} = Example→Generalization(E)
      if BlockedByCriteria(U, G_E, M_GE, M_EU)
        D = D + E
      else return L_E
  return Example→Label(LeastBlocked(D))
```

Figure 5: ALIGN's top-level training and testing procedures.

[2] In this paper, categories are mutually exclusive, and some training and testing examples have a null label (i.e., they are confusers).

specify criteria about *extra* entities that aren't represented in the positive case while remaining embedded in the case. For these NPCIs, ALIGN replaces each skolem with a variable, and constrains each variable so that it cannot bind to any entity from the positive example that entered into the near-miss mapping. Thus, a NPCI such as `(touches j (AnalogySkolemFn x))` is translated to capture the hypothesis that *there cannot be something extra that touches j,* as follows (*cannot* is implicit because it is an exclusion hypothesis):

```
(and (different i ?skolem)
     (different j ?skolem)
     (different k ?skolem)
     (different l ?skolem)
     (touches j ?skolem))
```

ALIGN discards near-miss pairs that are *explained away* by existing hypotheses associated with the positive example.

In practice, hypotheses produced from a single comparison can be over-specific, and must be revised to be practically useful. We describe this process next.

Revising Hypotheses with Analogical Generalization

ALIGN maintains one SAGE generalization context for every (non-*null*) label encountered, and each training example is added to the generalization context corresponding to its label, if any. If SAGE assimilates the example into a generalization, its associated hypotheses are generalized to refer to the entities in the generalization. Generalized hypotheses are pruned if they include conditions not true of all examples assimilated into the generalization (i.e., expressions with $p < 1.0$ for inclusion hypotheses, and $p > 0$ for exclusion hypotheses). Figure 4 (bottom) demonstrates pruning an inclusion hypothesis.

ALIGN uses generalized hypotheses to block labels and explain away new near-misses. An extra analogical translation step is required to project these hypotheses from the generalization to an unlabeled or negative example, via the positive (assimilated) example. The degree to which a failed hypothesis blocks a label is weighted using the size of the generalization it is associated with, with the intuition being that hypotheses that persist after more generalization operations are more accurate, all else being equal.

Since SAGE can produce multiple clusters from the positive examples of a single concept, ALIGN can maintain alternative sets of hypotheses for a given concept, resulting in a disjunctive category structure. Structural similarity (via analogical retrieval) determines which disjunct(s) get tested against a given unlabeled example.

Classification via Analogy

To classify an unlabeled example, ALIGN retrieves similar labeled examples from memory. Those retrieved examples that have been assimilated during learning are exchanged for their associated generalizations. Starting with the most similar case, ALIGN tests each of the case's associated hypotheses by:

1. Translating the hypothesis to refer to entities in the unlabeled example, using the entity correspondences of the best mapping.
2. Testing whether the translated condition holds. If an exclusion hypothesis holds or an inclusion hypothesis fails to hold (skolems count as failures), do not infer that label.

If these hypotheses are consistent with the new example, ALIGN classifies the new example with the retrieved label. Otherwise, ALIGN iterates to the next retrieved example. This is important for distinguishing similar categories.

Because we assume that the set of concepts is collectively exhaustive, ALIGN conducts repeated retrievals during classification until it finds an unblocked label. If no unblocked label is found after 3 retrievals, then the label of the most highly supported retrieval is chosen. Support is determined by subtracting the cumulative weight of the inconsistent hypotheses from that of the consistent hypotheses. Since *null*-labeled retrievals cannot have associated hypotheses, they have neutral (0) support.

Evaluation

To evaluate the extension of analogical generalization with near-misses, we ran two classification tasks under different conditions: (1) *ALIGN* is the full system described above; (2) *Prototypes* is *ALIGN* without near-miss analysis; and (3) *Examples* is *ALIGN* without near-misses and *also* without analogical generalization, so classification is reduced to similarity-based retrieval over the library of training examples. For moderately high similarity thresholds (0.6-0.9), we expected Prototypes to outperform Examples and ALIGN to outperform both.

Arches: 8	Bridges: 4	*False arches:* 8
Skeletal arms: 4	Triangles: 4	*False triangles:* 4
Skeletal legs: 4	Quadrilaterals: 4	*False quads:* 4

Table 1: A dataset of sketched concepts. "False" categories were negative examples of all categories.

Experiment 1

ALIGN was compared with the Prototypes and Examples conditions in a classification task involving objects sketched in CogSketch. There were 44 sketches distributed over 6 mutually exclusive labels, where 16 of the sketches had *null* labels (i.e., no positive labels) but were potential near-misses for some of the concepts (e.g., *false arches* are nearly arches) as summarized in Table 1. The cases produced by CogSketch each contained, on average, 4.5

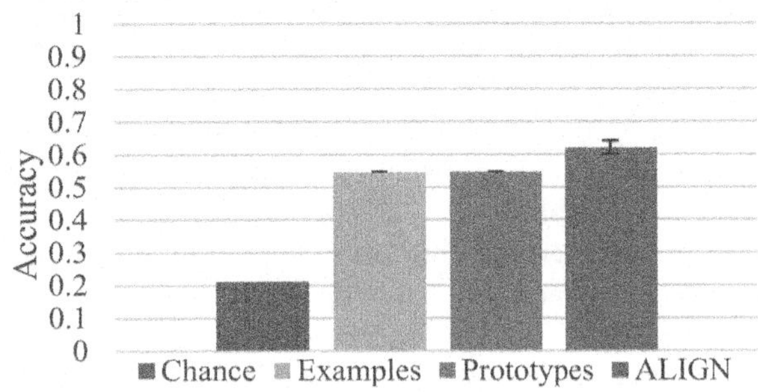

Figure 6: Classification performance of ALIGN compared to Examples and Prototypes.

unique entities and 31 facts. The task was to choose one or none of the 6 labels, with chance at 21% accuracy. Performance was evaluated via 4-fold cross-validation. Statistical significance was measured using a one-tailed, paired t-test. The similarity threshold for ALIGN was set to 0.8. This was also the assimilation threshold used for the Prototypes condition.

Results

Figure 6 shows the results of Experiment 1. The Prototypes and Examples approaches performed identically at 55% accuracy, well above chance ($p < 0.01$). ALIGN demonstrated a 7% improvement over these conditions ($p < 0.01$).

Experiment 2

This experiment evaluated classification performance in a task involving geospatial concepts. Examples were circled on a Freeciv map using CogSketch as described above. The dataset consisted of 60 examples evenly distributed over 6 mutually exclusive and collectively exhaustive categories: *Isthmus*, *Peninsula*, *Strait*, *Bay*, *Archipelago* and *Island*. The cases produced by CogSketch each contained, on average, 8 unique entities and 60 facts. 10-fold cross-validation was used. ALIGN was compared to the Prototypes approach over a range of similarity thresholds. At a threshold of 1, both reduce to Examples.

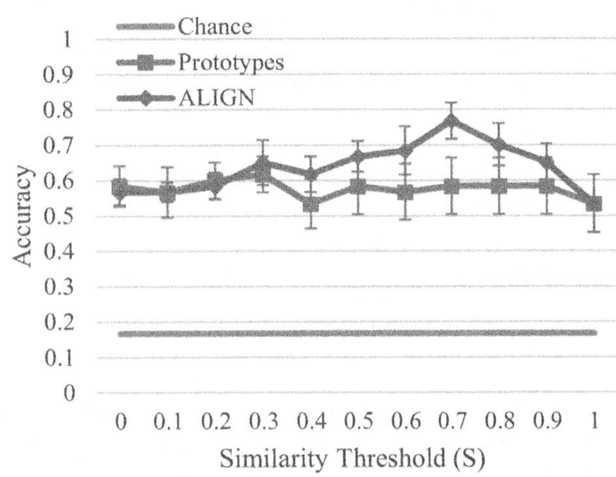

Figure 7: Classification accuracy on a geospatial dataset.

Results

As shown in Figure 7, ALIGN achieved a peak accuracy of 77%, significantly outperforming the Prototypes peak performance of 62% ($p < 0.05$). The Prototypes condition where similarity threshold (S) is 1 is by definition the Examples condition, since $S = 1$ effectively prevents generalization and near-miss analysis. Here, Examples performed significantly worse than ALIGN with an accuracy of 53% ($p < 0.05$), which was not significantly different from the peak of Prototypes.

Discussion

This data demonstrates that extending analogical generalization with near-misses can improve classification for spatial concepts represented as structured, qualitative descriptions. The interaction between the similarity threshold and the marginal benefit of near-misses suggests that there is a "sweet spot" for comparison; when the threshold is too low, more distant near-miss comparisons are generated, resulting in more hypotheses, most of which are incidental differences and should be pruned. When the similarity threshold is too high, the generalizations in SAGE end up smaller in size and more numerous, providing less basis for pruning bad hypotheses.

Using analogical generalization alone (Prototypes) did not significantly improve performance over simple retrieval (Examples) as we expected. The identical performance in Experiment 1 is likely related to the size of the categories; out of a group of four bridges, at least three must be sufficiently similar for two to generalize in the training set and a third to match with the resulting prototype during classification. Also recall that Experiment 1 contains examples without any positive label, which are not given a chance to generalize. Thus, their incidental similarities to other categories are not suppressed.

Related Work

ALIGN is capable of learning with relatively few examples. It requires orders of magnitude fewer examples than existing connectionist models (e.g., Elman 1998; Krizhevsky, Sutskever, and Hinton 2012). We believe ALIGN makes more realistic demands.

The IDeAL system (Bhatta and Goel 1997) learned by analogy over structured representations similar to those used by ALIGN, but it was applied to a design problem-solving task instead of recognition. Its retrieval mechanism indexed previous designs by their function, whereas retrieval in ALIGN uses domain-general similarity-based retrieval. IDeAL learned generic teleological mechanisms by comparing a correct solution provided by a teacher to designs retrieved from memory – similar to near-miss discovery in ALIGN – but it relied on design-specific background knowledge to abstract the appropriate aspects from the design pair. Hypothesis production in ALIGN is domain-general, so instead it relies on finding similar positive examples to properly refine its hypotheses.

Cleuziou, Martin and Vrain (2003) described an inductive logic programming (ILP) approach to learning disjunctive concepts that bore similarities to ALIGN. Positive examples were clustered into *subconcepts* according to a similarity measure, and a separate conjunctive definition was learned for each subconcept based on the negative examples. Its representations, similarity metric, and hypothesis generation were all based in first order logic; the rules learned contained logical variables and were tested deductively, in contrast with the hypotheses here, which are embedded in learned models and tested via analogical projection. Winston (1982, 1986) also explored learning rules from analogies, producing logical rules via generalizing on one example. His if-then rules and censors were functionally similar to our inclusion and exclusion hypotheses, respectively.

Another analogous approach is K-Means+ID3 (Gaddam, Phoha, and Balagani 2007), which cascaded k-means clustering and ID3 decision trees for anomaly detection. While their approach used feature-vector data, it shared the idea that rule-based class boundaries can apply better when trained locally in some similarity space.

Conclusions and Future Work

This paper describes ALIGN, a concept learning model that extends analogical generalization with near-misses. It is capable of automatically finding its own near-miss examples, and we have shown evidence from two experiments that near-misses significantly improve performance over analogical generalization and retrieval alone. We plan on experimenting with ALIGN in other domains, as well as expanding the range of concepts in sketched domains.

Acknowledgements

This material is based upon work supported by the Air Force Office of Scientific Research under Award No. FA2386-10-1-4128.

References

Bhatta, S., & Goel, A., 1997. Learning generic mechanisms for innovative strategies in adaptive design. *The Journal of the Learning Sciences* 6(4), 367-396.

Cleuziou, G., Martin, L., & Vrain, C., 2003. Disjunctive learning with a soft-clustering method. In *ILP'03: 13th International Conference on Inductive Logic Programming*, 75–92.

Elman, J., 1998. Generalization, simple recurrent networks, and the emergence of structure. In *Proceedings of the Twentieth Annual Conference of the Cognitive Science Society*. Mahwah, NJ: Lawrence Erlbaum Associates.

Falkenhainer, B., Forbus, K., & Gentner, D., 1989. The structure-mapping engine: Algorithm and examples. *Artificial Intelligence* 41(1), 1-63.

Forbus, K., Gentner, D., and Law, K., 1995. MAC/FAC: A model of similarity-based retrieval. *Cognitive Science* 19, 141-205.

Forbus, K. D., Usher, J., Lovett, A., Lockwood, K. and Wetzel, J., 2011. Cogsketch: Sketch understanding for cognitive science research and for education. *Topics in Cognitive Science* 3.

Gaddam, S., Phoha, V., & Balagani, K., 2007. K-Means+ID3: A novel method for supervised anomaly detection by cascading k-means clustering and ID3 decision tree learning methods. *IEEE Transactions on Knowledge and Data Engineering* 19(3).

Gentner, D., & Namy, L., 1999. Comparison in the development of categories. *Cognitive Development* 14, 487-513.

Gentner, D., 1983. Structure-mapping: A theoretical framework for analogy. *Cognitive Science* 7(2), 155-170.

Krizhevsky, A., Sutskever, I., and Hinton, G. E., 2012. Imagenet classification with deep convolutional neural networks. *Advances in Neural Information Processing Systems*, 1097-1105.

Kuehne, S., Forbus, K., Gentner, D. and Quinn, B., 2000. SEQL: Category learning as progressive abstraction using structure mapping. *Proceedings of CogSci. 2000.*

Lovett, A., Forbus, K., and Usher, J., 2010. A structure-mapping model of Raven's Progressive Matrices. *Proc. of CogSci 2010.*

Lovett, A., & Forbus, K., 2011. Cultural commonalities and differences in spatial problem solving: A computational analysis. *Cognition* 121, 281-287.

Markman, A. B., & Gentner, D., 1996. Commonalities and differences in similarity comparisons. *Memory & Cognition* 24(2), 235-249.

Muggleton, S., & De Raedt, L., 1994. Inductive logic programming: Theory and methods. *Journal of Logic Programming* 19-20, 629-679.

Sagi, E., Gentner, D., & Lovett, A., 2012. What difference reveals about similarity. *Cognitive Science* 36, 1019-1050.

Siddiqi, K., Shokoufandeh, A., Dickinson, S. J., and Zucker, S. W., 1999. Shock graphs and shape matching. *International Journal of Computer Vision* 30, 1-24.

Smith, L., & Gentner, D., 2014. The role of difference-detection in learning contrastive categories. *Proceedings of CogSci. 2014.*

Winston, P. H., 1970. Learning structural descriptions from examples. Ph.D. diss., MIT, Cambridge, MA.

Winston, P. H., 1982. Learning new principles from precedents and exercises. *Artificial Intelligence* 23(12).

Winston, P. H., 1986. Learning by augmenting rules and accumulating censors. In *Machine Learning: An Artificial Intelligence Approach* 2, 45-62. Morgan-Kaufman.

Yin, P., Forbus, K., Usher, J., Sageman, B. and Jee, B., 2010. Sketch Worksheets: A Sketch-based Educational Software System. *Proceedings of the 22nd Annual Conference on Innovative Applications of Artificial Intelligence.*

Automatic Ellipsis Resolution: Recovering Covert Information from Text

Marjorie McShane & Petr Babkin
Rensselaer Polytechnic Institute
{margemc34, petr.a.babkin}@gmail.com

Abstract

Ellipsis is a linguistic process that makes certain aspects of text meaning not directly traceable to surface text elements and, therefore, inaccessible to most language processing technologies. However, detecting and resolving ellipsis is an indispensable capability for language-enabled intelligent agents. The key insight of the work presented here is that not all cases of ellipsis are equally difficult: some can be detected and resolved with high confidence even before we are able to build agents with full human-level semantic and pragmatic understanding of text. This paper describes a fully automatic, implemented and evaluated method of treating one class of ellipsis: elided scopes of modality. Our cognitively-inspired approach, which centrally leverages linguistic principles, has also been applied to overt referring expressions with equally promising results.

Introduction

The grammatical process of ellipsis – the non-expression of semantic content – increases the efficiency of natural language communication by people but introduces challenges for machine processing. For example, the final clause in sentence (1)[1] will be of little use to an intelligent agent until and unless it is decorated with metadata indicating that what the toddler *could* do is *teach illiterate women to read and write.* (In this and subsequent examples, elided categories are indicated by [e] and their sponsors – i.e., the material used to recover their meaning – are italicized.[2])

(1) Aid workers in war-ravaged Kabul were stunned when a toddler from a poor family offered to *teach illiterate women to read and write* – and then promptly proved he could [e].

This paper reports an implemented and evaluated method of automatically resolving elided scopes of modality, which expands upon the preliminary work reported in McShane et al. 2012b. The work is novel because ellipsis has been left largely untreated by natural language processing (NLP) systems (Spenader and Hendriks 2005), being resistant to the currently prevalent methodological preference for supervised machine learning. The closest point of comparison is Hardt's (1997) VP ellipsis system; however, whereas that system requires a perfect (manually corrected) syntactic parse as input, ours does not rely on any manually provided prerequisites. Other comparisons require the leap from elided to overt referring expressions; Lee et al. 2013 provides a nice overview of the current state of the art in resolving those.

The key point about ellipsis that has been overlooked is that while resolving some instances does require sophisticated semantic and pragmatic reasoning, not all cases are so difficult. Leveraging linguistic insights, our system automatically detects which instances of ellipsis it can resolve with high confidence and treats only those, supplementing each resolution decision with a corpus-attested measure of confidence that will contribute to an intelligent agent's evaluation of whether it has understood the meaning of a language input sufficiently to act in response to it.

The work is being carried out within the OntoSem language processing system of the OntoAgent cognitive architecture (McShane and Nirenburg 2012). OntoAgents are cognitively simulated, language-endowed intelligent agents that are being configured to collaborate with people in task-oriented applications, such as the prototype Maryland Virtual Patient physician training system (Nirenburg, McShane and Beale 2008). OntoAgents carry out deep semantic and pragmatic language analysis, yielding ontologically grounded text meaning representations that populate agent memory and subsequently support agent reasoning (McShane et al. 2012a; McShane, Nirenburg and Beale, Submitted).

Research and development in the OntoAgent paradigm seeks to balance the socio-economic necessity of near-term utility with the scientific goal of fundamentally solving

[1] Most examples are from the Gigaword corpus (Graff and Cieri 2003), which we used for system testing and evaluation.

[2] The inflectional form of the head of the sponsor is irrelevant since, in reality, an elided *meaning* is recovered based on the *meaning* of the sponsor. For discussion of the term *sponsor,* see Byron 2004, p. 16.

problems of artificial intelligence. In this spirit, we simultaneously work toward preparing OntoAgents to fully interpret every text input, on the one hand, and to leverage well-selected "lightweight" strategies to meet near-term goals, on the other. Our work on ellipsis detection and resolution is a good example of how those strategies can interact over time. First we configure a lightweight – though linguistically and cognitively inspired – strategy that offers useful, near-term results, albeit with incomplete coverage; then we incorporate more knowledge-intensive analysis methods, as needed, to expand coverage.

Linguistic Background

"Modality" refers to a class of meanings that can scope over a proposition (cf. recent work on sentiment analysis, e.g., Pang and Lee 2008). A given proposition can be scoped over by many different types of modal meanings, as shown by the italicized strings in (2). In addition, multiple modalities can scope over a proposition, as shown by (3).

(2) The US *has <has not, might have, cannot have, should not, might, wants to, does not want to, seems to have, could not have, is believed to have, failed to*, etc.> sign(ed) the treaty.

(3) The US might have to sign the treaty.

The microtheory of modality in OntoSem distinguishes ten types of modality: epistemic, belief, obligative, permissive, potential, evaluative, intentional, epiteuctic, effort, and volitive (Nirenburg and Raskin 2004). Values of each modality can be realized in language by various words and phrases: e.g., **volitive**: *want to, not want to*; **permissive**: *may, may not*; **epiteuctic**: *succeed in, fail to*. Each modal meaning has a scope that represents the event(s) the meaning applies to. The scope can be overtly specified or elided; if elided, it must have a *sponsor* that allows the reader/hearer to reconstruct the unexpressed meaning.

Although sponsors for elided referring expressions – like sponsors for any referring expression – are most accurately understood as semantic entities rather than text strings, the latter can serve as a proxy which is, on the one hand, sufficient for some applications and, on the other hand, a strong first step toward the more involved analysis needed to arrive at full semantic resolution. For example, in (4) the elided category refers to a different instance of *sending* a different set of *children* abroad than is indicated in the sponsor clause – a phenomenon known as *sloppy coreference* (Fiengo and May 1994).

(4) Better-off parents could *send their children abroad for English education* but poorer families could not [e].

In the system implementation reported here, the ellipsis treatment is deemed correct if the system (a) correctly detects the ellipsis and (b) selects the leftmost verbal element of the sponsor, which might be a the head of the sponsoring proposition (like *send* in (4)), or a modal or non-modal matrix verb scoping over the proposition. The notion of "leftmost verbal element" of the sponsor requires further comment.

When the sponsor-containing clause includes one or more matrix verbs, they can either be included in or excluded from the sponsor: e.g., in (4) the modal element *could* must be excluded from the sponsor. For both semantic and functional reasons, matrix verbs can be usefully divided into two subclasses: modal (*can, could, expect to,* etc.) and non-modal (*agree, ask, avoid, beg, challenge, choose,* etc.), which are treated differently by the system.

When *modal* matrix verbs appear in the sponsor clause, the decision of whether to include them in, or exclude them from, the sponsor is guided by a half dozen modality correlation rules of the following type:

- If the sponsor clause contains *effort* or *volitive* modality and the ellipsis-licensing modality is *epiteuctic* or *epistemic*, the sponsor should exclude the sponsor-clause modality: John wanted to *ski* and did [e].
- If the sponsor clause contains any number of modalities with the outer one being *epistemic* (indicating negation) and the ellipsis-licensing modality being *epistemic* (e.g., *do, don't*), then all modalities are included in the sponsor except for the outer epistemic: John didn't *want to try to ski* but Mary did [e].

When *non-modal* matrix verbs occur in the sponsor clause, they are usually excluded from the sponsor, e.g., *refused to* in (5). However, if that non-modal matrix verb is scoped over by modality, then it is included in the sponsor, e.g., *ask* in (6).

(5) Mylonas refused to *reveal* the ransom paid for his release, although police sources did [e].

(6) He wanted to *ask* me to come but didn't [e].

This rather coarse-grained rule set has been under refinement since the evaluation reported here, with results to be reported separately.

Although resolving reference to a text string does not address the issue of sloppy coreference – one of the most studied aspects of ellipsis in theoretical linguistics – it has a significant practical benefit: the system requires as input only a raw (not manually corrected) syntactic parse along with several readily sharable word lists and rule sets. In other words, this system is ready to be incorporated into application systems, or could easily be reimplemented in other environments.

The Engines

The system takes as input our indexed version of the Gigaword corpus (Graff and Cieri 2003) and consecutively launches the following processing engines.

Modal scope ellipsis detector. This engine extracts elliptical contexts of interest by finding verbal modal elements (e.g., *can, won't*) that are directly followed by a hard discourse break, defined as a period, semi-colon or colon. This maximally lightweight detection strategy achieves high precision at low cost, but at the expense of recall.

Syntactic analyzer. The sentences that are hypothesized to contain modal-scope ellipsis are processed by the Stanford dependency parser (version Stanford-corenlp-2012-01-08; de Marneffe, MacCartney and Manning 2006), whose output serves as input to our rule-based resolution strategy.

Elliptical "phrasal" detector. The first ellipsis resolution strategy seeks configurations that can be treated like open patterns, i.e., multi-word expressions (phrasals) containing a combination of fixed and variable elements, such as *wherever NP *can, all the N (that) NP *can,* and *everything (that) NP *can* (the notation **can* refers to any inflectional form of the verb, such as *could, cannot,* etc.). All of the phrasals treated so far function as adverbials, so a simple resolution strategy – selecting the preceding verbal element as the sponsor – works quite well. For example, sentence (7) matched the pattern *what NP *can* and correctly indicated that the sponsor was *say*.

(7) Vincent Schmid, the vicar of the cathedral, said prayer and music would *say* what words could not [e].

Simple parallel configuration detectors. A key linguistic insight guiding our approach is that *syntactically simple* contexts that show specific types of *structural parallelism* provide high predictive power without the need to resort to deep semantic or pragmatic analysis. Let us define what we mean by *structural parallelism* and *syntactic simplicity*.

Structural Parallelism. Each structurally parallel context contains an ellipsis clause directly preceded by a conjunct that is syntactically connected to in one of three ways that can be loosely described as exhibiting syntactic parallelism: coordination (be it of clauses or verb phrases), parataxis, and certain types of main/adverbial clause pairs. The Stanford parser calls these dependencies "conj" (8), "parataxis" (9) and "advcl" (10), respectively. For each example, the key dependencies are indicated, and, for readability, the word-number indices output by the parser are included only when needed for disambiguation. As mentioned earlier, only the leftmost element of the sponsor is italicized.

(8) They *kept* attacking and we didn't [e].
conj(kept, did)

(9) In one walk, they *used* poles; in the other, they didn't [e].
parataxis(used,did)

(10) Oakland's Barry Zito took the victory, *hurling* eight innings as Santana did [e].
advcl(hurling, did)

The motivation for exploiting syntactic parallelism to predict ellipsis resolution derives both from the well-documented linguistic effects of parallelism (e.g., Goodall, 2009; Hobbs and Kehler 1998; McShane 2000, 2005; McShane and Beale, Submitted) and successful results of our experiments.

Syntactic simplicity. The predictive power of parallel configurations decreases significantly if the conjuncts – particularly the first – contain relative or subordinate clauses because such elements provide additional candidate sponsors for the elided verb phrase. For example, if we rewrite corpus-attested (11) such that the first clause includes several embedded clauses, as in (11a), it becomes necessary to carry out sophisticated reasoning about the world to determine which preceding verb is the leftmost constituent of the sponsor: *autographed? broken? playing? left?*

(11) Bush *autographed* a steady stream of memorabilia, but Garciaparra, his hand in a cast, could not [e].

(11a) Bush *autographed* a steady stream of memorabilia, but Garciaparra, who had broken his wrist playing soccer the day before he left for the conference, could not [e].

We operationalized the notion of "simple parallel" configurations in terms of the output of the Stanford parser. Configurations are deemed "simple parallel" if they contain: (a) exactly one instance of a *conj, advcl* or *parataxis* dependency – which we call "whitelisted" dependencies – that links the modal element licensing the ellipsis with an element from the sponsor clause; (b) no instances of a "blacklisted dependency" – i.e., *ccomp, rcmod, dep* or *complm* – which indicate various types of embedded verbal structures that complicate matters by offering competing candidate sponsors; (c) one or more instances of a "graylisted" dependency, defined as an *xcomp* or *aux* dependency that takes as its arguments matrix and/or main verbs from the sponsor clause. The parse for sentence (12) includes one whitelisted dependency, ***conj****(wanted, did),* and three graylisted dependencies: ***xcomp****(wanted, try),* ***xcomp****(try, start),* ***xcomp****(start, juggle).*

(12) John wanted to *try* to start to juggle and did [e].

Although graylisted dependencies make sponsor clauses more complicated, and although contexts containing them can offer more than one reasonable resolution for the ellipsis (in (12), either *try* or *start* could be interpreted as the left-hand constituent of the sponsor), the added complications can be managed by the rule sets for treating sponsor-clause matrix verbs described above.

We configured 6 search patterns to detect and resolve simple parallel configurations. Three of them do not permit modal verbs in the sponsor clause, though non-modal matrix verbs are permitted: Simple Conjunction NoMod (8, above), Simple Parataxis NoMod (9), Simple Adverbial Clause NoMod (10). The other three simple parallel configurations contain one or more modal verbs in the sponsor clause, as well as, optionally, non-modal matrix verbs: Simple Conjunction Mod (13), Simple Adverbial Clause Mod (14) and Simple Parataxis Mod (no corpus examples of the latter were found).

(13) Fans in other countries could *apply* on the Internet, but fans in the host nation could not [e].
Whitelisted: **conj**(apply-6, could-17).
Graylisted: **aux**(apply-6, could-5)

(14) I tried to *drive* hard as I could [e].
Whitelisted: **advcl**(drive, could)
Graylisted: **xcomp**(tried, drive)

Although "simple parallel" configurations do not represent a large percentage of elliptical examples in the corpus, when they are found, they offer quite confident predictions about the ellipsis sponsor.

Less Simple Parallel Configuration Detector. In an attempt to increase recall, we experimented with relaxing the notion of "simplicity" in syntactically parallel configurations by permitting the parse to contain a single extra whitelisted dependency (*conj, advcl, parataxis*) or a single blacklisted dependency (*ccomp, rcomd, dep, complm*). The goal was to operationalize the intuition that, although having many extra candidate sponsors due to syntactic complexity would dramatically reduce the predictive power of the engine, having just one additional point of complexity might not be too detrimental, especially if we could classify the most benign types of additional dependencies. For example, in (15), the whitelisted dependency that establishes the parallelism used to resolve the ellipsis is ***advcl****(exploded, did)*, and the "extra" whitelisted dependency that can be ignored is ***parataxis****(thrown, exploded)*.

(15) Two of the devices were thrown over a security fence; one *exploded*, while the other did not [e].

A combination of introspection and corpus analysis suggested that the most benign additional dependency was *parataxis*. So for this precision-oriented system run, we included just two "less simple parallel" configurations: Simple Adverbial Clause Mod and Simple Adverbial Clause NoMod, each with one additional parataxis dependency.

Non-Parallel, Closest Modality Detector. This engine does not seek structural parallelism; instead, it walks back through the text and seeks the first modal verb, hypothesizing that it might be "paired" with the ellipsis licensor and therefore point to the sponsor. (16) is an example correctly resolved by this strategy: *could* is the most recent modal verb, which is stripped from the sponsor due to the modality-correlation rules described above.

(16) Rivard and Cosworth's Steve Miller both said they could *build* an Indy only engine similar to Mercedes for next year if they must [e].

This concludes the description of the current state of our ellipsis detection and resolution system. The output of the system is a set of examples that the system (a) believes include modal-scope ellipsis prior to a hard discourse break, and (b) believes it can, with high confidence, resolve, with "resolution" defined as indicating the leftmost verbal element of the sponsor. We next describe an evaluation exercise that both validates the utility of the approach and provides pattern-level (rather than corpus-level) confidence metrics for systems that might employ the results.

Evaluation, Analysis, Lessons Learned

Our original research goals included learning as much as possible about realizations of modal-scope ellipsis in the Gigaword corpus; building a robust system to treat those phenomena; and detailing a plan of work to expand the system and cover residual phenomena. To assess our progress, we carried out a combined evaluation and glassbox analysis of the linguistically motivated hypotheses described above and the engines we used to implement them. Evaluation was carried out by a graduate student judge whose decisions were selectively checked by a senior developer. Evaluation results are presented below. We are confident that launching our engines on other comparable corpora would yield similar results.

Evaluating elliptical "phrasals". Of the 18,298 Gigaword sentences that were identified as having modal-scope ellipsis before a hard discourse break, the system detected 486 unique examples that it believed matched one of our phrasal configurations. We randomly selected about 1/3 of those – 161 examples – to be manually evaluated. Among those, there were 8 detection errors (nominals, like *a can*, were mistaken for verbs), yielding a detection accuracy of

95%. Of the 153 actually elliptical examples, 147 were resolved correctly, yielding a resolution accuracy of 96%.

Evaluating parallel and non-parallel configurations. The system detected 1,814 unique Gigaword inputs that it believed matched one of the "simple parallel", "less simple parallel" or "non-parallel" configurations. All of these were manually evaluated. There were 24 ellipsis detection errors, yielding a detection accuracy of 98%. The actually elliptical 1,790 examples were evaluated for resolution accuracy, with results as shown in Table 1.

Table 1. Evaluation results for non-phrasal configurations. Fractions were rounded down. P1/P2: phases 1 and 2 of testing.

Pattern	Exs.	MatrixVerb Err. (P1/P2)	Misc. Err.	Precision (P1/P2)
Simp.Conj.Mod	238	2 / 2	1	98 / 98 %
Simp.Conj.No.Mod	364	83 / 48	15	73 / 83 %
Simp.Adv.Cl.Mod	132	3 / 3	2	96 / 96 %
Simp.Adv.Cl.No.Mod	662	16 / 10	53	89 / 90 %
Simp.Para.No.Mod	54	0	4	92 / 92 %
Less.Simp.Parallel	15	0	2	80 / 80 %
NonParallel	325	8 / 5	60	79 / 80 %

Column 2 indicates the number of examples that matched each configuration listed in Column 1. Columns 3 and 4 show error tallies, with 4 indicating miscellaneous errors and 3 reflecting errors in which a matrix verb should have been stripped from the sponsor but was not. In phase 1 of testing (P1), we had not yet incorporated the non-modal-matrix-verb stripping rules described above, so, e.g., the system selected *refused* rather than *reveal* as the head of the sponsor for example (5). The phase 2 system (P2), by contrast, incorporated that rule and correctly treated this, and many other, cases of non-modal matrix verbs. We cite this example of stepwise system enhancement to show the natural progression of glassbox testing/evaluation in a knowledge-based system. Naturally, the phase 2 evaluation statistics reflect only the introduction of globally applicable rules, not instance-level tweaks that would have undercut the overall validity of the evaluation results.

One source of residual errors related to processing sponsor-clause matrix verbs results from the parser's misinterpretation of certain matrix + complement constructions. Details aside, for some matrix verbs, if the logical subject of the complement clause is a full NP (*She urged* ***the crowd*** *to disperse peacefully*), the parser fails to establish the expected xcomp dependency between the matrix verb (*urged*) and its complement (*disperse*). However, if that full NP is replaced by a pronoun (*She urged* ***them*** *to disperse peacefully*), the expected xcomp dependency is returned. We have experimented with working around this error by automatically replacing full NPs in such configurations by pronouns, but the workaround is not yet reliable enough for inclusion in the system. As a sidebar, we consider the incorporation of such workarounds a necessary response to real-world constraints, and a much better option than building systems that rely on prerequisites that cannot be automatically supplied.

Space does not permit exhaustive reporting of our error tracking, but let us mention just three types of errors that are easily remedied. First, our modality correlation rules, which initially only applied to verbs, should be extended to adjectives and nouns that convey modal meanings, such as *opportunities* (which conveys potential modality) in (17). Second, topicalization strategies in the sponsor sentence, such as *NP copula* ***to*** V_{INFIN} (18) can be exploited in new detection/resolution patterns.

(17) I had my opportunities to *break* and I didn't [e].

(18) The first target was to *qualify* for the Asian Cup and we did [e].

Third, we hypothesize that the performance of the non-parallel pattern will improve dramatically if we introduce two types of linguistically motivated constraints: (1) the pattern will accept only semantically strong correlations between the ellipsis licensing modal and the most recently encountered modal: e.g., *tried...failed* and *could...couldn't* will be treated, but *believe...want to* will not; (2) the system will evaluate only the most recent verbal structure to determine if it contains such a modal element, it will not be permitted to skip over candidate sponsors in search of a modal. Both of these constraints will reduce recall in favor of precision. Further research is needed to determine how to judiciously expand recall without unacceptable losses in precision.

In contrast to these more easily remedied errors is the hard residue of difficult phenomena, such as contexts in which the actual sponsor is located outside of the window of coreference. Typical evaluation setups would manually remove such instances, but we include them in our results to accurately portray how the system can perform when launched, unaided, on open text.

System enhancement is continuing in two stages. We are currently: implementing the three easy fixes just described; enhancing the ellipsis-detection process to significantly increase recall; expanding the inventory of phrasal configurations and the lists of non-modal matrix verbs; improving our matrix stripping rules to more precisely cover specific combinations of modal and non-modal matrix verbs; investigating how our current rule sets apply to VP ellipsis sponsored by a non-modal verb (*I went because she advised me to [e]*); and redefining "resolution" to include the entire span of the sponsor rather than just the leftmost element. Our practical strategies will continue to rely on minimal preprocessing requirements, making the resulting approach and system widely applicable.

The next stage of system enhancement – moving toward the type of full interpretation discussed in McShane et al. 2012b – will rely on the semantic and pragmatic analysis engines of the OntoSem environment. For example, we will seek other types of non-parallel configurations that offer strong predictive power, including those that leverage semantic constraints; we will seek linguistically motivated methods of loosening the definition of "simplicity" in simple parallel configurations to increase system recall; and we will investigate how reference resolution for subjects can inform the more precise reconstruction of elided categories in terms of instance vs. type event coreference and strict vs. sloppy argument coreference. We must emphasize that all of these 2nd stage enhancements will involve analysis and algorithms that pertain not only to elided categories but to overt referring expressions as well. For example, the overt referring expressions *do it* and *do that*, as well as some uses of pronominal *this, that* and *it,* refer to propositions, and detecting their sponsors involves the same reasoning as detecting the sponsors for elided VPs. Based on our past work in resolving overt and elided *nominal* referring expressions (McShane and Nirenburg 2013; McShane and Beale, Submitted), we hypothesize that the resolution algorithms for overt and elided v*erbal* referring expressions will largely overlap.

Discussion

The system described here treats an important subset of elliptical phenomena – elided scopes of modality – in fully automatic mode. The approach is primarily knowledge-based in that it leverages linguistic observations involving syntax, semantics and discourse, but it uses only readily available resources: the Stanford dependency parser, several word lists, and lightweight engines that match input sentences to ellipsis resolution patterns and then resolve the ellipsis.

Our main claims are: (1) that treating *some* instances of difficult linguistic phenomena is preferable to avoiding difficult phenomena wholesale; (2) that configuring systems that can work in fully automatic mode – from detecting which phenomena will be treated, to treating them and approximating the system's confidence in each answer – is preferable to configuring systems that require manually prepared input, such as annotated corpora; and (3) that incorporating knowledge-based methods into intelligent agent systems in practical, readily extensible ways offers the best balance between near-term utility and long-term progress.

The main motivation for our overall program of research is to develop cognitively plausible intelligent agents. Work reported in this paper is no exception, which is made manifest along several lines. First, the ellipsis detection and resolution strategies incorporate well-attested linguistic phenomena, such as syntactic parallelism effects, a well-motivated inventory of modal meanings and their lexical realizations, and predictable semantic correlations between modal meanings (*try…fail; can…cannot*).

Second, the approach reflects a practical interpretation of the principle of least effort, which arguably underpins much of human behavior. It is unlikely that a person engages in deep semantic and pragmatic analysis to resolve the ellipsis in a sentence like *Mary napped but I didn't [e]*; instead, this is more likely involves a cognitively cheaper, ready-made resolution strategy that can be implemented, for example, through analogical reasoning. We implement this strategy by first leveraging cheap, high-confidence "phrasals" (lexicalized patterns), which are ready-made, combined solutions to ellipsis detection and resolution problems. Next, we invoke more compositional but still very high-confidence patterns; and so on, covering ever more cases but with ever higher processing demands, lower precision and lower confidence. This progression from "ready-made solution" to "fully compositional analysis" is prominent across all text understanding modules of OntoSem.

Third, the necessity of resolving elided categories is absolutely central to artificial intelligent agent systems, particularly if they are to participate in dialog applications, since dialog prominently features a broad array of elliptical phenomena. In other words, ellipsis cannot wait until the next pendulum swing of preferred methods in NLP brings explanatory modeling back into the focus of the field.

Fourth, in order for intelligent agents to collaborate effectively with people, they need to be able to independently evaluate their confidence in their own language understanding. The approach described here offers detailed, pattern-level confidence metrics, which should be of much greater utility to intelligent agents than a single, corpus-level measure.

Finally, this work will contribute directly to the functioning of agents in the OntoAgent architecture, as they attempt to arrive at the full meaning of every utterance as input to subsequent reasoning and action.

Acknowledgments

This research was supported in part by Grant N00014-09-1-1029 from the U.S. Office of Naval Research. All opinions and findings expressed in this material are those of the authors and do not necessarily reflect the views of the Office of Naval Research. Thanks to Ben Johnson for his work on an early implementation of this system.

References

Byron, D. 2004. Resolving Pronominal Reference to Abstract Entities. PhD Dissertation, University of Rochester. Available as Technical Report 815, University of Rochester Computer Science Department.

de Marneffe, M., MacCartney, B., and Manning, C. D. 2006. Generating Typed Dependency Parses from Phrase Structure Parses. In Proceedings of the 5th International Conference on Language Resources and Evaluation (LREC).

Fiengo, R., and May, R. 1994. *Indices and Identity.* Cambridge, Mass.: The MIT Press.

Graff, D., and Cieri, C. 2003. English Gigaword. Linguistic Data Consortium. Philadelphia.

Goodall, G. 2009. *Parallel Structures in Syntax: Coordination, Causatives and Restructuring*. Cambridge University Press.

Hardt, D. 1997. An Empirical Approach to VP Ellipsis. *Computational Linguistics* 23(4): 525-541.

Hobbs, J., and Kehler, A. 1998. A Theory of Parallelism and the Case of VP Ellipsis. In Proceedings of the 36th Annual Meeting of the Association for Computational Linguistics (ACL-98), pp. 394-401.

Lee, H., Chang, A., Peirsman, Y., Chambers, N., Surdeanu, M., and Jurafsky, D. 2013. Deterministic Coreference Resolution Based on Entity-Centric, Precision-Ranked Rules. *Computational Linguistics* 39(4): 885-916.

McShane, M. 2005. *A Theory of Ellipsis*. Oxford University Press.

McShane, M. 2000. Hierarchies of Parallelism in Elliptical Polish Structures. *Journal of Slavic Linguistics* 8: 83-117.

McShane, M., and Beale, S. Submitted. Reference Resolution for Intelligent Agents: A Focus on Confidence. Submitted to *Journal of Language Modelling.*

McShane, M., Beale, S., Nirenburg, S., Jarrell, B., and Fantry G. 2012a. Inconsistency as a Diagnostic Tool in a Society of Intelligent Agents. *Artificial Intelligence in Medicine*, 55(3): 137-48.

McShane, M., and Nirenburg, S. 2012. A Knowledge Representation Language for Natural Language Processing, Simulation and Reasoning. *International Journal of Semantic Computing* 6(1).

McShane, M., and Nirenburg, S. 2013. Use of Ontology, Lexicon and Fact Repository for Reference Resolution in Ontological Semantics. In Oltramari, A., Vossen, P., Qin, L., and Hovy, E. (eds.), *New Trends of Research in Ontologies and Lexical Resources*. Springer, pp 157-185.

McShane, M., Nirenburg, S., and Beale, S. Submitted. The OntoSem Text Understanding System. Submitted to *Advances in Cognitive Architectures.*

McShane, M., Nirenburg, S., Beale, S., Johnson, B. 2012b. Resolving Elided Scopes of Modality in OntoAgent. *Advances in Cognitive Systems,* vol. 2, Dec. 2012.

Nirenburg, S., McShane, M., and Beale, S. 2008. A Simulated Physiological/Cognitive "Double Agent". In Beal, J., Bello, P., Cassimatis, N., Coen, M., and Winston, P. (eds.), Papers from the AAAI Fall Symposium, "Naturally Inspired Cognitive Architectures," Washington, D.C., Nov. 7-9. AAAI technical report FS-08-06, Menlo Park, CA: AAAI Press.

Nirenburg, S., and Raskin, V. 2004. *Ontological Semantics.* Cambridge, Mass.: The MIT Press.

Pang, B., and Lee, L. 2008. Opinion Mining and Sentiment Analysis. *Foundations and Trends in Information Retrieval* 2: 1–135.

Spenader, J., and Hendriks, P. 2006. Combining Multiple Information Sources for Ellipsis. *Research on Language and Computation* 4(4): 327-333.

Inference Graphs: Combining Natural Deduction and Subsumption Inference in a Concurrent Reasoner

Daniel R. Schlegel[a] and **Stuart C. Shapiro**[b]
[a]Department of Biomedical Informatics
[b]Department of Computer Science and Engineering
University at Buffalo, Buffalo NY, 14260
<drschleg,shapiro>@buffalo.edu

Abstract

There are very few reasoners which combine natural deduction and subsumption reasoning, and there are none which do so while supporting concurrency. Inference Graphs are a graph-based inference mechanism using an expressive first–order logic, capable of subsumption and natural deduction reasoning using concurrency. Evaluation of concurrency characteristics on a combination natural deduction and subsumption reasoning problem has shown linear speedup with the number of processors.

1 Introduction

Inference Graphs (IGs) are a graph-based inference mechanism using an expressive first–order logic (FOL), capable of subsumption and natural deduction (ND) reasoning using forward, backward, bi-directional (Shapiro, Martins, and McKay 1982), and focused reasoning (Schlegel and Shapiro 2014a), all using concurrency. In this paper we will focus our discussion on the ability of IGs to combine ND and subsumption reasoning using concurrency, a combination which no other system provides.[1]

ND is a proof–theoretic reasoning method which makes use of a set of introduction and elimination rules for each logical connective. Subsumption is a reasoning method which allows the derivation of knowledge about entire classes of entities from knowledge about other classes, without needing to introduce instances. Subsumption reasoning is most commonly associated with description logics (DLs) (Baader et al. 2010). It is often missing from first order reasoners because of the lack of non–atomic conceptual descriptions (Woods 1991).

There have been many ND reasoners over the years, and reasoning using subsumption is increasingly popular. The combination of these two techniques allows for more sophisticated reasoning about entire classes of entities. We know of only two reasoners which combine the two techniques, namely, ANALOG (Ali and Shapiro 1993; Ali 1994) — which is an ancestor of this work — and PowerLoom (USC Information Sciences Institute 2014). Unlike PowerLoom, IGs use a single graph structure to represent inference paths, whether they be for subsumption or ND. Neither ANALOG nor PowerLoom support concurrency.

IGs derive their ability to reason using both ND and subsumption largely from the logic they implement: a Logic of Arbitrary and Indefinite Objects ($\mathcal{L}_A$). $\mathcal{L}_A$ is a first–order logic which uses quantified terms instead of quantified formulas with universally and existentially bound variables. There are two types of quantified terms: arbitrary and indefinite. Arbitrary terms replace universally quantified formulas, and indefinite terms replace existentially quantified formulas. Both types of quantified terms are structured, having a set of *restrictions* which the quantified term satisfies. A quantified term subsumes another quantified term if their sets of restrictions are appropriately related (further detailed in Section 3.1). For example, an arbitrary term, a_1, subsumes another arbitrary term, a_2, if the restriction set of a_1 is a subset of that of a_2. Using this relationship, one can derive new information about a_2 from information about a_1, without introducing or knowing about any individuals which are instances of a_1 or a_2. This feature is the essence of subsumption reasoning.

$\mathcal{L}_A$ allows for forming expressions that use propositional connectives and quantified terms. Propositional connectives can be reasoned about using ND, while quantified terms can be reasoned about through subsumption reasoning. IGs allow the use of concurrency in both types of inference.

In Section 2 we will discuss $\mathcal{L}_A$ and some KR concerns. The IG formalism implementing $\mathcal{L}_A$ is presented in Section 3. Section 4 will discuss the IG concurrency model. Finally, Section 5 presents an evaluation of IG performance.

2 Background

2.1 A Logic of Arbitrary and Indefinite Objects

$\mathcal{L}_A$ is a FOL designed for use as the logic of a KR system for natural language understanding, and for commonsense reasoning (Shapiro 2004). The logic is sound and complete, using ND and subsumption inference. Throughout this paper we will assume the deductive rules implemented are the standard rules of inference for FOL, though the actual implementation uses set-oriented connectives (Shapiro 2010),

[1]This paper is an extended and updated version of (Schlegel and Shapiro 2014c). Parts of it are adapted from (Schlegel and Shapiro 2013) and (Schlegel 2014). A conception of IGs using only ground predicate logic can be seen in (Schlegel and Shapiro 2014b).

which subsume the standard rules.

The logic makes use of arbitrary and indefinite terms (collectively, quantified terms). Quantified terms are structured — they consist of a quantifier indicating whether they are arbitrary or indefinite, a syntactic variable, and a set of restrictions. The range of a quantified term is defined by the conjunction of its set of restrictions. A quantified term q_i has a set of restrictions $R(q_i) = \{r_{i_1}, \ldots, r_{i_k}\}$, each of which make use of q_i's variable, v_i. Indefinite terms may be dependent on one or more arbitrary terms $D(q_i) = \{d_{i_1}, \ldots, d_{i_k}\}$. The structured nature of quantified terms allow them to satisfy Woods's requirement that a logic for subsumption have non–atomic conceptual descriptions. We write an arbitrary term as `(every` v_{q_i} $R(q_i)$`)` and an indefinite term as `(some` v_{q_i} $D(q_i)$ $R(q_i)$`)`.[2] The structured nature of quantified terms syntactically differentiates them from universally and existentially quantified variables familiar in first–order predicate logic (FOPL).[3]

Semantically, arbitrary and indefinite terms are also different from FOPL's universally and existentially quantified variables. Instead of reasoning about *all* members of a class, $\mathcal{L}_A$ reasons about a *single* arbitrary member of a class.[4] For indefinite members, it need not be known *which* member is being reasoned about, the indefinite member itself can be reasoned about. Indefinite individuals are essentially Skolem functions, replacing FOPL's existential quantifier.

To our knowledge, the only implemented systems which use a form of arbitrary term are ANALOG (Ali and Shapiro 1993) and Cyc (Lenat and Guha 1990), though arbitrary objects themselves were most famously defended by Fine (Fine 1983) after being attacked by Frege (Frege 1979). The logic of $\mathcal{L}_A$ is based on those developed by Ali and by Fine (Fine 1985a; 1985b), but is different — notably it is more expressive than ANALOG. It is designed with computation in mind, unlike Fine's work, which omits key algorithms.

Since an arbitrary term represents an arbitrary entity, there are no two arbitrary terms with the same set of restrictions. Occasionally it is useful to discuss two different arbitrary members with the same restrictions, so we provide the special restriction `(notSame` $q_{j_1} \ldots q_{j_k}$`)` for this purpose.

2.2 Knowledge Representation

In the tradition of the SNePS family (Shapiro and Rapaport 1992), propositional graphs are graphs in which every well-formed expression in the knowledge base, including individual constants, functional terms, atomic formulas, or non-atomic formulas (which we will refer to as "rules"), is represented by a node in the graph. A rule is represented in the graph as a node for the rule itself (henceforth, a *rule node*), nodes for the argument formulas, and arcs emanating from the rule node, terminating at the argument nodes. Arcs are labeled with an indication of the role (*e.g.*, antecedent or consequent) the argument plays in the rule, itself. Every node is labeled with an identifier. Nodes representing individual constants, proposition symbols, function symbols, or relation symbols are labeled with the symbol itself. Nodes representing functional terms or non-atomic formulas are labeled `wft`*i*, for some integer, *i*. Every SNePS expression is a term, hence `wft` instead of `wff`. An exclamation mark, "`!`", is appended to the label if it represents a proposition that is asserted in the KB. Arbitrary and indefinite terms are labeled `arb`*i* and `ind`*i*, respectively. No two nodes represent syntactically identical expressions; rather, if there are multiple occurrences of one subexpression in one or more other expressions, the same node is used in all cases. Propositional graphs are built incrementally as terms are added to the knowledge base, which can happen at any time.

Quantified terms are represented in the propositional graph just as other terms are. Arbitrary and indefinite terms also each have a set of restrictions, represented in the graph with special arcs labeled "restrict", and indefinite terms have a set of dependencies, represented in the graph with special arcs labeled "depend."

Each term in the knowledge base has a semantic type, itself existing within an ontology of semantic types which the user can add to. Only terms of type Proposition may be asserted (taken to be true) in the knowledge base. Generic terms are terms which contain either other generics, or arbitrary terms, and analytic generic terms are tautological generics built from the restrictions of an arbitrary term.

3 Combining Natural Deduction and Subsumption in IGs

IGs are an extension of propositional graphs. To propositional graphs, IGs add directed message passing *channels* wherever inference (ND or subsumption) is possible. Channels are built within rules and generic terms, and wherever terms *match* each other. Inference messages, containing substitutions, pass forward through channels. Nodes for rules collect and combine messages. When a received or combined message satisfies an inference rule it *fires*, sending more messages onward through the graph through its outgoing channels.

To motivate the discussion, we introduce an example inspired by the counter–insurgence domain, first only in the logical syntax of $\mathcal{L}_A$, and in a later subsection, using an IG.

```
;; A person is arrested if and only if
;;  they are held by a another person
;;   who is a corrections officer.
(iff
  (Arrested (every x (Isa x Person)))
  (heldBy x (some y (x)
              (Isa y Person)
              (Isa y CrctnsOfcr)
              (notSame x y))))

;; A person is detained if and only
;;  if they are held by another person.
```

[2] The syntax we use is a version of CLIF (ISO/IEC 2007).

[3] In many papers and books FOL and FOPL are used interchangeably. Here this is not the case — $\mathcal{L}_A$ and FOPL are both members of the class of FOLs, but $\mathcal{L}_A$ is not FOPL.

[4] This is in contrast to DLs, which reason about classes. DLs have two languages: one to discuss classes, another to discuss instances; $\mathcal{L}_A$ uses a single language to discuss instances and arbitrary individuals.

```
(iff
  (Detained (every x (Isa x Person)))
  (heldBy x
          (some y (x) (Isa y Person)
                      (notSame x y))))

;; A person is either detained,
;;  on supervised release, or free.
(xor
  (Detained (every x (Isa x Person)))
  (onSupervisedRelease x)
  (Free x))

;; A person who is not free
;;  has travel constraints.
(hasTravelConstraints
  (every x (Isa x Person)
           (not (Free x))))

;; A person who has been captured,
;; has been arrested.
(Arrested (every x (Isa x Person)
                   (Captured x)))
```

It will then be asked of the system if captured persons have travel constraints:

```
(hasTravelConstraints
  (every x (Isa x Person) (Captured x)))
```

This can be derived by recognizing that the arbitrary person who is captured, is a person (a subsumptive relationship), then applying rules in the KB which apply to persons. For example, since a person is arrested if and only if they are held by another person who is a corrections officer, then a *captured* person is arrested if and only if they are held by another person who is a corrections officer.

3.1 The Match Process

Whenever a term is added to the graph, it is matched with all other terms. A term, t_i, matches another term, t_j, if t_i and t_j unify,[5] if each substitution of one quantified term for another in the created substitutions follow appropriate subsumption rules, and if t_i is the same type, or a subtype of t_j. The match process is a way to identify more specific terms which may share their instances with more general ones. For example, consider that some person who is a corrections officer is still a person.

When t_i and t_j are unified, instead of producing a most general unifier, a factorization is produced which contains bindings for each of the terms being unified. While this is described in (McKay and Shapiro 1981), the main idea is that as unification is performed, instead of forming a single substitution, form two – σ_i and σ_j – such that all and only quantified terms in t_i are given bindings in σ_i, and all and only quantified terms in t_j are given bindings in σ_j. During this process, we treat quantified terms as simple variables without considering their restriction sets.

[5]We avoid pairwise unification using an approach similar to (Hoder and Voronkov 2009)

Once t_i and t_j have unified, we must determine in which direction(s) (if either) their substitutions are compatible in their subsumption relationship and in type. To define our notion of subsumption formally, we say:

1. an arbitrary, arb_i, subsumes another, arb_k, if $\forall r_{i_j} \in R(arb_i), \exists r_{k_l} \in R(arb_k)$ such that r_{i_j} matches r_{k_l},
2. an arbitrary, arb_i, subsumes an indefinite, ind_k, if $\forall r_{i_j} \in R(arb_i), \exists r_{k_l} \in R(ind_k)$ such that r_{i_j} matches r_{k_l}, and
3. an indefinite, ind_i, subsumes another, ind_k, if $\forall r_{k_j} \in R(ind_k), \exists r_{i_l} \in R(ind_i)$ such that r_{k_j} matches r_{i_l}.

If t_i and t_j unify, and for each substitution pair $t_l/v_l \in \sigma_i$, t_l has type equal or lower than v_l, and if t_l is a quantified term, v_l subsumes t_l, then we call t_i an *originator*, and t_j a *destination*, and add the 4-tuple $< t_i, t_j, \sigma_i, \sigma_j >$ to the set of matches to return. If t_i and t_j unify and for each substitution pair $t_l/v_l \in \sigma_j$, t_l has type equal or lower than v_l, and if t_l is a quantified term, v_l subsumes t_l, then we call t_j an *originator*, and t_i a *destination*, and add the 4-tuple $< t_j, t_i, \sigma_j, \sigma_i >$ to the set of matches to return. So, 0, 1, or 2 4-tuples are the result of the process.

3.2 Communication Within the Network

The results of the match process are used to create some of the *channels* in the graph. Channels are a pre-computation of every path that inference might take. Each channel starts at an originator node, and terminates at a destination. Each node has channels to every node that it can derive and to every node that can make use of inference results that the originator has derived. *Messages* are sent through the channels. Messages come in several types, and either communicate newly inferred knowledge (*inference messages*) or control inference operations (*control messages*).

Channels In addition to the originator and destination, each channel has a type and contains three structures — a valve, a filter, and a switch. Valves control the flow of inference; filters discard inference messages that are irrelevant to the destination; and switches adjust the variable context of the substitutions that inference messages carry from that of the originator to that of the destination.

There are three types of channels — i-channels, g-channels, and u-channels. I-channels are meant to carry messages that say "I have a new substitution of myself you might be interested in", and u-channels carry messages that say "you or your negation have been derived with the given substitution." G-channels are i-channels, but used only within generic terms.

Definition 3.1. A *channel* is a 6-tuple $< o, d, t, v, f, s >$, where o is the originator, d is the destination, t is the type, v is the valve, f is the filter, and s is the switch. ■

A filter serves to stop messages with irrelevant substitutions from flowing through a channel. The filter ensures that the incoming message's substitution is relevant to d by ensuring that, for every substitution pair t_f/y in the destination bindings, there is a substitution pair t_s/y in the passing message substitution such that either $t_f = t_s$ or t_s is a specialization of t_f, determinable through one-way pattern matching. If a message does not pass the filter, it is discarded.

Switches change the substitution's context to that of the destination term. The switch applies the originator binding substitution to the term of each pair in the passing message substitution. This adjusts the substitution to use quantified terms required by the destination. The updated substitution is stored in the passing message.

Valves control inference by allowing or preventing messages from passing to the destination.

Definition 3.2. A *valve* is a pair $< (open|closed), wq >$ where the first position indicates whether the valve is opened or closed, and wq is a waiting queue.[6] ■

When an inference message is submitted to a channel, it first is sent through the filter, then the switch. Should the message pass the filter, it will eventually reach the valve. The valve, depending on whether it is open or closed, allows the message to pass or prevents it from doing so. If a reached valve is closed, the message is added to that valve's waiting queue. When a valve is opened, the items in the waiting queue are sent on to the destination.

Channels are built between any two nodes which match each other. All channels from the match operation are i-channels, since they communicate new substitutions for the originator, which the destination may be interested in.

Channels are built in several other locations as well: within rules, generic terms, and quantified terms. Each of these channels is simpler than those created from the match process, as their filters and switches are no-ops.

Within rules, i-channels are built from each antecedent to the node for the rule itself, and u-channels are built from the rule node to each consequent. This allows the antecedents to inform the rule of newly satisfying substitutions, and it allows the rule node to send substitutions produced when the rule fires to its consequents.

A generic term, g, is defined recursively as a term that is a parent of one or more arbitrary terms $a_1, \ldots, a_n$, or one or more other generic terms, $g_1, \ldots, g_m$. Each a_i and g_k has an outgoing g-channel to g. This allows substitutions to begin at the arbitrary terms, and be built up successively as higher level generic terms are reached.

Arbitrary terms have i-channels from each restriction to the arbitrary itself. This allows arbitrary terms to find instances of themselves through the combination of substitutions from terms matching each restriction.

In Figure 1 the IG for the example is shown, with channels drawn as specified. For example, `wft2` has an i-channel to `wft3!` and `wft3!` has a u-channel to `wft2`, indicating that `wft2` may want to share a substitution it has with `wft3!`, and `wft3!` might derive `wft2`. Additionally, `wft19!` has an i-channel to `wft2`, indicating that `wft2` may be interested in `wft19!`'s assertional status and substitution.

Messages Messages of several types are transmitted through the IG's channels, serving two purposes: relaying derived information and controlling the inference process. A message can be used to relay the information that its

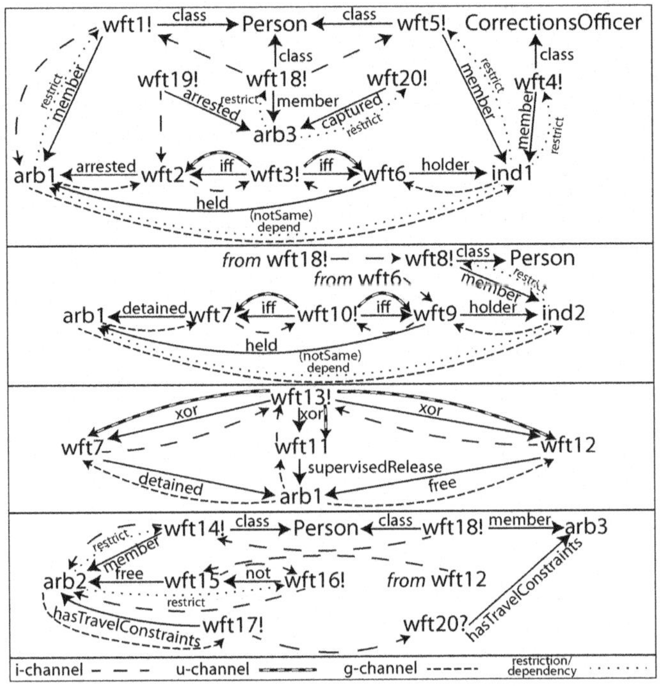

Figure 1: The IG for the example, split into four segments for easier reading. The top IG segment contains propositions meant to mean that a person is arrested if and only if they are held by a another person who is a corrections officer (`wft3`), and that the arbitrary captured person is arrested (`wft19`). The second segment contains the rule that a person is detained if and only if they are held by another person (`wft10`). The third segment contains the rule that a person is either detained, on supervised release, or free (`wft13`), and the final segment contains the generic proposition that a person who is not free has travel constraints (`wft17`), along with the question of whether the arbitrary person who is captured has travel constraints (`wft20`). Channels and restrictions/dependencies for quantified terms are drawn according to the key at the bottom of the figure.

origin has a new asserted or negated substitution instance (an `i-infer` or `g-infer` message), or that it has found a substitution for the destination to now be asserted or negated (`u-infer`). These messages flow forward through the channels, and are called inference messages. Control messages flow backward through channels, controlling inference: `backward-infer` messages open valves, and `cancel-infer` messages close them.

Definition 3.3. A message is an 8-tuple:

$$< pri, subst, type, pos, neg, fNS, t?, fwd? >$$

where: *pri* is the priority of the message (discussed further in Section 4); *subst* is a substitution; *type* is the type of message; *pos* and *neg* are the are the number of known true ("positive") and negated ("negative") antecedents of a rule, respectively; the *fNS* is the *flagged node set*, which contains a mapping from each antecedent with a known truth value to its truth value; $t?$ indicates whether the message regards a

[6] This is a simplified conception of a valve which does not account for the dynamic nature of backward inference. See (Schlegel 2014) for more on this topic.

true or negated term; and *fwd?* indicates whether this message is part of a forward inference process. ■

3.3 Inference by Combining Messages

Inference in the IG is essentially the combination of messages, and the determination of whether a resulting combination satisfies the requirements of a deductive rule, quantified term, or generic term.

Two messages, m_1 and m_2 may be combined if they are compatible – that is, if their substitutions and flagged node sets are compatible. We say that two substitutions, $\sigma = \{t_{\sigma_1}/v_{\sigma_1} \ldots t_{\sigma_n}/v_{\sigma_n}\}$ and $\tau = \{t_{\tau_1}/v_{\tau_1} \ldots t_{\tau_m}/v_{\tau_m}\}$, are compatible if whenever $v_{\sigma_i} = v_{\tau_j}$ then $t_{\sigma_i} = t_{\tau_j}$, and that two flagged node sets are compatible if they have no contradictory entries (that is, no antecedent of the rule is both true and false).

Two messages that are compatible are combined in the following way. Let

$$m_1 = < pri_1, subst_1, type_1, pos_1, neg_1, fNS_1, t?_1, fwd?_1 >$$

and

$$m_2 = < pri_2, subst_2, type_2, pos_2, neg_2, fNS_2, t?_2, fwd?_2 >$$

where m_2 is the most recently received message. The combined message, m_3, combines m_1 and m_2 as follows:

$$m_3 = < max(pri_1, pri_2), merge(subst_1, subst_2), nil, |posEntries(fNS_3)|, |negEntries(fNS_3)|, fNS_3, nil, or(fwd?_1, fwd_2) >$$

Some fields in m_3 are made *nil*, to be later filled in as necessary. The combined flagged node set, fNS_3, is the addition of all entries from fNS_2 to fNS_1.

Messages may be combined efficiently using several different data structures. Which structure is used depends on the logical operation a specific node performs. The approaches include a tree-based approach called a P-Tree, a hash-map based technique called an S-Index, and a default combinatorial algorithm (see (Choi and Shapiro 1992)). The result of the combination process is a set of new messages seen since just before the message arrived at the node. The newly created messages are added to the node's cache, and examined to determine if the conditions of the node are met to send out further messages. If the message arriving already exists in the cache, no work is done. This prevents re-derivations, and can cut cycles.

The *pos* and *neg* portions of the messages in the new combined set are used to determine if the conditions of the node are satisfied. For a rule node, this determines whether the rule may fire. For example, for a conjunctive rule to fire, *pos* must be equal to the number of rule arguments. A disadvantage of this reasoning approach is that some rules are difficult, but not impossible, to implement, such as negation introduction and proof by cases. For the non-rule-node combination nodes, this process determines if an instance has been found, by waiting until *pos* is equal to the number of required restrictions or subterms.

The restrictions of an arbitrary term arb, represented by analytic generic terms with i-channels to arb, are taken conjunctively. Therefore, messages from restrictions must be combined in arb as they are available. When a message m has been received or created via combination such that $m_{pos} = |R(q)|$, where m_{pos} is the number of positive antecedent instances in the message, it is considered to be an instance of the arbitrary, and is sent onward to any generic terms the arbitrary is part of. In the example this is evident in `arb2`, which has two restrictions: `wft14!` and `wft16!`. Only when both of these terms report to `arb2` with compatible substitutions can the combined substitution be sent to `wft17!` for instantiation of the generic.

As discussed earlier, a generic term, g, is defined recursively as a term that is a parent of one or more arbitrary terms $a_1, \ldots, a_n$, or one or more other generic terms, $g_1, \ldots, g_m$. As instances are discovered by a_i and g_k, substitutions for those instances are sent to g via the appropriate i-channel to g. g combines these substitutions should they be compatible, and sends out resulting messages. Unlike arbitrary terms where all restrictions must be satisfied for an instance to be made, generics require instances for only as many compatible subterms as are available.

In the example, we can now derive that the arbitrary captured person has travel constraints. Messages flow forward from `wft18!` (through `wft1!` and `arb1`), and from `wft19!` to `wft2`, which then satisfies `wft3!`, deriving a generic instance of `wft6` – the arbitrary captured person is held by a corrections officer. We derive the arbitrary captured person is detained by messages flowing from `wft6`, and `arb1` (through `ind2`) to `wft9`, which satisfies `wft10!` and derives a generic instance of `wft7`. The message from `wft7` satisfies the `xor` rule `wft13!`, allowing a negated instance of `wft12` to be derived – captured persons are not free. Finally we learn that the arbitrary captured person has travel restrictions since messages from `wft18!` (through `wft14!`), and from `wft12` (through `wft15` and `wft16!`) satisfy `arb2`, allowing a message to be sent asserting `wft20` (through `wft17!`).

4 Concurrency

The structure of IGs lends itself naturally to concurrent inference. Any number of nodes in the graph may process messages simultaneously without fear of interfering with any others. Only when a single node receives multiple messages must those messages be processed synchronously. This synchronous processing is necessary because the message caches are shared state. We need not concern ourselves with the actual order in which the messages are processed, since the operation is commutative, meaning there is no need to maintain a queue of changes to the message cache.

In order to perform inference concurrently, the IG is divided into *inference segments* (henceforth, *segments*). A segment represents the inference operation — from receipt of a message to sending new ones — which occurs in a node. Valves delimit segments, as seen in Figure 2. When a message passes through a valve a new *task* is created — the application of the segment's inference function to the message. When tasks are created they enter a global prioritized queue, where the priority of the task is the priority of the message. Tasks are removed from the queue and executed as processors become available. When a task is executed, inference is performed, and any newly generated messages are sent toward its outgoing valves for the process to repeat.

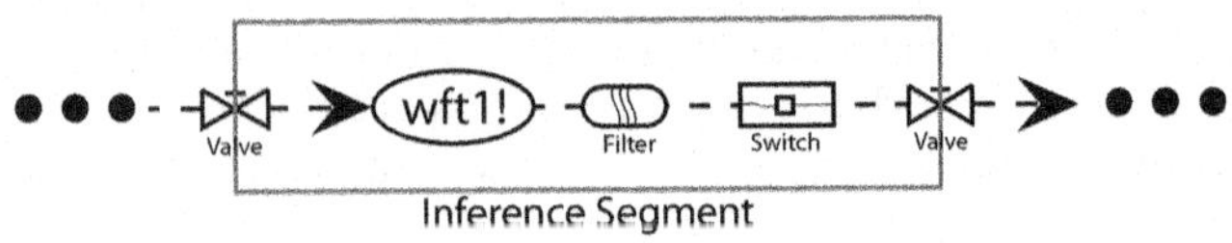

Figure 2: A single inference segment.

The goal of any inference system is to infer the knowledge requested by the user. If we arrange an IG so that a user's request (in backward inference) is on the right, and channels flow from left to right wherever possible (the graph may contain cycles), we can see this goal as trying to get messages from the left side of the graph to the right side of the graph. We, of course, want to do this as quickly as possible.

Every inference operation begins processing inference messages some number of levels to the left of the query node. Since there are a limited number of tasks that can be running at once due to hardware limitations, we must prioritize their execution, remove tasks that we know are no longer necessary, and prevent the creation of unnecessary tasks. Therefore,

1. Tasks relaying newly derived information using segments to the right are executed before those to the left.
2. Once a node is known to be true or false, all tasks still attempting to derive it are canceled, as long as their results are not needed elsewhere, and in all channels pointing to it that may still derive it, valves are closed.
3. Once a rule fires, all tasks for potential antecedents of that rule still attempting to satisfy it are canceled, as long as their results are not needed elsewhere. Valves are closed in channels from antecedents that may still satisfy it.

All `cancel-infer` messages have the highest priority. Then come `i-infer` and `u-infer` messages. `backward-infer` messages have the lowest priority, decreasing at each step backward through the graph. As `i-infer` and `u-infer` messages flow closer to the goal, they get higher priority, but their priorities remain lower than that of `cancel-infer` messages.

5 Evaluation

We have aimed to combine ND and subsumption reasoning within a system which supports concurrency. We have not implemented the fastest known algorithms for procedures such as subsumption, due only to research agenda. For this reason, the most interesting measure of the performance of IGs is the concurrency characteristics.

We evaluated the performance of IGs in backward inference, as it is the most resource intensive type of inference IGs can perform, and most fully utilizes the scheduling heuristics. To do so we used graphs of chaining and-entailments, meaning for each implication to derive its consequent, all its antecedents had to be true. Each entailment had bf antecedents, where bf is the branching factor, and a single consequent. Each antecedent and consequent made use of the same single arbitrary term, a, containing a single restriction.[7] Each consequent was the consequent of exactly one rule, and each antecedent was the consequent of another rule, up to a depth of d entailment rules. Exactly one consequent, cq, was not the antecedent of another rule. A single instance of each leaf node was asserted which made use of an arbitrary which was subsumed by a. We tested the performance of the system in backchaining on and deriving a term subsumed by cq.

Since we backchained on a term subsumed by cq, this meant terms subsumed by every rule consequent and antecedent in the graph would have to be derived. This is the worst case of entailment. The timings we observed are presented in Table 1.[8] This experiment showed that speedup grows linearly[9] as more CPUs are involved in inference.

Table 1: Inference times using 1, 2, 4, and 8 CPUs for 100 iterations in an IG with $bf = 2$ and $d = 7$.

CPUs	Inference Time (ms)	Speedup
1	229551	1.00
2	123015	1.87
4	65783	3.49
8	36013	6.38

Experiments testing the effect of depth and branching factor showed no statistically significant effect. All results were found to be very similar to those of (Schlegel 2014) which tested ND reasoning alone.

6 Conclusion

IGs are the only inference mechanism which combine ND and subsumption reasoning, and support concurrency. Inference is performed through a message passing architecture built upon propositional graphs. IGs derive their ability to perform both types of inference from a logic, $\mathcal{L}_A$, which uses structured quantified terms. Evaluation of concurrency characteristics on a combination ND and subsumption reasoning problem has shown linear speedup with the number of processors.

7 Acknowledgements

This work has been supported by a Multidisciplinary University Research Initiative (MURI) grant (Number W911NF-09-1-0392) for "Unified Research on Network-based Hard/Soft Information Fusion", issued by the US Army Research Office (ARO) under the program management of Dr. John Lavery.

[7] Adjusting the number of arbitrary terms or restrictions used has a very small impact, as calculation of instances is performed only once per arbitrary, and the arbitrary or arbitraries need to be shared by all nodes to perform meaningful inference.

[8] Tests were performed on a Dell Poweredge 1950 server with dual quad-core Intel Xeon X5365 processors and 32GB RAM. Each test was performed twice, with the second result being used.

[9] $y = 0.764x + 0.32$, $R^2 = 0.9986$

form accurate path integration with noise-free velocity inputs. However, their study still suffers from some major constraints. Firstly, the CAN-based grid cell model itself is insufficient to build a cognitive map, lacking the important recurrent interactions with place cells (Bonnevie et al. 2013). Secondly, it remains unknown whether the actual self-motion and visual inputs can drive a model for error corrections to construct cognitive maps.

In this work, we aim to develop a computational model integrating visual cues, place cells and velocity-coupled grid cells for building cognitive maps. We use one dimensional continuous attractor network (CAN) to model head direction cells, as in (McNaughton et al. 2006; Zhang 1996), to encode orientations of the robot and will not discuss it in detail. Our strategy is based on the principle that velocity-coupled grid cells play the role of path integrator while place cells encode the output of path integration (Moser, Kropff, and Moser 2008). To the best of our knowledge, this is the first model in which visual inputs, place cells and velocity-coupled grid cells contribute together to build spatial cognitive maps of indoor environments on a mobile robot.

Cognitive map mechanisms have continuously inspired important implications in robotic mapping and navigation. In (Burgess et al. 1997), the model was coupled strongly to the biology of place cells, and showed how place cell firing can enable mapping and navigation in a miniature mobile robot. Multimodal integration of visual place cells and grid cells was proposed to enhance robot localization (Cuperlier, Quoy, and Gaussier 2007; Jauffret, Cuperlier, and Gaussier 2012). Most models have been tested only in laboratory environments and cognitive maps have not been built in these models. RatSLAM (Milford and Wyeth 2008), made a significant progress in emulating the spatial navigation ability of the hippocampal system, being able to build a semi-metric topological map in a real large area. (Tian et al. 2013) extended to use an RGB-D sensor to built cognitive maps for robot navigation. However, path integration in these works was performed by a heuristic method that makes an appropriately displaced copy of place cell activities, which sacrifices biological fidelity.

In summary, this work makes the important progress in the following two aspects:

1. The proposed entorhinal-hippocampal model, in which place cells, velocity-coupled grid cells and visual inputs contribute together to building cognitive maps simultaneously, presents the closest biological fidelity. It provides an embodied substrate to verify neural activities of the entorhinal-hippocampal circuitry found in neurobiological experiments, e.g., in laboratory rats.

2. The spatial cognitive system built on a mobile robot provides a practical robotic mapping and navigation approach. It would motivate more practical developments on neuro-inspired robotic spatial cognitive systems in real environments.

Methods

Architecture

Figure 1 shows the system architecture to build cognitive maps on a mobile robot platform. The robot consists of a Pioneer 3-DX mobile base, an RGB-D sensor and a laptop with an Intel(R) Core(TM) i7-3740 CPU with 16GB RAM. The front wheels of the base are equipped with encoders that provide raw odometry data and the RGB-D sensor is mounted on the front-top of the base to capture visual RGB-D images of environments. The robot's locations and orientations are encoded in place cell and head direction cell population activities, respectively. The system includes four major steps: (1) Self-motion of the raw odometry data is used to generate and drive the velocity-coupled grid cell activities. (2) A Hebbian learning algorithm is applied to learn the strengths, i.e., the weights, between place cell and gird cell population activities and determine computation of place cell activities, which path-integrate self-motion during map building. (3) Visual images are used for correcting the accumulative errors associated with the path integration and resetting when loop closures are detected. (4) A cognitive map is updated during the building process.

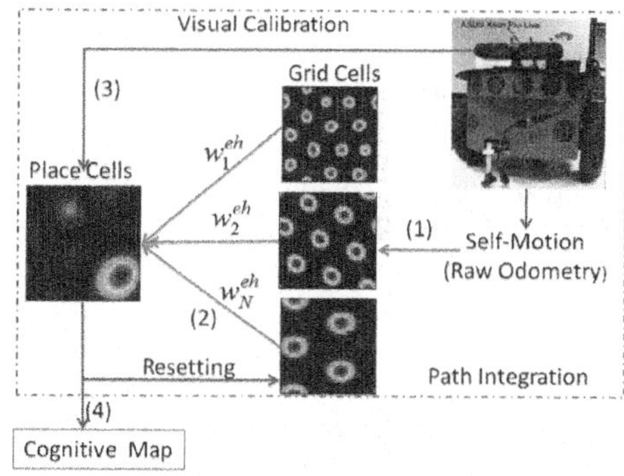

Figure 1: System architecture. Steps (1)-(4) are explained in text.

From Grid Cells to Place Cells

There are mainly two general models to describe grid cell formation, i.e., oscillatory interference (Burgess 2008; Zilli and Hasselmo 2010) and CAN (Fuhs and Touretzky 2006; Burak and Fiete 2009). In an oscillatory interference model, grid cells exhibit theta phase precession during the theta cycle, acutely vulnerable to subtle changes in the phase of underlying oscillation. In a CAN model, neurons are often arranged in a 2D neural sheet. Recurrent connectivity among the neurons in a neural sheet with a global inhibition leads random patterns of population activity to spontaneously merge to organized 'bumps' of grid cell population activity (Burak and Fiete 2009). The bumps are envisaged to move as the animal moves from one place to another. A grid cell response is obtained by summing the firing activity of a single neuron over a full trajectory. The most remarkable progress of (Burak and Fiete 2009) is to accurately integrate velocity inputs into grid cell models. In this work, we use a simplified CAN model to generate and drive velocity-coupled grid cell population activities.

As in (Burak and Fiete 2009), the dynamics of rate-based neurons in a 2D neural sheet is specified by:

$$\tau ds_i/dt = \left[\sum_j W^g_{ij} s_j + B_i\right]_+ - s_i \qquad (1)$$

where $[\cdot]_+$ denotes a threshold-linear function that leaves positive arguments unchanged and sets negative ones to zero. W^g_{ij} is the synaptic weight from neuron j to neuron i in a neural sheet. $\sum_j W^g_{ij} s_j$ is the inhibitory recurrent input to neuron i, s_i is the synaptic activation of neuron i and τ is the time-constant of neuron response. If the length of a neural sheet is n, there will be n^2 neurons in the network. Each neuron i has a preferred direction θ_i (W, N, S or E). The feed-forward excitatory input B_i to neuron i, defined by:

$$B_i = 1 + \alpha \hat{\mathbf{e}}_{\theta_i} . \mathbf{v}_t \qquad (2)$$

where $\hat{\mathbf{e}}_{\theta_i}$ is the unit vector pointing to θ_i. $\mathbf{v}_t$ is the velocity at time t. W_{ij} is defined as follow:

$$W^g_{ij} = W^g_0(\mathbf{x}_i - \mathbf{x}_j - l\hat{\mathbf{e}}_{\theta_j}) \qquad (3)$$

with

$$W^g_0 = g_{exc}\mathbf{e}^{-\gamma|\mathbf{x}|^2} - \mathbf{e}^{-\beta|\mathbf{x}|^2} \qquad (4)$$

where g_{exc} is the gain which modulates the size of grid cell population activities and l is the shift in the outgoing weights. λ determines the spacing of the activity in a neural sheet. We use $\gamma = 1.1\beta$, $\beta = 3\lambda^{-2}$.

As mentioned in (Fuhs and Touretzky 2006), one grid cell population activity in one neural sheet is not sufficient to perform path integration as it results in ambiguities in location representations. Hence, multiple layers of neural sheet with various scales and orientations are required to encode unique locations in a space. Each neural sheet represents one grid cell population activity. In our implementation, λ and g_{exc} are uniformly sampled to generate multiple grid cell population activities. A hippocampal place cell population activity is defined as a weighted sum of a selective subset of grid cell population activities, i.e., a subset of neural sheets, with a global inhibition to balance the grid cell excitations:

$$p_i(r) = A\left[\sum_{j=1}^{N} w^{eh}_{ij} s_j(r) - C_{\text{inh}}\right]_+ \qquad (5)$$

where A and C_{inh} are the gain and the global inhibition of the place cell network. N is the layers of neural sheet. w^{eh}_{ij} is the synaptic weight connecting from grid cell population activity j to place cell population activity i. r is the current location of the robot. C_{inh} affects the number of peaks by clustering the place cell population activities and is set as $B * max(p_i(r))$. B is used to control the peaks of the place cell population activities. To generate one major peak of the place cell population activities, we need to learn a synaptic weight distribution to determine a proportion of grid cell population activities with overlapping activity bumps at a single location (Si and Treves 2009; Savelli and Knierim 2010). This can be accomplished by either a linear summation of a subset of grid cells with certain spatial frequencies or Hebbian learning methods. Oscillatory interference based grid cell models are normally suitable for the linear summation method (Solstad, Moser, and Einevoll 2006). In this work, we instead apply competitive Hebbian learning to find a subset of CAN-based grid cell population activities to compute the corresponding place cell population activity for cognitive map building, as defined by:

$$dw^{eh}_{ij}/dt = kp_i(s_j - \langle s_j \rangle) \qquad (6)$$

where k is the learning rate and $\langle\cdot\rangle$ is the mean of the grid cell activities. The learning rate k permits the formation of place cell population activities during the first few minutes of exploration. In our implementation, we set it as 0.00005 experimentally. In addition, we constrain $w^{eh}_{ij} \geq 0$ to prevent the weights becoming negative. Eq. (6) implicates that the sum over all weights is kept constant. Thus, small weights can be reduced by weight competition. According to the Oja's rule (Oja 1982), we further normalize the weights as $\sum_{j=1}^{N}(w^{eh}_{ij})^2 = 1$ to prevent the some neurons always winning the competition (Rolls, Stringer, and Elliot 2006).

The right-hand side of Eq. (6) determines the direction of weight changes: if the current grid cell population activity is greater than mean of the afferent population activities, the synapse is potentiated; otherwise, it is depressed. Eq. (6) allows to detect grid cell population activities with spatial coincidence from multiple layers of neural sheet. Figure 2 shows the evolution of the synaptic weights of the 80 layers of neural sheet during the first 5 minutes of the session. All the synaptic weights were initially assigned to $1/80$. It can be observed that by the competitive Hebbian learning algorithm, a small portion of the synaptic weights remained positive while a large portion of them converged to zero across the session. Thus, only a small subset of grid cell population activities will be selected to form one major peak of place cell population activities.

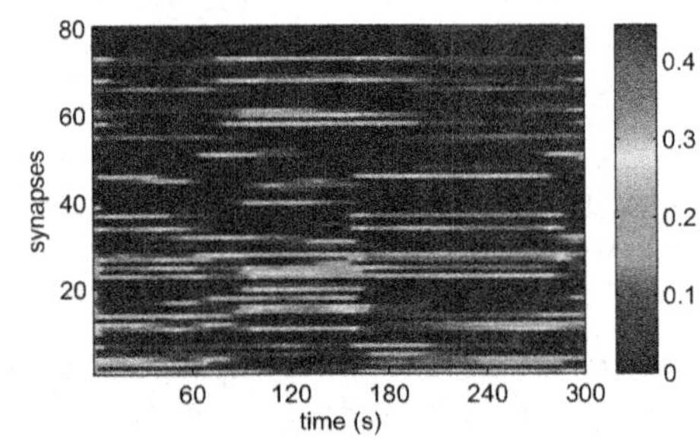

Figure 2: Evolution of synaptic weights.

Effects of Learning Parameters

In this section, we evaluate the effects of Hebbian learning parameters on place cell activities. Learning the synaptic weights between gird cells and place cells is important to determine the contributions of grid cell population activities to generating place cell population activities which encode the robot's locations for cognitive map building. The size and the layers of neural sheets, the spacing of grid cell population activities in one neural sheet by λ and the gain g_{exc} mainly affect the formation of the place field activities. Obviously, if the value of λ increases, the spacing of the grid cells will also increases, thus leading fewer peaks of the place cell population activities. Fig 3 and 4 show how the size of neural sheet and the layers of neural sheet affect the learning results. In these two examples, g_{exc} is both set as 1.0. It can be observed that with the same λ and the layers of neural sheet, the larger the size of the neural sheet, the fewer the number of the major peaks of the place cell population activities. At the same time, with the same λ and the same size of the neural sheet, larger number of the the layers of neural sheet reduces the number of the major peaks of the place cell population activities.

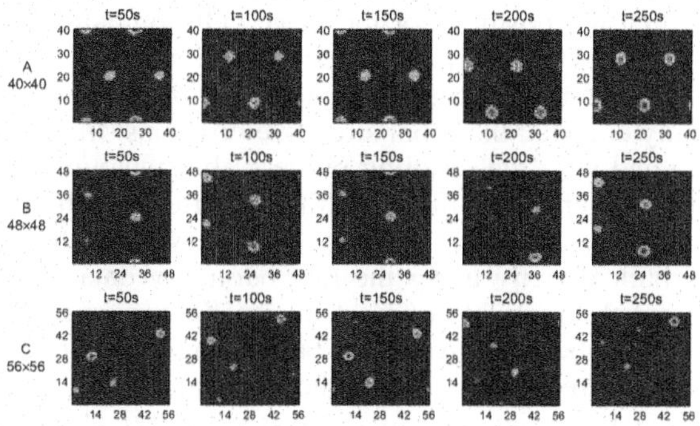

Figure 3: Larger size of the neural sheet leads to fewer peaks of the place cell population activities. Row A to C represent the results of 40×40, 48×48 and 56×56, respectively.

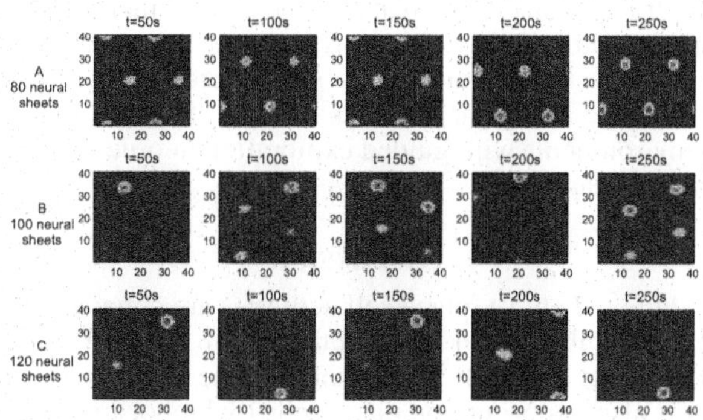

Figure 4: More grid cells reduce the number of the major peaks of the place cell population activities. Row A to C represent the results of 80, 100 and 120, respectively.

Different values of g_{exc} will also lead to different place cell population activities. Fig 5 shows the results in which g_{exc} was sampled from [1, 1.1]. It can be observed that the Hebbian learning results are much better than those when g_{exc} is set to 1.0, as shown in Row A in Fig 3 and 4. However, it is non-trivial to determine an optimum. In our current implementation, it was set experimentally. Furthermore, to deal with the presence of the multiple peaks, one solution is that we can increase the value of B to reduce the numbers

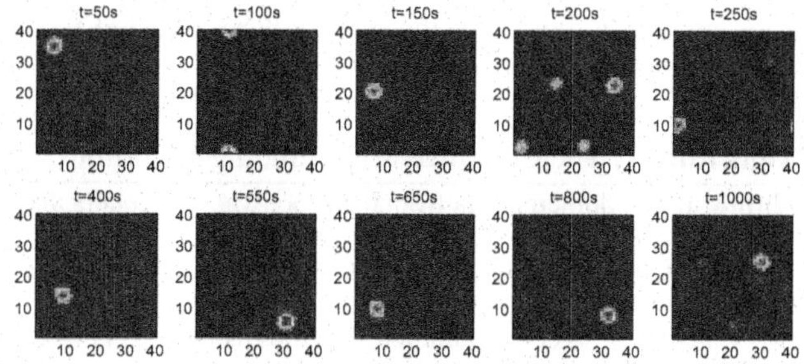

Figure 5: Place cell population activity generated from grid cell population activities with g_{exc} sampled from [1, 1.1].

of peaks. However, from our experiments, we have observed that the major peak of the place cell population activities exists consistently during the entire session even in the case of multiple peaks. Thus, this property of the proposed method guarantees that cognitive maps can be correctly built using various scales of grid cell networks.

Visual Calibration and Map Building

Evidence has revealed that when a rat returns to a familiar environment, the path integrator should be reset in order to adjust to the perceived environment (Moser, Kropff, and Moser 2008; Fuhs and Touretzky 2006). However, it remains unclear that how the brain senses and transforms external sensory inputs into an internal cognitive map (Burak and Fiete 2009). In our implementation, we use RGB-D images as visual cues to correct the path integration errors and reset the place cell population activities as well as the associated grid cell population activities at the previous locations and directions when loop closures are detected. Depth information can avoid ambiguity caused in 2D images and it is invariant to lighting conditions, in which many similar indoor scenes become distinguishable. A comparison between the image profiles is performed for each pair of incoming RGB and depth frames (Tian et al. 2013) for loop closure and new scene detection.

Our cognitive map contains a set of spatial coordinates that the robot has experienced in its past travels, as shown in Fig 6. The robot's spatial coordinates are calculated from the place cell population activities which are generated from a subset of grid cell population activities using Eq. (5). Nodes in the cognitive map are constructed by associating the major peak of the place cell population activities with corresponding visual cues, locations and denoted as visual experiences. These visual experiences serve as visual cues for loop closure detection. **Algorithm** 1 shows the cognitive map building process. The incoming visual inputs are compared with the historical visual experiences. If the latest input matches the previous visual experiences, it is considered as a familiar scene which had been seen previously by the robot. The status of the grid cell population activities and the place cell population activity are then reset to the previous matched visual experiences. The current visual input and the matched visual experience are merged to one experience. Otherwise, a new visual experience is created. Once a loop closure is detected, the map will be adjusted to the recalled visual experiences.

Algorithm 1: The Cognitive Map Building Algorithm

Input: Raw odometry data from the robot wheel encoders and visual images from the RGB-D sensor
Output: Cognitive map
Begin:
- Calculate grid cell population activities using Eq. (1)-(4).
- Calculate place cell population activities using Eq. (5).
- Obtain one major peak of place cell population activities using Eq. (6).
- Perform visual profile comparison.
  if The incoming visual input matches the previous visual experiences,
  then Perform resetting and map correction.
  else Create a new visual experience.
  end if

End:

Experimental Analysis

We aim to build a cognitive map for a large office environment of $35m \times 35m$ on a mobile robot to validate the effectiveness of the proposed model. Table shows the parameters setting. The mobile robot is commanded to make a complete exploration of the indoor environment (the exploration process is shown in the accompanying video).

Fig.6 shows the experimental results. Row A shows the dead-reckoning map obtained from the robot odometry. Obviously, this map can not represent the environment properly. Row B shows the cognitive map built by the proposed computational model. With visual inputs, the system can successfully perform loop closure detection and and correct the odometry drift. Finally it generates a cognitive map which encodes both topological and metric information. In Row C, the blue dotted line shows the real trajectory traveled by the robot, and the red crosses indicate the firing locations of the grid cell located at (20,20) in the 21th layer of the neural sheets. Row D shows the corresponding rate map. To generate the rate map, a spatial smoothing algorithm using a Gaussian kernel, as described in (Hafting et al. 2005), is adopted with a bin size of $0.5m \times 0.5m$.

From the experiment, we have observed that before the first loop closure was detected, the cognitive map was the same as the raw map built directly using the raw odometry data. When the loop closure was detected (i.e., the robot detected a scene which it had traveled.), resetting was performed and the map was corrected according to the recalled visual experiences. Fig. 7 demonstrates an example of loop closure detection and path integration resetting process. Fig. 7(a) and (b) show the constructed map and corresponding place cell population activities at t=15 seconds. When t=265 seconds, the incoming visual input matched with the previous visual experience (t=15 seconds) and a loop closure was thus detected (Fig. 7(c)). Immediately, the system corrected the map (at t=267.5 seconds), as shown in Fig. 7(e). Correspondingly, the grid cell population activities and the place cell population activities were reset to the visual experience at t=15 seconds. Fig. 7(f) show the result of resetting the place cell population activities at t=265 seconds (Fig. 7(d)) to the previous position and direction of the visual experience at t=15 seconds (Fig. 7(b))[1]. It should be noted that the positions of the place cell population activities in Fig. 7(b), (d) and (f) are not the same as those in the cognitive map because the place cell population activities only encoded the robot's relative positions. In addition, before and after the resetting process, the synaptic weights remained unchanged, thus resulting in different activities at t=15 seconds and 267.5 seconds. As observed, the final raw maps built directly using the raw odometry data failed to represent the real environment due to the accumulated errors, while the cognitive maps built using path integration resetting correctly represented the environment with associated visual experiences. Fig. 8 shows that the final cognitive map correctly represented the spatial representation of the robot's exploring space.

Parameter	Setting
Shift in Outgoing Weights l	2
Size of Neural Sheet	40×40
Time-Constant of Neuron Response τ	10ms
Periodicity of the Formed Lattice λ	$[13, 21]$
Gain g_{exc}	$[1, 1.1]$
Parameter B	0.5
Layers of Neural Sheet N	80
Learning Rate k	0.00005

Table 1: Parameter Setting

Throughout the map building process, the grid cells spiked at regular intervals along the robot trajectory, displaying grid-like property. Compared to the regularly tessellating triangle structure spanning the environment observed from the grid cells in rat's entorhinal cortex region (Hafting et al. 2005), the responses of a single grid cell in our simulation were at regular intervals because the robot explored the environments with guided exploration in order to build a complete map.

Discussion

As addressed above, place cell activities are generated from a selected subset of grid cell activities. In a recent research (Bonnevie et al. 2013), it is found that the formation of grid cells is also dependent on place cells by hippocampal back-projections. In our model, grid cells interact with place cells. First, due to the ambiguous location representations in grid cells, the resetting process was performed on place cells, leading to the corresponding resettings of grid cells. Second, the competitive Hebbian learning used in this work also implicates that grid cells interact with place cells.

In most existing experiments (Burak and Fiete 2009; Zilli and Hasselmo 2010), the velocity inputs are extracted from ground-truth trajectories recorded by an allothetic tracking system. However, for animals or autonomous mobile robots, the accumulated errors are inevitable. In our model, the velocity inputs were extracted from idiothetic wheel encoders,

[1]The resetting results of grid cells are not shown in the paper.

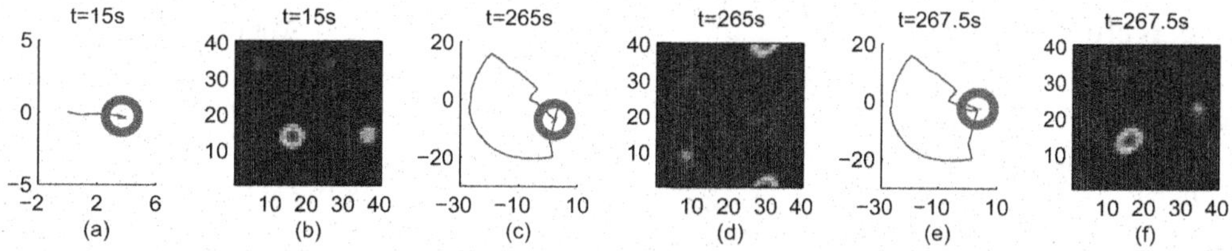

Figure 7: Loop closure detection and path integration resetting. The red circle indicates the robot's current position.

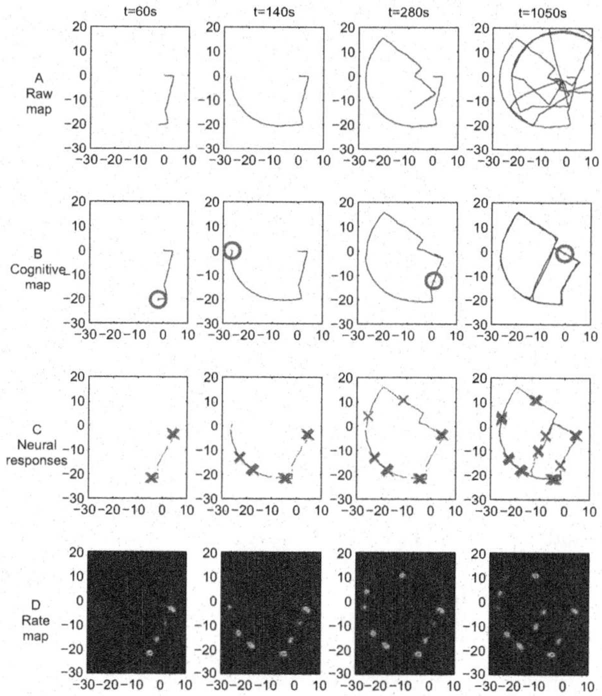

Figure 6: Neural responses in the map building process.

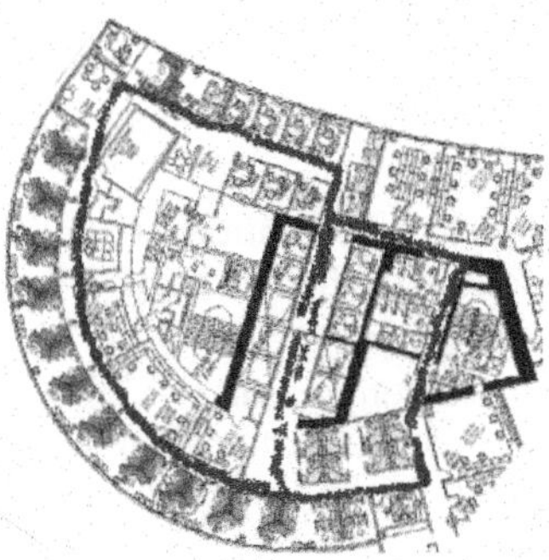

Figure 8: The final cognitive map (in blue) superimposed on the office layout.

which are self-generated signals and the accumulated errors are reflected in raw odometry data, to generate and drive CAN-based grid cell population activities. Together with the visual information captured from the RGB-D sensor for loop closure detection and map correction, our cognitive map model is able to produce accurate representation of the environment in contrast to what constructed from the raw data.

Neural Sheet	Memory(MB)	Time (Second)
32 × 32	66	450
40 × 40	217	1638
48 × 48	564	2304
56 × 56	1180	10913
64 × 64	2192	21988

Table 2: Weights for various neural sheets

For computational efficiency, we use a small scale network with a sheet of 40×40 neurons and N is 80. We have conducted experiments with large scale of grid cell networks, such as 64×64, which can still build accurate cognitive maps. However, it is found that the CAN-based grid cell model is computationally inefficient and not scalable. With larger n, the generation time and the memory storage of the recurrent synaptic weights increase dramatically. Table shows the times and memories to generate and store the recurrent synaptic weights of 80 layers of neural sheet with various sizes of the neural sheet. It can be seen that for only 80 grid cell population activities with a sheet of 64×64, it requires around 6 hours to generate and 2.2G memory to store the recurrent synaptic weights. To simulate large scale networks, using scalable neuromorphic hardware (Furber et al. 2014; Merolla et al. 2014) could drive the way.

Our cognitive map model will contribute to developing innovative robotic spatial cognition approaches (Huang, Tang, and Tian 2014; Milford, Wiles, and Wyeth 2010). Compared to the traditional probabilistic SLAM algorithms, the proposed method tracks the neural activities, which encode locations and orientations with regard to the robot in a cognitive map. The advantage is that poses and related view information can be efficiently associated with the cognitive map for efficient robot navigation and localization without modeling uncertainties of landmarks.

Conclusion

In this paper, we proposed a novel entorhinal-hippocampal model which is able to build cognitive maps simultaneously by integrating activities of place cells and grid cells with real visual inputs. The mobile robot embedded with the spatial cognitive model was able to accurately map the environment. Such a model will facilitate to investigate neural mechanisms of spatial cognition in a non-intrusive way. Furthermore, it will inspire innovative robotic approaches for mapping, localization and navigation, etc.

References

Bonnevie, T.; Dunn, B.; Fyhn, M.; Hafting, T.; Derdikman, D.; Kubie, J. L.; Roudi, Y.; Moser, E. I.; and Moser, M.-B. 2013. Grid cells require excitatory drive from the hippocampus. *Nature neuroscience* 16(3):309–317.

Burak, Y., and Fiete, I. R. 2009. Accurate path integration in continuous attractor network models of grid cells. *PLoS computational biology* 5(2):e1000291.

Burgess, N.; Donnett, J. G.; Jeffery, K. J.; John, O.; et al. 1997. Robotic and neuronal simulation of the hippocampus and rat navigation. *Philosophical Transactions of the Royal Society of London. Series B: Biological Sciences* 352(1360):1535–1543.

Burgess, N. 2008. Grid cells and theta as oscillatory interference: theory and predictions. *Hippocampus* 18(12):1157–1174.

Cuperlier, N.; Quoy, M.; and Gaussier, P. 2007. Neurobiologically inspired mobile robot navigation and planning. *Frontiers in neurorobotics* 1.

Domnisoru, C.; Kinkhabwala, A. A.; and Tank, D. W. 2013. Membrane potential dynamics of grid cells. *Nature* 495(7440):199–204.

Fuhs, M. C., and Touretzky, D. S. 2006. A spin glass model of path integration in rat medial entorhinal cortex. *The Journal of Neuroscience* 26(16):4266–4276.

Furber, S. B.; Galluppi, F.; Temple, S.; and Plana, L. A. 2014. The spinnaker project. *Proceedings of the IEEE* 102(5):652–665.

Hafting, T.; Fyhn, M.; Molden, S.; Moser, M.-B.; and Moser, E. I. 2005. Microstructure of a spatial map in the entorhinal cortex. *Nature* 436(7052):801–806.

Huang, W.; Tang, H.; and Tian, B. 2014. Vision enhanced neuro-cognitive structure for robotic spatial cognition. *Neurocomputing* 129:49–58.

Jauffret, A.; Cuperlier, N.; and Gaussier, P. 2012. Multimodal integration of visual place cells and grid cells for robots navigation. In *Second Symposium on Biology of Decision Making*, 136–145.

McNaughton, B. L.; Battaglia, F. P.; Jensen, O.; Moser, E. I.; and Moser, M.-B. 2006. Path integration and the neural basis of the'cognitive map'. *Nature Reviews Neuroscience* 7(8):663–678.

Merolla, P. A.; Arthur, J. V.; Alvarez-Icaza, R.; Cassidy, A. S.; Sawada, J.; Akopyan, F.; Jackson, B. L.; Imam, N.; Guo, C.; Nakamura, Y.; Brezzo, B.; Vo, I.; Esser, S. K.; Appuswamy, R.; Taba, B.; Amir, A.; Flickner, M. D.; Risk, W. P.; Manohar, R.; and Modha, D. S. 2014. A million spiking-neuron integrated circuit with a scalable communication network and interface. *Science* 345(6197):668–673.

Milford, M., and Wyeth, G. 2008. Mapping a suburb with a single camera using a biologically inspired slam system. *Robotics, IEEE Transactions on* 24(5):1038–1053.

Milford, M. J.; Wiles, J.; and Wyeth, G. F. 2010. Solving navigational uncertainty using grid cells on robots. *PLoS computational biology* 6(11):e1000995.

Monaco, J. D., and Abbott, L. F. 2011. Modular realignment of entorhinal grid cell activity as a basis for hippocampal remapping. *The Journal of Neuroscience* 31(25):9414–9425.

Moser, E. I.; Kropff, E.; and Moser, M.-B. 2008. Place cells, grid cells, and the brain's spatial representation system. *Neuroscience* 31(1):69.

Oja, E. 1982. Simplified neuron model as a principal component analyzer. *Journal of mathematical biology* 15(3):267–273.

O'Keefe, J., and Dostrovsky, J. 1971. The hippocampus as a spatial map. preliminary evidence from unit activity in the freely-moving rat. *Brain research* 34(1):171–175.

O'keefe, J., and Nadel, L. 1978. *The hippocampus as a cognitive map*, volume 3. Clarendon Press Oxford.

Rolls, E. T.; Stringer, S. M.; and Elliot, T. 2006. Entorhinal cortex grid cells can map to hippocampal place cells by competitive learning. *Network: Computation in Neural Systems* 17(4):447–465.

Savelli, F., and Knierim, J. J. 2010. Hebbian analysis of the transformation of medial entorhinal grid-cell inputs to hippocampal place fields. *Journal of neurophysiology* 103(6):3167–3183.

Si, B., and Treves, A. 2009. The role of competitive learning in the generation of dg fields from ec inputs. *Cognitive neurodynamics* 3(2):177–187.

Solstad, T.; Moser, E. I.; and Einevoll, G. T. 2006. From grid cells to place cells: a mathematical model. *Hippocampus* 16(12):1026–1031.

Taube, J. S. 2007. The head direction signal: origins and sensory-motor integration. *Annu. Rev. Neurosci.* 30:181–207.

Tian, B.; Shim, V. A.; Yuan, M.; Srinivasan, C.; Tang, H.; and Li, H. 2013. Rgb-d based cognitive map building and navigation. In *Intelligent Robots and Systems (IROS), 2013 IEEE/RSJ International Conference on*, 1562–1567. IEEE.

Tolman, E. C. 1948. Cognitive maps in rats and men. *Psychological review* 55(4):189.

Zhang, K. 1996. Representation of spatial orientation by the intrinsic dynamics of the head-direction cell ensemble: a theory. *The journal of neuroscience* 16(6):2112–2126.

Zilli, E. A., and Hasselmo, M. E. 2010. Coupled noisy spiking neurons as velocity-controlled oscillators in a model of grid cell spatial firing. *The Journal of neuroscience* 30(41):13850–13860.

Proceedings of the Twenty-Ninth AAAI Conference on Artificial Intelligence

An Association Network for Computing Semantic Relatedness

Keyang Zhang [1] and **Kenny Q. Zhu** [2]
Shanghai Jiao Tong University, Shanghai, China
[1]keyangzh@gmail.com, [2]kzhu@cs.sjtu.edu.cn

Seung-won Hwang
POSTECH, Pohang, Republic of Korea
swhwang@postech.ac.kr

Abstract

To judge how much a pair of words (or texts) are semantically related is a cognitive process. However, previous algorithms for computing semantic relatedness are largely based on co-occurrences within textual windows, and do not actively leverage cognitive human perceptions of relatedness. To bridge this perceptional gap, we propose to utilize free association as signals to capture such human perceptions. However, free association, being manually evaluated, has limited lexical coverage and is inherently sparse. We propose to expand lexical coverage and overcome sparseness by constructing an association network of terms and concepts that combines signals from free association norms and five types of co-occurrences extracted from the rich structures of Wikipedia. Our evaluation results validate that simple algorithms on this network give competitive results in computing semantic relatedness between words and between short texts.

Introduction

Computing semantic relatedness between two words (or texts) is a fundamental task in natural language processing, artificial intelligence and information retrieval. Strictly speaking, semantic relatedness is a more general notion than semantic similarity as it captures not only closeness between two objects within a type hierarchy (e.g., river and stream), but also any other relations (e.g., river and boat) (Budanitsky and Hirst 2006). Traditionally, semantic similarity has been computed either within some lexicon (Jarmasz 2003; Resnik 1995; Jiang and Conrath 1997; Lin 1998) or by comparing the distributional properties of contexts (Deerwester et al. 1990; Gabrilovich and Markovitch 2007; Hassan and Mihalcea 2011). On the other hand, semantic relatedness has been largely modeled by co-occurrences within a window in a large text corpus.

For both similarity and relatedness, co-occurrences play a central role, hence how they are extracted and combined can significantly influence the quality of relatedness computation. So far, dozens of similarity functions (McGill 1979) have been proposed for IR, all of which involving co-occurrences in one way or another, but few achieve satisfactory results on both similarity and relatedness. The reason for such limited success, we argue, is that, since similarity and relatedness are ultimately human perceptions and thus evaluated against human annotated scores, simple window-based co-occurrences, often contaminated with noises, offer insufficient signals to match the human perception. In other words, there exists a perceptional gap between the relatedness perceived by humans and the co-occurrences we collect from text corpora.

As a human perception signal to bridge such gap, we consider a well-studied psychological process called *free association*. In free association, a person is given a *cue* word and is asked to produce the first word that comes to her mind as the *response*. Previously, a number of free association experiments by psychologists resulted in a few data sets called *free association norms*. Table is a fragment of the free association norms collected by the University of South Florida (Nelson, McEvoy, and Schreiber 2004), known as *Florida Norms* from now on.

Table 1: The strongest reponses to the cue word "river"

Cue	Response	Strength
river	lake	15/150
river	stream	15/150
river	water	9/150
river	flow	8/150
river	boat	7/150
river	canoe	7/150

Each row of the data contains a cue word, a response word and the strength of the association (a fraction of the people who responded with this pair of association in the experiment). The free association norms can be viewed as a network in which nodes are the words, and edges carry the strengths. One can see that edges in this network connect both similar pairs (e.g., river and stream) and related ones (e.g., river and boat), which seems ideal for computing semantic relatedness. However, this network suffers from two limitations. First, the number of cue words in these datasets ranges from 100 to 5000, which means only the most common English words are covered and the scale of such a network is too small for predicting the relatedness score between two arbitrary words. Second, due to the cost of free association experiments, the number of human subjects is usually small. A cue word is typically presented to a few dozens to 1000 subjects, yielding a few dozens unique responses. Thus the free association network is fairly sparse.

In this paper, we propose a novel approach to construct a large-scale, comprehensive association network of English terms and concepts by combining semantic signals from both free association norms and Wikipedia. Wikipedia is a large, high-quality text corpus from which co-occurrences can be drawn. In the past, people primarily extracted co-occurrences between terms within the Wikipedia article body. Instead, we leverage the rich structure within Wikipedia, to extract 5 types of co-occurrences, which are then aggregated into a single, universal association strength score by learning from the strengths of the free association norms. Such scores are used to weight the edges in the proposed association network. This network can be thought of as an expanded, smoothed version of the free associate network, and can be used to simulate how an average human being associates one concept to another in her mind. We would then use this association network to compute the semantic relatedness between terms and short texts.[1]

In summary, this paper makes three main contributions.

1. We extract 5 different types of co-occurrences from Wikipedia and construct a "synthetic" association network by training on free association norms (Section);
2. We empirically show that free association is a competent alternative source of knowledge for computing semantic relatedness, and our "synthetic" association network effectively simulates free association and resolves its limitations (Section and Section);
3. We propose algorithms to compute semantic relatedness based on the constructed association network , which outperform state-of-the-art methods (Section).

Our Approach

In this section, we first define the proposed *association network*, then show how to populate such a network. We then propose algorithms to compute relatedness using this network, and finally conclude with some discussions.

Association network

A *super node* s represents a set of synonymous terms and their corresponding Wikipedia concepts (or article pages), denoted as (T, C), where T is a set of terms and C is a set of Wikipedia concepts. For example, $(\{apple, apples\}, \{Apple, Apple\ Inc.\})$ is one such super node. Given a term t, we can generate a super node s by Algorithm 1. $def_c(t)$ returns a set of Wikipedia concepts defining t, while $def_t(c)$ returns a set of terms defined by c. We say t is defined by c if t, as an anchor text, links to c at least 10% of the time, and c is being linked from t at least 10% of the time. We found the results to be insensitive to the value of 10%, which was empirically determined.

Our association network is a weighted directed graph $G(V, E)$, with $w(e)$ denoting the weight of edge e ($e \in E$). Each vertex in the graph is a super node s, and an edge

Algorithm 1 Generate super node

function BOOTSTRAP(term t)
  $T \leftarrow \{t\}, C \leftarrow \{\}$
  while T or C is updated **do**
    for $t \in T$ **do**
      $C \leftarrow C \cup def_c(t)$
    for $c \in C$ **do**
      $T \leftarrow T \cup def_t(c)$
  return (T, C)

$e(u, v)$ ($u, v \in V$) indicates u can associate to v, with strength $w(e)$. For all $u \in V$, strength is normalized:

$$\sum_{v \in V} w(u, v) = 1 \quad (1)$$

Network construction

Given a set of terms T_0, we populate an association network $G(V, E)$ in two steps: first determine the vertex set V in our network, and then determine edge set E and estimate the association strengths for edges in the network.

To determine the vertex set V of our association network G, we run Algorithm 1 for every $t \in T_0$, such that the set of all output super nodes is V. Algorithm 1 ensures V to have the following property [2]:

Lemma 1 *Each term t in T_0 appears in exactly one vertex of G, and no two vertices share an identical concept c.*

To determine the edge set E of our association network and the association strength of each $e \in E$, we tap into five types of co-occurrences in Wikipedia to compute five association strength scores, which are then integrated by a linear weighted sum, where the weight parameters are trained using free association norms labeled by human beings.

These five types of co-occurrences are sentence level co-occurrences (*slc*), title link co-occurrences (*tlc*), title gloss co-occurrences (*tgc*), title body co-occurrences (*tbc*), and category level co-occurrences (*clc*). Examples of these co-occurrences are shown in Figure 1.

Specifically, *slc* refers to the co-occurrence of two terms in one sentence, such as *water* and *precipitation. tlc* refers to the co-occurrence of a page's title and an anchor text in the page, such as *river* and *lake*, *river* and *precipitation. tgc* refers to the co-occurrence of a page's title and an unlinked term in the *gloss*, or the definition paragraph of this page, such as *river* and *stream. tbc* refers to the co-occurrence of a page's title and an unlinked term in the body paragraphs, the paragraphs except for gloss, such as *river* and *water. clc* refers to the co-occurrence of two concepts in some category page, e.g., the concepts *Lake* and *Stream* co-occur in the category page "Bodies of water". As described above, slc is between two terms, clc between two concepts, and the other three between a concept and a term. For all these types of co-occurrences, we first map the term or the concept to the corresponding super node, and then count the frequency.

[1] In this paper, we use "short text relatedness" and "short text similarity" interchangeably.

[2] The proof of this lemma is given at http://adapt.seiee.sjtu.edu.cn/~keyang/assoc/.

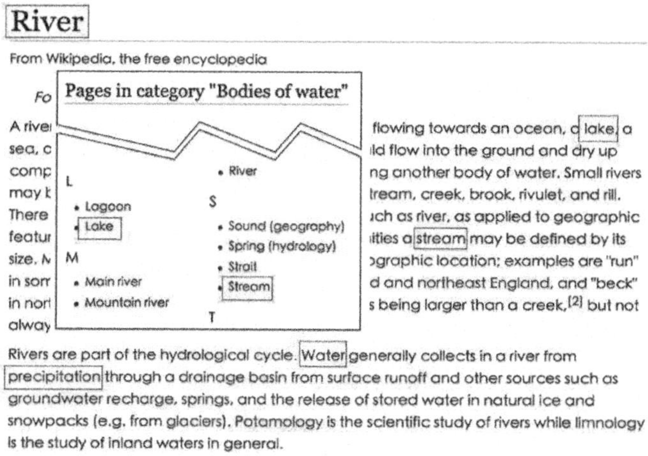

Figure 1: Five types of co-occurrences in Wikipedia

For each type of co-occurrences denoted as τ, where $\tau \in \{slc, tlc, tgc, tbc, clc\}$, we model the association strength from u to v after the measure proposed in (Wettler 1993) in (2). Here, α is an exponent parameter between 0 and 1. $p_\tau(u)$, $p_\tau(v)$ and $p_\tau(u,v)$ is computed as $\frac{f_\tau(u)}{N_\tau}$, $\frac{f_\tau(v)}{N_\tau}$ and $\frac{f_\tau(u,v)}{N_\tau}$ respectively, where $f_\tau(u)$, $f_\tau(v)$ is the occurrence frequencies of u, v, $f_\tau(u,v)$ is the co-occurrence frequency of u and v, and N_τ is the total number of tokens for a particular τ. We defer the discussion of the choice of α till Section .

$$r_\tau(u,v) = \frac{p_\tau(u,v)}{p_\tau(v)^\alpha p_\tau(u)} \tag{2}$$

$r_\tau(u,v)$ is normalized to $w_\tau(u,v)$:

$$w_\tau(u,v) = \frac{r_\tau(u,v)}{\sum_v r_\tau(u,v)} \tag{3}$$

We perform a case study to examine the different capabilities of capturing associated pairs by the five types of co-occurrences. We compare the normalized association strength $w_\tau(u,v)$ for every τ and the result is shown in Figure 2. u is set to be the super node of *river*, and v's are the super nodes of 5 terms most associated with *river*, as shown in Table . We observe the following: i) *slc* is distributed more uniformly among the pairs than others ii) only river-lake and river-stream have *clc*, as lake and stream are in the same type hierarchy as river iii) *tlc*, *tgc* and *tbc* capture the terms explaining or describing river, basically all the terms except for boat in this case. This shows that even though *slc* has been widely used in the literature, reflecting related terms of locality, other types of co-occurrences, though less studied, have complementary strength in terms of capturing associated pairs.

We then integrate the five types of $w_\tau(u,v)$ into a single strength score: $w(u,v) = \sum_\tau \theta_\tau w_\tau(u,v)$. We mimic human perception of relatedness in determining how to aggregate co-occurrences. Specifically, we train the weights θ_τ through a linear regression on the Florida Norms.

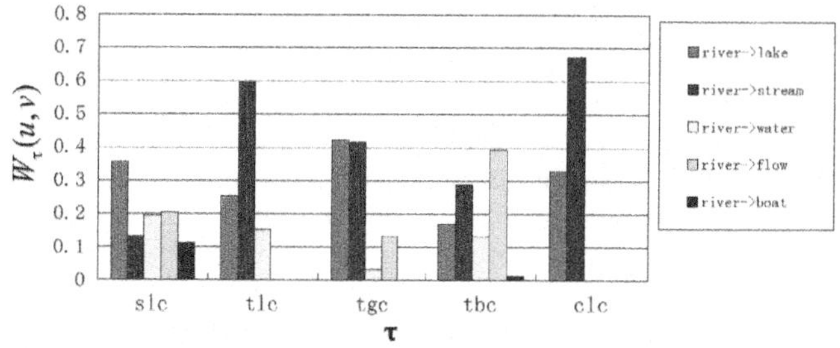

Figure 2: Comparison of $w_\tau(u,v)$ for different τ

We first use the terms appearing in Florida Norms as T_0 to determine the super node set V. Then we use every cue-response pair in Florida Norms as a training instance, with the label being the association strength computed form the norms. For every training instance we map the two terms into their corresponding super nodes u and v, and calculate $w_\tau(u,v)$ for every τ as its features. When performing linear regression, we impose the constraints that $\sum_\tau \theta_\tau = 1$, $0 < \theta_\tau < 1$ for all θ_τ, and that the intercept term must be equal to 0. The parameters θ_τ are then used to combine the different $w_\tau(u,v)$ regardless of the given T_0: As $\sum_\tau \theta_\tau = 1$ holds true, it is easy to attest that the combined strength score $w(u,v)$ meets the requirement of (1). An edge $e(u,v)$ exists if and only if $w(u,v) > 0$.

Relatedness computation

We now present how to leverage the constructed network for computing relatedness between terms and between short texts. In both algorithms, the intention is to leverage the latent *bridge* vertices between two observed vertices to provide supportive information in relatedness computation. The weight of a bridge vertex x, with respect to an unordered pair of vertices $\{u,v\}$, is defined as in (4).

$$W_{\{u,v\}}(x) = \max(w(u,x) \times w(x,v), w(v,x) \times w(x,u)) \tag{4}$$

For term relatedness computation, we first map any given term t to its corresponding vertex u in the association network. The relatedness between any vertex u and itself is always defined to be 1: $relate(u,u) = 1$. To compute relatedness between two vertices u and v, our baseline algorithm is to add up the weights of the edges between u and v:

$$relate(u,v) = w(u,v) + w(v,u) \tag{5}$$

This algorithm captures the intuition that if u associates more strongly to v or vice versa, u and v are often more related (see Table). As validated later in Section , despite its usefulness and intuitiveness in detecting related pairs, this algorithm leverages insufficient signals from the association network and hence obtains sub-optimal accuracy, especially when the association network is sparse. Thus, we propose a revised algorithm as a natural extension to the baseline:

$$relate(u,v) = w(u,v) + w(v,u) + \sum_{x \in V} W_{\{u,v\}}(x) \tag{6}$$

This algorithm captures the intuition that if u associates more strongly to v, directly or indirectly (via some bridge vertices), or vice versa, u and v are often more related.

For the short text relatedness computation, we abstract a given text as a bag of super nodes, i.e., a vector with each dimension being a super node and weight in that dimension being the occurrence frequency of the terms mapping to this super node. While cosine similarity could be directly computed to measure if two text vectors are similar or not, it suffers from low accuracy as semantically similar texts do not necessarily share identical or synonymous terms with each other. Therefore, we expand the original vectors before computing cosine similarity between two vectors, by adding bridge vertices identified through our association network as new dimensions. Algorithm 2 shows how we convert the original vector vec_0 to the expanded vector vec_+, where K is a parameter controlling the extent of the expansion (i.e., higher K means more expanded vertices).

Algorithm 2 Expand vector

```
function ExpandVector(network G(V, E), vector vec_0, integer K)
    vec_+ ← vec_0
    for u, v ∈dimension set of vec_0 and u ≠ v do
        V_K = top K vertices in V sorted by W_{u,v}
        for x ∈ V_K do
            vec_+(x) ← vec_+(x) + 1
    return vec_+
```

Discussion

Instead of disambiguating the term occurring in a Wikipedia page to one of its concepts and defining each vertex to be a disambiguated concept in the association network, we choose to define each vertex to be a super node, comprising multiple concepts for a term. That is because, even though it is possible to disambiguate a term in Wikipedia pages by taking advantage of contextual information, such a task is more difficult on the free association norms, where virtually no context is available. Even worse, the two end-to-end tasks (term and short text relatedness) also inherently lack context information to perform reliable disambiguation.

When computing the association strength between two super nodes u and v, the parameter α needs to be chosen to instantiate the general form shown in (2). One natural choice is to set α to be 0, which turns the formula into conditional probability, i.e., the probability of observing v, given u. However, it is argued previously (Wettler 1993; Washtell 2009) that the conditional probability measure does not take into consideration the general frequency of the response word and therefore tends to bias toward highly frequent words, such as function words. As a result, we follow (Wettler 1993) to set α to be 0.66, which, according to them, perform the best in estimating word association.

Our algorithms for relatedness computation are for showcasing the power of the association network, and thus many other algorithms can be developed to take advantage of the full potential of the association network.

Experimental Results

This section primarily evaluates two association networks, one constructed only using the original free association norms (denoted as AN_{free}), and the other constructed through the approach proposed in Section (denoted as AN_{wiki}). The results on AN_{free} show the usefulness as well as limitations of free association norms, while the results on AN_{wiki} validate the added benefits of Wikipedia structures in working around the two limitations of AN_{free}, leading to better performance in semantic relatedness computation tasks. [3]

Data sources and statistics

The original Florida free association norms data contains 5,019 cue words (which form the set of *normed words*) and a total of 72,176 cue-response pairs. 63,619 of these pairs contain responses that are also normed words. These pairs are called *normed pairs* with known forward (cue-to-target) and backward (from target-to-cue) strengths.

Our baseline association network, AN_{free}, is made up of the 5019 normed words as vertices and the 63,619 normed pairs as directed edges. Each edge carries a normalized weight $w(u, v)$, which is proportional to $Pr(v \mid u)$, Note, in AN_{free}, each word forms a super node by itself, as we aim to evaluate usefulness of the original free association norms, without depending on additional knowledge (e.g., Wikipedia) to construct super nodes.

Our proposed synthetic association network, AN_{wiki}, consists of 17,469 vertices (super nodes) and 107M directed edges. This network is constructed using the 20,000 most common English words (with stop words removed) as given T_0, and using a Wikipedia dump from July, 2014.

Our test set for evaluting term relatedness is the well-known *WordSimilarity-353* (Finkelstein et al. 2002) (a.k.a. WS-353 with 353 word pairs),

For testing short text similarity, we use the well-known public set *Li30* (Li et al. 2006), comprising 30 pairs of short texts. A newly constructed dataset STSS-131 (O'shea, Bandar, and Crockett 2013) is used to tune the parameter K decribed in Algorithm 2.

AN_{free} v.s. AN_{wiki}

To illustrate the usefulness of free association network, as well as its limitation in semantic relatedness computation, we create WS-227, a subset of WS-353, in which all words belong to some vertex in AN_{free}.

The baseline algorithm with (5) as its metric is denoted by AN^0, while the revised algorithm with (6) as its metric is denoted by AN^+. We apply AN^0 and AN^+ using AN_{free} and AN_{wiki} on WS-227 and WS-353, and compare the performance measured in Spearman correlation with two other well-known algorithms, namely LSA (Deerwester et al. 1990) and ESA (Gabrilovich and Markovitch 2007), in Table 2. The result for LSA is obtained from the widely

[3] A demo of our system is available at http://adapt.seiee.sjtu.edu.cn/~keyang/assoc/.

used online portal[4], while the result for ESA is obtained from ESAlib[5].

We observe the following: 1) AN^{+}_{free} performs better than LSA and ESA on WS-227, despite its relatively small size, which suggests that free association can be useful in computing semantic relatedness. 2) However, when tested on WS-353, due to its limited vocabulary, AN^{+}_{free} shows a drastic degrade in performance, which reflects one of its primary limitations. Conversely, AN_{wiki}, of a larger lexical coverage, performs consistently well on both WS-227 and WS-353. 3) Due to AN_{free}'s another limitation, sparseness, AN^{0}_{free} exhibits sub-optimal performance on both WS-227 and WS-353; while AN^{+}_{free} shows a significant improvement as the sparseness problem is alleviated by leveraging the latent bridge vertices. 4) Though the best performance is obtained by AN^{+}_{wiki}, its advantage over AN^{0}_{wiki} is not large. We argue that it is because by reverse-engineering the association strength into an aggregation function of a vector of structured co-occurrence, AN_{wiki} alleviates sparseness by enabling to infer the edge weights missing in AN_{free}.

Table 2: Spearman correlation on two WS datasets

Methods	WS-227	WS-353
LSA	0.542	0.579
ESA	0.727	0.744
AN^{0}_{free}	0.645	0.476
AN^{+}_{free}	0.752	0.512
AN^{0}_{wiki}	0.758	0.785
AN^{+}_{wiki}	**0.782**	**0.813**

Prediction of free association

In this experiment, we evaluate if AN_{wiki} can be used to predict free association strengths given by humans. We compute Spearman correlation between scores predicted by a number of competing methods (Washtell 2009) and the human association strength computed from the Kent's free association norms (1910). Our method is just mapping the two terms to vertex u and v, and assigning $w(u, v)$ as predicted association strength.

As is shown in Table 3, AN_{wiki} does a reasonable job in simulating free association, compared with other common approaches. And as a reference, the Spearman correlation between the human labeled scores of Kent dataset and those of the Minnesota dataset (Jenkins 1970) using the same set of cue words is 0.4, which can be viewed as an upper bound for computer-based systems.

End-to-end tasks: term & short text relatedness

Table 4 compares AN_{wiki} with a number of previous approaches on the term relatedness computation using WS-353 dataset. Our association network achieves state-of-the-art results on correlation with human scores.

[4]http://lsa.colorado.edu/

[5]http://ticcky.github.io/esalib/

Table 3: Association Prediction

Methods	Spearman
Cond. Prob.	0.31
SCI	0.34
PMI	0.28
Dice/Jaccard	0.32
AN_{wiki}	**0.37**

Table 4: Spearman correlation on WS-353 dataset

Methods	Spearman
Resnik (1995)	0.353
LSA-Landauer (1997)	0.581
Lin (1998)	0.348
Roget-Jarmasz (2003)	0.415
ESA-Gabrilovich (2007)	0.75
Agirre (2009)	0.78
Reisinger (2010)	0.77
SSA-Hassan (2011)	0.629
TSA-Radinsky (2011)	0.80
CLEAR-Halawi (2012)	0.810
Xu (2014)	0.683
AN_{wiki}	**0.813**

Table 5 shows that our association network outperforms all existing approaches by significant margins on short text similarity task.

Recall that, Algorithm 2 is parameterized by K determining the extent of expansion. Our reported results use $K = 10$, empirically tuned based on STSS-131 dataset.

Table 5: Pearson and Spearman correlation on Li30 dataset

Methods	Pearson	Spearman
STASIS-Li (2006)	0.816	0.813
LIU (2007)	0.841	0.854
LSA-OShea (2008)	0.838	0.871
STS-Islam (2008)	0.853	0.838
Omiotis-Tsatsaronis (2010)	0.856	0.891
WSD-STS-Ho (2010)	0.864	0.834
SPD-STS-Ho (2010)	0.895	0.903
SSA-Hassan (2011)	0.881	0.878
LDA-Guo (2012)	0.842	0.866
WTMF-Guo (2012)	0.898	0.909
WTMF+PK-Guo (2013)	0.902	–
AN_{wiki}	**0.942**	**0.940**

Effects of different co-occurrences and free association training

In this experiment, we compare an association network built from only sentence-level co-occurrences (slc), an association network with 5 types of co-occurrences uniformly combined (uniform), and our proposed network, which comes with weights trained from free association norms. Table 6 gives rise to these observations: i) AN_{wiki}(uniform) outperforms AN_{wiki}(slc) by a large margin on both tasks, which shows that the four additional types of co-occurrences are useful in capturing signals not available in slc; ii) AN_{wiki} further improves the results from AN_{wiki}(uniform) by a substantial margin, which shows that signals tapped from free association norms can indeed benefit semantic relatedness computation tasks.

Table 6: Several variants of AN_{wiki}

Methods	WS-353	Li30
AN_{wiki}(slc)	0.734	0.884
AN_{wiki}(uniform)	0.766	0.903
AN_{wiki}	**0.813**	**0.942**

Execution time

Average execution time for computing the relatedness score for a pair of terms in WS-353 is $10.3ms$, and for a pair of short texts in Li30 is $465.3ms$. The time and space consumption can be further reduced by filtering out edges with insignificant weights. Experiments show that by removing up to 90% of the edges, the accuracy in both term and short text relatedness remains virtually constant, and at the same time the execution time for a pair of terms and a pair of short texts are reduced to $1.4ms$ and $19.1ms$, respectively.

Related Work

In this section, we introduce a number of studies in *semantic relatedness computation* and related work in *free association*.

Previous approaches to semantic relatedness pursue two main directions, of using hand-crafted lexical taxonomies like WordNet (Miller 1995) or Roget's Thesaurus (Roget 1911) as semantic knowledge, or of employing probabilistic approaches to decode semantics based on large corpora.

The first approach of using hand-crafted resources proposes knowledge-based measures that tap into the properties of their underlying structure to compute semantic relatedness (Roget 1911; Lin 1998; Leacock and Chodorow 1998; Hirst and St-Onge 1998; Jiang and Conrath 1997; Resnik 1995; Wu and Palmer 1994). Though showing potential in such tasks like term relatedness computation, this approach requires to construct manually curated lexical resources and thus cannot easily scale to larger lexical coverage or to a new language.

On the other hand, the second approach of using corpus-based measures, instead of relying on human-organized knowledge, utilize the contextual information and patterns observed in large corpus to construct semantic profiles for words. Latent Semantic Analysis (LSA) (Deerwester et al. 1990) was an original approach to leverage word co-occurrences from a large corpus of text, and "learns" its representation by applying Singular Value Decomposition to the words-by-documents co-occurrence matrix. Explicit Semantic Analysis (ESA) (Gabrilovich and Markovitch 2007) as well as Salient Semantic Analysis (SSA) (Hassan and Mihalcea 2011) were proposed to incorporate large amounts of human knowledge such as Wikipedia into word relatedness computation. They both represent a word as a concept vector, where each dimension corresponds to a Wikipedia concept. Later, Temporal Semantic Analysis (TSA) (Radinsky et al. 2011) considered that words have different meanings over time and extended the concept vector with a temporal dimension. To bridge the corpus-based measures with knowledge-based measures, Constrained LEArning of Relatedness (CLEAR) (Halawi et al. 2012) was proposed to learn word relatedness based on word occurrence statistics from large corpora while constraining the learning process by incorporating knowledge from WordNet. Some recent works like (Mikolov et al. 2013) used machine learning techniques to compute continuous vector representations of words from large datasets , shown to perform better than LSA for preserving linear regularities among words.

Some models aim particularly at solving the similarity problem between two sentences, or two short texts (Guo and Diab 2012; 2013; Ho et al. 2010; OShea et al. 2008). WSD-Based Sentence Similarity (Ho et al. 2010) was proposed to compute the similarity between two sentences based on a comparison of their actual meanings by integrating word sense disambiguation. WTMF (Guo and Diab 2012) was proposed to model the missing words in the sentences as a typically overlooked feature to address the sparseness problem for the short text similarity task.

All the existing semantic relatedness models mentioned above, though leveraging some useful signals from hand-crafted lexical taxonomies or large corpus text, fail to actively take advantage of the human perception signal in semantic relatedness computation. Our approach, by effectively bridging this gap using signals in the well-studied psychological process of free association, outperforms state-of-the-art models in both word and short text relatedness tasks.

Free association is a task requiring human participants to produce the easily associated word for the given cue word, to tap into human perception acquired through world experience (Nelson, McEvoy, and Schreiber 2004). Mining the signals contained in this cognitive process is made possible by several collections of free association norms (Nelson, McEvoy, and Schreiber 2004; Kent and Rosanoff 1910; Jenkins 1970; Kiss et al. 1973), which are typically collected by researchers in phychology and cognitive science. As the Florida Norms is the largest collection available, and also the most recent in time, we choose to use it as our primary source of human perception to be combined with signals from Wikipedia.

Conclusion

We synthetically build an association network, by aggregating Wikipedia signals, using free association as a training data. Our evaluation results validated that our proposed framework reaches state-of-the-art in a standard benchmark for term relatedness computation and outperforms all other state-of-the-arts for short text similarity computation by a significant margin.

Acknowledgement

Kenny Q. Zhu, the contact author, was supported by NSFC grant 61373031 and NSFC-NRF Joint Research Program. Seung-won Hwang was supported under the framework of international cooperation program managed by NRF of Korea (2014K2A2A2000519). This work received contributions from Kailang Jiang and Jinyi Lu.

References

Agirre, E.; Soroa, A.; Alfonseca, E.; Hall, K.; Kravalova, J.; and Pasca, M. 2009. A study on similarity and relatedness using distributional and wordnet-based approaches. In *NAACL'09*.

Budanitsky, A., and Hirst, G. 2006. Evaluating wordnet-based measures of lexical semantic relatedness. *Computational Linguistics* 32.

Deerwester, S. C.; Dumais, S. T.; Landauer, T. K.; Furnas, G. W.; and Harshman, R. A. 1990. Indexing by latent semantic analysis. *JASIS* 41(6).

Finkelstein, L.; Gabrilovich, E.; Matias, Y.; Rivlin, E.; Solan, Z.; Wolfman, G.; and Ruppin, E. 2002. Placing search in context: the concept revisited. *ACM Trans. Inf. Syst.* 20(1).

Gabrilovich, E., and Markovitch, S. 2007. Computing semantic relatedness using wikipedia-based explicit semantic analysis. In *IJCAI*.

Guo, W., and Diab, M. 2012. Modeling sentences in the latent space. In *ACL*.

Guo, W., and Diab, M. T. 2013. Improving lexical semantics for sentential semantics: Modeling selectional preference and similar words in a latent variable model. In *HLT-NAACL*.

Halawi, G.; Dror, G.; Gabrilovich, E.; and Koren, Y. 2012. Large-scale learning of word relatedness with constraints. In *KDD*.

Hassan, S., and Mihalcea, R. 2011. Semantic relatedness using salient semantic analysis. In *AAAI*.

Hirst, G., and St-Onge, D. 1998. Lexical chains as representations of context for the detection and correction of malapropisms. In *WordNet: An Electronic Lexical Database*.

Ho, C.; Murad, M. A. A.; Kadir, R. A.; and Doraisamy, S. C. 2010. Word sense disambiguation-based sentence similarity. In *ACL*.

Islam, A., and Inkpen, D. 2008. Semantic text similarity using corpus-based word similarity and string similarity. *TKDD* 2(2).

Jarmasz, M. 2003. *Roget's Thesaurus as a Lexical Resource for Natural Language Processing*. Ph.D. Dissertation, Ottawa-Carleton Institute for Computer Science.

Jenkins, J. J. 1970. The 1952 minnesota word association norms. *Norms of word association*.

Jiang, J., and Conrath, D. 1997. Semantic similarity based on corpus statistics and lexical taxonomy. In *Intl. Conf. on Res. in Computational Linguistics*.

Kent, G. H., and Rosanoff, A. J. 1910. *A study of association in insanity*. American Journal of Insanity.

Kiss, G. R.; Armstrong, C.; Milroy, R.; and Piper, J. 1973. An associative thesaurus of english and its computer analysis. *The computer and literary studies*.

Landauer, T. K.; Laham, D.; Rehder, B.; and Schreiner, M. E. 1997. How well can passage meaning be derived without using word order? a comparison of latent semantic analysis and humans. In *CogSci*.

Leacock, C., and Chodorow, M. 1998. Combining local context and wordnet similarity for word sense identification. *WordNet: An electronic lexical database* 49(2).

Li, Y.; McLean, D.; Bandar, Z. A.; O'shea, J. D.; and Crockett, K. 2006. Sentence similarity based on semantic nets and corpus statistics. *TKDE* 18(8).

Lin, D. 1998. An information-theoretic definition of similarity. In *ICML'98*.

Liu, X.; Zhou, Y.; and Zheng, R. 2007. Sentence similarity based on dynamic time warping. In *ICSC*.

McGill, M. 1979. An evaluation of factors affecting document ranking by information retrieval systems. Tech. Rep., Syracuse Univ , School of Information Studies.

Mikolov, T.; Chen, K.; Corrado, G.; and Dean, J. 2013. Efficient estimation of word representations in vector space. *arXiv preprint arXiv:1301.3781*.

Miller, G. A. 1995. WordNet: A lexical database for english. *Commun. ACM* 38(11).

Nelson, D. L.; McEvoy, C. L.; and Schreiber, T. A. 2004. The university of south florida free association, rhyme, and word fragment norms. *Behavior Res. Methods, Instruments, & Computers* 36(3).

O'shea, J.; Bandar, Z.; and Crockett, K. 2013. A new benchmark dataset with production methodology for short text semantic similarity algorithms. *TSLP* 10(4).

OShea, J.; Bandar, Z.; Crockett, K.; and McLean, D. 2008. A comparative study of two short text semantic similarity measures. In *KES-AMSTA*.

Radinsky, K.; Agichtein, E.; Gabrilovich, E.; and Markovitch, S. 2011. A word at a time: computing word relatedness using temporal semantic analysis. In *WWW*.

Reisinger, J., and Mooney, R. J. 2010. Multi-prototype vector-space models of word meaning. In *NAACL*.

Resnik, P. 1995. Using information content to evaluate semantic similarity in a taxonomy. In *IJCAI'95*.

Roget, P. M. 1911. *Roget's Thesaurus of English Words and Phrases*. HarperCollins New York.

Tsatsaronis, G.; Varlamis, I.; and Vazirgiannis, M. 2010. Text relatedness based on a word thesaurus. *JAIR* 37(1).

Washtell, J. 2009. Co-dispersion: A windowless approach to lexical association. In *EACL*.

Wettler, M, R. R. 1993. Computation of word associations based on the co-occurrences of words in large corpora. In *the 1st Workshop on Very Large Corpora*.

Wu, Z., and Palmer, M. 1994. Verbs semantics and lexical selection. In *ACL*.

Xu, C.; Bai, Y.; Bian, J.; Gao, B.; Wang, G.; Liu, X.; and Liu, T.-Y. 2014. Rc-net: A general framework for incorporating knowledge into word representations. In *CIKM*.

Computational Sustainability and Artificial Intelligence

Influence-Driven Model for Time Series Prediction from Partial Observations

Saima Aman
Department of Computer Science
University of Southern California
Los Angeles, California
Email: saman@usc.edu

Charalampos Chelmis and **Viktor K. Prasanna**
Department of Electrical Engineering
University of Southern California
Los Angeles, California
Email: {chelmis, prasanna}@usc.edu

Abstract

Applications in sustainability domains such as in energy, transportation, and natural resource and environment monitoring, increasingly use sensors for collecting data and sending it back to centrally located processing nodes. While data can usually be collected by the sensors at a very high speed, in many cases, it can not be sent back to central nodes at a frequency that is required for fast and real-time modeling and decision-making. This may be due to physical limitations of the transmission networks, or due to consumers limiting frequent transmission of data from sensors located at their premises for security and privacy concerns. We propose a novel solution to the problem of making short term predictions in absence of real-time data from sensors. A key implication of our work is that by using real-time data from only a small subset of *influential* sensors, we are able to make predictions for *all* sensors. We evaluated our approach with a large real-world electricity consumption data collected from smart meters in Los Angeles and the results show that between prediction horizons of 2 to 8 hours, despite lack of real time data, our influence model outperforms the baseline model that uses real-time data. Also, when using partial real-time data from only $\approx 7\%$ *influential* smart meters, we witness prediction error increase by only $\approx 0.5\%$ over the baseline, thus demonstrating the usefulness of our method for practical scenarios.

Introduction

Low cost wireless sensors are increasingly being deployed in large numbers for performing monitoring and control in many sustainability domains such as in smart electric grids, transport networks, and natural resource and environment monitoring. These sensors are located at geographically dispersed locations and periodically send back acquired data to centrally located processing nodes (Ciancio and Ortega 2005) via wireless links and the Internet (Chong and Kumar 2003). They include sensors for monitoring natural resource and environment such as biodiversity and atmosphere (Lozano et al. 2009); smart meters for measuring energy consumption (Simmhan et al. 2013), (Marascu et al. 2013); loop detectors installed under pavements for recording traffic (Pan, Demiryurek, and Shahabi 2012); and meters on wind turbines that record wind speed and turbines' power output (Bullis 2014).

Due to several factors, data from all sensors is not available at central nodes in real-time or at a frequency that is required for fast and real-time modeling and decision-making. For example, wind turbines record data every few seconds, but transmit data every five minutes to far-off research centers for use in forecasting algorithms (Bullis 2014). *Physical limitations* of existing transmission networks, such as latency, bandwidth and high energy consumption (Ciancio and Ortega 2005) are key factors that limit the frequency of data transmission from sensors to central nodes (Bouhafs, Mackay, and Merabti 2012). Sometimes, consumers may also limit frequent transmission of information from sensors located at their premises for *security and privacy* concerns (McDaniel and McLaughlin 2009).

All these situations reflect the ***partial data problem***, *where only partial data from sensors is available in real-time*, and complete high resolution data become available only periodically, generally one or more times a day. Without addressing this problem, traditional solutions risk degradation in performance and inaccurate interpretation of generated insights. For instance, time series prediction methods are adversely affected by the prediction horizon length, and in the case of partial data, the effective prediction horizon for those sensors for which data is unavailable in real-time becomes larger, which in turn leads to detrimental increase in prediction error. Thus, the time series approach cannot be used for accurate predictions, for example, for up to 8 hours ahead. A possible approach - as we propose in this paper - is to develop creative solutions using data from a small subset of sensors selected on the basis of some heuristics or learning methods, while minimizing information loss resulting from leaving out data from remaining sensors. The intuition behind this approach is the fact that sensors located spatially close to each other or sensing activities driven by similar schedules - such as those on an academic campus or traffic on high density roads - are likely to be correlated. If this information can be leveraged, it will obviate the need for real-time transmission from *all* sensors to the central nodes, and thereby reduce the load on the transmission network. Also, it would make it simpler to add new sensors without straining the network.

We distinguish *partial data* from *missing data*, which is arbitrary unavailability of data at random time periods due to diverse factors, whereas partial data is systematic unavailability of data for known time periods for a known subset of smart meters, due to non-transmission of data in that period. While selective missing data is lost, partial data becomes available when batch transmission occurs, and can be used to re-train our models.

In this paper we address the partial data problem in the context of smart electricity grids, where high *volume* electricity consumption data is collected by smart meters at consumer premises and securely transmitted back to the electric utility over wireless or broadband networks. There, they are used to predict electricity consumption and to initiate curtailment programs ahead of time by the utility to avoid potential supply-demand mismatch. Partial data problem arises when data from smart meters is only partially available in real-time. To address this, we propose a two-stage solution: first, we learn the dependencies among time series of different smart meters, then, we use data from a small subset of smart meters which are found to have high *influence* on others to make predictions for all meters. Our main contributions are:

1) We leverage dependencies among time series sensor data for making short term predictions with *partial real-time data*. While time series dependencies have been used previously, the novelty of our work is in extending the notion of dependencies to discover *influential* sensors and using real-time data only from them to do predictions for *all* sensors.

2) Using real-world electricity consumption data, we demonstrate that despite lack of real time data, our prediction models perform comparably to the baseline model that uses real-time data, thus indicating their usefulness for practical sustainability domain scenarios.

Related Work

Many predictive modeling methods are designed for ideal scenarios where all required data is readily available. For example, time-series prediction methods such as Auto-Regressive Integrated Moving Average (ARIMA) (Box and Jenkins 1970) and Auto-Regressive Trees (ART) (Meek, Chickering, and Heckerman 2002) require observations from recent past to be readily available in real-time to make short-term future predictions. However, this assumption does not hold true for many sensor-based applications involving "big data" that is only *partially* available in real time. The solutions proposed to address this problem can be categorized into two types: 1) Reduce the volume of transmitted data by techniques such as data compression (Marascu et al. 2013), (Razzaque, Bleakley, and Dobson 2013), data aggregation (Karimi, Namboodiri, and Jadliwala 2013), model-driven data acquisition (Deshpande et al. 2004), and communication efficient algorithms (Sanders, Schlag, and Muller 2013); 2) Estimate missing real-time data by techniques such as interpolation based on regression (Kreindler and Lumsden. 2006), or through transient time models that use differential equations to model system behavior (Cuevas-Tello et al. 2010). Main challenge with these methods is that estimates depend on the accuracy of models and interpolation errors get propagated to subsequent analysis and decision-making steps. Another method for estimation is using spectral analysis of time series, though it is a more complex and involved process that is suitable only for periodic time series (Bahadori and Liu 2012). We use an orthogonal approach where instead of trying to estimate missing real-time data, we first discover *influential* sensors and then do predictive modeling using real time data from only these sensors.

Our approach involves learning dependencies among time series data from different sensors. Several techniques have been proposed to learn dependencies among time series data; the more popular among them are based on cross-correlations (Box and Jenkins 1970) and Granger Causality (Granger 1969). The latter has gained popularity in many domains such as climatology, economics, and biological sciences due to its simplicity and robustness (Bahadori and Liu 2012). It is however time consuming for evaluating pairwise dependencies when large number of variables are involved. Lasso-Granger (Arnold, Liu, and Abe 2007) is proposed to provide a more scalable and accurate solution. In our work, we leverage the Lasso-Granger method to discover dependencies among time series from different sensors, and then identify influential sensors based on these dependencies.

Our work brings the much needed focus to efficient data collection methods for sustainability domains. In smart grid, data streams from thousands of sensors are monitored for predictive analytics (Balac et al. 2013), and demand response (Kwac and Rajagopal 2013). With large scale adoption of smart meters, most cities would soon have millions of smart meters recording electricity consumption data every minute. For utilities, real-time data collection from meters all over a city would be prohibitive due to limited capacity of current transmission networks. Such scenarios necessitate development of alternative methods, such as ours, that could work with only partial data that is available in real-time.

Preliminaries

Consider a large set of sensors $\mathcal{S} = \{s_1, ..., s_n\}$ collecting real-time[1] data. Due to network bandwidth constraints, only some of these sensors can send data back to the central node in real-time, while the rest send the collected data in batches every few hours (Fig. 1). The problem we address is to use this *partial data* to make predictions for *all* sensors.

Problem Definition Given a set of sensors $\mathcal{S}$ with time series outputs $\{x_j^i\}, j = 1, ..., t, i = 1, ..., n$, make short-term predictions $\{x_j^i\}, j = t+1, ..., t+h, i = 1, ..., n$ for each sensor $s_i \in \mathcal{S}$, when readings $\{x_k^o\}, k = t-r+1, ..., t$ for $o \in \mathcal{O}$ are unavailable for a subset $\mathcal{O}$ of sensors, $\mathcal{O} \subset \mathcal{S}$.

For simplicity, we assume all time-series sensor outputs to be sampled at the same frequency and be of equal length.

We *hypothesize* that we can learn dependencies in past time series outputs from sensors and use them to identify the set of sensors that are more helpful in making predictions for

[1]In the context of this paper, data collected at 15-min intervals are considered real-time, even though our models would be applicable (with even greater impact) to data at smaller resolutions.

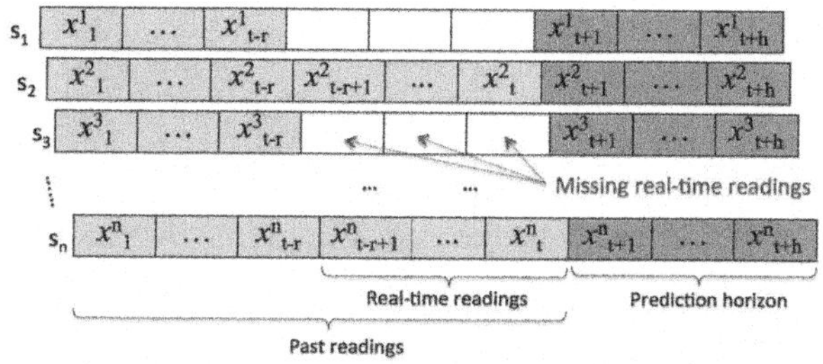

Figure 1: Some sensors can send readings to a central node in real-time, while the rest send every few hours resulting in partial real time data.

other sensors, so that we can collect real-time readings from only these sensors.

Definition 1 *A **dependency matrix** $\mathcal{M}$ is an $n \times f$ matrix, where each element $\mathcal{M}[i,j]$ represents the dependence of time series $\mathcal{T}_i$ on time series $\mathcal{T}_j$.*

Here, n is the number of sensors and f is the number of features used for each sensor.

Definition 2 *The **influence** $\mathcal{I}^k$ of a time series $\mathcal{T}_k$ is defined as the sum of all values in the column k in the dependency matrix $\mathcal{M}$.*

$$\mathcal{I}^k = \sum_{j=1}^{n} \mathcal{M}[j,k] \tag{1}$$

Definition 3 ***Compression Ratio**, $\mathcal{CR}$ is defined as the ratio between the total number of sensor readings that would be required for real-time prediction and the number of readings actually transmitted from selected influential sensors for prediction with partial data.*

$$\mathcal{CR} = \frac{\sum_{i=1}^{n} |\mathcal{P}_i|}{\sum_{i=1}^{n} |\mathcal{P}_i| - \sum_{o\in\mathcal{O}} |\mathcal{P}_o|} \tag{2}$$

where $\mathcal{P}_i$ is the sequence of past values from sensor s_i used for prediction and $|\mathcal{P}_i|$ is the length of this sequence; $\mathcal{O}$ is the subset of sensors with unavailable real-time readings and n is the total number of sensors. For simplicity, we consider same length l of past values for all sensors. Hence, $|\mathcal{P}_i| = l, \forall i$ and above equation can be simplified as $\mathcal{CR} = \frac{n}{n-|\mathcal{O}|}$.

Methodology

We propose a two-stage process, where we first learn dependencies from past data and determine influence for individual sensors, and then use this information for selecting influential sensors for regression tree based prediction.

Influence Discovery

We cast the problem of making predictions for a sensor $s_i \in \mathcal{O}$ in terms of recent real time data from other sensors as a regression problem. In ordinary least squares (OLS) regression, given data $(\mathbf{x}^i, y_i), i = 1,2,...,n$, the response y_i is estimated in terms of p predictor variables, $\mathbf{x}^i = (x_{i1},...,x_{ip})$ by minimizing the residual squared error.

We identify sensors that show stronger *influence* on other sensors using the Lasso Granger method. We thus use Lasso Granger as a novel way for feature selection. The lasso method is used in regression for shrinking some coefficients and setting others to zero by penalizing the absolute size of the coefficients (Tibshirani 1996). The OLS method generally gives low bias due to over-fitting but has large variance. The Lasso improves variance by shrinking coefficients and hence may reduce overall prediction errors (Tibshirani 1996).

Given n sensor outputs in form of time series $\mathbf{x}^1, \mathbf{x}^2, ..., \mathbf{x}^n$, with readings at timestamps $\mathbf{t} = 1,...T$, for each series $\mathbf{x}^i$, we obtain a sparse solution for coefficients $\mathbf{w}$ by minimizing the sum of squared error and a constant times the L1-norm of the coefficients:

$$\mathbf{w} = \arg\min \sum_{t=l+1}^{T} \left\| x_t^i - \sum_{j=1}^{n} \mathbf{w}_{i,j}^T \mathcal{P}_t^j \right\|_2^2 + \lambda \|\mathbf{w}\|_1 \tag{3}$$

where $\mathcal{P}_t^j$ is the sequence of past l readings, i.e., $\mathcal{P}_t^j = [x_{t-l}^j, ..., x_{t-1}^j]$, $\mathbf{w}_{i,j}$ is the j-th vector of coefficients $\mathbf{w}_i$ representing the dependency of series i on series j, and λ is a parameter which determines the sparseness of $\mathbf{w}_i$ and can be determined using cross-validation method.

Influence Model (IM)

We first learn the dependency matrix $\mathcal{M}_j$ for each day as follows. Each sensor's data is split into a set of q daily series $\{\mathcal{D}_j^i\}_{i=1,...,n, j=1,...,q}$. Longer time series data is usually non-stationary, i.e., the dependence on preceding values changes with time. Splitting into smaller day-long windows ensures stationarity for time series data in each window. Dependency matrix is re-calculated daily to account for changes in influence over time. Weights for daily series for each day are calculated using eqn. 3. The weight vectors $\mathbf{w}_i$ form the rows of the dependency matrix $\mathcal{M}$. We set diagonals of the dependency matrix to zero, i.e., $\mathcal{M}[i,i] = 0$ in order to remove self-dependencies and simulate the case of making prediction without a sensor's own past real-time data. Given $\mathcal{M}$, *influence* $\mathcal{I}$ of all series can be calculated using eqn. 1.

Predictions for a given day are based on training data from a previous *similar* day sim. We consider two cases of similarity: 1) *previous week* - same day in the preceding week, which captures similarity for sensor data related to periodic (weekly) human activities; 2) *previous day*, which captures similarity for sensor data related to human activities and natural environments on successive days.

We apply a windowing transformation to the daily series $\{\mathcal{D}^i\}$ in both training and test data to get a set of $\langle$predictor, response$\rangle$ tuples. Given time-series $\mathbf{x}$ with k values, the transformation of length l results in a set of tuples of the form $\langle (x_{t-l+1}, ..., x_t), x_{t+h} \rangle$ such that $l \le t \le k-h$.

The prediction model for a sensor s_i is a regression tree (Breiman et al. 1984) that uses predictors from all sensors with non-zero coefficients in the dependency matrix learned from a similar day, i.e., predictors are taken from $\{\mathcal{D}^k\}, \forall k : \mathcal{M}_{sim}[i,k] \neq 0$. Since $\mathcal{M}[i,i] = 0$, sensor s_i's own past values are not used as predictors. Hence, *a key benefit of this model is that we are able to do predictions for a sensor in*

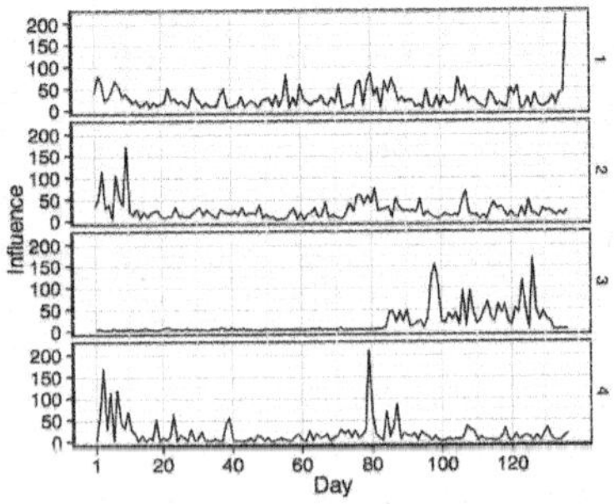

(a)

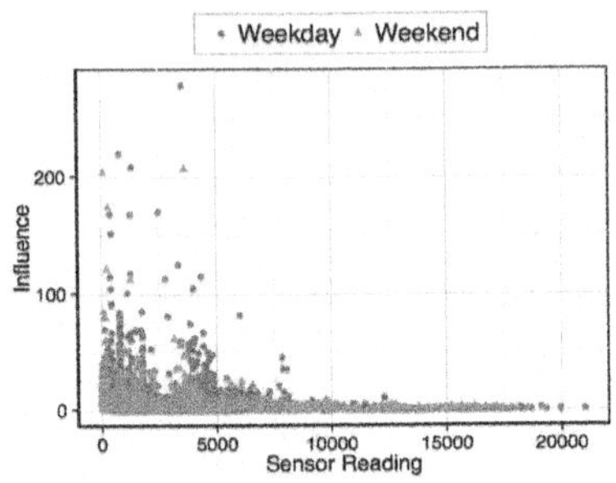

(b)

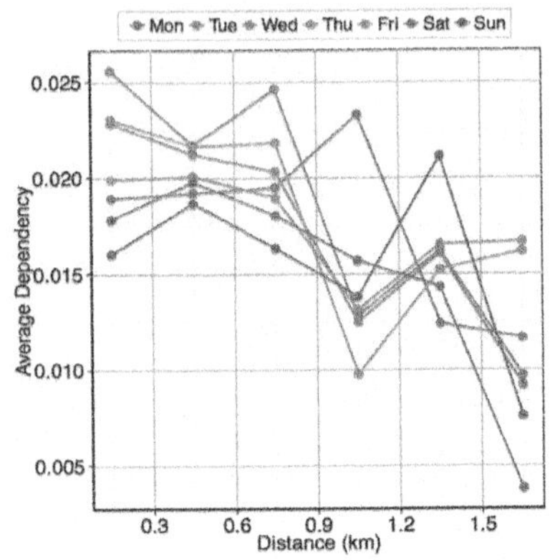

(c)

Figure 2: Influence/dependency w.r.t (a) time, (b) size, and (c) distance: higher values observed for weekdays than for weekends.

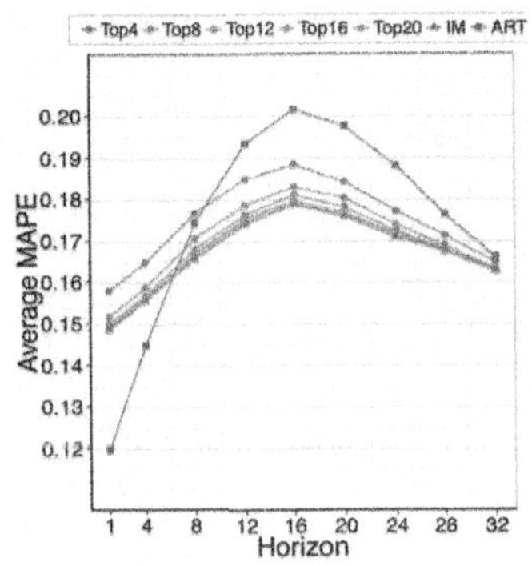

(a)

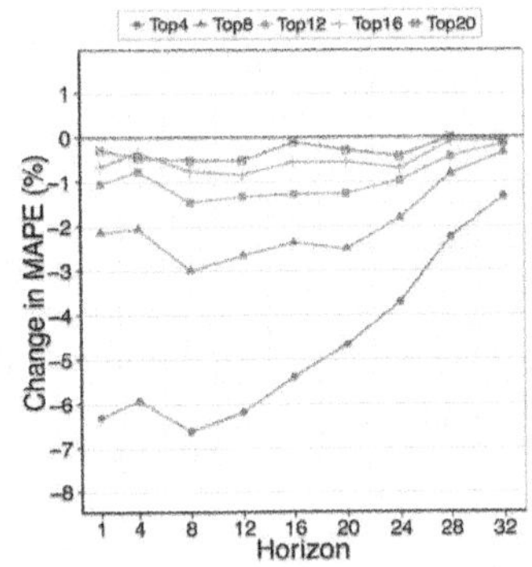

(b)

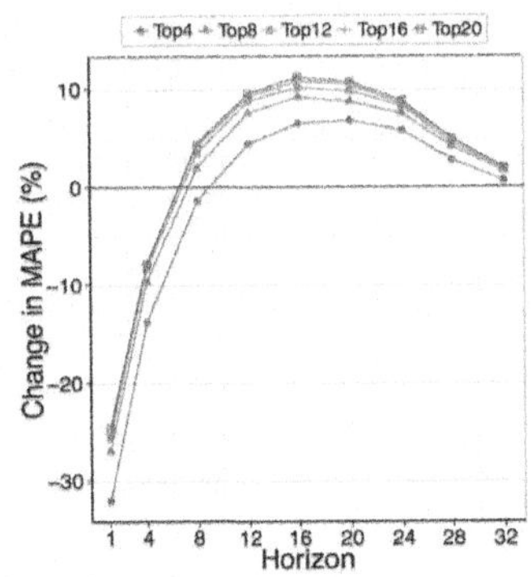

(c)

Figure 3: LIM's performance: (a) MAPE; and percentage change in MAPE with respect to (b) IM and (c) ART. (Negative change implies increase in error.)

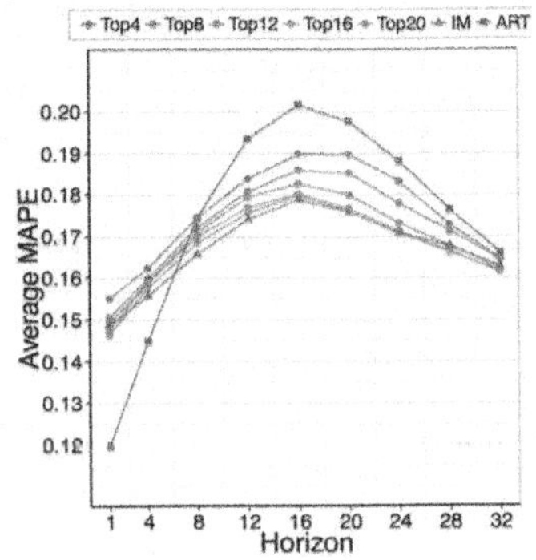

(a)

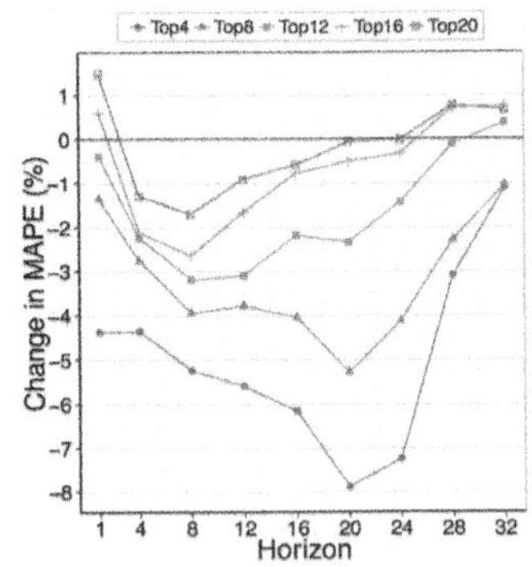

(b)

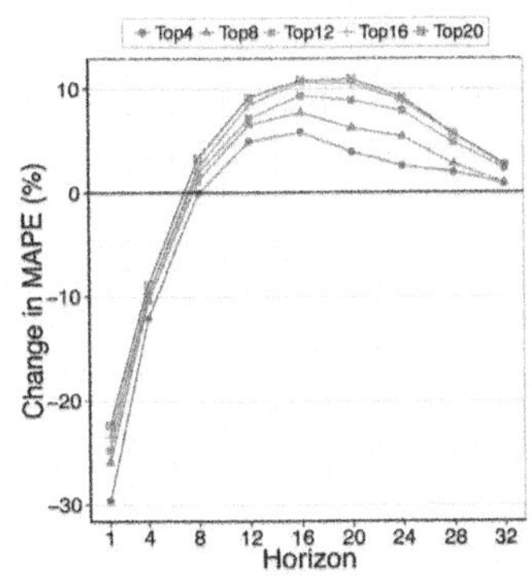

(c)

Figure 4: GIM's performance: (a) MAPE; and percentage change in MAPE with respect to (b) IM and (c) ART. (Negative change implies increase in error.)

absence of its own past values by using past values of its influential sensors.

Local Influence Model (LIM)

In the previous section, we discussed how IM resolves the problem of partial data availability by using influential sensors (a small subset of sensors) to transmit data in real time. However, without restricting the number of influential sensors, the subset of influential sensors considered by IM may include the total number of sensors. Next, we discuss a policy to ensure that only a fraction of sensors is considered for real-time predictions. For each sensor s_i, we sort the corresponding row $\mathcal{M}[i,]$ in the dependency matrix and consider only readings from the top τ_l sensors in this model.

Global Influence Model (GIM)

In LIM, because local influencers are selected for *each* sensor, overall it may still require real-time data from a large number of sensors, thus defeating the goal of getting real-time data from only a few influencers. Thus, we are interested in finding *global* influencers. Using dependency matrices $\mathcal{M}_j$, we calculate daily influence $\mathcal{I}_j^i$ for each sensor s_i as described in equation 1. After sorting the sensors based on their influence values, we consider only readings from the top τ_g sensors in the influence model.

Experiments

Datasets

1) Electricity Consumption Data[2]: collected at 15-min intervals by over 170 smart meters installed in the USC campus microgrid (Simmhan et al. 2013) in Los Angeles.
2) Weather Data: temperature and humidity data taken from NOAA's (NOAA 2013) USC campus station, linearly interpolated to 15-min resolution.

Performance Comparison

We evaluate our models for up to 8 hour-ahead prediction[3]. Given the short horizon, the length of previous values used was set to 1-hour. Out of two choices of similar day for training, previous week and previous day, we found previous week to perform better.

Baseline Model We use the Auto-Regressive Tree (ART) Model as the baseline. Our proposed models are also based on regression tree concept so ART provides a natural baseline to compare performances. ART uses recent observations as features in a regression tree model and has been shown to offer high predictive accuracy on a large range of datasets (Meek, Chickering, and Heckerman 2002). ART's main advantage is its ability to model non-linear relationships in data, which leads to a closer fit to the data than a standard autoregressive model. We implement a specialized $ART(p, h)$ model that uses recent p observations of a variable for making h interval ahead prediction. While ART uses a variable's own recent observations, our models only use other variables' observations to make predictions.

Evaluation Metric We used MAPE (Mean Absolute Percentage Error) as the evaluation metric, as it is a relative measure and therefore scale-independent (Aman, Simmhan, and Prasanna 2014). MAPE $= \frac{1}{n}\sum_{i=1}^{n}\frac{|x_i - \hat{x}_i|}{x_i}$ where x_i is the observed value and $\hat{x}_i$ is the predicted value.

Influence Variation

Fig. 2(a) shows influence variation for the top 4 influencer sensors. Given this variation, we decided to *re-calculate influence for each day* in our experiments, rather than use a static value calculated over a large number of days. Fig. 2(b) shows the distribution of influence for each sensor with the size of sensor readings. It is interesting to note that buildings with smaller consumption values have higher influence.

[2]Available from the USC Facilities Management Services.

[3]Smart Grid applications such as Demand Response usually require up to 6 hours ahead predictions (Aman, Simmhan, and Prasanna 2014).

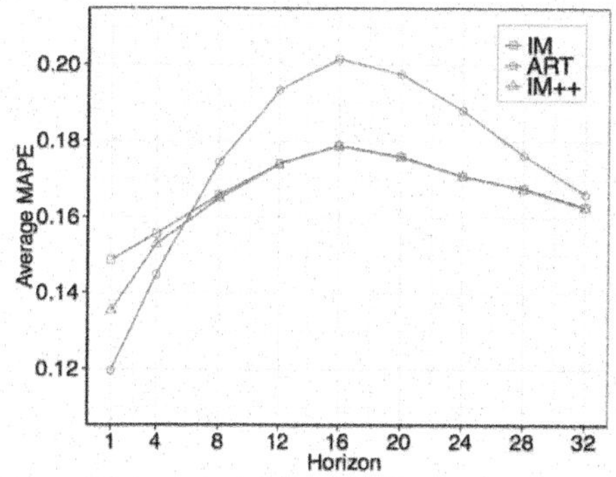

Figure 5: Prediction performance: partial data vs. complete data. For ART, recent values used as predictors at the time of prediction become increasingly ineffective for longer horizons, when IM's use of more recent real-time values of other sensors become more useful.

Also, influence for weekdays is higher possibly due to more activity and movement of people between buildings.

Fig. 2(c) shows average dependency decreasing with increase in the distance between the sensors. This validates our intuition about greater dependency among closely located sensors. This can be attributed to greater movement of people between neighboring buildings, and hence greater dependency in their electricity consumption. Also, there is more movement on weekdays, hence we observe that average dependency is higher for weekdays than for weekends.

Prediction Performance

Fig. 5 shows prediction errors of the *influence model*, averaged over all days and for all sensors. ART performs well up to 6 intervals (1.5 hour), as due to the very short prediction horizon, electricity consumption is not expected to drastically change from its previous 4 values. ART performs well as it has access to real-time data. Instead, IM achieves comparable accuracy despite the lack of real-time data. IM's accuracy also increases with the prediction horizon, where it consistently outperforms ART. While increase in IM's error is subdued, ART's error increases rapidly with increasing horizon implying that the previous 4 values used as predictors at the time of prediction become increasingly ineffective for predicting values beyond 1.5 hours ahead in time. Here, *more recent real-time values of other sensors become more useful predictors than a sensor's own relatively older values.* That IM achieves good accuracy despite the lack of real-time data is an important result and its main advantage.

For comparison, we used an additional baseline (shown as IM++ in Fig. 5), where we include both other sensors' real-time data as well a sensor's own real-time data. IM++ outperforms IM initially, but beyond 2 hours its performance is similar to that of IM. This implies that even in absence of a sensor's own data, IM can achieve same results as when this data is available, again indicating its advantage.

For *local influence model* (Fig. 3(a)), we consider real-time values from top τ influential sensors for each sensor ($\tau = 4, 8, 12, 16, 20$). ART performs well initially due to very short prediction horizon, but its errors increase rapidly

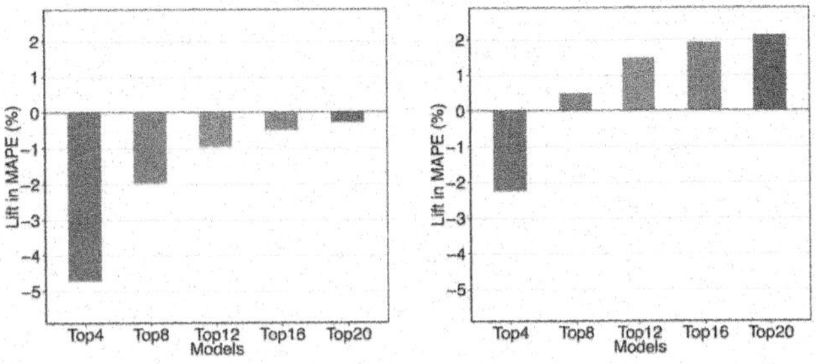

(a) (b)

Figure 6: Lift in MAPE for LIMs w.r.t (a) IM and (b) ART. Positive lift is observed w.r.t. ART beyond Top 8. (Positive lift indicates reduction in MAPE.)

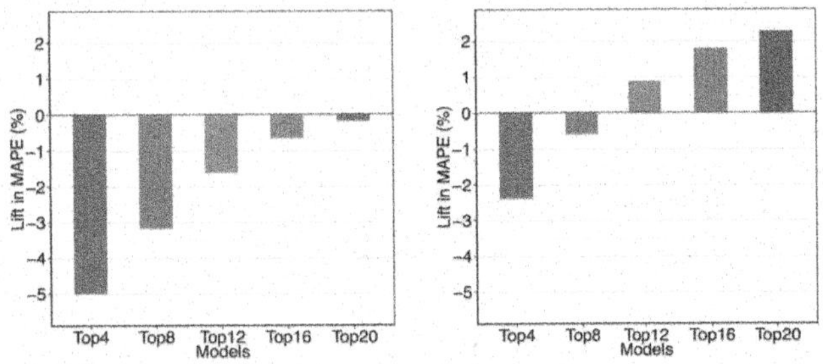

(a) (b)

Figure 7: Lift in MAPE for GIMs w.r.t (a) IM and (b) ART. Positive lift is observed w.r.t. ART beyond Top 12. In (b) Only $\approx 0.5\%$ increase in prediction error over ART is witnessed while using just top 8 ($\approx 7\%$) of smart meters.

with increasing horizon. *The LIMs show performance comparable to IM, while using real-time values from fewer sensors.* Using increasingly fewer predictors increases the prediction error for LIMs, but only slightly. LIM's performance deteriorates compared to IM in terms of percentage change (Fig. 3(b)) with increasing horizon. This can be the effect of very few sensors remaining influential over longer horizons. When averaged over all horizons, we observe 4.71% increase in error compared to IM for Top 4 model which comes down to 1.97% increase for Top 8 and less than 1% increase for Top 12, 16, and 20 models (Fig. 6(a)). We observe that beyond 1-2 hour horizon, all LIMs outperform ART (Fig. 3(c)) as for ART, the *effective horizon* now includes the prediction horizon and the unavailable real-time data. When averaged over all horizons, we observe that for Top 4, there is an increase in error by 2.24%, but for Top 8 (and Top 12, 16, 20), the error actually decreases (Fig. 6(b)) with respect to ART. Thus, we conclude that for this dataset, we need at least 8 influential sensors for each sensor to improve performance over the baseline.

The *global influence model* uses real-time values from only top τ influential sensors selected globally for *all* sensors ($\tau = 4, 8, 12, 16, 20$) GIM outperforms ART beyond 8 intervals (Fig. 4(a)). However as the number of predictors is reduced when moving from Top 20 to Top 4 model, we observe that increase in errors is more pronounced for GIM (Fig. 4(a)) than for LIM (Fig. 3(a)) as the number of unique influential sensors is significantly lower in the case of GIM as compared to LIM and IM. *While LIM used influential sensors selected separately for each sensor, GIM uses the same set of influential sensors for all sensors and still achieves comparable performance.* Top 20 and Top 16 GIMs outperform IM (Fig. 4(b)) for 1 interval ahead and later for 28 and 32 intervals. This could be due to the large number (20 and 16) of predictors selected in these models overlapping with those of IM. This is further supported by the average result over all horizons, where both Top 20 and Top 16 models show less than 1% increase in errors compared to IM (Fig. 7(a)). We also observe that all GIMs outperform ART beyond 12 intervals, i.e., 3 hour horizon (Fig. 4(c)). When at least 12 influential sensors are available, improvements are observed over the baseline across all horizons (Fig. 7(b)). We also found that as compression ratio (eqn. 2) was increased from 5 to 30, increase in MAPE was only by $\approx 1\%$. *GIM is able to provide a practical solution using real-time values from only a small fraction of sensors, thus achieving great compression ratio.*

Conclusion and Future Work

We address the *partial data problem* in sustainability domain applications that arises when data from all sensors is not available at central nodes in real time, either due to network latency or data volume, or when transmission is limited by the consumers for security and privacy reasons. Standard models for short term predictions are either unable to predict or perform poorly when trying to predict with partial data. We propose novel *influence* based models to make predictions using real-time data from only a few influential sensors, and still provide performance comparable to or better than the baseline. Thus, we provide a practical alternative to canonical methods - which assume real-time data availability for all sensors - for dealing with unavailable real-time readings in sensor streams. These models are generalizable to applications in several domains, and provide a simple and interpretable solution that is easy to understand and apply for domain experts.

Future extension of this work is towards a two stage process for influence discovery, guided by heuristics, and by a combination of local and global selection of influential sensors to further improve prediction performance. Another direction of research is for scenarios when time series data from different sensors is not sampled at equally spaced time intervals resulting in irregular time series.

Acknowledgments

This material is based upon work supported by the United States Department of Energy under Award Number DEOE0000192, and the Los Angeles Department of Water and Power (LA DWP). The views and opinions of authors expressed herein do not necessarily state or reflect those of the United States Government or any agency thereof, the LA DWP, nor any of their employees.

References

Aman, S.; Simmhan, Y.; and Prasanna, V. 2014. Holistic measures for evaluating prediction models in smart grids. *IEEE Transactions in Knowledge and Data Engineering* PP(99).

Arnold, A.; Liu, Y.; and Abe, N. 2007. Temporal causal modeling with graphical granger methods. In *International conference on Knowledge discovery and data mining (KDD'07)*. ACM.

Bahadori, M. T., and Liu, Y. 2012. Granger causality analysis in irregular time series. In *SIAM International Conference on Data Mining (SDM 2012)*. SIAM.

Balac, N.; Sipes, T.; Wolter, N.; Nunes, K.; Sinkovits, R. S.; and Karimabadi, H. 2013. Large scale predictive analytics for real-time energy management. In *IEEE International Conference on Big Data*.

Bouhafs, F.; Mackay, M.; and Merabti, M. 2012. Links to the future: communication requirements and challenges in the smart grid. *IEEE Power and Energy Magazine* 10(1).

Box, G. E. P., and Jenkins, G. M. 1970. *Time series analysis, forecasting and control*. Holden-Day.

Breiman, L.; Friedman, J.; Stone, C. J.; and Olshen, R. A. 1984. *Classification and regression trees*. CRC press.

Bullis, K. 2014. Smart wind and solar power. *MIT Technology Review*.

Chong, C., and Kumar, S. P. 2003. Sensor networks: Evolution, opportunities, and challenges. *Proceedings of the IEEE* 91.

Ciancio, A., and Ortega, A. 2005. A distributed wavelet compression algorithm for wireless multihop sensor networks using lifting. In *IEEE International Conference on Acoustics, Speech, and Signal Processing (ICASSP'05)*.

Cuevas-Tello, J. C.; Tiňo, P.; Raychaudhury, S.; Yao, X.; and Harva, M. 2010. Uncovering delayed patterns in noisy and irregularly sampled time series: an astronomy application. *Pattern Recognition* 43(3).

Deshpande, A.; Guestrin, C.; Madden, S. R.; Hellerstein, J. M.; and Hong, W. 2004. Model-driven data acquisition in sensor networks. In *International conference on Very large data bases (VLDB 2004)*.

Granger, C. W. J. 1969. Investigating causal relations by econometric models and cross-spectral methods. *Econometrica* 37(3):424–438.

Karimi, B.; Namboodiri, V.; and Jadliwala, M. 2013. On the scalable collection of metering data in smart grids through message concatenation. In *IEEE International Conference on Smart Grid Communications (SmartGridComm)*.

Kreindler, D. M., and Lumsden., C. J. 2006. The eects of the irregular sample and missing data in time series analysis. *Nonlinear dynamics, psychology, and life sciences* 10(2).

Kwac, J., and Rajagopal, R. 2013. Demand response targeting using big data analytics. In *IEEE International Conference on Big Data*.

Lozano, A. C.; Li, H.; Niculescu-Mizil, A.; Liu, Y.; Perlich, C.; Hosking, J.; and Abe, N. 2009. Spatial-temporal causal modeling for climate change attribution. In *ACM SIGKDD International Conference on Knowledge Discovery and Data Mining (KDD'09)*. ACM.

Marascu, A.; Pompey, P.; Bouillet, E.; Verscheure, O.; Wurst, M.; Grund, M.; and Cudre-Mauroux, P. 2013. Mistral: An architecture for low-latency analytics on massive time series. In *IEEE International Conference on Big Data*.

McDaniel, P., and McLaughlin, S. 2009. Security and privacy challenges in the smart grid. *IEEE Security and Privacy* 7(3).

Meek, C.; Chickering, D. M.; and Heckerman, D. 2002. Autoregressive tree models for time-series analysis. In *2nd International SIAM Conference on Data Mining (SDM)*. SIAM.

NOAA. 2013. Quality Controlled Local Climatological Data Improvements/Differences/Updates.

Pan, B.; Demiryurek, U.; and Shahabi, C. 2012. Utilizing real-world transportation data for accurate traffic prediction. In *IEEE International Conference on Data Mining (ICDM'12)*.

Razzaque, M. A.; Bleakley, C.; and Dobson, S. 2013. Compression in wireless sensor networks: A survey and comparative evaluation. *ACM Transactions on Sensor Networks* 10(1).

Sanders, P.; Schlag, S.; and Muller, I. 2013. Communication efficient algorithms for fundamental big data problems. In *IEEE International Conference on Big Data*.

Simmhan, Y.; Aman, S.; Kumbhare, A.; Liu, R.; Stevens, S.; Zhou, Q.; and Prasanna, V. 2013. Cloud-based software platform for data-driven smart grid management. *IEEE Computing in Science and Engineering*.

Tibshirani, R. 1996. Regression shrinkage and selection via the lasso. *Journal of the Royal Statistical Society, Series B* 58(1).

Proceedings of the Twenty-Ninth AAAI Conference on Artificial Intelligence

Sharing Rides with Friends: A Coalition Formation Algorithm for Ridesharing

Filippo Bistaffa and **Alessandro Farinelli**
Department of Computer Science
University of Verona
Verona, Italy
{filippo.bistaffa,alessandro.farinelli}@univr.it

Sarvapali D. Ramchurn
Electronics and Computer Science
University of Southampton
Southampton, UK
sdr@ecs.soton.ac.uk

Abstract

We consider the Social Ridesharing (SR) problem, where a set of commuters, connected through a social network, arrange one-time rides at short notice. In particular, we focus on the associated optimisation problem of forming cars to minimise the travel cost of the overall system modelling such problem as a graph constrained coalition formation (GCCF) problem, where the set of feasible coalitions is restricted by a graph (i.e., the social network). Moreover, we significantly extend the state of the art algorithm for GCCF, i.e., the CFSS algorithm, to solve our GCCF model of the SR problem. Our empirical evaluation uses a real dataset for both spatial (GeoLife) and social data (Twitter), to validate the applicability of our approach in a realistic application scenario. Empirical results show that our approach computes optimal solutions for systems of medium scale (up to 100 agents) providing significant cost reductions (up to −36.22%). Moreover, we can provide approximate solutions for very large systems (i.e., up to 2000 agents) and good quality guarantees (i.e., with an approximation ratio of 1.41 in the worst case) within minutes (i.e., 100 seconds).

1 Introduction

The concept of real-time ridesharing, where people arrange one-time rides at short notice with their private cars, is rapidly shifting the way people commute for their daily activities. Companies such as *Uber* or *Lyft* allow users to quickly share their positions and arrange rides with other people they know/trust within minutes, hence providing a credible alternative to standard transportation systems (such as taxis or public transport). A clear trend for such companies is to build a community of users, where commuters can rate drivers/passengers, and then use such information to automatically form groups of commuters that know/trust each other.

Following this trend, here we focus on providing an approach that, given the desired starting points and destinations of a community of commuters, can share cars to lower associated transportation costs (i.e., travel time and fuel), while considering the constraints imposed by the social network that connects such commuters. We call this problem the Social Ridesharing (SR) problem.

In particular, we provide a model for the SR problem casting this as a Graph Constraint Coalition Formation (GCCF) problem, where commuters (i.e., riders and drivers) form coalitions (i.e., join in a car) meeting the constraints imposed by the social network (i.e., users prefer to join a car with their friends). Specifically, following relevant literature on GCCF (Myerson 1977; Voice, Ramchurn, and Jennings 2012), we consider a coalition to be *feasible*, only if the commuters involved in such coalition form a connected subgraph of the social network.

Recently, (Kamar and Horvitz 2009) addressed the computational aspects related to ridesharing, proposing an interesting model to evaluate ridesharing plans, on which we base our model for SR. However, such work is mostly focused on incentive design aspects for ridesharing while here we focus on the optimisation problem posed by SR. Moreover, they do not consider the role of the social network in their work. Now, the optimisation problem related to coalition formation (i.e., Coalition Structure Generation) has been addressed by several researchers throughout the years (Sandholm et al. 1999; Service and Adams 2011; Rahwan, Michalak, and Jennings 2012; Shehory and Kraus 1998). Consequently the relevant literature offers a wealth of optimal solution techniques as well as approximate algorithms that can provide quality guarantees. However, as pointed out in (Voice, Ramchurn, and Jennings 2012), all such algorithms do not consider graph constraints that limit feasible coalitions, hence they can not be applied to the GCCF problem as their behaviour for such specific problem is not well defined.

Recently, several approaches have been explicitly designed to deal with the GCCF problem (Voice, Ramchurn, and Jennings 2012; Voice, Polukarov, and Jennings 2012; Bistaffa et al. 2014). Among these approaches, here we consider as a solution technique the CFSS algorithm proposed in (Bistaffa et al. 2014) which, unlike previous approaches, can provide approximate solutions with quality guarantees for large-scale systems (including thousands of agents). Hence, this approach is particularly suitable for SR, in which good solutions for a large number of agents are needed in near real-time. On the other hand, one key element for the efficiency of such approach is the possibility of finding an effective and efficient bounding function to prune significant part of the search space. Now, such a bounding function is easy to provide only for specific characteristic functions which can be decomposed into a sum of monotonic and anti-monotonic functions ($m + a$). Unfortunately, the SR problem does not exhibit such a property, hence we significantly extend the CFSS algorithm to provide solutions for large-scale systems (e.g., up to 2000 agents) in this scenario.

In more detail, this paper advances the state of the art in the following ways:

- We provide a formalisation of the ridesharing optimisation problem as GCCF.
- We significantly extend the state-of-the-art approach for solving GCCF to provide optimal solutions, as well as approximate solutions with quality guarantees for large-scale systems.
- We evaluate our approach with realistic datasets, i.e., GeoLife from Microsoft Research for the geospatial data and Twitter for social networks. Results show that our approach computes optimal solutions in minutes for systems including up to 100 agents, and provides approximate solutions for systems including up to 2000 agents, with good quality guarantees (i.e., with an approximation ratio of 1.41 in the worst case).

In what follows, we first provide necessary background on the GCCF problem and on the CFSS algorithm, then we describe our model of the SR and our solution technique. Finally we present the results of our empirical evaluation.

2 Background

The purpose of this section is twofold. First, in Section 2.1 we define the GCCF problem. Second, in Section 2.2 we provide some background on the state of the art algorithm for solving GCCF, namely the CFSS algorithm.

2.1 GCCF Problem Definition

A *coalitional game* or *characteristic function game*[1] consists of a finite set of players $\mathcal{A}$ and a characteristic function $v : 2^{\mathcal{A}} \to \mathbb{R}$, that maps each coalition $C \in 2^{\mathcal{A}}$ to its value, describing how much collective payoff a set of players can gain by forming a coalition. A coalition structure CS is a partition of the set of agents into disjoint coalitions. The set of all coalition structures is $\Pi(\mathcal{A})$. The value of a coalition structure CS is assessed as the sum of the values of its composing coalitions:

$$V(CS) = \sum_{C \in CS} v(C) \quad (1)$$

The *coalition formation problem* (Shehory and Kraus 1998; Sandholm et al. 1999) (or *coalition structure generation problem*) takes as input a coalitional game and aims at identifying CS^*, the most valuable coalition structure, i.e., $CS^* = \arg\max_{CS \in \Pi(\mathcal{A})} V(CS)$.

Now, given a graph $G = (\mathcal{A}, E)$, where $E \subseteq \mathcal{A} \times \mathcal{A}$ is a set of edges between agents, representing their relationships (i.e., friendship), (Myerson 1977) considers a coalition C to be feasible if all of their members are connected in the subgraph of G induced by C. That is, if for each pair of players from $a, b \in C$ there is a path in G that connects them without going out of C. Given a graph G the set of feasible coalitions is

$$\mathcal{FC}(G) = \left\{ C \subseteq \mathcal{A} \;\middle|\; \begin{array}{l}\text{The subgraph induced by } C \text{ on } G \\ \text{is connected}\end{array} \right\}.$$

Consequently, a graph constrained coalition formation (GCCF) game is a coalitional game together with a graph G, where a coalition C is considered feasible if $C \in \mathcal{FC}(G)$. In GCCF games a coalition structure CS is considered feasible if each of its coalitions is feasible, i.e.,

$$\mathcal{CS}(G) = \{CS \in \Pi(\mathcal{A}) \mid CS \subseteq \mathcal{FC}(G)\}.$$

Hence, the goal for a GCCF problem is to identify CS^*, which is the most valuable coalition structure, i.e., $CS^* = \arg\max_{CS \in \mathcal{CS}(G)} V(CS)$.

After the definition of the GCCF problem, we now present the state of the art algorithm to solve it, namely the CFSS algorithm.

2.2 CFSS

CFSS (Bistaffa et al. 2014) is based on the concept of *edge contraction* on the graph G, which represents the merging of the coalitions associated to its incident vertices. Such an operation can be used to generate the entire search space $\mathcal{CS}(G)$ and organise it as a rooted tree $\mathcal{T}_G$, which can be traversed with polynomial memory requirements in order to find the optimal solution. Each feasible coalition structure $CS \in \mathcal{CS}(G)$ is represented only once, one per each node of $\mathcal{T}_G$, by means of a *2-coloured graph* G^c, in which the nodes of G^c represent the coalitions of CS and the edges are marked either in green (i.e., such edge can still be contracted) or in red, meaning that a previous contraction of that edge has already been done, and its endpoints must not be in the same coalition in the following phases of the algorithm. Figure 1(a) shows an example of a 2-colour graph in which edge $(\{A\}, \{D\})$ is red: hence, in any subsequent step of the algorithm it is impossible to contract it. This marking ensures that each feasible coalition structure is represented in $\mathcal{T}_G$ without any redundancy. In particular, given a node $\mathcal{T}_G$ representing a feasible coalition structure CS, its children are assessed contracting each green node in the corresponding 2-colour graph G^c. We refer to the subtree of $\mathcal{T}_G$ rooted at CS as $\mathcal{ST}(CS)$.

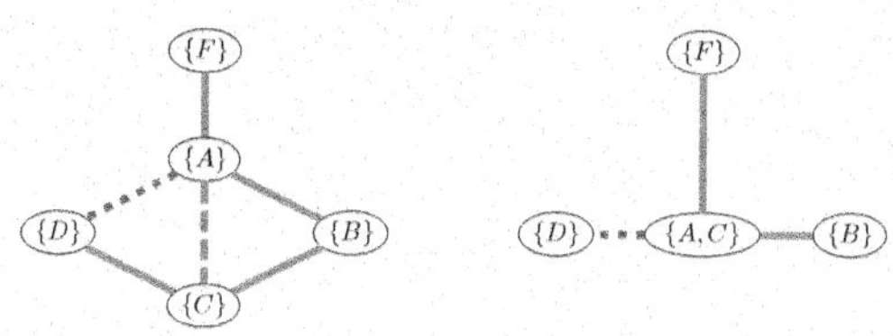

Figure 1: Example of a green edge contraction.

In the next section, we show how we represent a Social Ridesharing (SR) problem as a GCCF problem.

[1]Note that, to be consistent with relevant literature (Myerson 1977), here we use the name game. However, we do not consider stability of coalitions and we do not address issues such as payment schemes for the agents, which are typical of mechanism design.

3 Social Ridesharing Model

In this section we define our model for the SR problem. In particular, we consider a set of riders $\mathcal{R} = \{r_1, \ldots, r_R\}$, where $R > 0$ is the total number of riders, and a non-empty[2] set of drivers $\mathcal{D} \subseteq \mathcal{R}$, containing the riders owning a car. Every driver $r_i \in \mathcal{D}$ can host up to $s(r_i)$ riders in his car, including himself, where the function $s : \mathcal{R} \to \mathbb{N}^0$ provides the number of seats of each car. If $r_i \notin \mathcal{D}$, then $s(r_i) = 0$. Given a set of riders $C \subseteq \mathcal{R}$, C is said to be *valid* if the following constraint holds:

Constraint 1. $|C| > 1 \implies \exists r_i \in C : s(r_i) \geq |C|$, *i.e., at least one rider has a car with enough seats for all the riders.*

Notice that such a constraint allows a rider $r_i \notin \mathcal{D}$ to be in a singleton. In fact, if the total number of available seats is less than the total number of riders in the system, such a rider might need to resort to public transport paying a cost $k(\{r_i\})$ for the ticket. Formally, the function $k : \mathcal{R}^0 \to \mathbb{R}^-$ provides such a cost, where $\mathcal{R}^0 = \{\{r_i\} \mid r_i \in \mathcal{R} - \mathcal{D}\}$ is the set of all the singletons excluding the drivers, as we assume that such riders always prefer to use their car w.r.t. public transport.

Now, in several ridesharing online services (e.g., *Lyft* and *Uber*) a commuter declares whether he is available as a driver or as a rider, hence the two sets are disjoint and a valid set of riders C contains at most one driver. Formally, the following additional constraint must hold:

Constraint 2. $|C \cap \mathcal{D}| \leq 1$, *i.e., the number of drivers per car can be at most 1.*

Notice that Constraint 2 is optional, but it holds in several established real-world services, arising from aspects of practical nature. Nonetheless, since our approach supports a more general model, it can also be applied to scenarios where such a constraint does not hold.

We consider a *map* of the geographic environment in which the SR problem takes place, represented by a connected graph $\mathcal{M} = (\mathcal{P}, \mathcal{Q})$, where $\mathcal{P}$ is the set of geographic points of the map and $\mathcal{Q}$ is a set of edges (each associated to a positive weight) among these points. In what follows, we assume that a path going through n points is represented as a tuple $P \in \mathcal{P}^n$, denoting as P^i the i-th point in such a tuple.

Each rider $r_i \in \mathcal{R}$ has to move from a starting point p_i^a, i.e., its pick-up point, to a destination point p_i^b in the map $\mathcal{M}$ and each car drives through a path that contains all the starting and destination points of his passengers. Not all paths are valid, and a *valid* path must fulfil two constraints to correctly accommodate the needs of all the passengers. Formally, given a valid set of riders C and a path P of n points, P is said to be *valid* if the following constraints hold:

Constraint 3. $\exists r_i \in C : s(r_i) \geq |C| \wedge P^1 = p_i^a \wedge P^n = p_i^b$, *i.e., P goes from the driver's starting point to its destination.*

Constraint 4. $\forall r_i \in C\, \exists x, y : P^x = p_i^a \wedge P^y = p_i^b \wedge x < y$, *i.e., for each rider, its starting point precedes its destination.*

Henceforth, we refer to the set of all valid paths for a given set of riders C with $\mathcal{VP}(C)$.

[2]If $\mathcal{D} = \varnothing$ the problem is trivial and it is not taken into account.

Following (Kamar and Horvitz 2009), we define the total cost $v(C)$ of a valid set of riders C as:

$$v(C) = \begin{cases} t(P_C) + c(P_C) + f(P_C), & \text{if } C \cap \mathcal{D} \neq \varnothing \\ k(C), & \text{otherwise.} \end{cases} \tag{2}$$

where P_C is the optimal path for C, and $t : \mathcal{P}^n \to \mathbb{R}^-$, $c : \mathcal{P}^n \to \mathbb{R}^-$ and $f : \mathcal{P}^n \to \mathbb{R}^-$ are negative[3] cost functions respectively representing the time cost, the cognitive cost[4] and the fuel cost of driving through a given path. We denote the sum of these three cost functions as *cost* $(\cdot)$. Notice that if $C \cap \mathcal{D} = \varnothing$, Constraint 1 imposes that C is formed by a single rider without a car, hence its cost is provided by $k(\cdot)$. Furthermore, P_C is defined as follows:

$$P_C = \arg\max_{P_i \in \mathcal{VP}(C)} cost(P_i) \tag{3}$$

Finally, as mentioned before, a key aspect of ridesharing is the presence of a social network G that restrict the formation of groups. Hence, our SR model considers the previous definition of *feasible* coalition from Section 2.1 and we define a valid set of agent as a set that does not violate Constraint 1 and whose members induce a connected subgraph on G.

Such SR problem can be easily translated into a GCCF problem, as each valid set of riders is indeed a coalition and $v(\cdot)$ provides its coalitional value. Hence, CS^* represents the optimal coalition structure which maximises the social welfare (i.e., minimises the total cost) for the system. However, the computation of the optimal path in Equation 3 represents a hard problem, which could be not solvable in realistic scenarios. Hence, in the next section we show how a reasonable assumption on the cost functions allows to reduce this complexity making such computation tractable.

4 Route computation

The computational complexity of Equation 3 derives from the lack of assumptions on the cost functions $t(\cdot)$, $c(\cdot)$ and $f(\cdot)$. However, in many urban scenarios the cost of driving through a path is determined by the length of the path itself, and longer paths usually result in higher costs. Hence, we assume that $t(\cdot)$, $c(\cdot)$ and $f(\cdot)$ are *antimonotonic* functions, i.e., given two paths P_i and P_j, if the length of P_i is greater than the length of P_j, then $t(P_i) < t(P_j)$, $c(P_i) < c(P_j)$ and $f(P_i) < f(P_j)$. Against this background, the following proposition holds:

Proposition 1. *If $t(\cdot)$, $c(\cdot)$ and $f(\cdot)$ are antimonotonic functions, the optimal path P_C for a set of riders C is the shortest path $P_i \in \mathcal{VP}(C)$.*

Proof. See Appendix. □

Given a path $P \in \mathcal{P}^n$, the function $best : \mathcal{P}^n \to \mathcal{P}^m$ is defined as $\bigoplus_{k=1}^{n-1} sp\left(P^k, P^{k+1}\right)$, where the function $sp(\cdot)$ provides the shortest path between two points, $\oplus$ represents the

[3]Since we consider a maximisation problem, we represent costs as negative values.

[4]Following (Kamar and Horvitz 2009), this cost represents the fatigue incurred by the driver during the trip.

concatenation of tuples and m is the number of points resulting from all such concatenations. The function $best(\cdot)$ can be computed efficiently in $O((n-1)\cdot(|\mathcal{Q}|+|\mathcal{P}|\log|\mathcal{P}|))$, assuming that $sp(\cdot)$ is implemented using Dijkstra's algorithm. Moreover, if $\mathcal{M}$ is an euclidean graph $sp(\cdot)$ can be computed in $O((n-1)\cdot|\mathcal{Q}|)$ with an A* algorithm.

Proposition 2. *Given a tuple of points T, $best(T)$ is the shortest path going through such points in order.*

Proof. See Appendix. □

Finally, given a set of riders C, we define $\mathcal{VT}(C)$ as the set of tuples which contains only and all the start and destination points of its riders (without repetitions) and which satisfy Constraints 3 and 4. Against this background, we prove the following theorem:

Theorem 1. *If $t(\cdot)$, $c(\cdot)$ and $f(\cdot)$ are antimonotonic functions, the optimal path P_C for a car C is P_C^*, the shortest among all paths in $\{best(P_i) \mid P_i \in \mathcal{VT}(C)\}$.*

Proof. See Appendix. □

Theorem 1 provides an affordable algorithm to compute the optimal path for a set of riders assuming that the cost functions are antimonotonic. Notice that its search space is $\mathcal{VT}(C)$, whose size is significantly smaller than $\mathcal{VP}(C)$ of Equation 3, and although being still exponential w.r.t. $|C|$, $|\mathcal{VT}(C)|$ is manageable for reasonably sized groups of riders. In fact, it is only 2520 for $|C| = 5$ (i.e., the number of seats of an average car).

In the following section, we detail how the CFSS algorithm, can be adapted to tackle the above defined problem.

5 CFSS for Ridesharing

In order to solve the SR problem, the original version of CFSS must be modified to correctly assess the additional constraints introduced in Section 3. In particular, to ensure that Constraints 1 and 2 hold, we must avoid the formation of coalitions which are not valid sets of riders. This can be achieved by avoiding the contractions of the green edges which would result in the violation of such constraints. Notice that such edges must be marked in red, even if we are not visiting the corresponding subtrees: in fact, this is equivalent to traversing such search spaces and discarding any possible solution they may contain, because such solutions would violate one of the above mentioned constraints.

A key enhancement for the efficiency of CFSS is the use of a branch and bound search strategy to prune significant parts of the search space. In (Bistaffa et al. 2014), authors provide a general bounding technique for a particular class of characteristic functions, namely $m+a$ functions.

Unfortunately, the characteristic function defined in Equation 2 is not an $m+a$ function, since it depends on P_C, and in particular on the actual position of the start and destination points of the riders. As an example, consider Figure 2, which shows the start and destination points for 3 riders, i.e., $\mathcal{R} = \{r_1, r_2, r_3\}$, in which only r_1 owns a car, i.e., $\mathcal{D} = \{r_1\}$. For simplicity, we assume that $v(C)$ is equal to the length of P_C, and $k(\{r_2\}) = k(\{r_3\}) = -1$.

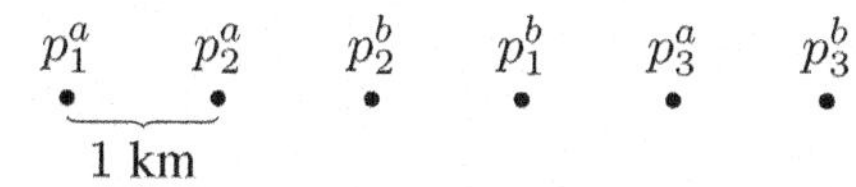

Figure 2: Example start and destination points for 3 riders.

In this example, $v(\{r_1\}) = -3$, $v(\{r_2\}) = -1$, $v(\{r_3\}) = -1$. However, we notice that p_2^a and p_2^b are actually part of the path travelled by r_1, hence it is reasonable for r_2 to join r_1 in the coalition $\{r_1, r_2\}$. In fact, $v(\{r_1, r_2\}) = v(\{r_1\}) = -3 > v(\{r_1\}) + v(\{r_2\}) = -3 - 1 = -4$. On the other hand, r_3 start and destination points are outside r_1's path,[5] hence ridesharing is not effective in this case: $v(\{r_1, r_3\}) = -7 < v(\{r_1\}) + v(\{r_3\}) = -3 - 1 = -4$. Notice that this particular characteristic function cannot be seen as the sum of a monotonic and an antimonotonic part, since it exhibits a monotonic behaviour for some coalition structures, i.e., $v(\{r_1, r_2\}) > v(\{r_1\}) + v(\{r_2\})$, while it is antimonotonic for some others, i.e., $v(\{r_1, r_3\}) < v(\{r_1\}) + v(\{r_3\})$.[6]

Hence, in the next section we provide alternative bounding techniques that can be used in our ridesharing scenario.

5.1 Bound Computation

Given a feasible coalition structure CS in our search tree, we now show how to compute an upperbound $M(CS)$ for the values assumed by the characteristic function in $\mathcal{ST}(CS)$, i.e., $M(CS) \geq V(CS_i)\ \forall CS_i \in \mathcal{ST}(CS)$. This value can be used to avoid visiting $\mathcal{ST}(CS)$ if $M(CS)$ is not greater than the current best solution.

First, we provide a method to compute $M(CS)$ in scenarios where Constraint 2 holds. In these environments it is not possible to merge coalitions both containing a driver, since only single riders not owning a car are allowed to join existing groups. Notice that the addition of a rider to car can only result in a greater cost, if we consider antimonotonic cost functions. Therefore, the sum of the costs of all the cars (i.e., all the coalitions containing a driver) can only increase after such an addition. More formally:

Proposition 3. *If $cost(\cdot)$ is an antimonotonic function and Constraint 2 holds, then $M(CS) = \sum_{C \in \mathcal{R}^d(CS)} v(C)$, where $\mathcal{R}^d(CS) = \{C \in CS \mid C \cap \mathcal{D} \neq \varnothing\}$.*

We now detail how to compute an upperbound without assuming Constraint 2. We define $\mathcal{S}_1$ as the set of the start and destination points of all the riders, i.e., $\{p_i \in \mathcal{P} \mid \exists r_j \in \mathcal{R} : p_i = p_j^a \vee p_i = p_j^b\}$, and $\mathcal{S}_2$ as the set of all the couples of different points in $\mathcal{S}_1$, i.e., $\{(p_i, p_j) \in \mathcal{S}_1 \times \mathcal{S}_1 \mid p_i \neq p_j\}$. Then, we define $\mathcal{S}_{1,a}(r_i)$ as the set of all the shortest paths from r_1's starting point to the start and destination points of any other rider, i.e., $\{P_i \in \mathcal{P}^n \mid P_i = sp(p_i^a, p_j)\ \forall p_j \in \mathcal{S}_1 : p_j \neq p_i^a\}$. Similarly, we define $\mathcal{S}_{1,b}$ considering r_1's destination point.

[5]The optimal path for $C = \{r_1, r_3\}$ is $P_C = (p_1^a, p_3^a, p_3^b, p_1^b)$.

[6]This notion of antimonotonic function should not be confused with the one previously defined for $t(\cdot)$, $c(\cdot)$ and $f(\cdot)$, which take paths as arguments, while characteristic functions are defined on coalition structures.

Also, we define $\mathcal{S}_{2,a}(r_i)$ as the concatenation of all the couples of shortest paths from r_1's starting point to the start and destination points of any other rider, i.e., $\{P_i \in \mathcal{P}^n \mid P_i = sp(p_i^a, p_j) \oplus sp(p_i^a, p_k)\ \forall (p_j, p_k) \in S_2 : p_j \neq p_i^a \wedge p_k \neq p_i^a\}$. Again, we define $\mathcal{S}_{2,b}$ considering r_1's destination point. Finally, we define $m : \mathcal{R} \to \mathbb{R}^-$ as:

$$m(r_i) = \begin{cases} \max\limits_{P_i \in \mathcal{S}_{1,a}} cost(P_i) + \max\limits_{P_i \in \mathcal{S}_{1,b}} cost(P_i), & \text{if } r_i \in \mathcal{D} \\ \max\limits_{P_i \in \mathcal{S}_{2,a}} cost(P_i) + \max\limits_{P_i \in \mathcal{S}_{2,b}} cost(P_i), & \text{otherwise.} \end{cases}$$

We can now state the following proposition:

Proposition 4. *If $cost(\cdot)$ is an antimonotonic function, then* $M(CS) = \frac{1}{2} \cdot \sum_{r_i \in \mathcal{R}^d(CS)} m(r_i)$.

Sketch of proof. See Appendix. □

These results allow us to bound $V(\cdot)$ in all the coalition structures in $\mathcal{ST}(CS)$. In the next section we detail how our bounding techniques, underlying our optimal branch and bound search strategy, can also be adapted to compute approximate solutions with quality guarantees.

5.2 Approximate Solutions

The bounding techniques described in previous section allow to prune significant parts of the search space, thus providing optimal solutions for system of significant size (i.e., up to 100 agents, see Section 6 for further details). However, a realistic application might involve community of thousands of agents, and, following the concept of real-time ridesharing, the system should be able to provide solutions in minutes. Consequently, for realistic applications approximate solutions must be considered. Now, following the approach proposed in (Bistaffa et al. 2014), the bounding techniques detailed above can be used to implement an approximate version the SR problem. In particular, we stop the search process after an amount of time t_s and compute the bound $M(CS)$ for all the leaf configurations of the search tree, the maximum among all these values is an admissible bound for the approximate solution found within t_s.

The quality of this approximate approach, together with a performance analysis of our optimal solution algorithm, will be object of our experimental evaluation, presented in the following section.

6 Experimental Evaluation

Having described and analysed our branch and bound approach for the SR problem, we now present the empirical evaluation. In what follows, we first present our evaluation methodology, then we discuss the achieved results.

6.1 Evaluation Methodology

The main goals of the empirical analysis are: i) to estimate the social welfare improvement when our ridesharing method is employed, ii) to evaluate the performance of our optimal algorithm in terms of runtime and scalability, iii) to evaluate the approximate performance and guarantees that our approach can provide when scaling to very large number of agents, i.e., up to 2000 agents.

Our experimental evaluation considers realistic datasets, both for spatial and social data. In particular, our map $\mathcal{M} = (\mathcal{P}, \mathcal{Q})$ is a realistic representation of the city of Beijing, with $|\mathcal{P}| = 8330$ points and $|\mathcal{Q}| = 13290$ edges, equivalent to an average resolution of a point every ~10 meters. This map has been derived from the GeoLife[7] dataset provided by Microsoft, which comprises 17621 trajectories with a total distance of about 1.2 million km, recorded by different GPS loggers and GPS-phones with a variety of sampling rates. This pool of trajectories is also adopted to sample random paths used to provide the start and destination points of the riders in our experiments. Moreover, in each experiment the graph G is a subgraph of a large crawl of the Twitter social graph completed in 2010. We adopted the Twitter dataset since it is freely available, free from privacy restrictions (unlike Facebook) and has been presented in a well established paper (Kwak et al. 2010). In particular, G is obtained by means of a standard algorithm (Russell 2013) to extract a subgraph from a larger graph, i.e., a breath-first traversal starting from a random node of the whole graph, adding each node and the corresponding arcs to G, until the desired number of nodes is reached. In our experimental evaluation there is no mapping between the trajectory data and the social graph, since they belong to independent projects.

In our experiments we adopt a cost model that only considers fuel expenses, i.e., $v(C) = K_{fuel} \cdot \overline{P_C}$, where $\overline{P_C}$ represents the length of P_C in km, $K_{fuel} = -0.0\overline{6}$ €/km (considering a fuel cost of -1 € per litre and an average consumption of 1 litre of fuel every 15 km) and $k(\{r_i\}) = -3$ € $\forall r_i \in \mathcal{R}$, which represents the average public transportation cost, i.e., a bus or a train ticket. Moreover, we assume that each car has a capacity of 5 seats, i.e., $s(r_i) = 5\ \forall r_i \in \mathcal{D}$.

All our experiments are done considering Constraint 2 (drivers always drive their cars), as it models many real-world online services, e.g., *Lyft* and *Uber*. Hence, we employ both the bounding techniques detailed in Section 5.1 and we take the minimum one, since both are admissible. Each experiment is repeated on 20 random instances, and we report the average and the standard error of the mean of the results. Our approach is executed on a machine with a quad-core 3.40GHz processor and 16 GB of memory.

6.2 Social Welfare Improvement

Here we consider the improvement of the social welfare (i.e., the cost reduction for the overall system) when using our automatic car formation approach as compared to the scenario in which every rider adopts its own conveyance (i.e., no ridesharing). This gives an indication of what gain can be achieved by the overall community when using our system for ridesharing. More formally, we define the social welfare improvement as $100 \cdot \left| \frac{V(CS^*) - V(\mathcal{R}^0)}{V(\mathcal{R}^0)} \right|$. Such an improvement is influenced by the percentage of drivers in the system (Figure 4), which determines the number of available seats and the number of riders which can share a ride without having to resort to public transport. Moreover, with more drivers it is more probable that a rider can join a car whose path is

[7] http://research.microsoft.com/en-us/projects/geolife

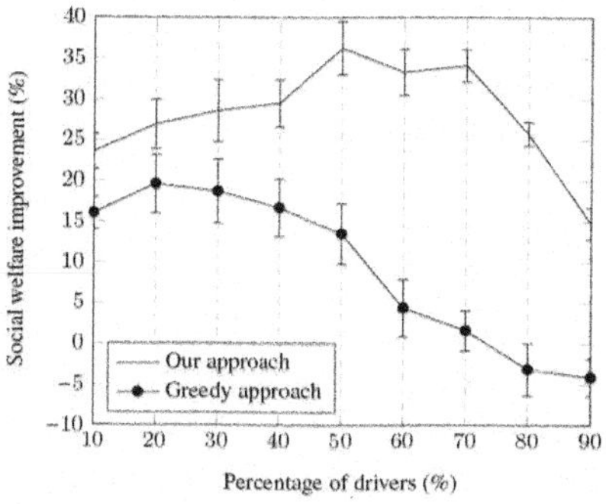

Figure 4: Social welfare improvement.

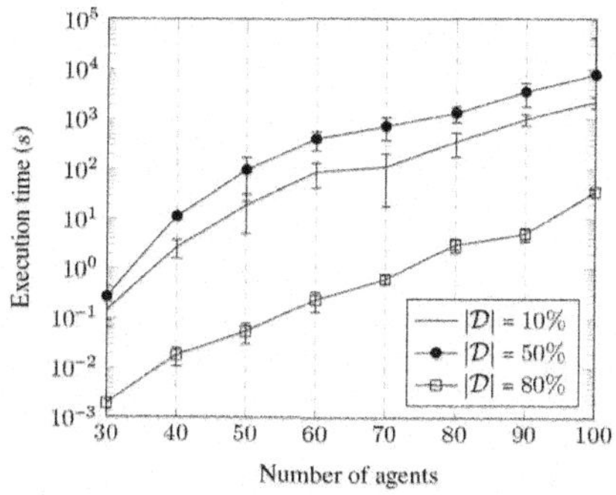

Figure 6: Runtime needed to compute the optimal solution.

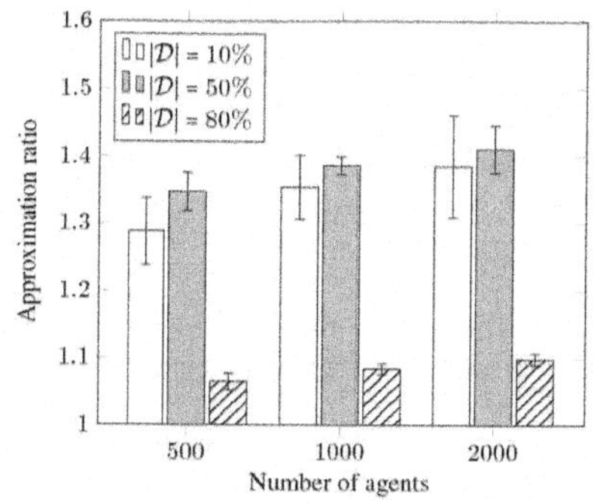

Figure 8: Approximation ratio of the solutions.

closer to him/her. On the other hand, if the majority of the riders own a car (i.e., > 80%), ridesharing is not very effective since too few riders without a car can benefit from sharing their commutes with a driver. In particular, when only the 10% of the total riders own a car, the average cost reduction (computed over 20 random instances with $|\mathcal{R}| = 50$ for each driver percentage) is −23.49%, reaching −36.22% when half of the riders owns a car.

To show the importance of an optimal approach, we benchmark our algorithm against a greedy one, in which every driver chooses its next stop as the closest among the destinations points of his current passengers and the starting points of the remaining riders. This choice is made considering the constraints imposed by the social network, avoiding the formation of unfeasible coalitions. As Figure 4 shows, our method allows superior cost reductions w.r.t. such a greedy approach, which can provide a maximum improvement of −19.55% for $|\mathcal{D}| = 20\%$. When the majority of the riders owns a car, such an algorithm provides solution whose costs are higher than the reference ones. In this scenario, where only few riders do not own a car, the greedy approach does not perform well since it might assign a rider to a sub-optimal coalition before considering the optimal one.

6.3 Optimal Performance

Figure 6 shows the runtime needed to compute the optimal solution when increasing the number of agents. Our approach is tested in 3 scenarios, i.e., with low (10%), medium (50%) and high (80%) percentage of drivers, showing that this parameter has a significant influence on the performance of our algorithm. In fact, the size of the search space is determined by the the number of available seats (reduced when such a percentage is low) and the number of riders without a car who can benefit from sharing their commutes (reduced when the majority of the agents owns a car), consistently with the behaviour of the social welfare improvement detailed in the previous section. Notice that, in any case, our approach can solve systems with 100 agents in a reasonable amount of time, i.e., about 2 hours at most for $|\mathcal{D}| = 50\%$. This runtime is suitable for services with day-ahead or week-ahead requests (e.g., *Lyft*). Such a performance is possible thanks to our bounding techniques (see Section 5.1), which allow to prune a significant part of the search space. In more detail, such techniques allow an average pruning of the 97.5% of the search space (resulting in an average runtime improvement of about 4 hours) on 20 random instances with $|\mathcal{R}| = 60$ and $|\mathcal{D}| = 50\%$.

6.4 Approximate Performance

Figure 8 shows the value of the approximation ratio (i.e., the ratio between the bound and the approximate solution) provided by our approach when used to solve large systems with $|\mathcal{R}| \in \{500, 1000, 2000\}$. In particular, we adopted the approximate technique explained in Section 5.2, stopping the traversal of the search tree after $t_s = 100$ seconds. Our experiments show that, for $|\mathcal{R}| = 500$ and $|\mathcal{D}| = 80\%$, the provided bound is only 6.65% higher than the solution found within the time limit, reaching a maximum of +29.92% when $|\mathcal{R}| = 2000$ and $|\mathcal{D}| = 50\%$. In the worst case, CFSS provides an approximation ratio of 1.41 and thus solutions that are at least 71% of the optimal.

7 Conclusions

We considered the Social Ridesharing problem, showing how it can be modelled as a GCCF problem and extending the state of the art algorithm for GCCF, i.e., CFSS, to solve it. Our empirical evaluation shows that our approach can lead to a cost reduction for the entire system that reaches the −36.22% and that our approximate technique can compute solutions for very large systems (i.e., up to 2000 agents) with good quality guarantees (i.e., with an approximation ratio of 1.41 in the worst case), hence being suitable for realistic applications.

Future work will look at extending our model to include more complex routing scenarios with traffic information, time constraints for riders as well as multi-hop ridesharing (Drews and Luxen 2013).

Acknowledgments.

This work was carried out as part of the ORCHID project funded by EPSRC (EP/I011587/1).

Appendix.

We report here the proofs of the propositions and the theorem stated in our paper.

Proposition 1. *If $t(\cdot)$, $c(\cdot)$ and $f(\cdot)$ are antimonotonic functions, the optimal path P_C for a set of riders C is the shortest path $P_i \in \mathcal{VP}(C)$.*

Proof. Since $t(\cdot)+c(\cdot)+f(\cdot)$ is an antimonotonic function, such a proposition follows as a direct consequence. □

Proposition 2. *Given a tuple of points T, $best(T)$ is the shortest path going through such points in order.*

Proof. By contradiction. Suppose there is a path P' going through all the points of T in order which is shorter than $best(T)$. Hence, there must exist two consecutive points in T, namely p_i and p_j, such that the subpath of P' going from p_i to p_j is shorter than the subpath of $best(T)$ going from p_i to p_j, which is a contradiction since it violates the definition of $best(T)$. □

Theorem 1. *If $t(\cdot)$, $c(\cdot)$ and $f(\cdot)$ are antimonotonic functions, the optimal path P_C for a car C is P_C^*, the shortest among all paths in $\{best(P_i) \mid P_i \in \mathcal{VT}(C)\}$.*

Proof. By contradiction. Suppose there is an optimal path $P' \neq P_C^*$. Then, P' must be shorter than P_C^* (Proposition 1). Since P_C^* is the shortest among all the paths going through all the tuples in $\mathcal{VT}(C)$ (Proposition 2), then it does not exists a tuple $T \in \mathcal{VT}(C)$ such that P' goes through all its points, which is a contradiction since T can be computed from P by removing any point which is neither a starting nor a destination point of a rider in C. □

Proposition 4. *If $cost(\cdot)$ is an antimonotonic function, then $M(CS) = \frac{1}{2} \cdot \sum_{r_i \in \mathcal{R}^d(CS)} m(r_i)$.*

Sketch of proof. This proof can be derived from the proof of the bound for the TSP problem with triangle inequality (Cormen et al. 2009; Brassard and Bratley 1996). □

References

Bistaffa, F.; Farinelli, A.; Cerquides, J.; Rodríguez-Aguilar, J.; and Ramchurn, S. D. 2014. Anytime coalition structure generation on synergy graphs. In *AAMAS*, pp. 13–20.

Brassard, G., and Bratley, P. 1996. *Fundamentals of Algorithmics*. Prentice-Hall, Inc.

Cormen, T. H.; Leiserson, C. E.; Rivest, R. L.; and Stein, C. 2009. *Introduction to Algorithms*. The MIT Press, 3rd edition.

Drews, F., and Luxen, D. 2013. Multi-hop ride sharing. In *SOCS*. AAAI Press.

Kamar, E., and Horvitz, E. 2009. Collaboration and shared plans in the open world: Studies of ridesharing. In *IJCAI*, pp. 187–194.

Kwak, H.; Lee, C.; Park, H.; and Moon, S. 2010. What is twitter, a social network or a news media? In *WWW*, pp. 591–600.

Myerson, R. B. 1977. Graphs and cooperation in games. *MOR* 2(3):pp. 225–229.

Rahwan, T.; Michalak, T.; and Jennings, N. R. 2012. A hybrid algorithm for coalition structure generation. In *AAAI*, pp. 1443–1449.

Russell, M. A. 2013. *Mining the Social Web*. O'Reilly Media, 2nd edition.

Sandholm, T.; Larson, K.; Andersson, M.; Shehory, O.; and Tohmé, F. 1999. Coalition structure generation with worst case guarantees. *AIJ* 111(1):pp. 209–238.

Service, T. C., and Adams, J. A. 2011. Constant factor approximation algorithms for coalition structure generation. *JAAMAS* 23(1):pp. 1–17.

Shehory, O., and Kraus, S. 1998. Methods for task allocation via agent coalition formation. *AIJ* 101(1-2):pp. 165–200.

Voice, T.; Polukarov, M.; and Jennings, N. 2012. Coalition structure generation over graphs. *JAIR* 45:pp. 165–196.

Voice, T.; Ramchurn, S.; and Jennings, N. 2012. On coalition formation with sparse synergies. In *AAMAS*, pp. 223–230.

Proceedings of the Twenty-Ninth AAAI Conference on Artificial Intelligence

Best-Response Planning of Thermostatically Controlled Loads under Power Constraints

Frits de Nijs and **Matthijs T. J. Spaan** and **Mathijs M. de Weerdt**
{f.denijs, m.t.j.spaan, m.m.deweerdt}@tudelft.nl
Delft University of Technology, The Netherlands

Abstract

Renewable power sources such as wind and solar are inflexible in their energy production, which requires demand to rapidly follow supply in order to maintain energy balance. Promising controllable demands are air-conditioners and heat pumps which use electric energy to maintain a temperature at a setpoint. Such Thermostatically Controlled Loads (TCLs) have been shown to be able to follow a power curve using reactive control. In this paper we investigate the use of planning under uncertainty to pro-actively control an aggregation of TCLs to overcome temporary grid imbalance. We present a formal definition of the planning problem under consideration, which we model using the Multi-Agent Markov Decision Process (MMDP) framework. Since we are dealing with hundreds of agents, solving the resulting MMDPs directly is intractable. Instead, we propose to decompose the problem by decoupling the interactions through arbitrage. Decomposition of the problem means relaxing the joint power consumption constraint, which means that joining the plans together can cause overconsumption. Arbitrage acts as a conflict resolution mechanism during policy execution, using the future expected value of policies to determine which TCLs should receive the available energy. We experimentally compare several methods to plan with arbitrage, and conclude that a best response-like mechanism is a scalable approach that returns near-optimal solutions.

Introduction

Reliable incorporation of decentralized renewable energy sources in power grids provides challenges for which Artificial Intelligence techniques can be employed. In order to take full advantage of wind and solar power, demand should follow their supply to maintain energy balance. The problem of how to influence the demand is called Demand Response, which we address using planning-under-uncertainty methodology. Planning to shift demands is most useful when storage capacity is available, offering flexibility by temporarily buffering energy. Unfortunately, large-scale electrical storage is unfeasible at the moment.

However, a large potential storage capacity can be found in the various heat buffers operated by consumers: houses, refrigerators and hot water reservoirs all need to be maintained at a certain temperature offset from the environment temperature, to which they decay over time. This requires constant action to counteract. The exact moment when these buffers are heated or cooled, however, can often be shifted. By storing more energy in the heat buffer now, we can later 'extract' this heat from the buffer in the form of reduced loads. In this sense, we may think of heat buffers controlled by thermostats as a kind of batteries (Hao et al. 2013). The storage potential in these batteries can be exploited through Demand Response.

These Thermostatically Controlled Loads (TCLs) can themselves be controlled automatically by the system operator. Existing work has mainly focused on using Control Theory to make an aggregation of TCLs closely follow an available power signal (Callaway 2009; Hao et al. 2013). There, control actions are applied every second, which requires the use of reactive systems. Their goal is to match both positive and negative fluctuations. This implies that the power available is always sufficient to cover demand, otherwise devices would begin to over- or under-perform.

Instead of using TCLs for balancing, we investigate the potential of TCLs for buffering temporary drops in power production, such as those caused by the fluctuations in renewable generation. These fluctuations typically occur on longer timescales (Koch, Zima, and Andersson 2009), potentially violating the consumers' comfort constraints if no preventive action is taken. To respond to fluctuations before they occur, we propose a planning approach with an objective to minimize the discomfort experienced by end-users.

In this paper we present a Power Constrained Planning (PCP) problem formulation, in which the deviation from the TCL setpoint is optimized under power availability constraints. For example for grids running in island mode, or when only (own) renewable energy may be used, the available power should be modeled as a constraint. We model this as a centralized planning problem with cooperative agents because in such scenarios the system operator and the TCL owners are both interested in a stable power supply, and hence their objectives align. Because in such cases power constraints may be too severe to guarantee comfort, we aim to *minimize* the total discomfort.

In order to solve the PCP problem, we model it as a Multi-agent Markov Decision Process (MMDP) (Boutilier 1996), in which each TCL is represented by an agent. However, as we are considering neighborhoods with hundreds of households, naively solving the resulting exponentially-sized MMDP will not suffice. In this paper, we show how we can exploit the fact that the only interaction among the agents is the allocation of available power. We decouple the problem and let each agent compute its own individual plan using a single-agent MDP. Combining the individual plans will result in a joint plan that might not be feasible due to power constraints. Hence, we introduce an arbitrage mechanism that ensures power constraints are respected by limiting the number of TCLs that can be switched on simultaneously. However, by in turn computing best-response policies and by learning the probability of being allowed to switch on, we compute scalable and effective solutions to the PCP problem.

We perform experiments on a small toy problem and on a larger test scenario. The toy problem allows us to clearly illustrate our ideas and to showcase the limited scalability of optimal centralized solutions. Using the larger scenario, we show that the best-response policies are able to scale to realistic problem sizes, while maintaining a solution quality that is near optimal.

Background

A thermostatic load is any device that is able to consume (electric) power for the heating or cooling of a body in relation to the outdoor temperature, such as refrigerators or central heating systems. The goal of the thermostat is to operate the device such that the temperature of the body remains as close as possible to a given setpoint at all times.

A Markov chain model of thermostats controlled by hysteresis controllers was presented by Mortensen and Haggerty (1988). In their model, the temperature of the body in the next time step $\theta_{i,t+1}$ is deduced from the current temperature $\theta_{i,t}$, the current outside temperature θ_t^{out}, a temperature input from the device θ_i^{pwr}, and a random temperature shift $\theta_{i,t}^{\text{rnd}}$ modeling exogenous actions such as opening a door. The hysteresis controller operates to keep the temperature within a deadband surrounding temperature setpoint $\theta_{i,t}^{\text{set}}$.

We use a similar model in this paper to make on/off decisions $m_{i,t}$ for every TCL i and for every discrete time period t. The length of such a period Δ, together with the thermal constants R_i (thermal resistance, °C / kW) and C_i (thermal capacitance, kWh / °C) determine how quickly the current temperature responds to the external factors through the fraction $a_i = \exp \frac{-\Delta}{R_i C_i}$, resulting in the model:

$$\theta_{i,t+1} = a_i \theta_{i,t} + (1 - a_i)\left(\theta_t^{\text{out}} + m_{i,t}\theta_i^{\text{pwr}}\right) + \theta_{i,t}^{\text{rnd}}. \quad (1)$$

Power Constrained Planning

We adapt the unconstrained model from the previous section into a Power Constrained Planning (PCP) problem. We use boldface characters to represent vectors of device parameters over all devices, i.e., $\boldsymbol{\theta}_t = [\theta_{1,t} \quad \theta_{2,t} \quad \cdots \quad \theta_{n,t}]$. Then, using the Hadamard product $\boldsymbol{b} = \boldsymbol{a} \circ \boldsymbol{\theta}_t \implies b_i = a_i \times \theta_{i,t} \quad \forall i$, we can define a state transition function to compute $\boldsymbol{\theta}_{t+1}$ as

$$f(\boldsymbol{\theta}_t, \boldsymbol{m}_t, \theta_t^{\text{out}}) = \boldsymbol{a} \circ \boldsymbol{\theta}_t + (1 - \boldsymbol{a}) \circ \left(\theta_t^{\text{out}} + \boldsymbol{m}_t \circ \boldsymbol{\theta}^{\text{pwr}}\right). \quad (2)$$

For simplicity, we keep random factor $\theta_{i,t}^{\text{rnd}}$ set to 0 for the planning phase, because we focus on distributions with expected value 0, and so that we can produce simpler optimal formulations.

With this function, we can define a planning problem using a given horizon h, the thermal properties of the n thermostatic loads with initial temperatures $\boldsymbol{\theta}_0$, the predicted outdoor temperature θ_t^{out}, and the predicted power constraint L_t. A solution is a device activation schedule that never switches on more devices than is allowed while minimizing cost function $c(\boldsymbol{\theta}_t)$. The entire planning problem becomes:

$$\begin{aligned} \underset{[\boldsymbol{m}_0 \ \boldsymbol{m}_1 \ \cdots \ \boldsymbol{m}_{h-1}]}{\text{minimize}} \quad & \sum_{t=0}^{h-1} c(\boldsymbol{\theta}_t) \\ \text{subject to} \quad & \boldsymbol{\theta}_{t+1} = f(\boldsymbol{\theta}_t, \boldsymbol{m}_t, \theta_t^{\text{out}}) \\ & \sum_{i=1}^{n} m_{i,t} \leq L_t \\ & m_{i,t} \in [0, 1] \qquad \forall i, t \end{aligned} \quad (3)$$

In this model power consumption is assumed to be constant within a time step, while in reality start-up transients occur when devices switch on. However, these occur only for a couple of seconds, after which consumption is constant, as is evident from measurements on heat-pump power consumption (van Lumig 2012, pages 25-28). We consider minute time scales, on which transients do not have a significant effect.

Due to the generality of the model, the controlled loads can have different objectives which can be expressed through the cost function. Besides typical functions such as the squared error $c(\boldsymbol{\theta}_t) = \sum_{i=1}^{n} \left(\theta_{i,t} - \theta_{i,t}^{\text{set}}\right)^2$ or maximum setpoint deviation $c(\boldsymbol{\theta}_t) = \max_i \left(\theta_{i,t} - \theta_{i,t}^{\text{set}}\right)$, we might imagine more application-specific functions. For example, a refrigerator may only incur high penalties when the temperature gets above a (thawing) threshold.

As a representative example of a cost function we use a variant of the squared error where minor (0.5 degrees) offsets incur no costs at all:

$$c(\boldsymbol{\theta}_t) = \sum_{i=1}^{n} \max\{0, \left|\theta_{i,t} - \theta_{i,t}^{\text{set}}\right| - 0.5\}^2. \quad (4)$$

We use this cost function because it has been shown in user studies that 90% generally acceptable comfort levels can be found in a small (2.5°C) band surrounding the ideal temperature (de Dear and Brager 1998). Additionally, it is implementable in mixed-integer programming constraints, and it imposes an intuitive notion of fairness; if even a single house is far from its setpoint, a large penalty is still incurred.

Optimal Solutions

To solve the PCP problem optimally, we can encode the formulation from Equation 3 as a mixed-integer program (MIP) with a minor reformulation. We introduce new variables $c_{i,t}$ and let $c(\boldsymbol{\theta}_t) = \sum_{i=1}^{n} c_{i,t}^2$. To ensure that these variables represent the correct cost values, we add the following constraints:

$$\begin{aligned} c_{i,t} &\geq 0 && \forall i,t \\ c_{i,t} &\geq \theta_{i,t} - \theta_{i,t}^{\text{set}} - 0.5 && \forall i,t \\ c_{i,t} &\geq -\theta_{i,t} + \theta_{i,t}^{\text{set}} - 0.5 && \forall i,t \end{aligned} \tag{5}$$

Alternatively, the problem can be modeled as a Multi-agent Markov decision process (MMDP) (Boutilier 1996). In our MMDP model we have a set of n agents that all have the same actions $\mathcal{A}$ available to them, and an agent-specific state $\mathcal{S}$. The transition function $T : \mathcal{S}^n \times \mathcal{A}^n \times \mathcal{S}^n \to [0,1]$ describes for each joint state and joint action pair $(\mathbf{s}, \mathbf{t})$ the probability of attaining joint state $\mathbf{s}'$. The agents are cooperating to maximize the collective system reward. Agents are rewarded for their actions in a certain joint state, through the reward function $R : \mathcal{S}^n \times \mathcal{A}^n \to \mathbb{R}$.

Concretely, we propose the following MMDP model for the optimization problem defined in Equation 3.

The continuous temperature is discretized into k non-overlapping states s_j each defining a temperature interval $[\theta_{s_j,\text{min}}, \theta_{s_j,\text{max}})$. In addition to this, there are two extrema states s_{min} and s_{max} ranging from $(-\infty, \theta_{s_1,\text{min}})$ and $[\theta_{s_k,\text{max}}, \infty)$ respectively, resulting in the following state space of an agent: $\mathcal{S} = \{s_{\text{min}}, s_1, s_2, \ldots, s_k, s_{\text{max}}\}$.

Each agent has two actions available to it: $\mathcal{A} = \{\text{off}, \text{on}\}$. The previous action is not part of the state because short-cycling of the devices is already prevented by the sufficient time between decisions.

The rewards assigned to the agents in each time step are the costs depending on how large the deviation from the set-point $\theta_{i,t}^{\text{set}}$ is:

$$\sum_{i=1}^{n} -\max\{0, |s_i - \theta_{i,t}^{\text{set}}| - 0.5\}^2. \tag{6}$$

The transition function from a state s to a state s' is derived by applying the Markov heat-transfer function $f(\theta, m) = \mathbf{a}\theta + (1 - \mathbf{a})(\theta_{\text{outside}} + m\theta_{\text{heating}})$ to the lower and upper values of the temperature range $[\theta_{s,\text{min}}, \theta_{s,\text{max}})$. This produces a new range $[\theta'_{\text{min}}, \theta'_{\text{max}})$ that may overlap the ranges of multiple discrete states $s_j, s_{j+1}, \ldots$. The degree of overlap determines the (uniform) probability of transitioning to each of these potential future states. The factored (per agent) transition function is thus probabilistic, in order to be consistent with the heat-transfer function:

$$\begin{aligned} \theta'_{\text{min}} &= f(\theta_{s,\text{min}}, m) \\ \theta'_{\text{max}} &= f(\theta_{s,\text{max}}, m) \\ T(s, m, s') &= \frac{\min(\theta_{s',\text{max}}, \theta'_{\text{max}}) - \max(\theta_{s',\text{min}}, \theta'_{\text{min}})}{\theta'_{\text{max}} - \theta'_{\text{min}}} \end{aligned} \tag{7}$$

The imposed power constraint L_t which limits the number of activated devices is then encoded in the joint transition function. The joint transition function specifies the cross product of all agents' action spaces $\mathcal{A}^n$. By removing those actions where the number of agents 'on' is more than L_t we obtain the required constraint.

The resulting MMDP is subsequently solved optimally using value iteration (Puterman 1994).

Decoupling, Arbitrage, and Best-Response

The only interaction among the TCLs is the allocation of the power availability. We therefore introduce a method that exploits this limited level of interaction as follows. First, we decouple the agents and let them find an individually optimal plan. Then we use an arbitrage mechanism upon execution to make sure that the agents together do not overuse the available power. Finally, we show how to let the agents coordinate their plans by simulating the arbitrage mechanism in advance, and performing a best-response to each other's policies. Each of these steps is discussed in more detail below.

First we completely *decouple* the agents, i.e., we factorize the MMDP by discarding the restriction L_t in the joint transition function. Then we solve a single-agent MDP for each agent separately.

Second, to overcome the problem that the agents' plans are no longer guaranteed to jointly stay within the power limit, we resolve the conflicts at policy execution using an *arbitrage mechanism*: in case too many devices want to switch on in a certain time step t, we iteratively search for the agent that expects to lose the least utility from switching off, and switch it off. This is repeated until the conflict is resolved. To determine which agent expects to lose the least utility by going from on to off we look at the difference between the planned utility scores in the value table.

Because this procedure is greedy and deterministic it risks getting caught in a local minimum. Thus, instead of always selecting the agent that expects to lose the least utility, we use the utility loss as a probability of being selected. A common probability distribution for fairly selecting between weighted alternatives is the logit equilibrium (McKelvey and Palfrey 1998).

Third, the plans for the single-agent MDPs take into account the effect of arbitrage and thereby indirectly of the plans of other agents by estimating how likely an agent is to be assigned such a constrained action. The following subsection describes how we arrive at good estimates of this probability.

Best-Response Planning for Arbitrage

The first step towards estimating the probability of being assigned energy is to take the pessimistic assumption that everyone always wants to make use of all available energy. Given this assumption, the probability of being able to activate the TCL is $p_{\text{on}}(t) = \frac{L_t}{n}$. This allows agents to detect potentially congested regions in time, but without knowing the actual level of congestion.

To estimate the actual demand in congested regions, we simulate policies computed in an earlier iteration and tally how much energy is requested. If energy is requested $\text{rq}_{\text{on},t}$

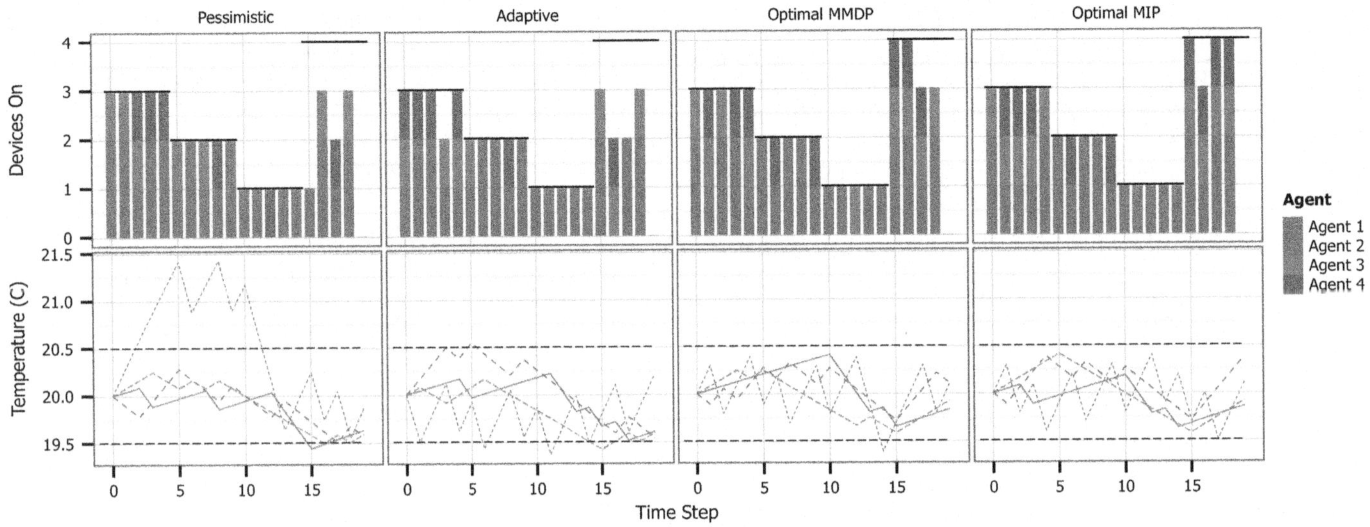

Figure 1: Activation scheme and agent temperatures in the example instance.

times in iteration i, then in the policy computation for iteration $i+1$ we assign probability $p_{\text{on}}(i,t) = \frac{L_t}{\text{rq}_{\text{on},i-1,t}}$, or $p_{\text{on}}(i,t) = 1$ if $\text{rq}_{\text{on},i-1,t} \leq L_t$.

Additionally, during periods where the expected demand is higher than the limit on the consumption, agents with a poor insulation level are much more likely to receive part of the available power. This is because those are the agents which incur a large potential error if they are skipped. Thus, agents that have a high degree of insulation are expected to make use of it by heating up before a constrained period. Such agents should learn that they will not receive power from arbitrage during constrained periods. To learn its relative probability of receiving power, each agent p_j counts $\text{rc}_{p_j,\text{on},i,t}$, the frequency with which his request for energy is granted in a time step t. Its probability then becomes $p_{\text{on}}(p_j,i,t) = \frac{\text{rc}_{p_j,\text{on},i-1,t}}{\text{rq}_{p_j,\text{on},i-1,t}}$.

Experimental Results on Small Instances

In order to demonstrate the value of the decomposition using arbitrage, we perform a number of experiments on small instances. These experiments are designed to show that:

1. Using individual probability to decompose the MMDP results in near-optimal performance on small instances.
2. Optimal solution methods do not scale beyond a handful of agents and a short horizon.

To investigate the behavior of the decomposition relative to the optimal solutions, we develop a toy instance with hand-crafted parameters resulting in a known optimal solution cost of 0. This instance has 4 agents, a horizon of 20 and $\theta^{\text{set}}_{i,t} = 20, \forall i, t$. In the first 5 time steps, 3 agents are allowed to switch on, in the next 5 time steps only 2 are allowed, followed by 5 time steps where only 1 is allowed. The final 5 time steps are unconstrained. Figure 1(top) illustrates the power constraints using black horizontal bars. Furthermore, the agents have insulation parameters chosen such that we know how frequently they need to switch on in order to keep the temperature within the deadband. In steady state agents 1 and 2 need to be on 75% of the time, while agents 3 and 4 need to be on 25% of the time.

We apply optimal MMDP and MIP solvers to this problem (with the MMDP creating plans for 9 distinct temperature states and $\theta_{\text{min}} = 18.5$, $\theta_{\text{max}} = 21.5$), as well as the arbitrage decompositions using the Pessimistic probability $p_{\text{on}}(t) = \frac{L_t}{n}$, and the decomposition using the Adaptive probability $p_{\text{on}}(p_j,i,t) = \frac{\text{rc}_{p_j,\text{on},i,t}}{\text{rq}_{p_j,\text{on},i,t}}$ (using 10 iterations, each with 10 simulations). The plans are subsequently evaluated using the planned decisions applied to the original continuous temperature function, Equation 1.

Because the optimal MMDP solver relies on a discretization of the temperature state, the level of discretization determines how likely it is to return optimal solution. Similarly, we expect the decompositions to not generate the optimal schedules. In particular, the pessimistic scheme is expected to strongly overheat several of the agents in the first 5 time steps, expecting heavy congestion in the subsequent middle 10 time steps. In contrast, the adaptive scheme should be able to detect that during the congested period agents 1 and 2 have much higher probability of switching on, promoting only agents 3 and 4 to pre-heat, limiting the error.

These expectations can be tested by looking at the cumulative error scores found in Figure 2 and the solutions generated by the four schemes in Figure 1. In Figure 1 we see that the optimal MIP is indeed able to keep all agents within the deadband simultaneously. It seems that the optimal MMDP suffers slightly from the low number of temperature states, which results in a small error w.r.t. optimal when agent 2 dips below 19.5 degrees in step 14.

Further, while the adaptive scheme stays close to the optimal, it is clear that the pessimistic approach is unable to find a good schedule. The reason for this can be seen in Figure 1: The second agent needs a lot of energy quickly, and

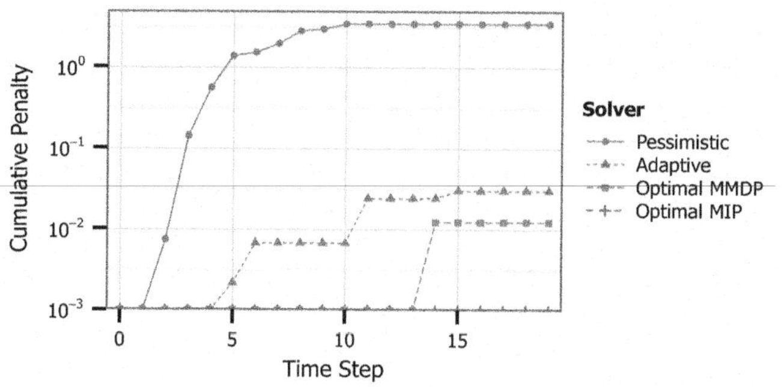

Figure 2: Cumulative penalty (log scale) in the example instance.

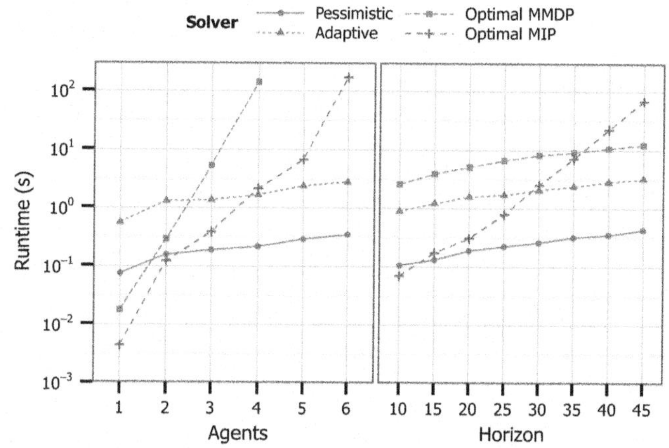

Figure 3: Scalability of the optimal and arbitrage methods for increasing agents and horizon, runtime on log scale.

expects it will be unlikely to receive it during the low power time steps. Therefore it strongly overheats before time 10. In contrast, the other methods are able to interleave agent 2 between the energy needs of the other agents. Hence, we conclude that we see all the expected behaviors.

For this small instance, all four considered formulations are able to return a solution within a reasonable amount of time (where solving the MMDP took the longest, at 12.5 minutes). However, we expect that the optimal formulations do not scale well, namely that their solving time grows exponentially with the instance size. On the other hand, the decoupled Pessimistic and Adaptive formulations are expected to grow in polynomial time, with the Adaptive formulation taking longer due to the iterative planning and simulation rounds.

We expect that both the MMDP and the MIP formulations grow exponentially in time with the number of agents, while we expect the MIP to additionally have exponential growth in the length of the horizon. The MMDP does not suffer from this because the Markovian property allows it to compute decisions iteratively, collapsing the computed decision sequences into a single expected value.

To evaluate the scalability we constructed a generator that builds instances which are similar to the example presented above, but with a variable number of agents and length of the horizon. We generated instances with the horizon fixed at 20 and the number of agents increasing from 1 to 6, and with the horizon from 5 to 45 and the number of agents fixed at 3 (10 instances per setting). In addition, we set the MMDP approach to use only 6 temperature states, and we imposed a run-time cut-off of 5 minutes. The average run-time performance is shown in Figure 3.

From the figure we can conclude that, indeed, the optimal methods are not scalable. Both methods appear to have run-time exponential in the number of agents, while the MIP also seems to have run-time exponential in the horizon.

Experimental Results on Real-World Instance

In the previous section, we show that the adaptive approach is able to stay close to the non-scalable optimal solutions in terms of solution quality. We expect that the adaptive approach is scalable to the size of typical real-world instances while maintaining near-optimal solution quality. To demonstrate this, in this section we apply it to a simulated neighborhood of 182 households equipped with heat-pumps. Their parameters are modeled to match measured performance (van Lumig 2012, page 60).

To determine if the solution quality is near optimal for this larger instance, we compare the pessimistic and the adaptive decomposition to a relaxation of the optimal MIP. This relaxation allows the devices to be switched on only partially. Because devices cannot be switched on partially, and because the decision time step granularity of 1 minute is the minimum to prevent short-cycling, it is not possible to implement the outcome of the relaxation. However, it is a lower bound on the optimal solution with binary activations.

In addition to this lower bound, we also compare our results with a hysteresis control solution that operates each house without look-ahead. For this control method we also perform arbitrage when required, by switching off units in order of their current temperature (hottest first).

For the instance, we model a two-day period during which a gradual decrease of the available power occurs starting from hour 6. At hour 20 the minimum capacity is reached and only 10 out of 182 heat pumps are allowed to be switched on. At the start of the second day, all devices can be switched on again. The households would all like to maintain an internal temperature of 21 degrees ($\theta^{\text{set}}_{i,t} = 21, \forall i, t$).

The decision frequency is set to once every minute. While it is unlikely that in a real-world scenario the power limit is known with such accuracy, this granularity allows each unit to switch just in time, and it also serves as a worst-case problem size to demonstrate scalability. Since the agents are now decoupled, we can solve the MMDP with much finer temperature discretization. For the adaptive decomposition we discretized temperature from 16 to 24 degrees over 80 states, resulting in bins of 0.1 degree width. Computed plans are again evaluated using the continuous temperature evolution (Equation 1) using a timescale of one second per time step (thus, a decision is held constant for 60 time steps in the simulation). Finally, in the simulation procedure the random component is enabled; for each house in every simulation

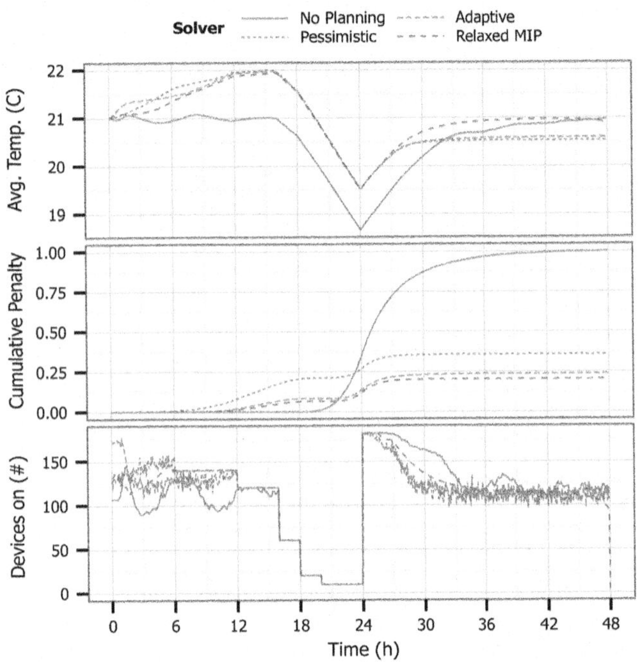

Figure 4: Average temperature, normalized cumulative penalty, and total load in the real-world instance.

step a value is drawn from the Gaussian distribution with mean 0 and standard deviation 0.01. Figure 4 presents the average indoor temperature, the normalized cumulative error and the number of devices switched on for this instance.

The cumulative penalty of the adaptive decomposition stays close to the MIP relaxation lower bound, which confirms our expectation that the adaptive decomposition stays close to optimal even in this larger instance. In addition we again see that the pessimistic decomposition heats up too much. This is evident from the cumulative penalty because the amount of error incurred above the deadband is higher than below it. Nevertheless, both planning solutions perform much better than the non-anticipatory control.

In addition, we can see in the graph of the average temperature (top) that the pessimistic decomposition starts heating earlier, which results in a larger number of devices switched on before the constraints kick in. In the graph showing devices switched on (bottom) we can also observe the gradual behavior of the relaxation versus the spiky discrete behavior of the decompositions.

Finally, it is important to note that computing the 182 policies for the adaptive decomposition took only 7.5 minutes, less time than it took the optimal MMDP solver to compute a solution for the four agent toy example. This demonstrates that the adaptive decomposition is indeed scalable to real-world instances.

Related Work

Mathieu et al. (2013) propose controlling thermostatic loads as arbitrage, essentially making them follow the inverse of a real-time price signal. They consider a control scenario where loads are only allowed to be controlled inside their deadbands, which is unobtrusive to the end-user. Their focus is on reducing the energy costs of consumers, under the assumption that sufficient power is available to maintain temperature inside the deadbands as required. They do not keep track of the states of individual devices in the planning and control phases, which causes a mismatch between their expected and actual performance, and limits applicability to relatively homogeneous collections of TCLs.

Stadler et al. (2009) present the dynamics of a system of setpoint controlled refrigeration units. Their results demonstrate that planning is necessary to get the most out of the storage capacity, which matches our observations.

A planning problem definition related to our own is presented by Bosman et al. (2012). The authors consider the planning of a fleet of MicroCHP units, so that their profit is maximized while the heat demand and minimum and maximum power production constraints are satisfied. The local search algorithm used first builds plans for each device individually using Dynamic Programming, which are then combined into a global plan and checked against the power constraints. If constraints are violated, the objective function of each house is updated and the devices replan until a feasible solution is found. Compared to our contribution the authors do not consider time-variable power constraints. Their heuristics are also much more computationally intensive, which limits their experiments to planning interval sizes and number of devices planned of 15 minute intervals over 24 hours and 100 units respectively, while requiring more than an hour of computation time.

Best-response planning has been used to coordinate routing and charging of electrical vehicles under uncertainty to minimize combined waiting and travel time (de Weerdt et al. 2013). Such behavior is quite natural for agents, and known to eventually converge to a stable situation in congested settings (Milchtaich 1996). This supports the idea that the presented approach may relatively easily transfer as well to situations with strategic agents.

Conclusions and Future Work

In this paper we investigate planning the activation of Thermostatically Controlled Loads (TCLs) for buffering for periods of low power availability. To this end we present a planning problem definition for the optimal control of Thermostatically Controlled Loads under power constraints. Because optimal solution methods do not scale on this problem definition, we propose a decoupling of the Multi-agent Markov Decision Process (MMDP) into an MDP per agent. At policy execution time, any conflicts that occur are resolved using an arbitrage mechanism, which greedily uses the policies to determine which agents benefit most from the available energy. By using a best-response planning process, agents are able to learn how likely they are to receive energy in a certain time step. From evaluating the adaptive decomposition on both large and small instances, we conclude that it is able to return near-optimal solutions while remaining scalable. This method therefore seems promising to control an aggregation of TCLs.

To extend this work we are considering two directions. On the one hand, we currently assume that the power production curve is known. In practice we do not know exactly how much power will be available for the TCLs in the future. Thus, we want to investigate planning TCLs under uncertainty. An advantage of the MDP framework is that it naturally allows for encoding uncertainty through the transition function, which makes the existing approach a promising starting point. On the other hand, we want to look into the addition of power quality constraints. Switching on many TCLs on a single feeder cable causes a large voltage drop for the last TCL in line. This can cause violations of the power quality norms, and risks damaging electric appliances. Hence, planning should be extended to take into account not just power but also voltage constraints in the grid.

Another interesting avenue of future work is the application of arbitrage and best-response to other planning problems. Because the MMDP framework considered is quite general, we expect the proposed techniques to apply as well to other problems where agents share a common infrastructure but otherwise do not have constraints in common.

Acknowledgments

Support of this research by network company Alliander is gratefully acknowledged.

References

Bosman, M.; Bakker, V.; Molderink, A.; Hurink, J.; and Smit, G. 2012. Planning the production of a fleet of domestic combined heat and power generators. *European Journal of Operational Research* 216(1):140–151.

Boutilier, C. 1996. Planning, Learning and Coordination in Multiagent Decision Processes. In *TARK*, 195–210.

Callaway, D. S. 2009. Tapping the energy storage potential in electric loads to deliver load following and regulation, with application to wind energy. *Energy Conversion and Management* 50(5):1389–1400.

de Dear, R. J., and Brager, G. S. 1998. Developing an Adaptive Model of Thermal Comfort and Preference. *ASHRAE Transactions* 104(1):145–167.

de Weerdt, M. M.; Gerding, E.; Stein, S.; Robu, V.; and Jennings, N. R. 2013. Intention-aware routing to minimise delays at electric vehicle charging stations. In Rossi, F., ed., *Proceedings of the International Joint Conference on Artificial Intelligence*, 83–89. AAAI Press.

Hao, H.; Sanandaji, B. M.; Poolla, K.; and Vincent, T. L. 2013. A Generalized Battery Model of a Collection of Thermostatically Controlled Loads for Providing Ancillary Service. In *Annual Allerton Conference on Communication, Control and Computing*.

Koch, S.; Zima, M.; and Andersson, G. 2009. Active Coordination of Thermal Household Appliances for Load Management Purposes. In *Symposium on Power Plants and Power Systems Control*.

Mathieu, J. L.; Kamgarpour, M.; Lygeros, J.; and Callaway, D. S. 2013. Energy Arbitrage with Thermostatically Controlled Loads. In *European Control Conference*, 2519–2526.

McKelvey, R., and Palfrey, T. 1998. Quantal response equilibria for extensive form games. *Experimental economics* 1(1):9–41.

Milchtaich, I. 1996. Congestion games with player-specific payoff functions. *Games and economic behavior* 13(1):111–124.

Mortensen, R., and Haggerty, K. 1988. A stochastic computer model for heating and cooling loads. *IEEE Transactions on Power Systems* 3(3):1213–1219.

Puterman, M. L. 1994. *Markov Decision Processes—Discrete Stochastic Dynamic Programming*. New York, NY: John Wiley & Sons, Inc.

Stadler, M.; Krause, W.; Sonnenschein, M.; and Vogel, U. 2009. Modelling and evaluation of control schemes for enhancing load shift of electricity demand for cooling devices. *Environmental Modelling & Software* 24(2):285–295.

van Lumig, M. 2012. Inventarisatie warmtepompmetingen WP1. Technical report, Laborelec.

FutureMatch: Combining Human Value Judgments and Machine Learning to Match in Dynamic Environments

John P. Dickerson
Carnegie Mellon University
dickerson@cs.cmu.edu

Tuomas Sandholm
Carnegie Mellon University
sandholm@cs.cmu.edu

Abstract

The preferred treatment for kidney failure is a transplant; however, demand for donor kidneys far outstrips supply. *Kidney exchange*, an innovation where willing but incompatible patient-donor pairs can exchange organs—via barter cycles and altruist-initiated chains—provides a life-saving alternative. Typically, fielded exchanges act *myopically*, considering only the current pool of pairs when planning the cycles and chains. Yet kidney exchange is inherently dynamic, with participants arriving and departing. Also, many planned exchange transplants do not go to surgery due to various failures. So, it is important to consider the future when matching.

Motivated by our experience running the computational side of a large nationwide kidney exchange, we present FUTUREMATCH, a framework for *learning to match in a general dynamic model*. FUTUREMATCH takes as input a high-level objective (e.g., "maximize graft survival of transplants over time") decided on by experts, then automatically (i) learns based on data how to make this objective concrete and (ii) learns the "means" to accomplish this goal—a task, in our experience, that humans handle poorly. It uses data from all live kidney transplants in the US since 1987 to learn the quality of each possible match; it then learns the *potentials* of elements of the current input graph offline (e.g., potentials of pairs based on features such as donor and patient blood types), translates these to weights, and performs a computationally feasible batch matching that incorporates dynamic, failure-aware considerations through the weights.

We validate FUTUREMATCH on real fielded exchange data. It results in higher values of the objective. Furthermore, even under economically inefficient objectives that enforce equity, it yields better solutions for the *efficient* objective (which does not incorporate equity) than traditional myopic matching that uses the efficiency objective.

Introduction

Chronic kidney disease is a life-threatening health issue that affects millions of people worldwide; its societal burden is likened to that of diabetes (Neuen et al. 2013). Damage from kidney disease can cause irreparable loss of organ function and, eventually, kidney failure. Such failure requires either continual dialysis or an organ transplant to sustain life.

The preferred treatment for kidney failure is transplantation. However, the demand for donor kidneys is far greater than supply. In the US alone, the waiting list for a kidney transplant had 101,956 patients as of November 18, 2014 (UNOS). Demand is increasing: for example, 36,395 people were added to the US national waiting list in 2013, while only 16,461 left it due to receiving a kidney.

Patients can receive a transplant organ from either a deceased or living donor. Roughly two thirds of transplanted kidneys are sourced from cadavers, while one third come from willing and healthy living donors. Patients who are fortunate enough to find a willing living donor must still contend with *compatibility* issues like blood type, tissue type, and other medical or logistical factors (as we discuss later in the paper). If a willing would-be donor is incompatible with a patient, the kidney cannot be transplanted.

Kidney exchange is a recent innovation that allows patients to swap willing but incompatible donors. Figure 1 shows a graphical representation of a small pool consisting of three patient-donor pairs, where an arrow from pair i to pair j means the patient at j is compatible with the donor at i. Also shown is an altruistic donor; such donors do not come with paired patients and are willing to donate a kidney without asking for one in return. The basic kidney exchange problem is then to recommend an optimal—according to some social welfare function—set of disjoint cycles and altruist-initiated chains in the graph.

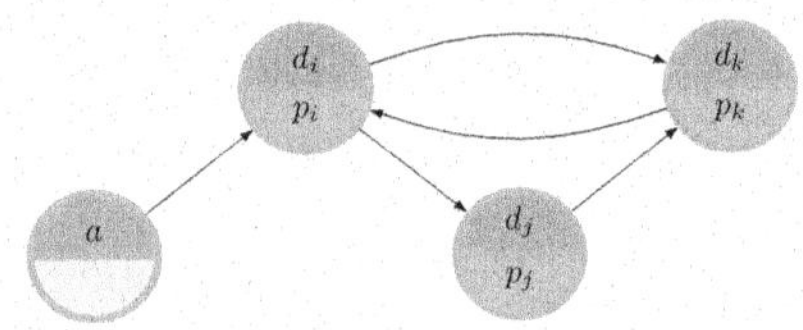

Figure 1: Tiny example kidney exchange pool with three patient-donor pairs and one altruistic donor.

Our Contributions

Fielded kidney exchange algorithms match patients and donors myopically, considering only the current state of the pool when deciding on a matching. However, kidney exchange is inherently dynamic, with patient-donor pairs and altruists arriving and departing the pool over time. Intuitively, the matching algorithm should take distributional information about the future into account when deciding what action to take now. Indeed, recent research has shown that such *dynamic* matching should result in increased overall social welfare (Awasthi and Sandholm 2009; Ünver 2010; Dickerson, Procaccia, and Sandholm 2012; Ashlagi, Jaillet, and Manshadi 2013; Anshelevich et al. 2013; Akbarpour, Li, and Gharan 2014; Anderson et al. 2015). However, most of that prior work has been either not computationally scalable or studied in simplified theoretical models, while here we study the problem in its full complexity and develop a computationally scalable methodology. Also, the prior work has focused mainly on maximizing the number of matches, while our approach is for any objective. Furthermore, many planned exchange transplants do not go to surgery due to various failures in the last few weeks before the operation (Ashlagi et al. 2011; Dickerson, Procaccia, and Sandholm 2013). That introduces a second form of dynamism. *The approach in this paper is the first to address both forms of dynamism.*

As a proof of concept for this paper, we learn a novel transplant quality predictor from a dataset consisting of all living-donor kidney transplant events in the US since Oct 1, 1987, and discover that some present-day features of living-donor transplants do not align with older results from deceased donation in the medical literature (Opelz 1985). This is noteworthy since today's exchange priority policies have largely been inherited from the United Network for Organ Sharing (UNOS) deceased-donor waiting list policies.

Motivated by our experience running the computational side of the UNOS nationwide kidney exchange that includes over 140 transplant centers (over 60% of the centers in the US), we present FUTUREMATCH, a general framework for learning how to match in dynamic environments. FUTUREMATCH separates the "means" from the "ends" of kidney exchange; it takes as input from human experts an overarching objective, and automatically learns a matching strategy to achieve this goal. We validate the framework on three example objective functions on real data drawn from the large, fielded exchange. We find that using FUTUREMATCH *even with economically inefficient objectives*—like maximizing the match size subject to equity constraints—results in significantly higher efficiency than myopic matching with the explicit objective of efficiency.

Kidney Exchange Model

The standard model for kidney exchange encodes a kidney exchange as a directed *compatibility graph* $G = (V, E)$ by constructing one vertex for each patient-donor pair in the pool (Roth, Sönmez, and Ünver 2004; 2005a; Roth, Sönmez, and Ünver 2005b). An edge e from v_i to v_j is included if the patient in v_j wants the donor kidney of v_i. A paired donor is willing to give her kidney if and only if the patient in her vertex v_i receives a kidney.

The weight w_e of an edge e represents the utility to v_j of obtaining v_i's donor kidney. A cycle c in the graph G represents a possible kidney swap, with each vertex in the cycle obtaining the kidney of the previous vertex. If c includes k pairs, we refer to it as a *k-cycle*. For example, the compatibility graph in Figure 1 includes two possible cycles: a 2-cycle between vertex v_i and v_k, and a 3-cycle consisting of vertices v_i, v_j, and v_k. In kidney exchange, cycles of length at most some small constant L are allowed—all transplants in a cycle must be performed simultaneously so that no donor backs out after his patient has received a kidney but before he has donated his kidney. In most fielded kidney exchanges, $L = 3$ (i.e., only 2- and 3-cycles are allowed).

Fielded kidney exchanges gain great utility through the use of chains (Montgomery et al. 2006; Rees et al. 2009). Chains start with an altruistic donor donating his kidney to a patient, whose paired donor donates her kidney to another patient, and so on. The compatibility graph in Figure 1 includes four possible chains: $\langle a, v_i \rangle$, $\langle a, v_i, v_j \rangle$, $\langle a, v_i, v_k \rangle$, and $\langle a, v_i, v_j, v_k \rangle$. Chains can be (and typically are) longer than cycles in practice because it is not necessary to carry out all the transplants in a chain simultaneously. There is a chance that a donor backs out of his/her commitment to donate—which has happened (albeit rarely) already in the United States. Cycles cannot be executed in parts because if someone backs out of a cycle, then some pair has lost a kidney (i.e., their "bargaining chip"). In contrast, if someone backs out of a chain, no pair has lost their bargaining chip (although it is unfortunate that the chain ends).

A *matching* M is a collection of disjoint cycles and chains in the graph G. The cycles and chains must be disjoint because no donor can give more than one of her kidneys. Given the set of all legal matchings $\mathcal{M}$, the (batch) *clearing problem* in kidney exchange is to find a matching M^* that maximizes some utility function $u : \mathcal{M} \to \mathbb{R}$. Formally:

$$M^* = \arg\max_{M \in \mathcal{M}} u(M)$$

The standard clearing problem for finite cycle cap $L > 2$ (even without chains) is NP-hard (Abraham, Blum, and Sandholm 2007). Abraham, Blum, and Sandholm (2007) took the first serious computational step toward solving the kidney exchange problem by providing a specialized branch-and-price-based (Barnhart et al. 1998) integer program solver; subsequent work by Dickerson, Procaccia, and Sandholm (2013; 2014) has increased solver speed and generality. We use an adapted version of that clearing algorithm as the batch clearing algorithm module in our framework (as we will discuss later).

In fielded kidney exchanges, one typically finds the maximum weighted cycle cover (i.e., $u(M) = \sum_{c \in M} \sum_{e \in c} w_e$). This *utilitarian* objective can favor certain classes of patient-donor pairs while marginalizing others, a phenomenon that we explore—and help alleviate—in this paper.

Proposed Method

We now present the FUTUREMATCH framework for learning to match in dynamic environments. We begin by motivating and describing the framework at a high level in the first subsection. In the following subsections we discuss the different parts of the framework in detail and how we instantiated them for kidney exchange.

The FUTUREMATCH Framework

We are interested in learning from demographically accurate data how to match *in the present* such that some overarching objective function is maximized over time. Scalability is important: heavy offline statistics can be computed and periodically updated, but the fielded clearing algorithm must run quickly (within minutes or at most hours).

Figure 2 graphically depicts the FUTUREMATCH framework. A domain expert (e.g., a committee of medical and legal professionals) begins by describing an overall objective function for the exchange. Even *measuring* this objective can be difficult: for example, if the goal is to maximize the number of days added to patients' lives via kidney transplantation, then calculating the relative quality of a proposed match requires knowing some notion of utility for each edge—representing a potential transplant—in the compatibility graph. We propose to learn this edge weight function $w : E \to \mathbb{R}^+$ from data, and give examples for a variety of objective functions later.

The learned weight function w is then fed into a parameterized (kidney exchange) simulator, calibrated by real data so that it mimics the underlying distribution. This generator in turn feeds training and test sets into a system for learning the *potentials* of element classes in the compatibility graph. Intuitively, given an element θ (e.g., vertex, edge, cycle, or chain type), a potential $P_\theta \in \mathbb{R}$ quantifies the expected utility to the exchange of that element in the future (Dickerson, Procaccia, and Sandholm 2012). Potentials are combined with w to quantify an edge-specific quality rating. Here, we learn potentials for the combinations of different blood types for pairs under each of the weight functions we define.

Finally, the fielded clearing algorithm incorporates the combined weight function w and set of potentials $\mathcal{P}_\Theta$ into its myopic weighted matching algorithm. This incorporation comes at very low or no cost to the runtime of the clearing algorithm; indeed, the final "potential-aware" input graph is simply a re-weighted version of the original compatibility graph, using the weights that encode the future.

In the rest of the section, we describe an in-depth implementation of FUTUREMATCH. Our goals are twofold: first, to show the general applicability and tractability of the framework, and second, to mimic a large fielded kidney exchange. Accomplishing this second goal, and leveraging our involvement with fielded kidney exchanges, sets the stage for adoption of sustainability-motivated technology that solves a problem clearly too difficult for humans—a success story for computational sustainability practitioners.

Encoding an Objective Function

We now discuss in depth the process of defining an objective for FUTUREMATCH. We do this in the context of kidney exchange, but note that the process is general.

The medical and legal communities in kidney exchange are concerned about a wide variety of match characteristics. In our experience, the most frequently discussed include the number of overall matches, the number of overall transplants, the quality of transplants, and whether or not to prefer specific subgroups in the exchange (children, sensitized patients, underrepresented ethnicities) and by how much. Other concerns could include notions of fair treatment among participating centers and minimizing legal exposure.

In this paper, we consider two different kidney exchange models—deterministic, where post-algorithmic match failures are not quantified in the optimization problem and failure-aware, where they are—and three matching objectives in each of the two models:

1. MAXCARD: Maximize the total number (i.e., cardinality) of patients who are algorithmically matched (in the deterministic model) or receive transplants in expectation (in the failure-aware model);
2. MAXCARD-FAIR: Maximize the total number of patients who are algorithmically matched (in the deterministic model) or receive transplants in expectation (in the failure-aware model), where "marginalized" patients are weighted in the objective by some constant factor β more than others; and
3. MAXLIFE: Maximize the total time algorithmically-matched (deterministic) or transplanted (failure-aware) donor organs will last in patients.

Each of these objectives amounts to setting weights on edges in the input graph (e.g., Figure 1). Next, we detail edge weighting algorithms for these example objectives.

In our experience, when committees debate priority points for today's exchanges, the discussions confound the goal and the means. For example, a goal could be to maximize matches and a means could be to prioritize sensitized patients because they are harder to match in the future. On the other hand, many argue that sensitized patients should be inherently preferred, and it seems that most do not make a clear distinction between means and ends. In contrast, FUTUREMATCH clearly *separates ends and means*. Our objective (i.e., the "end") lives in the space of weights on edges, which the committee can clearly debate. On the other hand, our framework automatically optimizes, via learning, the potentials (the "means") that are used as the means for enabling the algorithm to make good future-aware failure-aware decisions. The committee does not need to debate these potentials, whose quantitative impact on performance is hard for a human to predict or even understand.

Defining MAXCARD and MAXCARD-FAIR. The MAXCARD-FAIR objective can be viewed as a generalized form of MAXCARD (that is, MAXCARD is just MAXCARD-FAIR with an empty set of vertices who are preferred by the objective). A natural weighted fairness rule, adapted from (Dickerson, Procaccia, and Sandholm 2014), adjusts edge weights by some re-weighting function $\Delta : E \to \mathbb{R}^+$. A simple example re-weighting function is multiplicative:

$$\Delta^\beta(e) = \begin{cases} (1+\beta)w_e & \text{if } e \text{ ends in } V_P \\ w_e & \text{otherwise} \end{cases}$$

Here, $V_P \subseteq V$ is the set of preferred vertices (we will define one such subset in the experiments). Intuitively, for some $\beta > 0$, this function scales the weight of edges ending in marginalized vertices by $(1+\beta)$. For example, if $\beta = 1.5$, then the optimization algorithm will value edges that result in a marginalized patient receiving a transplant at 250% of their initial weight (possibly scaled by factors such as edge failure probability or chain position, as we discuss later).

For any $M \in \mathcal{M}$, let M' be the matching such that every edge $e \in E$ has augmented weight $\Delta^\beta(e)$. Then the MAXCARD-FAIR utility function u_Δ is defined in terms of the

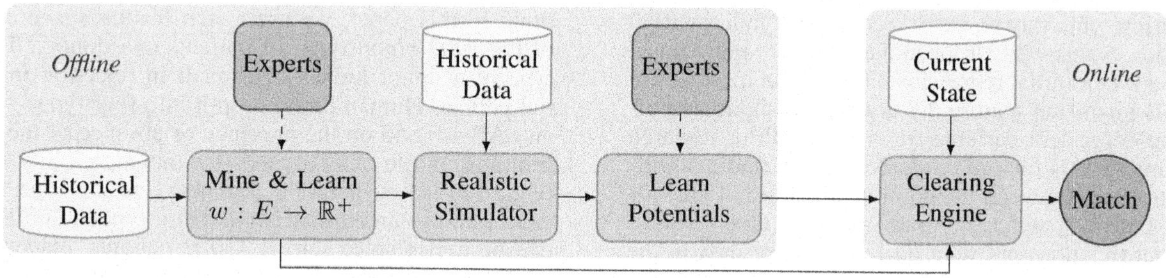

Figure 2: The FUTUREMATCH framework.

utilitarian MAXCARD utility function u applied to the augmented matching M', such that $u_\Delta(M) = u(M')$. In the experiments, we vary the parameter β to empirically quantify its effects on each of the three objective functions.

Optimizing for MAXLIFE via learning to predict graft survival from data. With the MAXLIFE objective we are interested in maximizing how long the transplanted kidneys, in aggregate, survive in the patients.[1] To do so, we must first determine an empirically sound estimate of the lifespan of a transplant as a function of donor and recipient attributes.

Delen, Walker, and Kadam (2005) compare a variety of techniques for predicting breast cancer survivability; unlike their study, we are interested in predicting the survival *length* of a kidney graft, as opposed to whether or not a patient survives treatment at all. Data mining models are also actively being developed to predict the risk of readmission for congestive heart failure patients (Meadem et al. 2013). Most related to our work is the Kidney Donor Profile Index (KDPI), which is currently under development by UNOS for use in the deceased donor allocation process (Kidney Transplantation Committee 2011). The KDPI score of a deceased donor kidney measures the estimated quality of the donor organ being allocated to the *average* recipient. In contrast, our predictor, which we will describe next, provides a unique quality score not just based on donor attributes but also based on attributes of the specific potential recipient.

We look at all 75,264 *living donor* transplant events in the US between October 1, 1987 and June 30, 2013. This data includes medical characteristics of the recipient and donor at the time of transplantation, as well as follow-up data regarding the health of the recipient and the recipient's new kidney; this follow-up data is updated at least annually.

Conditioned on a kidney graft being marked as failed in our dataset, the average graft lifetime is about 1912.7 days, or slightly over 5 years. However, due in large part to the marked increase in kidney failure since the late 1980s, nearly 75% of grafts in the dataset are not marked as failed. This occurs because either (i) the recipient is still alive with a functioning donated kidney or (ii) the recipient has died, but for a non-kidney-failure-related reason. Thus, we use *survival analysis* to estimate the lasting power of a graft.

Features of both the recipient and donor have a large effect on graft survival. For example, tissue type (HLA) testing measures the closeness of match between antigens in the cells of a donor and patient. Figure 3 gives a Kaplan-Meier estimator of the survival functions of (i) kidney transplants resulting from a donor and recipient being a perfect HLA match and (ii) those resulting from imperfect HLA matchings. Clearly, a kidney that is a perfect tissue type match is more desirable than an imperfectly matched one; indeed, the model estimates a median survival time of 5808 days for a perfect match compared to 4300 for an imperfect match. A log-rank test revealed that the difference between the two distributions was significant ($p \ll 0.0001$).

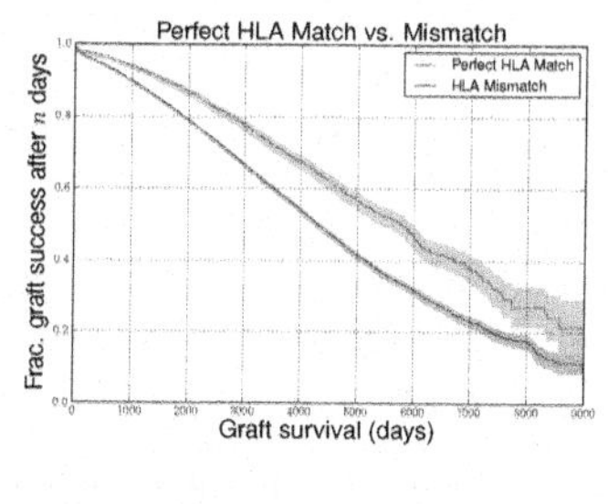

Figure 3: Kaplan-Meier estimator of survival functions, 95% confidence intervals.

In our experiments, we use a Cox proportional hazards regression analysis to explore the effect of multiple features on survivability. At a high level, this method regresses the survival time of the graft against explanatory features of the donor and recipient. More specifically, define the *hazard* H at time t days after a transplant as follows:

$$H(t) = H_0(t) \times \exp(b_1 X_1 + b_2 X_2 + \ldots + b_k X_k) \quad (1)$$

Here, each X_i is a predictor variable corresponding to a single feature of the donor or recipient, and $H_0(t)$ is a baseline hazard rate at time t for a recipient with $X_i = 0$ for $i \in \{1, \ldots, k\}$. Then $H(t)$ represents the instantaneous risk of graft failure at time t. We want to learn this function.

To begin, we include the following features: recipient age, difference in donor and recipient's age, donor HLA profile, recipient HLA profile, donor and recipient blood type compatibility. The HLA profile of a donor or recipient is separated into three integral features—HLA-A, HLA-B, and HLA-DR—that can take values in $\{0, 1, 2\}$, representing 0, 1, or 2 mismatches. By separating the general HLA mismatch feature into three separate mismatch features, we complicate (but increase the power of) the model (Opelz 1985); this separation is motivated by evidence that mismatches at the HLA-A, -B, and -DR level have varyingly negative impact on survival.

We ran a Cox proportional hazards regression on this unpruned feature space. This used 74,244 live donor transplan-

[1] Another objective would be to maximize aggregate increase in life duration. This would involve subtracting out the expected life duration without a transplant from the expected life duration with the transplant, and could incorporate the possibility of additional transplants after graft failure.

tations during which there were 18,714 graft failures (920 live donation events were dropped due to one or more missing features). Our initial regression showed that increases in the HLA-B mismatch feature did not have a significant effect on the dependent variable ($p = 0.22$). Prior research from the mid-1980s on *cadaveric* donation found a significant relationship between the combined feature of HLA-B and HLA-DR mismatches on graft outcome (Opelz 1985); we find that this does not hold on living donor data in the present. After selecting significant variables in this initial run—that is, all of the attributes previously discussed *except* HLA-B mismatch—we re-ran a Cox proportional hazard regression. Results are reported in Table 1.

feature	$\exp(b_i)$	$\text{SE}(b_i)$	z	p
recipient age	1.00753	0.0008	9.715	$< 2 \times 10^{-16}$
age diff.	1.00525	0.0007	7.766	8.10×10^{-15}
HLA-A	1.05273	0.0120	4.297	1.73×10^{-5}
HLA-DR	1.08680	0.0119	6.984	2.86×10^{-12}
ABO incomp.	1.37871	0.0748	4.295	1.74×10^{-5}

Table 1: Learned weights via Cox regression after feature pruning for statistical significance.

Table 1 gives the standard error, z-score, and corresponding p-value for each of our pruned features; each clearly has a statistically significant effect on graft survival. To interpret the results, as an example first consider the HLA-DR feature. We see that $\exp(b_{\text{HLA-DR}}) \approx 1.087$; recalling Equation 1, a unit increase in the HLA-DR mismatch feature will result in a factor of 1.087 increase over the baseline hazard rate. Varying either recipient age or the difference in donor and recipient age was also statistically significant, with a unit increase in recipient age having a larger effect on the hazard rate. As might be expected, blood type compatibility plays the largest role in hazard rate, where an incompatible (and thus heavily immunosuppressed) transplant has a factor 1.379 increase over the base hazard rate.

Using this data, we can estimate $S_e(t)$, the survival probability at time t for a potential transplant $e \in E$ between a recipient and donor with features x_i^e, as follows: $S_e(t) = \exp\left(-H_0(t) \times \sum_i x_i^e b_i\right)$. Building on this, we define a weight function $w : E \to \mathbb{R}^+$ as $w(e) \propto \exp\left(-\sum_i x_i^e b_i\right)$. Intuitively, the weight function w assigns higher relative weight to edges with lower risk, in turn biasing the optimizer toward transplants with longer expected graft survival.

Learning the Potentials

The weight function w defined above quantifies how useful an edge is *in the present.* To complement this, *potentials* quantify how useful an element of the graph (an edge, 2-cycle, etc.) is expected to be in the future. This idea was initially proposed by Dickerson, Procaccia, and Sandholm (2012); we build on their work but use a better learning algorithm (theirs did not converge, while ours did) for determining the potentials, and a significantly more realistic distribution of training and test instances.

First, we select a set Θ of features representing different element types in the pool. Then, for each element type θ, assign some value $P_\theta \in \mathbb{R}$ that represents the expected potential usefulness of that kind of element to the pool over time. In this paper, we use a rich feature space consisting of the *ABO blood types* of patients and donors. The blood type of a donor kidney can result in rejection in a potential patient. Human blood is split into four types—O, A, B, and AB—based on the presence or absence of the A and B proteins. While other reasons for incompatibility also exist (e.g., due to sensitization, sickness, etc.), a type O kidney can be transplanted into any patient; type A and B kidneys can be transplanted into A and B patients, respectively, or an AB candidate; and type AB kidneys are limited to only type AB patients. This imposes a natural partial ordering on blood types; for example, it seems that an O-donor is somehow more "valuable" than an A-donor because she has no blood type restriction. Our automatically learned potentials agree with this, as we will now discuss.

There are $4 \times 4 = 16$ combinations of patient and donor blood types, and 4 possible blood types of altruists. So, we have 20 different kinds of vertices. We want to learn a potential for each of those 20 vertex types. Formally, the types of vertex are $\Theta_{\text{ABO}} = \{\text{O-O}, \text{O-A}, \ldots, \text{AB-B}, \text{AB-AB}\} \cup \{\text{O}, \ldots, \text{AB}\}$, and we want to learn values P_θ for $\theta \in \Theta_{\text{ABO}}$.

We combine the learned potentials P_θ with the weight function w learned earlier using a function $f_w : E \to \mathbb{R}$. It balances the *myopic* value of an edge encoded by w with the *future value* of an edge encoded by potentials. The idea is that the revised weight, f_w, of an edge is its immediate value if matched minus the potentials of its vertices because if those vertices are matched now, they cannot contribute to future matches. Specifically, $f_w(e) = w(e) \cdot (1 - P_{\theta_d} - P_{\theta_p})$, where d and p are the vertices adjacent to edge e.

We use SMAC (Hutter, Hoos, and Leyton-Brown 2011), a state-of-the-art model-based algorithm configuration tool that searches through a parameter space to optimize a given objective. SMAC guides its navigation in the space of parameter vectors by constructing a model that predicts algorithm performance as a function of the parameters. It uses the model to select promising parameter vectors and tests them against the incumbent parameter vector.

In our setting, the parameter vector is the vector of potentials. At each parameter vector that SMAC navigates to, we run a large number of trials of our simulator of a kidney exchange to see how the batch matching algorithm would perform in a dynamic setting using that parameter vector. That performance number is then fed back to SMAC, and SMAC navigates to the next parameter vector to continue the search. We learned potentials in two models—*deterministic*, where post-algorithmic match failures are not quantified in the optimization problem and *failure-aware*, where they are—using a realistic dynamic simulator we built based on historical data from the UNOS kidney exchange (Kidney Paired Donation Work Group 2013).

Experiments

We validated FUTUREMATCH experimentally on data from the UNOS nationwide kidney exchange. We explore the effect each of the three objectives—MAXCARD, MAXCARD-FAIR, and MAXLIFE—has on a variety of metrics under FUTUREMATCH and under myopic deterministic matching, which is the fielded state of the art. The latter does not take edge failure or learned potentials into account during optimization; as described earlier, it finds a maximum weight matching (i.e., for each chain or cycle c, $u(c) = \sum_{e \in c} w_e$) during each period separately.

In the fairness-weighted experiments, we adapt our matching algorithm using the re-weighting function Δ^β described earlier. The preferred set of vertices V_P includes those with a pediatric or highly-sensitized patient. These preferences are commonly used in kidney exchanges, albeit not in sophisticated, quantitative ways. For kidney exchange it has explicitly been articulated that pediatric patients should be preferred not only because they have a lot of life left (barring their kidney disease) but also because having poor kidney function stunts growth. Similarly, some patients are *highly sensitized*, which means they are extremely unlikely to be medically compatible with a random organ. For these patients, finding a kidney is difficult (UNOS). The percentage of highly-sensitized patients in fielded kidney exchanges is high; over 60% of the patients in the UNOS kidney exchange are highly sensitized. In fielded exchanges, both of these "marginalized" patient types are prioritized. We quantitatively explore how this should be done and what the impact is.

Results. We compare FUTUREMATCH against a baseline of myopic deterministic matching under each of the objectives. Conservatively, statistical significance was determined using the Wilcoxon signed-rank test, which is a nonparametric alternative to the paired t-test. Table 2 shows the median expected gain in the overall number of transplants from using FUTUREMATCH under each of the objectives. Each column labeled $|V| = k$ corresponds to a simulation over k patient-donor pairs and altruists; we test over increasing values of k because kidney exchanges (both in the US and worldwide) are still expanding toward their steady-state sizes.

Table 2 (top) shows that the two objectives that do not regard fairness—MAXCARD and MAXLIFE—significantly beat myopic deterministic matching under the same objective. Interestingly, so too does MAXCARD-FAIR for low values of β. As β increases, the gain in *overall* number of transplants decreases (although it never drops below the deterministic matching algorithm with significance). This decrease in overall gain is incurred because marginalized patients, who (i) generally have lower in-degree, and (ii) have a higher probability of match failure, are being weighted more than easier-to-match pairs.

Table 2 (bottom) explores this tradeoff between fairness and efficiency explicitly. For the fairness-agnostic and lightly fairness-preferring objectives, a relative loss of a few marginalized transplants is realized—although this loss of marginalized transplants is always less (typically much less) than the overall gain in transplants. Increasing the optimizer's preference for marginalized patients results in statistically significant gains in the number of marginalized transplants at *no* statistically significant loss in the overall expected number of transplants. In fact, for a middle ground around $\beta = 2$, FUTUREMATCH often shows statistically significant gains in *both* overall transplant and marginalized transplant counts—a clear win over myopia.

Our experiments support the following conclusions:

- FUTUREMATCH under MAXCARD and MAXCARD-FAIR with low $\beta = 1$ results in a significant increase in the *overall* number of transplants compared to myopic, at the cost of a smaller decrease in the number of *marginalized* transplants.
- FUTUREMATCH under MAXCARD-FAIR with high β results in a significant increase in *marginalized* transplants, at *no cost* to the overall number of transplants under myopic matching.
- For a middle ground around $\beta = 2$, FUTUREMATCH can result in both more overall expected transplants and more marginalized transplants.

We note that we are *not* making policy recommendations; rather, we are giving a proof of concept that our framework can effectively balance conflicting wants in an exchange. Indeed, the exact fairness quantification β that most effectively balances efficiency and fairness is a function of the underlying graph dynamics, which vertices are considered marginalized, and the ethical and legal wants of an exchange. All of these dimensions can be effectively encoded, validated, compared, and fielded through FUTUREMATCH.

Conclusions

We presented FUTUREMATCH, a framework for learning to do complex matching in a general dynamic model. The framework addresses a computational sustainability problem directly uses data mining and optimization in many of its modules. Motivated by our experience running the computational side of a large nationwide kidney exchange, we showed how to instantiate FUTUREMATCH to mimic an exchange under three different matching objectives and under two models of kidney exchange. We validated FUTUREMATCH on real data drawn from 94 match runs of the US nationwide exchange, and found that dynamic matching results in statistically significant increases in each of these objectives. Perhaps most critically, we showed that the framework yields better efficiency *and* better fairness than deterministic myopic matching algorithms—which are the status quo class of algorithm in practice.

Acknowledgments

This material was funded by NSF grants IIS-1320620, CCF-1101668, and IIS-0964579, and by the Department of Defense (DoD) through the National Defense Science & Engineering Graduate Fellowship (NDSEG) Program. This work used the Extreme Science and Engineering Discovery Environment (XSEDE), which is supported by National Science Foundation grant number OCI-1053575; specifically, it used the Blacklight system at the Pittsburgh Supercomputing Center (PSC). We thank Intel Corporation for machine gifts, and thank Christos Faloutsos, Katrina LaCurts, Evangelos Papalexakis, and Keith Winstein for comments.

This work was supported in part by Health Resources and Services Administration contract 234-2005-370011C. The content is the responsibility of the authors alone and does not necessarily reflect the views or policies of the Department of Health and Human Services. The authors also thank Ruthanne Leishman, Elizabeth Sleeman, Darren Stewart, and the rest of the UNOS KPD Pilot Program staff.

References

Abraham, D.; Blum, A.; and Sandholm, T. 2007. Clearing algorithms for barter exchange markets: Enabling nationwide kidney

Total	$\|V\| = 300$ Gain	p	$\|V\| = 400$ Gain	p	$\|V\| = 500$ Gain	p	$\|V\| = 600$ Gain	p	$\|V\| = 700$ Gain	p	$\|V\| = 800$ Gain	p	$\|V\| = 900$ Gain	p
MAXCARD	+2	✓	+4	✓	+5	✓	+6	✓	+10	✓	+11	✓	+13	✓
MAXCARD-FAIR, $\beta = 1$	+1	✓	+4	✓	+6	✓	+8	✓	+9	✓	+11	✓	+12	✓
MAXCARD-FAIR, $\beta = 2$	+1		+2	✓	+3	✓	+3	✓	+5	✓	+6	✓	+10	✓
MAXCARD-FAIR, $\beta = 3$	+1		+0		+3	✓	+1		+1	✓	+3	✓	+2	
MAXCARD-FAIR, $\beta = 4$	-1		+1		+1		+1		+3	✓	+3		+2	
MAXCARD-FAIR, $\beta = 5$	+0		+0		+1		+1		+1		+2		+3	
MAXLIFE	+2	✓	+3	✓	+6	✓	+8	✓	+7	✓	+11	✓	+9	✓
Marginalized														
MAXCARD	-2	✗	-2	✗	-3	✗	-4	✗	-6	✗	-7	✗	-9	✗
MAXCARD-FAIR, $\beta = 1$	-1	✗	-1	✗	-1	✗	-2	✗	-3	✗	-3	✗	-5	✗
MAXCARD-FAIR, $\beta = 2$	+0		+0		+1	✓	+1	✓	+2	✓	+1		+1	
MAXCARD-FAIR, $\beta = 3$	+1	✓	+1	✓	+3	✓	+3	✓	+3	✓	+5	✓	+4	✓
MAXCARD-FAIR, $\beta = 4$	+1	✓	+2	✓	+3	✓	+4	✓	+4	✓	+5	✓	+5	✓
MAXCARD-FAIR, $\beta = 5$	+1	✓	+2	✓	+3	✓	+4	✓	+5	✓	+7	✓	+5	✓
MAXLIFE	-1	✗	-3	✗	-3	✗	-5	✗	-6	✗	-6	✗	-9	✗

Table 2: Median gains in expected total number of transplants (top table) and total number of marginalized transplants (bottom table) under FUTUREMATCH. A ✓ represents statistical significance (Wilcoxon signed-rank test, $p \ll 0.01$).

exchanges. In *Proceedings of the ACM Conference on Electronic Commerce (EC)*, 295–304.

Akbarpour, M.; Li, S.; and Gharan, S. O. 2014. Dynamic matching market design. In *Proceedings of the ACM Conference on Economics and Computation (EC)*, 355.

Anderson, R.; Ashlagi, I.; Gamarnik, D.; and Kanoria, Y. 2015. A dynamic model of barter exchange. In *Annual ACM-SIAM Symposium on Discrete Algorithms (SODA)*.

Anshelevich, E.; Chhabra, M.; Das, S.; and Gerrior, M. 2013. On the social welfare of mechanisms for repeated batch matching. In *AAAI Conference on Artificial Intelligence (AAAI)*, 60–66.

Ashlagi, I.; Gilchrist, D. S.; Roth, A. E.; and Rees, M. 2011. Nonsimultaneous chains and dominos in kidney-paired donation—revisited. *American Journal of Transplantation* 11(5):984–994.

Ashlagi, I.; Jaillet, P.; and Manshadi, V. H. 2013. Kidney exchange in dynamic sparse heterogenous pools. In *Proceedings of the ACM Conference on Electronic Commerce (EC)*, 25–26.

Awasthi, P., and Sandholm, T. 2009. Online stochastic optimization in the large: Application to kidney exchange. In *Proceedings of the 21st International Joint Conference on Artificial Intelligence (IJCAI)*, 405–411.

Barnhart, C.; Johnson, E. L.; Nemhauser, G. L.; Savelsbergh, M. W. P.; and Vance, P. H. 1998. Branch-and-price: Column generation for solving huge integer programs. *Operations Research* 46(3):316–329.

Delen, D.; Walker, G.; and Kadam, A. 2005. Predicting breast cancer survivability: A comparison of three data mining methods. *Artificial Intelligence in Medicine* 34(2):113–127.

Dickerson, J. P.; Procaccia, A. D.; and Sandholm, T. 2012. Dynamic matching via weighted myopia with application to kidney exchange. In *AAAI Conference on Artificial Intelligence (AAAI)*, 1340–1346.

Dickerson, J. P.; Procaccia, A. D.; and Sandholm, T. 2013. Failure-aware kidney exchange. In *Proceedings of the ACM Conference on Electronic Commerce (EC)*, 323–340.

Dickerson, J. P.; Procaccia, A. D.; and Sandholm, T. 2014. Price of fairness in kidney exchange. In *International Conference on Autonomous Agents and Multi-Agent Systems (AAMAS)*, 1013–1020.

Hutter, F.; Hoos, H.; and Leyton-Brown, K. 2011. Sequential model-based optimization for general algorithm configuration. In *Proc. of LION-5*, 507–523.

Kidney Paired Donation Work Group. 2013. OPTN KPD pilot program cumulative match report (CMR) for KPD match runs: Oct 27, 2010 – Apr 15, 2013.

Kidney Transplantation Committee. 2011. OPTN concepts for kidney allocation.

Meadem, N.; Verbiest, N.; Zolfaghar, K.; Agarwal, J.; Chin, S.-C.; and Roy, S. B. 2013. Exploring preprocessing techniques for prediction of risk of readmission for congestive heart failure patients. In *Data Mining and Healthcare (DMH), at International Conference on Knowledge Discovery and Data Mining (KDD)*.

Montgomery, R.; Gentry, S.; Marks, W. H.; Warren, D. S.; Hiller, J.; Houp, J.; Zachary, A. A.; Melancon, J. K.; Maley, W. R.; Rabb, H.; Simpkins, C.; and Segev, D. L. 2006. Domino paired kidney donation: a strategy to make best use of live non-directed donation. *The Lancet* 368(9533):419–421.

Neuen, B. L.; Taylor, G. E.; Demaio, A. R.; and Perkovic, V. 2013. Global kidney disease. *The Lancet* 382(9900):1243.

Opelz, G. 1985. Correlation of HLA matching with kidney graft survival in patients with or without cyclosporine treatment: for the collaborative transplant study. *Transplantation* 40(3):240–242.

Rees, M.; Kopke, J.; Pelletier, R.; Segev, D.; Rutter, M.; Fabrega, A.; Rogers, J.; Pankewycz, O.; Hiller, J.; Roth, A.; Sandholm, T.; Ünver, U.; and Montgomery, R. 2009. A nonsimultaneous, extended, altruistic-donor chain. *New England Journal of Medicine* 360(11):1096–1101.

Roth, A.; Sönmez, T.; and Ünver, U. 2004. Kidney exchange. *Quarterly Journal of Economics* 119(2):457–488.

Roth, A.; Sönmez, T.; and Ünver, U. 2005a. A kidney exchange clearinghouse in New England. *American Economic Review* 95(2):376–380.

Roth, A.; Sönmez, T.; and Ünver, U. 2005b. Pairwise kidney exchange. *Journal of Economic Theory* 125(2):151–188.

United Network for Organ Sharing (UNOS). http://www.unos.org/.

Ünver, U. 2010. Dynamic kidney exchange. *Review of Economic Studies* 77(1):372–414.

Temporal Smoothness Prior

Given the fact that for each device i, $|\mathbf{1}^\top \boldsymbol{c}_i(t) - \mathbf{1}^\top \boldsymbol{c}_i(t+1)|$ is zero except at times when it turns on or off and the fact that such switching does happen at a small number of time instants compared to the entire time period, we would like to minimize the objective function

$$\rho_3(\{\boldsymbol{c}(t)\}_{t=1}^T) = \sum_{i=1}^{L} \sum_{t=1}^{T-1} |\mathbf{1}^\top \boldsymbol{c}_i(t) - \mathbf{1}^\top \boldsymbol{c}_i(t+1)|. \quad (18)$$

Notice that the above cost function allows to change the active powerlet within a dictionary of each device without paying penalty, only counting if the device gets on or off.

Disaggregation Optimization

Considering all the constraints and priors studied so far, we propose to solve the optimization program

$$\begin{aligned} &\min \lambda\, \rho(\{\boldsymbol{c}(t)\}_{t=1}^T) + \sum_{t=1}^{T} \ell(\bar{\boldsymbol{y}}(t) - \boldsymbol{B}\boldsymbol{c}(t)) \\ &\text{s.t.}\ \ \mathbf{1}^\top \boldsymbol{c}_i(t) \leq 1,\ \ \boldsymbol{c}_i(t) \in \{0,1\}^{N_i},\ \forall t, i. \end{aligned} \quad (19)$$

where the composite prior on the coefficients is defined by

$$\begin{aligned} \rho(\{\boldsymbol{c}(t)\}_{t=1}^T) \triangleq & \sum_{t=1}^{T} \rho_1(\boldsymbol{c}(t) + \eta \sum_{t=1}^{T} (\rho_{2a}(\boldsymbol{c}(t)) + \rho_{2b}(\boldsymbol{c}(t))) \\ & + \eta' \rho_3(\{\boldsymbol{c}(t)\}_{t=1}^T), \end{aligned} \quad (20)$$

where $\eta, \eta' > 0$ are regularization parameters and $\ell(\cdot)$ denotes the loss function. Typically, we choose $\ell(\cdot) = \|\cdot\|_1$, which provides robustness to robustness to errors, transients and unmodeled dynamics. Once we solve the optimization program (19) and obtain $\boldsymbol{c}^*(t)$, we estimate the energy consumption of each device at time t by $\hat{\boldsymbol{y}}_i(t) = \boldsymbol{B}_i \boldsymbol{c}_i^*(t)$.

Experiments

In this section, we evaluate our proposed energy disaggregation framework on the real-world REDD dataset (Kolter and Johnson 2011), a large publicly available dataset for electricity disaggregation. The dataset consists of power consumption signals from six different houses, where for each house, the whole electricity consumption as well as electricity consumptions of about twenty different devices are recorded. The signals from each house are collected over a period of two weeks with a high frequency sampling rate of 15kHz. We exclude House 5 data from our experiments, since, for the majority of devices, it contains very few or no events in the entire recording period. We refer to our method as Powerlet-based Energy Disaggregation (PED) algorithm.

Experimental Settings

Since our framework can work with both high-frequency and low-frequency signals and given the fact that low-frequency sampling is more practical, less costly and more challenging, we use the low-frequency sampling rate of 1Hz. To learn the dictionary of powerlets for each device in a house, we use the first week of recorded electricity signals for training and use the rest of data for testing. We choose a window size of $w = 15$. It is important to note that a small window size results in lower performance, due to overemphasizing transients when building the dictionary, while a large window size results in having different dynamics or operation modes of a device within a given window, hence obtaining lower performance. With a sampling rate of 1Hz, typically, $w \in [10, 50]$ corresponds to temporal windows that capture transients and contain electricity from a single operation mode. We model each device as a mixture of dynamical systems of the form (8), where we set the model order to be $m = 3$ (the experimental results are robust to other choices of m around this value). We use our subset selection scheme in (7) to extract about 20 powerlets for each device. Thus, we obtain a compact dictionary $\boldsymbol{B}$ in our method, which typically consists of a few hundred powerlets. In order to perform disaggregation using the optimization program (19), we set $\lambda = 30$ and $\eta = \eta' = 1$ and use the prior that kitchen appliances typically work together (without this prior we obtain between 3% and 5% lower performance). To implement (19), we use the standard integer programming solver of MOSEK. With $w = 15$ and 400 powerlets and without the temporal smoothness prior, it takes about 12 seconds to perform disaggregation on a temporal window of 15 seconds. As a result, our method can perform disaggregation in real-time. However, it is important to mention that we can make use of the standard convex relaxation by using the constraint $\boldsymbol{c}_{ij} \in [0,1]^{N_i}$ instead of binary constraints on $\boldsymbol{c}_i$ elements and solve the resulting problem using faster algorithms such as ADMM or Proximal methods. However, since the integer programming formulation is our desired formulation that, given the compact size of our dictionaries, can be solved efficiently, we choose not to use convex relaxations in this paper. We leave investigating convex relaxations of our desegregation optimization for future work.

Once we solve the disaggregation optimization for the test aggregate electricity signal in a house, we compute the disaggregation accuracy, similar to (Kolter and Johnson 2011), by

$$\text{disaggregation acc} = 1 - \frac{\sum_{t \in \mathbb{W}} \sum_{i=1}^{M} \|\hat{\boldsymbol{y}}_i(t) - \boldsymbol{y}_i(t)\|_1}{2 \sum_{t \in \mathbb{W}} \|\bar{\boldsymbol{y}}(t)\|_1}, \quad (21)$$

where $\mathbb{W} \triangleq \{1, w+1, 2w+1, \ldots\}$ and the 2 factor in the

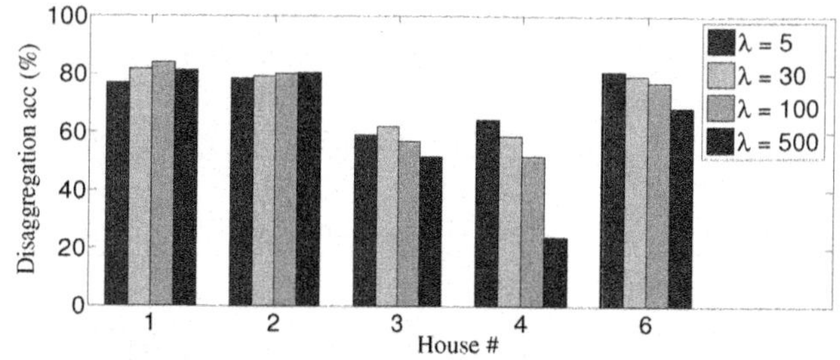

Figure 2: Effect of the regularization parameter λ on the disaggregation accuracy of our proposed algorithm for houses in the REDD dataset.

Table 1: Energy disaggregation accuracies (%) of different algorithm over the six different houses in the REDD dataset.

	House 1	House 2	House 3	House 4	House 6	Total
Simple Mean	41.4%	39.0%	46.7%	52.7%	33.7%	42.7%
FHMM	71.5%	59.6%	59.6%	**69.0%**	62.9%	64.5%
PED (proposed)	**81.6%**	**79.0%**	**61.8%**	58.5%	**79.1%**	**72.0%**

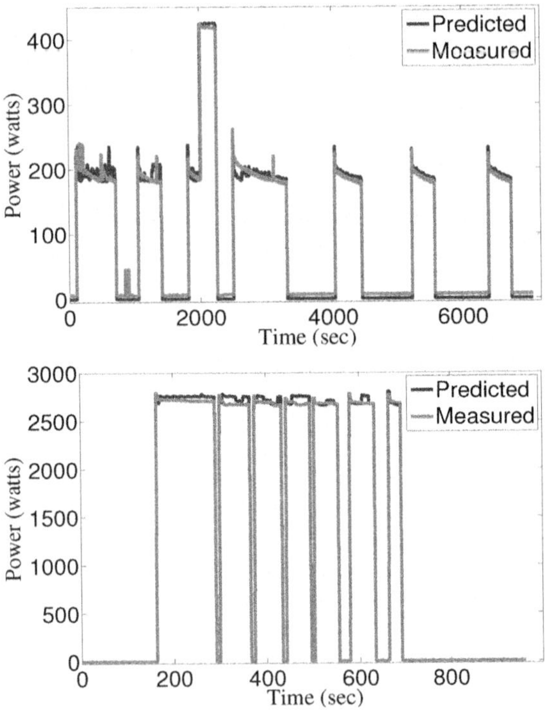

Figure 3: Actual and estimated electricity consumption of refrigerator (top) and washer-dryer (bottom) for House 1 using our proposed framework.

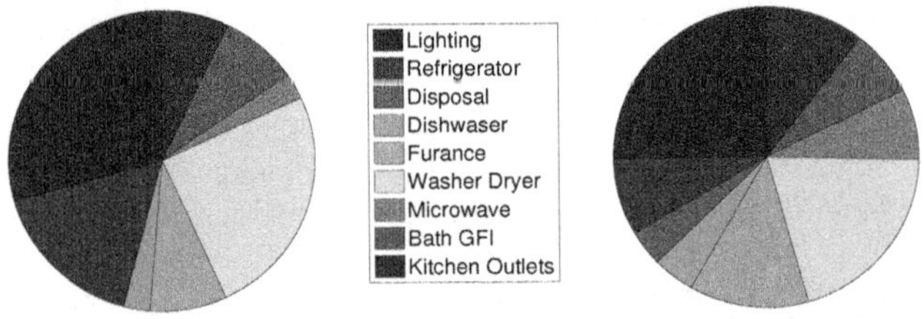

Figure 4: Pie charts showing actual energy consumption (left) and predicted energy consumption by our framework (right) for different devices in House 3 during one week.

denominator comes from the that that the absolute value results in "double counting" errors. We compare our method with the FHMM algorithm (in its supervised setting) (Kolter and Johnson 2011) and a Simple Mean prediction algorithm, which estimates the total consumption percentage of each device and predicts that the whole electricity signal breaks down according to this percentage at all times.

Experimental Results

Figure 2 shows the disaggregation results of our algorithm for different houses as a function of the regularization parameter λ in the proposed optimization program (19). Notice that for a large range of the regularization parameter, $\lambda \in [5, 100]$, our algorithm performs well. However, for large values of λ, the performance can decrease, as the accuracy results for House 4 shows. This comes from the fact that by putting higher emphasis on the device-sparsity, i.e., having a smaller number of operating devices in the disaggregation results, the optimization prefers to set the contribution of devices with small consumption to zero.

Table 1 shows the disaggregation results for all the six houses in the REDD dataset, with $\lambda = 30$ in our method. Notice that our algorithm performs significantly better than FHMM and the naive Simple Mean on the dataset, achieving about 7.5% higher accuracy overall. This comes from the fact that we have modeled and separated the two steps of learning a dictionary and performing disaggregation, focusing separately on a convex method for learning the desired dictionary of powerlets and on the desired disaggregation formulation. On the other hand, FHMM learns a dictionary using EM, which is prone to local optima, and uses approximate inference for disaggregation.

Figure 3 shows the actual and estimated energy consumption, obtained by our method, for two devices in the House 1. Notice that our method perfectly captures transients and different steady states in each device, thanks to our effective approach for building the powerlets dictionary, and achieves a close prediction to the actual energy consumption. Finally, Figure 4 shows the Pie charts corresponding to the actual and the predicted energy consumption by our algorithm for the House 3 over one week. Notice that the predicted consumption of our method is close to the actual consumption, achieving 81.8% accuracy. In fact, this accuracy is much higher than the one reported in Table 1 for House 3. This comes from the fact that while predicted consumption can be different from actual consumption at each time instant, e.g., due to prediction lag, if we aggregate the predictions over a longer time period, such errors decrease and we often obtain much higher accuracy.

Conclusions

In this paper, we proposed a new algorithm for energy disaggregation which consists of the two steps of learning a dictionary of power consumption signatures and a disaggregation optimization. To address the first step, we modeled each device as a mixture of dynamical systems, computed dissimilarities between energy snippets of each device using the learned models, and generalized state-of-the-art convex subset selection schemes to deal with sequential data in order to find signature power consumptions for each device. Collecting powerlets from all devices in a dictionary, we proposed an optimization program for disaggregating a whole energy signal by incorporating several priors such as device-sparsity, knowledge about devices that do or do not work together, and temporal smoothness. Finally, by experiments on a real energy dataset, we showed that our framework provides promising results for energy disaggregation.

Investigating convex relaxations of our proposed integer program for desegregation and their efficient implementation are the subject of our ongoing research. In addition, investigating conditions on the powerlets, under which our proposed optimization recovers the true disaggregation of a given aggregate signal, is the subject of our current theoretical analysis.

Acknowledgment

E. Elhamifar and S. Sastry are supported by grants ONR N000141310341, ONR N000141210609, ONR N000140910230, DARPA FA8650-11-1-7153. This work is supported by NSF CPS:Large:ActionWebs award number 0931843, TRUST (Team for Research in Ubiquitous Secure Technology) which receives support from NSF (award number CCF-0424422), and FORCES (Foundations Of Resilient CybEr-physical Systems) which receives support from NSF (award number CNS-1239166).

References

Aharon, M.; Elad, M.; and Bruckstein, A. M. 2006. K-SVD: an algorithm for designing overcomplete dictionaries for sparse representation. *IEEE Trans. on Signal Processing* 54(11):4311–4322.

Berges, M.; Goldman, E.; Matthews, H. S.; and Soibelman, L. 2010. Enhancing electricity audits in residential buildings with non-intrusive load monitoring. *Journal of Industrial Ecology: Special Issue on Environmental Applications of Information and Communications Technology* 14(5).

Darby, S. 2006. The effectiveness of feedback on energy consumption. *Technical report, Environmental Change Institute, University of Oxford.*

Dempster, A.; Laird, N.; and Rubin, D. 1977. Maximum likelihood from incomplete data via the EM algorithm. *Journal of the Royal Statistical Society* 39(1).

Elhamifar, E.; Sapiro, G.; and Sastry, S. S. 2014. Dissimilarity-based sparse subset selection. *under review in IEEE Transactions on Pattern Analysis and Machine Intelligence.*

Elhamifar, E.; Sapiro, G.; and Vidal, R. 2012. Finding exemplars from pairwise dissimilarities via simultaneous sparse recovery. *Neural Information Processing Systems.*

Froehlich, J.; Larson, E.; Gupta, S.; Cohn, G.; Reynolds, M.; and Patel, S. 2011. Disaggregated end-use energy sensing for the smart grid. *IEEE Pervasive Computing* 10(1).

Ghahramani, Z., and Jordan, M. I. 1997. Factorial hidden markov models. *Machine Learning* 29(2-3).

Gupta, S.; Reynolds, S.; and Patel, S. N. 2010. Electrisense: Single-point sensing using emi for electrical event detection and classification in the home. *Conference on Ubiquitous Computing.*

Hart, G. 1992. Nonintrusive appliance load monitoring. *Proceedings of the IEEE* 80(12).

Kim, H.; Marwah, M.; Arlitt, M.; Lyon, G.; and Han, J. 2011. Unsupervised disaggregation of low frequency power measurements. *In Proceedings of theSIAM Conference on Data Mining.*

Kolter, J. Z., and Jaakkola, T. 2012. Approximate inference in additive factorial hmms with application to energy disaggregation. *International Conference on Artificial Intelligence and Statistics.*

Kolter, J. Z., and Johnson, M. J. 2011. Redd: A public data set for energy disaggregation research. *SustKDD Workshop on Data Mining Applications in Sustainability.*

Kolter, J. Z.; Batra, S.; and Ng, A. Y. 2010. Energy disaggregation via discriminative sparse coding. In *Advances in Neural Information Processing Systems.*

Laughman, C., and Leeb, S. 2003. Advanced non-intrusive monitoring of electric loads. *IEEE Power and Energy.*

Mairal, J.; Bach, F.; Ponce, J.; Sapiro, G.; and Zisserman, A. 2008. Supervised dictionary learning. *NIPS.*

Neenan, B., and Robinson, J. 2009. Residential electricity use feedback: A research synthesis and economic framework. *Technical report, Electric Power Research Institute.*

Wytock, M., and Kolter, J. Z. 2014. Contextually supervised source separation with application to energy disaggregation. In *AAAI Conference on Artificial Intelligence.*

Ziefman, M., and Roth, K. 2011. Nonintrusive appliance load monitoring: Review and outlook. *IEEE Transactions on Consumer Electronics* 57(1).

Pattern Decomposition with Complex Combinatorial Constraints: Application to Materials Discovery

Stefano Ermon
Computer Science Department
Stanford University
ermon@cs.stanford.edu

Ronan Le Bras
Department of Computer Science
Cornell University
lebras@cs.cornell.edu

Santosh K. Suram, John M. Gregoire
Joint Center for Artificial Photosynthesis
California Institute of Technology
{sksuram, gregoire}@caltech.edu

Carla P. Gomes, Bart Selman
Department of Computer Science
Cornell University
{gomes,selman}@cs.cornell.edu

Robert B. van Dover
Department of Materials Science and Engineering
Cornell University
rbv2@cornell.edu

Abstract

Identifying important components or factors in large amounts of noisy data is a key problem in machine learning and data mining. Motivated by a pattern decomposition problem in materials discovery, aimed at discovering new materials for renewable energy, e.g. for fuel and solar cells, we introduce CombiFD, a framework for factor based pattern decomposition that allows the incorporation of a-priori knowledge as constraints, including complex combinatorial constraints. In addition, we propose a new pattern decomposition algorithm, called AMIQO, based on solving a sequence of (mixed-integer) quadratic programs. Our approach considerably outperforms the state of the art on the materials discovery problem, scaling to larger datasets and recovering more precise and physically meaningful decompositions. We also show the effectiveness of our approach for enforcing background knowledge on other application domains.

Introduction

In recent years, we have seen an enormous growth in data generation rates in many fields of science (Halevy, Norvig, and Pereira 2009). For instance, in combinatorial materials discovery, scientists search for new materials with desirable properties by obtaining measurements on hundreds of samples in a single batch experiment using a composition spread technique (Ginley et al. 2005; Narasimhan, Mallapragada, and Porter 2007). Providing computational tools for automatically analyzing and for determining the structure of the materials formed in a composition spread is an important and exciting direction in the emerging field of Computational Sustainability (Gomes 2009). For example, this approach has been successfully applied to speed up the discovery of new materials with improved catalytic activity for fuel cell applications (Gregoire et al. 2010; van Dover, Schneemeyer, and Fleming 1998) and of oxygen evolution catalysts with applications to solar fuel generation (Haber et al. 2014). Long-term solutions to several sustainability issues in energy and transportation are likely to come from break-through innovations in materials (White 2012), and computer science can play a role and provide support to accelerate new materials discovery (Le Bras et al. 2011).

To accelerate the discovery of new materials, materials scientists have developed high-throughput experimental procedures to create composition-spread libraries of new materials, a process that can be intuitively understood as generating an enormous number of compounds in a single experiment by mixing different amounts of a small number of basic elements (Takeuchi, van Dover, and Koinuma 2002). The promising libraries are then characterized using X-ray diffraction to determine the underlying crystal structure and composition. Specifically, a set of X-ray diffraction signals are sampled at n different material compositions, each one corresponding to a different mixture of some basic elements. A key problem in materials discovery is called the *phase map identification problem*, defined as finding $k \ll n$ basic phases (basis functions that change gradually with composition, in terms of structure and intensity), such that all the n X-ray measurements can be explained as a mixture of the k basic phases. The decomposition is subject to physical constraints that govern the underlying crystallographic process.

The *phase map identification* is effectively a source separation or spectral unmixing problem (Berry et al. 2007) where the sources are the k non-negative, basic x-ray diffraction signals and each observation is a non-negative combination of these k sources. Therefore, a standard approach from the literature is non-negative matrix factorization (NMF) (Long et al. 2009). Nevertheless, this approach overlooks the physical constraints from the crystal formation. For example, it does not guarantee connectivity of the "phase regions" in the phase map, nor can it handle basis patterns that are slightly changing ("shifting") as the crystal lattice constants change. Recent development (Kusne et al. 2014), while not enforcing these constraints *per se*, have shown to be resilient to peak shifting for example. To obtain physically meaningful decompositions, researchers (Le Bras et al. 2011; Ermon et al. 2012) have looked at constraint programming formulations that can incorporate all the necessary constraints. The down side of these approaches is that they are fully discrete (they require a discretization of the data through peak detection) and they cannot directly deal with continuous measurement data. On the other side of the spectrum with respect to NMF, the unsupervised nature is lost, and scalability becomes an issue as, for example, in a fully discrete problem there is no notion of gradient anymore. In addition, these approaches are not robust to the presence of noise in the data, as noise considerably impacts the efficiency of their filtering and propagation mechanisms.

In this work, we aim to achieve the best of both worlds by bridging the previous approaches and providing a new hybrid formulation, where we integrate additional domain knowledge as additional constraints into the basic NMF approach. We introduce CombiFD, a novel pattern decomposition framework that allows the specification of very general constraints. These include constraints used with some matrix factorization and clustering approaches (such as non-negativity or partial labeling information) as well as more general ones that require a richer representation language, powerful enough to capture more complex, combinatorial dependencies. For example, we show how to encode complex a-priori scientific domain knowledge by specifying combinatorial dependencies on the variables imposed by physical laws. We also propose a novel solution technique called AMIQO (**A**lternating **M**ixed **I**nteger **Q**uadratic **O**ptimization), that involves the solution of a sequence of (mixed-integer) quadratic programs. We solve these optimization problems using state-of-the-art combinatorial optimization techniques. Overall, our constrained factorization algorithm clearly outperforms previous approaches: it scales to large real world datasets, and recovers physically meaningful and significantly more accurate interpretations of the data when prior knowledge is taken into account.

Framework

Given n data points $a_i \in \mathbb{R}^m$, each one represented by an m-dimensional vector of real-valued features, we represent the input data compactly as a matrix $A \in \mathbb{R}^{m \times n}$, each column corresponding to a data point and each row to a feature. In the context of the *phase map identification*, A corresponds to the n observed X-ray diffraction patterns, each of them as a vector of m scattering intensity values.

We are interested in low-dimensional representations which can approximate the input data A by identifying its essential components or factors. Namely, for a given number k of basic phases, we want to approximate A as $A \approx WH$, where $W \in \mathbb{R}^{m \times k}$ represents k basic phases (or phase patterns) and $H \in \mathbb{R}^{k \times n}$ the combination coefficients at each data point. This problem belongs to the family of low-rank approximation problems, an important research theme in machine learning and data mining with numerous applications, including source separation, denoising, compression, and dimensionality reduction (Berry et al. 2007).

Low-Rank Approximation

Given a non-negative matrix $A \in \mathbb{R}^{m \times n}$ and a desired rank $k < \min(n, m)$, we seek matrices $W \in \mathbb{R}^{m \times k}$ and $H \in \mathbb{R}^{k \times n}$, $H, W \geq 0$ that give the best low rank approximation of A, i.e. $A \approx WH$. Typically this is formulated as the following optimization problem:

$$\min_{W,H} ||A - WH||_2 \quad (1)$$

where $W \in \mathbb{R}^{m \times k}$ is a matrix of *basis vectors* or *patterns* and $H \in \mathbb{R}^{k \times n}$ the *coefficient* matrix. The symbol $|| \cdot ||_2$ indicates (entry-wise) Frobenius norm.

This basic problem can be solved by the so-called truncated Singular Value Decomposition (SVD) approach, which produces the best approximation in terms of squared distance. It can be computed efficiently and robustly, obtaining a representation where data points can be interpreted as linear combinations of a small number of basis vectors.

In many applications input data are non-negative, for instance representing color intensities, word counts (Tjioe et al. 2008) or x-ray scattering intensities in our motivating application. The basis vectors computed with an SVD, however, are generally not guaranteed to be non-negative, and this leads to an undesirable *lack of interpretability*. For example, it is not possible to interpret an image as the superposition of simpler patches, or an X-ray diffraction pattern as the composition of several basic compounds when obtaining negative values for some of the basis vectors or the coefficients. To overcome this limitation, researchers have introduced the NMF approach, which explicitly enforces non-negativity constraints on the basis vectors and coefficients.

While non-negativity is a very common constraint in many domains, in some applications we have additional valuable *a priori* information on the features (each feature corresponds to a row of A and W). For instance, we might also know *a priori* an upper bound on the value of some features, or that two Boolean features are incompatible, or that non-negativity only holds for a subset of the features. In particular, in our materials science domain basis, vectors (patterns) correspond to chemical compounds and their underlying crystal structures. For chemical systems in thermodynamic equilibrium, the compositional variation of the concentration and lattice parameters of each compound follow well-defined rules, from which constraints on the coexistence and variation of basis patterns can be defined (Le Bras et al. 2011; Ermon et al. 2012). While some constraints such as non-negativity can be individually enforced in some approaches, others such as connectivity and the complex rules defining shifting basis patterns (see below for details) have not been considered before. To the best of our knowledge, there is no general factor analysis framework that can handle the *combination* of all these constraints. This motivates the definition of the following general pattern decomposition subject to combinatorial constraints problem.

CombiFD: Pattern Decomposition with Combinatorial Constraints

Given a (general) matrix $A \in \mathbb{R}^{m \times n}$ and a desired rank $k < \min(n, m)$ we seek matrices $W \in \mathbb{R}^{m \times k}$ and $H \in \mathbb{R}^{k \times n}$ that minimize $||A - WH||_p$ where $p \in \{1, 2\}$ and $|| \cdot ||_p$ is an entry-wise norm (e.g. $p = 2$ corresponds to the Frobenius norm). Moreover, the factors need to satisfy an additional set of J linear inequality constraints, possibly requiring binary or integer variables. This is formalized as the following optimization problem:

$$\begin{aligned} \underset{W,H,x,b}{\text{minimize}} \quad & ||A - WH||_p = f(W, H) \\ \text{subject to} \quad & C[\text{vec}(W), \text{vec}(H), x, b]^T \leq d \\ & b_i \in \{0, 1\},\ i \in [1, N]. \end{aligned} \tag{2}$$

where $x \in \mathbb{R}^M$ is a vector of additional real-valued variables, b is a vector of N binary variables, $d \in \mathbb{R}^J$, $C \in \mathbb{R}^{J\times(mk+nk+M+N)}$ and $\text{vec}(\cdot)$ denotes vectorization (stacking a matrix into a vector). That is, we have J linear inequalities involving the entries of W, H, x and b, with coefficients given by C and right-hand side given by d. As Integer Linear Programming is well known to be NP-complete, very general constraints can be encoded by appropriately choosing C and d. These additional (combinatorial) constrains are extremely useful to encode prior knowledge we might have about the domain. These include non-negativity ($W, H \geq 0$), upper bounds ($W_{i,j} \leq u$), sparsity (see Example 1), semi-supervised clustering (see Example 2) as well as many others. Other examples of intricate constraints can be found in the experimental section below.

Example 1: L_0 sparsity Suppose we want to explicitly formulate a sparsity constraint on the coefficient matrix. That is, we want to find W, H such that $A \approx WH$ and each column of H has at most S non-zero entries, i.e. $||H_i||_0 \leq S$ where H_i is the i-th column of H. For instance, in a topic modeling application where the basis vectors correspond to topics, this constraint ensures that each document can have at most S topics. This can be encoded as follows:

$$\begin{aligned} \min_{W,H,b} \quad & ||A - WH||_2 \\ \text{s.t.} \quad & b_{i,j} \geq h_{i,j}, \sum_j h_{i,j} = 1, \sum_i b_{i,j} \leq S \\ & b_{i,j} \in \{0, 1\}\ i \in [1, k], j \in [1, n] \end{aligned} \tag{3}$$

which can be easily rewritten more compactly in the form (2) by selecting appropriate C and d (in this case, $M = 0$ and $N = kn$).

Example 2: Semi-Supervised Clustering As an example, in a semi-supervised clustering problem, we can easily include partial labeling information as constraints on H, e.g. enforcing Must-Link or Cannot-Link constraints (Liu and Wu 2010; Basu, Davidson, and Wagstaff 2008; Choo et al. 2013). Suppose we have prior information on P_{ML} pairs of data points $ML = \{(i_1, j_1), \cdots, (i_{P_{ML}}, j_{P_{ML}})\}$ that are known to belong to the same cluster (Must-Link) , and p_{CL} pairs of data points $CL = \{(i_1, j_1), \cdots, (i_{p_{CL}}, j_{p_{CL}})\}$ that are known not to belong to the same cluster (Cannot-Link).We encode this prior knowledge into our CombiFD framework as follows:

$$\begin{aligned} \min_{W,H,b} \quad & ||A - WH||_2 \\ \text{s.t.} \quad & W, H \geq 0, \sum_j h_{i,j} = 1, \sum_i b_{i,j} \leq S \\ & b_{i,j} \geq h_{i,j},\ b_{i,j} \in \{0, 1\}\ i \in [1, k], j \in [1, n] \\ & b_{i,i_s} = b_{i,j_s}\ i \in [1, k], (i_s, j_s) \in ML \\ & b_{i,i_s} + b_{i,j_s} \leq 1\ i \in [1, k], (i_s, j_s) \in CL \end{aligned} \tag{4}$$

Related work

Many low rank approximation schemes are available, including QR decomposition, Independent Component Analysis, truncated Singular Value Decomposition, and Nonnegative Matrix Factorization (Berry et al. 2007).

While these basic methods are unsupervised, there is a growing interest in incorporating prior knowledge or user guidance into these frameworks (Zhi et al. 2013). For example, in semi-supervised clustering applications, user guidance is often given by partial labeling information, which can be incorporated using hard constraints (Liu and Wu 2010; Basu, Davidson, and Wagstaff 2008; Choo et al. 2013). Typical constraints used in this case are Must-Link and Cannot-Link, enforcing that two data points must or cannot be in the same cluster, respectively. For example, (Hossain et al. 2010) present an integrated framework for clustering non-homogenous data, and show how to turn Must-Link and Cannot-Link constraints into dependent and disparate clustering problems. Recently, researchers have also considered interactive matrix factorization schemes for topic modeling that can take into account user feedback on the quality of the decomposition (Choo et al. 2013) (topic refinement, merging or splitting) and semi-supervised NMF with label information as constraints (Liu and Wu 2010). Constraint clustering (Basu, Davidson, and Wagstaff 2008) is another example of this approach. Alternatively, regularizations or penalty terms are also used to obtain solutions with certain desired properties such as sparsity (Hoyer 2004; Cai et al. 2011), convexity (Ding, Li, and Jordan 2010), temporal structural properties and shift invariances (Smaragdis 2004; Smaragdis, Raj, and Shashanka 2008).

Most of the work in the literature is however confined to a single type of constraints or simple conjunctions, which limits their usability. With CombiFD, we propose a new approach for finding a low dimensional approximation of some data (decomposition into basic patterns) that is able to incorporate not only existing types of constraints but also more complex logical combinations.

Constrained Factorization Algorithm

Solving the general CombiFD optimization problem (2) is challenging for two reasons. First, the objective function is not convex, hence minimization is difficult even in the presence of simple non-negativity constraints (Berry et al. 2007). Second, we are allowing a very expressive class of constraints, which can potentially specify very complex, intricate dependencies among the variables. Unfortunately, general nonconvex mixed-integer non-linear programming has not seen as much progress as their linear (MILP) and quadratic (MIQP) counterparts, and most approaches are either application specific or do not scale well. Even in the presence of simple constraints (as it is the case for NMF), the problem is rarely solved to optimality and in practice heuristic approaches are used. Yet, simple heuristic approaches such as multiplicative update rules (Lee and Seung 1999), which is one of the most widely used algorithms, do not apply to our case due to the integer variables. Similarly, projected gradient techniques cannot be directly applied here (Lin 2007). We therefore introduce a new approximate technique called AMIQO which exploits the special structure of the problem and takes full advantage of advanced MIQP optimization techniques from the OR literature.

To solve the general CombiFD optimization problem (2), we introduce AMIQO (**A**lternating **M**ixed **I**nteger **Q**uadratic **O**ptimization) with pseudocode reported as Algorithm 1. AMIQO is an iterative two-block coordinate descent procedure enhanced with sophisticated combinatorial optimization techniques beyond the standard convex optimization methods. In fact, the key advantage of our CombiFD framework is that for either H or W fixed, problem (2) is a mixed-integer quadratic program.[1] Mixed-integer quadratic programs have been widely studied in the operations research literature, and we can leverage a wide range of techniques that have been developed and are implemented in state-of-the-art mixed-integer quadratic programming (MIQP) solvers such as IBM CPLEX. These integer programs do not have to be solved to optimality, and it is sufficient to improve the objective function with respect to the factorization found at the previous step (which is used to warm-start the search). Notice that when there are no binary variables ($N = 0$), the optimization problems in the inner loop of AMIQO correspond to standard quadratic programs that can be solved efficiently, even in the presence of (linear) constraints in the form (2), which are more general than non-negativity. AMIQO is inspired by the seminal work of Paatero and Tapper who initially proposed the use of a block coordinate descent procedure for NMF (Paatero and Tapper 1994), and was later followed upon by a number of researchers, including an unconstrained least squares version (Berry et al. 2007), and solution techniques based on projected gradient descent (Lin 2007), Quasi-Newton (Kim, Sra, and Dhillon 2007), and Active-set (Kim and Park 2008). However, our approach is novel in that it uses a mixed integer solver in each coordinate descent step, and is the only one that can take into account combinatorial constraints, guaranteeing feasibility of the solution at every iteration even in the presence of intricate combinatorial constraints.

Algorithm 1 AMIQO

```
Find feasible W^0, H^0, x^0, b^0 for (2)          ▷ Use MIP solver
for j = 0, ··· , t − 1 do
    W^{j+1}, x̃^{j+1}, b̃^{j+1} ← argmin_{W,x,b} f(W, H^j) s.t. (2)
    and H = H^j                                     ▷ Use MIQP solver
    H^{j+1}, x^{j+1}, b^{j+1} ← argmin_{H,x,b} f(W^{j+1}, H) s.t.
    (2) and W = W^{j+1}                             ▷ Use MIQP solver
end for
return W^t, H^t
```

We summarize the properties of AMIQO with the following proposition:

Proposition 1. *Let W^j, H^j be as in Algorithm 1. If (2) is feasible, the following two properties hold: 1) For all j, $0 \leq j \leq t$, the optimization problems in the inner loop of the algorithm are feasible and (W^j, H^j, x^j, b^j) is feasible for (2). 2) The objective function $||A - W^j H^j||_p$ is monotonically non-increasing, i.e. $||A - W^j H^j||_p \geq ||A - W^{j+1} H^{j+1}||_p$*

Theorem 1. *AMIQO run on CombiFD problem (4) with $S = 1, ML = CL = \emptyset$ is equivalent to k-means.*

Proof. See Appendix for both proofs. □

Although the objective function is monotonically non-increasing, AMIQO is not guaranteed to converge to a global minimum. This is consistent with the hardness of problem (2). More specifically, the quality of the final solution found might depend on the initialization of W^0 and H^0. This issue is common to other standard matrix factorization algorithms, and several heuristic initialization schemes have been proposed to mitigate the issue (Albright et al. 2006). Nevertheless, in our experimental evaluation, the initialization did not play a major role, and we typically converged to the same solution, regardless of the initial conditions.

Experiments – Encoding domain knowledge as additional constraints

In order to show the generality of our approach, we provide experimental results on three application domains, with increasingly more complex constraints capturing a-priori domain knowledge. We start with semi-supervised clustering with partial labeling information, i.e. simple Must-Link and Cannot-Link constraints. We then consider another clustering problem, where we include more complex logical constraints on the features, describing higher-level biological knowledge. Finally we consider our motivating application: the phase map identification problem.

Clustering with partial labeling information

NMF has become a popular approach for clustering, with application domains ranging from document clustering (Shahnaz et al. 2006) and graph clustering (Kuang, Park, and Ding 2012) to gene expression data clustering (Tjioe et al. 2008). Cluster membership is determined by the coefficient matrix H, which reflects how each data point decomposes into the basis vectors.

There are several ways to obtain hard clustering assignments (binary indicators) from the coefficient matrix H (real valued). We follow (Ding, Li, and Peng 2008) and normalize the matrix H so that the entries can be interpreted as the posterior probability $p(c_s|d_j)$ that a data point j belongs to cluster s. Specifically, we let $D_W = diag(\mathbf{1}^T W)$ and estimate the cluster membership probability as $p(c_s|d_j) \propto [D_W H]_{sj}$. As a result, a data point j is assigned a cluster $s^*(j)$ such that $s^*(j) = argmax_s [D_W H]_{sj}$.

We consider a semi-supervised clustering task where we assume to have some prior information on the labels (equivalently, on the cluster assignment) of a subset of datapoints. Specifically, we assume to have information about pairs of data points, which should either belong to the same cluster (Must-Link) or not (Cannot-Link). This information is obtained using standard labeled datasets from the UCI repository (Bache and Lichman 2013) for which a ground truth clustering is known. To generate various amounts of prior

[1] For $p = 1$, it simplifies to a mixed-integer linear program.

knowledge, we randomly select P pairs of data points, using their labels to specify a MustLink or CannotLink constraint.

We compare our CombiFD formulation of the problem (4) with two previous approaches from the literature: CNMF (Constrained NMF) (Liu and Wu 2010) and NMFS (NMF-based semi supervised clustering) (Li, Ding, and Jordan 2007). The first approach is based on enforcing non combinatorial constraints on H, while the second approach captures the ML and CL constraints using penalty terms in a modified objective function which is then approximately minimized using multiplicative updates.

We report in Figure 1 the accuracy obtained using these methods as a function of the amount of supervision, i.e. the number of Must-Link or Cannot-Link constraints used. Accuracy is defined as in (Liu and Wu 2010) and corresponds to $AC = 1/n \cdot max_\sigma \sum_{i=1}^{k} |r_i \cap c_{\sigma_i}|$, where $\sigma : 1..k \to 1..k$ is a bijection mapping clusters r_i to ground-truth classes c_j. Namely, each cluster is assigned a label such that the labeling best matches the ground truth labels. Note that the accuracy can be computed efficiently using, for example, the Hungarian algorithm.

Results are averaged over 100 runs. We see that CombiFD significantly outperforms the competing techniques across all levels of prior knowledge. Intuitively, this is because by properly taking into account the combinatorial nature of the problem, CombiFD can automatically make logically sound inferences about the data: for example, we can take into account transitive closure (i.e., if a and b must link, and b and c must link, then a and c must link as well) and other logical implications. The deeper reasoning power and greater accuracy provided by AMIQO however involves a small computational overhead, with a typical runtime in the order of a couple of minutes for AMIQO versus a few tens of seconds for the competing techniques.

Clustering with more complex prior knowledge

In this experiment, we consider the Zoo dataset from UCI (Bache and Lichman 2013). This is a dataset of 101 animals, each one represented as a vector of 17 non-negative features (e.g. whether it has hair or not, whether it has feathers or not, or its number of legs). There are 7 class labels.

We solve the clustering problem using our CombiFD approach (2), where we enforce non-negativity as well as additional constraints capturing some well known biological facts. Specifically, we enforce the following constraints on the basis vectors using our CombiFD framework: $\neg(HasMilk \wedge HasEggs)$, $HasFeathers \to HasEggs$, and $\neg(HasFeathers \wedge HasHair)$. Since we are not aware of any other matrix factorization technique that can take into account this kind of complex, logically structured prior knowledge, we compare with standard NMF (problem (1)), which is a totally unsupervised technique.

Table 1 reports the accuracy (defined as before) and runtime of the two approaches averaged over 100 runs. The results show that the CombiFD approach, which incorporates a limited amount of logically structured prior knowledge, significantly improves the accuracy of standard NMF, while still running within seconds using AMIQO.

Approach	**Accuracy**		**Time (*seconds*)**	
	Avg.	Std. Dev.	Avg.	Std. Dev.
NMF	0.72	0.08	**1.84**	0.1
CombiFD	**0.82**	0.05	4.06	0.8

Table 1: Accuracy and runtime of NMF vs. CombiFD on the UCI Zoo dataset for 100 runs.

Spectral Unmixing for Materials Discovery

We first present how to incorporate complex constraints capturing some of the key physical laws that govern the data-generating process for the phase map identification problem.

Sparsity: According to the so-called Gibbs phase rule, under equilibrium conditions at fixed temperature and pressure, there can be mixtures of at most M phases occurring at each data point (chemical composition) in a library involving M basic elements. This is encoded as $||H_s||_0 \leq M$, for $s \in [1, k]$ as in (3).

Shifting: Each basis pattern may be slightly stretched by a different amount for each composition sample. Indeed, chemical alloying within a given compound may alter the crystal lattice constants, leading to a systematic shift (as a function of composition) of peak positions in the measured X-ray patterns. For isotropic lattice expansion and signals measured versus the scattering vector magnitude, the peak shifts are proportional to the peak positions, corresponding to a linear stretch of the signal. Therefore, we use Qk basis vectors, where k are free and $(Q-1)k$ are constrained to be shifted versions of the free basis vectors. This is encoded as follows: $A_{i,j} = interpolate(A_{\lfloor i/(1+\ell\gamma)\rfloor, zQ}, A_{\lceil i/(1+\ell\gamma)\rceil, zQ})$ for $j = zQ + \ell$, $z \in [0, k-1]$, $\ell \in [1, Q-1]$, where γ is a constant for the shifting granularity and $interpolate(x, y)$ denotes linear interpolation between x and y. By choosing Q to be no smaller than the ratio of the maximum peak shift and the minimum peak width (a known value for a given experiment), a linear sum of the Q mutually-constrained basis patterns can accurately model each instance of the shifting phase pattern.

Connectivity: The compositions at which a phase (or basis) is observed should form a connected region in composition space, and its lattice parameters should vary smoothly across the region. Hence we build a graph $G = (V, E)$ with n vertices (one vertex per data point) and edges between sample points that have similar compositions. Let $G(H_\ell)$ be the subgraph induced by the vertex set $V(H_\ell) = \{i : H_{\ell,i} > 0\} \subseteq V$ (the set of vertices where phase ℓ is used). We want to enforce $G(H_\ell)$ is connected for $\ell = 1, \cdots, k$. The first formulation we consider is flow based. Intuitively, this flow-based encoding defines a flow for each phase ℓ that can only pass through vertices where the phase is present. There is a source node that injects positive flow in the network, and there is some outgoing flow at every vertex where a phase is used. In order to satisfy flow conservation, there has to be a path from the source to any other node belonging to the same phase in the network. This constraint enforces connectivity but it can be expensive to include in the MIQP formulation when there is a large number of points.

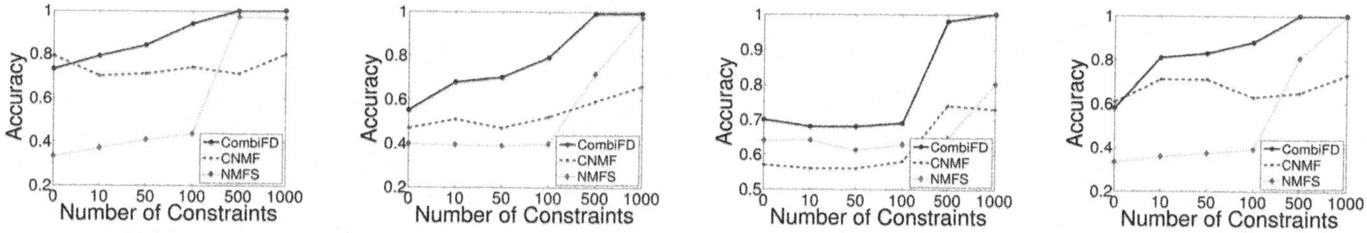

(a) Iris (b) Wine (c) Ionosphere (d) Seeds

Figure 1: Accuracy as a function of the amount of prior knowledge. CombiFD (solid blue line) clearly outperforms competing techniques across all levels of supervision (number of constraints).

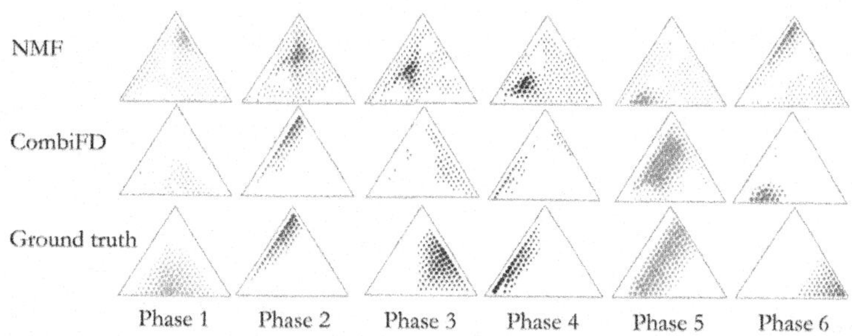

Figure 2: Results of NMF (top row), CombiFD (middle row), and ground truth (bottom row) for the Al-Li-Fe oxide system. In each row, each one of the 6 plots corresponds to the map of the concentration of a basis pattern (crystal phase). The size of each dot is proportional to the phase concentration estimated at that point from the coefficient matrix H. It can be seen that standard NMF overlooks the physical constraints, e.g. there are often mixtures of more than 3 basis patterns and the phase regions are disconnected. CombiFD recovers accurately all the phases except for the last one.

We therefore also consider the following variation. For all triples of points v_1, v_2, v_3 that lie on a straight line (in this order) in the composition space, and for every phase ℓ, we enforce the constraint that $h_{\ell,v_2} \geq \min\{h_{\ell,v_1}, h_{\ell,v_3}\}$. Although these constraints do not strictly enforce connectivity, they are simpler and often strong enough that the solution obtained is actually connected.

We consider synthetic data from (Le Bras et al. 2014), generated from the Aluminium(Al)-Lithium(Li)-Iron(Fe) oxide system and for which the ground truth is known. This dataset has 219 points and 6 underlying phases, where each phase has up to 42 diffraction peaks. We report in Fig. 2 the data interpretation obtained using regular NMF, CombiFD and the ground truth. On average, the number of iterations of AMIQO is about 8, with runtimes ranging from minutes to a few hours. We can see that although we cannot recover exactly the ground truth solution, our interpretation obtained considering prior domain knowledge is much more accurate. For example, using NMF the sparsity constraint is violated for many sample points. In terms of evaluation metric we adapt the previous definition of accuracy to the case of soft cluster assignment, to reflect the fact that a sample point might be assigned to multiple clusters. Namely, we define $AC = 1/n \cdot max_\sigma \sum_{i=1}^{k} |r_i \cap c_{\sigma_i}|/|r_i \cup c_{\sigma_i}|$. Note that this metric does not explicitly reflect the amount of violated combinatorial constraints, which would be interesting to evaluate in future work. We report the results in Table 2. Overall, CombiFD outperforms NMF, confirming the visual that incorporating prior knowledge indeed improves the accuracy of the interpretation. Compared with the previous constraint programming formulation (SMT) (Ermon et al. 2012), the CombiFD algorithm exhibits much better scalability, allowing us to quickly analyze more realistic sized datasets with hundreds of sample points in a few hours. In fact, SMT could not find solutions after 20 hours on all instances but one.

Finally, we show results obtained with CombiFD on a real dataset (Fe-Bi-V oxide system, Fig. 3). While the phase map is unknown for this system, Fig. 3 shows the excellent match between the phase 1 basis pattern from the CombiFD solution and the pattern of the known $Bi_4V_2O_{11}$ phase (Bergerhoff and Brown 1987). Chemical alloying of Fe into this compound, of the form $Bi_4V_{2-x}Fe_xO_{11-x}$, has also been observed, which may be related to the identification of this phase 1 basis pattern over a wide composition range in the library (Vannier et al. 2003). The results of Fig. 3 demonstrate the ability of CombiFD to identify well-connected phase regions from experimental data, and further investigations are underway to evaluate the presence of minority phases with weak signals in this composition library.

Conclusions

The ability to integrate complex prior knowledge into unsupervised data analysis approaches is a rich and challenging research problem, pervasive in a variety of domains, such as scientific discovery. In particular, the motivating appli-

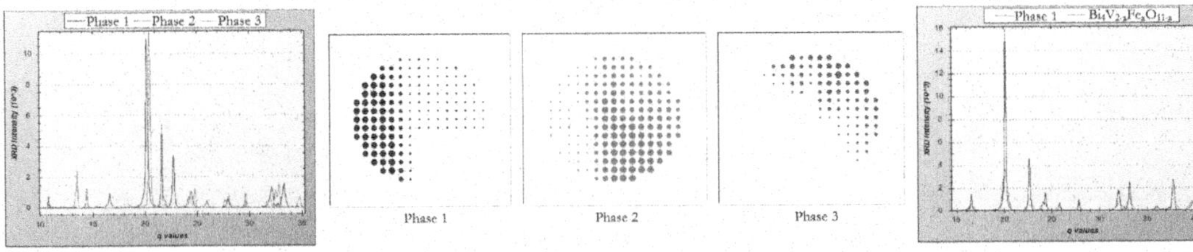

Figure 3: Results obtained with CombiFD and 3 phases (k=3) on the Fe-Bi-V oxide system. The X-ray diffraction data was collected at the SLAC National Accelerator Laboratory. The plot on the left shows the patterns of the 3 phases for low values of q (10-30 nm^{-1}), while the center 3 diagrams indicate where each phase appears. The right plot shows how one (recovered) phase matches a phase from the literature.

Parameters		Accuracy		
n	m	**NMF**	**CombiFD**	**SMT**
28	650	0.65	0.86	**0.96**
60	300	0.68	**0.77**	*t.-o.*
60	650	0.66	**0.75**	*t.-o.*
219	300	0.64	**0.73**	*t.-o.*
219	650	0.64	**0.73**	*t.-o.*
219	100	0.64	**0.75**	*t.-o.*
219	200	0.63	**0.73**	*t.-o.*

Table 2: Accuracy of NMF vs. CombiFD vs. SMT for different instances of the Al-Li-Fe oxide system. *t.-o.* indicates a time-out after 20 hours of CPU time.

cation of this work is the discovery of new fuel cell and solar fuel materials, thereby addressing pressing issues in sustainability such as the need for renewable and clean energy. We introduced CombiFD, a novel factor-based pattern decomposition framework that significantly generalizes and extends prior approaches. Our framework allows the specification of general constraints (including combinatorial ones), which are used to specify a-priori domain knowledge on the factorization that is being sought. These include traditional constraints such as non-negativity as well as more intricate dependencies, such as the ones coming from known phase behavior of chemical systems. We introduced a general factorization algorithm called AMIQO, based on solving a sequence of (mixed-integer) quadratic programs. We showed that AMIQO outperforms state-of-the-art approaches on a key problem in materials discovery: it scales to large real world datasets, it can handle complex, logically structured prior knowledge and by including prior knowledge into the model, we obtain significantly more accurate interpretations of the data. There are many directions to further extend our work, namely concerning representation formalism to capture other combinatorial constraints, with good performance/runtime trade-offs, as well as other algorithms to solve the combinatorial optimization problem.

Acknowledgments

Work supported by the National Science Foundation (NSF Expeditions in Computing award for Computational Sustainability, grant 0832782, NSF Inspire grant 1344201 and NSF Eager grant 1258330). Experiments were run on an infrastructure supported by the NSF Computing research infrastructure for Computational Sustainability grant 1059284. In collaboration with the Energy Materials Center at Cornell (emc2), an Energy Frontier Research Center funded by the U.S. Department of Energy (DOE), Office of Science, Office of Basic Energy Sciences (Award No. DE-SC0001086). Research conducted at the Cornell High Energy Synchrotron Source (CHESS) is supported by the NSF and the National Institutes of Health/National Institute of General Medical Sciences under NSF award DMR-0936384. Based upon work performed by the Joint Center for Artificial Photosynthesis (JCAP), a DOE Energy Innovation Hub, supported through the Office of Science of the U.S. Department of Energy (Award No. DE-SC0004993). Use of the Stanford Synchrotron Radiation Lightsource, SLAC National Accelerator Laboratory, is supported by the U.S. DOE, Office of Science, Office of Basic Energy Sciences under Contract No. DE-AC02-76SF00515.

Appendix: Proofs

Proof of Proposition 1 The proof is by induction. Suppose (W^j, H^j, x^j, b^j) is feasible for (2) (the base case $j = 0$ holds by construction). It follows that (2) augmented with the additional constraint $H = H^j$ is still feasible, and therefore $\min_{W,x,b} f(W, H^0)$ subject to (2) and $H = H^j$ admits an optimal solution $W^{j+1}, \tilde{x}^{j+1}, \tilde{b}^{j+1}$. Since $W^{j+1}, H^j, \tilde{x}^{j+1}, \tilde{b}^{j+1}$ is feasible for (2), it follows that (2) augmented with the additional constraint $W = W^{j+1}$ is also feasible. Therefore, $\min_{H,x,b} f(W^{j+1}, H)$ subject to (2) and $W = W^{j+1}$ admits an optimal solution $H^{j+1}, x^{j+1}, b^{j+1}$. It also follows that $W^{j+1}, H^{j+1}, x^{j+1}, b^{j+1}$ is feasible for (2). Finally, since we are optimizing at every step, it follows that $||A - W^j H^j||_p \geq ||A - W^{j+1} H^j||_p \geq ||A - W^{j+1} H^{j+1}||_p$.

Proof of Theorem 1 The initial (feasible) values of H^0, b^0 can be seen as an initial (hard) assignment of data points to clusters, where data point i belongs to cluster s if $b^0_{s,i} = 1$. The optimal solution for $\min_{W,b} f(W, H^j)$ subject to (2) and $H = H^j$ is to choose each column W to be the centroid of the data points assigned to the corresponding cluster by b^j at iteration j, i.e. for each s set the s-th column of W to be $w_s = 1/(\sum_i b_{s,i}) \sum a_i b_{s,i}$ (non-negative because the data points are assumed to be non-negative). An optimal solution for $\min_{H,b} f(W^{j+1}, H)$ subject to (2) and $W = W^{j+1}$ can be found by assigning each data point i to the cluster whose centroid w_s is closest to data point a_i, i.e. setting $h_{s^*(i),i} = b_{s^*(i),i} = 1$ where $s^*(i) = \arg\min_s ||w_s - a_i||_2$. These operations exactly correspond to k-means clustering initialized with the hard cluster assignment given by b^0.

References

Albright, R.; Cox, J.; Duling, D.; Langville, A.; and Meyer, C. 2006. Algorithms, initializations, and convergence for the nonnegative matrix factorization. Technical report, NCSU Tech Report.

Bache, K., and Lichman, M. 2013. UCI ML repository.

Basu, S.; Davidson, I.; and Wagstaff, K. 2008. *Constrained clustering: Advances in algorithms, theory, and applications*. CRC Press.

Bergerhoff, G., and Brown, I. 1987. Crystallographic databases. *International Union of Crystallography, Chester* 77–95.

Berry, M. W.; Browne, M.; Langville, A. N.; Pauca, V. P.; and Plemmons, R. J. 2007. Algorithms and applications for approximate nonnegative matrix factorization. *Computational Statistics & Data Analysis* 52(1):155–173.

Cai, D.; He, X.; Han, J.; and Huang, T. S. 2011. Graph regularized nonnegative matrix factorization for data representation. *PAMI, IEEE Transactions on* 33(8):1548–1560.

Choo, J.; Lee, C.; Reddy, C. K.; and Park, H. 2013. Utopian: User-driven topic modeling based on interactive nonnegative matrix factorization. *Visualization and Computer Graphics, IEEE Transactions on* 19(12):1992–2001.

Ding, C. H.; Li, T.; and Jordan, M. I. 2010. Convex and semi-nonnegative matrix factorizations. *Pattern Analysis and Machine Intelligence, IEEE Transactions.* 32(1):45–55.

Ding, C.; Li, T.; and Peng, W. 2008. On the equivalence between non-negative matrix factorization and probabilistic latent semantic indexing. *Computational Stat. & Data Analysis* 52(8):3913–3927.

Ermon, S.; Le Bras, R.; Gomes, C. P.; Selman, B.; and van Dover, R. B. 2012. Smt-aided combinatorial materials discovery. In *SAT 2012*, 172–185. Springer.

Ginley, D.; Teplin, C.; Taylor, M.; van Hest, M.; and Perkins, J. 2005. Combinatorial materials science. In *AccessScience*. McGraw-Hill Companies.

Gomes, C. P. 2009. Computational sustainability: Computational methods for a sustainable environment, economy, and society. *The Bridge* 39(4):5–13.

Gregoire, J. M.; Tague, M. E.; Cahen, S.; Khan, S.; Abruna, H. D.; DiSalvo, F. J.; and van Dover, R. B. 2010. Improved fuel cell oxidation catalysis in pt1-xtax. *Chem. Mater.* 22(3):1080.

Haber, J. A.; Cai, Y.; Jung, S.; Xiang, C.; Mitrovic, S.; Jin, J.; Bell, A. T.; and Gregoire, J. M. 2014. Discovering ce-rich oxygen evolution catalysts, from high throughput screening to water electrolysis. *Energy Environ. Sci.* 7:682–688.

Halevy, A.; Norvig, P.; and Pereira, F. 2009. The unreasonable effectiveness of data. *Intelligent Systems, IEEE* 24(2):8–12.

Hossain, M. S.; Tadepalli, S.; Watson, L. T.; Davidson, I.; Helm, R. F.; and Ramakrishnan, N. 2010. Unifying dependent clustering and disparate clustering for non-homogeneous data. In *SIGKDD*, 593–602. ACM.

Hoyer, P. O. 2004. Non-negative matrix factorization with sparseness constraints. *Journal of ML Research* 1457–1469.

Kim, H., and Park, H. 2008. Nonnegative matrix factorization based on alternating nonnegativity constrained least squares and active set method. *SIAM* 30(2):713–730.

Kim, D.; Sra, S.; and Dhillon, I. S. 2007. Fast newton-type methods for the least squares nonneg. matrix approx. problem. In *SDM*.

Kuang, D.; Park, H.; and Ding, C. H. 2012. Symmetric nonnegative matrix factorization for graph clustering. In *SDM*, 106–117.

Kusne, A. G.; Gao, T.; Mehta, A.; Ke, L.; Nguyen, M. C.; Ho, K.-M.; Antropov, V.; Wang, C.-Z.; Kramer, M. J.; Long, C.; et al. 2014. On-the-fly machine-learning for high-throughput experiments: search for rare-earth-free permanent magnets. *Scientific reports* 4.

Le Bras, R.; Damoulas, T.; Gregoire, J. M.; Sabharwal, A.; Gomes, C. P.; and Van Dover, R. B. 2011. Constraint reasoning and kernel clustering for pattern decomposition with scaling. In *CP*. 508–522.

Le Bras, R.; Bernstein, R.; Gregoire, J. M.; Suram, S. K.; Gomes, C. P.; Selman, B.; and van Dover, R. B. 2014. A computational challenge problem in materials discovery: Synthetic problem generator and real-world datasets. In *AAAI*.

Lee, D. D., and Seung, H. S. 1999. Learning the parts of objects by non-negative matrix factorization. *Nature* 401(6755):788–791.

Li, T.; Ding, C.; and Jordan, M. I. 2007. Solving consensus and semi-supervised clustering problems using nonnegative matrix factorization. In *Data Mining, 2007. ICDM 2007. Seventh IEEE International Conference on*, 577–582. IEEE.

Lin, C.-J. 2007. Projected gradient methods for nonnegative matrix factorization. *Neural comp.* 19(10):2756–2779.

Liu, H., and Wu, Z. 2010. Non-negative matrix factorization with constraints. In *Twenty-Fourth AAAI Conference*.

Long, C.; Bunker, D.; Karen, V.; Li, X.; and Takeuchi, I. 2009. Rapid identification of structural phases in combinatorial thin-film libraries using x-ray diffraction and non-negative matrix factorization. *Rev. Sci. Instruments* 80.

Narasimhan, B.; Mallapragada, S.; and Porter, M. 2007. *Combinatorial materials science*. John Wiley and Sons.

Paatero, P., and Tapper, U. 1994. Positive matrix factorization: A non-negative factor model with optimal utilization of error estimates of data values. *Environmetrics* 5(2):111–126.

Shahnaz, F.; Berry, M. W.; Pauca, V. P.; and Plemmons, R. J. 2006. Document clustering using nonnegative matrix factorization. *Information Processing & Management* 373–386.

Smaragdis, P.; Raj, B.; and Shashanka, M. V. 2008. Sparse and shift-invariant feature extraction from non-negative data. In *ICASSP*, 2069–2072.

Smaragdis, P. 2004. Non-negative matrix factor deconvolution; extraction of multiple sound sources from monophonic inputs. In *Indep. Component Analysis and Blind Signal Separation*. 494–499.

Takeuchi, I.; van Dover, R. B.; and Koinuma, H. 2002. Combinatorial synthesis and evaluation of functional inorganic materials using thin-film techniques. *MRS bulletin* 27(04):301–308.

Tjioe, E.; Berry, M.; Homayouni, R.; and Heinrich, K. 2008. Using a literature-based nmf model for discovering gene functional relationships. *BMC Bioinformatics* 9.

van Dover, R. B.; Schneemeyer, L.; and Fleming, R. 1998. Discovery of a useful thin-film dielectric using a composition-spread approach. *Nature* 392(6672):162–164.

Vannier, R.; Pernot, E.; Anne, M.; Isnard, O.; Nowogrocki, G.; and Mairesse, G. 2003. $Bi_4V_2O_{11}$ polymorph crystal structures related to their electrical properties. *Solid State Ionics* 157(1):147–153.

White, A. 2012. The materials genome initiative: One year on. *MRS Bulletin* 37(08):715–716.

Zhi, W.; Wang, X.; Qian, B.; Butler, P.; Ramakrishnan, N.; and Davidson, I. 2013. Clustering with complex constraints-algorithms and applications. In *AAAI*.

Learning Large-Scale Dynamic Discrete Choice Models of Spatio-Temporal Preferences with Application to Migratory Pastoralism in East Africa

Stefano Ermon
Stanford University
ermon@cs.stanford.edu

Yexiang Xue
Cornell University
yexiang@cs.cornell.edu

Russell Toth
University of Sydney
russell.toth@sydney.edu.au

Bistra Dilkina
Georgia Tech
bdilkina@cc.gatech.edu

Richard Bernstein
Cornell University
rab38@cornell.edu

Theodoros Damoulas
NYU CUSP
td47@nyu.edu

Patrick Clark
USDA Research Service
pat.clark@ars.usda.gov

Steve DeGloria
Cornell University
sdd4@cornell.edu

Andrew Mude
International Livestock Research Institute
a.mude@cgiar.org

Christopher Barrett
Cornell University
cbb2@cornell.edu

Carla P. Gomes
Cornell University
gomes@cs.cornell.edu

Abstract

Understanding spatio-temporal resource preferences is paramount in the design of policies for sustainable development. Unfortunately, resource preferences are often unknown to policy-makers and have to be inferred from data. In this paper we consider the problem of inferring agents' preferences from observed movement trajectories, and formulate it as an Inverse Reinforcement Learning (IRL) problem . With the goal of informing policy-making, we take a probabilistic approach and consider generative models that can be used to simulate behavior under new circumstances such as changes in resource availability, access policies, or climate. We study the Dynamic Discrete Choice (DDC) models from econometrics and prove that they generalize the Max-Entropy IRL model, a widely used probabilistic approach from the machine learning literature. Furthermore, we develop SPL-GD, a new learning algorithm for DDC models that is considerably faster than the state of the art and scales to very large datasets.

We consider an application in the context of pastoralism in the arid and semi-arid regions of Africa, where migratory pastoralists face regular risks due to resource availability, droughts, and resource degradation from climate change and development. We show how our approach based on satellite and survey data can accurately model migratory pastoralism in East Africa and that it considerably outperforms other approaches on a large-scale real-world dataset of pastoralists' movements in Ethiopia collected over 3 years.

Introduction

A useful and important tool in developing sensible policies for productive land use and environmental conservation is a set of micro-behavioral models that accurately capture the choice process of agents in the system. This is particularly true when we wish to analyze behavioral responses under as-yet unobserved states of the world, such as under alternative policy regimes or climate change. However specifying and fitting suitable models in settings with complex spatio-temporal aspects raises important research challenges, including the "curse of dimensionality" associated with handling large state spaces, and capturing the agents' preferences.

We tackle these issues specifically in the context of migratory pastoralism in the Borena plateau, Ethiopia, which is an exemplar of both the technical aspects of the problem we have in mind, and a setting with crucial policy relevance. Migratory pastoralists manage and herd livestock as their primary occupation. They face uncertainty over shocks to resource availability from drought and climate change, conflict, and disease. During semi-annual dry seasons they must migrate from their home villages to remote pastures and waterpoints, which can be modeled as selection amongst a discrete set of camp sites.

In this movement choice problem the pastoralists face a key tradeoff: they want to locate at the most abundant resource points (measured by observable water and forage), but movement (measured by distance) carries energy costs. Scouting out resource abundance on an ongoing basis also carries effort costs. How they balance these factors affects their response to changes that affect resource abundance (climate change, resource degradation and renewal, waterpoint maintenance), and distance (creation of new waterpoints, land use restrictions). A suitably fitted model of individual preferences over movements yields a number of opportunities for policy-relevant simulation analyses. Policy-makers regularly face decisions over land use controls (e.g., zoning for housing, farmland, parkland), waterpoint maintenance (many of the waterpoints in the system are man-made and require ongoing investment) and herd re-stocking after droughts, among others. With the parameters governing pastoralists' individual decisions over movement in hand, we will be able to modify exogenous characteristics of the system such as land access, waterpoint presence, or herd sizes, and simulate predictions about behavioral responses.

Our goal is to develop a model to capture the planning decisions made by the herders. The model must be structural, meaning that its parameters provide intuitive insights into the decision-making process, as well as generative, meaning that it can potentially be used to simulate behavior under new circumstances such as changes in resource availability, access policies, or climate. This raises key challenges due to the relatively large choice set and complex state space.

While methods for structural estimation of behavioral models have been known in economics since at least the 1980s (Rust 1987), methods for estimation in complex spatio-temporal settings are still in their infancy. In parallel, there is a growing literature in computer science under the name of inverse reinforcement learning (IRL), see e.g. (Ng and Russell 2000; Kolter and Ng 2009; Taylor and Stone 2009). While often motivated by a different set of modeling problems, IRL shares the objective of fitting the agent's choice function. In this paper, we study the Dynamic Discrete Choice models from Econometrics, which are widely used in economics (Aguirregabiria and Mira 2010) and engineering (Ben-Akiva and Lerman 1985) but have received little attention so far in the computer science literature. In fact, we show an interesting connection: under some conditions, Dynamic Discrete Choice models generalize the Max-Entropy IRL Model (Ziebart et al. 2008), a widely used approach from the Machine Learning literature. Despite the numerous applications in the economics literature there has been little effort on developing scalable algorithms for learning DDC models on very large datasets. In this paper we fill this gap by developing SPL-GD, a new learning algorithm for Dynamic Discrete Choice models that is considerably faster than the state of the art and scales to very large datasets. Our technique combines dynamic programming with stochastic gradient descent, which is often used to scale machine learning techniques to massive datasets (Bottou and Bousquet 2008).

Our method allows us to infer micro-behavioral models in complex spatio-temporal settings. We apply it in the context of migratory pastoralism in the Borena plateau, Ethiopia. The available data includes surveys from 500 households; static geospatial map layers including village and road locations, ecosystem types, elevation and other terrain features; a dynamic greenness index (NDVI) from satellite sensing; locations of wells, ponds, and other water points identified by interview, field exploration, and satellite imagery; and GPS collar traces of 60 cattle from 20 households in 5 villages, at 5-minute intervals collected over 3 years. The GPS traces are our primary source of information regarding behavior and resource use. We show that using our approach with this data we can accurately model pastoralist movements, and considerably outperform other approaches, including a Markov model and the Maximum Entropy IRL model.

Problem Definition

We consider planning problems represented as *finite* Markov Decision Processes (MDP). Formally, an MDP is a tuple (S, A, P, r, η) where S is a finite set of states, A is a finite set of actions, P is a finite set of transition probabilities and $r : S \mapsto \mathbb{R}$ is an (immediate) reward function (the more general case $r : S \times A \mapsto \mathbb{R}$ can also be handled), and $\eta \in [0, 1]$ is a *discount factor*. If an agent executes an action $a \in A$ while in a state $s \in S$, it receives an immediate reward $r(s)$ and it transitions to a new state $s' \in S$ with probability $P(s'|s, a)$.

Planning. Let the planning horizon T be the (finite) number of time steps that the agent plans for. A plan is represented by a *policy*, where a policy is a sequence of decision rules, one for each time step in the planning horizon. A policy π is called *Markovian* if, for each time step t in the planning horizon, the decision rule $\pi_t : S \to A$ depends only on the current state s_t. If the MDP is deterministic, i.e. $P(s'|s, a) \in \{0, 1\}$, a policy is equivalent to a sequence of T actions (or alternatively states) for each possible initial state. We define the *value* of a policy π from an initial state $s \in S$ as $v^\pi(s) = \mathbf{E}^{s,\pi}\left[\sum_{t=0}^{T-1} \eta^t r(s_t)\right]$, which is the expected value of the discounted total reward when the initial state is $s_0 = s$ and the action taken at time t is chosen according to π.

The goal in a probabilistic planning problem (also known as optimal control or reinforcement learning) is to compute a policy π that maximizes the value function $v^\pi(s)$ for a given MDP, a problem that is widely studied in the literature (Puterman 2009; Bertsekas 1995; Powell 2007).

Inverse Planning Problem

In an inverse planning problem, also known as inverse reinforcement learning (Ng and Russell 2000) or structural estimation of an MDP (Rust 1987), the goal is to identify an MDP that is consistent with observed planning choices made by a rational agent. Specifically, we assume that we are given a state space S, an action set A, transition probabilities P and we want to find a reward function r (intuitively, capturing preferences of the agent over states), which *rationalizes* the observed behavior of an agent. For finite state spaces, the reward function can be represented as vector of real numbers $\mathbf{r} \in \mathbb{R}^{|S|}$, where each component gives the reward for one state. For large state spaces, it is common (Ng and Russell 2000; Ziebart et al. 2008; Powell 2007; Kolter and Ng 2009) to assume linear function approximation of the reward function r, relying on state-based features:

$$r(s) = \theta \cdot \mathbf{f}_s,$$

where $\mathbf{f}_s$ is a *given* feature vector of size m for each state $s \in S$ and $\theta \in \mathbb{R}^m$ is an *unknown* parameter vector to be estimated.

In many practical settings, we do not know the agent's policy π, but can observe the agent's trajectories, i.e. sequences of states from S that are visited, from which we can try to infer the agent's rewards and policy (also known as imitation learning). Specifically, we observe K finite sequences $\mathcal{S} = \{\tau^1, \cdots, \tau^K\}$ of state-action pairs made by the agent. For simplicity of exposition, we assume all sequences have length T, $\tau^k = (s_0, a_0)^k, (s_1, a_1)^k, \ldots, (s_{T-1}, a_{T-1})^k$, where $s_t \in S$ and $a_t \in A$.

If we assume that the trajectories are obtained by following a policy π^*, i.e. for each trajectory k and for each time step t, $(s_t, a_t)^k$ is such that $a_t = \pi^*(s_t)$, then a further natural modeling assumption that captures the rationality of the agents is that the policy π^* is an optimal policy with respect to the (unknown) reward function r (existence of an optimal policy is guaranteed, see (Puterman 2009; Bertsekas 1995)). Formally, this means that the expected policy value is such that $v^{\pi^*}(s) \geq v^{\pi}(s), \quad \forall s \in S, \quad \forall \pi$. Unfortunately, this formulation is known to be ill-posed because it is clearly under-determined. For example, if the reward function $r(\cdot) \equiv 0$, the optimality equation is satisfied by any policy π^*. Additional modeling assumptions are needed to resolve this ambiguity. One option is to introduce a margin (Ng and Russell 2000; Ratliff, Bagnell, and Zinkevich 2006), maximizing the difference between the reward from the optimal policy and its alternatives (Ng and Russell 2000).

Since our final goal is that of informing policy-making, we take a probabilistic approach and focus on *generative models* that can be used to simulate behavior under new circumstances such as changes in resource availability and policies. In the probabilistic approach, we assume the data (i.e., the observed trajectories $\mathcal{S}$) are samples from a family of probability distributions, which depend on the unknown reward function, allowing for suboptimal behavior. Estimating the reward function becomes a statistical inference problem. Notable approaches include Maximum entropy IRL (Ziebart et al. 2008) from the AI literature and Dynamic Discrete Choice models (Rust 1987) from the econometrics literature. We start by reviewing Maximum Entropy IRL (MaxEnt-IRL), which is the most closely related to our approach, and then review logit Dynamic Discrete Choice models (logit DDC), which will be the foundation for the work developed in this paper.

Maximum Entropy Inverse Reinforcement Learning Instead of assuming that the given trajectories follow an optimal policy, Ziebart et al. (Ziebart et al. 2008) assume that each observed trajectory $\tau^k = (s_0, a_0)^k, (s_1, a_1)^k, \ldots, (s_{T-1}, a_{T-1})^k$ is an i.i.d. sample from a probability distribution [1]:

$$P_\theta^{ME}(\tau^k) = \frac{\exp(U_\theta(s_0^k, \cdots, s_{T-1}^k))}{\sum_{\mathbf{s}'} \exp(U_\theta(\mathbf{s}'))} \tag{1}$$

where $U_\theta(s_0, \cdots, s_{T-1}) = \sum_t r(s_t) = \sum_t \theta \cdot \mathbf{f}_{s_t}$ and the sum is over are all possible trajectories of length T starting from state s_0. In this way, trajectories with higher total reward U are more likely to be sampled, but it is possible to observe sub-optimal behavior, specifically trajectories that do not provide the highest possible total reward. We can then recover the reward function by solving $\theta^*_{ME} = \arg\max_\theta \prod_{k=1}^K P_\theta^{ME}(\tau^k)$ to find the maximum likelihood estimate of the model parameters. The optimization problem is convex for deterministic MDPs, but not in general for stochastic MDPs (Ziebart et al. 2008).

[1] For simplicity, we report the above equation for a deterministic MDP and refer the reader to (Ziebart et al. 2008) for the general stochastic MDP case.

Dynamic Discrete Choice Modeling We will again assume that the decision makers do not always take optimal actions. This can be motivated by thinking about additional features (beyond the vector $\mathbf{f}_s$ we consider) that are taken into account by the agent but are not included in our model, hence giving rise to a behavior that is apparently not rational based on the data. When this effect is modeled as random noise affecting the decision process with an extreme value distribution, it gives rise to another stochastic model for the observed trajectories called logit Dynamic Discrete Choice (Rust 1987).

Specifically, in the dynamic discrete choice model it is assumed that at each step, the decision maker will not take the action with the largest future discounted utility, but instead will sample an action based on the following recursion:

$$V_\theta(s, a, T-1) = \theta \cdot \mathbf{f}_s, \quad \forall s \in S, \quad \forall a \in A \tag{2}$$

$$V_\theta(s, a, t) = \theta \cdot \mathbf{f}_s + \tag{3}$$

$$\eta \sum_{s' \in S} P(s'|s, a) \cdot \log\left(\sum_{a' \in A} \exp(V_\theta(s', a', t+1))\right)$$

The probability of choosing action a in state s at time t is defined as

$$p_\theta^{DC}(s, a, t) = \frac{\exp\left(V_\theta(s, a, t)\right)}{\sum_{a'} \exp\left(V_\theta(s, a', t)\right)} \tag{4}$$

$$P_\theta^{DC}(\tau^k) = \prod_{t=0}^{T-1} p_\theta^{DC}(s_t^k, a_t^k, t)$$

The model is then fitted to the data $\mathcal{S}$ by setting θ as to maximize the likelihood of the observed transitions:

$$\theta^*_{DC} = \arg\max_\theta \prod_{k=1}^{K} \prod_{t=0}^{T-1} p_\theta^{DC}(s_t^k, a_t^k, t)$$

$$= \arg\max_\theta \log\left(\prod_{k=1}^{K} \prod_{t=0}^{T-1} p_\theta^{DC}(s_t^k, a_t^k, t)\right) \tag{5}$$

We will use the following notation for the log-likelihood function: $L_\theta^{DC} = \log\left(\prod_{k=1}^K \prod_{t=0}^{T-1} p_\theta^{DC}(s_t^k, a_t^k, t)\right) = \sum_{k=1}^K \sum_{t=0}^{T-1} \log p_\theta^{DC}(s_t^k, a_t^k, t)$ and $L_\theta^{DC}(s, a, t) = \log p_\theta^{DC}(s, a, t)$.

The objective function is optimized using gradient descent (Rust method, (Rust 1987)). The exact gradient can be computed by differentiating the likelihood expression (5) with respect to θ. The objective is generally not convex/concave (Rust 1987).

An Equivalence Relationship

Although on the surface the Maximum Entropy IRL model (1) and the Dynamic Discrete Choice model (4) appear to be very different, we prove the models are equivalent under some conditions:

Theorem 1. *For finite horizon deterministic MDPs, under the MaxEnt-IRL and logit DDC with $\eta = 1$, for any trajectory $\tau = (s_0, a_0), (s_1, a_1), \ldots, (s_{T-1}, a_{T-1})$ we have:*

$$P_\theta^{ME}(\tau) = P_\theta^{DC}(\tau).$$

Proof. See (Ermon et al. 2014). □

Since the log likelihood (1) for the Maximum Entropy IRL model is concave, we also have the following Corollary:

Corollary 1. *For deterministic MDPs and $\eta = 1$, the log likelihood (5) for logit DDC is concave.*

If we allow the discount factor η to be a free parameter, the class of DDC models are therefore strictly more general than MaxEnt-IRL models for *deterministic MDPs*. Note that using a discounted total reward (with $\eta < 1$) to score paths in the MaxEnt-IRL model (1) is not very meaningful, because the effect is that of putting more "weight" on the transitions occurring at the beginning of the trajectories. In the extreme case $\eta = 0$, only the first action taken matters with respect to scoring paths. On the other hand, DDC models are meaningful even for $\eta = 0$, and they simply become "static" discrete choice models where *at each step in the trajectory* agents are only considering the reward collected at the next time step.

Learning Discrete Choice Models at Scale

The standard method for learning Discrete Choice Models (solving the optimization problem (5)), is to use gradient descent as in (Rust 1987). This approach starts with a random initial θ, and iteratively updates θ following the gradient direction, until convergence. Intuitively, one has to iteratively solve a planning problem with the current estimate of the reward function (current θ), compare the results with the data (actual trajectories $\mathcal{S}$), and update the parameters as to make the predictions match the empirical observations. Convergence can be improved using (truncated) quasi-Newton techniques such as the BFGS algorithm (Liu and Nocedal 1989), which is considered one of the best algorithms for unconstrained optimization. However, since the objective (5) is generally not convex, the method might get trapped in local optima.

Unfortunately, this technique is also not very scalable. In fact, evaluating the likelihood L_θ^{DC} of the data (and computing its gradient with respect to θ), is required in every iteration of the procedure, and this requires the computation of $V_\theta(s, a, t)$ for every $\forall t \in \{0, \ldots, T-1\}$, $\forall s \in S$ and $\forall a \in A$. Following a Dynamic Programming approach, computing $V_\theta(s, a, t)$ from the end of the horizon towards the beginning, results in complexity $O(T(|A| + |S|^2|A|^2))$ *per iteration*. This approach can be very expensive as a subroutine even for moderately sized MDPs.

Simultaneous Planning and Learning

Fitting the model using the gradient is expensive for large datasets and complex MDPs because at every iteration we have to: 1) go through the entire dataset, and 2) fill a Dynamic Programming (DP) table containing the $V_\theta(s, a, t)$ values. The first problem is ubiquitous in large scale machine learning, and a very popular and successful solution is to use stochastic gradient methods (Bottou and Bousquet 2008; Duchi, Hazan, and Singer 2011; Roux, Schmidt, and Bach 2012). The key idea is to trade off computational cost and accuracy in the computation of the gradient, which is approximated looking only at a (randomly chosen) subset of the training data. Unfortunately, in our case we still need to fill the entire Dynamic Programming table even to compute the gradient for a small subset of the training data. To overcome both scalability issues at the same time, we introduce a new scalable learning algorithm, called SPL-GD (**S**imultaneous **P**lanning And **L**earning - **G**radient **D**escent). Our technique uses approximate gradient estimates which can be efficiently computed exploiting the dynamic structure of the problem. We report the pseudocode of SPL-GD as Algorithm 1.

The key observation is that the log-likelihood from (5) can be decomposed according to time as $L_\theta^{DC} = \sum_{t=0}^{T-1} L_\theta^{DC}(t)$, where $L_\theta^{DC}(t) = \sum_{k=1}^{K} L_\theta^{DC}(s_t^k, a_t^k, t)$ represents the contribution from all the transitions from time t. Further notice from (4) and (3) that $L_\theta^{DC}(t_0)$ and its gradient $\nabla L_\theta^{DC}(t_0)$ depend only on $V_\theta(s, a, t')$ for $t' \geq t_0$.

Rather than updating θ using the full gradient $\nabla L_\theta^{DC} = \sum_{t=0}^{T-1} \nabla L_\theta^{DC}(t)$ (which requires the computation of the entire DP table), in SPL-GD we simultaneously update the current parameter estimate θ (Learning) *while we iterate* over time steps t to fill columns of the DP table (Planning). Specifically, while we iterate over time steps t from the end of the time horizon, we use an approximation of $\nabla L_\theta^{DC}(t)$ to update the current parameter estimate θ. After each update, we continue filling the next column of the DP table *using the new estimate* of θ rather than discarding the DP table and restarting.This introduces error in the estimates of $\nabla L_\theta^{DC}(t)$ because we are slowly annealing θ through the recursive calculation. However, we observe that with a small learning rate λ_j, the gradient estimates are sufficiently accurate for convergence. Notice that for $\eta = 0$ (if the discount factor is zero, the MDP is static) the bias disappears and SPL-GD corresponds to fitting $K \cdot T$ logistic models using a variant of mini-batch stochastic gradient descent (with a fixed ordering) where training data is divided into mini batches according to the time stamps t.

Empirical results In Figure 1 we report a runtime comparison between Algorithm 1 and the state-of-the-art batch BFGS (with analytic gradient, and approximate Hessian). The comparison is done using a small subset of our Borena plateau dataset (one month of data, $T = 30$) and the MDP model described in detail in the next section. We use a learning rate schedule $\lambda_j = \frac{1}{\sqrt{j}}$. We see that our algorithm is about 20 times faster than BFGS, even though BFGS is using approximate second-order information on the objective function. The advantage is even more significant on datasets covering longer time periods, where more gradient estimate updates occur per iteration.

Algorithm 1 SPL-GD ($\mathcal{S} = \{\tau^1, \cdots, \tau^K\}, \{\lambda_j\}$)

Initialize θ at random
for $j = 0, \cdots, M$ **do**
    for $t = T - 1, \cdots, 0$ **do**
        if t = T-1 **then**
            $V(s, a, T-1) = \theta \cdot \mathbf{f}_s, \quad \forall s \in S, \quad \forall a \in A$
            $\nabla V(s, a, T-1) = \mathbf{f}_s, \quad \forall s \in S, \quad \forall a \in A$
        else
            $V(s, a, t) = \theta \cdot \mathbf{f}_s + \eta \sum_{s' \in S} \left(\log\left(\sum_{a' \in A} \exp(V(s', a', t+1))\right)\right) P(s'|s, a), \quad \forall s \in S, \quad \forall a \in A$
            $\nabla V(s, a, t) = \mathbf{f}_s + \eta \sum_{s' \in S} \left(\frac{\sum_{a' \in A} \exp(V(s', a', t+1)) \nabla V(s', a', t+1)}{\sum_{a' \in A} \exp(V(s', a', t+1))}\right) P(s'|s, a), \quad \forall s \in S, \quad \forall a \in A$
        end if
        for $k = 1, \cdots, K$ **do**
            $\nabla L^{DC}(s_k^t, a_k^t, t) = \nabla V(s_k^t, a_k^t, t) - \frac{\sum_{a'} \exp\left(V(s_k^t, a', t)\right) \nabla V(s_k^t, a', t)}{\sum_{a'} \exp\left(V(s_k^t, a', t)\right)}$
            $\theta \leftarrow \theta + \lambda_j \nabla L^{DC}(s_k^t, a_k^t, t)$
        end for
    end for
end for
return θ

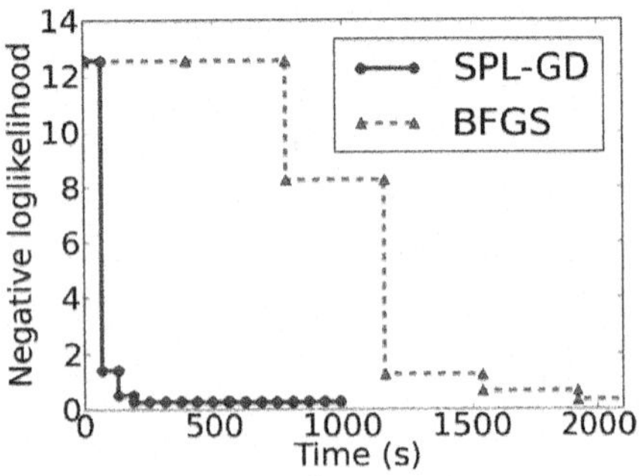

Figure 1: Runtime comparison between SPL-GD and BFGS. SPL-GD converges much faster than BFGS.

Modeling Pastoral Movements in Ethiopia

Our work is motivated by the study of spatio-temporal resource preferences of pastoralists and their cattle herds in the arid and semi-arid regions of Africa. Our overall goal is to develop a model for the planning decisions made by the herders, which is the focus of this paper, as well as the individual movements and consumption patterns of the cattle. This model must be *structural*, meaning that its parameters provide intuitive insight into the decision-making process, as well as *generative*, meaning that it can potentially be used to simulate behavior under new circumstances such as changes in resource availability, access policies, or climate.

Available Data: The available data includes survey data from individual households in the Borena plateau, Ethiopia; static geospatial map layers including village and road locations, ecosystem types, elevation and other terrain features; a dynamic greenness index (NDVI) at 250m × 250m (NASA LP DAAC 2014); locations of wells, ponds, and other water points identified by interview, field exploration, and satellite imagery; and GPS collar traces of 60 cattle from 20 households in 5 villages, at 5-minute intervals over sub-periods spread over 3 years. The GPS traces are our primary source of information regarding behavior and resource use.

State Space: The first modeling choice is the time scale of interest. Behaviorally, cattle could change movement patterns over minutes, while herding plans are likely to be made on a daily basis, though these might require multiple segments due to travel, sleep, etc. At the top level, the pastoralists migrate to remote camps as required to maintain access to nearby resources, as conditions change seasonally. While the end goal is a coupled model that incorporates these three scales (minutes, days, seasons), we have begun by focusing primarily on the migration decisions, which we represent as a decision whether to move to an alternate camp location each day. We extracted a list of observed camp locations by clustering the average GPS locations of the herds during the nighttime hours, across the entire time horizon for which we have collected data. There were nearly 200 camps that exhibited migration. We denote $C = \{c_1, c_2, \ldots, c_m\}$ the set of identified camping sites.

Features: We model the suitability of each campsite $c_i \in C$ as a function of a number of time-dependent features, which are generally selected data items listed above in their raw form and meaningful functions of those data. The features we considered are: distance from home village (a closer campsite might be more desirable than one far away), distance from major road, 8 variants of distance from closest water-point (based on different estimates of the seasonal availability of different classes of water points), and 2 representations of the greenness/vegetation index each intended to capture different spatio-temporal characteristics (normalized spatially over the Borena plateau region and temporally over 13 years of data).

MDP Modeling: We model each household as a self-interested agent who is rationally taking decisions as to optimize an (unknown) utility function over time. Intuitively, this utility function represents the net income from the economic activity undertaken, including intangibles. In our model, each household is assumed to plan on a daily basis the next campsite to use, so as to optimize their utility

Method	Fold 1		Fold 2		Fold 3		Fold 4	
	LogLik.	Moves (191)	LogLik.	Moves (85)	LogLik.	Moves (78)	LogLik.	Moves (116)
Markov	-8864.5	2209.8	-1807.8	372.2	-7265.7	1756.0	-4570.2	1214.1
MaxEnt IRL	-1524.4	424.6	-787.7	293.8	-796.7	339.7	-1004.2	299.4
Discrete Choice	**-1422.1**	**102.5**	**-657.8**	**104.9**	**-643.4**	**115.9**	**-911.3**	**94.9**

Table 1: Data log-likelihood and predicted total number of movements along all trajectories, evaluated in cross-validation on the held-out data, for each model. The actual number of camp movements is given in parentheses.

Figure 2: Trajectories (color denotes household), camps (circles), and waterpoints (triangles) for one village. Heavier trajectory lines illustrate movements in a one-month period during the wet season; faded lines denote movements during other times. Labels and other details omitted for privacy.

function looking ahead over the entire time horizon T. Formally, we model the problem as a Markov Decision Process as follows. Let $D = \{0, \cdots, T-1\}$. The action set is $A = C$, where each action corresponds to the next campsite to visit. We use an augmented state space $S = C \times C \times D$, where visiting a state $s = (c, c', t)$ means moving from camp c to c' at time t. This allows us to model the variability of the features over time and to incorporate information such as the distance between two campsites as state-based features. The MDP is deterministic, with transition probabilities $P((c_1', c_2', t)|(c_1, c_2, k), a) = 1$ iff $t = k+1$, $c_1' = c_2$, $c_2' = a$, and 0 otherwise. This means that if the agent transitioned from c_1 to c_2 at time k, and then takes action $a = c \in C$, it will transition from c_2 to c at time step $k+1$. We furthermore assume a utility function that is *linearly dependent* through θ in the features available to our model, and possibly additional information not available to the model. At present, we do not model competition or interactions between different households.

We then extract sequences of camping locations from the GPS collar data. These can be interpreted as K finite sequences of state-action pairs $\mathcal{S} = \{\tau^1, \cdots, \tau^K\}$ in our MDP model. A static illustration of the movements, camps and water points is shown in Figure 2. Our goal is to infer θ, i.e. to understand which factors drive the decision-making and what are the spatio-temporal preferences of the herders.

Results

We consider the dynamic discrete choice model, the maximum entropy IRL model and, as a baseline, a simple Markovian model that ignores the geo-spatial nature of the problem. For the Markov model, the assumption is that pastoralists at camp c_i will transition to camp c_j with probability p_{ij}. Equivalently, trajectories $\mathcal{S}$ are samples from a Markov Chain over C with transition probabilities p_{ij}, where the maximum likelihood estimate of the transition probabilities $\widehat{p}_{ij}$ is given by the empirical transition frequencies in the data, with Laplace smoothing for unobserved transitions.

We fit and evaluate the models in 4-fold cross-validation, in order to keep data from each household together, and stratify the folds by village. Training using SPL-GD on the entire 3-year dataset takes about 5 hours (depending on the initial condition and value of η), as opposed to several days using BFGS. We choose η in cross-validation with a grid search, selecting the value with the best likelihood on the training set.

We report results in Table 1. In addition to evaluating the likelihood of the trained model on the held-out test set, we also report the predicted number of transitions; although none of the models are explicitly trying to fit for this, it gives a sense of the accuracy and was used for example in (Kennan and Walker 2011).

The simple Markov model dramatically overfits, failing to generalize to unobserved camp transitions, and performs extremely poorly on the test set. The other models based on an underlying MDP formulation perform much better. We see that Dynamic Discrete Choice outperforms MaxEnt IRL: allowing the extra flexibility of choosing the discount factor does not lead to overfitting, and leads to improvements on all the folds. These results suggest that the features we consider are informative, and that considering discount factors other than $\eta = 1$ (as in the MaxEnt IRL model) is important to capture temporal discounting in the herders' decisions. The trained model recovers facts that are consistent with our intuition, e.g. herders prefer short travel distances, and allows us to quantitatively estimate these (relative) resource preferences. This provides exciting opportunities for simulation analysis by varying the exogenous characteristics of the system.

Conclusions

Motivated by the study of migratory pastoralism in the Borena plateau (Ethiopia) we study the general problem of inferring spatio-temporal resource preferences of agents from data. This is a very important problem in computational sustainability, as micro-behavioral models that capture the choice process of the agents in the system are crucial for policy-making concerning sustainable development.

We presented the Dynamic Discrete Choice model and showed a connection with Maximum Entropy IRL, a well known model from the machine learning community. To overcome some of the limitations of existing techniques to learn Discrete Choice models, we introduced SPL-GD, a novel learning algorithm that combines dynamic programming with stochastic gradient descent. Thanks to the improved scalability, we were able to train a model on a large dataset of GPS traces, surveys, and satellite information and other geospatial data for the Borena plateau area. The model obtained is generative and predictive, and outperforms competing approaches. As a next step, we plan to start using the model for for policy-relevant simulation analyses, as well as to couple it with optimization frameworks to allocate limited resources under budgetary constraints.

Acknowledgments

We gratefully acknowledge funding support from NSF Expeditions in Computing grant on Computational Sustainability (Award Number 0832782), the Computing research infrastructure for constraint optimization, machine learning, and dynamical models for Computational Sustainability grant (Award Number 1059284), Department of Foreign Affairs and Trade of Australia grant 2012 ADRAS 66138, and David R. Atkinson Center for a Sustainable Future grant #2011-RRF-sdd4.

References

Aguirregabiria, V., and Mira, P. 2010. Dynamic discrete choice structural models: A survey. *Journal of Econometrics* 156(1):38–67.

Ben-Akiva, M. E., and Lerman, S. R. 1985. *Discrete choice analysis: theory and application to travel demand*, volume 9. MIT press.

Bertsekas, D. 1995. *Dynamic programming and optimal control*, volume 1. Athena Scientific Belmont, MA.

Bottou, L., and Bousquet, O. 2008. The tradeoffs of large scale learning. In *Advances in Neural Information Processing Systems*, volume 20, 161–168.

Duchi, J.; Hazan, E.; and Singer, Y. 2011. Adaptive subgradient methods for online learning and stochastic optimization. *The Journal of Machine Learning Research* 12:2121–2159.

Ermon, S.; Xue, Y.; Toth, R.; Dilkina, B.; Bernstein, R.; Damoulas, T.; Clark, P.; DeGloria, S.; Mude, A.; Barrett, C.; and Gomes, C. 2014. Learning large-scale dynamic discrete choice models of spatio-temporal preferences with application to migratory pastoralism in East Africa. Technical report, Department of Computer Science, Cornell University.

Kennan, J., and Walker, J. R. 2011. The effect of expected income on individual migration decisions. *Econometrica* 79(1):211–251.

Kolter, J. Z., and Ng, A. Y. 2009. Regularization and feature selection in least-squares temporal difference learning. In *Proceedings of the 26th annual international conference on machine learning*, 521–528. ACM.

Liu, D. C., and Nocedal, J. 1989. On the limited memory bfgs method for large scale optimization. *Mathematical programming* 45(1-3):503–528.

NASA LP DAAC. 2014. MOD13Q1. Vegetation Indices 16-Day L3 Global 250m.

Ng, A. Y., and Russell, S. J. 2000. Algorithms for inverse reinforcement learning. In *ICML*, 663–670.

Powell, W. B. 2007. *Approximate Dynamic Programming: Solving the curses of dimensionality*, volume 703. John Wiley & Sons.

Puterman, M. L. 2009. *Markov decision processes: discrete stochastic dynamic programming*. John Wiley & Sons.

Ratliff, N. D.; Bagnell, J. A.; and Zinkevich, M. A. 2006. Maximum margin planning. In *Proceedings of the 23rd international conference on Machine learning*, 729–736. ACM.

Roux, N. L.; Schmidt, M.; and Bach, F. R. 2012. A stochastic gradient method with an exponential convergence _rate for finite training sets. In *Advances in Neural Information Processing Systems*, 2663–2671.

Rust, J. 1987. Optimal replacement of GMC bus engines: An empirical model of harold zurcher. *Econometrica: Journal of the Econometric Society* 999–1033.

Taylor, M. E., and Stone, P. 2009. Transfer learning for reinforcement learning domains: A survey. *The Journal of Machine Learning Research* 10:1633–1685.

Ziebart, B. D.; Maas, A. L.; Bagnell, J. A.; and Dey, A. K. 2008. Maximum entropy inverse reinforcement learning. In *AAAI*, 1433–1438.

Proceedings of the Twenty-Ninth AAAI Conference on Artificial Intelligence

A Nonparametric Online Model for Air Quality Prediction

Vitor Guizilini[1] and **Fabio Ramos**[1,2]
[1]National ICT Australia (NICTA),
[2]School of Information Technologies, The University of Sydney, Australia.

Abstract

We introduce a novel method for the continuous online prediction of particulate matter in the air (more specifically, PM10 and PM2.5) given sparse sensor information. A nonparametric model is developed using Gaussian Processes, which eschews the need for an explicit formulation of internal – and usually very complex – dependencies between meteorological variables. Instead, it uses historical data to extrapolate pollutant values both spatially (in areas with no sensor information) and temporally (the near future). Each prediction also contains a respective variance, indicating its uncertainty level and thus allowing a probabilistic treatment of results. A novel training methodology (Structural Cross-Validation) is presented, which preserves the spatio-temporal structure of available data during the hyperparameter optimization process. Tests were conducted using a real-time feed from a sensor network in an area of roughly 50×80 km, alongside comparisons with other techniques for air pollution prediction. The promising results motivated the development of a smartphone applicative and a website, currently in use to increase the efficiency of air quality monitoring and control in the area.

Introduction

Real-Time Air Quality Forecast (RT-AQF), although a fairly new discipline in atmospheric sciences, represents one of the most far-reaching developments and practical applications of science and engineering (Zhang et al. 2012a). Numerous studies (Phalen and Phalen 2011; Greenbaum et al. 2001) show that even acute (short-term) exposure to high level of air pollutants may pose serious health consequences, such as eye irritation, difficulty breathing, pulmonary, cardiovascular health effects and premature death. Chronic (long-term) exposure may lead to cancer, premature death and damage to the body's immune, neurological, reproductive and respiratory systems. The US. Environmental Protection Agency (EPA) has set air quality standards for six air pollutants: sulfur dioxide (SO_2), nitrogen dioxide (NO_2), carbon monoxide (CO), ozone (O_3), lead (Pb) and particulate matter with aerodynamic diameters less than or equal to 10 μm (PM10) and 2.5 μm (PM2.5). Despite these efforts, air pollution is estimated to kill 3 million people worldwide, and PM pollution in particular has been directly linked to excess deaths in many countries.

The first RT-AQF techniques were developed in the 1970s, based largely on empirical or statistically trained models (McCollister and Wilson 1975; Wolff and Lioy 1978). The sophistication level of such models increased considerably over time to address challenges, such as nonlinearity (Ryan 1995). The development of 3-D numerical air quality models (AQMs) on urban, regional and global scales (Zhang et al. 2012a) also led to significant performance improvements, introducing systems that account for meteorology, emissions, chemistry and removal processes (Zhang 2008; Russel and Dennis 2000). Another performance leap was due to the first real-time data repositories (U.S. EPA 2009), providing effective platforms for continuously communicating air quality conditions and forecasts to the public via the internet and other medias.

Broadly speaking, techniques for RT-AQF can be divided into three categories (Wayland 2002):

Criteria Schemes: Employ rules-of-thumb or thresholds to predict the future state of air quality. For example, if the temperature forecast if above 30°C, then a photochemical smog event will occur. Another example, often surprisingly robust, is persistence, which means assuming that the air quality tomorrow will be similar to today's (U.S. EPA 2003).

Deterministic methods: Attempt to simulate the underlying chemical and physical process of air pollution production. Usually requires a lot of computational power, and takes into consideration variables such as meteorological conditions, gaseous and particle emissions, chemical reactions and nature of surface (Zhang et al. 2012a; Zhang 2008),.

Nonparametric models: An increasingly popular approach that makes predictions based on patterns in past meteorological, traffic and air quality data, using regression or neural network systems. For example: multiple non-linear regression relations for radiation and temperature might be use to predict peak ozone concentrations (Athanasiadis et al. 2003; Marchant and Ramos 2012; Athanasiadis and Mitkas 2004).

A detailed list of different methods currently used throughout the world can be found in (Cope and Hess

2005). Current state-of-the-art (Zhang et al. 2012b) include 3-D online-coupled meteorology-chemistry models, based on global and regional CTMs (Chemical Transport Models) that enable a better understanding of mechanisms for pollutant formation and development of emission control strategies. Extension to these models include their coupling with urban models (traffic and/or local pollutant dispersion) or a CFD model for urban/local scale applications.

The deterministic approaches rely on parametric models that must be carefully constructed by experts according to which phenomenon is being studied. A balance must be reached between complexity and computational power, which imposes a limit to how many variables can be incorporated, as well as their mutual correlations. This work takes a different approach and looks into RT-AQF from a machine learning perspective, with historically accurate measurements being used to extrapolate the value of a target variable (particulate matter concentration) both in time (the near future) and space (where there are no sensor measurements). In fact, this approach is particularly useful in such problems due to their chaotic nature: the number of contributing factors is so high that no deterministic model will ever be able to capture all its nuances, and even minor imprecisions on initial conditions will produce vastly different outcomes.

Commonly used methods include classification and regression trees (Burrows et al. 1995), artificial neural networks (Perez and Reyes 2006), fuzzy logic (Shad et al. 2009) and variations of the Kalman Filter (van der Wal and Janssen 2000; Zolghadri and Cazaurang 2006). This paper introduces the use of Gaussian processes as a machine learning tool for air quality forecast, and develops a novel framework for the training and continuous update of the nonparametric model over spatio-temporal data. This framework is able to learn periodical patterns in previous measurements in order to probabilistically predict their values in unobserved areas of the input space, as well as gradually adapt to new behaviors as more information is incorporated into the starting model. A novel training methodology is proposed, named *Structural Cross-Validation*, that is shown to improve accuracy by minimizing an error function while maintaining the spatio-temporal structure of available data. We also explore the use of other environmental variables, such as temperature, humidity and wind, to improve the accuracy of PM10 and PM2.5 predictions.

Overview on Gaussian Processes

The task of estimating air pollutant values from historical data can be seen as a regression problem, where available information is extrapolated to areas of the input space with no direct measurements. While most current approaches use a carefully developed model involving different relevant variables and their correlations, there is a limit to how many variables can be used, and a limit to how complex these correlations can become before the resulting model is rendered computationally unfeasible.

We opted here to go in a different direction and use a nonparametric model, in particular a Gaussian Process (Rasmussen and Williams 2006), to generate the transformation function between inputs and outputs. This approach eliminates the need to explicitly define a model, using instead previous measurements to extract patterns and then extrapolate this information to new, unobserved areas of the input space. This allows for greater flexibility and generality, and we show how to maintain computational complexity under check while achieving a good approximation of the underlying function.

Inference

We start with a set of N observations $\mathbf{y} = \{y_n\}_{n=1}^N$ and its corresponding spatio-temporal coordinates $X = \{\mathbf{x}_n\}_{n=1}^N$, where $\mathbf{x}_n = \{x, y, t\}_n$ contains latitude, longitude and time components. The goal is to estimate a continuous transformation function $f(\mathbf{x}_n)$ between inputs and outputs, thus allowing inference to be performed in unknown regions of the input space. The closer these regions are to the available data, the more accurate the final estimation will be, as it is to be expected.

This proximity is defined by a covariance function $k(x_i, x_j)$, or kernel, which imposes a metric that quantifies how close any two input points are to each other. From this covariance function the covariance matrix K is generated, with components $K_{ij} = k(\mathbf{x}_i, \mathbf{x}_j)$. Inference on a test point $\mathbf{x}_*$ is then of the form:

$$\bar{f}_* = m(\mathbf{x}_*) + K_{*N}\tilde{K}_{NN}^{-1}(\mathbf{y} - m(X)) \tag{1}$$

$$v_* = K_{**} - K_{*N}\tilde{K}_{NN}^{-1}K_{N*}, \tag{2}$$

where $\tilde{K}_{NN} = K_{NN} + \sigma_n^2 I$ is the covariance matrix K_{NN} disturbed by zero-mean Gaussian noise of variance σ_n^2 and $m(.)$ is a mean function selected as part of the nonparametric model. The covariance function parameters θ_k, the mean function parameters θ_m and the noise level σ_n, compose the hyperparameter set $\theta = (\theta_k, \theta_m, \sigma_n)$ that defines the GP model. These values can be optimized based on available data by maximizing a certain objective function, usually the log-marginal likelihood (Rasmussen and Williams 2006) due to its balance between complexity and data fit that avoids overfitting.

Covariance Functions

As stated previously, the choice of covariance function plays a pivotal role in the predictive power of a nonparametric model. For the particular case of air pollutant prediction (or any environmental phenomenon), we are particularly interested in temporal trends, that repeat over time in a cyclical manner. For this reason, two different covariance functions were selected, the *Matérn* 3/2 (Eq. 3) and the *Periodic* (Eq. 4), the first to account for short and medium-term trends and the second to account for cyclical patterns:

$$k_{MT} = \theta_v^2 \left(1 + \frac{\sqrt{3}r}{\theta_l^2}\right) \exp\left(-\frac{\sqrt{3}r}{\theta_l^2}\right), \tag{3}$$

$$k_{PR} = \theta_v^2 \exp\left(\frac{-2\sin^2\left(\frac{r}{\theta_p}\right)}{\theta_l^2}\right). \tag{4}$$

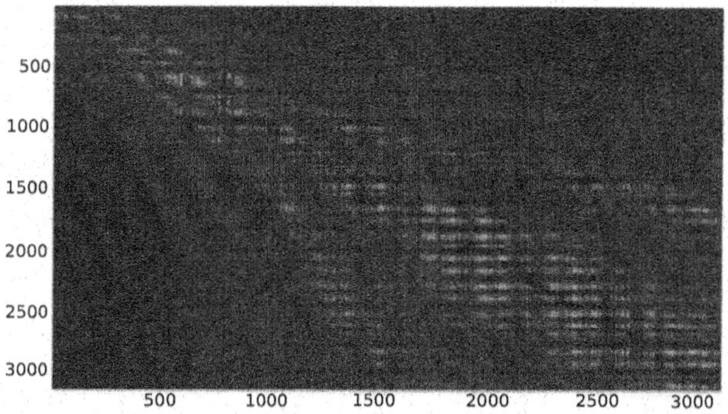

Figure 1: Example of the covariance matrix K, based on Eq. 5. The diagonal area is more closely related, due to the temporal Matérn covariance function, and the various waves indicate different periodic cycles, that gradually lose strength due to decay. The chess pattern is due to spatial correlation, that distantiates points that are physically far away.

In the above equations, $r = |\mathbf{x}_i - \mathbf{x}_j|$ is the distance between input points and the various θ parameters compose the covariance function coefficients θ_k that will be optimized during the training stage. The final spatio-temporal covariance function (Fig. 1) is then of the form:

$$k = \left(k_{MT}^{xy} + k_{MT}^{xy}\right) \times \left(k_{MT}^{t} + \sum_{p=1}^{P} k_{MT}^{t} k_{PR}^{t(p)}\right). \quad (5)$$

We can see that the spatial and temporal components of the covariance function are calculated separately and multiplied at the end. Spatially, two Matérns account for short and medium-scale behavioral changes in air pollutant concentration, while temporally there is one Matérn for short-term trends and a series of Periodics to model cyclical patterns. Each Periodic, in turn, is multiplied by a Matérn to account for decay, where the effects of old behaviors slowly fade away as the time interval increases.

Frequency Analysis

Every signal, no matter its complexity, is composed of basic waves, and as more waves are used to represent it, the closer the approximation becomes to the original. However, it is impossible to use all frequencies to describe a signal, and therefore it is necessary to select which ones are more relevant to the application at hand. Also, while the GP framework is capable of learning specific frequency parameters (the θ_p in Eq. 4), it is vital that a good initial estimate is provided due to the presence of local maxima in the objective function.

For this reason, a frequency analysis (Terras 2011) is first conducted on the available data to find its wave components in descending order of relevance (Fig. 2). The first P components are used as starting values for the periodic hyperparameters, and further optimized during the training stage. The upper limit for the number of frequencies used by the nonparametric model is given by the increase in hyperparameter quantity, that affects training times and may create overfitting scenarios.

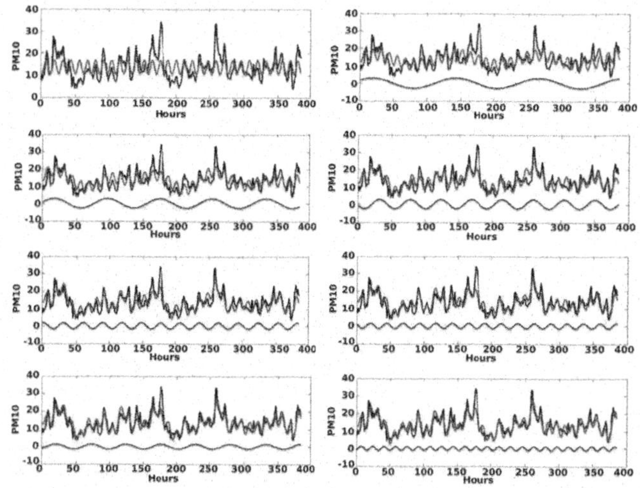

Figure 2: Frequency analysis on hourly measurement of air pollutant concentrations. Starting from the top left, each image incorporates a new frequency into the estimate (blue line), and it is possible to see how the resulting approximation (red line) starts to resemble the true signal (black line).

Sub-sampling

A common drawback in the standard GP derivation (as in most machine learning algorithms) is the computational cost, that scales cubically with the number of training points. This imposes a limit to the amount of available data that can be maintained for training and inference purposes, which is especially detrimental to this application due to the presence of periodic functions that could in theory go back months or even years in time.

For this reason, a novel sub-sampling method is proposed, which exploits the cyclical nature of periodic covariance functions to remove data that will be less correlated to the test points (Fig. 3). This can be achieved by setting up a threshold level δ for the correlation value that is deemed relevant, and discarding all points that fall below this threshold:

$$\{X, \mathbf{y}\}_{PR}^{t(p)} = \left\{(\mathbf{x}, y)_n \mid k_{PR}^{t(p)}(\mathbf{x}_n, \mathbf{x}_*) > \delta\right\}_{n=1}^{N}. \quad (6)$$

Since the periodic hyperparameters are known (albeit changing during the training stage), they can be used to determine these intervals without the need to calculate every correlation. The resulting subset can then be efficiently obtained by means of simple comparisons between the temporal components:

$$\{X, \mathbf{y}\}_{PR}^{t(p)} = \left\{(\mathbf{x}, y)_n \mid \bigcup_{i=1}^{M} d(t_* - pi, t_n) < \theta_l h(p)\right\}_{n=1}^{N}, \quad (7)$$

where $d(x, y) = |x - y|$, M is the number of historical periods to be considered and $h(p)$ is the interval of hours considered, which is itself a function of p (empirically we determined $h(p) = \sqrt{p}$ to be a suitable interval function). This process is repeated for each periodic covariance function, generating the subset $\{X, \mathbf{y}\}_{PR}^{t} = \bigcup_{p=1}^{P} \{X, \mathbf{y}\}_{PR}^{t(p)}$ that is

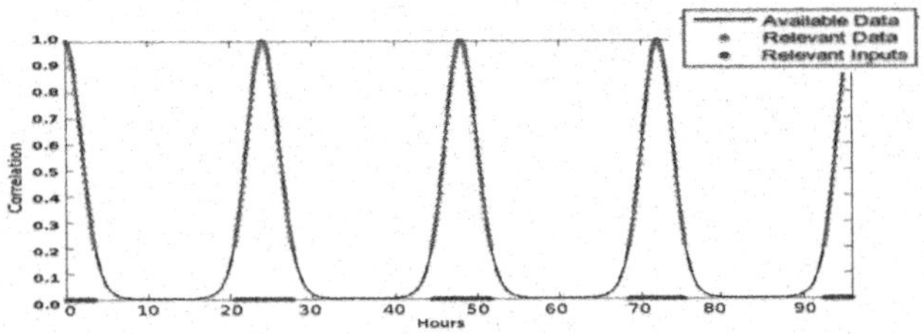

Figure 3: Example of subsampling, for a periodic covariance function with a period $\theta_p = 24$ hours and length-scale $\theta_l = 0.5$. With this configuration, only roughly 30% of the points are used during training and inference.

most correlated to the test points given the necessary computational constraints. This method is particularly useful with longer periods and smaller length-scales, since this configuration tends to create sharp peaks with larger areas of virtually no correlation.

Training Methodology

The aforementioned sub-sampling method, while effective in decreasing the amount of data used for inference, has the drawback of being sensitive to the test point coordinates, since correlation is calculated in relation to that particular timestep. For this reason, we propose a novel training methodology that not only exploits this behavior to produce models optimized for different future predictions, but also maintains during training the same spatio-temporal structure available for inference. We also propose a technique to incorporate extra environmental variables into the prediction of air pollutant concentrations, by combining individually trained base models.

Structural Cross-Validation

The proposed training methodology resembles the traditional Cross-Validation (CV) approach, in the sense that an error function between ground-truth and estimates is minimized. However, this minimization is conducted while maintaining the same spatio-temporal structure that will be available during inference. We start from the design assumption that, during the inference stage, at each timestep k two actions are performed:

1. **Update:** New available measurements are incorporated into the nonparametric model:

$$\{X, \mathbf{y}\}^{1:k} = \left[\{X, \mathbf{y}\}^{1:k-1}, \{X, \mathbf{y}\}^{k}\right] \tag{8}$$

2. **Prediction:** A new estimate set is obtained for h timesteps into the future (Eqs. 1 and 2):

$$f_*^{k+h} = \mathcal{GP}(\mathbf{x}_*^{k+h} | \{X, \mathbf{y}\}^{1:k}, \theta^k). \tag{9}$$

By constantly adding new information to the nonparametric model, we ensure that predictions will always be at a fixed distance h from available data, and thus will have similar variance values. Gaps in data (such as sensor failure) are treated naturally by an increase in variance values, that is restored to normal levels once new information becomes available.

For the training stage, each estimate also contains its respective ground-truth, which allows for a third step:

3. **Error Calculation:** The estimate set is compared to their respective ground-truths, according to an error metric $e(.,.)$, and a measure of accuracy ζ is produced:

$$\zeta^k = e(f_*^{k+h}, \mathbf{y}^{k+h}). \tag{10}$$

A diagram of the proposed Structural Cross-Validation algorithm is depicted in Fig. 4. Initially, the available data is divided into two subsets: *starting model* $\{X, \mathbf{y}\}^{1:S}$ and *evaluation data* $\{X, \mathbf{y}\}^{S+1:N}$. Each training step is performed by incrementally (1) incorporating evaluation data from the current timestep into the starting model; (2) performing inference on evaluation data from h timesteps ahead; and (3) comparing these estimates to the actual measurements to generate error values. The accumulated error $\zeta = \sum_{k=S+1}^{N} \zeta^k$ quantifies the adequacy of the current nonparametric model, and is minimized using standard gradient-descend techniques.

Note that, while the final model can be used to perform inference at any spatio-temporal coordinate, it will be optimized for the timestep h used during training. This allows the generation of specific models for different timesteps, that will provide better estimates than a generic one. The same training process can be maintained during the inference stage, taking advantage of the interval between timesteps to further optimize the hyperparameters based on new information. This allows the nonparametric model to gradually adapt to new behaviors and forget old ones, a vital characteristic for long-term usability.

Extra Variables

Here another issue is explored: the incorporation of extra variables into the nonparametric model for the prediction of air pollutant concentrations. Several environmental factors, such as temperature, humidity and wind, may be responsible for changes in air pollutant concentrations, and therefore could be used to improve estimates. A straightforward approach would be the use of multiple-output GPs (Boyle and Frean 2005), but this would create an even bigger computational cost, due to the need of simultaneously maintain all variables and their correlations.

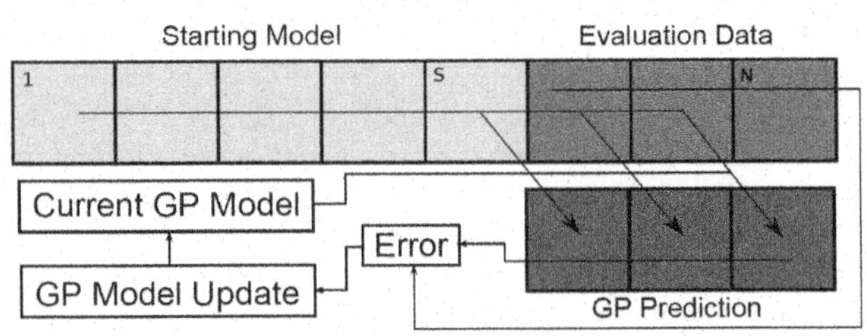

Figure 4: Diagram of the Structural Cross-Validation technique.

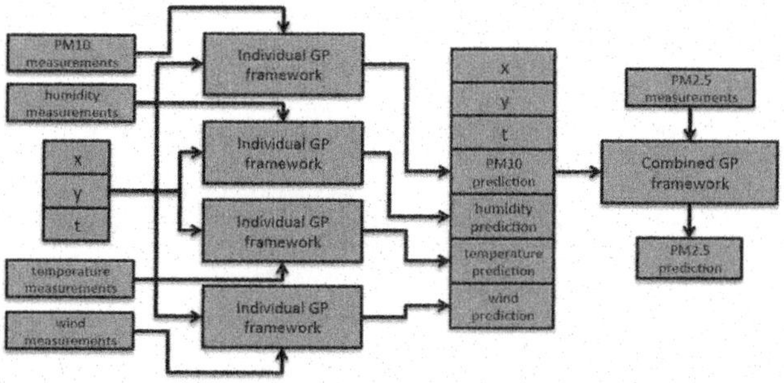

Figure 5: Diagram of the framework for incorporating extra variables.

Because of that, we propose a layered model that combines different base models to increase the amount of information available for inference, without significantly affecting computational time and memory requirements. A diagram of this layered model is depicted in Fig. 5, for the particular case of using PM10, humidity, temperature and wind to predict PM2.5 concentrations. Each one of these extra variables receives the measurements coordinates $\mathbf{x} = \{x, y, t\}$ and their respective ground-truth to produce its own base model. The predictions from these base models are used to augment the input vector for the combined model, which is then trained based on its own ground-truth information. During inference, further optimization can be performed individually for each base model, and afterwards the new estimates are used to further optimize the combined model.

Experimental Results

Tests were conducted using a sensor network composed of 14 sensors, covering an area of roughly 50×80 km. All sensors provide hourly measurements of PM10, temperature (TP), humidity (HM) and wind (WD), and three of these

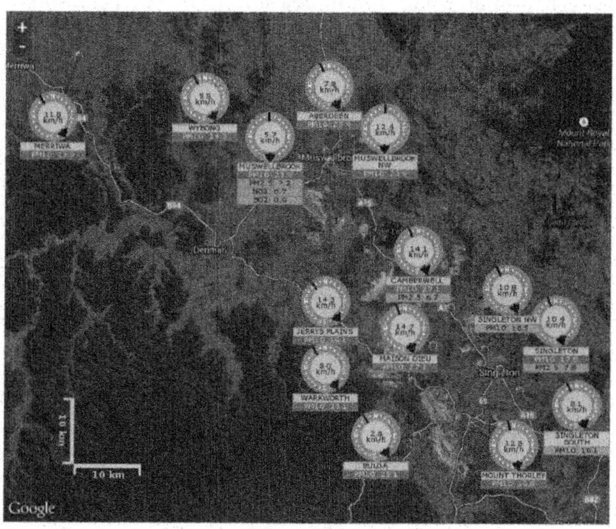

Figure 6: Sensor network used during experiments.

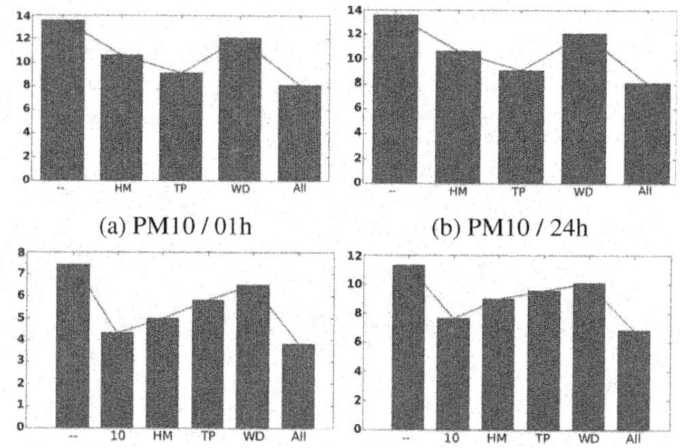

(a) PM10 / 01h (b) PM10 / 24h

(c) PM2.5 / 01h (d) PM2.5 / 24h

Figure 7: Performance improvement given by the incorporation of extra variables, according to the error metric used during optimization (average over 1 month period).

sensors also provide hourly PM2.5 measurements. The goal was to generate predictive estimates for 1 and 24 hours into the future, as well as in the area surrounding the sensors. In all experiments, a time interval of 3 months was used for training (2 for the starting model and 1 for evaluation), with initial periods of 24, 48, 168 and 672 hours. As new data is incorporated, old data is removed at the same rate. Priority was given to sudden increases in pollutant concentration, since these are the relevant behaviors in air quality control. It is worthy noting that RT-AQF models notoriously struggle with hourly and daily estimates, usually performing better in larger time-scales.

A different base model was trained based on each of these variables, and then combined to generate the final models for PM10 and PM2.5 (PM10 measurements were also used to improve PM2.5 estimates). The improvement generated by the incorporation of each extra variables can be seen in Fig. 7, as well as the improvement generated by the inclusion of all of them. We can see that, for PM10, adding temperature produced the largest improvement, while for PM2.5 it was the introduction of PM10 estimates, followed by humidity. In all cases, the combined model was capable of greatly improving performance, roughly doubling accuracy by maintaining base models of extra variables.

Another way of quantifying the improvement proportioned by the incorporation of extra variables is with QQ-plots; a graphical method for comparing two probability distributions, by plotting their quantiles against each other. If the two distributions are linearly related, the points in the QQ-plot will approximately lie on a line, and any non-linearity will generate deviations. The QQ-plots for base and combined models are shown in Fig. 8, where we can see that the introduction of extra variables is indeed capable of approximating the prediction and measurement distributions. As expected, the algorithm performs less accurately in areas of high pollution value, since these are sporadic and the non-parametric model does not have enough samples for a robust

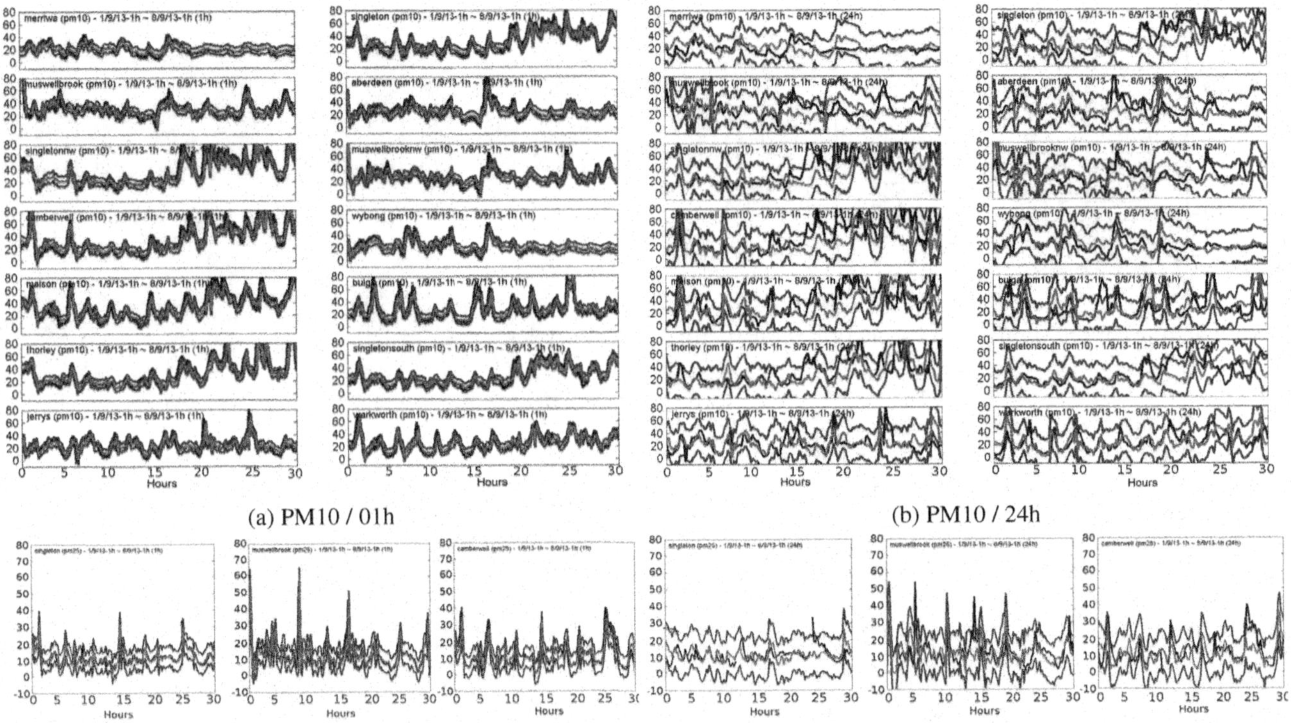

(a) PM10 / 01h (b) PM10 / 24h

(c) PM2.5 / 01h (d) PM2.5 / 24h

Figure 9: Comparison between GP estimates (red line) and actual sensor measurements (black line), within two standard deviations (blue lines) over the course of 1 month.

estimate. A quantitative comparison between these results and other approaches is given in Table 1.

The progression of predictions over time, for each sensor, can be seen in Fig. 9, alongside the actual measurements and the corresponding 95% confidence boundaries. As expected, 1 hour predictions are very accurate, and this performance decreases as we move away from test data. Note that the estimates are still within the confidence boundaries, indicating that the nonparametric model is able to correctly gauge the accuracy of its own predictions. These estimates can then be used to prevent high peaks in air pollutant concentrations by taking cautionary measures in areas of highest probability of reaching hazardous thresholds.

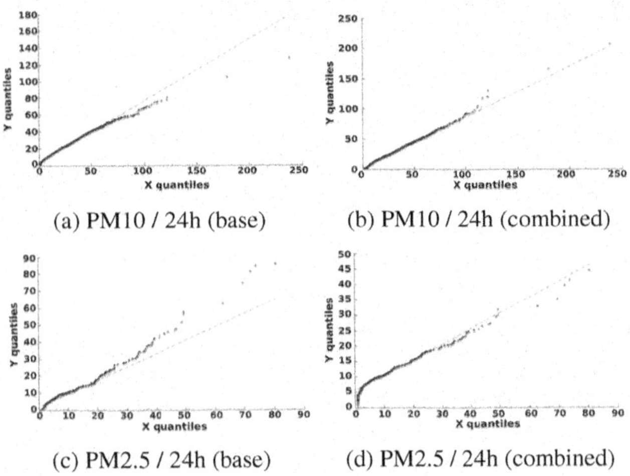

(a) PM10 / 24h (base) (b) PM10 / 24h (combined)

(c) PM2.5 / 24h (base) (d) PM2.5 / 24h (combined)

Figure 8: QQ-Plots for PM10 and PM2.5.

Poll. / # hours	SCV-GP	PERS	FITC	CART
PM10 / 1h	**8.48**	14.67	10.42	9.91
PM10 / 24h	**13.21**	22.09	18.29	17.27
PM2.5 / 1h	**3.92**	6.89	5.11	4.83
PM2.5 / 24h	**5.05**	11.93	9.98	9.11

Table 1: Root Mean Square Error comparison between the proposed algorithm (SCV-GP) and the persistent approach (PERS), a sparse GP implementation (FITC, (Quinonero-candela, Ramussen, and Williams 2007)) and decision trees (CART, (Breiman et al. 1984)). The same extra variables were used in all experiments (where applicable).

Conclusion

We presented a novel algorithm for the online prediction of air particulate matter (PM10 and PM2.5) that relies on a nonparametric model to extract patterns from historical data and uses this information to estimate future behaviors, both spatially and temporally. This is a purely nonparametric approach, without any assumptions regarding the physical and chemical aspects of air pollution, and therefore could be readily applied to any spatio-temporal predictive scenario. It scales linearly to the number of extra variables, and is able to incorporate new information as it becomes available. The probabilistic nature of GPs allows the generation of uncertainty values alongside the estimates in an intuitive manner that can be easily understood by the final user. In future work we intend to explore the use of mobile sensors, as a way to maximize coverage without the need to increase the network size. More powerful modeling techniques will also be explored, such as nonstationarity and heteroscedasticity.

Acknowledgements

NICTA is funded by the Australian Government through the Department of Communications and the Australian Research Council through the ICT Centre of Excellence Program.

References

Athanasiadis, I. N., and Mitkas, P. A. 2004. An agent-based intelligent environmental monitoring system. *CoRR.*

Athanasiadis, I. N.; Kaburlasos, V. G.; Mitkas, P. A.; and Petridis, V. 2003. Applying machine learning techniques on air quality data for real-time decision support. In *In: First International NAISO Symposium on Information Technologies in Environmental Engineering (ITEE'2003*, 24–27. ICSC-NAISO Publishers.

Boyle, P., and Frean, M. 2005. Multiple output gaussian process regression. Technical report, University of Wellington.

Breiman, L.; Friedman, J.; Olshen, R.; and Stone, C. 1984. *Classification and Regression Trees.* Monterey, CA: Wadsworth and Brooks.

Burrows, W. R.; Benjamin, M.; Beauchamp, S.; Lord, E. R.; McCollor, D.; and Thomson, B. 1995. CART Decision-Tree Statistical Analysis and Prediction of Summer Season Maximum Surface Ozone for the Vancouver, Montreal, and Atlantic Regions of Canada. *Journal of Applied Meteorology* 34:1848–1862.

Cope, M. E., and Hess, G. D. 2005. Air quality forecasting: a review and comparison of the approaches used internationally and in australia. *Clean Air and Environmental Quality* 39:39–45.

Greenbaum, D. S.; Bachmann, J. D.; Krewski, D.; Samet, J. M.; White, R.; and Wyzga, R. E. 2001. Particulate air pollution standards and morbidity and mortality: case study. *Americal Journal Epidemiology* 154(12 Suppl):S78–90.

Marchant, R., and Ramos, F. 2012. Bayesian optimisation for intelligent environmental monitoring. In *IROS*, 2242–2249. IEEE.

McCollister, G., and Wilson, K. 1975. Linear stochastic models for forecasting daily maxima and hourly concentrations of air pollutants. *Atmospheric Environment* 9:417–423.

Perez, P., and Reyes, J. 2006. An integrated neural network model for PM10 forecasting. *Atmospheric Environment* 40(16):2845 – 2851.

Phalen, R., and Phalen, R. 2011. *Introduction to Air Pollution Science.* Jones and Bartlett Learning.

Quinonero-candela, J.; Ramussen, C. E.; and Williams, C. K. I. 2007. Approximation methods for gaussian process regression.

Rasmussen, C. E., and Williams, K. I. 2006. *Gaussian Processes for Machine Learning.* The MIT Press.

Russel, A., and Dennis, R. 2000. Narsto critical review of photochemical models and modeling. *Atmospheric Environment* 34:2283–2324.

Ryan, W. F. 1995. Forecasting ozone episodes in the baltimore metropolitan area. *Atmospheric Environment* 29:2387–2398.

Shad, R.; Mesgari, M. S.; abkar, A.; and Shad, A. 2009. Predicting air pollution using fuzzy genetic linear membership kriging in GIS. *Computers, Environment and Urban Systems* 33(6):472 – 481.

Terras, A. 2011. *Fourier analysis on finite groups and applications.* Cambridge University Press.

U.S. EPA. 2003. Technical assistance document for reporting of daily air quality - air quality index (AQI). Technical report, Environmental Protection Agency, Office of Air Quality Planning and Standards, Research Triangle Park, NC.

U.S. EPA. 2009. Technical assistance document for reporting of daily air quality - air quality index (AQI). Technical report, Environmental Protection Agency, Office of Air Quality Planning and Standards, Research Triangle Park, NC.

van der Wal, J., and Janssen, L. 2000. Analysis of spatial and temporal variations of PM 10 concentrations in the netherlands using kalman filtering. *Atmospheric Environment* 34(22):3675 – 3687.

Wayland, R. 2002. Communicating real-time and forecasted air quality to the public. *Environment Management.*

Wolff, G. T., and Lioy, P. J. 1978. An empirical model for forecasting maximum daily ozone levels in the northeastern united states. *Journal of Air Pollution Control Association* 28:1034–1038.

Zhang, Y.; Bocquet, M.; Mallet, V.; Seigneur, C.; and Baklanov, A. 2012a. Real-time air quality forecasting, part i: History, techniques, and current status. *Atmospheric Environment* 60:632–655.

Zhang, Y.; Bocquet, M.; Mallet, V.; Seigneur, C.; and Baklanov, A. 2012b. Real-time air quality forecasting, part ii: State of the science, current research needs, and future prospects. *Atmospheric Environment* 60:656–676.

Zhang, Y. 2008. Online coupled meteorology and chemistry models: History, current status, and outlook. *Atmospheric Chemistry and Physics Discussions* 8:1833–1912.

Zolghadri, A., and Cazaurang, F. 2006. Adaptive nonlinear state-space modelling for the prediction of daily mean PM10 concentrations. *Environmental Modelling and Software* 21(6):885 – 894.

Power System Restoration With Transient Stability

Hassan Hijazi and **Terrence W.K. Mak** and **Pascal Van Hentenryck**
NICTA and Australian National University
7 London Circuit, Canberra, ACT 2601, Australia
{Hassan.Hijazi,Terrence.Mak,Pascal.Vanhentenryck}@nicta.com.au

Abstract

We address the problem of power system restoration after a significant blackout. Prior work focus on optimization methods for finding high-quality restoration plans. Optimal solutions consist in a sequence of grid repairs and corresponding steady states. However, such approaches lack formal guarantees on the transient stability of restoration actions, a key property to avoid additional grid damage and cascading failures. In this paper, we show how to integrate transient stability in the optimization procedure by capturing the rotor dynamics of power generators. Our approach reasons about the differential equations describing the dynamics and their underlying transient states. The key contribution lies in modeling and solving optimization problems that return stable generators dispatch minimizing the difference with respect to steady states solutions. Computational efficiency is increased using preprocessing procedures along with traditional reduction techniques. Experimental results on existing benchmarks confirm the feasibility of the new approach.

Introduction

Power system restoration is a key ingredient in defining the self-healing property of the future smart grid. Restoration plans are generated automatically using smart optimization procedures, reducing the cost and the inconvenience caused by blackouts. A restoration plan consists in a set of repair actions, such as connecting or disconnecting a line. The primary objective is to isolate faulty equipments while maximizing the percentage of load recovery. The problem has a time dimension related to the ordering of the repair actions. This ordering has a direct influence on the load recovery over time. It is, for instance, natural to favor early load recoveries. This captures the essence behind the Restoration Ordering Problem which is at the core of this paper. Traditionally, this problem is addressed with simplifying assumptions, e.g., ignoring ramping rates of generators but, most importantly, disregarding transient stability during line switching. Incorporating operational limits on transient states is computationally challenging, as they are defined using partial differential equations (PDEs). Existing discrete optimization tools cannot deal with such non-algebraic expressions. In our context, this refers to the ability to reason about the power system transient states over a short period of time (e.g., a few seconds) after the line closing.

In this work, we focus on capturing the dynamics of generator rotor angles as a measure of transient stability related to switching operations in transmission networks. Our contributions are based on a few key ideas:

1. We use rotor angle stability, a traditional metric to assess the transient stability of a system, and the classical model of generator dynamics based on the Swing equations (Kundur, Balu, and Lauby 1994).
2. We capture transient states through a discretization of the dynamics model, including a nonlinear formulation of the power flow equations on these transient states.
3. For each restoration step, we define an optimization model that finds a transient-stable generator dispatch minimizing the difference with respect to the steady state solution. This ensures that the size of the blackouts increase as little as possible while ensuring transient stability.

More generally, this paper can be viewed as a novel, hierarchical approach to the optimization of complex hybrid dynamic systems. Given a static version of the models, the key idea relies in adjusting optimal steady-state solutions taking into account the system dynamics. The overall computational tractability is thus improved.

Related Work

Our work is closely related to the transient-stable optimal power flow problem, which was first proposed by Gan et al. (Gan, Thomas, and Zimmerman 2000). The problem was later extended to multi-contingency settings in (Yuan, Kubokawa, and Sasaki 2003). Both approaches utilize the swing equation to reason on transient stability. Our work is also related to techniques improving stability during transmission loop closures in normal operating conditions, e.g., techniques on reducing rotor shaft impacts and standing phase angles (Martins et al. 2008; Ye and Liu 2013; Ketabi, Ranjbar, and Feuillet 2002; Hazarika and Sinha 1999).

To the best of our knowledge, this work represents the first attempt to incorporate transient stability into full power restoration schemes and to optimize generator dispatches and load pickups as additional degrees of freedom.

Background

In this section, we introduce our notations and discuss the Restoration Ordering Problem (Van Hentenryck, Coffrin, and Bent 2011; Coffrin and Van Hentenryck 2014b).

Nomenclature

N	Set of buses in the power grid
$N(n)$	Set of buses connected to bus n
$L \subseteq N \times N$	Set of lines
$G \subseteq N$	Set of generators in the power grid
$G(n)$	Set of generators at bus n
$D \subseteq N$	Set of demands in the power grid
$D(n)$	Set of demands at bus n
R	Set of damaged components to repair
$S_{ij} = p_{ij} + iq_{ij}$	Power flow for line $< i, j >$
$y_{ij} = g_{ij} + ib_{ij}$	Line admittance for line $< i, j >$
$Y = G + iB$	The Y-bus admittance matrix
$V_i = v_i \angle \theta_i$	Voltage magnitude and phase angle at bus i
θ_{ij}, v_{ij}	Shorthand for $\theta_i - \theta_j$ and $v_i - v_j$
$\overline{x}, \underline{x}$	Upper and Lower bound on x

The Restoration Ordering Problem

This section introduces the main notations used in the paper and formalizes the Restoration Ordering Problem (ROP) (Van Hentenryck, Coffrin, and Bent 2011; Coffrin and Van Hentenryck 2014b). The ROP takes as inputs the topology of the network $\mathcal{PN}$ and the set R of damaged components to be repaired. Its main goal is to find the best ordering of the repairs in R in order to recover the loads in the network as quickly as possible. The intuition underlying the ROP is depicted in Figure 1. The ROP only reasons about steady states, each of which corresponds to a restoration action. Moreover, at each step, the ROP searches for a steady state that maximizes the served load, which can be expressed as a power flow sub-problem. In other words, the ROP searches over sequences of $|R|$ steady states and aims at finding the sequence maximizing the served load over time. This paper focuses on transmission line restorations for simplicity (i.e., $R \subseteq L$) but the ROP can be generalized easily to other components (Van Hentenryck, Coffrin, and Bent 2011).

Model 1 shows a simplified Mixed-Integer Nonlinear Program for the ROP. Its two main set of decision variables are the variables z_{rl} and l_{ri}: Binary variable z_{rl} specifies whether line l is operational at step r and variable l_{ri} represents the percentage of served load at bus i for step r. The remaining variables are the traditional power flow variables. There are $|R|$ copies of these variables (and the associated constraints), one for each restoration step.

The objective function (O.1) maximizes the load restored over time. Constraints (C.1.1–C.1.2) ensures that exactly only one line is repaired at each step. Constraints (C.2.1–C.2.2) enforce power conservation on nodes while constraints (C.2.3–C.2.8) implement the AC steady-state power flow equations and the thermal limits on transmission lines (i.e., constraints (C.2.5) and (C.2.8)). Constraints (C.2.3–C.2.5) are conditional to the appropriate line being operational.

Model 1 AC Restoration Ordering Problem

Inputs:

$\mathcal{PN} = \langle N, L, G, D \rangle$	- Power network
$R \subseteq L$	- Damaged items
p_i^l, q_i^l	- Active/reactive power loads on bus i

Variables: $(0 \leq r \leq |R|)$

$z_{rl} \in \{0, 1\}, \forall l \in R$	- Operating state of line l at step r
$l_{ri} \in [0, 1], \forall i \in D$	- load percentage of load i at step r
$\theta_{ri} \in (-\infty, \infty), \forall i \in N$	- bus angle at step r
$v_{ri} \in (\underline{v}_i, \overline{v}_i), \forall i \in N$	- bus voltage magnitude at step r
$p_{ri}^g \in (0, \overline{p}_i^g), \forall i \in G$	- Active injection of generator i
$q_{ri}^g \in (\underline{q}_i^g, \overline{q}_i^g), \forall i \in G$	- Reactive injection of generator i
$p_{rij} \in (-\overline{S}_{ij}, \overline{S}_{ij})$	- Active flow from i to j
$q_{rij} \in (-\overline{S}_{ij}, \overline{S}_{ij})$	- Reactive flow from i to j

Maximize

$$\sum_{r=0}^{|R|} \sum_{i \in D} \overline{p}_i^l l_{ri} \tag{O.1}$$

Subject to: $(0 \leq r \leq |R|)$

$$\sum_{l \in R} z_{rl} = r, \tag{C.1.1}$$

$$z_{(r-1)l} \leq z_{rl}, \qquad \forall l \in R, r \neq 0 \tag{C.1.2}$$

$\forall i \in N$:

$$\sum_{j \in G(i)} p_{rj}^g - \sum_{j \in G(i)} p_j^l l_{rj} = \sum_{j \in N(i)} p_{rij} \tag{C.2.1}$$

$$\sum_{j \in G(i)} q_{rj}^g - \sum_{j \in G(i)} q_j^l l_{rj} = \sum_{j \in N(i)} q_{rij} \tag{C.2.2}$$

$\forall i, j : \exists l \in R$ between buses i and j

$$p_{rij} = z_{rl}(g_{ij} v_{ri}^2 - v_{ri} v_{rj}(g_{ij} \cos(\theta_{rij}) - b_{ij} \sin(\theta_{rij}))) \tag{C.2.3}$$

$$q_{rij} = z_{rl}(-b_{ij} v_{ri}^2 - v_{ri} v_{rj}(g_{ij} \sin(\theta_{rij}) - b_{ij} \cos(\theta_{rij}))) \tag{C.2.4}$$

$$p_{rij}^2 + q_{rij}^2 \leq \overline{S}_{ij} z_{rij} \tag{C.2.5}$$

$\forall i, j : \exists l \in L - R$ between buses i and j

$$p_{rij} = g_{ij} v_{ri}^2 - v_{ri} v_{rj}(g_{ij} \cos(\theta_{rij}) - b_{ij} \sin(\theta_{rij})) \tag{C.2.6}$$

$$q_{rij} = -b_{ij} v_{ri}^2 - v_{ri} v_{rj}(g_{ij} \sin(\theta_{rij}) - b_{ij} \cos(\theta_{rij})) \tag{C.2.7}$$

$$p_{rij}^2 + q_{rij}^2 \leq \overline{S}_{ij} \tag{C.2.8}$$

The ROP is computationally challenging. On the one hand, it suffers from the combinatorial explosion of ordering problems. On the other hand, the non-convex power flow equations represent a major computational challenge in cold-start contexts (Stott, Jardim, and Alsac 2009; Overbye, Cheng, and Sun 2004). The first difficulty is typically addressed using greedy algorithms, large neighborhood search, and/or randomized adaptive decompositions (Bent and Van Hentenryck 2007; Van Hentenryck, Coffrin, and Bent 2011). The second difficulty is avoided by convexifying the nonlinear power flow equations, e.g., using linear approximations (Van Hentenryck, Coffrin, and Bent 2011; Coffrin and Van Hentenryck 2014a; 2014b), or quadratic relaxations (Coffrin et al. 2014; Hijazi, Coffrin, and Van Hentenryck 2013).

Transient Stability for Restoration Planning

Prior work on power restoration has largely focused on computing optimal restoration plans maximizing load recovery over steady states. However, in practice, these restorations

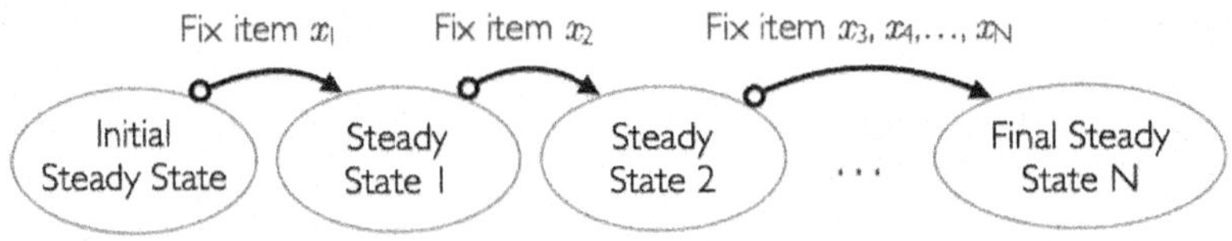

Figure 1: A diagram illustrating a sequence of steady states generated by Restoration Ordering Problem

may not always be feasible as there could be violations of operational limits, safety limits, and stability limits (Adibi and Kafka 1991). The ROP only captures such operational limits as algebraic constraints over steady states, e.g., thermal limits imposed by Constraint C.2.5 in Model 1. It does not capture limits on transient states. Hence, it is possible to derive restoration actions that are not transient stable (Kheradmandi and Ehsan 2004), thus increasing the size of the blackout. Adding constraints on the steady states (Mak et al. 2014) can reduce this possibility. This paper goes one step further by incorporating the system dynamics, which we now present the system dynamics before describing the overall approach.

Rotor Dynamics and Swing Equations

The general form for computing power system dynamic response (Kundur, Balu, and Lauby 1994; Yuan, Kubokawa, and Sasaki 2003) after a disturbance is usually written as follows:

$$\dot{x} = f(x, y)$$
$$0 = g(x, y)$$

where $g(\bullet)$ represents a set of algebraic equations describing the power transmission network and $f(\bullet)$ represents a set of first order differential equations describing the internal dynamics of network equipments. Vector x captures the short-term dynamic variables and y is a vector of algebraic state variables. Given an initial condition for variables x and y, we can compute a set of transient states over time by using equations $f(\bullet)$ and $g(\bullet)$. To incorporate rotor angle stability, we first introduce the "classical" model of generator dynamics corresponding to the Swing equations (Kundur, Balu, and Lauby 1994) (for implementing $f(\bullet)$):

$$\frac{d\delta_i}{dt} = \omega_i - \omega_0$$
$$\frac{2H_i}{\omega_0}\frac{d\omega_i}{dt} = p_i^m - p_i^e - D_i\omega_i$$

where $H_i, \delta_i, D_i, \omega_i$, and ω_0 respectively denote the inertia constant, the rotor angle, the damping coefficient, the current angular velocity, and the nominal angular velocity of a generator i (which is assumed constant for all generators at 50Hz/60Hz). On the right hand side of the equation, p_i^m and p_i^e are the mechanical and electrical powers acting on the rotor of generator i. In the Swing equations, δ_i and ω_i are short-term dynamic variables (i.e., the x-vector above) and p_i^m and p_i^e are algebraic state variables (i.e., the y-vector above). In steady states, the mechanical power is assumed to be equal to the electrical power and the rotor angle of all generators remains constant. Once a disturbance occurs, the electrical power changes and there is a difference between mechanical and electrical power. Hence, the rotor angle of generators changes according to the Swing equation. Figure 2 shows a the rotor swings after the closure of a transmission line for a 3-bus example. The y-axis shows the rotor angle (in degrees) of the generators and the x-axis shows the time in seconds after the line closing.

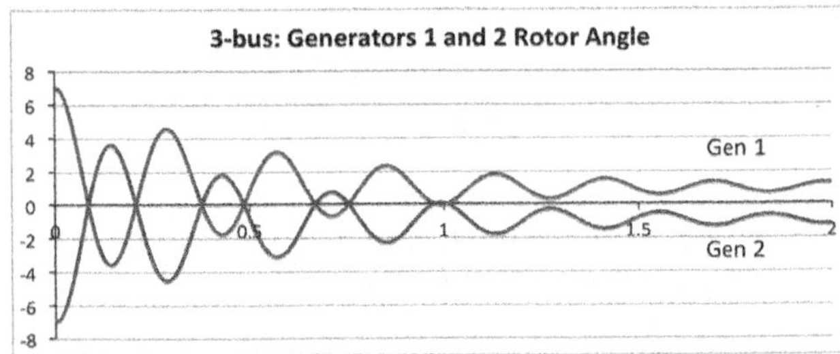

Figure 2: Rotor swings during transmission loop closures

To implement the Swing equations in optimization tools, we perform a trapezoidal discretization over a given time horizon ($1 \leq t \leq T$) (Gan, Thomas, and Zimmerman 2000). This leads to the following discretized equations, $\forall i \in G, 1 \leq t \leq T-1$,

$$\delta_{it+1} - \delta_{it} - \frac{\Delta}{2}(\omega_{it+1} + \omega_{it}) = 0 \tag{1}$$
$$\omega_{it+1} - \omega_{it} - \frac{\Delta}{2}(a_{it+1} + a_{it}) = 0 \tag{2}$$
$$a_{it+1} - \frac{\omega_0}{2H_i}(p_{i1}^e - p_{it+1}^e - D_i\omega_{it}) = 0 \tag{3}$$

with the following initial conditions at $t = 1$,

$$\omega_{i1} = 0, a_{i1} = 0 \tag{4}$$

where δ_{it}, ω_{it}, a_{it}, and p_{it}^e are the rotor angle, the angular velocity, the angular acceleration, and the electrical power of generator i at time step t, $1 \leq t \leq T$. Δ is a constant representing the time interval between every time step.

To increase rotor stability, (Gan, Thomas, and Zimmerman 2000) suggest to bound at all time steps the difference between the rotor angle of a generator δ_{it} and a reference angle δ_t^r representing the Center Of Inertia (COI):

$$\delta_t^r = \frac{\sum_{i \in G} H_i\delta_{it}}{\sum_{i \in G} H_i}, 1 \leq t \leq T \tag{5}$$

The stability constraints then become:

$$\forall i \in G, 1 \leq t \leq T : -\overline{\delta} \leq \delta_{it} - \delta_t^r \leq \overline{\delta} \tag{6}$$

where $\overline{\delta}$ represents the bound constant to be determined.

AC Power Flow Equations Over Time

The set of algebraic constraints $g(\bullet)$ include the AC power flow equations characterizing power transmission and passive network equipments (Liu and Thorp 2000). Two admittance matrices define the line properties and the load characteristics, before and after a line switch, resp. Y^o and Y^c. The AC power flow equations are then specified as follows, $\forall\, i \in N, 2 \leq t \leq T$,

$$\sum_{j \in N} [V_{it}V_{jt}(G^c_{ij}\cos(\theta_{ijt}) + B^c_{ij}\sin(\theta_{ijt}))] = \sum_{j \in G(i)} p^e_{jt} \quad (7)$$

$$\sum_{j \in N} [V_{it}V_{jt}(G^c_{ij}\sin(\theta_{ijt}) - B^c_{ij}\cos(\theta_{ijt}))] = \sum_{j \in G(i)} q^e_{jt} \quad (8)$$

with the following initial conditions for $t = 1$:

$$\sum_{j \in N} [V_{i1}V_{j1}(G^o_{ij}\cos(\theta_{ij1}) + B^o_{ij}\sin(\theta_{ij1}))] = \sum_{j \in G(i)} p^e_{j1} \quad (9)$$

$$\sum_{j \in N} [V_{i1}V_{j1}(G^o_{ij}\sin(\theta_{ij1}) - B^o_{ij}\cos(\theta_{ij1}))] = \sum_{j \in G(i)} q^e_{j1} \quad (10)$$

In the classical generator model, every generator i is defined as an internal bus connected to a terminal node with transient reactance X_i and constant voltage V^g_i. The rotor angles δ_{it} are then treated as bus phase angles. Note that we ignore the reactive power flow constraints for transient states (i.e., when time $t > 1$) (Liu and Thorp 2000). For all $i \in G, 1 \leq t \leq T$,

$$p^e_{it} = \frac{V^g_i V_{it}}{X_i}\sin(\theta_{it} - \delta_{it}) \quad (11)$$

with the following extra condition on time step $t = 1$,

$$q^e_{i1} = \frac{V^2_{i1}}{X_i} - \frac{V^g_i V_{i1}}{X_i}\cos(\theta_{i1} - \delta_{i1}) \quad (12)$$

The last part corresponds to boundary conditions representing safety/operating limits. For the initial state at $t = 1$, for all $i \in G$ we have,

$$0 \leq p^e_{i1} \leq \overline{p}^e_i, \underline{q}^e_i \leq q^e_{i1} \leq \overline{q}^e_i, \underline{V}^g_i \leq V^g_i \leq \overline{V}^g_i \quad (13)$$

For all time steps t, we have,

$$\forall i \in N : \underline{V}_i \leq V_{it} \leq \overline{V}_i \quad (14)$$

$$\forall i \in G : -\overline{\theta} \leq \delta_{it} - \theta_{it} \leq \overline{\theta} \quad (15)$$

$$\forall \langle i,j \rangle \in L : -\overline{\theta} \leq \theta_{it} - \theta_{jt} \leq \overline{\theta} \quad (16)$$

Let us emphasize that this formulation allows voltage magnitudes to fluctuate at every transient time step t. This may naturally lead to other stability issues. In order to avoid drastic fluctuations, we add the following constraints bounding their magnitude for all time steps.
$\forall\, i \in N, 1 \leq t \leq T - 1$,

$$V_{it} - \overline{V^\Delta} \leq V_{it+1} \leq V_{it} + \overline{V^\Delta}. \quad (17)$$

A Non-Linear Program for Stability Enhancement

Given the set of constraints (1)-(17) defining the transient behavior of the system, we now introduce Model 2 for stability enhancement after a line-switching operation. An optimal solution in Model 2 guarantees a transient-stable switching with generator dispatches that minimize the distance to the original steady-state solution.

Model 2 Transient Stable Line Closing Model

Inputs:

$\mathcal{PN}$	- Power network
Y^o, Y^c	- Admittance matrix before and after line closing
p^T_i, q^T_i	- i^{th} generator active/reactive target dispatch,
X_i, H_i, D_i	- transient reactance, inertia, and damping constant
$f_q = \frac{\omega_0}{2\pi}, \Delta, T$	- Grid frequency, integration step, time horizon
$\overline{\delta}, \overline{V^\Delta}$	- Maximum rotor swing and voltage fluctuations

Variables: ($\forall t : 1 \leq t \leq T$)

$\forall i \in N$,

θ_{it}	- Terminal bus angle
V_{it}	- Bus voltage

$\forall i \in G$,

V^g_i	- Internal bus voltage
p^e_{it}, q^e_{it}	- Generator active and reactive injection
$\delta_{it}, \omega_{it}, a_{it}$	- Generator rotor angle, velocity, and acceleration
δ^r_t	- Rotor angle reference index

Minimize

$\sum_{i \in G}[(p^e_{i1} - p^T_i)^2 + (q^e_{i1} - q^T_i)^2]$ - Distance from target dispatch

Subject to:

Equations (1) - (17)

Simplification and Kron Reduction

In Model 2, the number of variables is O($|N|T$). The model dimension can be reduced by constructing a smaller equivalent network and computing the corresponding admittance matrices. Since a line closing only affects a subset of connected complements in the network, we disregard islands that are not related to the current switching. An admittance preserving reduction known as Kron reduction (Ward 1949) is then performed. This technique removes all buses that are not under study by translating their properties into new lines. In our case, since we are only interested in rotor dynamics, Kron reduction is used to remove all non-generator buses. This results in two admittance matrices Y^o and Y^c representing the reduced network before and after line closing. The number of variables in Model 2 is then O($|G|{\cdot}T$), where G represents the number of generators on the island corresponding to the line closings. Figure 3 shows an example of Kron reduction on a 6-bus network with three generators (G1 to G3), three loads (L1 to L3), and five transmission lines. After performing the Kron reduction, only three buses (with generators) are left. Three virtual transmission lines are constructed and loads L1 to L3 are re-adjusted to maintain an equivalent transfer admittance and power flows.

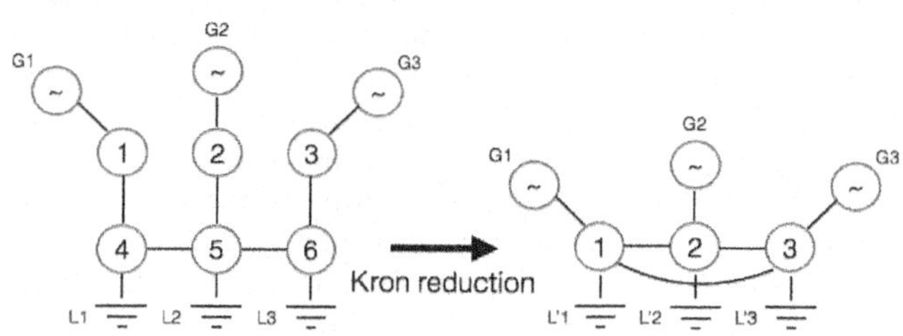

Figure 3: An example network illustrating Kron reduction

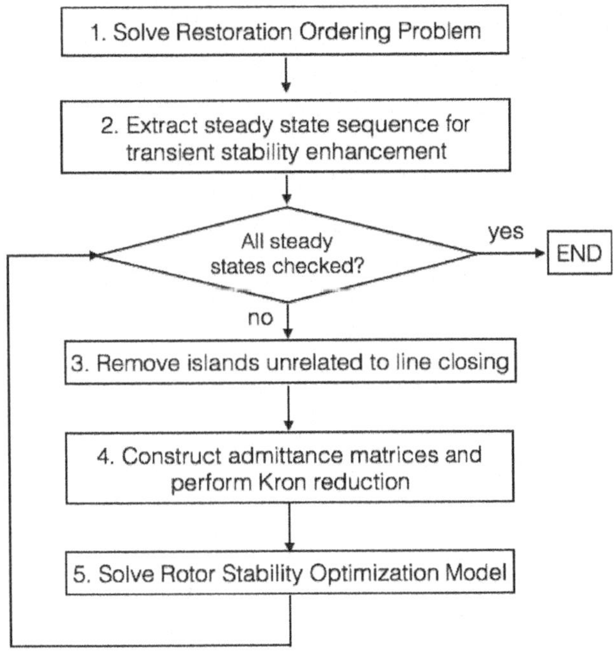

Figure 4: Flow chart for the stability enhancement routine

Kron reduction is inspired by Kirchhoff's Current Law (KCL) (Kundur, Balu, and Lauby 1994). Given an admittance matrix Y, a vector of voltages V, and a vector of current injections I, the KCL law (in matrix form) states that:

$$I = YV$$

Since the current injections will be zero for non-generator buses, we can use Gaussian elimination to delete corresponding rows from the system of equations. This will allow us to generate a reduced Y-bus matrix representing the network. Following the Gaussian elimination, we obtain the following set of equations allowing to remove a non-generator bus n from the network.

$$\forall i, j \in N - \{n\} : Y_{ij}^{'} = Y_{ij} - \frac{Y_{in}Y_{nj}}{Y_{nn}}$$

Stability Enhancement Routine

Figure 4 presents our overall approach to power restoration with transient stability. Step 1 solves the ROP to obtain a restoration plan defined as a sequence of steady states. Since this solution may be computed using approximation techniques, it may be necessary to convert the potentially non-AC feasible steady states into AC feasible solutions. A standard load flow procedure can be used in the conversion process. Step 2 extracts the sub-sequence of steady states corresponding to line switchings within an energized island. One can safely ignore lines connecting two islands as this is covered by standard approaches (e.g., monitoring periodic oscillations of the phase angle variables or using a synchronization check relay)(Kundur, Balu, and Lauby 1994). Steps 3 and 4 remove islands which are not related to the line-switching operations and perform a Kron reduction (as discussed in the last section) in order to reduce the size of Model 2. Finally, our optimization model is run in Step 5 to find generator dispatches that ensure transient stability during the switching operations.

Experimental Results

We now present experimental results to demonstrate the benefits of the proposed approach. The experimental results study whether the steady states returned by the ROP are transient-stable under various increasingly strict rotor angle limits and for various reactance values. They also study the magnitude of changes in generator dispatches to ensure transient stability, i.e., how close the transient-stable dispatches p_{i1}^e and q_{i1}^e and the target dispatches p_i^T and q_i^T are. Our model is implemented in AMPL (Fourer, Gay, and Kernighan 2002; AMPL 2014), and uses Ipopt 3.11 (Wächter and Biegler 2006) as a nonlinear solver. We have tested our model on 5 MATPOWER benchmarks (Zimmerman, Murillo-S andnchez, and Thomas 2011). Note that the ROP was solved using the utilization heuristic (Coffrin, Van Hentenryck, and Bent 2012).

Table 1 presents experimental results for various generator reactances and maximum rotor swing limits $\overline{\delta}$. The table presents aggregate results obtained by summing up all the objective values after solving Model 2 for all of the restoration steps (after filtering and simplification). Hence, each value provides a measure on the degree of dispatch (measured in per-unit (Kundur, Balu, and Lauby 1994)) required to obtain transient stability. In other words, larger values indicate large adjustments in dispatch. The table also indicates, in parentheses, the number of restoration steps in which Model 2 is not solved by IPOPT within one hour. Note that, in general, a rotor angle limit of 90 degrees is considered acceptable, the goal of the current experiment is to push the limits on this bound as far as possible.

The results indicate that the steady-state dispatches are in general transient-stable except for the 39-bus and 57-bus benchmarks. Fortunately, in general, it is possible to ensure transient stability with minor changes in generator dispatches. The changes in dispatch increases with stricter limits on rotor angles. In extreme cases, where the bound is set to 1 degree, IPOPT fails to find transient stable dispatches for the 14-bus, 39-bus, and 57-bus benchmarks. This indicates that adjusting generator dispatch may not be sufficient for an arbitrary degree constraint, but those limits are extremely strict.

Overall, the results show that the proposed approach produces transient-stable restoration plans with minimal adjustments in generator dispatches. These adjustments are however necessary to guarantee transient stability, highlighting the benefits of the proposed approach.

Conclusion

Automated power restoration is a key component in future smart grids. Finding the optimal restoration plan is only one step towards system recovery. Guaranteeing transient stability of all switching operations is equally critical. In this paper, we propose an algorithmic procedure for validating

Table 1: Generator total dispatch adjustments on 5 Matpower benchmarks ($T = 400, \Delta = 0.005$)

	6 Bus				14 Bus				30 Bus			
	Maximum Rotor Swing				Maximum Rotor Swing				Maximum Rotor Swing			
Gen. Reactance	90	40	10	1	90	40	10	1	90	40	10	1
0.02	0.00002	0.00002	0.00002	0.17967	0.00000	0.00000	0.00000	6.53902	0.00004	0.00003	0.00004	2.91547
0.06	0.00003	0.00003	0.00003	0.10593	0.00000	0.00000	0.00000	8.67193	0.00004	0.00003	0.00004	3.07084
0.10	0.00003	0.00002	0.00002	0.00843	0.00000	0.00000	0.00000	8.18311	0.00004	0.00004	0.00004	3.76922
0.14	0.00002	0.00003	0.00002	0.30335	0.00000	0.00000	0.00000	6.09923 (1)	0.00004	0.00005	0.00004	4.17696
0.20	0.00003	0.00003	0.00003	1.01248	0.00000	0.00000	0.00000	3.66457 (3)	0.00004	0.00004	0.00004	4.07680

	39 Bus				57 Bus			
	Maximum Rotor Swing				Maximum Rotor Swing			
Gen. Reactance	90	40	10	1	90	40	10	1
0.02	0.00001	0.00001	20.52951	7.95879 (6)	0.00000	0.00000	0.66260	131.39311
0.06	0.00001	0.00001	81.80927 (1)	0.00002 (7)	0.00000	0.00000	1.36766	1.12417 (21)
0.10	0.42052	0.28436 (1)	78.24781	48.13747 (5)	0.23766	0.23766	39.33088	1.14312 (21)
0.14	0.49691	0.49698	60.35684	41.99449 (5)	0.68299	0.67222 (1)	73.84672	1.26118 (21)
0.20	0.00002	0.00002	34.26957	69.35875 (3)	0.83704	0.83744	120.01411 (1)	1.41655 (21)

and enhancing transient stability of such restoration plans. Stability is measured using the nonlinear dynamic swing equations corresponding to rotor angles of power generators. Computational scalability is then improved using preprocessing and reduction routines. Numerical experiments are carried on state-of-the-art benchmarks, assessing the scalability of the approach and validating the stability results.

Acknowledgement

The authors would like to thank David Hill and Ian Hiskens for many interesting discussions on power restoration. NICTA is funded by the Australian Government through the Department of Communications and the Australian Research Council through the ICT Centre of Excellence Program.

References

Adibi, M., and Kafka, R. 1991. Power system restoration issues. *IEEE Computer Applications in Power* 4(2):19–24.

2014. AMPL. AMPL Optimization: http://www.ampl.com.

Bent, R., and Van Hentenryck, P. 2007. Randomized adaptive spatial decoupling for large-scale vehicle routing with time windows. In *AAAI'07*, 173–178.

Coffrin, C., and Van Hentenryck, P. 2014a. A linear-programming approximation of AC power flows. *Informs Journal on Computing* 26(4):718–734.

Coffrin, C., and Van Hentenryck, P. 2014b. Transmission system restoration: Co-optimization of repairs, load pickups, and generation dispatch. In *Proceedings of the 18th Power Systems Computation Conference (PSCC'14)*.

Coffrin, C.; Hijazi, H.; Lehmann, K.; and Van Hentenryck, P. 2014. Primal and dual bounds for optimal transmission switching. In *Proceedings of the 18th Power Systems Computation Conference (PSCC'14)*.

Coffrin, C.; Van Hentenryck, P.; and Bent, R. 2012. Last-Mile restoration for multiple interdependent infrastructures. In *AAAI'12*, 455–463.

Fourer, R.; Gay, D. M.; and Kernighan, B. W. 2002. *AMPL: A Modeling Language for Mathematical Programming*. Cengage Learning.

Gan, D.; Thomas, R.; and Zimmerman, R. 2000. Stability-constrained optimal power flow. *IEEE Transactions on Power Systems* 15(2):535–540.

Hazarika, D., and Sinha, A. 1999. An algorithm for standing phase angle reduction for power system restoration. *IEEE Transactions on Power Systems* 14(4):1213–1218.

Hijazi, H.; Coffrin, C.; and Van Hentenryck, P. 2013. Convex quadratic relaxations of nonlinear programs in power systems. In *Optimization Online: http://www.optimization-online.org/DB HTML/2013/09/4057.html*.

Ketabi, A.; Ranjbar, A.; and Feuillet, R. 2002. New approach to standing phase angle reduction for power system restoration. *European transactions on electrical power* 12(4):301–307.

Kheradmandi, M., and Ehsan, M. 2004. Dynamic analysis of transmission line connection in restoration of interconnected power systems. In *Electrical and Computer Engineering, 2004. Canadian Conference on*, volume 3, 1621–1624.

Kundur, P.; Balu, N. J.; and Lauby, M. G. 1994. *Power system stability and control*. McGraw-hill New York.

Liu, C.-W., and Thorp, J. 2000. New methods for computing power system dynamic response for real-time transient stability prediction. *Circuits and Systems I: Fundamental Theory and Applications, IEEE Transactions on* 47(3):324–337.

Mak, T. W. K.; Coffrin, C.; Van Hentenryck, P.; Hiskens, I. A.; and Hill, D. 2014. Power system restoration planning with standing phase angle and voltage difference constraints. In *Proceedings of the 18th Power Systems Computation Conference (PSCC'14)*.

Martins, N.; De Oliveira, E.; Moreira, W.; Pereira, J. L. R.; and Fontoura, R. 2008. Redispatch to reduce rotor shaft impacts upon transmission loop closure. *IEEE Transactions on Power Systems* 23(2):592–600.

Overbye, T. J.; Cheng, X.; and Sun, Y. 2004. A comparison of the AC and DC power flow models for LMP calculations. In *Proceedings of the 37th Annual Hawaii International Conference on System Sciences.*

Stott, B.; Jardim, J.; and Alsac, O. 2009. DC power flow revisited. *IEEE Transactions on Power Systems* 24(3):1290–1300.

Van Hentenryck, P.; Coffrin, C.; and Bent, R. 2011. Vehicle routing for the last mile of power system restoration. In *Proceedings of the 17th Power Systems Computation Conference (PSCC'11).*

Wächter, A., and Biegler, L. T. 2006. On the implementation of an interior-point filter line-search algorithm for large-scale nonlinear programming. *Mathematical Programming* 106(1):25–57.

Ward, J. B. 1949. Equivalent circuits for power-flow studies. *Transactions of the American Institute of Electrical Engineers* 68(1):373–382.

Ye, H., and Liu, Y. 2013. A new method for standing phase angle reduction in system restoration by incorporating load pickup as a control means. *International Journal of Electrical Power & Energy Systems* 53:664–674.

Yuan, Y.; Kubokawa, J.; and Sasaki, H. 2003. A solution of optimal power flow with multicontingency transient stability constraints. *Power Systems, IEEE Transactions on* 18(3):1094–1102.

Zimmerman, R.; Murillo-S andnchez, C.; and Thomas, R. 2011. MATPOWER: Steady-state operations, planning, and analysis tools for power systems research and education. *IEEE Transactions on Power Systems* 26(1):12 –19.

Aggregating Electric Cars to Sustainable Virtual Power Plants: The Value of Flexibility in Future Electricity Markets

Micha Kahlen and Wolfgang Ketter
Erasmus University Rotterdam
Burgemeester Oudlaan 50, The Netherlands
{kahlen,wketter}@rsm.nl

Abstract

Electric vehicles will play a crucial role in balancing the future electrical grid, which is complicated by many intermittent renewable energy. We developed an algorithm that determines for a fleet of electric vehicles, which EV at what price and location to commit to the operating reserve market to either absorb excess capacity or provide electricity during shortages (vehicle-2-grid). The algorithm takes the value of immobility into account by using carsharing fees as a reference point. A virtual power plant autonomously replaces cars that are committed to the operating reserves and are then rented out, with other idle cars to pool the risks of uncertainty. We validate our model with data from a free float carsharing fleet of 500 electric vehicles. An analysis of expected future developments (2015, 2018, and 2022) in operating reserve demand and battery costs yields that the gross profits for a carsharing operator increase between 7-12% with a negligible decrease in car availability (<0.01%).

Introduction

In its World Energy Investment Outlook 2014, the International Energy Agency estimates that over the next 20 years a cumulative investment of $53 trillion is required worldwide to limit the concentration of greenhouse gases in the atmosphere to 450 parts per million of CO_2 (International Energy Agency 2014). First concrete steps in that direction require European Union member states to have a 30% renewable content by 2030; especially intermittent wind and solar power is subsidized (The European Parliament and The Council of the European Union 2009). These large scale penetrations of volatile renewable energy sources pose a challenge to the stability of the electrical grid as their production is inflexible to changing demand and difficult to forecast (Kassakian and Schmalensee 2011). This complicates balancing the grid and providing sufficient energy to consumers at all times, thereby increasing the chance of blackouts.

Smart grids offer an information based solution that utilizes the transition from data poverty to data richness in the electricity sector. According to Malhotra, Melville, and Watson this also paves the way for real-time control of energy use for many devices. Important in that regard are electric vehicles (EV) which have storage capacities that can contribute to solving the imbalance problem. The EVs are charged when wind and solar sources produce energy, and they make energy available to the grid when those energy sources are unavailable, called vehicle-to-grid (V2G). Together they constitute a *virtual power plant* (VPP), which are distributed power sources that are centrally coordinated to support flexible energy supply. Specifically we look at very short term (seconds to minutes) integration of demand and supply on the operating reserve market. We combine real-time information from electric cars about their location, usage, and battery storage, with information from reserve markets in an algorithm to optimally allocate EV capacity. This algorithm, which we call *FleetPower*, makes an explicit trade-off between benefits from offering cars for rental and using them for balancing the grid in real-time which was not considered in previous research (Vytelingum et al. 2011; Voice et al. 2011). To the best of our knowledge this is the first study that uses real driving, charging, and locational data of 500 EV in 54 urban districts. The data for this study was provided by the Daimler AG.

Background and Literature

This section describes and explains relevant research and the general setting of balancing renewable energy sources. First the embedment in the trading agent literature in a sustainability context will be given. Consequently, we will describe the operating reserve market in more detail from where the VPP sources its revenues. Finally, we will position our research within the literature on EVs and the carsharing context.

Agent-based Sustainable Society

Previous research employed intelligent trading agents to act on behalf of consumers in decentralized electricity markets. A prominent example is the Power Trading Agent Competition (Power TAC) where brokers compete to attract customers and purchase electricity on their behalf (Ketter, Collins, and Reddy 2013). The realism of the platform was demonstrated by Ketter, Peters, and Collins. Similarly to other brokers such as defined by Urieli and Stone and

Reddy and Veloso we outline a broker that acts on behalf of carsharing fleets only and focuses on the operating reserve market. We take advantage of particulary high electricity prices on the operating reserve market that stem from real-time changes in electricity demand and production. In a similar vein to Ketter et al. who make real-time pricing decisions based on economic regimes, we make real-time decisions for renting out a specific EV or turning it into a VPP. Another example of the benefits of agents in decentralized electricity markets is illustrated by Ramchurn et al..

Operating Reserves: Balancing the Electrical Grid

If at any point in time there is a difference in the quantity of electricity produced and consumed, the electricity market has to be regulated in real-time to maintain stability. This is coordinated by electronic auctions, specifically first-price sealed-bid auctions, in which participants make *offers* to generate electricity, called positive operating reserves, or *bids* to absorb and consume electricity, called negative operating reserves. The balancing responsible party accesses these offers and bids as needed in the merit order (cheapest resources are used first) to keep the market in an equilibrium. This mechanism gains importance with increasing levels of intermittent renewable energy, as production depends on exogenous factors such as the weather. Especially battery storage is valuable in this regard because it has no ramp-up costs and time. Ramp-up costs and time to start-up generators are significant for base load power plants. EVs possess large electrical batteries that are almost instantly scalable. Previous research proposed to use this capacity to offer balancing services to the grid (Vytelingum et al. 2011; Peterson, Whitacre, and Apt 2010; Schill 2011).

Electric Vehicles and Carsharing

Carsharing and especially the free float carsharing model, where the car can be picked up and dropped off anywhere, contribute to more sustainable ways of transport in terms of construction, operation, and decomposition of mobility systems. Firnkorn and Müller find that even under a pessimistic scenario, free float carsharing has a significantly positive effect on carbon emissions.

Charging many EVs in the same neighborhood at the same time will overload transformers and substations quickly (Kim et al. 2012; Sioshansi 2012). Previous research has addressed this issue by proposing smart charging. Smart charging means to charge EVs at times when the grid is less congested to complement peaks in electricity consumption. Drivers are incentivized to shift their charging, yielding significant peak reductions (Valogianni et al. 2014). An extension of smart charging is the V2G concept which was mentioned in the introduction. Regarding the technical feasibility it should be noted the standard of the International Electronical Commission ICE 62196 supports V2G. A study by Vytelingum et al. looked at the savings a household can make with a battery exposed to variable pricing at the energy wholesale market and found that efficient use of the battery would save 14% in utility costs and 7% in carbon emissions. Other studies find yearly benefits per EV of \$ 10-120 (Peterson, Whitacre, and Apt 2010) and \$ 176-203 (Schill 2011). Within this research stream there are two conflicting opinions regarding the economic feasibility of the V2G concept. Peterson, Whitacre, and Apt contend that relatively low yearly benefits per EV would not justify a widespread roll out. Kahlen, Ketter, and van Dalen, however, argued that V2G would enable volatile renewable energy sources to be suitable for mainstream usage. Tomic and Kempton show that the profitability depends on the target market; the larger the variations in the electricity price the higher the profitability.

Previous research greatly contributed to this topic, however under the unrealistic assumption that driving patterns are known in advance. So they consider a static system, whereas in reality it is a complex sociotechnical system (Geels 2004). Users have valuations for being mobile that differ over time and conflict with market interests (Vytelingum et al. 2011; Tomic and Kempton 2007). We approach this problem from a sociotechnical perspective by appropriating valuations for mobility from price and demand for the EVs in a carsharing context. Besides, in contrast to our work, previous studies have used either very small fleets or data from combustion engine vehicles which have a longer range and are not subject to range anxiety, the fear of stranding with an empty battery.

Model Description

At the core of this research is the development of an algorithm that decides how to deploy EVs, and its evaluation in a simulation environment. A simulation approach is most suitable for this purpose as we are dealing with a complex system that would be prohibitively expensive to build. It would be difficult to manipulate a variety of parameters to find the optimal market equilibrium. A simulation approach helps to refine the algorithm, which is driven by business needs from its environment that was discussed in the introduction, and applying knowledge from existing agent-based approaches.

Virtual Power Plant Decision Support: FleetPower

The algorithm, which we call FleetPower, decides which EVs should be deployed as part of a VPP, which EVs should be charged, and which EVs should be made available for rental for one time interval ahead in real-time. This applies only to EVs that are parked at a charging spot for the time under consideration.

Individual Car Performance Indicators. FleetPower calculates the expected profit performance indicator (PPI) for a specific EV i over time interval t (see Equation 1). Therefore it maximizes expected profits over renting (rental benefit RB), charging (negative regulation benefit NRB), and turning the car into a VPP (positive regulation benefit PRB).

$$PPI_{t,i,l} = \max(RB_{t,i,l}, NRB_{t,i,l}, PRB_{t,i,l}) \quad (1)$$

For a table of notation including measurement units see Table 1. The expected profits for renting (RB) car i during interval t parked at location l is estimated with a multiple linear regression model (see Equation 2). The regression is based on the probability with which a car gets rented out (a)

and the storage capacity available (q). The probability to be rented out at a given location varies over every quarter of an hour and differs for each day of the week. As rental benefits are generally much higher than benefits from PRB and NRB a car that was predicted not to be rented out when it actually was rented out will be much costlier than the other way around. To account for these asymmetric misclassification costs, we use the upper confidence interval as predictor for RB. The level of confidence depends on the magnitude of the asymmetric misclassification costs. During rentals the battery is used and depreciation costs (D) as well as electricity costs for charging (C) for the expected difference in the battery state before and after driving (ΔQ) are taken into account.

$$RB_{t,i,l} = \beta_1 + \beta_2 a_{t,l} + \beta_3 q_{t,i} - \left[D + \left(\frac{C}{\epsilon}\right)\right] \Delta Q_{t,i} \quad (2)$$

where:

$$\Delta Q_{t,i} = \beta_4 + \beta_5 a_{t,l} + \beta_6 q_{t,i} \quad (3)$$

If an EV is parked at a charging station FleetPower has the option to charge the car. In this respect the negative regulation benefit (NRB) is defined as the quantity with which the battery of car i at interval t can still be charged with (Ψ) and the bid price for negative operating reserves (P^{neg}), which differs per EV i and time interval t (see Equation 4). More specifically the quantity that the battery can still be charged with (Ψ^{neg}) in time interval t takes into account the amount of electricity stored in the battery Q and the charging speed γ, which is defined by $\Psi^{neg}_{t,i} = \min((\Omega_i - Q_{t,i}), \gamma\Delta t)$. As this option would replace the costs for charging, we add the opportunity benefit of not having to pay for charging fees (C). In other words the NRB is the difference between what one would pay with a common electricity tariff and the negative operating reserve market price.

$$NRB_{t,i} = \Psi^{neg}_{t,i}(P^{neg}_{t,i} - C) \quad (4)$$

The bidding price is determined by the cost that would be incurred to charge the EV with the regular electricity tariff C and charging inefficiency ϵ, the expected rental profits RB, and profit margin μ^{neg} which maximizes overall profits for the time intervals t in the test data set (see Equation 5). Note that if P^{neg} is too high, the market will instead choose a cheaper bid and consequently there is no NRB for that time period.

$$P^{neg}_{t,i} = -\frac{C}{\epsilon} + RB_{t,i,l} + \mu^{neg}_t \quad (5)$$

In a similar vein an EV could also contribute to a VPP. The electricity stored (Ψ^{pos}) in EV i that can be accessed within time interval t and the offered selling price for positive operating reserves (P^{pos}) specify the positive regulation benefit (PRB). The electricity available for a VPP (Ψ^{pos}) at time interval t based on the amount of stored electricity Q and the discharging speed δ is expressed by $\Psi^{pos}_{t,i} = \min(Q_{t,i}, \delta\Delta t)$. Besides also the cost for battery wear out is depreciated (D) over its effective use and the costs for charging C, including inefficiency ϵ, are taken into account. Moreover the opportunity costs of not being able to rent out the EV (RB) due to its commitment to a VPP in the current interval t and recharging it thereafter are considered (see Equation 6). Opportunity costs for recharging apply only if the next lessee cannot complete his expected trip with the reduced capacity from the VPP ($(Q_t - \Psi^{pos}_{t,i}) < \Delta Q_{t+j}$). The discharging inefficiency (η) also plays an indirect role as the amount of electricity consumed from the battery Ψ^{pos} is larger than the amount sold by $\frac{\Psi^{pos}}{\eta}$.

$$PRB_{t,i} = \Psi^{pos}_{t,i}\left[P^{pos}_{t,i} - \left(D + \frac{C}{\epsilon}\right)\right] - \sum_{j=1}^{\frac{\Psi^{pos}_{t,i}}{\delta t}} (RB_{(t+j),i,l} \mid (Q_t - \Psi^{pos}_{t,i}) < \Delta Q_{t+j}) \quad (6)$$

The offered selling price (P^{pos}) is composed of the depreciation cost (D), charging costs (C) including inefficiencies (ϵ), opportunity costs for rental and recharging time (RB) if the battery has insufficient capacity ($(Q_t - \Psi^{pos}_{t,i}) < \Delta Q_{t+j}$) for the lessee's purposes, and margin μ^{pos} which maximizes overall profits for the time intervals t in the test data set (see Equation 7).

$$P^{pos}_{t,i} = D + \frac{C}{\epsilon} + \sum_{j=1}^{\frac{\Psi^{pos}_{t,i}}{\delta t}} (RB_{(t+j),i,l} \mid (Q_t - \Psi^{pos}_{t,i}) < \Delta Q_{t+j}) + \mu^{pos}_t \quad (7)$$

FleetPower Decision Making at the Fleet Level. While it is important for lessees to rent a car at a specific location, the location within a city is less relevant for operating reserves. Rather than deciding for each EV individually where it should be deployed, we estimate an overall quantity for negative and positive operating reserves. This quantity comes from different EVs across the city and could switch within a time interval (t) from one EV to another if it is rented out.

Therefore we do not simply sum up the storage of each individual EV (Ψ) that could be committed to a VPP, but we correct this amount for the risk pooling effect (RPE). The risk pooling effect refers to better forecasts on the fleet level than at the individual car level. That means we predict how much overall storage should be used for positive and negative operating reserves. Then these amounts are allocated back to the individual EVs. This is why a VPP outperforms several EVs in isolation. The estimation for each operating reserve at the fleet level is based on a linear regression model with two independent variables. The first independent variable is the quantity of electricity available after the previous interval in the EVs (Ψ^{neg}/Ψ^{pos}) where the performance indicator suggested to charge (Equation 8) or turn the EV into a VPP (Equation 9). The second independent variable consists of the amount of electricity available in EVs where the performance indicator suggested negative or positive regulation in the last time interval, but where it would have been more profitable to rent out the EV. The term s refers to safety

Table 1: Table of Notation.

Variable	Description	Unit
a	Rental probability	$\frac{\%}{100}$
D	Battery depreciation cost	\$/kWh
d	Distance EV_i to closest EV	km
C	Electricity price (industry average)	\$/kWh
i	Specific EV	tag
I	Total number of EVs ($\sum i$)	
l	Location	ZIP code
P	Bid/offer price to buy or sell electricity from reserve market	\$/kWh
Q	Amount of electricity stored in an EV	kWh
q	Battery state of charge (Q/Ω)	$\frac{\%}{100}$
s	Safety stock	kWh
t	Time interval	index
Δt	Duration of a time interval	15 minutes
β	Regression parameter	
γ	Charging speed	kW
δ	Discharging speed	kW
ϵ	Charging inefficiency	$\frac{\%}{100}$
η	Discharging inefficiency	$\frac{\%}{100}$
μ	Margin on the bid/offer price	\$
Ψ	Electricity accessible within time interval	kWh
Ω	Maximum battery capacity	kWh

stocks that determine the trade-off between the risk of not renting out a car and missing out on potential profits on the reserve markets. The safety stocks (in combination with Equation 8 and 9) determine how many cars should not be committed as reserves. The optimization of the safety stock was done over the 7 week training period with the objective to maximize the overall profit. The safety stock grows with the asymmetric misclassification costs discussed in the previous section.

$$RPE_t^{neg} = \beta + \beta_{n^{neg}} \sum_{i=1}^{I} (h(x) * \Psi_{t-1,i}^{neg}) + \beta_{r^{neg}} \sum_{i=1}^{I} (j(x) * \Psi_{t-1,i}^{neg}) - s \quad (8)$$

$$RPE_t^{pos} = \beta + \beta_{n^{pos}} \sum_{i=1}^{I} (k(x) * \Psi_{t-1,i}^{pos}) + \beta_{r^{pos}} \sum_{i=1}^{I} (m(x) * \Psi_{t-1,i}^{pos}) - s \quad (9)$$

where:

$$h(x) = \begin{cases} 1, & if \quad PPI_{t-1,i} = NRB_{t-1,i} \\ 0, & otherwise \end{cases} \quad (10)$$

Table 2: Descriptive Statistics Car2Go Dataset.

Description	Value
EV type	Smart Fortwo Electric
Max. battery capacity (Ω)	16.5 kWh
Electricity costs (C)	0.1155\$ (Band IC)
Battery depreciation cost (D)	0.13 \$/kWh (2015) 0.067 \$/kWh (2018) 0.034 \$/kWh (2022)
Charging speed (γ)	3.6 kW (linear)
Discharging speed (δ)	13.2 kW (linear)
Charging inefficiency (ϵ)	96% (Reichert 2010)
Discharging inefficiency (η)	97.4%
	Min. / Avg. / Max.
EVs available (a)	13% / 85% / 97%
Rental revenues	4.89 \$ / 20.04 \$ / 322.34 \$

$$j(x) = \begin{cases} 1, & if \quad PPI_{t-1,i} = NRB_{t-1,i} \\ & and \quad RB_{t-1,i} > NRB_{t-1,i} \\ 0, & otherwise \end{cases} \quad (11)$$

$$k(x) = \begin{cases} 1, & if \quad PPI_{t-1,i} = PRB_{t-1,i} \\ 0, & otherwise \end{cases} \quad (12)$$

$$m(x) = \begin{cases} 1, & if \quad PPI_{t-1,i} = PRB_{t-1,i} \\ & and \quad RB_{t-1,i} > PRB_{t-1,i} \\ 0, & otherwise \end{cases} \quad (13)$$

The actual allocation of individual cars is done in the order of profitability according to PPI, until the respective overall quantities $\sum_{i=1}^{I} \Psi^{neg} - RPE^{neg}$ and $\sum_{i=1}^{I} \Psi^{pos} - RPE^{pos}$ are reached. Each quantity is submitted to the operating reserve market at the average price from Equations 5 and 7 weighted by the quantities for the individual prices respectively.

Design Evaluation: Evidence from a Real World Setting

In order to assess the economic viability of the above described algorithm in practice, we apply it to the carsharing service Car2Go of the Daimler AG. We use a seven week time period from 08.11.2013 till 27.12.2013 as a training data set (bootstrap period). From this training set the expected values for the average driven kilometers, rental time, rental profit, and rental probabilities at each time are used to train the model. The last four weeks from 28.12.2013 to 24.01.2014 are used to evaluate the model.

Carsharing Operator: Car2Go

The free floating fleet of Car2Go in Stuttgart, Germany consists of 500 EVs. These EVs are distributed over 54 zip codes of Stuttgart and its surrounding area. Members pay for this service on a use basis only (per minute and km above a threshold of 50 km) and are incentivized to return EVs to a charging station when the battery status is below 30% by rewarding them with 20 free driving minutes.

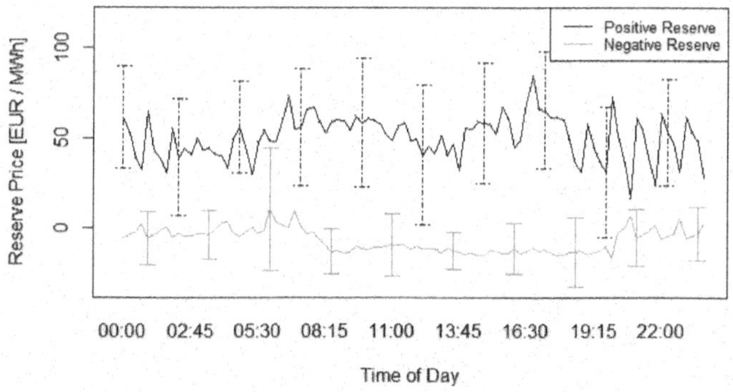

Figure 1: Daily Operating Reserve Prices from 08.11.2013 to 24.01.2014.

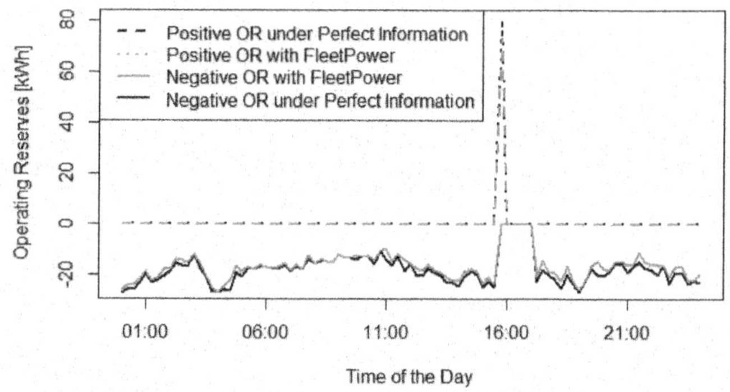

Figure 2: Virtual Power Plant Output for the 5th of January 2014.

The carsharing operator shared data with us for the availability of EVs with a granularity of 15 minutes. This data contains the unique car name, the geo coordinates where the car is parked, the street name and zip code of that location (l), the state of charge of the battery (Q), and whether the EV is currently charging. Based on this information we can infer how long the EV was rented, how many kilometers were driven, and how much revenues were earned as rental benefit (RB). For an overview of the dataset see Table 2.

Secondary Operating Reserves: Transnet BW

As illustrated in the section Operating Reserves EV storage is particularly suited for the secondary operating reserve, due to its fast response requirement. Therefore we use auction data on secondary operating reserves to determine the prices for balancing at each point in time. We use the data from regelleistung.net, the German operating reserve operator for the region of Transnet BW (see Figure 1). Note that even though the profits from renting out EVs are higher on average, the commitments on the operating reserve markets take precedence over renting because a severe penalty is imposed for not living up to commitments. As a consequence rental profits that occurred in the dataset, while the algorithm committed these EVs to the VPP, are opportunity cost. Only if another, available EV was in the immediate vicinity this car was assumed to be taken instead. Immediate vicinity is interpreted as if customers were willing to walk to another car if it is less than normally distributed with a mean of 250 meters and a standard deviation of 100 meters away (d) as calculated with the haversine formula (Robusto 1957).

Fitting the Model to the Case

We train the model for the expected rental benefit (Equation 2) from 7 weeks of Car2Go rental data. It suggests that being at a place and time where EVs frequently get rented out has a strong positive impact, and lower battery levels have a negative impact on rental profits. To account for the asymmetric payoff from rental (average benefit per rental is \$ 20.04) and operating reserves (average benefit is \$ 0.40) we use the upper 99% confidence level to overstate the rental benefit accordingly.

After we have fitted the model for the individual performance indicators to the Car2Go case, we can train the fleet level decision making model with information from the individual EVs. At popular time intervals, and therefore adjacent intervals, fewer cars (stored electricity) are available but many will be rented out. In a similar way the stored electricity is positively related to the number of EVs rented out in the previous time interval. In this case we use both an upper 99% confidence interval and a safety stock s of 56 and 33 kWh respectively for positive and negative operating reserves which was optimal during the test period.

Operating Reserve Markets: Design for Flexibility

Current operating reserve markets use dedicated idle capacity as operating reserves which are committed a week in advance. It is not only inefficient to have that much idle reserve, but it is also not fit to balance a market with large capacities of decentralized energy sources. Therefore we propose and use an alteration of the market design. In this design power comes from a critical mass of flexible, absorptive generation and storage capacity, rather than having fixed commitments one week in advance. This has the advantage that battery storage can offer additional reserves to the market to meet growing demand. Note that this market design is not risk free. It depends on the availability of sufficient flexible absorption and generation capacity, like storage in batteries that is elastic to price changes.

Analysis and Discussion

Over the four week hold out period the algorithm made 154,445 EV management decisions, of which it decided in 75,813 instances to turn an EV into a VPP (49%). Of these 75,813 instances only 89 were for providing positive regulation capacity and 75,724 instances were for providing negative regulation capacity. In 109 of these instances a lessee wanted to rent an EV while it was committed as a VPP; in 69 of these instances there was a car in walking distance. That means that we had to refuse lessees in 40 instances over the four week time period translating into a gross profits reduction of 0.125%. At the same time the algorithm traded 61 MWh on the operating reserve market, increasing the gross

Table 3: Sensitivity Analysis for Different Balancing Needs and Battery Technology Developments.

	Balancing Need Today	**Balancing Need x2**	**Balancing Need x3**
Battery Technology 2015	↑ 7.18% gross profit	↑ 8.75% gross profit	↑ 11.44% gross profit
Battery Technology 2018	↑ 7.20% gross profit	↑ 8.90% gross profit	↑ 11.81% gross profit
Battery Technology 2022	↑ 7.23% gross profit	↑ 9.05% gross profit	↑ 12.11% gross profit

profits of Car2Go by about 7.18% assuming capital costs are 60% of rental revenues (industry average). This increase is significant at the 0.01 significance level (p-value 0.002). The negative operating reserves account for virtually all the increased gross profit (99.8%). This can be traced back to the high battery costs, which are higher than the average positive operating reserve price. When we compare this to a case in which Car2Go has perfect information on future usage of EVs, we see that FleetPower makes almost optimal decisions. With perfect information they would increase gross profits by about 8%. The relatively high accuracy of FleetPower can mostly be attributed to the risk pooling by substituting committed EVs for operating reserves with other available EVs if a lessee wants to rent a specific EV. If we were to make this decision for each EV individually, we would increase gross profits by only 0.07%. One can conclude that using FleetPower is significantly more profitable then only renting out EVs and comes close to a scenario where the fleet owner has perfect information. Figure 2 illustrates at which times of the day FleetPower turns EVs into a VPP and how much output it produces. Most of the day the EVs provide negative reserve capacity, but at 16.00 PM the market price is high enough for the VPP to provide positive reserve capacity.

Planning for Change: A Sensitivity Analysis

In order to assess how rapid developments in the energy sector will influence the decisions and their profitability in the future, we consider three scenarios for future balancing needs. In the first scenario we consider the current market need for balancing, in the second scenario we consider market prices when the balancing need goes up twofold, and in the third scenario we consider market prices when the balancing need goes up threefold. The scenarios are derived by multiplying the balancing demand per time interval by 2 and 3 respectively, which increases volatility proportionately along the merit order. Besides the balancing requirements, also a change in the costs of battery technology is expected. This is due to a large investment in battery technology not only for EV but also laptops, mobile phones, and other applications. We consider three scenarios for the battery depreciation costs. The first scenario of 0.13$/kWh is likely to be achieved by 2015, the second scenario of 0.067$/kWh is likely by 2018, and the 3rd scenario of 0.034$/kWh is likely by 2022 (US Department of Energy 2013).

As expected we see a steady increase in profits for fleet owners with increasing balancing needs and decreasing battery costs from initially a 7.18% gross profit increase to 12.11% under the 2022 scenario. At first glance it might seem as if the increase in the balancing need is more decisive than the battery technology. However, battery costs only have an influence on positive operating reserves, which account for about 0.2% today and 14% under the 2022 scenario. Therefore the impact appears relatively minor, but it increases as the positive operating reserves play a bigger role. For an overview of the gross profit increases for the individual scenarios see Table 3. While under current conditions it would hardly be economical to base positive operating reserves on EV storage only, it does make sense in the 2022 scenario. In that case about every 20th person would need to have an EV that participates, but is not dedicated to the operating reserves. Under these circumstances one could retire all peaking power plants in the secondary operating reserve market, reducing the peak to average ratio by 4.5%. The peak to average ratio is the bottleneck in the electrical grid and determines its efficiency. When we relate this to increasing energy efficiency, we find that despite efficiency losses when charging and discharging EVs, the overall efficiency achieved by retiring peaking power plants offsets these losses and increases overall system efficiency.

Conclusion and Future Work

In this study we have proposed and evaluated the agent-based algorithm FleetPower which enables companies with EV fleets to participate in the operating reserve market next to renting out electric vehicles (EV). It continuously makes the decision whether a specific EV at a specific location should be available for rent, or to sell part of its energy storage as negative or positive operating reserve. The algorithm makes this decision based on forecasts for revenues from rental, positive, and negative operating reserves and aggregate EV availability in VPPs with an accuracy above 99%. We show that using EV for operating reserves enhances gross profits of the EV fleet owner by 7.18%, but that the market design of the operating reserves needs to change for more flexibility to tap into the potential of large scale storage of EVs. V2G currently accounts for only a marginal proportion of these additional profits, while 99.8% are due to negative operating reserves. With a rising need for balancing capacity and decreasing battery costs, also V2G will account for a higher share (14%) of the increase in gross profits by 2022. In total the gross profits for EV fleet owners could go up by as much as 12.11% by 2022. With this algorithm it is possible to replace carbon intensive generation capacity with clean energy storage in the future, which increases system efficiency (peak to average ratio) by 4.5%.

In future research we will analyze the influence of seasonality on the ability of EVs to replace peaking power plants. In addition we expand the analysis with tow cities in the US and NL to account for different levels of renewable energy sources. Finally we plan to implement the broker in Power TAC to compete with and benchmark against other brokers.

References

Firnkorn, J., and Müller, M. 2011. What will be the environmental effects of new free-floating car-sharing systems? the case of car2go in ulm. *Ecological Economics* 70(8):1519–1528.

Geels, F. 2004. From sectoral systems of innovation to socio-technical systems: Insights about dynamics and change from sociology and institutional theory. *Research policy* 33(6):897–920.

International Energy Agency. 2014. *World Energy Investment Outlook*. Paris, France: OECD/IEA.

Kahlen, M.; Ketter, W.; and van Dalen, J. 2014. Agent-coordinated virtual power plants of electric vehicles. In *Proceedings of the 13th International Conference on Autonomous Agents and Multiagent Systems (AAMAS 2014)*, 1547–1548.

Kassakian, J. G., and Schmalensee, R. 2011. The future of the electric grid: An interdisciplinary mit study. Technical report, Massachusetts Institute of Technology. ISBN 978-0-9828008-6-7.

Ketter, W.; Collins, J.; Gini, M.; Gupta, A.; and Schrater, P. 2012. Real-time tactical and strategic sales management for intelligent agents guided by economic regimes. *Information Systems Research* 23(4):1263–1283.

Ketter, W.; Collins, J.; and Reddy, P. 2013. Power TAC: A competitive economic simulation of the smart grid. *Energy Economics* 39(0):262–270.

Ketter, W.; Peters, M.; and Collins, J. 2013. Autonomous agents in future energy markets: The 2012 Power Trading Agent Competition. In *AAAI Conference on Artificial Intelligence*, 1298–1304.

Kim, E.; Tabors, R.; Stoddard, R.; and Allmendinger, T. 2012. Carbitrage: Utility integration of electric vehicles and the smart grid. *The Electricity Journal* 25(2):16–23.

Malhotra, A.; Melville, N.; and Watson, R. 2013. Spurring impactful research on information systems for environmental sustainability. *MIS Quarterly* 37(4):1265–1274.

Peterson, S.; Whitacre, J.; and Apt, J. 2010. The economics of using plug-in hybrid electric vehicle battery packs for grid storage. *Journal of Power Sources* 195(8):2377–2384.

Ramchurn, S.; Vytelingum, P.; Rogers, A.; and Jennings, N. 2011. Agent-based control for decentralised demand side management in the smart grid. In *Proc. of 10th Int. Conf. on Autonomous Agents and Multiagent Systems - Innovative Applications Track (AAMAS 2011)*, 5–12.

Reddy, P., and Veloso, M. 2011. Learned Behaviors of Multiple Autonomous Agents in Smart Grid Markets. In *AAAI Conference on Artificial Intelligence*, 1396–1401.

Reichert, S. 2010. Considerations for highly efficient bidirectional battery chargers for e-mobility. In *E-Mobility. Technologien, Infrastruktur, Maerkte*, 5. Leipzig: VDE-Verlag.

Robusto, C. 1957. The cosine-haversine formula. *American Mathematical Monthly* 64(1):38–40.

Schill, W. 2011. Electric vehicles in imperfect electricity markets: The case of Germany. *Energy Policy* 39(10):6178–6189.

Sioshansi, R. 2012. OR Forum-Modeling the impacts of electricity tariffs on plug-in hybrid electric vehicle charging, costs, and emissions. *Operations Research* 60(3):5060–516.

The European Parliament, and The Council of the European Union. 2009. Directive 2009/28/ec of the eurpean parliament and of the council on the promotion of the use of energy from renewable sources and amending and subsequently repealing directives 2001/77/ec and 2003/30/ec. *Official Journal of the European Union* L 140(1):16–62.

Tomic, J., and Kempton, W. 2007. Using fleets of electric-drive vehicles for grid support. *Journal of Power Sources* 168(2):459–468.

Urieli, D., and Stone, P. 2014. TacTex13: A champion adaptive Power Trading Agent. In *AAAI Conference on Artificial Intelligence*, 1447–1448.

US Department of Energy. 2013. EV everywhere grand challenge blueprint.

Valogianni, K.; Ketter, W.; Collins, J.; and Zhdanov, D. 2014. Effective management of electric vehicle storage using smart charging. In *AAAI Conference on Artificial Intelligence*, 472–478.

Voice, T.; Vytelingum, P.; Ramchurn, S.; Rogers, A.; and Jennings, N. 2011. Decentralised control of micro-storage in the smart grid. In *AAAI Conference on Artificial Intelligence*, 1421–1427.

Vytelingum, P.; Voice, T.; Ramchurn, S.; Rogers, A.; and Jennings, N. 2011. Theoretical and practical foundations of Large-Scale Agent-Based Micro-Storage in the smart grid. *Journal of Artificial Intelligence Research* 42:765–813.

Energy Usage Behavior Modeling in Energy Disaggregation via Marked Hawkes Process

Liangda Li[1,2] and **Hongyuan Zha**[1,2]
[1]Software Engineering Institute, East China Normal University, Shanghai, China
[2]College of Computing, Georgia Institute of Technology, Atlanta, GA, USA

Abstract

Energy disaggregation, the task of taking a whole home electricity signal and decomposing it into its component appliances, has been proved to be essential in energy conservation research. One powerful cue for breaking down the entire household's energy consumption is user's daily energy usage behavior, which has so far received little attention: existing works on energy disaggregation mostly ignored the relationship between the energy usages of various appliances across different time slots. To model such relationship, we combine topic models with Hawkes processes, and propose a novel probabilistic model based on marked Hawkes process that enables the modeling of marked event data. The proposed model seeks to capture the influence from the occurrence and the marks of one usage event to the occurrence and the marks of subsequent usage events in the future. We also develop an inference algorithm based on variational inference for model parameter estimation. Experimental results on both synthetic data and three real world data sets demonstrate the effectiveness of our model, which outperforms state-of-the-art approaches in decomposing the entire consumed energy to each appliance. Analyzing the influence captured by the proposed model provides further insights into numerous interesting energy usage behavior patterns.

Introduction

Energy conservation has become a critical issue in modern society and data analysis methodology has recently been applied to the analysis of energy consumption patterns in households. Several prior studies (Darby 2006; Neenan and Robinson 2009; Wytock and Kolter 2014) have shown that consumers, i.e., household members are more likely to conserve their energy usage when provided with breakdown energy consumption records. However, such fine-grained energy consumption data is not readily available, since it requires numerous additional meters installed on individual appliances. Therefore there has been much interest in the data analysis problem of energy disaggregation — the task of taking a whole-house energy signal and separating it into its component appliances. One powerful cue for breaking down the entire household's energy consumption is user behavior in energy usage(Baptista et al. 2014), which is known to be a major factor in determining the energy consumption in households. Such *energy usage behaviors* can include: how users perform their daily routines, how they share the usage of appliances, and users' habits in using certain types of appliances. Understanding such energy usage behaviors will significantly increase the accuracy of estimating the usage time of each appliance, which consequently benefits the energy disaggregation task.

Despite of the importance of energy usage behaviors, they have not received enough attention in the recent literature, especially how a user's current energy usage behavior influences his/her or other people's future usage behavior. Modeling such influence is important due to the following two reasons: 1) energy usage behaviors rarely depend on the current time slots only. One's energy usage behaviors in the previous time slots also exert a significant impact. For instance, a user's usage time of washing machine can be different from day to day, but his/her sequential behaviors in clothes washing are always similar: first using the washer, and then the dryer. 2) under many circumstances, a user's behavior is not just determined by himself/herself, but influenced by other members in the same household. For example, when parents wake up earlier than usual in the morning, they may also wake up their children earlier than usual. Another instance is that two household members are not able to use the bathroom at the same time, and consequently one member has to postpone his/her usage of the bathroom. Thus, to understand energy usage behaviors, appropriate modeling of influence among the energy usage behaviors of different users in the same household across different time slots is essential.

Unfortunately, the influence between energy usage behaviors is hard to model directly, since the state-of-the-art smart-grid data rarely records the number of household members, and the exact timestamp when a certain member uses a certain appliance. Since the energy consumption of each appliance is relies on the user behavior, we turn to modeling the relationship between the energy usages of different appliances across different time slots, and expect that such relationship will be able to reveal the influence between the energy usage behaviors of different users in the same household. We want to emphasize that such relationship has so far been largely ignored by existing works on energy disaggregation (Kolter, Batra, and Ng 2010; Kolter and Jaakkola 2012; Parson et al. 2012). Those works mostly focus on the distribution of energy consumption of each appliance alone. They either learned the energy usage patterns of each appliance within a certain period (for instance, a week), or studied the influence between energy usage patterns from one time slot to the next. Recent works discussed the dependency between appliances in the same time slot only (Kim et al. 2011). More importantly our method, while modeling the influence between energy usage patterns, also pays attention to the relationship between the energy usages of different appliances across different time slots.

One main challenge in modeling the influence among various appliances across different time slots is how to model the influence between *marked* events, which is defined to be events with marks that contain detailed information of the corresponding event. Under our scenario of energy disaggregation, events are the usage of a certain appliance in a certain time slot, while their marks are the amount of consumed energy. We leverage the general idea of marked point process for our modeling purpose (Rasmussen 2013). Specifically, we propose a novel probabilistic model named marked Hawkes process (M-Hawkes) based on the combination of multivariate Hawkes processes and topic models. This M-Hawkes is designed to model how the occurrence and the mark of an event *together* influence the occurrence and the mark of subsequent events in the near future. In the proposed M-Hawkes model, the topic model part models the distribution of marks of observed events, designed to find user behavior patterns underlying the amount of consumed energy of each appliance in each time slot, while the Hawkes process part models the occurrences of observed events, and captures the influence between different appliances under different energy usage behavior patterns across different time slots.

In a nutshell, our major contributions include: (1) We fully utilize both temporal and energy amount information in addressing the energy disaggregation task, emphasizing the analysis of the underlying energy usage behavior patterns; (2) We consider the relationship among the energy consumption of different appliances across different time slots, which existing works failed to model; (3) We propose a novel probabilistic model that combines Hawkes processes with topic models, which enables the modeling of the influence from the occurrence and the mark of an event to the occurrence and the mark of subsequent events in the future.

Problem Definition

Let us consider a typical scenario in energy disaggregation, where M appliances are used in a sequence of N time slots $T = \{t_n, n = 1, \ldots, N\}$. Multiple appliances can be used simultaneously in one time slot, and certain appliance is not necessarily always in use. Our paper considers the unsupervised setting, i.e., we only observe the total amount of consumed energy X_n in each time slot n, while the amount of consumed energy $x_{m,n}$ of each appliance m used in that time slot is unavailable. The target of energy disaggregation is to predict each $x_{m,n}$ based on the observed T and X.

Instead of straightforwardly predicting $x_{m,n}$ from X_n, we introduce a set of latent variables $\{Y_{m,n}\}$ to denote whether the m-th appliance is used in the n-th time slot, and turn to solving a much easier problem first: which appliances are in use in each of the time slot. The basic intuition is that the usage of one appliance raises the probability of the usage of related appliances (including itself) in the near future. For instance, people are very likely to use dryer after using washing machine. Such self- & mutually exciting nature coincides with the *self- & mutually exciting* property of the multi-dimensional Hawkes process, i.e., the occurrence of one event in the past will trigger events happening in the future.

Multi-dimensional Hawkes Process

The multi-dimensional Hawkes process is a class of self- or mutually-exciting point process models (Hawkes 1971), which are widely used to describe data that are localized at a finite set of time points $\{t_1, \ldots, t_N\}$ (Schoenberg 2010). Formally, the multi-dimensional Hawkes process on an event cascade $\{t_l\}_{l=1}^N$ is defined to be a M-dimensional point process with the intensity of the m-th dimension given by:

$$\lambda_m(t) = \mu_m + \sum_{t_l<t} \alpha_{m_l,m}\kappa(t - t_l)$$

Here μ_m denotes the base intensity of the m-th dimension, $\kappa(t - t_l)$ is a time-decaying kernel, while $\alpha_{m,m'}$ denotes the infectivity from events in the m-th dimension to events in the m'-th dimension. Hawkes process has been widely used in applications, such as earthquake prediction (Ogata 1988), sales modeling (Yan et al. 2015; Errais, Giesecke, and Goldberg 2010), Asset management (Yan et al. 2013), search behavior modeling (Li et al. 2014), crime modeling (Stomakhin, Short, and Bertozzi 2011), and armed conflict analysis (Mangion et al. 2012; Li and Zha 2013).

In our tasks, building a multi-dimensional Hawkes process on Y relates the inference of m-th appliance usage state in the n-th time slot $Y_{m,n}$ with that of other appliances in different time slots, thus can be expected to sharply raise the inference accuracy.

Marked Hawkes Process

Although the (multi-dimensional) Hawkes process has been proved to be effective in modeling the influence between event occurrences in many applications, we find it unable to completely solve our energy disaggregation problem. For one thing, the total amount of consumed energy in each time slot has not been utilized; for another, it only predicts whether an appliance is in use rather than the energy it consumes. A better solution is modeling marked events instead of normal events, where the mark of an event refers to those additional features other than the temporal information that describes the event.[1] In energy disaggregation, *taking the*

[1]A mark can be the casualty of an armed conflict event, the magnitude of an earthquake event, and in our application, the consumed energy of an appliance usage event.

usage of an appliance in a time slot as an event, the corresponding amount of consumed energy is actually the mark of that event. Such marked events are very common in current social networks, as the descriptions of events are usually available.

Since the marks of an event are very likely to be described by numerous features — a vector with each feature represented by continuous or categorical variables, directly modeling the relationship between marks and occurrences of different events is difficult. One widely used effective solution is the topic model, which clusters all observed marks into several topics/categories, with similar marks in the same category.

To enable the modeling of marks of events in Hawkes processes, we further introduce a new set of latent variables $\{Z_{m,n,k}\}$ to denote whether the marks of an event from the m-th dimension, whose occurrence is previously denoted by $Y_{m,n}$, belongs to the k-th category/topic, we propose the following novel multi-dimensional Hawkes process to model the entire event sequence, with the intensity of an event from the m-th dimension occurring in time slot t whose intensity can be written as: whose intensity can be written as:

$$\lambda_m(t) = \mu_m + \sum_{t_l<t} \sum_{m'} Y_{m',l} \sum_{k,k'} Z_{m,n,k} Z_{m',l,k'} \beta_{m,m',k,k'} \kappa(t - t_l). \tag{1}$$

Here the base intensity μ_m captures how often an event from m-th dimension happens spontaneously, while $\beta_{m,m',k,k'}$ models the degree of *influence* between a event from dimension m with marks of category k to a event from dimension m' with marks of category k'. Notice that the proposed new Hawkes process can handle events with multidimensional marks, while in our application, only a single dimension, the amount of consumed energy, is used.

According to the definition of $Y_{m,n}$, we have $Y_{m,n} = \text{HawkesProcess}(\lambda_m(t_n))$. Thus the proposed new Hawkes process straightforwardly models the influence between the occurrence and the mark pattern membership of past events and those of the current event. Assume each appliance has K energy consumption patterns with the k-th pattern denoted as $\theta_{m,k}$, the entire amount of consumed energy in the n-th time slot X_n can be approximated by $\sum_m Y_{m,n} \sum_k \theta_{m,k} Z_{m,n,k}$. The approximation itself does not provide much evidence for the inference of Y and Z, and the learning of θ. However, by constructing a multi-dimensional marked Hawkes process on Y and Z, we relate the inference of $Y_{m,n}$ and $Z_{m,n}$ with that of other appliances in different time slots, thus the inference/learning accuracy can be expected to be increased.

Finally, we present our generative model that produces the entire energy consumption as follows:

- Draw a vector μ of length M that denotes the base intensity of each appliance and a $MK \times MK$ infectivity matrix β that denotes the degree of influence between different appliances under different consumption patterns.
- For each appliance m,
  - draw a K dimensional vector θ_m, where each dimension indicates a single energy consumption pattern of the appliance.
  - draw a K dimensional membership vector $\pi_m \sim \text{Dirichlet}(\alpha)$.
- For the n-th time slot,
  - For the m-th appliance in the n-th time slot,
    * Draw whether it will be used by $Y_{m,n} \sim \text{HawkesProcess}(\lambda_m(\cdot))$, where the intensity λ_m is defined as in Eqn (1);
    * Draw the user energy usage pattern membership $Z_{m,n} \sim \text{Multinomial}(\pi_m)$;
    * Draw the amount of consumed energy of device $x_{m,n} \sim Y_{m,n}\text{Gaussian}(\sum_k \theta_{m,k} Z_{m,n,k}, \sigma)$;[2]
  - Calculate the total amount of consumed energy in the n-th time slot $X_n = \sum_m x_{m,n}$.

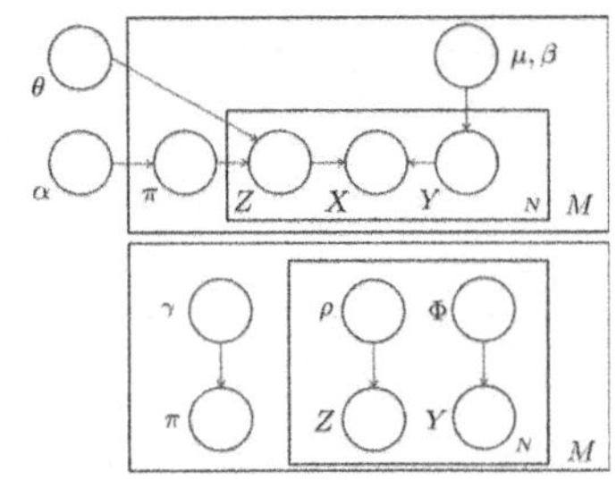

Figure 1: Graphical model representation of M-Hawkes and the variational distribution that approximates the likelihood. The upper figure shows the graphical model representation of M-Hawkes, while the lower figure shows the variational distribution that approximates the likelihood.

Note that in our M-Hawkes model, the number of appliances that can be simultaneously used in the same time slot is constrained by the total amount of consumed energy at that time. Such a constraint not only benefits the inferring of energy usage patterns of each appliance, but also enables the modeling of several events occurring in the same time slot, which existing Hawkes models hardly handled.

Under our M-Hawkes model, the joint probability of data $T = \{N(\cdot)\} = \{\{t_n\}_{n=1}^N\}$, $X = \{\{X_n\}_{n=1}^N\}$ and latent variables π, Y, Z can be written as follows:

$$p(T, X, \pi_{1:M}, Y, Z|\alpha, \theta, \mu, \beta) = P(T, Y|Z, \mu, \beta) \prod_n P(X_n|Y_n, Z_n, \theta)$$
$$\prod_n \prod_m P(Z_{m,n}|\pi_m) \prod_m \prod_n P(Y_{m,n}|\pi_m) \prod_m P(\pi_m|\alpha).$$

Inference

In this section, we derive a mean-field variational Bayesian inference algorithm for our proposed M-Hawkes model.

Variational Inference

Under M-Hawkes model, given observations of both temporal information $T = \{N(\cdot)\} = \{\{t_n\}_{n=1}^N\}$ and consumed energy X of energy consumption event sequences, the log-likelihood for the complete data is given by $\log p(T, X|\mu, \beta, \alpha, \theta)$. Since this true posterior is hard to

[2]In our experiments, we use a constant σ.

infer directly, we turn to variational methods (Blei and Jordan 2005), whose main idea is to posit a distribution over the latent variables with variational parameters, and find the settings of the parameters so as to make the distribution close to the true posterior in Kullback-Leibler (KL) divergence.

$$q(\pi_{1:M}, Y, Z|\gamma_{1:M}, \Phi, \rho_{1:N}) = \prod_m q_1(\pi_m|\gamma_m) \prod_m \prod_n q_2(Y_{m,n}|\phi_{m,n}) q_2(Z_{m,n}|\rho_{m,n})$$

where q_1 is a Dirichlet, q_2 is a multinomial, and $\{\gamma_{1:M}, \Phi, \rho\}$ are the set of variational parameters. We optimize those free parameters to tighten the following lower bound $\mathcal{L}'$ for our likelihood:

$$\log p(T, X|\mu, \beta, \alpha, \theta) \geq E_q[\log p(T, X, \pi_{1:M}, Y, Z|\alpha, \theta, \mu, \beta)] - E_q[\log q(\pi_{1:M}, Y, Z)]. \quad (2)$$

Isolating terms containing λ in Eqn (2), we have

$$\mathcal{L}_h = \sum_{m=1}^{M} \sum_n E_q(\log \lambda(Y_{m,n})) - \sum_{m=1}^{M} \int_0^T E_q(\lambda(s))ds, \quad (3)$$

as the partial likelihood on temporal data assuming consumption pattern distribution is known. On one hand, we have $\sum_{m=1}^{M} \int_0^T E_q(\lambda(s))ds = \sum_{m=1}^{M} b_m \beta_{m,m'k,k'} + T \sum_{m=1}^{M} \mu_m$. Here

$$b_{m,m',k,k'} = \sum_{n=1}^{N} \sum_{l=1}^{n-1} r_{m,m',lnkk'} (K(t_n - t_l) - K(t_{n-1} - t_l)),$$

where $K(t) = \int_0^t \kappa(s)ds$, and we define function $r_{m,m',lnkk'} = \phi_{m',l} \rho_{m,n,k} \rho_{m',l,k'}$. On the other hand, in order to update each Hawkes hyper-parameter μ and β independently, we adopt the strategy in (Yang and Zha 2013), and break down the log sum $E_q(\log \lambda(t_n))$ based on Jensen's inequality as:

$$\mathbb{E}_q(\log(\lambda_m(t_n))) \geq \eta_{m,nn} \log(\mu_m) - \eta_{m,nn} \log(\eta_{m,nn}) + \sum_{l=1}^{n-1} \sum_{m',k,k'} \eta_{m,m',lnkk'} \log(r_{m,m',lnkk'} \beta_{m,m',k,k'} \kappa(t_n - t_l)) - \sum_{l=1}^{n-1} r_{m,m',lnkk'} \eta_{m,m',lnkk'} \log(\eta_{m,m',lnkk'}),$$

where $\{\eta\}$ is a set of branching variables constrained by:

$$\eta_{m,m',lnkk'} \geq 0, \ \eta_{m,nn} + \sum_{l=1}^{n-1} \sum_{m',k,k'} r_{m,m',lnkk'} \eta_{m,m',lnkk'} = 1.$$

Under a coordinate descent framework, we optimize the lower bound as in Eqn (2) against each variational latent variable[3] and the model hyper-parameter. For variational latent variables, we have the following process

- update rules for ρ's as:

$$\rho_{m,n,k} \propto \exp(\sum_m (\Psi(\gamma_{m,k}) - \Psi(\sum_k \gamma_{m,k})) + \log([X_n - \sum_{m' \neq m, k' \neq k} \phi_{m',n} \rho_{m',n,k'} \theta_{m',k'}]_+) - \log(\phi_{m,n} \theta_{m,k}) + \sum_{l=1}^{n-1} f_{l,n} + \sum_{l'=n+1}^{N_m} f_{n,l'}),$$

where we define

$$f_{l,n} = \sum_{m',k'} (\eta_{m,m',lnkk'} \phi_{m',l} \log(\frac{\beta_{m,m',k,k'} \kappa(t_n - t_l)}{\eta_{m,m',lnkk'}}) - \phi_{m',l}(K(t_n - t_l) - K(t_{n-1} - t_l))) \rho_{m',l,k'}$$

- update rules for γ's as:

$$\gamma_{m,k} = \alpha_k + \sum_n \rho_{m,n,k};$$

- update rules for ϕ's as:

$$\phi_{m,n} \propto \exp(\eta_{m,nn} \log(\mu_m) - \log(\sum_k \rho_{m,n,k} \theta_{m,k}) + \log([X_n - \sum_{m' \neq m, k} \phi_{m',n} \rho_{m',n,k} \theta_{m,k}]_+) + \sum_{l=1}^{n-1} \sum_{m',k,k'} \eta_{m,m',lnkk'} \log(b_{mm',lnkk'}) + \sum_{l=n+1}^{N} \sum_{m',k,k'} \eta_{m',m,nlkk'} \log(b_{mm',nlkk'})).$$

where $b_{mm',lnkk'} = r_{m,m',lnkk'} \beta_{m,m',k,k'} \kappa(t_n - t_l)$.

- and update rules for η as:

$$\eta_{m,nn} = \frac{\mu_m}{\mu_m + \sum_{l=1}^{n-1} \sum_{m',k,k'} b_{mm',lnkk'}},$$

$$\eta_{m,m',lnkk'} = \frac{\beta_{m,m',k,k'} \kappa(t_n - t_l)}{\mu_m + \sum_{l=1}^{n-1} \sum_{m',k,k'} b_{mm',lnkk'}}.$$

Learning

We use a variational expectation-maximization (EM) algorithm (Dempster, Laird, and Rubin 1977) to compute the parameters in our M-Hawkes model. This variational EM algorithm iteratively approximates the posterior by fitting the variational distribution q and optimizes the corresponding bound against the parameters.

In updating α, we use a Newton-Raphson method, since the approximate maximum likelihood estimate of α doesn't have a closed form solution. The Newton-Raphson method is conducted with a gradient and Hessian as follows:

$$\frac{\partial \mathcal{L}'}{\partial \alpha_k} = N(\Psi(\sum_k \alpha_k) - \Psi(\alpha_k)) + \sum_m (\Psi(\gamma_{m,k}) - \Psi(\sum_k \gamma_{m,k})),$$

$$\frac{\partial \mathcal{L}'}{\partial \alpha_{k_1} \alpha_{k_2}} = N(\mathbb{I}_{(k_1=k_2)} \Psi'(\alpha_{k_1}) - \Psi'(\sum_k \alpha_k)).$$

The maximum likelihood estimation of *energy usage pattern* θ can be derived through calculating the first derivative of lower-bound $\mathcal{L}'$ against corresponding parameters. We obtain the update formulas given as follows:

$$\theta_{m,k} = (\mathbf{A}^T \mathbf{A})^{-1} \mathbf{x}.$$

where $\mathbf{A} = [\phi_{m,n} \rho_{m,n,k}]_{n,mk}$ is a matrix of size $n \times mk$, and $\mathbf{x} = [X_n]_n$ is a vector of length n.

To obtain the approximate maximum likelihood estimation of Hawkes hyper-parameters, we optimize the lower bound as in Eqn (2) against each hyper-parameter, and update μ and β independently with closed-form solutions as:

$$\beta_{m,m',k,k'} = \frac{1}{b_m} \sum_{n,l<n} r_{m,m',lnkk'} \eta_{m,m',lnkk'}, \ \mu_m = \frac{1}{T} \sum_{n=1}^{N} \eta_{m,nn}$$

[3]Here we categorize branching variables η as variational latent variables.

In real world scenario β is usually a sparse matrix, as influence only exist in limited pairs of appliances and patterns. Thus to select effective influence and avoid overfitting, we enforce the sparsity of β by imposing lasso type of regularization as $\|\beta\|_1$, and employ the widely used alternating direction method of multipliers (ADMM) (Boyd 2010; Li and Zha 2014) to address the constraint optimization problem.

Our variation inference algorithm, named Marked-Hawkes (M-Hawkes), can be interpreted intuitively in the following way. The mark pattern distribution γ of each appliance is determined by both the topic/pattern prior and the pattern assignment of each appliance at each time slot. The probability ϕ of an appliance m used in the n-th time slot is jointly determined by: (a) other appliances used in the current time slot; (b) how likely an appliance was used spontaneously; (c) the influence from the occurrence and the mark pattern of past events to the current occurrence; and (d) the influence from the occurrence and the mark pattern of future events to the current occurrence. The energy consumption pattern ρ of an appliance m used in the n-th time slot is jointly determined by: (a) the pattern prior of this appliance; (b) the mark patterns of other appliances; (c) past/future influence to the current mark pattern.

In our mean-field variation inference algorithm, the computational cost of inferring variational variables is $O(NM^2K^2)$. The computational cost of the estimation of topic hyper-parameters is $O(NM^2K^2 + M^3K^3)$. The computational cost of the estimation of Hawkes hyper-parameters is $O(N^2M^2K^2)$, which can be reduced to $O(NM^2K^2)$ by only considering the influence in temporally-close time slots. Thus the total computational cost of our algorithm is $O(NM^2K^2 + M^3K^3)$. Since in real-world scenarios, influence exists only among limited pairs of appliances and patterns, M^2K^2 can be reduced to some much smaller constant, thus the above cost can be viewed as linear in the number of events or time slots.

Experiments

We evaluated our M-Hawkes model on both synthetic and real-world data sets, and compared the performance with the following baselines:

Hawkes: This is a normal multi-dimensional Hawkes process that models the occurrence of events only and no marks of events;

AFAMAP: This method proposed an approximation inference algorithm, named Additive Factorial Approximate MAP, to efficiently solve the additive factorial hidden Markov model by looking at the observed difference in consumed energy, and incorporating a robust mixture component that can account for unmodeled observation (Kolter and Jaakkola 2012).

NIALM: This method, named non-intrusive load monitoring, iteratively separated individual appliances from an aggregate energy consumption record, and updated prior models of general appliance types for each specific appliance instance (Parson et al. 2012).

Synthetic data

Data Generation. Given parameters $(M, N, K, \alpha, \theta, \mu, \beta)$, the synthetic data is sampled according to the proposed generative model. Here each element μ_m and $\beta_{m,m,k,k'}$ are randomly generated in $[0.5\hat{\mu}, 1.5\hat{\mu}]$ and $[0.5\hat{\beta}, 1.5\hat{\beta}]$ respectively before the simulation. In addition, α is a vector of size K, where the element α_k is generated in $[0.5\hat{\alpha}, 1.5\hat{\alpha}]$ before the simulation. Our synthetic data are simulated with two different settings:

- `Small`: $M = 10, N = 120, K = 3, \hat{\mu} = 0.01, \hat{\beta} = 0.5, \hat{\alpha} = 0.1, \hat{\theta} = 10$. Simulations were run 1,000 times using the pre-generated parameters μ, β;
- `Large`: $M = 50$, $N = 10{,}000$, $K = 5$, $\hat{\mu} = 0.01$, $\hat{\beta} = 0.5$, $\hat{\alpha} = 0.1$, $\hat{\theta} = 10$. Simulations were run 10 times.

To test the robustness of our method, we add two types of noise to the original synthetic data:

`Event Noisy`: We generate additional 10% of total number of events randomly in the time window of each already sampled event sequence, and add them to the sequence;

`Mark Noisy`: Instead of using the simulated X_n as the consumed energy at the n-th time slot, we use a noisy value X'_n which is obtained by adding Gaussian noise on X_n:

$$X'_n = \max(0.1e + 1, 0)X_n, \; e \sim \mathcal{N}(0, \sigma'). \tag{4}$$

The default value of σ' is set to be 1.

Evaluation metrics. We consider the following evaluation metrics: 1) first, we compare the average log predictive likelihood on events falling in the final 10% of the total time

Table 1: Inference and Estimation of M-Hawkes on Synthetic data

Data set	MAE(μ)	MAE(β)	MAE(Y)	MAE(Z)
S-Synthetic	0.065	0.197	0.9251	0.9432
S-E-Noisy	0.077	0.281	0.9042	0.9229
S-M-Noisy	0.092	0.313	0.8847	0.9085
L-Synthetic	0.148	0.346	0.8718	0.8942
L-E-Noisy	0.163	0.353	0.8503	0.8642
L-M-Noisy	0.187	0.386	0.8284	0.8372

"S-" stands for data setting `Small`, "L-" stands for `Large`, "E-" stands for `Event Noisy`, and "M-" stands for `Mark Noisy`.

Table 2: Log Predictive Likelihood on Both Synthetic and Real-world Data

Data set	M-Hawkes	Hawkes	AFAMAP	NIALM
S-Synthetic	-96.23	-136.26	-104.28	-108.63
S-E-Noisy	-109.21	-148.32	-120.94	-125.27
S-M-Noisy	-116.93	-161.24	-134.27	-140.05
L-Synthetic	-152.39	-194.38	-168.03	-173.26
L-E-Noisy	-165.82	-208.43	-181.46	-186.85
L-M-Noisy	-171.47	-224.06	-186.94	-191.27
Smart*	-145.39	-182.55	-157.83	-160.35
Pecan	-192.17	-234.88	-209.12	-216.43
REDD	-171.37	-210.26	-182.37	-187.51

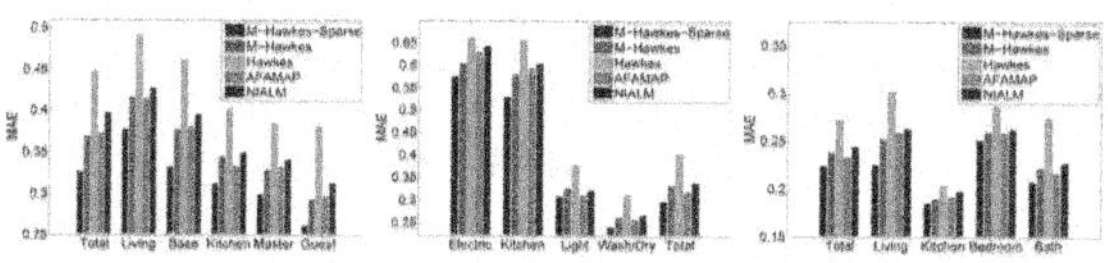

(a) Smart* (b) REDD (c) Pecan

Figure 2: Performance Comparison of Energy Disaggregation on Real World Data Sets.

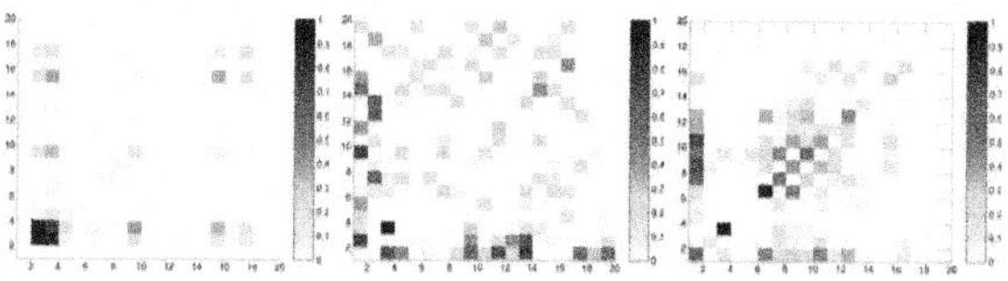

(a) Smart* (b) REDD (c) Pecan

Figure 3: Energy Usage Pattern on Real World Data Sets. Indice of significant appliances: Smart*: 2-lamp, 3-ac, 4-fan, 9-toaster, 15-refrigerator, 17-microwave. REDD: 1-main, 6-dishwaser, 15-kitchen_outlets, 17-light, 19-washer-dryer. Pecan: 1-ac, 2-dishwasher, 13-microwave, 16-refrigerator.

of each event cascade; 2) next we compare the average relative distance between the estimated parameters and ground-truth ones by Mean Average Error (MAE). For instance, the MAE of parameter β and $\frac{1}{M}\sum_m |\frac{\mu_m - \hat{\mu}_m}{\mu_m}|$, which we denote as $\mathrm{MAE}(\beta)$. 3) finally, we measure the performance of energy disaggregation by the MAE between the ground-truth consumed energy of each appliance $x_{m,n}$ and the estimated consumed energy $\hat{x}_{m,n}$, which is calculated based on the inferred $\rho_{m,n}$ and the estimated $\hat{\theta}_m$.

Inference and Estimation. Table 1 evaluates both the accuracy of our proposed variational inference algorithm in parameter estimation and latent variable inference on the synthetic data. We find that, on the small synthetic data, M-Hawkes can recover the Hawkes parameters μ and β very well, and accurately estimate the model's hyper-parameters. On the large synthetic data, M-Hawkes's performance on parameter estimation becomes worse. The shapely increased number of appliances makes the event occurrence prediction more difficult, and further affects the learning of users' energy usage behavior patterns. On both noisy data sets, M-Hawkes's performances in both inference and estimation become worse. We also find that the performance of energy disaggregation become worse with respect to the increase of the number of appliances, which shapely increases the complexity of the problem.

Real-world Data

We also conducted extensive experiments on two real-world data sets. The first data set is Smart* (Barker et al. 2012), which is a high-resolution data set from three homes including over 50 appliances.. The second data set is Reference Energy Disaggregation Dataset (REDD) (Kolter and Johnson 2011). This data set comprises six houses including around 20 appliances. The third data set is Pecan Street [4]. This data set collects one-minute resolution disaggregated data for 450+ homes including around 20 appliances, dating from late 2012 to early 2014.

Model Fitness. Table 2 shows the log predictive likelihood on energy consumption falling in the final 10% of the total time of data. According to Table 2, M-Hawkes fits both synthetic and real-world data better than alternative probabilistic models. The comparison on synthetic data is meaningful since we add noise into it. AFAMAP performs better than the normal multi-dimensional Hawkes process, which shows the importance of modeling marks of events besides the occurrences. On both noisy data sets, the performances of all models become worse. However, the decrease of the performance of M-Hawkes is smaller than baselines, which demonstrates the robustness of our proposed model. Thus when the usage timestamps and the amounts of consumed energy of some appliances are misrecorded, M-Hawkes performs better in energy disaggregation, and learns energy usage behaviors better.

Performance on Energy Disaggregation. To illustrate the effectiveness of the proposed model in energy disaggregation, we compare it with all baselines measured by $\mathrm{MAE}(X)$. Here we use M-Hawkes-NS to denote the M-Hawkes model with no sparsity constraint on Hawkes hyper-parameter β. According to Figure 2, M-Hawkes performs at least 5% better than all compared methods with comparable time costs. Also, M-Hawkes outperforms compared methods on all categorized appliances. Such results demonstrate the importance of modeling the relationship between the consumed energy of different appliances across different time slots. M-Hawkes's advantage over M-Hawkes-NS illustrates that only a limited number of dependencies exist between appliances in real world energy consumption.

Energy Usage Behavior Pattern Analysis. Based on the parameters learned by the proposed M-Hawkes model, we analyze the energy usage behavior patterns detected in real world energy consumption. According to Figure 3, influences exist in only limited pairs of appliances. Moreover, the degrees of those influences are very different. In the Smart* data, the influence between lamp and ac is greater than those between all other pairs of appliances. The influence between refrigerator and microwave is greater than that between refrigerator and toaster, which implies that people are more likely to cook food using microwave than toaster. Notice that Smart* data only recorded significant energy consumptions of refrigerator, which makes its usages easily detectable. In addition, the self-influence on some appliances, such as ac, are also very significant. The interpretation is that those appliances are often used for a long time continuously. The results on REDD also show that rarely used appliances, such as dishwaser and washer-dryer influence much less other appliances than those frequently used appliances, such as light and kitchen outlets. Moreover, the influence between a certain pair of appliances is not always symmetric. In Pecan, the influence from refrigerator to microwave is greater than the influence from microwave to refrigerator. One explanation is that people are used to open refrigerator to fetch food

[4]http://www.pecanstreet.org/

before turn on the microwave to cook them. We also find such phenomenon in Smart* data.

Conclusion and Future Work

In this paper, we formulated the task of energy disaggregation into the modeling of marked event sequences. Our paper presented a probabilistic model that integrates topic models with Hawkes processes to capture the influence from the occurrence and the mark of an event to the occurrences and the marks of future events. In future work, it would be interesting to consider other marks, e.g., the attributes of appliances, into this framework, and investigate the performance of M-Hawkes in other domains. In addition, we'll attempt to directly model the behavior of users instead appliances, and the influence inbetween.

Acknowledgments

This work is supported in part by NSF IIS-1116886 and NIH R01 GM108341.

References

Baptista, M.; Fang, A.; Prendinger, H.; Prada, R.; and Yamaguchi, Y. 2014. Accurate household occupant behavior modeling based on data mining techniques. In *Proceedings of the Twenty-Eighth AAAI Conference on Artificial Intelligence, July 27 -31, 2014, Québec City, Québec, Canada.*, 1164–1170.

Barker, S.; Mishra, A.; Irwin, D.; Cecchet, E.; Shenoy, P.; and Albrecht, J. 2012. Smart*: An open data set and tools for enabling research in sustainable homes. In *Proceedings of the 2012 Workshop on Data Mining Applications in Sustainability (SustKDD 2012), Beijing, China.*

Blei, D., and Jordan, M. 2005. Variational inference for dirichlet process mixtures. In *Bayesian Analysis*, volume 1, 121–144.

Boyd, S. 2010. Distributed optimization and statistical learning via the alternating direction method of multipliers. *Foundations and Trends in Machine Learning* 3(1):1–122.

Darby, S. 2006. The effectiveness of feedback on energy consumption. *Technical report, Environmental Change In- stitute, University of Oxford.*

Dempster, A. P.; Laird, N. M.; and Rubin, D. B. 1977. Maximum likelihood from incomplete data via the EM algorithm. *Journal of the Royal Statistical Society. Series B (Methodological)* 1–38.

Errais, E.; Giesecke, K.; and Goldberg, L. R. 2010. Affine point processes and portfolio credit risk. *SIAM J. Fin. Math.* 1(1):642–665.

Hawkes, A. G. 1971. Spectra of some self-exciting and mutually exciting point processes. *Biometrika* 58:83–90.

Kim, H.; Marwah, M.; Arlitt, M. F.; Lyon, G.; and Han, J. 2011. Unsupervised disaggregation of low frequency power measurements. In *SDM*, 747–758. SIAM / Omnipress.

Kolter, J. Z., and Jaakkola, T. 2012. Approximate inference in additive factorial hmms with application to energy disaggregation. In *Proceedings of the Fifteenth International Conference on Artificial Intelligence and Statistics, AISTATS 2012, La Palma, Canary Islands, April 21-23, 2012*, 1472–1482.

Kolter, J. Z., and Johnson, M. J. 2011. Redd: A public data set for energy disaggregation research. In *Proceedings of the SustKDD workshop on Data Mining Applications in Sustainability.*

Kolter, J. Z.; Batra, S.; and Ng, A. Y. 2010. Energy disaggregation via discriminative sparse coding. In *Advances in Neural Information Processing Systems 23: 24th Annual Conference on Neural Information Processing Systems 2010. Proceedings of a meeting held 6-9 December 2010, Vancouver, British Columbia, Canada.*, 1153–1161.

Li, L., and Zha, H. 2013. Dyadic event attribution in social networks with mixtures of hawkes processes. In *Proceedings of the 22nd ACM International Conference on Conference on Information; Knowledge Management*, CIKM '13, 1667–1672. New York, NY, USA: ACM.

Li, L., and Zha, H. 2014. Learning parametric models for social infectivity in multi-dimensional hawkes processes. In *Proceedings of the Twenty-Eighth AAAI Conference on Artificial Intelligence, July 27 -31, 2014, Québec City, Québec, Canada.*, 101–107.

Li, L.; Deng, H.; Dong, A.; Chang, Y.; and Zha, H. 2014. Identifying and labeling search tasks via query-based hawkes processes. In *Proceedings of the 20th ACM SIGKDD International Conference on Knowledge Discovery and Data Mining*, KDD '14, 731–740.

Mangion, A. Z.; Dewarc, M.; Kadirkamanathand, V.; and Sanguinetti, G. 2012. Point process modelling of the afghan war diary. *PNAS* 109(31):12414–12419.

Neenan, B., and Robinson, J. 2009. Residential electricity use feedback: A research synthesis and economic frame- work. *Technical report, Electric Power Research Institute.*

Ogata, Y. 1988. Statistical models for earthquake occurrences and residual analysis for point processes. *Journal of the American Statistical Association.* 83(401):9–27.

Parson, O.; Ghosh, S.; Weal, M.; and Rogers, A. 2012. Non-intrusive load monitoring using prior models of general appliance types. In *Proceedings of the Twenty-Eighth AAAI Conference on Artificial Intelligence, July 22 -26, 2012, Toronto, Canada*, 356–362.

Rasmussen, J. G. 2013. Bayesian inference for hawkes processes. *Methodology and Computing in Applied Probability* 15(3):623642.

Schoenberg, F. 2010. Introduction to point processes. *Wiley Encyclopedia of Operations Research and Management Science* 616–617.

Stomakhin, A.; Short, M. B.; and Bertozzi, A. L. 2011. Reconstruction of missing data in social networks based on temporal patterns of interactions. *Inverse Problems.* 27(11).

Wytock, M., and Kolter, J. Z. 2014. Contextually supervised source separation with application to energy disaggregation. In *Proceedings of the Twenty-Eighth AAAI Conference on Artificial Intelligence, July 27 -31, 2014, Québec City, Québec, Canada.*, 486–492.

Yan, J.; Wang, Y.; Zhou, K.; Huang, J.; Tian, C.; Zha, H.; and Dong, W. 2013. Towards effective prioritizing water pipe replacement and rehabilitation. In *Proceedings of the Twenty-Third International Joint Conference on Artificial Intelligence*, IJCAI '13, 2931–2937. AAAI Press.

Yan, J.; Zhang, C.; Zha, H.; Gong, M.; Sun, C.; Huang, J.; Chu, S.; and Yang, X. 2015. On machine learning towards predictive sales pipeline analytics. In *Proceedings of the Twenty-Ninth AAAI Conference on Artificial Intelligence.*

Yang, S., and Zha, H. 2013. Mixture of mutually exciting processes for viral diffusion. In *Proceedings of the 30th International Conference on Machine Learning (ICML-13)*, volume 28, 1–9.

Proceedings of the Twenty-Ninth AAAI Conference on Artificial Intelligence

HVAC-Aware Occupancy Scheduling

BoonPing Lim, Menkes van den Briel, Sylvie Thiébaux
Optimisation Research Group, NICTA
Research School of Computer Science, ANU
{first.last@anu.edu.au}

Scott Backhaus, Russell Bent
Defense Systems and Analysis Division
Los Alamos National Laboratory
{backhaus,rbent}@lanl.gov

Abstract

Energy consumption in commercial and educational buildings is impacted by group activities such as meetings, workshops, classes and exams, and can be reduced by scheduling these activities to take place at times and locations that are favorable from an energy standpoint. This paper improves on the effectiveness of energy-aware room-booking and occupancy scheduling approaches, by allowing the scheduling decisions to rely on an explicit model of the building's occupancy-based HVAC control. The core component of our approach is a mixed-integer linear programming (MILP) model which optimally solves the joint occupancy scheduling and occupancy-based HVAC control problem. To scale up to realistic problem sizes, we embed this MILP model into a large neighbourhood search (LNS). We obtain substantial energy reduction in comparison with occupancy-based HVAC control using arbitrary schedules or using schedules obtained by existing heuristic energy-aware scheduling approaches.

1 Introduction

Heating, ventilation and air-conditioning (HVAC) systems are responsible for 20% of the USA total energy consumption (Pérez-Lombard, Ortiz, and Pout 2008) and account for one hundred billion dollars/year electrical expenditure. These high energy costs together with rising environmental pollution levels call for innovative computational sustainability research focused on improving energy management in buildings.

Recent studies show that building HVAC consumption can be significantly reduced by adopting occupancy-based control strategies that exploit measured or predicted occupancy information (Erickson et al. 2009; Agarwal et al. 2010; West, Ward, and Wall 2014). For instance, model *predictive* control strategies determine supply air flow rate and temperature over longer time horizons so as to optimise energy consumption, whilst remaining within air flow and temperature bounds that reflect the predicted occupancy of various building zones (Goyal, Ingley, and Barooah 2013).

Another recent research line investigates the *proactive* control of *occupancy* in order to minimise HVAC consumption (Kwak et al. 2013; Majumdar, Albonesi, and Bose 2012; Pan et al. 2012). Many office and university buildings offer some scope for occupancy control via their room booking and scheduling systems. For instance meetings, exams, use of special purpose rooms, and other short-term activities can be scheduled to occur at times and in rooms that are beneficial from an energy standpoint. Unfortunately, existing occupancy scheduling approaches assume conventional HVAC control strategies (Kwak et al. 2013). Moreover, since reasoning using explicit models of the HVAC and the building is computationally expensive, they typically adopt suboptimal scheduling strategies guided by proxies for the optimisation criterion. One such proxy is the minimisation of the number of rooms used and of the time gap between successive meetings; it is used to guide the search towards solutions that take advantage of thermal inertia and schedule meetings to take place back-to-back in as few rooms as possible (Pan et al. 2012; Majumdar, Albonesi, and Bose 2012).

This paper presents an approach which aims at combining the strengths of the above research directions. A naïve combination would be to schedule occupancy in a first phase using existing methods, and then control HVAC based on this occupancy schedule. In contrast, we model and solve the *joint* HVAC control and occupancy scheduling problem. This results in an integrated approach whose benefits exceed the naïve superposition of both of its parts, as the scheduling fully exploits the capabilities of the underlying occupancy-based HVAC control across available times and locations.

In more detail, the joint problem we consider is that of deciding the respective times and locations (rooms) of a set of meetings or similar activities, as well as the HVAC supply air temperature and air flow rate for each zone and time, in such a way as to optimise the overall HVAC consumption over a long time horizon. The schedule complies with the HVAC and building dynamics models, and with comfort and air-flow rate bounds that depend on the scheduled zone occupancy. It also satisfies typical meeting scheduling constraints, including constraints on meetings times, on meeting locations (e.g. room capacity, equipment availability), and on participant attendance conflicts. Once built, such a schedule can be used in any building equipped with an occupancy-based HVAC controller by simply complementing the occupancy forecast (Mamidi, Chang, and Maheswaran 2012) with the occupancy information captured in the schedule. Our approach can even be used with a conventional HVAC control system by constraining the bounds on supply air flow rate/temperature and the temperature setpoints to be those found in the optimal solution to the joint problem.

To ensure the existence of a feasible control (for adequately sized HVACs) and improve on current occupancy-based HVAC control practices, we introduce a standby mode enabling the HVAC to re-activate at night if this is necessary to meet the temperature bounds of an early morning meeting or results in reduced consumption. To address the challenges caused by the presence of non-linear HVAC control constraints, we relax them in a principled way to obtain a mixed-integer linear (MILP) model guaranteed to provide a lower bound on the objective function. To tame the problem complexity further and scale to large problems, we combine the MILP model with Large Neighbourhood Search (LNS). LNS destroys parts of the schedule and MILP repairs them.

Our experiments illustrate the circumstances under which the standby mode is beneficial, demonstrate the approach's scalability, and show the superiority (over 50% consumption reduction) of our joint MILP model compared to heuristic scheduling solutions and to more naïve integrations of meeting scheduling and occupancy-based HVAC control.

To summarise, the main contributions of the paper are: a) an efficient MILP model for occupancy-based HVAC control which can be used in a range of applications, b) a scalable and effective approach to occupancy scheduling which exploits the capabilities of HVAC control and c) experiments showing a substantial reduction in energy consumption over the state of the art.

2 Occupancy-Based HVAC Control

This section introduces the occupancy-based HVAC control aspects of our MILP model. Section 3 will cover the scheduling aspects. We describe in turn the type of HVAC system we focus on along with the objective function we consider, the bounds the control must comply with, the effect of the control on the building thermal dynamics, and the linear relaxation of the non-linear constraints.

Our HVAC control model builds on well-accepted work by Goyal et al. (2012; 2013), but introduces a number of significant changes required to be suitable as a subcomponent of our more complex joint scheduling and control model. Notably, the control model studied by (Goyal, Ingley, and Barooah 2013) is a purely continuous *non-linear* model which does not consider occupancy. Our experiments using the IPOPT solver (Wächter and Biegler 2006) revealed that this model is impractical for our application, in terms of both memory and run-time requirements. In contrast, our model is an efficient linear model that incorporates discrete variables to capture occupancy and our standby mode.

2.1 VAV System and Objective Function

Following Goyal et al. (2013), we consider variable-air-volume (VAV) based HVAC systems, which are widely deployed in commercial buildings. With such systems, the building is divided into a number of zones (or locations) $L \subseteq \mathbb{N}$, each of which can be an individual room or a group of rooms. To simplify notation, we assume that each zone corresponds to a single room. Figure 1 shows a schematic of a VAV system connected to two building zones.

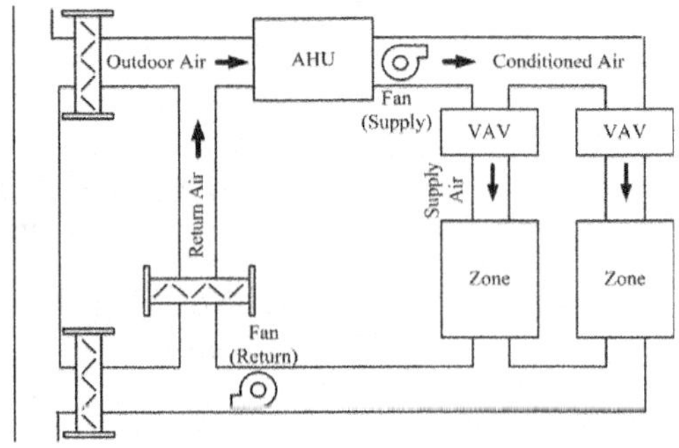

Figure 1: VAV System with Two Zones

Let $K = \{1 \dots n\}$ be a finite set of discrete time steps considered over the optimisation horizon. For simplicity, we assume that successive time steps are separated by a fixed duration $\Delta t \in \mathbb{R}^+$; that is, $\forall k \in K$, we have $t_k \in \mathbb{R}^+$ and $t_k - t_{k-1} = \Delta t$. The objective is to minimise the total energy consumed over the optimisation horizon:

$$\text{minimise: } \sum_{k \in K} e_k \tag{1}$$

where e_k is the energy consumed at time step k:

$$e_k = p_k \times \Delta t \qquad \forall k \in K \tag{2}$$

The power p_k is consumed by the three main operations shown in Figure 1 and detailed below: the air conditioning operation performed centrally by the air handling unit (AHU) consumes p_k^{Cond}; the fan operation, also performed centrally, consumes p_k^{Fan}; and the reheating operation performed locally at each zone $l \in L$ by the zone's VAV unit consumes $p_{l,k}^{Heat}$ at each zone:

$$p_k = \left(p_k^{Cond} + p_k^{Fan} + \sum_{l \in L} p_{l,k}^{Heat} \right) \qquad \forall k \in K \tag{3}$$

Air Conditioning Operation. The air handling unit (AHU) admits a mixture of outside air at temperature T_k^{OA} and return air, and conditions it to a pre-set conditioned air temperature T^{CA} (usually 12.8C). The conditioned air is then distributed through the supply duct to the VAV unit at each zone. The AHU consumption p_k^{Cond} is the power consumed in cooling the total air flow required. Let $a_{l,k}^{SA}$ denote the air flow rate required by location l at time step k and C^{pa} the heat capacity of air at constant pressure (1.005 kJ/kg·K):

$$p_k^{Cond} = C^{pa} \left(T_k^{OA} - T^{CA} \right) \sum_{l \in L} a_{l,k}^{SA} \quad \forall k \in K \tag{4}$$

Fan Operation. The supply fan, driven by a variable frequency drive, maintains a constant static pressure in the supply duct. When the opening of the VAV dampers increases to pull in more air flow into the conditioned space (resp. decreases to pull less air flow), the fan speeds up (resp. slows down). The fan consumption is the power consumed to push the total air flow required through the supply duct, which is proportional to the sum of the air flow rates $a_{l,k}^{SA}$ required over all locations. Let β be the fan coefficient (0.65):

$$p_k^{Fan} = \beta \sum_{l \in L} a_{l,k}^{SA} \qquad \forall k \in K \tag{5}$$

Reheating Operation. Each zone l has a VAV unit connected to the supply duct. The unit is equipped with continuously adjustable valves and reheat coils. These enable regulating the air flow rate $a_{l,k}^{SA}$ into the zone and modulating the supply air temperature $T_{l,k}^{SA}$ to maintain the zone temperature within given bounds, if necessary by reheating the supply air. Here we consider the power $p_{l,k}^{Heat}$ consumed by the reheating process to heat the supply air from the conditioned temperature T^{CA} to an appropriate location supply air temperature $T_{l,k}^{SA}$.

$$p_{l,k}^{Heat} = C^{pa}(T_{l,k}^{SA} - T^{CA})a_{l,k}^{SA} \quad \forall l \in L, k \in K \quad (6)$$

Decision Variables. The two key HVAC decision variables are the supply air flow rate $a_{l,k}^{SA}$ and temperature $T_{l,k}^{SA}$ at each location $l \in L$ and time step $k \in K$. We determine an optimal control for these variables, given occupancy information and bounds on supply air temperature, supply air flow rate, and room temperature during vacant and occupied periods. Below we will introduce a third decision variable ($w_{l,k}$) to decide when the HVAC should activate at night, which in turn will influence the bounds. When taking the HVAC control model in isolation, the building occupancy is an *input* to the model. When we integrate scheduling to the model in Section 3, occupancy will become a *variable*.

2.2 Temperature and Air Flow Bounds

We now model the constraints on the temperature, supply air temperature and supply air flow rate in each location, as a function of the location occupancy and the time of the day. We introduce the auxiliary variable $T_{l,k} \in \mathbb{R}$ representing the *actual* temperature in location $l \in L$ at time step $k \in K$, and the boolean input $z_{l,k}$ which is true iff l is occupied at time step k. When a location is not occupied, its temperature can lie freely within a wide temperature range $[T^{unocc,lb}, T^{unocc,ub}]$, whilst the temperature is otherwise constrained to lie within a more restricted comfort range $[T^{unocc,lb} + C^{lb}, T^{unocc,ub} - C^{ub}]$, where C^{lb} and C^{ub} are appropriate constants. This constraint is expressed as follows: $\forall l \in L, k \in K$

$$T^{unocc,lb} + C^{lb} z_{l,k} \leq T_{l,k} \leq T^{unocc,ub} - C^{ub} z_{l,k} \quad (7)$$

Further, the supply air temperature and flow rate at each location are constrained in a way that depends on the HVAC operating mode at the current time step. We have two operating modes: *active* and *standby*. Let $K^s \subseteq K$ be the set of time steps that fall within standard operating hours (6am to 6pm). During standard hours ($k \in K^s$) the HVAC is always in active mode. The supply air temperature $T_{l,k}^{SA}$ at location l must fall within $[T^{CA}, T^{SA,ub}]$. The supply air flow rate $a_{l,k}^{SA}$ must fall within $[a_l^{SA,lb}, a^{SA,ub}]$ where the upper bound is the air flow rate obtained when the dampers are fully open, and the lower bound is a constant (depending on the area size of the location and on the return air ratio) necessary to ensure that the minimal fresh outside air requirements are met. This yields the constraints:

$$T^{CA} \leq T_{l,k}^{SA} \leq T^{SA,ub} \quad \forall l \in L, k \in K^s \quad (8)$$

$$a_l^{SA,lb} \leq a_{l,k}^{SA} \leq a^{SA,ub} \quad \forall l \in L, k \in K^s \quad (9)$$

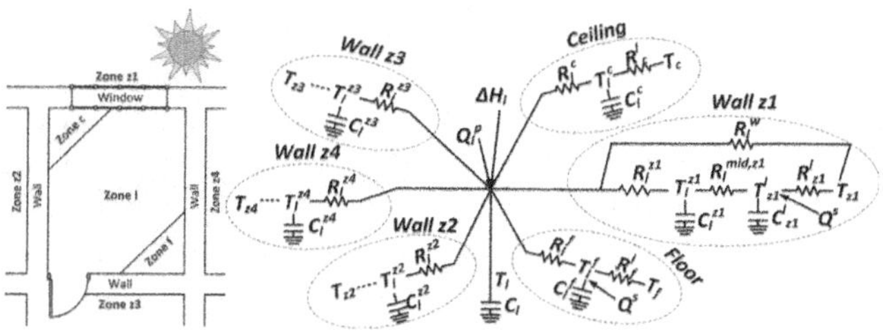

(a) Zone (b) Lumped-RC Network

Figure 2: Thermal Model

Outside business hours ($k \in K \setminus K^s$), the HVAC is in stand-by mode and will only activate if this enables or lowers the cost of satisfying a future constraint. For instance, it could activate at night and benefit from the low outside night temperature to more cheaply cool the supply air to meet the temperature bounds in (7) for an early morning meeting. Note that this is different from conventional operations where HVACs are always off outside hours; as our experiments will show, the standby mode enables model-predictive approaches to occupancy-based control to meet constraints and save energy. The decision of whether or not HVAC activation is required by location l is represented by the boolean decision variable $w_{l,k}$. The presence of these boolean variables makes our model a mixed-integer model. When $w_{l,k}$ is true, the supply air flow rate and temperature are constrained to lie within $[T^{CA}, T^{SA,ub}]$ and $[a_l^{SA,lb}, a^{SA,ub}]$, respectively, and when $w_{l,k}$ is false, $a_{l,k}^{SA}$ is set to zero and the value of $T_{l,k}^{SA}$ is irrelevant (and for simplicity may as well also be zero). This is captured by the following constraints:

$$T^{CA} w_{l,k} \leq T_{l,k}^{SA} \leq T^{SA,ub} w_{l,k} \;\; \forall l \in L, k \in K \setminus K^s \quad (10)$$

$$a_l^{SA,lb} w_{l,k} \leq a_{l,k}^{SA} \leq a^{SA,ub} w_{l,k} \;\; \forall l \in L, k \in K \setminus K^s \quad (11)$$

2.3 Building Thermal Dynamics

Having defined the space of decisions as the supply air flow rate $a_{l,k}^{SA}$, the supply air temperature $T_{l,k}^{SA}$ and the HVAC activation requirement $w_{l,k}$ at each location and time step, we now model the impact of these decisions on the building thermal exchanges. To model the thermal dynamics of the building, we adopt a computationally efficient lumped RC-network (Gouda, Danaher, and Underwood 2000) which incorporates the thermal resistance and capacitance of each zone and between adjacent zones, as well as the solar gain and the internal heat gain in each zone – in particular the heat gain arising from occupancy. For the sake of simplicity, we ignore humidity and infiltration.

The principles behind the model are represented in Figure 2. Figure 2a shows the zone structure that we adopt. Zone l is separated by a wall and a window from zone $z1$ and by a wall from zones $z2$, $z3$, and $z4$, which could represent either indoor or outdoor zones. It is also separated by the ceiling and floor from zones c and f which are above and below zone l, respectively. Zone l has a capacitance C_l that models the heat capacity of the air in the zone. It also has a solar gain $Q^s_{l,k}$ and heat gain $Q^p_{l,k}$ at time step k. Moreover, the inner (resp. outer) wall separating l from zone $z \in Z = \{z1, z2, z3, z4, f, c\}$ has a capacitance C^z_l (resp. C^l_z), resistance R^z_l (resp. R^l_z), and temperature $T^z_{l,k}$ (resp. $T^l_{z,k}$) at time step k. The window has a resistance R^w_l. Finally, the internal node between the inner and outer walls separating l from $z \in \{z1, z2, z3, z4\}$ has a constant resistance $R^{mid,z}_l$. Capacitances, resistances, solar gain, and (in this section) occupant heat gain are inputs to the model whilst temperatures are auxiliary variables. The interaction between zones is modeled using a lumped RC-network. Specifically, we use 3R2C for walls separating two zones, 2R1C for the ceiling and floor and 1R for windows. The lumped network for Figure 2a is given in Figure 2b.

The lumped network translates into a set of coupled difference equations which can be summarised as follows. The first difference equation defines the temperature $T_{l,k}$ in zone l at time step k as a function of the location, inner walls, ceiling, floor and outdoor temperatures at the previous time step, of the heat gain $Q^p_{l,k-1}$ at the previous time step and of the enthalpy $\Delta H_{l,k-1}$ of the location due to the supply air:

$$\frac{C_l}{\Delta t}(T_{l,k} - T_{l,k-1}) = -\left[\sum_{z \in Z} \frac{1}{R^z_l} + \frac{1}{R^w_l}\right] T_{l,k-1} + \sum_{z \in Z} \frac{T^z_{l,k-1}}{R^z_l} + \frac{T^{OA}_{k-1}}{R^w_l} + Q^p_{l,k-1} + \Delta H_{l,k-1} \tag{12}$$

The heat gain $Q^p_{l,k}$ is simply the heat gain q^p generated per person (75W), times the number of occupants $pp_{l,k}$:

$$Q^p_{l,k} = q^p \times pp_{l,k} \tag{13}$$

Ignoring humidity, the enthalpy is defined as follows:

$$\Delta H_{l,k} = C^{pa} a^{SA}_{l,k} (T^{SA}_{l,k} - T_{l,k}) \tag{14}$$

The remaining difference equations define the temperatures $T^z_{l,k}$ and $T^l_{z,k}$ of the inner and outer walls at time step k as a function of each other and of the location temperature $T_{l,k-1}$ at the previous time step. Taking $z = z1$ in the example of Figure 2a:

$$\frac{C^l_{z1}}{\Delta t}(T^l_{z1,k} - T^l_{z1,k-1}) = -\left[\frac{1}{R^l_{z1}} + \frac{1}{R^{mid,z1}_l}\right] T^l_{z1,k-1} + \frac{T_{z1,k-1}}{R^l_{z1}} + \frac{T^{z1}_{l,k-1}}{R^{mid,z1}_l} + Q^s_{k-1} \tag{15}$$

The definition of $T^{z1}_{l,k}$ is symmetrical except for the absence of solar gain Q^s_{k-1}. The equations for the other walls, and the ceiling and floor are similar, so we omit them here.

2.4 MILP Relaxation

Observe that the model as presented so far is a mixed-integer *non-linear* (MINLP) model. This is because of the bilinear terms $a^{SA}_{l,k} T^{SA}_{l,k}$ and $a^{SA}_{l,k} T_{l,k}$ in Equations 6 and 14. From a computational standpoint, it is better to relax these equations so as to obtain a MILP for which effective solvers exist that are guaranteed to return a lower bound on the globally optimal MINLP objective. To obtain a suitable MILP, we use the linear programming relaxation of bilinear terms introduced by McCormick (1976). This relaxation introduces a new variable v for the bilinear term xy together with four inequalities that define its convex envelope using the bounds $[\underline{x}, \overline{x}]$ and $[\underline{y}, \overline{y}]$ on each of the two variables involved:

$$\begin{aligned} v &\geq \underline{x}y + \underline{y}x - \underline{x}\underline{y} \\ v &\geq \overline{x}y + \overline{y}x - \overline{x}\overline{y} \\ v &\leq \underline{x}y + \overline{y}x - \underline{x}\overline{y} \\ v &\leq \overline{x}y + \underline{y}x - \overline{x}\underline{y} \end{aligned}$$

Hence, our MILP model is obtained by replacing the bilinear terms $a^{SA}_{l,k} T^{SA}_{l,k}$ and $a^{SA}_{l,k} T_{l,k}$ in Equations 6 and 14 with new variables and adding the corresponding convex envelope definitions. The relevant bounds are:

- $a^{SA}_{l,k} \in [\underline{a}^{SA}_{l,k}, \overline{a}^{SA}_{l,k}] = \begin{cases} [a^{SA,lb}, a^{SA,ub}] & \text{for } k \in K^s \\ [0, a^{SA,ub}] & \text{for } k \in K \setminus K^s \end{cases}$
- $T^{SA}_{l,k} \in [\underline{T}^{SA}_{l,k}, \overline{T}^{SA}_{l,k}] = \begin{cases} [T^{CA}, T^{SA,ub}] & \text{for } k \in K^s \\ [0, T^{SA,ub}] & \text{for } k \in K \setminus K^s \end{cases}$
- $T_{l,k} \in [\underline{T}_{l,k}, \overline{T}_{l,k}] = [T^{unocc,lb}, T^{unocc,ub}]$ for $k \in K$

This concludes the description of our MILP model for occupancy-based HVAC control. Given the occupancy $pp_{l,k}$ and $z_{l,k}$, and the external temperature T^{OA}_k, it controls the supply air flow rate $a^{SA}_{l,k}$ and temperature $T^{SA}_{l,k}$ and decides when a location requires HVAC activation $w_{l,k}$ out of the standby mode, in such a way as to optimise the total energy consumption $\sum_{k \in K} e_k$. The strengths of this model are its integration of realism and computational efficiency, its adequacy as a component of occupancy scheduling and other more complex models, and its optional ability to activate out of the standby mode when this improves consumption.

3 Occupancy Scheduling

Until now, zone occupancy over time was a model input. We now present our joint HVAC control and meeting scheduling model, in which occupancy is a decision variable.

Let $M \subseteq \mathbb{N}$ be a set of meetings to be scheduled to take place at the locations in L during the time horizon K. Each meeting $m \in M$ is characterised by the following inputs: its duration $\tau_m \in \mathbb{N}$ (number of time steps), the set of allowable time steps $K_m \subseteq K$ at which it can start, the set of allowable locations $L_m \subseteq M$ at which it can take place, and its set of attendees $P_m \subseteq A$, for some appropriate set of attendees A. In addition, let $N \subseteq 2^M$ be the set of meeting sets which have at least one attendee in common, that is $N = \{M_i \subseteq M \mid \forall m, m' \in M_i, P_m \cap P_{m'} \neq \emptyset\}$. In practice, only all pairs of incompatible meetings are needed. Note that the sets K_m and L_m can be used to encode a variety of situations, such as room capacity requirements and availability of special equipment such as video conferencing, as well as time deadlines for the meeting occurrence and attendee availability constraints.

The main scheduling variable is the boolean decision variable $x_{m,l,k}$ which is true iff meeting $m \in M$ is scheduled to take place at location $l \in L_m$ starting at time step $k \in K_m$. The scheduling part of the model interacts with the HVAC control part via the auxiliary variables $z_{l,k}$, which, as before, is true iff location l is occupied at time step k, and $pp_{l,k} \in \mathbb{N}$, which, as before, represents the number of occupants at location l at time step k. These terms are used in Equations 7 and 13, respectively, but are now variables rather than inputs.

The set of MILP scheduling constraints are the following. The first constraint ensures that all meetings are scheduled to occur exactly once within the range of allowable locations and start times:

$$\sum_{l \in L_m, k \in K_m} x_{m,l,k} = 1 \quad \forall m \in M \tag{16}$$

The second constraint ensures that if a location is occupied by a meeting then it is exclusively occupied by this meeting during its entire duration:

$$\sum_{\substack{m \in M, k' \in K_m \\ \text{such that} \\ l \in L_m \text{ and } k - \tau_m + 1 \leq k' \leq k}} x_{m,l,k'} \leq z_{l,k} \quad \forall l \in L, k \in K \tag{17}$$

As a result, no two meetings can occupy the same location at the same time step. Observe that (17) also determines the occupancy variable $z_{l,k}$ used in the occupancy-based HVAC control part of the joint model.

The following constraint establishes the number of occupants $pp_{k,k}$ of each location l at each time step k:

$$\sum_{\substack{m \in M, k' \in K_m \\ \text{such that} \\ l \in L_m \text{ and } k - \tau_m + 1 \leq k' \leq k}} x_{m,l,k'} \times |P_m| = pp_{l,k} \quad \forall l \in L, k \in K \tag{18}$$

This is used in equation 13 to establish the internal heat gain arising from occupancy.

Finally, the last constraint ensures that meetings with an intersecting attendee set cannot overlap in time:

$$\sum_{\substack{m \in \nu, l \in L_m, k' \in K_m \\ \text{such that} \\ k - \tau_m + 1 \leq k' \leq k}} x_{m,l,k'} \leq 1 \quad \forall k \in K, \nu \in N \tag{19}$$

Our joint HVAC control and occupancy scheduling model is simply obtained by adding equations 16-19 the HVAC control model given by equations 1-15 (with 6 and 14 linearised). The model optimises the total energy consumed not only over the HVAC decision variables $a^{SA}_{l,k}$, $T^{SA}_{l,k}$ and $w_{l,k}$ as before, but also over the scheduling decision variables $x_{m,l,k}$. A building occupancy-based HVAC controller need only use the schedules $x_{m,l,k}$ produced. A conventional controller may instead use the bounds on room temperature and supply air flow rate/temperature determined by equations 7, 10 and 11 as setpoints.

This concludes the description of our joint HVAC control and occupancy scheduling model. The next section experimentally investigates its benefits in terms of energy reduction, in comparison with more naïve integrations of scheduling and HVAC control. Section 5 shows that by embedding this model into a large neighbourhood search, we can scale to timetabling problems of practical relevance.

4 Benefits of the Model

Our experiments aim at explaining the usefulness of the standby mode and at demonstrating that our HVAC-aware scheduling model leads to significant consumption reduction (50% to 70% in our experiments) when compared to occupancy-based HVAC control using arbitrary schedules or energy-aware schedules generated by heuristic methods. Experiments are conducted over 5 summer days with a row of 4 co-located zones, each consisting of a single 60 m^2 room with a capacity of 30 people. The zones differ by a high or low value for their thermal resistance and capacitance. The two end zones have three outside walls and the middle two zones have two. The duration between successive time steps is Δt = 30min, giving more than enough time for thermal effects to occur. Shorter durations did not significantly affect the results. The input data and parameters are available from the first author. The MILP models are solved using Gurobi 5.6 (2014). All experiments were conducted on a cluster consisting of 2× AMD 6-Core Opteron 4184, 2.8 GHz with 64 GB of memory.

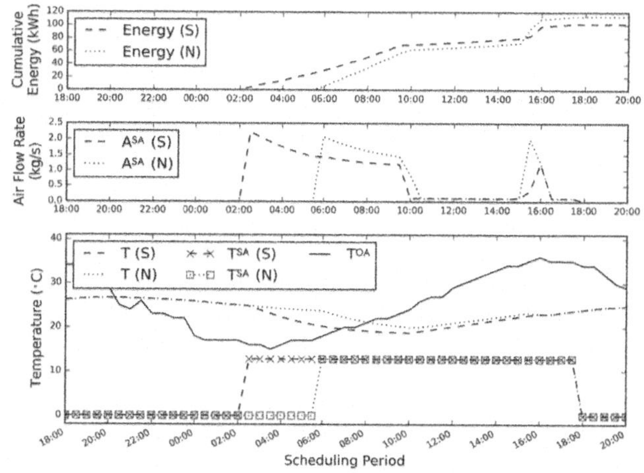

Figure 3: HVAC control with and without standby mode.

4.1 Usefulness of Standby Mode

We start by illustrating the usefulness of the standby mode. In conventional operations, HVACs are usually switched on a few hours prior to start of business (6am) and are turned off in the evening (6pm) and at night. Model predictive control strategies are capable of pre-cooling a zone, but only when the HVAC is switched on. Our standby mode enables the HVAC to self activate outside business hours to provide additional pre-cooling when this is beneficial. Because HVAC consumption is highly dependent on the temperature gap between the outdoor temperature and the conditioned air temperature, pre-cooling at night, when the outdoor air temperature is cooler, can reduce energy consumption. The following experiment shows that such pre-cooling can be beneficial not only for early morning meetings, but also, more surprisingly, for late afternoon meetings.

Figure 3 compares the operations of the HVAC optimally controlled by the model in Section 2 with standby mode (S) and without standby mode (N). For this experiment, a single meeting is scheduled to occur between 16:00-17:00 in a given zone on a given day. Observe that when the HVAC is running with the standby mode enabled, it activates as early as 02:30 and pushes between 2.2 and 1.2 kg/s of supply air at 12.8 C to bring down the zone temperature to approximately

19°C by 09:00. Between 02:30 and 6:00, the outdoor temperature lies between 15 and 17°C, which is about 2-4°C higher than the 12.8°C conditioned air temperature. Without the standby mode, supply air is pushed into the room at a higher average rate between 2.0 and 1.5 kg/s right after the HVAC is turned on at 06:00, which, as the outdoor temperature is higher at that time (18-22°C), requires a higher rate of energy consumption. During the day, the zone temperature increases slightly due to the daytime thermal gain, and at 15:00, one hour before the meeting starts, the room is pre-cooled again. This time, the standby-mode enabled HVAC requires cooling about half the amount of supply air, which brings significant energy savings since the outside temperature is around 36°C. Altogether, the standby mode reduces consumption by 11.9% (12kWh) on this example.

As shown above, a standby-mode-enabled HVAC can be effective in areas with high diurnal temperature variation. In addition to decreasing energy consumption, it can provide pre-cooling at off-peak electricity cost. For organisations that are charged by electricity suppliers according to their peak consumption, another benefit of the standby mode is that it can help smooth the peak that is regularly observed at the start of the operating hours.

4.2 Joint Model vs Simpler Models

Whilst the standby mode is beneficial, the much larger gains in our approach stem from the joint model: we now compare our joint model with simpler approaches representative of the existing literature on occupancy-based HVAC control and energy-aware meeting scheduling, and observe a 50%-70% energy consumption improvement. Specifically, we consider a set of timetabling problems derived from the PATAT (2002) Melbourne University dataset and compare the optimal (O) solutions produced by the joint model in Section 3, with those produced by giving arbitrary (A) schedules and heuristic (H) energy-aware schedules as input to the HVAC control model in Section 2. Several authors have argued that scheduling meetings back to back in as few rooms as possible is a suitable heuristic that takes advantage of thermal inertia to reduce energy consumption (Kwak et al. 2013; Majumdar, Albonesi, and Bose 2012; Pan et al. 2012). In line with this, the heuristic we compare to minimise the number of rooms used and the time gap between meetings in these rooms, subject to the scheduling constraints 16-19.[1] In all three cases (A,H,O), we run the HVAC control model with standby mode (S) and without it (N), resulting in six different methods labeled AN, AS, HN, HS, ON, OS, where for example, HS denotes HVAC control with standby mode using heuristic schedules.

To examine problems with different degree of constrainedness, we extracted 70 problem instances from the PATAT dataset, consisting of 40 instances of 10 meetings each, 20 instances of 20 meetings each, and 10 instances of 50 meetings each. All meetings have up to 30 attendees, a 1.5h duration and an allowable time range of one or two random days (09:00-17:00) within the 5 days of the experiment.

The AN/AS results are obtained by selecting, for each instance, an arbitrary schedule consistent with the scheduling constraints 16-19 in Section 3 and using it as input to the occupancy-based HVAC control model in Section 2. Similarly, the HN/HS results are obtained by selecting the schedule optimising the heuristic among those consistent with the scheduling constraints, and using it as input to the occupancy-based HVAC control model. The ON/OS results are obtained by solving the joint model for each instance.

Table 1 shows, for each of the 6 approaches, the average energy consumption per room over the 70 instances, and the percentage excess consumption taking OS as the baseline. The results show a clear improvement as we move from arbitrary schedules (AN/AS), that are currently the norm with room booking systems, to energy aware schedules (HN/HS), and a much greater improvement when these schedules take into account the capabilities of occupancy-based HVAC control (ON/OS). The interactions between the various scheduling constraints, the thermal dynamics of the building and the HVAC control are so complex that heuristic methods can only achieve a fraction of the performance of the global optimisation methods enabled by our MILP model. As expected, the gain conferred by the standby mode decreases as we move to schedules that make better time and location decisions. Similarly, we observed that for more constrained problems (e.g. with 50 meetings), the standby mode is more effective, because there is a greater likelihood that meetings need to be scheduled in rooms that require higher cooling load which the standby mode can mitigate by pre-cooling.

5 Scaling to Large Problems

MILP enables us to easily manage the tightly constrained interactions between meeting scheduling and its direct impact on energy consumption. However, it only allows us to solve small problem instances in reasonable time. To scale to problem sizes that universities face when scheduling exams, we developed a hybrid solution that embeds the MILP model into a large neighbourhood search (LNS) (Shaw 1998).

LNS is a local search metaheuristic, which iteratively improves an initial solution by alternating between a destroy step and a repair step. The main idea behind LNS is that a large neighbourhood allows the heuristic to easily navigate

Strategy	Average energy consumption (kWh)	Excess consumption vs. baseline
AN	212.14	74.84%
AS	199.94	64.78%
HN	184.26	51.86%
HS	177.32	46.14%
ON	124.13	2.30%
OS	121.34	baseline

Table 1: Comparison of arbitrary (A), heuristic (H), and optimal (O) scheduling strategies over HVAC with (S) and without (N) standby mode.

[1] Majumdar et al. (Majumdar, Albonesi, and Bose 2012) observe that the single most important predictor of performance is good match between the room capacity and the size of the meetings. However this does not play a role in our experiments since all four rooms have the same capacity.

Proceedings of the Twenty-Ninth AAAI Conference on Artificial Intelligence

Data Analysis and Optimization for (Citi)Bike Sharing

Eoin O'Mahony[1], **David B. Shmoys**[1,2]
Cornell University
Department of Computer Science[1]
School of Operations Research and Information Engineering[2]

Abstract

Bike-sharing systems are becoming increasingly prevalent in urban environments. They provide a low-cost, environmentally-friendly transportation alternative for cities. The management of these systems gives rise to many optimization problems. Chief among these problems is the issue of bicycle rebalancing. Users imbalance the system by creating demand in an asymmetric pattern. This necessitates action to put the system back in balance with the requisite levels of bicycles at each station to facilitate future use. In this paper, we tackle the problem of maintaing system balance during peak rush-hour usage as well as rebalancing overnight to prepare the system for rush-hour usage. We provide novel problem formulations that have been motivated by both a close collaboration with the New York City bike share (Citibike) and a careful analysis of system usage data. We analyze system data to discover the best placement of bikes to facilitate usage. We solve routing problems for overnight shifts as well as clustering problems for handling mid rush-hour usage. The tools developed from this research are currently in daily use at NYC Bike Share LLC, operators of Citibike.

1 Introduction

Bike-sharing systems are a cost effective way of promoting a sustainable lifestyle in urban areas. The number of bike-sharing systems has more than doubled since 2008 (Larsen 2013). These systems generally consist of stations where users can take out or drop off bikes, and may return a bike to a free dock at any station. New York City launched the largest bike-sharing system in North America, Citibike, in May 2013 with over 300 stations and 5000 bikes. The system has been a success with ridership approaching 40000 trips per day. With this success comes a set of management problems. Chief among these is the issue of system imbalance; bikes become clustered in certain geographic areas which leaves other areas devoid of bikes; for example, the traders wake up early in their East Village apartments, rapidly deplete the supply of bikes there, and then overwhelm the capacity for docks in the Wall Street area. This system imbalance necessitates moving bikes around the city to put the system back in balance. This is achieved either by trucks, as is the case in most bike-share cities, or other bicycles with trailers, as is being tested in New York.

Operators of bike-sharing systems have limited resources available to them, which constrains the extent to which rebalancing can occur. Hence, this domain is an exciting application for the field of computational sustainability. Based on a close collaboration with NYC Bike Share LLC, the operators of Citibike, we have formulated several optimization problems whose solutions are used to more effectively maintain the pool of bikes in NYC. There is an expanding literature on operations management issues related to bike-sharing systems, but the problems addressed here are particularly suited to the complex blend of human and system constraints that are present for Citibike. For these problems, we shall present results utilizing different approaches: integer programming formulations that can typically be solved (at scale) by off-the-shelf integer programming solvers, and heuristic approaches that yield good solutions quickly.

We begin by tackling the problem of how best to use system data to plan for usage. That is, we want to place bikes at stations to handle the surge in usage experienced during rush-hours. We approach the issue of inferring true demand for trips and use these amounts to better plan for system usage. From these computations we know both when and where bikes are needed and progress to answering the question: how do we get them there?

We focus on two very different rebalancing problems. First, we tackle rebalancing the system during rush-hour, developing novel methods for optimizing rebalancing resources. During rush-hour, system usage is high, rendering large truck routes unreliable as the system state might shift dramatically before the route is completed. Traffic is also at its peak during rush hour, which greatly limits the ability of trucks to move easily through the city; this motivates the use of bike trailers instead of large trucks. The nature of the mid-rush balancing requires a drastically different approach than the one used for the overnight problem. Our goal is not to maintain system balance but to ensure that users are never too far from either a bike or a dock. To achieve this, we formulate a clustering problem that yields stations in the city for which rebalancing resources can be targeted.

We then tackle the problem of moving bikes around the city overnight. Overnight the system experiences low usage and as a consequence stockage levels are relatively constant. Traffic is also at its lowest during these hours resulting in trip times being both reliable and short. This allows a rebalancing plan spanning the overnight shift to be computed and executed without fear of users making it redundant or counterproductive. We formulate an optimization problem whose goal is to produce a series of truck routes to get the system as balanced as possible during the overnight shift. We provide both theoretical results as well as an empirical approach to this problem based on a (relatively) tractable integer programming formulation. The combination of these two approaches yields a fast method of obtaining high quality solutions that can be used in practice.

2 Related Work

Due to the increasing importance of bike-sharing programs, and the operational difficulties in managing them, a great deal of attention has been focused on a variety of problems that relate to bike-sharing. In particular, work such as (Raviv, Tzur, and Forma 2013), (Contardo, Morency, and L.-M. Rousseau 2012), (Schuijbroek, Hampshire, and van Hoeve 2013), (Chemla, Meunier, and Calvo 2013) and (Shu et al. 2013) focus on the problem of (overnight) rebalancing. (Raviv, Tzur, and Forma 2013) tackles the problem of finding truck routes and plans for how many bikes to move between stations. The paper minimizes an objective function tied to both the operating cost of the vehicles as well as penalty functions relating to station imbalance. The models provided are benchmarked on instances from both the Paris and Washington DC bike-share systems. (Schuijbroek, Hampshire, and van Hoeve 2013) combines both finding service level requirements for stations with planning truck routes to keep stations rebalanced. They use a clustering based heuristic for routing on data from Boston and Washington DC to produce truck routes. (Rainer-Harbach et al. 2013) take a local search approach to finding both routes for trucks and the number of bikes to be collected or dropped off at each station. (Contardo, Morency, and L.-M. Rousseau 2012) identify that a different rebalancing approach needs to be taken during rush hours. They formulate flow problems on space-time networks. Solutions are generated using a combination of Dantzig-Wolfe decomposition and quickly generated upper and lower bounds. (Chemla, Meunier, and Calvo 2013) solves the static rebalancing problem, where a plan of where to move bikes is created. They provide a branch-and-cut algorithm for a problem realization and a tabu search to find heuristic solutions. (Shu et al. 2013) uses a time-flow formulation combined with stochastic modeling to tackle the problem of rebalancing. These papers tackle the rebalancing problem in a way that is similar to traditional inventory management and package routing problems, for example (Anily and Bramel 1999), (Archetti et al. 2007) and (?). However, in our work we approach the problem in a manner closer to orienteering problems (Vansteenwegen, Souffriau, and Oudheusden 2011), (Chekuri, Korula, and Pál 2012). Our work also handles full size instances; both in terms of number of stations and trucks considered. Much of the previous work has focused on instances for which two or three trucks are available. Furthermore, our work builds on the understanding of the practicalities of running Citibike, in their current state, it is much simpler operationally to simply have trucks go to an overloaded station, fill the truck with bikes, and then deposit all of them at a (sufficiently) depleted station.

Other work creates models to analyze bike-sharing systems, specifically (Nair et al. 2013), (Vogel and Mattfeld 2011), (Kaltenbrunner et al. 2010) and (Lin and Yang 2011). This work focuses on modeling how users will impact the system, detecting usage patterns from behavior. This insight into usage patterns is used to create stochastic models representing system usage. (Vogel and Mattfeld 2011) classifies stations based on their usage patterns, identifying stations used by commuters, tourists, etc. (Garca-Palomares, Gutirrez, and Latorre 2012), (Martinez et al. 2012) and (Romero et al. 2012) aim to optimize the placement of stations in bike-sharing systems.

Our work provides fundamentally different models of bike rebalancing compared to previous approaches: for mid rush-hour rebalancing, we focus on a covering problem viewpoint, closely tied to the very small number of pairs of stations that can be rebalanced by bike trailers; for overnight rebalancing, we focus on full truck-load routes that give rise to an problem of covering a bipartite graph with sufficiently short alternating paths. These models are driven by observations obtained by our collaboration with New York Bike Share LLC., the operators of Citibike.

3 Data Analytics for Bike Share Systems

Our earliest goal for the collaboration with NYC Bike Share LLC was to make their planning and decision making *data driven*. Specifically, it is crucial to use the data available to understand how the system is being used and where usage is putting stress on the system. The first problem we tackled was the problem of rush-hour planning. Weekday rush-hours (6am-10am and 4pm-8pm) account for the majority of bike trips taken in New York. Although mostly symmetric over the course of a day, each rush-hour period in isolation is highly asymmetric. In fact we observe many extremes of behavior with some areas of the city having a large outflow of bikes and other areas having a large inflow of bikes. To deal with this surge we aimed to answer the following question: suppose we could click our fingers and have the system in any state before the morning and evening rush hours, what would that state be? To answer this question we used a number of methods, each of which raises deeper questions about the analysis of bike-share usage.

Planning for Rush-Hour Usage To plan for a rush-hour we need to know where we expect bikes to be taken from and areas where we expect they will accumulate. We also need to identify stations that are *self-balancing*, specifically their flow of bikes *in* is roughly equal to their flow of bikes *out* thus requiring no rebalancing actions. Out first approach to discover the ideal system state before the morning and evening rush-hours relied on clustering stations based on their observed usage. The intuition is that stations that experience similar behavior during rush-hours will belong to the same cluster, we then analyzed the type of behavior typical of each cluster and label the cluster with a desired level. These levels are used to inform the operators of Citibike where bikes need to be placed to anticipate user demand.

This approach has been highly successful, by using the fill levels generated by this computation the operations team at NYC Bike Share have been able to tailor their rebalancing operations to best serve the heavy rush-hour usage. However, although successful this method has a number of limitations. Specifically there is a weakness related to exploitation versus exploration. This method is slow to react to shifts in usage, to illustrate this we will consider an example that happened at a station in Brooklyn. The station was initially self-balancing with low usage, thus it was assigned a low fill level. However, over time the behavior of this station shifted to become a consumer of bikes. This change was not reflected in its level as there were never enough bikes placed there for high usage to be recorded. This station was identified by chance and this experience led us to believe that there might be others in a similar situation. This caused us to consider the question, assuming we could keep each station stocked with bikes and spaces, what would a typical day's usage look like? This question is, in essence, what is the true demand for bikes in the system?

Computing Demand for Bikes Although system data gives us information on each ride taken by users in New York these data might not be a true reflection of the actual demand in the system. Consider a bike-share station at Penn Station in the evening rush hour. A huge number of commuters want to return bikes and take a train from the station. However if we were to not rebalance this station it would quickly fill up and we may observe a fraction of the trips that could have happened. This motivates the computation of the underlying demand. Knowing the demand for bikes and docks in the system allows us to plan more effectively for usage.

Observed trip data differs from the true demand due to censoring, that is stations being empty or full preventing users taking or returning bikes at the station. For many days we may observe zero trips for a time period but perhaps this is related to the station being empty/full. These outage windows are highly consistent as the morning and evening rush-hour behavior patterns are similar from day to day, meaning that the same stations are empty at the same time almost every day. However due to rebalancing operations we have days where we managed to replenish these stations with bikes or remove excess bikes. Out aim is to rely on rebalancing operations having had sufficient impact to give us data for most stations.

Consider a matrix of observations, O,where O_{ij} is equal to the number of bikes out on day i at time j and a level matrix, L, where L_{ij} is the number of bikes at the station on day i at time j. We use the average number of trips for each time window as a lower bound on the true demand. The lower bounds we produce are first order approximations of the true demand. Consider the impact of changing operations to facilitate these demands, this could easily drive more ridership as people see the system becoming more reliable.

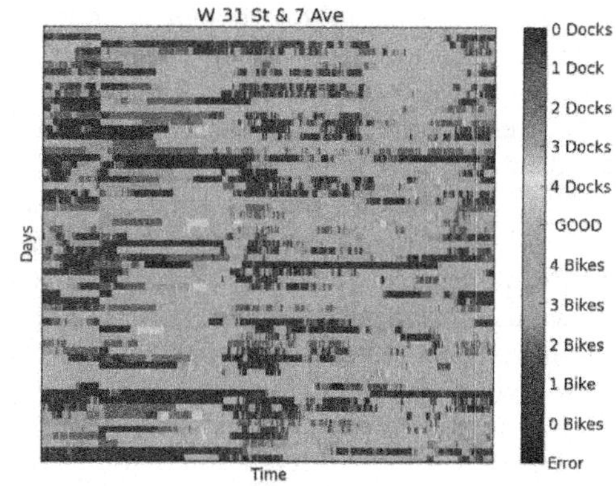

Figure 1: Example mask matrix for a Penn Station bike-share station over 60 days.

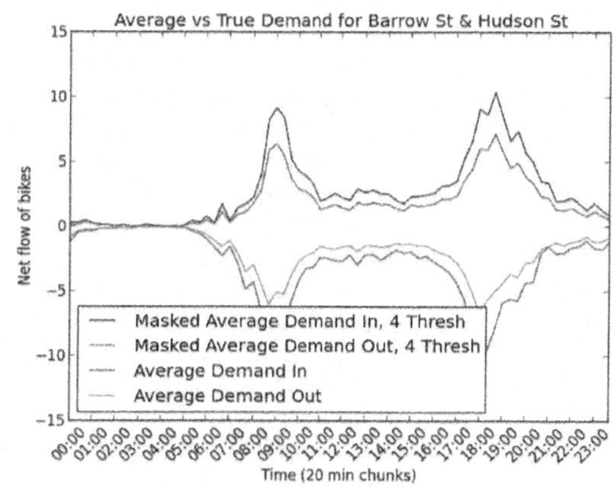

Figure 2: Example of the two lower bounds on true demand for a station in the West Village.

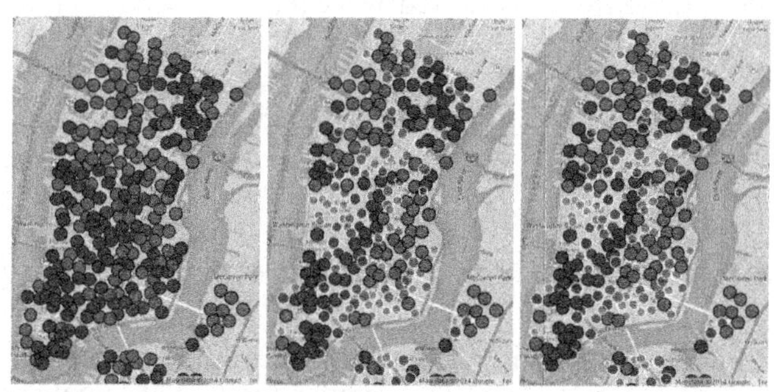

Figure 3: Morning levels assigned based on different cost functions. From left to right, minimizing max gap, minimizing the sum of the gaps, minimizing the sum of the gaps squared all with six thousand bikes. The color of stations corresponds to fill percentage, blue to 10%, red to 90% and purple to 50%.

To compute more accurate lower bounds on demand we need to take censoring of demand into account; to do this we mask the observed trip matrices, removing elements where the corresponding level element is at zero. That is lower bound on true demand of bikes out at time j, $T^o_j = avg_i(O_{ij}|L_{ij} > 0)$ This in essence ensures that zeroes that occur in the observed matrix are actual zeroes and not just zeroes due to outages. Due to broken bikes and broken docking points we use a soft outage number, that is considering a station to have a stockout if the number of bikes or docks drops below a given threshold. In practice, the correct value for this threshold is between two and five. An example of such a mask matrix for one of the Penn Station locations is shown in Figure 1. Using a threshold of four, the bounds on true demand flows for a West Village station are shown in Figure 2. From this figure we can see that the lower bound obtained by the mask matrix is larger in both magnitude and duration throughout the rush-hours.

Optimizing Resource Allocation Under the assumption that the lower bounds we have computed are a good proxy for the underlying user demand, optimization of management decisions for the system becomes possible. We can frame the question of how many bikes to place at a station before the rush hour as an optimization problem. Given, for each station, the expected number of bikes in and out of the station for each minute of the rush hour, the station capacities and the number of bikes that can be deployed into the system we solve an optimization problem where for each station we decide the number of bikes placed there, $X_s \in \{0...c(s)\}$ (where $c(s)$ is the capacity of the station). Given a budget of bikes B we need to ensure that $\sum_s X_s \leq B$. We then minimize some objective function $J(X)$, the structure of which impacts the quality of the solution to the problem. One initial candidate is to compute the net flow from the lower bounds for each station and look at the smallest and largest value for this curve over the rush hour. These values are the maximum imbalance the flow at the station will create. We can then penalize a station's level for being too far under or over these values. This penalty can take the form of minimizing a quadratic function of the differences, minimizing the sum of the differences or minimizing the maximum difference. Given for each station, s, the net flow curve at each time t as f^s_t, minimizing the maximum difference can be solved by the integer program below.

$$\min D \tag{1}$$

$$s.t. \quad \sum_s X_s \leq B \tag{2}$$

$$\forall s \quad D \geq X_s + \min_t f^s_t \tag{3}$$

$$\forall s \quad D \geq c(s) - X_s - \max_t f^s_t \tag{4}$$

$$\forall s \quad X_s \in \{0...c(s)\} \tag{5}$$

$$D \geq 0 \tag{6}$$

Minimizing the sum of the differences and the sum of the differences squared take similar forms with auxiliary variables recording the amounts that each station is under- and over-served, i.e., by constraints (3, 4). These auxiliary variables are then summed or squared and summed. It is important to put a lower bound of zero on the difference variables since we concern ourselves only with trips missed. Solutions to the optimization problem produced by Gurobi (Gurobi Optimization 2014) using these three objective functions are shown in Figure 3. Both minimizing the sum and sum of squared worse case imbalances result in a solution that matches operator intuition about the system.

4 Rebalancing

Having computed the desired fill levels for stations before the morning and evening rush-hours, as well as analyzing their behavior during these rush-hours, we address the problem how to get them there? We take different approaches for both planning for the rush-hour surge and managing this surge in ridership. Both our approaches are novel and drastically different from existing work.

Mid-Rush Rebalancing

The morning and evening weekday rush-hours account for the majority of trips taken on New York's bike-share system. Usage is extremely high during these periods and asymmetric; that is, the net flow of bikes out of many stations is largely positive or largely negative and often matched by an opposite symbol flow in the complementary rush-hour period. From observation of data, the net flow of stations can be computed. The behavior of stations from one day's rush-hour to the next is very consistent, allowing us to classify them as either producers, consumers or balanced stations.

Our goal during the rush hour is to ensure that users of the system are not too far from either a bike or a dock. A criterion close to this is contained within the contract that requires the operator of Citibike to maintain a specified level of quality of service in a range of aspects; fines are imposed for failing to meet certain levels. We will focus rebalancing resources on covering the critical areas of the city and will be able to rebalance only a small subset of stations. Using historical data that indicate which stations accumulate bikes (producers) and which lose bikes (consumers), we want to ensure that each producer station is close to a producer station that will be rebalanced, and that each consumer station is close to some rebalanced consumer station. To rebalance a consumer station, bikes must be delivered to it, ideally from a producer station where bikes need to be removed for rebalancing. We select producer and consumer stations to rebalance, pairing them up so that rebalancing is achieved for both producer and consumer simultaneously.

In NYC, most of the mid-rush rebalancing is done by special bicycles outfitted with trailers that can hold a few Citibikes, typically three; due to the nature of this resource, the most effective plan is to designate certain pairs of stations (i.e., with one producer and one consumer) to be targeted for mutual rebalancing. These pairs must be sufficiently close, so that the bicycles can be moved effectively within the narrow timeframe of a quickly transpiring rush hour. These considerations gave rise to the following optimization model:

Definition *Mid-Rush Pairing Problem* We are given a complete undirected graph $G = (P \cup C, E)$ with a non-negative metric distance function $d(e), \forall e \in E$, as well as an integer k, and an integer T; the goal is to select two subsets, $P' \subseteq P$ and $C' \subseteq C$ such that $|P'| = |C'| \leq k$, such that there exists a perfect matching in $\{e \in E : d(e) \leq T\}$ between P' and C' which minimizes $\max(\max_{p \in P} d(p, P'), \max_{c \in C} d(c, C'))$ We define $d(p, P')$ to be the distance between p and the closest point in P' to it.

Integer Programming Formulation Similar to the case of the k-center problem, (Hochbaum and Shmoys 1985), the objective function is determined by exactly one edge length. Thus there are only a polynomial number of possible optimal values - $|P|^2 + |C|^2$. For each potential optimal value, we either verify its infeasibility (by showing that the IP is infeasible) or we have a solution.

$$\sum_{u \in V} x_u \leq k, \qquad \forall V \in \{P, C\}; \tag{7}$$

$$\sum_{u \in V:(u,v) \in E_V} y_{(u,v)} = 1, \qquad \forall v \in V, \quad \forall V \in \{P, C\}; \tag{8}$$

$$y_{(u,v)} \leq x_u, \qquad \forall (u,v) \in E_V, \quad \forall V \in \{P, C\}; \tag{9}$$

$$\sum_{c \in C:(p,c) \in E_M} m_{(p,c)} = x_p, \qquad \forall p \in P; \tag{10}$$

$$\sum_{p \in P:(p,c) \in E_M} m_{(p,c)} = x_c, \qquad \forall c \in C; \tag{11}$$

$$x_u \in [0,1], \qquad \forall u \in V; \tag{12}$$

$$y_{(u,v)} \in \{0,1\}, \quad \forall (u,v) \in E_P \cup E_C; \tag{13}$$

$$m_{(p,c)} \in \{0,1\} \qquad \forall (p,c) \in E_M. \tag{14}$$

In the integer linear programming formulation of the Mid-Rush Pairing Decision Problem, we wish to decide if there is a feasible solution in which each producer is served within a distance of d_P and each consumer within d_C, and that the paired nodes are within input threshold T; we let E_P be those pairs $(u, v) \in P \times P$ for which $d(u, v) \leq d_P$, E_C be those pairs $(u, v) \in C \times C$ for which $d(u, v) \leq d_C$, and let E_M be those pairs (u, v) such that $d(u, v) \leq T$. In the IP formulation, there exists a 0-1 decision variable x_u for each $u \in P \cup C$ to indicate whether (or not) that node is selected as one of the $2k$ paired stations; there is a 0-1 decision variable $y_{(u,v)}$ for each $(u, v) \in E_P \cup E_C$ to indicate whether node v is served by node u in the pairing. Finally, we have a 0-1 decision variable $m_{(p,c)}$ for each $(p, c) \in E_M$ to indicate whether producer p and consumer c are paired. Hence, we get the integer programming relaxation as shown above. We implemented the above model in Gurobi, by using a bisection search over the space of possible objective functions we were able to solve instances from New York in under a minute. We believe this performance to be due to the high quality of the LP relaxation of the above IP, in most cases the LP relaxation is integral.

Overnight Rebalancing

The majority of rebalancing operations occur overnight. From our analysis of system data and underlying demand we have computed the desired state of the system for start of the morning rush-hour. Previous work has attempted to compute routes for rebalancing trucks that allow a fully general pattern of pickups and drop-offs, and specify the number of bikes to be collected from and dropped to each station. We take a different approach that is motivated by working closely with the operators of the New York bike-sharing system. We restrict ourselves to moving truckloads of bikes. With this restriction, we formulate a model to optimize the use of a given-size fleet of rebalancing trucks. We derive an IP formulation that is reasonably tractable for fleets with a small number of trucks, and then provide a heuristic approach that takes advantage of the fact that the IP finds high quality solutions for the 1-truck special case.

During the overnight rebalancing shift, the goal is to get the system ready for the morning rush hour. We aim to have all stations at their desired level as specified by a balancing plan. Often this is an unrealistic demand as the resources available are inadequate to achieve this. This motivates the problem of getting the system as close as possible to this state with the resources available. To achieve this, we compute a set of routes for rebalancing trucks that optimize the number of stations rebalanced. We limit these routes to move only full truckloads of bikes. Previous approaches have focused on the number of bikes to move between stations. From analyzing system state at the beginning of the overnight shift we observed that it is desirable to move only full trucks of bikes. A full truck of bikes is, in most cases, enough to bring a station to the required level. Also, the travel time in Manhattan can dominate the loading time of a truck, making it desirable from an operational standpoint to move only full truck loads of bikes. Finally, the simplicity of the instructions needed to implement full truckload routes is an important element in the practicality of this approach. Using these observations, we formulate the problem as trying to find a set of truck routes that rebalances as much of the system as possible in the time available. We route trucks in a bipartite graph, where one node set consists of stations with a surplus of bikes and the other of stations with a deficit of bikes. We now formally define the *Overnight Rebalancing Problem*. The intuition for this model is that we want to have routes for trucks that alternate between surplus and deficit stations. The distance between a surplus and a deficit station takes into account both the travel time and loading/unloading time. The time limit is determined by the length of a shift operated by rebalancing staff.

Definition *Overnight Rebalancing Problem* We are given a complete bipartite graph $G = (P \cup M, E)$, a number of trucks T, a non-negative metric distance function $d(e)$ for each $e \in E$, and a distance limit L, and the aim is to find T vertex-disjoint paths $\mathscr{P}$, each starting in P and ending in M, such that $\forall p \in \mathscr{P}, \sum_{e \in p} d(e) \leq L$, so that the total number of vertices visited by at least one path is maximized.

Empirical Solution Given the importance of having the bike-share system in a good state before the morning rush hour it is crucial to quickly produce high quality routes for the overnight rebalancing shift. To achieve this we tackled the Overnight Rebalancing Problem from an empirical perspective.

$$\max \sum_{t\in\{1,\dots,T\}} \sum_{v\in P\cup M} z_v^t \qquad \text{subject to} \quad (15)$$

$$\sum_{p\in P} r^t_{(d_{start},p)} = 1 \qquad \forall t \in \{1...T\} \quad (16)$$

$$\sum_{m\in M} r^t_{(m,d_{end})} = 1 \qquad \forall t \in \{1...T\} \quad (17)$$

$$\sum_{u\in\mathcal{N}(v)} r^t_{(u,v)} = \sum_{u\in\mathcal{N}(v)} r^t_{(v,u)} \qquad \forall v \in P\cup M, \forall t \in \{1...T\} \quad (18)$$

$$\sum_{e\in \bar{E}} r^t_e \cdot d(e) \leq L \qquad \forall t \in \{1...T\} \quad (19)$$

$$\sum_{t\in\{1,\dots,T\}} z^t_v \leq 1 \qquad \forall v \in P\cup M \quad (20)$$

$$\sum_{u\in P\cup M} r^t_{(u,v)} = z^t_v \qquad \forall v \in P\cup M, \forall t \in \{1...T\} \quad (21)$$

$$f^t_e \leq r^t_e \cdot |P\cup M| \qquad \forall e \in \bar{E}, \forall t \in \{1...T\} \quad (22)$$

$$\sum_{u\in\mathcal{N}(v)} f^t_{(u,v)} = \sum_{u\in\mathcal{N}(v)} f^t_{(v,u)} + z^t_v \qquad \forall v \in P\cup M, \forall t \in \{1...T\} \quad (23)$$

$$r^t_{(u,v)} \in \{0,1\} \qquad \forall (u,v) \in \bar{E}, \forall t \in \{1...T\} \quad (24)$$

$$f^t_{(u,v)} \in \{0...|P\cup M|\} \qquad \forall (u,v) \in \bar{E}, v \neq d_{end}, \forall t \in \{1...T\} \quad (25)$$

$$z^t_v \in \{0,1\} \qquad \forall v \in P\cup M, \forall t \in \{1...T\} \quad (26)$$

One approach to solving the Overnight Rebalancing Problem is to formulate it as an integer program; we give a formulation for which standard IP software typically computes high-quality solutions for modest-sized inputs within reasonable time bounds. Given the input graph $G = (P \cup M, E)$, we construct an augmented (directed) graph $\bar{G}$: we start with the input bipartite graph, bidirecting its edges, and add a start *depot* vertex d_{start} as well as a finish *depot* d_{end}. In addition to two directed copies of each edge $(u,v) \in E$, there is an edge from d_{start} to each vertex in P and an edge from each vertex in M to d_{end}. Let $\bar{E}$ denote the augmented set of edges, and for each $u \in P \cup M$, we let $\mathcal{N}(u)$ denote the set of vertices v for which there exists an edge $(u,v) \in \bar{E}$. In constructing an integer programming formulation, there will be three type of integer variables. First, there are 0-1 variables z_v^t that indicate whether the truck $t \in \{1,\dots,T\}$ rebalances node v. We also have a set of 0-1 variables $r^t_{(u,v)}$ that indicate whether the edge (u,v) is on the route traversed by truck t, $t = 1,\dots,T$. Hence, we have flow conservation constraints (16), (17), and (18), which ensure, respectively, that the path starts at a node in P, ends at a node in M, and that whenever the path enters a node, it must exit that node as well. Similarly, it is natural to have the length constraint (19) to upper bound the length of the path, and disjointness constraint (20) to ensure that at most one truck rebalances a given node v. Finally, it is clear that the node v is visited by t, if there is some edge $e = (u,v)$ for which $r_e^t = 1$; hence, we get the constraints (21).

However, if one considers the feasible solutions to just these constraints, then it is easy to forget that a feasible 0-1 solution for r^t might not correspond simply to a path, but to a path plus a collection of cycles. The role of the final set of variables is to enforce that the only nodes that are serviced by t are those nodes on the path indicated by r. For each edge $e = (u,v) \in \bar{E}$, where $u \in d_{start} \cup P \cup M$, and $v \in P \cup M$, the integer variable f_e^t counts the number of nodes in $P \cup M$ yet to be traversed in its path (and so, for example, if the path for truck 1 rebalances 8 nodes, starting node $u \in P$, then $f^1_{(d_{start},u)} = 8$). First, each variable f_e^t is positive (and of course is at most $|P \cup M|$) only when r_e^t is 1; this is enforced by constraints (22). Finally, if the count entering node v is ℓ, then the count exiting it $\ell - 1$ (provided the truck traverses node v); this is exactly captured by the constraint (23). And notice the effect of this constraint on a potential cycle selected by the variables r; its corresponding f value must decrease by 1 for each edge traversed in the cycle, but clearly this is impossible. Hence, this additional set of flow variables and constraints preclude the possibility of selecting cycles.

Heuristic Approach As the number of trucks increases, the time it takes to solve the IP increases. From experimental results shown below, one truck is solvable by the IP, whereas larger number of trucks require more than the modest time limit given to the solver. This leads us to investigate a heuristic approach to the problem, specifically a greedy algorithm. In this greedy algorithm, we repeatedly solve the IP for one truck, and then remove those vertices from the graph and solve again. Removing the vertices covered by the route is valid, since the bipartite graph is complete, and once chosen no other truck will be able to use the removed vertices.

Framing this optimization problem as a covering problem allows us to analyze properties of the greedy heuristic. In this case we are choosing a subset from a ground set of all possible truck routes, paths starting in P, ending in M of distance at most L, to cover another set, the set of all vertices. Given a subset of truck routes, the number of vertices covered is equal to twice the number of (p,m) pairs covered by trucks, where each p and each m can appear in at most one pair. To compute this, consider ordering the truck routes and take all pairs defined by the first route. For all subsequent routes, if a vertex on the route has already been visited we shortcut the pair it belongs to in the route and continue. We observe that this objective function is submodular (Lemma 4.1). This property allows a greedy approach, where at each step the best possible route for a truck is taken, to yield a $(1 - \frac{1}{e})$ solution, as shown in Nemhauser, Wolsey and Fisher (Nemhauser, Wolsey, and Fisher 1978).

Typically, when maximizing a submodular function over a finite ground set, at each stage the element from the set that increases the objective function the most is added. However, in this case, the ground set is exponential in size requiring a different approach than iterating through the elements of the ground set. Given a problem instance, it is clear that solving the problem for one truck yields the best route from the ground set. For the following iterations, by removing routes we have already taken, the best route for one truck is equal to the best element from the ground set to add. Thus solving the 1-truck IP to find the best route at each stage gives us a $(1 - \frac{1}{e})$ approximation to the original problem (though albeit without any guarantee on how efficient the algorithm is).

Lemma 4.1 *The function mapping a set of paths of length at most L that start in P and end in M to the number of (p,c)*

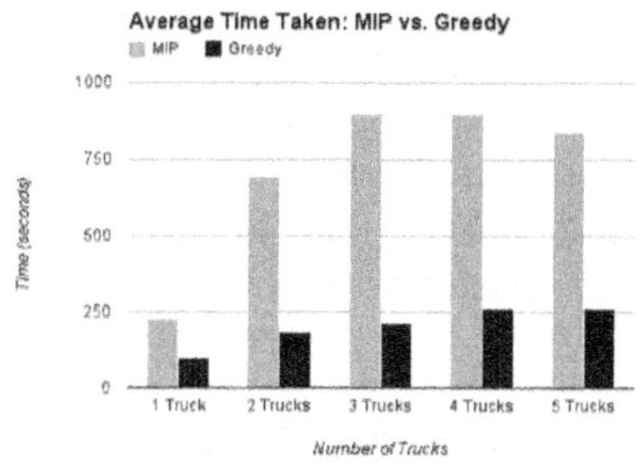

Figure 4: Average time taken by the IP and greedy approaches for different numbers of trucks on real instances.

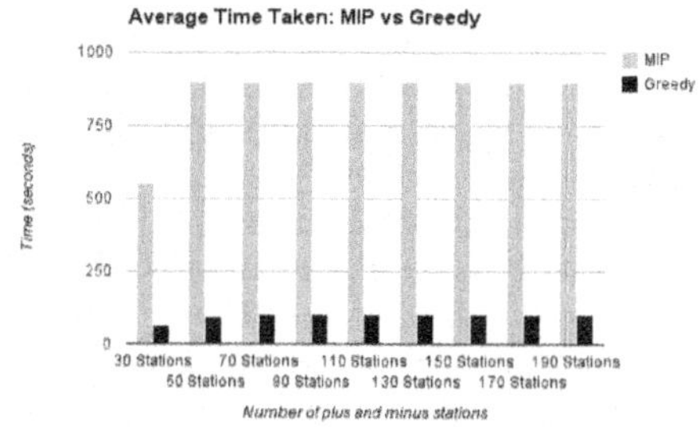

Figure 6: Average time taken by the IP and greedy approaches for different instance sizes in random instances.

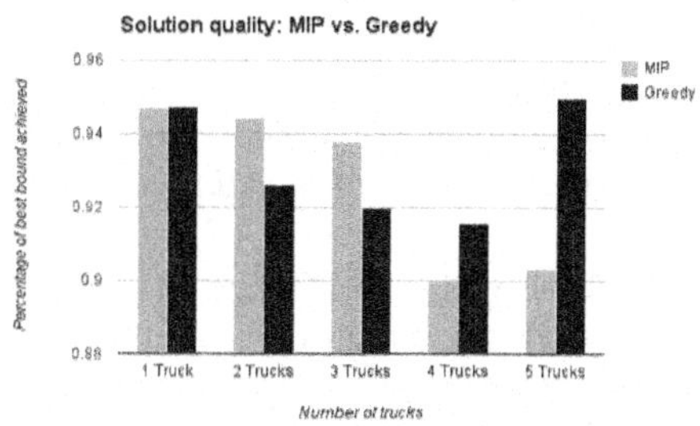

Figure 5: Solution quality found by the IP and greedy approaches for different numbers of trucks on random instances.

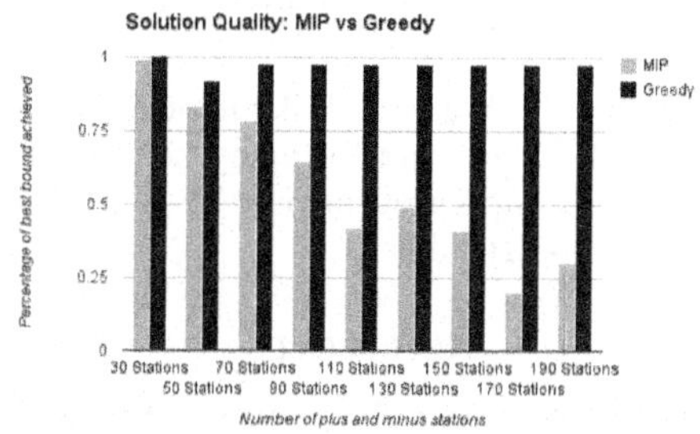

Figure 7: Solution quality found by the IP and greedy approaches for different instance sizes in random instances.

pairs (where each p and each c can appear in at most one pair) visited by at least one path is monotone submodular.

Proof Consider adding a path to the set of paths and re evaluating the objective function. There can be no decrease in the objective function as we are not removing any paths. Given two sets of paths A, B with $A \subseteq B$ we can not gain more by adding another path to B than by adding it to A as any pairs visited by A are visited in B and shortcutting that must take place in A must take place in B.

Experimental Results We tested the integer programming approaches on real world instances gathered from actual system data. We implemented the IP in Gurobi (Gurobi Optimization 2014) and carried out a number of experiments. The experiments were run on Linux machines with 2 Intel x5690s running at 3.46GHZ, a 128GB SSD and 96GB RAM. To generate the real world instances we took a series of system snapshots of the system state at the 8pm start of the overnight shift during June 2013. We used a standard plan for the system state at the start of the morning rush hour to compute the stations that make up the bipartite graph, specifying the surplus and deficit nodes P and M. The instances typically had 50 P vertices and 50 M vertices. With station location GPS information, we can compute an estimated travel distance between the stations. For each instance we vary the number of trucks available for rebalancing and analyze both the runtime taken by the solver as well as solution quality; in total, the data set contained 50 instances. We ran the IP with a 900 second cutoff and restricted the greedy to use only 300 seconds for each greedy call to the IP. The results can be seen in Figures 4 and 5. From this it is clear that as the number of trucks increases, the greedy approach produces higher quality solutions in less time than the IP. In Figure 5 we compare the solutions returned by both methods to the best bound found by the solver in 900 seconds. It is interesting to note that although one can solve the 1-truck inputs to optimality (say, with an hour of computation time), it is typically the case that this only shows the incumbent solution to be optimal.

We also conducted experiments on randomly generated instances where we fix the number of trucks at 5 (a realistic number of available trucks) and we vary the number of P and M vertices. The results of this experiment are shown in Figures 6 and 7. Again the greedy approach outperforms the MIP. The performance of the greedy solution, both in terms of time taken and solution quality allows it to be used in practice.

5 Conclusion and Future Work

In this paper, we provide a novel way of thinking about bike rebalancing in bike-share systems. Our models are motivated by operational constraints and observations gleaned from a close collaboration with bike-share operators. We provide solution methods for our models that are sufficient to provide high quality, usable solutions to real world instances from New York City as well as providing provable guarantees on solution quality. Solutions to the mid-rush rebalancing problem are already in use in New York and the tools developed to solve the Overnight Rebalancing Problem are currently being integrated into the truck dispatching system. Our approaches provide "the overarching vision for how we like our system to look," according to Citibike director of operations Michael Pellegrino (Wald 2014).

The collaboration with New York Bike Share LLC. is ongoing: a wealth of other operational challenges remain to be tackled, such as optimizing battery replacement for stations and developing models for future system expansion. Furthermore, we are continuing to improve the solution methods for the models presented in this paper, refining both the computational results as well as improving the models through feedback from people in the field.

Acknowledgments We would like to acknowledge Shane Henderson and Lior Seeman for many helpful discussions. This research was supported in part by NSF grants CCF-0832782 and CCF-1017688.

References

Anily, S., and Bramel, J. 1999. Approximation algorithms for the capacitated traveling salesman problem with pickups and deliveries. *Naval Research Logistics (NRL)* 46(6):654–670.

Archetti, C.; Bertazzi, L.; Laporte, G.; and Speranza, M. G. 2007. A branch-and-cut algorithm for a vendor-managed inventory-routing problem. *Transportation Science* 41(3):382–391.

Chekuri, C.; Korula, N.; and Pál, M. 2012. Improved algorithms for orienteering and related problems. *ACM Transactions on Algorithms* 8(3):23.

Chemla, D.; Meunier, F.; and Calvo, R. W. 2013. Bike sharing systems: Solving the static rebalancing problem. *Discrete Optimization* 10(2):120 – 146.

Contardo, C.; Morency, C.; and L.-M. Rousseau. 2012. Balancing a dynamic public bike-sharing system. Technical Report CIRRELT-2012-09, Université de Montréal, Montréal, Canada.

Garca-Palomares, J. C.; Gutirrez, J.; and Latorre, M. 2012. Optimizing the location of stations in bike-sharing programs: A GIS approach. *Applied Geography* 35(1?2):235 – 246.

Gurobi Optimization, I. 2014. Gurobi optimizer reference manual.

Hernndez-Prez, H., and Gonzlez, J. J. S. 2007. The one-commodity pickup-and-delivery traveling salesman problem: Inequalities and algorithms. *Networks* 50(4):258–272.

Hochbaum, D. S., and Shmoys, D. B. 1985. A best possible heuristic for the k-center problem. *Mathematics of Operations Research* 10(2):180–184.

Kaltenbrunner, A.; Meza, R.; Grivolla, J.; Codina, J.; and Banchs, R. 2010. Urban cycles and mobility patterns: Exploring and predicting trends in a bicycle-based public transport system. *Pervasive and Mobile Computing* 6(4):455 – 466. Human Behavior in Ubiquitous Environments: Modeling of Human Mobility Patterns.

Larsen, J. 2013. Bike-sharing programs hit the streets in over 500 cities worldwide. *Earth Policy Institute*.

Lin, J.-R., and Yang, T.-H. 2011. Strategic design of public bicycle sharing systems with service level constraints. *Transportation Research Part E: Logistics and Transportation Review* 47(2):284–294.

Martinez, L. M.; Caetano, L.; Eir, T.; and Cruz, F. 2012. An optimisation algorithm to establish the location of stations of a mixed fleet biking system: An application to the city of lisbon. *Procedia - Social and Behavioral Sciences* 54(0):513 – 524. Proceedings of {EWGT2012} - 15th Meeting of the {EURO} Working Group on Transportation, September 2012, Paris.

Nair, R.; Miller-Hooks, E.; Hampshire, R. C.; and Bušić, A. 2013. Large-scale vehicle sharing systems: Analysis of Velib. *International Journal of Sustainable Transportation* 7(1):85–106.

Nemhauser, G.; Wolsey, L.; and Fisher, M. 1978. An analysis of approximations for maximizing submodular set functions. *Mathematical Programming* 14(1):265–294.

Rainer-Harbach, M.; Papazek, P.; Hu, B.; and Raidl, G. R. 2013. Balancing bicycle sharing systems: A variable neighborhood search approach. In Middendorf, M., and Blum, C., eds., *EvoCOP*, volume 7832 of *Lecture Notes in Computer Science*, 121–132. Springer.

Raviv, T.; Tzur, M.; and Forma, I. 2013. Static repositioning in a bike-sharing system: models and solution approaches. *EURO Journal on Transportation and Logistics* 2(3):187–229.

Romero, J. P.; Ibeas, A.; Moura, J. L.; Benavente, J.; and Alonso, B. 2012. A simulation-optimization approach to design efficient systems of bike-sharing. *Procedia - Social and Behavioral Sciences* 54(0):646 – 655. Proceedings of {EWGT2012} - 15th Meeting of the {EURO} Working Group on Transportation, September 2012, Paris.

Schuijbroek, J.; Hampshire, R.; and van Hoeve, W.-J. 2013. Inventory rebalancing and vehicle routing in bike sharing systems. *Tepper School of Business* Paper 1491.

Shu, J.; Chou, M. C.; Liu, Q.; Teo, C.-P.; and Wang, I.-L. 2013. Models for effective deployment and redistribution of bicycles within public bicycle-sharing systems. *Operations Research* 61(6):1346–1359.

Vansteenwegen, P.; Souffriau, W.; and Oudheusden, D. V. 2011. The orienteering problem: A survey. *European Journal of Operational Research* 209(1):1 – 10.

Vogel, P., and Mattfeld, D. C. 2011. Strategic and operational planning of bike-sharing systems by data mining - a case study. In Bse, J.; Hu, H.; Jahn, C.; Shi, X.; Stahlbock, R.; and Vo, S., eds., *ICCL*, 127–141. Springer.

Wald, C. 2014. Wheels when you need them. *Science* 345(6199):862–863.

Towards Optimal Solar Tracking: A Dynamic Programming Approach

Athanasios Aris Panagopoulos
Electronics and Computer Science,
University of Southampton, UK
ap1e13@ecs.soton.ac.uk

Georgios Chalkiadakis
Electronic and Computer Engineering,
Technical University of Crete, Greece
gehalk@intelligence.tuc.gr

Nicholas R. Jennings
Electronics and Computer Science,
University of Southampton, UK
nrj@ecs.soton.ac.uk

Abstract

The power output of photovoltaic systems (PVS) increases with the use of effective and efficient solar tracking techniques. However, current techniques suffer from several drawbacks in their tracking policy: *(i)* they usually do not consider the forecasted or prevailing weather conditions; even when they do, they *(ii)* rely on complex closed-loop controllers and sophisticated instruments; and *(iii)* typically, they do not take the energy consumption of the trackers into account. In this paper, we propose a policy iteration method (along with specialized variants), which is able to calculate near-optimal trajectories for effective and efficient day-ahead solar tracking, based on weather forecasts coming from online providers. To account for the energy needs of the tracking system, the technique employs a novel and generic consumption model. Our simulations show that the proposed methods can increase the power output of a PVS considerably, when compared to standard solar tracking techniques.

Introduction

In recent decades, a large number of photovoltaic systems (PVSs) have been integrated into the electricity grid. A PVS's power output depends mostly on the irradiance incident on the PV module and its operating temperature: in general, PVSs favor lower operating temperatures and greater levels of incident solar irradiance. In this context, *solar tracking (ST)* techniques can be used to orient the system towards the greatest possible levels of incoming solar irradiance. Depending on location and season, ST can increase the PVS power output by up to 100% (Mousazadeh et al. 2009).

The effectiveness of the ST technique used is therefore crucial for the overall efficiency of the PVS. Now, *active*[1] ST relies on electrical motors to move the PVS. The motors are driven by a controller that operates in a *closed-loop* or in an *open-loop* fashion (i.e., with or without making use of any feedback, respectively). Typical open-loop trackers are the *chronological* trackers, which follow the sun based on a chronological model of its motion (Reda and Andreas 2004). Although simple, they do not take into account the forecasted or prevailing weather conditions (e.g., the degree of cloud coverage). On the other hand, closed-loop controllers take the weather conditions into account, but they usually depend on expensive and sophisticated instruments (Lynch and Salameh 1990). On top of that, existing closed-loop controllers typically do not take into account the energy consumption caused by the tracking itself, nor do they consider the system's maintenance cost; they simply greedily turn the system towards the perceived highest irradiance values. For a review of ST techniques see (Mousazadeh et al. 2009).

In this work we develop novel *low-cost* ST techniques that can be used in both an *open-loop* or a *closed-loop* manner. We do not make use of expensive equipment or sensors, but the backbone of our approach is the estimation of the optimal trajectories a day before, based on weather forecasts coming from online providers for free. To this end, we employ a recently developed web tool, RENES (Panagopoulos et al. 2012), that predicts the power output of a PVS given available weather forecasts (www.intelligence.tuc.gr/renes). These predictions form the reward dynamics of a *policy iteration (PI)* technique we devise. The technique, *Solar Tracking Policy Iteration (STPI)*, alternatively optimizes over action sub-spaces. Although optimizing over sub-problems in an alternating fashion is a generally common concept elsewhere (Bezdek and Hathaway 2002), this is the first time that such an optimization technique is proposed for MDPs.

Importantly, the method makes use of a novel *tracking system consumption model* we develop (and which can be extended to account for maintenance and other costs). The method is appropriate for *dual-axis* (i.e., employing two axes of rotation) tracking, and is shown to be much more efficient than the, also sensor-less, *chronological* ST. We also provide four additional control methods: a PI method specialized for *single-axis tracking*, two near-optimal *myopic* methods (one specialized for *single-axis* and one for *dual-axis*) which we detail later, and a method that enables us to define the next-day-optimal positioning for any fixed-orientation (yet re-adjustable) PVS operating within the geographical region of a given weather station. The efficiency of the latter is higher than positioning the system according to *yearly-optimal* fixed-orientation estimates, and the method can be easily extended to define the *weekly-optimal* PVS orientation. Moreover, our methods are shown to improve the power output of a PVS even when compared to closed-loop *sensor-based* ST. Last but not least, all our methods come

[1] *Passive* ST, usually based on thermal expansion effects, is less common (Mousazadeh et al. 2009), and hence not considered here.

with guarantees of near-optimality.

Although dynamic programming can naturally find the optimal solution to the ST problem, this paper is the first to propose such an approach. This is probably due to the fact that an appropriate reward model had not been devised until now (due to the lack of free and ready-to-use power output estimates, and an appropriate consumption model). We resolve this issue, and thus contribute to the state-of-the-art, as follows: first, we employ the recent method of (Panagopoulos et al. 2012) to get PVS power output estimates;[2] and, second, we devise here, for the first time, a generic, parameterizable tracker power consumption model.

Our simulation results show that our approach outperforms all benchmark methods (i.e., chronological, sensor-based and/or fixed-orientation). Though we evaluate our approach via simulations involving the popular *azimuth-altitude dual axis trackers* (AADAT) and *vertical single axis trackers* (VSAT), we note that it can be used in conjunction with many other ST systems (e.g., *tilted axis*, or *horizontal single axis*). Finally, it is worth noting that our next-day policy comes complete with an expected PVS power output estimation. This is crucial for the smooth integration of PVSs into the electricity grid—since it is essential that short-term predicted PVS production estimates are available, notwithstanding their intermittent nature (Ramchurn et al. 2012).

Background

The total irradiance G_T falling on an arbitrarily oriented surface, consists of the *beam* G_B, *sky-diffuse* G_D and *ground-reflected* G_R components (Luque and Hegedus 2011) :

$$G_T = G_B + G_D + G_R \tag{1}$$

Usually, the cosine effect is used to model the variations of the G_B component, as seen in Eq. 2 below:

$$G_B = G_B^{max} \cos\theta_s \tag{2}$$

where θ_s is the angle between the normal to the surface and the direction to the sun (as seen in Fig. 1) and G_B^{max} is the incident beam irradiance when the surface is oriented normally to the incoming radiation (i.e., $\theta_s = 0°$). G_B^{max} is the maximum beam irradiance that the PV module can orient to, and depends on weather conditions and solar position.

Now, the G_D component varies according to Eq. 3 which assumes that every point of the celestial sphere emits light with equal radiance (Liu and Jordan 1961):

$$G_D = G_D^{max}(1 + \cos\beta)/2 \tag{3}$$

where β is the inclination angle of the surface and G_D^{max} is the incident diffuse irradiance for $\beta = 0°$. G_D^{max} is the maximum diffuse irradiance that the PV module can orient to, and depends on weather conditions and solar position.

Finally, the G_R component is modeled by Eq. 4 which assumes that the ground is horizontal, of infinite extent, and reflects uniformly to all directions (Luque and Hegedus 2011):

$$G_R = G_R^{max}(1 - \cos\beta) \tag{4}$$

[2]We note here, that one could alternatively use the work of (Chakraborty et al. 2012), which, however, unlike RENES, does not come with a ready-to-use web tool, and requires the availability of historical PVS-specific production output data.

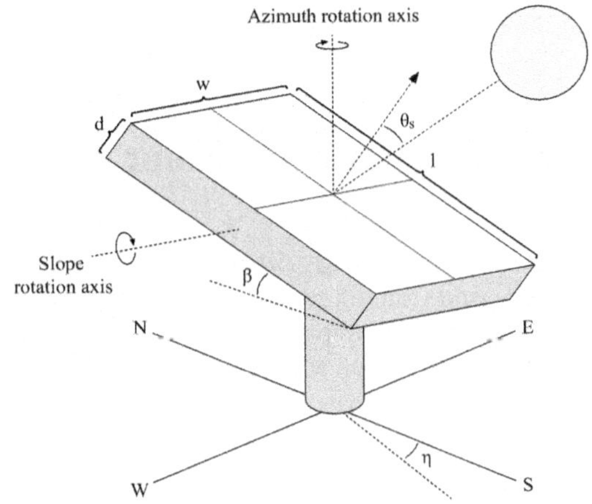

Figure 1: Abstract AADAT (in VSAT β is fixed)

where G_R^{max} is the maximum reflected irradiance that the PV module can orient to (for $\beta = 90°$), and depends on weather conditions and solar position.

In our work we focus on both *AADAT* and *VSAT* tracking systems. The AADAT has two degrees of freedom, rotating over a slope (elevation) and an azimuth axis. An abstract AADAT is illustrated in Figure 1. The VSAT rotates only over the azimuthal axis, while its slope angle is kept fixed.

Typically, the movement allowed in tracking systems is constrained within a certain range in both the azimuthal and elevation axis. We henceforth denote the allowed azimuthal and elevation angular range by r_{Az} and r_{Sl} respectively.

The possible slope and azimuth orientations of a dual axis system consists of a discrete number of possible positions within the allowed range at each rotation axis, depending on the tracker step size. Now, a misalignment of $\pm 1°$ causes only a minor drop of $\sim 0.015\%$ in the incident beam irradiance G_B (cf. Eq. 2). Thus, small misalignments are not a concern for typical commercial systems.

The controller step-size (i.e., the system's minimum angular displacement) θ gives rise to two sets of distinct possible orientation positions for the PVS (one such set per axis of movement). We denote these by K, the set of azimuth orientation positions, and by Λ, the set of possible positions on the elevation axis. In particular, we have $|K| = \lfloor r_{Az}/\theta \rfloor + 1$ and $|\Lambda| = \lfloor r_{Sl}/\theta \rfloor + 1$. The time required for a minimum displacement θ to occur is denoted by δ; its value is assumed constant in our model, in order to maintain a fixed mean angular velocity for every minimum displacement.

Now, the controller requires some time to interact with the PVS, and it takes the system some time to execute the controller commands. For simplicity, the controller in our model is synchronous, meaning that any two consecutive controller-system interactions are separated by a fixed-length time interval Δ. A natural choice is to pick a Δ length that is sufficient to move the PV panel at any orientation starting from an arbitrary position (i.e., $\Delta \geq \delta \cdot max(|K| - 1, |\Lambda| - 1)$), and small enough so as the environmental conditions do not change abruptly during this interval.

Hence, the operation time of a PVS is naturally divided

into a number of equal time intervals of length Δ each. Letting Δ_{Day} stand for the day-length (i.e., the time between sunrise and sunset), the required controller-system interactions are contained in a set I, with $|I| = \lceil \Delta_{Day}/\Delta \rceil$. Note that each interaction corresponds to a specific *time-step* or *interaction id* τ; and that these interactions are sufficient to orient the PV panel to any orientation right after the sunrise, and to move it back to the initial position after the sunset.

A Dynamic Programming Approach

The aim of our work is to calculate optimal ST trajectories for the day ahead, based on available weather forecasts—which can actually come from online providers for free. To this end, we employ dynamic programming and, in particular, an intuitive *policy iteration* technique (and variants).

Defining the MDP

The problem is naturally modeled as a fully observable, finite-horizon, discrete-time Markov decision process (MDP) corresponding to an $\langle S, A, P, R\rangle$ tuple as follows:

First, S is a finite set of *states*, where each state $s \in S$ corresponds to a tuple $\langle \kappa_s, \lambda_s, \mathbf{w_s}\rangle$ with $\kappa_s \in [1, |K|]$ denoting the azimuth orientation position, $\lambda_s \in [1, |\Lambda|]$ denoting the slope orientation position, and $\mathbf{w_s}$ standing for the vector of *stochastic weather condition variables* which are required to calculate the MDP reward dynamics (i.e., prevailing wind speed and direction, relative humidity, temperature, and sky conditions). As such, $|S| \geq |K \times \Lambda|$. The value of each state depends on the $\tau \in [1, |I|]$ time-stamp at which the state is visited—that is, $|I|$ represents the horizon for our problem. Note that the time-stamp τ at which s is visited is sufficient to extract all necessary information regarding the *non-stochastic environmental conditions* (i.e., the solar position angles) relevant to s and τ. Therefore, these do not have to be explicitly included in the state representation.

Then, A is a finite set of *actions*, with each action $a \in A$ positioning the PVS to some specific orientation. Thus, a corresponds to tuple $\langle \kappa_a, \lambda_a\rangle$, with $\kappa_a \in [1, |K|]$ and $\lambda_a \in [1, |\Lambda|]$. Hence, we have $|A| = |K \times \Lambda|$.

The *transition model* P defines the $P(s, a, s')$ probability that taking action $a = \langle \kappa_a, \lambda_a\rangle$ in state s will lead to s'. Thus, given a particular action a at a state s, for the successive state s' we will have: $\kappa_{s'} = \kappa_a$, $\lambda_{s'} = \lambda_a$; while the transition probabilities will depend entirely on the $P(\mathbf{w'_s}|\mathbf{w_s})$ ones. Note that in the case that $\mathbf{w'_s}$ is independent of $\mathbf{w_s}$ we will not have a *probabilistic transition model*, but rather a *probabilistic reward model*. Hence, in that case, $\mathbf{w_s}$ can be omitted from the state representation and expected reward values can be extracted directly from the controller interaction id, τ, at which s is visited. The same holds if only non-probabilistic weather forecasts are available.

Finally, R is a *reward model* determining the $R_a(s, s')$ reward received for a transition from state s to s' after taking action a. This reward is the energy produced during the time between two consecutive controller interactions, minus the energy consumed due to the movement of the tracker throughout this interval. Thus:

$$R_a(s, s') = Prod(s, s') - Cons(s, s') \tag{5}$$

where $Prod(s, s')$ and $Cons(s, s')$ are functions estimating the energy produced and consumed as a result of the PVS system moving from s to s' (after some action a taken at s).

Calculating $Prod(s, s')$ is straightforward, assuming that the PVS power output is steady throughout a time interval Δ between two consecutive controller interactions:

$$Prod(s, s') = \frac{(Pwr(s) + Pwr(s'))}{2}\Delta \tag{6}$$

where $Pwr(s)$ stands for the PVS power output at state s. In our work, the $Pwr(s)$ estimates are provided by RENES, given the PVS orientation (i.e., κ_s,λ_s), the particular time of day (derived based on τ and used to estimate the solar position angles), the (fixed for a given system)) PV characteristics, as well as the stochastic weather conditions in $\mathbf{w_s}$.

Consumption model A distinct contribution of our work is the construction of a generic and parameterizable solar tracker consumption model. With an arbitrary displacement corresponding to an aggregation of minimum angular displacements on each one of the rotation axes, we calculate the consumption of an arbitrary displacement as the (efficiency-weighted) sum of the consumptions corresponding to these minimum angular displacements. Now, in order to maintain a fixed mean angular velocity for every minimum angular displacement θ, every such θ is assumed to follow a simple trapezoid motion profile with three motion phases (of equal time duration): *(1)* an *angular acceleration phase*, *(2)* a *constant angular velocity phase*, and *(3)* an *angular deceleration phase*. As such, the consumption for θ is calculated as the sum of the consumption for all three motion types in sequence. Then, the system consumption $Cons(s, s')$ is:

$$Cons(s, s') = \frac{1}{c_{eff}}\left(\sum_{1}^{|\kappa_s-\kappa_{s'}|} Cons_\theta^{az} + \sum_{1}^{|\lambda_s-\lambda_{s'}|} Cons_\theta^{sl}\right) \tag{7}$$

where c_{eff} stands for the efficiency factor of the tracking system. This corresponds to the mean efficiency of the motors, multiplied by the mean efficiency of the gears, and is further reduced to best fit all other secondary losses of the system during a displacement. $Cons_\theta^{az}$ and $Cons_\theta^{sl}$ represent the consumption of every minimum angular displacement θ over the azimuth and slope (elevation) axis respectively. Their values are calculated by the following equations:

$$Cons_\theta^{az} = \sum_{\mu=1}^{3}(\alpha_\mu \mathcal{I}_{A_{(\theta,\mu)}} - T^w_{A_{(\theta,\mu)}})\theta_\mu \tag{8}$$

$$Cons_\theta^{sl} = \sum_{\mu=1}^{3}(\alpha_\mu \mathcal{I}_S - T^w_{S_{(\theta,\mu)}})\theta_\mu \tag{9}$$

where θ_μ and α_μ stand for the angular displacement and acceleration for each one of the motion phases, and can be computed as $\theta_1 = \theta_3 = \theta_2/2 = \theta/4$, and $\alpha_1 = -\alpha_3 = 9\theta/2\delta^2$ and $\alpha_2 = 0$. Now, $\mathcal{I}_{A_{(\theta,\mu)}}$, $\mathcal{I}_S$, $T^w_{A_{(\theta,\mu)}}$ and $T^w_{S_{(\theta,\mu)}}$ stand for the *moment of inertia* and wind *torque*, for the azimuth and slope axis respectively.

For the slope rotation, the moment of inertia is independent of the azimuthal orientation, and, assuming the panel is a cuboid, can be given by $\mathcal{I}_S = \frac{m}{12}(l^2 + d^2)$ (Myers 1962), where m stands for the mass of the panel, and l and d for the length and thickness of the panel as seen in Fig. 1. Note, however, that the azimuthal motion occurs simultaneously with the slope one. Hence, T_S^w, T_A^w and $\mathcal{I}_A$ are not constant during the motion. Nevertheless, due to the very small displacement corresponding to each motion phase, these quantities were assumed constant and equal to their value at the beginning of each motion phase.

For the azimuthal rotation, the moment of inertia depends on the slope orientation. Assuming that the panel is a cuboid, the moment of inertia for the azimuthal rotation given a particular slope angle β can be computed as follows:

$$\mathcal{I}_A = \frac{m}{12}\left(l^2\cos^2(\beta) + d^2\sin^2(\beta) + w^2\right) \qquad (10)$$

where w stands for the *width* of the panel.

We also modeled the PVS aerodynamics, estimating the torque on the rotation axes due to the incident wind as $T_X^w = \frac{1}{2}\rho w l^2 V^2 c_X$, where $X \in \{A, S\}$, ρ denotes the *air density*, V the prevailing *wind speed*, and c_A and c_S denote the non-dimensionalized slope and azimuth *moment coefficients*, respectively. These coefficients depend on the orientation of the system. The air density was estimated based on the *local pressure*, the *relative humidity*, and the *temperature*, based on standard meteorological equations (Picard et al. 2008). The moment coefficients are calculated based on *wind direction* and *system orientation*, as in (Roos 2012).

Optimal Solar Tracking

With the above MDP at hand, the *optimal ST policy* can be derived by solving the corresponding Bellman optimality equation (Sutton and Barto 1998). However, due to the size of the state and action spaces (typically $|I| \cdot |S| \cdot |A| > 4$Bn, without even considering $\mathbf{w_s}$),[3] the optimal tracking policy for the day-ahead cannot be computed exactly in realistic settings applications. Rather, it can only be approximated. To this end, we have devised several approximation methods, which we now proceed to describe.

Approximation Methods

We now describe the approximation techniques we developed in order to compute effective ST policies.

Solar Tracking Policy Iteration method (STPI)

We devised a policy iteration (PI) approximation technique to compute a beneficial ST policy. The technique interweaves two distinct PI procedures, which are used in an alternating fashion. The first PI procedure, *SlopePI*, considers an arbitrary input policy for the above MDP, e.g., a myopic one. It then attempts to improve that policy, in a usual PI fashion, but assuming a *fixed azimuthal policy*, π_κ. Given this fixed π_κ policy, it computes the respective optimal slope-positioning policy, π_λ. The output policy is then fed in a second PI algorithm, which estimates an optimal (given π_λ) azimuth-positioning policy, π_κ. The process repeats until convergence, or until some computational or time limit is reached. By combining the derived policies computed for each axis, we can derive a ST policy. The same PI algorithm can be readily employed for single axis tracking, with the action selection process for the static axis (the slope one, in the case of VSAT) considering only a set of fixed possible orientations for the whole motion (so as to estimate the best possible fixed slope angle for VSAT tracking during the next day). The overall PI technique is shown in Alg. 1, while Alg. 2 describes the PI process to derive a slope policy (the PI for deriving an azimuthal policy is entirely similar). Note that STPI effectively alternates between solving MDPs with state-action spaces which are orders of magnitude smaller than that required by the original problem formulation. Though there are no formal guarantees for convergence to the optimal policy,[4] the technique is intuitive, and exhibits good behavior in practice. We note here again that, surprisingly enough, this is the first time that an approach that alternatively optimizes over MDP action subspaces is proposed for optimal policy approximation.

That said, the choice of the initial policy used is crucial for the efficiency of any policy iteration algorithm (Sutton and Barto 1998). The initial policy we use is a *myopic* one, which maximizes power output alone (disregarding any associated repositioning costs). Now, the tracking consumption of a PVS is a very small fraction of its production (typ-

Algorithm 1 "Alternating" Policy Iteration for ST

```
procedure STPI(π)
    Initialize π_λ and π_κ based on π
    while π_λ and π_κ are not stable do
        π_λ ← SLOPEPI(π_λ, π_κ)
        π_κ ← AZIMUTHPI(π_κ, π_λ)
    Derive π' by combining π_κ and π_λ
    return π'
```

Algorithm 2 Slope Policy Iteration

```
procedure SLOPEPI(π_λ, π_κ)
  while π_λ is not stable do
    for all τ ∈ I in descending order do
      for all s ∈ S that can emerge based on π_κ at τ do
        a ← ⟨κ_a = π_κ(s,τ), λ_a = π_λ(s,τ)⟩
        V_τ(s) ← Σ_{s'} P(s,a,s') (R_a(s,s') + V_{τ+1}(s'))
    for all τ ∈ I (in any order) do
      for all s ∈ S that can emerge based on π_κ at τ do
        π_λ(s,τ) ← argmax_λ Σ_{s'} P(s,a,s')(R_a(s,s')+
          V_{τ+1}(s')), where a = ⟨κ_a = π_κ(s,τ), λ_a = λ⟩
  return π_λ
```

[3]In more detail, for a day with 12 daylight hours (i.e., $\Delta_{Day} = 12\ hours$); a typical system (like the one considered in our evaluation) with $r_{Az} = 270°$, $r_{Sl} = 63°$ and $\theta = 1.8°$ (at each axis); and a control interval of 5 min (i.e., $\Delta = 5\ min$), there will be: $|I| = \lceil \Delta_{Day}/\Delta \rceil = 144$, $|A| = |K| \cdot |\Lambda| = \lfloor r_{Az}/\theta \rfloor + 1 \cdot \lfloor r_{Sl}/\theta \rfloor + 1 = 5,436$, $|S| \geq |K| \cdot |\Lambda| \Rightarrow |S| \geq 5,436$, and, hence, $|I| \cdot |S| \cdot |A| \geq 4,255,213,824$.

[4]Intuitively, however, since each iteration improves on the current policy, STPI is expected to converge to a fixed point.

ically less than 1% (Mousazadeh et al. 2009)). As such, the *myopic policy* is essentially a *near-optimal* one, achieving over 99% of the optimal performance. Moreover, any gains achieved by a method that lowers consumption is typically accompanied by costs due to lower production. Hence, the near-optimality guarantees of the myopic policy are even stronger; and they are *inherited by STPI*, as any derived improved policy cannot be worse than the initial one. We now describe how to derive the myopic policy.

Myopic method

We define the *myopic policy* in this domain as a method that maximizes power generation only. As such, we can modify the MDP reward function to account for the PVS power output only: $R_a(s, s') = Prod(s, s')$. Given the fact that all possible PVS orientations are accessible from any state, it is clear that the optimal policy in this modified MDP is equivalent to the one that chooses the action that gives the maximum expected reward for the next time interval.

Now, the power output of a PVS increases proportionally to incident irradiance. In order to maximize the incident G_T we need to maximize the sum $G_B + G_D + G_R$ as seen in Eq. 1. Moreover, as seen in Eqs. 3 and 4, G_D and G_R components vary from their maximum based only on the slope angle of the PV module. On the other hand, Eq. 2 illustrates that the G_B component varies from its maximum based on the incident angle, which for any given sun position depends on the slope and azimuth angle of the PV module. In particular, G_B reaches its maximum as the incident angle reaches zero (i.e., when the azimuth and slope angle of the PV module are the same as the azimuth and slope angle of the sun). As such, fixing the azimuth angle to follow the sun azimuth, ensures that we are always able to track the maximum G_T (for any weather conditions). The only thing that we need to do is to optimize the PVS slope angle at every time step, so that we balance the G_T components and get the maximum expected G_T. For (vertical) single axis tracking, the problem is further simplified into following the sun over the azimuth (and just defining the best next-day fixed slope orientation).

Next-Day-Optimal Fixed-Orientation

In the context of this work, we also propose and calculate the *next-day-optimal fixed PVS orientation*, by simply evaluating the whole space of possible orientations, given the next-day weather prediction. The derived orientation is suitable for any fixed-orientation (yet re-adjustable) PVS operating within the geographical region of a given weather station. Moreover, next-day-optimal fixed positioning can also be used by trackers in the case of scheduled power cuts. We note that this method can also be extended for weekly-optimal or some hours-optimal positioning, as needed.

Simulation Experiments

In order to evaluate our methods we simulated a PVS located at Chania, Crete, and estimated its output energy gain from employing each one of our methods. We chose Crete for our evaluation due to the great degree of PVS penetration on this sunny Greek island.[5] Moreover, this choice ensures that RENES provides accurate PVS power output predictions (Panagopoulos et al. 2012). That said, we note that considering locations with lower sunshine and greater wind speeds for our evaluation, would only favor our methods (as suggested by our evaluation results with "fictional" weather data below). Now, our simulations were performed for 8 different daily weather patterns; 4 of them corresponding to actual, real days, and 4 of them fictional. Moreover, we compared our methods against additional baseline methods we implemented for this purpose: *chronological VSAT* and *AADAT*, and a *yearly optimal fixed-orientation* system.

In more detail, the *chronological* AADAT calculates the sun positions as prescribed in the work of (Reda and Andreas 2004), and then orients the PVS so as to point towards the sun, irrespective of weather conditions. For the *chronological* VSAT, we used the same procedure to calculate the PVS azimuthal positions; while the slope angle was fixed to its yearly optimal value for VSAT tracking, given the location's latitude, as prescribed in (Li et al. 2011). Finally, we used the equations provided in (Chang 2009) to calculate the yearly optimal slope position for *fixed-orientation* south-facing panels at our location of interest.

The Simulated Photovoltaic System and Dataset

We modeled a typical $72m^2$ system (i.e., $w = 6.0m$, $l = 12.0m$, $d = 0.20m$) with $270°$ of azimuthal motion range, and $63°$ of elevation motion range. The system weight was set to $2500kg$. The modeled system was limited to provide a *step-size* of $\theta = 1.8°$ at each axis, which could lead to a maximum misalignment of $\arccos(\cos^2(\theta))/2 \simeq 1.27°$, corresponding to a G_B drop of $\sim 0.025\%$. The time δ required for a minimum displacement θ to occur, was set to $1s$, and the interval between two consecutive controller interactions was set to $\Delta = 5min$. As the efficiency of the motors and gears depends on the speed and load at all times (Burt et al. 2008), we used a mean efficiency of 30% for both[6] which leads to consumption that is close to the reported practical value for such systems (Mousazadeh et al. 2009).

For the purposes of our research, archival weather data was accumulated from the *weather underground* website (www.wunderground.com) regarding four different days at our location of interest. Specifically, we accumulated archival weather data for the $20/03/2011$ equinox, the $22/09/2012$ equinox, the solstice of $21/06/2012$, and the solstice of $21/12/2008$. These days are noted from now on as day 1, 2, 3 and 4 respectively. As there is a 30-minute gap between consecutive archival weather data, we use linear interpolation to meet the model's time interval requirements. Furthermore, as we are interested in the prevailing conditions within a $\Delta = 5min$ interval, all variables are assumed constant and equal to their mean value within that interval.

In particular, the acquired meteorological variables are:

[5] $\sim 60MW$ of installed PV power, corresponding to $\sim 7\%$ of Crete's energy production and $\sim 70\%$ of the total Greek islands' installed PV power (Public Power Corporation of Greece).

[6] Based on data provided at www.acosolar.com; and users.ece.utexas.edu/~valvano/Datasheets.

Dataset		Fixed-Orientation		Single Axis ST (VSAT)			Dual Axis ST (AADAT)		
	Day	Year-Opt	Next-Day-Opt	Chronological	Myopic	STPI	Chronological	Myopic	STPI
Real	1	31.520 (-)	**32.448** (-)	32.533 (.027)	32.791 (.019)	**32.794** (.015)	32.021 (.061)	33.033 (.078)	**33.070** (.037)
	2	49.736 (-)	**50.275** (-)	52.036 (.029)	52.042 (.028)	**52.046** (.023)	51.624 (.063)	52.326 (.087)	**52.360** (.049)
	3	67.301 (-)	**68.921** (-)	71.037 (.039)	72.977 (.057)	**72.985** (.048)	73.434 (.091)	74.003 (.106)	**74.027** (.080)
	4	11.736 (-)	**11.748** (-)	11.623 (.019)	11.738 (.031)	**11.754** (.010)	11.465 (.037)	11.788 (.059)	**11.822** (.021)
Fictional	1	31.520 (-)	**32.448** (-)	32.530 (.030)	32.784 (.026)	**32.790** (.019)	31.899 (.183)	32.730 (.381)	**32.972** (.121)
	2	49.736 (-)	**50.275** (-)	52.034 (.031)	52.040 (.030)	**52.045** (.023)	51.515 (.172)	52.034 (.379)	**52.247** (.156)
	3	67.301 (-)	**68.921** (-)	71.018 (.059)	72.961 (.074)	**72.977** (.055)	73.264 (.261)	73.706 (.404)	**73.862** (.237)
	4	11.736 (-)	**11.748** (-)	11.615 (.026)	11.729 (.041)	**11.751** (.010)	11.411 (.090)	11.567 (.280)	**11.747** (.032)

Table 1: Simulation results (all values are in kWh, and correspond to PVS net energy gain; tracking consumption in parenthesis).

relative humidity, *temperature*, *wind speed*, *wind direction*, and *qualitative cloud coverage observations* (appropriately transformed to quantitative values, as in Panagopoulos et al. (2012)). The observed general weather patterns of the days examined is as follows. The general pattern for *Day 1* consists of several transitions in the cloud coverage levels (moving from mostly sunny to scattered clouds, then to mostly cloudy, and back to mostly sunny); the general weather pattern for *Day 2* consists of a simple transition in the cloud coverage levels, from mostly cloudy to clear sky; there was a clear sky throughout *Day 3*; while *Day 4* was a day with (almost) full cloud coverage.

Now, though only four, these days exhibit weather patterns that are quite distinct from each other, thus enabling us to test the model under a wide range of meteorological conditions at our location of interest. However, throughout these four days, the prevailing wind speed value was quite low. Given the fact that power consumption grows with *high* prevailing wind speed, we decided to test the system with fictional wind data. We thus created four additional, "fictional" days, with exactly the same weather conditions as their real counterparts—apart from the wind, whose speed was set to *60 km/h*. That value corresponds to a typical maximum wind speed that a PVS can withstand without a need to orient itself to a safe position (Peterka and Derickson 1992).

In the absence of probabilistic weather forecasting reports (and respective online providers) we used deterministic archival weather data for both the weather predictions and ground-truth. As such, in our experiments, the accuracy of the weather forecasts does not affect the efficiency of our methods. We note here, that in the absence of weather prediction uncertainty, the evaluation results of the proposed low-cost *Myopic* method are equivalent to a tracking system where an expensive sensors arrangement along with a closed-loop controller is used to orient the solar panel towards the maximum incident solar irradiance. As such, by comparing *STPI* against *Myopic* we effectively compare our sensor-less, low-cost STPI against sensor-based ST.

The Results

The evaluation results of the experiments are collectively reported in Table 1. All energy values are in kWh, and correspond to PVS net energy gain. Tracking consumption is also reported inside parenthesis (when applicable).

In all experiments, our methods clearly outperform the baseline ones. It is also worth noting that, in general, as the system's degrees of freedom are increased, so do the positive system efficiency effects from using our methods (i.e., compared to fixed-orientation systems, the net energy gain increases when using *Myopic* or *STPI* with one rotation axis; and it increases even more when using these methods with two axes of rotation). By contrast, the benefits from using chronological ST often decrease when moving from fixed-orientation to one and, further on, to two rotation axes, as the additional system abilities are not fully exploited.

Regarding the methods' individual performance, not surprisingly, *next-day optimal fixed-orientation* significantly outperforms the yearly optimal one. In addition, *Myopic* gives a significant advantage over chronological tracking, in both VSAT and AADAT, as it also considers the weather conditions. At the same time, *STPI* does consistently better than *Myopic*, even though not by a wide margin. This low improvement margin is not surprising: in an appropriately designed, sizable PVS, like the one used in our simulations, the tracking consumption is *much* lower than the energy produced (less than 1% (Mousazadeh et al. 2009)). Thus, the net energy gains achieved by methods that take consumption into account, are not expected to differ dramatically from those achieved by methods that maximize power generation notwithstanding consumption needs. This fact is confirmed from our evaluation results: an improvement from using *STPI* instead of *Myopic* is present in all days and tracking systems, but is more substantial for high prevailing wind speeds, and especially for dual-axis tracking. However, over time (i.e., within a long operating time window and/or for clusters composed of many PVSs put together), even small improvements like the ones observed are significant. Even for an average-sized PV park of 2MW nominal power, one would be able to, annually, gain over €1500 more by using *STPI*, compared to *Myopic* (and over €10000 compared to chronological AADAT). Moreover, smaller PVSs (or not very efficiently designed ones) would exhibit a higher consumption over production ratio, and thus a higher expected improvement from using *STPI*, which attempts to approximate the optimal policy. Of course, the net gain is expected to further improve if the actual optimal policy is computed. However, *Myopic* is already near-optimal, as argued above; and, when compared to *Myopic*, *STPI* is shown in our simulations to already be achieving higher net energy gains and substantially lower consumption (of up to $\sim$90% reduction).

As a final note, *STPI* is expected to yield increased benefits when one considers a more detailed consumption model. In particular, the tracking cost is not limited to the motor consumption; there is also the maintenance cost, which should, ideally, also be taken into account. Moreover, real-world buy and sell energy prices will most probably have different values. These requirements can be readily incorporated in our model, by simply modifying Eq. 5. Specifically, for a grid-connected PVS, Eq. 5 can be replaced by:

$$R_a(s, s') = Prod(s, s')p^s - Cons(s, s')p^b - (t^{op}c_m) \quad (11)$$

Here, c_m denotes maintenance cost given operating time t^{op}, and p^s and p^b denote the sell and buy energy prices.

Conclusions and Future Work

In this work, we formulated ST as a dynamic programming problem. The exact solution to this problem would provide the optimal ST trajectories. However, for reasons of computability, we approximate the optimal solution by a policy iteration method (along with specialized variants) which utilizes available weather forecasts—that can actually come from online providers for free. Importantly, our methods make use of a generic and parameterizable tracker power consumption model we put forth. All our methods come with near-optimality guarantees, and we demonstrated their efficiency against commonly employed conventional ST techniques (i.e., chronological, sensor-based, and/or fixed-orientation). As such, our methods can serve as the basis for the development of web-based tools for efficient predictive ST. Future work includes incorporating additional details in our model (as, e.g., demonstrated by the suggested use of Eq. 11 above). Furthermore, we aim to modify our methods to account for additional tracking systems (such as pole trackers), and to consider weather forecasts updates throughout the operation day, in real-time.

Acknowledgements We thank Andonis Mitidis (Univeristy of Florida) and Kostas Lagogiannis (University of Edinburgh) for comments and fruitful discussions. We also acknowledge funding from the UK Research Council for the ORCHID project, grant EP/I011587/1.

References

Bezdek, J. C., and Hathaway, R. J. 2002. Some notes on alternating optimization. In *Advances in Soft Computing AFSS 2002*. Springer. 288–300.

Burt, C. M.; Piao, X.; Gaudi, F.; Busch, B.; and Taufik, N. 2008. Electric motor efficiency under variable frequencies and loads. *Journal of irrigation and drainage engineering* 134(2):129–136.

Chakraborty, P.; Marwah, M.; Arlitt, M. F.; and Ramakrishnan, N. 2012. Fine-grained photovoltaic output prediction using a bayesian ensemble. In *Association for the Advancement of Artificial Intelligence (AAAI) 2012*.

Chang, T. P. 2009. The suns apparent position and the optimal tilt angle of a solar collector in the northern hemisphere. *Solar Energy* 83(8):1274–1284.

Li, Z.; Liu, X.; and Tang, R. 2011. Optical performance of vertical single-axis tracked solar panels. *Renewable Energy* 36(1):64–68.

Liu, B., and Jordan, R. 1961. Daily insolation on surfaces tilted towards equator. *Solar Energy* 10:53.

Luque, A., and Hegedus, S. 2011. *Handbook of Photovoltaic Science and Engineering*. Wiley.

Lynch, W. A., and Salameh, Z. M. 1990. Simple electro-optically controlled dual-axis sun tracker. *Solar Energy* 45(2):65–69.

Mousazadeh, H.; Keyhani, A.; Javadi, A.; Mobli, H.; Abrinia, K.; and Sharifi, A. 2009. A review of principle and sun-tracking methods for maximizing solar systems output. *Renewable and Sustainable Energy Reviews* 13(8):1800–1818.

Myers, J. A. 1962. *Handbook of Equations for Mass and Area Properties of Various Geometrical Shapes*. NAVWEPS report 7827. U.S. Naval Ordnance Test Station.

Panagopoulos, A.; Chalkiadakis, G.; and Koutroulis, E. 2012. Predicting the power output of distributed renewable energy resources within a broad geographical region. In *European Conference on Artificial Intelligence (ECAI) 2012*, 981–986.

Peterka, J. A., and Derickson, R. G. 1992. Wind load design methods for ground-based heliostats and parabolic dish collectors.

Picard, A.; Davis, R. S.; Gläser, M.; and Fujii, K. 2008. Revised formula for the density of moist air (cipm-2007). *Metrologia* 45(2):149.

Ramchurn, S.; Vytelingum, P.; Rogers, A.; and Jennings, N. R. 2012. Putting the "smarts" into the smart grid: A grand challenge for artificial intelligence. *Communications of the ACM*.

Reda, I., and Andreas, A. 2004. Solar position algorithm for solar radiation applications. *Solar Energy* 76(5):577–589.

Roos, T. H. 2012. A wind loading correlation for an isolated square heliostat part 2: Moments and side forces.

Sutton, R., and Barto, A. 1998. *Reinforcement Learning: An Introduction*. A Bradford book. Bradford Book.

Risk Based Optimization for Improving Emergency Medical Systems

Sandhya Saisubramanian and **Pradeep Varakantham** and **Hoong Chuin Lau**
School of Information Systems, Singapore Management University
80 Stamford Road, Singapore 178902
{sandhyas, pradeepv, hclau}@smu.edu.sg

Abstract

In emergency medical systems, arriving at the incident location a few seconds early can save a human life. Thus, this paper is motivated by the need to reduce the response time – time taken to arrive at the incident location after receiving the emergency call – of Emergency Response Vehicles, ERVs (ex: ambulances, fire rescue vehicles) for as many requests as possible. We expect to achieve this primarily by positioning the "right" number of ERVs at the "right" places and at the "right" times. Given the exponentially large action space (with respect to number of ERVs and their placement) and the stochasticity in location and timing of emergency incidents, this problem is computationally challenging. To that end, our contributions building on existing data-driven approaches are three fold:

1. Based on real world evaluation metrics, we provide a risk based optimization criterion to learn from past incident data. Instead of minimizing expected response time, we minimize the largest value of response time such that the risk of finding requests that have a higher value is bounded (ex: Only 10% of requests should have a response time greater than 8 minutes).
2. We develop a mixed integer linear optimization formulation to learn and compute an allocation from a set of input requests while considering the risk criterion.
3. To allow for "live" reallocation of ambulances, we provide a decomposition method based on Lagrangian Relaxation to significantly reduce the run-time of the optimization formulation.

Finally, we provide an exhaustive evaluation on real-world datasets from two asian cities that demonstrates the improvement provided by our approach over current practice and the best known approach from literature.

Introduction

Emergency Medical Systems (EMS) – which aim to provide timely care to victims of sudden and unforeseen accidents, injuries or illnesses – are an integral part of the health care system. Saving a few seconds in responding to an incident can save a human life and due to this reason, many major cities around the world invest heavily in building emergency response systems that can reduce response time of ERVs.

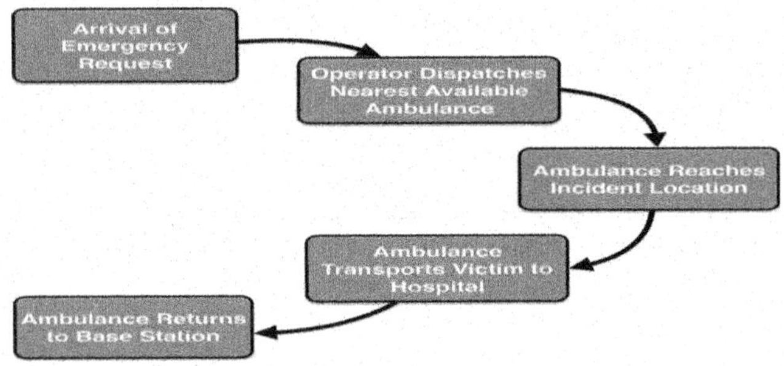

Figure 1: Process Flow

Increasing the fleet size of ERVs continuously to meet the varying demand and performance benchmarks is not practically feasible and hence research in EMS has focussed on optimizing the utilization of existing emergency vehicles. In this paper, we specifically focus on ambulances. However, the formulations and mechanisms developed are applicable to other emergency response settings. Figure 1 provides the sequence of events in responding to an emergency request.

The significance of optimization in EMS is best illustrated by the rich research history it bears. The existing research has specifically focussed on the twin problem areas of: ambulance allocation and reallocation to base locations and ambulance dispatch to incidents. A survey of the existing approaches (Brotcorne, Laporte, and Semet 2003) highlights that much of the previous work in EMS has been on dispatch of ambulances from the base locations (Schmid 2012; Andersson and Värbrand 2007; Ibri, Nourelfath, and Drias 2012). While dispatch is an important research problem, given the practical difficulty of ascertaining the criticality of an emergency request over phone, in many EMS systems, ambulance dispatch procedure is fixed wherein the requests are served in the order of their arrival and from the nearest base location that has an idle ambulance. Furthermore, dispatch problem can only be simplified with a good allocation of ambulance to locations. Hence, our focus in this paper is on the first problem area of EMS – ERV allocation and reallocation to the base locations.

In this paper, we focus on ambulance allocation and dynamic reallocation for the entire ambulance fleet and not for an individual ambulance (Maxwell et al. 2010). To facilitate the detection of patterns and avoid heuristic worst case planning (Andersson and Värbrand 2007), we employ a data-driven approach, similar to the work by (Yue, Marla, and Krishnan 2012). Ironically, even though target metrics and actual evaluation of EMS are based on the notion of bounded risk (Hong Kong 2009; Australia 2013; Ontario 2013; Singapore 2013; Wales 2014; NFPA 2010), researchers have focussed on optimizing other metrics such as expected response time (Yue, Marla, and Krishnan 2012; Schmid 2012). We address this discrepancy by considering the risk based optimization criterion and that is also the main distinction from existing work.

In addition to the greedy mechanism[1] by (Yue, Marla, and Krishnan 2012), existing work has provided heuristic search based mechanisms for computing allocation (Gendreau, Laporte, and Semet 2001) based on modelling as a coverage problem. On the contrary, we focus on a scalable approximation approach with guarantees on learned allocation to learn from past data. To that end, our main contribution is an optimization formulation that provides novel insights on enforcing resource capacity constraints for a continuous time line using scalable linear constraints. Furthermore, by employing intuitions from Sample Average Approximation (Pagnoncelli, Ahmed, and Shapiro 2009), we enforce the risk constraint using discrete variables and a linear constraint. In order to achieve scalability that will assist in live decision support, we also develop a partition technique based on Lagrangian relaxation.

We evaluate the effectiveness of our techniques on real-world ambulance data sets from two large cities in Asia. The experimental results show that in addition to outperforming the best known approach in the literature (Yue, Marla, and Krishnan 2012), our approach is able to reduce the response time by at least a few minutes over current practice.

Motivation: Ambulance Allocation

Formally, ambulance allocation problem for a given set of requests is given by the tuple:

$$\langle \mathcal{R}, \mathcal{B}, \mathcal{A}, \mathbf{T}, C, \alpha \rangle$$

The set of emergency requests is given by $\mathcal{R}$ and any emergency request, r in $\mathcal{R}$ is defined as the tuple $\langle t, s, h \rangle$, where t is the arrival time, s is the source location of the emergency and h is the nearest hospital to serve the request. The set of base locations is given by $\mathcal{B}$ and the set of ambulances is given by $\mathcal{A}$. $\mathbf{T}$ is a two dimensional vector providing the time taken to travel between any two locations in the city and this information is typically obtained from mapping services like google maps. More specifically, T_{l_1,l_2} is the time taken to travel from l_1 to l_2. C_l provides the maximum number of ambulances that can be stationed at base location l.

The goal is to compute an allocation, $\mathbf{a}$ of ambulances to base locations, that has the least value of response time, such that the percentage of requests exceeding that response time is less than the tunable input paramater, α. We refer to this response time as the α-response time. Since a request can be served from more than one base locations, the MILP formulation to determine the "right" allocation of ambulances to base locations such that the α-response time is reduced, becomes challenging.

MILP formulation for Ambulance Allocation

We now provide a Mixed Integer Linear Program (MILP) formulation for ambulance allocation. A detailed discussion on major assumptions made in the formulation and how they can be relaxed are presented in the latter section. Table 1 provides the variables and constants that are employed in the formulation.

The goal of the linear formulation is to minimize a response time value δ by addressing the following challenges:

1. **Ensuring that the probability of exceeding δ is bounded by α:** This is a chance constraint:

   $$Pr(\delta^r \geq \delta) \leq \alpha$$

   where δ^r is the response time for request r and probability is computed over the set of requests $\mathcal{R}$.

   Insight 1 *Since we have a discrete set of requests, we can use the technique adopted in Sample Average Approximation (SAA) (Pagnoncelli, Ahmed, and Shapiro 2009; Varakantham and Kumar 2013) to provide an equivalent set of linear constraints as follows:*

   $$z^r \in \{0,1\}, z^r \geq \frac{\delta^r - \delta}{M}, \quad \forall r \in \mathcal{R} \quad (1)$$

   $$\frac{\sum_r z^r}{|\mathcal{R}|} \leq \alpha \quad (2)$$

   It should be noted that the variable z^r is set to 1 if δ^r is greater than δ and 0 otherwise. Therefore, sum of all z^r variables divided by total number of requests gives the percentage and hence should be less than α.

2. **Computing available ambulances at each location l, at the point of arrival of request r:**

   Insight 2 *Since the set of requests are known before hand, by computing binary constants, $F_l^{q,r}$, we can compute number of available ambulances using a linear constraint on the binary variables* $\mathbf{y}$ *as shown in Equation 3.*

   $$a_l^r = a_l - \sum_{q \in \mathcal{R}, q.t < r.t} y_l^q \cdot F_l^{q,r}, \forall r \in R, l \in \mathcal{B} \quad (3)$$

Variables/ Constants	Definition
a_l	Number of ambulances at l
a_l^r	Number of ambulances at l when r arrives
y_l^r	Binary variable that indicates if request r is served by an ambulance from l.
$F_l^{q,r}$	Binary constant indicating whether an ambulance at l, if deployed to serve request q, will be available to serve the next request r

Table 1: Notation

[1] Unlike for expected response time objective (Yue, Marla, and Krishnan 2012), the learning problem for a given set of requests when optimizing with bounded risk notion is not sub-modular. Hence, greedy mechanism is also a heuristic and does not provide any quality guarantees.

$$a_l^r \geq 0, \quad \forall r \in R, l \in \mathcal{B} \tag{4}$$
$$a_l \leq C_l, \quad \forall l \in \mathcal{B} \tag{5}$$
$$\sum_l a_l = |\mathcal{A}| \tag{6}$$

For each location, constraint 3 computes the number of idle ambulances based on the number of ambulances still serving previous requests(second part of right hand side)[2]. Constraints 4,5,6 ensure number of ambulances is a whole number and is within the capacity of the location, while also preventing any violation of the fleet size.

3. **Preventing service of a request when there are no ambulances available**: This is achieved by using a logical constraint that sets y_l^r variables for all locations to be zero.
$$\sum_l y_l^r = min(1, \sum_l a_l^r), \qquad \forall r \in \mathcal{R} \tag{7}$$
4. **Computing response time given y variables**: We can only ensure that the response time has a lower bound using the following constraint. However, in conjunction with objective and bounded risk constraint, response time for every request is equivalent to the lower bound.
$$\delta^r \geq \sum_l (y_l^r \cdot \mathbf{T}_{l,r.s}) + (1 - \sum_l y_l^r) \cdot M \quad \forall r \in R \tag{8}$$

Constraints 1-8 along with an objective of "$\min_{\mathbf{a}} \delta$" form the complete MILP. Henceforth, we refer to the response time δ, as α-response time for the given set of requests, $\mathcal{R}$.

Partitioning the Request Set for Scalability

The computational complexity of the MILP introduced in the previous section increases rapidly with increase in the number of requests (Figure 6). To counter this computational complexity, we exploit the notion of independence among requests. A formal definition of dependence of requests is presented below using the binary vector, **F**.

Definition 1 *Two requests q and r are **dependent** if there exists at least one location l for which* $F_l^{q,r} = 1$.

The dependency between requests is with respect to being served by an ambulance from the same base location. We pursue a two step approach to identify and exploit independence between requests:

1. Identify the minimum set of requests, say $\mathcal{G}$ in the request set $\mathcal{R}$, that if removed can create ξ independent partition sets of the request set with $\cup_{k \leq |\xi|} \xi_k = \mathcal{R} \setminus \mathcal{G}$
2. Given the independent partitions and the new set of requests $\mathcal{R} \setminus \mathcal{G}$, we compute one ambulance allocation (and not one ambulance allocation for each partition) that works across the independent partitions by using the well known technique of Lagrangian dual decomposition(LDD) (Fisher 1985)[3].

For (1), in the case of dynamic reallocation of ambulances for a small interval of time (say 4 hours), we only consider

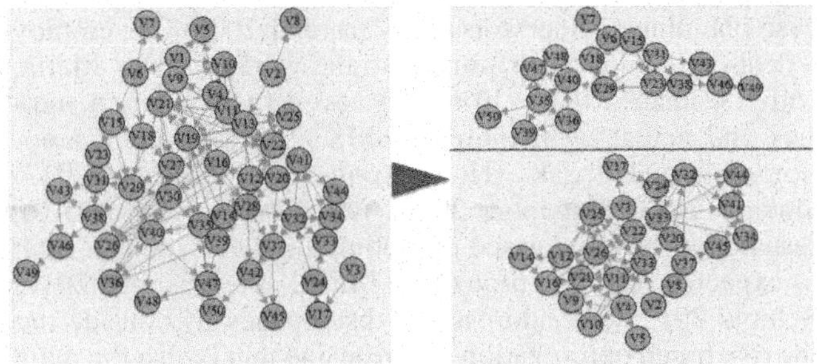

Figure 2: Partition of requests on a real request set

requests for those 4 hours on multiple different days in creating the request set. Hence, all these requests over different days are naturally independent. In the more interesting case of static allocation, there may not exist an exact partition across days. Figure 2 provides a small example of requests (taken from data set) and their connectivity (obtained from **F**). In such cases, we adopt minimal separator algorithm (Shen and Liang 1997) to provide the partitions and correspondingly get the number of requests to be removed. In the example of Figure 2, we had to remove 12% requests to obtain the two partitions. Even though we remove requests, it is possible to maintain the risk bound of the original problem and obtain a conservative estimate of the optimal α response time by increasing the risk bound to $\alpha + \epsilon$[4], where ϵ corresponds to the percentage of requests that are removed. This provides a conservative estimate, because we assume that all ϵ% of requests will have a response time higher than the optimal in the original.

An updated optimization corresponding to partitions, ξ is:

$$\min \sum_{k \leq |\xi|} \delta_k$$
$$s.t. \; Pr(\delta_k^r \geq \delta_k) \leq \alpha + \epsilon, \qquad \forall r \in \xi_k, k \leq |\xi| \tag{9}$$
$$a_{l,k}^r = a_{l,k} - \sum_{q \in \xi_k, q.t < r.t} y_{l,k}^q \cdot F_{l,k}^{r,q}, \; \forall r, k, \forall l \in \mathcal{B} \tag{10}$$
$$a_{l,k} \leq C_l, \qquad \forall l \tag{11}$$
$$\sum_l a_{l,k} = |\mathcal{A}|, \qquad \forall k \tag{12}$$
$$a_{l,k}^q \geq 0, \qquad \forall r, l, k \tag{13}$$
$$\sum_l y_{l,k}^r = min(1, \sum_l a_{l,k}^r), \qquad \forall r, k \tag{14}$$
$$\delta_k^r \geq \sum_l (y_{l,k}^r \cdot T_{l,r.s}) + (1 - \sum_l y_l^r) \cdot M, \; \forall r, k \tag{15}$$
$$a_{l,k} = n_l, \forall k, l \tag{16}$$

In the above optimization problem, we employ n_l to ensure all partitions have the same allocation of ambulances. Constraint 16 ensures that allocations across partitions are equal.

Dual Decomposition

Except for constraint 16, all the other constraints are defined

[2]Please refer to supplementary file for steps to compute F value.

[3]Please refer to the supplementary material for a background on Lagrangian dual decomposition.

[4]It should be noted that there may be no solution once the risk value is increased to account for the removed requests. In such a case, we can only get a heuristic approximation with this algorithm.

$$
\begin{aligned}
&\min \delta_k \\
&s.t.\ Pr(\delta^r_k \geq \delta_k) \leq \alpha + \epsilon, && \forall r \in \xi_k && (19)\\
&a^r_{l,k} = a_{l,k} - \sum_{q \in \xi_k, q.t < r.t} y^q_{l,k} \cdot F^{r,q}_{l,k}, && \forall r, \forall l \in \mathcal{B} && (20)\\
&a_{l,k} \leq C_l, && \forall l && (21)\\
&\sum_l a_{l,k} = |\mathcal{A}| && && (22)\\
&a^q_{l,k} \geq 0, && \forall r, l && (23)\\
&\sum_l y^r_{l,k} = min(1, \sum_l a^r_{l,k}), && \forall r && (24)\\
&\delta^r_k \geq \sum_l (y^r_{l,k} \cdot T_{l,r.s}) + (1 - \sum_l y^r_l) \cdot M, && \forall r && (25)
\end{aligned}
$$

Table 2: SOLVESLAVE(k)

on a specific partition. Hence, we obtain the Lagrangian by dualizing constraint 16:

$$\mathcal{L}(\lambda) = \min_{\mathbf{a}_k, \mathbf{n}} \sum_{k \leq |\xi|} \delta_k + \sum_{l,k} \lambda_{l,k} \cdot (a_{l,k} - n_l)$$

or alternatively

$$= \min_{\mathbf{a}} \Big(\sum_{k \leq |\xi|} \big[\delta_k + \sum_l \lambda_{l,k} \cdot a_{l,k}\big]\Big) - \min_{\mathbf{n}} \sum_{k \leq |\xi|, l} \lambda_{k,l} \cdot n_l$$

Since n_l is unbounded, the overall optimization will be unbounded. The equivalent bounded optimization for calculating $\mathcal{L}(\lambda)$ is:

$$\min_{\mathbf{a}} \Big(\sum_{k \leq |\xi|} \big[\delta_k + \sum_l \lambda_{l,k} \cdot a_{l,k}\big]\Big)\ s.t. \sum_{k \leq |\xi|} \lambda_{k,l} = 0, \forall l \quad (17)$$

If we use an update rule for λ that ensures the constraint 17 is always satisfied, then $\mathcal{L}(\lambda)$ decomposes over the individual partitions. Table 2 provides the slave optimization problem corresponding to each partition k.

Update of Price Variables——————
In order to ensure that dualized constraint violations are minimized, the final optimization at the master is: $\max_\lambda \mathcal{L}(\lambda)$ and we solve this optimization using sub-gradient descent on λ. Combining the update required for sub-gradient descent and for satisfaction of constraint 17, we have the following update rule:

$$\lambda^{t+1}_{l,k} = \tilde{\lambda}^{t+1}_{l,k} - \sum_k \frac{\tilde{\lambda}^{t+1}_{l,k}}{\sum_k \tilde{\lambda}^{t+1}_{l,k}} \ \&\& \ \tilde{\lambda}^{t+1}_{l,k} = \lambda^t_{l,k} + \gamma^t \cdot a_{l,k} \quad (18)$$

Primal Extraction from Dual Solution, $\{\mathbf{A}_k\}_{k \leq |\xi|}$———
Let the dual solution values be $\{\mathbf{A}_k\}_{k \leq |\xi|}$, once all the slave optimization problems are solved. When the ambulance allocations across the partitions are not equal, the obtained dual solution is not a feasible primal solution. However, all the following derived allocations are feasible solutions given the dual solution: $\langle \mathbf{A}_1, \mathbf{A}_1, \cdots, \mathbf{A}_1 \rangle$, $\langle \mathbf{A}_2, \mathbf{A}_2, \cdots, \mathbf{A}_2 \rangle, \ldots$. Amongst all these solutions, we take the one which provides the least value of α-response time as the primal solution for the current iteration. α-response time for a given ambulance allocation, $\mathbf{A}_k$ for a partition q is obtained by replacing all occurrences of $a_{l,q}$ with $A_{l,k}$ in SOLVESLAVE(q);

Algorithm 1 provides the pseudo code for the overall procedure of Lagrangian dual decomposition. We stop our lagrangian approach when the duality gap (difference between the primal and dual value) falls below a tunable value,μ.

Algorithm 1: SolveLDD()

```
Initialize: λ⁰, it ← 0 ;
repeat
    ∀k : d_k, A_k ← SOLVESLAVE(k)
    Update prices according to Equation 18
    p, A_p ← EXTRACTPRIMAL ({A_k}_{k≤|ξ|});
    it ← it + 1;
until [p − Σ_{k≤|ξ|} d_k] ≤ μ;
return p, A_p
```

Dynamic Reallocation

When there exists a strong pattern of requests coming through in a few hours, it is beneficial to alter the allocation computed from a large set of requests. For instance, on a wednesday or friday night, there is high chance of emergency events occuring near areas with clubs as there are large gatherings of people due to ladies' night or weekend. By using request sets for the next few hours from multiple days, SOLVELDD() can be used to obtain a new allocation. While such a modification is applicable, there are practical concerns: (a) only a few ambulances are available for allocation at that time step; and (b) ambulances could spend a significant time moving between base locations without serving requests.

Therefore, we consider reallocating ambulances by minimizing movements with respect to existing allocation of ambulances. This ensures that many ambulances do not remain unavailable for long while undergoing reallocation. We introduce a penalty parameter p, that is calculated as the difference between the orginal allocation and the planned reallocation. This penalty paramater helps to keep a check on drastic changes to the existing allocation and to ensure better α-response time with minimal movement of ambulances. Users can adjust the input parameter Γ which serves as upper bound for the penalty parameter p, to balance performance and reallocation of the fleet. We add the following constraints to achieve the reallocation with minimal movement. a_l denotes the number of ambulances at l, obtained by previous allocation and n_l denotes the number of ambulances at l after reallocation.

$$p = \sum_l (n_l - a_l); \quad p \leq \Gamma \quad (26)$$

Experimental Results

We perform experiments on real world data by varying parameters to make the following performance comparisons:

- Risk based optimization (RBO) and the current practice (response time observed from the data).

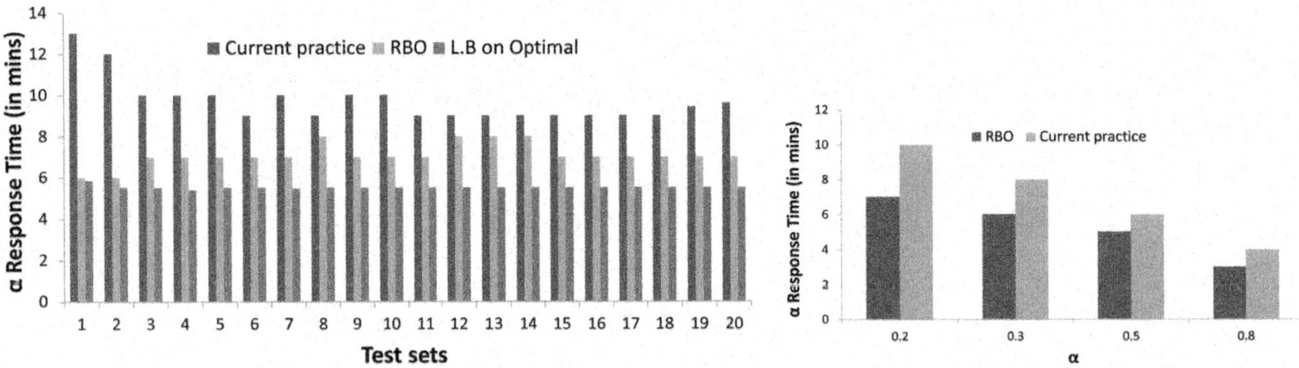

(a) Results on multiple test sets (b) α response time comparison

Figure 3: RBO Vs Current practice

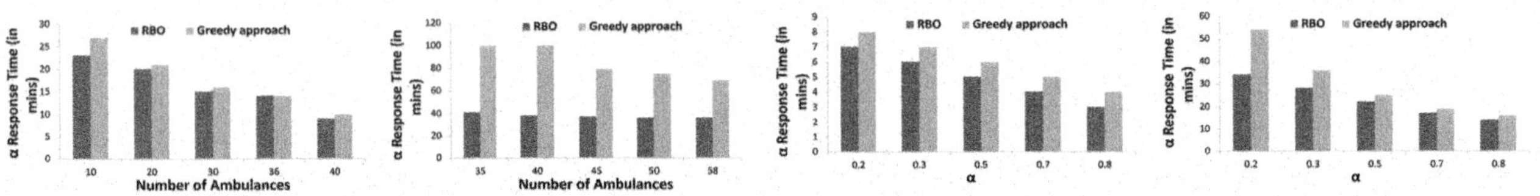

(a) Dataset1: Effect of fleet size (b) Dataset2: Effect of fleet size (c) Dataset1: Effect of α (d) Dataset2: Effect of α

Figure 4: RBO Vs Greedy approach

- RBO and the best known approach for ambulance allocation in the literature(Yue, Marla, and Krishnan 2012).
- RBO with and without LDD.
- Dynamic reallocation and static allocation.

We experiment with two data sets, namely Dataset1 and Dataset2 obtained from two asian cities. Dataset2 is adopted from (Yue, Marla, and Krishnan 2012). Both these datasets provide information about emergency requests over a sustained period of time (1 year). An emergency request consists of the time of request arrival, incident location and hospital location for the request. We also have information about number of ambulances, categories of ambulances, base locations etc.

The metrics employed for performance comparisons include the: α response time (α-rt), percentage of requests with response time less than 15 minutes[5] and run time. An $\alpha - rt = 8$ when $\alpha = 80\%$ indicates that at least 80% of the requests are served with response time ≤ 8 minutes. Given the number of cities that employ α response time as the performance indicator for emergency medical systems (Hong Kong 2009; Australia 2013; Ontario 2013; Singapore 2013; Wales 2014; NFPA 2010), we also use that as our main evaluation criterion. RBO (Risk Based Optimization) represents the approach introduced in this paper, "CP" refers to current practice and "Greedy" denotes the greedy approach (Yue, Marla, and Krishnan 2012).

In making a comparison, we always consider a training set and test set. Training sets are used to obtain an allocation and testing sets are used to evaluate such an allocation. To calculate the α response time on the test set using the obtained allocation, we use the standard dispatch technique, wherein a request that arrives first is serviced and by an available ambulance nearest to the incident location. Unless otherwise stated, the default settings of the experiments are $\alpha = 0.2$, fleet size of dataset1 = 40 and fleetsize of datatset2 = 58. The experiments involving RBO refer to RBO with LDD.

RBO vs Current practice——————
Figure 3(a) plots the α-rt for 20 different test sets from Datatset1, that were created from requests on different days. An allocation for RBO was computed from a training data set consisting of requests spread over a week. In addition to comparing with CP, we also compare with an approach, wherein we use RBO to compute an allocation on the test set requests. As it can be expected, this approach will provide a lower bound on the optimal α-rt, as test set requests are assumed to be known in advance. We observe that results from RBO are always better than CP, with the difference as much as 6 minutes in some occasions. Furthermore, results from RBO are typically closer to the lower bound on optimal α-rt than to the results from CP.

Figure 3(b) presents the results of our approach on Dataset1 in comparison with current practice, when α is increased. On Y-axis, we provide the α-response time for both our approach and current practice. The α response time values reduce as α is increased for both approaches, since risk reduces as α is increased.The key result however is that RBO was able to provide lower α-response time value than CP for all values of α. In some instances, this difference was as high as 3 minutes. Since we did not have sufficient information to compare our approach with the current practice on dataset2, we restrict the compar-

[5]Fitness measure employed in (Yue, Marla, and Krishnan 2012)

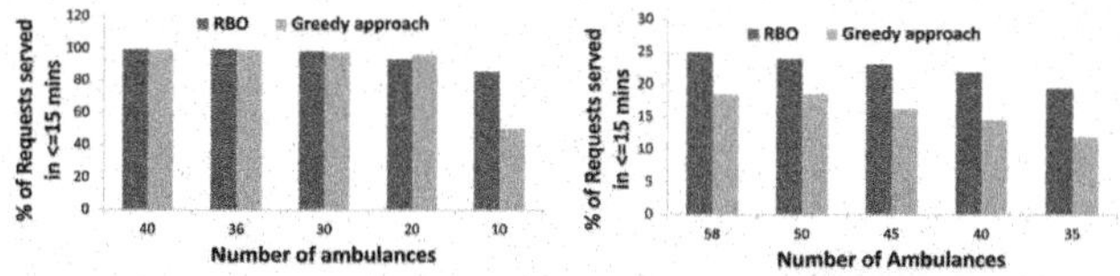

(a) Dataset1 (b) Dataset2

Figure 5: α response time $\leq$ 15 minutes

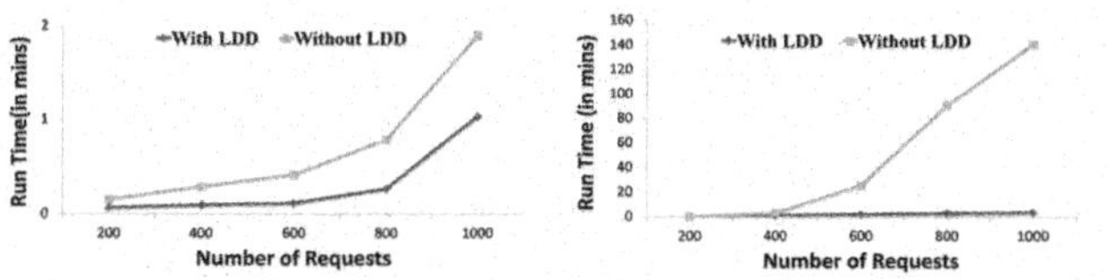

(a) Dataset1 (b) Dataset2

Figure 6: Run time comparison

ison of our approach against the current practice to datatset1.

RBO vs Greedy——————

Figure 4 presents the results with respect to the α-rt metric on both the datasets. Figure 4(a)-(b) compare α-rt performance as fleet size is varied on both the datasets. Irrespective of the fleet size, we observe that RBO performs better than greedy. The difference is particularly significant on Dataset2. Figure 4(c)-(d) compare the α-rt performance as α is increased. We again observe that RBO performs better than Greedy. Previously, the metric employed in evaluating the "Greedy" technique of (Yue, Marla, and Krishnan 2012) is the maximum number of requests with a response time less than 15 minutes. Figure 5 shows the % of requests served within the metric by our approach in comparison with the greedy approach on both the datasets. As can observed from the graph, RBO outperforms greedy by atleast 20% on all instances of dataset2.

RBO with and without LDD——

From figure 6, we demonstrate the reduction in runtime when LDD is used in conjunction with the MILP. While the time taken by RBO with LDD increases linearly, the time taken by RBO without LDD increases exponentially for Dataset2. However, on Dataset1 for same number of requests in the training set,while LDD provides a difference, it is not significant. This is because the run time depends on how densely populated the requests are on the time line.

Dynamic Reallocation——

To allow for "live" reallocation of ambulances and to determine the significance of dynamic reallocation, we apply RBO with minimal movements constraints (constraint 26) on both datasets. By varying the upper bound Γ of the penalty parameter p , we observe the effect on the performance when a fraction of the fleet is used for reallocation.

Figures 7(a) and (b) provide the α-rt on Dataset1 and Datatset2 for different reallocation intervals and different percentage of ambulances available for reallocation (Γ). When $\Gamma = 0$, no ambulances are allowed for reallocation and hence this result gives us the result of existing allocation for that interval of time. We observe that as we increase the Γ value, we allow more ambulances to be reallocated and the α response time either reduces or remains the same as that of static allocation in most cases.From figure 7(c) and (d), we observe that our reallocation technique provides better results than the greedy reallocation apporach over the three reallocation intervals.

In some cases, dynamic reallocation did not improve α-rt (as shown in Figure 7) and in few other scenarios (not shown here), the α-rt with dynamic reallocation was worse than with the static allocation. Hence, identifying when and where dynamic reallocation is helpful and is an important problem for future work.

Discussion and Future Work

In this section, we discuss some of the important assumptions made in the paper. First, in the MILP formulation for ambulance allocation, we assumed that if there is no ambulance to serve a request when it arrives, then the optimization problem assigns a large value of response time or equivalently it is considered as not served. However, in practice, the dispatcher would wait for a grace time (ex: 5-10 minutes) before considering the request as unserved. This can be trivially implemented in our model by modifying the definition of $F_l^{q,r}$ to consider the grace time. That is to say, for a grace time of 5 minutes, $F_l^{q,r}$ is set to 0 if request q finishes within 5 minutes after arrival of request r.

Second, after serving a request, ambulances return to the respective base locations from where they were dispatched to serve the request. We can potentially allocate ambulances after the victim has been delivered to the hospital. Exploiting on the fly allocation may or may not be an opportunity depending on how the requests arrive. Understanding when and where on the fly allocation is useful, is an important problem and we intend to explore it in the future.

Third, in dynamic reallocation, it is advisable to not move the same ambulance repeatedly over two locations. Since we cannot identify individual ambulances in our model(as we consider homogenous fleet), this criteria cannot be explicitly handled by our model. However, it is possible to have a more specific penalty constraint, wherein ambulance movement from different base locations are penalised differently.

Finally, while we assume that all ambulances can cater to all requests, certain very specific requests such as cardiac emergencies will need ambulance with specialized cardiac support system. In such cases, allocation and dispatch of ambulances should be based on the type of request. To perform this, additional information about the type of illness should be considered in the definition of emergency request. With minor modifications to our MILP, we can address such specific constraints.

Acknowledgements

We thank the anonymous reviewers for their valuable feedback. This research is supported by the Singapore National Foundation under its International Research Centre @ Singapore Funding Initiative and administered by the IDM Programme Office, Media Development Authority (MDA).

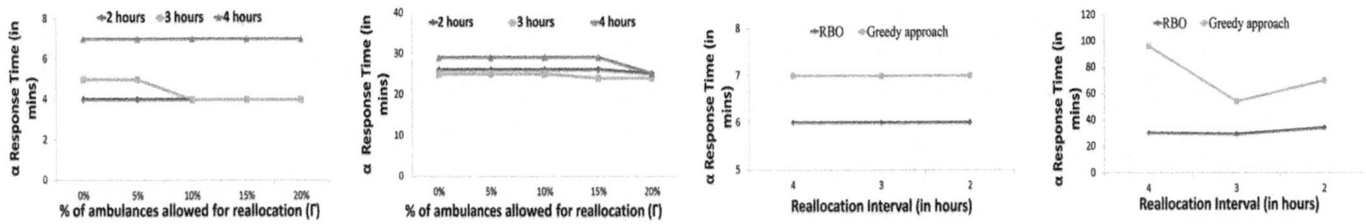

(a) Dataset1: Effect of Γ (b) Dataset2: Effect of Γ (c) Dataset1: Effect of Reallocation Interval (d) Dataset2: Effect of Reallocation Interval

Figure 7: Dynamic Reallocation results

References

Andersson, T., and Värbrand, P. 2007. Decision support tools for ambulance dispatch and relocation. *Journal of the Operational Research Society* 58:195–201.

2013. Western australia emergency response standards. http://www.parliament.wa.gov.au/publications/tabledpapers.nsf/displaypaper/3910362aee83dcb07812912948257b880016bbc6/$file/362.pdf.

Beraldi, P.; Bruni, M.; and Conforti, D. 2004. Designing robust emergency medical service via stochastic programming. *European Journal of Operational Research* 158(1):183 – 193.

Bertsekas, D. P. 1999. *Nonlinear programming*. Athena Scientific.

Boyd, S.;Xiao, L., and Mutapcic, A. 2003. Subgradient methods.

Brotcorne, L.; Laporte, G.; and Semet, F. 2003. Ambulance location and relocation models. *European Journal of Operational Research* 147(3):451 – 463.

Charnes, A., and Cooper, W. W. 1959. Chance-constrained programming. *Management Science* 6(1):pp. 73–79.

Fisher, M. L. 1985. An applications oriented guide to lagrangian relaxation. *Interfaces* 15(2):10–21.

Gendreau, M.; Laporte, G.; and Semet, F. 2001. A dynamic model and parallel tabu search heuristic for real-time ambulance relocation. *Parallel computing* 27(12):1641–1653.

2009. Hong kong emergency response standards. http://www.hkfsd.gov.hk/eng/performance.html.

Ibri, S.; Nourelfath, M.; and Drias, H. 2012. A multi-agent approach for integrated emergency vehicle dispatching and covering problem. *Eng. Appl. Artif. Intell.* 25(3):554–565.

Kumar, A.; Wu, X.; and Zilberstein, S. 2012. Lagrangian relaxation techniques for scalable spatial conservation planning. In *Proceedings of the Twenty-Sixth Conference on Artificial Intelligence*, 309–315.

Liu, Y.; Yuan, Y.; hui Li, Y.; and Pang, H. 2013. A chance constrained programming model for reliable emergency vehicles relocation problem. *Procedia - Social and Behavioral Sciences* 96(0):671 – 682.

Maxwell, M.; Restrepo, M.; Henderson, S.; and Topaloglu, H. 2010. Approximate dynamic programming for ambulance redeployment. *INFORMS Journal on Computing* 22(2):266–281.

2010. National fire protection association of united states. http://www.nfpa.org/codes-and-standards/standards-development-process/safer-act-grant/nfpa-1720.

2013. Ontario emergency response standards. http://www.auditor.on.ca/en/reports_en/en13/304en13.pdf.

Pagnoncelli, B.; Ahmed, S.; and Shapiro, A. 2009. Sample average approximation method for chance constrained programming: theory and applications. *Journal of optimization theory and applications* 142(2):399–416.

Rajagopalan, H. K.; Saydam, C.; and Xiao, J. 2008. A multiperiod set covering location model for dynamic redeployment of ambulances. *Comput. Oper. Res.* 35(3):814–826.

Schmid, V. 2012. Solving the dynamic ambulance relocation and dispatching problem using approximate dynamic programming. *European Journal of Operational Research* 219(3):611–621.

Shen, H., and Liang, W. 1997. Efficient enumeration of all minimal separators in a graph. *Theoretical Computer Science* 180(12):169 – 180.

2013. Singapore emergency response standards. http://www.scdf.gov.sg/content/scdf_internet/en/general/publications/_jcr_content/par/download/file.res/SCDF_Quality_Service_indicators.pdf.

Varakantham, P., and Kumar, A. 2013. Optimization approaches for solving chance constrained stochastic orienteering problems. In *Algorithmic Decision Theory*. Springer. 387–398.

2014. Wales emergency response standards. http://wales.gov.uk/statistics-and-research/ambulance-services/?lang=en.

Yue, Y.; Marla, L.; and Krishnan, R. 2012. An efficient simulation-based approach to ambulance fleet allocation and dynamic redeployment. In *Proceedings of AAAI Conference on Artificial Intelligence (AAAI)*.

Predisaster Preparation of Transportation Networks

Hermann Schichl*
Faculty of Mathematics
University of Vienna, Austria

Meinolf Sellmann
IBM Research
Yorktown Heights, NY, U.S.A.

Abstract

We develop a new approach for a pre-disaster planning problem which consists in computing an optimal investment plan to strengthen a transportation network, given that a future disaster probabilistically destroys links in the network. We show how the problem can be formulated as a non-linear integer program and devise an AI algorithm to solve it. In particular, we introduce a new type of extreme resource constraint and develop a practically efficient propagation algorithm for it. Experiments show several orders of magnitude improvements over existing approaches, allowing us to close an existing real-world benchmark and to solve to optimality other, more challenging benchmarks.

Earthquake Preparation

We consider a real-world pre-disaster planning problem that was introduced in (Peeta et al. 2010). Given a transportation network, where links are subject to probabilistic failure, the task is to use a limited budget to decrease the failure probability on selected links such that the overall expected shortest-path distance between a number of origin/destination pairs (OD-pairs) is minimized. The original model assumes independence between the failures of links. Consequently, a priori an exact standard stochastic programming approach would need to consider an exponential number of scenarios. Therefore, the approach in (Peeta et al. 2010) solves the problem without guarantees on the quality of the solution. Exploiting value-interchangeability, a symmetry-notion from constraint programming, only very recently (Prestwich, Laumanns, and Kawas 2013; 2014) were able to reduce the number of scenarios massively to a point where the benchmark introduced in (Peeta et al. 2010) could be solved to optimality within a number of minutes.

The idea of combining scenarios that all lead to the same value for the random variable considered (in our case: the sum of all expected shortest path lengths between all origin/destination pairs) is very interesting for scenario generation in general. We build on this idea and formulate the predisaster planning problem as an integer programming problem with a very simple constraint structure and a heavily non-linear objective. Due to the binary nature of investment decisions the problem is obviously not convex. Furthermore, we will show that it is hard to approximate and also neither sub- nor super-modular. We then introduce a new type of extreme resource constraint and develop a practically effective propagator which allows us to solve the existing benchmark instances in milliseconds, two to three orders of magnitude faster than existing methods. This then paves the way for tackling harder benchmark instances which consider several orders more non-interchangeable scenarios as well as correlated failure probabilities.

Problem Definition and Complexity

Definition 1. *We are given an undirected graph $G = (N, E)$ with a node set $N = \{1, \dots, n\}$ and an edge set $E = \{\{i,j\} \mid i,j \in N, i < j\}$. Furthermore, we are given four functions. An a priori survival probability function $s : E \to [0,1]$, a survival probability after investment function $v : E \to [0,1]$, an edge length function $l : E \to \mathbb{N}$, and a cost of investment function $c : E \to \mathbb{N}$. Finally, we are given a budget limit $C \in \mathbb{N}$, as well as node pairs $(o_1, d_1), \dots, (o_k, d_k) \in N^2$ and penalties $M_{o_h,d_h} \in \mathbb{N}$ for disconnecting the OD pair (o_h, d_h).*

Given a set $I \subseteq E$, we denote with $p_I : E \to [0,1]$, with $p_I(i,j) = v(i,j)$ if $\{i,j\} \in I$ and $p_I(i,j) = s(i,j)$ otherwise, the survival probabilities after investing in links in I. We consider the probability space (Ω, P_I) where $\Omega = \{F \mid F \subseteq E\}$ and P_I is the unique probability measure with $P_I(F) = \prod_{\{i,j\}\in F} p_I(i,j) \prod_{\{i,j\}\notin F}(1 - p_I(i,j))$. Finally, for all $o, d \in N$ let us denote with $\mathrm{SPL}^{\mathrm{I}}_{\mathrm{o,d}} : \Omega \to \mathbb{N}$ a random variable over (Ω, P_I) such that $\mathrm{SPL}^{\mathrm{I}}_{\mathrm{o,d}}(F)$ returns the shortest-path length from o to d in the weighted graph (N, F, l), and $M_{o,d}$ if no path from o to d exists in (N, F) (we omit a formal definition of shortest paths due to limited space).

The Predisaster Transportation Network Preparation Problem (PTNP) consists in selecting a subset $I \subseteq E$ of links to invest in such that $\sum_{\{i,j\}\in I} c(i,j) \leq C$ and $\sum_{h=1}^{k} \mathrm{E}(\mathrm{SPL}^{\mathrm{I}}_{\mathrm{o_h,d_h}})$ is minimized.

The PTNP is a probabilistic version of the deterministic problem class of survivable network design problems (SNDPs). Node- and link-survivable network design prob-

*This research was supported through grant P22239-N13 by the Austrian Science Foundation FWF.

lems have important applications in supply chain design, telecommunication network design (Kerivin and Mahjoub 2005), and wildlife preservation (LeBras et al. 2013). The SNDP helps to design networks that keep their functionality in case of the failure of a small number of links or nodes. The PTNP, on the other hand, optimizes networks for maximal survivability in case of a disaster that may simultaneously affect many links and nodes at the same time.

Later we will also study variants of this problem where we consider correlations between link failures (change in definition of P_I) or where we change the objective and minimize the expected maximum relative length increase $\max_{h=1}^{k}\{\mathrm{E}(\mathrm{SPL}^{\mathrm{I}}_{\mathrm{o_h,d_h}})/\mathrm{SPL}^{I}_{o_h,d_h}(E)\}$ or where we minimize the sum of squares of these values $\sum_{h=1}^{k}\left(\frac{\mathrm{E}(\mathrm{SPL}^{\mathrm{I}}_{\mathrm{o_h,d_h}})}{\mathrm{SPL}^{I}_{o_h,d_h}(E)}\right)^2$.

Theorem 1. *The PTNP is APX-hard and, unless $P = NP$, cannot be approximated for any constant relative error guarantee.*

Proof. Reduction from Steiner trees (omitted). □

Thus, not only is the PTNP NP-hard, it cannot even be approximated. Moreover:

Theorem 2. *The PTNP is neither sub- nor super-modular.*

Proof. Assume there is just one OD-pair, connected by two paths, the first consists of two edges a and b, the second has just one edge c which directly connects origin and destination. All edges have length 1, a priori survival probability 0, and survival probability 1 after investment. Investing in a by itself results in no improvement, yet after investing in b investing in a helps. This is a case of increasing returns. However, after investing in b and c, investing in a is again useless as the shortest path, going directly via edge c, is already guaranteed to exist. This is a case of diminishing returns. □

Formulation as Non-linear Integer Program

Therefore, pre-disaster planning is hard and does not exhibit some of the standard structural backdoors which would lead to reasonably practically efficient algorithms. Consequently, (Peeta et al. 2010) used a best-effort approach to tackle the problem. (Prestwich, Laumanns, and Kawas 2013), on the other hand, considered scenario bundles which led to the first provably optimal solutions for the Istanbul benchmark introduced in (Peeta et al. 2010).

We propose a non-linear integer programming model. There is only one constraint in the problem, and that is the limit on the budget which is exhausted linearly by the binary investment decisions. Our objective is to state the problem in the form

$$\text{minimize } f(x_1,\dots,x_m) \text{ such that} \sum_{i=1}^{m} x_i c_i \leq C,$$

where m is the number of links in the graph, $x_1,\dots,x_m$ are binary variables with $x_i = 1$ if and only if we invest in the link i, c_i is the investment cost on link i, and C is our total available budget. To achieve this simple structure we need to formulate the objective function f which, given the investment decisions, computes the sum of the expected shortest path lengths over all OD-pairs.

Assume that, for each OD-pair (o,d), we know the list $P_1,\dots,P_r$ of all simple paths from o to d, ordered by increasing path lengths. Then, we can compute the expected shortest path length for this pair by summing up, over all paths P_i in the list, the product of the length of P_i times the probability that all links in P_i survive while, for all paths P_j with $j < i$, at least one edge in P_j does not survive. That is, rather than considering scenarios and computing the shortest paths given a scenario, we directly compute the probability that a given path determines the shortest-path length, thus bundling all scenarios that lead to the same shortest path (compare with (Peeta et al. 2010)).

The objective becomes simpler if we reorder events. Let us denote with $l(P_i)$ the length of path P_i and with $p_i(x_1,\dots,x_m)$ the probability, given the investment decisions $x_1,\dots,x_m$, that at least one edge in each path $P_1 \dots P_{i-1}$ does *not* survive. To simplify the notation, let us also set $l(P_0) = 0$ and $l(P_{r+1}) = M_{o,d}$, where $l(P_r) \leq M_{o,d} \in \mathbb{N} \cup \{\infty\}$ is the penalty for losing all connections between o and d. Then the expected shortest-path length for the pair (o,d) is

$$\mathrm{E}(\mathrm{SPL}_{o,d}^{\{i \mid x_i=1\}}) = \sum_{i=1}^{r+1}(l(P_i) - l(P_{i-1}))p_i(x_1,\dots,x_m),$$

and it holds $f(x_1,\dots,x_m) = \sum_{(o,d)} \mathrm{E}(\mathrm{SPL}_{o,d}^{\{i \mid x_i=1\}})$. Our task thus reduces to

- computing the r shortest simple paths between o and d which have length lower than $M_{o,d}$, and
- computing the terms $p_i(x_1,\dots,x_m)$.

For the first task we conduct a simple best-first search in the given graph, whereby we prune paths that have no chance of obeying the threshold $M_{o,d}$ using shortest-path distances to the destination (see (Sellmann 2003b)) as well as those that are not simple (meaning that no node is visited more than once).

Our second task is a bit more involved. In $p_i(x_1,\dots,x_m)$, to assess the probability that the first $i-1$ paths are all blocked, we enumerate all disjoint events where this is the case. To keep the objective somewhat reasonable in size, we will need to find mutually disjoint blocking events which quickly partition all possible cases.

Assume we have to compute the term $p_{i+1}(x_1,\dots,x_m)$ and we have the list of paths $P_1,\dots,P_i$. We can view these paths as sets of links. Then, each blocking event will select at least one element in each set, one link for each path that is failing. Therefore, we are actually looking for set covering solutions: The sets to be covered are the paths, and the elements in the sets are links in the graph. Once we arrive at this view it is easy to devise a very simple yet surprisingly effective greedy heuristic to enumerate all mutually exclusive events which will block paths $P_1,\dots,P_i$: In each step we select a link that will cover as many paths as possible that are currently not covered, with ties broken randomly.

Once all paths are covered, we store the respective set of links. Then we backtrack our last decision and decide *not* to include this link this time. Then, we try to add other links to achieve a full cover. If we find a new cover, we store the set of all links in the cover, *as well as the set of links we actively decided not to include*. The latter is necessary to ensure that the probabilistic events, whose cumulated probability we are aiming to assess, are mutually disjoint. Only then can we simply add their probabilities to arrive at the joint probability $p_{i+1}(x_1, \ldots, x_m)$.

Of course, we can improve this greedy tree-search enumeration by adding early pruning whenever it is clear that a full cover can no longer be achieved down a branch. Moreover, the independence of link failures allows us to stop the generation of covers early when each remaining link can only cover at most one path currently not covered. Then, for each such path, we can assess the probability of its failing as 1 minus the product of all survival probabilities of remaining links on this path. The probability of all remaining paths being covered is then simply the product of these values.

Despite these improvements, the entire procedure may appear prohibitively expensive. However, it turns out that it is extremely efficient in practice. For the real-world Istanbul scenario introduced in (Peeta et al. 2010), for example, we find 24 shortest paths total for five OD-pairs. To formulate the entire objective, using the greedy strategy described above, we need to consider a mere 156 covers in total. Not only is this number of covers less than the 341 remaining scenarios which are eventually considered in (Prestwich, Laumanns, and Kawas 2013), but also the entire computation of these scenarios takes milliseconds compared to 5 minutes reported in (Prestwich, Laumanns, and Kawas 2013).[1] Most importantly, we arrive at a non-linear integer program with an extremely simple constraint structure which we are going to exploit in the next section.

Extreme Constraints

We established that our pre-disaster planning problem is neither sub- nor super-modular. However, we make a simple observation: In order to achieve a minimal shortest path length it never hurts to invest in another link if the budget allows us to do so. Consequently, we only need to consider selections of links to invest in which *fully exhaust our budget*. By that we do not mean that there is necessarily no money left, but that the remaining money would not suffice to invest in any additional link. Formally, we introduce the following extreme constraint for linear resources.

Definition 2. *Given n binary variables $x_1, \ldots, x_n$, costs $c_1, \ldots, c_n \in \mathbb{N}$, and a budget $C \in \mathbb{N}$, the* $\text{ExtremeLinearResource}(x_1, \ldots, x_n)$ *constraint is true if and only if $\sum_i x_i c_i \leq C$ and $\forall i: \ x_i = 0 \rightarrow c_i > C - \sum_j x_j c_j$.*

Before we study this constraint and develop a propagator, let us briefly compare it to other constraints. For optimization problems, in CP so-called global optimization constraints are considered. Prominent examples are the allDifferent constraint with costs (Régin 1999; Focacci, Lodi, and Milano 1999; Régin 2002; Sellmann 2002), the knapsack constraint (Trick 2001; Sellmann 2003a; Trick 2003), the shorter path constraint (Sellmann 2003b; Sellmann, Gellermann, and Wright 2007), or the not-too-heavy spanning tree constraint (Dooms and Katriel 2006; 2007).

Typically these constraints consider a particular constraint in conjunction with a bounded (often linear) objective. That is, apart from enforcing the basic constraint (allDifferent, bounded linear resource, directed path, spanning tree, etc) these optimization constraints merely consider a bound on the objective, yet they do not require an *optimal* assignment. This also explains some rather unusual names, such as shorter path instead of shortest path constraint, or not-too-heavy spanning tree instead of minimum spanning tree constraint. The reason why bounds are considered rather than optimal assignments is that there may be other constraints in the problem which prohibit solutions that would be optimal with respect to the basic constraint in isolation. For the problem at hand, we can enforce the extreme variant of the linear resource constraint. We believe that the same idea can also be applied in many other applications and for classical combinatorial optimization problems, e.g., in bin packing.

Theorem 3. *Achieving generalized arc-consistency (GAC) for the ExtremeLinearResource Constraint is NP-hard.*

Proof. We reduce Number Partitioning to GAC on ExtremeLinearResource. Given n natural numbers $a_1, \ldots, a_n$, we need to decide whether there exists a set $I \subseteq \{1, \ldots, n\}$ such that $\sum_{i \in I} a_i = S$ with $S = \left\lfloor \frac{\sum_{i=1}^n a_i}{2} \right\rfloor$. We construct an ExtremeLinearResource constraint over $n+1$ binaries with weights $a_1, \ldots, a_n$ associated with $x_1, \ldots, x_n$ and 1 associated with x_{n+1}. The budget capacity is S.

Now, we must filter 0 from the domain of x_{n+1} if and only if the number partitioning instance has no solution: Assume that 0 must be filtered from the domain of x_{n+1}. This means that there is no way of fully exhausting the resource (without overfilling!) using the first n items with weights $a_1, \ldots, a_n$. Consequently, there is no solution to the number partitioning problem. On the other hand, if there is no way of exhausting the budget exactly, then in any selection of items that obeys the budget constraint there is always room to add item x_{n+1}. Consequently, GAC must infer that $x_{n+1} = 1$ and thus filter value 0 from the domain of x_{n+1}. □

Theorem 4. *GAC for the ExtremeLinearResource constraint is achievable in pseudo-polynomial time $O(n^2 C)$, where n is the number of items and C the available budget.*

Proof. We set up a three-dimensional dynamic program (DP): the first dimension is the item index (size $n+1$), the second is the index of a skipped item with smallest weight (size $n+1$) and the last dimension is the total weight of the selection (size C). Then, node $N_{i,m,k}$ is reached by branching on items $1, \ldots, i$ such that ($m = 0$ or ($x_m = 0$ and $c_m \leq \{c_j \mid 1 \leq j \leq i, \ x_j = 0\}$)) and $\sum_{j=1}^{i} x_j = k$. The construction starts at node $N_{0,0,0}$. Now, we iterate through

[1] All experiments were conducted on 1.6 GHz Intel Core i7 Q170 machines with a 4-core CPU, 6 MB cache, and 12 GB RAM, running 64-bit Fedora 20. The code was compiled with g++ 4.8.3 and full optimization. No external software was used.

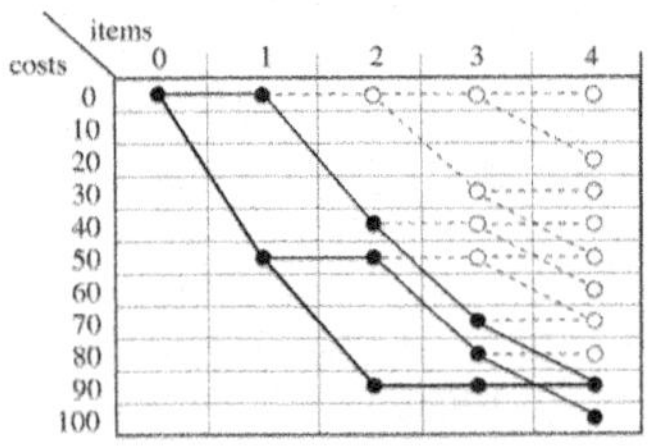

Figure 1: Illustration of the two-dimensional dynamic program with four items with costs 50, 40, 30, and 20, the budget limit is 100. Dashed lines and hollow nodes depict nodes and edges which are removed. In the situation shown no values can be filtered from variable domains. However, after deciding, e.g., not to invest in link 2, it is immediately inferred that we must invest in links 1, 3 and 4.

layers $i = 1, \ldots, n$: For all existing nodes $N_{i-1,m,k}$, if 0 is in the domain of x_i, we add a directed edge to (the potentially new) node $N_{i,h,k}$ where $h = m$ if $m > 0$ and $c_h \geq c_m$, and $h = i$ otherwise. This edge corresponds to branching on $x_i = 0$. If 1 is in the domain of x_i, and if $k + c_i \leq C$, we add an edge from $N_{i,m,k}$ to (the potentially new) node $N_{i+1,m,k+c_{i+1}}$. This edge corresponds to branching on $x_i = 1$. Finally, we remove all nodes and adjacent edges from where we cannot reach any node $N_{n,m,k}$ with $c_m + k > C$. As a result, we only retain nodes and edges on paths from $N_{0,0,0}$ to some node $N_{n,m,k}$ with $c_m + k > C$. These paths directly correspond to feasible solutions to the ExtremeLinearResource constraint. Following the filtering based on dynamic programs introduced in (Trick 2001), if and only if there is no edge that corresponds to branching on $x_i = b$ (with $b \in \{0, 1\}$) on layer i, then and only then b can and must be removed from the domain of variable x_i. □

In summary, we have found that the ExtremeLinearResource constraint is NP-hard to filter exactly, but it is hard in the nicest possible way, allowing us to filter the constraint in pseudo-polynomial time.

In practice, we may wish to limit the size of the dynamic program a bit further. To eliminate a factor n in the complexity, we can keep a record on an upper bound on the smallest cost skipped on any path to a node and a lower bound on the slack left in the budget on any path to the leaf-level. Then, whenever we are guaranteed that the smallest item skipped has cost lower or equal the remaining slack in the budget we can remove a node and analogously also edges in the dynamic program. Filtering variable domains then works exactly as before (see Figure 1).

To achieve this, at each node we record two values, SKIP and SLACK. At level $i \in \{0, \ldots, n-1\}$ and budget $k \in \{0, \ldots, C\}$ the following recursion equations govern: $\text{SKIP}_{0,k} = \infty$, $\text{SLACK}_{n,k} = C - k$,

$$\text{SKIP}_{i+1,k} = \max\{\text{SKIP}_{i,k-c_i}, \min\{\text{SKIP}_{i,k}, c_i\}\}, \text{ and}$$

$$\text{SLACK}_{i,k} = \min\{\text{SLACK}_{i+1,k+c_i}, \text{SLACK}_{i+1,k}\},$$

whereby we discard values from consideration which do not belong to feasible nodes and edges in the dynamic program.

Instance	Solution	Value	ELR	LR
B_1-Low	{10,17,21,22,23,25}	83.0801	0.03	0.14
B_2-Low	{4,10,12,17,20,21,22,25}	66.1877	0.05	2.22
B_3-Low	{3,4,10,16,17,19–22,25}	57.6802	0.11	16.51
B_1-High	{10,17,21,22,23,25}	212.413	0.03	0.11
B_2-High	{4,10,12,17,20,21,22,25}	120.083	0.08	2.18
B_3-High	{3,4,10,16,17,19–22,25}	78.4017	0.11	17.1

Table 1: Istanbul Benchmark Results

This heuristic filtering algorithm comes with no theoretical guarantees, but it runs in $O(nC)$ and it may only miss very few filtering opportunities in practice, thus making it a favorable choice within a practical solution approach. We will use this algorithm in the following experiments.

Experimental Results

Using the ExtremeLinearResource constraint, we conduct a plain branch-and-bound to find the optimal investment for our pre-disaster planning problem: At each search node, we first perform constraint filtering. Then, we compute a dual (since we are minimizing: lower) bound on the objective simply by assuming that we could invest in all links undecided so far. As branching heuristic, we branch on highest cost investments first.

Istanbul Earthquake Preparation

We test this algorithm on the Istanbul benchmark introduced in (Peeta et al. 2010): We are expected to move casualties after an earthquake from highly affected areas, as determined in the Japan International Cooperation Agency Report (2002), to areas with large medical support capacities. The task is to minimize the sum of the expected shortest-path distances for five OD-pairs. In the first set of three instances B_1-Low, B_2-Low, and B_3-Low, the penalty for experiencing a disconnect for an OD-pair is 31, 31, 28, 19, and 35, respectively. This is to model the costs of airlifting injured people to regions with properly equipped medical facilities.

In the corresponding instances with the suffix -High, the penalty for a disconnect is 120, for all five OD-pairs. It is important to note that neither (Peeta et al. 2010) nor (Prestwich, Laumanns, and Kawas 2013) consider paths that exceed the low penalties, even when the penalty of a disconnect is high. The total number of paths considered is, in both papers, 24. In B_1 the total budget is 10% of the budget needed to invest in all links in the network, in B_2 it is 20%, and in B_3 it is 30%. The exact survival probabilities before and after investment are given in (Peeta et al. 2010). These values were determined by structural engineers using domain-specific information, as summarized in the 2003 Master Earthquake Plan of the Istanbul Municipality. The independent failure probabilities on the network links as well as the fact that investment decisions affect probabilities itself render this problem a very hard stochastic optimization problem.

In Table 1 we show the results. We give the optimal solutions and corresponding objectives for all six benchmark instances, as well as the run-times in seconds based on non-linear integer programs, once using the ExtremeLinearResource constraint (ELR), and once using a standard

LinearResource constraint (LR) which limits the budget but does not enforce that we exhaust it to a point where we could not afford any other investment. In both cases we use the same dual bound and the same branching strategy.

The new extreme constraint results in speed-ups of up to two orders of magnitude. Moreover, overall our approach massively outperforms the previously published approaches. Both algorithms in (Peeta et al. 2010) and (Prestwich, Laumanns, and Kawas 2013) run for ca. 5 minutes on each instance, whereby the first gives approximate results only. The AI-based non-linear optimization approach, on the other hand, finds six solutions and proves their respective optimality in less than half a second for all six instances *together*. Note that this time includes everything, the computation of the shortest paths up to the penalty values, the coverings and set-up times of the non-linear integer programs, as well as their solution based on the ExtremeLinearResource constraint. The new approach thus runs three orders of magnitude faster than the previous state-of-the-art.

Comparing with the solutions given in (Prestwich, Laumanns, and Kawas 2013), we find that our solution to B_2-High has a slightly higher expected path length than the one given in that paper. The reason for this is that the solution given there actually violates the 20% budget constraint. Indeed, our solutions show that the optimal investment decisions for the low and high penalties are *exactly the same.* The objective value differs, of course, but the links in which to invest are identical.

To challenge the new method, we considered three other problem variants. In the first *all paths* up to the penalty of 120 may serve as shortest paths. Doing so results in tripling the number of paths considered, which jumps from 24 to 72, roughly 15 different evacuation routes for each OD-pair. The number of scenarios that our approach considers also jumps, from 156 to 8,491. For B_1 the new approach now requires 8 seconds, for B_2 22 seconds, and for B_3 26 seconds. Considering more paths obviously increases the complexity of the problem, as the scenarios which result in the same shortest routes become harder and harder to represent compactly. This confirms the same finding in (Prestwich, Laumanns, and Kawas 2013). Curiously, looking at the solutions, we find that the optimal investment decisions are again the very same as the ones given in Table 1. In practice this justifies simplifying problem instances by considering paths up to a relatively low threshold only as budget constrained investment decisions are hardly affected by considering large numbers of sub-optimal paths.

In the second and third variants of the benchmark we consider different objectives: First, instead of considering the sum of all expected shortest-path lengths we minimize the maximum path length. Since some OD-pairs are much closer together than others, we normalize the penalty for each OD-pair by dividing by the length of the shortest path for this pair. Therefore, we minimize the maximum expected percent increase relative to the shortest path for each OD-pair. The final variant minimizes the sum of squares of these expected ratios rather than their maximum.

Run-times in seconds and optimal solutions are given in Table 2. We observe that these objectives do not make the

Instance	Solution	Value	ELR	LR
B_1-max	{19–22,28}	1.99401	0.01	0.11
B_2-max	{9,16,20,21,22,25}	1.57278	0.01	3.4
B_3-max	{4,7,10,12,16,17,19–22,25}	1.30401	0.03	20.9
B_1-squ	{10,17,21,22,23,25}	15.0528	0.03	0.14
B_2-squ	{4,10,12,17,20,21,22,25}	9.29439	0.06	2.33
B_3-squ	{3,4,10,16,17,19–22,25}	6.67251	0.08	18.3

Table 2: Istanbul Benchmark Variants

overall problem harder for the AI-based approach. This is interesting since the sum of squares would be much harder to model as a traditional two-stage stochastic program. On the larger instances, the use of the extreme version of the linear resource constraint leads to over 500-fold speed-ups over the traditional constraint. Overall, the new approach does not only work significantly faster than existing approaches, it also offers much greater flexibility regarding the exact choice of objective function.

Bay Area Earthquake Preparation

With the introduction of the ExtremeLinearResource constraint, the Istanbul benchmark instances, which were impossible to solve to optimality 18 months ago, no longer pose much of a problem. We therefore introduce a new, even more challenging benchmark set. Based on the Highway Evacuation Plan of the Federal Highway Administration (FHWA) we consider the emergency mass transportation highway evacuation network for the California bay area (Vásconez and Kehrli 2010)).

The scenario again considers the possibility of an earthquake, whereby in this case we assume that most urban infrastructure, housing as well as utilities (water, gas, and electricity), would be destroyed, thus requiring large numbers of citizens to leave the bay and flee to lesser populated areas to the North and East (see Figure 2). The challenge is to mass evacuate people from San Francisco (node 2), Berkeley/Oakland (node 7), Palo Alto/Mountain View (node 16) and Santa Clara/San Jose (node 18), each to any one of five possible evacuation points: Petaluma (node 0), Vallejo (node 19), Benicia (node 20), Antioch (node 6), or Tracy (node 15). Failure probability and cost models follow a similar logic as in the Istanbul benchmark, with highest costs and highest failure probabilities for bridges, whereby we assume that some positive failure probability persists even after in-

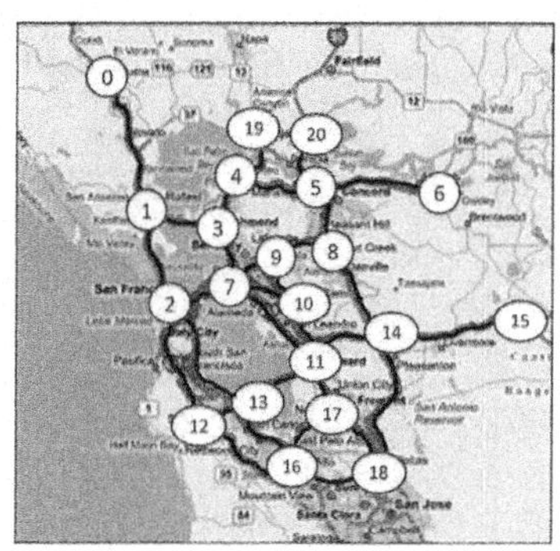

Figure 2: Bay Area Highway Mass Evacuation Network

vesting in a link. Budgets are again limited to 10%, 20%, and 30% of the cost of investing in all links in the network, denoted by subfixes, E_1, E_2, and E_3.

Note that budgets that would allow investment in 30% of all possible investments are improbable, we consider them here to test the limits of the approaches developed. In practice, less than 10% are much more realistic. Moreover, while the size of the networks considered in these and the Istanbul instances may appear small at first, it is important to stress that real-world evacuation networks are fortunately small: Roads with intersections and one lane roads are not suitable for mass evacuations. Cars break down, accidents happen, and even via a multi-lane freeway we can maximally evacuate 2,000 cars per lane and hour. Consequently, in areas with millions of people investment decisions focus on designated mass evacuation routes only. Nevertheless, computationally these problems are still extremely hard, because the search space grows exponentially in the number of network links, and the objective function is highly non-linear which massively increases the complexity even for evaluating a given investment plan.

For each of the four areas to be evacuated we now face roughly 20 possible evacuation routes. The model considers 81 paths and 16,196 covers total. That is over 100 times the number of scenarios than we needed to consider for the Istanbul benchmark. In Table 3 we minimize again three different objectives as before: sum of all expected shortest path lengths (-sum), maximum percent increase (-max), and sum of squared percent increases in expected shortest path length (-squ). We observe similar trends as before, minimizing the maximum percent increase in expected shortest path length is easiest, the other two objectives are roughly equally hard, whereby the Bay Area instances are clearly harder than the Istanbul instances. Overall, even when having to consider two orders of magnitude more scenarios, we can still solve each instance in a few seconds.

We wanted to see how far we could push this approach and considered a -High variant for this benchmark as well. In these instances, we consider 351 evacuation routes, on average more than 85 per evacuation area. This leads to over 3 million scenarios that need to be considered, roughly 20,000 times (!) the number of scenarios considered for the Istanbul benchmark. Just computing the non-linear objective function for this problem takes over 80 seconds. For the 10% budget limit we can solve this problem to optimality in 2 minutes, for 20% in 4 minutes, and for 30% in 6 minutes.

Since improved upper bounds on the objective result in better pruning, we used the ExtremeLinearResource constraint and the monotonicity of the objective function to derive a primal heuristic for finding good feasible points before we start the branch and bound procedure. Using this heuristic, solution times for the most difficult Bay Area -High variants reduce to 2.1, 4.5, and 12.8 seconds, respectively, plus 80 seconds each for constructing the objective function. After constructing the objective, roughly equal time is spent between the primal heuristic and the branch and bound.

Instance	Solution	Value	ELR
E_1-sum	{3,6,8}	58.0981	1.85
E_2-sum	{3,6,8,9}	55.9286	3.5
E_3-sum	{3,6,7–10,12,27,28}	54.7743	4.5
E_1-max	{3,6,8}	1.94013	1.21
E_2-max	{3,6,8,9}	1.67574	1.35
E_3-max	{1,3,6,8,9}	1.59876	1.55
E_1-squ	{3,6,8}	8.4507	1.72
E_2-squ	{3,6,8,9}	7.51121	3.4
E_3-squ	{0,3,5,6,7–10,12,27}	7.1024	4.4

Table 3: Bay Area Benchmark

Instance	Solution	Value	ELR
E_1-low	{6,8,12,27}	57.921	3.2
E_2-low	{3,6,8,9}	55.935	4.45
E_3-low	{3,6–10,12,27,28}	54.719	6.97
E_1-high	{6,8,12,27}	61.518	140
E_2-high	{6,8,9,10,27}	58.614	180
E_3-high	{3,6–12,27}	57.172	400

Table 4: Bay Area Benchmark with Correlation

PTNP With Failure Correlation

Next, we considered scenarios where link failures are *correlated*. We believe this is a very important aspect in practice: Bridges of the same construction type may exhibit similar resistance depending on the strength and frequency of shock waves. Links of same orientation may show some correlation, as shock waves hit them equally longitudinally or crosswise. Low ocean drives may sink under the water level or could be flooded by Tsunamis which would affect them equally. All these effects may correlate failure probabilities.

We model correlated link failure distributions by means of Bayesian networks. The variables modeling the investment decisions are binary value nodes $X_i, i = 1, \ldots, k$ of the network, as are the nodes $L_j, j = 1, \ldots, n$ that describe the failure probabilities of the links. The Bayesian network is required to be *monotone* in the sense that for all variable vectors X and $\overline{X}$ with $X \leq \overline{X}$ and all pairwise disjoint subsets I, J, K all conditional link failure probabilities satisfy $\mathrm{P}(L_K|L_I, \hat{L}_J, X) \geq \mathrm{P}(L_K|L_I, \hat{L}_J, \overline{X})$, i.e., that the probability for simultaneous failure of the links in K, given that the links in I fail and those in J survive, reduces if additional investments are made. This is a generalization of the concept of monotonicity of Bayesian networks as, e.g., discussed in (van der Gaag, Bodlaender, and Feelders 2004).

The monotonicity of the Bayesian network implies that the monotonicity of the objective is retained. This and the budget constraint are the two primary sources for inference in our approach. Consequently, the AI-based approach handles these problems as well. Table 4 shows that we can efficiently handle such correlated distributions as well, both with low and high cutoff thresholds.

Best-Effort Solutions

To assess how the approach scales with increased network sizes we took the Istanbul benchmark and successively refined the network by splitting every edge into m sub-edges, simulating that instead of a single investment decision on every edge m investment decisions can be taken independently of each other. Of course, the investment costs are chosen in such a way that they add up to the original cost for investing into the unsplit link, and the survival probabilities of the sub-links are ensured to be consistent with the original survival probabilities for the unsplit link. We expect that solution times show some form of exponential increase with increasing number of investment decisions to be taken. In Table 5 in three columns we show the solution times in seconds of the full branch and bound proving global optimality, the primal heuristic, which usually finds a solution deviating not more than 5% from the global optimum, and a simplified primal heuristic, which usually finds a solution within 15% of the global optimum. Due to the stochastic nature of the PTNP the size of the sample space for computing the expected values increases exponentially with the number of links, so in the biggest case just the evaluation of the objective function at a single point takes more than one second.

We find that the full branch and bound scheme works well up to about 150 decision variables, the expensive heuristic up to about 600 decision variables, and the simplified heuristic up to about 900 decision variables. For investment decision problems like ours runtimes of about 4 hours of computation time are completely acceptable in practice. These experiments thus show that we can effectively solve real-size PTNP problems, especially when keeping in mind that in reality instances hardly reach sizes bigger than the Bay Area instances.

Conclusion

We developed a novel AI-based solution method for the pre-disaster network preparation problem. We formulated the problem as a highly non-linear integer programming problem and developed a practically efficient propagator for the extreme linear resource constraint. Based on this approach we were able to effectively close the Istanbul benchmark, with run-time improvements over the best existing methods of three orders of magnitude. We then considered an even more challenging set of benchmark instances with five-orders of magnitude more scenarios, larger network sizes, and with and without link failure correlation. We showed that the AI approach is flexible and efficient enough to also solve these instances in affordable time.

$\#edges$	Branch and Bound	Heuristic	Simple Heuristic
30	0.03	0.01	0.01
60	0.54	0.21	0.01
90	25.8	1.73	0.07
150	13777	26	0.67
210	—	129	2.45
300	—	1227	10.7
600	—	13695	253
900	—	—	1628

Table 5: Istanbul Subdivision Benchmark Results

References

Dooms, G., and Katriel, I. 2006. The minimum spanning tree constraint. In *Principles and Practice of Constraint Programming-CP 2006*. Springer. 152–166.

Dooms, G., and Katriel, I. 2007. The "not-too-heavy spanning tree" constraint. In *Integration of AI and OR Techniques in Constraint Programming for Combinatorial Optimization Problems*. Springer. 59–70.

Focacci, F.; Lodi, A.; and Milano, M. 1999. Cost-based domain filtering. In *Principles and Practice of Constraint Programming–CP'99*. Springer Berlin Heidelberg. 189–203.

Kerivin, H., and Mahjoub, A. R. 2005. Design of survivable networks: A survey. *Networks* 46(1):1–21.

LeBras, R.; Dilkina, B. N.; Xue, Y.; Gomes, C. P.; McKelvey, K. S.; Schwartz, M. K.; Montgomery, C. A.; et al. 2013. Robust network design for multispecies conservation. In *AAAI 2013*.

Peeta, S.; Sibel Salman, F.; Gunnec, D.; and Viswanath, K. 2010. Pre-disaster investment decisions for strengthening a highway network. *Computers & Operations Research* 37(10):1708–1719.

Prestwich, S. D.; Laumanns, M.; and Kawas, B. 2013. Value interchangeability in scenario generation. In *Principles and Practice of Constraint Programming*, 587–595. Springer.

Prestwich, S. D.; Laumanns, M.; and Kawas, B. 2014. Symmetry breaking for exact solutions in adjustable robust optimisation. In *ECAI 2014*, 741–746.

Régin, J.-C. 1999. Arc consistency for global cardinality constraints with costs. In *Principles and Practice of Constraint Programming–CP'99*. Springer Berlin Heidelberg. 390–404.

Régin, J.-C. 2002. Cost-based arc consistency for global cardinality constraints. *Constraints* 7(3-4):387–405.

Sellmann, M.; Gellermann, T.; and Wright, R. 2007. Cost-based filtering for shorter path constraints. *Constraints* 12(2):207–238.

Sellmann, M. 2002. An arc-consistency algorithm for the minimum weight all different constraint. In *Principles and Practice of Constraint Programming-CP 2002*, 744–749. Springer.

Sellmann, M. 2003a. Approximated consistency for knapsack constraints. In *Principles and Practice of Constraint Programming–CP 2003*, 679–693. Springer.

Sellmann, M. 2003b. Cost-based filtering for shorter path constraints. In *Principles and Practice of Constraint Programming–CP 2003*, 694–708. Springer.

Trick, M. A. 2001. A dynamic programming approach for consistency and propagation for knapsack constraints. In *3rd international workshop on AI and OR techniques in Constraint Programming for Combinatorial Optimization Problems (CP-AI-OR)*, 113–124.

Trick, M. A. 2003. A dynamic programming approach for consistency and propagation for knapsack constraints. *Annals of Operations Research* 118(1-4):73–84.

van der Gaag, L. C.; Bodlaender, H. L.; and Feelders, A. 2004. Monotonicity in bayesian networks. In *Proceedings of the 20th conference on Uncertainty in artificial intelligence*, 569–576. AUAI Press.

Vásconez, K. C., and Kehrli, M. 2010. Highway evacuations in selected metropolitan areas: Assessment of impediments. Technical Report FHWA-HOP-10-059, Federal Highway Administration, Office of Transportation Operations, Washington, DC 20590.

SmartShift: Expanded Load Shifting Incentive Mechanism for Risk-Averse Consumers

Bochao Shen
CCIS
Northeastern University
Boston MA, 02115
ordinary@ccs.neu.edu

Balakrishnan Narayanaswamy
Computer Science and Engineering
University of California, San Diego
La Jolla CA, 92093
muralib@cs.ucsd.edu

Ravi Sundaram
CCIS
Northeastern University
Boston MA, 02115
koods@ccs.neu.edu

Abstract

Peak demand for electricity continues to surge around the world. The supply-demand imbalance manifests itself in many forms, from rolling brownouts in California to power cuts in India. It is often suggested that exposing consumers to real-time pricing, will incentivize them to change their usage and mitigate the problem - akin to increasing tolls at peak commute times. We show that risk-averse consumers of electricity react to price fluctuations by scaling back on their total demand, not just their peak demand, leading to the unintended consequence of an overall decrease in production/consumption and reduced economic efficiency. We propose a new scheme that allows homes to move their demands from peak hours in exchange for greater electricity consumption in non-peak hours - akin to how airlines incentivize a passenger to move from an over-booked flight in exchange for, say, two tickets in the future. We present a formal framework for the incentive model that is applicable to different forms of the electricity market. We show that our scheme not only enables increased consumption and consumer social welfare but also allows the distribution company to increase profits. This is achieved by allowing load to be shifted while insulating consumers from real-time price fluctuations. This win-win is important if these methods are to be embraced in practice.

Introduction

Power utilities worldwide face at least two major challenges. The first is *Peak Demand* - a period in which the demand for power is significantly higher than average. In order to satisfy a large peak demand, utilities (generation/distribution companies) have to make large capital investments including new 'peaking' generation stations, larger capacity lines, transformers, and operational expenditures including expensive purchases of electricity on the "spot market" (Harris 2006). For example, it is estimated that a 5% lowering of demand would have resulted in a 50% price reduction during the peak hours of the California electricity crisis in 2000-2001 (International Energy Agency 2003). As a result of the quadratic dependence between resistive losses and transmitted current, peaks also lead to substantial energy wastage. The second challenge faced by power utilities is that of *Supply-Demand* imbalance. (Borenstein 2002) states that "the difficulties that have appeared in California and elsewhere are intrinsic to the design of current electricity markets, in which demand exhibits virtually no price responsiveness and supply faces strict production constraints".

Research at the intersection of computer science and economics has established that incentives are a powerful way to allocate scarce resources (Courcoubetis and Weber 2003). Incentive mechanisms incorporating information exchange require back and forth communication between the consumers and the producers. Conventional electricity infrastructure is not designed to support such a dialog, instead relying on unilateral actions by the producers such as price-regulation and load-shedding. Fortunately, the introduction of new communication (Sood et al. 2009) and control (Farhangi 2010) infrastructure will allow increased consumer participation in the smart grid.

Traditionally, economists and electricity companies have focused on pricing as a mechanism to solve these two problems in a systematic way. However, homes and small businesses have an inherent and systemic requirement for stable electricity costs (Chao 2010). It is understood that "Consumers generally shy away from markets when products are complicated, supply is uncertain, prices are volatile, and information is lacking" (Chao 2012). We demonstrate that exposing *risk-averse* consumers to the actual real-time costs of electricity production, will result in a reduction in aggregate demand leading to reduced revenue for the generators and distributors with potential knock-on effects for the economy at large. At the same time, the volatility of real-time pricing can have strong effects on grid stability (Roozbehani, Dahleh, and Mitter 2012). A second concern with real-time pricing, is that consumer prices may increase (Allcott 2009) or net electricity consumption may decrease (Allcott 2011), depending on the model. We initiate the study of a new model of incentives and utility-customer interaction. To reduce volatility, whilst yet accounting for end-user constraints (e.g., washer must be run only during the day), we introduce an inter-temporal characteristic to the customer 'bidding' language. More importantly, we ensure that the customer and the utility will both be no worse off under our scheme than under flat-rate pricing. Our mechanism, SmartShift, does this by rewarding consumers who shift consumption with increased allocations for the same cost. Consumers are paid in kind and not cash, advantaging both the consumer and the producer. For real-world adoption it is critical to devise mutually beneficial schemes, such as Smartshift, that increase the economic pie within the world of electrical power.

We design consumer-supplier interaction protocols that respect the physical constraints and characteristics of the grid. Such protocols must account for realistic models of consumer behavior and requirements, while being computationally tractable to allow practical implementation in grids with millions of customers. Our main contributions are:

- SmartShift - a novel incentive mechanism, consistent with utilities' obligation to serve (Chao 2012), that allows risk-averse homes to move their demands from peak hours in exchange for greater electricity consumption in non-peak hours (SmartShift section).
- demonstration of the practical benefits of SmartShift through extensive simulations (Simulations section).
- characterization of the computational complexity of SmartShift (SmartShift section).
- formalization of the folklore that purely price driven approaches have negative consequences in a world with risk-averse consumers (SmartShift section).

Pricing in electricity markets - background

We study a market model with distribution companies (or utilities - the suppliers of electricity) and customers (consumers of electricity), each of whom is exposed to different prices, with associated risks and properties.

Prices seen by customers: *Flat-rate pricing* is the de-facto standard for retail electricity, where every unit costs the same fixed amount. Homes for example prefer this, particularly since, unlike businesses that may experience revenues in line with consumption growth, they have a strong inbuilt preference for stability in the costs. However, flat-rate pricing lacks any incentive for households to make rational usage decisions, especially during peak hours. We show that under flat-rate pricing risk-averse consumers will have high welfare due to lack of volatility but, (1) it cannot eliminate the peak load problem, since there is no slot-wise price differentiation, and as a result (2) the distribution company may face profit fluctuations.

With *real-time pricing*, peak reduction is achieved by charging consumers higher rates when the overall electricity load is high, encouraging them to reduce consumption (Mohsenian-Rad and Leon-Garcia 2010). However, as we will discuss in more detail, the fluctuating nature of market prices will discourage consumption by risk-averse consumers, while also being known to increase grid volatility (Roozbehani, Dahleh, and Mitter 2012). Real-time pricing will result in a decrease of the absolute total consumption of electricity (Di Cosmo, Lyons, and Nolan 2012) and consequently, total revenue of the distribution company (utility). Participation in most voluntary real-time pricing (RTP) programs has decreased, in particular "Between 2000 and 2003, half of all programs in existence prior to 2000 lost 25% or more of their participants, while only two programs saw participation increase" (Barbose, Goldman, and Neenan 2004), likely due to price volatility.

Prices seen by the distribution company: The time varying market, procurement or generation price of electricity can be modeled in different ways. The price can be modeled as *endogenous* or *exogenous*. We use the term *Endogenous Market Price* to denote a price that depends on the total electricity consumption at each time slot. This can be a useful model in situations where the number of consumers is relatively large, with their total consumption affecting market price. The resulting price is typically modeled as a quadratic function of the total electricity consumption; the quadratic or piecewise quadratic nature of generation and distribution cost curves is usually due to a multiplicity of fuel sources and generation modes. See (Wood and Wollenberg 2012; Harris 2006) for detailed justification of this common model.

Exogenous Market Prices are independent of the actions of the distribution company, its customers or their consumption. This is usually the case when the number of the responding consumers are relatively small, or if there is a large background electricity load which dominates an endogenous market price. In this case, we can just treat the real-time market price as a random variable independent of the decisions made by customers. See (Harris 2006; Chao 2012; Roozbehani, Dahleh, and Mitter 2012) for some justification and analysis of this stochastic pricing model.

Shortcoming of purely price driven approaches: We prove, in the exogenous price model, both that (i) risk-averse consumers have a lower expected social welfare and that (ii) the distribution company gets lower expected revenue under real-time pricing when compared to flat-rate pricing. On the other hand, we point out that the distribution company never makes a loss under real-time pricing, but can incur losses with some probability under flat-rate pricing. This leads us to develop a scheme with the advantages of both.

Our approach

We propose *SmartShift*, an expanded load shifting mechanism, where consumers are incentivized to shift their electricity load from peak-time to non-peak-time in exchange for an expanded electricity load, while still incurring the same cost. Since consumers self select, their social welfare (of consuming electricity) is non-decreasing under this scheme. Observe that from a pragmatic stand-point the unit of a home allows for the effective use of an in-kind incentive as a tool of behavior change. A single appliance/user may not be able/willing to consume the incentive, but an aggregate of a household will be able to more effectively consume the incentive via coordination among the household members (de Vries 2008).

In addition to the development of a new in-kind incentive model, our work is distinguished by a focus on computational issues. We prove that, in the *endogenous price* model, calculating the optimal shifted load is NP-complete for both real-time and flat-rate pricing. In contrast, we show in the *exogenous price* case that we can calculate the optimal shifted load in polynomial time.

We prove that employing *SmartShift* increases the expected profit of the distribution company both under real-time pricing and flat-rate pricing. We employ numerical experiments to show that it also decreases the probability of scenarios where the distribution company incurs losses, i.e. its risk. Thus, in the exogenous price model the use of *SmartShift* with flat-rate pricing provides a solution to the problems of *Peak Load* and *Supply-Demand* imbalance; the resulting electricity load allocation simultaneously increases consumers' social welfare, and distribution companies' profits and thus is a win-win solution.

Related Work

Evidence from the use of sophisticated usage-based pricing schemes (Courcoubetis and Weber 2003) indicates there is a strong case to be made for managing a grid via incentive schemes. Price based congestion control schemes in the power systems literature (often based on successful protocols developed for internet congestion control (Keshav and Rosenberg 2011)) that discourage consumption when the grid is loaded, fall into four basic categories: 1. day ahead or time-of-use (TOU) pricing, 2. dynamic pricing, 3. back-off strategies and 4. tâtonnement (or negotiation).

TOU pricing (particularly when users have significant storage, patience or flexibility) leads to the herding problem, where large amounts of consumption are shifted to low price regions creating new peaks (Carpenter et al. 2012). Dynamic pricing, as we discuss, can lead to uncertainity and reduced consumption by risk-averse customers. Randomized back-off type approaches, where users back-off on consumption when the grid is loaded (motivated by CSMA protocols developed for wireless communication), require trust that the agent will respond as expected to signals. This is not incentive compatible (Basar et al. 1995) as the response strategies are unverifiable and it is in the agents' interest to choose small back-off windows which allow them to consume electricity with minimum inconvenience. In Tâtonnement (Walker 1987), consumption agents and the distribution company exchange both price information and consumption profile information until convergence. While they were not explicitly categorized as such, tâtonnement forms the basis of much work in this area including (Mohsenian-Rad et al. 2010; Vytelingum et al. 2010; Li, Chen, and Low 2011; Ilic, Xie, and Joo 2011). Since typical distribution grids could have millions of users and tens of millions of devices, computational complexity is of paramount importance (Jain et al. 2013). In this context, the use of in-kind incentives and attention to computational complexity and risk-aversion makes our model and analysis novel.

Market Model Description

We now describe the overall electricity market model, explain the roles of the generation factory, the distribution company and the end consumers. We describe the two pricing mechanisms of the distribution company and then explain the two models for the market price of electricity: (1) Endogenous Market Price; (2) Exogenous Market Price.

Generation companies generate electricity, which is purchased by distribution companies. They then transfer it to the (n) end consumers, and charge for this service. The distribution company payes a price per unit of $p_m^{(t)}$ in time slot t, and must decide how to charge users - i.e. decide on a pricing mechanism.

We assume that both the distribution company and the end consumers know the statistical properties of the market price $p_m^{(t)}$. For the gaussian model we use, the mean μ_m and the standard deviation σ_m suffice. This can be learned, for example, based on the long run price history. In the short term, i.e. over the period of a single billing cycle, say a day, only the distribution company is assumed to know the market price $p_m^{(t)}$. A billing cycle is assumed to consist of k slots and without loss of generality we index t in the next billing cycle as $1 \leq t \leq k$. In this work, we study the market behavior (i.e. social welfare, revenue, etc) in the short term given the known long term statistical information.

At the beginning of each (short term) billing cycle, the distribution company will anounce the specific pricing mechanism. The prices seen by the consumers, $p_c^{(t)}$ will then be (1) *real-time pricing*: $p_c^{(t)} = p_m^{(t)}$; (2) *Flat-rate pricing*: $p_c^{(t)} = \mu_m$, where μ_m is the mean of $p_m^{(t)}$.

Risk-averse consumers: utility, valuation: Each consumer i has a valuation function $V_i^{(t)} : x_i^{(t)} \rightarrow R$ which reflects the value consumer i receives when she consumes $x_i^{(t)}$ units of electricity at time slot t. In general, the valuation function could be any concave increasing function and all the results in this paper continue to hold at a qualitative level. For sake of concreteness, we assume that consumers' valuation function $V_i^{(t)}(\cdot)$ has the form $V_i^{(t)} = \alpha_i^{(t)} \log x_i^{(t)}$.

Intuitively, the marginal value of consuming a additional unit of electricity will increase more slowly given the increased consumption of electricity. $\alpha_i^{(t)}$ can be seen as a parameter specific to consumer i that pegs the logarithmically increasing valuation curve to the value that consumer i puts on consuming $x_i^{(t)}$ units of electricity at time slot t.

Under flat rate pricing, consumer i estimates her net utility $U_i^{(t)}$ of consuming $x_i^{(t)}$ units of electricity at time slot t by $U_i^{(t)} = V_i^{(t)} - \mu_c x_i^{(t)}$.

As explained earlier, under uncertain real time pricing, consumers tend to be *risk-averse*. Risk-averse consumers will take the additional risk of price fluctuation into consideration when they estimate their net valuation, i.e., the net utility function for risk-averse consumers should be revised as $U_i^{(t)} = V_i^{(t)} - (\mu_c + \lambda_i \sigma_c) x_i^{(t)}$; σ_c is the standard deviation of the price $p_c^{(t)}$ and μ_c is it's average over the k time slots. σ_c represents the degree of price fluctuation; λ_i ($\lambda_i \geq 0$) quantifies the level of risk-aversion of consumer i. Specifically, $\lambda_i = 0$ captures the situation where consumer i is risk-neutral while $\lambda_i < 0$ models the risk-averse consumer ($\lambda_i > 0$ models the risk-seeking consumer, a type rarely seen in markets).

Electricity consumption, social welfare and profit: We apply our incentive mechanism to the two different pricing mechanisms - real-time and flat-rate - of the distribution company and analyze the resulting market behavior.

Real-time pricing: The distribution company charges the consumers a time varying price of $p_c^{(t)} = p_m^{(t)}$ over the time slots of the billing cycle. Clearly, $\mu_c = \mu_m$ and $\sigma_c = \sigma_m$. With predictions (possibly gleaned from long run observations) of the mean and variance of the real-time electricity price, a rational consumer will consume $x_i^{(t)}$ units of electricity so as to maximize the net utility $U_i^{(t)}$. By the first order derivative condition $\mathrm{d}U_i^{(t)}/\mathrm{d}x_i^{(t)} = 0$, the net utility $U_i^{(t)}$ at time slot t is maximized when $x_i^{(t)*} = \alpha_i^{(t)}/(\mu_m + \lambda_i \sigma_m)$. Thus, risk-averse consumers will consume less electricity when the real-time market price has a large standard deviation (large fluctuations and uncertainty in price).

Flat-rate pricing: The distribution company charges the end consumers a fixed price $p_c^{(t)} = \mu_m$ over the time slots of the billing cycle. Since the consumers know that they will be charged a flat-rate price equal to the mean of the market price they will infer that $\mu_c = \mu_m$ and $\sigma_c = 0$ and will respond by consuming the amount $x_i^{(t)*} = \alpha_i^{(t)}/\mu_m$ (even though they are risk-averse).

Social welfare of consumers: After each consumer is charged price $p_c^{(t)}$ at time slot t, the actual net utility she receives is $U_i^{(t)\prime} = V_i^{(t)} - p_c^{(t)} x_i^{(t)}$. And, the social welfare W of all the consumers is $W = \sum_{t=1}^{k} \sum_{i=1}^{n} U_i^{(t)\prime}$.

The **profit** η that the distribution company gains is $\eta = \sum_{t=1}^{k} \sum_{i=1}^{n} (p_c^{(t)} - p_m^{(t)}) x_i^{(t)}$. $\eta < 0$ means that the distribution company incurs losses with respect to its expected margins; $\eta > 0$ means that the distribution company profits. Note that in general, in a monopoly, a company can ensure profits by overcharging (increasing $p_c^{(t)}$ arbitrarily. In that case η quantifies the difference to expected profits. In addition, in most markets, electricity companies are at minimum semi-regulated and required to fix an operating margin. We avoid these complications by setting $p_c^{(t)} = p_m^{(t)}$.

Recall that the market price $p_m^{(t)}$ can be either endogenous or exogenous.

Endogenous market price: When the total consumption of a group of end consumers is large enough to dominate the overall electricity load of the grid, then the cost of generating electricity depends on those end consumers' total consumption. So does the market price $p_m^{(t)}$. Concretely, we assume $p_m^{(t)}$ has the form: $p_m^{(t)} = Q(\sum_{i=1}^{n} x_i^{(t)})$, and in particular that $Q(\cdot)$ has a quadratic form, i.e. $Q(x) = ax^2 + bx + c$. In this case, due to the convex nature of the problem, the market equilibrium is the fixed point of the interaction between the consumers and the supplier. It can hence be computed iteratively: starting with an initial estimate for mean μ_m and standard deviation σ_m, the end consumers respond with their electricity demand $\{x_i^{(t)}\}$. Based on this response, i.e. $\{x_i^{(t)}\}$, the endogenous market prices are generated by the quadratic function $Q(\sum_{i=1}^{n} x_i^{(t)})$. These prices are then used as input for the next round of computation until convergence is achieved.

Exogenous market price: When the total consumption of a group of end consumers is too small to meaningfully affect the overall electricity in the grid, then the market price $p_m^{(t)}$ can be assumed to be independent of consumers' consumption. Under the exogenous model, we assume $p_m^{(t)}$ $(1 \leq t \leq k)$ are independent random variables drawn from a normal distribution $p_m^{(t)} \sim N(\mu_m, \sigma_m^2)$.

SmartShift

SmartShift is an alternative, expanded load shifting, incentive mechanism that addresses the challenges of peak demand and the supply-demand imbalance detailed in the Introduction. In order to guide the design of our mechanism, we first ask ourselves two questions: (1) What incentivizes the consumers to shift their electricity load? (2) What goal will the distribution company achieve after it offers the incentivies to the consumers? The answer to these two questions will provide a win-win solution to both consumers and the distribution company. We then study how to achieve the optimal solution under (1) Endogenous (2) Exogenous market price.

What is the incentive for consumers to shift load?: Each rational consumer i will only agree to shift her consumption $x_i^{(s)}$ from time slot s to time slot t, if her valuation does not decrease. This gives us the following result,

Theorem 1. *With the same payment p_0, consumer i will have no decrease in utility, if she shifts $x_i^{(s)}$ from time slot s to time slot t with expansion, which results in an expanded load of $m_i^{(s\to t)} x_i^{(s)}$ at time slot t. The necessary and sufficient condition, therefore is for the expansion ratio $m_i^{(s\to t)}$ to satisfy the following:*

$$m_i^{(s\to t)} \geq \max\{\exp(\frac{(\alpha_i^{(s)} - \alpha_i^{(t)}) \log x_i^{(s)}}{\alpha_i^{(t)}}), 1\}. \quad (1)$$

The proofs of all the theorems in this paper can be found in (Shen, Narayanaswamy, and Sundaram 2014). This gives us a lower bound on the expansion ratio of a consumer. How close a user's expansion ratio is to her baseline is a measure of her *tolerance* or flexibility. The smaller the required expansion ratio, the greater the tolerance. Conversely, the larger the expansion ratio the more intolerant is the consumer of the slot change.

What is the benefit to the distribution company?: The distribution company will agree to shift consumer i's load $x_i^{(s)}$ from time slot s to slot t with an expansion ratio $m_i^{(s\to t)}$ for the same payment only if it benefits the distribution company to do so. For load $x_i^{(s)}$, the distribution company obtains a profit $\eta = (p_c^{(s)} - p_m^{(s)}) x_i^{(s)}$. After the expanded load shifting to time slot t, the profit becomes $\eta' = p_c^{(s)} x_i^{(s)} - p_m^{(t)} m_i^{(s\to t)} x_i^{(s)}$. So long as $p_m^{(s)} > p_m^{(t)} \cdot m_i^{(s\to t)}$, the distribution company stands to increase its profit $(\eta' - \eta > 0)$ and hence will agree to the expanded load shifting.

Our expanded load shifting incentive mechanism, SmartShift, meets both these requirements and is supported

Protocol 1 The message exchange protocol for SmartShift

STEP 1: The distribution company and the end consumers exchange information, or observe common historical data, to achieve consensus on the long term mean μ_m and standard deviation σ_m of the market price.
STEP 2: The n end consumers communicate their consumption $\{x_i^{(t)}|1 \leq i \leq n, 1 \leq t \leq k\}$ over the next period of k time slots, and their expansion ratios (which must be satisified if their loads would be shifted) $\{m_i^{(s\to t)}|1 \leq i \leq n, 1 \leq s \leq k, 1 \leq t \leq k\}$ to the distribution company.
STEP 3: The distribution company computes the optimal load shifting and communicates the resulting load allocation to the end consumers.

by Protocol 1 that exchanges messages between the distribution company and the end consumers.

We now study how to achieve optimal load shifting in both cases - endogenous and exogenous prices.

Endogenous market price: optimal load shifting

Theorem 2. *Computing optimal load shifting under endogenous market price is (weakly) NP-complete.*

We make a further comment, for the special setting where the consumption of electricity is discrete, i.e. users may shift entire appliances or units but not arbitrary amounts. In this setting it is not hard to create examples, where an equilibrium (in terms of prices and load distribution) may not exist. Suppose utilities and prices are such that, if a user doesn't consume a unit of electricity then the resultant lower price makes it favorable for her to in fact consume the unit; but, in doing so, the load is driven up and along with it the price (which is dependent quadratically on the load) thus making it unfavorable to consume the additional unit. Thus, determining endogenous prices with all or nothing or discrete consumption is an inherently hard problem where an equilibrium may not exist.

Exogenous market price: optimal load shifting In the exogenous market price case, the load shifting will never affect the market price $\{p_m^{(t)}\}$. To achieve the optimal load shifting, for each consumer i, her load $x_i^{(s)}$ should be shifted to the time slot $t^* = z_i^{(t)}$ at which $p_m^{(t^*)} \cdot m_i^{(s\to t^*)}$ is the minimum over all time slots $\{t^*\}$. Computing optimal load shifting under exogenous market price, as Alg. 2, runs in $O(nk^2)$ time.

Exogenous market price: real-time vs flat-rate: We now study how the two pricing mechanisms (real-time pricing and flat-rate pricing) have different performance on social welfare, revenue and profit in the model of exogenous market price. Specifically, we have the following theorems:

Theorem 3. *Given exogenous market prices, the expected social welfare W in real-time pricing is less than the expected social welfare W' in flat-rate pricing.*

Theorem 4. *Given exogenous market prices, the expected revenue R_{RT} in real-time pricing is less than the expected revenue R_{FR} in flat-rate pricing.*

Theorem 5. *Given exogenous market prices, real-time pricing always leads to a zero profit ($\eta_{RT} = 0$), while flat-rate pricing leads to a zero profit in expectation ($E(\eta_{FR}) = 0$).*

Algorithm 2 Optimal load shifting under exogenous market price

Input: $\{x_i^{(t)}|1 \leq i \leq n, 1 \leq t \leq k\}$, $\{m_i^{(s\to t)}|1 \leq i \leq n, 1 \leq s \leq k, 1 \leq t \leq k\}$.
Output: $\{z_i^{(t)}|1 \leq i \leq n, 1 \leq t \leq k\}$.

```
for each consumer i do
    for each time slot t do
        z_i^(t) ← argmin_{1≤t'≤k} {m_i^(t→t') p_m^(t')};
    end for
end for
```

(Recall that profit and loss refer to money gained or lost beyond the expected or pre-set margins.)

Theorem 5 shows that under real-time pricing the distribution company always achieves the anticipated profit per electricity unit; under flat-rate pricing the distribution company achieves the anticipated profit per electricity unit on average (in expectation). In other words, under flat-rate pricing the distribution company will sometimes incur a loss. This actually happens roughly about 50% of time, if the exogenous market price is assumed to be drawn from a normal distribution. In summary, flat-rate pricing mechanism has the advantage of encouraging consumers to consume the electricity (larger social welfare) they need without being constrained by considerations of price risk, but this risk is then shifted to the distribution company which could incur losses, i.e. $\eta < 0$, in some cases. However, we show, using simulations, that employing our expanded load shifting incentive mechanism, SmartShift, with flat-rate pricing reduces the probability of such (loss-incurring) scenarios.

Simulations

We evaluate SmartShift using a real-time electricity load data set from *Smart** (Barker et al. 2012). Through numerical experiments, we then study how our expanded load shifting mechanism can improve the performance over flat-rate pricing while providing a win-win solution to both the distribution company as well as the consumer.

We obtain **real-time electricity load** $\{x_i^{(t)}\}$ from the *Microgrid Data Set* (Barker et al. 2012) which includes average real power usage (kilowatts) at one minute sampling rate from 400 homes for 24 hours ($k = 24$). We average the (per minute) sampled data points per hour to get the hourly averaged electricity usage. We filter out households with zero power usage resulting in $n = 395$ profiles.

We simulate the **real-time market price** $\{p_m^{(t)}\}$ using a normal distribution $N(\mu_m, \sigma_m^2)$ motivated by the model of (Roozbehani, Dahleh, and Mitter 2010). We obtained similar results for other ditributions. We fix μ_m and vary σ_m to study how the fluctuation of the price will affect the market. We generate **valuation coefficients** $\{\alpha_i\}$ as follows: We assume that the electricity load profiles are generated under a flat-rate pricing model with mean price $\mu_p = 50$. Thus, $\alpha_i^{(t)} = x_i^{(t)} \cdot \mu_p$. Similar results were obtained with other

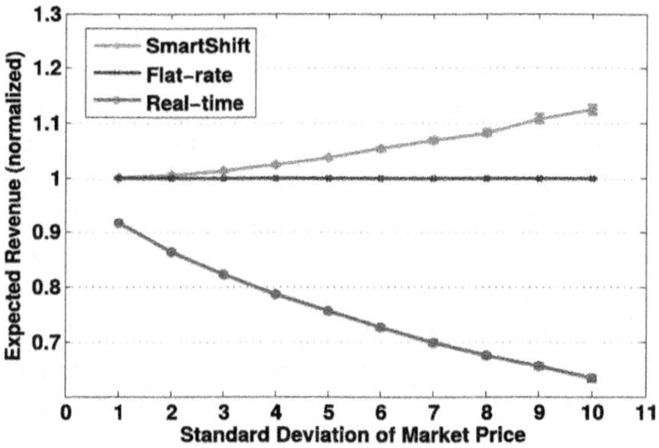

Figure 1: Normalized revenue vs price volatility

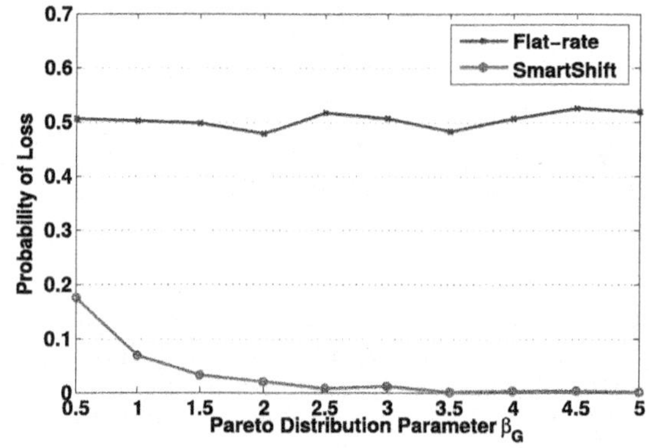

Figure 2: Loss probability vs consumer tolerance

settings. We draw the **risk-aversion parameter** $\{\lambda_i\}$, from a Pareto distribution as follows:

$$f_{pdf}(\lambda_i) = \frac{\beta_R \cdot \lambda_{min}}{\lambda_i^{\beta_R+1}} \tag{2}$$

where f_{pdf} gives the probability density function for the Pareto distribution; λ_{min} sets the minimum value for λ_i; β_R controls how much of the probability mass is close to λ_{min}, when β_R is larger, there is a larger probability mass of λ_i that is close to λ_{min}. To generate the **expansion ratio** $\{m_i^{(s\to t)}\}$, we first use Eq. 1 to calculate the minimum value $m_{i,min}^{(s\to t)}$. Then, we draw $m_i^{(s\to t)}$ from a Pareto distribution:

$$f_{pdf}(m_i^{(s\to t)}) = \frac{\beta_G \cdot m_{i,min}^{(s\to t)}}{(m_i^{(s\to t)})^{\beta_G+1}} \tag{3}$$

As before, the larger β_G is, the larger the probability that $m_i^{(s\to t)}$ is close to the minimum expansion ratio $m_{i,min}^{(s\to t)}$. Thus, β_G controls the dispersion in the tolerance of risk-averse consumers; the larger β_G is the more tightly concentrated is the population around a high tolerance level.

Risk-aversion and pricing mechanism: In all our simulations, each point is averaged over 100 repeated experiments. 95% confidence interval is also shown. In Figure 1, we draw the risk-aversion parameter $\{\lambda_i\}$ from the Pareto distribution, Eq. (2), by setting $\beta_R = 1$ and $\lambda_{min} = 1$. These are fixed for subsequent repetitions. Figure 1 shows that, while real-time pricing induces risk-averse consumers to contract usage with increased volatility (Theorem 4), SmartShift increases total revenue by simultaneously buffering consumers from price shocks and exploiting the increased volatility to more optimally shift the load.

In Figure 2, we fix the fluctation of the price by setting $\mu_m = 50, \sigma_m = 5$, but vary the tolerance of the consumers by varying the β_G from 0.5 to 5 with step size of 0.5. For each β_G, we sample a set of prices from normal distribution $N(\mu_m, \sigma_m^2)$ where $\mu = 50, \sigma_m = 5$, then sample the $\{m_i^{(s\to t)}\}$ from Eq. (3) with the fixed $\{m_{i,min}^{(s\to t)}\}$ and the varying β_G. We show that the larger β_G is (i.e. the more tightly clustered consumers are around a high tolerance level) the less the probability of the distribution company incurring a loss $\eta < 0$. This relationship follows from the fact that when the desired expansion ratio $m_i^{(s\to t)}$ is small, it is more probable for the expanded load shift to be satisfied.

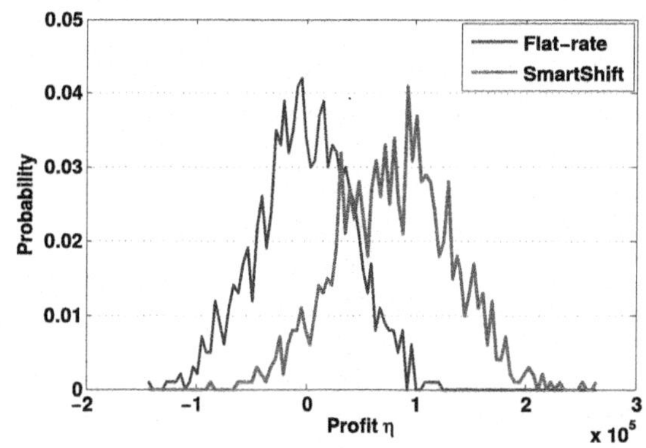

Figure 3: Probability density function of profit

In Figure 3, we fix the price fluctuation, risk-aversion and tolerance of the consumers. We sample prices from $N(\mu_m, \sigma_m^2)$ where $\mu_m = 50, \sigma_m = 5$, risk-aversion from Eq. (2) where $\beta_R = 1, \lambda_{min} = 1$, and tolerance from Eq. (3) where $\beta_G = 1$ and $m_{i,min}^{(s\to t)}$ computed by Eq. (1). By sampling 1000 sets of prices, we compute the profit η distribution. Figure 3 shows that the probability mass moves to the right after applying SmartShift. This also demonstrates that SmartShift reduces the probability of the distribution company incurring a loss ($\eta < 0$).

Conclusion

We have presented a general incentive-based mechanism, SmartShift, for reducing the load on the electricity grid. Our scheme grants users increased consumption in exchange for reducing their usage in peak periods. We have shown analytically that SmartShift under flat-rate pricing is a win-win for both consumers (increased social welfare) and producers (enhanced profits). SmartShift has elements of algorithms for iterative price setting (Mohsenian-Rad et al. 2010; Jain et al. 2013) with the added features of in-kind incentives and a slot-pairwise bidding language. A separate study of each these effects is of interest.

References

Allcott, H. 2009. Real time pricing and electricity markets. *Harvard University*.

Allcott, H. 2011. Rethinking real-time electricity pricing. *Resource and Energy Economics* 33(4):820–842.

Barbose, G. L.; Goldman, C. A.; and Neenan, B. 2004. A survey of utility experience with real time pricing. 127.

Barker, S.; Mishra, A.; Irwin, D.; Cecchet, E.; Shenoy, P.; and Albrecht, J. 2012. Smart*: An open data set and tools for enabling research in sustainable homes. In *Proceedings of the 2012 Workshop on Data Mining Applications in Sustainability (SustKDD 2012)*.

Basar, T.; Olsder, G. J.; Clsder, G.; Basar, T.; Baser, T.; and Olsder, G. J. 1995. *Dynamic noncooperative game theory*, volume 200. SIAM.

Borenstein, S. 2002. The trouble with electricity markets: Understanding California's restructuring disaster. *The Journal of Economic Perspectives* 16(1):191–211.

Carpenter, T.; Singla, S.; Azimzadeh, P.; and Keshav, S. 2012. The impact of electricity pricing schemes on storage adoption in ontario. In *e-Eenergy*.

Chao, H.-p. 2010. Price-responsive demand management for a smart grid world. *The Electricity Journal* 23(1):7–20.

Chao, H.-p. 2012. Competitive electricity markets with consumer subscription service in a smart grid. *Journal of Regulatory Economics* 41(1):155–180.

Courcoubetis, C., and Weber, R. 2003. *Pricing Communication Networks: Economics, Technology and Modeling*. Wiley.

de Vries, J. 2008. *The Industrious Revolution: Consumer Behavior and the Household Economy, 1650 to the Present*. Cambridge University Press.

Di Cosmo, V.; Lyons, S.; and Nolan, A. 2012. Estimating the impact of time-of-use pricing on Irish electricity demand. MPRA Paper 39971, University Library of Munich, Germany.

Farhangi, H. 2010. The path of the smart grid. *IEEE Power and Energy Magazine* 8(1):18–28.

Harris, C. 2006. *Electricity Markets: Pricing, Structures and Economics*. Sussex, England: Wiley.

Ilic, M.; Xie, L.; and Joo, J. 2011. Efficient coordination of wind power and price-responsive demand Part I: Theoretical foundations. *IEEE Transactions on Power Systems* 26(4):1875–1884.

International Energy Agency. 2003. The power to choose - enhancing demand response in liberalised electricity markets findings of IEA demand response project.

Jain, S.; Balakrishnan, N.; Narahari, Y.; Hussain, S. A.; and Voo, N. Y. 2013. Constrained tâtonnement for fast and incentive compatible distributed demand management in smart grids. In *Proceedings of the fourth international conference on Future energy systems*, 125–136. ACM.

Keshav, S., and Rosenberg, C. 2011. How internet concepts and technologies can help green and smarten the electrical grid. *ACM SIGCOMM Computer Communication Review* 41(1):109–114.

Li, N.; Chen, L.; and Low, S. 2011. Optimal demand response based on utility maximization in power networks. In *IEEE Power and Energy Society General Meeting*, 1 –8.

Mohsenian-Rad, A.-H., and Leon-Garcia, A. 2010. Optimal residential load control with price prediction in real-time electricity pricing environments. *Smart Grid, IEEE Transactions on* 1(2):120–133.

Mohsenian-Rad, A.; Wong, V.; Jatskevich, J.; Schober, R.; and Leon-Garcia, A. 2010. Autonomous demand-side management based on game-theoretic energy consumption scheduling for the future smart grid. *IEEE Transactions on Smart Grid* 1(3).

Roozbehani, M.; Dahleh, M.; and Mitter, S. 2010. On the stability of wholesale electricity markets under real-time pricing. In *49th IEEE Conference on Decision and Control (CDC), 2010*, 1911–1918.

Roozbehani, M.; Dahleh, M. A.; and Mitter, S. K. 2012. Volatility of power grids under real-time pricing. *Power Systems, IEEE Transactions on* 27(4):1926–1940.

Shen, B.; Narayanaswamy, B.; and Sundaram, R. 2014. SmartShift: Expanded Load Shifting Incentive Mechanism for Risk-averse Consumers. http://www.ccs.neu.edu/home/ordinary/papers/CCIS-NU-TR31-2014.pdf. [Northeastern University Technical Report: CCIS-NU-TR31-2014].

Sood, V.; Fischer, D.; Eklund, J.; and Brown, T. 2009. Developing a communication infrastructure for the smart grid. In *Electrical Power & Energy Conference (EPEC), 2009 IEEE*, 1–7. Ieee.

Vytelingum, P.; Voice, T.; Ramchurn, S.; Rogers, A.; and Jennings, N. 2010. Agent-based micro-storage management for the smart grid. In *AAMAS*, 39–46.

Walker, D. 1987. Walras's theories of tatonnement. *The Journal of Political Economy* 95(4):758–774.

Wood, A. J., and Wollenberg, B. F. 2012. *Power generation, operation, and control*. John Wiley & Sons.

Proceedings of the Twenty-Ninth AAAI Conference on Artificial Intelligence

Incentivizing Users for Balancing Bike Sharing Systems

Adish Singla
ETH Zurich
adish.singla@inf.ethz.ch

Marco Santoni
ElectricFeel Mobility Systems
marco@electricfeel.com

Gábor Bartók
ETH Zurich
bartok@inf.ethz.ch

Pratik Mukerji
ElectricFeel Mobility Systems
mukerji@electricfeel.com

Moritz Meenen
ElectricFeel Mobility Systems
meenen@electricfeel.com

Andreas Krause
ETH Zurich
krausea@ethz.ch

Abstract

Bike sharing systems have been recently adopted by a growing number of cities as a new means of transportation offering citizens a flexible, fast and green alternative for mobility. Users can pick up or drop off the bicycles at a station of their choice without prior notice or time planning. This increased flexibility comes with the challenge of unpredictable and fluctuating demand as well as irregular flow patterns of the bikes. As a result, these systems can incur imbalance problems such as the unavailability of bikes or parking docks at stations. In this light, operators deploy fleets of vehicles which re-distribute the bikes in order to guarantee a desirable service level. Can we engage the users themselves to solve the imbalance problem in bike sharing systems?

In this paper, we address this question and present a crowdsourcing mechanism that incentivizes the users in the bike repositioning process by providing them with alternate choices to pick or return bikes in exchange for monetary incentives. We design the complete architecture of the incentives system which employs optimal pricing policies using the approach of regret minimization in online learning. We investigate the incentive compatibility of our mechanism and extensively evaluate it through simulations based on data collected via a survey study. Finally, we deployed the proposed system through a smartphone app among users of a large scale bike sharing system operated by a public transport company, and we provide results from this experimental deployment. To our knowledge, this is the first dynamic incentives system for bikes re-distribution ever deployed in a real-world bike sharing system.

Introduction

A Bike Sharing System (henceforth BSS) is a new concept of public transportation offering citizens a flexible and green alternative as well as complementing the slow and crowded transportation in urban areas. This mobility trend had an exponential growth over the last years, and, as of June 2014, over 700 cities actively operate automated bike sharing systems deploying an estimate of 800,000 bikes worldwide (Meddin and DeMaio 2014). BSSs increase the user's commuting flexibility by allowing her to pick up or drop off a bike at any station and let her decide the duration of the trip without any prior planning or reservation. Indeed, this flexibility is the key factor for the success of BSSs.

Balancing problem. This flexibility also poses a number of new challenges for the BSS operators. The demand is often unpredictable, asymmetric and fluctuating throughout the day. Other factors such as altitude differences, weather conditions or events in the city can cause irregular or asymmetric rental demands and flow of bikes. As the number of available bikes and parking spots at any bike station in the system is limited, satisfying the forthcoming demand with such limited resources is a major challenge and recurrent problem for BSS operators. A BSS user would experience an unsatisfactory quality of service when attempting to rent or drop off a bike at an empty or full station respectively. Meeting the demand for bikes and free docks requires an extensive logistic work and poses major operational costs to the operators. Thus, fleets of vehicles (or trucks) are deployed to re-distribute bikes among stations to balance the system out (Büttner, Mlasowsky, and Birkholz 2011).

Incentivizing users. Apart from the large operational costs, deploying trucks for the re-distribution goes against the green concept of BSS. Can we engage the users of such systems and provide them incentives to contribute re-balancing the system? Termed as *crowdphysics* by Sadilek, Krumm, and Horvitz (2013), this class of crowdsourcing systems requires users to sequence or synchronize physical actions in time and space, and can lead to building self-sustainable systems. The goal of building such a system presents several challenges including: *i)* the system's large scale in terms of user base as well as number of stations, *ii)* the fluctuating demand over time that needs to be taken into account while determining problematic stations, *iii)* the unknown personal costs of the users and their strategic behavior potentially aiming at maximizing their profit, *iv)* the budget constraints of how much can be spent on incentives and *v)* a user-friendly interface to make such a system appealing (*e.g.*, through a smartphone app). Building such a self-sustainable and crowd-powered bike sharing system is the key idea we explore in this paper. While we focus on BSSs, similar problems arise in other domains (*e.g.*, car sharing or rerouting users on over-booked flights) and our methodology is applicable to these systems as well.

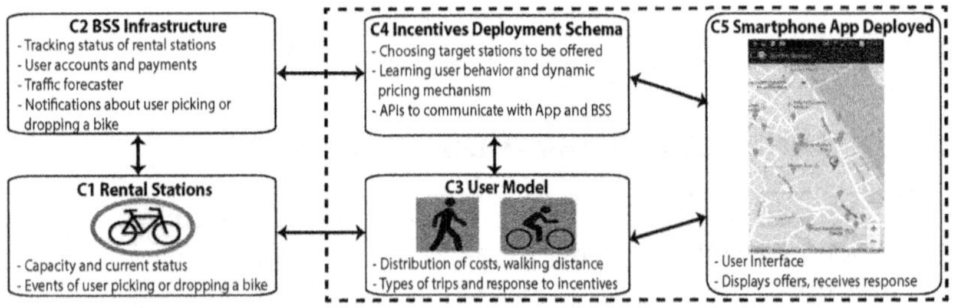

Figure 1: Overview of the system, our contributions are shown in the dotted box

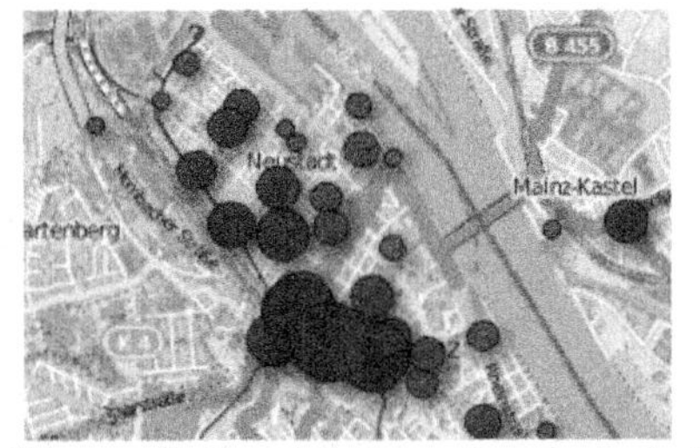

Figure 2: Spatial dist. of accepted offers

Overview of our system

In this paper, we design the complete architecture of an operating incentives system for engaging users in the bike-repositioning effort (see Figure 1). In collaboration with a company operating large scale bike sharing systems, we deployed our system on a real-world BSS in a city of Europe[1]. In Figure 1, the components *C1 Rental Stations* and *C2 BSS Infrastructure* correspond to the rental stations, the hardware and software infrastructure of the public bike sharing system. These components involve tracking all the user activities such as picking or dropping the bikes, managing user accounts and the payment system.

The main components that we designed and built include *C3 User Model*, *C4 Incentives Deployment Schema* (IDS) and *C5 Smartphone App*. The IDS is the central component in the overall design that handles the user's requests through *C5 Smartphone App*. The request includes input such as the user's target station and type (i.e., bike pick up or drop off). The IDS communicates with the BSS Infrastructure to evaluate the current and predicted status of the stations, and then decides whether to offer incentives to the user by requesting a change in her pickup or drop-off location. In order to maximize the efficiency under given budget constraints, we design dynamic pricing mechanisms using the approach of regret minimization in online learning that can learn over time about the optimal pricing policies. We consider the users as strategic agents who may untruthfully report information about their personal cost and location to maximize their profit. We model the full rental process of the user and her reaction to incentives in the component *C3 User Model*. In summary, our main contributions are as follows:

- We design the complete architecture of an incentive system with the goal of enabling self-sustainable, crowd-powered and greener bike sharing systems.
- We build an incentive deployment schema that interacts with the users and BSS infrastructure, decides about offering incentives, and learns from past interactions.
- We validate our assumptions by surveying BSS users, and demonstrate the effectiveness of our approach via a detailed BSS simulator. We report on our experience deploying our system via a smartphone app integrated with a real-world BSS.

Related Work

Truck-based repositioning in BSS. The problem of asymmetric flow, imbalance and repositing of the vehicles has been studied in generic vehicle sharing systerms that could involve cars or bikes (Cepolina and Farina 2012; Kek et al. 2009; Clemente et al. 2013; Nair and Miller-Hooks 2011; Correia and Antunes 2012). Regarding BSS's balancing problem, a substantial literature (Rainer-Harbach et al. 2013; Pfrommer et al. 2014; Raviv and Kolka 2013; Chemla, Meunier, and Wolfler Calvo 2013; Schuijbroek, Hampshire, and van Hoeve 2013; George and Xia 2011) introduced bike repositioning policies based on trucks. The user dissatisfaction function introduced by Raviv and Kolka (2013) measures the performance of a BSS station and provides the quality of a repositioning. Nair et al. (2013) provides a detailed quantitative analysis of the repositioning strategies for Vélib', the BSS in Paris.

Crowd-based repositioning in BSS. Recent literature has investigated crowd-based BSS balancing policies (Fricker and Gast 2012; Waserhole, Jost, and Brauner 2013; Pfrommer et al. 2014; Chemla, Meunier, and Pradeau 2013; GoDCgo 2011) to study the potential of influencing BSS users by offering incentives that could improve balancing of the system. In Paris, Vélib' runs a static incentive schema that offers users 15 extra free minutes each time they return a bike to an elevated station (Vélib' 2014). However, in contrast, our proposed mechanism is dynamic and can efficiently take into account the current state of the system to decide where and what incentives to offer. Pfrommer et al. (2014) also introduced a dynamic pricing mechanism using model-based predictive control principles. Our pricing mechanism, in contrast, is based on an efficient and provably near-optimal online learning framework. Furthermore, we build an operating end-to-end system integrated with a real-world BSS for deployment, and we investigate the incentive compatibility of our approach.

The Model

We now formalize the problem addressed in this paper.

BSS. There are m stations in a city denoted by the set $\mathcal{S} = \{s_1, s_2, \dots, s_m\}$. We denote the number of bikes available at time t at station s as $v(s,t)$. Along the lines of Pfrommer et al. (2014), we split every day into 12 slices $h \in \mathcal{H}$ of two hours each, where a time of the day t is mapped to the corresponding time-slice using $h(t)$. The demand of rentals from station s_i to station s_j within time-slice h is modeled as a discrete random variable z which represents a count of the number of trips with probability density function $\tau(z|s_i, s_j, h)$. We denote $\hat{z}(h)$ to represent the estimate

[1]Bike sharing operator MVGmeinRad in Mainz, Germany.

of the total number of trips within time-slice h. The BSS infrastructure has a proprietary demand forecaster that can predict the future demand of incoming and outgoing traffic at the stations and is made available to us through their APIs. See (Côme and Oukhellou 2012; Kaltenbrunner et al. 2010; Borgnat et al. 2011; Froehlich, Neumann, and Oliver 2009; Han, Côme, and Oukhellou 2014) for possible approaches.

Quality of service. The goal of a bike repositioning policy is to prevent customers' dissatisfaction about not finding an available bike or a parking slot. Waserhole, Jost, and Brauner; Chemla, Meunier, and Pradeau; Fricker and Gast (2013; 2013; 2012) have proposed metrics aiming at maximizing the number of trips or minimizing the number of problematic stations. However, these metrics fail to capture the dissatisfaction experienced by BSS users. We adopt the measure of service level proposed in Pfrommer et al. (2014):

$$\text{Service level} = \frac{\text{Potential customers} - \text{No-service events}}{\text{Potential customers}}$$

where the number of no-service events corresponds to the customers who could not rent a bike at an empty station or failed to return their bike at a full station.

Truck-based re-positioning policies. The BSS operator allocates a fixed daily budget B that can be used by the truck-based policy. The BSS company where we deployed our incentives system uses its proprietary re-positioning policy. See (Chemla, Meunier, and Pradeau 2013; Raviv and Kolka 2013) for possible approaches.

User model. Consider a user (or customer) u at location l_x^u interested in an action $x \in \{pick, return\}$, i.e., pick up or drop off a bike. We assume that, by default, the user would consider the nearest station to her location to perform the action, given by $s_x^u \leftarrow \arg\min_{s \in \mathcal{S}} d(l_x^u, s)$, where d measures the distance between two locations. The incentives system encourages users to shift their pickup or drop-off stations to contribute balancing the BSS. For simplicity, we assume that the user u is willing to walk to another station up to a maximum distance γ^u, and, within this radius, her cost for the additional effort is constant given by c^u. She is not willing to walk for distance more than γ^u despite of any offer by our incentive system. We validate these assumptions through a survey study with real BSS customers. In our model, the costs of the users are *i.i.d.* sampled from an underlying *unknown* distribution f. We let $F : [c_{\min}, c_{\max}] \rightarrow [0, 1]$ denote the cumulative distribution function (CDF) of costs or "cost curve", unknown to the system.

Suppose a user u at location l_x^u, going to station s_x^u, is offered an alternate station s_x^* for a payment of p^*. We model her reaction to this incentive as an indicator function:

$$\mathbb{1}^u_{\text{accept}}(l_x^u, s_x^*, p^*) = \begin{cases} 0 & \text{if } \gamma^u < d(l_x^u, s_x^*) \text{ or } p^* < c^u \\ 1 & \text{otherwise} \end{cases}$$

which takes value 0 or 1 when the user rejects or accepts the offer, respectively. We remark that the information about user cost c^u and her true location l_x^u is private to the user and may vary among users. We consider the users as strategic agents who may untruthfully report their private information about the location l_x^u or private cost c^u to maximize their profit. For simplicity of the mechanism design, we use $\hat{\gamma}$ to represent the maximum distance for the whole population, and we obtain its estimate through a user survey.

Procedure 1: Incentives Deployment Schema (IDS)

Input: *user* u; *location* l_x^u; $x \in \{pick, return\}$;
Output: Offer: station s_x^*; price p^*;
Parameters: *radius* $\hat{\gamma}$;
begin
  if HASINCENTIVESPENDING(u) **then**
    return null;
  candidate stations $C \leftarrow \mathcal{S}$;
  default target $s_x^u \leftarrow \arg\min_{s \in \mathcal{S}} d(l_x^u, s)$;
  foreach $s \in C$ **do**
    s.status $\leftarrow$ PROBLEMATIC(s);
    if $d(l_x^u, s) > \hat{\gamma}$ **then**
      $C = C \setminus \{s\}$;
    if $x = return$ & $s.status \neq$ EMPTY **then**
      $C = C \setminus \{s\}$;
    if $x = pick$ & $s.status \neq$ FULL **then**
      $C = C \setminus \{s\}$;
  if $s_x^u \in C$ **OR** $C = \emptyset$ **then**
    return null;
  $s_x^* \leftarrow \arg\min_{s \in C} d(l_x^u, s)$;
  $p^* \leftarrow$ PRICINGMECHANISM();
  Output: s_x^*, p^*;

Incentivizing users for repositioning. We study an incentive system as an alternative to truck-based re-distribution in BSSs. We propose a dynamic incentives schema that computes incentives each time a user makes a new request. The BSS operator regularly allocates a budget $B(h)$ for time batch h, and the goal of the incentives schema is to exploit the budget efficiently. Therefore, if a user u makes a request at time t for action type x, a dynamic algorithm is responsible to select the alternate station s_x^* and compute the value of the incentive p^* based on the following inputs: *i)* reported location of user l_x^u, *ii)* current status of the system: $v(s,t)\,\forall s \in \mathcal{S}$, *iii)* near-future demand $\tau(z|s_i, s_j, h)\,\forall s_i, s_j \in \mathcal{S}$, *iv)* budget available, and *v)* information about historical interactions with users.

Our goal is to design a system that is *i)* budget-feasible, i.e., operates under strict budget constraints, *ii)* efficient in terms of improvement in quality of service for a given budget, *iii)* incentive-compatible (truthful), i.e., it is in best interest of users to reveal true information, and *iv)* can deal with unknown user costs and learn pricing policies over time.

The Incentives System

We now present the various components of our incentives system and discuss its properties.

Incentives Deployment Schema

Procedure 1 illustrates the *Incentives Deployment Schema* (IDS) that handles the users' requests forwarded by the deployed smartphone app. For each request, the IDS gets as input the user identifier u, the action type $x \in \{pick, return\}$ and the user's reported location l_x^u. Based on the user input and the current status of the system, IDS computes the offer that consists of the alternative target station s_x^* and the offered price p^*. Initially, the IDS ensures that the user does not have any pending incentive, i.e., an incentive offer that she recently accepted but did not accomplish yet. Then it creates a set of candidate stations that are within the maximum walking distance $\hat{\gamma}$ from l_x^u and are "problematic", i.e. full or empty. The problematic status of the stations is based on input from the APIs of the BSS infrastructure that provides the current status $v(s,t)$ as well as the forecast of future traffic. The IDS also takes into account the pending incentives associated with each station while updating the status that additionally accounts for future traffic.

Once the IDS has filtered the candidate stations, it selects as target station s_x^* the one closest to reported location l_x^u. Then, it sends a request to the *pricing mechanism* to obtain the price p^* to be offered. This offer is displayed to the user on the smartphone app. If the user accepts, the IDS registers this incentive offer as pending until she accomplishes the assigned task or it expires after a prefixed amount of time.

Pricing Mechanism DBP-UCB

The main challenges in designing an optimal pricing mechanism are due to the limited and dynamically changing budget (B) as well as pool size of users to make offers to (N) and the unknown "cost curve" F. Additionally, the mechanism has to compute the offers in an online setting with only limited interaction with the users in terms of the information that can be received from them for learning. First, let us consider an offline setting where the cost curve F is known and $\{p_0(=c_{min}), \dots, p_i, \dots, p_K(=c_{max})\}$ be the set of available prices that the mechanism can offer. In this case, the optimal truthful mechanism denoted by OPT-FIX, is to offer a fixed price p^{OPT} (Singer 2010) given by:

$$p^{\text{OPT}} = \arg\max_{p} \min\left\{F(p), \frac{B}{N \cdot p}\right\} \quad s.t.\ p \in \{p_0, \dots, p_K\} \tag{1}$$

Now, in case of unknown F, we can cast the problem as that of online learning of the optimal price. Note that, $F(p)$ simply denotes the probability of getting an acceptance from the user when offered price p. In particular, we are interested in designing mechanisms based on the posted-price model where the mechanism makes a price offer p and the user simply says "yes" or "no" to the offer, instead of soliciting the user's bid. In a learning framework, the mechanism can make different price offers over time to different users, and use the binary feedback of acceptance to learn an estimate of $F(p)$. There is an inherent explore-exploit trade off here of exploring (or learning) about different, potentially suboptimal, prices and exploiting the estimates of $F(p)$ to offer the price that appears best. Multi-armed bandits (MAB) (Lai and Robbins 1985) provide a natural formalism for tackling this problem, considering the prices as actions (or arms) with unknown stochastic reward given by the function $F(p)$. In the MAB framework, the performance of a mechanism is measured in terms of its "regret" R_n, i.e., the cumulative loss of the mechanism w.r.t. the optimal fixed price p^{OPT} after n iterations. The goal is to design a "no-regret" mechanism that learns to perform competitively, i.e., the average regret w.r.t. n goes to zero $\lim_{n\to\infty} R_n/n = 0$. However, note that in contrast to standard MAB settings, here actions have different

Procedure 2: Pricing Mechanism DBP-UCB

Input: *start time* t_0; *prices* $\{p_0, \dots, p_i, \dots, p_K\}$;
Output: Price p^n at iteration n;
Initialize:
- $n = 0; h^0 = h(t_0);$ ▷ First batch
- $B = B(h^n); B^n = B; N = 2 \cdot \hat{z}(h^n);$
- $N_i^n = 0; F_i^n = 0; \forall i \in [0, \dots, K]$ ▷ Value estimates

foreach *request by user at time* t **do**
  if $h^n \neq h(t)$ **then**
    $h^n = h(t);$ ▷ New time batch
    $B^n = B^n + B(h^n); B = B^n;$ ▷ More budget
    $N = 2 \cdot \hat{z}(h^n);$ ▷ Trips estimate from forecaster
  $\tilde{F}_i^n = F_i^n + \sqrt{\frac{2\cdot\ln(n)}{N_i^n}};$ ▷ Same as in BP-UCB
  $i^n = \arg\max_i \min\left\{\tilde{F}_i^t, \frac{B}{N\cdot p_i}\right\}\ s.t.\ p_i \le B^n;$
  Output: Offer price $p^n = p_{i^n}$ at iteration n;
  Feedback: Observe acceptance decision y^n;
  Update Variables:
  - $B^{n+1} = B^n - p^n \cdot y^n; F_{i^n}^{n+1} = F_{i^n}^n + \frac{(y^n - F_{i^n}^n)}{(N_{i^n}^n + 1)};$
  - $N_{i^n}^{n+1} = N_{i^n}^n + 1; h^{n+1} = h^n; n = n + 1;$

  Wait for new user request;

costs and there is a budget constraint.

For static settings where the budget (B) and the number of users (N) is known and fixed in advance, Singla and Krause (2013) designed a no-regret mechanism BP-UCB that is budget feasible, truthful and has fast convergence rates. This scenario does not correspond to the incentives system we are interested in as, in this context, the pricing mechanism has to operate continuously throughout time, is allocated new budget in time batches and the number of users coming to the system is dynamic. In this light, we design our mechanism DBP-UCB (Dynamic Budgeted Procurement using Upper Confidence Bounds), illustrated in Procedure 2, as a dynamic variant of BP-UCB. The key idea we use is that the learning process of the mechanism can be decoupled from the constraints on B and N. While the parameters B and N change dynamically at the onset of each time batch, it carries over the estimates of $F(p)$ across batches, ensuring DBP-UCB maintains the convergence properties of BP-UCB.

At a high level, the mechanism DBP-UCB operates as follows. At the onset of each new time batch h, the mechanism is provided with an additional budget $B(h)$ by the BSS operator. Furthermore, the number of participants N for a batch is approximated by the expected number of trips $\hat{z}(h)$ taking place in the corresponding batch h estimated by the BSS forecaster. In particular, the expected number of rentals is multiplied by two as the user may interact with the incentives system both to pick and return a bike. The mechanism sequentially interacts with users in discrete steps denoted by n. Let B^n be the budget at iteration n, N_i^n be the number of times p_i price has been offered so far, and F_i^n be the current estimate of the cost curve for prices $\forall i \in [0, \dots K]$. The mechanism also maintains upper confidence bounds on F_i^n

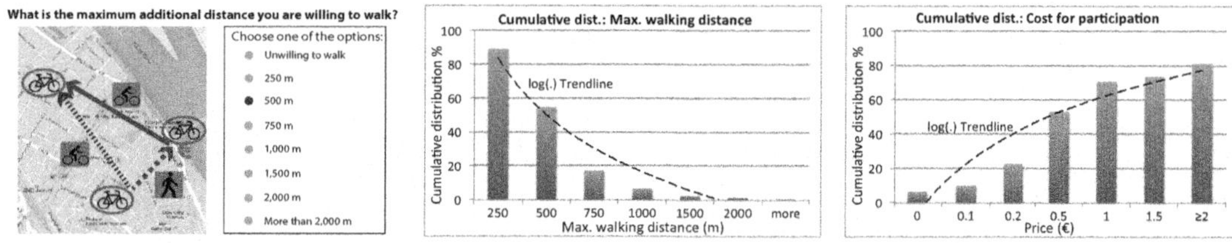

(a) Sample survey question (b) Dist. of max. walking distance γ^u (c) Dist. of costs c^u

Figure 3: Survey study with customers of a real-world BSS[1] in a city of Europe where we deployed our incentive system

denoted as $\tilde{F}_i^n$, representing the optimistic estimates of F at iteration n, and used to compute the optimal price p^n to offer. The mechanism receives the binary feedback y^n which is then used to update the estimates for price p^n.

Truthfulness of Incentives System

As the system users may act strategically, it is important to analyze the truthfulness of the IDS to understand the real-world performance of the proposed system. Each user has a private cost c^u and location l_x^u and we now discuss the truthfulness of our system w.r.t. these two dimensions of the users' private information. The mechanism DBP-UCB is based on the posted-price model, where it is in the user's best interest to truthfully accept the offer whenever the offered price is higher than the private cost c^u. Furthermore, given the large scale of the system, the interaction with a single user does not significantly affect the learning behavior of the mechanism, thus making it behave truthfully in real-world BSSs.

Let us now analyze the truthfulness of IDS w.r.t the location information. One crucial aspect here is that no incentives are offered when the user's default station s_x^u is already among the candidate stations. This notably improves the efficiency (by over 50% in our simulations) of the IDS by avoiding to pay out incentives for stations that the user would have taken anyways. We discuss the implications of this on the truthfulness of IDS below. If the system has no way to infer s_x^u, the user may indeed act strategically by misreporting to obtain an incentive that would have not been offered otherwise. In the real deployment of our system, instead of allowing the user to declare her current location (l_x^u), it is directly retrieved from the deployed mobile-app which provides localization features. Based on this location information, the user's default pickup station can directly be inferred. This technical solution does not directly apply to the bike drop-off scenario where users explicitly declare their target location. However the drop-off location could potentially be inferred based on user's historical trips, making the system incentive-compatible in real-world deployments.

Experimental Evaluation

In this section, we carry out extensive experiments to understand the practical performance of our system.

Datasets and Experimental Setup

First, we describe our datasets and the BSS simulator.

Historical BSS dataset. For our simulations, we used a historical dataset from Boston's Hubway, made publicly available by the Boston Metropolitan Area Planning Council[2]. The Hubway dataset contains data collected between 28th July, 2011 and 1st October, 2012 with rich information about 95 stations, 694 bicycles, 552,030 rentals, and snapshots of the status of the BSS at regular intervals.

Survey study. We did a survey study among the customers of a real-world BSS[1] in a city of Europe where we also deployed our system. Our goal is to validate the realism of our model, as well as to obtain realistic statistics about the distribution of users' personal costs c^u and of their maximum walking range γ^u. The participants were asked generic questions about their rental behaviors (*e.g.*, purpose and duration of the trips) and then we introduced them to the proposed incentives system asking various questions to elicit their preferences about private cost and walking distance. Figure 3(a) illustrates a survey question, and the distributions obtained from the survey for γ^u and c^u are shown in Figures 3(b) and 3(c) respectively. Note that the survey also contained an additional choice of "unwilling to walk" or "unwilling to participate at any cost" that accounted for roughly 20% of the response for both questions.

Simulator. We built a complete simulator of a real BSS based on Hubway's historical data as well as the survey data from customers. Each simulation starts by taking a snapshot of the status of the BSS, i.e., the number of bikes at each station retrieved from the historical dataset and runs the simulation for a total of 30 days. The BSS simulator generates users' trip events by sampling from the distribution learnt from the historical data. Lastly, the simulator associates each rental to a user with cost c^u and γ^u sampled from the distributions obtained from the survey. For the TRUCKS, we used the myopic greedy policy as defined by Chemla, Meunier, and Pradeau (2013). Using the idea of *dynamic* (during rush hours) and *static* (during off hours) repositioning from Raviv and Kolka (2013), our policies operate in time from 12:00 p.m. and 3:00 p.m, and then from mid-night to morning. We assume that the trucks entail a fixed cost of 50 € per hour to the system and the policy allocates the number of hours based on the total budget.

Results

We now discuss the findings from our experiments.

Varying budget. We compare the performance of different policies by varying the allocated budget. We envision that the operators would deploy the incentives system in parallel to

[2]http://hubwaydatachallenge.org/.

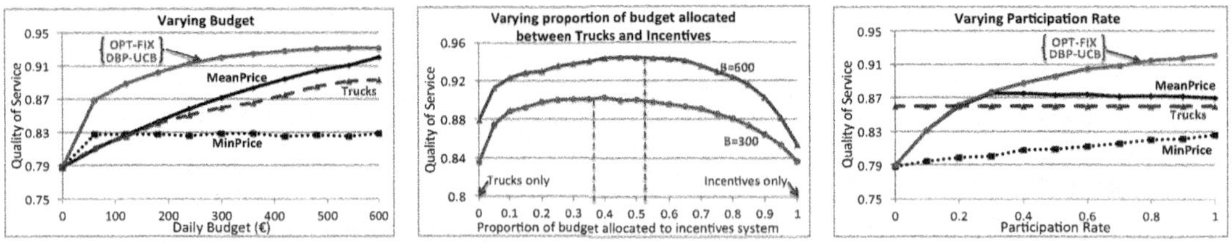

(a) Varying budget (b) Budget tradeoff (c) Varying participation

Figure 4: Simulation results based on historical data of Hubway BSS[2] and survey data from customers of real-world BSS[1]

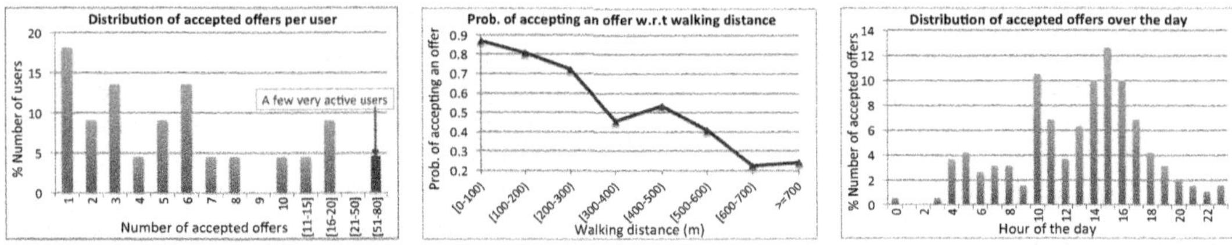

(a) Dist. of accepted offers per user (b) Prob. of acceptance w.r.t walking (c) Dist. of accepted offers over day

Figure 5: Results from deployment of our system through smartphone app on a real-world BSS[1] in beta-test phase for 30 days

existing TRUCKS repositioning rather than as standalone policy. To take this into consideration, we compare the policies when deployed in addition to an already running TRUCKS policy allocated with 150 €, (i.e., equivalent of 3 hours of trucks that would run between 12:00 p.m. and 3:00 p.m). Apart from comparing to TRUCKS, we also compare our proposed system with IDS running different baseline pricing mechanisms instead of DBP-UCB: i) MINIMUM mechanism selects the minimum price available c_{min}; ii) MEAN mechanism offers the mean price obtained from the user's cost distribution. Our results in Figure 4(a) indicate that the proposed IDS with DBP-UCB pricing mechanism compares favorably w.r.t. TRUCKS, as well as other baseline pricing mechanisms. The performance of DBP-UCB almost matches OPT-FIX, as it converges very fast to the optimal price in less than a day of simulation time. Note that allocating more budget B to TRUCKS is simply equivalent to running policy with total of $B + 150$ € budget.

Budget tradeoff between IDS and TRUCKS. This experiment aims to understand how to trade off budget investment between TRUCKS and the incentives system. Figure 4(b) illustrates that the best service levels are achieved when the two repositioning services are run in complement to each other, and shows the high potential of adding our incentives system to the existing BSS infrastructure. In fact, these two policies have complementary effects. While the trucks tackle the imbalances at a macro level by moving the bicycles from a part of the city to the other, the effect of the incentives system is rather dynamic and at a micro level, incorporating the traffic flow and fluctuating demands.

Varying user participation. The previous experiments assume that all the BSS customers participate in the incentives system. However, this assumption may not hold in reality, especially in the testing phase of the system. With the same setup as used in Figure 4(a), we vary the participation rate of users between 0% and 100%, with budget fixed at 300 €. Figure 4(c) illustrates that the proposed system can surpass standalone TRUCKS policy with 20% participation.

Deployment

We deployed our incentives system on a real-world BSS in a beta-test phase for a period of 30 days in a city of Europe, in collaboration with a large scale bike sharing company[1]. We designed a smartphone app as an interface between the users and the incentives system. The system itself was integrated with the BSS infrastructure through their APIs. The participants were offered monetary incentives for the bike pickup scenario, with payments directly transferred to the customer accounts. Given the small pool of participants in the testing phase limiting the process of learning, we adopted a simple pricing mechanism based on OPT-FIX. Using the approximate users' cost distribution, denoted as $\tilde{F}$, obtained through the survey study, we computed the approximation of the optimal price $\tilde{p}^{\text{OPT}}$ using Equation 1 by replacing F with $\tilde{F}$. We now present the findings from this deployment.

Participation. Figure 5(a) represents the histogram of the number of incentives obtained by each participant. The result shows that most participants collected five or less incentives each while few particularly active users collected more than 50 incentives each.

Reaction to incentives. In total, the acceptance rate of the incentive offers over all participants was about 60%. Here, the rejection of an offer corresponds to the case of a user rejecting an incentive to pick up a bike at an offered target station and starting a rental somewhere else. Furthermore, as we recorded the information about the user's location when an offer is made, we can compute the distance that the users were required to walk for a given offer. Figure 5(b) shows the probability of an offer being accepted as decreasing with respect to the distance to be walked and matches closely with the survey data in Figure 3(b).

Time and space distribution. Figure 5(c) shows that incentives were not collected equally throughout the day, but most incentives were collected during the afternoon and at late morning. In Figure 2, the diameter of each station is proportional to the number of incentives collected by users at that station. The map shows that the majority of incentives were paid out at stations in the city center.

Conclusions

There is much potential in intelligent and self-sustainable systems that incentivize and empower their users to actively engage in the system processes. In this paper, we presented the architecture of an incentives system to engage BSS users in the bike repositioning process. We worked in collaboration with a bike sharing company, designed and built a working system integrated with the BSS infrastructure. We investigated the incentive compatibility of our system, and also designed a dynamic pricing mechanism DBP-UCB to optimize the efficiency of the incentives system. We evaluated the proposed system through extensive simulations using historical and user survey data, and deployed it through a smartphone app for a period of 30 days.

Acknowledgments. We'd like to thank bike sharing operator MVG-meinRad for promoting the surveys and trial to their customers, and ElectricFeel Mobility Systems for providing access to their software platform and infrastructure for running the trial. This research is supported in part by SNSF grant 200021_137971 and Nano-Tera.ch program as part of the Opensense II project.

References

Borgnat, P.; Abry, P.; Flandrin, P.; Céline, R.; Rouquier, J.-B.; and Fleury, E. 2011. Shared bicycles in a city: a signal processing and data analysis perspective. *Advances in Complex Systems* 14:415–438.

Büttner, J.; Mlasowsky, H.; and Birkholz, T. 2011. Optimising Bike Sharing in European Cities - A Handbook.

Cepolina, E. M., and Farina, A. 2012. Urban car sharing: An overview of relocation strategies. *WIT Transactions on the Built Environment* 419–431.

Chemla, D.; Meunier, F.; and Pradeau, T. 2013. Self-service bike sharing systems: simulation, repositioning, pricing.

Chemla, D.; Meunier, F.; and Wolfler Calvo, R. 2013. Bike sharing systems: Solving the static rebalancing problem. *Discrete Optimization* 10:120–146.

Clemente, M.; Fanti, M. P.; Mangini, A. M.; and Ukovich, W. 2013. The vehicle relocation problem in car sharing systems: modeling and simulation in a petri net framework. In *Application and Theory of Petri Nets and Concurrency*. Springer. 250–269.

Côme, E., and Oukhellou, L. 2012. Model-based count series clustering for Bike-sharing system usage mining, a case study with the Vélib' system of Paris. *Transportation Research-Part C Emerging Technologies* 22:88.

Correia, G. H. d. A., and Antunes, A. P. 2012. Optimization approach to depot location and trip selection in one-way carsharing systems. *Transportation Research Part E: Logistics and Transportation Review* 48:233–247.

Fricker, C., and Gast, N. 2012. Incentives and regulations in bike-sharing systems with stations of finite capacity. *arXiv preprint arXiv:1201.1178* 1–25.

Froehlich, J.; Neumann, J.; and Oliver, N. 2009. Sensing and Predicting the Pulse of the City through Shared Bicycling. *Twenty-First International Joint Conference on Artificial Intelligence (IJCAI-09)* 1420–1426.

George, D. K., and Xia, C. H. 2011. Fleet-sizing and service availability for a vehicle rental system via closed queueing networks. *European Journal of Operational Research* 211:198–207.

GoDCgo. 2011. Capital Bikeshare's Reverse Rider Rewards. http://www.godcgo.com/reverse-rider-rewards.aspx.

Han, Y.; Côme, E.; and Oukhellou, L. 2014. Towards Bicycle Demand Prediction of Large-Scale Bicycle Sharing System. In *Transportation Research Board 93rd Annual Meeting*.

Kaltenbrunner, A.; Meza, R.; Grivolla, J.; Codina, J.; and Banchs, R. 2010. Urban cycles and mobility patterns: Exploring and predicting trends in a bicycle-based public transport system. *Pervasive and Mobile Computing* 6:455–466.

Kek, A. G. H.; Cheu, R. L.; Meng, Q.; and Fung, C. H. 2009. A decision support system for vehicle relocation operations in carsharing systems. *Transportation Research Part E: Logistics and Transportation Review* 45:149–158.

Lai, T. L., and Robbins, H. 1985. Asymptotically efficient adaptive allocation rules. *Advances in applied mathematics* 6(1):4–22.

Meddin, R., and DeMaio, P. 2014. The Bike-sharing World - First Week of June 2014. http://bike-sharing.blogspot.ch/2014/06/the-bike-sharing-world-first-week-of.html.

Nair, R., and Miller-Hooks, E. 2011. Fleet Management for Vehicle Sharing Operations. *Transportation Science* 45:524–540.

Nair, R.; Miller-Hooks, E.; Hampshire, R. C.; and Bušić, A. 2013. Large-Scale Vehicle Sharing Systems: Analysis of Vélib'. *International Journal of Sustainable Transportation* 7:85–106.

Pfrommer, J.; Warrington, J.; Schildbach, G.; and Morari, M. 2014. Dynamic Vehicle Redistribution and Online Price Incentives in Shared Mobility Systems. *IEEE Intelligent Transportation Systems Magazine*.

Rainer-Harbach, M.; Papazek, P.; Hu, B.; and Raidl, G. R. 2013. Balancing bicycle sharing systems: A variable neighborhood search approach. In *Evolutionary Computation in Combinatorial Optimization*. Springer. 121–132.

Raviv, T., and Kolka, O. 2013. Optimal inventory management of a bike-sharing station. *IIE Transactions* 45(10):1077–1093.

Sadilek, A.; Krumm, J.; and Horvitz, E. 2013. Crowdphysics: Planned and Opportunistic Crowdsourcing for Physical Tasks. *SEA* 536–545.

Schuijbroek, J.; Hampshire, R.; and van Hoeve, W.-J. 2013. Inventory rebalancing and vehicle routing in bike sharing systems.

Singer, Y. 2010. Budget feasible mechanisms. In *FOCS*, 765–774.

Singla, A., and Krause, A. 2013. Truthful incentives in crowdsourcing tasks using regret minimization mechanisms. In *WWW*, 1167–1178.

Vélib'. 2014. How it works: Vélib'. http://en.velib.paris.fr/How-it-works/Stations.

Waserhole, A.; Jost, V.; and Brauner, N. 2013. Pricing techniques for self regulation in Vehicle Sharing Systems. *Electronic Notes in Discrete Mathematics* 41:149–156.

A Simulator of Human Emergency Mobility following Disasters: Knowledge Transfer from Big Disaster Data

Xuan Song†, Quanshi Zhang†, Yoshihide Sekimoto†, Ryosuke Shibasaki†, Nicholas Jing Yuan‡ and Xing Xie‡

†Center for Spatial Information Science, The University of Tokyo, Japan

‡2Microsoft Research, P.R. China

{songxuan,zqs1022,sekimoto,shiba}@csis.u-tokyo.ac.jp, {nicholas.yuan,xing.xie}@microsoft.com

Abstract

The frequency and intensity of natural disasters has significantly increased over the past decades and this trend is predicted to continue. Facing these possible and unexpected disasters, understanding and simulating of human emergency mobility following disasters will become the critical issue for planning effective humanitarian relief, disaster management, and long-term societal reconstruction. However, due to the uniqueness of various disasters and the unavailability of reliable and large scale human mobility data, such kind of research is very difficult to be performed. Hence, in this paper, we collect big and heterogeneous data (e.g. 1.6 million users' GPS records in three years, 17520 times of Japan earthquake data in four years, news reporting data, transportation network data and etc.) to capture and analyze human emergency mobility following different disasters. By mining these big data, we aim to understand what basic laws govern human mobility following disasters, and develop a general model of human emergency mobility for generating and simulating large amount of human emergency movements. The experimental results and validations demonstrate the efficiency of our simulation model, and suggest that human mobility following disasters may be significantly more predictable and can be easier simulated than previously thought.

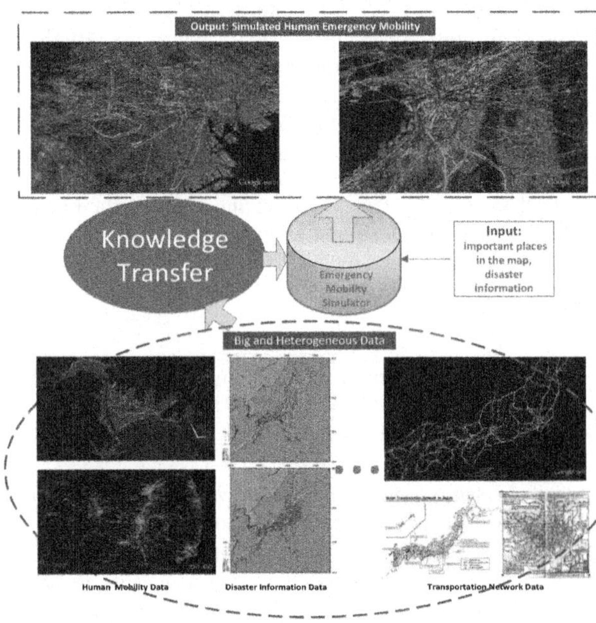

Figure 1: **Can we simulate human emergency mobility for any disaster, any place and any people?** By mining big and heterogeneous data, we aim to discover general knowledge and understand what basic laws govern human mobility following disasters. Can we develop a general model of human emergency mobility for generating or simulating large amount of human emergency movements following different disasters?

Introduction

Japan is one of the countries most affected by natural disasters. Two out of the five most expensive natural disasters in recent history have occurred in Japan, costing huge economic loss and large number of people death in the years 2011 and 1995 only. Meanwhile, according to Japan Meteorological Agency, there were over 10681 earthquakes above intensity one entire Japan in 2011 year only. These severe natural disasters usually cause large population movements and evacuations. Hence, understanding and simulating these movements following disasters are critical for planning effective humanitarian relief, disaster management, and long-term societal reconstruction. However, such kind of research is very difficult to be performed due to the fact that there is no reliable approach for accurately sensing human mobility. Recently, however, people's mobile phone data, GPS trajectories data, location-based online social networking data, and IC card data have emerged and increased explosively. The explosive increasing of these human mobile sensing data becomes the "Big Data", and offers a new way to circumvent methodological problems of earlier research for human behavior modeling because they offer high temporal and spatial resolution, are instantaneously available, have no interview bias, and provide longitudinal data for very large populations. Recenly, Song *et al.* (Song et al. 2014a; 2014b) collected data from 1.6 million GPS users in Japan

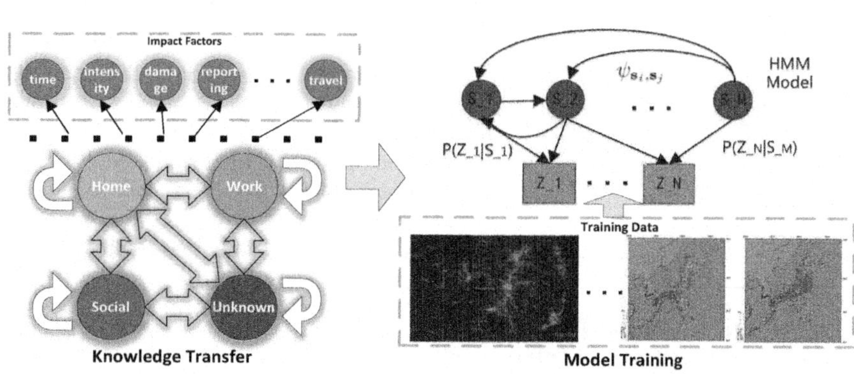

Figure 2: **Knowledge transfer and model development.** We model human activities and mobility following disasters as the random transition through its home, working location, social relationship as well as some unknown places (e.g. shelters or hotels), and the transition process will be impacted and influenced by various disaster factors. We develop a HMM based model, and utilize the big and heterogeneous data to train its parameters.

to mine and modeling human mobility during the 2011 Great East Japan Earthquake and Fukushima nuclear accident, and developed a model for predicting human behavior and mobility. However, due to the uniqueness of this disaster, their model is difficult to be applied to some different disasters (e.g. small scale one) and the places not affected by this disaster. Furthermore, their model can only be applied to the specific person that has the historical GPS records in the database. Meanwhile, due to the privacy concern, such kind of data is usually very sensitive and difficult to be published or released for further research purpose. Therefore, in this research, we aim to: *(1) discover knowledge from big disaster data and understand what basic laws govern human mobility following disasters. (2) develop a general model of human emergency mobility for generating or simulating large amount of human emergency movements following different disasters.*

In this paper, we collect big and heterogeneous data to capture and analyze human emergency mobility following different disasters in Japan (as shown in Figure 1). By mining these big data, we find that: even though human movement and mobility patterns following disasters have a high degree of freedom and variation, the majority of human mobility is based on random movement between a small set of important places. Hence, we model human activities and mobility following disasters as the random transition through its home, working location, social relationship as well as some unknown places (e.g. shelters or hotels). But the transition process will be impacted and influenced by various factors, such as intensity of earthquake, damage level, news reporting, current time, travel distance, travel time and etc. We develop a general model of human emergency behavior, and use the collected big human mobility data and disaster information data to learn how these factors will influence people's decisions. Finally, given a series of important places of people, disaster information and transportation network of the city or country, our training model can randomly simulate or generate human mobility following this disaster. Our work will have the following key characteristics that make it unique in the world:

- **Big and heterogeneous data:** 1.6 million users' GPS records in three years, 17520 times of Japan earthquake data in four years, news reporting data, transportation network data and etc.
- **A general model of human emergency mobility:** our model can randomly simulate or generate human mobility following disasters, it can be applied to any people, any place and any disaster.

The remainder of this paper is structured as follows: Section 2 introduces our big and heterogeneous data source. Section 3 describes the knowledge transfer from data and model development. Section 4 provides the details on human emergency mobility simulation and generation. Experimental results are presented in Section 5. Related work is briefly reviewed in Section 6, and the paper is finally summarized in Section 7.

Heterogeneous Data Source

In this research, we utilize big and heterogeneous data source to understand human mobility following disasters, and they can be summarized as follows:

- Human mobility data: we collected GPS records of approximately 1.6 million anonymized users throughout Japan from 1 August 2010 to 31 July 2013. To manage these data, we utilized five computer to build up a Hadoop cluster, which contained 32 cores, 32GB memory, 16TB storages, and was able to run 28 tasks at the same time. It can provide indexing, retrieval, editing and visualization services.
- Disaster information data (earthquake and tsunami): we collected 17520 times of earthquake data throughout Japan from 1 January 2010 to 31 December 2013. These data contains occurrence time, earthquake hypocentral location, earthquake magnitude, earthquake intensity for impacted places, damage level (1-7) (e.g. destroyed buildings and people death by the earthquake or tsunami) and etc.

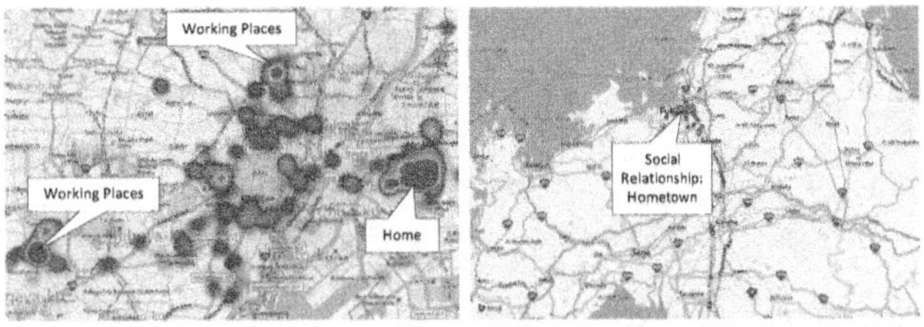

(a) Distribution of geographic location on woking days

(b) Distribution of geographic location on important holidays

Figure 3: **Distribution of geographic location for one of the authors.** This figure shows the distribution of geographic location for specific person (one of the authors of this paper) during normal times. The color denotes the probability of staying location of this person at a specific time period; warmer ones indicate higher probability. Figure (a) shows this distribution on working days, and Figure (b) shows the cases on some important holidays (e.g. national holiday, New Year Festival, Christmas day).

- Disaster reporting data: we collected government declarations as well as news reports from mainstream medias in Japan and all over the world for large-scale disasters (e.g 2011 Great East Japan Earthquake). Based on these information, we empirically divided these reporting and declarations into four levels to measure the disasters, e.g. one level means not serious from the reporting, and four level means extremely serious.
- Transportation network data: we collected the road network data and metro network data of main cities in Japan. These data contains road structure and POI information.

Knowledge Transfer and Model Development

By performing some empirical analysis on human mobility data following disasters, we find that: even though human movement and mobility patterns following disasters have a high degree of freedom and variation, the majority of human mobility is based on random movement between a small set of important places, such as home location, working location, social relationship (friends' house, hometown and etc.) and some unknown places (e.g. shelters, hotels and etc.). Meanwhile, these mobility patterns will also be impacted and influenced by various kinds of factors (as shown in Figure 2). For instance, if a small earthquake with low intensity occur at midnight, people may stay at home and go back to sleep. In contrast, if a big earthquake occur at midnight and cause some building destructions, people may screw out of the house and find some safe places to stay, but they need to consider the travel distance or travel time. But if a very huge earthquake (such as 2011 Great East Japan Earthquake) occur and become the composite disaster accompanied with many negative news reporting, people may leave their living city and find a safe place (e.g. hometown) far from the disaster. Hence, in this section, we aim to understand how these factors will influence and govern human mobility following disaster, and extract general knowledge of human disaster behaviors by mining big and heterogeneous data.

Important Places Discovery

To model and understand human behavior and mobility following disaster, we need to discover and recognize important places in peoples daily life, e.g. home, working places, and places of important social relationships (e.g. hometown, parents, relatives and good friends). In this research, we utilized the mobility data to compute distribution of geographic location (X. Song and Shibasaki 2013b) for individual people (as shown in Figure 3). Based on the analysis of this distribution with time, it is easy for us to find and recognize some important places of individual people. For example, the highest frequency staying place by daylight on working day is usually peoples working place, and the one in night is usually peoples home (as shown in Figure 3-a). Meanwhile, some high frequency visited places on the weekend and some important holiday (e.g. national holiday, New Year Festival, Christmas day) are recognized as the peoples important social relationships (as shown in Figure 3-b).

Model Development and Learning

Preliminaries: Consider a set of individual people's activities $Activity = \{act_1, act_2, ..., act_n\}$ after the disasters, and each activity $act_i = \mathbf{l}_1 \rightarrow \mathbf{l}_2 \rightarrow ... \rightarrow \mathbf{l}_m$ denotes a series of m location transfer with the disaster information. Each location $\mathbf{l}$ is a tuple in the form of $\mathbf{l} =< uid, time, label, latitude, longtitude, distance, intensity, damage, reporting >$, where uid is the id of people, $time$ is the current time, $label$ specify the people's important places, such as home location, working location, places of important social relationships and unknown places. Here, $latitude$ and $longtitude$ specify the geographic position of this location, $distance$ is the distance from the earthquakes, $intensity$ is the seismic or intensity scale of the earthquake at this location, $damage$ is the damage level of this location, and $reporting$ is the government declarations and news reporting level. Therefore, our goal is to learn a general model from $Activity$. Given a series of people's important places and disaster information, we want to randomly simulate or generate people's location transition sequences with the probability.

HMM based Model: In this study, given a set of disaster information $\mathbf{Z} = \{\mathbf{z}_1, \mathbf{z}_2, ...\mathbf{z}_N\}$, such as intensity of earthquake, damage level, news reporting, current time, travel distance, travel time, we model human activities and mobility following disasters as the random transition through a series of state $\mathbf{S} = \{\mathbf{s}_1, \mathbf{s}_2, ..., \mathbf{s}_M\}$, such as home location, working location, social relationship, some unknown places. In this study, we use hidden Markov model (HMM) (J. Ye and Cheng 2013; Zucchini and MacDonald 2009) to model dependency between these states, and the overall behavior model with its graphical representation is shown in Figure 2.

In our study, the following three key parameter components of HMM model need to be learned: (1) initial state probability $\phi_{\mathbf{s}_i}$ for each hidden states $\mathbf{s}_i \in \mathbf{S}$; (2) state transition probability $\psi_{\mathbf{s}_i,\mathbf{s}_j}$ from the hidden states $\mathbf{s}_i$ to $\mathbf{s}_j$; and (3) state-dependent output probability $P(\mathbf{z}_j|\mathbf{s_i})$, which determines the probability of the people's mobility $\mathbf{z}_j \in \mathbf{Z}$ given the hidden behavior state $\mathbf{s}_i \in \mathbf{S}$.

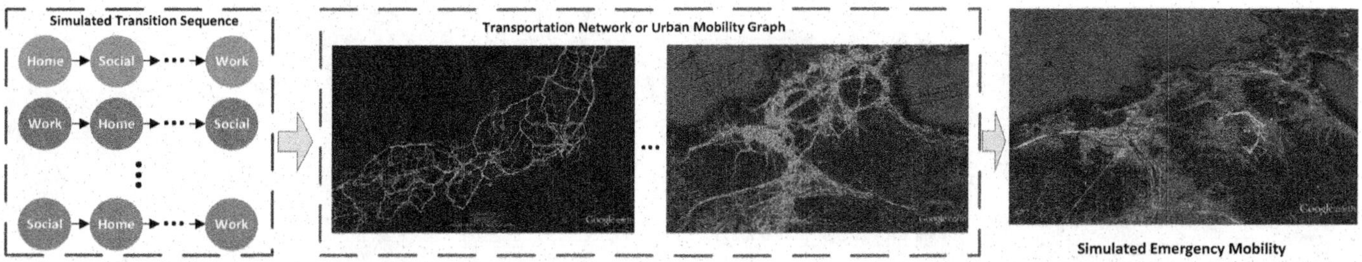

Figure 4: **Emergency mobility simulation.** Based on our training HMM model, we randomly simulate the location transition sequences. Then we utilize the transportation network or pre-trained urban mobility model to plan the traveling routes, and finally generate the human emergency movements following disasters.

Model Learning: To learn the overall behavior model, we need to estimate the key parameters of HMM as the discussion above, and a suitable solution is to use EM approach which aims at maximizing the likelihood of the location transfer sequences. In our study, the overall likelihood should be summed over all possible location transfer through the underlying hidden states, and is able to be computed by:

$$P(\mathbf{Z}_{1:T}) = \sum_{\mathbf{S}_1=\mathbf{s}_1}^{\mathbf{s}_M} \cdots \sum_{\mathbf{S}_T=\mathbf{s}_1}^{\mathbf{s}_M} \phi_{\mathbf{S}_1} \prod_{t=2}^{T} \psi_{\mathbf{S}_{t-1},\mathbf{S}_t} \prod_{t=1}^{T} P(\mathbf{Z}_t|\mathbf{S}_t). \tag{1}$$

Here, we assume the HMM is time-homogeneous, and state transition probabilities and state-dependent output probabilities do not change with time t.

According to (Zucchini and MacDonald 2009), we reformulate Equation (1) as:

$$P(\mathbf{Z}_{1:T}) = \Phi \mathcal{P}_{\mathbf{Z}_1} \Psi \mathcal{P}_{\mathbf{Z}_2} \ldots \Psi \mathcal{P}_{\mathbf{Z}_T} \mathbf{1}^\top, \tag{2}$$

which is expressed by matrix multiplications to reduce the computational cost. Here, Φ is a $1 \times M$ initial state distribution vector, Ψ is a $M \times M$ hidden state transition matrix where $\Psi_{ij} = \psi_{\mathbf{s}_i,\mathbf{s}_j}$, and $\mathcal{P}_{\mathbf{Z}_T}$ is a $M \times M$ diagonal matrix with $P(\mathbf{Z}_t|\mathbf{s}_i)$ on the diagonal and other entries as 0. Then we can use Baum-Welch algorithm (Baum et al. 1970) to estimate the hidden state transition probabilities and the state-dependent output probabilities.

To decide the right number of hidden states M in learning the HMM, we use *Bayesian Information Criterion* (BIC) (Schwarz and others 1978) to evaluate the HMM with different state numbers, and a smaller BIC value always leads to better model fitness.

Emergency Mobility Simulation

Given a series of important places of people and the disaster information, we aim to randomly simulate and generate its emergency mobility following this disaster (as shown in Figure 4). There are mainly two stages for the simulation process: (1) based on the training HMM behavior model, we randomly generate location transition through its important places; (2) given the location transition sequences, we use the transportation network or pre-trained urban mobility graph (Song et al. 2014a) to plan the traveling routes. Hence, in this section, we will present details on how to simulate human emergency mobility following different disasters.

Location Transition Simulation

To randomly generate person's location transition sequence following disasters, we utilize particle filter (Doucet, Godsill, and Andrieu 2000) approach to simulate this process. The basic idea behind a particle filter is very simple. Starting with a weighted set of samples $\{w_t^{(k)}, \mathbf{s}_t^{(k)}\}_{k=1}^K$ approximately distributed according to $p(\mathbf{s}_{t-1}|\mathbf{z}_{t-1})$, new samples are generated from a suitably designed proposal distribution $q(\mathbf{s}_t|\mathbf{s}_{t-1}, \mathbf{z}_t)$. To maintain a consistent sample, the new importance weights are set to

$$w_t^{(k)} \propto w_{t-1}^{(k)} \frac{p(\mathbf{z}_t|\mathbf{s}_t^{(k)})\psi_{\mathbf{s}_t^{(k)},\mathbf{s}_{t-1}^{(k)}}}{q(\mathbf{s}_t^{(k)}|\mathbf{s}_{t-1}^{(k)}, \mathbf{z}_t)}, \sum_{k=1}^{K} w_t^{(k)} = 1. \tag{3}$$

Hence, the overall simulation process is present as follows:

1. Initialization:
Generate K weighted set of samples $\{w_t^{(k)}, \mathbf{s}_t^{(k)}\}_{k=1}^K$ from the learnt initial state probability $\phi_{\mathbf{s}_i}$ of our trained HMM.

2. Resampling:
Resample K particles from the particle set $\mathbf{S}_t$ using weights of respective particles.

3. Location Transition Simulation:
Simulate the state transition of the particle set $\mathbf{S}_t$ with the learnt transition probability $\psi_{\mathbf{s}_i,\mathbf{s}_j}$ of our trained HMM.

4. Weighting:
Recalculate the weight of $\mathbf{S}_t$ by using Equation (3). Here, we utilize the learnt observation model $P(\mathbf{Z}_{1:t}|\mathbf{S}_t)$ of our trained HMM as the proposal distribution in Equation (3).

5. Behavior Selection :
Select person's transition behavior by finding the highest weight one in the particle set $\mathbf{S}_t$.

6. Iteration:
Iterate Steps 2, 3, 4, and 5 until convergence.

Mobility Simulation

Given the location transition sequences of people following disasters, there are two ways to simulate its traveling routes. For the small earthquakes, we can directly use the transportation network (e.g. road network data and metro network) of cities to plan people's traveling routes. But for the large-scale earthquakes, the public transportation systems are usually unavailable. Hence, we use the pre-trained urban mobility graph (Song et al. 2014a) to plan the traveling routes (as shown in Figure 4).

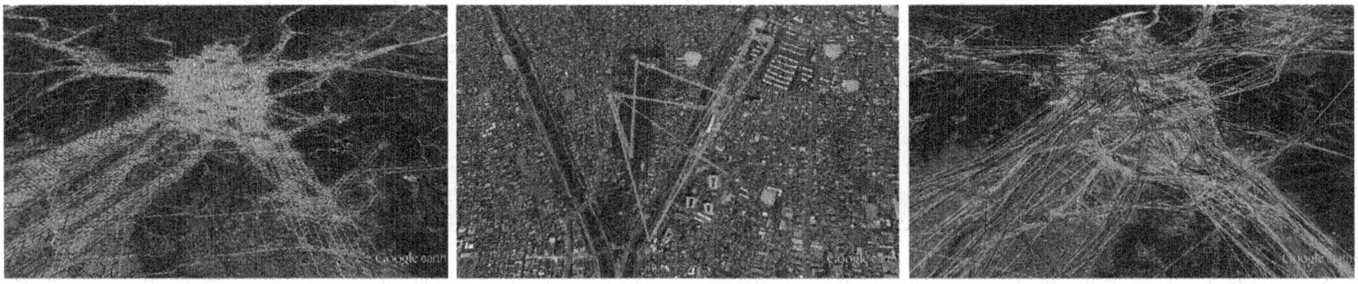

(a) Urban mobility graph for Kyoto (b) Simulation results of single person (c) Simulation results of large number of persons

Figure 5: **Visualization of simulation results.** This figure shows the example of our simulation results for Kyoto. Here, we use the pre-trained urban mobility model to plan the routes. Fig.a shows the urban mobility graph of Kyoto. Fig.b shows the example of simulation results for the single person. Fig.c shows the example of simulation results for large number of persons in Kyoto.

To effectively plan people's traveling routes by considering various disaster factors, we train a decision model by using Markov Decision Process (MDPs) (Puterman 1994). In our problem, the transportation network or urban mobility graph provide us a deterministic MDP, the nodes are able to be seem as *state*, the edge is the *action*, and the *path* is the people's movements following the earthquake. These movements are parameterized by their path feature $\mathbf{f}_\zeta$. For instance, a person's movements can be described by: travel through node A ($dens = 0.37$, $type = residential$) to node B ($dens = 0.58$, $type = commercial$), and finally stayed in node C ($dens = 0.75$, $type = administrative$) with route 1 ($frq = 0.37$, $time = 0.58$) ($A \rightarrow B$) and route 2 ($frq = 0.29$, $time = 0.62$)($B \rightarrow C$), where $dens$ is the region population density, $type$ the region types (e.g. residential, commercial and etc.), frq the travel frequency of the route, $time$ is the travel time of the route. Hence, we need to utilize all the population trajectories to train a MDPs model that is able to optimally demonstrate these people's movements after the earthquake. Obviously, this is an *Inverse Reinforcement Learning* problem. In this study, we utilize the *Maximum Entropy Inverse Reinforcement Learning* algorithm (B. D. Ziebart and Dey 2008b; 2008a) to train the overall decision model.

Finally, given person's location transition sequence, its mobility can be easily simulated by performing the Markov model route planning. In our study, we assume that people usually will find a safe and fast route (e.g. high frequency visited route and low travel time) for evacuation following the disasters. Hence, we employ the route planning using the destination-conditioned Markov Model (Simmons et al. 2006). This model recommends the most probable route satisfying origin and destination constraints.

Experimental Results

Based on the disaster information data (space and time), we selected human movements (GPS trajectory) in 24 hours following each earthquake from our human mobility database, and the selected geotropical regions were the places where the earthquake intensity was above one. These GPS trajectories, the related disaster information and the disaster reporting information formed the training and testing dataset. We randomly selected 80% of the data for the model training, and used the remaining 20% data for testing and evaluation. We then converted the GPS trajectories in the training set to the sequence of important places transition as the discussion in Section 3 to prepare the training samples. In the training process, we found that the majority of training data were from some very small-scale earthquake (e.g. earthquake intensity is below 3). To balance the training samples of large and small scale disasters, we randomly selected 20% data from small-scale disasters set, and use them with large-scale disaster data to form the new training sample dataset. In this section, we present experimental results and evaluation of model for human emergency mobility simulation.

Simulation Results

To simulate human emergency mobility following disasters, users need firstly to select the important places in the map, and then input the disaster information (e.g. occurrence time, earthquake hypocentral location, earthquake intensity at this region, damage level and etc.), and our simulator can automatically simulate possible movements of this person. To show the performance, here we used the real information in the testing dataset as the input. Figure 5 shows the sample results of our simulator. From Fig.5-b, we can see that our simulation results are very similar the real movements of this person following a specific disaster.

Performance Evaluation

Evaluation metrics: To evaluate the accuracy of the simulated mobility of people, we used three different metrics discussed in (B. D. Ziebart and Dey 2008a). The first compared the model's most likely simulated trajectory (trajectory with the highest probability) with the actual demonstrated trajectory in the testing set and evaluated the amount of route distance shared. The second shows what percentage of the testing trajectories match at least 90% (distance) with the model's simulated one. The final metric measures the average log probability of mobility in the training set under the given model.

Table 1: Performance Evaluation

Algorithm	Matching	90% Matching	Log-Prob
Our Model	65.26%	45.33%	-7.13
MF	58.23%	39.62%	-7.97
GM	51.22%	33.16%	-8.21
PMM	63.18%	42.69%	-7.33

Baseline models: We considered three non-trivial baseline models for comparison. (1) *Most Frequented Location Model (MF)*: For every hour of the day, this model simulates the most likely (most frequent visited) place of a particular people. Despite its simplicity, this model is very strong baseline. Lu *et al.* (X. Lu and Holme 2012) also used this model to predict population mobility after the 2010 Haitian earthquake. (2) *Gaussian Model (GM):* This model has been proposed by Gonzales *et al.* (MC. Gonzalez and Barabasi 2008), and it models human movements as a stochastic process centered around a single point. This model is static in time and captures the scale of a person's movements more than anything else. (3) *Periodic Mobility Model (PMM):* This model is built on the intuition that the majority of human movement is based on periodic movement between a small set of locations. As the state-of-the-art methods, it has been proposed by Cho *et al.* (E. Cho and Leskovec 2011), which is able to predict the locations and dynamics of future human movements. For training these baseline models, we retrieved the GPS data in three months from our mobility database by using person ID in the testing set, and use them to train the final model. Then, we used these baseline models to predict human next visited places following the disasters, and then used the transportation network to plan the final traveling routes of people.

Performance evaluation: We compared the performance of our model with the performance of the baselines, and table 1 shows their performance. The baseline models are trained by particular people's historical movements, and can only be applied to specific person. In contrast, our model is a general mobility model, and can be applied to any person. From this table, we can see that the performance of our model is very similar to PMM model, and has a much better performance than the other two models. Obviously, our simulator is more powerful for simulating human emergency mobility than these competing methods that are used for predicting or simulating human mobility during normal times.

Related Work

Recently, a number of studies on human mobility patterns during disasters have been proposed (M. Moussaid and Helbing 2009; Hahm and Lee 2009), mainly focusing on small-scale and short-term emergencies (e.g. crowd panics and fires). However, research on the dynamics of population movements on a national scale during large-scale disasters (e.g. earthquakes, tsunamis, and hurricanes) is very limited (X. Lu and Holme 2012), likely the result of difficulties in collecting representative longitudinal data in places where infrastructure and social order have collapsed (JP. Bagrow and Barabasi 2011; L. Bengtsson 2011) and where study populations are moving across vast geographical areas (X. Lu and Holme 2012). Recently, the big auto-mobile sensor data (e.g. mobile phone data, GPS data, location-based social network data and etc.) offer a new way to analyze and model population movements for very large populations (CM. Song and Barabasi 2010; MC. Gonzalez and Barabasi 2008; X. Lu and Holme 2012; JP. Bagrow and Barabasi 2011; C. Song and Barabasi 2010; N. Eagle and Lazer 2009). Meanwhile, human mobility or trajectory data mining (Backstrom, Sun, and Marlow 2010; Giannotti et al. 2007; E. Cho and Leskovec 2011; J. Ye and Cheng 2013; Z. Li and Nye 2010; Scellato, Noulas, and Mascolo 2011; X. Song and Shibasaki 2013a; 2013b; Yuan et al. 2013) have become a very hot topic in various research fields.

More Recently, Song *et al.* (Song et al. 2014a; 2014b) collected the data from 1.6 million GPS users in Japan to mine and model population evacuations or mobility during the 2011 Great East Japan Earthquake and Fukushima nuclear accident, and demonstrated that the prediction of large population movements or individual person after large-scale disaster was possible. However, due to the uniqueness of this disaster, their model is difficult to be applied to the places outside of Japan or places not affected by this disaster. Furthermore, their model can only be applied to the specific person that has the historical GPS records in the database. Thus, in this research, we firstly propose a general model of human emergency mobility that can be applied to any people, any place and any disaster.

Conclusion

In this paper, we collect big and heterogeneous data to capture and analyze human emergency mobility following different disasters in Japan, and develop a general model of human emergency mobility for generating or simulating large amount of human emergency movements following disasters. The experimental results and validations demonstrate the efficiency of our simulation model, and suggest that human mobility following disasters may be easier simulated than previously thought.

We note the limitations within our study. Because our training data was very huge, we found that with the increasing amount of training data, the performance of our model will face some bottlenecks. In the future, we will try to build up Deep Belief Net and utilize the deep learning technology to model large amount of human emergency movements.

Acknowledgements

This work was partially supported by Grant-in-Aid for Young Scientists (26730113) of Japan's Ministry of Education, Culture, Sports, Science, and Technology (MEXT), Grant of Microsoft Research, Grant of Japan's Ministry of Land, Infrastructure, Transport and Tourism (MLIT), and DIAS/GRENE project of MEXT. We specially thank ZENRIN DataCom CO., LTD for their supporting.

References

B. D. Ziebart, A. Maas, J. B., and Dey, A. K. 2008a. Maximum entropy inverse reinforcement learning. *Proc. of AAAI Conference on Artificial Intelligence (AAAI)* 1433–1438.

B. D. Ziebart, A. Maas, J. B., and Dey, A. K. 2008b. Navigate like a cabbie: Probabilistic reasoning from observed context-aware behavior. *Proc. of Ubicomp.* 322–331.

Backstrom, L.; Sun, E.; and Marlow, C. 2010. Find me if you can: improving geographical prediction with social and spatial proximity. In *Proceedings of the 19th international conference on World wide web*, 61–70. ACM.

Baum, L. E.; Petrie, T.; Soules, G.; and Weiss, N. 1970. A maximization technique occurring in the statistical analysis of probabilistic functions of markov chains. *The annals of mathematical statistics* 164–171.

C. Song, T. Koren, P. W., and Barabasi, A. 2010. Modelling the scaling properties of human mobility. *Nature Physics* 6:818–823.

CM. Song, ZH. Qu, N. B., and Barabasi, A. 2010. Limits of predictability in human mobility. *Science* 327:1018–1021.

Doucet, A.; Godsill, S.; and Andrieu, C. 2000. On sequential monte carlo sampling methods for bayesian filtering. *Statistics and computing* 10(3):197–208.

E. Cho, S. A. M., and Leskovec, J. 2011. Friendship and mobility: User movement in location-based social networks. *Proc. of ACM SIGKDD* 1082–1090.

Giannotti, F.; Nanni, M.; Pinelli, F.; and Pedreschi, D. 2007. Trajectory pattern mining. In *Proceedings of the 13th ACM SIGKDD international conference on Knowledge discovery and data mining*, 330–339. ACM.

Hahm, J., and Lee, J. 2009. Human errors in evacuation behavior during a traumatic emergency using a virtual fire. *Cyberpsychol Behavior* 12:98–98.

J. Ye, Z. Z., and Cheng, H. 2013. What's your next move: User activity prediction in location-based social networks. *Proc. of SIAM International Conference on Data Mining (SDM)*.

JP. Bagrow, D. W., and Barabasi, A. 2011. Collective response of human populations to large-scale emergencies. *Plos ONE* 6.

L. Bengtsson, X. Lu, A. T. R. G. J. v. S. 2011. Improved response to disasters and outbreaks by tracking population movements with mobile phone network data: A post-earthquake geospatial study in haiti. *PLoS Medical* 8.

M. Moussaid, S. Garnier, G. T., and Helbing, D. 2009. Collective information processing and pattern formation in swarms, flocks, and crowds. *Top Cogn. Sci.* 1:469–497.

MC. Gonzalez, C. H., and Barabasi, A. 2008. Understanding individual human mobility patterns. *Nature* 453:779–782.

N. Eagle, A. P., and Lazer, D. 2009. Inferring friendship network structure by using mobile phone data. *Proc. of the National Academy of Sciences of USA (PNAS)* 106:15274–15278.

Puterman, M. L. 1994. *Markov Decision Processes: Discrete Stochastic Dynamic Programming*. Wiley-Interscience.

Scellato, S.; Noulas, A.; and Mascolo, C. 2011. Exploiting place features in link prediction on location-based social networks. In *Proceedings of the 17th ACM SIGKDD international conference on Knowledge discovery and data mining*, 1046–1054. ACM.

Schwarz, G., et al. 1978. Estimating the dimension of a model. *The annals of statistics* 6(2):461–464.

Simmons, R.; Browning, B.; Zhang, Y.; and Sadekar, V. 2006. Learning to predict driver route and destination intent. In *Intelligent Transportation Systems Conference, 2006. ITSC'06. IEEE*, 127–132. IEEE.

Song, X.; Zhang, Q.; Sekimoto, Y.; and Shibasaki, R. 2014a. Intelligent system for urban emergency management during large-scale disaster. In *Twenty-Eighth AAAI Conference on Artificial Intelligence*.

Song, X.; Zhang, Q.; Sekimoto, Y.; and Shibasaki, R. 2014b. Prediction of human emergency behavior and their mobility following large-scale disaster. In *Proceedings of the 20th ACM SIGKDD international conference on Knowledge discovery and data mining*, 5–14. ACM.

X. Lu, L. B., and Holme, P. 2012. Predictability of population displacement after the 2010 haiti earthquake. *Proc. of the National Academy of Sciences of USA (PNAS)* 109:11576–11581.

X. Song, Q. Zhang, Y. S. T. H. S. U., and Shibasaki, R. 2013a. Intelligent system for human behavior analysis and reasoning following large-scale disasters. *IEEE Intelligent Systems* 28:35–42.

X. Song, Q. Zhang, Y. S. T. H. S. U., and Shibasaki, R. 2013b. Modeling and probabilistic reasoning of population evacuation during large-scale disaster. *Proc. of 19th SIGKDD conference on Knowledge Discovery and Data Mining (KDD)* 1231–1239.

Yuan, J.; Zheng, Y.; Xie, X.; and Sun, G. 2013. T-drive: Enhancing driving directions with taxi drivers' intelligence. *Knowledge and Data Engineering, IEEE Transactions on* 25(1):220–232.

Z. Li, B. Ding, J. H. R. K., and Nye, P. 2010. Mining periodic behaviors for moving objects. *Proc. of ACM SIGKDD* 1099–1108.

Zucchini, W., and MacDonald, I. L. 2009. *Hidden Markov models for time series: an introduction using R*. CRC Press.

Real-Time Predictive Optimization for Energy Management in a Hybrid Electric Vehicle

Alexander Styler and Illah Nourbakhsh

Abstract

With increasing numbers of electric and hybrid vehicles on the road, transportation presents a unique opportunity to leverage data-driven intelligence to realize large scale impact in energy use and emissions. Energy management in these vehicles is highly sensitive to upcoming power load on the vehicle, which is not considered in conventional reactive policies calculated at design time. Advancements in cheap sensing and computation have enabled on-board upcoming load predictions which can be used to optimize energy management. In this work, we propose and evaluate a novel, real-time optimization strategy that leverages predictions from prior data in a simulated hybrid battery-supercapacitor energy management task. We demonstrate a complete adaptive system that improves over the lifetime of the vehicle as more data is collected and prediction accuracy improves. Using thousands of miles of real-world data collected from both petrol and electric vehicles, we evaluate the performance of our optimization strategy with respect to our cost function. The system achieves performance within 10% of the optimal upper bound calculated using *a priori* knowledge of the upcoming loads. This performance implies improved battery thermal stability, efficiency, and longevity. Our strategy can be applied to optimize energy use in gas-electric hybrids, battery cooling in electric vehicles, and many other load-sensitive tasks in transportation.

Introduction

The advent of hybrid and electric vehicles yields a compelling new platform for artificial intelligence. These vehicles offer numerous high-level control opportunities managing state of charge, power fulfillment, battery temperature, and various other internal systems. As sensing and computation become cheaper, more complex intelligent controllers can be utilized to manage these high-level tasks in real-time. Intelligent control in these systems can yield improved energy efficiency, reduced emissions, and increased vehicle longevity.

In this work we demonstrate a data-driven adaptive optimization approach to manage energy in a passenger vehicle in real-time. Cheap sensing technology allows rich state data to be measured continuously, including GPS coordinates, speed, and power load. This state data can be leveraged to make real-time predictions of upcoming load based on prior observed state and load data. Given a set of independent sample load predictions, our approach calculates optimal controls in real-time with respect to the distribution defined by that set.

With accurate predictions, our approach produces near-optimal control decisions in hybrid vehicles, improving on existing fixed and reactive policy architectures. The load predictions are based on prior observed data, so the performance improves over the lifetime of a vehicle as more trips are recorded. Over time, data set coverage improves and unique trips become less likely. In practice, frequent commutes and errands comprise the majority of trips for many drivers and upcoming load is easily predicted. Continually collecting trip data over the lifetime of the vehicle enables long-term adaptation to changing routes, driver behaviors, and traffic trends.

We evaluate our optimization approach on a simulated hybrid battery-supercapacitor energy management task. In this vehicle, an electric battery acts as the primary energy source for vehicle range and operation. A supercapacitor is coupled to the system and acts as a small, highly efficient buffer. Either can be used to power the electric motor or receive energy from regenerative braking. The task is to minimize the sum of the current-squared on the battery pack, which helps improve battery pack longevity and thermal stability. The supercapacitor can be pre-charged from the battery before high-power loads such as steep hills or rapid accelerations. This task is analogous to other hybrid vehicle energy sourcing tasks, but is highly sensitive to prediction or control error due to the small size of the buffer.

We compare our predictive system to an prescient optimal controller that is given the upcoming demand *a priori*. Using real world data collected over thousands of miles of trips in several U.S. states, we test each control system in a hybrid electric vehicle simulation that can replay each trip. We compare a batch system that has all other data available to make predictions and an adaptive system that has only prior data chronologically and grows its data set over time.

Related Work

The rapid adoption of hybrid electric vehicles (HEVs) has sparked a great interest in the application of learning and intelligence to this domain. Several works have demonstrated that optimization of energy management in HEVs, using *a priori* knowledge of the power loads, results in superior performance over fixed reactive algorithms. The works show that either dynamic programming (Mosbech 1980) (Oprean et al. 1988) (Brahma, Guezennec, and Rizzoni 2000) or optimal control theory (Lyshevski and Yokomoto 1998) (Delprat, Guerra, and Rimaux 2002) can be used to effectively determine an upper bound on performance. The success of these retrospective optimizations highlights the importance of combining power load information with optimization techniques. These efforts motivated our approach to combine predictions of power loads with a dynamic programming optimization that can execute in real-time.

For real-time controllers, successful control has been demonstrated using rule-based and fixed point policies. An overview of existing HEV control strategies and papers is well covered in (Salmasi 2007). Rule based and reactive control can be successful using fuzzy logic controls or parameter optimization, but generally do not approach the bound provided by retrospective optimization. A popular approach to HEV control, known as Equivalent Consumption Minimization Strategy (ECMS), calculates future fuel expenditure required to offset the present battery energy expenditure. Fixed approaches are somewhat successful, but adaptive ECMS has been shown to perform very well for charge-sustaining mode (Musardo et al. 2005). These approaches are limited to charge sustaining mode. For plug-in HEVs, utilizing the full range of battery energy can pose significant improvement to fuel consumption, but at the cost depending on charge recovery from the grid while the car is parked. To optimally exploit charge depletion in a plug-in HEV, the total trip energy use and charging opportunities must be known.

Optimization of the energy management tasks using only the present vehicle state has limited potential for success. Driver variability and decision making has a large impact on the inputs and performance of these tasks. Work has shown that variability between drivers is significant (Ericsson 2000), and these variabilities have a large impact on vehicle operation (Holmén and Niemeier 1998) (LeBlanc et al. 1995). Additionally, researchers have shown that driver mood and behavior yield significant variability to load (De Vlieger, De Keukeleere, and Kretzschmar 2000). Due to the influence of the driver, optimization of vehicle management tasks ideally consider the total system including both the vehicle and driver. For instance, fuzzy logic controllers accounting for driver behavior patterns or trip type have shown marked improvement over reactive control (Langari and Won 2005), simply by tessellating categories of driver control and trip classification into a small number of discrete categories.

The importance of power loads and driver behavior for optimization has led many researchers to explore the potential of prediction. Significant work exploring the use of stochastic Markov chains to model driver behavior has achieved remarkable success (Opila et al. 2013) (Liu and Pentland 1997). These Markov chains can then be used to generate value functions and control policies using stochastic dynamic programming. While some work trains the Markov chains on a fixed set of federal driving data, the implementation by Cairano allows dynamic adaptation to new driving data over the life of the vehicle (Di Cairano et al. 2014). Furthermore, the work demonstrates that the optimization programming can be pushed offline, with simple table lookups at run-time

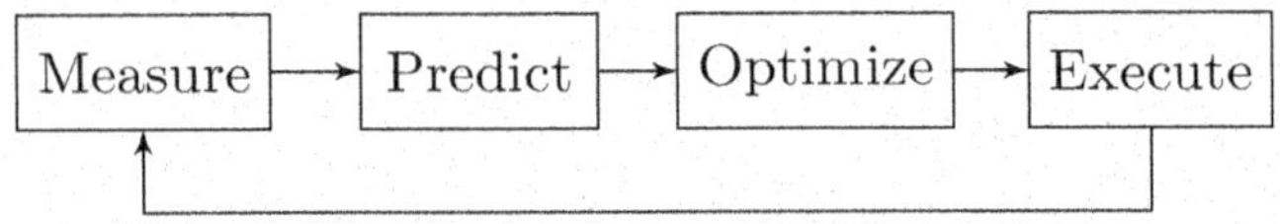

Figure 1: System Diagram of Control Loop. This four step process loop runs continuously, generating new controls as quickly as can be calculated. Changes in the measured state result in new predictions that are then used to calculate new controls.

to achieve rapid control. This leveraging of past data, real-time optimal control, and dynamic adaptation inspired similar goals for our system.

While these approaches use single stochastic Markov chains, work has shown that training examples are more informative as separate independent experts (Styler and Nourbakhsh 2013). Selecting a set of local predictions, based on vehicle state, can achieve better performance than global solutions or averaged solutions. The set of predictions maintains information about uncertainty of the upcoming load, while avoiding the averaging effects of a single stochastic Markov chain. We use a similar kNN matching approach to load prediction. Our optimization approach exploits these independent predictions to achieve real-time optimal control.

We extend prior work by creating a solution that can achieve real-time optimal control with respect to distributions defined by sets of predictions. We present a complete, dynamic system that learns driver behavior, traffic trends, and routes to optimize towards efficiency, longevity, or emissions.

Algorithm

The control algorithm chooses discrete controls based on its sensor readings of the vehicle state and environment. Due to the high frequency of changing inputs and demands on a vehicle, the algorithm must be able to react quickly in real-time. It operates as a simple control loop described in the diagram shown in Figure 1. The vehicle state measurement is an instantaneous snapshot of the vehicle state, and does not directly inform an optimal control decision. However, this state measurement can be informative of the upcoming loads. The algorithm matches the present state to similar historical states in its dataset. Recorded power loads that followed each of these historical states are used as predictions of upcoming load on the vehicle. Given these sample predictions, and a candidate set of discrete controls, and a cost function, the algorithm calculates the one-step optimal control that minimizes expected cost-to-go. This control is executed continuously while the process repeats, until a new control is calculated, as shown in Algorithm 1. Fast computation is important to achieve rapid, responsive controls that can react to new information.

If the actual upcoming sequence of power loads were known *a priori*, the cost-to-go function would be an accurate representation of total cost that would be incurred over the remainder of a trip given a state and control. Choosing the cost-to-go minimizing control at each timestep would be

Algorithm 1 High-Level Control Algorithm. The feature vector, x_t, is matched to historical states to get a weighted set of predictions, $\{Z_0, w_0\}...\{Z_k, w_k\}$. The corresponding precomputed cost-to-go functions J_i are fetched for each prediction Z_i. The control u_t that minimizes the one step cost plus the expectation of cost-to-go is executed

loop
  $x_t \leftarrow$ COMPUTEFEATUREVECTOR($sensorvalues$)
  $\{Z_0, d_0\}...\{Z_k, d_k\} \leftarrow$ KNN(x_t, k)
  $w_0...w_k \leftarrow 1/d_0...1/d_k$
  $w_0...w_k \leftarrow$NORMALIZE($w_0...w_k$)
  $\{J_0...J_k\} \leftarrow$ LOOKUPCTGFUN($Z_0...Z_k$)
  $\{u_t\} \leftarrow$ ARGMIN$_u(c(x_t, u) + \sum_i w_i J_i(x'_i, t+1))$
  EXECUTE(u_t)
end loop

optimal, barring any discretization error. For a predictive controller, it is unlikely that a single prediction would accurately describe the upcoming load. A set of weighted predictions is used to account for noise and uncertainty inherent in the driving domain from intersections, traffic, or driver behavior. These weighted predictions define the predicted distribution of upcoming load. When they are in agreement, the algorithm will be very aggressive with its controls due to the certainty of the distribution. When the predictions disagree, however, the controls will be more conservative to mitigate the uncertainty. For example, when a vehicle approaches an uncertain intersection, the controls will be conservative, considering each likely possibility. As the intersection is decided, confidence increases and the controls can be more aggressive.

Computing a cost-to-go function using Dynamic Programming can be very expensive as the number of states, controls, or timesteps increases. However, most vehicles have significant downtime, often overnight, which yields plenty of opportunity for offline computation. Our optimizer utilizes this explicitly by computing cost-to-go function tables offline that are simply referenced at run-time. This allows the agent to use rapid interleaved planning and execution without sacrificing solution quality.

State Measurement

The algorithm initially takes a measurement of the present vehicle state. The state space can consist of many potential features that can be measured with a handful of cheap sensors. Features accessed from the vehicle computer include speed, acceleration, and power demand. GPS coordinates, bearing, and time of day require external sensors. Such features are invaluable to make load predictions in vehicles. Hybrid and electric vehicles can also provide information on battery state of charge, temperature, and current load. Additional meta-features, such as recent variance in acceleration, may be calculated if needed. The system architect should instrument the vehicle and select the features necessary to make informed predictions using historical data. This feature vector representing the instantaneous vehicle state is then passed to a prediction system. More features that inform the upcoming duty can yield better predictions and performance.

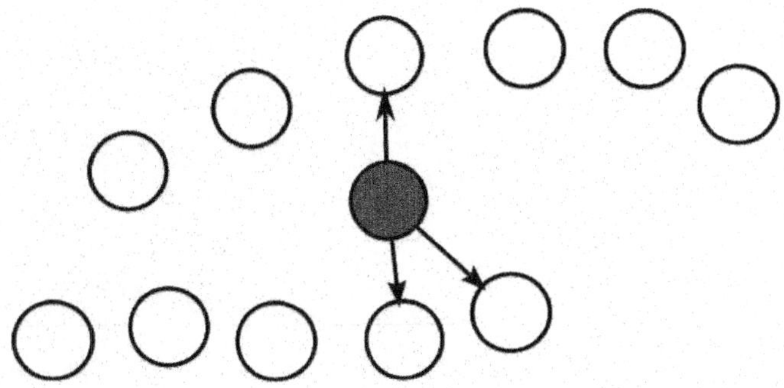

Figure 2: Example kNN State Matching. In this 2D example, the present state, in gray, matches to the three closest training examples in white. These states are from historical trips, and each contains an index into a specific time in that trip.

Load Prediction

Given this state feature vector, the algorithm then make predictions of the vehicle's upcoming power load. These predictions are difficult to calculate analytically, requiring a known route, topology data, driver behavior, and traffic information. Instead, the algorithm uses prior observed loads from previous trips as predictions. The present state vector is matched to similar states in the dataset, and the observed loads that followed those similar states are used as predictions. This is only accurate if upcoming load is informed by the instantaneous state vector. This assumption is central to the success of the algorithm: if the state measurement is independent of the upcoming load, the predictions will be useless.

The prediction step matches the present vehicle state to historical training data using a nearest neighbor comparison, as shown in Figure 2. The dataset is searched to find the k states that have the lowest weighted Euclidean distance, d, to the present state, x:

$$d = \sqrt{w_1(x_1 - z_1)^2 + ... + w_m(x_m - z_m)^2} \tag{1}$$

For each training state, z, the distance is computed in the feature space of dimensionality m. Each feature has an importance weight, w, that can be defined by the architect or tuned using a simple optimizer such as gradient descent. The features should be normalized to be on the same scale so that the relative weights have physical meaning when inspected.

Each of the k matches is assigned an importance weight calculated as the inverse of this distance. Therefore, training states with very similar features to the present state will have high importance weight associated with their prediction. The distance function can be modified to suit the application, but non-linear distance functions can preclude many kNN algorithms. For our linear distances, a standard kd-tree approach is used to minimize computation time for matching. The predictor returns the importance weight and indices identifying the source trip and time index for each training state match. Each of these indices references an exact point in time in a prior trip in the dataset, for which all power load data has been recorded. These weighted predictions are then passed to the optimizer system.

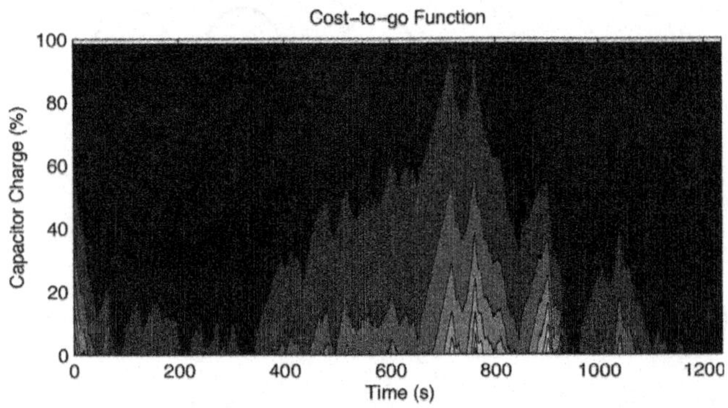

Figure 3: Example Cost-To-Go Function. The function encodes the expected cost-to-go for a given state at each timestep. Brighter values represent higher cost-to-go. In this example, an empty capacitor at 700s will result in very high cost being incurred.

Control Optimization

Given a set of predictions, we want to choose the optimal control that minimizes expected cost-to-go. For a discrete set of controls and discrete timesteps, a brute force approach that tests each control at each timestep is exponential in the lookahead time and quickly becomes intractable. Instead, for each separate prediction, we compute the cost-to-go function, $J(x,t)$, for each task state, x, and timestep, t, using Dynamic Programming and the Bellman Equation:

$$J(x,t) = \min_{u}[c(x,t,u) + \gamma J(x',t+1)] \tag{2}$$

Here, γ is a discount factor, x', denotes the state resulting from executing the control, u, and c represents the one-step cost function. The state transition function, H, is calculated using the predicted load, L_t, at each timestep in simulation:

$$x' = H(x,u,L_t) \tag{3}$$

For our tested domain, x is the state of charge of the capacitor. Our transition function is a simple model that calculates the change in state of charge for a given load power, L_t, and charging power, u.

An example cost-to-go function is shown in Figure 3. Using Dijkstra's Algorithm, computing this function and calculating all the state transitions requires $O(X*U*T)$ simulations, where X is the number of states, U the number of possible controls, and T the number of timesteps. It is unrealistic to compute these functions for multiple predictions at run-time.

However, each training example, or prior trip, has a fixed sequence of loads and thus fixed transitions. Therefore, this cost-to-go function can be precomputed offline and stored for each trip. For typical state and timestep resolutions, this can be done overnight with reasonable simulation complexity. At run-time, the fixed cost-to-go function for each trip matched by the predictor is simply loaded from memory. This pushes the bulk of optimization computation offline as these cost-to-go functions do not need to be computed on-the-fly.

Given a set of weighted predictions, $\{Z_0, w_0\}...\{Z_k, w_k\}$, and a starting state, x, the algorithm calculates the expected cost-to-go of each candidate discrete control and selects the best:

$$u_t = \arg\min_{u} c(x,t,u) + \mathbb{E}_Z[J(x',t')]$$
$$u_t = \arg\min_{u} c(x,t,u) + \sum_i (w_i J_i(x',t')) \tag{4}$$

Here, J_i represents the cost-to-go function for prediction Z_i and w_i denotes its weight; x' and t' represent the resulting state and timestep when executing control u given the state transition function for that prediction. The resulting u_t is the one-step cost-to-go optimal control with respect to the set of weighted predictions. As the cost-to-go and transition functions are precomputed offline, very little computation is required at each timestep.

Execution

The selected control that minimizes the expected cost-to-go is then executed. The control loop repeats, starting with a new state measurement, to calculate the next control.

Training

After a trip is complete, the observed data is added to the the training dataset. This training occurs offline when the vehicle is not in use, so as not to monopolize computational resources. This continual training enables the vehicle to adapt to new routes, traffic patterns, or driver behaviors.

For a trip, the vehicle states measured at each timestep are added to the kNN tree. Then, the loads over the course of the trip are used to calculate the state transition function. Using Dynamic Programming, this transition function is used to calculate the cost-to-go function, $J(x,t)$, at each state and timestep. This function is then added to the database to be referenced at run-time.

Experiment

We test performance on a simulated prototype hybrid electric vehicle (EV), using real-world power data from drivers. The simulated vehicle combines a high-power supercapacitor with a high-energy battery pack. The optimization task is to minimize current-squared on the battery pack by leveraging the capacitor as a buffer. We implement our algorithm and compare its performance at various parameterizations to an prescient optimal controller that has *a priori* knowledge of upcoming power loads. We additionally compare the performance of dynamic learning with leave-one-out batch learning.

Data Collection

To evaluate our algorithm, we used a dataset of real-world trips collected daily from a set of volunteer drivers. We needed repeated data collected from individual vehicles so we could test long-term learning and prediction. We constructed the dataset by instrumenting eight different petrol vehicles

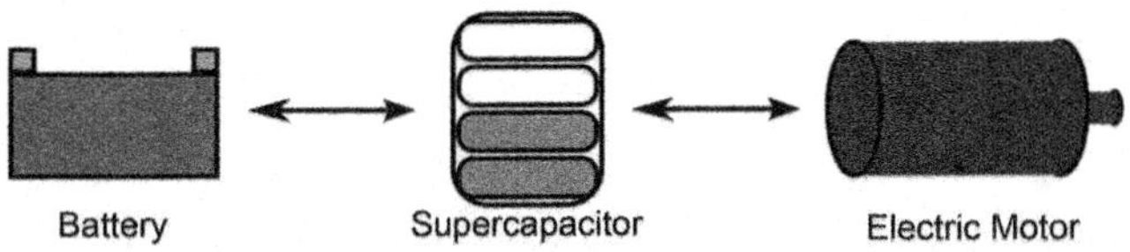

Figure 4: Simplified Diagram of Supercapacitor Buffer. The supercapacitor in this hybrid electric vehicle system can act as a buffer on the battery pack.

with sensors and collecting data from them over the course of ten months.

This data was run through a standard longitudinal vehicle model to calculate the expected power loads on an EV battery pack at each timestep. The model was calibrated using three different EVs by collecting real-world power load data at the terminals of their battery packs. The EVs were instrumented in the same way as the petrol vehicles, and the model was tuned to minimize RMS error between the calculated power load and observed power load. Validation and explanation of this model and data can be found in our previous work (Styler et al. 2011).

State data was recorded every second, limited by the frequency of the data supplied by the GPS receiver. The state data recorded from the vehicles include GPS coordinates, time, elevation, speed, acceleration, and power load. Using this data, we can simulate our algorithm on each of these vehicles.

Hybrid Electric Vehicle Prototype

The hybrid EV prototype combines a battery and supercapacitor to create a heterogeneous energy pack, as shown in Figure 4. This pack can handle high power loads with ease while offering high energy density for sufficient driving range. The supercapacitor pack in this prototype EV has a much higher power density than the battery pack. This allows it to meet high power demands, such as rapid accelerations or regenerations, with great efficiency. However, these supercapacitors have very low energy density, and cannot be used for long before depletion. The battery pack is extremely energy dense but performs poorly at high power loads. Under high load, such as accelerating up a hill, the battery pack generates a significant amount of heat and loses efficiency due to the Peukert Effect. External cooling systems also require additional energy, reducing overall vehicle efficiency.

Ideally, the supercapacitor would handle all high power loads, and the battery pack would only handle low power loads and low power charging of the capacitor. Intelligent predictive control is needed to optimally pre-charge or discharge the capacitor. For the simulated hybrid EV prototype, the control lever is the total power drawn from the battery. Any excess or shortage of power, with respect to the demanded power load, is handled by the supercapacitor buffer. This allows the vehicle to charge or discharge the supercapacitor, while meeting the driver power demands, with a single control variable.

Cost Function and Setup

The system architect defines a degree of freedom for control and an objective cost function to minimize. For this experiment, the algorithm will control the charging and discharging of the capacitor by controlling battery pack output. It is constrained to meet all demands created by the driver and to operate within the safety limits of the energy pack.

To minimize high power loads on the battery, the one-step cost function calculates the square of current on the battery given the voltage, V_t

$$c(x,u,t) = \frac{u}{V_t}^2 \tag{5}$$

The difference between the battery power output, u, and the load demand is handled by the supercapacitor. The battery power output can be constrained if the supercapacitor is at or near its charge limits.

The total cost incurred for a trip is the integral of the current squared from the battery over time. Using this cost function results in the desired behavior of pre-charging of the capacitor during idle or low power loads in order to handle upcoming high power loads later. This will result in lower thermal output and possibly longer longevity of the battery, but neither are modeled in the scope of this work.

The state feature vector used for our prediction is:

$$\begin{vmatrix} GPS & Bearing & Time & Day \\ Speed & Acceleration & EnergyUsed & \end{vmatrix} \tag{6}$$

The frequency of control decisions for the simulation is set to $1Hz$, to match the frequency of the state data contained in a dataset. In an actual implementation, it can operate at higher frequency if the sensors measuring vehicle state can supply new information faster.

Each driver dataset is tested independently and the results are combined into a single performance measure.

Results

We test and analyze the performance in our simulator using the real-world data. We compare performance against an upper bound calculated by a prescient optimal controller with *a priori* knowledge of the upcoming load. We also compare to a simple buffer method and a controller optimizing against the mean of the weighted predictions. We compare varying number of predictions k with a fixed $50Wh$ capacitor size. We also show sensitivity to varying capacitor size with a fixed $k = 7$. Finally, we compare the dynamic dataset that grows chronologically with a leave-one-out batch dataset of all the data.

Performance Comparison

The results of various methods are compared with the algorithm, shown in Figure 5. The baseline represents the total cost incurred for a battery pack without a supercapacitor. The buffer method only stores regenerated energy and spends it as soon as possible. It simply demonstrates an additional baseline with no intelligent control, and is not meant to reflect the performance of fixed point or reactive policies.

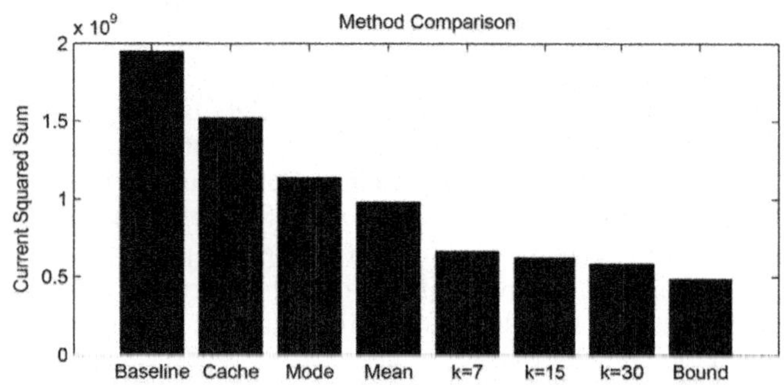

Figure 5: Comparison of Methods. This shows the improvement in current squared for each method over the baseline. High number of predictions, such as $k = 30$, approach the upper performance bound. Marked improvement over mean or mode predictions is observed.

The mode method only uses the single most likely prediction for optimization, and it is thus more subjective to prediction error and noise. The mean method averages the load predictions of $k = 7$ neighbors into a single prediction and calculates the optimal control. Due to this combination of predictions at run-time, offline computation of the cost-to-go function is not possible and the algorithm cannot run in real-time. These approaches serve as an indication of the limits of approaches that do not consider uncertainty.

We observe the predictive algorithm achieves $> 91\%$ of the performance improvement possible with $k = 30$.

Sensitivity

The sensitivity of performance to number of neighbors and capacitor size was tested. The number of neighbors increases performance, with diminishing returns, at the cost of marginal computation time. The size of the supercapacitor affects the ability to buffer large demands and the sensitivity of the algorithm to prediction error.

The sensitivity to the number of neighbors is shown tangentially in Figure 5. Here we observed improved performance as k increases, but with diminishing returns. Each additional neighbor has a lower importance weight attached to the prediction. As k increases, these weights become insignificant to the overall optimization and have negligible effect on the control outcome.

Supercapacitor size greatly affects the performance of the agent, shown in Figure 6. Excessively large capacitors have significant headroom, allowing control mistakes to occur with little penalty to overall performance. As the capacitor size is reduced, the algorithm is more susceptible to prediction error, and mistakes in control from inaccurate predictions can incur significant cost. The performance relative to the optimal prescient agent is shown at six sizes, $\{5, 10, 50, 100, 200, 1000\}$ Wh.

Dynamic Performance

The performance results shown so far were calculated using a batch leave-one-out cross validation (LOOCV) test. For each trip tested, every other trip in the dataset is used as training

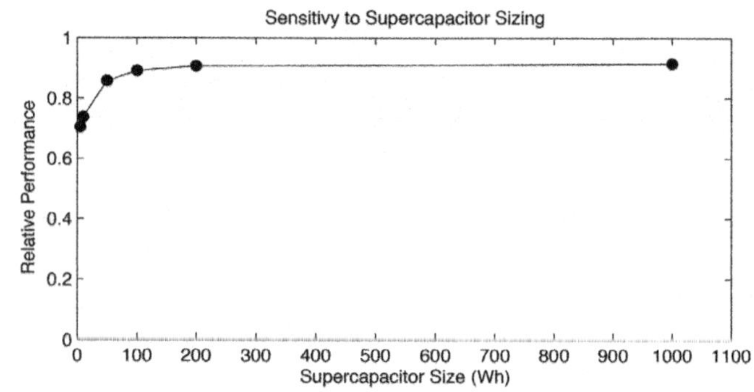

Figure 6: Sensitivity to Supercapacitor Size. The graph shows the sensitivity of performance to the capacitor size. Larger capacitors are less sensitive to prediction error as the large buffer allows for many mistakes.

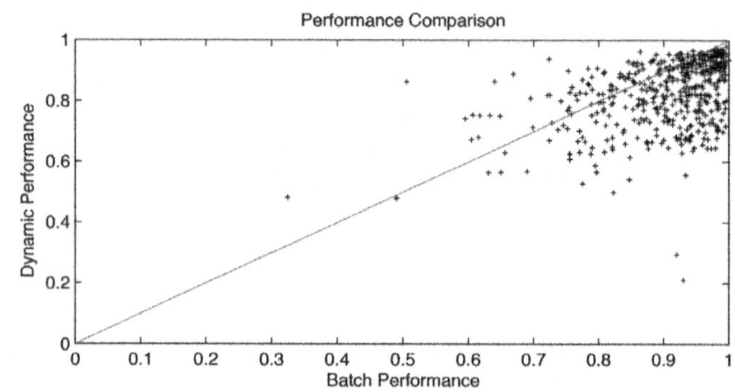

Figure 7: Performance Comparison of Batch and Dynamic Systems. The graph compares individual trip performance using the batch or dynamic learners. In most cases the batch learner performs better due to better coverage.

data. This eliminates any possible bias effects due to data ordering or dataset division, but demonstrates results after months of driving data has been collected. To evaluate the dynamic performance, we also tested how well the algorithm performs through a simulated lifetime of the vehicle. The data was tested chronologically, in the order it was collected, and each trip was added to the training data after testing.

The results comparing the batch performance to the dynamic performance are shown in Figure 7. Each point represents the performance of a trip, relative to an optimal upper bound, for the batch and dynamic case. The majority of trips perform better in the batch case, with more training data, and only a few outliers perform significantly better in the dynamic case due to noise.

Future Work

The next extension to this work is implementation on a high fidelity plug-in HEV simulator. A common problem in plug-in HEV control is sustaining charge over the course of a trip, so electric power is always available. Our algorithm can predict charging events to optimally deplete the battery when appropriate. Also, it can optimally distribute the use of electric power between charging cycles. This extension would allow the direct comparison of this approach to many existing methods.

Other sustainability domains sensitive to spatiotemporal loads may also be optimized by leveraging past data. One such possible application is HVAC control in an office building, where human behavior patterns influence load.

Conclusions

In this work, we have demonstrated we can achieve real-time near-optimal control of an energy management task by leveraging predictions from prior data. A dynamic system can constantly improve performance by expanding the dataset to improve data coverage. Future uncertainty and prediction error will bound the performance of this approach.

Our optimization approach, the independent combination of the cost-to-go functions at run-time, allows almost all computation to be done offline. A handful of simulations, a tree search, and a few table lookups are computed at run-time, which can be done faster than real-time on even modest hardware. This real-time prediction and optimization approach achieves performance close to retrospective optimizations using *a priori* knowledge of the upcoming power loads.

In simulation, we achieved $> 91\%$ of the improvement achieved by the prescient upper bound. This performance is excellent and suggests our optimization approach could be successful for other high-level vehicle optimization tasks.

We have demonstrated the potential for data-driven intelligence and real-time optimization in this transportation sustainability task. Our approach could be used for other load-sensitive sustainability problems with adequate predictions. The environmental implications of this work can be realized with further research.

Acknowledgments

The authors gratefully acknowledge the contributions of BMW, Bosch, Bombardier, Google, the ChargeCar team, the CREATE Lab, our data volunteers, and reviewers. This material is based upon work supported by the National Science Foundation under Grant No. (0946825).

References

Brahma, A.; Guezennec, Y.; and Rizzoni, G. 2000. Optimal energy management in series hybrid electric vehicles. In *American Control Conference, 2000. Proceedings of the 2000*, volume 1, 60–64. IEEE.

De Vlieger, I.; De Keukeleere, D.; and Kretzschmar, J. 2000. Environmental effects of driving behaviour and congestion related to passenger cars. *Atmospheric Environment* 34(27):4649–4655.

Delprat, S.; Guerra, T. M.; and Rimaux, J. 2002. Control strategies for hybrid vehicles: optimal control. In *Vehicular Technology Conference, 2002. Proceedings. VTC 2002-Fall. 2002 IEEE 56th*, volume 3, 1681–1685. IEEE.

Di Cairano, S.; Bernardini, D.; Bemporad, A.; and Kolmanovsky, I. 2014. Stochastic mpc with learning for driver-predictive vehicle control and its application to hev energy management. *Control Systems Technology, IEEE Transactions on* 22(3):1018–1031.

Ericsson, E. 2000. Variability in urban driving patterns. *Transportation Research Part D: Transport and Environment* 5(5):337–354.

Holmén, B. A., and Niemeier, D. A. 1998. Characterizing the effects of driver variability on real-world vehicle emissions. *Transportation Research Part D: Transport and Environment* 3(2):117–128.

Langari, R., and Won, J.-S. 2005. Intelligent energy management agent for a parallel hybrid vehicle-part i: system architecture and design of the driving situation identification process. *Vehicular Technology, IEEE Transactions on* 54(3):925–934.

LeBlanc, D. C.; Saunders, F.; Meyer, M. D.; and Guensler, R. 1995. Driving pattern variability and impacts on vehicle carbon monoxide emissions. *Transportation Research Record* (1472).

Liu, A., and Pentland, A. 1997. Towards real-time recognition of driver intentions. In *Intelligent Transportation System, 1997. ITSC'97., IEEE Conference on*, 236–241. IEEE.

Lyshevski, S. E., and Yokomoto, C. 1998. Control of hybrid-electric vehicles. In *American Control Conference, 1998. Proceedings of the 1998*, volume 4, 2148–2149. IEEE.

Mosbech, H. 1980. Optimal control of hybrid vehicle. In *Proc., International Symp. on Automotive Technology & Automation (ISATA80)*, volume 2, 303–320.

Musardo, C.; Rizzoni, G.; Guezennec, Y.; and Staccia, B. 2005. A-ecms: An adaptive algorithm for hybrid electric vehicle energy management. *European Journal of Control* 11(4):509–524.

Opila, D. F.; Wang, X.; McGee, R.; and Grizzle, J. 2013. Real-time implementation and hardware testing of a hybrid vehicle energy management controller based on stochastic dynamic programming. *Journal of Dynamic Systems, Measurement, and Control* 135:021002.

Oprean, M.; Ionescu, V.; Mocanu, N.; Beloiu, S.; and Stanciu, C. 1988. Dynamic programming applied to hybrid vehicle control. In *Proc. of the International Conf. on Electric Drives (ICED 88)*, volume 4, D2.

Salmasi, F. R. 2007. Control strategies for hybrid electric vehicles: Evolution, classification, comparison, and future trends. *Vehicular Technology, IEEE Transactions on* 56(5):2393–2404.

Styler, A., and Nourbakhsh, I. 2013. Model predictive control with uncertainty in human driven systems. In *Twenty-Seventh AAAI Conference on Artificial Intelligence*.

Styler, A.; Podnar, G.; Dille, P.; Duescher, M.; Bartley, C.; and Nourbakhsh, I. 2011. Active management of a heterogeneous energy store for electric vehicles. In *Integrated and Sustainable Transportation System (FISTS), 2011 IEEE Forum on*, 20–25. IEEE.

CPSIA information can be obtained
at www.ICGtesting.com
Printed in the USA
BVOW09s2305160217
476430BV00008B/37/P